The New York Times
Film Reviews
1987-1988

The New York Times
Film Reviews
1987-1988

𝕿imes BOOKS / ⓖⓟ

Times Books & Garland Publishing, Inc. / New York 1990

Library of Congress Catalog Card Number: 70-112777

ISSN 0362-3688
ISBN 0-8240-7590-0

Manufactured in the United States of America

Contents

Foreword

In 1970, THE NEW YORK TIMES FILM REVIEWS (1913-1968) was published. It was a five-volume set, containing over 18,000 film reviews exactly as they first appeared in The Times.

The collection was accompanied by a sixth volume, an 1,100 page computer-generated index, which afforded ready access to the material by film titles, by producing and distributing companies, and by the names of all actors, directors, and other persons listed in the credits.

Further volumes appeared in 1971, 1973, 1975, 1977, 1979, 1981, and 1983 reproducing the reviews that were printed in The Times during the years 1969-1970, 1971-1972, 1973-1974, 1975-1976, 1977-1978, 1979-1980, 1981-1982, 1983-1984, and 1985-1986; the present volume carries the collection through 1988. The index as originally conceived was incorporated into the 1969-1970, 1971-1972, 1973-1974, 1975-1976, 1977-1978, 1979-1980, 1981-1982, 1983-1984, 1985-1986 volumes and the present volume.

New compilations will be published periodically to keep the collection constantly updated.

BEST FILMS

Articles listing the best and award-winning films published in The Times appear at the end of each year's reviews. These include the awards of the Academy of Motion Picture Arts and Sciences and the "best films" selections of The New York Times and the New York Film Critics.

The New York Times
Film Reviews
1987

WISDOM, written and directed by Emilio Estevez; director of photography, Adam Greenberg; film editor, Michael Kahn; music by Danny Elfman; produced by Bernard Williams; released by the 20th Century-Fox Film Corporation. At Ziegfeld, Avenue of the Americas and 54th Street; Baronet, 59th Street at Third Avenue; 23d Street West Triplex, between Eighth and Ninth Avenues. Running time: 108 minutes. This film is rated R.

Karen Simmons	Demi Moore
John Wisdom	Emilio Estevez
Lloyd Wisdom	Tom Skerritt
Samantha Wisdom	Veronica Cartwright
Williamson	William Allen Young
Cooper	Richard Minchenberg

By VINCENT CANBY

John Wisdom, played by the possibly talented Emilio Estevez, who also wrote and directed the movie, is in a no-win situation. Though he's an intelligent, clean-cut, high-school-educated man of 23, he can't get a decent job because of his police record. As a teen-ager, Wisdom once got drunk with his friends and stole a car, a felony for which he was put on probation for four years.

Now his past haunts him. Being honest, he always acknowledges his record when he applies for white-collar positions and always is turned down. He's even dismissed from his job as a janitor because, says his boss, he's overqualified and lacks the love required for cleaning offices and lavatories.

According to "Wisdom," which opened yesterday at the Baronet and other theaters, society has left open only one route to the young man — crime, but what sort of crime? In what should be a funny sequence (but isn't), he considers, in turn, kidnapping, arson and murder, none of which really interest him. Like so many of his contemporaries, including beauty-contest winners, Wisdom is most interested in that vaguely generalized group termed people.

Suddenly he has it. He'll hold up banks and, instead of taking money, he'll destroy mortgage records, thus freeing all those little guys on whom the lending institutions are foreclosing in the economic squeeze of the mid-80's.

•

Most of "Wisdom" is played as cut-rate, populist comedy — Wisdom and his girlfriend, Karen (Demi Moore), being hailed by the public for their unorthodox, philanthropic exploits in robbing banks throughout the Southwest. Soon, however, things go wrong for the do-gooders, possibly because no one could think of a lighthearted way to get them out of their mess.

Mr. Estevez is far more at ease as an actor than as a writer or director, though he's certainly as competent as most people making television movies. The problem is that "Wisdom" is aggressively boring, either because one can predict everything that's going to happen and exactly how it will look on the screen or because the concept of the film eventually seems even more confused than the title character.

After devoting the second half of the movie to pretty images of himself and Miss Moore on their socially conscious joyride, Mr. Estevez, as Wisdom, is heard on the soundtrack saying something to the effect that the public was wrong to see the pair as romantic heroes. Under the circumstances, that thought comes a bit late.

The performances aren't especially good or bad. Mr. Estevez and Miss Moore are photogenic, and Tom Skerritt and Veronica Cartwright, as Wisdom's worried, well-meaning parents, are no less bland than their roles.

•

The R-rated movie is titled "Wisdom," but by the end it's become "Bonnie and Clunk."

1987 Ja 1, 9:5

Demi Moore and Emilio Estevez play bank robbers in "Wisdom," a contemporary adventure story written and directed by Mr. Estevez.

FILM VIEW

JANET MASLIN

Unlikely Casting Can Reward Actor and Audience

It happened when audiences watched Jane Fonda bask in a bathing suit in "On Golden Pond," and it will happen again when they see her get out of bed in "The Morning After," Sidney Lumet's nimble and very entertaining new thriller: a moment of detachment, a pause during which the viewer inevitably thinks more about the real Miss Fonda than her role. Gee, but her legs look great. She's in such good shape that even her *feet* look trim. No question about it, those workouts pay off. And incidentally, isn't she just a little too fit for Alex Sternbergen, a.k.a. Viveca Van Loren, the run-down, alcoholic actress she's supposed to be playing?

Yes, definitely. So the audience's attention will be drawn to the artifice through which this fine performance of Miss Fonda's is achieved. Her hair is bleached a weak, frowzy shade of blonde, and she often appears in glaring light that ages her greatly; in the early scene that shows her waking up from a night she can't even remember, she pantomimes a hangover so monumental that the daylight actually hurts. A makeup wizard has given her runny, bloodshot eyes, and Miss Fonda herself supplies the harsh voice, the proclivity for little lies and the messy, unstable temperament that the role requires. Still, she's somewhat out of place. She was even out of place in "On Golden Pond" playing Henry Fonda's prickly daughter — and she *was* Henry Fonda's prickly daughter, after all.

That Miss Fonda appears to be playing against type here is no detriment to "The Morning After." As a matter of fact, it's part of the fun. It's a reminder that actors need not be wholly credible to be effective, and that a performance need not be stylized or abstract to make good use of a certain inherent falseness. Playing against type, as Miss Fonda did in "Klute" and again does here, can be a risky business: it can mean Sylvester Stallone playing a country singer (as he did in "Rhinestone") or Bill Murray as a mystic ("The Razor's Edge") or Mary Tyler Moore as a sheltered, stay-at-home young wife ("Just Between Friends"). But this kind of chancy casting, when done well, has unexpected advantages.

• • •

It becomes a way of including the audience in the fiction being constructed, of inviting viewers to share and enjoy the deception to which they are privy. Used cleverly, this kind of unlikely casting becomes a confidence that the audience and the film makers can share. "The Morning After" has a shrewd, smart-talking screenplay ("She's got a record — assault with a deadly weapon. Did you know that when you married her?" "It's *why* I married her"). It also has an attractively light touch, but what really holds the interest is the playful sparring that links Miss Fonda with Jeff Bridges, who plays a redneck ex-policeman very much her junior. The gamesmanship extends well beyond the two actors and their roles here, since in addition to fooling one another they are also fooling us.

Every film star brings the memory of other roles to each new one, but those echoes needn't always be powerful. They are, though, for Mr. Bridges, who — as in "Against All Odds" and "Eight Million Ways To Die" — is once again playing the hard-boiled but implacable suitor in a story of intrigue. That he manages to bring such a different physical style to each role is part of the enjoyment

Among current examples of chancy casting are Willem Dafoe, above, as the saintly Sergeant Elias in "Platoon"; Jane Fonda, top right, as the run-down, alcoholic actress Alex Sternbergen in "The Morning After" and Blythe Danner as the hard-working, old-fashioned Jewish mother in "Brighton Beach Memoirs."

of watching him; the awareness of those earlier performances actually heightens this one instead of undermining it.

It's especially true with Miss Fonda that the memory of earlier roles, particularly the more prim ones, adds an extra dimension to the more dissolute woman she plays here. If in "Klute" Miss Fonda took a more defiant posture, almost daring the audience to accept her as a prostitute, in "The Morning After" she takes a more relaxed, playful approach. If you're willing to believe that Jane Fonda would live on cigarettes and Thunderbird, the film seems to say, well, let's see what else you can be talked into.

Blythe Danner isn't any less at home as an old-fashioned Jewish mother than Jane Fonda is as a dissipated ex-starlet, but it's almost an even match. In "Brighton Beach Memoirs," which is one of the few Neil Simon works to adopt an explicitly ethnic tone, Miss Danner is certainly an unexpected presence. She brings not the least bit of built-in ethnic style to a role that could so easily be played as a caricature. As the kind of high-strung, hard-working, proudly ascetic parent whose nagging is her most visible means of showing affection, she seems to be newly inventing what could have been a stock character.

There's a little dialect, which is not the most successful part of the performance, and there are a few standard mannerisms. But most of the character is less automatic, growing out of Mr. Simon's dialogue and Miss Danner's forthright, unfettered interpretation. The mother, her overworked husband and her widowed sister are all played by actors of no distinct ethnicity. Miss Danner, Judith Ivey and Bob Dishy have been neutrally cast, and by some lights even miscast. But for that very reason, they allow Mr. Simon's memories of a Depression-era Jewish household to stand on their own. By contrast, Jonathan Silverman fits like a glove into the role of the story's wise-cracking young protagonist. This feels more like type-casting, and more like overkill.

In Oliver Stone's "Platoon," a key bit of casting against type provides the film with one of its boldest strokes. The film's young protagonist, Chris Taylor, finds himself torn between two rival sergeants, the vicious, amoral Barnes and the saintly Elias, two friends whose sharply contrasting codes of ethics eventually bring them into conflict. The players Mr. Stone has chosen for the roles are Willem Dafoe, a fine actor whose handsome face is so menacing that he has inevitably been cast (in Walter Hill's "Streets of Fire" and William Friedkin's "To Live and Die in L.A.") as the scariest of villains; and Tom Ber-

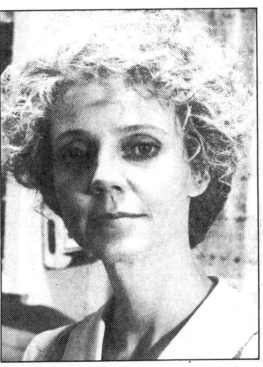

enger, a nice-guy type. The hitch is that Mr. Dafoe plays the saint and Mr. Berenger, made up with disfiguring facial scars, plays the unprincipled killer.

The eventual confrontation between these two would have been shocking anyhow, but it is made all the more so by this casting coup. Both of these usually-typecast actors emerge from "Platoon" with whole new careers in store, and both perform brilliantly in their surprising roles. Even better, the entire fighting unit of "Platoon" is made up of actors cast against the familiar war-film conventions, which contributes greatly to the uniqueness of "Platoon" within that genre. By contrast, the Marine unit in Clint Eastwood's "Heartbreak Ridge" is exactly what might be expected, the usual band of misfits and miscreants who are whipped into shape by a sergeant (Mr. Eastwood) who's determined to make men out of them. The big guy is big, but he turns

out to be no match for the sergeant. The small, feisty, rebellious type (Mario Van Peebles) turns out to be the best raw material in the bunch. Et cetera.

Finally, there's Richard Gere, an actor who seems to bring a certain built-in attitude with him to whatever roles he plays. This isn't star quality, exactly, but it's a self-conscious aloofness that makes his King David peculiarly like his American Gigolo. In "No Mercy," however, Mr. Gere appears to be approaching his role as a Chicago policeman somewhat differently. It's a tough-guy part, but the tough guy wears his heart on his sleeve, particularly after he falls in love with the beautiful blonde (Kim Basinger) to whom he has been handcuffed, a blonde who is the moll of a Louisiana gangster.

Mr. Gere seems to approach this character more openly and emotionally than he does most, to be playing against his own self-proclaimed type. And the results are refreshing and unexpected. In production notes for the film, Mr. Gere cites the late John Garfield as an influence, and that admiration is apparent on the screen, in the less studied, more spontaneous and distinctly un-Gerelike poignancy that he brings to this seemingly hardboiled role. Incidentally, the film's director, Richard Pearce, has also cast the gangster's role a bit unexpectedly and done it with perfect élan. The part is played by the Dutch actor Jeroen Krabbé, normally a much more sophisticated type who makes a very stylish figure here. Yes, the gangster does disembowel his victims, after all. But Mr. Krabbé sees to it that he stands elegantly straight, wears a formidable-looking outfit and coolly addresses those he is about to knife as "my friend." So the nastiest of roles is cast unpredictably, and played with unanticipated flair. ■

1987 Ja 4, II:17:1

Snapping at Heels

THE CITY AND THE DOGS, produced and directed by Francisco J. Lombardi; screenplay (Spanish with English subtitles) by Jose Watanabe, based on the novel by Mario Vargas Llosa; director of photography, Pili Flores Guerra; released by Cinevista. At Film Forum 1, 57 Watts Street. Running time: 133 minutes. This film has no rating.

Poet	Pablo Serra
Lieutenant Gamboa	Gustavo Bueno
Jaguar	Juan Manuel Ochoa
Colonel	Luis Alvarez
Slave	Eduardo Adrianzen
Teresa	Liliana Navarro
Arrospide	Miguel Iza

By JANET MASLIN

SELDOM has any work of Latin American literature traveled successfully to the screen, with the notable exception of Manuel Puig's "Kiss of the Spider Woman," a novel whose author had the movies very much in mind. It may be that the dense, sometimes hallucinatory style of these works, with their abruptly shifting points of view, keeps them permanently out of any film maker's reach. Certainly that's the case with "The City and the Dogs," a film by Francisco J. Lombardi, based on Mario Vargas Llosa's 1962 novel, "The Time of the Hero." Mr. Lombardi has made a creditable attempt to translate the novel, but its irony, its complexity and its richness of style simply elude him.

"The City and the Dogs," which opens today at the Film Forum 1, presents Mr. Vargas Llosa's tale of a military academy in Lima, Peru, a place that in the author's mind takes on mythic dimensions. The cadets at the college are known by the most formidable of nicknames — Jaguar, the Slave; the Poet. And their code of honor is enforced in the most brutal and merciless manner, as they punish one another for real and imagined transgressions. Indeed, an early scene in "The City and the Dogs" underscores the vast differences between this portrait of military-school life and the more conventional ones with which American audiences are familiar. Two younger cadets, being hazed by older ones, are made to crouch on the ground and behave like dogs in a mating ritual, while in the background we see casual glimpses of other cadets being walked on leashes, confined inside a ring of fire and hung upside down.

The story concerns a fatal error made by the cadet called Esclavo. (The film's subtitles, which are so poor that they consistently misspell "cigarette," neglect to translate this as Slave.) A timid and dutiful sort, the Slave (Eduardo Adrianzen) finds himself unable to tolerate the detention that is enforced on the cadets after one of them steals a set of exam questions. The Slave's frustration has to do with his longing for a pretty girl named Teresa (Liliana Navarro), who has barely noticed him.

The Slave implores the Poet (Pablo Serra), who has earned that nickname partly by writing love letters and pornographic stories for his classmates, to go see Teresa in his place, and the Poet finds his loyalty greatly tested. It is even further strained by the activities of the Jaguar (Juan Manuel Ochoa), a feral-looking classmate who functions as a kind of gangland chief within the school's confines. As the Jaguar's activities are gradually exposed, and as he and the Slave come into conflict, the Poet must examine his own conscience and redefine his own morality.

Mr. Lombardi has directed his film in a blunt, literal style that has narrative force but not much more. Life at the academy, richly and unpredictably detailed by Mr. Vargas Llosa, has little depth and few surprises here, so that its allegorical dimension all but disappears. However, the film proceeds engrossingly despite its very leisurely pace, and the casting is effective. Mr. Serra makes a stalwart, reflective Poet, and Mr. Ochoa makes his face a mask of coldness and corruption as befits the Jaguar. Gustavo Bueno is also memorable as the lieutenant who is the students' stern taskmaster, and in some ways is the story's pivotal character.

"The City and the Dogs" is earnest and involving, but it isn't a film that can easily stand on its own. It may well send audiences back to Mr. Vargas Llosa's novel for a keener sense of the academy, its inhabitants and the battles they must wage.

1987 Ja 7, C20:5

Down Home

MY SWEET LITTLE VILLAGE, directed by Jiri Menzel; screenplay (Czechoslovakian with English subtitles) by Zdenek Sverak; cinematography by Jaromir Sofr; music by Jiri Sust; distributed by Circle Releasing Corporation. At 68th Street Playhouse, at Third Avenue. Running time: 100 minutes. This film is rated PG.

Townspeople keep an eye on an itinerant artist in the Czechoslovak film "My Sweet Little Village"—"I only want to have one small 'bourgeois' theme," says Jiri Menzel, its director, "that being decent can be beautiful."

Otik	Janos Ban
Pavek	Marian Labuda
Skruzny	Rudolf Hrusinsky
Mrs. Pavek	Milena Dvorska
Rumlena	Ladislav Zupanic
Turek	Petr Cepek
Mrs. Turek	Libuse Safrankova
Kaspar	Jan Hartl
Odvarka	Evzen Jegorov
Kunc	Oldrich Vlach

By VINCENT CANBY

THERE'S no irony in the title of "My Sweet Little Village," Jiri Menzel's bucolic comedy that opens today at the 68th Street Playhouse. The movie, which has been chosen by Czechoslovakia as its nominee for the Oscar as this year's best foreign-language feature, seems to define the problems faced by a film maker in a society where everything's perfect. Bliss can be as boring as decadence.

The setting is a picturesque Czechoslovak village that could have been ordered from a catalogue. It comes equipped with assorted livestock and poultry, including a rooster that announces each dawn offscreen (and is, possibly, a pre-recorded sound effect), and by a bunch of eccentric characters, who laugh and eat and gossip and scowl and, on occasion, noisily disagree with each other.

More or less at the center of the film, and probably the owner of the title's possessive pronoun, is a middle-aged medical doctor who prefers to prescribe common sense instead of medicine and who, being a poet at heart, has an accident (minor and comic) every time he takes his car on the road.

There are also a pretty young wife, her young lover and her jealous older husband; a downy-cheeked farm boy, painfully in love with the village schoolmarm; a sweet-tempered, mentally retarded young man who's tall and skinny, and his boss, a tubby, short-tempered truck driver who acts as Oliver Hardy to the slow-witted fellow's Stan Laurel.

Though it means to be cheering, "My Sweet Little Village" is Mr. Menzel's most melancholy work. It's by far the slickest and least engaging film (at least, among those shown here) by the man who received the foreign-language Oscar for his first film, "Closely Watched Trains" (1967). Unlike Milos Forman and Ivan Passer, his contemporaries, who chose to work in the West after the overthrow of the liberal government in 1968, Mr. Menzel elected to remain in Czechoslovakia, where, in addition to being a film director and actor, he was a director of satiric theater.

There's no way of knowing exactly how Mr. Menzel would have developed as a film maker had he left Czechoslovakia, or had he been able to work at home in a less restrictive atmosphere. Possibly he would have made exactly the same kinds of films.

Whatever the reasons, the Menzel films have become increasingly small and slight and sort of unctuous. They are "warm," but it's canned heat. It's as if he were reworking the same impulses that went into "Closely Watched Trains" and his rueful, Renoiresque second film, "Capricious Summer," though without urgency and without references to the world around him.

"My Sweet Little Village" is third-rate Renoir and second-rate Forman — that is, the Milos Forman who made "The Firemen's Ball." It's all sunlight and no shadows, so that even its occasionally funny gags seem flat and its moments of pathos unearned.

"My Sweet Little Village," which has been rated PG ("Parental Guidance Suggested"), contains some partial nudity and one seduction scene.

1987 Ja 9, C6:5

ASSASSINATION, directed by Peter Hunt; screenplay by Richard Sale; director of photography, Hanania Baer; film editor, James Heckert; music by Robert O. Ragland and Valentine McCallum; produced by Pancho Kohner; released by The Cannon Group Inc. At UA Twin, Broadway at 49th Street; Manhattan Twin, Third Avenue at 59th Street; 86th Street Twin, at Lexington avenue. Running time: 88 minutes. This film is rated PG-13.

Jay Killian	Charles Bronson
Lara Royce Craig	Jill Ireland
Fitzroy	Stephen Elliott
Charlotte Chang	Jan Gan Boyd
Tyler Loudermilk	Randy Brooks
Reno Bracken	Erik Stern
Senator Bunsen	Michael Ansara
Briggs	James Staley
Polly Sims	Kathryn Leigh Scott
Osborne Weems	James Acheson

By VINCENT CANBY

In "Assassination," which opened yesterday at the UA Twin and other theaters, Charles Bronson, who may outlast the Mount Rushmore sculptures, plays the chief of security for the nation's newest First Lady. "What's she like?" he asks on Inauguration Day. "Let's just say," replies a friend, "that you're going to miss the hell out of Nancy Reagan."

The new First Lady, played by Jill Ireland (Mrs. Bronson), is initially a major pain. She's also none too bright. She's the last person in Washington to realize that someone "close" to her is trying to kill her. She doesn't cotton to this fact until there have been several explosions in her vicinity and a number of innocent people have been killed.

Says Mr. Bronson, as he tries to explain the gravity of her situation, "That yacht was definitely blown up premeditatively."

Most of "Assassination" takes place on the road as the First Lady flees Washington, incognito, first pursued — and then willingly accompanied — by Mr. Bronson. Somehow the assassin always knows where they are. This is possibly because, though they flee from the south lawn of the White House to Indiana and the Far West, there are always the same mountain peaks in the background as there were in the District of Columbia.

You could say that it's all like some terrible dream. People run, but they don't move. Gunmen shoot at each other at point-blank range — and miss. The dialogue also suggests nightmares. "Oh, what a relief," the First Lady says after one or another close call, or, when she's really had a fright, "I'm still shaking."

In spite of the noisy explosions with which the film is scored, "Assassination" has a majestic, slightly arthritic pace that's almost soothing. The screenplay was written by Richard Sale, who's been writing movies for over 40 years, and directed by Peter Hunt, who directed television's "Last Days of Pompeii" and, before that, "On Her Majesty's Secret Service," the first and last James Bond film to star Richard Lazenby.

The story makes no sense whatsoever and most of the performances are awful, but that's not important in a Charles Bronson vehicle. His is an implacable movie presence, quite unlike any other. It's good to know that he's still in there, squinting at the bad guys and occasionally dispatching them with as little effort as possible.

1987 Ja 10, 13:1

THE KINDRED, directed by Jeffrey Obrow and Stephen Carpenter; screenplay by Mr. Carpenter, Mr. Obrow, John Penney, Earl Ghaffari and Joseph Stefano; director of photography, Mr. Carpenter; edited by Mr. Penney and Mr. Ghaffari; music by David Newman; produced by Mr. Obrow; released by F/M Entertainment. At RKO Warner, Broadway at 47th Street; Olympia, Broadway and 107th Street, and other theaters. Running time: 91 minutes. This film is rated R.

John Hollins ....David Allen Brooks
Dr. Phillip Lloyd .... Rod Steiger
Melissa Leftridge ....Amanda Pays
Sharon Raymond ....Talia Balsam
Amanda Hollins ....Kim Hunter
Hart Phillips ....Timothy Gibbs
Brad Baxter .... Peter Frechette
Cindy Russell ....Julia Montgomery
Nell Valentine ....Bunki Z
Harry ....Charles Grueber

By CARYN JAMES

There are precisely two spirited scenes in "The Kindred" — Kim Hunter's entire role. She rises above this horror film's near-total banality as a dying scientist pleading with her son to end her secret experiment. He must destroy her notebooks, the "Anthony journals," she warns John. When he asks, "Who's Anthony?" she practically rises out of her deathbed to cry, "Your brother!" and soon dies, without explaining.

Now John, also a scientist, is surprised enough to find that he has a brother, but the real shock awaiting him is that Anthony is a hybrid monster — a cross between tissues John has donated to his mother's work and some unidentified marine life form, all mixed up and given life in the lab Mom has set up in her son's old room at home. And though it takes John half the film to discover his sibling's identity, the audience knows almost from the start, for "The Kindred" is more of a hybrid than Anthony. The five writers and two directors credited with piecing it together have come up with a disjointed, jigsaw-puzzle movie that is constantly announcing its borrowed characters and subplots and special effects.

There's the group-of-people-in-a-lonely-country-house plot, as John,

his girlfriend and several friends go to his mother's house to destroy her research. There's romance, because John has invited along a beautiful, mysterious stranger who makes his plain girlfriend jealous. There's the half-human monster hiding in the cellar (he may be John's brother, but he looks like a blood relative of the dragonlike creature in the "Alien" films, only with lots of slithering octopus tentacles). And there's a horror plot that keeps us predicting quite accurately when the mad brother in the

basement will crash through the floorboards and attack his visitors.

The special effects are gruesome enough (after Anthony has attacked one woman, we watch her change into a fishy creature, complete with gills, who resembles Linda Blair in "The Exorcist"). But those few episodes are not much help in a film with the dragged-out pace of a television soap opera and the limpest of human conflicts. The evil scientist who wants to kidnap Anthony and continue the experiments is played by Rod Steiger,

who speaks his few lines through clenched teeth as he walks through a cameo role that's too laughable to be truly villainous.

Maybe "The Kindred," which opened yesterday at the RKO Warner and other theaters, was meant to be a sinister horror tale of genetic engineering gone haywire, but it turned out to be a silly story about a not-too-bright guy who learns about sibling rivalry the hard way.

1987 Ja 10, 13 :1

Ricky Francisco

A scene from the Oliver Stone film—Coming out of a long tradition that includes everything from "Battleground" to "The Green Berets," "it uses a number of war-movie conventions, but so effectively that it's as if they'd been reinvented."

FILM VIEW

VINCENT CANBY

'Platoon' Finds New Life in the Old War Movie

" I kept thinking about all the kids who got wiped out by 17 years of war movies before coming to Vietnam to get wiped out for good," Michael Herr remembers in "Dispatches," his book of Vietnam memoirs published in 1977.

"Most combat troops," he goes on, "stopped thinking of the war as an adventure after their first few firefights, but there were always the ones who couldn't let that go. . . A lot of correspondents weren't much better. We'd all seen too many movies, stayed too long in Television City, years of media glut had made certain connections difficult.

". . . even after you knew better you couldn't avoid the ways in which things got mixed, the war itself with those

parts of the war that were just like the movies, just like 'The Quiet American' or 'Catch-22'. . . just like all that combat footage from television. . ."

In "Living Room War," his 1969 collection of essays, Michael J. Arlen takes exception to those who were saying at that time that television was making "the hazards of [the Vietnam] war. . . 'real' to the civilian audience." Those hazards, he suggests, are "also made less 'real' — diminished, in part, by the physical size of the television screen, which, for all the industry's advances, still shows one a picture of men three inches tall shooting at other men three inches tall. . ."

Whether the images are 30 feet tall or three inches, movies and television work on us in similar ways. The images are drugs whose side effects aren't immediately recognized. They do inform us, but with whatever "truth" they hold to be self-evident, which may be Rambo's or Walter Cronkite's.

Movies and television can make the wildest fiction look like fact, and lethal facts look as harmless as fiction. Even at their most reasonable, movies and television must distort their subjects to the extent that they find esthetic order in chaos, conferring on events a romantic vision or, at least, a comprehensible overview. They put at a safe distance those unmentionable, unrecognized things that otherwise are allowed to enter our minds only as nightmares.

Now, nearly 12 years after the fall of Saigon and nearly 20 years after the particular time it recalls, comes Oliver Stone's "Platoon," the best fiction film yet made about the fighting in Vietnam. Here's an exceptionally good, serious, foot-soldier's view of the war that, in spite of its sense of desolation, could well inspire the fantasies of some future generation of American soldiers.

It's something of a circle. As the film maker's imagination shapes his movies, those movies shape our imaginations. Thus, as Mr. Herr writes, the war itself gets mixed with those parts of the war that are just like the movies.

• • •

Though "Platoon" is a far cry from John Wayne's gung-ho "Green Berets," it's still a work of fiction. It comes out of a long tradition of "war" movies — everything from "Battleground" to (don't laugh) "The Green Berets." It also uses a number of war-movie conventions, but so effectively that it's as if they'd been reinvented.

"Platoon" finds in the experiences of the members of a single platoon of soldiers some equivalent to just about every horror story we've ever read about Vietnam, including the My Lai massacre. This is the license that can be granted to a film that — until its final few minutes — so rigorously keeps its eye at ground level.

It shares with its soldiers the pervasive physical discomforts of heat, damp, insects and exhaustion that, somehow, are made bearable by (because they seem less important than) their fear. Never before, I think, have I seen in a war movie such a harrowing evocation of fear, which functions like adrenaline but feels like a headache, the kind that rises and falls but never quite disappears. As much as anything that actually happens in combat, it's day-to-day fear — the will to survive, attached to the awareness that there's no earthly reason one has to — that alters the psyche.

Mr. Stone's achievement is not in the creation of a new kind of war movie but in the degree to which he rediscovers new life in the old, which he virtually redefines by cleaning away the debris that has accumulated over the years.

• • •

"Platoon" is a lean film, beginning with its dusty, hazily golden opening shots on a Vietnam airstrip, where new arrivals from the States are being deposited from a giant transport plane that looks like a World War II LST, though one that magically flies. Very little is specifically stated. Mr. Stone doesn't have to announce his meaning (though he eventually does, in the film's only major lapse of judgment). The film's talk is mostly to the point of what's happening, or might happen, or *can't* happen, which is what most vividly describes the soldiers' boredom.

Its three principal characters are Chris Taylor (Charlie Sheen), the young college dropout, who's the film's hesitant mouthpiece, and the two sergeants who have effectively split the platoon between them. They are Barnes (Tom Berenger), a seriously out-of-control, life-sized, clay-footed version of the "fighting machine" Sylvester Stallone glorifies in "Rambo," and Elias (Willem Dafoe), a man no less tough than Barnes, but whose tours of duty have transformed him into a soft-spoken, almost embarrassed prophet of doom.

The other members of the platoon don't wear labels that immediately characterize them. They take some time to get to know and, even then, they tend to merge, not as stereotypes but as the same sorts of men. "Two years of high school, mostly poor and unwanted... They're the bottom of the barrel, and they know it," is the way Chris Taylor describes them. The differences that finally do distinguish them are all the more prized and moving for being so finely graded.

Mr. Stone appreciates the singularity of the grunts without italicizing them. It's part of the film's revivifying mystery that when the members of this particular platoon find themselves on the verge of wiping out an entire village, the identities of the men who cave in to the hysteria (and of those who hang back) haven't been predictable.

"Platoon" is about war as seen by men for whom the only goal is daily survival. There are no great issues here, no debates about good and evil. It's about fighting for anonymous pieces of jungle, to hold positions that may well include the enemy, in a landscape of code names and numbers, where there are no points on the compass. It's to the film's credit that it manages to bring moral order to this confusion without celebrating it.

Whether or not this is what the public wants to see, I've no idea. At Loew's Astor Plaza the other weekday afternoon, there was a small but noisy claque that kept trying to respond to the film's reluctant heroes, and to its grim battle footage, as if "Platoon" were really another "Rambo." It wasn't easy. The My Lai-like sequence began promisingly, but the resolution clearly left some of the claque unsatisfied.

Does "Platoon" romanticize its grunts? I suppose it does, at least to the extent that all movies somehow lend larger-than-life importance to whomever they acknowledge. There are also occasional moments when Mr. Stone allows a self-conscious image to repeat an idea that requires no amplification — as in the Christ-like image of a betrayed American soldier being crucified, not on a cross but by bullets.

Not having been in Vietnam, I've no idea how accurate "Platoon" is in some of its details. Is the ratio of black "grunts" to white grunts correct, and does Mr. Stone soften the bitterness of racial antagonisms? Someone else can answer those questions. Anyone who fought in Vietnam will bring to the film a set of expectations far different from those of someone for whom Vietnam was, first, the living room war, then the war of written recollections and, most recently, the war as refought in the case of Westmoreland v. CBS.

It must say something about the American public's feelings toward the entire Vietnam experience that it's taken this long for the producers of a commercial film to attempt to make such a movie. As fine as they were, both "Apocalypse Now" and "The Deer Hunter" more or less floated above the concerns of the American foot soldiers and saw the war in terms of mythology. "Rambo" and Chuck Norris's two "Missing in Action" films jumped the gun, giving us revisionist views of a war whose sad end had scarcely been admitted by movies — with the exception of "The Deer Hunter" — in the first place.

Clint Eastwood's new film, the hugely popular war-comedy, "Heartbreak Ridge," acknowledges the Vietnam defeat, but then goes on to buck us up with a reenactment of our military triumph in Grenada. If I interpret "Heartbreak Ridge" correctly — and I'm not sure it makes complete sense — it seems to suggest that the only wars we can win from now on must be of the scale of the invasion of Grenada.

I've no way of knowing, but I suspect that in any future, nuclear-free engagements, the men who fight it will, in their fantasies, be seeing themselves not as any member of "Platoon's" Bravo company but as good old Clint. Mr. Eastwood still exemplifies the glamour that, in most of our war movies to date, disguises the true consequences of mortality. There's very little glamour in "Platoon."

■

1987 Ja 11, II:21:1

Befriending a Mugger

TOUCH AND GO, directed by Robert Mandel; written by Alan Ormsby, Bob Sand and Harry Colomby; director of photography, Richard H. Kline; film editor, Walt Mulconery; music by Sylvester Levay; produced by Stephen Friedman; released by Tri-Star Pictures. At the Coronet, 59th Street and Third Avenue. On Friday, the film will open at the Criterion, Broadway at 45th Street, and Movieland Eighth Street, at University Place. Running time: 111 minutes. This film is rated R.

Bobby Barbato	Michael Keaton
Denise DeLeon	Maria Conchita Alonso
Louis DeLeon	Ajay Naidu
Jerry Pepper	John Reilly
Dee Dee	Maria Tucci
Gower	Richard Venture
Lester	Max Wright
McDonald	Michael Zelniker
Levesque	Jere Burns
Lupo	D. V. deVincentis

"**T**OUCH AND GO" is a dismally ineffective, would-be sentimental movie about a professional hockey star (Michael Keaton) who befriends a tough little street urchin (Ajay Naidu), after the urchin tries to mug him, then falls in love with the boy's unwed mom (Maria Conchita Alonso). The film, which opens today at the Coronet, was shot mostly in Chicago, where it's set and which also stands in for a brief sequence in Minneapolis.

Except for the Chicago skyline, everything in "Touch and Go" looks phony. This includes the performances of Mr. Keaton, Miss Alonso and Mr. Naidu, as well as the extremely tasteful set decoration of Miss Alonso's tenement apartment, which appears to have been done by Marshall Field & Company. At the end of the film as at the beginning, the actors seem to be meeting each other for the first time.

Most of the people connected with "Touch and Go" have done better work, including Mr. Keaton (in "Johnny Dangerously"), Miss Alonso (in "Moscow on the Hudson") and Robert Mandel, the director, who also did "F/X."   *VINCENT CANBY*

1987 Ja 14, C20:5

Eyeful

THE BEDROOM WINDOW, directed by Curtis Hanson; screenplay by Mr. Hanson, based on the novel "The Witnesses" by Anne Holden; director of photography, Gil Taylor; edited by Scott Conrad; music by Michael Shrieve and Patrick Gleeson; produced by Martha Schumacher; released by De Laurentiis Entertainment Group. At U.A. Twin, Broadway at 49th Street; U.A. East, 85th Street and First Avenue; Gemini Twin, 64th Street and Second Avenue; Loews 84th Street Sixplex, at Broadway; 23d Street West Triplex, near Eighth Avenue. Running time: 111 minutes. This film is rated R.

Terry Lambert	Steve Guttenberg
Denise	Elizabeth McGovern
Sylvia	Isabelle Huppert
Collin	Paul Shenar
Quirke	Carl Lumbly
Henderson's Attorney	Wallace Shawn
Jessup	Frederick Coffin
Henderson	Brad Greenquist
State Attorney Peters	Robert Schenkkan

By VINCENT CANBY

ONE rainy night after leaving an office party early, Terry Lambert (Steve Guttenberg), a young, cheerfully on-the-loose Baltimore bachelor, returns to his apartment. There, by prearrangement, he meets his boss's sexy young wife, Sylvia (Isabelle Huppert), who's also managed to slip away from the festivities. Both having had too much to drink, they proceed to consummate what, for some time, has been a vague yen.

Later, while Terry is in the bathroom, Sylvia hears screams from the street. She looks out the window to watch in helplessness as a man beats a woman with the apparent intent of killing her. Sylvia calls for Terry, who doesn't hear, and tries without success to open the window. Sylvia can do nothing. Finally, some other people who've heard the screams rush out to save the woman. The attacker, who's had as good a look at Sylvia as she's had at him, flees.

Neither Terry nor Sylvia thinks much about the incident until the next day when they learn that, an hour after the scene in the street, another young woman in the neighborhood was beaten, raped and strangled. What should they do?

In "The Bedroom Window," Curtis Hanson's new suspense thriller, Sylvia insists that she do her civic duty, but without compromising her marriage. She persuades Terry to go to the police and, coached by her, give them a description of the man and the details of the struggle.

Isabelle Huppert and Steve Guttenberg star in the Curtis Hanson mystery-thriller "Bedroom Window," about a man accused of murder.

Being on a high generated by this new affair, Terry agrees to Sylvia's plan. However, one thing goes wrong after another, and it isn't long before Terry himself, abandoned by the faint-hearted Sylvia, is the chief suspect in what subsequently becomes a series of murders.

"The Bedroom Window," directed and adapted by Mr. Hanson (from Anne Holden's English novel), begins with what sounds like a terrific idea. The movie itself also starts off with a good deal of expertise.

Mr. Hanson's previous work as a director ("Losin' It") and as writer ("Never Cry Wolf") appears to have taught him a lot about how movies work. Just about all the information the audience needs to know is briskly and efficiently delivered with a minimum of dialogue in that opening sequence.

After that, however, watch out.

•

Mr. Hanson runs out of invention almost immediately. To push this story to the point where Terry, the innocent and good Samaritan, finds himself in serious jeopardy, Mr. Hanson is forced to impose on him several totally absurd decisions that forever cut the audience loose from its commitment to both character and situation.

It's something that Alfred Hitchcock — though he loathed what he called "the plausibles" — would never have allowed to happen. Either Hitchcock wouldn't have given the audience time to question plausibility, or he would have found some way of making the irrational appear, at least for the moment, utterly rational. This is beyond Mr. Hanson.

"The Bedroom Window," which opens today at the Gemini and other theaters, is reminiscent of "Blood Simple," another slick film made by young film makers for whom craft is all, but who don't seem to give a hoot as to what it's all about. The only thing "The Bedroom Window" seems

to be about is movie making — that is, it's about putting pieces of film together to create momentary effects that needn't signify anything at all. Sometimes this is called "pure cinema." Sometimes, in fact, it's pure nonsense.

When the craft is devoted to a plot as brilliantly constructed as Agatha Christie's "Witness for the Prosecution," the effect is exhilarating. Characters take vivid shape from circumstances. However, when reason is permitted to enter, illusion vanishes.

•

In addition to the opening sequence, "The Bedroom Window" has a couple of other moments that define what the rest of the movie should be, but isn't. One is a funny, cannily constructed courtroom scene in which Wallace Shawn, playing a slyly menacing defense attorney, tears Terry Lambert's second-hand testimony to shreds. Most of the time, however, Mr. Hanson either tips us off to the surprises to come, or attempts to create suspense by devices learned in Film Making I, including the car that won't start at a key moment.

One result is that the characters in "The Bedroom Window" are little more than well-dressed wraiths. They're weightless, translucent phantoms who seem to have emerged from the television screen. They're functions of a not-great story. They talk and fight and make love, but they define nothing, represent nothing. They have no past or future. It's significant that the audience never really knows what sort of upwardly mobile job Terry Lambert has.

This kind of movie making puts a terrible burden on the actors. They have to supply their own substance from the personalities they bring to the movie set. Mr. Guttenberg is an attractive performer, but he can't carry something of this order. He's nice and perplexed, and that's about it. Miss Huppert's character is somewhat more interesting but, to make it-

self known, it has to fight its way through her heavily French-accented English, which tends to make every line of dialogue sound the same.

Elizabeth McGovern is even more dimly seen, playing the serial killer's would-be first victim, who eventually becomes Terry Lambert's ally. In the film she's identified only as a cocktail waitress. However, to make the story work a little better, I like to think that, off-screen, she's studying international law at George Washington University. Though she's an excellent actress, Miss McGovern can't easily play a woman with nothing on her mind except overtime and tips.

1987 Ja 16, C6:4

English Melodrama

DEFENSE OF THE REALM, directed by David Drury; written by Martin Stellman; cinematographer, Roger Deakins; music by Richard Harvey; produced by Robin Douet and Lynda Myles; released by Hemdale Releasing Corporation. At Cinema 1, Third Avenue at 60th Street. Running time: 96 minutes. This film is rated PG.
Nick Mullen................................Gabriel Byrne
Nina Beckman ....Greta Scacchi
Vernon Bayliss ....Denholm Elliott
Dennis Markham ....Ian Bannen
Victor Kingsbrook ....Fulton Mackay

"**D**EFENSE OF THE REALM," which opens today at the Cinema 1, is an English melodrama about an ambitious young Fleet Street reporter, a cynical older Fleet Street reporter who drinks too much, the bombing of an embassy in Ankara, Turkey, a prominent Labor Party official who frequents the same London call girl as a diplomat from a Communist country, and a couple of young men who are trying to escape from prison.

It's also about the ruthless tactics of daily journalists and about a giant, apparently Tory-sponsored cover-up conspiracy so complicated that the movie never can adequately explain it, or, at least, explain how the Ankara bombing fits in.

"Defense of the Realm" (a very grand title for such a small movie) was written by Martin Stellman and directed by David Drury, and stars, among others, the usually fine Denholm Elliott as the hard-drinking reporter.

Here Mr. Elliott looks so puzzled and behaves so impatiently that you might think he'd been trying to make sense of the script. It's not a great performance but he's better than anyone else, including Gabriel Byrne, who plays the younger reporter, and Greta Scacchi ("Heat and Dust"), as the secretary to the Labor Party fellow.

The movie is a breathless but largely incomprehensible mess.

•

"Defense of the Realm," which has been rated PG ("Parental Guidance Suggested"), contains some vulgar language.   VINCENT CANBY

1987 Ja 16, C6:5

Busybodies

COMIC MAGAZINE, directed by Yojiro Takita; screenplay (Japanese with English subtitles) by Yuya Uchida and Isao Takagi; photography by Yoichi Shiga; edited by Masatsugi Kanazawa; music by Katsuo Ono; a Zune Keisatsu Production with Kitty Films and New Century Producers.

At Lincoln Plaza 2, Broadway and 63d Street. Running time: 120 minutes. This film has no rating.
With: Yuya Uchida, Yumi Asou, Hiromi Go, Beat Takeshi, Yoshio Harada, Taiji Tonoyama, Masahiro Kuwana, Rikiya Yasuoka, Tsurutaro Kataoka, Daisuke Shima, Kazuyoshi Miura, Pussycat Club.

"Comic Magazine" was shown as part of last year's New Directors/ New Films Series. Following are excerpts from Vincent Canby's review which appeared in The New York Times April 13, 1986. The film opens today at the Lincoln Plaza 2, Broadway and 63d Street.

BEHIND the opening credits, during which we see a man receiving a touch-up haircut, a stern voice on the soundtrack warns that "sex in the theater is strictly forbidden." If it's funny — and it is — it's because the narrator has raised the possibility of sex, which probably wasn't on too many people's minds anyway, only to deny it.

This is also pretty much the method used by the new generation of paparazzi who are the subject of Yojiro Takita's "Comic Magazine" ("Komikku Zasshi"), a nasty, rude, invigoratingly satiric Japanese comedy.

The film's form is picaresque, and its wandering hero is an ambitious, solemn-faced television journalist named Kinameri, played wonderfully well by Yuya Uchida, who also wrote the screenplay (with Isao Takagi).

The film that it most resembles is Federico Fellini's "Dolce Vita," though Kinameri, unlike Marcello Mastroianni's reporter, remains resolutely unsentimental. Kinameri also remains forever outside the events he's covering, most of which, apparently, are based on actual stories that riveted Japanese television viewers two years ago.

•

At one point, the doggedly persistent Kinameri, his portable mike in hand, accompanied by his camera crew, corners in a barroom the notorious Kazuyoshi Miura, the Japanese businessman accused of murdering his wife and implicated in the death of his mistress. Mr. Miura (who plays himself in the film, quite winningly) objects to Kinameri's line of questioning ("Why would you want to kill your wife?" or something similar). He suggests that the reporter is not only impolite but is also ignoring his (Mr. Miura's) basic human rights.

Quick as a flash, Kinameri, whose approach to a story is always frontal, says it's Mr. Miura who's being impolite and who's ignoring Kinameri's basic human rights as well as those of the television audience. Most of Kinameri's interviews are adversarial. During a funeral ceremony, he creeps up on the grieving mother of a murdered child to ask the woman if she knew her daughter was a prostitute.

Kinameri, as played by Mr. Uchida, remains a kind of dour Everyman of the "new" Japanese journalism. His work hours are such that he seldom sees his wife. His average breakfast is a sandwich made up of one folded-over slice of white bread, filled with jam and vitamin pills. Though his heroes are Bob Woodward and Carl Bernstein ("All the President's Men"), Kinameri is serving — more or less willingly — a life sentence devoted to the trivial and, at best, the sensational.

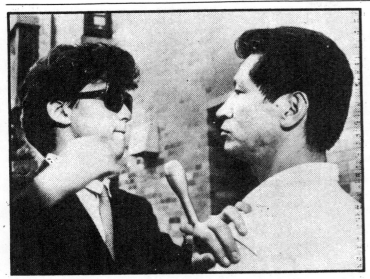

Shima Daisuke and Yuya Uchida, the star and co-writer of "Comic Magazine"—"I consider my movie making an extension of rock 'n' roll."

Mr. Uchida the writer, and Mr. Takita, the director, never attempt to impose an artifical dramatic line on "Comic Magazine." Nor do they impose some kind of supposedly rewarding emotional growth on Kinameri. It's enough that we see the events as they are seen by Kinameri who, though he increasingly longs for the serenity of his own private life, isn't about to give up the second-rank celebrity enjoyed by television journalists.

"Comic Magazine" is a scurrilously funny picture of a technologically advanced society with an insatiable appetite for what's largely irrelevant.

1987 Ja 16, C14:6

Doubtful Prognosis

CRITICAL CONDITION, directed by Michael Apted; screenplay by Denis Hamill and John Hamill; story by Denis Hamill and John Hamill and Alan Swyer; director of photography, Ralf D. Bode; edited by Robert K. Lambert; music by Alan Silvestri; produced by Ted Field and Robert Cort; released by Paramount Pictures. At Loews State, Broadway and 45th Street; Orpheum, 86th Street near Third Avenue; Loews 34th Street Showplace, near Second Avenue, and other theaters. Running time: 90 minutes. This film is rated R.

Eddie/Kevin	Richard Pryor
Rachel	Rachel Ticotin
Louis	Rubén Blades
Stucky	Joe Dallesandro
Maggie	Sylvia Miles
Dr. Foster	Bob Dishy
Chambers	Joe Mantegna
Intern	Bob Saget
Box	Randall (Tex) Cobb
Helicopter Junkie	Garrett Morris

By JANET MASLIN

RICHARD PRYOR impersonates a doctor in "Critical Condition," a frantic mess of a movie that tries to offer a microcosmic view of modern medicine. It takes place in a New York City hospital during a power failure, and has a screenplay by John and Denis Hamill, whose last big idea was about the graffiti-writing Robin Hood of "Turk 182!"

This one is only slightly better, and even the direction by Michael Apted ("28 Up," "Coal Miner's Daughter") lacks its customary incisiveness. No one in "Critical Condition," which

Richard Pryor

opens today at Loews State and other theaters, is working at top form, least of all Mr. Pryor, who looks haggard and agitated much of the time. Still, the film does have an interesting cast and an energetic tempo. And it's good for the occasional laugh, as when, early in the film, Mr. Pryor's fast-talking huckster announces his desire to build a 32-screen cineplex with 18 seats per screen. An earlier project, an "offshore shopping mall," has fallen through.

The potential investors for this scheme turn out to be gangsters, and Mr. Pryor accidentally winds up in jail. Attempting an insanity plea, he tries barking like a dog and finding wildly erotic possibilities in some Rorschach inkblots, but it's no use. Hospital authorities are about to return him to prison when a hurricane intervenes, and he is inadvertently provided with a chance to escape. To do that, he must pretend to be the new doctor in charge of the hospital, and help shepherd the place though a night without electrical power.

•

The screenplay provides for a large assortment of stock characters, but the roles have been imaginatively cast: Rubén Blades as the orderly who becomes Mr. Pryor's sidekick, Bob Dishy as a doctor who worries constantly about malpractice, even

Sylvia Miles in the relatively restrained role of a head nurse. Bob Saget is nicely earnest as the first-year intern who may be the only competent medic on the premises, and Joe Dallesandro, as a mad-dog killer, has a nostalgic opportunity to take his shirt off and snarl. Rachel Ticotin makes a great-looking hospital administrator, and Joe Mantegna fumes comically as her boss. He winds up tied to a chair and used as an oversized Ping-Pong paddle on the psychiatric ward.

Altogether, though, there is too much going on, and not enough mirth or insight to accompany it. And this is the kind of film whose hero can change his luck, reassess his world view and fall in love, all in a single night. Mr. Pryor can handle that well enough, but there are certainly other things he does better.

1987 Ja 16, C16:4

Cultural Cannibalism

WANTED DEAD OR ALIVE, directed by Gary Sherman; written by Michael Patrick Goodman and Brian Taggert and Mr. Sherman; director of photography, Alex Nepomniaschy; edited by Ross Albert; music by Joseph Renzetti; produced by Robert C. Peters; released by New World Pictures. At the National, Broadway and 44th Street; 23d Street West Triplex, between Eighth and Ninth Avenues, and other theaters. Running time: 104 minutes. This film is rated R.

Nick Randall	Rutger Hauer
Malak Al Rahim	Gene Simmons
Philmore Walker	Robert Guillaume
Terry	Mel Harris
Danny Quintz	William Russ
Louise Quintz	Susan McDonald
John Lipton	Jerry Hardin
Patrick Danahy	Hugh Gillin
Dave Henderson	Robert Harper

"WANTED: DEAD OR ALIVE" was a 1958 television series starring Steve McQueen. It has now, in the process of becoming a feature film, lost its colon, and that's not the half of it. Even to those of us who have become more or less used to the cultural cannibalism that passes for inventiveness these days, the film "Wanted Dead or Alive," which opens today at the National and other theaters, will seem outstandingly unnecessary. It's not that the television show was sacrosanct; all it really had to recommend it was Mr. McQueen. It's just that producers wanting to make another latter-day urban "Rambo" should at least be expected to come up with something of their own.

It is mentioned casually in one scene, to the tune of some old-timey harmonica music, that Nick Randall, the new film's hero, is supposed to be the great-grandson of Josh Randall,

Rutger Hauer

the bounty hunter played by Mr. McQueen. Beyond that, and Nick's career as a latter-day bounty hunter who works quietly for the police in Los Angeles, the new film has nothing to do with its supposed predecessor. It involves Nick in the hunt for a wily Arab terrorist named Malak Al Rahim after Malak blows up a Los Angeles movie theater in which more than a hundred men, women and children were at a matinee of "Rambo" itself. There may be those who fail to see this in the calamitous light that is intended.

Nick Randall is played by Rutger Hauer, who will run his career into the ground by taking more such roles. Mr. Hauer, who is Dutch, has improved his American accent to the point where it sounds innocuously flat and seems to be emanating from somewhere other than his body, but in any case there is little for him to say. He is required mostly to shoot and sneer, and he does this in a wearily one-note way. "He's the best there is at a job he hates," say the posters for this film. If he doesn't care, why should we?

"Wanted Dead or Alive" has a dim, grubby look and a mostly anonymous cast, though Gene Simmons makes another stab at super-villainy in the role of Malik. Robert Guillaume appears as an old pal of Nick. When confronted with a blood-smeared locker into which Nick has just poured some buckshot (there was an Arab terrorist inside it at the time), he shakes his head with fond bemusement. Mr. Guillaume is better than the rest of the cast, but he has no more reason to be here than the chance to utter some words that couldn't be said on "Benson," his hit television series.

JANET MASLIN

1987 Ja 16, C17:2

FILM VIEW

Animation Turns For the Worse

They come from two different worlds: she is a serene thoroughbred, he's a street-smart scoundrel with radical ideas. They meet through friends and fall in love, and he does what he can to show her the world. "Aw, come on, kid, start building some memories," he urges. But she wants a stable and conventional life, while he wants freedom to

"Pinocchio" (1940)— "characters that really come alive."

roam. He scorns her fondness for "life on a leash."

Will she be able to compromise? Will he be able to commit? Does it matter that they're only dogs? No, it does not, for "Lady and the Tramp" remains one of Disney's most enduring classics, and one that speaks charmingly and articulately to audiences of all ages. It's a children's film full of recognizable characters and situations, rendered in cleverly anthropomorphic terms that in no way diminish their realism. It's both entertaining and instructive. It's a great deal sweeter than any film for older audiences would dare to be, and yet it never seems saccharine. It presents a world that can be troubling, but also one in which order can be discovered, and it focuses very strongly on the importance of home and family. It is, in short, the kind of children's film they simply don't make any more.

Like it or not, there's only one conclusion to be drawn about the state of the animated children's film: it is in terrible decline. While animation contines to evolve as an ever more sophisticated art form (the recent New American Animation show at the Film Forum, featuring the highly innovative work of Jane Aaron, Robert Breer and Marion Selwood, was particularly encouraging in that regard), children's animation seems to grow less and less creative.

The animation itself has in most cases become much cruder, despite the help of computers, than it was when done painstakingly by hand. Contrast "The Care Bears Movie" (1985) with Disney's "Pinocchio" (1940) and you'll see the difference between characters that blink and bob their heads and characters that really come alive. More important, though, is the shift in content. For every Disney film focusing on a child's need for his parents or on rivalry with a sibling — as a number of them subtly did — today brings the adventure of a tiny warrior, dressed in garish pastels, with a mission to save the galaxy. These films have premises that are as wishy-washy as they are messianic — the avowed mission of the Care Bears is "to help everyone share their feelings with others" — but they are hardly without commercial appeal. What modern child wants to watch a puppet like Pinocchio when he or she can have She-Ra, the Princess of Power?

This Christmas, "An American Tail" provided the latest illustration of how far afield children's animation has gone. Directed by Don Bluth and presented by Steven Spielberg, "An American Tail" certainly represents a technical improvement over much current animation; indeed, its execution is good enough to hold an audience's interest even if the narrative never did. The film's protagonist, Fievel the Mouse, is a lively and spirited little creature. He is, however, seldom either very boyish or very mouselike in his mannerisms, without any of the distinctive personality we have come to associate with cinematic rodents.

In the film, Fievel flees from Russia to America, becomes separated from his parents, makes new friends in the New World, attends a political rally and then embarks on something like a race war, in which the mice of New York plot to drive all cats into the Hudson (and onto a steamer bound for Hong Kong). Eventually, he is reunited with his family, but neither that nor anything else in "An American Tail" has much emotional impact. The style of the film is much too conventionally childish to interest

parents in the audience, and yet the content probably eludes many children. To make matters worse, the mouse campaign against all catdom features big-fanged, red-eyed cats and a torchlight mouse parade toward a haunted-looking structure by the pier. At the Criterion Center, where I saw the film, one child howled piteously throughout the cat-versus-mouse episodes. Of course, children are often scared by animated films and may indeed consider that part of the fun. But the frightening scenes are usually more limited (like the sequence in which boys become donkeys in "Pinocchio"), more markedly exaggerated and more understandable on children's own terms than those in "An American Tail."

How can material like this hold a candle to the Disney animation on which my generation was raised? When I saw "Lady and the Tramp" last week, it was every bit as fresh and bewitching as it had seemed 32 years earlier, during its first release. (It seems highly unlikely that today's children will be looking back as fondly three decades hence on Fievel, let alone He-Man, the Care Bears, My Little Pony or Rainbow Brite.) What's more, it seemed to be an entirely satisfying experience for the adults in the Guild audience, most of whom were there alone. There were only two children in the theater at the show I attended, and they were greatly outnumbered by nostalgic grown-ups.

● ● ●

What makes "Lady and the Tramp" so magical? It is not even generally acknowledged to be one of Disney's very best. Certainly "Pinocchio" has the edge when it comes to the animators' virtuosity, and it's "Dumbo" (1941) that can still move any audience to tears. (Remember lonely little Dumbo's visit to the cage in which his mother is incarcerated, and the loving way she picks him up and cradles him in her trunk?) And of course, for its bravura showmanship and grand ambitions, there is always "Fantasia" (1940), Disney's most conspicuous venture into the realm of the abstract. But the 1955 "Lady and the Tramp," coming well after the studio's early-40's heyday, showcases the homier aspects of the Disney opus, and does so enchantingly.

The quality that most distinguishes the film's chief characters is their sheer dogginess, which is rarer than one might think among cartoon canines. When Lady first appears as a young puppy, she scampers and frolics and refuses to be left alone, in a lifelike and wholly irresistible manner any pet-owner will recognize. She is finally allowed onto her owners' bed "just for tonight," and there is then a witty cut to the full-grown Lady, still sleeping contentedly in exactly the same spot. Her owners, who are so sugary the dog mistakenly thinks their names are "Darling" and "Jim Dear," proclaim Lady to be the very light of their life, a situation that changes drastically once they discover they are expecting a baby.

"Lady and the Tramp" deals with sibling rivalry particularly well: it depicts Lady's resentment at all the love lavished on the new baby, and then lets her reconcile her feelings, embrace the baby and move on to other things. Just when the baby's arrival threatens to destroy her happiness, Lady meets Tramp, a rakish character who's highly critical of Lady's middle-class existence. "I bet they've got a lid on every trash can and a fence around every tree," he says scornfully of the picture-perfect neighborhood where Lady lives. "I wonder what the leash-and-collar set does for excitement." Tramp does what he can to show Lady a more adventurous life, and she does what she can to tame his wandering ways. In the end, the experience seems highly beneficial for both of them.

●

It's true that "Lady and the Tramp" rigidly enforces sexual stereotypes in a manner that's bound to have an influence on children; Lady is so demure, pretty and house-

bound, Tramp so jaunty and free. But that effect is more than balanced by the sheer wealth of imagination on display here. The dog characters are at once so canine and so human; the backgrounds are so ingenious and changeable (in one scene, as Lady recounts the way her owners are neglecting her, the cozy arch of their fireplace becomes the rain-pelted doorway of a doghouse even as she speaks to Jock and Trusty, her long-time admirers). When the Disney animators take the trouble to bring a wolfhound or a goldfish or a pair of witchy Siamese cats to life, they do it with the utmost panache. In "Pinocchio," the animators weren't afraid to let 20 cuckoo clocks go off simultaneously in Gepetto's crowded toy workshop; that particular sequence will always be a marvel. Nowadays, you're lucky if the musclebound He-Man will talk and flex his eyebrows at the same time.

One more difference between the vintage style of children's animation and today's has to do with its palette. There are pastels in "Lady and the Tramp," especially on Lady's human mother and in the flower garden where Lady happily uproots a tulip from time to time. But they are used almost ironically, and as part of a much larger scheme. And the range of colors varies greatly from scene to scene, being both decorative and highly expressive of mood. In Disney's heyday, the visual look of an animated film could be even more ambitious than that, as in the simple, bold landscapes in "Dumbo," which have something of an Expressionist quality.

But today, colors are apt to be either fiercely primary, as in scenes depicting one cosmic battle or another, or sickeningly sweet. The Care Bears, for instance, live in a pastel paradise called Care-A-Lot; they have heart-shaped noses and footpads, and they even blow heart-shaped bubbles. Then there's little Rainbow Brite, whose name says it all. Are moods really this simple, are problems this readily solved, are emotions this easy? Does life afford such limited choices? The great Disney animators didn't think so. Our children shouldn't have to, either. ∎

1987 Ja 18, II:19:1

Sad Sack

THE HOUR OF THE STAR, directed by Suzana Amaral; screenplay (in Portuguese with English subtitles) by Miss Amaral and Alfredo Oroz, based on the novel by Clarice Lispector; cinematography by Edgar Moura; released by Kino International. At Film Forum 1, 57 Watts Street. Running time: 96 minutes. This film has no rating.
Macabéa	Marcelia Cartaxo
Olimpico	José Dumont
Glória	Tâmara Taxman
The Fortuneteller	Fernanda Montenegro
The Boss	Umberto Magnani

By JANET MASLIN

THE heroine of "The Hour of the Star" is a doomed innocent, a young woman so naïve and unworldly that she is first seen wiping her nose on the collar of her blouse. She works as a typist in Rio de Janeiro, living in one cramped room with several roommates. Yet she is so lonely that she likes riding the subway, just for the sake of companionship. Part of what she enjoys on these train rides is the chance to stand next to men, with whom she otherwise has little contact. As a holdover from her sheltered girlhood, she still dresses and undresses under the bedcovers.

A man wearing sunglasses does seem to be staring at her one day as she eats her favorite meal of a hot dog and Coca-Cola. But when he begins walking toward her, she realizes that the sunglasses are no affectation and that the man is blind. Later on, when she does finally find a suitor, he isn't much better: a vain, ignorant metalworker who describes her petulantly as "a hair in my soup" and who will offer to buy her coffee only if she pays for her own milk, in case it costs extra.

"The Hour of the Star," directed by Suzana Amaral, is based on the novella of the same name by Clarice Lispector, the Ukrainian-born writer who spent much of her life in Brazil. The book's heroine, named Macabéa, is the creation of a meddlesome male narrator named Rodrigo S. M., who gives the book its philosophical dimension but also intrudes incorrigibly upon her story (in order to better understand Macabéa, he announces, he will sleep less, dress more shabbily, and give up sex, football and all human contact).

•

This narrator is able to consider Macabéa's plight from a variety of perspectives, analyzing her life even as he invents and describes it. On film, this is more difficult to do, and in any case Miss Amaral barely at-

In Disney's "Lady and the Tramp" (1955), above, "the quality that most distinguishes the chief characters is their sheer dogginess."

Fievel the Mouse, left, the star of "An American Tail" (1986), lacks "any of the distinctive personality we have come to associate with cinematic rodents."

tempts it. So she is left with Macabéa's sketchy story alone. Though its heroine can be captivating in her innocence and melancholy, Miss Amaral's film never regards her from any illuminating perspective. It chooses the easier path of simply pitying Macabéa for her wretchedness and romanticizing her for the same reason.

"The Hour of the Star," which opens today at the Film Forum, de-

tails Macabéa's misery most effectively. Indeed, the film's earliest sections are its most powerful, as they sketch a character whose ignorance is almost too great to be believed and whose aspirations are heartbreaking. As played with extraordinary unselfconsciousness by Marcelia Cartaxo, Macabéa is perpetually red-nosed and as unglamorous as any film heroine has ever been. Indeed, there's a great deal of sophistication to a performance so utterly plain. Without

condescending to the character, Miss Cartaxo can make it credible that Macabéa feels unreasonably passionate about guava preserve and cheese, or that she listens studiously to a radio station to learn random facts, like the period of time it would take a fly traveling in a straight line to circle the planet.

The title refers to Miss Lispector's ironic conception of death as the ultimate starring role and to Macabéa's secret vision of herself as a movie queen ("Did you know that Marilyn Monroe was the color of peaches?" she asks her suitor one day). It also denotes an ending that suffers especially from the absence of a directorial voice and which crystalizes the film's patronizing vision of the person at its center. While Macabéa's humanity might be expected to emerge and blossom under the camera's scrutiny, the reverse actually happens: strange and affecting at first, she becomes more and more of a sad statistic as the film progresses.

Is Macabéa's destiny wholly determined by her poverty and ignorance? Are there really, as Miss Lispector writes, "thousands of girls like this girl from the Northeast to be found in the slums of Rio de Janeiro," girls who "aren't even aware of the fact that they are superfluous and that nobody cares a damn about their existence?" Is Macabéa's story simply "the unremarkable adventures of a girl living in a hostile city" and nothing more? Miss Lispector's book struggles more successfully with these questions. But in Miss Amaral's intriguing and finally frustrating film, Macabéa, for all her uniqueness, is allowed to become the bland embodiment of a socioeconomic stereotype.

1987 Ja 21, C22:1

Jose Dumont and Marcelia Cartaxo in "The Hour of the Star."

SWEET COUNTRY, produced, written and directed by Michael Cacoyannis, based on the novel by Caroline Richards; director of photography, Andreas Bellis; edited by Mr. Cacoyannis and Dinos Katsourides; music by Stavros Xarhakos; released by Cinema Group. At Sutton, Third Avenue at 57th Street. Running time: 150 minutes; This film is rated R.

Anna	Jane Alexander
Ben	John Cullum
Eva	Carole Laure
Paul	Franco Nero
Monica	Joanna Pettet
Juan	Randy Quaid
Mrs. Araya	Irene Papas
Mr. Araya	Jean-Pierre Aumont
Father Venegas	Pierre Vaneck

By VINCENT CANBY

THE suffering of destitute, undernourished, ignorant and despairing peons amounts to nothing when compared to the ghastly emotional distress suffered by those liberal members of the haute bourgeoisie who care deeply about mankind.

This is the astonishing (if unintended) message of Michael Cacoyannis's "Sweet Country," a spongy indictment of the United States-approved military coup that, in 1973, overthrew Chile's legally elected Marxist president, Salvador Allende.

Carole Laure stars in Michael Cacoyannis's "Sweet Country," a drama about the impact of politics on relationships in Chile in the 1970's.

The film, opening today at the Sutton Theater, is set mostly in Chile on the day of — and in the months immediately after — the coup, which it recalls entirely through the delicate sensibilities of a bunch of well-dressed, well-heeled Chileans and Americans.

Mr. Cacoyannis, best-known for his film version of Nikos Kazantzakis's "Zorba the Greek" (1964), not only directed "Sweet Country," but also wrote the screenplay, adapting it from the 1979 novel by Caroline Richards, an American who lived in Chile during and after the Allende administration.

I've not read the novel, but the movie should be about as welcome to Allende supporters as a C.A.R.E. package of fleece-lined mittens in Uganda.

The only representative of the lower orders to appear in "Sweet Country" is a despicable, illiterate, fascist military policeman, played by Randy Quaid in one of Mr. Cacoyannis's many casting coups. Mr. Quaid may have accepted this unlikely role in a noble effort to — as actors say — "stretch" himself.

When, leering at the young woman he intends to rape, Mr. Quaid drawls, "Mah name is Wan" (meaning "Juan"), the sound of talent snapping might be heard all the way from Santiago, Chile, to Houston, Tex.

At the center of the movie is Anna (Jane Alexander), a sweet, as yet politically dozy North American woman. Anna has come to Allende's Chile with her doctor-husband, Ben (John Cullum), with the vague intention of escaping "the crassness, complacency and pace" of life in the States. On the evening of the day of the coup, Anna begins to awaken. She knows that something is wrong. She's so upset that she has to force herself to sip the celebratory champagne being poured by her wealthy fascist neighbors.

Very quickly Ben and especially Anna find themselves up to their necks in the new leftist underground movement, largely through their friendship with the members of a patrician Chilean family who love justice more than life itself. They include

the father (Jean-Pierre Aumont), the mother (Irene Papas) and the two beautiful daughters (Joanna Pettet and Carole Laure).

It isn't long before Anna has become an activist, meeting in a chic couturier's back room with other activists, including a murderous nun. The latter declines to drive the getaway car in an assassination plot by explaining that she thinks someone else would be more suitable, "someone with a less dubious Vatican record than a left-wing nun."

Sex plays a bigger role in this revolution than politics. In addition to Mr. Quaid's lechery, there also are a rape and a couple of meaningful extramarital relationships, including Anna's with a French-Canadian intelligence agent, played by Franco Nero. Miss Laure, who takes off her clothes in virtually every film she makes, disrobes twice in "Sweet Country," each time to dramatize some awful, new, fascist humiliation.

With the exception of Miss Pettet's, all of the performances are terrible, but they only match the material. You don't often hear dialogue of a flat-footedness to equal Mr. Cacoyannis's work here. Lines like "Don't touch me. I'm dirty" (after a rape), or Anna's anguished, "It's all so unreal!" (toward the end), demonstrate a reckless disregard for the funnybone.

If you remember the events of 1973 as they were happening, or even Costa-Gavras's sorrowful, dramatically riveting "State of Seige," you know that this isn't exactly a subject guaranteed to make someone slap his knees in merriment. Yet this is what Mr. Cacoyannis achieves with "Sweet Country," a movie that successfully trivializes everything it means to hold most dear and near.

1987 Ja 23, C6:5

A film review yesterday of "Sweet Country," by Michael Cacoyannis, misidentified a film by Costa-Gavras on the 1973 military coup in Chile that overthrew President Salvador Allende Gossens. The Costa-Gavras film was titled "Missing."

1987 Ja 24, 3:2

The documentary "Package Tour" follows a group of Hungarian Jews on a pilgrimage to the concentration camp where they were sent during World War II.

Hell Remembered

PACKAGE TOUR, a documentary directed by Gyula Gazdag; in Hungarian with English subtitles; director of photography, Elemer Ragalyi. At the Public Theater, 425 Lafayette Street. Running time: 75 minutes. This film has no rating.

By JANET MASLIN

THEY might be at a college reunion, standing by the old brick buildings and walking through the wrought-iron gate, talking about the past. But the gate is infamous, with its sign that reads "Arbeit Macht Frei." And the place is Auschwitz, where many of these elderly Hungarian visitors were once imprisoned. They are now returning politely as tourists, paying heed to the No Smoking sign as they walk through the crematorium. "Package Tour," a simple and very affecting documentary by Gyula Gazdag, is a record of the memories and emotions that this pilgrimage arouses.

"Package Tour," which opens today at the Public Theater, relies on neither newsreel footage nor voiceover narration to summon the past. It is all there in the faces of these visitors, and even in their conversation. "Where were you deported from?" replaces "Where are you from?" as a more or less casual inquiry. The visitors point to the various spots where they remember last seeing friends or loved ones. The voice of a German-speaking tour guide momentarily startles them as they enter the camp. "Most people here already know all this" explains their own young Hungarian-speaking guide, as the German man tries to launch into a description of Auschwitz and its history.

The stories told by these survivors are not substantially different from other stories in other Holocaust documentaries. But the immediacy of their surroundings prompts these people to recall the smaller points, the horrendous yet also mundane details that give their stories especially great impact. One woman, whose injuries flared up 40 years later and prevented her from making the trip, is interviewed at home and describes in grisly detail the circumstances by which she was evaluated by Dr. Josef Mengele, as he decided which prisoners would join work details and which were headed for immediate death. Sent to the latter group, she was saved by a young soldier who let her go back to the original line, and 10 minutes later she found herself before Mengele all over again. He was busy talking, didn't remember her, and sent her to the work group. "The worst 10 minutes of my life," she says.

•

The film's central question, that of why these people have chosen to return, is answered indirectly but eloquently. They are seen placing flowers on memorials, picking flowers, looking for the names of relatives on lists of the dead. Of course, the urge to honor lost friends and relatives is a profound one. But several men in the group also talk about the impact of the Holocaust on organized Judaism, and the ways in which its demoralizing effects linger on.

"Package Tour" attempts to assess the damage. At the end of the film, it is revealed that a young girl taken by her parents on the tour refused to be photographed. She was frightened by what she saw, and did not want her schoolmates to know she was Jewish. Some of the older people in the group, looking back in bewilderment at their own passivity and helplessness, are also re-experiencing their own fears. But most seem to have made the trip not only as mourners but also as survivors, in a spirit of quiet affirmation.

1987 Ja 23, C7:1

A Way Out

THE FRINGE DWELLERS, directed by Bruce Beresford; written by Mr. Beresford and Rhoisin Beresford, based on the novel by Nene Gare; director of photography, Don McAlpine; edited by Tim Wellburn; music by George Dreyfus; produced by Sue Milliken; released by Atlantic Releasing Corporation. At the Baronet, 59th Street and Third Avenue. Running time: 98 minutes. This film is rated PG.

Trilby	Kristina Nehm
Mollie	Justine Saunders
Joe	Bob Maza
Noonah	Kylie Belling
Bartie	Denis Walker
Phil	Ernie Dingo
Charlie	Malcolm Silva
Hannah	Marlene Bell
Audrena	Michelle Torres
Blanchie	Michele Miles

WITH "The Fringe Dwellers," Bruce Beresford, whose American films have been a mixed bag ranging from "Tender Mercies" to "King David," returns to his native Australia to make a small, graceful, low-keyed drama about the lives of contemporary aborigines.

Set in and around the shantytown inhabited by aborigines on the edge of a remote country village, the film is principally about Trilby Comeaway, a pretty, unsmiling young woman who longs to better her life by moving to the big city. As played by Kristina Nehm with impatience alternating with stony reticence, Trilby is something of a heroic character — tough, calculating, relentless and self-aware, ready to do anything to achieve her goals.

She's also a mystery to the other members of her family, who are more inclined to take life as it comes and not to question fate too closely. Trilby's mother, Mollie, an expansive, jolly woman, helps the family finances through her poker skills. Her father, Joe, talks big but hates work. He also has a fondness for booze. Her older sister, Noonah, training to be a nurse, is the most responsible one, while her little brother, Bartie, as unsmiling as Trilby, expresses himself through his precocious drawings.

•

Though nothing in "The Fringe Dwellers" comes as much of a surprise, the film displays the kind of bare-boned intelligence that amounts to respect toward its characters. It never slops over into special pleading. From first to last, the movie maintains an unexpected reserve. This is the result as much of Mr. Beresford's disciplined handling of the actors and of the material, as of the economical screenplay, adapted by the director and his wife, Rhoisin Beresford, from a novel by Nene Gare.

"The Fringe Dwellers," which opens today at the Baronet theater, is also a very sad film. Though it never openly acknowledges the fact — it doesn't have to — the film is never unaware that Trilby's search for equality and assimilation, and the price she pays for them, marks the inevitable, absolute end of an entire culture. Mr. Beresford doesn't weep or show us a lot of picturesque folkways. He simply says this is the way the world is going — take note.

The movie also provides some plum roles for the members of its mostly aboriginal cast. In addition to Miss Nehm, they include Justine Saunders as Mollie, Bob Maza as Joe, Kylie Belling as Noonah and Denis Walker as Bartie. They're all first-rate.

VINCENT CANBY

1987 Ja 23, C13:3

Mother and Child

SCENE OF THE CRIME, directed by André Téchiné; screenplay (in French with English subtitles) by Mr. Téchiné, Pascal Bonitzer and Oliver Assayas; camera, Pascal Marti; edited by Martine Giordano; music by Philippe Sarde; produced by Alain Terzian. At Lincoln Plaza, Broadway at 63d Street. Running time: 90 minutes. This film has no rating.

Lili	Catherine Deneuve
Grandmother	Danielle Darrieux
Martin	Wadeck Stanczak
Thomas	Nicholas Giraudi
Maurice	Victor Lanoux
Grandfather	Jean Bousquet
Alice	Claire Nebout
Father Sorbier	Jacques Nolot

"Scene of the Crime" was shown as part of last year's New York Film Festival. Following are excerpts from Janet Maslin's review, which appeared in The New York Times Sept. 27, 1986. The film opens today at the Lincoln Plaza, Broadway at 63d Street.

ANDRE TECHINE'S elegant thriller "Scene of the Crime" is alive with danger and sexual possibility, in a manner reminiscent of Claude Chabrol. Though its setting is rural, it is never bucolic, not for a moment. The film begins as a young boy takes a bicycle ride, and no sooner has he stopped to pick a flower — a sprig of oleander, which is poisonous — than he is accosted by a stranger. The man has no money, and he orders the boy to get him some and return with it by nightfall. The boy is too frightened not to do as he is told.

From this beginning, Mr. Téchiné sets in motion a suspenseful, and at several points genuinely shocking, series of events. They involve the boy's family life as much as they involve the man in the forest — and, as the drama progresses, they bring these elements irrevocably together. Mr. Téchiné is able to rotate the various elements of the film's psychological puzzle with exceptional poise.

The boy, Thomas (Nicholas Giraudi), lives with his mother (Catherine Deneuve) and grandmother (Danielle Darrieux) in a household where the balance of power is constantly shifting. Thomas's father, Maurice (Victor Lanoux), who is separated from the boy's mother, also lives nearby. It is gradually revealed that the mother, Lili, needed to escape the stifling effects of her union with Maurice, though he continues to want her. Lili now runs a nightclub that is situated on a lake, perched just at the water's edge.

•

"Scene of the Crime," which has been handsomely photographed by Pascal Marti, is essentially about Lili, and about the deepest aspects of her love for her son. It is the occasion for another subtle, superbly controlled performance from Miss Deneuve, who is becoming a more and more resourceful actress as she grows older. Miss Deneuve begins the film with the dulled, dutiful look of a woman whose life holds no surprises, and she dresses in provincial clothing that makes her look as plain as possible (that isn't very plain). But as the film progresses, and her life is thrown into turmoil, she begins to come alive. Through the course of the ordeal she suffers during the story, she takes on a harried, desperate look that actually makes her more beautiful.

Mr. Téchiné's technique is showy, but it works. Whether he is framing an image of mother and son at a window or projecting old family movies onto Lili and Maurice as they grapple or offering quietly startling glimpses of the nightclub by the water, the director makes every shot matter. And if the film is finally slightly less than the sum of its parts, that's only because the parts are so well chosen and so striking.

1987 Ja 23, C14:1

An Era's Voices

RADIO DAYS, directed and written by Woody Allen; director of photography, Carlo Di Palma; edited by Susan E. Morse; produced by Robert Greenhut; released by Orion Pictures corporation. At New York Twin, Second Avenue and 66th Street; 34th Street Showplace, between Second and Third Avenues; 84th Street Six, at Broadway. Running time: 90 minutes. This film is rated PG.

Rocco	Danny Aiello
Biff Baxter	Jeff Daniels
Sally White	Mia Farrow
Joe	Seth Green
Fred	Robert Joy
Mother	Julie Kavner
New Year's singer	Diane Keaton
Irene	Julie Kurnitz
Ceil	Renee Lippin
Rabbi Baumel	Kenneth Mars
Abe	Josh Mostel
"Silver Dollar" emcee	Tony Roberts
Masked Avenger	Wallace Shawn
Father	Michael Tucker
Roger	David Warrilow
Bea	Dianne Wiest
Narrator	Woody Allen
Mrs. Silverman	Belle Berger
Mr. Zipsky	Joel Eidelsberg
Latin band leader	Tito Puente

By VINCENT CANBY

RADIOS once came in two basic models of wooden cabinets. The table-top, sheathed in oak or mahogany veneer, looked like a small, peak-roofed sentry box, with Romanesque or Gothic arches in front of the sometimes gold-flecked fabric masking the speaker.

The table-top radio added a certain tone to any suite of living-room furniture, though certainly not as much as the majestic console, the big, heavy floor-model that was a prized piece of furniture in its own right.

For most of us who were born before World War II — or even during the war's early days — it's sometimes difficult to realize that these extraordinary objects are now antiques, and that the material that poured from their speakers constituted a singular, if short-lived, popular art. We didn't have to *look* at the radio — though we always did — to be swept up by the voice of the unknown diva on "The Major Bowes Amateur Hour," the awful dooms facing "Little Orphan Annie," the arcane knowledge possessed by contestants on "Name That Tune," the adventures of "The Lone Ranger," or the gaiety of the annual New Year's Eve festivities at the Roosevelt Hotel, presided over by Guy Lombardo. We didn't see a wooden cabinet, often scratched and scuffed, its speaker-fabric punctured by children who'd wanted to discover what was going on inside.

Instead we saw a limitless universe, created entirely out of voices, music and sound effects that liberated each mind in direct relation to the quality of its imagination. When Uncle Bob (or Ted or Ray) promised to send a shooting star over the house to mark a young-listener's birthday, the young listener, who had hung out the window for an hour without seeing the star, questioned not Uncle Bob (or Ted or Ray), but his own eyesight.

What's sometimes referred to as the golden age of radio — roughly from the mid-30's through the mid-40's — holds a privileged position in the memories of most of us who grew up with it. Radio wasn't outside our lives. It coincided with — and helped to shape — our childhood and adolescence. As we slogged toward maturity, it also grew up and turned into television, leaving behind, like dead skin, transistorized talk-radio and nonstop music shows.

It's this brief and, in hindsight, enchanted period that Woody Allen remembers in his most buoyant, comic and poignantly expressed of memoirs, titled, with his unflagging, poetic exactitude, "Radio Days."

"Radio Days," which opens today at the New York Twin and other theaters, is as free in form as it is generous of spirit. It's a chronicle of a family during the radio years, as well as a series of short-short stories. These follow, one after another, like the tales of Scheherazade, if Scheherazade had been a red-headed little Jewish boy in the Rockaways, born poor, star-struck, infinitely curious, and seriously incompetent as a juvenile criminal.

The little boy, Joe (Seth Green), whose recollected thoughts are spoken on the soundtrack by Mr. Allen, is so happily lost in the world of radio that he scarcely notices the Depression around him. He has "Breakfast With Irene and Roger," who hobnob with the rich and famous (and talk about it the next morning), and he knows the true, inside story of Sally White (Mia Farrow), of "Sally White and Her Great White Way," who's radio's most glamorous Broadway gossip columnist. He enjoys the intense arguments about the stars: "He's a ventriloquist on radio. How do you know he doesn't move his lips?"

The boy's first loyalty is to the Masked Avenger (Wallace Shawn), a Green Hornet-sort of radio vigilante who, at the moment of triumph, says heartily, "It's off to jail for you! I hope you enjoy making license plates!"

To buy the Masked Avenger's "secret-compartment ring," Joe helps himself to donations intended for the "Jewish Homeland Fund." This leads to a good deal of physical stress in a confrontation with his parents and his rabbi, who compete with each other for the right of beating the boy senseless (in the middle of which Joe solemnly addresses the rabbi as "My faithful Indian companion").

Joe is, indeed, surrounded by stress and aggravation, from morning to night. "Turn off the radio," screams his mother (Julie Kavner). "Why should I?" says the boy. "*You* listen to it." "That's different," she says. "Our lives are ruined anyway." Radio is Joe's Camelot.

Never has Mr. Allen been so steadily in control, as "Radio Days" slides from low blackout sketch to high satire to family drama that's as funny as it is moving.

One of the film's many performances-without-price is Dianne Wiest's as Joe's ever-hopeful, unmarried Aunt Bea, who's attracted to the wrong men mostly because they're the only ones available. On a foggy night, while parked at Breezy Point, a particularly promising suitor hysterically abandons Bea when he hears the news that the Martians have landed in New Jersey.

•

"Radio Days" is so densely packed with vivid detail of place, time, music, event and character that it's virtually impossible to take them all in in one sitting. Carlo Di Palma is again responsible for the stunning photography, and Santo Loquasto for the production design.

Among the memorable presences who fill the screen there are old Mrs. Silverman, who has a fatal heart attack — her teacup halfway to her lips — after watching a white woman kiss a black man, and gentle Mr. Zipsky who, without warning, has a breakdown and takes a meat cleaver to his neighbors. Also: genial Uncle Abe (Josh Mostel), who goes next door to complain to the radical neighbors, playing their radio on the high holy days, and returns several hours later as a confirmed Marxist.

The members of the huge cast are uniformly splendid. Many, like Tony Roberts, Danny Aiello and Jeff Daniels, are familiar from earlier Allen films, while others, like David Warrilow and Tito Puente, are new.

The film is nothing if not generous with — and to — its talent. Miss Farrow is hilariously common-sensical as the ambitious cigarette girl ("*Who is Pearl Harbor?*" she asks in bewilderment on Dec. 7, 1941), and Diane Keaton, on the screen only a few minutes, helps to bring the film to its magical conclusion with a lovely, absolutely straight rendition of "You'd Be So Nice to Come Home to." It's New Year's Eve, 1943, and Mr. Allen's radio days are as numbered as those of Proust's old Prince de Guermantes.

"Those voices," says the narrator by way of a benediction, "grow dimmer and dimmer."

At this point I can't think of any film maker of Mr. Allen's generation with whom he can be compared, certainly no one at work in American movies today. As the writer, director and star (even when he doesn't actually appear) of his films, Mr. Allen works more like a novelist who's able to pursue his own obsessions, fantasies and concerns without improvements imposed on him by committees.

At this point, too, his films can be seen as part of a rare continuum. Each of us has his favorite Allen movie, but to cite one over another as "more important," "bigger," "smaller" or "less significant" is to miss the joys of the entire body of work that is now taking shape. "Radio Days" is a joyful addition.

Mr. Allen, our most prodigal cinema resource, moves on.

"Radio Days," which has been rated PG ("Parental Guidance Suggested"), includes some mildly vulgar language and double-entendres.

1987 Ja 30, C1:1

Slinks and Arrows

OUTRAGEOUS FORTUNE, directed by Arthur Hiller; written by Leslie Dixon; director of photography, David M. Walsh; edited by Tom Rolf; music by Alan Silvestri; produced by Ted Field and Robert W.

Mia Farrow, Tony Roberts, Dianne Wiest and Danny Aiello (from left) are part of the large cast in Woody Allen's new film, "Radio Days," which opens today.

Brian Hamill

Cort; released by Touchstone Pictures. At Ziegfeld, Avenue of the Americas at 54th Street; Coronet, Third Avenue and 59th Street; 23d Street West Triplex, between Eighth and Ninth Avenues; Bay Cinema, Second Avenue at 32d Street. Running time: 92 minutes. This film is rated R.

Sandy	Bette Midler
Lauren	Shelley Long
Michael	Peter Coyote
Stanislov Korzenowski	Robert Prosky
Atkins	John Schuck
Frank	George Carlin
Weldon	Anthony Heald

By JANET MASLIN

IF Redford and Newman were chasing their man and had tracked him to a little shack somewhere, would they stop to check their makeup before breaking down the door? Probably not — and certainly not with the delicious aplomb shown by Shelley Long and Bette Midler in "Outrageous Fortune," which opens today at the Ziegfeld and other theaters. Since "Outrageous Fortune" is a buddy film starring two women, and since it is sure to be a hit, it will undoubtedly prompt speculation that two-women buddy films are now the genre to beat. Maybe so — but that's not why this one works. It works because Miss Midler and Miss Long are hilarious, both separately and together.

Another thing that works is Leslie Dixon's screenplay, which has energy, wit and a supreme confidence that's just this side of bluster. Miss Dixon's story starts small and spirals higher and higher, reveling in each unlikely new turn of fate. In terms of implausibility, the events in "Outrageous Fortune" rate about a 12 on a scale of 10, but that's part of the fun. So are the screenplay's cattiness and its feminism, which are cheerfully relaxed. It's the latter that generates the terrific title, which would go nicely with plenty of adventure films but in this case signifies both wild goings-on and one heroine's desire to play Hamlet.

That's the wish of Lauren, a straight-backed, high-minded aspiring actress played by Miss Long as a variant of her "Cheers" character on television. Miss Long, who hasn't before found a film vehicle to suit her nearly so well, does this bluestocking role to perfection, and grates horribly against Miss Midler, who is at her own raucous best as Sandy, another would-be actress of a decidedly less sophisticated stripe. They meet in the class of a renowned acting teacher, a class for which Lauren has had to wheedle money from her parents, who are afraid to let her into their apartment building for just this reason. (She winds up having to ask for money through the intercom at the front door.) Sandy has no plans to take the class, but she does so just to annoy Lauren. She winds up with a scholarship, too.

To further guarantee that these two will take a resounding dislike to each other, Miss Dixon's screenplay involves them with the same man, a schoolteacher (played by Peter Coyote) who seems much too good to be true. And is. Once the man disappears — under circumstances that are as suspicious as circumstances get — they reluctantly embark upon a merry chase. From a New York tenement to a mesa in New Mexico, and into the clutches of both the C.I.A. and the K.G.B., the two of them bound from adventure to adventure, cementing their friendship along the way.

Chase films as antic as this have a way of wearing out their welcome.

Shelley Long and Bette Midler on the run in the comedy "Outrageous Fortune."

But "Outrageous Fortune" consists of one good setup after another, and it turns out to be much more than the sum of its parts. As directed by Arthur Hiller, it has a light tone, a steady pace and an enjoyable professionalism that help take the edge off the material's occasional lapses. For instance, there's an autopsy-room scene that might have been toned down, not because it's graphic but because it's stupidly rude. And there's no excuse for letting the heroines throw heaps of money to distract their pursuers even one time, let alone twice.

What helps to hold the film together is the kind of humor that grows out of the characters themselves, not merely from the situations in which they find themselves. Miss Midler has flawless phrasing and timing when it comes to delivering just about any vulgarity, and she can get laughs simply by walking across a room. But her best gag here has to do with an apartment that's perfectly in keeping with the woman she plays. As for Miss Long, her priggishness is most delightful when it falls apart, as in a scene that has her impersonating a police officer and trying to convince a couple of thugs that she's holding a gun on them. Her change of attitude is a hard act to follow, but Miss Midler keeps up her end of things by marching up to these confused captives and frisking them.

"Outrageous Fortune" also has the two leads' actressy aspects to keep it going. Though not as knowing as "Tootsie" about the life of the none-too-successful actor, it lets Lauren, Sandy and the audience enjoy the spectacle of two tyros using what they learned in school. In one scene, a person they're attempting to fool with fake middle-European accents actually commends them for their energy, if not for their talent. And Miss Dixon, after introducing the acting-school aspect of the story, actually remembers to keep using it, creating a consistency that's not half as commonplace as it might seem. Just when the film has finally and inevitably degenerated into chase scenes, she's able to pull one last trick out of her hat.

"Outrageous Fortune" is light entertainment, and in this case that's a compliment. It's lighter than air.

1987 Ja 30, C5:1

Sad Smile

MES PETITES AMOUREUSES, written and directed by Jean Eustache; in French with English subtitles; director of photography, Nestor Almendros; edited by Françoise Belleville, Alberto Yaccelini and Vincent Cottrell; music by Theodore Botrel; produced by Pierre Cottrell. At the Public Theater, 425 Lafayette Street. Running time: 110 minutes. This film has no rating.

Mother	Ingrid Caven
Daniel	Martin Loeb
Girl	Jacqueline Dufranne
Client	Maurice Pialat
José	Dionys Mascolo
Boss	Pierre Edelman

IN many ways "Mes Petites Amoureuses," Jean Eustache's 1974 French film opening today at the Public, looks as if it had been meant to answer anyone who'd been less than enchanted by the director's "Mother and the Whore," one of the more antagonizing films presented at the 1973 New York Film Festival.

"The Mother and the Whore" is a long (3 hours and 35 minutes), humorless contemplation of the relations between men and women as primarily revealed in extended exchanges of pithy, aphoristic dialogue spoken by Jean-Pierre Léaud, Bernadette Lafont and Françoise Lebrun. "Mes Petites Amoureuses" is something else — a short (less than two hours), almost taciturn film that wears a smile (though a sad one) behind the impassive expression of Daniel, its adolescent hero.

Daniel, played by Martin Loeb with stern diffidence, is a slightly younger first cousin to François Truffaut's Antoine Doinel. He's the way Antoine might have been when Antoine was somewhere between "The 400 Blows" and "Love at 20." Daniel isn't exactly unwanted, but he's nobody's principal concern. He's also a vast reservoir of unexpressed feelings.

He spends his time being shuttled between a Paris suburb, where he lives with his loving but preoccupied grandmother, and a small town in

Martin Loeb, at center, stars in the French drama "Mes Petites Amoureuses," about an adolescent boy's discovery of sex.

southwestern France, where he shares a tiny apartment with his mother and her Spanish lover. Traveling from one home to the other, Daniel carries a small suitcase that looks as if it were made of cardboard and contained only a change of socks.

•

"Mes Petites Amoureuses" would initially seem to owe an unconscionable amount of its inspiration to the Truffaut films. Daniel's mother (Ingrid Caven) behaves decently as long as Daniel doesn't make demands that come between her and her lover, who in turn, isn't unkind to the boy, but neither is he especially interested in him.

Though Daniel loves school and its camaraderie, his economically pressed mother doesn't hesitate to force him to get a job instead. Like Antoine Doinel, Daniel is obsessed by sex, and much of "Mes Petites Amoureuses" is devoted to his confused responses to girls, including one wordless (though quite successful) encounter in a movie theater.

As were so many films of the 60's and early 70's, "Mes Petites Amoureuses" is studded with movie references. Like "Stolen Kisses," it even opens with the voice of Charles Trenet singing a romantic ballad on the soundtrack.

However, Mr. Eustache's narrative method is quite different from Truffaut's in the Doinel cycle. It more closely resembles the Truffaut of "Small Change." "Mes Petites Amoureuses" alternates between being anecdotal and simply a record of the observations of a very special sensibility. It's less like a piece of finished fiction than a series of terse, precisely worded entries in a notebook.

This is both the style of the film and its charm. Mr. Eustache, who was widely respected in France, made one more feature, "Une Sale Histoire" (1978), and four shorts before his death in 1981 at the age of 43.

VINCENT CANBY

1987 Ja 30, C16:1

OPERA DO MALANDRO, directed by Ruy Guerra; screenplay (Portuguese with English subtitles) by Chico Buarque, Orlando Senna and Mr. Guerra, based on the play "Opera do Malandro" by Mr. Buarque; director of photography, Antonio Luis Mendes; edited by Mair Tavares, Ide Lacreta and Kenout Peltier; play dialogue, music and lyrics by Mr. Buarque; produced by Marin Karmitz and Mr. Guerra and M. K.2 Productions-France-Austra Brazil, T. F. 1 Films Productions France and Ministère de la Culture; released by the Samuel Goldwyn Company. At Cinema Studio 1, Broadway and 66th Street. Running time: 105 minutes. This film has no rating.

Max	Edson Celulari
Lu	Claudia Ohana
Margot	Elba Ramalho
Tigrao	Ney Latorraca
Otto Strudell	Fabio Sabag
Geni	J. C. Violla
Satiro Bilhar	Wilson Grey
Victoria Strudell	Maria Silvia
Fiorella	Claudia Gimenez
Fichinha	Andrela Dantas
Doris Pelanca	Ilva Nino
Dorinha Tubao	Zenaide

"Opera do Malandro" was shown as part of last year's New York Film Festival under the title "Malandro." Following are excerpts from Janet Maslin's review, which appeared in The New York Times Sept. 27, 1986. The film opens today at the Cinema Studio I, Broadway and 66th Street.

Ney Latorraca and Edson Celulari appear in the Brazilian musical "Opera do Malandro," set among the nightclubs and bordellos of Rio de Janeiro in 1941.

SHE'S dressed like the schoolgirl Gigi, but she's singing a samba. The group of white-suited hoodlums is supposed to be dancing in formation, but each moves in a slightly different direction. The gangster hero delivers one of his longer musical soliloquies in a men's room, sashaying past the row of urinals. No doubt about it: if the Brazilian film "Malandro" has the look of a 40's big-studio musical, it's also got more than a few idiosyncrasies.

"Malandro" was directed by Ruy Guerra, who demonstrates more admiration for vintage Hollywood than rhythm in his blood. Set in Rio at the time of Pearl Harbor, his film intermingles gangsters, bar girls, a Nazi sympathizer named Otto Strudell and a hero called Max Overseas in a suitably flimsy but elaborate plot, which also throws Max together with Otto's beautiful daughter.

•

The film's looks, which ought to be everything, aren't particularly handsome or even trim. But at least Mr. Guerra's homage — the film specifically invokes "Scarface" and "Casablanca," and there are dozens of visual allusions — is more good-humored than slavish. In keeping with the Latin score, the players always seem more languid than the fiery passions that the lyrics describe. The editing and choreography are sufficiently at odds with the music to make this a nice try rather than pure enchantment, but it is never less than amiable. And it does have an earthy, fun-loving, distinctly Brazilian personality of its own.

1987 Ja 30, C6:5

ALLAN QUATERMAIN AND THE LOST CITY OF GOLD, directed by Gary Nelson; screenplay by Gene Quintano, based on the novel by H. Rider Haggard; director of photography, Alex Phillips; edited by Gary Griffen and Dan Loewenthal; music by Michael Linn; produced by Menahem Golan and Yoram Globus; released by the Cannon Group Inc. At the Warner Twin, Broadway at 47th Street; the Manhattan Twin, Third Avenue at 59th Street; the 86th Street Twin, at Lexington Avenue. Running time: 103 minutes. This film is rated PG.

Allan Quatermain	Richard Chamberlain
Jesse Huston	Sharon Stone
Umslopogaas	James Earl Jones
Agon	Henry Silva
Swarma	Robert Donner
Nasta	Doghmi Larbi
Nyleptha	Aileen Marson
Sorais	Cassandra Peterson
Robeson Quatermain	Martin Rabbett
Dumont	Rory Kilalea

By JANET MASLIN

The credits for "Allan Quatermain and the Lost City of Gold," from the never-bashful Cannon Films, tell us that the film is "based on H. Rider Haggard's best-selling classic novel." That's sweet, but it isn't entirely accurate, since the new film is really based on Steven Spielberg's Indiana Jones sagas. Even the music is as similar as is legally possible. And while this second Quatermain film, in what is rather wishfully intended as a series, hasn't got much to recom-

Richard Chamberlain and Sharon Stone search for a missing man in the African wilderness in Gary Nelson's "Alan Quatermain and the Lost City of Gold," a sequel to the 1985 "King Solomon's Mines"

mend it, it's of minor academic interest. Those who take the Spielberg special effects for granted are sure to learn a lot by watching these same tricks done badly.

So when the floor parts to reveal a booby trap in "Allan Quatermain," which happens repeatedly, the floor wobbles like the plywood that it probably is. When the *earth* parts, it looks more like plywood covered with straw. And when the spears shoot out of the ground to signal *another* of the endless array of traps, someone beneath the set has a devil of a time retracting them smoothly. Even the trained snakes aren't quite as professional here.

•

Fortunately, Richard Chamberlain is professional and then some, since the film would otherwise be virtually unwatchable. As the title character, he wears a hat with leopard trim and says things like, "I've seen some amazing things in my life, but never *anything* to compare with this!"

•

The cast also includes James Earl Jones and Sharon Stone as two of Quatermain's sidekicks and Robert Donner as a third, a turban-wearing Indian who is repeatedly made fun of for his cowardice. Martin Rabbett plays Mr. Chamberlain's younger brother and looks a good deal like him. The film was shot in Zimbabwe and features a large horde of spear-

carrying extras; otherwise, most expenses were spared. The Lost City of Gold itself looks like a movie producer's very new, very large and very unattractive villa. "Allan Quartermain and the Lost City of Gold," which was directed by Gary Nelson, may be slightly under-exposed throughout. If not, then the Warner Twin, one of the theaters where the film opened yesterday, needs a new bulb in its projector.

●

"Allan Quartermain and the Lost City of Gold" is rated PG ("Parental Guidance Suggested"). It contains some scantily clad starlets and some violence.

1987 Ja 31, 14:5

FILM VIEW

JANET MASLIN

Woody Allen Savors the Details

There's a moment of pure happiness in Woody Allen's new "Radio Days" in which the narrator's Cousin Ruthie appears with a towel on her head, doing a little dance. Though not the Latin fireball type — Cousin Ruthie ordinarily wears white anklets and spends time gossiping with her mother about the neighbors — she has done what she can with this improvised turban and some junk jewelry. With a smile of tremendous satisfaction, she is prancing and swaying to Carmen Miranda's "South American Way" and lip-synching the song perfectly. And when two of Ruthie's male relatives wander into this scene and see what she's doing, they understand. In the same spirit of delight *they* begin lip-synching, delivering the "Ai-yi's" right on cue.

The scene is wonderful not just for Ruthie's dancing but for what it illustrates so viscerally about popular art's ability to brighten lives. Mr. Allen has touched on this many times before, most notably in "The Purple Rose of Cairo," but in "Radio Days" he gives it his full attention. In "Radio Days," which is set between the late 30's and 1944, the radio is heard constantly and its influence is everywhere. It affects everything, from the outcome of a date to the aftermath of a robbery. In one scene, it even makes a palpable difference in the way a father feels about his child.

Mr. Allen has always made a point of defining his characters in esthetic and intellectual terms as well as dramatic ones. Particularly in his films from "Annie Hall" onward, he has taken care to let audiences know not just what characters do but also what they see and hear and read. These details have an indelible effect: will anyone forget that Annie Hall and Alvy Singer were waiting to see "The Sorrow and the Pity" at the Beekman when they got into the argument about (and including) Marshall McLuhan? Or that Isaac, the television writer Mr. Allen played in "Manhattan," counted Flaubert's "Sentimental Education" and the second movement of Mozart's Jupiter Symphony — not to mention Groucho Marx and Willie Mays — among his reasons for living?

Mr. Allen's references to art, ideas and pop cultural artifacts aren't always this conspicuous. Indeed, they grow less and less so as he becomes more amazingly assured with each new film. It happens, in "Hannah and Her Sisters," that Mia Farrow is seen reading Richard Yates's "Easter Parade," a novel about two sisters and their life-long rivalry, but Mr. Allen does nothing to call attention to that detail; it is simply there. Nor is it necessary to know that the Gershwin songs in "Manhattan" comment so aptly on the action ("Someone to Watch Over Me" for the night when Isaac finds himself falling for the abrasive intellectual played by Diane Keaton, "But Not for Me" in his final encounter with the schoolgirl Tracy) to sense their profound effect on the film's mood.

It can be argued that this is little more than cultural name-dropping, in keeping with the comfortable, tasteful settings in which Mr. Allen's affluent characters often live; he has sometimes been accused of creating Yuppie porn. But Mr. Allen clearly has at least as much enthusiasm for low art as for high, and the lower the better: spotlight-ing a balloon sculptor, a dressed parrot and a blind xylophone player, as Mr. Allen did in "Broadway Danny Rose," is surely the act of a genuine aficionado. Even when Mr. Allen's taste for pop cultural anomalies seems cruel, as it sometimes does in that film, it is redeemed by the obvious sincerity of his affection. Are "Mairzy Doats" and "Tico Tico," both of which turn up in "Radio Days," great songs? Maybe not, but there's something deliriously silly about them, something capable of generating the most innocent sort of joy. "Radio Days" is a jubilant yet graceful salute to that innocence.

Like "Brighton Beach Memoirs," "Radio Days" is set in Brooklyn during World War II, and the domestic scenes in the two films have some slight similarity (though Mr. Allen's film, with its ravishing cinematography and outstandingly witty costume and production design, is by far the better looking). It may well be that "Brighton Beach Memoirs" uses period radio broadcasts in its soundtrack, but if so, they aren't memorable in the slightest. But in "Radio Days," the large extended family of the nameless boy narrator (Mr. Allen's voice is heard on the soundtrack) cares passionately about what it hears. Everyone has a favorite show: Uncle Abe (Josh Mostel) loves the crazy sports stories ("He had one leg and one arm, but more than that he had *heart*..."), while his wife Ceil, admires a certain ventriloquist ("How do you know he's not movin' his lips?" Uncle Abe wants to know). And the young narrator adores a swashbuckling hero called the Masked Avenger. This is radio, so the Masked Avenger is played by — who else? — Wallace Shawn.

If the people in the film define themselves somewhat by their radio favorites, they also can't help but note the contrast between the real world and the one they hear about. "I suppose you woulda been happier married to Rita Hayworth?" asks Aunt Ceil, who's lying in bed eating chocolates with her hair in curlers at the time. And Uncle Abe doesn't exactly have an answer. Over the breakfast dishes in Rockaway, the narrator's mother listens to a couple of swells named Roger and Irene, who dine in their Manhattan townhouse while recounting the previous night's round of parties, dropping names like "Moss" and "Cole."

Unlike Cecilia, the movie fan played by Mia Farrow in "The Purple Rose of Cairo," this mother (played by Julie Kavner) doesn't reflect moonily that "the people were so beautiful — they spoke so beautifully and they did such romantic things!" She's bemused but not starstruck, being too busy to enjoy the luxury of such intoxicating reveries. "Radio Days" gives as much weight to the real world as to the imagined one, and that's why it is able to be so funny, never turning sad. In this film, Mr. Allen's characters don't experience as a reproach the exaggerated glories celebrated by pop culture. They view them with an amusement that heightens their daily lives. And the only wistfulness that colors the film is the narrator's regret that these lovely daydreams are a thing of the past.

●

Even the film's rare tragic notes have a hopeful quality, thanks to radio's power to stir the emotions. As the narrator's father listens to the live news accounts of a disaster involving a small child, he stops in mid-spanking to embrace his own son. Hours later, in his and many other households and public places, listeners are seen silently following the story and remembering how much they care for their own loved ones.

And the story of the narrator's marriage-minded Aunt Bea, who is

Brian Hamill

Dianne Wiest and Robert Joy in "Radio Days"

played with such sweetness and intelligence by Dianne Wiest, is also somehow inspirational, in spite of Bea's many radio-related disappointments. (Her look of dejection and then acceptance with one suitor, when the radio plays his dead fiancé's favorite songs, makes for one of the film's finest moments.) When all else fails, Bea finds reason to rejoice in something as simple as forming an impromptu conga line with her sisters around the dining room table. Even now, the narrator remains deeply grateful to her for such revelations as "The Donkey Serenade." (Dick Hyman, the musical supervisor responsible for several dozen extremely well-chosen songs plus a very hummable laxative jingle, is — with no pun intended — one of the film's unsung heroes.)

Mr. Allen embraces these memories of a more ingenuous popular culture in an uncommonly wholehearted way. Even a shot of young girls' saddle shoes, swaying at a soda fountain to the music of a romantic boy crooner, can be extraordinarily expressive, and the narrator's first view of the Radio City Music Hall is so lovingly depicted that it becomes a moment of pure rapture (Frank Sinatra is heard singing, and "The Philadelphia Story" is on the screen). On one of the film's most beautiful sets, a nightclub roof in Times Square surrounded by fabulous pop artifacts made of neon, the film's group of radio swells gather on New Year's Eve, to welcome in 1944 (back home, the narrator's family is bringing in the New Year with Hoffman's soda). The radio stars contemplate the fleetingness of their fame, and "the truth is, with the passing of each New Year's Eve, those voices do seem to grow dimmer and dimmer," Mr. Allen says. But that hardly seems true. His "Radio Days" is a tribute that revives them, understands both their triviality and their value, and insures they will be heard for a long time to come. ■

1987 F 1, II:21:1

Not 'Fake Modest'

FILMING OTHELLO, directed by Orson Welles; camera, Gary Graver; edited by Marty Roth; music by Francesco Lavagnino and Alberto Barbaris; produced by Klaus Hellwig and Juergen Hellwig. At Film Forum 1, 57 Watts Street. Running time: 90 minutes. This film has no rating. WITH: Mr. Welles, Micheal LacLiammoir, Hilton Edwards.

By VINCENT CANBY

THROUGHOUT his lifetime, Orson Welles seems to have ached to be as resoundingly immodest as he deserved to be without feeling guilty about it.

Micheal (sometimes spelled Michael) MacLiammoir, who played Iago to Welles's Othello in Welles's classic 1952 film adaptation, once wrote of Welles: "He knew that he was precisely what he himself would have been if God had consulted him on the subject at his birth. He fully appreciated and approved of what had been bestowed and realized that he couldn't have done the job better himself; in fact, he would not have changed a single item."

The word modesty, or one of its variants, seems to have cropped up a lot in Welles's conversations toward the end of his life. It's there on the

book jacket of Barbara Leaming's 1985 biography, "Orson Welles," in which the subject urges the writer to make herself a character in the biography. "I think it's a wonderful way to do a biography," she quotes him as saying, "particularly because you are telling, excuse the expression, a rather dense story. I can be frank with you without sounding fake modest, but you're talking about — alas — some kind of legend."

•

In "Filming Othello," his entertaining and revealing 1978 film memoir opening today at the Film Forum, Welles, standing in the corner of a studio, greets the audience with a few remarks about Shakespeare's play, which is, he notes, "something more than a masterpiece." In fact, it's a work of such magnitude that he can only ask with humility, "Where does that leave a mere movie maker?"

A few moments later, he asks, "Is my movie good or bad?" He says he really doesn't know. Again, he doesn't want to sound "fake modest," but since the film is still being shown after 30 years, he assumes "it still has some life in it." He then goes on to quote some mostly very ecstatic comments on the film.

This was ever one of the more charming aspects of Welles in such appearances. Con artist and raconteur, magician and movie master, he always managed to call attention to his genius by apologizing for somehow being thrust into a position (against his will) in which even to deny genius was to acknowledge it. There is much of this in "Filming Othello," and it's all part of the rather dense portrait of the man that emerges from the 90-minute film, directed, of course, by the man himself.

•

Commissioned for West German television, "Filming Othello" was to have been the first in a projected series in which Welles would discuss his individual films and how they came to be what they are. He never got to the second in the series, which was to have been about "The Trial," but "Filming Othello" is so good it makes one long for more. Not more of the same, exactly, for Welles wouldn't have repeated himself with film. Having worked his way through his charm with "Filming Othello," he would, I suspect, have moved on to a different kind of consideration of "The Trial."

This isn't to say that "Filming Othello" is only charm. It's a fascinating collage made up of various things, including some re-edited footage from the magnificent opening sequence of "Othello." More or less at the center of the memoir is a luncheon reunion at which Welles, a sometimes brilliantly funny Mr. MacLiammoir and a patiently funny Hilton Edwards, who played Brabantio in "Othello," discuss the play, Coleridge, the film, Dostoyevsky, Lord Olivier, Dante and envy as opposed to jealousy, which Welles, ever-ready with an aphorism, calls "the seasickness of passion."

As time touches memory and reorders facts, Welles, the editor of his life as well as of film, inserts into this luncheon footage some shots of himself, photographed later but seemingly at the same luncheon, making comments that give the discussion more point than it might have had otherwise. The screen is "a dead thing," Welles says on another occasion. One has to work to make it exciting enough to grab the mind and the imagination, which is what he's doing here much of the time.

"Filming Othello" is full of priceless anecdotes, some of which Welles has told before in a slightly different form, about the problems that had to be solved during the approximately four years it took to make his movie. Money was always running out, and actors were sent home. When the film, which had initially been conceived as an Italian-French co-production, finally arrived at the 1952 Cannes Film Festival (where it shared the grand prize), it was officially Moroccan, which presented problems to festival functionaries responsible for finding the score for the Moroccan national anthem.

There also are clips from Welles's 1977 appearance before a Boston audience of young film aficionados, as he answers questions about "Othello." He's in marvelous shape and thoroughly enjoying himself. During this encounter, he says he wishes he weren't looking back but forward to "Othello."

"Promises," he says, "are much more fun than explanations."

At the end of this rich recollection, one walks out of the theater eager to see "Othello" again. However, as is so often the way with movies above a certain age, Welles's "Othello" is not currently available. For unreported reasons, it is, in the picturesque language of lawyers, "tied up."

1987 F 4, C24:3

Mating Rituals

BLACK WIDOW, directed by Bob Rafelson; written by Ronald Bass; director of photography, Conrad L. Hall; edited by John Bloom; music by Michael Small; produced by Harold Schneider; released by 20th Century-Fox Film Corporation. At Criterion Center, Broadway between 44th and 45th Streets; Sutton, 57th Street at Third Avenue; 34th Street East, near Second Avenue; 23d Street West Triplex, between Eighth and Ninth Avenues; Embassy 72d Street, at Broadway. Running time: 100 minutes. This film is rated R.

Alexandra	Debra Winger
Catharine	Theresa Russell
Paul	Sami Frey
Ben	Dennis Hopper
William Macauley	Nicol Williamson
Bruce	Terry O'Quinn
Sara	Lois Smith
Michael	D. W. Moffett
Ricci	Leo Rossi
Shelley	Mary Woronov
Irene	Rutanya Alda
Shin	James Hong
Etta	Diane Ladd
Herb	David Mamet

By VINCENT CANBY

BOB RAFELSON'S "Black Widow," with its good, flashy star-performances by Debra Winger and Theresa Russell, comes on with the seductiveness of an expensive perfume that inevitably evaporates before the night is over.

However, though it promises more than it can ever deliver, this classy-looking melodrama is soothing, in the way that luxe can be, as well as redeemingly funny, in part, at least, for not becoming mired in its own darker possibilities.

"Black Widow," which opens today at the Sutton and other theaters, is about the curious relationship between Alexandra (Miss Winger), a lonely, self-deprecating woman who works as an investigator for the Justice Department, and Catharine (Miss Russell), a beautiful, utterly confident young woman who marries rich, older men, loves them briefly and then kills them (without pain) for their money.

Ronald Bass, who wrote the screen-

play, and Mr. Rafelson, the director, set up this initial situation with wit and skill. They cross-cut between scenes from Catharine's first two happy marriages and those in which Alexandra, everybody's pal (and nobody's sweetheart), sits in her grimly functional Washington office, sorting through statistics on her computer terminal. Alex longs for excitement. Catharine makes her own.

•

Alex's antennae go up when, in less than a year, she comes upon two cases of death attributed to a phenomenon known as Ondine's curse — perfectly healthy men of late middle age drop dead of heart failure. The failures of the heart aren't what interest Alex as much as the coincidence that both men were exceedingly wealthy and married to much younger women.

Even that might not be cause for alarm in real life but, in a movie such as this, Ondine's curse is said to be such a rare occurrence that Alex is prompted to look further. In each instance, she finds, the widow grieved long enough for the estate to be settled, turned all of its assets into cash and then, pulling herself together, took the money and ran.

•

Alex traces Catharine to Seattle. Having been the pampered sex kitten of a toy tycoon (now dead) in Dallas, and the elegant, socially acceptable wife of a New York publisher (now dead), Catharine has changed identities yet again. She's now sharing her concern for the preservation of American Indian cultures with her new husband, a mild-mannered philanthropist, played with very comic understatement (and a perfect American accent) by Nicol Williamson.

Still later the trail leads to Hawaii where, at last, Alex and Catharine come face to face with each other and with a rude, possibly crazy private detective (James Hong, a hilariously unorthodox scene stealer). Alex also meets Catharine's latest fiancé, a rich, sad-eyed Frenchman (Sami Frey), who wants to build a resort hotel on the trembling edge of an active volcano where to spend one night would loosen the tusks of an elephant, to say nothing of the molars of tourists.

•

In no time at all, each woman is aware of the other's identity, though neither appears willing to act on that knowledge. For several weeks, Alex and Catharine live in a dangerously steamy stasis that has nothing much to do with their so-called real lives. It's time out for both of them. They share clothes, confidences (carefully edited) and even a man. The possibility of a sexual attraction is there, but more urgent is the glimpse each gives the other of another existence.

It's one of the film's most decent surprises that their mutual attraction is comprehensible, which is as much due to the particular screen presences of the two actresses as to the material and the direction.

Miss Winger possesses the gift of seeming always to have hidden reserves of feeling that might erupt in chaos at any minute. Even here, playing what is essentially another variation on her "Legal Eagles" role of ambitious career woman, she manages to suggest a life of order being lived at risk.

Miss Russell comes into her own in "Black Widow" after a number of

Debra Winger

Theresa Russell

Roddy McDowall

films ("The Last Tycoon," "Straight Time" and "Insignificance," among others), in which her fine performances were neutralized either by those of other actors or by the murkiness of the material. Mr. Rafelson gives her the opportunity to be a film's alluring (Kathleen Turner-like) center, and she makes the most of it. She's an unusual-looking actress. With her small, thin-lipped cat-mouth, turned down at the edges, she at first suggests the sort of pouty sexiness that France made a movie requisite some years ago.

Yet Miss Russell also has a clear-eyed sweetness that adds unexpected dimension to the homicidal Catharine. The film is stuffed with good performances by other actors (some of whom are on and off before you know it), including Dennis Hopper, Lois Smith, Mary Woronov, Diane Ladd and David Mamet, the playwright.

"Black Widow" demands credulity before it's absolutely necessary, and it grinds to a slow if desperate resolution, but it has some other important things going for it that make it very easy to take.

1987 F 6, C3:1

Chills and Shivers

DEAD OF WINTER, directed by Arthur Penn; written by Marc Shmuger and Mark Malone; director of photography, Jan Weincke; film editor, Rick Shaine; music by Richard Einhorn; produced by John Bloomgarden and Mr. Shmuger; released by M-G-M Entertainment Company. At Paramount, Broadway and 61st Street; Tower East, Third Avenue and 71st Street, and other theaters. Running time: 108 minutes. This film is rated R.
Julie Rose/Katie McGovern/Evelyn .... Mary Steenburgen
Mr. Murray .... Roddy McDowall
Dr. Joseph Lewis .... Jan Rubes
Rob Sweeney .... William Russ
Officer Mullavy .... Ken Pogue
Officer Huntley .... Wayne Robson
Roland McGovern .... Mark Malone

By JANET MASLIN

THE star plays three women, one of them mostly dead. The setting is a huge, isolated mansion filled with unnerving decorating touches, like the polar bear in the parlor. The town is the kind of place where they give you free goldfish when you buy gas, and nobody thinks that's peculiar. And the villain likes to tell eerie little stories about President McKinley, which are lies. When a director approaches Gothic horror with this much enthusiasm, the results are bound to be as merry as they are frightening. So audiences for Arthur Penn's "Dead of Winter" are in for a hair-raising treat.

Mr. Penn reportedly was asked to take over the direction of this film in midstream, a couple of weeks after shooting began; it had previously been the project of the co-writer and co-producer Marc Shmuger, a friend of Mr. Penn's son. Whatever its genesis, "Dead of Winter" has been made with a steady hand. The screenplay is inelegant but lively, and the direction gives the material a wicked edge. When Roddy McDowall, as an extremely solicitous villain, heads up a staircase with a glass of milk on a silver tray, even non-Hitchcock fans will see some humor in the situation.

"Dead of Winter," which opens today at Loews Tower East and other theaters, isn't campy or self-mocking; it's a lot more clever than that. It begins with the attention-getting device of sending a mysterious woman into an isolated train station on New Year's Eve to retrieve a money-filled briefcase — too full to close, a nice touch — from a locker. She returns edgily to her car, and Mr. Penn gives the audience its first little frisson with some New Year's Eve noise-makers. That's just a warm-up for the real shock, since the woman is promptly murdered and her corpse maimed, in a suitably picturesque way.

The film next moves to New York, where an aspiring actress named Katie McGovern (Mary Steenburgen) is ready to answer a casting call. The advertisement solicits a "leading lady type, must be willing to travel." Katie is told she may just land the part if she follows the very polite Mr. Murray (Mr. McDowall) upstate for a video screen test, though neither this nor anything else about Mr. Murray arouses her suspicions. She joins him for a ride to the much-too-secluded home of the wheelchair-bound Dr. Joseph Lewis (Jan Rubes), a psychiatrist-producer. Psychiatrist-producer? Like all good, dutiful horror heroines, Katie doesn't question this or anything else until she finds that Murray and the doctor, the mansion's only other occupants, have stolen her driver's license and thrown it onto a roaring fire.

●

Well, it goes on. And on. And it is kept moving by Mr. Penn's prowling, mischievous camera and Miss Steenburgen's delightfully sporting approach to the horror that surrounds her. Miss Steenburgen, suitably mysterious in the opening scenes and then spunkily energetic as the ever-hopeful Katie, winds up playing a number of scenes with herself and doing it exceptionally well. It is always possible to tell which of three different women she is from the look on her face rather than her clothing — which is a good thing, since the clothing becomes deceptive after a while. The triple-role device is carried to a thoroughly enjoyable wild extreme.

As a too-polite duo, Mr. McDowall and Mr. Rubes come close to "My Dear"-ing Miss Steenburgen to death before attempting other methods; there's one particularly nice moment in which they greet her video screen test with a creepy little round of applause. Thanks to the obligatory heavy sedatives, severed phone wires, secret doorways (Mr. Penn gets a great shot while introducing one of these) and moving corpses, the cat-and-mouse game is kept going for a long time.

The material is never credible, nor does it pretend to be; that's part of the fun. Anyone who could locate a missing person using clues like two goldfish and a covered bridge is working well outside the bounds of normal mystery lore.

1987 F 6, C4:3

Mary Steenburgen portrays an aspiring actress caught between two blackmailers in "Dead of Winter."

Rock as Life

LIGHT OF DAY, written and directed by Paul Schrader; director of photography, John Bailey; film editor, Jacqueline Cambas; music by Thomas Newman; produced by Rob Cohen and Keith Barish; released by Taft Entertainment Pictures. At National, Broadway and 44th Street; Gemini Twin, 64th Street and Second Avenue; 84th Street Sixplex, at Broadway; 86th Street Twin, at Lexington Avenue; Movieland Eighth Street, at University Place, and other theaters. Running time: 107 minutes. This film is rated PG-13.
Joe Rasnick ....Michael J. Fox
Jeanette Rasnick ....Gena Rowlands
Patti Rasnick .... Joan Jett
Bu Montgomery .... Michael McKean
Smittie .... Thomas G. Waites
Cindy Montgomery .... Cherry Jones
Gene Bodine .... Michael Dolan
Billy Tettore .... Paul J. Harkins
Benji Rasnick .... Billy Sullivan
Benjamin Rasnick .... Jason Miller

THERE'S a make-or-break moment in Paul Schrader's "Light of Day" in which Joan Jett, the hard-rock singer-guitarist who plays a similar type of musician in the film, announces, "I've been tryin' to live my life by an idea!" Part of the audience is sure to find this ridiculous — and not without reason, since the character she plays is an unmarried, unfit mother who spends most of her time in high-decibel dives. But another part will understand what both Miss Jett and the film are getting at. The idea of which she speaks is rock-and-roll at its most raw, rock-and-roll in its purest form.

"Light of Day," which opens today at the RKO National Twin and other theaters, is Mr. Schrader's attempt to place a gritty, unglamorous rock saga in a grassroots setting. It employs not a single rock-video editing trick, which is very much to Mr. Schrader's credit. And it has a good feeling for the club scene in which Miss Jett, playing Patti Rasnick, and Michael J. Fox, as her younger brother, Joe, try to make a living with their struggling band. What it doesn't have is any genuine forward movement. The rock story, which is intriguing but aimless, is later grafted onto the tale of family problems that provides the film with its melodramatic conclusion. Otherwise, it would have nowhere to go.

As in "Blue Collar" and "Hardcore," Mr. Schrader shows himself capable of launching the action in a powerhouse style. Once again, that forcefulness deteriorates as the film progresses. As "Light of Day" introduces Joe and Patti and places them in a Cleveland working-class setting,

Joan Jett and Michael J. Fox portray sister and brother rock musicians in "Light of Day."

Mr. Schrader initially displays a toughness and realism that will hold any audience's attention; the film's clear, strong visual style and its night-and-day contrasts further heighten its impact. These things only heighten the disappointment when "Light of Day" runs out of steam.

•

"Light of Day" pits Joe and Patti, who live together with Patti's 4-year-old son, Benji (Billy Sullivan), against their parents, their employers and the world in general. By day, Joe works in a metal-pressing plant making Charles and Diana commemorative trays (they're Andy and Fergie trays by the time the film is over), while Patti tries more free-form work, like petty theft. As the film opens, they pay a visit to the pious, proper mother (Gena Rowlands) who's entirely incapable of communicating with them, and the weakling father (Jason Miller) whom neither of them respects. This visit is disastrous enough to show why they prefer the comfort of their own more squalid surroundings.

Their band, the Barbusters (which also includes the wisecracking Michael McKean and a couple of others), will travel anywhere and work for almost nothing, just for the chance to play. The film follows the Barbusters on the road for a while, then reaches a key juncture when Joe, Patti, Patti's son and her boyfriend of the moment go to the supermarket. Patti takes some steaks and slips them into her son's clothing, encouraging the boy to help her steal. Joe sees this happen. But he doesn't try to interfere immediately. And when he does register his objection, he does it in a roundabout way. Mr. Fox is very appealing here, and makes it clear that he will be well suited to dramatic roles when the right ones come along. But his performance here is limited by the screenplay, which keeps Joe a relatively passive character, still under his sister's childhood spell.

Miss Jett is good too, snapping her way angrily through confrontational scenes and musical ones alike, and taking a sentimental turn just when the story does. And Miss Rowlands is genuine and affecting, though it's never exactly believable that she is Joe and Patti's mother. Mr. Schrader's screenplay greatly favors the younger characters, giving their parents a bad case of the Middle American blahs. Mother watches "Donahue," and quotes him at the dinner table. Dad says: "We got a good life, me and her. We don't talk much, we don't go out much, but I can't complain."

Bruce Springsteen wrote the rousing title song and reportedly took the phrase "Born in the U.S.A." from an earlier draft of Mr. Schrader's screenplay. It's possible, even from the finished film, to see what he and Mr. Schrader might share. One of the monologues included on Mr. Springsteen's recent live album describes his boyhood dream of becoming a rock-and-roller and proving something to his family, to himself, to the world; those ambitions are described in terms of musical triumph, not money or fame. "Light of Day" wants to embody a similar dream, but it pulls its punches. Mr. Schrader may have started out to make a film about the fiercest, most incorruptible stirrings of young talent. But he wound up making a soap opera along the way.

•

"Light of Day" is rated PG-13 ("Special Parental Guidance Suggested for Those Younger Than 13"). It contains some strong language.
JANET MASLIN

1987 F 6, C4:3

Voodoo Odyssey

AMULET OF OGUM, directed by Nelson Pereira dos Santos; written (Portuguese with English subtitles) by Mr. dos Santos, based on a story by Francisco Santos; cinematography by Helio Silva; film editors, Severino Dada and Paulo Pessoa; music by Jards Macale; produced by Regina Films. At Public Theater, 425 Lafayette Street. Running time: 117 minutes. This film has no rating.
Gabriel	Ney Sant'Anna
Severiano	Jofre Soares
Eneida	Annecy Rocha
Dr. Barauna	Emmanuel Cavalcanti
Blind Singer	Jards Macale
Gabriel's mother	Maria Ribeiro
Francisco Santos	José Marinho

"AMULET OF OGUM," opening a limited run today at the Public Theater, is the sort of folkloric though sophisticated film that was so beloved by members of Brazil's "new cinema" in the late 1950's and 60's.

The film's director, one of the founders of Cinema Novo, is the highly regarded Nelson Pereira dos Santos, best known in this country for his poetic "Vidas Sêcas" ("Barren Lives," 1963) and, more recently, for "How Tasty Was My Little Frenchman" (1971) and "Memoirs of Prison" (1984).

Mixing Christian and voodoo beliefs, "Amulet of Ogum" is a fable of death and resurrection about a poor boy from Brazil's poverty-stricken northeast at loose in the underworld of Rio de Janeiro. Having been confirmed in the rites of Ogum, Gabriel, played by Ney Sant'Anna (the director's son), exists in a state of grace, having what's called "a closed body" that protects him from physical harm.

Gabriel quickly catches the attention of the gang boss. The boy is young, handsome, none too bright but singularly bulletproof. Though he's a successful hit man, he remains innocent until, at last, he attempts to strike out on his own.

•

Gabriel's peculiar odyssey — which takes him from innocence to sin to salvation — is as much a musical as a religious journey, the film being scored, from beginning to end, with folk music and Brazilian versions of more ordinary pop material. "Amulet of Ogum" is at its best when it's most delirious with sound and visual imagery. Shooting on a modest budget, Mr. dos Santos has made every cruzeiro count. However, the film's symbolism may escape audiences who don't share its frame of references.

"Amulet of Ogum," made in 1975, is performed in appropriately florid style by just about everyone except young Ney Sant'Anna, who keeps a heroic cool about him, which is fitting for a figure of such import.
VINCENT CANBY

1987 F 6, C4:3

COME AND SEE, directed by Elem Klimov; screenplay (Russian with English subtitles) by Mr. Klimov and Ales Adamovich, based on "The Story of Khatyn" and other war stories by Mr. Adamovich; director of photography, Aleksei Rodionov; music by Oleg Yanchenko; production companies, Belarusfilm and Mosfilm Studios. At Bleecker Street Cinema, 144 Bleecker Street. Running time: 142 minutes. This film has no rating.
Florya Gaishun	Aleksei Kravchenko
Glasha	Olga Mironova

By WALTER GOODMAN

THE terrible central event of "Come and See," which takes up about a quarter of the 2-hour, 22-minute Soviet movie now at the Bleecker Street Cinema, is the burning of a Byelorussian village by German invaders in 1943. A line on the screen tells us that hundreds of villages in the Soviet republic east of Poland were destroyed, their people annihilated. The history is harrowing and the presentation is graphic; you feel it through your body as villagers are packed into a barn to be incinerated.

Powerful material, powerfully rendered by the director and co-writer Elem Klimov, yet the scene goes on for so long with such heavy-handed intrusions that you are left with a feeling of being worked on — which means the effects have stopped working. So it is with the movie as a whole, which won a grand prize at the 1985 Moscow international film festival.

In episodes that shift, sometimes subtly, sometimes startlingly, from down-in-the-mud realism to a dreamlike state, a boy named Florya endures the German invasion. His family is slaughtered; a friend, a beautiful young woman who wants only love and babies, is raped; he joins the partisans, is captured and nearly killed. He is our witness to the savagery of the Nazi onslaught against the peoples of Eastern Europe. But it becomes evident early on that young Florya, played by a grimacing Aleksei Kravchenko, serves Mr. Klimov mainly as a body through which he can display his directorial powers.

The inherent conflict between the director and the character with whom the audience is expected to identify becomes most troubling in a climactic scene that is poundingly effective taken by itself but makes no sense at all from Florya's point of view. We are asked to believe he has a vision of Hitler's career, running backward in time, from the German invasion to Adolf as babe in arms. You don't have to be unduly literal minded to realize as the newsreels are driving in reverse that this is not the vision of a peasant lad who hasn't been to the movies much. It's a moviemaker's tour de force.

•

Olga Mironova and Alexei Kravchenko appear in Elem Klimov's "Come and See," a Russian drama set during the Nazi invasion of Byelorussia.

After years of running into troubles with his country's film authorities, Mr. Klimov was elected president of the Soviet Film Makers Union last May, a beneficiary of Mikhail S. Gorbachev's experiment in glasnost, or openness. Possibly the unorthodox style of "Come and See" would bother some cultural commissar, but there is little in its content to offend the authorized Soviet view of World War II. The partisans are comradely; the Germans are pulp villains, sadistic, cowardly, fanatic. "Inferior races spread the microbe of Communism," declares one whose particular mission is to kill Russian infants. Not only does an SS officer drag a woman by her hair on the way to her fate worse than death but he also pauses to light a cigarette. Mr. Klimov can't leave bad enough alone.

The ending is a dose of instant inspirationalism. The camera makes its way through the forest to the accompaniment of a choir that soars and soars until we get a glimpse of the heavens, not the most original moment in the movie. Yet scene for scene, Mr. Klimov proves a master of a sort of unreal realism that seeks to get at events terrible beyond comprehension. He shows what he can do particularly after Florya has been deafened by bombs and we seem to be inside the boy's head, with the sounds of the outside world overwhelmed by his panting breaths; everything turns distant and ominous. Ominous enough without Mr. Klimov's intrusions, at the expense of his own unquestionable talent.

1987 F 6, C4:4

War's Postmortem

THE ASSAULT, directed and produced by Fons Rademakers; screenplay (Dutch with English subtitles) by Gerard Soeteman, based on the novel by Harry Mulisch; director of photography, Theo van de Sande; edited by Kees Linthorst; music by Jurriaan Andriessen; released by the Cannon Group Inc. At Cinema 1, Third Avenue at 60th Street. Running time: 149 minutes. This film is rated PG.
Anton Steenwijk ....Derek de Lint
Anton, as a boy ....Marc van Uchelen
Truus Coster/Saskia de Graaff
                      Monique van de Ven
Cor Takes ....John Kraaykamp
Fake Ploeg ....Huub van der Lubbe
Mrs. Beumer ....Elly Weller
Karin Korteweg ....Ina van der Molen
Father Steenwijk ....Frans Vorstman
Mother Steenwijk ....Edda Barends
Peter Steenwijk ....Caspar de Boer
Mr. Korteweg ....Wim de Haas
Karin, as a young girl ... Hiske van der Linden

By JANET MASLIN

IT is an ordinary day in the Netherlands during January 1945, or a day as ordinary as an occupied nation can know. The Steenwijk family, having pulled down its blackout shades and had its paltry dinner, is at the end of a reasonably peaceful evening. Then shots are heard. A well-known and hated collaborator has been assassinated in front of the house next door, and his body has been moved to the Steenwijk's, who will now be held responsible for the crime. Seconds later, Nazi troopers are heard. Father Steenwijk remains seated at the table, his head bowed, as they break down the door.

"The Assault," which opens today at Cinema 1, follows the subsequent life of Anton Steenwijk, who as a boy of about 12 years old witnessed this horror. His mother, father and brother were executed, and their house burnt to the ground. Anton himself was treated with unaccountable kindness, relatively speaking. He was given hot chocolate and a warm uniform by his captors, and eventually placed with relatives in Amsterdam. And on the night of the killings he was detained overnight in a dark cell with a woman saboteur who makes a lasting impression. She warns him never to forget what happened to his parents, or why.

The rest of Fons Rademakers's 2½-hour film constitutes an earnest postmortem, sketched by a slow and heavy hand. As a grown man, Anton (Derek de Lint) returns to the scene of the crime and talks to his former neighbors. He has a heated confrontation with the collaborator's son. He marries twice, once to a woman who greatly resembles the jailed Resistance fighter (and is in fact played by the same actress, Monique van de Ven). He talks to every remaining participant in the events of that terrible night, and does what he can to make sense of the crime.

•

Mr. Rademakers, who also directed "Max Havelaar," attempts to integrate Anton's experience with the world events of his lifetime. So Anton's encounter with the collaborator's son is set against the backdrop of a 1956 anti-Communist rally, and a 1966 episode in his life is introduced by newsreel footage of Vietnam. When Anton finally reaches a moment of acceptance and understanding, it happens to him at an antinuclear rally, at which both his children coincidentally happen to be present. But these scenes give the film a symmetry that is largely unearned, since it is otherwise somewhat choppy and narrow. Not even the personal drama of Anton's hardship has much real impact.

Mr. de Lint is a handsome actor with a pained, serious expression that never changes. He isn't able to make the film's later sections as compelling as the outrage with which it opens, and neither is Mr. Rademakers. Crammed as it is with detail, and fixed as it is on Anton's history, "The Assault" still remains unfocused. Mr. Rademakers seems unwilling to come to a strong conclusion, or even a distinct one, and that vagueness is reflected throughout the film.

And the voice-over narrator who keeps the audience apprised of Anton's deductive process is no help. He also announces, with much the same solemnity and in the same newsy you-are-there style, that "in Lucca, Tuscany, he buys a summer house" and that "like an autumn leaf, despair flutters inside him."

"The Assault" is rated PG ("Parental Guidance Suggested"). It contains some violent episodes.
            JANET MASLIN

1987 F 6, C8:1

Low Aim

FROM THE HIP, directed by Bob Clark; screenplay by David E. Kelley and Mr. Clark, story by Mr. Kelley; director of photography, Dante Spinotti; edited by Stan Cole; music by Paul Zaza; produced by René Dupont and Mr. Clark; released by De Laurentiis Entertainment Group. U.A. Twin, Broadway and 49th Street; Manhattan Twin, Third Avenue at 59th Street. Running time: 112 minutes. This film is rated PG.
Robin Weathers .... Judd Nelson
Jo Ann .... Elizabeth Perkins
Douglas Benoit ....John Hurt
Craig Duncan .... Darren McGavin

Judd Nelson, Richard Zobel and Ray Walston star in Bob Clark's "From the Hip," about a young lawyer seeking professional stardom.

Larry ....Dan Monahan
Steve Hadley ....David Alan Grier
Roberta Winnaker ....Nancy Marchand
Phil Ames ....Allan Arbus
Raymond Torkenson ....Edward Winter
Matt Cowens ....Richard Zobel

"FROM THE HIP" goes out of joint in its first couple of minutes, when Judd Nelson pours ice-cold water over his attractive bedmate (Elizabeth Perkins) in order to get her out of bed and to work on time. In another 20 minutes, cold water has been poured on credibility by the yells, insults and prancings of Mr. Nelson, who is supposed to be a super-smart young lawyer. Instead of getting him ejected posthaste from the courtroom and his classy Boston law firm, the antics bring him success.

Unlawyerlike outrageousness is the joke in Bob Clark's one-joke comedy, which starts today at the U.A. Twin and other theaters. Mr. Nelson plays Robin (Stormy) Weathers, one year out of law school and determined to make a name for himself by hook or crook: "I'm about to compromise my values, I think." This fellow is supposed to be pushy yet likable, obnoxious yet charming. Under the assault-and-battery direction of Mr. Clark, Mr. Nelson manages half the job.

Whatever the audience may think, the other characters in the movie find Stormy a riot. The spectators at his trials, including the high-paid partners in his law firm who evidently have nothing better to do, cheer his nonsensical speeches to the jury. It's a laugh-and-applause claque. Clear the courtroom!

•

As the script would have it, Stormy gets himself assigned to a seemingly unwinnable case, defending an arrogant professor ("a cross between Charles Manson and William Buckley") who is charged with having murdered a prostitute; the evidence is all against him. John Hurt plays the professor with saturnine scorn, overcoming the polysyllabic language he must utter, Hollywood's notion perhaps of how intellectuals talk. Even he, however, can't conceal the hoariness of the climax.

Unfortunately, most of the screen time is devoted to Mr. Nelson, alternating between cockiness and conscience, the voice of which is the pretty Miss Perkins: "Just go out there and be a good guy." Their scenes together will remind you of other forgettable movies. "I love you," says she. "I know, it keeps me going," says he. Hold them for contempt of audience.

"From the Hip" is rated PG ("Parental Guidance Suggested"), owing mainly to the profanity the hero uses in the courtroom.
            WALTER GOODMAN

1987 F 6, C10:4

Bare Bones

ONE WOMAN OR TWO, directed by Daniel Vigne; screenplay (French with English subtitles) by Mr. Vigne and Elisabeth Rappeneau; director of photography, Carlo Varini; edited by Marie-Josèphe Yoyotte; music by Kevin Mulligan, Evert Verhees and Toots Thielemans; a Hachette Première/Philippe Dussard S.A.R.L./FR3 Films/D.D. Productions Production. At the Paris, Fifth Avenue and 58th Street. Running time: 97 minutes. This film is rated PG-13.
Julien Chayssac ....Gérard Depardieu
Jessica Fitzgerald ....Sigourney Weaver
Mrs. Heffner ....Dr. Ruth Westheimer
Pierre Carrière ....Michel Aumont
Constance ....Zabou
Gino ....Jean-Pierre Bisson
Alex ....Yann Babilée
The Mayor .... Maurice Barrier
Patrick .... Robert Blumenfeld
Maxwell .... Michael Goldman

HARD as it is to believe, the brilliant director of "The Return of Martin Guerre" has now made an idiotic comedy about a paleontologist, some women and some bones. The bones, being silent, have a definite advantage over the other players.

Daniel Vigne's "One Woman or Two," which opens today at the Paris, turns out to be a "Bringing Up Baby" of sorts for the indefatigable Gérard Depardieu. He's an actor who can do almost anything, but he can't turn himself into a Gallic Cary Grant. Mr. Depardieu plays a daffy scientist who discovers a two-million-year-old woman and dubs her "the first Frenchwoman," saying things like "feel the femininity of her cute little skull?" He falls halfway in love with this elusive creature and dubs her "Laura," thus making needless reference to a film much better than this one.

When the scientist enthusiastically builds a life-sized, 4-foot, 8-inch clay likeness of Laura and begins whispering sweet nothings to it, the statue looks alarmingly like Dr. Ruth Westheimer, who is herself in the film. She plays a daffy American philanthropist with an interest in paleontology, and when she meets Laura, she falls to her knees and exclaims, "My God, thank you for this prrrezious moment!" Dr. Ruth will never be mistaken for an actress, but she does have pep.

•

Also on hand is Sigourney Weaver, as a disdainful American advertising executive who speaks finishing-school French and seems to begin most sentences with "Je déteste." Miss Weaver looks very chic and behaves very standoffishly, though the film seems intended as a happy-go-lucky farce.

Aside from serving as the scientist's love interest, she is on hand as a focus for the anti-American attitudes with which the film abounds. Miss Weaver's character plans crassly to use Laura as a marketing gimmick to

sell a perfume called "French Lady." Her boss in New York, intended as an even more archetypical Yank, has an office decorated with a Superman likeness and a gold lamé E. T. He speaks loudly and wears plaid pants. "Here in the U.S., everything is dollars and cents," someone confides to the scientist when he finally visits New York and witnesses a French Lady rock video in the making.

There are occasional hints that Mr. Vigne may have had something more substantial in mind, like letting Laura's story cast some light on the

present. But for the most part, any hints of intelligence are as buried as the first Frenchwoman herself is when the story begins.

•

"One Woman or Two" is rated PG-13 ("Special Parental Guidance Suggested for Those Younger Than 13"). It contains brief nudity and some sexual innuendoes.

JANET MASLIN

1987 F 6, C18:1

FILM VIEW

VINCENT CANBY

In the Dark, It's Reality That Woos the Audience

In the opening sequence of Sidney Lumet's "Morning After," Alex Sternbergen (Jane Fonda) a once-promising, still-beautiful, former Hollywood starlet, awakens with a terrible hangover, sharing a bed with a man she doesn't know, who has a kitchen knife stuck in his chest. What will she do or, for that matter, what *should* she do? There's no point in summoning the paramedics — even Dr. DeBakey couldn't help this one. The man is dead.

It's an attention-grabbing way to start a movie. If Alex doesn't immediately call the cops, which would be the sensible way to behave (and would, of course, end the movie right there), she'd better have a bloody good excuse or the audience will turn away from her.

We may not have learned much from movies but, having sat through many earlier "Morning Afters," we do know that a lot of muddle (and film time) can be avoided by making a clean breast to the police of even the most embarrassing facts.

• • •

Audiences tend to assume an adversarial role in relation to films. As much as we want to be fooled, we don't want to be fooled at the expense of whatever common sense we possess. We must be coaxed, courted and seduced into abandoning our connection to the world outside the theater. We give up this connection with reluctance, always temporarily, and as soon as we spot something arbitrary or phony, we use it as an excuse to flee the cracked reality of the fiction.

This is probably because, whether we admit it or not, the grasp we have on our own lives is already fugitive enough. We can't afford to waste energy justifying the carelessness and disorder in the lives of others. Though each of us has a different threshold of disbelief, there's always a point — possibly just around the next bend of the story — at which we might simply say, "Enough."

Alex Sternbergen does *not* call the police. She's repelled by the sight of the blood she's been sleeping next to, but she seems to be equally interested in the high-tech décor of the unfamiliar loft apartment in which she finds herself. She manages to dress without getting the blood from her hands onto her clothes. She pours herself a healthy drink to settle her nerves, and then washes her hands. She makes one phone call (to the husband from whom she's amicably estranged) and leaves, only to return some hours later to clean up her fingerprints and the mess in general.

Demonstrating a sense of humor that later becomes clearly manifest, Mr. Lumet and James Hicks, who wrote the "Morning After" screenplay, take a big risk by challenging the audience's credulity so early in the film. The average movie that aims to tell a whopper is more discreet. If it slips into implausibility later on, it's usually out of desperation. Yet the risk taken by Mr. Lumet and Mr. Hicks pays off.

The explanation for Alex's reluctance to go to the police isn't great, but it's serviceable: she's an alcoholic with a long history of blackout spells. She has a record of sorts with the Los Angeles Police Department (for having once been booked for assault with a deadly weapon), and she thinks that she just might have stabbed the guy.

Even more important to the eventual success of "The

Morning After" are the effortlessly funny performances by Miss Fonda and Jeff Bridges, as a redneck ex-cop who befriends Alex Sternbergen, the hip look of the film and sharpish tone of screenplay. As plots of whodunits go, "The Morning After" is pretty simple-minded (there are only two possible suspects) but, through one bit of sleight of hand after another, Mr. Lumet manages to divert our attention from its cracked reality.

Suspense melodramas aren't the only kinds of films to which we lug our built-in plausibility meters. Some part of the mind of even the most faithful, least demanding moviegoer is ever ready to protect itself from emotional involvement through disbelief. Comedies that are more physically spectacular than funny (following the lead of the seminal "Ghostbusters") turn off some of us, though certainly not everybody.

So does a historical film containing a few unintended anachronisms in period detail or dialogue. Yet I also remember going along with the overwrought, apparently fictional Russian roulette sequences in Michael Cimino's "Deer Hunter." These outraged many people for good reason but, at least to me, they dramatized a psychological despair more important to the point of the film than the fact that such contests never actually happened.

People who've put down their money to see a film or a play initially want to believe, or they wouldn't be there. Mike Nichols is reported to have said once that when the curtain goes up on the first act of any play, the audience will enthusiastically put up with almost anything, including five minutes of utter silence in the pitch dark, in anticipation of unknown delights to come. However, if those delights don't materialize, the natives will become quickly, sometimes dangerously restless.

•

As members of the audience, we are friendly adversaries, but never more adversarial than when watching the kinds of films-of-situation at which Alfred Hitchcock excelled, and to which "The Morning After" is a distant cousin. There's no room in such movies for the sort of sentiment or characterization that can sometimes carry movies that are even more implausible and less intelligently plotted.

In "Hitchcock," François Truffaut's still incomparable book about

the craft of film making, Truffaut notes at one point:

"The art of creating suspense" (which he defines as "the stretching out of anticipation") "is also the art of involving the audience, so that the viewer is actually a participant in the film. In this area of the spectacle, film making is not the dual interplay between the director and his picture, but a three-way game in which the audience, too, is required to play."

The problem is that, given half a chance, the audience won't play.

Truffaut also writes that "while Hitchcock maintains that he is not concerned with plausibility, the truth is that he is rarely implausible. What he does, in effect, is to hinge the plot around a striking coincidence, which provides him with the master situation."

Everything in a Hitchcock film, including each character, exists to serve the story. If, however, the character, to serve the story, must behave in some uncharacteristic way, the audience will sever all relations with the film.

This is what eventually happens in "The Bedroom Window," the new suspense-melodrama written and directed by Curtis Hanson, a film maker who clearly knows what he's up to. In this film, however, he's hampered by casting that's less than ideal and by a lapse in plausibility that, three-quarters of the way through, effectively sets the audience free.

Mr. Hanson's screenplay, adapted from a novel by Anne Holden, uses a situation that could well have intrigued Hitchcock: a married woman, involved in an adulterous affair, looks out the window of her lover's apartment one night to see a man in the street below brutally beating a young woman with the seeming intent of raping and killing her. She gets a good look at the man, who's finally scared away before doing much

20

Jeff Bridges and Jane Fonda in "The Morning After"— Sleight of hand diverts attention from its cracked reality.

more damage than badly scaring his victim.

The next day, when she hears that later another woman in the same neighborhood was, in fact, murdered, the adulterous but public-spirited wife insists that her lover report to the police to give her evidence as if it were his own.

So far, so good. Hitchcock, too, would have appreciated the lengths to which this not-quite-noble wife goes to see justice done, though without wrecking her marriage to a very rich man. In no time at all, the young, more or less innocent lover, who thus perjures himself, becomes the prime suspect in what turns out to be a series of rape-murders committed by the same man.

The film's casting is weak — neither Steve Guttenberg nor Isabelle Huppert has enough screen presence to give substance to the characters of the clandestine lovers who, without apology, exist to serve the film's situation. Even this isn't very important until Mr. Hanson's inspiration runs thin and, to keep the film from ending too soon, he forces Mr. Guttenberg to withhold information for no plausible reason whatsoever.

This is a pity, since "The Bedroom Window" has had, until then, so much going for it. The film's opening sequence is a model of Hitchcockian concision, as is a funny-scary courtroom sequence in which Mr. Guttenberg's testimony is successfully ripped to shreds by a defense lawyer (played with friendly venom by Wallace Shawn).

•

More than any other kind of film, the suspense-melodrama is only as good as its final 30 minutes. Even if these fail, the audience probably won't walk out. We all want to find out what happens next, but our hearts will be elsewhere.

American would-be imitators of Hitchcock usually fall short much in the way that Mr. Hanson does in "The Bedroom Window," by a sudden failing of invention. European directors

become sidetracked by allowing their characters to have serious lives of their own, almost apart from the plot. This is the distracting aspect of André Téchiné's "Scene of the Crime," an enjoyable but ultimately disorienting film in which the characters, who inhabit a soft-focused, idealized vision of the French provinces, are far more complex than the situations they are supposed to serve.

The most important of these characters are a beautiful, independent woman (Catherine Deneuve), who's left her husband (Victor Lanoux) to pursue her own career as the owner of a disco, and her troubled, 13-year-old son (Nicolas Giraudi), who lives with his mother and possibly loves her too well.

•

The film is so rich with characters (including those of Miss Deneuve's parents, played by Danielle Darrieux and Jean Bousquet) that the melodramatic events that change their lives can never measure up to their stature. The events (involving two escaped convicts) aren't implausible, exactly. However, because they're of a different if not lesser order of fiction, they allow the audience to pull back in bewilderment. What are a couple of ordinary escaped convicts doing in a classy movie like this?

They're there to realize Mr. Téchiné's attempt to make a Hitchcock film of "substance" — which is to deny the substance that exists in Hitchcock's mastery of the most economic of cinema styles. Next to outright implausibility, the most sure-fire way of alienating an audience's commitment to a film is an evident aspiration to upgrade a supposedly lesser art.

Though we think we're relaxing when we're watching a movie, we're in constant battle. To be defeated by it — to be won over by its reality — is the sweet surrender. ■

1987 F 8, II:21:1

My Brother's Keeper

THE GOOD FATHER, directed by Mike Newell; written by Christopher Hampton, based on the novel by Peter Prince; photography by Michael Coulter; edited by Peter Hollywood; music by Richard Hartley; produced by Ann Scott; released by Skouras Pictures. At 57th Street Playhouse, Avenue of the Americas and 57th Street. Running time: 90 minutes. This film is rated R.

Bill Hooper	Anthony Hopkins
Roger Miles	Jim Broadbent
Emmy Hooper	Harriet Walter
Cheryl Miles	Fanny Viner
Mark Varner	Simon Callow
Mary Hall	Joanne Whalley
Jane Powell	Miriam Margolyes
Leonard Scruby	Michael Byrne
Bill's Son	Harry Grubb

By VINCENT CANBY

THOUGH he makes a good living as a marketing executive with a London publishing house, Bill Hooper (Anthony Hopkins) lives in self-imposed squalor in a dingy bed-sitter near some railroad tracks. Bill, divorced and the father of a small son, is furious with the world and everybody in it, especially with the self-sufficient Emmy, his former wife, who now lives with another man, and even with the child, whom he blames for coming between the parents.

On a day when he has visiting rights, he keeps his son in the park until the bored little boy is blue with cold. "Why didn't you take him back to your place?" says Emmy. "How could I?" says Bill. "You have my flat."

He rides a motorcycle around London and stares out at people through the thick plastic shield of his crash helmet, even when he's not on the bike. In the company of old friends, he's a raw nerve. Bill Hooper is an avid collector of injustices and betrayals, including those of others.

In "The Good Father," Mike Newell's intense, short-focused, very good new English film, Bill Hooper takes it upon himself to help a friend in need. At a party he chances upon a weepy, somewhat drunk Roger Miles (Jim Broadbent), a professor with not much money who's mourning the loss of his child. The child's not dead, but Roger's wife is planning to move to Australia with their son and her lesbian lover.

Bill is astonished at Roger's flabbiness. "You're going to let her do that?" Well, says Roger, he doesn't want to cause a fuss, and, well, he still loves his wife. Whatever makes her

happy will make him happy — sort of. Roger, clearly, is someone who needs assistance.

"The Good Father," which opens today at the 57th Street Playhouse, is about Bill Hooper's rehabilitation when he becomes involved in affairs that appear to be outside his own. He finds Roger the best legal aid available and promises to pay for it himself. As the bewildered Roger looks on, Bill encourages the lawyer in a vicious attack on the morals of the wife Roger still loves.

Bill becomes almost human again. When he learns that Emmy's lover has left, his interest in sex revives. He starts an affair with a pretty, much younger woman and makes plans to move into a new, large, upscale flat. In Christopher Hampton's excellent screenplay (adapted from a novel by Peter Prince), that, however, is only a part of Bill Hooper's story.

"The Good Father" is full of ironic surprises. It's the kind of "small" film that, by recording so accurately the minute details of particular lives, also manages — without effort — to evoke the larger, mostly unseen context in which these lives are led: the England of Margaret Thatcher and a society that now only dimly remembers the excitement and urgency of the political commitment of the 1960's.

•

Any sense of isolation is that of its self-absorbed characters, not of the film. Mr. Newell, who directed "Dance With a Stranger," and Mr. Hampton keep strictly to the matters at hand without straining to impose either sentimental or cosmic import on them.

The result is a consistently absorbing drama, wonderfully well acted by Mr. Hopkins, who moves through the film as if wired with enough explosives to wipe out half of London. At any minute, he might blow. It's a brilliant, exacting characterization, the only reservation being that it's initially so persuasive that the resolution may come as a bit of a stretch. Perhaps not.

Giving him fine support are Mr. Broadbent, who looks and acts like an English Randy Quaid, and Simon Callow (the vicar in "Room With a View"), who has several piercingly funny scenes as the barrister for whom no tactics can be so dirty that they aren't as rewarding emotionally as they are professionally. The women's roles, though uniformly sympathetic, are not so rich, possibly

Anthony Hopkins, right, and Harry Grubb in a scene from "The Good Father."

because "The Good Father" is very much a movie about the fallibility of men, middle-class and lowercase.

1987 F 11, C23:1

Dueling Biceps

OVER THE TOP, directed by Menahem Golan; screenplay by Stirling Silliphant and Sylvester Stallone, story by Gary Conway and David C. Engelbach; director of photography, David Gurfinkel; film editors, Don Zimmerman and James Symons; music by Giorgio Moroder; produced by Mr. Golan and Yoram Globus; Warner Brothers presents a Cannon Group, Inc./Golan-Globus Production. At Criterion Center, Broadway at 45th Street; 86th Street Twin, at Lexington Avenue; Manhattan Twin, 59th Street and Third Avenue; Eighth Street Playhouse, at Avenue of the Americas. Running time: 92 minutes. This film is rated PG.

Lincoln Hawk	Sylvester Stallone
Jason Cutler	Robert Loggia
Christina Hawk	Susan Blakely
Bob (Bull) Hurley	Rick Zumwalt
Michael Cutler	David Mendenhall
Tim Salanger	Chris McCarty
Ruker	Terry Funk

By JANET MASLIN

IT took colossal crust — more specifically, it took Sylvester Stallone — to make a film that is largely about arm-wrestling. It isn't that exciting to watch, and it's not the sport of kings, either. But Mr. Stallone saw the potential for something Rockylike in this subject, as indeed he sees it everywhere. So "Over the Top," which opens today at the Criterion and other theaters, tells of a modest, bashful trucker named Lincoln Hawk — Mr. Stallone sure can write names for himself — whose gift for arm-wrestling may just take him to the top.

The screenplay, by Mr. Stallone and Stirling Silliphant, doesn't even make sense. A lot of it has to do with Hawk's efforts to win back the love of his estranged 12-year-old son Michael (David Mendenhall), whose mother (Susan Blakely) kept the boy away from Hawk but changed her mind when she became mortally ill. The boy exists partly as a plot expedient and partly as a sounding board for Hawk's philosophy, which is garbled even by Mr. Stallone's standards. Winning isn't everything, Hawk teaches the boy, though it's pretty clear he lives for little else. And even if you lose, you can lose like a winner; that's good, too. But whatever you do, never give up. The boy is able to parrot this right back to his father by the time the story is over.

Mr. Stallone assumes a humble air, as the trucker whose work is never fully documented; it may be that he only drives to the gym and the hair salon. The star has been very nicely groomed, and has developed biceps worth showing off — a lucky thing, since they're on camera most of the time. Menahem Golan, who directed "Over the Top," concentrates admiringly on the Stallone physique and later branches out to pay similar attention to a number of huge, mean-looking galoots, who play the cream of the world's arm-wrestling talent. Some of the final arm-wrestling matches, pitting Mr. Stallone against these behemoths, feature slow-motion photography, abundant grunts and horrid little crunching sounds.

•

Mr. Stallone has also given himself a rich adversary in the form of Robert Loggia, who plays Hawk's powerful father-in-law. Poor Mr. Loggia must grapple with absolutely hopeless dialogue ("Do you actually think

you can get away with what you've done?") and endure the humiliation of having Mr. Stallone drive a truck through the gates of his mansion and across the lawn. This is the kind of film in which the mansion's front lawn includes lots of white statuary, and Mr. Stallone breaks it all. The film seems to advocate reason as a good first approach to any problem, and all-out destruction as the next best thing.

"Over the Top," which is one of Mr. Stallone's more muddled efforts but by no means a flop on the order of "F.I.S.T." or "Rhinestone," includes a phenomenal number of plugs for various products. Brut cologne, Adidas sportswear and the Las Vegas Hilton are featured prominently and often. There are smaller but unmistakable plugs for Pepsi-Cola, Duracell batteries and many others.

•

"Over the Top" is rated PG ("Parental Guidance Suggested"). It includes some strong language.

1987 F 12, C21:2

Dummy Love

MANNEQUIN, directed by Michael Gottlieb; written by Edward Rugoff and Mr. Gottlieb; director of photography, Tim Suhrstedt; film editor, Richard Halsey; music by Sylvester Levay; produced by Art Levinson; released by Twentieth Century Fox; presented by Gladden Entertainment. At Gotham, Third Ave. at 58th St.; 86th St. E., at Third Ave.; National, Broadway and 44th St. Running time: 90 minutes. This film is rated PG.

Jonathan Switcher	Andrew McCarthy
Emmy	Kim Cattrall
Claire Timkin	Estelle Getty
Richards	James Spader
Felix	G. W. Bailey
Roxie	Carole Davis
B. J. Wert	Stephen Vinovich
Armand	Christopher Maher
Hollywood	Meshach Taylor
Emmy's mother	Phyllis Newman

SOMETIMES it's possible to find out everything you need to know about a film in the first minute or two. It's possible with "Mannequin," anyhow. "Mannequin," which opens today at the National and other theaters, starts with an animated credit sequence that looks suspiciously like a Saturday-morning cartoon. Then it has a cute title. ("Edfu, Egypt. A really long time ago. Right before lunch.") Next there's a scene between a pretty young mummy and what seems, oddly enough, to be her Jewish mother. This scene is played comically but isn't funny.

After this, there's a cut to the real story, which takes place in the present and is about a young man falling in love with the department-store mannequin he has helped manufacture. Nothing necessarily wrong with that, except that the soundtrack begins playing the obligatory pop standard (in this case, the Temptations' "My Girl") before the action can even get started. That's that. The remaining hour and a half of the film are about Jonathan (Andrew McCarthy), his mannequin (Kim Cattrall), and the hubbub they create at a Philadelphia department store. The idea is that together, the boy and mannequin create window designs so brilliant they set the world on its ear.

As co-written and directed by Michael Gottlieb, "Mannequin" is a state-of-the-art showcase of perfunctory technique. No attempt has been made to integrate the detachable rock video sequence — in which boy and mannequin dash through the department store, turning up in lots of

different outfits — into the rest of the story. There is an *effort* to stage a serious love scene between the two of them, but at one recent screening it drew more laughs than the would-be humor. In place of a real story, there is just the spectacle of stock characters being put through their paces to fill up the time.

•

Several of those stock characters play upon racial and sexual stereotypes, and a few are drawn along obnoxiously homophobic lines. One screamingly effeminate store employee drives a pink Cadillac with a license plate that reads BAD GIRL. And the credits list "Effete Executive" as one of the minor characters.

The Cadillac-driving figure is at least played with some energy by an actor named Meshach Taylor, and in fact a few of the minor players give signs of being funnier than their material. (Carole Davis, who was a nagging record-company functionary in "This Is Spinal Tap," is Jonathan's nagging girlfriend here.) Mr. McCarthy is capable of charming nonchalance but has little occasion to display it here. And Miss Cattrall just beams excitedly, paying no particular attention to anything around her. It's never a disappointment when the mannequin, which comes to life only intermittently, turns back into wood.

•

"Mannequin" is rated PG ("Parental Guidance Suggested"). It includes some sexual innuendoes and some undraped mannequins.

JANET MASLIN

1987 F 13, C8:6

84 CHARING CROSS ROAD, directed by David Jones; screenplay by Hugh Whitemore, based on the book by Helene Hanff; originally adapted for the stage by James Roose-Evans; director of photography, Brian West; edited by Chris Wimble; music by George Fenton; produced by Geoffrey Helman; released by Columbia Pictures. At Baronet, 59th Street and Third Avenue. Running time: 99 minutes. This film is rated PG.

Helene Hanff	Anne Bancroft
Frank Doel	Anthony Hopkins
Nora Doel	Judi Dench
Maxine Bellamy	Jean De Baer
George Martin	Maurice Denham
Cecily Farr	Eleanor David
Kay	Mercedes Ruehl
Brian	Daniel Gerroll
Megan Wells	Wendy Morgan
Bill Humphries	Ian McNeice
Ginny	J. Smith-Cameron
Ed	Tom Isbell

Anne Bancroft

By VINCENT CANBY

WORKING carefully and with the least sleazy of intentions, some very good people have taken Helene Hanff's popular epistolary memoir, "84 Charing Cross Road," which records the New York writer's 20-year correspondence with a London bookshop, and made a movie guaranteed to put all teeth on edge, including George Washington's, wherever they might be.

The film "84 Charing Cross Road," which opens today at the Baronet, has a screenplay by Hugh Whitemore ("Stevie"), was directed by David Jones ("Betrayal") and stars Anne Bancroft, who's equally at ease in drama ("The Pumpkin Eater") and farce (the remake of "To Be or Not to Be"), and who may be the only leading lady in America today with the ability to cross one eye without moving the other.

Playing opposite Miss Bancroft is the estimable Anthony Hopkins, as

Anthony Hopkins portrays a British dealer in rare books in David Jones's "84 Charing Cross Road," derived from a stage adaptation of Helene Hanff's autobiography.

the mild-mannered English bibliographer at Marks & Co. with whom she corresponds. It's a modest performance in an exceedingly dim role, and of interest only when seen alongside the actor's spectacular work in the just-opened "Good Father."

•

The result of this high-powered collaboration is a movie of such unrelieved genteelness that it makes one long to head for Schrafft's for a double-gin martini, straight up, and a stack of cinnamon toast from which the crusts have been removed.

It's not as if everyone concerned couldn't have known the quality of the gruel before they plunged into it. The book was the basis for a London television show in 1975 and, as adapted by James Roose-Evans, was a play that was successfully put on in London in 1981. A 1982 New York production closed after 96 performances.

Now as then, "84 Charing Cross Road" is about a lot less than it pretends to be. Front and center, from start to finish, is a wraith of a character. She is Helene Hanff (Miss Bancroft), a struggling New York writer who is equally — heedlessly — in love with England and literature, though all the audience comprehends is a rather peculiar passion for leather bindings, not what's in them. The film's Helene might feel just as passionately about baseball cards and, in the blunt way Miss Bancroft performs, this would make somewhat more sense.

•

The film is a seemingly unending series of non-epiphanies. The first comes in 1949 when, standing on Madison Avenue, thumbing through a copy of her beloved Saturday Review of Literature, Helene spots an advertisement for Marks & Co., Antiquarian Booksellers. Miss Bancroft reacts in the manner of an all-too-sincere actress playing Bernadette having her first vision.

Thus begins her pen-pal relationship with Frank Doel (Mr. Hopkins) and the other dear people at Marks & Co. As they supply her with books, she supplies them with slangily affectionate letters in which she pours out her heart about the joys of acquiring and feeling previously owned copies of Hazlitt, Stevenson, Pepys, de Tocqueville, Chaucer, Landor, Woolf and Newman ("dear, goofy John Henry"), among others.

The film crosscuts between the letters (hers to them and theirs to her) in which hardly anything of importance is revealed. She sends them packages of food, which they receive with weepy gratitude, in return for which they send her gifts that bring on the kind of teary-eyed smiles a mother directs at her son-the-doctor.

•

To the extent that any substance is revealed through these exchanges, Helene is a wan woman with apparently no other life. We're told that she writes television scripts ("Ellery Queen," "The Hallmark Hall of Fame," short stories). All the audience sees, however, is a domiciled shopping-bag lady who likes to fondle her books and, when she opens them, to chain-smoke cigarettes and to drink so much gin she wouldn't remember much of anything she reads anyway.

This Helene has very few friends. The film treats the emptiness of her life with the delicacy of an undertaker. It maintains utmost discretion. At one point the camera, in panning across her cluttered apartment, sees

the photograph of a naval officer on which the camera lingers for maybe half a second. Is he a dead fiancé? A brother? Admiral Nimitz? One shouldn't ask.

From time to time, Helene does display a certain amount of nerve, as when she ridicules those great (and cheap) old Modern Library Giant editions that allowed several generations of Americans to grow up halfway educated without having to fawn on Marks & Co. in London. Even her wisecracks are meager: "I hope 'madam' doesn't mean over there what it means over her," she writes to Frank in one of her early letters. He smiles fondly.

Twee is the English word for it.

•

"84 Charing Cross Road," which has been rated PG *("parental guidance suggested"), includes some genteely vulgar language.*

1987 F 13, C10:4

Going Over the Score

DUET FOR ONE, directed by Andrei Konchalovsky; screenplay by Tom Kempinski and Jeremy Lipp and Mr. Konchalovsky, based on the play by Mr. Kempinski; director of photography, Alex Thomson; edited by Henry Richardson; produced by Menahem Golan and Yoram Globus; released by the Cannon Group Inc. At Cinema I, Third Avenue at 60th Street. Running time: 107 minutes. This film is rated R.

Stephanie Anderson	Julie Andrews
David Cornwallis	Alan Bates
Dr. Louis Feldman	Max von Sydow
Constantine Kassanis	Rupert Everett
Sonia Randvich	Margaret Courtenay
Penny Smallwood	Cathryn Harrison
Leonid Lefimov	Sigfrit Steiner
Totter	Liam Neeson
Anya	Macha Meril
Mrs. Burridge	Janette Newling

Alan Bates and Julie Andrews star in Andrei Konchalovsky's "Duet for One," based on the West End play about a concert violinist afflicted with multiple sclerosis.

By JANET MASLIN

IT took half a dozen extra characters and a very large tree to open up Tom Kempinski's two-character play "Duet for One" and bring it to the screen. But the focus is still Stephanie Anderson, a brilliant violinist (modeled, to some extent, on the cellist Jacqueline Du Pré) who is married to a celebrated conductor and has multiple sclerosis. Stephanie's illness becomes an occasion for her to re-examine her life as she describes it to Dr. Louis Feldman (Max von Sydow), a psychiatrist who is something of a friend and fan. It also becomes an occasion for Mr. Kempinski to elicit the audience's pity in a far too easy and automatic way.

"Why should I die such a horrible death?" Stephanie asks in Andrei Konchalovsky's film "Duet for One," which opens today at Cinema I. "Was I so terrible? Was this music so terrible?" A good deal of the screenplay, which is by Mr. Kempinski, Mr. Konchalovsky and Jeremy Lipp, is as disingenuous as that, and as needlessly coy.

•

But "Duet for One," for all its sogginess and contrivance, is a compelling vehicle, particularly for a star who fits the material as well as Julie Andrews does. The idea of a Julie Andrews role these days hardly conjures up the chipperness of her early career, since Miss Andrews has lately been effective as a quietly exasperated, somewhat queenly heroine reluctantly facing up to mortality. Here, even more so than in "That's Life!," Miss Andrews finds the opportunity to draw on previously underused aspects of her talent. Her performance is often a good deal better than the material.

Surrounding Stephanie, and providing her with an opportunity to confront separate aspects of her life, are her husband, David Cornwallis (Alan Bates), and a household full of friends and retainers. There is the hotheaded Constantine Kassanis (Rupert Everett), Stephanie's violin protégé and a passionate young man

who cannot help speaking the truth; Constantine makes Stephanie face up to the waning of her musical abilities.

There is Penny Smallwood (Cathryn Harrison), the pretty secretary on whom David is growing more and more dependent as his wife drifts away; because of Penny, Stephanie must deal with her feelings of jealousy, too. There is even a maid named Anya (Macha Meril) with whom Stephanie can discuss sexual frustration.

•

Finally, as Stephanie grows angrier and more self-destructive, there is a junkman named Totter (Liam Neeson) with whom she has an affair. It's typical of both the material's bluntness and Mr. Konchalovsky's that the junkman has a wife who dresses garishly and that he spends evenings singing in a neighborhood pub. (As Stephanie begins debasing herself, the music on the soundtrack descends rather snobbishly to include a pop song and a big-band number.) All these developments are terrifically tidy, as is the story's ending. They do little to alleviate the essential talkiness of the material.

Miss Andrews is much more powerful a presence than anyone else in the cast, though Mr. Everett has a few amusingly spirited moments as Constantine. Though the material is episodic and fragmented, Miss Andrews is forceful and affecting enough to keep it together. Mr. Konchalovsky, working at a much less feverish pitch than he did with "Runaway Train," gives the film a stately look befitting its refined and affluent heroine, and does better in establishing her external surroundings than her inner state.

A couple of dream sequences are worked in gracefully, but too many of Stephanie's thoughts are made visible by devices like the above-mentioned tree. A reminder of Stephanie's marriage, her lost youth, the life that will go on after she is gone — the tree is made to take on much more weight than its branches can easily bear.

1987 F 13, C10:4

On the Border

NO MAN'S LAND, directed by Alain Tanner; screenplay (French with English subtitles) by Mr. Tanner; photography by Bernard Zitzerman; edited by Laurent Uhler; music by Terry Riley; produced by Mr. Tanner and Marin Karmitz; production companies, Filmograph; M.K.2 Productions in association with Westdeutscher Rundfunk/Channel Four Television/Film on Four International/Télévision Suisse Romande/Films A2. At the Public Theater, 425 Lafayette Street. Running time: 110 minutes. This film has no rating.

Paul	Hugues Quester
Madeleine	Myriam Mézières
Jean	Jean-Philippe Ecoffey
Mali	Betty Berr
Lucie	Marie-Luce Felber
Hitchhiker	Maria Cabral
First French policeman	André Steiger
Second French policeman	Jacques Michel
Informer	Teco Celio
Banker	Jean-Pierre Malo

"No Man's Land" was shown as part of the 1985 New York Film Festival. Following are excerpts from Vincent Canby's review, which appeared in The New York Times Oct. 5, 1985. The film opens today at the Public Theater, 425 Lafayette Street.

ACH of the four principal characters in Alain Tanner's "No Man's Land" wants to be someplace else.

Madeleine, who runs a disco on the French-Swiss border, dreams of going to Paris to pursue a singing career. Her lover, Paul, who makes his living smuggling money, gold and goods across the border, plans to emigrate to Canada. Mali, a pretty young Algerian woman who lives in France and works in Switzerland, would like to be anywhere except where she is. Louis, born on a Swiss farm and trained as a clockmaker, would give anything to leave his mistress, Lucie, and move in with Mali.

Not for nothing is the film titled "No Man's Land," which, of course, refers not only to the strip of land between the French and the Swiss customs stations, through which the characters are constantly passing, but also to their states of mind.

Thus, what we have here is an all-too-explicit metaphor that traps Mr. Tanner's drama as effectively as his characters are trapped by their lives. Once you've understood the title, there's no place for the film to go that you can't anticipate long before the gloomy, none-too-bright young characters.

Mr. Tanner is Switzerland's most interesting, most gifted film maker, but his best films ("La Salamandre," "The Middle of the World," "Jonah Who Will Be 25 in the Year 2000") have all been made in collaboration with John Berger, the English novelist and critic.

Without Mr. Berger's assistance, Mr. Tanner's films, like this one, tend to be completely humorless and cold, memorable only for their picturesque landscapes and cloud formations. "No Man's Land" has a cast of attractive young actors and a soundtrack score by Terry Riley, the American minimalist composer who's been strongly influenced by Indian music. The music is actually the most interesting thing in the movie.

1987 F 13, C14:6

African Fables

FACES OF WOMEN, written, directed and produced by Désiré Ecaré; in French with English subtitles; directors of photography, François Migeat and Dominique Gentil; edited by Giselle Miski, Mme. Djé-djé

and Nicholas Barrachin; a Films de la Lagune (Abidjan) Production with the assistance of the French Ministry of Foreign Affairs; released by New Yorker Films. At the Lincoln Plaza Cinema, Broadway and 63d Street. Running time: 105 minutes. This film has no rating.

Bernadette	Eugénie Cissé Roland
Kouassi	Sidiki Bakaba
N'Guéssan	Albertine N'Guéssan
Brou	Kouadio Brou
Affoue	Mahile Véronique

WITH: Carmen Levry, Anny Brigitte, Alexis Leatche, Désiré Bamba, Fatou Sall and the Adioukrou people of Lopou village

ESIRE ECARE'S "Faces of Women," opening today at the Lincoln Plaza Cinema, is a technically rough, cheerfully rude, folkloric comedy about the status of women in the Ivory Coast, where Mr. Ecaré was born and raised. It is, in fact, two separate fables with a common frame, that of a street festival where the singing and dancing is nonstop.

In the first story, a bored wife is accused by her tyrannical farmer-husband of having an affair with his younger brother, a nattily dressed layabout. The wife isn't, but would like to. At her wit's end, she takes ka-rate lessons in order to best her husband physically.

The highlight of the fable is a long erotic scene in which the layabout seduces the wife's best friend as the young woman is bathing in the river. Aside from suggesting what the unhappy wife is missing, this sequence hasn't much to do with the rest of the fable, but it's beautifully photographed. Mr. Ecaré is as casual about the film's narrative line as his characters are about the truth.

●

The second, much more poignant story is about Bernadette, a large, imposing though illiterate woman who supports her lazy husband, her Europeanized daughters and a large number of assorted relatives with her successful fish-smoking business.

Bernadette, who has 200 employees, would like to open a small restaurant in Abidjan, more or less for the fun of it, and goes to the bank to take out a loan. To her shock she finds that she can't. She has no assets, nothing that would be acceptable as collateral. Her business, she's told, is all cash-flow, a concept she doesn't com-prehend. Everything she makes in profit is spent on luxuries by her hangers-on. Says her husband piously, "Women aren't meant to understand such things."

●

With the help of her eldest daughter, a very pretty, sharp-tongued, elegantly dressed young woman, Bernadette takes her first steps toward liberation. If she has her way, her favorite niece will become a cadet at St. Cyr. Eugénie Cissé Roland, who plays Bernadette, has a sort of grandeur about her that's also genuinely funny.

"Faces of Women" is the first feature by Mr. Ecaré, who began shooting in 1973 and finished 12 years later. Made on a shoestring, with post-synchronized sound, "Faces of Woman" is also a one-movie record of a film maker's development. The style of the fable about Bernadette is far more sophisticated and subtle than the opening segment, which sometimes seems to be the film diary of a movie maker in search of a subject.
VINCENT CANBY

1987 F 13, C22:1

FILM VIEW

JANET MASLIN

Comedies Without Laughs Merit Cries of Protest

s of this writing, about $71 million has been spent nationwide on tickets to see "The Golden Child," starring Eddie Murphy. If ticket prices are assumed to be $6 in all parts of the country (though they're sometimes lower), and if discounts for various age groups are overlooked, that gives a low estimate of at least 11,833,333 tickets sold. Even if one quarter of these viewers were recidivists paying "The Golden Child" return visits, that would still mean approximately 8,874,999 men, women and children have seen this film. It may be that not one of them has laughed while watching it, not even once.

If that's an exaggeration, it's slight. Audiences sit through "The Golden Child" in near-total silence, and only occasionally does the film elicit any reaction. They watch, in what can only be bewilderment, as exotic locations, fake-looking stunts and incomprehensible special effects parade wearily across the screen. They may chuckle at Mr. Murphy's very infrequent wisecracks — some of the humorous material was reportedly added when the film was almost finished, to give it a much-needed boost — but none of the jokes is memorable. Nor is anything else about "The Golden Child," but that need not slow its momentum. It's already in orbit, and now it can stay there.

Thanks to those attendance figures, "The Golden Child" has been firmly established as a comedy hit. By the time it reaches television and ascends to the home video market, where it can linger in perpetuity, it may be billed as a comedy classic. It can sit right there, on a shelf beside "Spies Like Us" and "Three Amigos" and "Ghostbusters" and "Legal Eagles," on the shelf reserved for Non-Movies of the 80's. And it will fit in perfectly: clerks will be able to recommend it to customers in good conscience. But this is a film that was never well liked, not even when it was new. Why does it deserve to live forever?

It's not "The Golden Child" itself that is at issue, or even the great tradition of big-name comedy-action-romance-dramas, dating back perhaps to "Silver Streak," of which it is part. It's the fact that no one cries foul. If patrons found that they were being left for two hours to look at a blank screen, they might well object. Yet "The Golden Child," which is the next best thing, elicits not a peep. The cinematic non-event is so commonplace today, and perhaps so inevitable a byproduct of film making by committee, that audiences are becoming numb. They don't enjoy themselves, but they don't bother to complain.

What's bringing them in to see "The Golden Child" in the first place? Obviously, it isn't word of mouth. Nor is it the film's premise, which has to do with Eddie Murphy's

traveling from Los Angeles to the gates of heli to save the child who embodies spiritual perfection and... (Can *anyone* mistake this for a first-draft story idea designed by film makers who knew exactly what they wanted?) It's probably just the sight of Mr. Murphy himself, peering down assuredly in his black leather hat, in a poster that promises at least some modicum of fun.

Paramount, which has done a much better job of marketing "The Golden Child" than making it, has also had unwarranted good results with the antic-looking Richard Pryor likeness being used to sell "Critical Condition," another moribund comedy. Both Mr. Murphy and Mr. Pryor have built up enough well-deserved good will with audiences to get away with any number of humorless transgressions. But how can audiences enjoy the sight of Mr. Pryor just going through the motions, as he does in "Critical Condition"? And how encouraged can they be by the news that Mr. Murphy's next film, due in May, will be called "Beverly Hills Cop II"? Of course it will be a hit; that goes without saying. It may even be wonderful. But if the rest of the film proves no more resourceful than its title, it may be Emperor's New Clothes time at the movies all over again.

When an audience is powerfully moved by the film

it's watching, the effect is unmistakable: just look at the faces in any theater where "Platoon" is playing. And when an audience genuinely appreciates a comedy, that, too, is easy to see. It's not just a matter of laughter; it's the openness and receptiveness on people's faces as they watch the screen. If you visited a theater showing "The Golden Child" and then one showing "Outrageous Fortune," the difference would be obvious before you even looked at the screen.

That difference is worth mentioning now because it will probably blur with time. "Outrageous Fortune" is funny and clever, but it's also slick enough to appeal mostly to a mainstream audience with a taste for proven formulas, the same audience at which "The Golden Child" is aimed. Neither of them has the spark and individuality of a "Radio Days," and both are aimed at a fairly low common denominator. How low? There's a commercial now on television for a word processor that corrects spelling mistakes, and the three examples of misspelling shown are "eet," "stob" and "mayir." The presumption is that anything more taxing might baffle viewers, and "The Golden Child" appears to have been made with similarly dim expectations of those who see it.

A film can attempt lowest-common-denominator humor and still deliver, to the satisfaction of one and all; look at "Crocodile Dundee." It's not the lack of sophistication that hurts "The Golden Child," but rather the lack of clarity and confidence. "Outrageous Fortune," which isn't any more daring, manages to set up the funny spectacle of two ill-matched, antipathetic women chasing a man who's cheated on both of them, and turn it into a crowd-pleasing adventure. The screenwriter, Leslie Dixon, has mentioned Francis Veber ("Les Compères") as a comedy writer-director she admires, right alongside Preston Sturges and Woody Allen, and Mr. Veber's influence on the finished film is very apparent. Comedies like "Les Compères" lay no claims to greatness, any more than "Outrageous Fortune" does. But they're bona fide fun, and that's enough.

It used to be true, in the days before video, that the line between a "Golden Child" and an "Outrageous Fortune" would be quickly and firmly drawn. People came out to see films more readily, and they were more inclined to form definite opinions and tell their friends. Nowadays, as the whole film-watching process becomes more gradual and less immediate, the funny film and the dud are more easily confused. By the time something

turns up on video or on television, the initial reaction it generated will be largely forgotten. And friends' opinions won't count for as much, because those friends may have waited to see it at home, too.

So as audiences sit still acquiescently for listless, joyless films like "The Golden Child," they doom themselves to more of the same. A passive acceptance of a film this feeble sends a message of encouragement to those who made it. That much has always been true, but thanks to the new technology, films can live on in perpetuity, and perpetuity has gotten longer. It's no longer just a matter of this spring's second run or next year's revival. Years hence, "The Golden Child" and others like it may still be floating around in one form or another. And a whole new audience may wonder why, since it wasn't funny and it wasn't good, it wouldn't go away.

●   ●   ●

Many readers have written to note that Annie Hall and Alvy Singer decided not to go to the Beekman Theater, winding up at the New Yorker, and that Rockaway is in Queens. Nice talk, they say, from someone discussing Woody Allen's scrupulous attention to detail. Mea culpa. ■

1987 F 15, II:19:1

Ancient Omelet

THE LEGEND OF SURAM FORTRESS, directed by Sergei Paradjanov and Dodo Abashidze; in Georgian with English subtitles; distributed by the International Film Exchange. At Film Forum 1, 57 Watts Street. Running time: 90 minutes. This film has no rating.

By WALTER GOODMAN

IN ancient Georgia, apparently, you had to break eggs not only to make an omelet, but to make a fortress, too. Anyhow, a basket of eggs, picturesquely mashed, is one of the ingredients that goes into "The Legend of Suram Fortress." But another ingredient, which remains a mystery until the end of the tale, is more crucial, since it provides the plot of the new movie from the Soviet Union, now at Film Forum 1.

The reputation of Sergei Paradjanov, who directed along with Dodo Abashidze, rests largely on "The Color of Pomegrantes," made almost 20 years ago, which will be shown at Film Forum beginning Feb. 27. The Soviet authorities found that movie "hermetic and obscure." In 1974, the director was convicted of homosexuality and spent the next four and a half years in confinement. It has been suggested that the release of "The Legend of Suram Fortress," which Mr. Paradjanov made in 1985, is evidence of a loosening up in Moscow.

It's a minimalist spectacle, an epic with a cast of tens. Lushly photographed in a way that both enhances and obscures, it tells of this fortress that refuses to stay up. Messengers report that the stone keeps crumbling, leaving Georgia open to the invaders: "I bring you bad news, Prince."

The story begins in ancient Tbilisi, when Durmishkan, a young servant of the King, is freed. He leaves Vardo, his betrothed, and sets off to make his fortune, which he does with the help of a mystically inclined peddler. Forgetting all about poor Vardo, Durmishkan marries and has a son called Zurab. Meantime, Vardo, who has been carrying a torch for Durmishkan (there are torchbearers aplenty here), has turned into a famed seer, and when the King sends Zurab, now a sturdy youth, to ask Vardo how to keep Suram standing, she reveals the secret ingredient.

Be assured that the story is not told in so straightforward a way. It's almost over before you can figure out what that initial egg-mashing was all about. The movie is a display of sumptuous austerity, dusty fields and hills suddenly bursting into the bright colors of a caravan, a carnival, the King's court. Mr. Paradjanov goes in for exotica and ritual. The formal framing doesn't let us forget that we are looking at legend, not life; often, a couple of animals are placed like bookends on either side of a centered figure or object to start a scene. The dancing is stylized, and the actors, assisted by not-always-comprehensible dialogue, make sure that no one will confuse them with real people.

"You haven't understood a thing," says Vardo to Zurab, a comment that I took personally. There are refer-

Eddie Murphy, at left, in "The Golden Child"—Despite its huge box-office grosses, audiences sit through this comedy in near-total silence. Above, Shelley Long and Bette Midler in the funny, clever "Outrageous Fortune."

ences to religious experiences, prayer and sin, absolution and redemption, which have something to do with the freedom of Georgia. There's St. George himself being pleaded with by maidens in chains to handle the dragon. The conclusion is suffused with whitewashed radiance and the swell of an organ.

Although Mr. Paradjanov has a reputation as a prankster, I don't think this is an elaborate joke. Still, it's not easy to take the subheads straight: "A Dream and Premonition of Death" or "First Love," a very brief episode about a girl who keeps saying she's a butterfly while her boyfriend keeps saying he's a grasshopper and flopping in the grass. And I could swear that the tune that runs through the movie is a variation of "Bei Mir Bist Du Schön." That's pretty funny for ancient Tbilisi.

1987 F 18, C18:5

Texas Towns

SQUARE DANCE, produced and directed by Daniel Petrie; screenplay by Alan Hines; director of photography, Jacek Laskus; edited by Bruce Green; music by Bruce Broughton; produced in association with NBC productions; released by Island Pictures. At Plaza, 58th Street, east of Madison Avenue. Running time: 112 minutes. This film is rated PG-13.

Dillard	Jason Robards
Juanelle	Jane Alexander
Gemma	Winona Ryder
Rory	Rob Lowe
Gwen	Deborah Richter
Frank	Guich Koock
Beecham	Elbert Lewis
Aggie	Charlotte Stanton
Dub Mosley	J. David Moeller
Dolores	Dixie Taylor

By VINCENT CANBY

AS anyone who took square dancing at summer camp knows, "home" is the position from which all steps originate and the spot to which a

Zade Rosenthal

Jane Alexander as Juanelle in "Square Dance."

dancer returns after do-si-do-ing. This is the signally simple metaphor that hangs over "Square Dance" like a heart-shaped, helium-filled balloon with a slow leak.

The film, directed by Daniel Petrie and adapted by Alan Hines from his own novel, is a sentimental journey into the kind of Texas landscapes that Horton Foote evokes with far more rigor and humor. It opens today at the Plaza theater.

"Square Dance" is all about home, in this case the Texas "scratch farm" owned by crusty old Grandpa Dillard (Jason Robards). Grandpa's wife is dead and his only child, Juanelle (Jane Alexander), has long since fled Twilight (for that, indeed, is the name of this small town) for the bright lights of Fort Worth.

The old man's only companion is God-fearing Gemma (Winona

Winona Ryder, as a girl seeking clues to her identity, and Jason Robards, as her cantankerous grandfather, star in Dan Petrie's "Square Dance."

Ryder), Juanelle's 12-year-old daughter, who sings in the church choir and seems perfectly happy until the appearance one afternoon of her mother, who's come to fetch her. The chain-smoking Juanelle, with her dyed hair, her junk jewelry and her short, tight denim skirt, appalls Gemma, who doesn't want to be liberated, especially by a jade like Juanelle.

Not long afterward, however, Gemma has a tiff with Grandpa and takes off for Fort Worth where, in a dim, no-man's land on the city's edge, she shares quarters above a garage with her mother and stepdad, Frank (Guich Koock).

●

In the course of "Square Dance," Gemma comes not only to know and love her rough-edged mom, whose heart is 24-karat-soft, but also to appreciate the place that, be it ever so humble, there's no other location like. She even becomes a woman, onscreen (though discreetly), and experiences the first hints of romantic and sexual love in an innocent relationship with an "older" man.

He is Rory (Rob Lowe), a mentally retarded fellow who hangs around the beauty shop where his mother and Juanelle work. Rory's idea of contentment is to chew on a button. As he has fantasies about being married to Gemma, she sees in him the sweetness that has somehow become lost in all of the other adults she knows.

There's a good deal more plot than this to "Square Dance," though nothing that happens comes as much of a surprise. It recalls "Tender Mercies," but lacks that film's beautifully realized sense of character, place and time. Mr. Hines is a native Texan, yet "Square Dance" is a movie that could have been inspired by attending to the films, plays and novels of other writers.

Miss Alexander, who's also the movie's co-executive producer, obviously likes her lady-within-the-tramp role, and plays it without going overboard, but also without being especially interesting. The same is true of Mr. Robards and Miss Ryder. It may be the material. The most arresting performance is Mr. Lowe's. The audience's attention is grabbed, if only to see whether he's going to go too far, which he doesn't. He's good, as are two other performers in small roles, Mr. Koock and Elbert Lewis, who plays an ancient friend out of Grandpa Dillard's childhood.

●

"Square Dance," which has been rated PG-13 ("Special Parental Guidance Suggested for Those Younger Than 13"), contains some partial nudity and explicit sexual references.

1987 F 20, C4:5

Turmoil

IRA, YOU'LL GET INTO TROUBLE, directed, produced and photographed by Stephen A. Sbarge; edited by Mark Rappaport; released by New Line Cinema. At the Thalia, 95th Street at Broadway. Running time: 85 minutes. This film has no rating.

By WALTER GOODMAN

YOUR response to "Ira, You'll Get Into Trouble" is likely to be related to your feelings about the student commotions of the late 1960's. Stephen A. Sbarge's cinéma vérité documentary, completed in 1970 and now at the Thalia, follows an attractive group of

New York City high schoolers who try to organize against what they view as a repressive establishment. We see them sitting-in rather ineffectually at the offices of the United Federation of Teachers, rallying, being chased by the police, putting out an underground newspaper and rapping, rapping, rapping.

The hand-held camera gets remarkably close to the young folks, whose hair is just as long as you remember and whose skirts are just as short. Mr. Sbarge, a sympathetic observer, picks up on their high spirits and makes as much as possible of what were so-so demonstrations by the standards of the time. But there's also plenty of hot air and self-romanticizing here.

The movie begins with the 1968 dispute over "community control" of schools, particularly in the Ocean Hill-Brownsville section of Brooklyn, which caused strikes, boycotts and much bad feeling between mostly white teachers and mostly black local activists — or agitators, depending on which side you were on. The students here came down on the side of the community-control forces and were particularly taken with the Black Panthers, then much in the news, whom they saw as leaders of a new American revolution.

The outlook and style of the band are seen best in a young man (call him Ira) on whom Mr. Sbarge focuses. Unstoppably articulate, not to say glib, he calls for student freedom from teachers, for whom his kindest epithet is "pigs," and is free with four-letter descriptions of most people over the age of 18. His purpose, in the watchword of the period, is to radicalize the young.

Like the other members of this largely white cadre, Ira is plainly destined for college. They form an elite that feels solidarity with the less privileged and aspires to lead others who "haven't reached some of the political conclusions we've reached" to a realization of how they are being kept down by capitalism and "the system."

"The system is killing us," says a fit-looking girl. When a boy remarks, "I really don't feel that I'm persecuted," it's a downer for the group; he seems to be betraying a faith. Catchphrases about "brainwashing" and "spirit crushing" pour from them, along with an abundance of "you knows."

Watching this zesty report (itself a product of the period), one wonders where all the boys and girls have gone. At a time of relative political passivity, you may find yourself regretting that the ideals that engaged them aren't bubbling very vigorously just now, or you may be relieved that the fashionable foolishness to which they were prone has subsided. That, to repeat, is likely to depend on your feelings about the 60's.

1987 F 20, C4:5

Indigestion

EAT AND RUN, directed by Christopher Hart; written by Stan Hart and Christopher Hart; director of photography, Dyanna Taylor; edited by Pamela S. Arnold; music by Scott Harper; produced by Jack Briggs; released by New World Pictures. At Waverly, Avenue of the Americas and Third Street. Running time: 85 minutes. This film is rated R.

Mickey McSorely	Ron Silver
Judge Cheryl Cohen	Sharon Schlarth
Murray Creature	R. L. Ryan
The Police Captain	John F. Fleming
Sorely McSorely	Derek Murcott
Pusher	Robert Silver
Grandmother	Mimi Cecchini

A BALD and very fat man, supposedly an extraterrestrial named Murray, stomps through "Eat and Run" devouring every Italian he meets, after which he belches loudly and spits out a button or two. "Eat and Run" doesn't get any funnier, and not much of it even measures up to that comic pinnacle. As co-written and directed by Christopher Hart, this comedy specializes in schoolboy humor at its most mirthlessly stupid. On those rare occasions when Mr. Hart does stumble onto something funny, he's apt to kill the joke by running it into the ground.

"Eat and Run," which opens today at the Waverly, does demonstrate a certain degree of technical proficiency. Mr. Hart attended the N.Y.U. Film School, so he knows how to do things like assemble a modest replica of the "Psycho" shower scene. What he lacks is any sense of staging or timing, not to mention the ability to rein in his worst impulses. "Eat and Run" repeats a bad-alliteration joke twice, a barroom joke three times, and an eating-too-much-cake joke too many times to count. The film's herpes-related humor is carried to excess, too.

R. L. Ryan, the actor who plays Murray, looks nicely incongruous when dressed as a Cub Scout, but is otherwise wasted. So is Ron Silver, the film's real star, who plays a detective and has to affect pseudo-hardboiled narration when talking about himself ("'I got a plan that cannot miss,' I said boldly"). This gag, like the others, is repeated ad nauseam. It's very hard to understand why "Eat and Run" was ever made.

JANET MASLIN

1987 F 20, C5:1

Poetic Politics

BARRAVENTO, directed by Glauber Rocha; script (Portuguese with English subtitles) by Rocha, Luis Paulino dos Santos and José Telles de Magalhaes; photography by Toni Rabattoni and Valdemar Lima; edited by Nelson Pereira dos Santos; produced by Braga Neto and Rex Schindler; production company, Iglu Films. At Public Theater, 425 Lafayette Street. Running time: 76 minutes. This film has no rating.
Firmino .... António Sampaio
Girl .... Luiza Maranhão
Fisherman .... Aldo Teixeira
Daughter .... Lucy Carvalho

"B ARRAVENTO" ("The Turning Wind"), opening today at the Public Theater, is the first feature by the highly regarded Brazilian director Glauber Rocha, who died at the age of 42 in 1981. The film, made in 1961, is about the efforts of Firmino, part revolutionary, part devil, to free the fishermen in his native Bahian village from capitalist exploitation and the religious superstition that prevents social change.

"Barravento" is an exceptionally beautiful work, shot in the dramatically filtered, black-and-white photography associated with Eisenstein's "Que Viva México!" and Flaherty's "Moana." In its use of dance and song within — and as comment on — the narrative, it parallels a number of films by Rocha's associates in Brazil's Cinema Nôvo movement. Even the fights are choreographed as if they were ballets.

It's also a far more tidy, far less flamboyant work than Rocha's later films, including "António das Mortes" (1968). These are so lavish in their use of legend, left-wing politics and obscure mysticism that they tend to be more popular at film festivals than with ordinary audiences.

There's nothing obscure about "Barravento." It's poetic but also completely straightforward in its revolutionary concerns. António Sampaio cuts a striking, sinuous figure as the comparatively sophisticated Firmino, who moves through the film as if he were a politically committed Sportin' Life. Nelson Pereira dos Santos, another notable Cinema Novo director ("Vidas Secas," "Amulet of Ogum"), acted as film editor for Rocha on "Barravento."

VINCENT CANBY

1987 F 20, C5:1

Father and Son

BILLY GALVIN, directed and written by John Gray; director of photography, Eugene Shlugleit; edited by Lou Kleinman; produced by Sue Jett and Tony Mark; released by Vestron Pictures. At 23d Street West Triplex, between Eighth and Ninth Avenues. Running time: 95 minutes. This film is rated PG.
Jack Galvin .... Karl Malden
Billy .... Lenny von Dohlen
Mae .... Joyce Van Patten
Nora .... Toni Kalem
Donny .... Keith Szarabajka
George .... Alan North
Nolan .... Paul Guilfoyle
Kennedy .... Barton Heyman

J ACK GALVIN, the title character's father in the family drama "Billy Galvin," likes to watch the Muppets on television. He calls people "Yardbird," and can't stand it when his wife forgets to close the kitchen cabinet door. These details, in John Gray's simple, big-hearted and essentially familiar film, are meant to say a good deal more about Jack's character than they actually do. But then, surprise is less central to "Billy Galvin" than sentiment, anyhow. Scratch any one of the principals — Billy, his parents, his barmaid girlfriend, kindly mentor or helpful roommate — and there's a wistful speech lurking just beneath the surface.

The setting is Boston, and the characters mostly Irish; a lot of them, like Jack (Karl Malden) and Billy (Lenny Von Dohlen), work in blue-collar construction jobs. This is a bone of contention between the Galvins, since the father wants his son to be an architect instead. He wants this so much that he refuses to give Billy work on the high-rise job for which Jack himself is a foreman. Jack even uses his union connections to keep Billy unemployed. But Billy wrangles his way in anyhow and tells his father, in a scene Mr. Gray films as a highly confrontational two-shot, that he won't back down.

It's not hard to anticipate the father-son rapprochement toward which "Billy Galvin," which opens today at the 23d Street West Triplex, is eventually headed. Nor is it hard to guess that both Jack and Billy, for all their tough talk, are softies at heart. As it turns out, Jack just wants a better life for Billy than the one he's had, and simply has a funny way of showing it. Billy, for his part, just wants to be like his dad. So Mr. Gray's screenplay must create a series of false flare-ups to maintain the illusion of conflict between these two, as well as tangential troubles between Billy and his sweetheart (Toni Kalem).

But it all progresses with surprising ease, in spite of the material's essential ordinariness. Mr. Gray's direction helps give his screenplay an energy it might otherwise lack, and most of the performers are relaxed and convincing. Though the oft-repeated idea that "Everything goes by so *fast*" threatens to give the film a maudlin streak, its tone is gentle and even mildly humorous. Mr. Malden and Mr. Von Dohlen are well-matched, sharing both stubbornness and affection. Their sincerity, and Mr. Gray's, are the film's greatest assets.

•

"Billy Galvin" is rated PG ("Parental Guidance Suggested"). It contains some strong language.

JANET MASLIN

1987 F 20, C8:5

The Rambo Game

DEATH BEFORE DISHONOR, directed by Terry J. Leonard; story and screenplay by John Gatliff and Lawrence Kubik; director of photography, Don Burgess; edited by Steve Mirkovich; music by Brian May; produced by Lawrence Kubik; released by New World Pictures. At Embassy 1, Broadway and 46th Street; Loews Orpheum, Third Avenue and 86th Street, and other theaters. Running time: 96 minutes. This film is rated R.
Burns .... Fred Dryer
Ramirez .... Joey Gian
Ruggieri .... Sasha Mitchell
James .... Peter Parros
Halloran .... Brian Keith
Ambassador .... Paul Winfield
Elli .... Joanna Pacula
Maude .... Kasey Walker
Jihad .... Rockne Tarkington
Amin .... Dan Chodos
Gavril .... Muhamad Bakri

By JANET MASLIN

T HE movies are looking for a few good men, to change the face of American foreign policy and out-Rambo Rambo in the process. The latest of these hopefuls is Gunnery Sgt. Jack Burns, who in "Death Before Dishonor" is a marine with a mission. Stationed in the fictitious Middle Eastern country of Jemal, Burns (Fred Dryer) must stand by helplessly while his commanding officer (Brian Keith) is kidnapped by Arab terrorists. The terrorists' actions, reprehensible as they are, exist chiefly as an excuse for Burns to do what he does best: get fighting mad.

"Death Before Dishonor," which opens today at the Embassy 1 and other theaters, isn't nearly as inflammatory as it would like to be. A lot of blood is shed and a lot of slogans spouted, but the effect is still strangely tame. It may just be that there's an art to this sort of film making after all, and that "Death Before Dishonor," which is of about the caliber of "Delta Force," is simply too perfunctory. Say what you like about Rambo, but at least he had style.

What Sergeant Burns has, in this film directed by Terry J. Leonard, is a physical advantage; he's a lot taller and tougher-looking than anyone around him. Mr. Dryer, who stars in the television series "Hunter," has a blunt look like Jack Nicholson's without any of the mischief or cunning. What he has instead is a capacity for cold, unblinking rage, never modulated by reason of any kind. The film seems to be cooling it heels while it waits to give Burns sufficient excuse to let loose.

In Nicosia, an Israeli ambassador and his family are murdered by two terrorists, one of whom — this is Hollywood, after all — is a machine-gun-toting cutie (Kasey Walker) in a tank top and tight black jeans. In Jemal, to which the story proceeds, there is another sexy villain, this one a news photographer (Joanna Pacula) working hand in hand with a group of what seem to be Palestinians. Meanwhile, back home, two of Burns's new re-

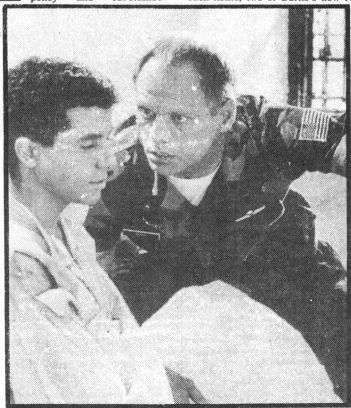

Yossi Ashdot is interrogated by Fred Dryer, a Marine counterterrorist specialist, in "Death Before Dishonor."

cruits are being initiated into the corps. To do this, they must chug a gallon or two of beer out of their helmets and stand by manfully while other marines pound gold insignia pins into the new recruits' chests, until they bleed.

•

Burns amuses his men with Marine humor, like a story about his being surrounded and greatly outnumbered in El Salvador. "So how'd you get away?" one of the younger men asks. "We didn't," Burns deadpans. "So what happened?" he is asked again. "We were killed — har har!" is the punch line. Don't get it? Then "Death Before Dishonor" may not be for you.

Those at whom it is aimed are those who will appreciate the little things, like the bumper sticker that reads "God, Guts and Guns Keep America Free," or the portrait of John Wayne in fighting regalia. They may also enjoy some of horrific touches, like the power drill with which the kidnapped officer and his driver are enthusiastically tortured. There is also plenty of tough talk to savor, like Burns's command to the pretty journalist to "Do me a favor and tell your terrorist friends this: Don't get us mad." And Paul Winfield, as the American Ambassador to Jemal, must firmly tell this same young woman that "the reality is, Miss, the United States does not and will not negotiate with terrorists." In view of recent events, that line's effect is different from what must have been intended.

The terrorists, depicted as worthless, lying scum, are led by a character named Abu Jihad, who is in fact played by an actor named Rockne Tarkington. Amazing.

1987 F 20, C10:1

To Have and to Hold

THE GOOD WIFE, directed by Ken Cameron; screenplay by Peter Kenna; director of photography, James Bartle; edited by John Scott; music by Cameron Allan; produced by Jan Sharp; released by Atlantic Releasing Corporation. At Loews 84th Street Six, at Broadway; U.A. Twin, Broadway and 49th Street, and other theaters. Running time: 97 minutes. This film is rated R.

Marge Hills	Rachel Ward
Sonny Hills	Bryan Brown
Sugar Hills	Steven Vidler
Neville Gifford	Sam Neill
Daisy	Jennifer Claire
Archie	Bruce Barry
Ned Hopper	Peter Cummins
Mrs. Gibson	Carole Skinner
Mrs. Jackson	Clarissa Kaye-Mason
Mr. Fielding	Barry Hill

"THE GOOD WIFE," set in the long-ago 1930's, is Marge Hills (Rachel Ward), an earnest, reliable friend to anyone in need in the rural New South Wales town where she lives with her husband, Sonny (Bryan Brown), a hard-working logger. When a baby's expected in the community, Marge becomes the unpaid midwife. She remembers birthdays. She's polite, cheerful and always has a nice word to say about everybody.

When first seen in "The Good Wife," the Australian film opening today at Loews 84th Street Six and other theaters, Marge is on her hands and knees, scrubbing the floor of the modest, immaculately-kept bungalow she shares with Sonny and, very soon, with Sonny's younger, loutish brother, Sugar (Steven Vidler).

Marge likes her husband. He's thoughtful and gives her security,

though he makes love with all the passion of — and somewhat more quickly than — someone brushing his teeth.

To tell the truth, which the movie stresses at some length, Marge lacks sexual fulfillment. She's not as shocked as you might expect when, out of Sonny's hearing one evening, Sugar looks up from his newspaper and says, "Marge, why can't we do what you and Sonny do?" Something stirs deep inside Marge. She says, "Why don't you ask Sonny?"

Sugar does, and Sonny, who needs his brother as much as he needs Marge, says, "O.K." It's O.K. for everyone except Marge. Alas, Sugar is even more fleet in bed than Sonny. Thus Marge is fair game when the smooth-talking, city-handsome Neville Gifford (Sam Neill) arrives in town to take over management of the local saloon. More out of boredom than anything else, Neville makes a blunt, half-hearted proposition to Marge that awakens her sleeping passions and, worse, her fantasies. The sweet, mild-mannered slavey suddenly becomes a half-crazed slave to her own titanic sexual obsessions.

"The Good Wife" was directed by Ken Cameron from an original screenplay by the Australian playwright Peter Kenna, who describes it as "a modern-day 'Madame Bovary.' " That's only partially true. Though "The Good Wife" is acted with restraint by Miss Ward and her co-stars, it also recalls Bette Davis's camp-classic "Beyond the Forest." "The Good Wife" isn't grotesque enough to be camp. It's never silly

even when overwrought. However, it's so full of underdeveloped material that, by the time you reach the end, you feel cheated. Perhaps it should have been a novel.

It may also be that Mr. Kenna's screenplay would have been better served had Mr. Cameron treated it in a grittier, less picturesque fashion, with fewer shots of ironically tranquil landscapes and dawns, and more attention to the rudeness of the characters, including poor Marge. These people are denatured James M. Cain people.

Miss Ward is an astonishingly beautiful woman, in a high-fashion way, and though she's also a good actress, she seems here to have been cast below her station. In her cheap, shapeless little cotton frocks, bought off the rack, she looks as if she were going to what the rich, during the Depression, used to call a hard-times party. There's intelligence in what she, Mr. Brown, Mr. Vidler and Mr. Neill do, but no overwhelming emotional conviction.

When you aren't absolutely convinced by a movie of this sort, the usual reaction is to laugh in the wrong places.
VINCENT CANBY

1987 F 20, C19:3

ALPINE FIRE, directed and written by Fredi M. Murer; in Swiss-German dialect; cameraman, Pio Corradi; edited by Helena Gerber; music by Mario Beretta; a Bernard Lang Production; presented by Vestron Pictures. At Cinema Studio I, 66th Street and Broadway. Running time: 117 minutes. This film is rated R.

Rachel Ward and Bryan Brown star in "The Good Wife," directed by Ken Cameron and set in the Australian countryside in 1939.

The Boy	Thomas Nock
Belli	Johanna Lier
The Mother	Dorothea Moritz
The Father	Rolf Illig
The Grandmother	Tilli Breidenbach
The Grandfather	Joerg Odermatt

LIKE its title, Fredi M. Murer's "Alpine Fire" is ultimately a lot more corny (and a lot less meaningful) than one wants to believe while watching it. The Swiss film is the first fiction feature to be made by Mr. Murer, who, until now, has specialized in documentaries, and who clearly knows how to photograph scenery and weather under difficult conditions.

Shot high in the Urner Deutsh region of the Swiss Alps — in spring, summer, fall and deepest winter — the movie is most interesting when it is simply recording the long, difficult, daily routines of an ancient farm family living at a precarious slant near the top of Europe. Mr. Murer doesn't get carried away by the spectacular mountainscapes, but they remain more riveting, even in the background, than the primal urges of the characters in the foreground.

These are a laconic, hard-bitten but loving father and mother, who married late in life, and their two children, the teen-aged, deaf son, called simply "the boy," and his pretty older sister, Belli, who acts as teacher to her younger brother.

Farming is difficult enough in the most benign terrain. On the side of a rocky Alp, isolated as much by nonstop chores as by geography, the members of this family face physical and psychological problems of an especially exotic kind. Until this particular year, they seem to have coped pretty well.

However, when the boy — as is said, in this sort of fiction — becomes a man, forbidden longings make themselves felt. Belli and the boy drift into a relationship that, under the circumstances, seems perfectly natural. However, it's not one that could easily be accepted by even far more sophisticated folk.

Though apparently made on a limited budget, and without stars, "Alpine Fire" is reminiscent of the "cinema of quality" against which the young turks of France's New Wave originally rebelled. I think of Jean Delannoy's "Symphonie Pastorale" (1948), initially because of the scenery. Yet there's also about "Alpine Fire" the sort of noble, trumped-up romanticism with which Mr. Delannoy and Jean Aurenche, his collaborator, treated problems fairly remote to the rest of us.

Alpine incest is an idea whose time has not yet come. It's also a subject of fairly limited application.

Though Mr. Murer's screenplay has built-in problems, he has cast and directed it with a good deal of skill, right up to its surreal ending, the only way out of a narrative from which there could be no other exit that wouldn't destroy all that's gone before. Rolf Illig and Dorothea Moritz give beautifully timed and controlled performances as the parents, and Johanna Lier remains sweetly mysterious as the doomed Belli. Thomas Nock is also persuasive as the boy.

Mr. Murer is evidently a man who knows how to direct actors as well as he knows how to take advantage of the elements. In "Alpine Fire," however, the elements and the scenery have a majestic beauty that overwhelms everything else.

"Alpine Fire" opens today at the Cinema Studio 1.   VINCENT CANBY

1987 F 20, C20:1

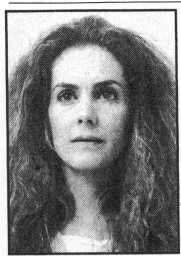

Julie Hagerty

Yuppie Muddle

BEYOND THERAPY, directed by Robert Altman; screenplay by Christopher Durang and Mr. Altman, based on the play by Mr. Durang; director of photography, Pierre Mignot; edited by Steve Dunn; music by Gabriel Yared; produced by Steven M. Haft; released by New World Pictures. At Guild 50th Street, west of Fifth Avenue; U.A. Gemini Twin, 64th Street and Second Avenue; Waverly Twin, Avenue of the Americas and Third Street; Loews 84th Street Six, at Broadway. Running time: 93 minutes. This film is rated R.

Prudence	Julie Hagerty
Bruce	Jeff Goldblum
Charlotte	Glenda Jackson
Stuart	Tom Conti
Bob	Christopher Guest
Zizi	Geneviève Page
Andrew	Cris Campion
Cindy	Sandrine Dumas
Le Gérant	Bertrand Bonvoisin

By VINCENT CANBY

PRUDENCE and Bruce, two yuppies who still have a few years left before hitting the age of mandatory retirement, are a match made not in heaven but in the personals column of New York magazine. Everything goes wrong when, after she answers his ad, they meet for the first time in a French restaurant.

Bruce admires her breasts and her contact lenses. Prudence likes the timbre of his voice. He likes *her* voice. She *loves* the Brut cologne he's wearing. "Thank you," says Bruce, "my male lover Bob gave it to me." At that point, Prudence begins to think she should leave, though she doesn't and the muddle increases.

Bruce tells her that she's both like a little girl and like a woman. Prudence: "How am I like a woman?" He says that she dresses like a woman and wears eye shadow like a woman. With utter sincerity she attempts to return the compliment: "You're like a man. You're tall. You have to shave." He also likes to cry, but she thinks men shouldn't cry "unless something falls on them," which Bruce calls sexist.

In Robert Altman's screen adaptation of Christopher Durang's stage farce "Beyond Therapy," Prudence and Bruce are a most winning misalliance as played by the singularly earnest and comic Julie Hagerty and Jeff Goldblum. She has a silent-screen heroine's stubborn innocence combined with the weary reason of someone who's been through the mill. He comes on with the eagerness of a lap dog that doesn't know it's the size of a Great Dane. When he's feeling frisky, people get squashed.

"Beyond Therapy," which opens today at the Guild 50th Street and other theaters, has a cast of good farceurs. In addition to Miss Hagerty and Mr. Goldblum, they are Tom Conti and Glenda Jackson, as the respective, totally mad analysts of Prudence and Bruce, and Christopher Guest ("This Is Spinal Tap") as Bruce's reluctantly abandoned lover, Bob.

Mr. Durang is not nice about analysts. Miss Jackson has enormous enthusiasm for her work, though she's inclined to say "porpoise" when she means "patient" and "dirigible" when she means "secretary." The analyst played by Mr. Conti is a lecher who spends part of each 50-minute hour making fun of Prudence, the other part trying to persuade her to go to bed with him.

What "Beyond Therapy" lacks — to a near-fatal degree — is the kind of inexorable logic that is the fuel of any farce and makes its loony characters so funny. In classic farce, no matter what the characters do, it's bound to turn out badly, not because the people are stupid but because they are obsessed by their own desperate needs.

Under Mr. Altman's wayward direction, "Beyond Therapy" has been transformed into a feature-length blur. There's no special logic at work. The performances are good, but the film has been assembled without an overriding sense of humor and style. It remains in bits and pieces.

It's possible to hear most of Mr. Durang's often priceless dialogue without ever quite understanding who's doing what to whom or why. The screenplay, written by Mr. Durang and Mr. Altman, adds one major character (that of Bob's "theatrical" mother, who remains an offstage presence in the play). This character could be funny, though the performance here is not. It isn't the screenplay that's cracked. It's Mr. Altman's production "improvements," which only get in the way of the straight and narrow farcical narrative line.

Cluttering up the landscape are subsidiary characters (mostly nonspeaking roles) who are supposed to be funny but who remain utterly mysterious. The film also suggests, though tentatively, that the two analysts have themselves been having a furious, anonymous affair, which is a good idea that has no real payoff.

Even more ambiguous and disorienting is the fact that the film seems to have been made in Paris, though the setting is Manhattan, which may make you feel as if you're having a breakdown while watching it. However, it does allow Mr. Altman to close with a shot that might be described as an anticlimactic epiphany.

If "Beyond Therapy" does nothing else — and it doesn't — it proves that farces don't need epiphanies, especially anticlimactic ones.

1987 F 27, C8:5

Sex as Power

WORKING GIRLS, directed by Lizzie Borden; screenplay by Miss Borden with Sandra Kay, story by Miss Borden; director of photography, Judy Irola; music by David van Tieghem; produced by Miss Borden and Andi Gladstone; released by Miramax Films. At 57th Street Playhouse, Avenue of the Americas and 57th Street. Running time: 90 minutes. This film has no rating.

Molly	Louise Smith
Lucy	Ellen McElduff
Dawn	Amanda Goodwin
Gina	Marusia Zach
April	Janne Peters
Mary	Helen Nicholas

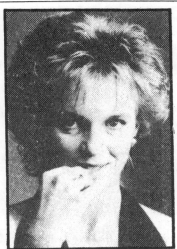

Louise Smith

ON its surface, Lizzie Borden's "Working Girls" seems to be a remarkably even-tempered view of prostitution, at least as practiced by the women who work in a small, expensive, immaculately maintained Manhattan bordello.

The "girls" themselves are a fairly unusual crew. They include Molly, a pretty Yale graduate with degrees in English literature and art history, and Dawn, a beauty who looks to be about 20 and is studying for a law degree. Nobody at this "club" has been kidnapped by white-slavers or lured away from home after being hooked on drugs. These women are there because the pay is good and the hours more or less what they make them.

"Working Girls," directed by Miss Borden and written by her and Sandra Kay, covers several days in the life of Molly, who, as played with Ivy League cool by Louise Smith, is a hooker entirely in command of her life as well as one with an appreciation for language. "I don't believe there's such a word as 'aphrodisiacal,' " she says when one of her customers attempts to describe a particularly exciting experience.

Molly has a stable relationship with her black female lover (who doesn't know about her "job") and her lover's small daughter. Sometime in the future she may become a professional photographer.

●

Most of the other women are equally at ease in their work, though April, who's 43 and now dealing cocaine as a sideline, seems to be in the life mostly to prove to herself that she still has the right stuff.

However, "Working Girls" is not quite as serene — and certainly not as passive — as it initially seems, and this is the film's achievement. Miss Borden, whose "Born in Flames" (1983) was militantly feminist, here adopts an entirely different approach.

"Working Girls," though a work of fiction, sounds as authentic as might a documentary about coal miners. The camera attends to the duties of the "girls" without apparent emotional response. Yet, as it watches them smile on their customers, build their egos and affect a totally bogus camaraderie with the men, it's ridiculing the poor slobs who must come to them with their fat wallets in search of pleasure and release.

Within the bounds of fairly conventional sex, the "girls" give the customers their money's worth. The work is grubby and exhausting but, ultimately, it's also a demonstration of women's power. Sex is a natural resource that, as long as the society remains as it is, might as well be exploited. Other feminists might object, but Miss Borden is worth listening to.

●

She's also a good, disciplined film maker. The movie, which is small in scope, is extremely well photographed by Judy Irola and looks almost self-effacing. There's no fanciness about the production. It's as straightforward as are "the girls" going about their business. The excellent cast includes Amanda Goodwin as Dawn, the would-be lawyer; Janne Peters as the aging April, and Ellen McElduff as the madam who puts great store by promptness, cleanliness and the value of a buck.

"Working Girls" opens today at the 57th Street Playhouse.

VINCENT CANBY

1987 F 27, C8:5

Heartland Hoops

HOOSIERS, directed by David Anspaugh; written by Angelo Pizzo; director of photography, Fred Murphy; film editor, C. Timothy O'Meara; music by Jerry Goldsmith; produced by Carter de Haven and Mr. Pizzo; released by Orion Pictures Corporation. At U.A. Twin, Broadway and 49th Street; Gemini Twin, 64th Street and Second Avenue; U.A. East, First Avenue and 85th Street; Loews 84th Street Six, at Broadway; 23d Street West Triplex, near Eighth Avenue. Running time: 115 minutes. This film is rated PG.

Coach Norman Dale	Gene Hackman
Myra Fleener	Barbara Hershey
Shooter	Dennis Hopper
Cletus	Sheb Wooley
Opal Fleener	Fern Persons
George	Chelcie Ross
Rollin	Robert Swan
Rooster	Michael O'Guinne
Mr. Doty	Wil Dewitt
Sheriff Finley	John Robert Thompson

WHO could resist a tiny Middle Western town where the barber shop is called Rooster's and the game of basketball is foremost on every mind? Probably no one, and the quaintly innocent "Hoosiers" is irresistible in much the same way. This film's very lack of surprise and sophistication accounts for a lot of its considerable charm. As written by Angelo Pizzo, directed by David Anspaugh, imbued with a convincingly old-fashioned look and acted in a friendly, forthright manner, "Hoosiers" seems about as sweetly unself-conscious as a film can be.

"Hoosiers," which opens today at the U.A. Twin and other theaters, is a sports drama about playing, competing and going the distance. But it presents those things simply, harkening back to a time well before "Rocky" was a gleam in Sylvester Stallone's eye. Based by Mr. Pizzo on a real David and Goliath episode in Indiana basketball history (the story of the 1954 Milan High School team), it tells the fictitious story of Coach Norman Dale (Gene Hackman), who in 1951 arrives in the remote hamlet of Hickory, Ind., a place where people have names like Opal and Cletus and Junior. "This place don't even appear on most state maps," says his fellow teacher Myra Fleener (Barbara Hershey), a straight-backed, guarded woman who is deeply suspicious of Coach Dale from the very start (though she eventually grows willing to go for long strolls through the farm country with him). "A man who

Gary Farr

Gene Hackman stars as a high school history teacher and basketball coach in
David Anspaugh's "Hoosiers," set in a small town in Indiana in 1951.

comes to a place like this, either he's runnin' away from somethin' or he has nowhere else to go," she says.

Sure enough, Coach Dale is running from an earlier career crisis in a much bigger league. And sure enough, this is his last chance. In addition to offering the coach a very clear shot at redemption, the story also introduces Shooter (Dennis Hopper), who has a phenomenal knowledge of basketball and also happens to be the town drunk. The coach's last chance turns out to be Shooter's last chance too, to regain his self-respect and also the love of his boy, who happens to be on the Hickory team. "Son — oh, I *wish* I could be there!" cries Shooter when the team stands on the brink of the state championship. It's a sentimental role, but Mr. Hopper manages to seem no less at home than he did in "Blue Velvet." That alone is enough to make his Oscar nomination (which is for this film) well deserved.

●

Mr. Hackman is exactly right for the role of Coach Dale, bringing shrewdness and a varied temperament to a man who might otherwise have seemed bland. Though the coach does scandalize Hickory with his unorthodox methods — ignoring the advice of a former coach, booting the local sheriff and Rooster out of practice sessions, and enlisting Shooter as his right-hand man — his approach is generally too helpful to seem shocking.

When the Hickory team, made of farm boys who've "probably never seen a building over two stories except in a photograph," according to the coach, go to the city for the championship competition, they are visibly unnerved by the sight of the big arena in which the game will take place. (All but one of the extremely clean-cut team members are played by non-actors from Indiana.) So the coach takes out his tape measure, and has the players measure some of the dimensions of the court, and reassures them that it is exactly equivalent to what they're used to. They are relieved; he may not be. "It is big!" he whispers excitedly a moment later.

"Hoosiers" isn't. It's a small film, and a very admirable one.

●

"Hoosiers" is rated PG ("Parental Guidance Suggested"). It contains some mildly rude language.
JANET MASLIN

1987 F 27, C10:3

Perchance to Dream

A NIGHTMARE ON ELM STREET 3: DREAM WARRIORS, directed by Chuck Russell; written by Wes Craven and Bruce Wagner; director of photography, Roy Wagner; edited by Terry Stokes; music by Angelo Badalamenti; produced by Robert Shaye; released by New Line Cinema. At Embassy 2, Broadway at 47th Street; Embassy 3, Broadway at 47th Street; Orpheum Twin, 86th Street near Third Avenue; Loews 84th Street Six, near Broadway; Eighth Street Playhouse, near Avenue of the Americas, and other theaters. Running time: 97 minutes. This film is rated R.
Nancy Thompson .... Heather Langenkamp
Kristen Parker .... Patricia Arquette
Max ....Larry Fishburne
Freddy Krueger .... Robert Englund
Dr. Elizabeth Simms .... Priscilla Pointer
Dr. Neil Goldman .... Craig Wasson
Elaine Parker ....Brooke Bundy
Joey ....Rodney Eastman
Phillip .... Bradley Gregg
Will .... Ira Heiden
Kincaid .... Ken Sagoes
Jennifer .... Penelope Sudrow
Taryn .... Jennifer Rubin

FREDDY KRUEGER is the most talkative of slashers, and also the most creative. In "A Nightmare on Elm Street 3: Dream Warriors," which opens today at the Embassy 2 and 3 and other theaters, he displays a great debt to Dali in concocting surreal visions for his prey. When Freddy enters the dreams of his teen-age victims, ordinary objects become armed and dangerous. A bathroom faucet may sprout claws like Freddy's and grab its victim. A mirror may snatch up someone passing by. A roasted pig may rear up from the dining room table and growl. Small wonder that one young woman gulps down undiluted instant-coffee crystals, in her efforts to avoid Freddy's idea of dreamland.

In the new film, directed by Chuck Russell (who co-wrote "Dreamscape"), a group of young people are brought together in the psychiatric ward of a hospital, united by Freddy's ability to enter their dreams. What they have in common, it develops, is a tie to the Elm Street of the first film, though no one explains why they never ran into one another on the block. In any case, they band together in an effort to fend off Freddy, whose method is to generate fantasies so awful they lure people to their deaths. In one such sequence, a young woman innocently watching late-night television is provoked to the point of suicide when she sees Dick Cavett turn into Freddy and attack Zsa Zsa Gabor.

The film's dream sequences are ingenious, and they feature some remarkable nightmare images and spe-

cial effects. Freddy may emerge as a giant man-eating serpent, or perhaps as a puppet come to life, maybe even as a beautiful woman who quite literally tongue-lashes and tongue-ties her prey. If his victim has a fondness for drugs, he may develop syringe-like fingers; for a person who is paralyzed, he may devise an extra-special wheelchair. Mr. Russell, directing a screenplay by Wes Craven and Bruce Wagner, keeps the visions varied and clever. Unfortunately, the overall film lacks the tight logic of its dream episodes. It's never quite clear when and how Freddy can enter a dream, how many people can see him simultaneously, how often he can kill off the same victim (some die, and some just wake up with a tell-tale scratch or two). Also, Mr. Russell mounts the nightmares a lot more effectively than he directs the actors in quieter moments. Craig Wasson is on the bland side as a doctor investigating the Freddy problem. And Heather Langenkamp, as a beautiful dream disorder expert who is an old hand at Freddy's game, hardly radiates the poise of a medical professional. If anything, she brings to mind the Miss America Pageant and its talent competition.

Some of the tormented teen-age roles are well played (Patricia Arquette as one haggard insomniac, Jennifer Rubin as another), and Priscilla Pointer is dependably good as a Freddy-proof doctor. But the real star is Freddy himself, brought scarily to life by Robert Englund. Freddy taunts his victims a lot more vocally and colorfully than most of his horror-film comrades; he's much better company than Jason ("Friday the 13th"), for example. Despite a subplot that involves a mysterious nun and finally labels him as "the bastard son of a hundred maniacs," he seems to be insult-proof, too. And indestructible. Though one of the more remarkable episodes reduces him to the status of a mere skeleton, the film ends with the obligatory frisson of foreboding. Freddy will be back.
JANET MASLIN

1987 F 27, C15:3

An Immigrant's Story

CLASS RELATIONS, directed and written and edited by Jean-Marie Straub and Danièle Huillet; in German with English subtitles; photography by William Lubtchansky; production companies, Janus Film and Fernsehen, Hessischen Rundfunk and NEF-Diffusion. At Public Theater, 425 Lafayette Street. Running time: 126 minutes. This film has no rating.

Karl Rossmann .... Christian Heinisch
Uncle Jacob .... Mario Adorf
Delamarche .... Harun Farocki
Chef .... Kathrin Bold
Brunelda ....Laura Betti

"Class Relations" was shown as part of the 1984 New York Film Festival. Following are excerpts from Vincent Canby's review, which appeared in The New York Times Oct. 7, 1984. The film opens today at the Public Theater, 425 Lafayette Street.

MORE than the films of any other directors, the minimalist works of Jean-Marie Straub and Danièle Huillet, his wife and collaborator, demand that one be in a mood so receptive that it borders on the brainwashed.

This is said by way of confession, for I've been fascinated by at least two of their films — "The Chronicle of Anna Magdalena Bach" and their adaptation of Arnold Schoenberg's "Moses and Aaron" — and been threatened with dreamless slumber by others.

Their latest, "Class Relations," based on Franz Kafka's first novel, "Amerika" (1912), is far less minimal than even "Moses and Aaron," but then it doesn't have Schoenberg on the soundtrack. There's also the problem that the Straubs' dry, deadpanned cinema is not really as well suited to this particular Kafka work as one might expect. Like the Straubs, Kafka resolutely refuses to evoke any kind of emotional identification in his audience. Yet "Amerika" is also far funnier than the Straubs can allow their movie to be.

Following the Kafka text with some fidelity, "Class Relations" is about the adventures of a young European immigrant named Karl Rossmann who, even before he gets off the boat in New York Harbor, discovers a land where everyone, namely Karl, is presumed guilty until proved innocent, which is impossible in the Kafka universe.

However, unlike Joseph K. in "The Trial," Karl is neither destroyed by his presumed guilt nor liberated by his ultimate acceptance of it. Karl Rossmann is infinitely practical and resilient as he moves with steadfast serenity from one unearned put-down to the next.

Though the Straubs do move their camera throughout these adventures, the camera somehow gives the impression that it would prefer to stay where it is. It's a cat that wants to sit in the sun. The minimalism is expressed in the impassive attitudes of the actors, and in the manner in which they deliver their dialogue, which sounds as if they were giving instructions on how to put on one's life jacket in case of an unscheduled landing at sea.

Robert Bresson does something similar, but the point in the Straubs' film is not to call attention to the distance between actor and dramatized circumstance, as in Bresson, but to deny the viewer any chance to respond in predictable ways.

Though Karl moves through America as an innocent, he's not filled with any crazy, Candide-like optimism. He's utterly, consistently rational, incapable of surprise and, when, at the end, he seeks relief by going off to the Nature Theater of Oklahoma, one may be sure he'll rise above whatever it turns out to be. Though always misjudged, Karl has no sense of guilt, and so the system doesn't terrify him. It simply doesn't work as well as it might.

The actors are unusually good.

Standouts are Christian Heinisch, who plays Karl with solemn, angelic patience; Mario Adorf, as Karl's expansive, inscrutable Uncle Jacob; Laura Betti, as a singer, and Kathrin Bold, as a cook who does her best to support Karl in the face of all of the nonevidence against him.

1987 F 27, C16:1

Dream Date

SOME KIND OF WONDERFUL, directed by Howard Deutch; written by John Hughes; film editors, Bud Smith and Scott Smith; director of photography, Jan Kiesser; produced by Mr. Hughes; released by Paramount Pictures. At Paramount, 61st Street and Broadway; Orpheum, 86th Street near Third Avenue; 34th Street Showplace, between Second and Third Avenues. Running time: 93 minutes. This film is rated PG-13.

Keith Nelson	Eric Stoltz
Amanda Jones	Lea Thompson
Watts	Mary Stuart Masterson
Hardy Jenns	Craig Sheffer
Cliff	John Ashton
Laura	Maddie Corman
Skinhead	Elias Koteas
Mia	Chynna Phillips
Shayne	Molly Hagan

By JANET MASLIN

JOHN HUGHES may be the only grown man in America capable of shaping an entire film, quite seriously, around a question of who will take whom to the prom. In films like "Sixteen Candles" and "The Breakfast Club" (which he wrote and directed) and "Pretty in Pink" (which he wrote and produced), Mr. Hughes's preoccupation with the most microscopic teenage problems has made him king of an entire genre, however inconsequential and small.

But at long last, the John Hughes method has paid off. "Some Kind of Wonderful," produced and written by Mr. Hughes and directed (as "Pretty in Pink" was) by Howard Deutch, has a much wider appeal than its predecessors. It has a light touch, a disarming cast, a well-developed sense of humor and a lot of charm. It also shows off, even better than the earlier films have, Mr. Hughes's keen understanding of the world his young characters inhabit and the ways in which they might behave. What would a ninth-grader do if her father poked his head into the classroom one day and said, "Hi, honey," in front of all her friends? That's simple. She'd scream.

"Some Kind of Wonderful," which opens today at the Orpheum and other theaters, is a much-improved, recycled version of the "Pretty in Pink" story. In both these films, an uncool, unpopular teen-ager from the wrong side of town becomes fixated on someone rich, heedless and good-looking, ignoring a best friend of the opposite sex whose attentions are sincere. In this case, it is Keith Nelson (Eric Stoltz) who tells his father, "I like art, I'm working at a gas station, my best friend is a tomboy. These things don't fly too high in the American high school." Yet Keith, outcast that he is, has developed a crush on Amanda Jones (Lea Thompson), who takes her name from the busy little princess of the Rolling Stones song.

Keith's best friend, and the one who really cares for him, is the tough, boyish Watts (Mary Stuart Masterson), who turns up in men's underwear and dogtags in one locker-room scene. Watts is prepared to sit by stoically while Keith makes a fool of himself over Amanda, occasionally offering

Eric Stoltz

the kind of hard-boiled, colloquial advice Mr. Hughes writes so well. "Chicks like her have one thing on their mind, and you don't make enough of it to matter to her," Watt says. When Keith counters that you can't tell a book by a cover, she points out, "Yeah, but you can tell how much it's gonna cost."

Keith's friendship with Watts, his home life with bewildered parents and precocious siblings, his standing among his schoolmates — all these things are established by Mr. Hughes and Mr. Deutch in a funny and involving way. It may well be that Mr. Hughes's work, which seems so much more controlled and less manic this time, is shown off to best advantage when filtered through a second party. In any case, "Some Kind of Wonderful" progresses comfortably and affectingly until it reaches what ought to be a dead end. As in "Pretty in Pink," Mr. Hughes gives his central character an impossible choice between two suitors, each of whom is made to seem appealing. But this film segues easily into near-fantasy, with an ending right out of a fairy tale.

Though parts of "Some Kind of Wonderful" are sketchy — there isn't much explanation of how Watts became so aggressively boyish, for example — the principals' acting fills in the gaps. Mr. Stoltz, who was seen (or not quite seen) as the facially deformed Rocky Dennis in "Mask," emerges as a handsome, self-possessed actor with a clear, steady gaze. If he doesn't seem precisely the school pariah, he does make Watts's crush understandable. And Mary Stuart Masterson turns Watts, who for all her black leather is something of a stock character, into a figure ennobled by her fierce longing. It's a touching and dignified performance, so much so that Miss Thompson's more superficial Amanda need not be seen as a villainess. The three leads work well together, particularly in the long sequence that has Keith and Amanda going on a carefully planned dream date, with Watts acting as their chauffeur. As the other two sit embracing on the stage of the Hollywood Bowl, with Watts watching miserably from a seat in the rear (the place is otherwise deserted), the film creates a perfect embodiment of every adolescent's nightmare.

Some of the smaller roles are also very well done, in the film's typically exuberant style. Maddie Corman is

amusingly brash as Keith's incorrigible kid sister. And Elias Koteas, as the hood who sits next to Keith in detention one day, has a chance to compare artistic efforts with the story's hero. "That," he says, pointing to an original drawing, "is what my girlfriend would look like without skin."

FILM VIEW

JANET MASLIN

Movie Bloodlines Lead To Rambo's Children

Films may not have the bloodlines that race horses do, but a hit has a way of leaving a trail. Its descendants are liable to be indirect, thanks to the singularity that makes it a hit in the first place, and to the riskiness of exact cloning (since the authorized clone is almost always a letdown, and the clone without the "II" in its title seldom stands a chance). So anyone who sets out deliberately to copy a hit will soon discover the elusive brilliance of the original, whether it's "E.T." or "Top Gun" or a $100 million-grossing dance movie. But that doesn't mean that the hit isn't, in its own way, able to spawn.

Once a film is installed in the pantheon of popular culture, as "Rambo" surely has been, its influence will be felt in a variety of ways. Yes, there is a "Rambo III" in the works, but that's almost beside the point; it's the oblique influence that is more telling. Very soon after the original release of "Rambo," another film showed a thin, bald man with a rag tied around his head, dressing up as Rambo for a costume party. It also became possible to send a Rambogram to a friend as a practical joke, delivered by some shirtless he-man with a knife in his teeth. At that point, the Rambo ripple effect had begun. And it continues. One of the few lonely jokes in the recent comedy "Mannequin" has to do with a security guard who has made "Rambo" the name of his bulldog.

Even in loftier circles, the aftereffects are still being felt. As was reported last week in these pages, academics across the nation are willing to examine Rambo's speech patterns, his body language, his politics and his resemblance to the President in an entirely serious manner. Someone has even taken the trouble to count the number of lines that Sylvester Stallone so laboriously mutters during the course of the film. Most of them aren't much longer than "Yup" or "Nope," and even the aphorisms are conspicuously terse ("To survive a war, you gotta *become* a war"), but altogether, there are 163.

Of course, "Rambo"-generated fallout can also be found on the screen. The hit's influence can easily be detected in "Death Before Dishonor," which has a Marine hero and a Middle Eastern setting but still employs the Rambo one-man-band approach to foreign policy problem-solving. And the success of "Rambo" also colors "Over the Top," Mr. Stallone's new saga of a triumphant arm-wrestler, even if the chief function of "Rambo" in this case is to cast a long shadow.

The "Rambo" influence can even been seen as playing some role in the box-office success of "Platoon," though Oliver Stone's view of events in Vietnam could not be more different from Mr. Stallone's. Yes, "Rambo" was an action film of almost cartoonlike simplicity, whereas "Platoon" is a thoughtful, visceral work that leaves its audiences devastated. But "Rambo" may have helped pave the way, if not for the making of "Platoon," then for its wide-scale acceptance.

Had "Platoon" arrived in the pre-"Rambo" era, it would certainly have been admired and respected, but it might well have been relegated to art-house status. "Rambo," the first down-to-earth Vietnam blockbuster aimed directly at the solar plexus, may have helped convince the widest possible audience that the memory of Vietnam and the prospect of an exciting hit film were not mutually exclusive. And if the two films' caliber or attitudes are in no way comparable, they don't have to be.

Just as "Kramer vs. Kramer" may have helped pave the way for the very different "Terms of Endearment" by making audiences receptive to emotionally wrenching parent-child subject matter, "Rambo" helped to create the climate in which "Platoon" currently thrives.

In that case, the effect is purely circumstantial, but no one could regard the overlapping of "Death Before Dishonor" with "Rambo" as a happy accident. Actually, the lineage of "Death Before Dishonor" is slightly more complicated, since it owes something to the "Dirty Harry" films as well, namely the specter of a tough-looking vigilante operating outside the law, supposedly for the sake of the community. But this established formula has been updated, thanks to "Rambo," and given a more militaristic angle. So Gunnery Sgt. Jack Burns (Fred Dryer), assigned to the fictitious Arab nation of Jemal, sits still for the American-hating antics of local terrorists only briefly before striking out on his own.

The incendiary trailer for "Death Before Dishonor" fits more flying bodies (mostly in Arab headgear) into two minutes' time than most films pack into two hours. But the finished film is surprisingly tame. Although Burns does launch a one-man war, grudgingly teaming up with Israeli anti-terrorist operatives but still doing most of the dirty work himself, he somehow lacks gusto. Mr. Dryer's characterization is just as cold, nasty and humorless as any "Rambo" fan could wish, but there's an extra dimension that the character lacks. The greased biceps? The flaming bazookas? The special "survival" knife (Rambo's ugly-looking instrument guaranteed to endanger the survival of anyone in its path)? Burns just doesn't have enough of a gimmick, and he doesn't have the crusading craziness that put Rambo on the map. Primitive as it was, "Rambo" had an intensity and personality that aren't easily matched.

That may well have occurred to Mr. Stallone himself in the wake of "Over the Top," his latest stab at creating a new character, and a film apparently not destined (on the evidence of its so-so opening grosses) for box-office immortality. As Mr. Stallone knows better than anyone, "Rambo" is a tough act to follow. And as he must also know, in watching the "Rocky" saga as it wanes, a character like either Rocky or Rambo has a limited life span in the public consciousness, especially if the character's story can be told in its entirety the first time around. So Mr. Stallone continues to devise new vehicles for himself. And "Over the Top" is one of his strangest.

•

Directed by Menahem Golan, the Cannon Films executive who must himself be somewhat mindful of "Rambo" (Mr. Golan also directed "The Delta Force," with Chuck Norris as more of a nice-guy vigilante), "Over the Top" is a film whose subtext is much more interesting than its surface. It presents the ever more glamorous, prosperous-looking Mr. Stallone — no wonder, since he was reportedly paid $12 million to do this — as a poor, humble truck driver named Lincoln Hawk. His two interests in life are his 12-year-old son Michael (David Mendenhall), who has been turned against his father by his mother's wealthy family, and the fine art of arm-wrestling. The film alternates bizarrely between arm-wrestling bouts and Mr. Stallone's own variation on "Kramer vs. Kramer." It's never clear which of these is meant to be the real lure.

In his paternal capacity, Mr. Stallone is forced to do a lot more talking than Rambo does (a big mistake) and to play teacher and mentor. He instructs the boy that winning isn't everything, which is not the lesson of earlier Stallone films, and tells him he can win arm-wrestling bouts just by trying harder than his adversary. (Luckily, the film does not follow Michael's efforts to get through later life with that maxim.) Hawk also teaches his son how to drive his enormous truck illegally, which seems to be some small nod to the vigilante spirit. And he rails against his rich father-in-law in a heated custody battle.

Finally, not because he seeks glory but because he needs money for a new truck, Hawk enters an arm-wrestling contest that pits him against the finest arm-wrestlers in the world. Since "Over the Top" is Mr. Stallone's baby, there's no need to guess whether the story ends in yet another triumph.

What's notable about "Over the Top" is the absence of Mr. Stallone's hit-making acumen, on which even some of his least attractive efforts have been able to trade. Poor trucker fights the establishment? An arm-wrestler claws his way to the top? A father fights for the love of his boy? It's all simple enough, but Mr. Stallone at his shrewdest has been even simpler. In the end, "Rambo" may be best remembered for such crude ingredients as its savage weaponry, bare-chested chic, primitive politics and tongue-tied understatement ("Do we get to win this time?"). It may be sooner rather than later that the sight of an oily, raging Rambo comes to look as sadly outmoded as a white-suited disco dancer on Saturday night. But for the moment, he continues to cast a very long shadow. ■

1987 Mr 1, II:21:1

Abuse of Power

BROKEN MIRRORS, written and directed by Marleen Gorris; in Dutch with English subtitles; photography by Frans Bromet; produced by Matthijs Van Heijningen; distributed by First Run Features. At Film Forum 1, 57 Watts Street. Running time: 110 minutes. This film is not rated.

Diane	Lineke Rijxman
Dora	Henriette Tol

By VINCENT CANBY

BY coincidence, two films have just arrived here that were made by women who see brothels, and the lives of the women who work in them, as signifying the lot of women in a political world in which men have all the power, at least until now.

Lizzie Borden's ironic "Working Girls," which opened last week at the 57th Street Playhouse, is about the women who work in a small, high-class Manhattan brothel that's run with the efficiency of a successful nail-and-skin-care center. Though it's a fiction film, "Working Girls" has the even tone of a rigorously disciplined documentary, which it otherwise doesn't resemble at all.

Opening today at Film Forum 1 is "Broken Mirrors," a 1984 Dutch film written and directed by Marleen Gorris, whose work is more fancified than Miss Borden's but far more conventional.

Crosscut with the stories of the women who work at Amsterdam's Club Happy House, which is just as garish as its customers expect it to be, is the tale of a serial killer who loathes women. He's a respectable, supposedly happily married businessman who kidnaps his victims, chains them to a bed in a remote concrete blockhouse and then starves them to death. He gets his kicks not from sex but from his power to humiliate and degrade, which, according to Miss Gorris, may be not very different from what goes on at the Club Happy House. Only somewhat more extreme.

If you agree with that idea, which vastly oversimplifies the nature of the exchanges that take place within the world's oldest profession, you pretty much have the entire point of "Broken Mirrors." Miss Gorris uses the nonsuspense story of the serial killer as a sort of hook to focus the audience's attention on her feminist concerns, which are a good deal less provocative than Miss Borden's.

"Broken Mirrors" has the manner of a movie that means to be art. The sequences relating to the serial killer have been bleached of the primary colors in which the goings-on at the Club Happy House have been photographed. The performances, however, are good, particularly that of Henriette Tol as a prostitute who knows exactly what she's doing, and when it's time to call it quits.

1987 Mr 4, C21:1

Siding Wars

TIN MEN, written and directed by Barry Levinson; director of photography, Peter Sova; film editor, Stu Linder; music by David Steele and Andy Cox; produced by Mark Johnson; presented by Touchstone Pictures; distributed by Buena Vista Distribution Company. At Cinema 2, Third Avenue at 60th Street; 84th Street Sixplex, at Broadway; Waverly, Third Street and Avenue of the Americas. Running time: 109 minutes. This film is rated R.

B. B.	Richard Dreyfuss
Tilley	Danny DeVito
Nora	Barbara Hershey
Moe	John Mahoney
Sam	Jackie Gayle
Gil	Stanley Brock
Cheese	Seymour Cassel
Mouse	Bruno Kirby
Wing	J. T. Walsh
Carly	Richard Portnow
Looney	Matt Craven
Bagel	Michael Tucker

By JANET MASLIN

TOE to toe, eyeball to eyeball, fin to fin — when the two feuding aluminum siding salesmen in "Tin Men" square off, they use every means available, Cadillacs included. Their battle alone would be enough to sustain an ordinary comedy, but Barry Levinson's richly textured new film also has a rueful nostalgia, a fine-tuned streak of con artistry, and the same hilarious, nit-picking small talk that colored "Diner," his first and best film — which is recalled, rivaled and in a few ways even outdone by this one.

Mr. Levinson's work does not lend itself to the one-sentence synopsis, which is one of the best things about it. It's at least as concerned with ambiance as it is with storytelling. So the new film shares with "Diner" a place (Baltimore), an approximate time (1963, while the earlier film was set in 1959), a hangout (the diner itself) and a couple of minor characters, and it also reprises the earlier film's lifelike, meandering conversational tone. Four years later, Mr. Levinson's characters are still voicing their opinions about things like the proper way to prepare eggs, the best act on "The Ed Sullivan Show" and the questionable realism of "Bonanza." And although the predominantly male characters in this film are older than their "Diner" counterparts, they do not approach such subjects with appreciably more sophistication. "They were older, but they didn't seem particularly responsible, so I was intrigued by that," Mr. Levinson has said about the real aluminum siding men from whom the film takes its inspiration.

"Tin Men," which opens today at Cinema 2 and other theaters, centers on the funny and wholly irrational fight that erupts between two of them. The fact that Bill (B. B.) Babowsky (Richard Dreyfuss) has put only one-sixteenth of a mile on his brand new blue Cadillac before the yellow Cadillac of Ernest Tilley (Danny DeVito) smashes into it is only nominally at the root of their warfare. It's also a clash of styles. B. B., who works for the optimistically named Gibraltar Aluminum Siding Company, favors shiny suits and fancies himself a consummate operator. Tilley, whose company is just as unscrupulous but a little less successful, is more crude. Aside from their occupations and their taste in automobiles, the two have little in common — until B. B. decides to torture Tilley further by chasing his wife. But the wife (Barbara Hershey) is dissatisfied, and Tilley not nearly as concerned with her as he might be. Things don't work out quite the way B. B. planned.

•

Mr. Levinson, whose real genius is for the little things, is able to say everything with props and settings, strange habits and casual remarks. Just as one of the numerous salesmen in "Tin Men" can explain quite sincerely how a smorgasbord table in a restaurant made him think about God, Tilley's wife, Nora, can quietly transfer her cookie jar, which is shaped like a sheep's head, from one man's home to the other's. It's a way of stating where her loyalties now lie, just as Tilley's way of expressing his thoughts about Nora is to make a malevolent inventory of everything she owns. Nobody can get the malicious mileage out of an exclamation like "toiletries!" that Mr. DeVito can.

"Tin Men" has a lot of good performances, just as "Diner" did; the coteries of oddball siding salesmen surrounding each of the two principals (among them Jackie Gayle, John Mahoney, Seymour Cassel, Bruno Kirby and Michael Tucker, who reprises a small "Diner" role) are at the film's very heart. But it also has an outstandingly fine and more substantial performance from Mr. Dreyfuss, who confirms the impression that his career has taken a radically different turn.

Mr. Dreyfuss, absent from the screen for a while before "Down and

Danny DeVito

Richard Dreyfuss

Out in Beverly Hills" and this film, is no longer the antic comic figure of his earlier days. He seems more seasoned, more dignified and no less funny. And the role of a suavely flim-flamming salesman suits him just as well as that of Duddy Kravitz did. Mr. Dreyfuss has a new stateliness that contrasts most amusingly with the mock-elegant outfits he sports here, and the tricks he plays on unsuspecting customers. Dropping matchbooks, waving cash rebates and pretending to be a magazine photographer are only a few of the professional secrets revealed in Mr. Levinson's first-rate screenplay. Production notes point out that all these ploys "are based on actual aluminum siding salesman pitches."

The heyday of these freewheeling characters didn't last; Maryland's Home Improvement Commission saw to that. So "Tin Men" reflects the wistful feeling of a golden age nearing its end. That air of regret also recalls "Diner" and is a shade more appropriate here, if only by virtue of the characters' age. But this film is more conscientiously plotted and a little less full, if only because it concentrates on two principals rather than a half-dozen. And Miss Hershey, appealing as she is, can't do much about the fact that her character matters only marginally in a film that is truly about men. They are men who sustain and annoy one another, men who get on one another's nerves and wouldn't have it any other way. Mr. Levinson understands them completely.

1987 Mr 6, C3:1

ANGEL HEART, directed by Alan Parker; screenplay by Mr. Parker, based on the novel "Falling Angel" by William Hjortsberg; director of photography, Michael Seresin; edited by Gerry Hambling; music by Trevor Jones; produced by Alan Marshall and Elliott Kastner; released by Tri-Star Pictures. At National Twin, Broadway and 44th Street; Tower East, Third Avenue and 71st Street; 84th Street Sixplex, at Broadway; Movieland Eighth Street, at University Place; Movie Center 5, between Powell and Douglass Boulevards. Running time: 113 minutes. This film is rated R.

Harry Angel ....Mickey Rourke
Louis Cyphre ....Robert De Niro
Epiphany Proudfoot ....Lisa Bonet
Margaret Krusemark ......Charlotte Rampling
Ethan Krusemark ....Stocker Fontelieu
Toots Sweet ....Brownie McGhee
Dr. Fowler ....Michael Higgins
Connie ....Elizabeth Whitcraft
Sterne ....Eliott Keener
Spider Simpson ....Charles Gordone
Winesap ....Dann Florek

from a sort of makeshift throne, is a guy named Louis Cyphre (Robert De Niro), a smiling though chilly fellow with enough oil on his hair to put a two-inch slick on the English Channel. He also has Fu Manchu fingernails and a fondness for silver-handled canes.

When Cyphre speaks to Harry, it sounds like a parody of fatherly concern. He's impatient, but he has all the time in the world for Harry. He's both solicitous and overbearing. He wants Harry — and no one but Harry — to track down a once-promising crooner named Johnny Favorite, who disappeared toward the end of World War II before paying off a debt.

There aren't that many sleazy divorce cases coming Harry's way that he can easily refuse the money. Then, too, he's intrigued. Indeed, why him?

In this fashion Mr. Parker, who's both the director and screenwriter, begins his now-notorious "Angel Heart," which, after the removal of 10 seconds of footage, recently received an R rating instead of the X

George Kontaxis

Lisa Bonet and Mickey Rourke star in Alan Parker's drama "Angel Heart."

By VINCENT CANBY

ALAN PARKER'S "Angel Heart" is set in 1955 in the very particular Manhattan of cheap walk-ups, unwashed windows and perpetual twilight inhabited by Harry Angel (Mickey Rourke), a private eye who specializes in gathering information for use in sleazy divorce cases. He talks tough but he's no Sam Spade. Harry exists in a self-imposed limbo, without a past or a future, which is all right with him.

Harry is understandably unsettled when a well-dressed lawyer shows up at his flea-bag office. The man offers Harry a large fee and a fat expense account to take on a missing-persons case. With all of the other detectives in town, why Harry? More out of curiosity than ambition, Harry travels up to Harlem to meet the lawyer's principal, whom he finds in a second-floor meeting room in a building that also houses an evangelical religious group.

The principal, who greets Harry

with which it was first slapped. The film opens today at Loews Tower East and other theaters.

As Harry's search takes him to Poughkeepsie, Coney Island and, finally, to New Orleans and the Louisiana bayou country, the movie itself evolves into an odd, utterly humorless fusion of private-eye melodrama and occult-horror film.

I've not read Mr. Parker's source material, William Hjortsberg's 1978 novel "Falling Angel," which, I'm told, is an affectionate and witty recollection of Sam Spade-Philip Marlowe literature, with the addition of supernatural elements.

Affection of any sort is totally lacking in this film adaptation. The only wit is supplied by Mr. De Niro, who delivers his lines, some of which are genuinely funny, with a comic daintiness that gives firm style to the otherwise murky, pointless narrative. Mr. De Niro's role, however, is small. He shows up just frequently enough to act as a built-in trailer for the rest of the movie, saying, in effect: "Stick around. It's going to get better." It doesn't.

Instead, it gets loonier and increasingly transparent as Harry finds himself up to his heart — and neck — in the company of a bunch of seriously committed devil worshipers. It isn't easy to take all this seriously, even as a metaphor. Among other things, "Angel Heart" might lead you to believe that in the business of buying and selling souls, it's the Devil who is short-changed.

•

As Harry goes from one clue to the next, he displays the persistence of a very dim door-to-door salesman who's the last one to know that he has no knack for the job. With the right role, Mr. Rourke is a good, interesting, vivid actor. Here he's suitably intense, but to such little effect you're likely to note that as 1955's Harry Angel, he sports the same two-day-old, male-model stubble (and "Miami Vice" wardrobe) he used for his 1986 character in "9½ Weeks."

What "Angel Heart" does have in some abundance is smashing-looking production design by Brian Morris and beautiful, moody camera work by Michael Seresin. It also has some horror-film special effects that, added to a long sex scene involving Mr. Rourke and Lisa Bonet (of "The Cosby Show"), contributed to the film's original X rating. The scene itself, in which supernatural blood drips down on the pair having sex on a bed, is still in the film. Gone, however, are brief, overhead shots of Mr. Rourke's X-rated buttocks.

In addition to Miss Bonet, who is very beautiful in a tiny but flashy role, the supporting cast includes Charlotte Rampling, who's somewhat more discreetly seen as a New Orleans psychic, of whom her father says: "Margaret was a strange kid. She was into tarot cards before she could read."

Mr. Parker ("Midnight Express," "Shoot the Moon," "Birdy") is an eclectic film maker. He seems to have no readily identifiable obsessions that define supposedly more serious directors. He's a very able technician who needs a good screenplay, which is what's missing here. In its bits and pieces, "Angel Heart" looks a lot better than it does when endured, without a break, from beginning to end.

1987 Mr 6, C5:1

Manmade Electricity

LETHAL WEAPON, directed by Richard Donner; written by Shane Black; director of photography, Stephen Goldblatt; edited by Stuart Baird; music by Michael Kamen and Eric Clapton; produced by Mr. Donner and Joel Silver; released by Warner Bros. At Criterion Center, Broadway at 45th Street; 84th Street Sixplex, at Broadway; Manhattan Twin, 59th Street east of Third Avenue; 86th Street Twin, at Lexington Avenue; Movieland Eighth Street Triplex, at University Place; Movie Center Five, 125th Street between Powell and Douglass Boulevards. Running time: 107 minutes. This film is rated R.

Martin Riggs..............................Mel Gibson
Roger Murtaugh ....Danny Glover
Joshua ....Gary Busey
The General ....Mitchell Ryan
Michael Hunsaker ....Tom Atkins
Trish Murtaugh ....Darlene Love
Rianne Murtaugh ....Traci Wolfe
Amanda Hunsaker ....Jackie Swanson
Nick Murtaugh ....Damon Hines

BEFORE the opening credits are over, a beautiful, half-naked blonde has snorted cocaine and jumped out the window of a high-rise building, landing on the roof of a parked car. Clearly, the makers of "Lethal Weapon,"

Danny Glover, top, and Mel Gibson in "Lethal Weapon."

someone called the General (Mitchell Ryan), with the help of the spooky blond henchman he calls "Mr. Joshua." Gary Busey, looking strikingly leaner and meaner in this role, gives it just the right unpleasant edge.

"Lethal Weapon" was directed by Richard Donner, whose tactics are lurid but effective. The film is all fast action, noisy stunts and huge, often unflattering close-ups, but it packs an undeniable wallop. The cartoonishness of his "Superman" and the busyness of his "Goonies" both contribute to this film's broad, volatile style. Like Riggs, Mr. Donner seems ready to stop at nothing. That can't help but command attention.

JANET MASLIN

1987 Mr 6, C7:1

Microcosmic

LILY TOMLIN, directed by Nicholas Broomfield and Joan Churchill; photography by Miss Churchill; editing by Mr. Broomfield; produced by Miss Churchill and Mr. Broomfield; made in association with Channel Four Television, Public Television Stations and the Corporation for Public Broadcasting. At Bleecker Street Cinema, 144 Bleecker Street. Running time: 90 minutues. This film has no rating.

"LILY TOMLIN" is an unusual, extremely patient, backstage record of how Lily Tomlin, Jane Wagner and their associates put together "The Search for Signs of Intelligent Life in the Universe," Miss Tomlin's smash-hit, one-woman Broadway play of the 1985-86 season.

The film, opening today at the Bleecker Street Cinema, is the work of Nicholas Broomfield and Joan Churchill, who co-produced and co-directed, with Miss Churchill responsible for the photography and Mr. Broomfield for the sound. The film was authorized, in that Miss Tomlin signed a contract with the film makers giving them creative control and theatrical and cable rights to the documentary.

In spite of this, and even after cooperating in the film's production over a two-year period, Miss Tomlin eventually sought — but failed to win — a court injunction against its release. Among her complaints was that she thought the film, which includes scenes from the play, would stand in the way of a pay-cable television sale of the play itself.

It's difficult to see what the fuss is about. As the judge wrote in denying the injuction, "For the Court, viewing the film (twice) has only enhanced interest in seeing the show in its entirety. (Parenthetically, for what it's worth, Ms. Tomlin, for whose creativity and talents the Court has great admiration, is most favorably presented in all aspects of the film, including the close-ups.)"

The Court, for what it's worth, is not a bad movie critic.

•

The one serious reservation about "Lily Tomlin" is that it's too reverential of the star and her "creativity." By one means and another, the film makers were clearly inhibited. There doesn't seem to be a seriously revealing, spontaneous moment in the entire film. From start to finish, Miss Tomlin is seen as if photographed through a bullet-proof plastic bubble, designed to protect her from the movie-making terrorists.

This isn't to say that there isn't much of interest in "Lily Tomlin," which there is, but that none of it is

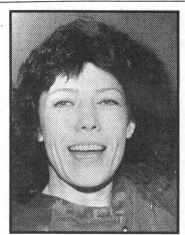

Lily Tomlin

uncalculated or surprising. Miss Tomlin was reportedly persuaded to cooperate with the film makers because, as an admirer of Ruth Draper, she was sorry there were no filmed records of how that great monologuist worked. Maybe now she knows why. It's possible that Miss Draper didn't like people inventorying all of the junk she had to go through before she found a small treasure.

"Lily Tomlin" is nothing if not discreet. We see Miss Tomlin conferring, for the benefit of the camera, with her writer, Miss Wagner, and with Peggy Feury, her drama coach. The camera is also on hand as the star tries out material before adoring audiences in Atlanta, San Diego and other cities. We hear her express anxiety that a key character in the play, that of the teen-ager Agnus Angst, is not coming together properly.

We see her do riffs on some of her well-known characters, including Mrs. Beasley, the liberated housewife, and Ernestine, the telephone operator. There also are clips from early, classically funny television shows in which she plays Ernestine as well as Edith Anne, the little girl who may be Miss Tomlin's most beautifully observed character.

•

The so-called backstage stuff, however, is only peripherally informative. Miss Tomlin has one of the world's most engaging smiles, but the talented woman behind it has no more individuality in the film than a reigning monarch as pictured on a postage stamp.

The film's best moment has nothing directly to do with Miss Tomlin, though it's obviously one that pleases Miss Churchill and Mr. Broomfield. It's the sight of Cheryl Swannack, Miss Tomlin's road manager, planted on a Broadway corner, shouting orders up to the painters who are in the process of creating a larger-than-life likeness of Miss Tomlin over Times Square. With the authority of a top sergeant, Miss Swannack tells them exactly where to place the left eye's twinkle. The painters seem also to have failed to connect the end of the nose to the eye.

By surmounting such crises is show-biz history made.

VINCENT CANBY

1987 Mr 6, C8:5

Friendships

WAITING FOR THE MOON, directed by Jill Godmilow; screenplay by Mark Magill; story by Miss Godmilow and Mr. Magill; director of photography, Andre Neau; edited by George Klotz; music by Michael Sahl; produced by Sandra Schulberg; released by Skouras Pictures Inc. At Cinema Studio 1, 66th Street and Broadway. Running time: 88 minutes. This film is rated PG.
Alice B. Toklas................Linda Hunt
Gertrude Stein..............Linda Bassett
Fernande Olivier.......Bernadette Lafont
Ernest Hemingway........Bruce McGill
Guillaume Apollinaire........Jacques Boudet
Henry Hopper.........Andrew McCarthy

By WALTER GOODMAN

"WAITING FOR THE MOON" plays touch and go with the relationship of Gertrude Stein and Alice B. Toklas, the famous pair who knew everybody who was anybody or likely to become somebody in avant-garde Paris in the 1920's and 30's. The script by Mark Magill offers snatches of a few days in 1936, out of order in an attempt perhaps to suggest the spirit of Stein's own "Cubist" writings. But whenever the movie, which opens today at Cinema Studio 1, threatens to touch on anything serious, it goes off to something else.

We see the sportive spinsters proofreading and picnicking picturesquely and mildly cavorting with friends such as Hemingway and Apollinaire, the French poet who died some 20 years before the time of the movie. The screenplay, based on a story by Mr. Magill and Jill Godmilow, who also directed, takes liberties with such facts in the interests of their narrative. Nothing wrong with that — if only there were more of a narrative to get interested in. The script is filled with allusions; the characters remain elusive.

•

Ms. Godmilow's direction is of the school, exemplified by public television's "American Playhouse" series, that assumes lethargy is arty. "Waiting for the Moon" drifts lazily, with the camera taking long rests on the faces of the principals. As Toklas, Linda Hunt continues her career of playing Linda Hunt. Linda Bassett, hair cut in the Steinian manner but decidedly prettier, relies on a secretive smile that conceals everything. It draws you in up to a point, at which you realize the enigma is not destined to be revealed.

Neither actress is able to develop a character out of the banter with which they have been supplied. They make small jokes, have small spats, enjoy small reconciliations. They even have a small baby to make small noises over. This high-powered pair comes off as cutely companionable. The deeper note beneath their light exchanges is the belief that Stein is terminally ill, and Toklas is distressed that her friend will not allow herself to be properly comforted. "Why is it so hard for you to appreciate me?" demands Toklas. Questions are raised but not answered. Much is suggested; nothing is explored.

•

A few of the scenes are lovely, in particular a midnight picnic during which the women and three friends join in on "The Trail of the Lonesome Pine," said to have been Stein's favorite song. Other scenes are either flimsy or awkward, particularly an episode of a drunken Ernest Hemingway posturing away like mad in a bordello. Turning maudlin, he tells Stein that Toklas is a saint, a very different description from the one he was to provide in "A Moveable Feast."

"Waiting for the Moon" does not argue this or any other matter. There are no disclosures about the women's sexual relationship, just hints as they cuddle each other, alternating in the roles of comforter and comfortee. You begin to long for a little prurience. Nor is there any opening up of Stein's mind. The failure of imagination here is not Gertrude Stein's.

•

"Waiting for the Moon" is rated PG ("Parental Guidance Suggested"), owing to a few naughty words.

1987 Mr 6, C14:5

Political Defense

NO END, directed by Krzysztof Kieslowski; screenplay (Polish with English subtitles) by Mr. Kieslowski and Krzysztof Piesiewicz; photography by Jacek Petrycki; edited by Krystyna Rutkowska; music by Zbigniew Preisner; production company, Zespoly Filmowe, Unit'TOR'; released by New Yorker Films. At Public Theater, 425 Lafayette Street. Running time: 108 minutes. This film has no rating.

Ulla Zyro	Grazyna Szapolowska
Antoni (Antek) Zyro	Jerzy Radziwilowicz
Joanna	Maria Pakulnis
Labrador	Aleksander Bardini
Jacek Zyro	Krzysztof Krzeminski
Darius	Artur Barcis

"No End" was shown as part of last year's New York Film Festival. Following are excerpts from Vincent Canby's review, which appeared in The New York Times Sept. 30, 1986. The film opens today at the Public Theater, 425 Lafayette Street.

"NO END," Krzysztof Kieslowski's 1984 Polish film that's only recently been made available abroad, is a dour, deadly serious contemplation of the effects of martial law on post-Solidarity Poland. Like some of Andrzej Wajda's work, it's also the sort of movie that can only be fully understood by someone with an intimate knowledge of the various twists and turns in recent Polish political history.

"No End" is about the efforts of Ulla, an English translator (whose most recent book is identified only as "the Orwell"), to come to terms with the death, from a heart attack, of her husband, Antek, a young, liberal lawyer. Ulla is full of loneliness and guilt. At the time he died, their marriage had not been going well, though for reasons not made very clear through the English subtitles.

Against her own best judgment, Ulla finds herself being drawn into a case Antek was handling at the time of his death. It's a risky case — the defense of a young strike organizer — that most lawyers won't touch. Labrador, who finally takes it, is a skillful opportunist. He's the man who taught Antek all the younger man knew about the law, though he himself chose to remain at a safe distance from cases of a political nature. Approaching his 70th birthday and forced retirement, Labrador accepts the defense of the young strike organizer as his swan song.

"No End" is a film that moves its characters arbitrarily around to make its points. Ulla, the mother of a loving child, becomes increasingly distraught as she sees the utter futility of her life reflected in Labrador's handling of the strike organizer's defense. The most interesting character is actually Labrador, who, in the film's best scenes, defines what he terms the "gray area" between compromise and selling out, ultimately persuading the young man to compromise to win a suspended sentence. Ulla responds to this victory in a way that "No End" simply cannot support.

According to the film's program notes, "The plot's progression along these two parallel lines generates a powerful metaphor for the walking corpse of liberalism in contemporary Poland."

1987 Mr 6, C17:2

And Baby Makes 3

RAISING ARIZONA, directed by Joel Coen; screenplay by Ethan and Joel Coen; photographed by Barry Sonnenfeld; edited by Michael R. Miller; music by Carter Burwell; produced by Ethan Coen; released by 20th Century-Fox. At the Beekman, Second Avenue at 66th Street. Running time: 92 minutes. This film is rated PG-13.

H. I.	Nicolas Cage
Ed	Holly Hunter
Nathan Arizona Sr.	Trey Wilson
Gale	John Goodman
Evelle	William Forsythe
Glen	Sam McMurray
Dot	Frances McDormand
Leonard Smalls	Randall (Tex) Cobb
Nathan Jr.	T. J. Kuhn
Florence Arizona	Lynne Dumin Kitei

By VINCENT CANBY

H.I. McDonough (Nicolas Cage), called "Hi," is a big, sincere oaf whose vocabulary is full of words and phrases he's picked up from reading magazines while serving time as a nonpaying guest of the state of Arizona. He's highly motivated, but in the wrong direction. When first seen in Joel and Ethan Coen's new comedy, "Raising Arizona," he is one of the state's most faithful recidivists.

Hi's weakness is the all-American "convenience store" that, at any hour of day or night, can be held up for a six-pack of beer, a pair of pantyhose, a package of bubble gum or cash. However, every time he pulls a job (with an unloaded gun), he's caught, tried and sentenced, serves a few months for what's called "rambunctious behavior" and is paroled, only to repeat the cycle.

Over the years of his recidivism, Hi develops an increasingly sentimental attachment for Edwina (Holly Hunter), called "Ed," the young police photographer in charge of mug shots at the pen. Ed is pretty in the flawed way of someone who always looks worried. If Hi's weakness is convenience stores, Ed's is unreliable men.

After being paroled for the third or fourth time, Hi proposes to Ed. They're married, settle down in a weedy trailer park and seem ecstatically happy, with Hi working in a sheet-metal plant and Ed pursuing her career in prison photography. Observes Hi on the soundtrack, "Ed rejoiced that my lawless days were over."

All of this is background information for the real business at hand in "Raising Arizona," and is presented in a very extended (about 10 minutes) pre-credit sequence. This promises a lot more than is ever delivered in the film, which opens today at the Beekman Theater.

"Raising Arizona" is the second feature by the Coen brothers, the film-making team whose flashy, neo-Hitchcockian "Blood Simple" caused a stir at the 1984 New York Film Festival. The Coens collaborate on their scripts, which are then directed by Joel and produced by Ethan. They're nothing if not knowledgable about films, as well as talented — up to a point.

•

At the long-delayed, actual beginning of "Raising Arizona," Hi and Ed are living in a marital bliss marred only by the news that they can't have a baby of their own. Because of Hi's prison record, they're also denied the right to adopt. With no other way out, they decide to help themselves to one of the quintuplets recently born to the wife of Nathan Arizona Sr., the king of a statewide empire of unpainted furniture and bathroom-fixture outlets.

They reason that, with five babies, the Arizonas wouldn't miss just one. Says Ed, her brow furrowed as usual, "They have more than they can handle, anyway."

Nathan Arizona is not unlike the hard-sell huckster played by Mr. Cage in "Peggy Sue Got Married" — a Crazy Eddie-type for whom pleasure is business. He has the Coens' best lines and, as played by Trey Wilson, exemplifies the implacable nuttiness that's missing in much of the rest of the film. Asked by a reporter if it's true that his son has been kidnapped by UFO's, Nathan, who sounds like the Great Gildersleeve, says sorrowfully, "Don't print that, son. If my wife reads that, she'll lose all hope."

Also very funny are Hi and Ed's best friends, Glen and Dot (Sam McMurray and Frances McDormand). Though they already have a batch of children of their own, they feel the need of a baby so strongly that they aren't above trying to blackmail Hi and Ed to acquire the purloined Nathan Arizona Jr.

The other subsidiary characters aren't nearly as much fun. They include a couple of escaped convict-brothers, surnamed Snopes in a jokey reminder of Faulkner's Yoknapatawpha County, and a motorcycle-riding goon who shows up out of nowhere to help the Arizona family locate Junior. In addition to this utterly pointless reference to the "Road Warrior" films, "Raising Arizona" also "quotes" from "Carrie," "Badlands" and, I suspect, from other movies I didn't immediately recognize.

•

When Jean-Luc Godard and François Truffaut did this sort of thing 25 years ago, it served as an affirmation of their regard for works too long unrecognized. It announced pride in what then seemed to be an arcane heritage. Today it seems mostly a film-school affectation, which is a major problem with "Raising Arizona." Like "Blood Simple," it's full of technical expertise but has no life of its own.

The Coens' screenplay has a lot of funny, raffish ideas in it, and it has been well cast, even down to T. J. Kuhn, who appears as Nathan Arizona Jr., and to the other babies who play his siblings. However, the direction is without decisive style. "Raising Arizona" has the manner of a Jonathan Demme film — say, "Handle With Care" or "Melvin and Howard" — directed by someone else. Its automobile chases are appropriately frantic, but they've been shot and edited with the kind of clumsiness that television producers try to cover up with laugh tracks.

Mr. Cage and Miss Hunter, who should carry the movie, go at their

Frances McDormand in a scene from "Raising Arizona."

roles with a tenacity that the film itself never makes adequate use of. They less often prompt spontaneous pleasure than the recognition that they're supposed to be funnier and more endearing then they manage to be. "Raising Arizona" may well be a comedy that's more entertaining to read than to see.

•

"Raising Arizona," which has been rated PG-13 ("Special Parental Guidance Suggested for Those Younger Than 13"), takes a lighthearted view of kidnapping.

1987 Mr 11, C24:5

Poetic Madness

MAN FACING SOUTHEAST, written and directed by Eliseo Subiela, in Spanish with English subtitles; photographed by Ricardo de Angelis; edited by Luis César d'Angiolillo; music by Pedro Aznar; produced by Luján Pflaum; released by Filmdallas Pictures. At Cinema 1, Third Avenue and 60th Street. Running time: 105 minutes. This film is rated R.

Dr. Julio Denis	Lorenzo Quinteros
Rantes	Hugo Soto
Beatriz (the Saint)	Inés Vernengo
Dr. Prieto	Rubens W. Correa
Hospital Director	David Edery
Mental Patient	Tomás Voth

DR. JULIO DENIS, a member of the psychiatric staff of a large Buenos Aires hospital, works too hard, which has begun to take its toll on his career and private life. His wife and children have left him. At the end of the day, Julio returns to his lonely apartment, looks at movies of a home life he no longer has, drinks too much Scotch and plays the saxophone.

At work he listens to the sad story of a young man who survived a suicide pact with a girlfriend. On the soundtrack, Julio wonders what would happen if he took and held the young man's hand, to show the patient that someone cares. He quickly realizes that's not what a doctor is supposed to do. He stares at the doomed patient and thinks, "Welcome to hell."

Julio is thus fair game for the mysterious patient who one day signs himself into the hospital. Rantes, the stranger, has the eerie serenity and dark good looks of a Velázquez saint, but he claims to be from another galaxy. This is a fairly common psychosis but, as their sessions continue,

Mystery Man Hugo Soto plays the role of Rantes and Ines Vernengo portrays The Saint in the drama "Man Facing Southeast." Written and directed by Eliseo Subiela, the Argentine film is set in a Buenos Aires psychiatric hospital where a routine check reveals an extra patient, Rantes, who says he has come from another planet to study the inhuman behavior of earthlings.

Julio finds his patient increasingly plausible, as does "Man Facing Southeast," Eliseo Subiela's Argentine film that opens today at Cinema 1.

Julio discovers that Rantes has the I.Q. of a genius. He's also a master organist. One night when Julio takes him to an open-air concert, Rantes steps forward and leads the orchestra to the astonished admiration of the conductor. Back at the hospital, the other patients are drawn to him as if he's a savior. In the afternoons, Rantes stands in the hospital courtyard, facing southeast, sending and receiving messages from "home."

●

As an example of Latin American fiction, "Man Facing Southeast" is lower-middle-brow García Márquez and bourgeois Borges. "Man Facing Southeast" is one of those sentimental films that find madness both poetic and romantic. Is Rantes what he says he is? The movie answers firmly, "Yes and no."

Mr. Subiela mixes his metaphors with a vengeance. Though Julio knows, at heart, that Rantes is psychotic, the doctor begins to see himself as Pontius Pilate to Rantes's outer-space Jesus. The movie goes along with this, picturing Rantes, at one point, as the Jesus in tableau vivant based on Michelangelo's Pietà. Rantes is also able to perform minor miracles.

At their most profound, the wit and wisdom of the screenplay sound like borrowings from a lesser J. B. Priestley play. The movie has the arty look of a book for the cocktail table. It's full of religious-type lighting, the sort that bathes silhouettes in golden halos. It also contains many fond, intense close-ups of the impassive face of Hugo Soto, the actor who plays Rantes, in which any truism can be read at will.

Lorenzo Quinteros appears as the exhausted Julio, a doctor who truly needs a rest, and Inés Vernengo as a

young woman who may or may not be Rantes's sister or even another extraterrestrial. "Man Facing Southeast" arrives in New York having received the International Critics Award at the Toronto Festival of Festivals last September. *VINCENT CANBY*

1987 Mr 13, C4:5

'Poetic Reporter'

SWIMMING TO CAMBODIA, directed by Jonathan Demme; written by Spalding Gray; photographed by John Bailey; edited by Carol Littleton; music by Laurie Anderson; produced by R. A. Shafransky; released by Cinecom. At Cinema Studio 1, 66th Street at Broadway. Running time: 87 minutes. This film has no rating.
WITH: Spalding Gray

By JANET MASLIN

IT would be wrong to think of "Swimming to Cambodia" as a one-man show, even though it captures the performance of a single artist, Spalding Gray, as he sits alone on an almost empty stage. For one thing, Mr. Gray's feature-length monologue brings people, places and things so vibrantly to life that they're very nearly visible on the screen. For another, this is a two-man undertaking, one that shows off both Mr. Gray's storytelling talents and Jonathan Demme's ability to frame them. This film's arrival in the wake of Mr. Demme's pioneering concert film "Stop Making Sense" and his jubilant, anarchic comedy "Something Wild" completes quite an amazing triple play.

"Swimming to Cambodia," which opens today at the Cinema Studio 1, is nothing it might be expected to be. Though Mr. Gray talks for an hour and a half and is the central figure in most of his stories, his egocentricity seems minimal. And he is never a bore. Nor is he inclined to speak with an ironic detachment, no matter how absurd or strange or painful the circumstances he describes. Mr. Gray, who has described himself at various times as a "poetic reporter" and a "wandering poet-bachelor-mendicant," seems a true adventurer. A tireless enthusiast, he sounds as eager to find meaning in his experiences as he is to reinvent them, and he is a delightful storyteller in the bargain.

"Swimming to Cambodia" revolves loosely around the fact that Mr. Gray played a small role in "The Killing Fields." It describes the conversation in which Mr. Gray listened to the director Roland Joffé talk about Cambodia's recent history. Mr. Gray then confessed: "I want to be very straight with you. I'm not very political; I don't know anything about the secret bombing; I've never voted in my life," and Mr. Joffé replied, "Perfect! We're looking for the American Ambassador's aide." Building outward from this central fact, Mr. Gray weaves in descriptions of the Thai settings where filming took place and the extracurricular activities in which he and various colleagues engaged.

What elevates this above the realm of small talk is Mr. Gray's roundabout — and peculiarly suspenseful — way of dramatizing the episode's moral and political repercussions. His own understanding of the horrific events in Cambodia was greatly intensified during his stay in Thailand, but Mr. Gray describes the raising of

his consciousness in a deceptively off-handed way. He may contrast the Gulf of Thailand with the Hamptons. Or his graphic and grotesquely funny description of a Thai brothel may be followed by talk of genocide under Pol Pot's rule. "Who needs metaphors for hell or poetry about hell?" he asks. "This really happened, here on this earth."

Such moments of quiet outrage are sobering. But Mr. Gray's comic, colloquial descriptions can be even more so. There is his talk, for instance, of "this weird bunch of rednecks called the Khmer Rouge," who "had been educated in Paris in the strict Maoist doctrine, except someone threw a perverse little bit of Rousseau into the soup. This made for a strange bunch of bandits, hanging out in the jungle living on bark, bugs, leaves and lizards, being trained by the Vietcong. They had a back-to-the-land, racist consciousness beyond anything Hitler had ever dreamed of. But they had no scapegoat other than the city-dwellers of Phnom Penh. They were like a hundred thousand rednecks rallying in New Paltz, N.Y., 90 miles above the city, about to march in."

That passage, and the entire two-hour version of "Swimming to Cambodia" that Mr. Gray has performed for live audiences, can be found in printed form. Engaging as it is on the page, it is even more so on screen, thanks in large part to Mr. Demme's extremely subtle contribution. Like Woody Allen's films, "Swimming to Cambodia" has an episodic and deceptively random structure, as if its various elements could be easily reshuffled. In fact, the material seems to have been been trimmed and rearranged with great care. Gone are some of Mr. Gray's angrier observations after the trip was over and some of his talk about specific individuals; meanwhile, the shifts in mood have been made especially sharp. Mr. Demme's cuts and camera movements are kept to a bare minimum, but they are very deft.

The monologue, punctuated by only a couple of well-chosen clips from "The Killing Fields," is pieced together from a couple of different performances of "Swimming to Cambo-

Spalding Gray

dia," which takes its title from Mr. Gray's thought that explaining the upheaval in that country "would be a task equal to swimming there from New York." But the transitions are mostly seamless. Or they would be were it not for the variations in Mr. Gray's hoarseness by the end of the performance, or the froth on his lips. These things are vivid reminders of the gargantuan energy that has gone into Mr. Gray's epic outpouring, an energy that will touch and transform anyone who hears it.

Laurie Anderson's rhythmic, intermittent score, John Bailey's crisp cinematography and Carol Littleton's unobtrusive editing greatly enhance the finished product. Mr. Gray emerges as the best raconteur, and least likely film star, this side of Andre Gregory and Wallace Shawn. And Mr. Demme once again positions himself on the cutting edge. He remains the American commercial cinema's most reliable and direct link to the avant-garde.

1987 Mr 13, C8:1

Australian Sojourn

KANGAROO, directed by Tim Burstall; screenplay by Evan Jones, from the novel by D. H. Lawrence; photography by Dan Burstall; edited by Edward McQueen-Mason; music by Nathan Waks; produced by Ross Dimsey; released by Cineplex Odeon Films. At the Paris, 58th Street and Fifth Avenue. Running time: 105 minutes. This film is rated R.

Richard Somers	Colin Friels
Harriet Somers	Judy Davis
Jack Calcott	John Walton
Vicki Calcott	Julie Nihill
Kangaroo	Hugh Keays-Byrne
Jaz	Peter Hehir
Struthers	Peter Cummins
O'Neill	Tim Robertson

D.H. LAWRENCE spent only two days in Sydney, Australia, when he arrived there in May of 1922. Yet he wrote several chapters about Sydney in "Kangaroo," the novel about Australia that he composed at a breakneck pace. Though Lawrence had no plans to document his Australian sojourn, he wound up writing 150,000 words in five weeks' time, giving his book an undeniable urgency. But the film version of "Kangaroo" is more staid, a calm and decorous work with a plot of no overwhelming interest. The one fiery thing about it is Judy Davis's performance, as a character modeled on Frieda Lawrence, the author's wife.

"Kangaroo," which opens today at the Paris, shapes a story of Australian politics to reflect more familiar Lawrentian ideas about love, loyalty, intellectual audacity and sexual expression. In that, it may sound a lot bolder than it happens to be. It follows a notorious British writer called Richard Somers, who is played by Colin Friels as a serious, tasteful shadow of Alan Bates's Lawrence figure in the far more audacious "Women in Love." Harassed in England, Richard embarks with his German-born wife, Harriet, to Australia, a place that he initially finds dauntingly dull. It seems, as he observes to her, to have "no inside life of any sort."

Richard learns otherwise when his neighbor, Jack Calcott (John Walton), introduces him to the title character, a general who leads a secret paramilitary organization. Committed to stifling Australia's nascent labor movement, Kangaroo urges Richard to become a mouthpiece for

Judy Davis

Tom Conti

this movement. "We need you," he says. "A country does not exist until it has found a voice." Later on, Kangaroo declares, "We shall force the serpent of the left to stir, and we shall stamp on it." Richard, he says, "can justify it to Australia. And to the world."

But Kangaroo, played by Hugh Keays-Byrne, seems mostly bluster, despite the violent confrontation to which his teachings eventually lead. And his pleas that Richard "love" him have none of the glowering masculine intensity that might give them some mystery. Instead, Kangaroo seems all empty swagger, and Mr. Friels's Richard becomes more timid bystander than intellectually vigorous observer. Only Miss Davis, as the prickly, challenging woman who seems more than a match for her husband, gives the story life. "For years, you rail against class distinctions," she tells him. "Then you come to a place where there aren't any and you can't stand it."

"Kangaroo" has none of Lawrence's intensity, but it does have something of a "Masterpiece Theater" patina. As directed by Tim Burstall, it has an attractive look and a polite, reasonable manner to which Lawrence himself never aspired.
JANET MASLIN

1987 Mr 13, C12:5

Miracle Worker

GOSPEL ACCORDING TO VIC, written and directed by Charles Gormley; music by B. A. Robertson; produced by Michael Relph; released by Skouras Pictures Inc. At the New Carnegie, 57th Street and Broadway. Running time: 92 minutes. This film is rated PG-13.

Vic Mathews	Tom Conti
Ruth Cancellor	Helen Mirren
Jeff Jeffries	David Hayman
Father Cobb	Brian Pettifer
Nurse	Jennifer Black
Headmaster	Dave Anderson
Brusse	Tom Busby
Doctor	Sam Graham
McAllister	Kara Wilson
MacKrimmond	Robert Paterson
Gibbons	John Mitchell

By WALTER GOODMAN

THE Blessed Edith Semple is causing a commotion at a parochial school in Glasgow named for her. One group, led by the school's baby-faced chaplain, is campaigning for her canonization, but discovers that the Vatican is not in the market for miracles just now. A church official expresses admiration for the Blessed Edith because she performed her solitary wonder around World War I and hasn't bothered anybody since: "One nice little miracle — and then off."

Most of the teachers at the school are willing to let the Blessed Edith lie, but some of them are indignant about what they believe to be lies in her behalf. The most indignant, in a perplexed way, is a gifted teacher of the ungifted named Vic: Not only are his successes with slow students being attributed to the intervention of the Blessed Edith, but she also seems to have afflicted him with supernatural powers. Such are the premises from which "Gospel According to Vic," the latest treat from Scotland, buzzes blithely off. It opens today at the New Carnegie.

If there is an actor who can compete with the blessed Tom Conti for quirky charm, bring him on. As Vic, mischief glitters in his soulful eyes; it sneaks through the cracks in his voice and the gaps in his reactions. Even in action, he seems bemused at the oddness of what he is about. Mr. Conti makes Vic a joy to be around, whether he is rousing his class to outbursts of educational hysteria or admiring the way Helen Mirren, the new teacher, fills out a skirt. Miss Mirren fills out her role admirably, too. Her spunky, ironically believing manner plays lightly off Mr. Conti's baffled skepticism.

Charles Gormley's zesty direction of his own irreverent script should raise all spirits except possibly the Blessed Edith. Every character is off-center — a doctor who conceals evidence of an apparent miracle because he is a nonbeliever and the chaplain who destroys the evidence because he believes so strongly he doesn't need it; the school's head and the local bishop, who can take a miracle or leave it, depending on how much trouble it causes; a schoolful of splendidly scruffy kids, all of whom want to be miracles.

To add salt to these nuts, Mr. Gormley throws in droll asides, such as a Hasid seen awaiting an audience in the Vatican, a journalist wearing tweeds and an earring, a Hell's Angel type up to his ears in a cast. And the lines are smart, too. "The Blessed Edith," says Miss Mirren, "is much admired by her admirers." When Vic isn't making rude remarks about St. Teresa, he is defending a boy who was caught masturbating: "He has to learn to do it in private like the rest of us." Any kid would be lucky to have such a teacher.

Although the movie fades away without resolving the question of what the Blessed Edith is up to, it ends with a good old heart-warming joke. "Gospel According to Vic" may not be a miracle, but it's definitely a blessing.

●

"Gospel According to Vic" is rated PG-13 ("Special Parental Guidance Suggested for Those Younger Than 13"), owing to some talk about sex and, possibly, to the prevailing spirit of irreverence.

1987 Mr 13, C13:1

Bargain Basement

EVERYTHING FOR SALE, written and directed by Andrzej Wajda; Polish with English subtitles; photography by Witold Sobocinski; music by Andrzej Korzynski; produced by Film Polski; released by New Yorker Films. At Public Theater, 425 Lafayette Street. Running time: 98 minutes. This film has no rating.

The director	Andrzej Lapicki
His wife	Beata Tyszkiewicz
Elzbieta	Elzbieta Czyzewska
Daniel	Daniel Olbrychski
Director's assistant	Witold Holtz
Teen-age girl	Malgorzata Potocka
An actor	Bogumil Kobiela
Forester	Tadeusz Kalinowski
Forester's wife	Irena Laskowska
Actress	Elzbieta Kepinska
Cameraman	Jozef Fuchs
Actor on stage	Wieslaw Dymny

THOUGH Andrzej Wajda's career has had its ups and downs, his position as Poland's premier film maker remains secure. He stunned the international film world with his early movies, including "A Generation" (1954), "Kanal" (1956) and "Ashes and Diamonds" (1958), and then, in the mid- to late-60's, went through a lean period in which he seemed to be making movies about everybody's concerns except his own. With "Landscape After Battle" (1970), Mr. Wajda rediscovered his own voice and sense of direction, and has gone on to make the more recent, mature masterworks "Man of Marble," "Danton" and "A Love in Germany."

All this is said by way of warning about "Everything for Sale," the 1968 Wajda film that opens today at the Public Theater.

"Everything for Sale" is a sorry mess — a movie supposedly made in homage to Zbigniew Cybulski, the phenomenally popular young Polish actor who was killed in 1967 while attempting to jump onto a moving train. Mr. Wajda obviously felt deeply about the actor, who became a star in his "Ashes and Diamonds" and appeared in over 40 films in 12 years.

Mr. Cybulski occupied a singular position in Poland's postwar culture. He was a pop star, a rebel and a symbol of the skepticism of youth. He was also a fine actor and a dynamic screen presence. To compare him with James Dean is to emphasize only a small part of his across-the-board appeal. Even Mr. Cybulski's tinted glasses — which he wore because of near-sightedness — became something of a political statement as well as a fashion note.

●

It's apparent that the actor's life and career inspire extremely mixed emotions in Mr. Wajda. However, few of these are sorted out in "Everything for Sale," a mind-bendingly trendy (late 60's-style) movie about the tribulations of a director attempting to make a movie with a Cybulski-like star who never shows up. By mixing (and confusing) scenes of the film itself with those from the movie within it, it's also making some not-very-interesting observations about the nature of "film" and reality.

At times, "Everything for Sale" looks like correspondence-course Fellini. At other times it's so soberly and rather meanly self-concerned that it's far more about the awful trials of being a famous, successful, living director than about the finality of being a famous, successful, dead actor, who, otherwise, is never characterized with any substance.

The philosophy of "Everything for Sale" would fit on the head of a pin, with room to spare for the Old and New Testaments. Or, as someone says when news of the offscreen actor's death is heard: "Today it's a tragedy. Tomorrow it's the story of a film."

It's also true that tomorrow never comes.
VINCENT CANBY

1987 Mr 13, C15:1

Goofy Gore

EVIL DEAD 2: DEAD BY DAWN, directed by Sam Raimi; written by Mr. Raimi and Scott Spiegel; photography by Peter Deming; edited by Kaye Davis; music by Joseph Lo Duca; produced by Robert G. Tapert; co-produced by Bruce Campbell; released by Rosebud Releasing Corporation. At Movieland, Broadway at 47th Street; Olympia Quad, Broadway at 107th Street; Coliseum Twin, Broadway at 181st Street; Movie Center 5, 125th Street between Powell and Douglass Boulevard. Running time: 85 minutes. This film has no rating.

Ash	Bruce Campbell
Annie	Sarah Berry
Jake	Dan Hicks
Bobby Joe	Kassie Wesley
Possessed Henrietta	Theodore Raimi
Linda	Denise Bixler
Ed	Richard Domeier
Professor Knowby	John Peaks
Henrietta	Lou Hancock

By CARYN JAMES

TALES of demonic possession are common, but the clever creators of "Evil Dead 2: Dead by Dawn" seem possessed by the ghosts of Moe, Larry and Curley. While Sam Raimi's 1983 "Evil Dead" winked at the conventions it played off — young couples stranded in a lonely cabin, possessed by evil spirits, surrounded by foggy moonlight — its sequel turns these clichés into hilariously silly, Three-Stooges-inspired slapstick. Think of Mr. Raimi, the director and co-writer, as a demented Moe, masterminding the scenario that turns a severed head and a chopped-off hand into slapstick props. Bruce Campbell, the star and co-producer, plays the resilient hero, Ash, whose body becomes a comic battlefield. When spirits possess his right hand, his hand attacks his head; he's Curley, forever slapping himself in the face. And Mr. Raimi's camera, like an overshadowed Larry, often takes on a disembodied life of its own, racing through the woods to give us the spirit's point of view. Highbrow it's not, but "Evil Dead 2" is one of the goofiest, goriest movies this side of the grave.

The demons first possess Ash's girlfriend, so he's forced to lop off his beloved's head with a shovel. The head flies away and sinks its teeth into Ash's hand, dangling like a pair of jokey chattering dentures. Mr. Campbell's quizzical raised eyebrow and some deflating lines reassure us that all the film's disgusting messes

Bruce Campbell

are just jokes. "I'm fine," Ash tells his mirror reflection after one nasty bout with evil, and the reflection answers: "We just cut up our girlfriend with a chainsaw. Does that sound fine?"

•

The supporting characters are gently satirized clichés: the local redneck and his girlfriend; the daughter of the cabin's owners, a prepp-ette in bermudas and knee socks who translates the lethal "Book of the Dead" and tries to take the curse off her mother (a vile creature locked in the fruit cellar). Ash even acts out a parody-Rambo rescue.

But "Evil Dead 2" doesn't sustain its crackpot wit. The effects that produce spectacular slimy-faced demons can become jarring set pieces. The girlfriend's headless body dances around in a lengthy scene that displays "look what I can do" amateurism. And near the end, the film abandons comedy altogether, going for geysers of blood and constant shrieks. After we've settled into a world where the monsters' Kelly green blood tells us not to be scared, it's too late for Mr. Raimi to pull the comic carpet out from under us and create some tension.

"Evil Dead 2," which opens today at Movieland and other theaters, is genuine, if bizarre, proof of Sam Raimi's talent and developing skill. But it is definitely not for the squeamish; its ideal audience would be full of Three Stooges fans with streaks of grotesque humor.

1987 Mr 13, C18:1

Sticky Wickets

PLAYING AWAY, directed by Horace Ové; screenplay by Caryl Phillips; photographed by Nic Knowland; edited by Graham Whitlock; music by Simon Webb; produced by Vijay Amarnani; released by International Film Exchange. At the Roy and Niuta Titus Theater 1, Museum of Modern Art, 11 West 53d Street, as part of the 1987 New Directors/New Films series. Running time: 100 minutes. This film is not rated.

Willie-Boy	Norman Beaton
Godfrey	Robert Urquhart
Majorie	Helen Lindsay
Derek	Nicholas Farrell
Stuart	Brian Bovell
Errol	Gary Beadle
Yvette	Suzette Llewellyn
Jeff	Trevor Thomas
Louis	Stefan Kalipha
Fredrick	Bruce Purchase
Robbo	Joseph Marcell
Viv	Sheila Ruskin
Kevin	Mark Barratt
Pat	Valerie Buchanan
Boots	Jim Findley
Mick	Julian Granger
Wilf	Ram John Holder
The Colonel	Patrick Holt

By VINCENT CANBY

"PLAYING AWAY," directed by the Trinidad-born Horace Ové, is a movie about the comic pretensions of social and political organisms — the kind of community-comedy at which British movie makers have excelled from "Tight Little Island" and "I'm All Right, Jack" through "A Private Function."

The new film is about the inevitable culture clash that takes place when the residents of a small, affluent, idyllically picturesque village in Suffolk invite a West Indian cricket team to participate in a match highlighting the village's "Third World Week."

In the course of the two-day weekend, the visitors — mostly Jamaicans who've immigrated to the rough-and-tumble Brixton section of London — remain ever unsurprised by the manners of their rich, rural hosts. The hosts, in their turn, are positively heroic in masking distaste with a show of sportsmanship, no matter how crudely some of the visitors behave.

In addition to the match that is the weekend's climax, there are the vicar's reception, at which the village band turns lilting Caribbean melodies into dirges fit for a viking's funeral; special Sunday-morning services in the ancient church; impromptu, boozy confrontations in the pub, and late-night connections on the grass.

•

It's a weekend of people falling over backward to be polite, of furiously short tempers, of tentative, romantic attachments and, possibly, of new understandings, though that's not at all certain.

"Playing Away" will be shown at the Museum of Modern Art tonight at 8:30 (and tomorrow at 1 P.M.) as one of the two opening attractions of the annual New Directors/New Films series, sponsored jointly by the Film Society of Lincoln Center and the museum's Department of Film. It helps get the festival off to a sane, safe and sweet start.

The big hurdle facing such comedies is that one can usually anticipate most of the crises as soon as one knows the film's main premise. "Playing Away" offers few surprises. The achievements of Mr. Ové, as director, and Caryl Phillips, who wrote the original screenplay, are those of characterization and emphasis. With the help of an excellent cast, the film makers bring to particular life nearly a dozen characters who never quite conform to expectations.

Melodrama is threatened and, without one's being aware of how it happens, it eases into comedy. Genteel lives are obliquely seen to be desperate and do-gooders to be much less silly than they initially sound.

•

Several performers dominate the film. Norman Beaton, the star of last year's "Black Joy," again plays a fast-talking, West Indian operator whose savoir-faire isn't threatened even when he has to replace one of his missing cricket players with a girlfriend. Trevor Thomas, who was the innocent, too-good-to-be-true hero in "Black Joy," has a smaller but more complex role in "Playing Away," as a

handsome young West Indian who has moved into the world of the white establishment.

Helen Lindsay is a delight as a club woman out of a Helen Hockinson cartoon — someone who is not unaware of the figure she cuts but still doesn't mind being laughed at in a good cause. Nicholas Farrell is also excellent as the captain of the village team, a guy who enjoys the company of one of his fellow players far more than he does his wife's.

"Playing Away" has the manner of a tale that should be told at the end of a halcyon summer day. It's witty and wise without being seriously disturbing for a minute.

1987 Mr 13, C19:1

Hard Knocks

BLACK AND WHITE, written and directed by Claire Devers, photographed by Daniel Desbois, Christopher Doyle, Alain Lasfargues and Jean Paul Da Costa; edited by Fabienne Alvarez and Yves Sarda; music by the Rhapsodes; produced by Films du Volcan, Ministère de la Culture. At the Roy and Niuta Titus Theater 1, in the Museum of Modern Art, 11 West 53d Street, part of the 1987 New Directors/New Films series. Running time: 80 minutes. This film has no rating.

Antoine	Francis Frappat
	Jacques Martial
	Josephine Fresson
M. Poland	Marc Berman
Night Watchman	Benoit Regent
Edith	Claire Rigollier
Hairdresser	Catherine Belkodja
Masseur	Arnaud Carbonnier

CLAIRE DEVERS'S "Black and White," which opens this year's New Directors/New Films series at the Museum of Modern Art, is most notable for its cool and businesslike approach to the bizarre concerns nondescript in outline, named Antoine (Francis Frappat) who is but little less fashionable health club. Along with the job as masseur of some of the athletes, and Antoine, who is white, attracts the interest of an extremely taciturn black masseur.

This is not an overtly sexual interest, although that element is doubtless there. It's more peculiar. It has to do with the masseur's inarticulated desire to administer ever more brutal body rubs, and Antoine's quiet eagerness to receive them. In terms of strangeness, it seems to go well beyond garden-variety sadomasochism, but its underlying elements go unexplored.

In any case, the rubs get rougher. The health club's charwoman begins to find blood on the floor. Meanwhile, Antoine's relationship with the woman who is either his wife or roommate becomes progressively worse. When he shows her, in a kind of character-revealing trick, to choose three creatures with which to compare herself, she picks a panther, an eagle and a whale. When she touches him one day, he flies into a rage and strikes her.

The rubs continue. Antoine is so badly bruised that he must make up stories about falling off a stepladder, and on one occasion he even swoons. It turns out that the masseur has actually broken bones, and so Antoine is hospitalized. But the masseur, who is by now a figure of considerable mystery, comes to spirit Antoine away. It would be unfair to tell where this all leads, but had it not been staged so affectlessly and filmed in such stark black and white, the film's ending would seem ridiculous. The rest would, too.

•

Ms. Devers, who won the Caméra d'Or at Cannes last year for the best first feature, does have a certain genuineness working in her favor. The events in "Black and White" are made to seem authentically weird, but the blankness that keeps them that way becomes tiresome after a while. Ms. Devers's technique, which far surpasses her choice of material, yields the occasional haunting image, like the sight of a discarded white doctor's coat floating on a river at night. However, "Black and White" is too elliptical to arouse much more than morbid curiosity, and it never escapes the great silliness bubbling just beneath its somber, neo-Gothic surface.

"Black and White" will be shown today at 6 P.M. and tomorrow at 3:30 P.M. at the Museum of Modern Art.

JANET MASLIN

1987 Mr 13, C20:4

Cortege

HEAT, directed by R. M. Richards; screenplay by William Goldman, based on the novel by Mr. Goldman; photographed by James Contner; edited by Jeffrey Wolf; music by Michael Gibbs; produced by Keith Rotman and George Pappas; released by New Century/Vista Film Company. At Ziegfeld, 54th Street between Avenue of the Americas and Seventh Avenue; Gotham Cinema, Third Avenue at 58th Street; 34th Street East, near Second Avenue; 23d Street West Triplex, between Eighth and Ninth Avenues. Running time: 101 minutes. This film is rated R.

Nick Escalante	Burt Reynolds
Holly	Karen Young
Cyrus Kinnick	Peter MacNicol
Pinchus Zion	Howard Hesseman
Danny Demarco	Neill Barry
Cassie	Diana Scarwid
Baby	Joe Mascolo
Felix	Alfie Wise

SO you think Charles Bronson is the most lethal object on two feet? That's because you haven't seen "Heat," which opens today at the Ziegfeld and other theaters. William Goldman has patched together a scenario based on his own novel to demonstrate that it's Burt Reynolds all the way. He plays Nick Escalante, a guy so tough that hunks twice his size turn to jelly at his frown, yet so lovable that little girls blow kisses at him.

Escalante, known as "Mex," is always ready to help a pal, even when it's a zonked-out party girl (Karen Young) who wants him to risk his life so that she can become a castrating female, no metaphor intended. That incident occurs early enough in this lugubrious movie, directed by R. M. Richards as though it were a funeral cortege for Mex's adversaries, so that you know Mex will come out all right and be able to give a crash course in courage to a young fellow (Peter MacNicol) who's rich enough not to need it. They pass the time trading tag ends of pop psychotherapy while you're waiting for Mex to start damaging bad guys again.

The setting is Las Vegas, where Mex wins and loses a lot of money in blackjack without getting too excited about it, and things work up tepidly to the big battle in a factory handily stocked with murderous devices. Things finally get hot when Mex's opponents are crushed, electrified, speared, fried and parboiled in slow motion. "I think I'm not here," says Mex. "My brain is somewhere else." Another thing about Mex — he's lucky. WALTER GOODMAN

1987 Mr 13, C33:1

THE NIGHT OF THE PENCILS, directed by Héctor Olivera; screenplay (Spanish with English subtitles) by Mr. Olivera and Daniel Kon, based on the historical essay by María Seoane and Héctor Ruiz Nuñez; photography by Leonardo Rodríguez Solís; edited by Miguel Mario López; music by José Luis Castineira de Dios; produced by Fernando Ayala; production company, Aries Cinematográfica Argentina S.A. At Roy and Niuta Titus Theater 1, 11 West 53d Street, as part of the New Directors/New Films series. Running time: 101 minutes. This film has no rating.

Pablo .... Alejo García Pintos
Claudia .... Vita Escardo
Horacio .... Pablo Novarro
Daniel .... Leonardo Sbaraglia
Panchito .... José Ma. Monje Berbel
Claudio .... Pablo Machado
María Claudia .... Adriana Salonia
Doctor Falcone .... Héctor Bidonde
Nelva de Falcone .... Tina Serrano
Raúl .... Lorenzo Quinteros

By CARYN JAMES

One of the sad recognitions to come from "The Night of the Pencils" is that its subject no longer shocks. Based on actual events, the film — about six Argentine high school students who disappeared in 1976, and a seventh who survived torture and imprisonment to tell their story — could easily have relied on ideological anger or sentimentality. But with harrowing accomplishment, Héctor Olivera confronts the grim dailiness of the teen-agers' prison existence.

In Mr. Olivera's acclaimed satire "Funny Dirty Little War," the comedy mirrored political alignments so tangled no one could quite sort them out. But with the inherently dramatic material of "The Night of the Pencils," he is shrewdly, adamantly realistic, and gains much emotional power from his restraint.

We first see the seven friends in the fall of 1975, when Isabel Perón's Government and Argentina's economy are about to collapse. With a passion reminiscent of students in the United States in the 60's, they agitate for lower bus fares. Mr. Olivera catches them at that tenuous moment in their lives when their boundless self-confidence is matched only by their deeply hidden insecurity. Pablo, the survivor, seems more boyish than his friends; he is infatuated with Claudia, the savvy daughter of a political family.

Typical adolescents, the girls giggle about boys and the boys roughhouse, but they are not political naïfs. The police have broken up their school dance, and have brought in mounted horsemen with swords to attack the crowd at the demonstration for the student bus pass. Claudia's father, a former Mayor who had once been imprisoned, tells her, "Nothing is free in politics. ... Be cautious." But his daughter's persistence, and the momentum of the film itself, ask "How?" Caution may not be possible, or even desirable, when faced with such brutal, irrational enemies.

Mr. Olivera builds his film on irony and contrast, so the visual beauty of the early scenes — the deep blue night in which cars and lights glisten — calls attention to the ominous unseen political dangers. In daylight, the once-beautiful, now crumbling buildings, including the high school itself, become emblems of a country falling apart, not knowing what to preserve from its past.

The turning point comes a short time after the military junta overthrows Isabel Perón; the six students are dragged from their beds, blindfolded and kidnaped by the police, who come to call the event "The Night of the Pencils." When Pablo himself is later imprisoned — there is, of course, no real reason for his being set apart — he hears that his friends have been tortured with a severity exceptional even by police-state standards. He is given electric shocks while jaunty radio music masks his cries.

Shaped by the students' experience, the focus of the film narrows. We are taken into their horrendously constrained world; they exist in tiny adjoining cells from which they can yell to but not touch or see one another. In relentless close-ups, we see the caked blood on their faces. We see their bodies become more and more emaciated, the underwear that passes for clothing reduced to filthy shreds.

Mr. Olivera makes just a few false moves. Heavy-handed music announces the arrival of the police. And when Pablo asks Claudia to go steady when they get out of prison, the scene is played for sentiment and youthful optimism rather than the desperate need to have and offer hope of a future.

"The Night of the Pencils" will be shown in the New Directors/New Films series at the Museum of Modern Art today at 8:30 P.M. and tomorrow at 1 P.M.

1987 Mr 14, 13:1

POSITIVE I.D., directed, written and produced by Andy Anderson; photography by Paul Barton; edited by Mr. Anderson and Robert J. Castaldo. At Roy and Niuta Titus Theater 1, 11 West 53d Street, as part of the New Directors/New Films series. Running time: 102 minutes. This film has no rating.

Julie Kenner .... Stephanie Rascoe
Don Kenner .... John Davies
Roy and Lieutenant Mercer ...Steve Fromholz
Dana .... Laura Lane
Melissa .... Gail Cronauer
Dr. Sterling .... Audeen Casey
Mr. Tony .... Matthew Sacks
Johnny .... Steven Jay Hoey
Scotty .... John Williamson
Katie Kenner .... Erin White
Mary Kenner .... April White
Vinnie DeStephano .... Terry Leeser

By JANET MASLIN

Unlike almost any other story of switched identities, Andy Anderson's "Positive I.D." pays no attention to the underpinnings of such an act. It concentrates on the mechanics, which, as Mr. Anderson sees them, can take on a life of their own.

"Positive I.D.," which will be shown today at 6 and tomorrow at 3:30 P.M. as part of the New Directors/New Films series, is about Julie Kenner (Stephanie Rascoe), a rape victim who seems badly shellshocked when the story begins. Evidently, the crime has been widely publicized. "That wasn't Mommy, that was someone who looked like Mommy," one of her children says, after catching a glimpse of her on television at a trial.

Julie pays scant attention to her husband or children, and concentrates most of her energy on taking frequent baths. She speaks little, and wants mostly to be alone. But as the film progresses, Julie begins to recover from her ordeal. She is just regaining her energies when an employee at her daughter's school demands a copy of the child's birth certificate, thus planting the seed of an idea. At the records bureau Julie, who lives in Texas, learns that birth certificates and death certificates are not cross-referenced there.

So she embarks upon an elaborate campaign to become someone else, a project that is presented here largely in terms of clever paperwork. Mr. Anderson, who works the occasional comic flourish into an otherwise methodical and suspenseful story, has

Julie pick her new identify partly on the basis of a dead woman's date of birth. If she can become four years younger in the process, why not?

●

"Positive I.D." recalls "Blood Simple" in its mixture of dark humor and the macabre. But it is also a good deal more matter-of-fact. The nuts and bolts of Julie's transformation take up most of the film and give it a slow pace, the payoff for which is presumably the final explanation for Julie's undertaking. However, there can't be much real surprise about what she has in mind. Mr. Anderson, who directed the earlier "Ritual" and "Point of View," sometimes reveals an irreverent, unpredictable side that could have been shown off more fully here to good advantage. The few such moments, as when Julie goes on shopping trips in her new incarnation or finds that she can't master the instructions on a television cooking show, give the film a helpful boost.

Mr. Anderson, who wrote, directed, produced and co-edited the film on a very small budget, displays a good deal of technical promise and attention to detail. He gives shorter shrift to the actors, who perform rather stiffly throughout. Miss Rascoe is reasonably convincing and makes Julie seem thoroughly engrossed in what she's doing. But she isn't given nearly enough chance to enjoy the masquerade.

1987 Mr 14, 13:1

HEY BABU RIBA, directed by Jovan Acin; screenplay (Serbo-Croatian with English subtitles) by Mr. Acin, from the memories of Petar Jankovic, George Zecevic and Mr. Acin; photography by Tomislav Pinter; edited by Snezana Ivanovic; music by Zoran Simjanovic; produced by Dragoljub Popovic and Nikola Popovic; production companies, Avala Film and Inex Film. At Roy and Niuta Titus Theater 1, Museum of Modern Art, 11 West 53d Street, as part of the New Directors/ New Films Series. Running time: 109 minutes. This film has no rating.

Esther .... Gala Videnovic
Glen .... Relja Bacic and Nebojsa Bakocevic
Sacha .... Marko Todorovic and Dragan Bjelogrlic
Kica .... Srdjan Todorovic and Milos Zutic
Pop Djordje Nenadovic and Goran Radakovic
Rile .... Milan Strljic and Dragomir Bojanic-Gidra

BY WALTER GOODMAN

IF "Hey Babu Riba" seems like an odd title for a movie from Yugoslavia, that's the point. Along with other American big-band numbers of the early 1950's, this ditty is a favorite of beautiful girl whom they call Esther in homage to Esther Williams — whose adventures are here related. What makes the movie, which will be shown at the Museum of Modern Art tonight at 6 and tomorrow at 8:30 P.M., much more interesting than a Serbian variation of "Stand by Me" is its political perspective.

Set in Belgrade in 1953, when Yugoslavia was in the throes of breaking away from the Soviet camp, "Hey Babu Riba" focuses on a once-privileged set that has found itself in difficulties under the Tito regime. Esther's father is a former Royalist officer who has fled to Italy; her mother is languishing for want of streptomycin. The father of one of her friends is in jail; another, a doctor, has been put out of business by socialized medicine. All are selling off cherished possessions to eke out an existence, and their "surplus living space" is being occupied by Communist Party favorites.

●

The director, Jovan Acin, was born in Belgrade in 1941, and his screenplay, drawn in part from his own memories, is about a generation entranced by American popular culture, from Glenn Miller to Levis, and by a Western spirit of freedom as well. Esther's boyfriends listen to the Voice of America, perform a zippy version of Miller's "American Patrol," kid around in English and despise all things Russian. They mock the "comrades" who are battening on the downfall of their parents. When

Gala Videnovic as Esther and Relja Bacic as Glen in "Hey Babu Riba."

they defeat a group of party types in a rowing competition, it's a victory for their class.

Although some of the events seem a little disjointed and the effort to tie up loose ends grows strained, the movie is alive with the energies of an unsettling period and the unsettled young. The foursome's loss of virginity, though a convention of rite-of-passage movies, is handled most amusingly. Esther's pregnancy is a more serious matter. The question is, by whom?

•

The young protagonists are amiable if a bit colorless. More flavorsome performances come from characters churned up by the postwar changes: a woman known as the vulture, who goes about trading nylons and powdered milk for the pianos and music boxes of the once-rich and as a sideline initiating their offspring into sex and cigarettes; a conscientious official who tries earnestly to persuade Esther to get her father to collaborate with the regime, and, especially, a rapacious apparatchik named Rile (Milan Strljic), a handsome blackguard who falls for Esther and is unscrupulous in his pursuit. One of the movie's good jokes is that Rile, ever on the make, had his wrists tattoed with pictures of Stalin and Lenin just before the break with Moscow; now he wears wristbands and is taking a crash course in English instead of Russian.

Incidentally, if you've been dying to hear "Comin' Round the Mountain" sung in Serbo-Croatian, here's your chance.

1987 Mr 15, 60:1

A Hard Row

A WOMAN ALONE, directed by Agnieszka Holland; screenplay (Polish with English subtitles) by Miss Holland and Maciej Karpinski; photography by Jacek Petrycki; edited by Roman Kolski; music by Jan Kanty Pawluskiewicz. At Roy and Niuta Titus Theater 1, 11 West 53d Street, as part of the New Directors/New Films Series. Running time: 110 minutes. This film has no rating.
WITH: Maria Chwalibog, Boguslaw Linda, Pawel Witczak, Krzysztof Zaleski and Bohdana Majda

By JANET MASLIN

THE life depicted in the Polish film "A Woman Alone" is unrelievedly grim. It is the life of Irena (Maria Chwalibog), an unwed working mother whose energies are being taxed to their limit. She lives in a small room with her young son Bob (Pawel Witczak), and must share a bed with him; mother and son are also harassed by their landlord. Her job as a letter carrier is so physically draining that she sometimes collapses under the weight of her sack. Her life seems to hold no satisfactions, not even small ones. Even when she bathes at home (where there is no indoor plumbing), she must do it with Bob's used bathwater.

And she has no real hope. Irena pays weekly visits to a dying aunt whom she hopes may leave her a small sum, but the trips exhaust her even further — and she winds up having to assume household expenses for the aunt, who is apparently a miser. She cannot turn to family, to friends, to her work or even to Bob for any comfort.

Agnieszka Holland, who directed "A Woman Alone" in 1981 (before making her German film, "Angry Harvest," which was shown in the New York Film Festival), begins with a step-by-step depiction of Irena's grueling daily routine. The film has a raw, documentary quality, making use of some hand-held footage, as it lays out the facts of Irena's life. But "A Woman Alone" is not solely about quiet hardship; it is about the breakdown that occurs as Irena reaches the end of her tether. As the film progresses, Irena's frustration mounts almost palpably, and her angry outbursts become more desperate. "All he can see is that I work like a mule and no one respects me, so why should he?" she exclaims about Bob at one point. More pointedly, she adds: "I don't know how to educate a child and make a good Pole out of him. All our values have been destroyed."

Sharply critical of the system that consigns Irena to her fate, the film follows her vain efforts to enlist the help of local Party officials in improving her housing. Not having joined Solidarity, she cannot seek help in that direction either. When an outside force does alter Irena's life, it arrives in the unlikely shape of a disabled mine worker (Boguslaw Linda) who is several years her junior. Odd, excitable and vaguely unsavory as this man is, he wants to help her. And Irena has no choice but to welcome help, from whatever quarter it may come.

•

"A Woman Alone," which will be shown tonight at 8:30 and tomorrow at 6:00 as part of the New Directors/New Films series, begins on as bleak a note as might be imagined. But it progresses to something even sadder, with a brief coda that is genuinely bizarre. Miss Holland, who elicits a moving performance from Miss Chwalibog, has shaped a painful portrait, not only of a single person but also of the larger forces that shape her fate.

1987 Mr 15, 61:1

Old Black Magic

WITCHBOARD, directed and written by Kevin S. Tenney; director of photography, Roy H. Wagner; edited by Daniel Duncan and Stephen J. Waller; music by Dennis Michael Tenney; produced by Gerald Geoffray; released by Cinema Group. At Criterion Center, Broadway and 45th Street; RKO 86th Street Twin, at Lexington Avenue; RKO Coliseum Twin, Broadway and 181st Street; Olympia Quad, Broadway at 107th Street; Movie Center 5, 125th Street between Powell and Douglas Boulevard. Running time: 91 minutes. This film is rated R.

Jim Morar	Todd Allen
Linda Brewster	Tawny Kitaen
Brandon Sinclair	Steven Nichols
Zarabeth	Kathleen Wilhoite
Lieutenant Dewhurst	Burke Byrnes
Mrs. Moses	Rose Marie
Lloyd	James W. Quinn
Dr. Gelineau	Judy Tatum
Wanda	Gloria Hayes
Malfeitor	J. P. Luebsen

By CARYN JAMES

THE one time I tried to use a Ouija board, the marker refused to move, and I tossed it aside after a few seconds. "Witchboard" convinces me I was right. Any movie that features a Ouija — or "witchboard," as we're told it's sometimes called — as a way for spirits to enter this world ought to offer the audience some guesswork. But the first feature written and directed by Kevin S. Tenney is as moribund as any Ouija I've ever seen.

There is a romantic triangle in the background: Brandon, a rich, handsome, unnaturally blond young man; Linda, his former lover, and Jim, Brandon's former best friend who happens to be Linda's present lover. In the greatest stretch of imagination the film calls for, we're asked to believe Jim did not steal Linda away from Brandon. Right. When Brandon brings his Ouija to a party at Jim and Linda's, they tune in a mass murderer named Malfeitor ("evildoer" in Portuguese, the film says) disguised as the spirit of a little boy killed 30 years before. Malfeitor possesses Linda until the two men in her life end their feud and team up to save her.

•

This film is so cheaply made that its grand special effect has a knife fly through the kitchen, and a conveniently open bottle of ketchup tips itself over; the ketchup drips on the knife to resemble blood, which the astute Linda takes as a bad sign. The dialogue is so unreal that when Jim tells his landlady (in a cameo by Rose Marie; I don't know why) to call an ambulance for Linda, instead of running for the phone she stops to ask, "Why, what happened?" The plot is so predictable that when the Ouija slowly spells out its answers, the scenes are less suspenseful than "Wheel of Fortune."

One good thing I can say about "Witchboard," which opened Friday at the Criterion Center and other theaters: Todd Allen as Jim doesn't overact. (Steven Nichols, as Brandon, and Tawny Kitaen, as Linda, do.) The very best I can say is that "Witchboard" should encourage struggling film makers. Watch it and think, "I can do better than that!"

1987 Mr 15, 61:1

FILM VIEW/Janet Maslin

Toward Maturity

JOHN HUGHES IS A MAN WITH FEW champions, and for good reason. His detractors would argue that he has made some of the most cavalier, sophomoric films in recent years, and they would be right. They could say that "Ferris Bueller's Day Off," for example, reaches a pinnacle of shameless pandering with its plot about a smug, self-congratulatory high school boy who decides to skip school by conning his witless parents into believing he is ill. This boy's idea of a meaningful gesture is encouraging a friend to wreck his father's Ferrari. His life is so privileged and unexamined that the thought of "Ferris Bueller's Day Off" being viewed as representative Americana by foreign audiences is frightening.

It could be noted that Mr. Hughes's "Weird Science" is almost as bad, and that even his Molly Ringwald trilogy — "Sixteen Candles," "The Breakfast Club," "Pretty in Pink" — treats teen-age concerns like dating, fashion and popularity as if they were matters of state. And his critics could certainly say that Mr. Hughes, who is somewhere in his mid-30's, is too old for this sort of thing. They would be right about that, too.

But to concentrate on this is to ignore the more important facts about Mr. Hughes: that he burst onto the scene with the hilarious screenplay for one film ("National Lampoon's Vacation") and the potentially funny idea for another ("Mr. Mom"); that he has since carved out a significant section of the moviegoing public and made it his own, with five films grossing a reported $200 million in three years' time; that he is now ready to set his sights on an older audience. And that his work, on the evidence of the current "Some Kind of Wonderful," is becoming more assured and developing a much wider appeal. Mr. Hughes will be someone to reckon with sooner or later. He may be already.

That Mr. Hughes did not actually direct "Some Kind of Wonderful" is almost beside the point. It was directed by Howard Deutch, who also did "Pretty in Pink," but both films were written by Mr. Hughes and fully reflect the Hughes point of view. What marks all of Mr. Hughes's films, first and foremost, is their lack of condescension to teen-age characters and their real understanding of how these characters feel. Much of "Sixteen Candles," for example, seems to come directly from the heart of a lovestruck, sullen, deliriously adolescent girl (played by Miss Ringwald). Mr. Hughes understands this girl's every thought. He knows that her reaction, for example, to the sight of visiting grandparents setting up shop in her bedroom would be a fine blend of affection and horror, and that mood is captured perfectly in Miss Ringwald's aghast expression.

These nuances, the ones that launched Mr. Hughes' career, are distinctly tiny, which is what makes them so real. They are also extremely localized and narrow, especially when compared to foreign-made films about characters of the same age. The stereotypical French teen-ager in films tends to be a young girl on the verge of sexual awakening, a process that may be helped along by a visiting uncle or an older friend of the family. The British teen-ager, by comparison, may be more concerned with economic and class issues. But most of the John Hughes adolescents care more about sex appeal than sex itself, and have no real money worries (even if they go to school with much wealthier peers). They care about high school status, about being liked and accepted and about the compromises that go into winning their friends' approval. These are things that have made Mr. Hughes's films fiercely engaging for adolescent viewers, especially American ones, and of very limited interest to anyone else.

But "Some Kind of Wonderful" is different. No less steeped in teen-age slang and teen-age mores than its predecessors, it manages to touch on far more universal emotions than "Pretty in Pink," which tells almost the same story. Both films are about a hero who's an outcast of sorts — in this case, a boy (played by Eric Stoltz) who likes art and works at a gas station — and who develops a crush on someone very popular and self-assured (Lea Thompson). This crush is followed closely by the hero's best friend, who in "Some Kind of Wonderful" is a drum-playing tomboy (Mary Stuart Masterson), and who, of course, is madly in love with him.

So beneath the up-to-the-minute flourishes that help sell the film to Mr. Hughes's long-standing admirers, there lurks a sweet, familiar love story any audience might enjoy, a story whose resolution is every bit as charming as it is unreal. The result is something much less dependent on little details, and more involving on the basis of a plot that might work just as well if the characters were older. Without losing his gifts for fast, funny dialogue or his eye for acting talent (for the most part, this film is particularly well cast), Mr. Hughes has taken a definitive step out of the genre he himself created.

Although the spottiness of his early work makes him more than capable of backsliding, this all bodes well for "She's Having a Baby," his film about young marrieds, which is due out this summer, and "Planes, Trains and Automobiles," a future project which is purportedly about two grown men.

Without question, "Some Kind of Wonderful" marks Mr. Hughes as someone to watch (and does the same for Mr. Deutch, though it's harder to identify his contribution). Be warned, though, that seeing this film may be a sobering experience in ways that Mr. Hughes never intended. At a suburban theater a week ago Saturday night, in just the kind of community Mr. Hughes makes films about, my friends and I were the only patrons not being dropped off by their parents for the 7:30 show.   1987 Mr 15, II:21:1

Out of Luck

THE REALM OF FORTUNE, directed by Arturo Ripstein; screenplay (Spanish with English subtitles) by Paz Alicia Garciadiego, based on a story by Juan Rulfo; photography by Angel Goded; edited by Carlos Savage; music by Lucía Alvarez; production company, Imcine/Conacine; released by Azteca Films. At Roy and Niuta Titus Theater 1, the Museum of Modern Art, 11 West 53d Street, as part of the 1987 New Directors/New Films series. Running time: 132 minutes. This film has no rating.
Dionisio Pinzón .... Ernesto Gómez Cruz
Bernarda Cutino/La Caponera ....
.... Blanca Guerra
Lorenzo Benavides ....Alejandro Parodi
La Pinzona ....Zaide Silvia Gutiérrez
Cara de Canario ....Margarita Sanz
Patilludo .... Ernesto Yáñez

By CARYN JAMES

DIONISIO PINZON seems the perfect hero for a dark comedy. A heavy, middle-aged peasant, he appears simple-minded, yet has enough dumb luck to leave behind his squalid shack — no running water but lots of religious gewgaws — and become wealthy by raising gamecocks. He happily marries a much-used woman who sings at sleazy carnivals, and finishes life as a crazed cardsharp, playing endless games in his near-empty mansion. But while Arturo Ripstein has been one of Mexico's more prominent directors for over 15 years, in "The Realm of Fortune" he gropes his way through Dionisio's mordantly promising history. The film, part of the New Directors/New Film Series, will be shown at the Museum of Modern Art today at 8:30 P.M. and tomorrow at 6 P.M.

Over two hours long, "The Realm of Fortune" meanders interminably through major and minor events; Dionisio works as a town crier, is blessed by a priest who cannot take his eyes off television, becomes childishly attached to a dying gamecock he rescues. Yet these episodes do not take off into Buñuel — or Fellini — land, as you expect they might (Mr. Ripstein was once an assistant to Buñuel.) They merely distort the shape of Dionisio's story, without substituting any surreal, antinarrative vision.

•

Mr. Ripstein creates strong, intentionally imprecise settings — the hot sun shines on a cornfield where the poor Dionisio buries his mother, and his future wife sings over the noise of the cockfights in tawdry, smoke-filled tents. Against these effective backdrops, though, Mr. Ripstein's tone wavers — now serious, now comic, now almost ironic — in a style so out of control that the characters are reduced to petty caricatures, and the film's ostentatious symbols and symmetries are emptied of meaning. When Dionisio, in his first flush of wealth, begins to wear dark glasses and a tacky black leather jacket, it is less a revelation of character than a momentary sight gag. "You have died on me — now what will I do?" he says to his mother's corpse. He repeats those words to his pet gamecock's corpse, and later to his wife's, but the parallels say nothing new about the selfish consistency beneath his changing fortunes. Based on a story by Juan Rulfo — whose dialogue and imagery often suggest great depth in peasant characters — the film feels as if it has lost the spirit of its source.

Under the baroque ornamentation of "The Realm of Fortune," there is a genuine tragi-comedy of an ignoble peasant who turns his back on simple

goodness, destroying himself and his family. Toward the end we get a glimpse of what that more consistent film might have been. Dionisio's once-glamorous wife wanders around their house in a shabby sweater, so neglected she talks to herself. Their teen-age daughter escapes into promiscuity. The desperation of these women and the dramatic tension between them is far more interesting than all Dionisio's adventures. It may be that he is, after all, a vapid character, defined in excruciating detail by a director who cannot convey his fascination with a banal man masquerading as an eccentric.

1987 Mr 17, C14:1

3 Generations

A PROMISE, directed by Yoshishige Yoshida; screenplay (Japanese with English subtitles) by Mr. Yoshida and Fukiko Miyauchi, from the novel "Rojuko Kazoku" by Shuichi Sae; photography by Yoshihiro Yamazaki; edited by Akira Suzuki; music by Haruomi Hosono; produced by Yasuyo Saito and Matsuo Takahashi; production companies, Seibu Saison Group, TV Asahi, Kinema Tokyo. At Roy and Niuta Titus Theater, 11 West 53d Street. Running time: 123 minutes. This film has no rating.
Ryosaku Morimoto ....Rentaro Mikuni
Tatsu .... Sachiko Murase
Yoshio .... Choichiro
Ritsuko .... Orie Sato
Takao .... Tetsuta Sugimoto
Naoko .... Kumiko Takeda
Saeko Nogawa ....Reiko Tajima
Inspector Tagami .....Tomisaburo Wakayama
Sergeant Miura .... Sakatoshi Yonekura
Takeya Nakamura .... Choei Takahashi
Noriko Nakamura ....Mieko Yuki

By JANET MASLIN

A CULTURE may reveal itself most fully through the things it fears. In the fine new Japanese film "A Promise," the pain and humiliation of senility take a terrible toll, not only on the elderly but also on the younger relatives whose lives are affected. "A Promise," about an elderly woman found dead in the house of her son and daughter-in-law, addresses the question of euthanasia, since the woman has almost certainly died at the hands of her loved ones. But it is even more disturbing as a study of ways in which the older generation's weakness and debility can affect the younger.

"A Promise" is a well-drawn portrait of an entire family in contemporary Japan, from the sheepish, overlooked grandparents to the harried parents to the children growing up on rock video. It has been directed by Yoshishige Yoshida in a cool, modern style that seems all the more merciless, under the circumstances. The rituals of Japanese life are seen as stripped of most of their meaning, existing only in the hollowest form. The legacy of order and fastidiousness brings no comfort, and when it comes to facing the unruliness of old age, it may even make life harder.

•

So 50-year-old Yoshi (Choichiro) and his wife Ritsuko (Orie Sato), who take care of Yoshi's parents, are even more unnerved than they might be by simple facts of the older couple's lives. It is Yoshi's mother, Tatsu (Sachiko Murase), who has become senile, and her lack of bladder control makes her otherwise quite reserved daughter-in-law especially upset. The younger woman's excessive revulsion, and the lack of inner resources it reveals, is not shared by Yoshi, but he suffers in his own way. The physical job of caring for his mother and dealing frankly with her frail, tiny body is almost more than he can bear.

For all the pain that "A Promise" explores, it also has moments of great tenderness and beauty, moments between two elderly actors (Ms. Murase and Rentaro Mikuni as her husband) who play their roles very movingly. The reality of their old age is sweetened by their shared memories of happier times. And Mr. Mikuni, who must embody varying degrees of senility as the story progresses, can make an extremely eloquent gesture out of simply staring quietly at an urban landscape. Choichiro is quite good also as a man whose own moral shortcomings are brought into play by this family crisis, and who somehow finds unexpected strength upon which to draw. The film devotes some attention to a police inquiry into the old woman's death, but that seems largely irrelevant. Most of it explores the event in a manner that is far more profound.

"A Promise," a heartbreaking film that is nonetheless one of the brighter lights of this year's New Directors/New Films series, will be shown tonight at 6 P.M. and tomorrow at 8:30 P.M.

1987 Mr 17, C14:4

Highway to Nowhere

REICHSAUTOBAHN, produced, written (German with English subtitles) and directed by Hartmut Bitomsky; camera, Carlos Bustamante; a Big Sky Film Production; presented in association with Goethe House, New York. At Film Forum 1, 57 Watts Street. Running time: 90 minutes. This film has no rating.

By WALTER GOODMAN

WHY did Hitler build the famed autobahn, Germany's thousands of kilometers of high-speed highway? To ease the unemployment that was afflicting the country in the 1930's? To provide fast transport to grease a sluggish economy? To make travel pleasanter for car owners? To serve military needs?

None of the above, according to the skeptically inclined "Reichsautobahn," a German documentary on the construction, use and disuse of the highways. It maintains that the autobahn was a luxury that suited Hitler's grandiose tastes and served his regime as a demonstration of Germany's technical prowess and national solidarity — "the will of a community." The propaganda by which this message was conveyed gives the documentary, which opens today at Film Forum 1, its most striking scenes.

If the anti-autobahn narrator can be believed, the unemployment rate was scarcely affected by hiring for the road-building; the roads proved too weak to bear heavy trucks; there were not enough privately owned cars to make much use of them for sightseeing and, when war came, the military chose other means of moving troops and equipment. But none of that was allowed to interfere with turning the autobahn into a symbol of growing German power and pride.

Although Hartmut Bitomsky, who produced, wrote, directed and edited, provides as much detail as anybody could ask for on how the roads were built, his deeper interest is in their political esthetic, the way their sweep

Hitler's Highway Black and white photography and Nazi engineering are on display in "Reichsautobahn."

and grandeur were used by Nazi propagandists to celebrate Hitler's genius and instill pride in the country. "Where Germany ends," said Hitler, "the potholes can begin."

Books, magazines, paintings, poems, radio programs and, of course, movies acclaiming the autobahn proliferated. America, too, would succumb to an infatuation with highways a couple of decades later, but the difference in spirit is instructive. The taste of the Goebbels propaganda machine for the portentous takes the form of awesome shots of workers looming like supermen, vistas of concrete disappearing into the horizon like speed itself, roads transformed by dramatic photography into "cultural monuments."

It's absurd, yet impressive. And there's the Führer shoveling energetically at the groundbreaking and then tooling along in an open car, accompanied by the usual swastikas and fawning officials, as section after section is opened. They were called "Adolf Hitler's roads." (Nazi propaganda was not known for a sense of humor, but there are some unintentionally funny episodes, particularly one short movie that features a fake Englishman who goes into raptures over the glorious autobahn.)

Adolf Hitler's roads, with their imposing bridges, were smashed during the German retreat at the end of the war, and this intelligently argumentative documentary ends with rubble that has yet to be cleared away and with an up-to-date traffic jam. Hitler seems to have been a couple of decades early. Germany needs more roads.

1987 Mr 18, C22:4

Pie in the Sky

WILD MOUNTAINS, directed by Yan Xueshu; screenplay (Chinese with English subtitles) by Mr. Xueshu and Zhu Zi, from the novella "Jiwowade Renjia" ("The People of Jiwowa") by Jia Ping'ao; photography, Mi Jiaqing; music by Xu Youfu; production companay, Xi'an Film Studio. At Roy and Niuta Titus Theater 1, The Museum of Modern Art, 11 West 53d Street, as part of the 1987 New Directors/New Films series. Running time: 100 minutes. This film has no rating.

Guilan	Yue Hong
Huihui	Xin Ming
Hehe	Du Yuan
Qiurong	Xu Shouli
Ershui	Tan Xihe
Ershen	Qiu Yuzhen

By JANET MASLIN

THE Chinese film "Wild Mountains" takes place in a rustic paradise fraught with problems that might be found anywhere: troubles about money, ambition, get-rich-quick schemes, idle gossip and marital discord. It concerns two married couples, the younger of them separated. Hehe (Du Yuan) has come to live with his brother Huihui (Xin Ming) and sister-in-law in a hut that is within clear view of the place where his beautiful wife Qiurong (Xu Shouli) lives with their baby. Hehe and Qiurong have quarreled about his dissatisfaction with simple peasant life and his eagerness to see the wider world.

For all its emphasis on crude simplicity, "Wild Mountains" seems conceived as a commercial entertainment, and an enjoyable one at that. The hard, chore-filled life of these peasants is presented with a glowing romanticism. And even at the end of each exhausting day, the characters retain their cheerfulness and good humor. The film's homespun humor ("Filthy! We could grow crops on you!") is delivered with a certain urbanity, by actors who seem markedly more sophisticated than the characters they play. None of this diminishes the film's rueful intelligence or its picturesque charm.

In "Wild Mountains," which was directed by Yan Xueshu, the scenery is the real star. The camera often takes time out to roam the landscape, which is quite spectacular. And the beauties of nature are celebrated at every turn, as is the work ethic. Quirong labors long and hard with her little son strapped onto her back, an arrangement that must be made doubly taxing by the baby's diaperless apparel. Guilan, Huihui's childless wife, cares for barnyard animals and teases her husband about the pigpen, which is the closest thing to an outhouse that the family has. Hehe argues with his brother about the peasant's lot and helps to dream up moneymaking ideas, the loveliest of which involves silkworms. Perhaps the worst plan, which is Hehe's alone, is to raise a passel of flying squirrels, on the theory that their droppings have medicinal value.

"Wild Mountains" eventually takes Hehe and Guilan on a trip to a small city, where they marvel at the souvenirs, the television and the other signs of modern civilization. This way of life impinges only indirectly on their mountain existence, but it signals a dissatisfaction that has far-reaching effects for all four principals. "Wild Mountains," acted in a hearty, life-affirming spirit that suits the direction, demonstrates considerable wisdom in presenting a discontent that could turn up anywhere, and the forces that may set it in motion.

1987 Mr 19, C26:4

A Murky Past

THE DARK SIDE OF THE MOON, directed by Erik Clausen; screenplay (Danish with English subtitles) by Mr. Clausen; photography by Morten Bruus and Jens Schlosser; edited by Ghita Beckendorff and Jack Thuesen; music by Robert Broberg; production company, Film-Cooperativet Danmark/Metronome Productions A/S for the Danish Film Institute. At Roy and Niuta

Titus Theater 1, Museum of Modern Art, 11 West 53d Street, as part of the 1987 New Directors/New Films series. Running time: 93 minutes. This film has no rating.

John	Peter Thiel
Maria Bianca	Catherine Poul Jupont
John's daughter	Christina Bengtsson
Husband	Kim Jansson
The Turc	Yavuzer Cetinkaya

WITH: Berthe Qvistgaard, Erik Truxa, Anne Nojgaard, Marianne Mortensen, Stig Hoffmeyer, Ramezan Arslan, Meliha Saglanmak, Roy Richards, Dogan Arslan and Elmas Yildiz

By VINCENT CANBY

ERIK CLAUSEN'S "Dark Side of the Moon" is a Danish film about a man named John who's released from prison after serving 16 years for an awful crime, the nature of which the film treats as a mystery long after it actually is.

The film will be shown at the Museum of Modern Art today at 8:30 P.M. and next Sunday at 1 P.M., in the New Directors/New Films series.

John is played by Peter Thiel, who looks like a younger, somewhat less tense Klaus Kinski, though he has every right to be raving mad. The moon and its reasonable facsimiles stalk John in and out of prison, in and out of flashbacks and especially in the gaudy nightclub where he finds work as a dishwasher. There's a round, full-moon-colored window, high above the nightclub stage, from which John can watch the show.

The headliner is a woman named Maria Bianca, who sings with the voice of a man and develops an interest in John. When she takes him back to her flat one night, she pretends to be caring for a baby in the next room, though the sounds John hears are those from a tape recorder. He flees.

However, he cannot flee his past. He seeks out his married daughter, who wants nothing to do with him. At another point he wanders through the now-closed factory where he worked for 10 years in charge of the machine shop. Mr. Clausen, whose fourth feature this is, has a liking for watery (or at least damp) landscapes, silhouettes, long shadows, the sounds of echoed footsteps and the shells of buildings as abandoned as John.

Mr. Clausen is a more accomplished technician than director and writer. His poetic images, though

Troubled Soul John Thiel, portraying a former prisoner, dwells on his past in the Danish film "The Dark Side of the Moon."

pretty, seldom have the effect of packing the movie with associated meanings and emotions. Instead they simply dress up a small, sad, dim story.

1987 Mr 19, C28:1

Satirizing the System

HOLLYWOOD SHUFFLE, directed and produced by Robert Townsend; written by Mr. Townsend and Keenen Ivory Wayans; director of photography, Peter Deming; edited by W. O. Garrett; music by Patrice Rushen and Udi Harpaz; released by the Samuel Goldwyn Company. At Embassy 3, Broadway at 47th Street; Metro Cinema, 99th Street and Broadway; Quad Cinema 2, 13th Street, between Fifth Avenue and Avenue of the Americas. Running time: 82 minutes. This film is rated R.

Bobby Taylor	Robert Townsend
Lydia	Anne-Marie Johnson
Bobby's mother	Starletta Dupois
Bobby's Grandmother	Helen Martin
Stevie	Craigus R. Johnson
Manvacum	Domenick Irrera
N.A.A.C.P. President	Paul Mooney
Producer	Lisa Mende
Mr. Jones	John Witherspoon
Donald	Keenen Ivory Wayans

By JANET MASLIN

HAVING appeared in "A Soldier's Story," "Streets of Fire," "Ratboy" and "American Flyers," Robert Townsend had established himself as a not bad, not terribly memorable black actor best suited to supporting roles. He might have remained one indefinitely, had he not had the temerity to challenge fate. Mr. Townsend raised $100,000, some of it as cash advances against his own credit cards, and used the money to co-write, produce, direct and star in a comedy about the very troubles he had encountered. Even if "Hollywood Shuffle" had been a dismal failure, the tale of its origins would have made a great story.

Happily, the film itself makes the story even better. "Hollywood Shuffle," which opens today at the Embassy 3 and other theaters, is an exuberant satire, uneven but tirelessly energetic, with the kind of comic bluster that can override any lapse. It's

Paul Slaughter

How to Succeed Robert Townsend, seen with Tammy Cates, is director and star of "Hollywood Shuffle," a comedy about a young black actor striving for success in the film industry.

funny, ragged, appealingly mean-spirited and very easy to like, even if it plays as a series of skits rather than a coherent whole. Mr. Townsend, who also does stand-up comedy, has devised a hit-and-run format that suits him well, and has tacked a series of daydreams and digressions onto a thin but barely noticeable story line. What the film lacks in structure it makes up for in reality-minded humor.

The plot has to do with an aspiring young actor named Bobby Taylor and his hopes of landing a leading role in a film; the digressions have to do with wear and tear on the psyches of Bobby and others like him. Who is their role model? Could the leading black television actor of Bobby's day really be the winged, beanie-clad star of "There's a Bat in My House," a television show that asks: "Can a black bat from Detroit find happiness with a white suburban family? He's half bat, half soul brother — but together he adds up to big laughs!" Is that too farfetched? Bear in mind, before answering, the existence of an actual television show, having its premiere this evening, about Snow White and Prince Charming living in the suburbs with their 20th-century children.

The film's principal complaint, demonstrated in an opening scene that has Bobby practicing the line "You done messed with the wrong dude, ba-by," is that the range of roles available to up-and-coming black actors is severely limited, to put it mildly. This idea is also borne out by the closing credits, which list a group of "Zombie Pimps" and another of "Eddie Murphy Types." The same cast members reappear over and over again in a number of similar capacities.

As Bobby watches classically trained actors turn up at casting calls to read lines like "Why you be gotta pull a knife on me? I be got no weapon," he all but despairs. And when he does manage to land a starring role as a jive-talking, Afro-wearing hoodlum, he feels even worse. Bobby's shame at selling out leads to a slave-film fantasy, in which Bobby plays the Stepin Fetchit role, and a day-dream about a black actors' school run by white teachers, who proudly teach them to swagger. Bobby even imagines starring in a two-man movie critics' show called "Sneakin' Into the Movies," in which he and a friend rely on a wider range of hand gestures than the usual thumbs up or thumbs down to express their opinions of films like "Amadeus" and "Dirty Harry." At the show's end, they are thrown out of the theater by an angry usher.

Mr. Townsend's one misstep is to sugarcoat some of those parts of the film involving women. He gives Bobby a mother (Starletta Dupois), a grandmother (Helen Martin) and a pretty, chaste girlfriend (Anne-Marie Johnson), who help to keep him from losing sight of his real values. Good as these actresses are, they slow down a film whose best scenes are its most biting. But the rest of the cast, including John Witherspoon and Mr. Townsend's co-screenwriter, Keenen Ivory Wayans, helps to sustain the satirical tone, and this quick, funny film never loses sight of its central point. The opportunities for black actors in Hollywood remain as limited as they ever were. But Mr. Townsend has taken aim at the industry's funny bone and struck a solid blow.

1987 Mr 20, C8:1

Moonlighting By day in "Burglar," Whoopi Goldberg is a San Francisco bookseller; by night, she turns to thievery. Her co-star in the Hugh Wilson comedy-mystery is Bob Goldthwait, portraying a poodle groomer who is her best friend.

Back on the Job

BURGLAR, directed by Hugh Wilson; screenplay by Joseph Loeb 3d, Matthew Weisman and Mr. Wilson, based on books by Lawrence Block; director of photography, William A. Fraker; edited by Fredric Steinkamp and William Steinkamp; music by Sylvester Levay; produced by Kevin McCormick and Michael Hirsh; released by Warner Brothers. At National, Broadway and 44th Street; Sutton, 57th Street and Third Avenue; 84th Street Six, at Broadway; 86th Street Twin, at Lexington Avenue; 84th Street Twin, 12th Street at Seventh Avenue, and other theaters. Running time: 100 minutes. This film is rated R.

Bernice Rhodenbarr	Whoopi Goldberg
Carl Hefler	Bob Goldthwait
Ray Kirschman	G. W. Bailey
Dr. Cynthia Sheldrake	Lesley Ann Warren
Carson Verrill	James Handy
Detective Todras	Anne DeSalvo
Detective Nyswander	John Goodman
Frankie	Elizabeth Ruscio
Graybow	Vyto Ruginis
Knobby	Larry Mintz

By VINCENT CANBY

THE further the screen version of "The Color Purple" recedes into history, the better it looks, especially Steven Spielberg's presentation of Whoopi Goldberg, the star of her first film in what became an Oscar-nominated performance.

Because of her talent, plus the fact she has no serious competition, Miss Goldberg is the premier black actress in American films today, but you wouldn't know it from her appearances since "The Color Purple." There have been "Jumpin' Jack Flash," a wan spy caper, and now the lamentable "Burglar," which opens today at the Sutton and other theaters.

What's happening to Miss Goldberg (with, I assume, her cooperation) is the kind of exploitation less often associated with people than with corporate takeovers. It's as if Miss Goldberg had been "acquired" by Hollywood, which set about to liquidate her assets as quickly and heedlessly as possible. Another movie as sloppy as "Burglar" and the actress will have no credit left.

In certain kinds of comedy, sloppiness isn't in itself all that damaging. It was virtually the comic style of the initial "Police Academy" film, which was directed by Hugh Wilson, who also directed "Burglar." Unlike "Police Academy," the new film is not about slobs. It's about doing a poor imitation of the kind of all-purpose packaging that helped make Eddie Murphy so successful in "Trading Places" and "Beverly Hills Cop."

Miss Goldberg, however, is a far grittier, far more decisive film personality than Mr. Murphy. The yuppie image that Mr. Murphy wears with such grace — though in various disguises — looks foolish on her.

•

In "Burglar," Miss Goldberg plays a retired San Francisco cat burglar who's blackmailed into returning — reluctantly — to her trade by a crooked cop, who wants $20,000 in cash and a mink coat for his wife. Even this so-called idea might be funny if the screenplay had really been written and not, as it appears to have been, talked into being at story conferences.

It's unfunny, nonsensical and, what's far worse, requires that Miss Goldberg behave like a performing bear. She's the only black person in an otherwise white world, an alien creature of unidentified origins and no apparent sexuality, someone who talks with Miss Goldberg's own tonal elegance, which, for comic effect, is sometimes instantaneously modified into a variety of street accents.

What Mr. Wilson and his associates attempt to do is to allow the star to do character riffs — within the context of a narrative — that approximate the sort of things she does as monologues in her one-woman show. Unfortunately, the demands of the story keep interfering so that Miss Goldberg never gets a chance to establish any identity whatsoever.

In "Burglar" she comes across as something of a freak, who apparently owns a bookshop (though she's seldom in it), and, among other things, was the boxing champ of the prison where she served time. She lives alone in a fancily decorated apartment overlooking San Francisco, and has, as her only friend, a dog-groomer, an asexual male who talks peculiarly. In this role, Bob Goldthwait, who was wonderfully funny in "Police Academy 2," is as lost as his co-star.

In addition to Miss Goldberg and Mr. Goldthwait, the cast of "Burglar" includes Lesley Ann Warren, who plays a greedy dentist so dumb she can't figure out how many days are in 72 hours. That sounds far more amusing than it plays. "Burglar" is a wasteland for everyone in it.

The one point it makes — loud and clear — is that if there are few movie roles of any substance for actresses, there are even fewer if the actress also happens to be black. Perhaps Miss Goldberg should take matters in her own hands like Robert Townsend, the young black actor who, fed up with the roles offered to him, made his own film, "Hollywood Shuffle" (review on page C8). She couldn't do worse than she's doing now.

1987 Mr 20, C10:4

Bad Bite

IN THE JAWS OF LIFE, directed by Rajko Grlic; screenplay (Serbo-Croatian with English subtitles) by Mr. Grlic and Dubravke Ugresic; photography by Tomislav Pinter; edited by Zivka Toplak; music by

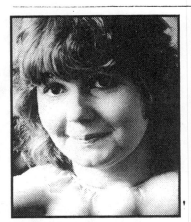

Vitomira Loncar

Brane Zivkovic; produced by Alexsander Stojanovic; production companies, Art Film, Croatia Film Jadran Film, Union Film and Kinematografi. At Roy and Niuta Titus Theater 1, the Museum of Modern Art, 11 West 53d Street, as part of the 1987 New Directors/New Films series. Running time: 96 minutes. This film has no rating.
WITH: Gorica Popovic, Bogdan Diklic and Vitomira Loncar

"IN THE JAWS OF LIFE," Rajko Grlic's 1984 Yugoslav comedy, is about two women — Dunja, a pretty, successful film maker, and Stefa, the fictional heroine of the television soap opera that Dunja is currently producing.

The public is much taken by the plump Stefa, who's self-conscious about being "fat" and is surrounded by people who never stop eating (though they never add an ounce). Stefa also has terrible luck with men, including an overweight Serbian gigolo who wears jazzy leopard-patterned briefs but talks a better game than he plays.

Framing these adventures from the film-within-the-film are the more seriously comic adventures of Dunja, who lives in a handsome, terraced apartment in the middle of Belgrade. The men in her life include a pompous literary critic, who feels he doesn't always have to read the books he pans; a physicist, who's young but not so young that living with his opera-singer mother (as he still does) is entirely healthy, and a rock musician, who calls himself Mick Jurec and is an aging remnant of the late 60's.

"In the Jaws of Life" will be shown in the New Directors/New Films series at the Museum of Modern Art today at 6 P.M. and tomorrow at 3:30.

The festival's program notes describe "In the Jaws of Life" as "bittersweet," but it seems far less sweet than plain bitter, and more bored with the lives it describes than it appears to understand. Though Dunja, who has created the character of Stefa, is aware of the resentments of her soap-opera heroine, Mr. Grlic never allows Dunja full expression of her own resentments, which, possibly, reflect his own.

Whether it means to be or not, I've no idea, but "In the Jaws of Life" is a very bleak comedy about people whose lives are at a dead end. Perhaps it's more political than an outsider can easily recognize. Whatever the reason, "In the Jaws of Life," though nicely acted, seems constrained and still unrealized, a movie with a lot more on its mind than it ever talks about.

VINCENT CANBY

1987 Mr 20, C15:1

Checkered Chinese

SLEEPWALK, directed by Sara Driver; screenplay by Ms. Driver and Lorenzo Mans, from a story by Ms. Driver and Kathleen Brennon; photography by Frank Prinzi and Jim Jarmusch; edited by Li Shin Yu; music by Phil Kline; production company, Ottoskop Filmproduktion GmBH, Munich, West Germany, and Driver Films Inc., New York; production team, Dave Bromberg, Dan Shulman, J. C. Hardin and Jane Weinstock. At Roy and Niuta Titus Theater 1, the Museum of Modern Art, 11 West 53d Street, as part of the 1987 New Directors/New Films series. Running time: 78 minutes. This film has no rating.
Nicole......................................Suzanne Fletcher
Isabelle ....Ann Magnuson
Jimmy ....Dexter Lee
Dr. Gou ....Steven Chen
Ecco Ecco ....Ako
DRUM/SING, directed by Gregor Nicholas. Running time: 22 minutes.

By CARYN JAMES

WHEN Chinese fairy tales impinge on the life of Nicole, a young woman in downtown New York, several things happen: her sexy French roommate becomes bald; her finger begins to bleed; an Oriental woman about to unravel these mysteries is killed. Nicole's half-Chinese son, a wise child, thinks the whole thing smells like almonds. Sara Driver's lyrical, witty "Sleepwalk" has the illogical sense of a dream, backed by the texture of everyday life. In her first feature, Ms. Driver blithely absorbs influences — from chiaroscuro to Surrealism to performance art — and spins them into her own vibrant, original style.

"Sleepwalk" begins with the theft of an ancient manuscript, which the sinister Dr. Gou asks Nicole to translate. She does, and soon life imitates these tales. Isabelle, the bald, vain roommate, is punished for her greediness, like the princess in the manuscript story who refused to give a bird a lock of her hair. Another tale warns, "Keep the child away from the man who smells like almonds." The child is clearly Nicole's son. But why does Dr. Gou lie on a bed of almonds, and why does Ecco Ecco, the Oriental woman, say "almonds, poison," as she points to the manuscript?

Ms. Driver, who co-wrote the screenplay, takes the incoherence of these events for granted. Despite its trappings of mystery and suspense, "Sleepwalk" is barely concerned with plot; what matters is the feel of this place where dreams meet reality. In a glance Ms. Driver captures the print shop where Nicole works, a grimy warehouse building where she and her hip-looking colleagues bend over computer terminals and drafting tables, intensely bored. On her way to a neighborhood bodega, Nicole sees a child throw a handful of stardust into the air; at least that's what it looks like.

Sara Driver, a graduate of the New York University Film School, has worked on Jim Jarmusch's three films. She produced his "Stranger Than Paradise," and he and Frank Prinzi did the dazzling camerawork on "Sleepwalk." Ms. Driver's film, though, is like a Jarmusch work turned upside-down and inside-out. Instead of his black-and-white photographic images, she works with light and shadow like a painter creating still lifes. Doors open and light slashes diagonally across darkened rooms; whole scenes seem painted from a palette of blues. And while Mr. Jarmusch's characters are downtrodden dreamers, Ms. Driver's are offbeat people who have dreams foisted on them.

Although "Sleepwalk" moves slowly, Ms. Driver keeps her images from becoming static or self-consciously artsy. The performance artist Ann Magnuson is colorful comic relief as Isabelle; she may lose her rich red hair and parade around much of the film looking like Daddy Warbucks, but she never drops her perfectly exaggerated French accent. Suzanne Fletcher's Nicole is methodical and laconic, a relatively ordinary center for her jumbled household, a perfect foil for the magic that appears before her.

"Sleepwalk" will be shown as part of the New Directors/New Films series at the Museum of Modern Art today at 8:30 P.M. and tomorrow at 1 P.M. It will be preceded by "Drum/Sing," a 1985 short from New Zealand featuring a performance by a group called From Scratch — a trio of percussionists who use drums and chimes, their hands, and occasionally their voices. This appeals to a rather specialized taste. "Drum/Sing" is an unimaginative 22 minutes, worth sitting through only to discover the freshness of "Sleepwalk."

1987 Mr 20, C15:1

LOYALTIES, directed by Anne Wheeler; screenplay by Sharon Riis, based on a story by Miss Riis and Miss Wheeler; photography by Vic Sarin; edited by Judy Krupansky; music by Michael Conway Baker; produced by Ronald Lillie and William Johnston. At Roy and Niuta Titus Theater 1, The Museum of Modern Art, 11 West 53d Street, as part of the 1987 New Directors/New Films series. Running time: 98 minutes. This film has no rating.
David Sutton ....Kenneth Welsh
Rosanne Ladouceur ....Tantoo Cardinal
Lily Sutton ....Susan Wooldridge
Beatrice ....Vera Martin
Leona ....Diane Debassige
Eddy ....Tom Jackson
Nicholas Sutton ....Jeffrey Smith
Naomi Sutton ....Meredith Rimmer
Jeremy Sutton
Alexander and Jonathan Tribiger
Robert Sutton ..Christopher Barrington-Leigh
Lisa ....Yolanda Cardinal

By VINCENT CANBY

"Loyalties," set in the small community of Lac la Biche in northwestern Canada, is a technically adequate Canadian film about the sustaining friendship that grows up between two very different kinds of women. The film will be shown in the New Directors/New Films series at the Museum of Modern Art today at 6 P.M. and tomorrow at 3:30 P.M.

Rosanne Ladouceur (Tantoo Cardinal), who's "mostly" of American Indian stock, is in her mid-30's, pretty (in the seasoned way of someone who's always worked hard) and accustomed to taking life as it comes. When Rosanne's boyfriend — the father of her children — gets drunk and beats up Rosanne in the bar where she works as a waitress, the boyfriend gets off scot-free and Rosanne loses her job.

Lily Sutton (Susan Wooldridge) is a well-groomed, very proper English-woman considered by her mother to have slipped on the social scale by marrying David (Kenneth Welsh), a medical doctor who has risen from the lower English orders. She's not yet a snob but, unlike Rosanne, who calls a spade a spade, Lily would prefer to use euphemisms, which is pretty much what's wrong with her marriage and her life.

At the start of the movie, Lily and her children are joining David in Lac la Biche, apparently to escape some unmentionable scandal in England.

To help the unemployed Rosanne, David hires her to work for the Suttons as au pair woman and unofficial family counselor. Inevitably, the unmentionable thing that drove the Suttons from England reappears in Lac la Biche.

"Loyalties" is the second feature to be directed by Anne Wheeler, who also collaborated with Sharon Riis on the story that Miss Riis adapted into the screenplay. There's nothing especially wrong with the movie, but then there's nothing very right, either.

Except for Miss Cardinal's performance as the earthy, intelligent Rosanne, "Loyalties" is utterly without distinguishing characteristics, either in its narrative or in the way it has been written and directed. Everything about the film — including the other performances, the photography, the local color, the schmaltzy soundtrack music and the interior décor — looks as if it had been ordered from a catalogue.

1987 Mr 21, 14:3

Examining Myths

A **HERO'S JOURNEY: THE WORLD OF JOSEPH CAMPBELL,** directed by William Free and Janelle Balnicke; photography by Erik Daarstad and H. J. Brown; edited by Yasha Aginsky; produced by Mr. Free. At Roy and Niuta Titus Theater 1, The Museum of Modern Art, 11 West 53d Street, as part of the 1987 New Directors/New Films Series. Running time: 58 minutes. This film has no rating.

AND:

DARK HAIR, directed by Midori Kurisaki; photography by Hideo Fujii and Fujio Morita; produced by Midori Kurisaki. At Roy and Niuta Titus Theater 1, The Museum of Modern Art, 11 West 53d Street, as part of the 1987 New Directors/New Films Series. Running time: 60 minutes. This film has no rating.
WITH: Senjaku Nakamura

By JANET MASLIN

AFFECTIONATELY profiled in the hourlong documentary "A Hero's Journey," the scholar and teacher Joseph Campbell seems a figure of heroic proportions. Along with outlining the basic tenets of Mr. Campbell's landmark theories concerning the universality of certain myths, the film touches on a protean life that is equally remarkable.

Mr. Campbell, a handsome and extremely charming man now in his 80's, describes the pattern of his intellectual development with offhanded ease. He speaks of his early fascination with American Indian lore, saying "I think that's where my life as a scholar began — I know it did." These tales, he found, "were symbolic stories that reconciled the Indians to the harsh reality of life." And they led the very young Mr. Campbell to contemplate the important role played by mythology in primitive cultures.

Once an altar boy in the Roman Catholic church, he found himself expanding religion into a larger mythological framework. An Atlantic crossing in the early 1920's led to a chance meeting with the philosopher Krishnamurti, under whose influence Mr. Campbell began to contemplate Eastern religions as well. And in Paris, he also located elements of a universal mythology in the works of Picasso, Matisse, Brancusi and other artists of the day.

By the time of the 1929 stock market crash, Mr. Campbell — who was also a saxophone player, an early surfer, and one of the fastest half-

A scene from Midori Kurisaki's film "Dark Hair."

milers in the world — was ready to spend five years reading. After that, he emerged to begin teaching at Sarah Lawrence College, where he appears to have been understandably popular with his female students, one of whom he married. Seen today, expounding on his ideas in a seminar at Esalen, Mr. Campbell is still surrounded by admiring young women. "A Hero's Journey," while providing a good introduction to his scholarly career, manages along the way to make this admiration seem wholly understandable.

Another of Mr. Campbell's fans is the film maker George Lucas, who is seen briefly at a testimonal event honoring the scholar. "Whether it is Odysseus, King Arthur or Luke Skywalker, the hero is the one who responds to the call of adventure," the film's narrator observes. Indeed, clips from "Star Wars" are used to illustrate some aspects of the universal heroic figure, as set forth in Mr. Campbell's comprehensive work "The Hero With a Thousand Faces." Among these, as the narrator explains, are a feeling of restlessness, the hearing of a call to action, a separation from family and home, the need for a mentor, and the entering into a dreamlike labyrinth where the hero's initiation will occur. The "Star Wars" excerpts are well used in demonstrating the far-reaching pop cultural ramifications of Mr. Campbell's theories.

As directed by William Free and Janelle Balnicke, "A Hero's Journey: The World of Joseph Campbell" is both serious and colloquial, which aptly suits Mr. Campbell himself.

•

On the same bill, and of more limited interest, is Midori Kurisaki's "Dark Hair," an examination of the importance of women's hair and hairdos in Japanese culture. Explaining the names and histories of various coiffures, and employing elaborate puppets to dramatize certain stories, "Dark Hair" reiterates the thought that "truly dark hair is life for a woman." Coming on the heels of a subject as riveting as Mr. Campbell, this study of hair and its meaning cannot help but seem small.

"A Hero's Journey" and "Dark Hair" will be shown tonight at 6 and tomorrow night at 8:30 as part of the New Directors/New Films series.

1987 Mr 22, 62:1

Life Is Extraordinary

A WOMAN FROM THE PROVINCES, directed by Andrzej Baranski; screenplay (Polish with English subtitles) by Mr. Baranski and Waldemar Sieminski, from a novel by Mr. Sieminski; photography by Ryszard Lenczewski; edited by Marek Denys; music by Henryk Kuzniak; production company, Oko Film Unit. At Roy and Niuta Titus Theater 1, Museum of Modern Art, 11 West 53d Street, as part of the 1987 New Directors/New Films Series. Running time: 104 minutes. This film has no rating.

Andzia	Ewa Dalkowska
Her Mother	Ryszarda Hanin
Jadzka	Bozena Dykiel
Celinka	Magdalena Michalak
The Acquaintance	Halina Wyrodek
Solski	Kazimierz Wichniarz
Andzia's Father	Aleksander Fogiel
Szczepan	Maciej Goraj
Henius	Jan Jankowksi
Siejwa	Hanna Giza

By WALTER GOODMAN

"A WOMAN FROM THE PROVINCES" finally works almost in spite of itself. The Polish movie, which will be shown at the Museum of Modern Art tonight at 9 and tomorrow at 6 P.M., creates a mosaic of a woman who did nothing more special than live out an arduous existence in a village. It takes a while, but the director, Andrzej Baranski, finds the truth in the truism that every closely observed life is extraordinary.

His screenplay, based on a novel by Waldemar Sieminski, begins with Andzia at age 60 watching television in a comfortable house and relecting chattily on everyday pleasures. We learn, in flashbacks, that she was widowed young and left with two babies; until late in life she had to do menial work to get by. Andzia is a survivor, without histrionics. Gradually, memories from a half-century come together to create this woman from the provinces. The tone is as subdued as the faded and sometimes fuzzy color; for a stretch or two you may find yourself growing impatient, but the unhurried pace, the unpressured manner prove faithful to the material.

•

Not every piece in the mosaic is a jewel. Mr. Baranski favors setting up scenes through the frame of a door or a window, with his actors assuming poses, a technique that draws attention to itself when we should be involved with Andzia. And some of the dialogue is plainly written with an eye to the ear of the audience. People say things to each other in a stilted manner to provide us with information. "I'm still single," announces Andzia's sister to an impetuous suitor, "but my sister has been married and widowed." The effect, again, is to rub in our role as auditors.

But then there are moments that sparkle. When the pretty young Andzia, wooed by two men, first rejects then settles for the less ardent, more conventional of them, the simple girl's conflicting desires and fears shine through. The seemingly trivial squabbles over money between the elderly Andzia and her husband assume crucial importance as we go back into her hard-working, skimping past, beginning with her mother taking the few pennies the child has earned by selling rags and tags to buy food for her ailing father.

•

What Mr. Barzanksi is after are not explosions but an accumulation of experiences. Politics is scarcely mentioned but is always present in the way that the need for money, food and security grinds away at lives that never range very far from fundamentals.

•

Missing is a convincing sense of place; most of the time Andzia's village seems uninhabited. As Andzia, the beautiful Ewa Dalkowska must go from 20 to 60, a demand that she meets best in its middle range. She's too womanly to pass as 20, and as the elderly Andzia, she looks overly fashionable. Nonetheless, by the end we feel we know her.

1987 Mr 22, 62:2

FILM VIEW/Vincent Canby

Big Screen Soloists

DON'T PANIC. IT SAYS MORE about the underutilized flexibility of films than about their uncertain financial state that the most entertaining new movie to arrive in New York since "Radio Days" is "Swimming to Cambodia," Spalding Gray's one-man performance piece directed for the screen by Jonathan Demme.

The question may well be asked: Is "Swimming to Cambodia" really a film? The unequivocal answer: Yes.

"Swimming to Cambodia" is an eccentric, personal, freely associating monologue about life, death, sex and love (and being a relentlessly observant bit-player in "The Killing Fields"), delivered by Mr. Gray, the 45-year-old actor, writer and professional raconteur. Though his features are vaguely WASPy and handsome, they also suggest those of a clown who's just taken off a red plastic nose and whiteface makeup.

From the start of the film until its end, 87 minutes later, Mr. Gray sits — unbudging — at a table on the small stage, addressing the audience at Manhattan's downtown Performing Garage. In the course of his alternately hilarious and poignant recollections, Mr. Gray moves around a bit in his chair, but he never even slumps in a dramatic way. In these restricted but relaxed circumstances, it would be a coup de théâtre if he just stood up.

He sips from a glass of water. Occasionally, using a teacher's wooden pointer, he directs attention to maps of Southeast Asia behind him. Every now and then Mr. Demme briefly lowers the lights, possibly to vary the look of the movie image and to separate Mr. Gray's thoughts about his girlfriend, Renee, from those on genocide and the Khmer Rouge. At other moments, to illustrate Mr. Gray's recollections of the production of "The Killing Fields" in Thailand, he shows clips from the finished film.

From time to time, we hear Laurie Andersons's evocative and haunting musical score, which sometimes helps to set an anecdote and, at other times, works in counterpoint.

"Swimming to Cambodia" is not for anybody who likes movies "juicy," the currently popular, vague, somewhat lubricious catchword for a narrative movie stuffed with not-fully-digested raw material and involving actors, incident, changes of locale and emotion.

■

"Swimming to Cambodia" isn't even minimalist as originally defined by the German director Jean Marie Straub's "Chronicles of Anna Magdalena Bach" and "Aaron and Moses," and eventually domesticated by Louis Malle's "My Dinner With Andre." Instead, "Swimming to Cambodia" belongs to that still evolving category of entertainment called the "concert film."

45

The concert film was, at first, just that: a filmed recording of a rock music concert, exemplified by Michael Wadleigh's "Woodstock" (1970). Eventually, however, the rock-concert film degenerated into the rock-concert-*promotion* film, mainly designed to publicize the album recorded during the filming of the concert.

The appearance of "Swimming to Cambodia" in theaters (instead of on free or even pay television) owes a lot to Richard Pryor. As he showed with "Richard Pryor Live in Concert" (1979), the public was more than willing to pay stiff admission prices to see a movie in which a single performer cavorts around a bare stage for 78 minutes.

With the exception of "Richard Pryor Live on the Sunset Strip" (1982), directed by Joe Layton and photographed by Haskell Wexler, the Pryor concert films haven't been notable for their cinematic style. The chief attraction was — at least, originally — the promise of seeing and hearing a Richard Pryor stand-up performance before it might be expurgated to conform to even the relaxed standards of pay television.

The Pryor films demonstrated that, when personality and material are right, a solo performer can fill the comparatively big screen of a theater (as well as the seats) just as effectively as the spectacle of intergalactic war.

The theater screen is far more adaptable than most producers appear to understand. Even as these producers ignore the possibilities of virtually every recent innovation in theater projection and sound technology, they've also allowed television producers to corner the market in solo performers. Today's movies aren't really big in terms of subject, screen size or the amount of visual information contained in any frame of film. At the same time they seldom realize their potential for intimacy of the sort demonstrated by Mr. Pryor's concert films, and now by "Swimming to Cambodia."

Most theatrical films exist in limbo, as if waiting their irrevocable call to the television and video cassette markets, which is why they're so boring. They have no distinct character.

"Swimming to Cambodia" represents a breakthrough, not toward the big and elaborate, but toward the small, lean and finely detailed. Mr. Demme, who was also responsible for the implacably straightforward Talking Heads concert film, "Stop Making Sense," has the great talent to be able to present his concert-film subjects without upstaging them.

With what appears to be deceptively little cinematic artifice, he allows Mr. Gray's alternately caustic and humanely funny performing presence to come through, undistorted, on the theater screen. Because the film does have its own identity, I've no doubt that "Swimming to Cambodia" will play with equal effect on television.

Whoopi Goldberg has now made three theatrical movies, but her best comedy "film" is still "Whoopi Goldberg," Mike Nichols's taped adaptation of her one-woman Broadway show, presented by Home Box Office. "Whoopi Goldberg" might well have had the theatrical life that, I suspect, awaits the incomparable "Swimming to Cambodia." □

1987 Mr 22, II:19:1

MY LIFE AS A DOG, directed by Lasse Hallstrom; screenplay (Swedish with English subtitles) by Mr. Hallstrom, Reidar Jonsson, Brasse Brannstrom and Per Berglund, based on a novel by Mr. Jonsson; cinematographer, Jorgen Persson; edited by Christer Furubrand and Susanne Linnman; music by Bjorn Isfalt; produced by Waldemar Bergendahl; a Svensk Filmindustri Picture. At Roy and Niuta Titus Theater 1, Museum of Modern Art, 11 West 53d Street, as part of the New Directors/New Films Series. Running time: 101 minutes. This film is rated PG-13.

Ingemar .... Anton Glanzelius
Uncle Gunnar .... Tomas von Bromssen
Mother .... Anki Liden
Saga .... Melinda Kinnaman

By VINCENT CANBY

WHEN left to his own devices, Ingemar Johansson is a most winning adolescent — skeptical, introspective, curious, trying earnestly to bring order out of nature's chaos. As played by 11-year-old Anton Glanzelius in Lasse Hallstrom's 1985 Swedish film "My Life as a Dog," Ingemar even looks unfinished. His forehead's too high for the rest of his face, and his eyes too small. Physically as well as emotionally, he's still in transit.

The trouble with "My Life as a Dog" is that too often it imposes an alien sensibility upon the boy, requiring that he behave in a way that adults can too easily identify as charming. "My Life as a Dog" is a movie with a split point of view.

Sometimes (especially in its funnier moments) it recalls the gravity with which François Truffaut remembered childhood. At other times, however, it suggests a 1980's variation on the prettified, idealized, sentimental view of kids favored by the Hollywood producers who made fortunes with Jackie Coogan, Jackie Cooper, Shirley Temple, Margaret O'Brien and their lesser spinoffs.

"My Life as a Dog" will be shown in the New Directors/New Films series at the Museum of Modern Art today at 6 P.M. and tomorrow at 8:30 P.M. It will begin a regular commercial engagement here in May.

As adapted by Mr. Hallstrom, Reidar Jonsson and two other collaborators from a novel by Mr. Jonsson, the film covers a crucial year in Ingemar's life, when, in additon to the storms of puberty, he must face the fact that his mother is dying of tuberculosis.

As much as he loves his mother (and his daydreams are full of poetic visions of her, accompanied by the sound of her uninhibited laughter), he seems always to be failing her. Ingemar and his older brother both mean well, but ordinary horseplay inevitably turns noisy and nasty when she's trying to sleep. When Ingemar is taken to the hospital to see her for what may be the last time, all he can say is that he's planning to buy her a toaster for Christmas.

In these moments, "My Life as a Dog" is funny and true and moving, as it also is when, on the soundtrack, he confides something of his philosophy for surviving from one day to the next: "You have to compare all the time — to get a distance on things." What's the good of being the first dog in space, he asks, if, like Russia's Laika, you wind up starving to death? How can a liver transplant be described as "successful" if the patient doesn't pull through? He ponders the meaning of a bus-train accident that leaves 6 people killed and 14 injured. He's fascinated by statistics.

The character possesses an honesty and rigor that the rest of the film would seem to deny. Too many of the things that happen to Ingemar are intended to be "cute." Inevitably, these sequences are seen not through the boy's eyes but through those of the film makers, including one sequence in which Ingemar is humiliated for his participation in a sex-education "lecture" given by an older friend in a woodshed.

Mr. Glanzelius gives a firm and wise performance as the determined, mostly unsmiling Ingemar, whose namesake's unexpected 1959 heavyweight championship victory over Floyd Patterson brings the film to its conclusion. There also are good contributions by Anki Liden as Ingemar's mother, Tomas von Bromssen as Ingemar's uncle (whose favorite song is the Swedish version of "Oh, What a Lovely Bunch of Coconuts"), and Didrik Gustavsson, as a bedridden old man who likes to listen to Ingemar read the copy in the corset ads in a mail-order catalog.

"My Life as a Dog" looks as pretty as a picture, which, in this case, is too pretty for its own good.

●

"My Life as a Dog," which has been rated PG-13 ("Special Parental Guidance Suggested for Those Younger Than 13"), includes scenes of adolescent sex play and vulgar language translated from the Swedish by the English subtitles.

1987 Mr 24, C14:3

Smiting and Smitten

MY FRIEND IVAN LAPSHIN, directed by Aleksei German; screenplay (Russian with English subtitles) by Eduard Volodarsky, based on the short stories of Yuri German; director of photography, Valery Fedosov; a Lenfilm Production. At Roy and Niuta Titus Theater 1, Museum of Modern Art, 11 West 53d Street, as part of the New Directors/New Films series. Running time: 100 minutes. This film has no rating.

Lapshin .... Andrei Boltnev
Adashova .... Nina Ruslanova
Khamin .... Andrei Mironov
Okoshkin .... Aleksei Zharkov
Patri Keyevna .... Z. Adamovich
Zanadvorov .... A. Filippenko

By WALTER GOODMAN

ONE'S sympathies are all with Aleksei German. The Soviet director has had his troubles with his country's authorities; movies that he made 10 and 20 years ago have only recently been released in the West. His fourth and latest effort, "My Friend Ivan Lapshin," which will be shown at the Museum of Modern Art as part of the New Directors/New Films series tonight at 8:30 and tomorrow at 6 P.M., is one of the first proscribed films to benefit from glasnost. Scheduled to open next month at the Cinema Studio, it is evidence that not every movie that has displeased the cultural commissars is a masterpiece.

The story, based on the tales of Mr. German's father, Yuri, is told by a barely glimpsed present-day narrator recalling what life was like in a small Russian village in 1937 when he was 9 years old. Sharing his family's apartment are three young policemen, led by Ivan Lapshin. Ivan, blankly played by Andrei Boltnev, is smitten with a touring actress and is out to smite a local murderer.

Mr. German's knack for visual authenticity provides the movie's main interest. Scene after scene, shot for the most part in the sepia of old photographs, catches the poverty and confusion of a hard time — the crowded apartment, the beat-up cars, the dreary town and its shabbily dressed people, the outbursts of desperation and nuttiness. In his treatment of a troupe of actors and some musicians jangling along on a flag-festooned little trolley, the director seems to have picked up some tricks from Fellini, but the spirit is very different. It's mostly complaint and bickering; only the policemen seem in good humor. People quarrel constantly about food and living space; a woman goes into hysterics over the loss of some gasoline.

Why was "Ivan" held back? Perhaps the leading character's rote response to every symptom of distress — "We'll clear the land of scum and build an orchard" — was taken by the Kremlin as a dangerous piece of irony. Perhaps Soviet officialdom would prefer a prettier version of life before the war. Perhaps they feared the confusion shown here might be taken as a comment on Stalin's rule. But the authorities are not pictured as particularly incompetent or unkind, just uninterested; if any sharper political criticism is implied, it is lost in the chaos the movie seeks to capture.

The scattered reminiscences, unrelated to the boy from whom they ostensibly originate and about whom we learn nothing, keep getting in the way of the rather casual plot, which has Ivan's best friend, a journalist, becoming involved with the actress and the murderer. Mr. German shows more consideration for his father's anecdotes (much is made of little practical jokes, youthful byplay, awkward accidents that add up to nothing) than for his audience's comprehension. You can hardly tell one policeman from another and often can't be sure where they are or what they are doing there.

The scenes between Ivan and the actress would be soap opera if there were not a shortage of soap, and his final shoot-out with the murderer, whom we scarcely meet, is pulp detective fiction in any language. Beneath the camouflage of the look of time past, "Ivan" is makeshift melodrama.

1987 Mr 24, C14:5

On the Road

BACKLASH, directed and produced by Bill Bennett; screenplay by Mr. Bennett, David Argue, Gia Carides, Lydia Miller and Brian Syron; photography by Tony Wilson; edited by Denise Hunter; music by Michael Atkinson and Michael Spicer; released by Samuel Goldwyn Company. At Roy and Niuta Titus Theater 1, Museum of Modern Art, 11 West 53d Street, as part of the New Directors/New Films series. Running time: 90 minutes.

Trevor Darling	David Argue
Nikki Iceton	Gia Carides
Kath	Lydia Miller
Lyle	Brian Syron
Mrs. Smith	Anne Smith
Mr. Smith	Don Smith
Waitress	Jennifer Cluff

By JANET MASLIN

THE Australian film "Backlash" begins with a brief, crude sequence in which a young aboriginal woman is attacked by her employer, an older white man whom she proceeds to murder and emasculate (we are later told) with a garden shears. How will the film, which is the second dramatic feature by Bill Bennett, make use of this episode? As it turns out, the focus shifts quickly from the murder to the man-and-woman police team assigned to escort the accused woman to her trial. Once these three begin their journey together, the film shifts gears entirely and becomes an odd hybrid, a whimsical, eccentric road movie with an element of mystery.

The older and wilder of the two police officers is Trevor Darling (David Argue), who resents his assignment and makes a point of insulting both his companions. His partner, Nikki Iceton (Gia Carides), does her best to ignore him and concentrate on her fiancé and her law studies, which isn't made any easier when Trevor decides to do headstands wearing little more than his gun belt and his underwear.

Their charge, named Kath (Lydia Miller), is initially silent much of the time, watching apprehensively as her two escorts trade nasty remarks. But gradually the three become used to one another. And when they find themselves stranded in a remote setting, bathing in a pond and sleeping in sheep-shearing pens, a certain rustic peacefulness begins to free them from their various ill humors. The film watches all three depart from their earlier roles, and establish new bonds on an entirely different footing.

"Backlash" eventually returns to the murder story, and to the prejudice and injustice that are shown to surround it. But these are the weaker aspects of a film that, at its best, recalls the picaresque Scottish comedies of Bill Forsyth, with their flair for the unexpected. Trevor plays with sheep shearings and imagines himself a magistrate. Nikki is teased relentlessly about her calorie counter, and Kath teaches the other two how to catch fish with a pair of stockings. In a roadside restaurant, one character asks a bored waitress whether the fish is fresh and is told, "Of course it's fresh, it's a specialty," even if later examination proves the fish is in the freezer.

"Backlash" has a homespun look and a refreshing spontaneity that easily make up for its lack of polish. If its efforts to examine questions of law and bigotry are less compelling than Mr. Bennett's flair for small, peculiar flourishes, it's an entertaining effort all the same, with a particularly good performance from the snappish, high-strung Mr. Argue.

"Backlash" is to be shown tonight at 6 P.M. and Saturday at 3:30 P.M. as part of the New Directors/New Films series.

1987 Mr 26, C14:4

Thought for Food

TAMPOPO, directed by Juzo Itami; screenplay (Japanese with English subtitles) by Mr. Itami; photography by Masaki Tamura; edited by Akira Suzuki; music by Kunihiko Murai; produced by Mr. Itami, Yasushi Tamaoki and Seigo Hosogoe. At Roy and Niuta Titus Theater 1, Museum of Modern Art, 11 West 53d Street, as part of the New Directors/New Films series. Running time: 114 minutes. This film has no rating.

Goro	Tsutomu Yamazaki
Tampopo	Nobuko Miyamoto
Man in white suit	Koji Yakusho
Gun	Ken Watanabe
Pisken	Rikiya Yasuoka
Shohei	Kinzo Sakura
Tabo	Mampei Ikeuchi
Master of ramen making	Yoshi Kato
Rich old man	Shuju Otaki
Mistress of the man in white suit	Fukumi Kuroda
Rich old man's mistress	Setsuko Shinoi
Girl catching oysters	Yoriko Doguchi
Supermarket manager	Masahiko Tsugawa

By VINCENT CANBY

"TAMPOPO," Juzo Itami's new Japanese film, is a satiric comedy about noodles — about their making, cooking, serving and consumption. It's about people who take noodles seriously, who read self-help books that, among other things, instruct the eater to regard the pork "affectionately" while "slurping" the noodles that have been "activated" by the soup.

In particular, the film is about Tampopo (the Japanese word for dandelion), a youngish widow who aspires to make, cook and serve the best noodles in any noodle shop in Tokyo, and about the people who help her on her way to the top. These include a truck driver-noodle connoisseur named Goro, who affects the mannerisms of Clint Eastwood, and a rich old man who loves noodles so much that, after he overindulges, a vacuum cleaner must be used to empty his stomach.

"Tampopo" will be shown in the New Directors/New Films series at the Museum of Modern Art today at 8:30 P.M. and on Saturday at 6 P.M.

Though it's not consistently funny (at least not to someone who, with a clear conscience, buys his noodles in plastic bags), "Tampopo" is one of the more engaging films to be shown in this year's series. It's also another example of the eccentric humor that has been showing up recently in Japanese films, most effectively in Yojiro Takita's "Comic Magazine" and Yoshimitsu Morita's "Family Game," both of which were introduced to this country in earlier New Directors/New Films series.

"Tampopo" is buoyantly free in form. It's as much an essay as it is a narrative — always ready to digress into random gags and comic anecdotes. These may not have much bearing on Tampopo and her noodle education, but they all have to do with food and with the Japanese love of ritual that has made an art of slurping noodles, arranging flowers, drinking tea and committing suicide.

The film's writer-director, Mr. Itami, who's also an actor (he played the father in "The Family Game"), seems to have a special fondness for the solemnity of the prose used by connoisseurs. His principal characters and even the bit players converse by exchanging the sentiments of food critics.

Noodles that aren't great are described as "sincere," and when Tampopo is on the verge of a noodle breakthrough, her admirer must say, in all frankness, that "they're beginning to have substance, but they still lack depth." "Noodles," says a man searching for the perfect phrase, "are synergetic things." Early in the film, the sight of a bowl of noodles is compared to a Jackson Pollock painting.

Some of the best moments are only distantly related blackout sketches, including one about a father who urges his children, "Keep on eating! It's the last meal Mom cooked" — while Mom lies on the floor in the kitchen, having just committed suicide out of boredom.

There is also a running gag about a food-oriented gangster whose last words to his moll are about yam sausage, and another sequence in which a little boy wanders through the zoo wearing a sign: "I only eat natural foods. Do not give me sweets or snacks."

Mr. Itami often strains after comic effects that remain elusive. The most appealing thing about "Tampopo" is that he never stops trying. A funny sensibility is at work here.

1987 Mr 26, C21:1

End of an Era

WITHNAIL AND I, directed and written by Bruce Robinson; photography by Bob Smith; edited by Alan Strachan; music by David Dundas; produced by Paul M. Heller; a Cineplex Odeon Films Release. At Roy and Niuta Titus Theater 1, Museum of Modern Art, 11 West 53d Street, as part of the New Directors/New Films series. Running time: 108 minutes. This film has no rating.

Withnail	Richard E. Grant
Marwood/I	Paul McGann
Monty	Richard Griffiths
Danny	Ralph Brown
Jake	Michael Elphick
Irishman	Daragh O'Malley
Isaac Parkin	Michael Wardle
Mrs. Parkin	Una Brandon-Jones
General	Noël Johnson
Waitress	Irene Sutcliffe

By VINCENT CANBY

THE place is London, where the swinging 1960's are coming to an end. Nearly gone is the decade of "The Yellow Submarine," "Hair," dropping out and turning on (preferably with money from home or an idependent income), of "Oh! Calcutta!" Mary Quant, free love, public sex, booze, "Blow-Up," pills to soar on and pills for the descent.

For a favored few, the 60's were one long time out. For even fewer, they were something to recycle and celebrate in music, movies and plays, as well as in the journalese of the new journalism. For the rest, much of what identified the period as the 60's existed in another dimension. One was aware that something special was happening, even though a lot of it was invisible to the naked eye.

"Withnail and I," the bracing new English comedy written by Bruce Robinson (who wrote "The Killing Fields") and his first film as a director, may also be the first film to contemplate the bilious aftermath of that brief, highly publicized, illusory era. The movie will be shown in the New Directors/New Films series at the Museum of Modern Art today at 8:30 P.M. and tomorrow at 1 P.M.

"Withnail and I" is not the whole story of the 60's. It's a small, wise, breezy footnote.

•

Marwood, who's the "I" of the title, and Withnail are young, would-be actors who wake up one morning to find only 90 days left in the decade. Their funds are low and their flat is hip-deep in the souvenirs and roach-infested debris of their earnest hedonism. On that awful morning, each must deal with a very real, *physical* hangover, which seems more like a foreclosure on the spirit.

Even in his pain, Withnail (Richard E. Grant) is elegant — tall, slim, vaguely Byronic, with something rude to say about everybody. Though he seems never to have acted very seriously, he has an agent and calls himself an actor, possibly because he assumes he looks like one. Marwood (Paul McGann) is more practical and, by comparison, commonplace. He's fed up with dirty dishes, the women who come and go, the dope pusher who drops by to talk about plans to become a toy manufacturer, and by aimlessness as a way of life.

Largely at Marwood's insistence, the two decide to spend a soul-cleansing weekend in the country in a primitive cottage borrowed from Withnail's uncle, Monty (Richard Griffiths). Things go horribly wrong from the start. They have no aspirin, and there's no place to buy any. The country is not what Withnail expected. "It's not like H. E. Bates," he says. "I thought they'd all be out drinking cider and discussing butter."

To keep warm, they must burn furniture in the fireplace. Because there's no food in the house, they contact a farmer for a chicken, which is delivered alive. "How do we make it die?" asks Withnail. Marwood takes care of this, only to have his friend say of the patchy corpse, "Shouldn't it be more bald?"

Matters aren't helped by the arrival of Monty, who, as a result of some hints dropped by his nephew, has developed a grand passion for the innocent Marwood. Monty, too, had once trod the boards, though, as he remembers when he's had too much wine, there's always "that morning when you wake up and say, 'Alas, I shall never play the Dane.' "

In his role as both writer and director, Mr. Robinson has the good sense to keep "Withnail and I" in short focus and specific in character and incident. Though Withnail and Marwood are always aware of the nature of the times they inhabit, the period details never become set decoration. "Withnail and I" isn't social history. It's about growing up, almost as if by accident.

It's also genuinely funny, especially Mr. Robinson's dialogue, though the accents of the actors occasionally make individual words unintelligible to the American ear. Mr. Grant, Mr. McGann and Mr. Griffiths are nothing less than neat or, as Andy Warhol would have said, super.

"Withnail and I" does credit to this year's New Directors/New Films series.

1987 Mr 27, C9:1

High and Low Life

STREET SMART, directed by Jerry Schatzberg; written by David Freeman; director of photography, Adam Holender; edited by Priscilla Nedd; music by Robert Irving 3d; produced by Menahem Golan and Yoram Globus; released by Cannon Films Inc. At U.A. Twin, Broadway at 49th Street; U.A. 86th Street East, between Second and Third Avenues; U.A. Gemini, Second Avenue at 64th Street; Quad Cinema, 13th Street, between Fifth Avenue and Avenue of the Americas. Running time: 96 minutes. This film is rated R.

Jonathan Fisher	Christopher Reeve
Punchy	Kathy Baker
Alison Parker	Mimi Rogers
Leonard Pike	Jay Patterson
Ted Avery	Andre Gregory
Fast Black	Morgan Freeman
Harriet	Anna Maria Horsford
Joel Davis	Frederick Rolf
Reggie	Erik King
Art Sheffield	Michael J. Reynolds

"STREET SMART" tells of a facile, blowhard journalist who's corrupt enough to fictionalize an entire feature story. But it is not the predictable tale of this man's lapse and subsequent redemption — and that's what makes it interesting. Instead, "Street Smart" follows Jonathan Fisher (Christopher Reeve) from his first misstep into the web of trouble spun out of his initial set of lies. It grows into an engrossing study of loose talk, weakness and seduction, played out in both the world of high-powered journalism and the seediest corners of Times Square.

"Street Smart," which opens today at the U.A. Twin and other theaters, centers on a shrewd writer who proves to be a lot less clever than he supposes. To satisfy an editor at a publication that sounds a lot like New York magazine, Jonathan concocts a wholly fictional profile of a Times Square pimp, whom he dubs Tyrone. (David Denby, New York's film critic, has noted that David Freeman, who wrote the script, faked his own such profile in that magazine some years ago.) Jonathan does this partly because he can't persuade real pimps to talk to him, and partly just because it's easy. In any case, the story is a big success. Tyrone becomes the toast of the town.

Everyone wants to meet him, start-

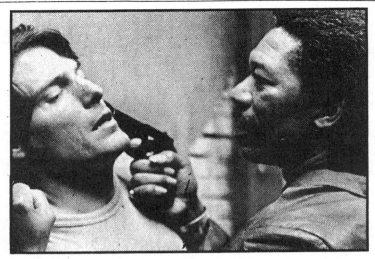

Christopher Reeve and Morgan Freeman, right, in "Street Smart."

ing with Jonathan's equally glib editor, played with a flurry of brittle energy by a dapper-looking Andre Gregory. More to the point, the district attorney's office, prosecuting a real pimp named Fast Black (Morgan Freeman), finds the Tyrone story of great interest. For reasons that are not made completely clear — one of several key plot problems with Mr. Freeman's otherwise ingenious screenplay — Jonathan has, after only chatting with a prostitute who knows Fast Black, inadvertently captured him so completely that the district attorney's office thinks he has met with the real McCoy. So Jonathan's editor wants Tyrone invited to dinner. And the attorney prosecuting Fast Black wants to subpoena Jonathan's notes.

•

The situation becomes even more compelling when Jonathan and Fast Black finally meet. Mr. Reeve, who manages the challenging job of giving a credible, unflattering performance as a man with very little backbone, is particularly good in the scene that has him quietly marveling at his own hipness while he and Fast Black, his new friend, drive around the city. And Morgan Freeman, who is extremely good, makes Fast Black a clever, hot-tempered manipulator who recognizes what a sucker he's found in clean-cut, upscale Jonathan. So when Jonathan immediately realizes that he can pass off Fast Black as the real Tyrone, he is by far the less shrewd of the two. It is Fast Black who's the better schemer, once he sees how much he can force Jonathan to do in support of his initial bogus story.

"Street Smart" winds up being a bit too smart for its own good, but it's compelling and complex. As directed by Jerry Schatzberg, it's a frankly lurid film capable of fine, unexpected subtleties. Mr. Schatzberg is able to orchestrate a hotel-room meeting between Jonathan and a feisty, knowing prostitute (played very memorably by Kathy Baker) so that it suggests the many different forms of seduction to which this opportunistic writer finally submits. He is able to intermingle the Times Square and glossy journalism worlds with a nicely understated irony. Even when the film goes too far, as in an overly obvious party scene mixing high life and low, or in an ending that unconvincingly affirms Jonathan's supremacy, it sustains a certain basic perceptiveness. The ways in which Jonathan slides

from one job into another, from one woman to her supposed opposite, from lies into truth and back again, are powerfully underscored.

Mr. Schatzberg, in addition to eliciting strong performances from actors in difficult roles, has given the film a palpably shifting moral climate and an evocative visual style; the set decoration says a lot about the various characters' illusions about themselves. "Street Smart" tells a disturbing story, and tells it well.

JANET MASLIN

1987 Mr 27, C8:1

On a Tear

BLIND DATE, directed by Blake Edwards; written by Dale Launer; director of photography, Harry Stradling; edited by Robert Pergament; music by Henry Mancini; produced by Tony Adams; released by Tri-Star Pictures. At the National, Broadway and 44th Street; the Gemini, 64th Street and Second Avenue; the 84th Street Sixplex, at Broadway; the Gramercy, 23d Street near Lexington Avenue. Running time: 95 minutes. This film is rated PG-13.

Socializing Bruce Willis and Kim Basinger star in the Blake Edwards comedy "Blind Date," about an executive who ignores a friend's warning not to give his date a drink before taking her to an important dinner.

Nadia Gates	Kim Basinger
Walter Davis	Bruce Willis
David Bedford	John Larroquette
Judge Harold Bedford	William Daniels
Harry Gruen	George Coe
Denny Gordon	Mark Blum
Ted Davis	Phil Hartman
Susie Davis	Stephanie Faracy
Muriel Bedford	Alice Hirson
Jordan the Butler	Graham Stark

By JANET MASLIN

THE perfect gag, as orchestrated with supreme professionalism by Blake Edwards, is something that proceeds in stages. It has a beginning, a middle, an end, and maybe even a postscript or two. The beginning is the anticipatory stage, as when Bruce Willis, playing the man in "Blind Date" who falls in love with a woman who should never drink, is seen with a hypodermic syringe, some whisky and a box of chocolates. The middle comes when the chocolates are delivered, and the young woman's mother soon remarks that her daughter seems to have eaten them all.

The end is the wild part, when the young woman, who by this time happens to be at her own wedding, goes out of control, which is something she has been doing to various degrees throughout this wickedly inventive farce. And the postscript, as with all the film's better comic setups, is the satisfying sense that yet another funny routine has been built, timed and executed with clockwork precision. Mr. Edwards, whose films are as different as the dismal "A Fine Mess" and the devastatingly funny "S.O.B.," can't always be counted on to deliver the comic goods. But when he's right on track, as he is in most of "Blind Date," he's an unbeatable farceur.

"Blind Date," which opens today at the National and other theaters, has a screenplay by Dale Launer, who wrote the equally witty and circuitously plotted "Ruthless People." Clearly, Mr. Launer is a formidable comic talent in his own right, and he and Mr. Edwards are well-matched. They have made "Blind Date" a charming feat of gamesmanship, a film that repeatedly asks the questions "can we top this?" and "how much worse can things get?" The respective answers are always "yes" and "a lot."

•

As the title suggests, the film is about a blind date that goes awry, but nothing proceeds in the ways that might be expected. The man is the overworked Walter Davis (Mr. Willis), an "assistant portfolio assessor" at a financial firm who needs to take the right woman to an important company dinner. His brother arranges an introduction to Nadia Gates (Kim Basinger), who's a knockout and seems very nice. Speaking shyly, wearing the kind of girlish hairdo Diane Keaton perfected, and looking as demure as anyone could in a form-fitting red suit, Nadia seems too good to be true. Why, the smitten Walter asks her, does such a lovely creature even have a free evening? Bad question.

The corporate dinner is for the benefit of a Japanese tycoon who has strict and traditional notions of womanly behavior. And the film is shrewd enough to let Nadia wreck the dinner and ruin Walter's career very early on, as a mere warmup to the ever-expanding mess that will follow. What does she do? Nothing stupid or vulgar, or else this would be comedy of a much lower order. She just disturbs a costly flower arrangement, delivers an impromptu lecture on California divorce law, and rips the pocket off one or two men's suits. After this, all is pocket-ripping pandemonium.

Mr. Willis is set up mostly as a straight man, though he does eventually have the chance to offer some party-wrecking one-upsmanship of his own. But Miss Basinger has the chance to prove herself a delightful physical comedienne, with a fluid grace that's most apparent when she's falling apart or falling down. One of the more ingeniously staged scenes has her arguing sleepily with Mr. Willis as she lies in a bed that he has kicked, so it is now at a diagonal. Satin sheets and the downward angle make the bed just slippery enough for Miss Basinger to have to wriggle incessantly while she struggles to speak.

"Blind Date" is farce of a traditional and even old-fashioned sort, but Mr. Edwards's complete enthusiasm for the form creates a comic style so avid that it's slightly surreal. Every prop exists to hit, startle or flummox someone at an unexpected moment. A man (Nadia's nasty ex-boyfriend, played by John Larroquette) drives through a pet shop and emerges, quite literally, with a monkey on his back. A butler displays a remarkable trick for coaxing a dog into its pen. And when a car plows into a flour warehouse there are great white billows in its wake, as if this were not a building but a gigantic bag. Comic possibilities are everywhere in "Blind Date," and the tireless Mr. Edwards leaves none of them unexploited.

•

"Blind Date" is rated PG-13 ("Special Parental Guidance Suggested for Those Younger Than 13"). It contains some strong language.

1987 Mr 27, C11:1

Sorrowful Subject

THE HANOI HILTON, written and directed by Lionel Chetwynd; director of photography, Mark Irwin; edited by Penelope Shaw; music by Jimmy Webb; produced by Menahem Golan and Yoram Globus; released by Cannon Films Inc. At the Coronet, 59th Street at Third Avenue. Running time: 130 minutes. This film is rated R.

P.O.W.'s David Anthony Smith and Michael Moriarty square off in "The Hanoi Hilton," about a group of American servicemen captured and held in the infamous Hoa Lo prison.

Lieutenant Commander Williamson	Michael Moriarty
Captain Hubman	Paul Le Mat
Major Fisher	Jeffrey Jones
Colonel Cathcart	Lawrence Pressman
Capt. Robert Miles	Stephen Davies
Major Oldham	David Soul
Captain Turner	Rick Fitts
Maj. Ngo Doc	Aki Aleong
Paula	Gloria Carlin

"THE HANOI HILTON," written and directed by Lionel Chetwynd, is an earnest but clumsy tribute to the heroism of the American servicemen — mostly officers — who were captured and held prisoner by North Vietnam during the long, desperate undeclared war we now refer to simply as Vietnam.

Mr. Chetwynd is aware that these men faced physical and psychological hardships unlike those faced by any other group of P.O.W.'s in the nation's history. The increasing unpopularity of the war at home obscured the prisoners' plight and confused the country's sense of loyalties. In many of the home-front debates over the war itself, the prisoners were, indeed, forgotten.

It's a big, tough, sorrowful subject, but Mr. Chetwynd finds no way to dramatize its singularity.

The movie, set mostly in a Hanoi prison, looks and sounds like something out of World War II, with American servicemen being cruelly abused by their small, sadistic, yellow captors. One new wrinkle: the presence in the prison of a Cuban interrogator — more vicious than even his North Vietnamese colleagues — who talks in the street jargon of Spanish Harlem in the 1980's, though the film is set in the 60's and early 70's. Without meaning to be, the movie comes across as racist, if only by default.

The drama itself, about how the individual prisoners react to [illegible] torture, depends so much on the [illegible] of these scenes that it ultimately has the effect of exploiting the spectacle of torture. "Aha," says the sadistic, Jesuit-schooled Vietnamese captor, "it's time for you to experience Room 18!"

Unlike "Platoon," in which the enemy remains vague and unseen, "The Hanoi Hilton" tries to characterize the Vietnamese, but only comes forth with secondhand stereotypes. It must be admitted, however, that the movie does no more justice to the characters of the prisoners than to those of the Vietnamese. Along the way, the movie also finds time to send up American peaceniks as represented by a bubble-headed actress wearing Jane Fonda's "Klute" haircut.

Though the film contains scarcely any action and though it's as sincere as a pledge of allegiance to the flag, its point of view is no less narrow than that of "Rambo."

Prominent in the cast, and doing as well as the simple-minded material allows, are Michael Moriarty and Paul Le Mat as captured American officers, Aki Aleong as the Vietnamese prison keeper and Gloria Carlin, who stands in for Miss Fonda.

"The Hanoi Hilton" opens today at the Coronet theater.

VINCENT CANBY

1987 Mr 27, C13:1

Pretty Familiar

PRETTYKILL, directed by George Kaczender; screenplay by Sandra K. Bailey; director of photography, Joao Fernandes; edited by Tom Merchant; music by Robert Ragland; produced by John R. Bowey and Martin Walters; released by Spectrafilm. At U.A. Twin, Broadway and 49th Street; Olympia Quad, Broadway and 107th Street; Coliseum, 181st Street and Broadway, and other theaters. Running time: 95 minutes. This film is rated R.

Sgt. Larry Turner	David Birney
Heather Todd	Season Hubley
Toni	Susannah York
Harris	Yaphet Kotto
Francie	Suzanne Snyder
Jacque Mercier	Germaine Houde
Lightnin' Boy	Gary Majchrizak

By WALTER GOODMAN

WHAT'S showing at the U.A. Twin and other theaters beginning today? Prostitutes with diction of gold: "My clients expect a certain level of style." A black-white cop team. Drug busts, kinky sex, mother love, murder and mayhem. You say you've seen it all before? Sure, but perhaps not so foolishly put together as in "Prettykill."

The screenplay by Sandra K. Bailey owes a lot to the inventions and conventions of other recent cop flicks, and the Canadian director George Kaczender, in his first American effort, doesn't let us forget it. The main events are the tracking down of a homosexual drug seller named Lightnin' Boy and a prostitute named Francie, who has a severely split personality, one-half of which is murderously inclined. ("Why is this happening to me?" asks Francie, and so may you.) Both personalities are played by Suzanne Snyder, who isn't much good at either. As a police lieutenant who can't do anything right, Yaphet Kotto is all wrong.

And if you can believe David Birney as the super-tough, super-conscientious, super-sweating cop ("I don't like what I do anymore. I don't like who I am.") and Season Hubley as the super-elegant prostitute who hardly ever sweats ("I don't like to keep the Ambassador waiting"), then, as the bad guy says, "You seen too many movies, man."

1987 Mr 27, C13:3

Basque Everyman

TASIO, directed and written by Montxo Armendariz; in Spanish with English subtitles; camera, José Luis Alcaine; edited by Pablo G. DelAmo; music by Angel Illarramendi; produced by Elias Querejeta. At the Public Theater, 425 Lafayette Street. Running time: 96 minutes. This film has no rating.

Tasio, adult	Patxi Bisquert
Tasio, adolescent	Isidro José Solano
Tasio, child	Garikoitz Mendigutxia
Paulina	Amaia Lasa
Brother of Tasio	Nacho Martinez
Friend of Tasio	José Maria Asin
Guard	Paco Sagarzazu
Tasio's father	Enrique Goicoechea
Tasio's mother	Elena Uriz

By NINA DARNTON

THE small Spanish village at the foot of the hills of Urbasa is in Basque country. It is psychologically as far from the Basque industrial center of Bilbao as it is from the trendy night life of fast-moving Madrid. Here Tasio, the hero of the first feature written and directed by the Basque film maker Montxo Armendariz, is born, matures, comes of age, takes a wife, raises his child.

The rhythms of this peasant village, mired in poverty and settled into the beauty of the surrounding hills and forests, are ageless. The film follows Tasio — whose poverty forces him to hunt for food in the hills, and whose heritage leads him to become a charcoalmaker. We see him as a barefoot child hunting for birds' nests, and as an adolescent, learning with pride how to stoke the smoldering coal stacks with safety, attending a village dance, struck by the beauty of a pretty young girl.

"Tasio" is undramatic and basically uneventful, but it is never boring. The director has skillfully intertwined the rhythms of local life with the rhythms of nature, and has counterbalanced the gentleness of family warmth with the harshness of life, the isolation and beauty of the landscape with the people who know how to make use of it, to draw a portrait of a fiercely independent free man.

Tasio grows into a man who is not lazy but cannot work for others. He supports his wife and child by hunting. But hunting with traps is illegal, and he must outwit the local warden as well as the occasional groups of civil guards whose three-pointed hats, a symbol of the hated authority of the central government, remind the viewer that this is indeed a Basque film. The government is portrayed as an impediment to freedom — an annoyance, but one that can be outsmarted.

"Tasio," which opens today at the Public Theater, is a production of Elias Querejeta, who has produced many of the films of Spain's premier film maker, Carlos Saura. The cinematographer, whose beautiful shots of the surrounding forest and portraits of the townfolk help to build an essential atmosphere, is José Luis Alcaine.

Mr. Armendariz has gone to great pains to create an authentic, highly detailed village atmosphere. He has assembled a cast whose rugged faces suggest, wordlessly, the hard quality of local life as well as its rewards in family unity and warmth. Particularly good is Patxi Bisquert, who plays Tasio as an adult and manages to convey unbendable independence alongside quiet sensitivity.

The film is slow, gentle, rhythmic — seducing the viewer without excitement, adventure or suspense. It gives some insight into a foreign and fascinating culture, and a glimpse into the nature of a free man.

1987 Mr 27, C15:1

Sexual Mélange

LAW OF DESIRE, written and directed by Pedro Almodóvar (in Spanish with English subtitles); photography by Angel Luis Fernández; edited by José Salcedo; a Cinevista Release. At Roy and Niuta Titus Theater 1, Museum of Modern Art, 11 West 53d Street, as part of the New Directors/New Films series. Running time: 100 minutes. This film has no rating.

Pablo Quintero	Eusebio Poncela
Tina Quintero	Carmen Maura
Antonio Benitez	Antonio Banderas
Juan Bermúdez	Miguel Molina
Ada, child	Manuela Velasco
Ada, mother	Bibi Andersen
Inspector	Fernando Guillen
Dr. Martin	Nacho Martinez
Antonio's mother	Helga Liné

PEDRO ALMODOVAR'S "Law of Desire" begins with a scene in which a film maker directs another man to perform a very graphic sexual act before the camera, a sequence in which the film maker's reactions are monitored as closely as the actor's. The film, it develops, will turn into a big hit for the film maker, who is already something of a celebrity. "Law of Desire" graduates from that sensationalized opening to a breezy study of the famous director Pablo Quintero (Eusebio Poncela), who lives quite the high life in modern Madrid. Casual drug use and casual homosexual encounters are all in a day's work for Pablo, who exists quite happily in a film devoid of moral opprobrium.

The few complications in Pablo's life involve his family tree. He has a sister, Tina, who used to be his brother and who has been transformed into a flaming femme fatale. Pablo is very loyal to Tina, and to the little girl named Ada (Manuela Velasco) whom she is raising. Ada's parentage is somewhat confusing, especially since her mother is also named Ada, and is played by a deep-voiced transsexual named Bibi Andersen. Tina, who is supposed to be the transsexual in the story, is played vivaciously by Carmen Maura, whose origins are apparently a lot less complicated.

•

"Law of Desire" follows Pablo into the trouble caused by Antonio (Antonio Banderas), a younger man who is fascinated by him, and whom he casually seduces. Antonio becomes obsessed with Pablo, and dangerously jealous of his steady lover, Juan. What ensues is a fairly conventional story of sexual intrigue and danger, made infinitely more complicated by the colorful personalities of all concerned. What it lacks in depth, "Law of Desire" makes up in surface energy, with a lively cast, a turbulent plot and a textbook-worthy collection of case histories.

On the evidence of the opening credits, Mr. Almodóvar is himself something of a celebrity in his native territory. Certainly he's capable of attention-getting forays into anything-goes behavior, and of a seriousness not easily mistaken for guilt or gloom. "Law of Desire" is an entertaining jumble, though it hardly needs the standard thriller elements on which it finally relies. Mr. Almodóvar works best when he is setting these lively characters in motion, and least well when the film's essentially conventional structure is revealed.

"Law of Desire" will be shown tonight at 6 and tomorrow at 8:30 P.M. as part of the New Directors/New Films series at the Museum of Modern Art.   JANET MASLIN

1987 Mr 27, C15:1

Explorations

THE ONLY SON, directed by Yasujiro Ozu; in Japanese with English subtitles; distributed by Films Inc. Running time: 87 minutes. This film has no rating.
I LIVED, BUT . . ., written (in Japanese with English subtitles) and directed by Kazuo Inoue; distributed by Shochiku Company Ltd. Running time: 118 minutes. This film has no rating. Both at Film Forum 1, 57 Watts Street.

By VINCENT CANBY

THE work and life of Yasujiro Ozu (1903-1963) are evoked with insight, intelligence and spirit in the splendid program opening today at the Film Forum 1. It's a double bill of "The Only Son" (1936), the Japanese film master's first "talkie" (he didn't want to rush into sound without knowing how to use it), and "I Lived, but . . ." (1983), a nearly two-hour documentary on Ozu's career made by his longtime associate, Kazuo Inoue.

It's apparent from "The Only Son"

that Ozu's concerns, as well as the formal austerity of his style, were as fully developed and disciplined in 1936 as they were to be when he made his last film, "An Autumn Afternoon," in 1962. Only French critics (as reported by Donald Richie, the film scholar) would dare to find Ozu's early films, including "The Only Son," "more imaginative filmically" than those he made toward the end of his life.

Ozu's extraordinary achievement is that even though his oeuvre is so homogenous, the films themselves remain so rich in psychological and social revelations. I doubt that anyone with any previous experience with Ozu could look at a minute or two of new footage without being able to identify the man who made it.

Ozu's style immediately proclaims itself: the fixed, unmoving camera, the fondness for so-called "tatami shots" (the camera seeing all from the point of view of a seated observer), sequences punctuated by shots of rooms, streets or landscapes from which all humans have fled, the use of simple, direct cuts between sequences as well as within scenes, the total absence of dissolves and overlapping shots. (They, Mr. Richie quotes Ozu as saying, "aren't part of cinematic grammar — they are only attributes of the camera.")

•

By reducing style to essentials (which, though plain, are far from minimalist), Ozu creates his cinema-of-character, in which nothing is allowed to interfere with the interior lives of his characters as seen in the pared-down, surface representation of those lives. Instead of putting us off, this lack of artifice is what draws us into an Ozu film, as if into a series of exotic caves we must explore without a map.

"The Only Son" is about sacrifice, loneliness and the accommodation of failed expectations. The time is 1923. A widow, who works in a spinning mill in the provinces, gives up her wages, savings and property to send her son to school in Tokyo — so he will be able to better himself. When she goes to visit him 14 years later, the son, phlegmatic but not a bad sort, is working as a teacher in a night school to support a wife and baby he hasn't bothered to tell his mother about.

They live in modest circumstance in a small house at the edge of an industrial wasteland. Says the son to his newly arrived mother, more or less in desperation, "You can see the municipal incinerator from here."

This synopsis cannot do justice to "The Only Son," which is anything but simple. Though Ozu never appears to be seeing a world beyond the tiny one inhabited by his characters, the Depression hangs over everything like a high, flat, gray cloud. The shape of the sun can be seen, but it gives no warmth.

•

The mother understands the realities of the times, but not her son's acceptance of his lot. She calls him a coward. He and his wife attempt to entertain her, but she nods off at the movies and has little interest in the tourist sights. She genuinely likes her daughter-in-law and grandson. Toward the end of her visit, she seizes on one small gesture by the son in an attempt to justify to herself all her years of self-denial. The film's final, desolate image reveals how successful she is.

Though Ozu's characters seem to be as passive as the film maker's way of appearing to sit back to allow events to happen, that passivity is as

deceptive in his characters as in his style. Just as there is rigor in the manner in which Ozu chooses to present his characters, the characters are full of active contradictions.

The surface is polite, almost placid, but there are wars being fought inside both the mother and her child in "The Only Son." Despair is at loggerheads with hope. Reality bullies its way into the dream of what might have been. Ultimately there is the appearance of acceptance, something that infuriated the younger Japanese film makers who followed Ozu, but who may have been missing the point.

Ozu's characters were never meant to be role models. Though utterly specific, they are aspects of the human condition. The worst criticism that can be aimed at Ozu is not passivity but the perfect symmetry of his narratives, which stresses the cyclical, soothing nature of life, as if to deny its inescapable bleakness.

The title of Mr. Inoue's documentary, "I Lived, but . . .," is a play on the titles of the series of successful silent-film comedies made by Ozu in the late 1920s and early 1930s ("I Graduated, but . . .," "I Flunked, but . . ." and "I Was Born, but . . ."). In the elegant colors of Ozu's last films, Mr. Inoue interviews dozens of Ozu's friends and associates — including Chishu Ryu, who appeared in "The Only Son" and many succeeding Ozu films over the years — as well as two of his brothers and a sister.

Taking his lead from Ozu, who had little interest in Freudian interpretation, Mr. Inoue avoids any analysis of the very rich biographical data, including the fact that the unmarried Ozu lived throughout his life with his beloved mother.

Instead, "I Lived, but . . ." is mostly concerned with his friendships with other film people and his work methods (Says one actor, "It's as if he were directing puppets, but puppets with a soul"). In one brief sequence, Ozu, a tall, patrician-looking man, recalls his early love of movies, though not of Japanese movies, which, he says, "were only about their stories." Because Mr. Inoue also includes nearly two dozen clips from Ozu films, "I Lived, but . . ." functions both as an introduction to, and a meditation on, the Ozu career.

This is a most special film program.

1987 Ap 1, C25:1

Designer Dungeon

CAPTIVE, directed and written by Paul Mayersberg; music by Edge and Michael Berkeley; produced by Don Boyd; released by Virgin-CineTel. At Cinema 3, 2 West 59th Street. Running time: 103 minutes. This film is rated R.
Rowena .... Irina Brook
Gregory .... Oliver Reed
Hiro .... Hiro Arai
D .... Xavier Deluc
Bryony .... Corinne Dacla

By VINCENT CANBY

MOVIES like Paul Mayersberg's "Captive" are as rare as peacocks' teeth, and even more precious. It's a movie that prompts questions worthy of our time: "Who designed his distressed-leather jacket?" "Was her dress bought off the rack?" "Where does he have his hair done?" "Are cement floors that are covered by two inches of water, traversed by Japanesy, wooden slats, really easy to live with? The reflections are lovely, especially at night, but how does one control the damp?"

"Captive," which opens today at Cinema 3, marks the absolute end of the 1960's — here is a designer's view of revolution.

If Mr. Mayersberg, who both wrote and directed "Captive," has anything on his mind, it's probably best not gone into. The film is a paralyzingly irrelevant, unintentionally hilarious fairy tale, a 1980's update of "Sleeping Beauty," cross-fertilized by the Patty Hearst story.

The snoozy "princess" is Rowena le Vay (Irina Brook), the bored, beautiful, pampered daughter of an international tycoon, Gregory le Vay (Oliver Reed), who mourns his dead wife by trying to re-create her in Rowena. Lonely, her ego-tank running on empty, Rowena mopes around her London palace all day, having occasional lovers, drinking too much and, when in the depths of despair, throwing a glass of Scotch at Daddy's Goya.

•

Unknown to Rowena, her awakening is at hand. Monitoring her every move is a gang of three — one terribly elegant young Frenchman called simply D, a handsome young Japanese fellow named Hiro, and the young Frenchwoman Bryony, who lives with D and Hiro and shares their passion for high-tech interior décor, boutique-radical clothes and old-fashioned sadomasochism, the kind that grandmother used to like.

Most of "Captive" is about Rowena's magical liberation after she's kidnapped by the gang of three and carried off to their garage apartment. It's not above a garage. It was a garage or, perhaps, an abandoned factory. Whatever it was, it's now one of those huge, glorious "spaces" so beloved by decorators and upwardly mobile clients. The kidnappers' purpose: to brainwash Rowena so that she can find out who she really is.

First they put her — handcuffed and hunched over, chin-to-knees — into a glossy white box, which sits in the middle of the living room and looks like something that a keg of Balenciaga might have come in. Later, they force water down her throat through a funnel and, when she begins to respond favorably, they hang her upside down from a rafter.

Happiness follows. Rowena enthusiastically joins the gang in a raid on an art gallery where, instead of Scotch, she throws acid at Daddy's Goya. She gets pregnant — more happiness. But then, as it must, the real world closes in. No matter that several people are finally dead, Rowena has learned how to tell Daddy where to put his money.

"Captive" is the first film to be directed by Mr. Mayersberg, who wrote the screenplays for "The Man Who Fell to Earth" and "Merry Christmas, Mr. Lawrence." He clearly needs supervision.

However, the film's blood lines are impeccable. Miss Brook is the daughter of Peter Brook and Natasha Parry, and Mr. Reed, long a celebrity in his own right, is the nephew of Sir Carol Reed. In most reviews, this sort of information wouldn't be worth repeating, but "Captive" is such a deliriously fatuous movie that one wants to treat it as a society note.

The cast members move through the film not as artists but as models, in, on, around and handling designer clothes, sheets, pillow cases, throw cushions, light fixtures, candles, handcuffs, revolvers (D's is wheat-colored, to match his hair) and even, I assume, designer hydrochloric acid.

1987 Ap 3, C8:1

Bouncer in Babylon

CLUB LIFE, directed, written and produced by Norman Thaddeus Vane, story by Bleu McKenzie and Mr. Vane; director of photography, Joel King; music by FM Songs (America) Inc.; released by Troma Inc. At Cine 1, 711 Seventh Avenue, near 47th Street. Running time: 92 minutes. This film is rated R.

Cal	Tom Parsekian
Tank	Michael Parks
Sissy	Jamie Barrett
Hector	Tony Curtis
Tilly	Dee Wallace
The Doctor	Ron Kuhlman
Butch	Pat Ast
1st Punk	Bruce Reed

By JANET MASLIN

"CLUB LIFE" may well be the only film ever to set a funeral scene inside a disco, with mourners lined up along the railings, and the coffin and floral arrangements set up on the lighted dance floor. So it's original, anyhow. It also includes a gangland murder shot in a hall of mirrors, and a love scene shot on a transparent waterbed filled with fish.

The plot concerns Cal McFarland (Tom Parsekian), who is nothing but a lowly motorcycle racer until someone tells him he looks like Evel Knievel, at which point he decides to go to Hollywood. He winds up at a club called the City, starting out as a parking-lot attendant but quickly working his way up to the job of bouncer. The City is a neon-lit phantasmagoria, very popular with dancers who might actually be more comfortable in motel rooms, considering their choreography. The club becomes Cal's entire world.

The place is owned by Hector (Tony Curtis), who serves as the film's resident philosopher as he fights to resist the mobsters who want to take the place over. "Take your Gucci shoes and walk out!" Hector shouts to them when they pay a visit. "The only way you're getting this club is over my dead body!" Even non-psychics in the audience may sense that Hector is headed for trouble.

The film is also about Hector's girlfriend, Tilly (Dee Wallace), once an aspiring singer, who asks the plaintive question, "You think it's fun, getting up with a hangover every day, going to bed with the sunshine?" The other principals are Cal's old sweetheart Sissy (Jamie Barrett), a small-town girl who quickly becomes a quasi-prostitute, and a senior bouncer named Tank (Michael Parks), who teaches Cal the tricks of the trade.

Tony Curtis in "Club Life."

"Club Life," which opens today at the Cine 1, was written, directed and produced by Norman Thaddeus Vane, whose chief interest is in the club setting. The film is too loud and busy to establish this in terms of character or conversation, so it concentrates strictly on the visual set, which is garish but attention-getting. The acting consists mostly of unfocused posturing, in a succession of scenes that could easily have been rearranged without losing any of their dramatic focus. Only Mr. Curtis is any better than the material, with a world-weary gravity that seems, in this context, like the last word in maturity.

1987 Ap 3, C9:1

POLICE ACADEMY 4: CITIZENS ON PATROL, directed by Jim Drake; written by Gene Quintano, based on characters created by Neal Israel and Pat Proft; director of photography, Robert Saad; film editor, David Rawlins; music by Robert Folk; produced by Paul Maslansky; released by Warner Brothers. At the Criterion Center, Broadway at 45th Street; the Manhattan Twin, 59th Street, east of Third Avenue; the UA East, First Avenue and 85th Street; the Eighth Street Playhouse, at Avenue of the Americas. Running time: This film is rated PG.

Mahoney	Steve Guttenberg
Hightower	Bubba Smith
Jones	Michael Winslow
Tackleberry	David Graf
Sweetchuck	Tim Kazurinsky
Claire Mattson	Sharon Stone
Callahan	Leslie Easterbrook
Hooks	Marion Ramsey
Proctor	Lance Kinsey
Captain Harris	G. W. Bailey

By JANET MASLIN

The Police Academy series seems to shoot for an ever younger crowd. The optimum viewer for "Police Academy 4: Citizens on Patrol," which opened yesterday at the Criterion Center and other theaters, would be a 10-year-old boy. Even better, it would be a whole pack of them. That's not to say the film isn't funny; it means only that the sense of humor being addressed is very specific. Stay away if drawing room farce is what you're after.

On the other hand, pigeon jokes, torn pants, spilled food jokes and cartoonish pratfalls are all handled with dependable (and predictable) dispatch. One of the film's more ambitious moments concerns a Port-o-San that is moved, without the knowledge of its occupant, to the middle of a football field.

"Police Academy 4," which was written by Gene Quintano and directed by Jim Drake, has a plot about recruiting citizen volunteers to help stop crime; this means an opportunity to enlarge the cast and a chance to put everybody through gag-filled basic training all over again. The new players, like the original ones (who are still here in full force), are limited to one-shtick roles and are sometimes even more limited than that. Steve Guttenberg is still the resident sweet-faced ringleader, and Michael Winslow is still making funny noises; G. W. Bailey, as the captain in charge of these miscreants, is still winding up with Mace sprayed in his armpits and other occupational injuries. Also in the cast is Bobcat Goldthwait, whose voice is his fortune and who sounds like the closest human approximation of fingernails being scraped across a blackboard.

1987 Ap 4, 12:5

Social Comedy

SOREKARA, directed by Yoshimitsu Morita; screenplay (Japanese with English subtitles) by Tomomi Tsutsui, based on the novel "And Then" by Soseki Natsume; camera, Yonezo Maeda; edited by Akira Suzuki; music by Shigeru Umebayashi; produced by Mitsuru Kurosawa and Sadatoshi Fujimine; art director, Tsutomu Imamura; released by New Yorker Films. At Lincoln Plaza Cinema, Broadway and 63d Street. Running time: 130 minutes. This film has no rating.

Daisuke	Yusaku Matsuda
Michiyo	Miwako Fujitani
Hiraoka	Kaoru Kobayashi
Father	Chishu Ryu
Umeko	Mitsuko Kusabue
Seigo	Katsuo Nakamura

By VINCENT CANBY

WATCHING Yoshimitsu Morita's "Sorekara" ("And Then") is like tuning in to the dream of a stranger. It's often very beautiful and exotic, but it remains teasingly remote, beyond the point of depth perception. Without the film's production notes (which aren't available to the ticket-buying public), I'm not at all sure I'd have had any reliable idea when it was taking place.

According to these notes, "Sorekawa" is set in Tokyo in 1909 and is based on a novel by Soseki Natsume, which was published in that year, when the modernization of Japan was well along though far from being universally accepted.

The film, which opens today at the Lincoln Plaza Cinema, is a social comedy, but it's written and directed with such discretion that it seems as if Mr. Morita has been too polite for his own good, much like the film's central character.

●

Daisuke (Yusaku Matsuda), the 30-ish younger son of a rich and powerful businessman, has broken away from his family to the extent that he lives in his own modest house, though the bills for it and for his servants are paid by the older brother who runs the family business.

Daisuke is a dedicated romantic. He reads. He responds to beauty. He looks down on trade and the new world of capitalism. With the arrogance of the very rich, he tells Hiraoka, a desperate, penniless, former classmate, that a career in business is only supportable if it's an extension of one's intellectual life.

Daisuke's serenity is disturbed when, after a separation of three years, he meets Michiyo, Hiraoka's wife, whom Daisuke loved without ever declaring himself. Instead, he had stepped aside to favor his friend. Now, however, Hiraoka has become an embezzler and philanderer and Michiyo a lonely, terminally sick woman. She has the self-effacing ways of the old-fashioned Japanese wife, but she doesn't hesitate to beg money from the rich — and essentially naïve — Daisuke. He falls in love all over again.

This is the fascinating, distantly seen center of the film, which, much like 1909 Japan, mixes old-fashioned conventions with some startling, utterly mysterious new mannerisms. As he demonstrated in his original and funny "Family Game," seen here in 1984, Mr. Morita is a major new talent in the Japanese cinema.

●

His movies look like those of no other contemporary director. He likes to interrupt what appears to be a straightforward narrative with surreal images, which sometimes have the function of question marks, sometimes of exclamation points. Some-

Of Love Miwako Fujitani stands at the apex of a love triangle in the Yoshimitsu Morita's "Sorekara."

times they look like so much decoration.

In "Sorekara" he uses a new (to me) device that certainly is startling, and maybe too startling: he somehow manages to freeze the foreground images while the background images continue to move. It doesn't add anything of importance to the meaning of the film, but it does call attention to the man who made it.

"Sorekara" is best when Mr. Morita seems to be doing least. The period details are evocative because they are not stressed. These include a grand garden party where the guests parade around in top hats, cutaways, white gloves and the kind of afternoon dresses that would not have been out of place at Buckingham Palace in 1909.

Japan's still insecure position in the Western scheme of things is touched on when three young men argue about politics. "Japan is in debt," says one. "We're inferior to Europe." Another says, "People try to keep up." There are references to a terrible "sugar scandal" that is currently shaking the Japanese business community, but, like the caller in "The Monkey's Paw," it remains forever offstage.

Along with Mr. Matsuda (who played the lunatic tutor in "The Family Game") as Daisuke, the excellent cast is headed by the venerable Chishu Ryu, one of the mainstays of Ozu's cinema, as Daisuke's old father. Miwako Fujitani and Kaoru Kobayashi play the film's two most interesting, most complex roles, those of the possibly duplicitous Michiyo and her opportunistic husband, Hiraoka.

Mr. Morita attempts to emphasize the universality of his story, and its associations to life in Japan today, with a narrative style that is so cool it seems almost distracted. In the program notes he says that though the film is set in 1909, the costumes and décor were purposely designed not to re-create a particular Meiji period but the sense of a "'Meiji culture,' as if making a science-fiction picture."

However, "Sorekara" is most successful when it's utterly specific — when Mr. Morita allows the audience to make up its own mind about universal applications.

1987 Ap 8, C23:1

Charlie Sheen

Travelogue

THREE FOR THE ROAD, directed by B. W. L. Norton; screenplay by Richard Martini and Tim Metcalfe and Miguel Tejada-Flores; story by Mr. Martini; director of photography, Steve Posey; edited by Christopher Greenbury; music by Barry Goldberg; production designer, Linda Allen; produced by Herb Jaffe and Mort Engelberg; released by New Century/Vista Film Company. At Ziegfeld, 54th Street between Avenue of the Americas and Seventh Avenue; Coronet, Third Avenue at 59th Street, and 23d Street West Triplex, between Eighth and Ninth Avenues. Running time: 90 minutes. This film is rated PG.

Paul.................................Charlie Sheen
Robin.....................................Kerri Green
T. S. ....Alan Ruck
Blanche ....Sally Kellerman
Missy.......................................Blair Tefkin
Senator Kitteredge ....Raymond J. Barry
Virginia ....Alexa Hamilton
Stu ....Bert Remsen
Clarence ....James Avery

"**T**HREE FOR THE ROAD," which opens today at the Ziegfeld and other theaters, has no fewer beer cans or car chases or know-nothing jokes than the usual teen-age adventure-comedy. But it does have a lot less personality than most, which is peculiar. The director, B. W. L. Norton, and the writers, Richard Martini, Tim Metcalfe and Miguel Tejada-Flores, display no idea whatsoever of how to keep a film moving or how to hold an audience's interest. Listlessness and sloppiness on this scale are truly depressing.

"Three for the Road" concerns the idealistic young Paul Tracy, who has political aspirations, and is asked by a senator he admires to escort the senator's difficult daughter, Robin, to her umpteenth reform school. He is joined for the trip by a friend named Tommy, who calls himself T. S., keeps a poster of Faulkner in his room and likes to ask female conquests the titles of the last books they've read. This is meant to establish him as either funny or literary, probably both.

In the role of T. S. is Alan Ruck, who played the obnoxious sidekick in "Ferris Bueller's Day Off" and is no less obnoxious here. Paul is played by Charlie Sheen, a handsome, serious actor who is simply not cut out for light comedy. Mr. Sheen brings his most formidable glower to delivering even the smallest of small talk. Robin is played by Kerri Green, who has a pixieish prettiness and very little to do except, in scenes like the one that has her eating with her feet in a fancy restaurant, things she might as well

have not done. Sally Kellerman plays Robin's mother with fire-breathing intensity and seems to have wandered into the wrong movie.

●

The three protagonists make their journey in the senator's ice-blue Mercedes-Benz, which is presented without irony or admiration, merely a sense of casual entitlement. Most of the action takes place on and around superhighways, so there isn't even much scenery. The direction is paceless, and the writing extraordinarily lazy. When Paul and T. S. are stranded without a car, for instance, the screenwriters have them stumble upon a passed-out drunk who happens to hold in his hand the key to a brand-new Porsche, which is parked nearby.

In addition to lacking imagination, the principals behave very stupidly. What does Paul do, scenes later, when two policemen and the now-awakened drunk pull up beside him at a stoplight, as he sits behind the wheel of the stolen car? He screeches to a start and makes an illegal wrong turn onto a one-way street, just in case they haven't noticed him. In only one area have the film makers displayed any resourcefulness: coming up with plot twists that will land the principals, particularly Mr. Sheen, in their underwear. Film students, take note.

●

"Three for the Road" is rated PG ("Parental Guidance Suggested"). It contains some vulgar language and mild suggestiveness.
JANET MASLIN

1987 Ap 10, C5:1

Big Lights, Bright City

THE SECRET OF MY SUCCESS, directed and produced by Herbert Ross; screenplay by Jim Cash and Jack Epps Jr. and A. J. Carothers; story by Mr. Carothers; director of photography, Carlo di Palma; edited by Paul Hirsch; music by David Foster; production designers, Edward Pisoni and Peter Larkin; released by Universal Pictures. At Orpheum, Third Avenue at 86th Street; 34th Street Showplace, west of Second Avenue; Movieland, Broadway and 47th Street; Gemini, Second Avenue at 64th Street; 84th Street Six, at Broadway, and Olympia Quad, Broadway at 107th Street. Running time: 109 minutes. This film is rated PG-13.

Brantley Foster ....Michael J. Fox
Christy Wills ....Helen Slater
Howard Prescott ....Richard Jordan
Vera Prescott ....Margaret Whitton
Fred Melrose ....John Pankow
Barney Rattigan ....Christopher Murney
Art Thomas ....Gerry Bamman
Donald Davenport ....Fred Gwynne
Jean ....Carol-Ann Susi
Grace Foster ....Elizabeth Franz

"**T**HE SECRET OF MY SUCCESS," directed with a lot of panache by Herbert Ross, is a comedy about the meteoric rise in the Manhattan business world of Brantley Foster (Michael J. Fox), who, when he leaves the Kansas farm, tells his worried mother, "I want to have a meaningful experience with a beautiful woman."

His mother remains uncertain. Did Brantley pack an iron? "You don't want to walk around wrinkled in New York." Says Brantley, who manages to implicate everybody in his own schemes, "I'm doing this for you, Mom, as much as for myself."

Hanging over "The Secret of My Success" is the long shadow of Frank Loesser's classic musical "How to Succeed in Business Without Really Trying," as adapted for the stage by Abe Burrows, Jack Weinstock and

Upwardly Mobile Michael J. Fox and Helen Slater try to get ahead in business in "The Secret of My Success."

Willie Gilbert from Shepherd Mead's comic novel. The memory of the Broadway show, and the film version, is heightened by the ebullient, all-out performance by the pint-sized Mr. Fox in the hustler's role, which was earlier played with somewhat more edge (and no less charm) by the pint-sized Robert Morse.

"The Secret of My Success" is, in fact, so reminiscent of the show that one keeps expecting it to take off with Mr. Loesser's great score. It never does, but the movie has its compensations.

●

In addition to Mr. Fox, these include Helen Slater ("Supergirl"), as the business whiz Brantley Foster successfully courts, and Margaret Whitton, as the boss's predatory wife, who also happens to be Brantley's aunt by marriage. "Gee," says Brantley, when she complains about her loveless marriage to a man only later revealed to be his uncle, "I just hope that when I'm his age I can wake up next to a woman as beautiful as you are."

As important as the performances and the screenplay's snappish lines is the film's glittery, glass-and-steel look. Here's a case in which the production design (by Edward Pisoni and Peter Larkin) and the camera-work by Carlo di Palma (Woody Allen's current cameraman) are integral to the film's comic point. The Manhattan that Mr. Ross shows us is a Kansan's fantasy city. It's H. G. Wells's "Things to Come" already arrived. That the city also looks gigantic and impersonal only makes the schemes of the characters seem funnier — for being so small and self-regarding.

The movie builds up a lot of good will early on, which is needed when the time comes to resolve its farcical complications. The screenplay, by Jim Cash and Jack Epps Jr. ("Top Gun" and "Legal Eagles"), and A. J. Carothers, runs low on invention toward the end. It's most fun when it's scene-setting, that is, introducing the routine at the huge conglomerate where Brantley hangs his hat and hopes. It's close to inspired when the ambitious Brantley finds himself leading two lives — as a mailroom boy who masquerades as a junior ex-

ecutive, making split-second, Clark Kent-like wardrobe changes in elevators.

When eventually, as it must, the story makes its demands on the characters, things slow down considerably. However, "The Secret of My Success" still leaves you with a good feeling about the idiocies of Big Business (which, according to recent news stories, is beginning to worry about the long-term effects of these caustic images).

"The Secret of My Success" opens today at the Gemini and other theaters.

●

"The Secret of My Success," which has been rated PG-13 ("Special Parental Guidance Suggested for Those Younger Than 13"), contains some funny though sexually explicit references. *VINCENT CANBY*

1987 Ap 10, C14:4

Julian Sands in the role of Percy Bysshe Shelley in "Gothic."

House Party

GOTHIC, directed by Ken Russell; screenplay by Stephen Volk; director of photography, Mike Southon; music by Thomas Dolby; edited by Michael Bradsell; music by Thomas Dolby; production designer, Christopher Hobbs; produced by Penny Corke; released by Vestron Pictures. At Cinema 1, Third Avenue at 60th Street. Running time: 90 minutes. This film is rated R.

Byron ....Gabriel Byrne
Shelley ....Julian Sands
Mary ....Natasha Richardson
Claire ....Myriam Cyr
Dr. Polidori ....Timothy Spall
Fletcher ....Andreas Wisniewski
Murray ....Alex Mango
Rushton ....Dexter Fletcher
Justice ....Pascal King
Tour Guide ....Tom Hickey
Mechanical Doll ....Linda Coggin
Mechanical Woman ... Kristine Landon-Smith

By VINCENT CANBY

DURING the summer of 1816, while he was in residence in a villa on the Swiss shore of Lake Geneva, Lord Byron, then 28, was host to his fellow poet Percy Bysshe Shelley, 24; Mary Godwin, Shelley's 19-year-old mistress, whom he later married; Mary's step-sister, Claire Clairmont, 18, who was pregnant with Byron's child, and John William Polidori, Byron's doctor and friend, who was 21.

In addition to the Byron-Clairmont daughter, named Allegra by her father, the tangled alliances of that

Natasha Richardson as Mary Shelley, in "Gothic."

summer produced two works of supernatural fiction: Mary Shelley's classic "Frankenstein," and Polidori's "Vampyre," which is supposed to have been one of the inspirations for Bram Stoker's "Dracula." The members of the group apparently liked to play "Can You Top This?" with homemade horror stories — Mary and Polidori being the only ones to finish theirs.

The director Ken Russell, the apostle who preaches that too much is never enough, has taken this footnote to literary history and boiled it down to one frenzied night of sadomasochistic seductions, séances, fights, drugtaking, hallucinations and spectacular special effects.

"Gothic," written by Stephen Volk, isn't always coherent, but it's as ghoulishly funny and frenzied as a carnival ride through "The Marquis de Sade's Tunnel of Love." The film opens today at the Cinema 1.

At one point the needy Byron is seen making love to a mute housemaid who, for the occasion, puts on a mask labeled Augusta (for Byron's beloved half-sister and mistress). At another point, Claire, who's had a convulsion during the séance, is found crawling around a dungeon floor, a rat dangling from her mouth, much like the unfortunate fellow in Tod Browning's 1931 "Dracula."

Everybody seems to have dreams that foretell the future, including Shelley's watery death when he goes down with his sailboat. As if to prepare us for the film's final revelation — that Mary went on to write "Frankenstein" — the friends argue whether God is the creator of man, or vice versa.

⦁

With one exception, the actors are little more than adequate, possibly because it's not easy to give a serious performance in these fun-house circumstances, speaking lines that are most effective when they can't be clearly understood. When they are understood, they are alarmingly inconsequential.

The exception is the beautiful Natasha Richardson, who doesn't seem tall as much as she seems mysteriously elongated, a flesh-and-blood wraith whose presence gives substance to Mr. Russell's dreams. Miss Richardson, the daughter of Tony Richardson and Vanessa Redgrave, has much of her mother's distinctive

quality — even in her line readings — though she never seems to be a carbon copy. She's an original with — I'd be willing to bet — a remarkable career ahead of her.

Don't go to "Gothic" expecting to be elevated. This is no reverie. It's a series of gaudy shock effects, an anthology of horror-film mannerisms that looks like a 60's LSD trip. If "Gothic" says anything about Byron, Shelley and their friends, it's just that anyone who trusted them with a summer rental had to be out of his mind.

As Mr. Russell sees them, both Byron and Shelley were rather like today's more notorious rock stars, and no more or less articulate in matters relating to God, life, death and other metaphysical concerns. They were passionate republicans who behaved like heedless aristocrats, with no interest whatsoever in living down reputations for sexual excesses and what now is called — unromantically — substance abuse.

When, at the start of the film, Shelley, Mary and Claire arrive by rowboat to visit Byron at the Villa Diodati, Shelley is pounced upon by 19th-century groupies hiding in the bushes. On the far side of the lake, a binocu-lared tour guide, surrounded by tourists, is pointing out Byron's villa and the window that's supposed to be his bedroom.

What's going on inside the villa would probably outstrip the imagination of even the most fevered fan. The film's imagination, after all, is supplied by Mr. Russell, the man who made "Women in Love," "The Music Lovers," "Tommy" and "Altered States," among others, in a cinema language of deepest purple.

Byron (Gabriel Byrne) greets his guests with the friendliness of a Count Dracula. "I've dreamt of this day since Piccadilly Terrace, when we argued metaphysics," he says, enchanted by the sight of the young blond Shelley (Julian Sands). Byron is already tired of Claire (Miriam Cyr), who makes the mistake of referring to his club foot as "cloven," in a failed joke about his diabolical ways.

Byron is also tired of Polidori (Timothy Spall), who loves him too. He seems to want Shelley, who is torn by his admiration for Byron, his love for Mary (Natasha Richardson), his affection for Claire and his need for laudanum. Nobody, however, has the strength to turn away from any sincerely offered sexual encounter.

The long night that ensues — a bedroom farce played for screams — is scored by a lot of old-fashioned thunder and lightning, plus Thomas Dolby's exceptionally evocative soundtrack music. It makes no more sense than most rock videos, but it's only boring when, every now and then, Mr. Russell and Mr. Volk feel that they have to touch base with the known facts of history.

1987 Ap 10, C16:3

Doubles

MAKING MR. RIGHT, directed by Susan Seidelman; written by Floyd Byars and Laurie Frank; director of photography, Edward Lachman; edited by Andrew Mondshein; music by Chaz Jankel; production designer, Barbara Ling; produced by Mike Wise and Joel Tuber; released by Orion Pictures Corporation. At Loews Paramount, 61st Street and Broadway; Loews Tower East, Third Avenue and 72d Street; 23d Street West Triplex, between Eighth and Ninth Avenues. Running time: 100 minutes. This film is rated PG-13.
Jeff Peters/Ulysses .... John Malkovich

Ann Magnuson

Frankie Stone .... Ann Magnuson
Trish .... Glenne Headly
Steve Marcus .... Ben Masters
Sandy .... Laurie Metcalf
Estelle Stone .... Polly Bergen
Dr. Ramdas .... Harsh Nayyar
Don .... Hart Bochner
Ivy Stone .... Susan Berman
Suzy Duncan .... Polly Draper
Bruce .... Christian Clemenson
Tux Salesman .... Robert Trebor

By JANET MASLIN

AS the credits for "Making Mr. Right" roll by, the film's barefoot heroine is seen driving her bright red convertible to the sound of a high-voltage pop song, shaving her legs and painting on lipstick as she goes. This is the kind of hot-blooded, fun-loving moment that Susan Seidelman, who also directed "Desperately Seeking Susan" and "Smithereens," manages best. In fact, Ms. Seidelman plays with clothes, knickknacks, pop tunes and crazily single-minded characters better than almost any other film maker around. Her "Desperately Seeking Susan" will long stand as the definitive guide to everybody who was anybody, and anything that was au courant, in the year in which it was made.

"Making Mr. Right" has a lot in common with its predecessor, right down to the gerund in its title. It has great costumes, a large and cleverly chosen cast, the same kind of jokey, throwaway stylishness and an equally convoluted plot involving two characters who, in some way, share the same identity. In this case, the setting is Miami Beach rather than downtown Manhattan, and the story has a science-fiction aspect, involving a dour, disagreeable inventor who creates an android in his own image. The android has been custom-designed to withstand a long, boring trip into deep space, but fate has other things in store.

The screenplay, by Floyd Byars and Laurie Frank, also involves an unmarried career woman named Frankie Stone (Ann Magnuson), who is hired to do public relations for the android and winds up becoming his good friend. Aside from Frankie, the film includes a number of other single women who are coping with the opposite sex as best they can, each looking for a man with just the right chemistry. There's no accounting for why some matches work and others don't. In the same way, there's no easy explanation why Ms. Seidelman's tried-and-true methods are less successful

here than they were last time.

It may simply be that she is not quite at home with this slightly less effervescent story idea, or with finding satirical potential in high-tech settings, or even with the principal characters here, than she was last time. In any case, "Making Mr. Right" aims for the carefree style of Ms. Seidelman's last film, and has much the same sense of whimsy and the same distinctive touch. But it's a little more labored, and a little less fun.

"Making Mr. Right," which opens today at Loews Tower East and other theaters, certainly has its moments. But most of them take place on the periphery of the central story, which involves the spunky Miss Magnuson, John Malkovich, and John Malkovich again. In a double role, Mr. Malkovich appears as both the grouchy Dr. Jeff Peters, who works for the large and Orwellian Chemtech Corporation and can't stand Frankie Stone, and as the wide-eyed Ulysses, who is so taken with Frankie that she quite literally makes his head — which is detachable — spin. Frankie, who dresses as a kind of executive cigarette girl and happens to be between romances when Ulysses and the doctor come along, has a lasting effect on them both.

Though Ulysses is meant to have a childlike charm, and to be a *tabula rasa* learning everything about the modern world by studying Frankie, the contents of Frankie's pocketbook and Phil Donahue, Mr. Malkovich actually seems more comfortable as the mean-spirited inventor. In that capacity, as Jeff, he has a date with a man-crazy fellow worker named Sandy (played by Laurie Metcalf, who's even funnier than she was as the sister-in-law in Ms. Seidelman's last film). This appointment, like most of Jeff's, is kept by Ulysses instead, and leads to one of the film's most inspired episodes. Another has Frankie taking Ulysses on a shopping trip, although here Ms. Seidelman resorts to the kind of anatomical jokes that wouldn't be funny coming from a male director making a film about women. They aren't funny coming from her, either.

"Making Mr. Right" adds up to somewhat less than the sum of its parts, but the parts are often delightful, particularly when Ms. Seidelman keeps them moving at a sufficiently furious pace. One subplot involves the wedding of Frankie's sister Ivy (played by Susan Berman, the star of "Smithereens") to a busboy, and features costumes by Rudy Dillon and Adelle Lutz that are the film's very zaniest, which is saying something. Ed Lachman's cinematography has a bright, colorful look bordering on the radioactive.

The casting by Risa Bramon and Billy Hopkins is a constant source of fun, with memorable supporting performances from Glenne Headly as Frankie's oversexed friend; Hart Bochner as her estranged husband, a soap-opera star; Ben Masters as the politician boyfriend whom Frankie has jettisoned after catching him in a clinch with Miss Little Havana; Harsh Nayyar as the suave Dr. Ramdas, who fancies himself quite a smoothie, and Robert Trebor as the bewildered salesman who has never fitted an android for a tuxedo before. And probably never will again.

"Making Mr. Right" is rated PG-13 ("Special Parental Guidance Suggested for Those Younger Than 13"). It contains some strong sexual innuendoes.

1987 Ap 10, C16:5

FILM VIEW/Janet Maslin

Business on the Big Screen

LUCKILY, NOT MANY OF US develop our business ethics by studying what we see on the screen. If we did, we might all be con artists or underworld kingpins or brilliant, ruthless executives held captive by our uncontrollable passions. Even now, when real-life headlines threaten to steal its thunder, Hollywood is as eager as ever to hold its mirror up to the business community. And the ways in which films depict businessmen and their scruples tell us a lot about the times in which we live.

"The man of virtue makes the difficulty to be overcome his first business, and success only a subsequent consideration." Confucius said that, but then Confucius would have understood very little about the 1980's in America. George Orwell came closer to the mark when he described the go-getter of the early 20's: "Get on! Make good! If you see a man down, jump on his guts before he gets up again." These, like Orwell's, are cutthroat times, but they have engendered their own brand of gentlemanly pragmatism.

On the evidence of the appealing and almost comically coldblooded new film "The Secret of My Success," today's version of the Horatio Alger method makes hard work only a secondary consideration. In this latter-day variation on "How to Succeed in Business Without Really Trying," enterprise, ambition and a keen eye for the shortcut count for a lot more. So Brantley Foster, the young would-be executive who comes to New York from the film's stylized idea of Kansas (a place where people sit placidly shucking corn while they talk), talks to his mother about penthouses and Jacuzzis, and promises her that

Hollywood's depiction of the ethics of moneymaking holds a mirror to our times.

he'll be coming home in his own plane. Thanks to a business miracle, he makes good on that promise in only a few weeks' time.

How does he do it? "All you really need is a little gumption, a willingness to work, some common sense and a brother-in-law who is vice president in charge of personnel," writes the humorist Dave Barry in his how-to manual "Claw Your Way to the Top." This turns out to be not too far afield of Brantley's actual method.

In fact, Brantley has an uncle who is the C.E.O. of a huge conglomerate, and this helps him to land a mailroom job. Brantley's extra idea is to appropriate an empty office, order up a nameplate and some stationery and invent an executive alter ego for himself so that he's able to hold down two jobs at the same time.

Of course, in this comedy directed by Herbert Ross, the two-identity plot sets up some predictable farce, with the irresistible Michael J. Fox, as Brantley, often getting caught during costume changes. And some of the humor stems from Brantley's friendship with a mailroom buddy, who refers to the executives as "suits" and announces "some-

thing happens to a man when he puts on a necktie — cuts off all the oxygen to his brain."

But despite these ties to the low-level job in which he might be expected to languish for at least a week or two, Brantley immediately sees himself as a man on the way up. And the movie actively celebrates his brashness. It applauds the ultimate connection between the double-breasted suits in which Brantley covertly dresses and the limousine-riding, opera-going lifestyle to which his efforts eventually lead.

"The Secret of My Success" regards business success as utterly glamorous, uncomplicated and in no way incompatible with standing up for the things one believes in; that makes it very much a movie of the moment. So does Carlo DiPalma's dazzling cinematography, which takes a sardonic yet admiring view of big, bold, depersonalized corporate architecture.

A sequence in which Brantley burns the midnight oil concentrates less on the work he is doing than on the stunning spires of the Chrysler and other buildings at night, which appear as beacons to this up-and-coming young man steering his course. This film is as frank a tribute to unbridled ambition as the movies have produced in years.

The aluminum siding salesmen of "Tin Men" are every bit as unscrupulous as Brantley, but that film wistfully depicts them as dinosaurs, with their very individualism on the verge of becoming obsolete. Brantley's wisdom has to do with studying corporate resources and fending off a hostile takeover.

These salesmen work on a smaller and more psychologically astute scale, discussing how a customer may be convinced of a salesman's honesty if the salesman, who is anything but honest, leaves a $5 bill on the floor and makes sure the sucker finds it.

Barry Levinson, who wrote and directed the film, loves these tactics for their very obsolescence and views good old-fashioned hoodwinking as an art about to be supplanted by the things for which Brantley stands. "Tin Men" winds up romanticizing the kind of entrepreneurial wiliness that exists for its own sake, and for the sake of sheer gamesmanship, without any larger corporate goal in sight.

More unusual than either of these perspectives, and more difficult to convey on the screen, is the ambivalence toward success and ambition depicted in "Street Smart," Jerry Schatzberg's engrossing film about a magazine reporter who fakes a feature story and must grapple with the consequences of that act.

He is not immediately caught in the lie; that would be too simple. Instead, he is further seduced, as he was by the easy rewards of writing an attention-getting profile, into carrying the deceit further and further.

The film's attitude toward this is never one of simple condemnation. It understands, or at least it tries to, that selling out in one's professional life can be a gradual and even subtle process, a slow deterioration that may not even be noticed until the individual is absolutely forced to take score. That too, like Brantley's method for making it, provides a timely lesson. □

1987 Ap 12, II:17:1

Samuel Beckett
Associated Press

Reclusive Writer

SAMUEL BECKETT: SILENCE TO SI-
LENCE, directed by Sean O'Mordha, and
KAREN BLIXEN, a documentary directed
by Nic. Lichtenberg, in Danish with English subtitles, at Film Forum 1, 57 Watts
Street. Running time: 98 minutes. This
film has no rating.

By WALTER GOODMAN

TO ask that a documentary
capture the vision of a great
writer is to ask too much.
What a sensitive documen-
tary can do, and what Sean O'Mordha's "Samuel Beckett: Silence to Silence" does admirably, is bring together the man's life and work in a
way that offers glimpses of how the
one flowed into the other. For those
who haven't read much about the singular Nobel Prize-winner, the documentary provides illuminating details of his childhood, school days and
his war years with the French resistance; for admirers, there are tantalizing snatches of his prose, poetry
and inimitable plays. "Samuel Beckett" can be seen at Film Forum for
the next two weeks.

If anything, Mr. O'Mordha approaches his task with overmuch
reverence. The sepulchral intonings
of the narrator, David Warrilow, re-
putedly the pre-eminent interpreter
of the Beckettian oeuvre, though hypnotic in their way, sometimes seem at
odds with the kidding-oneself spirit in
much of the work. Similarly, several
of the accompanying visual images
are weighted with the sort of self-conscious significance that the writer
himself often mocks and that the intelligent text, written by Richard Ellmann and Declan Kiberd, sensibly
shuns. They call his prose, most aptly,
"sumptuous minimalism" and tell of
his obsession with "people in the last
ditch," characters "who live on the
edge of nonbeing." Where his friend
James Joyce wanted to get everything into his work, he seems bent on
taking everything out. In the world
according to Samuel Beckett, we find
"language and humor pitted against
grief and silence."

●

The documentary's reclusive subject, who cooperated in its making
(though not to the extent of allowing
himself to be photographed), provided the Beckettesque title and a few
recollections. He told the director
that between the completion of his

trilogy of novels, "Molloy," "Malone
Dies" and "The Unnameable," and
the start of "Waiting for Godot" in
1948, he was not so much bogged
down as "fogged down." He also permitted the filming of the original
manuscript of "Godot." For anyone
who cherishes that wordshed of a
work, the sight of the playwright's
tiny, tidy handwriting, in French, in a
school copybook, written through on
one side of each page and then back,
the other way, on the other side, is a
little like looking at the original Declaration of Independence.

Among other pleasures are clips
from several plays, including "Happy
Days," "Endgame" and "Krapp's
Last Tape," with such performers as
Billie Whitelaw, Jack McGowran and
Patrick Magee, and photographs of
the writer and his family over the
years, evidence that the voice of age
once had the body of a youth.

Also on the bill at Film Forum is a
short and rather silly interview with
Karen Blixen, or Isak Dinesen, made
in 1953, and an hourlong portrait of
William Carlos Williams, which was
not available for review.

1987 Ap 15, C22:1

Believe It or Not

HEAVEN, directed by Diane Keaton; cinematography by Frederick Elmes and Joe
Kelly; edited by Paul Barnes; music by
Howard Shore; produced by Joe Kelly; released by Island Pictures. At New Carnegie, 57th Street and Broadway. Running
time: 80 minutes. This film is rated PG-13.

"HEAVEN," a film by Diane
Keaton, is the cinema
equivalent of a book
that's discounted to
$19.95 before Christmas with the
warning that it will be $50 after. If you
respond to that kind of come-on, you
may respond to "Heaven."

The movie is a comparatively lavish documentary that means to be an
inquiry into how various people con-
ceive of heaven, hell, death and other
related matters. Because the tone of
the film is dumbfoundingly silly,
"Heaven" becomes, instead, a conceit imposed on its subjects. It's patronizing toward those who do "believe." It exploits those unsuspecting
others who aren't sure why they're
being interviewed or what they're
supposed to say. It offers more hip
types the chance to giggle and mug in
front of the camera, and their friends
the chance to giggle as they watch
them.

The questions asked by Miss Keaton, the interviewer as well as the director, carry built-in answers. The
fundamentalists describe heaven
with the authority of cartographers
who've been there and returned. A
few people are sincerely vague. One
of the film's photogenic "found objects" is a small, frail, elderly Los
Angeles woman who describes
heaven as all "clouds, trees, birds
twirping and angels flying around —
half a dozen angels." A little boy fills
up his screen time by saying that it's
"all white, like marshmallows."

One young woman reports that
Jesus is alive and well and living in a
Pakistani commune in London. Don
King, the fight promoter, comes on to
say something not very memorable,
but a movie is a movie and publicity
is publicity.

Mr. King is the only so-called celebrity in the film, if you don't count the
celebrity of Victoria Sellers, the
daughter of Peter Sellers and Britt

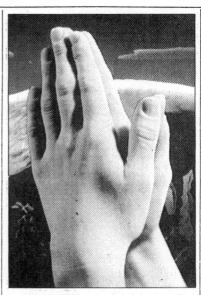

Looking Up Paradise after death
— its existence, its appearance, its
life styles — is explored in an
assortment of interviews in the
documentary "Heaven."

Ekland, and of her boyfriend, Kenny
Ostin, the son of Mo Ostin, the head of
Warner Brothers Records. They are
among the gigglers.

●

None of the interviewees, including
Miss Keaton's parents and her sister,
are identified on camera, so that even
knowing who's who becomes something of an "in" trivia game. More
than anything else, "Heaven" looks
like the sort of film that might have
been made by Mary Wilke, the fragile, know-it-all neurotic Miss Keaton
played in Woody Allen's "Manhattan." One's torn between wanting to
kick the film and wanting to protect it
from wasting all this money.

The interviews are supplemented
with lots of old film clips from, among
other things, "The Green Pastures,"
"Metropolis," a lot of defenseless
Hollywood junk and religious-promo-
tional films.

As off-putting as the movie's tone
(and, perhaps, contributing to it) is
the elaborate production. It's full of
self-consciously pretty pictures that
say a lot less about their subjects
than about the people responsible for
the camera work, the production design (the principal "set" suggests
something for a Vogue magazine
fashion spread), the lighting and
graphics, the special effects, the editing and the music.

Just what the movie is attempting
to say, I've no idea. Possibly it's back-
ing up Henry Adams's "Mont-Saint-
Michel and Chartres," if only indirectly, by recording the emotional
and spiritual confusion that are the
residue of a time when the world was
unified by faith. Possibly not.

"Heaven" opens today at the New
Carnegie.

●

*"Heaven" is rated PG-13 ("Special
Parental Guidance Suggested for
Those Younger Than 13"), perhaps
because of its treatment of religion.*
                               VINCENT CANBY

1987 Ap 17, C8:5

Tai-Chi Tarzan

WILD THING, directed by Max Reid; screenplay by John Sayles; story by Larry
Stamper and Mr. Sayles; director of
photography, Rene Verzier; music by
George S. Clinton; edited by Battle Davis
and Steven Rosenblum; production designer, Ross Schorer; produced by David Cal-
loway and Nicolas Clermont; released by
Atlantic Releasing Corporation. At Quad
Cinema, 13th Street between Fifth Avenue
and Avenue of the Americas. Running
time: 92 minutes. This film is rated PG-13.

Wild Thing	Rob Knepper
Jane	Kathleen Quinlan
Chopper	Robert Davi
Trask	Maury Chaykin
Leah	Betty Buckley
Wild Thing 10 years old	
	Guillaume Lemay-Thivierge
Free/Wild Thing at 3 years	Robert Bednarski
Winston	Clark Johnson
Father Quinn	Sean Hewitt
Rasheed	Teddy Abner
Lisa	Cree Summer Francks
Paul	Shawn Levy

WHO is "Wild Thing"?
What is he? A legend in
his time and place, that's
what. The time, alleg-
edly, is the present, the place, "the
zone," a surreal section of town peopled by crooks and crazies.

Since the zonies did not see the
beginning of Max Reid's movie,
which opens today at the Quad Cinema, they don't know that at age 3,
Wild Thing watched his hippie
mother and father being gunned
down by a bad guy and a crooked cop,
that he was raised by a batty bag lady
who turned him off the Establishment, and that with the help of tai chi,
homemade bows-and-arrows, innate
jungle agility and a bare chest, he
grew to be Tarzan of the creeps.

How Wild Thing (Rob Knepper)
rescues and discovers sex with the
shapeliest social worker anybody
ever came across on a dark night in
the ghetto (Kathleen Quinlan) and
how he wreaks vengeance on the bad
guys is the stuff of John Sayles's
comic-book script. Mr. Sayles, a
writer and director of note ("Return
of the Secaucus Seven"), was
awarded a MacArthur Foundation
"genius" grant in 1983. Maybe this is
his joke on the Establishment.

Mr. Reid's direction is nearly incoherent in places, a relief from the coherent passages. The acting generally suits the material. The most
frightening moment comes at the
end, when we learn that Wild Thing
lives, which is to say that if the gross
is sufficient, he will be swinging unstoppably across the nation's screens
again before you can say, "Get down
from there!"

●

*"Wild Thing" is rated PG-13 ("Spe-
cial Parental Guidance Suggested for
Those Younger Than 13"), probably
because of its violence.*
                               WALTER GOODMAN

1987 Ap 17, C13:1

Precocious Primate

PROJECT X, directed by Jonathan Kaplan;
screenplay by Stanley Weiser; story by
Mr. Weiser and Lawrence Lasker; director of photography, Dean Cundey; edited
by O. Nicholas Brown; music by James
Horner; production designer, Lawrence G.
Paull; released by 20th Century-Fox Film
Corporation. At Criterion Center, Broadway at 45th Street; Gotham Cinema, Third
Avenue at 58th Street; 23d Street West Triplex, 333 West 23d Street; 86th Street East,
at Third Avenue; 34th Street East, 241
East 34th Street; 84th Street Six, at Broadway. Running time: 107 minutes. This film
is rated PG.

Simian Signs Matthew Broderick, as a young airman assigned to a top-secret program, befriends a communicative chimpanzee in "Project X."

Jimmy	Matthew Broderick
Teri	Helen Hunt
Dr. Carroll	Bill Sadler
Robertson	Johnny Ray McGhee
Sgt. Krieger	Jonathan Stark
Col. Niles	Robin Gammell
Watts	Stephen Lang
Dr. Criswell	Jean Smart
General Claybourne	Chuck Bennett
Hadfield	Daniel Roebuck
Airman Lewis	Mark Harden
Major Duncan	Duncan Wilmore

By WALTER GOODMAN

HOW much you enjoy "Project X" depends on how much monkeying around you can take. As somebody says, "There are monkeys all over the place." The stars of this show, upstaging Matthew Broderick all the way, are a chatter of chimpanzees, an aptitude of apes. They play experimental animals at an Air Force base in Florida who are taught to fly an airplane (in simulated circumstances) as a prelude to the final, but final, experiment.

"Project X," which opens today at the Criterion Center and other theaters, is a young folks' story, a sweet-natured boy-and-his-chimp tale (even the bad guys aren't all that bad), with a dose of Animal Liberation to give the impression that something of current significance is going on.

Although Stanley Weiser's screenplay starts in the jungle, it doesn't beat around the bush. Mr. Broderick, as a young Air Force private named Jimmy, gets attached to the newest, brightest little experimental subject, named Virgil, who has enjoyed three years of advanced schooling with a pretty psychologist named Teri (Helen Hunt) at the University of Wisconsin. Teri is cute, though not as cute as Jimmy, and Virgil is cuter and maybe smarter than both his adopted parents put together. He's a prodigiously fast learner, can communicate through sign language and is easy to cuddle. Yes, Virgil is adorable, and you can't help rooting for Jimmy when he defies the brass to save the little guy from the ultimate experiment.

The director, Jonathan Kaplan, lays on the animal antics without stint; it's a one-ring circus. The way

he tugs at our sympathy for the poor smart beasts may remind you of a house pet scratching away for attention. And in case you're left in any doubt about how you're supposed to be reacting, James Horner's insistent musical score directs audience emotions like a traffic cop. You may begin to feel you're the experimental subject. Much cleverer is the camerawork of Dean Cundey, particularly in the climactic moments of simulated flying. The scenes of the primate Luddites busting up all that high-tech experimental paraphernalia are natural cheer-rousers, and the movie's final takeoff is all anybody could ask.

To get back to the story's significance, the case is made by Jimmy, in a plea to higher-ups, that the experiments are not really necessary. If he is right, then the issue is moot — Let the monkeys go! But suppose that the sacrifice of some monkeys will enhance the well-being of some humans? That is the question with which Animal Liberationists must grapple. Be assured there is no grappling in this cockles-warmer, not even between Mr. Broderick and Miss Hunt.

●

"Project X" is rated PG ("Parental Guidance Suggested"), owing presumably to the possibly frightening effects of those final experiments on the cute monkeys.

1987 Ap 17, C15:1

Feet of Clay

THE FESTIVAL OF CLAYMATION, directed by Will Vinton and others; an Expanded Entertainment Release of an International Tournee of Animation Presentation. At Bleecker Street Cinema, 144 Bleecker Street; Metro Cinema, 99th Street and Broadway. Running time: 90 minutes. This film has no rating.

"CLAYMATION" is the name imposed by Will Vinton on his technique for making animated movies with clay figures. It's a clunky word, appropriate to what is often a clunky form. A 90-minute sampler of the Vinton group's work over the past several years, "The Festival of Claymation," can be seen starting today at the Bleecker Street and Metro Cinemas.

The most instructive item, called, yes, "Claymation," shows how the three-dimensional animation process proceeds, from the coloring and modeling of the clay to the use of the camera. Each frame of film requires scores of tiny changes in the little sculpted figures to create the illusion of movement. Is it worth all the bother? The results have an earthy color and plenty of texture; what they don't have is the airiness of more conventional types of animation. They are solid, but not pretty.

The most successful of these samples is "Dinosaur." This brief rundown of a couple of hundred million prehistoric years benefits from an amusing script by Susan Shadburne and from the applicability of the clay to the creatures' lumpish forms and plodding gait. "Dinosaur" is evidently aimed at schoolchildren, and seems on target. There's also a mildly amusing retelling of Mark Twain's celebrated tale of the celebrated jumping frog of Calaveras County. The other shorts have less to commend them. "The Great Cognito" demonstrates that a stand-up comedian and a laugh track can be as annoying in clay as in the flesh; "A

Christmas Gift" is drenched in seasonal sentiment; the unappealingly titled "Vanz Kant Danz" features an unappealing chorus line of pigs that only reminds you of how much better the Disney people did this sort of thing. Kan't Klay Danz?

Also on the bill are several commercials, including the currently popular "I Heard It Through the Grapevine" plug for California raisins. If sitting through commercials for Domino's pizza, Cap'n Crunch and Kentucky Fried Chicken is your idea of a good time, enjoy.

The samples are tied together by a couple of dinosaurish-looking figures, named Rex and Herb, takeoffs on television's movie reviewers. It's not a bad gag to have them squabbling about the show's little segments in the jargon of their trade ("artsy, pretentious, psuedo-intellectual"), but the joke is overworked, and like other ingredients of this festival, the pair is no more of a pleasure to be around on the big screen than on the small one.

WALTER GOODMAN

1987 Ap 17, C16:1

Pure Oxygen

PRICK UP YOUR EARS, directed by Stephen Frears; written by Alan Bennett, based on the book by John Lahr; director of photography, Oliver Stapleton; edited by Mick Audsley; music by Stanley Myers; art director, Philip Elton; produced by Andrew Brown; released by the Samuel Goldwyn Company. At Lincoln Plaza 1 and 2, 63d Street and Broadway. Running time: 111 minutes. This film is rated R.

Joe Orton	Gary Oldman
Kenneth Halliwell	Alfred Molina
Peggy Ramsay	Vanessa Redgrave
John Lahr	Wallace Shawn
Anthea Lahr	Lindsay Duncan
Elsie Orton	Julie Walters
William Orton	James Grant
Mrs. Sugden	Janet Dale
Mme. Lambert	Margaret Tyzack
Brian Epstein	David Cardy

By VINCENT CANBY

LIKE John Lahr's 1978 biography of Joe Orton, the English playwright, the screen adaptation of "Prick Up Your Ears" comes immediately to the harrowing point: Kenneth Halliwell's hammer-murder of Orton, his lover and friend; his own suicide, and the subsequent discovery of the bodies.

"Joe Orton and Kenneth Halliwell were friends," Mr. Lahr writes in the first paragraph. "For 15 years, they lived and often wrote together ... They shared everything except success. But on Aug. 9, 1967, murder made them equal again."

Mr. Lahr's book goes on to examine Orton's life in relation to the small body of viciously funny, sometimes brilliant plays (including "Entertaining Mr. Sloane," "Loot" and the posthumously produced "What the Butler Saw") that had suddenly made him a major influence in the English theater.

By the time one reaches the end of the Lahr biography, one has not only admiration for Orton's extraordinary, unsentimental education, but also some understanding of his craft and why the plays, which at first so scandalized London's West End, swept through the theater with the giddy effect of pure oxygen. They cleared a stuffy head with laughter. As Orton was a product of his times, he helped to shape those that followed.

The film, unlike the book, goes on to record little more than the facts of the Orton life, the mere existence of the plays and the terrible effect that success had on what was, in reality, a marriage in which one partner, Orton, at first nurtured by the mind and body of the other, goes on to discover his own, absolutely separate identity.

Except for Orton's overnight success in the theater, and except for the most particular circumstances of the playwright's death, the story of the Orton-Halliwell relationship probably doesn't seem much different from those of many heterosexual unions, or even of nonsexual relationships of, say, teachers and students, foremen and machinists, editors and reporters and, on a short-term basis, of taxi drivers and their fares.

However, not many of these wind up in page 1 stories that report the number of hammer blows imprinted on the victim's head. There's a large difference between a murder-suicide and a noisy row that ends in the divorce court, a summary dismissal from one's place of employment or a hearing in front of the taxi commission. The Orton-Halliwell story isn't exactly universal in its application, and to treat it as such, if only by default, is not to do it justice.

"Prick up Your Ears," which opens today at the Lincoln Plaza 1 and 2, is short on point if long on credentials.

The film was written by Alan Bennett, the actor ("Beyond the Fringe"), playwright ("Habeas Corpus"), television writer ("An Englishman Abroad") and screenwriter ("A Private Function"), and directed by Stephen Frears, whose last film was the seriously funny "My Beautiful Laundrette."

●

It has a very good cast, headed by Gary Oldman, who, as Orton, looks remarkably like the playwright and surpasses his fine work as Sid Vicious in "Sid and Nancy"; Alfred Molina as the initially arrogant and finally self-victimized Halliwell, one of the least endearing roles any actor could take on, and Vanessa Redgrave as Peggy Ramsay, Orton's tough, practical theatrical agent.

Wallace Shawn appears as Mr. Lahr, in Mr. Lahr's capacity as investigative reporter. However, he's less a character than a plot function, designed to bring together the film's chronologically fractured structure. Julie Walters ("Educating Rita") plays Orton's working-class mother.

The film covers the main events of the Orton life in a manner that is nothing less than distracted. One has little understanding of the fatal intensity — and need — that kept Orton and Halliwell together. Because the film is either unable or unwilling to deal with the plays, the audience is left to discover wispy reminders of the Orton style, manner and method in isolated scenes from so-called real life.

A couple of these are very good, as when Orton and his sister get the giggles during their mother's funeral. When Orton notices that his mother has been laid out without her plate, he can't resist saying: "What a shame. She was very proud of her teeth." After the funeral, he purloins the plate, which he later slips as a prop to an actor about to go on stage in his hit play "Loot." (However, movie audiences, who've never seen the play, will completely miss the point of the joke.)

●

Gary Oldman as Joe Orton and Alfred Molina as Kenneth Halliwell in "Prick Up Your Ears"

In another short, pertinent scene, he maliciously and hilariously sends up Brian Epstein (David Cardy), the Beatles manager (now dead), when Epstein objects to the homosexual innuendoes in the screenplay Orton has written for the singing group.

The film is almost perfunctory in recalling one of the key Orton-Halliwell collaborations — when, in the late 1950's and early 1960's, having nothing better to do, they began to steal and deface library books by adding their own rude, obscene, sometimes very funny jacket copy and illustrations. The manic enthusiasm with which they threw themselves into this entirely private political gesture-artistic endeavor (which resulted in six-month prison terms for each) virtually defines their claustrophobic relationship. You can't tell this from the film.

Nor do you get much idea of the social-political climate. The movie introduces the Festival of Britain, which celebrated Britain's return to a peacetime economy, and at another point, the coronation of Queen Elizabeth II is seen on a television screen. However, no vital connection is made between Orton's work and the world in which he lived. Except for the occasional topical reference, "Prick Up Your Ears" could be taking place in limbo.

"Prick Up Your Ears" is more effective in dramatizing the sexual games played by Orton and Halliwell, including Orton's brazenly frank encounters in the men's rooms of London, which both fascinated and enraged his friend.

As played by Mr. Oldman, Orton has a lot of bitchy, self-assured charm, while Mr. Molina's Halliwell is a sad, seemingly impotent Dracula, right from the beginning of their friendship. Miss Redgrave is refreshingly staunch and common-sensical in a film that — like those about Yukio Mishima and Dorothy Stratten — probably would never have been made had the life it records not ended with such picturesque violence.

1987 Ap 17, C17:1

Teen-Age Revolt

SUMMER CAMP NIGHTMARE, directed by Bert L. Dragin; screenplay by Mr. Dragin and Penelope Spheeris, based on the novel "The Butterfly Revolution" by William Butler; director of photography, Don Burgess; edited by Michael Spence; music by Ted Neeley and Gary Chase; art director, Barry Franenberg; produced by Robert T. Crow and Emilia Lesniak-Crow; released by Concorde. At Coliseum, 181st Street and Broadway. Running time: 90 minutes. This film is rated PG-13.

Mr. Warren	Chuck Connors
Franklin Reilly	Charles Stratton
Chris Wayne	Harold (P) Pruett
Donald Poultry	Adam Carl
John Mason	Tom Fridley
Heather	Melissa Brennan
Stanley Runk	Stuart Rogers
Hammond Pumpernil	Shawn McLemore
Debbie	Samantha Newark

By CARYN JAMES

THOUGH it sounds like a slasher film, "Summer Camp Nightmare" is an earnest little rip-off of "The Lord of the Flies." This version of adolescence-turned-evil relies on the heavy political symbolism a 15-year-old might take to heart — and look back on at 16 with embarrassment.

Despite his years as "The Rifleman," Chuck Connors seems uneasy as the superstrict director of an isolated boys' camp. As Mr. Warren, he rigs the television so it picks up only a religious channel; he locks boys away in a special cabin as punishment for normal behavior and calls the nearby girls' camp off-limits. Soon a power-hungry teen-age counselor — the one who smiles demoniacally at the camera — leads a revolt; the boys lock the adults away and take over both camps. Before any adults reappear, there are two murders and a rape.

This slow walk from bad summer days into nightmare violence calls for some finesse — otherwise the story will veer off into the ludicrous or lurid. Bert L. Dragin doesn't take the cheap shots here, but he does take all the obvious ones, directing his first film as if the characters' actions explained themselves. The revolutionary counselor, meant to be so charismatic, is a smirky, neo-con rich boy who somehow gains control and turns fascist (there's even a firelight rally where the kids chant their allegiance to him). I'm not convinced the other kids would talk to this guy, much less follow him.

"Summer Camp Nightmare," which opens today at the Coliseum, was written by Mr. Dragin and Penelope Spheeris (as the director of "Suburbia" and "The Boys Next Door," she has shown more feeling for young 1980's rebels), based on a 1961 novel called "The Butterfly Revolution" — which was also the film's working title and one that captures perfectly its stilted sincerity.

The spirited actors — especially Adam Carl as a misfit electronics whiz who becomes the film's conscience — deserve much better. And the teen-age audience, weaned on John Hughes's realism, may have already outgrown this old chestnut about kids' inhumanity to kids.

1987 Ap 17, C30:5

Pastoral Quirks

PADRE NUESTRO, directed by Francisco Regueiro; screenplay (Spanish with English subtitles) by Angel Fernández Santos and Francisco Regueiro; director of photography, Juan Amoros; edited by Pedro Del Rey; art director, Enrique Alarcón; produced by Eduardo Ducay and Julián Marcos; released by International Film Exchange. At Embassy 72d Street, at Broadway. Running time: 90 minutes. This film has no rating.

Cardenal	Fernando Rey
Abel	Francisco Rabal
Cardenala	Victoria Abril
María	Emma Penella
Valentina	Amelia de la Torre
Jeronima	Rafaela Aparicio
Blanca	Lina Canalejas
El Papa	José Vivo
Lolita	Yolanda Cardama
Sagrario	Luis Barbero
Guevines	Francisco Vidal
La Muda	Diana Peñalver
Monja	María Elena Flores

By WALTER GOODMAN

BENEATH the austere compositions of "Padre Nuestro" beats an operatic heart. The eccentric, alluring Spanish movie, which opens today at the Embassy 72d Street, begins in the Vatican with a witty and humane conversation between the down-to-earth Pope, who is rather possessive about his connections to heaven, and an important cardinal who has learned he has less than a year to live. The nononsense faith they share runs through all that follows.

The Cardinal (Fernando Rey) wants to go home again, back to the village that his family owns and that he left 30 years before. There are accounts to settle. Still living out the fate to which his desertion consigned them are the woman he made pregnant; their daughter, who has turned into a beautiful cocaine-sniffing whore known as the Cardinaless; a granddaughter who likes to run with the sheep; an unmarried brother (Francisco Rabal), an atheist with sex problems; their pious, pampered, potty matriarch, and the rich vineyards that supply the church with its most prized consecrated wines — at a big loss to the family.

•

How the Cardinal goes about sorting things out is the stuff of "Padre Nuestro." The conversations between Mr. Rey and Mr. Rabal sing; the two pros give superlative performances full of shadings and surprises. One of their duets takes place at a billiard table where the Cardinal, a toothpick slanting sportily from his lips, shows he hasn't lost his touch since the match was broken off three decades ago. In the old Cardinal you can detect the seductive charm and vanity of the young man, chastened by years of prayer and reflection but by no means subdued.

The brothers mistrust each other in a loving way yet are much alike. Both are tough moralists with soft spots for human weakness. Both have inherited the spirit of their womanizing father and have paid heavily for it. The funniest scene in a tale that moves in an unforced way between drama or melodrama and comedy comes when the brother confesses the nature of his sexual weakness and the Cardinal gives him a simple if slightly painful remedy.

The camera of Juan Amoros catches the beauties of the village, enabling us to see, along with the Cardinal, what he gave up by leaving. Whether his real sin was the fornication or the desertion, the distress it caused comes through palpably. Under the direction of Francisco Regueiro, who collaborated on the inventive screenplay, the villagers are often odd but never unbelievable.

Whether the Cardinal's return improves matters for those who should have been his loved ones or made things worse remains unsettled as the dying prelate has his last conversation with the Pope. The impossibility of undoing what has been done may be what His Holiness was trying to get across at the start of an ingratiating movie that offers no big message but lots of small ones about affection, responsibility and settling accounts.

1987 Ap 22, C24:1

No Windows

THE HOUSEKEEPER, directed by Ousama Rawi; screenplay by Elaine Waisglass, based on the novel "A Judgement in Stone," by Ruth Rendell; director of photography, David Herrington; edited by Stan Cole; music by Paul Zaza; produced by Harve Sherman; released by Castle Hill. At Cine 1 and 2, Seventh Avenue and 48th Street; Baronet, Third Avenue at 59th Street. Running time: 96 minutes. This film has no rating.

Eunice Parchman	Rita Tushingham
George Coverdale	Ross Petty
Jackie Coverdale	Shelley Peterson
Bobby Coverdale	Jonathan Crombie
Melinda Coverdale	Jessica Steen
Joan Smith	Jackie Burroughs
Norman Smith	Tom Kneebone

"THE HOUSEKEEPER," based on Ruth Rendell's Edgar-winning suspense novel, is neither good enough to support Rita Tushingham's carefully considered performance as a closet psychotic nor bad enough for one to accept its mindless horrors for their own entertaining sake.

Miss Tushingham ("A Taste of Honey," "The Knack," "Dr. Zhivago"), in her first new film to be seen here in years, plays poor Eunice Parchman, a working-class Englishwoman who grows up seriously disturbed when her teachers and parents fail to recognize her dyslexia. Not being able to read or write, Eunice turns into a repressed Medea who, on the outside, seems only to be acutely shy and frumpish.

After her father dies suddenly of asphyxiation (Eunice has held a pillow over his face until he stopped breathing), she accepts a job in America as housekeeper to an upper-middle-class doctor and his family. Needless to say, she hasn't mentioned her small disability to her future employers, nor is she the sort of person to seek help on her own.

•

The Canadian film, opening today at the Baronet and other theaters, is the first theatrical movie to be directed by Ousama Rawi (Miss Tushingham's husband), whose previous experience is as a cameraman and a director of commercials and shorts. This is apparent throughout "The Housekeeper." It has a clean, completely impersonal look and is performed by actors who (with the exception of Miss Tushingham) behave as if they're in a somewhat bizarre, feature-length detergent commercial.

All of these other characters oversell either their sitcom "ordinariness" or, like the friend who pushes

Rita Tushingham

Eunice over the edge at the end, their eccentricities.

Miss Tushingham's performance exists in a different dimension. It's not a great role, but she invests it with a dark, fearful spirit summoned — seemingly — out of thin air.

VINCENT CANBY

1987 Ap 24, C7:1

A Private War

EXTREME PREJUDICE, directed by Walter Hill; screenplay by Deric Washburn and Harry Kleiner, story by John Milius and Fred Rexer; director of photography, Matthew F. Leonetti; film editor, Freeman Davies; music by Jerry Goldsmith; production designer, Albert Heschong; produced by Buzz Feitshans; released by Tri-Star Pictures. At Astor Plaza, Broadway and 44th Street; Sutton, 57th Street at Third Avenue; 86th Street Twin, at Lexington Avenue; Movieland Eighth Street Triplex, at University Place; 84th Street Sixplex, at Broadway, and other theaters. Running time: 104 minutes. This film is rated R.

Jack Benteen	Nick Nolte
Cash Bailey	Powers Boothe
Maj. Paul Hackett	Michael Ironside
Sarita Cisneros	Maria Conchita Alonso
Sheriff Hank Pearson	Rip Torn
Sgt. Larry McRose	Clancy Brown
Sgt. Buck Atwater	William Forsythe
Sgt. Declan Patrick Coker	Matt Mulhern
Sgt. Charles Biddle	Larry B. Scott
Sgt. Luther Fry	Dan Tullis Jr.

By JANET MASLIN

ACTORS get leaner and meaner when they work for Walter Hill. The sun shines down with an angrier glare. The gunfire is sharper, the insults more ambitious, and the only gentle sounds are those of womenfolk, as they (vainly) importune their tough guys to stay. In this hard-boiled universe, nothing is too nasty: not a bomb inside a bunny rabbit, or a point-blank surprise shot to someone's forehead, followed by the offhanded comment "I liked him, too." If Mr. Hill, whose best films have a genuinely hard-boiled glamour, never intends this as parody, neither is he ever more than a hair away.

Mr. Hill's films, like "The Warriors" and "Streets of Fire" and now "Extreme Prejudice," are often more intent on being reckoned with than being liked or understood. At times, that can make their storytelling look complicated and their bravado rather thin. But even at their silliest, they never fail to command a certain awe. No one else does what Mr. Hill can do, though it may well be that no one else wants to.

Set in Texas and across the border into Mexico, "Extreme Prejudice" is one of his more vigorous efforts. It has a bold, bright look and a crisp tempo, propelling the action from one shootout to another until it finally reaches the most violent of its crescendos. By the time it has arrived at this last stage, the film is so close to being ludicrous that it's hard to know whether it is deteriorating or ascending.

•

"Extreme Prejudice," which opens today at Loews Astor Plaza and other theaters, has a story co-written by John Milius (with Fred Rexer), who is himself a creditable candidate for King of the Cowboys and who seems to be entirely on Mr. Hill's wavelength. The film (the screenplay is by Deric Washburn and Harry Kleiner) concerns two childhood friends who find themselves on opposite sides of the law. Jack Benteen (Nick Nolte)

Nick Nolte

has grown up to become a tough-as-nails Texas Ranger, while his old pal Cash Bailey (Powers Boothe) wears an attention-getting white suit and controls local drug trafficking across the Mexican border.

Jack and Cash, who square off for some memorable name-calling at various points in the story, are ably matched, and both actors bring a lot of squinty-eyed, cold-blooded enthusiasm to their roles; Mr. Boothe even manages to find some measure of cynical, malevolent humor. Mr. Nolte winds up with more of the coolly businesslike dialogue, with lines like "He died goin' forward, that means a hell of a lot down here." Some of the talk is also obscured by Mr. Hill's way of encouraging the cast to speak without any unclenching of teeth.

The supporting players are memorable-looking and photogenic, and they are caught up in a whole extra plot about supposedly dead ex-soldiers who engage in a covert mission on Jack Benteen's turf. All of this is complicated, and clear exposition is not Mr. Hill's strong suit, but he does make it move. The cold, clear cinematography by Matthew F. Leonetti is also helpful, especially when Mr. Hill stages shootouts to make Sam Peckinpah seem a pacifist by comparison. Rip Torn makes a great if brief appearance as another Texas Ranger, and Maria Conchita Alonso has the extraordinarily thankless role of a woman torn between Jack and Cash. When Cash suggests, during one of the two men's fights, that she rip some clothes off to provide "motivation," it's hard to know whether to laugh. Or spit nails. Or cry.

1987 Ap 24, C8:5

Fish Story

L'ANNEE DES MEDUSES, written and directed by Christopher Frank, based on his novel; in French with English subtitles; cinematography by Renato Berta; edited by Nathalie Lafaurie; music by Alain Wisniak; art director, Jean-Jacques Caziot; produced by Alain Terzian; distributed by European Classics. At the Paris, Fifth Avenue and 58th Street. Running time: 110 minutes. This film has no rating.

Chris	Valérie Kaprisky
Romain	Bernard Giraudeau
Claude	Caroline Cellier
Vic	Jacques Perrin
Marianne	Béatrice Agenin
Dorothée	Betty Assenza
Miriam	Charlotte Kadi
Pierre	Pierre Vaneck
Lamotte	Philippe Lemaire
Peter	Antoine Nikola

Ah, civility. Where but on the French Riviera could the concept of mother-daughter toplessness be greeted with such heavenly nonchalance? Christopher Frank's "Année des Méduses," which opens today at the Paris, is about a beautiful, voluptuous teenager (Valérie Kaprisky) and mother (Caroline Cellier) who vacation together in an atmosphere of utterly casual exhibitionism. The beach is glamorous, the clientele well heeled, and no one spends a nickel on swimwear. So the women are forever rolling things down or peeling things off, and the men never bat an eye. The film's cast does include a couple of pre-adolescent boys, but sadly, their reaction to these goings-on is left unrecorded.

"L'Année des Méduses" might have been about a number of things. It might have addressed the mother-daughter competitiveness that could reasonably be expected to arise in these surroundings, or it might even tackle the story of Salome, which is invoked from time to time. But the true subject here is the bathing-suit shortage. Like the recent "Betty Blue," Mr. Frank's new film, for all its pretensions, is about its heroine's anatomy and little more.

Miss Kaprisky, as a vixen named Chris, has two ways of looking: annoyed and available. She is in the latter mode most of the time, particularly when flirting with men who are interested in her mother. (Chris also has a father — but he is at home working during much of the story, so Chris and her mother, Claude, are left to their own discretion, which is just about nonexistent.) Chief among these is the rakish, shrewd Romain (Bernard Giraudeau), who specializes in luring topless bathers to his boat and then lending them to his friends. When one of the film's minor characters finds herself cynically ill-used in this way, she begins looking sheepish and wearing heavier clothing, which is the film's way of conveying shame.

•

The film chronicles Chris's escapades and her studied abandon, which becomes more and more aggressive as she encounters some minor disappointments. For one thing, her chic, soignée mother (Miss Cellier has something like a Stéphane Audran role) is quite popular in her own right, which prompts Chris to tell her that, at 38, she is simply too old. For another, Romain seems more interested in the mother than he is in Chris, which prompts an angry confrontation. Romain's cool denunciation of Chris in the film's climactic moments seems designed to add a sociological dimension, suggesting that a life of bourgeois respectability is even emptier than one of total promiscuity. This outburst brings Romain a form of retribution that must have seemed a lot more like poetic justice in Mr. Frank's novel, on which the film is based, than it does on the screen.

Voyeurism may have its rewards, and Mr. Frank's film does hold the attention. But it hardly casts any new light on the plight of the poor, misunderstood Lolita, who has seldom seemed more spoiled and petulant than she does here. Miss Kaprisky, who starred with Richard Gere in the remake of "Breathless," makes it clear that she is a sex star, not an actress. There's a big difference between the two. JANET MASLIN

1987 Ap 24, C9:1

Monkey Love

LINK, directed and produced by Richard Franklin; screenplay by Everett De Roche; director of photography, Mike Malloy; edited by Andrew London; music by Jerry Goldsmith; production designer, Norman Garwood; released by Cannon Films. At Thalia SoHo, 15 Vandam Street. Running time: 103 minutes. This film is rated R.

Dr. Steven Phillip	Terence Stamp
Jane Chase	Elisabeth Shue
Link	Locke
David	Steven Pinner
Dennis	Richard Garnett
Tom	David O'Hara
Bailey	Kevin Lloyd
Taxi Driver	Joe Belcher

By WALTER GOODMAN

It's the season of the chimp. Last week brought us a screenful of the cute critters in "Project X," and starting today the Thalia SoHo is offering Richard Franklin's smart-monkey movie, "Link." Link may not be King Kong, but he's one champ chimp. As played by a primate named Locke (trained by Ray Berwick, who was responsible for the flights of Hitchcock's "Birds"), Link is an ape-of-all-work in the isolated mansion of an anthropologist (Terence Stamp). Link's response to the appearance of a student assistant (Elisabeth Shue) is as macho as the next fellow's. Not only is Miss Shue more resourceful than Fay Wray in "King Kong," she is a lot more robust; one glimpse of her as she steps into the bath is enough to give Link ideas about a meaningful relationship.

The clever screenplay by Everett De Roche keeps us uncertain for the first half of the movie: Which are the menaced characters and which the menacers? What about that unpleasant type who arrives to take away Link and gives Miss Shue an appraising look? What about those ferocious wild dogs out there on the heath? And is the anthropologist slightly absent-minded, or slightly sadistic? It isn't very nice of him to call the 45-year-old Link "a broken-down circus act" in the old guy's hearing, and can Miss Shue be correct about the intelligence tests he gives his apes being "culturally biased?"

Mr. Stamp turns in a shrewdly ambiguous performance; he could be a dedicated scientist or a mad one, or both. Does Miss Shue need protection from him or from the muscular Link, who can upend a truck if upset, or wrench an unfriendly arm from its socket? We can see she is making a mistake when she cuddles Imp, the baby chimp, causing Link to go ape. And she surely is riskily remiss in disregarding the rules laid down by the anthropologist (where *can* he have disappeared to?) for maintaining dominance over the resident beasts.

•

The script may be taken as a wry comment on romantics who attribute superior qualities to all animals except the human sort. In the second half, when "Link" settles into an old-fashioned maiden-monster movie, Mr. Franklin accelerates the action, turning up the tension degree by devious degree. Before you know it, everybody is missing but Link. Mike Malloy's camera abets by offering, at appropriate moments, an ape's-eye view of the world.

Link, or Locke, lights up his scenes, as he joins the anthropologist in lighting up a Havana, cooks the telephone in the microwave oven, raises his arms in triumph over his mastery of fire and carries a torch for the luscious Miss Shue with a smoldering desire and threat that are recognizably human.

1987 Ap 24, C10:4

FOREVER, LULU, written, produced and directed by Amos Kollek; director of photography, Lisa Rinzler; edited by Jay Freund; production manager, Sarah Green; released by Tri-Star Pictures. At Coronet, 59th Street at Third Avenue. Running time: 86 minutes. This film is rated R.

Elaine	Hanna Schygulla
Lulu	Deborah Harry
Buck	Alec Baldwin
Diana	Annie Golden
Robert	Paul Gleason
Herself	Dr. Ruth Westheimer
Alphonse	Raymond Serra
Pepe	George Kyle
Archie	Harold Guskin
Larry	Amos Kollek
Harvey	Charles Ludlam

By VINCENT CANBY

Things are tough all over. The otherwise great Hanna Schygulla, last seen here in Andrzej Wajda's magnificent "Love in Germany," now turns up as the front woman for a dim little comedy called "Forever, Lulu," which opens today at the Coronet.

The film was written, produced and directed by Amos Kollek, who earlier made "Goodbye, New York," but whose chief claim to fame is still the fact that he's the son of Teddy Kollek, the Mayor of Jerusalem. Mr. Kollek seems to be under the impression that he's making a raffishly eccentric, Manhattan comedy in the Susan Seidelman manner. For Ms. Seidelman, whose current film ("Making Mr. Right") is only her third, this must signal her arrival in the big time. For Mr. Kollek, this may signal his departure.

"Forever, Lulu" has the disheveled manner of a movie made by people living out of suitcases in a bus station. Everything's messy and nothing quite fits. Mr. Kollek's screenplay, stuffed with secondhand satire, is about Elaine Hines (Miss Schygulla), a youngish German woman who lives in poverty on the Lower East Side. By day she works as a secretary for a toilet-seat manufacturer and, at night, tries to write a great American novel about a youngish German woman who lives in poverty on the Lower East Side, etc.

Elaine's adventures suggest a forgetful child's impression of Ms. Seidelman's "Desperately Seeking Susan." They involve a mob murder, a couple of satchels full of cash, and a punkish-blond mystery woman who slips around the edges of the film as if she were Madonna, though she's actually played by Deborah Harry.

At one point, when Elaine has become rich, famous and celebrated as a best-selling author, she's interviewed on television by Dr. Ruth Westheimer, playing herself. Dr. Ruth should be more careful. In a movie as sloppily directed as this, people can get stepped on.

Alec Baldwin, who appears as a policeman smitten by Elaine, and Paul Gleason, as Elaine's married former lover, give decent performances, though the other members of the supporting cast are fairly dreadful. These include Mr. Kollek himself and Charles Ludlam.

Miss Schygulla is neither good nor bad. She's simply present and accounted for.

1987 Ap 24, C10:4

Bringing Out the Beast

MY DEMON LOVER, directed by Charles Loventhal; screenplay by Leslie Ray; director of photography, Jacques Haitkin; edited by Ronald Roose; music supervisor, Kevin Benson; production designer, Brent Swift; produced by Robert Shaye; released by New Line Cinema. At Embassy 2, Broadway at 47th Street; New York Twin, Second Avenue and 66th Street; 34th Street Showplace, between Second and Third Avenues. Running time: 86 minutes. This film is rated PG-13.

Kaz	Scott Valentine
Denny	Michelle Little
Fixer	Arnold Johnson
Charles	Robert Trebor
Captain Phil Janus	Allen Fudge
Sonia	Gina Gallego
Man in Healthfood Store	Calvert DeForest
Grady	Eva Charney
Chip	Dan Patrick Brady

"My Demon Lover" is about a young man who turns into a wild animal in the presence of the opposite sex, and it's a movie to bring out the beast in us all. Its hero and heroine, Kaz (Scott Valentine) and Denny (Michelle Little), are as painfully cute as their names, with Denny, when she first appears, wearing a bowler hat and jauntily toting a loaf of French bread. After they meet at a health-food restaurant, Kaz starts using Fruitburger as an affectionate nickname. Charles Loventhal's frenetic direction would barely suit a sitcom, let alone a film that also sets out to scare.

Mr. Loventhal and the screenwriter, Leslie Ray, use the man-turns-into-demon device to try out a wide, tired and thoroughly illogical array of makeup tricks, each one sillier than the last. It would seem as if a film this busy couldn't possibly bore its audience, but that's not the case.

The best that can be said for "My Demon Lover," which opens today at the Embassy 2 and other theaters, is that the film makers have worked overtime shuffling characters, locations and wrinkled latex masks with horns. Mr. Valentine, who appears in the masks, plays a supposedly charming vagrant who has been mysteriously cursed and appears to borrow almost all of his screechy, importunate mannerisms from the comedian Bobcat Goldthwait, who handles them a lot better. At other times Mr. Valentine merely widens his eyes and pretends, none too convincingly, to be adorable.

Miss Little is in a constant tizzy, and she never calms down. Neither she nor anyone else pays heed to the larger implications of Kaz's condition or worries unduly when he turns into a large, motherly woman whose head is full of yellow goo. The settings range from Greenwich Village, where the spunky Denny has her cluttered career-girl apartment, to Central Park, where the action moves to a huge, ominous hilltop castle. By the time the castle appears, it seems no less irritating or misplaced than anything else.

•

"My Demon Lover" is rated PG-13 ("Special Parental Guidance Suggested for Those Younger Than 13"). It contains some sexual suggestiveness. JANET MASLIN

1987 Ap 24, C14:1

THE BROTHERS QUAY: LEOS JANACEK: INTIMATE EXCURSIONS, 30 minutes; **THE CABINET OF JAN SVANKMAJER,** 13 minutes; **THE EPIC OF GILGAMESH,** 11 minutes; **STREET OF CROCODILES,** 20 minutes, based on the writings of Bruno

Schulz; music by Leszek Jankowski. At Film Forum 1, 57 Watts Street. This film has no rating.

By VINCENT CANBY

"THE BROTHERS QUAY" is the umbrella title for the four animated Surrealist films (in which miniature objects are photographed in stop-motion) that make up the program opening today at the Film Forum 1. The Brothers Quay are, in fact, the American-born, London-based film makers, Timothy and Stephen (identical twins). The Quays, who started out as graphics designers, are now specialists in clever cinematic nightmares inspired by the fears, frights and longings of others.

The individual films are "Street of Crocodiles" (1986), based on material by Bruno Schulz, a Polish Surrealist writer shot in the street by a Gestapo officer in 1942; "Leos Janicek: Intimate Excursions" (1983), which attempts to find visual references in the correspondence of Leos Janacek, the Czechoslovak composer; "The Cabinet of Jan Svankmajer" (1984), a tribute to the Czechoslovak film animator, and "The Epic of Gilgamesh" (1985), inspired by the Babylonian myth.

Surrealist films aren't meant to be interpreted in the systematic manner of a foreign language. One reads into them what one will, and, in this case, if one has any knowledge of the source material, what one can. The Quay films have the initial impact of monstrous, extremely personal visions of disorder, set in a pocket-sized universe where effects have little to do with causes.

On occasion the images are beautiful. They're always strikingly vivid. Hell looks like a 19th-century steel mill as imagined by Rube Goldberg. Pins can dance. Screws unscrew themselves to screw themselves into a host-substance at a different location. Moths and grasshoppers are the size of 747 jumbo jets. An opera diva has a wire body and the head of a pigeon. The mostly monochromatic backgrounds have the delicacy of old etchings.

No matter what the source material of the particular film, the images don't vary much in style — or in the associations they evoke — from one film to the next. Thus each film might be more effective if seen separately, and in contrast to something more conventional in manner and content. Seen in a group, as these are being presented by the Film Forum, they blur to the point where they begin to look like one long roll of bizarre, animated wallpaper.

1987 Ap 29, C19:4

Maverick Purist

ROSA LUXEMBURG, written and directed by Margarethe von Trotta; in German and Polish with English subtitles; edited by Dagmar Hirtz; music by Nicholas Economou; produced by Eberhard Junkersdorf; art direction, Bernd Lepel and Karel Vacek; released by New Yorker Films. At Lincoln Plaza 3, Broadway and 63d Street. Running time: 122 minutes. This film has no rating.

Rosa Luxemburg	Barbara Sukowa
Leo Jogiches	Daniel Olbrychski
Karl Liebknecht	Otto Sander
Luise Kautsky	Adelheid Arndt
Clara Zetkin	Doris Schade
Kostia Zetkin	Hannes Jaenicke
August Bebel	Jan-Paul Biczycki
Mathilde Jacob	Karin Baal
Paul Levi	Winfried Glatzeder

Barbara Sukowa in the title role of "Rosa Luxemburg"

By VINCENT CANBY

WHEN she was murdered in Berlin on the night of Jan. 15, 1919, Rosa Luxemburg — flippantly referred to as Red Rosa by both friends and enemies — had been one of the leading figures of the European left for over 20 years. She was 49. Two weeks earlier, the woman who preached unity in the ranks (though she'd angrily broken away from the German Social Democrats five years before), joined with the members of her splinter group, the Spartacists, to found the German Communist Party.

Her death was probably as much of a relief to Lenin and the Bolsheviks in Moscow, whom she relentlessly criticized for their autocratic programs, as it was to her former comrades in the Social Democratic Party, who authorized the purge of the ultraleft Spartacists and orchestrated the cover-up of her murder.

Rosa Luxemburg is one of the most fascinating figures in modern European political history, and today one of the least known, at least in the United States. In both East and West Germany her name is usually invoked in ways that carefully omit those aspects of the Luxemburg creed that don't fit the political fashions of the moment.

She was a purist. She clung to Marx's teachings (as she perceived them) when Lenin, in Russia, and Bernstein, in Germany, were rewriting the master to fit their own particular needs. She believed in the dictatorship of the proletariat but said that no cause could justify the taking of one innocent life.

There's no way Margarethe von Trotta's seriously conceived new film, "Rosa Luxemburg," which opens today at the Lincoln Plaza 3, can set the record straight on this complex woman. No film could.

Even Elzbieta Ettinger, the author of a new biography ("Rosa Luxemburg," published by Beacon Press), admits the impossibility of telling the *entire* story. "There is no such thing as 'definitive biography,'" Miss Ettinger writes in her preface. "A biography is always a selection and therefore a biographer is always 'biased.'"

Miss von Trotta's film, with a fine, soberly intelligent performance by Barbara Sukowa (the seductive star of Rainer Werner Fassbinder's "Lola"), is a first-rate introduction to an extremely complicated personality. It's necessarily simplified, as well as biased on behalf of those aspects of Luxemburg that will speak most clearly to today's audiences.

The movie concentrates on her abhorrence of violence, though her own Spartacists were not exactly nonviolent. It dramatizes her pacifism and her break with the German Social Democrats when, at the start of the war, they embraced the Kaiser's militarism, thus abandoning the concept of the international brotherhood of the proletariat. (In 1915 she suggested a new ending for "The Communist Manifesto": "Workers of all countries unite in peacetime, but in war — slit one another's throats!")

Miss von Trotta and Miss Sukowa try to emphasize Luxemburg's womanliness, though her lovers, in the film as in her life, never are a match for her. Leo Jogiches, her first and greatest love (a fiery revolutionary who answered her passionate letters with political tracts), is played by the excellent Polish actor Daniel Olbrychski as a handsome, dimly seen weakling. The other men are ciphers.

The film is, surprisingly, most effective when Luxemburg is alone, either in one of her many prison cells, with her thoughts being heard on the soundtrack, or speaking on the political platform. The Luxemburg words are still rousing, whether she is describing her idea of "spontaneous revolution" (as opposed to revolution imposed on the masses by the intelligentsia) or heaping sarcasm on revisionist members of the Social Democratic Party.

Miss Sukowa, whose pronounced jaw here seems to be made of steel (though the rest of her is desperately frail), delivers the speeches with such conviction that Luxemburg's apparent failure at the end becomes genuinely moving.

Otherwise, however, this Luxemburg appears to exist in a community of strangers. Miss von Trotta simply hasn't the means or the time to characterize the people around her. The film's fractured chronology doesn't help. Missing, too, is a sense of Luxemburg's many contradictions, which, as much as her love life and her longing for conventional domesticity, make her such an alluring subject for the biographer.

•

Though she was a spectacular demonstration of the liberated woman, she had little interest in organized feminism. She preferred to devote herself to "larger" issues. She was a Polish-born Jew who, as a child, had survived a pogrom and, throughout her life, suffered other forms of anti-Semitism. Yet she saw the Jewish cause as only another expression of the dreaded nationalism that divided the working classes and kept them in bondage. In one way or another, at one point and another, she succeeded in alienating just about everybody.

The film is rich with period detail, though Miss von Trotta never allows this to get in the way. The film has a clean, uncluttered look. In spite of the narrative ellipses and the simplification of issues, there's never any doubt that "Rosa Luxemburg" is about a most remarkable woman.

1987 My 1, C10:5

Like a Man Asleep

THE ELEMENT OF CRIME, directed by Lars von Trier; screenplay by Mr. von Trier and Niels Vorsel; photography by Tom Elling; edited by Thomas Gislason; music by Bo Holten; production, Per Holst Filmproduktion in cooperation with the Danish Film Institute; a Reel Movies International/Metro Cinema release. At Metro 2, 99th Street and Broadway. Running time: 104 minutes. This film has no rating.
Fisher ....Michael Elphick
Osbourne ....Esmond Knight
Kramer ....Jerold Wells
Kim ....Me Me Lei
Grandfather ....Preben Lerdorff Rye
Housekeeper .... Astrid Henning-Jensen
Judge ....Ghota Andersen

"THE ELEMENT OF CRIME," opening today at the Metro 2, is a film noir that's murky without being terribly mysterious.

The English-language Danish film is set in a Europe where the sun never shines at some near-future time when the Continent has become a giant wasteland of photogenic junkyards, trash heaps and mud puddles. Fisher (Michael Elphick), a retired police inspector, is called back from Cairo to solve a series of murders of young girls.

In his pursuit of truth, he seeks the help of his old mentor, Osbourne (Es-

mond Knight), who once wrote a book titled "The Element of Crime." This supposedly seminal study of antisocial behavior puts forth the idea that, to track down a criminal, one must assume the criminal's point of view. Like his mentor before him, Fisher assumes the criminal's point of view only too well.

•

"The Element of Crime" is the first feature to be directed by Lars von Trier, who has clearly looked at many other people's films, including Orson Welles's "Touch of Evil" and Sir Carol Reed's "Third Man," though without learning much about dialogue or narrative.

Fisher wanders through the movie's watery, surrealistic landscapes like a man asleep, which he is (he's telling his story under hypnosis), painstakingly uncovering clues the size of billboards. As he approaches the awful truth, his soundtrack narration seriously deteriorates. "I couldn't stay in Halberstadt," he says toward the end. "It's always 3 o'clock in the morning. Do you know what I mean?"

We do. We do.

The film's only claim for attention is the unusual camerawork by Tom Elling, who's photographed it in what initially appears to be a golden sepia. However, every now and then isolated objects will register in bold primary colors against the monochromatic backgrounds. The effect is interesting without being especially pertinent. *VINCENT CANBY*

1987 My 1, C11:1

Growing Pains

MY LIFE AS A DOG, directed by Lasse Hallstrom; screenplay (Swedish with English subtitles) by Mr. Hallstrom, Reidar Jonsson, Brasse Brannstrom and Per Berglund, based on a novel by Mr. Jonsson; cinematographer, Jorgen Persson; edited by Christer Furubrand and Susanne Linnman; music by Bjorn Isfalt; produced by Waldemar Bergendahl; a Svensk Filmindustri Picture. At Lincoln Plaza 2, Broadway and 63d Street. Running time; 101 minutes. This film has no rating.
Ingemar ....Anton Glanzelius
Uncle Gunnar ....Tomas von Bromssen
Mother ....Anki Liden
Saga ....Melinda Kinnaman
Aunt Ulla ....Kicki Rundgren
Berit ....Ing-Marie Carlsson

"My Life as a Dog" was shown as part of this year's New Directors/ New Films series. Following are excerpts from Vincent Canby's review, which appeared in The New York Times March 24. The film opens today at Lincoln Plaza 2, Broadway at 63d Street.

WHEN left to his own devices, Ingemar Johansson is a most winning adolescent — skeptical, introspective, curious, trying earnestly to bring order out of nature's chaos. As played by 11-year-old Anton Glanzelius in Lasse Hallstrom's 1985 Swedish film "My Life as a Dog," Ingemar even looks unfinished. His forehead's too high for the rest of his face, and his eyes too small. Physically as well as emotionally, he's still in transit.

The trouble with "My Life as a Dog" is that too often it imposes an alien sensibility upon the boy, requiring that he behave in a way that adults can too easily identify as charming. "My Life as a Dog" is a movie with a split point of view.

Sometimes (especially in its funnier moments) it recalls the gravity with which François Truffaut remembered childhood. At other times, however, it suggests a 1980's variation on the prettified, idealized, sentimental view of kids favored by Hollywood producers.

As adapted by Mr. Hallstrom, Reidar Jonsson and two other collaborators from a novel by Mr. Jonsson, the film covers a crucial year in Ingemar's life, when, in addition to the storms of puberty, he must face the fact that his mother is dying of tuberculosis.

As much as he loves his mother (and his daydreams are full of poetic visions of her, accompanied by the sound of her uninhibited laughter), he seems always to be failing her. When Ingemar is taken to the hospital to see her for what may be the last time, all he can say is that he's planning to buy her a toaster for Christmas.

In these moments, "My Life as a Dog" is funny and true and moving,

as it also is when, on the soundtrack, he confides something of his philosophy for surviving from one day to the next: "You have to compare all the time — to get a distance on things." What's the good of being the first dog in space, he asks, if, like Russia's Laika, you wind up starving to death? He ponders the meaning of a bus-train accident that leaves 6 people killed and 14 injured. He's fascinated by statistics.

The character possesses an honesty and rigor that the rest of the film would seem to deny. Too many of the things that happen to Ingemar are intended to be "cute." Inevitably, these sequences are seen not through the boy's eyes but through those of the film makers.

Mr. Glanzelius gives a firm and wise performance as the determined, mostly unsmiling Ingemar, whose namesake's unexpected 1959 heavyweight championship victory over Floyd Patterson brings the film to its conclusion.

1987 My 1, C16:1

FILM VIEW/Janet Maslin

Blake Edwards: Laughs Amid The Brickbats

THE TOMATOES ARE AGAIN flying, as they always do with the advent of a new Blake Edwards film. For a director who specializes in light farce, Mr. Edwards certainly can generate a lot of ill humor. "Ever been steered by a critic to a movie you ended up actively despising?" asks Amram Whiteman of New York City, one of numerous annoyed readers. "Enjoy it I didn't. . .a car crashes into a store twice or even three times (I don't remember which). Funny? I don't think so. A waiter is tossed in a swimming pool. Funny? Not on your life. Pocket ripping also leaves me quite cold."

Mr. Whiteman is hardly alone in responding to "Blind Date" this way. One fellow critic maintains that the lack of close-ups accounts for what he takes to be the film's failed humor, while the clerk at my local video store has been warning customers away from "Blind Date" months before it even comes out on tape. "The actors are from television, and the writing is the worst ever," he volunteered the other day. One of the film's few champions is a 5-year-old boy, the son of a colleague, who particularly loved the swimming pool and car crash scenes. He also liked one in which Bruce Willis, as a rude party guest, catapults an olive into a fellow celebrant's cleavage. Now why, among viewers 5 and over, does Mr. Edwards always manage to raise so many hackles, even with a film as relatively benign as this?

With a career that spans 30 years and is surely one of the most checkered in Hollywood history, Mr. Edwards has yet to establish anything like a loyal following. And for good reason: no Edwards film, however entertaining, has ever failed to make its audience wince here and there, with the wrong actor, the wrong song, the too-garish setting or the too-dumb gag. Nor is his style even distinctive enough to win him admirers. "Many people confuse Edwards's films with the works of other directors, such as George Roy Hill," note Peter Lehman and William Luhr, authors of a critical study of the Edwards oeuvre. "Others associate him with several Julie Andrews musicals with which he had nothing to do, although late in his career he did, in fact, marry that actress."

■

Mr. Edwards is on his third wind now, after his early hits ("Operation Petticoat," "Breakfast at Tiffany's," "Experiment in Terror" and "Days of Wine and Roses"), and his mid-60's Pink Panther period (starting with "The Pink Panther" in 1964, which Messrs. Lehman and Luhr feel "began a new, mature phase in his career"). After a string of fabulous disasters ("The Party," "Darling Lili") and an entire decade spent in eclipse, Mr. Edwards has lately bounded back with a vengeance: "10," "S.O.B.," "Victor/Victoria," "Micki and Maude" and now "Blind Date" mark his remarkable resurgence as a comedy director, while the more controversial "That's Life!" sounded a newly reflective note. Of his recent films, only "A Fine Mess" last year is, by anyone's standards, irredeemable.

So the 1980's have been good to Mr. Edwards. But his is not a style for this decade, and that's part of the problem. There's a dated quality to his films, even when they touch on reasonably daring subjects (like transvestism in "Victor/Victoria," bigamy in "Micki and Maude"). And when the story is more ordinary, as it is in "Blind Date," things can seem even creakier. "Blind Date" is about a financial analyst who must bring just the right woman to impress his colleagues at a business dinner; he finds a date who is beautiful, nervous, shy and not to be trusted in the presence of alcohol. She proceeds to wreck his career and, after that, his life, as the film becomes an ever-escalating comedy of errors.

This is familiar Edwards territory, and one of the film's satisfactions, aside from its selection of well-staged pratfalls, is a certain knowledge of what lies in store. Props will fly apart and bean innocent bystanders; food will fly; strangers will tiptoe through one another's boudoirs, as they have in half the films Mr. Edwards has made. If this isn't the most innovative type of comedy under the sun, it's one of the most reliable. And the things that hurt "Blind Date" — the blandness of Bruce Willis in the leading role (especially compared with Kim Basinger, who emerges as a fine physical comedienne), the leisurely pace, the element of repetition — do little to diminish the sheer escapism, the reassuring silliness, that this kind of humor provides.

There are waves of fashion in comic film making as there are in anything else, and right now this brand of humor could not be more outmoded. Mr. Edwards has often tried to examine sexual stereotypes and sexual malaise, for example. But even a comic misfire like Susan Seidelman's "Making Mr. Right," in which a single woman falls in love with an android, seems more current than a "Victor/Victoria," in which Julie Andrews's role of a woman playing a man playing a woman is more intriguing than credible. And lately, the emphasis has been on sitcom-inspired humor, with its safe and synthetic style (as in "Outrageous Fortune" and "The Secret of My Success"). Mr. Edwards's full-blown, perfectly predictable approach is as far removed from these formulaic hits as it is

Bruce Willis and Kim Basinger, left, misdirect the champagne in "Blind Date."

For many, this veteran director's comedies are subjects for scorn.

from "Raising Arizona," something closer to comedy's cutting edge.

■

But Mr. Edwards perseveres, however unevenly. He can still plant a cockroach in a restaurant ("Victor/Victoria") or a bigamist's two wives in the same waiting room ("Micki and Maude") with a singular flair. His "Blind Date," with its energetic sight gags and boudoir farce, is more of the same. Comedy like this, never really fashionable in the first place, can't even go out of style. □

1987 My 3, II:19:1

Pre-AIDS Abandon

THE ALLNIGHTER, directed and produced by Tamar Simon Hoffs; screenplay by M. L. Kessler and Miss Hoffs; director of photography, Joseph Urbanczyk; edited by Dan M. Rich; music by Charles Bernstein; production designer, Cynthia Sowder; released by Universal Pictures. At the Plaza, 42 East 58th Street and other theaters. Running time: 92 minutes. This film is rated PG-13.

Molly	Susanna Hoffs
Val	DeDee Pfeiffer
Gina	Joan Cusack
C.J.	John Terlesky
Killer	James Anthony Shanta
Mickey Leroi	Michael Ontkean
Sergeant MacLeish	Pam Grier
Connie Alvarez	Kaaren Lee
Mary Lou	Janelle Brady

By JANET MASLIN

WATCH enough exploitation films about sun-loving, fun-loving teens and you become accustomed to a certain level of benign idiocy. But even by that standard, "The Allnighter" is outstandingly dim. It concerns graduation eve at a California college, though none of the students seems clever enough to graduate from driving school. The principals are three bubble-headed women who room together, and the film could be accused of sexism if their male counterparts were not equally dumb.

"The Allnighter" stars Susanna Hoffs, who fortunately has another, much more successful career as lead singer with the Bangles, and the film's producer, director and co-writer is her mother, Tamar Simon Hoffs. At best, it's a family affair. Miss Hoffs plays Molly, who, amazingly enough, is the college valedictorian. On this particular evening, she has no time to worry about preparing her speech, being more concerned with how to tell C. J. (John Terlesky), who is a walking work of calendar art, that she likes him.

●

When the film's other characters want to communicate similar thoughts, they simply show up on one another's doorsteps carrying bottles of champagne and hop into bed with pre-AIDS abandon. But Molly, who unlike her two friends does *not* find herself mistaken for a prostitute and hauled off to jail later in the story, is more subtle than that. So it takes her and the film nearly two hours to get the point across.

One of Molly's roommates is Val (DeDee Pfeiffer, sister of Michelle), a dizzy blonde engaged to a supposedly terrible fiancé who seems not much worse than the other males in the film, though he is not blond. The other is Gina (Joan Cusack, sister of John), who looks and dresses like a kind of Girl George and is using her video camera to make a home movie about her friends. Mrs. Hoffs should not make jokes about film making. Also in the cast, wasting her time, is the gorgeous Pam Grier.

"The Allnighter" opened Friday at local theaters, among them the Criterion Center 5, which has a screen so small (about 5 by 7 feet) that it provides all the disadvantages of watching television and none of the comforts of home.

●

"The Allnighter" is rated PG-13 ("Special Parental Guidance Suggested for Those Younger Than 13"). It includes off-color language and a few sexual episodes.

1987 My 4, C16:1

Peter Ustinov in a scene from "Memed, My Hawk."

Feudal Turkey

MEMED MY HAWK, written and directed by Peter Ustinov, based on the novel by Yashar Kemal; director of photography, Freddie Francis; edited by Peter Honess; music by Manos Hadjidakis; produced by Fuad Kavur; released by Filmworld. At Guild 50th Street, at Rockefeller Plaza. Running time: 104 minutes. This film is rated PG-13.

Abdi Aga	Peter Ustinov
Ali Safa	Herbert Lom
Memed	Simon Dutton
Rejeb	Denis Quilley
Jabbar	Michael Elphick
Hatche	Leonie Mellinger
Lame Ali	Vladeck Sheybal
Kerimoglu	Michael Gough
Sergeant Asim	Walter Gotell

By CARYN JAMES

PETER USTINOV has a style like no other. Blustery, with eyes rolling and voice rumbling, his characters may have a political edge but they are conceived in the broad strokes of a vaudevillian. That farcical manner may be the one least suited to the story of a young man who rebels against the feudal lord of his Turkish village in 1923, yet the style pervades "Memed, My Hawk," written and directed by Mr. Ustinov and starring him.

He plays Abdi Aga, the owner of five villages, who pretends he can read and who rides in a car pulled by horses; his villagers, he complains, are "too ignorant to connect two wires" and start the motor. Memed, the idealistic hero, flees the village with his lover, Hatche, who had been chosen as the bride of Abdi Aga's repugnant nephew. Chased and forced into a shoot-out with the aga's men, Memed kills the nephew and joins the brigands in the nearby hills, while Hatche is imprisoned for the murder. Memed is determined to save Hatche and destroy Abdi Aga.

•

"Memed, My Hawk," based on the novel by Yashar Kemal, one of Turkey's most important writers, ought to embody its theme of political resistance in the characters' conflicts and actions. But the people on screen speak in aphorisms meant for the audience; they never reach one another. An old rebel tells Memed: "Allah is very busy. It is hard to get his attention." And a member of the aga's household says, "I hate Abdi Aga as only a servant can hate a master." They are not people, but walking, talking symbols.

Mr. Ustinov is so talented and professional that his film is always smoothly competent. The washed-out browns and grays of the rocky hills and caves reflect the villagers' constricted lives; he refuses to prettify or poeticize their landscape or their long history of servitude. (The film was shot in Yugoslavia because the Turkish Government refused permission to make it there.) There are some elegant, understated small roles. Vladeck Sheybal is a weasely looking rebel, and Michael Gough, the British character actor, a wise and slippery carpet merchant, though the better-known stars, Herbert Lom and the late Siobhan McKenna, have parts so slight they nearly disappear.

What's wrong with the film is what's missing from it — the texture of village life held in feudalism's dying grasp, the sparks of anger and love that would allow us to feel Memed's passion, the subtlety that would convince us of Abdi Aga's fear. "Memed, My Hawk," which opened Friday at the Guild, may be concerned with poverty and oppression, but it feels as stately and painless as a second-rate costume drama.

•

"Memed, My Hawk," is rated PG-13 ("Special Parental Guidance Suggested for Those Younger Than 13"). It includes some rear-view nudity.

1987 My 4, C17:1

Dead and Undead

CREEPSHOW 2, directed by Michael Gornick; screenplay by George A. Romero, based on stories by Stephen King; directors of photography, Dick Hart and Tom Hurwitz; edited by Peter Weatherly; music by Les Reed; produced by David Ball; released by New World Pictures. At Embassy 1, Broadway and 46th Street; U.A. East, First Avenue and 85th Street; Bay Cinema, Second Avenue at 32d Street. Running time: 92 minutes. This film is rated R.

Ray Spruce	George Kennedy
Martha Spruce	Dorothy Lamour
Annie Lansing	Lois Chiles
Rachel	Page Hannah
The Hitchhiker	Tom Wright
The Creep	Tom Savini

THE ghoulish campfire-tale premises of Stephen King's stories are often a lot more memorable than their particulars, but Mr. King almost always provides more follow-through than "Creepshow 2," a three-section omnibus film based on his writing. As directed by Michael Gornick, with a screenplay by George A. Romero, "Creepshow 2," which opened Friday at the Embassy 1 and other theaters, has three suitably grisly ideas that are only glancingly developed. The episodes are marginally interesting, but each is a little too long. And each could be fully explained in a one-sentence synopsis.

The first is about a cigar-store Indian that comes to life to avenge the murders of a kindly storekeeper and his wife, played by George Kennedy and Dorothy Lamour, at the hands of three hoodlums. After some initial nastiness, as the hoodlums rob the store and harass and kill the elderly couple, the horrific effects begin. A headdress-wearing, tomahawk-wielding silhouette is seen stalking the robbers individually. He winds up with a particularly apt souvenir of his adventures, and there are some nice special effects as the statue comes to life.

The second story concerns four teen-agers who steal off for an afternoon swim at a pond that, unbeknownst to them, is the home of a man-eating oil slick. The slick actually belches as it swallows the last of its good-looking young snacks.

Finally, Lois Chiles plays an adulterer who hits a hitchhiker with her Mercedes while hurrying home to her husband, only to discover that the hitchhiker will not die. Mr. King turns up briefly as a truck driver in this segment, which seems to intend some element of social commentary since the driver is well-heeled and white and the undead hitchhiker (Tom Wright) is a black man. In any case, they go up in a puff of smoke before the tale is over.

"Creepshow 2," which can't really compare with its predecessor, also contains some very poorly animated footage designed to connect the three stories. These animated scenes are aimed at a younger audience than the rest of the film seems to be.

JANET MASLIN

1987 My 4, C17:1

Mayhem in Midlife

MALONE, directed by Harley Cokliss; screenplay by Christopher Frank, from the novel "Shotgun" by William Wingate; director of photography by Gerald Hirschfeld; edited by Todd Ramsay; music by David Newman; production designer, Graeme Murray; produced by Leo L. Fuchs; released by Orion Pictures Corporation. At Criterion Center, Broadway at 45th Street; Eastside Cinema, Third Ave. at 55th Street; Orpheum, Third Ave. and 86th St.; 23d St. West, between Eighth and Ninth Avenues. Running time: 92 minutes. This film is rated R.

Malone	Burt Reynolds
Delaney	Cliff Robertson
Hawkins	Kenneth McMillan
Jo Barlow	Cynthia Gibb
Paul Barlow	Scott Wilson
Jamie	Lauren Hutton
Harvey	Philip Anglim
Calvin Bollard	Tracey Walter

By WALTER GOODMAN

WHAT is it about a Burt Reynolds movie these days that gives you the feeling of having seen it before, once or a dozen times? Maybe it's the role into which Mr. Reynolds seems to have settled — a master of mayhem in midlife crisis. The big guy has grown weary of killing, but no matter where he goes, there are baddies who require it.

This time around, in "Malone," which is now occupying the Criterion Center and other theaters, Mr. Reynolds is a defector from the Central Intelligence Agency, looking for a peaceful spot out West, when he runs into a high-level conspiracy by a right-wing crazy to take over the country. Christopher Frank's screenplay, adapted from William Wingate's novel "Shotgun," is a variation on the homesteader-vs.-cattle-baron standard; the just-folks Barlows are being strong-armed by the powerful Delaney, who consorts with Senators and quotes Jefferson and, of all people, Henry James. Malone, a descendant of Shane, doesn't talk much.

•

Mr. Reynolds is slow to anger. It takes a full 20 minutes before a local bully makes the mistake of taunting him into showing what he can do. *Whack! Crack! Grunt! Groan!* After that, it's just a question of the ways devised for Malone to kill off one by one the regiment of skilled and well-armed operatives in Delaney's employ. Mr. Reynolds handles the assignment like a pro; you can hardly tell he's acting.

Douglas Curran

Burt Reynolds in "Malone."

Nobody could make "Malone" believable, but the director, Harley Cokliss, makes it watchable. He is fortunate in his cast. Cliff Robertson, as the obsessed Delaney, delivers his slogans in behalf of Patriotism with the same air of single-minded sincerity that he has brought to his commercials for A.T.&T. Kenneth McMillan is sheepishly bullying as a sold-out sheriff; Lauren Hutton is playful as Malone's playmate, who incidentally has the mission of killing him; Philip Anglim does an oily number as a Delaney henchman, and Scott Wilson and Cynthia Gibb are the down-home Barlows. Of particular note is the communications center operated by the plausible Mr. Robertson; he's learned a lot from those commercials.

1987 My 4, C17:4

Jock Calendar

CAMPUS MAN, directed by Ron Casden; screenplay by Matt Dorff, Alex Horvat and Geoffrey Baere; screen story by Mr. Dorff and Mr. Horvat; director of photography, Francis Kenny; edited by Steven Polivka; music by James Newton Howard; production designer, David Gropman; produced by Peggy Fowler and Jon Landau; released by Paramount Pictures. At U.A. Twin 1, Broadway and 49th Street. Running time: 94 minutes. This film is rated PG.

Todd Barrett	John Dye
Brett Wilson	Steve Lyon
Dayna Thomas	Kim Delaney
Molly Gibson	Kathleen Wilhoite
Cactus Jack	Miles O'Keeffe
Katherine Van Buren	Morgan Fairchild
Professor Jarman	John Welsh
Charles McCormick	Josef Rainer
Mr. Bowersox	Dick Alexander

THE look and sound of "Campus Man," which has found its way into the United Artists Twin and other theaters, mark it as a production done on the cheap, which is appropriate to this little anecdote about a business major at Arizona State who produces a jock calendar featuring his best friend, a champion diver, and so jeopardizes the friend's amateur standing. Also splashing around here are a tough moneylender and, yes, a couple of pretty girls. As the hustling entrepreneur, John Dye is indistinguishable from the other cutely coiffed young fellows who find their way into such movies. Steve Lyon, as the athlete, has plenty of opportunity to show off his biceps and pecs. Except for a few diving scenes, Ron Casden's direction offers no distractions. It took three people to patch together the made-for-music-video screenplay.

"Campus Man" is rated PG ("Parental Guidance Suggested"), owing to some rude language and a shower-room glimpse of male buttocks. WALTER GOODMAN

1987 My 4, C17:1

Sentimental Journey

HEARST METROTONE NEWSREEL SHOW, directed by Robert Rosen; original films produced by the Hearst Corporation, 1929-1940; distributed by the U.C.L.A Film and Television Archive. At Film Forum 1, 57 Watts Street. Running time: 100 minutes. This film has no rating.

By WALTER GOODMAN

ONE sets out on a journey through the 1930's via newsreels of the decade, with trepidation; what begins with chorus girls tap dancing on roller skates must end with the fall of France and the bombing of Britain.

In its giddy way, "Hearst Metrotone Newsreel Show," a 100-minute selection of the items that kept audiences entertained between the main feature and the B-feature in the days when moviegoing was an expedition, takes us down the slide from hokum to horror. The chorines would never stop tapping, but their simple rhythms would be overwhelmed by the discordant sounds of Depression, drought, strikes and wars around the world.

The newsreels now running at Film Forum 1 were donated to the Film and Television Archive of the University of California at Los Angeles in 1981 and have been compiled by Michael Friend of the American Film Institute. Moviegoers of a certain age will find nostalgia aplenty, as the deep-voiced narrators utter resonant clichés about baseball players (Gehrig and Ruth), gangsters (Capone and Dillinger) and royals (the Duke and Duchess of Windsor — "a love story of the ages"). How young they all look. Calvin Coolidge, we are informed, in scenes of his funeral, is "gone but not forgotten" and "will live in the hearts of his countrymen." The Senate investigations of big business don't, alas, seem dated, although the politicians bluster a little more than they tend to do in these cool-image days.

•

Sports, society and show biz were the staples of the newsreels, along with disasters (there's the Hinden-

burg going down in flames), animals (from baby monkeys to a chaotic bullfight) and Presidents. That's Herbert Hoover explaining to assembled Boy Scouts that "Together with his sister, the boy is the most precious thing in American life." The clips of Hoover and Roosevelt speak volumes about the change of spirit emanating from the White House after 1933.

The war photography, from Africa, China, Spain and finally Europe, is striking, reminding us of the daring work done by battlefield cameramen in the ferocious 40's. The narration is coy — no hint of who the aggressor is in Ethiopia, or whom the Spanish refugees are fleeing. By the end of the decade, however, the newsreels are frankly propagandistic, promoting military preparedness and aid to Britain ("Yes, Britain can take it!"), as well as treating Roosevelt with cult-of-personality adulation. It's particularly startling in light of the anti-Roosevelt and isolationist line of the Hearst newspapers for much of the period.

Among the show's incidental treats are glimpses of 93-year-old John D. Rockefeller assuring the Depression-ridden nation that "prosperity always returns and will again" and handing out a few coins; Primo Carnera, briefly the heavyweight champion, trying to act tough; Al Smith exchanging his derby for a 10-gallon hat, and the very young Robert Kennedy making what may have been his first public address.

1987 My 6, C18:1

Family-Man Killer

THE STEPFATHER, directed by Joseph Ruben; screenplay by Donald E. Westlake, story by Carolyn Lefcourt, Brian Garfield and Mr. Westlake; director of photography, John Lindley; edited by George Bowers; music by Patrick Moraz; production designer, James William Newport; produced by Jay Benson; released by New Century/Vista Film Company. At Gemini, Second Avenue at 64th Street. Running time: 90 minutes. This film is rated R.

Henry Morrison, Jerry Blake, Bill Hodgkins	Terry O'Quinn
Stephanie Maine	Jill Schoelen
Susan Blake	Shelley Hack
Dr. Bondurant	Charles Lanyer
Jim Ogilvie	Stephen Shellen
Al Brennan	Stephen E. Miller
Karen	Robyn Stevan
Paul Baker	Jeff Schultz
Art Teacher	Lindsay Bourne

JERRY BLAKE (Terry O'Quinn) is first seen in a bathroom, showering, shaving, changing his clothes and significantly altering his appearance. He has just killed his family. When he

is finished washing, Blake descends the stairway to the living room, walks past the bodies and strides confidently out into the street on his way out of town. Actually, Jerry Blake is not his name yet. He will become Jerry Blake in his next life, in the next pleasant small-town setting with the next family he plans to murder.

With that beginning, "The Stepfather," which opens today at the Gemini, most certainly gets your attention. In fact, the film's entire premise is an unusually rich and promising one. Imagine a man who, for whatever reason, is both enchanted and enraged by the notion of a happy family, a man whose warring impulses lead him to marry and remarry, to kill and kill again. In Jerry Blake's case, the fascination with idealized family life runs so deep that he spends a lot of his time building a birdhouse, the miniature replica of a picture-perfect suburban dwelling. "You all right, sweetheart?" Jerry asks his wife after belting her so hard he bloodies her mouth.

But with all its potential for horror, psychological acuity and even humor, "The Stepfather" has an ordinary side, too. As written by Donald E. Westlake (from a story by Mr. Westlake, Carolyn Lefcourt and Brian Garfield) and directed by Joseph Ruben (who also made the intriguing "Dreamscape"), "The Stepfather" is too often disappointingly thin. The film need not provide a full account of Blake's psychosis to be credible, but it does cry out for more insight than Mr. Ruben offers. Without that, the story becomes forced and insubstantial. It even loses much of its ability to scare.

•

Just after the opening sequence, Jerry Blake is seen one year later, firmly ensconced in the bosom of a whole new family. How did he get there? There is never much explanation of how he came so quickly to marry Susan (Shelley Hack) and become a doting stepdad to her teen-age daughter, Stephanie (Jill Schoelen), or of how these two have managed to forget the husband and father who died. There is simply the spectacle of Jerry going through his family-man motions: bringing home a new puppy, presiding edgily over holiday dinners, calling his stepdaughter Pumpkin. Of course, this is meant to seem empty, in view of what Jerry ultimately has in mind. But it winds up feeling even more shallow than Mr. Ruben may have intended it to.

In its attempts at black humor and attention to small-town propriety, "The Stepfather" is indebted to Hitchcock's "Psycho" and "Shadow of a Doubt"; its happy-family fixa-

tion recalls "The Shining" by Kubrick, as does one episode that finds Stephanie trapped inside a bathroom with a crazed, sweet-talking Blake outside the door. Otherwise, though, the film isn't nearly suggestive enough, and its separate episodes never merge into a coherent portrait of Blake. Without knowing why Blake is driven to behave as he does, or even how he handles the particulars, it's difficult to take him seriously. And if "The Stepfather" doesn't stand up as a psychological thriller, neither is it a full-fledged horror story since its scares are predictable and are saved for the last few minutes.

•

Still, there's a lot to admire in Mr. Ruben's ambition, if not always in his execution. "The Stepfather" aspires to an intricacy and irony not often found outside the work of Hitchcock and his most skilled imitators; it's as clever in its construction as it is unremarkable in execution. The actors are sometimes bland, but they seem well aware of what Mr. Ruben has in mind. And they do their best with difficult roles. For instance, how can Miss Hack convey trust in this peculiar, brand-new spouse without seeming an utter fool? It isn't easy, but she manages it somehow.

Mr. O'Quinn does a creditable job of switching gears between bizarre, obsessive pleasantries, Chamber of Commerce platitudes and the enraged muttering that precedes his violent outbursts. Miss Schoelen radiates suspicion, as well she might. As a psychiatrist, Charles Lanyer serves as a strange kind of doppelgänger for Blake, and Stephen Shellen is as appealing as a ghost from Blake's past, a man determined to stop him. Of course, he isn't easily stopped, nor is he easily forgotten. For all the film's drawbacks, Blake emerges as a classically polite and convention-minded monster, an all-American killer who, like Norman Bates's mother, wouldn't hurt a fly.

JANET MASLIN

1987 My 8, C9:1

A Snake Stars

STEELE JUSTICE, directed and written by Robert Boris; director of photography, John M. Stephens; edited by John O'Connor and Steve Rosenblum; music by Misha Segal; production designer, Richard N. McGuire; produced by John Strong; released by Atlantic Releasing Corporation. At U.A. Twin, Broadway and 49th Street; 23d Street West Triplex, near Eighth Avenue; Movie Center 5, 125th Street between Powell and Douglass Boulevard, and other theaters. Running time: 95 minutes. This film is rated R.

John Steele	Martin Kove
Tracy	Sela Ward
Bennett	Ronny Cox
Reese	Bernie Casey
Harry	Joseph Campanella
Gen. Bon Soong Kwan	Soon-Teck Oh
Cami	Jan Gan Boyd
Kelso	David Froman
Kay	Sarah Douglas

"STEELE JUSTICE" isn't designed as a comedy, but it does earn high marks for inadvertent humor. This is thanks in part to the writer and director, Robert Boris, whose "Oxford Blues" was no laughing matter but who this time has tried to meld "Rambo" with "Miami Vice," throwing in a touch of the Chippendale's calendar. The last is evoked by the presence of Martin Kove, the big, burly, smirking fellow in the title role.

Mr. Kove wears a Band-Aid across the bridge of his nose during much of

Eye on the World
Benito Mussolini is one of the historical figures seen in the "Hearst Metrotone Newsreel Show," a feature-length compilation of newsreels from 1929 through 1940.

the film, and it is by far the most expressive thing on his face. "Steele Justice," which opens today at the U.A. Twin and other theaters, does feature a nice performance from the Sinaloan milk snake in the cast, but there is substantially worse work from everyone else.

•

The action begins in Vietnam, where Mr. Kove, as John Steele, appears as a small boy's idea of a living, breathing Rambo doll, wearing elaborate war paint and flexing his muscles at the enemy. Years later, the same evil Vietnamese officer who taunted Steele in the opening sequence has turned up as a drug kingpin in Los Angeles, and Steele is still without a shirt. Indeed, one episode depicting a vicious attack on Steele's best friend and his family positions Steele in the bathtub as the shootings occur, so that he can race into the street as decoratively as possible, wearing only his blue jeans.

Steele's friend is then simultaneously referred to as "murdered" and "fighting for his life in the hospital." In any case, he leaves behind a sweet young daughter who wears pigtails but looks at least 15 years older than she is supposed to be. At one point, this daughter sits down at the piano and appears to play Beethoven without moving her hands.

Other comic highlights include the shooting of a dance team engaged in making a horrible rock video and Steele's attempts to reverse the effects of a poison dart. He rips off his shirt, sucks the wound, attacks it with a knife, then cauterizes it with a hot frying pan, thus making both movie and medical history.

JANET MASLIN
1987 My 8, C12:4

Emptiness and Death

RIVER'S EDGE, directed by Tim Hunter; written by Neal Jimenez; director of photography, Frederick Elmes; edited by Howard Smith and Sonya Sones; music by Jurgen Knieper; production designer, John Muto; produced by Sarah Pillsbury and Midge Sanford; released by Island Pictures. At Baronet, 59th Street and Third Avenue. Running time: 99 minutes. This film is rated R.

Layne	Crispin Glover
Matt	Keanu Reeves
Clarissa	Ione Skye Leitch
Samson	Daniel Roebuck
Feck	Dennis Hopper
Tim	Joshua Miller
Maggie	Roxana Zal
Tony	Josh Richman
Mike	Phil Brock
Jamie	Danyi Deats

By JANET MASLIN

THE generation gap, as revealed in Tim Hunter's bitter and disturbing new film, "River's Edge," is the thing that divides Samson (Daniel Roebuck) and Feck (Dennis Hopper). Long ago, Feck murdered his girlfriend — but he lived to regret it, and the killing has made him a crazy, desperate loner, a hermit who keeps an inflatable party doll as his only companion. Samson is younger, calmer, and very different. As the film begins, Samson has just strangled a young woman who said something unpleasant about his mother. He doesn't regret it; in fact, he doesn't feel a thing.

"River's Edge," which opens today at the Baronet, is about the anomie of Samson and his friends in the face of this inexplicable violence. Their reaction is so casual that it comes as a

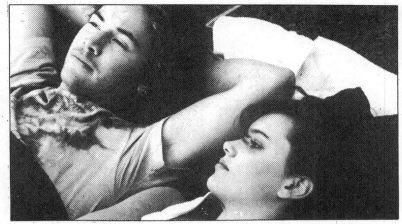

Growing Up
Keanu Reeves and Ione Skye share a quiet moment in "River's Edge," Tim Hunter's drama about reaction among a group of teen-agers to the murder of a schoolgirl by one of their friends.

shock. After an opening scene depicting a tough-looking boy named Tim throwing his sister's favorite doll into a river, and another in which Samson sits beside the body of a young woman named Jamie, it develops that 12-year-old Tim (Joshua Miller) has seen Samson commit the crime. It also develops that for Tim, Samson's act isn't much different from his own. Tim accosts Samson, tells him what he knows, and then asks for some drugs. It's as simple as that.

Later on, when Samson (who is nicknamed John) tells his school friends what he's done, they are only slightly more concerned. They think he is joking. So he shows them Jamie's body, over which Mr. Hunter's camera lingers time and again during the film, as if to try to summon something from the audience that the characters themselves do not feel. The sight of the body, and the suggestion that their classmate Jamie has been raped as well as strangled, is only marginally more upsetting for Jamie's girlfriends than it is for the boys.

Though the girls are a little more worried about the etiquette of the situation — most specifically, about whether to tell the police — the whole group of Jamie and Samson's peers remains surprisingly calm. "River's Edge" is about their sincere, bewildered efforts to grasp the difference between killing a doll and killing a person, and about the audience's own efforts to understand how any amount of drug taking and parental indifference can induce this kind of stupor.

As he demonstrated in "Tex," Mr. Hunter has an extraordinarily clear understanding of teen-age characters, especially those who must find their own paths without much parental supervision. But the S. E. Hinton story for that film is a great deal more innocent than this one, and a lot more easily understood. While Mr. Hunter retains his ear for adolescent dialogue (the screenplay is by Neal Jiminez) and his eye for the aimless, restless behavior of these characters, neither he nor we can easily make the necessary leap to understand their casualness about Samson's crime. That Mr. Hunter is brave enough to avoid easy moralizing and easy explanations finally makes his film harder to fathom.

Much of "River's Edge" — which is based on several actual incidents, especially one in Northern California — is acted with utter conviction by a fine and largely unknown young cast. But the uncertain conceptions of a few key characters are damaging, especially that of Layne, who in his confusion becomes Samson's accom-

plice. Layne thinks himself more daring than his classmates, and without question he is more stoned. That leads him to conclude that loyalty to Samson is the only practical option. Samson and Jamie were both friends, he reasons, but it is Samson who's still alive and needs support. This is the film's key moral position, but it is explicated cartoonishly by Crispin Glover, who makes Layne a larger-than-life caricature and creates a noisy, comic impersonation instead of a lifelike character. Nor does it help that one of the film's other moral polarities comes from a 60's-minded, hipper-than-thou schoolteacher who declares, "We took to the streets and made a difference!" To his bored, jaded 80's high-school students, this kind of self-righteousness makes no sense at all.

Most of the performances are as natural and credible as the ones in "Tex," with Mr. Roebuck a sad and helpless figure as Samson, and Keanu Reeves affecting and sympathetic as Tim's older brother; a different kind of generation gap already exists between these two, and the threat of fratricide between them leads to the film's most frightening confrontation. The ravishing Ione Skye Leitch (daughter of the singer Donovan) seems convincingly troubled as the character who must wonder why she feels more watching television tragedies than she does about her dead friend. And Mr. Hopper, whose scenes with the party doll ought to be thoroughly ridiculous, once again makes himself a very powerful presence. For better or worse, Mr. Hopper is back with a vengeance.

Though its Midwestern locale and lower socioeconomic stratum give it a different setting, "River's Edge" shares something with Bret Easton Ellis's "Less Than Zero," a novel that is also full of directionless, drug-taking teen-age characters who are without moral moorings and left entirely to their own devices. This is as chilling to witness as it is difficult to dramatize, if only because at their centers these lives are already so empty.

1987 My 8, C28:4

Infertile Field

GARDENS OF STONE, directed by Francis Coppola; screenplay by Ronald Bass, based on the novel by Nicholas Proffitt; director of photography, Jordan Cronenweth; edited by Barry Malkin; music by Carmine Coppola; producion designer, Dean Tavoularis; produced by Michael I. Levy and Mr. Coppola; released by Tri Star Pictures. At Paramount, 61st Street and Broadway; Tower East, Third Avenue and 71st Street; Movieland Eighth Street Triplex, at University Place. Running time: 112 minutes. This film is rated R.

Clell Hazard	James Caan
Samantha Davis	Anjelica Huston
Goody Nelson	James Earl Jones
Jackie Willow	D. B. Sweeney
Homer Thomas	Dean Stockwell
Rachel Feld	Mary Stuart Masterson
Slasher Williams	Dick Anthony Williams
Betty Rae	Lonette McKee
Lieutenant Webber	Sam Bottoms
Pete Deveber	Elias Koteas
Colonel Feld	Peter Masterson
Mrs. Feld	Carlin Glynn

By VINCENT CANBY

IN the initial sequence of "Gardens of Stone," Francis Coppola's screen version of Nicholas Proffitt's novel, the camera observes the procedures of a military funeral at Arlington National Cemetery with dispassionate, reportorial efficiency.

Against rolling green lawns covered by long, neat rows of white headstones and, here and there, clumps of fine old trees heavy with foliage, a funeral cortege moves toward a new grave site — the honor guard, the caisson bearing the flag-draped coffin, the riderless horse, followed by mourners.

The day is cloudless and still. There is comfort in this natural beauty and in the discipline of the rituals, even in the commands barked to the seemingly faceless members of the honor guard. As if in a reverie, these isolated sounds give way to those of helicopter rotors chopping the air, of voices heard on walkie-talkies, of the desperation and chaos of battle.

Then, as arbitrarily, the sounds of ceremony reassert themselves. A bagpiper plays. Words of consolation are spoken. Before the coffin is lowered into the grave, the flag is removed, folded and presented to the widow, "at the request of the President."

•

In these moments in which the peace of the present is layered with desolation from the past, and in a few other sequences that come later, there is an emotional resonance in "Gardens of Stone" that is otherwise remarkably absent. Though a seriously conceived film about the American experience in Vietnam, "Gardens of Stone" has somehow wound up having the consistency and the kick of melted vanilla ice cream.

The movie, set in 1968 and 1969, attempts to examine the meaning of the Vietnam War entirely through the eyes of the members of the "Old Guard," the stateside-based elite Army unit whose duties include Presidential escorts and military funerals at Arlington. The problem is that these men, though decent, aren't very interesting as described by the film. Their world is small and arid.

James Caan, second from left, in Francis Coppola's new "Gardens of Stone"

There's no sense of contrast between what they do in what they call "the garden," and the hopeless war being fought overseas. When they talk, it's mostly in the sentimental-obscene language of service-comedy palship.

Chief among these men in Sgt. Clell Hazard (James Caan), a decorated veteran of World War II, Korea and two Vietnam tours, a man with 27 years of service who now finds himself at war with the Army he thinks of as his family.

Hazard opposes the war, not on political grounds — he has no sympathy with the peaceniks and marches on the Pentagon — but because it's a war "without a front, with nothing to win and no way to win it." The ultimate loser, he feels, must be the Army itself.

At the start of "Gardens of Stone," Hazard has been living in a kind of furious stasis. Abandoned some years before by his wife and son, he attends to his ceremonial job during the day and, in his off hours, depends on the company of Sgt. Maj. Goody Nelson (James Earl Jones).

•

Things change with the arrival of Jackie Willow (D. B. Sweeney), a recruit who happens to be the son of a man with whom Hazard served in World War II and Korea. In Willow, Hazard sees not only the son his wife has taken from him, but also the exemplification of the young, gung-ho soldier the Army is systematically destroying in a cause that is as lost as it's unpopular. Willow longs to see action and, at last, he does.

Clell is the film's only fully realized character and Mr. Caan, in his first movie in five years, plays him with humor and intensity, like the veteran he now is. There's exhaustion, disappointment and confusion written into his still-strong features.

However, the performance is largely wasted in "Gardens of Stone," about which it would be praise to say that it has too many things on its mind. In fact, it's simply unfocused and clumsily composed. There's occasional poignancy but, too often, what are supposed to be dramatic confrontations are just exchanges of plot information.

In adapting the Proffitt novel, Ronald Bass hasn't written a screenplay but a collection of synopses for three or four films. In addition to the relationship between Clell and Jackie Willow, the film is also about Clell's affair with an antiwar newspaper reporter (Anjelica Huston), and Jackie's romance with the daughter (Mary Stuart Masterson) of a colonel who doesn't approve of her alliance with an enlisted man.

It's a mystery why Mr. Coppola, one of the most efficient writers in Hollywood, came to direct such a screenplay, one that's alternately lame and utterly confusing. Possibly he tried to improve things, but the movie builds to no point. It unravels. There's not a shred of feeling between Clell and young Jackie Willow, a character to which Mr. Sweeney brings no distinctive personality. He's a foolish zero. Largely because of their screen presences, there are found moments of emotion in some of the Caan-Huston encounters, which, in terms of their characters, are unbelievable.

Mr. Jones, almost Buddha-shaped in this film, is likable as Clell's best friend, but it's the sort of role that wouldn't have been out of place in "The Phil Silvers Show." Miss Masterson and her real-life parents, Carlin Glynn and Peter Masterson (who play her parents in the film), contribute a bit of class.

The most important missing ingredient is Mr. Coppola. "Gardens of Stone" is, finally, so commonplace that one longs for even the inappropriate grandeur of "Rumble Fish" and "The Outsiders."

1987 My 8, C32:1

FILM VIEW/Vincent Canby

Gun Movies

IT'S TIME TO COME TO THE DEFENSE of the American moviegoing public, too often and too glibly characterized as a collective cretin with the taste of a 12-year-old and the brain of a gnat. In fact, the American moviegoing public is incredibly sophisticated. It's an organism so sensitive that, within a few weeks, it can discern the difference between Sylvester Stallone in "Rambo," stripped to the waist and carrying enough live ammo to refight the Vietnam War, and Sylvester Stallone in "Over the Top," in which the fully dressed star plays an arm wrestler with heart.

An arm wrestler? *Heart*? If Sylvester Stallone fans want heart they'll stay home, drink beer and watch "The Cosby Show."

In spite of the title and its associations with World War I and trench warfare, and in spite of Mr. Stallone's successful recent appearances in "Rocky" and "Rambo" movies, the American public did not buy "Over the Top." It opened in February and died in April, a record only "Howard the Duck" could envy. Mr. Stallone has gotten the message. Principal photography on "Rambo III" begins in September.

Even more impressive is the way the public is differentiating among "Lethal Weapon," "Extreme Prejudice" and "Malone," three violent action movies whose virtues and vices can be appreciated by only the most discriminating. To the rest of us, each is cut from the same bolt of polyester.

"Lethal Weapon" is about two tough Los Angeles police detectives who, after following a lot of false leads and racking up a high body count, bust a drug ring. "Extreme Prejudice" is about a tough Texas Ranger who, after following a lot of false leads and racking up a high body count, busts a drug ring. "Malone" is offbeat, being about a former law officer who busts a ring of fascists planning to take over the Government.

However, the politics of "Malone" are merely décor. All three films are equally about guns — handguns — their beauty in repose, how to use and abuse them and what people look like when they're shot — fatally in the head or chest or merely wounded with shots to the side or to a limb or a digit.

Yet "Lethal Weapon" is a smash hit and "Extreme Prejudice" is extremely iffy, while "Malone" seems to have been judged a loser by its distributors even before it arrived in town.

■

"Malone," starring Burt Reynolds, who's usually a popular guy with a gun, was booked into one of the tinier (250-seat) auditoriums in the Criterion Center on Times Square, which, you might think, would be heart of "Malone" country. Apparently not. At the first show on opening day, one could have played paddleball in the theater without appearing to be unruly. Mr. Reynolds plays the title character, Malone, who, like Mel Gibson in "Lethal Weapon," is a lethal weapon in himself. In effect, Malone *is* a gun.

My problem with these films is that I have to work hard to appreciate their subtle differences. "Malone" was filmed mostly in the scenic Northwest, so the backgrounds don't look like those either in "Extreme Prejudice," which is set in Texas and Mexico, or in "Lethal Weapon," set in Los Angeles. "Malone" also features Lauren Hutton as sex interest for Mr. Reynolds, though she's on and off the screen in a jiffy.

"Extreme Prejudice" is, I suspect (though I'm not entirely sure), movie making of a slightly higher order. It was directed by Walter Hill ("The Warriors," "Streets of Fire"), with a melodramatic humorlessness that, being unsupported by the screenplay, is frequently funnier than he seems to realize.

Nick Nolte plays the dedicated Ranger and Maria Conchita Alonso is the mistress he neglects in favor of his life with his gun. "Jack," says Miss Alonso at a critical moment in their relationship, "I have to know where you and me are going, and how long it takes to get there." Such talk gets her nowhere. She runs off to her former lover (Powers Boothe), who's also Jack's former best friend, turned drug smuggler.

The showdown, a badly edited parody of the "blood ballet" that climaxed Sam Peckinpah's classic "Wild Bunch," reunites the two buddies and their guns while Miss Alonso looks on — helplessly, of course.

■

"Lethal Weapon," directed with a good deal of intentional humor by Richard Donner, opens by cross-cutting between the off-duty lives of its two hero cops. Danny Glover plays the 50-year-old head of a Bill Cosby household, complete with wisecracking kids, a pretty, understanding wife, who's a terrible cook (joke-joke, nudge-nudge), and a pretty house that looks unlived in.

His white partner, Mr. Gibson, a suicidal widower, sits alone in a trailer, getting drunk and fondling his service revolver. At one point he sticks the barrel in his mouth — and the camera cuts to a close-up of his finger on the trigger. Though this is the opening scene of the movie, and reason tells one that he can't commit suicide *yet*, Mr. Gibson has such intensity as an actor that it's a legitimately scary moment.

■

After that, "Lethal Weapon" isn't exactly downhill. It's cross-country, through a landscape of simulated mayhem and brutality, featuring the same car chases that one has

'Lethal Weapon,' 'Extreme Prejudice' and 'Malone' are all about weapons and their beauty.

seen in the other films. There's no sex whatsoever. The most erotic gesture in "Lethal Weapon," as in "Extreme Prejudice" and "Malone," is the way that the rear end of every automobile sways from side to side, like Marilyn Monroe's hips, after making a short, tire-screeching turn.

Being about nothing more than their stories, these movies have even demystified guns. Symbolism can't survive in such arid circumstances. A gun is now loved and envied because it's a gun, representative of absolutely nothing except its own gunliness. We may be poorer for that.

1987 My 10, II:17:1

Paradise Lost

HOT PURSUIT, directed by Steven Lisberger; screenplay by Mr. Lisberger and Steven Carabatsos, story by Mr. Lisberger; director of photography, Frank Tidy; editd by Mitchell Sinoway; production designer, William J. Creber; produced by Pierre David; released by Paramount Pictures. At Embassy 4, Broadway and 47th Street; Guild 50th Street, at Rockefeller Plaza; Orpheum Twin, 86th Street near Third Avenue. Running time: 93 minutes. This film is rated PG-13.

Dan Bartlett	John Cusack
Lori Cronenberg	Wendy Gazelle
MacLaren	Robert Loggia
Bill Cronenberg	Monte Markham
Buffy Cronenberg	Shelley Fabares
Victor Honeywell	Jerry Stiller
Ginger Cronenberg	Dah-Ve Chodan

By CARYN JAMES

"HOT PURSUIT" begins with the tragedy of a failed chemistry test, which keeps a prep school senior, Dan Bartlett, from joining his girlfriend and her family on a Caribbean cruise. Danny is a levelheaded scholarship student, and his romance with Lori is an attraction of opposites. She is a rich girl distinguished by her ability to talk and smile at the same time and her tendency to practice cheerleader splits at any moment. Unexpectedly, the chemistry teacher shows up in Dan's room and lets the lovelorn A student out of the makeup test so he can go on the trip; the teacher has a 16-year-old daughter of his own and, he says, pretty girls don't like to be let down. (These adults aren't understanding about their kids' love lives; they're saintly.)

•

As Dan scrambles to catch up with Lori's family, he is always a step behind in a series of shamefully predictable near misses: after flying to the Caribbean, he is waylaid by drugged-out islanders, done in by a bottle of rum and caught in a suspenseless storm at sea. In the final, silliest plot twist, he challenges the murderous pirates who try to take over the family's charter boat.

Now this lame teen-aged adventure is the last thing you'd expect from Steven Lisberger, who wrote and directed "Tron," the 1982 film that featured computer-generated people. Whatever its failings, "Tron" was at least innovative. But as director and

co-author of "Hot Pursuit," Mr. Lisberger must have used the low-budget teen-movie handbook as a primer. He found an attractive young hero (John Cusack, best known for his role in Rob Reiner's "Sure Thing") who doesn't yet have the flair to carry a bad film. He lined up the requisite minor television stars (Monte Markham and Shelley Fabares as Lori's parents) and truly wasted a talent (Robert Loggia as a strange old salt). He took a slapdash script and set it in a locale that could be any sunny island. "Hot Pursuit," which is now at the Guild 50th Street and other theaters, is just what you'd expect from such a stale formula: a misadventure in paradise that makes "Gilligan's Island" look like "The Night of the Iguana."

•

"Hot Pursuit" is rated PG-13 ("Special Parental Guidance Suggested for Those Younger Than 13"). It includes a scene in which Danny joins in with the cheerful drug-smoking islanders.

1987 My 11, C14:5

Sand Castles

ISHTAR, written and directed by Elaine May; photography by Vittorio Storaro; edited by Stephen A. Rotter, William Reynolds and Richard Cirincione; music by John Strauss; production designed by Paul Sylbert; produced by Warren Beatty; released by Columbia Pictures. At Ziegfeld, Avenue of the Americas and 54th Street; Sutton, 57th Street and Third Avenue; 34th Street East, near Second Avenue; Art Greenwich Twin, 12th Street and Seventh Avenue. Running time: 105 minutes. This film is rated PG-13.

Lyle Rogers	Warren Beatty
Chuck Clarke	Dustin Hoffman
Shirra Assel	Isabelle Adjani
Jim Harrison	Charles Grodin
Marty Freed	Jack Weston
Willa	Tess Harper
Carol	Carol Kane
Mr. Clarke	David Margulies
Emir Yousef	Aharon Ipale
Mrs. Clarke	Rose Arrick
Abdul	Fuad Hageb
Dorothy	Julie Garfield

By JANET MASLIN

THERE are parts of "Ishtar" that could have been directed by anyone — anyone equal to the demands of a

On the Road
·Dustin Hoffman and Warren Beatty star in "Ishtar" as two singer-songwriters booked for an engagement in the Middle East, where they become enmeshed in political intrigue.

big-name, big-scenery adventure, anyone capable of herding large crowds of extras across the screen. But there are also parts that could have been directed only by Elaine May. One of these finds Chuck Clarke (Dustin Hoffman), a writer of horrible songs, being cradled in the arms of Lyle Rogers (Warren Beatty), a songwriter of equivalent talent who is Chuck's partner in crime. Chuck is in the midst of attempting suicide, but he has become distracted, as usual, by the artistic possibilities inherent in his situation.

"I'm finally on the ledge, I'm finally on the edge of my life ...," Chuck croons tentatively, singing pretty much the way he writes. Just then, Lyle arrives to talk him down. Chuck is *not* a failure, Lyle insists, no matter how things might appear. "Hey, it takes a lot of nerve to have nothing at your age, don't you understand that?" Lyle asks vehemently. "Most guys would be ashamed and just say, 'The hell with it.' You say, 'I'd rather have nothing than settle for less.'"

This is pure Elaine May — astute, fine-tuned neurotic humor from the woman who, in her screenplay with Mr. Beatty for "Heaven Can Wait," could explain a woman's shriek at the sight of her insufficiently dead husband with one of the all-time great lines. ("She just saw a mouse?" "No, before. Outside. But she relives it.") There may not be enough of Miss May's readily identifiable comic style in her screenplay for "Ishtar," which is also saddled with a busy, unwieldy plot and a good deal of monotony in its middle sections. But certainly there is some of it, and a little of Miss May's wit goes a long way.

It's impossible to discuss "Ishtar," which opens today at the Ziegfeld and other theaters, without noting the extravagant rumor-mongering that has surrounded its making. Much has been said about the film's enormous cost (undisclosed, but somewhere in the vicinity of $40 million), its delayed release and Miss May's reported fussiness in casting her camels and shaping her sand dunes. Thanks to Miss May's perfectionism and the sizable egos of her two male stars, it was noisily anticipated that this version of a Bob Hope-Bing Crosby "Road" movie might amount to a "Road to Ruin."

•

But "Ishtar" isn't "Heaven's Gate." It isn't "Heaven Can Wait," either, since it lacks the self-destructiveness of the former and the latter's more effortless charm. It's a likable, good-humored hybrid, a mixture of small, funny moments and the pointless, oversized spectacle that these days is sine qua non for any hot-weather hit. The worst of it is pain-

less; the best is funny, sly, cheerful and, here and there, even genuinely inspired.

The film's budget may well be a matter of outtakes and overtime, since the huge expense doesn't show up on the screen. Did it take Miss May, for one desert scene, 50 attempts to get the right shot of big, fat, patient-looking vultures flopping down next to her stars? If it did, it was worth it, because she got scene-stealing vulture behavior in the end. "No, no, no — not dead, just resting!" Lyle angrily tells them, while Chuck voices some memorable disbelief at the way these birds do business. Miss May has a way of letting the same basic attitudes carry over to anyone, feathered or otherwise, anywhere.

The segments that begin and end "Ishtar" involve Chuck and Lyle and their songwriting, and are infinitely more interesting than the middle hour concerning the fictitious Middle Eastern nation of the title. In New York, Lyle is seen as a Good Humor man too busy rhyming the names of flavors to stop his truck for customers. Chuck performs at an Italian restaurant where the waiters have a way of bumping into him while he sings. Their songwriting partnership is encapsulated in a montage of quick snippets, so that no one song goes on for more than a line or two. The timing here is just right, and the songs (mostly by Paul Williams and Miss May) just awful. Mr. Hoffman and Mr. Beatty perform them as badly as Bill Murray would, which is high praise.

After Carol Kane and Tess Harper — seen only momentarily and visually well matched as the hapless women in Chuck and Lyle's lives — have walked out on them, the two men take an overseas job. Their agent (played with just the right weariness by Jack Weston) has suggested "the hotel where the American journalists stay in Honduras — the last act left because they got nervous about the death squads, but there's nothing to worry about if you don't go out in the countryside." He also mentions North Africa, and the singers choose Ishtar, which turns out to be the one place where their talents are even remotely appreciated. However, the film becomes sillier and duller once it gets there. Some of the slower portions involve Isabelle Adjani, who may be playing a Shiite Moslem terrorist but still has the closest thing to a Dorothy Lamour role.

As handsomely as the film has been photographed by Vittorio Storaro, it never develops a memorable visual style or even a sharp sense of place. Ishtar remains a vague setting, and it is made even more so by too-frequent, too-noticeable cutting in every scene. What saves the Ishtar episode is the presence of Charles Grodin,

who once again perfectly embodies one of Miss May's deadpan opportunists — a man whose utter cynicism never diminishes his sincerity in the slightest. Mr. Grodin plays a C.I.A. agent who recruits Mr. Hoffman (the plot has become hopelessly overcomplicated by now) with a fine mixture of casualness and chicanery. With a shrug, Mr. Grodin offers him "$150 a week — it's not much, but you can't really put a price on Democracy."

Mr. Hoffman and Mr. Beatty make a good team; they have an easy, friendly rapport, and they don't even need the running gag about Mr. Beatty's being the less attractive of the two. Both look older, more careworn and a little weary, which is just right for the film's purposes, as are their calculatedly unflattering costumes. If neither does his best work here, Mr. Hoffman has a nice abandon and Mr. Beatty a studiedly oafish, self-effacing charm. There are moments, if only a few of them, when the two actors and Miss May seem to be in perfect alignment. "He'd rather just sit there than move when you ask him; he'd rather get shot!" Mr. Hoffman cries in exasperation about a stubborn camel. "Actually, I kind of admire that," says Mr. Beatty. Mr. Hoffman considers that for a moment, then acknowledges, "Me, too."

•

"Ishtar" is rated PG-13 ("Special Parental Guidance Suggested for Those Younger Than 13"). It contains some rude language and very brief nudity.

1987 My 15, C3:1

Comedy of Terrors

MONSTER IN THE CLOSET, directed and written by Bob Dahlin; story by Mr. Dahlin and Peter L. Bergquist; director of photography, Ronald W. McLeish; edited by Raja Gosnell and Stephanie Palewski; music by Barrie Guard; production designer, Lynda Cohen; produced by David Levy and Mr. Bergquist; at U.A. Twin, Broadway and 49th Street. and other theaters. Running time: 92 minutes. This film is rated PG.
Richard Clark	Donald Grant
Diane Bennett	Denise DuBarry
Dr. Pennyworth	Henry Gibson
Father Finnegan	Howard Duff
General Turnbull	Donald Moffat
Sheriff Ketchum	Claude Akins
The Professor	Paul Walker
Scoop Johnson	Frank Ashmore
Old Joe	John Carradine
Margo Crane	Stella Stevens
The Monster	Kevin Peter Hall

By WALTER GOODMAN

FOR about 20 minutes, "Monster in the Closet" seems about to break out as a spoof not only of "Aliens" and such, but also of anything else that happened to pop into the head of its writer and director, Bob Dahlin — from health food to insect lib. Most of the characters remind you of somebody. There's a reporter named Clark, who becomes a sexual object when he takes off his glasses; a bespectacled kid, known as "the professor," who's a gadget whiz; a garrulous Nobel laureate whose white hair

sprouts like Einstein's, and of course the gurgling, growling, snarling, slurping monster that closets a sexy coed, a seeing-eye dog and an obnoxious movie child before the credits roll. There are informative captions: "The Building Next Door. Two-Seventeen P.M. The Shower."

All right, so it's a touch broad. But just as we're getting into the spirit, Mr. Dahlin runs out of gags and gas and substitutes fireworks. Once the cops and the Army are brought in and all that firepower is directed at the poor monster, the movie is gunned down by the conventions it set out to kid. The joke self-destructs. There are still some laughs, as the good guys woo the monster with a xylophone, but the pursuit goes on for too long and the humor trails behind.

•

The movie, which opens today at the U.A. Twin and other theaters, is well cast. Donald Grant and Denise DuBarry make an agreeable couple as, respectively, the cub reporter with the special eyes and the whiz kid's mother. Among the familiar faces are Henry Gibson as the old scientist; Donald Moffat as a blustering general; Stella Stevens, taking a long and constantly interrupted shower; Claude Akins as a tabacco-chewing sheriff who doesn't trust his aim; John Carradine as a crochety blind codger, and Howard Duff as a crucifix-wielding priest who has seen "Dracula" and "King Kong" too many times. The main unfamiliar face is that of Kevin Peter Hall as the monster, which, like lots of humans, can't resist a walk-in closet.

•

"Monster in the Closet" is rated PG ("Parental Guidance Suggested"), probably owing to some earthy language.

1987 My 15, C9:1

With a Smile

PERSONAL SERVICES, directed by Terry Jones; written by David Leland; director of photography, Roger Deakins; edited by George Akers; production designer, Hugo Luczyc-Wyhowski; produced by Tim Bevan; released by Vestron Pictures. At Cinema II, Third Avenue at 60th Street. Running time: 103 minutes. This film is rated R.
Christine Painter	Julie Walters
Wing Commander Morton	Alec McCowen
Shirley	Shirley Stelfox
Dolly	Danny Schiller
Rose	Victoria Hardcastle
Timms	Tim Woodward
Sydney	Dave Atkins
Mr. Popozogolou	Leon Lissek
Mr. Marsden	Benjamin Whitrow

CHRISTINE PAINTER, the heroine of "Personal Services," seems to slip into her career in prostitution by accident. When the film begins, Christine (played by Julie Walters, the star of "Educating Rita") is working as a waitress and apparently making some extra money by subletting apartments to prostitutes. So she is party to what they do, but somehow thoroughly indignant whenever their clients appear and misunderstand her own role ("What do you think I am?" she snaps furiously at one polite, elderly man.) One day, though, the rent is due and Christine has no money. She seemingly has no recourse when the landlord suggests he take it out in trade, and after that, the rest is history.

An opening disclaimer announces that "Personal Services" is fiction,

Not a Home

Alec McCowen and Julie Walters are principals in ''Personal Services,'' about a waitress who becomes the proprietor of suburban brothel catering to an eminent clientele.

By JANET MASLIN

I N the interval between ''Beverly Hills Cop'' and ''Beverly Hills Cop II,'' Axel Foley, the brash young police detective from Detroit, has been on at least one fishing trip with Billy Rosewood (Judge Reinhold), John Taggart (John Ashton) and Andrew Bogomil (Ronny Cox), his friends on the Beverly Hills force. Some other things have happened as well. Axel has. become, in the mind of the nation if not in his own, the supreme practitioner of inspired back talk, the wise guy against whom all others are measured. To anyone who saw the first film, Eddie Murphy's endlessly resourceful Axel is now no stranger to the ways of Beverly Hills, and no novice at manipulating them to his own comic advantage.

A true sequel to ''Beverly Hills Cop'' might have made good use of Axel's past experience, or at least have acknowledged it somehow. But ''Beverly Hills Cop II,'' which opens today at Loews Astor Plaza and other theaters, is not an extension of the original story; it's a clone. As such, it's quite a skillful one, repeating the first film's better setups and recalling it as freely and often as possible. Mr. Murphy even wears his same old T-shirt, and of course he's funny in the same old ways, whether he's impersonating a Caribbean psychic or commandeering a mansion by pretending to be a building inspector.

So the new film has at least some of its predecessor's appeal. But it can't match the first film's novelty, or recapture the excitement of watching a great comic character like Axel Foley as he first came to life. That's the liability facing all but the most imaginative sequels: the chance that the original work's very originality was its greatest virtue. Lively as it is, ''Beverly Hills Cop II'' can't help but suffer from the lack of any originality at all.

It might seem as though ''Top Gun'' and the ''Beverly Hills Cop'' story were sufficiently different to require different directorial styles. But they aren't, at least not in the minds of the producers Don Simpson and Jerry Bruckheimer, for whom the worldwide grosses of those films (over $300 million each) must seem stylish and then some. So the producers have transferred Tony Scott, who directed ''Top Gun,'' to Axel Foley's territory. And Mr. Scott has done what he can to prove that megamovies of the rock video age are essentially interchangeable anyhow. ''Beverly Hills Cop II'' has hit songs (or at least they will be), loud action sequences, flashy cuts among eyecatching but unrelated visual images, and a steady, upbeat pace. That it lacks airborne fighting footage is almost beside the point.

''Beverly Hills Cop II'' begins exactly the way the first film did, with Mr. Murphy in Detroit in the midst of an undercover scam. However, he is now wearing the fanciest of wardrobes and driving a Ferrari, which effectively cuts any tie to reality in the film's first few minutes. Supposedly, the Detroit police department has paid for all of this, in an effort to help

---

and that it is not the life story of Cynthia Payne, the British madam whose brothel was raided in 1978 and who subsequently became a celebrity. However, the titles say that events in Miss Payne's life inspired the story, and she is credited as a consultant. Miss Payne apparently catered to older men with kinkier tastes, but she ran an establishment that was as well liked for its homeyness as for its prurience. The film does what it can to echo Miss Payne's pragmatism and her down-to-earth bawdiness, but it seems less comfortable with the essence of her line of work than she was.

•

''Personal Services,'' which opens today at Cinema II, was directed by Terry Jones of Monty Python, so it is hardly surprising that Mr. Jones mines this material for its humor. The screenplay, by the talented writer, director and actor David Leland (who co-wrote ''Mona Lisa''), also focuses on the comic aspects of Christine's career. The film finds its humor in naughtiness, in the humiliations to which Christine's clients happily subject themselves, and in her own breezy, raunchy way of discussing their goings-on. One of Christine's most obscene anatomical discussions takes place in a restaurant with two women who are friends of hers, the elder and frumpier of whom leafs through sewing patterns as the talk goes on.

This dowdy, sweet-looking lady, who serves as Christine's maid and assistant, turns out to be a man. And that is only one of many peculiar circumstances Christine manages to take in stride. Her clientele consists of staid, mousy-looking men who enjoy dressing up — as schoolboys, in bikinis and dog collars, in rubber — and Christine is seen matter-of-factly administering spankings and so on; she gets perhaps her greatest fun from the group of ''slaves'' who insist on doing her garden work and paying her for the privilege. The film sees all this as a kind of thrilling schoolboy silliness, and it seems to have almost nothing to do with real sex or real prostitution.

There are times, though, when ''Personal Services'' seems needlessly coy, as when Christine is hired by her first client and complains when he asks her to wear red lipstick, thinking it looks tarty; the real tartiness of the situation is left unmentioned. There are also moments of unhelpful sentimentality, as when Christine daydreams over women's magazines depicting a life of wellheeled propriety, and has fantasy assignations with the handsome young man who would presumably take her away from all this. Both the film and Christine, as played with an engaging

---

brassiness by Miss Walters, are too hardboiled for such lapses.

•

There are also a few episodes that carry more emotional weight than the film can comfortably handle, no matter how devil-may-care its attitude. One of these has Christine helpfully sending her adolescent son, and then her widowed father, to the same one of her employees on the same afternoon, and pausing between rounds to embrace both the men in her life. This is too awkward to be funny, and the film is otherwise too superficial to make it deliberately unsettling.

For the most part, though, ''Personal Services'' is as dauntless, lively and inexhaustible as Christine herself. Miss Walters gives an energetic, blustery performance and makes quite a credible businesswoman, saying things like ''It's just like a Tupperware party, really, but I sell sex instead of plastic containers.'' That's the attitude to which the film resolutely clings, but at least it's an attitude conducive to humor. Mr. Jones has a keen eye for the ludicrousness of certain situations, and keeps the film fast and funny when he sticks to specifics. His efforts to pinpoint a larger hypocrisy, as in a closing scene identifying Christine's most frequent clients, are less successful.

The casting is mostly quite good, with Danny Schiller perfectly lovely as the sweet old lady and Shirley Stelfox drolly funny as an employee who spends a lot of her time dressed as a prim-looking governess. Alec McCowen, as a retired military man who becomes one of Christine's backers, spends a little too much time romping about crazily in ladies' underwear. But at least he, like everyone else in the film, seems to know how to have a good time.

JANET MASLIN

1987 My 15, C4:5

Forecast: Fair

GOOD WEATHER, BUT STORMY LATE THIS AFTERNOON, directed by Gérard Frot-Coutaz; written (French with English subtitles) by Mr. Frot-Coutaz and Jacques Davila; distributed by Coralie Films International. Running time: 85 minutes. This film has no rating. At Film Forum 1, 57 Watts Street.

Jacqueline .... Micheline Presle
Jacques .... Claude Piéplu
Bernard .... Xavier Deluc
Brigitte .... Tonie Marshall

By WALTER GOODMAN

''G OOD WEATHER, but Stormy Late This Afternoon'' is a sort of tribute to Micheline Presle, a French

---

actress who came to international attention in 1947 when she starred with Gérard Philipe in ''Le Diable au Corps.'' Gérard Frot-Coutaz, who directed and collaborated on the screenplay for ''Good Weather,'' his first feature, loses no chance to display Ms. Presle's still attractive face and offers her plenty of opportunity to show her stuff, from comedically cracked to sadly sexy. The pleasant movie, which opens today at Film Forum 1 (whose modest marquee may not be able to accommodate the windy title), is a slice-of-middle-aged-life that goes from soup to soap.

At issue is Jacqueline (Ms. Presle), a retired teacher in her mid-50's, who seems determined to drive herself and everybody around her, particularly her husband (Claude Piéplu, another familiar face of French cinema) batty. She nags interminably about routine matters, worries a lot about chickens, lapses into meandering monologues about her family, lives on pills and whines about her unhappy condition: ''I'm no good for anything anymore.''

When the couple's handsome son, Bernard (Xavier Deluc), pops in for lunch with a leggy blonde in a handkerchief-sized dress (Tonie Marshall), we learn what's at the bottom of Mamma's problems. She dolls up for the occasion, refuses to remember the girlfriend's name and bursts in on the couple's sex play with a refreshing glass of orangeade. Bernard acts more like a lover than a son, and she blossoms at his touch. The poor fellow is so lost in his Oedipal complex that he can't find his way to matrimony with the eager blonde.

•

If this sounds a touch obvious, c'est dommage. The movie, which moves somewhat unsteadily between the sensitive and the sentimental, is at its most original when Ms. Presle is in her comic mode, examining their prospective lunch — ''This chicken is strange'' — or joining in a nostalgic song with Mr. Piéplu, who gives a subtle performance as the unsubtle husband.

''Good Weather'' offers sharp details of middle-class existence in a suburban high-rise, affection for people whose lives seem to be all in the past and bursts of humor. But more is signaled than developed. Like Bernard, the talented Mr. Frot-Coutaz seems to have been unable to break away from his fixation with Ms. Presle.

1987 My 20, C20:3

Rodeo Redux

BEVERLY HILLS COP II, directed by Tony Scott; screenplay by Larry Ferguson and Warren Skaaren, story by Eddie Murphy and Robert D. Wachs, based on characters created by Danilo Bach and Daniel Petrie Jr.; director of photography, Jeffrey L. Kimball; edited by Billy Weber, Chris Lebenzon and Michael Tronick; music by Harold Faltermeyer; production designer, Ken Davis; produced by Don Simpson and Jerry Bruckheimer; released by Paramount Pictures.

Eddie Murphy and Judge Reinhold in "Beverly Hills Cop II."

Axel pass as a plausible high roller. Yet his boss, Inspector Todd (Gil Hill), balks at advancing him expense money once Axel decides to return to California to help his old friends. All of the key original actors, like Mr. Hill, have returned this time, and the screenplay (by Larry Ferguson and Warren Skaaren) works hard to give them more to do.

Axel's arrival in Beverly Hills is greeted by exactly the same kinds of touristy shots — Rodeo Drive, the Beverly Hills Hotel — that showed up in the first film. And soon he is embroiled in a complicated plot that, like the first film's, pits him against cool, merciless Teutonic villains. Chief among these are Jürgen Prochnow as an evil kingpin and Brigitte Nielsen as his coldblooded assistant. The six-foot-tall Miss Nielsen is a walking photo opportunity, and Mr. Scott happily cuts from stylized images of her to other attention-getters, like shattering glass or galloping race horses. The rock-video imperative, the need to keep all images as vibrant and nonverbal as possible, is especially noticeable in Miss Nielsen's scenes.

For all the flash, it's Mr. Murphy that audiences will come to see, and Mr. Murphy whose manic impersonations are the film's only raison d'être. To his credit, Mr. Murphy always manages to make his riffs seem new. And Axel's delight at his own extravagant rudeness remains his funniest attribute, never more so than in the particularly contrived scene that brings Axel, crazy Billy Rosewood and the wonderfully long-suffering John Taggart to the Playboy mansion. (The new film is more noticeably misogynist than its predecessor, and more intent on cheesecake, which is where the crowd of volleyball-playing bunnies come in.) To hear Mr. Murphy cry "Hef!" — with just the right mix of impudence, wit and sheer reckless bravado — is to remember why Axel Foley became the toast of Beverly Hills in the first place.

1987 My 20, C28:1

Correction

A movie review of "Beverly Hills Cop II" on Wednesday omitted the film's rating. It is R.

1987 My 25, 3:1

Toothy Charm

THE CHIPMUNK ADVENTURE, directed by Janice Karman; written by Miss Karman and Ross Bagdasarian; music by Randy Edelman; produced by Mr. Bagdasarian; released by the Samuel Goldwyn Company. At Embassy 4, Broadway and 47th Street; 23d Street West Triplex, at Eighth Avenue; 86th Street Twin, at Lexington Avenue. Running time: 76 minutes. This film is rated G.
With the voices of: Ross Bagdasarian, Janice Karman, Dody Goodman, Susan Tyrell, Anthony DeLongis, Frank Welker, Nancy Cartwright, Ken Sansom, Charles Adler, Philip Clark, George Poulos and Pat Pinney

WHAT sort of film walks a thinner line than the animated children's musical, catering as it does to two such disparate age groups, each so easily bored? At least "The Chipmunk Adventure," which opens today at Embassy 4 and other theaters, tries to interest both parents and children and does a reasonably good job. For the parents, there are references to high finance, bored jet-setters and Pierre Cardin socks. For the children, there are pleasant, colorful Chipmunks on a round-the-world tour. And for both there is music, including a Chipmunk-style rendition of "Woolly Bully" and a nice, sentimental hymn to Mother.

"The Chipmunk Adventure" is the work of Ross Bagdasarian — son of Ross Bagdasarian Sr., the Chipmunks' original creator — and his wife, Janice Karman. It is animated in standard Saturday-morning cartoon style, so that the non-Chipmunk characters look lifeless and the backgrounds never move. However, if its visual sophistication is slight, it has other charms. The Chipmunks — the ringleader Alvin, the brainy Simon and the always-hungry little Theodore — are a lot less saccharine than the Care Bears, and they behave like real boys. Their supporting cast in this, their first feature film, includes three ponytailed girl Chipmunks and an extremely adorable baby penguin.

•

The Chipmunks are left alone when Dave Seville, their human guardian, goes on a trip abroad. And they soon fall into the clutches of a pair of evil foreigners named Klaus and Claudia.

The Chipmunks are conned into embarking on an around-the-world balloon race, which is actually part of Klaus and Claudia's diamond-smuggling operation. To get the Chipmunks to do this, the glamorous villains offer a $100,000 prize to the winner, and suggest that the boys compete against the girls. Parents may be surprised at the enthusiasm shown by both all-too-modern Chipmunk teams for that large cash prize.

The balloon trip means a lot of scenery, and children will doubtless enjoy animated glimpses of llamas, windmills, famous landmarks and so on. There is also an enjoyable dance number featuring animated cobras, and a couple of homages to Mr. Bagdasarian's late father. He was the composer of such novelty hits as "Witch Doctor" and "Come on a My House," and both are included here.

JANET MASLIN
1987 My 22, C10:5

Anthropology 101

THE PORNOGRAPHERS, directed by Shohei Imamura; screenplay (Japanese with English subtitles) by Mr. Imamura and Koji Numata, story by Akiyuki Nozaka; cinematography by Shinsaku Himeda; music by Toshiro Mayuzumi; produced by Shohei Imamura, Jiro Tomoda and Issei Yamamoto; distributed by East-West Classics. At Film Forum 2, 57 Watts Street. Running time: 128 minutes. This film has no rating.
Subuyan Ogata	Shoichi Ozawa
Haru Matsuda	Sumiko Sakamoto
Elderly Executive	Ganjiro Nakamura
Banteki	Haruo Tanaka
Keiko Matsuda	Keiko Sakawa
Koichi Matsuda	Masaomi Kondo
Detective Sanada	Akira Nishimura

By JANET MASLIN

THE large carp that presides over parts of Shohei Imamura's "Pornographers" is only one of many testaments to Mr. Imamura's real and piquant eccentricity. The carp watches over a widow named Haru (Sumiko Sakamoto), and she believes it to be the embodiment of her dead husband. It jumps, or at least she thinks it does, when it disapproves of her behavior. It seems to jump frequently in the presence of Subu (Shoichi Ozawa), Haru's lover. In any case, Mr. Imamura has any number of opportunities to stage shots near the carp, through the carp tank and from the carp's point of view.

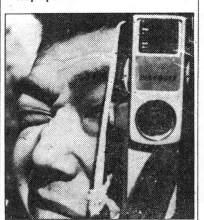

Sex for Sale Eight-millimeter pornographic film makers are the subject of "The Pornographers," by the Japanese director Shohei Imamura.

"The Pornographers," which opens today at the Film Forum 2, has a bizarrely matter-of-fact tone and a great many flashes of dark humor. It's at least as engaging as it is obscure. Subu, who is one of three pornographers to whom the title refers, conducts his covert film-making business with a pragmatism that seems quite strange under the circumstances, and with an utter lack of lasciviousness or lust. He regards it as something like charitable work, and he himself seems part monk, part entrepreneur.

It's difficult to know what goes through Subu's head when he recruits a young mother to play the role of a virgin, or prepares to stage a schoolgirl-in-uniform routine for an elderly client. What's clearer is that Subu's career and his life with Haru and her teen-age daughter Keiko (after whom he does tacitly lust) are both full of little frustrations. Mr. Imamura, who subtitled this film "An Introduction to Anthropology," explores a much seedier and more offbeat side of Japanese life than usually can be found on the screen. Made in 1966, "The Pornographers" was well ahead of its time.

•

Mr. Imamura, who often frames his images in intriguing and unexpected ways, can be as wrenching as he is bleakly funny. Haru's eventual decline into madness (and into the carp's life) strikes a sobering chord, as does Subu's guilty erotic fixation on a childhood scar of Keiko's and the accident that caused it. The ending of the film, which takes place some time after the main action and presents the culmination of Subu's creative efforts, is haunting in its own way. "Into each hair I've poured all my pain," he observes, while crafting his ironic masterpiece.

The actors are supremely diffident, as suits Mr. Imamura's detached style, and the film's tone is quietly ironic. A scene in which a customer puzzles over his new "G.I. cut" in Haru's barbershop is no less consequential than the one in which Subu muses, "I guess I'm fascinated by the pathos of being a man."

1987 My 22, C10:5

Underprivileged

ENEMY TERRITORY, directed by Peter Manoogian; screenplay by Stuart Kaminsky and Bobby Liddell, story by Mr. Kaminsky; director of photography, Ernest Dickerson; edited by Peter Teschner; music by Sam Winans and Richard Koz Kosinski; production design by Medusa Studios; produced by Cynthia de Paula and Tim Kincaid; released by Empire Entertainment Company Inc. At U. A. Twin, Broadway and 49th Street, and other theaters. Running time: 89 minutes. This film is rated R.
Barry	Gary Frank
Will	Ray Parker Jr.
Parker	Jan-Michael Vincent
Elva Briggs	Frances Foster
The Count	Tony Todd
Toni Briggs	Stacey Dash
Chet	Deon Richmond
Barton	Tiger Haynes
Mr. Beckhorne	Charles Randall
Haj	Peter Wise
Psycho	Robert Lee Rush

By WALTER GOODMAN

THE territory at issue in "Enemy Territory" is a graffiti-stricken project somewhere in New York City. After dark, it is prey to the Vampires, a hissing teen-age gang whose members can bust down armor-plated, multi-locked-and-bolted doors with a nudge. They have more guns than the Contras and are led by the Count, a creature so vicious that he smashes an old lady's glasses, which doesn't stop that game soul from spraying the street with an automatic weapon when required.

The Count is rhetoric-mad, in a san-

Ray Parker Jr.

guinary vein: "Tonight we taste blood!" he howls. "Vampire blood will not go unavenged!" Probably an out-of-work actor.

•

As night falls, an insurance sales-man makes a call in the building and has the darndest time getting out, even with the help of several coura-geous folks, including a petite 17-year-old who can lay out three or four hoodlums with a flick of her fist when annoyed. As somebody says, "This stuff just keeps getting thicker."

This slum of a movie, directed on the cheap by Peter Manoogian, opens today at the U. A. Twin and neighbor-hood theaters. It's enough to bring down property values in any neigh-borhood.

1987 My 22, C7:1

Noodle Mania

TAMPOPO, directed by Juzo Itami; screen-play (Japanese with English subtitles) by Mr. Itami; photography by Masaki Ta-mura; edited by Akira Suzuki; music by Kunihiko Murai; produced by Mr. Itami, Yasushi Tamaoki and Seigo Hosogoe. At Cinema Studio 1, Broadway at 66th Street. Running time: 114 minutes. This film has no rating.
Goro .... Tsutomu Yamazaki
Tampopo .... Nobuko Miyamoto
Man in white suit .... Koji Yakusho
Gun .... Ken Watanabe
Pisken .... Rikiya Yasuoka
Shohei .... Kinzo Sakura
Tabo .... Mampei Ikeuchi
Master of ramen making .... Yoshi Kato
Rich old man .... Shuju Otaki
Mistress of the man in white suit
.... Fukumi Kuroda
Rich old man's mistress .... Setsuko Shinoi
Girl catching oysters .... Yoriko Doguchi

"Tampopo" was shown as part of this year's New Directors/New Films series. Following are excerpts from Vincent Canby's review, which appeared in The New York Times March 26. The film opens today at Cinema Studio 1, Broadway at 66th Street.

"TAMPOPO," Juzo Itami's new Japanese film, is a sa-tiric comedy about noodles — about their making,

cooking, serving and consumption. It's about people who take noodles seriously, who read self-help books that, among other things, instruct the eater to regard the pork "affection-ately" while "slurping" the noodles that have been "activated" by the soup.

In particular, the film is about Tampopo (the Japanese word for dandelion), a youngish widow who as-pires to make, cook and serve the best noodles in any noodle shop in Tokyo, and about the people who help her on her way to the top. These in-clude a truck driver-noodle connois-seur named Goro, who affects the mannerisms of Clint Eastwood, and a rich old man who loves noodles so much that, after he overindulges, a vacuum cleaner must be used to empty his stomach.

Though it's not consistently funny (at least not to someone who, with a clear conscience, buys his noodles in plastic bags), "Tampopo" is another example of the eccentric humor that has been showing up recently in Japa-nese films, most effectively in Yojiro Takita's "Comic Magazine" and Yo-shimitsu Morita's "Family Game."

"Tampopo" is buoyantly free in form. It's as much an essay as it is a narrative — always ready to digress into random gags and comic anec-dotes. These may not have much bearing on Tampopo and her noodle education, but they all have to do with food and with the Japanese love of ritual that has made an art of slurp-ing noodles, arranging flowers, drink-ing tea and committing suicide.

The film's writer-director, Mr. Itami, who's also an actor (he played the father in "The Family Game"), seems to have a special fondness for the solemnity of the prose used by connoisseurs. His principal charac-ters and even the bit players con-verse by exchanging the sentiments of food critics.

Noodles that aren't great are de-scribed as "sincere," and when Tam-popo is on the verge of a noodle break-through, her admirer must say, in all frankness, that "they're beginning to have substance, but they still lack depth." "Noodles," says a man searching for the perfect phrase, "are synergetic things." Early in the film, the sight of a bowl of noodles is compared to a Jackson Pollock paint-ing.

Some of the best moments are only distantly related blackout sketches, including one about a father who urges his children, "Keep on eating! It's the last meal Mom cooked" — while Mom lies on the floor in the kitchen, having just committed sui-cide out of boredom.

Mr. Itami often strains after comic effects that remain elusive. The most appealing thing about "Tampopo" is that he never stops trying. A funny sensibility is at work here.

1987 My 22, C17:1

Children's Crusade

AMAZING GRACE AND CHUCK, directed by Mike Newell; written and produced by David Field; director of photography, Rob-ert Elswit; edited by Peter Hollywood; music by Elmer Bernstein; released by Tri Star Pictures. At the 68th Street Play-house, at Third Avenue. Running time: 115 minutes. This film is rated PG.
President .... Gregory Peck
Russell Murdock .... William L. Petersen
Chuck Murdock .... Joshua Zuehlke
Amazing Grace Smith .... Alex English
Pamela .... Frances Conroy
Lynn Taylor .... Jamie Lee Curtis

Taking a Stand Gregory Peck portrays the President of the United States in "Amazing Grace and Chuck," about a little boy whose principles create a national movement.

IMAGINE what a thrill it is for Chuck Murdock (Joshua Zuehl-ke), a Montana schoolboy, to find the President of the United States right there in his bedroom. The President is a genial, movie-starrish fellow with a folksy manner — actual-ly, he's Gregory Peck — and he has come to discuss nuclear disarma-ment. He wants to see if his plans to negotiate a treaty with the Soviet Union meet with 12-year-old Chuck's approval.

How exactly did Chuck come to wield this kind of influence? It all started at a Little League game. Chuck had recently been taken on a tour of a missile base with his class-mates, and the sight of a Minuteman 3 upset him terribly. So did the ghastly thought that if his little sister were to drop a fork simultaneously with a nuclear explosion, she would be vaporized by the time the fork hit the floor. So Chuck decided to make the only kind of statement available to him. A star baseball player, he refused to pitch at an important Little League game.

The story of Chuck's gesture made the wire services. It was seen by Amazing Grace Smith (Alex English, the professional basketball star, a Denver Nugget), who plays a Boston Celtic. Amazing decided to follow Chuck's lead, and also to move to Montana. He was soon followed there by two Miami Dolphins, a number of other well-known athletes, and even-tually the President himself.

Now surely there is no one among us who would not like to see an intelli-gent, cogent film addressing itself to children's fears about the nuclear threat. But "Amazing Grace and Chuck," which opens today at the 68th Street Playhouse, is much too silly and farfetched for that. It should be said, to the film's credit, that at least it avoids the "Rocky-Karate Kid" route of finding personal aggrandize-ment under every stone, and that Mr. Zuehlke plays Chuck as a thoughtful, serious and very modest boy. But en-tirely too much of the film is grounded in a visual and moral para-dise, where the sky is not cloudy all day.

•

Mike Newell's two best-known films, "Dance With a Stranger" and "The Good Father," are about the bit-terest forms of warfare between the sexes. If Mr. Newell's name did not appear in the opening credits for

"Amazing Grace and Chuck," there would be absolutely no way of identi-fying this direction as his. The film's style is as doggedly ordinary as its story is preposterous. The screenplay (by David Field, who was also the producer) starts with a simple prem-ise and winds up spiraling away more crazily than the wildest science fic-tion.

Among the loonier developments are a plot against Amazing Grace by an evil industrialist; a late-night threatening call to the industrialist from the President; a visit to one of Chuck's Little League games by the President and the Soviet Premier; and a nationwide vow of silence on the part of children, who are follow-ing Chuck's example. "The thing that's beginning to concern me is this silent children thing — it's new," a Cabinet minister says.

Along with Mr. Zuehlke, who is so precocious and somber, and Mr. Eng-lish, who is nothing if not sincere, the cast includes William L. Petersen as Chuck's father, a National Guard fighter pilot who is none too patient with his son's antics, and Jamie Lee Curtis as Amazing's agent and confi-dante. Miss Curtis looks pert and seems totally at sea.

•

"Amazing Grace and Chuck" is rated PG ("Parental Guidance Sug-gested"). It contains some mildly off-color language. JANET MASLIN

1987 My 22, C30:4

ERNEST GOES TO CAMP, directed by John R. Cherry 3d; screenplay by Mr. Cherry and Coke Sams; directors of photography, Harry Mathias and Jim May; edited by Marshall Harvey; music by Shane Keis-ter; produced by Stacy Williams; released by Touchstone Pictures. At the Guild 50th Street, 33 West 50th Street; the Embassy 2, Broadway and 47th Street; the Embassy 72d Street Twin, at Broadway; the Bay, Cinema, Second Avenue at 32d Street; the 23d Street West Triplex, between Eighth and Ninth Avenues; the Eastside Cinema, Third Avenue at 55th Street; the UA East 85th Street, at First Avenue; the Coliseum, Broadway and 181st Street. Running time: 90 minutes. This film is rated PG.
Ernest P. Worrell .... Jim Varney
Nurse St. Cloud .... Victoria Racimo
Sherman Krader .... John Vernon
Old Indian Chief .... Iron Eyes Cody
Bronk Stinson .... Lyle Alzado
Jake .... Gaillard Sartain
Eddy .... Daniel Butler
Bobby Wayne .... Patrick Day

By CARYN JAMES

How would you like to spend 90 minutes with Crazy Eddie? "Ernest Goes to Camp" is a lot easier on the eardrums, but you get the idea: Take a character well known from televi-sion commercials, spin him off into a feature film and destroy that fuzzy line between commercials and enter-tainment.

As Ernest P. Worrell, better known as Vern's neighbor, Jim Varney has appeared in hundreds of local com-mercials around the country. Ernest is a wide-eyed, wide-mouthed yokel, constantly sticking his head in Vern's window and his nose in Vern's busi-ness, telling the helpless, always un-seen neighbor what soft drink or car or mattress to buy. He is the kind of well-meaning pain in the neck who can be amusing for about 30 seconds, and then only because you're not Vern.

John R. Cherry 3d, the advertising executive who invented Ernest and directed all those commercials, also directed and co-wrote "Ernest Goes to Camp," his first movie. Well, it's not so much a movie as a marketing decision; it seems based on the prem-

Country Living A mummylike Jim Varney, as Ernest P. Worrell, portrays a counselor in "Ernest Goes to Camp."

ise that no success should go unexploited.

Will adults leave home to see a very long commercial? We won't really know, because Mr. Cherry has come up with a kiddie film set in summer camp, cleverly aiming his campaign to market Ernest at an audience of unsuspecting children. Minimal plot, cartoon characters, instant movie.

At Kamp Kikakee, Ernest is a handyman-turned-counselor in charge of half a dozen delinquent boys who look awfully clean-cut and well bred to begin with. The point is made, again and again, that these baby punks just need some love and attention. And Ernest can save them, for while his look and manner are the same as on television — Mr. Varney may never escape Ernest after this — here he is a lonely guy with a pathetic know-it-all swagger.

The plot is simple: Some evil building contractors try to dupe an old Indian into signing over the campgrounds, and Ernest plans to save the day. But the movie is really about sight gags. How many times can Ernest mug at the camera or get attacked by animals and insects?

There have been worse ideas for innocuous summer films, but not many worse executions. The slapstick is tame and predictable. The characters and their inspirational message are served up as neatly — there's no avoiding this — as if they were in commercials.

In one energetic scene Ernest and his gang fight off the contractors by using flaming arrows, flying food and attack turtles, each one sent off in its own little parachute. But that doesn't make up for all the obvious comedy and the maudlin theme. "Ernest Goes to Camp" opened yesterday at the Guild 50th Street and other theaters. It's such a pesky film, now I know how poor Vern feels. ●

"Ernest Goes to Camp" is rated PG. It has a couple of fires and fight scenes, but the film should not be disturbing. Very young children, however, might be warned not to copy the dangerous stunts.

1987 My 23, 15:4

Dilemmas and Fun

THE SECOND VICTORY, directed and produced by Gerald Thomas; screenplay by Morris West; director of photography, Alan Hume; edited by Leslie Healey; music by Stanley Myers; production designer, Harry Pottle; released by Filmworld Distributors Inc. At Cinema 1, Third Avenue at 60th Street. Running time: 95 minutes. This film has no rating.

Major Hanlon	Anthony Andrews
Dr. Huber	Max Von Sydow
Karl Fischer	Helmut Griem
Dr. Sepp Kunzli	Mario Adorf
Anna Kunzli	Birgit Doll
Max Holzinger	Wolfgang Reichmann
Traudl Holzinger	Renee Soutendijk
Liesl Holzinger	Immy Schell
Rudi Winkler	Gunther Maria Halmer

By WALTER GOODMAN

"THE SECOND VICTORY" is a brisk action movie abounding in colorful characters, picturesque scenery and the homilies of Morris West, who wrote the screenplay based on his novel. The adroitly plotted tale, which opens today at Cinema 1, takes place in 1945. No sooner does Anthony Andrews, as a British major with a conscience as big as the Alps, arrive to head the Occupation forces at a scenic Austrian town than his sergeant is killed. The search for the killer begins what Mr. West has conceived as a morality tale of justice, vengeance and mercy, but don't let that spoil your enjoyment.

Part of the fun is watching a Continental cast overact under the direction of Gerald Thomas. There's Helmut Griem laying on tough charm as a police chief who is determined to save the murderer (Jacques Breuer), who has been driven mad by what he endured on the Eastern Front. A few minutes of Mr. Breuer doing his crazy number, and any jury would prescribe instant commitment. There's shifty Mario Adorf, as a sometime British agent who made a fortune by misappropriating Jewish property during the war; now he is into classy smoking jackets and snifters of brandy. There's Gunther Maria Halmer being sinister as a doctor who is trying to escape punishment for what he did when he was "the butcher of Dachau." This baddie is also an atheist with unorthodox sexual preferences.

There's a wise priest (Wolfgang Preiss), who was the major's teacher years ago when the young fellow thought he might like to be a monk. Father Albertus sometimes speaks in italics: "You wanted to be an angel of mercy and you're forced to be a policeman." There's the village doctor (Max Von Sydow), a good person. And there are a couple of women (Birgit Doll and Renee Soutendijk) who comfort the major as he deals with what the screenplay keeps insisting are big moral dilemmas. In case anybody has missed the message, the climactic confrontation between the major and the murderer takes place in a church.

Mr. West and Mr. Thomas keep the plot bubbling. Not all the dialogue is top drawer ("He killed my uncle, and now I'm carrying his child"), and some of the close-ups of narrowing eyes and twisting mouths may remind you of the silents. (Messrs. Andrews and Von Sydow are relatively restrained.) But if you can take the grimaces as part of the show, like the masks in a morality play, you may get a kick out of them. Which is more than can be said for Mr. West's theological pretentions.

1987 My 27, C22:3

Heedless Passion

DEVIL IN THE FLESH, directed by Marco Bellocchio; screenplay (Italian, with English subtitles) by Mr. Bellocchio and Enrico Palandri, with the collaboration of Ennio de Concini; photography by Giuseppe Lanci; edited by Mirco Garrone; music by Carlo Crivelli; production managers, Angelo Barbagallo and Stefano Bolzoni; an Italian/French co-production of LP Films SRL/Istituto Luce/Films Sextile/FR3 FilmProduction. At Plaza, 58th St., east of Madison Ave. Running time: 110 minutes. This film is rated X.

Giulia Dozza	Maruschka Detmers
Andréa Raimondi	Federico Pitzalis
Mrs. Pulcini	Anita Laurenzi
Giacomo Pulcini	Riccardo de Torrebruna
Dr. Raimondi	Alberto di Stasio
Mrs. Dozza	Anna Orso
Don Pisacane	Claudio Botosso
Mrs. Raimondi	Catherine Diamant
The Terrorists	
	Lidia Broccolino, Stefano Abbati

By VINCENT CANBY

WHEN Raymond Radiguet was 14 years old, he asked Guillaume Apollinaire to read some of his poetry. Apollinaire didn't much like it, but cushioned his criticism. "Don't despair, sir," he said. "Remember Arthur Rimbaud didn't write his masterpiece until he was 17."

Radiguet began *his* masterpiece — the romantic novel "Le Diable au Corps" ("Devil in the Flesh") — when he was 17 or 18 and published it in 1923, the year he died of typhoid fever at the age of 20. Helped no doubt by what's been described as "American-style" publicity, and by Radiguet's liaison with Jean Cocteau, "Le Diable au Corps" was an instant success.

It's also been an enduring one, at least in France. With Alain-Fournier's "Le Grand Meaulnes," the Radiguet classic is discovered by youthful readers with the same kind of excitement that American college students come upon Ernest Hemingway, J. D. Salinger and Kurt Vonnegut.

Its World War I story, about the passionate affair of an adolescent boy and an older woman married to a French soldier at the front, is no longer as shocking as it once was. However, its cynicism (early critics found it unpatriotic) continues to speak to successive generations of restless young people at odds with inherited tradition.

In 1947, Claude Autant-Lara made the definitive film version, written by Jean Aurenche and Pierre Bost, starring Micheline Presle and introducing Gérard Philipe, who, though 25, looked like a teen-ager. Autant-Lara and his associates treated the material with such fidelity that the French Ambassador to Belgium walked out of a screening at a 1947 film festival in Brussels, and the film only arrived in this country two years later with a small cut.

The new "Devil in the Flesh" opening today at the Plaza Theater is something else entirely. Marco Bellocchio, the Italian director ("Fists in the Pocket," "Leap Into the Void," among others), has made no attempt to adapt the Radiguet original. Instead, he uses it loosely, more or less as inspiration for a contemporary romantic drama in which he once again explores his favorite themes — family relationships and the individual's relationship to the society that represses him.

It's a very mixed bag. This "Devil in the Flesh" is photographed in bright, shiny, primary colors, which (intentionally, I suspect) give everything, even the characters, the look of plastic. It's also more studiously erotic than anything Radiguet (or Autant-Lara) would have dared, yet so self-consciously theoretical that it has almost no emotional impact. It's like a chic, upscale picture-magazine with captions that are sometimes banal, sometimes incomprehensible

Federico Pitzalis, left, and Maruschka Detmers in "Devil in the Flesh."

and, on occasion, provocatively literate.

Mr. Bellocchio's "Devil in the Flesh" is about a teen-ager named Andréa (played by Federico Pitzalis, who looks a lot like an Italian version of the young Gérard Philipe) and Giulia (Maruschka Detmers), a beautiful, possibly schizophrenic young woman only a few years older than Andréa. Giulia, who's given to wild, unprovoked giggles, is not easily fathomable, either to Andréa or the audience. The daughter of an army officer assassinated by members of the Red Brigades, she's engaged to a terrorist standing trial for murder and sabotage.

Giacomo (Riccardo de Torrebruna), the terrorist, turns state's evidence and confesses to Giulia that as a complete mediocrity, he longs for the bourgeois life. Giulia, who seems to have been getting bored with him anyway, throws herself into her affair with Andréa with a ferocity that would consume most real-life teenagers.

Adding very Bellocchio-like complications to the situation is the fact that Giulia is a former patient of Andréa's father, a Freudian analyst, and may have had an affair with him.

•

The most persuasive character in the film is neither Andréa nor Giulia, but Mr. De Torrebruna's Giacomo, who exemplifies the exhausted, commonplace end of the rebellious 1960's. Giacomo is on screen only briefly, but his hymn to the joys of dreary, ordinary life is the movie's darkest, funniest moment.

Miss Detmers, a Dutch-born French actress (her Italian dialogue was dubbed by someone else, though her giggle is her own), and Mr. Pitzalis, a nonprofessional actor, are mainly photogenic, at least partially because Giulia and Andréa are romantic nonentities.

Giulia is somewhat more interesting for her beauty and for her startlingly heedless behavior. Whenever Giacomo or Andréa begins to talk in earnest with her, she has a habit of interfering with the speaker's clothing.

This "Devil in the Flesh" has gained a certain notoriety (and its X rating) for a short scene in which she performs fellatio on Andréa while he's telling her the story of Lenin's return to St. Petersburg in the spring of 1917. The scene isn't exactly offensive, nor is it especially necessary. It's not funny in the way of something that's utterly gratuitous — Mr. Bellocchio is too good a film maker for that. However, by being so specific, the scene successfully interrupts whatever dramatic line the film has previously established.

Just because the movie never sweeps you up in any emotional or intellectual way, it's possible to enjoy Mr. Bellocchio's stylistic mannerisms, including his fondness for long, uninterrupted takes that allow scenes to build naturally though, ultimately, to no great point.

Fairly early in the film there's a sequence in Giacomo's courtroom where a pair of unrepentant terrorists make love in full view of the spectators. The gesture is intended as the ultimate insult to the state, and it has its desired effect to the extent that it turns the courtroom upside down. Like Giacomo, those unidentified lovers remain in the memory far more vividly than Giulia and Andréa.

"Devil in the Flesh" is a movie that consistently upstages itself.

1987 My 29, C3:1

Zarah Leander

Adulation ·

MY LIFE FOR ZARAH LEANDER, a documentary directed, written, edited, photographed and produced by Christian Blackwood. At Public Theater, 425 Lafayette Street. Running time: 90 minutes. This film has no rating.
WITH: Zarah Leander, Paul Seiler, Margot Hielscher, Douglas Sirk, Michael Jary, Bruno Balz and Harold Prince

By JANET MASLIN

A FEMALE impersonator named Armand does a nightclub impression of Zarah Leander in Christian Blackwood's new film, a study of the German film star and the most ardent of her fans. But he cannot begin to match the freakishness of Miss Leander's own presence, which is captured in a variety of film clips here. The legendary "dark" voice that made Miss Leander famous was uncannily deep, and her posturing could be correspondingly muscular. Even at her comeliest, in Douglas Sirk's 1937 films "To New Shores" and "La Habanera," Zarah Leander looked and sounded very much like a man.

This made her extremely popular in Nazi Germany, as did the hearty, strenuous manner in which she could deliver even a seductive love song. Although she left Germany during World War II and returned to her native Sweden, Miss Leander never overcame her reputation as a Nazi favorite. She didn't get along with Goebbels, she later maintained in a television interview. But she found him "an interesting man" who had "a good sense of humor and interesting timing — everything else he did is none of my business." Miss Leander, who died in 1981 and whose appearance had by then changed dramatically for the worse, made numerous comeback attempts but never regained her former glory.

But in the eyes of some, she remained royalty. She can have had no more devoted a fan than Paul Seiler, who is the other subject of "My Life for Zarah Leander," which opens today at the Public Theater. The wan, bespectacled Mr. Seiler keeps a Zarah Leander shrine in his home in Germany, complete with 8-by-10 glossy photograph and a chair he' bought at auction (he weeps openly when remembering that Miss Leander's underthings were sold publicly at the same time). Mr. Seiler first heard Miss Leander's singing as a 7-year-old in 1943, met her in 1955 and subsequently did what he could to become her devoted servant. "She al-

ways wanted someone around to do something for her, and I accepted that," he says.

•

"My heart was beating fast, but I wasn't in love with her," Mr. Seiler recalls about an early meeting. "There was nothing erotic about it." Mr. Seiler, who, like many of Miss Leander's other devotees, is a homosexual, explains her as a figure with whom a man might easily identify. And Miss Leander herself, in interview footage, displays a kind of campy fragility ("They all think I'm strong. In my films I play those roles, but I'm not that way").

Asked about Miss Leander's appeal, men and women who knew her described her allure in the most glowing terms. "She was so breathtaking that people stopped dead in their tracks," one man declares. "I saw a woman fainting at the sight of her." The producer and director Harold Prince remembered thinking her almost unrecognizable "primarily because she was so heavy," and described something "bulldoggish" about her. "But she had enormous glamour," he says.

For Mr. Seiler, though, this goes way beyond ordinary adulation; in fact, the film's title refers to his avowed willingness to give his life for the star. When a critic attacked her and hurt Miss Leander's feelings, Mr. Seiler marched to the critic's office and dumped his entire collection of Leander memorabilia upon the man's desk. He reflects solemnly upon the importance of such gestures. "Without me, without us, there wouldn't be any stars," he observes. And he also questions the morality of abject devotion to a woman whose reputation has a black mark or two. Discussing the star's wartime attitudes with his friend Armand, Mr. Seiler asks, "But doesn't that hurt your love for Zarah?" Armand doesn't really see why it should.

Mr. Blackwood captures the ghoulishness of such star-worship, albeit with a little less wit or detachment than Gore Vidal brought to "Myra Breckinridge." He treats Mr. Seiler as perhaps a more fascinating figure than most viewers will find him, and adds some truly unnecessary footage of Mr. Seiler and Armand drinking champagne toasts to Armand's nightclub act. Zarah Leander herself remains a sad and shadowy figure, but the film does offer bizarre and compelling proof that she lives on.

1987 My 29, C8:1

SUMMER HEAT, directed by Michie Gleason; screenplay by Mr. Gleason, based on the novel "Here to Get My Baby Out of Jail" by Louise Shivers; director of photography, Elliot Davis; edited by Mary Bauer; music by Richard Stone; production design by Marsha Hinds; produced by William Tennant; released by Atlantic Releasing Corporation. At the Coronet, 59th St. at Third Ave. Running time: 90 minutes. This film is rated R.
Roxy .... Lori Singer
Aaron .... Anthony Edwards
Jack .... Bruce Abbott
Ruth .... Kathy Bates
Will .... Clu Gulager
Baby .... Jessie Kent
Strother .... Noble Willingham
Bass .... Nesbitt Blaisdell
Neb .... Matt Almond
Georgeanna .... Jane Cecil
Aunt Patty .... Miriam Byrd-Nethery
Callie .... Jessica Leigh Mann
Raider .... Michael Mattick
Mr. Tatie .... Conrad McLaren

THE beautiful, slinky Lori Singer moves like a sleepwalker through "Summer Heat," barely shaking her

Marriage in Turmoil In "Summer Heat," Lori Singer and Anthony Edwards star as a young couple whose relationship is rocked by the arrival of a handsome drifter.

mane of back-lighted hair. As a sheltered young wife and mother in rural North Carolina tobacco country, she is called upon to knead, scrub, mend and otherwise convey the becalmed monotony of her life. "Summer Heat," adapted from Louise Shivers's much more imaginatively titled novel "Here to Get My Baby Out of Jail," is about the forces that overtake this young woman and reshape her life when a handsome stranger comes to town. It may sound torrid, but on the page it was larger than that, strongly evocative of a place, a time (1937) and an entire way of life. On the screen, it's like watching tobacco grow.

As written and directed by Michie Gleason, "Summer Heat" is serious, reverent and good-looking, but it lacks assurance. The pacing is uniformly flat and the script is a string of one-idea scenes; sometimes a whole episode seems designed to allow a character to deliver a single line. Miss Singer's listlessness is no help, and it is something very different from the ingrained passivity of Roxy, Miss Shivers's heroine. Roxy is the wife of a farmer named Aaron (Anthony Edwards) and has a daughter named Baby, and at 20 or so, her life is entirely circumscribed; she has no future. Roxy's father (nicely played by Clu Gulager) runs the local funeral home, which somehow seems a warmer and more comforting place than Aaron's farm.

When Jack Ruffin (Bruce Abbott) appears, Roxy doesn't so much fall in love with him as sense a change in the wind. "Well, I thought I cared something about him," Miss Shivers's Roxy said much, much later, after the events at Aaron's farm became a matter of public record. "I never cared a whole lot." Simple and seductive as this story seems, Roxy's passivity and her larger imprisonment make it a lot more difficult to dramatize than the romance-novel version of the same events would be.

"Summer Heat" has a carefully achieved rustic look and a few flashes of vitality, as when Jack first appears in town under a Clark Gable movie marquee, or when Roxy tells her amorous husband "Aaron, sometimes I think you're just doin' this cause you can't think of anything better to do." But as the story picks up momentum and moves toward its violent denouement pitting Aaron against Jack, the film loses more and more steam. Roxy's numbness remains impenetrable, even when her life becomes the stuff of headlines.

"Everyone in the world has some kind of secret," a relative tells her. "But everyone doesn't get found out and have their picture put in the paper."

JANET MASLIN

1987 My 29, C8:4

'Unfinished Business'

VIVECA LINDFORS is the writer, director and star of "Unfinished Business," which looks and sounds like a monodrama, though there are a number of other speaking parts in it. The film, a project of the Directing Workshop for Women, of the American Film Institute, is an intensely self-absorbed, self-referential work about Helena (Miss Lindfors), a great actress attempting to come to terms with herself and her dedication to the theater, thus "to justify my time on earth."

That's not easy. It takes a lot of self-analytical talk by Helena and the people around her, especially her former husband, Ferenzy (Peter Donat), a great actor who left Helena for a younger woman and his own theater in Berlin. The setting is Helena's theater in Southern California during a festival of international theater companies.

Miss Lindfors uses the camera to examine herself with a relentlessness that is often less a revelation than an imposition. We're given great close-ups of her face and her body, clothed and unclothed. She spares herself (and the audience) nothing to do with the ravages of time, though her magnificent bone structure preserves the outline of the facial beauty that originally took her to Hollywood in the mid-1940's.

The confrontations between Helena and Ferenzy are not super. At best, their dialogue is full of lines from terrible plays as yet (one hopes) unwritten. "Revenge and betrayal!" one of them shouts at the other. "You throw those words around like fireflies." Mostly the dialogue just sort of accumulates. The line, "What's happening?" is immediately followed by "What's happening to us?"

The subsidiary characters include Helena's grown son (James Morrison), who gets to speak the kind of line that self-destructive amateur dramatists never seem to be able to cut out of a script. "I'm so sick and

tired of theatrical moments in real life," he says at one point.

The pictorial quality is fuzzy, being a transfer to film from the original tape. "Unfinished Business" opens today at the Public Theater on a double-bill with Fritz Lang's "Moonfleet" (1955), in which Miss Lindfors appears with Stewart Granger, George Sanders and Joan Greenwood.

VINCENT CANBY

1987 My 29, C8:4

Big-Time Small Town

ATHENS, GA. — INSIDE/OUT, directed and written by Tony Gayton; director of photography, James Herbert; edited by Adam Wolfe; music by various composers; produced by Bill Cody. At Waverly 1, Avenue of the Americas and Third Street. Running time: 82 minutes. This film has no rating.

A NUMBER of the musicians seen in "Athens, Ga. — Inside/Out" point to Pylon as the best band in town, but Pylon isn't even operational any more. The group, according to one member, "just decided to quit while we were still having a good time." Formerly art students, the band members now hold odd jobs; the lead singer, a dynamo on stage, works in a copying shop. "But I never planned on being a musician, so it's no big loss in my life," she said. Bear in mind that Pylon, having played several shows with U2 and begun to get some big-city bookings, stood on the verge of stardom while throwing in the towel.

In Athens, Ga., which is the subject of Tony Gayton's bright, scrappy new documentary, this kind of attitude makes more sense than it might in other places. The musicians who are interviewed and perform in concert sequences display a uniformly easy-going attitude toward mainstream success. Some of them have made it (like the B-52's, senior statesmen of the Athens scene, and R.E.M.), and some have little chance. But they all share an appreciation for the friendly and comforting cultural atmosphere of Athens, and for the energy and eccentricity that have put the place on the map.

"Paint sacred art!" the Rev. Howard Finster says his finger — or, rather, a little painted face that appeared on his finger — told him one day. "I'm no professional, not me," he replied. "How do you know?" asked the finger. And Mr. Finster said to himself "How *do* I know?" So he began making primitive paintings, full of faces like the little one on the finger, and eventually a group he thought of as "Peepin' Heads" asked him to do an album cover. Actually, it was Talking Heads, and the cover won an award for Mr. Finster, who is better and better known as a primitive artist these days. Mr. Finster fits very comfortably into the Athens scene.

In fact, "Athens, Ga. — Inside/Out" recalls "True Stories," the film starring and directed by David Byrne of Talking Heads; though it has none of the ironic detachment, it has much the same fondness for strange real-life phenomena. This is even evident in the wide range of hybrid musical styles Athens has produced, from punk rockabilly to after-the-fact hippie to rock-and-roll Irish lament. The groups heard here, all of them as lively off stage as on, include the Bar-B-Q Killers (named for a local criminal), the Flat Duo Jets (whose

crazed-looking lead singer should consider a movie career), the Kilkenny Cats and the Squalls. None of them sounds imitative of any of the others.

Mr. Gayton takes a vigorous and appreciative look at all of this, and his film has a refreshingly homemade feeling; it's as likably odd and unpretentious as Athens itself. If the film dwells too long on such minor details as how and where the musicians acquired their equipment, it's also nicely free-form. The participants are invited to show off their favorite Athens phenomena, and they do it with gusto. One points out his Elvis Presley bathroom, decorated with all sorts of Elvis memorabilia, including what looks like a tiny doorstop by Mr. Finster, a work entitled "Elvis at 3." Another notes that "Maxie's down the road is the only township that I know of that has an apostrophe in its name." And everyone sings the praises of Walter's Restaurant. Athens is the kind of place where Walter can keep an "M.B." plaque on his counter, and explain that it means "Master of Barbecue."

JANET MASLIN

1987 My 29, C14:1

Pastoral Symphony

SALVATION!, directed by Beth B; screenplay by Beth B and Tom Robinson; director of photography, Francis Kenny; edited by Elizabeth Kling; music by new Order, Cabaret Voltaire, The Hood and Arthur Baker; production design, Lester Cohen; produced by Beth B and Michael H. Shambert; distributed by Circle Releasing Corp. At the Bleecker Street Cinema, at LaGuardia Place. Running time: 80 minutes. This film is rated R.

Rev. Edward Randall	Stephen McHattie
Lenore Finley	Dominique Davalos
Rhonda Stample	Exene Cervenka
Jerome Stample	Viggo Mortensen
Oliver	Rockets Redglare
Stanley	Billy Bastiani

By VINCENT CANBY

IN the late 1970's Beth B and Scott B began making Super-8, home-movie spectacles for the entertainment of their friends in the downtown music and art scenes. Five years ago they went all-out for their 16-millimeter send-up of Big Business, "Vortex," which was shown at the New York Film Festival.

Now, on her own, Beth B has directed "Salvation," a comparatively ambitious (35-millimeter), mini-budgeted satire of television evangelists so topical that it could have been made yesterday, which is also the way it looks.

With Beth B, however, slapdash is very much a part of her comic style. It's as if she and her associates

Stephen McHattie in "Salvation."

agreed that more carefully considered thought and imagination would obscure (and possibly ennoble) the sleazy subject being satirized.

•

"Salvation," opening today at the Bleecker Street Cinema, has its share of wonderfully tawdry, privileged moments separated by long, flat intervals, which are devoted either to information necessary to the plot, or to music-video material. The only consistent thing in the movie is its exuberantly expressed, very dim view of the quality of American life.

According to Beth B, she became interested in television evangelism two years ago when she attended what she calls an "evangelist superconference" at the Rev. Jerry Fallwell's headquarters in Lynchburg, Va. Out of that initial encounter with the new religious proselytizers came her screenplay (written with Tom Robinson) about the Rev. Edward Randall (Stephen McHattie), a young, handsome, sexually repressed pastor of a ministry-of-the-air in desperate need of better ratings.

The answers to the pastor's prayers are provided by a blackmailer named Jerome Stample (Viggo Mortensen), an out-of-work shipyard worker looking for a fast

Preachers

Exene Cerrenka appears in "Salvation!," about television evangelists.

Directorial Debut Viveca Lindfors directed and acted in "Unfinished Business," a drama about family relationships, with Peter Donat.

buck; Jerome's wife Rhonda (Exene Cervenka), who eventually finds her calling as the pastor's co-star (described as "the next Shirley Mac-Laine"), and Rhonda's sister Lenore (Dominique Davalos), an over-the-hill nymphet who quite enjoys the pastor's sado-masochistic games.

The maddening thing about "Salvation" is the way it always falls short of realizing the explosive laughs that remain buried just beneath the surface. The movie sets up a farcical situation, such as the pastor's first encounter with the sexy Lenore, and then allows the comic possibilities to dwindle away in what looks to be desperate improvisation. Its attention span is short.

The film is prescient, but only randomly funny. The soundtrack score, rudely satiric on its own, often overwhelms the images. There's a good deal of invention in the settings, including the Stamples' awful little house with the American flag and the Disney figures in the front yard, as well as in the performances by Miss Davalos, Mr. Mortensen and Miss Cervenka.

Mr. McHattie is exceptionally good as the wayward, bigoted pastor. The performance is so intense — and so legitimate — that it threatens to bust the film apart, which it might have done if "Salvation" weren't so loosely organized that there's nothing much to bust apart anyway.

1987 My 31, 51:1

Good Guys and Bad

THE UNTOUCHABLES, directed by Brian De Palma; written by David Mamet; director of photography, Stephen H. Burum; edited by Jerry Greenberg; music by Ennio Morricone; art director, William A. Elliott; visual consultant, Patrizia Von Brandenstein; produced by Art Linson; released by Paramount Pictures. At Embassy 1, Broadway and 46th Street; New York Twin, Second Avenue and 66th Street; 34th Street Showplace, between Second and Third Avenues; 84th Street Six, at Broadway; Embassy 2, Broadway and 47th Street; 86th Street Twin, at Lexington Avenue; Movie Center 5, 125th Street between Powell and Douglas Boulevard. Running time: 120 minutes. This film is rated R.

Eliot Ness	Kevin Costner
Al Capone	Robert De Niro
Jim Malone	Sean Connery
George Stone	Andy Garcia
Oscar Wallace	Charles Martin Smith
Frank Nitti	Billy Drago

By VINCENT CANBY

"THE UNTOUCHABLES," Hollywood's latest big-budget, high-concept, mass-market reworking of material not entirely fresh, has more endings than Beethoven's Fifth, but it's also packed with surprises, not the least being that it's a smashing work. It's vulgar, violent, funny and sometimes breathtakingly beautiful. After this "Untouchables," all other movies dealing with Prohibition Chicago, Al Capone and the lawmen who brought him to justice (for income tax evasion) must look a bit anemic.

The film, opening today at the New York Twin and other theaters, is of such entertaining order that it almost redeems Hollywood's current reputation for idiotic profligacy and total irrelevance.

Taking as their source material the 1957 book "The Untouchables," written by the G-man Eliot Ness with Oscar Fraley, as well as the popular television series starring Robert Stack, the producers have somehow

Al Capone, played by Robert De Niro, second from left, in a courtroom confrontation with Eliot Ness, portrayed by Kevin Costner, second from right, in "The Untouchables."

managed to assemble a movie that has its own distinctive personality. It can't have been easy, considering the idiosyncratic talents involved.

The playwright David Mamet ("Sexual Perversity in Chicago," "Glengarry Glen Ross") wrote the first-rate, very Mamet-sounding screenplay, which has been directed by Brian De Palma as if on a dare. Mr. De Palma ("Carrie," "The Fury," "Scarface") always goes too far, but this time it's more or less the scheme of the movie.

In addition to being a jazzed-up version of the old-fashioned cops-and-robbers movie, "The Untouchables" also represents a confrontation you don't often see in movies of this sort. On one side there's a worldly Neapolitan sensibility, represented by the movie's Al Capone (and, perhaps, by Mr. De Palma). On the other side, there's the puritanical, WASP-y ethic that originally brought on Prohibition in an attempt to legislate American morals and, in failing, substantially altered American life, not for the better. In much the same way, the florid look of the film is at war with the cautionary tale being told.

These polarities are exemplified in the film through the rich performances by Robert De Niro, who, speaking Mr. Mamet's lines, creates a viciously mythic Al Capone, and by Kevin Costner as the young, blandly handsome Eliot Ness who, by the end of the film, is no longer as straight as the arrow he once was.

Mr. Costner, whose scenes were cut out of "The Big Chill" and who had small parts in "American Flyers" and "Silverado," went into "The Untouchables" as a vaguely familiar face. He comes out of it a new star with his own, very particular screen presence. Like Montgomery Clift, whom he sometimes resembles, Mr. Costner projects a haunted quality that adds unexpected dimension to what could have been a fairly commonplace role.

Equally fine is Sean Connery as Jim Malone, the only "good" cop in Mayor (Big Bill) Thompson's pervasively corrupt Chicago. For that reason, Jim Malone is walking a beat as a patrolman when Eliot Ness enrolls him in the elite corps of crime-busters known as "the untouchables." In any other movie, this, too, would be a pretty ordinary role but, as written by Mr. Mamet, directed by Mr. De Palma and played by Mr. Connery, Jim Malone becomes something like the original on which all similar roles were patterned.

"The Untouchables" is often bloody and outrageous, but never quite as bloody and outrageous as Mr. De Palma's "Scarface," an updated revision of the 1932 Howard Hawks classic with Paul Muni. In "The Untouchables," Mr. De Palma is constantly teetering on the edge of offensiveness to credibility, conventional concepts of decency and movie manners. He opens with a dizzy overhead shot (the camera looking down on Al Capone holding a press conference while he has his nails manicured), and never really lets up until after the film's great set-piece (a shootout in Chicago's Union Station), which should — but doesn't — end the film.

In between there's virtually an anthology of De Palma shock effects, including an especially devious sequence in which the horror comes from witnessing the execution of a man already dead. Occasionally, the director really does go too far, at one point by opening up "The Untouchables" into a kind of mock-Western. When Eliot Ness and his associates stake out the Canadian border to catch an incoming shipment of illegal booze, the movie looks more like 1870 than 1930, which is, I'm sure, intentional.

Mr. De Palma and his cameraman, Stephen H. Burum, the film's "visual consultant," Patrizia Von Brandenstein, and the art director, William A. Elliott, make extensive use of locations to be found only in Chicago, including the exterior of Louis Sullivan's magnificent Auditorium Hotel and Theater (now Roosevelt University). The gaudy lobby of the old Balaban & Katz Chicago Theater serves as the lobby of Capone's hotel, and the Rookery, remodeled by Frank Lloyd Wright in 1907, serves as the headquarters of the Chicago police.

The excellent supporting cast includes Charles Martin Smith, as the Government accountant whose idea it is to nab Capone on a tax rap; Andy Garcia, as a member of "the untouchables" who has changed his surname to Stone to hide his Italian heritage, and Billy Drago, as Frank Nitti, a Capone lieutenant who carries a gun permit hand-written by the Mayor.

Though the bootleg era has been done to death in movies and on television, Mr. De Palma and Mr. Mamet rediscover it, not necessarily as it was, but as it's perceived in legend shaped by a certain amount of amused skepticism. In spite of its title, "The Untouchables" is an original.

1987 Je 3, C17:1

Poor Little Rich Boy

MORGAN STEWART'S COMING HOME, directed by Alan Smithee; screenplay by Ken Hixon and David Titcher; director of photography, Richard Brooks; edited by Robert Lederman; musical supervisor, Peter Afterman; production designer, Charles Bennett; produced by Stephen Friedman; released by New Century/Vista Film Company. At U.A. Twin, Broadway at 49th Street; U.A. Gemini Twin, 64th Street and Second Avenue, and other theaters. Running time: 96 minutes. This film is rated PG-13.

Morgan Stewart	Jon Cryer
Nancy Stewart	Lynn Redgrave
Tom Stewart	Nicholas Pryor
Emily	Viveka Davis
Jay Springsteen	Paul Gleason
General Fenton	Andrew Duncan
Ivan	Savely Kramorov
Garrett	John David Cullum

By CARYN JAMES

IF energy and charm were enough to rejuvenate the poor-little-rich-boy story, Jon Cryer could have saved "Morgan Stewart's Coming Home." In "Pretty in Pink," he even managed to make a character named Ducky believable — he was the misfit who pined for Molly Ringwald and laughed at himself before anyone else did. But Mr. Cryer can't yet carry a film on the strength of his snaggletoothed smile, and the people and events around him in "Morgan Stewart" lack the quirky feel of real life.

As Morgan, Mr. Cryer plays the teen-aged son of plastic parents — a wimpy senator and his monstrously ambitious wife. They beg off Thanksgiving dinner because they'd rather do the "Donahue" show, but call their son home from prep school when it's time to puff up the Senator's family-man image in his re-election campaign. All Morgan wants, of course, is a little love. All he gets are marching orders from his father's slimy campaign manager.

As he searches for affection, Morgan finds a rich little poor girl named Emily (Viveka Davis, whose character is too wise and wacky to be true, but whose enthusiasm matches Mr. Cryer's) and they conspire to save Morgan's innocent father from political ruin at the hands of a dirty trickster. The film is loaded with predictable turns, including a lame running joke about the broken English the Stewarts' Russian butler speaks. Don't ask why a Russian is working for a United States senator; this is one innocent politician. In fact, politics are beside the point here. If they mattered, Lynn Redgrave's role as Morgan's aloof, power-behind-the-throne mother, Nancy, complete with some Nancy Reaganish ensembles, would be awfully heavy-handed. But with no political edge, she's just a misunderstanding Mom, and the greatest challenge for Ms. Redgrave is keeping up her adept American accent.

"Morgan Stewart's Coming Home," now playing at the U.A. Twin and other theaters, looks like a made-for-television movie, and is so sitcom-family wholesome that when Morgan and his girlfriend change out of some freezing, drenched clothes and jump in a hot shower together, they keep their underwear on. It's hard to imagine any adult sitting through this movie without dozing off or cracking up, but it's a harmless enough fantasy, and if Jon Cryer's career takes off — he's due in at least two more films, "Dudes" and "Superman IV" — "Morgan Stewart" may find a place in the archives as an early little movie in which the star wasn't nearly matched by the material.

•

"Morgan Stewart's Coming Home" is rated PG-13 ("Special Parental Guidance Suggested for Those Younger Than 13"). There's that delicate shower scene and some indelicate language.

1987 Je 4, C16:4

The Low Road

QUIET HAPPINESS, directed by Dusan Hanak; screenplay (Czechoslovak with English subtitles) by Mr. Hanak and Ondrej Sulaj; director of photography, Viktor Svoboda; distributed by International Film Exchange. Film Forum 1, 57 Watts

Street. Running time: 89 minutes. This film has no rating.
Sonia .... Magda Vasaryova
Emil .... Robert Koltai
Dr. Macko .... Jiri Bartoska
Dr. Galova .... Jana Brejchova

FILM FORUM 1 began a week-long festival of seven recent Czechoslovak films yesterday that will be shown in rotation. Dusan Hanak's "Quiet Happiness," the only one of the seven I've seen, will be shown nightly at 8, while three of the six others will make up the rest of each day's bill.

"Quiet Happiness" is a short-focused, emotionally pinched film that has been described as "an Eastern European 'Unmarried Woman.'" It's about Sonia (Magda Vasaryova), a pretty, love-starved nurse who, in the course of the movie, gets up enough nerve to leave her husband, a slob-bish electrician, and then to have the baby of her weak-willed, handsome married lover.

•

As written by Mr. Hanak and Ondrej Sulaj, Sonia is not a very interesting or even appealing figure. It's difficult to understand how she ever came to marry her husband, whom she treats quite badly, or what she can offer her lover except long, soulful, slightly resentful glances. The camera examines Miss Vasaryova's face in many fond close-ups, but fails to come up with any reasonable answers.

The saddest, most convincing thing about the film is the banality of Czechoslovak society, which one sees, almost as if by accident, in the corner of each film frame. One begins to suspect that this is not exactly intentional when, half-way through, the film quotes from Liv Ullmann's memoirs, seemingly under the impression that Miss Ullmann is Simone de Beauvoir.   *VINCENT CANBY*

1987 Je 4, C17:1

Sees All, Knows All

SHADEY, directed by Philip Saville; written by Snoo Wilson; director of photography, Roger Deakins; edited by Chris Kelly; music by Colin Towns; production designer, Norman Garwood; produced by Otto Plaschkes; released by Skouras Pictures, Inc. At Quad Cinema, 13th Street between Fifth Avenue and Avenue of the Americas. Running time: 90 minutes. This film is rated PG-13.
Oliver Shadey .... Antony Sher
Dr. Cloud .... Billie Whitelaw
Sir Cyril Landau .... Patrick Macnee
Carol Landau .... Leslie Ash
Captain Amies .... Bernard Hepton
Dick Darnley .... Larry Lamb
Lady Constance Landau . Katherine Helmond
Shulman .... Jon Cartwright
Carl .... Jessie Birdsall

MAYBE "Shadey" is meant to be a spoof on formula movies. Snoo Wilson, who wrote the British feature that opens today at the Quad Cinema, has tossed elements of many formulas into his brew — science-fiction, spy thriller, screwball comedy, black humor, political satire, psychosex, fantasy and more — and mixed ill. The result has little fizz and leaves a sourish aftertaste.

Oliver Shadey is a young fellow with the gift of seeing things that ordinary people can't see and putting them on film. A useful tool, that, for British intelligence, which would like to inspect Soviet submarines close up, and the peaceably inclined Shadey is put to work for his country against his

Antony Sher

will. All Shadey wants is to be a woman, but he lacks the money for the operation. How he manages to achieve his desire on the cheap is the jest of a plot that does not bear recounting.

Shadey is played by a newcomer to feature films, Antony Sher, of the Royal Shakespeare Company and trying awfully hard to be cute. Accompanying his new face are several familiar faces from television. Patrick Macnee, of "The Avengers," plays a big-business man who trades Shadey to the intelligence service for a suite of offices. Katherine Helmond, of "Soap," plays his crazy wife. Bernard Hepton, of John le Carré's "Smiley" series, manages to eke a glimmer of humor from the role of an unintelligent operative. Billie Whitelaw, known for her interpretations of Samuel Beckett's plays, is entirely wasted as Shadey's mannish handler.

The director, Philip Saville, has a knack for muddle. "Shadey" is a cheerless comedy, a chill-less thriller, a charmless fantasy. Swallow at your own risk.

•

"Shadey" is rated PG-13 ("Special Parental Guidance Suggested for Those Younger Than 13"), owing to some sexual hanky-panky and one scene of violence.

WALTER GOODMAN

1987 Je 5, C10:1

Postwar Scenes

THEATER IN RUINS, directed by Irmgard von zur Muehlen; screenplay (German with English subtitles) by Dieter Hildebrandt; produced by Bengt von zur Muehlen; narrated by Erich Schwarz; distributed by Chronos-Film. At Thalia SoHo, 15 Vandam Street, between Avenue of the Americas and Seventh Avenue. Running time: 56 minutes. This film has no rating. Interviews with: Friederich Luft, Hans Borgelt, Boleslaw Barlog, Ita Maximowna, Hildegard Knef and Klaus Schwarzkopf

By WALTER GOODMAN

HARDLY had Nazi Germany died in 1945 than Berlin's theaters began to come to life. The need for diversion seemed almost as great as any of the other many needs of the residents of a destroyed and conquered city. People lined up at box offices, much as they lined up for water or fuel, some having walked for two or three hours to see a production of "The Gay Pari-

sienne." "Theater in Ruins," Irmgard von zur Muehlen's absorbing documentary now at the Thalia SoHo, begins at that point and goes on to tell, with clips and stills from productions of the time, how the re-emergent theater was divided, along with the rest of Berlin, into political zones.

The Russians were first off the mark as patrons of the arts, subsidizing German and Soviet plays and occasionally an American work, such as William Saroyan's "Time of Your Life," which seemed to contain an acceptable message about America. They set up a culture club called the Seagull, where theater folk could get a hot meal; we see a Soviet officer straight-facedly promising a freedom that German artists had not known for almost a decade.

Makeshift theaters sprouted all over the city. Some Jewish directors and actors who had fled the Nazis returned. One of the first postwar productions was of Lessing's "Nathan the Wise." In the hard winter of 1945, actors rehearsed in overcoats, musicians wore gloves, audiences covered themselves with blankets.

•

As political divisions hardened, the West countered on the cultural front with productions of French, British and American works, including Thornton Wilder's "Skin of Our Teeth," whose chronicle of a family enduring disaster after disaster had special meaning to Germans of 1945. The Western occupying powers blacklisted actors who performed in an anti-American play. The Russians took umbrage at a production of Sartre's anti-Communist "Dirty Hands," and were further irritated by "The Flies," with its warnings against the power of the state. By the 1950's Bertolt Brecht had settled in East Berlin and set up the Berliner Ensemble to do his didactic dramas, while in the Western half of the city European and American intellectuals were calling for freedom. The split was complete.

Such is the history sketched by "Theater in Ruins," based on a book by Hans Borgelt. At less than an hour, the documentary is too short to do more than suggest the influence of politics on postwar culture, and for those who do not understand German, scenes from the plays, presented without subtitles, are more tantalizing than illuminating. You leave the movie wanting more, yet remembering those early shots, of a defeated people emerging from their shelters to an uncertain future — and eagerly filling any space that might serve as a theater. The idea of it is so moving that you may even forget to ask yourself what all those writers, directors, actors and members of the audience were doing during the war.

1987 Je 5, C10:4

Ya Big Lug

HARRY AND THE HENDERSONS, directed by William Dear; written by Mr. Dear, William E. Martin and Ezra D. Rappaport; director of photography, Allen Daviau; edited by Donn Cambern; music by Bruce Broughton; production designer, James Bissell; produced by Richard Vane and Mr. Dear; released by Universal Pictures. At Movieland, Broadway at 47th St.; New York Twin, Second Ave. and 66th St.; 34th St. Showplace, between Second and Third Avenues; 84th St. Six, at Broadway. Running time: 105 minutes. This film is rated PG.
George Henderson .... John Lithgow
Nancy Henderson .... Melinda Dillon

Sarah Henderson ....Margaret Langrick
Ernie Henderson ....Joshua Rudoy
Harry ....Kevin Peter Hall
Jacques Lafleur .... David Suchet
Irene Moffitt .... Lainie Kazan
Dr. Wallace Wrightwood .... Don Ameche
George Henderson Sr. ....M. Emmet Walsh
Sgt. Mancini ....Bill Ontiveros
Dirty Harry Officer ....David Richardt

By VINCENT CANBY

Attention must be paid when a movie is as aggressively awful as "Harry and the Hendersons," though it's so pin-headed that it could be the last of its inbred line. It's not likely to spawn.

The film, produced by Steven Spielberg's Amblin Entertainment, is such a witless rehash of Mr. Spielberg's own "E. T." that one begins to wonder how that classic ever came to be made. In "Harry and the Hendersons," the "creature," later to be named Harry, is the legendary Bigfoot, the towering, hairy half-man, half-beast that stalks the mountains of the Pacific Northwest and provides copy for supermarket newspapers. If he exists, he can sue for defamation of character.

It's the conceit of William Dear, the director and co-author of the screenplay, that a sitcom family unit (one impulsive dad, one patient mom and one wretched child of each sex) runs over Bigfoot while driving back to Seattle in its station wagon after a camping trip. For reasons not easy to follow, the Hendersons decide to take the domestic King Kong home, possibly to sell the carcass. When it turns out he isn't dead, they nurse him back to health and attempt to keep his existence a secret. Most of the film's jokes are about Harry's smell and size. He desperately needs a bath and a deodorant, and he's so big and heavy that he breaks chairs, floors and ceilings.

•

Harry is played by a 7-foot-2-inch actor, Kevin Peter Hall, in what appears to be a slightly altered Chewbacca suit. However, it's not his looks or reputed smell that offend — it's his unctuous manner, which is that of the film itself. Harry is so sentimental he'd weep at the sheer, sweet wonderfulness of a Crazy Eddie television commercial. Tears of gratitude well up in his eyes when someone *doesn't* swat him. Unlike E. T., who regards the world with a sophisticated if kindly dubiety, Harry, who's meant to be lovable, is simply dumb. He's the ad-man's dream of the perfect consumer. He'd buy anything.

His abject adoration of the boorish Hendersons and their plastic way of life is not satiric. In the way of sitcoms, "Harry and the Hendersons"

sanctifies the values of an imagined American society that's never looked quite as scarily empty-headed as it does here.

Mr. Spielberg's own films about Middle America are never this vacuous, perhaps because his visions are based on first-hand observation of people and places. His movies are somehow related to the real world.

There's a sharp, comic edge even to an all-out horror film on the order of "Poltergeist." "Harry and the Hendersons," which opens today at the 34th Street Showplace and other theaters, is based not on life but other people's fictions.

The cast includes John Lithgow, Melinda Dillon and Don Ameche, who've demonstrated their talents in

other movies and needn't be held accountable here.

•

"Harry and the Hendersons," which has been rated PG *("Parental Guidance Suggested"), includes some vulgar language.*

1987 Je 5, C14:5

FILM VIEW/Janet Maslin

Excess Baggage

ORDINARILY, UPON ENTERING a movie theater, you check your baggage at the door. That baggage consists of whatever nonessential information you may have picked up concerning the fiscal, professional or amorous peculiarities of those who made the film, or miscellaneous tidbits that are even more marginal. Was so-and-so lately sighted with a baby and a stroller in Central Park? Is movie star X being outrageously overpaid? Does Y produce nothing but surefire spinoffs? It's seldom fair to keep such data in mind while watching a film. More to the point, it's seldom helpful.

But there are times when an awareness of outside information is inevitable, and at these times a little judgment is in order. Does it matter, as you watch Brian De Palma's great-looking "Untouchables," that this immensely entertaining gangster film must have been very costly to make? Or that part of the budget went into paying Bob Hoskins's salary after Robert De Niro replaced him as Al Capone? The latter fact is worth noting, but it does nothing to diminish the sweeping malevolence of Mr. De Niro's delightful performance in the role. And the former point, the one about the budget, should have little real bearing upon anyone's enjoyment of the film. If anything, it summons the satisfaction of seeing money well spent.

■

Certainly no one who has not spent the last month on the moon can watch "Ishtar" without money in mind. Did it really cost $51 million? Were Warren Beatty and Dustin Hoffman each paid actors' salaries of $5 million or so? Didn't Elaine May waste an extraordinary amount of film, or time, or catering costs, or *something* to run up a tab that high? Doesn't all this bespeak a dreadful unprofessionalism and cast an inescapable shadow over the finished product?

You would think, to read the most outraged and dismissive accounts of "Ishtar," that it does. However, behind that smokescreen of spurious and/or irrelevant information lurks an amazingly inoffensive film, and one that happens, at times, to be very funny indeed. It is undoubtedly funnier than, say, the Dan Aykroyd/Chevy Chase version of the same story would have been, and a $30 or $40 million budget for a film starring those two might not raise eyebrows anywhere. Yet something about this particular combination of personalities, or about Miss May's famously dilatory working habits, has turned "Ishtar" into the debacle of the hour. It's hard to believe that those who compare it with classic megabuck flops like "Heaven's Gate" and "Howard the Duck" could realistically equate the ordeals of sitting through either of those films with the lighthearted pleasures of this one.

The most salient fact about Columbia Pictures' "Ishtar," though, is that it isn't costing you or me or anyone else who is not a Coca-Cola stockholder a dime. A terribly overpriced restaurant meal may be cause for consumer complaints, but the same $6 that gets you into "Ernest Goes to Camp" or "Meatballs III" or "Evil Dead 2" will get you into "Ishtar," too. So the offense, if it exists, is not against us. And the implications of the failure of "Ishtar," if indeed it turns out to be a failure — it may well have a second chance on cable and on video cassette, long after the present furor is forgotten — will not be terribly broad. Mr. Beatty may look less foolproof as a producer. Another studio may think twice before giving Miss May — who could certainly make funny films at half the price, or even at a tenth — carte blanche. And maybe the stars will think twice about accepting other singing roles, although I personally do not think they should.

■

So the excess information audiences may bring to "Ishtar" is unnecessary at best. But the case of "Beverly Hills Cop II" is different. Here, too, is a film that cannot be watched in a vacuum, even though it would improve if it could. Joke for joke, scene for scene, pound for pound, this sequel would seem almost as funny as the original film if the original film had not been — well, *original.*

But it was. And the sequel is nothing more than a calculating knock-off, however skillfully the copying has been done. It's apparent right from Mr. Murphy's first scene in the new film, which is almost exactly the same as his first scene in the *old* film, that strict imitation, augmented by attention-getting rock video effects, is what the producers Don Simpson and Jerry Bruckheimer ("Flashdance," "Top Gun") and the director Tony Scott ("Top Gun") have in mind.

Just Visiting
John Lithgow and Don Ameche star in "Harry and the Hendersons," a comedy about a typical family in the Pacific Northwest that takes in an unusual house guest

Ralph Nelson

Our path to a film is often paved with reports and gossip that may or may not be relevant.

Anyone with a memory will be at least faintly aware of the strong similarities between the two films; anyone who watches a tape of "Beverly Hills Cop" within a month of seeing the new film will find the resemblance astonishing. Does this matter? It certainly does. This kind of knowledge isn't excess baggage; it happens to be extremely germane. Because if Elaine May and Warren Beatty are individuals who make films very infrequently, and who work in idiosyncratic ways, Simpson and Bruckheimer amount to a cottage industry, and a very influential one at that. Their hit-making techniques have once again proven phenomenally successful in commercial terms — in its first weekend, "Beverly Hills Cop II" took in $33 million, or nearly 3½ times what "Ishtar" grossed in two weeks. So those techniques are bound to be imitated. And a box-office affirmation of methods this shameless will have lasting implications for us all.

It's not that "Beverly Hills Cop II" isn't funny. It's just that, when the excess baggage is taken into account, it's no laughing matter.

□

1987 Je 7, II:24:1

15 Minutes

ANDY WARHOL, directed by Lana Jokel; photographed by Mark Woodcock, Roger Murphy and Miss Jokel; produced by Michael Blackwood; a Michael Blackwood Production. Running time: 53 minutes. This film has no rating. At the Public Theater, 425 Lafayette Street.

By JANET MASLIN

THE friends, critics and colleagues who discuss Andy Warhol and his career in Lana Jokel's 1973 documentary say much the same things that obituary writers observed about him in February. At the time this film was made, the perception of Mr. Warhol as a brilliant manipulator, a dedicated voyeur and man of keen commercial judgment was already in place.

So were the thoughts — expressed here by a critic, David Bourdon, and a film maker, Emile de Antonio — that there might be more effort and radicalism to Mr. Warhol's work than met the eye. As was the idea, voiced by Harold Rosenberg, an art critic, that "the primary creation of Andy Warhol is Andy Warhol himself."

"Andy Warhol," a short (53-minute) profile opening today at the Public Theater, features a good deal of Mr. Warhol himself, glancing craftily at the camera as he says such things as: "I don't think people really like art. It's just displayed nicely in museums." Mr. Warhol is also seen at the Factory, supervising the production of early issues of Interview, and in the country, playing with a dog in a garden. These casual scenes contrast markedly with the film's more studied interview footage, in which he concentrates more carefully on being Andy Warhol. At one point, after having talked animatedly for a while, he says "I think I could stare for 10 minutes without blinking" and proceeds to adopt the more familiar, blank-faced Andy Warhol mien.

●

The film also includes clips from various Warhol films, including the sequence from "Lonesome Cowboys" in which two wranglers practice ballet exercises, using a hitching post as a barre. Of particular interest are the comments of Mr. de Antonio, who speaks perceptively and somewhat tartly about Mr. Warhol's obsession with celebrity, and who finds as much interest in Mr. Warhol's methods as in the work itself. Mr. Bourdon discusses the ways in which early Warhol drawing prefigured the later work, and analyzes the deceptive simplicity of the latter.

This documentary, which does its best to be comprehensive about the Warhol career, has a rambling, unstructured style that befits Mr. Warhol's own approach to film making. (Interviewed here, Henry Geldzahler, then the Metropolitan Museum's curator of 20th-century art, talks of how he sat in a chair smoking a cigar before a running movie camera while Mr. Warhol, who shot enough of this footage for an entire feature, made phone calls in another room.) The film also incorporates comments from Clement Greenberg, Barbara Rose and other art critics, and sounds a variety of different notes about Mr. Warhol, from the flippant to the unexpectedly astute. When Mr. Warhol remarks that "Culture is slowly disappearing" — a process to which he undoubtedly contributed — it is both.

1987 Je 9, C20:1

THE BELIEVERS, directed by John Schlesinger; screenplay by Mark Frost, based on the book "The Religion" by Nicholas

Practitioner Martin Sheen portrays a police psychologist involved in the investigation of a series of murders in New York City in John Schlesinger's occult thriller "The Believers."

Conde; director of photography, Robby Müller; edited by Peter Honess; music by J. Peter Robinson; production design, Simon Holland; produced by Mr. Schlesinger, Michael Childers and Beverly Camhe; released by Orion Pictures Corporation. At National, Broadway and 44th Street; Manhattan Twin, 59th Street and Third Avenue; Orpheum, 86th Street near Third Avenue; 84th Street Six, at Broadway; 23d Street Triplex, between Eighth and Ninth Avenues; Bay Cinema, Second Avenue at 32d Street; Movie Center 5, 125th Street, between Powell and Douglas Boulevards. Running Time: 100 minutes. This film is rated R.

Cal Jamison	Martin Sheen
Jessica Halliday	Helen Shaver
Chris Jamison	Harley Cross
Lieut. Sean McTaggert	Robert Loggia
Kate Maslow	Elizabeth Wilson
Donald Calder	Harris Yulin
Dennis Maslow	Lee Richardson
Marty Wertheimer	Richard Masur
Mrs. Ruiz	Carla Pinza
Tom Lopez	Jimmy Smits

By VINCENT CANBY

WHEN Stephen King sits down to write "Carrie" or "Children of the Corn" or some other work of the horrible occult, you can bet that, somewhere down deep, he enjoys and even believes what he's doing. Writers can't easily fake the sort of enthusiasm and concentration that are apparent in Mr. King's hugely popular novels and stories, in which good and evil lock harps and horns in matches that, more often than not, end in tie decisions.

Enthusiasm and concentration are both dismally lacking in "The Believers," opening today at the Manhattan Twin and other theaters. It's an absurd, especially cheerless movie about child-sacrificing devil-worshippers who've slipped out of Africa and, via East Harlem, have come down into midtown Manhattan to infiltrate the ranks of the white establishment. In addition to everything else that's wrong, "The Believers" is more than a little bit racist.

John Schlesinger has directed Mark Frost's not-great screenplay (based on Nicholas Conde's book, "The Religion") as if he were a tourist on a day trip to an exotic ghetto. The movie is full of snaps of picturesque voodoo ceremonies utilizing fresh chicken blood, decapitated cats and, ultimately, small boys.

Mr. Schlesinger, the man who made "Darling," "Midnight Cowboy," "Sunday, Bloody Sunday" and "The Falcon and the Snowman," may not believe this nonsense, though the movie pretends to.

When you hear bongo drums, you know the devil isn't far off. An evil unguent causes the eruption on its victim of a frightful sore that emits more insects than the trunk of a decaying redwood tree. A man who appears to have a bad case of ulcers actually has a belly full of snakes. Humble, God-fearing folk clutch their rosaries and crucifixes and fight the powers of one graven image with those of another.

●

"The Believers" has none of the wit and ambiguous charm of "Rosemary's Baby" — it's far too explicit and commonplace. It doesn't have the passion of "The Exorcist," which, though lurid, was, at least consistent in its mythology.

Even more unforgivable, particularly to anyone who cherishes Mr. King's wildest nightmares, is the film's total humorlessness and clumsy plotting. "The Believers" moves so slowly, and with such unwarranted deliberation, that you might think that the movie makers were trying to build a home stereo with English-language instructions imported from Taiwan. Nobody seems to know what to do next, except the actors.

They say their hysterical, less-than-inspired lines ("What kind of a monster did *that*?" is typical) and get off fast.

Among the more prominent members of the cast are Martin Sheen, as a psychologist who wrestles with the forces of darkness for the life of his son; Helen Shaver, as his girlfriend; Robert Loggia, as an overwhelmed police inspector; Malick Bowens, as the devil's personnel manager (a black man who wears what appear to be grey-blue contact lenses), and Harris Yulin, as a business tycoon who has welcomed a take-over bid from the ultimate foreign power.

1987 Je 10, C22:5

Tristeza

CHILE: HASTA CUANDO?, directed and produced by David Bradbury; in Spanish with English subtitles; cinematographers, David Knaus and Peter Schnall; distributed by Filmmakers Library. Running time: 57 minutes.
PAINTED LANDSCAPES OF THE TIMES, directed by Helene Klodawsky; cinematographer, Judy Irola; produced by Miss Klodawsky and Liette Aubin; distributed by First Run Features. Running time: 26 minutes. At Film Forum 1, 57 Watts Street. These films are unrated.

By WALTER GOODMAN

IN 1985, under the pretext of covering a music festival, David Bradbury, an Australian documentary maker, led a camera team to Chile to report on the state of the opposition to the regime of Gen. Augusto Pinochet 12 years after the coup that brought him to power. Mr. Bradbury, alas, found nothing new. The scenes of the police breaking up political demonstrations with water cannons, tear gas and clubs have become only too familiar in Chile, as in much of the rest of the world. "Chile: Hasta Cuando?" ("Chile: Until When?") offers a close-up view of the continuing resistance and repression in one of South America's enduring dictatorships.

It is a partisan view. The admiring attention devoted to Communist activists and critical asides about the role of United States officials and companies in support of the regime place Mr. Bradbury on the political left. However, he also lets us hear from non-Communist opponents of General Pinochet, including elements of the Roman Catholic Church, trade unionists and a spokesman for the Christian Democrats. Their peaceful efforts to wrest reforms from the Government have not gotten very far.

The division in Chile is presented along class lines. The poor, Mr. Bradbury reports, are getting poorer and more defiant: "People have lost their fear because of their hunger."

●

The most chilling interviews here are with an affluent couple, supporters of the regime. The husband, a businessman, says, "This is a government that lets you do what you want under political rules." He adds, as an aside, "The only freedom you don't have is political." His wife, skeptical of reports of torture by the military, asks, "Why torture somebody when you can shoot them?" The singer, John Denver, interviewed at a cocktail party during the music festival, opines that things are getting better.

Mostly, we hear from the wives, parents and children of people who have "disappeared"; some have been missing for years after being picked up in raids by security men or vigilantes. While Mr. Bradbury's team was in Chile, two prominent Communists were kidnapped and killed, and the documentary reaches its climax with shots of their funeral, which brought together all segments of the opposition. The authorities later admitted, under pressure, that army officers had been responsible for the murders; the punishments were light. Life in Chile goes on pretty much as it has since 1973. The question in the title remains open.

The hourlong "Chile: Hasta Cuando do?" is accompanied at Film Forum 1 by "Painted Landscapes of the Times," Helene Klodawsky's half-hour documentary on the "journalistic paintings" of Sue Coe. Miss Coe maintains that her ferocious drawings of skulls and skeletons and contorted figures expose the hidden "truth" about the world, which is essentially that the rich are beating up on the poor. She spells the President's name "Raygun." Admirers of her work will probably admire the movie.

1987 Je 10, C24:5

Giving Devil His Due

THE WITCHES OF EASTWICK, directed by George Miller; screenplay by Michael Cristofer, based on the book by John Updike; director of photography, Vilmos Zsigmond; edited by Richard Francis-Bruce; music by John Williams; production designer, Polly Platt; produced by Neil Canton, Peter Guber and Jon Peters; released by Warner Bros. At Criterion Center, Broadway and 45th Street; 84th Street Six, at Broadway; Beekman, Second Avenue at 65th Street; Gramercy, 23d Street near Lexington Avenue; Movieland Eighth Street, at University Place; Movie Center 5, 125th Street, between Powell and Douglass Boulevards. Running time: 122 minutes. This film is rated R.

Daryl Van Horne	Jack Nicholson
Alexandra Medford	Cher
Jane Spofford	Susan Sarandon
Sukie Ridgemont	Michelle Pfeiffer
Felicia Gabriel	Veronica Cartwright
Clyde	Richard Jenkins
Raymond Neff	Keith Joakum
Fidel	Carel Struycker

Jack Nicholson

By JANET MASLIN

JOHN UPDIKE performed his own bit of deviltry when he concocted "The Witches of Eastwick," a novel filled with such delicious mischief that it seems made for the movies. With its three small-town New England witches, all divorced or conveniently widowed (one has "permanized" her husband "in plastic and used him as a place mat") and its latter-day devil, an extremely eligible bachelor who adores synthetics and Pop Art, Mr. Updike's story has great comic possibilities. It also has enormous visual appeal, since the witches are apt to do things like unstring pearl necklaces or conjure up thunderstorms to express their pique.

Furthermore, it's sexy, being the story of how the playfully diabolical Darryl Van Horne lures all three witches into his hot tub for extended sybaritic celebrations. But from the film maker's standpoint, "The Witches of Eastwick" is also something of a trap. Its best moments are decidedly uncinematic, recording the innermost thoughts of the various characters or the remarkable auras they perceive around one another, not to mention those extended hot-tub scenes. More importantly, Mr. Updike's own genius for astonishingly fine-tuned description dwarfs anything a camera can do.

●

So in making a film of "The Witches of Eastwick," George Miller (director of the "Mad Max" films) and the playwright Michael Cristofer (who wrote "The Shadow Box") have had to start from scratch. They have radically altered things, and their film resembles Mr. Updike's novel only remotely; even the characters' names have been rearranged and spelled differently. In the face of such sweeping changes, comparisons with Mr. Updike's book would be invidious, unfair and unnecessary if the film's own sense of purpose were clear. But it isn't; in fact, it's not even clear for whom the film is intended.

"The Witches of Eastwick," which opens today at the Beekman and other theaters, brings a broad, obvious, punchy style and a lot of special effects that are much too frail to support this kind of gimmickry. The chief thing that has been lost, for all the levitating and vomiting and so on, is the sense of witchiness itself. Mr. Updike's witches knew their own

powers, and their shrewdness was a large part of the fun. But in the film, it's never clear what Alexandra (Cher), Sukie (Michelle Pfeiffer) and Jane (Susan Sarandon) know about the supernatural, or even about one another. These three characters are conceived here only in the sketchiest way. All we know is that they are a hairdresser's delight, with their respective cascades of black, blond and reddish curls, and that they have collectively made a wish for Mr. Right.

●

This brings them Daryl Van Horne, in the form of Jack Nicholson, whose high spirits and madman antics are always a treat, even when they've become more or less familiar. The film's flamboyant, mock-elegant costumes for Mr. Nicholson are more or less novel, as are some of the settings; it can't help but be fun watching him float in an inflatable pool zebra while spitting cherry pits into a huge silver bowl. A lot of what he does here recalls "The Shining," but the reprise is enjoyable.

Mr. Nicholson has the chance to deliver three wildly excessive amorous pitches, one tailor-made for each witch, and an inspired tirade asking why God created the opposite sex ("So what do you think? Women — a mistake? Or did He do it to us on purpose?!"). Typical of the film's excesses is the fact that this tantrum, so exuberantly delivered, is followed by an ugly, unnecessary fit of vomiting in a church.

Like a lot of the magical events that occur here, the vomiting is none too well explained. In the book, Mr. Updike's witches decide to torment an obnoxious neighbor (with whose husband one of them is having an affair) by putting feathers, straw and various household sweepings into a container and forcing this bewildered woman to spit them out.

In place of this, the film offers Veronica Cartwright as a shrill hysteric who spits pits as the witches eat cherries. But the performance is overwrought, the sexual motive is missing and the effect is as puzzling as it is unpleasant.

Even when the witches and Van Horne embark upon a tennis game in which magic clearly governs the ball, it's not entirely clear who is doing what to whom. And a lot of the tricks have been appropriated at random and simply reassigned to different characters or different situations.

"The Witches of Eastwick" does have enough flamboyance to hold the attention, directed as it has been by Mr. Miller in a bright, flashy, exclamatory style. But beneath the surface charm there is too much confusion and the charm itself is gone long before the film is over. Though the performers are eminently watchable, the sight of all three women flouncing naughtily in their lingerie, or marching about in unison, effectively renders the whole thing rather silly. In any case, none of them seem a match for Mr. Nicholson's self-proclaimed "horny little devil." As battles of the sexes go, this is barely a scrimmage.

1987 Je 12, C3:4

The Beast Without

PREDATOR, directed by John McTiernan; written by Jim Thomas and John Thomas; director of photography, Donald McAlpine; edited by John F. Link and Mark Helfrich; music by Alan Silvestri; production designer, John Vallone; produced by Law-

On the Prowl In "Predator," Arnold Schwarzenegger, as a professional soldier, leads a mission in search of guerrilla captives in the Latin American jungle.

rence Gordon, Joel Silver and John Davis; released by 20th Century-Fox Film Corporation. At National, Broadway and 44th St.; Warner, Broadway and 43d Street; Gotham Cinema, Third Avenue at 58th Street; 86th Street East, between Second and Third Avenues; Embassy 72d Street, at Broadway; Movieland Eighth Street, at University Place. Running time: 106 minutes. This film is rated R.

Dutch	Arnold Schwarzenegger
Dillon	Carl Weathers
Anna	Elpidia Carrillo
Mac	Bill Duke
Blain	Jesse Ventura
Billy	Sonny Landham
Poncho	Richard Chaves
General Phillips	R. G. Armstrong
Hawkins	Shane Black

"PREDATOR" starts out as a second cousin to "Rambo" and "Missing in Action," with Arnold Schwarzenegger (as Maj. Dutch Schaefer) leading a covert mission to find military operatives missing in Latin America. After 45 long minutes, he and his cohorts (among them Carl Weathers) find an enemy camp and conduct a raid. "Knock, knock," says Mr. Schwarzenegger, kicking down the door to a hut. "Stick around," he says, running somebody through with a sword.

The missing men are found, but they have been brutally butchered, and the camera lingers lovingly on the carnage. Then "Predator" turns into a monster movie. It seems that the troops are being stalked by a large thing, played by Kevin Peter Hall, who also plays the large thing in "Harry and the Hendersons." It looks like a man-sized lizard, can disguise itself like a chameleon, contains high-tech computer components and has dreadlocks on its head. Something for everyone.

●

As Mr. Schwarzenegger demonstrated in "The Terminator," he is much better at playing such creatures than at wrangling with them, though in this film he does the latter. The last part of the film concentrates on man-to-monster battles through the jungle. Care to guess who wins?

"Predator," which opens today at the National and other theaters, is alternately grisly and dull, with few surprises, though the creature's face, when finally revealed, has an interesting claw configuration where its mouth ought to be. The habitat is a good deal more interesting than the action, since it contains both floristy-looking palm fronds and large, deciduous trees that have produced some autumn leaves. The film was shot in Mexico.   JANET MASLIN

1987 Je 12, C6:4

Gold Diggers

MILLION DOLLAR MYSTERY, directed by Richard Fleischer; screenplay by Tim Metcalfe and Miguel Tejada-Flores and Rudy De Luca; photographed by Jack Cardiff; film editor, John W. Wheeler; music by Al Gorgoni; production designer, Jack G. Taylor Jr.; produced by Stephen F. Kesten; released by De Laurentiis Entertainment Group. At Criterion Center, Broadway and 45th Street; Gemini Twin, 64th Street and Second Avenue; U.A. East, 85th Street and First Avenue; Movieland Eighth Street, at University Place; Movie Center 5, 125th Street between Powell and Douglass Boulevards. Running time: 95 minutes. This film is rated PG.

Sidney Preston	Tom Bosley
Tugger	Royce Applegate
Dotty	Pam Matteson
Fred	Mack Dryden
Bob	Jamie Alcroft
Stewart Briggs	Rick Overton
Barbra Briggs	Mona Lyden
Quinn	Kevin Pollak
Officer Gretchen	Gail Neely
Lollie	Wendy Sherman
Rollie	Eddie Deezen
Slaughter	Rich Hall

LEGEND has it that Dino De Laurentiis was walking down the street one day when he saw a line of people buying lottery tickets. If a movie could capture the excitement of this experience, he reasoned, it might be a big hit. We are fortunate that he was not passing a bank robbery or a natural disaster when inspiration struck.

So Mr. De Laurentiis made "Million Dollar Mystery," a film in which $4 million disappears and only $3 million is found. The remaining $1 million is still missing, and clues to its whereabouts are contained in the film. There are also clues in packages of Glad Bags, which is co-sponsoring the giveaway. But you needn't see the film or buy the bags to find the money. The official sweepstakes entry form — which has several clues that are not readily detectable in the movie — can be obtained by writing to Million Dollar Mystery Movie, Official Entry Form Request, P.O. Box 802568, Chicago, Ill. 60680.

•

The fine print on this entry form reveals that the winner will not be chosen until next January. The money "is not physically hidden, it is only hidden in the movie." If more than one entrant guesses the correct answer, a drawing will be held to select a winner. The winner's "name and likeness may be used for advertising and publicity for this and similar promotions without further compensation." The winner will receive a free trip to Los Angeles to pick up the prize. "Trip will be scheduled based upon the availability of Mr. De Laurentiis."

I hate to make the film itself an afterthought, but that's what it is. All things considered, it could be a lot worse. "Million Dollar Mystery," directed by Richard Fleischer, is a harmless copy of "It's A Mad, Mad, Mad, Mad World" without the stars. A few young comedians have some funny moments, among them Rich Hall as a would-be Rambo, Peter

Pitofsky as a man who goes wild after tasting toxic waste and Kevin Pollak as a policeman who can imitate Peter Falk, Bill Cosby and Woody Allen.

"Million Dollar Mystery" opens today at the Gemini and other theaters. Remember, money isn't everything.

•

"Million Dollar Mystery" is rated PG ("Parental Guidance Suggested"). It includes some rude language.
                              JANET MASLIN

1987 Je 12, C6:4

A Long Walkabout

BURKE AND WILLS, directed by Graeme Clifford; written by Michael Thomas; director of photography, Russell Boyd; edited by Tim Wellburn; music by Peter Sculthorpe; production designer, Ross Major; produced by Mr. Clifford and John Sexton; released by Hemdale Releasing Corporation. At Cinema 1, Third Avenue at 60th Street. Running time: 140 minutes. This film is rated PG-13.

Robert O'Hara Burke	Jack Thompson
William John Wills	Nigel Travers
Julia Matthews	Greta Scacchi
John King	Matthew Farger
Charley Gray	Ralph Cotterill
William Brahe	Drew Forsythe
Tom McDonagh	Chris Haywood
Dost Mahomet	Monroe Reimers

By WALTER GOODMAN

TWO hours and 20 minutes may not seem excessive for a 3,700-mile trek across an untracked Australia, yet you may find yourself fidgeting in the course of the new Australian movie based on that adventure. Despite Russell Boyd's stunning photography and a big, burly, bushy-bearded performance by Jack Thompson as Burke, leader of the 19th-century expedition, "Burke and Wills," which opens today at Cinema 1, runs short of plot even before the explorers run short of water.

Robert O'Hara Burke and William John Wills set out "to conquer the country" on Aug. 20, 1860, along with 17 other men plus horses, camels and supplies. As re-created by Michael Thomas's screenplay, Burke is a forceful, impetuous and fatally wrongheaded leader. Wills, played somewhat diffidently by Nigel Travers, is more reflective, much more the English gent, and no match for Burke when it comes to taking command. Unfortunately, after setting up their potentially clashing personalities, the story settles for tepid disagreement and bouts of good fellowship. The most emotional moment in the movie is the death of Burke's horse. Greta Scacchi, as a singer who keeps telling Burke how much she adores him, can't compete.

•

Another piece of the plot has to do with the expedition's prosperous organizers who hold back desperately needed help. Here, the director, Graeme Clifford, seems to be encouraging obvious performances, presenting the upper strata of Melbourne as Victorian caricatures in order to rub in the falseness of civilized life.

Out in authentic nature, by contrast, the heroes are more human, except perhaps for that fellow who keeps his jacket buttoned and his cravat tied even on the hottest days. We know the days are hot, because excerpts from Wills's diary tell us periodically of temperatures above 100 degrees (and no shade). It's like tuning into an all-weather radio sta-

Jack Thompson

tion. The climax gets more exciting, with near misses between survivors and rescuers, but that is followed by a stagy ending that refuses to end.

The most evocative element of "Burke and Wills" are the tribesmen, who move like shadows along the expedition's way, part of the land that the white men have set out to exploit. The observation of a young soldier that the country is, after all, the black man's, seems a gesture to present-day sensibilities, yet each time the natives appear, in the often surprising editing of Tim Wellburn, the movie sounds a deeper note.

Except for a couple of diversions — a cricket game in the wilderness, a chorus of "Hark the Herald Angels Sing" to celebrate Christmas in the desert — it's a hard and not unfamiliar journey, particularly on the way back for the four men who make it to the gulf. Lots of sun and not enough water or food and too many rats and lizards and bursts of craziness on the cruel sands. "Thirsty work!" as somebody says. Oops, there goes another camel.

•

"Burke and Wills" is rated PG-13 ("Special Parental Guidance Suggested for Those Younger Than 13"). It includes a mild sex scene.

1987 Je 12, C10:1

Faster, Faster

THE MOST BEAUTIFUL, directed by Akira Kurosawa; screenplay (Japanese with English subtitles) by Mr. Kurosawa; cinematography, Joji Ohara; music by Seichi Suzuki; art direction, Teruaki Abe; produced by Motohiko Ito. At Cinema Village, 22 East 12th Street. Running time: 85 minutes. This film has no rating.

Watanabe	Yoko Yaguchi
Mizushima	Takako Irie
The Director	Takashi Shimura
Sanada	Ichiro Sugai
Workers	Koyuri Tanima, Toshiko Hattori

THOUGH it was only Akira Kurosawa's second feature, "The Most Beautiful" (1944), a propaganda film meant to boost Japan's industries at the height of the war, is an interesting footnote to the Japanese master's later career. The star is Yoko Yaguchi, who later married Mr. Kurosawa and remained his wife until her death during the production of the recent "Ran."

Considering the wartime conditions under which it was made, and the se-

verely limited dramatic possibilities offered by the form, "The Most Beautiful" is surprisingly personal. The film is a semi-documentary about the all-out efforts of a group of high school girls to increase the output of lenses at their optical plant. Chief among the young women is Watanabe (Miss Yaguchi), who is as driven to meet her production goals as one of Mr. Kurosawa's later samurai warriors is driven by his sense of honor.

Though stuffed with uplifting mottos ("Better character means better production," "It's not a matter of pride but of responsibility"), the movie has a lean, uncluttered look and a temper that's anything but hysterical. Watanabe's girlfriends are idealized to the point where they cause an uproar when their increased production quotas are set at only 50 percent of the men's instead of at two-thirds. Watanabe's passion for perfection goes beyond patriotism and becomes an obsession that almost kills her.

Mr. Kurosawa clearly has contradictory feelings about such behavior. Though "The Most Beautiful" is set almost entirely in the lens plant and the women's dormitory where the workers live, Mr. Kurosawa manages to give us a sense of what's happening elsewhere, as in references to the battles at Tarawa and Kwajalein, reported with no special fervor.

                          VINCENT CANBY

1987 Je 12, C14:5

Artificial Stars

THE PUPPETOON MOVIE, animated by Peter Kleinow; voice direction, screenplay and editing by Arnold Leibovit; music by Buddy Baker; director of photography, Gene Warren Jr.; produced by Mr. Leibovit; an Expanded Entertainment Release of an International Tournee of Animation Presentation. At Bleecker Street Cinema, 144 Bleecker Street. Running time: 80 minutes. This film has no rating.

By CARYN JAMES

IT'S hard to resist a movie that lists a Gumby maker and a Gumby adviser in the credits. The familiar little green fellow leads off "The Puppetoon Movie," introducing this collection of nine films by George Pal; animated shorts from the 1930's and 40's, their technique influenced the creators of similar characters from Gumby to the Pillsbury Doughboy.

Pal, who died in 1980, may be better known as the producer or director of pioneering science-fiction films such as "War of the Worlds" and "The Time Machine." But he also masterminded these cartoonlike films, in which the camera shoots hundreds of minutely different three-dimensional objects rather than drawings.

•

Though Pal's puppetoons seem strikingly artificial today, these stiffly moving toys take on a quaint, stylized charm as they emerge from the past, full of music and brilliant color, with flashes of wit and politics. A big-band crooner sings "Harbor Lights" on an ocean liner, against a glistening skyline that makes us marvel at the visual beauty Pal achieved. Busby Berkeley-type dancers are shot from above; Sleeping Beauty wakes to the sound of a radio as Prince Charming drives up in a flashy car.

Pal's political concerns are evident

On the Move Animation by the Academy Award-winning George Pal (1908-1980) is the subject of "The Puppetoon Movie."

in "The Tulips Will Always Grow" (a reminder that Pal, who was born in Hungary, fled Europe during World War II), in which a Dutch boy and girl survive the destruction of their windmill and their tulip garden by fascists.

But while the tulips spring up magically in row after row, our awe at this once-new technique fades fast; soon we're apt to yearn for some narrative continuity, and to be distracted by the unnatural movement of the puppets as their mouths gape and their eyes roll around. Eventually, even some of the classic Pal shorts — such as "Tubby the Tuba," with Victor Jory telling the story of the tuba who longs to play a melody — are reduced to curiosities; like Cinerama travelogues or early 3-D movies, they needn't do more than exploit what was then an innovation.

•

Arnold Leibovit, who produced "The Puppetoon Movie," also wrote its cutesy narrative frame: Gumby returns in this long chair, joined by Mr. Peanut, the monster from the movie "Gremlins" and dozens of other characters who are puppetoon descendants. "George made it possible for all of us to be stars," says Speedy Alka-Seltzer.

Clearly, "The Puppetoon Movie" is a labor of love, burdened with all the weight of that cliché; it's a hagiography that inadvertently does a disservice to Pal. He may have kept his Puppetoons short for practical reasons — those hundreds and thousands of figures were exorbitantly expensive — but he did, after all, mean them to last a few minutes. Stringing them together in this long chain creates feature-length demands they were never meant to carry. Despite its moments of irresistible charm, "The Puppetoon Movie," which opens today at the Bleecker Street Cinema, is more a film archivist's dream than an entertainment.

1987 Je 12, C18:1

DANCES SACRED AND PROFANE, directed, produced and edited by Mark Jury and Dan Jury; based on books of Charles Gatewood, a photographer and anthropologist; photography by Dan Jury; music by Larry Gelb; a presentation of Valley Filmworks; produced by Thunder Basin Films. At the Waverly, Avenue of the Americas at Third Street. Running time: 80 minutes. This film has no rating.

Charles Gatewood is a photographer and anthropologist who specializes in "subcultures." On the evidence of "Dances Sacred and Profane," Mark and Dan Jury's documentary about Mr. Gatewood, he is drawn particularly to Mardi Gras revels, gatherings of nudists and sex clubs. Bare breasts, elaborately tattooed bodies and bizarre behavior are featured in his work, and in the movie.

Addressing those who may find his subject matter "revolting and disgusting," Mr. Gatewood asserts that it "tells us something about ourselves." He sees "important statements being made there," about "liberation through excess" and "some kind of actualization of transcendence."

The Mardi Gras material is only a way of working up to the documentary's main subject — a 57-year-old Silicon Valley salesman whose original name was Roland Loomis, who calls himself Fakir Musafar and whom Mr. Gatewood calls "a modern primitive" and "an astronaut of inner spaces." Mr. Loomis, or Mr. Musafar, sticks long needles here and there into his body — a practice known as "piercings," which he is sure he first tried in a prior existence, perhaps in India. Mr. Gatewood characterizes its practitioners as "a sub-sub-subculture." Mr. Musafar induces Mr. Gatewood to lie on a bed of nails. Mr. Gatewood finds it uncomfortable.

The big scene of "Dances" takes place in the Wyoming hills, where Mr. Musafar, assisted by an "apprentice shaman," goes through the Sioux sundance ritual that Richard Harris pretended to endure in the movie "A Man Called Horse." It's a way, we are told, of attaining a spiritual experience through suffering.

First, the two men, naked except for a few eagle feathers, armbands, garlands and tattoos, attach themselves by pins through their chests to a rope slung over a branch of a cottonwood tree and sway back and forth for two or three hours until their flesh is ripped. That's called the "ripping flesh ceremony."

Then, Mr. Musafar hangs from the tree for 20 minutes on a rope attached to iron hooks that go through holes in his chest. On his return to earth, he reports, "I was up there with the creators of the universe."

"Dances Sacred and Profane," which opened yesterday at the Waverly, is unrated. It should appeal to people who like seeing a man twisting slowly in the wind.

WALTER GOODMAN

1987 Je 13, 13:1

FILM VIEW/Vincent Canby

Into the Dark Heartland

"RIVER'S EDGE," DIRECTED BY TIM Hunter from an original screenplay by Neal Jimenez, is the year's most riveting, most frightening horror film, even if it doesn't really belong in the same category with any acknowledged classics of the genre. Metaphysics has nothing to do with "River's Edge," though, like "Dracula," it's a tale of the undead.

In this case, the undead are not victims of the notorious Transylvanian émigré. They're Middle American high school students, spaced out on the utter fatuousness of life at a time when no one they know is in need of jobs, housing, food, clothing, medical care, educational facilities, transportation or appliances — major or minor.

There hasn't been an American movie of quite the same ferocity since Terrence Malick's "Badlands," a fictionalized version of Charles Starkweather's 1958 murder spree through the Middle West, or "Over the Edge," Jonathan Kaplan's fine, seldom-seen melodrama about life in a model American community, written by Mr. Hunter and Charlie Haas. As social criticism, "River's Edge" is far more scathing than Dennis Hopper's "Easy Rider," which went out in search of America and found nothing there except bigotry.

In the America explored by Mr. Jimenez and Mr. Hunter, bigotry might be welcome. It would be a sign of life if someone cared enough to feel anything, including hate.

Mr. Jimenez was inspired by mostly by the 1981 news story out of Milpitas, Calif., about a high school student who raped and murdered his girlfriend, left her in a gully and then bragged about it to his friends. When they refused to believe him, he escorted them to the scene of the crime.

Later, friends brought other friends to look. No one seems to have been shocked or outraged or frightened, only convinced. For two days, the murder remained an open secret without anyone's calling the police.

Eventually someone did. The young murderer was given a sentence of 25 years to life, and several of his friends were convicted as accessories to the crime.

Taking this raw material, Mr. Jimenez has written a screenplay that has the effect of a surreal comedy, about a society that's reached the absolute end of commitment to — or interest in — anything, set in a time without moral obligations, when the quick and the dead have at long last achieved the same body temperature.

Unlike either "Badlands" or "Easy Rider," "River's Edge" doesn't have a dominant central figure, which is both its weakness and its possibly unintentional daring. Mr. Jimenez and Mr. Hunter don't provide the members of the audience with much in the way of hints as to how they're supposed to react. We're left on our own to make up our minds as we see fit.

To the extent that "River's Edge" has a sympathetic character, he's Matt (Keanu Reeves), the young man who finally does call the police but who, when asked to explain why it took him so long, is genuinely baffled. "I don't know," he says. The unbelieving cop asks him what he felt when he saw the body of the girl, someone he'd known since grade school. Matt, furrowing his brow, replies, "Nothing."

On the surface, anyway, Matt isn't very different from his best friends, Samson (Daniel Roebuck), the slobbish, beer-drinking kid who commits the murder (and doesn't care who knows it), and Layne (Crispin Glover), a mind-scrambled speed freak who enthusiastically takes on the self-imposed responsibility of saving the apathetic Samson. When Matt asks why he bothers, Layne points out that although both Samson and the dead girl were his friends, Samson, being alive, is the one who needs help.

It has to do with loyalty, friendship and honor, Layne explains with the manic excitement of someone who suddenly finds himself in the middle of a movie. After talking about loyalty, honor and friendship (as if he'd just seen "Top Gun"), Layne makes the kind of mental leap peculiar to amphetamine addicts: "Why do you suppose the Russians are gearing up to take us over?" Matt can't answer.

Everyone in "River's Edge" is either emotionally comatose or hopelessly out of date. In the classroom, Matt and his friends listen with boredom as their teacher talks with passion about the social accomplishments of 1960's radicals. He could be describing life in ancient Rome. The only person who has some idea of what's going on is Feck (Dennis Hopper), a gimpy, mind-wasted, former Hell's Angel who is the community's chief source of drugs.

Feck lives in a shabby bungalow on the edge of town, where he tends his marijuana plants and shares his solitude with a life-sized, inflatable sex doll named Ellie. He initially agrees to hide Samson since he (Feck) feels a kinship with the boy. Feck once murdered the woman he loved.

Sometime later, in the manner of one war veteran talking to another, Feck asks Samson if he also loved his victim. Samson's reaction: "Oh, she was O.K."

Feck is disgusted — what is the world coming to? There are times when "River's Edge" is almost funny in the way of a 1980's update of "Tobacco Road."

Like Mr. Malick, in his screenplay for "Badlands," Mr. Jimenez and Mr. Hunter decline to offer any explanations for the behavior that's been witnessed. They simply describe it in lean, unemphatic detail, helped by the members of a splendid cast who, except for Mr. Hopper, are still little known.

'River's Edge' is a fierce exploration of the emptiness of Middle American life.

Explanations depend almost entirely on the emotional and intellectual experience one brings into the theater.

Unlike "Badlands," a far more romantic movie (and one that was a flop at the box office when it was released in 1973), the very bleak "River's Edge" is turning into an unexpected hit, which may tell us something about the times, though just what, I'm not sure. Whatever the reasons, it's so effective that it has a way of implicating all other, lesser movies in the horror it dramatizes with such insistent, chilly detachment.

■

After seeing "River's Edge," it's difficult to sit through (as I did) "Harry and the Hendersons," the latest production from Steven Spielberg's movie factory, without wanting to blame Mr. Spielberg and his associates for Western civilization's imminent decline and fall.

That's putting a possibly unfair burden on situation comedies in general and, in particular, on the Spielberg-factory film. "Harry and the Hendersons" is, after all, an apparently harmless "E.T." ripoff, about an idealized Middle American family that attempts to make a house pet of Bigfoot, the legendary half-man half-beast who's supposed to stalk the mountains of the Pacific Northwest.

However, "Harry and the Hendersons," which reduces the mysteries of life to soothing, sitcom dimensions, could be just the sort of movie that would have contributed to the dread sense of aimlessness that afflicts the kids in "River's Edge." You can't grow up watching an average of 30 to 50 hours a week of life-as-it-should-be (but never is), without beginning to resent the fact that something important is missing in your own existence.

The teen-agers in "River's Edge" drink beer and smoke dope but probably don't see themselves as much different from the high school kids they watch on television (or in "Harry and the Hendersons") coping with clumsy dads, worried moms and bratty little brothers and sisters.

The difference between the reality of their lives and the lives they see on television and in movies appears only to be one of degree. The kids on television and in the movies succeed in having fun. They get into embarrassing but painless scrapes. They make out. When they touch home base, they trade sarcastic but loving quips with Mom, Dad and Bratty Sibling. They live on an earth where the sky is an unvarying, ideal shade of blue (unless the plot calls for rain).

In "River's Edge," the sky is always overcast. Matt's worried mom seems to think she's behaving like the idealized worried mom in "Harry and the Hendersons," except that she has a live-in boyfriend who's not much older than her son, and her biggest worry is Matt's stealing her marijuana. When Matt is confronted by his bratty younger brother, Matt must cope not with a witticism, but with a loaded gun.

What happens in "River's Edge" is not something one wants to know about. It's as if one could suddenly see around that corner where, according to some economists, there waits a global depression to make the 1930's look like a mini-recession. The achievement of Mr. Jimenez and Mr. Hunter is that although "River's Edge" is colder than death, one attends to it, mesmerized, not through emotional identification but through recognition of its landscape. □

1987 Je 14, II:23:5

Furry Friends

BENJI THE HUNTED, written and directed by Joe Camp; director of photography, Don Reddy; edited by Karen Thorndike; music by Euel Box and Betty Box; wild animals furnished and trained by Steve Martin's Working Wildlife; special cougar work by Sled Reynolds and Gideon; Cub Mom, Maureen T. Hughes; produced by Ben Vaughn; distributed by Buena Vista Pictures Distribution. At Guild 50th Street, at Rockefeller Plaza. Running time: 93 minutes. This film is rated G.

Benji	Himself
Frank Inn	Himself
Hunter	Red Steagall
TV Director's Voice	Joe Camp
Producer's Voice	Steve Zanolini
Countdown Voice	Karen Thorndike
Newscaster	Nancy Francis
Engineer's Hand	Ben Vaughn
TV Cameraman	Mike Francis

By JANET MASLIN

WHO but Benji would dare to work with co-stars like these? In "Benji the Hunted," which opens today at the Guild, he appears with four adorable blue-eyed cougar cubs, who become his charges when their mother is killed by a hunter. Benji feeds them, carries them about in his teeth and protects them from such other cast members as a timber wolf and a Kodiak bear. Also in the film are ferrets, raccoons and one extremely brave frog, whose job is to be played with by the cougars. It took 23 cougar cubs (because they grow so quickly) to fill the four cougar roles.

All this activity is set in the wilds of Washington and Oregon, where Benji is lost after a fishing accident. The film begins with a newscaster who reports that "one of America's most huggable heroes" is missing, and makes a reference to Joseph Conrad, which seems seriously out of place under the circumstances. Anyway, Benji spends the rest of the film in the woods, embarking upon the doggie equivalent of an Outward Bound program. Joe Camp, who directed, cuts occasionally to the helicopter that is searching for Benji, but mercifully spares the audience any details of the rescue operation.

●

The film contains almost no dialogue — just an excessive amount of bland, elevator-type music and the spectacle of Benji performing various tricks. All things considered, Benji's ability to hold the viewer's interest is remarkable, as is his sweetness with the cubs and his fearlessness with larger, predatory types. Adults are likely to stay alert, and any child who has so much as petted a poodle will probably find the animal footage irresistible.

Occasionally, Mr. Camp, who also wrote the screenplay, runs into potentially sticky situations. Will Benji have to upset his young fans by killing anything to eat? No, he won't, since Mr. Camp conveniently comes up with a hunter and his stock of game birds. (Benji steals them and feeds them to the cubs, while he himself dubiously licks a raspberry.) And how will Benji defend himself and the cubs against the nasty-looking wolf who is the story's villain? Luckily, one action scene sends the wolf flying off a cliff, either the victim of his own misjudgment or perhaps a suicide.

Special technical credits for the film include such unusual designations as "Special Cougar Work" and "Cub Mom." The blue-skied mountain scenery, as photographed by Don Reddy, is quite pretty.

1987 Je 17, C18:6

Proboscis Opus

ROXANNE, directed by Fred Schepisi; screenplay by Steve Martin, from the play "Cyrano de Bergerac" by Edmond Rostand; director of photography, Ian Baker; edited by John Scott; music by Bruce Smeaton; production designed by Jack DeGovia; produced by Michael Rachmil and Daniel Melnick; released by Columbia Pictures. At Ziegfeld, Avenue of the Americas and 54th Street; Coronet, Third Avenue and 59th Street; 34th Street, near Second Avenue; Waverly Twin, Avenue of the Americas and Third Street. Running time: 106 minutes. This film is rated PG-13.

C. D. Bales	Steve Martin
Roxanne	Daryl Hannah
Chris	Rick Rossovich
Dixie	Shelley Duvall
Chuck	John Kapelos
Mayor Deebs	Fred Willard
Dean	Max Alexander
Andy	Michael J. Pollard
Ralston	Steve Mittleman
Jerry	Damon Wayans
Trent	Matt Lattanzi

By JANET MASLIN

BEHIND the clownish make-up, Steve Martin gives a sweet and serious performance as a latter-day Cyrano de Bergerac in "Roxanne." It's easy to see why Mr. Martin, who wrote the film and served as its executive producer, was moved to re-invent this role. The turnabout of identities must have intrigued him, with one man writing love letters in the name of another; stories about confused identities have attracted Mr. Martin a number of times before. The star-crossed romance must have been appealing, too, since Mr. Martin conveys hopeless longing very well. And the nose itself is a perfect prop for a man who began his career with a fake arrow through his head, a man who has since evolved from a coolly absurdist stand-up comic to a fully formed, amazingly nimble comic actor.

In "Roxanne," which opens today at the Coronet and other theaters, Mr. Martin plays C. D. Bales, a fire chief whose grace and gallantry recall Edmond Rostand's hero even more keenly than does the length of his nose. The setting, which is as much a part of the film's appeal as Mr. Martin's thoroughly charming performance, is the gorgeous, homey-looking little town of Nelson, Wash. (the film was actually shot in British Columbia), which becomes a kind of character in its own way.

Mr. Martin strides through Nelson with the proud bearing of an inveterate outcast, a man who has long since learned to field the kinds of insults he inevitably attracts. Most of the film's nose jokes are collected in one key sequence that has Mr. Martin challenging a barroom bully to choose a number off a dartboard; Mr. Martin promises to make up as many funny-nose insults as that number dictates. The bully chooses 20, and Mr. Martin spins out 20 rejoinders, as promised. Among them: "It must be wonderful to wake up in the morning and smell the coffee — in Brazil" and "I'd hate to see the grindstone."

Mr. Martin's screenplay is big-hearted and funny. But it's also very light; this is the no-fault version of "Cyrano," the one in which no one really suffers much and things work out happily in the end. Since the story's tragic dimension is gone, the film must depend on Mr. Martin's comic versatility, which seems boundless, and on the romantic chemistry he generates with the title character, a glamorous astronomer played by Daryl Hannah. Miss Hannah is lovely, and more spirited here than she's been in other roles. But the script makes a joke of how various Nelson residents confuse astronomy and astrology, and for all the efforts to make Miss Hannah look solemn and brainy (she conspicuously wears glasses in a number of scenes), it's not hard to see how that mistake is made. In any case, neither she and Mr. Martin nor she and Rick Rossovich, as the good-looking lummox with whom she is initially smitten, set off many sparks.

As directed by Fred Schepisi, "Roxanne" is a thoroughly pleasant, down-to-earth romantic comedy that never entirely takes flight, though it picks up immeasurably whenever Mr. Martin is on screen. He is able, more completely than even the location photography or the set design, to create a rich sense of place simply by the way he strolls jauntily through the town. The various houses and restaurants seen in the film have the comfortable, upscale clutter of situation-comedy settings, but Mr. Martin humanizes them just by being there. Another oddly realistic presence is that of Shelley Duvall, who fits surprisingly well into the role of Mr. Martin's level-headed pal and confidante.

Along with the funny firehouse gags that turn up frequently (Michael J. Pollard is very well cast as the oddest of the firefighters) and the best of the verbal quips ("What's a light year?" "Same as a regular year only

Skin Deep
Steve Martin and Daryl Hannah square off in "Roxanne," an updated version of "Cyrano de Bergerac."

it has less calories"), "Roxanne" also is memorable for the florid letters Mr. Martin's C. D. composes and the speeches he delivers in a similar vein. Coming from anyone else, a bit of excess like "Why should we sip from a teacup when we can drink from a river?" would be ruinous. But Mr. Martin actually makes it touching. The pathos and illusion he creates are most notable in a scene that has him visiting a plastic surgeon, trying on a succession of handsome noses that look very much like Mr. Martin's actual one. The performance has been so convincing that it's startling to remember that the tree-branch proboscis isn't real.

•

"Roxanne" is rated PG-13 ("Special Parental Guidance Suggested for Those Younger Than 13"). It includes some off-color remarks and brief nudity.

1987 Je 19, C3:4

Childhood's End

WITHNAIL AND I, directed and written by Bruce Robinson; photography by Bob Smith; edited by Alan Strachan; music by David Dundas; produced by Paul M. Heller; a Cineplex Odeon Films Release. At Carnegie Hall Cinema, Seventh Avenue between 56th and 57th Streets. Running time: 108 minutes. This film is rated R.

Withnail	Richard E. Grant
Marwood/I	Paul McGann
Monty	Richard Griffiths
Danny	Ralph Brown
Jake	Michael Elphick
Irishman	Daragh O'Mallery
Isaac Parkin	Michael Wardle
Mrs. Parkin	Una Brandon-Jones
General	Noel Johnson
Waitress	Irene Sutcliffe

"Withnail and I" was shown as part of this year's New Directors/New Films Series. Following are excerpts from Vincent Canby's review, which appeared in The New York Times March 27. The film opens today at the Carnegie Hall Cinema, Seventh Avenue between 56th and 57th Streets.

THE place is London, where the swinging 1960's are coming to an end. For a favored few, the 60's were one long time out. For even fewer, they were something to recycle and celebrate in music, movies and plays, as well as in the journalese of the new journalism. For the rest, much of what identified the period as the 60's existed in another dimension. One was aware that something special was happening, even though a lot of it was invisible to the naked eye.

"Withnail and I," the bracing new English comedy written by Bruce Robinson (who wrote "The Killing Fields") and his first film as a director, may also be the first film to contemplate the bilious aftermath of that brief, highly publicized, illusory era.

"Withnail and I" is not the whole story of the 60's. It's a small, wise, breezy footnote.

Marwood, who's the "I" of the title, and Withnail are young, would-be actors who wake up one morning to find only 90 days left in the decade. Their funds are low and their flat is hip-deep in the souvenirs and roach-infested debris of their earnest hedonism. On that awful morning, each must deal with a very real, physical hangover, which seems more like a foreclosure on the spirit.

•

Even in his pain, Withnail (Richard E. Grant) is elegant — tall, slim, vaguely Byronic, with something rude to say about everybody. Though he seems never to have acted very seriously, he has an agent and calls himself an actor, possibly because he assumes he looks like one. Marwood (Paul McGann) is more practical and, by comparison, commonplace. He's fed up with dirty dishes, the women who come and go, the dope pusher who drops by to talk about plans to become a toy manufacturer, and with aimlessness as a way of life.

Largely at Marwood's insistence, the two decide to spend a soul-cleansing weekend in the country in a primitive cottage borrowed from Withnail's uncle, Monty (Richard Griffiths). Things go horribly wrong from the start. They have no aspirin, and there's no place to buy any. The country is not what Withnail expected. "It's not like H. E. Bates," he says. "I thought they'd all be out drinking cider and discussing butter."

To keep warm, they must burn furniture in the fireplace. Because there's no food in the house, they contact a farmer for a chicken, which is delivered alive. Matters aren't helped by the arrival of Monty, who, as a result of some hints dropped by his nephew, has developed a grand passion for the innocent Marwood. Monty, too, had once trod the boards, though, as he remembers when he's had too much wine, there's always "that morning when you wake up and say, 'Alas, I shall never play the Dane.'"

In his role as both writer and director, Mr. Robinson has the good sense to keep "Withnail and I" in short focus and specific in character and incident. Though Withnail and Marwood are always aware of the nature of the times they inhabit, the period details never become set decoration. "Withnail and I" isn't social history. It's about growing up, almost as if by

accident.

It's also genuinely funny, especially Mr. Robinson's dialogue, though the accents of the actors occasionally make individual words unintelligible to the American ear.

1987 Je 19, C10:1

Provocation

A VIRUS KNOWS NO MORALS, directed, written and produced by Rosa von Praunheim; in German with English subtitles; photographed by Elfi Mikesch; edited by Mr. von Praunheim and Michael Schäefer; music by Maran Gosov and the Bermudas. At the Public, 425 Lafayette St. Running time: 82 minutes. This film has no rating.

Rudiger	Rosa von Praunheim
Christian	Dieter Dicken
Dr. Blut	Maria Hasenaecker
Student	Christian Kesten
Carola	Eva Kurz
Therapist	Regina Rudnick
Mother	Thilo von Trotha

SPEAKING of AIDS, as does everyone in Rosa von Praunheim's brave and vicious "A Virus Knows No Morals," a sadistic research doctor (a woman) says, "The best defense is shame." Someone else says that acquired immune deficiency syndrome is psychosomatic. A Marxist declares that AIDS victims "are the proletariat of tomorrow." The owner of a gay bathhouse, who himself has AIDS, suppresses the distribution of so-called safe sex literature.

Mr. von Praunheim (born Holger Mischwitzki), is a scratchy, angry film maker with something rude to say about everybody. Since the 1970's, the German director has served as the unrelenting conscience of the gay liberation movement. In "It's Not the

Richard E. Grant, Richard Griffiths and Paul McGann share a meal in "Withnail and I."

Homosexual Who Is Perverse, but the Situation in Which He Lives" (1970), he ridiculed homosexuals who sought tolerance instead of a self-awareness that would allow them to function usefully to change society.

In "A Virus Knows No Morals," which opens today at the Public Theater, he's as caustic about AIDS victims who don't hesitate to pass it on as he is about measures intended to comfort victims and to limit the spread of the disease. Mr. von Praunheim's films look cheaply made and more or less pasted together, which works in their favor and is very much part of a their conscious style. Technical niceties would only dilute the savagery of his social satire.

•

To the extent that "A Virus Knows No Morals" has a narrative, it's about Rudiger (Mr. von Praunheim), the bathhouse owner, and his lover, Christian (Dieter Dicken), a music student, and the various cartoon characters they meet in the course of Rudiger's terminal illness. These include a female therapist who urges Rudiger "to prepare for pain as if it were beauty." There's also a woman who tries to seduce a bisexual man as if she were trying to save the universe. "I want a baby by a gay man," she says, "before they die out."

Society's response to AIDS is to set aside the island of Helgoland as a quarantine center, equipped with housing, medical and recreational facilities, and run according to a speeded-up calendar. In recognition of the limited life expectancy of the victims, Christmas will be observed once a month.

Mr. von Praunheim doesn't pretend to have answers to the questions that are raised. The point of "A Virus Knows No Morals" is to provoke, embarrass and enrage — to persuade people to think. Someone suggests that as the hippie culture led to drugs, and as the 1960's student revolutionary movements led to terrorism, gay liberation led to AIDS. Mr. von Praunheim is clearly sending up this thinking, as well as the behavior that prompted it.

Among agitprop film makers, Mr. von Praunheim is very rare. He doesn't traffic in false hopes or positive images. He deals in doom. "A Virus Knows No Morals" has been called a black comedy, but it's much rougher than that. When a chorus of male transvestites — wearing nurses' gowns and grotesque makeup — sings cheerfully, "You have your fate in your hands," the effect isn't funny but profoundly disturbing. "A Virus Knows No Morals" is armed camp.

VINCENT CANBY.

1987 Je 19, C10:4

Swept Again

SUMMER NIGHT, directed and written (in Italian with English subtitles) by Lina Wertmuller; director of photography, Camillo Bazzoni; music by Bixio; art director, Enrico Job; produced by Gianni Minervini for A.M.A. Film, Leone Film and Medusa Distribution with the collaboration of Reteitalia S.p.a. Released by New Line Cinema. At Cinema 1, Third Ave. at 60th St. Running time: 88 minutes. This film has no rating.
Fulvia .... Mariangela Melato
Beppe .... Michele Placido
Miki .... Roberto Herlitzka
Turi .... Massimo Wertmuller

By VINCENT CANBY

LINA WERTMULLER'S newest comedy, "Summer Night With Greek Profile, Almond Eyes and Scent of Basil," isn't as bad as her "End of the World in Our Usual Bed on a Night Full of Rain" (1978), but it's not even in the same universe with her "Swept Away by an Unusual Destiny in the Blue Sea of August" (1975). The once galvanizingly funny Italian director has run out of ideas, though not words.

"Summer Night," opening today at Cinema 1, is a half-baked variation on the classic "Swept Away." In that exuberant romantic farce, you may remember, Mariangela Melato, as a rich, spoiled capitalist, and Giancarlo Giannini, as a dedicated Communist deckhand (as well as a practicing male chauvinist pig) exploded the theories of Karl Marx by falling furiously in love (and playing sadomasochistic games) while shipwrecked on a desert island.

The new comedy repeats that situation without any of the original's zest, wit, humanity or politics. "Summer Night" is chicly boring, though extremely well dressed (gowns by Valentino, chains by Bulgari). It's a blurry farce about Fulvia (Miss Melato), a beautiful, high-handed billionaire, who turns the tables on a notorious terrorist-kidnapper, Beppe (Michele Placido), by kidnapping and holding *him* for ransom.

The settings, including a magnificent villa in Sardinia, have far more character than the people, including Miss Melato's Fulvia. In the Hercules-handsome, bubble-brained Beppe, the movie has an empty center, due equally to the way in which the role has been written and to the colorless performance by Mr. Placido.

Miss Melato's role is not much weightier, but at least the actress registers as a screen presence. When she sweeps through the sets and around the supporting members of the cast, she demonstrates a certain amount of authority. Mr. Placido has all of the personality of the winner of a Steve Reeves look-alike contest.

1987 Je 19, C12:6

Turnabout

Mariangela Melato, in the role of an immensely wealthy industrialist, arranges the kidnapping of a terrorist in Lina Wertmuller's "Summer Night."

Carry-On

LUGGAGE OF THE GODS, directed and written by David Kendall; director of photography, Steven Ross; edited by Jack Haigis; music by Cengiz Yaltkaya; art director, Joshua Harrison; produced by Jeff Folmsbee; released by General Pictures. At Eighth Street Playhouse, at Avenue of the Americas. Running time: 80 minutes. This film has no rating.
WITH: Mark Stolzenberg, Gabriel Barre and Gwen Ellison

"LUGGAGE OF THE GODS" is an extremely modest comedy about the effects on the members of a North American Stone-Age tribe when, by chance, a jet airplane dumps cargo in its vicinity. It's full of fairly predictable culture-clash jokes involving such things as transistor radios, spear guns, canned food and hats decorated with plastic fruit.

The film is a first feature, written and directed by David Kendall on a budget of practically nothing, photographed entirely on locations in New York, at city parks and near Bear Mountain. Mr. Kendall demonstrates somewhat less ingenuity in his humor than in his efficient use of the limited budget. Comparisons with "The Gods Must Be Crazy," which it recalls to its own disadvantage, are said to be unfair. According to the film's production notes, "Luggage of the Gods" was made at approximately the same time as the South African film and, thus, was not inspired by it in any way.

"Luggage of the Gods" opens today at the Eighth Street Playhouse.

VINCENT CANBY

1987 Je 19, C12:6

FILM VIEW/Janet Maslin

De Palma Breaks The Mold

WE HAVE ALL SEEN OUR SHARE OF heartless remakes, films made in a spirit of cannibalism and apparently for no better reason. They're part of the recycling blight that afflicts all aspects of popular culture in a period, like this one, that has no distinct identity of its own. So it's possible for a new record that sounds almost precisely like a 20-year-old record to be a Top-40 hit all over again. At the movies, this can mean knockoffs as mindless and random as the recent "Wanted: Dead or Alive," which had absolutely nothing to do with the television series from which it took its title.

Or it might mean the Tom Hanks version of the French comedy "The Tall Blond Man With One Black Shoe," which for some reason was entitled "The Man With One Red Shoe." Does this signify a certain contempt for the audience, a presumption that the viewer cannot remember the original film or television program or comic strip and also finds words like "Black," "Red" and "Blond" confusing? You be the judge — and remember that another French comedy, "Three Men and a Cradle," is now being remade as "Three Men and a Baby," in case American audiences cannot be trusted to know what a cradle is for.

In a time of rampant, empty remaking, it follows that Brian De Palma would be a prime offender. It's well known that he loves to borrow. It's also known that he borrows in stylish but often senseless ways, and that he has a penchant for lifting Alfred Hitchcock's most ingenious effects and transferring them to contexts in which they mean nothing (consider his use, in "Body Double," of the famous "Vertigo" 360-degree kiss shot to link bland characters who, far

In 'The Untouchables,' he has made a completely original film from familiar materials.

from being obsessed with one another as the originals were, actually seem rather bored). Mr. De Palma's remake of "Scarface," while less derivative than his Hitchcock-inspired thrillers, was crazily lurid in its own way and became even more so as it moved along. So there's every reason to expect that in making "The Untouchables," a film whose title so clearly evokes the old television series, Mr. De Palma would draw upon his own worst instincts.

Instead, "The Untouchables" is by far the most complete and successful film Mr. De Palma has made. It's his most coherent work, as well as his most emotionally accessible. And it has a moral dimension that involves the audience even more fully than the abundant action does. Mr. De Palma's flamboyant visual style has never been so thoroughly in the service of content. And his most notable homage here, to the baby carriage scene from Eisenstein's "Battleship Potemkin," is exceptionally witty and well chosen. Even if "The Untouchables" is nominally a remake, it's one that breaks the mold. This remake is a complete original.

Set in 1930, with the principal characters in lavish Giorgio Armani gangster gear, "The Untouchables" is in fact quite contemporary. It never aspires to the angry, hard-boiled style of earlier gangster dramas, serving instead as an extravagantly handsome latter-day morality play, as well as an exciting action film. Al Capone, who is embodied so entertainingly by Robert De Niro, is seen as the consummate businessman, a ruthless and almost comically bighearted killer (told, during an emotional moment at the opera, that his men have killed one of the key Untouchables, he smiles through his tears). A self-proclaimed "peaceful man," this Capone can move from smooth talk to unreasoning violence in a split second, as he does in the dinner-table scene that brings the film's most shocking outburst. At another moment, he reasons in his most amicable but threatening tones that if someone robs him, "I'm gonna say he stole, not talk to him about spitting on the sidewalk."

Eliot Ness, such a one-note tough guy in the television version, has become a clean-cut family man whose very decency is almost a joke. "Let's do some good!" he cries while leading his first raid against bootleggers. "I am very proud of you!" Ness's wife writes, in a note she gives him on the day he starts his new job. Ness actually chuckles when he reads this, and says to a co-worker, "Nice to be married, huh?" Capone, meanwhile, takes his breakfast in bed at a hotel where the lingerie-clad cuties chase the gangsters down the front stairs to say goodbye.

Ness, who is played with apparent blankness (and in fact considerable subtlety) by Kevin Costner, seems at first no match for the blissfully amoral Capone. But Ness changes as the film progresses, and the evolution of his character is beautifully delineated. A key event is Ness's meeting with Malone, a cynical, worldly Chicago cop who becomes Ness's mentor; Sean Connery's fine performance as Malone provides the film with its moral center. This first encounter, so adroitly written by David Mamet (it's impossible to imagine anyone better suited to writing this screenplay), establishes Malone as shrewd, honest and a maverick, the ideal man to teach Ness the ways of the world.

"I have become what I beheld, and I am content that I havedone right," Ness proclaims modestly and memorably, once the events in the film have forced him to fight Capone and his men more violently than Ness would have liked. When asked to assess his own role in the war against Capone, Ness puts it this way: "I just happened to be there when the wheel went round." A hero like Ness and an attitude like that are most unusual in today's climate of self-aggrandizing characters who care at least as much for recognition and glory as they do for goodness itself. Wistful as it is about a man like Ness and his singularity, "The Untouchables" is never nostalgic; if anything, it turns his decency, a refreshingly new tactic, into something for which mere violence and venality are no match. If this Ness recalls any kind of earlier film figure, it is not the honest policeman but that quintessential loner and idealist, the heroic cowboy.

The producer of "The Untouchables" has said that audiences seem to be unusually tolerant of this film's violence, perhaps because they care so much the characters that the bloodshed never seems exploitative. That's true, and it's another unusual element, given the conventions of the day. We have become unaccustomed to seeing characters as well played and well developed as these Untouchables (the other two, aside from Ness and Malone, are Andy Garcia's calm,

smiling rookie and Charles Martin Smith's nervous accountant) actually die; we're used to thinking that for likable characters there's always a second chance (in its most extreme form, this is the Bobby Ewing syndrome). But deadly things do happen in "The Untouchables," and Mr. De Palma makes them extremely moving. He also makes them suspenseful and surprising, since the calamity that is most frequently and ominously telegraphed is the one that never happens.

The film's pièce de resistance is its baby carriage sequence, the one that plays jokingly on "Potemkin" but also shows off Mr. De Palma's bravura technique to its best advantage. All the film's best elements — the grand settings, the clever editing, Ennio Morricone's rousing score — come into play as Ness waits in a deserted railway station to stop a key Capone lieutenant from boarding a train. The suspense builds and builds through a number of false alarms, after which a woman with a crying baby asks Ness to help her take the little boy's carriage up a flight of stairs. Because of the kind of man Ness is, we know he must help her. Because of the kind of film this is, we know the Capone man will arrive at the same time. What we don't know, and what makes this particular homage so deft, is what Ness or any of the others will do when the shooting begins.

There's a vast difference between recycling the past and simply evoking it. "The Untouchables" does the latter, and it evokes Mr. De Palma's own past as much it does as anyone else's. Certainly there's a hint of John Ford in the bracingly beautiful outdoor sequence that would be wildly incongruous in any other gangster film but seems inspired here; certainly the lavish sets and costumes suggest many a high-priced period production. But the pulp vitality and the bold flourishes — Mr. De Palma shoots three different scenes under cathedral-like domes, sometimes using wide-angle shots, and none of it seems excessive — are very much the director's own. They're a direct outgrowth of his earlier style, a style that has often seemed rootless, showy, maddeningly erratic and even self-destructive. This time, indeed for the first time, it works perfectly. □

1987 Je 21, II:19:5

First Steps

GROWING PAINS: NUMBER ONE, written and directed by Dyan Cannon; a project of the American Film Institute's Directing Workshop for Women. Running time: 48 minutes.
The Principal............................Allen Garfield
CLASS, directed by Michael Kinberg. Running time: 9 minutes.
PHOTO ALBUM, directed by Enrique Oliver; distributed by Flower Films. Running time: 14 minutes.
MADE IN CHINA, directed by Lisa Hsia; distributed by Filmmakers Library. Running time: 28 minutes. These films have no rating.

AWKWARDNESS and embarrassment are the common denominators that unite the four short films on the Film Forum 1's "Growing Pains" program, films that benefit greatly from being in one another's company. Sentiments like these, when viewed with the bemused spirit that these very different films somehow share, take on a disarming candor.

From Dyan Cannon's 1976 "Number One," the first and longest film in the program, with its humorous look at schoolchildren sharing sexual confidences in a bathroom, to Lisa Hsia's 1985 "Made in China," in which the film maker examines her own family's recent history, the films view potentially painful experiences as a source of rueful humor. In "Number One," two little boys and girls goad one another into disrobing (one of the girls is the chief instigator of this) and then pay the price, in the form of numerous scoldings from their various parents and teachers.

The children, who are filmed charmingly by Miss Cannon in a stylized sepia blur (she herself supplies the off-screen voice of an angry mother), seem to have been directed rather than scripted, so that they bring their own giggles and improvisations to material that readily invites them. If Miss Cannon's view of a repressed and punitive adult world seems narrow, her own merry understanding of the children and their feelings more than makes up for that.

Also very good is Miss Hsia's film, in which she faces up to the contradictions inherent in her own upbringing. Raised by her prosperous Chinese-American family in the most conventionally American way — snapshots show Miss Hsia and her siblings on camping trips and so on — Miss Hsia thought of Chinese culture as something to be experienced only on Sundays, when her family habitually went out for Chinese food. So when she ventured to Beijing to live with cousins there, she found the experience thoroughly unnerving. Would she be taken for an "honored foreign guest" or a native? Would she have any trouble observing the law of the land? What would she tell relatives who asked about disco dancing and the price of motorcycles in the West? "Made in China" is as inventive as it is frank, with Miss Hsia using old photographs, footage of herself in Beijing and even jokey animated sequences to tell this story.

Also on the program are two much shorter films: "Class," Michael Kinberg's collection of schoolroom images, which conveys a restless mood and impersonal atmosphere that are instantly recognizable; and "Photo Album," Enrique Oliver's studiedly irreverent and overly snappy look at his own Cuban relatives and the illusions to which they cling.

JANET MASLIN

1987 Je 24, C18:4

Show and Tell Dyan Cannon, seen with some of her subjects, is represented by her film "Number One" in "Growing Pains," a program of four shorts about growing up.

Rick Moranis as Dark Helmet in Mel Brooks's "Spaceballs."

Sci-fi Sendup

SPACEBALLS, directed by Mel Brooks; written by Mr. Brooks, Thomas Meehan and Ronny Graham; director of photography, Nick McLean; edited by Conrad Buff 4th; music by John Morris; production designed by Terence Marsh; produced by Mr. Brooks; released by Metro-Goldwyn-Mayer Pictures Inc. At Loews Paramount, Broadway at 61st Street; Loews Tower East, Third Avenue and 71st Street; 23d Street West Triplex, between Eighth and Ninth Avenues, and other theaters. Running time: 96 minutes. This film is rated PG.

President Skroob and Yogurt	Mel Brooks
Barf	John Candy
Dark Helmet	Rick Moranis
Lone Starr	Bill Pullman
Princess Vespa	Daphne Zuniga
King Roland	Dick Van Patten
Colonel Sandurz	George Wyner
Radar Technician	Michael Winslow
Voice of Dot Matrix	Joan Rivers

By JANET MASLIN

THERE was a strong enough hint of self-mockery to the original "Star Wars" to place it well beyond a parodist's easy reach. Nonetheless, it remains an attractive target. In the wake of the original film's 1977 release came "Hardware Wars," a very funny short film that substituted household appliances — irons, toasters, whatever — for the familiar spacecraft and filmed them in the same imposing way. Now, on a much grander scale, there is Mel Brooks's "Spaceballs," an ambitious sendup of "Star Wars" and everything it has come to stand for.

"Spaceballs," which opens today at Loews Tower East and other theaters, has the makings of a hilarious skit, which makes its feature-length running time its most serious flaw. Stretched out to fill an hour and a half's worth of screen time, Mr. Brooks's vision of "Star Wars" and its underlying silliness cannot help but wear thin. But "Spaceballs" has none of the aggressively unfunny humor that has marred some of Mr. Brooks's other recent efforts, and its spirits remain consistently high. If it isn't likely to generate what Mr. Brooks himself refers to as "Spaceballs II: The Search for More Money," neither is it anything less than gentle, harmless satire that occasionally has real bite.

Every now and then, "Spaceballs" produces the kind of out-of-film experience that has given Mr. Brooks's best work its distinctively surreal dimension. While the soundtrack music doesn't emanate from an off-camera orchestra here, as it did in "Blazing Saddles," Mr. Brooks manages to call attention to the film-making process itself at every opportunity. More particularly, he emphasizes the ephemeral nature of the marketing process, which for a film like "Spaceballs" may be the very heart of the matter anyhow. So the official "Spaceballs" towel, shaving cream, place mat and flame thrower ("A Children's Toy") are very much in evidence, not to mention the lunch box and the coloring book. And halfway through the film, when the action bogs down, the characters watch themselves on the "Spaceballs" video cassette to find out what happens next.

•

An opening title crawl explains that war now wages between the planet Spaceball and the planet Druidia, adding that "If you can read this, you don't need glasses." Mr. Brooks, who produced, directed and co-wrote the film (with Thomas Meehan and Ronny Graham), then cuts to a slow look at what is undoubtedly the longest heap of intergalactic hardware ever captured on film, right down to its bumper sticker. He then introduces his own version of the "Star Wars" crew, including a princess (Daphne Zuniga) whose distinctive hairdo turns out to be a pair of detachable earmuffs, and a C-3PO who has the voice of Joan Rivers.

John Candy, outfitted with a pair of movable ears, plays a canine character, and Rick Moranis has the funniest role, that of a peculiarly infantile Darth Vader type who plays with tiny "Spaceballs" dolls when he thinks no one is looking. There is also a commander called Colonel Sandurz (George Wyner), who is on hand mostly so that someone can say, "What's the matter, Colonel Sandurz — chicken?"

In addition to concentrating on "Star Wars" itself, "Spaceballs" tosses in gibes at the expense of other recent science fiction; there is a "Star Trek" sight gag, a visit to the "Planet of the Apes" and some understandable foreboding when John Hurt ("Alien") puts in an appearance. There are also some long slow stretches, during which Mr. Brooks tries too hard to stick to the standard plot requirements. But every so often, "Spaceballs" comes up with something that's sure to be remembered, like the invention of "Perri-air," which comes out of cans and is consumed by the elite on an increasingly airless planet. "There is absolutely no air shortage whatsoever," declares Mr. Brooks to the televison cameras as he plays President Skroob, leader of the planet Spaceball, and gulps Perri-air on the sly.

•

"Spaceballs" is rated PG ("Parental Guidance Suggested"). It contains the mildly off-color jokes that are the sine qua non of any Mel Brooks comedy.

1987 Je 24, C23:1

War Is Hell

FULL METAL JACKET, produced and directed by Stanley Kubrick; screenplay by Mr. Kubrick, Michael Herr and Gustav Hasford, based on the novel "The Short Timers," by Mr. Hasford; edited by Martin Hunter; director of photography, Douglas Milsome; music by Abigail Mead; production designer, Anton Furst; released by Warner Bros. At National, Broadway and 44th Street; Manhattan Twin, 59th Street east of Third Avenue; Eighth Street Playhouse, west of Eighth Street; Cinema Studio, Broadway at 66th Street; 86th Street East, between Second and Third Avenues. Running time: 118 minutes. This film is rated R.

Private Joker	Matthew Modine
Animal Mother	Adam Baldwin
Private Pyle	Vincent D'Onofrio
Gunnery Sergeant Hartman	Lee Ermey
Eightball	Dorian Harewood
Cowboy	Arliss Howard
Rafterman	Kevyn Major Howard
Lieutenant Touchdown	Ed O'Ross

By VINCENT CANBY

MORE than any other major American film maker, Stanley Kubrick keeps to his own ways, paying little attention to the fashions of the moment, creating fantastic visions that, in one way and another, are dislocated extensions of the world we know but would prefer not to recognize.

The best Kubrick films — "Lolita," "Dr. Strangelove," "2001," "A Clockwork Orange" and "Barry Lyndon" — are always somewhat off-putting when first seen. They're never what one has expected. No Kubrick film ever immediately evokes the one that preceded it. Yet it's so distinctive that it can't be confused with the work of any other director.

Though the general public couldn't care less, this can be infuriating to anyone who wants to be able to read a film maker's accumulated body of work as if it were a road map leading to some predetermined destination. As movie follows movie, the Kubrick terrain never becomes familiar. You drive at your own risk, confident only that the director has been there before you.

"Full Metal Jacket," Mr. Kubrick's harrowing, beautiful and characteristically eccentric new film about Vietnam, is going to puzzle, anger and (I hope) fascinate audiences as much as any film he has made to date. The movie, opening today at the National and other theaters, will inevitably be compared with Oliver Stone's "Platoon," but its narrative is far less neat and cohesive — and far more antagonistic — than Mr. Stone's film.

•

Like "The Short Timers," Gustav Hasford's spare, manic novel on which it is based, the Kubrick film seems so utterly reasonable that one doesn't initially recognize the lunacies recorded so matter-of-factly. The film is a series of exploding boomerangs. Just when you think you can relax in safety, some crazed image or line or event will swing around to lodge in the brain and scramble the emotions.

"Full Metal Jacket" is closer in spirit to Francis Coppola's "Apocalypse Now," even if it has none of the mystical romanticism of the Coppola film in either its text or physical production. However, lurking just off-screen, there's always the presence of Mr. Kubrick, a benign, ever mysterious Kurtz, who has come to know that the only thing worse than disorder in the universe is not to recognize it — which is, after all, the first step toward understanding and, possibly, accommodation.

Disorder is virtually the order of "Full Metal Jacket," whose pivotal character, Private Joker (Matthew Modine), the narrator of the novel, wears a peace symbol on his battle fatigues and, on his helmet, the slogan "Born to Kill." Disorder is also there in the structure of the film itself.

"Full Metal Jacket" is divided into two parts, which at first seem so different in tone, look and method that

Matthew Modine as Private Joker in "Full Metal Jacket."

they could have been made by two different directors working with two different cameramen from two different screenplays. Only the actors are the same. Part of the way in which the movie works, and involves the audience, is in its demand that the audience make the sudden leap to the seemingly (but far from) conventional battle scenes in Vietnam, which conclude the film, from its flashily brilliant first half, set in the Marine Corps boot camp at Parris Island, S.C.

•

Though Mr. Modine's Private Joker, a humanist in the process of being permanently bent by the war, provides the film with its center, the poetically foul-mouthed Gunnery Sergeant Hartman (Lee Ermey) is the film's effective heart, giving terrifying life to "Full Metal Jacket" long after he has left the scene and the film has moved on to Vietnam.

Sergeant Hartman is a Marine "lifer," a machine whose only purpose is to turn the soft, half-formed young men who arrive at Parris Island into killers without conscience. There's no nonsense that he's doing it for the men's own good. Everything is made subordinate to "the corps," to which end the recruits are humiliated, beaten, exhausted, tricked, lied to, subjected to racial slurs and drilled, constantly drilled, physically and psychologically.

They recite by rote creeds, prayers and obscene couplets intended to detach them from all values from the past. On Christmas they sing "Happy birthday, dear Jesus," and laugh at their own impertinence. They sleep with their rifles, to which they've been ordered to give girls' names. The training is a kind of ecstatic, longed-for washing of brain and body, defined by Mr. Kubrick in a succession of vignettes so vulgar and so outrageous that one watches in hilarity that, boomerang-like, suddenly returns as shock and sorrow.

The effect of this part of the film, photographed and played with an unnatural cleanliness that reflects the nature of the training iself, is so devastating that one tends to resist the abrupt cut to Vietnam, where order is disorder and truth is simply a matter of language. At one point Private Joker, who has become a Marine combat correspondent, respectfully notes that henceforth "search and destroy" missions are to be described as "sweep and clear." The landscape is lunar. Even the sky is a different color.

⬤

Though the first half seems complete in itself, the point of "Full Metal Jacket" is made only through the combat mission that ends the film in the ruins of the city of Hue, which, as seen by Mr. Kubrick, is both a specific place and the seat of judgment for all that's gone before. Sergeant Hartman's ghost looks on.

The performances are splendid. Mr. Modine ("Birdy," "Mrs. Soffel," "Streamers") must now be one of the best, most adaptable young film actors of his generation. The film's stunning surprise is Mr. Ermey, a leathery, ageless, former Marine sergeant in real life. He's so good — so obsessed — that you might think he wrote his own lines, except that much of his dialogue comes directly from Mr. Hasford's book, adapted by the novelist with Mr. Kubrick and Michael Herr ("Dispatches"). Note with admiration Vincent D'Onofrio, who plays a hopelessly overweight Parris Island recruit who turns himself into Sergeant Hartman's most dedicated student.

"Full Metal Jacket" is not without its failed inspirations. A series of tele-

vision "interviews" with battle-worn marines suggests a different, simpler, more obvious kind of movie. Some jokes intended to appall are just jokes: "How do you manage to shoot women and children?" "Easy. You don't lead them so far." It sounds as if it's been said many times before, but that could also be the point.

Not for Mr. Kubrick is location shooting in the Philippines or Thailand. Since the early 1960's, he has lived and worked in England, where he created his own, very particular Vietnam locations for "Full Metal Jacket." They're otherworldly. They don't match expectations, any more than the narrative does. They are, however, utterly true to a film of immense and very rare imagination.

1987 Je 26, C3:1

Just the Facts, Ma'am

DRAGNET, directed by Tom Mankiewicz; written by Dan Aykroyd, Alan Zweibel and Mr. Mankiewicz; director of photography, Matthew F. Leonetti; edited by Richard Halsey and William D. Gordean; music by Ira Newborn; production designed by Robert F. Boyle; produced by David Permut and Robert K. Weiss; released by Universal Pictures. At Warner Twin, Broadway and 43d St.; New Carnegie, 57th St. and Broadway; Gemini, Second Ave. at 64th St.; U.A. East, First Ave. at 85th St.; 84th St. Six, at Broadway; Art Greenwich Twin, 12th St. and Seventh Ave. Running time: 110 minutes. This film is rated PG-13.

Friday	Dan Aykroyd
Streebek	Tom Hanks
Whirley	Christopher Plummer
Gannon	Harry Morgan
Connie Swail	Alexandra Paul
Emil Muzz	Jack O'Halloran
Jane Kirkpatrick	Elizabeth Ashley
Jerry Caesar	Dabney Coleman
Enid Borden	Kathleen Freeman
Mayor Parvin	Bruce Gray
Granny Mundy	Lenka Peterson

THE surprise about "Dragnet," described by its director, Tom Mankiewicz, as "a comedic homage to one of the classic television shows," is not that it's less than an unalloyed delight, but that it manages to be funny at all. The film opens today at the Gemini and other theaters.

The new, updated parody, starring Dan Aykroyd (as the nephew of the original Sergeant Friday), and Tom Hanks as his hippie partner in the Los Angeles Police Department, has some real laughs, though they don't come in clusters. They're as isolated and lonely as stoplights in the suburbs.

Considering the age of the material, as well as its relentless recycling (even now, in current radio and television commercials), it's some sort of wonder there's anything left to which to pay a comedic homage.

By the time that Jack Webb's long-running television series finally called it quits (for the second time) in 1970, there had also been two feature

films based on the Webb characters and the show had become a parody of itself. This new "Dragnet" is actually sloppier in its initial conception than in its execution.

⬤

You can't *hate* a movie in which Mr. Aykroyd's uptight Sergeant Friday says of Los Angeles's soft-core smut king, "How could Jerry Caesar build a modern Gomorrah smack in the city where they recorded 'We Are the World'?" There are also an imported compact automobile described as on "the cutting edge of Serbo-Croatian technology," and an unscrupulous television evangelist (Christopher Plummer) who giggles too much.

Mr. Aykroyd and Mr. Hanks play well together, but the funniest performance in the film is that of Dabney Coleman, as the smut king (who lisps). Somewhat less diverting are the car chases and the time out necessary to explain the throwaway story. The summer movie season has officially arrived.

⬤

"Dragnet," which has been rated PG-13 ("Special Parental Guidance Suggested for Those Younger Than 13"), includes some vulgar language and one sequence, meant to be cautionary, in which Mr. Hanks declines to make love to the young woman sharing his bed because he has run

Dorian Harewood being wounded during the Tet offensive in Stanley Kubrick's new film, "Full Metal Jacket."

out of condoms. Very young children may well think that the box he shakes is empty of cigarettes.

VINCENT CANBY

1987 Je 26, C3:1

Midi Melodrama

JEAN DE FLORETTE, directed by Claude Berri; screenplay (in French with English subtitles) by Mr. Berri and Gérard Brach from the novel by Marcel Pagnol; original dialogue by Mr. Pagnol; director of photography, Bruno Nuytten; edited by Arlette Langmann, Hervé de Luze and Noëlle Boisson; music by Jean-Claude Petit; production designer, Bernard Vezat; a Renn Productions/Films A2/RAI 2/DD Productions production; released by Orion Classics. At the Paris, Fifth Avenue and 58th Street. Running time: 122 minutes. This film is rated PG.

César Soubeyran	Yves Montand
Jean de Florette	Gérard Depardieu
Ugolin	Daniel Auteuil
Aimée	Elisabeth Depardieu
Manon	Ernestine Mazurowna
Pique-Bouffigue	Marcel Champel
Philoxène	Armand Meffre

GET ready to binge.

Claude Berri's four-hour, two-part screen adaptation of Marcel Pagnol's epic, two-part Provençal novel, published under the collective title of "L'Eau des Collines" ("Water of the Hills"), is going to be irresistible.

That's if "Jean de Florette," the first of the two films, is any indication — and there's no reason to suppose that it isn't. Here's the kind of exuberant, French Midi, melodramatic comedy that no one has successfully brought off since Pagnol himself made "César" (1936), which, with "Marius" and "Fanny," constitutes the Pagnol "Marseilles Trilogy." (I exclude Jean Renoir's Midi films. They remain incomparable.)

"Jean de Florette" stars Gérard Depardieu, a fine new actor named Daniel Auteuil and Yves Montand (in the role of his career) in a peasant tale of money, property, duplicity and greed, which is nothing if not colorful while miraculously avoiding the merely picturesque. It's also the most enjoyable, most canny feature-length "preface" in the history of the cinema.

It may be that television's miniseries are making us more polite and docile these days. I can't recall ever having walked out of a movie theater with the same mixture of satisfaction and anticipation as I did when I left the screening of "Jean de Florette," which, even if ripe with narrative, doesn't quite stand on its own.

Though the films were made at the same time on a marathon, nine-month shooting schedule in the South of France, they are being released here separately, as they were in France. "Jean de Florette," opening today at the Paris, will be followed later this year by "Manon des Sources" ("Manon of the Springs"), which is not a true sequel but, in fact, the rest of the story.

"Jean de Florette" is set in the 1920's, in the beautiful, forbiddingly arid hills 30 or so miles north of Marseilles but light-years away in terms of manners and habits. With "Manon of the Springs," it's a tale of Dickensian shapeliness about a rich, proud farmer, César Soubeyran (Mr. Montand), who, unmarried and childless, schemes with Ugolin (Mr. Auteuil), his nephew and heir, to acquire the only property in the district to possess a functioning spring.

When he dies, César wants to leave behind an orchard "that's like a cathedral," but there can be no orchard, or no flower farm (Ugolin's plan), without the spring.

The scheme begins with the inadvertent murder of the coveted property's irascible old owner and proceeds to the carefully planned deception of the foolish, earnest young man who inherits the farm and who, instead of selling it, decides to settle down there. Unknown to the heir, Jean de Florette, his acquisitive neighbors have stopped up the spring.

Jean, a postal clerk from the city, is played by Mr. Depardieu with a humpback and a sweet, alert, 19th-century faith in progress-through-knowledge. He arrives to take up residence with his young wife, Aimée (Elisabeth Depardieu), who's a former opera singer; their small daughter, Manon (Ernestine Mazurowna), and a library of self-help books on agriculture.

Jean is a terrifically winning character, romantic and hard-working. He also drinks too much and is fatally self-confident. He's no match for the wily César and the younger Ugolin, who, if left to his own devices, would probably have been won over by Jean's innocence and helped him.

Mr. Montand's César, who's said to dominate "Manon of the Springs," remains on the edges of "Jean de Florette" as, with a clear conscience, he enthusiastically stage-manages what turn into terrible events. The physically formidable Mr. Depardieu successfully disappears inside the naïve, ambitious, former postal clerk, and Mr. Auteuil's Ugolin, who seems to be almost retarded at first, emerges as a man of essential decency that fails.

All of the performances, like the characters, are rich without being quaint. The Midi landscapes are magnificent through the seasons. Mr. Berri tempts fate by borrowing the film's musical theme from Verdi

Sygma/Etienne George

Daniel Auteuil and Yves Montand undertake a conspiracy in "Jean de Florette."

Gérard Depardieu in "Jean de Florette," opening today at the Paris.

("La Forza del Destino"), which puts a great load onto the tangled narrative and, from time to time, almost flattens it.

Yet Mr. Berri's control remains sure and firm. "Jean de Florette" has the delicacy or something freshly observed. It's so good that one needn't be ashamed of escaping into its idealized if harsh and rocky world.

•

"Jean de Florette," which has been rated PG ("Parental Guidance Suggested"), contains two scenes of violence that could trouble extremely young children.

VINCENT CANBY

1987 Je 26, C3:1

Small-Town Standoff

STRAIGHT TO HELL, directed by Alex Cox; screenplay by Dick Rude and Mr. Cox; director of photography, Tom Richmond; edited by Dave Martin; production designer, Andrew McAlpine; produced by Eric Fellner; released by Island Pictures. At Cinema 1, Third Avenue at 60th Street. Running time: 86 minutes. This film is rated R.

Norwood .... Sy Richardson
Simms .... Joe Strummer
Willy .... Dick Rude
Velma .... Courtney Love
Karl .... Zander Schloss
Poncho .... Del Zamora
Sal .... Luis Contreras
Mr. Dade .... Jim Jarmusch
George .... Miguel Sandoval
Fabienne .... Jennifer Balgobin
I. G. Farben .... Dennis Hopper
Sonya .... Grace Jones
Hives, the Butler .... Elvis Costello

AFTER he directed "Sid and Nancy," the mercurial Alex Cox (who also made "Repo Man") reportedly needed a change of pace. So he co-wrote and directed "Straight to Hell," a low-budget, freewheeling parody that amounts to one long private joke. On Sergio Leone's main set in Almería, Spain — with traffic visibly whizzing back and forth in the background — Mr. Cox has assembled a cast of colorful punk miscreants and turned them loose. The result is a mildly engrossing, instantly forgettable midnight movie.

There are some cameos here: Elvis Costello silently serves coffee, which in the film's scheme of things is a precious substance, from a silver tray. Dennis Hopper, in the company of Grace Jones, turns up as a touristy-looking entrepreneur, and Miss Jones

wears ordinary hair for the first known time. The director Jim Jarmusch appears as a growling Mr. Big. None of this is even halfway as amusing as it sounds.

On the evidence of his earlier films, Mr. Cox is clearly a director of great promise, but he needs material worth working with. And in "Straight to Hell," which opens today at Cinema 1, he has none. Using deliberately hackneyed dialogue ("Louise, I thought you loved me." "I don't know what love is") and a mixture of every costume style this side of outer space, Mr. Cox stages a small-town standoff involving bank robbers, a pregnant moll, a local gang (played by the Irish group the Pogues) and assorted stock characters, like the jealous storekeeper and his gorgeous, faithless wife. There's a great deal of whimsy at work here, about 10 tons' worth in all.

JANET MASLIN

1987 Je 26, C8:5

FILM VIEW/Vincent Canby

Sex Can Spoil The Scene

ABOUT THREE-QUARTERS OF THE WAY through "Devil in the Flesh," Marco Bellocchio's updated Italian variation on Raymond Radiguet's 1923 French novel set during World War I, Mr. Bellocchio takes a carefully considered leap toward artistic freedom but lands in an esthetic void. A hardcore sex sequence, which might initially have seemed a bold decision, turns out to have been a fatal gaffe.

One's involvement in the film, and in Mr. Bellocchio's ideas about politics, sex, power and repression — none too consistent or profound up to that point of the movie, anyway — is suddenly superseded by a curiosity about the mechanics of film making, or, at least, about the mechanics of making *this* film.

Mr. Bellocchio's "Devil in the Flesh" isn't to be confused with the Radiguet novel or with Claude Autant-Lara's romantic, melancholy 1947 screen version, in which Micheline Presle plays the older, married woman with whom the teenage Gerard Philippe falls wondrously in love.

The new "Devil in the Flesh" is set in an economically fat, contemporary Italy, where the battles being fought aren't against any foreign enemy, but against demons within. These are externalized as bourgeois hypocrisy, lower-middle-class morality and, of course, the Red Brigades who, if they hadn't existed in real life, would have had to be invented by Italian movie makers for the convenience of their film industry.

Mr. Bellocchio's lovers are Andrea, the teen-age son of a classic (and neurotic) Freudian analyst, and Giulia, who's somewhat older than Andrea and far more emotionally needy. Giulia, whose father was assassinated by the Red Brigades, is engaged to a mild-mannered terrorist on trial for his life when she meets the precocious, sophisticated Andrea. Already bored by her fiancé's dreams of bourgeois domesticity, as well as by his mother's suffocatingly protective presence, Giulia throws herself into her affair with the boy.

Sometimes Giulia seems quite mad, and probably is — being so frightfully repressed by society and by its tiresome taboos against everything from small, essentially harmless fibs to sexual intercourse in public places. Giulia is meant to seem a strange, wild thing, even if seriously disturbed. Because she is played by the seductively beautiful Maruschka

An explicit act in 'Devil in the Flesh' turns rather conventionally intellectualized European fiction into a documentary.

Detmers, the audience tends to go along with her and with Andrea's heedless infatuation with her.

The two meet clandestinely at all hours of the day and night. In a series of poetically lighted, discreetly photographed scenes they make abandoned love in various nooks and crannies of the apartment that Giulia is to share with her future husband. The mother-in-law-to-be understands all in silent fury. Andrea's father, who himself has a letch for Giulia (a former patient), tries to register disapproval, but without ever telling Andrea to quit. After all, the father is a Freudian, which in Mr. Bellocchio's book means that he's a dinosaur in the world of modern therapists.

Finally the movie, like the increasingly desperate Giulia, loses its mind completely. While Andrea, in response to her childlike plea that he tell her a story, spins a yarn about Lenin's return to St. Petersburg in the spring of 1917, Giulia performs fellatio on the boy. The act is not suggested. It's explicit.

Unlike the camera during all of the other love-making scenes, which have been staged (through inexplicit images) to create a sense of erotic need and satisfaction, the camera butts into the action, like the director of a porn film, to show the audience things that only a pushy third party would ever see.

∎

There are no doubles for the actors. One's first response makes one feel approximately 14 years old: "Gee whiz, they're actually doing it!" Then one begins to wonder how it was staged. Did the actors really want to do it? (Apparently.) Was there a large crew watching? (No. According to the program notes, the actors were left alone with a running camera.) What about AIDS? (The film was made two years ago, before, it seems, anybody in Italy was thinking about so-called safe sex in relation to acquired immune deficiency syndrome.)

"Devil in the Flesh," which, until then, has been a rather conventionally intellectualized, European fiction film, has suddenly become something else entirely — a documentary. Its leading characters are not Andrea and Giulia but the actors who play them, and because the characters disappear, so does the fiction the sequence was meant to illuminate.

In the late 1960's and early 1970's, when the sexual revolution began and, among other things, pornographic movies became a taxable industry, there were sage predictions that it was only a matter of time before anything, including hardcore porn sequences, could be included in legitimate fiction films. The now comparatively tame-looking "Last Tango in Paris" appeared to be leading in that direction and, up to a point, the predictions were correct.

The language heard on the screen today approximates (and sometimes outdoes) what can be heard on any street. Total nudity no longer surprises. Just about any sexual practice, involving any combination of the sexes, can be simulated in sometimes quite graphic detail (as in the current "Prick Up Your Ears"), without necessarily shattering what in the theater is called "the fourth wall," that invisible scrim that forever separates the audience from the stage.

Efforts begun in the theater of the 1960's to include the audience in the stage action (as in "Hair") now seem self-conscious and ultimately self-defeating. Audiences don't want to be stepped on or hugged or kissed by members of Actors Equity invading the auditorium. When we go to the theater or to see a film, we don't need to be convinced of reality, but of illusion. Reality is what we make of it.

"Devil in the Flesh" is a serious movie, and seriously mistaken, though not because of any breach in what, in the language of cant, is called "common decency."

Mr. Bellocchio demonstrates that, for the foreseeable future, explicit sex on stage or the screen remains far different from explicit sex painted or sculpted or described in the language of the fiction writer. It's not a reimagining or an evocation of anything. It's recorded, documented fact, which destroys illusion as thoroughly as hairpieces that don't fit, scenery that wobbles when bumped into and dumb dialogue ("Why am I telling you all this?"). ☐

1987 Je 28, II:18:5

NEW YORK/John Gross

'Untouchables' Lurches Between Playing It Straight and Playing It Cool

BRIAN DE PALMA MIGHT have made a movie about Al Capone, but instead he decided to make a movie called "The Untouchables." In its title and its choice of a hero, the G-man Eliot Ness, it salutes the famous television series that can still be found doing the rounds late at night, recalling the black-and-white simplicities of the 1950's and early 60's, and which even at the time looked back to the simplicities of a still earlier epoch.

Mr. De Palma's films are well known for their perverse streak, to put it no more strongly than that. His screenwriter, David Mamet, takes a notoriously disenchanted view of the American scene. Given the two men's reputations, there was an unusual amount of curiosity before the movie opened about how they would handle their venerable material. Prohibition Chicago, yes; but a bang-bang television program that had had Walter Winchell as its resident moralist? Surely Mr. De Palma and Mr. Mamet weren't going to be wholly in earnest.

■

In the event, the most unexpected thing about the movie, it has been generally agreed, is how straight they have decided to play it. There are local twists and limited turns (and there is no Walter Winchell); but critics who came hoping to see an ironical reworking of the old G-man legend have been sent away disappointed.

True, Kevin Costner, in an engaging portrayal, makes Eliot Ness more human and less of an automaton than Robert Stack was on television. But he is still the same intrepid crusader. If he learns how to bend the rules in the course of his crusade, we feel that he is still inwardly incorruptible, and if he eventually dispatches a hardened killer when he doesn't absolutely have to, it is only after being subjected to maximum provocation.

He has also been fitted out with a wholesome young family, and at one point he teases his adoring wife about calling their new son "John Edgar." But we can be sure that it is the most playful of jokes. John Edgar Hoover is still in his heaven.

Not, of course, that the film is anywhere near as unsophisticated as this may make it sound. Mr. De Palma's direction is bold and ingenious, and he contrives some electrifying little touches.

Capone at the opera, for example, watching "I Pagliacci" while two of his henchmen are carrying out a killing for him in another part of town. After the performance, champagne is brought on (the references to alcohol in this movie about Prohibition are both sparing and carefully judged); one of the singers, still wearing his makeup and his clown's costume, raises his glass with a plump smile that suddenly makes him seem like

an effete double of the overweight Capone, who is an untiring performer himself, and who knows how to clown, too.

It is imaginative moments like these that make "The Untouchables" disconcerting. How could anyone who had dreamed them up expect us to swallow the more simple-minded elements in the movie? And some of those elements are very simple-minded indeed.

There are the scenes with the eager, toothy, bespectacled little accountant, for instance, who keeps insisting that the way to get Capone is on income-tax violations. No one will listen to him; even Ness wears a patronizing smile. But he keeps plugging away (won't *anyone* listen?); he also runs cheerfully amok with a shotgun when he realizes that the gangsters are actually killing people, and eventually comes to a gory end in the line of duty (but then he always did look a bit expendable).

The effect of such scenes is to make us wonder whether anything in the film can be taken seriously. There are other scenes that ought, in principle, to make a direct assault on our feelings. A little girl has been blown up by a gangster's bomb, and her mother comes to see Ness when his morale is at its lowest, to assure him that she has faith in him. A poignant enough incident, you might suppose; certainly there is no hint of caricature about the way it is presented. Yet invisible quotation marks hover round it, and most of the other outwardly straightforward scenes in the movie, lending an ironic distance.

For much of its length, in fact, "The Untouchables" seems to have been made in a spirit of pastiche, with mildly absurdist undertones. Other sequences, by contrast, are exercises in extravagance and self-indulgence. An ambush on the Canadian border turns into a scene from a Western; a baby carriage (with a baby inside it) goes bouncing down the staircase during a shootout at a railroad terminus, and obliging commentators won't fail to recall the Odessa Steps sequence in " he Battleship Potemkin."

Between mock seriousness and directorial trickiness, what remains? A few episodes are genuinely exciting. Sean Connery invests Malone, the veteran patrolman whose help Ness enlists, with more authority than the part deserves. (In conception Malone — the one good apple in the Police Department barrel — is just as much of a comic-strip character as the other members of Ness's team.) There are suavely filmed sequences making the most of Chicago landmarks, grandiose interiors, rich period detail.

But none of this, while it keeps you watching, is enough to compensate for the lack of a commanding central myth. Much cruder gangster films have projected far more emotional power.

If there is a mythic dimension to the movie, it can only be the one provided by Robert De Niro in his portrayal of Capone. Mr. De Niro plays the part with relish — a Capone who cultivates his image and enjoys the limelight, a prima donna who has the press eating out of his hand and who delivers accomplished after-dinner

speeches (though he is liable to round off the evening with a display of psychopathic fury).

The gangster as great communicator — it is a novel interpretation, and as far as it goes an arresting one. But it doesn't sufficiently allow for the Napoleonic element in Capone (the Capone of cinematic myth, that is, not the real man), and it doesn't permit him to dominate the action as ferociously as he does in most movie versions of the legend. Its strengths are primarily those of comedy.

There is nothing wrong with that in principle, and De Niro himself turns in a satisfyingly sardonic performance. But elsewhere the humor of the movie has a way of being not so much cruel as brutish. In one scene, Malone blows out the brains of a gangster whom he pretends to be interrogating, in order to persuade another gangster to talk. What the second gangster doesn't know is that first gangster is already dead. But the audience knows, and the laughter that greeted the incident on the evening I saw the movie was as ugly as the incident itself.

In the end, for all its virtuosity, "The Untouchables" has something hollow about it. You feel that it is a product of Hollywood's decadence, that it is playing cleverly and self-consciously with energies that it doesn't naturally possess. ☐

1987 Je 28, II:31:1

Road Warrior

EL COCHECITO, directed by Marco Ferreri; screenplay by Mr. Ferreri and Rafael Azcona; cinematography by Juan Julio Baena; music by Miguel Asins Arbo and Mr. Ferreri; produced by Pedro Portabella. Released by Kino International Corporation. At Film Forum 2, 57 Watts Street. Running time: 88 minutes. This film has no rating.
Don Anselmo......................................José Isbert
Don Lucas ....José A. Bepe
WITH: Pedro Porcel, María Luisa Ponte, José Luis López Vázquez.

By WALTER GOODMAN

ALL Don Anselmo wants is a motorized wheelchair. The problem is that there's nothing wrong with his legs, and his prosperous but parsimonious son, the lawyer, refuses to indulge him. The drastic steps the old fellow takes to stop walking and start riding constitute the plot of "El Cochecito" ("The Little Coach"), Marco Ferreri's 1960 movie, which is having its American premiere at Film Forum 2.

Mr. Ferreri is best known for "La Grande Bouffe," a satire about Franco's Spain in which several gourmands dine themselves to death. "El Cochecito," too, has its satiric edge — almost everybody, even likable Anselmo, is utterly self-centered; when Anselmo goes out of his way to reunite a pair of young lovers, it's an aberration. You'll need patience, but as the little tale develops, the movie offers a quirkily rueful look at the loneliness and longings of age.

Don Anselmo, played most cunningly by José Isbert, wants the motorized wheelchair so he can go buzzing around town with his invalid pal Don Lucas and join in the races for the handicapped. Since his wife's death, Anselmo has been drifting pointlessly about the big crowded

Zade Rosenthal

Charles Martin Smith, Kevin Costner, Sean Connery and Andy Garcia in Brian De Palma's screen hit, "The Untouchables."

apartment that serves as home for his extended family and offices for his son and son-in-law. For him, it's just a way station to the cemetery. The motorized wheelchair promises freedom.

It takes a while, almost half the movie, for Mr. Isbert to work his manic charm and the story to come into focus. As the plot veers this way and that, like one of the wheelchairs on a first outing, you may find yourself wondering what Mr. Ferreri is up to; some of the encounters are so casual as to be perplexing. The black-and-white movie seems to be fighting itself — black humor clashing with light sentiment.

But Anselmo and the others grow on you. The pleasures here lie in the vividness of the characters, never caricatures. The family members, grumpy Don Lucas, the bossy servant to a rich invalid, the avuncular wheelchair salesman, the shrewd woman to whom Anselmo sells his late wife's jewels — they're all real people in

real places. And by the end, the chuckles of recognition have built up to cheers for Anselmo's desperate defiance.

1987 Je 29, C18:2

INNERSPACE, directed by Joe Dante; screenplay by Jeffrey Boam and Chip Proser, story by Mr. Proser; director of photography, Andrew Laszlo; edited by Kent Beyda; music by Jerry Goldsmith; production designer, James H. Spencer; produced by Michael Finnell; released by Warner Brothers. At the Criterion Center, Broadway and 45th Street; the Sutton, 57th Street and Third Avenue; the Art Greenwich Twin, 12th Street at Seventh Avenue; the 86th Street Twin, at Lexington Avenue; the 84th Street Six, at Broadway; the 23d Street West Triplex, at Eighth Avenue. Running time: 118 minutes. This film is rated PG.

Lieut. Tuck Pendleton	Dennis Quaid
Jack Putter	Martin Short
Lydia Maxwell	Meg Ryan
Victor Scrimshaw	Kevin McCarthy
Dr. Margaret Canker	Fiona Lewis
Mr. Igoe	Vernon Wells
The Cowboy	Robert Picardo
Wendy	Wendy Schaal

Family Feud

Jose Isbert and Maria Luisa Ponte star in "El Cochecito," a black comedy from Spain about a dispute among relatives.

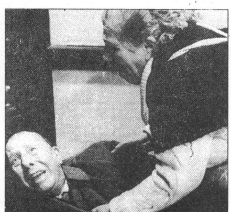

By JANET MASLIN

WHEN Mel Brooks, in his current "Spaceballs," refers to a planned sequel called "Spaceballs II: The Search for More Money," he is more or less joking. When the makers of "Innerspace" leave their film without a real ending, and instead with a plug for the sequel that has apparently been planned, they are not. It takes great confidence to think of a second film before the first is even finished; either that, or it takes great nerve. In any case, "Innerspace," which opens today at the Criterion and other theaters, has all the brashness of a hit, if not all the luster.

"Innerspace" was directed by Joe Dante, who also directed "Gremlins" (that film was written by Chris Columbus and, irony of small ironies, Mr. Columbus's own "Adventures in Babysitting" also opens today). It has been made in a style best described as enthusiastic. The story, by Chip Proser (who co-wrote the screenplay with Jeffrey Boam), must have looked great on paper, and is slightly less great on screen, thanks to the breathless way in which the various story elements have been crammed together. Mr. Dante is better able to convey an excitement about all the wild things that befall his characters than a clear and steady sense of just what is going on.

"Innerspace" is about a scientist who becomes miniaturized and travels through the body of another man. But if the idea recalls "Fantastic Voyage," the film itself owes more to "All of Me," with Martin Short given the fine comic opportunity to play a man whose body is taking instructions from elsewhere, and Dennis Quaid as the microbe-sized scien-

Dennis Quaid in "Innerspace."

tist giving the orders.

Mr. Quaid, as a Navy man named Lieut. Tuck Pendleton, is participating in an experiment that means to shrink him and inject him into the bloodstream of a rabbit. But thanks to the maneuverings of microchip thieves in Silicon Valley, something goes wrong. And he winds up inside of Mr. Short, who plays a hypochondriac supermarket clerk named Jack Putter. Mr. Short, with more to do here than he had in "Three Amigos," will doubtless find an even better film role some day, since he spends a lot of time playing a sentimental straight man here. He does have one opportunity to cut loose with a remarkable little dance, though. And in one of the film's better special-effects scenes, his face turns to quivering rubber.

One of the film's subplots has Jack beginning to fall for Tuck's girlfriend Lydia (Meg Ryan), a glamorous reporter; another has Kevin McCarthy and Fiona Lewis leading a band of industrial spies who hope to learn the secrets of miniaturization and make them their own. This leads, in one of the better trick sequences, to the two spies' being compressed to the size of small children, so that one has to stand atop another in order for them to make a telephone call. This is the sort of visual gamesmanship that "Innerspace" might be expected to deliver. And there are some memorable special-effects episodes, notably one involving Jack's stomach acid and another in which Jack and Tuck manage to share a drink.

Mr. Dante also directed "Explorers," the science-fiction fantasy that culminated in the remarkable sight of extraterrestrial creatures sitting in space watching the earthly television shows, becoming a repository for the worst of our junk. His view of pop culture seems both mischievous and appreciative, and there are times when his film conveys that with great buoyancy (fittingly enough, one of its key scenes takes place in a shopping mall). At other times it has a busy and perfunctory tone, one that might have been alleviated by a more streamlined screenplay and a sharper sense of why any of this should matter. We shouldn't have to wait for "Innerspace II" for that.

•

"Innerspace" is rated PG ("Parental Guidance Suggested"). It includes a couple of mildly suggestive scenes.

1987 Jl 1, C17:1

Wild in the Streets

ADVENTURES IN BABY-SITTING, directed by Chris Columbus; written by David Simkins; director of photography, Ric Waite; edited by Fredric Steinkamp and William Steinkamp; music by Michael Kamen; production designer, Todd Hallowell; produced by Debra Hill and Lynda Obst; released by Touchstone Pictures. At Embassy 2, Broadway at 47th Street; Baronet, Third Avenue and 59th Street; Bay Cinema, Second Avenue at 32d Street; Waverly Twin, Avenue of the Americas at Third Street; Embassy 72d Street Twin, at Broadway. Running time: 100 minutes. This film is rated PG-13.

Chris	Elisabeth Shue
Sara	Maia Brewton
Brad	Keith Coogan
Daryl	Anthony Rapp
Joe Gipp	Calvin Levels
Dawson	Vincent D'Onofrio
Brenda	Penelope Ann Miller
Dan	George Newbern
Pruitt	John Ford Noonan
Mike	Bradley Whitford

IMAGINE the terrors that await nice kids from an affluent suburb when a series of mishaps forces them to visit downtown Chicago at night, with no better chaperone than their feisty blond baby sitter. This is what "Adventures in Baby-Sitting," which opens today at the Baronet and other theaters, asks its audience to do. The kids meet such exotic types as gangsters, thieves and blues musicians, and everyone they encounter is delighted to make them the center of attention (the gangsters chase them; a car thief befriends them; the musicians invite them to sing). It's hard to know whether naïveté this overwhelming is deliberate or accidental.

To be fair, "Adventures in Baby-Sitting" is determinedly cute, and its pep may well be appreciated by anyone with a frame of reference as narrow as the film makers' own. It's clear from the film's opening moments that pep is all that matters here anyhow. Elisabeth Shue, who is

spunky and attractive as the baby sitter in question, is first seen lip-synching to a rock song just as Tom Cruise did in "Risky Business," a touch designed to wake up viewers if not dazzle them with originality. Every time the action starts to flag, the director, Chris Columbus, throws in another hit song.

After Chris (Miss Shue) is hired to watch Brad (Keith Coogan) and Sara (Maia Brewton), she gets a call from her friend Brenda (Penelope Ann Miller), who has attempted to run away from her stepmother. Trapped at the bus station, surrounded by homeless people who are bothering her, Brenda is now having second thoughts and begs Chris to come to her rescue. So Chris piles her two charges and their busybody friend Daryl (Anthony Rapp) into the family station wagon, and off they go. It only takes one flat tire on the highway to launch the film's nightlong series of adventures.

•

In the course of a single evening, Chris rethinks her values, ditches one boyfriend and finds another one; Brad becomes more mature; Sara has a tiny epiphany with her favorite comic-book hero. The kids witness a violent assault, visit some gangsters' headquarters, become kidnap victims, attend a fraternity party and scale a skyscraper from the outside. Mr. Columbus knows how to keep things moving, all right. But neither he nor the screen writer David Simkins, in their efforts to pack every imaginable kind of scene into this humble story, has the faintest idea of where to stop.

Appearing briefly late in the film, in the role of Sara's comic-book hero Thor, is Vincent D'Onofrio, who here looks like a muscular blond Adonis. Mr. D'Onofrio is barely recognizable as the helpless, overweight recruit who makes such a startling impression in Stanley Kubrick's "Full Metal Jacket."

•

"Adventures in Baby-Sitting" is rated PG-13 ("Special Parental Guidance Suggested for Those Younger Than 13"). It contains some strong language.

1987 Jl 1, C24:3

SLEEPWALK, directed by Sara Driver; screenplay by Ms. Driver and Lorenzo Kathleen Brennon; photography by Frank Prinzi and Jim Jarmusch; edited by Li Shin Yu; music by Phil Kline; production company, Ottoskop Filmproduktion GmBH, Munich, West Germany, and Driver Films Inc., New York; production team, Dave Bromberg, Dan Shulman, J. C. Hardin and Jane Weinstock. At the Bleecker Street Cinema, at La Guardia Place, and the Carnegie Screening Room, Seventh Avenue and 57th Street. Running time: 78 minutes. This film has no rating.

Nicole	Suzanne Fletcher
Isabelle	Ann Magnuson
Jimmy	Dexter Lee
Dr. Gou	Steven Chen Ecco
Ecco Ecco	Ako

"Sleepwalk" was shown as part of this year's New Directors/New Films series. Following are excerpts from Caryn James's review, which appeared in The New York Times March 20. The film opens today at the Bleecker Street Cinema, at La Guardia Place, and the Carnegie Screening Room, Seventh Avenue and 57th Street.

WHEN Chinese fairy tales impinge on the life of Nicole, a young woman in downtown New York,

several things happen: her sexy French roommate becomes bald; her finger begins to bleed; an Oriental woman about to unravel these mysteries is killed. Nicole's half-Chinese son, a wise child, thinks the whole thing smells like almonds. Sara Driver's lyrical, witty "Sleepwalk" has the illogical sense of a dream, backed by the texture of everyday life. In her first feature, Ms. Driver blithely absorbs influences — from chiaroscuro to Surrealism to performance art — and spins them into her own vibrant, original style.

"Sleepwalk" begins with the theft of an ancient manuscript, which the sinister Dr. Gou asks Nicole to translate. She does, and soon life imitates these tales. Isabelle, the bald, vain roommate, is punished for her greediness, like the princess in the manuscript story who refused to give a bird a lock of her hair. Another tale warns, "Keep the child away from the man who smells like almonds." The child is clearly Nicole's son. But why does Dr. Gou lie on a bed of almonds, and why does Ecco Ecco, the Oriental woman, say "almonds, poison," as she points to the manuscript?

Ms. Driver, who co-wrote the screenplay, takes the incoherence of these events for granted. Despite its trappings of mystery and suspense, "Sleepwalk" is barely concerned with plot; what matters is the feel of this place where dreams meet reality.

Ms. Driver, a graduate of the New York University Film School, has worked on Jim Jarmusch's three films. She produced his "Stranger Than Paradise," and he and Frank Prinzi did the dazzling camerawork on "Sleepwalk." Ms. Driver's film, though, is like a Jarmusch work turned upside-down and inside-out. Instead of his black-and-white photographic images, she works with light and shadow like a painter creating still lifes. Doors open and light slashes diagonally across darkened rooms; whole scenes seem painted from a palette of blues. And while Mr. Jarmusch's characters are downtrodden dreamers, Ms. Driver's are offbeat people who have dreams foisted on them.

Although "Sleepwalk" moves slowly, Ms. Driver keeps her images from becoming static or self-consciously artsy. Ann Magnuson is colorful comic relief as Isabelle; she may lose her rich red hair and parade around much of the film looking like Daddy Warbucks, but she never drops her perfectly exaggerated French accent. Suzanne Fletcher's Nicole is methodical and laconic, a relatively ordinary center for her jumbled household, a perfect foil for the magic that appears before her.

1987 Jl 3, C5:1

FILM VIEW/Janet Maslin

Inside the 'Jacket': All Kubrick

STANLEY KUBRICK'S "FULL METAL JACKET" establishes its grip on the viewer's attention instantaneously, with an opening scene in which young recruits are shorn by an off-screen Marine Corps barber, while a corny, lulling song is heard in the background ("Kiss me goodbye and write me when I'm gone/Goodbye sweetheart, hello Vietnam"). The scene would be ordinary, even a cliché, were it not for the look on the young men's faces. In their eyes we see absolutely nothing: no apprehension, no bravado, not even blind obedience, only the emptiness of clay ready to be molded.

The sense of sheer animal helplessness, conveyed with the seeping white light, uncluttered frames and daunting angles of which Mr. Kubrick is a master, is a shock. It's also a challenge to the audience to remain mindful of these men's humanity, despite the brutal and dehumanizing ordeal to which they will be subjected.

■

This opening scene is something else as well: It's an announcement of the cool, merciless perspective of Stanley Kubrick, whose directorial distance from the inner workings of his characters has always been extraordinary. In "Full Metal Jacket," that distance allows Mr. Kubrick to take a frighteningly clinical view of the process by which fighting men are molded. He presents the gradual and deliberate assault on individuality and privacy that is basic training; the connections between sex and aggression; the combat soldier's ultimate and even stirring realization that he has left his better nature far behind him. Mr. Kubrick's vision of this process is infinitely more troubling and singular than the one set forth in Oliver Stone's "Platoon."

Comparisons between these two films are as specious as they are inevitable, for their directors appear to have aimed for very different effects. But "Platoon," as the film that has most definitively brought the Vietnam experience home for moviegoing America, stands as a kind of box-office landmark, and "Full Metal Jacket" appears at least superficially to cover similar terrain. Harrowing as both of these films are, their effects are very different. "Platoon" conveys the day-to-day physical experience of men at war with exceptional realism, while "Full Metal Jacket" has a more abstract and typically (for Mr. Kubrick) elliptical style. While "Platoon" develops a relatively conventional narrative, "Full Metal Jacket" has a separate prologue (as "2001" did) and a less linear structure in which storytelling is less central than the distinct, indelible images Mr. Kubrick has created.

If "Platoon" accompanies its brutal realism with the en-

Adam Baldwin and Matthew Modine in action

nobling sounds of Samuel Barber's "Adagio for Strings," "Full Metal Jacket" takes the opposite tack. It scores the sharply poetic imagery to be found here with the most soulless and banal American popular songs imaginable, from "These Boots Are Made for Walking" to "Surfin' Bird" (Mr. Kubrick, with his use of a children's song in the film's last scene, even manages the kind of heavy irony that would sink anyone else, and that in his hands becomes bone-chilling.) Perhaps most important, "Platoon" is a film that anticipates and manipulates every response that its audience has. "Full Metal Jacket," while no less wrenching, allows no easy catharsis, no comfortable understanding. In that, it has more in common with Mr. Kubrick's own work than it does with any other film about the Vietnam War.

◼

It's a mistake to look to Mr. Kubrick's films for easily encapsulated attitudes; even his earlier war film "Paths of Glory" (1957) was strikingly anomalous for its time. "The Shining" is no ordinary horror film, any more than "2001" is a simple, reductive vision of life in space. Mr. Kubrick, in adapting material as varied as Anthony Burgess's "Clockwork Orange," Stephen King's "Shining," Thackeray's "Barry Lyndon," Nabokov's "Lolita," Terry Southern's "Dr. Strangelove" and now Gustav Hasford's "Short-Timers," the novel on which his new film is based, has always extracted and shaped elements from these books into films that are never slavishly faithful to their sources. What finally matters, in his films, is less their identifiable ideas than their vast and genuine staying power. The pure mystery of his monolith (in "2001"), the stark, empty corridors of his haunted hotel (in "The Shining,"), the exquisite and ironic perfection of his 18th-century landscapes (in "Barry Lyndon") are as elusive as they are unforgettable.

The basic training episode in "Full Metal Jacket" will have that same long-lasting impact, as will the extended combat sequence, near the film's end, that culminates in a transcendent image of war and its horror. In between, briefly, the film (co-written by Michael Herr, Mr. Hasford and Mr. Kubrick) takes a journalistic tone that only underscores how much more haunting Mr. Kubrick's work is when he avoids the verbal and the literal. When American soldiers try to explain their feelings about the Vietnamese people, the war itself, even the landscape (it's a land without horses, the Texan nicknamed Cowboy complains), they are only echoing what we already know. But when Mr. Kubrick films a group of soldiers gathered around a writhing prisoner, in the ruins of a structure that's as much like a temple as a military headquarters, with the full import of their role made clear to all of them, he creates a visual epiphany that no viewer could forget, and no combat journalist could easily equal.

Even more involving, in its way, is the basic training episode that serves as a prelude to the events in Vietnam. Basic training, with its grueling workouts and its colorfully obscene invective, is as basic a convention as the war film has; we've all seen this before. But we haven't seen it done as it's done here. Mr. Kubrick devotes about 45 relentless minutes to a process that is as overwhelming for the audience as it must be for the recruits. And in doing that, he also takes care to maintain the viewer's critical distance.

So the audience can experience what is being done to these men and think about it, too: about the way the drill sergeant (played by Lee Ermey, himself a former Marine sergeant and a man with extraordinary lungs) deliberately violates every racial, sexual and personal taboo as he hectors his men, infantilizing them (he makes them sleep holding their rifles, march holding their genitals) so as to reconstruct them along different lines. The title refers to a shell casing, a kind of model for the tough, hollow fighter who will emerge from this ordeal; it's also a reference to the misfit in the group (a figure of astonishingly real anguish, as played by Vincent D'Onofrio) for whom this training most conspicuously backfires.

No one who sees "Full Metal Jacket" will easily put the film's last glimpse of Mr. D'Onofrio, or a great many other things about Mr. Kubrick's latest and most sobering vision, out of mind.

A caller has pointed out that Eliot Ness was not, as I inadvertently suggested two weeks ago, actually approached for help by the woman struggling with her baby carriage in that film's train station scene. As he so neatly put it, "A true hero doesn't have to be asked." □

1987 Jl 5, II:17:5

Love Story

KARMA, directed and produced by Ho Quang Minh; screenplay (Vietnamese with English subtitles) by Mr. Minh and Nguy Ngu, based on a story by Nguy Ngu; photography by Tran Dinh Muu and Tran Ngoc Huynh; music by Trinh Cong Son. At Film Forum 1, 57 Watts Street. Running time: 100 minutes. This film has no rating.
Binh .... Tran Quang
Nga .... Phuong Dung
Tri .... Le Cung Bac
Binh's mother .... Ba Nam Sa Dec
Van .... Thuy An

By JANET MASLIN

UNLIKE the Western-made films that have regarded Vietnam as a hellish, bewildering landscape, a terra incognita in which American soldiers are set adrift, Ho Quang Minh's "Karma" regards it as home. The Hanoi-born Mr. Minh, now a naturalized Swiss citizen, made his film in and around Ho Chi Minh City, as Saigon is now named, working with a Vietnamese cast and crew. Deserts and beaches are seen here more frequently than the predictable jungle scenery, and the film's psychic landscape is as unconventional, at least by Western standards, as its physical one.

The war is remote in this drama set between 1968 and 1972 (and based on a Vietnamese short story entitled "The Wounded Beast" by Nguy Ngu, who co-wrote the screenplay). But its effects are inescapable, and they can be seen everywhere, particularly in the embittered face of Binh (Tran Quang), the story's hero. Binh, once missing in action and presumed dead, has returned to find that his beautiful young wife, Nga, has betrayed him and has become a bar girl who befriends visiting soldiers. Nga and the other bar girls seen in the film seem bored, aristocratic and coolly contemptuous of their companions, again in opposition to the usual clichés.

At Film Forum I, where "Karma" opens today, it has been described as "'Platoon' turned inside out," but there's a touch of television soap opera to it, too. As Nga, Phuong Dung is glamorous but amateurish, and she seems to be summoning thoughts of dead puppies when the screenplay requires her to grieve for Binh's lost love. The dashing Tran Quang is better, but it's difficult to make this small, melodramatic love story support the entire weight of the war. The film's incidental scenes, like those showing life at the bar or the process by which Binh's genteel family is forced from its home in the name of relocation, are much more successful than those concentrating on Binh's rage and Nga's regret.

If an American influence manifests itself in the soap-opera aspects of "Karma," there are also attempts at Japanese delicacy, particularly in the final symbolic representations of Nga's remorse. More impressive than the occasional artiness of "Karma" (it begins with a dream sequence set in the dunes) is the velvety black and white photography, which is exceptionally fine.

1987 Jl 8, C22:5

Working-Class War

THE WHISTLE BLOWER, directed by Simon Langton; screenplay by Julian Bond, based on the novel by John Hale; director of photography, Fred Tammes; edited by Bob Morgan; production designer, Morley Smith; produced by Geoffrey Reeve; released by Hemdale Releasing Corporation. At 68th Street Playhouse, at Third Avenue. Running time: 110 minutes. This film is rated PG.

Michael Caine

Frank Jones	Michael Caine
Lord	James Fox
Bob Jones	Nigel Havers
Cynthia Goodburn	Felicity Dean
Sir Adrian Chapple	Sir John Gielgud
Bill Pickett	Kenneth Colley
Bruce	Gordon Jackson
Charles Greig	Barry Foster
Secretary to the Cabinet	David Langton

By JANET MASLIN

A NUMBER of killings occur during "The Whistle Blower," Simon Langton's film about a British spy ring. But there is only one gun to be seen here, glimpsed briefly in one of the film's last scenes, and for the most part it stays inside a drawer. "The Whistle Blower" eschews the usual equipment to be found in spy stories, and the usual attitudes too. While its intrigue plot is indeed suspenseful and tight, this film's real focus is on British society and its stratification. Mr. Langton, Julian Bond, the film's screenwriter (who also wrote "The Shooting Party") and an outstandingly fine cast explore these distinctions deftly.

The film traces the efforts by one man, Frank Jones, an office-equipment salesman played by Michael Caine, to unravel the intrigue that has enveloped his idealistic young son. Bob Jones (played by Nigel Havers, who was young Lord Lindsey in "Chariots of Fire") works as a Russian translator in the Government office where a fellow employee has recently been convicted of spying. When Frank comes to visit him on his birthday, the son voices his dissatisfaction.

He loves the Russian language, Russian literature, and hates using his expertise to study tapped telephone conversations by Communist Party officials. He hates feeling, when the Bolshoi Ballet comes to town, "the certainty that the K.G.B. man is sitting in the bloody prop corner." He hates the climate of mistrust and suspicion in which his work is done. "Their secret world has put out the light of the ordinary world," he says.

Bob sees a number of his colleagues perish under peculiar circumstances, as part of the aftermath of the spy scandal. When he himself has a suspicious accident, his father cannot help but try to find out what happened. Frank, a widower and Korean War veteran who values "the quiet life at the end of the day," is gradually enraged and astonished by what he learns of his son's fate and the circumstances that have shaped it. And he is goaded into action by the air of secrecy that surrounds even Bob's friends and co-workers. "We've got our jobs and our futures too, you know," one woman responds to inquiries from this bereaved man.

"The Whistle Blower," which opens today at the 68th Street Playhouse, has been directed in a swift, economical and nicely detailed style by Mr. Langton; only in its final scenes, when the underlying cynicism gives way to obviousness, does the film loosen its grip. As based on a novel by John Hale, it has an intricate plot that hinges indirectly on matters of class and position. These little issues arise everywhere: in the way an elderly aristocrat tries to commandeer a parking place from an impudent left-wing journalist (Kenneth Colley), in Frank's meeting with an old wartime buddy (Barry Foster) who has come up in the world; in the attitude of a high-born British Intelligence official (James Fox) toward those who are less so. Mr. Fox, addressing a more working-class colleague in a scene that takes place at the races, manages to give orders without meeting the other man's eyes at all.

At the pinnacle of the film's social microcosm is Sir Adrian Chapple, a gentlemanly Government leader played by Sir John Gielgud as the full embodiment of the screenplay's disillusionment. By contrast, Mr. Caine plays Frank as a resolutely ordinary man, a firm believer in stability and the simple virtues. Frank, at first shocked by his son's daring to complain about a steady job, eventually has his thinking reshaped by the hard facts that unfold before him. Mr. Caine captures this process in its every small nuance, conveying the man's bitterness, his quiet anguish and above all his tenacity.

As headed by Mr. Caine, who gives a full and affecting performance well above his usual high level, the film's entire cast is a marvel. Every last role in this complex and crowded story is well played; even the walk-on parts, the police detectives and office workers, become memorable. Like the actors, the varied and believable sets contribute greatly to the film's crisp and definite manner, helping to shape the small, tense universe in which the action unfolds. "It's a flight from reality," one character says about the world of espionage. But as evoked so well here, it has a reality of its own.

•

"The Whistler Blower" is rated PG ("Parental Guidance Suggested"). It contains some violence, most of it implicit, and mildly strong language.

1987 Jl 10, C4:2

Elements of Intrigue

THE SQUEEZE, directed by Roger Young; written by Daniel Taplitz; director of photography, Arthur Albert; edited by Harry Keramidas; music by Miles Goodman; production designer, Simon Waters; produced by Rupert Hitzig and Michael Tannen; released by Tri-Star Pictures. At Criterion Center, Broadway and 45th Street; Gemini, 64th Street and Second Avenue; 84th Street Sixplex, at Broadway; Movieland Eighth Street Triplex, at University Place. Running time: 102 minutes. This film is rated PG-13.

Harry Berg	Michael Keaton
Rachel Dobs	Rae Dawn Chong
Titus	Meat Loaf
Tom T. Murray	John Davidson
Rigaud	Ronald Guttman
Gem Vigo	Leslie Bevis
Joe	George Gerdes

Michael Keaton

T HERE'S nothing about Michael Keaton that says movie star. But Mr. Keaton, with his ordinary looks, permanent scowl and diffident manner, has in the past been able to carry entire films (most notably "Mr. Mom") with his quick wit and casual, smart-alecky delivery. He would certainly do the same for "The Squeeze," which opens today at the Gemini and other theaters, if there were anything to carry. As it is, Mr. Keaton languishes half-heartedly in a colorful, expensive-looking comedy-action-romance-drama that's just about entirely empty.

•

In "The Squeeze," directed in high television style by Roger Young ("Lassiter"), Mr. Keaton plays an artist who designs sets for discothèques, so the screenplay by Daniel Taplitz must be credited with at least some originality. And one of the film's first scenes has a cat nibbling on a severed finger, so the story is not without elements of intrigue. However, there's a problem with overkill throughout. Beginning with the finger and Mr. Keaton's ostensible artwork (an immense dinosaur made of exposed circuitry and embedded with dozens of television sets), the film starts out big and tries to get bigger. Soon it has incorporated shrunken heads, a scheme for winning the lottery, the Staten Island Ferry and even Meat Loaf, who plays a thug.

Also in the film is Rae Dawn Chong, who teams up with Mr. Keaton for a lot of pointless chase scenes accompanied by too-loud music. John Davidson plays a corrupt and wildly exaggerated game show host, which will either seem funny or not, depending on whether you know he's been the host of "Hollywood Squares."

•

"The Squeeze" is rated PG-13 ("Special Parental Guidance Suggested for Those Younger Than 13"). It contains some bedroom innuendoes and strong language.

JANET MASLIN

1987 Jl 10, C24:1

REVENGE OF THE NERDS II: NERDS IN PARADISE, directed by Joe Roth; written by Dan Guntzelman and Steve Marshall, based on characters created by Tim Metcalfe, Miguel Tejada-Flores, Steve Zacharias and Jeff Buhai; director of photography, Charles Correll; edited by Richard Chew; music by Mark Mothersbaugh and Gerald V. Casale; production designer, Trevor Williams; produced by Ted Field, Robert Cort and Peter Bart. At the Gotham Cinema, Third Avenue at 58th Street; the 86th Street East at Third Avenue; Embassy 72d Street at Broadway;

Robert Carradine in "Revenge of the Nerds II: Nerds in Paradise."

the Criterion, Broadway at 45th Street, and Movieland Eighth Street, at University Place. Running time: 81 minutes. This film is rated PG-13.

Lewis	Robert Carradine
Booger	Curtis Armstrong
Lamar	Larry B. Scott
Poindexter	Timothy Busfield
Sunny	Courtney Thorne-Smith
Wormser	Andrew Cassese
Ogre	Donald Gibb
Roger	Bradley Whitford
Buzz	Ed Lauter
Aldonza	Priscilla Lopez

By JANET MASLIN

If you've seen one nerd — a four-eyed, egg-headed individual with a plastic pencil holder in his breast pocket and a song in his heart — have you seen them all? That is the question loosely posed by "Revenge of the Nerds II: Nerds in Paradise," which opened yesterday at the Movieland and other theaters. And the answer is probably no, since this film is at least slightly more varied than the average fraternity-boy comedy.

Of course, disgustingness is the nerds' stock in trade. And while that may count for a lot in "Animal House" circles, it will not endear them to viewers at large.

"Nerds in Paradise" follows the flat-footed, horribly dressed members of Lambda Lambda Lambda fraternity to Fort Lauderdale, where they attend an interfraternity council meeting and are shunned by one and all. Booted out of the nice hotel where the rest of the group is staying, the Tri-Lambs, led by arch-nerd Lewis Skolnick (Robert Carradine), wind up in a dump that is the last word in squalor. Unfortunately, it's also the last words in ethnic insults, since the atmosphere is Hispanic, the proprietor is a Carmen Miranda type (played by Priscilla Lopez) and the boys' rundown accommodations are dubbed the "Ricky Ricardo Suite."

Even for nerds, the leading characters are a motley crew. Mr. Carradine (who wears flip-up sunglasses and a belt just under his armpits) is likable, mostly for the gasping hee-haw of a laugh he has perfected. And some of the lesser nerd characters are also appealing. But there's nothing good that Larry B. Scott can do with the script's stereotypically limp-wristed homosexual character. And Curtis Armstrong, with an overwritten slob's role that has him leering at coeds, belching ostentatiously and picking his nose, manages to overact even that.

The nerds' rap number, in which they sing of nerd pride, is probably the high point of this whole endeavor.

1987 Jl 11, 18:4

FILM VIEW/Janet Maslin

Only Ankle Deep in Adventure

SOMETIMES EVEN FILMS ABOUT adventure, about discovery, about wondrous technological triumphs have a way of seeming small. It's a function of the particular universe that is being explored. If that universe is effectively no larger than, say, a suburban backyard, there isn't much to be unearthed no matter how energetic the digging. A film about a wild, mysterious creature from parts unknown cannot have much magic if all the creature (Harry) wants is to go home with an all-American family (the Hendersons), raid the refrigerator and lounge in the easy chair.

Since so many of today's adventure films are aimed at younger and more suggestible segments of the audience, and since so many of the adventures themselves are essentially about nothing, there is often reason to wonder what really is being conveyed. Whatever message "Harry and the Hendersons" means to get across — that Bigfeet need to be loved? that they're just like you and me? — it communicates a terrible flimsiness about the Hendersons and their lives. Parts of the Henderson house actually fall off when Harry knocks into them, and this is presented as pure fun. If anything, it's chilling.

■

Like the current "Adventures in Babysitting" and "Innerspace," "Harry and the Hendersons" is directed in a punchy, exclamatory, neo-Spielbergian style by a director, William Dear, who has spent time under Mr. Spielberg's wing. A few of these protégés — most notably Robert Zemeckis, director of "Back to the Future" — have used the wry fondness for middle American life and the vigorous, emphatic camera movements that are Mr. Spielberg's trademarks and made them part of something new. But too often, these films' persistent pep, sitcom settings and enthusiastically farfetched premises are all they have to offer. Scratch the surface of this much senseless activity and there may be nothing underneath.

Nothing, that is, except the spectacle of film makers scrambling frantically to the head of the class. When a director and screenwriter crowd in as many different kinds of calamities as Chris Columbus and David Simkins have in "Adventures in Babysitting," they seem more intent on wowing each other, or potential employers, than on wooing the viewer. "Adventures in Babysitting" is crammed to its very rafters. It tells of gangsters, derelicts, thieves, fraternity boys and blues musicians, all of whom pay a disproportionate amount of attention to the nice, well-heeled suburban white kids at the center of the story. In following these kids on their bold journey into downtown Chicago, the film flips through so many different kinds of adventure scenes that it seems more like a trailer, a catalogue, even a résumé than a story.

Perhaps it's this emphasis on speed and showiness that leads Mr. Columbus, who wrote the equally high-voltage "Gremlins," "The Goonies" and "Young Sherlock Holmes," to take the film's more latent content so lightly. When affluent white kids quake at the thought of inner-city life and then find all their prejudices comically reinforced, how funny is that, really? Would the all-black audience at a blues club really stop everything and demand that the white kids,

Beneath the roiling surface of some of the current crop of supposedly exciting movies lies nothing at all.

who stumble inadvertently onto the club's stage, sing a little song?

■

To be fair, this scene is good-natured fun, the film's young stars are likable and at least "Adventures in Babysitting" is lively. But it's a narrow-minded romp about characters who are shallow and proud of it, characters who may never venture any farther from what's safe and familiar than they do during this story. It's hard to see how exploits this tame can be called, even ironically, "adventures" at all.

Notwithstanding its story about miniaturization, "Innerspace" isn't quite this small. Its leading man, as played by Dennis Quaid, is just raucous enough to pass for a grown-up with personality. As the innocent bystander into whose body the microbe-sized Mr. Quaid is injected, Martin Short displays real sweetness and comic style. And the premise is intriguing: We've seen tiny travelers sailing through the human body before (in "Fantastic Voyage"), but they haven't enjoyed the close, companionable relationship Mr. Short forms with Mr. Quaid who, through the use of various high-tech devices, is able to converse with him. In one scene, Mr. Quaid even persuades Mr. Short to down some liquor so they can amicably share a drink.

"Innerspace" would appeal more completely to the amateur scientist in each of us if it were content to stick to this two-man experiment and the havoc it creates. Certainly the possibilities are endless, and the representations of Mr. Short's innards exert a great fascination. In fact, making his character a confirmed hypochondriac is one of the screenplay's wittier touches.

■

But "Innerspace" doesn't have the confidence to keep things simple or leave well enough alone. It throws in industrial spies, a Middle Eastern operative dealing in stolen technology, a supermarket staff and a beautiful reporter who gives the two heroes something in common. All of this has the effect not of amplifying the basic story but of smothering it. The action that takes place inside Mr. Short is finally much more far-reaching than the standard chases and other, more conventionally ambitious escapades that occur around him.

Real adventure, despite the implied lessons of films like these, doesn't always mean bigger, faster or more flamboyant events. Sometimes it just means sidestepping the familiar and facing up to the unknown. □

1987 Jl 12, II:19:1

Keith Coogan, Maia Brewton and Elisabeth Shue in "Adventures in Babysitting"

Rhapsody

GOOD MORNING, BABYLON, directed by Vittorio and Paolo Taviani, based on an idea by Lloyd Fonvielle; story and screenplay by the Tavianis in collaboration with Tonino Guerra; director of photography, Giuseppe Lanci; edited by Roberto Perpignani; music by Nicola Piovani; production supervisor, Tommaso Calevi; produced by Giuliani De Negri; released by Vestron Pictures. At Cinema 1, Third Avenue at 60th Street. Running time: 115 minutes. This film is rated PG-13.

Nicola	Vincent Spano
Andrea	Joaquim De Almeida
Edna	Greta Scacchi
Mabel	Desiree Becker
Bonanno	Omero Antonutti
D. W. Griffith	Charles Dance
Moglie Griffith	Berangere Bonvoisin
Grass	David Brandon
Thompson	Brian Freilino
La Veneziana	Margarita Lozano
Duccio	Massimo Venturiello
Operat Irlandese	Andrea Prodan

By JANET MASLIN

THE rosy style of Paolo and Vittorio Taviani, with its radiant physicality and its intoxicating sense of magic, has most often been used to create cinematic folk tales ("The Night of the Shooting Stars," "Chaos," "Padre Padrone") about Italian peasantry. It is considerably less at home in the Hollywood of 1916, the backdrop against which the Tavianis' "Good Morning, Babylon" unfolds. Never has Hollywood, a place more commonly viewed with cynicism and awe, been romanticized this rhapsodically. It took the Tavianis to view a tale of two immigrant stonemasons, who work on the sets for D. W. Grif-

Charles Dance as D. W. Griffith in "Good Morning, Babylon."

fith's "Intolerance," as a parable concerning brotherhood, honor, filial loyalty and the very essence of art.

So there are moments when "Good Morning, Babylon," which opens today at Cinema 1, seems to have taken leave of its senses entirely, and these moments occur more and more frequently as the film proceeds. But "Good Morning, Babylon," which is described as "an American fable," gets off to a charming start. It finds two brothers, Andrea (Joaquim De Almeida) and Nicola (Vincent Spano), at work with the rest of their siblings on a church restoration in their native Tuscan village. Their father, whose approval means everything to his sons, later singles out these two for particularly high praise.

Just as the Tavianis discover a raw, earthy humor in the family rivalry thus engendered, so do they also give a rich, painterly beauty to a scene of the many brothers at dinner. The Tavianis' gorgeous visual effects are achieved almost offhandedly, with a casualness that's even comic, so that a scene of Andrea and Nicola at work in a pigpen is no less ravishing than anything else in the film. Having broken loose from their family and traveled to America — the voyage is encapsulated by a tin plate's sliding from brother to brother as they travel on rolling seas — Nicola and Andrea work their way west. As they go, they take something of the Tavianis' Italy with them, from the stunning landscapes these film makers can find anywhere to one brother's way of making a rude, defiant gesture to an offending vulture.

•

When the brothers reach San Francisco and help complete the magnificent Italian Pavilion for the Exposition there, "Good Morning, Babylon" begins to invoke the presence of D. W. Griffith, and begins to go wrong. Griffith, seen here as one of the reigning visionaries of his day, might be expected to dominate the film, but he never achieves that kind of stature. Instead, he's presented as a good-humored lightweight, boasting with bizarre precision that he can make a film "300 times better" than one that has impressed him, or playing the great man to his adoring wife. "Are you thinking of your old idea?" she asks, in the awkward, artificial tone that characterizes much of the Tavianis' screenplay. "'Intolerance' — I can always tell when it crops up in your head." Though he is wryly impersonated by Charles Dance, this

Griffith, who ultimately hires the brothers to build elephants for his Babylon set and becomes a jocular father figure for them, too frequently plays the fool.

In Hollywood, the brothers find rivals who challenge their manhood ("We are the sons of the sons of the sons of Michelangelo and Leonardo!" one brother angrily declares. "Whose sons are you?"). They also encounter two ripe, acquiescent nymphs named Mabel (Desiree Becker) and Edna (Greta Scacchi), whose claims to hard-heartedness are belied by their sunny good looks. "Remember, we promised each other we only go out with directors or producers," one tells the other, but they soon fall for the brothers' evident charm. In one scene, each man proudly offers his future bride a firefly he has caught for her, and the moment would seem ludicrous if it weren't also so sweet. The film's playful tone allows for some mockery of these courtship rituals anyhow, as when Nicola writes a love letter telling Edna she is "as beautiful as a snowy mountain," and the phrase "snowy mountain" becomes a joke all over town.

•

Enjoyable as it initially is, "Good Morning, Babylon" passes the point of no return when it begins to celebrate the burgeoning film industry's great fellowship, to sentimentalize these early days and to make unsuccessful attempts at interweaving the brothers' lives with the larger story around them. The film's very loveliness begins to seem wildly inappropriate, as do its occasional flashes of solemnity. And toward the very end, as the film attempts bolder and bolder strokes of plot development with ever crazier leaps, the Tavianis' expertly crafted bubble just about bursts. Neither their feelings about film making nor their feelings about brotherhood, surely this film's two main subjects, come through clearly.

"Good Morning, Babylon" has been acted with just the right earnestness, by a cast whose slightest hint of flippancy might have scuttled the entire thing. Mr. Spano, in a marked departure from earlier street-smart roles, plays the proud, diligent and oddly childlike Nicola particularly well.

"Good Morning, Babylon" seems a strange departure for the Tavianis, until it becomes clear — all too clear — that they have not departed at all.

1987 Jl 15, C18:5

Silent Heroes Vincent Spano and Joaquim De Almeida star in "Good Morning, Babylon"

Dreamdrome

EAT THE PEACH, directed by Peter Ormrod; screenplay by Mr. Ormrod and John Kelleher; director of photography, Arthur Wooster; edited by J. Patrick Duffner; music by Donal Lunny; production designer, David Wilson; produced by Mr. Kelleher; released by Skouras Pictures Inc. At 57th Street Playhouse, at Avenue of the Americas. Running time: 98 minutes. This film has no rating.

Vinnie	Stephen Brennan
Arthur	Eamon Morrissey
Nora	Catherine Byrne
Boots	Niall Toibin
Boss Murtagh	Joe Lynch
Sean Murtagh	Tony Doyle
Bunzo	Takashi Kawahara
Vicky	Victoria Armstrong
Mrs. Fleck	Barbara Adair

PETER ORMROD'S "Eat the Peach" is a fictional film, but it's based on the kind of true story no one could ever invent. Mr. Ormrod, who formerly worked in television, came across a man named Connie Kiernan who had brought his dream to life in his own backyard, and taken his inspiration from "Roustabout," the Elvis Presley movie. Mr. Kiernan, like Elvis in that film, was fascinated with the Wall of Death, this being a cylindrical track for motorcyclists who like to do their riding horizontally. There amid the car parts, the chickens and stray cats beside his house, he had to have one of his very own.

So Mr. Ormrod turned this into the story of Vinnie (Stephen Brennan) and his brother-in-law Arthur (Eamon Morrissey), two unemployed factory workers whose whimsy knows no bounds. After a Japanese-owned computer company has closed up shop in the Irish border town where they live, Vinnie and Arthur begin giving their collective imagination free rein. Cyclists already, and living in the midst of the kind of "vast industrial bog" (as described by Mr. Ormrod's co-writer, John Kelleher) whose very emptiness fires the imagination, they develop the cyclodrome idea. Or rather it develops itself, for the racetrack plan has soon taken on a life of its own.

•

Financing their plan sends Vinnie and Arthur into a life of smuggling various goods across the Northern Irish border. It also leads to Vinnie's very nearly blowing up the house he shares with an understandably disgruntled wife and daughter. These developments, and the grand opening that has friends and neighbors standing by in polite terror as the rickety Wall of Death quakes and wobbles, are more to the point than the two men's hopes, dreams or determination. There's an air of futility that pervades their project, and indeed the entire film, since it's essentially about people who think big, mean well and accomplish very little.

"Eat the Peach," which opens today at the 57th Street Playhouse, is presented by Jonathan Demme, and it's easy to see something of Mr. Demme's own sensibility at work here. The film's eccentric, single-minded characters, its lackadaisical wit and its love of the peripheral recall Mr. Demme's own "Handle With Care," though that film's comic potential was far more fully realized than this one's.

Mr. Ormrod's direction has a quick, throwaway manner that's appealing, and his oddball secondary characters — the would-be promoter who affects mannerisms he thinks are American, the local politician who gets caught up in Vinnie and Arthur's schemes —

Stephen Brennan

give the film a nicely unpredictable air. But finally, Mr. Ormrod's own view of the characters seems indistinct, a problem made larger by their scheme's less than triumphant outcome. Whether Mr. Ormrod regrets their misfire or applauds their optimism isn't entirely clear.

Mr. Brennan and Mr. Morrissey are extremely amiable, though, and the film has a nicely idiosyncratic manner. There can't help but be something attractive about heroes who see the magic in junkheaps, and visions of fame and glory everywhere. .   *JANET MASLIN*

1987 Jl 17, C6:1

To Serve and Protect

ROBOCOP, directed by Paul Verhoeven; written by Edward Neumeier and Michael Miner; director of photography, Jost Vacano; edited by Frank J. Urioste; music by Basil Poledouris; production designer, William Sandell; produced by Arne Schmidt; released by Orion Pictures. At National Twin, Broadway and 44th Street; D. W. Griffith, 59th Street, east of Third Avenue; Orpheum, Third Avenue at 86th Street; 84th Street Six, at Broadway; Nova, Broadway and 147th Street; Movie Center 5, 125th Street between Powell and Douglass Boulevards. Running time: 103 minutes. This film is rated R.

Murphy/Robocop	Peter Weller
Lewis	Nancy Allen
The Old Man	Daniel O'Herlihy
Jones	Ronny Cox
Clarence	Kurtwood Smith
Morton	Miguel Ferrer
Sergeant Reed	Robert DoQui
Leon	Ray Wise
Johnson	Felton Perry
Emil	Paul McCrane

By WALTER GOODMAN

IF it's violence you're after, "Robocop," now showing at the National and other theaters, gives full value. In his first American movie, Paul Verhoeven, a Dutch director ("Soldier of Orange"), doesn't let the furiously futuristic plot get in the way of the flaming explosions, shattering glass and hurtling bodies. Everything's constantly on the move in this movie full of camera tricks and computer tricks; if you glance away, chances are you'll miss somebody being blown away. Fortunately, the victims of the hand-held cannons that everybody shoots at everybody else take so long dying that you have plenty of time to enjoy their pain. When a baddie goes crashing into a toxic-

Laurel Moore
Peter Weller as "Robocop."

waste tank, he not only staggers out looking hideous, but staggers on and on, getting hideouser and hideouser.

Robocop (Peter Weller, well hidden) is an armored and computerized Galahad created by a sinister security company. He walks like Godzilla and shakes off shells like the tank the Army wishes it had. He was a good Detroit cop named Murphy before he was demolished by a gang of real bad guys led by a sadist (Kurtwood Smith). Only Murphy didn't quite die; there was a little piece of human memory inside the armor. So we have here a variation on the part-man-part-monster genre, except that this monster is programmed to enforce the law; he knows when and where a crime is being committed and can see through walls. The glitch is he's also been programmed not to go after the security-company biggies.

Humor glimmers amid the mayhem. One of the many final shootouts is between Robocop and ED 209 (ED stands for "enforcement droid"), a hulking klutz of a robot who can't do anything right. Robocop's crime-busting techniques are funny if you don't mind how the criminal's body gets busted in the process. Jost Vacano's camera finds a particularly droll point of view in a men's room. And periodically, a happy pair of television anchorfolk pops up to deliver news of the latest disaster at such popular Detroit spots as the Lee Iacocca Elementary School. They break for a commercial for a product called Nukem, which comes with a warranty.

The plot, in case you need a respite, involves a corporate vice president (Ronny Cox) who is in cahoots with the bad guys, and another executive (Miguel Ferrer) who is a cocaine-sniffing decadent. Is that meant to be a comment on big business? Don't worry about it. Whatever may have been in the minds of the writers, Edward Neumeier and Michael Miner, has more trouble emerging from Mr. Verhoeven's sizzling battles than poor Murphy does from his robosuit.

1987 Jl 17, C10:1

A Will's Power

PING PONG, directed by Po Chih Leong; written (Chinese with English subtitles) by Jerry Liu, based on an idea by Po Chih Leong; director of photography, Nick Knowland; edited by David Spiers; music

by Richard Harvey; production designer, Colin Pigott; produced by Malcolm Craddock and Michael Guest; released by Samuel Goldwyn Company. At Carnegie Screening Room, 887 Seventh Avenue, at 57th Street; Bleecker Street Cinema, 144 Bleecker Street. Running time: 95 minutes. This film has no rating.

Mike Wong	Davip Yip
Elaine Choi	Lucy Sheen
Mr. Chen	Robert Lee
Ah Ying	Lam Fung
Siu Loong	Victor Kan
Cherry	Barbara Yu Ling
Alan Wong	Ric Young
Alan's Wife	Victoria Wicks
Uncle Choi	Stephen Kuk
A Chee	Rex Wei
Jimmy	Hi Ching

FLAVORFUL glimpses of London's Chinatown — the back alleys of restaurants, a gambling den, a traditional funeral — promise something tasty from "Ping Pong," but the main dish doesn't live up to the starters.

The director, Po Chih Leong, has been making features in Hong Kong for the past decade, not that you'd know it from the bowl of chop suey being served at the Bleecker Street Cinema and the Carnegie Screening Room. The main ingredient is the effort of a young English-bred Chinese woman (Lucy Sheen) to settle the estate of a rich old rake named Sam Wong. His will is an attempt to reconcile Chinese tradition with up-to-date London style, and Miss Sheen begins to feel like "a bleeding Ping-Pong ball" as she is batted about by the heirs.

•

Her biggest problem is Sam's son, Mike, who has been left his father's restaurant on condition that he run it along traditional lines, which doesn't appeal to this swinging Anglophile. The other conflicts, be warned, are equally interesting.

There are a few funny touches, such as a trash can filled with Chinese travel brochures outside the Chinese Embassy, but mostly the movie is not funny or touching or much of anything. Anyhow, matters seem to work out all right, don't ask me why, and Miss Sheen ends up dressed like a Chinese heroine of old, sitting in a tree. It's just barely scrutable.

WALTER GOODMAN

1987 Jl 17, C10:6

Rita or Raquel?

LA GRAN FIESTA, directed by Marcos Zurinaga; screenplay (Spanish, with English subtitles) by Ana Lydia Vega and Mr. Zurinaga; photography by Mr. Zurinaga; edited by Roberto Gándara; music by Angel Peña; produced by Mr. Gándara; released by Zaga Films. At Lincoln Plaza 3, 63d Street and Broadway. Running time: 105 minutes. This film has no rating.

José Manuel	Daniel Lugo
Attorney Vázquez	Miguelángel Suárez
Don Manolo González	Luis Prendes
Raquel Cordelia González	Cordelia González
Rita Laura Delano	Laura Delano
Master of Ceremonies	Raúl Carbonell Jr.
Angel Luis	Carlos Augusto Cestero
Don Miguel de la Torre	Raúl Dávila
Poet	Raul Julia
Judge Cropper	E. G. Marshall
Don Antonio Jiménez	Julián Pastor

IT'S 1942 and a big night in San Juan, P.R., where the casino is being turned over to the United States Navy. Among the guests at the farewell party is José Manuel, the son of Don Manolo González. José Manuel's marriage to Rita, the daughter of Don Miguel de la Torre, is about to be announced. But José

Island Intrigue Raul Julia, in the role of a poet, puts in an appearance in "La Gran Fiesta," Marcos Zurinaga's drama of politics, romance and family relations set in a glittering casino in Puerto Rico during the early days of World War II.

Manuel loves Raquel and has no sooner given the bad news to Rita than he learns that his father, Don Manolo, has been falsely accused by his partner, Don Antonio Jiménez, of being involved in anti-American activities. José Manuel can save his father from the clutches of ambitious District Attorney Vázquez only by getting the influential Don Miguel to intercede on the family's behalf. But that means giving up Raquel and marrying Rita. What will José Manuel do?

Such is the predicament raised in "La Gran Fiesta," the first full-length movie from Puerto Rico. It's the sort of story where conspirators talk loud enough so they can be overheard by somebody behind a potted plant. Every now and then, the orchestra breaks into song, allowing the camera a chance to circle the ballroom, catching the principals and featured players looking anxious or sad or conspiratorial. In case anybody isn't sure what's going on, the lyrics help. "I see myself in your pupils," the soloist croons, and the camera goes to Rita, who is telling José Manuel, "Your eyes tell me you're going to lie." Back to the crooner: "Don't look at me that way anymore."

Marcos Zurinaga, who directed and helped write the script, stretches every scene till you can see right through it. For dramatic purposes, there's a climactic blackout and a dance where people have to change partners. Many of the lines seem to have been collected from old B-flicks: "Not now, Vázquez, can't you see I'm busy?" "How can I face them all?" "You've sunk as low as one can sink." There are many references to political intrigue, but they are pretty obscure, not that it matters one way or the other. Raul Julia does a mystifying turn as a flashy young drunk who makes a speech, and E. G. Marshall, playing a judge, spends most of his time shooting pool. If you want to know what José Manuel decides about Rita and Raquel, you'll have to go to the Lincoln Plaza 3.

WALTER GOODMAN

1987 Jl 17, C17:1

Equal Time

RITA, SUE AND BOB TOO, directed by Alan Clarke; written by Andrea Dunbar; photography by Ivan Strasburg; edited by Steve Singleton; music by Michael Kamen; produced by Sandy Lieberson; released by Orion Classics. At Cinema 2, Third Avenue at 60th Street. Running time: 95 minutes. This film is rated R.

Bob	George Costigan
Rita	Siohban Finneran
Sue	Michelle Holmes
Michelle	Lesley Sharp
Aslam	Kulvinder Ghir
Sue's Father	Willie Ross
Sue's Mother	Patti Nicholls
Lee	Paul Oldham
Michael	Bryan Heeley

By JANET MASLIN

"**U**NCEREMONIOUS" does not begin to do justice to the manner in which Bob, Sue and Rita inaugurate their romance. "Romance" isn't exactly right, either. Sue and Rita have been baby-sitting at Bob's when his wife, Michelle, suggests he drive them home. Bob is more than accommodating. He takes these two teenage girls to a deserted spot, begins leering at them and is more than a little amazed when they leer right back.

It's clear immediately that Sue and Rita — played with heart, humor and substance by two game, burly-looking actresses, Michelle Holmes and Siobhan Finneran — are a down-to-earth duo. From the back seat of the car, Rita complains noisily that Sue's deflowering in the front seat is taking too long. Also, Rita wants to listen to the radio, which is one of many things that ought to cool Bob's ardor. Another is the fact that Rita, without being any too nice about it, demands equal time.

Bob's interest does not abate, and so the affair continues. "I wonder if he'll bring us here again," muses Rita. "Oh, he will," Sue replies knowingly, with a hint of the matronliness that is already so evident in these rambunctious schoolgirls. "Make no mistake about that."

•

"Rita, Sue and Bob Too," a British film that opens today at Cinema 2, may have the makings of a naughty romp, but it's no more genuinely carefree than the heroines themselves. The housing project in which Rita and Sue live is a squalid place — Sue's father is an abusive drunk, her mother very vocal in her hatred for him — and it's enough to make the brand-new, cookie-cutter suburban street on which Bob lives sufficient to turn the girls' heads. That the ménage à trois, which begins so inauspiciously, creates so much trouble has more to do with everyone's underlying misery than it does with bad luck or bad judgment.

Alan Clarke, drolly directing Andrea Dunbar's thoroughly unsentimental screenplay, seems to use the two girls' sauciness as a rebellion against the conformity that is everywhere around them (Mr. Clarke can even find something funny in the way a teacher drones "Thank you, thank you" when collecting papers from his class, or in the sight of the two girls bobbing mindlessly on a sofa as they watch rock videos). But beneath its dry humor is a sad story. It's too bad the film couldn't be tougher about that, since it ends on a cheerful note that, under the circumstances, seems thoroughly unconvincing. But if the film is about how Sue and Rita finally find their niche, then the ending does make for a certain symmetry.

Mr. Clarke plays up the fun-loving

Michelle Holmes in "Rita, Sue and Bob Too."

aspects of the material effectively enough to create a sly, absurdist tone. Bob's wife, Michelle (played in an effectively deadpan manner by Lesley Sharp), may be hurt by her husband's transgressions, but she demonstrates this by jumping up and down on one of his light-colored suits and by making such a noisy scene at the housing project that one of Rita and Sue's neighbors does deep-knee bends in his excitement. Bob grows ever more confounded by all this trouble. Sue, who at one point withdraws from the threesome, takes up with a Pakistani suitor (sweetly played by Kulvinder Ghir) who thinks she ought to visit his homeland. Sue thinks otherwise. When he takes her to a Pakistani film in which the heroine dances on broken glass to protect her boyfriend, he asks Sue if she would do the same for him. "Would I 'ell!" says she.

"Rita, Sue and Bob Too" takes place in a world where small-mindedness carries at least as much weight as sex appeal. When Bob, Sue and Rita attempt a night on the town, they go to a club where the revelers listen to bawdy music-hall numbers and dance a loosely modified version of the bunny hop. Also happening to be there is one of Bob's staunchly middle-class neighbors, who can't wait to bustle up the walk to that cookie-cutter house and tell Michelle what she's seen.

1987 Jl 17, C18:1

JAWS: THE REVENGE, directed and produced by Joseph Sargent; written by Michael de Guzman, based on characters created by Peter Benchley; director of photography, John McPherson; edited by Michael Brown; music by Michael Small; production designer, John J. Lloyd; released by Universal Pictures. At Movieland, Broadway and 47th Street; N.Y. Twin, Second Avenue and 66th Street; 34th Street Showplace, between Second and Third Avenues; 84th Street Six, at Broadway. Running time: 99 minutes. This film is rated PG-13.

Ellen Brody	Lorraine Gary
Michael	Lance Guest
Jake	Mario Van Peebles
Carla	Karen Young
Hoagie	Michael Caine
Thea	Judith Barsi
Louisa	Lynn Whitfield
Sean	Mitchell Anderson

By CARYN JAMES

Before we join the Brody family in the fourth part of the "Jaws" saga, here's what's happened in our story so far. Dad survived a few chilling shark attacks in the original "Jaws," rescued his two sons from another great white in the tepid "Jaws II,"

and let's not even think about the laughable "Jaws 3-D." The question is: Why hasn't this family moved to Nebraska?

Well, whether they're trusting souls or just fools who can't take a hint, "Jaws the Revenge" finds Ellen Brody still on Amity Island with her grown son Sean. Her husband, the police chief played by Roy Scheider, is dead (his heart attack, Ellen says, was caused by fear of the shark). Suddenly a great white chomps on Sean's boat, and the grieving Ellen heads to the Bahamas to visit her older son, Michael, and his family. Sharks have never appeared in those warm waters, says Michael, a marine biologist. Call it mother's intuition, but Ellen suspects a vengeful shark family is trailing her own. Guess who's right?

This might have been good family feuding, but nothing kills a sequel faster than reverence, and "Jaws the Revenge" has a bad case of "Jaws I" worship, beginning with lingering shots of Roy Scheider's photo hanging in the Amity Police Department and running through Ellen's sepia-toned memories from the first film. Joseph Sargent, the director, has turned this into a color-by-numbers version of Steven Spielberg's original "Jaws."

●

What's missing from "Jaws the Revenge," which opens today at Movieland, N.Y. Twin and other theaters, is the intensity of the first film, where the characters were truly quirky and the action was focused on the man versus shark battles — not quite a mythic feud, but more than a soggy version of the Hatfields and McCoys.

Mr. Sargent and the screenwriter, Michael de Guzman, make some sincere but lame attempts to create characters who are more than fish bait. Ellen is courted by a scruffy pilot, inspiring some Oedipal jealousy in Michael. The pilot has an eccentric's name, Hoagie, but even Michael Caine can't turn him into more than a shaky subplot device.

And we get some effective Spielberg-type close-ups of the shark's mouth leaping out of the water, the better to disguise the fact that it's a mechanical shark. But we know what's coming too well; there's not much surprise when the shark shows

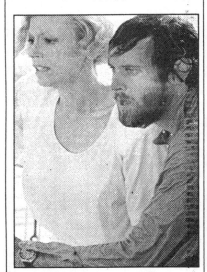

Feeding Time Lorraine Gary and Lance Guest are pitted against the customary voracious shark in "Jaws The Revenge."

Michael Caine in "Jaws."

up and takes a few bites out of Michael's boat, Hoagie's seaplane and a couple of non-Brodys.

Lorraine Gary has some affecting moments as Ellen, but "Jaws the Revenge" is mild and predictable, the very things an adventure movie should never be.

●

"Jaws the Revenge" is rated PG-13, ("Parental Guidance Suggested for Those Younger Than 13"). There are the inevitable gory scenes, some very graphic, of people devoured by the shark.

1987 Jl 18, 15:4

A Tragic Experiment

THE SEA AND POISON, written and directed by Kei Kumai, based on the novel by Shusaku Endo; in Japanese with English subtitles; photography by Masao Tochizawa; music performed by the Tokyo Symphony Orchestra; produced by Kanou Otsuka. At Film Forum 1, 57 Watts Street. Running time: 123 minutes. This film has no rating.

Suguro	Eiji Okuda
Toda	Ken Watanabe
Professor Gondo	Shigeru Kamiyama
Professor Hashimoto	Takahiro Tamura

EARLY in "The Sea and Poison," the harrowing Japanese movie now at Film Forum 1, a surgical team performs a lung operation on a young woman. It is probably the most graphic view that most of its audience will ever have had of the scalpel and forceps doing their work, and you may find yourself joining the young intern Suguro, who confesses, "Today

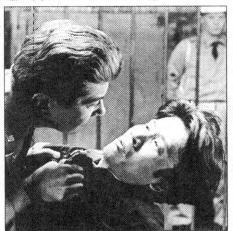

in the operating room, I had to close my eyes."

That episode prepares us for another operation, the climactic scene in which a captured American pilot is subjected to vivisection experiments. Again, there is the feeling of being trapped in an operating room; you can't watch, but you can't stop watching. In these scenes, the director, Kei Kumai, proves himself a master of a kind of super-realism.

Mr. Kumai's script, drawn from a novel by Shusaku Endo, is less gripping. Mr. Endo based his controversial work on an atrocity committed in the spring of 1945 by doctors at the University of Kyushu medical department. Under orders of the military, they performed fatal experiments on eight American fliers. Twenty-five of those involved were convicted of war crimes.

Mr. Kumai tells the story through three participants in the operation — two interns (including Suguro, sympathetically played by Eiji Okuda) and a nurse. Their reasons for cooperating — careerism, weakness, jealousy — smack of a kind of fiction that doesn't rise to its momentous subject. Perhaps the characters were better developed and more convincing in Mr. Endo's novel.

At the end, Suguro's friend Toda (Ken Watanabe) says, "You never know what those who would punish us would do if they were placed in the same position." Resonant words, but there's not enough here to back them up. And Mr. Kumai seems to lose control altogether whenever military types are brought on; the American interrogator seems to have been borrowed from Japan's wartime propaganda movies, and the cackling Japanese officers from Hollywood's.

When he is directing his camera at the operating table or into hospital wards or along the hospital's heavily shadowed corridors, however, Mr. Kumai is very much in charge. His vision, in black and white, is strong, steady, serious. The poignantly beautiful image we are left with, the residue of the experiment on the operating-room floor being washed away to the sea, suggests the depths of a deeply troubling theme.

WALTER GOODMAN

1987 Jl 22, C18:3

California Dreamers

SUMMER SCHOOL, directed by Carl Reiner; screenplay by Jeff Franklin; story by Stuart Birnbaum, David Dashev and Mr. Franklin; director of photography, David M. Walsh; edited by Bud Molin; music by Danny Elfman; production designer, David L. Snyder; produced by George

Remembrance

"The Sea and Poison," a Japanese film based on actual events in the spring of 1945, recounts the decision of Japanese doctors to perform experimental surgery, leading to certain death, on captured American pilots.

Shapiro and Howard West; released by Paramount Pictures. At the Criterion Center, Broadway and 45th Street; Orpheum Twin, 86th Street near Third Avenue; Gotham Cinema, Third Avenue at 58th Street; Metro Twin, Broadway and 99th Street. Running time: 98 minutes. This film is rated PG-13.

Freddy Shoop	Mark Harmon
Robin Bishop	Kirstie Alley
Phil Gills	Robin Thomas
Francis (Chain Saw) Gremp	Dean Cameron
Dave Frazier	Gary Riley
Alan Eakian	Richard Horvitz
Rhonda Altobello	Shawnee Smith
Larry Kazamias	Ken Olandt
Anna-Maria Mazarelli	Fabiana Udenio
Pam House	Courtney Thorne-Smith

By JANET MASLIN

CARL REINER, as a school official who gets lucky with the lottery, disappears at the very beginning of "Summer School," and in doing so he has the right idea. However, Mr. Reiner also directed this strained, rambling teenage comedy, so he can hardly be thought of as getting away scot-free. "Summer School" opens today at the Criterion Center and other theaters.

Set in California, "Summer School" is about a laid-back, surf-loving teacher named Shoop (Mark Harmon) and the band of high school miscreants who ruin his summer vacation. Normally a gym teacher, Shoop is impressed into teaching something he knows only sketchily — English — to a group of slow learners. There's a separate little subplot for each character — the pregnant girl (Shawnee Smith) who wants Shoop to accompany her to Lamaze class, the boy (Ken Olandt) who moonlights as a stripper, the pretty 16-year-old blonde (Courtney Thorne-Smith) who wants to move into Shoop's apartment. There's also a story line about Shoop's chasing the arch, patronizing teacher (Kirstie Alley) in the classroom next door, though her off-putting manner makes Shoop's interest a mystery.

Mr. Harmon has an easygoing attractiveness, but neither he nor anyone else seems comfortable with the film's antic pace. And for all its busyness, this comedy has no real focus, ricocheting from character to character with wearying abandon. Sloppy camera work and editing further contribute to the overall messiness. A scene in which the class's buxom Italian exchange-student (Fabiana Udenio) peels off her clothes to reveal a bikini is followed by a brief scene in which she's wearing shorts again.

The film's only bright idea is a duo named Chain Saw (Dean Cameron) and Dave (Gary Riley), who love horror films and instigate grisly but imaginative practical jokes, like pretending to be attacked by bunnies when the class makes a field trip to a petting zoo. These two, both nicely played, devote their essay on the person they most admire to the makeup wizard Rick Baker and do a first-rate Siskel and Ebert imitation.

●

"Summer School" is rated PG-13 ("Special Parental Guidance Suggested for Those Younger Than 13"). It contains a lot of strongly off-color language, gory special effects and a film clip from "The Texas Chain-saw Massacre."

1987 Jl 22, C22:1

Brief Candle

LA BAMBA, written and directed by Luis Valdez; director of photography, Adam Greenberg; edited by Sheldon Kahn and Don Brochu; music by Carlos Santana and Miles Goodman; production designer, Vince Cresciman; produced by Taylor Hackford and Bill Borden; released by Columbia Pictures. At Embassy 3 and 4, Broadway and 47th Street; Plaza, 58th Street east of Madison Avenue; 86th Street Twin, at Lexington Avenue; 23d Street West Triplex, at Eighth Avenue, and other theaters. Running time: 106 minutes. This film is rated PG-13.

Ritchie Valens	Lou Diamond Phillips
Bob Morales	Esai Morales
Connie Valenzuela	Rosana De Soto
Rosie Morales	Elizabeth Peña
Donna Ludwig	Danielle von Zerneck
Bob Keene	Joe Pantoliano
Ted Quillin	Rick Dees
Buddy Holly	Marshall Crenshaw
Jackie Wilson	Howard Huntsberry
Eddie Cochran	Brian Setzer

By JANET MASLIN

WE already know as much about Ritchie Valens's brief life as we learn from "La Bamba," the film biography that traces his early love of music, his dizzying rise to stardom and his tragic death in a plane crash. We know these things less specifically from Valens's own story than as conventions of this film and others like it, among them "The Buddy Holly Story" and "Sweet Dreams," the biography of Patsy Cline.

Films like these — and "La Bamba" parallels "The Buddy Holly Story" very closely, since Valens and Holly had similar temperaments and died in the same accident — are better admired for their innocence and simplicity than faulted for their lack of sophistication. They don't make excessive claims for the people being profiled, concentrating if anything on the ordinariness the characters rose above. They don't attempt any more complex trajectory than the thrilling rise to fame, followed by the terrible irony of life cut off in its prime. They are made in the same eager, admiring spirit that marked their heroes' or heroines' love of popular music. At their best, they bring that music to life all over again.

"La Bamba," which opens today at the Plaza and other theaters, is the gentlest of these biographies; it takes its cue from Valens himself. Born Ricardo Valenzuela, a Mexican-American raised in California, Valens was apparently a dutiful son and a cleancut, hard-working schoolboy. He grew up poor, and in 1957 he was still picking fruit to help support his family. In 1958 he changed his name. He had three top-10 records, among them "Donna" and the title song. His career was only eight months old when, in 1959, at the age of 17, he died.

It's a sad story, but "La Bamba" doesn't make the mistake of being morbid. It concentrates instead on Valens's nice-guy side and on his love of rock-and-roll. Luis Valdez, who wrote and directed "La Bamba," also devotes a lot of attention to Valens's competitive relationship with his half-brother, Bob Morales (Esai Morales), but Bob is a one-note boorish character — he drinks, picks fights, sells drugs, steals Valens's girl and then mistreats her — and this part of the film is its weakest. It's much better in capturing the Chicano world from which Valens came, and the music (performed vibrantly on the soundtrack by Los Lobos) that he made.

●

A film like this is quite naturally a showcase for its star, and as Valens, Lou Diamond Phillips has a sweetness and sincerity that in no way diminish the toughness of his onstage persona. The role is blandly written,

Rocking
Lou Diamond Phillips portrays the 50's rock singer Ritchie Valens in Luis Valdez's biographical film "La Bamba."

but Mr. Phillips gives Valens backbone. He's a strong, sympathetic figure even when saying things like "My dreams are pure rock-and-roll" or "One of these days I'm going to buy you the house of your dreams, Mom." Lines like these abound in Mr. Valdez's screenplay, but they're so predictable they have a certain charm. The same might be said for Valens's romance with Donna (Danielle von Zerneck), about whom he wrote so mournful a song.

Mr. Valdez gives "La Bamba" enough warmth to make up for its conventionality, as well as a strong feeling for Valens's Chicano roots. It's also good in a lengthy segment re-enacting one of Alan Freed's legendary rock-and-roll shows, with Brian Setzer, Howard Huntsberry and Marshall Crenshaw doing rousing impersonations of Eddie Cochran, Jackie Wilson and Buddy Holly, respectively. Their brief performances look hard to beat, but when Mr. Phillips's Valens strides onto the stage and sings his version of the Mexican folk song "La Bamba," he tops them all. Though the film moves on awkwardly to depict the fatal plane crash, its real culmination is right there, in Valens's onstage triumph.

●

"La Bamba" is rated PG-13 ("Special Parental Guidance for Those Younger Than 13"). It includes brief partial nudity and some profanities.

1987 Jl 24, C4:3

Headstrong, Heartsick

WISH YOU WERE HERE, written and directed by David Leland; photographed by Ian Wilson; edited by George Akers; music by Stanley Myers; production manager, Caroline Hewitt; produced by Sarah Radclyffe; released by Atlantic Releasing. At Lincoln Plaza 1 and 2, 63d Street and Broadway. Running time: 90 minutes. This film is rated R.

Lynda	Emily Lloyd
Hubert	Geoffery Hutchings
Eric	Tom Bell
Dave	Jesse Birdsall
Dr. Holroyd	Heathcote Williams

HER name is Lynda and she's as much of a problem as she can possibly be. What's more, she seems to like it that way. This pretty and precocious 15-year-old girl (Emily Lloyd) is a constant source of worry and annoyance to her widowed father, and she does everything she can to dismay him, from bicycling through town with her skirts hiked up to raucously inviting a group of men to compare her legs with Betty Grable's. Lynda's cheekiness would seem more gratuitous if her unhappiness were not also abundantly clear.

"Wish You Were Here," which opens today at the Lincoln Plaza 1 and 2, has a brazen, defiant quality very much like Lynda's. Both the character and the film are more affecting than they initially seem. "Wish You Were Here" marks the directorial debut of David Leland, who is also an actor and co-wrote the sharp-edged screenplay for "Mona Lisa." In addition, he wrote the recent "Personal Services." Mr. Leland's directorial style, like his writing, is full of mischief; he begins this film with the sight of Lynda as a schoolgirl wearing a gas mask, and with an elderly woman in a Shirley Temple costume tap-dancing alone by the sea. But beneath its archness lies something genuine and affecting.

Still, Mr. Leland's heroines maintain their breeziness through thick and thin. In "Wish You Were Here," Lynda remains seemingly unscathed by many of the misadventures that befall her, misadventures that almost always involve men. Except for the one episode that has her frying the hair of a volunteer model at hairdressing school — and it was her father, after all, who hoped she would take up hairdressing — Lynda saves her most self-destructive behavior for various suitors. She has an affair with a self-consciously suave young bus conductor, who wears bright yellow pajamas to bed and smokes cigarettes from a holder, and then betrays her. She has another affair with a coolly sinister older man who is her father's friend.

She is at her spikiest in a wickedly funny scene that has her visiting a psychiatrist (Heathcote Williams), whom her father hopes will put an end to Lynda's free use of profanities. The doctor, whose desk is covered with likenesses of monkeys, calmly asks Lynda to go through the alphabet and say every rude word she can think of that begins with each particular letter. She cooperates — and then some. But he is stymied when Lynda gets to the F's and insists that she cannot think of anything at all.

●

As the title suggests, "Wish You Were Here" is about longing. In this, it takes a solidly analytical view that contrasts oddly with its surface flippancy. Lynda misses the mother who died when she was 11 — various flashbacks, including the one with the gas mask, show Lynda at this traumatic stage of her life — and her defiance takes on pathos when seen in this light. By the film's end, Lynda's attempts to work out feelings of be-

Emily Lloyd in "Wish You Were Here," at Lincoln Plaza.

trayal and abandonment have been replaced by the jaunty, affirmative stance she takes when assuming the role of motherhood on her own.

There's a patness and a clinical quality to this evolution. But most of the time Mr. Leland's idiosyncratic wit makes it more interesting than that, and less predictable. Lynda's wild outbursts — toward the end of the film, she insults her lover and denounces her father in the genteel tea room where she works as a waitress — are as entertaining as they are cathartic, and Miss Lloyd delivers these strings of epithets as colorfully as Mr. Leland writes them. Miss Lloyd is captivating, managing to seem both feisty and fragile, and capturing the full emotional range of this complicated young girl.

"Wish You Were Here" has a quaint, inviting period look — the year is 1951, the setting a British coastal village — and a cast that's well attuned to Mr. Leland's brand of cleverness. The actors, particularly Tom Bell as Lynda's older lover, have a changeable quality, a playfulness and a sly reserve that are very much in keeping with the film's overall style.   *JANET MASLIN*

1987 Jl 24, C7:2

Postpartum Exchange

MIX-UP, directed by Françoise Romand; photography by Emile Navarro; edited by Maguy Alziari; music by Nicolas Frize; produced by Dominique Rouchand and Jacques Merlino in association with Antenne 2 and with the participation of the Ministry of Culture. At Thalia SoHo, 15 Vandam Street. Running time: 60 minutes. This film has no rating.

"Mix-Up" was shown as part of last year's New Directors/New Films series. Following are excerpts from Vincent Canby's review, which appeared in The New York Times April 4, 1986. The film opens today at the Thalia SoHo, 15 Vandam Street, and will be shown today and tomorrow only.

ONE day in November 1936, in a Nottingham, England, nursing home, two respectable, middle-class, expectant mothers, Margaret Wheeler and Blanche Rylatt, as yet unknown to each other, were each delivered of a daughter. Twenty years later, it was generally agreed by all of the interested parties, including the daughters who'd been raised as Valerie Wheeler and Peggy Rylatt, that a terrible muddle had been made. Each mum had been sent home with the other's baby.

Taking this true story, a nightmare that haunts every new mother, Françoise Romand, a French director, has made "Mix-Up," which she describes as "documentary-fiction." Whatever it is in fact, "Mix-Up" is a deliciously oddball movie, told mostly in interviews that look like no other "talking heads" images you'll see in any documentary.

Mrs. Wheeler, an articulate, intense woman, was apparently the first one to suspect that something was wrong, even before she had left that nursing home 50 years ago. She remembers today that the baby she was shown as being her own was suspiciously long and skinny. She also was not reassured by the efficiency of the nursing home, especially when she received telegrams, flowers and letters addressed to Mrs. Rylatt.

After seeing the Rylatt baby, Mrs. Wheeler was convinced that an unintentional switch had been made, though her husband, Charles, and Fred and Blanche Rylatt were inclined to think she was going through some kind of postpartum panic. In the years that followed, the Wheelers and the Rylatts kept in touch by mail, entirely at the insistence of Margaret Wheeler, who kept sending the Rylatts bundles of snapshots of the child she was raising, grudgingly (in spite of herself), as her own.

•

The movie never discovers exactly what happened in the nursing home. Instead of seeking to fix responsibility, the film recalls — through interviews that are sometimes sad and occasionally lunatic — how the six people most concerned were affected by, and dealt with, a situation that is farcical in fiction but tragical in real life.

Mrs. Wheeler's campaign to establish the truth became, she says, an "enriching" crusade. For her unintentionally adopted daughter, Valerie, a tall, patrician woman, the entire experience was a subliminal horror story. She sensed, early on, that her "mother" did not regard her as her own, but as someone a little less than the equal of the rest of the Wheeler children.

The more conventional Mrs. Rylatt raised her Peggy "Rylatt" with as much love as she gave her other children, one of whom, today, uses his interview to discuss his commitment to the Jehovah's Witnesses.

•

In these scenes, the film traces the steps by which the truth dawned on the Wheelers and the Rylatts — Fred Rylatt died in 1975. The principal characters are surprisingly candid, intelligent and very game. With the exception of Mrs. Wheeler, they're all a little bit embarrassed to find themselves at the center of what sounds like the synopsis for a hilarious if cruel comedy.

This is something that Miss Romand manages to suggest without ever condescending to her subjects or ridiculing their situation. The director and her cameraman, Emile Navarro, often photograph their interviewees in such a way that the movie looks as if it had been designed by a high-tech graphics artist. This, however, isn't window dressing. It calls attention to the distance between the bizarre events being recalled and the perfectly rational, ordinary world in which the story was played out.

"Mix-Up," which was made for television, does go on for somewhat longer than the material can easily sustain, but it's the work of a film maker of original vision.

1987 Jl 24, C12:6

SUPERMAN IV: THE QUEST FOR PEACE, directed by Sidney J. Furie; screenplay by Lawrence Konner and Mark Rosenthal; story by Christopher Reeve, Mr. Konner and Mr. Rosenthal; director of photography, Ernest Day; music by John Williams; production designer, John Graysmark; produced by Menahem Golan and Yoram Globus; released by Warner Bros. At Criterion Center, Broadway at 45th Street; Manhattan, Third Avenue at 59th Street; Movieland Eighth Street, at University Place; Bay Cinema, Second Avenue at 32d Street; 86th Street East, at Third Avenue; Movie Center 5, 125th Street between Powell and Douglas Boulevards. This film is rated PG.

Superman/Clark Kent	Christopher Reeve
Lex Luthor	Gene Hackman
Lois Lane	Margot Kidder
Lenny	Jon Cryer
Lacy Warfield	Mariel Hemingway
Perry White	Jackie Cooper
Jimmy Olsen	Marc McClure
Nuclear Man	Mark Pillow

By JANET MASLIN

Part of the fun of each Superman film has always been that opening credit crawl, with its hilariously grandiose lettering and its stately pace. In "Superman IV: The Quest for Peace," which opened yesterday at the New Carnegie and other theaters, the credits zip by in a shaky manner, trailed by billows of unsightly glitter. This is a bad sign.

What's more, the Superman flying sequences, which were spectacular in the first film, look chintzy in this one, and the special effects are perfunctory, too. (Superman repairs some damage to the Great Wall of China with a single brief glance.) The cinematography is so sloppy that Superman's turquoise suit is sometimes green.

Luckily, there's more to "Superman IV" than looks. Christopher Reeve is still giving this character his all, and especially in his bumbling Clark Kent incarnation he remains delightful. (Clark pretends he can't hit a baseball in one scene, then bats it into outer space when no one's looking.) Also back, and also a treat, is Gene Hackman as the gleefully malevolent Lex Luthor. Jon Cryer does a funny turn as Luthor's obnoxious nephew.

The women in Superman's life — Margot Kidder as the sexy, earnest Lois Lane (who still doesn't get the full picture where Superman is concerned) and Mariel Hemingway as a glamorous new love interest for Clark — also add some spice. One prolonged sequence here has Clark/Superman courting exhaustion as he meets both of them for a double date.

Miss Hemingway plays Clark Kent's new boss, the daughter of an unscrupulous mogul (Sam Wanamaker) who takes over The Daily Planet and tries to turn it into a sleazy tabloid. ("Summit Kaput — Is World On Brink?" asks one banner headline, illustrated by a photo of a girl in a bathing suit.)

•

This film's social conscience, which fortunately is presented with a minimum of self-righteousness, also leads Superman to the United Nations, where he makes a speech and promises to rid the world of nuclear weapons. He is then seen gathering missiles into a gigantic mesh shopping bag, spinning it around and flinging it into the sun, where it explodes. The Superman series gets more and more whimsically outrageous as it goes along.

The cast wears costumes that are swanky but very strange, and the dialogue is also unexpectedly funny at times, as when Luthor pronounces Superman a workaholic and advises him to "stop and smell the roses." There's also a new character, a solar-powered blond titan (Mark Pillow) created by Luthor as a rival for Superman, to keep the action moving. Threadbare as it's beginning to look, the Superman series hasn't lost its raison d'être. There's life in the old boy yet.

•

"Superman IV: The Quest for Peace" is rated PG ("Parental Guidance Suggested"). It contains some minimal violence and rude language.

1987 Jl 25, 13:2

Carry On, James

THE LIVING DAYLIGHTS, directed by John Glen; screenplay by Richard Maibaum and Michael G. Wilson; director of photography, Alec Mills; edited by John Grover and Peter Davies; music by John Barry; production designer, Peter Lamont; produced by Albert R. Broccoli and Mr. Wilson; released by MGM/UA. At Astor Plaza, 44th St. and Broadway; 84th Street Six, at Broadway; 34th Street Showplace, between Second and Third Aves.; New York Twin, Second Ave. and 66th St.; Orpheum, 86th St. near Third Ave. Running time: 130 minutes. This film is rated PG.

James Bond	Timothy Dalton
Kara Milovy	Maryam d'Abo
Gen. Georgi Koskov	Jeroen Krabbé
Brad Whitaker	Joe Don Baker
Gen. Leonid Pushkin	John Rhys-Davies

Conflict

Gene Hackman, as the villainous Lex Luthor, squares off against Christopher Reeve, as the Man of Steel, in Sidney J. Furie's "Superman IV: The Quest for Peace,"

By JANET MASLIN

IT'S a tough job, keeping the world's waiters and butlers and bathing beauties apprised that he takes his martinis "shaken, not stirred." But somebody has to do it, and in "The Living Daylights" — a great title, from a 1966 Ian Fleming short story — that somebody is Timothy Dalton. Mr. Dalton, the latest successor to the role of James Bond, is well equipped for his new responsibilities. He has enough presence, the right debonair looks and the kind of energy that the Bond series has lately been lacking. If he radiates more thoughtfulness than the role requires, maybe that's just gravy.

There are times, though not too many of them, when this James Bond seems to take things awfully seriously. One of the many death-defying stunts in "The Living Daylights" finds 007 in an airplane being piloted by Kara Milovy (Maryam d'Abo), the beautiful Czechoslovak cellist who becomes his latest flame. Kara has bungled the job, and is about to fly the plane into a mountain when Bond grabs the controls and takes over. Before saving the day, he wastes one precious moment on the kind of seething slow burn that was never part of the old James Bond personality, and is very noticeable in the new one.

Mr. Dalton, who trained at the Royal Academy of Dramatic Arts and has had a lot of experience playing Shakespeare, has a more somber, reflective acting style than the ones Bond fans have grown used to; he's less ironic than Sean Connery, less insistently suave than Roger Moore. Instead, Mr. Dalton has his own brand of charm. His Bond is world-wearier than others, but perhaps also more inclined to take the long view (as well he might, after all these years). In any case, he has enthusiasm, good looks and novelty on his side.

In "The Living Daylights," the 16th James Bond feature, Bond becomes embroiled with a wily Soviet defector (Jeroen Krabbé), a ruthless American arms dealer (Joe Don Baker), the leader of a group of Afghan freedom fighters (Art Malik) and the head of the K.G.B. (John Rhys-Davies). The way in which all this happens is complicated but engrossing, and it takes the action from Gibraltar to Vienna to Tangier, and finally to Afghanistan. So "The Living Daylights," which opens today at Loews Astor Plaza and other theaters, is appropriately scenic, and it keeps moving. But its pace can be tiring, since there are few dramatic highs or lows, merely the endless string of crises that help to keep Bond in business. Two hours and 10 minutes' worth of such crises make the film a little too long.

One major change in the formula has made 007 less of a ladies' man this time; he is even heard diplomatically telling a hotel manager that he will forgo his usual suite in favor of one with two bedrooms. The relatively chaste courtship he conducts with Kara may disappoint some fans, but making the role less compulsively lecherous also makes it a lot easier to play. Mr. Dalton, while less rakish than his predecessors, handles the romantic subplot charmingly, though Miss d'Abo greatly overdoes the naïveté. It's a little disconcerting, to find them clip-clopping through Vienna in a horse-drawn carriage, behaving like a couple en route to the senior prom.

Supporting characters count for a lot in Bond films, and this cast is a good one; Mr. Krabbé, as a cheerfully unprincipled turncoat, and Mr. Baker, who gets a lot of comic mileage out of the arms dealer's gung-ho boyishness, are both very enjoyable. The direction, by John Glen, has the colorful but perfunctory style that goes with the territory, and it's adequate if uninspired. At this late date, the James Bond formula doesn't require much modification. Keeping it afloat, as "The Living Daylights" succeeds in doing, is accomplishment enough.

●

"The Living Daylights" is rated PG ("Parental Guidance Suggested"). It includes some brief nudity.

1987 Jl 31, C3:5

Lupine Lover

THE WOLF AT THE DOOR, directed and produced by Henning Carlsen; screenplay by Christopher Hampton, story by Mr. Carlsen and Jean-Claude Carrier; cinematography by Mikael Salomon; edited by Janus Billeskov Jansen; music by Roger Bourland; released by International Film Marketing. At Cinema 3, 59th Street at the Plaza Hotel. Running time: 92 minutes. This film is rated R.

Paul Gauguin	Donald Sutherland
August Strindberg	Max Von Sydow
Annah	Valérie Moréa
Mette Gauguin	Merete Voldstedlund
Juliette Huet	Fanny Bastien
Judith Molard	Sofie Graboel
William Molard	Jean Yanne
Ida Molard	Ghita Norby

By WALTER GOODMAN

AT first sight, as he struts haughtily through the streets of Paris beneath a broad-brimmed straw hat, behind a macho mustache, throwing a small secret smile to a pretty girl along his route, Donald Sutherland's Paul Gauguin might be returning in triumph from his two years in Tahiti. But the hat is ratty as well as natty, the way his paintings are loaded on the cart being trundled before him hints that not everybody considers them masterpieces, and his eyes carry anxiety as well as arrogance. We soon learn that he has only four francs in his pocket.

So starts "The Wolf at the Door," the Danish-French co-production now at Cinema 3, about the difficult period, 1893 to 1895, that the painter spent in Paris before returning to the island where his art and his libido had flourished. This is the third Gauguin, or facsimile, I've seen on screen: George Sanders played the character inspired by the painter in "The Moon and Sixpence" and Anthony Quinn played him in "Lust for Life"; Mr. Sutherland's portrayal is by far the most compelling.

The 45-year-old Gauguin's two passions are painting and girls 30 years younger than himself. To his art, he is indomitably true, to women unfailingly faithless. He had fled his Danish wife, Mette, and five children, and his French mistress and their child to go to Tahiti and has now left his 13-year-old Tahitian "wife" to return to Paris, where he accepts the gift of a Javanese gamine, Annah (beautiful Valérie Moréa, who seems to have sprung straight from a Gauguin canvas).

The story follows the facts, as Gauguin tries with little success to break into the Parisian art market and disports himself with his pals and his girls. But how to turn this interlude into a movie? The device used by the scriptwriter, Christopher Hampton, adapter of "Les Liaisons Dangereuses," is Ida Molard, the teen-age daughter of some friends of Gauguin. Mr. Hampton places the painter's bedroom in the Molard apartment, close enough to Ida's so that the shrieks from his lovemaking sessions with Annah and his mistress (Fanny Bastien) can stir longings in the girl's budding bosom, which she shows off for Gauguin's and the audience's enjoyment. Ida also serves as occasional narrator, telling us how and what Gauguin is feeling. "As every day passed, he was being frozen out of France," says this 14-year-old, whose good luck it is to have her lines written for her by Mr. Hampton.

But lovelorn Ida (Ghita Norby) isn't interesting enough to hold attention. The perspective is off. Her most useful function is to listen enraptured as Gauguin talks about himself. Mr. Sutherland's casual yet proud telling of the fable of the wolf and the dog, which gives the movie its double-edged title, makes a particularly powerful few moments. (Degas, an early admirer, said Gauguin painted like a wolf; La Fontaine reminds us that the wolf does not wear a collar.)

As is only appropriate for a movie about Gauguin, "The Wolf at the Door" offers plenty of color. Henning Carlsen's direction, although sometimes drifting, comes alive in such scenes as an amusing painting auction where most of the bidding is done by Gauguin's impoverished cronies and his one brief meeting with Mette (Merete Voldstedlund), which is heavy with memories of love and desertion. Max Von Sydow, giddily bewigged, makes an engagingly eccentric August Strindberg, whose conversations with Gauguin ought to be more provocative than they are, considering their attitudes toward women. You are left with the feeling that Mr. Hampton is holding back. But Mr. Sutherland gives his all, and that's a lot, a sensitively shadowed portrait of the artist as a middle-aged man.

1987 Jl 31, C8:5

Body Language

A MAN IN LOVE, directed by Diane Kurys; original screenplay by Miss Kurys, with co-adaptation by Olivier Schatzky; director of photography, Bernard Zitzermann; edited by Joele Van Effenterre; music by Georges Delerue; art director, Dean Tavoularis; produced by Michel Seydoux, Camera One and Alexandre Films; released by Cinecom Pictures. At Cinema 1, Third Avenue at 60th Street. Running time: 108 minutes. This film is rated R.

Adrift
Donald Sutherland portrays Paul Gauguin during the uneasy year he spent in Paris between trips to Tahiti in Henning Carlsen's "Wolf at the Door."

Steve	Peter Coyote
Jane	Greta Scacchi
Michael	Peter Riegert
Harry	John Berry
Bruno	Vincent Lindon
Pizani	Jean Pigozzi
Sam	Elia Katz
De Vitta	Constantin Alexandrov
Paolo	Michele Melega
Dr. Sandro	Jean-Claude de Goros
Julia	Claudia Cardinale
Susan	Jamie Lee Curtis

"A MAN IN LOVE" is an unaccountably bad film from Diane Kurys, who at other times (with "Peppermint Soda" and "Entre Nous") has seemed one of the most promising new directors around. The story centers around a very important American film star played by Peter Coyote, which is to say that "A Man in Love" is misconceived from the very start.

Mr. Coyote is never convincing as the sort of fellow who draws a large, adoring throng of reporters when he deigns to reveal the plans for his latest project. But at the beginning of "A Man in Love," he announces to the assembled multitudes that he will be making a biographical film about the Italian writer Cesare Pavese. Solemnly, Mr. Coyote describes the details of Pavese's life, right up to the point when he ingests a lethal dose of sleeping powder. "And he drinks. And he waits. And he dies," Mr. Coyote says with glum relish. From this, and from the rest we see of "Pavese," it's pretty clear that the finished product will be keeping them away in droves.

"A Man in Love," which is Miss Kurys's first English-language film and which opens today at Cinema 1, is about the romance that springs up between the big star Steve Elliott (Mr. Coyote) and the beautiful young actress who is cast as his co-star. She is Jane Steiner (Greta Scacchi), who is first seen vacationing prettily in Tuscany with her gorgeous mother (Claudia Cardinale) and alcoholic father (John Berry). The father, a hack journalist, later turns up on the set at the Cinecittà studio in Rome after Jane is hired for "Pavese," and he pesters Steve Elliott for an interview. Steve says no, and Jane has the kind of tantrum which, in a film like this, can really pique a man's interest. "Who do you think I am?" he asks Jane angrily. "Who do you think you are?" she counters. The screenplay, by Miss Kurys and Olivier Schatzky, has a persistently tin ear.

●

The point, once Steve and Jane get down to business, seems to be that glamorous movie people can't help falling for one another when they're on location, eagerly forsaking the realities of everyday life and letting their lives and art intertwine. This will not be news to anyone who has

On the Set
Peter Coyote and Jamie Lee Curtis are among the stars of Diane Kurys's "Man in Love," about a famous actor who falls for a bit player.

ever seen a movie set or François Truffaut's "Day for Night," or even a soap opera or two. Still, Miss Kurys presents it as revelation, which gives her film a painfully self-evident quality all the way through. The only refreshingly unaffected character is Michael (Peter Riegert), who accurately describes his role as "Steve's slave." Michael takes a cheerfully resigned approach to duties like lounging around the swimming pool, keeping Jane away from Steve's wife, Susan (Jamie Lee Curtis), and remaining at the dinner table alone when Steve and Jane abruptly disappear and go off to bed. When this happens, Michael petulantly calls out for dessert.

Miss Kurys directs the bedroom scenes with more enthusiasm than she brings to the rest of "A Man in Love," and indeed, they are the film's only real means of attracting an audience. Miss Scacchi's languid abandon in these scenes is enough to make up for her more awkward manner elsewhere. But Miss Kurys's way of playing life-versus-art tricks with the audience can be annoying, as when Steve begins to embrace Jane, then suddenly begins howling and curls up into a fetal position; this is then shown to be a scene from the film within the film, though it's directed in an entirely inappropriate way. There are far too many indications throughout "A Man in Love" of Miss Kurys's eagerness to find more in this material than is actually there.

In the last reel, the focus suddenly shifts to Jane's mother, whose white blood-cell count has been mentioned ominously throughout, and to Jane's attempt to write down an account of her feelings. Here and only here does "A Man in Love" at all resemble Miss Kurys's other, better, less strenuously commercial work.

JANET MASLIN

1987 Jl 31, C10:6

True Grit

SINGING ON THE TREADMILL, directed by Gyula Gazdag; written by Mr. Gazdag and Miklos Gvorffy; camera by Elemer Ragalyi; music arranged by Ferenc Gyulai Gaal; produced by Mafilm-Hunnia Studio. In Hungarian with English subtitles. At the Public Theater, 425 Lafayette Street. Running time: 76 minutes. This film has no rating.

Mr. Dezso	Ewald Schorm
Mr. Rezso	Istvan Iglodi
Anna	Lili Monori
Peter	Robert Koltai
Boszi	Judit Pogany
Odon	Sandor Halmagyi
Kati	Mari Kiss
Joska	Zoltan Papp
Tini	Eszter Csakanyi
Rudi	Laszlo Helyey
Elvira	Hedi Temessy
Patko	Lajos Oze
Ageless Goddess of the Operetta	Hanna Honthy

"SINGING ON THE TREADMILL" is a frolic with an edge — which may be why it was banned by the Hungarian authorities for a decade after it was made in 1974. Gyula Gazdag, who directed and did some of the writing, has blended the froth of operetta and the grit of reality into a concoction that is creamy on the outside, tart on the inside. It can be savored, with subtitles, at the Public Theater.

Although incoherence is the essence of this show, there is a plot of sorts: a couple of showbiz sharpies are trying to create an edifying musical extravaganza about four couples squabbling over possession of a dilapidated house in Budapest. The impresarios do their casting in a stricken countryside where the population is engaged in carrying out hard labor or in evading it. "The condition of happiness," sing the pair, "is trust in us" — the refrain of the state planner.

But the young folks who are assigned the leads refuse to act the way good citizens are supposed to act; they keep jumping from their real personas to their musical roles and back again. When they are not smooching, they're smacking each other around; instead of trying to fix up their exceedingly leaky premises, they mope, complain and in general are poor models of comradeship. One woman keeps committing suicide, not that that keeps her down for very long.

●

It's a delicious romp. Every time realism gets in the way of Socialist Realism, the principals break into song and dance. "Don't take advantage of my weakness," sings a damsel, and her beau sings back, "Your weakness sets me on fire." The musical numbers, bathed in a roseate glow or set behind pouring rain or around an enormous statue of Eros, with odd characters wandering by, are campily catchy. A lovelorn bureaucrat and a bedraggled fortuneteller do their big duet in water up to their chins.

The message of the lyrics is unfailingly upbeat — "Sweet love blossoms in our hearts" — and your heart goes out to the performers, who have so little to sing about. The whole cast and an army of fiddles deliver a rhapsody to "The Birches of Buda." Proclaiming "We all love each other," the young couples race through fields where peasants are endlessly, fruitlessly at work. Everybody joins in a Latin-beat celebration, for no evident reason, of Mount Popocatépetl. Mr. Gazdag, clearly infatuated with the musicals he is kidding, finds little to sing about in real-life Hungary.

Everywhere the lovers go, they are shadowed by pipe-smoking men in dark suits and bowlers, and a treadmill is much in evidence.

The grand finale brings together the entire cast, fitted out in costumes from every operetta ever staged in the Austro-Hungarian Empire. There is rejoicing: "This nice free life is finally ours." But the glow turns to melancholy during a prolonged fadeout in pink — Mr. Gazdag's final and very effective comment, with the chorus swaying mechanically and the principal players smiling, desperately smiling.

WALTER GOODMAN

1987 Jl 31, C11:1

People Are Strange

THE LOST BOYS, directed by Joel Schumacher; screenplay by Janice Fischer and James Jeremias and Jeffrey Boam, story by Miss Fischer and Mr. Jeremias; director of photography, Michael Chapman; edited by Robert Brown; music by Thomas Newman; production designer, Bo Welch; produced by Harvey Bernhard; released by Warner Bros. At Criterion Center, Broadway at 45th Street; Movieland Eighth Street, at University Place; Coronet, Third Avenue at 59th Street; 84th Street Six, at Broadway; 86th Street Twin, at Lexington Avenue; Movie Center 5, at 125th Street and Douglass Boulevard. Running time: 98 minutes. This film is rated R.

Michael	Jason Patric
Sam	Corey Haim
Lucy	Dianne Wiest
Grandpa	Barnard Hughes
Max	Ed Herrmann
David	Kiefer Sutherland
Star	Jami Gertz
Edgar Frog	Corey Feldman
Alan Frog	Jamison Newlander
Paul	Brooke McCarter
Dwayne	Billy Wirth

By CARYN JAMES

FILL a bathtub with holy water and garlic, load a plastic water pistol and aim at the vampires. In "The Lost Boys," Joel Schumacher's hip, comic twist on classic vampire stories, practical reactions to the unnatural seem normal. These lost boys are not Peter-Pan innocents, but teen-agers who dress like rock stars, roar through town on motorcycles and happen to fly through the air and drink blood. The hero is a boy who's trying to save his older brother before the brother becomes a total vampire and before their mom comes back to see what a mess the house is.

"The Lost Boys" is to horror movies what "Late Night With David Letterman" is to television; it laughs at the form it embraces, adds a rock-and-roll soundtrack and, if you share its serious-satiric attitude, manages to be very funny.

Dark Doings
Assorted vampires capture the attention of Dianne Wiest and Corey Haim in "The Lost Boys."

When Lucy, a just-divorced mother (Dianne Wiest), and her two sons move to the California coastal town of Santa Carla, the local vampire pack seems no more or less sinister than the aging hippies, homeless scavengers and other eccentrics crowding the boardwalk. Who would guess that David, the smirking gang leader with the platinum hair, is more than an ordinary punk kid? But soon David (Kiefer Sutherland; no one smirks with more conviction) enlists Lucy's older son as part of his gang, and Michael (Jason Patric) enters their underground cavern where a huge poster of Jim Morrison looks down on the vampire band. Michael drinks a little wine; well, it might be blood, but there's peer-group pressure and he's after David's girlfriend, so he takes a chance.

●

Especially in these early scenes, "The Lost Boys" adores the playful fashions of kids who echo the long hair of their 60's parents or mimic the leather-and-spikes style of punk rockers. But this is more than a richly photographed look at Dracula's stylized sons. The film searches out the menacing undercurrents in ordinary things, capturing the eeriness of neon-bright amusement parks and grotesque fun-house faces. As the Doors' "People Are Strange" plays wittily in the background, the movie seems to ask how we can separate the seriously strange from the harmless, garden-variety wackos.

Its humor comes from an absolutely straightfaced response to the suburban undead — they're just Santa Carla's version of a youth problem. When Michael starts lusting for blood and fading out in mirrors, Sam reacts like any normal younger sibling. "My own brother is a blood-sucking vampire," he yells, "You wait till Mom finds out." Such lines could have been too cute or coy, but Corey Haim, a picture of wide-eyed mouth-gaping innocence, carries them off with perfect naturalness and expert comic timing. Sam calls his mother home from a dinner date ("Mom, I think we have to have a real long talk about something"), while Michael, flying out the window, picks up the other phone to reassure her things are just fine. Suspicious of everyone, Sam even worries about Lucy's new beau (Edward Herrmann), a mild-mannered guy who wears nerd-loud shirts. "What if my Mom's dating the head vampire?"

Mr. Haim is enormously appealing as Sam, determined to prevent Michael from making his first kill and turning into a vampire for good. Sam's friends, Edgar and Alan Frog, say "Kill your brother; you'll feel better," but instead Sam, Michael and the Frog brothers decide to go after the vampire gang. There is a major battle featuring some clever special effects — vampires hanging by their toes from rafters, vampires fighting in the air — and striking views of the transformed boys, white-faced and fang-toothed. (Michael Chapman's photography, especially in the night scenes, is full of glittering contrasts.) But at every turn Mr. Schumacher opts for comedy over horror, and the finale is relentlessly funny.

The director of "St. Elmo's Fire,"

Mr. Schumacher has a feel for how young people act and talk, though the screenwriters make the other actors strain. They give Dianne Wiest dopey-mom lines and make her father, Barnard Hughes, a caricature of a feisty old Grandpa.

"The Lost Boys," which opens today at the Criterion and other theaters, doesn't reinvent vampire history; it's not timeless, but timely, sardonic and shrewd.

1987 Jl 31, C21:1

FILM VIEW/Janet Maslin

Summer Serves Up Its Sleepers

THIS SUMMER'S TWO MAIN SLEEPERS TURN out to be "Robocop," which has already attracted a sizable action audience, and "La Bamba," which should draw a smaller but no less attentive music-loving crowd. On the surface, a violent, futuristic police fantasy and a sweetly nostalgic rock-and-roll biography would appear to have nothing in common, but in a way these films have similar appeal. Each offers slight but distinct variations on a formula that is comfortingly familiar. Each creates its own little universe, a world that is enveloping and complete.

And each has a clear, reductive moral dimension, a very simple sense of right and wrong. Of course, "Death Wish" had that too, so moral directness isn't automatically attractive. But when it's accompanied by the right degree of modesty, as it is in both these instances, it can be compelling indeed.

Neither "Robocop" nor "La Bamba" takes place on a grand scale, and that's another thing that makes them likable. These aren't films that aspire to greatness, and they wouldn't be sleepers if they did. Each is a small-scale film with a big imagination, a one-note fantasy that in its own way is very pure. Neither is a seamless work or a technological marvel, but each has a powerful sense of purpose. And whether it's the vision to dream up the last word in police revenge fantasies or the urge to re-create the innocence and excitement of early rock-and-roll days, a sense of purpose can be a wonderful thing.

■

In "Robocop," the Dutch director Paul Verhoeven has combined the grimly futuristic mood of a "Blade Runner" with the masculine ethos of a vintage western. This is the

'Robocop' and 'La Bamba' share decent characters whose triumph is irresistible.

story of a man who becomes a machine. But it's also about a man who loses and reclaims his identity.

His name is Murphy, and he's a Detroit cop who is inadvertently sacrificed to the corrupt business interests that are seen — in the "near future," when "Robocop" takes place — as ruling that city. "I say good business is where you find it," says Ronny Cox, as a top officer of the company that plans to manufacture robots to augment the city's embattled police force. When a demonstration model accidentlly opens fire inside a corporate board room, shooting a lower-level em-

ployee to smithereens, this mishap is deemed "only a glitch." In this moral climate, where the television sets spew forth an endless barrage of idiocy and the billboards proclaim, "The future has a silver lining," Murphy is ambushed and tortured to death by a band of vicious hoodlums. His body is then secretly reclaimed and put to use by the robot manufacturers, who turn him into a part-human, part-mechanical prototype of their newest model.

Robocop turns out to be a strong, hard-working and polite addition to the police force, and if this were a Superman film he would be as a local hero. But "Robocop" is about revenge and restitution, not glory. It follows Robocop, who is such an innocent that he actually eats baby food, through the slow process by which his memory and past re-emerge. And it waits patiently for his realization of who he was, how he suffered and what he can do to right the score.

Unlike most of the other screen avengers we've been seeing, Robocop isn't a free agent. That's one of the film's many clever touches. Robocop, from whose high-tech point of view several key scenes are shot, has been programmed with a secret directive that keeps him very much under his manufacturers' thumbs, and that paves the way for an extremely satisfying trick ending. So Mr. Verhoeven, working from a screenplay by Edward Neumeier and Michael Miner, is able to incorporate human sentiments and high-tech capabilities into this single ingenious figure, and play them off against each other in a thoroughly involving way. In addition to being a fascinating visual invention — Peter Weller's face, when he finally removes his Robocop helmet, is framed so eerily against its mechanical backdrop that it actually seems to float — Robocop embodies a well-drawn moral dilemma. Will he serve as an extension of the corrupt entrepreneurs who made him, or will he become his own man?

■

In "La Bamba," the aspiring rock singer played by Lou Diamond Phillips faces no such confusion, since his only goals are to sing, play, be good to his friends and family and buy a nice house for his mother some day. This is all very simple, and it's conceived, acted and framed that way. But "La Bamba," like "Robocop," builds up to the spectacle of a decent and naïve character who at long last, despite formidable obstacles, achieves a bittersweet triumph. It, too, makes that final triumph irresistible.

Mr. Phillips is a real find, not only for the decency and sturdiness he brings to the film's early segments but for the way he changes so excitingly in its climactic scene. It is here that the 17-year-old Ritchie Valens, heretofore presented as a nice boy and a friendly fixture in the Chicano community that is the film's other real focus, suddenly comes into his own. When Mr. Phillips's Ritchie takes the stage at a lovingly re-created late-50's rock show (Eddie Cochran, Jackie Wilson and Buddy Holly are the acts seen preceding him), he abruptly sheds his polite veneer and becomes fiercely animated, a thrilling embodiment of the music that he loves. When a small film culminates in such a big moment, it doesn't seem small any more. □

1987 Ag 2, II:23:5

Love and Justice

STAKEOUT, directed by John Badham; written by Jim Kouf; director of photography, John Seale; edited by Tom Rolf; music by Arthur B. Rubinstein; production designer, Philip Harrison; produced by Mr. Kouf and Cathleen Summers; released by Touchstone Pictures. At Embassy 2, Broadway at 47th Street; Beekman, 65th Street and Second Avenue; 23d Street West Triplex, between Eighth and Ninth Avenues; Bay Cinema, Second Avenue at 32d Street; Embassy 72d Street Twin, at Broadway. Running time: 115 minutes. This film is rated R.

Chris Lecce	Richard Dreyfuss
Bill Reimers	Emilio Estevez
Maria McGuire	Madeleine Stowe
Richard (Stick) Montgomery	Aidan Quinn
Phil Coldshank	Dan Lauria
Jack Pismo	Forest Whitaker
Caylor Reese	Ian Tracey
Captain Giles	Earl Billings

By WALTER GOODMAN

FROM the flounderings in a fish factory early in "Stakeout" to its scalp-buzzing sawmill climax, John Badham's

new movie delivers excitement, humor and good nature. The director uses the conventions of the action-comedy in so adroit a way that you may even forget the hundred other films you've seen lately about a couple of cops kidding around with each other in between battling the bad guys. You can catch "Stakeout" at the Beekman and other theaters.

The detectives here are Chris and Bill (Richard Dreyfuss and Emilio Estevez). They are assigned the overnight watch of the house of Maria (Madeleine Stowe), the sometime girlfriend of an escaped murderer (Aidan Quinn). Complications arise when Chris and Maria meet and take to each other more than suits the situation. Before you know it, Chris becomes the object of his own surveillance, giving Mr. Dreyfuss plenty of opportunity to crawl under the bed and tumble out of the window. He's the Caucasian male in the pink beach hat seen skulking away from the premises; his is the drowsy voice on the wiretap. Meantime, the ruthless

Richard Dreyfuss, left, and Emilio Estevez in "Stakeout."

escaper and an accomplice are on their way to Seattle for what we know will be a final smasheroo not just for justice but for love.

Familiar? Sure — but filled with fillips. Still reeking from the fish fight, our guys are summoned to meet a finicky F.B.I. man who will not remind anybody of Elliot Ness. Chris's efforts to hide his identity from Maria, whom the boys are pleased to discover does not weigh 313 pounds as reported, brings back happy memories of the knockabout movies of the 1930's, when characters went into contortions pretending to be somebody else. Ogling Maria through a telescope while talking to her on the phone, Chris bursts out, "Your food is burning!" And then has to explain how he knew.

This cop team is a pleasure to be around. "I'm in love," Chris tells Bill after meeting Maria. "I have to face up to my heterosexuality. But don't worry, you'll be provided for." We even find ourselves enjoying the gross-out competition between these big kids and the daytime shift. Mr. Dreyfuss and Mr. Estevez are so at ease with each other that the concocted situation begins to seem natural, in a nutty way. Even mean Mr. Quinn shows an engaging side; he's boyish enough so you can see what the wholesome Maria might once have seen in so bad a dude.

When Mr. Badham decides to lay on a car chase or a dose of violence, you can count on a zinger. But the quiet scenes, too, are taut. What gives "Stakeout" its special lift are the people. Credit the deft performances, Jim Kouf's amiable script and, especially, John Badham's easy balancing of boyish banter and hectic heroics.

1987 Ag 5, C21:1

Sangre O-Plus

VAMPIRES IN HAVANA, written, directed and designed by Juan Padrón; in Spanish with English subtitles; principal animators, José Reyes, Mario García Montes and Noël Lima; music by Rembert Egues; distributed by the Cinema Guild. At Film Forum 1, 57 Watts Street. Running time: 80 minutes. This film has no rating.

T
O most grown-ups, "Vampires in Havana," the Cuban-made animated feature now at Film Forum 1, is likely to seem like kid stuff, but it's a bit rough for little kids. Which sort of narrows the potential audience.

Done in bright colors and brash spirits and set in 1930-ish Havana, "Vampires" tells the tale of Pepito, a trumpet-tooting grandson of Dracula, who has been brought up on a secret formula that enables him to survive in the sun. But two bands of unscrupulous vampires — a European cartel and a Chicago mob — are after the formula, so look out, Pepito. If that weren't enough, our hero is also being chased by the Cuban dictator, General Machado, who catches the spunky little guy in bed with voluptuous Signora Machado.

It's all very hip, with takeoffs on gangster-movie types and Latin lovers, but the animation is nothing special and many of the jokes are standard crash-and-splat stuff. The exceptions, such as the toasts drunk in vintage O-Plus blood, tend to be repeated. The freshest turn shows an audience of cartoon figures being scared by human beings on a movie screen, and the ending, when Pepito sings out the secret formula over Radio Vampire International, has a happy beat. The 14- to 16-year-old crowd may not get the anticapitalist message, but they might be tickled by the fangs. *WALTER GOODMAN*

1987 Ag 5, C23:1

High Hopes

NADINE, written and directed by Robert Benton; director of photography, Nestor Almendros; film editor, Sam O'Steen; music by Howard Shore; production designer, Paul Sylbert; produced by Arlene Donovan; released by Tri Star Pictures. At Gemini Twin, 64th Street and Second Avenue; 84th Street Six, at Broadway; Movieland Eighth Street, at University Place. Running time: 88 minutes. This film is rated PG.
Vernon Hightower .... Jeff Bridges
Nadine Hightower .... Kim Basinger
Buford Pope .... Rip Torn
Vera .... Gwen Verdon
Renee .... Glenne Headly
Raymond Escobar .... Jerry Stiller
Dwight Estes .... Jay Patterson
Boyd .... William Youmans
Cecil .... Gary Grubbs
Floyd .... Mickey Jones

By VINCENT CANBY

N
ADINE and Vernon Hightower are Splitsville. The time is the early 1950's, but theirs is not a separation that would interest Walter Winchell. It's not even news in Austin, Tex., where Nadine is a hairdresser in the Alamo Beauty Shop and Vernon runs a losing proposition called the Bluebonnet Lounge, the sort of roadhouse that does six dollars and change on a busy night.

Though romantically disadvantaged, Nadine (Kim Basinger) and Vernon (Jeff Bridges) are very winning characters. They are the flip sides of the tormented lovers in Sam Shepard's "Fool for Love," unencumbered by a past that includes anything more serious than Vernon's failed get-rich-quick schemes and Nadine's desire to lead a life of bourgeois respectability. They are the high-school homecoming queen and the football hero 12 years after graduation and not a minute brighter.

In "Nadine," Robert Benton's easily identifiable, very amiable new comedy, Nadine and Vernon find themselves up to their eyeballs in lunatic events that constantly threaten to overwhelm them as well as the movie. However, they're always saved in the nick, not by fate (or plot) but by Mr. Benton's commitment to character, and by his inability to go for more than three or four

Jeff Bridges

minutes without coming up with a line of dialogue or a bit of business that immediately separates the work of a first-rate artist from that of a hack.

"Nadine" opens today at the Gemini and other theaters.

•

At the beginning of the film, Nadine is pregnant but, standing on her pride, she won't tell Vernon. She's refusing to sign the divorce papers until he gives her a new Buick with white sidewalls, well knowing that Vernon, in his present state of economic collapse, couldn't even afford the sidewalls. Then, too, she's jealous of Vernon's new girlfriend, Renee (Glenne Headly). By chance, Renee works in the accounts receivable department at the Lone Star Brewery where Vernon's account grows monthly. Says Vernon, by way of explaining his tardiness, "I'm good for it, but it's just that all my money is

Kim Basinger in the title role in "Nadine."

tied up in . . . assets and stuff."

Nadine and Vernon are initially brought back together by murder. Nadine has had the bad luck to be in the office of a sleazy photographer, trying to retrieve some "art studies" for which she posed, when the photographer is murdered. Making a second attempt to get the pictures, she and Vernon find, instead, evidence of a major real-estate scam, which Vernon decides to cut himself in on.

Mr. Benton is not particularly comfortable in laying out the details of the scam. This functions as the film's McGuffin — the coded message or top-secret plans on which Alfred Hitchcock's espionage films often relied but which were, in themselves, beside the point and utterly meaningless.

In "Nadine" the scam is the convenience that throws Nadine and Vernon into a series of extremely unlikely slapstick situations, most often in confrontation with a local Mr. Big played with exuberantly nasty good humor by Rip Torn. The couple is kidnapped, threatened with rattlesnakes, besieged in an empty house and, finally, the object of a chase through a junkyard where, at one point, they hide in the explosives shack.

•

In Mr. Benton's best films, from "Bad Company" (written with David Newman) and "The Late Show" through "Places in the Heart," characters are revealed entirely through events that grow out of character. In "Nadine," the wild events appear to have been imposed on the characters. One result is that "Nadine" lurches from one comic set piece to the next, without the airy self-confidence that renders logic superfluous.

What makes the film enjoyable and funny is not its strained zaniness, but the utter seriousness with which Nadine and Vernon and everyone else in the film attempt to cope with an unreasoning landscape. Says Vernon to Nadine, while he's being beaten to a pulp in an unequal fight: "Don't worry, honey. I'm on a roll." The phrase may be an anachronism, but the emotion isn't.

All of the performances are excellent, especially those of Miss Basinger, who played the tragic side of Nadine in the film version of "Fool for Love," and Mr. Bridges, even when the movie appears to cut away from *them* to what's being done to them. In addition to Mr. Torn and Miss Headly, who has one of the film's funniest scenes, the fine supporting cast includes Jerry Stiller, memorably priceless as the lewd photographer, Mickey Jones as one of Mr. Torn's slow-witted goons, and Gwen Verdon, who could have done more if she'd had the material.

●

"Nadine," which has been rated PG ("Parental Guidance Suggested"), includes some scenes of violence and vulgar language.

1987 Ag 7, C8:3

Boutique Clique

HAPPY NEW YEAR, directed by John Avildsen; written by Warren Lane, director of photography, James Crabe; production designer, William Cassidy; produced by Jerry Weintraub; released by Columbia Pictures. At Quad Cinema, 34 West 13th Street; New Carnegie, 57th Street and Seventh Avenue. Running time: 86 minutes. This film is rated PG.

Nick	Peter Falk
Charlie	Charles Durning
Carolyn	Wendy Hughes
Jewelry Store Owner	Tom Courtenay

"**H**APPY NEW YEAR" didn't look very original or very funny back in 1973, when the original French film, written and directed by Claude Lelouch, opened in New York. The curious thing about the American remake, opening today at the Quad and New Carnegie Cinemas, is that although it's no better, it's certainly not worse.

Mr. Lelouch's screenplay, about a couple of aging Paris hoods who attempt to loot the Van Cleef & Arpels shop in Cannes, has been transposed to Palm Beach. The Carlton Hotel is now the Breakers and Van Cleef & Arpels has been turned into Harry Winston, which does *not* have a shop in Palm Beach. Warren Lane's screenplay sticks pretty closely to Mr. Lelouch's. John Avildsen is the director.

Though the story now seems just that much more tired than it did then, the new film has the advantage of good comic performances by Peter Falk, as the brains of the jewel heist, Charles Durning, as his partner, and Wendy Hughes, the Australian actress, as the classy Palm Beach shop owner who falls for Mr. Falk. Lino Ventura, Charles Gérard and Françoise Fabian were the original stars.

The new version also has the advantage of the comic presence of Tom Courtenay, who plays the fastidious manager of the jewelry store and shares the film's funniest moments with Mr. Falk. These are the sequences in which Mr. Falk cases the store disguised, alternately, as a doddering Palm Beach socialite and the socialite's flirtatious, battleship-shaped sister.

It's first-rate revue-sketch material. Everything else is vamping for time.

"Happy New Year," which has been rated PG ("Parental Guidance Suggested"), includes some vulgar language. VINCENT CANBY

1987 Ag 7, C10:6

THE GIRL, directed and produced by Arne Mattsson; screenplay by Ernest Hotch; director of photography, Tomislav Pinter; edited by Derek Trigg; music by Alfi Kabilio; released by Shapiro Entertainment. At 57th Street Playhouse, 110 West 57th Street; Bleecker Street Cinema, 144

Bleecker Street. Running time: 104 minutes. This film has no rating.

John Berg	Franco Nero
Eva Berg	Bernice Stegers
Pat/The Girl	Clare Powney
Lindberg	Frank Brennan
Hans	Mark Robinson
The General	Clifford Rose
Viveca	Lenore Zann
Peter Storm	Christopher Lee
Antonio	Sam Cook

Franco Nero

"**T**HE devil is a woman, still.
That seems to be the point of "The Girl," the truly awful English-language Swedish melodrama opening today at the 57th Street Playhouse and the Bleecker Street Cinema. The movie is a heavy-breathing, flesh-baring Brigitte Bardot film made 30 years too late, without Brigitte Bardot, about an amoral, 14-year-old schoolgirl who seduces men as easily as she murders them or takes off her clothes.

●

Appearing as her victims are Franco Nero, the Italian actor, who plays a Swedish lawyer, and Frank Brennan, the Irish-born actor, who plays a Swedish newspaper reporter. The 14-year-old Swedish girl is played by Clare Powney, who is English, clearly not 14 and appears to have studied acting with Pia Zadora.

Most of the film was photographed in Italy. The producer-director was Arne Mattsson, who *is* Swedish.

VINCENT CANBY

1987 Ag 7, C10:6

Sugary Purée

THE CARE BEARS' ADVENTURE IN WON-DERLAND, directed by Raymond Jafelice; screenplay by Susan Snooks and John De Klein, story by Peter Sauder; Care Bears character development supervised by Ralph Shaffer, Linda Edwards and Tom Schneider; picture editor, Evan Landis; director of animation, John Laurence Collins; music by Maribeth Solomon; produced by Michael Hirsh, Patrick Loubert and Clive A. Smith; released by Cineplex Odeon Films. At Art Greenwich Twin, Seventh Avenue at 12th Street; Manhattan Twin, Third Avenue at 59th Street; 34th Street East, 241 East 34th Street; Movieland, Broadway at 47th Street; Columbia Cinema, Broadway at 103d Street. Running time: 75 minutes. This film is rated G.

Grumpy Bear	Bob Dermer
Swift Heart Rabbit	Eva Almos
Brave Heart Lion/Dum	Dan Hennessey
Tenderheart Bear	Jim Henshaw
Good Luck Bear	Marla Lukofsky
Lotsa Heart Elephant	Luba Goy
White Rabbit	Keith Knight
Alice	Tracey Moore
Wizard	Colin Fox

By CARYN JAMES

I'VE seen many drawings of the Mad Hatter, from Tenniel's classic to Disney's cartoon, but never dreamed he resembled a gnome and was the exact color of Pepto-Bismol. That's how he looks, though, in "The Care Bears' Adventure in Wonderland," the third feature film starring characters who started out as toys and became sincere cutesy-poo cartoons.

Popsicle-colored bears and bunnies, the Care Bears and Care Bear Cousins have teeny little heart-shaped noses and tiny little sing-songy voices and they really really believe caring can change the world! Had enough? This jumbled story borrows bits and pieces from Lewis Carroll — a White Rabbit here, a Jabberwocky there — and throws them into the Care Bears blender.

An evil wizard kidnaps the princess of Wonderland and the Care Bears are called to the rescue. Half their contingent searches for the princess, while the other half finds a look-alike, an ordinary girl named Alice, to im-

Grumpy Bear is one of the animated stars of "The Care Bears' Adventure in Wonderland."

---

personate her in the meantime. Along the way, the Care Bears and Alice run across a Cheshire cat who sings a forgettable rap song while changing his psychedelic-colored spots and a policeman-caterpillar who stands on top of a mushroom directing traffic. These sugary crayon purées flit on and off the screen; the movie is paced so it won't strain the attention span of a 6-month-old, but there is nothing to spark a child's imagination.

●

Maybe the Care Bears creators really really believe that a movie *for* children should look and sound as if it were made *by* children. The drawings could have been lifted from a child's coloring book: the blocks of bright green are trees; the ones with pink hearts or purple squares colored on them are trees in Wonderland. Nothing in the background ever moves and the characters blink their eyes to signify motion.

What's the differences between the Care Bears television show on Saturday morning and "The Care Bears' Adventure in Wonderland," which opens today at the Manhattan Twin and other theaters? The movie is longer, and you will have to pay money to see it — about as much as it appears the producers spent to make it. But the film ends in true Care

Bears fashion, with a moral: "You are as special as you think you are," a Care Bear tells Alice. Not always; the Care Bears creators are a lot less special than they pretend.

1987 Ag 7, C21:1

WHO'S THAT GIRL, directed by James Foley; screenplay by Andrew Smith and Ken Finkleman; story by Mr. Smith; director of photography, Jan DeBont; edited by Pembroke Herring; music by Stephen Bray; production designer, Ida Random; produced by Rosilyn Heller and Bernard Williams; released by Warner Brothers. At the Ziegfeld, 141 West 54th Street; the Art Greenwich Twin, Greenwich Avenue at 12th Street; the Sutton, Third Avenue at 57th Street. Running time: 92 minutes. This film is rated PG.

Nikki Finn	Madonna
Loudon Trott	Griffin Dunne
Montgomery Bell	Sir John Mills
Wendy Worthington	Haviland Morris
Simon Worthington	John McMartin
Mrs. Worthington	Bibi Besch
Detective Bellson	Robert Swan
Detective Weston	Drew Pillsbury
Raoul	Coati Mundi
Benny	Dennis Burkley
Buck	James Deitz

By VINCENT CANBY

No big-budget movie takes less than two years from the time it's conceived until it arrives, in one form or another, in front of the public. The odd thing about "Who's That Girl," the new comedy starring Madonna, is that it looks as if it might have achieved its fairly modest goals had the people making it spent just 15 more minutes thinking about what they were doing.

Or, possibly, too many people spent more than 15 minutes contributing ideas on how to improve someone else's work. Perhaps a few more minutes of silent introspection would have helped.

Whatever happened, two things are clear: Madonna, left to her own devices and her own canny pace, is a very engaging comedian, and the screenplay, by Andrew Smith and Ken Finkleman, contains a lot of raffishly funny ideas that get lost in the busyness of the physical production.

"Who's That Girl" opened yesterday at the Ziegfeld, where the crowd was not large but devoted (the man in front of me brought his skate board), and other theaters.

●

The story, which qualifies as screwball, is about 24 consciousness-raising hours in the life of Loudon Trott (Griffin Dunne), a yuppie Manhattan lawyer who's about to marry his boss's beautiful, frightfully rich, debutante daughter, Wendy Worthington (Haviland Morris). On the day before the ceremony, Dad Worthington (John McMartin) asks Loudon to do him one little favor, that is, pick up a young woman, Nikki Finn, from the prison where's she been serving a four-year murder sentence and put her on a bus to Philadelphia.

Nikki Finn (Madonna) is a fast-talking amalgam of Bo-Peep, Marilyn Monroe and Calamity Jane. She's perfectly willing to get on the bus, she tells Loudon, just as soon as she finds the rat who framed her.

Involved in the ensuing mayhem are a handsome, 160-pound cougar, the "baby" that Nikki elects to bring up, a magnificent Rolls-Royce Corniche convertible that, in the course of the 24 hours, is reduced to scrap, a pair of musical-comedy crooks and a pair of earnest New York cops assigned to tail Nikki and Loudon.

●

When Madonna's no-nonsense pragmatism isn't being twisted into poses of lovable eccentricity, the actress is sexy and funny and never for a minute sentimental. At times she looks amazingly like Marilyn Monroe, but the personality is her own, more resilient and more knowing. As the WASP-y sleeping prince, Mr. Dunne ("After Hours") gives the most stylishly comic performance of a career that's been largely underrated by the public. Though he seems to be Madonna's foil, he provides the movie with its backbone, even in its most ludicrous moments. He may well be one of the most truly sophisticated straight men in the business today.

Mr. McMartin and the statuesque Miss Morris are almost as good, though at least part of the effect of Miss Morris's performance may come from the running gag of which she's the subject. Every time Loudon gets into a taxi, the driver at some point announces that he's had Loudon's fiancée in his cab. So what's the big deal, asks Loudon. "You gave her a ride." The inevitable reply, "I didn't say I gave her a ride. I said I had her in my cab."

The film is very short on outright guffaws. Its funniest moments are not the elaborately choreographed chases, not the big confrontation scenes nor even the scenes in which the cougar does some remarkable tricks. The laughs are almost all pe-

ripheral, as when Madonna explains why Cartier's *expected* her to shoplift the gold cigarette case on the counter. "They're in business to sell jewelry," she says. "They use gold cigarette cases as loss-leaders."

•

"Who's That Girl," which has been rated PG ("Parental Guidance Suggested"), includes some vulgar language.

1987 Ag 8, 16:1

BACK TO THE BEACH, directed by Lyndall Hobbs; screenplay by Peter Krikes and Steve Meerson and Christopher Thompson, based on characters created by Lou Rusoff; story by James Komack; director of photography, Bruce Surtees; edited by David Finfer; music by Steve Dorff; production designer, Michael Helmy; produced by Frank Mancuso, Jr.; released

by Paramount Pictures. At Criterion Center, Broadway and 45th Street; Gramercy, 23d Street near Lexington Avenue; Loew's 84th Street Six, Broadway at 84th Street; Gotham Cinema, 3d Avenue at 58th Street. Running time: 90 minutes. This film is rated PG.

The Big Kahuna	Frankie Avalon
Annette	Annette Funicello
Sandi	Lori Loughlin
Michael	Tommy Hinkley
Bobby	Demian Slade
Connie	Connie Stevens
Zed	Joe Holland
Mountain	David Bowe
Troy	John Calvin

By CARYN JAMES

Annette Funicello, fresh from her peanut-butter commercials, plays a cheery Ohio Mom who practically force-feeds Skippy sandwiches to her teen-aged son. Frankie Avalon is her car-salesman husband — he was the Big Kahuna, the world's greatest surfer — who takes the family back to the scene of all those 60's Beach Party movies. Annette gets to sing and dance in a pink polka-dot bathing suit with matching headband. Frankie gets to flirt with Connie Stevens. There's even a guest appearance by the Cleavers — Wally, June and the Beaver. So with all this self-parody floating around, why isn't "Back to the Beach" funny?

Maybe for sheer silliness nothing can match the originals: "Muscle Beach Party" or "Bikini Beach," or any of the other movies where Frankie and Annette fight, she makes him jealous, they kiss and make up — and only kiss, because they're not married and they're good kids. Meanwhile, the surfers triumph in some petty feud with a black-leather motorcycle gang.

In "Back to the Beach," Frankie and Annette go to California to visit their daughter, Sandi. They fight, she makes him jealous, they kiss and make up — and only kiss because they have to move on to the next scene, a confontation with the black-leather punks who have won their son's allegiance. Everything is resolved in the big Surf Off competition.

•

Once, the Beach Party formula must have seemed like a teen-age fantasy, but the movies have aged so badly they now play on television or video like goofy messages from outer space. In "Back to the Beach," the only message from from outer space is Pee-Wee Herman's rendition of "Surfin' Bird." ("Bird, bird, bird. Bird is the word.") He does the lyrics justice. The rest is a series of telegraphed jokes that will fulfill your worst fears. When Annette's son complains about all that peanut butter and she offers a change, can't you guess she means chunky instead of plain? How many stiff-hairdo jokes can you stand? And when Don Adams appears, it's painful; you know he's going to say, "Would you believe ...?", and he takes so long to get it over with.

"Back to the Beach" opened yesterday at the Criterion Center and other theaters. But if you catch a television commercial for it, or the rock video that's on television, you'll get the joke and see the most this movie has to offer.

•

"Back to the Beach" is rated PG, ("Parental Guidance Suggested"). There is some mildly bad language, but children are more likely to be bored than to witness anything naughty.

1987 Ag 8, 16:5

Dolph Lundgren as He-Man, left, and Billy Barty as Gwildor in "Masters of the Universe."

MASTERS OF THE UNIVERSE, directed by Gary Goddard; screenplay by David Odell; director of photography, Havania Baer; film editor, Anne V. Coates; visual effects producer, Richard Edlund; music by Bill Conti; production designer, William Stout; produced by Menahem Golan and Yoram Globus; released by the Cannon Group Inc. At the Warner Theater, Broadway at 47th Street; the UA Gemini, Second Avenue at 64th Street; the Waverly, Avenue of the Americas at Third Street; the Coliseum, Broadway at 181st Street; Movie Center 5, 125th Street between Powell and Douglass Boulevards; the Cosmo, 116th Street between Lexington and Third Avenues, and the Nova, Broadway at 147th Street. Running time: 106 minutes. This film is rated PG.

He-Man	Dolph Lundgren
Skeletor	Frank Langella
Evil-Lyn	Meg Foster
Gwildor	Billy Barty
Julie Winston	Courteney Cox
Detective Lubic	James Tolkan
Sorceress	Christina Pickles
Kevin	Robert Duncan McNeill
Man-at-Arms	Jon Cypher
Teela	Chelsea Field

By WALTER GOODMAN

Off the toy counter and onto the big screen flies He-Man, biceps rippling, pecs glistening, to do battle with evil Skeletor, colored waves flashing from every perverse pore, over who will be master of the universe. Specifically at stake in "Masters of the Universe," which can be found at the Warner and other theaters, is possession of the Cosmic Key, invented by the cute dwarf Gwildor, which can transport you anywhere in any galaxy. He-Man and his allies, Man-at-Arms and Teela, whose close-fitting battle suit reveals almost as much as He-Man's, find themselves in Colby,

Calif., where they get involved with a couple of teen-agers and are pursued by Skeletor's minions and a local cop. If you liked the toy, you'll love the movie.

Everybody flies around and fires off colored jolts of electricity. Skeletor has the numbers, but his troops, got up like clones of Darth Vader, are rotten shots. Their weapons make a Fourth of July sparkler show, but they almost never hit anybody. He-Man, meantime, is blowing them away wholesale. It's relatively bloodless combat; the villains go up in lights and that's that. The most satisfying scene is the destruction of a music store filled with synthesizers and amplifiers.

You don't get to see as much of Frank Langella, who plays Skeletor, as you do of Dolph Lundgren, who plays He-Man, but the bad guy has the good lines. "I must possess all or I possess nothing," intones Skeletor. "Assemble the mercenaries." "The Alpha and the Omega. Death and Rebirth." "I am not in the giving vein this day." Sure he is; it's not every day an actor gets to spout such stuff.

Finally, as He-Man and Skeletor get ready for their climactic face-off, Skeletor announces, "Let this be our final battle!" If you can believe that, you'll have no trouble believing the rest of it.

•

"Masters of the Universe" is rated PG ("Parental Guidance Suggested"), probably because of the battles.

1987 Ag 8, 50:1

FILM VIEW/Walter Goodman

Anguished Artists

THE REAPPEARANCE ON screen of Paul Gauguin, in "The Wolf at the Door," is evidence of the enduring appeal to movie makers of the lives of artists. And why not? The 19th-century artist, that superbly suffering figure, challenger of convention, unbudgeably independent, holding to his unique vision despite the scorn of a philistine society, enduring poverty in his, yes, garret, solaced only by adoring and available serving girls and society women, is the hot stuff of romantic drama. If the fellow is slightly cracked or behaves outrageously, so much the better. Cut off an ear like van Gogh, and it's a highbrow "Blue Velvet." Leave your family like Gauguin, and your chances of being memorialized take a leap.

And so we've grown up with handsome composers, hair flying as they assault their Steinways, and handsome writers, hair flying as they dip their nibs or attack their Remingtons with crazed expressions. They are always in a hurry because they don't want to miss that rendezvous across town with some stockbroker's art-loving wife, who gets the creative juices churning.

But maybe there's more to it. Like movie reviewers and other hangers-on, movie makers are artists manqués in the sense that after starting out with dreams of personal creation, they have been reined in by all the constraints that, we have been taught by their movies, the true artist finds unbearably chafing. Except, perhaps, for the most despotic directors, accommodation is the essence of movie collaboration, and accommodation is anathema to the sort of artist cele-

There is something about suffering artists that never fails to entrance movie makers and audiences.

brated in movies down the decades, from Rembrandt in 1936 to Gauguin in 1987. He won't give an inch. To his rebellious spirit, as it has been celebrated for us, it's all or nothing. A Rembrandt may run an atelier, but not everything produced there is a Rembrandt. Gallery owners are exploiters, critics are enemies, other painters are likely to be rivals and the public is a great insensitive ignoramus.

By paying his tribute to a misunderstood, ill-appreciated painter, then, the movie maker may be paying homage to the aspirations and illusions of youth, the dreams of following his own, special Muse into whatever attic or bedroom she might lead. He may even be identifying with his subject, a self-flattering, ego-boosting endeavor. That helps to explain the appeal of the Gauguin saga, versions of which have found their way onto the screen three times: W. Somerset Maugham's "Moon and Sixpence," Irving Stone's "Lust for Life," in which Gauguin played second brush to van Gogh, and now, "The Wolf at the Door," the most sensible of the lot.

Gauguin has everything going for him as a movie maker's artist. He's broke; he's irresistible to women, especially very young and photogenic ones, and when he has had enough, he discards them. He's both bohemian and intellectual; he carouses with a rakish crowd and talks ideas with August Strindberg. And above all, he is totally, irrevocably committed to his work, which, you can bet, is insufficiently appreciated by the sort of people who buy pictures. There is no life for him outside of painting, and no painting except in his own daring way. So he suffers, but he also has a swell time.

"The Wolf at the Door" is a superior exam-

Donald Sutherland as Paul Gauguin in "The Wolf at the Door"

ple of the genre, reasonably faithful to the facts of the case, picturesque and sustained by Donald Sutherland's intriguing portrayal of Gauguin. But it still falls short of its goal. What all artist-movies are searching for is the quintessential creator, the unquenchable spark, the divine or demonic drive that sets our genius apart from the generality of mankind. It's the internal quality that everyone is after, not the easiest thing for the camera, master of the external, to capture.

That accounts for all those piano-pounding, typewriter-banging passages in movies about composers and writers, as though physical exercise expresses internal commotion. Painters may not make as much noise, but they have the virtue of being in a visual line of work, just like the movie makers, so in "The Wolf at the Door" we are shown the artist's paintings, in hopes that they may illuminate the way to his soul. His palette is reflected in the movie's colors, and the casting has plainly been done with reproductions of his models at hand. The yellow wall is Gauguin yellow, his Javanese mistress is a replica of his Tahitian subjects.

But there's still the problem of capturing the creative process. The actual work of painting, even action painting, isn't all that exciting. Even if you do it on your back, like Charlton Heston up there splashing away at the ceiling of the Sistine Chapel in "The Agony and the Ecstasy," the audience's mind may drift. What is Moses doing in a church anyhow? And upside down at that? Not, let's hope, scribbling graffiti where Pope Julius can't get at it.

■

So how do you show the artist converting his vision to canvas? Thank your lucky Muse: Mr. Sutherland never raises brush to eyeball to squint out a perspective the way movie-artists have done since the invention of moving pictures. But he does have a way of narrowing his eyes and staring at his model, letting us know that he is peering beneath the skin, through the bones, into the very nature of corporeality. O.K., but we've seen impersonators of Rembrandt, van Gogh, Toulouse-Lautrec, Dante Gabriel Rossetti, Caravaggio, not to mention Michelangelo or Moses, giving out with equally intense stares on screen, and it doesn't add a jot to what you can find in their work.

One difficulty may lie in the movie makers' effort to be true to the facts. In "The Wolf at the Door," for example, Christopher Hampton, a classy writer, as demonstrated by "Les Liaisons Dangereuses," allows himself to build up the role of a 14-year-old French girl, making her more important to Gauguin than she probably was and central to the movie. But otherwise, he restricts himself pretty much to what the painter actually did during his interlude in France between 1893 and 1895. He tried to sell his paintings, hooked up with a tame monkey and that wild Javanese girl and had his foot broken by sailors. The result is earnest and intelligent, but the artistic impulse remains elusive.

For that, imagination may serve better than a gesture at biography, even movie biography, which is generally half fiction. Let the writer make up his own artist. I'm thinking in particular of "The Horse's Mouth," my favorite artist-movie. Based on Joyce Cary's exuberant novel about Gulley Jimson, a painter in search of a wall, with a brilliant performance by Alec Guinness, who also did the adaptation, it caught the obsession that drives the artist. You left the movie convinced that Gulley had to paint those walls.

Unless you care to play the psychoanalytic game, that's all the explanation we can hope for, as close as we can get to the divine madness. The artist of our dreams is possessed; he may be totally nuts, but he's a hero. If medals were given out for the sort of risks he takes, he'd have a shinier chest than Ollie North. Movie makers can't help sympathizing with his battle, and given some talent in the telling, neither can the descendants of the audiences that rejected his work. Which is why we will keep seeing movies about artists.

1987 Ag 9, II:19:1

Power Plays

NO WAY OUT, directed by Roger Donaldson; screenplay and story by Robert Garland, based on the novel "The Big Clock" by Kenneth Fearing; director of photography, John Alcott; edited by Neil Travis; music by Maurice Jarre; production designer, Dennis Washington; produced by Laura Ziskin and Mr. Garland; released by Orion Pictures Corporation. At Loews Paramount, Broadway at 61st St.; Guild 50th Street, 33 West 50th St.; Tower East, Third Ave. at 71st St.; Gramercy, 23d St. near Lexington Ave. Running time: 114 minutes. This film is rated R.

Tom Farrell	Kevin Costner
David Brice	Gene Hackman
Susan Atwell	Sean Young
Scott Pritchard	Will Patton
Senator Duvall	Howard Duff
Nina Beka	Iman
Marshall	Fred Dalton Thompson

S. Karin Epstein

Sean Young, left, and Kevin Costner in "No Way Out."

By VINCENT CANBY

THOUGH its title has been used before, and though its story about a political conspiracy and cover-up is guaranteed to bring out the plausible in the least rational of moviegoers, "No Way Out" has the exuberance of something freshly conceived. It's so effective, in fact, that when it's all over, you might want to sit through the beginning again just to see if the end is justified by the means. I suspect that it is.

"No Way Out," which has nothing to do with Joseph L. Mankiewicz's 1950 film about racial bigotry, is a most entertaining, twisty melodrama about the abuses of power, trust, friendship *and* women in contemporary Washington. Nothing in it is quite as it looks. However, it's apparent from the long, stunning, single-take aerial sequence, which is seen behind the opening credits, that Roger Donaldson, the director, and Robert Garland, who wrote the screenplay, have an overall view of things fixed in their minds.

The movie also benefits from the performances of an expert cast headed by Kevin Costner, who is the center of gravity within "No Way Out" as he is in "The Untouchables," and Gene Hackman, who's leaner, sharper, *better* than he's been in years. Equally fine are two comparatively new faces, Will Patton, who won an Obie for his performance in Sam Shepard's "Fool for Love," and Sean Young, a seriously funny, very beautiful young woman who's been seen in other films, including "Dune," but who from now on will never again be confused with the scenery.

"No Way Out" should do for Miss Young what "The Untouchables" did for Mr. Costner, that is, establish her as a screen personality whose singularity goes way beyond good looks. To date, Miss Young's best work has all been done for television, in the American Playhouse's memorable "Under the Biltmore Clock," adapted from an F. Scott Fitzgerald story, and as Rosemary Hoyt in the mini-series adaptation of Fitzgerald's "Tender Is the Night." She's now a screen presence in her own right.

●

Mr. Garland's screenplay is adapted from a Kenneth Fearing novel, "The Big Clock," made into a 1948 film by John Farrow, about a powerful publisher who frames his assistant for a murder that he has committed and that the assistant is investigating.

"No Way Out" is a far more complex, far more far-fetched piece of business, but so wittily conceived and presented that one wants to go with even the wilder imaginings of the flow.

The central situation is more or less this: one night, in a jealous rage, the Secretary of Defense (Mr. Hackman) accidentally murders his mistress. An elaborate cover-up scheme, involving the existence of a possibly mythical Russian "mole" in the Defense Department, is devised by the secretary's aide (Mr. Patton). Assigned to conduct the in-department investigation is Mr. Costner, a naval hero and the secretary's intelligence liaison man, who, by chance, is the only other person in Washington to know of the Secretary's guilt.

More of the plot cannot be honorably disclosed except that as Mr. Costner goes about the investigation, he finds that he himself is becoming the chief suspect, with no one to turn to for help. It's a fairly classic (and familiar) situation, made involving by characters and characterizations of a plausibility seldom seen in this sort of fiction.

●

Mr. Costner's career naval officer is both true-blue and ambitious, caught up in a series of amoral power-plays that he initially supports. He's an enthusiastic participant in Washington's social-political games, especially in an affair with a

Fred Dalton Thompson in "No Way Out."

mysterious beauty (Miss Young) who has no visible means of support, lots of high-ranking friends and, like Kay Kendall, a sense of humor and a gift for self-parody. They meet at an inaugural ball and, less than an hour later, are making love in the back of a limousine that though stretched, is still cramped quarters. Only afterward do they exchange names. Unlike most screen lovers, they seem to connect.

Mr. Hackman's Defense Secretary has the weary brusqueness of an Administration man who's convinced that the only impediment to good government is Congressional interference. He's particularly, winningly sarcastic about a powerful Senator whose chief cause is a prototype "phantom submarine," undetectable by sonar but so huge that, as the secretary says, it would make a very visible lump in the middle of any ocean. The wormiest, sharpest person on the scene is Mr. Patton, who, as his boss panics, assumes powers that even the Secretary wouldn't claim.

"No Way Out" recoups the reputation of Mr. Donaldson, the Australian-born director, who first came to international prominence with "Smash Palace," produced in New Zealand, and then made "The Bounty" and "Marie: A True Story." The new film, the last to be photographed by John Alcott (who died shortly after finishing it), looks suitably serious, but it has an unmistakable satiric momentum that carries the audience safely over some of the melodrama's thinner patches of ice.

"No Way Out" opens today at the Loews Paramount and other theaters.

1987 Ag 14, C3:1

With the Wave

NORTH SHORE, directed by William Phelps; screenplay by Tim McCanlies and Mr. Phelps; story by Mr. Phelps and Randal Kleiser; music by Richard Stone; produced by William Finnegan; released by Universal Studios. At Movieland, Broadway at 47th St.; New Carnegie, Broadway and 57th St.; New York Twin, Second Ave. and 66th St. Running time: 92 minutes. This film is rated PG.

Rick	Matt Adler
Chandler	Gregory Harrison
Kiani	Nia Peeples
Turtle	John Philbin
Vince	Jerry Lopez

"**N**ORTH SHORE," which opens today at the Movieland and other theaters, is about surfing on Oahu's north coast, where, apparently, more perfect waves break per annum than anywhere else in the world. It's about young Rick (Matt Adler), who is torn between a career as a professional surfer and pursuing his studies on an art scholarship in New York. "I know you love surfing," says his mom, "but don't throw away your career."

It's not revealing too much to report that at the end of the film, Rick makes what the film thinks is the right choice but, from the evidence we see, is a terrible mistake. He goes to New York. In less than a year, he'll be turning out five sunsets a day for sale in galleries along the Avenue of the Americas.

In the meantime, "North Shore" serves as a pre-teen-age landlubber's guide to big-time surfing, to the young men who do it and to the young women who watch them from shore, including one who says to her boyfriend at the end of a long day, "Let's find a beach where we can talk." The movie follows Rick, who learned how to surf in a "wave-tank" in Arizona, as he is instructed in the finer points of the art by Chandler, an older man of 30.

•

Chandler is a "soul surfer," meaning that he goes with the wave. Just the opposite is what's known as the "hot-dog surfer," who cuts up the wave, though, from shore, they all look pretty much alike. Chandler teaches Rick that a wave breaks in water that is half as deep as a wave is tall. A pretty Hawaiian girl, Kiani, teaches him to wrap a piece of lava rock in a tea leaf, put it on the altar and his wish will come true.

The surfing footage is fairly routine until the film's climax, a contest featuring some spectacular shots of surfers seen *beneath* the overhang of breaking waves. Otherwise, the surfing, writing, direction and performances are of a caliber to interest only undiscriminating adolescents.

•

"North Shore," which has been rated PG ("Parental Guidance Suggested"), includes some vulgar language.   VINCENT CANBY

1987 Ag 14, C6:6

Popularity

CAN'T BUY ME LOVE, directed by Steve Rash; written by Michael Swerdlick; director of photography, Peter Lyons Collister; edited by Jeff Gourson; music by Robert Folk; production designer Donald L. Harris; produced by Thom Mount; released by Touchstone Pictures. At Embassy 3, Broadway at 47th Street; Manhattan Twin, 59th Street east of Third Avenue; 86th Street East Twin, between Second and Third Avenues; Art Greenwich Twin, 12th Street and Seventh Avenue; Embassy 72d Street Twin, at Broadway. Running time: 94 minutes. This film is rated PG-13.

Ronald Miller	Patrick Dempsey
Cindy Mancini	Amanda Peterson
Kenneth Wurman	Courtney Gains
Barbara	Tina Caspary
Chuckie Miller	Seth Green
Mrs. Mancini	Sharon Farrell
Patty	Darcy De Moss

By CARYN JAMES

"**C**AN'T BUY ME LOVE" is a nerd's dream come true, as a self-described "social leper" discovers what it

costs to be a high-school hero: $1,000. For that fee, Cindy, the head cheerleader, pretends to date Ronald, who is so out of it he can't sit at the same lunch table as Cindy's friends. A little hair mousse, a few oversized jackets and nearness to Cindy make Ronald the senior-class "heartbreaker," all in one short month.

Patrick Dempsey and Amanda Peterson are appealing as these star-crossed yuppies: his cool-guy reputation grows, and he abandons his loyal, misfit old friends; she turns out to be a closet poet who values individuality. Though eventually they're saddled with preachy lines about being true to yourself — no irony here, the film just wags its finger and tells us money can *not* buy you love — Ronald is more likely to say, "I realize what a jerk I became." The grammar is a little fancy but that's almost the way real people talk.

This not-quite-outrageous premise is nearly believable and sometimes charming, so the film is just like a dozen others about who asks whom to

Patrick Dempsey

the prom. Michael Swerdlick, the writer, and Steve Rash, the director (best remembered for "The Buddy Holly Story" and forgotten for the Chevy Chase flop "Under the Rainbow"), waste a chance to make the much deeper, funnier movie that strains to break through.

•

The subterranean humor emerges, for instance, at a school dance, when Ronald nervously jerks his hands and jumps around the dance floor, and the rest of the kids follow; they're all dancing an African ritual Ronald picked up when he mistook an educational television show for "American Bandstand." (Nerdiness dies harder than he thought.) The point is too obvious, but the scene is handled with flair and true comic pacing.

What's more intriguing is the desperation we see in Ronald's face as he spends another Saturday night with his nerdy friends, playing cards, drinking root beer, ready to jump out of his skin because he passionately wants to be in the right clique. Why does popularity mean so much to him?

That question haunts every scene, but "Can't Buy Me Love" is lazy and confused about the answer. If Ronald learns his neat little lesson about love, why is he rewarded with a happy ending that reunites him with Cindy and the cheerleading crowd? If

Cindy now knows how empty popularity is, why doesn't she dump her hypocritical girlfriends, who put the moves on Ronald?

"Can't Buy Me Love," which opens today at Embassy 3 and other theaters, has an identity crisis that's a mirror-image of Ronald's own. He thinks he wants popularity at any price, though he's really a sincere guy. The film thinks it wants to be sincere, when all it truly wants is to be popular, just like the other kids' movies, so it sells off its originality.

•

"Can't Buy Me Love" is rated PG-13 ("Special Parental Guidance for Those Younger Than 13"). There are some four-letter words and one seduction scene.

1987 Ag 14, C13:1

Invasion

MONSTER SQUAD, directed by Fred Dekker; written by Mr. Dekker and Shane Black; director of photography, Bradford May; edited by James Mitchell; music by Bruce Broughton; production designed by Albert Brenner; produced by Jonathan A. Zimbert; released by Tri-Star Pictures. At Criterion, Broadway at 45th St.; the Gotham, Third Ave. at 58th St.; 34th Street East, near Second Ave.; Metro Twin, Broadway and 99th St., and other theaters. Running time: 81 minutes. This film is rated PG-13.

Sean	Andre Gower
Patrick	Robby Kiger
Del	Stephen Macht
Count Dracula	Duncan Regehr
Frankenstein	Tom Noonan
Horace	Brent Chalem
Rudy	Ryan Lambert
Phoebe	Ashley Bank
Eugene	Michael Faustino
Emily	Mary Ellen Trainor
Wolfman	Carl Thibault
Gill-Man	Tom Woodruff Jr.
Mummy	Michael MacKay

THE best thing about "The Monster Squad" is the ad campaign, a series of wanted posters for Count Dracula, the Wolfman and other anti-social types. These can be seen in most subway stations for the cost of a token.

The movie itself, opening today at the Criterion and other theaters (where the price of admission is considerably more), is a silly attempt to crossbreed an Our Gang comedy with a classic horror film, which usually means that both genres have reached the end of the line.

For the record, the film was directed by Fred Dekker and written by him with Shane Black. It's set in Anytown, U.S.A., where a group of plucky youngsters, none characterized except for the fat boy, are the only people to realize that their community has been invaded by "real" monsters. These include Count Dracula, Frankenstein's monster, the Wolfman, the Mummy and the Creature from the Black Lagoon, who have come together to represent evil in the pinch-penny Armageddon that ends the movie.

•

The comedy is cheerless. The performances are either inept or unlovably coy. Though the previous film credits ("Star Wars," "Aliens," among others) of the special-effects people are impressive, "The Monster Squad" looks like a feature-length commercial for a joke store that sells not-great, rubber monster masks.

The movie also has a certain amount of nerve in introducing a Holocaust survivor as the one fellow in town who recogizes, Dracula and his pals for what they are.

●

"The Monster Squad," which has been rated PG-13 ("Special Parental Guidance for Those Younger Than 13"), includes vulgar language and some sequences that could scare already emotionally troubled 4-year-olds.   VINCENT CANBY

1987 Ag 14, C15:1

Friends in Trouble

COLEGAS, written and directed by Eloy de la Iglesia. Released by Opalo Films. At the Thalia SoHo, 15 Vandam Street. Running time: 117 minutes. This film has no rating.

Antonio	Antonio González
Rosario	Rosario González
José	José Luis Manzano
Rogelio	Enrique San Francisco
Mother	Queta Claver

ELOY DE LA IGLESIA is a prolific Spanish movie maker (21 movies in 20 years) who is not well known in the United States. "Colegas" ("Pals"), now at the Thalia SoHo on a double bill with "El Diputado," his only other work to be commercially distributed in this country, should do nothing to change that situation.

Here's the story: José and Antonio, who live in a project in the slums of Madrid, are best friends, and Antonio's sister, Rosario, is José's girlfriend. When Rosario discovers she is pregnant, the youths, who can't find jobs, try to raise $400 for an abortion by such means as hustling in the steambaths and robbing a store. Deep down, they are too good to be much good at such lines, but desperate for money, they get involved with a professional crook, who is so bad that he robs convents — and so begins the loving threesome's *real* troubles.

●

It's a juvenile tale, told in a juvenile way. Mr. de la Iglesia goes in for shockers — a masturbation scene, an aborted abortion, the painful technique used by the boys to conceal bags of cocaine. The acting is as rudimentary as the dialogue, which the director helped write. "There's no other way out," somebody says. Don't give up; the exits are plainly marked.
WALTER GOODMAN

1987 Ag 14, C15:1

LIVING ON TOKYO TIME, directed by Steven Okazaki; screenplay by John McCormick and Mr. Okazaki; photography by Mr. Okazaki and Zand Gee; edited by Mr. Okazaki; produced by Lynn O'Donnell and Dennis Hayashi; released by Skouras Pictures. At Lincoln Plaza Cinema, Broadway at 63d St. Running time: 83 minutes. This film has no rating.

Kyoko	Minako Ohashi
Ken	Ken Nakagawa
Mimi	Mitzie Abe
Carl	Bill Bonham
Michelle	Brenda Aoki
Lana	Kate Connell
Richie	John McCormick
Nina	Sue Matthews
Jimbo	Jim Cranna
Warren	Alex Herschlag
Lambert	Keith Choy
Sheri	Judi Nihei
Lane	Lane Nishikawa

By WALTER GOODMAN

WHETHER the twain can meet is the issue addressed in "Living on Tokyo Time," the twain

Mismatched
Cultural contrasts are emphasized in "Living on Tokyo Time" when Ken Nakagawa, as a third-generation Japanese-American, marries Minako Ohashi, an immigrant from Japan.

being Kyoko, a young Japanese woman who comes to San Francisco with a desire "to have independent American experience," and Ken, a Japanese-American youth with the accent on American. He knows no Japanese, she knows little English, but that doesn't stop them from getting married so that she can stay in the United States.

Steven Okazaki, who directed as well as helped write the screenplay and work the cameras for his first feature, does better with the accessories than with the main plot. Ken (Ken Nakagawa) plays in a hard-rock group, whose leader explains that what counts is not how well you strum the guitar but how vigorously you assault it. Ken's buddies at the flower warehouse, where he sweeps up, give out with the wisdom of the West regarding sex. Ken's father is a thoroughly assimilated and self-absorbed health nut, especially partial to broccoli. The thing Ken likes best, next to his guitar, is junk food — that is, until he hooks up with Kyoko (Minako Ohashi).

She seems to symbolize an exotic heritage to him, but any sensible man, Oriental or Caucasian, would fall for so winsome a little woman, who phrases her English sentences so earnestly. Alas, she doesn't reciprocáte. Why? That's the mystery. Despite the device of having Kyoko write letters home and reflect for the audience's sake on Ken's unreciprocated affection, you may leave the Lincoln Plaza Cinema — where the film opens today — a little uncertain about what has been going on in their household.

●

Even with the communication gap between the traditions of the East and the loose ways of the West, however, it's clear enough what Kyoko means when she says, "Mr. Ken, I would like to sleep with myself tonight, please." Gentle, patient Ken, of course, replies, "No, problem." But he's hoping that things will work out the way they do in Japanese movies about arranged marriages: "Something really bad happens, and they fall in love."

Beside the local color of the San Francisco Japanese-American scene, amusingly sketched here, the pair is pallid. Ken is laid back to the point of somnoience, and Kyoko tends to repeat herself. "I cannot speak my feelings in English," she says. To judge by the translations of her letters, she doesn't do much better in her native tongue.

The scenes are brief, but the movie seems long. No confrontations, no

highs. Despite plenty of rock music, "Living on Tokyo Time" doesn't have much of a beat. Mr. Okazaki, who has up to now made only documentries, appears to have been trying for a light-hearted comedy with contemporary ballast. He's produced a leaden zeppelin.

1987 Ag 14, C20:1

DISORDERLIES, directed by Michael Schultz; written by Mark Feldberg and Mitchell Klebanoff; cinematographer, Rolf Kesterman; produced by Mr. Schultz, George Jackson and Michael Jaffe; released by Warner Brothers. At neighborhood theaters. Running time: 85 minutes. This film is rated PG.

The Fat Boys	
Ralph Bellamy	
Tony Plana	
Anthony Geary	

By CARYN JAMES

You like the Fat Boys or you don't, but they are what they are: three huge (the thin one is a couple of hundred pounds) rap music stars. Either way, you won't get much of what they're famous for in "Disorderlies," a blatant attempt to cross over from rap to mainstream comedy that virtually leaves the group's music behind. Instead, they are dropped into a comedy-suspense plot that's a very cut-rate blend of "Miami Vice" and the Three Stooges.

The Fat Boys play Brooklyn-born orderlies hired away from the country's worst nursing home by Winslow, the sleazy, debt-ridden nephew of an aged, ailing Palm Beach millionaire. The nephew hopes the disorderlies

will speed along his inheritance, but they blunder their way into restoring the old man's health. Desperate, Winslow tries to murder his uncle and frame the boys.

Michael Schultz, the director of last year's rap film, "Krush Groove," also directed and co-produced "Disorderlies." He seems to think the Fat Boys are natural comedians, but who knows? There's no evidence of it in this film, where slapstick means that one or another Fat Boy falls in a swimming pool, falls off a horse or hits another Fat Boy in the face.

●

There are many curious choices involved with "Disorderlies," which opened yesterday at the Criterion and other theaters, such as Ralph Bellamy's decision to play the wealthy old man, as if to cap his career with a bad joke. And there is no possible reason for the way Anthony Geary looks as the nephew; his trademark curls are gone, replaced by short, bristly yellow hair that makes him look — and apparently act — remarkably prissy.

But the strangest choice of all is to ignore the Fat Boys' fans, who might have liked to hear them rap in more than one scene, and to aim "Disorderlies" at an audience that probably doesn't know — and on the basis of this, shouldn't care — who the Fat Boys are.

●

"Disorderlies" is rated PG ("Parental Guidance Suggested"). There is some strong language and a glimpse of nudity.

1987 Ag 15, 13:1

FILM VIEW / Walter Goodman

Prankster Pals

SO WHAT'S THE SPECIAL KICK of "Stakeout," John Badham's new movie about a team of detectives assigned to keep an eye on the house of an all-time bad guy's sometime girlfriend? Not exactly a novel plot or situation — cop teams are a drug on the movie and television markets; they're due for a bust — and you don't have to have second sight to predict love at first sight between one of the cops at least and the shapely woman under surveillance.

What came to mind, however, as I found myself getting into the big kids' kidding around, was not the latest fashion in tough-guy smash-and-grabbers but the adventure movies of another time, on which many of us grew up. I'll always think of them as boys' movies because they seemed to speak especially to us boys or to the boy in us adults, and "Stakeout" gives the same sort of pleasure. The buddy banter between Richard Dreyfuss and Emilio Estevez as the cops, the attitude toward the woman in the case, the schoolyard or locker room low jinks punctuated by he-man action took me back to the great movie year of 1939 and "Gunga Din."

No, I'm not rating "Stakeout" up there with what may be the best boys' movie ever made. Still, there are family resemblances. A

From 'Gunga Din' to 'Stakeout,' buddies involved in good-natured mischief have proved an irresistible mix.

lot of time in "Gunga Din" is given to joshing around by Cary Grant, Douglas Fairbanks and Victor McLaglen. The humor is more clunky than classy, but it gets across the sort of good fellows they are, the youthful camaraderie that will serve them so well when they come under fire or fall into the enemy's clutches. Sophistication wasn't wanted here. What we wanted was to see the big guys acting like mischievous kids, having the sort of fun that we daydreamed we might have when we grew up, even though we knew that these heroes never would grow up.

So it is with the cops in "Stakeout." The practical jokes that the daytime and nighttime surveillance teams play on each other are, to be kind, crude, the sort of stuff you're supposed to grow out of in junior high school. (Remember the fake little telescopes that left a black ring around your eye?) These guys have not been subdued by maturity; they speak for boyhood — and for a boyhood of buddydom, without rough edges. They show us what "best friend," that prized phrase of adolescence, can mean.

There is never any question of their heterosexuality, however. Women are there to be rescued and reverenced. Despite the advances in sexual explicitness, the heroes' attitudes are not all that different from Douglas Fairbanks's attitude toward Joan Fontaine. Mr. Dreyfuss is as worshipful as any Victorian gent. He falls at first glimpse. (Granted, that glimpse of Madeleine Stowe reveals aspects that you never got to see of Ms. Fontaine, dolled up from neck to toes in a fashion designer's vision of a memsahib. And Miss Stowe, a woman of the 1980's, comes on the way girls used to only in boys' dreams. Nonetheless, like Ms. Fontaine, she behaves in a generally more grown-up way than any of the men around.)

The big kids in "Stakeout," moreover, lack the sadistic inclinations that infect movie cops these days. Who can imagine happy-go-lucky Cary or gallant Doug inflicting pain for the pleasure of it? Sure, the Dreyfuss-Estevez team is tough, and the enemy is merciless, but you never get the feeling that these lawmen are looking for opportunities to blow people away. These are wholesome, softhearted guys. Mayhem is forced on them; they are the kind of cops who would rather let a hundred criminals escape than endanger the life of a single innocent passer-by. Wouldn't Cary and Doug, even confronted by so sinister an adversary as Eduardo Cianelli, do the same?

Now, all this could be interpreted as a put-down of a concocted comedy-adventure entirely lacking in social overtones or psychological undertones. Mr. Dreyfuss is a little miffed when the woman in his life walks out, taking everything, including the bedroom curtains, but his main problem is trying to get some sleep with the light and street noises pounding into the room. He's not bedeviled by horrible nightmares about Vietnam. It's a relief being around him, not having to worry that really he identifies with the bad guy or has a mother fixation or might go beserk at the sound of a telephone — but a complex character he's not.

The question is, how much complexity do we need or want in a boys' movie? Seeing "Gunga Din" today may arouse more complicated feelings than it did in 1939, when the British Empire was standing against Hitler. The white man's burden celebrated by Rudyard Kipling has taken on different meanings, most of them unpleasant, and the sight of Sam Jaffe scampering loyally about as the ragged water boy who sacrifices himself to keep the sun from setting on her Majesty's realm does not go down well. Once it brought a lump in the throat; now, if you take it seriously, the gorge may rise.

But why take it seriously? One of the annoying things about some adventure movies these days is the affectation that they have something to say about crime or society or the human condition. "Robocop," for a recent example, contains some huggermugger about corporation types corrupting everything; it's a thin excuse for laying on the violence, which is what that movie is mainly about.

Mr. Badham is no slouch at violence, but his good guys aren't parading around asking for some crook to make their day. "Stakeout" is about something else, a couple of comical heroes who do battle because duty demands it, peacefully-inclined Joes who would rather fool around than fight. Just like Cary and Doug and Vic. □

1987 Ag 16, II:19:1

Moon, Spoon, June

WHERE THE HEART ROAMS, produced, directed and edited by George Paul Csicsery; cinematography by John Knoop; composer, Mark Adler; released by New Yorker Films. At Film Forum 1, 57 Watts St. Running time: 80 minutes. This film is not rated.

By VINCENT CANBY

A T its best, there's something sad and, one might even venture to say, ineffable about George Paul Csicsery's "Where the Heart Roams," a good, informative documentary-feature about romance novels, the women who write and edit them and the women who, by buying and reading them, have turned paperback junk into a $300 million-a-year industry.

Mr. Csicsery doesn't make fun of the women — he doesn't have to. That's the sad part. It's ineffable because the sight of so many people devoting themselves so earnestly to such easily parodied wish-fulfillment leaves one nearly speechless. The film opens today at the Film Forum 1.

Chelley Kitzmiller, a Southern California housewife, is the film's centerpiece. Some years ago Mrs. Kitzmiller read her first romance novel, Rebecca Brandywyne's "Sweet Savage Love," and became addicted. She now reads them by the dozens. In 1983

she helped organize something called the Love Train, an Amtrak special, to take romance-novel readers and authors from the West Coast to New York, with stops in between, to attend the second annual Romantic Book Lovers' Conference. The ride east, and the conference itself, are, more or less, the film's raison d'être.

Though Mrs. Kitzmiller is the centerpiece of the film, Barbara Cartland, the queen mother of the romance industry, comes on several times in a film-stealing cameo. Mrs. Cartland ("I give women beauty and love") is an eye-blinding presence. Now in her mid-80's, she's always dressed in kewpie-doll splendor (pale blue tulle, feathers of a color no bird ever grew and more jewelry than is absolutely necessary except for one's own coronation). She has written 362 romance novels that have sold more than 350 million copies. When she speaks, romance readers and writers pay heed, though, apparently, they are now going their own way.

"I am the best-selling author in the world, according to the Guinness Book of Records," Mrs. Cartland announces right off, holding an armful of roses and staring at the camera through lashes dewy with makeup. She's appalled by the current trend toward more explicit sex in romance novels. "It's soft porn, which is really a mistake," she says. How does a woman hold her man? It's perfectly simple, according to Mrs. Cartland. "You have to make his prison, which is his home, more attractive."

On board the Love Train, romance novelists give pointers to readers who want to write their own books and get a cut of the pie. One woman tries to justify romance novels from a feminist point of view. This means mostly that today's heroines have important jobs and fall madly, heedlessly in love with men six feet tall whose jobs, though important, may not be as important as those of the heroines.

About the sex scenes in one book, a reader says with enthusiasm, the author "takes you up to a certain point without going all the way. She leaves you with a good feeling; a *clean* feeling."

At the conference in New York, the movie attends writers' seminars on "the texture of kisses" and "sensuality." When the authors turn up to autograph copies of their works for devoted readers, Mrs. Kitzmiller stands patiently in line, though, by the end of the film, it seems apparent that she may be growing tired of her role as a foremost reader and would desperately like to become, instead, a foremost writer.

Crosscut with these scenes are interviews with Ted Kitzmiller, Chelley's husband, and Gina, her daughter. Gina admits that once her mom became hooked, the housework was pretty much left to her. Ted is seen relaxing at home in front of a fireplace, over which hangs a shotgun and a pair of antlers from a fairly small beast. At first, he says, he thought his wife's addiction was silly, but he's proud of her success in organizing the Love Train, even if she never writes her own romance novel. "After all," he says of the acclaim given Mrs. Kitzmiller for the Love Train, "how many people get their names in Newsweek, much less their pictures?"

"Where the Heart Roams" is as much about barren lives as it is about living happily ever after, but Mr. Csicsery, using terrific restraint, never overstates the obvious. It can't have been easy.

1987 Ag 19, C17:1

J. Giannini

Janet Dailey, left, and Barbara Cartland, right, leading authors of romance novels, with Kathryn Falk, an organizer of the Romantic Book Lovers' Conference.

Watch Your Step

DIRTY DANCING, directed by Emile Ardolino; written by Eleanor Bergstein; director of photography, Jeff Jur; choreography by Kenny Ortega; music by John Morris; edited by Peter C. Frank; produced by Linda Gottlieb and Ms. Bergstein; released by Vestron Pictures. At Gemini Twin, Second Avenue at 64th Street; National Twin, Broadway at 44th Street; 86th Street East Twin, near Second Avenue; 57th Street Playhouse, at Avenue of the Americas; 23d Street West Triplex, near Eighth Avenue; Loews 84th Street Six, at Broadway. Running time: 86 minutes. This film is rated PG-13.

Frances (Baby) Houseman	Jennifer Grey
Johnny Castle	Patrick Swayze
Jake Houseman	Jerry Orbach
Penny Johnson	Cynthia Rhodes
Max Kellerman	Jack Weston
Lisa Houseman	Jane Brucker
Marjorie Houseman	Kelly Bishop
Neil Kellerman	Lonny Price
Robbie Gould	Max Cantor

By VINCENT CANBY

IN their time, almost all forms of popular American music and dancing, from the foxtrot and the tango through rock-and-roll and all of its variations, have scandalized the members of an older generation, whose own sexuality had earlier been liberated by tamer means. As music, lyrics and dance steps have become more and more sexually explicit, fathers and mothers from coast to coast have felt alienated, and worried that pop music was leading their children straight to hell. As it was with the bunny hug, danced to a ragtime tune in 1910, so is it today when Madonna sings "Papa Don't Preach."

This culture generation gap has produced its own Hollywood genre. Most of these films have been quickies on the order of "Don't Knock the Rock" (1957) and "Twist Around the Clock" (1962), but there have occasionally been more ambitious if not much better films (Herbert Ross's "Footloose," 1984). Though music is the subject of each film, sex is the subtext. In the final reel, generations reconcile; initially stuffy oldsters end

up rocking, rolling or twisting the night away, showing the young that, though creaky of joint and infirm of body, they can still do "it."

"It" is also the subject of "Dirty Dancing," which opens today at the National and other theaters.

"Dirty Dancing" is a nicely bittersweet genre movie set at Kellerman's Mountain House, a Grossinger's-like Catskills resort hotel, in the summer of 1963. President Kennedy was still alive, America's stake in Vietnam had not yet become divisive, and socially conscious young people were going on freedom marches in the South and joining the Peace Corps.

•

The film is about Frances Houseman (Jennifer Grey), nicknamed Baby, a pretty middle-class teen-ager who finds her adult identity in her first love affair — with Johnny Castle (Patrick Swayze), the hotel's dance instructor. For a girl of Baby's conventionally liberal, Jewish background (she's planning to study "third world economics" in college), Johnny, a young man from the wrong side of the tracks, exemplifies the freedom expressed through a new and as yet socially unacceptable form of dancing. This "dirty dancing," a phrase used only in the film's title, features a lot of steamy body contact and pelvic thrusts, which unleash emotions supposedly left withered by mambos and cha-cha-chas.

Taking a formula that is itself creaky of joint and infirm of body, Eleanor Bergstein, the writer, and Emile Ardolino, the director, have made an engaging pop-movie romance of somewhat more substance than one usually finds in summer movies designed for the young.

I suspect that one's responses to "Dirty Dancing," to its period details, even to its state of mind, will depend on the associations one brings into the theater. What is undeniable, however, is a basic decency of feeling, shaped, in part, by the film's obligations to its optimistic genre.

Baby, as written by Miss Bergstein and played by Miss Grey ("Ferris Bueller's Day Off"), is no bubble-brained teen-ager, but a bright, inquisitive young woman who's on her way to being her own person. Miss Bergstein is much better on creating character than in re-imagining formula events. Baby's liberation comes through her forbidden association with the womanizing Johnny Castle, after his partner, Penny (Cynthia Rhodes), becomes pregnant and Baby agrees to substitute for her in a mambo demonstration at another hotel.

•

There's a really quite awful subplot about Penny's abortion, financed by

money that Baby has borrowed from her conventionally liberal doctor-father, and about the arrogant young Ivy League fellow who is responsible for Penny's condition.

Given the limitations of his role, that of a poor but handsome sex-object abused by the rich women at Kellerman's Mountain House, Mr. Swayze is also good. He's even convincing when he must admit, in one of the film's lesser moments, that "the reason people treat me like nothing is because I am nothing." He's at his best — as is the movie — when he's dancing.

The movie makes a lot of good use of period music, to which some not very evocative new songs have been added. The dancing itself, especially

Patrick Swayze and Jennifer Grey in "Dirty Dancing."

the dirty dancing, choreographed by Kenny Ortega, looks very contemporary, or, at least, as contemporary as "Saturday Night Fever," but it has a drive and a pulse that give the film real excitement. Though the film takes place in 1963, just a year after the twist was all the rage, the twist itself seems already to have come and gone at Kellerman's Mountain House. The women's clothes also look surprisingly mid-80's and, in 1963, would anybody have used the term "wimp"?

These anachronisms aren't especially important, except that Miss Bergstein has been so specific about the film's period. She seems to want "Dirty Dancing" to be seen as a fond goodbye to a comfortable, *liberal* American way of life before the country was radicalized by the assassination of President Kennedy and by the increasingly bitter anti-Vietnam War movement. That's loading a small movie with rather more than it can carry without a lot of highly detailed program notes.

"Dirty Dancing" works best when it's most direct and unpretentious. It has the kind of sweet simplicity that somehow always eludes John Hughes ("Sixteen Candles," "Pretty in Pink," "Ferris Bueller's Day Off"). Mr. Ardolino, whose background is in theater and television dance films, doesn't clutter the film with extraneous, sentimental detail, nor even with too much colorful (and familiar) detail about life in your usual Catskill resort hotel. He also obtains excellent performances from his cast, which, in addition to Miss Grey, Mr. Swayze and Miss Rhodes, includes Jerry Orbach, as Baby's father; Jack Weston, as the owner of Kellerman's, and Lonny Price, who is especially funny as Mr. Weston's arrogant, wimpish grandson.

•

"Dirty Dancing," which has been rated PG-13 ("Special Parental Guidance Suggested for Those Younger Than 13"), includes some vulgar language and a lot of dancing that is comparatively erotic.

1987 Ag 21, C3:4

Small Pleasures

THE BIG EASY, directed by Jim McBride; written by Daniel Petrie Jr. and Jack Baran; director of photography, Alfonso Beato; edited by Mia Goldman; produced by Stephen Friedman; released by Columbia Pictures. At Embassy 1, Broadway and 46th Street; Manhattan Twin, 59th Street east of Third Avenue; 34th Street East, near Second Avenue; Waverly Twin, Avenue of the Americas at Third Street; Metro Cinema, 99th Street and Broadway. Running time: 101 minutes. This film is rated R.

Remy McSwain	Dennis Quaid
Anne Osborne	Ellen Barkin
Jack Kellom	Ned Beatty
Detective Dodge	Ebbe Roe Smith
Detective DeSoto	John Goodman
Detective McCabe	Lisa Jane Persky
Lamar	Charles Ludlam
Cannon Di Moti	Marc Lawrence

REMY MCSWAIN (Dennis Quaid) is a tough, fast-talking New Orleans police detective who isn't above accepting free meals from all-too-obliging restaurants. They're the perks that go with the job. Anne Osborne (Ellen Barkin) is a pretty, sexually repressed assistant district attorney, assigned to investigate police corruption. Remy and Anne are made for each other, or would have been if "The Big Easy" were the sophisti-

cated comedy it could have been.

The first third of "The Big Easy," in which Remy attempts to seduce the not entirely unwilling Anne, has the frantic pacing and something of the hard-boiled humor of Howard Hawks's classic "His Girl Friday." After that, however, "The Big Easy" must attend to a frequently inscrutable story about a New Orleans drug war, most of which takes place off-screen but which successfully upstages the attractive leading characters.

"The Big Easy" was directed by Jim McBride ("David Holzman's Diary," the American remake of "Breathless"), who one day is going to come up with a commercial movie that works all the way through, and not just in patches. The screenplay, by Daniel Petrie Jr. and Jack Baran, has a number of funny lines and situations, but the end result looks fiddled with by people attempting to "fix" things.

•

Whoever fixed "The Big Easy" has fixed it by making essential story points fuzzy, and by pouring soundtrack music over it under the mistaken impression it was a hot fudge sundae. The movie opens today at the Embassy 1 and other theaters.

If one doesn't demand narrative coherence, it's possible to enjoy "The Big Easy" for the performances of Mr. Quaid ("Innerspace," "The Right Stuff"), who's acquiring a Jack Nicholson kind of comic self-assurance, and Miss Barkin ("Down by Law," "Tender Mercies"), who can be equally funny when the material allows.

The supporting cast includes the ever-reliable Ned Beatty, that excellent character actor Marc Lawrence and, in a small role, Charles Ludlam,

Ellen Barkin in "The Big Easy."

best known as the founder, principal playwright and star of New York's Ridiculous Theatrical Company. Mr. Ludlam, who died this year, is hilarious as a lawyer ever-willing to sink lower in society if it means winning the case. *VINCENT CANBY*

1987 Ag 21, C6:3

Agoraphobia

INSIDE OUT, written by Robert Taicher and Kevin Bartelme; directed by Mr. Taicher; director of photography, Jack Wallner; edited by David Finfer; music by Peer Raben; produced by Sidney Beckerman; released by Hemdale Releasing Corporation. At Cinema 2, Third Avenue at 60th Street. Running time: 87 minutes. This film is rated R.

Jimmy Morgan	Elliott Gould
Jack	Howard Hesseman
Amy	Jennifer Tilly
Verna	Beah Richards
Leo Gross	Dana Elcar

By WALTER GOODMAN

TALK about bad luck! In the space of about a week, Jimmy Morgan learns that he has lost his shirt in the stock market (a real trick these days), has his pants and underwear removed by a crooked business associate and takes a bath betting on boxing and football (even *college* games). Not only that, but Jimmy's estranged wife notifies him that she is taking his adored 11-year-old daughter to Chicago.

Now, Jimmy is not about to go to Chicago. In fact, he is not about to step outside his New York apartment. He communicates with the world by telephone and television, both of which operate nonstop, does his jogging to a simulated jogging scene on the tube, has Chinese food and cocaine delivered, is serviced by a house-calling barber and manicurist, gets dressed only for the latest stocker, and blows up when an old friend on a visit from California invites him out to dinner.

Why can't Jimmy Morgan leave his apartment? Well, it's a very comfortable apartment, and he has a dependable cleaning lady. Also, when he gets up enough courage to open his terrace door for a sniff of air, the street noises blow him right back inside, with palpitations. There's always a police siren howling in Jimmy's neighborhood. Jimmy yells at his friend that the streets are filled with criminals.

And get this — the man plays with toy trains.

•   •

That's about as much insight into Jimmy's coping difficulties as the synthetic screenplay for "Inside Out"

Entangled Dennis Quaid stars in "The Big Easy" as a police lieutenant who falls in love with an assistant district attorney investigating corruption in his department.

Elliott Gould

by Robert Taicher and Kevin Bartelme provides. Which leaves it up to Elliott Gould, as Jimmy, to look shaky and stricken, except when he is operating his remote-control devices for television and telephone. They give Jimmy the illusion that he is in control of his world, but anybody can see how remote he is. His most meaningful relationship in this difficult period is with a bum who takes shelter in the hallway; Jimmy communicates with him over the intercom and orders croissants delivered to him for breakfast.

The movie, which opens at Cinema 2 today, slogs from disaster to ordained disaster to a disastrously soggy ending, with dialogue as bankrupt as Jimmy's business and as ungiving as his bookie. "Jimmy, how can you do this to yourself?" asks his friend. Don't blame Jimmy. The main technique used by Mr. Taicher, who directed, for getting into Jimmy's feelings is to push the camera smack into his star's unshaven face, as though it might squeeze out emotion like a juicer. That puts a strain on Mr. Gould, who has to show panic with his eyes a lot of the time, like a heroine in the silents. Considering the little help he gets from script, director and most of the cast, he suffers manfully. At moments you might even bet that he understands the character. But you'd be safer with college football.

1987 Ag 21, C11:1

GARBAGE PAIL KIDS, written by Melinda Palmer and Rod Amateau; directed and produced by Mr. Amateau; director of photography, Harvey Genkins; released by Atlantic Releasing Corporation. At East Side Cinema, Third Ave. at 53d St.; Cinema 42, Seventh Ave. at 47th St.; Movie Center 5, 235 W. 125th St. Running time: 100 minutes. This film is rated PG.

Captain Manzini	Anthony Newley
Dodger	Mackenzie Astin
Tangerine	Katie Barberi

By CARYN JAMES

Where is Miss Manners when you need her? If only she'd been there to break up the big fight scene, when some vile children go on a rampage — one clears the room with nearly fatal flatulence, another vomits on her enemies.

These dirty fighters are the heroes of "The Garbage Pail Kids Movie," an attempt to cash in on the popularity of the bubble gum cards and stickers featuring the Garbage Pail Kids characters — dozens of them, all with extreme attitude problems.

As Captain Manzini, Anthony Newley owns a mysterious antique shop, where a 14-year-old boy named Dodger works. Dodger is infatuated with Tangerine, who is beautiful and at least old enough to drive. Her jealous boyfriend, Juice, scuffles with Dodger in the antique shop, where they overturn a garbage can full of green slime.

•

The next thing Dodger knows he's surrounded by seven repugnant little humans like Messy Tessie, whose nose is constantly running down her face, onto her fingers and on anyone else who happens to be nearby. Her pal, Valerie Vomit, saves her special skills for the grand finale fight scene, but Windy Winston makes a big entrance; he jolts Dodger to consciousness by turning his back and directing some foul air in the poor boy's face. Ali Gator is half-boy, half-alligator, which at least gives him half an excuse for his bad behavior.

The kids help Dodger win Tangerine's friendship, and the ostensible point is that beauty is only skin deep. I prefer Keats's "truth is beauty," so let's be honest: "The Garbage Pail Kids Movie" is gross-out humor for children, cynically packaged with goody-goody morals that wouldn't convince the most naïve parent or child.

Mr. Newley might as well be winking at the audience when he says, "We cannot choose the way we look, but we can choose the way we behave," because no one questions these kids' behavior. We're not shown incurable illness or even terminal ugliness here. Messy Tessie does not need sympathy; she needs a handkerchief. Get Windy Winston to a good gastroenterologist, but don't tell me he's shunned because he's funny looking.

•

None of this humor has even the repulsive gusto of John Belushi gorging himself in "Animal House." Antisocial body language is the film's real point, but it's snuck in, the way a small child might blurt out a bad word and giggle.

The production is truly beyond help. The kids are portrayed by 3- and 4-foot-tall adults wearing puppet-like heads that make for expressionless faces. When the kids run off to a movie theater the scene looks as if it was shot in someone's basement; when they land in the State Home for the Ugly (now *there's* a satirical idea gone to waste), it looks like an abandoned warehouse. "The Garbage Pail Kids Movie" is enough to make you believe in strict and faraway boarding schools.

"The Garbage Pail Kids" is rated PG, but it may be too repulsive for children or adults of any age.

1987 Ag 22, 14:5

FILM VIEW/Vincent Canby

In Search of Madonna's Persona

Ebet Roberts

Madonna on screen, at top, and Madonna in concert—Hollywood hasn't tapped the talent.

ON THE EVENING OF THURSDAY, AUG. 6, approximately 10,000 people, according to police estimates, crowded into the lower section of Times Square to watch the arrival of Madonna for the premiere of her new film, "Who's That Girl." The next day, at noon, at the first regularly scheduled performance of the film at the 1,151-seat Ziegfeld Theater, I counted less than 60 people in the house when the show began.

In this age of electronically enhanced personality, fame may be fleeting, but it doesn't disappear overnight. It took Tiny Tim more than a decade to fade away and the Sex Pistols a couple of years (and one murder). "Howard the Duck" lasted four weeks. Madonna was as big an attraction on Fri-

day at noon as she had been on Thursday evening but, apparently, her stardom on records, in music videos, in concert and as a free show in Times Square is *not*, as they say, translating to the box office of movie theaters.

With its usual bluntness, Variety stated the facts. "Who's That Girl," the trade paper reported last week, is "a loser."

Ever since she first came on the music scene three years ago, there's been a certain amount of hype surrounding the ascent of Madonna — actually Madonna Louise Veronica Ciccone from Bay City, Mich. — to the top of the record charts. The voice is small, the musicianship not super and the personality a kind of electronically enhanced variation on those of other people.

Yet that was then and this is now, when Madonna, the singer and knockout music-video performer, and, more recently, movie actress, has developed a public personality that is decidedly and wittily her own. Largely through the sexy, parodistic music videos directed by Mary Lambert, and Susan Seidelman's "Desperately Seeking Susan," her first theatrical feature, Madonna has shaped up as a character in her own right.

∎

She's a knowing, shrewd, pragmatic young woman, a performer of invigorating energy who still looks a lot like Marilyn Monroe, even with short hair, but who has much more in common with the enthusiastic, unembarrassed, comic tartiness of Jean Harlow, somehow let loose on the streets of New York in the 80's.

Little of this would you be able to guess from "Who's That Girl," the film, which is halfway over before the "real" Madonna emerges, and none at all from the "Who's That Girl" music video, which, though its purpose is to promote the film, promotes everything that's least attractive about it.

What you're witnessing is a film career that's terrifically promising, drain-wise. You might even suspect that there's a Cyndi Lauper "mole" among her advisers, someone bent on wrecking a career before it's decently gotten started and gained any momentum.

"Who's That Girl" doesn't duplicate the folly of last year's "Shanghai Surprise," in which Madonna was cast against type (as a missionary in pre-World War II China), before that portion of the theatrical movie audience that doesn't see music videos knew what her type was supposed to be.

"Who's That Girl," in fact, is a good deal better than its own distributors thought it was when they refused to screen it in advance to the press. It's

Hollywood should study Madonna as she's been defined in her best videos.

an 80's comedy that qualifies as screwball, with a promisingly nutty screenplay by Andrew Smith and Ken Finkleman.

∎

It's about a yuppie Manhattan lawyer, played straight and very comically by Griffin Dunne, whose assignment is simply to pick up Madonna, newly paroled on a murder rap, at a prison gate and put her on a bus to Philadelphia. The 45-minute drive turns into 24 hours of lunacy involving a wild cougar, mobsters, a society wedding, an interview with the fussy members of a co-op board, car chases and larceny at Cartier's.

Under the direction of James

The star in her new movie, "Who's That Girl"

By CARYN JAMES

CHEECH MARIN'S "Born in East L.A." is enormously good-natured — exactly the wrong tone for a comedy that needs all the rambunctious lunacy it can get. Instead, this story of an American mistakenly deported to Mexico as an illegal alien is amiable and plodding, the very last things you'd expect from Cheech, with or without Chong.

As a team, Cheech Marin and Tommy Chong have starred in several uneven movies, but their films never lacked a manic edge; the men may drive around Los Angeles in circles, but crazy disorientation is their style. On his own as writer, director and star of "Born in East L.A.," Mr. Marin is surprisingly cautious.

Based on his video parody of Bruce Springsteen's "Born in the U.S.A." Mr. Marin's idea is full of comic potential. When Rudy Robles is picked up by the immigration authorities in a factory raid, his family is out of town and his wallet home on the mantel; in Mexico with no money and no proof of his United States citizenship, he can only connive his way back across the border.

•

In Tijuana, Rudy tries to scrape together money for an illegal ride back by working as a shill for a sleazy American club owner (Daniel Stern) and moonlighting as a street musician. There are a few funny bits: Rudy tries to teach some Oriental men how to blend into the Los Angeles Mexican community, so they strut around and learn to say "Waa'sappenin'?" Back home, Rudy's mother has covered their phone with a garish, eye-blinking photo of Jesus; when Rudy calls for help, the only one around is his not-too-bright cousin, who thinks the voice on the answering machine is heavenly, and understands only that Jesus is in Tijuana. The film is desperate for a dozen other outrageous ideas to enliven the scenario.

The movie's strength is in Mr. Marin's appealing performance as Rudy, a straight-arrow cousin of the laid-back, dope-smoking character he usually plays. Mr. Marin may be a greatly underrated actor. As writer and director he tries so hard to be zany, convincing and eventually serious about the poverty that leads so many Mexicans to cross the border, that you find yourself rooting for the movie to pick itself up. But "Born in East L.A.," which opened Friday at Movieland and other theaters, never does, as if all that effort simply buried Cheech Marin's antic side.

1987 Ag 24, C14:5

BACKLASH, directed and produced by Bill Bennett; screenplay by Mr. Bennett, David Argue, Gia Carides, Lydia Miller and Brian Syron; photography by Tony Wilson; edited by Denise Hunter; music by Michael Atkinson and Michael Spicer; released by Samuel Goldwyn Company. At Cinema Studio, Broadway, at 66th Street. Running time: 90 minutes.

Trevor Darling	David Argue
Nikki Iceton	Gia Carides
Kath	Lydia Miller
Lyle	Brian Syron
Mrs. Smith	Anne Smith
Mr. Smith	Don Smith
Waitress	Jennifer Cluff

Foley, and also, perhaps, of the producers, Madonna plays the first half of the movie at a fever pitch of inappropriate (for her) mannerisms, including an adenoidal accent, a supposedly comic, "little girl" walk, shrewish temper tantrums and coy facial expressions, none of which has anything to do with the sophisticated, self-aware Madonna of music videos and concert stage. In the second half of the film, when she's allowed to play at her own insinuating pace, Madonna at last emerges and is a delight.

The "Who's That Girl" music video catches none of this quality at all, concentrating instead on the hysterically off-putting personality that the star is required to play in the early scenes. It appeals neither to people who've never seen her before nor to anyone who's admired the sometimes brazenly erotic and funny performer Madonna is in her best music videos.

■

It may be, as has been suggested by my colleague Jon Pareles, that there's simply too much "free" Madonna available on television, in her music videos, for the star to attract fans to movies theaters that charge as much as $6 a ticket. Movies, too, are not the "events" that her sell-out concert appearances are. Yet she's never even been seen dancing and singing in a movie. Hollywood has busily been giving a *new* image to

someone whose initial image hasn't yet been formed, at least as far as movies are concerned.

Before Madonna makes another film, her producers might do well to study the creature as she's been defined in her best music videos. Chief among these is the extraordinarily provocative, impressionistic "Open Your Heart," which, in a brisk, haiku-like 4 minutes and 22 seconds, presents Madonna as every adolescent boy's wildest, sweetest fantasy. It's a tiny, comic, sexy classic, directed by Jean-Baptiste Mondine, photographed by Pascal Lebegue, with smashing production design by Richard Sylbert ("Carnal Knowledge," among other films).

In Madonna, Hollywood has a potent, pocket-sized sex bomb. So far, though, all it does is tick. □

1987 Ag 23, II:17:5

Border Dispute

BORN IN EAST L.A., written and directed by Cheech Marin; director of photography, Alex Phillips; edited by Don Brochu; music by Lee Holdridge; produced by Peter MacGregor-Scott; released by Universal Studios. At Movieland, Broadway at 47th St.; New York Twin, Second Ave. at 66th St. Running time: 98 minutes. This film is rated R.

Rudy	Cheech Marin
Javier	Paul Rodriguez
Jimmy	Daniel Stern
Dolores	Kamala Lopez
McCalister	Jan Michael Vincent

Cheech Marin in "Born in East L.A."

"Backlash" was shown as part of this year's New Directors/New Films series. Following are excerpts from Janet Maslin's review, which appeared in The New York Times on April 13. The film opens today at the Cinema Studio, Broadway at 66th Street.

THE Australian film "Backlash" begins with a brief, crude sequence in which a young aboriginal woman is attacked by her employer, an older white man whom she proceeds to murder and emasculate (we are later told) with a garden shears. How will the film, which is the second dramatic feature by Bill Bennett, make use of this episode? As it turns out, the focus shifts quickly from the murder to the man-and-woman police team assigned to escort the accused woman to her trial. Once these three begin their journey together, the film shifts gears entirely and becomes an odd hybrid, a whimsical, eccentric road movie with an element of mystery.

The older and wilder of the two police officers is Trevor Darling (David Argue), who resents his assignment and makes a point of insulting both his companions. His partner, Nikki Iceton (Gia Carides), does her best to ignore him and concentrate on her fiance and her law studies, which isn't made any easier when Trevor decides to do headstands wearing little more than his gun belt and his underwear.

Their charge, named Kath (Lydia Miller), is initially silent much of the time, watching apprehensively as her two escorts trade nasty remarks. But gradually the three become used to one another. And when they find themselves stranded in a remote setting, bathing in a pond and sleeping in sheep-shearing pens, a certain rustic peacefulness begins to free them from their various ill humors. The film watches all three depart from their earlier roles, and establish new bonds on an entirely different footing.

"Backlash" eventually returns to the murder story, and to the prejudice and injustice that are shown to surround it. But these are the weaker aspects of a film that, at its best, recalls the picaresque Scottish comedies of Bill Forsyth, with their flair for the unexpected. Trevor plays with sheep shearings and imagines himself a magistrate. Nikki is teased relentlessly about her calorie counter, and Kath teaches the other two how to catch fish with a pair of stockings. In a roadside restaurant, one character asks a bored waitress whether the fish is fresh and is told, "Of course it's fresh, it's a specialty," even if later examination proves the fish is in the freezer.

"Backlash" has a homespun look and a refreshing spontaneity that easily make up for its lack of polish. If its efforts to examine questions of law and bigotry are less compelling than Mr. Bennett's flair for small, peculiar flourishes, it's an entertaining effort all the same, with a particularly good performance from the snappish, high-strung Mr. Argue.

1987 Ag 27, C18:3

MATEWAN, written and directed by John Sayles; director of photography, Haskell Wexler; edited by Sonya Polonsky; music by Mason Daring; produced by Peggy Rajski; released by Cinecom Entertainment Group and Film Gallery. At Cinema 1, Third Avenue at 60th Street. Running time: 132 minutes. This film is rated PG-13.

Joe	Chris Cooper
Danny	Will Oldham
Elma	Mary McDonnell
Few Clothes	James Earl Jones
Hillard	Jace Alexander
Sephus	Ken Jenkins
C. E. Lively	Bob Gunton
Ludie	Gary McCleery
Hickey	Kevin Tighe
Griggs	Gordon Clapp
Bridey Mae	Nancy Mette
Sid	David Strathairn
Cabell	Josh Mostel
Hardshell	John Sayles

By VINCENT CANBY

TAKING as his source material an especially bitter and bloody confrontation between West Virginia coal miners and the company that owned their souls in 1920, John Sayles has made a film with the sweetness and simplicity of an Appalachian ballad.

"Matewan," opening today at Cinema 1, is so direct in its sympathies and so unsophisticated in its methods that it seems to be an intrusion on our awareness of everything that's happened to complicate the American labor movement between then and now.

Yet it's this awareness that gives "Matewan" its poignancy and separates it from the old, optimistic, in-unity-there-is-strength movies made in the 1930's. Mr. Sayles understands that there *is* strength in unity, but his film is seen in the context of more than 60 years of labor history, which had included the growth of giant unions vulnerable to corruption, and, more recently, a political climate in which union-busting causes little outrage.

Mr. Sayles, possibly our foremost independent film maker ("The Return of the Secaucus Seven," "The Brother From Another Planet"), is also independently skeptical. He recognizes that good intentions sometimes leave as many victims dead on the street as greed.

•

"Matewan" borrows its title from the name of the small mining community in the West Virginia hills where, in the opening sequence, the Stone Mountain Coal Company is attempting to smuggle in a couple of boxcars full of black laborers to break the threatened strike. Like the Italian immigrants who have already been brought to Matewan, the black miners haven't known of the strike possibility until their arrival.

Also on the train is Joe Kenehan, a lone union organizer. As written by Mr. Sayles, and as played with a sense of patient mission by Chris Cooper, Joe Kenehan is a figure of mythic proportions, part Joe Hill, part Jesus Christ. His task: to give direction to the miners' negotiations and to prevent the kind of sabotage and violence that would give the company an excuse to bring in their goons. That he must fail is the film's distantly heard, mournful theme.

Though Mr. Sayles takes a long view of the events — for all of the passions expressed, the movie is almost chilly — there's never any doubt where his sympathies lie. The characters are either good or evil. They're the idealized figures portrayed in the Government-sponsored murals that, during the Depression, were painted in post offices and other public buildings from one end of the country to the other.

They include a hard-working, staunch widow-lady (Mary McDonnell); her 15-year-old son (Will Old-

Mr. Sayles, left, with Chris Cooper, who plays the union organizer

ham), a fiery lay-preacher who manages to find pro-union parables in the gospels; a great, bearlike man (James Earl Jones), who casts his lot with the strikers; a smarmy, union-sympathizing bar owner (Bob Gunton), who's a company fink; Matewan's police chief (David Strathairn) and mayor (Josh Mostel), who heroically stand up against the company; the town's lone hooker (Nancy Mette), turned to her trade after being widowed in a mine accident, and the company's two principal goons (Kevin Tighe and Gordon Clapp).

In addition to writing and directing the film, Mr. Sayles also appears in a brief scene as a fire-breathing, Red-baiting, fundamentalist preacher, which is about as close as "Matewan" ever gets to a comic moment.

•

There's not a weak performance in the film, but I especially admired the work of Mr. Cooper, Mr. Tighe, Miss McDonnell, Miss Mette, Mr. Gunton, Mr. Strathairn and Mr. Mostel. They may be playing Social-Realist icons, but each manages to make something personal and idiosyncratic out of the material, without destroying the ballad-like style.

For the most part, Haskell Wexler's photography doesn't go overboard in finding poetry in the images. The film was made on a comparatively small budget, entirely on West Virginia locations, and looks better than most profligate Hollywood films. The limited budget does occasionally show in scenes that might better have been reshot for narrative continuity and common sense. Though, by 1920, John L. Lewis and his United Mine Workers of America were formidable presences on the labor scene, neither is mentioned in the course of the film — a most curious omission.

Mr. Sayles's screenplay goes back to Shakespearean fundamentals in its use of such devices as purloined letters and conversations overheard by chance. I suspect, however, that this seeming artlessness is a conscious choice. It's another example of the long-lost innocence that "Matewan" bravely celebrates, without embarrassment and without apologies to contemporary fashions in film.

•

"Matewan," which has been rated PG-13 ("Special Parental Guidance Suggested for Children Younger Than 13"), contains several scenes of violence and some vulgar language.

1987 Ag 28, C3:4

Penal Servitude

MAID TO ORDER, directed by Amy Jones; written by Miss Jones, Perry and Randy Howze; director of photography, Shelly Johnson; edited by Sidney Wolinsky; music by Georges Delerue; produced by Herb Jaffe and Mort Engelberg; released by New Century/Vista Film Company. At Sutton, 57th Street and Third Avenue; U. A. East, 85th Street and First Avenue; 23d Street West Triplex, near Eighth Avenue. Running time: 95 minutes. This film is rated PG.

Jessie Montgomery	Ally Sheedy
Stella	Beverly D'Angelo
Nick McGuire	Michael Ontkean
Georgette Starkey	Valerie Perrine
Stan Starkey	Dick Shawn
Charles Montgomery	Tom Skerritt
Audrey James	Merry Clayton

IN "Maid to Order," Ally Sheedy plays the kind of girl who's waited all her life to be told to clean up her room. She's cast as Jessie Montgomery, a world-class brat who's turned from an heiress into a maid by her fairy godmother (Beverly D'Angelo), and who benefits immeasurably from this transformation. Story ideas don't get much older than this, but "Maid to Order" — which opens today at the Sutton and other theaters — is fun anyhow.

Tough Times
Ally Sheedy stars in Amy Jones's "Maid to Order," a Cinderella-in-reverse tale of a rich girl transformed into a domestic servant.

'Everyone involved radiates real enthusiasm, Amy Jones's direction is buoyant, and Ally Sheedy looks great in a uniform.

Owing equal debts to "Down and Out in Beverly Hills" and "It's a Wonderful Life," "Maid to Order" begins by presenting Jessie in her native habitat. She's very rich and bored, bored, bored. She borrows money from her father's servants, then wastes it on aimless nights on the town (one of which finds Jessie on stage in a nightclub dancing along to a vintage rock song that happens to be about moral accountability; there are moments when this film seems ready to break through its own frivolousness with a more sobering message. Soon after this, Jessie is annoyed to find herself arrested on a drug charge, an event that places her fate in the hands of her fairy godmother.

Wittily played by Miss D'Angelo (hers are among the film's many amusing costumes), the godmother sentences Jessie to life as a maid ("I did not spend six years in junior college to be a maid!" she complains). Jessie then finds herself placed with the worst family in Malibu. These are the Starkeys, Stan (Dick Shawn) and Georgette (Valerie Perrine), who can count racism among their numerous bad qualities; they hire and keep the incompetent Jessie only because she's white. Stan is a show-business promoter of sorts, and one of the film's timelier subplots has him staging a charity benefit that's actually just a means of hyping one of his clients. As for Georgette, she dresses frighteningly and hoards tin foil.

●

Once it reaches the Starkey household, the film alternates between mild satire and potentially dangerous sentimentality; there's an awful lot of emphasis on how sweet, decent and big-hearted Jessie's fellow servants are. But the downstairs cast is very likable, with Michael Ontkean as the handsome chauffeur and the singer Merry Clayton as a motherly cook. And as for upstairs, Miss Perrine and especially Mr. Shawn are quite hilarious. The targets are easy but the roles well drawn, as is everything about the Starkey household. It contains, among other things, a rack for the owners' collection of Walkmen and an enormous portrait of Elvis on one wall. "From Europe!" Mr. Shawn says proudly as he points out one decorative artifact.

Miss Sheedy's petulant manner and her air of faint distaste for her surroundings are just right for this role. And she shows herself to be an able physical comedienne, even if a little bit of Jessie does go a long way. Miss Jones, who also made the moodier "Love Letters" with Jamie Lee Curtis, proves herself capable of a much lighter touch. Her target, the beastliness of the rich and famous, is one of the broadest ones imaginable, but it won't ever go out of style.

●

"Maid to Order" is rated PG ("Parental Guidance Suggested"). It includes some rude language and brief nudity. JANET MASLIN

1987 Ag 28, C6:1

Father Gumshoe

THE ROSARY MURDERS, directed by Fred Walton; screenplay by Elmore Leonard and Mr. Walton, based on the novel by William X. Kienzle; director of photography, David Golia; edited by Sam Vitale; music by Bobby Laurel and Don Sebesky; produced by Robert G. Laurel; released by New Line Cinema. At Embassy 3, Broadway and 47th St.; Loews New York Twin, Second Ave. and 66th St.; 84th St. Six, at Broadway; Movieland Eighth St. Triplex, at University Pl. Running time: 101 minutes. This film is rated R.
Father Koesler .... Donald Sutherland
Father Nabors .... Charles Durning
Lieutenant Koznicki .... Josef Sommer
Pat Lennon .... Belinda Bauer
Javison .... James Murtaugh
Detective Harris .... John Danelle
Father Killeen .... Addison Powell
Sister Ann Vania ....Kathleen Tolan
Detective Fallon .... Tom Mardirosian
Irene Jimenez .... Anita Barone

A LARGE segment of Detroit's Roman Catholic clergy has been attacked and murdered by a crazed killer, yet there's only one sneaker-wearing priest on the trail. That is the premise of "The Rosary Murders," a well-meaning but plodding thriller with a screenplay co-written by Elmore Leonard, who's ordinarily so much faster on his feet. The story, based on a novel by William X. Kienzle, gives the impression of having been a lot more clever on the page. In fact the denouement, when at long last it arrives, reveals the killer to have staged quite an elaborate scheme, and its complexity comes as a surprise. Neither he nor anyone else in the film seems capable of that much ingenuity.

In "The Rosary Murders," which opens today at Loews New York Twin and other theaters, Donald Sutherland plays the affable and iconoclastic Father Koesler, a priest with some decidedly modern ideas about his calling. He adopts an informal manner, reveals unmistakable disappointment when a favorite nun announces her intention to leave the order and marry, and is willing to baptize an illegitimate child after a fellow priest, Father Nabors (Charles Durning), refuses to do so. And when the string of murders begins, it is to Father Koesler that the killer turns. In a plot twist reminiscent of Hitch-

Donald Sutherland

cock's "I Confess," the killer appears in church early in the film to taunt Father Koesler with the news of his exploits.

Though the police (led by Josef Sommer) are nominally involved in finding the killer, Father Koesler seems to be investigating alone. His only real assistant is Belinda Bauer, as the kind of glamorous newspaper reporter who paces when she talks, tosses her hair a lot and never takes notes.

The film's only suspenseful episode finds Father Koesler alone in a house with the killer, though it would be physically impossible to direct such a sequence *without* a nerve-tingling frisson or two. ("The Rosary Murders" was directed by Fred Walton, who co-wrote the screenplay.) There is also a little inadvertent humor in the scene that has Father Koesler interrogating a nun who has taken a vow of silence, as she passes notes to him in the confessional. His questions are about the fate of a teen-age girl, and even the silent nun — who must repeat one of her answers by underlining it a few times — seems stunned at the remarkable slow-wittedness of her interrogator.

JANET MASLIN

1987 Ag 28, C12:3

Uphill Battle

HAMBURGER HILL, directed by John Irvin; written by Jim Carabatsos; director of photography, Peter MacDonald; edited by Peter Tanner; music by Philip Glass; produced by Marcia Nasatir and Mr. Carabatsos; released by Paramount. At Orpheum, Third Ave. and 86th St.; Astor Plaza, Broadway and 44th St.; 34th St. Showplace, between Second and Third Aves.; 84th St. Six, at Broadway; Movie Center 5, 125th St., between Powell and Douglass Blvds. Running time: 94 minutes. This film is rated R.
Languilli.....................................Anthony Barrile
Motown .... Michael Patrick Boatman

Courtney Vance

Washburn	Don Cheadle
Murphy	Michael Dolan
McDaniel	Don James
Frantz	Dylan McDermott
Galvin	M. A. Nickles
Duffy	Harry O'Reilly
Gaigin	Daniel O'Shea
Doc	Courtney Vance
Lieutenant Eden	Tegan West

NO movie is simply what's on the screen. Much of what we see is what we bring into the theater. American critics saw "Platoon" as antiwar. When it was shown at Cannes last year, European critics, especially the French, read it as a glorification of American jingoism.

Some audiences find Stanley Kubrick's "Full Metal Jacket" perfunctory and uncharacterized. Others think it's the most profoundly considered film yet made about the import of Vietnam and all militarism.

I've no doubt that there'll be similarly divergent interpretations of, and opinions about, John Irvin's "Hamburger Hill," a well-made Vietnam War film that narrows its attention to the men of a single platoon in a specific operation. The film opens today at the Astor Plaza and other theaters.

Unlike "Platoon," which does pretty much the same thing, "Hamburger Hill," written by Jim Carabatsos, refuses to put its characters and events into any larger frame. It could have been made a week after the conclusion of the operation it recalls, which is both its strength and weakness, depending on how you look at it.

●

On May 10, 1969, the troops of the 101st Airborne Division began their assault on a hill numbered 937. Ten days later, after huge casualties, the hill was taken. The enemy bunkers were destroyed and the hill was ultimately abandoned. Whether or not the taking of the hill was worth the high price paid for it, the film doesn't say, though, by not taking a position, "Hamburger Hill" may be read in such a way as to seem hawkish.

This, however, is to oversimplify the movie to fit one's own politics. Mr. Irvin and Mr. Carabatsos also make some discomforting points about the antiwar movement at home, which, while directed at the war and political leaders, and not at the men fighting it, did result in ugly experiences for soldiers whose only aim was to survive to come home.

None of the soldiers in "Hamburger Hill" questions what he's

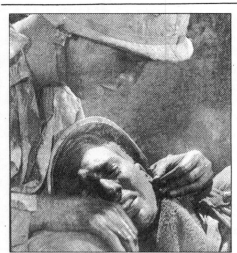

Don McCullin

Combat

Dylan McDermott comforts a wounded comrade, played by Anthony Barrile, in John Irvin's "Hamburger Hill," about a 10-day battle during the Vietnam War.

doing in Vietnam. He's there. That's the only reality that matters. In fear, fatigue and desperation, the men psyche themselves up by repeating, in a kind of auto-brainwashing chorus: "It don't mean a thing. It *don't* mean a *thing!*" The film leaves it up to the audience to decide if the war was, from the start, disastrous and futile, or if it was sabotaged by those same bleeding-heart liberals who figure so prominently in the oeuvre of Sylvester Stallone.

"Hamburger Hill" is most effective as a physical re-creation of the sights and sounds of the battle of Hill 937. The movie was made with the Defense Department's full cooperation, which isn't obtained easily (and certainly not for antiwar films), as well as the Defense Department of the Philippines. Mr. Irvin has had to work hard to resist the temptation to use these resources to create a film so.spectacular, so arresting to look at, that its abstract visual beauty would overwhelm the brutal truth of the combat.

He succeeds, but it couldn't have been easy. Not since "Apocalyse Now," which functions on a surreal level far beyond the reach of "Hamburger Hill," has there been spectacle to equal the scenes showing the dropping of phosphorus bombs in the jungle. What a great Fourth of July! As if to balance the seductiveness of this awesome pyrotechnical display (which is also a part of war), Mr. Irvin doesn't spare the audience shots of soldiers with heads blown off, guts spilling out and arms shot away. In effect, he's saying grimly: "Some glory. Some Fourth of July."

•

The film is far less effective as personal drama. In attempting to avoid stereotypes, "Hamburger Hill" winds up with the members of its platoon being largely interchangeable, which isn't helped by the casting of actors who tend to look so alike that it's difficult to tell one man from another. The characters' idiosyncracies are mostly small. They blend together. This may be realism of a sort, but it also has the effect of denying each man his eccentric due as well as his heroism.

As he has already demonstrated in such different sorts of films as "The Dogs of War" and "Turtle Diary," Mr. Irvin is an excellent director of actors. However he does it, they appear to respond to him. It's not that the actors don't know what they're doing here, but that the material is too self-effacing for the actors' own good.

Two actors who do have good material, and make the most of it, are Courtney Vance, as the platoon's snappish, highly articulate medic, and Dylan McDermott, as the platoon's exhausted sergeant. Mr. Vance is particularly fine. The narrative picks up weight and momentum every time he comes on the screen. Also good is Tegan West, who plays yet another young, raw lieutenant who must depend on the patience of his men. This may be at least partially because the role has become such a familiar, thankless one that any variation is welcome.

VINCENT CANBY.

1987 Ag 28, C16:5

Dry Spy

THE FOURTH PROTOCOL, directed by John Mackenzie; screenplay by Frederick Forsyth; director of photography, Phil Meheux; edited by Graham Walker; music by Lalo Schifrin; produced by Timothy Burrill; released by Lorimar Motion Pictures. At Coronet, Third Avenue at 59th Street; Waverly Twin, Avenue of the Americas at West Third Street; Ziegfeld, 54th Street near Avenue of the Americas. Running time: 120 minutes. This film is rated R.

John Preston	Michael Caine
Petrofsky	Pierce Brosnan
Vassilieva	Joanna Cassidy
Borisov	Ned Beatty
Brian Harcourt-Smith	Julian Glover
Sir Bernard Hemmings	Michael Gough
General Karpov	Ray McAnally
Sir Nigel Irvine	Ian Richardson
George Berenson	Anton Rodgers

By JANET MASLIN

IT might reasonably be expected that the sight of two Soviet spies assembling a nuclear device, which they plan to detonate near an American Air Force base in Britain to fake an accident that could destroy NATO, would be more than a little chilling. But in "The Fourth Protocol," which opens today at the Ziegfeld and other theaters, even the threat of Armageddon has a business-as-usual air. Espionage stories as crisp as this one have a way of finding exceptional fascination in the ordinary, but in the process they may reduce the unimaginable to its nuts and bolts. So the spies constructing the bomb go about their work with the solemn intensity of Maytag repairmen — nothing more, nothing less.

"The Fourth Protocol" has a screenplay by Frederick Forsyth, adapting his best-selling novel into a coolly efficient thriller with an octo-

Michael Caine

pus of a plot. It was directed by John Mackenzie ("The Long Good Friday"), who knows how to strike a note of drily controlled understatement and tell a convoluted story well. The plot concerns a decent and dependable British agent named John Preston (played by Michael Caine, himself the very embodiment of competence), who is first seen helping to entrap a double agent operating within the British foreign service. Later on, after Preston irritates his superiors enough to find himself transferred to a different department, it involves him in a race to thwart the bomb-wielding Soviet spies.

The principal spy is played by Pierce Brosnan, an odd choice for the role. Mr. Brosnan's good looks convey the proper dash — there's always a lock of hair draped charmingly across his forehead, and the cornflower-colored car he drives goes nicely with his eyes — but these just aren't looks that could kill. Yet he is cast as the ruthless and weirdly repressed Major Petrofsky, whose mission it is to move to an apartment right beside that American air base and create the above-mentioned stir. Another plot tentacle involves the internecine K.G.B. maneuverings that have helped send Petrofsky to Britain in the first place.

•

While it isn't possible to care any more about the film's many characters than they do about one another, there's a lot to like about the actors themselves. The credits list 64 speaking roles, and a great many of them are memorable. As the double agent whom Preston stalks early in the story (staging a burglary in the man's house and then trailing him to a pizza restaurant, where classified documents are concealed in the take-out boxes), Anton Rodgers passes convincingly from vast confidence to utter humiliation; Ian Richardson is supremely icy as the agent who traps and interrogates him. The robustly beautiful Joanna Cassidy has a thankless but attention-getting role. And Ray McAnally is subtle and shrewd as a Soviet general well versed in bending other Soviet generals to his will. It's one of the film's wittier touches to cast distinctly non-Soviet types in these roles (Ned Beatty plays another) and let them speak with twangy American accents.

"The Fourth Protocol" is an entertaining, better-than-average variation on a format that has long since

stopped offering anything new. Mr. Mackenzie's direction is economical and tight, but there's only so much that he can do. Pacing a story like this one means busily intercutting the various plot strands and pausing, every so often, for the obligatory blood on the snow. Beyond these carefully spaced flare-ups, the surprise is minimal, the suspense controlled and the threat of violence never very real.

1987 Ag 28, C19:1

HOUSE II: THE SECOND STORY, written and directed by Ethan Wiley; director of photography, Mac Ahlberg; edited by Marty Nicholson; produced by Sean S. Cunningham; released by New World Pictures. At Warner, Broadway at 43d Street; Orpheum, 86th Street at Third Avenue; Columbia Cinema, Broadway at 103rd Street; Movie Center 5, 125th Street between Powell and Douglass Boulevards; Coliseum Twin, Broadway at 181st Street. Running time: 88 minutes. This film is rated PG-13.

Jesse	Arye Gross
Charlie	Jonathan Stark
Gramps	Royal Dano
John	Bill Maher
Bill	John Ratzenberger
Kate	Lar Park Lincoln
Lana	Amy Yasbeck

By JANET MASLIN

"Say, honey, did you hear a noise in the attic?" "House II: The Second Story" might be expected to be that kind of film, but it's not.

Nor is it even much like the original "House," which was funnier and more whimsical than run-of-the-mill horror quickies and also managed to make a little sense. "House II," written and directed by Ethan Wiley, is unapologetically silly right from the start, with an opening sequence about a baby who is given away by his parents; after which the parents are murdered by a ghost. And what does this prologue have to do with the rest of the story? Practically nothing.

The baby does reappear, having grown up to be Jesse McLaughlin (Arye Gross, who was the life of the party in "Soul Man" but has little to do here). And he is seen driving up to the house in which the earlier action took place, a monstrous stone·pile that bears no resemblance to the house in the earlier film (the two stories are not connected). After this, there is not a line of dialogue to explain what Jesse and his girlfriend are doing there, whether they're really moving in or just visiting, or whether they plan to stay.

In any case, they do stick around, and the action gets goofier as it goes along. In short order, Jesse and a friend have dug· up the grave of Jesse's great-great-grandfather in their search for a magical artifact, and resurrected the old man (Royal Dano) in the process. Bored after 70-odd years in seclusion, he wants to party. Meanwhile, Jesse finds a rain forest in an upstairs room, does battle with a dinosaur and brings home a baby pterodactyl as a pet. Some friends from the music business arrive in search of a recording contract. Someone holds a Halloween party, at which Jesse's mummy of a great-grandfather fits in just fine. Every now and then a specter does rear its head, but this isn't a true horror film at all.

It means to be funny, with a cast including several talented young comedians (among them Bill Maher, as a record business exectuvie), but it's not. John Ratzenberger of "Cheers" has one of the film's few amusing sequences when, in the role of an electrician, he arrives to solve the house's

John Ratzenberger in "House II: The Second Story."

many problems. "Looks like you've got some kinda alternate universe in there or something," he remarks, peering through a huge hole in the wall.

"House II" opened yesterday at a number of theaters, including the newly refurbished Warner theater, where the day's first show began half an hour late. The reason, patrons were told if they asked, was that some trailers were being spliced onto the film, and one of those trailers turned out to be for "House II" itself. It presented all of the so-called highlights, making the film itself an afterthought. At best.

•

"House II" is rated PG-13 ("Special Parental Guidance Suggested for Children Under 13.") It includes some violence and rude language.

1987 Ag 29, 11:1

Jazz Master

SONNY ROLLINS: SAXOPHONE COLOSSUS, produced and directed by Robert Mugge. At the Bleecker Street Cinema, 144 Bleecker Street, as part of the Greenwich Village Jazz Festival. Running time: 101 minutes.

By JON PARELES

"SONNY ROLLINS: SAXOPHONE COLOSSUS," which has its New York premiere today at the Bleecker Street Cinema, is a sandwich of two documentaries, neither related to the classic 1956 album "Saxophone Colossus."

One is a performance from Saugerties, N.Y., from August 1986 that's interspersed with bits of biography and comment from Mr. Rollins, his wife, Lucille, and three jazz critics. The second is a full-length premiere, in Tokyo, of a Concerto for Tenor Saxophone and Orchestra, with themes and solos by Mr. Rollins and orchestrations by Heikki Sarmanto, who conducts the Yomiuri Symphony Orchestra. Together, the film offers plenty of Mr. Rollins's ebullient, sardonic, warmhearted, virtuosic saxo-

phone playing, in contexts that are by turns congenial and, unfortunately, fairly stilted.

Since the 1950's, Mr. Rollins has been acclaimed as one of jazz's greatest improvisers; when he's good, he's remarkable. He can spin out chorus upon chorus with a combination of logic, wit, ambition, dizzying speed and self-imposed challenges.

The film starts with one of those solos, a 15-minute tour de force on "G-Man"; Mr. Rollins touches down on the tune's riff now and then, only to spring further and higher each time. He alludes to basic blues; he builds far-flung harmonic sequences; he breaks into hyper-speed melodies; he sustains notes until they seem about to burst.

•

But the rest of the film can't match that momentum. When he speaks, Mr. Rollins is thoughtful, downright modest: "I'm always trying to improve myself," he says. Mr. Rollins and the critics sketch a biography; there are more selections from the Saugerties concert, including one in which Mr. Rollins jumps from the stage and, we find out later, fractures a heel. And there's a brilliant clip from 1963, with a Rollins quartet that was pushing be-bop to its limits, that makes a viewer long for more archival Rollins.

Instead, there's the saxophone concerto, not one of Mr. Rollins's better vehicles. It's a pastiche of Rollins themes, Tchaikovsky and Copland that evokes Hollywood soundtrack music. Mr. Rollins pours out notes and figurations, but he fights a losing

David Gahr
Sonny Rollins

battle against the orchestral clichés. And the film's director and producer, Robert Mugge, breaks up the music's momentum by separating the movements with interviews and mixing performance footage with a Tokyo travelogue, as if he's never seen an electronic billboard before.

"Saxophone Colossus" isn't the definitive Rollins film, but there's enough music to show why Mr. Rollins belongs in the jazz pantheon.

1987 S 1, C14:4

Banality of Evil

FLAMES IN THE ASHES, directed by Haim Guri and Jacquot Erlich for the Ghetto Fighters' House; in Yiddish and Hebrew with English subtitles; produced by Monia Avrahami. At Film Forum 1, 57 Watts Street. Running time: 90 minutes. This film has no rating.

By JANET MASLIN

THE Holocaust engendered forms of courage that are not easily documented or understood. As one voice asks in "Flames in the Ashes," which opens today at Film Forum 1, "Who is more heroic, one who goes in the woods to fight with a gun or one who decides to go that last road and die with his family?"

This film, part of an Israeli-produced trilogy, examines Jewish resistance in all its many forms. It does this by going right to the source, employing original footage of the ordinary events of the Holocaust, if the word ordinary can be used at all. These glimpses, drawn from rare archival footage (mostly taken by Germans, a closing title notes), are enormously affecting for their very unremarkableness. To see a group of Jews being calmly evacuated from their village, ushered by businesslike German guards and trailed by a few family dogs, is to understand a great deal about how rarely Jewish resistance blossomed and how miraculous it was when it did.

Like Lucy Dawidowicz's seminal book "The War Against the Jews 1933-1945" (1975), "Flames in the Ashes" places the ostensible lack of resistance in a much larger context. The off-camera voices of survivors attest to the victims' inability to comprehend the full extent of their plight. "What relationship is there between these events and an ordinary, normal human life?" one speaker asks. The film also documents the prisoners' feelings of guilt and helplessness, the eagerness of some to trust their captors and hope for the best, their worries of reprisals against family members and their fears of the community at large. "We were more afraid of the Poles than of the Germans," says one. As another puts it: "We were the loneliest people in the world."

•

The role played by the camera itself is all too apparent in the downcast, humiliated faces of well-dressed prisoners — perhaps only recently captured — who must endure its unwelcome gaze. Some of the other footage looks surprisingly undramatic, though, with people seen boarding the trains almost as if they were leaving for long, peaceful vacations. The film is especially successful in bringing home the human cost of this unimaginable horror, of turning the faceless, numberless victims into neighbors, relatives and friends. Without dwelling unduly on the confiscated snapshots of victims in happier times, the film makers convey a strong sense of the everyday lives that were interrupted.

"Flames in the Ashes" was made by Haim Guri and Jacquot Erlich for the Ghetto Fighters' House, as a companion to "The 81st Blow" and "The Last Sea," two of their other films. While by no means a seamless or polished documentary, it is one with a great sense of urgency. And when at long last it chronicles the emergence of organized Jewish resistance ("I became an animal — all I wanted was revenge," one voice says), it takes on

a note of triumph. As the faces of the young men and women who fought are seen on the screen, the words of a poem ("Testament") by Rachel Auerbachk are heard: "Let us not mourn them, but love them as though they were among us."

1987 S 2, C22:5

Mal Appétit

BUFFET FROID, directed and written (in French with English subtitles) by Bertrand Blier; photography by Jean Penzer; edited by Claudine Merlin; music by Johannes Brahms; produced by Alain Sarde; a Sara Films/Antenne 2 co-production; released by Interama. At Public Theater, 425 Lafayette Street. Running time: 95 minutes. This film has no rating.

Alphonse Tram.....................Gérard Depardieu
Inspector ....Bernard Blier
Murderer ....Jean Carmet
Widow ....Geneviève Page
Accountant ....Michel Serrault
WITH: Dénise Gence, Carole Bouquet, Jean Benguigui and Jean Rougerie

By VINCENT CANBY

IN "Buffet Froid" ("Cold Cuts"), his 1980 French film opening today at the Public Theater, Bertrand Blier ("Get Out Your Handkerchiefs," "Ménage") makes a fatal mistake. "Buffet Froid" is an absurdist comedy that is less meaningless and less irrational than fashionably foolish.

It begins well. In fact, it begins a little like Edward Albee's short classic, "Zoo Story": late at night, on the nearly empty platform of the spankingly clean Paris Metro, a possibly homicidal bum (Gérard Depardieu) approaches a dapper, middle-aged man (played by Michel Serrault, who's unbilled in the cast) and attempts to engage him in conversation.

The man does not want to talk. "You look like an accountant," says the bum, whose name is Alphonse Tram. "I *am* an accountant," says the man. Alphonse says he wants company. The man says that he doesn't. Alphonse produces a knife, which subsequently disappears. The man finally escapes the sycophantic, menacing Alphonse by jumping on a train as the doors are closing.

Sometime later Alphonse discovers the man lying in the passageway of another Metro station, dying, with Alphonse's knife sticking out of his stomach. The two men continue to argue. Before expiring, the man gives Alphonse his money, saying something to the effect that Alphonse might as well have it.

•

Alphonse goes home to his wife, with whom he lives in a brand-new Paris apartment building. They are, as yet, the only tenants. "How was your day?" asks his wife. "Nothing special," says Alphonse, who reports the encounter with the now-dead accountant. His wife agrees that it's just one of those things and puts Alphonse's bloody knife into the dishwasher.

"Buffet Froid" unravels still more absurdities, more meaningless encounters and more murders, all treated with the same straight face that tells us that the only logic is illogic and (I'm afraid) that we're all beyond feeling. The characters speak of having nightmares, but Mr. Blier clearly believes life is such a nightmare that no one can tell the difference anymore. Unlike Luis Buñuel, especially in his "Discreet Charm of the Bourgeoisie," Mr. Blier finds no redeeming, illuminating humor in the situation. "Buffet Froid" is awfully glum.

Mr. Depardieu, the most engagingly ambivalent presence in the modern cinema, gives "Buffet Froid" an import not really justified by Mr. Blier's material. The other lost souls he encounters are played by the director's actor-father, Bernard Blier (as a police inspector who believes that a murderer is less dangerous out of prison than in); Jean Carmet, as a shy murderer of women (whose whimpers remind him of birdsong in the country), and Geneviève Page, as a happy widow.

"Buffet Froid" is well titled. It's a meal composed entirely of side-dishes. There's no main course, and when the meal is over, you're still waiting for something serious to eat. The movie is a collection of random sketches in the service of no dominant idea.

There are some wonderfully absurdist moments in Mr. Blier's farce "Ménage," including a scene in which a pair of rich, bored Parisians help the burglars who are ransacking their apartment, but "Ménage" is more truly absurdist when its characters think they're being most logical. The people played by Mr. Depardieu, Mr. Blier and Mr. Carmet in "Buffet Froid" aren't especially logical, and they're too self-aware and too inclined to self-pity to be either believable or funny.

1987 S 4, C5:4

Tripe à la Mode

BLOOD DINER, direction and screenplay by Jackie Kong; director of photography, Jurg Walther; edited by Thomas Meshelski; music by Don Preston; production designer, Ron Petersen; produced by Jimmy Maslon; released by Lightning Pictures. At Eighth Street Playhouse, at Avenue of the Americas. Running time: 90 minutes. This film has no rating.

Michael Tutman	Rick Burks
George Tutman	Carl Crew
Mark Shepard	Roger Dauer
Sheba Jackson	LaNette La France
Connie Stanton	Lisa Guggenheim
Chief Miller	Max Morris
Little Michael	Roxanne Cybelle

By CARYN JAMES

THE only question worth asking about "Blood Diner" is: How bad can an exploitation movie be and still get released in theaters? The story is dim-witted enough. Two brothers retrieve their demented uncle's brain from the grave and follow its command: get body parts from various women and stitch them together into one body that an evil goddess can inhabit. The brothers own a restaurant, so the spare parts get put in the stew.

Don't think for a second, though, that "Blood Diner," which opens today at the Eighth Street Playhouse, is at all similar to "Eating Raoul" or any other real movie. It pretends to have a comic plot, but that's just a shabby excuse for the brothers to hack up naked women. The production is conspicuously low-budget, and the dubbing, lighting and continuity are pathetically amateurish, but none of that matters. This is not a real movie; it's celluloid swill.

1987 S 4, C6:5

Soul Music

A BROTHER WITH PERFECT TIMING, directed by Chris Austin; with Abdullah Ibrahim and Ekaya; at the Bleecker Street Cinema, 144 Bleecker Street, as part of the theater's Jazz Film Series. Running time: 90 minutes. This film has no rating.

By JON PARELES

WHEN he left South Africa in the 1960's, Abdullah Ibrahim took Cape Town with him. The city's mixture of African, Arabic, Oriental and European cultures echoes in the music he writes for his septet, Ekaya; there are spirituals, slow-rolling South African marabi rhythms, American jazz (especially Thelonious Monk and Duke Ellington), African traditional melodies, even the samba rhythms that Mr. Ibrahim traces to Africa.

In "A Brother With Perfect Timing," Mr. Ibrahim — a dignified, almost solemn figure at the piano — reveals himself as a casually charismatic storyteller, serious but never pompous. "This film is not a biography," the opening titles declare, after they give the salient dates in Mr. Ibrahim's story. It is, instead, an articulate, self-told portrait, echoed in music from Ekaya, his band of saxophones, brass and rhythm section.

●

Mr. Ibrahim recalls his childhood, talks about the traditional underpinnings of his music and a few of its spiritual implications, explains a little of the thought behind titles like "Tuan Guru" (an exiled Indonesian Moslem teacher) and "Water From an Ancient Well," and denounces apartheid with quiet determination: "We have to get this revolution done and finished." He also tells a joke or two. And without meaning to show off, he demonstrates parts of his music he doesn't show in concert — singing a North African song, for instance, as he drums cross-rhythms on his thighs.

Occasionally, the film visualizes Mr. Ibrahim's reminiscences, showing a boy and a young man in Cape Town itself, with a sense of understatement that just narrowly avoids looking arty or presumptuous. But for the most part, Mr. Ibrahim and his music are sufficient to give a well-rounded view of a musician for whom exile means both pain and inspiration.

"A Brother With Perfect Timing" will be shown today and Thursday at the Bleecker Street Cinema.

1987 S 4, C8:4

ERNIE ANDREWS: BLUES FOR CENTRAL AVENUE, produced and directed by Lois Shelton. With Ernie Andrews, Dolores Andrews, Buddy Collette, Harry (Sweets) Edison and others. Running time: 50 minutes. At the Bleecker Street Cinema, 144 Bleecker Street, as part of the theater's Jazz Film series. This film has no rating.

By JON PARELES

"The record shows I stood the blows," says Ernie Andrews, the blues singer, who tells his own story in "Ernie Andrews: Blues for Central Avenue," playing at the Bleecker Street Cinema as part of the Jazz Film series there. Central Avenue is where jazz sizzled in Los Angeles in the 1930's and 40's. Mr. Andrews, and others who were there, reminisce about big bands, after-hours clubs,

gambling, bathtub gin and the segregation that was a fact of life. There's plenty of nostalgia, but there's also the kind of gritty detail that's left out of too many jazz memoirs.

On Central Avenue, where there are now vacant lots and buildings for sale, there were jazz clubs such as the Club Alabam, Brothers and the Gayety Jungle Room. Stepin Fetchit, one habitué recalls, used to drive up to the door of a club with a train of six Cadillacs in various colors; another recalls that Don Robey, owner of Duke Records, would leave when he lost too much at gambling, fly to Texas for more money, and come

Ernie Andrews

back to a game still in progress.

Mr. Andrews, who was born in 1930, made his first hit while still in high school — and his last, "Don't Let the Sun Catch You Cryin'," while still in his teens. He sang with the bands led by Andy Kirk, Benny Carter and, in the 1950's, Harry James, but his career waned after World War II. Like many other singers, he had also signed a recording contract he came to regret. As he talks about his reversals, and as he sings the blues in recent performances, the pain in his eyes is unmistakable. But his voice still trumpets his vitality.

●

Sharing the bill at the Bleecker Street Cinema are two shorter blues films. "An American Songster: John Jackson" is an easygoing, 30-minute profile of Mr. Jackson, a country-blues singer who was discovered at a gas station in Fairfax, Va., playing fingerpicking Piedmont blues. Michelle Paymar and Roberta Grossman's 23-minute "Sippie" is about Sippie Wallace, the salty urban blues singer and songwriter known as the "Texas Nightingale," who first recorded in 1923.

1987 S 5, 11:1

House of Cards

FAMILY BUSINESS, direction and screenplay by Costa-Gavras, from the book by Francis Ryck; in French with English subtitles; director of cinematography, Robert Alazraki; edited by Marie-Sophie Dubus; music by George Delerue; art direction by Eric Simon; produced by Michele Ray-Gavras; released by European Classics. At Cinema 2, Third Avenue at 60th Street. Running time: 98 minutes. This film has no rating.

The Father	Johnny Hallyday
The Mother	Fanny Ardant
Faucon	Guy Marchand
Francois 1	Laurent Romor
Francois 2	Remi Martin
Martine 1	Juliette Rennes
Martine 2	Caroline Pochon

By VINCENT CANBY

COSTA-GAVRAS, the Greek-born French director, makes political thrillers of more effective style than anyone else at work today. Helping himself to dark chapters from contemporary history, he simplifies facts and shapes events to his own ends. He constructs movies that seethe with passion in the cause of justice and, incidentally, are whopping good suspense-melodramas, which is what most outrages those critics who stand to his political right. Nobody would give a hoot about the politics of such movies as "State of Siege" and "Missing" if they weren't so bloody entertaining.

Like many artists who excel in one field, Mr. Costa-Gavras longs to do other things. In 1980 he explored existential, romantic angst in "Clair de Femme," in which Romy Schneider and Yves Montand smiled at each other a lot, in elegant sets, and discussed the impossibility of love in fruity aphorisms. It was a disaster of hilarious proportions.

"Family Business," opening today at the Cinema 2, is something of an improvement. It's not an outright disaster; it's a cheerless bore.

The film is a comedy-drama about an upwardly aspiring middle-class family of burglars. Dad (Johnny Hallyday) and his best friend Faucon (Guy Marchand) go about their business of breaking and entering and cracking safes with the dedication of skilled performers. Mom (Fanny Ardant) explains to her young son that Dad and Faucon are like acrobats who "work without an audience and no net."

As the boy, François, grows into his teens, he longs to join the family business. Mom and Dad won't hear of it. François threatens to go to the cops. Mom and Dad care less about the boy's blackmailing tactics than his eagerness to learn. François goes on to become something of a star safecracker. The family buys a house on the Riviera. Mom gets her longed-for cello.

●

That's more or less the central situation of "Family Business," which fails not because of its mixture of comedy and melodrama but because Mr. Costa-Gavras hasn't made up his mind what the movie is about, and the characters in his screenplay aren't strong enough to point the way. Nothing much is made of the fact that Mom has married beneath her — she comes from the landed aristocracy — and drinks too much (out of worry and fret) or that Dad rather ruthlessly sabotages poor Faucon's desire to have a family of his own.

The characters are as dimly seen as the twilight world they inhabit. The movie might have been funnier and more dramatic if Dad had been a successful, non-union plumber.

The actors bring nothing to their roles. Mr. Hallyday, best known as a popular singer, registers as a cypher. Miss Ardant works hard to create a character out of thin air, as does Mr. Marchand (so fine as the chauvinist husband in "Entre Nous"), but they are utterly lost in the clutter of a kind of fiction for which Mr. Costa-Gavras has no talent whatsoever.

1987 S 6, 66:2

Johnny Hallyday as Dad in "Family Business."

THE RETURN OF RUBEN BLADES, produced and directed by Robert Mugge. With Rubén Blades and Seis del Solar, and Linda Ronstadt. At the Bleecker Street Cinema, 144 Bleecker Street, as part of its Jazz Film series. A Mug-Shot Production, in association with Channel Four (U.K.). Running time: 82 minutes. This film has no rating.

By JON PARELES

Rubén Blades, more than most popular singers, is a public, political figure. His lyrics are addressed to all of Latin America, urging self-determination and an end to outside intervention; his ambitions, as he says in a careful statement during the film "The Return of Rubén Blades," showing tonight at the Bleecker Street Cinema, might well encompass running for "the highest office" in his native Panama. They also involve reaching past the Spanish-speaking salsa audience to North America and beyond, but doing so on Mr. Blades's own terms — not an easy proposition.

On and off stage, Mr. Blades is articulate and even literary; he is also thoroughly politic, measuring almost every statement. And because the documentary is strictly present-tense, there's little sense of where Mr. Blades's music and his convictions came from, beyond his reminiscences of the United States presence on the Panama Canal.

"The Return of Rubén Blades" follows the singer to Harvard, where he gets his master's degree in international law; to his old neighborhood in Panama; to California for a recording session with Linda Ronstadt, and to New York for a performance at S.O.B.'s. The music is a joy, as danceable as it is intelligent, and Mr. Blades makes every nuance count; he's sly for the picaresque story of "Pedro Navaja," earnest for the pan-American anthems "Muevete" ("Move It," a tune by Los Van Van, a Cuban band, with new anti-apartheid lyrics by Mr. Blades) and "Buscando América" ("Searching for America"). Seis del Solar, Mr. Blades's band, mixes salsa, jazz and electronic

keyboards; at one point, Mr. Blades scat-sings a trombone-like solo, perhaps a token of his old connection with Willie Colón's band.

"The Return of Rubén Blades" captures Mr. Blades's charisma and his sincere engagement with issues outside music. But in taking him solely at face value, it misses the chance to explore issues raised by Mr. Blades's music and his career. The other film on the Bleecker Street bill, "Machito: A L ," provides some of th . Blades's modern music.

1987 S 7, 9:3

A Conversion

GOSPEL ACCORDING TO AL GREEN. Written, directed and produced by Robert Mugge. With Al Green, Willie Mitchell, Ken Tucker. Running time: 94 minutes. At the Bleecker Street Cinema, 144 Bleecker Street, as part of the Jazz Film series. This film has no rating.

By JON PARELES

ONE night after a concert at Disneyland, the soul singer Al Green had a conversion experience. He woke up in his hotel room, feeling as he never had before or since, shouting "Hallelujah!" Over the next two years, he vacillated between what he calls "a million-dollar career" and his calling to sing gospel music. After a spurned lover dumped boiling grits on him and then shot herself, Mr. Green bought himself the Full Gospel Tabernacle Church in Memphis, gave up his secular love songs and turned to the gospel full-time.

That's the story behind "Gospel According to Al Green," a documentary now playing at the Bleecker Street Cinema as part of the Jazz Film series. Robert Mugge's handsome film presents Mr. Green's inspired singing and lets him explain just why he's performing "Amazing Grace" instead of "Can't Get Next to You."

Mr. Green and Willie Mitchell, who produced Mr. Green's early-1970's soul hits, both recall the singer's early triumphs. Mr. Mitchell shows the studio where they worked and explains how one of Mr. Green's best songs, "Let's Stay Together," was recorded with an in-studio audience of local "winos." He seems disappointed that Mr. Green left secular music behind.

•

"If I must set it down — my career and the money and the popularity and the ladies — then I will," Mr. Green muses. Guitar in hand, he also talks about his early career, the incidents that changed his life and his ambitions. "I shall be one of the greatest evangelists in the world — in the world!"

Along with the on-camera interview, a performance on an intimate scale, the documentary presents Mr. Green at work, in a fine concert at an Air Force base and, even better, preaching from the pulpit in Memphis. At the base, where Mr. Green tells the audience, "Even the commanding officers here have a commanding officer," feet tap and women scream. And at his church, where he delivers a sermon that's one long crescendo, listeners clap, cry and dance as they get the spirit.

Throughout the film, there is extraordinary singing and performing; Mr. Green now puts the Memphis soul grooves he made with Willie Mitchell

Al Green in "Gospel According to Al Green."

at the service of traditional gospel songs. As Mr. Green, now a minister, explains, he also took "the ingenuity, the class, the charisma, the steps, the movement, the hesitation, the way to be curious" from his days as a rock performer. And his effect on listeners hasn't changed much from his soul-music days. "Gospel According to Al Green" captures his full wattage — and that's saying a lot.

1987 S 9, C18:5

Massacre in Lebanon

DEADLINE, directed by Nathaniel Gutman; story and screenplay by Hanan Peled; directors of photography, Amnon Salomon and Thomas Mauch; edited by Peter Przygodda; produced by Elisabeth Wolters-Alfs; released by Skouras Pictures. At Eastside Cinema, Third Avenue at 55th Street; U. A. East, 85th Street at First Avenue; Eighth Street Playhouse, near Avenue of the Americas. Running time: 99 minutes. This film is rated R.

Don Stevens	Christopher Walken
Linda Larson	Marita Marschall
Mike Jessop	Hywel Bennett
Hamdi Abu-Yussuf	Arnon Zadok
Yessin Abu-Riadd	Amos Lavie
Samira	Ette Ankri
Bernard	Martin Umbach
Abdul	Moshe Ivgi
Bassam	Sason Gabay
Habib	Shahar Cohen

"DEADLINE," which opens today at the Eastside Cinema and other theaters, is a singularly inept attempt to make dramatic and political sense of the war in Beirut. Set in the Lebanese capital in 1983, "Deadline" stars Christopher Walken as Don Stevens, who's a supposedly hot-shot American television journalist, though he's not above borrowing material from other reporters.

Nathaniel Gutman, the director, and Hanan Peled, who wrote the screenplay, see the war as a confrontation between the extremist factions of the Palestine Liberation Organization and the Christian Phalangists, with the moderate Israelis caught in between. The film was shot in Jaffa, Israel, and concludes with the massacre of civilians in the Palestinian refugee camps by the Phalangists.

According to the screenplay, Don Stevens, who's learned of the coming massacre, warns the Israelis, but too late for them to stop the terrible events, though they try. The way the movie presents the Israeli forces —

they look like a rather large body of concerned archeologists — they wouldn't have been able to alter the course of history anyway.

The film is a mess.

VINCENT CANBY

1987 S 11, C4:4

Gender Swap

HE'S MY GIRL, directed by Gabrielle Beaumont; screenplay by Taylor Ames and Charles F. Bohl; director of photography, Peter Lyons Collister; edited by Roy Watts; production manager, Fred Wardell; produced by Lawrence Taylor Mortorff and Angela Schaprio; released by Scotti Brothers Pictures Inc. At Cine 42, 216 West 42d Street, and Cine 1, Seventh Avenue and 48th Street. Running time: 104 minutes. This film is rated PG-13.

Reggie/Regina	T. K. Carter
Bryan	David Hallyday
Tasha	Misha McK
Lisa	Jennifer Tilly
Simon Sledge	Warwick Sims
Mason Morgan	David Clennon
Sally	Monica Parker

T.K. CARTER has nice legs, which is a lucky thing because they come in handy for his starring role in "He's My Girl." Mr. Carter plays Reggie, the best friend and would-be manager of an aspiring singer named Bryan (David Hallyday). Reggie enters Bryan's name in a contest being held by an MTV-like video station and they win, but there's a catch — Bryan must be accompanied on his free trip to Hollywood by a female date. Bingo! Arriving at the airport in Los Angeles are smallish blond Bryan and Regina, the towering, outspoken black woman who is Reggie's new alter ego. This is hardly the small-town Missouri couple that the video station had in mind.

It must have taken monumental energy to keep the subsequent action going for an hour and three-quarters; certainly it takes monumental stupidity on the part of other characters, who are never allowed to guess what Reggie is up to. Tasha (Misha McK), who works for the video station, likes Reggie but thinks he may be two-timing her with her new friend Regina, for example. Mason (David Clennon) from the video station thinks Regina is a hot number. Regina must fend off the Swedish beautician who wants to remove that little moustache. There's more along these lines.

"He's My Girl" is at least made relatively painless by Mr. Carter, who is happily overconfident and even convincing in his role. Beyond that, the film has little to recommend it. Mr. Hallyday (son of the French singing stars Johnny Hallyday and Sylvie Vartan) is pleasant but unremarkable in a non-written role; as Bryan's new girlfriend, Jennifer Tilly looks like a Modigliani but speaks in an itty-bitty voice that gets irritating; Miss McK, who has experience in soap operas and commercials, smiles much too tirelessly. Gabrielle Beaumont, the director, has a predictable sitcom style but not a polished one.

"He's My Girl" opens today at the Cine 42 and Cine 48, no doubt making only a brief pit stop before heading off for the home-video horizon. It concludes with a particularly dumb set of titles making non-funny jokes about what became of the various characters after the story ended.

•

"He's My Girl" is rated PG-13 ("Special Parental Guidance Suggested for Those Younger Than 13"). It contains brief nudity and occasional strong language.

JANET MASLIN

1987 S 11, C5:1

A 'Person Friday'

I'VE HEARD THE MERMAIDS SINGING, directed, written and edited by Patricia Rozema; produced by Miss Rozema and Alexandra Raffe; director of photography, Douglas Koch; music by Mark Korven; released by Miramax Films. At 68th Street Playhouse, at Third Avenue. Running time: 81 minutes. This film has no rating.

Polly Vandersma .... Sheila McCarthy
Gabrielle St.-Peres .... Paule Baillargeon
Mary Joseph .... Ann-Marie McDonald
Warren .... John Evans
Japanese Waitress .... Brenda Kamino
Critic .... Richard Monette

IN its opening scenes, Patricia Rozema's "I've Heard the Mermaids Singing" displays a certain amount of engaging whimsy. Polly Vandersma places herself in front of a home-video camera to tell us her story. Polly is 31 years old, a self-described "person Friday" who's been called "organizationally impaired" by the agency that finds her employment as a "temp." Polly can't type. Her mind wanders.

Polly is the sort of young woman whose heart leaps up when she beholds diners through a restaurant window "talking, laughing and interfacing." Sitting in a Japanese restaurant, before a table that's footstool-high, she doesn't know where to put her legs. Polly is innocent beyond belief. Yet she's so slyly and self-mockingly played by Sheila McCarthy, a very good new Canadian actress, that belief is willingly suspended. For about 40 minutes.

Whimsy is unreliable. Like a jolly drunk in a bar, it can turn suddenly aggressive. Very soon Polly's innocence loses its charm, and watching this movie is like being cornered by a whimsical, 500-pound elf.

•

"I've Heard the Mermaids Singing," written, directed and co-produced by Miss Rozema as her first feature, is the story of Polly's increasingly unhappy adventures among a bunch of fraudulent Canadian intellectuals.

Self-effacing, as always, Polly falls in love with Gabrielle (Paule Baillar-

Sheila McCarthy

geon), the beautiful, patrician owner of an art gallery. Gabrielle is amused by Polly and hires her as a permanent assistant, but she's too preoccupied by her own artistic aspirations as well as by another lover (Ann-Marie McDonald) to take Polly seriously.

The movie, which opens today at the 68th Street Playhouse, takes itself more seriously than the screenplay warrants. As it turns out, of course, Polly understands far more about the function and meaning of "art" than Gabrielle and all of her jargon-spouting, art-world pals put together.

Before Miss Rozema's aspirations toward seriousness are clearly and hopelessly evident, "I've Heard the Mermaids Singing" promises a good deal of fun. Miss Rozema has a sense of humor that should be protected. The fact that the film was made on a budget of $262,000 is an accomplishment all by itself. Most of all, though, "I've Heard the Mermaids Singing" is notable for bringing Miss McCarthy to the attention of the movie public. She's a find.

VINCENT CANBY

1987 S 11, C8:1

Welsh Fable

COMING UP ROSES, directed by Stephen Bayly; written (in Welsh with English subtitles) by Ruth Carter; director of photography, Dick Pope; edited by Scott Thomas; music by Michael Storey; designer, Hildegard Bechtler; produced by Linda James; released by Skouras Pictures. At Cinema Studio 2, 66th Street and Broadway. Running time: 90 minutes. This film is rated PG.

Trevor .... Dafydd Hywel
Mona .... Iola Gregory
Gwen .... Olive Michael
June .... Mari Emlyn
Eli Davies .... W. J. Phillips
Dino .... Glan Davies
Sian .... Gillian Elisa Thomas
Dave .... Ifan Huw Dafydd
Pete .... Rowan Griffiths
Mr. Valentine .... Bill Paterson
Councillor .... Clyde Pollitt

By VINCENT CANBY

"COMING UP ROSES," a Welsh film with English subtitles, is a low-key comedy that isn't exactly

at odds with its landscape, the economically depressed town of Aberdare in south Wales, but rather upstaged by it.

With the shutdown of the local coal mine, everyone in Aberdare is either out of a job or about to be. Finance companies are foreclosing on houses, automobiles, furniture and television sets. The last Aberdare theater, the Rex, has been sold, possibly to become a parking lot. Old Mr. Davies, the Rex's longtime manager, is dying even more rapidly than the town. All he looks forward to is a decent funeral and a proper headstone.

On top of everything else, the rain never stops in Aberdare. The damp and the chill are tangible.

Against this convincingly bleak background, Stephen Bayly, the American-born, longtime British resident, who directed the movie, attempts to make something sweetly daffy of the efforts of two former employees of the Rex to protect the theater from demolition and to persuade someone to reopen it.

•

Trevor Jones (Dafydd Hywel), once the Rex's projectionist and now its janitor, and Mona (Iola Gregory), the former usher and candy butcher, are gallant, unlikely saviors. Trevor is so passive and mild-mannered that he spends much of the movie trying to raise money to pay off on the house, telly and motorbike belonging to his former wife and her new boyfriend. Mona, who loves Trevor, attempts to win his heart through his stomach, but she's a notoriously bad cook. People retch at her table. These are funny but very tiny inspirations.

"Coming Up Roses," written by Ruth Carter, possesses more intelligence and sardonic humor than is ever effectively realized on the screen, in part because the director and the writer have so rooted the film in reality that it never takes on a fictional life of its own. The lunatic plan (growing mushrooms in the dark of the Rex) by which Trevor and Mona hope to save their fortunes is far less interesting than what we see happening in Prime Minister Thatcher's Britain outside the theater.

Though all of the performances are good, the characters aren't big or engaging enough to dominate the general gloom. One keeps wanting to see less of the earnestly comic, under-achieving Trevor and Mona and more of what's going on in Wales-at-large. Trevor and Mona are meant to be valiant. In fact, they just get in the way.

•

"Coming Up Roses," which opens today at the Cinema Studio 2, is also somewhat fuzzy in its thinking.

Though it says a lot of disparaging things about television as a substitute for movies, and though we see a video rental store across the street from the Rex, "Coming Up Roses" ignores the economic squeeze put on movie theaters by both television and video. It finds romance in attempts to turn back the clock in a way that both Mr. Bayly and Miss Carter understand to be doomed. After all, "Coming Up Roses" was financed in part by S4C, the Welsh-language television channel.

•

"Coming Up Roses," which has been rated PG ("Parental Guidance Suggested"), includes some mildly vulgar language in the English subtitles.

1987 S 11, C9:1

Dafydd Hywel

The Troubles

A PRAYER FOR THE DYING, directed by Mike Hodges; screenplay by Edmund Ward and Martin Lynch, based on the book by Jack Higgins; director of photography, Mike Garfath; music by Bill Conti; production designer, Evan Hercules; produced by Peter Snell; released by the Samuel Goldwyn Company. At Manhattan Twin, 59th Street east of Third Avenue; Carnegie Hall Cinema, Seventh Avenue and 57th Street; Art Greenwich Twin, 12th Street and Seventh Avenue; 84th Street Six, at Broadway. Running time: 104 minutes. This film is rated R.

Martin Fallon .... Mickey Rourke
Jack Meehan .... Alan Bates
Father Da Costa .... Bob Hoskins
Anna .... Sammi Davis
Billy .... Christopher Fulford
Liam Docherty .... Liam Neeson
Siobhan Donovan .... Alison Doody
Jenny .... Camille Coduri

By JANET MASLIN

THE things that attract attention in "A Prayer for the Dying" are not the things that should. How could a thriller starring Mickey Rourke, Alan Bates and Bob Hoskins so distract its audience with accents, costumes and hairdos that effectively upstage the cast? The most striking aspects of Mr. Rourke's performance (as a reluctant Irish Republican Army terrorist) are the reddish hue of his hair and the harsh brogue, so different from his normally buttery voice that it almost sounds dubbed. Meanwhile, Mr. Hoskins looks equally out of place in a cleric's robes. And Mr. Bates, as a sleek, ruthless gangster, sports hair that grows thicker and darker with each passing year.

"A Prayer for the Dying," which opens today at the Carnegie Hall Cinema and other theaters, has been roundly renounced by some of its participants, but its problems appear to have been built in right from the start. Chief among them is an essentially conventional approach to what might have been an arresting story. Based on the best-seller by Jack Higgins, the film outlines the plight of Martin Fallon (Mr. Rourke), who is seen watching the accidental destruction of a school bus as the film begins. Fallon is a terrorist grown weary of bloodshed, and he flees from Belfast to London as the film begins. He is followed there by two I.R.A. agents assigned either to kill him or to bring him home.

Fallon can obtain a passport from the gangster Jack Meehan (Mr. Bates), but in exchange he must commit one last murder. He is observed

Mickey Rourke

in the act by Father Da Costa (Mr. Hoskins), and Meehan then decrees that Fallon also kill the priest. But Fallon has another idea: he confesses his crime before Father Da Costa can stop him, thus silencing him by taking advantage of the priest's holy vows. Meanwhile, Fallon also becomes involved with the priest's blind, innocent niece, Anna (Sammi Davis), who just loves the way he plays the church organ.

•

"A Prayer for the Dying" was directed by Mike Hodges, better known for such early films as "Get Carter" and "Pulp" than for more recent efforts such as "Flash Gordon." While this film, initially at least, has a brisk style and an edgy rhythm, it becomes ever more sentimental as it goes along. A heavy overlay of Bill Conti's music second-guesses much of the action, and the actors must do things (like Mr. Rourke's romancing the blind niece) that can't even have looked good on the page. The questions of how much terrorism is too much and what a life of violence can do to the soul are never effectively raised as the film deteriorates into a series of unsurprising confrontations.

Even so, the actors seem to enjoy their showy roles, particularly Mr. Bates, whose Meehan dresses nattily and conducts his business out of a funeral home. Capable of unexpected generosity to a little old lady who reminds him of his mother, Meehan can also order the brutal torture of one of his men a moment later, adding, "I want him back at work tomorrow morning." Mr. Bates seems to be enjoying this greatly, and Mr. Hoskins brings his customary conviction to the role of the feisty priest. Only Mr. Rourke, who prowls glumly through the film, seems seriously dispirited — and, like the man he plays, seriously out of place.

1987 S 11, C11:1

Ooze and Glop

THE CURSE, directed by David Keith; written by David Chaskin; director of photography, Robert D. Forges; edited by Claude Kutry; music by John Debney; production designer, Frank Vanorio; produced by Ovidio G. Assonitis; released by Trans World Entertainment. At Criterion, Broadway and 45th Street; Orpheum, Third Avenue at 86th Street; Movie Center Five, 125th Street, between Powell and Douglass Boulevards; Essex, Grand Street, off Essex Street; Nova, Broadway and 147th Street. Running time: 100 minutes. This film is rated R.

Zachary	Wil Wheaton
Nathan Hayes	Claude Akins
Frances	Kathleen Jordan Gregory
Mike	Steve Davis
Alice	Amy Wheaton
Cyrus	Malcolm Danare
Dr. Alan Forbes	Cooper Huckabee
Carl Willis	John Schneider

ON a thundery night in Tellico Plains, Tenn., the sex-hungry wife (Kathleen Jordan Gregory) of a Bible-quoting farmer (Claude Akins) finds what she needs in the arms of a hairy-chested handyman. Before you can say, "Abstain from fleshly lusts," a flaming ball or egg or something falls to earth, contaminates the water, rots fruit, spoils people's complexions and turns chickens and humans homicidal. That, in an eggshell, is "The Curse," the week's entry in the suppuration stakes. Wil Wheaton and Amy Wheaton play a young brother and sister whom all the infected people, livestock and vegetables are out to get. David Keith directed from a screenplay by David Chaskin; they're asking for boils. If you need to see the worms, sores and nasty oozing glop for yourself, they're at the Criterion and other movie houses.

WALTER GOODMAN
1987 S 11, C13:4

Touring Argentina

SERA POSIBLE EL SUR: UN VIAJE POR ARGENTINA DE LA MANO DE MERCEDES SOSA, directed by Stefan Paul; in Spanish with English subtitles; cinematographers, Hans Schalk, Hans Warth and Jorge Casal; film editor, Hildegard Schroeder; produced by Gerd Unger and Chris Sievernich; an Arsenal Film Production. At the Public, 425 Lafayette Street, as part of the Festival Latino. Running time: 76 minutes. This film has no rating.

By JON PARELES

"**S**ERA POSIBLE EL SUR: Un Viaje por Argentina de la Mano de Mercedes Sosa" ("The South Will Be Possible: A Trip Through Argentina With Mercedes Sosa"), showing tonight as part of the Festival Latino at the Public Theater, is a passable documentary about a magnificent performer. Mercedes Sosa, born in the Andes in 1935, is a voice of Latin America's conscience. In her native Argentina, she is treated with a combination of reverence and pop-star adulation.

Miss Sosa's songs are anthems for peace, democracy and individual dignity, blending traditional music and heartfelt messages in a style she helped to create, the Latin American "nueva canción" ("new song"). She has a sumptuous voice, rich with melody and sheer conviction, and she often accompanies herself on a drum, playing Andean rhythms. From 1979 to 1982, she was exiled by Argentina's military dictatorship, and when she returned she was treated as a national heroine.

Stefan Paul, a West German director, followed Miss Sosa on a 1984-85 tour that covered the entire country, from the Andes to Patagonia. "Será Posible el Sur," named after a song about the legacy of Argentina's years of dictatorship, grew into an odd combination of concert documentary, travelogue and agitprop.

•

Miss Sosa is a large, rounded woman with chiseled Andean features and jet-black hair. On stage, she is serious yet spirited, wearing Andean-style clothes and sometimes putting down her drum to dance a zamba across the stage. She gets an uproarious response; as a stadium full of listeners sings along with her every word in Buenos Aires, she beams. In Patagonia, she arouses pop pandemonium, with the audience surging to the stage and reaching for her outstretched hand, and when she walks through a marketplace the public swarms around her.

Beyond Miss Sosa's songs, however, the film gives a sketchy impression of her. Miss Sosa had traveled all over Argentina before her exile, and it seems likely that the film maker had hoped to elicit a few words about each region, but her few on-camera monologues are disappointingly general. And given the breadth of Miss Sosa's repertory — she has been performing since she was 15 years old — it's a shame to have songs repeated in the course of the film.

Instead of Miss Sosa's perspective, the film presents gorgeous outdoor footage of the Argentine countryside: tobacco fields, mountain stonescapes, tremendous waterfalls and wildlife from pampas horses to Patagonian seals. There is also good-hearted but hectoring narration; it seems unnecessary to say, for instance, that Latin America's hopes rest with its children. Even so, "Será Posible el Sur" shows clearly how music can carry a nation's hopes, and it provides a good preview for Miss Sosa's concert at Carnegie Hall on Oct. 15.

1987 S 11, C15:1

The Woo-Woo Kid

IN THE MOOD, direction and screenplay by Phil Alden Robinson; story by Bob Kosberg, David Simon and Mr. Robinson; director of photography, John Lindley; edited by Patrick Kennedy; music by Ralph Burns; production designer, Dennis Gassner; produced by Gary Adelson and Karen Mack; presented by Kings Road Entertainment and Lorimar Motion Pictures. At the Baronet, Third Avenue at 59th Street. Running time: 98 minutes. This film is rated PG-13.

Ellsworth (Sonny) Wisecarver	Patrick Dempsey
Judy Cusimano	Talia Balsam
Francine Glatt	Beverly D'Angelo
Mr. Wisecarver	Michael Constantine
Mrs. Marver	Kathleen Freeman
The Judge	Peter Hobbs
Carlo	Tony Longo
Uncle Clete	Douglas Rowe
Chief Kelsey	Ernie Brown

By JANET MASLIN

WHATEVER Ellsworth (Sonny) Wisecarver's secret may have been, it is not revealed by "In the Mood," a well-meaning but terribly cute comedy about his romantic exploits. As a 14-year-old schoolboy in the spring of 1944, Sonny made headlines by eloping with a 21-year-old mother of two children, and he later ran off with another older woman, the wife of a marine. These adventures won him widespread publicity and such wonderful nicknames as What-a-Man Wisecarver and the Woo-Woo Kid. The actual Mr. Wisecarver, now older and wiser and living in California, has been quoted as saying, "Hell, I wasn't doing anything any other kid my age wasn't doing at the time."

Maybe not. But clearly, the real Sonny was a prodigy of sorts, so the film makes a mistake in presenting him as a sexless naif. As played by Patrick Dempsey, he's a very nice, rather sad-eyed innocent whose hangdog expression does little to explain why women found him irresistible. And Mr. Dempsey offers a steady stream of voice-over commentary, in the manner of Neil Simon's Eugene Jerome, which is neither funny enough nor revealing enough to give the film any momentum. If the events depicted in "In the Mood" were not in fact based on Sonny's true story, they wouldn't be credible for a second.

•

Sonny is first seen shyly romancing 21-year-old Judy Cusimano (Talia Balsam), who lives with a man in his 30's and longs for the company of her contemporaries. "What's it like being married to somebody that old?" Sonny asks sympathetically. It's dreadful, Judy says, and besides they aren't even married anyhow; soon after that, she and the virginal Sonny are off to a wedding chapel, which leads to Judy's arrest for felonious child-stealing. "You take Sinatra and have yourself a swoon," Judy told reporters at the time. "I'll take Sonny Wisecarver." The screenplay's best lines are those that no one could have made up.

Its worst are those that seem designed to undercut the idea of Sonny's rakishness completely, as when, at his wedding to Judy, he sighs, "This is so much better than the ninth grade!" Later on, after a judge labels him an "oversexed punk," he has developed no more noticeable charm when it comes to romancing Francine Glatt (Beverly D'Angelo), who is his neighbor at a rooming house; their flirtation begins when Francine barges into the communal bathroom while Sonny is using the facilities. Once again, it seems that the real events must surely have had more magic.

"In the Mood," which opens today at the Baronet, may be intended as a different kind of love story anyhow. As written and directed by Phil Alden Robinson, it reserves its greatest warmth for the era in which the action takes place. And the 1940's are indeed affectionately recreated here, with big-band music, elaborate costumes and well-chosen billboards in the background everywhere. At their best, these details are ingenious. Sonny even stops at a movie theater playing "Ants in Your Plants" and "Hey Hey in the Hayloft," two nonexistent films that any fan of Preston Sturges's "Sullivan's Travels" will fondly remember.

•

"In the Mood" is rated PG-13 ("Special Parental Guidance Suggested for Those Younger Than 13"). It includes a few mildly suggestive scenes.

1987 S 16, C27:1

Skid Row

STREET TRASH, directed by Jim Muro; screenplay by Roy Frumkes; director of photography, David Sperling; edited by Dennis Werner; music by Rick Ulfik; production designer, Rob Marcucci; produced by Mr. Frumkes; released by Lightning Pictures. At Eighth Street Cinema, at Avenue of the Americas. Running time: 91 minutes. This film has no rating.

Bill the Cop	Bill Chepil
Fred	Mike Lackey
Bronson	Vic Noto
Frank Schnizer	R. L. Ryan
Nick Duran	Tony Darrow
Doorman	James Lorinz

"STREET TRASH," now befouling the Eighth Street Cinema, is the stuff that civil-libertarian nightmares are made of. It claims no redeeming social value, and you don't have to be a Supreme Court nominee to question whether the Founders could have foreseen anything like it when they wrote the First Amendment.

The mayhem takes place in a skid-row junkyard, which is about right. Several denizens fall victim to a beverage called Tenafly Viper; one gulp and you turn into an action painting. In between these meltdowns there are dismemberments, disfigurements and a gang rape, from which the writer, Roy Frumkes, tries to squeeze hilarity. Surprisingly, there is a funny postscript — an encounter between a Mafia hood and a cool young guy (deadpanned by James Lorinz) — but by then you may not feel like laughing.

The director, Jim Muro, learned the trade in a course that Mr. Frumkes gives at the School for Visual Arts. Some testimonial. Mr. Muro is 22 years old. The movie seems to have been made by a much younger man.

WALTER GOODMAN

1987 S 16, C27:3

In Your Eye

GAP-TOOTHED WOMEN, produced, directed and photographed by Les Blank; edited by Maureen Gosling; distributed by Flower Films. Running time: 30 minutes.
MISS ... OR MYTH?, directed by Geoffrey Dunn and Mark Schwartz; photographed and edited by Mr. Schwartz; produced by Mr. Dunn, Mr. Schwartz and Claire Rubach; distributed by the Cinema Guild. At Film Forum 1, 57 Watts Street. Running time: 60 minutes. These films have no rating.

By VINCENT CANBY

BEAUTIFUL women or, rather, the differing ideas of what constitutes beauty in women are the shared theme of the two excellent documentaries that open today at the Film Forum 1.

"Miss ... or Myth?," directed by Geoffrey Dunn and Mark Schwartz, is a straightforward, 60-minute reportorial account of the Miss California beauty pageant and of its counterpageant, the feminist Myth California contest.

Topping the Film Forum program is Les Blank's 30-minute delight, "Gap-Toothed Women," which looks at and listens to women who happen to have a slight space between their two upper front teeth and feel just fine about it.

In documenting the history of the Miss California contest at Santa Cruz and of the Miss America pageant to which all Miss Californias go with hopes and busts held high, Mr. Dunn and Mr. Schwartz can't entirely avoid sending up the whole idea of American beauty pageants. Satire is built into the institution itself. As is known by anyone who's ever watched the Miss America show on television, nothing is much funnier or more disturbing than the intensity of the carefully rehearsed sincerity displayed by the women who participate.

Using a lot of archival footage to set the scene, "Miss ... or Myth?"

crosscuts between the Miss California contest of 1985 and the counterpageant that was organized to ridicule what feminists see as the false values of all such contests. The film makers discover that sincerity is shoulder-deep on both sides, and that it's not all phony. "Miss ... or Myth?" doesn't go for easy laughs.

Lisa Davenport, Miss California of

Ann Simonton after her arrest during anti-pageant demonstration in "Miss ... or Myth?"

1985-86, at first takes a very haughty view of the women who have so noisily expressed their dissatisfaction with the official pageant. "I hate to say this," she says (and then says it), "but they are not the example of womenhood I would like to follow. Many of them are fat. They don't take care of themselves. They're not even clean."

The principal spokeswoman for the opposition is Ann Simonton, a successful model as a teen-ager who, at 19, was gang-raped and now sees beauty pageants as promoting values that encourage rape in a society that debases women. As the climax of her protest (during which the counterdemonstrators chant "Dress meat, not women"), Miss Simonton puts on a bathing suit made out of pork ribs and slabs of other kinds of raw meat and splashes the steps of the pageant hall with a plastic bag of her own blood.

Eventually, even Miss Davenport seems to have some second thoughts. She recalls filling out her Miss America application form and feeling compelled to note that she once suffered from bulimia, though she credits the Miss America program with helping her to get over it.

Lee Ann Meriwether, who was Miss California of 1954 and Miss America of 1955, defends beauty pageants without whitewashing them. Other defenders of the Miss America contest talk about the pageant's scholarship program. Another woman calls it the "original" women's lib movement. Perhaps the most effective testimony is offered by Debra Johnson, an unsuccessful contestant at the 1985 Miss California contest, who politely points out that in 62 years no "woman of color" has ever won the California pageant.

"Miss ... or Myth?" also never lets the audience forget that the business of beauty pageants is business, the promotion of commerce (supermarkets, products, real estate developments) through the promotion of a comparatively narrow idea of beauty.

•

"Gap-Toothed Women" is something else entirely. The film is another common-sensical, inspiriting paean to the mystery and variety of ordinary experience by one of our most original film makers. Mr. Blank ("Garlic Is as Good as 10 Mothers," "Werner Herzog Eats His Shoe," "Burden of Dreams") is here honoring women who have come to terms with a slight physical imperfection that, in various societies, has been looked upon as the essense of beauty, as a sign of sexual appetite, as a mark of God's favor and, more recently (in this country), as being Howdy Doody-like.

The exuberant interviewees include Lauren Hutton, the model and movie actress; Miranda Bergman, the San Francisco muralist; Dori Seda, the underground cartoonist, and Shirley Sawyer, a belly dancer from Berkeley, Calif., whose leukemia is in remission. In addition to gap-teeth, which have affected each interviewee differently, these women have senses of humor and proportion that make them extraordinarily good company. More or less in passing, without half-trying, "Gap-Toothed Women" also becomes a celebration of womanhood.

1987 S 16, C28:3

Always 'It'

ORPHANS, directed and produced by Alan J. Pakula; screenplay by Lyle Kessler, based on his play; director of photography, Donald McAlpine; film editor, Evan Lottman; music by Michael Small; production designer, George Jenkins; released by Lorimar Motion Pictures. At Coronet, Third Ave. at 59th St. Running time: 115 minutes. This film is rated R.

Harold	Albert Finney
Treat	Matthew Modine
Phillip	Kevin Anderson
Barney	John Kellogg
Man in Park	Anthony Heald

By VINCENT CANBY

IN the lively precredit sequence of "Orphans," Alan J. Pakula's screen version of Lyle Kessler's one-set play, a skinny young man with a manic bounce to his walk approaches a suit-and-vest type sitting on a bench in Central Park. Treat (Matthew Modine), the intruder, sits down beside the suit-and-vest and immediately asks if the fellow has any pictures of his family. The mind inhabiting the suit and vest does some split-second calculations:

Anyone sitting alone on a bench in Central Park should be on his guard. People get mugged in Central Park. Yet as a contributor to liberal causes, and as a believer in the essential if theoretical decency of man, he must resist the terrible tendency of New Yorkers always to be fearful of strangers. He tells himself not to be so uptight.

The man takes out his wallet and shows the stranger pictures of his children. Several seconds later the younger man pulls a knife on the suit-and-vest, grabs his wallet and, in the scuffle that ensues, slashes his victim's arm. Treat starts to run away but is angered because the suit-and-vest howls as if mortally wounded when, in fact, he has only a superficial

cut.

Treat returns to the man, hurriedly attempts to tie a tourniquet around the arm, but is angered even more because the man doesn't seem to appreciate Treat's risky humanitarianism. Treat, who has a short fuse, is always being misunderstood by the people he robs.

•

Most — but certainly not all — of the rest of "Orphans" is confined to the rundown old house on the edge of Newark that Treat shares with his seemingly retarded younger brother, Phillip (Kevin Anderson), and the benign, mysterious Chicago gangster, Harold (Albert Finney), who moves in with the brothers. "Orphans" has nothing more to do with the man in the park, being, instead, about the odd redemption of Treat and Phillip by the alternately threatening and paternal Harold.

The unusual accomplishment of Mr. Pakula and Mr. Kessler, who adapted his one-set play for the screen, is that they've actually enriched the possibilities of the original comedy-drama by opening it up. "Orphans," which starts today at the Coronet theater, never quite overcomes the play's final anticlimaxes, but it's still a very successful example of the stage-to-film transfer of a play that seemed to be the sort that demanded its original, claustrophobic setting.

Even more important, this film adaptation provides a field day for its three remarkable stars and, in turn, for the audience that beholds them. "Orphans" could be subtitled "Actors Acting." The performances by Mr. Finney, Mr. Modine and Mr. Anderson aren't self-effacing. That is, the actors don't entirely disappear inside their roles. One watches them with the same sort of wonder with which one attends a performance by an opera singer hitting notes never heard before. The actors don't vanish, but seem to stand just a little to the side of the characters, as delighted as we are by what they're able to do.

This is extremely risky and rare in movies, but it works here. For all the grittiness of its milieu and the ferocity of the emotions expressed, "Orphans" is no more realistic than "The Magic Flute." The joy one feels is prompted not through identification with its tale, but by the spectacle of three very different actors taking promising material and realizing so many funny, contradictory and moving meanings in it. "Orphans" only goes flat when Mr. Kessler must take time to explain what has earlier been far more richly dramatized.

•

Mr. Finney's Harold is a great bear of a man, first seen in a seedy Newark bar doing a drunken song-and-dance routine. Treat picks him up, thinking possibly to separate Harold from his fancy jewelry. Once they are back at the house, Treat discovers that Harold is also carrying a fortune in negotiable stocks and securities. Treat, whose mind works quickly but clumsily, decides that he and Phillip will hold Harold for ransom, a plan that goes so far awry that Harold is soon the boys' employer-guru.

Just how Harold transforms their lives, and even their house, is not as important as the interaction of the three men in a series of crazily comic confrontations. For years Phillip, a house-bound wild-child, has pretended to be simple-minded and illiterate to provide Treat with someone to protect. About the only way the

Matthew Modine

brothers communicate is through an unending game of tag, in which Phillip is always "it." Treat, in turn, has convinced himself that he and Phillip can survive only by turning their backs on a society that exists to be regularly mugged.

Harold, reared in an orphanage about which he reminisces at whisky-soaked length, is a con artist at the end of his rope. He's both sentimental and tough as nails, and sets about to liberate these two would-be goons. Among other things, he convinces Phillip that he's not (as Phillip thinks) allergic to fresh air, and teaches Treat how to recognize and control his feelings. More exhaustive interpretations of the material, involving what Mr. Pakula (in the program notes) describes as "male bonding" and "parenting," underrate and oversimplify the most interesting aspects of Mr. Kessler's play.

Mr. Anderson, who has played the role of Phillip in the Chicago and New York productions of the play, as well as in London with Mr. Finney, is very much the equal of his two, better-known (until now) co-stars. That's saying a lot since Mr. Finney and Mr. Modine (wearing a close-cropped haircut left over from "Full Metal Jacket") have never been better. The supporting roles are also beautifully done by Anthony Heald, as the man on the park bench, and John Kellogg, as the receiver of Treat's stolen property.

Mr. Pakula's achievement is in making a film that's simultaneously theatrical *and* cinematic. "Orphans" honors both worlds.

1987 S 18, C3:1

FATAL ATTRACTION, directed by Adrian Lyne; screenplay by James Dearden; director of photography, Howard Atherton; edited by Michael Kahn and Peter E. Berger; music by Maurice Jarre; production designer, Mel Bourne; produced by Stanley R. Jaffe and Sherry Lansing; released by Paramount Pictures. At Paramount, 61st Street and Broadway; Tower East, Third Avenue and 71st Street; 34th Street Showplace, between Second and Third Avenues. Running time: 121 minutes. This film is rated R.

Dan Gallagher	Michael Douglas
Alex Forrest	Glenn Close
Beth Gallagher	Anne Archer
Ellen Gallagher	Ellen Hamilton Latzen
Jimmy	Stuart Pankin
Hildy	Ellen Foley
Arthur	Fred Gwynne
Joan Rogerson	Meg Mundy
Howard Rogerson	Tom Brennan
Martha	Lois Smith

YEARS hence, it will be possible to pinpoint the exact moment that produced "Fatal Attraction," Adrian Lyne's new romantic thriller, and the precise circumstances that made it a hit. It arrived at the tail end of the having-it-all age, just before the impact of AIDS on movie morality was really felt. At the same time, it was a powerful cautionary tale. And it played skillfully upon a growing societal emphasis on marriage and family, shrewdly offering something for everyone: the desperation of an unmarried career woman, the recklessness of a supposedly satisfied husband, the worries of a betrayed wife. What's more, it was made with the slick, seductive professionalism that was a hallmark of the day.

"Fatal Attraction," which opens today at the Paramount and other theaters, is a thoroughly conventional thriller at heart, but its heart is not what will attract notice. As directed by Mr. Lyne, who also made "9½ Weeks" and "Flashdance," it has an ingeniously teasing style that overrules substance at every turn. Mr. Lyne, who displays a lot more range this time, takes a brilliantly manipulative approach to what might have been a humdrum subject and shapes a soap opera of exceptional power. Most of that power comes directly from visual imagery, for Mr. Lyne is well versed in making anything — a person, a room, a pile of dishes in a kitchen sink — seem tactile, rich and sexy.

That kitchen sink is quite literally thrown into the torrid romance of Dan Gallagher and Alex Forrest, played by Michael Douglas and Glenn Close, neither of whom has previously given off much heat in other roles. However, Mr. Lyne's handiwork transforms them into a convincingly passionate pair. The change in Miss Close is especially startling, with the witchy blond tendrils and hard, steady gaze that make her character so seductive and finally so frightening. She first meets Dan at a party, then at a weekend business meeting, and after that Mr. Lyne toys luxuriantly with the viewer's expectations. In a film of his, even Miss Close's signaling Mr. Douglas to wipe some cream cheese off his nose during the meeting can have a remarkable charge.

•

It's raining after the meeting. Her umbrella works, his doesn't. He suggests they have a drink somewhere, and they do, and what happens after

Michael Douglas

Andy Schwartz

that is no surprise, nor is it made out to be any of Dan Gallagher's doing. His wife, who happens to be gorgeous and perfect (as played by Anne Archer, whose glamorous presence does a lot to make the extramarital affair seem unlikely), happens to be away for the weekend. So what does he do? He doesn't bother to resist, that's all. Audiences who saw the seduction coming will also see its byproduct, a streak of persistence and vindictiveness from the woman who considers herself wronged. As in "Play Misty for Me," still a classic of this genre, this spurned lover's pique becomes ever more terrifying as the film progresses. Most of her tricks are unsurprising, but they are unnerving anyway, so effectively does Mr. Lyne create the happy Gallagher family that Alex means to destroy. The film becomes more predictable and violent as it goes along, but at least one of her methods, having to do with the Gallaghers' search for a storybook house in the suburbs, is indeed ingenious.

"Fatal Attraction" provides some textbook examples of how to scare an audience even when the audience knows what's coming (though there's one final touch that's inexcusable). It also offers a well-detailed, credibly drawn romantic triangle that's sure to spark a lot of cocktail-party chatter. The fact that Dan Gallagher's home life seems so happy only makes matters more interesting, as does the film's refusal to explain him. It's even difficult to tell anything about this man's inner life from Mr. Douglas's performance, and that may be the point. He doesn't understand it either.

Contributing greatly to the film's success are a nicely direct screenplay by James Dearden, warmly handsome photography by Howard Atherton, a thoroughly credible production design by Mel Bourne and a wonderful and unaffected performance by Ellen Hamilton Latzen, who plays the Gallaghers' daughter.

JANET MASLIN

1987 S 18, C10:5

Do Not Adjust Your Set

AMAZON WOMEN ON THE MOON, directed by Joe Dante, Carl Gottlieb, Peter Horton, John Landis and Robert K. Weiss; screenplay by Michael Barrie and Jim Mulholland; director of photography, Daniel Pearl; edited by Bert Lovitt, Marshall Harvey and Malcolm Campbell; production designer, Ivo Cristante; produced by Mr. Weiss; released by Universal Pictures. At Movieland, Broadway at 47th Street; New York Twin, Second Avenue and 66th Street; 34th Street Showplace, between Second and Third Avenues.; 84th

Consequences

Glenn Close appears with Michael Douglas and Anne Archer in Adrian Lyne's "Fatal Attraction," a thriller about a pathological obsession born of a sexual encounter.

Street Six, at Broadway. Running time: 85 minutes. This film is rated R.

Brenda	Michelle Pfeiffer
Captain Nelson	Steve Forrest
Butch	Joey Travolta
Don Simmons	David Alan Grier
Karen	Rosanna Arquette
Jerry	Steven Guttenberg
Harvey Pitnik	Archie Hahn
Griffin	Ed Begley Jr.
George	Matt Adler
Mr. Gower	Ralph Bellamy
Mary Brown	Carrie Fisher

WHY tamper with perfection? The tinny, low-budget science-fiction epics that turn up on late-night television have the kind of innocence and silliness that don't grow on trees, so the idea of duplicating these classics seems doomed from the very start. But the makers of "Amazon Women on the Moon," which opens today at Loews New York Twin and other theaters, knew no fear. Nor did they know much about taste, concentration, restraint or any of the other virtues that might have bogged them down.

The result: an anarchic, often hilarious adventure in dial-spinning, a collection of brief skits and wacko parodies that are sometimes quite clever, though they're just as often happily sophomoric, too. As an added bonus, there's the film-within-a-film of the title, complete with intrepid space commander (Steve Forrest), spacesuit-wearing pet monkey and dopey assistant (Joey Travolta, who's especially funny) who just can't wait to reach the moon and tear off a hunk of that green cheese.

To the extent that this comic anthology has any structure at all, it's set up as a late-night television showing of "Amazon Women on the Moon," with the film clips regularly interrupted by authentic-looking skips, scratches, burns and tears. Sometimes this leads to a commercial, sometimes a separate skit, sometimes back to the feature itself, but there's really no telling where "Amazon Women" is going, and that's part of the fun. There are 20 separate skits here, made by five different directors, and if their quality varies greatly at least the pace is quick. The least inspired sketches quickly give way to ones that are better.

•

Among the high points are a look at the Son of the Invisible Man, who, as played by Ed Begley Jr., is something of an embarrassment to his neighbors. He thinks he's perfected his father's magic formula, and no one has the heart to tell him otherwise. So the patrons at the local bar sit patiently while he — naked, Invisible Man-style

Living It Up
Carrie Fisher stars in "Amazon Women on the Moon," a comedy directed by Joe Dante, Carl Gottlieb, Peter Horton, John Landis and Robert K. Weiss.

— rearranges the checkers on the checkerboards and cackles madly at his own wit. Then there's George (Matt Adler), the bashful teen-ager who tries to purchase a certain brand of condom from his kindly neighborhood druggist (played to the hilt by Ralph Bellamy), and finds out he's gotten much more than he's bargained for. Every young man's worst nightmare comes true as he finds his face on a billboard and his praises sung by a marching band. Another recurring presence in the film is Don (No Soul) Simmons (David Alan Grier), a man with a congenital defect that makes him sing songs like "Blame It on the Bossa Nova" and "Tie a Yellow Ribbon 'Round the Old Oak Tree."

The film's five directors show off very different predilections, the most noticeable being Joe Dante's taste for the macabre. Among Mr. Dante's contributions are a television show postulating wild premises, like the idea that Jack the Ripper may also have been the Loch Ness monster (Mr. Dante illustrates this with a giant sea serpent in a bowler hat and necktie, giving the most awful leer to a London prostitute). There is also a two-man team of critics who devote their show to analyzing the life of one particular viewer, Harvey Pitnik, and deem it worthless. This gives Harvey a fatal heart attack and leads into another of Mr. Dante's skits, with the Pitnik funeral staged as a celebrity roast.

The film's best sight gags come from Robert K. Weiss, who deserves kudos for the inspired idiocy of his "Amazon Women" segments and for bits like "Silly Pâté," advertising an elegant snack that can also be used to copy comic strips. John Landis does best with the Don Simmons scenes and least well with an extended, unfunny episode about a man who is attacked by his furniture and appliances. This is the film's inauspicious beginning sequence, but it compensates along the way, either as a final sketch — after the closing credits, so stick around — in which Carrie Fisher plays an innocent from the Midwest who is corrupted by New York ways. "Which one is Cole Porter?" she asks sweetly, surrounded by middle-aged gangsters in their underclothes.
JANET MASLIN
1987 S 18, C12:6

TOUGH GUYS DON'T DANCE, directed and written by Norman Mailer; photography by George Kohut; edited by Debra McDermott; music by Angelo Badalamenti; production designer, Armin Ganz; produced by Menahem Golan and Yoram Globus; released by Cannon Films Inc. At New York Twin, Second Avenue at 66th Street; 23d Street West Triplex, between Eighth and Ninth Avenues; 84th Street Six, at Broadway. Running time: 109 minutes. This film is rated R.
Tim Madden	Ryan O'Neal
Madeleine	Isabella Rossellini
Patty Lareine	Debra Sandlund
Regency	Wings Hauser
Wardley Meeks 3d	John Bedford Lloyd
Dougy Madden	Lawrence Tierney
Big Stoop	Penn Jillette

"I KEEP saying to myself," muses Tim Madden, "death is a celebration." Tim (Ryan O'Neal), ex-con, ex-bartender and would-be writer, does a lot of rather portentous musing in "Tough Guys Don't Dance," Norman Mailer's Cape Cod film noir that, with a body count of five murders and two suicides, turns out to be a fairly continuous celebration, though of what is not always apparent. Of mortality, perhaps. Maybe of movie making. Possibly of Provincetown, Mass., where the film was shot and which, no matter how hard Mr. Mailer tries, never seems more dangerous than a picturesque seafood restaurant that sells day-old lobsters.

More often, "Tough Guys Don't Dance" appears to be a celebration of the energy, the chutzpah, the imagination and, frequently, the misjudgment of Mr. Mailer. The novelist, essayist and playwright not only adapted his own quickie novel for the screen, but also, with evident pleasure, went on to direct it.

"Tough Guys Don't Dance," which opens today at the New York Twin and other theaters, is an easy movie to laugh at, but that is to deny how much genuine if loopy fun it is to watch. There's a singular mind behind this work, but it's refracted through a foreign substance: film.

Mr. Mailer is *not* a born film maker, nor has he picked up much expertise along the way, either as a moviegoer or from his experience as the director of several improvised, entertainingly offbeat 16-millimeter films of the late 1960's, including "Beyond the Law." Watching "Tough Guys" is a lot like listening to Mr. Mailer as he extemporizes about movies, posing good questions, which he may or may not answer, and making random observations that are sometimes to the point and sometimes utterly opaque.

"Tough Guys" is Mr. Mailer (winner of the National Book Award and the Pulitzer Prize, and one of the giants of American letters) amusing himself with a genre that people with a tiny fraction of his talent do far more effectively than he ever will. Like a collector's stamp, it's of interest for its imperfections, including its boldly embraced implausibilities, its narrative confusion, plus those political and social meanings that Mr. Mailer may read into it but that remain invisible to the rest of us.

Tim Madden, the "I" of the soundtrack narration, is a second-generation Mailer hero who sounds like a second-generation Sam Spade after he's OD'd reading Norman Mailer.

At the beginning of "Tough Guys," Tim wakes up with a terrible hangover in the fancily decorated, Provincetown house he shares with his rich, sluttish wife, Patty Lareine, who's recently left him. He has a brand-new tattoo on his arm and remembers nothing of the night before.

As the day goes on, it becomes clear that someone was murdered in or near his white Porsche and that the victim, whose severed head he finds in his marijuana stash in the Truro woods, may be either Patty Lareine or the woman he picked up the night before while drinking at the Widow's Walk, which looks like the kind of dive that would be notorious for its popovers and Indian pudding.

Tim has thought much about murder as some kind of ultimate gesture, but he's almost sure he's not capable of it. After all, when he was working as a chauffeur for Patty Lareine and Wardley, her previous husband, who was Tim's classmate at Exeter (am I going too fast?), Patty had wanted him to murder Wardley but he couldn't go through with it.

If the movie is occasionally difficult to follow, it's because so much plot has taken place before the movie begins, necessitating flashbacks that go on so long you don't remember whether you're in a flashback, have returned to the present, or are in a flashback within a flashback, which is probably why Mr. Mailer finally decided to use the very literary soundtrack narration.

In addition to Tim and Patty Lareine (nicely played by the newcomer Debra Sandlund as an arsenic-laced cupcake), the other principal characters are Dougy Madden (Lawrence Tierney), Tim's Irish bartender dad, who's dying of cancer; Wardley (John Bedford Lloyd), who looks and sounds like George Plimpton playing a Tennessee Williams character; Madeleine (Isabella Rossellini), one of Tim's former loves, and Regency (Wings Hauser), Provincetown's psychotic Acting Chief of Police.

There are also several scroungy subsidiary characters whom the movie rejects as if they were organ transplants from another time, place and movie. Mr. Mailer never successfully transforms the pretty, genteel Provincetown locations into a fictional setting worthy of his baroque vision and complex plot. The latter involves a lot of double- and triple-crosses, a multimillion-dollar cocaine deal, two decapitations, wife-swapping, orgiastic parties and ghosts of the American past.

Mr. O'Neal and the other actors don't have an easy time of it, but they all seem to be having a ball, playing out the author's violent fantasies and saying lines that teeter on the knife-edge between literature and lunacy. This is what Mr. Mailer intended, but it's not something that American movie audiences (and critics) are used to.

"Tough Guys Don't Dance" is not the high point of the Mailer career, but it's a small, entertaining part of it.
VINCENT CANBY

1987 S 18, C14:1

Just Kids

THE PRINCIPAL, directed by Christopher Cain; written by Frank Deese; director of photography, Arthur Albert; edited by Jack Hofstra; music by Jay Gruska; produced by Thomas H. Brodek; released by Tri-Star Pictures. At Criterion Center, Broadway and 45th Street; Gemini Twin, 64th Street and Second Avenue; 84th Street Six, at Broadway; Orpheum Twin, 86th Street near Third Avenue; Coliseum, Broadway and 181st Street; Movieland Eighth Street, at University Place; Movie Center 5, 125th Street between Powell and Douglass Boulevards. Running time: 109 minutes. This film is rated R.
Rick Latimer	James Belushi
Jake Phillips	Louis Gossett Jr.
Hilary Orozco	Rae Dawn Chong
Victor Duncan	Michael Wright
White Zac	J. J. Cohen
Raymi Rojas	Esai Morales
Baby Emile	Troy Winbush

By WALTER GOODMAN

IF you think New York's public schools have problems, you haven't been to Brandel High, the locale of "The Principal," which opens today at the Criterion Center and other theaters. This joint makes the Blackboard Jungle look like Rye County Day. Since most of the inmates, who pass their time im-

Partners Isabella Rossellini and Ryan O'Neal star in "Tough Guys Don't Dance," a film-noir comedy about drugs, police corruption, love and murder, directed by Norman Mailer and based on his novel.

bibing reefer smoke and loud noises from their boom boxes, necking, negotiating drug sales and beating up on one another, have been kicked out of other schools, expulsion holds no fears. Also, they lack a healthy self-image. As one says, "Garbage never leaves the dump."

In comes a new principal, who was promoted to the post as punishment for polishing a car with a baseball bat. This role model drinks too much, rides a motorbike and isn't good at holding jobs or wives or his temper. Brandel is his last chance: "I wanna make a school out of this place!" Will Rick Latimer be able to clean up the toilets and his own self-respect? Will he be able to inspire the time-serving teachers? Will he be able to face down Victor Duncan, the leader of the gang that terrorizes the premises? Anybody who has trouble answering those questions gets left back and has to watch the movie twice.

Although James Belushi can't make the title character believable, he brings snap to the role. By his side through the commotion is Louis Gossett Jr., as the school's security chief. Mr. Gossett is always a sturdy presence, but it's time he took off his sunglasses and started looking around for parts that give him a chance to be something besides sturdy. Michael Wright, as Victor Duncan, works hard at being tough on the outside and jelly on the inside. "I can blow you away anytime I want, man," says Victor. "Is that what you want?" replies Rick. Pause, as this registers. Also hanging around are baddies of two races and a couple of kids who prove to be O.K. deep down.

•

If you can swallow the premise, you may be able to digest the scene in which Mr. Belushi roars to the rescue of a pretty and conscientious teacher (Rae Dawn Chong), who is in the throes of being raped in a deserted classroom. The principal rides his bike up steps and along corridors and through doors to get to class while the rapist is still fumbling. Frank Deese's script is as rudimentary as the lyrics that pound through the hallways, and Christopher Cain's direction provides no surprises.

"Who do you think you are?" Mr. Gossett asks Mr. Belushi, "Dirty Harry or somebody?" That's about it. If in the inevitable showdown, the principal doesn't beat the baddest kid into submission, Brandel will not be redeemed. By now, Rick is no doubt ready for new challenges. Is New York ready for a school chancellor who can wield a baseball bat while riding a motorbike?

1987 S 18, C14:6

Scathing and Devoted

MAURICE, directed by James Ivory; screenplay by Kit Hesketh-Harvey and Mr. Ivory, based on E. M. Forster's novel; director of photography, Pierre Lhomme; edited by Katherine Wenning; music by Richard Robbins; production designer, Brian Ackland-Snow; produced by Ismail Merchant; released by Cinecom Pictures. At Paris, 58th Street west of Fifth Avenue. Running time: 135 minutes. This film is rated R.

Maurice	James Wilby
Clive	Hugh Grant
Alec	Rupert Graves
Dr. Barry	Denholm Elliott
Mr. Ducie	Simon Callow
Mrs. Hall	Billie Whitelaw
Lasker-Jones	Ben Kingsley
Mrs. Durham	Judy Parfitt
Anne Durham	Phoebe Nicholls
Risley	Mark Tandy
Dean Cornwalis	Barry Foster

By JANET MASLIN

STATELY and tasteful, supremely confident, proud of its Anglophilia and shameless in its devotion to the upper crust, the Merchant-Ivory style of literary adaptation by now owes at least as much to Ralph Lauren as to E. M. Forster or Henry James. That's no small part of its appeal. The Merchant-Ivory "Maurice," based on Forster's long-unpublished novel about a young man's coming to terms with his homosexuality, further perfects the approach that has worked better and better with each new film, particularly "The Bostonians" and "A Room With a View." Seriousness and intelligence are certainly part of these successes, but a keen sense of the exquisite also goes into making Merchant-Ivory magic.

If audiences take away a sole representative image from "Maurice," it might well be the sight of handsome, moody young Clive Durham (Hugh Grant) resting his head voluptuously upon the knee of Maurice Hall's white flannel trousers. Or it might be the image of clever young Cambridge undergraduates in their heavy tweeds, studying from well-worn leather volumes and resting their polished shoes on weathered Oriental rugs. It could even be the elegant English country house where Clive and his family hunt and stroll and dress for dinner, a world so convincingly rendered that the house very nearly feels drafty. In settings like these, the film makers' mixture of voyeurism and social criticism becomes all the more delectable.

The novel "Maurice" is a good choice, and that's half the battle. Like "The Bostonians" and "A Room With a View," "Maurice" paints a subtly scathing portrait of polite society, a portrait affording many opportunities for cameo acting triumphs. The novel's focus is predominantly on the inner life of the title character, but the film, while faithful, is broader. Moving slowly, with a fine eye for detail, it presents the forces that shape Maurice as skillfully as it brings the character to life.

•

"Maurice," which opens today at the Paris, gets immediately to the point, with an opening scene in which a preposterous teacher (Simon Callow, so deft at playing the fool) draws diagrams illustrating what he calls "the sacred mystery of sex" for the title character, then a thoroughly bewildered young schoolboy. When next seen, Maurice (James Wilby) has arrived at Cambridge and grown into a pleasant, stolid-looking fellow who seems vaguely uneasy in the company of his peers. The Cambridge scenes are gloriously nostalgic, capturing an era gone by (the year is 1909) and the headiness of bright, articulate students in their prime. Maurice himself, though a bit warier than the others, seems especially exhilarated by these surroundings.

James Ivory's direction ably conveys Maurice's growing attraction to Clive Durham, a dashing fellow who is then by far the more adventuresome of the two. Clive declares his love and proposes a close platonic bond with Maurice, stopping short of what classmates call "the unspeakable vice of the Greeks"; in this collegiate atmosphere, the two can easily enjoy the fondest of friendships. Later on, Maurice's affection grows more intense. On one occasion, when

Hugh Grant

Clive becomes ill, Maurice's eagerness to take care of him prompts sarcasm from Clive's doctor and the suggestion that his family amuse him with a pretty young nurse.

Though Forster's novel, begun in 1913 but not published until 1971, follows Maurice's efforts to conceal, cure and finally embrace his homosexuality, its key character is the chameleonlike Clive, who imagines that his own feelings for other men are but a passing fancy. The film watches Clive evolve from the coy, seductive figure who wins Maurice's heart into a pillar of the community; Clive eventually marries, renounces his past and expects his friend to do the same. If Mr. Grant, so good in the film's early sections, becomes less plausible as a self-important country squire, that's very much the point. Clive embodies all the conservatism and complacency, not to mention all the hidden desire, that Forster saw as most repressive in the English society of his day.

•

Maurice is ultimately the freer spirit, and Mr. Wilby (who has his first leading role here) captures the slow evolution of that freedom. A reserved actor capable of surprising vibrancy, he very convincingly presents Maurice's dilemma. The screenplay, by Mr. Ivory and Kit Hesketh-Harvey (rather than Mr. Ivory's frequent collaborator Ruth Prawer Jhabvala), takes its only liberties with the novel in emphasizing the repressive climate in which the story takes place. One such episode now shows Risley, the character based on Lytton Strachey, being arrested and tried for the very behavior Maurice is struggling to avoid.

Among the story's livelier events are Maurice's attempts to seek medical help, with Denholm Elliott as a physician who finds Maurice's confession intolerable and Ben Kingsley quite hilarious as the cigar-smoking American hypnotist who attempts to cure him. (He advises "exercise in moderation — a little tennis, or stroll about with a gun.") Billie Whitelaw is uncharacteristically befuddled as the mother who understands her "Morrie" not at all, and Barry Foster suitably stern as the dean who can do nothing to quell his students' extracurricular interests. Rupert Graves is grittily authentic as the gamekeeper who provides the story with what even Forster regarded as an unconvincingly happy ending.

"Maurice" unfolds with its own rhythm, at a languid, leisurely pace that makes the small details as noticeable as the major ones. It doesn't race, but neither does it meander. Mr. Ivory and Ismail Merchant have long since learned to breathe life into their material without excessive reverence, in a manner that is as decorous as it is dramatic. As might be expected, the costumes, settings and cinematography are once again ravishing.

1987 S 18, C18:5

Il Catalogo E Questo

THE MOZART BROTHERS, directed by Suzanne Osten; screenplay and story (Swedish with English subtitles) by Etienne Glaser, Miss Osten and Niklas Radstrom; camera by Hans Welin and Solveig Warner; edited by Lasse Hagstrom; music by Wolfgang Amadeus Mozart and Bjorn Json Lindh; produced by Bengt Forslund; distributed by First Run Features. At Cinema Studio, Broadway at 66th Street. Running time: 111 minutes. This film has no rating.

Walter	Etienne Glaser
Flemming/Mozart's ghost	Philip Zanden
Fritz	Henry Bronett
Eskil/Don Giovanni	Loa Falkman
Marian/Donna Elvira	Agneta Ekmanner
Ia/Donna Anna	Lena T. Hansson
Olaf/Don Ottavio	Helge Skoog
The Stone Guest	Krister St. Hill
Lennart/Leporello	Rune Zetterstrom
Therèse/Zerlina	Grith Fjeldmose
Switchboard Operator	Malin Ek

"I DON'T like singing and I hate opera," says the intense, beady-eyed Walter to the astonished members of the company he's about to direct in a new production of Mozart's "Don Giovanni."

Walter loathes "a theater that doesn't understand silence." To make the point that Lorenzo da Ponte's plot is ridiculous, "with all of those exits and entrances for no reason whatsoever," Walter picks up the libretto and drops it on the floor of the rehearsal hall.

The assembled singers stare at the mangled manuscript, and gasp. They're facing a rough trip.

Thus begins "The Mozart Brothers," Suzanne Osten's witty, sometimes hugely funny Swedish comedy that has the form of a feature-length sketch about the trials endured by an opera company at war with its formidably avant-garde director.

•

"The Mozart Brothers," opening today at the Cinema Studio, may not be totally comprehensible to anyone who doesn't share Miss Osten's affection for the Don, and for those restless, maverick directors who set out to rethink the classics, both in the theater and opera.

The surprising thing about "The Mozart Brothers" is that although Miss Osten is sending up the iconoclastic Walter, played with absolute conviction by Etienne Glaser (who also co-wrote the screenplay), she makes his nuttiness seem admirable. This is no silly exercise in anti-intellectualism.

It's a charming amalgam of "Don Giovanni" itself, soaring bits and pieces of which we hear and see in the course of the uproarious rehearsals, and the backstage battling and politicking by which Walter eventually brings everyone around to his frequently re-thought inspirations.

To begin with, Walter decides that da Ponte made a mistake in the opera's opening scene, in which the Don murders the father of Donna Anna. Instead, as Walter stages it, it is the father who kills the Don, the

Etienne Glaser plays an innovative stage director in "The Mozart Brothers."

story of the opera being the moment of death during which the Don's life whips by as a dream play.

Quoting Samuel Beckett ("Woman gives birth straddling the grave"), Walter announces that the setting will be a great, muddy cemetery, which presents certain physical problems when the singers try to move around the set without sinking up to their hips. Bored with actors attempting to "act" erotic, Walter leads his cast in exercises in which they search for their own eroticism.

•

He appears to give in when the singers object to playing their roles totally bald, but he fights the musicians, and their union representatives, when they refuse to perform onstage as members of the moralizing chorus.

Watching the proceedings with amused, gratified wonder is the tattered ghost of Wolfgang Amadeus himself.

My only objection to this robust, though delicately detailed film is the title, which Miss Osten means to be a reference to the Marx Brothers' "Night at the Opera." That's another kind of comedy entirely, and to recall it in connection with this movie undercuts the invigorating originality of Miss Osten's work.

VINCENT CANBY

1987 S 18, C21:1

The Battle of Jericho

THE PICKUP ARTIST, written and directed by James Toback; director of photography, Gordon Willis; edited by David Bretherton and Angelo Corrao; music by Georges Delerue; produced by David L. MacLeod; released by 20th Century-Fox. At Criterion Center, Broadway, between 44th and 45th Streets; Gotham Cinema, Third Avenue at 58th Street; 86th Street Twin, near Second Avenue; Movieland Eighth Street, at University Place; Metro Twin, 99th Street and Broadway. Running time: 85 minutes. This film is rated PG-13.

Randy Jensen	Molly Ringwald
Jack Jericho	Robert Downey
Flash	Dennis Hopper
Phil	Danny Aiello
Nellie	Mildred Dunnock
Alonzo	Harvey Keitel
Mike	Brian Hamill
Karen	Tamara Bruno
Rae	Vanessa Williams
Jack's Student	Angie Kempf
Stan	Robert Towne
Floor Manager	Jilly Rizzo

WATCH the actors' lips as they deliver their lines in "The Pickup Artist," which opens today at the Criterion Center and other theaters, and you'll sometimes see them mouthing words that didn't make it into the finished film. Something seems to have happened en route to the screen. "The Pickup Artist" is extremely brief — under 90 minutes — and a good deal tamer than the earlier works of James Toback, who wrote "The Gambler" and directed "Fingers," "Love and Money" and "Exposed," films not known for the kind of nice-guy romantic humor he displays this time. It's hard to know how "The Pickup Artist" started out, but there must have been more to it than now meets the eye.

Robert Downey stars as Jack Jericho, who makes a career of comparing women to various works of art and seems to have a not-bad track record, under the circumstances. He plies his trade up and down Columbus Avenue, operating out of a red convertible equipped with a ready-made ticket, in case he must park quickly in an emergency. After a period of observing Jack Jericho's methods, the film introduces him to Randy Jensen (Molly Ringwald), who's a lot better at this sort of thing than he is. Randy allows herself to be propositioned, shares a quick and rather dispassionate tryst in his convertible, and then refuses to give him her phone number.

On the fringes of all this, brandishing a fly-swatter, is Dennis Hopper, who plays Randy's alcoholic father and seems a lot more in keeping with Mr. Toback's earlier work. So does Harvey Keitel, as a businessman-gangster to whom Randy's father owes money; nobody can slam a door quite as ferociously as Mr. Keitel can. Randy has ideas about how to raise the sum and pay back the debt, rejecting the gangster's suggestion that she sleep with a very rich Colombian who is mad for her. "For me, sex and money just don't mix," Randy says.

•

The film roams from the Upper West Side to Coney Island to Atlantic City, maintaining a lighthearted style that doesn't quite match the hints of obsessiveness in Mr. Toback's screenplay. For one thing, Jack and Randy are meant to connect instantaneously with the kind of urgency that never comes through here; when Jack finally talks about love as a gamble, the speech seems a good deal more passionate than the action that has preceded it. For another, Mr. Downey is likable but lacks the fast-talking hucksterism that ought to go

Modern Ways
Molly Ringwald co-stars with Robert Downey in James Toback's romantic comedy "The Pick-Up Artist."

Brian Hamill

with his character. When delivering Jack Jericho's trademark pickup speeches, he never sounds entirely comfortable.

Miss Ringwald seems much more assured and less pouty than she has in earlier films, projecting the sweetness and confident sensuality that the role demands. Among the film's other assets are a lively rock soundtrack (with a title song written by Stevie Wonder) and a supporting cast including Mildred Dunnock, who gives a brief, lovely performance as Jack's grandmother. Hovering on the periphery in very small roles are Vanessa Williams, Jilly Rizzo and Robert Towne, among many others.

•

"The Pickup Artist" is rated PG-13 ("Special Parental Guidance Suggested for Those Younger Than 13"). Notwithstanding that altered dialogue, it still contains some strong language. JANET MASLIN

1987 S 18, C23:1

Sneak-a-Peek

LADY BEWARE, directed by Karen Arthur; written by Susan Miller and Charles Zev Cohen; director of photography, Tom Neuwirth; edited by Roy Watts; music by Craig Safan; produced by Lawrence Taylor Mortorff and Tony Scotti; released by Scotti Brothers Entertainment Industries Inc. At Cinema 2, Third Avenue at 66th Street; Columbia Cinema, 103d Street and Broadway; 86th Street East, at Third Avenue. Running time: 108 minutes. This film is rated R.

Katya Yarno	Diane Lane
Jack Price	Michael Woods
Mac Odell	Cotter Smith
Lionel	Peter Nevargic
Thayer	Edward Penn
Nan	Tyra Ferrell

THE stars of "Lady Beware" find each other through a shared interest in shop-window dummies. Diane Lane is a window dresser for a Pittsburgh department store whose creativity takes kinky turns, like spritzing Reddi-Wip on a mannequin's limbs. Michael Woods is turned on by her displays, including the décolletage she reveals as she is setting them up.

Much of this movie, which opens today at the Cinema 2 and other theaters, is devoted to Mr. Woods stalking Miss Lane. He talks dirty to her on the telephone, breaks into her mailbox, peeps at her taking a bath (a sight worth the peeping, not only for Miss Lane's endowments but also because she bathes by candlelight and sips champagne between scrubs) and

at her lovemaking, leaves messages in blood on her mirror, uses her toothbrush, seduces her lingerie and commits other nuisances.

•

Mr. Woods, a slickly coiffed villain with a hairy chest and a designer 8 o'clock shadow, has a family of his own; he cuddles his little daughter and takes out his sexual frustrations on his wife. Miss Lane, who acts distraught, scared or angry as required, or as the mood strikes, finally gets her own back in a denouement as clunky as the title. By then Karen Arthur, the director, seems to have given up trying to understand what is going on, for which you can't blame her. As for Miss Lane and Mr. Woods, if they have an inkling of why they are behaving so peculiarly, they are no more forthcoming about it than the dummies that surround them.

WALTER GOODMAN

1987 S 18, C23:1

Lives of the Party

HEY BABU RIBA, directed by Jovan Acin; screenplay (in Serbo-Croatian with English subtitles) by Mr. Acin, from the memories of Petar Jankovic, George Zecevic and Mr. Acin; photography by Tomislav Pinter; edited by Snezana Ivanovic; music by Zoran Simjanovic; produced by Dragoljub Popovic and Nikola Popovic; production companies, Avala Film and Inex Film. At Embassy 72d Street 2, at Broadway. Running time: 109 minutes. This film is rated R.

Esther	Gala Videnovic
Glen	Relja Bacic and Nebojsa Bakocevic
Sacha	Marko Todorovic and Dragan Bjelogrlic
Kica	Srdjan Todorovic and Milos Zutic
Pop Djordje Nenadovic and Goran Radakovic	
Rile	Milan Strljic and Dragomir Bojanic-Gidra

"Hey Babu Riba" was shown as part of this year's New Directors/New Films Series. Here are excerpts from Walter Goodman's review, which appeared in The New York Times March 15. The film opens today at the Embassy 72d Street 2, at Broadway.

SET in Belgrade in 1953, when Yugoslavia was in the throes of breaking away from the Soviet camp, "Hey Babu Riba" focuses on a once-privileged set that has found itself in difficulties under the Tito regime. Esther's father is a former Royalist officer who has fled to Italy; her mother is languishing for want of streptomycin. The father of one of her friends is in jail; another, a doctor, has been put out of business by socialized medicine. All are selling off cherished possessions to eke out an existence, and their "surplus living space" is occupied by Communist Party favorites.

What makes the movie much more interesting than a Serbian variation of "Stand By Me" is its political perspective. The director, Jovan Acin, was born in Belgrade in 1941, and his screenplay, drawn in part from his own memories, is about a generation entranced by American popular culture, from Glenn Miller to Levis, and by a Western spirit of freedom as well. When Esther's boyfriends defeat some party types in a rowing competition, it's a victory for their class.

•

The young protagonists — whom we meet again after life has taken its toll — are amiable if a bit colorless.

More flavorsome performances come from characters churned up by the postwar changes: a woman known as "the vulture," who goes about trading nylons and powdered milk for the pianos and music boxes of the once-rich, and as a sideline initiating their offspring into sex and cigarettes; a conscientious official who tries earnestly to persuade Esther to get her father to collaborate with the regime, and, especially, a rapacious apparatchik named Rile, a handsome blackguard who falls for Esther and is unscrupulous in his pursuit. One of the movie's good jokes is that Rile, ever on the make, had his wrists tattooed with pictures of Stalin and Lenin just before the break with Moscow; now he wears wristbands and is taking a crash course in English instead of Russian.

Incidentally, if you've been dying to hear "Comin' Round the Mountain" sung in Serbo-Croatian, here's your chance.

1987 S 18, C24:1

HOTEL COLONIAL, directed by Cinzia TH Torrini; screenplay by Enzo Monteleone, Miss Torrini and Robert Katz; director of photography, Giuseppe Rotunno; edited by Nino Baragli; music by Pino Donaggio; production manager, Paolo Lucidi; produced by Ira Barmak; released by the Orion Pictures Corporation. At 23d Street West Triplex, between Eighth and Ninth Avenues. Running time: 107 minutes. This film is rated R.

Marco Venieri	John Savage
Irene Costa	Rachel Ward
Carrasco	Robert Duvall
Werner	Massimo Troisi
Mario Anderson	Claudio Baez
Captain Santillana	Federico Gonzales
Mendoza	Daniel Santa Lucia
Bartender	Carlos Romano
Inmate	Carlos de Leon
Indian Girl	Isela Diaz

By VINCENT CANBY

Robert Duvall, John Savage and Rachel Ward star in "Hotel Colonial," which has the coherence and style of a Joseph Conrad story translated from English to Polish to Italian, then back to English, and updated to the 1980's. Something has been lost along the way.

The screenplay was written by Enzo Monteleone, who adapted it from his own story with the help of Cinzia TH Torrini, the film's director, and Robert Katz. It makes no sense whatsoever. However, this much is apparent:

Mr. Savage plays a totally Americanized Italian who goes to Bogotá,

Robert Duvall

Colombia, to collect the body of his brother, described on a television news broadcast as "the famed Italian terrorist," who has apparently committed suicide. When Mr. Savage arrives in Bogotá, which (for the mysterious purposes of this film) appears to be as flat as a pancake and far removed from any mountains, he discovers that the body is not his brother's. One thing leads to another and he learns that the famed Italian terrorist is dealing in drugs and, for recreation, slaughters monkeys and Indians.

Don't ask me why. I'm just reporting the facts.

Miss Ward appears as a member of the staff of the Italian Embassy in Bogotá and speaks with an Italian accent, which is better, as assumed accents go, than Mr. Duvall's, which is supposed to be the sort of Spanish accent that might be spoken by a famed Italian terrorist masquerading as a famed Colombian drug dealer.

The screenplay further asks us to believe that Mr. Savage would not recognize his brother simply because his brother wears a reddish toupee and speaks with a Spanish accent to hide his nonexistent Italian accent. On the basis of what can be seen in the finished film, Miss Torrini's direction is extremely fanciful. This is the sort of movie in which a character opens a fridge door and finds a flashback where the cartons of milk are stored. You might think that wee people inhabit the fridge, though, in fact, the explanation is much more simple: The editing is terrible.

"Hotel Colonial," which opened yesterday at the 23d Street West Triplex, was photographed mostly in Vera Cruz, Mexico, which looks exactly like Vera Cruz, Mexico, almost from start to finish.

1987 S 19, 16:3

All-Day Sucker

HELLRAISER, written and directed by Clive Barker; director of photography, Robin Vidgeon; edited by Richard Marden; music by Christopher Young; production designer, Mike Buchanan; produced by Christopher Figg; released by New World Pictures. At Warner, Broadway at 47th Street. Running time: 95 minutes. This film is rated R.

Larry	Andrew Robinson
Julia	Clare Higgins
Kirsty	Ashley Laurence
Frank	Sean Chapman
Frank the Monster	Oliver Smith
Steve	Robert Hines

By VINCENT CANBY

CLIVE BARKER, England's answer to Stephen King as a bestselling author of horror tales, branches out into film direction with "Hellraiser," a gooey horror movie in

which the main monster, gelatinous anyway, seems to have been dunked in simple syrup. It oozes and drips without thought for what it does to the floors, possibly because it's supposed to be a boorish creature from the beyond.

The tale itself is a variation on the legend of Pandora's box. In this instance the box promises its owner "ultimate pleasure," though, once opened, it unleashes the hounds of hell, who prattle about pleasure and pain being one.

The film, set in England, is mostly about the unhappy consequences when an otherwise uncharacterized young man (Sean Chapman), having opened the box and been reduced to a dripping, blood-sucking wraith, persuades his sister-in-law (Clare Higgins), to get him fresh bodies, including, if necessary, that of his brother (Andrew Robinson), who's also her husband.

Mr. Barker is no more successful in making the big leap from literature to film than Norman Mailer. He's cast his film with singularly uninteresting actors, though the special effects aren't bad — only damp.

"Hellraiser" opened Saturday in Manhattan theaters, including Cineplex Odeon's Warner Theater, formerly the Rialto, where, at the first show, the projector broke down briefly during the first of three trailers that preceeded the feature. When the show resumed, the picture was frequently out of focus and jiggled as if set on a nervous knee. Smoking is not allowed in the auditorium though that, apparently, doesn't always stop

Andrew Robinson in principal role of "Hellraiser."

the enjoyment of marijuana, the scent of which had to compete with

that of the real butter Cineplex Odeon pours on its popcorn.

"Hellraiser," which is stuffed with images of various body parts, sometimes hanging on meat hooks, isn't especially sickening. It's the smells in the auditorium that test the sensitivity of stomachs.

1987 S 20, 85:5

Remembrance Nebojsa Bakocevic and Gala Videnovic are two of the teen-age friends who are the focus of Jovan Acin's "Hey Babu Riba," set in Belgrade during a period of political turbulence of the 1950's.

Havana Homecoming

PARTING OF THE WAYS, written and directed by Jesús Díaz; in Spanish with English subtitles; director of photography, Mario García Joya; produced by Humberto Hernández; distributed by the Cinema Guild. At Film Forum 1, 57 Watts Street. Running time: 90 minutes. This film has no rating.

Susana	Veronica Lynn
Reinaldo	Jorge Trinchet
Ana	Isabel Santos
Aleida	Beatriz Valdés

By WALTER GOODMAN

THE opening situation of "Parting of the Ways" is fraught with possibilities. A woman who fled Fidel Castro's Cuba returns after 10 years to visit the son she and her husband left behind. He was 16 years old, draft age, and so denied permission to emigrate with his family. Now, still occupying the old family apartment in Havana, he is married and comfortable with the regime. Here are the makings of a politically consequential drama, of special interest to a North American audience because it comes from Cuba.

But having set up all manner of potential conflict, Jesús Díaz's movie, now at Film Forum 1, lapses into a domestic weepie. The son (Jorge Trinchet) still harbors feelings of having been abandoned by the parents he loved. The mother (Veronica Lynn) tries to assuage her guilt and buy her way back into his affection with suitcases stocked with gifts and memories stocked with the old country club days. His wife (Beatriz Valdés) disdains the gifts, resents the memories and is jealous of Ana (Isabel Santos), the cute young cousin with whom her husband grew up and who has come along on the visit.

The reactions are plausible but elementary; they beg for probing. Mr. Díaz keeps taking us to the threshold, then drawing back. The dramatic episodes, played out on a single day almost entirely in the big old apartment (which it is difficult to believe the teen-aged son was permitted to keep in housing-short Havana), are mainly closeup duets — mother and son, cousin and son, son and wife. It becomes claustrophobic. When son and cousin go up to the roof, you want to

Returning

Veronica Lynn and Jorge Trinchet appear in Jesus Diaz's "Parting of the Ways" ("Lejania"). The psychological drama from Cuba explores the complicated and controversial issue of exiles returning for family visits.

take a deep breath of the sea air along with them. The camera's intimacy isn't backed up by the script; we're close but not deep. You keep feeling there must be more going on than Mr. Diaz dares to search for; the actors work hard but don't have enough to work with. Their encounters, though affecting at moments, go on too long for what they reveal. When the climactic husband-wife confrontation hinges on whether he enjoyed a tumble with his cousin, we're in sitcom country.

●

The politics is reduced to capitalist materialism versus Communist wholesomeness. Son is briefly tempted by Mother's stock of jeans, tape recorders, watches, cameras. Daughter-in-law is stalwart: "I won't stand for her waving dollars in my face." There are problems in Cuba, Son concedes at Mother's invitation to complain, but "nobody is out of work or can't see the doctor or go to school." Mother, showing slides of her house and expensive car, becomes a caricature of a Miami matron, all consumer and part racist, a Wicked Witch of the North out to seduce a young worker.

We are promised explanations, particularly from a videotape made by the father shortly before his death, of how doting parents could have deserted their child. But when Father speaks, he explains nothing. Maybe that's Mr. Diaz's judgment on the original sin. "Nobody can understand what you did, lady!" declares the daughter-in-law. A natural reaction but short on illumination.

1987 S 23, C22:6

How to Be Nice

THE PRINCESS BRIDE, directed by Rob Reiner; screenplay by William Goldman, based on his novel; director of photography, Adrian Biddle; film editor, Robert Leighton; music by Mark Knopfler; production designed by Norman Garwood; produced by Andrew Scheinman and Mr. Reiner; released by the 20th Century-Fox Film Corporation. At Beekman, 65th Street

and Second Avenue; Guild 50th Street, 33 West 50th Street; New Carnegie, 57th Street and Broadway: Gramercy, 23d Street between Park and Lexington Avenues; Embassy 72d Street, at Broadway. Running time: 100 minutes. This film is rated PG.

Westley................................Cary Elwes
Inigo Montoya ....Mandy Patinkin
Prince Humperdinck ....Chris Sarandon
Count Rugen ....Christopher Guest
Vizzini ....Wallace Shawn
Fezzik ....André the Giant
The Grandson ....Fred Savage
The Princess Bride (Buttercup)
....Robin Wright
The Grandfather ....Peter Falk
The Impressive Clergyman ....Peter Cook
The Albino ....Mel Smith
Valerie ....Carol Kane
Miracle Max ....Billy Crystal

By JANET MASLIN

"THE PRINCESS BRIDE" is framed as a story told to a sick little boy, and the child is thoroughly skeptical — who wouldn't be? Here is a full-length fairy tale full of fanciful characters, madcap adventures and a lot of other things surely not to every taste. But "The Princess Bride" has sweetness and sincerity on its side, and when it comes to fairy tales, those are major assets. It also has a delightful cast and a cheery, earnest style that turns out to be ever more disarming as the film moves along. Even the little boy, who's a tough customer, is eventually won over.

"The Princess Bride," which opens today at the Beekman and other theaters, was adapted by William Goldman from his 1973 novel, which purports to be a conveniently abridged version of a children's book the author loved in his youth. The film version has been streamlined even more drastically, so that the heroine — an innocent beauty named Buttercup — has been introduced, disappointed in love and affianced to the wrong man before the first five minutes are over. That's all right; there's a lot more of the story left, and the look-alike blond Buttercup (Robin Wright) and her true love Westley (Cary Elwes) are on the dull side anyway. In the world of fairy-tale royalty, that's very much as it should be.

So Buttercup is engaged to the grandly supercilious Prince Humperdinck (Chris Sarandon), whose intentions are not the best and whose henchman, Count Rugen (Christopher Guest), prides himself on a "deep and abiding interest in pain." But before landing in their clutches, Buttercup is kidnapped by a strange threesome: a gleefully wicked ringleader (Wallace Shawn), a giant (André the Giant) and the dashing Spanish swordsman Inigo Montoya (Mandy Patinkin), who, like most of the story's characters, is just too big-hearted for his own good. "You seem a decent fellow — I hate to kill you," he tells one rival. There ensues vigorous duel to the death, but even this ends with a kindly little conk on the head.

●

It's hard to imagine that anyone besides Rob Reiner, whose other films (even the mercilessly funny "This Is Spinal Tap") have displayed such a fundamental *niceness*, could have handled "The Princess Bride" so comfortably. This material might easily have lent itself to broad parody or become too cute for its own good. But Mr. Reiner presents it as a bedtime story, pure and simple. The film's style is gentle, even fragile, with none of the bold flourishes that might be expected but with none of the silliness either. Its look is modest — even the high-flying adventure

From top, André the Giant, Mandy Patinkin and Wallace Shawn bungle a kidnapping in "The Princess Bride."

scenes have a mild quality — but "The Princess Bride" has a unifying conviction. Mr. Reiner seems to understand exactly what Mr. Goldman loves about stories of this kind, and he conveys it with clarity and affection.

"The Princess Bride" has been well cast, with each of the actors managing to remain within the bounds of the storytelling framework and still make a strong impression. With the possible exception of Mr. Shawn, whose comic appearances in tough-guy parts are becoming rather familiar, the actors are all skillfully matched to their roles. Mr. Patinkin, who is particularly good, turns out to be a fine swashbuckler, albeit not a very clever one; his heroic presence is somehow only enhanced by a halfway-impenetrable Spanish accent. Mr. Sarandon, always a fine villain, struts elegantly and displays his own brand of sinister charm. Mr. Guest is the very embodiment of cold-blooded evil until one unexpectedly funny duel scene, and Peter Cook appears briefly but memorably as a cleric performing a ceremony of, as he pronounces it, "mawwidge."

Billy Crystal and Carol Kane, made up to have a collective age of about 400, bicker energetically as a miracle maker and his nagging wife; as the film's other romantic duo, Miss Wright and Mr. Elwes are properly picturesque. Among the film's most appealing elements are a score by Mark Knopfler and the pleasantly intrusive presence of Peter Falk, who appears as a grandfather reading "The Princess Bride" to his grandson and interrupts the fairy-tale action every now and then. Mr. Falk doesn't do much more than make a great ceremony out of the act of reading, but that's enough.

●

"The Princess Bride" is rated PG ("Parental Guidance Suggested"). It has a few rude moments and some

minor violence, but there's nothing in it to keep children of any age away.

1987 S 25, C10:5

Hack License

YOU TALKIN' TO ME? screenplay and direction by Charles Winkler; director of photography, Paul Ryan; edited by David Handman; music by Joel McNeely; produced by Michael Polaire; released by United Artists. At Eastside Cinema, Third Avenue at 55th Street; Movieland Eighth Street, Eighth Street and University Place. Running time: 97 minutes. This film is rated R.

Bronson Green ....Jim Youngs
Peter Archer ....James Noble
Thatcher Marks ....Mykel T. Williamson
Dana Archer ....Faith Ford
Judith Margolis ....Bess Motta
Kevin ....Rex Ryon
James ....Brian Thompson
Alan King ....Alan King

By CARYN JAMES

AS this schizophrenic film begins, a dark-haired, intense New York actor, deeply entrenched in Robert De Niro worship, sits in an old movie theater watching "Taxi Driver." Bronson Green (Jim Youngs) sees himself stepping into the De Niro role as the obsessed, violent Travis Bickle, and Mr. Youngs gets to live out every young actor's fantasy. He looks the camera in the eye and jeers, "You talkin' to me? You talkin' to *me*?" Let's just say Robert De Niro does it better.

That, of course, is one of the points of "You Talkin' to Me?" which starts as a sardonic take on struggling actors. Looking around his room at posters for "Raging Bull" and "The King of Comedy," Bronson asks his idol, "Bobby, what do you think about moving to L.A.?"

When he hits the coast, Bronson gets a job as a taxi driver but spends most of his time being rejected by casting agents because he's too dark-haired and too intense. So he becomes a blond and develops a laid-back attitude that depends on calling people "dude."

●

This may sound funnier than it is, because Charles Winkler, who wrote the screenplay and directed, can't seem to decide how satirical to be and often settles for being condescendingly explicit. Bronson is even saddled with a puffed-up speech about why he acts — "for that moment when men become heroes."

But being tone-deaf is the least of Mr. Winkler's problems. Soon a series of made-in-storyland coincidences turns the movie into a self-important comment on racism and reduces social criticism to a cheap trick. The newly blond Bronson meets an attractive woman (they make eye contact on the freeway) whose father owns a religious television network.

Bronson becomes the network's spokesman for "The pure truth. The white truth." The job makes him a bit uneasy because his best friend, Thatcher, is a black man starting his own career as a model. When the racist media baron sees Thatcher's image on a billboard promoting milk, a big finish is very obviously on the way. By then you might be longing for that sort-of-satire about "Bobby." It was flat-footed, but at least it didn't overdose on a deadly blend of pomposity and plot-twisting.

"You Talkin' to Me?" which opens today at the Eastside Cinema and the Movieland Eighth Street, was made on a fairly small budget (less than $1 million) but with lots of help. Mr. Winkler, the production notes tell us, shot some scenes in the office of his father, the producer Irwin Winkler. The younger Mr. Winkler began his career as a teen-aged production assistant on Martin Scorsese's "New York, New York," and Mr. Scorsese gave him permission to restage some scenes from "Taxi Driver" here. No wonder Mr. Winkler has such trouble with his perspective on Hollywood; he's on the inside looking in.

1987 S 25, C14:1

Action and Slurs

CHINA GIRL, directed by Abel Ferrara; screenplay by Nicholas St. John; director of photography, Bojan Bazelli; edited by Anthony Redman; music by Joe Delia; production designer, Dan Leigh; produced by Michael Nozik; released by Vestron Pictures. At National Twin, Broadway and 44th Street; 86th Street East Twin, near Second Avenue; Columbia Cinema, Broadway at 103d Street; Movie Center 5, 125th Street between Powell and Douglass Boulevards. Running time: 89 minutes. This film is rated R.

Alberto (Alby) Monte	James Russo
Tony Monte	Richard Panebianco
Tyan-Hwa	Sari Chang
Johnny Mercury	David Caruso
Yung-Gan	Russell Wong
Tsu-Shin	Joey Chin
Maria	Judith Malina
Gung-Tu	James Hong
Perito	Robert Miano
Nino	Paul Hipp

SLEAZE has few champions, but Abel Ferrara is one of them, having made some of the liveliest exploitation films (among them "Ms. 45" and "Fear City") in recent years. Mr. Ferrara has since gone on to direct some episodes of "Miami Vice," where his brand of lurid, high-style glamour fits in perfectly. His films are outlandish by their very nature, and what could be more so than "China Girl," a blatant mix of "Romeo and Juliet," "Mean Streets" and "West Side Story" played out among very young, barely verbal Chinese and Italian street gangs? It would be gratifying to report that Mr. Ferrara had made a coup of this, but the odds against it are daunting. Instead, "China Girl" amounts to a cult item and a nice try.

Mr. Ferrara's touch is unmistakable — who else would film a dying man crawling into the arms of his mother and concentrate on the torn, bloody leg being dragged up a flight of stairs rather than the emotions of either party? And who else would hew so relentlessly to the rain-soaked-street, neon-in-the-puddles look? Or bring this romance to its predictably unhappy ending with the image of corpses lying hand in hand? There's a lot to like about this kind of bravado, but still not enough to catapult Mr. Ferrara into the mainstream. Then again, "China Girl" makes no stab at broad acceptance anyhow, which is another of its better qualities.

•

"China Girl," which opens today at the National and other theaters, hardly exists on the verbal level; Mr. Ferrara still doesn't have much idea of what to do with actors other than to let them fight with one another. It tells of Tony (Richard Panebianco) and Tyan (Sari Chang), who meet at a dance — where else? — and quickly strike up the kind of pure, beautiful romance that outrages everyone they know. The love scenes are of much

less interest than the brawls, and indeed the latter occur more frequently. The screenplay by Nicholas St. John seems concerned only with action and ethnic slurs, though it does stop to let one of Tony's cohorts address him as Gandhi for refusing to engage in one more rumble.

"China Girl" has intermittent flashes of virtuosity, though not enough of them to offset the film's slow, ordinary stretches or its essential silliness. Still, Mr. Ferrara remains a man to watch.

JANET MASLIN

1987 S 25, C16:6

Rolling a Three

THE BIG TOWN, directed by Ben Bolt; screenplay by Robert Roy Pool, based on the novel "The Arm" by Clark Howard; director of photography, Ralf D. Bode; film editor, Stuart Pappé; music by Michael Melvoin; production designer, Bill Kenney; produced by Martin Ransohoff; released by Columbia Pictures. At Embassy 1, Broadway and 46th Street; Sutton, 57th Street and Third Avenue; 86th Street Twin, near Lexington Avenue; 23d Street West, at Eighth Avenue; Metro Twin, 99th Street and Broadway. Running time: 110 minutes. This film is rated R.

J. C. Cullen	Matt Dillon
Lorry Dane	Diane Lane
George Cole	Tommy Lee Jones
Mr. Edwards	Bruce Dern
Ferguson Edwards	Lee Grant
Phil Carpenter	Tom Skerritt
Aggie Donaldson	Suzy Amis
Sonny Binkley	David Marshall Grant
Carl Hooker	Don Francks

IT'S the great American theme: a small-town boy seeks his fortune in the big city. In this case he's the best crapshooter at the local garage and he heads off to "The Big Town" of Chicago in 1957, where he makes a pile of money and has to choose between two women: a married stripper and an unmarried mother with a heart of gold. So it's not Horatio Alger. More to the point, this huge cliché of a movie isn't even a distant relation of films like "The Color of Money," which can actually make you root for hustlers. "The Big Town" only proves we've gone back to the 1950's one time too many.

There must be some behind-the-scenes explanation for what went wrong, but the evidence of the movie's failures is right there on the screen. Matt Dillon, who has shown some charm and flair in earlier films (such as "The Flamingo Kid"), can only look brooding as J. C. Cullen, the young man who rolls the dice and can figure the odds so well he becomes known as "Cully the Arm." We might be able to sympathize with him if we could find a coherent character to sympathize with. But he is not quite innocent and not very wise, not quite dynamic amd certainly not charming. He is easily defined by what he's not, because the whole film seems to have crucial pieces missing.

•

My favorite nonsense sequence goes like this: Cully and the stripper, Lorry Dane (Diane Lane), act out one of the coldest, least erotic sex scenes in recent movies; she's leaning against the bar in the strip club and he gives new meaning to the word quick. Next, they're walking down the street arm in arm, nuzzling each other (could this be love?), when we cut to a shot of Cully alone in his bed, where he gets a phone call from his mother with bad news from home. You can try to construct your own, better-built movie from the hints

Matt Dillon

thrown around here (Clark Howard's novel "The Arm," on which the story is based, may hold some of the missing pieces). But the director, Ben Bolt — who has directed many television shows in England and the United States, and so should know better — won't give you much to work with.

Lee Grant and Bruce Dern play the couple whose gambling stable Cully joins, and they both look as miserably stiff as any top-rate professional actors can. Tommy Lee Jones, as Lorry Dane's husband, doesn't have to do more than look sleazy and menacing, so he glowers and wears shiny silk shirts and a dollar-sign tie clip. Remarkably, Suzy Amis makes the young mother, who dreams of becoming one of the first women to be a disk jockey, someone to care about; Ms. Amis is obviously bringing more to the role than the screenplay has given her.

Like the actors, the music and other 1950's trappings resemble tacky artificial decorations hung on the story. They don't do much to convince us this is another time and place. In fact, "The Big Town," which opens today at the Sutton and other theaters, seems full of 1980's people crazily caught up in 1950's nostalgia, as if they've dropped by some We-Love-Elvis costume party and can't wait to get back home.

CARYN JAMES

1987 S 25, C20:4

High Mortality

BEST SELLER, directed by John Flynn; written by Larry Cohen; director of photography, Fred Murphy; film editor, David Rosenbloom; music by Jay Ferguson; production designer, Gene Rudolf; produced by Carter De Haven; released by Orion Pictures. At Astor Plaza, Broadway and 44th Street; Manhattan Twin, 59th Street and Third Avenue; Orpheum, Third Avenue and 86th Street; 34th Street Showplace, between Second and Third Avenues; 84th Street Six, at Broadway. Running time: 110 minutes. This film is rated R.

Cleve	James Woods
Dennis Meechum	Brian Dennehy
Roberta Gillian	Victoria Tennant
Holly Meechum	Allison Balson
David Madlock	Paul Shenar
Graham	George Coe
Mrs. Foster	Ann Pitoniak
Cleve's Mother	Mary Carver
Monks	Sully Boyar
Annie	Kathleen Lloyd
Cleve's Father	Harold Tyner

IN "Best Seller," written by Larry Cohen and directed by John Flynn, Brian Dennehy plays Dennis Meechum, a Jo-

seph Wambaugh-like Los Angeles cop who moonlights as the author of best-selling books about police work.

After the long pre-credit sequence, which is set in 1972 and, unfortunately, tips the mystery to come, the film formally begins 15 years later when Meechum, still on the force, is being badgered by his publishers for a new book. However, the poor man has had a writing block ever since his wife died of cancer. Enter Cleve (James Woods), a stylishly dressed young psychotic who makes Meechum the sort of offer every blocked writer dreams of.

Cleve confesses to the cop that for years he's been the hit man for Kappa Industries, a hugely successful conglomerate that has risen to the top of American business mostly, it seems, through the bumping off of United States Senators, accountants with loose lips and balky competitors. Cleve wants Meechum to write a book exposing Kappa and its chief executive officer, David Madlock (Paul Shenar), with whom the hit man has had a falling out.

Meechum is not stupid. He knows the book will be a best seller. He agrees to do it and, with Cleve's assistance, sets about certifying the facts.

"Best Seller" is about the curious relationship that grows up between the two men who, we are asked to believe, come to respect each other. If you can buy that, you may also buy the rest of the movie even though, from the very beginning, you're likely to be ahead of every plot twist and assassination.

In spite of its good cast and high mortality rate, "Best Seller," which opens today at the Manhattan Twin and other theaters, is as tepid as it's inept.

Mr. Cohen, the writer-director of such horror films as "It's Alive" and "It's Alive II," has another monster in Cleve, but Cleve's not really as interesting as the murderous newborn baby who lays waste Los Angeles in "It's Alive."

•

Lorey Sebastian

On the Job
James Woods plays a corporate hit man out for revenge in "Best Seller," co-starring Brian Dennehy and directed by John Flynn.

"Best Seller" aspires to make a political statement about American business practices, but simply trivializes its nightmarish view of capitalism rampant. Mr. Flynn and Mr. Cohen appear to have worked hard to create a movie totally without suspense, humor, plausibility, charm, excitement, wit and substance.

VINCENT CANBY

1987 S 25, C24:1

Lovelorn

DARK EYES, directed by Nikita Mikhalkov; screenplay (Italian with English subtitles) by Alexander Adabachian and Mr. Mikhalkov, with the collaboration of Suso Cecchi D'Amico, based on the short stories by Anton Chekhov; director of photography, Franco de Giacomo; edited by Enzo Meniconi; music by Francis Lai; production supervisor, Vittorio Noia; produced by Silvia D'Amico Bendico and Carlo Cucchi; released by Island Pictures. Tonight at Alice Tully Hall at 7:30 and Avery Fisher Hall at 9, as part of the 25th New York Film Festival. Tomorrow the film opens at Cinema 1, Third Avenue at 60th Street. Running time: 118 minutes. This film has no rating.

Romano	Marcello Mastroianni
Elisa	Silvana Mangano
Tina	Marthe Keller
Anna	Elena Sofonova
Elisa's Mother	Pina Cei
Pavel	Vsevolod Larionov
The Governor of Sisoiev	Innokenti Smoktunovski
The Lawyer	Roberto Herlitzka

By VINCENT CANBY

NIKITA MIKHALKOV'S "Dark Eyes," tonight's convivial opening attraction of the 25th New York Film Festival at Lincoln Center, is both enchanting and enchanted, a triumph composed of seemingly irreconcilable contradictions.

"Dark Eyes" is — technically — a pastiche, but it has the manner of something freshly conceived. It's Russian to the core, yet much of it is set in Italy and its star is the matchless Marcello Mastroianni. It's a wise, ruefully funny Chekhovian comedy, though Chekhov did not write it. It takes one into a turn-of-the-century world that's as casually prescient as those of "The Three Sisters" and "Uncle Vanya," without for a minute seeming to be.

Though it's about a man with the soul of an artist and the manner of a buffoon, about the man's abandoned aspirations and doomed love affairs, as well as about the heedless follies of the new European bourgeoisie, "Dark Eyes" is consistently exhilarating. In the steadfast resolve of a fellow who's an utter failure, it dramatizes a truly Chekhovian concept of comedy.

"Dark Eyes" will be shown twice tonight at Lincoln Center and will start its regular commercial engagement tomorrow at Cinema 1.

Like John Huston, Mr. Mikhalkov, best known here for "Slave of Love" and "Oblomov," is an eclectic film maker who manages to honor his source material. In "Dark Eyes," the Russian director borrows freely from four Chekhov stories, mostly from "The Lady With the Little Dog" and "The Name-Day Party," to create an original work that Chekhov would never have written.

•

The film begins and ends aboard a Mediterranean steamer en route to Italy from Greece. Romano (Mr. Mastroianni), a garrulous Italian fellow with frayed cuffs and the flush of an alcoholic, corners a Russian passenger, in the ship's saloon, and more or less pins down the stranger while he reminisces about the great, lost love of his life, a young Russian woman he met some years ago at an Italian spa.

In what is virtually a single, chronological flashback, Romano recalls his ironic downfall. It all began to go wrong, he remembers, at his wife's birthday party, at which point the film cuts to an earlier time and a huge estate in the Italian countryside.

The day is hot and still. People wander about the lawn. They play croquet. Elisa (Silvana Mangano), Romano's wife, attempts to attend to her duties as hostess while coping with the news that the family fortune may have been wiped out. Guests drink tea, eat strawberries and gossip. Small boys in sailor suits run about making too much noise. Boredom is in the air. Worry is only partly disguised. During the afternoon's musicale, Elisa cannot sit without fidgeting.

Romano is no help to her. The once-promising student of architecture, who "had the luck to marry an heiress," has long since given up any idea of a career. Seduced by money, Romano has accepted his position as consort and court jester. In the course of this party, he makes a fool of himself to amuse the children, flirts half-heartedly with his bird-brained mistress (Marthe Keller) and sneaks off for a nap. At the end of the day, Romano is so exhausted he feels he must go away for a few weeks "to take the waters."

•

"Dark Eyes" is as much about the lost marriage of Romano and Elisa as it is about Romano's love for Anna (Elena Sofonova), the young Russian woman he meets at the spa and with whom, initially, he begins an affair just to pass the time. He doesn't find Anna especially interesting "physically," though he feels there is something "pure" about her. Back home, Romano can't get Anna out of his mind. Under the pretense of selling a newly patented process for the manufacture of unbreakable glass, Romano sets off for Russia to find Anna.

Mr. Mastroianni's remarkable performance, both heartbreaking and farcical, sets the tone for "Dark Eyes," whose emotional landscape is as broad and rich as its physical terrain. The screenplay, by Alexander Adabachian and Mr. Mikhalkov "with the collaboration of Suso Cecchi D'Amico," makes astonishingly successful and intelligent use of the Chekhov material. Mr. Mikhalkov and his collaborators have folded key elements from "The Name-Day Party" into "The Lady With the Little Dog," borrowing from another tale, "Anna Around the Neck," for the substance of Anna's character, and taking inspiration from "My Wife" to arrive at their own conclusion.

The screenplay can be faulted only for being more shapely than Chekhovian, but then this is a movie, not a short story.

Though Mr. Mastroianni's performance is one of the highlights of his career, those by the other actors are almost in his league. Miss Sofonova, a beautiful, new young Russian actress, is both innocent and willful as the not completely naïve Anna. Miss Mangano's Elisa is as complex as Mr. Mastroianni's Romano, while Miss Keller, trapped for too many years in sudsy romantic roles, is here revealed to be a comic actress of sweet, rare humor.

•

Occasionally (especially in the spa sequences) Mr. Mikhalkov's vision appears to have been unduly influenced by the style of Federico Fellini, possibly because the orchestrations

A scene from "Dark Eyes," starring Marcello Mastroianni, hatless behind the seated woman.

make Francis Lai's soundtrack score sound uncomfortably like one by Nino Rota. There also are times when the lip-synching of the Italian dialogue is off. These are minor reservations. That the film is the work of a singular, very Russian artist, a man with a profound appreciation for his sources, is apparent throughout, from the indolent luxury of the great party scene until the final, elegant shot of the beloved Anna.

In one of the film's sharpest, funniest sequences, the dignitaries of a small provincial Russian city turn out to welcome Romano and his unbreakable-glass patent. The bewildered, love-sick Romano is celebrated as the town's first foreigner and the harbinger of the "new" Russia of "progress, prestige and population increase." Possibly inspired by "Uncle Vanya" is the ridiculous madman who attacks Romano and begs him not to build the factory that must eventually spoil Russia's great rivers, forests and streams.

In everything he wrote, Chekhov's sense of the future was as strong as his feeling for the past. The future existed in the commonplace world around him. Working today, Mr. Mikhalkov has access to hindsight, but he never allows himself to see more than the master felt instinctively, in his thoroughly Russian bones.

1987 S 25, C26:5

A TAXING WOMAN, written and directed by Juzo Itami; in Japanese with English subtitles; photographed by Yonezo Maeda; edited by Akira Suzuki; music by Toshiyuki Honda; produced by Yasushi Tamaoki and Seigo Hosogoe; presented by Itami Production and New Century Producers. At Alice Tully Hall, as part of the 25th New York Film Festival. Running time: 127 minutes. This film has no rating.

Ryoko Itakura .... Nobuko Miyamoto
Hideki Gondo .... Tsutomu Yamazaki
Hanamura .... Masahiko Tsugawa
Ishii .... Hideo Murota
Tsuyuguchi .... Shuji Otaki
Taro Gondo .... Daisuke Yamashita

By VINCENT CANBY

"Violence," says a Japanese gangster bidding a dramatic if temporary farewell to a confederate in handcuffs, "is obsolete. Today we go to prison for tax evasion."

The fine art of underreporting income, and the equally fine art of nabbing those who do, is the all-embracing subject of "A Taxing Woman," the solemnly funny new satire by Juzo Itami, the Japanese director whose comic meditation on noodles,

"Tampopo," is still playing first-run here at the Cinema Studio.

"A Taxing Woman" will be shown at the New York Film Festival at Lincoln Center at noon today and at 9:30 P.M. tomorrow.

It's now clear that Mr. Itami is one of the most original, most free-wheeling sensibilities in movies today — either at home in Japan or abroad. He's robust in a way that we seldom think of as characteristically Japanese. Like "Tampopo," this new movie has a narrative of sorts, and several vividly sketched characters, but "A Taxing Woman" is as much a densely detailed essay on contemporary Japanese manners as it is conventional fiction.

Mr. Itami has the self-assurance and the eye of a born film maker and the mind of the kind of social critic who more often expresses himself in prose. In any other discipline it would be too much to call his work Swiftian, but in movies, where social criticism of this quality is virtually nonexistent, Mr. Itami's sarcasm deserves high praise.

•

At the center of "A Taxing Woman" is Ryoko Itakura (Nobuko Miyamoto), who, after her divorce, has gone to work in the Japanese equivalent of the Internal Revenue Service to support herself and her 5-year-old son. A seemingly ordinary middle-class woman who wears her hair in a Louise Brooks bob and is self-conscious about her freckles, Ryoko suddenly finds her true calling as a tax inspector.

To all outward appearances, she's pretty, mild-mannered and shy, but on the trail of fraud she has the cool, unjudgmental tenacity of a bird dog with a nose for the second set of books. After serving her apprenticeship successfully terrorizing the aged proprietors of mom-and-pop stores, Ryoko moves into the big time: organized crime. She's promoted to an ultramodern task force whose principal target is Hideki Gondo (Tsutomu Yamazaki), a suave but gimpy fellow who operates what are called "adult motels" and who specializes in acquiring parcels of real estate from owners who don't want to sell. During the initial phases of the tax inquiry, Ryoko and Gondo are drawn to each other in a wacky variation on the sentimental movie about the cop who falls for the criminal. In Ryoko's case, however, it's evident that there could never be any real contest between infatuation and duty.

•

Mr. Itami is astonished by Japan's

Two workers at the Radium Dial Company's factory in Ottawa, Ill., in a scene from "Radium City," a documentary by Carole Langer.

staggering affluence and by a materialism so unembarrassed and so aggressive that it has polarized society. On one side are those people — including moms, pops and hoodlums — whose sole interest is in hanging onto the money they've made. On the other side are those selfless, comradely functionaries dedicated to seeing that the Government gets its cut of the melon. Nothing else matters.

The movie is thick with the inscrutably complex methods of tax evasion and with the high-tech methods of the law-enforcement officers. When, at long last, Ryoko and her fellow operatives close in on Gondo's empire, it's with enough precision, planning and Japanese-made electronic equipment to take not only Grenada but also Barbados and Tobago. The people in "A Taxing Woman" think small but on a grand scale.

The film is more witty than laugh-out-loud funny. "A Taxing Woman" doesn't possess the lyrically oddball footnotes that make "Tampopo" so special. Yet Mr. Itami is a man in touch with the world in which he lives and with the passions of his obsessed characters, which is why Ryoko and Gondo, though inflexible, are so appealing.

Miss Miyamoto (in private life, Mrs. Itami), who plays the ambitious noodle maker in "Tampopo," and Mr. Yamazaki, the philosophizing, noodle-loving truck driver in the earlier film, are wonderfully single-minded and deadpan comics.

"A Taxing Woman" also looks terrific, from its arresting opening shot — an image of a dying old man, past all but infantile needs — to its final, bitter sequence in which Gondo and Ryoko meet for the last time. The setting is a great, deserted baseball park that, in the context of the rest of the

movie, could possibly be the prototype for a brand-new export.

1987 S 26, 9:1

RADIUM CITY, directed and produced by Carole Langer; photography by Luke Sacher; edited by Ms. Langer and Brian Cotnoir; music by Timmy Cappello. At Alice Tully Hall, as part of the 25th New York Film Festival. Running time: 110 minutes. This film has no rating.

By JANET MASLIN

It must have sounded like a good job at the time, painting luminous numbers onto the faces of clocks. In old photographs, the teen-age girls who worked at the Radium Dial Company's factory in Ottawa, Ill., during the 1920's look happy, and they also look prosperous, since the pay was high. The work was even challenging, since it took skill to fill in the outlined numbers properly. The better to master this intricately detailed painting, the workers were encouraged to lick their brushes.

The consequences were dreadful and, as documented by Carole Langer in "Radium City," as far-reaching as the wildest nightmare. Many of the women developed radium-related cancer and of these, most died young; Miss Langer establishes that quickly because it is, in a terrible way, the very least of Ottawa's troubles. Or in any case just the beginning, for Miss Langer's film tells a tale that gets worse at every turn. "Radium City" outlines the complex aftermath of these events with as full an awareness of social and political consequences as medical ones. What emerges is as chilling a real-life horror story as anyone could imagine.

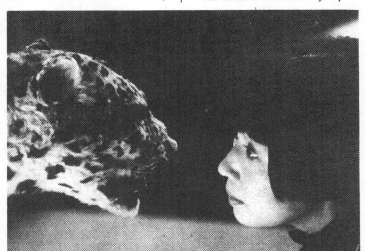

Nobuko Miyamoto in a scene from "A Taxing Woman."

After the Radium Dial workers began to get sick, according to the film, a lawsuit brought pressure to bear upon the company. With that, it closed and then re-opened under the name Luminous Processes in another part of town. The young women, though more apprehensive, kept on working. ("At 19, nobody asks questions about how dangerous anything is, you just take the job because you need it," said one of the women interviewed.) This was during the Depression, and with World War II Luminous Processes grew even more unassailable. Its president met with Albert Einstein and President Roosevelt about helping the war effort, and Luminous began using its facilities to turn out polonium, for possible use in atomic bombs.

Meanwhile, the death toll continued to rise, and an ever-greater shroud of mystery surrounded Ottawa. Three elderly women recall the death of their sister and the doctors' efforts to have her buried immediately, in the middle of the night, before an autopsy could be performed.

•

After the war, the Atomic Energy Commission began research into conditions in Ottawa, a town whose cemetery is still highly radioactive. (The three elderly women say they were told it would be centuries before their sister's body, which had been exhumed from its grave at the time of filming and sent elsewhere for tests, would lose its radioactivity.) Most of the results of their research remained secret. And in 1968 the original Radium Dial Company building was torn down, after having been used as a meat locker for a while. One woman said that of the family that ran the meat locker, all but one has since died of cancer.

Pieces of the building were scattered throughout the town and used as landfill. One man shows off the old counter he scavenged from the wreckage and installed in his basement. Another shows the spot where he kept an ornament from the building until a year ago, when someone took it away for tests. The spot is empty, but it still sets a geiger counter to ticking. So does much of the town. It has a high rate of birth defects, and the pets are sickly. One hunter was alarmed to bag a severely disfigured, tumor-covered deer.

"Radium City" is as much about the townspeople's efforts to deal with these ghastly facts as with the facts themselves. In addition to outlining the anger and grief of some residents, it also focuses on the fearfulness and boosterism of others.

The Mayor, who politely plays down the problem in an interview with Miss Langer, is also seen on a videotape (made by a local man named Ken Ricci, who serves as a geiger-counter-carrying vigilante) of a city council meeting, introducing a discussion of how to dismantle the now-abandoned Luminous Processes building with the news that anyone asking rude questions will be escorted out by the police. Not surprisingly, in view of this, the town's efforts to dispose of radioactive waste have been ineffectual. Carelessly hosing down factory sites has spread the problem even further, contaminating the water supply.

•

The people of Ottawa express varying degrees of resignation, bitterness and confusion, emotions that are brought into even sharper relief by the glimpses Miss Langer offers of the hardships in their lives.

A deeply religious woman whose young son has cancer talks about faith and frustration. The boy's eyes widen when his mother mentions a moment in which she felt that perhaps God ought to take him quickly.

A woman whose sister has Down's Syndrome recalls her mother, who worked in the radium factory and also had two miscarriages. Her mother used to say that "it's not who you know, but what you do as a person that counts in this life," she recalls. "And a few months before she died, she looked at me and said 'It's not what you know, it's *who* you know.' And it was really sad."

"Radium City" is about more than an isolated calamity. (And it's by no means isolated. An abandoned radium factory in Woodside, Queens, owned by the same family that ran the Ottawa plants, is currently under investigation.) The film is about the desire for independence that led those teen-age girls to the plants in the first place, about facing up to hardship and about the dangers of being too well-bred to ask questions. Miss Langer's tone is more accusatory than objective, and at times more sentimental than it needs to be, but the story she tells makes those lapses understandable. It is a story too important to be ignored.

"Radium City" will be shown tonight at 6 P.M. as part of the New York Film Festival.

1987 S 26, 9:4

DIARY FOR MY LOVED ONES, directed by Marta Meszaros; screenplay (Hungarian with English subtitles) by Miss Meszaros and Eva Pataki; director of photography, Miklos Jancso Jr.; edited by Eva Karmento; music by Zsolt Dome; set design, Eva Martin; a Mafilm-Budapest Studio production. At Alice Tully Hall, as part of the 25th New York Film Festival. Running time: 135 minutes. This film has no rating.

Juli	Zsuzsa Czinkoczi
Magda	Anna Polony
Janos	Jan Nowicki
Grandpa	Pal Zolnay
Grandma	Mari Szemes
Erzsi	Erzsebet Kutvolgyi
Anna Pavlovna	Irina Kuberskaia
Natasha	Adel Kovacs

By WALTER GOODMAN

The strongest scenes of "Diary for My Loved Ones" come in the form of Soviet and Hungarian newsreel footage — a victory celebration after World War II, Stalin being acclaimed and mourned, mass rallies and meetings laying down the current party line. Among the onlookers at several of these events, we glimpse the movie's main characters, skillfully interpolated into history. That merger is the essence of Marta Meszaros' forceful evocation of the early 1950's, when the Communist world was compelled to come to terms with its Stalinist past.

This diary from Hungary, which is being shown at the Film Festival at 3 P.M. today and again at 6:15 P.M. on Tuesday, is a continuation of "Diary for My Children," which was shown at the festival in 1984. Plainly autobiographical, it picks up in 1950, when Juli, the diarist, is 18 and determined to become a movie director. She is at once a victim and a beneficiary of Stalinist rule. Her father, an important Hungarian Communist with whom she lived in exile in Moscow, was purged in 1938; her beloved surrogate father Janos was arrested and jailed after the war, along with many other veterans returning from the West. But she owes her acceptance by a film school in Moscow to her great aunt, a thoroughly Stalinist official.

We see Juli's political development through her work, beginning with a typical piece of agitprop ("We vow to fight the imperialists!") and concluding with a documentary about demoralized Hungarian peasants that proves too realistic for the socialist realists who run her school. There's no missing the point, but Miss Meszaros is less successful in getting at Juli's internal development. The story, so explicit politically, is dramatically elusive. People tend to deliver speeches at each other and strike attitudes, often to highly obtrusive music. "How can you love a man who betrayed our cause?" the aunt demands of Juli. "They were crimes, not errors," declares Janos. "The perpetrators must be called to account."

There's an operatic quality here, notably in a clumsy champagne-swilling party scene, that is very much at odds with the movie's no-nonsense documentary aspect. When Janos is finally released from prison, we see the sky and hear angelic sounds. Juli (reticently played by Anna Polony) is an onlooker, who bursts out now and then in defiant speeches for which we have not been prepared. Miss Mezaros, who wrote the screenplay with Eva Pataki, seems a bit shy about letting us see some pages of the diary.

The anguish of the period is personified by Janos, a faithful Communist imprisoned in deference to Stalin's paranoia. Tortured and drugged, he testifes against a former comrade. After Stalin's death, he tries to take up his cause again, having made a then fashionable progression — "Condemnation, rehabilitation, appointment" — but is burdened by guilt for his betrayal and the beatings inflicted by his captors.

•

The passion of "Diary" comes from Miss Meszaros's determination to do justice to history and to its victims. She is merciless in her references to the party hacks in Hungary who shifted course according to the prevailing winds from Moscow. When a bureaucrat informs Juli that her father has been posthumously rehabililtated, you can imagine him delivering news of an execution in exactly the same bland way.

In answer to the question posed by Janos, "How could this have happened?", we are shown a society beaten down by an imposed ideology, where hero worship is substituted for ordinary human feelings and people prosper and perish by political whim. Lies are pounded in from every side: Guards at prison camps greet visitors with the word, "Freedom." To overcome the tawdriness of it all takes a character like Anna Pavlovna, a star actress who handles busybody commissars by offering them signed pictures of herself.

This section of the diary ends with the Budapest uprising of 1956. Juli, in Moscow, is unable to get permission to go home, and we leave her clutching unhappily at the bars of the Hungarian Embassy. Bars are a recurring visual theme of this tough picture of an imprisoned nation. Its appearance now is confirmation of significant change in Hungary, which we may learn more about in the next installment of Juli's diary.

1987 S 26, 12:3

Correction

A film review on Saturday about "Diary for My Loved Ones," shown at the New York Film Festival, misidentified the actress who played Juli. She is Zsuzsa Czinkoczi.

1987 S 29, A3:1

JACKIE CHAN'S POLICE STORY, directed by Jackie Chan; screenplay by Edward Tang; edited by Peter Cheung; music by Kevin Bassinson; art director, Wan Fat; produced by Edward Tang; released by Golden Harvest. At Alice Tully Hall, as part of the 25th New York Film Festival. Running time: 89 minutes. This film has no rating.

Kevin Chan	Jackie Chan
Selina Fong	Bridget Lin
May	Maggie Cheung
Tom Koo	Cho Yuen
Inspector Wong	Bill Tung
Frankie	Kenneth Tong
Superintendent	Lam Kok Hung

The New York Film Festival pays homage tonight at 9 to Hong Kong's Jackie Chan, Asia's most popular movie star, with the showing of "Jackie Chan's Police Story" at Alice tully Hall. The film will be shown again on Sunday at 2 P.M.

Noblesse oblige, as they say in the Bronx.

If you happen to miss either of these screenings, you can catch up with more or less the same kind of thing on virtually any day of the week on 42d Street, where comic kung-fu movies are treated not as cinematic epiphanies but as unpretentious comedies for people whose minds, like their feet, wander when not nailed to the floor.

The festival's program notes describe Mr. Chan, who is both the director and star of "Police Story," as "a combination of Buster Keaton and Clint Eastwood," which says less about Mr. Chan than it does about the festival's gift for unhinged hyperbole. This is not the actor's American debut. He has been seen here in Burt Reynolds's "Cannonball Run" and, in 1980, in the Hong Kong-made "Big Brawl," among others.

•

In "Police Story," set in Hong Kong, Mr. Chan plays an ace cop who is shyly clumsy around women. In the course of the story, about drug traffickers, Mr. Chan gets three separate birthday cakes thrown into his face, and participates in several elaborately staged gun fights and car chases. These are mildly amusing, though less amusing than the dubbed English dialogue that recalls, without meaning to, Woody Allen's egg-salad spy epic, "What's Up, Tiger Lily?"

Mr. Chan has nothing in common with either Buster Keaton or Clint Eastwood. He is more like a scaled-down, oriental Sylvester Stallone, with energy and a willingness to smile fondly at himself.

"Police Story" is of principal interest as a souvenir of another culture.

Just to make sure that Lincoln Center audiences know they're still in high-toned surroundings, "Police Story" shares its program with the National Film Board of Canada's short, "Pas de Deux," an elegantly photographed dance film by the estimable Norman McLaren.

VINCENT CANBY

1987 S 26, 12:3

Not by Turgenev

A MONTH IN THE COUNTRY, directed by Pat O'Connor; screenplay by Simon Gray, based on a novel by J. L. Carr; director of photography, Ken Macmillan; edited by John Victor Smith; music by Howard Blake; art director, Richard Elton;

Colin Firth plays a World War I veteran in "A Month in the Country."

produced by Kenith Trodd; released by Film Four International. At Alice Tully Hall, as part of the 25th New York Film Festival. Running time: 96 minutes. This film has no rating.

Birkin	Colin Firth
Moon	Kenneth Branagh
Mrs. Keach	Natasha Richardson
Reverend Keach	Patrick Malahide
Douthwaite	Tony Haygarth
Ellerbeck	Jim Carter
Col. Hebron	Richard Vernon
Kathy	Vicky Arundale

By JANET MASLIN

PAT O'CONNOR'S direction broadens and illuminates "A Month in the Country" even as the writing — a screenplay by Simon Gray, from the novel by J.L. Carr — strives to tie up any loose ends. Indeed, Mr. O'Connor, whose first feature was the haunting "Cal," does a great deal to keep an eloquent but small film from seeming even smaller.

"A Month in the Country" (which has no connection with the Turgenev work of the same name) is set in a tiny Yorkshire village called Oxgodbody, where a shell-shocked World War I veteran named Birkin (Colin Firth) arrives to work on uncovering a medieval painting on the wall of a local church. When Birkin first appears, it is in the midst of a torrential downpour, and Mr. O'Connor's establishing shots of the village in the rain do a lot to foreshadow the restorative powers of this simple, beautiful setting. Birkin's acute stammer and his nervous tics attest to his need to recuperate from a wartime ordeal, and the film follows his progress.

The screenplay displays competing tendencies toward tidiness and inconclusiveness, as well as an orderly, theatrical manner of bringing supporting characters onto and off the screen. Birkin's mission to restore the painting, set forth in the will of a local benefactress, reveals a mystery that Birkin then proceeds to solve, a mystery having to do with the painter himself. He is helped in this work by Moon, an archeologist who (at the behest of that same benefactress) has pitched a tent nearby and is searching for the remains of one of the benefactress's ancestors. Meanwhile, the church's vicar, Keach (Patrick Mala-

hide), opposes Birkin's efforts on the grounds that a painting in church will distract parishioners, and Keach's lovely wife gravitates toward Birkin. The wife is played by Natasha Richardson, Vanessa Redgrave's daughter, whose presence is mesmerizing and whose mannerisms are uncannily like her mother's. She has that same shyly lopsided grin and that same bold, penetrating gaze.

On its own, this material might seem far more neat and comfortable than it does in Mr. O'Connor's hands. But his direction lends it a strong sense of yearning, as well as a spiritual quality more apparent in the look of the film than in its dialogue. As in "Cal," Mr. O'Connor is especially good at emphasizing the characters' separateness from one another, as well as their unarticulated longing. The sense of unfulfilled desire and incommunicable sorrow give "A Month in the Country" great pathos, and the screenplay's trimness does set the stage for a transcendent final scene.

Though Mr. O'Connor seems less in tune with this material than with the Northern Irish tragedy of "Cal," he gives particular power to the story's elements of religion and doubt. He also gives moments that might have seemed precious — like a flirtatious speech by Mrs. Keach about roses — a sweetness that is real. So does the enormously self-possessed Miss Richardson, plucking a white rose and handing it to Birkin with great aplomb. "They bloom till autumn," she says of a favorite rose. "So you'll know when summer's over, because I usually wear one of the last in my hat." Not many actresses could deliver a line like that, as Miss Richardson does, without seeming the least bit coy.

"A Month in the Country" will be shown today at 4:30 and tomorrow at 9:15 P.M. as part of the New York Film Festival.

1987 S 27, 67:1

FILM VIEW/Janet Maslin

Slickness as Art

WITHOUT SPOILING ANY OF the thrills in Adrian Lyne's new thriller, it's possible to discuss the sequence in "Fatal Attraction" that finds a mother suddenly separated from her child. The mother has reason to suspect that her daughter may be in jeopardy, and so she is seen searching frantically for the little girl. Now, this ought to be enough: the mother's anxiety is the foremost emotion on anyone's mind. But Mr. Lyne also intercuts glimpses of the little girl's whereabouts. In a different sort of film, those glimpses would destroy any possibility of suspense.

Here, they only heighten the excitement. The child may not be in imminent danger, but she *is* doing something that looks great on camera and mixes quite nicely with the desperate-mother shots. So Mr. Lyne cuts back and forth between these two elements, dispelling any intense identification with the mother but greatly enhancing the energy level of the episode. That's the method of "Fatal Attraction": superficial effects achieved with great excitement and with a deftness that really is impressive. Mr. Lyne's shrewdness and professionalism should not be taken lightly.

We may not choose to embrace such virtues wholeheartedly, but neither should we dismiss them out of hand. Like anything else, slickness can be achieved with varying degrees of proficiency, and Mr. Lyne happens to be exceptionally good at what he does. "Fatal Attraction," shot in and around New York City, has a strong, inviting style and a high degree of concentration, with a refreshing lack of arbitrariness. There's never the feeling here that scenes — like the Seattle fish-packing and log-rolling episodes in John Badham's "Stakeout" — were thrown in because of the film's locale, not because they

With its energy and high gloss, Adrian Lyne's thriller is forceful enough to suspend disbelief as it hurtles along.

advance the story. Nor is there a sense of well-worn clichés being put through their weary paces; though its story is essentially familiar, "Fatal Attraction" is anything but a formula film.

Like another recent thriller, the equally red-hot "No Way Out," "Fatal Attraction" is forceful enough to suspend disbelief as it hurtles along, and so well acted that it transcends its own potential limitations. "No Way Out" might have been mere cloak-and-dagger nonsense in the hands of a director less clever than Roger Donaldson, and "Fatal Attraction," without Mr. Lyne, would have been a violence-edged soap opera and nothing more. Instead, each of these films displays an energy and high gloss that, at a time when so much film making is so dully workmanlike, are worth a lot.

The foremost thing that "Fatal Attraction" does for Mr. Lyne is to dispel the impression that his is a talent for soft-core porn effects and nothing more. Yes, Mr. Lyne could ogle Jennifer Beals in leotards (in "Flashdance") and run an ice cube over an undraped Kim Basinger (in "9½ Weeks") in emptily high style; each of those films was oddly impersonal, with character defined solely in terms of physical characteristics. "Fatal Attraction" is no less tactile or visually alluring than Mr. Lyne's earlier films ("Foxes" is another), but it's the first one to give equal time to its male characters or to focus much interest on personality.

Once again, the film's principals — a successful lawyer (Michael Douglas), his gorgeous and uncomplicated wife (Anne Archer) and the desperately lonely career woman (Glenn Close) with whom he has an affair — are defined more by where they go, what they own and what they wear than by what they say. But that seems rather apt, in view of the characters' own lack of introspection. "Fatal Attraction," which very convincingly depicts an affair between the career woman and the lawyer, is a morality tale for people who've lost touch with their own morals, and as such it amounts to a fascinating Rorschach test for the audience. Why does the lawyer, who appears happily married, have an affair with the career woman? Why does she cling to him so tenaciously? How does the wife fail to notice? A pat explanation of any of these things would sink the film, but Mr. Lyne's emphasis on surface details only lends it greater interest.

So the sequence in which Alex Forrest (Miss Close) and Dan Gallagher (Mr. Douglas) begin their affair is a marvel of ambiguity. After teasing the audience with the prospect of this illicit romance — and with the startling transformation of Miss Close into a magnificent flirt — Mr. Lyne shepherds them to a romantic restaurant, where James Dearden's artfully direct dialogue suspends all responsibility for what is about to happen. "I don't think having dinner with anybody is a crime," Dan says. "Not yet," Alex answers. A moment later, he asks why Alex has no date that Saturday night, and she admits to just having canceled one in his honor. "Does that make you feel good?" Alex asks. And Dan, who's a lawyer, answers carefully with a double negative of sorts: "It doesn't make me feel bad."

"Fatal Attraction" makes its audience look for visual manifestations of the things its characters don't know how to say. When Dan is at home with his happy family, there are only a mild sloppiness and a hint of cramped-apartment claustrophobia (plus the mindless sitcom on the television screen) to hint at dissatisfaction. Later on, he makes no outward show of guilt when he returns home — but he does take a shower under the shadow of his daughter's huge inflatable toad. Skin deep as it is, this kind of film making has never been more appropriate, or more timely. It's perfect for an age in which appearances are all, in which visceral responses count for more than considered ones, and in which a hint of dissatisfaction is beginning to make itself felt. And Mr. Lyne, on the evidence of "Fatal Attraction," is its master

□

1987 S 27, II:22:1

Midlife Crisis

THE THEME, directed by Gleb Panfilov; screenplay (Russian with English subtitles) by Mr. Panfilov and Aleksandr Chernivsky; director of photography, Leonid Kalashnikov; music by Vadim Bibergan; art director, Marksen Gaukman-Sverdlov; released by International Film Exchange. At Alice Tully Hall, as part of the 25th New York Film Festival. Running time: 100 minutes. This film has no rating.
Sasha Nikolayeva .... Inna Churikova
Kim Yesenin .... Mikhail Ulyanov
The Gravedigger .... Stanislav Lyubshin
Igor .... Yevgeny Vesnik
Jr. Lieut. Sinitsyn .... Sergei Nikonenko
Svetlana .... Nataliya Selezyova
Mariya Aleksandrova Yevgeniya Nechayeva

By WALTER GOODMAN

IF your heart sinks at the prospect of a movie about a writer in midlife crisis, take heart again. In "The Theme," which plays tonight and tomorrow night at the Film Festival, Gleb Panfilov, the Soviet director, gives the old subject a shot of imagination that sends it skipping around like a kid.

The midlifer at risk here is Kim, a once successful, still acclaimed playwright who knows he hasn't written anything worth writing for years. As played with sardonic wit by Mikhail Ulyanov, Kim is a tough veteran of the literary wars who can no longer swallow the praise that is still poured over him. This "guy with the shopworn face" has been around too long and knows himself too well. "Why am I alive?" he keeps moaning. "What do I write plays for?" But he often follows up such affectations with a self-mocking retort. If you mention writer's block, he's likely to knock your block off.

The movie gets started at a smart pace, as Kim is driving with his pal Igor, another hard-drinking writer, and an adorable and adoring bubblehead named Svetlana to Igor's house outside Moscow. The camera keeps its distance, and we hear the banter between the men, with pauses for Kim to try out on himself the artificial lines he is planning to put in the mouth of the hero of his proposed play about a 12th-century ruler. They have a run-in with a policeman in which the writers make sure the young fellow appreciates how well connected they are. By the time they get to their destination, we know a lot about Kim and something about the privileged situation of successful writers in the Soviet Union.

•

Their chattery hostess, Mariya Aleksandrova, a schoolteacher who wears a medal and exasperates Kim with her classroom compliments for celebrating "our truly wonderful Soviet society," invites her friend Sasha (played by the director's lovely wife and favorite star, Inna Churikova) to join them for dinner. Sitting quietly amid the nonstop nonsense, Sasha seems to see right through Kim.

The dinner scene, written, directed and acted with tremendous verve, is full of tidbits: the not entirely friendly rivalry between the two friends; the blatherings of Svetlana trying to defend Kim from any touch of criticism; the fatuous praise of Mariya Aleksandrova, and, as main course, Sasha's quiet honesty, in which Kim reads hard truths about himself that send him slightly wild. "I'm a lousy playwright!" he bursts out, drawing the usual reassuring remonstrances, only to have Sasha remark, "I think he's right."

The two meet again, in a cemetery, a lovely scene where the seemingly restrained Sasha becomes rapturous over the verses of a dead and little-known peasant poet, "a poor spirit" who has captured her imagination. By comparison with his simple heartfelt lines, so feelingly recited by Sasha, Kim's project seems utterly fake. The dead man becomes another rival for Kim, who by now is in love or thinks he is. He is so disconnected from honest feelings, however, that he can't be sure.

•

The climactic scene finds Kim hidden in Sasha's kitchen, eavesdrop-

Michael Douglas and Glenn Close as the illicit lovers in "Fatal Attraction"

ping as she makes a desperate farewell to her departing lover. It's a funny situation yet a grave one; Mr. Panfilov balances humor and grief most adroitly. Kim is overpowered by what he overhears; all that has happened to him, as a writer and a man, during his years of success, comes crashing home.

In its last minute or two, this rich movie goes out of control in a misconceived effort to tie things up. A letdown — but it can't take away from the performance of Miss Churikova, developing from quiet sadness, to enthusiasm to passion, or from the character of Kim, so Russian yet sharing plenty of qualities with Western literary lions, or from the inventiveness of Mr. Panfilov, who delivers acute little asides on Soviet society along the way.

It's probably the scene in which Sasha's lover, also a writer, renounces his homeland ("Everything's a lie here!") that caused the Soviet authorities to hold up the release of this spirited work after its completion in 1980. We can thank glasnost for the chance to see it at the Film Festival or at the Lincoln Plaza Cinema, where it opens Oct. 16.

1987 S 28, C18:1

Cheerful Despair

BARFLY, directed by Barbet Schroeder; written by Charles Bukowski; director of photography, Robby Muller; edited by Eva Gardos; production designer, Bob Ziembicki; produced by Mr. Schroeder, Fred Roos and Tom Luddy; released by the Cannon Group, Inc. At Alice Tully Hall, as part of the 25th New York Film Festival. Running time: 100 minutes. This film is rated R.

Henry	Mickey Rourke
Wanda Wilcox	Faye Dunaway
Tully	Alice Krige
Detective	Jack Nance
Jim	J. C. Quinn
Eddie	Frank Stallone
Janice	Sandy Martin
Lilly	Roberta Bassin
Grandma Moses	Gloria LeRoy
Ben	Joe Unger
Rick	Harry Cohn

By VINCENT CANBY

BARBET SCHROEDER, the French producer best known for his association with Eric Rohmer, infrequently directs films, but when he does, they're worth the long intervals between. It could be that being a producer is Mr. Schroeder's protective cover.

Nobody expects him to direct a new movie every 18 months. He's too busy producing the work of others. In the meantime he can take all the time he wants preparing his own films, including "More" (1969), a sunlit romance of doomed drug addicts, and "General Idi Amin Dada" (1976), his spellbinding documentary about the former dictator of Uganda, a man as madly obsessed as any of the creatures in the director's fiction films.

Mr. Schroeder's latest is "Barfly," his first American film and another not easily categorized movie that may be, I think, some kind of small, classic one-of-a-kind comedy. One thing is sure: "Barfly," in spite of its occasionally stomach-turning details, is *not* a tragedy — and it will invite anyone who says so to step into the alley.

"Barfly" will be shown at the New York Film Festival at Lincoln Center today at 9:30 P.M. and on Sunday at 4:30 P.M. It will open its commercial engagement here later this year.

Though it's set within the world of the seriously down-and-out in Los Angeles and is about people who are at the end of their ropes, "Barfly" somehow manages to be gallant and even cheerful. It has an admirably lean, unsentimental screenplay by Charles Bukowski, the poet laureate of America's misbegotten, a big, broad, mesmerizing performance by Mickey Rourke and one by Faye Dunaway that rediscovers the reserves of talent that, in recent years, have been hidden inside characters who wear designer wardrobes and sleep masks.

As Henry Chinaski, Mr. Rourke has a lot of the seedy, insinuating charm of Dustin Hoffman's Ratzo Rizzo in "Midnight Cowboy." Henry, the Bukowski surrogate figure, is a part-time writer and full-time drink-cadger who frequently gets beaten senseless in boozy brawls. Some area of his face seems always to be swollen. His knuckles remain perpetually skinned. The way he hustles down a street, Quasimodo-like (though he has perfectly normal legs), one can feel the pain in his ribs.

Henry is not a conventional movie's idea of a drunk. His alcoholism isn't "Lost Weekend"-instructive. It's far more insidious. He has no remorse for a life left behind, and he doesn't fall down or suffer blackouts. Throughout the long days and nights at the Golden Horn, a neighborhood bar just this side of Skid Row, he drinks only enough to maintain his easily wounded dignity. He's like a frigate bird hanging in the wind over the same patch of earth.

•

Though "Barfly" makes some half-hearted passes at explaining alcoholism as a way of dealing with life's pervasive second-rateness, it remains, for the most part, serenely above such paperback psychiatry. Mr. Bukowski and Mr. Schroeder are content simply to observe the minute, grotesque, hilarious details of the behavior of Henry and the other patrons of the Golden Horn — with respectful interest and amusement that never slop over into condescending compassion.

"Barfly" has the form of a vividly remembered vignette about several tumultuous days that almost (but not quite) change Henry's life. First there is his encounter with Wanda Wilcox (Miss Dunaway) who, though rather classily pulled together, is no less of a barfly than Henry and who, like him, has no particular past. Henry can't quite believe his good fortune when Wanda responds to him, scabby knuckles, dirty fingernails, filthy T-shirt and all.

Wanda tells him she likes the cockiness of his walk. He also talks in an unusual way, affecting a kind of W. C. Fields drawl to say things Wanda's never heard before. When she asks him solemnly if he doesn't hate people, he thinks before he answers, "No, but I feel better when they're not around." In the society Wanda keeps, this is rare wit.

In fact, Henry is light years ahead of Wanda in the brain department. Her recognition of this is to her credit, even as she admits that, if another man comes along with a fifth of whisky, she'll go off with him. Though the movie never makes a big deal of it, Wanda is far more lost than the resilient Henry will ever be.

•

Their new, very edgy relationship is complicated by the arrival of Tully (Alice Krige), a pretty, rich, uppercrust patron of arts who wants to publish one of Henry's short stories in her literary magazine.

Mickey Rourke in "Barfly."

This is pretty much the so-called plot of "Barfly." The film deals not in event but in the continuing revelation of character in a succession of horrifying, buoyant, crazy confrontations of barflies, bartenders, police and other representatives of the world of the sober. Mr. Bukowski's dialogue is not only richly funny but, when Henry quotes his own writings, it's also compelling. There's a kind of courtly nobility about Henry that Mr. Schroeder appreciates.

The story of Henry and Wanda doesn't come to a conclusion. The movie seems to withdraw from *it*. At the end of another raucous night at the Golden Horn, Robby Muller's discreet camera pulls back from the bar and out the front door without interrupting the lives that have been recorded.

Note also the performances of J. C. Quinn as Henry's bartender friend, Frank Stallone as the mean-tempered bartender who can never resist yet another fight with Henry in the alley and, as some of the Golden Horn regulars, Sandy Martin, Roberta Bassin, Gloria LeRoy, Joe Rice and Julie (Sunny) Pearson. Each one is memorable.

1987 S 30, C18:1

Image First

BAD BLOOD, directed and written by Léos Carax; in French with English subtitles; photography by Jean-Yves Escoffier; edited by Nelly Quettier and Hélène Muller; a Films Plain Chang-Soprofilms-FR3 Films Production. At Alice Tully Hall, as part of the 25th New York Film Festival. Running time: 105 minutes. This film has no rating.

Alex	Denis Lavant
Anna	Juliette Binoche
Marc	Michel Piccoli
Hans	Hans Meyer
Lise	Julie Delpy
The American Woman	Carroll Brooks
Boris	Hugo Pratt
Charlie	Serge Reggiani

By WALTER GOODMAN

THE pictures are in charge in Léos Carax's "Bad Blood," which plays at the New York Film Festival at 6:15 P.M. tonight and Friday. Most of the scenes seem to have been improvised in the interests of a striking shot, and the characters are in thrall to the camera. In this, his second feature, Mr. Carax lives up to his billing as "the natural heir of Jean-Luc Godard," showing a taste for under-

ground types and milieus, an inventive eye and a tolerance for tedium.

The plot is simpler than it appears. Alex (Denis Lavant), a small-time Paris hustler with very fast hands and a cigarette growing from between his lips, is inveigled into a superheist by Marc (Michel Piccoli) and Hans (Hans Meyer). In need of thousands to pay off the sinister "American woman," they plan to steal a virus culture from a big chemical company. The virus works against a fast-spreading and often fatal disease, STB, which strikes people who "make love without love."

An ailment with a moral. But Mr. Carax, who also wrote the murky script, doesn't show much concern for its consequences. One minor character appears to have been infected, but we are left to guess how come or so what. As for that big heist, when it finally comes off, the movie goes surrealistic, losing whatever crime-story tension has been built up. Instead of showing how Alex does the job, Mr. Carax lays on visual effects, such as an overhead shot of a squad of cops assuming a geometrical pattern for the camera's benefit.

It's the images, as cinéastes like to call them, that drive Mr. Carax. Some are stunners, in particular a dizzying rescue by parachute. It's so exciting and has so little to do with the plot that you can't help suspecting the characters were sent up in the plane solely so the photographer, Jean-Yves Escoffier, could do his stuff. Mr. Carax shows a special liking for overhead shots, shots of people racing or dancing past gritty walls, mirror shots and closeups of faces with fuzzy figures visible in the background. Since many of the prolonged closeups are of the beautiful Juliette Binoche (who plays Anna, Marc's languorous mistress and the love of Alex's life), they are not unpleasing. But who is that pretty woman in white who keeps wandering silently through and why is she weeping?

Mr. Carax makes much of speed ("I long for the kiss of speed," says Alex) and dramatic plays of light. But while the screen flashes and flickers, little else is happening. Not all his reflecting tricks can make the half-hour conversation between Anna and Alex seem less than three hours long, since neither they nor anybody else in the movie is coherent.

There are some funny moments: Alex does a vaudeville routine that ends with vegetables pouring onto his head; he and Anna kid around with shaving-cream beards; Halley's Comet is blamed for both a hot spell and a snowstorm; Hans gets all dolled up to go on the heist; a police inspector pauses in midaction to lament that his children never call him. You may wonder at such times whether "Bad Blood" is meant as parody of the whole film noir line.

The American woman (Carroll Brooks) is strictly-camp, and the amount of cigarette puffing is a smoking joke. However, the determinedly doleful tone defies laughter. When Alex turns on the radio and says, "Let's listen and let our feelings flow as they will" or "I feast my eyes to feast my dreams" or "Mutual love is a short circuit," we seem to be meant to take him seriously.

The main set, the apartment where the bare-chested criminals do their plotting, is on a street steeped in shadows, except for a couple of big abstract paintings at the far end. If it's symbols you're after, that's a pretty good one for this movie, touches of color in the gloom.

1987 S 30, C20:5

Literary Ambrosia

BABETTE'S FEAST, directed by Gabriel Axel; screenplay (Danish and French with English subtitles) by Mr. Axel from a novel by Isak Dinesen; cinematography, Henning Kristiansen; edited by Finn Henriksen; music by Per Norgard; production company, Just Betzer, Panorama Film International in cooperation with Nordisk Film A/S and the Danish Film Institute. At Alice Tully Hall, as part of the 25th New York Film Festival. Running time: 105 minutes. This film has no rating.

Babette	Stéphane Audran
Martine (old)	Birgitte Federspiel
Filippa (old)	Bodil Kjer
Martine (young)	Vibeke Hastrup
Filippa (young)	Hanne Stensgard
Lorenz Lowenhielm (old)	Jarl Kulle
Lorenz Lowenhielm (young)	Gudmar Wivesson
Achille Papin	Jean-Philippe Lafont
Lady from the court	Bibi Andersson

By VINCENT CANBY

TAKING a longish tale, "Babette's Feast," from Isak Dinesen's last collection, "Anecdotes of Destiny" (1958), Gabriel Axel has made a very handsome, very literary movie that does justice to the precision of the Dinesen prose, to the particularity of her concerns and to the ironies that so amused her.

"Babette's Feast" will be shown at the New York Film Festival at Lincoln Center tonight at 9:15 and on Monday at 6:15 P.M.

What with the English subtitles that translate the Danish dialogue and soundtrack narration, one spends almost as much time reading "Babette's Feast" as watching it. Subtitles, under most circumstances, are simply a necessary intrusion. In this case, however, they have the effect of subtly amplifying the distinctive voice of the storyteller, who can make great leaps forward and backward in time without destroying the commanding unity of the tale. Dinesen is just offscreen throughout.

"Babette's Feast" is set in the second half of the 19th century on Denmark's remote Jutland coast, in a small fishing village whose most notable inhabitants are a fervent Protestant pastor and his two beautiful, pious daughters. Martine and Filippa. Mindful of their responsibilities to their father and his reformist mission, each daughter turns down a beloved suitor. Martine's is a young officer, Filippa's a famous French opera star who has been vacationing on the Jutland coast.

After their father's death, the two young women slip into unmarried middle age, carrying on the pastor's work with saintly dedication. One night, in the middle of a terrible storm, Babette (Stéphane Audran) turns up at their door, battered by weather and circumstances, and carrying a letter of introduction from Filippa's opera singer, now old and retired. Having lost both her husband and son in the Paris Commune, Babette, he explains, needs political sanctuary. He begs the sisters to take her in. The sisters, who are nearly penniless, accept Babette's offer to act as their unpaid housekeeper.

In time, Babette becomes an indispensable though ever enigmatic member of the household. Her Roman Catholicism is politely ignored. She brings order and efficiency to the sisters' lives as defenders of their father's aging flock, which, over the years, has become split by old grievances and jealousies. Babette cooks, cleans, washes and sews, always remaining aloof and proud, at a distance from her benefactors.

All of this is by way of being the prelude to the film's extended, funny and moving final sequence, a spectacular feast, the preparation and execution of which reveal Babette's secret and the nature of her sustaining glory.

It's not telling too much to report that this glory is Art — in Babette's case, a very special God-given talent. "Babette's Feast" is an affirmation of Art as the force by which, in the words of the old pastor (who never quite realized what he was saying), "righteousness and bliss," otherwise known as the spirit and the flesh, shall be reconciled.

•

Mr. Axel, a film maker new to me who has worked as much in France as in Denmark, treats the Dinesen text with self-effacing but informed modesty. The understated courage of the characters, the barren beauty of the landscape and, finally, the unexpected appearance of salvation are all effortlessly defined in images and language that reflect the writer's style — swift, clean, witty and elegant.

Miss Audran dominates the movie in the same way that Babette takes charge of the sisters' household and the village. The actress is still one of the great natural resources of European films.

The beautiful Birgitte Federspiel, remembered from Carl Dreyer's classic, "Ordet," appears as the older Martine and Bodil Kjer as the older Filippa. Jean-Philippe Lafont plays the expansive opera singer and Bibi Andersson is seen in a cameo role as a patron of the arts. Every member of the cast is excellent.

A note of caution: do not see "Babette's Feast" on an empty stomach. Before the film ends, the feast itself, which includes, among other things, fresh terrapin soup, quail in vol-au-vents, blinis, caviar and baba au rhum, may drive you out to the nearest three-star restaurant. It could be a dangerously expensive evening.

1987 O 1, C22:5

The Inner Man

THE BELLY OF AN ARCHITECT, directed and written by Peter Greenaway; director of photography, Sacha Vierny; edited by John Wilson; music by Wim Mertens; produced by Colin Callender and Walter Donohue. At Alice Tully Hall, as part of the 25th new York Film Festival. Running time: 108 minutes. This film has no rating.

Stourley Kracklite	Brian Dennehy
Louisa Kracklite	Chloe Webb
Caspasian Speckler	Lambert Wilson
Io Speckler	Sergio Fantoni
Flavia Speckler	Stephania Cassini
Frederico	Vanni Corbellini
Julio	Alfredo Varelli
Caspetti	Geoffrey Coppleston
Pastarri	Francesco Carnelutti

By JANET MASLIN

STOURLEY KRACKLITE (Brian Dennehy), the central figure in Peter Greenaway's "Belly of an Architect," is at one point seen reflected in the central panel of a triptych mirror in his Rome apartment, wearing a blood-red robe and flanked by multiple Xerox copies of classically sculpted abdomens, copies he has made from photographs of Roman statuary. It's a perfect moment, or at least the kind of perfect moment Mr. Greenaway favors: orderly, symmetrical and obscure, offering great compositional beauty but no compelling reason why its riddles require solution.

At another point in the film, Mr. Greenaway considers the fact that the British one-pound note bears not just a likeness of Sir Isaac Newton but also of some apple blossoms, which constitute a veiled reference to gravity. It's an interesting fact but also a self-contained one, and it's just the kind of information that floats untethered throughout the film.

Without question, Mr. Greenway deserves credit for naming his hero Stourley Kracklite, calling his villain Caspasian Speckler, and using his film to celebrate Rome and its architecture with such elegance and discernment. But "The Belly of an Architect" may have as much to do with one man's intestinal maladies as with art, beauty, obsession, permanence and mortality, subjects to which it also pays some attention. It's hard to know. And watching the film's visual obsessiveness — with architectural shapes and symmetry, with cool, stationary long shots, even with the marble surfaces and deep, velvety tones that give it visual texture — becomes an ever less rewarding pursuit as the measure of the film's solipsism becomes known.

•

Kracklite, a renowned American architect, is first seen making love to his wife, Louisa (Chloe Webb), on a train bound for Rome, where he will live for nine months while staging an exhibition in honor of the French architect Etienne-Louis Boulée, a man who never traveled. The trip marks not only the birth of Kracklite's tribute but also the conception of a Kracklite heir, though this is not discovered until later in the story. When it is, Kracklite wants to know on which side of the border the child was conceived; such are his and the film's passion for detail.

While in Rome, Kracklite becomes more and more obsessed by Boulée, by architecture and by his own innards, which begin to bother him. He rails against Louisa suspects her of trying to poison him (an idea, like many of Kracklite's, generated by proximity to ancient Roman culture), and develops the belly fixation that induces him to study many photographs of Louisa's belly, the Emperor Hadrian's and his own. Mr. Greenaway accompanies these developments with dialogue rich in gamesmanship ("Are you a modern architect?" "No more modern than I should be") and with an extraordinary succession of studied, perfectly composed images. There is almost always an archway in the center of the frame. And in the center of that archway is, almost invariably, Kracklite.

Mr. Greenaway brings a welcome playfulness to some of this, as when he fuses the film's concerns with ancient art and bodily deterioration into the figure of a man who surreptitiously chips the noses off statues (and has quite a collection). However, there's nothing do be done with the film's essential elusiveness, and in any case Mr. Greenaway seems to prefer it that way. "The Belly of an Architect" does have a humanizing element in the form of Mr. Dennehy, who brings a robust physicality to Kracklite without missing the essentially cerebral nature of the role; this is one of the best things he has done. And as the highly undependable Louisa, quite unrecognizable from her "Sid and Nancy" role, is Chloe Webb, who's full of taunting flirtatiousness and speaks in a sleepwalker's tone.

"The Belly of an Architect" will be shown tonight at 6:15 and Saturday at 3 as part of the New York Film Festival.

1987 O 1, C22:5

Togetherness

LIKE FATHER LIKE SON, directed by Rod Daniel; screenplay by Lorne Cameron and Steven L. Bloom; story by Mr. Cameron; director of photography, Jack N. Green; edited by Lois Freeman-Fox; music by Miles Goodman; production designer, Dennis Gassner; produced by Brian Grazer and David Valdes; released by Tri Star Pictures. At Criterion Center, Broadway and 45th Street; Gemini Twin, 64th Street and Second Avenue; 84th Street Sixplex, at Broadway; U.A. East, 85th Street and First Avenue; Movieland Eighth Street Triplex, at University Place. Running time: 97 minutes. This film is rated PG-13.

Dr. Jack Hammond	Dudley Moore
Chris Hammond	Kirk Cameron
Ginnie Armbruster	Margaret Colin
Dr. Amy Larkin	Catherine Hicks
Dr. Armbruster	Patrick O'Neal
Trigger	Sean Astin
Lori Beaumont	Cami Cooper
Rick Anderson	Micah Grant

By CARYN JAMES

"LIKE FATHER LIKE SON" has a road map of a plot: thanks to an Indian brain-transference serum, a middle-aged doctor and his teen-age son trade minds but not bodies. It's easier to believe such a potion exists than to imagine anyone could make this movie live, but Dudley Moore and Kirk Cameron are so clever and charming as the mismatched pair that they turn a potential dud into a sweetly engaging film.

Jack (Mr. Moore) is a widower whose idea of fun is lecturing his son on the flow of blood. Chris (Mr. Cameron) may flunk biology because he can't bear to dissect a frog. So when Jack accidentally shakes some brain-serum in his Bloody Mary — how it got on the kitchen shelf is plausible but beside the point — the reversal is too neatly set up: Mr. Moore has to act like a sweet-faced, unsophisticated high-school senior, and Mr. Cameron has to act like a surgeon. Jack will destroy his son's popularity, and Chris ruin his father's chance to be the hospital's chief of staff.

Played too broadly, these reversals would be a waste. But both Mr. Moore and Mr. Cameron strike the right balance between wild exaggeration and poker-faced acceptance, always suggesting the real-life awkwardness of seeing through someone else's eyes.

Mr. Moore has perfected the knack of keeping his characters — from Arthur to the love-obsessed hero of "10" — on the edge of farce; however frenetic and slapstick his behavior, there's enough restraint and intelligence in his eyes to convince you this outrageous man might exist. As a 16-year-old, he gets to jump on the table and shout along with MTV and to disrupt a board meeting by trying to chew bubble gum and smoke a cigarette at the same time. But he also captures the confusion, the thoroughly baffled expression, of a teenager forced to make believe he's an eminent physician.

•

Surprisingly, Mr. Cameron (who stars in the television series "Growing Pains") keeps pace; he must have observed his co-star awfully well. As Chris arrives at school with a middle-aged mind, he is posture-perfect, with a slight swagger that recalls Mr. Moore's walk. And Mr. Cameron doesn't overplay the outrageousness of taking his son's girlfriend to a heavy-metal concert, where he stiffly, thoughtfully observes, "These chords are all very similar."

Switch

In "Like Father Like Son," Dudley Moore portrays a father who reverses roles with his son.

To enjoy this movie, you have to overlook a lot of irritations that get in the way of the genuine silliness. The minor characters are unredeemably predictable. There is an idealistic doctor (Catherine Hicks) whose love interest in Jack seems to have been edited out so only its ghost remains; and there is the chief of staff's wife (Margaret Colin) who offers her body to Jack's and causes Chris's mind to thank heaven. Rod Daniel (who directed the early Michael J. Fox film "Teen Wolf") manages to shoot himself in the foot several times by including some music-video-type scenes — Mr. Moore goes shopping and runs a track meet — that are wasted because they have no flair at all.

This sloppiness keeps "Like Father Like Son," which opens today at the Gemini and other theaters, from being first-rate; it never fulfills its potential for being a shrewd satire of cross-generational manners (though it comes a lot closer than 1977's "Freaky Friday," in which Barbara Harris and Jodie Foster pulled a similar mother-daughter brain trade). But this slick movie proves how much fun it can be to watch first-rate actors challenge our credulity and rise above a second-rate script.

•

"Like Father Like Son" is rated PG-13 ("Special Parental Guidance Suggested for Those Younger Than 13"). It contains a few rough words and one early scene of an injured man that might be a bit intense for very small children.

1987 O 2, C8:5

Strange Happenings

ANNA, directed by Yurek Bogayevicz; screenplay by Agnieszka Holland; story by Mr. Bogayevicz and Mr. Holland; director of photography, Bobby Bukowski; edited by Julie Sloane; production designer, Lester Cohen; produced by Zanne Devine and Mr. Bogayevicz; released by Vestron Pictures. At Alice Tully Hall, as part of the 25th New York Film Festival. Running time: 95 minutes. This film has no rating.

Anna	Sally Kirkland
Daniel	Robert Fields
Krystyna	Paulina Porizkova
Directors	
Gibby Brand and John Robert Tillotson	

By JANET MASLIN

A NUMBER of hard-to-believe things happen right at the beginning of "Anna," a first film directed by Yurek Bogayevicz and written by Agnieszka ("Angry Harvest") Holland. No. 1: though the title character, a once-celebrated Czechoslovak actress

(played by Sally Kirkland), lives amid the kind of gloomy décor in which one might expect to find an elderly lady, she emerges as a leggy, chic-looking creature. No. 2: also emerging, apparently from a mud puddle near the Brooklyn Bridge, is an even leggier and more chic-looking figure dressed in rags.

No. 3: the latter clutches Anna's home address in her hand and turns out to be a wildly devoted young fan named Krystyna, just off the plane from Czechoslovakia. She arrives at Anna's door just after Anna has left, and still (4) tracks Anna to the audition for which she is headed. At the audition, a group of terrible actresses try out, as Anna literally and figuratively towers over them. But these awful actresses win roles in a big hit play about women (5). And Anna (6) lands only an understudy's role.

Krystyna introduces herself to Anna, then collapses in a faint because she hasn't eaten in three days (this isn't hard to believe, it's just predictable). Anna takes Krystyna in to live with her (7). Krystyna begins to change; her brown teeth turn white after only one trip to a friendly dentist (8). Meanwhile, Anna, who rues her own failure, continues to encourage Krystyna (9) in her path to instant stardom (10). And the whole thing turns out to be an "All About Eve" variation in which Eve is just too nice (11 through 55) for words.

•

A cliché-load this hefty is no less irritating with a Middle European accent than it would be any other way, despite Miss Kirkland's immensely dignified presence and the obvious glamour of Paulina Porizkova, the

star fashion model who plays Krystyna. Miss Porizkova is gorgeous, and she also has a spry, unpredictable manner that works well on the screen, but the film seems too determined to turn her into Audrey Hepburn, making her do things with which not even Miss Hepburn, at her most elfin, could get away. What happens when Anna coaxes Krystyna into traveling to the Hamptons — of which she has never heard (56) — to catch the eye of a very famous director? Nothing compromising (57). And the director drives her home the next day in his limousine, drinking champagne (actually, this seems likelier than most of the film's other events). And when Krystyna steps out of the car, smiling as usual, a crowd of children gather around because they love her (I've stopped counting).

In addition to its falseness, "Anna" also sounds a note of self-pity about Anna's overlooked brilliance and her faded career. She went to jail in 1968, after the Soviet invasion of her homeland, for speaking out against the new regime. Her husband was out of the country at the time. Since then, Anna has lived in dispiriting exile, while he has gone from being Czechoslovakia's most renowned film director to a man who makes rock videos (oh, all right — 59). He rejects Anna when he sees her, but when one of Anna's old films is shown to a near-empty house, there he is in the theater (60).

•

Incidentally, "Anna" offers a glimpse of this film and a few looks at the play in which Anna is not quite appearing. But the former isn't good enough to explain Anna's great reputation, and the latter is much more foolish than it needs to be. Glimpses like this are always problematic. Unless the larger film is itself unassailable, there's a danger of letting the pot call the kettle black.

"Anna" will be shown tonight at 9:15 and Sunday at 7 P.M. at Alice Tully Hall as part of the 25th New York Film Festival.

1987 O 2, C11:1

Small Friends

BIG SHOTS, directed by Robert Mandel; written by Joe Eszterhas; director of photography, Miroslav Ondricek; edited by Sheldon Kahn, William Anderson and Dennis Virkler; music by Bruce Broughton; production designer, Bill Malley; produced by Joe Medjuck and Michael C. Gross; released by 20th Century-Fox Film

Sally Kirkland, left, and Paulina Porizkova portray Czechoslovak émigré actresses in New York in "Anna."

Corporation. At Gotham, Third Avenue at 58th Street; 86th Street East, at Third Avenue; Criterion, Broadway at 45th Street; Eighth Street Playhouse, at Avenue of the Americas; Columbia Cinema, Broadway at 103d Street. Running time: 90 minutes. This film is rated PG-13.

Obie	Ricky Busker
Scam	Darius McCrary
Dickie	Robert Joy
Keegan	Robert Prosky
Doc	Jerzy Skolimowski
Johnnie Red	Paul Winfield
Mom	Brynn Thayer
Dad	Bill Hudson
Uncle Harry	Jim Antonio
Alley	Andrea Bebel

IF all those movies about black-white teams of hero-adventurers strike you as kid stuff, you haven't seen anything yet. "Big Shots," which opens today at the Criterion and other theaters, is kid stuff with *kids*.

Young white Obie (Ricky Busker) from the Chicago suburbs loses his beloved dad and finds himself in the inner city where he hooks up with young, black street-smart Scam (Darius McCrary), also apparently fatherless. Trying to get back Obie's watch, a gift from Dad that was ripped off by toughs, the team has run-ins and crash-ins with a nasty pawnbroker, a couple of murderous drug dealers and some confused cops.

•

Believe it or not, amid the car chases, affection sprouts between the boys ("He's the best friend I ever had," says Obie of Scam) and oozes out on all sides. Mr. Busker and Mr. McCrary may have talent; it's hard to tell through the moist lines and the claptrap reactions dropped on them by Robert Mandel, the director. You haven't seen so much palm-slapping since Sunday afternoon football.

Paul Winfield brings a few nice moves to the part of a soft-hearted fence, but the character is too pat for much movement. "Big Shots" is billed as a comedy, which is no doubt why the youngsters are got up in oversize fedoras and shades.

•

"Big Shots," which is rated PG-13 ("Special Parental Guidance Suggested for Those Younger Than 13"), has a lot of street talk and a few killings.
WALTER GOODMAN

1987 O 2, C17:1

Australian Soap

THE RIGHT HAND MAN, directed by Di Drew; screenplay by Helen Hodgman; story developed by Steven Grives; director of photography, Peter James; edited by Don Saunders; music by Allan Zavod; production designer, Neil Angwin; produced by Mr. Grives, Tom Oliver and Basil Appleby; released by Filmdallas Pictures. At Carnegie Hall Cinema, Seventh Avenue and 57th Street. Running time: 101 minutes. This film is rated R.

Harry Ironminster	Rupert Everett
Ned Devine	Hugo Weaving
Dr. Redbridge	Arthur Dignam
Lady Ironminster	Jennifer Claire
Sarah Redbridge	Catherine McClements
Sam	Ralph Cotterill
Violet Head	Adam Cockburn
Lord Ironminster	Tim Eliott

By WALTER GOODMAN

THE special thing about Harry Ironminster, the hero of "The Right Hand Man," is that he suffers from diabetes. It's 1860, when languishing figures of fiction usually expired from weak lungs, but this is Australia.

Harry has other troubles. His main passion, along with the doctor's daughter, is his horses, and even before the credits roll, he loses control of a spirited matched pair; his father, Lord Ironminster, is killed, and Harry, who proves to be amputation prone, loses his right arm. In need of somebody to exercise the horses and the doctor's daughter, he hires Ned Devine, the driver of a 12-horse stagecoach that comes crashing through the movie from time to time. What happens then can be learned at the Carnegie Hall Cinema.

These upper-class Aussies talk this way: "Why do I not recover?" "Is it to do with his wasting disease?" "My sleeve is empty, but my hand, it reaches out and touches you." "This marriage would not have been perfect as a marriage between us should have been." "It seems, Harry, we have reached an impasse." "These visits must cease." Just as you're getting used to their mouthfuls, the young lord tells his new coachman, "I'd like to finalize our arrangement." Was 19th-century Australia as decadent as that?

Why, you may ask, doesn't rich young Harry go off to London where, as the doctor's scientifically minded daughter informs him, a researcher is having some success in helping diabetics? He's just too tired to think about it. And he'd hate to be parted from his horses.

The cast does earnest combat with Helen Hodgman's romance-magazine script. Rupert Everett makes a weary and rather wearying hero, but then he is supposed to be wasting away. Catherine McClements, as the doctor's daughter, is a lively new presence from Australia who may be given less foolish things to do in her next movie. Jennifer Claire plays Lady Ironminster as though she were trying out for "Dynasty"; still, what is to be done with a character who dines at a baronial table and spends the whole movie worrying about "the death of the Ironminster name"? The burden of being toughly, softly romantic as the right-hand man is too heavy for Hugo Weaving.

Di Drew, the director, also seems to be fighting the story. With the help of Peter James's camera, he gives us a rough-and-tumble Australian town, scrubby outdoors, smoky indoors. (The flow of blood during the amputations may be a wee excessive.) But the efforts at realism keep dissolving into chuckles. The ending is a howl. It could be a case of the left hand not knowing what the right hand is doing.

1987 O 2, C13:1

Racism as Humor

SURF NAZIS MUST DIE, directed by Peter George; screenplay by Jon Ayre; director of photography, Rolf Kesterman; edited by Craig Colton; music by Jon McCallum; produced by by Robert Tinnell; released by Troma. At Waverly Twin, Third Street and Avenue of the Americas, and Cine 42, 42d Street near Seventh Avenue. Running time: 95 minutes. This film is rated R.
Mama Washington ....Gail Neely
Leroy Washington ....Robert Harden
Adolf ....Barry Brenner
Eva ....Dawn Wildsmith
Mengele ....Michael Sonye
Hook ....Joel Hile

TROMA INC., the small independent company responsible for outstandingly irreverent features made on budgets that are lower than low, is in a good position to make films that are cheap, impudent and funny. But two out of three won't do. And "Surf Nazis Must Die" isn't funny in the slightest, the title notwithstanding. It's a standard, thoroughly stupid gang-war exploitation film intercut with occasional low-energy surfing footage, featuring characters named Adolf, Eva and so on who chant slogans, wear swastikas on their wetsuits and burn surfboards from time to time. Not even the actors' relatives will find this interesting.

"Surf Nazis Must Die," which opens today at the Waverly and Cine 42, doesn't even have a sufficiently well-developed punk sensibility to pay off. Even its sexism is perfunctory, although its racism is more developed and passed off as a kind of humor. A black man named Leroy (Robert Harden) is killed by the beach Nazi gang, and after that his pistol-packin' mother declares war. As the mother, Gail Neely is a good deal better than Barry Brenner, who plays the rabble-rousing Adolf and isn't even a decent speaker.

There are those who will take offense at the mere existence of a film that toys with such material. They're right.   *JANET MASLIN*

1987 O 2, C24:5

CHUCK BERRY HAIL! HAIL! ROCK 'N' ROLL, directed by Taylor Hackford; photography by Oliver Stapleton; edited by Lisa Day; concert production designer, Kim Colefax; produced by Stephanie Bennett; production Company, Delilah Films Production; released by Universal Pictures. At Alice Tully Hall, as part of the 25th New York Film Festival. Running time: 118 minutes. This film is rated PG.
WITH: Chuck Berry, Keith Richards, Linda Ronstadt, Julian Lennon, Robert Cray, Eric Clapton, Etta James, Little Richard, Bruce Springsteen and Jerry Lee Lewis.

Period Piece

Rupert Everett and Catherine McClements star in "The Right Hand Man," about a wealthy young man in 19th-century Australia.

By JANET MASLIN

A 60th-birthday tribute to the great rock innovator Chuck Berry may sound like an occasion for celebration., But Taylor Hackford's documentary "Chuck Berry Hail! Hail! Rock 'n' Roll!" is anything but a valentine.

The portrait of Mr. Berry, compiled from concert footage, conversations with him and interviews with many other rock-and-roll greats, presents an irascible and difficult figure, a man who's bitter about the past and so stubborn about the present that the film's subject, rather than its director, appears to be holding the reins.

Mr. Berry's new autobiography is a great deal more forthcoming about his life than the film is, and a desire to promote the book may be one of Mr. Berry's reasons for keeping the film makers on a short leash. He's smart about finances, too.

●

So this portrait of Mr. Berry is downbeat, and in some ways incomplete; it's very different from what might have been expected. But in its own way, Mr. Hackford's film is revealing. Mr. Berry's flair for colorfully odd syntax ("There were two girls in particular who came to mold the cast that gave shape to my heart," he writes, in a book that's as lively about his love life as it is about music) comes through here, as do a number of his eccentricities; after all these years, he still tours a lot, travels without luggage and plays with a different band in each city to keep expenses down. Bruce Springsteen recalls having backed up Mr. Berry many years ago, without the singer's even bothering to tell his musicians what keys to use. Mr. Springsteen laughingly recalls the panic of having to work this way, and Mr. Berry's rallying cry: "Play for that money, boys!"

In a lounge apparently built by Mr. Berry near his home — the film is not much good on particulars — a group of musicians is seen rehearsing for the birthday concert, led by Keith Richards, one of the Rolling Stones guitarists, who is the film's unsung hero. It's clear that Mr. Richards is having to buck tremendous difficulty in organizing this tribute, and the film captures several little spats between him and Mr. Berry, with Mr. Berry insisting angrily that he's going to play exactly as he likes; if it doesn't sound right in Mr. Hackford's film, too bad.

"He's given me more headaches than Mick Jagger, but I still cannot dislike him," says Mr. Richards, who is also very interesting in analyzing the roots of Mr. Berry's music. "The

Celebration

The 60th birthday concert of the rock pioneer Chuck Berry is the subject of "Chuck Berry Hail! Hail! Rock 'n' Roll," a documentary directed by Taylor Hackford.

more you find out about him, the less you know."

●

Some of the concert footage is good, some of it (like Julian Lennon's self-consciously filling in for his father to sing with Mr. Berry) less so. In addition, there are interviews with figures like Roy Orbison, the Everly Brothers, Jerry Lee Lewis, Bo Diddley and Little Richard (for whom Mr. Berry's patience seems just about to wear thin). On the evidence of these veterans, neither time nor rock-and-roll does very well by its heroes. Mr. Berry is also heard reminiscing angrily about the racism and payola of the old days, and about never receiving proper royalties.

The film contains very little information about Mr. Berry's background, and clearly that's his choice. There are no titles or voice-overs. Each Berry relative is allowed just a single one-sentence appearance, and the singer's wife, Themetta, is allowed to speak for only 10 seconds or so before Mr. Berry orders Mr. Hackford to turn off the camera. When Mr. Hackford tries to ask about his prison record, Mr. Berry does the same thing. He's a living legend, and one very tough customer.

"Chuck Berry Hail! Hail! Rock 'n' Roll!" will be shown tonight at 9 and tomorrow at 2, as part of the New York Film Festival.

1987 O 3, 10:5

UNDER SATAN'S SUN, directed by Maurice Pialat; screenplay (French with English subtitles) by Sylvie Danton and Mr. Pialat, from the novel by Georges Bernanos; photography by Willy Kurant; edited by Yann Dédet; art director, Katia Vischkof; produced by Daniel Toscan du Plantier; production companies, Erato Films, Films A2, Flach Films, Action Films, Sofica Investimage, Sofica Creations with the participation of the National Center of Cinematography. At Alice Tully Hall, as part of the 25th New York Film Festival. Running time: 97 minutes. This film has no rating.
Donissan ....Gérard Depardieu
Mouchette ....Sandrine Bonnaire
Menou-Segrais ....Maurice Pialat
Cadignan ....Alain Artur
Gallet ....Yann Dédet
Mouchette's mother ....Brigitte Legendre
Malorthy ....Jean-Claude Bourlat
Horse-trader ....Jean-Christophe Bouvet
Quarryman ....Philippe Pallut
Msgr. Gerbier ....Marcel Anselin
Marthe ....Yvette Lavogez
Havret ....Pierre D'Hoffelize

By JANET MASLIN

Maurice Pialat directs in an ordinary-looking style, yet he approaches film making in an extremely unconventional way. That paradox is more apparent than ever in "Under Satan's Sun," the film that won this year's top prize at the Cannes Film Festival and was roundly booed for doing so.

When Mr. Pialat approaches more psychological subjects, as he has in such films as "A Nos Amours," "Lou-lou" and "Police," his deceptively straightforward manner and his ability to suspend judgment can have the look of naturalism (though his scrutiny is so keen that it becomes extraordinarily penetrating over a period of time).

But "Under Satan's Sun" is about faith, and it's a more difficult, mysterious film in every way. Even so, Mr. Pialat has employed as plain a directorial style as ever. So the miraculous, the visionary and the diabolical fuse here in a film that grapples simply and powerfully with the unknown.

•

Adapted from a novel by Georges Bernanos (author of "Diary of a Country Priest" and "Mouchette," both filmed by Robert Bresson), "Under Satan's Sun" begins with a dialogue between two priests. Donissan (Gérard Depardieu) and his superior, Menou-Segrais (played by Mr. Pialat, who is also an accomplished actor), are nominally discussing Donissan's future, though this is merely the starting point for a typically rigorous and complex theological debate. The film's screenplay, adapted by Mr. Pialat with a scenario by Sylvie Danton, is outstandingly literate and also very dense. The interplay between Donissan, once a poor student and now a priest who gravely doubts his own ability, and the more knowing Menou-Segrais immediately establishes the moral and theological debate that rages throughout the film.

Mr. Depardieu, bulky in his cleric's robes and surprising in his earnestness, at first seems far removed from the more robust and libidinous figures he usually plays. Flagellating himself, and suffering in the hair shirt he insists on wearing (despite Menou-Segrais's urging that he not), he seems misplaced. But Mr. Depardieu is able to turn his oversize, lumbering frame into the battlefield on which a remarkable war of the spirit is waged and to embody the essential innocence of a man caught between theological absolutes. This battle, as staged by Mr. Pialat, is both metaphysical and matter-of-fact; no struggle between good and evil has ever been staged with so little fanfare.

•

Donissan's fate is shaped by a woman named Mouchette, played by Sandrine Bonnaire, who, like Mr. Depardieu, has also done astonishing work in other films by this director. When Mouchette first looms seductively and a little dangerously on the screen, she seems to be speaking to Donissan, though she is in fact visiting a wealthy older man named Cadignan, who is her lover; allowing scenes to run together in this way is only one of Mr. Pialat's methods of keeping his audience subtly off-balance. Mouchette's frightening instability is quickly established and made utterly convincing by Miss Bonnaire's outstandingly unaffected presence. And soon Mouchette has committed murder.

By the time Donissan encounters her, late in the film, he knows more about her than she does about herself. Donissan (though Mr. Pialat makes no point of emphasizing this) can detect sin without effort and is as open to evil as he is to good. "God twice let me see through a body to a soul," he says of these miracles, but their price is high. During a nightlong pilgrim-

age made by this troubled priest, he meets and converses with an enraged satanic figure; somehow, by making this representation so ordinary, Mr. Pialat makes it all the more diabolical. "You are marked now with the sign of my hatred," this stranger says in parting.

Though it deals with theology and rises to a stunning test of faith, "Under Satan's Sun" has a thoroughly secular style. That's one of the many things that make it fascinating. It's a work of great subtlety, some difficulty and tremendous assurance, one that demands and deserves close attention.

"Under Satan's Sun" will be shown at noon today and 9:15 P.M. Wednesday as part of the New York Film Festival.

1987 O 3, 13:1

ANITA — DANCES OF VICE, directed and produced by Rosa von Praunheim; screenplay (in German with English subtitles) by Mr. von Praunheim and H. Limpach; photography by Elfi Mikesch; edited by Mike Shepherd and Mr. von Praunheim; music by Konrad Elfers, Rainer Rubbert, Alen Marks and Ed Lieber; production companies, Road Movies and ZDF. At Alice Tully Hall, as part of the 25th New York Film Festival. Running time: 85 minutes. This film has no rating.
Anita Berber ....Lotti Huber
WITH: Ina Blum and Mikael Honesseau

By VINCENT CANBY

Rosa von Praunheim's "Anita — Dances of Vice" is a surprisingly tame movie to be made by the German director responsible for "It's Not the Homosexual Who Is Perverse, Rather the Situation in Which He Lives" (1970) and "A Virus Knows No Morals" (made in 1985 and released here this year). The former is a memorably savage satire on gay liberation conformism, while the latter is a grim examination of what might be called gay liberation's aftermath, in the era of acquired immune deficiency syndrome.

"Anita — Dances of Vice" is a fanciful homage to the instinctive, unstructured revolutionary in the person of Anita Berber (1899-1928), the notorious German dancer who, with her partner, Sebastian Droste, came to represent the decadence of 1920's Berlin with their nude dancing, their cocaine habits and their uninhibited sex lives.

The film will be shown at the New York Film Festival at Lincoln Center at 6 P.M. today and 9:30 P.M. tomorrow.

Mr. von Praunheim (whose real name is Holger Mischwitzki, and who was born in Latvia in 1942) approaches the legend of Anita Berber obliquely through the fictitious story of elderly, tub-shaped Mrs. Kutowski (Lotti Huber), an irrepressible schizophrenic who, claiming to be Berber, goes around contemporary Berlin talking dirty and taking off her clothers in public places.

•

Having been locked up in a psychiatric hospital, Mrs. Kutowski makes passes at the female nurses and recalls Berber's tumultuous career in hallucinatory flashbacks (in which Ina Blum plays Berber). In all ways she refuses to behave. "Why don't you pretend that you're Helen Keller or Doris Day?" says an exhausted therapist. Mrs. Kutowski is especially vicious to another patient, whom she calls Rosa Luxemburg and who goes on at boring length about the need for political action.

"I want to shock the philistines," says the old lady. "I'm bored with

politics. I live for the moment."

Mr. von Praunheim clearly admires the free, anarchic spirit of the foul-mouthed mad woman, played with great gusto by Miss Huber, who looks a bit like the older sister of Divine, the drag queen star of John Waters's movies. Yet neither she nor the Anita Berber we see in the parody-flashbacks is shocking or outrageous enough to provoke the audience, many of whom (at the press preview I attended) walked out on the film.

The director several times makes the unexceptional point that Berlin's decadence, exemplified by the behavior of Berber, softened up the Ger-

man philistines for events to come. "We need a strong leader," they are heard saying more than once. This seems much too simple and unequivocal a theme for a satirist of Mr. von Praunheim's already demonstrated perverse gifts.

The film's single best moment has nothing to do with politics at all. It comes when a male patient is complaining about the food and the medical care in the psychiatric ward. "I don't know when I'll get out," he says forlornly. He thinks a moment, then adds, "I'm not even sure I'm here."

1987 O 3, 15:1

FILM VIEW/ Vincent Canby

Ah, Sweet Mystery

BURIED NEAR THE CENTER OF the multipart comedy "Amazon Women on the Moon," an uneven series of sketches sending up late-night television, there's a small, priceless plum. It's "Son of the Invisible Man," an intentionally washed-out black-and-white film parody with Ed Begley Jr. as Jack Griffin Jr., the son of the late, demented scientist played by Claude Rains in the 1933 movie.

Swathed in bandages and wearing dark glasses, Jack Griffin Jr. announces to a skeptical friend that he's perfected his father's formula for invisibility. "But," cautions the friend, "your father went crazy." Jack Griffin Jr. says he's been taking the formula for two weeks and has never been more sane. At which point he unwraps himself, strips down to the buff and proceeds to play those mischievous pranks that so mystified the characters in the original film.

The only catch is that he's *not* invisible.

∎

The patrons in a small, Hollywood-English pub respond to Jack Griffin Jr. with patience. "Oh, dear," the barmaid announces when she hears him on the stairs, "here comes the invisible man again." The naked scientist enters and goes around the room lifting beer mugs, upsetting checkerboards, throwing darts, all the while giggling hysterically at the astonishment he believes he's causing.

The sketch lasts no more than a few

How do actors survive their apprenticeships to accomplish the extraordinary feats they occasionally do?

minutes but, in addition to being very funny on its own, it's also a very funny, perceptive commentary on acting, both as art and as self-delusion. An actor doesn't have to be crazy like Jack Griffin Jr., but he must possess the same monomaniacal, sometimes utterly misplaced confidence in the truth of what he's doing. That he may be just a fellow making an ass of himself can't enter his mind, or he'd chuck everything in favor of programming computers.

It remains a mystery to me how actors survive their apprenticeships to accomplish the extraordinary feats they occasionally do. Equally mysterious, to *them*, must be the differing responses of the members of their audiences who, in fact, don't play fair. Audiences do not remain constant.

They also have furious prejudices that only an analyst could unravel. I once had a friend, otherwise well adjusted, who disliked Rosalind Russell so intensely he wouldn't walk under a marquee with her name on it. It wasn't an especially inconvenient phobia, like the fear of public places. It didn't demand treatment, but it had little to do with the actress's talent or with anything in particular she'd ever done.

All of us, I suspect, including actors, have our own Rosalind Russells, if not to the same degree.

To each performer, in each different role, we also bring a set of expectations that, in the course of a performance, varies in reaction to circumstances over which the actor has little control. In "The Seven-Per-Cent Solution," "Apocalypse Now," "The Great Santini" and "Tender Mercies," Robert Duvall has shown that he's one of America's most skilled and resourceful actors.

Yet, after one has watched him fool around in such junk movies as "The Lightship" and the current "Hotel Colonial," expectations dwindle. Mr. Duvall didn't write or direct those movies. His worst crime: attempting to make a living in an uncertain business, supported, perhaps, by a misplaced conviction that he can turn sow's ears into utilitarian purses.

Because most movies have the *appearance* of realism, we tend to equate a performance with the way an actor looks. It's only in recent years that audiences have become aware of the art of the kind of acting that doesn't seem to be acting — the art of Gary Cooper, Clark Gable and James Stewart, carried forward in time by Steve McQueen and, more recently, by Kevin Costner. Yet, our appreciation for this seemingly non-acting performance tends to leave us unprepared for the spectacle of actors unashamedly acting up a storm.

We accept Dustin Hoffman's subtly inventive, risk-taking performance in "Tootsie" in large part because he wears a dress, which tells us he's playing someone he isn't. We know that he knows that he's giving a performance, as we do when actors and actresses win Oscars for flashy, cast-against-type performances as alcoholics, nymphomaniacs or characters who require that the performer wear a lot of makeup.

Yet when we watch the robust, very actorly work of the unmadeup Matthew Modine, Albert Finney and Kevin Anderson in Alan Pakula's "Orphans," movie audiences have a way of rejecting the bifocal image of actors exercising their talents, barefaced, while creating oversized characters of a kind we usually see only on the stage. That, however, is the fun of the film. Because "Orphans" (adapted by Lyle Kessler from his own play) doesn't mean to be everyday realism, the effect is as rare on the screen as it is exhilarating. Only Laurence Olivier and Alec Guinness, both of whom have a fondness for makeup, have gotten away with this sort of theatricality with any regularity in the past.

■

Another kind of performance, eliciting an entirely different audience response, is that of Marcello

Mastroianni, who plays the Italian but quintessentially Chekhovian hero of Nikita Mikhalkov's "Dark Eyes." Beginning with "La Dolce Vita" (1959), his first major hit in this country, Mr. Mastroianni has been building up an enormous amount of re-

Oversized characters provide the fun in 'Orphans.'

spect, affection and enlightened good will with smoothly sophisticated performances in a large number of exceptionally good films, including "8½," "Divorce — Italian Style," "A Special Day" and "La Nuit de Varennes."

The performance in "Dark Eyes"

Mickey Rourke in "Barfly"—"one of the year's funniest, gutsiest performances"

is highly theatrical, though it seems to be without artifice, and it's doubly rewarding. It demonstrates the fullness of a talent that has become enriched with time, and it somehow manages to exceed expectations. For some years now, there's never been any doubt that Mr. Mastroianni is one of finest film actors of our time, but he's still capable of surprise.

It takes decades to build up the kind of good will Mr. Mastroianni now enjoys, and good will is something that Mickey Rourke, still at the beginning of his career, desperately needs today.

Because Mr. Rourke has made his share of clinkers, including "9½ Weeks" and "A Prayer for the Dying," it may not be easy for audiences, including critics, to recognize the intelligence of his successfully inventive performance in Barbet Schroeder's rough, entertaining new vignette of a movie, "Barfly," shown at the New York Film Festival last week and scheduled to be released here later this year.

As an aggressively unrepentant drunk and barroom brawler, Mr. Rourke gives one of the year's funniest, gutsiest performances. It's bigger and wilder than life, though not in the stage tradition of the performances in "Orphans." Mr. Rourke never seems to stand outside his role. He's buried inside it and inside the compelling, scroungy realism of the movie itself.

Because he's the type of actor who isn't afraid to go too far, Mr. Rourke has, in the past, often looked as self-absorbed and ridiculous as the blithely naked Jack Griffin, Jr. in "Son of the Invisible Man." In "Barfly," the calculated recklessness pays off. Mr. Rourke's in complete command of his technique.

How fickle, literal-minded audiences respond to it is anybody's guess. □

1987 O 4, II:23:1

NEAR DARK, directed by Kathryn Bigelow; written by Eric Red and Miss Bigelow; director of photography, Adam Greenberg; film editor, Howard Smith; music by Tangerine Dream; production designer, Stephen Altman; produced by Steven-Charles Jaffe; released by F-M Entertainment. At Criterion, Broadway and 45th Street. Running time: 95 minutes. This film is rated R.

Caleb	Adrian Pasdar
Mae	Jenny Wright
Jesse	Lance Henriksen
Severen	Bill Paxton
Diamondback	Jenette Goldstein
Loy	Tim Thomerson
Homer	Joshua Miller
Sarah	Marcie Leeds
Deputy Sheriff	Kenny Call

By CARYN JAMES

IS "Near Dark" a mainstream commercial movie, tinged with blood, about an Oklahoma farm boy seduced and abducted by vampires? Or is it a fast-money thriller with artsy photography, about rowdy bloodsuckers who live like bikers and drive by night?

Kathryn Bigelow, who directed and co-wrote the script (with Eric Red, writer of the sadistic cult film "The Hitcher"), searches desperately for a style, and tosses into the pot touches of film-noir lust, some cornpone family sentiment, blue-colored nights, overexposed days, orange suns that race across the screen, and enough blood and violence so "Near Dark" can be sold as a horror film but not enough to risk its R rating. You might call this the scattershot school of film making.

Caleb, a young man with a pickup truck, is dazzled by Mae, a beautiful stranger. They kiss — in slow motion — and suddenly she bites his neck. Presto, his eyes are rimmed with slightly more eyeliner than Michael Jackson's; he's a vampire.

●

Caleb staggers toward home, but he's swooped off the field by Mae's grungy little vampire band — a violent young man, a middle-aged couple and a young boy — as they pull him into their Winnebago. For the next half-hour or so the film could be a casebook study of vampire transformation, as the nightstalkers cross state lines in stolen vans, dodging the sun. Mae must teach Caleb to kill; meanwhile, he lives off blood sucked from her wrists, in scenes that emphasize the sexual thrill of vampirism without requiring the couple to take off any clothes.

Eventually there's action. The vampires take over a seedy bar, drink their fill from the murdered customers, and drop the movie's few intentionally witty lines ("I hate it when they ain't been shaved," is one after-meal comment). They have a gunfight with the Kansas state police, who do the most damage by shooting holes in the walls of a bungalow and letting rays of sunshine in. And Caleb is reunited with his dad and little sister, who have tracked him down. After last-minute plot twists, there's a Hollywood happy ending.

Ms. Bigelow's too-studied compositions — Caleb in silhouette riding a horse toward the camera — clash with her unstudied approach to the characters' looks. Some vampires walk around with a little blood around their mouths, but it's as if they're messy eaters — disgusting but not exactly horrifying. Vampires go up in unconvincing special-effects flames. The result of being pushed and pulled through the confusing styles of "Near Dark," which opened yesterday at the Criterion Center and other theaters, is simple exhaustion.

1987 O 4, 67:2

Age-Old Story

MELO, directed by Alain Resnais; screenplay (French with English subtitles) by Mr. Resnais from a play by Henry Bernstein; photography by Charlie Van Damme and Gilbert Duhalde; edited by Albert Jurgenson and Jean-Pierre Besnard; music by Philippe-Gérard; art director, Jacques Saulnier; produced by Marin Karmitz; production companies, MK2 Productions and Films A2; released by European Classics. At Alice Tully Hall, as part of the 25th New York Film Festival. Running time: 112 minutes. This film has no rating.

Romaine Belcroix	Sabine Azéma
Christiane Levesque	Fanny Ardant
Pierre Belcroix	Pierre Arditi
Marcel Blanc	André Dussollier
Dr. Remy	Jacques Dacqmine
Priest	Hubert Gignoux
Yvonne	Catherine Arditi

By VINCENT CANBY

IN every film he's ever made, Alain Resnais has been exploring cinema techniques with such invention that technique has sometimes become the end instead of the means. One remembers (sometimes with pleasure, but often with impatience) the look and sound of "Hiroshima, Mon Amour," "Last Year at Marienbad" and "Providence" more vividly than what, finally, the spiffy style was intended to illuminate.

There are striking exceptions: "Nuit et Brouillard," his early (1955), evocative short film about the Holocaust, and three memorable features, "La Guerre Est Fini," "Stavisky" and "Mon Oncle d'Amérique," in each of which the particular manner of the film is simply another aspect of the concerns on the mind of Mr. Resnais.

His latest work is "Mélo," which, though it appears to be limpid, is as maddening as "Marienbad." It's not obscure, but it's difficult to understand what it is about the project that so fascinates this most sophisticated and intellectual of French film makers.

"Mélo" will be shown at the New York Film Festival at Lincoln Center tonight at 9:15 and tomorrow at 6:15 P.M.

"Mélo" is taken from Henry Bernstein's 1929 Parisian romantic melodrama, which has already been filmed four times , including twice as "Dreaming Lips" with Elisabeth Bergner as the star (in 1932 in German and in 1937 in English), and in German again with Maria Schell in 1952.

The play, as big a hit in New York in 1931 as it had been in Paris in 1929, appears to have been an exceptionally well-crafted example of a sort of "boulevard drama" that was a commonplace of the theater of the 20's. At the time it opened, critics in Paris and New York noted Bernstein's unusual adaptation of movie techniques to the stage. Like a film, the play was composed of a number of scenes in various locations, some very short and without dialogue, which must have seemed revolutionary in a theater where only musicals and agitprop epics enjoyed such freedom.

The film festival's program observes that Mr. Resnais has made "the most cinematic of films" not by opening it up but "by closing in on it." In fact, Mr. Resnais seems to have filmed the already opened-up text pretty much as it was written by Bernstein (the film carries no credit for a screenwriter). He has closed in on it only to the extent that he never allows the movie audience to forget that what they're watching is meant to be a representation of a stage piece.

Though the camera moves in for close-ups from time to time, the sets and lighting are intentionally artificial. A curtain falls between acts, and scenes are played in extended, fluid, unbroken takes that evoke the theatrical experience. Unfortunately, the film's opening scene sets such a high standard that nothing that follows can come up to it.

One watches "Mélo" with the attention split between the events being portrayed and the exceedingly poised, stylized method by which they are being presented. There is, finally, the suspicion that the Bernstein play isn't worth all of the care and thought that have been expended on this unusually handsome, emotionally arid production. The film is given to more theorizing than the material can bear.

The central situation is this: In a Paris suburb in 1926, Romaine Belcroix (Sabine Azéma), the pretty, kittenish wife of Pierre (Pierre Arditi), meets and falls carelessly in love with Marcel (André Dussollier), Pierre's best friend from their days at the music conservatory. While Pierre, a pianist, has married and become a contented, second-rate musician, Marcel is now a star of the international concert stage, as famous for his romantic adventures as for his virtuosity on the violin.

The affair that begins casually turns into a passion so grand that neither Romaine nor Marcel is willing to end it. Romaine, who can't bear to abandon the adoring Pierre, decides to poison him, and probably would succeed except for the nosiness of a doctor. She takes the only way out, which leads to a final scene of reconciliation between the two men that was regarded by the play's original critics as a coup de théâtre.

Something has been lost along the way, possibly because Romaine's two loves, as written by Bernstein and as played by Mr. Dussollier and Mr. Arditi, now seem to be such sticks. Everyone talks very well. As in theater, the characters are always at a little distance from the emotions they're expressing. Their passion is abstract.

Miss Azéma seems consciously to recall Louise Brooks in look and manner. The actress, seen here earlier in Bertrand Tavernier's "Sunday in the Country," comes close to bridging the gap between style and content. She's a bright, vibrant presence, both a quintessential figure of 1920's drama (a woman liberated only to be able to face destruction) and a specific character of willful charm.

Chief among the supporting players is Fanny Ardant. Strong, tall, slightly forbidding actress that she is, she invests her small role with more ominous, mysterious import than was ever written into it.

Like all of his work, "Mélo" is, I suspect, exactly the movie Mr. Resnais set out to make. It doesn't necessarily represent a failure of achievement, but one of communication with someone who doesn't share what, in "Mélo," seems to be his princess-and-the-pea sensibility.

1987 O 5, C19:5

Focus on Two Actresses

JOAN OF ARC AT THE STAKE, directed by Roberto Rossellini; written (in Italian with English subtitles) by Paul Claudel; photography by Gabor Pogany; edited by Jolanda Benvenuti; music by Arthur Honegger. At Alice Tully Hall, as part of the 25th New York Film Festival. Running time: 76 minutes. This film has no rating.

Joan of Arc	Ingrid Bergman
Brother Domenico	Tullio Carminati
Heurtebise	Augusto Romani
Mme. Botti	Agnese Dobbini
The Donkey	Gianni Avolanti
Bailiff	Gerardo Gaudioso
Peasant	Silvio Santarelli
Priest	Aldo Terrosi
Second Peasant	Luigi Paolillo

and

THE HUMAN VOICE, directed and written (in Italian with English subtitles) by Roberto Rossellini, from a one-act play, "La Voix Humaine," by Jean Cocteau; photography by Robert Juillard; edited by Eraldo Da Roma; music by Renzo Rossellini; produced by Roberto Rossellini for Tevere Film. At Alice Tully Hall, as part of the 25th New York Film Festival. Running time: 35 minutes. This film has no rating.
WITH: Anna Magnani

By VINCENT CANBY

THE 10th anniversary of the death of Roberto Rossellini, the master innovator of the Italian cinema, will be marked by the New York Film Festival tonight at 9:15 with the retrospective showing of two films virtually unknown in this country.

They are the 35-minute "Human Voice" (1948), Rossellini's adaptation of Jean Cocteau's one-character play, starring Anna Magnani, and the 76-minute "Joan of Arc at the Stake" (1954), Rossellini's interpretation of the Teatro San Carlo (Naples) stage production of the Arthur Honegger oratorio, text by Paul Claudel, starring Ingrid Bergman. Though students of Rossellini's works will not want to miss the program, the films are of less importance as cinema than as examples of the director's enthusiasm for odd forms, and as tributes to the two actresses who were so important to his professional and private life.

It may be that "The Human Voice" is more beloved by the actresses who get the chance to play it than to any members of the audiences who must sit through it. The one-act drama is no longer the stunner it once seemed. It's the sort of vehicle that wins an actress "tour de force" raves, largely because she gets a chance to laugh, cry, be alternately brave and bitchy, gallant and distraught, in the course of a series of interrupted telephone conversations with a departed lover.

Miss Magnani is quite remarkable and Rossellini's camera celebrates her in long, graceful takes, in close-ups and long shots, which treat the character with a gravity that the audience can be excused for not sharing. Miss Magnani never intentionally overwhelms Cocteau. However, being naturally a strong actress, her increasing desperation eventually takes on the scale of the grief of Medea, which only serves to make the woman she's playing seem absurdly, tiresomely small and self-absorbed.

Rossellini's "Human Voice" was originally intended to be a companion piece to "The Miracle," the once-scandalous Rossellini film, written by Federico Fellini and starring Miss Magnani with Mr. Fellini, about a simple-minded peasant woman who believes that she's immaculately conceived a child by St. Joseph. When "The Miracle" finally arrived in this country in 1950, it was the most notorious segment of "Ways of Love," a three-part film that also included Jean Renoir's "Day in the Country" and Marcel Pagnol's "Jofroi."

After last week's press screening of the Rossellini program, Isabella Rossellini, the director's daughter, corrected the festival's statement that

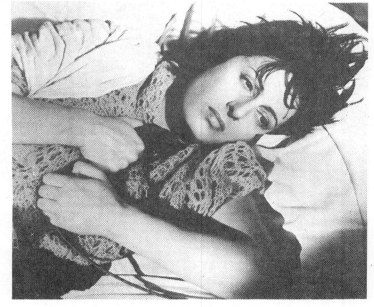

Anna Magnani in "The Human Voice."

"Joan of Arc at the Stake" had been filmed during a performance in front of a Teatro San Carlo audience. Instead, she said, it was filmed during the oratorio's engagement in Naples, but not with an audience on hand.

What Lincoln Center audiences will see is difficult to appreciate except as an example of film preservation. The movie, apparently, was once thought to be lost. Historians have worked mightily to re-create a new print from footage not in the best of condition. Even after a lot of upgrading, the original Gevacolor is no more than a kind of all-embracing greenish haze, marked here and there by slashes of bright colors. The soundtrack also is not great and, though the subtitles are adequate, it's not easy to follow the Claudel text.

As Joan, the oratorio's principal nonsinging role, Miss Bergman looks achingly young and beautiful. The camera moves around freely, sometimes peering down on a scene from a catwalk above the stage. One can see Rossellini's attempts to make this into cinema rather than filmed theater, but it's difficult to agree with him (as quoted by the French film historian Georges Sadoul) that "it is neorealism in the sense that I've always aimed at it."

The filmed oratorio is supplemented by black-and-white newsreel coverage of the Naples stage production's opening night, out front and backstage.

1987 O 6, C14:3

Real Life

LINDSAY ANDERSON: THE EARLY DOCUMENTARIES: THURSDAY'S CHILDREN, written and directed by Lindsay Anderson and Guy Brenton; photography by Walter Lassally; narrated by Richard Burton. Running time: 21 minutes.
EVERY DAY EXCEPT CHRISTMAS, written and directed by Mr. Anderson; produced by Leon Clore and Karel Reisz; photography by Mr. Lassally. Running time: 37 minutes.
THE SINGING LESSON, directed by Mr. Anderson, with the participation of the Warsaw Dramatic Academy. Running time: 20 minutes. At Film Forum 1, 57 Watts Street. These films have no rating.

By WALTER GOODMAN

THERE may be a more moving film in town than "Thursday's Children," but don't count on it. Lindsay Anderson's 1953 documentary runs only 21 minutes, every one of which produces a lump in the throat or a leap of the heart.

Mr. Anderson and Guy Brenton take us to the Royal School for the Deaf at Margate, England, to watch teachers leading children who have never heard a sound into a world of words. The tone is as low-keyed as the teaching, which is done mainly through games; we see the children, aged 4 to 7, getting into the spirit of "jump," "fall," "run." Now and then, the soundtrack is shut off; we see a teacher mouthing words and we hear what the children hear — silence. We share the joy of their successes without being able to forget their lifetime apartness.

The teachers are patient and efficient, the children eager, apparently aware that when they touch a teacher's face as she utters a sound, they are on their way to being able to talk to each other. "Speech is coming," says the narrator, Richard Burton,

and we root for the kids as they struggle to learn a word by remembering what it feels like when they say it. And when, finally, the word is spoken, it is not always recognizable. Thursday's child, says the nursery rhyme, has "far to go." Watching these bright-eyed girls and boys burst from their silence into games and stories, your own eyes are likely to grow a little moist.

•

This fine documentary, which won an Academy Award, is one of three on the current Film Forum 1 program by Mr. Anderson, better known for his features "This Sporting Life," "If" and "O Lucky Man!" It is followed by "The Singing Lesson," a diverting look at a student recital at the Warsaw Dramatic Academy, made in 1967. Nothing is lost in translation since there is very little of that. Although some of the interpolated pictures of crowd scenes in Warsaw seem forced, the performances themselves, set simply against a white wall, are energetic and amiable.

The longest piece, almost 40 minutes, is "Every Day Except Christmas," a report on Covent Garden in 1957, when it was still the center of London's fruit, vegetable and flower trade. Walter Lassally's strong photography concentrates on the camaraderie of the market's workers, beginning at midnight, when produce from all over England begins to arrive, and going on through the night, as apples, mushrooms, roses and much more are carried into the huge market by dray, hand, trolley, and set up on display, to the arrival of buyers in the early hours and the carting of goods to waiting trucks and cars. There's much bustle and banter, breaks for a cig and a cuppa and some singing on the job. A Salvation Army band marches through.

Although paid for by the Ford Motor Company, "Every Day Except Christmas," a product of England's free-cinema movement, is a celebration of the working class. The market jobs take strength, agility, delicacy and cooperation. The workers respect one another, and before the long night is over, they have earned our respect, too.

1987 O 7, C21:1

A Derailed Yuppie

BABY BOOM, directed by Charles Shyer; written by Nancy Meyers and Mr. Shyer; director of photography, William A. Fraker; film editor, Lynzee Klingman; music by Bill Conti; production designer, Jeffrey Howard; produced by Miss Meyers; released by United Artists Pictures. At 84th Street Six, at Broadway; 34th Street Showplace, between Second and Third Avenues; New York Twin, Second Avenue and 66th Street; Embassy 1, Broadway at 46th Street, and other theaters. Running time: 103 minutes. This film is rated PG.
J. C. Wiatt .... Diane Keaton
Dr. Jeff Cooper .... Sam Shepard
Steven Buchner .... Harold Ramis
Fritz Curtis .... Sam Wanamaker
Ken Arrenberg .... James Spader
Hughes Larrabee .... Pat Hingle
Elizabeth Wiatt
                Kristina and Michelle Kennedy

By JANET MASLIN

"BABY BOOM" isn't much more than a glorified sitcom, but it's funny, and it's liable to hit home. The reason: a devilishly good performance by Diane Keaton as the kind of high-energy, nail-spitting female ex-

ecutive who strikes fear into the hearts of everyone she meets. As the sort of woman who answers a middle-of-the-night phone call by mumbling, "I'm in a meeting; take a message," Miss Keaton's J. C. Wiatt embodies all that is bloodcurdling about today's success-crazed young professionals. Lest anyone consider this a sexist premise, rest assured that J. C.'s live-in male companion ("We both eat, sleep and dream our work — that's why we're together," says she) is even worse.

"Baby Boom," which opens today at the 84th Street Six and other theaters, envisions a predictable but amusing set of adventures for J. C. once her hard-boiled business persona begins falling apart. That happens because she inherits a baby through the sort of plot twist that automatically destroys the film's already slight claims to authenticity. The baby's parents were killed; J. C. is the child's only living relative; the little girl is brought all the way from England and delivered to J. C. before she can say no; the only people who want to adopt her are awful. The screenplay, by Charles Shyer and Nancy Meyers (Mr. Shyer directed), wastes no more energy than that on explaining this outlandish twist of fate.

In any case, J. C. is ill prepared for such an inconvenience. She's not a woman with time to spare. (The film shows J. C. and her live-in mate, played by Harold Ramis, grudgingly allocating four minutes for sex one evening before going right back to their reading.) So she tries to check the baby in a coatroom when she has a business lunch; she fastens a diaper with electrical tape; she cooks the baby a fashionable little pasta dinner and then, when the baby gets pasta all over herself, tries to handle the mess with household cleaner.

•

When it comes to this sort of detail, "Baby Boom" is as funny as it is contrived. And Miss Keaton has a wonderfully maniacal gleam in her eye each time she masters some new baby-related trick. The film also does well when it pokes fun at the high-pressure world of the New York child, a world in which bewildered tots attend strenuous gym classes while their parents wail over private-school rejections. Eventually, all of this leaves J. C.'s glamorous career in ruins (James Spader is effectively unctuous as the bright young thing campaigning for her job). And J. C. is seen crumpled on the steps in front of her high-rise office building in tears.

At this point the film makes a ridiculous error, sending J. C. off to a little Vermont town to lead a simpler life.

Merger

In "Baby Boom," Diane Keaton portrays a businesswoman whose progress is disrupted when she inherits a child, played by the twins Kristina and Michelle Kennedy.

It becomes all too clear that neither J. C. nor the makers of the film would know a little Vermont town if it bit them — or a simpler life, either. Not long after buying a picture-perfect house, sight unseen, though an ad in The New York Times Magazine (the film is a lot funnier when it shows a pre-baby J. C. daydreaming about this in New York than actually doing it), she uses produce from her own orchard to develop a classy little recipe for baby applesauce. And soon there is talk about marketing this stuff and landing it in every supermarket in America — so much for simplicity. It doesn't help that every blossom in the Vermont town appears to have come directly from the florist, or that Sam Shepard turns up as a conveniently lonely small-town bachelor.

Without Miss Keaton — or even with Miss Keaton, in one of her more fluttery incarnations — none of this would be believable for a second. Even so, it isn't especially likely. But Miss Keaton's comically exaggerated toughness and absurd self-confidence make the performance a delight. For an hour or so, at least, "Baby Boom" is wicked enough to have a real edge. Someone like J. C. Wiatt might not think so, but someone like J. C. Wiatt might not have time for a movie anyhow.

•

"Baby Boom" is rated PG ("Parental Guidance Suggested"). It includes occasional strong language.

1987 O 7, C24:5

Ancient Tale

YEELEN, directed, written and produced by Souleymane Cissé; in Bambara with English subtitles; photography by Jean-Noël Ferragut and Jean-Michel Humeau; edited by Dounamba Coulibaly, Andrée Davanture, Marie-Catherine Miqueau, Jenny Frenck and Seipati N'Xumalo; music by Michel Portal, with the participation of Salif Keita. At Alice Tully Hall, as part of the 25th New York Film Festival. Running time: 105 minutes. This film has no rating.
The son .... Issiaka Kane
The young Peul woman .... Aoua Sangare
The father .... Niamanto Sanogo
The Peul King .... Balla Moussa Keita
The mother .... Soumba Traore
The uncle .... Ismaila Sarr
The young boy .... Youssouf Tenin Cissé
The Komo chief .... Koke Sangare

By CARYN JAMES

IN "Yeelen" a writer and director from Mali, Souleymane Cissé, re-creates the pre-modern world of the Bambara culture, where the only hint of the industrial age is the presence of a blacksmith.

In this world where rituals have life or death results, a father tracks his son across the landscape of yellow dust and parched ground; the young man journeys to his wise old uncle, bringing a magic fetish, a brilliant stone that will unlock the spiritual secrets his father hoards. "Yeelen" means "brightness," and the symbolic stone's bright light suggests knowledge and power.

For all this mythic potential, though, watching "Yeelen" is a curiously flat experience. Mr. Cissé (whose films have also been shown in the 1980 New Directors/New Films series and at the 1983 New York Film Festival) blends invented images with near-documentary talking heads; he makes no concessions to anyone who wants narrative clues, more action or prettier imagery than the son's methodical journey offers. Instead he presents the culture as he imagines it was lived and demands that we confront it. "Yeelen" is so true to its own vision that at times it seems impenetrable to anyone else's.

As we follow the father and son — the father burns a chicken and invokes the gods; the son steals a tribal chief's wife — Mr. Cissé inadvertently reminds us that the line between the ritual and the static is often a shaky one.

Characters explain their beliefs and actions to each other at length; their recitations might be akin to Greek tragedy but we only know them through laughably translated subtitles. Sometimes the English is too modern — "Do me one more favor" — and sometimes it strains for an elevated tone. "Sacred crossroads. I sing for my spiritual mother," is sung by "cantors" (a correct word with all the wrong connotations).

The words matter because while Mr. Cissé's stark images, his washed-out greens against a gray sky, can be impressive, they aren't meant to carry the film, which withholds its visual magic until the last few minutes. The constant images of men roaming across the arid ground are true to the film's setting, but come to seem as barren as the landscape itself.

At the very end, Mr. Cissé's images are stunning. The son and father confront each other, each with a magic stone, and the fetishes pour out rays of light that meet and slowly turn the screen white. Jumping ahead in time, the son's own small son discovers two pure white orbs buried in the sand, as if his father and grandfather have been cystallized into the knowledge the child holds in his hands. But "Yeelen" forces us to endure our own long journey toward these last bright symbolic scenes — little reward for the struggle through an uneven film that is finally too skimpy to sustain the mythic weight it takes upon itself.

"Yeelen" will be shown at the New York Film Festival tonight at 9:15 and Saturday at noon.

1987 O 8, C37:1

Holding Court

HOROWITZ PLAYS MOZART, a film by Albert Maysles, Susan Froemke and Charlotte Zwerin; photography by Mr. Maysles and Don Lenzer, with Vic Losick and George Bottos; edited by Pam Wise; produced by Miss Froemke and Peter Gelb; a Peter Gelb Production; released by Columbia Artists. At Alice Tully Hall, as part of the 25th New York Film Festival. Running time: 50 minutes. This film has no rating.

By WALTER GOODMAN

SINCE his return to the American concert stage in 1985, Vladimir Horowitz has become a documentary perennial. "Vladimir Horowitz, the Last Romantic," celebrated his first recital in the United States in more than two years. His much publicized visit to the Soviet Union was commemorated on television in "Horowitz in Moscow." And showing tonight at 6:15 at the New York Film Festival is "Horowitz Plays Mozart," a filming of his first studio recording with a symphony orchestra in 35 years.

Like "The Last Romantic," the new work is a product of a Maysles documentary team, in this case Albert Maysles, Susan Froemke and Charlotte Zwerin. Their "direct cinema" technique — no script, hand-held camera — doesn't add much to an event that is taken up largely by a pianist at the piano. You can see the flying fingers and accompanying fiddling and the flourishes of the conductor almost any week on public television.

Music lovers may be annoyed by the breaks between movements of the Concerto No. 23 in A, with the Orchestra of La Scala led by Carlo Maria Giulini. But this is a recording session (actually two sessions, though you wouldn't know that from this example of cinéma vérité), and it is diverting to learn that the great man is capable of racing the orchestra. As the diplomatic recording producer puts it, "Mr. Horowitz rushes a little ahead."

•

You get the feeling, as the star cracks small jokes (he asks his page turner, "You know what you're doing here?") and uses pauses in the piano part to wave his arms conductorlike, that he is not unaware of the camera. Here, as in the earlier documentaries, he seems to fancy himself as a sit-down comic.

Between movements, he receives the press. "Always the same question," says his wife, Wanda Toscanini Horowitz, when he is asked what he thinks of the newer pianists. She advises him to take the Fifth Amendment. He accepts her advice on that one, but when he is asked his opinions of American orchestras, he plunges in with a preference for the Cleveland Orchestra over the Chicago Symphony ("not so good") and writes off the New York Philharmonic as "terrible." The lately redone Carnegie Hall, he says, is "spoiled." For him, "There's too much resonance." This mildly pleasant movie could use more resonance.

•

Also on the Film Festival bill is "Young in Heart," a half-hour tribute by Sue Marx and Pamela Conn to the love affair of a couple of octogenarians. It's sweet and short, a little too sweet and not quite short enough. Louis paints portraits; Reva paints flowers. They have suffered deep losses before finding each other. "It's very lonely being in bed by yourself," says Reva. You can't help wishing them well as a couple, even as you bid them farewell with relief.

A still shorter piece — a couple of minutes short — opens the program. Put together by Anita Thacher, it's a reading by Blythe Danner of Elizabeth Bishop's poem "One Art," a good poem that gains nothing from the banal photography.

1987 O 8, C37:1

La Ronde

L'AMI DE MON AMIE, directed and written by Eric Rohmer; in French with English subtitles; photography by Bernard Lutic; edited by Luisa Garcia; music by Jean-Louis Valéro; produced by Margaret Ménégoz; production company, Les Films du Losange; released by Orion Classics. At Alice Tully Hall tonight and tomorrow, as part of the 25th New York Film Festival. Running time: 102 minutes. This film has no rating.

Blanche	Emmanuelle Chaulet
Léa	Sophie Renoir
Adrienne	Anne-Laure Meury
Fabien	Eric Viellard
Alexandre	François-Eric Gendron

By VINCENT CANBY

SPECIFIC places, at specific times of year, have always been key to the methods and the manners of Eric Rohmer's splendidly singular comedies. In "My Night at Maud's," the wintry, non-picturesque streets and chilly apartments of the city of Clermont-Ferrand had the effect of prompting characters to argue long into the night, as if to stay out of cold, lonely beds. The lush, midsummer Annecy countrysides in "Claire's Knee" were an overwhelming aphrodisiac to an otherwise rational man. In "Pauline at the Beach," the sunlit crispness of the Normandy coast, at the end of the season, required that the characters stop talking around points and come to decisions before facing another autumn at loose ends in Paris.

Mr. Rohmer, the most cerebral, most morally committed of French directors, is also the one who seems most aware of the particular influences of geography and meteorology on people. In a Rohmer movie, the physical world, including architecture, describes the life of the mind.

The spectacular satellite city of Cergy-Pontoise, designed by the Argentine architect Ricardo Bofill, is the unbilled co-star of "L'Ami de Mon Amie" ("My Girlfriend's Boyfriend"), Mr. Rohmer's small, perfectly achieved new addition to the series of films he calls "Comedies and Proverbs." The film will be shown at the New York Film Festival tonight at 6:15 and tomorrow at 9 P.M.

From what Mr. Rohmer shows us, Cergy-Pontoise is a kind of underpopulated, modernist amalgam of Bath, a French co-op city and a Disneyworld. The old world — Paris — hovers on the horizon.

Mr. Rohmer, as much as the intense, well-meaning, sometimes seriously muddled lovers in the film itself, is fascinated and rather charmed by this bold architectural attempt to create, at one blow, a perfect environment: office and apartment buildings of glass, steel and reinforced concrete, separated by strategically located plazas and parks, along with shopping areas, 15 television channels, three legitimate theaters, restaurants, a couple of manmade lakes and other recreational facilities.

Mr. Rohmer remains resolutely unhorrified by it all. He appreciates this particular example of urban planning, while sometimes finding it as exotic as an Eskimo village and as funny as a miniature golf course.

Cergy-Pontoise was designed for community. "It's like a village," Fabien says to Blanche about Cergy-Pontoise, after running into Blanche near a shopping center several times within the same afternoon. Fabien is the lover of Léa, Blanche's best friend.

Fabien and Blanche, who scarcely know each other, feel guilty as well as pleased at these chance encounters, dictated not by fate but by the satellite-city's layout. In addition, Blanche is more than a little troubled because Léa has confided that she's tired of Fabien, and wishes she could leave him "in easy stages." Léa thinks that Blanche and Fabien would make a fine match.

Blanche, however, thinks she's in love with Alexandre, an engineer with the local power-and-light company, a man so handsome and self-assured that women chase *him.* In the course of one idyllic summer in this architectural paradise, Blanche, Fabien, Léa and Alexandre scheme to achieve their own ends without damaging friendships. That they will succeed is no surprise. The fun of "L'Ami de Mon Amie" is watching how close they come to the edge of failure, and the manner in which Cergy-Pontoise reveals character and rules choices.

The solemn Blanche, played by Emmanuelle Chaulet, an extremely pretty new actress making her film debut, loves the arid newness of Cergy-Pontoise. She's lonely but, most of the time, she's as confident that she'll find the ideal man as she is that grass will eventually be planted in the satellite city's unfinished plazas. Fabien (Eric Viellard), who considers himself an all-around sportsman, courts Blanche by taking her wind-surfing on a small man-made lake where the winds seldom get up to eight miles an hour. Wind-surfing here is mostly a matter of being able to stand up on utterly placid water.

Léa (Sophie Renoir, a brunette beauty) keeps making halfhearted attempts to leave Cergy-Pontoise, and keeps returning. In Paris, Alexandre (François-Eric Gendron) would be just another good-looking bureaucrat. In Cergy-Pontoise, he's a celebrity.

"L'Ami de Mon Amie" looks and sounds serene, but there are summer storms threatening within. Don't be put off by being aware of the click of heels on floors, the whisper of mild breezes, of the silences between earnest and frequently misunderstood confidences. Listen to what's being said. Everyone talks very well but often at hilarious cross purposes. Mr. Rohmer must be the master of the oblique love scene, in which two people who care terrifically for each other manage to convince each other that they are not in love.

Blanche refuses to understand her own emotions, but she sees everything else clearly. Talking about Cergy-Pontoise's manmade beach on a crowded Saturday, Blanche says — referring to the overpowering smell of hot dogs — that being there is like traveling in a foreign country. She puts up with things in Cergy-Pontoise that she wouldn't tolerate anywhere else.

"L'Ami de Mon Amie" is as clean and functional in appearance as the satellite city, but it's full of unexpected delights. As usual, every member of Mr. Rohmer's cast is very good, but Miss Chaulet may well be a brand-new star. Don't go anticipating a laugh a minute. A friend of mine emerged from the press screening claiming the movie was 16 hours long. I guessed about 90 minutes. In fact, it's 102 minutes; they are all wonderful.

1987 O 9, C4:5

Aussie Angst

DOGS IN SPACE, directed and written by Richard Lowenstein; director of photography, Andrew De Groot; edited by Jill Bilcock; musical director, Ollie Olsen; produced by Glenys Rowe; released by Skouras Pictures Inc. At 57th Street Playhouse, 110 West 57th Street. Running time: 108 minutes. This film has no rating.

Sam	Michael Hutchence
Anna	Saskia Post
Tim	Nique Needles
The Girl	Deanna Bond
Luchio	Tony Helou
Chainsaw Man	Chris Haywood

By CARYN JAMES

A BETTER title for "Dogs in Space" might have been "Sid and Nancy Meet the Secaucus Seven." This is a story about 60's survivors in 1978, drugged-out musicians who look and sound as if they're straight from the 80's. The large cast of men and women live in a communal house in Melbourne, a 60's relic where garbage fills the fireplace and huge joints are passed around. Richard Lowenstein, an Australian writer and director, jumps from person to person, snippet to snippet, cuts now and then to the group's flickering television screen, and constantly overlaps music and multiple conversations. The background is energetic; too bad the foreground is just as chaotic.

We're supposed to care about Sam, lead singer of a rock group called Dogs in Space, and his girlfriend, Anna. Her hair is dyed platinum; his is hennaed red. He has more talent than anyone else in the house, and she has more brains.

•

Michael Hutchence, lead singer of the rock group Inxs, plays Sam, pasty-faced and strung-out, a perfect self-absorbed 60's type: he grabs food from other people's plates, crawls on the floor wrapped in a blanket, pouts, snarls, demands attention and chalks it all up to creativity. Mr. Lowenstein presents this as part of Sam's charm — men indulge him, women adore him and no one says, "Sam, wash your hair" — but the portrayal is effective anyway.

Anna (Saskia Post) has that mid-80's, retro-50's, early-Madonna style. She looks mournful when Sam first shoots her up with heroin; she smiles proudly when she sees him onstage. So much for character development. This is a film of surfaces, where a frown and a smile stand for everything that is, or isn't, going on inside.

•

In fact, Anna's reaction to Sam's performance is intriguing. Buried inside this jumbled film must be a view of the offstage life that feeds that onstage moment. We're watching a man who carries his raucous persona into real life, and a woman so enraptured by the image she can't see its danger.

But Mr. Lowenstein — whose work includes many rock videos and "Strikebound," a film about Australian miners — prefers sensory overload to coherence. The music, by a variety of Australian bands, is a white-noise backdrop or a too-literal statement. ("The clocks stand still, rooms for the memory" is Sam's version of an elegy.) Like Sam and Anna, "Dogs in Space," which opens today at the 57th Street Playhouse, has talent, intelligence and no idea what to do with them.

1987 O 9, C7:1

Love and Money

SURRENDER, written and directed by Jerry Belson; director of photography, Juan Ruiz Anchia; film editor, Wendy Greene Bricmont; music by Michel Colombier; produced by Aaron Spelling and Alan Greisman; released by Warner Bros. At 84th Street Six, at Broadway; Sutton, Third Avenue at 57th Street; Criterion, Broadway at 45th Street; Movieland Eighth Street, at University Place; Bay Cinema, Second Avenue at 32d Street; 86th Street Twin, at Third Avenue. Running time: 96 minutes. This film is rated PG.

Daisy Morgan	Sally Field
Sean Stein	Michael Caine
Marty Caesar	Steve Guttenberg
Jay Bass	Peter Boyle
Ronnie	Julie Kavner
Ace Morgan	Jackie Cooper

JERRY BELSON, who wrote and directed "Surrender," almost certainly has a better idea of what this film is about than any audience will. It may be heartfelt, but it's confused. It starts out as a satire about love and money, with Michael Caine as an unlucky-in-love celebrity author who's paying alimony and palimony too. But it then develops into a too-cute romance centering on Sally Field, who fends off her rival suitors with a snappiness Doris Day would envy. Miss Field is spunky, all right, but she's always better in more serious roles, ones that present fewer opportunities for the kind of bottom-wriggling and eye-rolling that she does here.

The production notes describe the film as "semi-autobiographical" and quote Mr. Belson as saying that "everything that happened in the movie happened to me." So perhaps he, like Sean Stein, the best-selling author played by Michael Caine, attended a party at which terrorists invaded, forced the guests to strip and then tied them together in pairs, which is how Mr. Caine and Miss Field get acquainted in the movie. If it really happened, then it was undoubtedly less strange in real life than it is on the screen. In any case, Mr. Caine's Sean, a wealthy man badly victimized by women, has soon devised an elaborate plot to keep Miss Field's Daisy from knowing that he has money.

Daisy is supposed to be an impoverished artist; in one of its occasional flashes of real cleverness, the film shows her working by day in a painting mill stamping out hotel-room artworks by the score. (Another ingenious moment has Mr. Caine confronted by two open elevators, one containing a gorgeous blonde, the other a man with a vicious dog; he hesitates only briefly before deciding that the Doberman's a better bet.) And she's supposed to be indifferent to money, but she lives with a young lawyer, played with the right whininess by Steve Guttenberg, who thinks of little else.

•

After the tying-up incident, which is an embarrassment to all concerned, she also hits it off with Sean, who is a nervous, bashful recluse and amounts to being one of the odder characters Mr. Caine has played. Here is an actor who can do anything, but frolicking on an airport runway with Miss Field, as part of a young-and-in-love montage, is just about his limit.

"Surrender," which opens today at the Criterion Center and other theaters, seesaws aimlessly as it plays out this triangular romance, pausing every now and then to work an element of comic avarice into the proceedings. By the time Daisy has won the lottery at Lake Tahoe and crawled into bed under a covering of $5 bills, the story threatens to become truly bizarre. But Mr. Belson's style is amiable, if sloppy — the film has been very unattractively shot — and it's certainly painless. Among the film's better elements are supporting performances by Peter Boyle, as a lawyer who wears quite a remarkable hairpiece for his courtroom appearances, and Julie Kavner, who's the ideal actress for any film requiring a big-hearted, wisecracking best friend.

•

"Surrender" is rated PG ("Parental Guidance Suggested"). It includes some sexual innuendoes.

JANET MASLIN

1987 O 9, C10:6

Schoolyard Standoff

THREE O'CLOCK HIGH, directed by Phil Joanou; written by Richard Christian Matheson and Thomas Szollosi; edited by Joe Ann Fogle; lighting consultant, Barry Sonnenfeld; music by Tangerine Dream; production designer, William F. Matthews; produced by David E. Vogel; released by Universal Pictures. At Movieland, Broadway at 47th Street; New York Twin, Second Avenue and 66th Street; 86th Street Twin, at Lexington Avenue; 23d Street Triplex, between Eighth and Ninth Avenues. Running time: 90 minutes. This film is rated PG-13.

Jerry Mitchell	Casey Siemaszko
Franny Perrins	Anne Ryan
Buddy Revell	Richard Tyson
Brei Mitchell	Stacey Glick
Vincent Costello	Jonathan Wise
Mr. Rice	Jeffrey Tambor
Detective Mulvahill	Philip Baker Hall
Mr. O'Rourke	John P. Ryan

"THREE O'CLOCK HIGH," which opens today at Loews New York Twin and other theaters, is as well made as a film about a schoolyard showdown can be. It's even better made than that, which is precisely the problem. The director, Phil Joanou, has turned every shot into a portentous marvel, from the close-up view of an earring going into an ear to the 360-degree spin around the schoolyard as the nice-guy hero (Casey Siemaszko) awaits his dreaded confrontation with the mean-spirited bully (Richard Tyson). Presumably this is all part of the joke, but as jokes go it's a grim one. Too much talent, when it's brought to bear on a subject this teensy, can be worse than no talent at all.

It's clear that Mr. Joanou could do as clever a job of shooting a bullfrog or a bowl of spaghetti as he does in maneuvering the characters here. It's also clear that a world view this narrow can quickly become stupefying, even tragic. Jerry Mitchell (Mr. Siemaszko) wakes up. He goes to school. He meets and upsets a new student who threatens to clobber him, and he spends the rest of the day worrying about how to escape. In the process, he wows his sex-starved teacher, wins the admiration of all the other smug, comfortable kids in his school and catches the eye of a wildly seductive glamour girl. That's it. That's all. Nothing else happens.

•

And Mr. Joanou has done such a beautiful job of gilding this dandelion that every shot looks wonderful, in the tireless, punchy, hyperkinetic style of teen-age comedies with nothing in mind and energy to spare. So a punch from the bully sends all the bookcases in a library careening, like so many well-placed dominoes. The film jabs so relentlessly at the viscera that the audience is never allowed to notice anything independently; if Mr. Joanou wants you to spot a license plate, for instance, he drives the car right into a floor-level camera.

Other things are less important, like the lighting (by Barry Sonnenfeld, the cinematographer who shot "Blood Simple"), which is especially lovely. There are actors here, too, but the human elements are almost an afterthought; it hardly matters what they do.

•

"Three O'Clock High" is rated PG-13 ("Special Parental Guidance Suggested for Those Younger Than 13"). It includes some strong language.

JANET MASLIN

1987 O 9, C16:3

Wartime Reverie

HOPE AND GLORY, written, produced and directed by John Boorman; director of photography, Philippe Rousselot; edited by Ian Crafford; music by Peter Martin; production designer, Anthony Pratt; released by Columbia Pictures. At Alice Tully Hall tonight and Sunday, as part of the 25th New York Film Festival. Running time: 112 minutes. This film is rated PG-13.

Bill	Sebastian Rice Edwards
Sue	Geraldine Muir
Grace	Sarah Miles
Clive	David Hayman
Dawn	Sammi Davis
Mac	Derrick O'Connor
Molly	Susan Woolridge
Bruce	Jean-Marc Barr
Grandfather	Ian Bannen

By JANET MASLIN

IT'S difficult to imagine anyone's remembrance of World War II as idyllic, but it's not impossible. In John Boorman's radiant "Hope and Glory," the autobiographical hero is a young boy of just the right age, humor and sensitivity to savor the adventure of which he finds himself a part.

The horror of war intrudes only intermittently into the London suburb where Bill (Sebastian Rice Edwards) and his family live. And when war does make its presence felt, it's often in unexpected ways: not just the burning houses and the scattered shrapnel, but also the German flier who parachutes into this street of identical row houses, surveys the crowd of neighbors and calmly lights a cigarette before being led off, by a local constable, through someone's vegetable garden. It takes a young boy to marvel at the strangeness of all this, and a skilled film maker to recall it so clearly and so sweetly.

Mr. Boorman, the director of films including "Point Blank," "Deliverance" and "The Emerald Forest," has never shown anything like this temperament before. But "Hope and Glory" has an invitingly nostalgic spirit and a fine eye for the magical details that a little boy might notice. There is the incident involving fish, for example, after Bill's mother, Grace, has moved the family to a house on the Thames owned by her parents, who named their other daughters Faith, Hope and Charity. On one oddly peaceful day in this lovely setting, Bill and his little sister are sent by their wildly eccentric grandfather to catch fish, and warned not to come home empty-handed. The children have tried and failed, and are ready to despair, when a bomb blast kills every fish in the vicinity, thus providing an odd form of salvation.

•

"Hope and Glory" manages to be warmly personal without being private in the least. The details that are mystifying, like the fact that a sign in front of Bill's house names the place "Bhm-tam," are no less baffling to young Bill than they might be to a viewer (Mr. Boorman explains, in an autobiographical note introducing the film's published screenplay, that he himself never knew what this sign at his parents' house meant, either). Neither the local atmosphere nor the family history seems at all remote, and Mr. Boorman makes the film seem open and involving at every turn. Right from the scene establishing young Bill's first awareness of war — which comes in the form of sudden quiet when every lawnmower stops working on a Sunday afternoon, as the radio announcement is made — the film maintains an eccentric, childlike viewpoint that holds its audience's attention.

The key figures in Bill's life are almost all women, which is another of the film's peculiarities. Chief among them are his sturdily courageous mother (played by Sarah Miles, who's a good deal less excitable here than she is in other roles) and the rebellious teen-age sister (Sammi Davis, who's especially fine) who creates a new crisis every day. From the film's rosy vantage point, the war is seen as having frightened and inconvenienced these relatives without much altering the essential pettiness of their daily lives, and from this the film derives a lot of its humor. There is bleakness, perhaps, in the carefully constructed view of Bill's mother and an old flame sharing a picnic on a beach, right next to the line of barbed wire there to fend off enemy frogmen. But there's also a comic aspect, and Mr. Boorman has managed to capture both without diminishing either.

"Hope and Glory" has a luminous look and a period feeling that's both unusual and convincing, to which Shirley Russell's costumes are a particularly key contribution. The ensemble acting is uniformly entertaining (Ian Bannen, as Bill's foxy Grandpa, is especially so), and the pacing almost dreamlike, as befits a reverie. The film's ending is especially sweet, affirming the boyish sense of wonder and bemusement that informs it all.

"Hope and Glory" will be shown tonight at 9:15 and Sunday at 3 P.M. as part of the New York Film Festival. It opens at the Baronet next Friday.

•

"Hope and Glory" is rated PG-13 ("Special Parental Guidance Suggested for Those Younger Than 13") and includes some sexually suggestive episodes.

1987 O 9, C23:1

Off Their Toes

DANCERS, directed by Herbert Ross; screenplay by Sarah Kernochan; cinematography by Ennio Guarnieri; edited by William Reynolds; music by Pino Donaggio; production designer, Gianni Quaranta; produced by Menahem Golan and Yoram Globus; released by The Cannon Group, Inc. At Plaza, Madison Avenue at 58th Street; 84th Street Six, at Broadway; Art Greenwich Twin, Seventh Avenue at 12th Street. Running time: 99 minutes. This film is rated PG.

Footloose
Alessandra Ferri and Mikhail Baryshnikov star in "Dancers," Herbert Ross's drama about a ballet troupe and its production of "Giselle."

Tony	Mikhail Baryshnikov
Francesca	Alessandra Ferri
Nadine	Leslie Browne
Patrick	Thomas Rall
Muriel	Lynn Seymour
Wade	Victor Barbee
Lisa	Julie Kent
Contessa	Mariangela Melato
Paolo	Leandro Amato

"COULD you try please to think of me as just a guy?" Mikhail Baryshnikov asks a sweet young ballerina in "Dancers." Well, all right, but in fact the character he plays here is a renowned ladykiller and legendary star. And could you try please to think of this as just a movie? That, too, would be difficult, since "Dancers," which opens today at the Plaza and other theaters, is something like a sequel to "The Turning Point." And something like an afterthought as well.

Mr. Baryshnikov, comfortably typecast as the most famous male dancer in the world, plays Anton (Tony) Sergeyev, who has arrived in an extremely picturesque part of Italy to supervise the filming of a production of "Giselle." It is one of the film's wittier touches to introduce Leslie Browne, the budding ingénue of "The Turning Point," as an older, wiser ex-lover of Sergeyev's who now has a baby in tow. Sounding a note of bitterness, she also gives the film its only non-fluff element, as a woman who knows Sergeyev's habits all too well. When a demure young innocent (Julie Kent) who has caught Sergeyev's eye gushes that she's never seen him before, except onstage, Miss Browne's Nadine snaps, "You're gonna wish you stayed in the audience."

•

Unlike "The Turning Point," which ingeniously interwove a love and knowledge of the dance world into a larger and more conventional story, "Dancers" has a harder time concocting a plot. That's apparent even from the title. Mr. Baryshnikov, looking introspective and wearing very deep shadows under his eyes, has some enjoyable scenes in which he works out the staging of "Giselle" with his troupe (played by members of the American Ballet Theater), and others in which he broods about his life and career. But beyond that, little happens, except for an attempt at romance with the very young Miss Kent, who looks like a Botticelli and sounds exactly as Mariel Hemingway did in "Manhattan." The second half of the film derives what story it has from a labored interworking of the story of "Giselle" with the tale of this non-affair.

Herbert Ross, who directed both

this film and "The Turning Point," conveyed the more galvanizing aspects of dance far better in the earlier film. The dance scenes there, presented as brief, impassioned excerpts, were truly electrifying, whereas this film's longer passages have less spark. The attempt to work some offstage drama into "Giselle" only flattens the dance scenes, and the backstage angles — a constant reminder of the film that Sergeyev is overseeing — are at times distracting. Still, "Dancers" bubbles over with nice scenery and vibrant performers, and for anyone passionately interested in the world of dance, it has a touristy charm.

•

"Dancers" is rated PG ("Parental Guidance Suggested"). It includes some sexual innuendoes.
                    JANET MASLIN

1987 O 9, C24:1

Triangle

SOMEONE TO WATCH OVER ME, directed by Ridley Scott; written by Howard Franklin; director of photography, Steven Poster; edited by Claire Simpson; music by Michael Kamen; production design by Jim Bissell; produced by Thierry de Ganay and Harold Schneider; released by Columbia Pictures. At Warner, Broadway and 43d Street; Manhattan Twin, 59th Street east of Third Avenue; 86th Street Twin, at Lexington Avenue; 34th Street East, near Second Avenue; 23d Street West Triplex, at Eighth Avenue; Metro Twin, 99th Street and Broadway. Running time: 106 minutes. This film is rated R.

Mike Keegan	Tom Berenger
Claire Gregory	Mimi Rogers
Ellie Keegan	Lorraine Bracco
Lieutenant Garber	Jerry Orbach
Neil Steinhart	John Rubinstein
Joey Venza	Andreas Katsulas
T. J.	Tony DiBenedetto

IN "The Duellists," "Alien" and "Blade Runner," Ridley Scott earned a reputation as something of a stylist, a director whose use of striking visual and aural decoration is integral to the meaning of his work.

However, "Someone to Watch Over Me," his new film, reflects less a sense of style than a dependence on a few, comparatively easy-to-achieve effects that pass for style — smoky interiors often lighted from below, lots of reflecting surfaces, nighttime exteriors of startling, liquid clarity, all supplemented by a music track that contrasts cocktail-piano pop and high-toned classical tidbits.

Beneath its elegant mask, "Someone to Watch Over Me" is a commonplace melodrama about Mike Keegan

(Tom Berenger), a happily married New York policeman, who has an affair with Claire Gregory (Mimi Rogers), the beautiful Manhattan millionaire whose body he's been assigned to guard. Claire has had the misfortune to witness a murder while attending the opening of a fashionable downtown art gallery, and the murderer (Andreas Katsulas) wants her dead before she can testify.

Claire finds all the precautions just *too, too boring,* but something draws her to the strong, handsome, lower-middle-class policeman, who knows nothing about modern art and thinks her friends are superficial. Mike, on his part, has never before met anyone like Claire — witty, sweetly careless about money and, when the chips are down, basically decent.

While Mike spends his nights in Claire's bed, instead of standing watch outside the door, Ellie (Lorraine Bracco), his pretty wife and the mother of his child, senses that, well, Mike is changing. Poor Mike thinks he loves both women. Poor Ellie, who looks and sounds like Debra Winger in-performance, is shocked and humiliated. Poor Claire could be murdered at any minute, and almost is.

Nothing that happens to these three people is moving or even exciting. To keep the movie going until its absurd ending, the character of the murderer is changed, midstream, from an ordinary, run-of-the-mill New York mobster into a crazed psychotic. Howard Franklin's screenplay plays less like a feature film than like the pilot for a failed television series about New York policemen.

"Someone to Watch Over Me" opens today at the 86th Street Twin and other theaters. The George and Ira Gershwin title song is sung on the soundtrack by Sting, Roberta Flack, and Gene Ammons, which may be more often than you want to hear it.
                    VINCENT CANBY

1987 O 9, C40:1

MAN ON FIRE, directed by Elie Chouraqui; screenplay by Mr. Chouraqui and Sergio Donati, based on the novel by A. J. Quinnell; director of photography, Gerry Fisher; edited by Noelle Boisson; music by John Scott; produced by Arnon Milchan; released by Tri-Star Pictures. At Embassy 4, Broadway and 47th Street; Eastside Cinema, Third Avenue between 55th and 56th Streets; Movieland Eighth Street Triplex, at University Place; Orpheum Twin, 86th Street near Third Avenue; Coliseum Twin, Broadway at 181st Street; Movie Center 5, 125th Street between Powell and Douglass Boulevards, and other theaters. Running time: 93 minutes. This film is rated R.

Creasy	Scott Glenn
Sam	Jade Malle
David	Joe Pesci
Jane	Brooke Adams
Michael	Jonathan Pryce
Ettore	Paul Shenar
Conti	Danny Aiello
Julia	Laura Morante
Satta	Giancarlo Prati

By CARYN JAMES

Agents and accountants around the world must be cackling mischievously and counting up their fees: here is a thriller set and shot in Italy, with a French director and American stars. You might not expect much from this commercial contrivance, but the first line of "Man on Fire" is even sillier than you'd guess. Nurses and doctors run around in slow motion; someone pulls a zipper over a dead man's face; suddenly there's a voice-over from the grave: "And so that's how I ended. A stiff in a body bag." Never mind that a late plot twist explains the ghostly voice; the line sets the tone for a movie that always seems about to slip into unconsciousness.

As we flash back in the stiff's memory, we see he is a bitter former C.I.A. agent named Creasy (Scott Glenn), who wants "to beat out the nightmare" of horrors he has seen. He takes a job as a bodyguard for a wealthy couple's 12-year-old daughter, Samantha, who immediately explains that she went to school in Greenwich Village. This gives her an excuse to speak English and to carry around "Of Mice and Men," comparing herself and Creasy to Steinbeck's George and Lenny. Eventually this literary child breaks through Creasy's tough-guy defenses.

•

His emotional breakthrough doesn't make him a better bodyguard, though. One day as Creasy drives Sam home, terrorists open the unlocked passenger door, drag her off and shoot him. As soon as Creasy's wounded leg is out of its bandages, he leaves his hospital bed and tracks down Sam's kidnappers as fast as he can limp.

Scott Glenn, who has been powerful in "The Right Stuff" and "Silverado," has less presence than usual here. Blink a few times and you'll miss Brooke Adams as Sam's mother, and Danny Aiello as the American ringleader of the Italian terrorists.

"Man on Fire," which opened yesterday at the Embassy 4 and other theaters, is so full of rain it looks like monsoon season on Lake Como, but that makes as much sense as anything else the director and co-writer Elie Chouraqui has imagined.

1987 O 10, 18:4

FIRE FROM THE MOUNTAIN, directed by Deborah Shaffer; photography by Frank Pineda; edited by Virginia Reticker; music by Charlie Haden; produced by Adam Friedson and Ms. Shaffer. At Alice Tully Hall, as part of the 25th New York Film Festival. Running time: 60 minutes. This film has no rating.

By WALTER GOODMAN

As long as "Fire From the Mountain" stays close to Omar Cabezas's notable book, subtitled "The Making of a Sandinista," the documentary makes a forceful case in behalf of the Nicaraguan revolution. Firing off news clips that document Mr. Cabezas's vigorous prose, the movie, which plays at 6 o'clock tonight at the New York Film Festival, contrasts the poverty of Nicaragua's campesinos with the gaudy display of the Somoza set that ruled the country for decades. It rubs in the role of United States Marines in bringing the Somoza family to power and Washington's role in keeping it there. We glimpse President Nixon and Nelson Rockefeller consorting with Anastasio Somoza Debayle. The footage of Somoza's national guardsmen beating protesters and the accounts of their victims demonstrate why the guard was so hated.

Mr. Cabezas, who joined the Sandinistas early and became a high official in the Ministry of the Interior after their victory, writes with special feeling of his early days in the mountains: "Loneliness is trying to forget the sound of cars, the longing for colors, longing for a woman, longing to see your family." Kathleen Weaver's vibrant translation is read with great drive by Tony Plana.

The scenes of triumph when in July 1979 the rebels entered Managua's

main square to the cheers of thousands are rendered rousingly. Once Somoza is toppled, however, the documentary, like the new Government itself, runs into difficulties. "Well, now what do we do?" asks a suddenly elevated former guerrilla. What the director Deborah Shaffer does for much of the final 20 minutes of her 60-minute movie is deliver commercials for the regime.

It's a Sandinista-eye view of the Sandinistas. The message is that they are being prevented from making Nicaragua a revolutionary model by United States aggression. As selected citizens declare they would rather die on their feet than live on their knees, you may hear echoes of the exhortations at the filmed rallies, where people sing folk songs and clap on cue. Mr. Cabezas's prose has not been improved by his official duties. Now he goes around exhorting coffee growers, "When you throw that little red bean into the sack, you're defending the people of Central America."

A little dissatisfaction is voiced about shortages, but they are attributed to understandable errors of planning or to the need to divert resources to fight the contras, who are accused of Somoza-like atrocities. We are informed that Nicaragua is today a democracy, operated in the interests of The People. "Is this a Communist country?" a voice, perhaps Ms. Shaffer's, asks. "No," comes the reply, "it's a free country." Reassured, Miss Shaffer, who won an Academy Award in 1985 for "Witness to War," her short documentary about Dr. Charlie Clements's work in El Salvador, lays on shots of pretty children and crippled war veterans playing basketball in wheelchairs and holding weapons, ready to defend their homeland. The beach photography at the end is a "Come to Nicaragua" trailer.

•

The program at the Film Festival opens with "The Centerfielder," an 18-minute tale of a poor imprisoned shoemaker under the Somoza dictatorship who keeps remembering his happier years as a baseball player. Ramiro Lacayo Deshon directs with a heavy hand, but it cannot have been easy to do otherwise with Robert R. Young's script, designed, the press material tells us, to show how the poor shoemaker learns "there is no centerfield in the political life of his country." The North American participant in this first Nicaraguan-United States co-production is the Common Sense Foundation, which appears to have a certain point of view about Nicaragua and also helped pay for "Fire From the Mountain."

1987 O 10, 19:4

HOUSE OF GAMES, directed by David Mamet; screenplay by Mr. Mamet, based on a story he co-wrote with Jonathan Katz; photography by Juan Ruiz Anchia; edited by Trudy Ship; music by Alaric Jans; production designer, Michael Merritt; produced by Michael Hausman; released by Orion Pictures. At Avery Fisher Hall, as part of the 25th New York Film Festival. Running time: 101 minutes. This film is rated R.

Margaret Ford	Lindsay Crouse
Mike	Joe Mantegna
Joey	Mike Nussbaum
Dr. Littauer	Lilia Skala
Businessman	J. T. Walsh
Girl with book	Willo Hausman
Prison ward patient	Karen Kohlhaas
Billy Hahn	Steve Goldstein
Bartender/House of Games	Jack Wallace
Bartender/Charlie's Tavern	Ben Blakeman
Poker Playrs	G. Roy Levin, Bob Lumbra, Andy Potok, Allen Soule

Lindsay Crouse and Joe Mantegna in "House of Games."

By VINCENT CANBY

QUITE early in "House of Games," David Mamet's entertaining, deadpan, seriocomic melodrama about con artists, there's a backroom poker game that sets the tone for everything that comes after.

Though the players could withdraw at any point, they don't, this being a serious game. Raises are seen, and raised again. The pot accumulates. "Everybody stays. Everybody pays," says the dealer. Tensions mount and tempers shorten like fuses burning in slow-motion. Somebody must be bluffing, and somebody must lose, though there's nothing in the book that says the bluffer must lose or that the best hand wins.

That's the fascination of this insidiously addictive game in which the loser, if he plays his cards right, takes all. It's also the fun of the film with which Mr. Mamet, poker player and Pulitzer Prize-winning playwright, makes a fine, completely self-assured debut directing his original screenplay. Sometimes he's bluffing outrageously, but that's all right too.

In movies, as in poker, it's not always what you do but the way you do it. Or, as they say around the poker table, "A man with style is a man who can smile."

•

In "House of Games" a lot of other things are said, some of them unintentional howlers. "You need joy!" says a psychoanalyst to a woman in need, as if prescribing a detergent. But there's also the scam expert who reasons: "We all gotta live in an imperfect world. I acted atrociously, but I do that for a living." The movie never goes so far wrong that it can't retrieve its illusions.

"House of Games" will be shown tonight at 8 at Avery Fisher Hall, closing the 25th New York Film Festival with a presentation in which expectations are fulfilled. The film begins its regular commercial engagement here Wednesday at the D.W. Griffith Theater.

With "House of Games" it's clear that Mr. Mamet not only knows exactly how he wants his work to sound, but also how it should look. Though photographed on location in Seattle, "House of Games" contains no easily identifiable landmarks, no tourist attractions.

The movie remains ambiguously, mysteriously dislocated, not to give the impression that the setting is Anycity, U.S.A., but to emphasize the banality of place to its particular characters. For the sorts of things that occupy them, one city is as good as another. They're not the sort of people who look at scenery. They're floaters.

•

New to this world is Margaret Ford (Lindsay Crouse), a successful, severely stylish psychoanalyst, author of the new best seller, "Driven," a series of studies of obsessive behavior. Through one of her patients, a compulsive gambler who's alternately suicidal and abusive ("You do nothing. This whole thing is a con game"), Margaret decides to investigate the world of crooked gamblers, swindlers and confidence men, possibly for a new book.

Her initially reluctant docent is Mike (Joe Mantegna), a smooth-talking fellow of indeterminate age who appears to have learned how to be sincere by practicing in front of a mirror. Except for his gift of gab, everything about Mike is slightly bogus, his anger as well as his cool. His facial expressions never quite match what he says but, for Margaret, this is his charm as well as his value. He's also a fund of arcane information and, as a reader of character, as good as any analyst.

Not much more can be reported without revealing the twists, turns and reversals by which "House of Games" proceeds. Mr. Mamet's screenplay builds much like a whopping-good poker game in which the stakes become so high that the players, having invested so much, can't afford to pull out. One may have reservations about the film's ending, but the ending, I suspect, was the point toward which the writer was aiming before he put one word to paper.

There'll be further reservations about the film's style, which has something of Mike's sincerity about it. It's deliberately artificial, which is both comic and scary. The sometimes very funny, bizarre Mamet dialogue is spoken in intense monotones, a manner designed to call attention to itself.

Yet one hears the words as if they were italicized. Mostly this works extraordinarily well, though there are times, especially when the camera comes in for a tight close-up on the speaker, when the artifice wears thin. One sees the actor within the character who is speaking the lines, as well as the man, just off-screen, who wrote the screenplay and is monitoring everything the actor does.

Though "House of Games" is not of the dramatic heft of the playwright's "American Buffalo" and "Glengarry Glen Ross," the screenplay is the first true Mamet work to reach the screen, and the direction illuminates it at every turn. Both Miss Crouse and Mr. Mantegna and the supporting actors, including Mike Nussbaum, J. T. Walsh and Steve Goldstein, are splendidly in touch, not only with character but also with the sense of the film.

Early in "House of Games," guns are produced, in effect, onstage. According to the rules of theater, guns, once produced, must be used. Though Mr. Mamet abides by the rules, don't be put off by that. "House of Games," the vision of a secure movie maker, is a wonderfully devious comedy.

1987 O 11, 94:1

FILM VIEW/Janet Maslin

Audiences Vs. Vexing Subjects

SLOW, TERRIBLE DEATH, GRISLY EXPERIments and seemingly irrevocable pollution of the environment are hardly things about which audiences automatically want to hear. But Carole Langer's "Radium City" hooked the crowd anyway, and when that happens, the film maker deserves as much praise for tact as for technique. The strategy involved in making difficult subjects palatable — and more than that, transfixing — is always of interest, even when it backfires rather than succeeds. Because backfire it can. Push viewers too hard in the direction of unpleasant, potentially distasteful material (say, the violent and epithet-filled "China Girl," or the inexcusable "Surf Nazis Must Die") and you push them right over the edge.

The early parts of Miss Langer's documentary, a film about the city of Ottawa, Ill., and the ghastly problems caused by a factory that made radium clock dials there, certainly look as though they may lose the audience quickly. The opening titles have a pious sound, and the camera lingers longer and more sentimentally than necessary upon the cemetery where the factory's workers now lie.

What's more, this sounds as if it will be a familiar type of sad story. And the presence of three sweet-voiced elderly ladies, offering rambling reminiscences of their late sister (one talks about a favorite dress from her childhood), hints that Miss Langer may have trouble sticking to the point. Another off-putting element is the lack of objectivity here, since Miss Langer makes no attempt to represent the position of Joseph A. Kelly Jr., whose family ran the factory.

However, Miss Langer directs with a firm hand. She swiftly moves beyond the all-too-familiar aspects of this horror story and breaks new ground, with an even more dismaying look at how Ottawa has dealt with its troubles since the original damage was done: The inability and unwillingness of some residents to face the facts and the carelessness with which radioactive material has been handled become even more appalling than the contamination itself. What's more, as Miss Langer dispassionately piles up evidence and the chronicle goes from bad to worse, it takes on a momentum that renders objectivity almost beside the point. It becomes harder and harder to imagine that there *is* another side to this story. (And as for Mr. Kelly's chance for equal time, he has lately refused to speak to reporters investigating a similar radium problem in Woodside, Queens, where his company owns another factory. The chances of his wanting to appear in a film like Miss Langer's appear slim.)

So Miss Langer, by taking this story well beyond the point at which most environmental atrocity stories stop, and by capturing the terrible ordinariness of Ottawa's reaction to extraordinary danger, entirely circumvents any resistance her viewers may initially feel. The story itself, surprising in its very bleakness, becomes too compelling to ignore. It helps that a couple of Ottawa residents — particularly Ken Ricci, who roams the town with his Geiger counter, functioning as a self-styled vigilante — sound a note of alarm and activism, since a unilaterally blind populace would be off-putting in its own way. A story like this badly needs some kind of hero, and Mr. Ricci fills the bill.

A story like "Barfly" needs a hero, too, and the surprise is that it really has one. Henry Chinaski, a figure largely modeled on the writer Charles Bukowski (author of the film's screenplay), is as messily dissipated a drunk as might be imagined. When first seen, he's brawling in the alley behind a favorite hangout, dripping blood into his slimy chin whiskers, but he also has a kind of serenity. He likes what he is, and it shows, even when he's bathing in a hydrant or wolfing down a 30-second meal. As played most inventively by Mickey Rourke, he has a regal bearing that's thoroughly comic under the circumstances, and a refreshing eagerness to make waves. "What they really need is a little hint of death," he says diabolically about a complacent young couple in a convertible. And, since it's his unusual luck to have a car at his disposal at that moment, he proceeds to butt them into the middle of a busy intersection.

■

With its debauched characters and its sodden atmosphere, "Barfly" has the potential to distance its audience; even the slightest hint of pathos would do the job. But Barbet Schroeder, who directed, makes as few apologies as Mr. Bukowski does. And the resulting film is so defiantly sleazy, so unsentimental and so cheerfully uncompromising that it demands to be taken on its own terms, as do the characters themselves. Amazingly, this look at the down and out is a lot more life-affirming than films that strive for that effect.

Though James Ivory's adaptation of E. M. Forster's "Maurice" isn't the sort of film to spark controversy, it, too, risks alienating any viewers who refuse to accept a homosexual love story. That, of course, is their problem and not the film's, but Mr. Ivory's skill in circumventing it is impressive. His "Maurice" is so richly decorative, and so unassailably tasteful, that it creates a backdrop of gentlemanly decorum; set against this, the romance almost amounts to a form of subversion. It becomes impossible for audiences not to appreciate this challenge to the status quo.

Finally, there's the more difficult case of "Chuck Berry Hail! Hail! Rock 'n' Roll," Taylor Hackford's documentary about the great musical pioneer and showman. The film has the look and structure of a simple tribute, replete with concert footage, but in fact it's something else. Mr. Berry emerges as an irascible, difficult figure, hard to know and made even more so by his refusal to speak frankly about certain things. But there's nothing about the film's conventional good-time format to allow for this toughness in Mr. Berry, and as a result, it's confusing. In presenting a difficult subject of any kind, a director must pave the way. □

1987 O 11, II:25:5

Macho Woman

VERA, directed, written and produced by Sérgio Toledo, in Portuguese with English subtitles; cinematography by Rodolfo Sanchez and Tercio G. da Mota; music by Arrigo Barnabé; production designer, René Silber. At Bleecker Street Cinema, at La Guardia Place. Running time: 92 minutes. This film has no rating.

Vera	Ana Beatriz Nogueira
Prof. Paulo Trauberg	Raul Cortez
Clara	Aida Leiner
Orphanage Director	Carlos Kroeber
Paizão	Cida Almeida
Telma	Adriana Abujamra
Helena Trauberg	Imara Reis
Izolda	Norma Blum
Librarians	Abram Faarc, Liana Duval

"VERA," the first feature film by a new young Brazilian director named Sérgio Toledo, is about an unhappy young woman, reared in a São Paolo orphanage, who becomes convinced she is a man inhabiting a female body. The tone of the film is serious, matter-of-fact, even-tempered.

Vera (Ana Beatriz Nogueira) is an independent spirit of intelligence and sensitivity. When she falls in love with Clara, a pretty co-worker in a library, she doesn't hesitate to express her feelings, much to the horror of the other woman. When Clara at last responds and indicates that she loves Vera as a woman, poor Vera, in turn, is horrified at the suggestion of a lesbian relationship. She is, after all, a man! The ironies accumulate as Vera begins to behave with all of the arrogance of the most macho Brazilian male.

•

Yearning
Ana Beatriz Nogueria and Aida Leiner star in the Brazilian film "Vera," about a woman longing to be a man.

Mr. Toledo is a writer and director of real potential, though he can't yet bring himself to go directly to the heart of a scene if it means sacrificing picturesques images or ruthlessly cutting out redundancies, such as the television images of destructive phallic symbols that punctuate the movie from start to finish.

Miss Nogueira, who in drag looks something like Alain Delon, is exceptionally good in the title role, for which she was named best actress at this year's Berlin Film Festival.

"Vera" opens today at the Bleecker Street Cinema.

VINCENT CANBY
1987 O 16, C4:5

Vintage Performances

THE WHALES OF AUGUST, directed by Lindsay Anderson; written by David Berry, based on his play; director of photography, Mike Fash; edited by Nicolas Gaster; music by Derek Wadsworth; production designer, Jocelyn Herbert; produced by Carolyn Pfeiffer and Mike Kaplan; An Alive Films production with Circle Associates Ltd. At Cinema 2, Third Avenue and 60th Street. Running time: 90 minutes. This film has no rating.

Libby Strong	Bette Davis
Sarah Webber	Lillian Gish
Mr. Maranov	Vincent Price
Tisha Doughty	Ann Sothern
Joshua Brackett	Harry Carey Jr.
Mr. Beckwith	Frank Grimes
Old Randall	Frank Pitkin
Young Randall	Mike Bush
Young Libby	Margaret Ladd
Young Tisha	Tisha Sterling
Young Sarah	Mary Steenburgen

By VINCENT CANBY

"BUSY, busy, busy," says Libby (Bette Davis), the elder of two ancient, widowed sisters who are sharing what could be their last summer on the Maine coast.

The target of Libby's sarcasm is Sarah (Lillian Gish), the sweet-natured younger sister who takes care of Libby, brushes her long white hair, lays out her clothes, finds her shoes, does the cooking, tends to the cottage, weeds the garden and, in her spare time, makes little cloth dolls shaped like koala bears to be sold at the end-of-summer benefit.

Sarah is a living saint, but her saintliness is of the unremitting kind that might drive anyone crazy, especially the way she inserts an insistent "dear" as a preface or postscript to every sentence directed to her older sister.

Says Libby after a long silence, "I wish we were back in Philadelphia."

"But, dear," says Sarah, "it would be hot in Philadelphia." Says Sarah, "It would keep you from being so busy."

Sarah can be sarcastic too. When Libby comes out with yet another nasty remark, Sarah acknowledges it with a deadpan, serene, "As you like to say, dear." Sarah's sarcasm is muted, casual. Unlike Libby, she has memories of a happy, sexually satisfying marriage. She's not caged in an arid darkness.

With its two beautiful, very different, very characteristic performances by Miss Gish and Miss Davis, who, together, exemplify American films from 1914 to the present, Lindsay Anderson's "Whales of August" is a cinema event, though small in scale and commonplace in detail. It's as moving for all the history it recalls as for anything that happens on the screen. Yet what happens on the screen is not to be underrated.

It's possible that "The Whales of August," opening today at Cinema 2, could not have been made by anyone except Mr. Anderson, the English director ("This Sporting Life," "If," "Britannia Hospital") whose profound appreciation (and knowledge) of screen history is commanded by a rigorous sensibility. This is no "On Golden Pond," the kind of sentimental sitcom that reaches for laughs by having its old folk talk the jargon of the young.

In its way, "The Whales of August" is tough, but it has a major flaw in that David Berry's adaptation of his stage play isn't strong enough for the treatment it receives from the director and his extraordinary actors. In addition to the film's two icons, the cast includes Ann Sothern, wonderful as the sisters' resilient, full-blooded Maine neighbor, and Vincent Price, as an old, mannerly (and broke) White Russian refugee, who may be as fraudulent as the skeptical Libby suspects.

Mr. Berry is no American Chekhov. Though minutely observed, the lives of Libby and Sarah evoke no landscape larger than this tiny Maine island to which they've been returning every summer since they were girls. There are references to lost childhoods, dead husbands, wars survived and estranged children, but the references are more obligatory than enriching. There's nothing really at stake in the course of the day we see in almost documentary detail. There's even some confusion about time.

The film opens with a black-and-white prologue in which the sisters and their best friend, eventually to be played by Miss Sothern, are introduced as teen-age girls. They later refer to friendships lasting 50 years. But if the old ladies are in their 80's — at least — that would mean they'd started coming to the island in their comparatively mature 30's.

Because the film operates most effectively by being literal, the raising of such basic questions obscures one's commitment to it.

The pleasure of "The Whales of August" comes from watching how Mr. Anderson keeps his two stars working in unison, though each works by totally different methods. Miss Gish, intuitive like Sarah, appears to be without guile, still something of the silent-screen innocent, but there's not a gesture or a line-reading that doesn't reflect her nearly three-quarters of a century in front of a camera. Scenes are not purloined when she's on screen.

Miss Davis is more than up to the competition, which comes to look like harmony. Her elegantly sculptured features rivet the attention. When she barks out an uncalled-for, rudely welcome comment, the familiar voice, an echo from both "The Little Foxes" and "Beyond the Forest," cuts through the stasis, not to overwhelm Miss Gish but to give her something to act with *and* against.

Much in the way that Libby and Sarah come to terms with their edgy, precarious existence, "The Whales of August" records the reconciliation of the cinema of D. W. Griffith (and its idealized view of women) and that of Hollywood's golden era, when women could be far less than perfect and

great actresses could be heard as well as seen.

Appearing in supporting roles are Harry Carey Jr., identified with the films of John Ford (one of Mr. Anderson's favorite American directors), as a Maine handyman, and Frank Grimes, who plays a cameo role as a real-estate salesman. Mary Steenburgen, Tisha Sterling (Miss Sothern's daughter) and Margaret Ladd are seen in the film's prologue.

"The Whales of August" takes its time. One has to accept its pacing, which is deliberate and careful, the way someone with brittle bones walks across a rocky patch of earth. Its rewards are unexpected and quite marvelous. When Miss Gish sits in front of a mirror, doing up her hair, we're seeing a character named Sarah girding herself for further battle with an impossibly demanding sister, as well a demonstration of how a movie works on all the memories we bring to it.

1987 O 16, C3:1

No Biz Like It

WEEDS, directed by John Hancock; written by Dorothy Tristan and Mr. Hancock; director of photography, Jan Weincke; edited by David Handman, Jon Poll and Chris Lebenzon; music by Angelo Badalamenti, Melissa Etheridge and Orville Stoeber; production designer, Joseph T. Garrity; produced by Bill Badalato; released by De Laurentiis Entertainment Group. At 84th Street Six, at Broadway; Movieland Eighth Street, at University Place; Gemini, 64th Street and Second Avenue. Running time: 115 minutes. This film is rated R.

Lee Umstetter	Nick Nolte
Claude	Lane Smith
Burt	William Forsythe
Navarro	John Toles-Bey
Carmine	Joe Mantegna
Bagdad	Ernie Hudson
Dave	Mark Rolston
Lazarus	J. J. Johnson
Lillian	Rita Taggart

By JANET MASLIN

THE nicest bunch of guys you could ever hope to meet turn up inside San Quentin at the start of "Weeds," which at first has the look of a prison drama. And Nick Nolte makes quite an entrance, appearing in the film's first scene as a would-be suicide who leaps from a balcony, breaks both his wrists and then tries hard to hang himself in the scene after that. There is the suggestion, initially at least, that "Weeds," which opens today at the Gemini and other theaters, will be grim, but it quickly takes an inspirational turn. Mr. Nolte's Lee Umstetter has a lifetime sentence and no possibility of parole, but he somehow finds the hope and wherewithal to launch a writing and directing career.

"Weeds" was directed and co-written (with Dorothy Tristan) by John Hancock, whose "Bang the Drum Slowly" was as improbably big-hearted about baseball as this film is about prison life and the theater. Mr. Hancock's methods seem outrageously heart-tugging at first, but they work. "Gimme a thick book — I don't care what it's about," Mr. Nolte's Umstetter growls at the prison librarian, and it's a short leap from "War and Peace" to the writing of the title play.

Later, it develops that Umstetter has recycled some of his reading (notably of Genet's "Deathwatch") in the writing of his play, but this does little to stop him. Umstetter, who from this point onward has not a hair

Bette Davis, left, and Lillian Gish in "The Whales of August."

Troupers
Nicke Nolte stars in "Weeds," as a convict who organizes a touring theater company of former convicts.

out of place, presides over auditions in which the biggest, toughest con in the place (Ernie Hudson) offers a rendition of "The Impossible Dream." He stages a production of "Weeds," most notable for the amazing resourcefulness of the prison makeup, prop and costume departments. He gazes out into the audience and sees an attractive woman named Lillian (Rita Taggart), who turns out to be an important drama critic and writes that this was "one of the most exciting evenings I've spent in any theater, anywhere." Umstetter writes her a letter, she answers it, and not long afterward he gets a pardon and moves in with her.

Umstetter reunites his band of prison buddies and forms a traveling theater group called the Barbed Wire Theater; all of them, it seems, share his enthusiasm for working on a play about their prison experiences instead of pursuing other work. "I'm so tired anyway of misusin' women!" one soon-to-be-ex-pimp says with a sigh. As this may suggest, "Weeds" is a fairy tale, but it's an appealing one, with a gentle humor (the ex-cons bicker furiously about the crimes to be listed in their official biographies) and a very likable cast. The film makes the most of its fanciful material, as when "Weeds" finally arrives Off Broadway and the waiters at Sardi's fret about the ice sculpture for the opening-night party. It comes out resembling Alcatraz, the wrong prison.

•

Mr. Hancock's direction is good enough to keep the story's improbability from taking over; though the film owes its inspiration to a real ex-convict, Rick Cluchey, and the San Quentin Drama Group, it has the feel of pure fiction. Fortunately, the glimpses of the theater company at work are credible enough to give the story some weight, and Mr. Nolte fits unexpectedly well into this experimental stage production, which has him howling, shouting and even singing and dancing. He combines a tough, hard-bitten manner with great reserves of energy and optimism for this role, and the result is a galvanizing performance.

Mr. Nolte also blends nicely into the excellent ensemble cast, which includes Lane Smith as the mild-mannered embezzler who becomes his second in command, John Toles-Bey as the reconstructed pimp, William Forsythe as a very dim shoplifter, and Joe Mantegna as the only professional actor in the group, who arrives in mid-production and brings a comic enthusiasm to this dramatically recreated world of crime. Like the

traveling actors, and perhaps the audience too, he can't help but find a crazy enjoyment in this shared adventure.

1987 O 16, C10:5

Gender Bending

TOO OUTRAGEOUS, directed and written by Dick Benner; director of photography, Fred Guthe; edited by George Appleby; music by Russ Little; produced by Roy Krost; released by Spectrafilm. At Waverly Twin, Avenue of the Americas and Third Street; 86th Street East, between Second and Third Avenues; Columbia Cinema, Broadway and 103d Street. Running time: 103 minutes. This film is rated R.

Robin Turner	Craig Russell
Liza Connors	Hollis McLaren
Bob	David McIlwraith
Luke	Ron White
Betty Treisman	Lynne Cormack
Lee Sturges	Michael J. Reynolds
Rothchild	Timothy Jenkins
Tony Sparks	Paul Eves
Manuel	Frank Pellegrino
Phil the Waiter	Jimmy James

TEN years have passed since "Outrageous" first arrived, and since then what have its characters been thinking about? Their careers. Robin Turner (Craig Russell), the hairdresser-turned-female impersonator who began his nightclub routine in the earlier film, is still playing in small clubs, and his devoted friend Liza Connors (Hollis McLaren) hasn't yet fulfilled her dream of becoming a famous writer. Together, they talk a lot about making it big and being somebody.

This second film brings them each a success of sorts, though Robin worries about whether fame and fortune are really good for him. "Too Outrageous" tells what happens after Robin is discovered by a pair of agents who are intent on making him a big star. The agents, particularly a woman named Betty (Lynne Cormack), gush idiotically about what great potential Robin has, and dream of revamping his act so antiseptically that they can bill him as "Canada's Comic Illusionist," instead of the specialty performer that he clearly is. Meanwhile, Robin gets even when he appears on a live talk show and delightedly lets the world know that its host is gay.

Like its predecessor, "Too Outrageous," which opens today at the Waverly and other theaters, exists mainly as a vehicle for Mr. Russell's impersonations. He turns up regularly on various stages, offering impressions of such figures as Sophie Tucker, Mae West, Bette Davis and

Barbra Streisand, with a Tina Turner imitation that constitutes one of the film's few nods to anything current. While "Too Outrageous" isn't a work of reportage or even realism, it's notable that the AIDS epidemic plays so small a role in the lives of the film's predominantly gay characters; it's mentioned once in passing early in the story, and it's later used tragically but conveniently, as a plot device to remind Robin that perhaps he ought to rethink his priorities. Otherwise, the various characters tumble coyly and, it seems, heedlessly into bed at first meeting, further underscoring the film's escapist mood.

•

Though the film seems intent on embroiling Robin Turner in a story, Mr. Russell works best when left to his own devices. He's better off wise-cracking and performing than he is anguishing over his professional future. He's funny, for instance, in cavorting with the devoted retinue that follows him everywhere, and in countering the new agent's suggestion that he impersonate Anne Murray (the deep voice is possible, he explains, but he's much too feminine to do that walk). Dick Benner, who wrote and directed the film in a very low-keyed and often clumsy style, too often forces Mr. Russell into more dramatic situations than readily suit him. And Miss McLaren, as the once-schizophrenic companion who seems to be managing quite nicely these days, really has no role left to play.

Along with Mr. Russell, who does a particularly good Tallulah Bankhead, the film also features a female impersonator named Jimmy James, who looks uncannily like Marilyn Monroe.

JANET MASLIN

1987 O 16, C12:1

Worm Monster

THE BLUE MONKEY, directed by William Fruet; screenplay by George Goldsmith; director of photography, Brenton Spencer; edited by Michael Fruet; music by Patrick Coleman and Paul Novotny; art director, Reuben Freed; produced by Martin Walters; released by Spectrafilms. At Lyric, 42d Street, between Seventh and Eighth Avenues; Movie Center 5, 125th Street and Seventh Avenue. Running time: 98 minutes. This film is rated R.

Det. Jim Bishop	Steve Railsback
Dr. Rachel Carson	Gwynyth Walsh
Dr. Judith Glass	Susan Anspach
Roger Levering	John Vernon
George Baker	Joe Flaherty
Sandra Baker	Robin Duke
The Creature	Ivan E. Roth

"BLUE MONKEY" isn't much more than a standard angry-larva story, but it has been cleverly directed by William Fruet, who knows how to give it a new look. To be sure, what happens in the film is essentially familiar, as a slimy little abomination appears, grows, hatches and goes on to terrorize everyone it meets. From the standpoint of plot, there isn't that much to tell.

But Mr. Fruet, the director of a number of other horror films, has given this one some imaginative touches — beginning with the title, since "Blue Monkey" isn't about a monkey at all. It's about a man-sized hermaphroditic insect, a creature that first appears as a wormlike parasite in the body of a kindly repairman that, accidentally touched a houseplant that, according to George Goldsmith's amusingly deadpan screenplay, came from "a

newly formed volcanic island just north of Micronesia."

The repairman is soon whisked off to the county hospital — which was once an insane asylum, of course — and the creature emerges from his body in a white, maggoty form. "Take this to pathology," decrees Susan Anspach, as a doctor whose icy, businesslike manner is itself a form of wit under these circum-

Steve Railsback

stances. Miss Anspach is a welcome figure here, as is the creature itself, a behemoth that actually hurtles quickly down the hospital corridors instead of lumbering heavily in standard horror-film fashion.

•

The creature (played by Ivan E. Roth, who gets top billing in the closing credits) is lurking quietly in the basement one day when a group of plucky little kids, patients in the hospital, try to hunt it down. As they chatter nervously about this adventure, one child confidently tells the others, "I think we're going to find a big blue monkey." The giant insect merely stands by patiently and takes this in.

A lot of "Blue Monkey," which opens today at the Lyric and Movie Center 5, is also too ordinary (i.e., too awash in dripping slime) to interest nonaficionados of its genre. And as a police detective who happens to be visiting the hospital when the fun begins, the leading man, Steve Railsback, can't do much more than play straight man to the giant bug. But the film's spooky blue lighting is ingenious, as is some of the pointedly familiar dialogue: "So conventional weapons are useless against it?" "When those eggs hatch, you're going to have a lot of hungry larvae!" "I think we'd better all stop talking and start looking for that thing right now!"

JANET MASLIN

1987 O 16, C12:6

Waiter's View

LONG LIVE THE LADY!, directed and written by Ermanno Olmi; in Italian with English subtitles; director of photography, Maurizio Zaccaro; music by Georg Philip Teleman; a co-production of RAI Channel 1/Cinemaundici with the collaboration of Istituto Luce; presented by RAI Radiotelevisione Italiana. At Carnegie Screening Room, Seventh Avenue at 57th Street. Running time: 102 minutes. This film has no rating.

Libenzio	Marco Esposito
Corinna	Simona Brandalise

Anna	Stefania Busarello
Mayo	Simone Dalla Rosa
Ciccio	Lorenzo Paolini
Pigi	Tarcisio Tosi
The Lady	Marisa Abbate
Man With the Mustache	Luigi Cancellara
Libenzio's Father	Alberto Francescato
Grandmother	Giovanna Vidotto
Priest	Luca Dorizzi
Clowns	Michele Authier, Graziella Menichelli

ERMANNO OLMI, the Italian director best known here for his neo-realist dramas ("Il Posto," "The Tree of Wooden Clogs," among others), adopts the mannerisms of Isak Dinesen in his latest work, "Long Live the Lady!" The film opens today at the Carnegie Hall Screening Room, inaugurating the theater's program devoted to unusual Italian films that honor the tradition of Roberto Rossellini.

"Long Live the Lady!" is a contemporary comedy-allegory that reveals itself in the manner of a fairy tale set in an enchanted castle. The "castle" is, in fact, a splendid Alpine hotel. Its princes, princesses, magicians and court jesters are members of an international conglomerate who have come together to talk business and pay their respects to the conglomerate's aloof, very old and all-powerful chief executive officer, the "lady" of the title.

The central character is Libenzio, a naïve, young, apprentice waiter brought to the hotel to serve at the convention's magnificent banquet. Libenzio observes all with the wide, surprised eyes of Jack at the top of the beanstalk. He marvels at the mysteries of the hotel's grand kitchen and wine cellars. He's schooled in the etiquette of proper serving techniques, taught about hygiene ("Body odors offend," he's told), and is propositioned by an imperious female guest.

•

Mr. Olmi cross-cuts between these scenes of Libenzio's education and the boy's memories of his peasant family, for whom his success as a waiter is of paramount importance. The members of the ruling elite behave, of course, abominably. The dinner guests don't bat an eye when one of their number suffers a heart attack at the table. The old lady's son (and presumed heir) is dissolute. Everyone is craven.

"Long Live the Lady!" is best when it's most oblique, when Libenzio still sees all as if in a child's dream, before the film tips its social-political concerns about, I think, Italy today. After that, it becomes very precious, a pretty conceit that's a good deal less interesting to think about than to look at. *VINCENT CANBY*

1987 O 16, C26:5

Gift-Wrapped

ISLANDS, a film by Albert Maysles, Charlotte Zwerin and David Maysles; camera, David and Albert Maysles; edited by Kate Hirson; music by Scott Cossu; produced by Susan Froemke and Joel Hinman; released by Maysles Films Inc. At Film Forum 2, 57 Watts Street. Running time: 58 minutes. This film has no rating.

By WALTER GOODMAN

"ISLANDS" offers, among other things, a case history of the politics of esthetics, the case being Christo, the artist whose fancy it is to swathe large areas in fabrics of various hues. Albert Maysles, Charlotte Zwerin and David Maysles put their lightweight cameras and sound equipment to humorous use as they accompanied Christo into lobbying sessions with the West German Social Democratic leader Willy Brandt (about covering the Reichstag), with the Mayor of Paris, Jacques Chirac, who has since also become Prime Minister (about covering the Pont Neuf), and with Miami officials (about creating floating borders made of "a marvelous silky fabric" for a group of islands in Biscayne Bay).

It's one of the Maysleses' sharper movies. The eavesdropping in Miami produces examples of the higher gobbledygook. "What led you to this mode of artistic expression?" one official inquires earnestly. Another finds the project "offensive conceptually," while a defender calls it "a pure poetical gesture." Christo, who looks like Woody Allen and sometimes sounds like him, if you can imagine Mr. Allen with a Bulgarian accent ("I come to that space and disturb that space") is exasperated by the resistance he encounters, even though he has offered to pay for the million-dollar project himself out of proceeds from his paintings. "If it were a backdrop for some multimillion-dollar Hollywood production," he explodes, "there would be no problem. They would burn the islands!"

"Put a pill in your mouth now," orders his wife, Jeanne-Claude, who goes along everywhere and sometimes speaks for him.

In time, the message from Miami gets through. As an official puts it in an apt metaphor, "We're looking for a flowback from that resource." The translation is, Miami wants $250,000, and Christo produces the flowback. "Thanks for the generosity invoked there," says the official, with a straight face.

•

The last half of the hourlong movie is given to the laying of 6.5 million square feet of bright pink fabric. It's quite a sight, scores of people pulling and pushing and splashing as Christo races around on land and in boat shouting instructions through a bullhorn. The camera is everywhere, including underwater, showing us how the design takes shape — and finally there it is, more or less "like marvelous waterlilies," as the exultant Christo describes the sight from a helicopter, to waterlily music. "Look that!" he cries. "Look that!" Thank the Maysles team for much better views than Miamians could have had during the two weeks in May 1983 when the display blossomed on their bay. Is it art? Well, it makes for a lively movie.

You can appreciate the attraction of Christo's big-scale creating for the Maysleses, who recorded his two earlier spectaculars in America's West, "Christo's Valley Curtain" and "Running Fence." One is tempted to say, "Only in America," but two years after the Miami exploit, Christo wrapped the Pont Neuf. The Reichstag has yet to be adorned, the Socialist Mr. Brandt having proved less effectual than the conservative Mr. Chirac, which may hold some sort of political comment. (The artist compares his Reichstag project with Picasso's doing Guernica in the real Guernica.)

"Islands" is being shown for two weeks at Film Forum 2, along with a Maysles "direct cinema" retrospective. Included among these documentaries without narration, sets or scripts are "What's Happening!," a droll beetle's-eye view of the Beatles' frenetic first trip to America in 1964, and "Salesman," a grimly absorbing profile of four door-to-door Bible salesmen; the exploitive "Gimme Shelter," focusing on a 1969 tour of the Rolling Stones that ended in a murder, and "Grey Gardens," a cruel intrusion into the lives of a pair of recluses in the Hamptons, as well as the complete Christo trilogy, which can be seen next Thursday to Oct. 24.

1987 O 16, C26:4

Live Paintings

THE 20TH INTERNATIONAL TOURNEE OF ANIMATION, a series of short films produced by Terry Thoren. At the Bleecker Street Cinema, at La Guardia Place. Running time: 95 minutes. These films are not rated.

By CARYN JAMES

AS Mondrian-like bars of color race up and down walls, and Matisse-inspired dancers sail across the screen, it becomes clear that the "20th International Tournée of Animation" is not a kiddy cartoon festival. An annual compilation of the best short animated films from around the world may sound hokey or stuffy, but this year's selections are stylish and sophisticated. They so often resemble paintings come to life that the tournée may appeal to art lovers as much as animation fans.

Some of the most conventional animation techniques, highly refined, are behind the most appealing shorts. Jane Aaron's "Set in Motion" is not a cartoon, but a film of one ordinary room, in which brightly colored paper and cloth shapes have been moved minutely from one shot to the next. Set in action, the rows of pink squares or blue stripes swim over ironing board and television like strange schools of fish. In "Carnival," Susan Young uses ink-brushed torsos and pastel costumes to create dancers in a Brazilian festival. And Terry Wozniak's "Garbage In, Garbage Out" sets a turquoise blue dragon loose to stomp on cars and unsuspecting pedestrians in a city Red Grooms could claim as his own; this bright comic setting is crumpled by the hand of the animator, which reaches in and restores us to the black-and-white, line-drawn world of reality.

•

Even the films with stronger narratives share this playful awareness of the shapes of art and the styles of animation. Bruno Bozzetto's fairy tale about a bug who falls in love with a woman and turns himself into a man is complete with little red hearts that fly out of the bug's body as a symbol of love. In Zoltan Lehotay's "Success," an endearing concert singer who happens to be a mouse sings to a full opera house that looks like a delicate watercolor sketch. As in traditional cartoons, bugs and animals may have our sympathies here — the stylized humans are clearly not meant to seem real — but there's nothing sentimental, not a trace of coyness in these animated creatures.

The greatest disappointments are the computer-generated films, whose creators seem so dazzled by their own advanced techniques that they have forgotten that an audience may not be intrigued by a daddy desk lamp who scolds a baby desk lamp, or a unicycle who dreams he is in the circus. These computer-created objects have all the cute "look at me, I'm almost human" self-consciousness that cartoon mice have lived long enough to outgrow. Clay animation often has the same self-importance, and you'd have to love the technique to sit through the 10-minute "Break," from the Soviet Union, about boxers made of clay. "Break" slows down the pace of the entire film. But until then — roughly two-thirds of the way through — the tournée, which opens today at the Bleecker Street Cinema, maintains its high energy, quick clipped pace and surprising variety. That's a much better record than most anthologies can claim.

1987 O 16, C28:1

HELLO MARY LOU, directed by Bruce Pittman; screenplay by Ron Oliver; director of photography, John Herzog; edited by Nick Rotundo; music by Paul Zaza; produced by Peter Simpson and Mr. Pittman; released by Samuel Goldwyn Company. At Movieland, Broadway and 47th Street; Coliseum Twin, Broadway and 181st Street; Essex, at Grand Street; Nova, Broadway and 147th Street; Movie Center Five, 125th Street, between Powell and Douglas. Running time: 96 minutes. This film is rated R.
WITH: Michael Ironside, Wendy Lyon, Justin Louis, Lisa Schrage, Richard Monette

By VINCENT CANBY

Eight minutes into "Hello Mary Lou, Prom Night II," the title character is flambéed at her moment of triumph, standing on the stage of the high school auditorium, about to be crowned 1957 prom queen.

Mary Lou was not a good girl, but she really didn't deserve to burn for it, or so she thinks. After waiting in her grave for an arbitrary 30 years, her spirit returns to Hamilton High to wreak havoc on the students preparing for yet another prom night, and, especially, on the two boys who were, indirectly, responsible for her accidental demise. By chance, one of the boys is now the school principal and the other a pious Roman Catholic priest.

"Hello Mary Lou" has nothing much to do with the original "Prom Night" (1980), except that it's somewhat more entertaining if female nudity, bizarre violence and comically deadpan special effects amuse you. It also has an unusually attractive cast headed by Lisa Schrage, who plays the wanton Mary Lou and has sapphire eyes, and Wendy Lyon, a natural, Sissy Spacek-blonde, who plays the contemporary teen-ager whose body is frequently possessed by the irresponsible Mary Lou. Michael Ironside is the principal and Richard Monette the priest, who learns, to his surprise, that showing a crucifix to an evil spirit is as chancy as waving garlic in front of an axe murderer.

The movie has one scary-steamy scene in the girls' locker room, another in which a girl disappears into a blackboard as if it were Alice's looking glass, and a Grand Guignol grand finale that lasts almost 20 minutes. Bruce Pittman, the director, and Ron Oliver, who wrote the screenplay, have constructed the movie as if it were a gourmet banquet for toddlers. From the first course to the last, it's all ice cream.

"Hello Mary Lou" opened yesterday at several Manhattan theaters, including the Movieland, where a skinny gray and white cat, a dedicated member of the theater's staff, restlessly stalks the aisles in search of nonpaying customers.

1987 O 17, 16:5

FILM VIEW/Vincent Canby

Festival '87 Was High on Style

A T THE AGE OF 25, THE ANNUAL New York Film Festival, which closed one week ago tonight at Lincoln Center, has been running almost as long as Johnny Carson's "Tonight Show," possibly for many of the same reasons. It has no overwhelming personality that turns audiences into fanatics who either love it or hate it. As Carson fans *like* him, festival audiences *trust* it. The festival exists to serve — to introduce and present acts of varying degrees of interest, which pay heed to contemporary fashions without, it seems, being subservient to them.

Like Johnny Carson, the festival is incurably middlebrow, which goes with the real estate, but it's also skeptical. When its selections are compared to "Fatal Attraction," "Stakeout," "Robocop" and the other films that dominate commercial theaters these days, they seem positively avant-garde.

Then, too, much in the way that the deceptively innocuous Johnny will slip the occasional zinger to Ron, Nancy or the Pope (followed by an innocent "There goes my invitation to the White House/Vatican"), the festival will show "Letter to Jane" or "Othon" or "Salo" or "Sid and Nancy" or, as this year, Rosa von Praunheim's "Anita — Dances of Vice."

These are the films that, by being boring, shocking or incomprehensible, prompt walkouts, which are something the festival is short of. Within reason, walkouts are to be encouraged. If nothing else, they prove that at least some members of the Lincoln Center audiences are still alive. They're not so inhibited by the solemnity of the hall or the ludicrously hyperbolic program notes that they've stopped thinking for themselves.

The 1987 festival wasn't a corker. There were no discoveries. Even the retrospective selections were comparatively tame. Out of circulation since 1972, "The Manchurian Candidate" (1962), the John Frankenheimer-George Axelrod adaptation of Richard Condon's novel, is as evilly funny as it ever was, though its politics now look inscrutable. (It seems to approve of political assassination, given the deserving victim.) Roberto Rossellini's "Joan at the Stake" (1954) and "The Human Voice" (1948) are footnotes to the career and the private life of a great film maker.

■

The most interesting debut at the festival wasn't that of an unknown talent, but the horizontal move of the playwright David Mamet making his debut as the director of his first feature film, "House of Games." Familiar personalities returned, and how one responded to them, including Alain Resnais ("Mélo") and Eric Rohmer ("L'Ami de Mon Amie"), was dictated as much by the past performances of these directors as by the new films themselves.

Do you groan or smile when Bob Hope makes one of his royal appearances with Johnny Carson? Do you turn quickly to MTV when Jerry Lewis comes out and humbly takes over "The Tonight Show"? By this time, the response to a new Rohmer or Resnais film is probably knee-jerk automatic.

Mr. Rohmer goes on year after year refining his small, brilliant, crystalline comedies of manners, each film a variation on the ones that have gone before. The pleasure in a Rohmer comedy is provided not by its revelation of a new sensibility, but by the surprises with which he continues to invest his work. (He also appears to have access to an unlimited supply of extraordinarily attractive, brand-new young actors — this year's find being Emmanuelle Chaulet.)

Mr. Resnais, whose "Muriel" was at the first New York festival, hasn't continued to make the same film over and over again, though his preoccupation with style-as-content remains steadfast. To this extent, "Melo" was running with the crowd at the 1987 festival. Never, in my memory, have there been so many films in one Lincoln Center show that either traded on their looks or so proudly proclaimed their lack of interest in what passes for realism in conventional movies. In theory this is all to the good. In practice, the results were mixed.

"Mélo," adapted from a now-creaky 1929

Though not a corker, this year's film festival was notable for David Mamet's debut as a director.

Henry Bernstein romantic melodrama that was a hit in New York and Paris, calls attention to its theatrical origins by being played as if on a stage, with prettily lit, three-sided sets and a curtain (painted) dropped between "acts." This admission of fakery, though initially interesting, does nothing to enrich (or excuse) the preciousness of the text.

■

"In the Belly of the Architect," directed by Peter Greenaway ("The Draughtsman's Contract"), about an architect dying in Rome, looks as if it were designed as a backdrop for a David portrait. It's all classic columns, cornices and pristine surfaces, without much of anything (at least, that I could understand) happening in the foreground.

There seems to be an intense desire to provoke outrage-through-décor in Mr. von Praunheim's "Anita — Dances of Vice." This is about a cheerily lewd old schizophrenic Berlin woman who goes around town taking off her clothes and claiming to be Anita Berber, the dancer notorious in the 20's for performing nude. However, the visual elegance of the film's hallucinatory flashbacks (to the Anita of the 20's) works against stylistic tackiness, sometimes known as camp, which, in earlier von Praunheim films, has been the director's most effective weapon against philistine values.

In both "A Taxing Woman," Juzo Itami's very modern comedy satirizing the "new" Japan, and Mr. Rohmer's "Ami de Mon Amie," a romantic comedy set in one of Paris's spanking-new satellite cities, the look of the film is integral to director's method and what the movie is all about.

Mr. Rohmer never goes inside his characters' heads. All we know of them we learn from physical appearances and what they say, which is often mistaken. The handsome facades and not-quite-finished landscaping of Cergy-Pontoise, where the film takes place, discreetly reflect the emotional predicaments of Mr. Rohmer's young characters. They've planned their lives carefully but, somehow, things never work out according to their blueprints. They live their lives like tenants in just-completed apartment buildings, forever making adjustments to sudden emergencies unforeseen by the architects.

From its opening sequence, in which a senile, dying old man is seen being nursed by his nurse, "A Taxing Woman" is stuffed with sights as bizarre as its heroine. She's a woman who finds her job as a tax collector terrifically fulfilling, whether she's scaring mom-and-pop shopkeepers or playing a cat-and-mouse game with a big-time mobster. The film's sometimes astonishing images are full of the same kind of sarcasm that Mr. Itami is directing toward Japan's newly triumphant materialism.

■

The festival's most securely stylized film was "House of Games," Mr. Mamet's melodramatic comedy about confidence artists for whom, as the film maker knows, style is all. Having written screenplays ("The Postman Always Rings Twice," "The Untouchables") for other directors, Mr. Mamet, this time in the director's chair, gets the opportunity to show us how he wants his work to look and sound onscreen. The result is an ironic nightmare in which a seemingly rational woman (Lindsay Crouse) finds herself increasingly committed to a deadly serious, if metaphorical, poker game.

The manner of the film is no more realistic than the situation. The outside world — a large American city — remains as faceless to us as to the characters, who exchange their lines in speeded-up, highly theatrical monotones. The camera is positioned to catch images as self-conscious and artificial as the tale being told.

Because Mr. Mamet expertly builds the suspense, what (in other films) passes for reality seldom intrudes. There's no time to think about it. From the beginning to very near the end, "House of Games" creates and sustains its own weird reality, which is something rarely accomplished by even far more experienced directors. The Pulitzer Prize-winning tyro has arrived. □

1987 O 18, II:25:1

Love and Death

A DEATH IN THE FAMILY, directed by Stewart Main and Peter Wells; written by Mr. Wells; photography by Alan Locke; edited by David Coulson; produced by James Wallace. Running time: 52 minutes. **JEWEL'S DARL,** directed by Mr. Wells; written by Anne Kennedy and Mr. Wells; photography by Stuart Dryburgh; edited by Stewart Main. Running time: 30 minutes. Both films are New Zealand productions and unrated. At Film Forum 1, 57 Watts Street.

By WALTER GOODMAN

THE death in "A Death in the Family" is that of a young New Zealand man named Andrew Boyd; the family is made up of the friends and lovers who tended him in July 1985, during his final days. Stewart Main and Peter Wells were two of those friends, and their drama, which opens today at Film Forum 1, is meant as a loving tribute to "Andy" as well as an effort to present his disease, AIDS, as a personal loss rather than a medical specter.

The ambition is thoroughly admirable, the subject inherently powerful, but the moviemakers' techniques convert what must have been a deeply felt experience into art-house affectations.

Using Caravaggio as a model, they give us a gallery of starkly lighted tableaux, with Andy as the Christ figure and his friends as grieving disciples. Despite the use of a hand-held camera, there is little spontaneity here, as we observe how the unflagging attentions to Andy over two weeks, from spooning his broth to washing his feet, strenghen the ties among the group.

The dialogue, often directed at the camera, is eulogy: "He was special," says one friend. "He looked after people." To which another adds, "Now it's our turn to look after him." There are embraces, clasped hands, intertwined fingers. "He brought us together," somebody says. The ultimate loss is reduced to a testimonial to homosexual bonding.

Messages are pounded in. Among those caring for Andy, by way of exception, is a doctor whom compassion has brought her from the hospital where she met him to the house in Auckland where he breathes his last. She carries her cute baby with her everywhere, placing the child on Andy's bed as she does her examining. "See," those scenes insist, "you can't get it that way." All right, but would any mother put her baby at even infinitesimal risk?

What drama there is in "A Death in the Family" comes with the intrusion of Andy's real family, which drove him away when his homosexuality became embarrassing. In case anybody might miss the point, it is enunciated for us: "No one's ever taken the time to say, 'We love you no matter what you are.' "

Father, Mother and pious brother learn from seeing how much the friends give Andy how little they gave him; it is a Christian homily. Although the straight family is patronized, their reactions provide some of the more affecting moments in a work that is intermittently moving, but ends in a flurry of flower petals, candles and clouds that seem designed to make grief ridiculous.

The Film Forum program begins with "Jewel's Darl," Peter Wells's mannered 30-minute visit with a male transvestite and his girlfriend. American audiences may have trouble catching the New Zealand dialect and slang, which could be a blessing.

1987 O 21, C24:5

Bandits

THE SICILIAN, directed by Michael Cimino; screenplay by Steve Shagan, based on the novel by Mario Puzo; photographed by Alex Thomson; edited by Françoise Bonnot; music by David Mansfield; production designer, Wolf Kroeger; produced by Mr. Cimino and Joann Carelli; released by 20th Century-Fox Film Corporation. At National Twin, Broadway and 44th Street; Gotham Cinema, Third Avenue at 58th Street; 86th Street East Twin, between Second and Third Avenues; Bay Cinema, Second Avenue and 32d Street; Columbia Cinema, Broadway and 103d Street. Running time: 115 minutes. This film is rated R.

Salvatore Giuliano	Christopher Lambert
Prince Borsa	Terence Stamp
Don Masino Croce	Joss Ackland
Aspanu Pisciotta	John Turturro
Prof. Hector Adonis	Richard Bauer
Camilla	Barbara Sukowa
Giovanna Ferra	Giulia Boschi
Minister Trezza	Ray McAnally

THOUGH it's a separate novel, Mario Puzo's "Sicilian" functions as an extended insert within his "Godfather" epic, being an elaboration on what happened during the two years that the young Mafioso heir Michael Corleone was hiding out in Sicily after his brush with the New York law.

"The Sicilian" is not about Michael, but about the real-life, now-legendary Sicilian bandit Salvatore Giuliano, whom, according to Mr. Puzo's vivid imagination, Michael was supposed to escort to sanctuary in America. Salvatore never quite made it. He was murdered in 1950, at the age of 27, by one of his own men — that is recorded history. The people and events that brought him to this end are what interested Mr. Puzo.

One must assume that's also what interested Michael Cimino, the director, and Steve Shagan, the writer, who are responsible (at least in name) for the screen adaptation opening today at the Gotham and other theaters.

The film is a mess, though hardly on the panoramic scale of "Heaven's Gate," for which Mr. Cimino was the chief architect. Instead, "The Sicilian" is an example of the much more mingy mess that results when front-office people start squabbling with movie makers, who may already be squabbling among themselves.

Some time ago Gore Vidal lost his suit to receive screenplay credit for the film (he can thank heaven for small favors), and in May of this year, Mr. Cimino sued to stop the producers from releasing their version of the movie, which is, I assume, the version we're now seeing.

●

However, it will be difficult for Mr. Cimino to convince anybody that this movie is more of a mess than the one that the director had in mind. It's just shorter. Unlike the colossal "Heaven's Gate," "The Sicilian" contains no spectacular sequences that boggle the eye, if not the mind. The people who recut it may have left the continuity in ruins, but there's no evidence to suggest that, in its original length,

Christopher Lambert

"The Sicilian" would have been anything other than a multinational joke.

The casting is a key. Christopher Lambert (the photogenic Tarzan in "Greystoke") plays Salvatore Giuliano, the Sicilian peasant, with a French accent, and looks and dresses, much of the time, as if he were the off-duty ski instructor to the crowned heads of Europe. As Aspanu, Salvatore's first cousin and best friend, John Turturro, the American actor, at least sounds *sort of* Sicilian.

Joss Ackland, the English actor, plays the island's Mafia chief with the Savile Row elegance of James Bond's boss, while Barbara Sukowa, the gifted German actress, appears as an American heiress, a Sicilian duchess by marriage who speaks, it seems, through someone else's voice box. A number of other performers also sound as if they'd been post-synchronized.

Mr. Cimino's fondness for amber lighting and great, sweeping camera movements are evident from time to time, but the film is mostly a garbled synopsis of the Puzo novel. It works on no level. Gone (along with the character of Michael Corleone) are the members of Salvatore's family, as well as any conviction that the bandit was a kind of flawed Sicilian Robin Hood.

For some idea of what Giuliano meant to Sicily, one has to go back to Francesco Rosi's stark, comprehensive "Salvatore Giuliano," released here in 1964. *VINCENT CANBY*

1987 O 23, C4:5

Porsche Pushers

NO MAN'S LAND, directed by Peter Werner; written by Dick Wolf; director of photography, Hiro Narita; edited by Steve Cohen; music by Basil Poledouris; production designer, Paul Peters; produced by Joseph Stern and Mr. Wolf; released by Orion Pictures Corp. At Embassy 2, Broadway and 47th St.; New York Twin, Second Ave. and 66th St.; 34th Street Showplace, between Second and Third Ave.; Embassy 72d Street, at Broadway; Movie Center 5, 125th St. between Powell and Douglass Blvds. Running time: 106 minutes. This film is rated R.

Benjy Taylor	D. B. Sweeney
Ted Varrick	Charlie Sheen
Ann Varrick	Lara Harris
Lieut. Vincent Bracey	Randy Quaid
Malcolm	Bill Duke
Frank Martin	R. D. Call
Lieut. Curtis Loos	Arlen Dean Snyder
Captain Haun	M. Emmet Walsh
Danny	Al Shannon

By CARYN JAMES

HOW many talented actors does it take to steal a Porsche? And how many times do you want to watch them do it in the space of an hour and a half? In "No Man's Land," it takes two — Charlie Sheen and D. B. Sweeney, who pilfer Porsches faster and more often than you can say "Miami Vice clone." Though set in Los Angeles, the film has a familiar, television look and feel — two handsome partners, cops, criminals, fast cars and a marginal romance. The twist in the buddy-car-chase formula is that here the good guys tend to blur into the bad.

Mr. Sweeney is Benjy, a rookie policeman — the good guy — who goes undercover as part of a stolen-car ring run by Mr. Sheen as Ted — the bad guy. Ted does not seem vile, because he's young, attractive and only steals Porsches. The real villains are the rival thieves, undistinguished types who are older and less attractive, who kill people and are not status-conscious about their stolen cars. Benjy, the middle-class cop, is easily seduced by Ted's high life of private clubs and fancy clothes, and just as easily seduces Ted's sister.

Though Randy Quaid, as Benjy's boss, gives a perfunctory lecture about the difference between right and wrong, the film's heart is clearly

Sidney Baldwin

Wheels Charlie Sheen and Randy Quaid star in "No Man's Land."

with the enticing Ted. As he drives off in a Porsche owned by someone with hopeless, easy-listening taste in music, he tosses a Jack Jones cassette out the window and says, "They deserve it."

"No Man's Land" isn't honest enough to maintain this cynicism — eventually Benjy will have to declare his loyalties — and even if it had the courage of its nonconvictions, it doesn't have the flair to turn high style into a reason for living. Peter Werner, who has directed some stylish television shows ("Moonlighting" episodes and the mini-series "L.B.J.: The Early Years") is competent but dull here. The endless car chases through parking garages and close-ups of the two friends talking seem conceived for a television-size scale and budget, then blown up to fill a larger screen. Mr. Sheen and Mr. Sweeney have risen to tougher roles in "Platoon" and "Gardens of Stone." In "No Man's Land," which opens today at the Embassy 2 and other theaters, they can relax and walk through roles no one expects to be surprising.

1987 O 23, C10:5

Life After Death

THE FUNERAL, written and directed by Juzo Itami; cinematography by Yonezo Maeda; edited by Akira Suzuki; music by Joji Yuasa; produced by Yasushi Tamaoki and Yutaka Okada. In Japanese with English subtitles. Released by New Yorker Films. At Lincoln Plaza Cinema 1, Broadway and 63d Street. Running time: 124 minutes. This film has no rating.
Wabisuke Inoue .... Tsutomu Yamazaki
Chizuko Amamiya .... Nobuko Miyamoto
Kikue Amamiya .... Kin Sugai
Shokichi Amamiya .... Shuji Otaki
Satomi .... Ichiro Zaitsu
Ebihara .... Nekohachi Edoya
Shinkichi Amamiya .... Koen Okumura
Ayako .... Chikako Yuri
The Priest .... Chishu Ryu

By VINCENT CANBY

JUZO ITAMI'S "Funeral" is a series of joyous contradictions. Here's a robust comedy whose subject is death, a film that is quintessentially Japanese though it recalls (without in any way imitating) the work of the quintessentially French Jean Renoir, and a

tough-minded satire that is almost always sweet.

The movie, which opens today at the Lincoln Plaza Cinema 1, is about the mad scramble of the members of one affluent, bourgeois family to honor ancient traditions in a Japan that worships its high technology, fast foods, instant replays, automobiles and labor-saving appliances as much as it does its ancestors.

Cultural revolutions aren't easy, especially in Japan, whose film makers tend to regard such changes with measured, tightly controlled emotions. Mr. Itami gives the impression of being as thoroughly, heartily amused as he is astonished.

Nobuko Miyamoto (Mrs. Itami) and Tsutomu Yamazaki, the stars of both "Tampopo" and "A Taxing Woman," also play the leading roles in "The Funeral," as a successful, happily married Tokyo acting couple whose with-it lives are suddenly interrupted by her father's death.

●

In the pre-credit sequence, Mr. Itami sets up everything to come by introducing us to the corpse-to-be, a cross, diabetic old man in a jogging suit, who stuffs himself with food, makes cruel jokes at his wife's expense, and then suffers a massive heart attack. He's not really a bad fellow, just impossible to live with.

In the manner of a skeptical documentary, "The Funeral" covers three days in the lives of Chizuko (Miss Miyamoto) and Wabisuke (Mr. Yamazaki), from the afternoon they receive the news of the old man's death until, on the third day, the corpse is finally cremated, the ashes buried and everyone can go home. In the meantime, they've had to deal with a succession of arcane responsibilities and small crises, as well as the logistics of a family reunion where children become easily tired and fidgety.

Acting as their guide is the extremely efficient suburban undertaker, a man who wears a rakish brown beret and behaves as if he were directing a movie. There's no end to the decisions that must be made. Should the corpse be put into a coffin at the hospital, or should it first be taken home, put to bed and, on the day of the wake, placed in the coffin? How much should the Buddhist priest be paid? What sort of clothes should the family wear at the various functions?

Answers to some of these questions are provided by a handy video cassette titled "The ABC's of the Funeral," which Wabisuke watches while whipping cream with a portable electric whisk. There are egos to be attended to, including that of the undertaker who boasts about his work on the corpse, "A really beautiful expression, I think." Says Wabisuke, "But his ear is changing color." There is also the corpse's older brother, a stingy tycoon who mourns for himself in mourning for his younger brother.

●

There are endless condolence calls during which the guests say reassuring things about "going quickly" and "not suffering long." In this case, they also recall the dead man's ferocity as a croquet-player. "How old was he?" asks the Buddhist priest (played by the venerable Chishu Ryu), who arrives at the house in a white limousine. "Sixty-nine," says Wabisuke. Replies the priest, "Getting into the 70's is hard but, once there, you're safe for a while."

Out of these minute, specific details of observable behavior, Mr. Itami

Tsutomu Yamazaki, left, and Nobuko Miyamoto in "The Funeral."

creates a moving, wonderfully rich picture of upper-middle-class family life in contemporary Japan.

The serenity of this occasion is threatened when one of Wabisuke's friends shows up with Wabisuke's young, birdbrained mistress, who quite quickly gets drunk and has a fit of the giggles. In the most Renoir-like sequence, the mistress more or less blackmails Wabisuke into making love to her in the woods behind the house, while Chizuko stands in a child's swing nearby.

Though "The Funeral," produced in 1984, is Mr. Itami's first film as a director, it's his third to be seen in New York, following "Tampopo," the noodle epic now at the Cinema Studio 2, and his newest comedy, "A Taxing Woman," which was one of the hits at this year's New York Film Festival.

●

Mr. Itami, at 54, is not exactly a stripling, but he's far and away the most exciting new film maker to burst onto the international scene in a decade. Burst may not be exactly the right word. That makes it sound as if he were some kind of skyrocket that could fade away at any minute. On the basis of his first three films, that seems unlikely.

Before becoming a director, he'd already had several successful careers — as an actor, a television talk-show host and an essayist. Yet he brings to film making the kind of enthusiasm one associates with the young, as well as an abundance of ideas (about practically everything) that can only be accumulated over time. He's simultaneously lavish (in his use of random anecdotes) and frugal — in that every frame of film is packed with information. He wastes nothing.

Miss Miyamoto and Mr. Yamazaki are again splendid, in roles that have absolutely nothing to do with their performances in "Tampopo" and "A Taxing Woman." Everyone in the film appears to respond to the material with an enthusiasm that matches the writer-director's. That would include the young man who, as the cremator at the end of the movie, solemnly discusses the mechanics of his job with the mourners. They listen, enrapt by his revelations about temperature settings. It also helps them to pass the hour-and-a-half it takes to reduce an ordinary human

body to ashes of the proper consistency.

Among other things at which he excels, Mr. Itami is a master at discovering humor and sadness within the boredom of others.

1987 O 23, C14:3

From the Stage

THE GLASS MENAGERIE, directed by Paul Newman; playwright, Tennessee Williams; director of photography, Michael Ballhaus; edited by David Ray; music by Henry Mancini; production design by Tony Walton; produced by Burtt Harris; released by Cineplex Odeon Films. At Carnegie Hall Cinema, Seventh Avenue and 57th Street. Running time: 134 minutes. This film is rated PG.
Amanda .... Joanne Woodward
Tom .... John Malkovich
Laura .... Karen Allen
Gentleman caller .... James Naughton

THERE have been entertaining film versions of Tennessee Williams's works ("Cat on a Hot Tin Roof"), and there have been important ones ("A Streetcar Named Desire"). But by and large, Williams's work has never traveled easily to the screen. The playwright himself claimed to favor only "The Roman Spring of Mrs. Stone," disparaging all the other films adapted from his writing, and he may have seen the matter more clearly than anyone else could.

Part of the problem in adapting Williams's plays to the screen is their essential theatricality, but perhaps it's also a question of scale. On the stage, or even to anyone who reads it, a play like "The Glass Menagerie" can seem circumscribed and sweeping at the same time. The claustrophobia of the setting is there, as the play unfolds in a cramped St. Louis apartment, but the larger world is also at hand — magically so. It's apparent in the characters' most poetic monologues and in their most fanciful daydreams. A stage setting can suggest this dichotomy in many ways, while a film, necessarily, is bound to be more limited and more literal.

As directed by Paul Newman, the new screen version of "The Glass Menagerie" is extremely faithful to the text, far more so than the 1950 version that starred Gertrude Lawrence and supplied a happier ending than Williams had in mind. It captures a production that originated in Williamstown, Mass., then traveled to the Long Wharf in New Haven, with Joanne Woodward as the pitiable yet powerful Amanda Wingfield and Karen Allen as her fragile daughter. It's a serious and respectful adaptation, but never an incendiary one, perhaps because the odds against its capturing the play's real genius are simply too great. In any case, this "Glass Menagerie" catches more of the drama's closeness and narrowness than its fire.

•

Miss Woodward makes a fluttery, garrulous Amanda, bustling about the apartment setting that becomes, in Tony Walton's design, especially cluttered and dim. The lamps themselves are obstacles, frequently com-

Karen Allen

ing between the actors and the camera, and even Miss Woodward's frizzy gray coiffure sometimes gets in the camera's way. The feeling of claustrophobia is indeed effective, but it's also unrelieved, which makes the production feel longer than it should.

Though Miss Allen at first seems rather robust for Laura, she has a lovely, delicate presence here, with the same kind of dark-eyed shyness Jane Wyman once brought to the role. Like Miss Woodward, Miss Allen has a way of seeming too sane and sturdy for the material, but both actresses approach their roles with great conviction. As the third member of the Wingfield family, Laura's brother, Tom, John Malkovich has the awkward task of switching from the pained, poetic style of the opening narration to a more lightly conversational tone, but he manages this gently and well. Though Tom can be seen as the play's most cryptic character, having been drawn by Williams in such intentionally incomplete terms, Mr. Malkovich brings him fully to life. And the fourth cast member, James Naughton, makes the gentleman caller a fine mixture of hucksterism and real feeling.

"The Glass Menagerie," which opens today at the Carnegie Hall Cinema, starts out stiffly and gets better as it goes along, with the dinner-party sequence its biggest success; in this highly charged situation, Miss Woodward's Amanda indeed seems to flower. But quiet reverence is its prevailing tone, and in the end that seems thoroughly at odds with anything Williams ever intended.

"The Glass Menagerie" is rated PG ("Parental Guidance Suggested"). It includes some moderately strong language.

JANET MASLIN

1987 O 23, C14:3

Deceitful Duo

THE KILLING TIME, directed by Rick King; screenplay by Don Bohlinger, James Nathan and Bruce Franklin Singer; director of photography, Paul H. Goldsmith; edited by Lorenzo De Stefano; music by Paul Chihara; production designer, Bernt Amadeus Capra; produced by Peter Abrams and Robert L. Levy; released by New World Pictures. At Embassy 1, Broadway at 46th St.; Orpheum, Third Ave. at 86th St.; Movie Center 5, 125th St., between Powell and Douglass Blvds.; Coliseum Twin, Broadway and 181st St. Running time: 96 minutes. This film is rated R.

Sam Wayburn	Beau Bridges
Brian	Kiefer Sutherland
Sheriff Carl Cunningham	Joe Don Baker
Laura Winslow	Camelia Kath
Jake Winslow	Wayne Rogers

JAMES M. CAIN casts a shadow over "The Killing Time," which opens today at the Embassy 1 and other theaters. Unfortunately, it isn't a very long one. In a quiet little seacoast town, the kind of place where one of the two sheriffs (Beau Bridges) calls everyone but his colleague (Joe Don Baker) "Ma'am," we are asked to believe that two of the film's four male principals can be contemplating deceit, frame-ups and cold-blooded murder. Talk about casting against type! Mr. Bridges turns out to be one of the schemers, and he's simply too nice for this sort of thing.

Not Kiefer Sutherland, as a drifter who impersonates the town's newly recruited deputy sheriff after shooting the real candidate in an opening scene. Good as he is, Mr. Sutherland is in grave danger of taking on one too many weirdo roles. In this setting, Mr. Baker, who is always a treat, has the only role that makes much sense. He's about to leave town and retire, and as a sign above his desk announces, he'd rather be fishing.

"The Killing Time" does include one scene in which an important clue is wrapped up with a dead fish. Aside from that, it offers little that's new.

JANET MASLIN

1987 O 23, C14:3

Courtroom Drama

SUSPECT, directed by Peter Yates; written by Eric Roth; director of photography, Billy Williams; edited by Ray Lovejoy; music by Michael Kamen; production designer, Stuart Wurtzel; produced by Daniel A. Sherkow; released by Tri Star Pictures. At Gemini, Second Avenue at 64th Street; Movieland Eighth Street, at University Place; Criterion Center, Broadway and 45th Street; 84th Street Six, at Third Avenue. Running time: 120 minutes. This film is rated R.

Kathleen Riley	Cher
Eddie Sanger	Dennis Quaid
Carl Wayne Anderson	Liam Neeson
Judge Matthew Helms	John Mahoney
Charlie Stella	Joe Mantegna
Paul Gray	Philip Bosco
Grace Comisky	E. Katherine Kerr
Morty Rosenthal	Fred Melamed

By JANET MASLIN

AS the coming attractions might put it, "Suspect" brings you Cher as you've never seen her, before. It

Advocate In "Suspect," Cher plays the role of a public defender assigned to represent a deaf, mute, homeless Vietnam veteran accused of murdering a young woman.

brings Cher as a smart, tough, no-nonsense Washington public defender who lives entirely for her work. She even wears glasses. And she turns out to be surprisingly credible in this role, certainly a lot likelier than anything else about Peter Yates's new courtroom thriller, a genre that's a lot less novel than it sounds.

"Suspect" can easily be accused of obvious and sloppy plotting, but it does have this performance to recommend it. It also has some good supporting acting, a mastery of the darkish, post-"Verdict," richly colored courtroom look and a nice way of stringing together exciting if not entirely related suspense scenes.

It includes, for example, spooky shots of the lawyer's deserted office at night, a razor-wielding derelict, a search through old legal files to unearth evidence of a cover-up and assorted loud, startling noises designed less to further the plot than to keep the audience on its toes. The direction is what used to be called "stylish," which means that Mr. Yates will begin with a shot of the Polar Bears' Club diving into icy waters in a scene whose point is the discovery of a body in a river.

•

"Suspect," which opens today at Criterion Center and other theaters, does suffer from a screenplay that's slangier and more smart-alecky than it needs to be. "Well then, it's your basic dog-and-pony show," says Cher's Kathleen Riley in one of too many remarks designed to establish her as fiercely professional and hard-boiled. Her dedication is tested throughout the film, first by a homeless client (Liam Neeson) who is deaf, mute and decidedly hostile, physically attacking his lawyer at the first opportunity. In a screenplay like this, which proceeds to show Kathleen taming and befriending this man, this amounts to proof positive that he is innocent of a murder charge.

Her dedication is also tested by a flirty juror, a Washington lobbyist named Eddie Sanger (Dennis Quaid) who will gladly do anything to advance his cause; an early scene

shows him seducing a Congresswoman to sway her vote on a key issue. For reasons that are never sufficiently clear, Sanger takes a keen interest in helping Ms. Riley exonerate the homeless man. Inconvenienced as he is by the courtroom setting, and later by the jury's having been impaneled, he plays detective and helps uncover the evidence that leads to a cover-up and to an ending that's nominally a surprise.

An extended silent sequence at a library, where Sanger has gone to help Ms. Riley find some information without realizing that the judge trying the case (John Mahoney) is also present, is the very model of skillful suspense editing. Ray Lovejoy does a letter-perfect job of intercutting all three parties and the various covert, duplicitous and suspicious glances that they exchange.

•

If "Suspect" amounts to less than the sum of its parts, those parts are often valuable on their own. In addition to Cher's crisply compelling performance and Mr. Quaid's enjoyably mischievous one, "Suspect" also has Philip Bosco doing an effectively sinister turn and Joe Mantegna as the prosecuting attorney who's none too impressed with Kathleen Riley's tactics. This performance, together with his fine work in the current "House of Games" and "Weeds," easily makes Mr. Mantegna the supporting actor of the hour.

1987 O 23, C14:3

Deviled Eggs

PRINCE OF DARKNESS, directed by John Carpenter; written by Martin Quatermass; director of photography, Gary B. Kibbe; edited by Steve Mirkovich; music by Mr. Carpenter, in association with Alan Howarth; production designer, Daniel Lomino; produced by Larry Franco; released by Universal Pictures. At Movieland, Broadway at 47th Street; Manhattan Twin, 59th Street, east of Third Avenue; Orpheum Twin, 86th Street between Third and Lexington Avenues; 23d Street West Triplex, at Eighth Avenue; Movie Center 5, 125th Street, between Powell and Douglass Boulevards. Running time: 89 minutes. This film is rated R.

Priest	Donald Pleasence
Brian	Jameson Parker
Birack	Victor Wong
Kelly	Susan Blanchard
Street Schizo	Alice Cooper

"HOW," someone asks in John Carpenter's "Prince of Darkness," "did the Vatican manage to keep this secret for 2,000 years?"

"This secret" is the revelation that Satan is not an abstraction, a convenient concept of evil, but a presence living in what looks to be a clear-plastic dispenser of aerated, lime-flavored Kool-Aid, found in the basement chapel of an abandoned Los Angeles church.

After waiting around for eons, he has decided to come out of the drink-dispenser and take charge of his realm. Doing battle with him are a Roman Catholic priest (Donald Pleasence) and a professor of advanced physics (Victor Wong), both windbags who could easily bore Satan into submission, along with some of the professor's young graduate students.

For two days and nights, it's nip and tuck. One by one, the graduate students get spritzed by the evil liquid and are turned into Satan's zombies, stalking the halls of the old church like pod people from "Invasion of the

Body Snatchers." Poor, pretty Kelly (Susan Blanchard) becomes the host-incubator for the Prince, losing, among other things, her perfect complexion.

"Prince of Darkness," which opens today at the Movieland and other theaters, is a surprisingly cheesy horror film to come from Mr. Carpenter ("Halloween," "Escape From New York," among others), a director whose work is usually far more efficient and inventive. Martin Quartermass, whose first screenplay this is, overloads the dialogue with scientific references and is stingy with the surprises. You may well suspect things are not going to go well when the movie spends its first 15 minutes intercutting between the opening credits and scenes introducing the characters.

None of the performances are super, though Alice Cooper, the onetime rock star, makes an arresting cameo appearance as a mean-spirited zombie who stands outside the church, intimidating anyone who looks through the window.

VINCENT CANBY

1987 O 23, C26:1

JOHN AND THE MISSUS, directed by Gordon Pinsent; screenplay by Mr. Pinsent, based on his novel; director of cinematography, Frank Tidy; edited by Bruce Nyznik; music by Michael Conway Baker; produced by Peter O'Brian and John Hunter; released by Cinema Group Pictures. At Quad Cinema 2, 13th Street, between Fifth Avenue and Avenue of the Americas. Running time: 98 minutes. This film is rated PG.

John Munn	Gordon Pinsent
Missus	Jackie Burroughs
Matt	Randy Follett
Faith	Jessica Steen
Fred Budgell	Roland Hewgill
Denny Boland	Timothy Webber
Tom Noble	Neil Munro

By JANET MASLIN

Despite its terrible title and the complete lack of fanfare with which it arrived at the Quad Cinema yesterday, the Canadian film "John and the Missus" is a fine little sleeper. Though it has a good-sized cast, it amounts to a one-man show. Gordon Pinsent, best known as a Canadian television actor, has adapted his own novel and written and directed this film, in which he also stars. Mr. Pinsent, who is himself from Newfoundland, is very much at home in this story of a tight-lipped, stubborn Newfoundland miner resisting the pressures of a changing world.

Set in a scenic coastal village, "John and the Missus" has a homespun and affectionate feeling for life in this remote place. Like the title character, who announces he's "taking the day off" after he is nearly killed in a mine collapse, the natives have a gift for understatement. Cop Cove, where the story unfolds, is a place where one silent look from a grieving woman will announce that her husband has died, and where the dead man's friends will sit almost casually in his bedroom, talking among themselves, while the funeral director dresses up the corpse. That is the extent of the townspeople's involvement in one another's lives.

•

The film explores John's angry reaction to the news that the copper mine in which he works will be closing, and that the Government would like the miners to re-locate elsewhere. The year is 1962, a time of critical change for Newfoundland's population, and a time when many families were indeed resettled.

The film, which also explores John's long, loving marriage (Jackie Burroughs plays his wife) and his relationship with his newlywed son (Randy Follett), ends with the sight of John and his wife sailing off to another town in their house, which John has put on a barge deciding to move it rather than abandon it.

"John and the Missus" unfolds slowly, in something like a television style (Mr. Pinsent has directed numerous television movies), but it has earnestness and conviction. It also has a nicely colloquial screenplay, as when John insists that if he moved away "they'd sell me shirts

Gordon Pinsent and Jackie Burroughs in "John and the Missus."

that don't keep out the wind." He also resists going to where "we'd be drinkin' out other people's cups, sayin' grace at other people's tables." Mr. Pinsent delivers these lines with the terse, hard-bitten understatement that they need.

•

"John and the Missus" is rated PG ("Parental Guidance Suggested"). It contains some rude language.

1987 O 24, 17:1

NIGHTFLYERS, directed by T.C. Blake; screenplay by Robert Jaffe, based on the novella by George R.R. Martin; director of photography, Shelly Johnson; edited by Tom Siiter; music by Doug Timm; production designer, John Muto; produced by Mr. Jaffe; released by the New Century/ Vista Film Company. At National, Broadway and 44th Street; Manhattan, Third Avenue at 59th Street; 23d Street W. Triplex, between Eighth and Ninth Avenues; Coliseum, 181st Street off Broadway. Running time: 93 minutes. This film is rated R.

Miranda	Catherine Mary Stewart
Royd	Michael Praed
D'Branin	John Standing
Audrey	Lisa Blount
Keelor	Glenn Withrow
Darryl	James Avery
Lilly	Hélène Udy
Eliza	Annabel Brooks
Jon Winderman	Michael Des Barres

By CARYN JAMES

"This ship is alive!," says a telepathic crewmember on a 21st century spaceship. "It's a seething malignant presence and it hates all of you!" The ship's captain, whose mother is a jealous computer, has a confession of his own: "Contact with humans will probably kill me." There you have the problem with "Nightflyers"; it is the talkingest movie ever to pose as a science-fiction adventure.

The story, from a novella by George R.R. Martin, has lots of potential for suspense, if not originality, as the crew is attacked on its home turf by an evil alien. The film makers seem to have studied "Aliens," but not carefully enough to notice that its fun is in the chase, as the audience discovers the bizarre truth by racing along with the action.

Before the plot of "Nightflyers" can creep ahead an inch, though, we hear the eight crewmembers sitting around talking. Is the ship's handsome captain human? Why does he appear to the crew as a hologram? When something does happen — a major explosion destroys the kitchen and severs the cook's fingers — they talk some more. Did a gas leak cause the explosion? Or is there something evil aboard this ship?

It is useless to blame T.C. Blake for directing "Nightflyers," because there is no T.C. Blake; the name is a pseudonym of Robert Collector, who directed the film but left before post-production work was completed. A more visible culprit is the producer and writer, Robert Jaffe, whose first screenplay 10 years ago, "The Demon Seed," also left too little to the imagination.

The cast is game, especially the rock singer Michael Des Barre as the tortured telepath, and Catherine Mary Stewart as the project coordinator, who has some tender moments with the hologram (Michael Praed).

But the whole film looks murky — the ship resembles a big blob of chocolate pudding — and the special effects are heavy on lasers; that is, they are ordinary. In a long, final action sequence the crewmembers put on spacesuits and fly away from the ship, battling the alien force. Compared to the rest of "Nightflyers," which opened yesterday at the National Twin and other theaters, this ending is lively. Compared to an adventure film with real adventures, it is nothing special.

1987 O 24, 17:1

FILM VIEW/Janet Maslin

The Perils of Tinkering

EVERY FILM REQUIRES ITS audience to make a leap of faith, but some leaps are longer than others. A *lot* longer. It isn't even a question of whether what we're seeing can literally be believed. One film may make its viewers accept the idea that a nobody from Palookaville can slug his way to the top of the boxing world, or that a schoolboy can travel backward in time to meet his parents as teen-agers; another may strain credulity with the sight of a simple soul making a visit to his neighborhood store. When a film persuades viewers to accept the incredible, it can provide escapism of the most liberating kind. But if it fails to be convincing about even the most mundane details, it may just lose its audience at the starting gate.

Attitude counts for a lot when it comes to setting forth the impossible. Sometimes, as in David Mamet's brilliantly manipulative "House of Games," a film's ideas about truth and deception may be its entire raison d'être, but the credibility issue usually manifests itself in more pedestrian terms. For instance, could a man imbibe "brain transference serum" in his Bloody Mary and switch personalities with his teen-age son? Maybe not. But can the genial, crowd-pleasing comedy "Like Father, Like Son" induce its audience

When it comes to suspending audience disbelief, some movies are more deft than others.

to believe and even enjoy this notion? It can, and knowing one is being cajoled into accepting something entirely implausible only heightens the fun.

Depending on the general frame of mind in which a film puts us, we may or may not be inclined to ask niggling questions. Does it matter to anyone watching "Fatal Attraction," for example, that Glenn Close's high-powered career woman seems to abandon her editor's job entirely once she starts stalking a married lawyer (Michael Douglas) on a full-time basis? Does anyone wonder how a woman capable of behaving so erratically managed to claw her way to the top in the first place? It hardly matters, because the film is otherwise so successful in touching on attitudes and emotions that audiences recognize as real. The larger authenticity here is powerful enough to sweep away any implausibility in its path.

On the other hand, Ridley Scott's similarly glossy "Someone to Watch Over Me," while only a little more farfetched in absolute terms, has a much harder time transporting its audience to a climate of romantic unreality. For one thing, "Fatal Attraction" presents its characters' affluence and attractiveness quite offhandedly, which is part of its appeal; by comparison, Mr. Scott's film revels much too energetically in its ostentation. And Tom Berenger, as a married police detective from Queens assigned to guard a filthy-rich socialite who seems to become physically ill at the sight of a gaudy necktie, has a none too sympathetic role. So when the script attempts stretch after stretch in explaining why Mr. Berenger always winds up with the night shift, and why he's saddled with the dirty job of escorting this beauty to black-tie parties, one is inclined to disbelieve. This film's mistake is in supposing that mere voyeurism is enough to fuel such an elaborate and unwieldy fantasy.

Sometimes a film abdicates its claim to any sort of realism right from the start, usually in the name of antic humor. When "Surrender" presents Sally Field as an impoverished artist, complete with raffish living quarters and the spunkiest attitude this side of Doris Day, it automatically invites skepticism (without generating anything in the way of compensatory humor). And when "Anna," the film about an émigré actress trying to make her way in America with the help of a gorgeous and devoted young protégée, tells its story in entirely clichéd terms, it loses all hope of being taken seriously. It's possible to imagine two women characters like these, and even to see pathos and humor in their situation, but the film around them is much too studiously adorable. It insists, for example, that the older actress is a great talent who can only get work as the understudy in an elaborate show about feminism, which is supposed to be a big Broadway hit.

Now "Weeds," which is also about the theater, is not an iota more likely than "Anna" in absolute terms. (That each of these films is loosely based on someone's real experience — so is "Surrender," for that matter — has no bearing on its plausibility. Credibility is a matter of what we're willing to accept, not of what we know to be true.) And yet "Weeds" is by far the more transporting experience, even though it makes a point of flaunting its unlikely side right away. No sooner has Nick Nolte, as a hardened criminal with a lifetime sentence at San Quentin, made his entrance with a couple of suicide attempts than he begins writing a play and forming a theater company. The toughest cons in San Quentin show up for auditions, singing "The Impossible Dream." This is so crazy that it catches the viewer off guard, but it's also apt, since impossible dreaming is the film's strongest

suit. And "Weeds" is consistent and well acted enough to sustain its farfetched optimism to the very end.

One of the hardest things to tolerate, where credibility is concerned, is a film that changes gears the way "Baby Boom" does, with an hour's worth of big-city humor at the expense of hard-boiled, tough-talking careerist types, followed by a Vermont section that defies belief at every turn. The country scenes are as ludicrous as the city ones are savvy, and the result is a disconcerting mix. When a film demonstrates, as Mr. Mamet's "House of Games" does, that it has a sure, steady grip on what its audience will or will not believe, then going along with its deceptions becomes a pleasure. But when it's clear that even the film makers aren't certain where their own artifice defies belief, it's time to worry. □

1987 O 25, II:23:1

Film: 'Positive I.D.'

"Positive I.D." was shown as part of this year's New Directors/New Films series. Following are excerpts of Janet Maslin's review, which appeared in The New York Times March 14. The film is playing at the Sutton, Third Avenue and 57th Street.

UNLIKE almost any other story of switched identities, Andy Anderson's "Positive I.D." pays no attention to the underpinnings of such an act. It concentrates on the mechanics, which, as Mr. Anderson sees them, can take on a life of their own.

"Positive I.D." is about Julie Kenner (Stephanie Rascoe), a rape victim who seems badly shellshocked when the story begins. The crime has been widely publicized. "That wasn't Mommy, that was someone who looked like Mommy," one of her children says, after catching a glimpse of her on television at a trial.

Julie pays scant attention to her husband or children, and concentrates most of her energy on taking frequent baths. She speaks little, and wants mostly to be alone. But as the film progresses, Julie begins to recover from her ordeal. She is just regaining her energies when an employee at her daughter's school demands a copy of the child's birth certificate, thus planting the seed of an idea. At the records bureau Julie, who lives in Texas, learns that birth certificates and death certificates are not cross-referenced there. So she embarks upon an elaborate campaign to become someone else, a project that is presented here largely in terms of clever paperwork.

"Positive I.D." recalls "Blood Simple" in its mixture of dark humor and the macabre. But it is also a good deal more matter-of-fact. The nuts and bolts of Julie's transformation take up most of the film and give it a slow pace, the payoff for which is presumably the final explanation for Julie's undertaking. However, there can't be much real surprise about what she has in mind.

Mr. Anderson, who wrote, directed, produced and co-edited the film on a very small budget, displays a good deal of technical promise and attention to detail. He gives shorter shrift to the actors, who perform rather stiffly throughout. Miss Rascoe is

reasonably convincing and makes Julie seem thoroughly engrossed in what she's doing. But she isn't given nearly enough chance to enjoy the masquerade.

1987 O 27, C16:1

An Unlikely Triangle

HELL WITHOUT LIMITS, directed by Arturo Ripstein; screenplay (Spanish with English subtitles) by Mr. Ripstein, based on the novel by José Donoso; cinematographer, Miguel Garzón; edited by Francisco Chiu; music by Joaquín Gutierrez Heras; distributed by Azteca Films. At Cinema Village, 22 East 12th Street. Running time: 110 minutes. This film has no rating.
La Manuela ....Roberto Cobo
Japonesita ....Ana Martín
Pancho ....Gonzalo Vega
La Japonesa ....Lucha Villa
Lucy ....Carmen Salinas

By VINCENT CANBY

ARTURO RIPSTEIN's "Hell Without Limits," the 1978 Mexican film opening today at the Cinema Village, looks and sounds as if it were based on an idea for a Luis Buñuel film, which had been made, instead, by someone completely unqualified for the job.

The setting is the small, destitute Mexican town of El Olivo, owned lock, stock and barrel by a tiny old tycoon who has turned off the electricity, hoping that everybody will move away so he can sell the land at a fancy profit. As the movie begins, the only people left in El Olivo are Manuel, called La Manuela, the aging homosexual owner of the town's brothel; Japonesita, his pretty daughter (conceived many years ago to win a bet), two dispirited whores and some shopkeepers.

On this particular morning, Manuel is in a tizzy. Pancho, the married, macho truck driver who's desired both by him and Japonesita, has returned to town, which, Manuel knows, means trouble. The last time Pancho came home, he tore Manuel's ruffled red evening gown so badly that Manuel is still patching it up.

•

Manuel, with his plucked eyebrows, swishy gestures and passion for Pancho, is doomed, but no more than his daughter and Pancho. Japonesita de-ludes herself with the fond dream that the electricity will be turned back on. Pancho really is obsessed by Manuel, which, when he realizes it, drives him into a frenzy of foreordained violence.

There's a lot more to the plot, all of it recounted with an unwarranted solemnity and no sense of the absurd. Mr. Ripstein, who prefaces the film with a quote from Marlowe's "Doctor Faustus," takes no distance from the material. He demonstrates no irony. He accepts his grotesque characters at face value. This has the effect of making them seem possibly more foolish than necessary, and the movie an unintentional, melodramatic howler.

1987 O 28, C25:1

Chaotic London

SAMMY AND ROSIE GET LAID, directed by Stephen Frears; screenplay by Hanif Kureishi; director of photography, Oliver Stapleton; film editor, Mick Audsley; producers, Tim Bevan and Sarah Radclyffe; production designer, Hugo Luczyc Wyhowski; released by Cinecom Entertainment Group. At Cinema Studio 1, 66th Street and Broadway. Running time: 100 minutes. This film is rated R.

Rafi	Shashi Kapoor
Rosie	Frances Barber
Alice	Claire Bloom
Sammy	Ayub Khan Din
Danny	Roland Gift
Anna	Wendy Gazelle

By VINCENT CANBY

ABOUT three-quarters of the way through "Sammy and Rosie Get Laid," there's a particularly rich, riotously busy montage, a succession of shots of urban decay, exuberant West Indian street singers and three separate sets of lovers who alternately reminisce and argue while, at the end of a long London night, they make their circuitous routes to bed. The tempo of the editing increases. Suddenly the screen splits — horizontally — and we see each of the three couples, layered, more or less, one pair atop another, simultaneously but in separate images, as they achieve transitory satisfaction. That's about all they can hope for.

The sequence virtually defines "Sammy and Rosie Get Laid," the second collaboration of Stephen Frears, the director, and Hanif Kureishi, the writer, whose first film together was the memorable "My Beautiful Laundrette."

Mr. Frears and Mr. Kureishi have composed "Sammy and Rosie" as if they were building a giant bonfire in a mock celebration of the achievements of contemporary British society and, by extension, of the civilized world. They throw everything on — love, death, sex, politics, violence. A lot of stuff doesn't easily burn, but there's also plenty that does.

•

The film's opening and closing shots are accompanied on the soundtrack by the voice of Prime Minister Margaret Thatcher, enunciating measured truisms about inner cities and great tasks yet to be done. In-between, there are half a dozen interlocking narratives, including one that features a maimed specter, the victim of political torture in a third world country. It's Marley's Ghost, walking the streets of today's London as an illegal alien.

The specter is too much, yet overstatement is the style of "Sammy and Rosie," which is about England in the 1980's and the heritage of a couple of hundred years of empire and colonialism. "Sammy and Rosie" opens today at the Cinema Studio 1.

The new movie is far less orderly than "My Beautiful Laundrette." At times it seems as if Mr. Kureishi, having observed the rules of conventional film making in his first produced screenplay, had decided to allow himself a few liberties in his second. "Sammy and Rosie" is at its best when it's teasingly oblique. Often, however, it's alarmingly blunt, especially when characters are permitted to say exactly what seems to be on the writer's mind, straight from his notebook.

Sammy (Ayub Khan Din) and Rosie (Frances Barber) behave like a couple out of the 60's. Their marriage is "open," built, they say with increasing lack of conviction, on "freedom, plus commitment." Though no national origins are ever mentioned, Sammy is a Pakistani, bred to be a hip Londoner. Rosie, a liberated Englishwoman, is writing a book on the social and political history of kissing. Sammy and Rosie are the sort of young people who attend the Royal Court and the latest cabaret theaters and seek out lectures on semiotics.

•

They also cultivate reverse chic. They have the means to live elsewhere, but they choose to remain in a rundown, multiracial London neighborhood where, as the film opens, the police have just accidentally shot and killed a 50-year-old black cleaning woman, mistaken for a 20-year-old black trumpeter. Like the good liberals they are, Sammy and Rosie regard as perfectly natural the tumultuous rioting and police confrontations that follow. "An affirmation of the human spirit," pronounces Rosie, and Sammy agrees, until his car is burned up.

The anarchy of their lives is accentuated by the arrival of Rafi (Shashi Kapoor), Sammy's elegantly mannered, Oxbridge-educated father who, for years, has played a major role in the fascist political regime in what is probably Pakistan. Having, it seems, been tossed out of office, Rafi has come "home" to his beloved England with his bags full of cash, determined to reconcile with Sammy and to renew his courtship of Alice (Claire Bloom), the middle-class Englishwoman whom he loved and abandoned when he was a young man.

As if these weren't enough principal characters for one film, Mr. Kureishi also includes a handsome young black man, Danny (Roland Gift), who sometimes ironically refers to himself as Victoria, and who

seeks out Rafi for political advice. (Just why a black revolutionary would go to someone popularly identified with a repressive fascist regime is never explained.)

Danny stays around to become Rosie's lover, while Sammy continues his affair with a pretty young American photographer, Anna (Wendy Gazelle), who's putting together an exhibition to be called "Images of a Decaying Europe."

The patrician Rafi is appalled by the way Sammy and Rosie live. "How's marriage?" he asks Sammy early on. Replies Sammy, "A scream." Rafi's as disgusted by the state of the England to which he's returned as he is by Sammy and Rosie's bohemian friends. Yet his renewed courtship of Alice only reminds him of his own failures as the once liberal politician who, in the name of necessity, became a willing tool of a dictatorship.

"Sammy and Rosie" is sometimes very funny, sometimes utterly opaque, and sometimes too direct for its own good, as when Rafi defends political expediency on the grounds that expediency is the lesson taught by empire. Alice sneers at Rafi as the representative of a regime that introduced flogging for minor offenses, nuclear capability and partridge shooting.

The movie doesn't exactly lack for characters, incidents and ideas, which is both its problem and its fascination. There's too much going on in Mr. Kureishi's screenplay for any one person or thing to be satisfactorily explored. Mr. Frears acknowledges this overabundance by making a movie that is, itself, overabundant in detail. It's almost breathless in its pacing. The film is constantly crosscutting between characters, events and scene-setting images. As each character is overwhelmed to a greater or lesser degree by contradictory impulses, so is the film.

All the performances are good, but Miss Bloom is superb as the simultaneously romantic, firmly commonsensical Alice. Compared to the others, Alice is a fairly plain character. She's also the bridge between an idealized past and the chaotic, multiracial present.

"Sammy and Rosie" is not an easy film to characterize. It's too ambitious for its own good, which isn't at all bad in an era when most movies are simply a succession of car chases.

1987 O 30, C5:1

Londoners
Frances Barber and Roland Gift appear in Stephen Frears's "Sammy and Rosie Get Laid."

Lowlifes of L.A.

FATAL BEAUTY, directed by Tom Holland; screenplay by Hilary Henkin and Dean Riesner; story by Bill Svanoe; director of photography, David M. Walsh; film editor, Don Zimmerman; music by Harold Faltermeyer; producer, Leonard Kroll; production designer, James William Newport; released by MGM-UA Distribution Company. At Loews Astor Plaza, 44th Street and Broadway; 34th Street Showplace, between Second and Third Avenues; Orpheum, Third Avenue and 86th Street; Movie Center 5, 125th Street between Powell and Douglass Boulevards; Essex, 275 Grand Street. Running time: 103 minutes. This film is rated R.

Rita Rizzoli	Whoopi Goldberg
Mike Marshak	Sam Elliott
Carl Jimenez	Rubén Blades
Conrad Kroll	Harris Yulin
Lieutenant Kellerman	John P. Ryan
Cecile Jaeger	Jennifer Warren
Leo Nova	Brad Dourif
Earl Skinner	Mike Jolly
Deputy Getz	Charles Hallahan
Raphael	David Harris
Zack Jaeger	James Le Gros

By JANET MASLIN

"FATAL BEAUTY" asks whether a woman can be just as loudly, obnoxiously macho as a man, and answers with a resounding yes. The woman is Whoopi Goldberg, the man Eddie Murphy, and the model is "Beverly Hills Cop," though that film had nothing like the incessant firepower of this one. Someone dies graphically, riddled with bullets and shuddering voluptuously at each shot, on the average of every five minutes or so.

Playing an undercover policewoman, Miss Goldberg's Rita Rizzoli finds frequent occasion to impugn the virility of some of her male adversaries and to threaten to castrate others. Fighting a female enemy, she belts the woman squarely on the jaw, then does it again — and a third time after that. Her conversation runs exclusively to insults, as when she arrives late somewhere, is asked jokingly whether she stopped to pick up a sailor and replies: "Yeah! I almost had one, too, but your mother beat me to him." The wisecracks and the swaggering are as unrelieved as the film's almost comically ecstatic gunplay. Someone must have figured audiences like things this way.

It isn't Miss Goldberg's fault, because Miss Goldberg is funny whenever she's given half a chance. She makes her entrance camouflaged as a prostitute, shambling along with the no-nonsense gait that's a dead giveaway, and her appearance is good for a laugh before she even opens her mouth. When she walks into a bar, drawing a greeting Dolly Levi would envy, it's clear that Rita Rizzoli is someone to be reckoned with. She's

Partners
Ruben Blades and Whoopi Goldberg, as narcotics squad detectives, star in "Fatal Beauty."

Peter Sorel

Tom Beck	Michael Nouri
Lloyd Gallagher	Kyle MacLachlan
Cliff Willis	Ed O'Ross
Ed Flynn	Clu Gulager
Brenda Lee	Claudia Christian
John Masterson	Clarence Felder

tough, she's smart, and her nerves never fail her. Neither she nor the film needs machine guns to get that point across.

•

But the guns and the moronic thugs are everywhere, in a plot that seems intended chiefly to keep the audience awake. As directed by Tom Holland and written by Hilary Henkin and Dean Riesner, the film concerns a deadly batch of tainted cocaine and the various lowlifes who spread the stuff, including one (Mike Jolly) who bites into a glass and spits out the bloody pieces, just to prove he means business. Brad Dourif, who plays another goon, has this kind of ghoulish behavior down to a science, but its appeal has definite limits. Also in the cast: Rubén Blades, affable but somewhat wasted as Rizzoli's partner, and Sam Elliott, none too comfortable in the role of a potential love interest. The film, which allows them one chaste kiss and an implied overnight visit, knows better than to push its luck.

"Fatal Beauty," which opens today at Loews Astor Plaza and other theaters, is busy and cartoonish enough to find an audience, but its attempts to copy "Beverly Hills Cop" are at times too shameless. The California setting, the hit-minded soundtrack and the star's beat-up old car are very much in the earlier film's mode, as are scenes in which Rizzoli forces her way into various posh households and lets the occupants know who's boss. Ignore this, if you can. It's better to watch Miss Goldberg, who appears in one sequence wearing a taffeta skirt with crinolines and affecting a girlish manner, simply emphasizing the vast differences between herself and the rest of the world, and making those differences work to her advantage.

1987 O 30, C8:5

Overcoming Infirmity

GABY — A TRUE STORY, directed by Luis Mandoki; written by Martin Salinas and Michael James Love; developed by Mr. Mandoki, as told to him by Gabriela Brimmer; director of photography, Lajos Koltai; film editor, Garth Craven; music by Maurice Jarre; art director, Alejandro Luna; producer, Pinchas Perry; released by Tri-Star Pictures. At 57th Street Playhouse, 110 West 57th Street. Running time: 114 minutes. This film is rated R.

Sari	Liv Ullmann
Florencia	Norma Aleandro
Michel	Robert Loggia
Gaby	Rachel Levin
Fernando	Lawrence Monoson
Luis	Robert Beltran
Fernando's Mother	Beatriz Sheridan
David	Tony Goldwyn
Carlos	Danny De La Paz
Gaby — 3 years old	Paulina Gómez

THE heroine of "Gaby — A True Story" has cerebral palsy, and she communicates by moving her big toe along an alphabet board, spelling out words that way. So in one scene, in which Gaby (Rachel Levin) looks upset, her devoted father (Robert Loggia) pulls up a chair, rolls off Gaby's sock and says, "So tell me — what's going on?"

Fortunately, Luis Mandoki's film is a lot less awkward than this, and a lot less deadpan, too. In its own way, it has energy and strength, once it gets past the clumsy business of establishing Gaby's situation, introducing her family members, and allowing the father to make a little speech about greatness triumphing over infirmity, with Beethoven as the case in point. Gaby doesn't need this kind of pep talk. She's a hopeful, humorous figure and also a bold one, never afraid to spell out cheeky replies to her teachers' questions and not beyond placing her one working foot in the right fellow's lap.

"Gaby — A True Story," which opens today at the 57th Street Playhouse, is based on the life of Gabriela Brimmer, who collaborated on the film and appears to be an astonishingly determined woman. Born in Mexico to parents who survived the Holocaust, Gaby had the good fortune to be raised by an extremely understanding nurse who became her permanent companion. As the film presents this, the nurse, Florencia Morales, was largely responsible for teaching Gaby to communicate. Her mother, Sari, as played here by Liv Ullmann, was a sympathetic figure but a somewhat remote one, whereas Florencia accompanied Gaby everywhere and acted as both caretaker and interpreter. The family relationship appears to have indeed been unusual. For one thing, it is Florencia more than Gaby who refers to Sari as "Mommy."

•

A superb performance by Norma Aleandro, the Argentine actress who starred in "The Official Story" (and has her first English-speaking film role here), is a real standout, and it contributes greatly to the film's verisimilitude. Miss Aleandro is a marvel, conveying both the shyness and the meddlesomeness of someone living in so symbiotic a situation, blushing angrily every time Gaby expects her to translate a remark that's rude. One of the things the film does best is to present the delicate way in which Florencia and Gaby's parents deal with life's little awkwardnesses. For instance, Gaby's sexual awakening, once she falls in love with a disabled schoolmate named Fernando (Lawrence Monoson), moves her mother

to quiet tears. The mother would have walked in on this scene, and perhaps interrupted it, but Florencia warns her not to; both these parental figures know how difficult it has been for Gaby to maneuver such a thing at all.

Norma Aleandro in "Gaby — A True Story."

It's to the credit of Miss Levin and Mr. Monoson that their handicaps seem thoroughly real; in fact, Mr. Monoson has played seemingly normal roles in films like "The Last American Virgin," but he does a fine job of simulating Fernando's symptoms. Miss Levin, who herself endured a bout of Guillain-Barré syndrome from which she has since recovered, is older than the adolescent Gaby but brings warmth and empathy to the role. Her performance has a blunt, unsentimental quality, and the film does too.

JANET MASLIN

1987 O 30, C10:4

Turning the Worm

THE HIDDEN, directed by Jack Sholder; screenplay by Bob Hunt; director of photography, Michael Haitkin; edited by Michael Knue; production designers, C. J. Strawn and Mick Strawn; produced by Robert Shaye, Gerald T. Olson and Michael Meltzer; released by New Line Cinema. At Embassy 1, Broadway and 46th Street; 86th Street East Twin, between Second and Third Avenues; Movieland Eighth Street Triplex, at University Place; Sutton, 57th Street and Third Avenue; 84th Street Six, at Broadway; Movie Center 5, 125th Street between Powell and Douglass Boulevards. Running time: 98 minutes. This film is rated R.

"**T**HE HIDDEN," opening today at the Embassy 1 and other theaters, is a jokey sci-fi horror movie about the desperate pursuit of a vile "thing" from outer space.

Though of slimy texture, the creature looks like a large caterpillar, about 18 inches long, which can be passed from one host-human to another through the mouth. Once ingested, it turns its host into a short-tempered, short-lived lunatic who doesn't hesitate to kill when crossed. This is, possibly, a metaphor for a very real disease, but I doubt that it will be read as such by audiences stuffing popcorn into their mouths.

•

The movie was written by Bob Hunt and directed by Jack Sholder. It stars Michael Nouri ("Flashdance"), as a tough Los Angeles detective who must say at one point, "I don't believe this," and Kyle MacLachlan ("Dune," "Blue Velvet"), as a human-looking alien from outer space, who's dedicated to destroying the creature.

The movie is mostly a series of automobile chases through Los Angeles, but there is also some humor. Human hosts to the creature all develop mad passions to drive red Ferraris. Mr. MacLachlan's alien-cop, who has a hangover after drinking too much beer, *chews* the Alka-Seltzer tablet.

Maybe you have to see it to get the full import. On second thought, maybe not. *VINCENT CANBY*

1987 O 30, C19:1

DEADLY ILLUSION, directed by William Tannen and Larry Cohen; written by Mr. Cohen; director of photography, Daniel Pearl; film editor, Steve Mirkovich; music by Patrick Gleeson; producer, Irwin Meyer; released by CineTel Films Inc. At Cine Twin, Seventh Avenue between 47th and 48th Streets; Movie Center Five, 125th and Seventh Avenue; Coliseum, 181st Street off Broadway. Running time: 90 minutes. This film is rated R.

Hamberger	Billy Dee Williams
Rina	Vanity
Jane Mallory/Sharon	Morgan Fairchild
Alex Burton	John Beck
Paul Lefferts	Joe Cortese
Costillion	Michael Wilding Jr.
Burton Imposter	Dennis Hallahan
Nancy Costillion	Allison Woodward
Gloria Reid	Jenny Cornuelle
Crazy Man in Gun Bureau	Joe Spinell

By VINCENT CANBY

There's an engaging bravado about "Deadly Illusion," a brassy suspense-melodrama that has the manner of a man who refuses to acknowledge that he's painted himself into a corner. Instead of standing there, wringing his hands and looking silly, he boldly walks away, ignoring the footprints left behind.

"Deadly Illusion," which is continually finding itself cornered, stars Billy Dee Williams as an unlicensed Manhattan private eye whose clients often die violently. It's not his fault; it's the sort of clients he attracts. In this case, he's hired by a Wall Street tycoon to murder his unwanted wife, only Billy Dee doesn't really intend to go through with it, but the wife he tries to warn turns out to be the wrong woman anyway.

•

Though the body count is high and much of the plot impenetrable, the performances by Mr. Williams and the other actors have a decent swagger to them. They include Vanity, the recording star, Morgan Fairchild, John Beck, Joe Cortese and Michael Wilding Jr. The movie makes good use of Manhattan during the Christmas-New Year's week, and features an outlandishly nutty fight high in the branches of the Rockefeller Center Christmas tree.

Like Satan, Larry Cohen never sleeps. The prolific writer and director of horror films ("It's Alive," among others) wrote the screenplay for "Deadly Illusion" and, with William Tannen, shares the directorial credit.

1987 O 31, 10:5

DERANGED, directed and produced by Chuck Vincent; screenplay by Craig Horrall; director of photography, Larry Revene; edited by James Davalos; music by Bill Heller; art director, Marc Ubell; released by Platinum Pictures Inc. At the Criterion, Broadway at 45th Street. Running time: 85 minutes. This film is rated R.

Joyce	Jane Hamilton
Frank	Paul Siederman
Maryann	Jennifer Delora
Sheila	Jill Cumer
Margaret	Loretta Palma
Darren	John Brett

By CARYN JAMES

Apparently Chuck Vincent, the producer and director of "Deranged," doesn't want to be thought of as a sleazy guy. The production notes delicately describe him as a maker of "quality porn" movies ("Jack and Jill," Parts I and II) whose latest is a straight suspense film. "Deranged" proves you can dress Mr. Vincent's films up but you can't take them out.

Joyce is prone to hearing voices "since Daddy died." When she is attacked by an intruder in her apartment, she kills him with a quick jab of her scissors. But she is, of all things, *deranged* (apparently Mr. Vincent doesn't want to be thought of as a subtle guy) so we know she won't call the police. She sits around her apartment, receiving an occasional visit from the deli deliveryman, reliving scenes from her past. Her old therapist, her vicious mother and her suicidal father all show up as visions in the apartment. This may not be psychologically astute, but it is conspicuously cheap; most of the movie takes place on a single set.

Eventually, real and imaginary dead bodies pile up — under the hall table, in the closet, in the bathtub — and we learn the nasty sexual secret that caused Joyce to be so very deranged. Actually, Mr. Vincent isn't a very secretive guy, so Joyce's beloved Daddy leers at his little girl all through the movie. None of this is very suspenseful or convincing. "Deranged," which opened yesterday at the Criterion Center, is not pornography, of high or low quality; it is just a sleazy, muddled movie that should have been kept in the can.

1987 O 31, 12:3

BROKEN NOSES, directed by Bruce Weber; camera, Jeff Preiss; edited by Phyllis Famiglietti; music by Julie London, Chet Baker, Robert Mitchum, Danny Small, Gerry Mulligan, Joni James and Ken Nordine; produced by Nan Bush in association with Steven Cohen and Kira Films. At Film Forum 1, 57 Watts Street. Running time: 75 minutes. This film has no rating.
With Andy Minsker.

By WALTER GOODMAN

BRUCE WEBER, known for his photographs of athletic looking fellows posed sexily in underwear advertisements, demonstrates in "Broken Noses" that shorts do not make the man.

In mostly black and white and without narration, he introduces us to Andy Minsker, once a Golden Gloves champion, now shepherding a teenage boxing team in Portland, Ore. With his muscular yet supple chest, bared through much of the movie, and his tough soft face, shaped by other men's fists, Mr. Minsker could be one of Mr. Weber's models, but he proves to be a lot more.

The camera angles in on face and chest as the boxer reminisces over the trophies he won as a lightweight amateur in the 1970's and early 80's, talks with his parents and stepparents, fools around with his boys, is happily embarrassed by the effusions of a waitress. His air of melancholy sweetness is echoed in the smoky airs of Julie London and Gerry Mulligan.

The most poignant scene in the movie, which opens today at Film Forum 1, is a halting conversation between the boxer and his father, whose own short ring career was an inspiration to the son. Both know now that the young man's championship days are behind; something went wrong in 1984, when he wasn't chosen for the United States Olympic team, leaving unfocused recriminations.

●

We learn enough about his boyhood — a broken family, a stepfather who beat him and his sisters so severely that he lost their custody ("A little pain builds character," says the stepfather), never enough money ("I'm not a great provider," his father concedes) — to be touched by the respect and affection the son shows for both sets of parents. His memory is kind, and it's almost too easy to conclude that this boyish man is trying to be for his boys the model that he sought when he was growing up.

Mr. Weber can be intrusive, like a fighter who is more interested in showing off his footwork than connecting. Most of the photographic essays he inserts tell little about his subject, and the intermittent use of color seems arbitrary. But he can be inventive, as demonstrated by a comical interview with a little kid who for no particular reason is seated atop the shoulders of a bigger kid, whom he torments. And the final essay is a knockout. To Joni James's "Too Young," we see shots of an exhibition match that tell everything about Mr. Minsker's attachment to his little battlers and their own game spirit.

One leaves the theater with the picture of them dancing and punching away to prove themselves to their trainer, who is at ringside punching along with them.

1987 N 4, C28:5

Confusing Mix

SLAMDANCE, directed by Wayne Wang; screenplay by Don Opper; director of photography, Amir Mokri; edited by Lee Percy; music by Mitchell Froom; production designer, Eugenio Zanetti; produced by Rupert Harvey and Barry Opper; released by Island Pictures. At Waverly Twin, Avenue of the Americas and West Third Street; Columbia Cinema, Broadway and 103d Street. Running time: 100 minutes. This film is rated R.

On the Run In "Slamdance," Thomas Hulce plays the role of a cartoonist pursued by hired killers after his lover is found murdered.

C. C. Drood	Tom Hulce
Helen Drood	Mary Elizabeth Mastrantonio
Jim	Adam Ant
Bobbie Nye	Millie Perkins
Yolanda	Virginia Madsen
Smiley	Harry Dean Stanton
Bean	Judith Barsi
Mrs. Bell	Rosalind Chao
Buddy	Don Opper
Gilbert	John Doe
Detective	Marty Levy

WAYNE WANG, the gifted Chinese-American film maker ("Chan Is Missing," "Dim Sum"), goes straight if quite gracefully to the bottom with his first mainstream movie, "Slamdance," a Los Angeles-based tale of corruption and cover-up that's less interesting for its characters than for its fancy décor and images.

C. C. Drood (Tom Hulce), an underground cartoonist being framed by the police on a murder rap, works in a studio that is a converted Turkish bath, which identifies him as offbeat. The mysterious woman (Millie Perkins) behind the conspiracy lives in one of those magnificent old Los Angeles mansions that even fixed-income millionaires can't afford. This certifies her power.

A quick shot of someone swimming in a pool recalls a David Hockney painting while another shot, the purpose of which now escapes me, is nothing less than a recollection of Rembrandt's "Anatomy Lesson." Put them all together and you have complete confusion, a movie without any identity whatsoever.

In addition to Mr. Hulce, who gets an opportunity to reprise his hysterical, "Amadeus" giggle at least once, and Miss Perkins, the cast includes Mary Elizabeth Mastrantonio, as the cartoonist's estranged wife; the rock performer Adam Ant, as an untrustworthy friend; Virginia Madsen, as a beautiful hooker, and Harry Dean Stanton, as a detective who's not entirely happy framing an innocent man.

The film's most arresting and absurd character — that of a suicidal hit man — is played by Don Opper, who wrote the screenplay.

"Slamdance" opens today at the Columbia Cinema and Waverly Twin.
VINCENT CANBY

1987 N 6, C10:5

Pink-Colored Glasses

RUSSKIES, directed by Rick Rosenthal; screenplay by Alan Jay Glueckman, Sheldon Lettich and Michael Nankin; director of photography Reed Smoot; edited by Antony Gibbs; music by James Newton Howard; production designer Linda Pearl; produced by Mark Levinson and Scott Rosenfelt; released by New Century Entertainment Company. At Manhattan Twin, 59th Street and Third Avenue; 23d Street West Triplex, between Eighth and Ninth Avenues; Metro Twin, Broadway at 99th Street. Running time: 98 minutes. This film is rated PG.

Mischa	Whip Hubley
Danny	Leaf Phoenix
Adam	Peter Billingsley
Jason	Stefan DeSalle
Diane	Susan Walters
Raimy	Patrick Kilpatrick
Sulock	Vic Polizos
Mr. Vandermeer	Charles Frank
Mrs. Vandermeer	Susan Blanchard
Sergeant Kovac	Benjamin Hendrickson
Mrs. Kovac	Carole King

ALL the dopey, daffy, dizzy fun of glasnost is captured by "Russkies," the heartburning adventure-comedy that opens today at the Manhattan Twin and other theaters.

The setting is Key West, Fla., during the Fourth of July holiday. When first seen, the film's three carefully integrated (two white, one black) all-American-boy heros (aged 11 through 15) are in their clubhouse reading comic books about a Rambo-like superman, Captain Slammer. It's not giving too much away to report that, when seen at the end of the movie, the boys are back in their clubhouse, reading (I kid you not) "War and Peace."

In between, Danny, Adam and Jason have found a shipwrecked Russian sailor named Mischa (Whip Hubley), who, in spite of his slight accent, is just a regular guy, after all. In the wake of some heavy ideological give-'n'-take ("What about Afghanistan?" asks Danny. "What about Vietnam?" asks Mischa), the boys take Mischa on a glorious one-day tour of Key West. "What means this Fourth July?" asks Mischa. They buy him a hip wardrobe, introduce him to a Big Mac cheeseburger and to Adam's beautiful sister, Diane, with whom it's love at first sight.

Says Mischa: "I think I know why your country is strong. You have conviction. You have energy as young men."

●

Glasnost is not a one-way street. The warmhearted Mischa teaches the boys that one doesn't have to be, in their word, "homo" to be able to express affection by throwing a comradely arm around a shoulder. "I have big family," says Mischa. "Always hug. Like bears, always hugging."

Nor does true glasnot run smoothly. A couple of Mischa's shipmates also are ashore, nosing around the local military base in search of the traitor who's going to sell them a highly classified secret device. When cornered, these two sailors don't hesitate to hold Mischa's teen-age friends hostage. At the same time, the boys must save Mischa from a terrible beating by a local Commie-hater. Thus we learn that there are good and bad folk everywhere.

However, the big glasnost test comes when young Danny's father, whose own father was shot by the Russians when they invaded Hungary in 1956, is introduced to Mischa.

Every now and then, "Russkies," a comic-book movie whose heart is in the right place, exhibits the lighter side of its comic-book sensibility, as when the American traitor decides not to sell the secret device to the Russians. "Call it corny," he says, "but I'm not selling out my country on the Fourth of July!"

"Russkies," directed by Rick Rosenthal, has the brightly colored look of a commercial for a high-fiber breakfast cereal, and even talks like one. "America," says the expansive Mischa, "takes such big bite of life! Such color! Such freedom!" The cast members, most of whom come out of television commercials and soap operas, have perfect complexions and capped teeth.

•

"Russkies," which has been rated PG ("Parental Guidance Suggested"), contains some mildly vulgar words. VINCENT CANBY

1987 N 6, C12:3

A Bond of Brothers

CRY FREEDOM, directed and produced by Sir Richard Attenborough; screenplay by John Briley, based on the books "Biko" and "Asking for Trouble" by Donald Woods; director of photography, Ronnie Taylor; edited by Lesley Walker; music by George Fenton and Jonas Gwangwa; production designer, Stuart Craig; released by Universal Pictures. At Ziegfeld, Avenue of the Americas and 54th Street; New York Twin, Second Avenue and 66th Street; 84th Street Six, at Broadway. Running time: 155 minutes. This film is rated PG.

Stephen Biko .... Denzel Washington
Donald Woods .... Kevin Kline
Wendy Woods .... Penelope Wilton
Jane Woods .... Kate Hardie
Dr. Ramphele .... Josette Simon
Kruger .... John Thaw
Father Kani .... Zakes Mokae
Evalina .... Sophie Mgcina

By JANET MASLIN

THE mantle of greatness does not fall lightly onto the heroes of Sir Richard Attenborough's epic film biographies. It is placed there by a heavy hand. A great statesman, as in the director's "Gandhi" or his new "Cry Freedom," about the murdered South African leader Stephen Biko, is apt to be bathed in beatific light as he delivers important speeches, and to be making speeches even when he talks with intimate friends. He will be surrounded by acolytes, who often nod their approval as one. When he moves the masses, thousands of people will appear on screen. And he will speak to them in clear, helpful, eminently instructive tones. Everyone else in the film will speak that way, too.

These are fine methods for delivering a civics lesson, which to some extent is what the Attenborough approach is all about. But for a film that aspires to entertain as well as educate, they are less helpful. Without forgetting how valuable it is that someone has had the courage to make serious and sincere films about important subjects, it must be noted that good intentions aren't everything. Although "Cry Freedom" has sweeping, scenic good looks and two fine performances to recommend it, not to mention the weight of moral decency on its side, what comes through most strongly is the ponderousness of the Attenborough style.

"Cry Freedom" has other problems as well, problems that arise from the fact that there is no Gandhi at its center. In "Gandhi," the director had a wonderfully irascible and inspiring character with which to work, a long and fascinating story to tell, and a wealth of unforgettable aphorisms with which to pepper the dialogue. Stephen Biko was a less flamboyant kind of hero, more the dedicated political theorist and less the colorful eccentric. Much less is known about him. And tragically, his story was a great deal shorter.

Biko's terrible death in 1977, at age 30, at the hands of South Africa's Se-

Denzel Washington

curity Police (who at first tried to maintain that Biko had willfully starved to death or died of self-inflicted head wounds, until an inquest determined otherwise), was in some ways the most important event of his career, since it so outraged and galvanized many of his countrymen. Yet "Cry Freedom" makes relatively little of this, and in fact makes relatively little of Steve Biko himself, allowing him to disappear before the film is even half over. The rest of the time, it chooses to concentrate on Donald Woods, the newspaper editor who was Biko's close friend and bravely defied South African authorities on Biko's behalf. In theory, shifting the focus makes some sense, since the Biko story is sketchy and downbeat, the Woods part more conventionally dramatic. In fact, it is most unfortunate that this film, with its potential for focusing worldwide attention on the plight of black South Africans, should concentrate its energies on a white man.

Oddly enough, there is a stronger sense of South African racism in the opening part of "Gandhi," with the great statesman then a young Indian lawyer who is astounded and indignant at his treatment by a white train conductor, than there is in "Cry Freedom." The new film, for reasons that are incomprehensible, soft-pedals the very issue it is nominally about. Steve Biko, played with great magnetism and given an air of true heroism by Denzel Washington (though the role is badly underdeveloped in John Briley's screenplay), talks at length about white oppression, as do his supporters. Donald Woods, played by Kevin Kline as a dashing, debonair liberal who evolves ever-so-gradually into an adventurer, talks about it, too. But talking is most of what happens here, since the Attenborough approach makes no distinction between merely stating an idea and demonstrating one through dramatic action.

Though the film contains several stupendous riot scenes (including one compressing several weeks' worth of fighting in Soweto, in 1976, into a day and ascribing the actions of black riot police to white ones), it devotes very little time to the day-to-day indignities created by apartheid. In any case, the white actors playing security police are so cartoonishly evil-looking that their actions hold little surprise.

•

"Cry Freedom," which opens today at the Ziegfeld and other theaters, is bewildering at some points and ineffectual at others, but it isn't dull. Its frankly grandiose style is transporting in its way, as is the story itself, even in this watered-down form. Opening with self-consciously journalistic footage of a 1975 police raid on the Crossroads settlement, near Cape Town, it quickly introduces Donald Woods to Steve Biko through the intervention of Dr. Ramphele (Josette Simon), a fiery woman closely associated with the banned black leader (Biko's reputation as a ladies' man is the sort of humanizing detail the film badly needs, and refuses to make use of). The two men meet and quickly become friends, although they are almost exclusively seen discussing important political questions, rarely engaging in the give-and-take that would make the friendship seem real.

Among the film's best scenes are those in which Mr. Woods attempts to intervene in his friend's behalf with James Kruger (John Thaw), the minister of police, who plays the cordial host when Mr. Woods visits him at home and then ruthlessly betrays him. Here, and in a scene when police officers try to search Biko's home and he asks them to stay outside and show him their warrant through a window, there is a sense of how mannerliness and brutality play equal roles in South Africa's unique chemistry.

The funeral of Biko has also been stirringly staged, with a huge cast of extras singing a black nationalist anthem. Mr. Washington is particularly good in the courtroom scenes that provide his character with an excellent forum. And the long segment devoted to a scheme by Mr. Woods and his wife, Wendy (Penelope Wilton), to escape the country with the manuscript of Mr. Woods's book about his friend's death, is engrossing in a more ordinary way, though it's much too long. The film's editing is so messy, and its concentration so erratic, that it neglects to mention what becomes of the family's black maid, who will surely be implicated in their getaway, and who is left behind.

"Cry Freedom" can also be admired for Ronnie Taylor's picturesque cinematography, and for a large supporting cast including many African actors (Zakes Mokae turns up as a priest). It can be admired for its sheer scale. Most of all, it can be appreciated for what it tries to communicate about heroism, loyalty and leadership, about the horrors of apartheid, about the martyrdom of a rare man. Although these thoughts don't come through clearly enough, they can still be heard.

•

"Cry Freedom" is rated PG ("Parental Guidance Suggested"). It includes some violent episodes.

1987 N 6, C14:3

The Endless Winter

FIRE AND ICE, directed, produced and photographed by Willy Bogner; edited by Petra Von Oelffen and Claudia Travnecek; music by various composers. At U. A. Eastside Cinema, Third Avenue and 55th Street; Cine 1, 711 Seventh Avenue, between 47th and 48th Streets. Running time: 83 minutes. This film is rated PG.

Suzy .... Suzy Chaffee
John .... John Eaves
Narrator .... John Denver

"FIRE AND ICE" must be the fanciest skiwear commercial ever made. Willy Bogner, who designed the costumes as well as directed, produced and wrote this fashion show, belongs to a prominent West German ski apparel family. He also filmed the ski scenes for a couple of James Bond movies. "Fire and Ice," which opens today at the U. A. Eastside Cinema and Cine 1, runs only 83 minutes, but unless you have a thing for snow, it's endless winter.

The sappy story, narrated by John Denver, follows John (the freestyle world ski champion John Eaves) as he follows Suzy (the United States Olympic ski team member Suzy Chaffee) to Aspen, fantasizing along the way (to headache music you can probably catch on MTV) about the two of them slaloming down the slopes together in their gorgeous garb. This they do skillfully and glitzily — and keep doing and doing, with an occasional break for breakdancing, hang gliding and windsurfing. If "Fire and Ice" were a James Bond movie, somebody would have blown up the spectacular scenery before the credits. Calling Spectre.

•

"Fire and Ice" is rated PG ("Parental Guidance Suggested"), probably because of a glimpse of lovemaking and a few expletives along the way.

WALTER GOODMAN

1987 N 6, C14:6

Down, Up, Down

MADE IN HEAVEN, directed by Alan Rudolph; written by Bruce A. Evans; director of photography, Jan Kiesser; edited by Tom Walls; music by Mark Isham; production designer, Paul Peters; produced by Raynold Gideon, Bruce A. Evans and David Blocker; released by Lorimar Motion Pictures. At Manhattan Twin, 59th Street and Third Avenue; Criterion Center, Broadway and 45th Street; Metro Cinema, Broadway and 99th Street; Art Greenwich Twin, 12th Street and Seventh Avenue. Running time: 102 minutes. This film is rated PG.

Mike Shea/Elmo Barnett .... Timothy Hutton
Annie Packert/Alley Chandler .... Kelly McGillis
Aunt Lisa .... Maureen Stapleton
Annette Shea .... Ann Wedgeworth
Emmett .... Debra Winger
Steve Shea .... James Gammon
Brenda Carlucci .... Mare Winningham
Ben Chandler .... Don Murray
Tom Donnelly .... Timothy Daly
Wiley Foxx .... Amanda Plummer
Truck Driver .... Neil Young
Stanky .... Tom Petty
Shark .... Ric Ocasek
Mario the Toymaker .... Tom Robbins

HEAVEN is the place where movie directors go to test their whimsy, and Alan Rudolph's whimsy doesn't need testing — he's got fancifulness to spare. In "Made in Heaven," which opens today at the Manhattan Twin and other theaters, Mr. Rudolph envisions a sweetly colored alternative to a black-and-white world. Mike (Timothy Hutton) is leaving behind a life of

Looking for Love Timothy Hutton and Kelly McGillis star in ''Made in Heaven'' as lovers who meet in the hereafter but must find each other again on earth.

almost comical bleakness when he dives into a river to save a woman and her children, losing his own dreary life in the process. The film blossoms into pastels when Mike arrives in a place where the décor is inviting, the scenery can be changed at will, and one's full potential can be realized in a wink. Mike's Aunt Lisa, with whom he is happily reunited, has developed into quite a good painter during her stay there.

While in heaven, Mike falls in love with Annie (Kelly McGillis), and dreams his way into a happy eternity spent in her company. But Annie is scheduled to be dispatched to Earth as a baby, and leave Mike behind. So Mike begs Emmett, who has an orange punk haircut and seems an unlikely candidate for man in charge, if he too can become an earthly infant. And Emmett grudgingly agrees (Emmett is in fact Debra Winger, doing a cameo that's quite astounding.) The catch: Annie and Mike have 30 years to rediscover one another in their new incarnations. And if they don't make it, they'll be miserable forever.

''Made in Heaven,'' which has the dreaminess, the heartfelt romanticism and the sense of tangled destinies that have colored many of Mr. Rudolph's other films (among them ''Choose Me,'' ''Trouble in Mind'' and ''Welcome to L.A.''), again confirms the director as one of the American cinema's most fascinating also-rans. Mr. Rudolph has yet to make a film that really goes anywhere, but there's every reason to expect that he eventually will, since his work has so much energy and such a distinctive mood. In the meantime, ''Made in Heaven'' has a disarming gentleness and a light, buoyant charm, not to mention a penchant for surprises. Mr. Rudolph, who seems to love mystery guests, has included the rock musicians Neil Young, Tom Petty and Ric Ocasek and the novelist Tom Robbins, in this film's large cast, along with many others.

The leading roles here are too playful to be played easily, but Mr. Hutton's unusual earnestness takes him far; Miss McGillis seems more rock solid than her character, but she

gives off a suitably angelic glow. Ann Wedgeworth, who has the fragile, fading loveliness of many of Mr. Rudolph's heroines, plays Mike's bereaved mother, and has the film's most deeply felt scene when she discovers him again.

●

''Made in Heaven'' is rated PG (''Parental Guidance Suggested''). It contains a brief sexual interlude.
JANET MASLIN

1987 N 6, C16:1

She's Alive!

HELLO AGAIN, directed by Frank Perry; screenplay by Susan Isaacs; director of photography, Jan Weincke; edited by Peter C. Frank and Trudy Ship; music by William Goldstein; production designer, Edward Pisoni; produced by Mr. Perry; released by Buena Vista Pictures. At Embassy 1, Broadway and 46th Street; Sutton, 57th Street and Third Avenue; 84th Street Sixplex, at Broadway; 23d Street West Triplex, between Eighth and Ninth Avenue; Bay Cinema, Second Avenue and 32d Street. Running time: 96 minutes. This film is rated PG.

Lucy Chadman	Shelley Long
Zelda	Judith Ivey
Kevin Scanlon	Gabriel Byrne
Jason Chadman	Corbin Bernsen
Kim Lacey	Sela Ward
Junior Lacey	Austin Pendleton
Regina Holt	Carrie Nye
Phineas Devereux	Robert Lewis
Felicity	Madeleine Potter
Danny Chadman	Thor Fields

"HELLO AGAIN'' is a high-concept comedy with a terminally low laugh content. This may be why the ads, which publicize the gimmick, are slightly funnier than the movie that must dramatize it.

''Hello Again'' is about a desperately clumsy Long Island housewife (Shelley Long) who dies ''cute,'' choking on a ''South Korean chicken ball.'' One year later, under the auspices of her eccentric sister, an amateur medium, she's brought back from the grave to deal with her stuffy husband (an ambitious plastic surgeon), his new wife (once her best friend) and the notoriety that attends any well-publicized resurrection.

The only startling thing about the movie is that it's the work of Frank Perry and Susan Isaacs, the director-writer team that earlier produced ''Compromising Positions,'' a painlessly funny mystery about the murder of an amorous dentist. Neither partner is in top form here. The dialogue is full of zippy lines such as ''I never thought I'd live to see the day'' and ''I wouldn't be caught dead in that dress.''

Miss Long, a good comedienne, is polite to the dialogue but is upstaged by the camera, which, when she's about to do something klutzy, frequently assumes a position that telegraphs the gag to come. The supporting cast includes Judith Ivey, Corbin Bernsen, Sela Ward, Gabriel Byrne, Austin Pendleton, Carrie Nye and, of all people, Robert Lewis, the theater director (''Teahouse of the August Moon''), actor, producer and teacher. Nobody does especially well.

The film opens today at the Embassy 1 and other theaters.

●

''Hello Again,'' which has been rated PG (''Parental Guidance Suggested''), contains some mildly vulgar language. VINCENT CANBY

1987 N 6, C21:1

Second Chance Shelley Long portrays a suburban housewife brought back to life a year after her death in Frank Perry's ''Hello Again.''

Back to School

HIDING OUT, directed by Bob Giraldi; written by Joe Menosky and Jeff Rothberg; director of photography, Daniel Pearl; edited by Edward Warschilka; music by Anne Dudley; production designer, Dan Leigh; produced by Jeff Rothberg; released by De Laurentiis Entertainment Group. At Criterion Center, Broadway and 45th Street; Eighth Street Playhouse, 52 West Eighth Street; Orpheum Twin, 86th Street near Third Avenue. Running time: 99 minutes. This film is rated PG-13.

Andrew Morenski	Jon Cryer
Patrick Morenski	Keith Coogan
Ryan Campbell	Annabeth Gish
Killer	Oliver Cotton
Clinton	Claude Brooks

IT'S surprising that ''Hiding Out,'' which opens today at the Criterion Center and other theaters, has so little high style, since its director is Bob Giraldi, one of the reigning kings of rock video. Mr. Giraldi, who also directs commercials, takes a fairly ordinary approach to this easygoing teen-age comedy about a stockbroker in his mid-20's who must pretend to be a high-school student. Why? Don't ask, because the screenplay doesn't offer much of an explanation. It only takes a few minutes before Jon Cryer, as the stockbroker, has dyed stripes into his hair, given away his expensive suit, and begun trying to keep up with the teen-age Joneses.

The jokes are mild, revolving around things such as Mr. Cryer's accidentally giving tax advice to the father of a teen-age girl he's dating, or his feeling out of place at the roller rink. But the material is pleasant enough, and Mr. Cryer is a good deal less strained here than he has been in other roles, affecting a natural manner and a good way with wisecracks. He seems a lot more self-possessed than the rest of the cast, which is as it should be, since the screenplay has his new classmates recognizing his leadership abilities and begging him to run for senior-class president. Within a week, he is the most popular student around. We might all do well to start high school at age 27.

The affable supporting cast includes Keith Coogan as Mr. Cryer's amusingly goofy young cousin, and Annabeth Gish as the teen-age beauty who inevitably catches his eye. The

film has a nice coda, after an idiotically climactic shootout in the high-school gym, suggesting that Mr. Cryer could have unexpected charm in more adult roles.

●

''Hiding Out'' is rated PG-13 (''Special Parental Guidance for Those Younger Than 13''). It contains some strong language.
JANET MASLIN

1987 N 6, C21:1

Dazzling Lighting

LESS THAN ZERO, directed by Marek Kanievska; screenplay by Harley Peyton, from the novel ''Less Than Zero'' by Bret Easton Ellis; director of photography, Edward Lachman; edited by Peter E. Berger and Richard Hornung; music by Rick Rubin; production designer, Barbara Ling; produced by Jon Avnet and Jordan Kerner; released by 20th Century-Fox. At Criterion Center, Broadway and 44th Street; Gemini Twin, Second Avenue and 64th Street; 86th Street East, near Second Avenue; Movieland Eighth Street Triplex, at University Place; Olympia 1 and 2, Broadway and 107th Street. Running time: 96 minutes. This film is rated R.

Clay	Andrew McCarthy
Blair	Jami Gertz
Julian	Robert Downey Jr.
Rip	James Spader
Bradford Easton	Tony Bill
Benjamin Wells	Nicholas Pryor
Elaine Easton	Donna Mitchell
Hop	Michael Bowen
Markie	Sarah Buxton
Patti	Lisanne Falk
Robert Wells	Michael Greene

THE smartest thing that the makers of ''Less Than Zero'' have done is the thing that they didn't do: stick very closely to Bret Easton Ellis's novel, no matter how trendy and best-selling that book may have been. For all its shock value, Mr. Ellis's story of bored, jaded, affluent California teens-agers would have been paralyzingly downbeat on screen, if not worse. Indeed, by the time it got to the book's scenes of ultimate depravity — the snuff film watched as casual entertainment, the gang-rape of a 12-year-old girl — a faithful film version would have cleared the house.

So Marek Kanievska, who previously directed ''Another Country,'' has come up with an interesting and largely successful equivalent. On screen, ''Less Than Zero'' is more exotic and less nihilistic, but its otherworldly quality has been preserved and even improved upon. When Clay (Andrew McCarthy) returns from an Eastern college for a Christmas visit to his former haunts, he seems to have arrived on a different planet. The holiday décor includes white trees, seasonal jelly beans, fake icebergs containing video monitors and gilded vegetables; Clay's party-going friends recline on frightening modern furniture and bask in hellish, eerily colored nightclub lighting.

Drugs are everywhere, although Clay avoids them — this is one of the many sanitizing improvements that have been made, along with eliminating the most vacantly promiscuous sexual encounters and turning Clay's bisexuality into lovelorn heterosexual passion. His old flame Blair (Jami Gertz), who in the novel accompanied Clay on an extended, gloomy drinking binge that passed for a kind of honeymoon, has now become a sensate being too. Completing the romantic triangle that the screenwriter, Harley Peyton, has drummed up to create more of a story is the dissipated Julian (Robert Downey Jr.), who is

Clay's best friend and Blair's new beau. Julian's escalating drug problems provide the film with its only real dramatic momentum.

At heart, the film version of "Less Than Zero," which opens today at the Criterion Center and other theaters, is deeply conventional, with its underlying notion that these young people's lives are ruined because their rich parents neglect them. However, Mr. Kanievska gives it a superficial stylishness that is quite spectacular; every scene revolves around one ingeniously bizarre touch or another (the lighting effects are especially dazzling), and the cumulative effect is as striking as it means to be. The persistent unnaturalness of the film's look (only rarely interrupted, though it needn't have been, by a naturally lighted outdoor scene to put the characters back in touch with some kind of reality) winds up being deeply disorienting, and very powerful. In this context, Mr. Kanievska can toss in something as unexpected as sentimental string music and only further amplify the overriding strangeness.

In addition, Mr. Downey gives a performance that is desperately moving, with the kind of emotion that comes as a real surprise in these surroundings. Mr. McCarthy is also good in the early scenes that have him detachedly watching his friends' deterioration, though in later, more urgent moments he shows some strain. James Spader, as a drug dealer, is the embodiment of pure corruption, and in the midst of all this, it's understandable that Miss Gertz looks at sea. Tony Bill is exactly right as Clay's self-involved father, who doesn't seem fully to have noticed that his son has come home.

JANET MASLIN

1987 N 6, C23:1

Masters of a Universe

STEEL DAWN, directed by Lance Hool; written by Doug Lefler; director of photography, George Tirl; edited by Mark Conte; music by Brian May; production designer, Alex Tavoularis; produced by Lance Hool and Conrad Hool; released by Vestron Pictures. At National Twin, Broadway and 44th Street; Coliseum Twin, Broadway and 181st Street; Essex, Essex and Grand Street; Movie Center 5, 125th Street, between Powell and Douglass Boulevards. Running time: 102 minutes. This film is rated R.

Nomad	Patrick Swayze
Kasha	Lisa Niemi
Sho	Christopher Neame
Tark	Brion James
Cord	John Fujioka
Jux	Brett Hool
Damnil	Anthony Zerbe
Lann	Marcel Van Heerden
Makker	Arnold Vosloo

By WALTER GOODMAN

EARLY in "Steel Dawn," a mysterious fighting man (Patrick Swayze) arrives at a hardpressed frontier farm run by a beautiful widow (Lisa Niemi), who has a spunky little son (Brett Hool), who soon grows attached to the stranger. No, the mysterious fighting man's name is not Shane; it is Nomad. And it is not the Old West; it is the new post-nuclear-war world beloved of new movie makers. Meridian is a barren place, but close enough to civilization so hard-working Ms. Niemi can maintain her million-dollar hairdo and her curve-fitted designer wardrobe.

A rich farmer named Damnil (An-

thony Zerbe) is trying to get control of other people's property just like rich ranchers did in the Old West. He believes, correctly, that it contains a source of water, and, as he announces in a British accent, whoever controls the water controls the valley. But the mysterious newcomer outbattles all the henchmen who Damnil sends against him, so Damnil hires the formidable warrior Sho (Christopher Neame), who also has a British accent, and by George, the two bruisers go at it with slashing swords and karate chops and whatever. There are no six-guns, but there is a chariot race and a supply of lightly clad women at the big Damnil place.

"Steel Dawn," now playing at the National Twin and other theaters, has been directed by Lance Hool to emphasize Mr. Swayze's biceps. The movie starts with the mysterious fighter standing on his head. Maybe it looks better that way.

1987 N 6, C33:1

MANON OF THE SPRING, directed by Claude Berri; screenplay (French with English subtitles) by Mr. Berri and Gérard Brach, from the novel "L'Eau des Collines" by Marcel Pagnol; director of photography Bruno Nuytten; edited by Geneviève Louveau and Hervé de Luze; music by Jean-Claude Petit; production designer, Bernard Vezat; produced by Pierre Grunstein; released by Orion Classics. At the Plaza, 58th Street near Madison Avenue. Running time: 113 minutes. This film is rated PG.

César Soubeyran	Yves Montand
Ugolin	Daniel Auteuil
Manon	Emmanuelle Béart
Bernard Oliver	Hippolyte Girardot
Aimée	Elisabeth Depardieu
Victor	Gabriel Bacquier
Baptistine	Margarita Lozano
Belloiseau	Lucien Damiani
Water Specialist	Tiki Olgado
Philoxène	Armand Meffre

By VINCENT CANBY

SEEING "Manon of the Spring" four months after having been thoroughly enchanted by "Jean de Florette" is like

going back to bed in an attempt to continue an interrupted dream. Sleep may come, but the dream is gone.

"Manon of the Spring," which opens today at the Plaza, is the conclusion of Claude Berri's two-part adaptation of Marcel Pagnol's epic novel of Provence, "L'Eau des Collines" ("Water of the Hills"), shot as one film but, because of the nearly four-hour running time, released as two. Now, after the fact, I can say with hindsight's irritating authority that "Jean" and "Manon" only work when seen in immediate succession, in their proper chronological sequence.

Because "Jean de Florette" is still playing at the Lincoln Plaza 3, this can be done with the aid of jogging shoes — the Plaza, on East 58th Street, being a decent intermission's trot from the Lincoln Plaza, on Broadway at 63d Street.

That "Manon of the Spring" makes little narrative sense on its own isn't surprising. The two films are, in fact, a single story of duplicity, greed and fatally crossed purposes, spanning a decade. What is unexpected is how much "Manon" depends on the manner, style and pacing so carefully established by Mr. Berri in "Jean de Florette."

Even when you know the story thus far, you may suffer the bends when you suddenly drop into "Manon of the Spring" after having been away from the rarefied, peasant atmosphere of "Jean de Florette" for even a couple of weeks. Without the overture and what, in effect, are the work's first three acts, which were provided by "Jean," "Manon" plays the way an opera libretto reads in a dim, close-to-the-floor, aisle light.

"Ten years later, Manon, now grown into untamed womanhood, lives in the grotto with Baptistine, the well-keeper, and tends her goats. One day Ugolin, who, with his wealthy

Emmanuelle Béart

uncle, César, had earlier connived to insure Manon's late father's failure as a farmer, chances upon the nubile Manon as she bathes in a mountain pool.

"Ugolin falls hopelessly in love with the maiden as, peering over a rock, he watches her dance uninhibitedly about the pool, accompanying herself on a harmonica. Unknown to him, Manon has given her heart to Bernard, the handsome young schoolteacher, whose knife she found on a hillside. Meanwhile, the childless César urges Ugolin to marry and have children, unaware (along with everyone else in the movie) that Manon is Ugolin's first cousin once-removed."

There's more — much, much more — to this particular libretto, which also involves conversations overheard on barren hillsides (which seem as congested as Times Square), people hiding behind bushes unseen by people who stare straight at them, and letters sent but never received (the old blame-the-postman plot-ploy). When Manon loses her hair ribbon in the vast acreage where her

Jami Gertz, Robert Downey Jr., center, and Andrew McCarthy in "Less Than Zero."

Yves Montand as César and Mr. Auteuil as Ugolin in Claude Berri's "Manon des Sources,"

Sygma

goats roam, it's immediately found by Ugolin, who sews it to the nipple of his left breast.

The events in "Manon of the Spring" are no more wildly melodramatic than those in "Jean de Florette" but, without the indoctrination provided by "Jean," the second film functions as a mean-spirited review of the first. Helping to prompt this reaction is Mr. Berri's frequent use, on the soundtrack, of a soaring theme borrowed from Verdi's "Forza del Destino." The movie is stuffed with cues for arias that are never heard.

The first film succeeds because it works slowly. With the deliberation of a 19th-century novel, "Jean de Florette" establishes its time and place (the mid-1920's in the hills above Marseilles), its peasant characters, their particular sense of community, their codes of honor, the arid feeling of the terrain, and even a sense of the weather, often equated with fate.

"Jean de Florette" has its own rhythm, which is beautifully reflected in the performances of Yves Montand as the wily old César, Daniel Auteuil as the simple-minded Ugolin and, in

particular, Gérard Depardieu, as the humpbacked Jean de Florette, who disappears from the narrative at the end of the first film.

"Manon" picks up the story in midstream. Seen by itself, it has no rhythm. It's a last act, which, without the buildup, is more hysterical than one can easily take. It's too busy dealing with events to have time for character. The performances of Mr. Montand and Mr. Auteuil remain splendid but unsupported. A calculated picturesqueness also shows through, especially in the casting of Emmanuelle Béart as Manon. Miss Béart is an elegant beauty who looks about as much like a goatherd as Catherine Deneuve in a promo for Chanel perfumes.

See "Manon" if you must find out what happens next — as I did. But you will certainly enjoy it more if you take the time to enter its world gradually, by seeing "Jean de Florette" just before. Otherwise, it's a huge anticlimax.

1987 N 6, C25:1

BLIND TRUST, directed by Yves Simoneau; screenplay by Mr. Simoneau and Pierre Curzi; director of photography, Guy Dufaux; edited by André Corriveau; music by Richard Gregoire; produced by Claude Bonin and Roger Frappier; released by Cinema Group Entertainment. At Quad Cinema, 13th Street and Fifth Avenue. Running time: 88 minutes. This film is rated PG.

Roxanne	Marie Tifo
Gildor	Pierre Curzi
Théo	Jacques Godin
Martial	Robert Gravel
Meurseault	Jean-Louis Millette
H. B.	Yvan Ponton
Robin	Eric Brisebois
Janvier	Jacques Lussier

By CARYN JAMES

In the men's room of a small coffee shop, a mannish-looking woman peeks from inside a stall and sees a burly security guard nuzzling a young blond waiter. These three will become central to the action of "Blind Trust," an intelligent thriller by Yves Simoneau, a Canadian director, and the confusions of gender in the men's room give a clue that the story will resonate with tangled relationships and thwarted plans. We enter a mirror world of betrayed trust when an undercover policeman, on Govern-

ment orders, persuades a just-released prisoner to rob an armored truck; the Government officials want some mysterious documents and the robbers will keep the cash. The prisoner, Théo, recruits his teen-age son, already a minor street-criminal, and his former cellmate, who now owns a theatrical scenery company. The cellmate brings in his old girlfriend.

•

Mr. Simoneau blends elements of film noir — a cop named Meurseault, weary of playing both sides of the fence, has a sinister, Peter Lorre glare — with the glitz of a heist caper as the robbers' ensemble relies heavily on disguises, switched cars and careful timing only to have many monkey wrenches thrown into their plan. The undercurrents of personal drama are effective, with Jacques Godin especially strong as Théo, who cannot live with the guilt of luring his son into a plan that goes awry and turns violent. If all the film's elements don't blend together into a glossy, high-concept whole, that's part of the point; in borrowing so freely from various genres, Mr. Simoneau seems intent on bucking the trend toward stylish, one-note thrillers. The film's single major flaw is its "Mission Impossible" type music, which simplistically yells "suspense movie" throughout.

"Blind Trust," which opens today at the Quad Cinema, does not set itself up to be a psychological drama, but its confused characters and thoughtful script by Mr. Simoneau and Pierre Curzi (who was featured in "The Decline of the American Empire" and plays Théo's cellmate here) make this small, entertaining film more than the sum of its borrowed parts.

•

"Blind Trust," which is rated PG ("Parental Guidance Suggested"), contains some violence.

1987 N 7, 13:1

DEATH WISH 4: THE CRACKDOWN, directed by J. Lee Thompson; screenplay by Gail Morgan Hickman; director of photography, Gideon Porath; music by Paul McCallum, Valentine McCallum and John Bisharat; production designer, Whitney Brooke Wheeler; produced by Pancho Kohner; released by the Cannon Group. At the Warner Twin, Broadway and 47th Street; UA East, First Avenue at 85th Street; 23d Street West Triplex, between Eighth and Ninth Avenues; Coliseum Twin, Broadway at 181st Street; Movie Center 5, 125th Street between Powell and Douglass Boulevards, and New Delancey, 62 Delancey Street. Running time: 92 minutes. This film is rated R.

Paul Kersey	Charles Bronson
Karen Sheldon	Kay Lenz
Nathan White	John P. Ryan
Ed Zacharias	Perry Lopez
Detective Reiner	George Dickerson
Detective Nozaki	Soon-Teck Oh
Erica Sheldon	Dana Barron
Randy Viscovich	Jesse Dabson

There is, oddly enough, a philosophical premise to "Death Wish 4." "Anyone connected to drugs deserves to die," says a rich man who wants Charles Bronson to wipe out all the drug lords in Los Angeles. "I need a few days to think about it," Mr. Bronson replies, as if he's a coy job applicant holding out for more money.

In fact, this is the man who avenged the murders of his wife, daughter and assorted friends in the previous "Death Wish" movies, a man who keeps an arsenal of weapons hidden in a closet behind his refrigerator, just in case. His girlfriend's teen-age daughter has just died from an overdose of cocaine, so why does he hesitate at all? Before long Paul Kersey, a k a. the Vigilante, is back in action shooting up the two largest drug rings in the city.

Why Kersey is presented as a hero rather than a sociopath is also something of a mystery, but the film makers' belief in a streetwise death penalty for drug dealers seems intended to give the audience license to settle back and enjoy the killings. The victims, both innocent and guilty, are all cartoon thin, so it's not as if real people are dying. In "Death Wish 4" murder is literally an amusement, with some of the more spectacular killings set in a flashy roller-skating rink and on a bumper-car ride.

Charles Bronson is an almost emblematic figure here, so no one thinks it's at all strange that the feared vigilante is a middle-aged architect known by the blue Toronado he drives. "Death Wish 4," which opened yesterday at the Warner Twin and other theaters, is as efficient and predictable as Kersey himself, and inoffensive as long as you can root for a sociopathic hero.   *CARYN JAMES*

1987 N 7, 14:1

FILM VIEW/Janet Maslin

Facts Don't Always Give the True Story

AS ITS TITLE MAKES CLEAR, and the film itself makes even clearer, "Gaby — A True Story" is about a real woman and her real travails. Gabriela Brimmer was born with cerebral palsy, and without command of any muscles except those in her left foot. That foot became her only means of communication: she could spell out words by pointing her big toe at an alphabet board. Ms. Brimmer, with the help of an extremely devoted nanny, was able to overcome this handicap in a very big way. She demanded to go to regular schools, attended the University of Mexico, adopted a child, and became the subject of a best-selling book in her native country. Now she's a film heroine as well.

But she's not the sort of heroine whom viewers can watch with the same equanimity they might bring to a purely fictional creation. Watching her (as played by Rachel Levin) is unsettling, not because of her disability but because of her palpable presence both on and behind the screen. Miss Brimmer supplied the film with a dedication and a few lines of narration, and worked with the director Luis Mandoki in telling her story. Whether or not she was physically present while the film was being made, she must have been a powerfully influential figure in

When a real person is the source or model for a film, a certain degree of distortion is inevitable.

the minds of Mr. Mandoki and all of his co-workers. And her impact, deliberate or otherwise, guarantees "Gaby — A True Story" a narrower range and more reverential style than a film less committed to so-called truthfulness might have had.

When a real person is the source or model for a film, a certain degree of distortion is inevitably created. It becomes impossible to ignore the self-image and sensitivities of this real person, and we begin making allowances accordingly. We may, as in "La Bamba," sense instinctively that the dead rock star's family members are being more gently treated than other characters in his story, perhaps because they spent time with the director or controlled rights to the material. Or it may be that the living subject of a biographical film (as in "Chuck Berry Hail! Hail! Rock 'n' Roll!") exerts an obvious control over what information finds its way into the finished product. It may simply be a matter of soft-pedaling unpleasant realities so as not to hurt anyone's feelings. Whatever the reason, films revolving around real individuals draw a distinction between what is authentic — technically faithful to the facts — and what is true.

The best of these films, even when they take liberties with facts, use real personalities to create a larger, more colorful reality than their source material may have had. On the other hand, when films are reverential about their models and slavish about their facts, they have a way of losing track of a larger truthfulness. Has this particular scene been included in the film because it's an essential part of the story? Or is it there simply because it happened to someone and that person would like it recorded for posterity? Like a lot of contemporary fiction, films made in the shadow of their real-life inspirations often have trouble distinguishing important information from simple memorabilia.

The audience's willingness to accept certain facts about real-life characters usually has more to do with a film's overall persuasiveness than with the facts themselves. The magnificent tawdriness of "Barfly" seems entirely honest, even though an earlier film about the poet Charles Bukowski, "Tales of Ordinary Madness," took similar material and made it ridiculous; what works here is the power of the acting and direction as much as the facts themselves. But an audience may watch the somewhat clumsier "Weeds" and wonder why it should believe that a suicidal convict could become a successful playwright and director, even if that did happen to the film's real-life model.

"Cry Freedom," Sir Richard Attenborough's new film about the South African anti-apartheid leader Stephen Biko and the white newspaper editor Donald Woods, keeps its real-life models very much on the audience's mind. That is as it should be, since Sir Richard obviously intends the film to have a reportorial quality, but it also happens in less welcome ways. The portrait of the martyred Mr. Biko (played stirringly by Denzel Washington) is both wholehearted and skimpy, without even the ordinary modicum of biographical touches. Beyond political rhetoric, which characterizes his conversation even in private, the Biko character says little, and he disappears fairly early in the film.

Pervading the rest of "Cry Freedom" is the question of why Mr. Woods's character has been made so much the more prominent of the two. We wind up knowing a lot more about Mr. Woods — about his family, about the David Bowie posters in his home and in his office — than we do about a revered South African leader, and it's impossible not to wonder why. Since Mr. Woods seems a much more self-effacing figure in his own book, "Biko," the film's priorities are even more puzzling. And Mr. Attenborough's talk-show comments about not wanting to preach to the converted, and about giving the story a positive quality by concentrating on a living figure rather than a murdered one, don't cast any more light.

"Cry Freedom" raises the persistent questions that haunt film making overshadowed by fact: how have the film makers been influenced by their real-life models? Would this same material make sense on the screen if it weren't true? And in this watered-down version, can it be considered true, anyway? The more direct approach taken by television movies is positively refreshing by comparison: an actress who's had a terrible illness plays herself in her own story, and the awkward presence of the real-life figure is exploited without shame. That's that. But for feature films, especially films about subjects this important, it's rarely that simple. □

1987 N 8, II:25:1

Sex and Death

SIESTA, directed by Mary Lambert; screenplay by Patricia Louisianna Knop, based on a novel by Patrice Chaplin; director of photography, Bryan Loftus; edited by Glenn A. Morgan; music by Marcus Miller; production designer, John Beard; produced by Gary Kurfirst; released by Lorimar Motion Pictures. At Embassy 72d Street at Broadway. Running time 97 minutes. This film is rated R.

Claire	Ellen Barkin
Augustine	Gabriel Byrne
Kit	Julian Sands
Marie	Isabella Rossellini
Del	Martin Sheen
Cabbie	Alexi Sayle
Conchita	Grace Jones
Nancy	Jodie Foster
Desdra	Anastassia Stakis
Roger	Gary Cady

By JANET MASLIN

"SIESTA" is the kind of excitingly bad, artily experimental film that has become an endangered species, and as such it can be greeted with more warmth than would otherwise be warranted. Bad? Arty? Here is how "Siesta" begins: with the image of Claire (Ellen Barkin) in a skimpy red dress lying motionless in a field of dead grass. The dead grass proves to be next to an airport runway because a plane passes almost directly above her. With this, Claire breathes a deep, heaving breath and springs to life.

She yanks up the red dress to examine her bruised, mud-caked body (and allow the camera one of many opportunities to do likewise). Then she runs away, pulls off the dress entirely, and washes away its mysterious bloodstains in a muddy river. She lies down to sunbathe. Vultures circle overhead.

Claire finds a taxi with tiger-skin upholstery and a lipstick in the back seat. We learn she is in Spain. There is a lecherous, male driver with metallic teeth. We learn that Claire thinks she may have killed somebody on the Fourth of July. And with that, the film begins to weave back and forth in time, encompassing several days before the crime and the period immediately after it. It examines Claire's resumed romance with an old flame (played by Gabriel Byrne), her career as a daredevil skydiver and the final stunt that sends her fleeing her husband and manager, Del (played jauntily by Martin Sheen, whose telephone answering machine has a recording that says he and Claire "aren't here right now — and if you don't know where we are, we should fire our publicist!").

•

"Siesta," which opens today at the Embassy 72d Street theater, was directed by Mary Lambert, who was previously best known for directing television commercials and Madonna videos; she will still be best known for these things after "Siesta" is gone. Still, Miss Lambert's first feature has a game, mischievous spirit and a ripe bohemianism that are appealing. This film, which addresses itself passionately to thoughts about sex and death, turns out to be both obvious and muddy simultaneously (no

mean accomplishment), but it also has enough colorful exoticism to do any perfume commercial proud. In its glossy, solemn and numbingly pretentious way, it's got high style.

Actors fare surprisingly well under such circumstances, almost as well as the stark Spanish scenery. Miss Barkin looks exquisitely ravaged and proves over and over again that she is in excellent physical condition. (She actually tightrope-walks in one scene, since her lover is a tightrope trainer.) Julian Sands and Jodie Foster are a charming surprise as two jaded British travelers who briefly join forces with Claire; Miss Foster does devilishly well with the mannerisms and speech of a petulant post-deb, while Mr. Sands makes a marvelously raffish playboy-artiste ("Ah, dog that I am!" he sighs delightedly at a compliment from a female companion.) Isabella Rossellini has less to do and Grace Jones has nothing to do in lesser roles, but they contribute to the film's nonchalant glamour. So does Miles Davis, who performs the haunting score.

1987 N 11, C23:3

Full Moon

HOWLING III, directed by Philippe Mora; screenplay by Mr. Mora, based on a novel by Gary Brandner; director of photography, Lou Irving; edited by Lee Smith; music by Allan Zavod; production designer, Ross Major; produced by Charles Waterstreet and Mr. Mora; released by Square Pictures. At Cine Twin, Seventh Avenue near 47th Street; Essex, at Essex and Grand Streets, and other theaters. Running time: 94 minutes. This film is rated PG-13.

Beckmeyer	Barry Otto
Jerboa	Imogen Annesley
Donny	Leigh Biolos
Thylos	Max Fairchild
Olga	Dasha Blahova
United States President	Michael Pate
Sharp	Ralph Cotterill
Kendi	Burnham Burnham
Spud	Alan Penney
Yara	Carol Skinner
Goolah	Jenny Vuletic

IF you see only one werewolf movie this year, you might as well make it "Howling III," Philippe Mora's not-altogether straight-faced howler on behalf of lycanthropes' liberation. Among other things, the Australian-made movie suggests there's nothing inherently evil about being a werewolf that a little human understanding wouldn't cure. Mr. Mora and his associates are blunt about it: this anti-werewolf hysteria must stop.

In the meantime, they're free to exploit it with a good deal of earnest levity. "Howling III" involves a tribe of indigenously Australian (marsupial) lycanthropes, a defecting Russian ballerina named Olga, who is herself a werewolf, and Beckmeyer, a hardworking, civil libertarian Australian professor, who has espoused the werewolf cause.

Other characters include Jerboa, a pretty young woman who runs away from her werewolf family and goes to Sydney, where she quickly lands a small part in a horror film; Donny, the film's assistant director, who falls

in love with her, and the President of the United States, who sounds as if he'd been born and bred in Australia but is *not* a werewolf.

•

Mr. Mora's story isn't as important as some of its individual scenes, especially one in which Jerboa gives birth, on camera, to Donny's child, who slips quite naturally into his mother's pouch. Though the werewolf baby, constructed by the special effects department, looks like a bald otter, Donny says happily, "It's great!" There's also a spiffy scene in which Olga, rehearsing on stage at the Sydney Opera House, starts to change into a werewolf in mid-dance.

The movie, which opens today at the Cine Twin and other theaters, squarely faces the fact that not all werewolves are benign. When cornered, they're inclined to overreact, sometimes violently. Otherwise they're just folks, and when "Howling III" isn't dealing in werewolf jokes, it comes very close to being a werewolf idyll.

•

"Howling III," which has been rated PG-13 ("Special Parental Guidance Suggested for Those Younger Than 13"), contains some bloody violence as well as the above-cited scene of werewolf-birth.

VINCENT CANBY

1987 N 13, C5:1

Arnold Schwarzenegger

Next Contestant . . .

THE RUNNING MAN, directed by Paul Michael Glaser; screenplay by Steven E. de Souza, based on a novel by Richard Bachman (Stephen King); director of photography, Thomas Del Ruth; edited by Mark Roy Warner, Edward A. Warschilka and John Wright; music by Harold Faltermeyer; production designer, Jack T. Collis; produced by Tim Zinnemann and George Linder; released by Tri-Star Pictures. At Embassy 2 and 3, Broadway and 47th Street; Loews 34th Street Showplace, between Second and Third Avenue; Loews 84th Street, at Broadway, and other theaters. Running time: 100 minutes. This film is rated R.

Ben Richards	Arnold Schwarzenegger
Amber Mendez	Maria Conchita Alonso
Laughlin	Yaphet Kotto
Damon Killian	Richard Dawson
Fireball	Jim Brown
Captain Freedom	Jesse Ventura
Dynamo	Erland Van Lidth
Weiss	Marvin J. McIntyre
Buzzsaw	Gus Rethwisch
Subzero	Prof. Toru Tanaka
Mic	Mick Fleetwood

By VINCENT CANBY

THE year is 2019. In the fascist state that America has become, Ben Richards (Arnold Schwarzenegger) is a helicopter pilot with the Federal police. One night, while on a routine patrol, he's ordered to terminate a food riot in Bakersfield, Calif. Some 1,500 unarmed women and children are running amok in search of nourishment.

When Ben refuses to obey, someone else takes command of the craft and does the job. The state puts the blame on Ben, who becomes known as "the infamous butcher of Bakersfield," and packs him off to prison.

All this (and even more) happens during the opening credits of "The Running Man," which has the manners and the gadgetry of a sci-fi adventure film but is, at heart, an engagingly mean, cruel, nasty, funny send-up of television. It's not quite "Network," but then it also doesn't take itself too seriously.

•

The title, "The Running Man," is the name of a hugely popular television program within the film. This is the ultimate game show by which the state-run television network keeps citizens docile and glued to their sets. Each week the Los Angeles-based presentation picks a notorious prisoner to be "it" in a game of hide-and-seek, during which the prisoner is hunted to the death by professional "stalkers."

Steven E. de Souza ("48 Hours") adapted the screenplay from a novel by Richard Bachman, the pseudonym of Stephen King. Whatever the screenplay's literary provenance, the film most vividly recalls the various movie adaptation of Richard Connell's story "The Most Dangerous Game" and Norman Jewison's ponderous sci-fi nightmare, "Rollerball."

"The Running Man," which opens today at the Embassy 2 and other theaters, is a good deal more fun, in a ghoulish sort of way.

The game itself, played out in a section of Los Angeles devastated by "the great quake of '97," features Mr. Schwarzenegger, Maria Conchita Alonso, Yaphet Kotto and Marvin J. McIntyre, as they face a series of larger-than-life stalkers equipped with flame throwers, electric saws and razor-edged hockey sticks. The stunts, special effects and timely escapes are flashily directed by Paul Michael Glaser, though fairly standard stuff.

•

The chief contribution of Mr. Glaser (once the Starsky of "Starsky and Hutch") and Mr. de Souza is their raffish, backstage vision of television in 2017, which is not much different, of course, from 1987. It all comes together in the person of Damon Killian (Richard Dawson), the viciously cheery, lady-kissing, ratings-obsessed emcee of the television show.

Mr. Dawson, who was the host of television's long-running "Family Feud" game show, is wonderfully comic as a fellow who'd star his own beloved dad as the "running man" if it would buy him a few points. His hair always perfectly blow-dried, his haberdashery immaculate, Mr. Dawson steals the movie as a personality composed of equal parts of Phil Donahue, Merv Griffin and Maximilien François Marie Isidore (Mickey) Robespierre.

He has a mean mouth but he smiles a lot and can think on his feet. When one of the musclemen on his staff doesn't respond fast enough to his orders, he sneers, "What's wrong, steroids made you deaf?" In the course of the show in which "the butcher of Bakersfield" is turning stalkers into mincemeat, he hastily adds the innocent Miss Alonso to the cast of runners. Her crime: She cheated on her college exams and had sexual relations with three different men in one year.

•

Mr. Dawson is given the film's best lines, but Mr. Schwarzenegger goes through the movie with disarming dauntlessness. In the fight scenes there is, as is usual in all Schwarzenegger vehicles, a heavy emphasis placed on the vulnerability of male genitalia. One guy here is sliced up the middle by the buzz saw, which doesn't easily fit with the good clean fun of the movie's satire.

The film tries to have it both ways, not always successfully. Like many such sci-fi movies, it's also loaded with tantalizingly subversive reflections on the state of contemporary society. It's the supposition of "The Running Man" that we could advance from this era of blissful, Government-approved deregulation to a police state within the professional lifetime of one Johnny Carson. You could almost say that "The Running Man" makes you stop and think.

1987 N 13, C10:5

Investigation of Art

HYPOTHESIS OF A STOLEN PAINTING, directed by Raoul Ruiz; screenplay (French with English subtitles) by Mr. Ruiz, from an idea of Pierre Klossowski; director of photography, Sacha Vierny; edited by Patrice Royer; music by Jorge Arriagada; released by Coralie Films International. Running time: 70 minutes.
The Collector .... Jean Rougeul
Visitor's voice .... Gabriel Gascon
and
DOG'S DIALOGUE, directed by Mr. Ruiz.
At the Bleecker Street Cinema, 144 Bleecker Street.

IN connection with the French Film Institute's retrospective devoted to the work of Raoul Ruiz, the Chilean-born fabulist, the Bleecker Street Cinema today presents the American premieres of "Hypothesis of the Stolen Painting," a 1978 feature, and the short, "Dog's Dialogue" (1977), both made in France, where the filmmaker now lives.

"Hypothesis," said to be inspired by the work of Pierre Klossowski, the French author, is a meditation on the meaning of art through an examination of the possible things that art leaves unsaid. It's a last, exhausted gasp on behalf of interpretation. Examined long and closely enough, any work of art, or even any Coca-Cola bottle, can be interpreted as meaning just about anything.

In "Hypothesis," an art collector attempts to reconstruct the content of a painting missing from a series of seven painted in 1889 by an artist named Frederic Tonnerre (a fictitious character borrowed, apparently, from Klossowski). With the help of a cast of actors, who reconstruct the paintings in a series of not especially memorable tableaux vivants, the collector must first make connections among the paintings that exist in order to establish the connections that are missing.

As he goes about his musings, the collector appears to uncover some of the reasons for what we are told was the great scandal caused by the paintings when shown in their own day. There are references to the Knights Templar, to strange rituals and to unspeakable perversions. The movie isn't private. If anything, its observations about art and life are too general. They have the oracular vagueness of Chinese fortune cookies. At least one viewer's mind wandered away from the film long before Mr. Ruiz had ended it.

A good deal more penetrable is the 18-minute "Dog's Dialogue," a funny, deadpan recollection of the lurid life and violent death of an unfortunate prostitute named Monique, recollected in still pictures and moving images, along with soundtrack narration that evokes tabloid journalism. Mr. Ruiz is reported to have been inspired by Latin American "photonovels."
                                VINCENT CANBY

1987 N 13, C15:1

Under the Microscope

CROSS MY HEART, directed by Armyan Bernstein, written by Mr. Bernstein and Gail Parent; director of photography, Thomas Del Ruth; edited by Mia Goldman; music by Bruce Broughton; production designer, Lawrence G. Paull; produced by Lawrence Kasdan; released by Universal Pictures. At Movieland, Broadway and 47th Street; Manhattan Twin, 59th Street near Third Avenue; 86th Street East, between Second and Third Avenues; 23d Street West Triplex, between Eighth and Ninth Avenues; Columbia Cinema, Broadway and 103d Street. Running time: 100 minutes. This film is rated R.

David .... Martin Short
Kathy .... Annette O'Toole
Bruce .... Paul Reiser
Nancy .... Joanna Kerns
Jessica .... Jessica Puscas
Parking attendant .... Lee Arenberg
Susan .... Corrine Bohrer
Waiter .... Jason Stuart
Woman outside restaurant .... Lori Hail
Stud .... Michael D. Simms

By JANET MASLIN

IF a date were a thing that could be examined under a microscope, then "Cross My Heart" offers some idea of what it might look like, warts and all. The entire film concentrates on the all-important third encounter between David (Martin Short) and Kathy (Annette O'Toole), an event that the film deems critical for several reasons. David and Kathy, who are thirty-ish, liked each other a lot on their first two dates. Each of them is very eager, and very nervous. Each has a few key biographical facts he or she would rather keep under wraps. And the third date, by this film's reckoning, is the one on which it's obligatory to go to bed.

So "Cross My Heart," which opens today at the Manhattan Twin and other theaters, has a good-natured premise and a degree of novelty, thanks to a pace that presents the date in something approximating real time. The entire evening unfolds in its every detail. The two participants are seen deciding what to wear, and discussing their trepidations with their respective seconds (Paul Reiser, who was so funny as the cautious, nit-picking member of the "Diner" crowd, and Joanna Kerns); later on, the film follows everything from what they order for dinner to the elaborate bargaining process that precedes their sexual encounter.

As directed and co-written (with Gail Parent) by Armyan Bernstein, "Cross My Heart" aspires to both comedy and candor. It finds the former in amusing intercutting between David and Kathy (especially in the extended prologue), and in juxtaposing things like Kathy's desire for a stable breadwinner with the fact that David has just been dismissed that very morning. And funny things do happen, as when David borrows his friend's apartment and then has to worry about what's in it, or when he hands his friend's car keys over to a total stranger, who he mistakenly thinks has something to do with valet parking. But later on, when the small talk reaches the AIDS-and-condoms level and the new lovers argue ad nauseam about commitment, the film bogs down. "Cross My Heart" starts well and then grows more and more ordinary, largely because it has been designed as a feature-length film in the first place. This material, however promising, would be better suited to an extended skit.

It's also true that the film's insistence on frankness eventually brings it a nagging, droning quality all too reminiscent of real-life evenings that go on too long. Fortunately, Martin Short makes a delightful leading man even when there's little for him to do. Mr. Short is equally at home with the screenplay's jokey and realistic aspects, and for a comic actor he's unusually comfortable with a romantic role. Miss O'Toole is less funny, as

Martin Short

is her role; Kathy turns out to be a woman with a past (and a small daughter to prove it), and a penchant for reading magazine pop-psychology quizzes out loud. Miss O'Toole more or less plays straight man, but she has both the voluptuousness and the air of worry that her role requires.

1987 N 13, C21:1

FILM VIEW/Vincent Canby

The Trouble With 'Freedom'

BEFORE HE WENT TO SOUTH AFRICA IN 1983 to see for himself what life under apartheid was like, Sir Richard Attenborough was a self-described "well-intentioned liberal," the sort who protests by not buying South African oranges. His heart was in the right place.

A somewhat more activist Attenborough is now on view in his new film, "Cry Freedom," a movie whose heart is also in the right place but that raises questions about some of the methods and, more important, the effectiveness of such earnest, socially committed film literature.

"Cry Freedom" is a peculiarly schizoid narrative devoted far less to the life of Stephen Biko, the angry South African black nationalist leader, died violently in police custody in 1977, than to that of Donald Woods, the white South African editor who became Biko's friend, championed his cause, helped publicize his death and, as a result, was officially "banned" by the Government. The film's source material is Mr. Woods's biography, "Biko," published in 1978, just after Mr. Woods escaped with his family to London from South Africa, and "Asking for Trouble," the editor's autobiography, published in 1980.

The production notes for "Cry Freedom" report that in 1983, Mr. Woods, "with many misgivings but at the urging of a mutual friend," had sent off copies of his two books to Sir Richard in the hope that he would make a movie of them. Sir Richard did, yet "Cry Freedom," the result, is not the first time the Woods story has been dramatized, with or without misgivings.

"Banned," a BBC teleplay starring Mark Kingston and Janet Suzman as Mr. Woods and his wife, Wendy, was shown here in July 1985 on the Arts & Entertainment cable network. The program, presented as part of the BBC's "Escape" series, is about the experiences of the Woods family, their persecution by the South African Government and their eventual break for freedom. This is pretty much what "Cry Freedom" boils down to, supplemented by extensive, sometimes physically impressive footnotes describing the brutality of the South African regime and you-are-there snippets of Biko's life and death.

Though the story would seem to contain the material for a truly rousing epic, "Cry Freedom" comes on so clumsily (and, at times, with such a casual, opportunistic disregard for facts and chronology) that it may alienate more audiences than it converts. On second thought, however, "Cry Freedom" may represent a calculated risk on Sir Richard's part.

Attenborough's simplification of history robs Stephen Biko's story of its power.

It could be that it will mostly alienate those members of the audience who know the facts and already share the film maker's anger with an intolerable situation. It's Sir Richard's odd achievement to have made an anti-apartheid movie that not only does *not* preach to the converted, but also angers them.

Sir Richard isn't an especially subtle movie director, but subtlety has been beside the point of his best films to date. "A Bridge Too Far" (1976) is a vivid, effective, all-star reenactment of the events that surrounded one of the costliest Allied disasters of World War II. The Oscar-winning "Gandhi" (1982) dramatizes the life of the remarkable Mahatma in big, broad, moving terms that capture the sense of the public figure, while carefully avoiding the potentially off-putting, private idiosyncrasies.

These movies are as simple and forthright as recruiting posters. "Cry Freedom" is neither simple nor forthright. Throughout the film, one has the feeling that Sir Richard and John Briley, the writer (who also did the "Gandhi" screenplay), are trying desperately to make a movie that keeps eluding them.

Under ideal circumstances they would possibly have made a movie about Stephen Biko's short life and abrupt death (he was 30 when he died), dramatizing, firsthand, what Biko described as the black heritage of humiliation under apartheid in South Africa. This seems to have been impossible for several reasons. Not a great deal is known about Biko's life and, though he preached a form of activism that was acceptable to white liberals, he wasn't yet a public figure outside South Africa.

Then, too, Sir Richard and his associates were making a movie designed to touch *white* audiences. What better way, they reasoned, than by showing the evils of apartheid through the eyes of a white South African, a former supporter of the regime, who himself is radicalized by the words and example of his new friend, Stephen Biko?

That sounds better than it plays in Mr. Briley's screenplay. Mr. Biko is presented in such saintly terms (he's first seen in the film bathed in the sort of aureole once reserved for Jesus) that he never seems quite real.

Though played with a good deal of force and charm by Denzel Washington, Biko never is anything more than an idealized mouthpiece. Even the circumstances of his death are given less time and emotional import than the domestic crises faced by the Woods family. As real and dangerous as these crises are, they have the effect of making the film's treatment of Biko look patronizing. It's a dramatic convenience, an excuse for the terrible decisions that must be faced by Donald and Wendy Woods and their children, who flee South Africa with only the clothes they have on their backs.

There's not much else to be said for an anti-apartheid movie that reaches its climax in an extended "escape" sequence out of second-rate adventure-melodrama. Will Donald Woods (Kevin Kline), disguised as a priest, get safely across that bridge, marking the border between South Africa and Lesotho, without being defrocked? Will Wendy Woods (Penelope Wilton) and the kids be able to meet him in Lesotho and fly to London?

Though Sir Richard obviously intends that we should have our hearts in our mouths at this point, a number of people with whom I saw the film were more worried about the fate of the black servant the Woods family had left behind in South Africa to face the police. What happened to her is never mentioned, though the movie concludes with an honor roll of the names of all black South African political prisoners who've died in prison in the last 25 years from various "natural" or "accidental" causes.

Like "Gandhi," "Cry Freedom" has some big spectacle scenes involving thousands of extras, but these are used more or less like production numbers in an extravagant if arthritic musical. The film opens with an impressive reenactment of the furious Government raid on the black Crossroads settlement in 1975. Stephen Biko's huge public funeral also commands attention because of the logistics involved in filming so many people. A reenactment of the rioting in Soweto, which began in June 1976 and set off a year of unrest in which 600 blacks were killed, is compressed into a single day's event, then tacked onto the end of the movie in a way to suggest that the disturbances were prompted by Biko's death in 1977.

In fact, the South African Government used black as well as white policemen to suppress the Soweto riots, though only white police are seen in the movie. Sir Richard apparently didn't want to confuse audiences and, possibly, he didn't want to offend Zimbabwe, where most of the movie was shot and whose Government put up $4 million of the film's $21 million budget. This "simplification" of history also robs the movie of a demonstration of the kind of profound humiliation Stephen Biko was fighting against — the system under which blacks can be co-opted by the white power structure to kill blacks.

When Sir Richard withholds or overlooks historical fact in "Gandhi," it has the effect of clarifying the complicated narrative without damaging it. In "Cry Freedom," the result is sometimes utter confusion.

Though the film makes much of Donald Woods's campaign to publicize Biko's death in the hands of the police, the result of that campaign is recalled by the movie only as a sort of afterthought. It comes as a flashback to the Biko inquest, which has been inserted into the escape sequence near the movie's end, prompted, it seems, by nothing more than the film maker's desperation.

Sir Richard has said that his purpose in making "Cry Freedom" was to move audiences to such a pitch that, at the end, they'll stand up and say, "This is intolerable."

Some people may actually do that. Others cannot be faulted for saying that the movie just isn't good enough.

□

1987 N 15, II:25:5

Dites-Moi Pourquoi

LA VIE EST BELLE, directed by Benoît Lamy and Ngangura Mweze; written (French with English subtitles) by Mr. Mweze, Maryse Léon and Mr. Lamy; director of photography, Michel Baudour; edited by Martine Giordano; music by Papa Wemba, Tshala Muana, Zaiko Langa Langa and Klody; produced by Mr. Lamy and Vera Belmont; released by Lamy Films. At Film Forum 1, 57 Watts Street. Running time: 85 minutes.

Kourou	Papa Wemba
Kabibi	Bibi Krubwa
Mamou	Landu Nzunzimbu
Nvouandou	Kanku Kasongo
Nzazi	Lokinda Mengi Feza
Mongali	Kalimazi (Riva) Lombume
Mama Dingari	Mazaza Mukoko
Cherie Bondowe	Mujinga Mbuji Inabanza
Nganga, the Lawyer	Bwanando Ngimbi
Emoro, the Dwarf	Tumba (Emoro) Ayila
Grandpa Kalle	Pépé Kalle
Nvouandou's Chauffeur	Alamba Engongo

By JANET MASLIN

"LA VIE EST BELLE" is a genial musical comedy film from Zaire, and there are two striking things about it: how very African it is, and how very African it is not.

In the former category, there is a plot about a rich man who visits a witch doctor to cure his impotency problems, and about the annoyance of his wife (Landu Nzunzimbu) when he marries a second woman who is much more beautiful than she. There is also the presence of Papa Wemba, a celebrated singing star in his native land, and the vibrantly colored native fabrics that the film's leading actresses wear. Their hairdos are astonishing as well, and vary greatly from scene to scene.

Less indigenously African is the sight of the rich man, Nvouandou (Kanku Kasongo), tooling through the streets of Kinshasa, Zaire's capital, in his showy Mercedes, or the décor of Nvouandou's lavish home, which looks a lot like a run-down, 50's-modern American motel.

"La Vie Est Belle," which was co-directed by a Zairian (Ngangura Mweze) and a Belgian (Benoît Lamy), takes an easy and humorous look at these seeming contrasts, and also presents the affable personality of Mr. Wemba, who if not superstellar is certainly a pleasant, unaffected actor and a disarming musician.

Mr. Wemba plays a ragged, humble rural fellow who dreams of becoming a singing star, and who catches the eye of Kabibi (Krubwa Bibi), a poor girl who happens to be a ravishing beauty. If you didn't know Mr. Wemba was the singing sensation of Zaire you might wonder what Kabibi sees in Kourou, the character he plays, since she is also being relentlessly pursued by Nvouandou. Credibility, however, counts for very little in a film mostly given over to street singing, mild comedy and local atmosphere.

With its sizable cast of supporting characters (including a smiling dwarf who peddles kebabs at the market and always seems to be singing the title song), "La Vie Est Belle" offers a good look at Zaire's nightlife. The film, which opens today at Film Forum 1, has a lot more technical polish than its plot suggests, and it has been handsomely photographed by Michel Baudour, with bright, flat tones that suit the sunny scenery.

1987 N 18, C21:1

Organizational Task

THE WANNSEE CONFERENCE, directed by Heinz Schirk; screenplay (German with English subtitles) by Paul Mommertz; director of photography, Horst Schier; edited by Ursula Mollinger; production designer, Robert Hofer-Ach and Barbara Siebner; a co-production of Infafilm GmbH Munich, Manfred Koryowski and Australian Television — O. R. F. and the Bavarian Broadcasting Corporation; released by Rearguard Pictures. At the Festival, 57th Street and Fifth Avenue. Running time: 85 minutes.

Hofmann	Robert Artzhorn
Muller	Friedrich Beckhaus
Eichmann	Gerd Bockmann
Leibbrandt	Jochen Busse
Luther	Hans W. Bussinger
Meyer	Harald Dietl
Stuckart	Peter Fitz
Buhler	Reinhard Glemnitz
Neumann	Dieter Groest

By VINCENT CANBY

HISTORIANS of the Holocaust appear to fall into one of two schools of thought these days. The more traditional "intentionalists" see a direct connection between Hitler's ideology, expressed in his anti-Semitic speeches of the 1920's as well as in "Mein Kampf," and the eventual implementation of the "final solution" during World War II.

The newer, revisionist, so-called functionalists believe that Nazi bureaucrats more or less stumbled onto the "final solution" as anti-Semitic policies intensified and that, in fact, the systematic murder of European Jews was initially the result of practical considerations rather than of consistent ideology.

Whatever the school of thought, all historians would seem to agree that a key date in what became the ultimate horror was Jan. 20, 1942, when Reinhard Heydrich, chief of the Nazi Security Police and Secret Service, convened a conference in the upper-class Berlin suburb of Wannsee. There, in a handsome, lake-side villa, Heydrich presided over an 85-minute meeting of 14 key representatives of the SS, the Nazi Party and Government bureaus. The purpose was twofold: to win support for what Heydrich described as "an organizational task unparalleled in history," that is, the extermination of 11 million Jews, and to share responsibility so broadly that, in effect, responsibility disappears.

Using the secretary's notes from this meeting, along with letters written by Hermann Goering and Adolf Eichmann (a meeting participant), and testimony by Eichmann at his 1961 trial in Israel, the director Heinz Schirk and the writer Paul Mommertz have reconstructed the Wannsee conference in a short (85-minute) feature that's unlike any other Holocaust film I've ever seen.

"The Wannsee Conference," which opens today at the Festival Theater, is mesmerizing for seeming to be so commonplace. It has the slightly unreal, breathless pacing of a Broadway comedy about a convention of soft-drink bottlers considering new distribution procedures. Once the setting and principal characters are established, the camera stays mostly in the conference room.

The meeting, dominated by the charm and efficiency of Heydrich (Dietrich Mattausch), is easy, generally light-hearted, though some participants are clearly bored. One man, Rudolf Lange (Martin Luttge), the commander of the Gestapo in Latvia (who has already earned his credentials by liquidating 100,000 Jews at Riga), drinks too much brandy and falls asleep. There are jokes and sardonic asides that produce laughter, sometimes more than a little forced. At one point, Eichmann (Gerd Bockmann) admits that he vomited after witnessing the gassing of a truck-load of Polish Jews. Heydrich defends him: "When we faint, we prove that we are human," but duty is duty. Heydrich flirts with the stenographer taking the minutes,

Dark Times Jochen Busse, Dietrich Mattausch and Hans W. Bussinger appear in "The Wannsee Conference," Heinz Schirk's dramatization of the Third Reich's meeting at which the decision was made to legalize the killing of Jews.

and offers her a job on his staff. Another man expresses polite distaste for the entire scheme. Word will leak out, he says. He already feels like a pariah and would prefer to fight at the front.

Heydrich points out that the matters at hand are part of the same war, and equally important. Charts are brought out showing how many Jews remain in each occupied country. They are the meeting's "production goals." Someone — the sort of fellow who prompts groans at such meetings for being tiresome about small details — raises the question of the Nuremberg Laws and their definition of "Jewishness."

•

Heydrich and Eichmann are firm. From now on there will be no more splitting of hairs. Anybody with any Jewish blood is a Jew. It simplifies the bookkeeping. There are sighs of relief. Heydrich is called to the telephone. Snacks are served, along with more brandy. Anecdotes are told. The meeting continues to its conclusion with far less trouble than Heydrich anticipated. He's buoyant at the end.

Mr. Schirk has directed Mr. Mommertz's packed screenplay with immense self-assurance and authority. His camera is not a passive observer. It roams the room with a will of its own. It pans from one speaker to the next, moves into a close-up, or cuts to a reaction shot with ever-increasing assertiveness. Though the manners and camaraderie of the participants are quite ordinary, the camera is not. Its movements are those of a restless, impotent ghost who sees all and can do nothing.

Mr. Schirk and Mr. Mommertz are clearly intentionalists. I've no idea how much the film makers have had to make up to fill gaps in the historical record. Historians will have to decide that. Aside from Heydrich, Eichmann and Lange, only a couple of the other participants are strongly characterized by what they say and do, though they remain without formal identity. This is maddening in a film so provocative that it sends one back to the history books in an attempt to find out who said what to whom.

The omission was apparently a conscious choice on Mr. Schirk's part. "The Wannsee Conference" avoids any "You Are There" portentousness. In being so seemingly breezy, it finds a voice for dealing with matters that are, after all, not unspeakable. This is the film's sorrowful accomplishment.

1987 N 18, C29:3

High to Low

THE LAST EMPEROR, directed by Bernardo Bertolucci; screenplay by Mark Peploe with Mr. Bertolucci; photography by Vittorio Storaro; edited by Gabriella Cristiani; music by Ryuichi Sakamoto, David Byrne and Cong Su; production designer, Ferdinando Scarfiotti; produced by Jeremy Thomas; released by Columbia Pictures. At Cinema 1, Third Avenue and 60th Street. Running time: 166 minutes. This film is rated PG-13.

Pu Yi	John Lone
Wan Jung	Joan Chen
Reginald Johnston	Peter O'Toole
The Governor	Ying Ruocheng
Chen Pao Shen	Victor Wong
Big Li	Dennis Dun
Amakasu	Ryuichi Sakamoto
Eastern Jewel	Maggie Han
Tzu Hsü	Lisa Lu
Pi Yu (3 years old)	Richard Vuu

By VINCENT CANBY

PU YI (1906-1967), the last Manchu emperor of China, came to the Dragon Throne at the age of 2 and some months. Four years later, the prince regent, Pu Yi's father, was forced to abdicate all imperial authority to republican forces. The boy-emperor continued to stay on in lonely, unreal splendor in Beijing's Forbidden City for another decade or so. He was attended by 1,500 eunuchs, the various members of his extended household, their hangers-on and, toward the end, by Reginald Johnston, his faithful and sometimes acerbic British tutor, a Scot with a deep admiration for Chinese civilization and nothing but ridicule for salvation-mongering Christian missionaries.

In the 1920's, supported by his huge private fortune, Pu Yi and his beautiful empress, nicknamed Elizabeth, accompanied by his secondary wife, were kicked out of the palace and moved to the port city of Tianjin. For a few years they carried on in what

was seen as heedless, high-style decadence in the foreign enclave.

In the 1930's, the Japanese, who sought to legitimize their hold on Manchuria, returned Pu Yi and his family to their Manchu homeland where, until the end of World War II, he reigned as the Japanese puppet-emperor of the new state of Manchuko. After the war, he spent five years in a Russian prison, testified against his former Japanese allies in the Tokyo war crimes trials, was repatriated to China and, after 10 years of re-education, was paroled as *Mr.* Pu Yi. At the time of his death, he was a park attendant in Beijing.

•

These are the bare facts of a quite extraordinary life lived by someone who seems to have been a most commonplace person. Pu Yi was an accident of meteorology, the calm, empty center of the political hurricane that was blowing around him and that defined his place in history. Pu Yi was a cipher compared to the remarkable characters who, in one way or another, shaped his life and modern China — Tzu Hsui, the old, ferocious Empress Dowager, who brought the boy to the throne and promptly died, and the mutually warring revolutionaries, Sun Yat-sen, Chiang Kai-shek and Mao Zedong.

With the exception of the Empress Dowager, who makes one brief but riveting appearance, none of the major figures in this immense drama appear in Bernardo Bertolucci's arthritic, occasionally spectacular new film, "The Last Emperor." If it were a more poetically conceived movie, one might respond to everything of consequence that is *not* on the screen. That's not easy when most of what we do see and hear is of such ordinariness. The movie would appear to share Pu Yi's severely limited experience of — and curiosity about — the world.

"The Last Emperor," written by Mark Peploe "with" (as the credits say) Mr. Bertolucci, may have been inhibited by the enormousness of its subject, and even by the apparently enthusiastic support of China, which acted as host to Mr. Bertolucci, his cast and production crew. This isn't a movie that could offend any political biases, except maybe those of Chiang Kai-shek.

The director was given access to some magnificent locations within the Forbidden City as well as elsewhere in China and Manchuria. When the screenplay calls for thousands of extras, there are thousands of extras on the screen. One assumes that all of the costumes, props and random historical references are authentic. The eye is frequently entertained, while

End of an Era Wu Tao and Joan Chen star in "The Last Emperor," Bernardo Bertolucci's film about Pu Yi, who was crowned in the Imperial City and ended his life as a gardener there.

the center of the screen remains dead.

"The Last Emperor" is like an elegant travel brochure. It piques the curiosity. One wants to go. Ultimately it's a let-down.

•

The film opens in 1950, with the return to China of Pu Yi (John Lone) as a war criminal. Thereafter the movie jumps awkwardly forward and back in its attempt to account for more than 50 years of the emperor's utterly passive life. Big scenes recall the boy's first (and last) encounter with the Empress Dowager (Lisa Lu), his acclamation as emperor and something of his pampered, artificial childhood.

The movie picks up momentum with the arrival in 1919 of his tutor, Reginald Johnston (Peter O'Toole). Though Johnston seems to have been a most interesting fellow in real life, both incurably romantic and fastidiously British, Mr. Peploe's screenplay freights him with a lot of factual information to speak as dialogue, but nothing much in the way of character.

The curious (to Westerners) mating customs of Chinese monarchs are reported with care. Wan Jung (Joan Chen), Pu Yi's bride, is seen as a woman of some spirit who quickly adopts an opium habit to the disgust of her husband. When the movie attempts to characterize the bored lives of Pu Yi and Wan Jung in Tianjin, "The Last Emperor" looks briefly very much like "The Conformist."

Lots of cocktails are drunk. In the middle of the afternoon, Pu Yi leans against the piano in a hotel dining room and croons "Am I Blue," while Wan Jung trades sapphic sallies with Eastern Jewel (Maggie Han), a young woman dressed in a leather flying suit.

"I'm a Japanese spy and I don't care who knows it," announces the decadent Eastern Jewel. The fact that Eastern Jewel was a real character, a Manchu princess executed after the war as a traitor, doesn't inspire the director to make her seem to be anything more than an out-take from an earlier Bertolucci film.

•

Mr. O'Toole rattles off his lines with speed and what often seems to be a comic disregard for what they mean. From time to time, when he must register a certain ineffable sadness, he enunciates each word as if it were a pearl, which it isn't. This is not a great performance. Somewhat better are Mr. Lone, Miss Chen, Miss Lu and Richard Vuu, who plays Pu Yi as a 3-year-old and looks angelic.

"The Last Emperor," which opens today at Cinema 1, works most effectively as an illustrated introduction to modern Chinese history. It contains just enough information to send one looking for "From Emperor to Citizen," Pu Yi's autobiography, which is the basis of the film. Other helpful books include Henry McAleavy's "Dream of Tartary," also a life of Pu Yi, and Reginald Johnston's own account of his years in China, "Twilight in the Forbidden City."

•

"The Last Emperor," which has been rated PG-13 ("Special Parental Guidance for Those Younger Than 13"), includes some scenes of violence and nudity.

1987 N 20, C3:4

Cleverly in Control

SIGN O' THE TIMES, directed by Prince; director of photography, Peter Sinclair; film editor, Steve Purcell; music by Prince; produced by Robert Cavallo, Joseph Ruffalo and Steven Fargnoli; released by Cineplex Odeon. At Warner, Broadway and 43d Street; Art Greenwich Twin, Seventh Avenue at 12th Street; 34th Street East, at Second Avenue; Movie Center 5, 125th Street between Powell and Douglass Boulevards; New Delancey, 62 Delancey Street. Running time: 90 minutes. This film is rated PG-13.
WITH: Prince, Sheila E., Sheena Easton

"SIGN O' THE TIMES," which opens today at the Warner and other theaters, is mostly a concert film, but it also plays like science fiction: a visit to the Prince planet, where life is strange indeed. And madly, viscerally exciting, peopled by red-hot, inexhaustible Princelings whose onstage excesses become the perfect backdrop for the star's own antics. Prince himself, this time with a retinue as crazily galvanizing as Sly Stone's, has never seemed more the man of vision, however fanciful and impudent that vision may be. Anyone who has not yet had occasion to take Prince seriously will find "Sign o' the Times" a real surprise.

The wide range of Prince's musicianship comes through much more clearly here than it did in "Purple Rain," with which "Sign o' the Times" shares a small degree of silliness, sloppiness and obscurity; for Prince, these things seem to go with the territory. The film highlights Prince's range by shifting abruptly from song to song, with no attempt at any real continuity. There are brief dramatic sections here and there, with members of the troupe performing little sketches as Prince, looking pensive behind his steel-rimmed glasses, takes it all in; these fragments don't exactly hold the film together. But Prince himself does, as master showman, remarkable musician, and skilled ringmaster of this three-ring circus.

The stage set resembles a seedy downtown bar district (the show was filmed in Rotterdam and Antwerp, cities along the route of Prince's European tour earlier this year), and beneath its flashing bar and hotel signs, Prince and his sidekicks writhe. And writhe some more. The choreography combines Prince's familiarly frank sensuality with an 80's version of go-go dancing, the latter best exemplified by an amazing new recruit named Cat, who could have a second career endorsing health clubs any time she'd like to. The gaudiness is still there, and the stylized outrageousness, but what's also readily apparent is the show's sophistication. The choreography is indeed clever at times, and throughout it all, it's clear that Prince is wholly in control.

Prince himself, wearing things that only Prince would wear (cutout matador suits with shirred seams up the back; a mad bellhop outfit; a white bunny-fluff coat as a witty touch to accompany "If I Was Your Girlfriend"), cuts an astonishing figure. Whether singing in falsetto or dancing flat on his back, tripping about in four-inch heels or singing simply with an acoustic guitar, he remains a tough, commanding performer with a sure sense of how to hold his audiences absolutely rapt. Among the highlights of the show are the long version of "Forever in My Life" and the playful "U Got the

Prince in "Sign o' the Times."

Look," performed with Sheena Easton and photographed somewhat more grainily than the rest of the footage. The film was obviously assembled in a hurry, and its seams show. But its energy never flags.

Another high point is "The Cross," an anthem in Prince's newly messianic spirit and an illustration of his way of updating 60's attitudes for an 80's audience. Peace symbols are everywhere throughout the show, as is a vaguely psychedelic mood (one of the sidemen is dressed as a doctor, with stethoscope; another seems to be playing Father Death). But the overriding motif is pure Prince. And Prince, whose ties to soul and jazz are clearer than ever before, whose willingness to embrace different musical forms seems to grow all the time, has never cast a stronger spell.

•

"Sign o' the Times" is rated PG-13 ("Special Parental Guidance Suggested for Those Younger Than 13"). Guidance is strongly suggested; it contains a great deal of lascivious posturing).
JANET MASLIN

1987 N 20, C14:1

Metamorphosis

TEEN WOLF TOO, directed by Christopher Leitch; screenplay by R. Timothy Kring, story by Joseph Loeb 3d and Matthew Weisman, based on characters created by Mr. Loeb and Mr. Weisman; director of photography, Jules Brenner; edited by Steven Polivka, Kim Secrist and Harvey Rosenstock and Raja Gosnell; music by Mark Goldenberg; art director, Peg McClelian; produced by Kent Bateman; released by Atlantic Entertainment Group. At Embassy 3, Broadway and 47th Street; U. A. East, 85th Street and First Avenue; Movie Center 5, 125th Street, between Powell and Douglass Boulevards. Running time: 95 minutes. This film is rated PG.
Todd Howard .... Jason Bateman
Professor Brooks .... Kim Darby
Dean Dunn .... John Astin
Coach Finstock .... Paul Sand
Uncle Harold .... James Hampton
Chubby .... Mark Holton
Nicki .... Estee Chandler

By CARYN JAMES

WHEN a clean-cut college student turns into a werewolf, he does unspeakable things. Nothing violent, but this monster cuts classes! He starts hanging around with a frivolous crowd — oh, no! college students who like to dance! — so his

jilted girlfriend confronts him in biology class. "They don't like you, only the wolf," she warns. Then she throws her frog at him.

If only this were a spoof: "Dobie Gillis Turns Into a Werewolf." Unfortunately, "Teen Wolf Too" is serious about being true to yourself and your school, and its idea of cleverness is throwing frogs in your face.

In the first "Teen Wolf," Michael J. Fox had an innocent charm as a high-school student confused by the family curse that sneaked up on him and turned him into a hairy but high-jumping basketball star. His cousin Todd, played in "Teen Wolf Too" by Jason Bateman, is a lot more jaded, and so is this insultingly calculated sequel.

Here is a script that takes Todd, an intelligent boy, to Hamilton University on a boxing scholarship, although he has never boxed before. It seems the coach knows the family secret, and before long Todd is turning into a wolf just the way his cousin did — with very few special effects. Todd's eyes turn red, his forehead bulges and suddenly there's a shot of some horrified onlooker. Cut back to Todd, now in full werewolf makeup.

No one expects realism from a movie called "Teen Wolf Too," which opens today at Embassy 3 and other theaters; still, the film makers could pretend to know what college is like, might try to liven up the kindly werewolf formula. But Mr. Bateman's dime-store werewolf hair is as unconvincing as the dear old Hamilton campus, where the students sing a hokey hymn to their school, where John Astin is the dean of men (yes, a dean of men in the 1980's) and students at a dance wear color-coordinated royal blue outfits, the better to show up in the inevitable "Teen Wolf" music video.

Mr. Bateman can be an exceptionally engaging actor. Last season he ran away with Valerie Harper's television series, now called "Valerie's Family." He deserves much better than this sloppy sequel.

•

"Teen Wolf Too" is rated PG ("Parental Guidance Suggested"), but there is nothing truly frightening about it. Even a scene in which Todd's girlfriend spends the night in his room is extremely discreet.

1987 N 20, C14:6

NUTS, directed by Martin Ritt; screenplay by Tom Topor and Darryl Ponicsan and Alvin Sargent, based on the play by Mr. Topor; director of photography, Andrzej Bartkowiak; edited by Sidney Levin; music by Barbra Streisand; production designer, Joel Schiller; produced by Miss Streisand; released by Warner Brothers. At Criterion Center, Broadway at 45th Street; 84th Street Six, at Broadway; Coronet, Third Avenue at 59th Street; 86th Street East Twin, between Second and Third Avenues; Waverly Twin, Avenue of the Americas and Third Street. Running time: 118 minutes. This film is rated R.
Claudia Draper .... Barbra Streisand
Aaron Levinsky .... Richard Dreyfuss
Rose Kirk .... Maureen Stapleton
Arthur Kirk .... Karl Malden
Dr. Herbert A. Morrison .... Eli Wallach
Francis MacMillan .... Robert Webber
Judge Stanley Murdoch .... James Whitmore
Allen Green .... Leslie Nielsen
Clarence Middleton .... William Prince

By JANET MASLIN

IN "Nuts," Barbra Streisand has the kind of downscale role that has been known to win Oscars, a role in which a star forsakes her usual cocoon for the mud streaks, the tattered clothes, the rude invective that prove she has grit. Luckily, Miss Streisand's performance is better than that, but it's the showboating aspects of "Nuts" that attract the most attention.

As Claudia Draper, a call girl who has killed a customer and is fighting to prove her sanity and win her right to stand trial, Miss Streisand never seems any crazier than the average fox. Though she bangs angrily on a water pitcher while others are talking, though she exhibits wild mood swings, though at one point she even hauls off and slugs her lawyer, her behavior is always more entertainingly overboard than demented. No matter; "Nuts" doesn't strive very hard for realism. From the first glimpse of one tawny, sun-streaked (albeit unwashed) coiffure in the crowd at the Women's House of Detention, it's clear that the sanity issue is never even in question, and that this is less a believable drama than a one-woman show.

Miss Streisand, who produced "Nuts," didn't direct it. And Martin Ritt, who is the director of record, didn't either. The film is almost entirely adrift. A group of three screen-

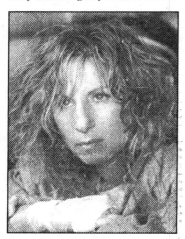

Barbra Streisand

writers — Tom Topor, Alvin Sargent and Darryl Ponicsan — are credited with adapting Mr. Topor's courtroom drama, but they have not succeeded in giving it any momentum at all. There are flashbacks to Claudia's past, but they only heighten the improbability of this woman's suddenly having snapped; there is a troubled family history, but it holds much less surprise that it's supposed to. There is also a glimmer of attraction between Claudia and her hard-working, put-upon lawyer, Aaron Levinsky (Richard Dreyfuss), but it is left largely undeveloped. A pity because Mr. Dreyfuss is sharp, honest, incisive and greatly underutilized in this supporting role.

The other key characters in "Nuts," which opens today at the Coronet and other theaters, are the white-haired elders who sit in judgment on the tormented Claudia, and who are responsible for her plight; such is the creakiness of Mr. Topor's original drama. They include Claudia's weak, sweet-faced mother (Maureen Stapleton), a smiling stepfather (Karl Malden) intent on keeping up appearances, a most unhelpful psychiatrist (Eli Wallach) and the judge in the case (James Whitmore), who has some nice moments reacting to Claudia's courtroom antics. Robert

Webber, as the prosecuting attorney, has his own chance to be flabbergasted when Claudia offers a detailed description of just what services she used to sell, and for how much. It's clear that she enjoys making him squirm.

Miss Streisand brings a lot of energy and mischief to moments like these, and her shrewd, well-delivered retorts provide the film with its liveliest moments. However, these flare-ups are relatively infrequent, and for the most part "Nuts" just drones along. The material is exceptionally talky and becalmed, the central question none too compelling, and the visual style distractingly cluttered. The uniformly yellowish-brown lighting becomes extremely oppressive, as does the use of extra reaction shots in court; when Claudia lashes out, the camera often takes care to study every face in the room. The props are at times also given more attention than necessary, since they cast no real light on Claudia's psyche. Nothing here does. Still, Miss Streisand, even in a ragged hospital gown, even taunting Mr. Dreyfuss with as much nastiness and raunch as she can muster, manages to be every inch the star.

1987 N 20, C16:6

Against the Odds

A BOY FROM CALABRIA, directed by Luigi Comencini; screenplay (Italian with English subtitles) by Mr. Comencini and Ugo Pirro, story by Demetrio Casile; director of photography, Franco Di Giacomo; edited by Nino Baragli; music by Vivaldi; produced by Fulvio Lucisano; an Italian-French Coproduction; Italian International Film-U.P. Schermo Video-Rome; Carthago Film S.R.L.-Canal Plus Productions General Image-Paris in collaboration with RAI Channel 1. At Carnegie Screening Room, Seventh Avenue and 57th Street. Running time: 106 minutes. This film has no rating.

Felice	Gian Maria Volonte
Nicola	Diego Abatantuono
Mariuccia	Therese Liotard
Mimi	Santo Polimeno
Crisolinda	Giada Faggioli
WITH: Jacques Peyrac, Enzo Ruoti, Jean Masrevery

LUIGI COMENCINI'S "Boy From Calabria," opening today at the Carnegie Screening Room, is an inoffensively sentimental Italian movie about a poor peasant boy's efforts to become a marathon runner, much to the horror of his hard-pressed father.

For most of the film, the cards are stacked against the boy, Mimi (Santo Polimeno). His father is cruel and arbitrary, but only because of his own tough life. Mimi has a friend in the community's rummy bus driver (Gian Maria Volonte), who urges on the boy with "exalting lies," intended to enlarge Mimi's horizons. The movie believes that men cannot live without fantasies.

•

The scenery is pretty and the outcome apparent from virtually the first scene. Young Mr. Polimeno gives a good, straightforward performance. Not so Mr. Volonte, who works very hard to appear to be both colorful and lovable, but succeeds in being neither. It's a Wallace Beery part.

Mr. Comencini is best known here for his "Bread, Love and Dreams," made in 1953. *VINCENT CANBY*

1987 N 20, C21:1

Sustaining Friendship

LOYALTIES, directed by Anne Wheeler; screenplay by Sharon Riis, based on a story by Miss Riis and Miss Wheeler; photography by Vic Sarin; edited by Judy Krupansky; music by Michael Conway Baker; produced by Ronald Lillie and William Johnston. At Quad Cinema, 34 West 13th Street. Running time: 98 minutes. This film is rated R.

David Sutton	Kenneth Welsh
Rosanne Ladouceur	Tantoo Cardinal
Lily Sutton	Susan Wooldridge
Beatrice	Vera Martin
Leona	Diane Debassige
Eddy	Tom Jackson
Nicholas Sutton	Jeffrey Smith
Naomi Sutton	Meredith Rimmer
Jeremy Sutton	Alexander and Jonathan Tribiger
Robert Sutton	Christopher Barrington-Leigh
Lisa	Yolanda Cardinal

"Loyalties" was shown as part of this year's New Directors/New Films series. Following are excerpts from Vincent Canby's review, which appeared in The New York Times March 21. The film opens today at the Quad Cinema.

"LOYALTIES," set in the small community of Lac la Biche in northwestern Canada, is a technically adequate Canadian film about the sustaining friendship that grows up between two very different kinds of women.

Rosanne Ladouceur (Tantoo Cardinal), who's "mostly" of American Indian stock, is in her mid-30's, pretty (in the seasoned way of someone who's always worked hard) and accustomed to taking life as it comes.

Lily Sutton (Susan Wooldridge) is a well-groomed, very proper Englishwoman considered by her mother to have slipped on the social scale by marrying David (Kenneth Welsh), a medical doctor who has risen from the lower English orders.

At the start of the movie, Lily and her children are joining David in Lac la Biche, apparently to escape some unmentionable scandal in England. To help the unemployed Rosanne, David hires her to work for the Suttons as au pair woman and unofficial family counselor. Inevitably, the unmentionable thing that drove the Suttons from England reappears in Lac la Biche.

•

"Loyalties" is the second feature to be directed by Anne Wheeler, who also collaborated with Sharon Riis on the story that Miss Riis adapted into the screenplay.

Except for Miss Cardinal's performance as the earthy, intelligent Rosanne, "Loyalties" is utterly without distinguishing characteristics, either in its narrative or in the way it has been written and directed. Everything about the film looks as if it had been ordered from a catalogue.

1987 N 20, C21:1

Times Sq. Twosome

HONEYMOON, directed by Patrick Jamain; screenplay by Mr. Jamain, Philippe Setbon and Robert Geoffrion; original story by Mr. Jamain and Mr. Setbon; photography by Daniel Diot; edited by Robert Rongier; music by Robert Charlebois; produced by Xavier Gelin and René Malo; released by International Film Marketing. At Cinema Village, 22 East 12th Street. Running time: 100 minutes. This film is rated R.

Cecile	Nathalie Baye
Zack	John Shea
Michel	Richard Berry
Sally	Marla Lukofsky
Novak	Peter Donat
Bill	Greg Ellwand

Barnes	Cec Linder
Sonny	Alf Humphreys
Garnier	Michel Beaune
Forrester	Arthur Grossner
Thelma	Adriana Roach

"HONEYMOON" was made in English, but it seems to have been designed as a cautionary tale for European audiences, a warning about hellish New York. It stars Nathalie Baye, and from the first shots of Miss Baye's trim little high-heeled legs making their way through ruffian-filled Manhattan, it's clear that this gentle French heroine is desperately out of place.

The plot, which is also rather desperate, concocts a terrible plight for this Cecile, whose lover Michel (Richard Berry) has most inconveniently landed in jail. She wants to visit him every day, but her visa has run out, and so she is forced — forced! — to marry a psychotic American (John Shea) whose name she finds through an agency. She is also forced to pay a fee for this privilege.

Soon her new husband, who was supposed to marry her in name only, has beaten a path to the door of her apartment, which seems to be in the sleaziest part of Times Square. To escape him, Cecile tries taking a room in a neighborhood hotel, which is even more horrid. He finds her anyhow. He insists on acting husbandly, saying things like "Darling, the neighbors." But Cecile is trapped in the city, and she has no money to escape, even though she finds a job slinging hash in a restaurant where a loudly dressed, horribly cute fellow waitress (Marla Lukofsky) becomes her friend and insists on calling her either "Cecil" or "Frenchy."

•

In this miserable setting, faced with one vulgarity after another, Cecille has no choice but to soften her resistance toward the groom, though it will surprise no one that this proves to be a bad idea. Only when the newlyweds are briefly getting along does the director and co-writer, Patrick Jamain, move the action to anywhere scenic — like the Brooklyn Bridge.

"Honeymoon," which opens today at the Cinema Village, is not helped by an extremely wooden screenplay; not even the American actors here are given comfortable-sounding dialogue. The camerawork is so wan it turns Times Square colorless, and Mr. Jamain hasn't the timing or the energy to manage even rudimentary thriller touches. Miss Baye tries hard, Mr. Shea tries too hard, and by and large the acting is dreadful. Not even the graffiti in the hall outside Cecille's slum apartment looks right.

JANET MASLIN

1987 N 20, C24:1

RENOIR, THE BOSS, directed by Jacques Rivette and André S. Labarthe; produced by Janine Bazin; production company, L'Institut National de l'Audiovisuel; in French with English subtitles; American version by Cheryl Carlissimo, Suzanne Fenn and Jackie Raynal; a Zanzibar Productions release. Running time: 60 minutes. This film has no rating. At Bleecker Street Cinema, 144 Bleecker Street, at La Guardia Place.
WITH: Jean Renoir and Marcel Dalio

"Jean Renoir, the Boss" was shown as part of the 1985 New York Film Festival. Following are excerpts from Vincent Canby's review, which appeared in The New York Times on Oct. 5, 1985. The film opens today at the Bleecker Street Cinema.

"JEAN RENOIR, THE BOSS," directed by Jacques Rivette and André S. Labarthe, was actually made in 1967 for a French television series titled "Film Makers of Our Times," but it had to wait 18 years before being equipped with English subtitles for the American market. Mr. Rivette and Mr. Labarthe don't attempt to cover the entire career of Renoir, who was to make only one more film, "The Little Theater of Jean Renoir," in 1969, before he died in 1979. Instead, they concentrate on what may be the quintessential Renoir film, "Rules of the Game" (1939), scenes from which are intercut with segments of an extended interview with the director.

Knowing the work as well as they do, the interviewers don't waste Renoir's time. Their questions are informed by their own knowledge of film making and their profound interest in — and appreciation for — the master's chef d'oeuvre. Renoir, in turn, responds to them enthusiastically, talking with humor, insight, ease, and with what might be described as modest, utterly candid self-assurance.

Mr. Rivette and Mr. Labarthe take Renoir through "Rules of the Game" from its inception (as a vague, very general idea about the state of French society after Munich), through the writing — Renoir had "The Marriage of Figaro" in the back of his mind — through the casting and then the changes and improvisations that were made while the film was shooting. They add a moving postscript in which they stage a reunion between Renoir and the film's star, Marcel Dalio, at the chateau that was the setting for the production. It's a splendid documentary.

1987 N 20, C23:1

FLOWERS IN THE ATTIC, directed by Jeffrey Bloom; screenplay by Mr. Bloom, based on the novel by V. C. Andrews; directors of photography, Frank Byers and Gil Hubbs; film editor, Gregory F. Plotts; music by Christopher Young; production designer, John Muto; produced by Sy Levin and Thomas Fries. At the National Twin, Broadway and 44th Street; the Columbia Cinema, Broadway and 103d Street; Movie Center Five, 125th Street, between Powell and Douglass Boulevards; the Coliseum Twin, Broadway and 181st Street. Running time: 95 minutes. This film is rated PG-13.
Grandmother ....Louise Fletcher
Mother ....Victoria Tennant
Cathy ....Kristy Swanson
Chris ....Jeb Stuart Adams
Cory ....Ben Ganger
Carrie ....Lindsay Parker
Father ....Marshall Colt
Grandfather ....Nathan Davis

By WALTER GOODMAN

The scary thing about "Flowers in the Attic," now playing at the National and other theaters, is that the novel by V. C. Andrews that inspired the movie has sold more than 4 million copies.

For readers who somehow missed the book, this is a story of four blond children — a couple of strapping teenagers named Cathy and Chris, who like to sleep in the same bed and keep the bathroom door open, and the little twins, Carrie and Cory. Mother's name is Corinne. If they have a cat, it could be called Cat.

This cute clan is disrupted by the death of father, whereupon mother (Victoria Tennant) takes them back to the family manse, whence she was kicked out 17 years ago, after marrying *her own uncle*. She plans to regain the love of her dying father and inherit his fortune.

The young folks are locked in and treated real mean by their grandmother (Louise Fletcher), who calls them "devil's spawn" and goes so far as to trim Cathy's golden locks. They spend most of their time in the attic, where their eyes grow cavernous from makeup. But what really gets to the kids is the realization that their own mother has been sprinkling arsenic on their cookies. Well, enough of that, lest, as little Cory, who eats more cookies than is good for him, puts it, "I'll have to thwow up."

On second thought, the scary thing about this movie, written and directed for minimum impact by Jeffrey Bloom, is that the book "Flowers in the Attic" was followed by four other horticultural horror shows, "Petals on the Wind," "If There Be Thorns," "Seeds of Yesterday" and "Garden of Shadows." There may be bitter fruit to come.

●

"Flowers in the Attic" is rated PG-13 (Special Parental Guidance Suggested for Children Under 13), probably out of concern for giving children bad dreams about wicked parents.

1987 N 21, 12:5

DATE WITH AN ANGEL, directed and written by Tom McLoughlin; director of photography, Alex Thomson; film editor, Marshall Harvey; music by Randy Kerber; production designer, Craig Stearns; produced by Martha Schumacher; a De Laurentiis Entertainment Group Release. At the Criterion Center, Broadway and 45th Street; the Gotham Cinema, Third Avenue at 58th Street; Movieland Eighth Street Triplex, at University Place. Running time: 105 minutes. This film is rated PG.
Jim Sanders ....Michael E. Knight
Patty Winston ....Phoebe Cates
Angel ....Emmanuelle Béart
Ed Winston ....David Dukes
George ....Phil Brock
Don ....Albert Macklin
Rex ....Pete Kowanko
Ben Sanders ....Vinny Argiro
Grace Sanders ....Bibi Besch

By JANET MASLIN

"Date With an Angel," which opened yesterday at the subterranean, shoeboxy Criterion 4 and other theaters, is about a breathtakingly lovely creature with feathers on her large, fluffy wings. Unfortunately, she's also got feathers in her head. The angel lands on earth and affixes herself to Jim Sanders (Michael E. Knight), a soon-to-be-married man. Jim feels he should resist her, but the angel spends the rest of the film gazing adoringly at him and following him everywhere.

The angel is played by Emmanuelle Béart, the extraordinarily beautiful star of "Manon of the Spring," and Miss Béart really does look the part. She's this film's greatest, not to say only, attraction, and it was no small accomplishment for the writer-director (Tom McLoughlin) to let her wear out her welcome.

With the advent of this creature, "Date With an Angel" unleashes Jim's jealous fiancée (played by Phoebe Cates, who gets to scream a lot), and Jim's three oafish friends, who chase the angel and want to become her personal managers, so they can market wing-backed T-shirts and other such stuff. Everyone's designs on the angel are purely innocent, which is less a display of virtue than a lack of imagination.

●

One scene has Jim and the angel visiting a Roman Catholic church, where a marijuana-smoking priest takes the whole thing in stride and a fat woman thinks she is seeing a miracle. This would seem like sacrilege if the whole thing were not so stupid.

The film's only amusing touch has Jim's future father-in-law, who makes a great show of adoring his daughter, happily deciding that the angel would make a better model for his cosmetics company; after all, business is business. Speaking of business, production notes reveal that the film makers were forced to interview, audition or screen-test five *thousand* actresses for the angel's role. It is a tough life.

●

"Date With an Angel" is rated PG ("Parental Guidance Suggested.") It contains some rude language, and the angel takes a bath.

1987 N 21, 14:5

FILM VIEW/Janet Maslin

Oh, for the Spice of Eccentricity

IN "NUTS," BARBRA STREISAND PLAYS A WOMAN who curses frequently, exhibits violent mood swings and lashes out angrily at those she loves. This behavior is supposed to convince an audience that a judge might find her certifiably insane, but by some latter-day, urban standards, it's really all in a day's work. The fact is that true craziness, however easy to spot on the street, is a rarity on the screen, and its absence grows more regrettable all the time. Unless one considers the systematic manufacture of prefab, predictable film product a form of institutionalized lunacy, the film business has rarely been more sanity-conscious than it is today.

In this climate, with so many conformist film characters wending their way through so many standard situations, any show of eccentricity stands out. It needn't be brilliant to qualify as an interesting change. In the 1970's, when oddity on screen was the rule rather than the exception, it was possible to carp that a "Quintet" (1979) or a "Three Women" (1977) might not be up to the high standards of Robert Altman, whose every film had its own original brand of idiosyncrasy. Nowadays, either of those films would look very daring indeed next to "Death Wish 4" or "Teen Wolf Too."

Craziness on the screen shouldn't be treasured inordinately, but it frequently has great exuberance and insinuat-

---

Beyond-the-pale behavior sometimes seems irresistibly romantic and brave.

---

ing power. Whether in its most extreme forms, as in Roman Polanski's "Repulsion," or at its most entertainingly extroverted, as in Sidney Lumet's "Dog Day Afternoon," beyond-the-pale behavior can seem wildly, irresistibly romantic, as well as brave. Strange behavior can also, whether in a "Sid and Nancy" or a "Taxi Driver," hold up a fun-house mirror to the conventions of so-called normal life, and thus serve a frightening and sardonic purpose as well.

Even the nonchalant bohemianism of Jim Jarmusch's "Stranger Than Paradise," one of the few genuinely eccentric American films in recent years, has the kind of force that supposedly saner films work much harder to achieve. Just the sight of one of Mr. Jarmusch's characters ambling down the street with her radio blaring, or another silently eating his TV dinner, is enough to establish Mr. Jarmusch's style as effortlessly peculiar. What's most striking, though, is the casualness of this film's characters in contrast, say, with the more orderly heroine of Andy Anderson's "Positive I.D." That film, about an unhinged woman who assumes a false identity to avenge a crime, seems much more crisply well-balanced than anything Mr. Jarmusch has done.

173

The point is that when anyone in today's practical-minded, dog-eat-dog film-making climate attempts a show of real unpredictability, attention should be paid. A "Less Than Zero," with its imaginative nightclub-nightmarish look and its envelopingly eerie modern lighting, deserves more credit for its unusual vision of high-gloss depravity than blame for the essential ordinariness of what lies underneath. Yes, we have seen other films about rich, neglectful Beverly Hills parents. And no, this film's anti-drug message is neither faithful to Bret Easton Ellis's blacker, more fashionably jaded novel nor particularly sincere (the film adopts the "Miami Vice" method, the high-glamour cautionary tone). However, the director, Marek Kanievska, has dared to depart substantially from a very popular book and has developed a visual approach that's as effective as it is unusual. Trivial as it is, this film's surface iconoclasm is very appealing.

■

Alan Rudolph long ago established his offbeat approach, and he occupies a singular cinematic niche. Although Mr. Rudolph has yet to make a film in which substance holds a candle to style, he remains a distinctive film maker whose work has its clear hallmarks. From "Welcome to L.A." to "Choose Me" to his new "Made in Heaven," Mr. Rudolph's films have had an exceptional fluidity bordering on pure shapelessness. But they've also had a sense of flow, of exotic characters ricocheting off one another in a frustrating world, of just-missed opportunities and of longing.

If Mr. Rudolph has ever done anything to make this vision more commercially accessible, that certainly isn't apparent on the screen. "Made in Heaven," more sugary than other Rudolph films but no less personalized, again confirms him as the sort of left-field film maker whose work provides an invaluable counterpoint to mainstream monotony. Even if none of Mr. Rudolph's films have entirely worked, each of them holds forth the promise of something much more audacious than what we're currently used to.

Out of the formidable miasma of rock video comes Mary Lambert, who has directed commercials and videos (most notably some of Madonna's) and now brings a similarly splashy approach to "Siesta," her debut feature. Madly pretentious as it is, "Siesta" is a hard film to take seriously, but in the present climate it's also a hard film not to like. Yes, Miss Lambert has used every mock-mysterious trick in the MTV book, and yes, a lot of the film's appeal has to do with Ellen Barkin's costume, or lack of same. But the advanced artiness of "Siesta" is so retrograde it seems newly entertaining. And the cast (most notably Miss Barkin, Jodie Foster and Julian Sands) is so untethered as to be having great fun.

Still, the most authentic craziness of the moment is to be found in "Barfly," a film about a man (the writer Charles Bukowski) with first-hand experience of a lunatic world, made by a man (Barbet Schroeder) who fully understands him. Unlike so many pretenders to eccentricity, these two seem to know whereof they speak. □

1987 N 22, II:23:5

PLANES, TRAINS AND AUTOMOBILES, directed by John Hughes; written by Mr. Hughes; director of photography, Don Peterman; edited by Paul Hirsch; music by Ira Newborn; produced by Mr. Hughes; released by Paramount Pictures. Running time: 90 minutes. This film is rated R.

Neal Page	Steve Martin
Del Griffith	John Candy
Chairman	William Windom
John Dole	Lyman Ward
Car rental clerk	Edie McClurg
Sue Page	Laila Robins

By JANET MASLIN

THE circuitous journey that is embarked upon in John Hughes's "Planes, Trains and Automobiles" is supposed to range from New York to Chicago, but its final destination is surprising. The two traveling companions, Neal Page (Steve Martin) and Del Griffith (John Candy), do indeed make it to the Windy City, but they also reach the place where confidences are voiced, insecurities are expressed and friendships are formed.

One need not be a student of Mr. Hughes's teen-oriented films (among them "Sixteen Candles" and "Some Kind of Wonderful") to sense that these are not usually the concerns of middle-aged traveling businessmen. However, Mr. Hughes conceives of this film's adult characters as lost adolescents, and seems to regard their mature status as a terrible burden that they will, with luck, be able to shed. So Mr. Martin, in the film's earlier sections, is the epitome of corporate stiffness, doing most of his acting with his cheek muscles and bristling murderously when someone steals a taxi from him at rush hour. The film is no more comfortable with this exaggerated version of grown-up reserve than it is with the misplaced, confessional pieties that color its conclusion.

The real trouble with "Planes, Trains and Automobiles," which opens today at Loew's Astor Plaza and other theaters, is simpler: there wasn't much of an idea here to begin with, and when Mr. Hughes works with non-teen-age characters he has smaller reserves of colloquial humor upon which to draw. It's harder to have one man complain that traveling with the other is "like going on a date with a Chatty Cathy doll" than it would be to have a teen-ager deliver that line. None of Mr. Hughes's earlier films have revolved around anything more complicated than prom dates and parent troubles and getting along with schoolmates, but they had a texture and authenticity that "Planes, Trains and Automobiles" lacks.

Mr. Martin and Mr. Candy are an easy twosome to watch even with marginal material, though, and the film is never worse than slow. In fact, it's even promising at first, with the bound-for-trouble promise of a quick trip home for Neal Page, who phones his wife to tell her he'll be there by 10. As a blow-by-blow anatomy of a horrid traveling experience, replete with flight cancellations, snowstorms and unscheduled detours, "Planes, Trains and Automobiles" has great potential, but it begins to meander once Neal and Del become a reluctant duo.

Neal detests the loud, tirelessly jolly Del on sight. But Fate forces them to share a plane ride, a hair-raising taxi trip and even a bed.

The great, embarrassed flurry of man-talk ("helluva game, helluva game!") with which these two leap out of bed the next morning is indeed funny, and the film does have its scattered moments. But too often, the audience has as much reason as Del and Neal do to wonder where, if anywhere, they are going.

1987 N 25, C19:1

Rowboats Passing

HOUSEKEEPING, directed by Bill Forsyth; screenplay by Mr. Forsyth, based on the novel "Housekeeping," by Marilynne Robinson; director of photography, Michael Coulter; edited by Michael Ellis; music by Michael Gibbs; production designer, Adrienne Atkinson; produced by Robert F. Colesberry; released by Columbia Pictures. At the Regency Cinema, Broadway at 67th Street. Running time: 117 minutes. This film is rated PG-13.

Sylvie	Christine Lahti
Ruth	Sara Walker
Lucille	Andrea Burchill
Aunt Lily	Anne Pitoniak
Aunt Nona	Barbara Reese
Helen	Margot Pinvidic
Sheriff	Bill Smillie
Principal	Wayne Robson
Mrs. Jardine	Betty Phillips
Mrs. Paterson	Karen Austin

By VINCENT CANBY

"HOUSEKEEPING," Bill Forsyth's fine adaptation of Marilynne Robinson's 1981 novel, is a clear-eyed, brow-furrowed, haunting comedy about impossible attachments and doomed affection in a world divided between two kinds of people.

On one side are those who live always in transit. They go through life as if they were passengers in leaky rowboats, riding out a permanent flood. They pass aimlessly through a succession of communities that, for them, remain as unknowable as the interiors of the houses whose roofs they float by.

Straddling the roofs, or hanging onto the upper branches of trees, sometimes looking exceedingly comic in their desperation, are the would-be survivors of the flood, those who persevere in their attempts to impose reason and order on random existence.

To the people in the rowboats they call out warnings of unknown dangers, only to be acknowledged by smiles or shrugs. The smiles and shrugs, roughly translated, mean that anything is better than living one's life hanging onto a tree.

●

"Housekeeping," set in the 1950's in a small Western town named Fingerbone, is about two sisters, Ruth, 15, and Lucille, 13, who've been raised by their grandmother after being abandoned by their voyaging mother. With the death of the old lady, who "spent all her life braiding hair and whitening shoes," the girls are briefly cared for by two fluttery great-aunts, and then by their mother's wandering sister, Sylvie (Christine Lahti).

Like their mother, whom they now barely remember, Sylvie is kind and sweet and always a little distant. The girls, in some panic, recognize the symptoms. Sylvie never takes off her coat. When Sylvie leaves the house her second morning home, Ruth and Lucille realize she's headed for the railroad station and another depar-

Sidetracked

Steve Martin and John Candy star as mismatched traveling companions in John Hughes's comedy, "Planes, Trains and Automobiles."

Joyce Rudolph

ture. They trail her and more or less coerce her into staying in town.

Life with Sylvie is unpredictable. It's just a little too unpredictable for the fastidious Lucille (Andrea Burchill), who'd like to live the way other people do. When Ruth (Sara Walker) or Lucille skips classes, Sylvie writes outrageously dramatic, transparently false descriptions of the illness. Says Ruth, the soundtrack narrator, "Sylvie's attitude toward truancy was unsatisfactory." Sylvie doesn't much care what the girls do during the day, as long as they don't hurt themselves.

•

Her own days are totally without structure. Sometimes she steals a boat and goes for long outings across Fingerbone's mountain lake, once returning with a fish sticking out of her pocket. She mortifies Lucille by snoozing, like a hobo, in the sun on a park bench in the middle of town. The housework goes undone. Sylvie never throws out old newspapers and has a peculiar fondness for tin cans, once she's soaked off the labels. Eventually, there are pretty stacks of shiny cans everywhere.

Sylvie takes no interest in her old acquaintances in Fingerbone, but talks with passing strangers, including a woman from South Dakota who, riding the rails, is en route to Portland for her cousin's execution.

"Why do you get involved with such trashy people?" says Lucille. "I wouldn't say 'trashy,'" Sylvie replies with utter calm. "*She* didn't strangle anybody." At the end of the day, Sylvie likes to sit in the dark.

•

About halfway through "Housekeeping," one may have the awful fear that the movie is going to turn into one of those sentimental comedies — so popular with the squarest Broadway audiences — about the lovability of essentially harmless, noisily self-proclaimed eccentrics.

There's no need to worry. "Housekeeping" is far too rigorously observed to slip into such nonsense. Further, in Sylvie, as written and di-

rected by Mr. Forsyth and as played by Miss Lahti, the film has someone who's neither harmless nor, in reality, merely eccentric. She's something quite other, possibly quite mad. Though one feels she could function in the world as Lucille wants to and the rest of us do, Sylvie elects not to, with a blithe manner that's initially engaging and, at the end, profoundly disturbing. She's a siren of the open road.

Miss Lahti, who was nominated for an Oscar for "Swing Shift," has the role of her film career to date, and she's spellbinding. Sylvie is a beauty even when she looks a mess. She enters the movie quietly, as if by a side entrance, so it takes some time to feel the strength of her presence, which, once established, dominates the film. When she's off-screen, one tends to worry about what she's up to. When she's on-screen, one searches for clues to what's going on in the seeming serenity of her mind.

"Housekeeping" is by far the most accomplished comedy yet made by Mr. Forsyth, the Scottish director who first came onto the international scene with "Gregory's Girl" and "Local Hero." Miss Robinson's novel has provided him with material in which the mysterious is an essential component of the mundane, and not simply a leavening agent. Though it's

full of moments of real sadness, "Housekeeping" is also startlingly funny.

Beginning with Miss Lahti, every member of the cast is special. However, pay special attention to Miss Walker, as the tall, gawky Ruth, who walks always with her head down, in shyness, and becomes mesmerized by Sylvie, and Miss Burchill, as the younger sister who longs, with breaking heart, to be totally, boringly ordinary.

Mr. Forsyth somehow manages to make us care equally for the sister who chooses to disappear in a passing rowboat, and the one who clings to the roof top, hoping the flood waters will recede.

•

"Housekeeping," which has been rated PG-13 ("Special Parental Guidance Suggested for Those Younger Than 13"), contains scenes of emotional complexity that could be frightening to very young children.

1987 N 25, C11:1

THREE MEN AND A BABY, directed by Leonard Nimoy; screenplay James Orr and Jim Cruickshank, based on "Trois Hommes et un Couffin" by Coline Serreau; director of photography, Adam Greenberg; edited by Michael A. Stevenson;

Fathers' Day

Tom Selleck, Steve Guttenberg and Ted Danson play three bachelors caring for a baby in Leonard Nimoy's "Three Men and a Cradle."

music by Marvin Hamlisch; production designer, Peter Larkin; produced by Ted Field and Robert W. Cort; released by Buena Vista Pictures Inc. At Embassy One, Broadway at 46th Street; Manhattan Twin, Third Avenue at 59th Street; Olympia Quad, Broadway at 107th Street; Embassy 72d Street, at Broadway and other theaters. Running time: 99 minutes. This film is rated PG.

Peter	Tom Selleck
Michael	Steve Guttenberg
Jack	Ted Danson
Sylvia	Nancy Travis
Rebecca	Margaret Colin
Patty	Alexandra Amini
Woman at Gift Shop	Francine Beers
Mary	Lisa Blair/Michelle Blair
Detective Melkowitz	Philip Bosco
Dramatic Actress	Barbara Budd

By JANET MASLIN

IT'S even clearer in the big, splashy, good-humored American version of "Three Men and a Baby" that it was in the French original (entitled "Three Men and a Cradle") that this story is about four babies, not just one. Aside from the infant girl left on their doorstep, the three fun-loving bachelors who grudgingly adopt her are children too. When the story begins, they have not a care in the world, just a life filled with revelry and a penthouse apartment that is a monument to their frolicsome ways. The American film makes this especially evident by filling the place with things like a jukebox and a pool table, the grownup equivalent of toys.

"Three Men and a Baby," which opens today at the Embassy 72d Street and other theaters, follows the French film as faithfully as it possibly can, and it too revolves around one lone idea: that there's humor in the spectacle of a grown man, heretofore ignorant of his own gentler nature, discovering that he can indeed administer formula and change diapers. The hilarity inherent in this has its limits, but it's a premise with enough timeliness and warmth to account for the first film's success. And in terms of success, this glossier, more effervescent remake will undoubtedly outstrip the original.

While preserving whatever bottled lighting there was to account for the magic in Coline Serreau's earlier film, "Three Men and a Baby" has taken on a brighter look, a grander setting and a more openly wisecracking tone. What it has lost is the funny, magisterial solemnity that Miss Serreau's three French bachelors could bring to the simplest aspects of baby care, and some of the humor that derived therefrom. When the infant made a mess on their sofa, these Frenchmen had no compunction about calling her a swine, while the attitude of their American counterparts is more laissez-faire. Either way, it all adds up to the same thing, and the spectacle of three grown men falling in love with their tiny charge

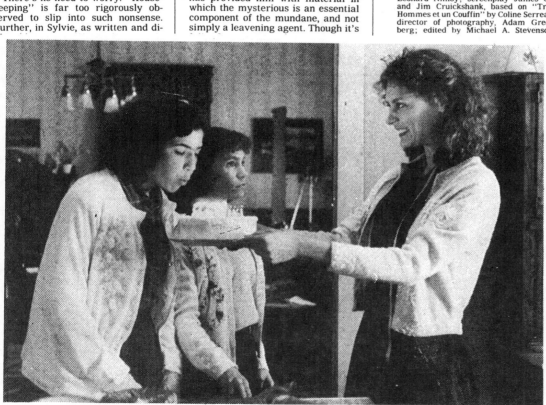

Sara Walker, left, Andrea Burchill, center, and Christine Lahti in a scene from "Housekeeping."

is heartwarming as ever.

•

The three bachelors, Peter (Tom Selleck), Michael (Steve Guttenberg) and Jack (Ted Danson), have had their occupations upgraded somewhat, and their scale of living greatly improved. Their shared apartment is now a palatial playhouse, and Jack is a globe-trotting, egocentric actor where his French counterpart was a mere flight steward. Either way, Jack has unknowingly fathered a child, and the baby is left at his doorstep just after he leaves for a lengthy trip overseas. So Jack's roommates, who initially refer to the child as "it," have no choice but to sharpen their baby-sitting skills.

"Three Men and a Baby" was directed by Leonard Nimoy, whose "Star Trek" direction gave little indication that he had the requisite sense of humor for this job. Happily, he does, and the film bubbles along in a funny if predictable way, with a lot more gags than the earlier film managed. "Angela! You look different, what happened?" cries the lady-killer of the trio, Jack, at the lavishly staged party scene that opens the film. "I'm dressed!" Angela replies. The screenplay, by James Orr and Jim Cruickshank, doesn't exactly take the high road, but it does have a dependable sense of fun.

Mr. Danson stands out as the cut-up among the three, even though the plot calls for him to be absent during a long middle section of the film. Mr. Selleck, as an architect who starts out resenting the newcomer, Mary (played by enchanting little twins, Lisa and Michelle Blair), but eventually takes her to a job site in a tiny pink hard hat, succeeds in melting before the audience's eyes. Mr. Guttenberg is a bit melty to begin with, trying harder than necessary to ingratiate, but he too fits winningly into this team. That none of these actors, except perhaps for Mr. Danson, has the powerful personality to carry a film alone only contributes to the easy, friendly team spirit that prevails.

Though the latter part of the story has been simplified, the film is still saddled with a cumbersome subplot about drug smuggling, and it still lacks any sense of the wider world (the effort to deal with the child's mother, essentially a walk-on character in both films, is especially weak here). However, some of the singularly American additions have been wittily done. In repeating the scene that has Peter going out to buy diapers, the joke becomes not just the bachelor's ignorance but the supermarket's staggering abundance of baby supplies. And where else would two bachelors, when they can't reach their roommate by telephone and rush home worriedly to find that he and the baby have been taking a shower, solve their problem by instantly having a new phone installed in the bathroom?

"Three Men and a Baby" has been given a new lease on life, and an enjoyable new lease at that. Whether it deserved or required any such thing is another matter.

"Three Men and a Baby" is rated PG ("Parental Guidance Suggested"). It contains brief bedroom scenes and some rude language.

1987 N 25, C24:3

BLIND, produced and directed by Frederick Wiseman; photography by John Davey; distributed by Zipporah Films Inc. At Film Forum 1, 57 Watts Street.

WITH: Students, teachers and staff of the Alabama School for the Deaf and Blind.

By VINCENT CANBY

FREDERICK WISEMAN, the lawyer turned film maker, made his first feature in 1967, the tough, harrowing, litigation-plagued "Titicut Follies," about life in the State Prison for the Criminally Insane at Bridgewater, Mass. It seems he's scarcely taken a day off since. In the last 20 years he's made 18 highly personal documentaries, most of them about institutions (hospitals, the police, the Army, meatpacking, among other subjects) that shape and define American life.

None of the Wiseman films I've seen to date initially appears to be quite as benign as his moving new film, "Blind," opening today at the Film Forum 1. The two-hour-plus feature is one of three that Mr. Wiseman has made about the work being done at the Alabama Institute for the Deaf and Blind at Talladega.

From the evidence presented by "Blind," which examines the education of sightless and vision-impaired children, the institute would seem to be exceptionally enlightened (and successful). However, as in virtually every Wiseman film, what's left unsaid and unseen in "Blind" is as important as anything that has reached the screen.

Mr. Wiseman and John Davey, his cameraman, apparently had free access to the classrooms. We see students from the age of 5 up learning to cope with physical handicaps as well as with more conventional courses in everything from English and music to civics (they read essays on "What America Means to Me," which often emphasize that America is *not* Russia).

•

A tiny boy named Jason makes his first solo voyage from a second-floor classroom to a classroom on the first floor, an adventure through corridors, around radiators and down stairways that, when one is blind, is as fraught with the unexpected as a descent from the Matterhorn.

The racially integrated children we see are, for the most part, unusually bright and responsive. It's only as the film proceeds that one realizes there are certain areas of school life about which Mr. Wiseman may have some doubts. In the office of the school's administrator there are references to William, who has what's described as "a tendency toward breaking and entering," for which he's being given the boot.

Another little boy, known as a troublemaker, is the subject of much discussion at a faculty meeting. The boy, it seems, delights in disrupting classes by, among other things, "rattling papers." There is talk about spanking him, though as one teacher points out, that's been tried in the past and hasn't been effective. The school's psychiatrist has no objections to trying it again. The boy, who has exhausted everyone's patience, begins to sound like a mini-member of the Red Brigades. It's a shock to see his solemn, impassive, totally defenseless face.

•

Since Mr. Wiseman never intrudes on his film, even as a voice on the soundtrack, we don't receive answers to questions that gnaw at the mind. Is spanking a regular part of the curriculum at this school that otherwise looks almost idyllic? We also see little

Evan Eames

A youngster learning to read in Frederick Wiseman's "Blind."

of the children's lives outside the classrooms and get only one quick view of their living quarters.

Like all Wiseman films, "Blind" remains in touch with the time and place beyond the immediate view of the camera, as when a teen-age boy talks to a counselor about his family problems. Is he bothered by the fact that his parents are divorced? In fact, he admits, his father has already left the woman for whom he left the boy's mother and is now living with someone else. The boy says it doesn't bother him, but he's still haunted by the wish they could get back together.

This is a reflection of the America of shopping malls, burger stands, service stations, run-down Main Streets, handsome, middle-class houses that we see at the beginning and the end of the film.

"Blind" opens with a sequence at a stock-car race track where the school's band gives a performancee before the start of the afternoon's events. The man responsible for "the race-track ministry" encourages the musicians. "Christ is the one who can fulfill you," he tells them. "You can find peace, happiness and contentment, whether you're blind or not." His blessing, spoken over the track's public address system: "Father, we ask that you be with this race, and that there be no injuries."

1987 D 2, C18:4

Bumbling Agents

THE TROUBLE WITH SPIES, directed, written and produced by Burt Kennedy, based on the book "Apple Spy in the Sky" by Marc Lovell; director of photography, Alex Phillips; music by Ken Thorne; production designer, José María Tapiador; released by De Laurentiis Entertainment Group. At Criterion Center, Broadway and 45th Street. Running time: 91 minutes. This film is rated PG.

Appleton Porter	Donald Sutherland
Harry Lewis	Ned Beatty
Mrs. Arkwright	Ruth Gordon
Mona Smith	Lucy Gutteridge
Jason Lock	Michael Hordern
Angus Watkins	Robert Morley
Captain Sanchez	Gregory Sierra
María Sola	Suzanne Danielle

THE TROUBLE WITH SPIES" has the manner of an overage tadpole that knows it will never be a frog. It's dour and gloomy, though it's supposed to be lighthearted. Somewhere along the line, a turn was missed.

The film, which opens today at the Criterion Center, is a dreadfully inept espionage comedy in which bumbling British agents bump unfunnily into bumbling Russian agents, mostly on the Mediterranean island of Ibiza. The cast includes Donald Sutherland, Ned Beatty, Michael Hordern, Robert Morley and, in what must have been one of her last film roles, Ruth Gordon, who died in 1985.

Burt Kennedy, who made some entertaining action films ("The War Wagon," among others) many years ago, wrote and directed it in 1984. "The Trouble With Spies" should be put back into its can and a heavy object placed on top, to prevent any further escapes.

•

"The Trouble With Spies," which has been rated PG ("Parental Guidance Suggested"), contains some mildly vulgar language.

VINCENT CANBY

1987 D 4, C5:1

Satire

REPENTANCE, directed by Tengiz Abuladze; written (in Georgian with English subtitles) by Nana Djanelidze, Tengiz Abuladze and Rezo Kveselava; director of photography, Mikhail Agranovich; music arranged by Nana Djanelidze; art director, Georgy Mikeladze; produced by Gruziafilm Studio. At Cinema Studio 1, Broadway and 66th Street. Running time: 145 minutes. This film has no rating.

Varlam Aravidze/Avel Aravidze	Avtandil Makharadze
Katevan Baratelli	Zeinab Botsvadze
Sandro Baratelli	Edisher Giorgobiani
Nino Barataelli	Katevan Abuladze
Guliko Aravadze	Iya Ninidze
Tornike	Merab Ninidze

By JANET MASLIN

THE skill with which "Repentance" has been made is sure to be eclipsed in importance by the very fact that it was made at all. The level of political self-criticism to be found in this Soviet film is so high, and the satire so scathing, that "Repentance" has been greeted as a phenomenon at home. For American audiences, it will seem almost equally startling. Yet "Repentance" also warrants attention for the flamboyant directorial style of Tengiz Abuladze, a man who favors surreal touches, unexpected leaps through time, and the blackest humor. "Repentance" would seem mordantly funny if its wit, like that of its central character, weren't also so cruel.

"Repentance," which opens today at the Cinema Studio 1, is a long, sprawling film with a style that is hardly seamless, yet Mr. Abuladze gives it a unifying vision. It centers on the mercurial figure of Varlam Aravidze, who was the mayor of a small Georgian village and is being buried as the film begins. As it turns out, he is gone but not forgotten, for his body reappears each morning in the garden of his son and daughter-in-law's unusually comfortable home. The body is positioned almost casually, propped against a tree, and is there each day no matter what precautions the townspeople take to trap it in its grave. Someone, it develops, wants to be certain that the mayor will not be left in peace.

That someone is a baker named Katevan Barateli, and much of the film is a flashback, presenting the story that she tells at her trial. It is the story of Varlam's long and sinister relationship with the people of his town, a relationship that begins on what appear to be friendly terms. Varlam likes to joke, even to play the clown. He professes to love art and music, to respect the importance of religion. But from the day of Varlam's inauguration, little Katevan's father, Sandro, a painter, sees danger coming. Soon after the first of his exchanges with the duplicitous mayor, Sandro has a dream that he and his wife are buried under newly plowed earth, with only their faces showing; watching them from the distance is Varlam, singing an aria.

•

Both the mayor and his grown son (in the film's later sections) are played by Avtandil Makharadze, an actor with a remarkable face. Mr. Makharadze would resemble Stalin even without the costumes and haircut he has been given here, and the addition of a small, vertical, Hitlerian black mustache only makes the effect that much more chilling. Mr. Makharadze perfectly embodies the mayor's mixture of hypocrisy and high-mindedness, evolving into an ever more deadly and corrupt figure as the story progresses. The persecution of Katevan's parents (the actor playing her father, Edisher Giorgobiani, has a Christ-like appearance) is depicted in specific detail, and Varlam's larger tyranny over the village is also presented. "If necessary, we'll catch a black cat in a dark room," says Varlam, "even if there's no cat there."

As its title suggests, the last part of "Repentance" concerns itself with contrition, as Varlam's descendants are forced to recognize his crimes; this section of the film is more ordinary than what comes before. Mr. Abuladze often illustrates Varlam's evildoing in lightheartedly surrealist terms that are, in this context, a real surprise, as when knights in armor appear in the background to support the black-shirted mayor in realizing his aims. Later on, when Sandro has been imprisoned — "exiled without the right to correspond," as his wife and daughter are told by a faceless official — he stands in a ruin overgrown by wildflowers while a man and woman at a white piano offer entertainment of a sort. Then the woman leaps back into position, replacing her blindfold and lifting her scales, for she turns out to be blind justice at its most unheeding. Imagery like this risks being terribly

Sovfoto (Abuladze)

Propped against a tree, the corpse of the evil Varlam fills his son, Avel, with terror in "Repentance."

heavy-handed, but Mr. Abuladze presents it with remarkable naturalness and ease.

The lessons of "Repentance" come through powerfully, but didacticism is not this film's foremost aim. It's a fine and accomplished work, as artful as it is sobering.

1987 D 4, C11:1

No Favors

STUDENT CONFIDENTIAL, written, produced, directed and edited by Richard Horian; director of photography, James Dickson; music by Mr. Horian; production designer, David Wasco; released by Troma. At Liberty, 42d Street, near Eighth Avenue; Movie Center 5, 235 West 125th Street. Running time: 95 minutes. This film is rated R.
Johnny Warshetsky .... Eric Douglas
Joseph Williams .... Marlon Jackson
Susan Bishop .... Susan Scott
Michael Drake .... Richard Horian
Elaine Duvat .... Elizabeth Singer
Jenny Selden .... Ronee Blakely

IT goes without saying that "Student Confidential" is bad, for it arrives by way of Troma Inc., the small company that has turned badness into an art form. Still, there are standards for everything, and this isn't the kind of bad film that's any fun.

Part of the problem is stupidity, or rather a lack of it: Richard Horian, who wrote, produced, edited and directed "Student Confidential" and further oversteps himself by serving as its star, insists on clipped, formal diction and stilted syntax at every turn. "Your use of innuendo is most disarming but not very subtle," says Mr. Horian, affecting an annoyingly mannered, huge-eyed naïveté to play

the guidance counselor at a very peculiar school.

The students include one ex-Playboy bunny (Susan Scott) and two mild-mannered brothers (Eric Douglas and Marlon Jackson) of better-known stars (Michael and Michael). So Mr. Horian ought to be credited with providing employment opportunities, but he hasn't done anyone any favors. "Student Confidential" isn't even the kind of raunchy, good-humored Troma embarrassment that actors like Kevin Costner ("Sizzle Beach, U.S.A.") or Vincent D'Onofrio of "Full Metal Jacket" ("The First Turn-On") get to live down later in their careers. If anyone here is on the verge of striking it big, it will indeed take hindsight to know.

•

In addition to being rather strange and (by Troma standards) arty, "Student Confidential," which opens today at the Liberty and Movie Center 5, is also dangerously slow. With its only focal point Mr. Horian's weird performance as the troubled, repressed counselor, the film must concentrate on nonsensical and protracted discussions revolving around each student's individual problems. About 15 minutes are devoted to the question of whether Miss Scott, whose face has supposedly been scarred in a terrible accident, should restyle her hair. _JANET MASLIN_

1987 D 4, C15:1

Universal View

A HERO'S JOURNEY: THE WORLD OF JOSEPH CAMPBELL, directed by William Free and Janelle Balnicke; photography by Erik Daarstad and H. J. Brown; edited by Yasha Aginsky; produced by Mr. Free. At the Eighth Street Playhouse, at Avenue of the Americas. Running time: 58 minutes. This film has no rating.

"A Hero's Journey: The World of Joseph Campbell" was shown as part of this year's New Directors/New Films series. These are excerpts from Janet Maslin's review, which appeared in The New York Times on March 22. The film opens today at the Eighth Street Playhouse.

AFFECTIONATELY profiled in the hourlong documentary "A Hero's Journey," the scholar and teacher Joseph Campbell seems a figure of heroic proportions. Along with outlining the basic tenets of Mr. Campbell's landmark theories concerning the universality of certain myths, the film touches on a protean life that is equally remarkable.

Mr. Campbell, who died on Oct. 30, is seen as a handsome and extremely charming man in his 80's, describing the pattern of his intellectual development with offhanded ease. He speaks of his early fascination with American Indian lore, saying, "I think that's where my life as a scholar began — I know it did." These tales, he found, "were symbolic stories that reconciled the Indians to the harsh reality of life." And they led the very young Mr. Campbell to contemplate the important role played by mythology in primitive cultures.

Once an altar boy in the Roman Catholic church, he found himself expanding religion into a larger mythological framework. An Atlantic crossing in the early 1920's led to a chance meeting with the philosopher Krishnamurti, under whose influence Mr. Campbell began to contemplate Eastern religions as well. And in Paris, he also located elements of a universal mythology in the works of Picasso, Matisse, Brancusi and other artists of the day.

•

By the time of the 1929 stock market crash, Mr. Campbell — who was also a saxophone player, an early surfer and one of the fastest halfmilers in the world — was ready to spend five years reading. After that, he emerged to begin teaching at Sarah Lawrence College, where he appears to have been understandably popular with his female students, one of whom he married. Seen in the film, expounding on his ideas in a seminar at Esalen, Mr. Campbell is still surrounded by admiring young women.

Another of Mr. Campbell's fans is the film maker George Lucas, who is

seen briefly at a testimonal event honoring the scholar. Indeed, clips from "Star Wars" are used to illustrate some aspects of the universal heroic figure, as set forth in Mr. Campbell's comprehensive work "The Hero With a Thousand Faces."

As directed by William Free and Janelle Balnicke, "A Hero's Journey: The World of Joseph Campbell" is both serious and colloquial, which aptly suits its subject.

1987 D 4, C18:1

Past as Prologue

WALKER, directed by Alex Cox; written by Rudy Wurlitzer; director of photography, David Bridges; film editors, Carlos Puente Ortega and Mr. Cox; music by Joe Strummer; production designer, Bruno Rubeo; produced by Lorenzo O'Brien; a Universal Picture. At Sutton, 57th Street and Third Avenue; Waverly, Avenue of the Americas at Third Street; Metro Twin, 99th Street and Broadway. Running time: 90 minutes. This film is rated R.
William Walker .... Ed Harris
Ephraim Squier ....Richard Masur
Maj. Siegfried Henningson Rene Auberjonois
Timothy Crocker ....Keith Szarabajka
Captain Hornsby .... Sy Richardson
Byron Cole .... Xander Berkeley
Stebbins ....John Diehl
Cornelius Vanderbilt .... Peter Boyle
Ellen Martin ....Marlee Matlin
Norvell Walker ....Gerrit Graham
James Walker ....William O'Leary
Yrena ....Blanca Guerra

By VINCENT CANBY

TAKING the true story of William Walker, the American adventurer who once ruled as the self-declared president of Nicaragua (1856-57), the director Alex Cox and the writer Rudy Wurlitzer have made "Walker," a hip, cool, political satire that's almost as lunatic as the title character.

The main difference is that the film intends to be funny while Walker, all five egocentric, puritanical feet of him, was fatally humorless. Though set in the mid-19th century, "Walker" is full of anachronisms, including Zippo lighters. At one point Walker's men are evacuated from a ticklish situation by a 1980's helicopter.

Mr. Cox and Mr. Wurlitzer apparently believe there's no point in wasting the hindsight conferred on them by time. Poor Walker couldn't see beyond the end of his nose, which is why his bold, blundering, occasionally brilliant campaigns ended in disaster.

For the film makers, Walker's invasion of Nicaragua, with 58 men and, initially, the enthusiastic support of Commodore Cornelius Vanderbilt ("I want that country stable!"), marked

the beginning of a new age in the relations between this country and Latin America. They also clearly believe that this "new age" continues with the United States' support of the Nicaraguan contras. Their case, like a Thomas Nast cartoon, is flip, irreverent, sparsely made and unkindly persuasive.

•

"Walker," which opens today at the Sutton and other theaters, doesn't pretend to be middle-of-the-road. It was produced with the complete cooperation of the Sandinista Government, mostly in Nicaragua where foreign intervention remains a vivid reality and not a memory of a colorful, bygone era.

It's difficult to realize today that the real-life Walker (1824-1860), who's now lucky to get a couple of paragraphs in an encyclopedia, was, briefly, one of the most celebrated public personalities of his time.

A qualified doctor, lawyer and journalist by the age of 24, Walker, like many of his contemporaries, wholeheartedly embraced the idea of America's "manifest destiny" as defined by John L. O'Sullivan in his U.S. Magazine & Democratic Review in 1845. "Our manifest destiny," O'Sullivan wrote, "is to overspread the continent allotted by Providence for the free development of our yearly multiplying millions."

The French describe people like Walker as chauvinist, after Nicolas Chauvin, who embraced Napoleon's imperial cause long after it was lost. The British term, jingoist (from the phrase "by jingo"), originated in a music-hall song popular at the time of the Crimean War. In this country, Walker and his kind were known as spread-eaglists.

•

Once they'd overspread the continent allotted by Providence, it seemed only natural to spread a little farther, first into Cuba and then into Mexico. This is where the film picks up Walker's story and where he first caught the attention of the American public and suffered his first defeat.

After failing to liberate Baja California from Mexico in 1854, Walker returned to this country to be tried (and acquitted) on charges of violating United States neutrality laws. The following year he took off for the west coast of Nicaragua to lend support to Nicaraguan liberals engaged in civil war with conservatives. In the ensuing confusion, he wound up as Nicaragua's president, as well as a mid-19th-century media phenomenon who almost persuaded President Pierce that Nicaragua should be annexed to the United States as a slave state.

Mr. Cox ("Repo Man," "Sid and Nancy") and Mr. Wurlitzer ("Two-Lane Blacktop") treat this extraordinary material not with solemn gravity but with deadpan amazement. "Walker" is the cinema equivalent of opéra bouffe. It's always sunny looking. The director shoots battle scenes that recall the slow-motion "blood ballets" from Sam Peckinpah's "Wild Bunch." Sometimes he speeds up the camera for comic effects that seem less jokey in Tony Richardson's "Tom Jones." Such affectations call attention to themselves, which, I suspect, is Mr. Cox's intention.

Giving the film coherence is its political conscience and the consistent intelligence of Mr. Wurlitzer's screenplay. The movie takes a few liberties with history (Walker and Vanderbilt never actually met, as they do in the film) and condenses time, but it somehow manages to make Walker into a quite engaging fanatic.

•

Parallels between Walker's patriotism and that of Lieut. Col. Oliver L. North, as presented in this summer's televised Iran-contra hearings, will inevitably be made. Yet they seem to be accidental, since the film had finished shooting several months before the hearings began. Ed Harris, who plays Walker, does have a lot of downhome charm, but he also had it when he played John Glenn in "The Right Stuff."

Mr. Harris may be a good deal taller than Walker ever was, but he has both the simplicity and the fervor to give substance to what might have been a line-drawing of a character. There's a kind of silent-film pathos in his scenes with Marlee Matlin (the Oscar winner for her performance in "Children of a Lesser God"), who plays his deaf but highly opinionated fiancée in the film's early sequences.

Once Walker arrives in Nicaragua, the movie becomes a breathless, neo-Brechtian, believe-it-or-not inventory of characters and events that must strike most Americans as outlandishly unbelievable, while many Central Americans may simply nod their heads in recognition.

Walker exhorts his men to act like the "honored guests" they are, then looks the other way as they run happily amok. The members of his motley crew retreat from a battle they've won. Walker talks about sacred trust, spiritual regeneration and freedom but finally, when cornered (after losing Vanderbilt's support), announces that he's found a solution to *his* country's economic problems: slavery.

•

Man of Destiny
In Alex Cox's "Walker," Ed Harris, at center, portrays William Walker, the 19th-century American who had himself declared President of Nicaragua.

Members of the excellent supporting cast, in addition to Miss Matlin, include Peter Boyle as Vanderbilt, Blanca Guerra as an aristocratic Nicaraguan beauty who seduces the priggish Walker, Gerrit Graham and William O'Leary as Walker's tagalong brothers, and Rene Auberjonois and Richard Masur as members of Walker's army.

"Walker" is witty, rather than laugh-out-loud funny. Without being solemn, it's deadly serious. It's also provocative enough to reach beyond — if not preach to — those who already are converted.

"Walker" is something very rare in American movies these days. It has some nerve.

1987 D 4, C36:1

HOME IS WHERE THE HART IS, directed and written by Rex Bromfield; director of photography, Robert Ennis; film editor, Michael Todd; music by Eric N. Robertston; art director, Jill Scott; produced by John M. Eckert; released by the Atlantic Entertainment Group. At Cine Twin, Seventh Avenue between 47th and 48th Streets. Running time: 94 minutes. This film is rated PG-13.
Belle Haimes .... Valri Bromfield
Rex Haimes .... Stephen E. Miller
Selma Dodge .... Deanne Henry
Carson Boundy ....Martin Mull
Martin Hart .... Eric Christmas
Art Hart ....Ted Stidder

By CARYN JAMES

When you have a plot in which 73-year-old twin brothers try to rescue their billionaire father from the roller derby queen turned nurse who kidnaps him with intent to marry — well, you pretty much have to go with the sheer stupidity of that idea. But in "Home Is Where the Hart Is," the writer and director Rex Bromfield makes comedy seem as moribund as Slim Hart, the near-speechless, heavily drugged 103-year-old object of this needless fuss. With no wild satire or lunatic frenzy to redeem it, "Home Is Where the Hart Is," which opened yesterday at the Cine Twin, never gets much funnier than its terrible punning title.

There should have been enough comic talent around to inspire Mr. Bromfield, who has made television documentaries in Canada and the United States. Valri Bromfield, (his sister), who plays the gold-digging Belle Haimes, sometimes puts comic freshness into tough-girl roles. Belle's sleazy lawyer, a guy with an oil-slick for hair, is played by Martin Mull, who often overcomes second-rate material. But neither does much with these worn-out characters.

•

As the twins, Eric Christmas and Ted Stidder resemble the old Yankee in Pepperidge Farm's television commercials and are quite appealing as they search for the man they still call Pappy. With their straightfaced deliveries, they might be playing feisty gents in some small British farce, but here they seem abandoned in a movie of their own. It's Leslie Nielson, as a sheriff named Nashvile Schwartz, who pulls off the best acting job. He makes it through this entire film, and does not look embarrassed once.

•

"Home Is Where the Hart Is" is rated PG-13 ("Special Parental Guidance Suggested for Those Under 13.") It contains four-letter words and other impolite language.

1987 D 5, 14:4

Baby Talk About Two Cultures

IN THE BLITHELY, DANGEROUSLY NONCONFORMist household in which Bill Forsyth's superb new "Housekeeping" unfolds, maintaining order may be a matter of sweeping the floating debris into closets while the flood waters surge knee-high. Or it might mean letting Darwinism prevail among the houseplants. "Fungus! D'you suppose she *grows* them?" exclaims a very proper lady from the local church, one of several sent to find out whether the woman of the house is a fit guardian for two young girls. What they discover, among other things, are giant mushrooms thriving in what is supposed to be a pot full of flowers.

This authentic chaos is a far cry from the controlled disarray to be found in "Three Men and a Baby," which embraces disorder with a good deal more caution. Both this film

'Three Men and a Baby' bears comparison to the French hit that inspired it.

and its French predecessor, Coline Serreau's "Three Men and a Cradle," are nominally about the confusion created in a three-man household once an uninvited infant appears on the doorstep. But their real focus is the conventionality that prevails there, baby notwithstanding.

Collectively, the six bachelors and two tots who appear in these two versions of the three men/baby story exemplify everything that is more or less normal in their respective cultures. What's interesting is that while the films are intentionally very similar, the differences between those cultures still come through. It is helpful, for purposes of this comparison, that these films are of equivalent merit, and that neither is anything more than light, agreeable farce. The American remake is the bigger and brighter of the two, with more jokes, but it lacks the comic solemnity of the French version, and it's slightly narrower in scope. In any case, no charges of tampering with genius can be leveled.

When the French film first struck box-office gold, there was talk of Miss Serreau directing the remake; the story of how this material found its way to Leonard Nimoy, who wound up directing it, would be worth hearing. So would the tale of how a decision was made to remake "Three Men and a Cradle" in the first place, since the French film speaks for itself and the American one copies it as closely as possible.

However, there are some interesting differences. Neither film goes out of its way to explain the circumstances by which three playboys have set up housekeeping together, but the French version is somewhat more comfortable with this unusual living arrangement. The three French bachelors seem to have banded together in self-defense; one of them is heard exclaiming irritably that no women are allowed in the apartment for more than a night at a time; this seems to have been an official rule of the roost. And their large Parisian apartment, with its air of fading majesty, seems an extravagance they may well have had to join forces to afford. By contrast, the American penthouse apartment is much more lavish, and just about everything in it (except for the vintage jukebox) is brand new. Though the American characters are supposed to be much more professionally successful than the French ones, the sheer excessiveness of their surroundings creates less an air of playboy sophistication than of childlike overindulgence.

■

While neither film deals very well with the question of what sort of mother would knowingly abandon her child to this trio, the French film is considerably more comfortable with the idea that the baby has a mother at all. It briefly attempts to illustrate that the mother, a flighty fashion model, is as hopelessly irresponsible as the airline steward (a mediocre film star in the American version) who fathered the child. In the American film the mother appears only for a moment, and she is welcomed almost as one of the boys. In its way, this development is a lot more peculiar than the French film's device of letting the mother fall peacefully asleep in her daughter's crib.

Another notable difference: the French child's startled grandmother (the baby was a complete surprise to all concerned) is simply too distracted to babysit. The American grandmother, played with tartness and wit by Celeste Holm, is a much more parental figure, and she is nobody's fool.

Both films are encumbered by an uninteresting drug-smuggling subplot and, not surprisingly, it is the American version that parlays this into a big, noisy chase scene that has little to do with the baby-oriented story. But the American film also lends itself to other visual flourishes, and its sight gags are a welcome addition to a plot that's essentially very thin. All three of the film's stars, Ted Danson, Tom Selleck and Steve Guttenberg, are ingratiating actors with a flair for television comedy timing, and they give the American film a much more jokey tone than its predecessor. The French story, particularly in its early stages, is instead told with an air of quiet outrage, as these fastidious bachelors endure the humiliation of watching the child do unspeakable things to their furniture. Each film contains its party scenes, but the bash that opens the remake exists mostly to establish the playboys' characters; it's fun, but gives no notion of the world around them. The French film doesn't either, but includes a dinner party in which one guest announces his intellectual disdain of infants, the young women register irritation at the bachelors' not paying them enough attention, and the baby's crying brings the party to an early close. Of course, this scene isn't in the American remake. An episode that really depicted a baby as unwelcome, unpleasant and even socially unacceptable would be un-American indeed. □

1987 D 6, II:23:5

Wartime Exploits

EMPIRE OF THE SUN, directed by Steven Spielberg; screenplay by Tom Stoppard, based on the novel by J. G. Ballard; director of photography, Allen Daviau; edited by Michael Kahn; music by John Williams; production designer, Norman Reynolds; produced by Mr. Spielberg, Kathleen Kennedy and Frank Marshall; released by Warner Brothers. At National Twin, Broadway and 44th Street; Regency Cinema, Broadway and 67th Street; Beekman, Second Avenue and 66th Street; 34th Street East, near Second Avenue; Movieland Eighth Street Triplex, at University Place. Running time: 145 minutes. This film is rated PG.
Jim .... Christian Bale
Basie ....John Malkovich
Mrs. Victor .... Miranda Richardson
Frank .... Joe Pantoliano
Jim's Father .... Rupert Frazer
Jim's Mother .... Emily Richard
Mr. Maxton ....Leslie Phillips

By JANET MASLIN

GOD playing tennis: that's what Jim Graham (Christian Bale), a privileged British schoolboy living in high colonial style in the pre-Pearl Harbor Shanghai of 1941, sees in one of his dreams. God taking a photograph: Jim thinks he sees that four years and seemingly several lifetimes later, as a starving, exhausted prisoner witnessing the brilliant light of the atomic bomb.

What transpires in between, the sweeping story of Jim's wartime exploits after he is separated from his family, is set forth so spectacularly in Steven Spielberg's "Empire of the Sun" that the film seems to speak a language all its own. In fact it does, for it's clear Mr. Spielberg works in a purely cinematic idiom that is quite singular. Art and artifice play equal parts in the telling of this tale. And the latter, even though intrusive at times, is part and parcel of the film's overriding style.

Yes, when Jim crawls through swampy waters he emerges covered with movie mud, the makeup man's kind; when he hits his head, he bleeds movie blood. It's hard not to be distracted by such things. But it's also hard to be deterred by them, since that same movie-conscious spirit in Mr. Spielberg gives "Empire of the Sun" a visual splendor, a heroic adventurousness and an immense scope that make it unforgettable.

•

There are sections of "Empire of the Sun" that are so visually expressive they barely require dialogue (although Tom Stoppard's screenplay, which streamlines J. G. Ballard's autobiographical novel, is often crisp and clever). Its first half hour, for example, could exist as a silent film — an extraordinarily sharp evocation of Shanghai's last prewar days, richly detailed and colored by an exquisite foreboding. Jim is first seen singing in a church choir (the Welsh hymn "Suo Gan" will echo again hauntingly later in the story), then gliding through crowded streets in his family's chauffeur-driven Packard. At home, he asks his parents off-handed questions about the coming war. When the three of them, elaborately costumed, heedlessly leave home for a party on the other side of the city, it's clear that their days there are numbered just from the way the Chinese servants wave goodbye.

•

That first glimpse of the choirboys will prompt audiences to wonder which of these well-groomed, proper little singers is to be the film's leading man. Mr. Bale, who emerges from the choir by singing a solo, at first seems just a handsome and malleable young performer, another charming child star. But the epic street scene that details the Japanese invasion of the city and separates Jim from his parents reveals this boy to be something more. As Mr. Bale, standing atop a car amid thousands of extras and clasping his hands to his head, registers the fact that Jim is suddenly alone, he conveys the schoolboy's real terror and takes the film to a different dramatic plane. This fine young actor, who appears in virtually every frame of the film and ages convincingly from about 9 to 13 during the course of the story, is eminently able to handle an ambitious and demanding role.

Once "Empire of the Sun," which opens today at the National and other theaters, follows Jim to the prison camp where he spends the duration of the war, it becomes slightly less focused. The pattern of events that occur within the camp is at times difficult to follow, in part because the emphasis is divided equally among so many different characters and episodes. When Mr. Spielberg — again, working almost without dialogue — outlines Jim's growing friendship with a Japanese boy from the airfield that adjoins the prison camp, or demonstrates Jim's profound respect for the Japanese pilots he sees there, the film takes on the larger-than-life emotional immediacy it seems designed for. But other episodes are less sharply defined. When Jim, who has proudly won his right to live in the American barracks, returns to the British camp in which he formerly lived, it takes a moment to remember why he's back — not because the motive is unclear, but because his depar-

ture from the one place and return to the other are separated by intervening scenes.

•

Still, there are many glorious moments here, among them Jim's near-religious experiences with the fighter planes he sees as halfway divine (in one nighttime scene, the sparks literally fly). And there is a full panoply of supporting characters, including Miranda Richardson, who grows more beautiful as her spirits fade, in the role of a married English woman who both mothers Jim and arouses his early amorous stirrings. It is the mothering that seems to matter most, for Jim's small satchel of memorabilia includes a magazine photograph of a happy family, a picture he takes with him everywhere. For a surrogate father, he finds the trickier figure of Basie (John Malkovich), a Yank wheeler-dealer with a sly Dickensian wit. Basie, who by turns befriends Jim and disappoints him, remains an elusive character, but Mr. Malkovich brings a lot of fire to the role. "American, are you?" one of his British fellow prisoners asks this consummate operator. "Definitely," Mr. Malkovich says.

"Gone With the Wind" is playing at the biggest movie theater in Shanghai when the Japanese are seen invading that city, and "Gone With the Wind" is a useful thing to remember. The makers of that film didn't really burn Atlanta; that wasn't their style. They, too, as Mr. Spielberg does, let the score sometimes trumpet the characters' emotions unnecessarily, and they might well have staged something as crazy as the "Empire of the Sun" scene in which the prisoners find an outdoor stadium filled with confiscated art and antiques and automobiles, loot that's apparently been outdoors for a while but doesn't look weatherbeaten in the slightest. Does it matter? Not in the face of this film's grand ambitions and its moments of overwhelming power. Not in the light of its soaring spirits, its larger authenticity, and the great and small triumphs that it steadily delivers.

1987 D 9, C25:1

Christian Bale as Jim Graham, a British schoolboy, in "Empire of the Sun."

Greed

WALL STREET, directed by Oliver Stone; written by Stanley Weiser and Mr. Stone; director of photography, Robert Richardson; film editor, Claire Simpson; music by Stewart Copeland; production designer, Stephen Hendrickson; produced by Edward R. Pressman; released by 20th Century-Fox Film Corporation. At Criterion Center, Broadway between 44th and 45th Streets; Gotham Cinema, Third Avenue at 58th Street; 86th Street East Twin, between Second and Third Avenues; Olympia Cinemas, Broadway at 107th Street; Movieland Eighth Street, at University Place. Running time: 120 minutes. This film is rated R.

Gordon Gekko	Michael Douglas
Bud Fox	Charlie Sheen
Darien Taylor	Daryl Hannah
Lou Mannheim	Hal Holbrook
Sir Larry Wildman	Terence Stamp
Carl Fox	Martin Sheen
Kate Gekko	Sean Young
Marvin	John C. McGinley
Ollie	Josh Mostel
Stone Livingston	Paul Guilfoyle
Realtor	Sylvia Miles
Mrs. Fox	Millie Perkins
Cromwell	Richard Dysart
Bidder at Auction	Richard Feigen
Artist at Auction	James Rosenquist

By VINCENT CANBY

OLIVER STONE'S "Wall Street" is a gentrified "Everyman," an upscale morality tale to entertain achievers who don't want to lose touch with their moral centers, but still have it all.

It's about Bud Fox (Charlie Sheen), a bright, blindingly ambitious young Wall Street broker who, on the strength of one insider tip, gains a spectacular career but loses his soul, at least temporarily. More important, it's also about Gordon Gekko (Michael Douglas), a corporate raider for whom "rich" isn't "$450,000 a year, but rich enough to have your own jet."

"Wake up, pal," Gekko tells Fox. "If you aren't inside, you're outside." Relying on information acquired by illegal hook and crook, Gekko buys up companies for peanuts and liquidates them for big bucks. "I create nothing," he says with his usual candor. "I own."

Gordon Gekko is a good character. He's ruthless, ironic and, under the circumstances, completely practical, and Mr. Douglas, in the funniest, canniest performance of his career, plays him with the wit and charm of Old Scratch wearing an Italian-designer wardrobe.

Somewhere toward the middle of "Wall Street," Gekko takes the microphone at the annual meeting of Teldar Paper, a company he's seeking to acquire, to deliver a pep talk on greed that — briefly — electrifies the movie. He sounds like Gore Vidal jazzing up the pages of The New York Review of Books.

"America has become a second-rate power," Gekko tells the Teldar shareholders. He cites the nation's horrendous trade imbalance and describes the backward state of domestic companies in competition with off-shore industry. Greed, he says, is all we have left, but greed is also what made America great. It's normal. It's healthy and it's what keeps the system going. By the time Gekko finishes, the stockholders in tennis shoes are cheering.

After that, "Wall Street" is all downhill.

Mr. Stone takes a dim view of the moral climate in which insider trading can flourish and corporate raiders are role models for the young. He comes out foursquare against a system that creates paper profits at the cost of diminishing products, services and jobs. Mr. Stone's heart is in the right place but, ultimately, his wit fails him. The movie crashes in a heap of platitudes that remind us that honesty is, after all, the best policy.

•

"Wall Street" isn't a movie to make one think. It simply confirms what we all know we should think, while giving us a tantalizing, Sidney Sheldon-like peek into the boardrooms and bedrooms of the rich and powerful.

The movie's subject is a potentially great one that demands the sort of brainy, brazen, unsentimental common sense that illuminates "Major Barbara" and "Heartbreak House."

Shaw could write heroes and heroines that are a match for brilliant villains. Even at its best, "Wall Street," which opens today at the Criterion and other theaters, is an unequal struggle. At its worst, it's a muddle.

Bud Fox, as written by Stanley Weiser and Mr. Stone, and as played by a spruced-up Charlie Sheen, is a softer, dopier version of Chris, Mr. Sheen's young soldier who's the conscience of Mr. Stone's far more effective, more efficient "Platoon." Like Chris in "Platoon," Bud Fox also has two "fathers" wrestling for his allegiance. In opposition to the magnetic, successful Gekko, there's Bud's dad, Carl (played by Martin Sheen, Charlie's real-life father), an airline mechanic and staunch union man who sees Gekko as the Evil One he is.

To those of us outside Wall Street, Bud's rise to the top looks remarkably easy and is, essentially, not very dramatic. However, Mr. Stone has dressed up the movie with an exceptionally handsome (and sometimes satiric) physical production, a pounding soundtrack score, a camera so restless and edgy that it defines Bud Fox's ambition better than the screenplay does, and a lot of fast talk and Big Business arcana that give the movie a certain excitement and tension.

When Mr. Douglas is not at the center of the screen, the movie loses its grit. There's a possibly very funny sequence in which we see Daryl Hannah, as a high-class interior designer ("I'd like to do for furniture what Laura Ashley did for fabrics"), spending thousands to give Bud Fox's new penthouse-condo a look of chic dishevelment. Yet the characters aren't sharply enough defined to make the situation caustic. The performances don't help. Mr. Sheen lacks the necessary, nervy intelligence and Miss Hannah has the screen presence of a giant throw pillow.

By trotting out such real-life Manhattan characters as James Rosenquist, the painter, and Richard Feigen, the art dealer, the movie appears to be celebrating the very world into which Bud Fox has moved, finally, with such qualms.

After he's reached the pinnacle of his gaudy success, Bud arises from the bed he's been sharing with Miss Hannah to address the Upper East Side dawn from his penthouse terrace. It's supposed to be a moment of solemn introspection, but when he asks the sun, "Who am I?," rude answers may come from the back of the theater. As in Cecil B. DeMille's biblical epics, wickedness is a lot more attractive than perfunctory moralizing.

The generally excellent supporting cast includes Sean Young ("No Way Out"), who appears in a couple of scenes as Mr. Douglas's wife.

The confusion at the heart of the film may be exemplified in the names with which Mr. Stone has saddled his two principal characters. The movie boils down to Fox versus Gekko. We're all supposed to understand that a fox is a flesh-eating mammal thought to be "sly and crafty" (Webster's phrase). But what about Gekko?

In fact, a gecko is a harmless tropical lizard. With suction-cup feet it can walk across ceilings and, though it looks as ferocious as a miniature crocodile (up to 8, 10 or 12 inches long), it mostly hides during the day, coming out at night to eat flies, mosquitoes and other insects. Its droppings are annoying, but the gecko is part of the natural order of things.

If Gordon Gekko is understood this way, then "Wall Street" is a lot more subversive than maybe even Mr. Stone realizes.

1987 D 11, C3:4

Mirth Amid Murder

THROW MOMMA FROM THE TRAIN, directed by Danny DeVito; written by Stu Silver; director of photography, Barry Sonnenfeld; edited by Michael Jablow; music by David Newman; production designer, Ida Random; produced by Larry Brezner; released by Orion Pictures Corporation. At Guild 50th Street, west of Fifth Avenue; Paramount, 61st Street and Broadway; D. W. Griffith, 59th Street and Third Avenue; 34th Street Showplace, between Second and Third Avenues; Movie Center 5, 125th Street, between Powell and Douglass Boulevards. Running time: 88 minutes. This film is rated PG-13.

Owen	Danny DeVito
Larry	Billy Crystal
Beth	Kim Greist
Momma	Anne Ramsey
Margaret	Kate Mulgrew
Lester	Branford Marsalis
Joel	Rob Reiner

By JANET MASLIN

THE film with the best title around (well, it certainly gets your attention) and the year's most memorable trailer (a single, extended breakfast-table scene, culminating in Danny DeVito's swatting Billy Crystal with a frying pan) is even funnier than it promised to be. It's "Throw Momma From the Train," Danny DeVito's highly unorthodox variation on Hitchcock's "Strangers on a Train," which Mr. DeVito has had the good grace to credit directly. Not every remake-meister bothers to do this, after all. And there are other signs of an underlying decency that helps make the film enormously likable without compromising its mean-spirited fun.

In "Throw Momma From the Train," which opens today at the Paramount and other theaters, it happens that Owen Lift (Mr. DeVito) sees the Hitchcock film at the suggestion of his writing teacher, Larry Donner (Billy Crystal), who is really in no position to give Owen suggestions at all. Larry is himself suffering from a bad case of writer's block, exacerbated by the fact that his ex-wife (Kate Mulgrew) has become a best-selling author and now goes on talk shows to discuss her "prisonlike marriage" and her huge success. Each of these things makes Larry crazy, especially the latter. But he is helpless to do anything about it until Owen sees the Hitchcock film and begins

saying "Crisscross!" the way Robert Walker did. An idea is born.

Owen has a mother he hates, played by Anne Ramsey as the ultimate grotesque. Miss Ramsey speaks in guttural tones that are sometimes indecipherable, but belts out insults and motherly pleasantries with equal enthusiasm. She's a mother who surely deserves the Pepsi-and-lye elixir Owen considers putting in her teacup, but she's also terribly difficult to kill. So Owen suggests the famous exchange-of-murders idea, whereby he will dispatch Larry's wife if Larry returns the favor. Owen travels to Hawaii (Mr. DeVito cuts an especially funny figure in the tropics), locates Larry's wife and then phones Larry surreptitiously to deliver his message. What happened? Larry asks. "I don't want to say it on the phone," Owen whispers. "All I can say is that I killed her last night."

While it would be a lot more criminal than anything Owen does to reveal the rest of the story, it's fair to say that "Throw Momma From the Train" has as much to do with writing as with murder. Its writer's-block jokes are especially inspired, particularly the one that finally gives Larry the motivation he has badly lacked, and the scene that ends the film on a very sweet note. Most inspired, however, is the teamwork between Mr. Crystal and Mr. DeVito, who make one of the oddest pairs imaginable but have a rapport that's a delight. And Mr. DeVito, who has directed numerous television programs, does a fine job of giving "Throw Momma From the Train" a clean, bright look, a quick pace and and a lot of wide-angle or overhead shots to make it suitably strange. Barry Sonnenfeld's cinematography is an additional plus, as is the visual wit with which various transitional shots are made.

As Owen, Mr. DeVito is such an odd combination of the childlike and the diabolical that he remains a captivating figure throughout the story. Mr. DeVito's comic timing is particularly enjoyable, since he has such a slow, steady, deliberate way of building up to outrageous behavior. Bubbling over with poison, Mr. DeVito nonetheless manages to suggest innocence. He's irresistible even when playing someone only a mother could love.

"Throw Momma From the Train" is rated PG-13 ("Special Parental Guidance Suggested for Those Younger Than 13"). It contains some rude language.

1987 D 11, C15:1

THE WILD PAIR, directed by Beau Bridges; screenplay by Joseph Gunn; story by Mr. Gunn and John Crowther; director of photography, Peter Stein; edited by Christopher Holmes and Scott Conrad; music by John Debney; production designer, Stephen M. Berger; produced by Paul Mason; released by Trans World Entertainment. At the Criterion, Broadway and 45th Street. Running time: 86 minutes. This film is rated R.

Joe Jennings	Beau Bridges
Benny Avalon	Bubba Smith
Colonel Hester	Lloyd Bridges
Captain Kramer	Gary Lockwood
Ivory	Raymond St. Jacques
Tucker	Danny de la Paz
Debby	Lela Rochon

"The Wild Pair," which sneaked into the Criterion and other theaters yesterday, is about an F.B.I. man (white) and a big cop (black) who join together to bring down a big drug pusher (black) and a sadistic ex-Marine colonel (white) who is on a private mission to save America from lesser races. The good guys are played by Bubba Smith and Beau Bridges, who also directed. Their relationship begins on a testy note but, before long, would you believe, they come to like and respect each other.

The bad guys are played by Lloyd Bridges and Raymond St. Jacques. Mr. Bridges gets a chance to spout about "a carefully devised plot by black and yellow races, supported of course by the Jews, to undermine the young people of this great nation." His followers appear to have been recruited less for their sharpshooting (they keep missing the good guys) than for their ability to fly out of windows and off porches.

There are car chases to the usual rock sounds, explosions, stabbings and so forth, as well as episodes in an X-rated movie, a topless bar, a massage parlor, a gambling den, a sex shop and so forth. Mr. Smith, who works with kids in his spare time, gets angry when the bad guys kill his girlfriend and his cat. A big moment comes when Beau Bridges spits into the face of Lloyd Bridges. Nothing Freudian. Movies like this spit into audiences' faces all the time.

WALTER GOODMAN

1987 D 12, 19:1

Ambition Is All

BROADCAST NEWS, written, produced and directed by James L. Brooks; director of photography, Michael Ballhaus; edited by Richard Marks; music by Bill Conti; production designer, Charles Rosen; released by 20th Century-Fox Film Corporation. At Coronet, Third Avenue at 59th Street. Running time: 133 minutes. This film is rated R.

Tom Grunick	William Hurt
Aaron Altman	Albert Brooks

Mommacidal
Anne Ramsey plays the title role and Danny DeVito is the son who asks a friend to kill her in "Throw Momma From the Train."

Laurel Moore

William Hurt and Holly Hunter portray a television news anchor and a producer in "Broadcast News."

Jane Craig	Holly Hunter
Ernie Merriman	Robert Prosky
Jennifer Mack	Lois Chiles
Blair Litton	Joan Cusack
Paul Moore	Peter Hackes
Bobby	Christian Clemenson
Martin Klein	Robert Katims

By VINCENT CANBY

THERE once was a time when big news events had the power to stun and, sometimes, to cause a certain amount of anxiety. Wars, earthquakes, airplane crashes, stock market busts, mass-murder sprees, kidnappings, duplicity in positions of public trust, political assassinations. These things could upset daily routine. They were reminders of the precariousness of the existence we tend to take for granted.

Today, having harnessed the atom, we're well on the way toward the taming of fate or, at least, our perception of random events as presented on the home television screen. Today, thanks to the warmth and sincerity of Dan and Peter and Jane and Connie, we might even accept — with little more than informed concern — the imminent end of the world: after the bang, we'll have these messages from the sponsors and then tomorrow's weather.

Television news-as-entertainment is the very funny, occasionally satiric subtext of "Broadcast News," the bright new comedy written and directed by James L. Brooks, with three smashing star performances by William Hurt, Albert Brooks and Holly Hunter. "Broadcast News" opens today at the Coronet.

In his first film since his Oscar-winning "Terms of Endearment," Mr. Brooks goes inside the offices and studios of the Washington bureau of a national television network to show us how things work. As exposés go, "Broadcast News" is gentle. It's far more amused than angry. Its wit is decently humane. It also says something about the pervasive nature of television that, although the subject is parochial, "Broadcast News" is no more or less arcane than "Miami Vice."

The movie is mainly concerned with the fortunes of three ambitious colleagues.

Tom Grunick (Mr. Hurt) is on his way up as an anchor. When he arrives at his new Washington berth, he is, by his own admission, "no good at what I'm being a success at." He can't write. He has no experience as a newsman. Yet he's making a fortune. What he does have, in addition to good looks, is a lot of savvy on how to use the camera.

Seen sitting at his anchor desk in a big fat close-up, Tom Grunick can take information being fed to him (via a hidden head-mike from the control room) and translate it into an expression of a singularly magnetic public personality. Cool, intelligent, caring. Off camera, Tom Grunick is earnest, well meaning, none too well informed. On camera he's the soul of Walter Cronkite inhabiting the physique of a matinee idol.

Aaron Altman (Albert Brooks) is an old-fashioned reporter. He's his own best legman. He's a quick study and possesses the kind of curiosity that equips him to cover just about any kind of story. He's a successful on-camera reporter, the sort who, without missing a beat, can switch from a story about equal opportunity employment to one about a war veteran.

More than anything else, Aaron Altman wants to be an anchor. However, when the lights are on him, behind that great, photogenic, immaculate desk in the news studio, Aaron Altman, Pulitzer Prize-winning reporter, goes to pieces. He sweats like a weight lifter and projects the charm of an unsuccessful salesman of used cars.

Jane Craig (Miss Hunter) is a pretty, brainy young woman who's obsessed with her work as a producer of television news spots. She's smart enough to know news from filler material and how best to present it. She's one of those women sometimes thought to be too smart for their own good, and sometimes she has to agree. When the head of the network

news division says, with a good deal of sarcasm, "It must be nice to always think you're the smartest person in the room," she replies, "No, it's awful."

●

The private lives of Tom, Aaron and Jane are scarcely more than slight interruptions in their careers. They exist entirely within their jobs. In the course of "Broadcast News," as the network goes through various upheavals, the three become emotionally involved in ways that would seem heartbreaking to people less ambitious. Here it's the material of high comedy.

Mr. Brooks's screenplay overstates matters both at the beginning of the film and at the end, with a prologue that strains to be cute and an epilogue that is just unnecessary. In between, however, the movie is a sarcastic and carefully detailed picture of a world Mr. Brooks finds fascinating and also a little scary.

Mr. Hurt, a most complicated actor, is terrific as a comparatively simple man, someone who's perfectly aware of his intellectual limitations but who sees no reason for them to interfere with his climb to the top. Miss Hunter, whose performance as the wife in "Raising Arizona" was lost in that film's comic frenzy, is a delight as a woman who at heart is quite satisfied to be liberated. Miss Hunter is a bit reminiscent of Debra Winger (who seems to be this year's role model for actresses) but is idiosyncratic enough to lend her own substance to the film.

●

As the fast-talking Aaron, Albert Brooks comes very close to stealing "Broadcast News." Mr. Brooks, who has directed and starred in three genially oddball comedies of his own (the most recent being "Lost in America"), is more or less the conscience of "Broadcast News."

Yet James Brooks, as this film's writer-director, has so balanced the movie that no one performer can run off with it. This would include Jack Nicholson, who makes a fine unbilled appearance as the network's star anchor from New York.

Mr. Brooks gives his characters the benefit of the doubt. Unlike stock figures, they can send themselves up. Says one reporter to another, "Would you tell a source you loved them just to get information?" The immediate response, "Yes," is followed by laughter all around. In fact, the question remains unanswered.

1987 D 16, C21:4

OVERBOARD, directed by Garry Marshall; written by Leslie Dixon; director of photography, John A. Alonzo; edited by Dov Hoenig and Sonny Baskin; music by Alan Silvestri; art directors, James Shanahan and Jim Dultz; produced by Alexandra Rose and Anthea Sylbert; released by Metro-Goldwyn-Mayer. At Warner, Broadway and 43d Street; 34th Street Showplace, between Second and Third Avenues; Gemini Twin, Second Avenue at 64th Street; Olympia Quad, Broadway at 107th Street. Running time: 115 minutes. This film is rated PG.

Joanna/Annie	Goldie Hawn
Dean Proffitt	Kurt Russell
Grant Stayton 3d	Edward Herrmann
Edith Mintz	Katherine Helmond
Billy Pratt	Michael Hagerty
Andrew	Roddy McDowall
Charlie	Jared Rushton
Joey	Jeffrey Wiseman
Travis	Brian Price
Greg	Jamie Wild
Captain Karl	Frank Campanella
Dr. Norman Korman	Harvey Alan Miller

Who Am I?
Goldie Hawn portrays a wealthy woman who loses her memory in "Overboard."

"OVERBOARD" is an apt title for a comedy that tries to show how the hard, brittle, thoroughly horrible exterior of an heiress named Joanna Stayton (Goldie Hawn) actually conceals a sweet, spunky, hardworking little homemaker and mom. All Joanna needs is a bout of amnesia to bring the better person within her to the fore.

While the prospect of watching Miss Hawn play a rude, nasty socialite is appealing (indeed, she has a wonderful time with this brief part of the role), and even the transformation to homebody is a funny idea, "Overboard" winds up taking things too far. By the end of the film, Miss Hawn has become just too virtuous to be any fun.

In "Overboard," which opens today at the Warner and other theaters, Joanna starts off aboard her yacht near the none-too-picturesque village of Elk Cove, Ore. The boat is stuck there while some repairs are being done, and this leaves Joanna even more bored and irritable than usual. So she torments Dean Proffitt (Kurt Russell), the carpenter she has hired to improve her closets, and then she refuses to pay his bill. Soon afterward, when Joanna accidentally falls overboard and develops amnesia, Dean has an opportunity to get even.

●

Ensconced in the local hospital as a "mystery woman," Joanna goes unclaimed for quite a while. Her husband, Grant (played by Edward Herrmann as an even sillier twit than he had to be), knows full well where Joanna is, but decides to take advantage of her memory loss. So does Dean, who claims her as his wife and takes her home to his messy shack and his four unruly children.

As written by Leslie Dixon (who wrote "Outrageous Fortune") and directed by Garry Marshall, "Overboard" is loaded with potential as long as it sticks to Joanna's comic revulsion at all this squalor, and her suspicion that she may be cut from different cloth. Dean really exacerbates matters by making up stories about how forward she was on their first date, and insisting that his oafish, beer-drinking buddy (played enjoyably by Michael Hagerty) is her high-school beau.

However, no one is content to leave well enough alone. Miss Hawn, now called Annie, must rise magnificently to her new responsibilities. After the initial funny complaints let up ("My life is like death, my children are the spawn of hell!" she shrieks at one point), the shack begins to look better and everyone's spirits improve. The place is clean. The kids behave. Store-bought marigolds sprout in the yard. Pretty soon, Annie is even self-possessed enough to go to school with "her" children and berate their teacher.

•

"Overboard," which sinks when it becomes this self-righteous, is clever enough to let love bloom spontaneously between Dean and his Annie, thus avoiding charges of sexism or white slavery. Though it starts on a note of enjoyable hostility between the two of them, the film soon aims for lighthearted romance. Mr. Marshall does a much better job with the feistier early scenes than with this subsequent mush, so the film does have a good first hour. But by the end, the process of getting Annie/Joanna back to her husband and mother (Katherine Helmond) and making her realize that money isn't everything is as laborious as lifting luggage (and incidentally, she's able to keep her money, no matter what). The film goes on much longer than it should.

The physical look of "Overboard" is also surprisingly dreary. Though the yacht scenes have some visual wit, particularly where Miss Hawn's outrageous costumes are concerned, John A. Alonzo's cinematography is conspicuously poor.

•

"Overboard" is rated PG ("Parental Guidance Suggested"). It includes some vulgar language.

JANET MASLIN

1987 D 16, C22:3

'That's Amore'

MOONSTRUCK, directed by Norman Jewison; written by John Patrick Shanley; director of photography, David Watkin; film editor, Lou Lombardo; music by Dick Hyman; production designer, Philip Rosenberg; produced by Patrick Palmer and Mr. Jewison; released by Metro-Goldwyn-Mayer. At Sutton, Third Avenue at 57th Street; 84th Street Six, at Broadway. Running time: 102 minutes. This film is rated PG.

Loretta Castorini	Cher
Ronny Cammareri	Nicolas Cage
Cosmo Castorini	Vincent Gardenia
Rose Castorini	Olympia Dukakis
Mr. Johnny Cammareri	Danny Aiello
Rita Cappomaggi	Julie Bovasso
Perry	John Mahoney
Raymond Cappomaggi	Louis Guss

By JANET MASLIN

THE moon hits your eye like a big pizza pie in "Moonstruck," and a lot of other things do too. "Moonstruck" is so heavily ethnic that it begins with Dean Martin's rendition of "That's Amore," and there's plenty more where that came from. With its accordion music, its bits of dialect and its love of opera (a key segment of the story unfolds at a Metropolitan Opera performance of "La Bohème"), "Moonstruck" clearly means to celebrate all things Italian. However, it creates the false but persistent impression that most of the people who made it have never been closer to Italy than, perhaps, Iowa.

"Moonstruck," which opens today

Cher and Nicolas Cage in "Moonstruck."

at the Sutton and other theaters, was directed by Norman Jewison, who may just be the Sir Richard Attenborough of light comedy. However, it offers further proof that Cher has evolved into the kind of larger-than-life movie star who's worth watching whatever she does. This time, she plays frumpy, which for Cher just means longer hems and a little gray in her hair. Those who wait for a Cinderella-like transformation will not be disappointed.

Cher also has what's supposed to be a comically heavy Brooklyn accent for her role as Loretta Castorini, who has a large, old-fashioned family and a job in a funeral parlor. As the film begins, Loretta becomes engaged to Johnny Cammareri, a doltish niceguy type played by Danny Aiello (in addition to Castorinis and Cammareris, there are also several Cappomaggis in the screenplay by John Patrick Shanley). Loretta is a widow, it develops. She's also the kind of woman who can explain that her first husband was run over by a bus in an utterly uninterested tone of voice.

•

Right after the marriage proposal — delivered in a crowded Italian restaurant with a lot of fuss about whether Johnny will kneel in his good suit — Johnny goes to Italy to see his dying mother and instructs Loretta to find his brother Ronny. This turns out to be Nicolas Cage, who has a role so awful that it's hard to know whom to blame. Ronny is a slob. He works stoking the oven in a bakery (as he describes the job, it's "sweat and sweat and sweat, and shove this stinkin' dough in and out of this hot hole in the wall!"). Ronny is also missing a hand, which he lost when Johnny came to see him years earlier and Ronny, lost in conversation, forgot to keep an eye on the bread slicer. It's impossible to tell whether this is supposed to be funny, but the film does carry a "Mr. Cage's Hand Design" credit for Eion Sprott.

The process whereby Loretta and Ronny fall in love is a lot less appealing than the large-family drama unfolding around the Castorinis' kitchen table (over which there is an ex-

tremely harsh, glaring light). Among the actors playing Loretta's older relatives are Julie Bovasso, Feodor Chaliapin Jr., Vincent Gardenia (as the father who spends much of the time listening to Vikki Carr sing "It Must Be Him") and Olympia Dukakis, who has a comic sourness to match Cher's and manages to have some good moments.

The title refers to one relative's theory that the full moon can make people wildly romantic, make them behave in wonderful, unpredictably crazy ways. Not crazy enough.

•

"Moonstruck" is rated PG ("Parental Guidance Suggested"). It contains a brief bedroom scene and minimal rude language.

1987 D 16, C22:3

Historical Movements

THE SPIRIT MOVES: A HISTORY OF BLACK SOCIAL DANCE ON FILM, Parts 1 and 2 directed and produced by Mura Dehn. Running time: 119 minutes.
IN A JAZZ WAY: A PORTRAIT OF MURA DEHN, directed by Louise Ghertler and Pamela Katz; distributed by Filmmakers Library. Running time: 30 minutes. At Film Forum 1, 57 Watts Street. These films have no rating.

By JENNIFER DUNNING

FOR many dancegoers, Mura Dehn is known, a little vaguely, as a woman who had something to do with film and black dancers. But the Film Forum is doing something about that, with a double feature consisting of "In a Jazz Way," a short film on Miss Dehn by Louise Ghertler and Pamela Katz, and a two-hour excerpt from "The Spirit Moves: A History of Black Social Dance on Film," a documentary by Miss Dehn. The program opens today for a two-week run at Film Forum 1.

"In a Jazz Way," shot in 1985, offers a tantalizing look at Miss Dehn. It has the look of a documentary that originally had more ambitious things

on its mind, but Miss Ghertler and Miss Katz do give us an undiluted dose of Miss Dehn, who died in February. We see her at her kitchen table, in her apartment in Washington Heights, reminiscing about her youth in Vienna and about her work recording and preserving the artistry of some of the great known and anonymous dancers of the Savoy Ballroom in Harlem.

Schooled in the dancing style of Isadora Duncan, Miss Dehn had been exposed to jazz in her native Russia, but she became a jazz fan when she met Josephine Baker in Paris in 1925. Judging by old film clips of her own work, Miss Dehn made fascinating use of jazz idioms to create her own unusual form of concert dance. She arrived in New York in 1930. "I wanted to come home," she says, "to be within my own land of dance. I was waiting to come."

•

"In a Jazz Way" does not attempt to give us a history of Miss Dehn's life and work, which included the formation of the Traditional Jazz Dance Company, a group of black entertainers active from 1932 to 1973. But we get a vivid sense of this vigorous, humane woman. There is some fairly stilted conversation with Alfred Liegens, the Savoy dancer and her teacher, but its tone is redeemed by a charming look at the two of them dancing expertly together in their old age. "One is lucky if, as a dancer, you have one or two good partners in your lifetime, like one or two good husbands," Miss Dehn observes.

She talks amusingly of her European counterparts' sour faces as they tried to "swallow the rhythmic pill" of jazz. Miss Dehn was more adventurous, a white woman moving unself-consciously into the Savoy with a movie camera and the reluctant permission of its manager. She analyzes the art of social dancing as being in part about knowing "how to hold your body and how to let it go." The truth of that observation is clear in all that we see, from the touching and funny sequence in where Miss Dehn films young break dancers of the 1980's to the sequences excerpted from "The Spirit Moves."

That film itself is overwhelming. Herbert Matter, Miss Dehn's chief cameraman, provides some striking silhouetted passages, sensitively using special effects to capture the excitement of the dance and music. But "The Spirit Moves" is at heart archival footage from the studio and the ballroom. Dance historians will learn much about the dance styles covered in the two hours shown here. We have, too, a living record of the men and women who forged those styles into an improvisational art form.

On another level, "The Spirit Moves" is a rare and vital social document. One can, for instance, see the truth of Miss Dehn's observation that the dances chronicle a time of prewar optimism for blacks, with the Lindy Hop, to the pessimism and disaffiliation of the postwar be-bop.

1987 D 16, C22:5

The Party's Over

THE DEAD, directed by John Huston; written by Tony Huston, based on the short story from the collection "Dubliners" by James Joyce; director of photography, Fred Murphy; edited by Roberto Silvi; music by Alex North; production designer, Stephen Grimes; produced by Wieland Schulz-Keil and Chris Sievernich; released

by Vestron Pictures. At Cinema 1, Third
Avenue and 60th Street. Running time: 83
minutes. This film is rated PG.

Gretta	Anjelica Huston
Gabriel	Donal McCann
Aunt Kate	Helena Carroll
Aunt Julia	Cathleen Delany
Mr. Brown	Dan O'Herlihy
Freddy Malins	Donal Donnelly
Mrs. Malins	Marie Kean
Mr. Grace	Sean McClory
Molly Ivors	Maria McDermottroe
Lily	Rachael Dowling
Miss Furlong	Katherine O'Toole
Miss Higgins	Bairbre Dowling
Bartell D'Arcy	Frank Patterson
Mary Jane	Ingrid Craigie

By VINCENT CANBY

"ONE by one we're all
becoming shades," says
Gabriel Conroy, looking
out into Dublin's bleak
winter dawn. Gretta, the wife he loves
and suddenly realizes he has never
known, lies asleep on the bed nearby.
His own life now seems paltry: "Better pass boldly into that other world,
in the full glory of some passion, than
fade and wither dismally with age."

These words are spoken toward the
end of "The Dead," John Huston's
magnificent adaptation of the James
Joyce story that was to be the director's last film.

Some men pass boldly into that
other world at 17. Huston was 81 when
he died last August. He failed physically, but his talent was not only
unimpaired, it was also richer, more
secure and bolder than it had ever
been. No other American film maker
has ended a comparably long career
on such a note of triumph.

"The Dead" and "Prizzi's Honor"
(1985), Huston's altogether different,
exuberantly melodramatic comedy,
comprise a one-two punch quite unlike anything I can remember in movies. Who would have thought the old
man had so much passion in him?

•

"The Dead" is so fine, in unexpected ways, that it almost demands
a re-evaluation of Huston's entire
body of work. Like most American
film makers of his generation, Huston
depended largely on what Hollywood
calls pre-sold properties, on novels
that had been published and plays
that had been produced. Of his 37
theatrical features, beginning with
"The Maltese Falcon" in 1941, all but
10 were adaptations.

The free-ranging restlessness of
Huston's mind is seen in his choice of
authors: B. Traven, Dashiell Ham-
mett, Herman Melville, Richard Condon, Rudyard Kipling, Noel Behn, the
fellows who wrote the Old Testament,
W. R. Burnett, Flannery O'Connor,
Malcolm Lowry and now (one might
think the most difficult of all) James
Joyce. It's not, however, just the variety of writers that's of interest but
also the particular material.

"The Dead," taken from "Dubliners," which was published in 1914,
may be the finest story in the collection, but it has, it would seem, just two
scenes, not much for a man who put
such store by conventional narrative.
The first scene, which lasts approximately an hour in the film, is the annual post-New Year's holiday party
given by two elderly Dublin sisters,
Kate and Julia Morkan, and their unmarried niece, Mary Jane.

•

Among the guests: the aunts'
favorite nephew, Gabriel Conroy, and
his wife, Gretta, a genial toper named
Freddy Malins and his domineering,
not completely disapproving mother,
some single young ladies who are
Mary Jane's music students, Mr.
Brown (an aging, gently skeptical

Protestant), a young man who is supposed to have the sweetest tenor in all
Dublin, and Molly Ivors, a politically
committed woman who twits the
Irish-born-and-bred Gabriel about his
fine English ways and affectations.

In the second scene, Gabriel and
Gretta are in the hotel room they've
taken for the night so they don't have
to make the long drive to their home
in the Dublin outskirts.

This is not exactly the material of
which epics are made. However, Huston and his elder son, Tony, who did
the immensely faithful adaptation,
discover the rich narrative line that
builds to the film's big, breathtaking
coda. Like Joyce's story, the movie
reveals itself with leisurely discretion
in bits of observed behavior and overheard conversation, which initially
seem as halt and illogical as Molly
Ivors's criticism of Gabriel.

The Huston camera moves about
the undistinguished, middle-class
Morkan drawing room, where there's
dancing before the banquet, as if it
were a guest looking for a place to sit
down. It seems to know everyone
slightly but no one especially well. It
attends to Aunt Kate, who worries
about the condition in which Freddie
Malins might turn up.

On the arrival of the Conroys, it
pays more attention to Gabriel
(Donal McCann), who frets about his
after-dinner speech, than to Gretta
(Anjelica Huston), who appears to be
a serenely self-assured wife and
mother. An amused Gretta tells the
aunts about Gabriel's insistence that
she wear galoshes. "Everyone on the
Continent is wearing them," says Gabriel. The aunts are properly amazed,
though they're not certain what galoshes are.

There are waltzes, with Mary Jane
providing the music at the piano.
Aunt Julia sings something by Bellini
in an ancient, sweet-flat voice that
reaches from a past no longer seen in
her face. Freddy Malins is overcome
with sentiment and goes on much too
long telling her that she's never
sounded better.

•

Mr. Grace recites a poem that
everyone agrees is beautiful, even if
the meaning of the words is not clear.
At dinner there is small talk about the
decline of opera in Dublin and about
the generosity of monks who sleep in
their coffins and pray for the salvation of all, even those not of the faith.
"Like free insurance," says Mr.
Brown.

At meal's end, in remarks preceding his toast to the three hostesses,
Gabriel chooses literary quotations
that aren't too highbrow. He speaks
with some feeling of Irish hospitality,
of traditions in danger of being lost, of
the memories of other such parties.
It's only later, when he and Gretta
are alone in the chilly hotel room, that
Gabriel understands exactly how
inescapable and unrelenting the past
continues to be.

Little by little, "The Dead" closes
in on Gabriel and Gretta Conroy. The
specific details accumulate, so that
the movie's final sequence becomes a
justification for everything that has
gone before. Revealed with stunning
forthrightness are the concerns that
have earlier been obliquely touched
on — the impermanence of all things,
including love, the impossibility of escaping the past, particularly the dead
who refuse to stay buried in their
country churchyards, and the relationship between the animate and
inanimate in Nature, which is not to
be understood, only accepted.

Sygma/Francois Duhamel

Donal McCann, Rachael Dowling, center, and Anjelica Huston in a
scene from John Huston's last film, "The Dead."

This remarkable sequence, in
which the film's third-person narrative slips into the first-person, has an
emotional impact not easily described. It's not sentimental. In the
way of any work of art, it's complete
in itself.

That Huston should have dared
search for the story's cinema life is
astonishing. That he should have
found it with such seeming ease is the
mark of a master.

The production is close to faultless,
from the camerawork of Fred Murphy, the production design of Stephen
Grimes (in collaboration with Dennis
Washington) and the costumes of
Dorothy Jeakins, to the performances by the exceptional cast, which
includes Helena Carroll and Cathleen
Delany as the aunts, Donal Donnelly
as the stewed Freddy Malins, Marie
Kean as his mother and Dan O'Her-
lihy as Mr. Brown. It's an ensemble
performance, but Miss Huston and
Mr. McCann must be the first among
equals.

Mr. McCann, at the beginning as
faceless as his character is indistinct,
grows into a figure of besieged grace.
The body sags but the spirit toughens.
Miss Huston is splendid, a figure of
such self-contained sorrow that it's
difficult to believe she was ever
Maerose Prizzi. Toward the end of
the party sequence, there's a shot of
her standing on the stairway in her
aunts' house, her face partly hidden,
listening to an unseen singer. Direction and performance are seamless in
an image that exemplifies the
achievement of this wonderful film.

"The Dead" opens today at the
Cinema 1.

•

*"The Dead," which has been rated
PG ("Parental Guidance Suggested"), contains some vulgarisms.*

1987 D 17, C19:4

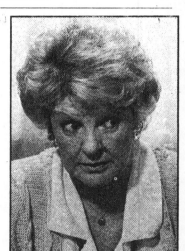

Elaine Stritch

Street; 84th Street Six, at Broadway; Art
Greenwich Twin, 12th Street and Seventh
Avenue. Running time: 82 minutes. This
film is rated PG.

Howard	Denholm Elliott
Stephanie	Dianne Wiest
Lane	Mia Farrow
Diane	Elaine Stritch
Peter	Sam Waterston
Lloyd	Jack Warden
Mr. Raines	Ira Wheeler
Mrs. Raines	Jane Cecil
Mrs. Mason	Rosemary Murphy

By VINCENT CANBY

"SEPTEMBER" is Woody Al-
len's riskiest film yet. It's a
small, tightly disciplined
drama about love, friend-
ship and family, set entirely within a
Vermont summer house at the end of
the season. People come and go to
destinations elsewhere, but the movie
remains inside the cottage, like a possibly hypochondriacal, invalid ghost.

There may be a world outside, but
the audience cannot see it. During the
day, the slatted wooden blinds are
drawn. At night, when the blinds are
open, there's only darkness. Brilliant
flashes of lightning reveal nothing.
This house could be drifting in the
universe that someone describes as
"haphazard, morally neutral and uni-
maginatively violent."

Close Quarters

SEPTEMBER, written and directed by
Woody Allen; director of photography,
Carlo Di Palma; edited by Susan E.
Morse; production designer, Santo Lo-
quasto; produced by Robert Greenhut; re-
leased by Orion Pictures Corporation. At
New York Twin, Second Avenue at 66th

Brian Hamill

Autumnal

Dianne Wiest and Mia Farrow star in "September," Woody Allen's intimate drama set in a Vermont home.

Within these restricted quarters six people play out an earnest, 24-hour game of injustice-collecting.

Lane (Mia Farrow) is still none too sure of herself after a suicide attempt some months before. She's restive with the continuing visit of her wise-cracking mother, Diane (Elaine Stritch), a playgirl-relic of the 1950's, and Diane's new husband, Lloyd (Jack Warden), a physicist. Diane's the sort of woman who raves on about the beauty of nature, picks great arm-fuls of flowers, then forgets to put them in water.

As usual, Diane has been taking over her daughter's life, including Peter (Sam Waterston), the advertis-ing copywriter who's rented Lane's guest house for the summer to complete a novel. Diane thinks Peter would be the ideal person to write her life's story. Lane is appalled at the prospect. One of the more flamboyant episodes in her mother's life is also hers or, as she tells Peter, "The story of a 14-year-old girl who kills her mother's lover is sleazy."

The other game players are Lane's best friend, Stephanie (Dianne Wiest), who's staying with Lane while having problems with her husband (off-screen in Philadelphia), and Howard (Denholm Elliott), Lane's older neighbor, a widower.

Howard loves Lane, who loves Peter, who loves Stephanie, who feels empty and who may love Peter but has obligations to her husband and children in Philadelphia.

Stripped to the bones of its narrative, "September" is less like Mr. Al-len's austere "Interiors" than like the diaphanous and lyric "Midsummer Night's Sex Comedy," but in a hair-shirt.

"September" is a difficult film to like initially, even while appreciating the scheme behind Mr. Allen's deci-sions. I stress "initially" because I had something of the same reaction at the opening of "Interiors," which, when I saw it again last year, seemed immeasurably more affecting. This was due — at least, in part — to modi-fied expectations and to an ear pre-pared to listen to dialogue that at first seemed funnier than it was meant to be.

The "September" that's being re-leased today is Mr. Allen's second version of a production he had virtu-ally completed when he decided to re-write and reshoot it, necessitating key cast changes. He's been reported as saying that he'd like to shoot it a third time. As it now plays, "Septem-ber" is chiefly interesting for its rela-tion to other Allen films, including "Hannah and Her Sisters," and for what it reveals about the interests and aspiration of America's most consistently venturesome film maker.

●

Even with its recollection of Lana Turner's Hollywood scandal in the 1950's, "September" is neo-Chekhov-ian. However, its characters come on the scene bearing very little baggage that one immediately believes, and nothing that suggests there is a world outside. It's not because the blinds are drawn, but because the charac-ters seem as new to each other as they are to the audience. With the ex-ception of Miss Stritch's Diane, they're so thin and frail that we don't even get a feeling of claustrophobia. The house is hermetically sealed, but it seems empty.

There's also a crucial point where the dramatic line goes wildly awry, when information of extraordinary import is introduced, but nothing more is made of it. It's as if Chekhov had decided to rewrite "Ghosts," without letting the ghosts out of the closet. It's not a lapse that can easily be explained by Miss Stritch's sigh-ing: "Let's not dwell on what's hap-pened before. It's over and done with."

The production design seems so far off that the characters have no rela-tion to the furniture and other objects in what is supposed to be a house of beloved memories. Everything looks to have been furnished by a decora-tor. Also, nobody eats. It's not neces-sary to show people at a table in a movie to believe that they eat, but here one suspects there's never been a meal prepared in the kitchen.

Coffee is drunk, and, on one occa-sion, tea for two is brewed from a sin-gle teabag, but it seems like stage business. Even the boozing looks un-real. People say they're drunk, though, from what they do and say, it's obvious that the bottles of Smir-noff are full of tap water.

●

Every now and then there's a line or a confrontation that suggests the life that's still missing from the screenplay. The physicist is seriously funny when he says the only thing more terrifying than the end of the world is the knowledge that it doesn't make any difference. Miss Farrow's despondent Lane also is suddenly, un-characteristically, self-aware when Stephanie asks her if she wants to die. "No," she says forlornly, "that's my problem. I've always wanted to live." This is true comedy.

Miss Stritch, in a beautifully con-trolled performance, delivers the film's best lines with rich irony. They describe a character who has been through the mill and has learned something. "You look in the mirror," she says, "and realize something is missing. Your future." The problems of the others, expressed in such state-ments as "You've been avoiding me" and "You make my head spin," are as minuscule as their imaginations. As is true of "Interiors," the women's characters are more finely drawn than those of the men, who, in performance, tend to behave like con-

sorts.

"September," which opens today at Loews 84th Street and other theaters, has big problems. However, Mr. Al-len's admirers will note the virtuosity of the director's use of the camera here. The film has been photographed in a series of long, fluid takes (with spare use of close-ups) that might serve as a guide to anyone contem-plating the screen adaptation of a stage play.

This is the way it should be done.

●

"September," which has been rated PG ("Parental Guidance Sug-gested"), includes mildly vulgar lan-guage.

1987 D 18, C3:1

Still Closer Encounters

BATTERIES NOT INCLUDED, directed by Matthew Robbins; screenplay by Brad Bird and Mr. Robbins and Brent Maddock and S. S. Wilson; story by Mick Garris; di-rector of photography, John McPherson; edited by Cynthia Scheider; music by James Horner; production designer, Ted Haworth; produced by Ronald L. Schwary; executive producers, Steven Spielberg, Kathleen Kennedy and Frank Marshall; released by Universal Pictures. At Movieland, Broadway at 47th Street; New York Twin, Second Avenue and 66th Street; U.A. East, First Avenue at 85th Street; 23d Street West Triplex, near Eighth Avenue; 84th Street Six, at Broad-way, and other theaters. Running time: 105 minutes. This film is rated PG.

Frank	Hume Cronyn
Faye	Jessica Tandy
Harry	Frank McRae
Marisa	Elizabeth Pena
Carlos	Michael Carmine
Mason	Dennis Boutsikaris
Sid	Tom Aldredge
Muriel	Jane Hoffman
Gus	John DiSanti
Kovacs	John Pankow
DeWitt	MacIntyre Dixon
Lacey	Michael Greene

"**N**O, they're not toys. You can't buy these things at Macy's!" cries one of the characters in "Batteries Not Included," describing the dinner-plate-size flying saucers that are the film's real stars. But even if the mer-chandise isn't readily at hand, toys are very much on the minds of all

concerned, since everything in the film has been designed in toymaker's terms. That includes the human char-acters, who are adults only in the way an 8-year-old might imagine them. Children may enjoy this, but their adult escorts will have a harder time. "Batteries Not Included," which opens today at the Movieland and other theaters, begins with a lengthy build-up to the saucers' arrival, which is of course the moment in which the film springs to life. Before that, it has been concentrating on the various residents of a soon-to-be-demolished East Village tenement. Each of these characters can be de-scribed in a single phrase, from the starving artist (Dennis Boutsikaris) to the hoodlum with a heart of gold (Michael Carmine) to the shy, kindly superintendent (Frank McRae) to the pregnant woman upstairs (Eliza-beth Pena). Children in the audience aren't apt to wonder why this woman isn't married. "Batteries Not Includ-ed" isn't the kind of film that prompts questions of any kind.

Luckily, the group also includes Hume Cronyn and Jessica Tandy as a beleaguered restaurant owner and his charmingly dotty wife, a woman whose senility seems to have left her in a state of grace. It is she who first spots "the little guys," as she calls them, when these electricity-seeking saucers arrive at the tenement and begin to save the day. They like to fix things, and so they come in very handy.

At first they look purely mechani-cal, but it turns out that the saucers have big, wistful eyes and like to af-fect the heart-rending blink. This is simply going too far. What's worse, they mate and have baby saucers, and the babies are easily confused with hamburgers, and ... Adults in the audience may well spend time wondering what to add to their Christmas lists by this point. It won't be saucer toys.

"Batteries Not Included" was di-rected by Matthew Robbins, with Steven Spielberg as executive pro-ducer. It's been well made and, espe-cially in Miss Tandy's case, acted with a sense of fun. But the time for this brand of fantasy may have come and gone.

●

"Batteries Not Included" is rated PG ("Parental Guidance Suggest-ed"). It contains some strong lan-guage.
JANET MASLIN

1987 D 18, C12:5

Citified

Jessica Tandy and Hume Cronyn play leading roles in "Batteries Not Included."

Secret Agent

LEONARD PART 6, directed by Paul Wei-land; story by Bill Cosby; screenplay by Jonathan Reynolds; director of photogra-phy, Jan DeBont; edited by Gerry Ham-bling; music by Elmer Bernstein; produc-tion designer, Geoffrey Kirkland; produced by Mr. Cosby; released by Co-lumbia Pictures. At Cine 1 and 2, Broad-way at 48th Street; Movie Center 5, 125th Street between Powell and Douglass Boulevards; Essex, 275 Grand Street. Run-ning time: 117 minutes. This film is rated PG.

Leonard	Bill Cosby
Frayn	Tom Courtenay
Snyderburn	Joe Don Baker
Giorgio	Moses Gunn
Allison	Pat Colbert
Medusa	Gloria Foster
Joan	Victoria Rowell

By CARYN JAMES

"**L**EONARD PART 6" has a James Bond, weapon-equipped car and soapsuds billowing down a stairwell in a scene Lucille Ball could romp through. Tom Courtenay is a gentleman's gentleman, in a role that owes a lot to Sir John Gielgud in "Arthur," and Gloria Foster is a villain who owes something to Tina Turner in "Mad Max: Beyond Thunderdome." If this comic stew were all of "Leonard Part 6," it would be a harmless, derivative holiday movie that children could giggle at and that would give anyone over the age of 10 a severe case of déjà vu. Because this is a backdrop for Bill Cosby, fans may expect some comic extravaganza from the television icon. But "Leonard" proves that even Bill Cosby makes mistakes.

As Leonard, Mr. Cosby plays a retired secret agent (his five earlier adventures, we're told, are too top secret to reveal) who runs a four-star restaurant, lives in opulence and is obsessive about his former wife. The Government needs him back because the power-mad Medusa Johnson is turning domestic pets and barnyard animals into vicious killers. With frogs that murder and rabbits that go for the throat, she plans to conquer the world.

But before he is lured out of retirement, we get a half-hour of Leonard at home, as if Cliff Huxtable from "The Cosby Show" had become fabulously wealthy but remained a simple dad at heart. He primps endlessly for a date with his ex-wife, telling Mr. Courtenay he hasn't been with a woman in the seven years since she left him. This we're meant to see as great devotion, not peculiarity. Leonard is just a family guy, but he doesn't have the mischievous glint in his eye that enlivens Cliff Huxtable, or for that matter Mr. Cosby's stand-up comedy routines.

When Leonard finally heads into action, we see some adventures that should have been funnier. Mr. Cosby, in a silver jumpsuit and pink ballet shoes, leaps his way out of danger with a push from some clumsy editing; you can see just where a real dancer's feet are spliced in. Many other incidents — Leonard has food dumped on his head — could only have been saved by the kind of high energy and visual inventiveness "Leonard" lacks. Mr. Cosby and the director, Paul Weiland, were reportedly at odds while filming "Leonard Part 6," which opens today at Cine 1 and other theaters, but there's plenty of blame for them to share. Mr. Weiland's direction, Mr. Cosby's story and Jonathan Reynolds's screenplay seem equally trite.

Mr. Cosby, a true comic expert, must know how tired "Leonard Part 6" is, and he even looks fatigued. When he asks his ex-wife, "If I save the world, will you move back in with me?," it's as if he's desperate to return to a modest domestic setting, where he's funnier, more innovative and much more successful.

•

"Leonard Part 6" is rated PG ("Parental Guidance Suggested"); there is a modest suggestion of public nudity by Leonard's daughter, and guarded references to sexual dalliances.

1987 D 18, C30:1

Hard Times

IRONWEED, directed by Hector Babenco; screenplay by William Kennedy, based on his novel; director of photography, Lauro Escorel; edited by Anne Goursaud; music by John Morris; production designer,

Jeannine C. Oppewall; produced by Keith Barish and Marcia Nasatir; released by Tri-Star Pictures. At Tower East, Third Avenue and 71st Street. Running time: 145 minutes. This film is rated R.

Francis Phelan	Jack Nicholson
Helen	Meryl Streep
Annie Phelan	Carroll Baker
Billy	Michael O'Keefe
Peg	Diane Venora
Oscar Reo	Fred Gwynne
Katrina	Margaret Whitton
Rudy	Tom Waits
Pee Wee	Jake Dengel
Harold Allen	Nathan Lane
Reverend Chester	James Gammon

By JANET MASLIN

EARLY in his novel "Ironweed," William Kennedy describes a visit made to a cemetery by the aging derelict Francis Phelan, whose mother and father and infant son are buried there. It is Halloween, and they are watching him, interested and bemused, from beyond the grave.

The infant Gerald, who was 13 days old when his father accidentally dropped him 22 years earlier, is a particularly piquant figure, and Mr. Kennedy describes him this way: "Gerald's grave trembled with superb possibility. Denied speech in life, having died with only monosyllabic goos and gahs in his vocabulary, Gerald possessed the gift of tongues in death. His ability to communicate and to understand was at the genius level among the dead. He could speak with any resident adult in any language, but more notable was his ability to understand the chattery squirrels and chipmunks, the silent signals of the ants and beetles, and the slithy semaphores of the slugs and worms that moved above and through his earth. . . .

"Gerald rested in his infantile sublimity, exuding a high gloss induced by early death, his skin a radiant white-gold, his nails a silvery gray, his clusters of curls and large eyes perfectly matched in gleaming ebony. Swaddled in his grave, he was beyond capture by visual or verbal artistry. He was neither beautiful nor perfect to the beholder but rather an ineffably fabulous presence whose like was not to be found anywhere in the cemetery, and it abounded with dead innocents."

Beautiful as this passage is, and as richly phantasmagorial, it comes as close to being entirely unfilmable as anything one might imagine. The same is largely true for the rest of Mr. Kennedy's book, so much of which takes place inside the mind of Francis Phelan or in the past. The superficial action of Mr. Kennedy's Pulitzer Prize-winning "Ironweed" is quite straightforward: in the autumn of 1938, Francis roams the streets of Albany, eking out his present-day existence and trying to come to terms with his past. They are exemplified, respectively, by his fellow derelict and longtime companion Helen and his wife, Annie, whom he abandoned after the baby died but must make his peace with now. Throughout the several days that the novel spans, Francis is also visited by a full panoply of ghosts.

•

But the real story of the film "Ironweed," which opens today at Loews Tower East, isn't the one that's on the screen. It's the tale of how Hector Babenco, the director, captured the harshness and pathos of life among Brazilian street urchins in "Pixote," made the brilliant "Kiss of the Spider Woman" on a shoestring, and thus earned his chance to play for big and,

as it turns out, crippling stakes. For despite its nearly two-and-a-half-hour running time, its superstar cast and its $23 million budget, Mr. Babenco's "Ironweed" is skeletal, a mere outline of Mr. Kennedy's far more resonant book. That Mr. Kennedy himself adapted the novel to the screen is only further evidence of how much more greatly film and literature diverge than those on either side of the fence often imagine.

Though "Ironweed" is a bleakly handsome, extremely well-acted film, its virtues are almost beside the point. The initial large question — that of why audiences in the market for a big-budget Christmas film should be drawn to anything as downbeat and actionless as this one — is never even addressed, let alone answered. "Ironweed" just is, that's all. It has a stubbornness that's akin to Francis Phelan's, but a good deal less justifiable.

As Francis Phelan, Jack Nicholson seems seldom to move, except in flashbacks that show Francis as a younger man. It's a fine performance, very true to the burned-out quality of a man confronting his own failures, but the overall effect is unavoidably glum. Mr. Nicholson makes himself almost unrecognizable at times, behind a grizzled beard and a despairing expression. And he rises to great heights of panic, of guilt and of self-justifying anger as the various ghosts from Francis's past come back — literally, wearing white suits — to haunt him. The performance is persuasive, but it's paralyzed by the absence of many real events in Francis's present-day story. When the film reunites him with his wife (Carroll Baker), son (Michael O'Keefe) and daughter (Diane Venora), the meeting comes too late in the story to have much impact. Besides, this sequence is made to look far too much like something off a greeting card.

○

Meryl . . . . . . as ever is a beauty. Miss Streep uses the role of Helen as an opportunity to deliver a stunning impersonation of a darty-eyed, fast-talking woman of the streets, an angry, obdurate woman with great memories and no future. There isn't much more to the film's Helen than this, and indeed the character may go no deeper, but she's a marvel all the same. Behind the runny, red-rimmed eyes, the nervous chatter and the haunted expression, Miss Streep is even more utterly changed than her co-star, and she even sings well. The sequence in which Helen entertains the real and imagined patrons of a barroom with a rendition of "He's Me Pal" is a standout.

Tom Waits and Jake Dengel are among the actors who play subsidiary derelicts, and it is in these minor characters that the film's Hollywood side really shows. From the real street children of "Pixote" to the movie bums who flaunt their down-at-the-heels mannerisms here, Mr. Babenco has surely come too long a way.

1987 D 18, C24:5

EDDIE MURPHY RAW, a concert film directed by Robert Townsend; written by Eddie Murphy; sketch written by Mr. Murphy and Keenen Ivory Wayans; director of photography, Ernest Dickerson; edited by Lisa Day; produced by Robert D. Wachs and Mr. Wayans. At Embassy 2 and 3, Broadway and 47th St.; Orpheum Twin, 86th Street near Third Avenue; Eighth Street Playhouse, at Avenue of the Amer-

Eddie Murphy

icas; Columbia Cinema, Broadway and 103d Street; Movie Center Five, 125th Street between Powell and Douglass Boulevards; Coliseum Twin, Broadway and 181st Street; Nova, 147th Street and Broadway. Running time: 91 minutes. This film is rated R.

By JANET MASLIN

At the Embassy 3, where "Eddie Murphy Raw" opened yesterday, even the ushers were laughing. And they, like everyone else in the place, had good reasons not to. The profanity is persistent, parts of Mr. Murphy's act are filthier than anything Richard Pryor ever attempted (like his adolescent impression of Mr. Pryor doing bathroom jokes), and when it comes to women and homosexuals, Mr. Murphy is clearly proud of his prejudices. Nonetheless, this feature-length concert film is hilarious, putting Mr. Murphy on a par with Mr. Pryor at his best.

The generation between the two is readily apparent, both in the routine that has Mr. Murphy mimicking his idol and in his long, scathing anecdote about a telephone call from Bill Cosby, who complained about the obscenity of Mr. Murphy's show. First of all, Mr. Murphy is a terrific parodist, doing a lethal Cosby imitation complete with long pauses and sententious phrasings. Second, he caps this brilliantly by reporting his own subsequent call to Mr. Pryor, who said he himself had received a similar dressing down. Do people like you? Mr. Pryor asked. Do you get paid? "Well, tell Bill I said have a Coke and a smile and shut up."

"Eddie Murphy Raw" has been filmed simply and invitingly by Robert Townsend, the director of "Hollywood Shuffle," who is very much in the actor-comedian's wavelength and does a subtle job of drawing the audience into the show. Mr. Murphy, a lot less interested in subtlety, does what he can to start fights between the couples in his nightclub audience by making wicked fun of sexual hypocrisy and insisting that infidelity is a way of life.

No remark of Mr. Murphy's can be printed here in unexpurgated form, but his observations about relations between the sexes are nothing if not keen. In particular, he applies this to his own life, elaborating at great length on why he isn't married and boiling the whole matter down to one simple cry: "Half!" Mr. Murphy's prosperity and superstar status clearly mean a lot to him, and it seems that a National Enquirer article about Johnny Carson's divorce settlements made a deep impression.

Mr. Murphy's idea of a solution to this is as funny as it is obnoxious; he imagines the most ignorant and unworldly of primitive African tribes-women, with a lot of talk about bones through the nose, and says this is the only sort of woman he would dare marry. He then provides a typically mean, and typically uproarious, impression of a female friend hectoring the new bride about community property. Nagging women figure as prominently in Mr. Murphy's act as unfaithful men do, but he makes fun of them with equal enthusiasm. One of Mr. Murphy's best bits is about the

wronged wife or girlfriend who gets even with her man by heading for the Bahamas, where she hooks up with a reggae-loving ladies' man Mr. Murphy calls Dexter St. Jacques.

Among the other memorable routines here are Mr. Murphy's thoughts about pop song lyrics of the 1980's — he translates Madonna's "Material Girl" into much more direct terms — and his impression of a macho Italian male who has just watched a "Rocky" film and sees it as an object lesson in race relations ("the worst white people fights," Mr. Murphy maintains, occur "around 'Rocky'-time"). There is also a wild and rather poignant impression of Mr. Murphy's father getting drunk and berating his mother with rules, regulations and garbled lyrics from old Motown songs.

1987 D 19, 18:4

FILM VIEW/Janet Maslin

Morality Tales for Our Time

IF LOOKS COULD KILL, TOM GRUNICK'S DASHING good looks would surely do it, because they're killing the business he's in. In "Broadcast News," Tom has been hired as a correspondent for a television network's Washington bureau solely on the strength of his telegenic qualities. His presence is a reproach to the more serious, less glamorous journalists who surround him. So they all wait for the inevitable moment of truth, the one that will expose him as just another pretty face.

The opportunity arrives when Tom, with absolutely no preparation or background knowledge, is asked to anchor a network special report on a terrorist attack overseas, and thus could well embarrass himself before audiences all across the nation. But that isn't what happens. In a more conventional film, Tom might get his comeuppance, but "Broadcast News" envisions a fate for him that's less harsh and perhaps a lot more realistic. And when an on-the-air embarrassment *does* occur, it happens to a character whose professional credentials put Tom's to shame.

It should be clear by now, in the year of "Fatal Attraction," that audiences are in the mood for morality plays, and that right now these lessons are best delivered in ambiguous terms. That makes them more suited to the uneasy tenor of the time, to the elements of opportunism and expediency that color decision making on and off the screen. While the occasional old-fashioned moral lesson does turn up from time to time — in "Overboard," Goldie Hawn plays a cold-hearted heiress who needs only a good conk on the head to rediscover simpler values — it's liable to seem terribly irrelevant. The most compelling allegories of the moment are those that address easy corruption, and do it in terms that a contemporary audience will understand.

When Brian De Palma, in "Scarface," wanted to show that Al Pacino's gangster character was over the edge, he set him in a house decorated like an enormous bordello and let the cocaine pile up in front of him like so much talcum powder. That may have been Mr. De Palma's sense of humor at work, but perhaps it also required this much exaggeration to make sure the audience knew this was depravity, not just business success. Oliver Stone's "Wall Street" doesn't have to go that far, but it, too, must ironically underscore the action from time to time in order to remind viewers where the evil lies. After all, Mr. Stone's film unfolds in such a casually

cutthroat business climate that it takes a while to realize the young protagonist's name is actually Bud. Everyone in the story seems to call one another Bud, Buddy or Pal.

■

What Tom Wolfe, in his new novel, "The Bonfire of the Vanities," calls "the sound of well-educated young white men baying for money on the bond market," is at first the background noise for "Wall Street," at the brokerage firm where young Bud has a low-level job. "Remember there are no shortcuts, son," says Hal Holbrook as a senior member of the firm, sounding just the kind of gassy, antiquated note this film doesn't need. Far more up-to-the-minute are the wisecracks of one of Bud's co-workers, who describes one master financier by saying, "Thirty seconds after the Challenger blew up, he was on the phone selling NASA short — Mr. Nice Guy!" In the world of "Wall Street," this is a compliment.

When the film moves to the corridors of power, it becomes genuinely witty for a while. It has to: if the office of the Boesky-like Gordon Gekko (played devilishly well by Michael Douglas) weren't designed so cleverly, the place might look more seductive than it should. But the black walls, the electronic gadgetry and the costly artworks conspire to be as off-putting as they are alluring, and the little nest (complete with sushi-making machine) that Bud wins for himself later in the film is even more so. Though "Wall Street" eventually takes a dive as precipitous as anything the stock market has done, descending into the worst sort of black-and-white moralizing, it manages for a long while to chart its characters' integrity indirectly. The expensive but slightly ghastly paintings that they buy, the details of their wardrobes — when Bud graduates to red suspenders, it's clear that he's a goner — say it all.

■

The irresistible "Broadcast News" tackles a tougher sort of moral dilemma and takes the unusual step of coming down on all sides of the fence. Jane Craig (Holly Hunter), a television producer, is an extremely dedicated professional, but her standards are unbearably high; she drives her co-workers crazy and at times weeps briefly for no reason. Aaron Altman (Albert Brooks) is a seasoned pro whose cynicism grows out of experience. When Aaron sees a newsman behaving hammily on camera, he cries out "Yes, please let's never forget — *we're* the real story." While his colleages watch a reporting segment that Aaron thinks is ridiculous, he asks "Mind if I turn on the news?"

The third element in what becomes a romantic triangle is Tom Grunick, whose slight doltishness is conveyed masterfully by William Hurt (in one scene, Mr. Hurt even *eats* in a slow-witted way), but who is never a simple target. "I'm no good at what I'm being a success at," he says early in the story. That very admission gives both Tom and the film more weight. So does the way the film's writer-producer-director, James L. Brooks, makes these characters too complex and appealing to allow easy judgments.

Ultimately, it's Tom and Jane who are most deeply at odds ("You could get fired for things like that," she tells him angrily about one transgression. "I got promoted for things like that," he replies). But the film's most brilliant and sobering touch is the brief epilogue that gives it the perspective of time. The idealism, the ambition and the cynicism that so enliven the story are now seen through the light of compromise, as the three principals move on to different sorts of lives. This film's most powerful moral lesson is its hint that moral lessons, of the sort that are dramatized here so affectingly, are rarely as clear-cut as they first appear. ▢

1987 D 20, II:25:5

Making (Air)Waves

GOOD MORNING, VIETNAM, directed by Barry Levinson; written by Mitch Markowitz; director of photography, Peter Sova; edited by Stu Linder; music by Alex North; production designer, Roy Walker; produced by Mark Johnson and Larry Brezner; released by Touchstone Pictures in association with Silver Screen Partners III. At Loews 84th Street Six, at Broadway. Cinema 2, Third Avenue at 60th Street. Running time: 120 minutes. This film is rated R.

Adrian Cronauer	Robin Williams
Edward Garlick	Forest Whitaker
Tuan	Tung Thanh Tran
Trinh	Chintara Sukapatana
Lieut. Steven Hauk	Bruno Kirby
Marty Lee Dreiwitz	Robert Wuhl
Sgt. Maj. Dickerson	J. T. Walsh
Gen. Taylor	Noble Willingham
Pvt. Abersold	Richard Edson
Phil McPherson	Juney Smith

By VINCENT CANBY

THE time of "Good Morning, Vietnam" is 1965. Adrian Cronauer (Robin Williams), an Armed Forces Radio disk jockey previously stationed in Crete, lands in Saigon to breathe a little life into the local programming. Until Cronauer's arrival, the AFR Saigon station has depended largely on the

Robin Williams in a scene from "Good Morning, Vietnam."

music of Mantovani and Percy Faith and helpful hints on how to withdraw books from the Army's lending libraries, interrupted from time to time by sanitized newscasts.

Though behind-the-lines sabotage is on the rise, and huge numbers of additional troops are arriving daily, the programming of the Saigon station reflects a prescribed sunniness that has less to do with the increasingly grim reality of Vietnam than with that of a giant rec room for preteens of the 1950's. At the top of the charts in this never-never land: "Around the World in 80 Days."

Within several days of taking over his dawn show, Adrian Cronauer has become the biggest, most controversial personality in Vietnam. Out the window have gone Mantovani, Percy Faith, Bing Crosby and Perry Como, to be replaced by the raucous laments and urgent innuendoes of James Brown, Martha Reeves and the Vandellas and Wayne Fontana, among others.

•

Between recordings, in his on-air monologues, Adrian Cronauer floats down the stream of his own manic consciousness. He talks about sex, the drama inherent in weather forecasts in the tropics, body functions, Army regulations, politics and Richard Nixon, then the former Vice President. At frequent intervals, he conducts interviews with characters inhabiting the dark side of his brain, including an Army fashion designer who's distraught about the material used for camouflage uniforms. "Why not plaids and stripes?" asks the petulant designer. "When you go into battle, clash!"

When in top form, Cronauer appears to be speaking in tongues, most of them all too familiar. At one time or another, he sends up just about every race, color, creed and sexual preference. The Army brass is upset, but his service listeners love him. Here, at last, is someone who knows the difference between a police action and a war. Reality has gained a pre-

carious beachhead.

"Good Morning, Vietnam," directed by Barry Levinson ("Diner," "Tin Men") succeeds in doing something that's very rare in movies, being about a character who really is as funny as he's supposed to be to most of the people sharing the fiction with him. It's also a breakthrough for Mr. Williams, who, for the first time in movies, gets a chance to exercise his restless, full-frontal comic intelligence.

•

Since making his film debut in Robert Altman's "Popeye" seven years ago, Mr. Williams has appeared in five movies, including George Roy Hill's "World According to Garp" and Paul Mazursky's "Moscow on the Hudson." Each film has had its endearing moments, but there was always the feeling that an oddball natural resource was being inefficiently used, as if Arnold Schwarzenegger had been asked to host "Masterpiece Theater."

Just how much of the fresh, cheeky Williams brilliance was going up the chimney can now be seen in "Good Morning, Vietnam."

The movie, which opens today at the Loew's 84th Street Sixplex and Cinema 2, is very much a star vehicle, but it's an exceptionally strong one. Mitch Markowitz's screenplay, based loosely on the experiences of a real-life Vietnam disk jockey, skids over a melodramatic subplot that would be fatal to any other movie.

Though Mr. Williams is the film's life as well as its conscience, Mr. Levinson knows how to present the star without exploiting him to a point of diminishing returns. "Good Morning, Vietnam" surrounds Mr. Williams with an especially strong cast of supporting actors, including two recruits from "Tin Men." They are Bruno Kirby, as a polka-loving officer who longs to replace Adrian Cronauer as the station's star disk jockey ("In my heart I know I'm funny," he says after his first disastrous broadcast), and J. T. Walsh, as

a sergeant major who's offended by Cronauer's loose ways with regulations.

Also commendable are Noble Willingham, who plays a remarkably free-thinking general, one of Cronauer's biggest fans; Forest Whitaker, as Cronauer's sidekick; Cu Ba Nguyen, as a Saigon bar-owner with a most singular sexual preference; Chintara Sukapatana, as a young Vietnamese woman whom Adrian lusts after, and Tung Thanh Tran, as her brother.

It's meant as praise for both the director and writer to say that several of the film's best sequences (aside from Mr. Williams's monologues) give every indication of having been improvised, though to what extent I've no idea. In one, Cronauer takes over an English class for Vietnamese civilians and proceeds to teach them the nuances lurking within the most commonplace American obscenities. In another, the disk jockey is suddenly confronted by his public in the persons of a truckload of soldiers heading into combat.

Mr. Levinson, who appreciates the Williams monologues as much as theater audiences will, provides them with a context that enriches their meaning without upstaging them, cross-cutting between Cronauer, broadcasting from his antiseptic radio studio, and the tormented, sometimes scenic Vietnamese countryside where his voice is being heard.

Make no mistake about it: Mr. Williams's performance, though it's full of uproarious comedy, is the work of an accomplished actor. "Good Morning, Vietnam" is one man's tour de force.

1987 D 23, C11:1

THE LONELY PASSION OF JUDITH HEARNE, directed by Jack Clayton; screenplay by Peter Nelson, from the novel by Brian Moore; director of photography, Peter Hannan; edited by Terry Rawlings; music by Georges Delerue;

production designer, Michael Pickwoad; produced by Mr. Nelson and Richard Johnson; released by Island Pictures. At 68th Street Playhouse, at Third Avenue. Running time: 110 minutes. This film is rated R.

Judith Hearne	Maggie Smith
James Madden	Bob Hoskins
Aunt D'Arcy	Wendy Hiller
Mrs. Rice	Marie Kean
Bernard	Ian McNeice
Father Quigley	Alan Devlin
Mary	Rudi Davies
Moira O'Neill	Prunella Scales
Edie Marinan	Aine Ni Mhuiri
Miss Friel	Sheila Reid

By JANET MASLIN

"THE Lonely Passion of Judith Hearne" is a solemn film about a spinster whose only excess is the wearing of mildly flamboyant bonnets, a woman who declares "It's only me!" when she enters a room and who asks for "just a soupçon of milk" with her tea.

In the film's very first scene, the little girl Judith has the joy snuffed out of her by an aunt (played by Wendy Hiller) who scolds her for giggling in church; the director, Jack Clayton, conveys Judith's feelings by watching her form a tiny tear. Years later, when Judith is grown, the film is no less ponderous or literal in unraveling the workings of her heart.

"The Lonely Passion of Judith Hearne," which opens today at the 68th Street Playhouse, has Maggie Smith in the title role, and she's good — almost too good, in fact. There's a suggestion of the actress's Miss Jean Brodie in her Judith Hearne, but this time the character is drawn in bolder strokes, and Miss Smith's subtlety only calls attention to the obviousness of the story.

Written by Peter Nelson and based on the much better novel by Brian Moore, "The Lonely Passion of Judith Hearne" presents Judith with what might be called one last chance at happiness. She moves into a Dublin boarding house where the proprietor's brother, James (Bob Hoskins), is also staying, having returned from a 30-year stay in America. He is dressed, as Judith observes to herself in a voice-over, "like a comedian in a music hall" (like everything else here, James's costumes are greatly overstated), but he seems interested in Judith and attracts her attention. "Well, don't faint, aunt dear — he noticed me today," Judith says to a framed photograph of her late relative. The screenplay is awkward enough to require such devices from time to time.

•

The story, about the raising and dashing of Judith's hopes, about her secret vice and about the crisis of faith that is provoked by events within the boarding house, is not without its lively turns, but the film's mood is so histrionic and grave that it has little life.

Mr. Hoskins, ordinarily such a sparkling, unaffected presence, is quite paralyzed by the crude Americanisms of his character, from the mustard-yellow outfits to the accent that makes his voice sound disembodied; the small talk in one scene actually has him naming the bridges in New York City to show off his knowledge of local color. Miss Hiller is commanding as the aunt, but some of her lines ("I want the cake, the cake, the cake ....") are utterly actor-proof, and Marie Kean, as the landlady, is made by the screenplay and the direction to seem more obvious than she need be. The film's only wild card is Ian McNeice, amusingly loutish and nasty as the landlady's overweight, stay-at-home son, who finds a little bit of himself in 17th-century poetry. The film would have benefited from more such wicked mischief.

1987 D 23, C15:1

A Cast of Voices

PINOCCHIO AND THE EMPEROR OF THE NIGHT, directed by Hal Sutherland; screenplay by Robby London, Barry O'-Brien and Dennis O'Flaherty, inspired by "The Adventures of Pinocchio" by Carlo Collodi; music by Anthony Marinelli and Brian Banks; produced by Lou Scheimer; released by New World Pictures. At Criterion, Broadway at 45th Street; New Carnegie, 57th Street and Broadway; Movie Center 5, 125th Street between Powell and Douglass Boulevards; New Delancey, 62 Delancey Street. Running time: 95 minutes. This film is rated G.

Scalawag	Edward Asner
Geppetto	Tom Bosley
Pinocchio	Scott Grimes
Twinkle	Lana Beeson
Bee-atrice	Linda Gray
Grumblebee	Jonathan Harris
Emperor of the Night	James Earl Jones
Fairy Godmother	Rickie Lee Jones
Gee Willikers	Don Knotts
Igor	Frank Welker
Puppetino	William Windom

By JANET MASLIN

DISNEY animation reached its pinnacle with "Pinocchio," and that film's finest moment is the scene in Geppetto's workshop when every single toy springs gloriously to life. In the new film "Pinocchio and the Emperor of the Night," by comparison, the toys in the workshop don't bother to move, and only one token tweety-bird flutters in the foreground. This is Saturday morning animation at best, and if presented as such it wouldn't seem worse than ordinary. But as a spinoff of the real "Pinocchio," to which it has virtually no connection (though the author Carlo Collodi gets an "inspired by" credit), it amounts to a form of bait and switch.

Although "Pinocchio and the Emperor of the Night," which opens today at the Criterion Center and other theaters, has a celebrity-filled cast — including Edward Asner, Don Knotts, Tom Bosley and James Earl Jones — you'd have to look at the credits to notice this star power. The voices are no more distinguished than the material, which has Pinocchio venturing near a sinister carnival and making friends with a number of brightly colored bugs. He also fixes his attention on a little wooden girl named Twinkle, who sings a cloying song. But the animation is so poor that it's difficult to tell who is a puppet, and who is not.

There are some sadly up-to-the-minute touches to "Pinocchio and the Emperor of the Night," not the least of them the fact that the 80's version of this once-childlike character now dreams of becoming a star. The direction, by Hal Sutherland, is also much more intrusive than the direction of the original film ever was; the camera frequently pans across static landscapes to compensate for what was once the animators' art. And now that Pinocchio has become a real boy, his fairy godmother, played by Rickie Lee Jones (who at least has a chance to sing), actually threatens him: "Don't forget, Pinocchio, if you take your freedom for granted you might lose it. You might even turn into a puppet again." As dirty tricks go, they just don't get any dirtier.

1987 D 25, C6:5

Troubled
Maggie Smith portrays a resident of a Dublin boarding house in "The Lonely Passion of Judith Hearne," co-starring Bob Hoskins.

Death and Apartments

RENDEZ-VOUS, directed by André Téchiné; written (French with English subtitles) by Mr. Téchiné and Olivier Assayas; director of photography, Renato Berta; edited by Martine Giordano; music by Philippe Sarde; production designer, Jean-Pierre Kohut-Svelko; produced by Alain Terzian; released by International Spectrafilm. At Bleecker Street Cinema, 144 Bleecker Street. Running time: 82 minutes. This film has no rating.

Nina	Juliette Binoche
Quentin	Lambert Wilson
Paulot	Wadeck Stanczak
Scrutzler	Jean-Louis Trintignant

By VINCENT CANBY

"RENDEZ-VOUS," opening today at the Bleecker Street Cinema, is a doomed love story of the kind of awfulness that can only be achieved by the French at their most solemn and irrelevant.

It's about Nina (Juliette Binoche), a pretty, headstrong young woman from Toulouse, who comes to Paris to be an actress and, with no experience whatsoever, lands a small role in a hit play. Still her life is incomplete. She's searching for meaning, as well as an apartment.

It's also about Quentin (Lambert Wilson), a young man with splendid cheekbones, who is performing in a hard-core pornographic take-off on "Romeo and Juliet." Quentin's problem is that his life is complete. Several years earlier, he became a star in his first play, a London production of the non-porn "Romeo and Juliet." Having had everything (including an apartment), he now seeks death.

Looking on as these two emotional midgets make love and torment each other are Scrutzler (Jean-Louis Trintignant), who directed Quentin in his London triumph, and Paulot (Wadeck Stanczak), an innocent who loves Nina with his own purity of heart and a list of available apartments. He's a real-estate agent.

The film was directed and written (in part) by André Téchiné, who has made some good films ("French Provincial," "Scene of the Crime") and some clinkers, of which this is a wanly, unintentionally funny example. Nothing in "Rendez-Vous" is supposed to be what it clearly is. Everything represents something else, even sex, which is going too far.

1987 D 25, C6:5

LORD OF THE DANCE/DESTROYER OF ILLUSION, directed by Richard Kohn; story and translation from the Tibetan by Mr. Kohn; director of photography, Jorg Jeshel; edited by Noun Serra; sound by

Barbara Becker; produced by Franz-Christoph Giercke; released by First Run Features. At Film Forum 2, 57 Watts Street. Running time: 113 minutes. This film has no rating.

By WALTER GOODMAN

For people who don't have to live there, Tibet is the most fascinating spot on earth, high amid the lost horizons of the Himalayas, aswirl with the cloudy mysteries and wisdom of the East. That fascination is sorely tested by "Lord of the Dance/Destroyer of Illusion," a conscientious documentary by Richard Kohn, an American student of Buddhist ritual, that opens today at Film Forum 2.

The filming took place in the autumn of 1984 in the Mount Everest area of Nepal, where a Tibetan lama, Trulshig Rinpoche, settled after

being driven from his native land during the Chinese Cultural Revolution. We encounter the lama — the 11th of that name, which means Precious Destroyer of Illusion — as he is presiding over the annual festival of Mani-Rimdu, during which, we are in-

formed by the soft-voiced narrator, monks become gods and do battle with malevolent spirits. The respectful narration is helpful about the details of the ceremony, but its significance, the search for "Buddhahood," remains as obscure as ever: "If your mind is pure, everyone is a Buddha. If your mind is impure, everyone is ordinary." The 100 or so resident monks are seeking to become Garwang Tojay-chenpo, Lord of the Dance — which explains the elaborate title, if little else.

•

The shooting took three weeks, and the 113-minute movie does not seem much shorter. Jorg Jeshel, the cinematographer, keeps his camera on the monks gathered at Thubten Choling Monastery as they go about their preparations, in particular the creation of a brightly colored mandala in sand. The final design of this symbol of the palace of the god is lovely, but the making of it, grain by grain, mantra by mantra, does not enthrall. After that, there is the ceremony, at which locals are invited to partake of magic pills for spiritual sustenance or "empowerment" and watch initiates in exotic garb do their slow dancing to drums, cymbals, horns and bells.

As the monks go "oom," we are told that they "have become Lord of the Dance," but what the outsider sees is a ragged chorus line. Maybe those pills are uppers; anyhow, watching the ritual without them is heavy on the eyes. For respite, the lens turns periodically toward the mountains, an acknowledgment of sorts that a camera is better suited to capturing the outer world than the inner.

Rites
A monk performs a drum dance in Richard Kohn's "Lord of the Dance," a documentary focused on the Tantric ritual of Tibetan Buddhist monks who have fled to Nepal to escape persecution.

As an anthropolitical record, "Lord of the Dance" will no doubt be of value to students of Tantric Buddhism, otherwise known as the Diamond Path to Enlightenment. For nonstudents, however, the path is ar-

L'Amour
Juliette Binoche stars in André Techiné's erotic drama "Rendez-Vous."

duous, the end shrouded. In his first effort at movie making, Mr. Kohn has attained accuracy at considerable sacrifice of general interest. Toward the blessed conclusion, Trulshig Rinpoche, a mild-looking, affable man, offers this piece of advice: "If you seek happiness for yourself, you can have everything in the world and still be unhappy. But if you seek happiness for others, you'll find happiness for yourself. That's the way it is." That's the way it is in fortune cookies, too.

1987 D 26, 14:4

Slow Motion

THE ROSE KING, directed by Werner Schroeter; written (German, Italian and Portuguese with English subtitles) by Mr. Schroeter and Magdalena Montezuma; director of photography, Elfie Mikesch; edited by Juliane Lorenz; produced by Mr. Schroeter and Mr. Lorenz with Futura-Film, Munich. At Film Forum 1, 57 Watts Street. Running time: 103 minutes. This film has no rating.

Anna...............................Magdalena Montezuma
Albert ....Mostefa Djadjam
Fernando ....Antonio Orlando

By VINCENT CANBY

WERNER SCHROETER'S "Rose King," opening today at the Film Forum 1, is one of those supposedly avant-garde films that aren't easy to write about without cracking up, but I'll try.

It's about a youngish man named Albert who lives near the Mediterranean on a rose farm with his mother, Anna. Albert, *I think*, is torn between a hopeless passion for his mother and one for Fernando, a young, moody hired hand who allows Albert to take liberties with him. The movie is full of long, static shots of a spider web, a single rose, a gun, a wood carving of the Virgin Mary, a movie projector and repeated shots of the actor who plays Fernando lying on a beach at night, naked, arms outstreched as if on a cross, or being tossed around by the heedless surf.

In between, Anna broods about Albert, and walks slowly from one room to another. All the characters walk slowly in "The Rose King," possibly because they, like the movie, aren't going anywhere.

Albert broods about Anna and says such things as "Mother, your love gave birth to my anguish." In addition to walking slowly from room to room, Albert also walks slowly to the barn, where he ties Fernando to a chair or sometimes removes Fernando's clothing, the better to bathe his body.

When Fernando is alone, he wanders around the church, taunting the Virgin Mary, apparently waiting for Albert to tie him up again. I say again, though this is the sort of film in which so many shots are repeated I'm not at all sure that anything happens more than once. The movie begins with an aphorism that is, possibly, intended to be funny: "If two children kiss, without knowing each other, one of them must die." It concludes — I'm sure I'm not giving away anything important — with a shooting and the crucifixion of a cat.

Mr. Schroeter has a formidable reputation in Europe. He composes his images as deliberately as a high-fashion photographer. The lighting is sometimes exquisite, and the soundtrack contains bits and pieces of canned classical music. The Film Forum bills Mr. Schroeter as the "enfant terrible of the new German cinema." At 42, he's not an enfant.

1987 D 30, C10:5

Critics' Circle Awards

"Broadcast News," James L. Brooks's romantic comedy about three ambitious young professionals working in television news, was voted the best film of 1987 by the New York Film Critics' Circle yesterday.

Mr. Brooks was also voted best screenwriter and best director. Holly Hunter, who plays the story's fiercely dedicated and much-pursued heroine, was voted best actress. Jack Nicholson, who has a small uncredited role in "Broadcast News" as well as starring roles in "Ironweed" and "The Witches of Eastwick," was voted best actor for his work in all three films.

Morgan Freeman was voted best supporting actor for his performance in "Street Smart," as a shrewd pimp who successfully manipulates a magazine reporter. Vanessa Redgrave was named best supporting actress for her performance as a wickedly catty literary agent in "Prick Up Your Ears." "My Life as a Dog" from Sweden was named best foreign film.

The group declined to vote a best documentary award this year. And it agreed that a best first feature award would be considered in future voting.

This year's prizes will be presented at the group's 53d annual awards ceremony on Jan. 24 at Sardi's restaurant.

"The Dead," John Huston's adaptation of the James Joyce story, was runner-up for the Best Film award. Michael Douglas, Anjelica Huston, William Hurt and Christine Lahti were among the actors who were close runners-up in the acting categories.

These are the 26 members of the New York Film Critics' Circle, and the publications for which they work:

David Sterritt, The Christian Science Monitor, chairman.
David Ansen, Newsweek.
Joy Gould Boyum, Glamour.
Dwight Brown, The Black American/The Hollywood Reporter.

Vincent Canby, The New York Times.
Kathleen Carroll, The Daily News.
Richard Corliss, Time.
Judith Crist, TV Guide.
David Denby, New York Magazine.
David Edelstein, The Village Voice.
Richard Freedman, Newhouse Newspapers.
Joseph Gelmis, Newsday.
Molly Haskell, Vogue/Playgirl.
J. Hoberman, The Village Voice.
Pauline Kael, The New Yorker.
Jack Kroll, Newsweek.
Mike McGrady, Newsday.
Janet Maslin, The New York Times.
Rex Reed, Coming Attractions.
Julie Salamon, The Wall Street Journal.
Andrew Sarris, The Village Voice.
John Simon, The National Review.
Peter Travers, People.
Armond White, The City Sun.
Bruce Williamson, Playboy.
William Wolf, The New York Observer.

1987 D 18, C28:2

The Year's Best

THE MOST IMPORTANT MOVIE news this year wasn't movies but business. More movies than ever went into release this year than at any time in recent memory. Distributors of video cassettes became an important source of production money. Box offices boomed, but often with movies that were interchangeable ("Robocop," "Stakeout," "Lethal Weapon," "Extreme Prejudice"). Theater chains were acquiring other theater chains so fast, so heedlessly, that it seemed possible one of them might accidentally acquire itself.

Not all of 1987's box-office hits were undeserving. Adrian Lyne's "Fatal Attraction" is not exactly "Marnie," but it has a lot of slick style and delivers just the kind of entertainment that's promised. The year's best comedy featuring a camel, Elaine May's crazily underrated "Ishtar," became the victim of its own publicity and big-budget backlash, which, I predict, will be forgotten in the future (see below).

The year's most majestic anticlimax must be "Cry Freedom," directed by Sir Richard Attenborough ("Gandhi"), the sort of worthy movie that appeals to one's conscience while sticking its hand in one's pocket. The year's worst movie? It's been erased from the memory bank.

Bernardo Bertolucci's "Last Emperor" seems to be haunting my mind with more vividness than I would have expected when I first saw it. It's not because of its travelogue aspects. The 360-degree "wrap-around" movie at China's pavilion at Disney World is a good deal more comprehensive in this respect.

"The Last Emperor" covers more than 50 years of modern Chinese history by focusing on the life of the one key figure who affected history the least. It's just possible that Mr. Bertolucci knew what he was doing: no single movie could dramatize so much history in any comprehensive way. By sticking to the story of Pu Yi, the passive, unremarkable, last Manchu ruler of China, the film makes us curious about everything that's going on in the outside world involving Sun Yat-sen, Chiang Kai-shek, Chairman Mao and the others.

"The Last Emperor" is a negative epic. It teases the memory as much for what it doesn't show as for what it does. It's not on the 10-best list, but it's something a lot of people should want to see.

Among the other deserving curios of the year are Suzanne Osten's "Mozart Broth-

Stanley Brock, Jackie Gayle and Danny De Vito in Barry Levinson's "Tin Men"

Mickey Rourke in Barbet Schroeder's "Barfly"—a small, classic, one-of-a-kind comedy

ers," the very funny Swedish sendup of an opera-hating, avant-garde theater director in the process of staging "Don Giovanni"; "Swimming to Cambodia," Spalding Gray's feature-length stage monologue, as preserved in the film directed by Jonathan Demme; and Claude Berri's "Jean de Florette" and "Manon of the Spring," one epic Marcel Pagnol film split into two two-hour parts — to its own detriment.

Not many documentaries reached theater screens in 1987, but among those that did, there were two splendid films about great film makers, "Filming 'Othello,'" Orson Welles's own, somewhat doctored recollection of how his 1951 classic was fabricated, piecemeal, and "Jean Renoir — the Boss," a film interview, conducted by Jacques Rivette and André S. Labarthe, in which the master talks about the conception and shooting of "Rules of the Game." They are musts for all film students.

A must for any student of human nature, or of Les Blank, is Mr. Blank's lyrical "Gap-Toothed Women," in which women discuss the slight space they have between their two upper front teeth, and how that space has af-

fected their perceptions of life. Mr. Blank is an American original.

For one reason and another these films did not make this year's 10-best list.

■

Those that follow, in alphabetical order, did:

"Barfly." Taking a spare, obscene, funny screenplay by Charles Bukowski, the poet laureate of America's misbegotten, Barbet Schroeder, the French director-producer, makes his American film debut with a movie that's a small, classic, one-of-a-kind comedy. Mickey Rourke stars as the Bukowski surrogate figure, a boozing, courtly poet who lives on the edge of sanity and Los Angeles's skid row. He and Faye Dunaway are most affecting as alcoholic lovers. They're two unseaworthy skiffs that pass in the night after a series of brief, alternately noisy and gentle collisions.

The movie is *not* about alcoholism, which it observes without pity, and without taking any high-toned moral stand. "Barfly" is about the spirit that survives in even the grubbiest bodies, in the grubbiest environments, inside a society where cleanliness, and two cars, are next to godliness.

"**The Dead.**" John Huston's last film, based on the James Joyce story, is also one of his greatest. Donal McCann and the incomparable Anjelica Huston are a Dublin (circa 1904) couple whose serene marriage is ruthlessly re-evaluated in the course of a single evening. The movie, written by Tony Huston, builds in the way of the story, through the accumulation of mundane details observed during a holiday dinner party, ending with a series of revelations that reach from middle-class Dublin to the outer banks of the universe.

Though small in physical scale, "The Dead" may be the biggest film Huston ever made. Coupled with the director's next-to-last film, the roller-coaster ride titled "Prizzi's Honor," it demonstrates the remarkable virtuosity of the man whose career began in 1941 with "The Maltese Falcon." It's the unequivocal "don't-miss" movie of the year.

"**Empire of the Sun.**" Steven Spielberg's high aspirations come very close to realization in this very moving, grandly staged adventure-epic about a boy and his war. The boy is Jim, played with uncanny presence by Christian Bale, 13. The war is the Japanese occupation of Shanghai, where, until Dec. 8, 1941, Jim has lived the comfortable colonial life with his English parents.

The movie is big in all the right ways. The scenes of civilian chaos preceding the occupation of Shanghai are stunning. It's also so intimate that it makes comprehensible Jim's admiration of his Japanese captors, during his crucial, harrowing years in the internment camp. Tom Stoppard did the excellent adaptation of J. G. Ballard's autobiographical novel. Supporting the star-performance by Mr. Bale, in whom Mr. Spielberg discovers the wit and guts of the young Jean-Pierre Leaud, are John Malkovich and Miranda Richardson, among others.

The movie appears to have been edited in a hurry — there are awkward gaps in the narrative line — but it's still a large winner.

"**Full Metal Jacket.**" Stanley Kubrick examines the methods by which ordinary, mostly decent young men can be turned into killing machines. The war just *happens* to be the late disaster in Vietnam, and the victims just *happen* to be United States Marine Corps recruits. However, without generalizing, the film's meaning is clear: this is the way that wars go.

Adapted by Mr. Kubrick and Michael Herr, from a novel by Gustav Hasford, the film initially looks to have been made by two different directors from two different screenplays. "Full Metal Jacket" requires the audience to make leaps in continuity and reasoning that pay off with its sorrowful ending. The uniformly fine cast includes Matthew Modine, Vincent D'Onofrio and Lee Ermey, who's unforgettable as a Parris Island gunnery sergeant.

■

"**House of Games.**" David Mamet, the idiosyncratic, Pulitzer Prize-winning playwright, makes a self-assured debut as the idiosyncratic director of his own screenplay, a serio-comic melodrama about con artists. Lindsay Crouse (Mrs. Mamet) and Joe Mantegna star as, respectively, a psychoanalyst and an ambitious hustler who offers to show her the ropes. The movie proceeds as if it were a poker game. As the cards are dealt, the stakes are raised until the point where no one can afford to withdraw.

Though the game is serious, every-

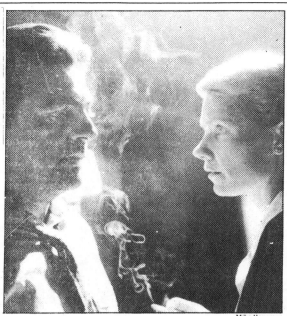
Mike Hausman
Joe Mantegna and Lindsay Crouse in David Mamet's "House of Games"— an original work

Christian Bale in Steven Spielberg's "Empire of the Sun"—a large winner.

Zade Rosenthal
Kevin Costner as Eliot Ness in "The Untouchables," directed by Brian De Palma

Ken Watanabe and Ryutaro Otomo in Juzo Itami's "Tampopo"—wise and funny

body is bluffing, including Mr. Mamet from time to time. The director's visual style and pacing are as Mamet-like as the writer's dialogue, which is as it should be. (It sometimes sounds as if the entire screenplay was written in italics.) "House of Games" is entertaining, bossy and original.

"**Housekeeping.**" Adapted from the Marilynne Robinson novel, this is Bill Forsyth's first film made entirely outside Scotland. It's an exuberant, disorienting comedy about two orphaned teen-age sisters and their different reactions to their odd Aunt Sylvie (Christine Lahti). The time is the 1950's and the place a small town in the Rockies called Fingerbone. Aunt Sylvie is more than odd. She's a hobo. Against her will, she agrees to settle down, *for a while*, to act as guardian to her nieces. The results

are funny and, to most of us who appreciate commonplace order, hair-raising.

The teen-age sisters are played with believably sweet intensity by Sara Walker and Andrea Burchill.

If there is justice in heaven, Miss Lahti and Anjelica Huston will be the major contenders for this year's best-actress Oscar.

"**Radio Days.**" Woody Allen is in top form in this freewheeling homage to the great, golden days of radio. The film takes the form of a family comedy, though it's frequently interrupted with wonderfully irrelevant anecdotes in which Mr. Allen gives us the inside dope on the fictitious (but usually recognizable) celebrities of the day. Seth Green plays Woody-the-boy with gravity, common sense and skepticism. Mr. Allen narrates.

Dianne Wiest, Mia Farrow, Diane Keaton and Josh Mostel are among the more prominent performers. As in all of Mr. Allen's films, it's not the length of the role that counts, but the role itself. Miss Keaton comes on only at the end, to sing, absolutely straight, "You'd Be So Nice to Come Home To." Bliss.

"**Tampopo.**" Juzo Itami emerges as one of Japan's most ebullient satirists with this, his second film, but the first to be released in this country. Actually, it was a tossup whether "Tampopo" should be on the 10-best list or "The Funeral," Mr. Itami's first film, which was released here after "Tampopo." Both are equally wise and funny. "Tampopo" may be slightly more adventurous in the way it manages to mix up the story of an aspiring noodle maker, Tampopo (played by Nabuko Miyamoto, who is

Mrs. Itami), and a lot of random comments on the manners and mores of contemporary Japan.

That Mr. Itami is not a two-shot director is demonstrated by his new comedy, "A Taxing Woman," shown at this year's New York Film Festival. It's still awaiting a commercial release.

■

"Tin Men." Barry Levinson, the man who made "Diner," has a keener ear for the hilarious banalities of American speech than any other film maker around today. He's also an expert director of serious comedy that doesn't take itself too seriously. The time is 1963 and the place is Baltimore (again). The film is mostly about the lunatic feud between two rather sleazy salesmen of aluminum siding, one suave and cool (up to a point), played by Richard Dreyfuss, the other (Danny DeVito) a hyperventilating kook. Under the skin, they are brothers.

Both actors are very funny as the sort of American males who, though they talk about women all the time, are much more comfortable pitted against other males. Barbara Hershey is terrifically patient as the woman who is more or less tossed from one to the other.

"The Untouchables." When I first heard that the old television series was going to be rehabilitated as a big-budget melodrama, I groaned. The groan was premature. As written by David Mamet and directed by Brian De Palma, this "Untouchables" is superior mass-market entertainment, fast, witty and appropriately shocking in the thoroughly conventional way of crime films.

Robert De Niro, as Al Capone, isn't on-screen all that much, but the performance is so big it dominates the movie and gives Kevin Costner, who's excellent as the true-blue Eliot Ness, someone to play off. However, Sean Connery will not be upstaged by either. His performance as a maverick (that is, honest) Chicago cop is the spine of the movie.

■

The 10 runners-up, in no special order of preference are:

Elaine May's "Ishtar," which possibly should have been made on a Hollywood back lot, but is no less funny for having been shot in North Africa; "Matewan," John Sayles's evocative folk ballad about a West Virginia coal miners' strike back in the days when, in unity, there was strength and, in strength, the promise of a better life.

Also, Margarethe von Trotta's "Rosa Luxemburg," another political film (but far more sophisticated than John Sayles's look back), with Barbara Sukowa as the determined Rosa; "Broadcast News," a charming romantic comedy, featuring some hilarious digs at television news as entertainment; "Orphans," Alan J. Pakula's smart adaptation of Lyle Kessler's play, notable for the performances of Albert Finney, Matthew Modine and Kevin Anderson.

Also, "Dark Eyes," Nikita Mikhalkov's exhilarating pastiche of four Chekhov stories, with Marcello Mastroianni front and center; "River's Edge," Tim Hunter's brutal recollec-

Combat in Stanley Kubrick's "Full Metal Jacket"— This is the way that wars go.

Brian Ham[...]

Mia Farrow in Woody Allen's "Radio Days"—the film maker in top form

tion of teen-agers in the land of the alienated and the emotionally dislocated; Alex Cox's "Walker," a jazzy, intentionally anachronistic biography of a 19th-century American adventurer running wild in Nicaragua, with

Ed Harris; "Good Morning, Vietnam," in which, for the first time in movies, Robin Williams gets a chance to demonstrate his full comic talents, under Barry Levinson's appreciative direction, and "The Whales of Au-

gust," Lindsay Anderson's gift to two great actresses, Lillian Gish and Bette Davis, who should thank him, Mike Kaplan (the producer who put it all together) and their lucky stars.

□

1987 D 27, II:23:1

Film Critics' Group Honors 'The Dead'

By JANET MASLIN

"The Dead," the work that marked the extraordinary synthesis of a great literary talent with a great cinematic one, was voted the best film of 1987 by the National Society of Film Critics yesterday.

In addition to honoring the late John Huston's adaptation of James Joyce's story, the group named Steve Martin the year's best actor for his tragicomic role in "Roxanne," which Mr. Martin adapted from "Cyrano de Bergerac." Emily Lloyd, a newcomer, was voted best actress for her performance as a feisty, rebellious teenager in "Wish You Were Here."

Both of the group's choices in the supporting acting categories came from the little-seen "Street Smart." Morgan Freeman, also named best supporting actor by the New York

Film Critics' Circle last month, was cited for his performance as a pimp who became involved with an unscrupulous journalist, and Kathy Baker was named best supporting actress for her performance as a prostitute.

'Hope and Glory' Wins 3

John Boorman received the best director and best screenplay awards for "Hope and Glory," his autobiographical film about a young British boy's World War II experiences.

Another award to "Hope and Glory" was the best cinematography prize, which was voted to Philippe Rousselot. The group declined to vote a best documentary award this year.

Among the runners-up were Albert Brooks, who placed second in the best actor category as well as third in the best supporting actor category for his performance in "Broadcast News," and Diane Keaton, who placed second

as best actress for her role in "Baby Boom."

The 39-member National Society of Film Critics, voting its 22d annual awards at the Algonquin Hotel yesterday, represents critics from New York, Boston, Los Angeles and other cities.

Under the chairmanship of David Kehr of The Chicago Tribune, the 34 members represented at yesterday's meeting also voted a special citation in tribute to Richard Roud, the former director of the New York Film Festival, whose unexpected ouster from his post in October has aroused great controversy. The citation read, "The National Society of Film Critics is pleased to honor Richard Roud for his invaluable contributions to the New York Film Festival and his vital role in introducing international cinema to the American audience."

1988 Ja 4, C18:1

Directors Guild Honors Bertolucci for 'Emperor'

By ALJEAN HARMETZ

Special to The New York Times

HOLLYWOOD, March 13 — Bernardo Bertolucci became the front-runner for the director's Oscar when he won the Directors Guild of Amer-

ica award for his opulent epic, "The Last Emperor," on Saturday night.

Only three times since the guild award was created in 1948 has the winner failed to capture the Academy Award as best director. The competition this year was particularly intriguing because two of the guild

nominees — James L. Brooks for "Broadcast News" and Steven Spielberg for "Empire of the Sun" — were not nominated by the academy. In what the audience took as a back-handed reference to the fact that he has never been nominated for an Academy Award, Mr. Spielberg mentioned that he has won guild nominations for six of his nine movies.

"This is a very nice welcome to a new member of the D.G.A.," said Mr. Bertolucci, whose "Last Emperor" details the sweeping changes in China during the 20th century by telling the life story of the boy emperor Pu Yi.

An Italian, Mr. Bertolucci said: "In the darkness of movie theaters, there are no more national identities. There are no more classes."

"Maybe I'm an idealist, but I still see movie theaters as big cathedrals," he continued, where people come to "dream the same dream together."

Television Honors

His comments have relevance to the Academy Awards, where none of the five nominees are American directors. The other nominees for both awards were Adrian Lyne, who is British, for "Fatal Attraction" and Lasse Hallstrom, from Sweden, for "My Life as a Dog." Mr. Bertolucci, Mr. Lyne and Mr. Hallstrom are joined in the race for the Oscar by a Canadian, Norman Jewison, for "Moonstruck," and another Englishman, John Boorman, for "Hope and Glory."

In the television honors that were also handed out during a dinner at the Beverly Hilton Hotel, Jud Taylor won the most prestigious prize, for dramatic specials, with "Foxfire," a movie about an old woman who must decide whether to move off her land.

The guild's highest honor, the D. W. Griffith award for outstanding achievement over a lifetime, went to Robert Wise, a former president of the guild and current president of the academy.

1988 Mr 14, C14:3

Dukakis and Connery Win Oscars For Best Supporting Performances

By ALJEAN HARMETZ

Special to The New York Times

LOS ANGELES, April 11 — For her performance as Cher's sardonic and sexy mother in "Moonstruck," Olympia Dukakis won an Oscar as best supporting actress at the 60th annual Academy Awards tonight.

Ms. Dukakis, a first cousin of the Democratic presidential candidate Michael Dukakis, was calm while she made the obligatory thank-yous. But then, raising the golden statuette in victory, she shouted, "Okay, Michael, let's go!"

The most popular winner early in

The New York Times

Billy Wilder

the evening was Sean Connery. His award as supporting actor for his portrayal of an honest Irish cop in "The Untouchables" had been telegraphed when he received a standing ovation as he emerged from colored smoke to present the award for visual effects. This was Mr. Connery's first nomination in 30 years as an actor, and he was awarded a second standing ovation when he walked majestically up to the stage to receive his Oscar.

Heading for what appeared to be a sweep, "The Last Emperor" won all the early awards for which it was nominated. Vittorio Storaro won for cinematography; Gabriella Cristiani for film editing; Ryuichi Sakamoto, David Byrne and Cong Su for best original music score; Ferdinando Scarfiotti for art direction, Bruno Cesari for set decoration, and Bill Rowe and Ivan Sharrock for sound.

Billy Wilder, a six-time Academy Award winner, received a seventh tribute from the Academy of Motion Picture Arts and Sciences tonight. This time, however, he did not have to wait in suspense.

Mr. Wilder, a writer, director and producer whose movies include "Some Like It Hot," "Sunset Boulevard" and "The Apartment," was given the Irving G. Thalberg Award, the Academy's highest honor. Named after the legendary boy genius of M-G-M, the award is bestowed on a film maker for his body of work. Given only 28 times in the Academy's 60 years of award presentations, the prize went to Steven Spielberg last year.

In the most expected win of the night, "(I've Had) The Time of My Life" from "Dirty Dancing" won as best song.

The award for visual effects went to "Innerspace," a comedy adventure voyage inside the human body.

The feature-length documentary award was won by "The 10 Year Lunch: The Wit and Legend of the Algonquin Round Table. The short documentary Oscar went to "Young at Heart," a tale of the romance between two painters who meet in their mid-80's. The film was co-produced by the daughter of one of the artists. The

Associated Press

Olympia Dukakis accepting her statuette at the Academy Awards ceremony last night, and Sean Connery in a scene from Brian DePalma's film "The Untouchables." They won Oscars for best supporting actress and actor.

SHORT FILM, ANIMATED, "The Man Who Planted Trees," Société Radio-Canada/Canadian Broadcasting Corporation; Frederic Back, producer.

SHORT FILM, LIVE, "Ray's Male Heterosexual Dance Hall" (Chanticleer Films).

DOCUMENTARY, FEATURE, "The 10-Year Lunch: The Wit and Legend of the Algonquin Round Table," Aviva Films; Aviva Slesin, producer.

DOCUMENTARY, SHORT SUBJECT, "Young at Heart," Sue Marx Films Inc.; Sue Marx and Pamela Conn, producers.

IRVING G. THALBERG AWARD, a special award given to a film maker for the body of his work. To Billy Wilder, writer and director.

award for animated film was won by "The Man Who Planted Trees," about a hermit who spent his life creating forests.

After 19 years at the Dorothy Chandler Pavilion in the Los Angeles Music Center, the awards ceremony was shifted to the Shrine Auditorium, a cavernous building with 6000 seats. The demand for tickets has escalated in recent years and the Shrine is almost double the size of the Pavilion.

The 4,523 voting members of the Academy are eligible to vote for the winners in most categories. However, no member is allowed to vote in the documentary, short film and foreign-language categories unless he certifies that he has seen all nominees.

The only nominations that are made by the Academy as a whole are those for best picture. Otherwise, the Academy is divided into 14 branches, and each branch nominates achievements in its own field. Thus, "Broadcast News" could get seven nominations, including a nomination for best picture, without its director, James L. Brooks, being nominated.

Actors comprise by far the largest branch. There are 1,267 actors, 257 art directors, 110 cinematographers, 257 directors, 181 film editors, 244 musicians, 203 short film makers, 317 in the sound branch, and 378 writers. The 320 executives, 349 producers, 287 public relations executives, and 353 members at large only nominate for best picture.

Excluding foreign language and documentary films, 263 movies were eligible for nomination for the 60th Annual Academy Awardsa. To be eligible, a film had to play at theaters in the Los Angeles area for seven consecutive days starting no later than Dec. 31, 1986.

Michael Douglas, nominated for an Academy Award for the first time, won the prize as best actor of 1987 for his performance as the cold-blooded corporate raider Gordon Gekko in "Wall Street." Mr. Douglas's father, Kirk, has been nominated three times for best actor, but has not yet won.

1988 Ap 12, C13:1

The New York Times
Film Reviews
1988

The Dogs Of '87

THE DECENT THING TO DO about the year's bad films used to be to let them go quietly. But that was in the days when a movie of no merit could be counted on to disappear into the oblivion from whence it came. Those days are gone, as anyone who regularly visits video stores must surely realize. It is now possible for a terrible film to resurface in a nice package that bears no memory-jogging information, just an indistinct title and the name of a star or two. With more new releases than ever, it takes a great barking dog of a bad film — an "Angel Heart," a "Who's That Girl?" — to stand out from the crowd.

Worst-film lists usually concentrate on spectacular examples like these; after all, "Angel Heart" had a character who wound up in a gumbo pot. But those are easy targets, and there's no real point in singling them out. Far more egregious are the two-week wonders, the films that were made for no real reason and have disappeared from theatrical release so quickly that they might just strike the home viewer's fancy. These are the ones that warrant a little warning.

Thanks to the ever-widening, more indiscriminate cable TV and video markets, 1987 brought more of these mediocrities than ever before. The films on the following list are just obscure and ordinary enough to turn up for a second chance, which they really don't deserve.

"Wanted Dead or Alive." This cheap, bloody action film masqueraded as a descendant of the old Steve McQueen television series, with which it had no legitimate connection. Rutger Hauer played a latter-day bounty hunter — nominally the "great-grandson" of the McQueen character — who investigated the bombing of a Los Angeles movie theater where "Rambo," this film's real inspiration, happened to be playing.

"Critical Condition." The screenplay for this thoroughly unfunny hospital comedy, with Richard Pryor, came from the writers of "Turk 182!" (another one to stay away from). The idea, about a huckster who's on the run from his enemies and winds up impersonating a doctor, was mildly amusing, but somehow Mr. Pryor was not. The star seemed unusually uncomfortable in the role.

■

"Allan Quartermain and the Lost City of Gold." Richard Chamberlain did his best Indiana Jones impersonation in a film whose sets and special effects were scene-stealingly chintzy, yet not quite bad enough to be fun.

"One Woman or Two." Though the film itself was calamitous, it could easily be made to look appealing with the right packaging.

George Kontaxis

Mickey Rourke plays a detective in "Angel Heart"—an easy target.

The director of "The Return of Martin Guerre" teamed Gerard Depardieu and Sigourney Weaver as a romantic duo, with Dr. Ruth Westheimer presumably providing that extra je ne sais quoi. Amazingly, Dr. Ruth wasn't bad, and Mr. Depardieu was.

"Over the Top." Sylvester Stallone chose arm-wrestling as his métier and flexed like crazy in the role of a simple trucker trying to win back the love of his son. The box-office failure of this film proved conclusively that even Stallone fans have their standards.

"Predator." So do Schwarzenegger fans, who did not much want to watch their hero battle a giant, computerized, half-invisible lizard.

"Mannequin." Teen-centric Hollywood hit its nadir with this vapid little comedy, its soundtrack laden with prefab pop songs, about a boy who brings a mannequin to life and frolics with her in a department store. The obligatory, detachable rock-video sequence wasn't even the worst of it.

"Eat and Run." A dreadful comedy about a fat extraterrestrial named Murray, who devours every Italian he meets. Stupid, and proud of it.

"Death Before Dishonor." Red-blooded Marines, led by the sneering tough-guy Fred Dryer (star of the television series "Hunter") warned Arab terrorists, "Don't get us mad." The services of John Milius ("Red Dawn") who does this kind of thing with a lot more gusto, were badly needed.

"Making Mr. Right." The director of "Desperately Seeking Susan," Susan Seidelman, assembled many similar ingredients here — great costumes, clever casting, throwaway style and an equally convoluted plot about two characters sharing the same identity — but everything went wrong. The idea of a perky career woman falling in love with a

John Clifford

In "Making Mr. Right" Ann Magnuson falls for an android.

male android proved only slightly less noxious than it would have been with the genders reversed.

"Three for the Road." A teen-age road movie entirely devoid of personality, which was also the problem with its star, Charlie Sheen. It followed the depressingly smug, monotonous exploits of two boys escorting a potential runaway (Kerri Green, an appealing actress in an awful role) across the country in her father's ice-blue Mercedes. In the 80's, this passes for an adventure.

"My Demon Lover." A boy who called his girlfriend "Fruitburger" would turn into a werewolf whenever they kissed. The peppy actors and ugly special effects were exceptionally ill-matched.

"The Allnighter." Susanna Hoffs of the Bangles starred in a teen-age comedy that looked all the more dangerously mindless in the age of AIDS. On graduation eve at a California college, various bubble-headed coeds and their male-model classmates did what they could to confuse true love with the one-night stand.

"Steele Justice." An inadvertent comedy about a bare-chested Vietnam veteran, back in the States and doing what he could to fight crime. Top acting honors went to the Sinaloan milk snake in the cast.

"Amazing Grace and Chuck." From Mike Newell, the director of "Dance With a Stranger," came this unaccountably naïve, somber fairy tale, about a schoolboy and an ex-basketball star banding together in the interest of nuclear disarmament. This film's good intentions dissolved in a cloud of wild improbabilities.

"Straight to Hell." Alex Cox, the versatile director of "Sid and Nancy," "Repo Man" and "Walker," proved how erratic he could be with

Charlie Sheen's performance adds little to "Three for the Road."

Mountains' Majesty

THE HORSE THIEF, directed by Tian Zhuangzhuang; screenplay by Zhang Rui; camera by Hou Yong and Zhao Fei; music by Qu Xiaosong; produced by Wu Tianming and Xian Film Studio. At Film Forum 1, 57 Watts Street. Running time: 88 minutes. This film has no rating.
WITH: Tseshang Rigzin, Dan Jiji, Jayang Jmco, Gaoba, Daiba, Drashi

By JANET MASLIN

THE Chinese film "The Horse Thief" is best watched as pure spectacle, since it unfolds almost entirely without benefit of dialogue. What little talk there is tends to be plain and to the point ("If only we had stew"). However, from the scenic and ethnographic standpoints the film is often quite arresting. Like the more dramatically compelling "Wild Mountains," another product of the Xian Film Studio in China, "The Horse Thief" concentrates on a primitive way of life, and captures it with a surprising degree of sophistication.

In this case, the setting is the harsh, barren landscape of Tibet, which on film has a stark beauty not unlike the landscapes of American westerns. It is here that the film's tribal drama of theft, ostracism and terrible retribution unfolds, although the director, Tian Zhuangzhuang (an iconoclastic graduate of the Beijing Film Academy), uses few conventional means of bringing these dramatic events to the forefront.

•

Instead, "The Horse Thief" proceeds as a series of tribal and Buddhist rituals, which are captured here wordlessly and in great detail. Much of the film's fascination lies in watching the funeral rites, or the tribal banishment, or the punishment in effigy that is meted out to Norbu (Tseshang Rigzin), the film's central character, after he commits the theft referred to by the title. The vultures, the cattle, the various animals herded by the tribesmen are part of the story's backdrop, set against majestic Tibetan scenery. Indeed, the film's mystical dimension is more evident in these sweeping tableaus than in the director's more awkward efforts to capture the experience of prayer.

"The Horse Thief," which opens today at the Film Forum 1, inaugurates that theater's series entitled "The Cutting Edge," which will present six selections by international film makers of unusual promise. The stark, forbidding beauty of "The Horse Thief" makes it a worthy choice for a program like this.

1988 Ja 6, C 15:1

---

this extended private joke. Dennis Hopper, Grace Jones, the director Jim Jarmusch and various rock performers acted out an Old West fantasy that was all too rich in whimsy.

"Adventures in Babysitting." This comedy about the horrors that befall clean-scrubbed, middle-class white kids who accidentally venture into the inner city at night affirmed every imaginable prejudice and preconception. The vogue enjoyed by such kiddie adventure films is officially over.

"Summer School." Carl Reiner's name and Mark Harmon's good looks promised a lot more high spirits than this washout actually delivered.

There were a lot more where these came from, sad to say. But all this naysaying warrants a little good news, too, and here it is: The year also produced some notable sleepers. Well worth watching for, just as the others are not, are:

"Dead of Winter," Arthur Penn's mischievous foray into the realm of Gothic horror, with a terrific three-way performance by Mary Steenburgen; "The Bedroom Window," directed by Curtis Hanson, was a creditable attempt at a Hitchcock-type thriller; "Some Kind of Wonderful," an unexpectedly charming adolescent comedy, directed by John Hughes; "The Whistle Blower," a beautifully acted British spy thriller, starring Michael Caine; "Scene of the Crime," André Techiné's sleek, suspenseful thriller, and "The Good Father," a keenly observed British drama, starring Anthony Hopkins and directed by Mike Newell, who thus made up for "Amazing Grace and Chuck."

Also: "Eat the Peach," the nicely eccentric story of two Irishmen with an impossible dream; "Maid to Order," a television-caliber comedy a lot more sprightly than most, and the horror film "The Blue Monkey," which had as much style and wit as the story of a big blue slug possibly could. □

1988 Ja 3, II:15:1

FILM VIEW/Vincent Canby

Big Talents vs. the Big Screen

FOR ONE REASON AND ANother, some great performers don't fit easily onto the motion picture screen. The camera wasn't kind to the Lunts in "The Guardsman" (1931), their first (and last) co-starring screen appearance. Somewhere between the movie set and the movie theater, the grace and elegant humor that were evident in all of their theatrical performances evaporated.

Ethel Merman could hold Broadway theatergoers in the palm of her hand, but when seen larger than life on a movie screen, she intimidated. Her good-humored, resilient brassiness suddenly became antagonizing. She didn't belt songs. She belted the audience. On television, Milton Berle was irresistible as a tireless, pushy top banana. In most of the movies he made, he was scaled down to play everybody's best friend. Hollywood never found a way to harness his effrontery.

Whoopi Goldberg, after a spectacular television debut in Mike Nichols's adaptation of her one-woman Broadway show, went on to win an Oscar nomination for her modest, sweet performance in "The Color Purple." Since then, she's been in a series of movie comedies so witless that she seems to be doing an extended fade-out, even as we watch.

"The Bill Cosby Show" is one of the biggest things ever to hit television, yet the box-office receipts for his new theatrical film, "Leonard, Part 6," are, according to Variety, "awful."

The news isn't all bad, however.

"Raw," Eddie Murphy's not-great concert film, has been a quick box-office smash, and Robin Williams, whose own concert films are pay-television classics, has his first, unequivocal theatrical hit in Barry Levinson's "Good Morning, Vietnam."

In just five years and five movies, Mr. Murphy has parlayed stardom as a television sketch artist and stand-up comedian, on "Saturday Night Live," into stardom as one of the most winning new leading men on the big screen. For Mr. Williams, the Juilliard-trained actor, movies have been more of an uphill slog, and may well continue to be.

■

That Mr. Murphy, who, as far as I know, has never been near an acting school, should be able to make the transfer from the small screen to the big one, without the effort and care visible in Mr. Williams's career, is what makes show biz so mysterious. The laws of alchemy are more reliable than those at work in the performing arts.

Following his discovery on television's "Mork and Mindy" series, Mr. Williams appeared in some decent movies, including Robert Altman's "Popeye," George Roy Hill's "World According to Garp" and Paul Mazursky's "Moscow on the Hudson." Yet the speed of thought and the maniacally poetic personality, which are the center of his one-man shows, were only evident in isolated moments.

Mr. Williams *can* impersonate Popeye. He *can* play a whimsically conceived writer named Garp, as well as an asylum-seeking Russian musician, but watching him in these movies is like watching a Concorde being driven from New York to Boston on the thruway. "Good Morning, Vietnam" is a cannily constructed star vehicle that allows Mr. Williams, as an Armed Forces Radio disk jockey in Saigon in 1965, to have it both ways: to play a fictional role, as a man of serious sensibility, and to perform, in character, a series of on-air, stream-of-consciousness monologues and other riffs that employ the particular gifts of a true show-biz original.

In tailoring this role to Mr. Williams's eccentric dimensions, Mr. Levinson and Mitch Markowitz, who wrote the screenplay, have liberated the star. It's as if he were making his big-screen debut. In passing, they've also discovered that the most singular aspect of the Williams personality — the searching, revved-up mind, the quality of which separates him from all other stand-up comedians — enriches the fictional drama that surrounds him. The Williams monologues don't stop the movie. They aren't like those gruesome interludes in Marx Brothers movies when Harpo plucks his harp or Chico fingers the piano. The monologues give "Good Morn-

Eddie Murphy, Robin Williams and Bill Cosby prove once again that not all stars are tailor-made for the movies.

ing, Vietnam'' its reason for being.

A problem remains: What does Mr. Williams do for an encore?

Mr. Williams is much more like the prickly, not comfortably caged Richard Pryor than is Eddie Murphy, who, possibly with hope, acknowledges Mr. Pryor's influence on his career. In "Raw," Mr. Murphy does a brilliant Pryor imitation but, later in the show, attempts to do a surreal, Pryor-type monologue that comes out sounding secondhand.

Mr. Williams, spinning wildly through the inner space of a monologue, gives every indication of speaking in tongues. He seems a man possessed, as does Mr. Pryor in his one-man shows. The performance is hilarious and a little scary. It's so intense that one feels that at any minute the creative process could reverse into a complete personality meltdown.

Like Mr. Pryor, Mr. Williams will probably always have trouble finding conventional fictional material that fits.

Not so Mr. Murphy, who has a redeeming blandness that will be as important to his big-screen career as his remarkable talents.

Blandness might seem an odd way to describe the star of "Raw," who spends much of his performance making unprintable remarks about women, homosexuals and body parts, while frequently clutching his own. He does a number of expert, sometimes vicious imitations of, in addition to Mr. Pryor, Bill Cosby, Stevie Wonder and Sylvester Stallone. He works freely in the borrowed styles of Mr. Pryor and of the ridiculed Mr. Cosby, partic-

ularly when he recalls stories from a middle-class childhood.

Mr. Murphy is such a terrifically smooth entertainer that he almost seems homogenized. He bears the same relation to Richard Pryor as Diana Ross does to Billie Holliday. One is an original. The other is a classy variation. As he has demonstrated in "48 Hrs." and the first "Beverly Hills Cop," Mr. Murphy is a movie natural. The camera that made fun of the Lunts adores him. He looks great, has a smile that won't quit and projects — in spite of the language — a thoroughly conventional, yuppie intelligence. When he's doing his stand-up concert routine, it seems first-rate acting rather than one-of-a-kind performing.

It's significant that the most passionate passages in "Raw" have nothing to do with race, homosexuals, childhood, body parts or even with his own sexual potency, which, possibly because it's played down in his fiction films, he talks about at great length here.

The real subject of "Raw" is money.

Mr. Murphy is earning at a phenomenal rate these days, and he wants to hang on to his loot. He asks the members of the audience to sympathize with him (and many do) for having arrived at a station in life where he can be sued for $12 million after a non-brawl in which he did not participate. He cites the terrible fate of Johnny Carson who, he says, was forced to give up half of a $300 million fortune to a wife under community property laws.

For a man of 26, who 10 years ago counted himself lucky to be making 30 bucks a week playing small comedy clubs, this, truly, is a fate worse than death. In his monologues, Richard Pryor is searching for an identity. He rummages around through the ruins of an unconventional childhood, various failed marriages, love affairs and life-threatening addictions. When he gets to the end, he's exhausted, and pretty much where he started.

In "Raw," Mr. Murphy, who neither smokes nor drinks and whose mother decorated his new 27-room mansion in New Jersey, seems to be searching for the name of the perfect tax lawyer. "Raw" exposes rather more of him than he may suspect. From the moment he appears on stage, behind a scrim in a silhouette that recalls Michelangelo's David, the audience knows it's in the presence of top-quality personality packaging. □

1988 Ja 10, II:21:1

You're on the Air

THE COUCH TRIP, directed by Michael Ritchie; screenplay by Steven Kampmann and Will Porter and Sean Stein, based on a novel by Ken Kolb; director of photography, Donald E. Thorin; edited by Richard A. Harris; music by Michel Colombier; production designer, Jimmie Bly; produced by Lawrence Gordon; released by Orion Pictures Corporation. At Astor Plaza, Broadway and 44th Street; New York Twin, Second Avenue and 66th Street; 34th Street Showplace, between Second and Third Avenues; 84th Street Six, at Broadway; Movie Center 5, 125th Street, between Adam Clayton Powell and Frederick Douglass Boulevards. Running time: 98 minutes. This film is rated R.
John Burns .... Dan Aykroyd
Donald Becker .... Walter Matthau
George Maitlin ....Charles Grodin
Laura Rollins ....Donna Dixon
Harvey Michaels ....Richard Romanus
Vera Maitlin ....Mary Gross
Lawrence Baird ....David Clennon

By VINCENT CANBY

IN "The Couch Trip," Michael Ritchie's new farce about radio sex therapists and assorted southern California con artists, Walter Matthau plays a comparatively small role, but in the way he looks and behaves he defines the movie's laid-back, ramshackle charm.

Mr. Matthau, wearing a conspicuously full head of jet-black hair, is first seen as a panhandler outside the Los Angeles airport as he solicits funds on behalf of "People for the Ethical Treatment of Plants." "Remember," he tells a would-be donor, "a man is never so tall as when he stoops to pet a plant."

The lines and situations in "The Couch Trip" aren't consistently first-rate, but the point of view is so engaging, and the performers so enthusiastically committed, that the movie makes willing co-conspirators of the members of the audience. Like Mr. Matthau, "The Couch Trip" can be good fun even when it's slouching around with nothing much to say.

Mr. Matthau is in excellent company. His co-stars are Dan Aykroyd as an Illinois mental patient who, through means I need not synopsize here, suddenly becomes the most popular radio sex therapist in the Los Angeles area, and Charles Grodin as the suicidal therapist whose place is so rudely usurped by the fast-talking Mr. Aykroyd.

The other loons include Richard Romanus as Mr. Grodin's slippery lawyer-manager, Mary Gross (formerly of "Saturday Night Live"), as Mr. Grodin's patient (up to a point) wife, and David Clennon, as a prison psychiatrist whose name and reputation are borrowed by Mr. Aykroyd. The one, possibly halfway sane character is played by Donna Dixon (Mrs. Aykroyd), as a psychiatrist who falls for the fraud played by her husband.

●

Gale Adler

Angst

Walter Matthau and Dan Aykroyd are seen in "The Couch Trip," about a psychiatrist and his patient.

"The Couch Trip," which opens today at the Astor Plaza and other theaters, has a story that means to be coherent but only works as a series of vaguely related sketches that get on and off fast. Near the beginning, there's a nifty one in which Mr. Aykroyd, trussed up in a straitjacket, manages to open a jar of candy and to conduct a telephone conversation without the use of his hands.

Also invigorating is the sight of Mr. Aykroyd, in a radio studio, as he fields questions from listeners on various sexual problems, answering with a four-letter bluntness that sends the show's ratings through the roof. At one point, he invites all his listeners to accompany him to a baseball game, segregating the crowds that turn up by their medical problems — "Nymphomaniacs in bus No. 1 with me."

Mr. Aykroyd's comedy style looks a lot looser than, in fact, it really is. Even when the material slides off into predictable routine, he carries on with such manic energy that one often doesn't notice that one is laughing with him and not at it. Mr. Grodin, one of the best farceurs in films or television, approaches farce from the opposite direction, never being more hilarious than when he's playing absolutely straight. Though they don't share many scenes in "The Couch Trip," their performances are nicely matched.

Overseeing all, mostly from the sidelines, is the revivifying presence of Mr. Matthau. He can find treasures in a single disapproving scowl that would elude most actors playing the uncut "Hamlet."

1988 Ja 15, C8:1

Mystery and Magic

EL SUR, directed by Víctor Erice; written by José Luis López Linares (Spanish with English subtitles), based on a story by Adelaida García Morales; cinematography by José Luis Alcaine; edited by Pablo G. del Amo; art director, Antonio Belizón; produced by Elías Querejeta and Chloe Productions; released by New Yorker Films. At Lincoln Plaza Cinema, Broadway at 63d Street. Running time: 94 minutes. This film has no rating.

Agustín	Omero Antonutti
Estrella (age 8)	Sonsoles Aranguren
Estrella (age 15)	Iciar Bollan
Julia	Lola Cardona
Milagros	Rafaela Aparicio
Doña Rosario	Germaine Montero
Irene Ríos/Laura	Aurore Clément
Irene Ríos's co-star	Francisco Merino
Casilda	María Caro

"EL SUR" ("The South"), opening today at the Lincoln Plaza Cinema, is the second feature by Víctor Erice, the Spanish director whose first film, "The Spirit of the Beehive," was one of the critical hits of 1976.

Like "The Spirit of the Beehive," the new work is a very somber recollection of childhood, seen mostly through the eyes of a young girl growing up in the aftermath of the Spanish Civil War. The time is the 1950's and the place a small walled town in the north of Spain where Estrella, the film's narrator, lives with her mother, Julia, and her adored father, Agustín, a medical doctor.

Estrella's early childhood is full of mystery and intimations of magic. Years before, she's been told, her parents fled the south after her father had a terrible fight with Estrella's grandfather. To Estrella, the south, which she knows only through picture postcards, is a land of sunny enchantment, and her father a bit like an exiled god, as well as a little scary. He spends long hours locked in the attic of their house, which is outside the walled town in an area called "no-man's land." He is, says Julia, "guarding his powers." As Estrella eventually learns, his powers are those of someone who can divine the sex of unborn babies.

•

When Estrella is a little older, Agustín instructs her in the art of divination. As she begins to learn about the war that divided her family and Spain, she also comes upon a much more personal secret that divides her father and mother.

As was Mr. Erice's method in "The Spirit of the Beehive," the new film reveals its concerns in small, seemingly unimportant details, much in the manner of a traumatized psychiatric patient. Every gesture is loaded with associated meanings. Objects are symbolic. Yet the emotional inhibitions, which had political significance in the first film, aren't particularly provocative here. The movie seems to whisper when there seems no reason why it can't speak in a normal voice.

"El Sur" is nicely acted by Omero Antonutti as Agustín and Iciar Bollan as the teen-age Estrella, though it lacks a dominating performance like that of Ana Torrent in "Beehive." Everything about "El Sur," including the highly theatrical lighting, is so artfully composed that it seems to be more about film making than characters or ideas.   *VINCENT CANBY*

1988 Ja 15, C 11:1

Unnatural Disaster

RETURN OF THE LIVING DEAD PART II, directed and written by Ken Wiederhorn; director of photography, Robert Elswit; edited by Charles Bornstein; music by J. Peter Robinson; art director, Dale Allan Pelton; produced by Tom Fox; released by Lorimar Motion Pictures. At Movieland, Broadway at 47th Street; U. A. East, 85th Street and First Avenue; 23d Street West Triplex, at Eighth Avenue; Metro Twin, Broadway at 99th Street, and other theaters. Running time: 89 minutes. This film is rated R.

Ed	James Karen
Lucy Wilson	Marsha Dietlein
Joey	Thom Mathews
Brenda	Suzanne Snyder
Tom Essex	Dana Ashbrook
Doc Mandel	Philip Bruns

YOU can't keep a gooey ghoul down. That's the message of "Return of the Living Dead Part II," which revives the creatures who enlivened (that may not be the right word) "Return of the Living Dead" but which has nothing to do with George Romero's 1968 cult favorite "Night of the Living Dead."

The main jokes in this jokey movie, written and directed on the cheap by Ken Wiederhorn, are squeezed from the lurchings of the gloppy creatures who ooze out of the town graveyard one night and the reactions of the goony townsfolk whose innards attract them. The living dead have a special taste for human brains; but all the people put together in this town would not make one satisfying meal.

Naturally, you can't kill the already dead, and you dismember them at your peril since the unattached heads and hands instantly develop hungers of their own and scramble after you. That's another joke. This noisy movie, now inhabiting Movieland and other theaters, is rated R, which means that the only people who can see it are those who ought to be too old for it.   *WALTER GOODMAN*

1988 Ja 15, C11:1

Sexual Skirmishes

PATTI ROCKS, directed by David Burton Morris; story and screenplay by Mr. Morris, Chris Mulkey, John Jenkins and Karen Landry, based on characters created by Victoria Wozniak; photographed and edited by Gregory M. Cummins; music by Doug Maynard; art director, Charlotte Whitaker; produced by Gwen Field and Mr. Cummins; released by Filmdallas Pictures. At the Waverly, Avenue of the Americas at Third Street. Running time: 86 minutes. This film is rated R.

Billy	Chris Mulkey
Eddie	John Jenkins
Patti	Karen Landry

By JANET MASLIN

BILLY REGIS (Chris Mulkey) is a ladies' man who likes to boast about his exploits, and Eddie (John Jenkins) is the friend who has heard it all. So when the two of them embark on an all-night drive to visit a girlfriend of Billy's in "Patti Rocks," it's a very long journey indeed. Billy describes his sexual adventures in rude, graphic detail; meanwhile, the more sensitive Eddie laments the breakup of his marriage. "Did your going out on June have anything to do with your splitting up?" Billy innocently wants to know.

As the dim, loudmouthed Billy and the cannier, more temperate Eddie busily embody a wide variety of attitudes about masculinity, they head for the apartment of Patti (Karen Landry), a place that becomes the crucible in which all their poses and prejudices are put to the test. The purpose of the trip is to inform Patti, who is pregnant, that Billy is a married man. But Patti's reaction is not what might be expected. She's annoyed, but at heart she doesn't much care. She wants the baby, but as for Billy, she can take him or leave him. Patti regards marriage as profoundly unglamorous anyhow. She's a free spirit. A simple snapshot of her child's father will suffice.

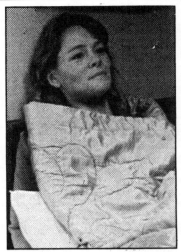

Karen Landry has the title role in "Patti Rocks."

"Patti Rocks," which opens today at the Waverly, was made by David Burton Morris as a sequel to his "Loose Ends," which was shown here in 1976 at the Whitney. But in fact it seems to hark back to an even earlier time. There's a late 1960's tone to both the attitudes espoused here and the awkward, even drab sincerity with which they are set forth. The film is interesting in its ambitions to the extent that it tries to contrast and exemplify so many sexual stereotypes and preconceptions. But its style is hopelessly ordinary without being particularly frank, and the level of insight displayed is hardly more engaging. Billy (talking about sexual conquests): "It's a rush — man, I need that." Eddie: "But do they need you?" Billy: "Who cares?" Or Patti, on the subject of her fierce independence: "I don't belong to anybody!"

Much of "Patti Rocks" is obvious in this way, but parts of it are genuinely strange: the scene in which Billy demands that Eddie immediately remove and lend him his underwear, or the scene in which a woman whom they encounter by the side of the road begins taunting Billy, demanding that he expose himself. At moments like this, "Patti Rocks" has more the air of a bad play than a bad film, though the difference is certainly moot. In any case, not until Miss Landry appears is it possible to glimpse what "Patti Rocks" has been after. Though her character is hackneyed and improbable, Miss Landry projects the subtlety and the furious energy that is so lacking in the story's earlier sections.

"Patti Rocks" is most notable for its exceptional earnestness and for what it might have been.

1988 Ja 15, C12:1

Smart-Alecky Duo

RENT-A-COP, directed by Jerry London; written by Dennis Shryack and Michael Blodgett; photography by Giuseppe Rotunno; film editor, Robert Lawrence; music by Jerry Goldsmith; production designer, Tony Masters; produced by Raymond Wagner; presented by Kings Road Entertainment Inc. At Criterion Center, Broadway and 45th Street; Manhattan Twin, 59th Street, east of Third Avenue; Coliseum Twin, Broadway and 181st Street; Movie Center 5, 125th Street between Powell and Douglass Boulevards. Running time: 96 minutes. This film is rated R.

Church	Burt Reynolds
Della	Liza Minnelli
Dancer	James Remar
Roger	Richard Masur
Beth	Dionne Warwick
Lemar	Bernie Casey
Pitts	Robby Benson
Alexander	John Stanton
Wieser	John P. Ryan

By WALTER GOODMAN

THE cop for rent in "Rent-a-Cop," which opens today at the Criterion and other theaters, is Burt Reynolds. He is reduced to taking a job as a security guard in a Chicago department store after a $2 million drug bust ends with everybody except him being blown away. It is during the busted bust, which starts things in brisk fashion, that he falls into the arms of Liza Minnelli, a rent-a-girl who was just doing business as usual in a nearby apartment when the bullets started to fly.

So far, O.K., but a movie like this, made up of the usual suspects — a tough chief cop, a millionaire chief crook, a sadistic murderer, a bantering black-white detective team — and the usual car chases and explosions soaked in a musical score that seems to be parodying the whole commotion, depends for specialness on the "magic" between the leads. That proves to be more elusive than the murderer. Mr. Reynolds does his customary number, but somewhat more sluggishly than usual; he produces no sparks. Ms. Minnelli, in better form, brings bounce to the proceedings with her portrayal of a spunky, scared hooker with a rough tongue and a heart of fluff.

She has plenty of reason to be scared. The bad guy on her trail (James Remar) looks like Robokiller when he puts on his working clothes; he shoots or knifes practically everybody who crosses his path, including Dionne Warwick, making a brief, unfortunately nonsinging appearance as a high-tech madam, and Richard Masur, who turns in a good perspiring performance as a cop gone bad.

•

There are a few funny scenes, notably an early one in which Mr. Reynolds, dressed up as Santa Claus, is distracted by a customer, a kid, a store manager and Ms. Minnelli as he tries to bring down a shoplifter. And a couple of slightly naughty exchanges

Targets

Liza Minnelli plays a former prostitute and Burt Reynolds the ex-policeman she enlists to protect her from a killer in "Rent-a-Cop."

offer Ms. Minnelli a chance at a punchline, which she delivers with snap. When Mr. Reynolds asks her to look away as he gets dressed, she retorts, "You got somethin' I haven't seen before, we'll donate it to science." Ms. Minnelli herself shows a lot of leg; Mr. Reynolds shows his chest. "What're you lookin' at?" he asks from the bathtub. "Nothin'," she cracks. "Thanks," he murmurs.

Such are the brighter points of a script that tends to be smart-alecky without being smart. As the movie goes on, the plot gets sloppy. Jerry London's direction is efficient but lacking in the touch or the material needed to mate a romantic comedy with a run-of-the-studio shoot-'em-down. On the evidence here, Ms. Minnelli, who manages to play along with the goings-on even while winking playfully at them, deserves better.

1988 Ja 15, C13:1

Places in the Country

STACKING, produced and directed by Martin Rosen; screenplay by Victoria Jenkins; director of photography, Richard Bowen; edited by Patrick Dodd; music by Patrick Gleeson; production design by David Wasco; released by Spectrafilm. At the Public, 425 Lafayette Street. Running time: 97 minutes. This film is rated PG.

Kathleen Morgan	Christine Lahti
Buster McGuire	Frederic Forrest
Anna Mae Morgan	Megan Follows
Gary Connaloe	Jason Gedrick
Dan Morgan	Ray Baker
Photographer	Peter Coyote
Clate Connaloe	James Gammon
Connie Van Buskirk	Kaiulani Lee

"STACKING," opening today at the Public Theater, is somewhat better than its title, which evokes nothing before one has seen the movie and not much more after. It refers to the operation by which bales of hay are collected and stacked together in one part of the field with the use of a large, tractorlike vehicle equipped with a forked scoop.

When "Stacking" begins, Dan Morgan, a farmer who makes a living stacking for others, has just had his

arm crushed while lying under his stacker trying to repair it. To his teen-age daughter, Anna Mae, this is a disaster, meaning they'll probably lose their farm. To Dan's wife, Kathleen, it could be a blessing. Kathleen hates the small Montana community where she has lived all her life, and hates having to work in Mom's Cafe to make ends meet. Kathleen wants to see the world outside.

When "Stacking" attends to gallant young Anna Mae, who, with a hired hand named Buster, vows to repair the stacker and save the farm, the movie plays rather like a denatured variation on Robert Benton's "Places in the Heart." Grit is celebrated. "Stacking" is also about poor Kathleen who dreams of far-off places, mostly, it seems, because a photographer, en route to California, came by one day on a motorcycle and took her picture.

"Stacking" is the sort of movie about which it's not easy to admit that it bored me silly. It means well and is sincere. It has a cast of good actors, headed by Christine Lahti as Kathleen, Megan Follows as Anna Mae and Frederic Forrest as Buster.

The characters in Victoria Jenkins's screenplay aren't stereotypical, but neither are they very interesting. Each is a collection of orderly speeches. The people don't seem attached to the landscape, but more like actors on a visit.

As directed by Martin Rosen, "Stacking" has a lot of pretty Montana scenery and a lot of not-great music on the soundtrack. Yet it has no real drive or personality of its own. It looks like a movie made as a cooperative venture by film students with a fairly fancy budget.

There's even something phony about all the fuss made about stacking, and about farming in general. Never once does the audience get a glimpse of the machine by which the new-mown hay is baled, thus to be ready for the stacker. After seeing "Stacking," you might suspect baling to be God's work.

•

"Stacking," which has been rated PG ("Parental Guidance Suggested"), includes some mildly vulgar language. VINCENT CANBY

1988 Ja 15, C15:1

Cautionary Tale

FOR KEEPS, directed by John G. Avildsen; written by Tim Kazurinsky and Denise DeClue; director of photography, James Crabe; edited by Mr. Avildsen; music by Bill Conti; production designer, William J. Cassidy; produced by Jerry Belson and Walter Coblenz; released by Tri-Star. At Criterion Center, Broadway and 45th Street; Gemini Twin, 64th Street and Second Avenue; Loews 84th Street Six, at Broadway; Movieland Eighth Street Triplex, at University Place. Running time: 98 minutes. This film is rated PG-13.

Darcy	Molly Ringwald
Stan	Randall Batinkoff
Mr. Bobrucz	Kenneth Mars
Mrs. Elliot	Miriam Flynn
Mrs. Bobrucz	Conchata Ferrell
Lila	Sharon Brown
Reverend Kim	Jack Ong
Wee Willy	Sean Frye

THERE was a time when unwanted teen-age pregnancy meant missing the senior prom, to say the very least. It was more of an inconvenience than it is in the thoroughly modern "For Keeps," which stars Molly Ringwald

Expecting
Molly Ringwald portrays a high-school girl whose future is complicated when she becomes pregnant in "For Keeps."

as a bright young mother-to-be. The problems created by adolescent pregnancy and early marriage are indeed set forth here, sometimes with the appearance of great candor. But in the final analysis, they are handled with all too remarkable ease. Its subject is nominally daring, but in spite of that, "For Keeps" proceeds with an amazing degree of caution.

This film's major revelation has nothing to do with the topic at hand. It's the fact that Miss Ringwald, despite the patness and oversimplification of the story, proves herself to be an even more versatile and captivating talent than she has before. There is nothing of Miss Ringwald's familiar pouty disdain to her performance as Darcy Elliott, a smart, popular small-town schoolgirl who can't believe the fix she's gotten into. Both she and her sweetheart, Stan Bobrucz (Randall Batinkoff), had big plans for college and careers, but we know

even before they do that things will go awry. The opening credits of John G. Avildsen's film intercut scenes of the young lovers with close-up documentary footage of the fertilization of an egg.

•

As this may suggest, "For Keeps," which opens today at Loews 84th Street Six and other theaters, has something of a nuts-and-bolts pragmatism in its approach. Each difficult stage of Stan and Darcy's story is outlined in realistic-sounding detail, after which it is somehow robbed of any sting. We are told, for instance, that the young parents-to-be have been going together for a long time and are deeply in love, so the stigma of teen-age promiscuity is gone. The issue of abortion is raised, but it is handled with kid gloves. Darcy's would-be sophisticate mother and Stan's religious, very old-fashioned parents ("Stretch marks are the badge of a real woman," Stan's father says) manage to be equally offended by their children's problem. Stan and Darcy fight and struggle and sacrifice in all the expected ways, but somehow — after all, Mr. Avildsen has "Rocky" and "The Karate Kid" to his credit — everything works out just fine.

Most of "For Keeps" is entirely predictable, but that should do little to diminish its interest for audiences of high-school age. Here again, Miss Ringwald is the very model of teen-age verisimilitude, and she's most impressive in making even the most hackneyed situations seem real. In fact, she's so good she's almost a problem. Mr. Batinkoff, while pleasant, is no real match for her, and the glowering parents who make their kids' lives miserable for a time are no real threat. There is the feeling that Miss Ringwald's Darcy can triumph over anything. But perhaps that's just what Mr. Avildsen had in mind.

•

"For Keeps" is rated PG-13 ("Special Parental Guidance for Those Younger Than 13"). It includes fairly frank talk about teen-age sex and a birth scene that may disturb very young viewers. JANET MASLIN

1988 Ja 15, C17:3

Snapshots
Christine Lahti and Megan Follows star in "Stacking," Martin Rosen's drama about a family on a Montana ranch whose lives are changed by a photographer.

FILM VIEW/Janet Maslin

80's Movies Take the Easy Route

LIKE SO MANY FILMS OF THE 1980'S, THE GOLDIE Hawn comedy "Overboard" offers something for everyone. To begin with, it presents the amusing spectacle of Miss Hawn impersonating a viciously bad-tempered heiress, striking terror into everyone she meets. After this satirical high-life phase, the film moves into its low-rent period, with an amnesiac Miss Hawn trapped in the squalid home of a carpenter (played by Kurt Russell), who intends to teach her a lesson. But it's an 80's-style lesson that the film has in mind.

The fun of watching Miss Hawn recoil at her newly reduced circumstances is quickly followed by a penitent stage, in which she begins to enjoy the simple life and rue the error of her earlier, ways. Then, finally, there comes the point at which the character must make a choice. Her mental fog lifts, her husband reappears to claim her and she must decide: will she be rich and wretched, or simple but poor?

Now a film like this could always be expected to end happily, regardless of the decade in which it was made. But "Overboard" is able to conclude on a note that's been especially typical of our time. The husband — please read no further if you wish to have the suspense preserved — turns out to be an obnoxious twit, and hence he is easily disposed of. The adoring carpenter and his four kids, having rearranged the heroine's values and taught her the joys of family life, offer a much sunnier alternative. But it turns out that the simple life need not be simple, since the heiress's fortune is still available. So this heroine, like so many of her 80's counterparts, manages to have it all.

A lot of recent films that appear to address moral dilemmas have managed to work out this way. But if the 80's as we knew them are indeed ending, the films that reflect the easy, undemanding moral climate of this period are about to seem very dated indeed. Audiences may be ready to sour on fairy-tale endings, even in fairy tales. (In "Batteries Not Included" — again, read no further if you'd like the ending to come as a surprise — a beloved tenement is demolished by a ruthless developer, then magically restored so that it's better than new.) So when a woman falls in love with her fiancé's younger brother, as Cher does in "Moonstruck," it may be deemed just too convenient for everyone to wind up as one big happy family. When an executive throws away her career for the chance to raise a child, as Diane Keaton did in "Baby Boom," it may not seem cricket for her to become even more high-powered and prosperous than ever as the head of a countrified, yuppified baby food concern.

Men have been just as apt to take the easy way out in these films as their female counterparts; only in the 80's could Charlie Sheen's young "Wall Street" go-getter wind up going to court but not necessarily to jail (and this only after the film spends an hour tantalizing its audience with ill-gotten gains). But it is in films about women, and especially in films about sexual mores, that the soon-to-be-obsolete 80's approach shows up most often. Having it all is by no means a women's problem exclusively, but for female characters it often exacts a higher toll. What this means, at a time when difficult questions are almost never taken seriously on screen, is late-80's films that are actually 50's films with a vengeance. Or *without* a vengeance, since the same troubles that might have brought a heroine of the 50's ostracism and grief are now taken in stride by her 80's counterpart.

There was a time when teen-age pregnancy meant instant tragedy on the screen (remember "Blue Denim"?). But that was before film characters became able to handle any and every type of problem. In "For Keeps," Molly Ringwald plays a high school senior who becomes pregnant by her first sweetheart, and the issues of abortion, teen-age marriage and forfeiting a career for child-rearing are all called into play. What's astounding about the film is how little real difficulty any of this creates. Although the manner of John Avildsen's film is thoroughly conventional — close your eyes and you can picture the young couple's dingy apartment, their fights with their parents, the scene in which the overwhelmed teen-age father and husband angrily tells his wife he's going "out" — its morality is anything but, since it lacks any element of real hardship. Not only do the lovebirds work out their problems without making unfashionably large sacrifices, but they even make it to the senior prom.

"Patti Rocks," essentially a three-character film that concerns itself entirely with relations between the sexes, also has a no-fault approach to the problem of an unplanned pregnancy, but at first glance the mood is more 60's than anything else. The heroine of the title, pregnant by her lover Billy and quite unperturbed about it, takes things perfectly in stride after Billy and his friend Eddie make an all-night pilgrimage to her apartment, arriving there to tell her that Billy is married. The film, which becomes a microcosm of sexual mores, contrasts Billy's constant, graphic sexual boasting with Eddie's more tempered, nice-guy approach. But above it all rises Patti, as a free spirit who views marriage as profoundly unglamorous and would much rather raise a child alone — no problem. The real hardships involved are as remote as the spectacle of Patti someday feeding her 3-year-old a peanut butter and jelly sandwich.

Some of this era's shrewdest films, like "Fatal Attraction," have made ambiguity between the sexes work to their advantage and played the angles brilliantly. But we may as well recognize the no-fault morality play as a temporary aberration, since its time is just about gone.

1988 Ja 17, II:18:5

Birger Malmsten and Eva Henning in "Three Strange Loves."

Between 30 and Death

THREE STRANGE LOVES, directed by Ingmar Bergman; written (in Swedish with English subtitles) by Herbert Grevenius, based on short stories by Birgit Tengroth; photography by Gunnar Fischer; a Janus Film, released by Kino International in association with the Swedish Information Service. At Film Forum 1, 57 Watts Street. Running time: 84 minutes. This film has no rating.

Rut	Eva Henning
Bertil	Birger Malmsten
Viola	Birgit Tengroth
Dr. Rosengren	Hasse Ekman
Valborg	Mimi Nelson
Raoul, the Captain	Bengt Eklund

By VINCENT CANBY

WATCHING Ingmar Bergman's "Three Strange Loves" now — 39 years after it was made — is like opening a time capsule whose contents are familiar though they're being seen for the first time. Titled "Torst" ("Thirst") in Swedish, the film opens today at the Film Forum in what is apparently its first New York theatrical engagement.

"Three Strange Loves" is Bergman's seventh feature. "Crisis," his first, was made in 1946. However, it's full of intimations of films to come, especially those about marriage after the initial excitement of sexual love has given way to boredom, followed by fear that this is all there is.

Already evident in "Three Strange Loves" is the master's self-assured, steely, stripped-down directorial style, which is even more remarkable considering the awkward structure of Herbert Grevenius's screenplay. The film is based on three short stories (written by Birgit Tengroth, who also appears in a supporting role) that have been more or less wrenched together without really fitting.

The central and by far the most typical story concerns the furiously unhappy marriage of Rut (Eva Henning) and Bertil (Birger Malmsten) who, when first seen, are tormenting each other during a night's stopover in Basel, en route to Stockholm after a vacation in Sicily. Rut and Bertil are in their early 30's, young enough to mind the loss of mutual passion and old enough to fear time's passage.

●

The weather is hot, and Rut cannot sleep. Small and lean, wearing only a cheap slip, she has the figure of the ballet dancer she once was. Rut appears to be no less bored by Bertil when he's asleep than when he's awake. She smokes, attempts unsuccessfully to read a German paper, and slams around the room trying to awaken him. Bertil simply draws the blanket over his head. At one point she begins to pack her suitcase, but thinks better of it. They're almost broke — she couldn't get very far on her own.

She lies back on the bed, smoking still another cigarette, and recalls what at first seems to be a happier time, an affair with Raoul, an army officer. Like everything else her mind now touches, this idyllic episode turns sour. Raoul announces rather late in their game that he's married, and when she reports she's pregnant he says she's a slut. The necessary abortion leaves her angry with Raoul, with Bertil and especially with herself.

Also moving in and out of the story of Rut and Bertil are Viola (Miss Tengroth), a desperate widow who, I think, was once Bertil's mistress; Dr. Rosengren (Hasse Ekman), Viola's sadistic psychiatrist, and Valborg (Mimi Nelson) who, like Rut, was once a ballet dancer. The screenplay cross-cuts among contemporary actions, flashbacks and dreams in its attempt to fuse the various stories, though the result is sometimes utter confusion. Key passages of dialogue are left untranslated by the English-language subtitles.

●

The excitement of the film comes from the mounting viciousness with which Bergman portrays the no-exit marriage of Rut and Bertil. There is astonishing, virtuoso economy in the way in which he works in these scenes, first in the Basel hotel room, and later aboard a night train crossing a ruined German landscape (the time is 1946). The movie is as tightly controlled, and as potentially explosive, as a one-set stage piece.

Though "Three Strange Loves" belongs to Bergman's social-realist period, there are vivid suggestions of hell aboard the noisy, steamy night train. Rut and Bertil can't escape even when it stops. They're besieged by clamoring, faceless masses demanding food at stations along the route. When they finally cling to each other, it doesn't signify reconciliation but a sudden, terrible awareness that there's no one else to turn to.

Even in his later, far more austere films, in which man wrestles with an uncaring universe, Bergman was never much more stoic — and grim.

1988 Ja 20, C20:1

Madrid Meander

HALF OF HEAVEN, directed by Manuel Gutiérrez Aragón; screenplay (Spanish with English subtitles) by Mr. Aragón and Luis Megino; director of photography, José Luis Alcaine; music by Milladoiro; produced by Luis Megino; released by Skouras Pictures, Inc. Running time: 127 minutes. This film has no rating.
Rosa .... Angela Molina
Grandmother .... Maragarita Lozano
Juan .... Antonio V. Valero
Delgado .... Nacho Martínez
Antonio .... Santiago Ramos
Ramiro .... Francisco Merino
Young Rosa .... Monica Molina
Olvido .... Carolina Silva
Don Pedro .... Fernando Fernán-Gómez

By WALTER GOODMAN

"HALF OF HEAVEN," the appealing Spanish movie that begins a run at the Lincoln Plaza Cinema today, is a quiet comedy, a low-temperature romance, a matter-of-fact fantasy. It's all about Rosa, a cheerful, affectionate, diligent girl who works her way up from the family farmhouse to running Madrid's most fashionable restaurant.

Rosa is luckier in business than in love. No sooner is she warned by her visionary grandmother to stay away from knife-grinders than she marries one and shortly finds herself a widow with a baby daughter. Rosa's father, driven batty by a houseful of women, threatens to take an ax to the child, but all works out for the best when Rosa is hired as a wet nurse to the infant son of Don Pedro, a hungry Madrid official who falls first for her rice pudding — "She feeds my son, she feeds me" — then for her.

The director, Manuel Gutiérrez Aragón, who also helped write the loose screenplay, tells the story in so unemphatic a way that it may take a while before you begin smiling at the flow of humor. The flow begins before the titles with big Grandma (Margarita Lozano) out in the fields, puffing blissfully on a stogie. Gradually the source of the bliss is revealed: Grandma is urinating, and the camera follows the stream until it joins a river. So much for Earth Mothers.

●

Angela Molina, the popular Spanish actress who plays Rosa as an adult, fetches fetchingly, but it's a bland role. Her feelings for the men who try

Getting Ahead
Margarita Lozano plays the role of a grandmother in "Half of Heaven," starring Angela Molina as an ambitious young woman who moves from the country to Madrid to open her own restaurant.

to get into her life are tepid and hazy. Happily, the people around her supply flavor. Grandma is a considerable presence even when she's just sitting around eating bread and butter. Rosa's daughter Olvido (Carolina Silva) inherits Grandma's prophetic talents and is more willing to act on them, for example, by feeding rat poison to her slovenly aunts.

Fernando Fernán-Gómez makes an engagingly eccentric Don Pedro, especially when delivering a grandiose and garbled official-lunch speech, which may be a takeoff on Spain's old guard or on such speeches worldwide. And Francisco Merino bustles drolly as a hustler who teaches Rosa the knack of buying cheap. He can always come up with a bargain price for the liver of a sheep that has fortunately been run over by the Andalusian Express. With his help, Rosa becomes "The Queen of Offal, the Empress of Innards."

Also taken with Rosa are a hypocritical bureaucrat and an affectionate student. Having managed to climb into Rosa's window one night, the student is busily engaged in warming her up when she departs abruptly to seek advice from Don Pedro, who thereupon benefits from the young fellow's amorous stokings. The stuff of farce is handled here in a gently funny way.

The tale is not as carefully served up as one of Rosa's banquets. You may find yourself wishing the service were not quite so relaxed, that the director would get on with it. But if you can adjust to the haphazard spirit, there is sustenance here in the quirky characters, amusing incidents and sly asides. The title, by the way, is said to come from a Chinese proverb about a woman being half of heaven — which may be taken as a comment on Confucius.

1988 Ja 21, C24:3

Concrete Overshoes

KING LEAR, directed and written for the screen by Jean-Luc Godard, based on the play by William Shakespeare; produced by Menahem Golan and Yoram Globus; released by the Cannon Group Inc. At Quad Cinema, 34 West 13th Street. Running time: 91 minutes. This film is rated PG.
William Shakespeare Jr. the Fifth
.... Peter Sellars
Don Learo .... Burgess Meredith
Cordelia .... Molly Ringwald
Norman Mailer .... Himself
Kate Mailer .... Herself
The Professor .... Jean-Luc Godard
Film Editor .... Woody Allen

By VINCENT CANBY

"Keep thou the napkin and go boast of this." — "Henry VI, Part III."

SEVERAL years ago, the Cannes Film Festival was brightened by the report that Menahem Golan, of Cannon Films, and Jean-Luc Godard had signed an agreement on a napkin calling for Cannon to produce an adaptation of "King Lear" to be written by Norman Mailer, directed by Mr. Godard, with Mr. Mailer in the title role co-starring with his daughter, Kate Mailer, as Cordelia.

Mr. Mailer did, indeed, write a legitimate update of the play in which Lear became Don Learo, a Mafia capo. In time, the film went into production in Nyon, Switzerland, though only for one day. On the second day, according to Mr. Godard, Mr. Mailer and his daughter flew back to the United States on the Concorde while "the daughter's boyfriend returned in economy."

Whatever happened to the napkin has not been recorded.

To meet his obligations, Mr. Godard eventually made a movie that opens today at the Quad Cinema.

●

This "King Lear" is a late Godardian practical joke, sometimes spiteful and mean, sometimes very beautiful, sometimes teetering on the edge of coherence and brilliance, often amateurish and, finally, as sad and embarrassing as the spectacle of a great, dignified man wearing a fishbowl over his head to get a laugh.

As one of his own principal characters, called the Professor, Mr. Godard doesn't put on a fishbowl in the film, but he does appear in punkish drag and in dark glasses from which dangle what appear to be ID tags and other assorted found objects, which may be to the point. The entire movie is a found object.

To the extent that "King Lear" has any structure, it's about William Shakespeare Jr. the Fifth (Peter Sellars), a spiky-haired young man who, notebook in hand, wanders in and around a post-Apocalypse Nyon hotel attempting "to recapture the works that have been lost," beginning with those of his famous ancestor. The time, we are told, is just after Chernobyl, which, as far as I know, wreaked environmental havoc but didn't destroy even one comic book.

In any case, the film is set in a cozy avant-garde void, frequently represented by Nyon's handsome, old-fashioned Beau Rivage Hôtel at the edge of a lake in the off-season when the trees are photogenically bare (and there are few tourists around to get in the way). Staying at the hotel are an old man named, Don Learo (Burgess Meredith) and his daughter Cordelia (Molly Ringwald).

Mostly the two just sit at a table in the otherwise empty dining room

Peter Sellars

looking glum and at loose ends. Occasionally they speak lines from the real "King Lear," which the eavesdropping Shakespeare records in his notebook. These, though they're random and brief, are so rich ("So we'll live, and pray, and sing, and tell old tales, and laugh at gilded butterflies.") and are so richly delivered by Mr. Meredith that they successfully destroy whatever interest one may have in the rest of the film.

Language like this has such an overwhelming life of its own that, alongside of it, Mr. Godard's familiar musings on words, either spoken or seen as graphics, seem much punier than need be. After making what is possibly the most lyrical film on language in the history of the cinema ("Le Gai Savoir," 1969), Mr. Godard has now made the silliest.

Ever frugal, Mr. Godard opens "King Lear" with a couple of scenes shot before the Mailers decamped, including one in which Kate Mailer asks her father why he's so obsessed by the Mafia. "I think the Mafia is the only way to do 'King Lear,'" he says. End of thought.

The movie is intercut with various title cards: "A Picture Shot in the Back" (apparently by the Mailers and Mr. Golan), "Fear and Loathing," "An Approach," "A Clearing" (which is repeated as "A cLEARing," get it?). Also intercut are stills of great film makers, references to Meyer Lansky and other mob figures, and a line to the effect that "by the late 60's, the entire country had been 'Vegasized.'" The wisp of yet another thought floats by and evaporates.

●

At one point Miss Ringwald, dressed in white, leads a black horse through some scenic underbrush and Mr. Meredith hops around with an emerald green butterfly net. Toward the conclusion, when it seems that Mr. Godard is at his wit's end, there's a brief sequence in a New York cutting room with Woody Allen. Looking awfully patient and wearing a black T-shirt with "Picasso" scrawled across the front, Mr. Allen is seen editing two pieces of film, first with safety pins, then a needle and thread.

To have won the cooperation of his excellent, seemingly uncomplaining cast, Mr. Godard remains in full command of his reputation as the most original film maker of his generation. Mr. Sellars (better known as a theater director), Miss Ringwald and, particularly, Mr. Meredith are remarkably good under terrible circumstances.

The most depressing thing about this Godard work is that it seems so tired, familiar and out of date. The movie's 1960's-ish worship of film as an end in itself, which was a mark of so many earlier, more ebullient Godard movies, now is lifeless. It's also surprising in that it comes from an artist who's been most daring and innovative in his experiments with video as the medium of the future.

•

"King Lear" is rated PG ("Parental Guidance Suggested"). It contains some vulgar language.

1988 Ja 22, C6:1

Lethal-Limbed Colonel

BRADDOCK: MISSING IN ACTION III, directed by Aaron Norris; written by James Bruner and Chuck Norris, based on characters created by Arthur Silver and Larry Levinson and Steve Bing; director of photography, Joao Fernandes; edited by Michael J. Duthie; music by Jay Chattaway; production designer, Ladislav Wilheim; produced by Menahem Golan and Yoram Globus; released by Cannon Films, Inc. At the National, Broadway and 44th Street; New York Twin, Second Avenue at 66th Street; Columbia Cinema, Broadway at 103d Street, and other theaters. Running time: 101 minutes. This film is rated R.

Braddock	Chuck Norris
General Quoc	Aki Aleong
Van Tan Cang	Roland Harrah 3d
Lin Tan Cang	Miki Kim
Reverend Polanski	Yehuda Efroni
Mik	Ron Barker
General Duncan	Floyd Levine
Littlejohn	Jack Rader
Thuy	Melinda Betron

By WALTER GOODMAN

LAST week, the Living Dead returned. Again. This week, it's Chuck Norris. As Col. Jim Braddock, in "Braddock: Missing in Action III," he returns to Vietnam to find his Vietnamese wife, who was unfortunately left behind at the fall of Saigon. On his prior trips, he rescued American prisoners of war; this time, he brings out a batch of Amerasian children, including the son he didn't know he had.

Wearing a worried expression beneath a week's worth of beard, Braddock knocks off what remains of the Vietnamese Army, already pretty well decimated by their earlier encounters. Leading the temporary survivors is a really nasty general who keeps yelling, "I got you, Braddock! You're finished, Braddock!" That's what he thinks. So swift are soft-hearted, lethal-limbed Braddock's moves that sometimes Communists plop over in agony without any visible contact between his foot or fist and their vital parts. Watching the Vietnamese missing their target and getting blown up wholesale, you can't figure out how with Braddock on active duty, the United States managed to lose in Vietnam.

Mr. Norris, who is almost as muscular as Sylvester Stallone and almost as expressive as Clint Eastwood, also helped write the script. You can practically see the balloons popping out of characters' mouths: "I don't step on toes, I step on necks!"

"I never thought we'd be coming back," says the colonel's pal, who plainly didn't take a look at the receipts from parts one and two. Aaron Norris directed, and the result is on view at the National and other theaters. As that general remarks before he meets the fate of all of Braddock's adversaries, "This has gone on long enough."

1988 Ja 22, C9:1

By the Book

PROMISED LAND, directed and written by Michael Hoffman; directors of photography, Ueli Steiger and Alexander Gruszynski; edited by David Spiers; music by James Newton Howard; production designer, Eugenio Zanetti; produced by Rick Stevenson; released by Vestron Pictures. At the Festival, 6 West 57th Street. Running time: 92 minutes. This film is rated R.

Davey Hancock	Jason Gedrick
Danny	Kiefer Sutherland
Bev	Meg Ryan
Mary	Tracy Pollan
Baines	Googy Gress
Pammie	Deborah Richter
Mr. Rivers	Oscar Rowland
Mrs. Rivers	Sondra Seacat
Circle K Clerk	Jay Underwood
Mrs. Higgins	Herta Ware

"PROMISED LAND" tries hard to win you over but finally wears you down with its sincerity. Michael Hoffman, the writer and director, seems determined to inject freshness into the old story about graduating seniors who discover life is hard after high school, but he transforms his best ideas and images into bludgeons. Nothing that follows is quite so ponderous as the opening sequence, though, a basketball game in the small Utah town of Ashville — a winning basket in slow motion, choral music in the background, the camera picking out each major character in close-up. They are called Davey and Mary and Danny, but are such types their names are superfluous. The basketball hero dates the cheerleader; the shy misfit wants to belong but can't.

It's a relief to escape this by-the-book setup and jump ahead two years. Now the basketball player (Jason Gedrick) is an Ashville cop; the cheerleader (Tracy Pollan) comes home from college knowing she must leave him behind for good. Meanwhile, the misfit (Kiefer Sutherland) has left town, become a rebel and married a raucous but lonely young woman with pink-red hair (Meg Ryan, in the only role with a touch of real-life unpredictability). As Davey and Mary agonize about their failing relationship, Danny and his wife hit the road back to Ashville in a big, old, pink-roofed Plymouth convertible, heading for the film's final confrontation. It is a melodramatic contrivance of people and time and place, which is not saved by the initial voice-over telling us this is based on a true story.

Mr. Hoffman (or perhaps it is his production designer, Eugenio Zanetti) has a feel for Ashville's dingy, ramshackle Victorian houses with limp lace curtains. But he goes too far, cramming Danny's family home full of Americana — a picture of George Washington, a pillow with the flag on it, everything short of a sampler that reads, "This is a movie about the broken American dream." Shot in Utah, the film has some spectacular images, of snow-covered plains with magnificent mountains in the background. But too often Mr. Hoffman seems to think a foggy, fuzzy look is atmosphere enough.

"Promised Land," which opens today at the Festival, was developed at the Sundance Institute, and Mr. Hoffman has ambition worth developing. But as a film maker he is less self-aware than one of his own characters. Mary says she *wants* to want small-town life, and realizes that is not the same as truly wanting it. Mr. Hoffman wants his film to be poignant, it seems, but doesn't see that is not the same as capturing the feeling on screen.

CARYN JAMES

1988 Ja 22, C13:1

Death of Innocence

THE GRAND HIGHWAY, a film by Jean-Loup Hubert; in French with English subtitles; director of photography, Claude Lecomte; camera, Jean Paul Meurisse; edited by Raymonde Guyot; music by Georges Granier; produced by Pascal Hommais and Jean François Lepetit; released by Miramax Films. At Paris, 58th Street, west of Fifth Avenue. Running time: 104 minutes. This film has no rating.

Marcelle	Anémone
Pelo	Richard Bohringer
Louis	Antoine Hubert
Martine	Vanessa Guedj
Claire	Christine Pascal
Priest	Raoul Billerey
Yvonne	Pascale Roberts
Solange	Marie Matheron

By CARYN JAMES

IN "The Grand Highway," the French director Jean-Loup Hubert gives us his romance with childhood innocence. The autobiographical story, set in a pretty peasant village in 1958, has the makings of a nostalgic glance backward, full of easy charm and sentimentality. Louis, an adorable 9-year-old, is sent from Paris to the country for three weeks while his mother has a baby. And though the film has its moments of cheap charm, it is unexpectedly rich in warmth, wit and intelligence. Through the child's eyes we are lured into an enchanted landscape, as lush as Monet's gardens, only to have Mr. Hubert insistently block this lyrical vision with a cold, adult look at his characters' disenchantment and at the harshness of peasant life. The result makes "The Grand Highway" more convincing, more charming.

Louis's naïveté is near total. He doesn't realize that his father has left his mother; he has never met Marcelle, the old friend of his mother with whom he is to stay, or her husband, Pelo. From the minute Louis and his mother arrive by bus on a blistering hot day, the child seems painfully vulnerable. Mr. Hubert's son, Antoine, plays Louis, captured in the last stages of boyhood, before a hint of puberty has appeared. With his wide eyes, pathetically narrow shoulders and skinny legs, Louis is the picture of heart-wrenching sweetness, who arrives to find Marcelle skinning a rabbit, scooping out its eye with a twist of her knife. Marcelle sees a treat for Louis's first supper; Louis sees a dead bunny.

Worn out and unhappy, the childless Marcelle does not have a clue about how to make Louis feel at home. She gives him a room overlooking the cemetery, where he sleeps in the bed of Pelo's dead grandmother, whose stern picture stares down at him. The room is full of spooky noises — some of them made by Pelo, calling out animal sounds to frighten the child. Marcelle's husband, it turns out, is coarse when he's sober and vicious when he's drunk. On another night Louis lies in bed and listens as Pelo tears up the room that was meant to be a nursery — their stillborn child was a boy who would have been Louis's age and whose room Marcelle has kept intact — and forces himself on his wife.

•

Marcelle and Pelo's hostile marriage is the unlikely backdrop for Louis's funny adjustment to country life. Soon he is climbing trees with his friend Martine, who is something of a flirt and a tease at age 10. Barefoot, wearing short red frocks, always sitting so her underpants show, Martine is the kind of girl who taunts Louis into climbing with her to the top of the

Antoine Hubert

steep church roof; there they urinate into the gutters and make the gargoyles spurt a stream onto a nun below.

As Louis and Martine gobble unripe apples, Martine's sister passes by with her boyfriend. "Don't blame me if you get sick," she says, and Martine shoots back, "Don't blame me if you get a baby." Then she drags Louis off to spy on the couple making love and later stands in the street mocking her sister — "Oh, oh," she says, barely suppressing a giggle — while we see the parish priest slowly walking up behind her.

With its misplaced boy hero, its deft blend of humor and sorrow, and especially in the playful friendship of Louis and Martine, "The Grand Highway" sometimes seems like a French version of "My Life as a Dog." But the hero of the Swedish film always had a mischievous gleam in his eye; Louis is more conventional, always guileless and baffled. Antoine Hubert is so natural that at first it seems he is not acting at all. (The director has said he created the character by observing his son.) But when Louis discovers his father has abandoned him, he reacts with such hurt and anger that Antoine Hubert is clearly a genuine actor.

•

Richard Bohringer (best known to American audiences as the hip but strange Gorodish in "Diva") turns the potentially trite and horrid Pelo into a strong, sympathetic man. He takes the boy fishing and to his carpentry shop, becoming the father-figure Louis yearns for. Mr. Bohringer, astoundingly straightforward, wards off all the clichés about good-hearted monsters and cruelty born of grief that lurk around the edges of the story.

The story, after all, is not what matters here. It is the atmosphere of Mr. Hubert's film that makes us feel we have entered his village, that the mismatched details of life there make sense, as they do when Martine picks the drunken Pelo up off the street and carts him home in a wooden wheelbarrow to their sweet-looking vine-covered cottage.

"The Grand Highway," which opens today at the Paris, was the top French-made film at the box office last year, and the No. 6 film overall (just behind "Beverly Hills Cop II"). Its appeal may be due to the superficial tug of emotions. But under its sweet nostalgia, Mr. Hubert's film is moving because he refuses to idealize the past or to ignore its bitterness.

1988 Ja 22, C17:1

A scene from "The Family"—Dining room squabbles upstage world tumult.

80 Years, One Address

THE FAMILY, directed by Ettore Scola; screenplay adaptation by Ruggero Maccari, Furio Scarpelli and Mr. Scola; director of photography, Ricardo Aronovich; edited by Francesco Malvestito; music by Armando Trovaioli; production designer, Luciano Ricceri; produced by Giorgio Scotton; a co-production of Les Films Ariane-Cinemax-FR3 Films Production (France), Massfilm S.R.L.-Cinecitta S.p.A-Rai Uno (Italy). At Cinema Studio 1, 66th Street and Broadway. Running time: 127 minutes. This film is rated PG.

Carlo	Emmanuele Lamaro/Andrea Occhipinti/ Vittorio Gassman
Carlo's Grandfather	Vittorio Gassman
Beatrice	Cecilia Dazzi/Stefania Sandrelli
Adriana	Jo Ciampa/Fanny Ardant
Giulio	Ioska Versari/Alberto Gimignani/Massimo Dapporto/Carlo Dapporto
Adelina	Consuelo Pascali/Ilaria Stuppia/Ottavia Piccolo

THE FAMILY," directed by the usually perceptive Ettore Scola, recalls 80 years in the life of a large, loving upper-middle-class Roman family. It begins in 1906 at the baptism of the baby Carlo, lying in the arms of his patrician grandfather (Vittorio Gassman) as the members of the family gather for a group photograph.

When the film ends, more than two hours later, Carlo, having been played by three other actors earlier, has become the spitting image of his grandfather, at least partly because Mr. Gassman makes a return appearance as his own grandson.

In the intervening years, Italy has survived World War I, the rise of Mussolini, the Spanish Civil War, World War II, the fall of Mussolini, Nazi occupation, Allied liberation, the sinking of the Andrea Doria and the marriage of Arthur Miller and Marilyn Monroe.

So does the movie, just barely, without ever leaving the big, roomy, comfortable apartment this family calls home and that, by 1986, must be a steal, rent-wise.

News of the outside world is smuggled in through casual bits of conversation, letters, references to occasional economic hardships and, finally, by television.

●

Except for the usual wear and tear of the years, the members of this family (who have no last name and who appear to age at different speeds) are born, grow up, love, mate and die with remarkably little fuss. One fellow is killed in Spain. Another becomes a prisoner of war in India.

Carlo, a professor of literature like his grandfather, marries a woman who adores him, instead of her more glamorous sister, whom he adores. No real problem, though. Carlo is honorable, as is his beloved Adriana, a concert pianist who, by the time the closing credits roll by, is being played by Fanny Ardant.

In Mr. Scola's best films ("La Nuit de Varennes," "A Special Day," "We All Loved Each Other So Much"), the characters possess their own particular eccentricities. Though tumultuous political events may be taking place around them, and may drastically alter their circumstances, the characters have identities of their own. The general scene is understood and made vivid in the way that it's refracted through the utterly specific.

"The Family," which opens today at Cinema Studio 1, has the manner of a film that was conceived as an idea: a family chronicle that unfolds entirely within a single set, thus to call attention to the blood ties that bind. The characters and events were thought up later.

Like "Le Bal," in which Mr. Scola examined a large patch of French history as played out within a Paris dancehall, "The Family" is too abstract — perfunctory, really — to be especially moving on its own. The changing period décor is almost as dramatic as anything that happens to Carlo and the members of the family.

Adding some excitement from time to time is the appearance of new actors, who take over the roles of aging characters much in the manner of runners in a relay race. Some actors look like the people they're replacing. Some don't.

The performances of Mr. Gassman, Miss Ardant, Stefania Sandrelli (who plays Carlo's wife) and the others are, like their roles, surprisingly colorless.

●

"The Family," which has been rated PG ("Parental Guidance Suggested"), includes a few mildly erotic scenes and vulgarisms.

VINCENT CANBY

1988 Ja 22, C11:1

FIVE CORNERS, directed by Tony Bill; written by John Patrick Shanley; director of photography, Fred Murphy; edited by Andy Blumenthal; music by James Newton Howard; production designer, Adrianne Lobel; produced by Forrest Murray and Mr. Bill; released by Cineplex Odeon. At Baronet, Third Avenue at 59th Street; Art Greenwich Twin, 12th Street and Seventh Avenue; Olympia, Broadway and 107th Street. Running time: 92 minutes. This film is rated R.

Linda	Jodie Foster
Harry	Tim Robbins
James	Todd Graff
Heinz	John Turturro
Mrs. Sabantino	Rose Gregorio
Melanie	Elizabeth Berridge

"FIVE CORNERS," opening today at the Baronet and other theaters, is about coming of age in the Bronx in the autumn of 1964, when student activists were listening to the Rev. Dr. Martin Luther King Jr., young women were still doing their darnedest to look like Jacqueline Kennedy and glue-sniffing was an acceptable way to attain a high.

Directed by Tony Bill, the film is based on John Patrick Shanley's first screenplay. Mr. Shanley's second screenplay serves as the basis for Norman Jewison's slickly homogenized current hit, "Moonstruck." This is worth noting, for although "Five Corners" often strains credulity (and patience), it almost always seems far more authentic than the saga of the lovelorn Cher in "Moonstruck."

The "Five Corners" screenplay is both overstuffed and underdeveloped. Mr. Bill's direction doesn't iron out unsightly bumps, but neither does it mute the voice of what often sounds to be a strong and original new screenwriter.

In a period of approximately 24 hours, "Five Corners" tells the stories of Linda (Jodie Foster), her sometime boyfriend James (Todd Graff) and Harry (Tim Robbins), who's about to go off to register voters in Mississippi. Their comparatively placid lives are thrown into chaos with the arrival back in the neighborhood of Heinz (John Turturro), a young psychotic who has been serving time for the attempted rape of Linda.

●

Mr. Shanley and Mr. Bill set their scene and introduce the characters with a good deal of humor and insight. There's a very funny early sequence in which a bored neighborhood Romeo pays two strangers five bucks to take his girlfriends off his hands. The movie hits just the proper note of comedy mixed with melodrama when two couples find themselves trapped, possibly fatally, in an elevator shaft.

It's not the elevator that finally does in the characters, but the mechanics of the plot, which, to keep things moving, demands that halfway intelligent people suddenly behave as if they'd lost their minds.

With the exception of Mr. Turturro and Rose Gregorio, who plays Heinz's equally demented mom, nobody in the otherwise excellent cast seems at home with his Bronx accent. Each speaks as if holding onto a tiger's tail with his teeth, which isn't easy. Miss Foster, more beautiful today than ever, doesn't look especially at home in her plain wash dresses, but the performance is a good one.

Equally intelligent are Mr. Graff, Mr. Robbins and Elizabeth Berridge, as a bubble-headed glue-sniffer who longs to settle down with a wedding ring and a husband. In their own separate category are Mr. Turturro and Miss Gregorio, who give "Five Corners" a larger-than-life, melodramatic dimension that ultimately makes the rest of the movie look small.　　　VINCENT CANBY

1988 Ja 22, C18:1

On Neither Side

SINGING THE BLUES IN RED, directed by Kenneth Loach; screenplay by Trevor Griffiths; director of photography, Chris Menges; edited by Jonathan Morris; music by Gerulf Pannach and Christian Kurnert; production designer, Martin Johnson; produced by Raymond Day; released by Angelika Films. At Quad Cinema, 34 West 13th Street. Running time: 110 minutes. This film has no rating.

Klaus Drittemann	Gerulf Pannach
Emma	Fabienne Babe
Lucy Bernstein	Cristine Rose
James Dryden	Sigfrit Steiner
Rosa	Eva Krutina
Lawyer	Robert Dietl
Marita	Heike Schrotter
Max	Stephen Samuel
Young Drittemann	Thomas Oehlke
Thomas	Patrick Gillert
Jürgen Kirsch	Heinz Diesling

By VINCENT CANBY

AT the age of 40, Klaus Drittemann, a writer and performer of protest songs, is given a one-way visa to leave East Germany for the West. Klaus has been in trouble with the authorities ever since the 1960's. He's a bristly character and has been a merciless critic of the East German Government for failures to realize its Marxist aspirations.

On the occasion of one of his earlier arrests, Klaus refused to recant or even to apologize. As he told his unhappy lawyer, "I have plans for this country." Henceforth, he's no longer allowed to perform.

When Klaus arrives in West Berlin, things aren't much better, even though he's enthusiastically welcomed by his recording company and by representatives of the West German and American Governments, which want to capitalize on what they choose to call his "defection." At a press conference, he makes rude remarks to the West German minister of culture about the "freedom" of the West German unemployed and of former Nazis occupying important Government positions.

Klaus is an unsmiling moralist. Like his father, a concert pianist who defected when Klaus was a boy, he's a man of stern principles. Yet, as played by Gerulf Pannach, a stocky, sardonic East German writer and performer whose own story parallels that of Klaus, he's a remarkably moving character. He persists in his refusal to believe there are only two choices left in this world, that is, to support either the East or the West.

•

Klaus Drittemann (whose last name translates rather too conveniently as "third man") is the central figure in "Singing the Blues in Red," opening today at the Quad Cinema. Though it was made mostly in Germany in German (with English subtitles), "Singing the Blues in Red" is an English film. It was written by Trevor Griffiths, who collaborated with Warren Beatty on the screenplay for "Reds," and directed by Kenneth Loach ("Kes," "Poor Cow," "The Game Keeper").

There's even something that's more English than German about the film's willingness to dramatize not a middle-road but a redefined, purified, pre-Stalinist left. It seems that for Mr. Loach and Mr. Griffiths, the divided city of Berlin, with its rampant consumerism on one side, and bumbling neo-socialism on the other, represents the truth not only of Germany, but also of a Britain where a divided left faces the triumphant Tory Government of Margaret Thatcher.

In pursuing Klaus's search for his long-lost father, who's finally found living under an assumed named in Cambridge, the narrative of "Singing the Blues in Red" becomes a bit tortured to make its points about power, whether in the hands of opportunists of left or right. The film contains a lot of skeletons jammed into one small closet. However, it also demonstrates an invigorating, completely independent moral perspective, which isn't very fashionable today and not easily dramatized.

"Singing the Blues in Red" is most effective when it's simply observing the details of Klaus's divided life before he leaves East Germany and, later, when he becomes the subject of a would-be publicity coup in West Berlin. Though the film's portrait of Western decadence is laid on with a trowel, it's also pretty funny. More important, Mr. Loach and Mr. Pannach succeed in communicating a lot of Klaus's feelings of anguish and loss, which go much deeper than the social-political satire.

In addition to Mr. Pannach, the excellent cast includes Cristine Rose, as the chilly, efficient American executive of the West German record company; Eva Krutina, as Klaus's mother, and Sigfrit Steiner, as his father.

Searching
Gerulf Pannache and Fabienne Babe star in Ken Loach's "Singing the Blues in Red," about an exiled East German musician seeking political and artistic freedom in the West.

Chris Menges ("The Killing Fields") is reponsible for the fine camerawork, including, I assume, that for some totally irrelevant flashbacks and dream sequences.

"Singing the Blues in Red" is straightforward and practical. It doesn't need these poetic flourishes.

1988 Ja 29, C8:5

Childhood Nostalgia

THE TREE WE HURT, directed and written by Dimos Avdeliodis; directory of photography, Philipos Koutsaftis; edited by Costas Fountas; music by Dimitris Papadimitriou; produced by Mr. Avdeliodis; released by Greek Film Center. At the Public Theater, 425 Lafayette Street. Running time: 75 minutes. This film has no rating.

Boy/Narrator	Yannis Avdeliodis
Runny-Nose Vangelis, the Cat Strangler	Nikos Mioteris
Boy/Narrator's Mother	Marina Delivoria
Man at head of funeral procession	Takis Agoris
Mad Seaman	Dimos Avdeliodis

By WALTER GOODMAN

IT'S summer 1960, in the picturesque Greek town of Chios, where people get around by donkey. School is ending, and a present-day narrator is calling up memories of the idyllic weeks he spent between fourth and fifth grades. They compose "The Tree We Hurt," an unassuming Greek movie that opens today at the Public Theater.

In the course of this brief holiday scrapbook, the boy assists his mother in cutting the bark of the gum tree — "the tree we hurt" — so the gum may drip out like tears or jewels. He frolics with a stray dog, joins in anouting on the beach, frees some trapped birds and is shot at by the bird catcher. He develops a crush on a pretty girl visitor. He and his best friend, Runny-Nose Vangelis, also known as the Cat Strangler, participate in funeral processions to earn a few coins. They splash in a tiny pool, eat ice cream and smoke a cigarette. With some other kids, they make war on wasps and pick on the local lunatic.

•

"So the days slipped by," a caption informs us. Dimos Avdeliodis, who wrote and directed and plays the lunatic, was born in Chios in 1952, which would make him close to the right age for this reminiscence, and it has the feel of autobiography. The mild adventures of his young heroes seem authentic in the manner of an unusually good home movie consisting of lightly connected episodes. There are lovely scenes, such as a line of women in white kerchiefs seated on donkeys moving between whitewashed buildings. The kids, who occasionally seem to be awaiting directions from off camera, are likable and fun to be with.

That's about it. Mr. Avdeliodis makes no effort to develop a story or propound a message, and his symbolism is not intrusive. "The Tree We Hurt," his first feature, may leave you feeling slightly unsatisfied, but you'd have to be W. C. Fields to kick a sun-splashed movie about kids and a dog and a cat and birds and donkeys.

1988 Ja 29, C11:1

Surreal Romp

MAMMAME, directed by Raul Ruiz; screenplay by Jean-Claude Gallotta and Mr. Ruiz; director of photography, Jacques Bouquin; edited by Martine Bouquin; music by Henry Torque and Serge Houppin; production designer, Mr. Ruiz; choreography by Mr. Gallotta; coproduced by Arcanal/Cinémathèque de la Danse, Maison de la Culture de Grenoble and Théâtre de la Ville de Paris; released by Pacific Film Archives. At Film Forum 2, 57 Watts Street. Running time: 65 minutes. This film has no rating.

WITH: Eric Alfieri, Mathilde Altaraz, Muriel Boulay, Christophe Delachau, Jean-Claude Gallotta, Pascal Gravat, Priscilla Newell, Viviane Serry and Robert Seyfried.

By JENNIFER DUNNING

"MAMMAME," which will be seen in its first New York screenings today and tomorrow at Film Forum 2, is the work of Raúl Ruiz, the Chilean expatriate film director, and Jean-Claude Gallotta, the French experimentalist choreographer. Mr. Ruiz is a surrealist. Mr. Gallotta is a fabulist. And the surprisingly immediate private worlds of these two enfants terribles of the arts are complementary here.

This filmed version of Mr. Gallotta's "Mammame" remains true to and even extends his dance, which fixes on the tribe of quirky, physically imperfect humans that has romped and nudged its way through other pieces by the choreographer. The dance is essentially a suite of duets in which one couple or another attempts to grab a few private moments together as members of the tribe engage in a series of small skirmishes, both sexual and tribal, taut and warily abandoned.

The child's cry for its mother suggested in the title is muted in this dreamlike film, which has few words and is set to a serviceable score by Henry Torque and Serge Houppin. But the dancers do surge and scamper fitfully through an overwhelming and incomprehensible environment for most of the film. And Mr. Gallotta

Footwork
In "Mammane," the director Raul Ruiz presents avant-garde dance, choreographed by Jean-Claude Gallotta.

"Mélo" was shown as part of last year's New York Film Festival. Following are excerpts from Vincent Canby's review, which appeared in The New York Times October 5, 1987.

MELO, directed by Alain Resnais; screenplay (French with English subtitles) by Mr. Resnais from a play by Henry Bernstein; photography by Charlie Van Damme and Gilbert Duhalde; edited by Albert Jurgenson and Jean-Pierre Besnard; music by Philippe-Gérard; art director, Jacques Saulnier; produced by Marin Karmitz; production companies, MK2 Productions and Films A2; released by European Classics. At Lincoln Plaza, Broadway and 63d Street. Running time: 112 minutes. This film has no rating.

Romaine Belcroix ....Sabine Azéma
Pierre Belcroix ....Pierre Arditi
Marcel Blanc ....André Dussollier
Christiane Levesque ....Fanny Ardant
Dr. Rémy ....Jacques Dacqmine
Priest ....Hubert Gignoux
Yvonne ....Catherine Arditi

By VINCENT CANBY

IN every film he's ever made, Alain Resnais has been exploring cinema techniques with such invention that technique has sometimes become the end instead of the means.

His latest work is "Mélo," which, though it appears to be limpid, is as maddening as "Last Year at Marienbad." It's not obscure, but it's difficult to understand what it is about the project that so fascinates this most sophisticated and intellectual of French film makers.

"Mélo" is taken from Henry Bernstein's 1929 Parisian romantic melodrama, which has already been filmed four times, including twice as "Dreaming Lips" with Elisabeth Bergner as the star (in 1932 in German and in 1937 in English), and in German again with Maria Schell in 1952.

The play appears to have been an exceptionally well-crafted example of a sort of "boulevard drama" that was a commonplace of the theater of the 20's. At the time it opened, critics in Paris and New York noted Bernstein's unusual adaptation of movie techniques to the stage. Like a film, the play was composed of a number of scenes in various locations, some very short and without dialogue.

Mr. Resnais seems to have filmed the already opened-up text pretty much as it was written by Bernstein (the film carries no credit for a screenwriter). He has closed in on it only to the extent that he never allows the movie audience to forget that what they're watching is meant to be a representation of a stage piece.

Though the camera moves in for close-ups from time to time, the sets and lighting are intentionally artificial. A curtain falls between acts, and scenes are played in extended, fluid, unbroken takes that evoke the theatrical experience. Unfortunately, the film's opening scene sets such a high standard that nothing that follows can come up to it.

One watches "Mélo" with the attention split between the events being portrayed and the exceedingly poised, stylized method by which they are being presented.

The central situation is this: In a Paris suburb in 1926, Romaine Belcroix (Sabine Azéma), the pretty, kittenish wife of Pierre (Pierre Arditi), meets and falls carelessly in love with Marcel (André Dussollier), Pierre's best friend from their days at the music conservatory. While Pierre, a pianist, has married and become a contented second-rate musician, Marcel is now a star of the international concert stage, as famous for his romantic adventures as for his

---

and Mr. Ruiz have in their individual ways turned dance over and coaxed it loose from familiar moorings.

•

Jacques Bouquin's photography and Mr. Ruiz's visual conception abolish the frame for dance that exists even in nonproscenium spaces. The camera moves up at the dancers from below them and low to the ground, and views them from high above, rather than at eye level. The dancers move in corridors and crannies that do not open out to anywhere. They are caught in compressed, concrete rooms perfect for forced confessions. And "Mammame" has an urgent, confessional feel, but made up of abstracted confessions made up of embraces and partings, small savageries and soothing caresses. Mr. Gallotta, the engineer of those "confessions," wanders through, popping up from time to time with a look of perplexed curiosity that enhances the streak of goofiness and Gallic insouciance that is generally and perversely present in his dances.

The dancers spring free a little, still compulsive, in a long stage-like space that appears to be part of an open-air theater, in which the company is enlarged by the dancers' shadows. Their sudden appearance on a beach at sunset is another freeing of sorts, but in this idyllic but fidgety apotheosis the film loses steam and becomes a puzzling and pretentious bore.

"Mammame" is accompanied by "From an Island Summer," a curiously sophomoric short film by Charles Atlas and Karole Armitage.

1988 Ja 29, C10:4

Why Oh Why Oh?

YOU CAN'T HURRY LOVE, written and directed by Richard Martini; directors of photography, Peter Lyons Collister and John Schwartzman; edited by Richard Candib; music by Bob Esty; produced by Jonathan D. Krane; released by Lightning Pictures. At Gemini Twin, 64th Street and Second Avenue; Cine Twin, Seventh Avenue near 47th Street; U.A. East, 85th Street and First Avenue; 23d Street West Triplex, at Eighth Avenue; Columbia Cinemas, Broadway at 103d Street. Running time: 92 minutes. This film is rated R.

Eddie Hayes ....David Packer
Skip ....Scott McGinnis
Peggy ....Bridget Fonda
Newcomb ....David Leisure
Marcie Hayes ....Luana Anders
Glenda ....Judy Balduzzi
Chuck Hayes ....Frank Bonner
Tony ....Anthony Geary
Mr. Glerman ....Charles Grodin
Kelly Bones ....Sally Kellerman
Rhonda ....Kristy McNichol
Tracey ....Danitza Kingsley
Miss Frigget ....Lu Leonard
Sparky ....Jake Steinfeld
Monique ....Merete

"YOU Can't Hurry Love," opening today at the Gemini and other theaters, is a very dim comedy about how funny and peculiar sunny Los Angeles is supposed to be to a square young man from Akron.

It's the first feature written and directed by Richard Martini, who apparently has connections. Appearing in throwaway cameos are Charles Grodin, Sally Kellerman and Kristy McNichol.

• •

The principal members of the cast are David Packer, as the lovesick Ohioan; Scott McGinnis (who looks like a young Nick Nolte), as Mr. Packer's more savvy cousin; David Leisure (who is funnier as the unreliable television spokesman for Isuzu automobiles), and Bridget Fonda (Peter's daughter), who plays a sympathetic employee of a dating service. A lot of other beautiful young women, often without clothes, dress the sets.

Miss Fonda sometimes resembles her aunt Jane, but never seems at ease attempting to act thin-air, which is something learned only with time and unhappy experience.

VINCENT CANBY

1988 Ja 29, C11:1

Eyeball to Eyeball

ANGUISH, directed by Bigas Luna; screenplay by Michael Berlin; director of photography, J. M. a Civit; edited by Tom Sabin; music by J. M. Pagan; production designer, Felipe De Paco; produced by Pepon Coromina; released by Spectrafilm. At Criterion, Broadway at 45th Street; Coliseum Twin, Broadway and 181st Street. Running time: 89 minutes. This film is rated R.

John..Michael Lerner
John's Mother ....Zelda Rubinstein

By CARYN JAMES

BIRDS fly around the room, and a little old lady with her hair in a bun croaks murderous orders at her son. John always does what Mama says, so he leaves the house, kills a couple of people and gouges out their eyes. He is, however, well raised enough to rinse off the eyeballs neatly in the victims' bathroom sinks.

There is a twisted but clever idea behind Bigas Luna's "Anguish," a film that wants to have its blood and deny it, too. With its Hitchcockian birds, psycho son and weird mama — as well as its evocation of the razor-slit eyeball in the surrealist classic "Un Chien Andalou" — Mr. Luna

---

Zelda Rubinstein

seems to have something more than schlock suspense on his mind.

Soon he reveals another layer of artifice; John and his mother (Zelda Rubinstein, the spooky psychic in "Poltergeist") are characters in "The Mommy," an intentionally hackneyed movie complete with badly dubbed foreign actors. As two teen-age girls in Los Angeles watch "The Mommy," one says it's "gross and disgusting." The other thinks her friend is a scared baby until a suggestible killer who has seen the film one time too many starts shooting up the moviegoers.

Mr. Luna weaves back and forth between "The Mommy" and the Los Angeles audience with some expertise; he at least keeps us alert and off guard. But his parodies of movie genres admire their sources too simply with too little thought. When the layers of fantasy are sorted out, Mr. Luna asks us to wallow in blood, to watch John wash off all those eyeballs, for no purpose. When the story pulls back from "The Mommy," it becomes as predictable, as gross and disgusting, as any quickie thriller about a murder rampage.

To argue that the film's mediocrity is its very point would be taking Mr. Luna's premise more seriously than his accomplishment, maybe more seriously than he intends. He does not play off ideas about fantasy and reality or about movies and the power of suggestion; he hands them to us, to make of them what we can. And we can make a better movie in our minds than the half-baked "Anguish," which opens today at the Criterion and Coliseum.

1988 Ja 29, C15:1

Correction

A list of credits in Weekend on Jan. 29 with a film review of "Anguish" misidentified the screenwriter. The film was written and directed by Bigas Luna.

1988 F 8, A3:1

virtuosity on the violin.

The affair that begins casually turns into a passion so grand that neither Romaine nor Marcel is willing to end it. Romaine, who can't bear to abandon the adoring Pierre, decides to poison him, and probably would succeed except for the nosiness of a doctor. She takes the only way out, which leads to a final scene of reconciliation between the two men that was regarded by the play's original critics as a coup de théâtre.

Something has been lost along the way, possibly because Romaine's two loves, as written by Bernstein and as played by Mr. Dussollier and Mr.

Arditi, now seem to be such sticks. Everyone talks very well. As in theater, the characters are always at a little distance from the emotions they're expressing.

Miss Azéma seems consciously to recall Louise Brooks in look and manner. The actress, seen here earlier in Bertrand Tavernier's "Sunday in the Country," comes close to bridging the gap between style and content. She's a bright, vibrant presence, both a quintessential figure of 1920's drama (a woman liberated only to be able to face destruction) and a specific character of willful charm.

Chief among the supporting players is Fanny Ardant. Strong, tall, slightly forbidding actress that she is, she invests her small role with more ominous, mysterious import than was ever written into it.

"Mélo" is, I suspect, exactly the movie Mr. Resnais set out to make. It doesn't necessarily represent a failure of achievement, but one of communication with someone who doesn't share what, in "Mélo," seems to be his princess-and-the-pea sensibility.

1988 Ja 31, 55:1

Nowhere in the film is there any hint that she's become psychotic *because* she's single and successful, nor is it suggested that she's single and successful because she's psychotic.

She's the flashiest character in the film, but she has the narrative function of a traffic accident. The make of the car is beside the point. What's important is that the accident serves to reaffirm the sanctity of the home, which, in this case, is also forgiving.

∎

FILM VIEW/Vincent Canby

Out of This World

IT ALL DEPENDS ON WHERE YOU'RE sitting. Some women argue that "Fatal Attraction" does the unmarried career woman a disservice in its lubricious exploitation of the character played by Glenn Close. The film, they say, is reactionary.

As I understand it, their responses are comparable to those of some men to "Three Men and a Baby," whose basic joke is based on the fondly held belief that all adult males are essentially 14 years old and wouldn't know one end of a baby from the other until the baby has, in the film's genteel word, "pooped."

For those who came in late, "Fatal Attraction" casts Miss Close as a Manhattan book editor who has a steamy weekend in town with Michael Douglas, a heretofore faithful husband whose wife and daughter are in the country.

When the weekend is over, Miss Close refuses to acknowledge the fling for what it was. She spends the rest of the movie becoming ever more unhinged as she terrorizes Mr. Douglas, his loyal (nonworking) wife and guiltless child.

"Fatal Attraction," according to the argument, endorses the suspicion that even when the career woman is successful, there's something so unnatural about her state that she's likely to turn into a homicidal maniac when she realizes how unfulfilled she really is. The point is also made that although Miss Close is made to pay for her adultery, the man in the case gets off scot-free, more or less.

Boys will be boys.

On the other hand, a number of men read "Fatal Attraction" as a cautionary nightmare, a persuasive argument against the one-night stand. "Boys will be boys," these men admit with what's meant to be disarming sheepishness, and boys should be careful.

"Boys will be boys" is, in fact, the repeated refrain in the ever-so-cute and bouncy song that is sung behind the ever-so-cute and bouncy opening credits for "Three Men and a Baby." The three "boys" are a Manhattan architect (Tom Selleck), a comic-strip artist (Steve Guttenberg) and an actor (Ted Danson), all of whom seem rather long in the tooth and financially well off to be sharing a Manhattan apartment for any speakable reason except the requirements of the story.

∎

In an era when most women work, at least part time, when most husbands share at least some of the household chores and when even

most unmarried adults are aware that babies, like pet pythons, poodles and Great Danes, poop, "Three Men and a Baby" evokes attitudes that go back at least several decades. Innocence of this sort today would seem to approach the pathological. Yet, as portrayed in "Three Men and a Baby," such innocence is clearly finding a huge and appreciative audience.

Between its opening in November and the end of the year, "Three Men and a Baby" earned (according to Variety) $45 million in rentals at American theaters, becoming the fourth most successful movie of 1987 (and still going strong in 1988).

The sexual revolution has come and gone, but most Americans continue to cling to stereotypical roles for men and women. "Three Men and a Baby" makes one feeble attempt to update itself when it has Mr. Selleck's girlfriend admit that she knows nothing more about babies than he does, but the film can't get off the hook so easily.

Bachelor fathers still tickle the funnybone, as does a bachelor mother (which was the title and subject of a Ginger Rogers hit nearly 50 years ago). In another 1987 release, "Baby Boom," Diane Keaton plays a high-powered, unmarried career woman thrown (comically, temporarily) for a loss when, like the "boys" in "Three Men and a Baby," she's saddled with someone else's child.

Though at the end of the film, after having learned how to appreciate motherhood, she elects to hang onto her career, it's also with the understanding that she's going to have both her career *and* the man (Sam Shepard) who'll make her complete.

As reflected in our mass entertainment, we remain staunch reactionaries, if not aggressive revisionists, though not always for the obvious reasons.

"Fatal Attraction," which is sure to be one of the year's big Oscar nominees, earned $60 million in 1987 (the third biggest money maker of the year) and, like "Three Men and a Baby," continues to do well at the box office. It is, I think, reactionary, but not because it slanders unmarried career woman.

Adrian Lyne, the director, and James Dearden, who wrote the screenplay, make it evident that the Glenn Close character is a special case. Her failing is not her sexual adventurousness. She's an emotional bandit from the start.

Once into the weekend affair, she doesn't turn into something she hasn't been before, but reveals herself to be a certifiable nut with a taste for serious violence and deceit, as well as for sex.

Calling "Three Men and a Baby" and "Fatal Attraction" reactionary is not to suggest that they're overtly political in the manner of "Rambo," "The Green Berets" or even the populist fables of Frank Capra.

Neither is it a necessarily pejorative term. Rather, it's to describe the kind of movies and television series that will always dominate our mass entertainment because they feed back to their audiences exactly the images the audiences have of themselves. If the images aren't especially honest, then they're the ones that audiences would wish were true.

"Fatal Attraction" is a brilliantly designed roller-coaster ride, and about as substantial. The scares are breathtaking though fleeting and, at the end, everyone (who matters) is O.K. The American home has been preserved. The upscale, urban American way of life, exemplified by the comparative luxe of the apartment where Mr. Douglas and his family live, has been endorsed. The movie questions nothing except a casual encounter with the wrong woman.

There are no loose ends.

"Three Men and a Baby" is equally reassuring. Nobody in the film (except the mother of the baby) has to worry about money or employment or career goals. There is no bomb in this universe, no war, no political scandal, no hungry, no homeless. We know this not because such things aren't shown, but because the fiction is so false, on its own terms, that it effectively denies the possibility of all other realities.

A work that is honest in its own terms (even one as supposedly artificial as "The Importance of Being Earnest" or as self-absorbed as "Tootsie") doesn't shut out the real world, but fits within it. Our most popular movies this year exist in limbo. □

1988 Ja 31, II:19:1

Medical War

HOXSEY: QUACKS WHO CURE CANCER?, produced and directed by Ken Ausubel; co-produced by Catherine Salveson. At Film Forum 1, 57 Watts Street. Running time: 100 minutes. This film has no rating.

By VINCENT CANBY

KEN AUSUBEL'S "Hoxsey: Quacks Who Cure Cancer?," opening today at Film Forum 1, is both sobersided and flamboyant, informative and incomplete, which is meant as praise since it's the sort of documentary that provokes strong, unexpected responses.

"Hoxsey: Quacks Who Cure Cancer?" is about medical politics, specifically about the long civil war between the organized medical profession, represented by the American

In Dispute Harry Hoxsey, whose purported herbal cancer remedy (first chanced on by his great-grandfather 80 years earlier) involved him in a 35-year war with the medical establishment that began in 1924, is the subject of "Hoxsey: Quacks Who Cure Cancer?" Ken Ausubel's documentary also deals with the politics of cancer treatment.

Medical Association (supported by the Federal Drug Administration), and independent practitioners, exemplified by Harry M. Hoxsey, who sell seemingly miraculous cancer cures.

Of all these practitioners, possibly the most successful and most colorful was Hoxsey. In 1924, Hoxsey, a former coal miner with an eighth-grade education, founded his first clinic, where he treated cancer with, among others things, a herbal tonic based on a formula handed down by his great-grandfather. Before his actvities were suppressed in the 1950's, Hoxsey owned a hugely successful private clinic in Dallas with branches in 17 states.

The film proceeds with what at first appears to be a deceptively disarming appreciation of Hoxsey. The Hoxsey story is recalled in old films of Hoxsey himself (who has the fast-talking manner of a carnival barker), in interviews with Mildred Nelson, the registered nurse who today carries on Hoxsey's work at a busy clinic in Mexico, and in the testimony of patients who say the Hoxsey treatments saved their lives.

The film examines Hoxsey's long-running battle with the A.M.A. and especially with its Dr. Morris Fishbein, against whom Hoxsey eventually won a slander suit. Among Hoxsey's charges against the A.M.A. was that it went after him only when he refused to sell its representatives the formula for his herbal brew. These accusations were never proved, but, according to the film, they fit the pattern of hanky-panky that later helped to discredit the A.M.A.'s official position toward other unorthodox practitioners.

"Hoxsey: Quacks Who Cure Cancer?" initially seems to be an unquestioning pro-Hoxsey treatise, but that's only Mr. Ausubel's method of revealing the true subject of the movie, which is greed and money as they have shaped medical politics in this country. The film doesn't spend much time dwelling on Hoxsey's failures (he himself died of cancer) or on Hoxsey himself (he also was apparently a successful oil man), nor does it go deeply into other, later so-called miracle treatments. The film hasn't the time or space.

Instead, it charts what it finds to be the gradual "liberalization" of the medical establishment's attitude toward cancer treatment that goes beyond surgery, radiation and conventional chemotherapy to include everything from diet and mental attitude to the sort of commonplace herbs in the Hoxsey tonic.

Everybody interviewed in this film makes claims that can't be easily supported. It isn't the claims that interest Mr. Ausubel as much as the policies of vested interests that, until now, have discouraged research into areas considered unorthodox by the medical community.

"Hoxsey: Quacks Who Cure Cancer?" is first-rate reportage.

1988 F 3, C21:4

Cultural Exchange

DISTANT HARMONY, directed by DeWitt Sage; director of photography, Miroslav Ondricek; edited by Oreet Rees, Coco Houwer and Sam Pollard; produced by John Goberman, Mr. Sage and Daniel Wigutow. At Carnegie Hall Cinema, Seventh Avenue at 57th Street. Running time: 87 minutes. This film has no rating.

By WALTER GOODMAN

LUCIANO PAVAROTTI and China make a formidable match in "Distant Harmony," a cheerful documentary about the tenor's tour of the country in June 1986. The director, DeWitt Sage, had the playful notion of playing off Western grand opera against traditional Chinese music and, in the course of these 85 highly entertaining minutes, reconciling them. So beginning today at the Carnegie Hall Cinema, you can hear a version of "O Sole Mio" performed on Chinese instruments while residents of Beijing do their morning exercises on screen.

On the Road Luciano Pavarotti's 1986 singing tour of China is recounted in DeWitt Sage's documentary "Distant Harmony."

Even more exotic, you can witness Mr. Pavarotti, hidden behind a marvel of a mask and a warrior's costume almost as colorful as the shirts he favors, take part in a Chinese operatic trio. This Western ear could detect no Italian accent.

Accompanying Mr. Pavarotti was the cast and crew of the Genoa Opera production of "La Bohème." Pavarottian high notes from the opera set off big bursts of applause. There are also recital performances of such standards as "Vesti la giubba" and shots of the China that Mr. Pavarotti apparently saw on his visit. If you have a low tolerance for cute kids, you may feel as though you have walked in on an official travelogue. But Miroslav Ondricek's photography is vivid, and the youngsters are appealing, whether singing little songs or doing a chorus number to a rock beat; their displays of acrobatics and martial arts are startling.

Mr. Sage finds diverting ways of making the point that East and West can meet. There is Mr. Pavarotti bicycling rythmically along to the strains of "La donna è mobile." (In a show of Chinese hospitality, the guest has the normally thronged thoroughfare pretty much to himself.) There he is coaching a local singer in the finer points of "Musetta's Waltz." And there he is sharing Italian song and Chinese pasta (the "first problem," one of the tour managers reports, is "food for Pavarotti") and then clapping exuberantly for a young Chinese cook who performs a delightful number in his own language.

If Mr. Pavarotti ever wears down, he does it off camera. (The complicated backstage preparations glimpsed here invite applause for the crew's energy, too.) Good will gets briefly out of hand, when in an interview the star expresses the belief that the Chinese people have achieved freedom, possibly drawing that optimistic assessment from the fact that they are free to applaud him.

The climax comes with Mr. Pavarotti, glistening white handkerchief unfurled, treating an audience of 10,000 at Beijing's Great Hall of the People to "Come Back to Sorrento." To judge by the response, old Sorrento can keep the pot on as high a boil in the East as it long has in the West. One of the singer's hosts points out that 100 or 200 million Chinese might have watched "La Bohème" on television, and asks, "Since the whole world likes these operas, why should we not like them?" Well, there may be reasons, but on the evidence of "Distant Harmony," if anybody can do away with culture clash, Luciano Pavarotti is the man.

1988 F 4, C15:1

Waking Nightmares

THE SERPENT AND THE RAINBOW, directed by Wes Craven; screenplay by Richard Maxwell and A. R. Simoun, inspired by the book by Wade Davis; director of photography, John Lindley; film editor, Glenn Farr; music by Brad Fiedel; production designer, David Nichols; produced by David Ladd and Doug Claybourne; released by Universal Pictures. At Movieland, Broadway at 47th Street; Manhattan Twin, 59th Street east of Third Avenue; 23d Street West Triplex, at Eighth Avenue; Metro Twin, Broadway at 99th Street; Movie Center 5, 125th Street between Powell and Douglass Boulevards; Essex, 275 Grand Street. Running time: 105 minutes. This film is rated R.
Dennis Alan .... Bill Pullman
Marielle Celine .... Cathy Tyson
Dargent Peytraud .... Zakes Mokae
Lucien Celine .... Paul Winfield
Mozart .... Brent Jennings
Christophe .... Conrad Roberts
Gaston .... Badja Djola

By JANET MASLIN

IT'S a long way from a Harvard ethnobiologist's thoughtful account of his search for exotic Haitian medicinal potions to a film with the advertising slogan "Don't bury me ... I'm not dead!" But in fact these two sides of "The Serpent and the Rainbow" aren't as different as they sound. Wade Davis's fascinating 1985 book is much more an adventure story than a scientific tract, and the film is the work of Wes Craven, whose horror credits ("A Nightmare on Elm Street," "The Hills Have Eyes") give an incomplete impression of his talents. This film amounts to Mr. Craven's crossover into the mainstream, even if it happens to be about zombies.

If "The Serpent and the Rainbow" never fully convinces its audience that the dead can walk, it's not for lack of trying. Nor is it without the efforts of an excellent cast, one that raises this far above the level of ordinary exploitation. Bill Pullman plays Dennis Alan, a raffish scientist who, like Mr. Davis, visited Haiti in hopes of learning the secrets of what the film calls "zombification" and got, more than he bargained for. Zakes Mokae is especially memorable as Alan's chief antagonist, the head of the dreaded Tontons Macoute security force, who displays menacingly bared teeth at all times, even when speaking — with the greatest sarcasm imaginable — of "happy, happy, happy island people."

This film, like much of Mr. Craven's other work, is about crossing the line that separates nightmare from reality, a line that seems especially thin in this setting. Handsomely photographed (in both Haiti and the Dominican Republic), and with a strong sense of spectacle, "The Serpent and the Rainbow" creates a climate in which voodoo seems very much at home. The ease with which seemingly rational characters slip into trancelike states is illustrated by Marielle Celine, a psychiatrist played by Cathy Tyson, the stunningly regal star of "Mona Lisa." While witnessing a voodoo dance ritual, Marielle becomes caught up in the dance as if possessed; later on, she brings a similiarly eerie abandon to a moment of sexual rapture.

Mr. Craven, whose "Elm Street" films slip frighteningly into and out of dream logic, builds this film's most alarming moments out of seemingly normal situations. A demure hostess at a dinner party may just offer a toast, grab a knife and then lunge at a man across the table, whose nightmare this happens to be; the people in this man's waking life may become interchangeable in his most hellish visions. Mr. Craven's attempts at such effects are always gripping, but here they are sometimes overpowered by the complexity of the material. The search for the zombifying elixir, the influence of the Tontons Macoute, the fall of the Duvalier dictatorship and the mysterious powers of voodoo sometimes run together in a manner less provocative than confusing.

"The Serpent and the Rainbow," which opens today at the Movieland and other theaters, also has a screenplay that often breaks its spell. When a dazed-looking, catatonic woman with a hairdo like Whoopi Goldberg's is identified as "a classic zombie" early in the story, for example, Alan is forced to remark rather superfluously "Well, she sure can't tell us anything." Things aren't much better when the talk turns philosophical, although a sorcerer named Mozart (nicely played by Brent Jennings) sounds the right note of mystery and menace. When Mozart crafts the zombie potion out of puffer fish and human skulls, the film sounds the note of ghoulishness for which Mr. Craven is best known; the same is true when Alan is tortured brutally by Mr. Mokae's memorable villain. At moments like this, the film's greatest unanswered question becomes why doesn't Alan just go home?.

1988 F 5, C3:4

Time Trials

JULIA AND JULIA, directed by Peter Del Monte; screenplay by Silvia Napolitano, Sandro Petraglia and Mr. Del Monte; story by Miss Napolitano and Mr. Del Monte; director of photography, Giuseppe Rotunno; edited by Michael Chandler; music by Maurice Jarre; produced by RAI-Radiotelevisione Italiana; distributed by Cinecom. At Embassy 3, Broadway at 47th Street; New York Twin, Second Avenue and 66th Street; 34th Street Showplace, near Second Avenue; Columbia Cinema, Broadway at 103d Street. Running time: 96 minutes. This film is rated R.
Julia .... Kathleen Turner
Paolo .... Gabriel Byrne
Daniel .... Sting
Paolo's Father .... Gabriele Ferzetti
Paolo's Mother .... Angela Goodwin
Carla .... Lidia Broccolino
Marco .... Alexander Van Wyk
Commissioner .... Renato Scarpa

"JULIA AND JULIA," opening today at the Embassy 3 and other theaters, is minor movie making, but it does prove two things: that Kathleen Turner has become the kind of star who can carry even third-rate fiction without losing her beautiful, voluptuous cool, and that high-definition tape (on which this was initially shot) can be transferred to film and look as good as anything shot on film to start with.

The movie itself is another matter. It's a not-very-spooky melodrama about an unfortunate American woman named Julia (Miss Turner) whose husband is killed (before the opening credits) in an automobile accident on their wedding day.

A few years later, Julia is living and working in silent sorrow in the picture-postcard pretty port of Tri-

este. One night she comes home to find that her husband (Gabriel Byrne) is not dead and that the two of them, with their small son, are living in elegant but not especially happy circumstances: He's become married to his career as a ship designer and she has taken a lover (Sting).

The grateful Julia goes along with all this, and tries to straighten out her marriage. Suddenly she's back in the world of her widowhood. Just when she thinks she knows what's going on, she's returned to the "other" life. Back and forth she goes — fate's plaything. Poor Julia thinks she must be going mad, mad, mad, but Miss Turner, who had a funnier run-in with time in "Peggy Sue Got Married," is always sane, sane, sane. Mr. Byrne and, in particular, Sting also are creditable.

Not so the movie, which was directed by Peter Del Monte, who also collaborated on the screenplay. "Julia and Julia" is "Twilight Zone" stuff. Giuseppe Rotunno was responsible for the crystal-clear, originally taped photography.

VINCENT CANBY

1988 F 5, C5:1

Private Lives

THE UNBEARABLE LIGHTNESS OF BEING, directed by Philip Kaufman; screenplay by Jean-Claude Carrière and Mr. Kaufman, adapted from the novel by Milan Kundera; director of photography, Sven Nykvist; film editor, Walter Murch; music by Mark Adler; production designer, Pierre Guffroy; presented by the Saul Zaentz Company. At Tower East, Third Avenue and 72d Street. Running time: 172 minutes. This film is rated R.
Tomas .... Daniel Day-Lewis
Tereza .... Juliette Binoche
Sabina .... Lena Olin
Franz .... Derek de Lint
The Ambassador .... Erland Josephson

By VINCENT CANBY

PHILIP KAUFMAN'S "Unbearable Lightness of Being" begins with much promise, as if it were a ribald fairy tale. "In Prague in 1968," says a title card, "there lived a young doctor named Tomas." Tomas (Daniel Day-Lewis) comes out of the operating room and goes straight to a pretty nurse waiting in the supply room.

"Take off your clothes," says Tomas. Forever altering one aspect of playing hard-to-get, the nurse does. On the other side of a frosted-glass window several other hospital employees watch Tomas's technique

with admiration.

"But the woman who understood him best was Sabina," says a second title card. The film cuts to Tomas and Sabina (Lena Olin) in a frenzied, thoroughly satisfying coupling on the platform bed in her studio — she's a painter.

Tomas and Sabina share a passion for acrobatic, technically ingenious sex that excludes serious emotional commitment but not nonstop conversation. That's the wonder of Tomas and Sabina. They can enjoy everything they're doing while always remaining a little detached. Each is like a movie critic who goes through his job with one part of his mind on the movie, while the part that's safely outside it criticizes the critic's reactions and prepares to tell all at any minute.

In the midst of ecstasy, the sweating, exultant Sabina tells Tomas, "You are the complete opposite of kitsch," though without defining the term. It makes no difference. It's clear that, to Sabina, whatever Tomas is doing, he's doing it right.

Tomas buzzes serenely through the world like a bumblebee, his eye on the next flower even before he has quite exhausted the one he's with.

A third title card: "Tomas was sent to a spa town to perform an operation." It's there that Tomas meets the

Kathleen Turner

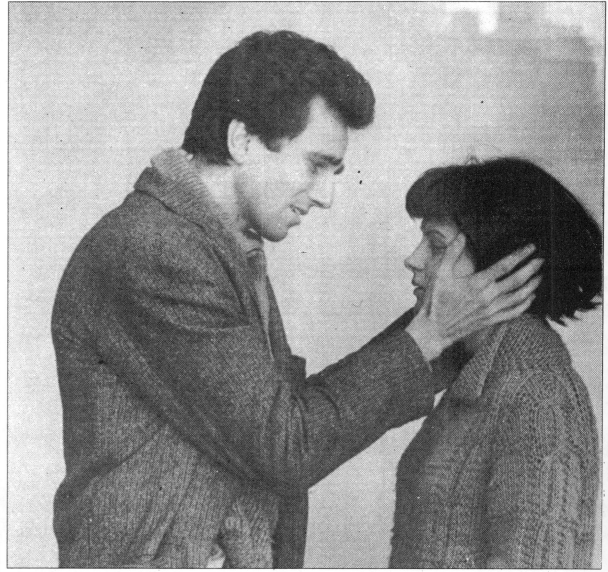

Daniel Day Lewis and Juliette Binoche in Philip Kaufman's adaptation of "The Unbearable Lightness of Being"

exceptional young woman who changes the course of his existence, forever altering one aspect of what has seemed to be his lightness of being.

She is Tereza (Juliette Binoche), a romantic waitress who falls profoundly in love with Tomas without knowing anything about him. She follows him back to Prague and, before he's aware of the consequences, he's allowing her to sleep the *entire* night in his bed, something that has always been against his rules. Soon they are married.

After that, "The Unbearable Lightness of Being" settles down to recapitulate the superficial events of Milan Kundera's introspective, philosophical novel with fidelity and an accumulating heaviness, as well as at immense length — nearly three hours. It's possible to read the book in less time.

The film opens today at Loews Tower East.

•

The novel, by the celebrated Czechoslovak writer who now lives in Paris, was adapted by Mr. Kaufman and Jean-Claude Carrière. Mr. Carrière is the French writer whose screenplays ("Belle de Jour," "The Discreet Charm of the Bourgeoisie," among others) for Luis Buñuel exemplify the seamless collaboration possible when a brilliant director meets a brilliant writer who knows the director's mind better than the director possibly does. Mr. Kaufman's most recent work was the fine, underappreciated adaptation of Tom Wolfe's "Right Stuff."

These credentials are worth noting. It's obvious that both Mr. Kaufman and Mr. Carrière understood the problems they faced in making a screen adaptation of a novel whose central character is really a never-seen, loquacious "I," representing the novelist spinning the tale. This "I" is both informally chatty and God-like. He doesn't participate in the story of Tomas, Sabina, Tereza and the others. He's looking down on them from a literary "above." When it suits him, he briefly enters the characters' minds and departs, a benign thief in the night.

Mr. Kundera entertains and instructs the reader. He also provokes responses that give point to commonplace misadventures set in momentous times. These are so unspeakably sad that the comic method seems the only civilized alternative to what would otherwise turn into kitsch, something sentimental and false.

Like brain surgeons removing a tumor, Mr. Kaufman and Mr. Carrière have excised the "I" from the screenplay. Whenever possible, they've saved bits and pieces of his observations, which have been reinserted as dialogue spoken by the characters, frequently with a good deal of awkwardness. The "voice" of the novel is gone. What remains is not exactly bowdlerized Kundera but, even with all the care, intelligence and eroticism that have gone into it, it's a bit zombie-like. It would be difficult to recognize if one hadn't known it when it was alive.

Mr. Kundera, whose citizenship was revoked after he left Czechoslovakia, dislikes having his novels and stories parsed for their politics. Yet everything he writes inevitably has strong political meaning, especially in relation to Czechoslovakia, which, landlocked and periodically overrun and cut up by invaders through the centuries, has somehow maintained its own identity.

"The Unbearable Lightness of Being" opens in 1968 during the thaw known as the "Prague spring," when everything in politics and the arts seemed possible after the long repression of the Stalinist winter.

As Tomas is drawn against his will into commitment to Tereza, he's also, briefly, drawn into politics. He writes an ironic essay about the morality of Czechoslovak Communist politicians who admit the errors of their Stalinist days without, like Oedipus, feeling the necessity of purging their guilt.

After the Soviet invasion, Sabina drives off to Switzerland, followed by Tomas and Tereza. When Tereza, feeling bereft with her womanizing husband in a strange country, returns to Czechoslovakia, Tomas follows. He remains committed to Tereza, though still unfaithful. His essay on Oedipus is recalled to haunt him. Tomas becomes a true political activist by remaining resolutely passive. This is the bittersweet joke.

I'm not sure how much of this comes through in the movie since, if one has read the novel, the impulse is to fill in the gaps. Photographed by Sven Nykvist, the film looks beautiful and authentic, but it's so monotonously paced that it seems to have been edited with the aid of a metronome. Although a good deal of the narrative has been excised, nothing has been condensed. The details of the lives of Tomas, Sabina and Tereza, recalled without Mr. Kundera's comments, don't fill the huge landscape provided by the film's extraordinary running time. It's literal without even being literary.

Mr. Day-Lewis, Miss Binoche and Miss Olin (who was spectacular in Ingmar Bergman's "After the Rehearsal") are surprisingly fine — both modest and intense as lovers whose private lives are defined by public events. The supporting cast includes Derek de Lint as one of Sabina's lovers; Erland Josephson in a tiny part, and (listed but unseen by me) Jan Nemec, the excellent Czechoslovak director whose "Report on the Party and Its Guests" came out during the "Prague spring."

Mr. Kaufman attempts to find a common denominator among the various accents by having everyone speak English with a Czechoslovak accent, but even these vary according to each actor's country of origin.

"The Unbearable Lightness of Being" is notably ambitious and it avoids kitsch. It understands Mr. Kundera, even as it fails to find picture-equivalents to his ideas.

1988 F 5, C8:5

Correction

Because of a computer error, the film review of "The Unbearable Lightness of Being" in Weekend yesterday included a phrase erroneously in the second paragraph. The passage should have read: " 'Take off your clothes,' says Tomas. After three seconds of playing hard-to-get, the nurse does. On the other side of a frosted-glass window several other hospital employees watch Tomas's technique with admiration."

1988 F 6, 3:2

LAND OF PROMISE, written and directed by Andrzej Wajda (in Polish with English subtitles), based on the novel by Wladyslaw Reymont; photographed by Witold Sobocinski, Edward Klosinski and Waclaw Dybowski; music by Wojciech Kilar; art direction by Tadeusz Kosarewica; distributed by Tinc Productions. At Cinema Village, 22 East 12th Street. Running time: 165 minutes. This film has no rating.
Karol Borowiecki .... Daniel Olbrychski
Moryc Welt ....Wojciech Pszoniak
Maks Baum .... Andrzej Seweryn
Anka .... Anna Nahrebecka

By CARYN JAMES

AT first glance, the mid-1970's seems like the least inventive phase in the career of Andrzej Wajda, the brilliant, prolific Polish director. His trilogy from the 50's, ending with the masterly "Ashes and Diamonds," assessed the emotional cost of World War II. In 1976, he would tear down Stalinist icons in "Man of Marble." But earlier in the decade, films such as "A Wedding" and "Land of Promise," both set in the 19th century, seemed to signal, if not a retreat from the political wars, at least an escape from the pressure of recent events.

"Land of Promise," the 1975 film that will have its first commercial run in New York at Cinema Village today and tomorrow, offers only a visual rest from contemporary battle. It has all the indirection you would expect of a defiant film maker whose work must pass Government censors and film boards (for years they rejected the idea for "Man of Marble"), all the accomplishment of one adept at portraying the personal drama of history.

Based on the 1898 novel by the Nobel laureate Wladyslaw Reymont, the film reveals the city of Lodz in the midst of industrialization. Three men who become partners to build a textile factory offer a microcosm of social classes and ethnic diversity, a neat balance that exists only in fiction. Karol is a Polish nobleman with diminished fortunes; Maks is a German whose father's old-time mill is failing; Moryc is a Jew who is valued, at times merely tolerated, for his business connections. The three first appear at a sunlit country estate, and even in this washed-out print we can tell that their world of exquisite beauty — cathedral-tall birches, expansive lawns, a huge white manor house — will vanish in the coming political turmoil.

•

The center of the trio is Karol, who articulates all too bluntly the thoughts of the greedy, youthful man of the future. He dismisses what he calls the "mummified gentry," which has left him penniless, while his father mourns for the "peaceful, simple, superior" life fading away. Daniel Olbrychski, a veteran of many Wajda films, gives Karol such controlled intensity that we almost believe he was the original of this stereotype.

Mr. Wajda seems to enjoy abandoning himself to 19th-century caricatures and narrative strategies, but his visual strength and authorial control redeem the story from its clichés. The partners, in top hats, drink champagne as they break ground for their factory; across the land, workers stream toward the other mills, dwarfed by buildings whose grayness is broken only by the pillars of black smoke that pour from them.

Such heavy-handed juxtaposition hasn't been done very well since Dickens, but Mr. Wajda makes it work because he is too smart to dwell on the smokestacks. He keeps moving his story ahead as the partners scheme to get more money and consider double-crossing one another, and as Karol wonders whether to betray his beautiful fiancée for a sim-

ple-minded, wealthy woman.

There are disturbing, graphic accidents in the factories, but like the images of poverty, the violence intrudes on more luxuriant and decadent images. In a theater, a heavy woman in clownish makeup rides a swing toward the audience and the camera flies with her, eventually picking out the three partners, who are busy spotting the women in the audience with the most jewels.

•

Not all of Mr. Wajda's 19th-century excesses sit comfortably in the 20th century. Too many secondary characters are stereotypes of Jews, especially a repulsive, piggish woman with whom Karol has an affair, and her merciless, vengeful husband. There is so little historical perspective on these characters that Mr. Wajda's own judgment seems to have failed him.

Though his film's narrative power is unquestionable, Mr. Wajda clearly wants to do more than replay history. Yet only in the final scene is there an unmistakable, overt reference to contemporary politics. When the now wealthy partners order police to shoot striking workers, Mr. Wajda is surely looking back to the 1970 protests in Gdansk, when Government troops fired on shipyard workers. The scene reverberates even more in hindsight, and points toward his 1981 film "Man of Iron," tracing the political movements that led to the creation of Solidarity.

"Land of Promise" remains a foray into the 19th century, but in spirit it is as political as any of Mr. Wajda's more pointed films. And if its artistry is finally too bound by the last century, it still bears the signature of a director whose every camera move has something to intrigue us.

1988 F 5, C13:6

New Pointillism

THE COMPUTER ANIMATION SHOW, a collection of animated films, produced by Terry Thoren; executive producers, Gary Meyer, Steve Gilula and Mr. Thoren; presented by Expanded Entertainment; an International Tournée of Animation Production. At Bleecker Street Cinema, at La Guardia Place. Running time: 90 minutes. This film has no rating.

HOW you gonna keep 'em down on the farm after they've seen Max Headroom? That question should have occurred to the producers of "The Computer Animation Show," a collection of computer-generated shorts that has plenty of technology but none of Max's sophisticated wit. Creatively, this film, which opens today at the Bleecker Street Cinema, is the equivalent of pointing a camera at Mr. Potato Head and making him move from side to side.

The selections are weighted toward television commercials — they include a singing pineapple and several cigarette ads from Malaysia — and reels put together by computer companies to display their work. There isn't much to intrigue the average moviegoer, who sees computer animation all the time but probably doesn't recognize it. The movie's centerpiece, for example, is the title sequence from Steven Spielberg's canceled television series "Amazing Stories." As a book flies through the air like a bat flapping its wings and a deck of cards spills like a waterfall into a top hat, a voice explains what computer animation is all about.

That lecturer's voice must have come from bad educational films, and its explanation is not as lucid as one by Peter Sorensen, a computer-magazine editor, in an article included in the press material. Simplified drastically, the article says computers are programmed to create images from millions of tiny dots — in principle, the way newspaper photographs are made — and the image is projected on a special monitor to be filmed.

•

This knowledge can make a short like "Déjà Vu" dazzling, momentarily. Flowers dance smoothly around a piano, dozens of balls bounce through the air, all in jewel-like colors that look painted but are computermade. That "gee whiz" attitude wears off before long, though, and we're left with 90 minutes of flying furniture and Neo-Classical sculptures that advertise products.

Because it is difficult to create computer images of humans (Max Headroom, in fact, is based on computer-enhanced videotape of a real actor), the film becomes unremittingly cute, overrun by toy cars and shiny robots. What's worse, much of "The Computer Animation Show" has tinny electronic music behind it, a careless effect that suits the movie's lopsided taste — too much technology, too little art. CARYN JAMES

1988 F 5, C14:5

Mating Rituals

SHE'S HAVING A BABY, directed, written and produced by John Hughes; director of photography, Don Peterman; music by Stewart Copeland; production designer, John Corso; released by Paramount Pictures. At Guild 50th Street, 33 West 50th Street; Paramount, 61st Street and Broadway; New York Twin, Second Avenue and 66th Street; 34th Street Showplace, between Second and Third Avenues. Running time: 106 minutes. This film is rated PG-13.

Jake Briggs .... Kevin Bacon
Kristy Briggs .... Elizabeth McGovern
Russ Bainbridge .... William Windom
Jim Briggs .... James Ray
Sarah Briggs .... Holland Taylor

FOR John Hughes's Ferris Bueller, it was only a day off; for his Jefferson (Jake) Briggs, it may be an entire life. In the first scene of "She's Having a Baby," which opens today at the Paramount and other theaters, Jake is seen marrying a woman he can barely stand, and this is only the beginning of his half-heartedness and disenchantment. He takes a dismal job in advertising. He moves to a sterile suburb. He winces at his wife's cooking. Jake seems bored with his entire existence, and as such he may be an even less sympathetic character than his teen-age antecedent.

"She's Having a Baby" is supposed to be about how Jake changes, but there's nothing in the first 98 percent of the film to indicate he's even capable of that. This character is shallow, smug and lazy, which is not to say Mr. Hughes can't make such qualities amusing; in the past, he has. But in this film's case, misanthropy in general and misogyny in particular are greater problems. Even when Jake, imagining his wife at death's door, is finally prompted to have some nice thoughts about her, there's no changing the fact that he hates his house,

Joyce Rudolph

Maturing Elizabeth McGovern and Kevin Bacon star in John Hughes's comedy "She's Having a Baby," about a newlywed couple confronting adult responsibilities.

neighbors, job, in-laws and everything else about his life.

•

Kevin Bacon is likable even when Jake is not, which is most of the time. But Elizabeth McGovern has a dreadful role that seems fatuous even by the standards of the 1950's, which is where this film's sense of social satire lies. (There is actually a fantasy sequence in which men with lawnmowers and women carrying trays of drinks do a little mock-suburban dance around the lawn sprinklers.) As Jake's wife, Kristy, Miss McGovern is made to seem a sexless, listless drone, an embodiment of domesticity at its most life-denying. However, while the film throws other women at Jake (most notably a fantasy creature with a European accent), it doesn't have the nerve to give him any more libido than his wife has.

Aiming at a target as easy as suburban sterility, "She's Having a Baby" might be expected to hit its mark every now and then. But the film's mood is simply too sour, despite the best efforts of a cast filled with appealing actors, a number of whom have had walk-ons in other Hughes efforts. Another modest plus is the pop-music soundtrack, which is as lighthearted as the comedy is leaden. When Jake and his wife have fertility problems and Kristy insists they take a more scientific approach to sex, Sam Cooke's "Chain Gang" is heard in the background.

•

"She's Having a Baby" is rated PG-13 ("Special Parental Guidance Suggested for Those Younger Than 13"). It includes some sexual references and strong language.
JANET MASLIN

1988 F 5, C18:1

Hard-Boiled Gumshoe

COP, directed by James B. Harris; screenplay by Mr. Harris, based on the novel "Blood on the Moon" by James Ellroy; director of photography, Steve Dubin; edited

by Anthony Spano; music by Michel Colombier; produced by Mr. Harris and James Woods; released by Atlantic Releasing Corporation. At Astor Plaza, Broadway and 44th Street; Gemini Twin, 64th Street and Second Avenue; Orpheum Twin, 86th Street near Third Avenue; Coliseum Twin, Broadway and 181st Street; Movie Center 5, 125th Street between Powell and Douglass Boulevards. Running time: 105 minutes. This film is rated R.

Lloyd Hopkins .... James Woods
Kathleen McCarthy .... Lesley Ann Warren
Dutch .... Charles Durning
Whitey Haines .... Charles Haid
Gaffney .... Raymond J. Barry
Joanie .... Randi Brooks
Bobby Franco .... Steven Lambert

JAMES WOODS is more frequently seen eating on-camera than just about any other actor, but he's so edgy and thin that there's nothing voluptuous about this behavior. If anything, it's borderline rude. So are Mr. Woods's smoking and his wisecracking; so is virtually everything else he does. Combine this taunting manner with the fierce, obsessive dedication Mr. Woods brings to almost any role and you have the makings of a perfect Elmore Leonard character, which Mr. Woods is bound to play some day. In the meantime, he has arrived as the detective hero of "Cop," based on James Ellroy's crime novel "Blood on the Moon."

In "Cop," which opens today at Loews Astor Plaza and other theaters, Mr. Woods plays the extremely hard-boiled Detective Sgt. Lloyd Hopkins, who is led by the long arm of coincidence onto the trail of a mass murderer. The character is a reasonable embodiment of certain detective-movie conventions, but the plot leaves a lot to be desired, especially since it devotes no more than 30 seconds' thought to the killer's motive or his history.

Instead, it throws in such rogue elements as a feminist poet who keeps pressed flowers sent by an imagined Mr. Right, and a corrupt policeman who deals in drugs and male hustlers. The film's unlikeliest moment comes when Hopkins, suspecting that this may be a mass-murder case, covers a table with photographs of various women who have been killed in the Los Angeles area. However did the police department find professional-looking 8-by-10 glossies of each one of these women, taken while they were *alive?*

•

"Cop" has some genuinely frightening moments early in its story, mostly when Mr. Woods attempts to play a family man who calls his little daughter "Penguin." Fortunately, his

James Woods

wife and child quickly take off for parts unknown, since this is one actor who should avoid kindly, fatherly gestures. For the rest of the story, his chief companion is Charles Durning, refreshingly droll as a fellow officer who marvels as much at Hopkins's ladykilling tactics as at his detective methods. The plot makes a crazy attempt to present Hopkins as a feminist — he has a horrible speech lamenting the lost innocence of the various streetwalkers and female crime victims he has encountered — but it spends even more time working cheesecake characters into the crime investigation. Lesley Ann Warren, who makes a remarkably slinky feminist poet, manages to be charming in an idiotic role.

For the most part, James B. Harris's direction is workmanlike and somewhat flat, but there are nice moments; one is the credit sequence, in which the off-screen voice of a man attempting to report a murder becomes unexpectedly funny as he encounters police-station bureaucracy. The film ends on a sharp note, too. Far and away the best thing about it is Mr. Woods, who served as co-producer and demonstrates a clear understanding of what makes great movie detectives great. Even in less-than-sparkling surroundings, he can talk tough with the best of them.
JANET MASLIN

1988 F 5, C19:3

FILM VIEW/Vincent Canby

Filming Childhood Isn't Kid Stuff

TOWARD THE END OF STEVEN Spielberg's "Empire of the Sun," there's a haunting sequence in which 13-year-old Jim Graham (Christian Bale), who has survived four years in a Japanese prisoner-of-war camp outside Shanghai, witnesses the first American air raid on the adjacent Japanese airfield.

Jim, the once-proper English schoolboy turned into P.O.W.-camp hustler, becomes hysterical with excitement, as well as torn by contradictory impulses. The raid means eventual liberation. Yet it's destroying the airfield that he and the other prisoners helped to build.

The dazzling spectacle of the raid is beyond anything he's ever imagined. A drab, day-by-day existence has magically become as full of possibilities as a dream. The bombs are real. The explosions and flames are of astonishing beauty. Jim can feel the heat and smell the exhaust of the attacking planes. Beside himself with awe, he runs back and forth across the top of a camp tower screaming encouragement, his feelings out of control and dislocated somewhere between infancy and ancient age.

In the thick of the raid, the camp's English doctor rushes up to the platform to retrieve the boy. Jim at first fights him off, then collapses, bewildered. His mind makes a 180-degree turn: he can't remember what his mother looks like, though he knows she has dark hair and that they were once planning to write a book on contract bridge.

"Empire of the Sun" is a grand adventure movie. It's also the best film ever made

'Empire of the Sun' is the best film ever made about childhood by a director born and bred in this country.

about childhood by a director born and bred in this country, where movie makers tend to take a safely revisionist view of childhood, one that's limited by expectations of what audiences want to believe about themselves.

In the work of Christian Bale, the English actor who ages from 9 to 13 in the course of the story, "Empire of the Sun" has a performance that sets the standard of achievement for this season's exceptionally ambitious group of performances by children.

These include Anton Glanzelius, 11, in Lasse Hallström's "My Life as a Dog"; the teen-age Gaspard Manesse and Rafael Fejto in Louis Malle's "Au Revoir les Enfants" (opening this week); Antoine Hubert, 9, and Vanessa Guedj (a worldly 10) in Jean-Loup Hubert's "Grand Highway"; Sebastian Rice Edwards, who's slightly older, in John Boorman's "Hope and Glory," and Lyndon Davies, who plays the 10-year-old Philip Marlow in Dennis Potter's splendid English miniseries, "The Singing Detective," directed by Jon Amiel.

I call these appearances "performances." However, I'm not at all sure that what we see these children do can be compared to the work of adult actors whose performances are the expression of their training and of their experiences, both as working actors and as veterans of the world they inhabit. (It may also be that, as an adult, I resist the uncomfortable thought that any child could have lived enough to be able to call up, and to put together, the kinds of sometimes harrowing associations that go into the work of older actors.)

In a recent interview with a New York Times reporter, Mr. Spielberg said that although "Empire of the Sun" was one of the most complicated movies he'd ever done, it was also one of his most efficient. The reason: Mr. Bale, who's in virtually every scene,

was inclined always to do his best work in the first take, and to grow increasingly artificial as the takes were repeated. Though Mr. Bale has had some training as an actor, the director relied less on the boy's conception of the role than on his ability to imitate the performance initially acted out by Mr. Spielberg.

∎

This doesn't underrate the child's contribution, including his intelligence, wit, looks and natural mannerisms, but it does explain why a handful of directors consistently obtain better, richer performances from children than do other directors.

Unlike the people responsible for the exuberantly cute performances that made stars of Gary Coleman, Ricky Schroder, Margaret O'Brien and (queen of them all) Shirley Temple, Mr. Spielberg, Mr. Malle and two or three other directors working today seek not to impose an alien, adult sensibility on the child. Instead, they somehow release the child's own sensibility in a way that works within the context of the script.

In the history of movies, the best, most memorable recollections of childhood have been evoked by children either who made their marks in one or two films (Henry Thomas of "E.T.," Bobby Henrey of "The Fallen Idol") or who quickly graduated to careers as adult actors (Elizabeth Taylor, Mickey Rooney, Judy Garland, Roddy McDowall).

The most obvious exception: Jean-Pierre Léaud, who grew up over a period of years onscreen in François Truffaut's series of autobiographical Antoine Doinel films, but whose adult performances have never had the dimension of those he did for Truffaut.

How children are portrayed in the movies we see depends as much on fashion and economics as it does on the abilities of directors and the malleability of the available children. I'm not talking about infants, who will always be in demand as props for use in movies about self-absorbed adults ("Three Men and a Baby," "Baby Boom," "Raising Arizona"). I'm talking about children pushing their way through the uncertain, often painful years from 5 to 15, give or take a year on either side. Television sitcoms see them as wisecracking, lovingly impertinent pseudo-adults. This vision pleases older audiences and gives younger audiences hip role models to follow. Theatrical films, like John Hughes's "Pretty in Pink" and "Ferris Buehler's Day Off," do their best to give back to the members of the teen-age audience the images they have of themselves, which, when the images are troubled, is quickly explained by the thoughtless behavior of the only vaguely seen adults.

Honest, less predictable visions of childhood are hard to sell to mass audiences (and thus not easily financed), as well as more difficult to make. They're the work of poets, not of journeymen contractors.

Childhood is rather like pain. It's easier to remember having gone through it than it is to relive the actual pain itself.

In retrospect, childhood becomes shapely, a series of neat causes and effects. In memory, the initially perceived chaos achieves order. Only a handful of movie makers have been able to reconstruct this period of change, growth and chaos with something approximating the original emotional impact. (Also, since most movie directors are men, most recollections are of boyhoods, in which girls play subsidiary roles.)

More than any other film maker,

Truffaut understood the concept of time held by children, for whom (as in his chef d'oeuvre, "Small Change") life is an unending present, without a past or a future until some extraordinary event. This is also understood by "My Life as a Dog" and "The Grand Highway," though both films impose a soothing, hindsight prettiness on the events recalled, which, in turn, is reflected to some extent in the performances of the child actors.

In "Hope and Glory," Mr. Boorman remembers his childhood in wartime England by imposing on his young surrogate hero a sense of adventure and innocence, which often seems as essentially sentimental as it is bogus. It's something perceived after the fact by the poet taking the awfully intrusive, long view.

∎

Mr. Malle does not take long views without being perfectly aware of what he's up to, nor does he pass them off as something else. His "Murmur of the Heart" is a romantic comedy about incest, culminating in the therapeutic, satisfying, one-night stand of a teen-age boy and his ravishing mother. In "Lacombe, Lucien" Mr. Malle tells the sorrowful tale of an ordinary, none-too-bright French farm boy who becomes a Nazi collaborator. "Pretty Baby," featuring the 12-year-old Brooke Shields in what's still her best film performance, deals with child prostitution.

In "Au Revoir les Enfants," the French director is remembering — after 40 years of introspection — a traumatic childhood event that never for a minute pretends to be the event exactly as it happened, but the event as the adult recalls it in an attempt to make sense of it. In the performances of his two young leading actors, Mr. Manesse and Mr. Fejto, there's a fine, merciless economy that perfectly serves the needs of the screenplay.

More than any other film maker at work in this country today, Mr. Spielberg appears to share Truffaut's un-

Only a handful of directors try to avoid imposing an alien, adult sensibility on child actors.

derstanding of childhood, though it's manifest in a series of mass-market entertainments that Truffaut could appreciate without ever imitating. The remarkable performances by Cary Guffey in "Close Encounters of the Third Kind," and by Henry Thomas and Drew Barrymore in "E.T.," were just trailers for Christian Bale's in "Empire of the Sun." Mr. Spielberg has pulled off a very American coup. He's made a $35 million adventure film that has the freshness and poignancy of something made in black and white, on a shoestring, in somebody's borrowed backyard.   □

1988 F 7, II:21:1

Fear of Sinking

CRAZY MOON, directed by Allan Eastman; written by Tom Berry and Stefan Wodoslawsky; director of photography, Savas Kalogeras; edited by Franco Battista; music by Lou Forestieri; art director, Guy Lalande; produced by Mr. Berry and Mr. Wodoslawsky; presented by Miramax Films, at the Festival, 6 West 57th Street. Running time: 90 minutes. This film is rated PG-13.

Brooks	Kiefer Sutherland
Anne	Vanessa Vaughan
Cleveland	Peter Spence
Alec	Ken Pogue
Mimi	Eve Napier
Anne's father	Sean McCann
Anne's mother	Bronwen Mantel

By CARYN JAMES

THE Festival Theater probably did not intend to have a mini-Kiefer Sutherland series. But after "Promised Land," the new coming-of-age-in-Utah film featuring the actor, last Friday it brought in "Crazy Moon," a 1986 Canadian movie in which he stars. You can't blame Mr. Sutherland for the lameness of either one. In fact, he and his co-star, Vanessa Vaughan, save "Crazy Moon" from its own worst tendencies. It keeps threatening to become "Children of a Lesser God Goes to High School."

Mr. Sutherland plays Brooks, a rebel who wears bow ties and listens to Tommy Dorsey music, who begs for attention by escaping into the big-band era. When he falls in love with a young deaf woman named Anne — here comes the plot twist that turns a script into a bad joke — she helps him overcome his fear of water and learn how to swim.

The movie, with its teach-a-lesson tone, reeks of simplistic psychology. Brooks lives in fantasyland because his rich father neglects him. Anne, who knows only sign language, learns how to speak in order to please him, and becomes independent enough to take off on her own.

●

But it's those swimming lessons that make the story ludicrous. We're meant to see that everyone is somehow handicapped, and with a little pluck can accomplish anything. Yet that pep-talking attitude glosses over the difference between learning to swim — no matter how deep Brooks's fears — and adjusting as a deaf person in a hearing world. It diminishes the problems of both characters, and cheapens the film's message.

Ms. Vaughan, who is deaf in real life, acts defiantly against this dreadful script, and gives Anne remarkable composure; she is the most level-headed, engaging character. Mr. Sutherland does some goofy turns when Brooks rides out of the past to pursue Anne in a motorcycle with a sidecar. But he is more convincing after he trades in his bow tie for a T-shirt.

The actors can't save the film from its lack of style, though. A movie that relies on the aura of the 30's and 40's should not put supermarket music next to "Blue Moon." If "Crazy Moon" is a little less laughable than it might have been, it is still a lot less moving than it intends.

●

"Crazy Moon" is rated PG-13 (Special Parental Guidance Suggested for Those Younger Than 13). There is some drug use and some blunt tips on seduction.

1988 F 8, C18:5

Hunter Sidney Poitier portrays an F.B.I. agent in "Shoot to Kill" whose pursuit of a ruthless murderer bound for Canada takes him into mountain wilderness.

Into the Woods

SHOOT TO KILL, directed by Roger Spottiswoode; screenplay by Harv Zimmel, Michael Burton and Daniel Petrie Jr.; story by Mr. Zimmel; director of photography, Michael Chapman; edited by Garth Craven and George Bowers; music by John Scott; production designer, Richard Sylbert; produced by Ron Silverman and Mr. Petrie; released by Touchstone Pictures. At Embassy 1, Broadway and 46th Street; Regency, Broadway and 67th Street; 23d Street West Triplex, near Eighth Avenue; D. W. Griffith, 235 East 59th Street; Coliseum, 181st Street and Broadway; Movie Center 5, 125th Street, between Powell and Douglass Boulevards. Running time: 106 minutes. This film is rated R.

Warren Stantin	Sidney Poitier
Jonathan Knox	Tom Berenger
Sarah	Kirstie Alley
Steve	Clancy Brown
Norman	Richard Masur
Harvey	Andrew Robinson
Ben	Kevin Scannell
Ralph	Frederick Coffin

By JANET MASLIN

IN the cool green mountains of the Pacific Northwest, a red-hot thriller unfolds. It's "Shoot to Kill," a film that marks the return of Sidney Poitier after a long absence from the screen, and a reappearance of good old-fashioned storytelling technique as well. This is essentially a formula film, and as such it's nothing fancy. But it has crisp, spare direction, enormous momentum and a story full of twists and turns. For anyone who thinks they don't make spine-tingling detective films the way they used to, good news: they've just made another.

"Shoot to Kill," which opens today at the Regency and other theaters, has beautiful scenery and a beauty of a gimmick, too. It begins with the attention-getting sight of a man in pajamas, bathrobe and house slippers racing into a San Francisco office building in the middle of the night. The man hastily scoops up two pounds of uncut diamonds and stuffs them into a bag, just before the police arrive. It develops that this man is a jeweler, that he is being blackmailed and that a vicious kidnapper is holding his wife hostage in their home. It's at this point that an F.B.I. agent, Warren Stantin (Mr. Poitier), a man of automatic and effortless authority, appears on the scene.

A tense, murderous confrontation ensues at the house, and the kidnapper — whose face we still have not seen — manages to escape. He finds a car and drives north, heading for the Canadian border. But he stops in the woods, and crosses paths with a tourist on a fishing trip. And so it happens that a group of five nice-guy fishermen and their plucky guide (Kirstie Alley), first seen singing "99 Bottles of Beer on the Wall," accidentally includes one crazed killer on the lam.

●

It's up to the audience to guess which one he might be, and the director, Roger Spottiswoode, doesn't make it easy. The five fishermen are particularly well cast, among them Richard Masur and Andrew Robinson (the latter's performance as the homicidal lunatic in "Dirty Harry" will forever make him a terrifying fellow). Mr. Robinson's presence is not the only echo of "Dirty Harry" in "Shoot to Kill," since something like that film's brisk, suspenseful manner is also evident here. So is its sense of an extended chase, as Stantin and a guide named Jonathan Knox (Tom Berenger) track the imperiled fishing party through the woods. It's only minimally troublesome that the plot has a couple of notable holes, or that the lethal-fisherman gambit is abandoned earlier than it might have been.

The kind of hostility and humor that arise between these ill-matched camping partners ("Ain't no elevators out here, Mister," the woodsman snarls upon meeting the city slicker) are easily anticipated. But Mr. Spottiswoode and the screenwriters (Harv Zimmel, Michael Burton and Daniel Petrie Jr.) make them fun anyhow. Of course, there's a scene with a moose and another with a bear; of course, there's a moment when Stantin is horrified to learn what Knox has cooked for dinner. (Roasted marmot.) These bits of levity are nicely mixed with the film's more heart-stopping episodes, like a sequence about crossing a very steep gorge on a very small handcar, supported by very unreliable-looking ropes.

●

Mr. Spottiswoode, who displayed a comparably electrifying style in his very different "Under Fire," eventually cuts to the chase — in this case, a brief car chase that comes very late in the story. It's the first real sign of ordinariness in an otherwise inventive film, so its conspicuousness is almost a backhanded compliment. But for the most part, Mr. Spottiswoode avoids the familiar and keeps this story exciting and fresh. He is greatly helped by the bracing outdoor look of Michael Chapman's cinematography, by the screenplay's taste for variety, and by John Scott's highly effective score.

Mr. Berenger, satisfyingly gruff, gets better with every new performance, and Miss Alley makes a smart, feisty heroine. But the main attraction is Mr. Poitier, still an actor who conveys immense star quality without resorting to much small talk. In fact, the whole film wastes very little time on idle conversation, preferring to define its characters through action. It does this simply, briskly and very well.

1988 F 12, C8:5

Love in Bloom Ann-Margret stars in "A Tiger's Tale," about a high-school senior and his girlfriend's mother.

Mother Love

A TIGER'S TALE, directed and produced by Peter Douglas; screenplay by Mr. Douglas, based on the book "Love and Other Natural Disasters" by Allen Hannay 3d; director of photography, Tony Pierce-Roberts; music by Lee Holdridge; production designer, Shay Austin; released by Atlantic Releasing Corporation. At 84th Street Six, at Broadway. Running time: 97 minutes. This film is rated R.

Rose	Ann-Margret
Bubber	C. Thomas Howell
Charlie	Charles Durning
Shirley	Kelly Preston
Claudine	Ann Wedgeworth
La Vonne	Angel Tompkins
Randy	William Zabka
Lonny	Tim Thomerson
Dr. Shorts	Steven Kampmann
Penny	Traci Lin

ORDINARILY you can tell a lot about a film from the names of its characters, and the principals in "A Tiger's Tale" include Rose Butts (Ann-Margret), Shirley Butts (Kelly Preston), Bubber Drumm (C. Thomas Howell), La Vonne (Angel Tompkins) and Claudine (Ann Wedgeworth). To be fair, this film, written, produced and directed by Peter Douglas (from a novel by Allen Hannay 3d), is a little better than that, but it does place excessive stock in rustic quirks and cracker-barrel humor. It's a romance, after all, in which the young hero declares to his older sweetheart that he's "stuck on you like a tick."

As the younger man who falls in love with his girlfriend's mother, Mr. Howell spends most of his time addressing Ann-Margret as "Ma'am," and fending off the pet tiger and several pet snakes that provide local color. Bubber is an aspiring veterinarian, and in one scene Mr. Howell tussles all too realistically with the tiger he keeps in his backyard. "How many armadillos you give him last night?" asks Charles Durning, wonderfully unflappable as Bubber's father. Two, Mr. Howell replies. "He was my tiger, I'd start givin' him four," Mr. Durning says.

Once Bubber meets Rose, who is a considerable eccentric in her own right (she likes to dress up and eat chop suey on her weekly Oriental nights), the film develops a little momentum but not much chemistry.

That Ann-Margret's knowing, voluptuous Rose might find herself in the arms of the young vet-to-be is difficult to believe; that he'd want her to, on the other hand, is easy. Ann-Margret may not be the American Jeanne Moreau, but she becomes an ever more stunning exemplar of the older woman's sexual magnetism as time goes by.

"A Tiger's Tale," which opens today at Loews 84th Street Six, is most notable for what it doesn't have: a heavy hand. The material has more than enough potential to become painfully silly, and Mr. Douglas's biggest accomplishment is making sure that doesn't happen. *JANET MASLIN*

1988 F 12, C9:1

Affair of the Heart

TRAVELING NORTH, directed by Carl Schultz; written by David Williamson, based on his play; director of photography, Julian Penney; edited by Henry Dangar; production designer, Owen Paterson; produced by Ben Gannon; released by Cineplex Odeon Films Inc. At Plaza, 58th Street, east of Madison Avenue. Running time: 98 minutes. This film is rated PG-13.

Frank	Leo McKern
Frances	Julia Blake
Freddie	Graham Kennedy
Saul	Henri Szeps
Helen	Michele Fawdon
Sophie	Diane Craig

"**T**RAVELING NORTH," opening today at the Plaza Theater, is a modest, essentially dreary Australian movie made bearable by the robust performance by Leo McKern in the star part.

Mr. McKern plays Frank, a widower and former Communist who, though he has long since left the party, still takes a radical line, mostly to disconcert his conventional associates. On his retirement as a construction engineer in Melbourne, he moves to Australia's tropical north in the company of Frances, a patrician, somewhat younger woman whose two grown daughters (Frank refers to them as Goneril and Regan) think she's making a big mistake.

As written by David Williamson, who adapted his own play for the screen, and as played by Julie Blake, Frances is rather a prig. She loves Frank though she quickly gets bored fishing with him and making do with a limited number of friends in the de facto retirement community. She's also remarkably unobservant about Frank.

•

At the very beginning of the movie, Frank has suffered a mild heart seizure that haunts every subsequent scene. It's not a question of what's going to happen but when. The film is halfway over, and Frank is huffing and puffing and looking pained with some frequency, before Frances is moved to ask, "Frank, what *is* the matter with you?"

"Traveling North" features the sort of dialogue that comes alive only when it is being bitchy, as when Frank hears that Frances's daughter and son-in-law have named their baby Tarquin. "Don't those idiots know who Tarquin was?" says Frank. "A Roman despot who raped everything in sight." It may not be Noël Coward, but in this context it sounds like wit.

Mr. Williamson's screenplay and the direction by Carl Schultz ("Careful, He Might Hear You") are full of decent sentiments without ever being surprising or especially moving.

•

"Traveling North," which has been rated PG-13 ("Special Parental Guidance Suggested for Those Younger Than 13"), contains some vulgar dialogue. *VINCENT CANBY*

1988 F 12, C10:1

Crash and Burn

ACTION JACKSON, directed by Craig R. Baxley; written by Robert Reneau; director of photography, Matthew F. Leonetti; edited by Mark Helfrich; music by Herbie Hancock with Michael Kamen; art director, Virginia Randolph; produced by Joel Silver; released by Lorimar Film Entertainment. At National Twin, Broadway and 44th Street; Orpheum Twin, 86th Street near Third Avenue; 34th Street East, at Second Avenue; Metro Twin, Broadway and 99th Street; Coliseum Twin, Broadway and 181st Street; Movie Center 5, 125th Street between Powell and Douglass Boulevards; Nova Theater, 147th Street and Broadway. Running time: 93 minutes. This film is rated R.

Action Jackson	Carl Weathers
Peter Dellaplane	Craig T. Nelson
Sydney Ash	Vanity
Patrice Dellaplane	Sharon Stone
Officer Kornblau	Thomas F. Wilson

"**A**CTION JACKSON" is named for a Detroit cop who is slow to take offense but when he does, gets out of the way. Played by Carl Weathers, a member of the highly-developed-upper-torso school of movie hero, he is after a power-mad automobile executive skilled in karate whose henchmen are killing off the leadership of the auto union. So much for redeeming social content. Sergeant Jackson has a degree from Harvard Law School, but he doesn't flaunt it; his snappy repartee comes straight from a junior high school locker room. Crashing through are several raffish characters whose acting doesn't get in the way of the stunts.

•

Like lots of kindred movies, "Action Jackson," which opens today at the National Twin and other theaters, is about shattered glass and fiery explosions. There may be a few more car bodies sent to the junk heap than usual, but, then, this is Detroit. The most visually compelling body belongs to Vanity, who plays a singer ("Can you kiss me?/Baby undress me"). She moves like grease in skirts that seem glued to her hips, which gives a person something to think about. *WALTER GOODMAN*

1988 F 12, C10:1

SCHOOL DAZE, directed, written and produced by Spike Lee; photographed by Ernest Dickerson; edited by Barry Alexander Brown; music by Bill Lee; production design by Wynn Thomas; released by Columbia Pictures. At Criterion Center, Broadway near 44th Street; 86th Street East, near Second Avenue; Quad Cinema, 34 West 13th Street; Columbia Cinema, Broadway at 103d Street; Movie Center 5, 125th Street near Douglass Boulevard. Running time: 120 minutes. This film is rated R.

Dap Dunlap	Larry Fishburne
Half-Pint	Spike Lee
Julian Eaves	Giancarlo Esposito
Jane Toussaint	Tisha Campbell
Rachel Meadows	Kyme

"**F**ROM the intimate, funny sexual battleground on which Spike Lee's "She's Gotta Have It" unfolded, Mr. Lee

On Campus Spike Lee wrote, directed and stars in "School Daze."

has moved on to bigger, bolder and messier ambitions. The new occasion is "School Daze," his scathing look at a fictitious white-financed, all-black college whose motto is "Uplift the Race."

This, in Mr. Lee's mind, is a place whose population is sharply divided: for every light-skinned, affluent sorority girl affecting blue contact lenses, there's a darker-skinned, poorer, less artificially coiffed classmate who bitterly resents such aspirations. The film labels these factions "wannabees" (as in "wanna be better than me") and, to give some indication of its level of malice, "jigaboos."

However, neither this anger nor Mr. Lee's daring is ever given free rein. Instead of a sharp satire or even an "Animal House" variation (since fraternity life is central to its story), "School Daze" is a collection of musical numbers, dramatic episodes, attempts at parody and cinematic wild cards, bound together only loosely by Mr. Lee's prevailing sense of outrage. This mixture would work better if an overall mood emerged more clearly, but the incisiveness comes and goes. For every tough-minded confrontation between the different student factions, "School Daze" is apt to offer a love scene less than vital to the plot, or an overlong musical scene whose effect is that of treading water.

•

"School Daze," which opens today at the Criterion Center and other theaters, is still the work of a brave, original and prodigious talent. And Mr. Lee remains his own best asset, this time appearing in the role of Half-Pint, a fraternity pledge who's had his head shaved and is subjected to numerous petty humiliations during the course of the story, all for the sake of fitting in. This seems particularly absurd and sophomoric to his older cousin Dap Dunlap (Larry Fishburne), who functions less as a character than as the film's conscience. It is Dap who demands that his classmates help force Mission College to divest itself of business interests in South Africa, even while they pay more attention to fraternity floats in the Homecoming parade.

Mr. Lee also invents a character named Julian (Giancarlo Esposito), who insists on being called "Big Brother Almighty" by his troops at

Gamma Phi Gamma, and who has a pronounced taste for the paramilitary, wearing black jodhpurs and swinging a billy club as he interrogates the pledges. Julian, who knows and cares nothing about events outside the Gamma universe, and Dap come to represent different polarities of black consciousness, with poor little Half-Pint caught between them. The film's greatest dramatic potential can be found here, but Mr. Lee never takes it very far. Instead, he's constantly playing the cut-up, switching to more lightweight material whenever tensions arise.

•

The film's mischievousness doesn't sting the way it should. When Mr. Lee sets the Gamma Rays — the frat boys' upwardly mobile girlfriends, who worry about things like bake sales — against the friends of Dap's girlfriend Rachel (Kyme) in a musical number about their rivalry, the two groups are choreographed much too similarly to suit the song's hostile tone; what's worse, their lyrics are sometimes unintelligible, and the number goes on much too long. Like the film's other musical sequences, this one is less barbed than it initially looks, and plays more like pointless entertainment than anything else. When Julian's girlfriend Jane (Tisha Campbell) and her friends pour on tight dresses and sing "I want you to know I'm not just for show," they aren't noticeably sending up Supremes-type singers. They're only imitating them, and not all that well.

The bravest parts of "School Daze" are those that pinpoint the uneasiness at its heart. When Dap and his friends go to a downtown fast-food restaurant and have an unfriendly encounter with a group of locals, for instance, they're face to face with an uncomfortable truth: the downtown blacks don't see them as apartheid-fighting crusaders, only as privileged college boys. Dap and his friends discuss this soberly on part of the drive home, but soon they're talking girls and school and fraternities all over again. And they're off the hook.

JANET MASLIN

1988 F 12, C11:1

Political Irony

LOS AMBICIOSOS, directed by Luis Buñuel; screenplay (Spanish with English subtitles) by Mr. Buñuel, Luis Alcoriza and Luis Sapin; director of photography, Gabriel Figueroa; edited by Rafael Ceballos; music by Paul Misrachi; produced by Raymond Borderie and Cinematografia Filmex S.A. Films Borderie. At the Public, 425 Lafayette Street. Running time: 97 minutes. This film has no rating.

Inés Vargas	María Félix
Ramón Vásquez	Gérard Philipe
Alejandro Gual	Jean Servais
Indarte	Víctor Junco
Colonel Olivares	Roberto Canedo
Carlos Barreiro	Andres Soler
Juan Cárdenas	Domingo Soler
López	Luis Aceves Castaneda

"**L**UIS BUNUEL said that "Los Ambiciosos" ("The Ambitious Ones"), also known as "La Fièvre Monte à el Pao," was not a good film, and he was right.

The French-Mexican co-production is about the futility of compromise, and is itself a demonstration of the kind of compromises that often beset big-budget, big-star co-productions. The movie was made in Mexico in 1959, just after "Nazarin" (1958) and

Gérard Philipe

just before "Viridiana" (1961), which marked the start of the master's late golden age that was to include "Tristana" and "The Discreet Charm of the Bourgeoisie."

"Los Ambiciosos" opens today at the Public Theater.

The movie is most notable in that it stars Gérard Philipe, speaking not-great dubbed Spanish (in what was to be his last screen performance before his death), playing opposite María Félix, the voluptuous, hugely popular Mexican actress.

•

In addition to Buñuel, three other writers (Luis Alcoriza, Luis Sapin and Charles Dorat) are credited with the screenplay. This may explain why "Los Ambiciosos" has such a busy though not especially complex narrative line.

The movie is one of Buñuel's most forthrightly political works, being about a young idealist (Mr. Philipe) who joins the staff of a notorious dictator in an attempt to humanize fascism from the inside. The outcome is inevitable, though, left to his own devices, Buñuel probably would not have given as much space to the idealist's love life as he gives to the man's moral confusion.

The setting is a fictitious South American country that stands in for Franco's Spain. Buñuel's ironies are pretty much overwhelmed by plot and by the uncharacteristically elaborate physical production. Always suspicious of spectacle, Buñuel much preferred to work on a small scale.

This is not vintage Buñuel, but Mr. Philipe is unexpectedly good as the muddled idealist. Miss Félix, a great Latin beauty, also does very well, her tendency to overstate emotion having been kept in check by the sly genius behind the camera.

VINCENT CANBY

1988 F 12, C13:1

Feminist Riddle

THE GOLD DIGGERS, directed and edited by Sally Potter; written by Lindsay Cooper, Rose English and Miss Potter; music by Lindsay Cooper; art director, Miss English; produced by Nita Amy and Donna Grey; released by Women Make Movies. At Thalia SoHo, 15 Vandam Street. Running time: 90 minutes. This film has no rating.

Ruby	Julie Christie
Celeste	Colette Laffont
Ruby's Mother	Hilary Westlake
Expert	David Gale
Expert's Assistant	Tom Osborn
Tap Dancer	Jacky Lansley

THERE are critics in Britain who have praised Sally Potter's "Gold Diggers" as "witty," "visually entrancing" and "an absorbing pleasure," and there may also be like-minded individuals on the planet Jupiter. But by any reasonable earthly standard, this thing — a 1983 oddity, sort of a feminist, deconstructionist, riddle-filled anti-musical, much of it set on the Icelandic tundra — is pure torture. Its only noteworthy attribute is the presence of Julie Christie, who embodies some sardonic notion of the archetypical unenlightened movie heroine through the ages. Like it or not, Miss Christie is infinitely better off playing such creatures straight than she is satirizing them here.

•

"The Gold Diggers," which opens today at the Thalia SoHo, begins with a black woman (Colette Laffont) and a white one (Miss Christie) outlining a vexing riddle ("Only in the darkness am I visible. You can see me but never touch me. I can speak to you but never hear you . . . who am I?"). One of them then maintains that since there are only 90 minutes to find an answer, "Time is short." This is laughable, under the circumstances. The camera goes on to explore a plotless configuration of bare Arctic landscapes, mock silent-movie scenes and caricatures of masculine behavior, and never has the clock moved more slowly. There is also about a 15-minute encounter between Miss Christie and a tap-dancing mime.

As for wit, "The Gold Diggers" does include a scene of male bearers carrying an iconographic woman in a sedan chair upon their shoulders. This is not a conscious allusion to Woody Allen's crucifix-parking dream sequence, but perhaps it should have been.

JANET MASLIN

1988 F 12, C22:1

Chagrin et Pitié

AU REVOIR LES ENFANTS, written, produced and directed by Louis Malle (in French with English subtitles); cinematography by Renato Berta; edited by Emmanuelle Castro; music by Schubert and Saint-Saëns; a French-German co-production: Nouvelles Editions de Films/M. K. 2. Productions/Stella Film GmbH/N. E. F. GmbH; released by Orion Classics. At Cinema 1, Third Avenue and 60th Street. Running time: 103 minutes. This film is rated PG.

Julien Quentin	Gaspard Manesse
Jean Bonnet	Raphaël Fejtö
Mme. Quentin	Francine Racette
François Quentin	Stanislas Carré de Malberg
Father Jean	Philippe Morier-Genoud
Father Michel	François Berléand
Joseph	François Négret
Muller	Peter Fitz
Boulanger	Pascal Rivet

By VINCENT CANBY

LOUIS MALLE'S "Au Revoir les Enfants" ("Goodbye, Children") is based on an event that took place during January 1944, when the French writer and director, then 12 years old, was attending a Jesuit boarding school near Fontainebleau. At the end of the Christmas holidays, in the middle of the scholastic year, there appeared at the school three new boys, one of whom became the young Malle's chief competitor for scholastic honors and then, briefly, his best friend.

Several weeks later, this boy, as well as the two other newcomers who were also Jewish, was arrested by the Germans and, with the school's headmaster, a priest, disappeared.

It has taken Mr. Malle more than 40 years to make "Au Revoir les Enfants." He grew up, attended the Sorbonne, became an assistant to Jacques Cousteau ("Le Monde du Silence") and went on to make his own series of often exceptional fiction and documentary films ("The Lovers," "Phantom India," "Murmur of the Heart," "Human, Much Too Human," "Lacombe, Lucien" and "Atlantic City," among others).

Every film that Mr. Malle made in those intervening years has been preparation for "Au Revoir les Enfants." Like "The Dead," which it resembles in no other way, it's a work that has the kind of simplicity, ease and density of detail that only a film maker in total command of his craft can bring off, and then only rarely.

•

"Au Revoir les Enfants," which opens today at Cinema 1, is a fiction film created out of memory and made tough by a responsible journalist's conscience. It's about life during the German Occupation of France, about being a bright, curious, rather privileged child, about growing up and, perhaps most important, about the compulsive need to find meaning, if not order, through recollection.

At the beginning of the film, Julien Quentin (Gaspard Manesse) is on a Paris railroad platform saying goodbye to his pretty mother before returning to school. He clings to her and weeps like a 6-year-old, and when she points out that this parting is not, exactly, forever, he doesn't hesitate to announce — haughtily — that he detests her.

Yet she encourages his childish behavior. "I'd like to dress up like a boy and join you," she says and hugs him. "Then we could be together and nobody would know." It's a splendidly ambiguous moment, the sort that films don't often contain. It may be the first time that Julien senses the end of childhood. The last thing that a 12-year-old boy wants is a boyhood pal who's actually his mother in knee-pants.

Julien is truculent in his initial encounters with the mysterious "new boy," Jean Bonnet (Raphaël Fejtö), who's considerably taller than he is and completely self-reliant. The new boy is given the bed next to Julien's in the dormitory. He attempts to be friendly, but Julien is wary.

"I'm Julien Quentin. Don't mess with me," is all that Julien will say at first. In the classroom Julien is jealous of the ease with which Jean answers questions. He's also baffled by Jean's indifference to gross insults, threats and practical jokes, which, according to the code of adolescents, are supposed to prompt outrage.

•

Little by little, Julien's curiosity gets the better of him. The two boys, who share a passion for books, become inarticulate friends, which still doesn't stop Julien from going through his friend's locker, where he discovers the secret of Jean's identity. His real name: Jean Kippelstein. A day or two later, Jean asks his older brother, "What's a 'Yid'?"

Mr. Malle never gets in the way of this story of friendship, betrayal and guilt. It's as if it were telling itself, rather than being recalled and composed by someone outside. The film attends to the daily routine of school life much the way Julien does, without noticing the things that will seem important only later, including the presence of the much despised Joseph.

Joseph (François Négret) is the school's runty, lame young kitchen helper, who supplies the boys with cigarettes and other black-market items in return for the food the boys receive from home. Though the relationship of the naïve, impressionable Julien and the exotic, martyred Jean is the focus of the film, Joseph is the film's catalyst, as well as its conscience.

Mr. Malle treats his young actors without condescension and they, in turn, respond with performances of natural gravity and humor. Most directors seem to go wrong when they attempt to recapture the way children behave and talk with each other when adults aren't around. Children in movies tend to become far brighter and more precocious than any children ever are. They are children remembered as we wish we had been. Mr. Malle never indulges this longing.

•

"Au Revoir les Enfants" remains utterly specific, which is why it's so moving without ever being sentimental. Though the action of the film covers only a few weeks, it seems (as it might to a child) to cover a lifetime. Not until the closing credits does Mr. Malle allow himself to take the long view. Not until then does everything we've seen begin to make the sense that Mr. Malle is just now coming to terms with.

Mr. Manesse and Mr. Fejtö are fine, but Mr. Négret is especially memorable as Joseph, who is a small, rich variation on the doomed farm boy in "Lacombe, Lucien." The excellent supporting cast includes Francine Racette, as Jean's bewitching mother; Stanislas Carré de Malberg, as Julien's worldly older brother, and Philippe Morier-Genoud, as the headmaster who, in one of the film's funnier moments, lectures a church full of well-heeled parents on the difficulties that a camel faces in passing through the eye of a needle.

•

"Au Revoir les Enfants," which has been rated PG ("Parental Guidance Suggested"), contains scenes that could be emotionally troubling to very young audiences.

1988 F 12, C15:1

SATISFACTION, directed by Joan Freeman; written by Charles Purpura; director of photography, Thomas Del Ruth; edited by Joel Goodman; music by Michel Colombier; production designer, Lynda Paradise; produced by Aaron Spelling and Alan Greisman; released by Twentieth Century Fox Film Corporation. At the Criterion Center, Broadway between 44th and 45th Streets; the Gemini 2, Second Avenue at 64th Street; the U.A. East, First Avenue and 85th Street; Olympia Cinemas, Broadway and 107th Street; the 23d Street West Triplex, at Eighth Avenue. Running time: 93 minutes. This film is rated PG-13.

Jennie Lee	Justine Bateman
Martin Falcon	Liam Neeson
May "Mooch" Stark	Trini Alvarado
Nickie Longo	Scott Coffey
Billy Swan	Britta Phillips
Daryle Shane	Julia Roberts
Tina	Debbie Harry
Frankie Malloy	Chris Nash

By CARYN JAMES

"Hey, guys!" That's Justine Bateman talking down and dirty as the lead singer of a female rock group called "Mystery" that tries to be the Bangles of the working class. There is one drug-addicted guitarist, one man-

Sygma

A scene from "Au Revoir les Enfants," recounting events during World War II at a Carmelite school south of Paris.

crazy guitarist, a thieving drummer and a token male keyboard player — a last-minute replacement who switches from Chopin to rock in a day. Only in Hollywood.

The members of this tough girl group might have been raised in Beverly Hills. As Jennie Lee, Ms. Bateman's singing is so distant from any human voice that the sound engineers must have been the busiest people on the film. And even though the band never plays one song from the 1980's (except a hokey ballad about leaves talking to trees, written for the movie) they get a summer-long gig at a beach resort.

There, they meet law students in madras pants, whose nerdy sense of fashion is not meant to extend to their taste in music, but I wonder. They do like it when the band sings, with all the energy of sleepwalkers, "Mr. Big Stuff/Who do you think you are?" Jennie Lee has a fling with a depressed older songwriter, who perks up long enough to write the hokey ballad.

There's nothing wrong with the acting that better material — preferably nonmusical — wouldn't solve. Ms. Bateman apparently wanted a

change from playing the bubble-headed Mallory Keaton on television's "Family Ties," so here is Jennie proving she's smart, giving her high-school valedictory speech: "We can make the kind of noise that's going to wake the world from its stagnant slumber." The class cheers.

So guys, "Satisfaction" is a typical, low-budget summer movie, where everyone has a hot romance, a good body and an expensive haircut. The mystery is why it opened yesterday at the Criterion and other theaters. My guess is that it will appear some summer evening on television; it happens to be an NBC Production, and NBC is the network of "Family Ties."

"Satisfaction" is rated PG-13 (Special parental guidance suggested for children under 13.) There is drug use and strong language.

1988 F 13, 15:1

Justine Bateman portrays one of five young people whose rock band is hired for the summer to play at a wealthy beach resort.

Sorry, Wrong Number

THE TELEPHONE, directed by Rip Torn; screenplay by Harry Nilsson and Terry Southern; director of photography, David Claessen; edited by Sandra Adair; art director, Jim Pohl; produced by Robert Katz and Moctesuma Esparza. New World Pictures and Odyssey Entertainment Ltd. present an Esparza/Katz Production in association with Hawkeye Entertainment Inc., At Cine 1, Seventh Avenue near 47th Street. Running time: 97 minutes. This film is rated R.

Vashti Blue	Whoopi Goldberg
Max	Severn Darden
Honey Boxe/Irate Neighbor	Amy Wright
Rodney	Elliott Gould
Telephone Man	John Heard

By CARYN JAMES

THE idea for "The Telephone" might have seemed great at around 3 in the morning, after a long night out.

"Let's put Whoopi Goldberg in a room and have her talk on the phone. She can play an out-of-work actress, invent crazy characters, make us laugh until we gradually see the dark side of her personality — she's a lonely, sexually frustrated woman wildly out of touch with reality. Terry Southern and Harry Nilsson can do the script."

Just before dawn that might not have seemed like a deadly blend of cute sentimentality and warmed-over hip. In some blurry-eyed state, it might even have seemed that "The Telephone" would resemble Ms. Goldberg's one-woman show, and be the kind of tour de force only she could carry off.

In the cold light of day, grown people in the movie business should have known better. They might as well have asked Ms. Goldberg to carry off reading the phone book. This is a cheap, labor-intensive idea for a movie, but no amount of manic invention could have saved it. "The Telephone" is as dull it is exhausting to watch. When Elliott Gould and John Heard pay brief visits to Ms. Goldberg's apartment, they do little to relieve the film's claustrophobia, but they offer some needed relief from her racing, steamroller monologues.

Ms. Goldberg no longer needs to prove she's versatile. The vignettes in her Broadway show were self-contained little narratives, based on fully formed personalities that ranged from a Valley Girl to a drugged-out man. But here, as she talks on her zebra-striped telephone, the stories are scattershot; half-finished raunchy jokes spoken with Japanese, Indian and Irish accents. She's rarely funny in her zany phase, and hits a real low when she does "The Dance of the Seven Flatulences." And she's awfully solemn when she falls apart over the husband who has left her. She actually stares into space and says, "God, why have you forsaken me."

The allusion to the Bible is not the only literary reference tossed around here, but the film doesn't even have the courage of its own pretentions. Its premise owes a lot to Jean Cocteau's play "The Human Voice," a one-woman drama in which a rejected woman talks to her former lover on the telephone. But the film is no hommage; it's just a steal. And when Ms. Goldberg calls the police to complain that a scene is missing from her videotape of Frank Capra's "Christmas in July," she doesn't believe Sgt. Samuel Beckett when he tells her there is no such movie. Ominous existential hints reside here; unfortunately they are spelled out at the end.

The truest, most sanely existential lines spoken during the film came from the audience on Friday night. "I want my money back," one person yelled, which encouraged another to say "I hope the film breaks." Because the movie skulked into town on Friday with absolutely no fanfare, there were fewer than a dozen people at the Cine 1.

Still, let's give Whoopi Goldberg some credit. She has not always chosen her films well, but she did sue New World Pictures to try to stop the release of "The Telephone." She claimed to have had approval of the final cut. She lost the suit, but it's hard to imagine that editing could have done much good here, so let's assume Ms. Goldberg just woke up a little too late.

1988 F 14, 77:1

Sexism on Film: The Sequel

By JANET MASLIN

WHEN THE CHARACTERS in John Hughes's "She's Having a Baby" catch a brief glimpse of the old "Dick Van Dyke Show" on television, the film sounds an amazingly nostalgic note. There, amid the sourness, petulance and misanthropy of Mr. Hughes's new comedy, are Rob and Laura Petrie, who led simple lives and fought over the silliest things. Despite it all, Rob and Laura were happy. And they liked each other infinitely more than Jefferson (Jake) Briggs (Kevin Bacon) and his wife, Kristy (Elizabeth McGovern), ever will.

"She's Having a Baby" is a work of extraordinary mean-spiritedness and misogyny, the story of a young man roped into marriage and the dreariest form of suburban life by a sexless, small-minded woman he can barely stand. It's a fine example of the revitalized sexism to be found in a number of today's films, yet along with most of them it has its inadvertent, even innocent side. It doesn't seem as if Mr. Hughes deliberately intended to generate this much bile, or to stray this far from the realistic teen-age comedies that made his reputation. He simply wrote about a slightly older character without modifying the adolescent state of mind.

So the authority figure in Jake Briggs's life — the person who, figuratively speaking, won't let him borrow the car — is not a parent but is instead a wife. That must be how

Despite the women's movement, some new works show that misogyny on film may be far from dead.

Mr. Hughes managed to make the most flagrantly sexist film in years.

For all its nastiness at Kristy's expense, "She's Having a Baby" generates more confusion than malice. In fact, it has an ingenuousness that seems emblematic of this particular moment. This is a time when sexism has begun to reappear in the movies after a long, uneasy hiatus, and is re-emerging in noticeably different form. Thanks to the initial power of the women's movement, cinematic sexism will never again be set forth as heedlessly as it was in the 1950's (which look like the Age of Reason compared with the stereotype- and prejudice-filled universe of Mr. Hughes's new film).

The return of sexually conservative behavior in the real world has meant a corresponding resurgence of sexual fantasy on the screen, and feminist pressure has lessened enough to clear the way for some notably demeaning imagery: for instance, the spectacle of Miss McGovern nagging her husband about decorating while he daydreams that a

Lena Olin in bowler and black lace in "The Unbearable Lightness of Being"

220

pretty, exotic blonde may make a pass at him. Yet the spirit of the women's movement remains powerful enough to prevent such visions from reaching the screen without some form of ancillary apology attached. This results, more often than not, in painfully mixed emotions. After Jake Briggs has spent an hour and a half sneering at his wife, he suddenly bursts into tears and realizes that this has been a happy life after all.

How can audiences fail to be confused by such mixed signals? And when it comes to confusion, what will those hapless viewers who have not read Milan Kundera's "Unbearable Lightness of Being" make of Philip Kaufman's sexually frank film adaptation of the book? On the page, one finds the artist Sabina, partner in what Mr. Kundera calls "erotic friendship" with the doctor named Tomas, a woman who is the embodiment of freedom, of Mr. Kundera's notion of lightness, of one half of the philosophical duality to be found in Tomas's nature. There on the screen, however, is the voluptuous actress Lena Olin in black lace underwear and a garter belt. That she wears the black bowler hat symbolizing her sexual hold over Tomas will probably not diminish the importance of the garter belt in anyone's mind.

Since so little of the questioning, playful tone of Mr. Kundera's book can be found in this slowly-paced film, and since the film discards the novel's way of examining events by pausing to raise questions about them, the sexual dynamics of the story inevitably become more prominent than they should. Tomas, after all, is a man with two slavishly devoted women in his life, neither of whom enjoys his unapologetic philandering; Tomas's opening remark to new women he meets is very often "Take off your clothes," and these lustful, obedient creatures are always happy to do as he says. Mr. Kaufman's fundamental seriousness is as apparent as Mr. Kundera's, and so the film cannot be accused of exploitativeness, yet it has that effect anyhow.

If this is backsliding, then when did it begin? How did Goldie Hawn, say, go from playing Private Benjamin to her present role in "Overboard," as a haughty woman who needs only a touch of amnesia to be turned into a household slave? One pivotal event in this evolutionary process was the success of "Blue Velvet," which was widely hailed for its frightening and fearless style. Less closely examined was the lingering effect of a film in which Isabella Rossellini performed much of her role stark naked, and was violently abused again and again by Dennis Hopper's character, a man so bizarre that his behavior could not possibly raise any rational objections. As a result of this, kinkiness in the art film had a new lease on life, and sexism in a serious context was respectable all over again.

So it has no longer been necessary to seek out films like the French "L'Année des Meduses," about the travails of a teen-age girl and her attractive mother vacationing on the no-bathing-suit French Riviera, for those interested in nudity on the screen. It is now just as apt to turn up in a "Siesta," the recent film starring Ellen Barkin as a woman who wandered through desert landscapes in and out of her red dress. ("Siesta" was the work of a woman director, Mary Lambert, who had made some rock videos and clearly cared more about pretentions than exploitation.)

It is far more common for a leading American star like Glenn Close (in "Fatal Attraction") or Kathleen Turner (in "Julia and Julia," though Miss Turner helped pioneer the comeback of such things with her more-or-less trail-blazing appearance in "Crimes of Passion") to surprise the audience with a flash of unexpected nudity in today's films

Ellen Barkin in "Siesta" — clothed and unclothed in the desert

that it was even five years ago. And even mainstream actresses like Miss Hawn (who takes a bath and wears some remarkable swimsuits in "Overboard") show renewed interest in kittenish roles.

Are the movies leading this recidivist wave, or merely reflecting a larger form of change? It's often difficult to distinguish intentional bias from the kind that simply reflects literary or sociological reality. Mr. Kaufman, after all, is being entirely faithful to Mr. Kundera's book, just as Oliver Stone in "Wall Street" may only be echoing the attitudes of the get-rich-quick culture that his film examines. Maybe it's customary in such circles to send a call girl dressed as a businesswoman to help a colleague celebrate a new professional arrangement; maybe the wives and girlfriends of Wall Street insiders are as vapid as the women who turn up in the film's beach house scene. (Certainly the men, exemplified by Michael Douglas as he rhapsodizes about the sunrise, aren't appreciably

better.) The best indication of what Mr. Stone intends here is probably his earlier "Salvador," which treats its female characters just as dismissively and has less of a satirical edge. In any case, right now the line between malicious and accurately observed misogyny appears especially thin.

The confusion bred by this is so rampant it can even be touching. In "Cop," James Woods plays an old-fashioned police detective but is shown to have some newfangled attitudes, too. Even while pursuing the various wildly-dressed hooker types who turn up frequently during the story, he must make speeches about the lost innocence of little girls and profess to read feminist poetry. This element of contrition deserves to be appreciated. But if it's a choice between the film's bisexual feminist poet character and its streetwalker in a purple spandex bodysuit, which one is the audience most apt to remember? □

1988 F 14, II:1:1

Ofelia Medina in "Frida."

A Flamboyant Artist

FRIDA, directed by Paul Leduc; in Spanish with English subtitles; director of photography, Angel Goded; produced by Manuel Barbachano Ponce; released by New Yorker Films. At the Film Forum, 57 Watts Street. Running time: 108 minutes. This film has no rating.

Frida	Ofelia Medina
Diego Rivera	Juan José Gurrola
Trotsky	Max Kerlow

By WALTER GOODMAN

FRIDA KAHLO'S death in 1954 at the age of 47 caused no great stir in the United States. In her native Mexico, however, she had been a celebrity, at least within radical political and artistic circles. About a year before, the first major exhibit of her paintings had been shown at Mexico City's Gallery of Contemporary Art. And for decades before that, she had been widely known as the somewhat flamboyant wife of Diego Rivera and as his comrade in Communist causes. "Frida," the Mexican movie that opens at Film Forum today, is an affectionate and affecting tribute to a colorful woman.

The director, Paul Leduc, shapes a series of bright tableaux, out of chronological order but flowing elegantly in a sort of order of the spirit. Playing Kahlo, Ofelia Medina grows older and younger scene by scene, as the movie drifts forward and backward in time. Now she is berating Rivera for enjoying an affair with her sister; now, much younger, she is in an energetic pillow fight with the sister and their father; now she is screaming during a miscarriage. Orientation is provided by references to the Spanish Civil War, the rise of Hitler, the dropping of the atom bomb.

Kahlo's existence, as pictured here, was one of painting and pain, of political and sexual passion. The pain began with a terrible bus accident, graphically dramatized, when she was 18. Her spine was fractured, her pelvis crushed, one foot broken. A few months before her death, her right leg had to be amputated. Confined often to bed or wheelchair, she surrounded herself with mirrors; her self-portraits grew out of those stretches of self-scrutiny. Many of them express physical pain, sometimes in a surreal way.

•

Yet she was anything but homebound. We see her marching behind the hammer and sickle through 20 years of political demonstrations. She appears also to have had the strength for several love affairs, with women as well as men.

There is little dialogue; the episodes speak eloquently without it. Some of them, accompanied by popular or folk music, sing. In one lovely sequence, Kahlo seems to float about her room in her wheelchair to the accompaniment of a happy tune. When dialogue is employed, as in an argument with a Stalinist painter, David Sequeiros, over the hospitality she and Rivera gave to the exiled Leon Trotsky, the language is stiff. Trotsky was one of Kahlo's conquests, which seems to have interfered only briefly with her adoration of Stalin. (The program at Film Forum begins with five minutes of home movies of Trotsky in Mexico, being visited by Kahlo and Diego Rivera. Nothing much happens, but the glimpse offers an opportunity to compare the look of the real Kahlo with the Kahlo re-created by Ms. Medina. The resemblance is remarkable, even to the mustache.)

"Frida" does not try to be a biography. (That is available in Hayden Herrera's 1983 book, "Frida.") What Mr. Leduc and Ms. Medina do is open up a life to us in the way that Kahlo herself attempted in her art. Whatever the real Kahlo was like, in their movie, she is vibrant.

1988 F 17, C18:5

Mixed Emotions

HIGH TIDE, directed by Gillian Armstrong; screenplay by Laura Jones; director of photography, Russell Boyd; edited by Nicholas Beauman; music by Mary Moffiatt and Ricky Fataar; production designer, Sally Campbell; produced by Sandra Levy; released by Tri-Star Pictures. At Lincoln Plaza 1, Broadway at 63d Street. Running time: 103 minutes. This film is rated PG-13.

Lilli	Judy Davis
Bet	Jan Adele
Ally	Claudia Karvan
Mick	Colin Friels
Col	John Clayton
Tracey	Monica Trapaga
Lester	Frankie J. Holden
Mary	Toni Scanlon
Jason	Marc Gray
Michelle	Emily Stocker

By JANET MASLIN

"HIGH TIDE" begins with shots of a cut-rate Australian Elvis impersonator, and rarely has an Elvis impersonator given off this much heat and light. This man's flash has nothing to do with his act, of course, and everything to do with the pop exuberance with which the director Gillian Armstrong (who made "Starstruck" in much the same spirit) captures him on screen. His feet tap; his lips curl; his hips wiggle like mad. Meanwhile, behind him, three singers in blond Cleopatra wigs and glittering green mermaid dresses smile and shimmy for all they're worth.

Now what has "High Tide," which opens today at the Lincoln Plaza 1, got to do with Elvis? Very little. And does it matter? Miss Armstrong's method here is often to seize upon seemingly tangential information and bring it vibrantly into focus, but she does this so well that she makes it work to her advantage. Despite the fact that it has familiar and even hackneyed material at its heart, "High Tide" has a lot of surface luster. It's much too highly charged, brilliantly photographed and well observed to seem ordinary.

Underneath one of those Cleopatra wigs in the opening scene, the film's heroine makes her unconventional entrance. At first glance, Lilli (Judy Davis) looks just like her two identically dressed fellow singers, but the irony of this is almost instantly clear. Lilli doesn't fit in, not here, not anywhere. A reckless, mocking, wildly irresponsible creature, Lilli is fired from her singing job almost as soon as the film begins. She isn't surprised, and she doesn't much care.

•

When her car breaks down, Lilli finds herself at a trailer park on the shore of a beautiful beach on the south Australian coast; this natural paradise is in fact a touristy spot called Eden. It is here that Lilli crosses paths with an adolescent girl named Ally (Claudia Karvan), with whom Lilli becomes fascinated. It isn't hard to guess why, and the film doesn't make much of a secret of it. Ally proves to be the daughter Lilli abandoned years earlier, when her husband died and her life began what has apparently been an uninterrupted downhill slide.

It is at this point that "High Tide," which has a screenplay by Laura Jones, begins to show its soap-opera side. Will Lilli and Ally reconcile? Will Lilli overcome the enmity of her mother-in-law Bet (Jan Adele), who raised the child and let her believe that Lilli was dead? Will Lilli turn her life around and become loving, caring and responsible? None of these questions are innately as interesting as the crackling way Miss Armstrong frames them, or the spiky, stubborn manner in which Miss Davis brings the character to life.

Miss Davis isn't an actress overly interested in making audiences like her; she never makes an ingratiating move when a difficult, challenging one will do. Even her appearance here — pale and unkempt, with blackish-red lipstick — conveys the character's rebellious, self-destructive side. Yet Miss Davis also suggests

Colin Friels and Judy Davis in "High Tide."

vast reserves of well-suppressed longing, and she is able to communicate all of Lilli's powerfully mixed feelings about her child in purely physical terms, simply by the way she watches the girl and the way she moves. Miss Davis has an extraordinarily vivid presence on the screen, and young Claudia Karvan is an excellent foil, saying little but registering all of the daughter's hope and apprehension. At every opportunity, Miss Armstrong surrounds each of them with tidal and aquatic imagery, suggesting the elusive, fluid quality of their affections.

Also notable is Russell Boyd's extravagantly beautiful cinematography. Among the good supporting players here are Colin Friels, as an earnest, kindly suitor of Lilli's, and the very hearty Miss Adele, who is deliberately made to seem out of synch with Ally and Lilli (ravishing beach and surf images are connected with these younger women, while the hefty Bet wears a rubber apron and hoses down the floor at a fish refinery). If these women are essentially familiar, and if the course of their story is finally unsurprising, Miss Armstrong makes them matter anyhow.

•

"High Tide" is rated PG-13 ("Special Parental Guidance Suggested for Those Younger Than 13"). It contains some strong language and sexual references.

1988 F 19, C5:1

R and R

A MONTH IN THE COUNTRY, directed by Pat O'Connor; screenplay by Simon Gray, from the novel "A Month in the Country" by J. L. Carr; director of photography, Ken Macmillan; edited by John Victor Smith; music by Howard Blake; production designer, Leo Austin; produced by Kenith Trodd; released by Orion Classics. At 68th Street Playhouse, at Third Avenue. Running time: 96 minutes. Rating: PG.

Birkin	Colin Firth
Moon	Kenneth Branagh

Mrs. Keach	Natasha Richardson
Reverend Keach	Patrick Malahide
Douthwaite	Tony Haygarth
Ellerbeck	Jim Carter
Colonel Hebron	Richard Vernon
Kathy	Vicky Arundale
Edgar	Martin O'Neil
Emily	Lisa Taylor

"A Month in the Country" was shown as part of last year's New York Film Festival. Following are excerpts from Janet Maslin's review, which appeared in The New York Times on Sept. 27. The film opens today at the 68th Street Playhouse, at Third Avenue.

PAT O'CONNOR'S direction broadens and illuminates "A Month in the Country" even as the writing — a screenplay by Simon Gray, from the novel by J. L. Carr — strives to tie up any loose ends. Indeed, Mr. O'Connor, whose first feature was the haunting "Cal," does a great deal to keep an eloquent but small film from seeming even smaller.

"A Month in the Country" (which has no connection with the Turgenev work of the same name) is set in a tiny Yorkshire village called Oxgodbody, where a shell-shocked World War I veteran named Birkin (Colin Firth) arrives to work on uncovering a medieval painting on the wall of a local church. When Birkin first appears, it is in the midst of a torrential downpour, and Mr. O'Connor's establishing shots of the village in the rain do a lot to foreshadow the restorative powers of this simple, beautiful setting. Birkin's acute stammer and his nervous tics attest to his need to recuperate from a wartime ordeal.

On its own, this material might seem far more neat and comfortable than it does in Mr. O'Connor's hands. But his direction lends it a strong sense of yearning, as well as a spiritual quality more apparent in the look of the film than in its dialogue. As in "Cal," Mr. O'Connor is especially good at emphasizing the characters' separateness from one another, as well as their unarticulated longing.

Though Mr. O'Connor seems less in tune with this material than with the Northern Irish tragedy of "Cal," he gives particular power to the story's elements of religion and doubt. He also gives moments that might have seemed precious — like a flirtatious speech by Mrs. Keach, the vicar's wife, about roses — a sweetness that is real. So does the enormously self-possessed Natasha Richardson, plucking a white rose and handing it to Birkin with great aplomb. "They bloom till autumn," she says of a favorite rose. "So you'll know when summer's over, because I usually wear one of the last in my hat." Not many actresses could deliver a line like that, as Miss Richardson does, without seeming the least bit coy.

"A Month in the Country" is rated PG ("Parental Guidance Suggested"). It contains some sexual references.

1988 F 19, C10:5

Natasha Richardson portrays a Yorkshire vicar's wife and Colin Firth a shellshocked art restorer.

Film: 'Stranded,' Sci-Fi

By JANET MASLIN

Sheriff Hollis McMann — we know he is Sheriff Hollis McMann because he shouts "This is Sheriff Hollis McMann!" into his megaphone before beginning every speech — arrives at the house where the kindly grandmother and her sweet teen-age granddaughter are being held hostage. "How many people are in the house with you?" he asks. "They're not, uh, *people*, Sheriff," the teen-age girl answers, thus providing "Stranded" with its only touch of anything resembling humor.

Science fiction is almost never as lifeless as "Stranded," which opened yesterday at the Embassy 3. The plot has to do with kindly extraterrestrials who hide out here briefly while running from political problems back home, but it unfolds at a snail's place and manages to be uneventful all the way through. A subplot about uneasy relations between the black sheriff and the gum-chewing white yahoos in his community (sample remark about the E. T.'s: "It wudn't like nuthin' I never seen before!") remains equally undeveloped. When the story is at long last over, grandma and granddaughter experience that peculiarly '80's epiphany of becoming briefly famous and giving an interview.

•

The creatures look as if they've had terrible past experiences with hairstyling mousse, and one of them likes the teen-age girl enough to stick around for a goodbye kiss. Even for those who believe love is where you find it, this is going too far. Humans in the cast include Joe Morton as the solemn sheriff, Ione Skye as the ingenue and Maureen O'Sullivan as the elderly lady who's much classier than this material deserves. None of them is photographed to good advantage, since virtually the entire film takes place in the dark.

Ads for "Stranded" have the temerity to describe it as "an experience you'll never forget." You're much more likely to forget it before it's over.

"Stranded" is rated PG-13 ("Special Parental Guidance Suggested for Children Under 13"). It contains violence and some strong language.

1988 F 20, 16:5

Where *Is* She?

FRANTIC, directed by Roman Polanski; written by Mr. Polanski and Gerard Brach; director of photography, Witold Sobocinski; film editor, Sam O'Steen; music by Ennio Morricone; production designer, Pierre Guffroy; produced by Thom Mount and Tim Hampton; released by Warner Brothers. At National, Broadway and 44th Street; Beekman, Second Avenue at 66th Street; 34th Street East, near Second Avenue; 84th Street Six, at Broadway; Movieland Eighth Street, at University Place. Running time: 120 minutes. This film is rated R.

Richard Walker	Harrison Ford
Sondra Walker	Betty Buckley
Michelle	Emmanuelle Seigner
Williams	John Mahoney
Gaillard	Gerard Klein

By JANET MASLIN

ALFRED HITCHCOCK would have appreciated the inexorable process whereby Dr. Richard Walker (Harrison Ford), a surgeon visiting Paris to address a convention and enjoy a kind of second honeymoon, is drawn into a web of intrigue. It is perhaps no accident that Dr. Walker's troubles begin in the shower. The quiet, brilliantly unremarkable opening sequence of Roman Polanski's "Frantic" follows the doctor and his wife, Sondra (Betty Buckley), as they take a taxi from the airport, check into their Paris hotel, call home to say they've arrived and prepare to work off their jet lag. The only tip-offs that anything may be amiss are the film's title and the presence of Mr. Polanski at the helm.

The doctor is in the shower when the phone rings; he sees Sondra answer it, watches her speak briefly, and can't quite hear what she's saying because of the sound of the running water. Nor can he make out the message she mouths in his direction. He's still showering and not paying much attention as Sondra next pulls a red garment out of her suitcase and wanders away. By the time he begins wondering who called and why, it's too late. Sondra has vanished without a trace, and "Frantic" has begun to live up to its title.

Hitchcock might have enjoyed the funhouse possibilities of such a disappearance, and the deeper ramifications of this man's desperate search. (He did precisely this in "The Man Who Knew Too Much," particularly the later version.) Mr. Polanski makes good use of these aspects of the story (written by him and Gerard Brach), but it is the doctor's mounting anxiety and frustration that most fully capture the director's imagination. These are the moods, after all, of Polanski films as diverse as "Repulsion," "Rosemary's Baby" and "Chinatown," all of which attest to his gift for approaching the most disturbing subjects in the most deceptively matter-of-fact way. "Frantic" generates its suspense precisely because it appears so reasonable, because it takes such a calm, methodical approach to

Harrison Ford

the maddening events that lure Dr. Walker into the maelstrom.

•

It's not entirely surprising that a film like "Frantic," which opens today at the Beekman and other theaters, eventually involves this guileless tourist with drug smugglers and international terrorists, with the more colorful fringes of Parisian nightlife, with a long-legged girl wearing black-leather motorcycle regalia. These, after all, can be almost standard ingredients for a story of intrigue. What's more unusual is the precise, understated way in which Mr. Polanski pieces the tale together, so that even the craziest development follows more or less sensibly 1rom whatever precedes it. There is, for instance, the point at which Dr. Walker has followed his trail of crumbs to the apartment of someone who turns out to be newly deceased. The doctor tries to flee immediately, but he sees a couple making love in the building's vestibule, steps back inside the apartment to wait until they're gone, and thus overhears the telephone message that provides the next piece of the puzzle.

"Frantic" doesn't just leapfrog from one corpse or lurid location to another; Mr. Polanski creates some of his most memorable moments by conveying the assorted petty annoyances that the doctor encounters. He doesn't speak French, so when he asks a florist whether he's seen Sondra in the neighborhood, the man thinks he's trying to send his wife roses. At the American Embassy, he's told to wait in line with all the other tourists whose spouses have *not* been kidnapped. At his hotel, he cannot even ask a question of the concierge without having to track the man to a weight-pumping machine at a gymnasium. Mr. Polanski has an unusually keen sense of the quiet fury such episodes might inspire.

He also takes a distinctly European view of this innocent abroad. Few American film makers would devote so little energy to worrying whether the doctor will deliver his speech on time, or to what will happen if professional colleagues spot him with that long-legged girl. The doctor doesn't worry either, partly because of his unflappable nature and partly because he is caught up in the film's prevailing atmosphere of temptation. Emmanuelle Seigner, as the reckless young beauty who joins forces with the doctor in his search, sports some remarkably devil-may-care outfits and an attitude to match. As such, she

manages to make the pressures on this happily married doctor even greater.

Harrison Ford, who appears to be doing his own dangerous stuntwork in this film as he clambers over Parisian rooftops, plays the doctor in a tough, cool, single-minded way. He's able to convey great determination, as well as a restraint that barely masks the character's mounting rage, and he makes a compelling if rather uncomplicated hero. Miss Buckley, whose appearance is brief, manages to behave as if nothing unusual were about to happen, which is no small achievement. Miss Seigner does what she's supposed to do, which is stop traffic. And Mr. Polanski, after a very long fallow period (though he has worked on the stage in Europe, his only film since "Tess" has been the disastrous "Pirates"), gives "Frantic" urgency and personality. He has succeeded in picking up the clever, unnerving thread of his earlier career.

1988 F 26, C3:4

Sand and Surf

ALOHA SUMMER, directed by Tommy Lee Wallace; screenplay by Mike Greco and Bob Benedetto, story by Mr. Greco; director of photography, Steven Poster; edited by James Coblentz, Jack Hofstra and Jay Cassidy; music by Jesse Frederick and Bennett Salvay; produced by Mr. Greco; released by Spectrafilm. At Criterion Center, Broadway between 44th and 45th Streets. Running time: 97 minutes. This film is rated PG.

Mike Tognetti	Chris Makepeace
Kenzo Konishi	Yuji Okumoto
Chuck Granville	Don Michael Paul
Lani Kepoo	Tia Carrere
Kimo Kepoo	Andy Bumatai
Amanda Granville	Lorie Griffin
Scott Tanaka	Scott Nakagawa
Jerry Kahani	Blaine Kia
Kilarney	Warren Fabro

"ALOHA SUMMER" features Bobby Darin songs, surfers, wholesome guys and their girls singing around a fire on a beach in Waikiki. An unironic memoir of six teen-aged friends in the summer of '59, it is more likely to inspire déjà vu about 50's movies than about the year Hawaii became a state.

A voiceover by Chris Makepeace takes us back to his character's adolescence, and gives away the movie's stilted tone. "By the end of the summer even Dad was calling us the Salty Six," he recalls. There's not a Dad in this film — maybe in creation — who would use that phrase. Besides, these six are not salty; they are thoroughly bland, despite their superficial variety.

Scott is the regular-guy islander, whose tradition-bound cousin, Kenzo, is visiting from Japan. They meet up with an Italian-American named Mike (Mr. Makepeace), and a rich, blond WASP named Chuck, who have come from the mainland. Then there are Jerry and Kilarney, referred to as the "Irish-Hawaiian brothers."

•

We're never told how these two got to be Irish and Hawaiian, though that bit of information might have helped fill out the movie's ostensible theme — breaking down racial and social barriers. We're meant to see the gang overlooking skin color and social class, growing beyond their parents' biases, but in fact the movie is built on predictable coming-of-age episodes. The boys do a lot of lusting after one another's sisters and face plenty of father-son conflicts; one of these erupts into a violent martial-

arts battle, as if the Karate Kid had dropped into the 1950's.

If the characters' problems are schematic, the resolutions are melodramatic — a smashed car, an accidental death and one last surfboard ride into a hurricane. A television report says the guys have headed into "the biggest killer surf ever to hit Hawaii." I guess we're supposed to think this is just a crazy end to one wild summer, but this movie lost any hint of suspense long before the hurricane hit. "Aloha Summer," which opens today at the Criterion Center, is empty nostalgia done for its own sake, set against some pretty pictures of waves. This is not unpleasant; it is uninteresting.

•

"Aloha Summer" is rated PG ("Parental Guidance Suggested"). It contains some violence.

CARYN JAMES

1988 F 26, C8:1

Sports Story

THE LAST MINUTE, directed by Pupi Avati; screenplay (Italian with English subtitles) by Pupi and Antonio Avati and Italo Cucci and Giuseppe Pirotte; director of photography, Pasquale Rachini; edited by Amedeo Salfa; music by Riz Ortolani; produced by Antonio Avati; A Duea Film and D.M.V. Distribuzione production in association with R.A.I. Channel 1. At Carnegie Screening Room, Seventh Avenue and 57th Street. Running time: 100 minutes. This film has no rating.

Walter	Ugo Tognazzi
Duccio	Diego Abatantuono
Di Carlo	Lino Capolicchio

IN the last minutes of "The Last Minute," we seem about to be treated to the big soccer match for which we have been prepared by the first hour and a half of the Italian movie that opens today at the Carnegie Screening Room. And, sure enough, the game starts — only the camera is facing the wrong way. Foul! We see the stands filled with rooters, the dugout with players, the press box with reporters; we see the stadium's passageways and locker rooms; what we don't see is the field. When the 17-year-old "yearling," who we know will save the game in the last minute, kicks the crucial goal, the news is brought to us by a radio announcer. It's enough to drive a fan to riot.

Instead of offering the rousing attacks and counterattacks of soccer, Pupi Avati's movie focuses on the routine downs and ups of a team manager (Ugo Tognazzi) whose troubles begin when his faltering club is taken over by a younger man with a high-priced hairdo. As Mr. Tognazzi scurries gamely around trying to rally support, we meet several athletes, trainers and hangers on, as well as the manager's neglected daughter, who has a crush on the team's untrustworthy star. Not one of these players scores. The script, which is supposed to be giving us an inside look at the workings of professional soccer, seems fixed. Game called on account of lost ball.

WALTER GOODMAN

1988 F 26, C10:5

THY KINGDOM COME, THY WILL BE DONE, a documentary directed, written, narrated and produced by Antony Thomas; director of photography, Curtis Clark. At the Waverly, Avenue of the Americas at Third Street. Running time: 107 minutes. This film has no rating.

By CARYN JAMES

A CONGREGATION sings a hymn — its members' heads thrown back, eyes closed, voices raised in ecstasy — and it seems they have surrendered their hearts to Jesus and their minds to their preachers. "Thy Kingdom Come, Thy Will Be Done," Antony Thomas's documentary about born-again Christians and the political right, is powerful enough to lead to that conclusion, and hectoring enough to make us aware of Mr. Thomas's own manipulation.

He is the writer, director, narrator and crusader of the film, bent on depicting the dangerous liaison between the far rights of religion and politics. He interviews fundamentalists and their ministers, sparingly selects television clips — Jerry Falwell pleading for money to help "little pregnant girls" — and warns of the values "the Christian right wishes to impose on the rest of America." He seems unaware that the film makes his point best when he lets the evidence speak for itself. What can you add to Jim Bakker's belief that he was "called from God to do television"?

Co-produced by England's Central Television network and PBS's "Frontline" series, the two-part film was withdrawn from the "Frontline" schedule last May, two months after Jim Bakker resigned. According to "Frontline," the documentary needed to be re-edited and updated for an American audience. The 90-minute film, which opens today at the Waverly and will air on PBS in April, has not caught up with any of the past year's evangelical-sexual scandals, but timeliness is not its major problem.

Mr. Thomas throws figures around casually (can we believe fundamentalists make up 40 percent of the American population?) and leaves huge holes in his argument about encroaching right-wing Christianity. His view of American society is so narrow that he forces us to doubt his assertions.

To discover who these born-again Christians are, for example, he interviews the most desperate souls — former drug addicts, a woman who was sexually abused from the age of 5, socially beaten people clinging to their church as to a life raft. They overwhelm the less dramatic, middle-class people who are as revealing in their attitudes ("My mother was a Christian and my dad an alcoholic") and as crucial to a study of religion's influence on politics.

●

When Mr. Thomas moves on to Heritage USA, the religious complex that Jim and Tammy Bakker built in South Carolina, he loses his best opportunity to explore the nexus of money, God and politics. In a shopping mall that resembles an old-time, small-town main street, he finds a talking doll that sings out an anti-abortion message: "God loved me before I was born."

But Mr. Thomas makes more of a fuss about the enclosed shopping area itself, a place without traffic or weather. "Nothing of the real America intrudes," he says, as if the real America were not blanketed with malls. He ignores the eerie outward resemblance between the Heritage **USA mall** and those thousands of others, one of the things that makes conservative Christianity acceptable to mainstream America.

Some sequences are so powerful that even Mr. Thomas's commentary cannot undermine them. One section effectively indicts the Bakkers for exploiting an 18-year-old named Kevin, who looks about 5, has withered arms and legs, and glides around in his wheelchair giving a tour of Kevin's House, a home for disabled children that remained empty months after its hurried completion. Kevin sounds spookily like a publicity agent, and before you know it he is on television appealing for money for the PTL. "They wouldn't ask if they didn't need it," he says.

●

Mr. Thomas doesn't say much about politics that isn't known already. And in the second half, he gives a simplistic view of the gulf between rich and poor. He focuses on Dallas, where H. L. Hunt's widow hosts a Bible-reading class for wealthy ladies while homeless men sleep in the street. As disturbing as that gulf is, Mr. Thomas does little to illuminate the problem of poverty or the political power of fundamentalists, whose strength cannot depend solely on the rich and the destitute.

Mr. Thomas's documentaries always come with a point of view. He is best known for his 1980 television film about the execution of a member of the Saudi royal family, "The Death of a Princess," which the Saudi Government tried to prevent from being shown in England. In "Thy Kingdom Come," it is worth sifting through his polemics to find those moments — richly photographed by Curtis Clark, who has done such feature films as "The Draughtsman's Contract"— that reveal much more than the speakers know.

1988 F 26, C11:1

Goodbye Cayumba

APPRENTICE TO MURDER, directed by R. L. Thomas; written by Alan Scott and Wesley Moore; director of photography, Kelvin Pike; edited by Patrick McMahon; music by Charles Gross; production designer, Gregory Bolton; produced by Howard K. Grossman; released by New World Pictures. At the Astor Plaza, Broadway at 44th Street; the Orpheum, Third Avenue at 86th Street; Movie Center 5, 125th Street between Powell and Douglass Boulevards. Running time: 94 minutes. This film is rated PG-13.
John Reese	Donald Sutherland
Billy Kelly	Chad Lowe
Alice Spangler	Mia Sara
Lars Hoeglin	Knut Husebo
Elma Kelly	Rutanya Alda
Tom Kelly	Eddie Jones
Clay Myers	Mark Burton
Irwin Myers	Adrian Sparks
Rufus	Tiger Haynes

THE film that announces for no good reason that it is "inspired by a true story" often lacks any authenticity of its own. Certainly that's the trouble with "Apprentice to Murder," which opens today at Loews Astor Plaza and other theaters and tells of strange goings-on in rural Pennsylvania, circa 1927. A mysterious neighbor begins showing signs of demonic power, and Donald Sutherland, pleasant but unremarkable as a nice-guy country doctor who is in fact conversant with these darker forces, takes up the cudgel on behalf of his community and does battle with the mystery man. He is aided by young Billy Kelly, who must say things like, "I ask of the spirit of Cayumba: Are you with us?"

●

Billy is played by an unremarkable, vaguely uncomfortable blond actor

Donald Sutherland

named Chad Lowe, whose family resemblance to brother Rob is the only thing that explains his presence here. The pretty young woman who (a closing title tells us) actually married Billy Kelly in real life is played by Mia Sara, who has an exotic loveliness but pays absolutely no attention to anyone she is supposed to be addressing. R. L. Thomas's direction is straightforward, ordinary and a little messy around the edges. In one scene, an actor in a room that is supposed to be ablaze shows not a single reflected trace of flickering light.

As for the screenplay, it seems unlikely that the rustic Pennsylvania youth of 1927 said things like: "Live for yourself. Take it before it's too late."

●

"Apprentice to Murder" is rated PG-13 ("Special Parental Guidance Suggested for Those Younger Than 13"). It includes violent and sexual episodes.   *JANET MASLIN*

1988 F 26, C14:1

Down-Home Drama

END OF THE LINE, directed by Jay Russell; screenplay by Mr. Russell and John Wohlbruck; director of photography, George Tirl; edited by Mercedes Danevic; music by Andy Summers; production designer, Neil Spisak; produced by Lewis Allen and Peter Newman, executive producer, Mary Steenburgen; released by Orion Classics. At Embassy 72d Street, at Broadway. Running time: 105 minutes. This film is rated PG.
Will Haney	Wilford Brimley
Leo Pickett	Levon Helm
Rose Pickett	Mary Steenburgen
Jean Haney	Barbara Barrie
Thomas Clinton	Henderson Forsythe
Warren Gerber	Bob Balaban
Everett	Kevin Bacon
Alvin	Michael Beach
Charlotte	Holly Hunter
Billy	Bruce McGill
Jeannie	Missy Platt
Chester	Carroll Dee Bland

THERE is a moment when "End of the Line" looks like a small miracle. However, that moment is extremely brief, and it occurs during the film's opening credits; no such impression ever comes again. Here in the cast of this unprepossessing small-town story are such singular actors as Mary Steenburgen, Holly Hunter, Kevin Bacon and Levon Helm, whose presence alone ought to be enough to hold the interest. But "End of the Line," which opens today at the Embassy 72d Street, is hopelessly mired in local color and unimaginative good intentions.

The ads for this film don't even name its director, Jay Russell; the actors are its main and possibly only attraction. The story (by Mr. Russell and John Wohlbruck) is set in the small town of Clifford, Ark., a place that is brought to life energetically at first, then effectively abandoned. Clifford's principal employer is the Southland Railroad, which has decided to shut down its operation in the town in favor of newfangled air freight, and this starts everyone a-thinkin'. Will Haney (Wilford Brimley, in overalls) decides to head for Chicago and talk that Southland boss man into changing his mind.

●

Ron Phillips

Wilford Brimley and Levon Helm as railroad men in "End of the Line"

Living dangerously, Will commandeers a railroad car and makes the trip along with Leo Pickett (Levon Helm), who is sort of the son he never had. The son he *did* have, Billy (Bruce McGill), sits at home in a body cast and is only one of many colorful figures on the Clifford front. Eventually, Will has a bad experience with the uppity young boss (Bob Balaban, doing a thoroughly unfunny obnoxious-yuppie impersonation) and appeals to his elderly father-in-law, who speaks Will's language. Despite this commendable resolution, audiences may wish that both Will and the film had stayed at home.

The dialogue is way too heavy on the hokum ("Rose saw the Gulf one time down in Mississippi. Said it was a real purty sight"). And so is Mr. Brimley, who if he keeps saying things like "Now we need five minutes of his time and by hell we aim to get it — please excuse my language!" is in grave danger of wearing out his salt-of-the-earth appeal. Mr. Helm, on the other hand, manages to seem a sweetly genuine country eccentric, and is even given a too-brief chance to sing. Miss Hunter sounds very much the way she did in the subsequent "Broadcast News" but looks entirely different, in her small role as Mr. Bacon's feisty but downtrodden ex-spouse. For his part, Mr. Bacon struts nastily and is much more interesting than he is in nice-guy roles. And Miss Steenburgen, the film's executive producer, hasn't nearly enough to do in her role as Mr. Helm's wife and Clifford's reigning beauty expert, though her costumes and hairdos may say it all.

•

"End of the Line" is rated PG ("Parental Guidance Suggested"). It doesn't contain much language stronger than "Dang!"

JANET MASLIN

1988 F 26, C15:1

Day of the Beehive

HAIRSPRAY, directed and written by John Waters; director of photography, David Insley; edited by Janice Hampton; art director, Vincent Peranio; produced by Rachel Talalay; released by New Line Cinema. At Embassy 2, Broadway at 47th Street; New York Twin, Second Avenue and 66th Street; 84th Street Six, at Broadway; Waverly Twin, Avenue of the Americas at West Third Street. Running time: 94 minutes. This film is rated PG.

Franklin Von Tussle	Sonny Bono
Edna Turnblad	Divine
Arvin Hodgepile	Divine
Amber Von Tussle	Colleen Fitzpatrick
Velma Von Tussle	Debbie Harry
Tracy Turnblad	Ricki Lake
Wilbur Turnblad	Jerry Stiller
Corny Collins	Shawn Thompson
Beatnik Girl	Pia Zadora

THE concept of Smell-o-Vision never really took hold in America's movie theaters, but it's very nearly a reality in John Waters's "Hairspray." During this bright, bouncy film's opening montage of early 60's teen-agers preparing their coiffures for a television dance program, it's almost possible to sniff the huge clouds of poison they spray onto their teased, empty heads. Such is the realism of "Hairspray," which is hardly the only film to recapture this period (roughly that of "American Graffiti") but may be the worst looking. That — a merry cavalcade of the period's most authentically awful props, fads and textiles — appears to be exactly what Mr. Waters was after.

Divine as Edna Turnblad in "Hairspray."

"Hairspray," which opens today at Loews New York Twin and other theaters, is the work of Mr. Waters at his most goofily benign. This time, the director of "Pink Flamingos" and "Female Trouble" has no need to deliberately offend, since the characters and costumes of "Hairspray" so handily do the job for him. There's no shade of mustard or chartreuse too awful to be re-created here, no figure of teen-age speech too stupid, no fad too trendy. (Assiduously doing the Mashed Potato is these kids' most thoughtful endeavor.) All of this gives "Hairspray" its own brand of hair-raising fun.

Mr. Waters isn't exactly a storyteller, but this isn't a film that depends on plot. All it's about is the rise to glory of Tracy Turnblad (Ricki Lake), a cheerful, overweight, bubbly teen who becomes a star on the "Corny Collins Show." (As Corny, Shawn Thompson has a very Dick Clark-like aplomb.) Once she wows the kids with her dancing talent, Tracy becomes the arch enemy of a blonde named Amber Von Tussle (Colleen Fitzpatrick), who's afraid Tracy may hurt her chances of becoming Miss Auto Show. Each of these girls has stage parents, with Sonny Bono and Debbie Harry aiding Amber's cause and, on Tracy's side, Jerry Stiller and the incomparable Divine.

•

As Tracy's mother, Divine barges through the film in a housedress and pin-curls, looking something like a wildly dressed refrigerator but sounding a lot more amusing. Divine also has another, smaller role, this time as the bigoted man who runs the television station that airs Corny's show. (In a man's suit, Divine manages to look only half-dressed.) One of the film's preoccupations is with the incipient civil-rights movement, with Tracy eventually leading a campaign to help integrate the "Corny Collins Show," which depends heavily on the music of black artists but refuses to allow black teens to dance on camera. However, Mr. Waters's general facetiousness creates such an odd mood in which to air these issues that this aspect of the story simply misfires.

So do such brainstorms as casting Pia Zadora in a beatnik's role, when the film sends Tracy and her friends a brief glimpse of the avant-garde in Baltimore (where the story takes place). And so do those performers who, like Miss Harry, make the mistake of camping it up in Mr. Waters's earlier style. This film is sillier, more ebullient and more innocent than that, without an overtly tongue-in-cheek manner. It isn't exactly deadpan, but it's a wildly colorful celebration of this bygone era, not simply a send-up.

The actors are best when they avoid exaggeration and remain weirdly sincere. That way, they do nothing to break the vibrant, even hallucinogenic spell of Mr. Waters's nostalgia.

•

"Hairspray" is rated PG ("Parental Guidance Suggested"). It includes a few mildly off-color remarks and nothing more.

JANET MASLIN

1988 F 26, C17:1

Course of True Love

ANGELE, directed and written by Marcel Pagnol, based on the novel "Un de Baumugnes" by Jean Giono; music by Vincent Scotto; produced by Films Marcel Pagnol; released by Interama. At the Public, 425 Lafayette Street. Running time: 136 minutes. This film has no rating.

Clarius Barbaroux	Henri Poupon
Philomène	Annie Toinon
Angèle	Orane Démazis
Saturnin	Fernandel
Amédée	Delmont
Albin	Jean Servais

By WALTER GOODMAN

MARCEL PAGNOL made "Angèle" in 1934, soon after the screen adaptations of his plays "Marius" and "Fanny" had spread his reputation as a chronicler of life in southern France. So why has "Angèle," one of Mr. Pagnol's first efforts as a movie director, not found its way into American theaters until now?

The answer may lie in a plot that was already dated 50 years ago. Angèle is a pretty, romantically inclined farm girl who is seduced by a city slicker. "Now I do what I want with her," he boasts to the guys at the bistro, and he proves as bad as his word by installing the poor young woman in a Marseilles brothel, where she becomes pregnant. "I sold my skin to get money," she sighs. When she comes back home, her embarrassed father ("I want nothing to do with that child!") locks mother and baby in a cellar, where they remain until freed by true love. It's a lot to swallow, yet even at more than two hours, Mr. Pagnol's sure touch for Provençal life and a juicy performance by the young Fernandel send it down with surprising ease.

As Angèle, petite and pretty Orane Démazis is appealing despite the improbability of her case, and strapping and even prettier Jean Servais manages to pump energy into the part of the honest mountain lad who turns her into an honest woman. It is Fernandel, however, as Saturnin, a soft-hearted if slightly feeble-minded farmhand, who lifts the movie out of the rut of its plot. At times, he seems to be trading on his cuteness, baring those big teeth, fluttering his eyelashes, but most of the way he is fun to be around as he conspires to bring Angèle and the mountain lad together.

The dialogue is a touch heavy with folk wisdom: "What's done tonight is done tomorrow." Mr. Pagnol's strengths, as in his other movies, are faithfulness to the light and rhythms of Provence and to the spirit of neo-realism. The cliffhanger here is not so much whether the hero will rescue Angèle in time as whether the director and actors can save the movie from its operatic scenario. With a little forebearance on the audience's part, they carry it off.

The Public Theater's Pagnol retrospective, inspired by the recent appearance of "Jean de Florette" and "Manon of the Spring," which are based on his work, begins tonight with "Angèle" and Alexander Korda's "Marius," from a Pagnol screenplay, and continues through March 17. You can see nine Pagnol movies, including the "Fanny" trilogy, starring Raimu and Pierre Fresnay, as well as "The Baker's Wife," "The Welldigger's Daughter," "Letters From My Windmill," "Topaze" and "Harvest."

1988 F 26, C19:1

A NIGHT IN THE LIFE OF JIMMY REARDON, directed and written for the screen by William Richert, based on the novel "Aren't You Even Gonna Kiss Me Goodbye," by Mr. Richert; director of photography, John J. Connor; edited by Suzanne Fenn; music by Bill Conti; production designer, Norman Newberry; produced by Russell Schwartz; released by the 20th Century-Fox Film Corporation. At Gemini, Second Avenue at 64th Street; U.A. East, Olympia, Movieland, 23d Street Triplex. Running time: 93 minutes. This film is rated R.

Jimmy Reardon	River Phoenix
Joyce Fickett	Ann Magnuson
Lisa Bentwright	Meredith Salenger
Denise Hunter	Ione Skye
Suzie Middleberg	Louanne
Fred Roberts	Matthew L. Perry
Al Reardon	Paul Koslo
Faye Reardon	Jane Hallaren
Mathew Hollander	Jason Court
Mr. Spaulding	James Deuter
Emma Spaulding	Marji Banks

By JANET MASLIN

"A Night in the Life of Jimmy Reardon" is hardly the first film about the sexual exploits of a very busy adolescent boy, and it won't be the last. But since it's the work of William Richert, director of the unforgettably nutty little masterpiece "Winter Kills," it's anything but standard issue.

Mr. Richert, who has based the film on a novel he wrote in 1963 at age 19, has done what he can to make this a more or less conventional coming-of-age story. In that he fails miserably, since conventionality is not his strong suit. Though this film can't match "Winter Kills" for inspired craziness, it does punctuate a seemingly ordinary story with welcome bursts of lunacy that are almost its saving grace. Even if Mr. Richert never overcomes the fundamental triteness of this material, he does what he can to keep it lively and off-balance at every turn.

The caliber of the acting varies so wildly (as it did in both "Winter Kills" and in the director's disappointing "Success") that this in itself should keep the audience on its toes. The story follows Jimmy, a recent high school graduate, through the few crucial hours that will help him decide what to do with his future, and through amorous encounters with several of the rich, spoiled and precociously worldly teen-age girls who are his friends. Some of the young actors, like River Phoenix as Jimmy and Meredith Salenger as his frisky nice-girl sweetheart, have trouble delivering Mr. Richert's arch dialogue in a believable way, but others seem better attuned to the director's world view.

Ione Skye seems supremely bored as a teen-age coquette capable of cheating on her steady beau while watching "Robin Hood" on television, and a knowing young actress named Louanne seems vastly to enjoy her role as the only female in Evanston, Ill., circa 1962, for whom Jimmy doesn't have time. Ann Magnuson, who does a marvelous job, is the very model of composure in her role as the worst friend Jimmy's mother (Jane Hallaren) ever had.

As in "Winter Kills," this story hinges on the son's making an 11th-hour discovery about his father, but this time the characters are too young and the story too obvious; there's no real element of surprise. "A Night in the Life of Jimmy Reardon," which opened yesterday at the Movieland and other theaters, prefers to startle its audience in much smaller ways, as when Jimmy tries to wangle some money out of his employer's mother (Marji Banks) and finds her to be one very sharp cookie, or when a young man in a white dinner jacket tries to impress the ladies with his sensitivity by reciting poetry and offering a harmonica rendition of "Streets of Laredo" at a country club dance.

1988 F 27, 20:1

Growing Up
River Phoenix confers with Matthew Perry while Anastasia Fielding looks on in "A Night in the Life of Jimmy Reardon."

Jews With Rhythm

A JUMPIN' NIGHT IN THE GARDEN OF EDEN, produced and directed by Michal Goldman; photographed by Boyd Estus; in English and Yiddish with English subtitles; distributed by First Run Features. At Film Forum 1, 57 Watts Street. Running time: 80 minutes. This film has no rating.
WITH: The Klezmer Conservatory Band and Kapelye

By WALTER GOODMAN

IN case the proclaimed revival of klezmer has somehow passed you by, you can catch up with the catchy music at "A Jumpin' Night in the Garden of Eden." Klezmer (the word comes from the Hebrew for musical instruments) had its origins in the Middle Ages and was popular in the shtetls of Eastern Europe. Itinerant bands of fiddlers, horn blowers and drummers were hired by Polish aristocrats to play their lively mishmash of Hebraic melodies and folk airs from every country where Jews had found themselves. Those poor Jews, a notch above beggars, must have had rhythm.

On stage in Michal Goldman's documentary at Film Forum 1 are two American klezmer bands, the Kapelye of New York City and the larger Klezmer Conservatory Band of Boston, whose members were recruited from the New England Conservatory of Music. (Although you don't have to be Jewish to play klezmer, Don Byron, a black clarinetist, remarks, "I'm always aware that I'm visiting.")

The young bandleaders, Henry Sapoznik (Kapelye) and Hankus Netsky (Klezmer) tell how they were drawn to the music by family members and 78 r.p.m. recordings from the 1920's, when that old klezmer spirit could be heard in the Yiddish theater. We see the groups rehearsing and letting loose on a New York street corner, at a simha for a couple of septuagenarians, at a klezmer camp in the Catskills and, in the Midwest, on the "Prairie Home Compan-

ion" radio show, where the studio audience was moved to dance in the aisles.

Charlie Berg, a drummer, describes the basic klezmer rhythm as an oy vay beat. Judy Bressler, the Boston group's vocalist, who learned Yiddish to sing the songs, delivers them with zest. Most tell stories: "The matchmaker came to grandpa ..." We also hear what may be contemporary commercial klezmer, belted by a Boston disk jockey who specializes in things Jewish: "If you wish to fill up your belly with the best of deli...."

Along with interviews with some old-timers who brought a semblance of klezmer with them from the old country, there are a few tantalizing stills and clips from movies of decades past. Today's klezmer mavens may not be strictly kosher, though they surely try, but listening to the scratchy comic, sentimental, sentimental-comic disks juxtaposed to their renditions, you appreciate that these young musicians are trying to recapture much more than just the tunes of a bygone time; they are after nothing less elusive than the spirit of a destroyed world. As one says, "Our old country is gone."

1988 Mr 2, C20:1

●

Back Page

SWITCHING CHANNELS, directed by Ted Kotcheff; screenplay by Jonathan Reynolds, based on the play "The Front Page" by Ben Hecht and Charles MacArthur; director of photography, François Protat; film editor, Thom Noble; music by Michel Legrand; production designer, Anne Pritchard; producer, Martin Ransohoff; released by Tri-Star Pictures. At Movieland Eighth Street, at University Place; Gemini, Second Avenue at 64th Street; Criterion, Broadway and 45th Street; Olympia, Broadway and 107th Street. Running time: 108 minutes. This film is rated PG.
Christy Colleran	Kathleen Turner
John L. Sullivan IV	Burt Reynolds
Blaine Bingham	Christopher Reeve
Roy Ridnitz	Ned Beatty
Ike Roscoe	Henry Gibson
Siegenthaler	George Newbern
Berger	Al Waxman
Warden Terwilliger	Ken James
The Governor	Charles Kimbrough

By VINCENT CANBY

SOME eccentric inspirations are better than others. In its own day, the idea of the safety pin sounded crazy as well as dangerous. There were also people who groaned when Howard Hawks decided to remake "The Front Page" with Rosalind Russell as Hildy Johnson. Not only did Hawks change Hildy from a man into a woman, but he introduced a love-hate *sexual* relationship between Hildy,

the star reporter of Chicago yellow journalism in the 1920's, and Hildy's manic, unscrupulous editor, Walter Burns.

Yet Hawks's "His Girl Friday" (1940) turned out to be an even more accurate, tougher and more hysterical screen adaptation of the newspaper farce than either the first "Front Page" movie in 1930 or Billy Wilder's 1974 adaptation.

Groans could also be expected more recently when Martin Ransohoff, the producer, announced still another variation on the Ben Hecht and Charles MacArthur stage classic. This one would retain the sex-change operation initiated by Hawks, while updating the time to the 1980's and substituting television reporters for the ink-stained wretches of the original.

The idea sounded awful and, as executed in "Switching Channels," it is.

The saving grace is that you don't have to admire "The Front Page," or even to have heard of it, to find the new movie an utter waste of time. It fails so successfully on its own that it makes the benign "Broadcast News" look like a work of seminal satire.

The film opens today at the Gemini and other theaters.

●

"Switching Channels," directed by Ted Kotcheff and written by Jonathan Reynolds, stars Kathleen Turner as the star reporter for the Chicago-based Satellite News Network, Burt Reynolds as her hard-driving boss (and ex-husband) and Christopher Reeve as the wimpish tycoon who wants to marry Miss Turner and take her to New York where she'll be anchor on something called "A.M. Manhattan."

Whether you go along with "Switching Channels" as a "fun" romantic comedy (which it apparently thinks it is) depends on whether you can swallow the idea that Miss Turner would be selling out in any measurable way by switching from SNN to "A.M. Manhattan." Though the movie tries to persuade us that she has made a name for herself by covering wars and revolutions, she appears most at home when doing dopey human-interest features, including one about the United States President's being serenaded by 1,500 kazoo players.

This scene, which begins "Switching Channels," is both pure and original. It's also one of the movie's only two (count them, *two*) successfully comic sequences, setting a standard never again to be achieved. The big problem seems to be "The Front Page" itself, which the movie makers hold onto as if it were a tiger's tail. They can neither let go of it nor make it into a credible comedy of the 80's.

Miss Turner is an astonishingly re-

Kathleen Turner

silent actress. In scene after scene of "Switching Channels," it's possible to see how entertaining she would be if the movie gave her half a chance. But she's always being undercut. She has no great rapport with Burt Reynolds, who acts less like an obsessed, power-driven editor than a movie star making an appearance on a talk show, trading quips and making sure that his hair remains in place. It is significant that his hair stylist receives screen credit, though hers doesn't.

Mr. Reeve, whose comic potential also goes unused, gives a good impression of an actor trying desperately to create a character who is square, in the Ralph Bellamy tradition, without losing his masculine sexiness. It's not easy. One foolish, unfunny, not-quite-inside joke has the man who played Superman revealed to be afraid of heights. Since much is made of the fact that Mr. Reeve is a manufacturer of sports equipment, one waits for the inevitable jock-strap joke as if approaching the gunshot that ends "Hedda Gabler." There's no avoiding it.

Some of the supporting characters do better. Ned Beatty, Charles Kimbrough and Ken James are good as anachronistic, 1920's-style Chicago opportunists, not above frying an innocent man in the electric chair to gain, or hold onto, political office. Not good at all is Henry Gibson, who plays this pawn as if he were hoping for an Oscar nomination. But then everybody connected with the movie seems utterly confused.

With the exception of a scene in which Mr. Gibson hides in a fancy copying machine (though the machine is no decent substitute for the rolltop desk of the original), the movie never finds the proper mixture of farce and melodrama that should be its style. It's all too nice and clean, like the manicured suburban industrial park where Satellite News Network has its broadcasting facilities.

•

"Switching Channels," which has been rated PG ("Parental Guidance Suggested"), contains vulgar language.

1988 Mr 4, C10:4

Yummy!

BABETTE'S FEAST, directed by Gabriel Axel; screenplay (Danish and French with English subtitles) by Mr. Axel from a novel by Isak Dinesen; cinematography, Henning Kristiansen; edited by Finn Henriksen; music by Per Norgard; production company, Just Betzer, Panorama Film International in cooperation with Nordisk Film A/S and the Danish Film Institute. At Cinema Studio, Broadway at 66th Street. Running time: 105 minutes. This film is rated G.

Babette	Stéphane Audran
Martine (old)	Birgitte Federspiel
Filippa (old)	Bodil Kjer
Martine (young)	Vibeke Hastrup
Filippa (young)	Hanne Stensgard
Lorenz Lowenhielm (old)	Jarl Kulle
Lorenz Lowenhielm (young)	Gudmar Wivesson
Achille Papin	Jean-Philippe Lafont
Lady from the court	Bibi Andersson

"Babette's Feast" was shown as part of last year's New York Film Festival. Following are excerpts from Vincent Canby's review, which appeared in The New York Times Oct. 1, 1987. The film opens today at the Cinema Studio, Broadway and 66th Street.

TAKING a longish tale, "Babette's Feast," from Isak Dinesen's last collection, "Anecdotes of Destiny" (1958), Gabriel Axel has made a very handsome, very literary movie that does justice to the precision of the Dinesen prose, to the particularity of her concerns and to the ironies that so amused her.

What with the English subtitles that translate the Danish dialogue and soundtrack narration, one spends almost as much time reading "Babette's Feast" as watching it. Subtitles, under most circumstances, are simply a necessary intrusion. In this case, however, they have the effect of subtly amplifying the distinctive voice of the storyteller, who can make great leaps forward and backward in time without destroying the commanding unity of the tale. Dinesen is just offscreen throughout.

"Babette's Feast" is set in the second half of the 19th century on Denmark's remote Jutland coast, in a small fishing village whose most notable inhabitants are a fervent Protestant pastor and his two beautiful, pious daughters, Martine and Filippa. Mindful of their responsibilities to their father and his reformist mission, each daughter turns down a beloved suitor. Martine's is a young officer, Filippa's a famous French opera star who has been vacationing on the Jutland coast.

•

After their father's death, the two young women slip into unmarried middle age, carrying on the pastor's work with saintly dedication. One night Babette (Stéphane Audran) turns up at their door carrying a letter of introduction from Filippa's opera singer, now old and retired. Having lost both her husband and son in the Paris Commune, he explains, Babette needs political sanctuary. The sisters, who are nearly penniless,

accept Babette's offer to act as their unpaid housekeeper.

In time, Babette becomes an indispensable though ever enigmatic member of the household. Her Roman Catholicism is politely ignored. She brings order and efficiency to the sisters' lives as defenders of their father's aging flock, which, over the years, has become split by old grievances and jealousies. Babette cooks, cleans, washes and sews, always remaining aloof and proud, at a distance from her benefactors.

All of this is by way of being the prelude to the film's extended, funny and moving final sequence, a spectacular feast, the preparation and execution of which reveal Babette's secret and the nature of her sustaining glory.

•

Mr. Axel, a film maker new to me who has worked as much in France as in Denmark, treats the Dinesen text with self-effacing but informed modesty. The understated courage of the characters, the barren beauty of the landscape and, finally, the unexpected appearance of salvation are all effortlessly defined in images and language that reflect the writer's style — swift, clean, witty and elegant.

Miss Audran dominates the movie in the same way that Babette takes charge of the sisters' household and the village. The actress is still one of the great natural resources of European films.

1988 Mr 4, C12:6

Gridlock

TRAFFIC JAM, directed by Luigi Comencini; screenplay (Italian, French, Spanish and West German with English subtitles) by Mr. Comencini, Ruggero Maccari and Bernardino Zapponi; photographed by Ennio Guarnieri; edited by Nino Baragli; music by Fiorenzo Carpi; art direction by Mario Chiari; produced by Silvio Clementellino; distributed by Cinetel. At Cinema Village, 22 East 12th Street. Running time: 116 minutes. This film has no rating. With: Annie Girardot, Fernando Rey, Miou Miou, Gérard Depardieu, Ugo Tognazzi, Marcello Mastroianni, Stefania Sandrelli, Alberto Sordi, Orazio Orlando, Gianni Cavina, Harry Baer, Angela Molina, Ciccio Ingrassia, Patrick Dewaere

"TRAFFIC JAM," Luigi Comencini's 1978 Italian film, begins as if it were going to be a light-hearted, satirical variation on Jean-Luc Godard's apocalyptic classic, "Weekend." Instead it becomes a very heavy, rather literal forecast of the decline and fall of capitalism through gridlock.

Caught in a 24-hour traffic jam, on a highway between Rome and Naples, are the members of an all-star European cast including Marcello Mastroianni, Gérard Depardieu, Annie Girardot, Patrick Dewaere, Angela Molina and Alberto Sordi. When the film sticks to comic anecdotes, before it starts telling the audience to shape up or ship out, "Traffic Jam" has a number of diverting moments.

As a vain movie star, Mr. Mastroianni is relaxed and extremely good company. Mr. Sordi also has his moments as a Socialist government minister who loathes the common people and doesn't want them urinating against the tires of his Jaguar. There's a funny, recurring shot of a hitchhiker who stands beside the

stalled traffic, holding out a card reading "Napoli."

During its last hour "Traffic Jam" turns solemn and doomy. There's a brutal gang rape, which prompts a character to ask forlornly why people can't love other people and fornicate "with love." A stalled trailer truck, loaded with new cars on the way to the salesrooms, says rather more than we need to hear about conspicuous consumption.

The film is pro-abortion, clean air and people who sing folk songs. It's firmly against any system that makes a poor man so desperate he'll exchange his pregnant wife's favors for a chauffeur's job at the Cinecittà movie studios. Mr. Comencini doesn't have a light touch.

"Traffic Jam" opens today at the Cinema Village.

VINCENT CANBY

1988 Mr 4, C14:6

Femme Fatale

AND GOD CREATED WOMAN, directed by Roger Vadim; written by R. J. Stewart; director of photography, Stephen M. Katz; edited by Suzanne Pettit; music by Thomas Chase and Steve Rucker; production designer, Victor Kempster; produced by George G. Braunstein and Ron Hamady; released by Vestron Pictures. At the Manhattan Twin, 59th Street and Third Avenue; Movieland, Broadway and 47th Street; Metro Twin, Broadway and 99th Street; Waverly Twin, Avenue of the Americas and Third Street. Running time: 100 minutes. This film is rated R.

Robin	Rebecca De Mornay
Billy Moran	Vincent Spano
James Tiernan	Frank Langella
Peter Moran	Donovan Leitch
Alexandra Tiernan	Judith Chapman
Timmy Moran	Jaime McEnnan
Blue	Benjamin Mouton
David	David Shelley

THERE are few real constants in this world, but surely Roger Vadim's gift for girl-watching looked like one of them. So it's sad to see Mr. Vadim's lecherous eye let him down. Whatever it was that possessed him to remake his 1957 "And God Created Woman," the film that launched Brigitte Bardot, it was not the discovery of a voluptuous and comparably kittenish new star. Mr. Vadim's leading lady this time is the thoroughly ordinary Rebecca De Mornay, who has all the self-interest her role requires but little of the sex appeal.

Actually, this "And God Created Woman," which opens today at the Manhattan Twin and other theaters, isn't a remake at all. In production notes for the film, Mr. Vadim points out that the plot and central character are quite different, and rightly notes that this does not matter since the original film hasn't been seen

much lately, and in any case is not remembered for its narrative. Incidentally, Mr. Vadim says that his reason for making the new film was to try to answer the question "What exactly is a young woman today?"

In this story, she's a prison inmate who dreams of performing her terrible hard-rock songs for all the world to hear. The plot, what there is of it, springs out of a little misunderstanding. One day, while Robin (Miss De Mornay) is in the midst of an escape attempt, she encounters a handsome carpenter named Billy Moran (Vincent Spano). She happens to be wearing only sweatsocks and sneakers at the time, so one thing leads to another. Billy then makes the not unreasonable assumption that Robin is interested in him, but he is wrong. After she persuades Billy to marry her so she can win her parole, Robin refuses to sleep with him again. Billy is not amused by this behavior.

•

The earlier film was also about a less-than-ideal wife, but Mr. Vadim has dispensed with the ending that had the husband finally smack her to help her come to her senses. He and the screenwriter, R. J. Stewart, have also added a subplot that involves Rebecca with a gubernatorial candidate (Frank Langella) in New Mexico, where the story takes place. The film contains relatively few bedroom scenes, which is odd in view of the fact that the story is about little else. It is perhaps worth noting that the characters often keep their socks on.

"And God Created Woman" has a slow pace, a trashy look and a notably poor sense of humor. The Donovan Leitch in the cast, in the small role of Billy's brother, is not the 60's folk-rock star but his teen-age son.

JANET MASLIN

1988 Mr 4, C22:4

Locked In

GIRL FROM HUNAN, directed by Xie Fei and U Lan; written (in Mandarin with English subtitles) by Zhang Xian, from the novel "Xiao Xiao" by Shen Congwen; cinematography, Fu Jingshen; edited by Zhang Lanfang; production design, Xing Zheng; produced by Don Yaping, from the Beijing Youth Film Studio; released by New Yorker Films. At Lincoln Plaza 1, Broadway and 63d Street. Running time: 99 minutes. This film has no rating.

Xiao Xiao (adult)	Na Renhua
Xiao Xiao (child)	Liu Qing
Hua Gou	Deng Xiaoguang
Chun Guan	Zhang Yu
Chun Guan's mother	Ni Meiling

"GIRL FROM HUNAN," one of the first films from China to receive commercial release in this country,

Romance
Rebecca DeMornay portrays an aspiring rock-and-roll singer who enters a marriage of convenience in "And God Created Woman."

From China

Na Renhua, playing a teen-age wife in an arranged marriage in turn-of-the-century China, carries her 6-year-old husband (Zhang Yu) in "Girl From Hunan."

is a plea for the rights of women as reflected in the sad consequences of the arranged marriage of a peasant girl, Xiao Xiao, 12, and a 2-year-old boy, Chun Guan.

The time is the early part of this century and the place a remote village where Xiao Xiao is brought by her uncle not realizing that the groom is a baby whom she'll be called upon to raise. Xiao Xiao is not a rebel. She accepts her lot, as her mother-in-law notes, takes care of her husband and works in the fields.

The years pass. Her breasts become full, as her mother-in-law notes. At age 16, Xiao Xiao is willingly seduced by a farmhand and becomes pregnant. Efforts to abort the baby fail. One night the terrified girl watches as the villagers drown a young widow who has been unfaithful to her husband. There is no question of executing the man. Instead, his legs are broken to make it more difficult for him to sneak around in the future.

"Girl From Hunan," which opens today at the Lincoln Plaza 1, is of more interest as a social-political document, or as ethnic cinema, than as art or entertainment. In China, a long shot of a nude woman about to be drowned, and the film's frank acknowledgement that lust exists, probably seem more sensational than they do here.

Xie Fei and U Lan, the directors, don't sentimentalize their story, and they treat Xiao Xiao, sweetly played by Na Renhua, with respectful reserve.

Yet the whole thing has the self-conscious manner of a travelogue. Manners and mores are examined and rituals attended to. Information is given. The misty landscapes are photographed in picturesque images that have nothing to do with poor Xiao Xiao's state of mind. They are scenery.

VINCENT CANBY

1988 Mr 4, C22:4

The Bad Old Days

THE HOUSE ON CARROLL STREET, directed and produced by Peter Yates; written by Walter Bernstein; director of photography, Michael Ballhaus; edited by Ray Lovejoy; music by Georges Delerue; production designer, Stuart Wurtzel; released by Orion Pictures Corporation. At Guild 50th Street, west of Fifth Avenue; Paramount, 61st Street and Broadway; New York Twin, Second Avenue and 66th Street; Art Greenwich Twin, 12th Street and Seventh Avenue. Running time: 101 minutes. This film is rated PG.
Emily .... Kelly McGillis
Cochran .... Jeff Daniels
Salwen .... Mandy Patinkin
Miss Venable .... Jessica Tandy
Alan .... Jonathan Hogan
Senator Byington .... Remak Ramsay
Hackett .... Ken Welsh
Stefan .... Christopher Rhode

By JANET MASLIN

"THE HOUSE ON CARROLL STREET" unfolds in a beautiful, clean city, a place of safe subways and balmy summer breezes, a peaceful, romantic urban landscape bathed in warm golden light. This place, strange and delightful as it may seem, is in fact New York. But the city's appearance (which is made spectacularly lovely by Michael Ballhaus's magical cinematography) is deceptive, for the time is 1951. The political climate is as sinister as the physical setting is serene.

The specter of McCarthyism rears its head immediately, in an opening scene that shows the demure young Life magazine photo editor Emily Crane (Kelly McGillis) being interrogated by a Senate committee. The committee's counsel, a vaguely Roy Cohn-ish figure named Ray Salwen (Mandy Patinkin), demands that she implicate her colleagues and reminds her that the photographs she chooses are "information received by *millions* of unsuspecting Americans." The film's atmosphere of paranoia and fear is thus quickly established, but almost as suddenly it becomes something else. And Emily, though still presented as the fiercely principled young professional, turns into Nancy Drew.

"The House on Carroll Street," which opens today at Loews New York Twin and other theaters, is more interesting for its good looks and presumably serious ambitions than for what it finally turns into, which is a silly suspense story speeding breathlessly from one wild coincidence to another. Dismissed from her Life job after the hearings, Emily is hired to read stories to a peppery old lady (Jessica Tandy). And before you can say "Rear Window," she has spied something suspicious in the house across the way. This peculiar activity involves none other than Salwen, her Senate committee tormentor, and a group of furtive-looking foreigners. Emily blunders just deeply enough into this intrigue to be tailed by the F.B.I., persecuted by Salwen and his cronies, and frightened by one stranger or another every time she turns around. Peter Yates, who directed from a screenplay by Walter Bernstein, is especially fond of startling the audience with loud noises.

●

Mr. Yates does his best to make "The House on Carroll Street" a stylish period thriller, but its more ambitious scenes get away from him. A chase through a bookstore is monotonously staged, and the pièce de résistance — a battle across the upper reaches of Grand Central Terminal

— becomes noticeably clumsy. Even such showy gestures as having Salwen describe the Red Menace by pouring ketchup onto a white tablecloth manage to lack visual flair, not to mention political sophistication. It hardly helps that whenever the plucky Emily is doing her eavesdropping, she's able to overhear something much too convenient, like "You'll be leaving on the Chicago Express, which departs at 6 o'clock."

Miss McGillis has been given a Breck Girl hairdo and a quaintly girlish wardrobe for this role, but she often seems considerably less fragile than the character, and no more interesting. (Emily is named for Emily Dickinson, whose poetry she loves, etc.) Miss McGillis also has the habits of purring her r's affectedly and of representing any strong emotion, from joy to fear, as an apparent readiness to burst into tears. In marked contrast to this is the funny, effortlessly natural Jeff Daniels, as the F.B.I. man who's assigned to follow Emily and of course becomes smitten. Mr. Patinkin, with his arms crossed, his hair slicked back and his face clenched in a tight, meaty smile, makes much more of his villain's role than the story ever does.

●

"The House on Carroll Street" is rated PG ("Parental Guidance Suggested"). It includes brief nudity.

1988 Mr 4, C23:1

Jailhouse Ghost

PRISON, directed by Renny Harlin; written by C. Courtney Joyner, original story by Irwin Yablans; director of photography, Mac Ahlberg; film editor, Ted Nicolaou; music by Richard Band and Eddie Surkin; produced by Irwin Yablans; released by Empire Entertainment. At Criterion Center, Broadway and 45th Street; Movie Center 5, 125th Street between Powell and Douglass Boulevards. Running time: 102 minutes. This film is rated R.
Sharpe .... Lane Smith
Burke .... Viggo Mortensen
Katherine .... Chelsea Field
Sandor .... Andre de Shields
Cresus .... Lincoln Kilpatrick
Lasagna .... Ivan Kane
Big Sam .... Tom (Tiny) Lister Jr.

By CARYN JAMES

"PRISON" has a generic, low-budget name, and for once you can judge a movie by its title. This prison-drama-meets-ghost-story, which opens today at the Criterion and Movie Center 5, turns out to be an object lesson in how cheaply and badly a film can be made.

We can predict the plot from the minute a man goes to the electric chair while a growling, nervous guard looks on. Twenty years later, a sudden phone call wakes the guard — his name, Sharpe, does not refer to his acumen — from the execution scene that haunts his nightmares. Now he's to be the warden of the very prison where that execution took place! You can almost hear the ghost of the innocent man — does anyone need to be told he was innocent? — cranking up in the wings.

●

He never quite enters, though, because in the film's cheapest touch the electrocuted man turns into an electric ghost. Sometimes he appears as a few blue lightning volts, and sometimes as a big blue light coming through a door. We know that's the

ghost because the blue lights are always followed by very big, very bad reaction shots, as if we are watching the silliest kind of acting class exercise. Today, pretend you're a vegetable! Next class, pretend you are scared by blue light!

There are other low-rent effects, such as barbed wire unrolling itself to strangle a man. But the only hint of suspense — and it's the slightest hint — comes from the handsome convict who risks his life to save another, and goes out of his way to be kind to his fellow prisoners. What's a nice, cute guy like this doing in prison? It's easier to figure out why he's in the movie than to guess why anyone would want to watch it.

1988 Mr 4, C33:1

MOVING, directed by Alan Metter; written by Andy Breckman; director of photography, Donald McAlpine; edited by Alan Balsam; music by Howard Shore; production designer, David L. Snyder; produced by Stuart Cornfeld; released by Warner Brothers. At the Criterion Center, Broadway and 45th Street; the Orpheum Twin, 86th Street and Third Avenue; the Manhattan Twin, 59th Street and Third Avenue; the 23d Street West Triplex, at Eighth Avenue; the Metro Twin, Broadway and 99th Street. Running time: 89 minutes. This film is rated R.
Arlo Pear .... Richard Pryor
Monica Pear .... Beverly Todd
Casey Pear .... Stacey Dash
Marshall Pear .... Raphael Harris
Randy Pear .... Ishmael Harris
Gordon Darnell Crawford .... Randy Quaid
Brad Williams .... Dana Carvey

By JANET MASLIN

Richard Pryor has been given the full Bill Cosby treatment for his role in "Moving," complete with charming family, fancy sweaters and brand-new Saab. Mr. Pryor plays Arlo Pear, a mass transit engineer who has been living in suburban splendor in New Jersey when a career change makes it necessary for him to relocate to Idaho. Nominally a comedy, this is in fact a horror story chronicling the hellish things that befall the Pear family's possessions en route, and documenting the general trauma of being uprooted.

Mr. Pryor doesn't really fit in here, but perhaps that's just as well. Sounding quiet, looking extremely thin and sporting a beard that changes shape from scene to scene, Mr. Pryor appears to be working at something less than full throttle, but every now and then some welcome hint of fury shows through. And by the end of the story he is ready to strike back at all the obnoxious, furniture-breaking movers and noisy neighbors who have tormented him, a move that is long overdue.

"Moving," which opened yesterday at the Criterion Center and other theaters, isn't anything out of the ordinary, but those who have shared at least some of these experiences ought to find it amusing. There is, for instance, the moving company that promises the Pear family the world, then sends a lone, elderly man who packs even the children's miniature toy cars individually; of course, he charges by the hour. There is the over-eager home buyer who forgets to ask certain basic questions, like whether a house's stairway to the second floor is included in the deal. There is the nice young man (played by Dana Carvey, who does the Church Lady on "Saturday Night Live") who applies for the job of driving the Saab out to Idaho, and apologizes profusely for being half a minute late. Only

after he [...] of the day [...]
Pears discover that the father is [...]
current cover boy on [...] of Psychology Today.

Randy Quaid [...]
role as a [...]
the Pears [...]
Rodney Dangerfield [...]
School [...] the work on the [...]
rector, Alice Mellon is [...]
fidence officer of a [...] bank [...]
cer to whom the Pears apply for a [...]
mortgage. Rodney Dangerfield [...]
as plus the Pears [...]
have perfected the art [...]
to be many a time [...]
less than 15 seconds. [...]
side is [...] that [...]
genial [...] that [...]
never stop [...]
does a lot to [...]
film makers [...]
feel like audiences [...]

[...] complete racial harmony.

The R rating for "Moving" seems
more a reflection of Mr. Pryor's past
than of this film's language, though
Andy Breckman's screenplay does include one or two R-caliber words. But
the Pears are so nice that whenever
they curse, they fine themselves a
quarter and contribute to the family
"swear jar." One of the film's funnier moments has Mrs. Pear
literally coolly laying down a wad of
cash in preparation for telling Arlo
what she thinks of Idaho.

1988 Mr 5, 16:4

Murder and Passion In the Hamptons

MASQUERADE, directed by Bob Swaim; written by Dick Wolf; director of photography, David Watkin; film editor, Scott Conrad; music by John Barry; production designer, John Kasarda; produced by Michael I. Levy; released by Metro-Goldwyn-Mayer Pictures, Inc. At Embassy 2, Broadway at 47th Street; 23d Street West Triplex, near Eighth Avenue; U. A. East, First Avenue and 85th Street; 84th Street Six, at Broadway. Running time: 90 minutes. This film is rated R.

Tim Whalan	Rob Lowe
Olivia Lawrence	Meg Tilly
Brooke Morrison	Kim Cattrall
Mike McGill	Doug Savant
Tony Gateworth	John Glover
Anne Briscoe	Dana Delany

By JANET MASLIN

The makers of "Masquerade" had
a great idea: put Rob Lowe in Top-
Siders. As the golden-boy skipper of a
racing yacht anchored off the Hamptons, Mr. Lowe has an appeal he
never manifested in earlier, sulkier
post-adolescent roles. This time, Mr.

S. Karin Epstein

All at Sea

In "Masquerade," Meg
Tilly portrays a wealthy
heiress and Rob Lowe
the yachtsman who
falls in love with her.

Lowe has the more interesting job of
playing Tim Whalan, whose good
looks, good manners and racing
record make him very much in demand, especially among those Hamptons residents who know about his
other, less obvious talents. In Tim's
case, still waters definitely run deep.

"Masquerade," which opens today
at the Embassy 2 and other theaters,
is about Tim's romance with the
naïve young Olivia Lawrence (Meg
Tilly), a lovely, guileless creature
who has only recently inherited several hundred million dollars. They
meet at a party, and without even
trying Tim sweeps Olivia off her feet.
"He's the first man I've ever been
comfortable with," Olivia tells a confidante, and she purrs to Tim that he
makes her sleep like a baby. All rosy
glow and deep contentment, Olivia
never thinks to wonder whether this
dreamboat may be planning to kill
her.

Bob Swaim, who also directed "La
Balance" and "Half Moon Street,"
makes the most of this situation. The
Hamptons look gorgeous, as do Tim
and Olivia themselves; every frame
of the film is rapturously pretty, and
bathed in the most flattering light.
The sets are both posh and attractive,
and Mr. Swaim knows exactly how to
film a dashing young yachtsman, the
wind in his hair and the surf flying by.
If he's less adroit with this film's
story of intrigue, that really is a secondary consideration.

●

There is indeed a plot on Olivia's
life, and Dick Wolf's screenplay
makes it an unduly complicated one.
Certain scenes here, particularly one
involving Tim, Olivia and her wicked,
drunken stepfather (John Glover),
don't add up even after all the pieces
are in place. But the murder scheme
exists chiefly as a way of testing Tim
and Olivia's feelings for each other,
and it is in bringing those feelings to
life that the film is at its best.

Miss Tilly makes a sweetly radiant
ingénue at first, then develops a sexier, more womanly side; she seems
so convincingly besotted with love
that in one scene Mr. Swaim films her
with her crucifix necklace noticeably
askew. (Mr. Swaim measures the
power of this couple's erotic bond by
the way they behave in the mornings
at breakfast, not by glimpses of the
night before.) Mr. Lowe is more of an
ice prince, and too many of the revelations about Tim's character come
from the dialogue rather than from
his behavior. But he makes a magnetic figure all the same.

●

Mr. Swaim has also cast the supporting roles quite well, so that the
film's incidental characters become

much more than mere pieces in the
puzzle. Kim Cattrall, much better
than she's been in films like "Mannequin" and "Tribute," brings a real
sultriness to the role of a bored wife
whose wealthy husband doesn't
watch her very closely; Dana Delany
sounds a surprisingly bitter note as a
woman from the wrong side of the
tracks who loses her chance to move
up. (In this film's scheme of things,
class consciousness is everywhere.)
Doug Savant, as a local police officer,
has the film's most peculiar role, but
he handles it with discretion. John
Barry's swelling score and David
Watkin's scenic cinematography contribute greatly to the rhapsodic mood.

Twice during the course of "Masquerade," couples go to the local
theater and come out happily declaring, "That was a *really* good movie!"
"Masquerade" won't elicit quite that
level of enthusiasm, but it'll come
close.
JANET MASLIN

1988 Mr 11, C8:5

A Hunt for a Killer, With Built-In Ironies

OFF LIMITS, directed by Christopher Crowe; written by Mr. Crowe and Jack Thibeau; director of photography, David Gribble; edited by Douglas Ibold; music by James Newton Howard; production designer, Dennis Washington; produced by Alan Barnette; released by 20th Century-Fox Film Corporation. At the National, Broadway and 44th Street; the Baronet, Third Avenue and 59th Street; the 86th Street East, at Third Avenue; the Bay Cinema, Second Avenue and 32d Street; the Columbia, 103d Street and Broadway; Movieland Eighth Street, at University Place. Running time: 101 minutes. This film is rated R.

Buck McGriff	Willem Dafoe
Albaby Perkins	Gregory Hines
Dix	Fred Ward
Nicole	Amanda Pays
Lime Green	Kay Tong Lim
Colonel Armstrong	Scott Glenn
Rogers	David Alan Grier

The story is nothing out of the ordinary: two tough-talking, super-
macho detectives are put on the trail
of a serial killer, a sadomasochist
who has been murdering prostitutes
and is sure to do it again. But the setting raises the ante, since it is the turbulent, troubled Saigon of 1968 in
which "Off Limits" unfolds. Here
things automatically become more
dangerous and perverse; here certain unavoidable ironies are built into
the situation. By rights, "Off Limits"
should never have been as conventional as it turns out to be.

But "Off Limits," which opens today at the Baronet and other theaters, is an unexpectedly standard
thriller. Though Christopher Crowe,
the director and co-writer, makes
some attempt to interweave glimpses
of the war and its effects into the
mystery plot, there are too many
lines like, "It's Tet; we've got a
cease-fire; don't worry about it," and
too few real surprises. One of the rare
ones is a foxy nun, played by Amanda
Pays, who says, "I find that wearing
my habit can be quite off-putting to
people." As a result of her field work
with the endangered prostitutes, Sister Nicole can talk quite unblushingly
about oral sex.

●

Interested in this nun, and even
more interested in finding the killer,
is Buck McGriff (Willem Dafoe), a
detective with the Army's Criminal
Investigations Division. His fellow
C.I.D. man is Albaby Perkins (Greg-

ory Hines), who chews gum most of
the time and can top even McGriff's
rampant machismo. Though the
screenplay, which is loaded with obscenities, hasn't given either of these
actors much of a character to work
with, they acquit themselves well on
the strength of sheer physical presence alone; Mr. Dafoe cuts a startling
figure under any circumstances, and
Mr. Hines a sympathetic one. Also excellent, in a cast that favors performers with a lean, mean look, are Fred
Ward as the master sergeant spear-
heading the investigation, Kay Tong
Lim as a dapper, sardonic Vietnamese police official, and Scott Glenn as
the craziest and most dangerous of
the suspects. The harrowing helicopter scene involving Mr. Glenn is
surely one of a kind.

The identity of the killer should not
surprise anyone familiar with stories
of this ilk, and indeed the writers
(Jack Thibeau, in addition to Mr.
Crowe) don't do that much to conceal
it. They have worked far harder in
coming up with a pretext for Sister
Nicole to turn up minus her habit,
wearing a slip, with her hair down.
JANET MASLIN

1988 Mr 11, C8:5

The Kid at the Office, The Old Man in School

VICE VERSA, directed by Brian Gilbert; written and produced by Dick Clement and Ian La Frenais; director of photography, King Baggot; edited by David Garfield; music by David Shire; production designer, Jim Schoppe; released by Columbia Pictures. At Loews Astor Plaza, 44th Street and Broadway; Orpheum Twin, 86th Street and Third Avenue; 34th Street Showplace, between Second and Third Avenues; Metro Twin, 99th Street and Broadway. Running time: 97 minutes. This film is rated PG.

Marshall	Judge Reinhold
Charlie	Fred Savage
Sam	Corinne Bohrer
Tina	Swoosie Kurtz
Robyn	Jane Kaczmarek
Turk	David Proval
Avery	William Prince

Luck doesn't get any worse than it
has for "Vice Versa," the twin of an
identically plotted film released only
a few months previously. Originality
isn't a factor for either this or "Like
Father, Like Son," since they both
owe a good deal to the earlier
"Freaky Friday," but timeliness undoubtedly is.

All things being equal, neither of
these films is appreciably better than
the other; the difference isn't one of
quality but of style. "Like Father,
Like Son" had Dudley Moore, who
brought a certain sly sophistication to
the role of a grown man with the mind
of a small boy, while "Vice Versa,"
which opens today at Loews Astor
Plaza and other theaters, has Judge
Reinhold, who concentrates more on
the innocent silliness of the situation.
Both of them have found gentle
humor in the plight of a grown man
sent off to junior high school while his
carefree, irresponsible, career-
wrecking son fills in for him on the
job.

Both films have the same sort of
prologue, detailing the discovery of a
magical potion ("Like Father, Like
Son") or icon ("Vice Versa") that
can effect an identity switch. In this
case, Mr. Reinhold plays a Chicago
department-store executive named
Marshall Seymour who is on a buying
trip to Bangkok when he accidentally
happens upon a stolen religious artifact and brings it home. Soon Mar-

Fred Savage, left, and Judge Reinhold as father and son in "Vice Versa."

shall has lost his driven, workaholic look and turned into his blithe 11-year-old son Charlie (Fred Savage). He fools around with the department-store merchandise, can't find his office and looks blank when his friends and co-workers use words like "feasible" and "enigma."

•

Charlie, for his part, barks orders at his teachers and summons limousines to drive him around town. "Is he famous?" someone asks the driver, upon seeing Charlie alight from his car. "He will be," the driver answers. "I'm gonna kill him."

Neither film had a mother figure on hand to witness the personality switch, but "Vice Versa" does give Marshall an ex-wife (Jane Kaczmarek) with whom Charlie usually lives. This presents the newly youthful Marshall with the danger of being shipped back to a woman he can't stand and forced to behave as her son. Beyond this, the screenplay by Dick Clement and Ian La Frenais doesn't do much with the story's darker possibilities, and it sounds a much too cloying note when both Charlie and his dad become sweet on the father's spunky girlfriend (Corinne Bohrer, in a Teri Garr role). Inevitably, they and the director Brian Gilbert coax this story along until it leads to a happy ending and heightened mutual understanding.

The film's best scenes are those between the goofily nonchalant Mr. Reinhold and the precociously stern Mr. Savage, however bluntly these moments call attention to the craziness of the premise. Of course, it is never explained why the father and son can't simply repeat their make-a-wish mistake immediately and return things to the status quo.

•

"Vice Versa" is rated PG ("Parental Guidance Suggested"). It contains some off-color language.

JANET MASLIN

1988 Mr 11, C12:6

The Final Bang, But No Whimpers

WHEN THE WIND BLOWS, directed by Jimmy T. Murakami; screenplay by Raymond Briggs, based on his novel; art direction, layout and animation by Richard Fawdry; music by various composers; produced by John Coates. At Eastside Cinema, Third Avenue at 55th Street. Running time: 81 minutes. This film has no rating.

Hilda's voice .... Dame Peggy Ashcroft
James's voice .... Sir John Mills

By VINCENT CANBY

James and Hilda Bloggs are living out their golden years in a modest, immaculately tidy cottage in a remote part of Sussex. James and Hilda are a staunch, lower-middle-class English couple, backbone-of-the-nation types whose faith in the future has remained undiminished since they stood up to the Jerries in 1940.

James spends his days puttering. Hilda keeps everything nice — cleaning, washing, ironing. It's a good life. They have each other, and, not far away, their son, Ron, Ron's wife, Beryl, and Baby Jim. From time to time James goes up to London to read the newspapers in the library. He likes to keep in touch.

One evening James returns with a pocketful of survival brochures and, over a cup of tea, announces, "There may be a pre-emptive strike." "Oh, no," says Hilda, "not another strike." No sooner is one strike settled than agitators start another.

James carefully explains that this strike will be different. A nuclear strike. "Well," says Hilda, "we'd best lay in supplies." James studies his Government literature and sets about to build, in the front room, what one brochure calls "an inner core, or refuge."

This is a sort of lean-to, constructed with doors placed at a 60-degree angle to the wall, where they'll have to remain for 14 days after the bomb goes off. Hilda says that at her age she certainly doesn't intend to use a chamber pot. Fallout or no fallout ("What *does* fallout look like, James?"), she will use the facility upstairs.

•

James and Hilda Bloggs are a most unlikely hero and heroine, and "When the Wind Blows" is a most unlikely entertainment. Here is an animated film (with live-action inserts) about the end of civilization, a subject much beloved by the makers of dreary, numbingly arty cartoons shown at film festivals.

"When the Wind Blows," opening today at the Eastside Cinema, is different. Though its point is as familiar as it is cautionary, it has a satiric, unsentimental identity of its own.

In a movie of this mixed-media sort, it's difficult to know who should be credited for its success. All I can do is name the names. Jimmy T. Murakami, last represented here by Roger Corman's "Battle Beyond the Stars," was the director, and Richard Fawdry was responsible for the animation and layout design. Possibly most important is the screenplay by Raymond Briggs, who adapted his own novel and who has a wonderfully comic way of turning a cliché inside out. Says James, as he cheerfully makes the cottage shipshape for a megaton blast: "After all, there's a war on, or almost."

Of immense help, too, are Sir John Mills and Dame Peggy Ashcroft, who supply the voices for James and Hilda. In most animated films, the "star" voices sound detached from the cartoon images that in no way evoke the actors. One of the magical things about "When the Wind Blows" is that Sir John and Dame Peggy bring the pudding-faced cartoon characters to life without calling attention to their own presences.

When the bomb drops before they're quite ready for it, James loses his temper with Hilda for, perhaps, the first time in their marriage. Hilda dawdles. "Come on, you stupid bitch," he yells and dives into the shelter. The first night in it is hell, and on the second day they can't resist exploring the mess inside the house and out: plaster everywhere, Hilda's curtains turned into brittle rags, the electricity and telephone out, the grass incinerated and a high dark haze hiding the sun. Says James at nightfall: "Hurry up, dear. We'd better get back into our inner core or refuge." Says Hilda, "Bang go a lot of people's holidays this year."

James promises that Emergency Services will come by with food. "Will it be like Meals on Wheels, dear?" asks Hilda. In time they both develop unsightly blotches on their legs and arms, which, James reassures her, "are a common complaint among the middle-aged." Hilda's gums begin to bleed. Says James, "I'll pop down to the chemist when the crisis pales into insignificance."

James and Hilda look on the bright side, right up to the end. Or, as James puts it: "It's bound to take it out of you. A shock like that."

Not since "Beyond the Fringe" has the English reputation for stoicism been so effectively sent up, and possibly never has it been sent up with such brutally funny seriousness.

1988 Mr 11, C19:1

An American Death In a Troubled Time

WHO KILLED VINCENT CHIN?, a film by Christine Choy and Renee Tajima; edited by Holly Fisher. Running time: 87 minutes. This film has no rating. At Roy and Niuta Titus Theater 1, Museum of Modern Art, 11 West 53d Street, as part of the New Directors/New Films series. Running time: 87 minutes. This film has no rating.

On a hot summer night in 1982, Vincent Chin, a young, thoroughly assimilated Chinese-American, was having a night out with his pals (white), celebrating the last days of his bachelorhood at a Detroit topless bar called the Fancy Pants. In the course of the evening, Mr. Chin got into a scuffle with another customer, Ron Ebens, an unemployed auto worker. Mr. Ebens and Michael Nitz, his stepson, left the Fancy Pants.

A little later, Mr. Ebens and Mr. Nitz cornered Mr. Chin outside a nearby McDonald's. While friends and strangers looked on, Mr. Nitz held Mr. Chin as Mr. Ebens beat him over the head with a baseball bat.

There's no doubt about what happened. As one witness puts it in "Who Killed Vincent Chin?," a good, solidly constructed new documentary by Christine Choy and Renee Tajima, "An auto worker, who was out of work, beat up a Chinese guy who he thought was Japanese."

There would also seem to be no doubt about who did it. Yet, by the end of their film, Ms. Choy and Ms. Tajima have so successfully analyzed this sudden, sad, fatal confrontation that almost everything except the Big Mac becomes implicated in the events.

"Who Killed Vincent Chin?" will be shown at the Museum of Modern Art tonight at 6, opening the 17th annual New Directors/New Films festival sponsored by the museum's department of film and the Film Society of Lincoln Center. It will be shown again at the museum tomorrow at 3:30 P.M.

"Who Killed Vincent Chin?" is about many things, including Detroit,

231

the economics of the automobile industry, the history of Oriental immigrants, blue-collar aspirations, American justice and the ways Americans talk. At one point, Mr. Ebens, who has an even-featured, open, clear-eyed American "look," sits beside his wife, Nita, on their living room couch and tries to recall his feelings about the killing. "I remember the next day was Father's Day," he says. "I sure felt silly."

The film makers also talk to Vincent Chin's mother, Mr. Chin's white boyhood friend who was with him the night of the death, friends and relatives of the defendants, topless dancers, policemen and people active in the campaign called "Justice for Vincent Chin." One defense lawyer is quick to admit that he himself drives a Japanese car, as if to certify that the crime had nothing to do with either race relations or economics.

There's even a clip from the Phil Donahue show in which Mr. Donahue, holding his microphone as if it were a religious object, gazes intently at a member of the "Justice for Vincent Chin" campaign and says, "Let me see if I see your strategy here."

•

As Ms. Choy and Ms. Tajima understand, so much talk threatens to obscure the fact that a killing took place. "I think the media blew it all out of proportion," says Mr. Nitz's girlfriend, who appears to be miffed at all the fuss. One of Mr. Ebens's fellow workers and drinking buddies sounds a lot like Harry Dean Stanton in "Repo Man": "In the plants you lead a very fast and hard life. You work hard and play hard. Ron fitted in real good."

Says Ron, who was known to have a drinking problem, "It was just like this was preordained to be."

Vincent Chin's mother talks about her early life in Detroit, when Chinese immigrants could not hope to work in the auto plants but, instead, serviced auto workers with laundries and restaurants. She was brought up to be inconspicuous and self-effacing in a white world. She always worried that her son was fooling himself when he assumed he had been accepted.

Using newsreel footage, Ms. Choy and Ms. Tajima set the story in the context of a Detroit attempting to cope with competition from overseas automobile makers, and with an unemployment rate of 17 percent. In one shot, auto workers trash a Japanese car in much the way Mr. Ebens and Mr. Nitz trashed Mr. Chin. By the time of the third trial related to the case, the question to be decided was whether the killing of Vincent Chin was premeditated, or could be excused as a sudden act of temper.

Unlike the law, the film makers never forget Vincent Chin himself.

VINCENT CANBY

1988 Mr 11, C22:3

Past vs. Present, The Palestinian Way

WEDDING IN GALILEE, directed by Michel Khleifi; screenplay (in Arabic, with English subtitles) by Mr. Khleifi; photography by Walther van den Ende; edited by Marie Castro Vasquez; music by Jean-Marie Senia; production companies: Marisa Films (Belgium)/LPA (France); released by Kino International. At the Roy and Niuta Titus Theater 1, Museum of Modern Art, 11 West 53d Street, as part of the New Directors/New Films series. Running time: 113 minutes. This film has no rating.

Anna Achdian

The Mukhtar	Ali M. El Akili
Officers	Makram Khouri, Juliano Mer Khamis
Bacem	Youssef Abou Warda
The Mother	Bushra Karaman
The Bride	Anna Achdian
Soumaya	Sonia Amar
The Groom	Nazih Akleh

By CARYN JAMES

"Wedding in Galilee" cannot help but seem exotic to Western eyes, as it lures us into a ritual wedding feast in a Palestinian village in Israel. Michel Khleifi, a writer and director who was born and raised in Nazareth and now lives in Brussels, relies on a wandering, Eastern-style narrative to depict Palestinian traditions threatened by 20th-century inroads.

His film is lyrical and extravagantly detailed when portraying the Palestinians. But because Mr. Khleifi turns simplistic and leaden whenever he points his camera at an Israeli, always viewed as the one-dimensional enemy, his often dazzling first feature is diminished by his insistently narrow vision.

Mr. Khleifi's sympathies are unexplored but instantly obvious. When the village leader, or mukhtar, decides his son must have a traditional wedding celebration that lasts through the night, he must ask the Israeli military governor for permission to break the curfew. The mukhtar wears a headdress and long robe, and with his weathered, impassive face is the picture of composed dignity. He faces an Israeli officer whom Mr. Khleifi presents as an ogre of injustice, who yells that the "extremist village" must be taught a lesson, who will lift the curfew only if he is present as the guest of honor at the wedding.

•

Though it unhinges his film, Mr. Khleifi's dismissive attitude toward the Israelis ironically frees him; he goes on to depict his Arab village in loving, almost anthropological detail.

White walls gleam against a wide, sun-baked landscape, and we can almost feel the hot wind blow during the wedding feast, as tradition mingles with its discontents. The village women ritually bathe and dress the bride, who will ride a blue-black horse through winding streets that look preserved from biblical times.

In this rich, nuanced setting, which Walther van den Ende has photographed with shocking brightness, the mukhtar's flirtatious teen-aged daughter wears jeans, and schemes to escape her old-fashioned life. Occasionally, Mr. Khleifi reminds us that young village men are plotting to kill the Israeli wedding guests. The mukhtar whispers hauntingly to his younger son: "Why do I want you to learn my story by heart? What I fear most for you is myself."

Just when it seems that Mr. Khleifi is composing a paean for his fading culture and preparing to kill off the characters he blames for its loss, the story loops back on itself. The bridegroom wants to kill his father, whose traditions are destroying him. An older man warns the young rebels that the repercussions for their violence will be too costly. The mukhtar repeats his question to his son, and it is doubly haunting.

•

The slow accumulation of details finally becomes deadening, though. The film's 113-minute length, not American expectations, makes the all-night wedding seem to unfold in real time. And when Mr. Khleifi turns his attention back to the Israelis, he resorts to crude symbols. The prize horse wanders onto an Israeli minefield. A female Israeli soldier is overcome by heat and taken inside by the Arab women; she soon discards her drab khaki uniform, seduced by their bright robes and jewels, in a scene that says more about Mr. Khleifi's view of women than it does about Arab or Israeli notions of femininity.

For all its flaws, "Wedding in Galilee" is a strong, rare example of Middle Eastern film making, and too vibrant artistically to be dismissed in the way Mr. Khleifi does his Israeli characters. Unlike more easily palatable films, it forces the audience to decide whether to separate politics and art, whether to accept the film on its creator's terms or not.

"Wedding in Galilee" will be shown at the Museum of Modern Art as part of the New Directors/New Films festival tonight at 8:30 and tomorrow at 1 P.M.

1988 Mr 11, C23:1

CALL ME MADAME directed by François Romand; written (French with English subtitles) by Anne Gallois; photography by Maurice Perrimond, assisted by Marc Seferchian; production company, I.N.A./TF1 with the participation of the Ministry of Culture and Communications. Running time: 52 minutes. This film has no rating.

NO APPLAUSE, JUST THROW MONEY directed and produced by Karen Goodman; cinematography by Buddy Squires; edited by Sara Fishko; production company, Simon & Goodman Picture Company. At Roy and Niuta Titus Theater 1, Museum of Modern Art, 11 West 53d Street, as part of the New Directors/New Films Festival. Running time: 28 minutes. This film has no rating.

By VINCENT CANBY

At the age of 55, Jean-Pierre Voidies had a sex-change operation. He had been a political activist, poet, novelist, husband of the bird-like Huguette Voidies and the father of one son, Jean-Noël. By his own account, Mr. Voidies was a member of the Underground during the Nazi occupation of France and was tortured by the Gestapo.

Today Ovida Delect, the former Jean-Pierre Voidies, is a dainty if strapping older woman, with the physique of a steam fitter and a voice to match. She's still a political activist, poet and novelist as well as the author of an autobiography, "Putting on the Dress." No longer the husband of Huguette, she is, instead, Huguette's lifelong companion and the cause of quite a lot of contradictory emotions in Jean-Noël, an earnest young man who continues to live at home and hopes to become a professional disk jockey.

•

Ovida Delect, both as she is and as she would like to appear before the world, is the subject of Françoise Romand's "Call Me Madame," a wonderfully oddball, 52-minute documentary that will be shown today at 6 P.M. in the New Directors/New Films Festival at the Museum of Modern Art. It will be repeated there at 3:30 P.M. tomorrow. On the same program is Karen Goodman's "No Applause, Just Throw Money," an exuberant, 28-minute celebration of New York City street performers.

Miss Romand makes documentaries that look like those of nobody else. Though she sticks to facts, they're often facts that few writers of supposedly serious fiction would dare to touch except under pseudonym. "Mix-Up," which introduced Miss Romand at the 1986 New Directors/New Films Festival, examined the tragicomic results of a long-running (20-year) real-life farce, begun when an English nursing home switched two babies and sent each mother home with the other's child.

If Miss Romand never seems to be ridiculing Ovida Delect, part of the reason must be that Miss Delect is such a forceful, enthusiastic collaborator, running the movie in much the way she runs her household. From her remarks about her politics and her activism, it's clear that she is not a nut. She's an unbudgeably self-confident presence.

At home, at a women's club meeting, standing in the prow of a rowboat

F. Ede

Huguette Voidies, left, and Ovida (formerly Jean-Pierre), in "Call Me Madame," a French documentary about a middle-aged poet who undergoes a sex-change operation.

and at a village memorial for the war dead, she enthusiastically recites her poetry, which sounds pretty awful in the English subtitles. In interviews, she attempts to define what femininity means to her ("openess, lightness, sweetness") and sees herself as a muse existing somewhere between sea and shore, which is how Miss Romand presents her at the beginning and the end of the film.

Dressed in gauzy white robes, Ovida sort of sports along a Normandy beach, waving her arms in a manner that looks like a distress signal, though it's meant to express the ineffable. "If I were a muse," says Ovida, "I'd rouse hordes of poets."

Ovida is not always easy to get along with. Life with her has taken its toll of Huguette, who frequently weeps when remembering why she was attracted to the young Jean-Pierre and fell in love with him. Jean-Noël recalls his shock when he first discovered his dad walking around the house in blue robes before the sex-change was complete. Says Jean-Noël, "I was the first victim." Says Huguette sadly, "Jean-Noël is an extension of the life that used to be."

Miss Romand talks to some of Ovida's fellow villagers, who are fairly caustic about the new woman, especially about her fastidious clothes. They still refer to "her" as "him." In one doleful shot, Ovida, quite pleased with herself, dances with a shy Huguette at a local fair. There's no question about who leads whom.

"No Applause, Just Throw Money" is an exceptionally cheerful montage of — according to the film's credits — 101 sidewalk performers, including magicians, musicians, dancers, singers, contortionists, fire-eaters, poets, mimes, unicyclists and one automatic human jukebox. City Hall should be in the debt of Karen Goodman, who produced and directed the film, and Sara Fishko, the editor. Here is a New York, N.Y., of friendliness, enthusiasm, élan and humor — the way it may never, ever have been in fact, but the way it can be in the movies.

1988 Mr 12, 14:4

Those in the Running Are Fast With a Slogan

THE GREAT RACEdirected by Jerzy Domaradzki; screenplay (Polish with English subtitles) by Feliks Falk; photography by Ryszard Lenczewski; edited by Miroslawa Garlicka; music by Jerzy Matula; production design, Tadeusz Kosarewicz and Barbara Komosinska; production company: Polish Television, "X" Film Unit. At Roy and Niuta Titus Theater 1, Museum of Modern Art, 11 West 53d Street, as part of the New Directors/New Films Series. Running time: 100 minutes. This film has no rating.

Stefan Budny	Tadeusz Bradecki
Radek Stolar	Jaroslaw Kopaczewski
Chairman	Leon Niemczyk
Wrzesien	Krzysztof Pieczynski
Janek Druciarek	Tadeusz Chudecki
Kazimierz Sosna	Tomasz Dedek
Fastyn	Cezary Harasimowicz
Jozef Butrym	Ryszard Jablonski
Romek Martyniuk	Edward Zentara

By WALTER GOODMAN

"The Great Race" is a metaphor for Poland in the 1950's — and possibly in 1988, too. Feliks Falk's screenplay centers on a "Peace Run" by model factory workers, high-producing farmers and zealous activists, thoroughly manipulated by Communist Party bureaucrats. The director, Jerzy Domaradzki, does not spare the satire. The sadly humorous movie, made in 1981 but held back under Poland's martial law, can be seen at New Directors/New Films tonight at 8:30 and tomorrow at 1 P.M.

The first entrant we meet is Stefan, a conscientious fellow who talks the party lingo: "Collective farms are a guarantee of prosperity." Stefan, good young Communist that he is, cannot understand why his father has been brought up on charges of being an imperialist agent; he is sure it must be a mistake and is determined to win the big race so that he can hand the country's President a letter asking for justice.

Hooking up with Stefan is Radek, an itinerant hustler, who enters the race mainly for the fun of disrupting it. Earnest Stefan is appalled when Radek steals the specially made sneaker of the front-runner, a quota-surpassing shipbuilder with flat feet. But that uncomradely act gives Stefan a shot at winning. Where the rules are rigged, Mr. Falk is suggesting, unscrupulousness is a virtue.

The tale is a bit strained, but the delivery is energetic and the comments pungent. As the exhausted runners go panting and limping by or drop out, a television announcer burbles on about the inspiration this "vanguard of youth" is giving to the peace-loving masses. The movie is awash with rousing song that may remind you of the Red Army Chorus, with exhortations ("Study Bolshevism and Show the Way to the Hesitant!") and with cadres of the Young Poles Union, in khaki shirts and red ties, chanting "Stalin! Stalin! Stalin!"

Pulling the strings is a cold-eyed careerist who makes sure that the *Long Live* and *Down With* banners are properly displayed and that the winner is of authentic working-class background and has an unblemished party record. "Our organization is like a mother," he coos. But this born fixer has not counted on the intrusion of the born spoiler, Radek. The funniest scene finds Radek spouting quickly learned tags from Marx in a campaign to seduce a buxom young comrade. She is a good sport. As his fingers go to work on the buttons of her blouse, she observes sensibly, "Human relations have to be separated from economics or we'll never get anywhere."

The performances, especially that of Jaroslaw Kopaczewski as Radek, are solid enough to ground the satire in reality. The digs at the displays of totally programmed spontaneity have application to many 20th-century regimes, from Mussolini's Italy to Sandinista Nicaragua. When "The Great Race" was recently shown in Moscow, we are told, the reception was enthusiastic. The Russians, like the Poles, have been there, and may be there still.

1988 Mr 12, 19:1

Far From Lazy After All These Years

KEEPING LOVE ALIVE, directed and produced by Stephen Garret and David Robinson; photography by Witold Stok; edited by Dai Vaughan and Jo Nott; musical director, Jonathan Cohen; production designer, Mark Thompson; production company, the Garrett Robinson Co. for Channel 4 TV. At Roy and Niuta Titus Theater 1, Museum of Modern Art, 11 West 53d Street, as part of the New Directors/New Films Series. Running time: 78 minutes. This film has no rating.

By VINCENT CANBY

"Keeping Love Alive" is a high-spirited, graceful performance by — and a suitably unfancified hommage to — Elisabeth Welch, the great American star of cabaret and musical comedy who, like Josephine Baker, Mabel Mercer and Ada (Bricktop) Smith, had to be recognized abroad to be recognized at home.

The film, produced and directed by Stephen Garret and David Robinson (the film critic for The Times of London), is the record of Miss Welch's one-woman show, photographed last year during two performances in London where, more than 50 years ago, Miss Welch was the darling of cafe society and, of greater importance to her, of such composers as Cole Porter and Noël Coward. More recently, Miss Welch performed her one-woman show Off Broadway in 1986 and, that same year, was nominated for a Tony for her work in "Jerome Kern Goes to Hollywood."

The film will be shown at the New Directors/New Films festival at the Museum of Modern Art, today at 8:30 P.M. and tomorrow at 6 P.M.

•

"Keeping Love Alive" is both oral history and a concert film. Miss Welch, now nearing 80 but looking much younger, stands onstage front and center and sings the songs associated with her remarkably long-lived career. There's a wooden stool behind her, but she can't be bothered with it. Between songs she reminisces about growing up in Manhattan with her black, Scottish and American Indian heritage, about her Broadway shows in the late 1920s, about Paris and London in the 1930s and 40s and, finally, about the arthritis she conquered in the 1970s with the help of surgery.

Like Mabel Mercer, Miss Welch doesn't waste gestures when she sings. She's certainly not immobile, but nothing she does distracts from the lyrics or comes between the song and the audience. She's an amused, enthusiastic high priestess serving the needs of the members of her sophisticated congregation. She and they know that although love doesn't last and its facsimile can be bought, one never gives up the pursuit.

Unlike Miss Mercer, who sat in a straight-backed chair when performing, Miss Welch doesn't give the impression that she's holding court. She appears to be singing for the pure joy of it. When she opens the show with the not-really-mournful "Why Was I Born?" her presence supplies the answer: to be standing there, on that very spot, that night, singing in a blue-spangled dress and defying time. The diction is delicately clear and precise. She wipes away the dirt and grime of the years to discover original meanings made fuzzy by the pollution of later performance styles.

•

Highlights of the repertoire include Porter's brilliant mock dirge "Miss Otis Regrets," Coward's "20th-Century Blues" and such standards as "It Had to Be You" and "I Can't Give You Anything but Love." Porter's "Love for Sale," which Miss Welch originally sang in the Broadway show, "The New Yorkers," would be the show-stopper, if movies could be stopped by anyone except the projectionist.

The film's manner is direct and always to the point of its star. Miss Welch is such an effective screen personality that even the cameraman's tight close-ups work. They invite us to look beyond the image to find the woman beneath. Miss Welch persuades us that we can.

In addition, we rediscover something of the temper of the times that also gave us Pound, Hemingway, Fitzgerald, Eliot, Elsa Maxwell, Hitler, the Duke and Duchess of Windsor and "Snow White and the Seven Dwarfs."

1988 Mr 13, 57:1

The Literal Keeper Of Hitler's Flame

THE CASE OF HERMAN THE STOKER, written and directed by Leszek Wosiewicz; photography by Andrzej Adamczak; edited by Jadwiga Lesniewicz; music by Lech Branski; production by Karol Irzykowski Film Studio. Running time: 23 minutes. This film has no rating.

A Deadly Game Of Life Imitating Life

SUNDAY PRANKS, directed by Robert Glinski; screenplay (Polish with English subtitles) by Mr. Glinski and Grzegorz Torzecki; photography by Jerzy Rekas and Grzegorz Torzecki; edited by Lucja Osko; music by Lech Branski; produced by Karol Irzykowski Film Studio. At Roy and Niuta Titus Theater 1, Museum of Modern Art, 11 West 53d Street, as part of the New Directors/New Films Series. Running time: 60 minutes. This film has no rating.

Half-Wit	Miroslawa Marcheluk
Caretaker	Stefan Szmidt
Caretaker's Wife	Emilia Krakowska

WITH: Daria Trafankowska, Halina Romanowska, Wojciech Skibinski and Jerzy Zass

By JANET MASLIN

Since "The Case of Herman the Stoker" makes some effort to penetrate the mind of its subject, a lot of it is about firewood. Leszek Wosiewicz's short film includes the information that birch logs are good for keeping bad thoughts away and for making a person ready to work. Maple, on the other hand, produces a more dynamic state of mind.

A man named Herman, who presumably contributed these observations (which are presented by two unseen narrators), learned to make fires when he worked at a mental institution. Later, once the patients were liquidated, it became a school for German officers during the days of the Third Reich. Herman was so sensitive to the nuances of firewood, and so adroit at making fires to suit particular personalities, that he came to hold a privileged position within the ranks of the regime; he eventually rose to the honor of building fires for the Führer himself. Hitler was a maple man.

•

An old man at the time this film was made, Herman (who died in 1985) is seen in brief, shadowy glimpses, and he is not interviewed directedly. Much of the time, the camera concentrates on forest imagery, on the ruined, abandoned building in which Herman can be found and on newsreel footage of the Third Reich at the height of its power. The narrator recites the story of Herman's career in eminently reasonable-sounding tones. Meanwhile, the camera observes burning logs, burning buildings and, eventually, burning people.

Irony is not this film's predominant note, though the camera does return regularly to the sight of a bird's nest atop an unused chimney, the single image that best encapsulates Herman's contribution to history. More haunting than even the facts of Herman's odd life, or the sight of him in utter obsolescence at the end of his days, is Mr. Wosiewicz's oblique meditation on the banality of evil and the highly original terms in which that meditation has been cast. "The Case of Herman the Stoker" is only nominally a documentary, and its indirect impact is much greater than what could have been achieved by more forthright methods. It is with the most chilling composure imaginable that the narrator says of Herman, "Keeping Hitler warm, he perfected his skill."

•

On the same bill is another Polish film, Robert Glinski's "Sunday Pranks," which offers a child's-eye perspective of totalitarianism. Set in 1953 on the day of Stalin's funeral, the film takes place in the courtyard of an apartment building, where a group of children mimic their elders in such games as lining one another up against the wall of a building and pretending to stage a mass execution. One particular child, a fat boy who is dressed in his Sunday best and claims to be going to the funeral, is an especially strong embodiment of the totalitarian ethos. "Sunday Pranks" has been handsomely photographed in stark black and white, but the action is unsurprising. When the children adopt a stray kitten and make it the center of their activities, it's all too clear that this pet's prospects for longevity are none too good.

"Sunday Pranks" and "The Case of Herman the Stoker" will be shown tonight at 6 o'clock and tomorrow night at 8:30 as part of the New Directors/ New Films series.

1988 Mr 13, 57:1

FILM VIEW/Vincent Canby

A Baltimorean Battles Bunkum

JOHN WATERS, BALTIMORE'S NEWest sage and the city's only full-time, live-in movie maker, loves Grace Metalious, fresh desk blotters, Glenn Gould, candy-filled bullets ("seven to a pack, 59 cents"), Pia Zadora, Flannery O'-Connor and the films of Randall Kleiser ("Blue Lagoon," among others). He hates slobbering dogs met in elevators ("Every time you make direct eye contact with these creatures, your I.Q. drops 10 points"), Hermann Hesse, "The African Queen," "people who ostentatiously hold their ears in New York subways," and iceberg lettuce ("the polyester of greens").

In "Crackpot," his collection of essays published by Macmillan two years ago, Mr. Waters says at one point that he has always wanted to sell out. "The problem is that nobody wanted to buy me."

All that may change with the current box-office success of his new film, "Hairspray," which would be too bad for those of us in the audience, as well as for any producer who did the buying. It's clear from both "Hairspray" and "Crackpot" that the compleat John Waters is a film maker *and* an essayist. You can't fully appreciate one without the other.

The times get what they deserve, and John Waters is a movie maker and a satirist for ours, someone almost totally obsessed by fashions, fads, celebrity, interior décor and hypocrisy, as well as by the awful difficulties in going too far when the limits of acceptabilty keep being pushed back to neutralize all would-be offenders.

However, it's significant that even Mr. Waters, who's made his reputation by dealing in bad taste, admits in "Crackpot" that "you can always think of ways to offend (AIDS, sickle cell anemia and rape jokes) but this would hardly be daring, only stupid." He adds, "Maybe the Golden Age of Trash is coming to an end."

Never fear.

Had Mr. Waters been in the time and place of Jonathan Swift, would he have dared write "A Modest Proposal," suggesting the eating of babies as a solution to the problems faced by the Irish economy? Probably not. Mr. Waters doesn't cut deep. He's a satirist of — and formed by — a culture that thinks it's waging a war on drugs by repeating the inspiriting, catchy slogan, "Just say no."

It's never a good idea for a satirist to reveal those subjects he believes to be out of bounds. It invites someone else to come along and satirize them successfully. It also removes the possibility of danger and suspense. Once we know the limits beyond which the satirist will not go, we feel profoundly cheated, as if someone had told us the ending of "Fatal Attraction."

Mr. Waters doesn't concern himself with the so-called larger issues, although, whether he knows it or not, he deals with them, sometimes hilariously, through his preoccupation with the detritus of our civilization. When and if the earth loses its ozone layer, and when all of us are walking around with hideous skin cancers that have transformed us into creatures from the Black Lagoon, scientists will be able to pinpoint what happened just by studying "Hairspray."

Coming after "Pink Flamingos," "Female Trouble" and "Polyester," Mr. Waters's new film is very much mainstream. It features no dog droppings ("Pink Flamingos") and is being presented without the aid of Odorama, the scratch-and-sniff card that was the new screen technique of "Polyester."

In a season in which most commercial movies are trash pretending to be something else, "Hairspray" looks like seminal cinema art. It's a genuinely satiric and (I hope my mouth won't be washed out with soap) sweet movie, which pretends to be trash. It's a frequently witty recollection of the early 1960's, viewed not in hindsight's soft, sometimes anachronistic focus (see "Dirty Dancing") but as if it were a sincere, if eccentric, appropriately garish, teen-age movie made in its own time.

Tracy (Ricki Lake) is a pretty, overweight, dancing (the Madison, the Mashed Potato, among others) fool, the daughter of Wilbur (Jerry Stiller) and Edna Turnblad (Divine), who put great store by being genteel. As described by her high school teacher, Tracy is "an upper-lower-class teen-ager." She has a beehive hairdo that won't quit and a burning ambition to become a star on "The Corny Collins Show," the local television spinoff of Dick Clark's afternoon dance program, as well as Miss Auto Show of Baltimore of 1962.

Tracy's principal rival is Amber Von Tussle (Colleen Fitzpatrick), who is fashionably slim and ferociously jealous, and whose consumption of hair spray, says her dad (Sonny Bono), eats up all the profits from his Tilt-a-Whirl. To add a dash of social uplift to the proceedings, which is what Sam Katzman, the B-picture producer, liked to do in the 1950's and 1960's, Tracy is a girl who fights to integrate the Corny Collins show, much to the horror of the ultraconservative Von Tussles.

Tracy's rise to celebrityhood is not easy, but neither is it especially difficult. "Hairspray" doesn't exactly get bogged down in plot. Instead, it's about the quality of American aspirations (then and now) as reflected in American movies. When Tracy becomes a Corny Collins star, the ecstatic Edna Turnblad envisions her as nothing less than a June Taylor dancer. The sky's the limit.

Mr. Waters loves the bizarre (he is reported to have an electric chair in his living room), as well as camp, but "Hairspray" is so circumspect that it could be adored by Edna Turnblad. As played by Divine, the 200-pound actor born Harris Glenn Milstead, Edna is a great, cheerful, eye-boggling cartoon. Even when her diet pills are wearing off, she's forever patient with her difficult daughter. She's the voice of reason in adversity ("Remember, you can't change the world's problems in a day"), though occasionally she does get exasperated ("Once again your hairdo has gotten you in hot water"). When the chips are down, though, she enthusiastically supports Tracy's leap toward stardom.

One of the film's funniest sequences takes place in the Hefty Hideaway ("Big Is Beautiful"), where both Tracy and Edna are able to purchase swinging fashions for the portly. Divine is equally funny, and hardly recognizable, as the bigoted owner of Corny Collins's television station.

Divine, the icon of the cinema of John Waters, died suddenly last week in Hollywood, and just as his singular talent was being widely recognized. Though he always resisted being identified as a female impersonator, it's what he did best as an increasingly self-assured actor. His barrel shape, teetering precariously atop high heels, defined Mr. Waters's risky comic method as much as any other image.

Divine dominates "Hairspray," even if his two roles are essentially supporting ones. However, young Miss Lake is no slouch when it comes to guarding scenes that might otherwise have been stolen by Divine. Miss Lake is an intense charmer. When she bubbles with excitement, she's both a character within the film and a comic mock-up of the steel-willed teen-age actress, circa 1960, doing her darndest to please.

With the exception of Pia Zadora, who makes a not-great cameo appearance, all the members of the cast are terrifically winning, becoming (and this is intended as praise) as much a part of the Waters landscape as the period music and dancing, the clothes, the vinyl-covered furniture and the all-important beehives.

Mr. Waters is a genuinely funny man. He's also an invigorating film critic. His essay on Jean-Luc Go-

234

dard's "Hail Mary," in "Crackpot," is one of the most perceptive reviews yet written about that curious movie. Further, his tone is on the mark when he's describing it: "When the Savior runs away, saying 'I must attend to my Father's work,' Joseph asks, 'When will he be back?' Mary answers in what must be the most hilarious line of the movie, 'Easter.'"

Writes Mr. Waters, "The bottom line: "Would Flannery O'Connor have liked 'Hail Mary'?"

He is equally articulate about the films of Marguerite Duras ("maddeningly boring, but really quite beautiful"), would love to see a museum do a retrospective devoted to nudist-camp films, and thinks that Liberace would have made the ideal homicidal loon in a "Texas Chainsaw" type of horror film. "Picture him chasing Drew Barrymore across a swamp with a buzzing chain saw and you can envision a mega-hit of staggering proportions."

He also has good advice for film students, who, he says, "waste too much time studying 'masterpieces.'" A much more practical syllabus: "Hit and Run Film Making," "Avoiding the Unions" and "To Hell with Completion Bonds."

Mr. Waters adores the tacky on screen, and loathes it in real life as represented by, among other things, the waiter who says, "Hi, my name is Bill. Can I help you?" His response: "I came here to *eat*, not to make friends. Just give me eggs and bacon and hold the biography." □

1988 Mr 13, II:23:1

More Questions Than Answers

Kenzo Okuzaki

THE EMPEROR'S NAKED ARMY MARCHES ON directed by Kazuo Hara; in Japanese with English subtitles; photography by Mr. Hara; edited by Jun Nabeshima; produced by Sachiko Kobayashi; production company, Shisso Production, Tokyo. At Roy and Niuta Titus Theater 1, Museum of Modern Art, 11 West 53d Street, as part of the New Directors/ New Films festival. Running time: 122 minutes. This film has no rating.
WITH: Kenzo Okuzaki

By VINCENT CANBY

The New Directors/New Films festival is presenting a number of unconventional documentaries, but none as alarming and significantly lunatic as "The Emperor's Naked Army Marches On," conceived by Shohei Imamura ("Vengeance Is Mine") and directed by Kazuo Hara as his first feature.

Its central figure is Kenzo Okuzaki, 65 years old, a World War II veteran who lives in Kobe with his pliant, uncomplaining wife, whom we later

learn is dying of cancer. At the start of the film, Kenzo has already spent 13 years 9 months in jail. His crimes: plotting to assassinate a former Prime Minister, attempting to hit the Emperor with lead pellets fired with a sling shot and distributing pornographic pictures of the Emperor to people outside a Tokyo department store.

Kenzo is a political activist. He's also a marriage broker. In an astonishing and funny precredit sequence, we see him delivering a wedding feast homily in which he recalls his years in jail and suggests that all countries and, indeed, all families are barriers to the true brotherhood of man. The bride and groom listen with eyes lowered, as if this were the sort of thing every bride and groom expected to hear on their wedding day.

●

"The Emperor's Naked Army Marches On" will be shown at the Museum of Modern Art at 8:30 tonight and 6 P.M. tomorrow.

From everything the audience sees, Kenzo Okuzaki is a certifiable psychotic, though "The Emperor's Naked Army Marches On" never addresses this suspicion. He's the sort of fellow who writes long, crazily incoherent letters to editors, confronts people on street corners and harangues them with a loudspeaker from his van. It could be that Mr. Hara thinks the psychotic state is the only sane response to the contradictions in contemporary Japanese society.

Whatever the film director thinks, he never says. Instead he follows Kenzo around Japan as the former soldier tries to get at the truth of something that happened more than 40 years ago — the execution of three of his army comrades when they were serving in New Guinea at the end of the war.

The audience never understands just why, at this late date, Kenzo decides to investigate these events, the details of which remain fuzzy. With Mr. Hara and a camera crew in tow, Kenzo calls on former officers and enlisted men he thinks were responsible for ordering the executions. There are suggestions that the men were condemned for desertion or for cannibalism. There's the further suggestion that they were executed to provide meat for their starving comrades.

Some of those interviewed treat Kenzo with respect and attempt to answer his questions. Others equivocate. Some contradict themselves. Through all the testimony, Kenzo behaves as if he had been appointed by God to act as His prosecuting attorney. At one point he starts beating an old man who is sick, while the old man's wife pleads: "No violence. No violence." The farce becomes dark and disorienting.

The cops are frequently called, and Kenzo often has to admit that there are some circumstances in which violence is called for. He says it with the stoicism of the true fanatic. At one point he decides he'd like to have his own jail cell in his house and drives off to the Kobe prison to get the measurements. When he's not allowed in, he goes into a tirade about the guards being "law's slaves, just like the Emperor."

●

It's difficult to understand "The Emperor's Naked Army Marches On" without knowing more of the facts than the film wants to give. It may be that there really are no more facts. What we see is all there is. In

that case, the film raises pertinent questions about the extent to which the presence of the camera "entraps" events that otherwise would never have occurred. In some documentaries, like this one, the questions are especially pertinent.

The most invigorating thing about "The Emperor's Naked Army Marches On" is its consistent irreverence. It doesn't mean to be polite or nice or soothing. It means to provoke and disturb — and let the devil take the hindmost.

A screen note at the end of the film reports that after photography was completed, Kenzo set out to assassinate one of his former Army comrades and, unable to get at him, shot and wounded the man's son instead.

He is now serving a 12-year prison sentence, seeming to be very happy, as well as satisfied that his wife died earlier than expected. Otherwise he would have had to worry about how to take care of her.

1988 Mr 15, C15:1

Recruiting Poster For Collective Action

THE BIG PARADE, directed by Chen Kaige; screenplay (Chinese with English subtitles) Gao Lili; cinematography by Zhang Yimou; edited by Zhou Xinxia; music by Qu Xiaosong and Zhao Quiping; art director, He Qun; production company, Xi-an Film Studio. At Roy and Niuta Titus Theater 1, Museum of Modern Art, 11 West 53d Street, as part of the New Directors/New Films festival. Running time: 94 minutes. This film has no rating.

WITH: Huang Xueqi, Sun Chun, Lu Lei and Wu Roufu

By WALTER GOODMAN

From the impressive overhead shots of troops assembling for a march-past in Beijing's huge central square on the 35th anniversary of the People's Republic of China, in October 1984, to the final slow-motion close-ups of them parading, the camera of Zhang Yimou commands "The Big Parade." The Chinese movie, directed by Chen Kaige and on view tonight at 6 o'clock and tomorrow at 8:30 P.M. as part of the New Directors/New Films festival, holds you by its photography even as you may be getting a bit restless at the Chinese version of the good old American boot-camp movie.

The youths are being trained to do their outfit proud on the big day. The drill is familiar. There's the tough squadron leader ("I bathe with sawdust and sleep on wood"), who is deeply concerned about his men. There's the self-promoting lad who learns something about working together with his comrades. There's the conscientious fellow who can't make it through training. There's the stuttering recruit who skips his mother's funeral to stay with the squad. There's the byplay among the young soldiers as they have their heads shaved: "Baldy! Baldy!"

The story is a combination of a boys' magazine tale and a recruiting document. Officers anguish over which of the soldiers must be eliminated before the parade. They raise questions like, "Must a recruit who makes an error be punished?" The squadron leader, who turns out to be a much softer type than we have seen lately in "Full Metal Jacket" or "An Officer and a Gentleman," reflects, "Do I really understand my sol-

diers?" You'd never catch Brian Donleavy worrying about something like that.

●

The pep talks and buddy-buddy exchanges and bouts of self-criticism are painfully earnest. "They used to say good men don't become soldiers," declares an officer. "That's not true any more." He exhorts his troops with a line from the national anthem: "Build a new Great Wall with our flesh and blood." A little heavy considering that all they are going to do is parade for a minute.

It's the photography that lifts "The Big Parade" out of the rudely fashioned trench of its story. Mr. Zhang keeps finding new angles from which to dramatize the disciplined cooperation that the movie preaches. He gives us fields of helmets and boots, ranks of expressionless profiles, orderly patterns of trucks and rifles, a military band at the ready, a snappy mass salute. The ordeal of the men when they are made to stand at attention for three hours in a summer sun is captured with excruciating immediacy; you can feel their pain through the shimmering heat. The downpour in which they must march is a bone-drencher. You may not be moved to join up, but you can't help coming away with a more direct understanding of the message of collective effort that the Chinese authorities are trying to drum into their countrymen.

1988 Mr 15, C16:5

What Lies Behind The Intense Eyes?

VINCENT: THE LIFE AND DEATH OF VINCENT VAN GOGH, directed, photographed, written and edited by Paul Cox; based on letters of Vincent van Gogh; music by Vivaldi, Rossini and Norman Kaye; produced by Tony Llewellyn-Jones for Illumination Films. At Film Forum 1, 57 Watts Street. Running time: 105 minutes. This film has no rating.

By CARYN JAMES

In one after another of van Gogh's self-portraits, he stares out at the viewer with intense, impenetrable eyes, eyes that seem to be floodgates holding his torrential emotions in check. "Vincent," Paul Cox's study of van Gogh's life and work, matches the intense surface of those self-portraits but contains little of their underlying power. As Mr. Cox propels van Gogh's own words and art at us with increasing speed, he keeps us at a fatal distance from the film, which aims to capture the artist's innermost point of view.

John Hurt reads from van Gogh's pensive, profusely descriptive letters to his brother Theo. Mr. Cox offers up dozens of the artist's sketches, drawings and paintings, accompanied by real-life landscapes as van Gogh might have seen them. There are reenacted scenes from the artist's life, but we see his face only as he painted it, hear only words he wrote.

Mr. Cox has chosen the letters to give a sense of van Gogh's development. He begins with the artist's youthful ambitions to be a clergyman, suggesting that this desire was a misplaced version of his true passion for line and color ("How lovely yellow is!" van Gogh writes). We hear familiar stories of the artist's poverty, of his unrequited love for his cousin and of his sojourn with a prostitute whom he thought of marrying as a gesture of Christian kindness. We follow van Gogh into his mad-

Van Gogh in an 1889 self-portrait.

ness; unlike his inquisitive neighbors in Arles, he writes, the asylum inmates at St.-Rémy possess "the discretion and manners to leave me alone." A gunshot signals his suicide in 1890 at the age of 37.

However intelligently the letters have been selected, the narration — Mr. Hurt begins it as a stiff recitation, which becomes more nuanced and tense — reduces van Gogh to the dimensions of a one-man Broadway show, the kind that races through a celebrated person's letters to hit all the high points of his life.

Fortunately, "Vincent," which opens today at the Film Forum 1, never loses sight of the life's work. The cinematography reveals the thick textures and swirling lines of van Gogh's flowering orchards, sunflowers and fields and, as much as film can, reproduces his range of burning yellows and miraculously deep blues. We see unfamiliar drawings of women at their needlework, as well as the unmistakable olive groves. But the film never brings us to that moment, achieved in first-rate biographies, when we suddenly understand how the life and mind of *this* artist came to bear on *that* specific work. Here the sense of creation comes in a backhanded way. When Mr. Cox films an orchard in bloom then cuts away to van Gogh's canvas, we notice how unrealistic, how truly transformed, the painter's vision is.

It is never clear how much Mr. Cox intends such discordances, though, for just as often he resorts to tacky, acted-out scenes. Here are actors dressed as peasants, gathered around a shabby dinner table, re-creating "The Potato Eaters." At such times, Mr. Cox seems desperate to liven up his film.

At others, it seems that the Dutehborn Australian director — his many features include "Cactus," shown at the 1986 New York Film Festival — is trying to break the bonds of the educational film genre to which "Vincent" belongs. The shots of van Gogh's cousin, for example, are grainy, as if Mr. Cox were playing with the texture of his film the way van Gogh did with his paint. But such scenes are half-hearted attempts, too rare and too obscure to be meaningful.

Van Gogh's paintings and letters are so full of genius that Mr. Cox's film never becomes dull, but it may be superfluous to anyone within range of the Metropolitan Museum of

Art and a bookstore, where the paintings and letters are easily found. "Vincent" remains a visually accomplished college classroom film, cerebral and worshipful to its core.

1988 Mr 16, C25:1

With God On His Side

LEVY AND GOLIATH, directed by Gérard Oury; screenplay (French with English subtitles) by Mr. Oury and Danièle Thompson; cinematography, Vladimir Ivanov and André Domage; edited by Albert Jurgenson; music by Vladimir Cosma; a Grange Communications-Jerry Winters Presentation; released by Kino International. At 68th Street Playhouse, at Third Avenue. Running time: 105 minutes. This film has no rating.

Moses Levy	Richard Anconina
Albert Levy	Michel Boujenah
Bijou	Jean-Claude Brialy
Goliath	Maxime Leroux
Malika	Souad Amidou
Brigitte Levy	Sophie Barjac

By WALTER GOODMAN

The notion must have seemed like a laugh riot: take a pure and pious Hasid and plop him onto the streets of Pigalle in the company of drug pushers, hookers and transvestites. Well, we've all seen worse; the problem here is that the heavy hand of Gérard Oury, who directed and collaborated on the script for "Levy and Goliath," knocks over credibility some time before Levy knocks over Goliath.

The meshugaas begins in Antwerp with a mix-up between bags of high quality cocaine and bags of ground industrial diamonds. Newly married Moses Levy, who can recite the Bible by heart, delivers the coke to the Renault factory in Paris and finds himself on the run from a gang of thugs led by a big, unpleasant character named Goliath. Moses is forced to shave his beard, cut his earlocks and consort with the heirs of Sodom and Gomorrah. He has on his side his assimilated brother, Albert, whose karate footwork comes in handy, a pretty Arab woman with whom he briefly shares a broom closet, and God, who appears to him in the form of steam and offers down-to-earth advice: "You smoke too much."

Richard Anconina makes an appealing Moses, particularly when figuring out a smart way to handle dumb Goliath. Jean-Claude Brialy does a robust "Cage aux Folles" turn as the head of an establishment where perversion is the norm. And an unidentified pig with a nose for cocaine snorts amusingly after the villains. There are puffs of fun, too, in the the cocaine dust wafting through the automobile plant and in the dazzling high enjoyed by sniffers of the diamond dust.

Mostly, however, there's more commotion than comedy in this French movie, which opens today at the 68th Street Playhouse — what with nasty bikers roaring after Moses, the young Hasid running around Paris picking up lessons in tolerance and the plot racing every which way except into unpredictability. When, finally, God reminds Moses that little David slew big Goliath with a stone, you can't help thinking of the West Bank these days, and that's enough to shut off laughter.

1988 Mr 17, C20:4

Greece, in Memory And in Metaphor

THE PHOTOGRAPH, directed by Nicos Papatakis; screenplay (Greek with English subtitles) by Mr. Papatakis; cinematography by Aris Stavrou and Arnaud Desplechin; edited by Delphine Desfons; music by Christodoulos Chalaris; production company, Greek Film Center/Ikones Ltd. At Roy and Niuta Titus Theater 1, Museum of Modern Art, 11 West 53d Street, as part of the New Directors/New Films festival. Running time: 102 minutes. This film has no rating.

WITH: Christos Tsangas, Aris Retsos, Zozo Zarpa, Christos Valavanidis and Despina Tomazani

By JANET MASLIN

The Greece that is seen in Nicos Papatakis's "Photograph" is a place of sharp contrasts, a land of majestic mountain scenery and crumbling, tacky modern construction. It is a fierce longing for this homeland that propels the story forward, and the longing takes an unusual form. A shy, decent and illiterate Greek furrier named Gerasimos Jiras has been living in Paris for many years when, in 1971, a young relative named Ilias arrives with some information and a get-rick-quick scheme. It is Ilias's idea to befriend and exploit the older man by revealing dire news about Gerasimos's stepparents, then he stumbles onto an even better plan.

Gerasimos is fascinated by a photograph that Ilias has brought with him, a picture of a pretty young woman who is a popular singing star back home. When Gerasimos asks about the picture, Ilias impetuously says that this is his 23-year-old sister, Joy. It isn't long before Gerasimos has asked Ilias to write her a letter in his behalf. Shrewdly, Ilias begins to develop an ever more elaborate correspondence between Gerasimos and Joy, abetted by a classically calculating mother back home who sends back the nonexistent Joy's letters with an authentic Greek postmark. Soon Gerasimos is so overcome by Joy's attentions that he asks her to be his bride.

"The Photograph," which manages to be both comic and sobering about these events, follows Ilias's plot as it escalates more and more crazily. Gerasimos sends Joy a photograph of himself standing beside a mink coat, in order to impress her; then he decides this isn't nearly enough. His house is not good enough to suit her, and so bit by bit he remodels the place according to Ilias's extremely detailed specifications (one letter from "Joy" says that it would be nice to have a kitchen on two levels, for example, and when a crew of French workmen arrives to renovate the place, Ilias pesters them mercilessly). It is both funny and worrisome when, as part of this undertaking, the roof falls in.

Eventually, when the house is perfect and Gerasimos has had everything covered in plastic to keep it that way, Ilias begins to feel the net closing in. There can be no more stalling; now he has no choice but to produce Joy. But by this time, Mr. Papatakis has skillfully moved the film further and further from the particulars of the photograph plot, so that the idea of Joy has come to represent both Gerasimos's idealized vision of his homeland and Ilias's more cynical view. The film ends on a note that is both poetic and cruel.

The actors in the two leading roles develop a memorably edgy rapport,

and seem to represent quintessential parts of the Greek character. The crafty, opportunistic and politically passionate Ilias contrasts powerfully with the sturdy, hard-working, fiercely intense older man. Mr. Papatakis's direction is forthright, but it proves to be a lot more subtle and wry than it initially appears. Though its story is simple, "The Photograph" is haunting and clever, the best Greek film to arrive here in many years.

"The Photograph" will be shown tonight at 6 P.M. and Saturday at 3:30 P.M. as part of the New Directors/New Films festival.

1988 Mr 17, C26:3

The Ordinary Lives Of Ordinary People

BELL DIAMOND, directed, filmed, edited and produced by Jon Jost; music by Jon English. At Roy and Niuta Titus Theater 1, Museum of Modern Art, 11 West 53d Street, as part of the New Directors/New Films festival. Running time: 96 minutes. This film has no rating.

Jeff	Marshall Gaddis
Cathy	Sarah Wyss
Haley	Terri Lyn Williams
Scott	Scott Andersen
Boss	Pat O'Connor
Laura	Kristi Jean Hager
Danny	Dan Cornell
Mick	Hal Waldrup
Ron	Ron Hanekan
Alan	Alan Goddard
The Counsellor	Anne Kolesar

By VINCENT CANBY

Jon Jost's "Bell Diamond" is about the seven-year marriage of Jeff, a Vietnam veteran, and Cathy, who live in Butte, Mont., in a house that is enviably full of waste space and seems to have been furnished with knickknacks won at a carnival.

As "Bell Diamond" opens, Jeff drinks beer, eats junk food and stares at a Brewers-Royals baseball game on television. In turn, Mr. Jost's camera stares at Jeff, waiting for some sign of life. The camera has the patience of a cat that knows it will be fed if it stares at the food cupboard long enough. Jeff doesn't move. The game continues. From the kitchen come sounds of plates being pushed around, which is what Cathy does when Jeff is staring at television.

One night, Cathy announces to Jeff that she's leaving him. "I don't want to live with you anymore," she says.

Jeff is astonished.

Says a woman to Cathy, "I just wish you two guys could work it out." Cathy: "He doesn't talk to me about anything." Cathy wants a baby but, it seems, Jeff can't give her one. It has something to do with Vietnam, but in what way is not clear.

This is pretty much the narrative of "Bell Diamond," the newest film by Jon Jost, described by the New Directors/New Films festival program notes as "probably this country's most unseen film maker," which is possible, though even that sounds like hyperbole. The notes also praise the film's "democratic respect for the extraordinariness of the ordinary" and calls it "the most public and touching work of a profoundly political film maker."

I report these appraisals as if I had a gun pointed at my head. Movies as earnestly unconventional and aggressively boring as Jon Jost's "Bell Diamond" put the members of the audience on the defensive. It's *supposed* to be boring, and we're supposed to see

236

beyond the boredom to the truth beyond. I can't, possibly because it's all too accessible.

"Bell Diamond," which is the name of a now-closed Butte copper mine, will be shown at the Museum of Modern Art today at 8:30 P.M. and on Saturday at 1 P.M.

As improvised by the actors who play them, Jeff and Cathy are meant to tell us something about the politically and emotionally depressed state of the current American scene. They seem, instead, to say more about the state of mind of a film maker hoping to find a movie in the course of making it.

•

Mr. Jost and the actors condescend to the inarticulate slob-characters. This is apparent when the film maker introduces the subject of "art," first in a reproduction of a George Bellows prizefight scene, which hangs on the wall of Jeff and Cathy's otherwise junk-filled house, and then in the remarks of an artist, a woman who lectures the intellectually needy Cathy about painting. Thomas Eakins's name is dropped ("Yeah, he's the one from Philadelphia").

Mostly, though, art is invoked in the prettiness of Mr. Jost's images of Butte. The city may be a forlorn place to the people who live there, but it's all too rich in the kinds of color and light contrasts that enchant the photographer. Such prettiness is an opiate.

1988 Mr 17, C30:1

Experiencing America

STARS AND BARS, directed by Pat O'Connor; screenplay by William Boyd, from his novel; director of photography, Jerzy Zielinski; edited by Michael Bradsell; music by Stanley Myers; production designers, Leslie Dilley and Stuart Craig; produced by Sandy Lieberson; released by Columbia Pictures. At Embassy 72d Street, at Broadway. Running time: 98 minutes. This film is rated R.

Henderson	Daniel Day-Lewis
Loomis Gage	Harry Dean Stanton
Sereno	Kent Broadhurst
Freeborn	Maury Chaykin
Beckman	Matthew Cowles
Irene	Joan Cusack
Teagarden	Keith David
Reverend Cardew	Spalding Gray
Cora	Glenne Headly
Melissa	Laurie Metcalf
Duane	Will Patton
Bryant	Martha Plimpton

By VINCENT CANBY

Toward the middle of "Stars and Bars," Henderson Dores (Daniel Day-Lewis), a New York art-auction-house representative, arrives in Atlanta to register at one of those multi-story theme parks that are now the fashion in hotels in this country. The room clerk, smiling, gives Henderson his key and says, "Follow the path through the atrium, then take the scenic elevator to the 35th floor."

It's another adventure for the impeccably tailored Henderson, an upper-middle-class Englishman for whom America is a coast-to-coast Disneyland. He makes his way through a man-made jungle of flora and chirping fauna to arrive at a boat landing. A smiling attendant greets him, draws up a canoe and directs him to paddle across to the elevator bank.

Henderson is *contained by* the canoe but, in the American sense, he's not really *into* it. Ever game, he attempts to cope with the paddle, his briefcase and the confusion caused by

Daniel Day-Lewis

the other canoes, each going in a different direction. He frowns slightly. The paddle seems very long and awkward. The canoes bump and get turned around. Traffic becomes snarled. Canoe-gridlock threatens. When he reaches the far side and the canoe capsizes, Henderson steps into the stagnant lagoon, into calf-high water, and strides toward dry floor as if crossing a street in Belgravia.

It's a short, virtually throw-away sequence that briefly recalls the elevated nuttiness of William Powell in "Libeled Lady" and Cary Grant in "Bringing Up Baby." It's also further confirmation that Daniel Day-Lewis ("My Beautiful Laundrette," "A Room With a View," "The Unbearable Lightness of Being") is well on his way to becoming the actor who really can do anything.

•

In "Stars and Bars," opening today at the Embassy 72d Street, he gives a heroically funny, high-style comedy performance that's up to its knees in slapstick.

Just how he pulls it off is not easily analyzed. His role, written by William Boyd, is a good one, and Pat O'Connor, the director who earlier did "Cal," appears to respond to him. Yet there's a streak of intense, cockeyed, singular sensitivity in Mr. Day-Lewis's performance that sets him apart from all his contemporaries, and keeps "Stars and Bars" in focus even when its comic points become a bit blunt.

The screenplay, adapted by Mr. Boyd from his own novel, is full of funny moments that, as the film proceeds, seem increasingly isolated from each other. "Stars and Bars" never gathers comic momentum. It's difficult to tell whether this is the result of the writing or the direction, or of some combination of each, even though the individual scenes sometimes work beautifully.

It may have something to do with the form. In "Stars and Bars" Mr. Day-Lewis plays yet another variation on the sophisticated European traveler in the land that, not by chance, gave us Oz and its phenomenally successful, phony wizard. Most of the people he meets are so broadly eccentric they could well inhabit another form of fiction.

•

"Stars and Bars" is about the education (and liberation) of Henderson Dores when he's sent into the Deep South to acquire a long-lost Re-

noir from Loomis Gage (Harry Dean Stanton), the patriarch of a relentlessly oddball, aristocratic Southern family. Complicating the negotiations are Henderson's New York fiancée, her teen-age daughter, another young woman with whom Henderson has recently fallen in love, and some New York lowlifes representing a competing auction house.

The excellent supporting cast, whose material never quite matches that given the star, includes Spalding Gray, Glenne Headly, Matthew Cowles, Maury Chaykin, Laurie Metcalf, Martha Plimpton, Joan Cusack and Will Patton. They're some of New York's finest.

Henderson Dores is no Tocqueville. He's too innocent. Criticism never passes his lips. He's also too polite and well bred ever to express anything but determined, sometimes delighted bewilderment, whether being attacked by a paranoid New Yorker or walking down Broadway wearing nothing but a piece of cardboard. Through it all, Mr. Day-Lewis remains a figure of true comic stature.

1988 Mr 18, C3:1

Plodding
In the Murk

Dennis Quaid

D. O. A., directed by Rocky Morton and Annabel Jankel; screenplay by Charles Edward Pogue; story by Mr. Pogue, Russell Rouse and Clarence Greene; director of photography, Yuri Neyman; edited by Michael R. Miller; music by Chaz Jankel; production designer, Richard Amend; produced by Ian Sander and Laura Ziskin; released by Touchstone Picturesu. At the Ziegfeld, Avenue of the Americas at 54th Street; the Coronet, Third Avenue at 59th Street; the Olympia Cinema, Broadway at 107th Street; the Gramercy, 23d Street between Park and Lexington Avenues. Running time: 100 minutes. This film is rated R.

Dexter Cornell	Dennis Quaid
Sydney Fuller	Meg Ryan
Mrs. Fitzwaring	Charlotte Rampling
Hal Petersham	Daniel Stern
Gail Cornell	Jane Kaczmarek
Bernard	Christopher Neame
Cookie Fitzwaring	Robin Johnson
Nicholas Lang	Rob Knepper
Graham Corey	Jay Patterson

By CARYN JAMES

"You just gave up, Dex," his estranged wife tells him. "I just quit," Dex tells his new girlfriend. And in case she didn't get it the first time, he explains it to her later: "I've been dead for four years now. I forgot to appreciate life."

Does this sound like dialogue from a suspense-filled thriller? The idea for "D.O.A." is a great one, borrowed from the 1949 Edmond O'Brien movie: a man is slipped a fatal, slow-acting poison, and has less than 48 hours to solve his own murder.

This updated version has Dennis Quaid, an actor with the spark and intelligence to carry off just about anything, as Dexter Cornell — English professor, blocked novelist, murder victim. Rocky Morton and Annabel

Jankel, who directed "D.O.A.," are the flashy, innovative creators of Max Headroom. Here they aim for a stylish mix of the 40's and 80's, beginning with a black and white homage to the older film, in which Mr. Quaid stumbles into a police station to report his own murder.

But all this talent is done in by Charles Edward Pogue's talky, obvious screenplay. He brings to the surface the original story's implied paradox — the emotionally dead man comes to life when he is actually dying — and along the way destroys all the fun.

•

Despite its sporadic noirish moments, "D.O.A." finds no style of its own. Cornell's office has a battered manual typewriter, an ancient electric fan and an answering machine — a mix that means absolutely nothing. Yet as Mr. Quaid tracks a half-dozen suspects through the murky plot, the film is too plodding to work as a straight old-fashioned thriller.

Daniel Stern is affably convincing as Cornell's best friend. But Charlotte Rampling, as a wealthy villain, shows less life than Max Headroom.

The only spirited touches are the scenes between Mr. Quaid and Meg Ryan as a freshman with a crush on Cornell, who becomes his sidekick and lover. She matches Mr. Quaid's ability to make third-rate dialogue sound better than it is, but even they can't make this sound better than second-rate.

"D.O.A.," which opens today at the Ziegfeld and other theaters, has to be one of the season's biggest disappointments.

1988 Mr 18, C8:5

Foreign Affairs

Marcello Mastroianni

THE TWO LIVES OF MATTIA PASCAL, directed by Mario Monicelli; screenplay (Italian with English subtitles) by Suso Cecchi D'Amico, Ennio De Concini, Amanzio Todini and Mr. Monicelli; director of photography, Camillo Bazzoni; music by Nicola Piovani; produced by Silvia D'Amico Bendicò and Carlo Cucchi; a co-production of RAI Channel 1, Antenne 2, Telemünchen, TVE, Channel 4, TRSI, Cinecittà, Excelsior Cinematografica. At the Carnegie Screening Room, Seventh Avenue at 57th Street. Running time: 120 minutes. This film has no rating.

Mattia Pascal	Marcello Mastroianni
Clara	Senta Berger
Paleari	Bernard Blier
Terenzio Papiano	Flavio Bucci
Adriana Paleari	Laura Morante
Romilda	Laura Del Sol
Malagna	Nestor Garay
Mino Pomino	Alessandro Haber
Pellegrinotto	Carlo Bagno
Veronique	Caroline Berg
Oliva	Clelia Rondinella
The Widow Pescatore	Rosalia Maggio
Silvia Caporale	Andrea Ferreol

Marcello Mastroianni has never had any trouble convincing us that he can charm any woman who catches his eye, and any audience along with her. He's doing it again in "The Two Lives of Mattia Pascal," a movie made for European television that opens today at the Carnegie Screening Room.

The director, Mario Monicelli, brings plenty of verve to this updating of Luigi Pirandello's novel. Like last year's "Dark Eyes," the story is told by Mr. Mastroianni in a long flashback. It begins when Mattia (Mr. Mastroianni) is about 40 years old. His father, a big man in a little town, has died, and the son finds himself fit for nothing except the opportune seduction. "Papa never wanted me to run things," he remarks, as he sprinkles a little salt on a cold chicken breast. Mattia is a man of affairs, but not the business sort.

Through nobody's doing but his own, he suddenly finds himself married to the woman coveted by his best friend, and is informed that he is the real papa of a bambino claimed by his crooked estate manager, who has, incidentally, ruined the estate. Mattia strolls forth to commit suicide, only "it's hard to jump into the water on such a freezing night." So, instead, he hops on a train that carries him to adventure, love, fortune and, for a time, the identity for which he was made: "No more Mattia Pascal, who I didn't like."

The women Mattia meets, all beauties, all individuals, are played with spirit by Senta Berger (Clara the prostitute), Laura Del Sol (Romilda the wife), Clelia Rondinella (Oliva the luscious peasant), Caroline Berg (Veronique the luck-bringing casino shill) and Laura Morante (the faithful Adriana). Whether the setting is a cemetery or a séance, a library or a casino, Mr. Monicelli, who directed "Big Deal on Madonna Street," lends it touches of truth and sly asides.

As for Mr. Mastroianni, trying without success to light a cigarette into the wind, nibbling a chocolate at the bedside of his wife, who has just suffered a miscarriage, making love over a washing machine, reverently following his car as it is being towed away, delicately dusting his own grave, he carries off his role lightly yet deeply. "I want to be me!" he declares at the end, as though he knew who that was. Mattia's is a tasty tale, delectably told.

WALTER GOODMAN

1988 Mr 18, C8:5

The Calculus Of Finite Differences

Edward James Olmos

STAND AND DELIVER, directed by Ramon Menendez; written by Mr. Menendez and Tom Musca; director of photography, Tom Richmond; edited by Nancy Richardson; music by Craig Safan; art director, Milo; produced by Tom Musca; released by Warner Brothers. At the National Twin, Broadway and 44th Street; Plaza, 58th Street east of Madison Avenue; Loews 84th Street Six, at Broadway; Art Greenwich Twin, 12th Street at Seventh Avenue. Running time: 103 minutes. This film is rated PG.

Jaime Escalante	Edward James Olmos
Fabiola Escalante	Rosana De Soto
Angel	Lou Diamond Phillips
Ramirez	Andy Garcia
Tito	Mark Eliot
Pancho	Will Gotay
Molina	Carmen Argenziano
Fernando Escalante	Bodie Olmos
Ana	Vanessa Marquez

By JANET MASLIN

Even those used to watching Edward James Olmos regularly in his "Miami Vice" role will have a tough time recognizing him at first in "Stand and Deliver," since Mr. Olmos has transformed himself so completely. His hair has been thinned and pasted unflatteringly across his pate; he looks heavier, wears glasses and has none of the complexion-improving makeup used for his television role. Mr. Olmos has turned himself into the complete embodiment of a hard-working, knowledge-loving public school math teacher whose greatest ambition is to see his students get ahead, and he has done this to inspiringly great effect. If ever a film made its audience want to study calculus, this is the one.

"Stand and Deliver," which opens today at the Plaza and other theaters, is a lot more fun than that may make it sound. Mr. Olmos, as the teacher named Jaime Escalante, has the viewer rooting for him all the way, and his classroom methods are anything but dull. He shows up with a chef's hat, some apples and a cleaver to teach fractions, for example. And he taunts the kids who won't pay attention with remarks like "Tough guys don't do math, tough guys deep-fry chicken for a living" and "Go to wood shop, make yourself a shoeshine box, you're gonna need it."

Teaching mostly Hispanic pupils at a high school in East Los Angeles, this man speaks directly to his students' hopes and fears. "There are some people in this world who assume you know less than you do because of your name and your complexion," he says, "but math is a great equalizer." Not surprisingly, they begin to love him, and they begin to love math, too. Lou Diamond Phillips, who's as good here as he was in "La Bamba," plays the group's biggest holdout, a boy named Angel who wears sunglasses and a hairnet and refuses to pay attention in class. But even he comes around eventually. Mr. Escalante, who knows a thing or two about teen-age pride, sneaks Angel extra textbooks so he won't have to be seen carrying books through the school corridors.

•

The students accomplish such miracles that "Stand and Deliver" plays a little like a fairy tale, even if it is based on a real story. However, Mr. Olmos makes it more than easy to understand why the students love their work and enjoy rising to the many challenges this hugely inventive teacher throws their way. Mr. Olmos seems to be living and breathing this role rather than merely playing it, and his enthusiasm really catches on.

Structurally, there's the slight problem of returning the film to its main course every time it makes a detour to examine the home life of one student or another. Ramon Menendez, who directed and co-wrote the film, is understandably eager to show why barrio kids have a hard time doing their homework, but these glimpses aren't much more than skin deep. When the film occasionally wanders in this way, one can hardly wait to get back to the tireless, wise-

cracking, one-of-a-kind Mr. Escalante for the next lesson.

•

"Stand and Deliver" is rated PG ("Parental Guidance Suggested"). It contains some profanity.

1988 Mr 18, C14:1

How Harry Got That Way

Geert Hunaerts

LOVE IS A DOG FROM HELL, directed by Dominique Deruddere; screenplay (Flemish with English subtitles) by Marc Didden and Mr. Deruddere; photography by Willy Stassen; edited by Ludo Troch and Guido Henderickx; music by Raymond Van Het Groenewoud; production design by Hubert Pouille and Eric Van Belleghem; production companies, Multimedia in cooperation with the Ministries for Culture of the Flemish and French Communities; released by Cineplex Odeon. At Roy and Niuta Titus Theater 1, Museum of Modern Art, 11 West 53d Street, as part of the New Directors/New Films series. Running time: 90 minutes. This film has no rating.

Harry Voss	Josse De Pauw
Harry Voss, age 12	Geert Hunaerts
Stan	Michael Pas
Jeff	Gene Bervoets
Bill	Amid Chakir
Princess	Florence Beliard
Mother	Karen Vanparys
Gina	Carmela Locantorc
Liza Velani	Anne Van Essche
Marina	Doriane Moretus

By WALTER GOODMAN

For a movie that starts with voyeurism, advances to acute acne and concludes with a bout of necrophilia, "Love Is a Dog From Hell" is a remarkably innocent romance. Dominique Deruddere, a 31-year-old Belgian director, found the idea for his first full-length feature in the stories of Charles Bukowski, an American writer with an underground reputation who did the screenplay for "Barfly." The funny, tender, surprising result can be seen at the New Directors/New Films festival tonight at 8:30 and Sunday at 6 P.M. at the Museum of Modern Art. (The program opens with "A Warm Reception in L.A.," by Vincent Cafarelli and Candy Kugel, a zippy five-minute singing cartoon about a writer whom nobody calls back.)

Mr. Deruddere, who collaborated with Marc Didden on the screenplay, first did a short movie based on Mr. Bukowski's account of a man making love to a dead woman, then worked his way back to the youth of the necrophiliac, here called Harry Voss. The interpretation of how Harry got that way is a bit pat, but the three matched sections of the final work are filled with such sympathy for his longings that they compel understanding.

We meet Harry in the 1950's, his handsome 12-year-old head bubbling with movie-screen romances, gor-

geous princesses kidnapped and rescued by dashing knights for the slow fadeout. Under the guidance of a slightly older friend, Harry makes contact with flesh-and-blood women but is defeated first by his shyness, then by his audacity. He learns only how to find solitary and unsatisfying relief for his so-far natural desires.

We meet him next as he is about to be graduated from high school. Still a romantic, he is now afflicted with as rotten a complexion as the movie screen has ever offered. He solaces himself by listening to love songs and writing love poems, especially to a coed named Liza. "I love her," he confesses to a pal. "I love them all!" The pal tries to fix him up, but even the most accommodating coed finds those pustules offputting.

And, finally, it is 1976, and Harry, "30 and broke," is something of a bum but no less the romantic. Again he has a pal to assist him in at last finding the woman of his dreams, beautiful, available, entirely and forever his. This one can't say no. "The best woman I've ever had," sighs Harry. "The kind you meet once in a lifetime." It's a comedy of desperation, with overtones of tragedy.

Mr. Deruddere draws fine performances from all parties, especially Geert Hunaerts as Harry the boy, and Josse De Pauw in his older incarnations. The episodes are no more than anecdotes really, but rich in incident, and the writing, photography (by Willy Stassen) and direction fill them with conviction.

•

The sexual cravings are explicit but never dirty. Mr. Deruddere has a patient way of letting an event register on Harry so that his reactions seem natural even at their most bizarre, as when he wraps his head in toilet paper to hide his acne and advances on the princess of the school dance like a helmeted knight. You can't help cheering for him.

As for that final scene, it is not at all macabre. The corpse is a beauty, and you may still find yourself cheering, at least a little, as Harry proves himself the lover he has always been deep down. The heart has its reasons.

1988 Mr 18, C15:1

Riparian Rights And Wrongs

Sonia Braga

THE MILAGRO BEANFIELD WAR, directed by Robert Redford; screenplay by David Ward and John Nichols, based on the novel by Mr. Nichols; director of photography, Robbie Greenberg; edited by Dede Allen and Jim Miller; music by Dave Grusin; art director, Joe Aubel; produced by Mr. Redford and Moctesuma Esparza; released by Universal Pictures. At Beekman, Second Avenue at 65th

Street. Running time: 115 minutes. This film is rated R.

Joe Mandragon	Chick Vennera
Sheriff Bernabe Montoya	Rubén Blades
Ladd Devine	Richard Bradford
Ruby Archuleta	Sonia Braga
Herbie Platt	Daniel Stern
Kyril Montana	Christopher Walken
Nancy Mondragon	Julie Carmen
Horsethief Shorty	James Gammon
Flossie Devine	Melanie Griffith
Charlie Bloom	John Heard
Amarante Cordova	Carlos Riquelme
Coyote Angel	Roberto Carricart

"The Milagro Beanfield War," Robert Redford's first film as a director since "Ordinary People," is a populist fable set in some beautiful New Mexican landscapes about one stubborn Chicano's battle against an uncaring system. It's as full of good intentions as a campaign to get out the vote.

For reasons not entirely clear, the decent, picturesque Chicanos of the Milagro Valley have been denied the right to irrigate their farms with water now being channeled to a huge development called the Miracle Valley Recreation Area. Instead of farms, the valley will soon be dotted with condominiums, golf courses, tennis courts and swimming pools.

When, by accident, an irrigation canal begins to drain onto his property, Joe, a handyman, comes to a fateful decision. He decides to borrow some of the water that once was his (and his father's, and his father's father's), to plant a small patch of beans in his side yard. Says Ruby Archuleta, who runs the local garage, "I always knew Joe couldn't go through life without attempting one great thing."

The word spreads through the Chicano community like wildfire, as gringos say. Ladd Devine, the head of the Miracle Valley project, is outraged. He imports a hired gun to restore order. Charlie Bloom, once active as a lawyer for political activists, knows that the Miracle Valley development will bring higher taxes, which will force the Chicanos to leave their homesteads. He throws in with Joe, Ruby and the others to protect their rights.

•

If "The Milagro Beanfield War" were more sharply focused, it might have had some of the primitive appeal of an old cattlemen-versus-the railroad western. However, the movie can't quite bring itself to be so crude and, in avoiding clichés, it avoids telling any particular story whatsoever.

The screenplay, by David Ward and John Nichols, based on Mr. Nichols's novel, is jammed with underdeveloped, would-be colorful characters, including a philisophical Chicano angel, who face a succession of fearful confrontations with the law that come to nothing. The narrative is a veritable fiesta of anticlimaxes, from the time the sun sets at the beginning of the film until it sets, yet again, behind the closing credits.

The film is very big on sunsets and sunrises. It also has a touristy appreciation for all manner of things folkloric. What it doesn't have is dramatic coherence or backbone. Even the villains are spineless.

•

The more prominent members of the cast include Chick Vennera as Joe, Sonia Braga of Brazil as Ruby, John Heard as Charlie Bloom, Christopher Walken as the hired gun, Daniel Stern as a New York University sociology student, Rubén Blades as the Chicano sheriff, Richard Bradford as Ladd Devine and Melanie

From Novel to Film Rubén Blades stars in "The Milagro Beanfield War."

Griffith as his wife. None of them have a great deal to do except look the part. The most riveting creature in the movie is a great white pig that does tricks on cue that would tax Lassie.

"The Milagro Beanfield War," which opens today at the Beekman Theater, is not Mr. Redford's finest hour.
    VINCENT CANBY
    1988 Mr 18, C17:1

Fraternity

DOMINICK AND EUGENE, directed by Robert M. Young; screenplay by Alvin Sargent and Corey Blechman, story by Danny Porfirio; director of photography, Curtis Clark; edited by Arthur Coburn; music by Trevor Jones; production designer, Doug Kraner; produced by Marvin Minoff and Mike Farrell; released by Orion Pictures Corporation. At Loews New York Twin, Second Avenue and 66th Street; Loews 84th Street Six, at Broadway; Waverly Twin, Avenue of the Americas at Third Street. Running time: 111 minutes. This film is rated PG-13.

Eugene Luciano	Ray Liotta
Dominick Luciano	Tom Hulce
Jennifer Reston	Jamie Lee Curtis
Larry Higgins	Todd Graff
Dr. Levinson	Robert Levine

Twelve seconds and a world of difference separate Dominick (Tom Hulce) and Eugene (Ray Liotta), fraternal twins whose mental abilities vary tremendously. Gino is a hardworking medical student, and his education is being paid for by Nicky, who is proud of being able to provide for his slightly younger brother. However, Nicky's own career is less distinguished, since he works cheerfully and at the height of his abilities as a garbage man. An accident that occurred when the twins were young has kept Nicky in a perpetually childlike state.

"Dominick and Eugene," which opens today at the New York Twin and other theaters, is a lot better than the standard-issue heartwarmer it may sound like. It's less sentimental than that, and the two leading actors do a superb job of bringing these characters to life. Mr. Liotta, such a menacing villain in "Something Wild," makes Gino a touchingly devoted figure, a man willing to sacrifice almost anything for his brother's welfare. His frustration at realizing that he can't protect Nicky from life's every problem is something Mr. Liotta makes very moving. And Mr. Hulce gives Nicky a happy, eager-to-please expression that clouds over immediately at the first hint that he may have misbehaved in any way; he

never makes a false or studied move. These two actors work wonderfully together, and the film emphasizes the warm, physical side of their brotherly bond.

•

As directed by Robert M. Young, "Dominick and Eugene" has a refreshing plainness and a welcome unwillingness to milk the story for more pathos than is warranted. It examines the brothers' growing realization that, at 26, they must become more independent of one another. But it accomplishes this by means of genuinely involving plot developments, along with a rather startling denouement. The screenplay by Alvin Sargent and Corey Blechman, from a story by Danny Porfirio, might seem more frankly manipulative were it not for the mutual love and concern conveyed by the two stars.

Jamie Lee Curtis makes a brief but winning appearance as a colleague of Gino's who's on her way to becoming part of the family, and Todd Graff is quite funny as the seedy nay-sayer who does everything he can to plant worries in Nicky's otherwise untroubled mind. ("It won't be long till you get a postcard from Atlantic City," he warns Nicky about his brother's having a girlfriend. " 'Having a great time. Glad you're not here.' "). This may be the only film that has ever ended with an upbeat, sunny montage showing garbage being collected.

•

"Dominick and Eugene" is rated PG-13 ("Special Parental Guidance Suggested for Those Younger Than 13"). It contains some profanity.
    JANET MASLIN
    1988 Mr 18, C20:1

All the Way Home

FIELD OF HONOR, directed by Jean-Pierre Denis; screenplay (French with English subtitles) by Mr. Denis, Hubert Au Petit, Christian Faure and Françoise Dudognon; photography by Miss Dudognon; edited by Geneviève Winding; music by Michel Portal art director, Marc Petitjean; produced by Chantal Perrin and Antoine Gannage; production companies, Baccara Productions/Palmyre Productions/Selena; released by Orion Classics. At Roy and Niuta Titus Theater 1, Museum of Modern Art, 11 West 53d Street, as part of the New Directors/New Films series. Running time: 85 minutes. This film has no rating.

Pierre Naboulet	Cris Campion
Henriette	Pascale Rocard
Arnaud Florent	Eric Wapler
The Child	Frédéric Mayer
The Mother	Marcelle Dessalles
The Peddler	André Wilms
Ernest	Vincent Martin
Pierre's Sister	Marion Audier
Florent's Father	Robert Sandrey
Florent's Mother	Lily Genny
Gang Leader	Louis-Marie Taillefer
Roger	François Segura

Jean-Pierre Denis's "Field of Honor" ("Champ d'Honneur") is a wistful tale about a young farmer from Périgord who goes off to fight in the Franco-Prussian War as the paid substitute for a rich man's son.

The film will be shown in the New Directors/New Films festival at the Museum of Modern Art tonight at 6 and on Sunday at 3:30 P.M.

Pierre Naboulet (Cris Campion), the farmer, never questions his lot. He is resigned and brave, and not even very surprised when he understands the bloody randomness of battle. He asks for and expects nothing from life, though he would prefer to

return home to his fiancée, Henriette.

Separated from his company in Alsace, Pierre comes upon the ruins of a farmhouse, where he finds a small German boy orphaned by the war. Together, communicating mostly in sign language, the two attempt to get back to the French lines.

•

"Field of Honor" is so muted that it's difficult to understand its point. The program suggests "the mystery of a world where the inevitable forever masquerades as happenstance." Yet nothing in this film can easily masquerade as happenstance, if only because it was ordered by Mr. Denis, who also wrote the screenplay. Instead, happenstance looks like the long arm of coincidence, which operates more often and more freely in fiction than in real life.

The movie is almost as resigned as Pierre. It observes all without visible emotion, including the contrast between the order of nature and the disorder of a landscape after battle. In this, it's reminiscent of John Huston's adaptation of "The Red Badge of Courage," though Pierre, who has no illusions about glory, is incapable of disillusion.

"Field of Honor" is a very handsome, muted work, nicely acted by Mr. Campion and Frederic Mayer, who plays the boy. It touches the feelings obliquely, like a reverie.
    VINCENT CANBY
    1988 Mr 18, C24:5

LITTLE NIKITA, directed by Richard Benjamin; screenplay by John Hill and Bo Goldman, story by Tom Musca and Terry Schwartz; director of photography, Laszlo Kovacs; edited by Jacqueline Cambas; music by Marvin Hamlisch; production designed by Gene Callahan; produced by Harry Gittes; released by Columbia Pictures. At Criterion Center, Broadway between 44th and 45th Streets; Gemini Twin, Second Avenue at 64th Street; Quad Cinema, 34 West 13th Street; Movie Center 5, 125th Street between Powell and Douglass Boulevards; Coliseum Twin, Broadway and 181st Street; Metro Twin, 99th Street and Broadway. Running time: 98 minutes. This film is rated PG.

Roy Parmenter	Sidney Poitier
Jeff Grant	River Phoenix
Richard Grant	Richard Jenkins
Elizabeth Grant	Caroline Kava
Konstantin Karpov	Richard Bradford
Scuba	Richard Lynch
Verna McLaughlin	Loretta Devine
Barbara Kerry	Lucy Deakins

Spy Story In "Little Nikita," Sidney Poitier, above, stars as an F.B.I. agent who sends a teen-ager, played by River Phoenix, into international espionage work.

239

Richard Benjamin's strategy in directing "Little Nikita" seems to have been to paper over the holes in the plot with routine moves from spy shows past, in hopes of making the improbable passable. Sidney Poitier, an F.B.I. agent again, gets onto a couple of K.G.B. "sleepers" named Richard and Elizabeth Grant, a very American couple in the southern California town of Fountain Grove, who have been waiting 20 years for the call to action from Moscow. It arrives in the form of Konstantin Karpov, who is out to get a former Soviet agent named Scuba, who has been killing off other Soviet agents in the United States as a way of blackmailing the Kremlin. "Your moment has come," announces Karpov.

Now, the Grants have a teen-age son, born Nikita but known as Jeff (River Phoenix), who is distressed to learn from Mr. Poitier, who just can't keep a secret, that "your parents are Russian spies." Soon the young fellow is yelling at them, "Truth has no meaning in this house."

Mr. Poitier's company is always agreeable, only in this case he is the most conspicuous undercover agent in the annals of the F.B.I. He practically forces people to catch onto him. But no more so than Karpov (Richard Bradford), who not only wears shades and talks with a Hollywood Russian accent, but also smokes Russian cigarettes. Even his hat looks Russian. This is farfetched stuff designed for the nearsighted.

•

The dialogue, too, is a touch familiar. "The man killed my partner," says the determined Mr. Poitier. "Nothing changes," says the cynical Karpov. The script sends Mr. Poitier out on an assignment that only his immediate boss knows about and puts him into bed with a plump guidance counselor mainly so that Jeff can burst in on them, for a laugh. In a burst of inventiveness, the final car chase is between a pickup truck and a trolley.

Since little that anybody does in this movie, which opens today at the Criterion Center and other theaters, makes much sense, it is a sort of achievement that Mr. Benjamin's direction, the music by Marvin Hamlisch and even the photography of the generally dependable Laszlo Kovacs leave nothing to the imagination.

•

"Little Nikita" is rated PG ("Parental Guidance Suggested"), owing to several killings and possibly the suggestion that one's parents might be Soviet moles.
WALTER GOODMAN
1988 Mr 18, C26:5

American Kitsch 101

O. C. AND STIGGS, directed by Robert Altman; screenplay by Donald Cantrell and Ted Mann, based on a story by Tod Carroll and Mr. Mann; director of photography, Pierre Mignot; edited by Elizabeth Kling; production designer, Scott Bushnell; produced by Mr. Altman and Peter Newman; released by MGM/UA Distribution Company. At Film Forum 2, 57 Watts St. Running time: 109 minutes. This film is rated R.

O. C.	Daniel H. Jenkins
Stiggs	Neill Barry
Randall Schwab	Paul Dooley
Elinore Schwab	Jane Curtin
Pat Coletti	Martin Mull
Sponson	Dennis Hopper
Gramps	Ray Walston
Wino Bob	Melvin Van Peebles

"O. C. and Stiggs," made by Robert Altman in 1984, deals with what may be one of the director's least favorite subjects: all-American boys. Mr. Altman's utter lack of sympathy for this film's two schoolboy protagonists (the screenplay is based on material from National Lampoon magazine) is unmistakable, and it's also liberating, so his satirical side is given unusually free rein.

The result: an enormous garage sale of a movie, cluttered with every imaginable form of junk to be found on the American scene. There is one family that favors cactus-shaped anything (including Jell-O), another that's insanely partial to lawn furniture, a third household that's a veritable monument to the South Seas. And around the film's edges there can be found an astonishing array of vanity plates, designer eyeglass frames, mermaid statuary and pastel-colored drinks. If we're indeed going to hell in a handbasket, as this film strongly suggests, then it may well be a beaded, gold-lamé handbasket with gilt trim.

The people in "O. C. and Stiggs" wend their way around the overabundant props, and try their best to sound various unusual notes of rebellion, while the two teen-age protagonists (played by Daniel H. Jenkins and Neill Barry) engage in a series of sophomoric pranks. Mr. Altman makes an asset of the boys' silliness, though, and shoots American high-school scenes in his own distinctive way (nothing looks quite normal, and the various props and displays glimpsed in the background are especially dopey).

•

The cast includes Dennis Hopper as a veteran who has confused Scottsdale, Ariz., with Southeast Asia, Paul Dooley as a wealthy businessman who is the butt of the boys' jokes, Jane Curtin as his wife, who imagines herself to be a secret tippler though her habits are an open secret, and Melvin Van Peebles as a local wino who seems to understand the boys better than anyone else does. Ray Walston plays the retired grandfather of one of the boys, happily entertaining anyone who'll listen with grisly memories of his days on the police force. He's especially proud of the time his partner said to him, after a shootout, "That guy's got more brains on the sidewalk than you've got in your whole head."

"O. C. and Stiggs" rambles a lot and doesn't have a full supply of the Altman alchemy, but it's certainly a lively, colorful satire; its notion of American artificiality runs so deep that the film begins and ends at a man-made surfing beach in the middle of the desert. Though it was not released by MGM/UA in 1984, it certainly should have been. It opens at the Film Forum 2 today.
JANET MASLIN
1988 Mr 18, C26:5

Mal de Famille

BEATRICE, directed by Bertrand Tavernier; screenplay (French with English subtitles) by Colo Tavernier O'Hagan; director of photography, Bruno de Keyzer; edited by Armand Psenny; music by Ron Carter; art director, Guy Claude François; produced by Adolphe Viezzi; released by Samuel Goldwyn

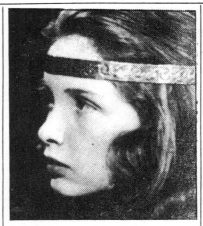

Courageous Beauty Julie Delpy plays the title role in "Beatrice."

Company. At the Paris, 58th Street west of Fifth Avenue. Running time: 128 minutes. This film is rated R.

François	Bernard Pierre Donnadieu
Béatrice	Julie Delpy
Arnaud	Nils Tavernier
François's mother	Monique Chaumette
Raoul	Robert Dhéry
Hélène	Michele Gleizer
Richard	Maxime Leroux

Bertrand Tavernier lays on plenty of medieval lifestyle in "Béatrice," possibly in an effort to distract us from its Gothic plot, compliments of Krafft-Ebing. The de Cortemare castle seems to have been decorated by the same firm that did the Majestic Theater — cold stone relieved by a swatch or two of material. The lighting, by torch, does not encourage reading, not that anybody in the place can read anyhow, but it does throw dramatic shadows. The inmates, got up in tatty finery, enjoy finger-licking banquets. People and animals are constantly bustling about the farmyard and through the spooky corridors, to jagged bits of music.

The ambiance is more solid than the goings-on. The French movie, which opens today at the Paris, begins with 10-year-old François de Cortemare stabbing to death his mother's lover. That's not the sort of thing a boy forgets, and when, 30 years later, François, bushy-bearded and fierce (Bernard Pierre Donnadieu), returns from the wars, he still has a low regard for women. Life hasn't gone well for François. Not only did he lose to the English, but his son Arnaud (Nils Tavernier) showed himself a coward. During François's years of imprisonment, his beautiful daughter, Béatrice (Julie Delpy), was forced to sell off his lands. Once home again, he spends most of his time humiliating Arnaud, abusing the resident wenches, insulting his mother, scaring his wife and, climactically, raping Béatrice.

It is difficult to judge the acting, since Colo Tavernier O'Hagan's script burdens the principals with such peculiar behavior and preposterous lines. The unforgiving François tells his mother: "The very sight of you smites any remaining joy." He laments, "My mother corrupted our blood, the devil drinks it up and my son howls in the night." Soon, François is howling in the night, too. Béatrice asks, in medieval lingo, "Whence comes this sorrow?" After informing Arnaud, "My father has sown the devil's seed," she requests that he kick her in the belly, please.

He obliges, maybe with more enthusiasm than sibling affection requires.

Other characters wander through, dragging significance like chains. There's a young woman who seems to have aspirations to sainthood and a boy, referred to as an "idiot," who knows sin when he sees it. Religious allusions pop up all over the castle, but nobody in the place has a prayer.
WALTER GOODMAN
1988 Mr 18, C25:1

A Film Director, Fondly Remembered

JOHN HUSTON AND THE DUBLINERS, directed and produced by Lilyan Sievernich; photography by Lisa Rinzler; edited by Miroslav Janek; music by Alex North; production company, Liffey Films. At Roy and Niuta Titus Theater 1, Museum of Modern Art, 11 West 53d Street, as part of the New Directors/New Films Series. Running time: 60 minutes. This film has no rating.

WITH: the cast and crew of "The Dead" by John Huston.

By JANET MASLIN

Dressed in the crisp, bright colors of his own paintings as he explores the mysteries of a 70-foot-long Chinese scroll, David Hockney effortlessly connects the past and the present, revealing himself to be a splendid art teacher in the process. In "A Day on the Grand Canal With the Emperor of China (or Surface Is Illusion but So Is Depth)," he delivers an extremely clear and articulate analysis of the manner in which the 17th-century scroll has been painted. Paying particular attention to ways in which the artist and his assistants used perspective, Mr. Hockney also draws comparisons with a later scroll of similar theme, in which Western influences are much more apparent. The conventional use of perspective in a Canaletto canvas provides another point of reference.

Philip Haas, who produced and directed the film, keeps the camera closely attuned to what Mr. Hockney has to say, and provides an apt visual accompaniment for his every comment. Marc Wilkinson's score is also helpful in building and sustaining the film's mood.

Mr. Hockney is often quite playful in his approach to the material, describing a tiny dumpling shop as a Mom and Pop operation and remarking that a figure of a monk reminds him "of my old friend Henry Geldzahler." But he is at his most serious and astute in examining the ways space is used and the eye encouraged to move. The film easily and subtly reveals at least as much about Mr. Hockney's own work as it does about the scrolls. And that makes Mr. Haas's indirect and unobtrusive approach to this contemporary figure all the more disarming.

•

On the same bill, "John Huston and the Dubliners" is a valentine to the late director and a relatively standard production film about his making of "The Dead." Much time is devoted to the actors' understandably admiring comments about Mr. Huston, and to the disposition of the prop department's fake snow. The film has the potential to seem ordinary, but it becomes touched with magic whenever the director makes his presence felt. Mr. Huston displays his characteristic gallantry and his keen attention to seemingly unimportant touches ("Don't worry about what you say, just keep talking," he tells one actor, and gives precise instructions for reading the line "Would you please pass the celery?"). He describes "The Dead" as "lacework," and this film makes the aptness of that description very clear.

When one player complains jokingly that "the most action we've had is breaking a wishbone," Mr. Huston replies: "Yes, that's true. But it depends what your idea of action is." Lilyan Sievernich's portrait of the artist reveals how very subtle Mr. Huston's own such ideas could be.

"A Day on the Grand Canal With the Emperor of China" and "John Huston and the Dubliners" will be shown tonight at 6 P.M. and tomorrow at 8:30 P.M. as part of the New Directors/New Films series.

1988 Mr 19, 8:3

A Chain Reaction Of Questions

SHAME, directed by Steve Jodrell; screenplay by Beverley Blankenship and Michael Brindley; photography by Joseph Pickering; edited by Kerry Regan; music by Mario Millo; production design by Phil Peters; produced by Damien Parer and Paul Barron. At Roy and Niuta Titus Theater 1, Museum of Modern Art, 11 West 53d Street, as part of the New Directors/New Films festival. Running time: 90 minutes. This film has no rating.

Asta Cadell	Deborra-Lee Furness
Tim Curtis	Tony Barry
Lizzie Curtis	Simone Buchanan
Tina Farrel	Gillian Jones
Norma Curtis	Margaret Ford
Danny Fiske	David Franklin
Sgt. Wal Cuddy	Peter Aanensen
Ross	Bill McClusky
Penny	Allison Taylor
Gary	Phil Dean
Bobby	Graeme (Stig) Wemyss
Andrew	Douglas Walker

By CARYN JAMES

It is easy to find soft-headed movies that pretend to be about women's roles in society, and much harder to come across a film as good as "Shame," a tough-minded Australian action story with a smart, sensitive, unsettling macho heroine. In the film's first minutes a black-clothed motorcyclist rides into a small town, takes off a helmet to reveal long, strawberry blonde curls and walks into a grimy bar asking for a room and a mechanic to fix her bike. Is she a tomboy or a femme fatale? A tourist or a drifter?

From then on the film provokes several new questions for every one it answers as it takes the B-level action genre seriously enough to turn it on its head and eventually shatter its limits. "Shame" will be shown as part of the New Directors/New Films festival at the Museum of Modern Art at 8:30 tonight and 1 P.M. tomorrow.

Stuck in town while she waits for spare bike parts, the heroine, Asta, is given a room by Tim Curtis, a mechanic. That night Tim's teen-age daughter is brought home, hysterical, angry and frightened. Lizzie has been raped by a gang of local teen-age boys who have terrorized and attacked other women in town. But even Lizzie's father doubts her story, buying into a thoughtless convention: the boys are just being boys, and the girls must have provoked them.

•

Asta believes and befriends Lizzie, confronts the gang members, teaches the women to stand up for themselves. But the film is never polemical or simple-minded. As Asta reveals bits about her life, she becomes more than the female reverse of a stereotypical male biker. She can

kick and claw her way out of trouble but more often uses her intellect and knowledge of the law to fight back. Deborra-Lee Furness, who plays Asta, looks strong but soft and resembles Judith Ivey.

Though the director, Steve Jodrell, plays off the action genre — two groups of women face off by throwing insults at each other in a supermarket — his style is distinct. "Shame" is less cartoonish than "Mad Max" and more exaggerated than Gillian Armstrong's current "High Tide," but it shares with those Australian films an atmosphere of open roads and wide landscapes as well as a distinct psychological undertow.

•

Mr. Jodrell makes us feel the barrenness of life in this town, where most of the women work in a pet-food factory with no hope of escape. And he has found actors whose faces express the thinness of their lives. Tim Curtis and his mother look like frail birds, so it is even more remarkable when Tim comes to his daughter's defense, when Lizzie's grandmother looks up to the night sky and confides an old desire to walk on the moon.

It would be easy, and expected, if Asta breezed through the town, dispensing good advice, vanquishing the bad guys. But "Shame" does not let anyone off that simply, for as it goes on it presents increasingly complex issues. What happens when the law won't keep the gang members away from Lizzie? When is violence the best, or the only, response to violence?

Finally the characters turn more violent, their story tragic and emotional. Action and true emotion rarely mix well, but Mr. Jodrell pulls off a relentless climax, always poised delicately between the exaggerated and the realistic.

His ending is especially troubling, undercutting the heroism we've been rooting for. Perhaps Asta has been heroic; perhaps she has also been wrongheaded and careless. "Shame" offers no answers, but its intelligent, distinctly styled way of framing the questions makes it one of the real finds of the New Directors festival.

It is preceded by Bill Plympton's macabre, comic "One of Those Days," an eight-minute animated film in which a man accidentally cuts off his nose shaving and finds that his day goes downhill from there. Mr. Plympton is one of the more talented, respected animators around, and his film is a suitably off-beat choice to accompany "Shame."

1988 Mr 19, 10:3

POLICE ACADEMY 5: ASSIGNMENT MIAMI BEACH, directed by Alan Myerson; written by Stephen J. Curwick, based on characters created by Neal Israel and Pat Proft; director of photography, James Pergola; film editor, Hubert C. de La Bouillerie; music by Robert Folk; production designed by Trevor Williams; produced by Paul Maslansky; released by Warner Brothers.

Highwater	Bubba Smith
Tackleberry	David Graf
Jones	Michael Winslow
Callahan	Leslie Easterbrook
Hooks	Marion Ramsey
Kate	Janet Jones
Proctor	Lance Kinsey
Nick	Matt McCoy
Harris	G. W. Bailey
Lassard	George Gaynes
Tony	René Auberjonois

By CARYN JAMES

If you've seen any of the previous "Police Academy" movies, there are

just a few things to say about "Police Academy 5: Assignment Miami Beach" that you don't already know.

First, Steve Guttenberg is not in this one, having gone on to richer things. But most of the cast is intact, including George Gaynes as the academy's kindly Commandant Lassard. He is being forced to retire, but first will be honored as Police Officer of the Decade at a convention in Miami. His former students, including Bubba Smith and Michael Winslow, go along.

That is almost too much plot for a "Police Academy" film, which tends to rely on gimmicks like jelly squirting out of a doughnut into someone's face. But there's more, a twist that brings "Police Academy 5," which opened yesterday at the Warner and other theaters, to its only point of intersection with Roman Polanski's "Frantic." It's the old switched suitcase routine.

•

The spaced-out Lassard picks up a lookalike bag full of stolen diamonds, and soon is kidnapped by the thieves. Their ringleader, René Auberjonois, is made up to look like a George Hamilton impersonator, with slicked-back black hair and a ton of bronzer.

This leads to a big rescue in the Everglades, and a line that pretty much sums things up. "You're one nutty old man," a kidnapper tells Lassard, and this is one nutty series, which revels in its own stupidity. Nowhere else would a character point a gun at a shark and snarl, "Desist and leave the swimming area now, mister!"

But the formula is pretty long in the tooth by now, and all the extra turns of plot can't disguise that.

"Police Academy 5" is rated PG. It contains some strong language.

1988 Mr 19, 13:3

FILM VIEW/Janet Maslin

Just Because It's True, Is It Art?

IN 1982, 18 STUDENTS FROM A HIGH SCHOOL IN EAST Los Angeles took the Advanced Placement exam in calculus and passed. They received college credit for their high school work. The next year, 31 students from the same school passed, and the number has climbed steadily ever since. Eighty-seven students passed the test in 1987.

This may not sound like the stuff of great screen entertainment, but it is the basis for "Stand and Deliver," an enjoyably uplifting classroom film about a teacher who keeps pencils in his breast pocket and inspires his students to do great things. Because there is a real incident at its heart, the film carries the increasingly popular "based on a true story" opening credit (rather than "inspired by a true story," an even fuzzier alternative). And a closing title reels off the exact test-passing data cited above.

Precisely what does this information contribute? Is it meant to make an otherwise skeptical audience stop questioning what it sees on the screen? Certainly "Stand and Deliver" contains enough authentic-looking touches — like the actual sight of students' pencils filling in the computer grid on a multiple-choice exam — to look like the real thing without benefit of any opening declaration: The differential equations that Edward James Olmos, as the teacher, regularly scrawls on his blackboard ought to be enough to do the trick.

And besides, today's real stories aren't easily separated from fiction most of the time. If an experiment were conducted and an audience watched "The Serpent and the Rainbow" without its "true story" title, would anyone suspect that a real Harvard University scientist named Wade Davis had gone to Haiti to study the mysteries of "zombification?" The exotic tortures and wild hallucinations that color Wes Craven's latest adventure into the unknown hardly have the ring of authenticity, no matter how fact-based they may be.

The same could be said for a number of recent films, like "Apprentice to Death," which starred Donald Sutherland as a strange rural doctor and mystic who eventually does battle with a demonic neighbor. Nothing but the film's opening and closing titles gives credence to the idea that anything like this could have happened in rural Pennsylvania in 1928.

Of course, there's nothing new about film makers using real incidents as the basis for their art. D. W. Griffith did it, and for that matter Shakespeare, too. The suggestion of historical accuracy can add a whole new dimension to any story, from "King Lear" to "Elvis and Me." And in most cases, that new dimension involves more than mere voyeurism. Knowing that a dramatic work has some kernel of truth automatically gives it added weight, even if it also sometimes makes the story more banal. A television film about a disabled athlete who triumphs in the Special Olympics or a father who terrorizes his family with his drinking problem can, if anything, be made *less* compelling by an awareness that it's based on real-life events. In these cases, after all, the film makers are selecting and glorifying life's most clichéd stories, rather than choosing to discover something new.

■

The popularity of the television docudrama has obviously begun making its presence felt on the big screen, as more feature films than ever before carry the "true story" declaration. And inevitably, it looks as though there's as much laziness as honesty involved. In the case of "Stand and Deliver," it's nice to know that real barrio students passed their real calculus exam; when it comes to a "Last Emperor," the knowledge that this is history come to life is an essential part of the film's mystique.

But there are less estimable films that rely on the "true story" mantle just as heavily and with much less good reason. Sometimes it's useful to ask what point there would be to watching a dutifully realistic film biography if it were only fiction or an otherwise-unconvincing adventure story if claimed to have an element of truth.

The "true story" title, when used too freely, is no longer a means of dispensing data; it becomes a way of short-circuiting the viewer's imagination. No longer is the job of letting a work of art take root in the imagination really necessary. And to take it one step further, as the masterminds behind a movie-meal tie-in scheme recently have, it is now possible to see a film and experience it in wholly tangible terms right afterward, by watching "Babette's Feast" and then eating it, too. What could be a more powerful encroachment of reality upon the imagination?

The "Babette's Feast" marketing staff deserves credit for a terrific idea, at least in commercial terms; after all, one of this film's chief effects is to work up its audience's appetite. There's no question that seeing the film and then sampling the restaurant Petrossian's version of its menu might make for a delightful evening. But what could be more different from the spirit of the film itself? Babette cooks her meal for a group of primly religious Danes so pleasure-denying that they vow not even to taste the food. And when she wins them over, her act is made more meaningful by a climate of austerity not usually found in expensive New York restaurants.

The film "Babette's Feast" is as much about art and sacrifice as it is about satisfaction. The meal, on the other hand, is about capturing the imaginary and holding it in one's hand. Enjoyable as this element of reality must be, surely it's better to let art make its full impact on its own. □

1988 Mr 20, II:21:5

Amphibian Exotic And Strange Country

CANE TOADS: AN UNNATURAL HISTORY, directed and written by Mark Lewis; production company, Film Australia. Running time: 46 minutes. This film has no rating. At Roy and Niuta Titus Theater 1, Museum of Modern Art, 11 West 53d Street, as part of the New Directors/New Films festival.

FEATHERS, directed and written by John Ruane; photography by Ellery Ryan; music by Louis McManus; produced by Timothy White. Running time: 48 minutes. This film has no rating.

Jack .... James Laurie
Bert .... Neil Melville
Fran .... Julie Forsyth
Doug .... John Flaus
Harold .... Angus Diamond

By JANET MASLIN

Pet or pest? This is the question posed by "Cane Toads: An Unnatural History," a short Australian documentary that's an absolute delight. It supplies the answers to every conceivable question the viewer may have about the species in question, and a few extras: What can the toad do for tourism? What sort of person goes out of his way to squash cane toads while driving? Who feeds his favorite toads cat food, or thinks they look nice in baby clothes?

Ugly even by toad standards, the cane toad is revealed to be an amazingly resourceful creature. It was imported to Australia from Hawaii in 1935 — to illustrate this, the director, Mark Lewis, shows glimpses of a train trip across Australia, from a toad's-eye view — in hopes that it would destroy a grub that threatened the sugar cane crop. However, the toads' lack of interest in eating grubs was matched only by their eagerness to multiply. There are now millions of cane toads in Queensland, descended from an original group of only 101. And as one of the film's interviewees puts it, "the total conquest of northern Australia is but a hop, skip and jump."

Mr. Lewis can hardly be blamed for having some fun at these creatures' expense. He displays a large statue of a toad on a pedestal as one Queensland resident explains why this would be a good tourist attraction, then makes the monument disappear as we learn that the measure was voted down. The bookbinder who sent the Prince and Princess of Wales a volume bound in toadskin for a wedding gift is allowed a chance to show off his wares. Mr. Lewis illustrates the toads' voracious and indiscriminate eating habits by filming one as it hungrily stalks a Ping-Pong ball. He underscores their unusual tenacity by depicting the mating ritual whereby the male attaches himself to the back of a female for a long period of time. "Strange that the male should be so intent as to fail to notice the female's condition," marvels one scientist, since the female lies squashed in the middle of a road and has been dead for hours.

"Cane Toads" is funny, but it's also well balanced; it captures the real danger that the toads pose to their new environment. Their skin secretes a deadly poison (which also doubles as a hallucinogenic drug for some Australians, the film reveals), and as a result they have caused great damage to other species. They have also multiplied at a frightening rate, which is why some of the Australians whom Mr. Lewis interviews have such enterprising ways of killing them. Staunchly on the toads' side, on the other hand, is one sweet-faced elderly woman who says, "If anyone tried to hurt one of my toads, there'd be a lot of noise and they'd realize I wasn't a lady."

●

On the same bill is another Australian film, "Feathers," adapted from Raymond Carver's short story about the city couple who spend a very odd evening at the home of their country friends. The farm couple have a peacock named Joey who seems very human, a baby named Harold who in some ways does not, and such odd collectibles as a plaster dental cast for the wife's new teeth, of which she and her husband are very proud. Written and directed by John Ruane, the film comes as close as it can to Mr. Carver's simple and ultimately quite mysterious tone, but too often it winds up seeming uninflected. Mr. Ruane does a creditable job and the actors are believable, but the film finds no visual equivalent for Mr. Carver's way of combining the very ordinary with the very strange.

"Feathers" and "Cane Toads: An Unnatural History" will be shown tonight at 6 o'clock and tomorrow night at 8:30 as part of the New Directors/New Films festival.

1988 Mr 21, C15:1

Tangled Emotions

LE JUPON ROUGE, produced and directed by Geneviève Lefebvre; screenplay (French with English subtitles) by Miss Lefebvre; photography by Ramón Suarez; edited by Josie Miljevic; music by Joanna Bruzdowicz; production companies: Antares Films, with the participation of the National Center of Cinema and the Ministry of Culture and Communications. At Roy and Niuta Titus Theater 1, Museum of Modern Art, 11 West 53d Street, as part of the New Directors/New Films festival. Running time: 90 minutes. This film has no rating.

Manuela .... Marie-Christine Barrault
Bacha .... Alida Valli
Claude .... Guillemette Grobon
Jean-Pierre .... Michel Favory
David .... Julian Negulesco
Dr. Glazman .... Gilles Segal
M. Smadja .... Michel Siksik

By VINCENT CANBY

That Americans do not have a corner on the manufacture of ludicrously bad, supposedly serious movies is demonstrated with unstoppable enthusiasm by "Le Joupon Rouge" (titled "Manuela's Loves" in English), the first feature by France's Geneviève Lefebvre. The writer-director, who has worked as a production assistant for François Truffaut, among others, should know better.

The film will be shown in the New Directors/New Films festival at the Museum of Modern Art today at 8:30 P.M. and tomorrow at 6 P.M.

Though "Le Joupon Rouge" means to be a celebration of the joys and sorrows of feminism, it's so mini-minded and self-important that it comes out looking like a travesty.

It's the story of the tangled emotional lives of three women: Manuela (Marie-Christine Barrault), a successful Paris fashion consultant in her late 40's; Bacha (Alida Valli), an old woman who, since her release from Ravensbruk, has devoted herself to those less fortunate, and Claude (Guillemette Grobon), a pretty, ambitious young theatrical designer.

●

For 20 years Manuela has pursued her own career while helping the noble Bacha by, it seems, typing the manuscripts of what are described as her "worthwhile books." Though Manuela has the occasional lover, she and Bacha are, to all intents and purposes, inseparable. They take vacations together. Manuela is always there when Bacha becomes depressed. Good works are an uphill struggle. Says a temporarily defeated Bacha, "My struggle to help that South African writer is getting nowhere."

People look up to Bacha. Students take notes when she announces, with a good deal of gravity, "Torture is a fundamental violation of human rights."

One evening when their good works are done, Bacha says to Manuela: "Come on. We'll get our minds off missing persons and apartheid by having dinner with Claude."

Truer words were never spoken.

●

Claude and Manuela, who share a passion for fabrics, textures and Bacha, fall madly in love and speak dialogue that would burn Barbara Cartland's heart. "Don't be afraid," Manuela tells Claude in their first romantic moment. "With women, everything is possible."

Bacha becomes furious. She has never thought of Manuela in "that" way. The old woman must take pills to sleep. Manuela tries to reconcile with Bacha by inviting her out to lunch. "Thanks," says Bacha, "but they need me at Amnesty."

At one point Bacha cries out, "I didn't survive Ravensbruk for *this!*" Only a movie of surpassing muddleheadedness could compare incarceration in a Nazi concentration camp with sexual jealousy, but there it is.

Miss Lefebvre may mean well, but she has no gift for realizing it. Her characters have less character than the handsome apartments they live in. The performances fit the material. Like Liv Ullmann, who shines in the films of Ingmar Bergman and then turns pale and drab in the movies of others, Miss Barrault is particularly vulnerable to her environment. She's the principal victim of "Le Joupon Rouge," though she seems never to stop smiling. Not since Maria Schell's has a smile meant to be sweet seemed so corrosive.

1988 Mr 21, C17:1

New-Age Family

FAMILY VIEWING, written and directed by Atom Egoyan; director of cinematography, Robert MacDonald; edited by Mr. Egoyan and Bruce MacDonald; music by Michael Danna; art director, Linda Del Rosario; production companies, Ego Film Arts, with the participation of the Canada Council, the Ontario Arts Council and the Ontario Film Development Corporation; released by Cinephile Ltd. At Roy and Niuta Titus Theater 1, Museum of Modern Art, 11 West 53d Street, as part of the New Directors/New Films series. Running time: 86 minutes. This film has no rating.

Stan	David Hemblen
Van	Aidan Tierney
Sandra	Gabrielle Rose
Aline	Arsinée Khanjian
Armen	Selma Keklikian
Aline's mother	Jeanne Sabourin
Van's mother	Rose Sarkisyan
Young Van	Vasag Baghboudarian

By JANET MASLIN

Video cameras and monitors watch over the characters in Atom Egoyan's "Family Viewing" with the patience and passivity of vultures, but without the enthusiasm. The advent of this modern technology seems to have drained all vitality out of the participants in Mr. Egoyan's very peculiar black comedy, and it's their listlessness that makes them so funny and sad.

A son affecting a great show of dutifulness, for example, arrives with flowers in hand to pay a visit to his mother in a nursing home, only to be told that the woman at whom he's gazing so lovingly is a complete stranger; his real mother was transferred to a different bed a long time earlier. The video equipment that watches over this and most other encounters in the film is clearly implicated as a key part of what has gone wrong with these people's lives.

●

Actually, the idea of lives gone wrong is more passionate than any judgment Mr. Egoyan musters. The film proceeds in a unique and utterly disaffected way, following the bizarre connections that link a teen-age boy named Stan (David Hemblen), his sexy stepmother and his dully unresponsive father. Everyone fights the battle against anomie, as when Stan complains, "Everything I do feels like I could be doing it or not, and it doesn't matter either way." "That's normal," his father reassures him. "Part of the age."

Also in the cast is a blithe young woman who makes a living delivering pornographic messages over the telephone, and who has grown to know Stan's family a lot better than anyone initially realizes. Much of the action finds Stan and this young woman at the nursing home where her mother and his grandmother are coincidentally living side by side, a lot more interchangeable than anyone initially realizes.

"Family Viewing" has an oddball humor and a sense of contemporary corruption that are very much its own. Its characters seem most alive when they are captured on videotape, and Mr. Egoyan even moves the main action onto videotape from time to time. (Stan's father, Van, works for a company that distributes the stuff, and so his apartment is a shrine to the art of living one's life on tape rather than through real experience.) The film's potential for absurdist humor is thus thoroughly exploited, but it takes on an added pathos when Stan begins struggling to preserve his few scraps of real feeling. He steals videotapes of the mother who abandoned him years earlier, thus angering his

father, who has been re-recording homemade porno footage over this material. And in an even more desperate move, Stan eventually steals his own grandmother, who seems immensely grateful to be freed from the film's impersonal, high-tech world.

●

"Family Viewing" seems hopelessly arch at first, but over time it develops real style and real feeling. Mr. Egoyan is well worth watching in the future. So is Aidan Hickey, whose grotesquely funny animated short "An Inside Job" is on the same bill. It depicts the travails of a dental patient, viewed only as a wide-open mouth and terrified tongue, whose real dentist is called away by a telephone call and whose guest dentist learned everything he knows by watching "The Treasure of the Sierra Madre," a film he thoroughly and hilariously misunderstands. Never trust a dentist carrying a tiny loot bag.

"Family Viewing" and "An Inside Job" will be shown tonight at 8:30 and tomorrow at 6 P.M. as part of the New Directors/New Films series.

1988 Mr 23, C20:5

Bounding, Bouncing, Slashing, Slaying

A CHINESE GHOST STORY, directed by Ching Siu-Tung; screenplay (in Chinese with English subtitles) by Yuen Kai Chi; cinematography by Poon Hang Seng, Sander Lee, Tom Lau and Wong Wing Hang; edited by Cinema City Company Ltd.; music by Romeo Diaz and James Wong; art direction by Yee Chung Man; produced by Tsui Hark. At Roy and Niuta Titus Theater 1, Museum of Modern Art, 11 West 53d Street, as part of the New Directors/ New Films series. Running time: 98 minutes. This film has no rating.

Lin Choi Sin	Leslie Cheung
Lit Siu Seen	Wong Tsu Hsien
Yin Chek Hsia	Wo Ma

By WALTER GOODMAN

If Gene Wilder undertook an all-Oriental takeoff on "The Night of the Living Dead," he might come up with something like "A Chinese Ghost Story." Ching Siu-Tung's spooky spoof, which plays at the Museum of Modern Art today at 6 and Friday at 8:30 P.M. as part of the New Directors/New Films festival, features a klutzy hero who keeps falling into pools and puddles; a supernatural seductress who slaughters her lovers on behalf of her evil master, Lord Black, who may be a woman; a fierce warrior-philosopher-mystic who demolishes opponents with magic firecrackers, and wall-to-wall off-the-wall special effects.

It's a scary medieval night at Lan Ro Temple, to which a young bill collector comes seeking shelter. This haunted hostel is home to a family of otherworldly presences as well as to the firecracker-flinging Taoist warrior, and before he knows it, the collector has plunged into love with a pretty woman who happens to be dead. The tale is not easy to follow, much less summarize, except to report that it's definitely a story of ghosts and definitely Chinese, made in Hong Kong. Mr. Ching, a specialist in the martial arts, does not show much patience for prolonged explanations and some of the captions seem intended to support a reputation for inscrutability: "She don't be interfering in reincarnation."

●

If there are any Eastern profundities emanating from the temple, this Westerner did not recognize them. The action consists almost entirely of the bill collector and the ghostly lady rescuing each other and the warrior rescuing both of them, usually by spectacular means. The main threat to all parties is an outsized tongue. Mr. Ching keeps his own tongue in his cheek, but everything else is let loose. It's 98 minutes of bounding and bouncing, flying and flailing, slashing and slaying. The wind whooshes something fierce, the light is an eerie blue, spirits appear out of nowhere and vanish into nothingness.

The kick you get from all this will depend on how exciting you find explosive exhibitions of extraterrestrial exercises. Exotic, too.

1988 Mr 23, C20:5

To Go or Not to Go

THE CHOICE, written and directed by Idrissa Ouedraogo; in tribal language with English subtitles; photography by Jean Monsigny, Sekou Ouedraogo and Issaka Thiombiano; edited by Arnaud Blin; music by Francis Bebey; production company, Les Films de l'Avenir, Ministère Français de la Coopération. At Roy and Niuta Titus Theater 1, Museum of Modern Art, 11 West 53d Street, as part of the New Directors/New Films Series. Running time: 80 minutes. This film has no rating.

WITH: Aoua Guiraud, Moussa Bologo, Assita Ouedraogo, Fatimata Ouedraogo, Oumarou Ouedraogo, Rasmane Ouedraogo, Salif Ouedraogo, Madi Sana, Ousmane Sawadogo

By CARYN JAMES

When a red Mack truck drives into a parched West African village bringing sacks of grain, we are prepared for an important and perhaps sadly familiar tale of tradition versus in-

From the Beyond
Ching Siu-Tung's "Chinese Ghost Story," to be seen at the Museum of Modern Art.

dustrialization in drought-stricken Africa. But there is nothing familiar about "The Choice," a beautifully composed, emotionally triumphant film from Burkina Faso that will be shown as part of the New Directors/New Films festival at the Museum of Modern Art tonight at 8:30 and tomorrow night at 6.

Without abandoning the stately, imagistic strengths of African cinema — qualities that often seem alien and dull to Westerners — the director, Idrissa Ouedraogo, has created a thoroughly accessible story.

This is a tale of love, jealousy and family bonds, set against the dislocation caused by the African famine. We follow one family: parents; their young son; their grown daughter, named Bintou, and her lover. They leave a village where sparsely spaced trees look like bundles of kindling, and stop in a town where the bazaar displays tote bags with "Paramount" written on them. There they sell their donkey and cart, and move on to a green land by a river bank, where they can grow food, playfully splash water, actually hear and feel a thunderstorm.

Moving slowly through this landscape, the characters look remarkably at home in the space the camera so carefully defines. Often they are centered in the picture, gracefully framed by tree trunks and branches. Then Mr. Ouedraogo will move in to extremely still closeups of their faces, which are often impassive, even at a family burial.

There are technical lapses — some glaringly overexposed shots, some scratchy film — but they only point out how generally accomplished the film is, as it reveals the strength of character held in reserve and captures the rich colors of the landscape.

Once the family has settled by the river, near another household, there are more complications. A man named Tigo wants to marry Bintou, and when she rejects him vows to take vengeance on her lover. Meanwhile, a friend of Bintou weeps when she looks at a photograph of her own lover, who has left her. Yet when he returns to her, she acts as coy as any woman in the world. "It's him, but I will ignore him," she says as he comes into sight.

By insisting on his characters' most universal emotions, drawing attention to what we share with them, Mr. Ouesdraogo also highlights what separates us. He forces us to look beyond the film's quiet surface, and to think again about his country's poverty.

For all its accessibility, this is hardly a narrative film by Western standards. There are none of the obvious breaks that indicate time has passed; rather, the state of Bintou's pregnancy, or the height of the crops, tells us months have gone by. "The Choice" may, in fact, be most interesting as an example of African film making. But in the way its calm surface so perfectly and paradoxically captures its characters' unsettled lives, it brings to our attention a most valuable film maker.

1988 Mr 24, C26:6

LE CAVIAR ROUGE, directed by Robert Hossein; screenplay (French with English subtitles) by Frederic Dard and Mr. Hossein, based on their novel; director of photography, Edmond Richard; edited by Sophie Bhaud; music by Claude-Michel Schoenberg and Jean-Claude Petit; art director, Jacques D'Ovidio; a French-Swiss co-production; Slotint S. A.-Television Suisse Romande and Philippe Dussart; distributed by Galaxy International Releasing Company Inc. At Festival, Fifth Avenue and 57th Street. Running time: 92 minutes. This film is rated PG.

Alex	Robert Hossein
Nora	Candice Patou
Yuri	Ivan Desny
Sibenthal	Maurice Aufair
Vaska	Constantin Kotlarow
Barrioff	Igor de Savitch
The Gator	Peter Semler

Whatever the ineffable quality that makes born movie actors of some people, it is entirely missing from the two dull leads who appear in "Le Caviar Rouge," which opens today at the Festival. This dreadfully solemn spy film, which is entirely without surprises, stars Robert Hossein (who also directed the film) and Candice Patou (Mr. Hossein's wife) as former lovers who once worked together as K.G.B. agents and have been brought together at an abandoned estate outside Geneva. "Geneva," a voice says as the film begins. "Subtle . . . cold . . . haunting . . . cruel as a seagull." There you have it, in a nutshell.

It turns out that the K.G.B. has con-structed an elaborate trap for these wily ex-partners. It arranges to isolate them in this gloomy old villa (from which the camera almost never escapes), apparently an abandoned Soviet consulate, and wait for them to betray each other. The spies are so crafty that it takes most of the film for one of them to spot a video camera, part of the surveillance equipment being manned by a large squad of K.G.B. operatives elsewhere in the building.

Mr. Hossein aspires to an existential murkiness and cuts with Ping-Pong regularity between himself and Miss Patou, which does nothing to boost the film's energy level. Production notes draw parallels between this and the work of Andrei Tarkovsky, but the only real similarity is the occasional background sound of running water.

•

"Le Caviar Rouge" is rated PG ("Parental Guidance Suggested"). It includes some violence.
JANET MASLIN
1988 Mr 25, C10:5

Coming of Age in the Army

By VINCENT CANBY

WHEN first seen in "Biloxi Blues," the movie, Eugene Morris Jerome is not, technically speaking, actually seen. He's an indistinct figure in the window of a World War II troop train. With more purpose than hurry, the train chugs across a broad, verdant American landscape, shimmering in the golden light of memory, as well as in the kind of humid, midsummer heat in which even leaves sweat. On the soundtrack: "How High the Moon."

In one unbroken movement, the camera swoops down and across time and landscape into a close-up of the ever-observant Eugene. He's headed for Biloxi, Miss., and basic training in the company of other recruits who, to his Brighton Beach sensibility, seem to have been born and bred under rocks.

They are Wykowski, Selridge, Carney and Epstein, the usual American cross-section. They're an exhausted but still tirelessly obscene crew given to communication by insults — rudely frank comments about each other's origins, intelligence, odors and anatomies. Says the voice of Eugene (Matthew Broderick), who has a would-be writer's way of stepping outside events to consider his own reactions to them: "It was hard to believe these were guys with mothers and fathers who worried about them. It was my fourth day in the Army, and I hated everybody so far."

It now seems as if the entire Broadway run of Neil Simon's 1985-86 hit play was simply the out-of-town tryout for the movie, which opens today at the Baronet and other theaters. However it came to be, "Biloxi Blues," carefully adapted and reshaped by Mr. Simon, is a very classy movie, directed and toned up by Mike Nichols so there's not an ounce of fat in it.

Here is one adaptation of a stage piece that has no identity crisis. "Biloxi Blues" is not a movie that can't quite cut itself loose from the past, and never for a minute does it aspire to be anything but a first-rate service comedy. With superb performances by Mr. Broderick, who created the role of Eugene on Broadway, and Christopher Walken, who plays Mr. Simon's nearly unhinged, very funny variation on the drill sergeant of movie myth, "Biloxi Blues" has a fully satisfying life of its own.

In one brief but key sequence, the camera watches Eugene and his buddies as they watch the Abbott and Costello classic "Buck Privates." The beautifully timed, low-comedy scene that so delights them continues to be funny in itself. It also helps to place "Biloxi Blues" in a very different movie-reality, in an Army that's racially segregated and in which ignorance and bigotry are the order, though, in hindsight, World War II remains the last "good war."

"Biloxi Blues" is about the education of Eugene Morris Jerome, who has three goals in life: to become a

BILOXI BLUES, directed by Mike Nichols; screenplay by Neil Simon, based on his play; director of photography, Bill Butler; edited by Sam O'Steen; music by Georges Delerue; production designer, Paul Sylbert; produced by Ray Stark; released by Universal Pictures. At Movieland, Broadway at 47th Street; Baronet, Third Avenue and 59th Street; U.A. East, First Avenue at 85th Street; Bay Cinema, Second Avenue at 32d Street; 23d Street West Triplex, at Eighth Avenue; Metro Twin, Broadway and 99th Street. Running time: 104 minutes. This film is rated PG-13.

Eugene	Matthew Broderick
Sergeant Toomey	Christopher Walken
Wykowski	Matt Mulhern
Epstein	Corey Parker
Selridge	Markus Flanagan
Carney	Casey Siemaszko
Hennesey	Michael Dolan
Daisy	Penelope Ann Miller

writer, to lose his virginity and to fall in love. Even if, through some warp in time, we'd never before heard of Neil Simon, the existence of this first-person memoir would reveal how Eugene succeeded in his chosen craft. "Biloxi Blues" recalls how he made out in the sex and romance departments while also growing up.

It makes no difference that there's never any doubt that he will make out. That's a given. The pleasure comes in witnessing Mr. Simon and Mr. Nichols as they discover surprises in situations that one might have thought beyond comic salvation.

•

Beginning with young Richard, the lovesick poet in Eugene O'Neill's "Ah, Wilderness!," would-be writer-characters in the American theater have been sneaking off to brothels virtually nonstop. However, not one of those earlier adventures equals the nuttiness of Eugene's with a Biloxi woman (Park Overall) who, on the side, deals in perfume, stockings, black lace panties and other items hard to find in a wartime economy. Says Eugene, "Do you sell men's clothing?"

There is also an idealized funniness in Eugene's sweet, tentative romance with a pretty Catholic girl (Penelope Ann Miller), who sends his head (and the camera) spinning. When she tells him that her name is Daisy, the delighted Eugene says that Daisy is the name of his favorite female character in fiction. Responds this no-nonsense Daisy, "Which one, Daisy Buchanan or Daisy Miller?"

Even more important are Eugene's relations with the other recruits, including the slobbish but pragmatic Wykowski (Matt Mulhern) and Selridge (Markus Flanagan), and especially Epstein, played by Corey Parker with seriously funny arrogance. Epstein is a young, bookish fellow with a delicate stomach and utter disdain for what people think.

Epstein serves as Eugene's conscience, but Eugene still can't bring himself to stand up for a fellow Jew: "Epstein sort of sometimes asked for it, but since the guys didn't pick on me that much, I just figured I'd stay neutral, like Switzerland."

Eugene's coming of age is sharpened in the film by having Eugene, rather than Epstein, become the key figure in the recruits' late-night showdown with the crazy Sergeant Toomey.

As Sergeant Toomey ("You're not fighting men yet, but I'd put any one of you up against a Nazi cocktail waitress"), Mr. Walken gets his best role in a very long time, possibly since "Pennies From Heaven." Mr. Broderick is wonderfully devious as a young man who's so taken by life's spectacle that he sometimes forgets he's a part of it.

As if he believed that a wisecrack left unspoken were a treasure lost forever, Eugene won't keep quiet. This is an endearing characteristic in Eugene but a problem in some of Mr. Simon's other works. "Biloxi Blues" is different. Mr. Nichols keeps the comedy small, precise and spare. Further, the humor is never flattened by the complex logistics of movie making, nor inflated to justify them.

"Biloxi Blues" is the second play in Mr. Simon's "Eugene trilogy," which begins with "Brighton Beach Memoirs" and ends with "Broadway Bound." It may not be as good a play as "Broadway Bound" but, with "The Heartbreak Kid," adapted from a Bruce Jay Friedman story, and "The Sunshine Boys," it stands as one of the three best films Mr. Simon has yet written.

•

"Biloxi Blues," which has been rated PG-13 ("Special Parental Guidance for Those Younger Than 13"), is full of uproariously vulgar language.
1988 Mr 25, C1:1

Grecian Snapshots

Jacqueline Bisset

HIGH SEASON, directed by Clare Peploe; written by Miss Peploe and Mark Peploe; director of photography, Chris Menges; edited by Gabriella Cristianti; music by Jason Osborn; production designer, Andrew McAlpine; produced by Clare Downs. Released by Hemdale Releasing Corporation. At D. W. Griffith, 235 East 59th Street. Running time: 104 minutes. This film is rated R.

Katherine	Jacqueline Bisset
Patrick	James Fox
Penelope	Irene Papas
Yanni	Paris Tselios
Basil Sharp	Sebastian Shaw
Rick	Kenneth Branagh
Carol	Lesley Manville
Chloe	Ruby Baker
Konstantinis	Robert Stephens

When people of wit and refined sensibilities try to work in a form that, somehow, seems beneath them, the result is likely to be as embarrassing as when a no-talent, stand-up comedian attempts Restoration comedy. This is the sense of "High Season," which pretends to be a romantic comedy with any number of quite serious subtexts.

The setting is the beautiful island of Rhodes, the residence of Katherine (Jacqueline Bisset), a successful if not economically self-sufficient photographer of ancient ruins and artifacts. Katherine lives with her pretty teen-age daughter in elegant poverty just a stone's throw from the studio of her estranged husband, Patrick (James Fox). He's a sculptor who, unlike Katherine, lives in the future. He makes big, boxy statues that have nothing to do with the glories that once were Greece.

The other characters include the very old Basil Sharp (Sebastian

In the Army
Matthew Broderick shares a treat with Penelope Ann Miller in "Biloxi Blues," directed by Mike Nichols and adapted by Neil Simon from his play about basic training in 1945.

Shaw), a famous art historian with a fondness for contemporary Greek lads; Yanni (Paris Tselios), a contemporary Greek lad out to make his fortune from tourism; his mother, Penelope (Irene Papas), who hates tourists, and a clumsy British agent (Kenneth Branagh) sent to the island to deal with a spy.

•

The movie, which opens today at the D. W. Griffith theater, is the first to be directed by Clare Peploe, who has worked in various capacities with some most impressive European directors. Among other things, she contributed to the screenplay of Michelangelo Antonioni's "Zabriskie Point." The screenplay for "High Season" is by Miss Peploe and her brother, Mark, who wrote Mr. Antonioni's "Passenger" and Bernardo Bertolucci's "Last Emperor."

By European standards, their credentials are impeccable. What they lack are senses of humor, spontaneity, fun and narrative, as well as (from the evidence here) any serious commitment to the matters they care about. The Peploes clearly take a dim view of the sort of voracious tourism that is laying waste much of the world, including Rhodes — understanding, too, the sad fact that tourism may be the only way the locals can make their livings.

Yet the movie functions as a sort of extension of tourism at its worst. For all their feeling for landscapes and tradition, Katherine and the other people in the film are so dopey they don't seem any better than the obviously gauche tourists the movie means to send up. The Peploes also make rather frivolous use of the story of a real-life English spy, Anthony Blunt.

The scenery is terrific, and, perhaps in the interests of authenticity, nearly everyone in the movie looks oversunned and dissipated. The exceptions are Miss Papas and Mr. Shaw, who gives the film's single performance of substance and intellect.

VINCENT CANBY

1988 Mr 25, C12:6

A NEW LIFE, written and directed by Alan Alda; director of photography, Kelvin Pike; edited by Wiliam Reynolds; music by Joseph Turrin; production designer, Barbara Dunphy; produced by Martin Bregman; released by Paramount Pictures. At Loews Paramount, 61st Street and Broadway; Loews Tower East, Third Avenue and 71st Street; Loews 34th Street Showplace, between Second and Third Avenues. Running time: 105 minutes. This film is rated PG-13.

Steve	Alan Alda
Mel Arons	Hal Linden
Jackie	Ann-Margret

Kay Hutton	Veronica Hamel
Doc	John Shea
Donna	Mary Kay Place
Judy	Beatrice Alda
Billy	David Eisner
Audrey	Victoria Snow

By JANET MASLIN

Alan Alda is an actor, a film maker and a person, of course, but he's also a state of mind. He's the urge, when one is riding in a gondola, to get up and start singing with the gondolier. He's the impulse to talk over an important personal problem with an entire roomful of concerned friends. He's the determination to keep looking up, no matter how many pigeons may be flying overhead. Mr. Alda's ideals may not be everyone's, but never let it be said that he doesn't make them crystal clear.

A film of Mr. Alda's is guaranteed to make you feel 10 years older, no matter what age you were when you went in. That's not entirely a negative thing, since it does have its soothing side. The middle-aged audience that made "The Four Seasons" a hit obviously enjoyed the feeling of recognition that comes with Mr. Alda's work, and that same audience may like the equally predictable "A New Life," which opens today at the Paramount and other theaters, almost as well.

This time, the focus is on the Giardinos, Steve (Mr. Alda) and Jackie (Ann-Margret), who have a trouble-free, relatively painless divorce after 26 years of marriage. Will they cope with the ordeal of dating? Will they find new mates? Will they get a new start? Mr. Alda's answers to these questions are in no way surprising, but his observations are bound to strike some viewers as all too realistic.

For the role of Steve, Mr. Alda sports unkempt curly hair, a graying beard and an angry, belligerent expression. It was Jackie who broke up the marriage, which is meant to explain his bad mood and also give him carte blanche for future girl-hunting. Abetted by a swinger friend named Mel (Hal Linden), Steve hits the singles circuit (where AIDS is magically not much of a consideration). But he doesn't forfeit the audience's sympathy by becoming involved with the trashy young women whom Mel sends his way. Steve is a sincere guy who's willing to learn from his mistakes, and he's looking for the real thing.

Jackie, who of course also has a best friend (Mary Kay Place) to help her re-enter the rat race, isn't sure she's looking for anyone at all. But she attracts the interest of a cute, enthusiastic, extroverted young artist (John Shea) who's a lot like Mr. Alda, only much younger. Meanwhile, Steve finally convinces himself that he's having a heart attack and winds up meeting a pretty young doctor (Veronica Hamel) who turns out to be Miss Right. When the two new couples finally meet, it is at the hospital, where Steve and Jackie's first grandchild has just been born.

Is it possible for people at their stage in life to make a new start? The film's answer is a resounding yes, though the future it creates for Steve looks a great deal brighter than what Jackie has in store for her. In any case, Mr. Alda transforms Steve from the selfish, angry sorehead he was at the start into the best Lamaze coach that any wife young enough to be her husband's daughter ever had. And Jackie gets that taste of independence that not every divorced woman in her 50's necessarily longs for.

•

Mr. Alda would not be Mr. Alda without managing a wrenching and authentic touch every now and then. "Did you ever think as long as we *lived* we'd have a conversation like this?" Steve asks Jackie, as they arrange to go to a singles' party in a TriBeCa loft. "Can I ask you a favor?" Steve's grown daughter (played by Beatrice Alda) asks when she learns her father will be having another child. "Spend some time with this one, O.K.?" These moments make "A New Life" affecting, but they are well outnumbered by scenes in which the principals and their cronies trade empty wisecracks, or simply yell at one another.

Most of the actors do exactly what might be expected, except for Miss Hamel, who has a welcome tartness, and Ann-Margret, who seems uncharacteristically subdued. No one looks his or her best, with the actors often oddly unkempt and the cinematography unflattering and dim. Mr. Alda is funniest when trying most actively to look terrible, as when he stands irritably in front of a television set, wearing a raincoat and eating with chopsticks from a tin take-out plate. Steve knows enough to realize this isn't very helpful, and the film finds some humor in his efforts to change. When he stops in front of a store window and stares wistfully at the mannequins, he isn't thinking about women; he's wondering if he would look any better in black leather pants. He doesn't.

•

"A New Life" is rated PG-13 ("Special Parental Guidance for Those Younger Than 13"). It contains sexually explicit language.

1988 Mr 25, C5:2

One-Way Ticket

SUBWAY TO THE STARS, directed by Carlos Diegues; script (Portuguese with English subtitles) by Mr. Diegues and Carlos Lombardi; photography by Edgar Moura; edited by Gilberto Santeiro; music by Gilberto Gil; art direction, Lia Renha; a French-Brazilian Col-Production: Chysalide Films (Paris) and CDK Produçoes (Rio de Janeiro); released by Filmdallas Pictures. At Lincoln Plaza, Broadway at 63d Street. Running time: 103 minutes. This film is rated R.

Vinicius	Guilherme Fontes
Freitas	Milton Gonçalves
Dream	Taumaturgo Ferreira
Eunice	Ana Beatriz Wiltgen
Father	Zé Trindade
Mother	Miriam Pires
Bel	Tanja Boscoli
Photographer	Flavio Santiago

Starting Over
Ann-Margret and Alan Alda star in "A New Life," Mr. Alda's romantic comedy about a couple who divorce after a long marriage.

By WALTER GOODMAN

"Subway to the Stars" makes stops at the slums and shanties, the dives and dumps of Rio de Janeiro. Yet when young Vinicius, the hero of Carlos Diegues's new crumbs-of-life movie, plays his saxophone, he can touch the stars. Not a novel notion, but Guilherme Fontes, with his soft, somewhat girlish face, brings such sweetness to the part of Vinicius, the invincibly hopeful musician, that the familiar character takes on a fresh and lovable spirit.

Vinicius's adventures, which can be followed starting today at the Lincoln Plaza theater, begin after a night of love in a car graveyard. His partner, Eunice, disappears, and he begins a search that gives Edgar Moura's camera an opportunity to put together an album of picturesque Rio that you won't get in brochures from the Brazilian travel office.

The vegetable market is a place of long hours, hard work, annoying customers and tedium; the dock is awash in garbage; the apartment that Vinicius shares with his uncle resembles a junkyard. In alleys, winos battle over a bottle. The subway is the most inviting public accommodation available to the poor. For Vinicius and the other residents of his beat-up housing project, the beauties of Rio are all in the distance; their day-to-day city is seedy and sleazy.

The story, which Mr. Diegues (who directed "Bye, Bye, Brazil") helped write, is a patchwork; some of the characters, like the hard-boiled cop who searches for Eunice, are merely sketched. What holds the movie together is the desperation of Rio's slum young, their efforts to break free with music, sex, drugs, crime, action, religion. One young woman spends a night going from man to man ("all good guys") in hopes of conceiving a child. The humor is mostly black; Vinicius and his best friend, Dream, are mugged on their way to commit a burglary, which, predictably, is bungled, with fatal consequences.

Mr. Diegues spares no sentiment for the older generation. Eunice's father is a drunk, her mother a television addict; Dream's blind mother is an affectionate burden. Vinicius's mother, who left him to make her own career as a stripper, gives her son the wisdom of the street — "Everyone sells what they have" — and wins his applause when she displays her wares. Gilberto Gil's music — a mixture of rock, jazz, pop and electronic sounds with a Brazilian flavor — catches the beat of the young, their willingness to try almost anything to spark their lives.

You may wish that Mr. Diegues and his co-writer Carlos Lombardi had taken more pains with the plot; the episodes don't connect very well. Perhaps, though, the lack of connection in these unsettled lives is the point. Whatever you decide about that, you'll find a vibrant movie-making intelligence glittering through "Subway to the Stars."

1988 Mr 25, C14:6

FRIENDSHIP'S DEATH, directed and written by Peter Wollen; photography by Witold Stok; edited by Robert Hargreaves; music by Barrington Pheloung; design by Gemma Jackson; produced by Rebecca O'Brien. At Roy and Niuta Titus Theater 1, Museum of Modern Art, 11 West 53d Street, as part of the New Directors/New Films festival. Running time: 86 minutes. This film has no rating.

Tilda Swinton

Sullivan	Bill Peterson
Friendship	Tilda Swinton
Kubler	Patrick Bauchau
Catherine	Ruby Baker
Palestinian	Joumana Gill

By CARYN JAMES

A lovely young woman named Friendship shows up in Jordan one day and tells a British journalist that she is an extraterrestrial peace envoy, a robot who took a wrong turn en route to M.I.T. The writer and director Peter Wollen might have created a fanciful backdrop for this science-fiction tale, but he chose a disturbingly real one. "Friendship's Death" is set in Amman in September 1970, when battles between Palestinian guerrillas and the Jordanian army were daily events, when several planes were highjacked to the Middle East and later bombed. But Mr. Wollen, who wrote the study "Signs and Meaning in the Cinema," is less concerned with these events than with how we remember them and invest them with meaning.

Early in the story, he shows television news film of a highjacked plane in flames. Sullivan, the journalist, says, "That's the image we all remember ... an image with all the meaning drained out of it," one that creates "a completely opaque curtain between us and history." As Sullivan and Friendship spend days discovering each other's prejudices and personalities, Mr. Wollen sets out to tear down that opaque curtain, to redefine our images of people and machines, of politics and civilized behavior. "Friendship's Death" will be shown as part of the New Directors/New Films festival at the Museum of Modern Art today at 10:30 and tomorrow at 8:30 P.M.

Sullivan begins as a journalistic cliché, stupidly eager to find danger, but a cliché with a sense of humor. "There are three versions of the truth," he tells Friendship. "The truth, my version and blatant lies." Friendship seems most human when she acts like a machine, warning Sullivan to type more gently instead of pounding away at his poor typewriter, which seems like "a very primitive and distant cousin" to her.

●

Unfortunately, these few glimpses of personality don't go very far. Both Friendship and Sullivan are rock-solid images, just as opaque as those Mr. Wollen rejects. Sullivan explains, "Politics is about maps, not people." When the displaced Friendship says, "I have every reason to identify with the Palestinians," Mr. Wollen underlines a point he had made obvious an hour before. Even the sexual undercurrent between man and alluring robot is talked to death.

It would take a lot of irony to send dialogue like this spiraling down into

the depths of meaning. These two characters even speak in a similar discursive manner. That similarity is part of the point, but the film might have been livelier if Friendship had been more human and Sullivan less robotic.

There are only two science-fiction touches, and the first picks up the film briefly. Some brightly colored objects — they look like children's plastic toys — are encoded with Friendship's voice and memories. Magically, they begin to glow and speak. Years later, Sullivan's daughter transfers one to videotape, and the film ends with Friendship's final message, a jumbled, wasted series of words and visual images, including a microscopic view of blood cells. But most of this pedestrian-looking film is confined to closed rooms, into which the surreal reality of war intrudes when armed guerrillas storm through a hotel room and begin shooting from the balcony.

●

This narrow scale is also part of Mr. Wollen's point. He was a cowriter on Michelangelo Antonioni's film "The Passenger," which sets a journalist traveling in search of his identity, back in memory and out on the open road. He has said "Friendship's Death" is like "a sequel" to the Antonioni film, only "enclosed and claustrophobic." That's a little like writing a sequel to "Moby-Dick," only set on land. It can be done, but why bother?

"Friendship's Death" will be preceded by "Sleepwalkers," an eight-minute black-and-white film that supposedly follows a couple through a kind of mating dance in an apartment, but that is really a routine study of light and shadows.

1988 Mr 25, C22:4

Playing for Pay

Anthony Michael Hall

JOHNNY BE GOOD, directed by Bud Smith; written by Steve Zacharias, Jeff Buhai and David Obst; director of photography, Robert D. Yeoman; edited by Scott Smith; music by Jay Ferguson; production designer, Gregg Fonseca; produced by Adam Fields; released by Orion Pictures Corporation. At Embassy 3, Broadway at 47th Street; Columbia Cinema, Broadway at 103d Street; 23d Street West Triplex, at Eighth Avenue; Essex, Essex and Grand Streets. Running time: 105 minutes. This film is rated PG-13.

Johnny Walker	Anthony Michael Hall
Leo Wiggins	Robert Downey Jr.
Wayne Hisler	Paul Gleason
Georgia Elkans	Uma Thurman
Coach Sanders	Steve James
Wallace Gibson	Seymour Cassel
Tex Wade	Michael Greene

If you wince when you hear that Chuck Berry's earthy "Johnny B. Goode" has been straightened out and reduced to the movie title "Johnny Be Good," wait till you hear the title character's full name. It's Johnny Walker, though his wholesome Mom and kindly Gramps don't seem like the sort of folks who would

name a boy after a bottle of Scotch. Johnny, in fact, is All-America, a high school football star who is the object of a fierce recruitment battle. Colleges will offer him anything — money, clothes, the coach's wife — to lure him to their team.

"I'm ready for college and corruption," Johnny tells one of the recruiters mobbing the family driveway, creating an eyesore with their polyester plaid sport coats. If only he had meant it, this might have been a savage satire.

And at moments it tries. Johnny visits campuses like Olde Tex, whose team is called the Horny Toads, and a glitzy California college called U.C.C., which has a steroid dispenser under a neon "Pharmacy" sign in the training room. But mostly the satire is as dated as the recruiters' plaid jackets, as lame as the Johnny Walker joke.

Though the film lurches between the earnest and the outlandish for a while, at heart it is not about corruption in sports, but about Making the Right Choice; it is an ethics lesson tacked onto an adolescent boy's fantasies.

●

Johnny, played by Anthony Michael Hall, is all wide-eyed innocence, a good kid even when he's supposed to be bad. He comes home from a visit to U.C.C. wearing a garish purple suit with gold threads running through it, and he looks as if he has been duped but not bought.

The film becomes refreshingly outrageous only when Robert Downey Jr. — back from the zombieland of "Less Than Zero" — is on screen as Johnny's best friend and flabby teammate, a guy angling to get a scholarship by association. (That's pretty much how this movie works, trading off on Chuck Berry's song title, which has nothing to do with the film.) Mr. Downey seems to belong in another, better movie, one that truly aims at the ripe issue of college recruiting scandals and that might let Johnny be bad.

Two of the screenwriters, Steve Zacharias and Jeff Buhai, also wrote "Revenge of the Nerds," so it's not surprising that they're more interested in tame teen-age fantasies than in social satire. As teen-age fantasies go, "Johnny Be Good," which opens today at the Embassy 3 and other theaters, won't put you to sleep, but it won't do much to stop you if you really want a nap.

●

"Johnny Be Good" is rated PG-13 ("Special Parental Guidance for Those Younger Than 13"). It has some nudity.   CARYN JAMES

1988 Mr 25, C29:1

Tale Told From Two Perspectives

LITTLE DORRIT, adapted for the screen and directed by Christine Edzard; photography by Bruno de Keyzer; edited by Olivier Stockman; music by Giuseppe Verdi, arranged by Michel Sanvoisin; produced by John Brabourne and Richard Goodwin. At Roy and Niuta Titus Theater 1, Museum of Modern Art, 11 West 53d Street, as part of the New Directors/New Films festival. Running time: 360 minutes. This film has no rating.

Arthur Clennam	Derek Jacobi
Mrs. Clennam	Joan Greenwood
Flintwinch	Max Wall
Affery	Patricia Hayes
Young Arthur	Luke Duckett
Flora Finching	Miriam Margolyes
Mr. Casby	Bill Fraser
Mr. Pancks	Roshan Seth

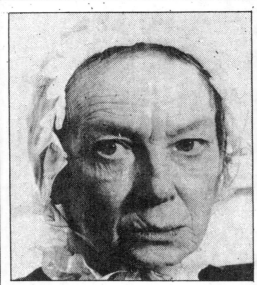

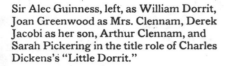

Sir Alec Guinness, left, as William Dorrit, Joan Greenwood as Mrs. Clennam, Derek Jacobi as her son, Arthur Clennam, and Sarah Pickering in the title role of Charles Dickens's "Little Dorrit."

Mr. F's Aunt	Mollie Maureen
Mr. Meagles	Roger Hammond
Minnie	Sophie Ward
Tite Barnacle	John Savident
Clarence Barnacle	Brian Pettifer
Daniel Doyce	Edward Burnham
Mr. Plornish	Christopher Whittingham
Mrs. Plornish	Ruth Mitchell
Old Nandy	Eric Francis
William Dorrit	Alec Guinness
Frederick Dorrit	Cyril Cusack
Little Dorrit	Sarah Pickering
Fanny	Amelda Brown
Tip	Daniel Chatto
Bob	Howard Goorney
The Dancing Master	Murray Melvin
Captain Hopkins	John McEnery
Mrs. Merdle	Eleanor Bron
Mr. Merdle	Michael Elphick
Sparkler	Simon Dormandy
Lord Decimus Barnacle	Robert Morley
The Bishop	Alan Bennett

By VINCENT CANBY

In this time of fast food for the mind as well as the body, the novels of Charles Dickens remain glorious anachronisms. No spare, slim stories they, padded out to novel-length by single lines of cryptic dialogue and a graphic designer's mutely beautiful, very wide margins.

Dickens wrote for a public that demanded its money's worth and he gave it to them — great, long, convoluted narratives, satirical and sentimental, so teeming with characters, events, and reversals of fortune that, even today, they defy what might be called "informed skimming." One keeps getting hooked, if only by the primal need to find out what happens next.

Dickens's work has been effectively ellipsized to serve as the basis for a few superior films of conventional length, including George Cukor's "David Copperfield" and David Lean's "Great Expectations." Until recent years audiences simply wouldn't sit still through the marathons that most Dickens novels would demand if done with the fidelity of, say, the Frank Perry adaptation of Joan Didion's "Play It as It Lays."

Television's mini-series have changed things. They have given us a taste for adaptations that approximate the *entire* content of a long work. They've also evolved into what is virtually a new dramatic form. They helped prepare Broadway audiences for the Royal Shakespeare Company's eight-and-a-half-hour version of "Nicholas Nickleby" (1981), and they prompt one to anticipate — with a good deal of excitement — Christine Edzard's six-hour adaptation of "Little Dorrit," the closing selection of this year's New Directors/New Films festival.

The British film will be shown at the Museum of Modern Art today in two parts, the first, titled "Nobody's Fault," at 1 P.M., and the second, "Little Dorrit's Story," at 8 P.M. The same schedule will be followed for the repeat showing tomorrow.

Six hours would seem to be more than ample time to recreate the manifold details of this (now) comparatively little read Dickens work, which George Bernard Shaw called "his masterpiece among many masterpieces," though critics of Dickens's day saw it as a rather vulgar piece of reformist propaganda.

The film's physical production must be one of the handsomest, most evocative ever given a Dickens novel, and the performances, by some of Britain's finest character actors, are as rich in baroque detail as anyone could hope when anticipating the film.

Yet Miss Edzard, the French-born designer and writer (she and her husband, Richard Goodwin, collaborated on the screenplay for "Tales of Beatrix Potter"), has imposed her own particular, maddening vision on the novel. Though she has kept to the original (mid-19th century) time and place (London and the Continent), she has elected to freight it with a modernist form that plays a lot less often than it lays, not exactly moribund, but also not doing much for the original.

●

Considering Dickens's penchant for subplots and extended narrative asides, the novel is straightforward, told in two parts ("Poverty" and "Riches") in chronological order. At its center is the curious love story of the middle-aged Arthur Clennam, brought up by a repressive, religious zealot of a mother, and the much younger, physically stunted, snow-pure Amy Dorrit ("Little Dorrit"), born and raised in the infamous Marshalsea debtors' prison by her mannered, blithely fraudulent old dad.

True, transforming love is not immediately recognized by Arthur. The 800-plus-page novel comes perilously close to The End and an Afterword before Arthur and Amy declare themselves. In the meantime, Dickens has given the reader a tumultuous portrait of a doomy, starchy, Protestant England, its unthinkable poverty, lunatic (under the circumstances) optimism, heedless bureaucracy, society snobs, celebrated swindlers and assorted, colorful low-lifes. Further complicating matters are a mystery relating to one major character's parentage and another mystery involving a sizable bequest that's been withheld from a rightful heir.

Dickens tells all this in his entertainingly garrulous manner as if sitting on a cloud, observing everything in the most minute, sometimes rueful, sometimes very comic detail. He doesn't much care for going into peoples' minds. He doesn't have to. Never at a loss for a caustic comment, he remains more of a reporter and social critic than a Freudian analyst.

Miss Edzard, who wrote the screenplay as well as directing the film, has chosen to reveal the novel by rearranging its two sections. In the first, we follow most of the novel's events as seen by Arthur Clennam (Derek Jacobi). It begins with Arthur's arrival home in London after 20 years in the Orient working for the family firm, and ends when, through unfortunate investments, he himself winds up a prisoner in the Marshalsea, from which he was instrumental in freeing Little Dorrit (Sarah Pickering) through an unexpected inheritance by her father, William (Alec Guinness).

●

Part Two goes back over these same events, while introducing some additional plot information, as seen through the eyes of Little Dorrit. The point, we are told in the film's program notes, is not a "Rashomon" examination of the impossibility of truth. Rather it seems to be an attempt to evoke two different, subjective points of view. Arthur, approaching a dour and loveless middle-age, sees a world that's grim and dour. Thus Part One is dimly lighted. The colors are dark. When it isn't raining, the sky is full of the debris of the Industrial Revolution.

Part Two is supposedly full of sunshine, light, bright colors. I say "supposedly" because, after several hours of watching, such subtleties tend to be overlooked unless one is terrifically bored. My problem with "Little Dorrit" is that, though increasingly restive, I was never bored. I was only aware that Miss Edzard's second telling of events really didn't serve Dickens *or* me. Subjective points of view are largely beside the point, especially in a film that otherwise seems to have so much spontaneous life.

Spun out and repeated in this fashion, the movie does a disservice to itself in the cause of a scheme that's of more interest in theory than in fact. It's exhausting.

That's the bad news.

The good is that "Little Dorrit" comes to vivid life just often enough to demand attention when one is beginning to think of other things that must be done. The cast is spectacular. The film is montage of memorable images, beginning with Miss Pickering's small, strained, pretty face that somehow remains soot-free. She's a Dickens heroine without silliness.

•

In addition to Mr. Jacobi's quietly staunch Arthur Clennam and Mr. Guinness's lordly William Dorrit, one must cherish the late Joan Greenwood as Arthur's terrible mother, Miriam Margolyes as Flora Finching (who speaks in woozily hilarious, nonstop paragraphs instead of phrases or even sentences), Max Wall as the evil Flintwinch, Patricia Hayes as Affery, Flintwich's wife, Roshan Seth as the rent collector, Pancks, and Eleanor

Bron as Mrs. Merdle, the social-climbing wife of Britain's financial wizard-of-the-moment. Until he goes broke, taking much of the country to ruin with him, Merdle is exalted as "the spirit of the age!"

Though inspired by two real-life financiers who failed, Merdle is still an eerily prescient Dickens creation. He's an axiom of greed. In mid-19th century London, Merdle takes the gentlemanly way out. In our society he'd be featured on magazine covers and, with the help of the willing ghost, would write a best seller, followed, possibly, by a television-movie sale.

1988 Mr 26, 11:1

least, the prerogatives of fiction, have multiplied the possibilities open to the makers of documentaries.

Among the first to demonstrate this freedom were Albert and David Maysles and Charlotte Zwerin in their seminal documentary feature, "Salesman" (1969). "Salesman" is fact, recorded as it happened, but the film — about the day-to-day life of a real-life Bible salesman on the skids — is as subjective and personal as a piece of fiction.

When "Salesman" was initially released, some critics worried about the extent to which the film makers may have (consciously or unconsciously) shaped the life they were photographing. Now those doubts seem almost beside the point. "Salesman" remains as vivid a document of the 1960's as any novel written in that time.

Today's documentary film makers no longer see themselves limited to works about socially and politically oriented events, issues and people. As the fiction writer may explore himself to understand the world, the documentary film maker often turns inward in order to see out. One of the funniest, most invigorating films of recent years is Ross McElwee's "Sherman's March," in which the young, garrulous director ponders his relations with women in general while drifting aimlessly through the South, meeting not women-in-general but some very specific, particular personalities.

As Françoise Romand shows in her "Call Me Madame," documentaries don't have to be about so-called "important" subjects to be important. It's enough, as in fiction, that the film maker is able to persuade us to share her (or his) curiosity, surprise or point of view. The result is an unusual variety of documentary films — including cockeyed, highly subjective essays, personal memoirs, comparatively conventional narratives and,

FILM VIEW/Vincent Canby

Fiction Fuels Documentary

IN ORSON WELLES'S "CITIZEN Kane," a journalist searches for the motivating force in the life of Charles Foster Kane, the newspaper tycoon. The result is a portentous "March of Time" type of documentary that, finally, misses the point. In Woody Allen's "Zelig," which poses as a documentary about the life and times of the notorious "Chameleon Man," the unmistakable figure of Mr. Allen (in the title role) is seen in old newsreel clip, peeking around Hitler to wave to a friend in the audience at a Nazi rally.

Inserted in Warren Beatty's "Reds" are interviews with Rebecca West, Henry Miller and Will Durant, among others, whose reminiscences about the Old Left give poignant historical perspective to the fictionalized story of the romance of John Reed and Louise Bryant.

Since the birth of movies, the documentary film form has been enriching our fiction films.

It's now apparent that fiction films, or, at

Françoise Romand at work on "Call Me Madame," about a Frenchman who underwent a sex-change operation

frequently, some combination of same.

Though the 17th annual New Directors/New Films Festival, ending today at the Museum of Modern Art, was not dedicated to documentaries, the documentary selections dominated the event, both by their quality and for their living testimony that the documentary is a far from moribund form.

In spite of the fact that few documentary films ever find theatrical release, and in spite of the fact that public television is virtually their only mass-audience outlet, documentary film makers carry on. Since it's not for the profits, something like love must be the spur.

As much as the print journalist, the documentary film maker deals in information that, it's assumed, will lead to truth. Today this information is being used in ways that probably would have baffled and disturbed such pioneers as Robert Flaherty ("Nanook of the North") and Louis de Rochemont, producer of "The March of Time" series. Very often, the film maker doesn't even allow himself to say what the truth is supposed to be. This is the "new documentary."

Consider these four films featured in the MOMA festival:

"The Emperor's Naked Army Marches On," in which Kazuo Hara, the Japanese director whose first feature this is, follows a clearly psychotic World War II veteran around Japan on what may be a wild goose chase.

The vet is attempting to fix the blame for the execution of three of his army comrades in New Guinea in 1945. With Mr. Hara's camera urging him on, he bullies and lies his way into the confidence of old comrades, delivers long, incoherent tirades against the Emperor and winds up (after the film was completed, we are told) serving a 12-year sentence in jail for attempted murder.

The movie has the chilly manner of a Peter Handke novel. Its "information" is presented as if it were raw material for us to make sense of, though, obviously, it's been edited by the film maker. It's clear that the making of the movie prompted much of the behavior we see, but the movie pretends to remain aloof from it. Time may or may not march on.

"Call Me Madame," by Françoise Romand, about a barrel-shaped, bespectacled, late-50-ish Frenchwoman named Ovida Delect, a poet, novelist and political activist who would probably have remained anonymous if she hadn't originally been he. Born Jean-Pierre Voidies, Ovida had a sex-change operation at the age of 55, by which she effectively abandoned Huguette, Jean-Pierre's wife, and Jean-Noel, the young man who was their son.

Miss Romand is the one-of-a-kind director who, in 1986, made "Mix-Up," the true story of two babies who were switched at the maternity hospital and lived 20 years with the wrong parents — the first documentary farce that I know of.

For "Call Me Madame" she seems to have had the run of the country house that Ovida Delect still shares with Huguette and Jean-Noel. Individually and together, each talks candidly about the changes in his/her life. Though the film is often very funny (Ovida is an iron-willed ham in front of the camera), it's also a desolate picture of a family forever smashed to smithereens in a most unusual way. The tone is friendly, nonjudgmental. Is this household really much different from many others? Perhaps not.

"The Case of Herman the Stoker," written and directed by Leszek Wosiewicz, a Polish director who considers the rise and fall of the Third Reich as he *imagines* it was seen by the man whose claim on history is that he made the fires for Hitler's fireplaces. Herman, who died in 1985, was interviewed by the director (off camera) and from time to time is is seen onscreen as a shadowy old man.

While Mr. Wosiewicz cuts between old newsreel footage (Hitler at his prime, happy, shirtless German youth batallions, dead bodies smoldering in shallow graves) and more recent shots of the ruins of Hitler's pleasure palaces, a voice on the soundtrack remembers Herman's thoughts (as ascribed to him by the director). Herman is fascinated by the therapeutic properties of various kinds of burning wood.

Beechwood stimulates careers, heals pimples and helps the digestion. Maple facilitates great feats. Oak possesses mystical properties. It "neutralizes harmful outside agents." Birch provides peace of mind.

It's no wonder that Herman gave careful consideration to the choice of wood he burned for Hitler. Keeping the Führer warm and well was his job. Herman "almost had all Europe under his command." He was astonished by the bomb plot on Hitler's life (why would anyone want to kill *Hitler*?) and astonished that, at the end, it all came to nothing. Long after the war, when Herman was an old man, his family teasingly described him as "all that's left of the Third Reich."

"Cane Toads: An Unnatural History," which is a deadly serious consideration of a potential ecological disaster that, much of the time, looks and sounds like an extended (46-minute) Monty Python sketch. The Australian film, shot by Mark Lewis, the director, in modest, self-effacing black and white, recalls the history of the cane toad, brought from Hawaii to Queensland in 1935 to destroy sugar cane grubs.

The toads couldn't have cared less about the grubs. "The life styles of the cane grub and the cane toad just didn't synchronize," says one scientist. Instead, they set about to destroy the continent's natural ecological balance.

Cane toads, some weighing as much as four pounds, are takeover toads. With their poison glands just behind their eyes, they kill all predators who would eat them, including domestic pets as well as snakes and other forms of wildlife. (The cane toad poison, boiled down, is the basis of a hallucinogen used by "cane toad drug abusers.") Some people keep cane toads as pets. An old lady, who looks like Michael Palin in drag, is soothed by their croaking calls at night. One man, otherwise humane, describes his satisfaction when he runs over a cane toad on the road. "They really go off with a bang," he says.

As was also demonstrated by the selections in the New Films/New Directors Festival, documentaries don't necessarily have to be "new" to command attention.

■

Two of the most satisfying festival films honored more familiar forms: "Keeping Love Alive," directed by Stephen Garrett and David Robinson, an unfancified, straightforward record of Elisabeth Welch's one-woman stage show, as performed by the cabaret star, now nearing 80, in London last year; and "Who Killed Vincent Chin?" directed by Christine Choy and Renee Tajima, an exploration of the sociopolitical background of the baseball-bat murder of a young Chinese-American in Detroit in 1982 by an unemployed auto worker who thought the victim was Japanese.

Even without easily accessible financing, and with few distribution outlets assured, independently-minded documentary film makers continue discover new frontiers. (A comprehensive review of contemporary work is promised by the 1988 Global Village Documentary Festival at the Public Theater, April 8-21. Among the directors: Jonathan Demme, Peter Watkins and Deborah Shaffer.)

The form is everlastingly elastic. As demonstrated by Claude Lanzmann's "Shoah" and Marcel Ophuls's "Sorrow and the Pity," it can embrace epic subjects or it can reveal the mysteries and idiosyncrasies of a single mind. This is the sort of documentary that is frequently denigrated as a "talking heads" movie. However, when the heads belong to Jean-Paul Sartre, Simone de Beauvoir and their friends ("Sartre Par Lui-Même"), it's not necessary to see feet, ankles, calves, knees, thighs, groins and torsos. Their existence, to the extent that anything can be said to exist, has already been established. □

1988 Mr 27, II:29:1

Things That Go Bump In the Night and Day

BEETLEJUICE directed by Tim Burton; screenplay by Michael McDowell and Warren Skaaren, story by Mr. McDowell and Larry Wilson; director of photography, Thomas Ackerman; edited by Jane Kurson; music by Danny Elfman; produced by Michael Bender, Larry Wilson and Richard Hashimoto; released by Warner Brothers. At the Criterion

Later On Michael Keaton appears as a ghost in "Beetlejuice."

Center, Broadway at 45th Street; the Manhattan Twin, 59th Street east of Third Avenue; Loews 84th Street Six, at Broadway; 34th Street East, near Second Avenue; Movieland Eighth Street Triplex, at University Place. Running time: 90 minutes. This film is rated PG.

Adam ....Alec Baldwin
Barbara .... Geena Davis
Betelgeuse ....Michael Keaton
Charles ....Jeffrey Jones
Lydia ....Winona Ryder
Juno ....Sylvia Sidney
Delia ....Catherine O'Hara
Otho .... Glenn Shadix

By JANET MASLIN

Anyone whose idea of high wit can be achieved with bizarre latex facial makeup and extra eyeballs in unexpected places will at least admire "Beetlejuice" for its ingenuity. Tim Burton, who also directed "Pee-Wee's Big Adventure," shows a keen grasp of preadolescent tastes in special effects (the weirder the better), pacing (illogical but busy) and comic constructs (only something incongruous, like people breaking into the "Banana Boat" song ("Day-O") for no reason, is funnier than something rude).

But for other audiences "Beetlejuice," which opens today at the Criterion Center and other theaters, is about as funny as a shrunken head — and it happens to include a few. The big joke here is death, since the film's principals are a cute young couple named Adam (Alec Baldwin) and Barbara (Geena Davis) who are killed as the story begins. These two immediately return as ghosts, but "Topper" this isn't; sophisticated spirit-world humor is hardly the order of the day. So dim are Adam and Barbara that he has trouble reading properly and they both require about 20 minutes' worth of not finding their reflections in mirrors to realize they're not precisely in the pink.

•

Adam and Barbara are horrified to find their rustic house sold to a group of fey, obnoxious New Yorkers who are a great deal more ghoulish than the ghosts themselves, and so they do what they can to haunt the place and scare the new owners away. They try severing their heads and so forth, but when the new owners shriek, it's only over the lack of closet space. Into the midst of this standoff rides Michael Keaton as the title character, a "bio-exorcist" who emerges from the grave determined to appall everyone as much as he possibly can. He does this much too well.

Elaborate as this sounds, there really isn't much plot here, only a parade of arbitrary visual tricks to hold the film together. Mr. Keaton, for instance, appears in one scene with a tiny carousel atop his head, bat-wings coming out of his ears and huge, inflatable arms that turn into mallets. At another point, when asked if he can be scary, he sprouts Medusa-like snakes atop his head. And when he spins his head in another scene, he complains, "Don't you hate it when that happens?"

•

Mr. Burton, who seems to take his inspiration from toy stores and rock videos in equal measure, tries anything and everything for effect, and only occasionally manages something marginally funny, like a bureaucratic waiting room for the dead packed with very peculiar casualties (that shrunken head is one of them). His actors, not surprisingly, are limited by the stupidity of their material. Winona Ryder makes a good impression as the new owners' daughter, a girl much creepier than the ghosts themselves, and Glenn Shadix does what he can as their very arch decorator, but as the owners Catherine O'Hara and Jeffrey Jones are made to behave as dopily as Mr. Keaton himself. To affirm this couple's status as bores, Dick Cavett and Robert Goulet appear as their friends.

•

"Beetlejuice" is rated PG ("Parental Guidance Suggested"). It includes rude language and gory special effects.

1988 Mr 30, C18:6

Hookers, Hustlers And Dear Old Dad

NIGHT ZOO, directed and written by Jean-Claude Lauzon; in French with English subtitles; director of photography, Guy Dufaux; edited by Michel Arcand; music by Jean Corriveau; produced by Roger Frappier and Pierre Gendron; released by Filmdallas Pictures. At Cinema 2, Third Avenue and 60th Street. Running time: 115 minutes. This film has no rating.

Marcel	Gilles Maheu
Albert	Roger Le Bel
Tony	Corrado Mastropasqua
George	Lorne Brass
Charlie	Germain Houde
American	Jerry Snell
Julie	Lynne Adams
Angelica	Anna-Maria Giannoti

By VINCENT CANBY

When first met, a young convict named Marcel (Gilles Maheu), sometimes called Stick, is being raped in his cell by his "birthday present," another convict acting on the orders of Marcel's associates in a drug operation gone sour. Marcel, it seems, double-crossed his associates, who are still on the outside and to whom he owes $200,000.

When Marcel gets out of prison and returns to his modish Montreal loft, which has a stunning river view, he has murder in his heart and an awful lot of listening to do. For the entire two years he's been away, his answering machine has been accepting messages. Who, the audience is allowed to ask, has been paying Marcel's telephone bill?

"Night Zoo," the French-Canadian film opening today at the Cinema 2, can't bother its pretty, solemn head with such practical matters. It's thinking of more important things, including Marcel's feral amorality as he fights his way through the zoo that is Montreal's demimonde of drug dealers, hookers, hustlers and crooked cops. "Night Zoo" is also about Marcel's need to reconcile with his dad, an exceptionally sentimental old windbag with a bad heart and a dream to go moose hunting with Marcel.

•

"Night Zoo," the first feature to be directed by Jean-Claude Lauzon, suggests that Mr. Lauzon overdosed on a double-bill of "Diva" and one of those television dramas of the 1950's that ends with the line, "I love you, Pop." It's all pretty ghastly, though its bogus tough-guy mannerisms are sometimes unintentionally funny.

In one especially lurid scene, Marcel rapes his former girlfriend, Julie, who has become a porn-parlor performer because he didn't return her phone calls. They are on a Montreal rooftop at night. A sliver of a moon looks down. After Marcel has had his way, to the accompaniment of the squeaks of chic leather outfits rubbing together, he sighs. What they *really* should do, he says, is get a band together and go to Australia.

Mr. Lauzon is not much good either at writing screenplays or in directing actors, but he sets the sleazy scene with a certain amount of photogenic style. The soundtrack score has an eerie appeal that is wasted here. If you can possibly hang on, don't walk out before the end. The film's final image, a variation on a Pietà, is a howler.

1988 Mr 30, C20:5

Memoirs of an Unseen Nerd

THE INVISIBLE KID, directed and written by Avery Crounse; director of photography, Michael Barnard; edited by Gabrielle Gilbert; music by Steve Hunter and Jan King; art director, Charles Tomlinson; produced by Philip J. Spinelli; released by Taurus Entertainment Company in association with Elysian Pictures. At Criterion Center, Broadway between 44th and 45th Streets; Columbia, Broadway and 103d Street; Movie Center Five, 125th Street between Powell and Douglass Boulevard. Running time: 96 minutes. This film is rated PG.

Grover Dunn	Jay Underwood
Milton McClane	Wally Ward
Cindy Moore	Chynna Phillips
Officer Chuck Malone	Mike Genovese
Donny Zanders	Nicolas deToth
Officer Terell	Thomas Cross
Principal Baxter	John Madden Towey
Dr. Theodore	Brother Theodore
Mom	Karen Black

By CARYN JAMES

Grover is a teen-age nerd, but will he stay nerdy for long? Of course not. He is the hero of "The Invisible Kid," a movie that proves you can cull every known cliché from successful teen adventure films and still come up with a bomb.

The story begins with bubbling green slime that is meant to make you say "yech" or "gross" but looks too plastic for that. When Grover accidentally adds a secret ingredient to this potion, it changes from toilet bowl cleaner to a magic powder that makes people invisible.

From that point on, Grover's family, friends and plot all line up in predictable order. His pal has big ideas for invisibility ("Let's at least sneak into the girls' locker room."). His mom is Karen Black, struggling to be kooky in another of her embarrassing cameos. And the beautiful girl next door (Chynna Phillips, who *does* resemble her mother, Michelle Phillips) will, of course, dump her basketball star boyfriend for Grover, whose nerdiness vanishes when he tosses away his black-rimmed glasses. (No one really needs glasses in movies.)

•

There are lots of tracking shots, in which the camera moves along empty high-school corridors to show an invisible person's point of view. The potion is constantly wearing off, leaving people in public without their clothes, though the camera never strays to areas that would risk the film's PG rating. There is more, but you get the idea.

"The Invisible Kid," which opened yesterday at the Criterion Center and other theaters, is especially painful to watch because it is the second film written and directed by Avery Crounse, whose first feature was an uneven but wildly original work called "Eyes of Fire" — part ghost story, part 18th-century morality tale. Here Mr. Crounse seems to go out of his way to level down his taste and aim at the mass audience. You can't blame him for trying to go commercial, but you might wish he'd had some flair for it.

•

"The Invisible Kid" is rated PG ("Parental Guidance Suggested"). There is some nudity.

1988 Mr 31, C16:4

Redemption Through Theft

Bernard Hill

BELLMAN AND TRUE, directed by Richard Loncraine; screenplay by Desmond Lowden and Mr. Loncraine, with Michael Wearing, based on a novel by Mr. Lowden; director of photography, Ken Westbury; edited by Paul Green; music by Colin Towns; production designer, Jon Bunker; produced by Mr. Wearing and Christopher Neame; released by Island Pictures. At Carnegie Hall Cinema, Seventh Avenue and 57th Street. Running time: 112 minutes. This film is rated R.

Hiller	Bernard Hill
The Boy	Kieran O'Brien
Salto	Richard Hope
Anna	Frances Tomelty
Guv'nor	Derek Newark
Donkey	John Kavanagh
Gort	Ken Bones
Peterman	Arthur Whybrow
Bellman	Peter Howell
Wheelman	Jim Dowdall

Bank heist stories ordinarily concentrate on the details and take a businesslike tone, but the British film "Bellman and True" could not be a greater departure from that. Though it catalogues the particulars of an elaborate theft, Richard Loncraine's dark, riveting, offbeat new gangster film is less about a robbery than about a man and boy who are unwittingly caught up in its machinations, and the ways in which this unlikely crisis binds them together.

The story begins with a computer systems engineer named Hiller (Bernard Hill) and his unnamed young stepson (Kieran O'Brien) as they move from one London hideout to another in hopes of avoiding gangsters, to whom Hiller is in debt for the sum of £1,000. Why should they want him so badly? It develops that the baby-faced, mockingly sweet Salto (Richard Hope) and a sidekick aptly named Gort (Ken Bones) have decided to capitalize on Hiller's access to computer records about the funds contained in a particularly busy bank near Heathrow Airport. But Hiller, unbeknownst to these hoods, is well on his way to self-destruction anyway. He has been drinking, has lost his job and has been left by his wife, who wrote in lipstick on a mirror this goodbye message: "Just boring."

•

The hoods find Hiller useful all the same, and they incarcerate him and the boy in a once-grand, now-dilapidated building. Mr. Loncraine, who favors vertiginous overhead shots and unsettling angles, gives this place a dangerous, claustrophobic feeling, despite its cavernous rooms. As the plan drags on, the boy grows ever more restless playing with toys that don't hold his interest and contending with an irritable gangster baby sitter, while Hiller hones his mechanical skills. The little car with a light-seeking cell that Hiller places between two equidistant candles becomes a tiny physical monument to his own frustration.

Finally, the hoods begin to make more active use of Hiller. They send him into the bank to do reconnaissance, instructing him: "Try not to behave like Michael Caine. Act natural." Hiller helps the ever-widening group of robbers to outsmart the bank's security system by staging one false alarm after another. Once the heist is set in motion, though, there are some inevitable surprises; the game turns deadly, and the gang must go on the run. Another of Mr. Loncraine's memorable images of maddening entrapment is the sight of the getaway car, a hardly inconspicuous gold Jaguar, ramming itself back and forth inside a small suburban alleyway because the driver has made a bad guess about its size.

"Bellman and True," which takes its title from the British song "D'ye Ken John Peel" and is based on a novel by Desmond Lowden, defies the conventions of bank heist stories in another way: it isn't about either money or encroaching doom. Though the story takes a bloody turn and the casualties run high, Hiller somehow flourishes in the midst of all this trouble. A defeated man as the story begins, an impatient and unhelpful companion to the young boy, he somehow discovers new reserves of canniness, self-respect and parental love. In the end, this is an unexpectedly upbeat and satisfying film, and its closing titles are a particularly appealing little surprise.

"Bellman and True," which opens today at the Carnegie Hall Cinema, is further evidence that the gangster story has become the preserve of British film makers in recent years. As with "The Long Good Friday" and "Mona Lisa," the world of crime is given a newly intriguing shadiness and a spark of sardonic w , even in a glum, murky climate of impending tragedy. And the story's colorful array of miscreants is played by an excellent cast of character actors from television and the stage.

•

Mr. Hill, who has played both John Lennon and Lech Walesa, is a quietly versatile actor who makes Hiller a mixture of self-destructiveness and hidden talents; Mr. Hope, as Salto, is insinuatingly sly.

Mr. Bones makes a memorable screen debut as the bullying Gort, and Frances Tomelty combines her character's jobs of hooker and baby sitter as well as she can. Derek Newark plays the worst of the thugs pitilessly, and Peter Howell is amusingly distinguished as the most elderly and eminent of the thieves. The 13-year-old Kieran O'Brien has a fine, unaffected presence as the needy young boy.

JANET MASLIN
1988 Ap 1, C4:4

The Visiting Team

PLAYING AWAY, directed by Horace Ove; screenplay by Caryl Phillips; photographed by Nic Knowland; edited by Graham Whitlock; music by Simon Webb; produced by Vijay Amarnani; released by International Film Exchange. At Cinema Studio 2, Broadway and 66th Street. Running time: 100 minutes. This film is not rated.

Willie-Boy	Norman Beaton
Godfrey	Robert Urquhart
Majorie	Helen Lindsay
Derek	Nicholas Farrell
Stuart	Brian Bovell
Errol	Gary Beadle
Yvette	Suzette Llewellyn
Jeff	Trevor Thomas
Louis	Stefan Kalipha
Fredrick	Bruce Purchase

"Playing Away" was shown as part of last year's New Directors/New Films festival. These are excerpts from Vincent Canby's review, which appeared in The New York Times March 13, 1987. The film opens today at the Cinema Studio 2, Broadway and 66th Street.

"Playing Away," directed by the Trinidad-born Horace Ove, is a movie about the comic pretensions of social and political organisms — the kind of community-comedy at which British movie makers have excelled, from "Tight Little Island" and "I'm All Right, Jack" through "A Private Function."

The new film is about the inevitable culture clash that takes place when the residents of a small, affluent, idyllically picturesque village in Suffolk invite a West Indian cricket team to participate in a match highlighting the village's "Third World Week."

In the course of the two-day weekend, the visitors — mostly Jamaicans who've immigrated to the rough-and-tumble Brixton section of London — remain ever unsurprised by the manners of their rich, rural hosts. The hosts, in their turn, are positively heroic in masking distaste with a show of sportsmanship, no matter how crudely some of the visitors behave.

•

In addition to the match that is the weekend's climax, there are the vicar's reception, at which the village band turns lilting Caribbean melodies into dirges fit for a viking's funeral; special Sunday-morning services in the ancient church; impromptu, boozy confrontations in the pub and late-night connections on the grass.

It's a weekend of people falling over backward to be polite, of furiously short tempers, of tentative romantic attachments and, possibly, of new understandings, though that's not at all certain.

The big hurdle facing such comedies is that one can usually anticipate most of the crises as soon as one knows the film's main premise. "Playing Away" offers few surprises. The achievements of Mr. Ove, as director, and Caryl Phillips, who wrote the original screenplay, are those of characterization and emphasis. With the help of an excellent cast, the film makers bring to particular life nearly a dozen characters who never quite conform to expectations.

•

Melodrama is threatened and, without one's being aware of how it happens, it eases into comedy. Genteel lives are obliquely seen to be desperate and do-gooders to be much less silly than they initially sound. "Playing Away" is witty and wise without being seriously disturbing for a minute.

1988 Ap 1, C4:4

Opera Hat Comique

THE MAN IN THE SILK HAT, written, produced, directed and narrated by Maud Linder; edited by Suzanne Baron and Pierre Gillette; music by Jean-Marie Senia; production company, Films Max Linder; a Media Home Entertainment Release; a Horizon Releasing Film; released by Kino International Corporation. At the Public, 425 Lafayette Street. Running time: 96 minutes. This film has no rating.

Featuring: Max Linder

Cinema students who missed "The Man in the Silk Hat" when it was shown on Channel 13 a year ago can catch up with it at the Public Theater, where it opens today.

The film is Maud Linder's homage to the art of her father, Max Linder (1883-1925), the dapper, innovative French film comedian whose work is often cited for its influence on Chaplin and Keaton. "The Man in the Silk Hat" contains clips from several dozen rarely seen one-reelers made between 1906 and 1916.

In addition, there are clips from his features, including the Hollywood-made "Three Must-Get-Theres," a parody of Douglas Fairbanks's "Three Musketeers," photographed, with the cooperation of Fairbanks, on the sets for the original film. "The Three Must-Get-Theres" was also seen in Miss Linder's earlier homage, "Max," shown at the Film Forum in 1980.

•

"The Man in the Silk Hat" is best when it presents the clips straight, and somewhat less effective when it uses the clips as if they were illustrations of Linder's life, which was far more troubled than this film cares to acknowledge. At the age of 42, Linder died with his young wife in what has sometimes been described as a suicide pact, and sometimes as a murder-suicide, when his daughter was less than a year old.

Linder's dapper screen presence — he looks like a cross between Marcello Mastroianni and Giancarlo Giannini — and his imaginative use of the camera can be fully appreciated only when seen in the context of the time in which he worked. Most of Linder's finest work was completed by the time Chaplin and Keaton hit their strides. Though he was accepted by the Hollywood community in the early 1920's, his films were not successful at the American box office.

"The Man in the Silk Hat" is charming as far as it goes. Linder's work has yet to be explored in relation to his life and to the films being made by others at the same time and afterward.
VINCENT CANBY
1988 Ap 1, C10:5

When God Gets Sick and Tired

Demi Moore in "Seventh Sign."

THE SEVENTH SIGN, directed by Carl Schultz; written by W. W. Wicket and George Kaplan; director of photography, Juan Ruiz Anchia; edited by Caroline Biggerstaff; music by Jack Nitzsche; production designer, Stephen Marsh; produced by Ted Field and Robert W. Cort; released by Tri-Star. At Criterion Center, Broadway and 45th Street; Gemini Twin, 64th Street and Second Avenue; Loews 84th Street Six, at Broadway; Movieland Eighth Street Triplex, at University Place; Movie Center 5, 125th Street, between Powell and Douglass Boulevards. Running time: 97 minutes. This film is rated R.

Abby Quinn	Demi Moore
Russell Quinn	Michael Biehn
The Boarder	Jürgen Prochnow
Lucci	Peter Friedman
Avi	Manny Jacobs
Jimmy	John Taylor
Dr. Inness	Lee Garlington
Penny	Akosua Busia

By VINCENT CANBY

"The Omen" isn't exactly one of the 10,000 best movies of all time, but it still towers above "The Seventh Sign," which also claims as its inspiration Revelation, the New Testament's apocalyptic, final book, written, according to the Columbia Encyclopedia, by "one John" in A.D. 95.

The Columbia entry adds, "Every period of Christian history has produced new (often bizarre) explanations of the book."

Movie makers are less interested in interpreting Revelation than in ransacking its enigmatic prophesies for bankable horror films. "The Omen" is about the frightfully disgusting things that happen when a pretty, bouncing baby boy, who is born to the wife of the United States Ambassador to the Court of St. James's, turns out to be the Antichrist himself.

"The Seventh Sign," opening today at the Gemini and other theaters, operates on a somewhat more mundane but no less apocalyptic level. It's also about the end of the world, brought about not by the Antichrist but by God, who is sick and tired of the mess we're making of things.

In the screenplay by W. W. Wicket and George Kaplan, the world's only hope for salavation is Abby (Demi Moore), a pregnant Los Angeles homemaker who, in an earlier incarnation, may have played a key role in the Crucifixion of Jesus. If plucky Abby can maintain hope *this time*, mankind may yet be saved. It's clear the writers have taken some liberties with their source material, so many, in fact, that the film's theology is even more opaque than Revelation's revelations.

"The Seventh Sign" is the work of Carl Schultz, best known here as the director of the Australian "Careful, He Might Hear You." It begins with a series of not easily explained natural disasters. Fish die by the millions off Haiti. A "terrorist village" in the Negev is found frozen in ice and reduced to the size of a movie maker's miniature set. The water of a river in Nicaragua turns to blood. Separately monitoring these events are a Roman Catholic priest (Peter Friedman) and a sad-faced man (Jürgen Prochnow) who wears civilian clothes and has a strange accent.

The priest reports back to a Vatican committee that, all signs to the contrary, the apocalypse has not begun. Says the chairman: "I will tell His Holiness. He will be quite relieved."

•

The sad-faced man, who later turns up in Los Angeles and calls himself David, tells Miss Moore that he originally came to earth as a lamb, but now he is a lion. Miss Moore starts having bad dreams. Her husband, Michel Biehn, can't help her — he's too busy defending a young man who murdered his mother and father, who were, in fact, sister and brother.

The world may well deserve being taught a lesson. It doesn't deserve a film as witless as this.

1988 Ap 1, C20:3

Moths to the Flame

Michael J. Fox

BRIGHT LIGHTS, BIG CITY, directed by James Bridges; screenplay by Jay McInerney, based on his novel; director of photography, Gordon Willis; edited by John Bloom; music by Donald Fagen; production designer, Santo Loquasto; produced by Mark Rosenberg and Sydney Pollack; released by United Artists. At Loews Astor Plaza, 44th Street, west of Broadway; Loews Orpheum, 86th Street near Third Avenue; Quad Cinema, 34 West 13th Street; Loews 84th Street Six, at Broadway. Running time: 110 minutes. This film is rated R.

Jamie	Michael J. Fox
Tad	Kiefer Sutherland
Amanda	Phoebe Cates
Megan	Swoosie Kurtz
Clara	Frances Sternhagen
Vicky	Tracy Pollan
Mr. Vogel	John Houseman
Michael	Charlie Schlatter
Alex Hardy	Jason Robards
Rittenhouse	David Warrilow
Mother	Dianne Wiest
Ferret Man	William Hickey

By JANET MASLIN

The hero of Jay McInerney's book "Bright Lights, Big City" didn't have a name, but he certainly had a voice. On the other hand, the film version calls its leading character Jamie Conway and allows him no real equivalent of the novel's astute, dry, nicely self-mocking second-person narration. "You are a republic of voices tonight," Mr. McInerney's hero tells himself at one juncture. "Unfortunately, that republic is Italy." Who could invent a visual or even conversational equivalent for that?

Mr. McInerney's book has rightly been compared with J.D. Salinger's "Catcher in the Rye" for its complete immediacy, its funny, vibrant and original style, its young man's view of responsibility and authority, and its underlying pain. When a book leaves its mark upon a generation in the way that these have, the movie-making impulse is seldom far behind. But in this case, it's a misguided one, at least to some degree. Too much of what makes "Bright Lights, Big City" so irresistible on the page — its knowing tone, its brisk rhythm, its droll wit and even its nonchalant, unassuming manner — simply cannot be translated to the screen.

That's the bad news, but there's good news too. The film version of "Bright Lights, Big City" directed by James Bridges, which opens today at Loews Astor Plaza and other theaters, seems to know precisely what it can and cannot do, and to work well within those limitations. It may not capture Mr. McInerney's novel completely or even succeed in standing on its own, but it does go a long way toward bringing the book to life. If Mr. McInerney's readers think it incomplete, they should also find it enjoyably familiar.

The film has a number of things working in its favor. For the most part, it's so well cast that fans of the novel will easily guess from the opening credits which actor has which role. Even the casting of small parts, like William Hickey of "Prizzi's Honor" as the strange fellow trying to peddle a ferret on the streets of New York, is exactly right. Gordon Willis's cinematography, Santo Loquasto's production design and Donald Fagen's coolly nocturnal music all contribute powerfully to the mood and settings of the story, which are evoked inventively. Since the story lurches unpredictably from the after-hours clubs where Jamie wrecks his health to the staid magazine offices where he is in the process of ruining his career, it took considerable versatility to capture this shifting atmosphere so well.

•

The film also manages to depict Jamie's self-destructiveness in an admirably nonjudgmental way, letting both the character and the audience come to their own conclusions; if the film were more moralistic, it would have nowhere to go, and if it were celebratory, it would seem hopelessly dated. Jamie's cocaine problem is simply a fact of his sleepless, high-voltage modern life, along with his drinking problem and his work problem and his problems about his wife and mother. The last two, presented fairly subtly in the novel, are more heavily emphasized here, exposing the naïve psychological underpinnings of Mr. McInerney's plot. Mr. McInerney, it should be noted, wrote the screenplay himself, and is no doubt the latest writer to learn the hard way how different films and fiction really are.

Michael J. Fox, looking not the least bit dissipated but wearing a con-

vincingly dazed, furtive expression, is the story's night-crawling hero. Mr. Fox is much better delivering funny lines than he is in this largely reactive role, but he is the sympathetic figure that the material needs. "Bright Lights, Big City" hardly has much of a story (which will be a problem for those unfamiliar with the novel); it simply follows Jamie through the series of exploits that finally create a crisis in his life and bring him to his senses. Some of that time is spent in nightclubs under the tutelage of his smug, indestructible, drug-hunting friend Tad Allagash (Kiefer Sutherland), and some of it is spent fact-checking in the offices of a New York magazine well known for its fastidious editorial practices.

The magazine scenes are the film's best, partly because the setting is unusual by movie standards, and partly because the comic aspects of all that nitpicking come through. An anecdote about how the magazine's stone-faced editor (John Houseman — the perfect choice) makes Jamie investigate the President's grammar has been preserved, as has Jamie's hard-luck assignment of having to place trans-Atlantic calls to check the facts in a wildly irresponsible story ("Where did you get this about the French Government owning a controlling interest in Paramount Pictures?"). Jason Robards makes a scene-stealing appearance as a hard-drinking veteran editor who remembers Faulkner fondly, to the extent that he remembers anything at all.

•

Dianne Wiest brings surprising emotion to the role of Jamie's mother, and Frances Sternhagen is suitably aghast as the editor who cannot believe Jamie has reversed certain accents and electoral districts in checking that article about France, but some of the other women's roles work less well. Swoosie Kurtz, as a co-worker, has the thankless job of sitting by in a worried, maternal manner while Mr. Fox recites an endless chunk of exposition. And Phoebe Cates is too giddy for the soulless fashion model who is Jamie's ex-wife. Tracy Pollan appears briefly but charmingly as a potential Miss Right.

The film ends as it begins, with a touch that faithfully recalls Mr. McInerney's novel. Mr. Bridges may not have breathed fire into this material, but he has preserved most of its better qualities. He has treated it with intelligence, respect and no undue reverence, assembling a coherent film that resists any hint of exploitation. Despite the story of debauchery and the potential for luridness, the fundamental decency of "Bright Lights, Big City" emerges as the film's signal quality.

1988 Ap 1, C22:5

Church vs. Godliness

Christine Boisson in "Sorceress."

SORCERESS, directed by Suzanne Schiffman; screenplay (French with English subtitles) by Pamela Berger and Miss Schiffman from a story by Miss Berger; cinematographer, Patrick Blossier; edited by Martine Barraque; music by Michel Portal; produced by Miss Berger, Annie Leibovici and George Reinhart. At 68th Street Playhouse, Third Avenue at 68th Street. Running time: 97 minutes. This film has no rating.

Etienne de Bourbon .... Tcheky Karyo
Elda .... Christine Boisson
The Curé .... Jean Carmet
Simeon .... Raoul Billerey
Cécile .... Catherine Frot
The Count .... Féodor Atkine
Agnès .... Maria de Medeiros
The Curé's Housekeeper .... Gilette Barbier
Madeleine .... Nicole Félix
Christophe .... Jean Daste
Martin .... Mathieu Schiffman
Young Etienne .... Michel Karyo
Village Woman .... Joelle Bernier

By WALTER GOODMAN

Like Bertrand Tavernier's recent "Béatrice," Suzanne Schiffman's "Sorceress" is set in France in the Middle Ages, but its spirit is in the Enlightenment. It is a parable about the clash between a dedicated healer and a dedicated pursuer of heretics, over whether God prefers to tend man's body or scourge his soul. The characters assume allegorical roles, and the resolution is meant to edify. The somewhat obvious yet intriguing movie, Miss Schiffman's debut as a director, opens today at the 68th Street Playhouse.

Into an isolated town, photographed with rough beauty by Patrick Blossier, strides Etienne de Bourbon, a well-born monk (Tcheky Karyo): "My task is to persuade the guilty to repent — or else be burned." It does not take him long to discover Elda, the "forest woman" (Christine Boisson), who wanders the glades collecting herbs for the treatment of everything from malarial fever to difficult childbirths to warts. "Her practices sound irregular," Etienne observes most ominously. He is outraged to learn that Elda leads the peasants in rites at a "sacred grove" in which the

intercession of "St. Guinefort," a legendary dog, is sought to save their babies.

This illiterate woman represents the spirit of scientific inquiry and Christian love. Etienne represents clerical obscurantism, "fierce, unblinking and blind," as the local priest (Jean Carmet) describes him. The priest stands for a Christianity with compassion for human weakness and ignorance, which Etienne only comes to appreciate the hard way.

•

The performances are better than the lines. Mr. Karyo's Etienne shows himself to be much more than a stock inquisitor, as his fanaticism is quelled by the evidence of Elda's honesty and knowledge and his growing sympathy for the townspeople's troubles. Miss Boisson manages to make Elda appealingly independent despite the burden of being right all the time. The script is not subtle. When the well-educated Etienne says, "I can learn nothing here," Elda replies, "I learn something here every day."

Miss Schiffman, who worked with François Truffaut for many years, keeps matters under control, even through a resolution that turns on a handy revelation and a quick psycho-spiritual fix. At its best, the rather programmatic screenplay, written by Miss Schiffman and Pamela Berger and based on a medieval manuscript, offers sharp comments on relations among church, aristocracy and peasantry. The good-hearted priest, dependent on the largesse of the local lord and unable to prevent the exploitation of the people, tolerates their resort to a pagan Christianity to relieve their misery. Mothers, babies and nourishing breasts are much in evidence as Miss Schiffman and Miss Berger pay 20th-century tribute to the women of the time, memorialized here as victims of sexual indignities and heroines of comfort and survival.

1988 Ap 1, C23:1

FILM VIEW/Janet Maslin

Wimps Sweeten The Screen

PRESIDENTIAL POLITICS ISN'T THE ONLY realm in which the wimp factor plays a role. It's also a consideration in film, for works like "The Milagro Beanfield War," in which a group of nice New Mexico townsfolk band together to outsmart a crass developer; "A New Life," the Alan Alda divorce comedy that pretends to have a cutting edge but is, in fact, colored by boundless optimism; "Dominick and Eugene," about a handsome young doctor making huge sacrifices to take care of his mentally deficient twin, and "Stand and Deliver," about a dedicated teacher who cares more about his students' math test scores than anything else in the world.

The wimp ethic — a celebration of the very sappiest good deeds and good intentions — is so unmistakable that it can be detected in the audience as well as on the screen. At the Beekman, where "The Milagro Beanfield

War" is playing, the daytime crowd has been polite, earnest looking and quite elderly; there were two major snoring incidents at last Friday's midafternoon show. And it was clear that the film's wimpier aspects were what this audience liked best. They enjoyed each new do-gooder character, delighted in the David and Goliath plot, admired the blue skies and postcard-perfect scenery. They laughed a lot at the abundant wimp humor.

Is this beginning to sound like an argument for bringing back Rambo (who *will* be returning soon, but that's another story)? It's not — it's worse. It's an acknowledgment that wimpiness, however contemptible, can also be secretly enjoyed, no matter how furtive one must be in finding excuses to do so. When the film maker does his best to avoid being maudlin, why not appreciate a story of brotherly love? Why not admire the math teacher's tireless dedication? Why resist the obvious charms of Robert Redford's colorful small-town fable? For that matter, why even resist the fullest flowering of wimp-mindedness, represented by Mr. Alda?

Each of these films faces its greatest challenge in attracting an audience in the first place — what teen-ager is going to tell his friends he was off watching "The Milagro Beanfield War" when he could have been seeing Rob Lowe? But the wimp trend grows ever harder to resist, and it surely has the numbers. Viewers looking for raunchy, uninhibited entertainment really have their work cut out for them and may be relegated to things like "Police Academy 5."

Even such pioneers of daring, off-color entertainment as Richard Pryor and John Waters have gone squeaky-clean with "Moving" and "Hairspray," respectively. And if those aren't wimpy enough, there are also such bighearted, soft-headed hits as "Moonstruck" and "Three Men and a Baby" to consider. Robin Williams talks a blue streak but behaves with conspicuous decency in "Good Morning, Vietnam," and then there's "Broadcast News," the hit sex comedy in which none of the three principals goes to bed with another.. The small boy's view of the world is currently popular, in films from "Hope and Glory" to "Vice Versa," and "Biloxi Blues" brings back Eugene Jerome, Neil Simon's quintessentially wimpy alter ego. Can there be any question that, right now, the wimp wields influence?

This isn't necessarily such bad news. Some of the films that most fully embody wimp attitudes are unabashed, retrograde fun. Mr. Redford's direction of "The Milagro Beanfield War" is as skillful as his work on "Ordinary People," albeit in a very different setting. And he also gives this film a gently comic tone that works unexpectedly well. The cast is good and the story a thoroughly satisfying morality play, but the wimp touches are there for anyone to see. Despite the title, hardly anyone gets hurt; even a beloved pet pig that is injured in the fracas turns out to be fine.

Melanie Griffith, as the tarty female companion of the wicked developer, is actually his wife, though any non-wimp film would make her his mistress. Sonia Braga, the Brazilian sex kitten, plays a small-town political firebrand and keeps her clothes on. The film's nice-guy tone is so prevalent that when a bulldozer goes off a cliff, one can't help thinking that it must have been a very old bulldozer, otherwise Mr. Redford wouldn't have condoned such wanton destruction. But however easy these things are to make fun of, they're also, secretly, rather nice.

So is "Dominick and Eugene," in spite of a premise sure to give hives to any wimp-hating viewer. Eugene (Ray Liotta) has dedicated his life to taking care of his good-hearted, simple-minded twin brother, Nicky (Tom Hulce), and the film explores both the love and the frustration that have bound them together. Both the actors are especially good, and they play their roles forthrightly, without any tendency to tearjerk. Nothing gets in the way of the story's emotional impact except for the subject itself, which is bound to keep some viewers out of the theater.

Alan Alda has come to represent the pure embodiment of cloying, life-affirming hokum, and yet Mr. Alda's "New Life" also has its secret charms. Yes, this story of divorce and romantic recovery is as old as the hoariest sitcom; yes, Mr. Alda's sensibility is unfailingly middle-aged. But this story, however predictable, does have its kernel of reality, and Mr. Alda has his dependable sense of humor. Even if "A New Life" doesn't raise more than mild chuckles, and even if half the moviegoing public wouldn't be caught dead watching such a thing, audiences may surreptitiously enjoy it. But they may want to visit the theater incognito, since wimp-watching is best done in secrecy. □

1988 Ap 3, II:26:5

Bonbons
Vanessa Redgrave and Tyler Butterworth star in "Consuming Passions," Giles Foster's black comedy about ineptitude in a British chocolate factory.

Secret Ingredient Is Awkward

CONSUMING PASSIONS, directed by Giles Foster; screenplay by Paul D. Zimmerman and Andrew Davies, based on a play by Michael Palin and Terry Jones; director of photography, Roger Pratt; edited by John Grover; production designer, Peter Lamont; produced by William Cartlidge; released by the Samuel Goldwyn Company and Euston Films. At the Paris, 4 West 58th Street. Running time: 100 minutes. This film is rated R.

Mrs. Garza	Vanessa Redgrave
Farris	Jonathan Pryce
Ian Littleton	Tyler Butterworth
Graham Chumly	Freddie Jones
Felicity	Sammi Davis
Ethel	Prunella Scales
Mrs. Gordon	Thora Hird
The Big Man	William Rushton
Dr. Forrester	John Wells
Dr. Rees	Timothy Wert
Mrs. Eggleston	Mary Healey

By VINCENT CANBY

"Mr. Farris," says an apprehensive Felicity Stubbs, who's the entire quality-control department at Chumley's Chocolates (est. 1887), "this new batch of chocolates has no nutritional value whatsoever."

Mr. Farris couldn't be more pleased. As he tells Graham Chumley, the nominal head of Chumley's since it was absorbed by Anglo Foods and Haulage: "We've taken the quality out of the product and put it where it belongs. In the advertising!"

"Consuming Passions," the new English satire opening today at the Paris Theater, takes a very dim view of rampant capitalism as exemplified by corporate takeovers and by the success story of a young, brainless innocent named Ian Littleton (Tyler Butterworth).

In the familiar tradition of many much better comedies, including "Kind Hearts and Coronets" and "I'm Alright, Jack," Ian makes one goof after another to bumble his way to the top. Most importantly, he accidently drops four employees into the giant Chumley's chocolate vat. Chumley's new chocs, called Passionelles, which have heretofore failed every possible taste test, suddenly become the rage of Britain.

●

The question posed by "Consuming Passions": how can a supremely conscienceless company continue to turn out its fortified chocolate treats without drawing unwanted attention to itself? (One answer is "By grinding up the unemployed," which more or less ends the joke.)

The question posed by anyone who sees the film: how could such a promisingly funny idea, and so many talented, intelligent people, have combined to make a film so breathlessly lame?

"Consuming Passions" is based on a play by Michael Palin and Terry Jones, two Monty Python regulars, and was written by Paul D. Zimmerman ("King of Comedy") and Andrew Davies. The director is Giles Foster, whose BBC Television credits include plays by Alan Bennett and the Ben Kingsley-Jenny Agutter "Silas Marner," broadcast here last year.

Heading the cast are Jonathan Pryce ("The Ploughman's Lunch," "Brazil"), who plays the venal Farris as a man with a whiplash-neck tic; Freddie Jones ("And the Ship Sails On") as the helpless Chumley; Sammi Davis as the sweetly stubborn Felicity Stubbs; the incomparable Prunella Scales ("Fawlty Towers," "Mapp and Lucia") as Chumley's secretary, and Vanessa Redgrave as a lusty Maltese-born earth mother, complete with a gold tooth and a tattoo.

The misuse of Miss Redgrave defines just about everything that's wrong with "Consuming Passions." As a woman widowed by an on-the-job accident at Chumley's, Miss Redgrave gives a very broad impersonation of Melina Mercouri overacting her heart out. The accent, the cascade of hair, the lamp-black eye makeup and the somewhat too-grand gestures are viciously funny and, in another movie, might be memorable. Here the impersonation seems to be without point and, to be unkind to Miss Mercouri, out of date.

Miss Scales is mostly a sight gag, dressed in eccentrically mod clothes and always eating a chocolate. Mr. Butterworth's innocent Ian is as colorless to the audience as he is to most of the other people in the movie. Only Mr. Pryce, whose material is somewhat better, gives a consistently comic performance.

"Consuming Passions" means well, but its clever ideas and lines are as random as iron filings waiting for a magnet to give them direction.

1988 Ap 6, C18:3

The Flow Of Blood and Life

FROM THE POLE TO THE EQUATOR, directed by Yervant Gianikian and Angela Ricci Lucchi; music by Keith Ullrich and Charles Anderson; co-produced by the film makers and ZDF-TV (West Germany); distributed by Museum of Modern Art. At Film Forum 1, 57 Watts Street. Running time: 96 minutes. This film has no rating.

By JANET MASLIN

To watch "From the Pole to the Equator" is to feel that one has seen a ghost — many ghosts, human and animal, from places all over the globe.

The spectral quality of this documentary is overwhelming. Two Italian film makers, Yervant Gianikian and Angela Ricci Lucchi, have drawn upon turn-of-the-century film from regions that were then fabulously exotic — the Arctic, India, Africa and less remote but equally striking settings in the Dolomites and the Caucasus — and assembled it at a sleepwalker's pace, with changeable color tints and a humming electronic score. The result offers haunting glimpses of a world in the process of being conquered.

"From the Pole to the Equator," which opens today at the Film Forum 1, draws upon the film archives of Luca Comerio (1874-1940), a pioneer of documentary film making who traveled widely and often recorded the interaction of people and animals; indeed, the abundant animal footage here is the contemporary film makers' most chilling material.

The killing of a polar bear by Arctic explorers is recorded in elaborate detail (the score, by Keith Ullrich and Charles Anderson, makes such events especially chilling). And later on, African tribesmen gather around a felled rhinoceros to remove its horns as a trophy for visiting white hunters. The animal's blood flowing in slow motion is incomparably eerie, as are other scenes in which captured or killed animals are offered up for the camera to examine. Surely Mr. Comerio had his own keen sense of the brutal effects wrought by European visitors in the areas he filmed, and Mr. Gianikian and Miss Ricci Lucchi heighten it even further. Their film ends with a cozy family scene of a well-dressed couple — we know nothing more about them, since there is no narration — playfully letting dogs have their way with a captive rabbit.

•

The archival footage used here also captures the quotidian life of far-flung regions, and "From the Pole to the Equator" gives this a dreamlike quality: uniformed African children being taught to make the sign of the cross, European women peering at a train going by, white-suited Indians walking a broad, shady avenue. The slow, sleepy quality of these images, only a shade more mobile than still photography, freezes them in the viewer's memory. The smallest, most ordinary gestures become indelible, like the sight of one Indian child grooming the hair of another. The first girl stares at the camera with the look of wonder, the self-consciousness and the trace of apprehension that seemed to greet Mr. Comerio in every setting.

Mr. Gianikian and Miss Ricci Lucchi create a subtle and disturbing momentum as they coax their film toward its concluding images of soldiers in combat. Some of these scenes are presented as tinted negatives, so scores of pale pink phantoms clamber over magenta hillsides on their way to destruction. This technique is as effective as it is unusual, and it creates a one-of-a-kind documentary of rare, insinuating power.

1988 Ap 6, C18:3

Breezy and Bloody

BAD DREAMS, directed by Andrew Fleming; screenplay by Mr. Fleming and Steven E. de Souza, based on a story by Mr. Fleming and Michael Dick, Yuri Zeltser and P. J. Pettiette; director of photography, Alexander Gruszynski; film editor, Jeff Freeman; music by Jay Ferguson; production designer,

Ivo Cristante; produced by Gale Anne Hurd; released by 20th Century-Fox Film Corporation. At the Criterion Center, Broadway and 45th Street; the 86th Street East Twin, near Second Avenue; the Waverly Twin, Avenue of the Americas near Third Street; the Olympia, Broadway and 107th Street; the Essex, 375 Grand Street; Movie Center 5, 125th Street, between Powell and Douglass Boulevards; the Coliseum, Broadway and 181st Street. Running time: 100 minutes. This film is rated R.

Cynthia	Jennifer Rubin
Dr. Alex Karmen	Bruce Abbott
Harris	Richard Lynch
Ralph	Dean Cameron
Dr. Berrisford	Harris Yulin
Connie	Susan Barnes
Lana	E. G. Daily
Gilda	Damita Jo Freeman
Ed	Louis Giambalvo
Miriam	Susan Ruttan

By VINCENT CANBY

After lying in a coma for nearly 14 years, Cynthia (Jennifer Rubin) wakes up in a psychiatric hospital looking remarkably healthy and beautiful, as well as far more serene than most of the people around her.

"If you want to feel into the 80's," says an edgy patient in Cynthia's therapy group, "you're at least one condo, two marriages and one yeast infection out of date."

Cynthia's problems appear not to be of the present, but of the past. She's the only survivor of Unity Fields, a commune whose other members died in a group-suicide pact under the direction of Harris (Richard Lynch), the Unity Fields guru. Now the certifiably dead Harris keeps appearing, sometimes as himself, sometimes as a ghastly, charred apparition, to urge Cynthia to join him; she's dawdled long enough.

This is the situation in the aptly titled horror film "Bad Dreams," the first feature to be directed (with a good deal of superficial style) by Andrew Fleming, a graduate of the New York University Film School, and written by him and Steven E. de Souza, also from the film school.

Most first-time novelists regurgitate their own childhoods. First-time feature-film makers, hoping to crash the theatrical movie market, look to other movies. "Bad Dreams," opening today at the Criterion and other theaters, is a breezy, bloody kind of amalgam of "The Breakfast Club" and "Nightmare on Elm Street."

It doesn't make a tremendous amount of sense, plot-wise, and it's instantly forgettable. However, it's amusing for as long as it lasts. Also, for a film of this genre, it has a cast of unusually good actors.

In addition to Miss Rubin and Mr. Lynch, they include Harris Yulin, as the man who runs the psychiatric hospital (where supervision is notably lax and the suicide rate rather high); Bruce Abbott, as the doctor who takes a personal interest in Jennifer, and Dean Cameron, Susan Ruttan and Damita Jo Freeman as some of the patients who make those therapy sessions as lively as the Oprah Winfrey show.

1988 Ap 8, C10:1

EIGHTEEN AGAIN, directed by Paul Flaherty; written by Josh Goldstein and Jonathan Prince; director of photography, Stephen M. Katz; film editor, Danford B. Greene; music by Billy Goldenberg; production designer, Dena Roth; produced by Walter Coblenz; released by New World Pictures. At Embassy 1, Broadway and 46th Street; Guild 50th Street, 33 West 50th Street; Loews New York Twin, Second Avenue and 66th Street. Running time: 99 minutes. This film is rated PG.

Jack Watson	George Burns
David Watson	Charlie Schlatter
Arnold	Tony Roberts
Madelyn	Anita Morris
Betty	Miriam Flynn
Robin	Jennifer Runyon
Charlie	Red Buttons

By JANET MASLIN

It's 10 P.M.: Do you know where your body is? If the latest bright idea to catch fire in Hollywood can be treated seriously, then perhaps your body is off following the dictates of someone else's mind. "Eighteen Again," which opens today at the Guild and other theaters, is the latest copycat variation on this theme, and thus far it's the one with the most problems. (Many thanks to the readers who have identified a popular boy's novel by F. Anstey, circa 1882, as one of the little-mentioned inspirations for this collective brainstorm.)

The trouble with a body-switching plot is that it may mean neither actor is all there. That's what happens in "18 Again," when an 81-year-old grandfather and his college-boy grandson change places.

Future students of this genre will undoubtedly probe both the philosophical issues involved (if a teen-age body with its father's mind allows the father's girlfriend to make a pass at him, has he done anything wrong?) and the methodology. Did the father-son or mother-daughter or owner-dog duo in question switch places because they drank a potion ("Like Father, Like Son")? Did they come into contact with a weird artifact ("Vice Versa")? Or did they simply hold hands, as the characters in this film do, while driving through a plate-glass window? Scholars are sure to compare the screenwriters' various ways of explaining this event, like this film's "I didn't ... I mean, I don't know — the accident! Somehow we got switched!"

•

In any case, the writers (Josh Goldstein and Jonathan Prince) and director (Paul Flaherty) ponderously establish that young David Watson (Charlie Schlatter) now has the mind of his grandfather Jack. But Jack — played by the amazingly spry 92-year-old George Burns, surely the man any audience has come to see — is in a coma. So most of the film follows Mr. Schlatter, a nervous actor who caps each line with an unnecessary, toothy grin, as he affects not-very-Burnslike mannerisms and smokes the older actor's trademark cigars. Mr. Schlatter, incidentally, is better than this in his small role as the hero's brother in "Bright Lights, Big City," where he's playing only one person.

Switched-On

George Burns portrays an 81-year-old who changes places with his teen-age grandson for two weeks in "18 Again!"

Mr. Burns is a welcome presence, and he offers amiable geriatric humor when he appears in person ("Look, I'd go out with women my own age, but there are no women my own age"). But he isn't on screen very much of the time. And his voice-over delivery of Jack-David's inner thoughts doesn't amount to much, either. For the most part, the film concentrates on Mr. Schlatter, and it has so little plot that a track meet and a fraternity party are among the biggest events that occur. References to Harry Truman and the Roaring Twenties are perhaps meant to appeal to an older audience, as is Red Buttons as Jack's friend, but "18 Again" isn't successfully aimed at anyone in particular. Anita Morris, who is excessive and obvious here even by her own standards, displays an extraordinary ability to perform any activity chest-first.

Advice to anyone contemplating body-switch tricks with a relative: treat "18 Again" as a cautionary tale, and stay where you belong.

1988 Ap 8, C12:1

Bewitched, Bothered And Bewildered

THE POINTSMAN, directed and produced by Jos Stelling; screenplay (in Dutch with English subtitles) by George Brugmans, Hans de Wolf and Mr. Stelling; photography by Frans Bromet, Theo van de Sande, Paul van den Bos and Goert Giltaij; edited by Rimko Haanstra; music by Michel Mulders; released by Vestron Pictures. At Lincoln Plaza 1, Broadway at 63d Street. Running time: 95 minutes. This film is rated R.

The Pointsman	Jim van der Woude
The Woman	Stephane Excoffier
The Engineer	John Kraaykamp
The Postman	Josse de Pauw
The Engineer's Assistant	Ton van Dort

A beautiful Frenchwoman in a chic red coat and black veiled hat makes a train trip across a bare, misty landscape. She naps; perhaps she dreams. The train stops, and she alights by mistake, arriving in a barren setting where only one other living being can be found. He is a brutish, almost comically bestial railroad employee who at first frightens her, then repels her, then somehow holds her in his thrall for an entire year.

There is no easy way to ascertain what the Dutch film maker Jos Stelling has in mind with "The Pointsman," and not much reason to try. "The Pointsman," which opens today at the Lincoln Plaza 1, is a mixture of strange, inchoate passions and even stranger Dutch humor, and there is little about it to capture the imagination. The characters and their actions are inscrutable, made even more so by the near-total absence of dialogue. The film's empty, mutable vistas (the exteriors were shot in Scotland) look good but evoke very little.

•

Jim van der Woude conveys the great changes that overtake the railroad employee when a woman whose luggage contains nothing but silky, feather-trimmed lingerie arrives in his bleak little world. Perhaps comically coarse at first (it's hard to tell), he ignores his new companion, concentrating on the rituals of his solitary life. On the night when the woman arrives, he dines by gnawing on a bone in wide-eyed rapture, savoring each bite and prolonging each belch. But the woman's presence eventually has its effect on him; in gradual stages, he smiles companionably, dresses up for an impromptu little party, and develops the sexual interest that seems to be the guiding impulse behind this entire parable.

Trigger-happy and jealous (one of the few other locals is a ludicrously flirty postman, played with some wit by Josse de Pauw), he eventually brings the story to a red-tinged climax involving both blood and many, many jars of preserved gooseberries. Such is the caliber of irony often displayed here.

Stephane Excoffier looks both beautiful and understandably bewildered, and Mr. van der Woude often shows himself capable of more subtlety than his role demands. Whether ingenuously wolfing down a meal or using a shrub for camouflage as he creeps up to spy on his cherished house guest, he has a wholehearted, intensely physical presence in this wearyingly cryptic role. The advertisments for "The Pointsman" that say "A beauty. A beast. And the world of trains" pretty much say it all.

JANET MASLIN

1988 Ap 8, C22:1

Armed and Dangerous

ABOVE THE LAW, directed by Andrew Davis; screenplay by Steven Pressfield and Ronald Shusett and Mr. Davis, story by Mr. Davis and Steven Seagal; director of photography, Robert Steadman; edited by Michael Brown; music by David Frank; production designer, Maher Ahmad; produced by Mr. Seagal and Mr. Davis; released by Warner Brothers. At National Twin, Broadway and 44th Street; Coronet, Third Avenue at 59th Street; Olympia, Broadway and 107th Street; Loews Orpheum, Third Avenue at 86th Street; 23d Street West Triplex, near Eighth Avenue; Movie Center 5, 125th Street between Powell and Douglass Boulevards; Coliseum Twin, Broadway and 181st Street. Running time: 104 minutes. This film is rated R.

Nico Toscani	Steven Seagal
Delores Jackson	Pam Grier
Sara	Sharon Stone
Salvano	Daniel Faraldo
Zagon	Henry Silva
Bartender	Ronnie Barron

Come the end of the year, "Above the Law" may well rank among the top three or four goofiest bad movies of 1988. The film, which opens today at the National and other theaters, is the year's first left-wing right-wing-movie. It's an action melodrama that expresses the sentiments of the lunatic fringe at the political center.

Here's a no-holds-barred exposé of a small group of Central Intelligence Agency crazies who have become unscrupulous drug traffickers to fi-

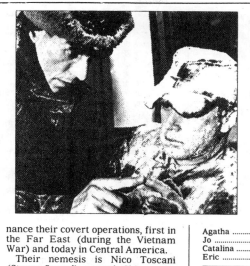

On the Rails
Jim van der Woude, in the title role of "The Pointsman," thaws out a frozen railroader, played by Ton van Dort.

nance their covert operations, first in the Far East (during the Vietnam War) and today in Central America.

Their nemesis is Nico Toscani (Steven Seagal), a tough Chicago detective and a former associate who turned his back on "the company" during the Vietnam War. In "Above the Law," Nico, who's also a Japanese-trained martial-arts expert, attempts to save the life of a United States Senator marked for assassination by the C.I.A. guys. The Senator is about to blow the whistle on the agents' drug dealings.

•

These charges sound familiar, as do references to "White House plumbers," but "Above the Law" is too confused to know how to use its inspirations. "You guys," says Nico to the C.I.A. creeps, "think you're above the law. Well, you're not above *mine*!" Stripped of his authority as a cop, Nico proceeds to lay waste his enemies, and a large part of Chicago, in his defense of the Constitution.

Nico is the sort of guy who might disagree with you, but he'd break your neck and shoot you through the heart to protect your civil rights.

The film was produced in Chicago and is composed of the sort of stuff (car chases, shootouts, kung-fu fights) that can be ordered from any movie-making catalogue. Its politics, however, are its own.

The true auteur of this nonsense appears not to be the director, Andrew Davis, but Mr. Seagal (which, according to the publicity material, is pronounced say-GAHL), who not only stars in the film, but also co-produced it with Mr. Davis, with whom he wrote the story.

Mr. Seagal is tall (6 feet 4 inches) but not terribly charismatic onscreen. Even when he walks, he's a still photograph. He looks like a seasoned (40-ish) runner-up in a contest for a job as an Armani model. In real life, we are told, he is a teacher of martial arts "in classes that stress spiritual values" and has been an "international security agent and bodyguard to several heads of state," whose names aren't mentioned.

VINCENT CANBY

1988 Ap 8, C26:4

A Suspicion Of Heterosexuality

SHE MUST BE SEEING THINGS, directed by Sheila McLaughlin; screenplay by Ms. McLaughlin; director of photography, Mark Daniels; film editor, Ila Von Hasperg; music by John Zorn; produced by Ms. McLaughlin; released by Ms. McLaughlin. At Film Forum 1, 57 Watts Street. Running time: 95 minutes. This film has no rating.

Agatha	Sheila Dabney
Jo	Lois Weaver
Catalina	Kyle Decamp
Eric	John Erdman

By JANET MASLIN

Sexual jealousy is the main force at work in Sheila McLaughlin's "She Must Be Seeing Things," but you'd never know it from the film's amiable, even dispassionate mood. Miss McLaughlin seems more concerned with contemplating this idea than with dramatizing it, and the same can be said for her film's exploration of various sexual stereotypes and its fascination with role-playing. A little more energy would have helped, however. As it is, "She Must Be Seeing Things" is a modest, agreeable and doubtless very personal film that never develops any real urgency.

"She Must Be Seeing Things," which opens today at Film Forum 1, is about the suspicions a lawyer named Agatha (Sheila Dabney) harbors about her more kittenish blond lover, an independent film maker named Jo (Lois Weaver). Agatha worries that Jo may be developing an interest in men, and there is evidence to suggest she is right.

One day when Agatha is straightening up Jo's messy apartment, she finds a diary filled with snapshots of various male friends who, on the evidence of the photographs, have an interest in Jo that is very like her own. So Agatha worries. She imagines things. She dresses in more mannish clothes and considers buying sex aids that will heighten her own masculine appeal. Meanwhile, Agatha gives Jo flimsy feminine lingerie, and Jo also uses clothes as a form of role-playing. None of this is presented with a sufficiently light touch to make it witty or with enough rigor to give it a genuinely interesting subtext.

Miss McLaughlin, whose ambitions often outstrip her technical skills, also gives "She Must Be Seeing Things" a film-within-a-film in which a 17th-century nun rebels against the convent and struggles with her own ideas about sexuality. The attempt to meld this into the story of Jo and Agatha, since Jo is in the process of making this film, is more well intentioned than successful. However, the film's two stars have a relaxed, believable rapport, and Miss Dabney in particular projects the wit and self-awareness of someone in the thrall of sentiments she knows to be wrongheaded, but just can't shake. The film is best when the two actresses simply convey the casual everyday quality of their characters' obviously happy love affair.

1988 Ap 13, C20:4

Rock-and-Roll Beat As East Meets West

Carrie Hamilton in "Tokyo Pop."

TOKYO POP, directed by Fran Rubel Kuzui; screenplay by Ms. Kuzui and Lynn Grossman; director of photography, James Hayman; film editor, Camilla Toniolo; music by Alan Brewer; production designer, Terumi Hosoishi; produced by Jonathan Olsberg and Kaz Kuzui; released by Spectrafilm. At U.A. Eastside, Third Avenue at 55th Street. Running time: 97 minutes. This film is rated R.

Wendy Reed	Carrie Hamilton
Hiro Yamaguchi	Yutaka Tadokoro
Grandfather	Taiji Tonoyoma
Dota	Tetsuro Tanba
Mother	Masumi Harukawa
Mama-san	Toki Shiozawa
Seki	Hiroshi Mikami
Mike	Mike Cerveris
Holly	Gina Belefonte

By WALTER GOODMAN

You don't have to be a fan of rock music to get a kick out of "Tokyo Pop," a wedding of American and Japanese youth cultures as seen through a fun-house mirror.

Carrie Hamilton plays Wendy Reed, a long-legged, not-too-successful vocalist from California who runs around Tokyo in a micro-miniskirt, patterned black stockings, boots, black leather jacket and a close-cropped head of peroxided hair. This not-so-frail Reed hooks up with a band leader (Yutaka Tadokoro, a rock favorite in Japan), who dreams of singing like Frank Sinatra. Ms. Hamilton and Mr. Tadokoro, both making their movie debuts, come through as sappily sweet kids beneath the know-it-all know-nothing rock poses. In the middle of a mutually incomprehensible conversation, Wendy says: "You know somethin'? You're really easy to talk to."

The movie, which opens today at the U.A. Eastside Cinema, was directed by Fran Rubel Kuzui, who also contributed to the rather mushy screenplay. Ms. Kuzui, an American, is married to a Japanese producer (Kaz Kuzui, a co-producer of "Tokyo Pop"), and her savvy about the territory where West meets East to a big beat gives the movie its rhythm and zing.

She brings on a goofy assortment of Tokyo rockers, who know as much English as it takes to shout out the monosyllables behind their music. (Mr. Tadokoro specializes in "Sure!") Wendy finds herself in "love hotels" with names like "C'est la Vie" and "Dream Castle" that feature emperor-sized beds and inspirational pornographic murals; a club where slightly looped middle managers brag about their status ("My company is the largest importer of farm equipment"); a Buddhist temple; an urban fishing pond, and a Dunkin' Donuts joint.

Among the cross-cultural characters who pass through are a kimono-clad elder, who makes his traditional obeisances behind a wall decorated with a blowup of the Beatles and reminisces about the cheering effects of boogie-woogie after World War II; his up-to-date son who runs a store that specializes in genuine plastic food; a club hostess with a grin as wide as the Pacific and a hairdo as high as Mount Fuji; a cigar-sucking, mah-jongg-playing "starmaker," who has evidently borrowed his persona from the moguls and Mafiosi he has seen in Hollywood movies.

The story has to do with whether mere money and acclaim are what the young folks really want and whether they can truly adapt to each other's ways. "Why do you have to be so Japanese?" demands Wendy, who has somehow become the most popular foreign singer in Japan. Will she never amount to more than a blond, round-eyed pop freak? But you don't need twain-meeting messages when Mr. Tadokoro gives out with "I Don' Wanna Letcha Go" or Ms. Hamilton delivers a rock rendition, with an all-Japanese backup, of "Home on the Range."

1988 Ap 15, C4:4

Turf Wars

COLORS, directed by Dennis Hopper; screenplay by Michael Schiffer; based on a story by Mr. Schiffer and Richard Dilello; director of photography, Haskell Wexler; film editor, Robert Estrin; music by Herbie Hancock; production designer, Ron Foreman; produced by Robert Solo; released by Orion Pictures. At Loews Astor Plaza, Broadway and 44th Street; Loews Orpheum, Third Avenue and 86th Street; Loews 84th Street Six, at Broadway; Gramercy, 23d Street and Lexington Avenue; Movie Center 5, 125th Street at Powell and Douglass Boulevards. Running time: 120 minutes. This film is rated R.

Danny McGavin	Sean Penn
Bob Hodges	Robert Duvall
Louisa Gomez	Maria Conchita Alonso
Ron Delaney	Randy Brooks
Larry Sylvester	Grand Bush
Frog	Trinidad Silva
Rocket	Don Cheadle
Bird	Gerardo Mejia
High Top	Glenn Plummer
Melindez	Rudy Ramos
Bailey	Sy Richardson

By JANET MASLIN

The ascension of Dennis Hopper from classic hipster to classic burnout to grand old man of the American cinema is at least as crazy as many of the things Mr. Hopper has done on the screen, but it's real. His new film, "Colors," proves this beyond doubt. "Colors," Mr. Hopper's look at violent Los Angeles street gangs and the police assigned to control them, has a superb eye for the poisonous flowering of gang culture amid ghetto life, and an ear to match; along with brilliant cinematography by Haskell Wexler, it's also got a fierce, rollick-

ing sense of motion. Though its story has the makings of standard stuff, and is sometimes sketchily told, nothing about "Colors" is ordinary.

"Colors," which opens today at Loews Astor Plaza and other theaters, has been accused of glorifying gang warfare, but its sense of frustration is much too powerful to support that claim. Equally strong is its sense of impending doom. The film introduces two L.A.P.D. officers assigned to track the gangs, and then builds its tension around the differences in their tactics and philosophies. The painful, unavoidable implication is that nothing can stop the gang mentality from perpetuating itself.

Bob Hodges (Robert Duvall) is the seasoned veteran who's learned a lot from long experience, while the hot-tempered newcomer Danny McGavin (Sean Penn) has learned nothing and knows it all. The difference between these two men is aptly summarized by a joke that is not repeatable here, but one that works very well in Michael Schiffer's screenplay. Mr. Hopper has assembled a huge cast of actors to play various racially-mixed gang members and street types, and all of them speak in realistic-sounding, tough-guy slang (the form of address "homes," short for "homeboy," is used as often as "man" was used in Mr. Hopper's "Easy Rider," and in much the same way). This adds greatly to its feeling of authenticity, even if the actors speak all at once or make very little sense. That, as the film makes clear, is part of the gang world, too.

What "Colors" does best is to create a sense of place and a climate of fear, to capture the vivid mark that gang life has left upon the downtown Los Angeles landscape. The look of this film, with its hard-edged, brightly sunlit urban settings and its constant threat of unanticipated motion, is genuinely three-dimensional and utterly enveloping. But the film has a narrative vagueness, too. Though it all comes together, most tragically, at the conclusion, "Colors" is less notable for its plot than for its chilling urgency and its sense of pure style.

Mr. Duvall, who gives a terrific performance and provides a solid, reassuring presence, is seen during the early parts of the film teaching his new partner the lay of the land. As the policemen and the camera cruise the streets warily, Hodges demonstrates that he knows better than to leap at every small provocation, and it's a lesson he imparts to everyone around him. "Hey kid, what's your heart beatin' for?" he asks a 14-year-old boy who's caught in a possible drug bust, and he leans down and gently feels the boy's chest as he speaks. McGavin, who favors more direct tactics, doesn't see the point of this at

first, nor does he have Hodges's talent for commanding respect from gang members. But by the end of the film, he's beginning to learn.

"Colors" depicts the continuing warfare between two rival gangs, who snipe at each other with shotguns from moving cars, and whose battle is taking a terrible toll. A mesmerizing early sequence finds members of the two groups in jail, separated by bars and sporting the red or blue rag-tag outfits that establish their identity, while the camera swims back and forth between them and rap music is heard above the general uproar.

•

The violence between these two groups is such a fact of their lives that they even have customs surrounding it, like the wearing of "In Memory of" gang shirts for a member's funeral. Some of these details go by in a blur, since it's not Mr. Hopper's style to emphasize any of the particulars, but they add significantly to the overall mood. Everything from a police crowbar emblazoned "May I Come In?" to a man who wears only underwear and a shower cap and seems desperately in love with a life-sized stuffed bunny contributes to the real and threatening atmosphere.

That none of the actors in "Colors" appear to be acting very strenuously is a great credit to the director, who keeps the film remarkably free of bogus-looking behavior. Mr. Penn keeps his muscle-flexing to a minimum and gives a tightly controlled performance; the rapport between the two principals is well-established. Among the actors playing gang members, who indeed look and sound believably tough, Glenn Plummer stands out as a hapless drug dealer who has the bad luck to antagonize Mr. Penn, and Grand Bush is memorable as a strong, silent king-pin. Trinidad Silva is also good as a kind of elder statesman, who wonders along with the policemen what this new generation is coming to. "Colors" is not without its occasional flashes of wry humor.

Mr. Hopper may be a great director of hip, street-smart male characters, but he's miserable when it comes to women. Maria Conchita Alonso, as a restaurant worker who becomes a girlfriend of McGavin's, conducts herself in admirable spitfire fashion but has a nonsensical role. The gang members' girlfriends are shown to have a much more thankless lot than even verisimilitude would require. And several scenes involve amazingly gratuitous nudity that, despite all the violence and the luridness, sounds this film's only real note of exploitation.

1988 Ap 15, C4:1

On Patrol

Sean Penn portrays a young Los Angeles policeman pitted against youth gangs in "Colors."

APPOINTMENT WITH DEATH, directed by Michael Winner; screenplay by Anthony Shaffer, Peter Buckman and Mr. Winner; director of photography, David Gurfinkel; film editor, Arnold Crust; music by Pino Donaggio; production designer, John Blezard; produced by Mr. Winner; released by Cannon Group. At Ziegfeld, Avenue of the Americas at 54th Street; U.A. Gemini, Second Avenue at 64th Street; Movieland Eighth Street, at University Place. Running time: 102 minutes. This film is rated PG.

Hercule Poirot	Peter Ustinow
Lady Westholme	Lauren Bacall
Nadine Boynton	Carrie Fisher
Colonel Carbury	John Gielgud
Emily Boynton	Piper Laurie
Miss Quinton	Hayley Mills
Dr. Sarah King	Jenny Seagrove
Jefferson Cope	David Soul
Lennox Boynton	Nicholas Guest
Carol Boynton	Valerie Richards

Peter Ustinov as Hercule Poirot in "Appointment With Death."

Michael Winner's "Appointment With Death," adapted from the Agatha Christie novel by Anthony Shaffer, Peter Buckman and the director, is not up to the stylish standard of the earlier all-star, Hercule Poirot mysteries, especially Sidney Lumet's "Murder on the Orient Express." The pleasures of the form are not inexhaustible, and this time the physical production looks sort of cut-rate.

Yet, compared to nearly everything else in this dreary movie season, "Appointment With Death" (which opens today at the Ziegfeld and other theaters) is like a month in the sun with old friends who, though traveling economy class, keep their good humor. They include Peter Ustinov (Poirot), Piper Laurie as a wealthy, hideously tyrannical mother whose children wish her quickly dead, and Lauren Bacall, Carrie Fisher, Hayley Mills, John Gielgud and Jenny Seagrove as some of the people whose lives she would gladly ruin. The time is 1937 and the main setting is Jerusalem, the principal stop on a Mediterranean cruise.

•

The scenery is exotic, the unraveling of the murders most perplexing, and the actors in enthusiastic form. Mr. Ustinov could — and possibly did — phone in his performance, but it barely shows. Miss Fisher somehow manages to suggest a subversive sense of humor even when saying straight lines.

Miss Laurie sets a high comic standard early in the film when told that her newly deceased husband changed his mind and left a second will. "Nonsense!" says the widow in a voice that would shatter crystal. "Elmer changed his mind only under *my* direction." You better believe it.

•

"Appointment With Death," which has been rated PG ("Parental Guidance Suggested"), includes very little that would disturb anybody of any age.   VINCENT CANBY

1988 Ap 15, C4:5

A Story of Friendship

ZELLY AND ME, directed by Tina Rathborne; written by Ms. Rathborne; director of photography, Mikael Salomon; film editor, Cindy Kaplan Rooney; production designer, David Morong; produced by Ms. Rathborne and Elliott Lewitt; released by Columbia Pictures. At 68th Street Playhouse, at Third Avenue. Running time: 87 minutes. This film is rated PG.

Zelly	Isabella Rossellini
Coco	Glynis Johns
Phoebe	Alexandra Johnes
Willie	David Lynch
Earl	Joe Morton

"Zelly and Me" might have worked as an exquisitely written novella, but it deals in feelings not easily ex-

Growing Up
Isabella Rossellini and David Lynch star in "Zelly and Me," about an 11-year-old orphan who is being raised by her possessive grandmother.

pressed in cinematic terms, and definitely not in the clunky, twee terms chosen by Tina Rathborne, the writer and director whose first theatrical feature this is.

The film, opening today at the 68th Street Playhouse, is about pretty little Phoebe (Alexandra Johnes), an orphan being raised by her rich, psychotically possessive grandmother, Coco (Glynis Johns), on a magnificent estate in the Virginia Tidewater. The time is 1958, for no special reason, I suspect, except that it's an attempt to remove a very fragile story from time and today's realities.

Coco alternately indulges Phoebe and humiliates her (by making the child get down on her knees to say she's sorry for non-felony crimes, including rudeness). One of the film's more awkward sequences is an elaborate wedding, staged with Coco's enthusiastic help, in which Phoebe's two favorite dolls, Waddles and Queenie, are joined in matrimony in a simple garden ceremony with the household staff in attendance.

●

Watching helplessly while Coco torments Phoebe is Mademoiselle (Isabella Rossellini), the little girl's French nurse, called Zelly for short. The film means for Zelly to be a force for good in Phoebe's life, but Zelly spends so much time kissing and hugging the child that one starts to wonder. Zelly also doesn't help things by filling Phoebe's imagination with stories of the martyrdom of Joan of Arc. All this is so heavily handled that one spends much of the film keeping an eye out for boxes of matches.

In a subplot of sorts, Zelly develops a relationship with Willie (David Lynch), a soft, shy sort of man who lives on the estate next door.

Whether he intended to be or not, Mr. Lynch, the director of "Elephant Man," "Dune" and "Blue Velvet," is a creepy sort of screen presence. Miss Rossellini and Miss Johnes aren't creepy, but one can never be sure just how nutty they're supposed to be, or on the way to becoming.

The footage is not entirely worthless. "Zelly and Me," which was shot in Virginia, is the next best thing to a Virginia Garden Club tour of two great, 18th-century Tidewater houses, Westover and White Marsh.

●

"Zelly and Me," which has been rated PG ("Parental Guidance Suggested"), includes material that could be emotionally disturbing to young children.

VINCENT CANBY

1988 Ap 15, C4:4

Sexless Romance, Horsy Obsession

RETURN TO SNOWY RIVER, directed by Geoff Burrowes; screenplay by John Dixon and Mr. Burrowes; director of photography, Keith Wagstaff; film editor, Gary Woodyard; music by Bruce Rowland; production designer, Leslie Binns; produced by Mr. Burrowes; released by Buena Vista Pictures. At Embassy 3, Broadway at 47th Street; Sutton, 57th Street at Third Avenue; 86th Street Twin, between Second and Third Avenues; Columbia Cinema, Broadway at 103d Street. Running time: 100 minutes. This film is rated PG.

Jim	Tom Burlinson
Jessica	Sigrid Thornton
Harrison	Brian Dennehy
Alistair Patton	Nicholas Eadie
Seb	Mark Hembrow
Hawker	Bryan Marshall
Patton	Rhys McConnochie
Jake	Peter Cummins
Mrs. Darcy	Cornelia Frances
Jacko	Tony Barry

By CARYN JAMES

There is a perfectly nonthreatening first love in "Return to Snowy River," between a boyish, handsome hero and a tomboyish, beautiful heroine. She has a stern, loving father. A handsome villain wants to marry her. But the strongest characters in this 19th-century Australian adventure are the horses. Wild horses stampede through emerald-green woods and glide in slow motion across a river. There are race horses, tame horses, dead horses, everywhere magnificent horses.

From its sexless romance to its horsy obsession, this sequel to 1983's "Man From Snowy River" might be a pre-adolescent's fantasy projected on the screen, a symptom of that time when riding the range in the Old West seems the height of unattainable glamour — all the more exotic if the ranch is half a continent away. Because it captures that prepubescent moment so precisely, "Return to Snowy River" is a warm, smart, though totally conventional family entertainment, the kind of film children may want to live in for a while and parents can sit through without squirming too much.

The original story ended with Jim Craig, a penniless mountain boy, vowing to return to claim his love, Jessica Harrison, a rich rancher's daughter. In the sequel he rides back to the Harrison ranch, having put together a herd of the best horses in all Australia. There he runs into competition for Jessica's hand in marriage, though not for her true affection. If he were more observant he might have noticed that her bad-tempered father, who was Kirk Douglas in the original, has turned into Brian Dennehy. (He can glower his way through this kind of role automatically.)

●

Each of the principals seems to be chasing most of the others at any given time. Jim chases Jess; Jess runs away; Mr. Harrison chases Jim. And when Jim points a gun at a wild stallion, a horse he set free in the first film, only a 10-year-old can really wonder if he will pull the trigger. But the plot is intentionally genre-bound, so suspense is beside the point.

What matters is that Jim (Tom Burlinson) has piercing blue eyes. Jessica (Sigrid Thornton, Mr. Burlinson's co-star in the first film) wears a vast amount of blue eyeliner — the better for them to stare down the rest of the world. All that blue complements the clear horizons, the panoramic views of mountains and valleys that are perpetually in the background. Those settings are too picturesque to seem real, but just right for a storybook tale.

Geoff Burrowes, who produced "The Man From Snowy River," directs its sequel by going for the obvious — close-ups of galloping hooves, overhead views of stampedes, plenty of orchestral brass announcing the scope and importance of the herds. But luckily, "Return to Snowy River," which opens today at the Sutton and other theaters, doesn't claim to be anything more than a big, old-fashioned melodramatic adventure. With so many nondescript or condescending children's films around, that is quite a lot to accomplish.

And for pure fantasy, it is hard to beat these lines spoken to Jessica by her father: "I was wrong and I was stupid. I'm sorry," words that countless preteens may dream of hearing every day.

●

"Return to Snowy River" is rated PG ("Parental Guidance Suggested"). It contains a bit of blood and violence and the death of a favorite horse.

1988 Ap 15, C8:1

Food for Thought

BRAIN DAMAGE, written and directed by Frank Henenlotter; director of photography, Bruce Torbert; film editors, James Y. Kwei and Mr. Hennenlotter; music by Gus Russo and Clutch Reiser; art director, Ivy Rosovsky; produced by Edgar Ievins; released by Palisades Entertainment. At Cine 1, Broadway and 47th Street; Lyric, 42d Street near Seventh Avenue. Running time: 95 minutes. This film is rated R.

Brian	Rick Herbst
Mike	Gordon Macdonald
Barbara	Jennifer Lowry
Morris	Theo Barnes
Martha	Lucille Saint-Peter

A brainless movie called "Brain Damage" opens today at Cine 1 and the Lyric. It's about an eel-like creature called Elmer that lives on fresh brains, straight from people's heads. Elmer attaches itself to a young fellow and keeps injecting him with a fluid that produces terrific highs and terrible withdrawal symptoms and turns him into a nut case. Written and directed by Frank Henenlotter, this oozer specializes in unspecial effects and unspeakable acting. Strictly for the brain damaged.

WALTER GOODMAN

1988 Ap 15, C16:5

Paris in the 20's

Keith Carradine is a painter in "The Moderns."

THE MODERNS, directed by Alan Rudolph; written by Mr. Rudolph and Jon Bradshaw; director of photography, Toyomichi Kurita; film editors, Debra T. Smith and Scott Brock; music by Mark Isham; production designer, Steven Legler; produced by Shep Gordon; released by Alive Film. At the Plaza, 58th Street at Madison Avenue. Running time: 126 minutes. This film has no rating.

Nick Hart	Keith Carradine
Rachel Stone	Linda Fiorentino
Bertram Stone	John Lone
Oiseau	Wallace Shawn
Libby Valentin	Genevieve Bujold
Nathalie de Ville	Geraldine Chaplin
Hemingway	Kevin J. O'Connor
L'Evidence	Charlelie Couture
Gertrude Stein	Elsa Raven
Alice B. Toklas	Ali Giron

By VINCENT CANBY

Since he made "Welcome to L.A." in 1974, Alan Rudolph has been demonstrating that a modest amount of talent and money, and a lot of nerve, can buy a certain degree of credibility and visual style.

"Remember My Name" and "Choose Me," among the other Rudolph works, are so pretty, so fey, so sincere and sometimes so simpleminded that they disarm criticism by appearing to take themselves far less seriously than audiences do. It's difficult to swat a comedy — even one that's not funny — that announces in every frame, "I'm just a sweet, small, inconsequential, *loving* movie about Life."

There are even some people who would praise him as a film maker of original and possibly profound sensibility.

●

To preserve this illusion, Mr. Rudolph should never have made "The Moderns," a project he nurtured for 12 years and describes, apparently with pride, as "the most rejected screenplay in Hollywood." The new film, used as a key to all that has gone before, unlocks the door to a room with nothing in it.

"The Moderns," opening today at the Plaza, is another Rudolph fable, this time set in Paris in the late 1920's, about artists, writers, art-forgers, collectors and, as set-dressing, characters labeled Ernest Hemingway, Gertrude Stein, Alice B. Toklas and, in what might be called an off-screen cameo, Maurice Ravel.

In the foreground are fictitious characters named Hart (Keith Carradine), a struggling painter who dabbles in unauthorized reproductions; Stone (John Lone), a nouveau riche collector who, we are told, made his vast fortune manufacturing condoms, and Oiseau (Wallace Shawn), a gossip columnist who dreams of flying off to become a columnist in Hollywood, which, in this film's view of the world, is the Paris of the future.

The women in their lives are Rachel (Linda Fiorentino), Stone's beautiful wife, beloved by Hart;

Libby Valentin (Genevieve Bujold), a former nun, now a gallery owner, and Nathalie de Ville (Geraldine Chaplin), a rich, wanton predator who uses men, women and a two-foot-long cigarette holder.

Just what the film is *really* about is anybody's guess. At times it seems to be seriously concerned with the doomed romance of Hart and Rachel Stone, who were lovers in an earlier time and place, including "a cave," not otherwise identified. It's also a lame sendup of "art" — if most people can't tell the difference between the original and a forgery, where does art come in? — set in a Paris that's part legend, part comic book.

The screenplay, written by Mr. Rudolph and Jon Bradshaw (who died before the film was made), is chock-full of self-conscious aphorisms ("It's easier to change your mind than your cafe"), terrible non-mots ("Art is only an infection. Some people get it and some don't"), and embarrassingly foolish jokes at the expense of Hemingway, Stein, Toklas and naïve tourists, none of whom Mr. Rudolph is in any position to make fun of. He has the sensitivity of someone who grew up knowing the market price of "bankable" paintings but nothing of their value.

•

"The Moderns," photographed by Toyomichi Kurita, looks good as long as Mr. Rudolph doesn't fancy it up, which he does constantly. He has a fondness for bleeding from sepia to color and back again for no particular purpose. He also likes tight close-ups, which only call attention to the void within. They ask the audience to find feelings and emotions that no one has bothered to write into the screenplay.

The way Mr. Rudolph uses overlapping dialogue suggests he learned his trade from a rug peddler. When we hear the dialogue of the next scene before the scene we're watching has left the screen, it's the voice of a director desperate to make a sale: "O.K., folks, this one isn't great, but hang on a minute. I have another right here you'll fall in love with!"

The actors are no better than their material, which defines itself. A woman of the world confides, "I detest the verisimilitude of Parisian life," and a distraught lover cries out, "Rachel, you can't walk in and out of people's lives like a stray cat." But then "The Moderns" is a movie that makes an afternoon with Gertrude and Alice more boring than a faculty tea. "Remember, Ernest," says Stein to Hemingway, "the sun also sets." But never soon enough on movies of such muddled aspirations.

1988 Ap 15, C21:1

A Deadly Business

PLAIN CLOTHES, directed by Martha Coolidge; screenplay by A. Scott Frank; director of photography, Daniel Hainey, film editors, Patrick Kennedy and Edward Abroms; music by Scott Wilk; production designer, Michel Levesque; produced by Richard Wechsler and Michael Manheim; released by Paramount Pictures. At neighborhood theaters. Running time: 98 minutes. This film is rated PG.

Nick Dunbar	Arliss Howard
Robin Torrence	Suzy Amis
Chet Butler	George Wendt
Jane Melway	Diane Ladd
Ed Malmburg	Seymour Cassel
Dave Hechtor	Larry Pine
Coach Zeffer	Jackie Gayle
Mr. Wiseman	Abe Vigoda
Mr. Gardner	Robert Stack
Daun-Marie Zeffer	Alexandra Powers

By JANET MASLIN

Unless they're uncommonly good, back-to-high school movies have a way of making audiences count the minutes till graduation, and certainly that's the case with "Plain Clothes." A little more complicated than most, and a little less interesting, "Plain Clothes" tries to combine a police investigation story with the usual classroom and locker-room stuff. Less would not necessarily have been more, but it would have been shorter.

"Plain Clothes" concerns a young-looking detective (Arliss Howard) who transforms himself into an old-looking student to investigate the murder of a teacher and a host of other complications. He does this at a school where everyone is willing to believe he is named Nick Springstein [sic] and distantly related to Bruce. His English teacher (Suzy Amis) seems to like him. So does a pretty blond girl in his class. Otherwise, nothing very notable happens, but among the nonessential sequences is a long one showing the school holding an elaborate springtime carnival and Nick being chosen May King.

•

Martha Coolidge has directed "Plain Clothes" in an adequate but mostly lifeless style, borrowing the Altmanesque device of having a stream of background remarks transmitted over the school's public-address system. Diane Ladd, Abe Vigoda, George Wendt, Seymour Cassel and Robert Stack are among the actors who get lost in the shuffle. "Plain Clothes" opened yesterday at the Cine 1 theater, on Seventh Avenue near 47th Street, which is open around the clock, so audiences can conceivably go see it in the middle of the night. It's impossible to imagine who would do this, or why.

1988 Ap 16, 18:1

Collectors

John Lone and Geraldine Chaplin portray aficionados of art in the Paris of the 1920's in "The Moderns," directed by Alan Rudolph.

Friends and Relations And Relationships

SOMEONE TO LOVE, directed and written by Henry Jaglom; director of photography, Hanania Baer; music by various composers; produced by M. H. Simonsons; an International Rainbow Picture. At Embassy 72d Street, at Broadway. Running time: 110 minutes. This film has no rating.

Danny's Friend	Orson Welles
Danny Sapir	Henry Jaglom
Helen Eugene	Andrea Marcovicci
Mickey Sapir	Michael Emil
Edith Helm	Sally Kellerman
Yelena	Oja Kodar
Blue	Stephen Bishop
Harry	Dave Frishberg

By WALTER GOODMAN

If you haven't been in a roomful of chatter about *relationships* lately and are aching for the experience, "Someone to Love" may be just the cure. Watching this latest effort of Henry Jaglom, who makes movies that feature his friends and relatives, is the next best thing to being trapped in a 1960's encounter session with people you'd just as soon not encounter.

Most of the movie, which opens today at the Embassy, takes place in an old Santa Monica theater where a director named Danny (Mr. Jaglom) is giving a Valentine's Day party for unmarried and divorced acquaintances. Among them are Sally Kellerman, playing an actress without an unmannered bone in her body; Andrea Marcovicci (Mr. Jaglom's close companion) playing Danny's close companion; Michael Emil (Mr. Jaglom's brother) playing Danny's brother, Mickey, and Orson Welles playing himself, in his last movie. The party consists of the guests, mostly show-business folk, being interrogated by Danny on their feelings about love, marriage and loneliness and being instructed to look directly into the camera.

•

Will Ms. Kellerman return to her husband? Will Ms. Marcovicci allow Danny to spend the night? ("I just learned to sleep by myself," she says while fending him off.) Will shy Mickey be able to pick up one of the good-looking women at the party? These matters are handled with an unfocused combination of mild satire and solipsistic sincerity. When Danny says, "I don't want this to be an egocentric experience," you can't be sure whether he is apologizing for his movie or kidding it.

Some of the humor may remind you of Woody Allen. (A man comes on to a woman over a bowl of nuts: "I could show you major major happiness. It goes way beyond this almond.") Or of a Nichols-May routine. (One single woman explains to another how to play one-person Scrabble.) Mr. Jaglom's direction benefits from close acquaintance and wry sympathy with the mating or nonmating games of his Hollywood set. As for the notion of a camera filming the camera that is filming the participants, who occupy the audience's place in the theater, by now it should be established that the feat of making a movie about making a movie is of interest mainly to the movie maker.

Perhaps Mr. Jaglom, who seems to view his works as personal documents, is confessing his own difficulty in dealing with *relationships* off camera. When the cameraman runs out of film at the same time Ms. Marcovicci runs out the door, Danny says and keeps on saying in what may be a reach for poignancy: "What do I do

Modern Life Orson Welles makes his final screen appearance in "Someone to Love," Henry Jaglom's exploration of love, commitment and alienation in the 1980's.

now? What do I do now?" Have an almond.

Mr. Jaglom can be amusing, particularly in his more frenetic moments, and Mr. Emil makes Mickey the one real person at the party. Welles, as ever, is a treat to watch and hear, even when he is reduced to pontificating about the sexual revolution. As for the rest, it's mainly life-style patois from interchangeable characters. A philosophic woman says, "Every freedom is hard to bear." Another says, "I don't feel alone because I feel connected to everybody." Thanks for sharing. Mickey, the only guest who seems to be eating anything, refuses to swallow what he calls "very silly, pretentious, indulgent nonsense." Yes, and saying doesn't make it less so.

1988 Ap 21, C20:4

Melanie Griffith

STORMY MONDAY, directed and written by Mike Figgis; director of photography, Roger Deakins; edited by David Martin; music by Mr. Figgis; production designer, Andrew McAlpine; produced by Nigel Stafford-Clark; released by the Atlantic Entertainment Group. At the Embassy 72d Street, at Broadway; the Gemini Twin, 64th Street and Second Avenue. Running time: 93 minutes. This film is rated R.

Kate	Melanie Griffith
Cosmo	Tommy Lee Jones
Finney	Sting
Brendan	Sean Bean

By JANET MASLIN

Mike Figgis happens to be a fledgling director whose reach is more than matched by his grasp, which is very lucky, since his "Stormy Monday" might have amounted to overreaching had it been handled with anything less than Mr. Figgis's absolute assurance. Here is the kind of neo-film noir plot that could easily seem mannered; here is a fragmented story that could easily add up to less than the sum of its parts. Here is an idiosyncratic setting — the waterfront nightclub district of Newcastle, England — that could easily have grown claustrophobic if it had not been filmed with so much feeling and skill.

But Mr. Figgis, who is a musician as well as a film maker, brings the place, the plot and the film's haunting characters vibrantly to life. What's more, he makes them irresistibly interesting. "Stormy Monday" is a sultry romantic thriller that holds its audience rapt with the promise of imminent danger, and is able to do this in an amazingly natural, unaffected way. Mr. Figgis, who wrote the film's original score, even manages to work some great blues songs into the jazz-tinged soundtrack, and to give the film a soulfulness matching that of the music.

As if this weren't enough, he's also gotten superb performances out of all four of his principals, who are fascinatingly mismatched. Despite this, the chemistry is there, for when Kate (Melanie Griffith) first meets Brendan (Sean Bean), she quite literally bowls him over. Kate, an American, has drifted into Newcastle at the behest of a powerful businessman named Cosmo (Tommy Lee Jones), who likes using her as a sexual lure in his dealings with other men, whereas Brendan has arrived in town with even less sense of purpose than that. Brendan gets a job in a nightclub run by the cool, insouciant Finney (Sting), and with this, the circle becomes complete. Cosmo has plans to pressure Finney to sell his club, and Kate and Brendan are caught between them. The narrative tightens slowly and inexorably, until it all most effectively comes together.

"Stormy Monday," which opens today at the Embassy 72d Street and the Gemini, tells its story very well (Mr. Figgis also wrote the screenplay), but it isn't the plot for which this film will be remembered. It's the haunting, deeply evocative mood that's most impressive, and Mr. Figgis modulates it beautifully. His direction, which is intensely stylish without any effort or strain, has a way of prompting rather than forcing the audience's interest, and a gift for arousing the viewer's curiosity. This isn't a trick that's done with mirrors; it's done through characters who are, for a film of this genre, exceptionally substantial and real.

The stellar Miss Griffith, with her sexy, singular blend of kittenishness and strength, is entirely at home here, making an irrevocably strong impression. So does Sting, whose quietly menacing performance in a character role is perhaps the film's biggest surprise. Mr. Jones makes Cosmo dangerous in a much more direct way, and he turns the ugly-American role that is the screenplay's thinnest into much more than a mere caricature. Mr. Bean is a wonderfully sturdy yet unassuming hero, giving Brendan exactly the right mixture of sweetness and suspicion. In the end, each of these four principals is appreciably changed by the events that unfold here, which makes for a very satisfying story, and for a great deal of eye-opening in a relatively short time.

Also in "Stormy Monday" are the various musicians (including a Cracow Jazz Ensemble, comically out of place during Newcastle's week-long, gimmicky celebration of all things American) and thugs and functionaries who give the film its abundant background texture. That these minor details are as well chosen as the major ones is yet further proof of Mr. Figgis's commanding new talent.

1988 Ap 22, C3:5

The Well-Heeled, Well Done

Lanah Pellay in "Eat the Rich."

EAT THE RICH, directed by Peter Richardson; written by Mr. Richardson and Pete Richens; director of photography, Witold Stok; edited by Chris Ridsdale; art director, Caroline Amies; produced by Tim Van Rellim; released by New Line Cinema. At Cinema 1, Third Avenue at 60th Street. Running time: 92 minutes. This film is rated R.

Commander Fortune	Ronald Allen
Jeremy	Robbie Coltrane
Sandra	Sandra Dorne
Jimmy	Jimmy Fagg
Spider	Lemmy
Alex	Lanah Pellay
Nosher	Nosher Powell
Fiona	Fiona Richmond
Ron	Ron Tarr

WITH: Linda and Paul McCartney and Miranda Richardson

"Excuse me," the elegantly dressed woman says to the waiter at Bastard's, the smart London supper club. "The baby panda, is it fried in honey?"

It isn't long before Bastard's has been taken over by revolutionaries, given a new name as well as a new menu that features the minced remains of earlier patrons. With the help of a staff of rude waiters, the place becomes an instant hit.

How this happens is related with engaging exuberance and a number of funny, low-comedy gags in "Eat the Rich," the new English comedy opening today at Cinema 1. Directed by Peter Richardson and written by him and Pete Richens, the film is apparently a byproduct of a bright new (to me, anyway) London group that calls itself the Comic Strip.

"Eat the Rich" looks and sounds very much like an upscale John Waters satire, reinforced by a strong political bias against Prime Minister Margaret Thatcher's Government and her Tory reign of affluence. Among the film's targets are Labor leaders who sell out, highly placed double agents and a hilariously crude, macho-Cockney Home Secretary (Nosher Powell), who settles a Middle East crisis by knocking two heads together. Later Nosher (which is also his character name) makes a pass at the Queen during a Buckingham Palace banquet.

•

The film's androgynous hero is Alex, played by Lanah Pellay, a transsexual who, though much thinner than Divine (the John Waters superstar who died recently), has Divine's ladylike way of delivering truisms ("Ron, we can't run away, but we can't hide either"). It is Alex who, after being fired from Bastard's, sets out to bring down the Government. "Hi," he says to a stranger, "we're starting a people's uprising. Do you fancy joining us?"

In no time at all a small, eccentric red brigade is formed.

The film's sensibility is very late-60's, and the physical production almost (but not quite) as handsome as something out of Jean-Luc Godard's pre-Maoist period. "Eat the Rich" looks deceptively haphazard, though keeping this sort of comedy on-target takes discipline, a willingness to throw out a lot of material before finding the stuff that works.

In the care of actors performing roles written to their order, most of the material is very easy to take. Most prominent in their support of Miss Pellay and Mr. Powell are Ronald Allen, as an intelligence chief sympathetic to revolution; Jimmy Fagg, as a terrorist with a weakness for ancient jokes, and Sandra Dorne, as Nosher's social-climbing wife, who has a fondness for musclemen and chocolate bonbons.

Among the "names" who make cameo apparances in the film are Paul and Linda McCartney and Miranda Richardson, who's very comic as a nasty civil servant.

VINCENT CANBY

1988 Ap 22, C4:4

Adolescent Angst

PERMANENT RECORD, directed by Marisa Silver; written by Jarre Fees, Alice Liddle and Larry Ketron; director of photography, Frederick Elmes; edited by Robert Brown; music by Joe Strummer; production designer, Michael Levesque; produced by Frank Mancuso Jr.; released by Paramount Pictures. At Embassy 3, Broadway at 47th Street; New York Twin, Second Avenue and 66th Street; 84th Street Six, at Broadway; 34th Street Showplace, between Second and Third Avenues. Running time: 90 minutes. This film is rated PG-13.

David Sinclair	Alan Boyce
Chris Townsend	Keanu Reeves
M. G.	Michelle Meyrink
Lauren	Jennifer Rubin
Kim	Pamela Gidley
Jake	Michael Elgart

Why should popular, talented, good-looking, success-bound David jump into the Pacific Ocean? If the writers of "Permanent Record" know, they are not telling. Anyhow, the event creates great distress among David's high school classmates, especially his best pal and musical collaborator, the sexpot whose favors he has been enjoying, and a shy, serious-minded girl who admires him. All are played by young folks dressed in jeans and acting-school mannerisms.

This assay into adolescent angst, unexcitingly directed by Marisa Silver, is clogged with lines such as: "Was there somethin' I coulda done?" "If only he'd told me." "I shoulda known. I shoulda been aware." "What happens when you die?" "Do you ever wonder?"

It makes you wonder. The implacable earnestness laid on by the script, which it took three people to put together, is not relieved by the nonstop songs, from rock-and-roll to Gilbert and Sullivan. The movie, which opens today at the Embassy 3 and other theaters, ends with everybody being so supportive you want to fall down.

•

"Permanent Record" is rated PG-13 ("Special Parental Guidance Suggested for Those Younger Than 13"), because of its subject matter.

WALTER GOODMAN

1988 Ap 22, C10:1

Into the Unknown In Lederhosen

BAGDAD CAFE, directed by Percy Adlon; screenplay by Percy and Eleonore Adlon and Christopher Doherty; director of photography, Bernd Heinl; edited by Norbert Herzner; music by Bob Telson; art director, Bernt Amadeus Capra; produced by Percy and Eleonore Adlon; released by Island Pictures. At Lincoln Plaza 1, 63d Street and Broadway. Running time: 91 minutes. This film is rated PG.

Jasmin	Marianne Sägebrecht
Brenda	CCH Pounder
Rudi Cox	Jack Palance
Debby	Christine Kaufmann
Phyllis	Monica Calhoun
Sal Jr.	Darron Flagg
Cahuenga	George Aquilar
Sal	G. Smokey Campbell
Muenchstettner	Hans Stadlbauer
Eric	Alan S. Craig

Imagine an enormous kewpie doll wearing a Bavarian business suit and you have some idea what Marianne Sägebrecht looks like in the opening moments of "Bagdad Cafe," a sequence explaining the circumstances by which this anomalous creature finds herself stranded in the American desert. There is an argument with a similarly dressed husband, and then a suitcase thrown out onto the sand. There is oom-pah music on the radio. There is an immense kewpie doll who looks terribly worried, for good reason.

The director, Percy Adlon, shoots this episode as showily as he possibly can. The camera observes it at a succession of odd angles, through color filters that change abruptly, with the dominant tone a yellowish-green reminiscent of badly deteriorating Technicolor stock. It's clear from this opening that Mr. Adlon, who directed the less antic and more piquantly odd "Sugarbaby," is this time willing to do just about anything for effect.

For a while, there appears to be some method to this, as a bizarre assortment of characters convene at the title locale. Both Bavarian visitors find their way to this dusty, dilapidated truck stop (albeit at different times), and they make the acquaintance of the natives, chief among them a furiously angry woman named Brenda (CCH Pounder) who is the proprietor of the place. Brenda has just had a fight with her husband, which gives her some common ground with Jasmin, as Miss Sägebrecht's character turns out to be called. The film watches, patiently and a bit incredulously, as Jasmin and Brenda gradually become friends.

•

"Bagdad Cafe," which opens today at the Lincoln Plaza 1, takes much more delight in the zaniness and variety of its characters than many viewers will. Mr. Adlon, who also is the co-producer and co-writer of the film, finds a tantalizing exoticism in all the wrong places, and seems most captivated by the fact that many of the film's characters are black (and a couple are American Indians, notably a local sheriff with long braids). That Jasmin can let her hair down, figuratively and literally, to become close to an irate black woman and her children is virtually the greatest miracle the film has to offer.

Mr. Adlon jokes briefly about his characters' racial attitudes, as when Jasmin first finds herself stranded among the local folks and imagines herself as a missionary in a stew pot, surrounded by dancing African tribesmen. But his awe at the differences between lederhosen-wearing Bavarians and the exaggeratedly crazy Americans in the film seems excessive. The denizens of the Bagdad Cafe include a retired Hollywood set painter who grins mysteriously at all times (played by Jack Palance, who looks remarkably fit), a tattoo artist, a backpacker who spends his time playing with a boomerang, and Brenda's various children, among them a daughter with an incongruous Valley Girl accent. The film doesn't do much more with these curiosities than marvel at them as it throws them together.

"Bagdad Cafe" is too slow-paced to work as a comedy, and its screenplay manages simultaneously to be both shapeless and pat (Jasmin likes to clean, and Brenda doesn't; Brenda has too many children, and Jasmin has none). It would be lost without Miss Sägebrecht, who luckily happens to be an actress of great if indescribable appeal. In "Sugarbaby," as a large, lonely woman who takes a handsome young man as the object of her overpowering affections, Miss Sägebrecht managed to be both emotionally immediate and cryptic, and she has a similar effect here. Though her Jasmin remains largely inscrutable, the character's lonely, affectionate nature and her capacity for magic come through.

"Bagdad Cafe" won the Berlin Film Critics' Ernst Lubitsch Award as best comedy of 1987, which may say more about the Berlin film critics than it does about the film.

◆

"Bagdad Cafe" is rated PG ("Parental Guidance Suggested"). It contains brief nudity.

JANET MASLIN

1988 Ap 22, C19:1

WHITE MISCHIEF, directed by Michael Radford; screenplay by Mr. Radford and Jonathan Gems; from the novel "White Mischief" by James Fox; director of photography, Roger Deakins; edited by Tom Priestley; music by George Fenton; produced by Simon Perry; production designer, Roger Hall; released by Columbia Pictures At Carnegie Hall Cinema, Seventh Avenue and 57th Street; Running time: 100 minutes. This film is rated R.

Alice	Sarah Miles
Broughton	Joss Ackland
Colville	John Hurt
Diana	Greta Scacchi
Erroll	Charles Dance
Nina	Geraldine Chaplin
Morris	Ray McAnally
Lizzie	Murray Head
Soames	Trevor Howard

By VINCENT CANBY

It's not easy being decadent, though intelligence isn't required. One must have a certain amount of time and money (or credit), an all-consuming self-interest and, whenever possible, an exotic setting in which to misbehave. Good looks, preferably beauty, also help, as well as the constitution of a goat.

This is pretty much the sum and substance of "White Mischief," Mi-

chael Radford's entertaining, sometimes perilously giddy screen variation on James Fox's 1982 investigative book. Like the book, some of whose facts it reshapes for its own purposes, the film is a recollection of a notorious murder case and the lives of a small, privileged group of upper-class colonials in Kenya in 1940 and 1941.

The basic facts are these: Early on the morning of Jan. 24, 1941, Josslyn Hay, 39 years old, the 22d Earl of Erroll and premier peer of Scotland, was found shot to death in his car a couple of miles down the road from the estate of Sir John Henry (Jock) Delves Broughton, 57, whose wife, Diana, 27, was planning to leave him to elope with the Earl.

Broughton was charged with the murder and stood trial. In Kenya at that time, virtually every other husband, and a couple of women, had compelling motives for dispatching the prowling peer, who is remembered as being as devastatingly attractive to men as he was to women, all of them married.

"White Mischief," which opens today at the Carnegie Hall Cinema, is like a classy, breathless backdate of "Life Styles of the Rich and Famous." The movie clearly disapproves of the sorts of things it reports. It's perfectly aware that, back home, a war was going on while these negligent aristocrats were safe in Kenya, swapping wives, drinking away their days and nights, shooting up and gunning down various endangered species, including one another. However, the movie doesn't allow a social conscience to spoil the voyeuristic fun.

"White Mischief," adapted for the screen by Mr. Radford and Jonathan Gems, never gets bogged down in analysis or even outrage. It deals in the looks of things and in behavior, exemplified in the seductive performance of Greta Scacchi as the chilly, ambitious Diana Broughton. Miss Scacchi ("Heat and Dust," "Good Morning Babylon") is a great beauty anyway, but with the ultra-blond hair she has here, and with her bright, hard, 1940's makeup, she defines both the character and the sort of film this is: brittle and often just a little too much.

Though Mr. Radford leaves no doubt about who he thinks killed the Earl of Erroll (the book never really commits itself), the film sticks close to the known facts of the odd marriage of Diana and Broughton (Joss Ackland), who make a prenuptial pact in which each promises not to hinder the other if he, or she, falls in love with someone else.

Within a few of weeks of their marriage and arrival in Kenya, where the financially pressed Broughton plans to farm, Diana has met and fallen in love with the charming Erroll (Charles Dance), who has no money but an impressive pedigree. Diana expects Broughton to honor their agreement and, for a while, it seems that he will. The night before Erroll's murder, Broughton toasts his wife and her lover at a jolly Champagne dinner at their Nairobi club.

"White [...] pts
to turn t[...] and
Erroll ir[...] -of-
the-cent[...] in-
terested[...] an-
ners of e[...] ety
known (s[...] ney
lived) as[...]

Social Set Greta Scacchi stars in Michael Radford's "White Mischief," based on an actual case of infidelity and murder in the British colony in Kenya during World War II.

Among their nearest and dearest friends: a morphine-addicted American heiress (Sarah Miles), who loves Erroll and animals (she appears at a polo match with a python draped around her shoulders); a forlorn wife (Geraldine Chaplin), also one of Erroll's former mistresses, who turns to her African help for companionship; Broughton's best friend (Trevor Howard, in his last screen role), who invites guests to spend the night and then spies on them after they've retired, and a wealthy, taciturn landowner (John Hurt) who, as they used to say, "has gone native."

As movie orgies go, the ones in "White Mischief" look comically underpopulated. In one short scene, we watch Diana, Erroll, Broughton and the rest of their set kicking up at a party where both sexes are wearing drag. Everyone appears exhausted. These things are probably intentional, but the movie's voice is so understated that it seems to have no voice at all. Instead, it often speaks through shock effects that are more absurd than satiric, including Miss Miles's overheated leave-taking of her former lover's body at the morgue.

Miss Scacchi, the film's true star, receives excellent support from Mr. Dance and Mr. Ackland, and from the other members of the large, somewhat underemployed cast.

1988 Ap 22, C20:1

A Small Boy's Story

THE STEAMROLLER AND THE VIOLIN, directed by Andrei Tarkovsky; written (in Russian with English subtitles) by Mr. Tarkovsky and Andrei Mikhailkov Konchalovsky; director of photography, Vadim Yusov; edited by L. Butuzova. At Film Forum 2, 57 Watts Street. Running time: 50 minutes. This film has no rating.

WITH: Igor Fomchenko, V. Zamansk, Nina Arkhangelskaya, Marina Adzhubei.

By WALTER GOODMAN

"The Steamroller and the Violin," which opens the Andrei Tarkovsky retrospective at Film Forum 2 today,

is in a much lighter mood than the works for which the Soviet director is celebrated. Mr. Tarkovsky, who died in 1986, was known for powerful, sometimes violent images and big, sometimes mystical symbols. This very early work, made in 1960 during his final year at the Moscow Film Institute and not shown in New York until now, is a small story told through the eyes of a small boy.

The focus is on a few hours that Sasha, a 7-year-old violin student, spends in the company of a steamroller driver named Sergei. Sasha, though spunky, is a privileged child who is picked on by the rougher kids in his apartment house. Sergei, who comes to his defense and lets him operate the steamroller, seems a sort of hero, a stand-in perhaps for the father who never appears. To Sergei, we sense, the boy represents a future that is beyond a mere worker.

•

It is a busy day for Sasha; besides driving the steamroller, he has a silent but meaningful encounter with a pretty girl in braids and a pink dress to whom he gives an apple. The influence on the young Tarkovsky of the classic short "The Red Balloon" is strong. Vadim Yusov's lyrical photography catches reflections from mirrors, windows, puddles. The world is broken up into mosaics. The rain comes down like a symphony; a wrecking ball does a ballet for Sasha and a building crumbles gracefully. "What am I to do with you, daydreamer?" asks his sternly affectionate music teacher. As plump, freckled Sasha plays his violin, light plays all about him. The world seems fresh and immensely inviting. This sweet work almost makes one regret that Mr. Tarkovsky left his playfulness behind as he plunged into weightier, sometimes murkier matters.

On the first Film Forum bill, along with "The Steamroller and the Violin," is "Nostalghia," made in 1983. Coming up: "Ivan's Childhood," which first brought Mr. Tarkovsky international attention, and "The Mirror" (1974); his last movie, "The Sacrifice," shown in this country a few weeks before his death, and, the final pairing, "Stalker" (1979) and the acclaimed 1965 "Andrei Rublev."

1988 Ap 22, C20:5

Performance Rebels

MONDO NEW YORK, directed by Harvey Keith; written by Mr. Keith and David Silver; director of photography, Leonard Wong; film editor, Richard Friedman; music by Johnny Pacheco and Luis Perico Ortiz; production designer, Jacquiline Jacobsen; produced by Stuart S. Shapiro; presented by International Harmony. At Quad Cinema, 13th Street west of Fifth Avenue. Running time: 82 minutes. This film has no rating.

WITH: Joey Arias, Rick Aviles, Charlie Barnett, Joe Coleman, Emilio Cubiero, Karen Finley, Phoebe Legere, Lydia Lunch, Ann Magnuson, Frank Moore, John Sex, Shannah Laumeister, Dean Johnson and the Weenies, and the Bodacious Ta-Ta's

By WALTER GOODMAN

Looking for a sampling of entertainments that are not listed in your run-of-the-mill going-out guide? It is available in "Mondo New York," which reaches into the East Village underground to dig up "performance artists" who present their bodies to be painted and enclosed in Saran Wrap, bite off the heads of mice, switch genders and rely on obscenities when they require a punchline. In its hunt for the outrageous, the movie also takes us to a cockfight, a purportedly authentic Haitian voodoo ceremony (this time a chicken gets its head bitten off), a simulated sadomasochistic party where the whips are waved to a Yiddish ballad and a dull affair that is supposed to be "a Chinese slave auction." It's 2 A.M. Is this where our children are?

The title is borrowed from "Mondo Cane," the 1963 Italian movie about bizarre behavior around the globe. This noisy 35-millimeter travelogue, directed by Harvey Keith, opens today at the Quad Cinema.

•

Leading the audience from loft to disco, along nighttime streets on which you would not want your sister to tarry, is a shapely, silent blonde (Shannah Laumeister). She seems to enjoy the more wholesome acts best but does not register a lot of emotion. A couple of the entertainers declare themselves against yuppie greed: "I tell you, Mr. Entrepreneur, that you're the reason that David's Cookies is a symbol of our culture." Karen Finley accompanies this rant by breaking raw eggs and smearing the results over her body. Joe Coleman, the mouse-head biter, sets a match to himself and explodes, but not permanently. Ann Magnuson, got up like a Dutch milkmaid, beats something that resembles a dead horse. If there is a theme here, it is camp rebellion.

Other stars of the show, household names in their own households, include Lydia Lunch, Phoebe Legere, Joey Arias and John Sex. Noises are provided by such groups as the Bodacious Ta-Ta's and Dean Johnson and the Weenies. The main laughs come from a couple of stand-up comics, Rick Aviles and Charlie Barnett, whose specialty is knocking every racial, religious and ethnic group in town. They do their stuff in Washington Square Park, which in this company makes them mainstream.

1988 Ap 22, C23:1

Manhunt

CASUAL SEX?, directed by Genevieve Robert; screenplay by Wendy Goldman and Judy Toll; based on the play "Casual Sex" by Ms. Goldman and Ms. Toll; director of photography, Rolf Kestermann; edited by Sheldon Kahn and Donn Cambern; music by Van Dyke Parks; production designer, Randy Ser; produced by Ilona Herzberg and Mr. Kahn; released by Universal Pictures. At Movieland, Broadway at 47th Street; Sutton, 57th Street and Third Avenue; Metro Twin, 99th Street and Broadway; 23d Street West Triplex, at Eighth Avenue. Running Time: 90 minutes. This film is rated R.

Stacy	Lea Thompson
Melissa	Victoria Jackson
Nick	Stephen Shellen
Jamie	Jerry Levine
Bianca	Sandra Bernhard
Vinny	Andrew Dice Clay
Ilene	Mary Gross
Megan	Valeri Breiman

The difference between something as up-to-the-minute as "Casual Sex?" and something as hopelessly retrograde as "Where the Boys Are" can be measured in language — clinical language, the kind the Thin Man would never have used to describe foreplay even if he'd had an inclination to describe it at all. So much for the way ideas of sophistication change from generation to generation. Take away the ostentatious candor, though, and "Casual Sex?" is "Where the Boys Are" all over again, with a plot about giddy young women at a sunny vacation spot, hunting. Their quarry is, for films of this kind, the eternal one: cute guys.

"Casual Sex?" started out on the stage, where it featured Wendy Goldman and Judy Toll (who have adapted their own material for the screen). The director, Genevieve Robert, has retained the stagey affectation of having the film's two principal characters talk to the camera from time to time, saying things like "Right now, we're both scared of being single and having sex." Aside from these confessional flourishes and the very infrequent bright remark ("It was the early 80's, and sex was still a good way to meet new people"), the film is as ordinary as it can be.

Visiting a California spa, the pert, determined Stacy (Lea Thompson, who's just right for this role) and her more glumly realistic roommate Melissa (Victoria Jackson, who has a dizzy charm and talks like a budding Selma Diamond) take up the chase. They set up headquarters in a hotel room outfitted with a gift basket of condoms, in one of the film's most conspicuous contemporary gestures.

•

But "Casual Sex?" proves not to be about promiscuity at all (the question mark is, of course, a dead giveaway, and it's mostly the use of words like "orgasm" that have earned the film its R rating). It's only about finding Mr. Right. Stacy wows everyone, Melissa strikes out, and eventually they both find happiness. Stacy is finally seen, years later, happily committed to someone with whom the film has never even shown her going to bed. Among the men in the cast, Andrew Dice Clay manages to be funny in what is definitely a Mr. Wrong role.

Opening today at the Sutton and other theaters, "Casual Sex?" is the kind of film in which Stacy can capture the attention of a handsome would-be songwriter at the spa, and the other guests can stand around oohing and aahing while he sings a love song in her honor. When it comes to fun-in-the-sun movie romances, some things never change.

JANET MASLIN

1988 Ap 22, C24:1

Jamaican Pantheon

COOL RUNNINGS: THE REGGAE MOVIE, directed, written, edited and produced by Robert Mugge; director of photography, Lawrence McConkey; music by various composers; presented by Sunsplash Filmworks Limited. At Cinema village, 22 East 12th Street. Running time: 105 minutes. This film has no rating.

Featuring: Third World, Rita Marley, Ziggy Marley, Gil Scott-Heron, Gregory Isaacs, Sugar Minott, Mutabaruka, Judy Mowatt, Alton Ellis, the Skatalites and others

By JON PARELES

The definitive reggae performance movie hasn't been made yet. "Cool Runnings: The Reggae Movie," filmed in Jamaica at the 1983 Reggae Sunsplash Festival, is an honorable attempt; the film maker, Robert Mugge, has also made documentaries about such worthy musicians as Al Green, Sonny Rollins and Rubén Blades. But "Cool Runnings," limited by middling performances and some poor technical choices, is for committed fans only.

The annual Sunsplash Festival assembles the reggae pantheon, but since the death of Bob Marley in 1981, reggae hasn't had a charismatic international symbol who can bring together its political and pop ambitions. One of the film's best performances, in fact, comes not from a reggae group but from Gil Scott-Heron, a New York-based singer who melds his hard-hitting funk song "The Bottle" with a danceable Puerto Rican guaganco.

There are other good, if not incendiary, segments of the film, which opens today at Cinema Village. Mutabaruka, a "dub poet" who performs with a band, delivers his angry, politicized lyrics bare-chested, with a long white chain between his wrists. Judy Mowatt sings a blithe, lilting song that insists, "Slave queen, remove the shackles from your mind." Gregory Isaacs, a sex symbol in Jamaica, teases the crowd with his "Night Nurse"; Sugar Minott sings a jazzy, free-form song that mixes political messages and come-ons. Bob Marley's wife, Rita Marley, and their son, Ziggy, who was then 14 years old, each make an appearance.

Unfortunately, Mr. Mugge didn't have a camera placed in the audience facing the stage, so the performers are shot from the sides, the back and below — not from the angle they were facing. Between songs are plugs for the festival and an embarrassing poem about reggae written, but not read, by Mr. Mugge.

1988 Ap 22, C36:5

A TIME OF DESTINY, directed by Gregory Nava; written by Mr. Nava and Anna Thomas; director of photography, James Glennon; film editor, Betsy Blankett; music by Ennio Morricone; production designed by Henry Bumstead; produced by Miss Thomas; released by Columbia Pictures. At the Gotham Cinema, Third Avenue at 58th Street; Loews 84th Street Six, at Broadway; the Quad Cinema, 34 West 13th Street. Running time: 115 minutes. Film is rated PG-13.

Martin	William Hurt
Jack	Timothy Hutton
Josie	Melissa Leo
Jorge	Francisco Rabal
Sebastiana	Concha Hidalgo
Margaret	Stockard Channing
Irene	Megan Follows
Ed	Frederick Coffin

"A Time of Destiny," opening today at the Gotham, is something of a first and, perhaps, a last.

It's a Basque-American soap opera set, alternately, in southern California and Italy during the final year of World War II, about Old World concepts of family and honor as challenged by New World manners. It's also about love, guilt, revenge, madness, divided loyalties and timely automobile accidents. The film was directed by Gregory Nava and written by him and Anna Thomas (Mrs. Nava), the team responsible for the earlier, more coherent "El Norte."

In its dizzy melodramatic intensity, "A Time of Destiny" is most reminiscent of the kind of B pictures the Italians used to turn out for domestic consumption in the 1940's and 50's. A friend of mine, a Cuban whose command of English wasn't great, was fascinated by the frequency with which the unhappy heroines of such films entered convents to become "nunks."

There are no nunks in "A Time of Destiny," but it's definitely a nunk movie, steeped in an Old European kind of Roman Catholicism.

William Hurt stars as the black-sheep son of a wealthy, southern California Basque immigrant (Francisco Rabal), who threatens to disown his pretty daughter (Melissa Leo) unless she comes home after eloping with a poor but decent young soldier (Timothy Hutton). For reasons not entirely rational, Mr. Hurt vows revenge on Mr. Hutton and gets himself assigned to Mr. Hutton's infantry platoon in Italy to do the deed.

The movie includes some big, unimpressive battle scenes, a number of orangey sunsets, a lot of comic-strip dialogue ("I'm going to get revenge!" "He's dead — he'll never forgive me now") and one memorable moment in which the silhouette of a gentle, southern California mountain range fades into the silhouette of a man lying on his death bed. The performances are not good.

"A Time of Destiny," which has been rated PG-13 ("Special Parental Guidance Suggested for Those Younger Than 13"), includes vulgar language. VINCENT CANBY

1988 Ap 22, C 29:1

LOVE IS A DOG FROM HELL, directed by Dominique Deruddere; screenplay (Flemish with English subtitles) by Marc Didden and Mr. Deruddere; photography by Willy Stassen; edited by Ludo Troch and Guido Henderickx; music by Raymond Van Het Groenewoud; production design by Hubert Pouille and Eric Van Belleghem; production companies, Multimedia in cooperation with the Ministries for Culture of the Flemish and French Communities; released by Cineplex Odeon. At the Waverly, Avenue of the Americas and Third Street. Running time: 90 minutes. This film has no rating.

Harry Voss	Josse De Pauw
Harry Voss, age 12	Geert Hunaerts
Stan	Michael Pas
Jeff	Gene Bervoets
Bill	Amid Chakir
Princess	Florence Beliard
Mother	Karen Vanparys
Gina	Carmela Locantore
Liza Velani	Anne Van Essche
Marina	Doriane Moretus

"Love Is a Dog From Hell" was shown as part of the recent New Directors/New Films festival. Following are excerpts from Walter Goodman's review, which appeared in The New York Times on March 18. The film opened yesterday at the Waverly, Avenue of the Americas at Third Street.

For a movie that starts with voyeurism, advances to acute acne and concludes with a bout of necrophilia, "Love Is a Dog From Hell" is a remarkably innocent romance.

Dominique Deruddere, a 31-year-old Belgian director, found the idea for his full-length feature in the stories of Charles Bukowski. Mr. Deruddere first did a short movie based on Mr. Bukowski's account of a man making love to a dead woman, then worked his way back to the youth of the necrophiliac, here called Harry Voss. The interpretation of how Harry got that way is a bit pat, but the three matched sections of the final work are filled with such sympathy for his longings that they compel understanding.

We meet Harry in the 1950's, his handsome 12-year-old head bubbling with movie-screen romances, but when it comes to flesh-and-blood women he is defeated first by his shyness, then by his audacity.

We meet him next as he is about to graduate from high school. Still a romantic, he is now afflicted with as rotten a complexion as the movie screen has ever offered. Even the most accommodating coed finds those pustules off-putting. And, finally, it is 1976; Harry, "30 and broke," is something of a bum but no less the romantic — and finally he finds the woman of his dreams, beautiful, available, entirely and forever his. And this one can't say no. It's a comedy of desperation, with overtones of tragedy.

Mr. Deruddere draws fine performances from all parties, especially Geert Hunaerts as Harry the boy, and Josse De Pauw in his older incarnations. The episodes are no more than anecdotes really, but rich in incident, and the writing (by Marc Didden and Mr. Deruddere), photography (by Willy Stassen) and direction fill them with conviction.

As for that final scene, it is not at all macabre, as Harry proves himself the lover he has always been deep down.

1988 Ap 23, 14:5

THE BLUE IGUANA written and directed by John Lafia; director of photography, Rodolfo Sanchez; edited by Scott Chestnut; music by Ethan James; production designer Cynthia Sowder; produced by Steven Golin and Sigurjon Sighvatsson; released by the Paramount Pictures Corporation. At Cine Twin, Seventh Avenue between 47th and 48th Streets; Cinema 2, Third Avenue at 60th Street, and 23d Street West Triplex. Running time: 90 minutes. This film is rated R.

Vince Holloway .... Dylan McDermott
Cora ....Jessica Harper
Reno ....James
Dakota .... Pamela Gidley
Yano .... Yano Anaya
Floyd ....Flea
Zoe the Bartender .... Michele Seipp
Detective Vera Quinn .... Tovah Feldshuh
Detective Carl Strick .... Dean Stockwell

By VINCENT CANBY

"The Blue Iguana," which opened yesterday at the Cinema 2 and other theaters, belongs to that genre of first feature most favored by film-school graduates. It's inspired not by life but by other movies. Whatever passion it possesses is the film maker's desire to make movies — *any* movies — before he has much of anything in mind to make movies about.

The writer and director of "The Blue Iguana" is John Lafia, who attended the film school at the University of California at Los Angeles. Mr. Lafia clearly knows good technical people and attractive performers. He also has a pleasantly oddball sensibility, which, in this case, is expressed in a comedy that looks like a talented film student's sendup of his homework.

"The Blue Iguana" was shot entirely in Mexico and is technically polished, even when the dialogue sounds as if it had been post-synchronized. Mr. Lafia and his associates seem to know how to stretch a peso, but the screenplay is what W. C. Fields used to call a moulage, "The Blue Iguana" is a mixture that embraces elements from private-eye movies, Sergio Leone westerns and caper comedies.

Its hero is Vince Holloway (Dylan McDermott), a contemporary bounty hunter or, as he calls it, "a recovery specialist" who deals in people and property. Vince talks terse, like Sam Spade and Philip Marlowe, and is supposed to be as tough as Clint Eastwood. He is sent to a small Mexican town to recover $20 million deposited in the town's principal industry, a bank that launders money for the mob and other antisocial types.

Among the people who cross his path are the beautiful queen of a nightclub (Pamela Gidley), who sings Marlene Dietrich's "Laziest Girl in Town" to a modern beat (and who manages to look like both Lauren Bacall and Cybill Shepherd); the beautiful owner of the bank (Jessica Harper), who loves money for itself; the town's cold-blooded Mr. Big (James Russo); an Elisha Cook-type of hood played by Flea (who actually does look like Elisha Cook), and a pint-size sidekick (Yano Anaya). Tovah Feldshuh and Dean Stockwell appear, briefly, as the pair of bizarre American detectives who dispatch Vince on his mission.

Every now and then there's a genuinely funny line ("I used to have so many friends I didn't have to see anyone twice"), but "The Blue Iguana" will be of most interest to film students who think they know as much about movies as Mr. Lafia.

1988 Ap 23, 18:2

THE UNHOLY directed by Camilo Vila; written by Philip Yordan and Fernando Fonseca; director of photography, Henry Vargas; edited by Mike Melnick; music by Roger Bellon; production designer, Mr. Fonseca; produced by Mathew Hayden; released by Vestron Pictures. At the National Twin, Broadway and 44th Street. Running time: 100 minutes. This film is rated R.

Lieutenant Stern .... Ned Beatty
Father Michael .... Ben Cross
Archbishop Mosely .... Hal Holbrook
Father Silva .... Trevor Howard
Luke ....William Russ
Millie ....Jill Carroll

By WALTER GOODMAN

So what in the name of heaven are Trevor Howard, Hal Holbrook, Ben Cross and Ned Beatty doing in "The Unholy," which was spirited into the Warner and other theaters yesterday? Well, it's like this. Mr. Cross is a young priest who does not know that he enjoys anti-Satanic powers, which ought to come in handy considering that the last two priests in his New Orleans church had their throats torn out by a mysterious force. Mr. Howard is a blind old priest, "a great scholar of demonology," who discovers that Mr. Cross is the Chosen One, destined to do battle with the Unholy One. Mr. Holbrook is an archbishop and Mr. Beatty is a cop.

The object of Mr. Cross's spiritual attentions is an unstable young woman named Millie, a waitress in a nightclub that seems to feature a ritual murder at every show. Although the screenplay by Philip Yordan and Fernando Fonseca makes nothing clear, it is possible that the Unholy One is seeking to get Millie's virginity along with her soul; she prefers to give at least one of them to Mr. Cross.

Camilo Vila's direction is on the labored side — ponderous movement accompanied by dirgelike music. The photography is as murky as the story, filling the screen with shadows that are periodically blasted by an unilluminating light. There's enough dry ice and tomato sauce laid on to supply a fast-food joint for a couple of years. The theaters may have to be exorcised, or at least aired out.

It will not give too much away, perhaps, to report that Satan, who sometimes takes the form of a nude redhead, really looks like a lizard. Mr. Cross finds himself crucified and tormented by the devil and lesser demons. He inquires, amid explosions and flames and windstorms and crashing glass, "Dear God, what is this You will have me do?" Mr. Howard, Mr. Beatty and Mr. Holbrook might have asked the same question.

"The Unholy" was Mr. Howard's last movie. If there is justice in heaven, he has gained admission despite it.

1988 Ap 23, 18:4

FILM VIEW/Janet Maslin

'Candidate' Runs Again And Wins

JOHN FRANKENHEIMER'S "MANCHURIAN CANdidate" is arguably the most chilling piece of cold war paranoia ever committed to film, yet by now it has developed a kind of innocence. There was so much that we had the good luck not to know in 1962, when the film was made; so much that, unluckily, we know now. A lone assassin, perhaps under the influence of a foreign government, can indeed shoot an American political leader. For that matter, so can a deranged housewife or a disgruntled movie fan. And the power of mind-control techniques, such an exotic part of this story, has been demonstrated by religious cults from Rajneeshpuram, Ore., to Jonestown.

Like much futuristic science fiction, Richard Condon's 1959 novel anticipated events that seemed eerie and prescient at the time and have now been surpassed by realities even stranger. However, this is not to suggest that the story has become dated. Mr. Frankenheimer's film, in re-release all year and now, at long last, in New York, retains its suspense, spookiness and ability to scare. And for every scene grown quaint, there are a dozen timelier than ever.

Though "The Manchurian Candidate" went, in the words of its writer and producer, George Axelrod, "from failure to classic without passing through success" and has long been out of circulation, it's about to make its mark all over again. And there are things about it to be seen in a new light. The story, for those fortunate enough to encounter it as a new experience, concerns a Korean war veteran, Raymond Shaw (Laurence Harvey), who comes home to a hero's welcome, and who has left a strikingly similar impression on each and every member of his wartime unit. Raymond Shaw, they say when asked, "is the bravest, kindest, warmest, most wonderful man I've ever known."

Not quite. Raymond Shaw is also the star of a collective nightmare these veterans share, and it takes the enterprising Ben Marco (Frank Sinatra), an Army buddy of Raymond's, to begin fitting the pieces together. As a stunning early sequence demonstrates, the entire group has been drugged, brainwashed and put in the service of a group of Russian and Chinese masterminds who plan to exploit their captives' helplessness. Raymond has been programmed to kill, and the others have been programmed to let him.

One thing not as apparent in 1962 as now is the singular wit of Richard Condon, whose later books "Winter Kills" and "Prizzi's Honor" became films more overtly funny than this one. However, the humorous side of Mr. Condon's conception is there in Mr. Axelrod's screenplay, which takes its best inspirations directly from the novel. It was Mr. Condon who imagined that a newspaper editor whom Raymond was sent to assassinate might be wearing his late wife's marabou-trimmed bed jacket at 4 in the morning; it was he who had the story's Joseph McCarthy-like Senator, Raymond's stepfather (James Gregory) and the willing pawn of his madly Machiavellian mother (Angela Lansbury), so inept as to have trouble remembering the exact number of Communists he had supposedly located inside the Defense Department. Mr. Condon imagined that a brainwashed man whose trigger mechanism was accidentally activated might overhear a suggestion to go jump in the lake — and take it at face value.

The film's most unusual sequence is its brainwashing footage, and it was Mr. Condon's notion that each American prisoner of war might be "under the impression that he had been forced to wait in a small hotel in New Jersey where space restrictions made it necessary for him to watch and listen to a meeting of the ladies' garden club." So Mr. Frankenheimer's brilliantly unsettling sequence shows the prisoners listening patiently to a talk about hydrangeas, sometimes delivered by a sweet-faced old lady in a straw hat and sometimes by a burly brainwashing expert named Yen Lo. This episode, in which Raymond's talents as a lethal weapon are demonstrated for a crowd of onlookers, becomes the group nightmare of which each of the veterans dreams some modified version. When a black soldier dreams it, the garden club ladies are all black.

Among the things that "The Manchurian Candidate" now seems most aptly to anticipate is the ability of television to distort images; one especially shrewd scene shows Raymond's stepfather delivering a rabble-rousing tirade while a television monitor in front of him presents his image at a noticeably different angle. Another is the enduring, dangerous power of reckless patriotism, demonstrated by Miss Lansbury's most fiery speeches and by the omnipresence of flags, eagles and likenesses of Abraham Lincoln. Miss Lansbury's unforgettable performance is terrifying on the political level, the Freudian level and quite a few levels in between.

Anomalous casting did a lot to make "The Manchurian Candidate" unique. Mr. Condon imagined a more communicative Raymond Shaw than the icy Laurence Harvey (and a more American one), but the actor's utter remoteness makes the character that much more unnerving. Frank Sinatra wasn't exactly right for the passionately intellectual Marco, either, but his performance worked very well. And the occasional inappropriate touches do as much to make

"The Manchurian Candidate" a classic as the clever ones. Where else will Mr. Sinatra ever be heard talking about "the novels of Joyce Cary" and "the ethnic choices of Arabs" to demonstrate his catholicity of interests? Where else will he ever be seen posing beside a copy of "Ulysses?" ☐

1988 Ap 24, II:23:5

A HUNGRY FEELING: THE LIFE AND DEATH OF BRENDAN BEHAN directed and produced by Allan Miller; photography by Don Lenzer; edited by Tom Haneke; narrated and songs sung by Liam Clancy; distributed by Frist Run Features. At Film Forum 1, 57 Watts Street. Running time: 85 minutes. This film has no rating.

By WALTER GOODMAN

Brendan Behan's life can be divided into three parts: his youthful years in an English jail for his activities in behalf of the Irish Republican Army; his writing, drawn largely from his experiences as a prisoner, and his prodigious boozing, which resulted in his death in 1963 at the age of 41. "A Hungry Feeling," Allan Miller's affecting documentary, which opens at Film Forum 1 today, tells his story through the people who knew him best — wife, brothers, I.R.A. comrades and fellow drinkers in the Dublin pubs, where he seemed most at home. We learn from his mother that it was his grandmother who gave him his first sip of stout.

Their recollections, interrupted now and then for an old I.R.A. battle song, are accompanied by dramatized excerpts from the three works that brought Behan international fame in the 1950's — the autobiographical "Borstal Boy," "The Quare Fellow" and "The Hostage" — and by newsreel clips of the writer holding forth (usually while holding a glass) and being carted off to jail after barroom rows. A brother recalls, "He got a great kick out of putting policemen's heads through Trinity College fence."

'Brendan was a theater himself," says Joan Littlewood, who first produced his plays, and indeed, he comes through as something of a stage Irishman who talked, sang and drank more than the men twice his size with whom he was wont to get into fights. Yet the glimpses of his writing, full of humor, humanity and rich prose, remind us of how big a talent lay behind the blather and the binges.

In all his works, Behan's heart and his pen went out equally to captors and captives, whom he saw as joined by common human sympathies. His success seems to have had a more destructive effect than jail. As though mocking his own celebrity, he appeared on television interviews both in Britain and the United States in a state of near stupefaction, flustering such veteran interviewers as Malcolm Muggeridge and Edward R. Murrow.

"A Hungry Feeling" is an affectionate look that does not gloss over its subject's weaknesses. One of Behan's old pals pictures him as a shy man who needed people but could not approach them without alcohol. As though warning against such pat interpretations, however, the Borstal boy himself tells a prison official, "I haven't any inhibitions, and my complexes are all in order." His long-suffering wife, Beatrice, sums up his final years: "Between his drinking and his talking, there was little left for anything else." That, this illuminating work confirms, was his tragedy and our loss.

1988 Ap 28, C20:3

CRITTERS 2: THE MAIN COURSE, directed by Mick Garris; written by D. T. Twohy and Mick Garris; director of photography, Russel Carpenter; edited by Charles Bornstein; music by Nicholas Pike; production designer, Philip Dean Foreman; produced by Barry Opper; released by New Line Cinema. At the Loews Orpheum Twin, Third Avenue at 86th Street, and other theaters. Running time 86 minutes. This film is rated PG-13.

Brad Brown	Scott Grimes
Megan Morgan	Liane Curtis
Charlie McFadden	Don Opper
Harv	Barry Corbin
Wesly	Tom Hodges
Mr. Morgan	Sam Anderson

By CARYN JAMES

Grovers Bend, like a twisted version of Grover's Corners in "Our Town," is a cozy, stage-set sort of place once visited by krites — criminal porcupines from outer space who tried to eat up the whole Brown family in "Critters." Two years later, "Critters 2: The Main Course" answers a question viewers may at last be ready to handle. Where do critters come from? It seems they are hatched from large green eggs that look like rotting avocados. And now it's Easter in Grovers Bend, where the simple townfolk paint the eggs in fancy colors and hide them for the kiddies on the church lawn.

Before the Easter service ends, the critters have hatched and they come out hungry. Anyone who believes those ugly eggs were imported European art objects probably deserves to be eaten by porcupines from another planet, but this sequel is so uninventive only the nasty people get eaten. The rest join in with the alien bounty hunters who have returned to finish off the krites, and with the heroic teen-ager, Brad Brown (Scott Grimes), who is back in Grovers Bend to visit his grandmother. (The rest of his family survived, but had the good sense to leave town and stay away from this movie.)

Is Brad's return connected to the new critter attack, the way Tippi Hedren seemed connected to Hitchcock's "Birds"? Not really. "Critters 2" piles up every stock movie idea you can remember about small-town heroism, macho sheriffs and alien invaders. But whenever it shows a glimmer of wit about those clichés, it leaps back to its safe, dull, derivative style. This film has all the wit of a townwide food fight, as the bounty hunters blast the critters out of a salad bar, lettuce and ketchup flying everywhere.

With their blood-red eyes and rows of pointy teeth, the critters look ugly enough, but they are as mechanical and cheaply made as "Critters 2," which opens today at Loews Orpheum and other theaters.

•

"Critters 2: The Main Course" is rated PG-13 ("Special Parental Guidance Suggested for Those Younger Than 13"). There is nudity and some repulsive, bloody deaths by critter attack.

1988 Ap 29, C6:6

Making Peace With a Memory

Barnard Hughes in "Da."

DA, directed by Matt Clark; screenplay by Hugh Leonard, from the play and novel "Home Before Night" by Mr. Leonard; director of photography, Alar Kivilo; edited by Nancy Nuttall Beyda; music by Elmer Bernstein; production designer, Frank Conway; produced by Julie Corman; released by Filmdallas Pictures. At the Paris, 4 West 58th Street. Running time: 102 minutes. This film is rated PG.

Da	Barnard Hughes
Charlie	Martin Sheen
Drumm	William Hickey
Young Charlie	Karl Hayden
Mother	Doreen Hepburn
Boy Charlie	Hugh O'Conor
Polly	Ingrid Craigie
Mrs. Prynne	Joan O'Hara
Young Oliver	Peter Hanly

By VINCENT CANBY

Ten years after Broadway gave Barnard Hughes a Tony Award for his rich, funny, affecting performance in Hugh Leonard's Irish comedy, "Da," movie audiences finally have the chance to see that performance in the screen adaptation opening today at the Paris theater.

"Da," once a tightly constructed, one-set memory play, has been "opened up" for the screen in fairly heavy-handed, unimaginative ways, but the life in the Hughes characterization remains undiminished by time or change of medium.

Da (Mr. Hughes) has always been a bit maddening to Charlie (Martin Sheen), his adoptive son, but he's even more impossible when Charlie, now a successful playwright, returns to the small Irish village of Dalkey to attend Da's funeral and close up the house. Da is dead but he won't lie down or shut up.

As Charlie goes about his supposedly somber tasks, tossing out mementos, letters, keys, souvenirs and all of the other debris that accumulate in a lifetime, Da keeps interrupting, not as a ghost but as a garrulous living presence. He butts into Charlie's mind with unasked-for advice and truisms, with offers of nice cups of tea and with biased recollections of events that are still painful to the middle-aged Charlie.

•

When Da isn't rewriting history to his own advantage, he may settle back in his easy chair and offer the kind of platitudes that earlier helped to drive Charlie from Ireland. "If the old heart hadn't given out on me the evening before last," Da observes with his usual cheery sagacity, "I'd still be alive today."

On the Broadway stage, "Da" was a sweet, fragile play given backbone by Mr. Hughes's performance and by the unrelieved intensity imposed on the events by the single, all-purpose playing area. Though "Da" moved around various settings in Dalkey, it was mainly tied to the small, claustrophobic house where Charlie grew up. In the confined physical space of the stage, the garrulous Da could drive anyone slightly mad.

The opened-up film gives geographic scope to the tale while it weakens the tension between father and son. It also reveals certain discrepencies between the characters as written and as played. As written, Charlie has always been mortified by Da's docile acceptance of his role in life as a faithful forelock-tugging gardener to "quality" (Protestant) folk.

Says Charlie, "If you ran into me Da with a motor car, he'd thank you for the lift." Charlie grows up angry and impatient, though the Da the audience sees is never a coward. He's terrifically good company and even iconoclastic as when, during the war, he loudly praises Adolf Hitler at the expense of Winston Churchill, much to the embarrassment of both Charlie and his mum.

•

In the film, Charlie's humiliations seem extremely small when compared to the love, companionship and good humor Da gave him over the years. Thus there's never really much at stake. At the beginning, especially, the movie lacks the bitterness that gives poignant perspective to a son's memories of his father.

As it goes along, however, the movie picks up momentum until, near the end, "Da" finally locates its emotional center, a love-hate relationship that is suddenly as moving as it's supposed to be. It's no accident, I suspect, that the movie is best when it moves the least, when the playing area is confined to the house where Charlie was raised.

Mr. Leonard, who adapted his play for the screen, and Matt Clark, the film's director, haven't been able to resist "improving" the play — somewhere near the middle of the film there's a terrible sequence involving a boy, his dog and a storm-tossed sea — but they haven't ruined it either. Most importantly, they have Mr. Hughes at the top of his form, being boastful, wheedling, majestic (when he has absolutely no right to be), senile and, without warning, self-aware (though not for long).

It's in the nature of the screenplay that none of the other characters come anywhere near Da, though the cast is a good one. Mr. Sheen is given some funny one-liners, but the role is essentially passive, as are those of Karl Hayden (Young Charlie) and Doreen Hepburn as Charlie's mother. William Hickey is excellent as young Charlie's fussy employer. "Da," however, is a one-man show.

•

"Da," which has been rated PG ("Parental Guidance Suggested"), includes some vulgar language.

1988 Ap 29, C10:1

Heaven Can Wait

WINGS OF DESIRE, directed by Wim Wenders; screenplay by Mr. Wenders and Peter Handke; director of photography, Henri Alekan; edited by Peter Przygodda; music by Jurgen Knieper; production designer, Heidi Ludi; produced by Mr. Wenders and Anatole Dauman; released by Orion Classics. At Cinema Studio 1, Broadway at 66th Street. Running time: 130 minutes. This film is rated PG-13.

Damiel	Bruno Ganz
Marion	Solveig Dommartin
Cassiel	Otto Sander
Homer	Curt Bois
Peter Falk	Peter Falk

By JANET MASLIN

Men have envisioned angels in many forms, but who besides Wim Wenders has seen them as sad, sympathetic, long-haired men in overcoats, gliding through a beautiful black-and-white Berlin on the lookout for human suffering? Like so many existential Clark Kents, the angels of "Wings of Desire" are mild-mannered, all-seeing individuals poised to assist those in need.

Some earthly beings can sense their presence, the children most keenly, but none really see or hear them as they perform their duties. A potential suicide with an angel draped compassionately against his shoulder may very well suppose he is alone. If the angels appear downcast, this partly results from a certain ineffectualness that is built into the job, since they cannot change fate but can only witness what it does to individual lives. It is this helplessness, as well as a longing for corporeal sensation, that ultimately gives an angel named Damiel (Bruno Ganz) the celestial equivalent of seven-year itch.

"Wings of Desire," which opens today at the Cinema Studio 1, has a loveliness of conception that, for a time, keeps it as feathery as an angel's wing. The early parts of the film trace the ordinary details of Damiel's working day, and the responsibilities he shares with a sort of teammate named Cassiel (Otto Sander). These angels may ride the subway, and listen in on each commuter's thought process, or they may find themselves in traffic, listening to a woman talk to the dog in her car. They may comfort a pregnant woman on her way to the hospital, or cradle the head of a wounded man.

They may also visit the library, which serves as a sort of headquarters, for the sheer pleasure of tuning in the cacophony of ideas to be found there. The most alluring thing about "Wings of Desire" is its vision of these angels as silent partners in almost all forms of human experience, be they physical or cerebral, violent or serene. In outlining the range of these angels' participatory role in the human sphere, Mr. Wenders presents the Berlin they inhabit as a stark, forbidding urban setting haunted by its own past, and brought warmly to life by the existence of this extra dimension. On those few occasions when Damiel's thoughts nearly turn him human, the black and white cinematography by the venerable Henri Alekan (who has worked with Charlie Chaplin, Abel Gance and Jean Cocteau) bursts into color.

The underlying conception of "Wings of Desire" is enchanting, but Mr. Wenders allows it to become terribly overripe. In a screenplay written by the director with Peter Handke, his earlier collaborator (on "The Goalie's Anxiety at the Penalty Kick"), the angels deliver an incessant flow of voice-over meditations, and so do the film's other characters — even Peter Falk, who plays himself in the uncharacteristically windy process of contemplating his own acting career.

Mr. Falk, supposedly in Berlin to make a World War II film, worries about whether he understands his role deeply enough, makes sketches, and broods in the screenplay's typically overblown fashion. While drawing an extra on the film set, he exclaims, "What a dramatic nostril!" Looking at an actor in costume, he muses, "Yellow star means death. Why did they pick yellow? Sunflowers. Van Gogh killed himself. This drawing stinks ..." Throughout the screenplay, there's a lot more where that came from.

The worst offender is a trapeze artist named Marion (Solveig Dommartin), the woman who at long lasts tempts Damiel to hang up his wings. Though her ultimate effect is to trivialize the film, Marion speaks loftily ("Where did time begin, and where does space begin?") and never seems to stop, except on those occasions when the camera lingers endlessly on her high-wire acrobatics. Marion embodies the sentimental, ponderously playful streak that is relatively recent in Mr. Wenders's films, and that does a lot to diminish the beauty of this one. When the characters quite literally wear wings, and when the director is willing to end a scene with a glimpse of someone juggling, the film's fundamental airiness turns very heavy indeed.

Startlingly original at first, "Wings of Desire" is in the end damagingly overloaded. The excesses of language, the ceaseless camera movement, the unyielding whimsy have the ultimate effect of wearing the audience down. The flashes of real delight that spring out of Mr. Wenders's visionary methods grow fewer and fewer as the film proceeds, and they are long gone by the time it nominally comes to life. Mr. Ganz, who conveys great yearning before reaching his decision "to take the plunge" and a charming eagerness thereafter, is left in a kind of limbo, and the film is, too. This comes as a relief of sorts, but it's also far less effective than must have been intended.

"Wings of Desire" is Mr. Wenders's most ambitious effort yet, and certainly radiates immense promise. But there's a relentlessness to the direction, which won the best-director award at Cannes last year, that keeps it earthbound.

•

"Wings of Desire is rated PG-13 ("Special Parental Guidance Suggested for Those Younger Than 13"). It contains some sexually suggestive material and fleeting nudity.

1988 Ap 29, C15:1

Bruce Willis in "Sunset."

SUNSET, screenplay and direction by Blake Edwards; story by Rod Amateau; director of photography, Anthony B. Richmond; edited by Robert Pergament; music by Henry Mancini; production designer, Rodger Maus; produced by Tony Adams; released by Tri Star Pictures. At the Criterion Center, Broadway and 45th Street, and other theaters. Running time: 105 minutes. This film is rated R.

Tom Mix	Bruce Willis
Wyatt Earp	James Garner
Alfie Alperin	Malcolm McDowell
Cheryl King	Mariel Hemingway
Nancy Shoemaker	Kathleen Quinlan
Victoria Alperin	Jennifer Edwards
Christina Alperin	Patricia Hodge
Captain Blackworth	Richard Bradford
Chief Dibner	M. Emmet Walsh

"Sunset," opening today at the Criterion and other theaters, is a Blake Edwards film that will keep dedicated film scholars busy for the next 50 years.

With all of the lightness of touch that pedants bring to the discussion of comedy, some will attempt to prove that "Sunset" is, indeed, funny, though there's not a single smile in it. Others will seek (and find) all sorts of keys to the true nature of the Edwards oeuvre, including "Darling Lili," his classic "Pink Panther" films, "10," "S.O.B." and "Victor/Victoria."

"Sunset" will leave everyone else close to speechless.

Mr. Edwards has always had a way of mixing flops in among his hits, but, in the past anyway, even his biggest flops ("The Tamarind Seed," "The Wild Rovers," "A Fine Mess") have had some redeeming nuttiness. "Sunset" is such a mess that, when I saw it, I thought the projectionist had misplaced a reel, though he hadn't.

The idea is an alluring one: the place is Hollywood and the time, 1929, just as sound is coming in. Tom Mix, the popular cowboy actor, is persuaded to star in a western, not as himself but as the legendary Wyatt Earp, to which end Earp is hired as a technical consultant. Complicating the making of the movie-within-the-movie is the murder of a prostitute, which involves the sadistic head of the movie company, his fearful wife, his lesbian sister, crooked cops, and the beautiful madam of the brothel.

•

Mr. Edwards's finished film remains little more than a fanciful idea, photographed. It's not quite a murder mystery, not quite a satiric send-up of Old Hollywood, not quite a comedy. It's a plot that unravels on its own, without characters, without *anything,* not even a point of view. It's a zombie.

Since there is no coherence to Mr. Edwards's screenplay, and the direction appears to be nonexistent, the actors cannot be faulted. Chief among these are James Garner (Wyatt Earp), Bruce Willis (Tom Mix), Mariel Hemingway (the madam), Malcolm McDowell (the studio chief), Patricia Hodge (his wife) and Kathleen Quinlan (as Tom Mix's girlfriend). *VINCENT CANBY*

1988 Ap 29, C13:1

A Scrapbook Of Various Lives

POWAQQATSI, directed by Godfrey Reggio; written by Mr. Reggio and Ken Richards; directors of photography, Graham Berry and Leonidas Zourdoumis, edited by Iris Cahn and Alton Walpole; music by Philip Glass; produced by Mel Lawrence, Mr. Reggio and Lawrence Taub; released by Cannon International. At Ziegfeld, 141 West 54th Street. Running time: 97 minutes. This film is rated G.

There are two kinds of dirt to be found in "Powaqqatsi": good dirt and bad. The former is the glistening mud that coats sinewy peasant laborers, outlining the contours of their lean bodies, caking their untroubled faces and their unencumbered feet. The latter is urban grime, part of the blight that afflicts these same simple souls when they fall under modern civilization's long shadow.

Godfrey Reggio, who directed this film, and the earlier head-trip "Koyaanisqatsi," magnifies this distinction until it achieves mountainous proportions, yet still he manages to see it in starkly one-dimensional terms. Though his film contains a wide variety of exotic images, many of them photographed in strikingly unusual ways, its cumulative point is a stunningly self-evident one.

The sensation of watching "Powaqqatsi," which opens today at the Ziegfeld, is that of being at an eternal World's Fair. The film maker's family-of-man approach involves the cross-cutting of parallel scenes from vastly different cultures around the globe, intermingled with the kinds of nature shots that demonstrate the marvelous capabilities of color film. A lot of this footage is impressive, as much for Mr. Reggio's enterprising way of finding unusual faces, places and artifacts as his gift for framing these glimpses in interesting ways. But these virtues have as much to do with coffee-table art as with cinema.

•

"Powaqqatsi" (its title, from two Hopi Indian words, is pronounced pow-ah-COT-see, and means something like "entity that consumes the life forces of other beings in order to further its own life") like "Koyaanisqatsi" (which was translated as "life out of balance"), has a long, ambitious and changeable score by Philip Glass. The music's varying degrees of jubilation and tension become one of Mr. Reggio's principal ways of editorializing; film speed is another, with the primitive imagery of the film's early sections photographed in rapt slow motion, and the later urban scenes sped up to an anxiety-ridden tempo. The slower scenes strive for a particularly hypnotic effect, as they reduce the motion of a hard-working calf muscle to its very components or capture every ripple on a body of water. Moments like this create the feeling that to watch the film in an entirely sober and lucid state of mind is to miss something essential.

What the film does best, especially in its introductory sections, is to convey a sense of the vastness and variety of the planet. The fact that the settings are not identified only serves to heighten their mystery. Capturing beautiful, remote sites in countries including Peru, Brazil, Kenya, Egypt and Nepal, Mr. Reggio splices together an extraordinary scrapbook, a resonant array of unspoiled scenery and uncomplicated lives.

Later on, in places like Hong Kong, he films the misery of urban existence, but even this is made strangely pretty. An unimaginably vast high-rise complex, for instance, may signify the most dehumanizing aspects of city dwelling, but it is photographed in an aerial shot that emphasizes its imposing symmetry.

"Powaqqatsi," which is the second part of a planned trilogy, reaffirms Mr. Reggio's diligence and sincerity, though it does not signficantly advance his achievement. Each of these films is sure to live forever in the minds of spelling-bee organizers everywhere. *JANET MASLIN*

1988 Ap 29, C20:4

I HATE ACTORS!, directed and screen adaptation (in French with English subtitles) by Gerard Krawczyk; based on the novel by Ben Hecht; director of photography, Michel Cenet; edited by Marie-Josephe Yoyotte; music by Roland Vincent; art director, Jacques Dugied; a co-production of Septembre Productions-Gaumont-Films A2. At 68th Street Playhouse, at Third Avenue. Running time: 91 minutes. This film is rated PG.

Orlando Higgens ....Jean Poiret
Mr. Albert ....Michel Blanc
J. B. Cobb .... Bernard Blier
Laurence Bison .... Michel Galabru
Elvina Bliss .... Pauline Lafont
Lieutenant Egelhofer .... Guy Marchand

The prevailing emotion that "I Hate Actors!" will arouse in most audiences is sympathy, for its cast is in an unenviable spot. Here, spouting the vintage, slangy dialogue of Ben Hecht's 1944 Hollywood novel, are Frenchmen. They try to pronounce names like "Miss Quackenbush." They argue the merits of American participation in the world war. They struggle with Hollywoodese, and lose badly — a line like "Chérie, vous êtes une star" simply lacks the proper snap. And they provide conclusive proof that French is not the preferred language for throwaway wisecracks, and never will be.

"I Hate Actors!" is a thoroughly puzzling first feature by Gerard Krawcyzk, whose presumable fondness for this material is not in any way borne out by his lifeless direction. Shot in black and white, and populated by a wide, vintage assortment of show-biz egomaniacs, the film has the look and feel of a comedy but absolutely no sense of humor.

Mr. Hecht's witticisms and his amusing character names ("Hercule Potnik," "Laurence Bison," "Miss Wondershake") are still here, as is the excessively complicated plot of his murder mystery. But they are presented without enthusiasm. And when Mr. Krawczyk does manage to set up a sequence competently, he has a habit of cutting away before the full effect has time to register. If this suggests that "I Hate Actors!" is fast-paced, it is not.

There is some minor interest in watching what the standard Hollywood elements of this story gain or lose in translation. The tawdry starlet Elvina Bliss (Pauline Lafont) is unusually chic, while the detective, Lieut. Egelhofer, has developed Guy Marchand's Gallic fall-guy manner. The studio head J. B. Cobb (Bernard Blier), who has many of the story's funnier lines, delivers them with authority but with none of the crassness that might be expected. The absence of crassness is the film's second biggest problem, since it indicates such poor feeling for the subject matter.

Chief among the other actors is Jean Poiret, who plays the central character — an agent — with charming but misplaced elegance. One of the film's many wrong numbers is a tacked-on 1981 Washington sequence that works a mention of President Reagan (seen in a television clip, which is dubbed into French) into the story. The film, which opens today at the 68th Street Playhouse, contains one lone joke that works, in which a pigtailed Chinese waiter is shown to have a very odd accent. "I never heard a Chinese speak Yiddish before," someone marvels. "Ssh," says the waiter's boss. "He thinks he's learning English."

●

"I Hate Actors!" is rated PG ("Parental Guidance Suggested"). It contains mild profanity.
JANET MASLIN
1988 Ap 29, C22:1

TWO MOON JUNCTION, directed by Zalman King; screenplay by Mr. King; written by Mr. King and Macgregor Douglas; director of photography, Mark Plummer; edited by

Marc Grossman; music by Jonathan Elias; production designer, Michelle Minch; produced by Donald P. Borchers; released by Lorimar Motion Pictures. At the 23d Street West Triplex, between Eighth and Ninth Avenues; Running time 104 minutes. This film is rated R.

April ....Sherilyn Fenn
Perry ....Richard Tyson
Belle ....Louise Fletcher
Sheriff Earl Hawkins ....Burl Ives
Patti-Jean .... Kristy McNichol
Chad ....Martin Hewitt
Delilah ....Juanita Moore
Senator Delongpre ....Don Galloway

Mrs. Delongpre ....Millie Perkins
Samantha ....Milla

"Two Moon Junction" is a breast-and-buttock show for the soft-porn set. On display at the National and other theaters is April, a Southern princess (Sherilyn Fenn) whose terrific sex urge compels her to take up with Perry, a carny (Richard Tyson). What these repellent people have in common are their great chests and

abundant hair. "You excite me so much I can't help myself," says Perry. "This has never happened to me before," says April.

Zalman King takes credit for writing and directing, and no one is fighting him for it. Louise Fletcher plays April's grandma, and Burl Ives plays a sheriff. Unlike the young folks, both keep pretty well covered up, in hopes probably that they won't be noticed.
WALTER GOODMAN
1988 Ap 30, 17:1

FILM VIEW/Janet Maslin

When the Harvest Is Random

SOME MONTHS AGO I FOUND MYSELF AT THE Quad Cinema for the first show of a film called "John and the Missus," which four other people had also come to see. Under the circumstances, this was astounding. Ads for the film offered little more than its dismal title and a photograph of unidentified workmen (they turned out to be miners) in an unidentified location (it turned out to be Newfoundland). The fine print indicated that the film's writer-director-star was Gordon Pinsent, possibly a household name in his native Canada but an unknown one here.

What's more, there was every sign that the four other patrons were there for recreational rather than professional purposes, since no one else appeared to be taking notes or staring longingly at his or her watch. When the film finally ended, it was all I could do to keep from asking the others why they were there.

The process whereby filmgoers decide what to see becomes more mysterious, intuitive and maddening every day. The must-see film featuring a film maker or actor whose work cannot be missed arrives nowadays only once in a blue moon. Otherwise, there's a large gray area into which most new films fall, a twilight zone in which indifference prevails. The really bad film is currently almost as rare as the really good one, but the so-so ones are everywhere.

How do most of these mediocrities draw a viewer out of the house? Since many of them are headed for the video cassette market almost immediately, the temptation to stay

Really bad films are almost as rare as really good ones, but the mediocre are everywhere.

home and wait must be very strong. By contrast, the urge to race out and see "Bad Dreams" (ad slogan: "It's a scream") or "Bagdad Cafe" (ad art: an assortment of actors sitting on a plate, with the slogan "100 percent of the minimum daily requirement") isn't apt to be overwhelming. And who can believe the claims made for less-than-hot properties like "The Seventh Sign," starring Demi Moore? Of this, an enterprising ad copywriter has declared: "The signs of a hit are everywhere. The momentum is growing. The excitement is building. The word is spreading. Millions of people are going to see the movie that everyone is talking about." "The Seventh Sign" happens to be doing decent business, but have you heard anyone mention it? Neither have I.

At press time, 17 films were scheduled to open this coming week, and there may well be more. They range from Ken Russell's "Salome's Last Dance," from Oscar Wilde's play, to "Dark Habits," from the Spanish film maker Pedro Almodovar ("Law of Desire"), about a nightclub singer hiding out

in a convent full of peculiar nuns, to "Slaughterhouse Rock," a film about Alcatraz-related nightmares that is not being screened for the press ahead of time (never a good sign). So if you choose one to see, will it be the one about the Jewish playwright and the Aryan actress in pre-World War II Austria (" '38: Vienna Before the Fall"), or the one in which Sean Penn is directed by his father ("Judgment in Berlin"), or the one about a latter-day Jack the Ripper ("Jack's Back")? "John and the Missus," which incidentally wasn't bad, would fit very nicely into this kind of so-what selection.

■

When it comes to detergents, at least you get a jingle; with films whose appeal is not immediately apparent, you're on your own. So here are several recommendations, bearing in mind that in times of rampant ordinariness, guts and originality become more precious than ever:

"Colors." A major surprise from Dennis Hopper, whose earlier directorial efforts have shown similar street-smart instincts but nothing like this kind of power. Edgy and exciting from beginning to end, "Colors" has been brilliantly photographed by Haskell Wexler and directed with an unfailing eye and ear for authenticity; in addition, it captures the explosive beauty of the Los Angeles barrio settings in which its story unfolds. The plot isn't always of paramount importance, and Mr. Hopper's direction of women is terrible, but his film's portrait of street gang members and their police adversaries vibrantly conveys the danger, dread and furious energy that shape their lives.

"Stormy Monday." Film noir seems to be the province of British directors these days, and the best of them approach this potentially hackneyed genre with new eyes. This film, like the earlier "Mona Lisa," presents characters living purely for the moment in an atmosphere tinged with menace, and makes them indelibly interesting. "Stormy Monday" is the work of Mike Figgis, a new film maker and former musician with an exceptionally confident, unaffected style. Fine performances are another great asset, from a strangely matched but incendiary cast including Melanie Griffith, Sting, Tommy Lee Jones and the film's attractively ingenuous leading man, Sean Bean.

"Bellman and True." The British also lead when it comes to small, quirky, beautifully acted dramatic films like this one, which traces the unlikely bond that arises between a stepfather and stepson during an elaborate bank robbery. A trim, accomplished film with a taste for the unexpected.

"Beetlejuice." MTV is currently featuring 10-second experimental films, and an entire generation of would-be new directorial talent may be watching. The possible result: more films like this one, in which the crazy effects are entirely, even deliberately unrelated. Still, the director, Tim Burton, has new tricks up his sleeve. And that's worth more than usual at a time when the transient, the interchangeable and the indifferent reign supreme. □

1988 My 1, II:23:1

Antipathy and Lust: Strange Bedfellows

MALA NOCHE, directed, produced and written by Gus Van Sant, based on a story by Walt Curtis; photographed by John Campbell. At Film Forum 1, 57 Watts Street. Running time: 78 minutes. This film has no rating.

Walt .... Tim Streeter
Johnny .... Doug Cooeyate
Pepper .... Ray Monge
Betty .... Nyla McCarthy

By VINCENT CANBY

Other people's obsessions are more often funny than tragic. As Feydeau understood, there's something innately farcical in the sight of an otherwise rational being in the pursuit of a doomed desire. It's a measure of the talent of Gus Van Sant that his "Mala Noche," opening today at Film Forum 1, remains as steadfastly, honestly grim as the Portland, Ore., skid row where most of it takes place.

Shot in atmospherically grainy black-and-white on a mini-budget of $25,000, "Mala Noche" is about Walt, a young man who runs a convenience store for down-and-outers when they can afford a pint of wine, a package of cigarettes or a bar of soap. Though he has a car and a furnished room, Walt doesn't live much above the subsistence level, but to the have-nots, Walt is as much of a capitalist as J. Paul Getty.

Walt's passion — and the unstated reason he hangs around skid row — is good-looking Mexican boys, immigrants who gravitate north to Portland to get as far away as possible from the border they've crossed illegally. Walt's particular passion is Johnny, a dour young Mexican who hates what he calls faggots and queers, though he will sleep with Walt for $25 but not for $15, which is all Walt has at the moment.

As Johnny remains unavailable, Walt becomes more and more fixed on the boy, who is 18 but, Walt notes with satifaction, "looks 16." Walt hands out small loans to Johnny and his two pals. He takes them for joy rides in his car. He accepts their insults and their horsing around, which, at any minute, could turn dangerous.

•

Walt doesn't care. He's prepared to take risks as he waits for Johnny to come around. In the meantime, he satisfies himself with Pepper, one of Johnny's friends who isn't so squeamish.

Walt acknowledges that he is exploiting the boys to a degree, but he tells himself he doesn't want to interfere with their lives or "buy" them, which is exactly what he is doing. When Pepper gets sick, Walt nurses him. Walt justifies himself by suggesting that the boys are, in turn, exploiting him, which the film seems to know to be nonsense.

I stress *seems* because the movie also appears to share Walt's infatuation. Whatever the film or Mr. Van Sant knows to be true, "Mala Noche" is a political parable that wouldn't offend a practicing Marxist.

It's also a very well-made movie, terse and to the point, nicely photographed by John Campbell and written and directed by Mr. Van Sant with sardonic humor. Says Walt after living with Pepper for a while, "They don't have any imagination about sex, but I guess it's not their fault." Doug Cooeyate and Ray Monge are the sex objects. Tim Streeter, who looks a bit like Richard Gere, gives an exceptionally intelligent performance as Walt, a man who is tough as nails up to a point and, beyond that, conniving, self-destructive and forlornly romantic.

1988 My 4, C20:5

The Seven Veils, Starring Lolita

SALOME'S LAST DANCE, direction and screenplay by Ken Russell; translated from the French by Vivian Russell; director of photography, Harvie Harrison; edited by Timothy Gee; art director, Michael Buchanan; produced by Penny Corke; released by Vestron Pictures. At Cinema 2, Third Avenue and 60th Street. Running time: 87 minutes. This film is rated R.

Herodias/Lady Alice	Glenda Jackson
Herod/Alfred Taylor	Stratford Johns
Oscar Wilde	Nickolas Grace
John the Baptist/Bosie	Douglas Hodge
Salome/Rose	Imogen Millais-Scott

By VINCENT CANBY

Like the bee to the buttercup, like the sledgehammer to the nail, Ken Russell was bound to get around to Oscar Wilde, not the Wilde of "The Importance of Being Earnest" or even of "The Picture of Dorian Gray," but the Wilde of the sulphurous, rhapsodic, simile-stuffed "Salome." This is the one-act play Wilde wrote in 1891 in French, the only language he thought pure enough for his vision of the primal encounter between John the Baptist and the unnamed (in the Bible) dancing daughter of Herodias, wife of Herod, King of Judea.

As it turns out, Mr. Russell may be the only man making movies today who could have found cinematic life in the old Wilde chestnut, now best remembered for the scandals surrounding its early productions (and its author), and for having served as the libretto for Richard Strauss's "Salome."

With his gifts for going too far, and with his almost childlike view of decadence (a blue-painted nipple here, a bare buttocks there, sometimes even a quick shot of full-frontal nudity!), Mr. Russell possesses just the right mixture of innocence, passion and theatrical intelligence the job requires. The new film deserves its place among the earlier Russell biographical extravaganzas, including "The Music Lovers" (Tchaikovsky), "The Savage Messiah" (Henri Gaudier-Brzeska) and "Gothic" (Lord Byron, P. B. Shelley).

Though his "Salome's Last Dance" is essentially a perfumed, comic stunt, Mr. Russell forces one to attend to (and to discover the odd glory in) the Wilde language, which, on the printed page, works faster than Valium.

•

The very short film (barely 87 minutes, though it will seem much longer to non-Russell fans) is a lively, typically Russellian treatment of the Wilde text, which, in its entirety, serves as the center of the film. Surrounding it is a fairly lugubrious, fanciful "frame": Wilde (Nickolas Grace) and his lover, Lord Alfred Douglas (Douglas Hodge), known as Bosie, arrive at a male brothel whose corpulent, gossipy proprietor, Alfred Taylor (Stratford Johns), has prepared a surprise for Oscar.

The surprise is a private production of "Salome," whose first public London production (Sarah Bernhardt was to star as Salome) has just been canceled by the Lord Chamberlain on the grounds that stage portrayals of Bibical characters are forbidden. In the performance that follows, Bosie plays John the Baptist, Alfred Taylor is Herod, a certain Lady Alice (Glenda Jackson) is Herodias and the brothel's pale, shy slavey, Rose (Imogen Millais-Scott), is the wanton Salome.

Mr. Russell's casting of Miss Millais-Scott as both Rose and Salome was a risk that pays off brilliantly. The actress, whose first film role this is, is not anybody's idea of the Salome of seven-veils notoriety. She's small, slight and blond, with a heart-shaped face and (here, anyway) a Cockney accent. But even when she seems (intentionally) to be having trouble plowing through lines that threaten to run on to eternity, she creates a vividly funny, quite legitimate Salome.

•

She is part-Lolita, part-Giulietta Masina and part Cecily from "The Importance of Being Earnest." Though Bosie's John the Baptist is not terrific, nor meant to be, there's a kind of teasing, spoiled petulance in her Salome that somehow holds the amateur theatrical together.

Mr. Russell makes sure this isn't easy. One of the actors on the stage suffers from flatulence. The action spills over from the stage into the drawing room where Oscar is lolling on pillows as he fondles a pageboy, covered from head-to-toe in gold body makeup. The female spear-carriers are topless. Even with all of these distractions, it's still possible to comprehend Wilde's play in which vice and virtue become so intertwined as to be indistinguishable.

Not so comprehensible (without program notes) is Mr. Russell's idea that, while watching this play, Oscar begins to see himself as John the Baptist and Bosie as the Salome whose pagan charms are to be his undoing. This may well be true, but the point isn't made on the screen.

Mr. Grace is not a very imposing Oscar Wilde, partly because Mr. Russell, like all scriptwriters writing dialogue for Oscar Wildes on the screen, insists on having the character speak in what sounds like snippets taken from the "Oxford Book of All-Too-Familiar Quotations." It's less a characterization than an impersonation. Miss Jackson's Herodias has a fine, steely elegance. Mr. Johns, as Herod (who is, after all, the central figure of the play), nearly steals the film from Miss Millais-Scott. He is first-rate.

"Salome's Last Dance" opens today at the Cinema 2.

1988 My 6, C8:5

When Paradise Is Passé

THE PROFOUND DESIRE OF THE GODS, a film by Shohei Imamura; screenplay (Japanese with English subtitles) by Mr. Imamura and Keiji Hasebe; cinematography by Masao Tochizawa; music by Toshiro Mayuzumi; produced by Imamura Productions/Nikkatsu Corporation; released by East-West Classics. At Film Forum 2, 57 Watts Street. Running time: 175 minutes. This film has no rating.

Nekichi	Rentaro Mikuni
Kametaro	Choichiro Kawarazaki
The Engineer	Kazuo Kitamura
Toriko	Hideko Okiyama
Uma	Yasuko Matsui
Ryugen	Yoshi Kato

By JANET MASLIN

The robust good looks of Shohei Imamura's 1968 Cinemascope epic "The Profound Desire of the Gods" only heighten the perverse quality of the action, and Mr. Imamura's ribald, casually comic direction has much the same effect. This three-hour film, which will begin the Film Forum 2's Imamura retrospective, makes an ideal introduction to the maverick qualities of this film maker's idiosyncratic style.

At some moments sounding a note of bizarre domestic comedy, and at other times attempting tragedy of mythic proportions, "The Profound Desire of the Gods" is nothing if not far-reaching. It unfolds on the tiny, remote island paradise of Kuragejima, in the Ryukyu Islands, and it concerns the Futori family, who are widely regarded as beasts by their neighbors. As the film demonstrates, there is a certain amount of justification for this. The Futori family history is rich with incestuous unions, forbidden practices and punishments from both fellow islanders and the gods.

So one of the family members, a man named Nekichi (Rentaro Mikuni), has been chained in a pit for his crimes; his sister and onetime lover, Uma (Yasuko Matsui), has become the much-abused mistress of the manager (Yoshi Kato) of a local mill. Another Futori is the wanton, feeble-minded Toriko (Hideko Okiyama), who scampers about happily in a burlap sack and is much too popular with the local men. There are also a venerable, mischievous grandfather and a grandson named Kametaro (Choichiro Kawarazaki), who remains understandably confused about his lineage. And there is a certain majesty to all this squalor, for the gods who founded Kuragejima are said to have been as incestuous as the Futoris themselves.

•

The early parts of the film unfold in a sunny, unhurried, halfway humorous style, as Mr. Imamura documents the peculiarities of the Futori household and conveys the elements of myth and superstition that color the islanders' lives. He does this in typically unpredictable fashion, often switching abruptly from the matter-of-fact to the fanciful with no warning. And there are frequent shots of the exotic sea and land creatures that live side by side with the islanders, suggestive of another dimension. Indeed, these glimpses of nature are specifically equated with divinity, and the film creates a strong sense of all-knowing, ever-present unseen

Cultural Clash

Choichiro Kawarazaki and Hideko Okiyama star in "The Profound Desire of the Gods," about the confrontation of primitive and modern societies.

powers. In one scene, the village storyteller sings · of Kuragejima's gods and goddesses to a group of children, while a snake slithers placidly in the foreground.

If the best parts of the films are those that convey the mixture of real and spiritual elements in the life of this unspoiled island, the more commonplace ingredient is a notion of civilization's corrupting influence. This takes the form of a subplot (which along with a fleeting reference to Vietnam is the only thing that makes the film seem dated) introducing a bespectabled engineer (Kazuo Kitamura) who has come from Tokyo to help modernize Kuragejima. Having no understanding of the local people's deep superstitious and religious convictions, this engineer is a ready source of low-keyed comedy as he tries to adapt his plans to the local customs.

The easygoing style in which these events unfold doesn't entirely pave the way for the divine retribution that is exacted from the Futoris by the film's conclusion, but in a way that makes these climactic events even more disturbing. Less successful is a coda that depicts the island five years later in its newly civilized state, with abundant Coca-Cola signs to overstate the point.

This film, and others in this well-deserved retrospective, amply emphasize the prophetic qualities of Mr. Imamura's work as well as the more erratic ones. Twenty years ago, he was helping to pioneer the break with traditionalism that has brought about such a flowering of iconoclastic Japanese cinema today.

1988 My 6, C10:1

Ordinary People, Extraordinary Risks

JUDGMENT IN BERLIN, directed by Leo Penn; screenplay by Joshua Sinclair and Mr. Penn, from the novel "Judgment in Berlin" by Herbert J. Stern; director of photography, Gabor Pogany; edited by Teddy Darvas; music by Karl Laabs; production designer Jan Schlubach and Peter Alteneder; produced by Joshua Sinclair and Ingrid Windisch; released by New Line Cinema. At the 68th Street Playhouse, near Third Avenue. Running time: 92 minutes. This film is rated PG.

Herbert J. Stern	Martin Sheen
Bernard Hellring	Sam Wanamaker
Judah Best	Max Gail
Uri Andreyev	Juergen Heinrich
Helmut Thiele	Heinz Hoenig
Edwin Palmer	Carl Lumbly
Guenther X	Sean Penn
Bruno Ristau	Harris Yulin

"Judgment in Berlin" (no relation to "Judgment at Nuremberg") is an account of the aftermath of a 1978 hijacking of a Polish airliner by an East German seeking asylum in the West. Helmut Thiele's appearance at Tempelhof Air Force Base in West Berlin was an embarrassment to the West Germans, so they tossed the case to the equally embarrassed Americans, who had no enthusiasm for punishing a refugee from the East but were bound by international treaty to crack down on hijackings. As an American official puts it, "State has a mess and Justice must clean it up."

A book about the hijacker's trial, written by Herbert J. Stern, the American judge who presided, serves as the basis for the movie that opens today at the 68th Street Playhouse. That's the trouble. In the miscast person of Martin Sheen (no relation to

Spencer Tracy), Judge Stern becomes the hero of the story. Perhaps the judge is being done an injustice, but the screenplay works so hard at delivering a shiny image that he becomes unappealing. Maybe he can appeal. The far-fetched speeches in which he presents himself as a lonely battler for Constitutional law against Nazi methods is the stuff of a stuffshirted self-promoter. The efforts to turn him into a regular sexy guy, with beautiful sexy wife and all, are strictly from Hollywood.

When the camera turns away from his preening honor toward the people involved in the actual escape, the story picks up. Leo Penn's direction, which seems programmed when Mr. Sheen is on screen, can be snappy. The courtroom jockeying is convincingly rendered by a superior cast that includes Sam Wanamaker as a flamboyant defense attorney; Harris Yulin as an American official; Heinz Hoenig as Helmut the hijacker, and Sean Penn, one of the director's sons, in a surprisingly strong climactic appearance as a surprise witness.

Even while telling the inherently moving story of ordinary people taking an enormous risk for freedom, however, the writers cannot resist churning out press releases to the American Way. The movie ends with smug summations that could have been lifted straight out of a Civics 101 textbook. Earlier, Helmut is made to declare, "I didn't come to Berlin to get the kind of trial we get in the East." Objection! Mr. Hoenig has already said it far better with the look on his face as he walked down the gangway that led to the West.

●

"Judgment in Berlin" is rated PG ("Parental Guidance Suggested"). It includes a little low-key sex and violence. WALTER GOODMAN

1988 My 6, C13:1

Inexorable Reality

Sunnyi Melles in the film "38: Vienna Before the Fall."

38: VIENNA BEFORE THE FALL directed by Wolfgang Glück; screenplay (in German with English subtitles) by Mr Glück, from the novel "This Too Was Vienna," by Friedrich Torberg; director of photography, Gerard Vandenberg; edited by Heidi Handorf; music by Gert Grund; production designer, Herwig Libowitzky; produced by Michael von Wolkenstein; released by East-West Classics. At Lincoln Plaza Cinema, Broadway at 63d Street. Running time: 96 minutes. This film has no rating.

Martin Hofmann	Tobias Engel
Carola Hell	Sunnyi Melles
Toni Drechsler	Heinz Trixner
Carola's Mother	Lotte Ledl
Frau Schostal	Ingrid Burkhard
Sovary, the publisher	Romuald Pekny

In a peaceful Viennese garden, a man and woman who have recently embarked on a love affair discuss the matters they care about most. He has found a good apartment, in a building he says Mozart often used to pass; will she move in? She has an offer to travel abroad for professional reasons; will he object too strenuously? And will their liaison survive such pressures? Entirely absorbed in these questions, the lovers remain oblivious to the gathering storm.

Wolfgang Glück's "38: Vienna Before the Fall" slowly and inexorably outlines the consequences of this blissful ignorance. Yet it never trades unduly upon the hindsight, irony and pathos that color this situation. Instead, it paints a credible picture of Martin Hofmann (Tobias Engel), a celebrated playwright who travels in Vienna's elite artistic circles and regards politics as an entirely different sphere. Proud of his reputation for controversy on the stage, Martin otherwise lives happily in a calm, rarefied world. As his friends grow increasingly fearful that their country will be annexed by Germany, Martin remains unwilling or unable to comprehend the danger.

"38: Vienna Before the Fall," which opens today at the Lincoln Plaza, gradually sets forth the evidence of change, and observes Martin's determination to look the other way. When Martin, who is Jewish, and his lover, a renowned Aryan actress named Carola Hell (Sunnyi Melles), move into their new home, there are noisy anti-Semitic mutterings from the building's porter; in discussions of the theater, there is a growing reluctance to mention the work of Jewish artists. Even the son of Martin's housekeeper expresses Nazi sympathies, but Martin seems to regard all of these lapses as more rude than threatening. Not even the efforts of a close friend, a newspaper editor, to dispel Martin's indifference and give him a clear warning really get through.

What makes the film interesting is its effort to see the Vienna of 1937 and 1938 though Martin's eyes. Proud,

stubborn and breathlessly in love with Carola, Martin fails to understand why he should not follow her to Berlin when she goes there for a theatrical engagement; it takes dramatic intervention on the part of the newspaper editor to save this playwright from himself. Carola, too, is dangerously headstrong, and her unfriendly remarks to admiring Gestapo officers only intensify the couple's problems. Because Martin, who was born Jewish but christened at an early age, has never previously come to terms with his own identity, he winds up doing so in the midst of this emergency. But even his most defiant gesture, in the end, is less courageous than blind.

Mr. Glück's telling of this story has some obvious touches, but it is graceful, too. And his vision of a society on the brink of destruction seems very deeply felt, especially since in this film the encroaching madness takes the form of a terrible calm. As played by Mr. Engel, a tall, perceptive-looking actor who conveys confidence and intelligence, the character of Martin becomes tragically understandable as a man who has long been protected by privilege. No stranger to political events elsewhere, he still finds it unimaginable that these forces can affect his own homeland. So when the annexation finally comes, and the persecution begins, Martin's sheltered, happy life leaves him classically ill-equipped to cope with disaster.

●

Though Carola is a less complicated figure, and though Miss Melles (who is in fact a stage actress) lacks the bearing and projection of a great star, she emerges as a sweet, sympathetic woman trying desperately to face the facts. When she is at one point offered a big movie role, perhaps as a concession from those nowplacated Gestapo officers, she sits with deep self-loathing and watches rushes of herself in a tap-dancing role; Carola cannot bear the irrelevance of such trivial work in such dreadful times. Later on, it is she who understands that the moment for defiance is past, even when Martin does not. Mr. Glück has a way of underscoring such revelations with too much music, but still the anguish comes through.

"38: Vienna Before the Fall" is a sad, decorous and gentle film with an unusual perspective, an attempt to understand inaction as a form of action and, perhaps, to see what cannot be seen. JANET MASLIN

1988 My 6, C17:1

Surprise Visit

JACK'S BACK, written and directed by Rowdy Herrington; director of photography, Shelly Johnson; editor, Harry B. Miller 3d; music by Daniel Di Paolo; production designer, Piers Plowden; producers, Tim Moore and Cassian Elwes; released by Palisades Entertainment. At Cine 1, 711 Seventh Avenue, near 47th Street, and other theaters. Running time: 95 minutes. This film is rated R.

John/Rick Wesford	James Spader
Christine Moscari	Cynthia Gibb
Dr. Sidney Tannerson	Rod Loomis
Jack Pendler	Rex Ryon

By CARYN JAMES

The world needs another movie about a copycat Jack the Ripper as much as it needs another Ripper, unless the film has the wit of "The Ruling Class" (Peter O'Toole as a nobleman who believes he's Jack), or the tautness of "Time After Time" (the Ripper chased through time by H. G. Wells). "Jack's Back" offers identical twins, silly coincidences and a huge red herring — a checklist designed to take the chill out of movie crime.

John Wesford, a young do-good doctor, discovers the modern Ripper's last victim (she was John's long-lost prom date; don't ask). When the Los Angeles police find John hanging from a noose, they think he's the repentant killer. Then his twin, Rick, turns up.

Rick has had a dream vision of his brother's murder. The police are skeptical, though not nearly as disbelieving as anyone who sees this film is likely to be. Rick ambles through most of the movie tracking down the killer, but not one episode is convincing or even entertaining. (Well, there is the scene when the Ripper sings "My Way" in the shower, but it's not worth waiting for.)

James Spader, effectively smarmy in "Less Than Zero" and "Wall Street," is wasted twice as the twins. "Jack's Back," which opens today at the Cine 1 and other theaters, is so dull it leaves you plenty of time to marvel at how a plot can be this rickety, how a production can look this shabby, and how the first-time writer and director Rowdy Herrington could borrow a story with so relentless a grip on our imaginations and in no time at all declaw it.

1988 My 6, C19:1

Amen!

Nanni Moretti in the film "The Mass is Ended."

THE MASS IS ENDED, directed by Nanni Moretti; screenplay (Italian with English subtitles) by Mr. Moretti and Sandro Petraglia; director of photography, Franco Di Giacomo; editor, Mirco Garrone; music by Nicola Piovani; produced by Achille Manzotti. At Carnegie Screening Room, Seventh Avenue and 57th Street. Running time: 94 minutes. This film has no rating.

Don Giulio	Nanni Moretti
Don Giulio's father	Ferruccio De Ceresa
Valentina	Enrica Maria Modugno
Don Giulio's mother	Margarita Lozano
Saverio	Marco Messeri
Cesare	Roberto Vezzosi
Gianni	Dario Cantarelli
Andrea	Vincenzo Salemme
Antonio	Eugenio Masciari

"The Mass Is Ended" begins with a young priest, Don Giulio, returning to his home in Rome after service on a picturesque island, only to find more problems than he can handle. They are mostly problems of the heart. The priest whom Giulio is replacing had to give up the pulpit when his love affair produced a child. A friend has become a recluse after breaking up with his lover. Another friend gets into trouble because of his fondness for boys. Giulio's father, who is given

to pondering whether there is such a thing as "universal love," leaves home to take up with a much younger woman. Giulio's unmarried sister is pregnant and intends to have an abortion. When she turns to him for comfort, the distraught Giulio tells her that if she goes ahead with her plan, "I'll kill you first and then myself."

The story is lightly told by Nanni Moretti, the director, co-writer and star, but we get to know none of these people; they are brought one after the other as means of overloading Giulio's circuits. Their seriatim confessions are as ordained as mass. Soon Giulio is so upset that he slaps his sister, picks on everybody else and skips shaving. He even puts his hand through a window. None of this is to be taken seriously, but it's not very comical either.

●

Mr. Moretti, who plays Giulio, has a pleasant manner, especially when he is running away from serious discussions to kick around a soccer ball with some youngsters. Other episodes, however — such as his awkward testimony at the trial of an old pal and an overextended scene of him being dunked in a trough in an argument over a parking space — just don't work.

The movie, now at the Carnegie Screening Room, ends in a bowl of Mamma Mia sentiment. "Why did you do it," Giulio demands of mama's corpse. "Who'll love me now?" There's a baptism, a wedding, some happy dancing to Nicola Piovani's juicy music, and off goes Giulio to a new assignment with fewer human beings to complicate things. We wish him well, but it doesn't much matter.

WALTER GOODMAN

1988 My 6, C18:6

Lawyer and Cop Join Forces

SHAKEDOWN, directed and written by James Glickenhaus; director of photography, John Lindley; edited by Paul Fried; music by Jonathan Elias; production designed by Charles Bennett; produced by J. Boyce Harman Jr.; released by Universal Pictures. At Orpheum, 86th Street near Third Avenue, and other theaters. Running time: 100 minutes. This film is rated R.

Roland Dalton	Peter Weller
Richie Marks	Sam Elliott
Susan Cantrell	Patricia Charbonneau
Nicky Carr	Antonio Fargas
Gail Feinberger	Blanche Baker
Michael Jones	Richard Brooks
Larry	David Proval

In "Shakedown," something fancy happens every 15 minutes or so, which is part of what makes the whole film so unremarkable. It becomes difficult to remember why the stolen police car being driven by the runaway thug, for example, has got upside-down amid the piles of burning rubble. Or why the roller coaster has run amok at Coney Island, or why the taxi has been impaled on the wrecking ball. The writer and director, James Glickenhaus, whose chief claim to fame is the earlier "Exterminator," would surely be lost without the sounds of screeching brakes and spraying gunfire at regular intervals.

Not all of "Shakedown" is as lurid as this. A lot of it is bogged down in exposition, with a plot about police corruption in which Peter Weller plays a legal aid lawyer named Ro-

land Dalton. In this, his last case before he begins work for his future father-in-law's Wall Street law firm, Dalton is assigned to defend a drug dealer (Richard Brooks) accused of killing a policeman in Central Park.

Dalton's nagging, acquisitive fiancée, Gail Feinberger (Blanche Baker), doesn't understand the first thing about his dedication to doing good. "Shakedown," which is full of ethnic stereotypes, also gives Dalton the chance to rekindle his utterly perfunctory affair with Susan Cantrell (Patricia Charbonneau), who happens to be the assistant district attorney on the case and the voice of his conscience, too. Susan urges him to stick with legal aid and not to forsake his values by selling out to the wealthy Feinbergers. However, she delivers this speech from her own very nice penthouse apartment with a big terrace and a full view of Central Park. This peculiarity goes unexplained.

The other star of "Shakedown," which opens today at the Orpheum and other theaters, is Sam Elliott, who plays a colorfully dissipated undercover cop named Richie Marks. First seen waking up in a round-the-clock movie theater on 42d Street (it is one of Mr. Glickenhaus's wittier touches to make the film on the screen a shoot-'em-up featuring armed ski jumpers), Marks quickly establishes himself as Dalton's alter ego, and together they hunt down the entrepreneurial policemen who are the story's villains.

●

Mr. Elliott, who seems to get better with age, has developed a grizzled look and an enjoyably wild gleam in his eye. Mr. Weller also demonstrates a maverick streak, though his is established mostly through loud neckties, a taste for Jimi Hendrix and an inappropriate tan. In Mr. Glickenhaus's screenplay, these are the sorts of things that pass for character traits. The dialogue tends to be aggressively heavy on the hackneyed ("You don't exactly look like chopped liver yourself") and the jive ("Is this gonna be some kind of female territorial doo-wop?").

Among the notable secondary aspects of "Shakedown" are the presence of memorable character actors like David Proval and Antonio Fargas in small roles, and a credit for "music composed, arranged and realized," which in this case seems a bit much.

JANET MASLIN

1988 My 6, C20:1

Screwball Caper

STICKY FINGERS, directed by Catlin Adams; written and produced by Miss Adams and Melanie Mayron; director of photography, Gary Thieltges; edited by Bob Reitano; music by Lisa Harlo, Jim Dyke and Ish; production design by Jessica Scott-Justice; released by Spectrafilm. At Loews New York Twin, Second Avenue and 66th Street. Running time: 96 minutes. This film is rated PG-13.

Hattie	Helen Slater
Lolly	Melanie Mayron
Evanston	Danitra Vance
Stella	Eileen Brennan
Kitty	Carol Kane
Diane	Loretta Devine
Sam	Christopher Guest
Marcie	Gwen Welles

"Sticky Fingers" is the work of a female director (Catlin Adams), female screenwriters (Miss Adams and Melanie Mayron) and a mostly female cast (including supporting players like Eileen Brennan, Gwen Welles and Carol Kane), but it's less feminist than dizzily feminine. The two leading characters, struggling musicians sharing a picturesquely shabby downtown flat, are as bubble headed as they can be. This is especially apparent after fate sends a suitcase full of money their way, courtesy of a drug-dealing friend (Loretta Devine) who asks them to watch it for an indefinite period. What do they do about this windfall? They shriek, they squabble and then they shop.

Helen Slater and Melanie Mayron, careening through the film in the kinds of zany "Desperately Seeking Susan"-inspired outfits that are fun as long as they're on somebody else, play the blithe Hattie and Lolly at a screwball pitch. To enhance this, Miss Adams often directs them to talk frenetically at the same time, and she establishes the characters' charming eccentricity with cute shots of their unusual shoes. A lot of care has gone into the film's earring wardrobe, too. So "Sticky Fingers" tries too hard, but it does have a fundamental good-naturedness that comes through.

Though the plot quickly deteriorates into standard caper material, with an added twist that makes the women constitutionally unable to keep money from slipping through their fingers, "Sticky Fingers" remains reasonably amiable. Miss Slater makes a dreamily distracted heroine who can turn comically tough at the oddest moments (as when she argues with her roommate over the proper use of kitchen sponges), and Miss Mayron tries hard to keep up her end of the twosome; in the supporting cast, Miss Brennan has some good moments as the roommates' uncharitable landlady, and Miss Kane

In the Money
Melanie Mayron and Helen Slater play struggling musicians who get their hands on a fortune in cash in "Sticky Fingers."

flutters nicely through the repeated scenes in which Hattie and Lolly are threatened with eviction.

Also in "Sticky Fingers," which opens today at Loews New York Twin, is Danitra Vance as the friend who assists Hattie and Lolly in their money-squandering schemes, and Christopher Guest, who's especially good as the boyfriend about whom Lolly has her doubts. For one thing, he has an old girlfriend (Miss Welles) who won't go away. For another, when he excuses himself from Lolly to have a confidential talk with this ex, he brings a baseball glove.

The lively visual style that might have brought "Sticky Fingers" out of its doldrums isn't here, as much of the film has been drably, and at times even ineptly, shot.

•

"Sticky Fingers" is rated PG-13 ("Special Parental Guidance Suggested for Those Younger Than 13"). It includes some rude language.
JANET MASLIN

1988 My 6, C28:5

Virginia Gothic

IN A SHALLOW GRAVE, written and directed by Kenneth Bowser, based on the novel by James Purdy; director of photography, Jerzy Zielinski; edited by Nicholas C. Smith; music by Jonathan Sheffer; production designer, David Wasco; produced by Mr. Bowser and Barry Jossen; released by Skouras Pictures, Inc. At Cinema 1, Third Avenue at 60th Street. Running time: 92 minutes. This film is rated R.

Garnet Montrose	Michael Biehn
Georgina Rance	Maureen Mueller
Quintas Pearch	Michael Beach
Potter Daventry	Patrick Dempsey
Edgar Doust	Thomas Boyd Mason

As "In a Shallow Grave" begins, World War II is still being fought. Garnet Montrose (Michael Biehn) returns from Guadalcanal so hideously scarred that people suck in their breath in shock when they see him.

Garnet lives as a recluse in the old Virginia farmhouse where he was born and brought up, tended only by a farmhand named Quintas (Michael Beach). Garnet is both overbearing and pathetic, writing love letters to the Widow Rance (Maureen Mueller), his childhood sweetheart who has been married twice in the meantime. The widow lives just down the road but she refuses to see her former lover.

Into this gothic atmosphere stumbles Potter Daventry (Patrick Dempsey), a young man on the run, who, as written, is more of a symbol than a character. Potter is rather like an idealized Tennessee Williams hero, both saint and sinner, as well as an instrument of salvation.

Directed by Kenneth Bowser, and adapted by him from the James Purdy novel, "In a Shallow Grave" is one of those movies that might be more tolerable on public television than at Cinema 1, where it opens today.

•

It is nicely acted, handsome looking and impenetrable. Mr. Bowser has structured it with the kind of heavy deliberation that tells us that nothing really means what it appears to mean. However, there's very little on the surface of the narrative that would lead us to search more deeply.

What is supposed to develop into a bizarre, three-way relationship in-

volving Garnet, the Widow Rance and Potter must be taken on faith. Because the widow is off-screen throughout most of the film, the audience sees only the possibility of a more conventional, two-way relationship between the soul-wounded vet and the drifter who appears to fall in love with him. This being a fable, nothing, of course, can really come of that.
VINCENT CANBY

1988 My 6, C21:1

An Uncoventional Singles Scene

DARK HABITS, directed and written (in Spanish with English subtitles) by Pedro Almodóvar; director of photography, Angel L. Fernández; edited by José Salcedo; production design by Pin Morales and Román Arango; released by Cinevista. At the Quad Cinema, 13th Street, west of Fifth Avenue. Running time: 95 minutes. This film has no rating.

Yolanda	Cristina S. Pascual
Mother Superior	Julieta Serrano
Sister Manure	Marisa Paredes
Sister Sin	Carmen Maura
The Marquesa	Mari Carillo
Sister Snake	Lina Canalejas
Chaplin	Manuel Zarzo
Sister Rat	Chus Lampreave
Mother General	Berta Riaza

By WALTER GOODMAN

When Yolanda's boyfriend dies of a dose of heroin laced with strychnine, with which she unknowingly supplied him, she seeks refuge from the police at the convent of the Holy Redeemers, dedicated to Our Lady of the Forsaken. Its motto: "Sin is our chosen path." There the nightclub singer-cum-junkie finds a home away from home.

The mother superior, whose cell is decorated with steamy photos of Hollywood sexpots, invites Yolanda to join in shooting up. Sister Manure trips on acid and has visions; Sister Rat of the Sewers writes soft porn ("The Call of the Flesh") under the name of Conchita Torres; Sisters Sin and Snake have their own outré avocations. Also on the premises is a chaplain who chain-smokes during mass, designs drop-dead gowns à la Cecil Beaton and may have something on with Sister Snake.

Such are the main residents of Pedro Almodóvar's "Dark Habits." (The more literal translation from the Spanish, "The Dark Hideout," has been changed for the sake of the pun.) Mr. Almodóvar, who has built a reputation in Spain in recent years for a bizarre sort of comedy, shows a taste for melodramatic lighting and perspectives, portentous music and sometimes grotesque close-ups — techniques often attached to movies that take religion seriously but employed here, more or less effectively, for satire.

•

This black comedy or light melodrama, which opens today at the Quad Cinema, does not go for belly laughs, but keeps you smiling at the innocence of the sinful nuns, as they appealingly carry on their appalling practices. When they pitch in to give a party, Sister Manure, who has been known to stick needles through her cheek at a whim, says: "I'll mortify myself. The crowd will love it."

The scattershot plot has to do with the mother superior's efforts, by blackmail and drug dealing, to maintain the convent despite the strong displeasure of the head of the order.

"It's been a while since we redeemed anyone," sighs the mother superior, who has sold off the convent's furnishings to keep her little band in coke — though her own preference is for heroin.

Mr. Almodóvar, who wrote as well as directed, does not quite bring the events together, but his wry attitude toward conventional morality is not lost, and the acting is sufficiently controlled to keep the characters from running away into farce. These coke-sniffing sisters come across as more innocent and pious and generous of spirit than their church superiors and lay benefactors. There is no preaching here, but when, with the forces of propriety cracking down on their disorderly order, the chaplain prays that they may continue to live "in the same healthy anarchy," you may find yourself uttering an amused amen.

1988 My 6, C28:5

Yesteryear's Lunacies

RIDERS OF THE STORM, directed by Maurice Phillips; screenplay by Scott Roberts; director of photography, John Metcalfe; edited by Tony Lawson; music by Brian Bennett; production designer, Evan Hercules; produced by Laurie Keller and Paul Cowan; released by Miramax Films. At Bleecker Street Cinema, 144 Bleecker Street at La Guardia Place. Running time: 92 minutes. This film is rated R.

Captain	Dennis Hopper
Tesla	Michael J. Pollard
Ace	Eugene Lipinski
Claude	James Aubrey
Ben	Al Matthews
Jerry	William Armstrong
Minh	Michael Ho
Sam	Derek Hoxby
Mrs. Westinghouse	Nigel Pegram

By VINCENT CANBY

In "Riders of the Storm," the anarchic spirit of the 1960's counterculture lives on in the persons of its stars, Dennis Hopper ("Easy Rider") and Michael J. Pollard ("Bonnie and Clyde"), and in its general attitude, which is suitably unkempt.

The time is supposed to be "the day after tomorrow," though it seems more like the day before yesterday. This has less to do with the failure of the movie makers' imaginations than with the speed with which last night's certified lunacies become this morning's rational behavior.

Willa Westinghouse, running as the Republican Party's first female Presidential candidate, stands every chance of winning. Mrs. Westinghouse is an image made to the order of what the pollsters have decided the voters want. In looks and manner she's a cross between Margaret Thatcher of Britain and Edna Everage, the well-upholstered, middle-class Australian matron who is one of Barry Humphries's most popular characters.

Mrs. Westinghouse says things that don't really sound outrageous anymore ("Moderation in the pursuit of peace is no virtue"). She constantly cites her own patriotism, her love of family and her hatred for Communism. Only once does she have self-doubt: "Is it possible to be a *Christian* warmonger?"

Unfortunately for the film, Mrs. Westinghouse isn't on the screen long enough. "Riders of the Storm" is mostly about the attempts of some renegade Vietnam veterans to sabotage her campaign. These fellows, under the command of Mr. Hopper, have been in the air (flying an ancient

B-29 bomber, a relic from World War II) since the end of the Vietnam War. The plane is equipped with all sorts of fancy electronic equipment that was originally designed to disseminate anti-North Vietnam propaganda in Southeast Asia.

In recent years the plane has been randomly flying around the United States interrupting establishment communications with something called the S and M Television network.

Like "Eat the Rich," another (much funnier) contemporary though very 1960-ish comedy, "Riders of the Storm" is an English film, shot largely in England with some location work in this country. It was written by Scott Roberts and directed by Maurice Phillips, a director of music videos.

Its spirit is stronger than its flesh. The jokes aren't great. Mr. Hopper wears funny hats, chews on a cigar and barks commands. Mr. Pollard, as the engineering genius aboard the plane, has little to do except smile subversively. The movie depends almost entirely on their physical presences to express its political attitude. The video effects are good.

1988 My 7, 12:3

The Universal Spice

SALSA, directed by Boaz Davidson; screenplay by Mr. Davidson and Tomas Benitez and Shepard Goldman, based on a story by Mr. Davidson and Eli Tabor; director of photography, David Gurfinkel; edited by Alain Jakubowicz; choreography by Kenny Ortega; production designer, Mark Haskins; produced by Menahem Golan and Yoram Globus. At the Criterion Center, Broadway and 45th Street; the U.A. East, First Avenue at 85th Street, and other theaters. Running time: 90 minutes. This film is rated PG.

Rico	Robby Rosa
Ken	Rodney Harvey
Rita	Magali Alvarado
Luna	Miranda Garrison
Lola	Moon Orona
Vicki	Angela Alvarado
Mother	Loyda Ramos
Chuey	Valente Rodriguez

By JANET MASLIN

Some myths exist in every culture, and evidently the one about the boy who disco-dances his way to greatness is one of them. "Salsa" presents the Latin version of this old standby, with Robby Rosa, a member emeritus of the kiddie-pop group Menudo, as the kid who can't be kept down. Mr. Rosa looks like a strutting, macho version of Michael Jackson, and the film's minimal plot is about all the women who can't help throwing themselves at him. At moments when the story attempts a more serious turn, yesterday's audience at the Criterion Center could be counted on to giggle.

As Rico, Mr. Rosa spends the film practicing his dance moves, flexing his muscles and threatening anyone who comes near his cute, frisky sister. His friends often remark that he loves salsa music better than anything, but this is not entirely true. It's more accurate that Rico (and the film) consider salsa a fine accompaniment to any other activity. Salsa can even be heard in the brief classroom scenes, despite the presence of nuns.

•

There is also a seduction scene in which Rico invites a new friend named Lola over to his room ("Great apartment, where's your bed?" asks she) and dims the lights, only to turn on the mirrored revolving ball that hangs from the ceiling and begin dancing up a salsa storm. Lola looks surprised by this, and even more so the next night when Rico is trading thumb rings with a former girlfriend named Vicki and angrily telling Lola to get lost. This is about as romantic as "Salsa" gets.

The film works salsa greats like Tito Puente into its dance club sequences, which are staged energetically and make a lot more sense than the narrative scenes. There is a subplot about a contest in which the best dancer at the club will win a trip for two to Puerto Rico. Bet on who'll win if you like, but don't bet on seeing any tropical scenery.

"Salsa" is rated PG ("Parental Guidance Suggested"). It contains a great many sexually suggestive scenes.

1988 My 7, 13:1

Blat, Blat, Blat, Thunk, Thunk, Thunk

DEAD HEAT, directed by Mark Goldblatt; written by Terry Black; director of photography, Robert D. Yeoman; edited by Harvey Rosenstock; music by Ernest Troost; production designer, Craig Stearns; produced by Michael Meltzer and David Helpern; released by New World Pictures. At the 86th St. Twin, at Lexington Avenue; Movie Center Five, 125th and Seventh Avenue; Running time: 87 minutes. This film is rated R.

Roger Mortis	Treat Williams
Doug Bigelow	Joe Piscopo
Randi James	Lindsay Frost
Dr. Ernest McNab	Darren McGavin
Arthur P. Loudermilk	Vincent Price
Rebecca Smythers	Clare Kirkconnell

There is one scene in "Dead Heat," now at the National and other theaters, that produces a cold sweat: A dead cop has a shootout with a dead bad guy. Blat blat blat go their guns; thunk, thunk, thunk go their torsos. Only nobody falls down. The prospect that they will keep it up forever is enough to chill even the professional moviegoer.

This sci-fi, low-tech comedy horror show, directed by Mark Goldblatt with the help of the usual specialists in disgusting effects, features Treat Williams, with the boyish smile, and Joe Piscopo, with the body-builder biceps, as a couple of cops who encounter criminals who cannot be mowed down by conventional methods. It's all part of some sort of eternal-life plot devised by creepy Vincent Price, which the screenwriter, Terry Black, has not quite figured out. When Mr. Williams is asphyxiated in the line of duty, his pals cook him under the resurrection microwave and he goes forth to outghoul the ghouls. "After all," somebody says in a reflective moment, "what separates life from death?" Not watching movies like this.

WALTER GOODMAN

1988 My 7, 13:1

FILM VIEW/Vincent Canby

'Beetlejuice' Is Pap for the Eyes

"**B**EETLEJUICE," WHICH IS quickly turning into a hit of serious proportions (it earned more than $9 million in its first three weeks of release), is a farce for our place and time. It's technically sophisticated and so amiable and well meaning that it seems rude to point out that, like some of our public figures, it is more of a bore to watch than to describe.

In the manner of most of the programming we see on television, "Beetlejuice" has been designed to be utterly painless. It passes in front of the eyes and is gone. In a society where the economic necessity is to please as many people as possible, the creation of something that doesn't offend has become an art.

Adam Maitland (Alec Baldwin, who looks and behaves rather like an un-neurotic William Hurt) and his wife, Barbara (Geena Davis, a full-lipped, dark-eyed beauty), are very much in love with each other, with their placid lives and with their big, comfortable old house in Connecticut. Within the first few minutes of the film, they are in a fatal automobile accident. Adam and Barbara are suddenly shades, confined to their house while trying to protect it and their privacy from the house's gauche new owners.

Even with the aid of the "Handbook for the Recently Deceased," Adam and Barbara are duds as ghosts. Haunting isn't easy. Adam and Barbara turn up in all sorts of ghastly incarnations, including headless and skinless, but the self-absorbed new owners look right through them. They receive no satisfaction from Juno (Sylvia Sidney), their caseworker. Juno has the patience of an employee in the Motor Vehicle Bureau. When they complain, she instructs them to go home and read the book.

Adam and Barbara are desperate. They turn to a renegade demon named Beetlejuice (Michael Keaton), a people exterminator who advertises his services on television ("Unhappy with eternity? Having trouble adjusting?").

■

It's at this point that "Beetlejuice" begins to take on life. Wearing a mothy fright wig and whitish makeup, Mr. Keaton recalls some worn-out but manic burlesque comic, a Bobby Clark of the hereafter, a leering, fast-talking lecher who admits that, after 600

years of celibacy, "I'm feeling a little anxious."

Even as I write this, I have the terrible feeling that I'm making "Beetlejuice" sound funnier than it is to sit through, which I have now done twice. Because the audiences at both matinees were small, I can only assume that attendance in the evenings and on weekends is huge.

It must also be that "Beetlejuice" is a comedy that desperately needs a laugh track, whether canned or the kind provided by a large audience that guffaws at special effects, levitation, grotesque monster makeup and ventriloquism. There wasn't a peep to be heard the first time I saw the film.

The only pleased grunts I heard the second time were my own, once when Mr. Keaton's Beetlejuice made an obscene gesture toward the innocent Barbara and another time when Adam and Barbara, visiting the headquarters of purgatory, are shown a fish tank full of bizarre creatures. The explanation: the creatures are lost souls — ghosts who have been exorcised ("That's death for the dead").

There are funny ideas in the screenplay, but either they are undeveloped by the writers or they are thrown away through what appears to be Tim Burton's shapeless direction. This may not be an oversight but, rather, the influence of a kind of television comedy show in which gags don't grow one out of another but succeed one another, randomly.

Such randomness is the style of Pee-wee Herman, the aging elf whose first feature, "Pee-wee's Big Adventure," was directed by Mr. Burton (and was also a big box-office hit). Mr. Keaton could have saved "Beetlejuice" for me, but he's really a supporting character, not on the screen long enough to pull things together. All he does is show up the genteel silliness of gags making fun of interior decorators, second-rate artists and, I suppose, the acute shortage of luxury housing everywhere.

"Beetlejuice" is, at least, painless. It is true to its own small ends.

"Sunset," written and directed by Blake Edwards, the only man in Hollywood who has claim to the title King of Comedy, is a disaster. Its pleasures aren't even random. There aren't any at all.

The initial idea seems to have been a good one: the imagined collaboration of the cow-

This is a time when the creation of movies that don't offend has become an art.

boy actor Tom Mix and the legendary lawman Wyatt Earp on the making of ambitious western in Hollywood in 1929.

The film's production notes make a great point of the fact that 1929 was a perilous time in Hollywood, when sound was coming in and a lot of stars were going out. Yet the released film makes no more than one passing mention of the advent of sound. "Sunset" is, instead, a heavily jocular murder mystery that calls upon Tom Mix (Bruce Willis) and Wyatt Earp (James Garner) to act as amateur sleuths.

That Mr. Edwards may have had another film in mind when he began to shoot "Sunset" is suggested by an unexplored reference to a real-life Hollywood scandal, as well as evidence that the movie was originally to have featured such personalities as Fatty Arbuckle and Laurel and Hardy, though they're nowhere to be seen here.

The film's continuity is so rough that, near the end, you might think a reel has been dropped by the projectionist. It hasn't.

One explanation for the mess is that Mr. Edwards was working against the clock to finish "Sunset" before the directors' strike last year. That's not good enough.   □

1988 My 8, II:19:1

Adult Threat, Childhood Terrors

LADY IN WHITE, directed and written by Frank LaLoggia; director of photography, Russell Carpenter; edited by Steve Mann; production designer, Richard K. Hummel; produced by Andrew G. La Marca and Mr. LaLoggia; released by New Century/Vista Film Company. At Coronet, Third Avenue and 59th Street, and other theaters. Running time: 112 minutes. This film is rated PG-13.

Frankie	Lukas Haas
Phil	Len Cariou

Angelo	Alex Rocco
Amanda	Katherine Helmond
Geno	Jason Presson
Mama Assunta	Renata Vanni
Papa Charlie	Angelo Bertolini
Melissa	Joelle Jacobi

By CARYN JAMES

Ghosts are rarely as intriguing as the people they haunt, so "Lady in White" has a shrewdly chosen focus. Its sympathetic, engaging, haunted hero is Frankie Scarlatti, a 9-year-old boy who sees the ghost of a murdered 10-year-old girl. Frankie is locked in a spooky school cloakroom on Halloween night in 1962, when he sees the apparition of Melissa and is nearly strangled himself. Though he is rescued, in the next months Melissa reappears, and their mysterious attacker, suspected of killing 11 children in a decade, is still on the loose.

Here are the bones of an ordinary ghost story. But the writer and director Frank LaLoggia brings them to life with exceptional vitality by giving Frankie his creator's own youth — an autobiographical Italian-American family, the embracing atmosphere of a small town in upstate New York.

The extended Scarlatti family — warm, funny, so real they make the characters in "Moonstruck" seem like impostors — includes Frankie's widowed father, wise-cracking older brother, foster uncle and Old World grandparents, who break into Italian when the slightest thing goes awry. When Mama Assunta sends Frankie off to school on Halloween morning, dressed in his Dracula cape and mask, there is nothing ominous in this sunny world — a touch that separates "Lady in White" from more conventional, simpler ghost tales.

This is a day full of comic details. Frankie skids his bike into wet cement. At his class's Halloween party, he reads a story he has written, in which a "prehysterical" monster haunts London. Mr. LaLoggia has the right feel for these scenes. "I really liked your story, Frankie," says a sincere little girl dressed as an angel. "I wish I was as weird as you."

Frankie's typical school days and loving family are an effective contrast to his strange, theatening encounters, but the child's traumas are not metaphorical. Mr. LaLoggia wants us to believe in ghosts as well as murder, to be lost in his equivalent of a Halloween tale that will keep us looking over our shoulders as we leave the movie theater. So, first he makes us believe in Frankie; then he shows us the ghosts from the child's point of view.

The hauntings could have been imagined by Frankie, whose room is cluttered with monster comics and werewolf models. Melissa, a translucent apparition, flies through the air. An eccentric recluse (Katherine Helmond) chases Frankie and his friends from an abandoned house. A white-robed woman haunts the bluff where Melissa died, and Frankie even runs through fog-filled woods. Only Frankie and his brother, Geno, ever see ghosts. But Mr. LaLoggia paces his story so quickly, and makes Frankie's perspective so convincing, that we never doubt the reality of the apparitions.

"Lady in White," which opens today at the Coronet and other theaters, has some serious flaws that threaten the film with self-destruction. The story is a flashback, in which Frankie, now a famous writer of suspense novels, returns home to Willowpoint Falls. Now and then we hear an

Eerie Beings Len Cariou co-stars with Katherine Helmond in "Lady in White," set in a small, idyllic-looking suburban town where a series of murders disturbs the peace.

overblown, discordant voiceover that makes the adult writer sound like a comedown from the child. ("Responsibility became my constant companion.")

When a black school janitor is accused of the murders, the heavy-handed subplot about 60's racism loads the film with more social weight than it can carry. And most damaging, we guess who the murderer is very near the film's beginning.

But Mr. LaLoggia glides over even the worst of these pitfalls, carried along by terrific performances. Lukas Haas, the wide-eyed Amish boy in "Witness," is totally natural as the sweet-faced Frankie. Alex Rocco is superbly controlled as the boy's father, a man whose love for his sons is always visible, yet never sentimental. And Jason Presson, as Geno, is everyone's taunting but affectionate older brother. Through them, Mr. LaLoggia creates an unusual, effective child's-eye-view of a sinister wide world, a restless afterlife, and the comforts of family.

●

"Lady in White" is rated PG-13 ("Special Parental Guidance Suggested for Those Younger Than 13"). It could be extremely frightening to children of any age. Some adults at a screening were quite chilled by the intensity of the ending.

1988 My 13, C10:3

Binding Pacifism To Aggression

Peter Phelps

THE LIGHTHORSEMEN, directed by Simon Wincer; screenplay by Ian Jones; director of photography, Dean Semler; edited by Adrian Carr; music by Mario Millo; production designer, Bernard Hides; produced by Mr. Jones and Mr. Wincer; released by Cinecom. At Cinema 1, Third Avenue at 60th Street. Running time: 110 minutes. This film is rated PG.

Dave	Peter Phelps
Tas	John Walton
Chiller	Tim McKenzie
Scotty	Jon Blake
Lieut. Gen. Sir Harry Chauvel	Bill Kerr

By VINCENT CANBY

"The Lighthorsemen" is a technically elaborate, artistically clumsy Australian film that tries to celebrate the heroism of 800 Australian mounted soldiers who triumphed over thousands of Turks and Germans at Beersheba, in southern Palestine, on Oct. 31, 1917. The battle was a key to the eventual Allied victory in the Middle East in World War I.

The film, opening today at Cinema 1, is not to be compared to Peter Weir's much tougher, less starry-eyed "Gallipoli." "The Lighthorsemen" is apparently a labor of love initiated by Ian Jones, who wrote the screenplay and is the co-producer of the film. Like many labors of love, the new movie is full of sincerity not easily appreciated by outsiders.

In what might originally have seemed a bold bid for the widest possible audience, the film takes as its hero a young Melbourne recruit named Dave (Peter Phelps), a natural horseman who is brave beyond words but simply cannot bring himself to shoot his fellow man. He drops out of the Lighthorsemen to become a heroic ambulance driver in the Beersheba campaign.

The result is a sort of pacifist-aggressive war adventure.

●

"The Lighthorsemen" tells the story of the battle in the experiences of Dave and three of his comrades, all of whom share a cheery Rover Boys heartiness that seems awfully smug. This is the kind of war movie in which someone is always getting down on one knee to draw an important diagram in the sand.

The music announces every event before it happens. Thus, just when you most expect it, a line of horsemen will suddenly rise up from behind the crest of a hill to be prettily silhouetted against the sky. The dialogue ("There is no joy in the defeat of an unworthy opponent") has the spontaneity of dispatches from headquarters.

None of the performances are really bad, but none are very good. Mr. Phelps looks a lot like Mel Gibson. Simon Wincer ("Phar Lap") was the director.

●

"The Lighthorsemen," which has been rated PG ("Parental Guidance Suggested"), includes the sort of mildly vulgar soldier language spoken when boys are on their own.

1988 My 13, C14:1

THE RECORD, directed and written by Daniel Helfer; in German with English subtitles; director of photography, Kay Gauditz; edited by Peter R. Adam; music by the Chance; a German/Swiss co-production by the Academy of Film and Television Munich and Cactus Film Zurich, with the assistance of the Berlin Film Fund, Bavarian Television Munich, Swiss Television Zurich and Cinéfilm Zurich. At the Public, 425 Lafayette Street.

Uwe Ochsenknecht in the film "The Record."

Running time: 92 minutes. This film has no rating.

Rico	Uwe Ochsenknecht
Banana	Laszlo I. Kisch
Bigi	Catarina Raacke
P. K. Wütrich	Kurt Raab

By JANET MASLIN

Rico Moreno (Uwe Ochsenknecht) has dark rings under his eyes, and no wonder: he's a pathological video addict with the James Dean and Marilyn Monroe posters to prove it. Rico and his best friend, Banana (Laszlo I. Kisch), have been busily running an ingenious movie-pirating operation, but even when he isn't working, Rico is apt to be glued to the set watching an old movie or perhaps the Academy Awards. As Daniel Helfer's "Record" begins, it appears as if this is enough to keep Rico happy.

But he does dream of an offshore broadcasting station, which would amount to the last word in video piracy and would cost a lot to launch. So a plan is born whereby Rico will try to set the world record for television-watching and then go on the road to repeat this stunt in video-mad places like Tokyo, presumably earning large promotional fees for his trouble. With this premise, Mr. Helfer launches a clever scheme of his own, creating a darkly funny parable. "The Record," which is this young Swiss director's first full-length feature, becomes the ultimate cautionary tale for anyone who's ever lacked the will power to turn off a game show, skip a few commercials or miss the last part of a late-night movie.

●

Rico winds up watching television for 10 days straight, and the movie documents his ordeal in every diabolical detail. The man from the Guinness Book of World Records arrives to wish him luck, and to set up a video camera that will monitor his every move and make sure he isn't dozing. He can take a fixed number of five-minute rest periods, but only if he flashes a sign stating this before the camera's unblinking eye. He can watch anything he likes, and he does — home video movies, porno films or documentaries about Arctic wildlife flicker before Rico's eyes interchangeably, and he seems not to care what he sees. This is the residue of the many years of television addiction that have turned Rico, as his girlfriend Bigi (Catarina Raacke) puts it, into "an optical trash can."

Gradually, Rico's indoor marathon takes its toll. His vision goes blurry. The rings beneath his eyes grow darker. He becomes desperate for images that look natural, and so Banana obligingly takes a video camera to the market and makes an impromptu film about fruit. Eventually things get so bad that Rico is identifying tearfully with an aquatic animal being slaughtered on one program, and turning blue when he sees a cold climate.

His identification with the world of video becomes so scarifyingly complete that he evolves into a human monitor. Even in the hospital, where this condition eventually lands him, Rico is unduly sensitive to anything remotely resembling a television screen. The film's statistic that 800 million people watch television eight hours a day may be exaggerated, but Mr. Helfer uses it to good and sobering effect. With the aid of this alarming figure, he turns "The Record" into a cogent, witty warning about the price of being part of that multitude.

"The Record," which opens today at the Public Theater, is well acted in an appropriately deadpan style, especially by Mr. Ochsenknecht, and its black-and-white cinematography is both good-looking and shrewd; in color, the film's overabundant television footage might well have become unbearable. As it is, this is a brief, clever film with a real point and a light touch. Rico's nightmare feels real, his exhaustion looks genuine, and Mr. Helfer seems to know whereof he speaks.

1988 My 13, C15:1

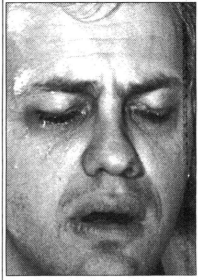

On Watch Uwe Ochsenknecht appears in "The Record" as a man determined to enter the Guinness Book of World Records by establishing a mark for nonstop television viewing.

the boat (John Laughlin) and work for the insurance man (Kim Cattrall). The trouble for which they are inevitably headed involves buried loot on an island near Cuba, but it also involves some notions of love, avarice and treachery that are right out of James M. Cain. Mr. Cain did it better.

Miss Dunaway appears to be taking her role perfectly seriously, which is a fine acting job right there. Miss Cattrall, after "Masquerade," does another good sex-kitten turn. But the men have more trouble; Mr. Travanti makes the insurance man (see James M. Cain on insurance men) even more boorish than he has to be, and Mr. Laughlin wildly overacts a dumb-hunk role. Ned Beatty appears with a scrupulously stained undershirt, a menacing sneer and an English accent that makes no less sense than anything else here.

1988 My 14, 16:5

Tax Cheats and a Japanese Nemesis

"A Taxing Woman" was shown as part of last year's New York Film Festival. Following are excerpts from Vincent Canby's review, which appeared in The New York Times Sept. 26, 1987. The film opens today at the Lincoln Plaza 1, Broadway at 63d Street.

"Violence," says a Japanese gangster bidding a dramatic if temporary farewell to a confederate in handcuffs, "is obsolete. Today we go to prison for tax evasion."

The fine art of underreporting income, and the equally fine art of nabbing those who do, is the all-embracing subject of "A Taxing Woman," the solemnly funny new satire by Juzo Itami, the Japanese director of the comic meditation on noodles, "Tampopo."

It's now clear that Mr. Itami is one of the most original, most free-wheeling sensibilities in movies today — either at home in Japan or abroad. He's robust in a way that we seldom think of as characteristically Japanese. Like "Tampopo," this new movie has a narrative of sorts, and several vividly sketched characters, but "A Taxing Woman" is as much a densely detailed essay on contemporary Japanese manners as it is conventional fiction.

Mr. Itami has the self-assurance and the eye of a born film maker and the mind of the kind of social critic who more often expresses himself in prose. In any other discipline it would be too much to call his work Swiftian, but in movies, where social criticism of this quality is virtually nonexistent, Mr. Itami's sarcasm deserves high praise.

At the center of "A Taxing Woman" is Ryoko Itakura (Nobuko Miyamoto), who, after her divorce, has gone to work in the Japanese equivalent of the Internal Revenue Service to support herself and her 5-year-old son. A seemingly ordinary middle-class woman who wears her hair in a Louise Brooks bob and is self-conscious about her freckles, Ryoko suddenly finds her true calling as a tax inspector.

To all outward appearances, she's pretty, mild-mannered and shy, but on the trail of fraud she has the cool, unjudgmental tenacity of a bird dog with a nose for the second set of books. After serving her apprenticeship successfully terrorizing the aged proprietors of mom-and-pop stores, Ryoko moves into the big time: organized crime. She's promoted to an ultramodern task force whose princi-

pal target is Hideki Gondo (Tsutomu Yamazaki), a suave but gimpy fellow who operates what are called "adult motels" and who specializes in acquiring parcels of real estate from owners who don't want to sell.

The movie is thick with the inscrutably complex methods of tax evasion and with the high-tech methods of the law-enforcement officers. When, at long last, Ryoko and her fellow operatives close in on Gondo's empire, it's with enough precision, planning and Japanese-made electronic equipment to take not only Grenada, but also Barbados and Tobago. The people in "A Taxing Woman" think small but on a grand scale.

The film is more witty than laugh-out-loud funny. "A Taxing Woman" doesn't possess the lyrically oddball footnotes that make "Tampopo" so special. Yet Mr. Itami is a man in touch with the world in which he lives and with the passions of his obsessed characters, which is why Ryoko and Gondo, though inflexible, are so appealing.

Miss Miyamoto (in private life, Mrs. Itami), who plays the ambitious noodle maker in "Tampopo," and Mr. Yamazaki, the philosophizing, noodle-loving truck driver in the earlier film, are wonderfully single-minded and deadpan comics.

"A Taxing Woman" also looks terrific, from its arresting opening shot — an image of a dying old man, past all but infantile needs — to its final, bitter sequence in which Gondo and Ryoko meet for the last time. The setting is a great, deserted baseball park that, in the context of the rest of the movie, could possibly be the prototype for a brand-new export.

1988 My 13, C14:3

Nobly Cheerful Despite Treachery

Faye Dunaway

MIDNIGHT CROSSING, directed by Roger Holzberg; written by Mr. Holzberg and Doug Weiser; director of photography, Henry Vargas; edited by Earl Wilson; production designer, Jose Duarte; produced by Mr. Weiser and Mathew Hayden; released by Vestron Pictures. Warner Theater, 43rd and Broadway; Eastside Cinema, Third Avenue at 55th Street. Running time: 104 minutes. This film is rated R.

Helen Barton	Faye Dunaway
Morely Barton	Daniel J. Travanti
Lexa Shubb	Kim Cattrall
Jeff Shubb	John Laughlin
Ellis	Ned Beatty
Captain Mendoza	Pedro de Pool
Miller	Doug Weiser

By JANET MASLIN

Of all the infirmities that actresses can suffer on the screen, blindness is one of the best. It affords the chance to be nobly cheerful even when, say, the star's husband is embracing one of his cute young employees right before the star's unseeing eyes. And the potential for suspense can be boundless, as "Wait Until Dark" made clear. So it's possible to understand what Faye Dunaway is doing playing a neglected wife in "Midnight Crossing," even though there's nothing but glaucoma to make the role worthwhile.

"Midnight Crossing," which opened yesterday at the Warner and other theaters, does have the makings of a good suspense plot, but in every other way it's badly bungled. The direction, by Roger Holzberg, is entirely without style, and Mr. Holzberg's screenplay is so flat that Miss Dunaway is at one point reduced to staring blankly and crying, "What's happening?" The script also abounds in platitudes ("Jeffrey, if this is what you really want, there's nothing to be ashamed of") and howlers (Husband to newly blind wife: "You can't let this get to you.") The story, which is also by Mr. Holzberg, deserved better.

The film follows a charter voyage by the blind ophthalmologist, Helen Barton (no one can accuse Mr. Holzberg of a light touch), her insurance-man husband of 20 years (Daniel J. Travanti) and the sexy young husband and wife who, respectively, run

Technological Intervention

MANIAC COP, directed by William Lustig; written and produced by Larry Cohen; edited by David Kern; music by Jay Chattaway; released by Shapiro Glickenhaus Entertainment Corporation. At the Criterion Center, Broadway at 45th Street; Movie Center 5, 125th Street between Adam Clayton Powell Boulevard and Frederick Douglass Boulevard. Running time: 92 minutes. This film is rated R.

WITH: Tom Atkins, Bruce Campbell, Laurene Landon, Richard Roundtree, William Smith, Robert Z'Dar and Sheree North

There was an intriguing half-minute during a showing of "Maniac Cop" yesterday, when the film broke. The flaring orange on screen at least livened up this amateurish effort about a monstrously strong uniformed policeman — or is he a civilian in costume? — who roams the streets of New York killing innocent people. The acting is stiff, the dialogue is stiffer and the action scenes are laborious. Even the presence of professionals like Sheree North and Richard Roundtree, in small roles, tend to diminish them rather than improve the film.

"Maniac Cop" opened yesterday at the Criterion Center and other theaters. With no advance screenings, no publicity agents pushing information about the people responsible for this disaster, it's hard to know where the film came from. That doesn't really matter, as long as it goes away soon.

CARYN JAMES

1988 My 14, 16:5

Into the Future To Change the Past

LIGHT YEARS, directed by René Laloux; screenplay adaptation by Isaac Asimov; edited by Simon Nuchtern; music by Jack Maeby, Bob Jewett and Gabriel Yared; produced by Bob Weinstein; released by Miramax Films. At Regency Cinema, Broadway and 67th Street. Running time: 79 minutes. This film is rated PG.

Ambisextra	Glenn Close
Airelle	Jennifer Grey
Metamorphis	Christopher Plummer
Sylvain	John Shea
Chief of the Deformed	Penn Jillette
Shayol	David Johansen
The Collective Voice	Terrence Mann

In the itty-bittiest print imaginable, the ads for "Light Years" indicate that Glenn Close, Christopher Plummer, Jennifer Grey and John Shea appear only in "starring the *voices of*" capacities. In other words, this is an animated film, and it wasn't made with these particular actors in mind.

Originally in French, the English-dubbed "Light Years" retains what must always have been a somber, self-important tone, as well as the topless, blue-skinned vixens who keep it from being ideal family fare. But the heavy-metal adolescent crowd that finds this appealing — along with character names like "Ambisextra," "Blaminhor," "Maxum," "Octum" and "Chief of the Deformed" — may be bored by the film's otherwise well-bred manner.

"Light Years," which opened yesterday at the Regency, is about a hero named Sylvain who lives for 1,000 years, which the film itself certainly will not do. Equipped with a pious subtext about technology gone mad, it follows Sylvain into the future so that he can change the past, a time-trick that has something to do with why the film's characters speak in dual tenses (for instance, "You are/ will be my friends.")

In the land of Gandahar, where Sylvain is prince, all is peace and harmony. The people are kind, the animals friendly, and the landscape rich in things like tuberous-looking blue trees producing bright red volleyball-sized fruit. René Laloux, who made the 1973 "Fantastic Planet," has a great affinity for anything as strange as this, and fills the film with bizarre mutants of all kinds. Foremost among these are a tribe whose members have too many body parts, randomly arranged (mouths on the kneecaps, extra limbs and faces in unusual places).

Anything that can be weirdly shaped or given an extra brain has had this done, but though the artwork is eccentric the animation is conventional and stiff. Isaac Asimov, who adapted the screenplay, has taken a comparably stilted tone. The exposition is both dull and overcomplicated, and the parade of creatures eventually seems limited. The actors, like Christopher Plummer playing a heap of pink protoplasm called Metamorphis, have the strangest roles of their careers.

JANET MASLIN

1988 My 15, 56:1

A Teen-Age Ghoul At Middle Age

FRIDAY THE 13th, PART VII — THE NEW BLOOD directed by John Carl Buechler; screenplay by Daryl Haney; director of photography, Paul Elliott; edited by Barry Zetlin; music by Harry Manfredini and Fred Mollin; production designer, Dick Lawrence; produced by Iain Paterson; released by Paramount Pictures. At Loews Astor Plaza, 44th Street and Broadway; Loews N.Y. Twin, Second Avenue and 66th Street, and other theaters. Running time: 90 minutes. This film is rated R.

Tina	Lar Park Lincoln
Nick	Kevin Blair
Mrs. Shepard	Susan Blu
Dr. Crews	Terry Kiser
Jason	Kane Hodder
Sandra	Heidi Kozak
Melissa	Jennifer Sullivan
Eddie	Jeff Bennett
David	Jon Renfield

By CARYN JAMES

The "Friday the 13th" series may have started as a slasher film and become a teen-age cult favorite, but somehow it has turned into a long-running serial about an odd but familiar neighborhood. Like the evil twin of Lake Wobegon, Crystal Lake is the little town that time forgot, where all the men are dead, all the women are dead and all the teen-agers are above ground — but not for long. Guest corpses come and go, but the malcontented star remains the same — Jason, the mass murderer in the hockey mask. This crazy kid tends to get chained at the bottom of the lake a lot, but he always surfaces in the summer to kill young lovers in the woods.

"Friday the 13th, Part VII — The New Blood," only wishes it had something really new to add to the formula. What it offers instead is a new kid in town, a Carrie clone named Tina, whose telekinetic powers should make her Jason's match.

When she was a child, Tina told her dad, "I hate you, I wish you were dead," and soon he was sleeping with Jason and the fishes at the bottom of the lake. Years later, she returns to the scene and tries to raise Dad from the lake. Up comes the waterlogged Jason. (Don't blame her; it's the kind of mistake any telekinetic teen-ager who killed her father might make.)

Though it's hard to guess how old Jason is in ghoul years, he seems to have hit middle age. There is a lot less blood, less screaming, less energy in this installment, as if Jason has become rather bored with his job. When the inevitable group of teen-agers gather in a lonely cabin for a birthday party, Jason goes through the motions — a knife through the throat here, an ax in the face there —

Crystal Lake's most durable citizen at work in "Friday the 13th, Part VII — The New Blood"

Michael Ansell

as if to say, "Let's get this over with so I can go back to the lake and take it easy."

All that slaughter, of course, leads to a rather dull final showdown, as Jason meets the Carrie clone, who telekinetically rips off the hockey mask to reveal his decomposing skull. (It's vile, but I've seen worse.)

"Friday the 13th, Part VII," which opened Friday at Loew's Astor Plaza and other theaters, should have gone for broke and invited Jason's pals to that birthday party. Freddy Krueger from Elm Street and that cute dog Cujo could have driven up to the lake in Christine the killer car. They'd have met Rocky and Rambo, Superman and Crocodile Dundee, all the serial stars. With any luck, they might have canceled one another out for good.

1988 My 15, 56:5

FILM VIEW/Janet Maslin

Dizzy Dames on New Whirl

THERE'S A BRIEF SCENE IN "Sticky Fingers" in which a woman is tinkering with a shelf on a window ledge that already holds a row of flowerpots. She's the kind of woman who giggles and shrieks and chatters too much while this job is being done. When it's finished, she steps back to admire her handiwork and, of course, the expected thing happens. She's been incompetent, and the flowerpots go splat.

Now, I personally would like nothing less than the sort of film in which this woman turns out to be a better, more commendable carpenter than any man. Still, it's distressing to witness the comeback of the dizzy dame. Silly, ineffectual women are back in fashion on the screen, and what's really peculiar about this phenomenon is its source. Most of the recent films we've seen about cute, bubbly, scatterbrained females have been the work of women directors.

Is this what anyone could have predicted not that many years ago when the scarcity of women film makers was being so widely lamented? And when Elaine May was accused (unfairly) of making cruel use of her daughter Jeannie Berlin in 1973's "Heartbreak Kid," could anyone have anticipated 1987's "Allnighter?"

This too was a mother-daughter film with a sunny setting, but what a difference. Tamar Hoffs, the mother, produced, directed and co-wrote the film that starred her daughter Susanna in a story of witless teen-agers on the prowl, seeking brief sexual flings in honor of their high-school graduation.

In its own way, this was much nastier than Miss May's unflattering shots of Miss Berlin

Ironically, most recent films about cute, scatterbrained females have been by women directors.

eating egg salad.

No one wants to believe that women film makers, given free rein, will seek out material like this, but the recent evidence has not been encouraging. The new breed of giddy female has picked up considerable popularity, and these characters have been proliferating faster than you can say "Madonna."

They aren't necessarily dimwitted, but they love to look that way; they tend to be extremely clever when it comes to things like shopping. Their raffishness is so intensive that achieving it is almost a full-time job. As a consequence, this leaves little time for being boy-crazy; they may be sexually predatory, but that has more to do with being modern than with liking men. Characters like these probably hold less erotic fascination for male viewers than they do for adolescent girls.

■

The women directors who make films about such figures — Susan Seidelman ("Desperately Seeking Susan," "Making Mr. Right"), Catlin Adams ("Sticky Fingers"), Genevieve Robert ("Casual Sex?") — undoubtedly see them as shrewd, but perhaps the audience gets another message. Because these women characters are so much more headstrong than their earlier, less-liberated prototypes, their daffiness becomes not just an affectation but a choice.

When the pert, successful Frankie Stone (Ann Magnuson), the heroine of "Making Mr. Right," is seen in that film's first frames, she is shaving her legs and putting on lipstick while driving her red convertible to the office. These characters' wildly self-contradictory impulses are defined in a single image.

When Frankie or the vacationing roommates Stacy (Lea Thompson) and Melissa (Victoria Jackson) in "Casual Sex?" talk about men, they can be obnoxiously clinical in a very deliberate way; much more clinical, in fact, than male characters would dare be about women in correspondingly mainstream movies.

This overbearing candor plus some visual flourishes — like the gift basket of condoms that winds up in Stacy and Melissa's hotel room — become a way of asserting the characters' modern side, but they also serve as a smoke screen for essentially retrograde values. If these women are aggressive enough about sex and independence, such films seem to say, then they have earned the right to be foolish in most other ways.

"Sticky Fingers," a more ambitious, better-intended dizzy-dame film than most, is one of the most unabashed recent examples of this credo. Its two best-friend characters, Hattie (Helen Slater) and Lolly (Melanie Mayron, who also co-wrote the script), are starving musicians sick and tired of being poor, so when the screenplay sends them a million-dollar windfall they are not in the mood for caution.

They embark on a wild spending spree, which could be funny no matter what the gender of the high rollers. But Miss Adams gives the film an almost all-female cast and treats crazy spending as a giddy, girlish vice, directing her two stars to shriek a lot, talk at the same time and squander money in exceptionally stupid ways.

■

While it's possible to see what sort of effervescence the film is aiming for, any light-hearted humor is dimmed by the sheer idiocy of this behavior. It's also hurt by the impression that Hattie and Lolly are meant to be regarded as backhandedly clever, since there are few real hints of crazy-like-a-fox thinking in anything they do.

"Sticky Fingers" clearly sees these characters as adorable; the likable side of its comic premise does come through. But it also trades heavily on the more charming aspects of playing dumb, and it's sure to make audiences wonder why a woman film maker would see things this way.

Miss Adams may be trying for deliciously offbeat humor, and her characters may not be any more birdbrained than the equivalent men. Still, in this case silliness is a part of the heroines' modus operandi, a quality they value and work hard to achieve. And while the film stresses their independence, it places equal emphasis on this fluffier side. For this current breed of film heroine, femininity and feminism may be almost interchangeable. □

1988 My 15, II:27:1

Bulletproof Daredevil

BULLETPROOF, directed by Steve Carver; screenplay by T. L. Lankford and B. J. Goldman; director of photography, Franci Grumman; edited by Jeff Freeman; music by Tom Chase and Steve Rucker; production designer, Adrian H. Gorton; produced by Paul Hertzberg; released by CineTeleFilms. At Criterion, Broadway at 45th Street; Loews 84th Street Six, at Broadway. Running time: 96 minutes. This film is rated R.

WITH: Gary Busey, Darlanne Fluegel, Henry Silva, Thalmus Rasulala and L. Q. Jones.

By CARYN JAMES

When the opening credits announce "Gary Busey is Bulletproof," you pretty much know what to expect. One of those daredevil cops who can only survive on film, Mr. Busey jumps into a shoot-out with a room full of gunrunners. They have piles of automatic weapons, he has a handgun, yet he escapes with a single bullet in his shoulder. Then he heads home to pluck the teeny bullet out with his tweezers. This is a fairly routine event for him, so he must also be infection-proof, but that medical mystery does not seem to interest the makers of "Bulletproof."

●

Instead, the film takes a sharper curve toward the silly. A Soviet-backed guerrilla force, made up of Cubans, Nicaraguans and some less specific Latin Americans, is massing in Mexico. For reasons the plot never makes clear, the United States Army intentionally lets the Communists capture a secret weapon called Thunderblast, which is a souped-up tank painted in black-and-white zebra stripes. Bulletproof — his name is McBain, but people address him as Bulletproof, even "Captain Bulletproof" — is sent to recapture Thunderblast. And what a coincidence! His former lover, a beautiful blond soldier named Devon, has been taken along with the tank.

How did Gary Busey come to this? It has been 10 years since he starred in "The Buddy Holly Story," and he seems to be drifting farther and farther from any role that might match his talent. In this one-note part his most startling characteristic is the unnatural blondness of his hair — the better to match Devon's, perhaps.

She, at least, has some wonderfully ludicrous lines. "I'll never sell out to you, scum," she tells the despicable guerrilla leader. "In your country you treat women like camels."

•

Steve Carver has directed "Bulletproof," which opened Friday at the Criterion Center and other theaters, as if he were putting together a jigsaw puzzle. He tries this piece, he tries that, he hammers in the pieces that don't quite fit.

1988 My 16, C13:1

Lost in the Stars

Val Kilmer in "Willow."

WILLOW, directed by Ron Howard; story by George Lucas; screenplay by Bob Dolman; director of photography, Adrian Biddle; edited by Daniel Hanley and Michael Hill; music by James Horner; production designer, Allan Cameron; produced by Nigel Wooll; executive producer, Mr. Lucas; released by Metro-Goldwyn-Mayer Pictures Inc. At Loews Tower East, Third Avenue at 71st Street, and other theaters. Running time: 124 minutes. This film is rated PG.

Madmartigan	Val Kilmer
Sorsha	Joanne Whalley
Willow	Warwick Davis
Queen Bavmorda	Jean Marsh
Raziel	Patricia Hayes
High Aldwin	Billy Barty
Kael	Pat Roach
Airk	Gavan O'Herlihy
Burglekutt	Mark Northover
Cherlindrea	Maria Holvoe
Kiaya	Julie Peters
Elora Danan	Ruth and Kate Greenfield

By JANET MASLIN

Today's films have a way of being supplanted overnight. However bright or ground breaking it may be, a new film can be followed in a flash by another that copies and comments on the first, and this process can repeat and repeat itself. So five or six stages of fantasy film making separate the 1977 "Star Wars" from the new "Willow," although George Lucas made his plans for both projects at roughly the same time. Even if the two sets of raw material had been of equal worth, "Willow" would inevitably lie under the long "Star Wars" shadow.

The startling thing about "Star Wars," after all, was its mixture of hip, knowing style and perfect innocence. Though every imaginable adventure-movie flourish found its way into Mr. Lucas's amalgam, "Star Wars" could simultaneously wink and marvel at the cinematic past. But as "Willow" now strives for a similar effect, even "Star Wars" has become fodder. So without anything like the earlier film's eager, enthusiastic tone, and indeed with an understandable weariness, "Willow" recapitulates images from "Snow White," "The Wizard of Oz," "Gulliver's Travels," "Mad Max," "Peter Pan," "Star Wars" itself, the Hobbit saga, Japanese monster films of the 1950's, the Bible and a million fairy tales.

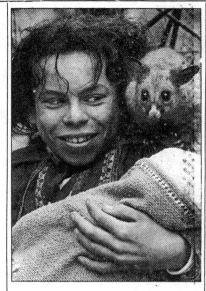

Wee Critters Warwick Davis plays the title role in "Willow," a fantasy by George Lucas about a mythical land inhabited by trolls, brownies and other tiny folk.

One tiny figure combines the best attributes of Tinkerbell, the Good Witch Glinda and the White Rock Girl.

As this may suggest, "Willow" is as vast as it is secondhand. Its scale is an advantage at a time when most other films seem unreasonably small; so is its easygoing sense of humor. And the attempt to stage another huge, ambitious fantasy has a certain nobility even when the film itself does not, so that "Willow" at least creates the sense that its audience is witnessing a legitimate cinematic event. For all but the most hardened fantasy fans, though, the effect will be less than all-enveloping. There is simply too much water over the dam since this idea took flight, and too little new under the sun.

•

And "Willow," which opens today at Loews Tower East and other theaters, doesn't have the perfect pitch of "Star Wars"; much of the time, it seems slightly askew. The title, for instance, suggests a beautiful, lissome heroine or perhaps a cherished tree, but it is in fact the name of a 3-foot 4-inch character (played by Warwick Davis) who doesn't even succeed in holding center stage. Willow is part of a tribe of neo-Munchkins called Nelwyns, and the film nominally centers on a mission that comes his way. A baby named Elora Danan (Kate and Ruth Greenfield) has been cast upon the waters after the evil Queen Bavmorda (Jean Marsh) hears the prophesy that this child will cause her downfall; then Willow finds the little girl and assumes the role of her protector. Bible scholars may well question the need for such novelty.

In any case, after its violent beginning, the film spends an enjoyable sojourn with several hundred Nelwyns, who live in igloo-like structures, are dwarfed by their own farm animals and rely on the teachings of a sorcerer named High Aldwin (Billy Barty, who's funny in this role). When the sorcerer tells Willow to follow his heart, he becomes the Obi-Wan Kenobi of a film that also has its Darth Vader, R2-D2, C-3PO and Princess Leia stand-ins. Much energy has gone into the creation of their names,

some of which (General Kael) have recognizable sources and others (Burglekutt, Cherlindrea, Airk) have only tongue-twisting in mind. Not even the names have anything like "Star Wars"-level staying power.

•

The plot is elaborate, as Willow teams up with a longhaired, barechested warrior named Madmartigan (Val Kilmer) to guard the baby, defeat the evil Queen and, in Madmartigan's case, indulge in amorous, pre-adolescent spatting with the evil Queen's daughter (Joanne Whalley). Among the film's more enjoyable features are some eye-catching, well-photographed mountain scenery; several disarming performances (Mr. Barty's; Julie Peters's as Willow's devoted wife) and some agreeably earnest ones (like Mr. Davis's Willow); unexpectedly convincing medieval-looking landscapes, and a sorceress character who starts out as a muskrat and evolves into many more animals before emerging as an elderly lady (Patricia Hayes).

Though "Willow" bears many signs of the Lucas imagination (Mr. Lucas wrote the story and was the film's executive producer), it has been directed by Ron Howard, whose approach is more matter-of-fact. Mr. Howard appears to have had his hands full in simply harnessing the special effects (like the two tiny characters who scramble around the principals' ankles) and keeping the plot straight, and he doesn't bring any particular color or personality to material that supposedly had these things to spare. However, it's more problematic that the direction doesn't always keep the action in clear focus. Even the battle scenes have been made so briskly businesslike that no particular details stand out in the pandemonium. And Willow, a pleasant but bland character, doesn't often inspire much sentiment, so the film lacks an emotional center. In place of this, it relies on so much overstatement and repetition that it's possible to grow tired even of the adorable baby.

•

"Willow" is rated PG ("Parental Guidance Suggested"). It contains violent scenes that are apt to frighten very young children.

1988 My 20, C8:4

Sibling Risibility

Stephen Kearney

RIKKY AND PETE, directed by Nadia Tass; screenplay by David Parker; director of photography, Mr. Parker; edited by Ken Sallows; music by Eddie Rayner; production designer, Josephine Ford; produced by Ms. Tass and Mr. Parker; released by Metro-Goldwyn-Mayer and United Artists. At Cinema 1, Third Avenue and 60th Street; Running time: 107 minutes. This film is rated R.

Pete	Stephen Kearney
Rikky	Nina Landis
Flossie	Tetchie Agbayani
Whitstead	Bill Hunter
Sonny	Bruno Lawrence
Ben	Bruce Spence

Not every road movie sends its characters off to do their rambling in a Bentley, but then "Rikky and Pete" is substantially out of the ordinary. A charmingly offbeat comedy from Australia, it breaks the road-movie tradition at every turn. The title characters are not runaway lovers or freewheeling pals; instead, they're a well-heeled brother and sister who've simply run out of options in Melbourne for the time being. So they take their mother's car and strike out for parts unknown. "I can remember when all of this was just open land," remarks Pete (Stephen Kearney) as they drive across an absolutely barren, dirt-brown desert.

"Rikky and Pete," which opens today at Cinema 1, hasn't much more sense of purpose than Pete himself, whose career as a mad inventor hasn't led to anything but trouble, or the somewhat less daydreamy Rikky (Nina Landis), who thinks that rehabilitating her crazy brother would be a real accomplishment. Enjoyably lackadaisical, full of odd characters and unexplained little surprises, the film simply trots along in the wake of its adventuring heroes.

Rikky becomes a street singer for a while, and Pete advances her career by identifying her as Eartha Kitt. Rikky and Pete develop a retinue of sorts, including one religious fanatic, one dogged policeman with a long memory for Pete's past exploits, and a selection of nutty, cheerful miners from the little outback town where the brother and sister decide to seek their fortune. Pete strikes up a romance with a beautiful Filipino geologist (Tetchie Agbayani) who has a knack for delightful malapropisms, most of which are unprintable. The family Bentley, inevitably, is cut in half and recycled.

Nadia Tass and David Parker, who made the earlier "Malcolm" and collaborate again on "Rikky and Pete" (she is the film's director and co-producer; he is writer, co-producer and cinematographer), have a wonderful way with sight gags and throwaway humor. "Just going to check out the African violets," says Pete at a family dinner back home in Melbourne, prompting a guest to remark, "I didn't know he was political." In fact, Pete *is* mildly political, or at least he's made a minor career out of baiting the police. In Melbourne, he used his Rube Goldberg-like inventing talents and his way with explosives to become something of a local legend, and when he reaches the outback little has changed. In one scene, Pete gets himself arrested, engineers his way onto the top of a moving paddywagon and stands there triumphantly as the vehicle drives through town, just so that two bewildered officers taking him to jail can be greeted with an unanticipated cheer.

The unassuming, witty manner of "Rikky and Pete" goes a long way toward making it likable, and so do the two stars. Mr. Kearney in particular has fine, offhanded charm and a lovely nonchalance, and the more rational, slightly exasperated Miss Landis makes a perfect foil. "Rikky and Pete," which has been saddled with perhaps the most uninviting ad slogan around ("The thing we do to prove we can do the things we do"), may be the season's nicest surprise.

JANET MASLIN

1988 My 20, C9:1

Deadly Masquerade

Uma Thurman

KISS DADDY GOOD NIGHT, directed by Peter Ily Huemer; screenplay by Mr. Huemer and Michael Gabrieli; director of photography, Bobby Bukowski; edited by Ila V. Hasperg and Ron Goldfinger; music by Don King and Arto Lindsay; production designer, Randy Benjamin; produced by Maureen O'Brien and William Ripka; released by A Beast of Eden Productions. At Variety Theater, 110 Third Avenue, between 13th and 14th Streets. Running time: 87 minutes. This film has no rating.

Laura	Uma Thurman
Sid	Paul Dillon
William B. Tilden	Paul Richards
Johnny	Steve Buscemi
Lara Tilden	Jennifer Lee Mitchell
Sue	Annabelle Gurwitch

By CARYN JAMES

Billed as "a film noir in living color," "Kiss Daddy Good Night" offers the expected seamy, noirish life that inevitably leads to murder. But its unexpected heroine is a more threatening version of Susan Seidelman's harmlessly crooked downtown women. Laura's life of petty crime owes something to "Smithereens" and "Desperately Seeking Susan," though she has an unusually intriguing modus operandi. She assumes an elaborate new identity, goes to clubs or art galleries, and puts the moves on the richest-looking man in the room. Back at his place, she slips something soothing into his drink, and while he's knocked out, she walks off with a few valuables — a 17th-century Italian dagger, a painting cut out of its frame, the cat.

During her lucrative nights of role-playing, Laura is followed back to her apartment. More funky than menacing, it is a place where Donald Duck cartoons play on television endlessly, where her friend Sid crashes while he tries to start up a new band. Her downstairs neighbor, an older man named William, is either a benevolent protector or a close relative of Humbert Humbert. He has an absent daughter named Lara, who looks like Laura, and they both have Lolita pouts.

"Kiss Daddy Good Night" will be shown at midnight tonight and tomorrow at the Variety theater. Setting itself up as a midnight cult film seems like the right way for this work to find its audience, one that values ambition and a quirky vision over polish. The director and co-writer, Peter Ily Huemer, creates a disorienting atmosphere that may have as much to do with a low budget as with style. The scenes are dark, often grainy, often with blue-tinged interiors. Exteriors look so murky that even familiar New York streets appear alien, as if they belonged in someone else's fantasy. (This is true even of a scene shot across the street from The New York Times.)

•

All this fakery — the sudden, blindingly bright shifts to daylight — can be turned to lively effect. But while "Kiss Daddy Good Night" has the ambitious strength of good independent film making, it also has the diffuseness that makes such works threaten to evaporate.

Ironically, the most ordinary part of the film, the murder plot, is the most compelling. The more inventive twist never quite works, because Laura (Uma Thurman) is too vaguely drawn to carry the noirish story. Sid (Paul Dillon) barely exists, though he takes up a lot of screen time searching for musicians. But Paul Richards makes William perfectly enigmatic and sinister.

"Kiss Daddy Good Night" is frustratingly uneven, but it might give relief to anyone sated with Hollywood gloss.

1988 My 20, C11:1

Just Hang Up

CALL ME, directed by Sollace Mitchell; written by Karyn Kay; director of photography, Zoltan David; edited by Paul Fried; music by David Frank; production designer, Stephen McCabe; produced by John E. Quill and Kenneth F. Martel; released by Vestron Pictures. At the Baronet, Third Avenue and 59th Street, and other theaters. Running time: 97 minutes. This film is rated R.

Anna	Patricia Charbonneau
Cori	Patti D'Arbanville
Alex	Sam Freed
Bill	Boyd Gaines
Jellybean	Steve McHattie
Switchblade	Steve Buscemi

"Call Me," the wrong number now at the Baronet and other theaters, is about Anna, who gets a panting phone call one night ("I want you, I want you, I want you."), which soon develops into an aural relationship as she and the caller share their fantasies about imaginative uses for an orange. The dirty talk is the more wholesome slice of Anna's story. The rest of the tale is about several creeps who are chasing her in the mistaken belief that she stole their money.

•

This is a movie that reviews itself. "It's just another awful New York story," says Anna's friend. The big scenes take place in grungy bars, luncheonettes, toilets and parking garages. There are references to junk food. "If this is your idea of a turn on," says Anna, "forget it." Karyn Kay wrote the dreary screenplay and Sollace Mitchell directed in the same spirit. "What a jerk I am!" confesses Anna. And she doesn't even have to watch. *WALTER GOODMAN*

1988 My 20, C11:1

Cat and Mouse

SATURDAY NIGHT AT THE PALACE, produced, directed and photographed by Robert Davies; screenplay by Paul Slabolepszy and Bill Flynn, based on Mr. Slabolepszy's play of the same name; edited by Carla Sandrock; production designer, Wayne Attrill; released by International Film Marketing; At the 68th Street Playhouse, at Third Avenue. Running time: 87 minutes. This film is rated R.

September	John Kani
Vince	Paul Slabolepszy
Forsie	Bill Flynn
Dougie	Arnold Vosloo
Roadhouse owner	Marius Weyers
Sally	Joanna Weinberg

Shot in the stark, underpopulated style of a drama seen on public television, the South African film "Saturday Night at the Palace" serves as a

Tense Times John Kani plays the manager of a hamburger emporium in "Saturday Night at the Palace," a drama set in Johannesburg that explores the turbulent life of contemporary black South Africans.

primer for the roots of that country's racial strife. It is, however, a very obvious and oversimplified work, essentially a three-character play that sustains a one-note quality all the way through. What gives the film energy is the sheer force of the inevitable, since it's clear from the first scenes that the three principals are on a collision course. Luckily, there's also a modicum of surprise to the film's violent and appalling resolution.

"Saturday Night at the Palace," which opens today at the 68th Street Playhouse, began as a play by Paul Slabolepszy, and Mr. Slabolepszy is cast in the film's most reprehensible role. He appears as Vince, an incorrigible white bully whose rage is as vast as it is unharnessed. Vince is first seen setting fire to the net on a soccer field, which is his way of protesting his having been dropped from the team. Later on, Vince and his roommate Forsie (Bill Flynn) attend a party where Vince chugs beer, taunts various men, and alternately abuses and seduces various women.

Meanwhile, a black restaurant worker named September (John Kani) is preparing for a trip home to the family he has not seen in two years. He is as decent and sweet as Vince is thuggish, and has made himself a great favorite with the restaurant's white manager. So September has the job of closing the place, but his two last customers turn out to be Vince and Forsie. The former is looking for trouble and, when he gets to the restaurant, he finds it. The latter, apparently a gentle fellow, becomes the man in the middle.

Mr. Slabolepszy, with his blond, belligerent good looks, does everything he can to be hateful, thrusting his chest forward with as much brutish confidence as he can muster. However, it's clear from the material that the audience is watching a sensitive, responsible fellow impersonating a raging ogre, and this necessarily calls attention to the theatricality of the performance. In addition, the screenplay by the playwright and Mr. Flynn deals in stereotypes so broad that they're almost unplayable, and Mr. Flynn in particular never seems entirely comfortable with his role. While Mr. Slabolepszy rails furiously against the innocent and Mr. Kani conveys September's dignity, intelligence and frustration, Mr. Flynn's position is less clear. Perhaps that's as it should be, since Forsie ultimately represents all that is uneasy and untenable about white South Africa's behavior toward blacks.

"Saturday Night at the Palace" was a success on the stage in South Africa, and the film version indeed has some power. But there's reason to wish it had been less crude. Too much of the dialogue is along the lines of "This isn't a *game* anymore, Vince," and Robert Davies's very plain direction does little to heighten the story's impact. The few glimpses of life among black workers in Troyeville, on the outskirts of Johannesburg, will make audiences wish the film conveyed a stronger visual sense of its setting. *JANET MASLIN*

1988 My 20, C16:1

From Normal Spouse To Ranting Maniac

WHITE OF THE EYE, directed by Donald Cammell; screenplay by China Cammell and Mr. Cammell, from the novel "Mrs. White" by Margaret Tracy; director of photography, Larry McConkey; edited by Terry Rawlings; music by Nick Mason and Rick Fenn; production designer, Phillip Thomas; produced by Cassian Elwes and Brad Wyman; released by Palisades Entertainment. At the Sutton, 57th Street at Third Avenue, and other theaters. Running Time: 111 minutes. This film is rated R.

Paul White	David Keith
Joan White	Cathy Moriarty
Mike Desantos	Alan Rosenberg
Mendoza	Art Evans
Phil Ross	Michael Green
Danielle White	Danielle Smith

"White of the Eye" could be described as a film about everything — about men and women, guilt and innocence, freedom and destiny — but then it could also be described as a film about nothing. It's the work of Donald Cammell, well known in 1970 as the co-director of "Performance" and best known as (in the words of one British journalist) an "occluded talent" since then.

Mr. Cammell, who has meanwhile directed rock videos and co-written an unpublished novel with Marlon Brando, has assembled another "Performance"-like array of mysterious images in "White of the Eye" — intense, veiny close-ups of eyeballs, or a shot of a desperate goldfish lying beached atop a lamb roast, signifying danger. But this time neither fortuitous timing nor elevating camerawork helps to invest such a miasma with meaning, and the results are pretentious, unsightly and vague. "White of the Eye" has a blurry, homemade look and a narrative so lackadaisical that by the second time a bored housewife has been the victim of a grisly murder, the earlier, similar killing has long been forgotten.

"White of the Eye," which opens today at the Sutton and other theaters, asks how a more or less normal husband and father (Paul White, played by David Keith) can evolve into a ranting maniac wearing Indian war paint, a samurai hairdo, and a huge band of explosives strapped across his chest. This would not be a burning question under any circumstances, but it's made especially absurd by the film's self-important manner. In "White of the Eye," a police detective can describe a gory crime scene as resembling a Picasso — not just any Picasso, but a late period Picasso at that. This same policeman (played by Art Evans) can also identify a group of ordinary-looking objects as signifying an ancient Indian compass. "Goes back to before the Vikings," he says with great nonchalance.

Cathy Moriarty, as Paul's wife, Joan, is equally impressive when it comes to casualness, since one scene finds her peeking behind some wood-work in her bathroom to discover a large array of body parts, each wrapped neatly in a paper bag. At this, Joan goes to the phone, calls a friend and asks her to mind the couple's young daughter, citing "marital problems" as the reason.

●

Miss Moriarty and Mr. Keith are both powerful presences here, but Mr. Cammell's elliptical direction keeps the material (a screenplay by the director and his wife, China, from a novel by Margaret Tracy) far out of reach. The characters are fundamentally incomprehensible, the timing way off (the denouement arrives half an hour too early), and the whole story ultimately just a 10-year detour in the life of Joan, who was on her way to Malibu when she first met Paul in the desert near Tucson, Ariz. These on-the-way-to-Malibu scenes have a grainy, high-contrast style that is meant to look very different from the rest of the film, but does not.
JANET MASLIN

1988 My 20, C22:5

Montage Movie

I DON'T GIVE A DAMN, directed by Shmuel Imberman; screenplay (in Hebrew with English subtitles) by Hana Peled, from the novel of the same name by Dahn Ben Amotz; director of photography, Nissim Leon Nitcho; edited by Atara Horenshtein; music by Benni Nagari; production designer, Shlomo Tzafrir; produced by Yair Pradelski and Israel Ringel; released by Trans World Entertainment. At Cinema 3, 2 West 59th Street. Running time: 90 minutes. This film is rated R.

Rafi	Ika Sohar
Nira	Anat Waxman
Maya	Leora Grossman
Eli	Shmuel Vilogeni
Amnon	Shlomo Tarshish
Yigal	DuDu Ben-Ze'ev

By WALTER GOODMAN

"I Don't Give a Damn" is a soapy Israeli movie composed of the residue of better movies past. It is about handsome Rafi (Ika Sohar), who is wounded in battle and loses the use of his legs. "My story ends here in the hospital," says Rafi. Promises, promises. There is at least an hour more to go, which he spends raging against his condition, breaking things and being mean to the people who want most to help him — relatives, friends, other patients and, especially, pretty Nira (Anat Waxman). This fellow is a world-class nudnik.

It was love at first motorbike ride between Rafi and Nira, and the energetic coupling they enjoyed in a sequence exactly like countless other such R-rated limb thrashings remains on Rafi's mind and torments him. It can never be that way for him again. When affectionate Nira arrives at the hospital with love and bagels (which look more like big pretzels), he yells, "Get out of my life, Nira!" And she yells back, "Cripple!" Maybe she should have brought chicken soup.

The director, Shmuel Imberman, spreads the schmaltz like a cholesterol salesman. The actors do not have a chance. When all those people start telling Rafi that he is closing himself off from possible aid and solace, it's like being at a convention of therapists. The scenes of him crashing around in his wheelchair will remind you of "Coming Home," but then, everything here will remind you of something you'd rather be seeing or would rather not have to see again. This sudser, which opens today at Cinema 3, has reportedly been a hit in Israel. Well, those things happen even between allies.

1988 My 20, C22:5

Updating 'A Night At the Opera'

ARIA written and directed by Robert Altman, Bruce Beresford, Bill Bryden, Jean-Luc Godard; Derek Jarman; Franc Roddam; Nicolas Roeg, Ken Russell, Charles Sturridge and Julien Temple; released by Miramax Films. At the Regency, Broadway and 67th Street; Quad Cinema, 34 West 13th Street, West of Fifth Avenue, and other theaters. Running time: 90 minutes. This film is rated R.

FEATURING: John Hurt, Teresa Russell, Nicola Swain, Jack Kayle, Marion Peterson, Valerie Allain, Buck Henry, Anita Morris, Beverly D'Angelo, Elizabeth Hurley, Peter Birch, Julie Hagerty, Genevieve Page, Bridget Fonda, James Mathers, Linzi Drew, Tilda Swinton, Spencer Leigh and Amy Johnson.

By JANET MASLIN

Giuseppe Verdi never cried out "I want my MTV," but he's gotten it anyhow. So have Wagner, Puccini and the other composers whose work has been given the rock-video treatment by 10 opera-loving film directors in "Aria," the composite film that opened yesterday at the Regency. The best of "Aria" isn't any more than cheerful kitsch, and a lot of it is junk. But the underlying idea, that of unleashing these film makers and encouraging them to set their flakiest daydreams to beautiful music, is at least as amusing as it is profane.

The best of the 10 segments is, perhaps predictably, the rare one without lofty pretensions. It's the skit involving an adulterous husband and wife who have both unwittingly scheduled their trysts for the same hideaway, California's blindingly garish Madonna Inn. Directed by Julien Temple, whose vast experience directing bona fide rock videos has given him better-than-average preparation for this job, it makes witty use of "Rigoletto," some of which even comes out of the mouth of an Elvis impersonator. Buck Henry, Anita Morris and Beverly D'Angelo romp mischievously through their brief roles.

On the other end of the spectrum is Bruce Beresford's film of a duet from "Die Tote Stadt" by Korngold in which a man imagines that his dead wife has returned to him. Mr. Beresford — who, along with the rest of the film makers, has evidently been encouraged to work high-toned nudity into the proceedings whenever possible — stages this with the two naked singers perched prettily on a bed. The lip-synching is terrible. And the delayed gratification, always a factor when opera singers stop the action to voice their emotions, is in this case almost a joke.

No less peculiar is Jean-Luc Godard's film set to Jean Baptiste Lully's "Armide." This segment is obscure even by Mr. Godard's standards, which is saying something; while it does derive loosely from the opera itself, the film maker's idea of setting the scene at a gymnasium among weight lifters who utterly ignore two swooning, casually naked young lovelies has its ludicrous side. So does Robert Altman's Grand Guignol approach to Jean Philippe Rameau's "Les Boréades," in which a band of gruesomely made-up extras (partly the cast of Mr. Altman's film "Beyond Therapy") plays an audience of lunatics. The most prettily pretentious segment of all is from Charles Sturridge, the director of "Brideshead Revisited," as he accompanies Verdi's "Forza del Destino" with black-and-white footage of children stealing and burning a Mercedes-Benz.

Ken Russell, avid as ever for both shock and titillation, has turned the "Nessun dorma" aria from Puccini's "Turandot" into a film inspired by the death of a friend; it begins with scenes of a beautiful woman being painted and ornamented, then turns into operating-room footage. Franc Roddam ("Quadrophenia") illustrates the "Liebestod" from Wagner's "Tristan and Isolde" with scenes of young lovers experiencing both passion and grief in Las Vegas, Nev., scenes that would look a lot like soft-core porn if they weren't such aggressively high art.

Bill Bryden casts John Hurt as a performer about to appear in "Pagliacci," in a series of scenes that are meant to connect the other segments, but don't. Derek Jarman has made a lyrical, uncharacteristically tame film in which an old woman recalls her youth, set to the "Depuis le jour" aria from Charpentier's "Louise." Nicolas Roeg, for reasons that are quite obscure, casts his wife, Teresa Russell, as King Zog of Albania and has her wear a mustache.

The work of a group of well-known still photographers, among them Annie Leibovitz and David Bailey, has been assembled in a closing montage that has a lot more punch than most of the film segments. This says quite a lot about the lightweight, superficial nature of the entire "Aria" method. Also on the bill, and perhaps the program's most inspired idea, is the Chuck Jones animated short "What's Opera, Doc?" in which Bugs Bunny appears as Brünnhilde, is chased by a spear-carrying Elmer Fudd and feigns a tragic death. It fits in perfectly with the rest of this pop pastiche.

1988 My 21, 54:3

Winner Lose All

THE SUICIDE CLUB, directed and produced by James Bruce; screenplay by Susan Kouguell and Carl Capotorto; director of photography, Frank Prinzi; music by J. Aaron Diamond; production designer, Stephen McCabe; released by Angelika Films. At the Cine Twin, Seventh Avenue between 47th and 48th Streets; Running time: 90 minutes. This film is rated R.

Sasha	Mariel Hemingway
Michael	Robert Joy
Cam	Lenny Henry
Nancy	Madeleine Potter
Cardinal	Michael O'Donoghue
Catherine	Anne Lange
Boyfriend	Christopher Lawford

By CARYN JAMES

A company that calls itself Suicide Productions Inc. really seems to be

High Stakes Mariel Hemingway stars in "The Suicide Club," about a group of friends who gamble for their lives.

asking for it. "The Suicide Club" won't really prove them wrong, but this Mariel Hemingway vehicle is not the truly terrible film you might expect. It appeared without advance press screenings after a couple of delayed opening dates.

Loosely suggested by a Robert Louis Stevenson story updated to the 1980's, Ms. Hemingway (one of the film's producers, with her husband, Steve Crisman) plays an heiress named Sasha. She is lured by a seductive stranger to a mansion where costume parties seem to be in constant progress, highlighted by a card game. The game's winner is obligingly killed.

Sasha, we're told and never begin to believe, is guilt-ridden because of her brother's suicide and is willing to escape her own empty life. But the parties seem to be the actual point of the film. Characters traipse around in vaguely baroque or Renaissance-looking clothes (interesting but cheesy-looking). Ms. Hemingway and Madeleine Potter, as the party's evil hostess, wear huge headdresses and subtly feud over the attentions of Lenny Henry, as Ms. Potter's adopted brother and lover.

All this sounds sort of Edgar Allan Poe-ish. And if the Stevenson story reads like second-rate Poe, the film's costumed masques are much closer to Roger Corman's B-movie versions — something that James Bruce, the film's director and a Louis Malle protégé, does not seem to realize. He does not have the flair to make these scenes either suspenseful or parodic (even though Michael O'Donoghue, like a ghost from the old "Saturday Night Live," prances around dressed as a cardinal). Neither high art nor low camp, "The Suicide Club" is much closer to a television movie of the week.

1988 My 21, 54:5

Apocalypse Later

WORLD GONE WILD, directed by Lee H. Katzin; screenplay by Jorge Zamacona; director of photography, Don Burgess; edited by Gary A. Griffen; music by Laurence Juber; production designer, Donald L. Harris; produced by Robert L. Rosen; released by Apollo Pictures. At the Warner Theater, 43rd and

Arid Action Bruce Dern portrays a survivor of a nuclear war that has ravaged the planet and made water a precious commodity, in "World Gone Wild."

Broadway; Running time: 94 minutes. This film is rated R.

Ethan	Bruce Dern
George Landon	Michael Paré
Angie	Catherine Mary Stewart
Derek Abernathy	Adam Ant
Ten Watt	Anthony James
Exline	Rick Podell

Mad Max mania is the guiding force behind "World Gone Wild," which opened Friday at the Warner theater and was greeted by only a curious few. At the very beginning of this standard-issue post-apocalyptic nightmare, a group of machine-gun-toting choirboys arrive at a desert commune full of over-the-hill hippies and proceed to mow down almost everyone in sight.

The time is the future, and the battle turns out to be over water, which has become the planet's most precious commodity. In films that are chips off the "Mad Max" block, isn't that always the way? The urban settings are dismal and dark, filled with rubble, and the populace is bestial and badly dressed. "World Gone Wild" at least aspires to some marginal humor, since it casts Adam Ant as the leader of the choirboys and has him read to them solemnly from the writings of Charles Manson. Bruce Dern is also a droll choice as the hippies' senior statesman, a fellow named Ethan who makes frequent wisecracks and takes so many drugs he can't be sure how much of this nastiness is real.

Michael Paré and Catherine Mary Stewart play the ingenue roles, to the extent that a story like this can have one. Miss Stewart plays the only remaining schoolteacher around, educating children from the only four books that are still in existence. One of these is "Iacocca."

JANET MASLIN

1988 My 22, 49:5

The Old College Try

SLAUGHTERHOUSE ROCK, screenplay by Ted Landon; directed by Dimitri Logothetis; director of photography, Nicholas Von Sternberg; edited by Daniel Gross; music by Mark Mothersbaugh and Gerald V. Casale; production design, Peter Paul Raubertas; produced by Louis George; released by Taurus Entertainment Company. At the Criterion, Broadway at 45th Street; other theaters; Running time: 97 minutes. This film is rated R.

Sammy Mitchell	Toni Basil
Alex Gardner	Nicholas Celozzi
Richard Gardner	Tom Reilly
Carolyn Harding	Donna Denton
Krista Halpern	Hope Marie Carlton
Jan Squires	Tamara Hyler
Jack	Steven Brian Smith
Marty	Ty Miller

"Slaughterhouse Rock" brings together the usual suspects of teen-age horror films: murder, rock music, sex, low budgets. Alex, a college student, is possessed by the spirit of a cannibal-ghost buried beneath Alcatraz, released from his grave by a dead rock star. In order to exorcise the spirit from his dreams, Alex and a half-dozen of his most foolhardy friends head for Alcatraz in the middle of the night, where they stumble over skeletons, corpses and many live rats. Alex's brother sprouts vampire fangs, the better to kiss his unsuspecting girlfriend.

There is always a way to improve on a stock formula, but "Slaughterhouse Rock," which opened yesterday at the Criterion Center and other theaters, manages to make these elements seem much worse and even more tired than they are. The only brief bright spot is Steve Brian Smith, who is amusing as Alex's wisecracking friend. According to the production notes, Mr. Smith, a stand-up comic, wrote many of his own lines. He should have written the others.

CARYN JAMES

1988 My 22, 49:5

NEW YORK/John Gross

Two New Movies Suggest That Shock Tactics Are Best Muted In a Work of Art

ONE OF THE MINOR OBsessions of the British writer Cyril Connolly was the murder of Lord Erroll in Kenya in 1941. But fascinating though he found the case (and officially, it has never been solved), there came a point when he couldn't help noting down his distaste for most of the characters involved.

"What a set!" he reflected, as he went through them one by one. Lord Erroll himself may have been the 22d earl, but he was also, in Connolly's view, a four-letter word. Sir Jock Delves Broughton, who was charged with shooting Erroll — his wife's lover — and acquitted, may have been the 11th baronet, but he was also a crook; and other leading players in the drama were variously summed up as drunk, sadistic, and dotty.

James Fox's account of the affair, "White Mischief," which he began writing under Connolly's tutelage, has now been made into a movie of the same name — or rather, it has provided the inspiration for a movie that differs from the book in a number of significant respects. Some of these are simply the result of the inevitable need to compress, but others are questions of emphasis and interpretation; and their general effect is to cast a romantic glow over the story, to soften the edges of the characters and make them out as more agreeable or more considerable people than they were.

This naturally means a loss of shock value, which, in principle, is a pity. But shock tactics in a work of art call for exceptional skill, and given the choice, it is usually better to play down sensationalism than to overindulge in it. Another new movie, Ken Russell's "Salome's Last Dance," provides an instructive example of what happens when a director puts his faith in unremitting excess.

The toning down of the "White Mischief" story is most obviously the case in the movie's characterization of Jock Delves Broughton. He is given a weight and a dignity in Joss Ackland's performance that the real baronet — if we are to believe the testimony collected by James Fox — was very far from possessing. But both Broughton's wife, Diana, and the insatiable Erroll have had their acts tidied up, too: there was something at once tougher and more tawdry about the originals.

I must confess to being of two minds about such changes. They make for a more generous film than you would have gotten if the director, Michael Radford, had aimed at a faithful transcript of the book. We are asked to believe that, with all their faults, these people are worth caring about. But since we are never quite persuaded that they *are* worth caring about, the final effect is one of hollowness. The film is well made and well acted; it moves forward briskly and evokes its period skilfully. But none of it reverberates or goes very deep.

Perhaps the film would have more of an impact if Mr. Radford (who also wrote the script, in collaboration with Jonathan Gems) had taken a more harshly realistic line. Perhaps we should have been shown the side of Erroll that enabled him to become a paid-up member of the British Union of Fascists, for example — admittedly only for a year or so, but he was a man in his 30's at the time, not a raw youth. Or possibly we should have been shown the actual circumstances of Broughton's death, which were somewhat more prosaic than those devised by the scriptwriters (in reality he died in a hotel in Liverpool, rather than on his estate in Africa), but no less grim.

Yet it is by no means certain that a more unsparing approach would have produced better results. Whenever the film tries too hard to document the dissolute ways of rich white settlers in Kenya 50 or 60 years ago — the socialite types who ran wild in the notorious "Happy Valley" region, at least — it tends to come unstuck.

Sarah Miles, who plays the no-holds-barred Alice de Janzé, has to bear most of the burden here, showing up at a polo match with a snake twined round her neck, or taking time out in the middle of a party for a quick jab with a hypodermic. There really was an Alice de Janzé (she was an American, whose money came from the Armour meat-packing fortune) and most of the tricks we see her getting up to are fully documented by James Fox. But in the movie they seem merely tiresome, and her constant would-be wicked little smile seems merely silly.

To be fair, there are one or two scenes of dissipation that work a good deal better — a listless party where it hardly seems to make any difference that the guests are all wearing drag, for example. But on the whole you feel grateful to Mr. Radford for his restraint, for not falling too greedily on the opportunities for outrageousness that Happy Valley offered. He has a much surer touch with the superior, rather Maughamish soap opera for which he mostly opts.

The Perils of Excess

In fact, it isn't quite as easy to be outrageous as some people suppose. Such is the chief, perhaps the only lesson to be derived from the films of Ken Russell, who has now turned his attentions to Oscar Wilde.

Most of us have known what to expect from Mr. Russell for a long time, but I tried to approach "Salome's Last Dance" with an open mind. After all, Wilde's "Salome" is such a gaudy piece of work that it might conceivably lend itself to the Russell treatment where Tchaikovsky and Byron and his other previous subjects have simply been maltreated and mauled.

Alas for my optimism. Mr. Russell can't leave well alone, even when he has a congenial text, and he is still intent on piling shock upon shock. He bombards us with nipples, body paint, green carnations, rude noises, anachronisms (cigarettes and fruit sundaes at the court of King Herod), sexual acrobatics, any amount of purple

Sarah Miles and Charles Dance in "White Mischief"—It is usually better to play down sensationalism than to overindulge in it.

mischief and crimson mischief. The participants in the revels include a trio of midgets dressed as Hasidim, and a Queen Herodias got up like Lady Macbeth.

Wilde himself makes an appearance, too. He is the one-man audience of the play within a play — for what we are watching is supposed to be the world premiere of "Salome," put on for the author's benefit in a brothel (with Wilde's lover, Lord Alfred Douglas, playing John the Baptist) after the censor has decreed that it cannot be presented in public.

Through the murk, you can vaguely make out some parallels between the drama on stage and Wilde's ill-fated private life. But they soon disappear amid a welter of luscious or sinister images, crude jokes and cheap whiz-bang thrills.

There are a few good strokes, although one of them is likely to be lost on most Americans. The plump brothel keeper who organizes the entertainment and takes the part of King Herod is played by Stratford Johns, an actor as irrevocably associ-

ated in Britain with his portrayal of a blunt detective inspector on television as Telly Savalas is with Kojak or Peter Falk with Columbo.

For anyone who has seen him in the role, he makes an even more startling apparition than he otherwise might, with his overripe mannerisms and heavily rouged cheeks. He turns in a powerful performance, too, as far as the chaotic conditions created by Mr. Russell permit: This is Herod with a touch of Hermann Goering.

If only Mr. Russell had been con-

tent to make a film of "Salome," he might have produced a rather good picture. As it is, the incessant shocks cancel one another out, and the vulgarities completely undercut the visual inventiveness. Mr. Russell does his best to whip up a good orgy, but watching the antics on screen I couldn't help recalling Henry James's comment to someone who told him that he had read a "daring" novel and been suprised to find how little it stirred him: "Ah, yes, the abysses are all so shallow." ☐

1988 My 22, II:43:1

FILM VIEW/Vincent Canby

'Patty' Launches a Major Star

CANNES, France

JUST 19 YEARS AGO VANESSA REDGRAVE, PERhaps one day to be known as the mother of Natasha Richardson, won the Cannes Film Festival's best-actress award for her bravura performance as Isadora Duncan, the dancer and all-American romantic who had a fatal fondness for long scarves. The film was Karel Reisz's "Isadora."

At this writing, one-third of the way into the 41st Cannes festival, it seems entirely possible that Natasha Richardson might win this year's best actress award for Paul Schrader's

"Patty Hearst," a biographical film that is less about an extraodinary character than about an extraordinary event.

Critics appear to be what is politely called divided by Mr. Schrader's movie, one of 22 films competing for the festival's grand prize. In cinematic terms, "Patty Hearst" is as spare and rigorous as a line drawing. However, there seems to be no argument about the exceptional quality of Miss Richardson's performance. The 25-year-old English actress is astonishingly fine as the Hearst publishing heiress who, in 1974, was kidnapped from her Berkeley, Calif., apartment by the self-styled Symbionese Liberation Army and wound up spending 18 months as an apparently enthusiastic, gun-toting member of the radical gang.

With "Patty Hearst," Miss Richardson, whose father is Tony Richardson, the director, acquires her own identity as a major actress on the international scene. From now on, her bloodlines need only be noted by "Who's Who in Film and Theater."

"Patty Hearst" is the first festival film to be seen so far that is worthy of being called controversial. It's a movie that gives value to legitimate argument. Before it was shown on

May 14, the festival had the air of a bizarre mass funeral, a hysterical event where the mourners were ready to trample each other to death to secure a place at the grave site.

The disgruntled critic for the newspaper Nice-Matin noted the festival's intention to be *pur et dur* (pure and difficult), and added that it was mostly *dur à avaler* (difficult to swallow). The early films have not been great.

There was the attempt to show a crowd pleaser on opening night, Luc Besson's "Big Blue," an elaborate, very expensive French film about deep-water free diving, shot in English, with Rosanna Arquette as its American star.

This was followed by even bigger anticlimaxes, including "El Dorado," another physically complex production, written and directed by Spain's Carlos Saura at huge cost on location in Costa Rica. Its only shocks were negative ones. Mr. Saura's reputation as a cinema original is based on his series of small-scale, poignant domestic dramas ("The Hunt," "La Prima Angelica," "Cria," among others), in which he dealt with life in Spain under the Franco regime in ways that somehow confounded the censors.

In "El Dorado," Mr. Saura chooses to tell the story of the same Lope de Aguirre who is the subject of Werner Herzog's mad, spectacular classic "Aguirre: The Wrath of God." Mr. Saura's Aguirre, played by Omero Antonutti, is finally no less obsessed than Mr. Herzog's, but both he and the movie are inert.

Considering Mr. Herzog's achievement, why would Mr. Saura want to devote so much time, effort and creative energy to the same story about the 16th-century Spanish adventurer who attempted to carve his own independent kingdom out of the Amazon jungles? One answer was to set some historical facts straight.

Also — and this is clearly apparent in the finished film — to draw parallels between then and now. Mr. Saura finds similarities between the politics of the Aguirre expedition, in which each succeeding leader either murders or is murdered by those who would follow him, and contemporary Latin American regimes in which coups d'état are virtually a constitutional obligation.

The fault with the film is not in its ideas, but in Mr. Saura's lethargic production. "El Dorado" is a series of dozy tableaux vivants in which characters, as in a pageant, confront each other, argue and then draw swords to spear each other. The Amazon has never flowed so slowly.

■

Germany's Margarethe von Trotta, whose last film was the successfully heroic and complex "Rosa Luxemburg," overreaches herself in a modern variation on Chekhov's "Three Sisters," called "Trois Soeurs" here and "Paura e Amore" in Italy, where it was made. To her credit, the idea seems not to have been hers originally, but one suggested by Angelo Rizzoli, the producer. Yet she took the bait.

Her three sisters are played by a French actress (Fanny Ardant), by Greta Scacchi, who spent her formative years in Australia, and by an Italian actress (Valeria Golino). The film is full of obvious, post-synchronized dubbing. This sort of thing is commonplace in European films, but it becomes downright eerie in a scene in which one of the sisters is shown as she watches television while a similarly Italian-dubbed Paul Henried and Bette Davis puff away on those two cigarettes he's just lit so suavely. The movie, set in the university town of Pavia, is more about 20th-century sisterhood than it is about Chekhov, though Ms. von Trotta dips into Chekhov to make her small point (Happiness does not exist. Only the attempt to achieve it is real).

Nobody longs to fly off to Rome, but, by the end, some members of the audience would have settled for Moscow.

In this context, Mr. Schrader's "Patty Hearst" is as bracing as a month in the country or, at least, as a couple of hours of good, old-fashioned, tasteless American prime-time television, which it resembles not at all. "Patty Hearst" is a truly tough movie. In the superficial respect that it deals with an actual event, involving actual characters living and dead, it recalls a television docudrama, but it's no more a docudrama than is Camus's "Stranger."

Mr. Schrader, and Nicholas Kazan, who wrote the screenplay, tell the harrowing story entirely from Patty's point of view. Yet they never attempt to enter her mind except in some brief, almost subliminal images in which Patty, during her weeks of isolation in a closet, feels as if she's being buried alive or begins to see distorted, nightmare visions of her past.

■

The film's Patty, which Ms. Richardson plays with a miraculously, accurate (and funny) California equivalent to the East Coast WASP accent, is a sweet, well-meaning but not exactly introspective member of the haute bourgeoisie. In captivity, she's as utterly passive as she seems to have been before her kidnapping. At the same time, there's a hint of steely invulnerability in that passivity. Mr. Schrader and Mr. Kazan do not fall into the television game of shaping Patty's story into some sort of upbeat moral tale of deprivation and redemption.

Their Patty seems to be an empty vessel. This has troubled a number of critics here who feel that the film thus lacks a moral frame to give it some larger meaning or application. This is also precisely why "Patty Hearst" is so profoundly scary and, in the breathtaking last scene, so moving. Empty vessels are people, too.

"Patty Hearst" has no neat answers. Instead it forces the audience to speculate about Patty's ordeal in ways that are flattering neither to Patty nor, more importantly, to the viewer. What would I have done? And, if it comes down to that, am I any less empty a vessel than Patty?

In remarks to members of the press after the screening, Mr. Schrader acknowledged that the story raises moral issues about which he himself still had some doubts. He also worried about criticism to the effect that the film appeared to make the members of the Symbionese Liberation Army look like some sort of gang that couldn't shoot straight, even though they did kill.

One thing about which he has no doubt, however, is that Patty Hearst received a raw deal in being brought to trial, prosecuted, convicted and imprisoned (though pardoned in 1979 by President Carter). It was, in a way, as much of a political act as (and a more serious political act than) Patty's voluntary association with the captors who had so effectively brainwashed her.

"Patty Hearst" is a cool, very laid back adult movie.

1988 My 22, II:21:5

A One-Man War In Afghanistan

RAMBO III, directed by Peter Macdonald; screenplay by Sylvester Stallone and Sheldon Lettich, from the novel by David Morrell; director of photography, John Stanier; edited by James Symons, Andrew London, O. Nicholas Brown, Edward A. Warschilka; music by Jerry Goldsmith; production designer, Bill Kenney; produced by Buzz Feitshans; released by Tri-Star Pictures. At the Loews 84th Street Six, Broadway at 84th Street; Criterion Center, Broadway at 45th Street, and other theaters. Running time; 104 minutes. This film is rated R.

Rambo .... Sylvester Stallone
Trautman .... Richard Crenna
Zaysen ....Marc de Jonge
Griggs ....Kurtwood Smith
Masoud ....Spiros Focas
Mousa ....Sasson Gabai

By JANET MASLIN

"The first was for himself," say the ads for "Rambo III." "The second was for his country. This time is for his friend." And the next may be for returning an overdue library book, but whatever John Rambo's reason for raising hell, there's one point that should never be misunderstood. John Rambo does *not* do these things because he enjoys them. He does *not* take any personal satisfaction in (to use just one small example) attaching a rope and a large rock to an adversary, then pulling the pin on a grenade so that it will explode as the man falls into an underground cave.

Fun for Rambo? Not at all. Rambo is revealed as a long-suffering, deeply religious person who would much rather be repairing the roof of a Thai monastery, which is what he's seen doing at the beginning of "Rambo III." However, "Rambo III" has a prologue of sorts, so that before the credits have even finished rolling Rambo is seen sweating, quivering and sneering his way through a stick-fighting match with a Thai opponent, as hundreds of local fans make bets and cheer.

"I just do that for a little extra money," Rambo explains modestly to his old friend Colonel Trautman

Sylvester Stallone is back as the action-film hero in "Rambo III," which opens today at the Criterion.

(Richard Crenna), who has come to recruit him for another one-man war, this time in Afghanistan. As Trautman quickly notes, and Rambo is far too self-effacing to mention, he gives the money he inevitably wins in such contests to the monks.

•

So "Rambo III," which opens today at the Criterion and other theaters, has a messianic streak, a pious tone and a bad tendency toward false modesty. But it also has a lot more. Even those who question Rambo's methods and his motives will have no choice but to acknowledge his very real accomplishments, along with those of Sylvester Stallone, who this time seems to know exactly what the global action-film audience would like to see. Mr. Stallone, having pumped his way to body-building perfection, has written (with Sheldon Lettich) for himself the latter-day narcissist's version of a John Wayne role, and forcefully re-invented the western to accommodate the character's munitions-mad, avenging-angel style.

Even though some parts of "Rambo III" are goofily idiosyncratic, the best of it is tried-and-true cowboy material, complete with cavalry charge. And modern special-effects technology, a huge budget and Mr. Stallone's own derring-do have conspired to let the film pack a wallop that no traditional western or war film could match. Everything here is larger than life, from Rambo's barrel-sized neck to the extent of his

wild-man bravado. When the lone Trautman and Rambo are cornered at the end of the film, their backs literally to the wall as an unbelievably large army of Soviet tanks and soldiers demand their surrender, Rambo's reply (unprintable here) has a real, if demented, grandeur. In every corner of the globe where "Rambo III" is seen, this moment is guaranteed to bring down the house.

"Rambo III" is dedicated "to the gallant people of Afghanistan," and it clearly intends that its politics be taken seriously. The plot sends Rambo into Afghanistan on a rescue mission after Trautman, who has been educating Afghan freedom fighters in the ways of Stinger missiles and is taken prisoner by a smirking, strutting Soviet colonel (Marc de Jonge). This casts Trautman in the unenviable role of political mouthpiece, as he lectures the colonel about Soviet foreign policy. And it makes the Afghan fighters, who are this film's noble Indians, entirely one-dimensional. "What we must do is stop this killing of our women and children," one fighter earnestly explains. And the film, for all its grandstanding, never goes any deeper.

•

Mr. Stallone has by now made Rambo parody-proof, since the character is every bit as laughable as he is grandiose; that's part of the fun. Rambo's self-important, weight-of-the-world manner and his taste for political posturing would make him

genuinely silly were they not counterbalanced by Mr. Stallone's startling, energetic physical presence and the film's stabs at self-mocking humor. ("That was close, John!" declares Trautman with supreme understatement, as yet another round of explosions nearly incinerate them.)

Still, the dialogue tends to be more inadvertently comical than necessary, laced with heavy sadism and predictable turns of phrase ("You've tried my patience long enough!"). The lines that are meant to stand out ("Who do you think this man is? God?" "No, God would have mercy. He won't") are often less memorable than the ones that aren't.

"Rambo III," directed by Peter Macdonald with a real flair for hard-hitting action scenes, is certain to pave the way for many more installments of the Rambo saga. And the scene against which the character's future exploits are measured may well be the one in which Rambo advances his study of amateur medicine, and adds mightily to his he-man credentials, by removing a spike from his side. Instead of pulling the spike out directly, he creates a second wound by forcing it through, then cauterizes both spots by lacing them with gunpowder. He then lights a spark. Don't try this at home.

1988 My 25, C15:1

Unique Gift For Inaction

CROCODILE DUNDEE II, directed by John Cornell; screenplay by Paul Hogan and Brett Hogan; director of photography, Russell Boyd; edited by David Stiven; music by Peter Best; production designer, Lawrence Eastwood; produced by John Cornell and Jane Scott; released by Paramount Pictures. At Loews Astor Plaza, Broadway at 44th Street; Manhattan Twin, Third Avenue at 59th Street; other theaters. Running time: 110 minutes. This film is rated PG.

Mick (Crocodile) Dundee ....Paul Hogan
Sue Charlton ....Linda Kozlowski
Walter Reilly ....John Meillon
Charlie ....Ernie Dingo
Rico ....Hechter Ubarry
Miguel ....Juan Fernandez
Leroy ....Charles Dutton
Brannigan ....Kenneth Welsh

The screen success of Mick (Crocodile) Dundee is based, quite literally, on nothing. Nothing is the thing that Dundee, in the disarming person of the Australian star Paul Hogan, does best. Mr. Hogan's calm, unflappable reactions to the various facts of New York City life were the comic foundation of "Crocodile Dundee," turning its mild, genial humor into box-office gold. It would be natural to expect more of the same from "Crocodile Dundee II," but the sequel often lacks the sense to leave well enough alone.

"Crocodile Dundee II," which opens today at Loews Astor Plaza and other theaters, is noticeably longer than the first film, and it's less enjoyably lazy. This time, stranded in New York, Dundee has begun to grow

Paul Hogan (left), Jerry Skilton and Steve Rackman in " 'Crocodile' Dundee II"

restless, and the film itself shows a comparable malaise. This is apparent right away, in the scene that shows Dundee up to his old outdoorsman's tricks, dynamiting fish in the middle of New York Harbor. The police arrive, and when they recognize Dundee they shake their heads with rueful admiration, as do a group of children in a playground scene moments later. It's a danger sign when a character is allowed to grow lovable in this way.

•

The plot — and that's the main trouble with "Crocodile Dundee II"; it *has* one — soon involves Dundee with a Colombian drug kingpin. This mastermind, named Rico (Hechter Ubarry), has kidnapped Sue (Linda Kozlowski), the stylish Newsday reporter with whom Dundee has now moved in. So the screenplay, by Mr. Hogan and his son Brett, must trump up a reason for the abduction, let Mick Dundee do a lot of worrying as proof of how much he loves Sue, and otherwise create too much unremarkable action and too much of an actor's role for Mr. Hogan, whose great gift is for offhand humor. Only late in the film, when he has returned to Australia and begun playing practical jokes involving bats and alligators, does Dundee have much chance to shine.

The film's first hour, the one set in New York, also has quite a touristy tone. There are urban caricatures for Dundee to marvel at, street scenes that would warm the heart of any travel agent, a tour of Bloomingdale's (where Dundee has a brief chance to use his woodsman's skills), and even an official tour guide showing off "the legendary New York City subway." Natives will find these touches at least as peculiar as they are picturesque.

Every so often, Mr. Hogan is given a chance to show off Dundee's unique gift for inaction, as when he copes with a stranger's suicide attempt by feigning absolute indifference to the man's problems and suggesting that he hurry up. These episodes are very welcome, since Mr. Hogan remains a likable fellow under any circumstances, even when John Cornell's direction is so slow it takes the snap out of the actor's comic timing. But too often, Mr. Hogan's amusing moments give way to the tedious, overacted exploits of the drug kingpin and his henchmen, who have their headquarters in a suburban mansion and who smirk endlessly about their ill-gotten gains. The kingpin remains a large part of the story even after Dundee and Sue have fled to Australia for a change of scene.

"Crocodile Dundee II" has been attractively photographed, if unremarkably directed, and it aims for affable, low-key escapism just as the first film did. But the earlier one had novelty to keep it going, and this time the novelty has begun to wear thin, even if Mr. Hogan remains generally irresistible. This time, he is so much more charming than anything else on the screen that no one in the cast (even Miss Kozlowski, who never brings much wit or glamour to her role) is a match for him. A man who's capable of leaving a three-foot, bandanna-wearing lizard as his calling card requires a less contrived, better designed vehicle for his talents.

•

"Crocodile Dundee II" is rated PG ("Parental Guidance Suggested"). It contains some strong language.
JANET MASLIN

1988 My 25, C15:3

Looming Shadows And Fancy Talk

THE TALE OF RUBY ROSE, written and directed by Roger Scholes; director of photography, Steve Mason; edited by Ken Sallows and Mr. Scholes; music by Paul Schutze; art director, Bryce Perrin; produced by Bryce Menzies and Andrew Wiseman; released by Hemdale. At the Cinema Village, 22 East 12th Street. Running time: 102 minutes. This film is rated PG.

Ruby Rose	Melita Jurisic
Henry Rose	Chris Haywood
Gem	Rod Zuanic
Bennett	Martyn Sanderson
Grandma	Sheila Florance
Cook	Sheila Kennelly
Tasker	John Mckelvey
Dad	Wilkie Collins
Mrs. Bennett	Nell Dobson

By WALTER GOODMAN

"The Tale of Ruby Rose" tries hard to live up to the mountains and mists of Tasmania's central highlands, where it is set in 1933, but the story cannot compete with the country's rugged grandeur. Ruby Rose makes her rough home in the wilderness with her trapper-skinner husband, Henry, and a young fellow whom they have adopted. Henry is not a bad sort beneath his unshaven cheeks, and Gem, the foster son, is a sensitive lad who gets upset by the trapper's trade. "I don't like to kill 'em," says Gem. "It's part of life, boy," says Henry. "Things grow and you kill 'em."

As for Ruby Rose, she wakes nightly in terror of the dark, which is filled with animal snorts and screams. She has a mystical or merely superstitious side, and is given to sprinkling around a whitish powder of some sort and painting the walls white to keep out the darkness. She says to herself: "Death roams in the dark. To keep away the dark is to keep away death." For a near illiterate woman, she sure talks fancy: "The dark has got into the heart. There is something that must be scoured."

That sort of populist pretentiousness, a burden on appealing Melita Jurisic, who plays Ruby Rose, pervades the camerawork, the lighting and the music. The rest of the cast is convincingly down to earth, and Roger Scholes, who wrote and directed the film, brings a documentary strength to scenes out among the animal snares, in a timber camp, at a recital by a touring soprano. But all those looming shadows and flying sparks and the straining after blank verse carry his movie away from reality without quite achieving legend.

Something draws Ruby Rose down to the valley, quite a journey for a young woman on foot, back to her father's house. There, she meets her old grandmother for the first time and they enjoy a romp together in a tin bathtub, a happy respite from the slogging story. Ruby Rose also learns what the trauma was that has kept her frightened all these years. The information may make her more comfortable with the dark, but it does not do much for her common sense, since she thereupon undertakes the trek back up to the highlands in a snowstorm, carrying a chair on her head.

Ruby Rose's tale, which is being played out at Cinema Village, is undernourished and overcooked, like the possums on which the household survives. The highs come mainly from the highlands.

"The Tale of Ruby Rose" is rated PG ("Parental Guidance Suggested.") It shows a few graphic glimpses of trapped animals.

1988 My 25, C18:6

The Immigrants' Tale

DRAGON CHOW, directed and co-written by Jan Schutte; screenplay by Thomas Strittmatter (in German, Mandarin, and Urdu with English subtitles); director of photography, Lutz Konerman; edited by Renate Merck; music by Claus Bantzer; production designer, Katharina Mayer-Woppermann; produced by Eric Nellessen; released by Novoskop and Probst films. At Lincoln Plaza, Broadway at 63d Street; Running time: 75 minutes. This film has no rating.

Shezad	Bhasker
Xiao	Ric Young
Rashid	Buddy Uzzaman
Herder	Wolf-Dieter Sprenger
Udo the cook	Ulrich Wildgruber

By JANET MASLIN

At the beginning of "Dragon Chow," the camera finds Shezad (Bhasker) on a dark street in Hamburg, West Germany, and follows him home. It's a great credit to the direction by Jan Schutte, whose first feature this sad, graceful and eloquent film is, that "Dragon Chow" generates immediate interest in this gentle soul and the question of where he may be going.

In the early hours of the morning, Shezad travels alone on the subway and arrives at a bus stop, where he meets a fellow Pakistani named Rashid (Buddy Uzzaman) and gratefully welcomes his friend's company for the rest of the ride home. Happily, they sing and converse in their native language.

Shezad and Rashid arrive at an uninviting, barrackslike welfare hotel filled with immigrant workers from many different lands. They share a room together, a room remarkably devoid of any souvenirs of their past lives. And yet the mood of "Dragon Chow" — which takes its name from the bouquets of flowers both Pakistanis sell in Hamburg bars, gifts that a reveler can bring home to appease a spouse — appears hopeful rather than grim. Shezad is a hard-working, quietly ambitious young man who dreams of making good in the restaurant business, and the film presents no immediate reason why such dreams cannot come true.

During the course of "Dragon Chow," which opens today at the Lincoln Plaza, Shezad shows himself to be a tireless worker. He finds a job in the kitchen of a Chinese restaurant, and gradually teaches himself to make better soup than the chef does. (This isn't hard; the chef is a tired, surly German who resents foreign labor and grudgingly teaches the staff such quasi-elegant locutions as "Would you like a drop of wine?") Eventually, Shezad both improves his culinary skills and develops a camaraderie with his fellow workers. He and a new Chinese friend named Xiao

(Ric Young) begin imagining what it would be like to run a place of their own.

There is only one cloud on the horizon, but it's a big one: the threat posed by the German immigration authorities, who treat illegal aliens with no mercy. The sweet-faced, balding, middle-aged Rashid is the first to suffer, and Shezad registers profound grief as he witnesses the fate that befalls his friend.

These foreign workers' terror of deportation is so great that an unemployed German stenographer named Monika becomes a key figure in their fantasies. One day Monika stops in the street to make a phone call, and asks the two Pakistanis to mind her shopping bags for a moment. Thrilled by this, they offer to buy her a cup of coffee and make polite conversation for a little while. As a parting gesture, they all stop in a photo booth and let the machine take a group picture, and then Monika says goodbye forever. Still, Shezad and Rashid think of her often, wondering whether either one of them could marry her and solve his problems.

"Dragon Chow," shot in black and white with a spare, simple camera style, brings its audience very close to these workers' hopes and worries without losing track of their essential foreignness, from German society and from one another. The Urdu conversations between Rashid and Shezad are deliberately not translated, and the restaurant scenes are almost entirely confined to the kitchen, with the diners seldom in view. The little victories that bring Shezad closer to success and security are presented with great feeling and extreme care. One of the film's best scenes depicts a dinner cooked by Shezad and Xiao for a group of fellow immigrants, who will then vote on whether a joint restaurant venture by the two men ought to be Pakistani or Chinese. The settling of this matter is as heartwarming as the story's final resolution is tragic.

"Dragon Chow" is aided greatly by the straightforward, modest quality of Mr. Schutte's direction and by lovely, uncomplicated performances in the leading roles. Bhasker and Mr. Uzzaman share a sweet, dignified demeanor that makes their performances all the more heartbreaking, and Mr. Young conveys a down-to-earth entrepreneurial spirit. Ulrich Wildgruber and Wolf-Dieter Sprenger are also good as two Germans, a cook and a hotel operator, who remain utterly indifferent to the problems facing these foreign workers.

1988 My 27, C10:5

Togetherness
Raul Julia portrays the leader of a religious cult in New Mexico in "The Penitent," directed by Cliff Osmond and co-starring Armand Assante.

THE PENITENT, written and directed by Cliff Osmond; director of photography, Robin Vidgeon; edited by Peter Taylor; music by Alex North; produced by Michael Fitzgerald; released by Cineworld Enterprises Corp. At Cine One, Seventh and 48th Street. Running time: 94 minutes. This film is rated PG-13.

Ramon	Raul Julia
Juan	Armand Assante
Celia	Rona Freed
Corina	Julie Carmen
Margarita	Lucy Reina
Mayor	Eduardo Lopez Rojas
Ramon's mother	Juana Molinero

By CARYN JAMES

"The Penitent" is melodramatic enough to culminate in a crucifixion and ludicrous enough so the victim's greatest ordeal on the cross seems to be a runny nose. At best, this garbled film is a study in unmotivated behavior.

Ramon (Raul Julia) has recently joined a two-century-old religious sect called "the penitente," which re-enacts Christ's Crucifixion every year. The victim is chosen by lot, tied to a cross, and left for a day in the blistering sun.

•

This penitent sect still exists, a title card tells us, in New Mexico, Colorado and northern Mexico, though we're left to wonder which of those areas contains Ramon's dusty little village. And that is the least of the film's questions.

Why has Ramon become a penitente? It has something to do with his dead father. Why does Celia (Rona Freed), the wife in Ramon's arranged marriage, run screaming into a corner, in a fit of overacting, whenever he tries to touch her? "She is young," the troubled Ramon tells his friend Juan (Armand Assante). Yet Celia looks to be in her 20's, and Ramon is old enough to know that muttering "Try not to be afraid" is not the best way to comfort a hysterical wife. But then, he's a man who believes in the power of will.

Juan squints in the sun, grins aimlessly and proves that a truly bad haircut — an extreme sort of crew cut — can make an attractive actor like Mr. Assante very unappealing. Yet Celia is seduced by the charmless Juan. Maybe it's the way he throws her into a lake, knowing she's afraid of water.

•

If there were a hint of religious conviction in "The Penitent," if Ramon were a spiritual being rather than a cipher, the story could have made sense. As it is, the film's excruciatingly long crucifixion ritual becomes a farce, full of easy, empty symbolism: Will Ramon or Juan be the sacrificial Christo? Who will carry the burden of sin, the guilty or the innocent? "The Penitent," which opens today at Cine 1, is a sham, a Harlequin romance lurking behind a facade of religion.

•

"The Penitent" is rated PG-13 ("Special Parental Guidance Suggested for Those Younger Than 13"). There are some gory scenes.

1988 My 27, C13:1

Where Nice Guys Finish Dead

WELCOME IN VIENNA directed by Axel Corti; screenplay by Georg Stefan and Mr. Corti (German with English subtitles); director of photography, Gernot Roll; edited by Ulrike Pahl and Claudia Rieneck; music by Hans Georg Koch; production designer, Fritz Hollergschwandtner; produced by Kurt Kodeal; released by Roxie Releasing. At Film Forum 1, 57 Watts Street. Running time: 121 minutes. This film is not rated.

Freddy Wolff	Gabriel Barylli
Sergeant Adler	Nicolas Brieger
Claudia Schutte	Claudia Messner
The Russian woman	Liliana Nelska
Treschensky	Karlheinz Hackl

By WALTER GOODMAN

"Welcome to Vienna" is remarkable for its fierce indictment of moral disarray in post-World War II Austria and for its gritty recapturing of 1945 Vienna, as people began to dig out of the rubble, black market operators bought chocolate bars from American soldiers and sold Mickey Mouse watches to Soviet soldiers, and careerists changed their politics to suit their new masters.

At the center of this tough Austrian movie, smartly directed by Axel Corti, are two American soldiers who had come to the United States as Jewish refugees and are now back in Europe as occupiers. Sergeant Adler, born in Berlin, is a Communist who makes a gesture at defecting to the East; when he is turned down by a disillusioned Soviet officer, he settles into enjoying the power of the occupier. "You can live a very decent life," he reflects, "without believing in anything." The more passive, more earnest Sergeant Wolff falls in love with an ambitious actress, Claudia Schutte, the daughter of a German intelligence officer who trades his knowledge of Soviet activities for refuge in the United States.

The sketchy plot serves mainly as an opportunity for the characters to reveal their weaknesses. Mr. Corti, who wrote the screenplay with Georg Stefan Troller, presents a city populated by admirers and beneficiaries of the Nazis and permeated with anti-

Home Again In "Welcome in Vienna," Gabriel Barylli portrays an Austrian-born G.I. who returns to his homeland at the end of World War II.

Semitism. When Wolff visits his family's old home, the people who took it over after its Jewish owners were forced to flee keep insisting on the legality of the proceedings. You can see the hatred, now mixed with fear, in their eyes. The prostitutes make cracks about "Jew boys" even as they solicit them. Everywhere, Wolff encounters distaste for "your kind." Even Claudia seems infected.

An anti-Nazi Austrian explains that if his new conservative party does not admit former Nazis, they will go off and create a right-wing movement of their own. He estimates that one-third of the country had Nazi sympathies and reminds Wolff, "The allies will not stay here forever." Adler permits a former SS officer to become a director in an American-run theater; his old uniform is used in a production of "The Skin of Our Teeth." Sabina's line, "Eat and be eaten," resonates.

The key figure is Treschensky, who begins as a German prisoner of war and ends as a cheerful wheeler-dealer. He describes himself as having been "somewhat of a Communist and somewhat of a Nazi — the only Nazi you'll find in Vienna now." When he is investigated, he handles the matter with a bribe. For Mr. Corti, the slippery, successful Treschensky is an emblem of "liberated" Austria. As Adler observes, "They just go on with the show without even bothering to change the cast." The tone here is bitter resignation.

The movie is diminished by the rather wan performance of Gabriel Barylli as Wolff. Even when he is finally roused to act against Treschensky, there is little force to him. Perhaps that is intentional, a statement by Mr. Corti, a prize-winning Austrian film maker who spent the war years out of his country, about the weakness of an honest man in so deeply corrupted a society. The statement gains power from the black-and-white photography of Gernot Roll and the art direction of Fritz Hollergschwandtner. "Welcome to Vienna," which opens today at the Film Forum 1, is the third part of a trilogy; the first two parts, "God Doesn't Believe in Us Anymore" and "Santa Fe," will be shown in July. As you leave the theater, you may find yourself thinking about Kurt Waldheim.

1988 Je 1, C17:1

When the Mob Goes Into Amusement

FUNLAND, directed by Michael A. Simpson; screenplay by Mr. Simpson, Bonnie Turner and Terry Turner; director of photography, William Vanderkloot; edited by Mr. Vanderkloot, Wade Watkins and Teresa Garcia; music by James Oliverio; produced by Mr. Vanderkloot and Mr. Simpson; released by Double Helix Films Inc. At the Cinema Village, 22 East 12th Street; Running time: 87 minutes. This film is rated R.

Angus Perry	William Windom
Bruce Burger	David L. Lander
Mike Spencer	Bruce Mahler
Mario DiMaurio/Bogie	Robert Sacchi
Doug Sutterfield	Clark Brandon
Denise Wilson	Jill Carroll
T. G. Hurley	Mike McManus
Kristin Cumming	Mary McDonough
Carl DiMaurio	Terry Beaver
Chad Peller	Lane Davies

By CARYN JAMES

Is Ronald McDonald beyond parody? The clownish hamburger spokesman has already taken a giant advertising step away from any ordinary circus character. Is there a fresh spoof of "The Godfather" left? Anything is possible, but the creators of "Funland" have tossed some trite satiric targets — organized crime, advertising, a psycho clown — into a grab bag, then lazily let them tumble out any old way.

This low-budget comedy has a fair amount of satiric potential. Bruce Burger (David L. Lander, best known as Squiggy on "Laverne and Shirley") is a clown-spokesman for a local pizza-burger franchise that has an advertising tie-in with an amusement park called Funland. Bruce converses with and through his faithful sidekick, a puppet named Peter Pepperoni. So it's no surprise that when a mob family takes over Funland and replaces him with the national Bruce Burger, the local Bruce goes haywire.

With his orange wig and chalk-white makeup, Bruce looks too much like a straightforward poor-man's version of Ronald McDonald to be a parody. The DeMaurio family doesn't spoof the endless "Godfather" spoofs; it simply apes them, from the father's mumbling Brando voice to the older son's tough-guy stance and the younger son's suave, businessman's persona.

•

"Funland" needs to raise the satiric stakes, to come up with more outrageous performances and ideas. Only Lane Davies, as the national Bruce — a Juilliard-trained actor who loathes children — puts a spark into what could have been another deadened stock character. And there is the DeMaurios' gleeful plan for a new ride, Celebrity Death and Disease, which would carry park patrons through various exhibits. "Here is Natalie Wood's rowboat," says a consultant, pointing to a scale model. The Elvis and John Lennon exhibits aren't far away. Not tasteful, but the scene has a comic edge that "Funland," which will be shown today and tomorrow at Cinema Village, otherwise misses.

1988 Je 1, C17:1

BIG, directed by Penny Marshall; screenplay by Gary Ross and Anne Spielberg; director of photography, Barry Sonnenfeld; edited by Barry Malkin; music by Howard Shore; production designer, Santo Loquasto; released by 20th Century-Fox Film Corporation. At the National Twin, Broadway at 44th Street; Gotham Cinema, Third Avenue at 58th Street; Running time: 104 minutes. This film is rated PG.

Tom Hanks, left, and Jared Rushton in "Big."

Josh	Tom Hanks
Susan	Elizabeth Perkins
MacMillan	Robert Loggia
Paul	John Heard
Billy	Jared Rushton
Young Josh	David Moscow
Scotty Brennen	Jon Lovitz
Mrs. Baskin	Mercedes Ruehl
Mr. Baskin	Josh Clark
Cynthia Benson	Kimberlee M. Davis
Freddie Benson	Oliver Block

By JANET MASLIN

When Henry Ford developed his Model T in 1903, there were Pierce, Packard, Stanley and various other cars already on the market, which only goes to show how little being first has to do with popular success. It's the small refinements, the careful streamlining and the sure sense of public taste that winnow the field and designate the best.

•

"Big," which opens today at the National and other theaters, is only the latest of several similar films in which grown-up bodies are taken over by children's minds. But its makers have built a better mousetrap in a number of important ways. Some day, should film scholars with time on their hands address themselves to this extremely minor phenomenon, they may note that "Big" is the first body-switching film to streamline its story so that there's only one changeling involved. This way, the film's young hero Josh Baskin (David Moscow) can become a bigger version of himself (Tom Hanks), instead of turning into his own father ("Like Father, Like Son" and "Vice Versa"), his grandfather ("18 Again!") or even a pet ("Oh, Heavenly Dog"). So there's no need to waste time and energy following around an extra body with, say, the looks of Chevy Chase but the brain of an old English sheepdog.

"Big" is also less coy than its fellows about the adolescent sexuality of its hero. At 13, Josh is old enough to experience sexual curiosity and even romantic stirrings about the women he meets in his newly grownup form. And "Big" handles this possibility gracefully instead of dodging it, as

some of the earlier films have taken pains to do. On the other hand, "Big" is also true to a 13-year-old boy's potential for indifference to the opposite sex, so that a woman who asks to spend the night with Josh may be invited, but only halfheartedly, to sleep over in the adjoining bunk bed.

•

As written by Gary Ross and Anne Spielberg and directed by Penny Marshall, "Big" also has a warmer, more engaging personality than its predecessors. Its success as a buoyant summer comedy will owe a lot to the cleverness with which the small details have been selected, from the opening shot of a video game (which tells the player he is in a cave surrounded by "the carcasses of slain ice dwarfs," thus nicely encapsulating the 13-year-old's sense of adventure) to the means by which the newly transformed Josh makes his first appearance. As Josh wakes up, the morning after having made a wish to an exotic-looking contraption at an amusement park, a pair of hairy legs emerge from his bed and a loud thud is heard as he drops to the floor. The next thing seen is Mr. Hanks, running frantically through Josh's room wearing too-small underwear with cartoon pictures on the back.

The role of a grown man with a young boy's mind has been a fine opportunity for each of the actors who have tried it, but in Mr. Hanks's performance, "Big" also has a distinct edge. Wide-eyed, excited and wonderfully guileless, Mr. Hanks is an absolute delight, and the film is shrewd in relieving him of the responsiblity to behave furtively and hide his altered condition. Once transformed, Josh tries to explain things to his mother, but she mistakes him for a burglar and chases him with a carving knife. So he has no choice but to head for the city and embark upon a new life, leaving his parents word that he has been kidnaped. One minor weakness in the screenplay is its forgetfulness about the kidnap story and various other loose ends.

•

It's a convention of films like this for the boyish man to do unexpectedly well in the grownup world, as straitlaced business colleagues respond encouragingly to his fresh ideas and his sense of wonder. Luckily, "Big" doesn't push this too far, but it does parlay Josh's computer expertise into a job at a toy company, where he whoops with glee over his first paycheck and tries to get it cashed as a $100 bill, 87 singles and a few dimes. Helped at first by his best friend, Billy (Jared Rushton), who is still 13 and a lot more savvy than Josh, he swiftly rises to the top. Soon Josh has his own office (bigger than the principal's, Billy exclaims) and a secretary to bring him junk food on a tray. The boss (Robert Loggia) has been impressed with Josh's romping through F.A.O. Schwarz, and this in turn creates deep resentment in a jealous co-worker (John Heard) and the sour, sophisticated Susan (Elizabeth Perkins), who is a fellow executive.

Once Susan, wearing a black cocktail dress, takes a spin on the trampoline in Josh's new apartment, it isn't hard to see which way the film is headed. But Miss Marshall minimizes the sentimentality and keeps things mercifully sweet. Miss Perkins is a bit chilly in this role even after she's meant to melt, but she becomes more girlish all the same, and the film celebrates this in an appealing way. Though "Big" ultimately turns on the notion that there's a hidden child in each of us, it manages to make this point with intelligence and taste. And the large pumpkin waiting at the end of Josh's Cinderella episode becomes an acceptable, even welcome thing.

"Big" features believable young teen-age mannerisms from the two real boys in its cast, and this only makes Mr. Hanks's funny, flawless impression that much more adorable. For any other full-grown actors who try their hands at fidgeting, squirming, throwing water balloons and wolfing down food in a huge variety of comically disgusting ways, this really is the performance to beat.

•

"Big" is rated PG ("Parental Guidance Suggested"). It includes off-color language and some sexual overtones.

1988 Je 3, C8:4

Into a Mystical World

John Savage in "The Beat."

THE BEAT, written and directed by Paul Mones; director of photography, Thomas DiCillo; edited by Elizabeth Kling; music by Carter Burwell; produced by Julia Phillips, Jon Kilik and Nick Wechsler; released by Vestron Pictures. At the Waverly Twin, Avenue of the Americas at Third Street; Running time: 98 minutes. This film is rated R.

Rex Voorhas Ormine	David Jacobson
Billy	Willliam McNamara
Kate	Kara Glover
Doug	Stuart Alexander
Vis	Marcus Flanagan
Dirt	David McCarthy
Danny	Reggie Bythewood
Auggie	Tony Moundroukas
Lon	Paul Dillon
Ian	Richard Eigen
Amy	Lisa Richards
Frank Ellsworth	John Savage

By CARYN JAMES

"The Beat" offers an unflinching view of New York street kids — raunchy, belligerent, unlovably tough. They live in run-down brick tenements in an area called Hellesbay (not subtle, but appropriate), and when they're not getting stoned they are disrupting classes at Osmo High. Their English teacher, Frank Ellsworth (John Savage), has an accent nearly as street-tough as his students', yet when he asks them to recite improvised poetry he gets the real-life nonreaction you might expect.

This gritty realism is the great strength of "The Beat," but even as we see the mounds of abandoned cars under crumbling bridges, the barren streets that define these kids' aimless lives, we hear a voiceover that smacks of the worst kind of adolescent poetry. "Ulcerous dragons dragged oozing scales along the pavement," says Rex, the new kid in Hellesbay. He is so immersed in his poetic fantasies that the neighbors call him retarded. Ellsworth champions Rex's creativity, and the school psychologist — a bow-tied fussbudget who wouldn't last a day in a merciless place like Osmo — thinks he is disturbed.

This sounds like a formula for a Hollywood-approved inspirational film like "Stand and Deliver," but "The Beat" breaks away from those stock patterns. Mr. Savage effectively underplays his role, and Paul Mones, the writer and director, concentrates on the misfit poet's effect on the street gang. "The Beat" wisely heads aways from the ordinary, then foolishly doesn't stop until it has gone beyond the bend of believability.

Rex resembles a mad poet, slouching and skulking along the corridors with a Rasputin-like gleam in his eyes. Eventually this maniacal guy in the nerdy green jacket lures the gang into his mystical world where they assume fictional roles such as princess-priestess and beggar. Suddenly, a street prophet is roaming the toughminded scene of "The Beat," in a contrast that might throw more experienced directors off balance.

"The Beat," which opens today at the Waverly, is Mr. Mones's first film, based on a story he wrote more than 10 years ago as a student. If the film has the passion of student work, it also shares Rex's adolescent pretensions, as if Mr. Mones is discovering alienation. He seems to admire Rex's indulgent poems (they were, after all, written by Mr. Mones), as much as his desire to create them. (Mr. Mones also has the English teacher call Whitman's "Song of Myself" "Song *to* Myself," so "The Beat" is a bad poetry lesson.) The film's style, at times so unsentimental, is often overwrought, with 360-degree camera swirls, close-ups of fiery-eyed youths. It shares, rather than mirrors, the hero's excesses.

As Rex skulks along chanting "the beat, the beat," he sounds less like a street-inspired rap singer — the obvious but credible parallel — than a bad performance artist. And as with failed performance art, it is finally easier to admire the creative energy and ambition behind "The Beat" than to sit through it. **1988 Je 3, C10:6**

Harvest Time Chevy Chase is cast in ''Funny Farm'' as a city dweller who escapes to the country to seek tranquility.

FUNNY FARM, directed by George Roy Hill; screenplay by Jeffrey Boam, from the novel by Jay Cronley; director of photography, Miroslav Ondricek; edited by Alan Heim; music by Elmer Bernstein; production designer, Henry Bumstead; produced by Robert L. Crawford; released by Warner Bros. At the National Twin, Broadway at 44th Street; Regency Cinema, Broadway at 67th Street; other theaters; Running time 99 minutes. This film is rated PG.

Andy	Chevy Chase
Elizabeth Farmer	Madolyn Smith
Sinclair	Joseph Maher
Bud Culbertson	Jack Gilpin
Brock	Brad Sullivan
Mayor Barclay	MacIntyre Dixon
Betsy Culbertson	Caris Corfman

Don't underrate amiability. Chevy Chase has built a successful movie career not on his comic gifts, which are considerable, but on his skill in seeming unstoppably good-natured, even on those rare occasions when he's supposed to behave like a rat.

The ad for ''Funny Farm,'' his new film opening today at the Regency and other theaters, features Mr. Chase, his mouth shaped into a moonlike grin, as the contents of an egg, smashed atop his head, drips down his face. There's no such shot in the movie, but it's an appropriate visual metaphor. ''Funny Farm'' is good-natured even when it's not funny.

•

The screenplay features material recycled from far better comedies, including ''Mr. Blandings Builds His Dream House,'' ''George Washington Slept Here'' and ''The Egg and I,'' as well as the Ma and Pa Kettle movies spun off from ''The Egg and I.'' It's about an up-scale city couple, Mr. Chase and Madolyn Smith, who abandon Manhattan to seek new and better lives in a New England community called Redbud. He is a sports writer who is going to write a novel, while she is planning to bear his children.

There are gags involving a Dutch door, a sheriff who is driven around in a taxi because he's flunked his driver's test, a rude postman and a number of eccentric neighbors one has met before. The film's several laughs come when Miss Smith sits down to read the first three chapters of Mr. Chase's novel, which, clearly,

is far worse than she could have expected. This scene appears to come from the heart.

The biggest surprise is that ''Funny Farm'' was directed by George Roy Hill (''The Sting,'' ''Slaughterhouse Five''). Mr. Hill is a comparatively classical director. He cannot have found it easy to make a comedy composed almost entirely of gags for which there are no buildups and, thus, no real payoffs. As a comedy style, it has the impatience of a child who plants radish seeds and then pulls up the first tiny sprouts to see how they're doing.

•

''Funny Farm,'' which has been rated PG (''Parental Guidance Suggested''), includes some mildly vulgar language. VINCENT CANBY

1988 Je 3, C14:6

Fate and Fascism

HISTORY, directed by Luigi Comencini; screenplay by Suso Cecchi D'Amico, Cristina Comencini and Luigi Comencini from the novel by Elsa Morante; director of photography, Franco Di Giacomo; edited by Nino Baragli; music by Fiorenzo Carpi; production designer, Paola Comencini; produced by Paolo Infascelli; released by Worldwide Distribution. At the Carnegie Screening Room, 887 Seventh Avenue, at 57th Street; Running time: 146 minutes. This film is not rated.

Ida	Claudia Cardinale
Remo, the innkeeper	Francisco Rabal
Useppe	Andrea Spada
Nino	Antonio Degli Schiavi
Cucchiarelli	Fiorenzo Fiorentini
Gunther	Tobias Hoesl
Carlo Davide	Lambert Wilson

By VINCENT CANBY

When Elsa Morante's ''History: a Novel'' was published in Italy in 1974, it was acclaimed by a number of critics as one of the great novels of the 20th century, on a par with the works of Joyce, Kafka and Proust, among others. American critics received the 1977 English translation with somewhat less enthusiasm.

''History,'' set in Rome and its outskirts between 1941 and 1947, is a very big, Dostoyevskian novel, full of moral debates and philosophical asides, about the terminally bleak existence of a group of characters victimized as much by Fate, which Morante calls History, as by fascism. The central figure is Ida, a school teacher who, being half-Jewish, lives in fear of persecution and in guilt for having always hidden her Jewish background.

•

At the start of the story, Ida is already the mother of a teen-age son when, after being raped by a German soldier, she gives birth to another boy, the epileptic Useppe. After nearly 600 pages, nobody, not even the family mongrel named Bella, has survived intact.

At least one American critic saw in ''History'' the material for a panoramic, grittily photographed, black-and-white movie on the order of Roberto Rossellini's neo-realist classic, ''Open City.'' Nobody could possibly have seen it as material for Luigi Comencini, best known as the director of gentle comedies (''Bread, Love and Fantasy,'' ''Bread, Love and Jealousy''), who is responsible for the film adaptation opening today at the Carnegie Screening Room.

The material appears to have been utterly beyond the talents (and, perhaps, the interests) of Mr. Comencini,

Time of Travail Claudia Cardinale plays the role of Ida, an Italian Jew who struggles in ''History'' to survive Nazi atrocities and Fascist rule.

who has told much of this dark tale as if it were the sort of soap opera in which cataclysmic events are mere inconveniences. With the exception of black-and-white newsreel footage, which is used from time to time to set the private story in history, the film is shot in color that is functional but characterless, which is the way that Mr. Comencini directs it.

•

As the war moves home to Rome, truly terrible things happen to Ida (Claudia Cardinale), to her teen-age son, Nino (Antonio Degli Schiavi), and to Useppe (Andrea Spada). The film records these things as if it didn't understand their meaning, or as if it preferred to ignore their profound effects. One might suspect that this was the director's ironic intention, except that, in the big scenes, he allows every member of the cast to overact dreadfully, as if to make up for the monotony of all that's gone before.

''History'' is also a technical mess. The movie is almost over before one learns that Ida is a schoolteacher. The scenes of Nino's adventures with the partisans are so clumsily constructed that there's never a surprise that hasn't been telegraphed. The movie is long, like the novel, but it has the manner of something that's been padded, rather than of something that has been packed with event and character. One longs for a few ellipses.

In a better movie, Miss Cardinale might have been a moving World War II variation on Mother Courage. The performers aren't even very good. Lambert Wilson, a respectable French actor, has a terrible time playing a pacifistic anarchist, who defects to the partisans, then becomes a drunk in remorse for having killed a German soldier.

A typically ''important'' Comencini touch: cross-cutting between a shot of an enraged partisan, who is kicking a wounded German soldier in the face, and a shot of a rather fake-looking yellow bird chirping sweetly on a branch above. This demonstrates the sensibility of someone who should be making television commercials.

1988 Je 3, C15:1

All Dressed Down With No Place to Go

Jeffrey Osterhage as Martin Clark in ''South of Reno.''

SOUTH OF RENO, directed by Mark Rezyka; screenplay by Mr. Rezyka and T. L. Lankford; director of photography, Bernard Auroux; edited by Marc Grossman; music by Nigel Holton and Clive Wright; production designer, Philip Duffin; produced by Robert Tinnell; released by Castle Hill Productions. At Movieland Eighth Street at University Place. Running time: 98 minutes. This film is rated R.

Martin	Jeffrey Osterhage
Anette	Lisa Blount
Hector	Joe Phelan
Willard	Lewis Van Bergen
Susan	Julia Montgomery
Brenda	Brandis Kemp
Louise	Danitza Kingsley
Manager of Motel	Mary Grace Canfield
Howard Stone	Bert Remsen

''South of Reno'' was written and directed by Mark Rezyka, whose previous experience has been in making music videos, most of them for heavy-metal bands. According to the production notes, Mr. Rezyka came up with the idea for this change of pace when someone asked him to think up a 30-minute story.

In its finished form, his film has even less plot than that, but it has been stretched to a running time of an hour and a half by means of pregnant pauses, slow pans of the desert horizon and scenes in which the film's hero, Martin Clark (Jeffrey Osterhage), sits staring at a television set that gets very bad reception. Even so, these garbled glimpses of ''Jeopardy'' and old movies are a lot more interesting than anything that happens to Martin in real life.

•

Striving for an aggressively arty look, and shooting every daytime scene under boringly bright-blue skies (though the cinematography by Bernard Auroux is quite crisp), Mr. Rezyka reveals Martin to be a troubled man. His wife, Anette (Lisa Blount), is fooling around with a garage mechanic named Willard (Lewis Van Bergen) in the isolated desert town where they live, and everyone but Martin knows all about this. After all, Anette can be seen wearing a trenchcoat, negligee and suspiciously new shoes (she has been shopping a lot, for a woman who complains of being stranded in the middle of nowhere) sitting in the dirt outside the motel room where she and Willard regularly meet. This is the kind of posing that the director favors.

Martin senses marital problems but is reluctant to do anything to rock the boat. He is, after all, so lonely that he routinely throws nails and broken glass onto the highway beside his mobile home, just for the chance to meet new people. Though Mr. Rezyka uses this device as an excuse to create acting roles for out-of-work centerfolds, and for Bert Remsen (as a man who has a flat tire changed by Martin and gives him a gun), this is a film in which next to nothing happens. The action scenes, like the one in which Martin gets drunk and drives his pickup truck to a place where he has created his own miniature neon Mecca, are more concerned with looking good than with expressing any form of thought.

•

It's impossible to tell what any of the cast members might do with a real story, but it's clear that Mr. Rezyka has no inclination to make his film move or his characters think. "South of Reno" opens today at the Eighth Street Movieland.

JANET MASLIN

1988 Je 3, C15:1

Cheating Hearts

PERFECT MATCH directed by Mark Deimel; screenplay by Nick Duretta, David A. Burr and Mr. Deimel; director of photography, Robert Torrance; edited by Craig A. Colton; music by Tim Torrance; produced by Mr. Deimel and Robert Torrance; released by Sandstar. At the Cine Twin, Seventh and 48th Street; Running time: 93 minutes. This film is rated PG.

WITH: Marc McClure, Jennifer Edwards, Diane Stilwell, Rob Paulsen and Karen Witter.

By VINCENT CANBY

"Perfect Match," which opened yesterday at the Cine 2, might be called "The (Video) Shop Around the Corner." Set in contemporary Los Angeles, "Perfect Match" is an extremely distant relative of Ernst Lubitsch's 1940 comedy about two lonely people who meet under false pretenses and fall in love in spite of themselves.

He (Marc McClure) is a small cog in the wheels of a conglomerate. She (Jennifer Edwards) works in a video shop and is in her 10th undergraduate year at the university. She doesn't want to move on. They meet through an ad in a personals column in which he has represented himself as a playboy-financier and she as a university professor.

Mark Deimel, the director, whose first film this is, succeeds in convincing the audience that the two odd-ball lovers are quite decent people. They are so decent, in fact, that they deserve much stronger, sharper comic material than is provided by the screenplay. The film's centerpiece is a long weekend at a mountain resort where, while skiing, horseback riding and camping, the lovers reveal themselves to be the frauds they are.

The actors are eager and willing, but the touch is heavy, heavy, heavy.

1988 Je 4, 12:3

A Second Childhood, But Bullets Are Real

THE WRONG GUYS, directed by Danny Bilson; screenplay by Paul De Meo and Mr. Bilson; director of photography, Frank Byers; edited by Frank J. Jimenez; music by Joseph Conlan; production designer, George Costello; produced by Charles Gordon and Ronald E. Frazier; released by New World Pictures. At Embassy 4, Broadway and 47th Street; Gemini, Second Avenue at 64th Street and other theaters. Running time: 96 minutes. This film is rated PG.

Louie Anderson
Richard .... Richard Lewis
Belz .... Richard Belzer
Franklyn .... Franklyn Ajaye
Tim .... Tim Thomerson
Duke Earle .... John Goodman

By JANET MASLIN

The arrested-development movie craze may have reached some kind of extreme with "The Wrong Guys," the story of five grown men who band together and re-live their Cub Scout days. Encouraged by Louie (Louie Anderson), whose mother was the group's original leader and whose house once boasted a display of different scouting knots mounted on the wall, the veterans of 1961's Den 7 reconvene for a wilderness adventure.

By the end of the film, they are back in uniform and being rescued by their mothers, several of whom grab their sons by the ears. But "The Wrong Guys," which was directed by Danny Bilson and opened yesterday at the virtually deserted Embassy 4 and other theaters, at least deserves credit for being less stupid and more cheerful than it could have been.

The cast can be described as unmistakably professional, with Richard Belzer, Tim Thomerson and Franklin Ajaye among the campers, and the mood is chipper if not exactly inspired. There's even something likable about the scouting songs that are heard over the credits, or about the deranged killer who sings "Tammy" while cleaning his machine gun.

This killer, who is named Duke Earle, mistakes the reunited scouts for F.B.I. men and pursues them, thus giving the film much more plot than it really needs. Otherwise, it develops only a few amusing contrasts between the characters' Cub Scout past and their latter-day habits, like wearing silk pajamas and taking sleeping pills.

•

"The Wrong Guys" is rated PG ("Parental Guidance Suggested"). It contains some mildly off-color language.

1988 Je 4, 12:3

On a Desert Island, Death Imitates Art

AMERICAN GOTHIC, directed by John Hough; screenplay by Burt Wetanson and Michael Vines; director of photography, Harvey Harrison; edited by John Victor Smith; music by Alan Parker; produced by John Quested and Christopher Harrop; released by Vidmark Entertainment. At Warner Twin, Broadway and 43d Street; Coliseum Twin, Broadway and 181st Street and other theaters. Running time: 90 minutes. This film is rated R.

WITH: Rod Steiger, Yvonne De Carlo, Michael J. Pollard, Fiona Hutchison and Sarah Torgov.

By CARYN JAMES

Rod Steiger is called Paw. Yvonne De Carlo is Maw. Try to imagine Grant Wood's wizened characters after they've binged on mashed potatoes and white bread for 40 years or so, and you'll find the only point of contact between the film "American Gothic" and the too-often-parodied painting. This cruel, painfully unfunny story is about Maw and Paw and their psychotic Bible-fearing family — two middle-aged sons and a middle-aged daughter, all three with the minds of children. They live with the daughter's mummified baby on an otherwise deserted island, so one can only guess at the inbreeding that has produced this crew.

There is no guesswork involved, though, when a plane carrying six young city types lands on the island.

The children send them, one by one, to that great slasher-movie in the sky. Sometimes they go in games: murder by swing and jump rope.

•

This may sound more satirical than it is, because John Hough has directed with the comic flair of a meat-packer slaughtering hogs. Michael J. Pollard has some genuinely funny moments as Woody, the balding son with the mischievous little boy's grin, but he seems to have landed from another planet, where actors have a better-developed sense of humor and self-parody.

"American Gothic," which opened yesterday at the Warner Twin, offers just a few meager possibilities for unintentional campy comedy. When Mr. Steiger addresses the camera as if he were reciting Shakespeare, he is truly, straightforwardly, hilariously bad — just what "American Gothic" deserves.

1988 Je 4, 12:6

Lethal Affinity

THE DRIFTER, written and directed by Larry Brand; photographed by David Sperling; edited by Stephen Mark; music by Rick Conrad; produced by Ken Stein; released by Concorde Pictures. At U.A. East, First Avenue at 85th Street; Criterion, Broadway and 45th Street and other theaters. Running time: 90 minutes. This film is rated R.

Julia .... Kim Delaney
Arthur .... Timothy Bottoms
Kriger .... Al Shannon
Trey .... Miles O'Keefe
Matty .... Anna Gray Garduno
Willie Munroe .... Loren Haines
Morrison .... Larry Brand

By CARYN JAMES

"The Drifter" was shot, its press material says, "in 17 days on a budget too low to mention." Here is a press release with more honesty than tact, and it is not encouraging. But there are worse things than competent formula films, and, as it turns out, many worse films around than "The Drifter." This is an unapologetic B-movie in the mold of Roger Corman, who was its executive producer.

The story of lust and murder begins with an old chestnut — a young woman driving on a lonely highway. Julia (Kim Delaney) picks up a mysterious, long-haired hitchhiker named Trey (Miles O'Keefe, from Bo Derek's "Tarzan"). He is handsome, scruffy, laconic, persistent. They make love on her motel-room floor by the blue light of a broken television; then she goes back to Arthur (Timothy Bottoms), her stable lawyer boyfriend.

Larry Brand, the film's writer and director, says he finished his script before "Fatal Attraction" was released, and we'll just have to take his word for it. In a clever gender twist, Julia gets the Michael Douglas role. Trey calls her at home, tracks her down at the office, insists on seeing her so he can stare into her eyes and mutter ominously, "When you make love with someone it's a forever thing."

But "The Drifter" has more in common with 40's film noir than with a glossy contemporary update like "Fatal Attraction." It is dark, slight, tightly focused on the stalked Julia and, after someone is murdered in her apartment, on a neat line-up of suspects. Trey is clearly too crazed with passion, and Arthur has his own sinister side. He has hired a spooky-look-

ing private detective, who tells him of Julia's fling. She has hired a goofy-looking private detective to help her stop Trey. Her detective is played by Mr. Brand (who knows how to hire cheap help). He faces her across a desk cluttered with wind-up toys, a photograph of Richard Nixon on the wall behind him. Would you trust any of these people?

The film's climax does not twist or surprise quite enough, does it move with the deft, quick motions this material demands. And though you couldn't call Mr. Brand original, he allows the genre's familiarity to work for him. "The Drifter," which opened Friday at the Criterion Center, carries its audience along effortlessly. And if Mr. Brand can create this modest, murderous diversion in 17 days for no money, think what he could do if he had, say, a month.

1988 Je 5, 59:1

Wanting It   Kevin J. O'Connor stars in Robert Frank and Rudy Wurlitzer's "Candy Mountain," about a young musician searching for fame and fortune.

What Now, Voyager?

CANDY MOUNTAIN, directed by Robert Frank and Rudy Wurlitzer; screenplay by Mr. Wurlitzer; director of photography, Pio Corradi; edited by Jennifer Auge; art directors, Brad Ricker and Keith Currie; produced by Ruth Waldburger; released by International Film Exchange, a Today Home Entertainment Company. At Quad Cinema, 13th Street, between Fifth Avenue and Avenue of the Americas. Running time: 91 minutes. This film is rated R.

Julius .... Kevin J. O'Connor
Elmore .... Harris Yulin
Al Silk .... Tom Waits
Cornelia .... Bulle Ogier
Archie .... Roberts Blossom
Huey .... Leon Redbone
Henry .... Dr. John
Winnie .... Rita MacNeil
Mario .... Joe Strummer

By CARYN JAMES

In an 80's twist on Jack Kerouac's myth of the open road, "Candy Mountain" presents the least self-reflective hero ever to hit the highway. Julius (Kevin O'Connor) is a sometime guitarist and a persistent con man, hired to track down a reclusive, brilliant guitar maker named Elmore Silk. The directors, Robert Frank and

Rudy Wurlitzer (who also wrote the screenplay), set Julius traveling on the fringes of society, for the film asserts, in its lighthearted, unpretentious way, that the spirit of our times can be found in those margins. It turns out to be a sardonic spirit, embodied in Julius's mercenary quest for a guru who refuses to dispense wisdom.

"How can you do the road with no car?" a toothless van driver asks Julius after his girlfriend drives off and leaves him stranded at an Esso station. He does it by pickup truck, school bus and jeep, wheedling rides, bumbling his way along Elmore's trail from New York through Canada to Nova Scotia. On the road, he encounters a series of eccentrics who never fall into total absurdity. (In a kind of subterranean joke, most are played by musicians, including Tom Waits and Leon Redbone, who give the film a bluesy-folksy score.)

Elmore's wealthy brother — Mr. Waits, wearing a garish golfing outfit — leads Julius to Elmore's daughter. She lives in a trailer near Niagara Falls, locked in a perpetual shouting match with her mean-spirited, wheelchair-bound husband (played by Dr. John, the singer and pianist whose real name is Mac Rebennack). Farther north, Julius drives a pickup into a boat parked in the middle of the road, and as punishment is locked in the room of a cabin for two days.

Robert Frank made his reputation in the 50's with "The Americans," a classic book of unprettified photographs, with an introduction by Kerouac, taken on Mr. Frank's own journey along the slightly off-kilter roads of the country. In 1959 his first film, "Pull My Daisy," established him as a chronicler of the Beats. But the narrative of "Candy Mountain," as fluidly cinematic as it can be, has more in common with Jim Jarmusch's current itinerent fringe dwellers than with Kerouac's generation. And though the film is full of bright, saturated colors — from orange leaves to Julius's lime-green sneakers — it does not contain a hint of self-conscious, artsy composition.

"Candy Mountain" resembles Mr. Frank's most famous photographs only in the way each glimpse of a character suggests a lifetime behind the moment we see. And the film resembles Mr. Wurlitzer's previous screenplays (most recently "Walker") in approaching history in a minor key. Working on a multilingual set, Mr. Wurlitzer directed the actors in English, while Mr. Frank set up the camera shots speaking German to the Swiss-German crew. The result is remarkably seamless.

After Julius's meanderings, it is risky for the directors to show us Elmore, but Harris Yulin gives a perfectly understated performance. So much less than Julius expected, he is much more than the audience could have hoped for. Shrewd, remote, dissipated and still handsome, Elmore is onto Julius and to himself. And though we have just witnessed the trail of dejection and bad blood Elmore has selfishly left behind, he seems wise.

The film avoids oracular statements, so when Elmore says, "Freedom doesn't have much to do with the road one way or another," it takes on the authority of simple truth. "Candy Mountain," which opens today at the Quad Cinema, seems to be a small, quirky film, but it easily assumes the weight, ambition and success that many larger films aim for and miss.

1988 Je 10, C6:5

In One Door And Out the Other

Lily Tomlin in "Big Business."

Bette Midler in "Big Business."

BIG BUSINESS, directed by Jim Abrahams; written by Dori Pierson and Marc Rubel; director of photography, Dean Cundey; edited by Harry Keramidas; music by Lee Holdridge; production designer, William Sandell; produced by Steve Tisch and Michael Peyser; released by Touchstone Pictures. At the National Twin, Broadway and 44th Street; the Gotham Cinema, Third Avenue at 58th Street, and other theaters. Running time: 91 minutes. This film is rated PG.

Sadie Shelton/Sadie Ratliff .... Bette Midler
Rose Shelton/Rose Ratliff .... Lily Tomlin
Roone Dimmick .... Fred Ward
Graham Sherbourne .... Edward Herrmann
Fabio Alberici .... Michele Placido
Chuck .... Daniel Gerroll

By VINCENT CANBY

It begins when an addled nurse in a small West Virginia hospital mixes up two pairs of newborn identical twins, sending each set of parents home with a mismatched pair of baby girls. By chance, both families name their twins Sadie and Rose, who, in a casting inspiration, grow up to be played by Bette Midler and Lily Tomlin.

This is the expectant premise of Jim Abrahams's "Big Business," which, though it never quite delivers the boffo payoff, is a most cheerful, very breezy summer farce, played to the hilt by two splendidly comic performers. The film opens today at the Cinema II and other theaters.

Sadie Shelton (Miss Midler) is the overbearing, ruthless chief executive officer of the family's Moramax company, a shining monument to corporate greed. Rose Shelton (Miss Tomlin) is her sister's loyal if fainthearted first lieutenant, a woman who would much rather be cooking or knitting than worrying about junk bonds.

Their sisters are Sadie and Rose Ratliff, raised in rural innocence in Jupiter Hollow, W.Va., a one-company town whose economic life is threatened when Moramax announces it is selling the Hollowmade Furniture Company to an Italian speculator.

As the predatory Sadie makes all the decisions for the twin sisters in New York, it is the ecology-minded, justice-seeking Rose Ratliff (Miss Tomlin) who is the dominant sister in West Virginia. Unlike the earnest Rose, Sadie Ratliff somehow feels out of place in Jupiter Hollow. She dreams of the big city and bright lights and couldn't care less about ecology.

It's Rose who organizes the town's protest to the takeover and drags her starry-eyed sister off to Manhattan, where, by glorious chance, the two sets of twins wind up in adjoining suites at the Plaza. The comic possibilities are not exactly numberless, but they are plentiful, more or less in relation to the number of doors (bedroom, bathroom, elevator) in any one scene. To complicate matters further, each sister has a suitor of sorts who, finally, finds happiness with a twin other than the one he started out with.

If Miss Midler gets most of the big laughs, that's pretty much built into the Dori Pierson-Marc Rubel screenplay, which depends as much on snappy one-liners as on mistaken identities.

Tippy-toeing around on perilously high heels, her top-heavy frame in ever-precarious balance, Miss Midler is a fiendish delight, both as Sadie Shelton cutting a pretty secretary down to size ("That dress looks like a blood clot"), and as her country sister, yodeling accompaniment to some West Indian street musicians on Fifth Avenue.

Compared with the two flamboyant Sadies played by Miss Midler, for whom polka dots may well have been invented, Miss Tomlin's two Roses are reserved but no less funny. There is a sly modesty in Miss Tomlin's characterizations that works as sweet counterpoint to Miss Midler's all-out clowning. In one of the best sequences in the film, the city Rose finds herself being happily courted by the country Rose's suitor, a miniature-golf champ played in fine, broad, down-home style by Fred Ward.

Also providing excellent farcical support are Edward Herrmann, as a stuffy, suit-and-vest type of corporate officer, and Michele Placido, as the handsome Italian speculator for whom the city Sadie falls after initially summing him up as "Eurotrash."

Dean Cundey's photography is so effective, and the editing so slick, that not until the movie is over does one wonder how the camera tricks were achieved. The film's writers and Mr. Abrahams, whose first solo credit this is (he co-directed "Airplane!" and "Ruthless People" with David and Jerry Zucker), sometimes do have trouble in characterizing the two sets of twins, allowing them to blend in such a way that the comic edge finally becomes blurred.

Yet the film moves at such a clip, and with such uncommon zest, that it's good fun even when the invention wears thin. "Big Business" is no "Comedy of Errors" (to which it is distantly related), which should be taken as praise.

"Big Business," which has been rated PG ("Parental Guidance Suggested"), contains some mildly vulgar language and situations.

1988 Je 10, C10:4

Family Conflicts

DADDY'S BOYS, directed by Joe Minion; screenplay by Daryl Haney; director of photography, David G. Stump; edited by Norman Hollyn; music by Sasha Matson; production design, Gabrielle Petrissans; produced by Roger Corman; released by Concorde. At Bleecker St. Cinema, 144 Bleecker Street. Running time: 85 minutes. This film is rated R.

Hard Times Set in the Great Depression and starring Laura Burkett and Daryl Haney, "Daddy's Boys" is about a father and his sons who rob banks and kidnap women.

Jimmy .... Daryl Haney
Christie .... Laura Burkett
Daddy .... Raymond J. Barry
Hawk .... Dan Shor
Otis .... Christian Clemenson
Madame Wang .... Ellen Gerstein
Axelrod .... Robert V. Barron
Traveling Salesman .... Paul Linke

The muse visits in many forms, but the desire to re-use a brothel set left over from "Big Bad Mama II" is not one of them. That was Roger Corman's inspiration for producing "Daddy's Boys," a cheaply made film that proves you often get exactly what you pay for.

Daddy is a whiner who lost his Oklahoma cornfields during the Depression, so he and his three sons drive around the country robbing banks and kidnapping women. This might have been fun if "Daddy's Boys" were at all clever in the way it steals from "Bonnie and Clyde" or "The Grapes of Wrath." But the dialogue is humorless, the pacing slow, the acting deadly.

The entire film looks contemporary, with colors too bright for the Depression, haircuts too modern for the period. So it's no surprise to learn, in articles included with the shameless press material, that "Daddy's Boys" was shot in less than three weeks, and its script thrown together in even less time than that.

Some talented people are involved. Joe Minion, a first-time director, wrote the script for Martin Scorsese's "After Hours." Among the brothers, Dan Shor has been impressive before, especially in John Huston's "Wise Blood." These two seem smart enough to overcome "Daddy's Boys," which will be shown at the Bleecker Street Cinema Friday and Saturday at midnight only — so much the better for the unsuspecting public.

CARYN JAMES

1988 Je 10, C13:1

High-Rise Hobgoblins

POLTERGEIST III, directed by Gary Sherman; written by Mr. Sherman and Brian Taggert; director of photography, Alex Nepomniaschy; film editor, Ross Albert; music by Joe Renzetti; production designer, Paul

Eads; produced by Barry Bernardi; released by Metro-Goldwyn-Mayer. At Warner, Broadway and 43d Street; Gramercy, 23d St. between Park and Lexington Avenues and other theaters. Running time: 97 minutes.

Bruce Gardner	Tom Skerritt
Patricia Gardner	Nancy Allen
Carol Anne	Heather O'Rourke
Tangina Barrons	Zelda Rubinstein
Donna Gardner	Lara Flynn Boyle
Scott	Kip Wentz
Dr. Seaton	Richard Fire
Kane	Nathan Davis

"Poltergeist III" is made much ghostlier by the death last February of its 12-year-old star, Heather O'Rourke, than by anything that happens on the screen. The setting this time is an impersonally modern high-rise building complex in Chicago, where little Carol Anne (Miss O'Rourke) has been packed off to live with her Uncle Bruce (Tom Skerritt) and Aunt Patricia (Nancy Allen). Carol Anne, who cried out the famous "They're *he-eere!*" that earned the first "Poltergeist" its place in history, is still being hotly pursued by whatever it is that blamed her family for building houses on a favorite graveyard.

The high-rise, where Uncle Bruce is in charge of building maintenance, is lined with mirrors that serve as veritable breeding grounds for Carol Anne's old friends. There's hardly a mirror that doesn't contain the false reflection of one persona non grata or another. But Gary Sherman, who directed and co-wrote the film, has no notion of creating a coherent universe through the looking glass. He is content with fiery or body-shattering effects, interspersed with irritating small talk and accidental humor. "Put dinner on a low flame, and *don't* forget the cilantro," snaps Carol Anne's psychiatrist (Richard Fire) at his wife as he goes off to make yet another house call.

"Poltergeist III," which opens today at the Warner and other theaters, suffers from bad casting and from the actors' having been encouraged to behave as if sampling an exciting new toothpaste; everyone smiles unreasonably, except when screaming. Zelda Rubinstein, still playing the story's diminutive, baby-voiced psychic, makes a stronger impression than anyone else in the film, or perhaps just a more peculiar one.

It is her unhappy task to educate the other characters about the restorative powers of love, uttering platitudes that are at least more articulate than the dialogue reserved for action scenes. Where is Donna (Lara Flynn Boyle), Uncle Bruce's pretty teen-age daughter? When her boyfriend, covered with icy slime, returns from the Other Side to answer this question, he replies: "In the garage. In the garage. *In the garage!!!*"

Perhaps that's why they call it "Poltergeist III."

JANET MASLIN

•

"Poltergeist III" is rated PG-13 ("Special Parental Guidance Suggested for Those Younger Than 13"). It contains some grisly special effects.

1988 Je 10, C17:1

HAIL HAZANA, directed by José María Gutiérrez; screenplay (Spanish with English subtitles) by José Samano and Mr. Gutiérrez, based on the novel "El Infierno y la Brisa" by José María Vaz de Soto; photography by Magi Torruella; edited by Rosa Salgado; produced by Mr. Samano; released by Stillman International. At Cinema Village, 22 East 12th Street. Running time: 97 minutes. This film has no rating.

Father Prefect	Fernando Fernán-Gómez
Headmaster	Héctor Alterio

WITH: José Sacristán, Gabriel Llopart, Luis Ciges, Enrique San Francisco

By WALTER GOODMAN

"Hail Hazaña!," made in Spain in 1978, when the memory of the Franco dictatorship was still fresh, may be taken as a parable of the country's political transformation. We are in a Roman Catholic boys' school, where each day begins with the neatly turned-out lads, in orderly columns, singing their anthem: "Beloved School, Second Home." No graffiti mar the walls, and the head of the school maintains surveillance through binoculars from an upstairs window.

But rebellion is afoot, incited by ideologically and sexually repressive measures. Discontent is expressed at first in small incidents — a broken window, a fire. The school director, a priest who fancies himself a master of adolescent psychology, quarrels with his prefect, a tough disciplinarian, over how to handle matters, and the boys take advantage of the disarray to mount a full-fledged rebellion. The revolutionary cry "Arriba Hazaña!" refers to Mañuel Azaña, a president of the pre-Franco Republic, about whom the students know nothing except that "he must be terrific, the way the priests hate him."

•

The movie's director, José María Gutiérrez, who also collaborated on the screenplay, builds convincingly to the rebellion, shrewdly exploring the divisions among the students as well as the faculty. Fernando Fernán Gómez as the prefect and Héctor Alterio as the head of the school never become outright villains; however benighted their outlook and actions, they truly care for the souls of their charges and are distressed and confused by the uprising. The students are by turns mischievous, frightened, daring and slightly cracked, as they commit small nuisances that smack of sacrilege and work themselves up to demands for sex education and a role in running things. They build a mass movement against compulsory mass.

The movie, now at Cinema Village, is especially sharp in its recognition of how readily rebels may resort to demagogy; in a mild way, a couple of the student leaders come to resemble the tyrants they are combating. Unfortunately, Mr. Gutiérrez's edifying anti-authoritarianism turns his movie soft. An up-to-date sort of priest (he wears mufti and smokes) takes over, makes reasonable concessions and gives the boys a say in their school's operations. The last 15 minutes become a civics lesson in democracy — much too rosy, but perhaps just what was needed for the Spain of the time.

1988 Je 10, C18:1

Custody Battle

Dietmar Prinz in title role in the film "Beethoven's Nephew."

BEETHOVEN'S NEPHEW, directed by Paul Morrissey; written by Mathieu Carrière and Mr. Morrissey, from a novel by Luigi Magnani; director of photography, Hanus Pólak; edited by Albert Jurgenson and Michèle Lauliac; music by Ludwig van Beethoven; art director, Mario Garbuglia; produced by Orfilm (Marita Coustet); released by New World Pictures. At the Plaza, 58th Street, east of Madison Avenue. Running time: 103 minutes. This film is rated R.

Beethoven	Wolfgang Reichmann
Karl van Beethoven	Dietmar Prinz
Johanna van Beethoven	Jane Birkin
Leonore	Nathalie Baye
Archduke Rodolphe	Mathieu Carrière
Anton Schindler	Ulrich Berr
Marie	Erna Korhel
Karl Holz	Pieter Daniel

Paul Morrissey's "Beethoven's Nephew," opening today at the Plaza, is something of a first: two different movies that unreel simultaneously on a single screen.

The first is the film as it is presented in the screenplay. This is the story of Ludwig van Beethoven's final years, when the composer became involved in a series of vicious court battles with his sister-in-law over the custody of his teen-age nephew, Karl, the son of his brother, Karl Caspar.

Though there has been speculation about the roots of Beethoven's obsession with Karl, including the suggestion of a homosexual relationship, no single cause has ever been substantiated. The screenplay, which the film maker asserts is scrupulously accurate, maintains a discreet distance from all such speculation.

•

However, the film, as photographed, is full of homoerotic nuances, even if they don't involve the increasingly deaf and emotionally troubled old man. Mr. Morrissey's camera ignores Mr. Morrissey's screenplay (written with Mathieu Carrière). Instead of attending to the facts, the camera just sort of hangs around, staring at Dietmar Prinz, who plays Karl.

Mr. Prinz, a young Viennese medical student, looks rather like a male version of Mariel Hemingway. He has a square jaw, blue eyes and wears spit curls and a ponytail. He is, one must admit, pretty. Maybe Mr. Prinz is acting sullen, or perhaps his mind is a blank. It's impossible to tell, even in the context of the so-called story. There's no doubt, though, that the camera adores his utterly expressionless face. It can't take its eyes off him. The camera subverts Beethoven's obsession and substitutes its own.

In the course of the film, Karl exchanges ambiguous glances with other young men who are almost as pretty. These include Karl's mother's lover, who also has blue eyes and wears his hair in 19th-century Viennese dreadlocks.

•

Meanwhile, the screenplay plods dutifully on with the facts as known: Beethoven gains custody of Karl, treats him like an underpaid secretary, finally is forced to send the boy off to boarding school and then promptly moves into a house across the street from the school. Karl becomes so distraught that he attempts suicide. When that doesn't work, he joins the army. About this time, Beethoven catches a cold. He dies.

In the past, Mr. Morrissey has made some weirdly engaging, offbeat movies, including "Flesh," "Trash" and, most recently, "Mixed Blood," each exhibiting a sense of humor that is nowhere to be seen in this one. There is, instead, a lot of Beethoven on the soundtrack and a number of handsome settings.

Most of the actors, beginning with Wolfgang Reichmann, who plays Beethoven, speak English with early-Arnold Schwarzenegger accents. The exceptions are Jane Birkin, who plays Karl's unhappy, much-maligned mother, and Nathalie Baye, who appears briefly as a French singer who takes her pleasure of Karl. *VINCENT CANBY*

1988 Je 10, C12:6

Cut to the Chase

Meg Ryan in "The Presidio."

THE PRESIDIO, directed and photographed by Peter Hyams; written by Larry Ferguson; edited by James Mitchell; music by Bruce Broughton; production designer, Albert Brenner; produced by D. Constantine Conte; released by Paramount Pictures. At the Embassy 2, 3 and 4, Broadway and 47th Street; Loews New York Twin, Second Avenue and 66th Street, and other theaters. Running time: 99 minutes. This film is rated R.

Lieut. Col. Alan Caldwell	Sean Connery
Jay Austin	Mark Harmon
Donna Caldwell	Meg Ryan
Ross Maclure	Jack Warden
Lieut. Col. Paul Lawrence	Dana Gladstone
Arthur Peale	Mark Blum

By JANET MASLIN

Sean Connery is a fine actor under any circumstances, but he doesn't do much acting in "The Presidio," which opens today at Loews 84th Street and other theaters. What he does is to recite his lines while staring over Mark Harmon's shoulder. For his part, Mr. Harmon does much the same thing, staring past Mr. Connery to deliver the other half of the leading men's back-and-forth banter in a style that the director Peter Hyams obviously intends as gutsy and crisp. There's a blowhard side to this tough stuff, too, since in one scene Mr. Connery fends off a large barroom bully using nothing but his thumb.

Mr. Connery doesn't often appear in uniform, and he doesn't often appear in roles this constricting. But in "The Presidio" he holds up the avuncular end of a standard-issue male buddy film, playing the gruff Lieut. Col. Alan Caldwell, who is teamed with the brash young police inspector Jay Austin (Mr. Harmon) when a jurisdictional dispute throws them together. Uniting to solve a murder that took place at the San Francisco military installation for which the film is named, they are also brought into conflict by Austin's wild passion for Caldwell's pretty daughter.

Ralph Nelson Jr.

Military Matters In "Presidio," directed by Peter Hyams, Sean Connery plays a provost marshal whose daughter is having an affair with a police detective with whom he is investigating a murder.

As Donna, the daughter, Meg Ryan first appears in an outfit that makes it extremely unlikely that she has spent any time around the Army base without coming to harm. But the screenplay explains that she had been away at boarding school until the month before. (Though it has some spark, Larry Ferguson's screenplay overstates and overexplains everything.) In any case, no sooner does she meet Austin than the high-stakes suggestive banter begins, and Donna recommends that they "cut to the chase." The chase, in this case, is an outdoor version of the strenuous "Fatal Attraction"-style sexual coupling that is in movie vogue at the moment, and it begins with Mr. Harmon stretched across a car hood. Someone is going to get hurt this way.

"The Presidio" proves to be no more real or moving in its love scenes than in any other way, since the material is so forced and the direction so intent on stylish overkill. Mr. Hyams, who is also the film's cinematographer, consistently takes a tricked-up approach to details that would better have been left alone. Arbitrary chase scenes are injected into the story at regular intervals; settings are colorful but largely irrelevant; the lighting effects are so showy they actually steal scenes. In the shot that finds Donna and Austin on their first date, the glowing lamp between them on the restaurant table is so attention-getting that it looks ready to talk.

Boosting the story in these and other artificial ways, Mr. Hyams dispels any hint of believability it may have had. It doesn't help that the mystery plot seems half-baked in the end, or that none of the actors appear entirely comfortable with their roles. Miss Ryan looks edgy and spends a lot of time tossing her hair. Mr. Harmon is easygoing and attractive, but his nice-guy manner belies his character's steely talk. Mr. Connery and Jack Warden, as an old Army buddy, share the kind of confessional drunk scene that no actor could salvage, in which they de-

cide that the nation is like a large house and the Army its Doberman Pinscher. Mark Blum makes a suitable villain, but it's never entirely clear what he or anyone else has done. Viewers interested in the Presidio itself, which serves as the backdrop for much of the story, would be just as well advised to take a guided tour.

1988 Je 10, C15:1

Documentary On Sex Change At the Age of 55

"Call Me Madame" was shown as part of this year's New Directors/New Films Series. Following are excerpts from Vincent Canby's review, which appeared in The New York Times March 12. The film, which is in French with English subtitles, opens today at the Public, 425 Lafayette Street.

At the age of 55, Jean-Pierre Voidies had a sex-change operation. He had been a political activist, poet, novelist, husband of the birdlike Huguette Voidies and the father of one son, Jean-Noël.

Today Ovida Delect, the former Jean-Pierre Voidies, is a dainty if strapping older woman, with the physique of a steam fitter and a voice to match. She's still a political activist, poet and novelist as well as the author of an autobiography, "Putting on the Dress." No longer the husband of Huguette, she is, instead, Huguette's lifelong companion and the cause of quite a lot of contradictory emotions in Jean-Noël, an earnest young man who continues to live at home and hopes to become a professional disk jockey.

Ovida Delect, both as she is and as she would like to appear before the world, is the subject of Françoise Romand's "Call Me Madame," a wonderfully oddball, 52-minute documentary that opens today at the Public on a bill with Miss Romand's earlier "Mix-Up."

Miss Romand makes documentaries that look like those of nobody else. Though she sticks to facts, they're often facts that few writers of supposedly serious fiction would dare to touch except under pseudonym.

If Miss Romand never seems to be ridiculing Ovida Delect, part of the reason must be that Miss Delect is such a forceful, enthusiastic collaborator, running the movie in much the way she runs her household. From her remarks about her politics and her activism, it's clear that she is not a nut. She's an unbudgeably self-confident presence.

At home, at a women's club meeting, standing in the prow of a rowboat and at a village memorial for the war dead, she enthusiastically recites her poetry, which sounds pretty awful in the English subtitles. In interviews, she attempts to define what femininity means to her ("openness, lightness, sweetness") and sees herself as a muse existing somewhere between sea and shore, which is how Miss Romand presents her at the beginning and the end of the film.

Ovida is not always easy to get along with. Life with her has taken its toll of Huguette, who frequently weeps when remembering why she was attracted to the young Jean-Pierre and fell in love with him. Says Jean-Noël, "I was the first victim." Says Huguette sadly, "Jean-Noël is an extension of the life that used to be."

Miss Romand talks to some of Ovida's fellow villagers, who are fairly caustic about the new woman, especially about her fastidious clothes. They still refer to "her" as "him." In one doleful shot, Ovida, quite pleased with herself, dances with a shy Huguette at a local fair. There's no question about who leads whom.

1988 Je 10, C16:6

Detachment And Despair In Europe

"Les Rendez-Vous d'Anna" was shown as part of the 1979 New Directors/New Films Series. Following are excerpts from Janet Maslin's review, which appeared in The New York Times on April 27, 1979. The film, which is in French with English subtitles, opens today at the Public Theater, 425 Lafayette Street.

The heroine of "Les Rendez-Vous d'Anna," described by the film's director, Chantal Akerman, as "a sort of mutant . . . perhaps a heroine of the future," is both so fearless and joyless she's almost a ghost. Anna, played with great care by Aurore Clément, is a young film maker traveling from city to city to promote her work. The movie spans several days and three countries, moving from one determinedly neutral setting to the next as it suggests a rootlessness that goes perhaps too far beyond freedom.

Anna meets a variety of people, listens closely to the long monologues they deliver and, upon rare occasions, volunteers tiny bits of information about herself. She seems engaged by everything and by nothing. She also seems, perhaps because of her attentive manner and regal bearing, to be in great demand as an audience and a lover. Everyone who encounters Anna wants more of her. But Anna isn't often generous with her feelings. Other people interest her, but then so do the shoes and leftover dinner she finds outside someone else's hotel-room door one evening.

Miss Akerman's film has a crisp, simple elegance at times, as the camera studies a hotel room or a train station with a patience like Anna's own. Miss Akerman's attention to detail is at times peculiarly excessive, as when Anna finds a strange man's necktie in her room and feels obliged to report that it is "on two hangers, on the left-hand side of the closet."

Most of the tales told to Anna cut right to the bone, to the very simplest level of despair, and yet the film's tone is too detached to seem bleak. If anything, the mood is mysteriously playful at times, as in a sweet, knowing sequence that shows an uncharacteristically lighthearted Anna singing a little song to one of her lovers. "A little sunshine can be so bright that it hurts," goes the refrain.

1988 Je 10, C13:1

FILM VIEW/Janet Maslin

Today's Alter Has a Smaller Ego

THE GROWN MAN WHO'S ACTUally a teen-ager, the housewife who revisits the senior prom, the white college student who pretends to be black and the high-powered executive who'd rather be making baby food have something in common. Like a surprising number of characters in recent film comedies, they share the same underlying secret, one that can be summed up this way: *I'm not really me.*

Who are they, then? Almost invariably, these films reveal their heroes and heroines to be surreptitiously younger, sweeter, more sensitive and more spontaneous — in other words, *nicer* — than they appear. While the character's public personality can go on to achieve stunning success in the business world, his private existence as, for example, a charmingly ingenuous mail-room boy, may underscore his likable side. That way, ambition, acquisitiveness and other potentially cold-blooded qualities can be made more acceptable, thanks to the invention of a secret life.

Of course, identity switching is nothing new, and comedies have always relied on it in various forms. But the 80's film versions have a peculiar spin, since they concern themselves so utterly with specific individuals and their own narrow worlds. When Preston Sturges' John Sullivan embarked on a secret life in "Sullivan's Travels," as a rich man impersonating a bum, he did it to find out how the other half lived. But no one in today's films experiences any comparable form of curiosity. When an 80's character changes age or sex or personality, the device is used mostly as a means of letting the hero find out more about himself.

Finding out becomes a matter of reconciling, more often than not, since today's characters show less interest in breaking out of sterile, conformist lives than in finding ways to make them more bearable. Benjamin Braddock's famous 1967 gesture of rebellion in "The Graduate" — breaking into church to whisk the woman he loved away from the altar and embark on an uncharted new course — would be unthinkable in times like these. Characters may complain, but they never truly break with convention. Today's version of a Benjamin Braddock might accept that job in "plastics" so fast it would make your head spin.

∎

But once installed, and having duly risen to the top as success-minded 80's characters invariably do, he might find himself in need of some secret escape valve, and that's where today's identity-switching fantasies come in.

Their escape-hatch value surely accounts for much of their popularity, even more so than Hollywood's time-honored way of letting great minds think alike. So the recent cluster of age-switching films — supplanting the time-switch ("Back to the Future," "Peggy Sue Got Married") and sex-switch ("Tootsie," "Victor/Victoria" and even "All of Me") variations on this theme — present men who enjoy all the privileges that accrue to successful professionals yet still, secretly, have the fun of behaving like little boys.

So they giggle on the job (Dudley Moore, as a doctor in "Like Father, Like Son"). They fool around with electric guitars (Judge Reinhold, playing a department store executive in "Vice Versa." Or as Tom Hanks does in "Big," they may even turn an adolescent's obsession with computers and toys into a career bonanza, should they be lucky enough to land a job that's made to order.

Mr. Hanks's Josh Baskin winds up working for a toy company, where the boss (Robert Loggia) is simply delighted by the playful high spirits of his newest employee. Even if the grown man's secret boyishness is treated as something he must hide from others, it becomes a source of enchantment for everyone he meets.

Ingenuousness, spontaneity and eagerness are seen as the keys to personal and professional success in these films, and the character often does better in his boyish mode than he has as a more tense and worried, more ordinary man. The fact that his friends and colleagues so enjoy his new incarnation is another way of saying that they liked him less as a hardened careerist, and indeed that seems to be the underlying point.

In "Big Business," the giddy identity-switching comedy that sends two sets of twins ricocheting through the Plaza Hotel, Bette Midler carries this to an especially hilarious extreme by playing both a screeching executive harpy and her sweet little sibling from the country, the latter first seen wearing a gingham dress and milking a cow. While the executive barks orders and strikes fear into her staff, her kinder, more generous alter ego also sashays across the screen, and

Laurel Moore

Lily Tomlin and Bette Midler in "Big Business"

thus has a powerfully mitigating effect.

Today's identity-switching premises aren't always designed to soften their characters' hard edges; sometimes they also bring hope and color lives that would otherwise be dull. So the New Jersey housewife played by Rosanna Arquette in "Desperately Seeking Susan" has the chance to blossom into an adventurous bohemian, and the old people in "Cocoon" are given a magical chance to shake off their infirmities and become young.

In "Micki and Maude," a man whose marriage has lost its spark finds an opportunity to reinvigorate himself with an extra wife, and in "Planes, Trains and Automobiles" Steve Martin's harried businessman finds himself enjoying unexpected friendship with John Candy, as a boyish new buddy.

Every member of the nouveau riche family of "Down and Out in Beverly Hills" finds some lively benefit in the presence of Nick Nolte's visiting derelict. Even the celestial branch of identity-change stories, from "Heaven Can Wait" to the recent "Made in Heaven," give their characters a new lease on earthly life once they pass through the pearly gates.

If Rockyism, the idea that streetwise, Everyman characters could turn dancing or boxing or karate into a route to wealth and fame, was the prevailing movie mind-set of the 1970's, we are now working our way out of that corner. Characters who've climbed to the top now find themselves wondering how to get back down. Even when they're as bubbly as "Big Business" or as innocent as "Big," today's comedies suggest a culture in which escapism takes the form of covert, no-risk daydreams of escape.

∎

Their characters, unlike Walter Mitty, dream of less instead of more; even more welcome than the film whose hero travels to other galaxies and conquers unknown worlds may be the smaller story of how someone ordinary gets through the day. And has fun — the great omission in the having-it-all 80's formula — in the process.

A lot of what makes "Big" appealing is the caliber of Tom Hanks's performance, the genial style of Penny Marshall's direction and the screenplay's wittier touches. But a lot of it is also the sight of Mr. Hanks really enjoying himself by playing with toys. Miss Marshall creates a remarkable image of paradoxical 80's existence when she pulls the camera back, in one nighttime scene, so that it looks through the windows of Josh Baskin's new loft, which he has stocked with junk food and furnished with playthings. (When the delivery men arrive, the secretly 13-year-old Josh is waiting for them with water balloons.)

There, seen through the windows, are Josh and his co-worker Susan (Elizabeth Perkins), who attended a black-tie party earlier in the evening and have perhaps come back to Josh's place for a tryst. The scene has a romantic feeling, but what are they doing? Having what is very possibly the best time they could have, just by jumping on a trampoline.

Susan has become a nicer, happier person by the time "Big" ends, and Josh has undoubtedly become wiser in certain ways. By the end of "Big Business," each of the twins' boyfriends has found a new, improved mate, a sweeter, more affectionate replica of the woman he knew before. Indeed, the popularity of the identity-switching premise may have a lot to do with the satisfying conclusion to which it's apt to lead: to a Cyrano (in Steve Martin's version of "Roxanne") who gets the girl, or to a bitchy heiress's discovery of the simple life (in "Overboard"), or to a man's becoming a better man (in "Tootsie") because he's been a woman. The ending may even be a moment of transcendent union, as it was when Steve Martin danced with Lily

Tomlin in "All of Me."

The endings of these films are often even happier than they look, since the miraculous transformation of a hard edged 80's character into a nicer, gentler alter ego has often been achieved at no cost. Rueful at the end of "Big," Josh Baskin is nonetheless much improved by his experiences and in any case this wistfulness is the exception rather than the rule. Identity-switching adventures tend to leave their characters fortified and invigorated, undaunted by lives they previously found taxing and ready to tackle the tasks before them with improved perspective and new enthusiasm. The audiences that have made these films so popular undoubtedly go home feeling that way, too. ☐

1988 Je 12, II:29:1

RIGHTS AND REACTIONS: LESBIAN AND GAY RIGHTS ON TRIAL, produced and directed by Phil Zwickler and Jane Lippman; photographed by Geoffrey O'Connor; edited by Miss Lippman; distributed by Tapestry International. Running time: 56 minutes.

OSCAR WILDE: SPENDTHRIFT OF GENIUS, produced and directed by Sean O'Mordha; written by Richard Ellman; narrator, Denys Hawthorne. Film Forum 1, 57 Watts Street. Running time: 60 minutes. These films have no rating.

By VINCENT CANBY

Homosexuality and the law is the shared theme of the two documentaries opening on a single bill today at Film Forum 1.

"Rights and Reactions: Lesbian and Gay Rights on Trial," by Phil Zwickler and Jane Lippman, is a straightforward record of the 1986 New York City Council hearings on the gay rights bill, which, after 16 years, was finally passed. Mr. Zwickler and Ms. Lippman are committed but self-effacing reporters who allow their subject to shape the film.

"Rights and Reactions," 56 minutes long, recalls the sometimes unruly hearings in the passionate testimony of the speakers, pro and con. Religious conservatives (Christian and Jewish) constantly interrupt the bill's supporters, who, speaking with impatience accumulated over the years, are (not surprisingly) far more persuasive.

The film is lean, functional and effective.

By comparison, "Oscar Wilde: Spendthrift of Genius" (60 minutes), produced and directed by Sean O'-Mordha, is fancified movie making that seems to be for people who, possibly, have never heard of Oscar Wilde. The screenplay is by Richard Ellmann, the author of the excellent Wilde biography that came out this year. It is filled with cradle-to-grave facts, all presented in an old-fashioned documentary style that you might have thought went out with "The March of Time."

Mr. O'Mordha takes his camera from Wilde's Irish birthplace to Trinity College in Dublin, Oxford University, London, Paris and Rome, while a high-toned narrator tells us what happened in each place and about the awful consequences. Every now and then an actor is employed to speak Wilde's more familiar lines in a self-conscious manner that would certainly not have pleased the author.

The film is informative and lugubrious.

1988 Je 15, C19:3

Take Me Out Susan Sarandon and Kevin Costner have a major league romance in a minor league town in "Bull Durham."

It's How You Play the Game

BULL DURHAM, directed and written by Ron Shelton; director of photography, Bobby Byrne; film editors, Robert Leighton and Adam Weiss; music by Michael Convertino; production designer, Armin Ganz; produced by Thom Mount and Mark Burg; released by Orion Pictures Corporation. At the Criterion Center, Broadway at 45th Street; the Loews New York Twin, Second Avenue and 66th Street, and other theaters. Running time: 115 minutes. This film is rated R.

Crash Davis	Kevin Costner
Annie Savoy	Susan Sarandon
Ebby Calvin (Nuke) LaLoosh	Tim Robbins
Skip	Trey Wilson
Larry	Robert Wuhl
Jimmy	William O'Leary
Bobby	David Neidorf
Deke	Danny Gans

By JANET MASLIN

"Bull Durham" is a film with spring fever, a giddy, playful look at life in baseball's minor leagues. The team on which it concentrates is the Durham, N. C., Bulls, but the film involves no person, team or chewing tobacco with the Bull Durham name, so the title is slightly puzzling. It would be unsporting to mention this if there weren't many other misfires of a similar nature: dialogue that strains to be colorful, indiscriminately piled-on pop songs, plot developments that aren't followed through on, and minor aspects of motivation that are never known.

It's a lucky thing that the film, like the players it celebrates, knows better than to stake too much on ability alone. Even luckier, it has more than enough spirit and sex appeal to get by. In fact, "Bull Durham" has a cast that's much too attractive to need the kind of overheated sexual grandstanding that the writer and director Ron Shelton (who previously wrote "Under Fire") insists upon. Brash but a little unsteady in his directing debut feature, Mr. Shelton has a way of overstating some things about these characters and leaving others bafflingly unsaid.

"Bull Durham," which opens today at the Criterion and other theaters, sets up a romantic triangle involving Annie Savoy (Susan Sarandon) with two baseball players, Crash Davis and (Nuke) LaLoosh (played by Kevin

Costner and Tim Robbins, both of whom might well have accepted these roles on the strength of the character names alone).

Annie, who narrates the film, is a baseball enthusiast with a difference: she keeps a shrine to the sport in her home, ponders odd facts linking baseball with religion (that there are 108 beads on a rosary, for instance, and also 108 stitches in a baseball), and each year chooses a player to become the beneficiary of her own highly unconventional brand of home instruction. It might be said that Annie is an aging groupie. But Mr. Shelton, who shows her lashing one new recruit to her bed and reading him Walt Whitman, presents her as a muse.

Miss Sarandon turns Annie into such a dish that the distinction hardly matters, sashaying through the film in off-the-shoulder outfits and delivering much more advice on the game of baseball than any of the Bulls ever dreamed he'd want to hear. Annie's protégé for this particular season is the talented, extremely dim (and extremely funny, thanks to Mr. Robbins) rookie she nicknames "Nuke," who is every tutor's dream.

Nuke follows Annie's every suggestion, right down to her idea of having him wear a black garter belt under his uniform while he pitches. That way, Nuke explains dutifully to a teammate, he can "keep one side of my brain occupied when I'm on the mound, thus keeping the other side slightly off-center, which is where it should be for artists and players." Good student that he is, Nuke has understandable nightmares about the pitfalls of following Annie's advice a little too far.

Crash Davis arrives on the scene as an older player assigned to keep Nuke from self-destructing, but he quickly emerges as the kid's antithesis in every way. Crash had the brains that might have made him great, but he didn't have the talent; he was good, but not good enough. And he can understand Annie a lot better than Nuke can, possibly better than she understands herself.

Mr. Shelton manages to make these qualities seem pat and hazy simultaneously, and there are too many times when it's difficult to be sure where Crash stands; when he picks a barroom fight with Nuke at the beginning of the film, for instance, the sequence is directed so slackly that it's momentarily hard to be sure whether the fight is a trick or the real thing. Kevin Costner, whose wary, elusive manner in other films has sometimes been mistaken for blankness, this time seems a good deal more definite than the material itself.

Mr. Costner, who is well on his way to becoming a full-fledged matinee idol, does a lot with this role all the same.

Mr. Costner gives Crash a shrewd, knowing manner so effortless that it's easily mistaken for nonchalance, and a flirty, confident style that Annie inevitably begins to appreciate. The attraction between them need not have led to the elaborate antics Mr. Shelton produces: Crash and Annie dancing around her apartment in kimonos (twice), or cavorting in the bathtub, or collaborating on an impromptu pedicure. Each of them, and particularly Mr. Costner, knows how to make a small amount of suggestiveness go a lot farther than this.

Another thing these actors do is to camouflage the material's seamier side. "I mean, it wasn't the first time I went to bed with a man and woke up with a note," says Annie at one point, but her past history is handled with

kid gloves. And Crash's professional status remains somewhat indistinct, so that he's neither a misguided winner nor the kind of resigned has-been played by Paul Newman in "Slap Shot," that classic comedy of second-rate sports. The best of "Bull Durham" has some of that film's loose-jointed, iconoclastic physical humor. It also has the charming if belabored notion that baseball, love, poetry and religion do indeed share common ground.

1988 Je 15, C20:5

Schism

Jodhi May in "A World Apart."

A WORLD APART, directed by Chris Menges; written by Shawn Slovo; director of photography, Peter Biziou; edited by Nicolas Gaster; music by Hans Zimmer; designer, Brian Morris; produced by Sarah Radclyffe; released by Atlantic Releasing Corporation. At Cinema 1, Third Avenue and 60th Street. Running time: 112 minutes. This film is rated PG.

Diana Roth	Barbara Hershey
Molly Roth	Jodhi May
Gus Roth	Jeroen Krabbe
Miriam Roth	Carolyn Clayton-Cragg
Jude Roth	Merav Gruer
Bertha	Yvonne Bryceland
Solomon	Albee Lesotho
Elsie	Linda Mvusi

By VINCENT CANBY

The title "A World Apart," refers to several things, including the insulated world of South Africa's white minority for whom each commonplace gesture of daily life becomes an act of overbearing political significance, an affirmation of the minority's own God-given (and Government-decreed) superiority. White South Africans don't ignore the members of the black majority, yet somehow they don't see them.

Apartheid, a state policy, is a trickster's magic spell that allows its supporters to hold two contradictory thoughts at the same time. Woe to anyone, white or black, who attempts to point out that this sort of thinking can lead only to breakdown and chaos.

"A World Apart" is about one white woman, Diana Roth (Barbara Hershey), who, in working clandestinely to correct what she sees to be an intolerable political situation, nearly wrecks the emotional life of her adoring daughter Molly (Jodhi May), 12.

•

The film presents two complex stories simultaneously, but in such a way that the political tragedy often appears to be used as a somewhat exotic background for everything happening in the foreground. Inevitably the importance given to one has the effect of diminishing, or at least restricting, the concern allowed the other.

"A World Apart," like Sir Richard Attenborough's "Cry Freedom," suggests that the white man's burden, which once was trade, education and the propagation of the Christian faith, is now to suffer selflessly on behalf of the world's benighted. In whatever way you look at these films, the white man still shoulders the burden, and still receives most of the sympathy.

"A World Apart," which marks the directing debut of Chris Menges, the Oscar-winning cameraman ("The Killing Fields," "The Mission"), was clearly one of the most popular films at this year's Cannes Film Festival. It won the Special Jury Prize (in fact, the festival's second prize) and Miss Hershey, Miss May and Linda Mvusi, who plays the family's black maid, shared the best actress award.

•

It's a beautifully acted, maddening movie that, while expressing all the right sentiments, never goes quite far enough. In this way, it soothes the consciences of white, liberal, middle-class audiences. It doesn't say anything that these audiences don't already know. It talks about Armageddon, but it reduces Armageddon to the vision of a sweet, baffled little girl who feels she's been abandoned by her mother.

"A World Apart" is said to parallel the childhood of its screenwriter, Shawn Slovo, whose parents, Joe Slovo, a lawyer, and Ruth First, a journalist, were active in the South African freedom movement. Miss Slovo sets the film in Johannesburg in 1963, shortly before her father went into exile and her mother was subjected to a series of arrests under the so-called 90-day law, allowing for prisoners to be detained without bail for up to 90 days.

Miss Hershey is splendid in the somewhat chilly role of the journalist. Diana Roth is the sort of ardent liberal (she's called a Communist by her enemies) who plows ferociously on, working for the betterment of the masses, while allowing her own children to fend for themselves.

Miss Hershey is so good that she even manages to suggest a cruel edge to Diana Roth. When she gives a "mixed" party at home, with music loud enough to rouse the neighbors, she is putting not only herself on the line, but also her family. There is something heedless about her that works against the cause she supports. The character is tough and intelligent but also so initially self-absorbed she doesn't understand the toll her activities are taking on those around her.

•

Young Miss May is remarkably fine as the child who, at an age when to conform is to succeed, suddenly finds herself without any real home life and ostracized by her friends at school. Mr. Menges also obtains stunning performances from the other children in the cast. The "world apart" is also that of childhood.

All of the blacks in the film are supporting characters, including Miss Mvusi's patient, wise maid and the nicely mannered freedom fighter played by Albee Lesotho. They are appreciated, certainly, but seen mostly as types. This is not much different from the way they are seen by the repressive South African Government.

On the basis of "A World Apart" (which, it must be emphasized, is far better than "Cry Freedom"), Mr. Menges is an efficient, intelligent director (especially in his handling of actors) but not a very exciting one.

The big scenes of black demonstrations are handsomely shot (the movie was made in Zimbabwe), but perfunctory, like the funeral of a murdered black freedom fighter. They

are more obligatory than moving. Mr. Menges treats the early departure of Diana's husband (and Molly's father) in much the same way. Gus Roth (Jeroen Krabbe) is less a character than a plot function.

"A World Apart" opens today at the Cinema 1.

1988 Je 17, C10:4

Holiday Dan Aykroyd co-stars with John Candy in "The Great Outdoors," about brothers-in-law whose rivalry leads to misadventures during a family vacation at a Wisconsin campground.

THE GREAT OUTDOORS, directed by Howard Deutch; written by John Hughes; director of photography, Ric Waite; edited by Tom Rolf, William Gordean and Seth Flaum; music by Thomas Newman; production designer, John W. Corso; produced by Arne L. Schmidt; released by Universal Pictures. At Movieland, Broadway and 47th Street; Beekman, 65th Street and Second Avenue, and other theaters. Running time: 90 minutes.

Roman	Dan Aykroyd
Chet	John Candy
Connie	Stephanie Faracy
Kate	Annette Bening
Buck	Chris Young
Ben	Ian Giatti
Cara	Hilary Gordon
Mara	Rebecca Gordon
Wally	Robert Prosky

The collective energy that has gone into making "The Great Outdoors," the comedy opening today at the Movieland and other theaters, probably wouldn't be enough to light a campfire. It's a film in which the raccoons, whose conversation is subtitled ("Rocks on top of the garbage cans." "That never works." "We'll just knock the cans over."), are funnier than the people.

"The Great Outdoors," which was directed by Howard Deutch, teams John Candy and Dan Aykroyd as brothers-in-law whose families spend a weeklong vacation together. But beyond that, very little happens. A bat gets into the cabin. A bear gets into the cabin. Leeches get into the rowboat. The dimply teen-agers, who are treated as another variety of wildlife, share a few tentative courtship scenes. Even these, the stock-in-trade of John Hughes, who wrote the film, seem terribly half-hearted.

Mr. Aykroyd, as the high-rolling brother-in-law of the two, wears an

Elvis impersonator's hairdo but otherwise hasn't much to do. Mr. Candy works harder, in a runaway water-skiing sequence and a steak-eating contest that represent the film's most refined humor. Though the film never becomes actively unfunny, neither does it do much more than tread water. The raccoons have a better time than the audience will.

•

"The Great Outdoors" is rated PG ("Parental Guidance Suggested"). It contains rude language and mild sexual suggestiveness.

JANET MASLIN

1988 Je 17, C12:6

Heights and Depths

Ozzy Osbourne

THE DECLINE OF WESTERN CIVILIZATION PART II: THE METAL YEARS, directed by Penelope Spheeris; director of photography, Jeff Zimmerman; edited by Earl Ghaffari; produced by Jonathan Dayton and Valerie Faris, released by New Line Cinema. At Eighth Street Playhouse, at Avenue of the Americas. Running time: 87 minutes. This film is rated R.

With: Joe Perry and Steven Tyler of Aerosmith; Alice Cooper; Gene Simmons and Paul Stanley of Kiss; Lemmy of Motorhead; Ozzy Osbourne; C. C. DeVille, Bobby Dall, Bret Michaels and Rikki Rockett of Poison, and other performers.

By JANET MASLIN

Even those who would never, without the urging of wild horses, dream of attending a film about the seamy world of heavy-metal music are sure to find Penelope Spheeris's "The Decline of Western Civilization Part II: The Metal Years" of unexpected interest. For one thing, Miss Spheeris has a way of asking just the right questions. Although the director does not appear on camera, she is very much a presence in the film, conveying a genuine interest that wins her subjects' trust, and perhaps tacitly goading them to new heights of outrageousness. But when it's time to ask bluntly about sex, drugs, ethics or economics, Miss Spheeris is ready to speak up.

"So what do you have to say to people who think your music maybe isn't all that original?" she asks. "Where do you see yourself in 10 years?" "What if you don't make it as a rock-and-roll star?" "Would you go out with a girl if she pays for some food if you didn't like her? Isn't that prostitution?" "Are you in it for the money?" Of Paul Stanley of Kiss, who has smugly arranged himself in a supine position for his interview with three lingerie-wearing groupies draped strategically around him, she inquires "Have you ever said to yourself 'I could fall in love with this groupie?'" Mr. Stanley flinches slightly and the girls look up, suddenly interested.

•

Soundscape Randy "O" of the rock group Odin is among the performers who appear in "The Decline of Western Civilization Part II: The Metal Years."

To say that Ozzy Osbourne functions as one of the film's chief voices of sanity may give some notion of what the other interviewees are like. Along with several of the other big-name luminaries who appear here, Mr. Osbourne conveys the impression that the measure of success in the heavy metal world is being able to budget a stay at the Betty Ford center. Newly rehabilitated himself, Mr. Osbourne is interviewed while puttering around a comfortable kitchen in his bathrobe, extolling his new abstemiousness yet still having trouble pouring orange juice into a glass. Compared with Steven Tyler of Aerosmith, who boasts about his musical and sexual talents and also declares, ". must've snorted up all of Peru," Mr. Osbourne indeed seems to be a simple soul.

On the other end of the spectrum and equally important to the film, are the heavy metal wanna-be's, the kids whose unguarded talk about their aspirations can be so revealing. "I don't want to be *like* Jim Morrison, but I want to go down in history like that," says someone unlikely to succeed. Another hopeful observes "I want to be extremely wealthy . . . to be remembered for the rest of my life and for my grandchildren's grandchildren's lives." Whatever love of music these aspirants may have — and the brief performance excerpts in the film are mostly loud and interchangeable — it is overshadowed by their eagerness for stardom, which they all view as inevitable.

•

Uniformly, those interviewed display a contempt for holding ordinary jobs, an unwillingness to contemplate anything between glory and the gutter and a blind faith that talent will find a way. Just as everyone Miss Spheeris asks cites sex as his or her favorite pursuit, they all express the same certainty that great success is just around the corner. What if it doesn't happen? "I don't believe that it won't because there's nothin' in this life you can't do" is a typical answer.

In Miss Spheeris's earlier hell-in-a-handbasket documentary, the original "Decline of Western Civilization" about punk rockers, the brainpower quotient was somewhat higher than it is among heavy-metal fans. That's one reason that the new film is both so funny and so sad. For all the amusingly fatuous remarks heard here — and Miss Spheeris has a great ear for these — the overriding dimness of most of the fans and musicians is frightening. The women are happy to be exploited, the men avid for new forms of self-destruction, and no one can see an inch beyond tomorrow.

The most startling sequence here is one in which a mother witnesses the death of her son. It hasn't happened yet, but from the way Chris Holmes of the group WASP drifts drunkenly on a swimming pool float, guzzling vodka out of the bottle, telling lurid groupie stories and marveling at how much older he looks than his 29 years, it's clear that Mr. Holmes is on a severe and deliberate downward spiral. Alongside sits his mother, silently taking all this in, until Miss Spheeris asks Mr. Holmes if he is an alcoholic. "Only when he's awake," the mother says.

❦

Miss Spheeris never makes direct moral judgments, but she suggests indirectly that many of those in the film share a craving for just the sort of help Mr. Holmes's mother fails to provide. Among the more pathetic scenes are the glimpses of young women competing for the attention of a club owner, Bill Gazzarri, a 60-year-old who claims he's like three 20-year-olds and works hard at using more obscenities than any of his young clientele. And behind some of the band members' bragging about taking financial advantage of female admirers ("it's kind of a rule that chicks don't really get in the house unless they have a sack of groceries with 'em") is a hint of real helplessness, which contrasts so markedly with the power-mad lyrics of heavy-metal songs.

"The Decline of Western Civilization II" opens today at the Eighth Street Playhouse, where it can be seen alone. But "This Is Spinal Tap" will be the perfect companion piece some day.

1988 Je 17, C14:4

Détente Comes To Chicago

RED HEAT, directed by Walter Hill; screenplay by Harry Kleiner and Mr. Hill and Troy Kennedy Martin, story by Mr. Hill; director of photography, Matthew F. Leonetti; edited by Freeman Davies, Carmel Davies and Donn Aron; music by James Horner; production designer, John Vallone; produced by Mr. Hill and Gordon Carroll. Released through Tri-Star Pictures. At Loews 84th Street Six, at Broadway; Loews Orpheum Twin, 86th Street near Third Avenue, and other theaters. Running time: 106 minutes. This film is rated R.

Ivan Danko	Arnold Schwarzenegger
Art Ridzik	James Belushi
Lou Donnelly	Peter Boyle
Viktor Rostavili	Ed O'Ross
Lieutenant Stobbs	Larry Fishburne
Cat Manzetti	Gina Gershon
Sergeant Gallagher	Richard Bright
Salim	J. W. Smith

The initial sequence of Walter Hill's "Red Heat" is set in the sexist unisex steamroom of a Russian foundry. The men in the steamroom — all of whom, including Arnold Schwarzenegger, appear to be past, present or future candidates for the Mr. Universe title — are dressed in loincloths. The women are naked.

Mr. Schwarzenegger is challenged by another man who says the film's

From Russia With Gun In "Red Heat," Arnold Schwarzenegger plays the role of a Russian homicide officer who journeys to Chicago to hunt for one of the Soviet Union's most wanted criminals.

star doesn't have the hands of a foundry worker. Those are fighting words. In the ensuing fracas, Mr. Schwarzenegger and his opponent go crashing through the steamroom window to carry on their fight in the snow.

In this way begins glasnost's first buddy movie.

●

"Red Heat, which is set mostly in the dirtier streets of Chicago, is about the grudging friendship that develops between Moscow's foremost homicide cop (Mr. Schwarzenegger) and his Chicago equivalent (Jim Belushi), when the Soviet officer comes to the States to extradite a notorious drug dealer.

The two men are, of course, the kind of opposites required of buddy movies. Mr. Schwarzenegger is a clean-living, self-sufficient stoic, appalled by the excesses of capitalism. Mr. Belushi is living testimony to what happens when a fellow has the freedom to choose between junk food and bean sprouts. He is an overweight slob but he is also canny, self-mocking and fast on his feet, which could go flat at any minute.

When the chips are down, as they are more or less throughout the movie, each man must respect the other.

"Red Heat" is a topically entertaining variation on the sort of action-adventure nonsense that plays best on television. Mr. Hill's touch is heavy when he takes himself seriously ("The Warriors," "Southern Comfort"). However, as he demonstrated in "48 Hours" and "Extreme Prejudice," he has a real gift for instantly disposable fantasy.

Though Mr. Belushi is the comedian of the film, the most consistently comic performance is given by Mr. Schwarzenegger. With jaw squared and face straight, he moves through the plot with the serenity of a battleship pushing its way through a fleet of sailboats. Even his Russian, translated by English subtitles, sounds as authentic as need be for this kind of thing.

"Red Heat" is otherwise noteworthy only for its climactic sequence, in

which Mr. Belushi and Mr. Schwarzenegger join forces to destroy many of the material rewards offered by the profit system, and the final shot, taken in Red Square in Moscow. Mr. Schwarzenegger, wearing his Russian policeman's uniform, stands at the center of the frame, apparently none the worse for his brief fling in the West.

"Red Heat" opens today at the Criterion Center and other theaters.

VINCENT CANBY

1988 Je 17, C14:5

The Reds, the Whites And Those in Between

Nonna Mordyukova in Aleksandr Askoldov's "Commissar."

COMMISSAR, directed by Aleksandr Askoldov; screenplay (in Russian with English subtitles) by Mr. Askoldov, based on "In the Town of Berdichev" by Vasily Grossman; camera, Valeri Ginzberg; music by Alfred Schnittke; produced by Gorky Studio. At Lincoln Plaza 3, 63d Street and Broadway. Running time: 105 minutes. This film has no rating.

Klavdia	Nonna Mordukova
Yefim	Rolan Bykov
Maria	Raisa Nedaskovskaya
Commander	Vasily Shukshin

WITH: Ludmila Volynskaya, Lyuba Katz, Pavlik Levin, Dima Kleinman, Igor Fishman, Marta Bratkova, O. Koveridze, L. Reutov, V. Shakhov.

By WALTER GOODMAN

Add "Commissar" to the remarkable series of Soviet movies that has been finding its way West after many years in the cinematic gulag. Completed in 1967 and not yet shown in the Soviet Union, it is the first and, as of now, the only movie made by Aleksandr Askoldov. As patrons of the Lincoln Plaza Cinema can at last confirm for themselves, "Commissar" is a brave, humane and powerful work.

"In the Town of Berdichev," the story by Vasily Grossman on which Mr. Askoldov based his screenplay, is the least impressive element of a virtuoso demonstration of movie making. In the aftermath of the Bolshevik Revolution, with the Reds still battling the Whites, a pregnant commissar in need of a home for the weeks before delivery is boarded with a poor Jewish family, the Magazaniks. "They think I'm Rothschild," grumbles sweetly cantankerous Yefim, a tinsmith with a beautiful wife on whom he dotes and six cute children.

●

Soon Klavdia the commissar, whom we first met as she condemned a miserable deserter to death, shows the softening influence of motherhood and proximity to the warm family life of the idealized Magazaniks. The transformation is a touch pat and Klavdia herself, though played with skilled restraint by the full-bodied Nonna Mordukova, never becomes a full-bodied character. Mr. Askoldov

plainly had more important things on his mind.

"Commissar" is a requiem for Soviet Jewry, not a popular subject among officially approved Soviet movie makers, writers or scholars. Yefim, who sings and dances away his poverty and his fears, is more a figure out of Sholom Aleichem than a model of the New Soviet Man. For him, in Rolan Bykov's thoroughly human portrayal, humor jigs hand in hand with misery. When he refers to Klavdia as "the Russian," this Jew defines his own position as an outsider in the country he happens to inhabit. He draws no distinctions between the Whites, though he knows they are anti-Semitic, and the Reds. "One group of rulers leaves," he says. "Another arrives." He cries, in words that were unutterable in the 1960's and still carry unhappy resonance: "Maybe some day Jews will live where they want." Yiddish is spoken here. Ideologically unacceptable.

The movie's power lies in image after stunning image displaying Mr. Askoldov's indebtedness to the great early Soviet directors. He can bring life to market days and to household chores, but realism, especially of the socialist sort, is too easy for his powers. Klavdia's struggles during a difficult delivery become the terrific heavings of a group of soldiers straining to push a ponderous gun wagon through sand. The approach of the White army is signaled by a tremendous hammering as the townsfolk nail up their windows. Although working with only a handful of characters, again and again Mr. Askoldov and his fine cinematographer, Valeri Ginzberg, find ways of dramatizing the turmoil that is shaking their lives.

Two scenes especially will be hard to forget. In one, three of the younger children wage a mock pogrom against their gentle older sister. "Dirty Yid!" they shriek. Carried away by their game, they tie the frightened girl to a swing, and in slow motion, which the director uses in several sequences to considerable effect, her body swings back and forth, an image of the eternal victim.

●

The most wrenching scene begins with a lovely interlude of all the Magazaniks dancing together as guns sound in the distance. Suddenly, the moment is transformed; now parents and children wear yellow stars as, followed by many other Jews, they move silently into darkness. We are supposed to be witnessing this grim revelation through Klavdia's mind, and it is a weakness of "Commissar" that nothing about the title character has readied us for such an example of compassionate foresight. Yet that seems a small fault in so largehearted a work. What stays with us is the vision that brought Mr. Askoldov 20 years of silence.

1988 Je 17, C16:4

Rolan Bykov, arms upraised, in the scene from "Commissar" that explains why Alexander Askoldov's film was threatened with destruction.

FILM VIEW/Vincent Canby

Is Rambo's Era Finished?

NOBODY MAKES STAR ENtrances to equal Sylvester Stallone's. As has become his custom, Mr. Stallone enters "Rambo III" in a succession of majestic pieces. He's assembled from huge, skin-tight close-ups of sepia-colored body parts: a muscular back, veined forearms, a chest so remarkably developed and symmetrically scarred that it looks like a terraced, defoliated Far Eastern rice paddy, seen from the air. When, finally, the camera pulls back to reveal Sylvester Stallone, full figure and flesh glistening, the moment demands obeisance.

These days, however, the grandeur in the way Mr. Stallone presents himself seems almost elegiacal.

Watching "Rambo III," we are witnessing a phenomenon that has already slipped into the past tense, though it appears to be taking place here and now.

"Rambo III" picks up the story several years after the end of "Rambo: First Blood Part II" (hereafter referred to as "Rambo II"), released three years ago. In the 1985 film, John Rambo, the alienated Green Beret vet played by Mr. Stallone, is persuaded to return to Vietnam to check out reports

that American servicemen are still being held prisoner 10 years after the end of hostilities. Rambo, in the course of his mission, single-handedly lays waste much of the countryside and most of the people in it.

He also secures the release of a dozen or so American POW's who, for no apparent reason except spite, have been kept in secret isolation by their sadistic Vietnamese captors, acting at the direction of even more sadistic Russian military advisers.

At the start of the new film, John Rambo has removed himself from life's commonplace arena and retired to Thailand. He is living a modest existence with Buddhist priests for whom, in his humble way, he gilds the towers of pagodas and, in his spare time, engages in the spectacular Thai sport of stick fighting. He does this, he explains, to pick up some extra change to give "ta da munx." "My war is ova," says John Rambo. He's now searching for inna peace.

With Rambo, as with most of us, inner peace must wait.

Rambo's old buddy, Colonel Sam Trautman (Richard Crenna), is captured by the Russians while on a clandestine mission in Afghanistan to arrange for the deliv-

ery of United States missiles to the freedom fighters. Earlier tales of Russian atrocities in Afghanistan (chemical warfare, the slaughter of innocent women and children) could not tear Rambo away from his Thai sanctuary.

However, when he hears of Trautman's capture, he suits up, which, in Rambo's case, means that he strips down — to pants, boots and an understated headband.

From that point onward, "Rambo III" is, in outline anyway, pretty much a rehash of "Rambo II," played in arid Afghan (in fact, Israeli) settings instead of Southeast Asian jungles. He crosses from Pakistan into Afghanistan and infiltrates the Russian base as if he were infiltrating Coney Island at noon on the Fourth of July.

Accompanying him are one freedom-loving Afghan patriot and one small, adoring, freedom-loving Afghan boy ("He's a boy, but he fights like a man"). Rambo saves Trautman and kills so many Russians that one boxcar could comfortably repatriate all of the Russian forces remaining in the country.

The battle scenes in "Rambo III" are evenly spaced and, like the chorus line in an old-fashioned musical, designed to wake up the teen-age equivalents to the butter-and-egg men in the audience. There are lots of explosions, aerial attacks, much creeping around enemy territory, the occasional hand-to-hand combats and, in one memorable sequence, a demonstration of how to rid yourself of a pesky spike that has been shot through your side. (You simply pour a little gunpowder in one end of the wound, light it and watch the spike fly out the other end.)

■

"Rambo III," which reportedly cost anywhere from $60-odd million to $80-odd million (depending on whether or not Mr. Stallone's fee is included), repeats the "Rambo II" formula, though there are notable differences in the mechanics of the two films and in the ways in which audiences look at them.

The differences are of a significance to suggest that Sylvester Stallone, like one of his greatest admirers, may well be a lame-duck cult hero. Time and fashion are passing him by.

Though "Rambo III," like its predecessor, is rated R, it is far less explicitly sadistic. The leering, cigarette-addicted Russian colonel in "Rambo III" does unmentionable things to poor Colonel Trautman, but the worst the audience sees is the colonel hanging by his wrists while his torturer swats him, sometimes like a beanbag but mostly with dire threats. This is tame stuff compared to the earlier film. In one sequence, Rambo, his nakedness hidden by a loincloth of biblical drape, is crucified across barbed wire. In another sequence, he is slowly sliced by a razor-sharp knife (hence the pretty chest scars evident in the new film). In still another, he is jolted with enough electricity to dim the lights in Moscow.

By contrast, the violence in "Rambo III" is consistently picturesque and impersonal, while the torture suggests nothing much more sickening than a fraternity initiation that has turned mean.

It's as if the enthusiastic demonstration of Russian sadism, which seemed O.K. during the height of the Reagan Administration's word war against "the evil empire," was now thought to be out of place, though for reasons the movie can't quite unsnarl.

The high point of "Rambo III" is dialectical. The insidious Russian colonel attempts to wheedle the trussed-up Trautman into revealing the place where the U.S. mis-

He could go to Nicaragua, but it would seem provincial.

siles will be delivered. "Come on," the Russian says in effect, "nobody will know if you squeal. We both want to get out of this place. You can understand the position I'm in." Replies Trautman, "Not on your tintype," or something in a more military vein. "We've had our Vietnam," he says. "Now it's your turn."

However, having gone that far, it seems possible that good old Trautman, the one man who appreciates the depth of Rambo's patriotic frustration, might go further and commiserate with the Russian about a war that the lily-livered parlor pinks back in Moscow won't allow the Russian army to win.

This mind set might also comprehend the eventual birth of a Russian Rambo, a pumped-up bear of a man who turns his back on Gorbachev's glasnost as the policy of sissies. Rambo-fashion, he goes back to Afghanistan to refight (and win) the lost war. In the process, he also frees Russian POW's held in captivity by Afghan freedom fighters under the direction of their American military advisers.

■

Mr. Stallone and Sheldon Lettich, who wrote the "Rambo III" screenplay, must have had some inkling of where the debate between the Russian colonel and Trautman might lead. They cut it off fast, but not before revealing that they have read and recorded the handwriting on the wall, though without acknowledging a word of it.

If, by chance, glasnost continues, the choices open to Rambo's particular kind of heroics are limited. Where can an internationally-minded vigilante go next? It looks as if the Ayatollah is going to make a peaceful departure from his own bed, so, for the time being, Iran is out as a venue.

Rambo could go down to Nicaragua and bang heads. Yet, after fighting a nascent World War III, Nicaragua would seem humiliatingly provincial, like taking the show on the road after a 10-year Broadway run. Also, any gung-ho movie about the Sandinistas and the contras will be a risky business until Oliver North and his associates settle their legal problems.

The awful truth: Rambo is out of date, which, I suspect, comes as no surprise to Mr. Stallone and his advisers.

■

It is, in fact, an eventuality for which Carolco, the production company that owns the Rambo character, has already made provision. Carolco's newest action-adventure movie is "Red Heat," an insinuatingly opportune attempt to reflect our new global manners. The movie, directed with a good deal of playfulness by Walter Hill, opened this past week at theaters near everybody.

Much like the recent Moscow summit, at which heads of state met to talk politely and sign agreements, while their first ladies smiled and exchanged discreet sarcasms to their aides, "Red Heat" is an amiable getting-to-know-you venture, quite in keeping with the post-Rambo era.

It's a dressed-up buddy film in which Arnold Schwarzenegger, as the

Moscow police department's foremost homicide cop, comes to the States to work with Jim Belushi, as his Chicago counterpart, to track down a Russian drug dealer. The narrative given is that the two men couldn't be more different. Instead of being black and white, heterosexual and homosexual, male and female, tall and short, they are American and Russian.

■

One is an iron-jawed, straight-thinking, clean-living product of a socialist system that only needs a little democratic slovenliness to be human. The other is a shrewd, streetwise slob who could use some of the Russian's self-discipline, if only to lose a little weight.

They quarrel a lot, but harmlessly. Each makes sarcastic remarks about the other's personal habits, mode of dressing and political system, yet, down deep, they come to something like mutual respect. In its mechanics, "Red Heat" is a standard police melodrama, and as much of a fairy tale as any Rambo movie. However, it's acted with unusual humor by its two stars, especially by Mr. Schwarzenegger, and, politically, it is, if not a stunning breakthrough, a relief.

Somebody over there obviously liked the project. The film ends with a panoramic view of Red Square with Mr. Schwarzenegger, safely returned from Sodom and wearing his Russian policeman's uniform, standing in the middle of Moscow. The shot, which must be something of a first, is like a big, broad, astonished grin. □

1988 Je 19, II:23:1

Not Just Anytime; Only When It's Funny

WHO FRAMED ROGER RABBIT, directed by Robert Zemeckis; screenplay by Jeffrey Price and Peter S. Seaman, based on the book "Who Censored Roger Rabbit?" by Gary K. Wolf; director of photography, Dean Cundey; film editor, Arthur Schmidt; music by Alan Silvestri; production designers, Elliot Scott with Roger Cain; produced by Robert Watts and Frank Marshall; released by Touchstone Pictures. At Ziegfeld, Avenue of the Americas at 54th Street; Coronet, Third Avenue at 59th Street, and other theaters. Running time: 96 minutes. This film is rated PG.

Eddie Valiant	Bob Hoskins
Judge Doom	Christopher Lloyd
Dolores	Joanna Cassidy
Roger Rabbit	Charles Fleischer
Marvin Acme	Stubby Kaye
R. K. Maroon	Alan Tilvern

By JANET MASLIN

In a parallel universe near a Hollywood movie studio, the Toons make the rules. Toons are movie actors who also happen to be cartoon characters, second-class citizens by Hollywood standards but a force to be reckoned with just the same. They have their own laws of physics, their own laws of gravity and their own distinctive sense of humor. So a Toon who's under the influence is apt to change color and spiral upward until he hits the ceiling. A Toon sent flying through a window leaves an exact silhouette. Toon shoes, if unpacked by accident, start to dance.

At the movie studio, where Toon stars like Dumbo work "for peanuts," in the words of one mogul who employs them, the collision between

Roger Rabbit and Bob Hoskins in "Who Framed Roger Rabbit."

Toon attitudes and those of the so-called real world leads to countless surprises. It also makes "Who Framed Roger Rabbit" a film whose best moments are so novel, so deliriously funny and so crazily unexpected that they truly must be seen to be believed.

Although this isn't the first time that cartoon characters have shared the screen with live actors, it's the first time they've done it on their own terms. So the Toons have one way of viewing the world, the humans another — and the director Robert Zemeckis, as the mastermind presiding over this wizardry, has an all-important overview. Mr. Zemeckis has directed a number of comedies about ordinary individuals who take that thrilling step into another dimension, from "Back to the Future" to "Romancing the Stone" and "I Wanna Hold Your Hand." Though it's long been clear that he's as much innovator as entertainer, Mr. Zemeckis has never before concocted anything quite as dizzying as this.

•

"Who Framed Roger Rabbit," which opens today at the Ziegfeld and other theaters, should be a delight for children of all ages except, perhaps, the ages of real children. It's hard to know what very young viewers will make of the Toons' refusal to maintain their lovable, parent-pleasing demeanor when the movie company's cameras cease to roll. The film's brilliant opening episode finds Roger Rabbit, a very Bugs-like invention, starring with a gurgling infant named Baby Herman in an animated sequence that's an inspired, hellish parody of the kind of cartoon that finds its humor in wanton destruction. Chasing the baby through a kitchen that expands unnervingly as the action becomes more frantic, Roger risks electrocution, flying knives and the many other insane hazards built into his line of work.

Then comes the cry of "Cut!" and the real film begins, with a live director berating Roger for seeing little birds when he should have seen little stars. Baby Herman speaks up in his real voice, a deep, masculine growl. And the camera follows Roger from the brightly colored cartoon set into the real world of 1947 Hollywood, making this transition with the supreme ease that is this film's greatest

achievement. However wildly inventive the Toon-human interchanges become, they are executed with the utmost sang-froid.

•

Roger has a problem, and his boss at the studio has a solution: Eddie Valiant (Bob Hoskins), a private detective, will be engaged to find out whether Roger's wife, Jessica, has been misbehaving. It is one small measure of the film's cleverness that Jessica, an animated bombshell who is a Rabbit only by marriage, looks and sounds so sultry (an uncredited Kathleen Turner supplies her speaking voice) that Roger and Eddie find her equally alluring. In any case, Eddie's search for clues about Jessica sends him stumbling onto something even bigger: a "Chinatown" scheme to corrupt an Eden of a Los Angeles, which according to the screenplay once had the greatest public transportation system in the world before a villain named Judge Doom (Christopher Lloyd) envisioned "wonderful, wonderful billboards reaching as far as they eye can see" beside the first freeway.

The film's only problem, and it's a minor one, is that the gumshoe plot of the screenplay by Jeffrey Price and Peter S. Seaman is relatively ordinary. Nothing else about the film can be described that way: not the startling visual tricks, not the Toon-related wit and not the remarkable Mr. Hoskins, who spends the entire film essentially talking to himself and still manages to give a performance that is foolproof. His Eddie is a gruff, lovable lug who nurses a terrible secret: a Toon killed his brother. "Just like a Toon to drop a safe on a guy's head," says another character sympathetically.

Talking to Toons, visiting the Toon universe (where everything sings) and even playing long scenes with the animated Roger handcuffed to his wrist, Mr. Hopkins makes his own very matter-of-factness funny. Another source of humor is his constant irritation with the Toons' odd habits, as when he shouts angrily at Roger, "Do you mean to tell me you could've taken your hand out of that cuff at any time?" "No, not any time," Roger explains patiently. "Only when it was funny."

"Who Framed Roger Rabbit" is a film with many, many stars. Some

are animated, making cameo appearances the way Betty Boop does, waiting tables at a nightspot where a human clientele watches Toons like Daffy and Donald Duck perform their stage show. ("Work's been kinda slow since cartoons went to color, but I still got it, Eddie," she confides.) Some are live actors, like Mr. Lloyd and Joanna Cassidy, who bring amusing conviction to the most improbable of roles. And many are offscreen: the hundreds of painters, animators, special effects technicians and other ingenious contributors whose work has been made to look so blissfully effortless. That's the most magical illusion of all.

1988 Je 22, C17:2

Punk Showdown

Jon Cryer in "Dudes."

DUDES, directed by Penelope Spheeris; written by J. Randal Johnson; director of photography, Robert Richardson; film editor, Andy Horvitch; music by Charles Bernstein; production designer, Robert Ziembicki; produced by Herb Jaffe and Miguel Tejada-Flores; released by Cineworld Enterprises Corporation. At Cine 1, Seventh Avenue and 48th Street. Running time: 90 minutes. This film is rated R.

Grant	Jon Cryer
Biscuit	Daniel Roebuck
Milo	Flea
Missoula	Lee Ving
Blix	Bill Ray Sharkey
Wes	Glenn Withrow
Jessie	Catherine Mary Stewart
Daredelvis	Pete Willcox

By JANET MASLIN

When the self-consciously hip central characters of "Dudes" leave New York for a cross-country journey, they make enemies in the heartland the way the heroes of "Easy Rider" did. Grant (Jon Cryer), Milo (Flea) and Biscuit (Daniel Roebuck) are inexplicably attacked by a band of outlaws led by the sneering Missoula (Lee Ving), who evidently doesn't like their punk-rock looks. In the aftermath of this ambush, which ends in murder, Grant and Biscuit vow to track down Missoula and exact revenge. The film presents this as a rite of passage for bored, city-bred rebels seeking a sense of purpose.

"Dudes," which opens today at the Cine 1, is the work of Penelope Spheeris, whose documentaries about comparable characters (both "Decline of Western Civilization" music films) have been more apt to ring true. Mr. Roebuck (who played the uncommunicative young killer in "River's Edge") and Mr. Cryer have a wholesomeness that doesn't entirely suit their characters. The clean-cut looks of Charlie Sheen and Maxwell Caulfield were more intriguing in Miss Spheeris's film about serial killers, "The Boys Next Door," than a comparable nice-guy manner is for these two innocents abroad.

•

"Dudes" has a more commercial tone than some of Miss Spheeris's earlier films, which is to say it's filled with scenic, largely unmotivated events and lacks conviction. Tongue-tied dialogue ("This country, man — it's like a Road Runner cartoon. Beep, beep!") is another problem. Still, there are enough eccentric touches to hold the interest, like the exuberantly vicious Mr. Ving in his villain's role, and the character calling himself Daredelvis (Pete Willcox), who has somehow worked a lot of Presley mannerisms into his act as a rodeo clown.

Among the film's most peculiar touches are its creeping niceness, which surfaces in charcters like Catherine Mary Stewart's spunky cowgirl, and the way Mr. Roebuck's skunk-striped hair sticks straight up six inches above his head as he travels through the wild West without hair spray.

1988 Je 24, C9:1

Israeli Life Through Arab Eyes

"Wedding in Galilee" was shown as part of the recent New Directors/New Films series. These are excerpts from Caryn James's review, which appeared in The New York Times on March 11. The film, in Arabic with English subtitles, opens today at the Film Forum 2, 57 Watts Street.

"Wedding in Galilee" cannot help but seem exotic to Western eyes, as it lures us into a ritual wedding feast in a Palestinian village in Israel. Michel Khleifi, a writer and director who was born and brought up in Nazareth, relies on a wandering, Eastern-style narrative to depict Palestinian traditions threatened by 20th-century inroads.

His film is lyrical and extravagantly detailed when portraying the Palestinians. But because Mr. Khleifi turns simplistic and leaden whenever he points his camera at an Israeli, always viewed as the one-dimensional enemy, his often dazzling first feature is diminished by his insistently narrow vision.

When the village leader, or mukhtar, decides his son must have a traditional wedding celebration that lasts through the night, he must ask the Israeli military governor for permission to break the curfew. The mukhtar, with his weathered, impassive face, is the picture of composed dignity. He faces an Israeli officer whom Mr. Khleifi presents as an ogre of injustice, who will lift the curfew only if he is present at the wedding.

Though it unhinges his film, Mr. Khleifi's dismissive attitude toward the Israelis ironically frees him; he goes on to depict his Arab village in loving, almost anthropological detail. White walls gleam against a wide, sun-baked landscape, and we can almost feel the hot wind blow during the wedding feast, as tradition mingles with its discontents.

In this rich, nuanced setting, which Walther van den Ende has photographed with shocking brightness, the mukhtar's flirtatious teen-aged daughter schemes to escape her old-fashioned life. Young village men plot to kill the Israeli wedding guests.

Just when it seems that Mr. Khleifi is composing a paean for his fading culture, the story loops back on itself. The bridegroom wants to kill his father, whose traditions are destroying him. An older man warns the rebels that the repercussions for their violence will be too costly.

The slow accumulation of details finally becomes deadening. The film's 113-minute length, not American expectations, makes the all-night wedding seem to unfold in real time. But for all its flaws, "Wedding in Galilee" is a strong, rare example of Middle Eastern film making, and too vibrant artistically to be dismissed in the way Mr. Khleifi does his Israeli characters.

1988 Je 24, C11:1

A Gothic World 'Come to Grief'

A HANDFUL OF DUST, directed by Charles Sturridge; screenplay by Tim Sullivan, Derek Granger and Mr. Sturridge, from the novel by Evelyn Waugh; director of photography, Peter Hannan; edited by Peter Coulson; music by George Fenton; production designer, Eileen Diss; produced by Mr. Granger; released by New Line Cinema. At Paris, 58th Street and Fifth Avenue. Running time: 117 minutes. This film is rated PG.

Tony Last	James Wilby
Brenda Last	Kristin Scott Thomas
Beaver	Rupert Graves
Mrs. Rattery	Anjelica Huston
Mrs. Beaver	Dame Judi Dench
Mr. Todd	Sir Alec Guinness
Marjorie	Beatie Edney
Jock	Pip Torrens
Dr. Messinger	Christopher Godwin
Mr. Graceful	Graham Crowden

By VINCENT CANBY

Evelyn Waugh's "Handful of Dust," published in 1934, seems to be a century removed from "Brideshead Revisited," which came out nine years later and is a far more conventional novel.

In "Brideshead Revisited," Waugh looks back with sorrow and a great sense of loss to a vanishing upper-class English society that, for all its excesses and eccentricities, molded Charles Ryder, the book's middle-class hero, into the man of grace and

In Decline

Kristin Scott Thomas and James Wilby appear in "A Handful of Dust," directed by Charles Sturridge and based on the Evelyn Waugh novel.

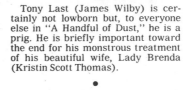

Getting Together
Anna Achdian, center, portrays the bride in "Wedding in Galilee," set in a Palestinian community disrupted by demonstrations and troubled by conflict between an Israeli governor and the village elder.

feeling he has become. "Brideshead Revisited" means exactly what it says. It was written with defiant elegance during the height of the war when England, stripped down and austere, was hanging on to its heritage by its teeth.

"A Handful of Dust" is something else, a last cry from the heedless 20's now turned into the depressed 1930's. It's a vicious, witty novel whose piercing romanticism remains largely unacknowledged by the author, who, instead of making moral judgments, describes the behavior of the privileged orders with precision and utter detachment. He seldom goes inside a mind.

When he does, most of the thoughts he discovers are never more profound than the cruel, snobbish, superficial things that people say to one another in the immaculately clipped dialogue. The novel's opening: " 'Was anybody hurt?' 'No one I am thankful to say,' said Mrs. Beaver, 'except two housemaids who lost their heads and jumped through a glass roof into the paved court.' "

•

In Waugh's comic novels, there's no sin worse than being either low born or unimportant. Waugh shares these prejudices up to a point.

Nothing is disguised in "A Handful of Dust," but it's as if Waugh felt that to reveal his emotions to the reader would be poor form. He was sending up a world in which the only thing more embarrassing than having feelings was the expression of them.

The vast differences between the two novels are demonstrated with a lot of erring good taste and misapplied intelligence in "A Handful of Dust," the screen adaptation directed by Charles Sturridge, the man who earlier directed the hugely popular "Brideshead" mini-series on television. The new film opens today at the Paris.

Tony Last (James Wilby) is certainly not lowborn but, to everyone else in "A Handful of Dust," he is a prig. He is briefly important toward the end for his monstrous treatment of his beautiful wife, Lady Brenda (Kristin Scott Thomas).

•

When first seen, Tony and Brenda seem to be the ideally happy couple that society takes them to be. They live at Hetton Abbey, one of the notable old county houses of England until 1864, when Tony's grandfather rebuilt it from top to bottom in ersatz Gothic. They have one beloved child, John, 7, and exist in enlightened penury since most of Tony's fortune goes for the upkeep of the great estate.

Growing restive with the genteel life in the country, Brenda slips into an affair with a London parasite, the somewhat younger John Beaver (Rupert Graves). Brenda has no illusions about Beaver. She knows that he is second rate and a snob. "No one likes you except me," she tells him at one point. "You must get that clear, and it's very odd that I should."

Beaver is a good-looking nonentity. He lives off last-minute invitations to luncheon parties, dinner parties and weekends in the country from which more desirable guests have suddenly had to excuse themselves.

Telling Tony she wants to study economics, Brenda takes a small London flat (brokered and furnished by Beaver's interior-decorator mother) to pursue her affair. She picks up all the bills. She takes Beaver into houses where he would otherwise never be received. When she falls in love with him, it is the act of a woman so willful that she assumes that her interest will transform a social slug into a man of importance.

Mr. Sturridge and Tim Sullivan and Derek Granger, who collaborated with the director on the screenplay, remain remarkably faithful to the novel. There don't seem to be a half-dozen lines that are not Waugh's. Yet the film is both too literal and devoid of real point.

Tony's fanatical devotion to Hetton Abbey (actually the Duke of Norfolk's Carlton Towers in Yorkshire) is not just an eccentricity, as it seems in the film. It is a commitment to a romantic ideal, to a system of exalting values, to trust, revealed in the novel in two remarkable paragraphs. In one of these, Tony comprehends the immensity of what has happened, realizing that because of Brenda's casual duplicity "an entire Gothic world had come to grief."

This is the heart and the horror of the novel, but it is nowhere to be understood in the movie, which, without it, is a rather chilly, plodding Gothic comedy of the 30's.

The casting of two of the principal characters is not perfect. Mr. Wilby, introduced in "Maurice," is tall and skinny and sort of bland. He looks the way Tony should but he comes close to being as tiresome as Brenda's friends find him. The movie never appreciates the other side of his seeming passivity.

Miss Scott Thomas is not bad, yet neither is she the breathtaking beauty that Brenda is. It's not possible to adore this Brenda and, at the same time, to be appalled by her. Her lack of a singular classiness also wipes out the effect of the nastiest recognition scene in all of English literature.

The third principal role is far more aptly cast. Mr. Graves, who was also in "Maurice," is a classic Beaver, always properly dressed, brushed and combed, his mouth ever at the edge of a pout, just the sort of bored young man who would mail a love letter that he'd somehow forgotten to finish.

Dame Judi Dench is also fine as Beaver's pushy mum, while Sir Alec Guinness makes another funnily errie appearance as the mysterious Mr. Todd, the half-Indian, half-Barbadian Englishman who, at the end, finds Tony in the Amazon jungles and nurses him back to health.

The single most stunning performance is that of Anjelica Huston. She flies into the film (in a biplane) around the midway point and takes command, much as her character does. She is Mrs. Rattery, a rich American woman who, no longer connected to any culture, speaks in what sounds like an aristocratic Englishman's idea of an American accent.

•

She and Mr. Wilby bring to vivid life the most effectively harrowing sequence in the film (which is also what it is in the novel).

The rich physical production, scored with much too much commonplace soundtrack music, is more in keeping with "Brideshead Revisited" than with the lean humors of "A Handful of Dust." Possibly the film should have been shot entirely in a studio in black and white. The luxuriant look, left under-described in the novel, dulls the cutting edge. The authentic, spectacular South American jungles, seen in sequences that begin and end the movie, add a wholesome, National Geographic touch that couldn't be less amusing.

•

"A Handful of Dust," which has been rated PG ("Parental Guidance Suggested"), contains a sequence involving the death of a child that could trouble very young children.

1988 Je 24, C14:1

FILM VIEW/Janet Maslin

Penelope Spheeris Finds the Heart of Rock

THE QUESTIONS MOST READILY raised by Penelope Spheeris's documentaries are those of how the film maker obtained her information and what she wanted it for. Delving into the world of punk rock for her first "Decline of Western Civilization" in 1980, and following with a look at heavy metal (in her current "Decline of Western Civilization II: The Metal Years"), Miss Spheeris is treading something of a new path. She's not exactly tackling subjects about which most potential viewers crave more data. Nor can the hostile, white male adolescent culture into which she ventures be a realm in which she herself, the mother of an 18-year-old daughter, is automatically welcome.

Yet Miss Spheeris obviously cares about and understands both the music and the people that her films are about; the candor with which her interviewees reveal themselves is proof of that. What's more, she sees beyond the dog collars and hears beyond the racket, locating some genuinely important matters at the heart of this material. "Decline II" in particular, with its emphasis on sex, money and substance abuse, depicts a world with its own caste system and its own visions of success, ideals apparently as dangerous to those who achieve them as to those who do not. It's remarkable that Miss Spheeris conveys this in such a detached yet sympathetic way, without voyeurism, and with so much clarity and humor.

Teen-age disaffection in its most extreme modern forms constitutes Miss Spheeris's real subject, and she has approached it in an unusually wide variety of ways. In addition to these documentaries, she has also made several narrative feature films about the same kinds of contemporary rebels, sometimes recycling documentary material and adapting it to suit fictitious characters. So Lee Ving of the rock group Fear, who is heard spewing insults at his audience during the first "Decline" (the crowd seems to like this as much as the music, and it's just as central to the act), plays the role of a vicious bully in "Dudes," which is the second film of Miss Spheeris to have opened here in the last two weeks. Mr. Ving was made for villainy, and he's at least as well suited to bad-guy acting roles as he is to punk posturing.

■

What's more, one of his colorful onstage comments from the first "Decline" film — a creative but somewhat bewildering obscenity — finds its way into "The Boys Next Door" (1986), where it is also delivered in haste and then marveled at a moment later. But even in this film, which is the best of Miss Spheeris's fiction features, there are aspects of adolescent nihilism that remain elusive. Charlie Sheen and Maxwell Caulfield, both unexpectedly good here, play two nice-looking, clean-cut kids who evolve into killers. The film traces this evolution in a series of convincing stages.

However, the real randomness and the scary apathy captured by Miss Spheeris's documentary camera cannot be matched by any invention of a grown-up, rational mind. When this film maker attempts, in her fiction work, to give her characters coherent thought patterns and parents who don't understand them, she loses some essential part of what makes her documentaries so star-

Gene Simmons of Kiss, center, in "The Decline of Western Civilization Part II"

tling. No invention can match the sight of a Los Angeles teen-age boy, with a shaved head and punk demeanor, declaring, "I hate cops to the *max*." Nor could any writer or director contrive anything as airily cold-blooded as the dead house-painter story recounted in the first "Decline," told by a young woman who found the man lying in her backyard and thought he was sleeping. When she kicked him, she found out otherwise. So she and a few friends got out the camera and posed for pictures with the corpse. "Didn't you feel sorry that the guy was dead?" Miss Spheeris asks. "No, not at all," the woman says blithely. "Because I hate painters."

There is a world of difference between this kind of punk posturing and the heavy metal ethos explored in "Decline II," which is the director's best work. Where the punks embrace violence, eschew materialism and run wild — a pack of dogs serves as a shadow of the teen-age principals in the 1984 "Suburbia" — the heavy metal crowd is less articulate and more motivated. Members of up-and-coming bands talk frankly about money and fame, and refuse to imagine anything as mundane as regular employment as an alternative to superstar status. If they don't make it big, say some of the interviewees, they may as well die. But this thought is delivered with childish petulance rather than anything as relatively considered as the punks' nihilism. The eagerness for power that's central to heavy metal lyrics has found its way into the fans' very daydreams.

At the top of the heap, Miss Spheeris finds the genre's smirking superstars, looking pampered and self-satisfied, inviting the viewer to eat his heart out. Their art, such as it is — and Miss Spheeris is smart enough to use considerably less music footage this time — is secondary to the cars, clothes, drugs and groupies that are heavy metal's real

measure of one's having arrived. Seen in this context, the misogyny and materialism espoused by would-be kings of the mountain amount to faint and ineffectual mimickry, but Miss Spheeris makes it funny.

Still, the young men who boast about being supported by women and the women priding themselves on groupie allure are seen clearly as potential casualties of this game.

Miss Spheeris no doubt regards herself as an enthusiast rather than an anthropologist, but the effect is the same. As studies of restrictive, self-contained cultures with their own strict habits and rules, both her "Decline" films are illuminating in unexpected ways. They say a great deal about how self-destructive adolescent behavior reflects the society that shapes it. And they show how a witty and perceptive film maker can take any subject and make it her own. □

1988 Je 26, II:21:1

Civil War

BEIRUT: THE LAST HOME MOVIE, directed and produced by Jennifer Fox; written by Miss Fox and John Mullen; cinematography, Alex Nepomniaschy; edited by Mr. Mullen; music by Lanny Meyers and Ziad Rahbani; released by Circle Releasing. At Film Forum 1, 57 Watts Street. Running time: 120 minutes. This film has no rating.

By CARYN JAMES

"Beirut: The Last Home Movie" begins in a New York subway, when Gaby Bustros steps on the J.F.K. Express and heads for a plane to the city she left 15 years before. "Shells have landed in my family's garden," she says, and we quickly follow her through the rubble of bombed-out

Front Lines
Despite the war all around them, members of a wealthy Lebanese family that has refused to leave home celebrate a marriage in "Beirut: The Last Home Movie."

Beirut, with clouds of smoke hovering over empty buildings, to arrive at her family's home — a 200-year-old house fronted by a huge marble staircase and filled with chandeliers and Oriental rugs.

This oasis, in one of the most desolate parts of Beirut, is the setting for Jennifer Fox's astute documentary about the Bustros family. Stubborn and apolitical, they remain in their ancestral home while the seemingly endless civil war surrounds them. Privileged and anomalous, they are a rich, psychological mystery, which Miss Fox turns into an consistently intriguing film.

Though we meet Gaby's widowed mother and 26-year-old brother, Fady, this is a story of three sisters. Mouna is the strong-willed oldest, who at 39 seems dour and lonely. Nyla, three years younger, appears so compliant she is without will at all. And Gaby, at 35, looks perpetually tired, with bags under her eyes. As the film progresses Gaby seems less sure of her purpose in returning — to convince her family they are foolish, if not suicidal, to remain in the house.

•

As the sisters address the camera — speaking, quite directly, to us — Miss Fox's narrative strategies are shrewd and subtle. She resists crass contrasts between the Bustroses' faded opulence and the war around them. Instead, she reproduces their points of view and duplicates their sense of enclosure; only occasionally does she leave the insular world of the house to show the streets outside. Eventually we see the sisters' children, and find their neighbors huddled in the house during a bombing, watching cartoons on television. It is mildly surprising that other people share the sisters' lives.

Only late in the film, off-handedly, do we learn that the Bustroses are Christians. Throughout, Miss Fox's tone is as free of politics and rhetoric as the Bustroses themselves. She leaves it to the audience to judge them as noble or self-indulgent.

Slowly, the film discovers a family hiding emotionally as well as physically. "Nobody wants to talk about the war, nobody wants to talk about money," Gaby complains. "I mean, nobody's wanted to talk about anything in this family, ever." Miss Fox gets them to talk about their comfortable childhood, their disbelieving reactions to the war, their tangled personal relationships. Here are children taking their cues from a cold-hearted father and an aloof mother.

•

When Mouna's future in-laws came to discuss wedding plans with her father, she recalls, she sat in another room reading "The Fountainhead."

"I was very happy to get married, but it wasn't enough for me to leave my book." When Fady says, "I didn't have the hate" or "the political view" to take part in the war on either side, his nonchalance makes us wonder whether everyone in the family is not, after all, a version of Mouna, who admits, "Every time there is something painful in my life I stop feeling."

Ultimately, the Bustroses' resistance to war and change becomes an oblique comment on the way Lebanon's civil war, after more than a dozen years, has become a way of life. "This is not the last party, not the last bombings, not the last anything," Nyla says after Fady's wedding, and by then we can feel the pull between common sense and the family's need to survive by creating their own reality.

Miss Fox's production notes explain her story's slightly fictionalized frame better than the film itself. Gaby returned to Beirut when the shelling of the garden took place, in April 1981. Miss Fox and her film crew only joined her six months later, after a brief visit by Gaby to New York. And Miss Fox describes Gaby's role as "the go-between" for the family and the crew, accounting for tensions the visitors must have caused in three months of shooting — intrusions the film itself never touches. Nonetheless, "Beirut: The Last Home Movie," which opens today at the Film Forum 1, remains a highly accomplished portrait of characters under siege despite themselves.

1988 Je 29, C19:1

Once Upon a Time

COMING TO AMERICA, directed by John Landis; screenplay by David Sheffield and Barry W. Blaustein, story by Eddie Murphy; director of photography, Woody Omens; film editor, Malcolm Campbell; music by Nile Rodgers; production designer, Richard MacDonald; produced by Robert D. Wachs and George Folsey Jr.; released by Paramount Pictures. At Loews Astor Plaza, at 44th Street west of Broadway; Loews Orpheum, 86th Street near Third Avenue, and other theaters. Running time: 115 minutes. This film is rated R.

Prince Akeem	Eddie Murphy
Semmi	Arsenio Hall
The King of Zamunda	James Earl Jones
Mr. McDowell	John Amos
The Queen of Zamunda	Madge Sinclair
Lisa McDowell	Shari Headley

By VINCENT CANBY

Eddie Murphy's new film has a good title, "Coming to America," a possibly funny idea (a black African prince travels incognito to New York to find a wife) and a screenplay that seems to have escaped its doctors before it was entirely well.

"Coming to America" is something new for Mr. Murphy. It is a romantic comedy, though nobody except the star seems aware of the fact.

On the evening of his 21st birthday, Prince Akeem (Mr. Murphy), heir to the throne of Zamunda, is introduced to the bride-to-be of his arranged marriage. She is as beautiful as he could wish, but having been raised to give way to the prince in all things, she's not his idea of fun and stimulation for the long haul.

When he orders her to disobey him, she lowers her eyes and dutifully says, "No." This could be the beginning of a crazy kind of Monty Python debate about the nature of disobedience, but the scene stops there. Instead, Akeem is given 40 days' grace

in which to sow some royal wild oats abroad.

•

Once in New York, accompanied by Semmi (Arsenio Hall), his aide-de-camp, Akeem goes underground in Queens in an attempt to escape the responsibilities of princeship. There are encounters with hookers, hustlers and deadbeats. There's also love at the first sight of Lisa McDowell (Shari Headley), the pretty daughter of a fellow who runs a fast-food restaurant, which, bearing his name, has the people at McDonald's in a suing mood.

Though "Coming to America" is a romantic comedy, John Landis, the director, and David Sheffield and Barry W. Blaustein, the writers, steer the film more often toward quick, in-and-out comic situations and gags that are only mildly funny. In part this is due to the fact that Mr. Murphy plays the prince with cheerful, low-keyed innocence that is completely legitimate, but is not supported by the short attention span of the screenplay. The romance is tepid.

•

"Coming to America" comes to life fitfully when it turns rude and raw, or when Mr. Murphy and Mr. Hall are allowed to throw themselves into the sort of sketch material that made Mr. Murphy a star on television.

Mr. Sheffield and Mr. Blaustein, who wrote material for Mr. Murphy on "Saturday Night Live," contribute some very brief, entertaining revue bits in which Mr. Murphy and Mr. Hall turn up as a number of other characters. Two of these are so off-the-wall and so disguised that one can only be sure who has been playing whom by watching the closing credits.

Mr. Hall, best known as an effusive talk-show host on television, seems most comfortable when he is doing his cameos, including one as the emotional Reverend Brown. James Earl Jones and Madge Sinclair, playing Akeem's regal parents, display consistent comic authority that's not evident in the rest of the movie. It's possible that Mr. Landis, the director of what is still Mr. Murphy's best comedy, "Trading Places," couldn't care less about consistency.

"Coming to America," which opens today at Loew's Astor Plaza and other theaters, even manages to work in those two ruthless old millionaires (Don Ameche and Ralph Bellamy) from "Trading Places." The gag, one of the film's better ones, is typical of "Coming to America" and can be instantly forgotten.

1988 Je 29, C20:5

Marriage Minded
In John Landis's "Coming to America," Eddie Murphy portrays an African prince who comes to New York in search of a bride. Arsenio Hall is his loyal, royal sidekick.

Bayou Kinfolk

Jill Clayburgh

SHY PEOPLE, direction and story by Andrei Konchalovsky; screenplay by Gérard Brach and Mr. Konchalovsky and Marjorie David; director of photography, Chris Menges; editor, Alain Jakubowicz; music by Tangerine Dream; production designer, Stephen Marsh; produced by Menahem Golan and Yoram Globus; released by the Cannon Group Inc. At 57th Street Playhouse, at Avenue of the Americas. Running time: 118 minutes. This film is rated R.

Diana	Jill Clayburgh
Ruth	Barbara Hershey
Grace	Martha Plimpton
Mike	Merritt Butrick
Tommy	John Philbin
Mark	Don Swayze
Paul	Pruitt Taylor Vince
Candy	Mare Winningham

By VINCENT CANBY

Though Diana Sullivan (Jill Clayburgh) is a successful Manhattan photojournalist, she is a dud as a single parent. Her pretty daughter, Grace (Martha Plimpton), who is 16 but looks older, snorts cocaine and is having an affair with one of her mother's former lovers. Diana feels vaguely alienated. She wishes her daughter would feel free to talk "things" over with her, but Grace is having too much fun.

Diana receives a commission from Cosmopolitan magazine to do a story about a long-lost branch of her family living in the Louisiana bayou. The trip seems a perfect excuse to get to know Grace again. She yanks Grace out of the Trinity School and takes the girl with her into an adventure that can't be easily believed, even when seen.

It's called "Shy People," and it was directed by Andrei Konchalovsky, the talented director who, as Andrei Mikhalkov-Konchalovsky, directed "Uncle Vanya" and "Siberiade" in his native Soviet Union, and, as plain Andrei Konchalovsky, directed "Maria's Lovers" and "Runaway Train" in this country.

"Shy People," which opens today at the 57th Street Playhouse, refers mostly to Diana's bayou kinfolk, whose literary cousins would be the Jeeter Lester clan over on Tobacco Road.

There is tough, gritty Ruth Sullivan (Barbara Hershey), the family matriarch and the widow of Diana's grandfather's brother, Joe, who married Ruth when she was 12 and is now presumed dead. Also living in and around the family's rubbish-strewn swamp compound are three of Ruth's four grown sons, each of whom has a problem.

Pauly "ain't altogether with us," meaning he is retarded. Mark has a short temper and a pregnant wife who wants a television set more than a baby. Tommy, for reasons never fully explained, is kept locked in the feed shed. Mike, the oldest son (always spoken of as "daid"), has forsaken the swamps to run the Pussycat Cafe in town.

Diana is initially delighted with the

picturesqueness of it all. She marvels at a primitive portrait of old Joe hanging over the mantelpiece. "It's like some combination of Grant Wood, Grandma Moses and Salvador Dali," she says with her usual lack of astuteness. Grace walks around in boredom, listening to her Sony Walkman.

Very quickly things go wrong. One day while Diana and Ruth are in town, Grace pulls out her coke stash to party with her cousins, goes (as one of the boys puts it) "all the way" with Tommy in the feed shed and then is attacked by Mark, who tries to rape her in a pool of lazily spilling honey.

Grace thinks he is being very fresh. She jumps into a boat and heads into the bayous, followed by an alligator. Back at the compound, Mark and Tommy are killing each other. Meanwhile, in town, Ruth is shooting customers at the Pussycat Cafe. Cut back to Grace as her boat sinks beneath her. Where is the alligator?

Though "Shy People" has been re-edited since I saw it at the 1987 Cannes Film Festival (where Miss Hershey was awarded the best-actress prize), it still contains more than its fair share of howlers. Yet these are less the result of dim incompetence than of an approach to film making that is intensely, crazily European.

The screenplay was written by the director with Gérard Brach, the veteran French screenwriter (Claude Berri's "Two of Us," among others), and Marjorie David, the only American. This is the same team that wrote "Maria's Lovers." Though the film (photographed by Chris Menges, mostly in Louisiana) reflects surface realities, it has the manner of something taking place on the moon.

American audiences will laugh at what they see to be its clumsiness. Miss Clayburgh's Diana is made to sound more like a fool than is absolutely necessary. (At one point she says to Ruth: "Don't you see? I can help you. I'm from Cosmopolitan magazine!") However, the more profound problem is Mr. Konchalovsky's approach to film making.

Having established time and place, Mr. Konchalovsky couldn't care less about plausibility. He is more interested in what the film is "about," no matter how awkwardly the story sits atop that subtext. "Shy People" is, first off, about a culture clash and value differences that are too obvious to be especially interesting to Americans.

•

In addition, the film is about the difference between people who are decisive and strong (the bayou Sullivans) and people who, like the civilized Diana and her daughter, are so indecisive they take stands on nothing whatsoever.

The film's central, most important character never appears. He is old Joe Sullivan, who, it turns out, was something less than the paragon whom Ruth continually cites. He used to beat her and, when really fired up, he would hang her by her heels, upside down, just for the fun of it. He was, Ruth finally admits, a sadistic tyrant but, when the bayou waters rose to flood levels, his terrible tyranny forced them to build the dikes that saved them all.

Uncle Joe Sullivan, you see, is (are you ready?) Uncle Joe Stalin.

Miss Clayburgh has the sort of terrible role (and worse dialogue) that no actress could play with conviction. Miss Hershey's performance is tech-

nically first rate, but limited in its effect by its melodramatic context. The other actors do what is expected of them. Mr. Konchalovsky's direction is as self-conscious as the screenplay and the frequently fancy images furnished by Mr. Menges (who went on to direct Miss Hershey in the current "A World Apart").

Most spectacular is Mr. Menges's long, single-take pan across the Manhattan skyline and down into its streets, which begins the film and is the best thing in it.

1988 Jl 1, C8:5

Murder at School

ABSOLUTION, directed by Anthony Page; screenplay by Anthony Shaffer; director of photography, John Coquillon; edited by John Victor Smith; production designer, Natasha Kroll; music by Stanley Myers; produced by Elliott Kastner and Danny O'Donovan; released by Trans World Entertainment. At D. W. Griffith, 235 East 59th Street; Quad Cinema, 34 West 13th Street. Running time: 96 minutes. This film is rated R.

Father Goddard	Richard Burton
Benji	Dominic Guard
Arthur	Dai Bradley
Blakey	Billy Connolly
Headmaster	Andrew Keir
Brigadier Walsh	Willoughby Gray

By CARYN JAMES

Richard Burton had a weakness for troubled clerics. From the high drama of "Becket" to the wonderfully trashy romance of "The Sandpiper," he really knew how to wrangle with his conscience. Whether he was playing the archbishop or the adulterous minister, his eyes grew piercing, his voice projected from deep in the diaphragm.

But he never learned when it was time to parody himself. How could he play "Exorcist II: The Heretic" with a straight face? And what did he see in "Absolution"? Here he tackled the hopeless role of Father Goddard, a teacher in a Roman Catholic boys' school, who is psychologically tortured when his favorite student confesses to murder.

"Absolution," which opens today at the D. W. Griffith and the Quad Cinema, was completed in 1979 — five years before Mr. Burton's death —

and never released in this country, supposedly because of legal problems. Whatever the cause, this film's obscurity should have been one of the great joys of Mr. Burton's late career.

•

Father Goddard and his handsome, arrogant student, Benji, both tend to persecute a boy named Arthur. It is not enough that Arthur is an oily-haired nerd with horn-rimmed glasses; he is forced to limp along wearing a leg brace as well. The claustrophobia and homoerotic undercurrents in the school are so predictable that it seems a relief when the plot turns to murder, until we discover what a creaky, talky plot it is.

The screenwriter, Anthony Shaffer, who also wrote the play "Sleuth," goes wild with Chekhov's rule that if a gun appears in Act I, it must later be fired. Here the gun is a religion lesson: a priest can never divulge the secrets of the confessional, even if the confessor is a murderer. 'o... en if the confessor is a murderer, Mr. Shaffer points out.

He then goes on to construct a plot that has all the suspense of a multiple-choice quiz. Maybe Benji has murdered someone, or maybe he's taunting Father Goddard by lying in confession, or maybe neither of the above. The choices go on. Maybe Benji has murdered again, he really means it this time, or maybe not.

•

Anthony Page's direction takes its cue from Mr. Shaffer's nothing-is-too-obvious school of drama. When Mr. Burton is ready to set off a fire alarm, Mr. Page makes sure to cut to the alarm first — just in case anyone might be surprised.

Given the general ineptitude that dominates "Absolution," it contains some fine, wasted performances. Dominic Guard keeps us guessing about Benji's motives. Dai Bradley is very effective as Arthur, who is both pesky and pathetic in his hero-worship of Benji. And Mr. Burton seems to take it all seriously, whether reciting poetry or scraping in the dirt for bodies. We can only hope he was laughing inside.

1988 Jl 1, C8:5

FILM VIEW

Toons Fly High

By VINCENT CANBY

MOVIE DISTRIBUTORS APpear to assume that, when summer arrives, the minds of their audiences go as soft as abandoned Eskimo Pies. At least, it looks that way. Schools are out. People are on vacation. Impulse theatergoing increases. Summer is a time for abbreviated, loose-fitting clothing and sloppy movies to match.

With the exception of a few holiday weeks in the winter, movie attendance peaks in the summer. However, it may not be because minds have gone soft, but because movies in summer once again become the social phenomenon they were before the age of television. There's a kind of license in summer moviegoing. It need not be justified.

If people will go to see almost anything in summer, there's no great impulse to release movies of more than routine interest or achievement. It helps, of course, but fewer distributors go broke underestimating what the public will pay to see in summer than in winter.

Thus the genuine surprise that the summer of '88 is starting off with the release of two of the best American films of the year to date. They are "Bull Durham," a smash hit that has come out of left field, and "Who Framed Roger Rabbit," the best, purest motion-picture fantasy since "E.T." Both comedies are so giddily entertaining that they almost wipe out the memory of one of the driest springs on record.

"Who Framed Roger Rabbit" is a movie of such pure, dizzy enchantment that one watches it from start to finish with a smile so wide that the facial muscles ache when it's over.

Though much of it was shot at the Elstree Studios in England and on English locations that doubled for American, and though Bob Hoskins, that fine English actor, is its star, "Who Framed Roger Rabbit" is a particularly American film, and one that could well become a classic. It is a generous, hysterical salute both to the great days of Hollywood's past and to its present, totally unexpected (at this point) vivacity and élan.

In the way that it combines cartoon and real characters within the same frame, in all sorts of slam-bang, overwrought intimacies, "Who Framed Roger Rabbit" is a technical marvel. Technical marvels, though, are something we take for granted. The dazzling accomplishment of "Who Framed Roger Rabbit" is something much more rare.

It is the creation of an utterly logical, imagined world where the physical laws that govern cartoon characters coexist with those that govern the rest of us. Roger Rabbit, flattened paper-thin under a toppled fridge, pops back into shape when the fridge is removed. Poor old Eddie Valiant (Mr. Hoskins), the seedy Los Angeles private eye who is the film's co-star, would remain forever squashed if hit on the head by a grand piano dropped from 15 stories up.

This is not only the method of "Who Framed Roger Rabbit" but also, in a way, what it's all about, though that shouldn't be stressed too much.

The setting is Los Angeles and the time is 1947, when the production of cartoon shorts for theaters was still profitable and Hollywood's biggest stars included, in addition to Gable and Tracy and Davis, the Mouses (Mickey and Minnie), Donald Duck, Daffy Duck, Dumbo, Tweety Bird and Roger Rabbit, among others. Roger is under contract to Maroon Studios, which has made a fortune in a cartoon series co-starring the hyperventilating Roger with Baby Herman, a gurgling, diapered tyke on-screen who, when off, is a whisky-voiced, cigar-smoking, 50-year-old skirt chaser.

It is the conceit of "Who Framed Roger Rabbit" that these cartoon actors, known as Toons, inhabit their own Hollywood enclave called Toontown. In 1947 Hollywood, Toons are treated in much the way that such black stars as Lena Horne, Hattie McDaniel, Stepin Fetchit and Eddie (Rochester) Anderson were once treated: separate and not very equal.

"Who Framed Roger Rabbit" is about the efforts of Eddie Valiant to clear Roger Rabbit when the star is accused of murdering the paramour of his sexy wife, Jessica, a hu-

man Toon with a loose reputation ("I'm not so bad. I'm just drawn that way").

Eddie is initially reluctant ("My brother was killed by a Toon"), but soon finds himself up to his ears in the caper. This involves blackmail, bribery, real estate fraud and a plan do away with Los Angeles's efficient, highly regarded public transportation company (the Red Car streetcar line), substituting for it a system of what the villain ominously calls "freeways."

The humans in "Who Framed Roger Rabbit" don't like Toons. Jealousy is part of it. Toons are born performers. Toons also can do things that would kill the rest of us. They survive electrocution, dismemberment, falls from airplanes, being roasted in ovens, run over by steamrollers and shot out of cannons through brick walls. Toons never die. They can only be destroyed when dropped into a solution (part turpentine, part benzine) known as "the dip."

The reason that "Who Framed Roger Rabbit" is so consistently cheering, even when the gags don't produce outright laughs, has to do with the unusual wit of the screenplay (by Jeffrey Price and Peter S. Seaman) and of the direction by Robert Zemeckis ("Back to the Future"). "Who Framed Roger Rabbit" is a film that has been thought through, beginning at the technical level and continuing up through the performances (by Mr. Hoskins and the others) and the emotional responses it prompts.

While I was watching it, I was reminded of the time when I saw Mel Brooks's "Young Frankenstein" with an audience composed of children aged from 6 or 7 to 14. Though much of the Brooks humor is intended for adults, the comic rhythm of the movie is so insinuating that even the youngest children screamed with helpless laughter at jokes that went flying over their heads. The same thing happens in "Roger Rabbit."

For the rest of us, "Roger Rabbit" is a delight in its own right as well as a revivifying recollection of the Golden Age of cartooning, when movie animation was a painstaking, not yet highfalutin art. Turning up in cameos and walk-ons are Betty Boop, Snow White, Goofy, Woody Woodpecker and a mincing, ladylike hippo from "Fantasia."

Among the film's highlights: a twin-piano concert by Donald Duck and Daffy Duck, which turns nasty and winds up a proper shambles, as well as the spectacular final sequence. In this, the usually resourceful Eddie Valiant, invading Toontown, finds himself in the kinds of terrifying situations (such as stepping into an elevator that isn't there) that, for Toons, are all in a day's work. That Eddie is not killed (crash, bam, splat) is due mainly to the ingenuity and resourcefulness of his new-found, boon Toon companions.

"Bull Durham" is something almost equally unusual, a rough, often uproarious, literate (to the extent that William Blake and Walt Whitman are mentioned) romantic comedy set in the world of minor-league baseball in the South, specifically, North Carolina. It was written and directed by Ron Shelton, whose only previous credits are as the writer of "Under Fire" and "The Best of Times."

At the center of it are three singularly weird and wonderful, potential washouts.

Annie Savoy (Susan Sarandon) is a part-time English teacher and full-time baseball groupie. At the start of each season, Annie chooses a promising rookie whom she can sleep with, and whose talents need to be honed to perfection by her knowledge of the game and of various mind-control exercises. Baseball wives would probably call Annie a tramp. She sees baseball as a religion and herself as its high priestess.

Ebby Calvin (Nuke) LaLoosh (Tim Robbins) is Annie's pick for the season, a big, good-natured, none-too-bright pitcher whose fastball is clocked at 95 miles per hour, though, if it doesn't miss the plate by miles, it's likely to hit the batter.

Crash Davis (Kevin Costner) is the old timer (he looks to be, at most, in his mid-30's), brought in to catch and, primarily, to take the rough edges off Nuke (a nickname that Nuke has picked for himself). Crash Davis has been through the mill. He has seen rookies like Nuke before and has pushed them into the big leagues where he himself once lasted, he admits, for about 15 minutes.

In the person of Mr. Costner (who is coming to have some of the screen heft of Gary Cooper, lightened by a nutty, screwball intensity), Crash functions as the conscience of the film, which is narrated (from time to time) by Annie. He's a great character, as eccentric in his way as the other two but never unaware. He's someone not often seen on the screen anymore, a hero of true stature.

Mr. Shelton, a one-time baseball pro himself, clearly knows the milieu and hasn't forgotten any of the oddballs and misfits he ever met. From the richness of the dialogue, it's also apparent that he has a natural writer's gift for letting the imagination run freely on its own, from whatever might have been the original inspirations. He's not tied down by plausibility.

As a director, he demonstrates the sort of expert comic timing and control that allow him to get in and out of situations so quickly that they're over before one has time to question them. Part of the fun in watching "Bull Durham" is in the awareness that a clearly seen vision is being realized. This is one first-rate debut.

Miss Sarandon has done some fine work in the past, including her performances in Louis Malle's "Atlantic City" and "Pretty Baby" too many years ago, but time is being good to her. She looks terrific and possesses the sort of comic authority one usually only recognizes on the stage, in a live performance. She takes control of the film, much in the way she handles both Nuke and Crash.

As the overconfident rookie, Mr. Robbins, heretofore a comparatively ordinary young leading man, has what could be the dream part of a career. It isn't likely that he'll again have a chance to be seen in the team locker room surreptitiously trying to put on a garter belt under a baseball uniform.

This is not a fetish, but just another one of Annie's ways of helping Nuke to get in touch with himself, "by keeping the mind off balance." Annie also has him breathing through his eyelids, though he can never be sure he's doing it right.

At long last, there are two new American films not to miss.   □

1988 Jl 3, II:1:3

LICENSE TO DRIVE, directed by Greg Beeman; written by Neil Tolkin; director of photography, Bruce Surtees; film editor, Wendy Greene Bricmont; music by Jay Ferguson; production designer, Lawrence G. Paull; produced by Jeffrey A. Mueller and Andrew Licht; released by the 20th Century-Fox Film Corporation. At the National, Broadway at 44th Street; the Plaza, 42 East 58th Street, and other theaters. Running time: 90 minutes. This film is rated PG-13.

Les	Corey Haim
Dean	Corey Feldman
Mom	Carol Kane
Dad	Richard Masur
Mercedes	Heather Graham
Charles	Michael Manasseri
Professor	Harvey Miller
Paolo	M. A. Nickles

By CARYN JAMES

Anyone old enough to have a license is probably much too old to be amused by "License to Drive," the comic adventure of a 16-year-old who fails his driving test and sneaks off on Saturday night in his grandfather's 1972 Cadillac. By morning he has driven around town with his drunken girlfriend passed out in the trunk and two friends howling in the passenger seats. It is proof of the candy heart beneath the film's reckless storyline that all this action seems at worst slightly naughty.

Early on, sweet-faced Corey Haim looks straight into the camera and asks: "An innocent girl. A harmless drive. What could possibly go wrong?" The scene offers one of the few hints that everyone involved knows exactly how predictable and formulaic the film is. But then, its ideal audience is a group that longs to be as old as its high-school characters, a group that hasn't been around long enough to grow tired of the car chases, romantic near-misses and "My dad's gonna kill me!" moments when fenders crumble and headlights shatter.

Though the plot and action never get better than a television movie of the week, the engaging cast brings much more style to the material than it deserves. As Les, who can't bear to pass up a date with a beautiful girl named Mercedes, Mr. Haim is exactly the good-but-mischievous son you'd expect from Richard Masur's solid Dad and Carol Kane's spacy Mom. Corey Feldman (who was also Mr. Haim's best friend in "The Lost Boys") is Dean, the more mischievous friend who goads Les to be his worst. The actors don't ever wink at the camera, but they realize that they're just this side of "Leave It to Beaver" and that it's not an unpleasant place to spend 90 minutes.

Throughout Les's long night, we know nothing bad will happen because, after all, this is a harmless summer comedy and because the film comes with built-in disclaimers. Les happens to be a very good driver who had a little trouble on the written part of his test. And Dean even warns his friend about the penalities for driving without a license. These kids never drive drunk; they don't do drugs; in the real world of teen-agers they're practically saints. And Les's understanding parents are straight from fantasyland. All is forgiven on Saturday morning after Les heroically drives his pregnant mom to the hospital. The car will only go in reverse, so Les's father, busy holding his wife's hand, lets his son drive to the hospital backwards.

"License to Drive," which opens today at the National and other theaters, is just as sweet, just as bland, as its unbelievable cartoonish world.

1988 Jl 6, C17:1

SHORT CIRCUIT 2, directed by Kenneth Johnson; written by S. S. Wilson and Brent Maddock; director of photography, John McPherson; edited by Conrad Buff; music by Charles Fox; production designer, Bill Brodie; produced by David Foster, Lawrence Turman and Gary Foster; released by Tri-Star Pictures. At Loews 84th Street Six, at Broadway; Criterion, Broadway and 45th Street and other theaters. Running time: 112 minutes. This film is rated PG.

Ben Jahrvi	Fisher Stevens
Fred Ritter	Michael McKean
Sandy Banatoni	Cynthia Gibb
Oscar Baldwin	Jack Weston
Saunders	Dee McCafferty
Jones	David Hemblen

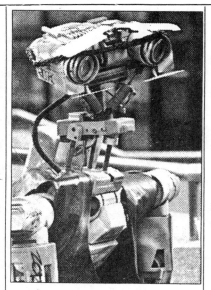

On the Loose

Robot No. 5 experiences life in the big city in "Short Circuit 2," Kenneth Johnson's sequel to the 1986 comedy.

"Short Circuit 2," a sequel to the 1985 comedy that became a best seller as a video cassette, is about the mechanically cute robot, now named Johnny Five, and his adventures in a big unnamed city that is, in fact, Toronto. It opens today at the Criterion and other theaters.

For anyone over the age of 6, the film is as much fun as wearing wet sneakers. The robot does some unusual things, but is singularly charmless. Even so, he is more appealing than the adult characters surrounding him. These include a supposedly comic Indian from India (Fisher Stevens), who speaks in malapropisms, a hustling but decent street vendor (Michael McKean), a pretty young woman (Cynthia Gibb) and Jack Weston, who plays a greedy bank executive.

The movie was written by S. S. Wilson and Brent Maddock, who wrote the first film, and directed by Kenneth Johnson. They all worked hard and spent a lot of money to come up with an automated toy that, on the screen, anyway, is harmless.

"Short Circuit," which has been rated PG ("Parental Guidance Suggested"), contains some situations that might be mildly distressing to especially timid tots.

VINCENT CANBY

1988 Jl 6, C18:5

Mortician Manqué

PHANTASM II, directed and written by Don Coscarelli; director of photography, Daryn Okada; edited by Peter Teschner; music by Fred Myrow with Christopher L. Stone; production designer, Philip J.C. Duffin; produced by Roberto A. Quezada; released by Universal Pictures. At Movieland, Broadway at 47th Street, and other theaters. Running time: 90 minutes. This film is rated R.

Mike	James Le Gros
Reggie	Reggie Bannister
The Tall Man	Angus Scrimm
Liz	Paula Irvine
Alchemy	Samantha Phillips
Father Meyers	Kenneth Tigar

There are some grotesquely stylish and scary moments in "Phantasm II," the sequel to a 1979 film that Don Coscarelli made as a precocious 25-year-old. Unfortunately, these episodes seem to take as long to arrive as the sequel did.

The best parts of "Phantasm II" have little to do with the returning heroes or the villain, called the Tall Man, and everything to do with the Tall Man's movie-derived methods of attacking the living and the dead.

He is a kind of mortician manqué. Instead of injecting bodies with embalming fluid, he shoots them full of something that looks suspiciously like bright yellow mustard. This, it seems, turns his victims into dwarfs wearing little brown monks' robes. These creatures, who show up periodically in the film, cluster around their victims and look a lot like the flying monkeys in "The Wizard of Oz." There are also wormy creatures that pop out of bodies, as in "Aliens." But the Tall Man's worst punishment is a flying silver ball, from the first "Phantasm," that looks like a Christmas tree ornament and conceals a kind of super-destructive Swiss Army knife that cuts and drills its way through a victim.

When 19-year-old Mike and his middle-aged friend, Reg, decide to do in the Tall Man for good, they are joined by a young woman named Liz. She and Mike have literally seen each other in their dreams, so it is a tender moment when they finally meet in an empty grave and fall into each another's arms. Mr. Coscarelli tries to keep things moving, deflating the horror with intentionally ludicrous scenes such as this, but the result is all too slow and labored.

When it succeeds, "Phantasm II," which opens today at the Movieland and other theaters, is slightly better than most horror films. Most of the time, you're left waiting for the dwarf-monks to show up.

CARYN JAMES

1988 Jl 8, C11:1

Two for the Road

LOOSE CONNECTIONS, directed by Richard Eyre; written by Maggie Brooks; music by Dominic Muldowney and Andy Roberts; produced by Simon Perry; released by Orion Classics. At Public Theater, 425 Lafayette Street. Running time: 90 minutes. This film has no rating.

Harry	Stephen Rea
Sally	Lindsay Duncan
Axel	Jan Niklas
Kaya	Carole Harrison
Kevin	Gary Olsen
Laurie	Frances Low
Supporter	Ken Jones

"Loose Connections," the 1983 English film that opens today at the Public Theater, is of main interest for having been directed by Richard Eyre, the director of the good, strong, politically provoking "Ploughman's Lunch" (1984), written by Ian McEwan.

"Loose Connections" is a politically aware romantic comedy about a pretty, committed feminist named Sally (Lindsay Duncan), a representative of the middle class, and her adventures on the European road with Harry (Stephen Rea), a rough, young male chauvinist out of Liverpool's working class.

In order to get a free trip to Germany, Harry answers Sally's ad for a German-speaking, mechanically adept person to drive with her to Munich, where she is to attend a conference on women's rights and problems. Sally originally had a female companion in mind, but settles for Harry, at least in part because he wears a large button reading "Gay."

Nothing happens in "Loose Connections" that isn't announced ahead of time, but the movie is very decently acted by Mr. Rea and especially by Miss Duncan, whom Broadway audiences saw in "Les Liaisons Dangereuses." She looks a little like a blond Diane Keaton, and has a lot of Miss Keaton's intelligence and sweet unpredictability.

The film, written by Maggie Brooks, is bright, articulate, gentle and completely unsurprising. Its best moment comes when Sally suddenly realizes that Harry has used her for his own ends. "I feel exploited!" she cries out in horror, which prompts Harry to launch into a funny, furious, self-serving diatribe about the sort of exploitation he has suffered through.

"Loose Connections" comes out firmly for unisex liberation.

VINCENT CANBY

1988 Jl 8, C11:1

Still Tipsy After All These Years

ARTHUR 2 ON THE ROCKS, directed by Bud Yorkin; written by Andy Breckman; director of photography, Stephen H. Burum; film editor, Michael Kahn; music by Burt Bacharach; production design by Gene Callahan; produced by Robert Shapiro; released by Warner Brothers. At Criterion Center, Broadway at 45th Street, and other theaters. Running time: 112 minutes. This film is rated PG.

Arthur	Dudley Moore
Linda	Liza Minnelli
Bert Johnson	Stephen Elliott
Susan	Cynthia Sikes
Hobson	Sir John Gielgud
Fairchild	Paul Benedict

By VINCENT CANBY

Seeing "Arthur 2 on the Rocks" is like meeting a once-ebullient, witty old friend who has let himself go to pieces. Arthur (Dudley Moore) still drinks too much, though now it's beginning to show. He looks vaguely unhealthy and is no longer funny.

Another Round

Dudley Moore, Cynthia Sikes and Stephen Elliott mix it up in "Arthur 2 on the Rocks."

Arthur won't shut up even when he has nothing to say. The formerly infectious cackle, with which he expresses appreciation of his own witticisms, sounds like the desperation of a man who realizes he has lost his audience, and has no idea why.

Arthur has become a clamorous bore.

"Arthur 2 on the Rocks," which opens today at the Criterion Center and other theaters, is a lame sequel to "Arthur" (1981), Steve Gordon's fine, featherweight, screwball comedy in which Mr. Moore courts and wins Liza Minnelli, playing a waitress named Linda, in spite of his $750 million inheritance.

Mr. Gordon, who died not long after writing and directing his only hit film, constructed the kind of self-contained, near-perfect comedy that defies further elaboration. His Arthur's drinking is funny because it is something that can be magically cured by the love of Linda, a relatively good woman who, when first met in "Arthur," is shoplifting. The earlier Arthur and Linda made a most endearing pair.

•

When they turn up in "Arthur 2 on the Rocks," the suspicion is that each is, in his or her own way, seriously sick.

The new movie begins with Arthur, again riding around New York in the back of his chauffeured Rolls, tormenting passers-by with drunken insults, which, this time, are not of the highest quality. As it turns out, he is hours late for an intimate dinner at Tavern on the Green with Linda, who, when he does arrive, is not at all surprised that he can hardly stand up.

That she still finds him funny no longer seems quite sane on her part. Linda has a reality problem to equal Arthur's. If this is what's been going on for the seven years of their marriage, it would seem more likely that' he would be in a hospital suffering delirium tremens, and she'd be in the psychiatric ward weaving wicker baskets.

The subject of plausibility would not arise if "Arthur 2 on the Rocks" had a life of its own. It doesn't. As written by Andy Breckman and directed by Bud Yorkin, it is a doughy, unimaginative spin-off beyond any saving by its two resourceful stars.

•

The story this time has something to do with their attempt to adopt a baby, and with a plan by the father of the debutante spurned by Arthur in the first film to blackmail Arthur into leaving Linda.

Sir John Gielgud was splendid in the first film as Arthur's Jeeves-like valet but, unfortunately, was killed off by Mr. Gordon. That doesn't stop Mr. Yorkin and Mr. Breckman. They rob the grave to bring back Sir John as a ghost in a not-great cameo.

Two performances are not bad. They are those of the deadpanned Paul Benedict, who plays Arthur's new, totally humorless valet, and the beautiful Cynthia Sikes, who, as Arthur's former fiancée, seems to have more common sense, as well as a greater sense of fun, than anyone else in this doomed endeavor.

"Arthur 2 on the Rocks," which has been rated PG ("Parental Guidance Suggested"), includes some mildly vulgar language.

1988 Jl 8, C8:1

Straddling Two Worlds

THE KITCHEN TOTO, directed and written by Harry Hook; director of photography, Roger Deakins; production designer, Jamie Leonard; supervising editor, Tom Priestley; music by John Keane; produced by Ann Skinner; released by the Cannon Group Inc., in association with British Screen and Film Four International. At Quad Cinema, 34 West 13th Street; D. W. Griffith, 59th Street, east of Third Avenue. Running time: 96 minutes. This film is rated PG-13.

Mwangi	Edwin Mahinda
John Graham	Bob Peck
Janet Graham	Phyllis Logan
Edward Graham	Ronald Pirie
D. C. McKinnon	Robert Urquhart
Mary	Kirsten Hughes
Dick Luis	Edward Judd

By CARYN JAMES

Harry Hook's subdued and powerful first film is a coming-of-age story loaded with history. Mwangi, a 12-year-old boy of the Kikuyu tribe, is a clear metaphor for Kenya's political development. Set in 1950, at the start of the struggle that would lead to independence from British rule 13 years later, "The Kitchen Toto" suggests how blacks such as Mwangi were doubly oppressed — by the white colonists and by the Mau Mau, the terrorist group that forced other Kikuyus to swear allegiance to them. But the film's beauty is in its refusal to treat Mwangi as a symbol. He is first an intelligent, curious, open-natured child, who becomes the ultimate victim, crushed between two cultures.

Though Mwangi's father, a minister, is threatened by the Mau Mau, he tells his congregation to renounce the oath that binds them to such violence. The Mau Mau break into the family's one-room hut at night, murder Mwangi's father, injure his mother and set fire to their home. Forced to earn money, Mwangi becomes the toto (Swahili for child) who helps out in the kitchen of John Graham, the white police chief.

Despite its eruptions into violence, the film focuses on ordinary personalities and minor daily brutalities. Graham's kindness — he is determined to help Mwangi and locate the men who attacked the family — is balanced by the cold-blooded attitudes of his wife and young son, Edward, who treat Mwangi as subhuman. Edward is a strange-looking child whose straw-colored hair, pale skin and narrow, suspicious eyes are a blatant contrast to Mwangi's wide-eyed curiosity about everything.

•

Mr. Hook's perspective and sympathy are always with Mwangi, who is played perfectly by Edwin Mahinda, who shows a remarkable, understated range of emotions. He cries silently when his mother leaves him at the Grahams. (Mr. Hook is not above lingering on those tears a bit too long.) But he has a strong child's resilience, and is soon traipsing through the woods with Edward, oblivious to the British boy's condescension. Edward loads his gun with ants and uses Mwangi for target practice; Mwangi gloats when the shot misses.

Eventually, of course, Mwangi recognizes his cruel treatment and his powerlessness. He learns to spit in a sandwich before serving it to a man who has tied him to a tree for a night, wrongly believing he is a poacher.

And soon the political undercurrents rise to engulf the Graham household, when Mwangi and another

End of Empire
Edwin Mahinda and Ronald Pirie are the stars of "The Kitchen Toto."

servant are taken to the woods and forced to swear allegiance to the Mau Mau. The film's major flaw is its lack of a fuller historical context in such scenes. Mr. Hook grew up in Kenya, where his father was a British colonel, so perhaps he did not see the need to explain that the Mau Mau's growing strength would culminate in the widespread, brutal murders in the next few years. For American audiences, the terrorists are likely to seem no more than isolated thugs who emerge from the woods, rather than part of a controversial, incendiary movement.

The devastating effect of the Mau Mau is painfully clear, however, when they attack the Graham house and cause Mwangi to be caught between his black and white masters. The rapid violence of the end might have turned to melodrama — someone is shot and the Grahams' baby is kidnapped — but it is redeemed by a moment of terrible recognition in Mwangi's eyes. He suddenly knows he has been trapped in a position from which he cannot escape.

Roger Deakins has photographed Kenya prettily, while avoiding a lush, over-romanticized Hollywood look. There are no large herds of animals racing across the screen here, just modest houses and cars and lawns set against a wooded green landscape. When the Mau Mau come in darkness, the scenes are threatening but never lurid.

"The Kitchen Toto," which opens today at the D. W. Griffith and Quad Cinema, is a perfectly controlled film that reverberates, very quietly, with political meaning.

•

"The Kitchen Toto" is rated PG-13 ("Special Parental Guidance for Those Younger Than 13"). It includes some bloody scenes.

1988 Jl 8, C12:5

Modern Magi

CAMMINA CAMMINA, written and directed by Ermanno Olmi; in Italian with English subtitles; cinematography and editing by Mr. Olmi; music by Bruno Nicolai; produced by RAI-Radiotelevisione Italiana-Scenario. At Thalia So-Ho, 57 Vandam Street. Running time: 150 minutes. This film has no rating.

Mel	Alberto Fumagalli
Rupo	Antonio Cucciarre
Kaipaco	Eligio Martellacci
The shepherd	Renzo Samminiatesi
Cushi	Marco Bartolini
Nohad	Lucia Peccianti
Woodsmen	
Guido Del Testa, Tersilio Gheilardini, Aldo Fanucci	
Arupa	Fernando Guarguaglini
Her companion	Anna Vanni
Astioge	Giulio Paradisi
Astioge's wife	Rosanna Cuffaro

"Cammina Cammina" was shown as part of the 1984 New York Film Festival. Following are excerpts from Vincent Canby's review, which appeared in The New York Times Oct. 4, 1984. The film opens today at the Thalia So-Ho, 15 Vandam Street, between Avenue of the Americas and Seventh Avenue.

Ermanno Olmi's "Cammina Cammina" ("Keep Walking, Keep Walking") opens with a good deal of exuberant promise as the peasants in a small village in northern Italy prepare to celebrate the Nativity by re-enacting the pilgrimage to Bethlehem of the wise men. There's a lot of rude pushing, shoving, laughing and general high spirits as the members of the pagaent's cast search for the right costumes and props.

All this comes before and during the opening credits, after which "Cammina Cammina" turns into a fairly straightforward movie about the journey of the Magi, based on New Testament stories as well as on legends that have accumulated over the centuries. The focus of the film is the priest, Melchior, called Mel in the film, and the trials faced by him and his flock as they follow the trail of the Christmas star over moor, mountain, field and fountain to the manger in the Holy Land.

Along the way they join forces with two other Magi, and have an unsatisfactory offscreen meeting with King Herod in Jerusalem, before beholding Mary, Joseph and the baby Jesus in Bethlehem.

Once Mr. Olmi forsakes the rural present for the mythical, rural past, the movie becomes almost intolerably solemn and tedious, though handsomely photographed in rugged Italian terrain and filled with the extraordinary faces of its nonprofessional actors.

Mr. Olmi seldom successfully dramatizes his paradoxes, which, ultimately, are reduced to an exchange between Mel and a follower toward the film's end. The follower berates Mel for having stolen away from Bethlehem in the middle of the night instead of staying to prevent Herod's massacre of the innocents. Says Mel, by way of explanation, "We shall build temples to celebrate the coming of God to earth." Replies his accuser, "Above all, you shall celebrate His death."

This is an interesting idea, but it comes too late to occupy the mind throughout the long succession of mostly impersonal, stately and awfully picturesque scenes that precedes it.

"Cammina Cammina" opens today at the Thalia So-Ho, 15 Vandam Street.

1988 Jl 10, 43:5

DEAD POOL, directed by Buddy Van Horn; screenplay by Steve Sharon; story by Mr. Sharon and Durk Pearson and Sandy Shaw; cinematography by Jack N. Green; edited by Ron Spang; music by Lalo Schifrin; produced by David Valdes; released by Warner Brothers. At the National Twin, Broadway and 44th

Law and Order Clint Eastwood appears for the fifth time as the police officer Dirty Harry Callahan in "The Dead Pool."

Street; the Sutton, 57th Street and Third Avenue, and other theaters. Running time: 91 minutes. This film is rated R.

Harry Callahan	Clint Eastwood
Samantha Walker	Patricia Clarkson
Peter Swan	Liam Neeson
Al Quan	Evan C. Kim
Harlan Rook	David Hunt
Molly Fisher	Ronnie Claire Edwards

By VINCENT CANBY

"The Dead Pool" is the fifth film in which Clint Eastwood has appeared as Harry Callahan, the San Francisco cop introduced in "Dirty Harry" in 1971. Harry is still the sort of guy who believes that if you spare the rod you spoil the psychopath. When in doubt, shoot.

Mr. Eastwood has now been playing Harry almost as long as Jean-Pierre Léaud played Antoine in François Truffaut's Antoine Doinel cycle. In much the same way that Mr. Léaud grew up on the screen, aging from 13 to 33 as the Truffaut surrogate figure, Mr. Eastwood has been developing into a cinema icon during the last 17 years.

At the same time, though, the Dirty Harry movies have been getting smaller. None is smaller than "The Dead Pool," which the tall, lean, sinewy actor drags behind him as if it were a toy duck. It quacks, slow or fast, depending on the speed at which it's pulled.

"The Dead Pool," which opens today at the Criterion and other theaters, possesses a couple of good jokes, but nothing can disguise the fact that it's a mini-movie in the company of a mythic figure.

The modest screenplay is mostly concerned with the troubles Harry faces when, as the result of the conviction of a Mafia boss (in which his testimony is crucial), he becomes a San Francisco celebrity. Harry is a private person. He detests publicity, as well as the television news people who pump it out, especially when he becomes the target of several assassination attempts.

There is a small mystery about who is trying to get rid of Harry. It could be the Mafia boss, or it could be the psychopath who has been murdering a group of people connected with a horror movie ("Hotel Satan"),

currently being filmed in the Bay Area. "The Dead Pool" takes its title from a game being played by the director, cast and crew of "Hotel Satan." This is a sort of lottery that involves a pool of names of people not expected to live out the year.

After Harry blows away four would-be assassins in the opening sequence, the film's body count mounts steadily, though the emphasis is more on comedy than on blood, guts, law and order.

"The Dead Pool" was directed by Buddy Van Horn, who earlier directed Mr. Eastwood's "Any Which Way You Can," and was written by Steve Sharon, but the film's personality is that of its star.

Among the supporting characters are a pretty television anchor (Patricia Clarkson) who comes to hate her job (and admire Harry) after he tells her to think about her responsibility to the public; an egotistical film director (Liam Neeson) beloved by auteurists; a know-it-all film reviewer (Ronnie Claire Edwards) who comes to no good end, and Harry's young Chinese-American partner (Evan C. Kim).

The only really inventive sequence is one in which Harry and his partner, riding in their unmarked car, are pursued up and down San Francisco's streets by a remote-controlled toy automobile packed with plastic explosives. It's the last word on the classic car chase in "Bullitt," which is still being imitated.

1988 Jl 13, C22:1

A Coin With One Side

THE LOVE SUICIDES AT SONEZAKI, directed and produced by Midori Kurisaki; in Japanese with English subtitles; photography by Kazuo Miyagawa; art direction by Akira Naito; distributed by R5/S8. At Film Forum 1, 57 Watts Street. Running time: 88 minutes. This film has no rating.

Head puppeteers
Tamao Yoshida and Minosuke Yoshida

"The Love Suicides at Sonezaki" (1981), opening today at Film Forum 1, is an adaptation of Monzaemon Chikamatsu's 18th-century bunraku

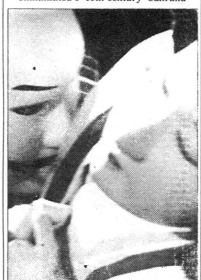

Tragic Romance The thwarted love of a businessman for a beautiful courtesan is portrayed in "The Love Suicides at Sonezaki."

puppet drama, filmed not in a bunraku theater but in realistic settings that are at odds with this most highly stylized theatrical form.

The film was directed by Midori Kurisaki and photographed by Kazuo Miyagawa, the veteran Japanese camerman who has worked with Kenji Mizoguchi ("Ugetsu") and Akira Kurosawa ("Rashomon," "Yojimbo"). Though "The Love Suicides" looks beautiful, the dramatic effect is diluted by the sight of real trees, real sky, real water.

Chikamatsu (1653-1724) turned to the puppet theater because he hated actors who attempted to "improve" his work. He might not have appreciated Miss Kurisaki's good intentions. In addition to location filming (in Kyoto), these include close-ups of the faces of the doll-actors that, in a bunraku theater, remain at a fixed distance from the audience. Such improvements spoil the theatrical spectacle. They also separate the physical artifice of the performance from the dramatic artifice of the play. "The Love Suicides at Sonezaki" is a death-obsessed tale about a young merchant and his faithful prostitute-mistress whose feelings for each other are so refined that they choose death before his dishonor.

Bunraku theater is performed by puppets, approximately three feet tall, each guided by three handlers dressed in black from head to foot. The presence of the handlers reinforces the fatalism of the drama. They are concerned angels, attending to their charges, easing their ways but helpless when it comes to changing events.

A much more satisfactory introduction to bunraku is provided by "The Lovers' Exile," a filmed record of a performance by the Bunraku Ensemble of Osaka, directed by Marty Gross, the Canadian film maker, and released here in 1981. In that film, photographed in a bunraku theater, one gets some sense of both the poetry and the mechanics of bunraku theater. They can't be safely separated.
VINCENT CANBY

1988 Jl 13, C22:1

Double-Crossing The Double-Crossers

A FISH CALLED WANDA, directed by Charles Crichton; written by John Cleese, original story by Mr. Cleese and Mr. Crichton; director of photography, Alan Hume; film editor, John Jympson; music by John Du Prez; production designer, Roger Murray-Leach; produced by Michael Shamberg; released by M-G-M Pictures Inc. At the Loews Tower East, Third Avenue and 71st Street, and the Loews Paramount, Broadway at 61st Street. Running time: 107 minutes. This film is rated R.

Archie	John Cleese
Wanda	Jamie Lee Curtis
Otto	Kevin Kline
Ken	Michael Palin
Wendy	Maria Aitken
George	Tom Georgeson
Mrs. Coady	Patricia Hayes

By VINCENT CANBY

The best thing about "A Fish Called Wanda" is the anticipation of it.

Here is an English caper-comedy written by and starring John Cleese, who is also its executive producer. It was directed by Charles Crichton, long associated with Ealing Studios and best remembered as the director of "The Lavender Hill Mob."

David James

Trolling Jamie Lee Curtis and John Cleese star in "A Fish Called Wanda," about a gang of jewel thieves who pull off a major heist.

Mr. Cleese's co-stars are Kevin Kline, a master of slapstick when he chooses to be; Jamie Lee Curtis, an actress so skilled she can locate the laughter in a simple reaction shot, or in a swivel-hipped walk away from the camera, and Michael Palin, Mr. Cleese's Monty Python associate, who specializes in chiropodists, suspect saviors and other servants of mankind.

The smaller roles are played by the sorts of actors who, in England, seem to be born as fully characterized, immediately identifiable nuts.

"A Fish Called Wanda," which opens today at the Paramount and Tower East Theaters, sounds great. Yet it plays like an extended lampshade joke.

It's not easy to describe the movie's accumulating dimness or to understand what went wrong.

Everyone knocks himself out to be funny. The worse the material becomes, the harder the actors work for increasingly less effect. Mr. Cleese, who has what is — technically, anyway — the romantic lead, gives himself a nude scene. Mr. Palin plays a man who is supposed to be comic because he stutters, not in the way of an upper-class twit but in the way of someone with a real problem. When all else fails, there are comic bits of business about armpits and bunions.

Beginning with cute character names, the screenplay is less than super. Four misfits come together to rob a London jeweler, and then spend the rest of the movie double-crossing each other. They are Wanda Gershwitz (Miss Curtis), a larcenous American woman; Otto West (Mr. Kline), whom Wanda introduces as her brother, though he is, like every other man in the film, a lover; Ken Pile (Mr. Palin), whose job, it seems, is simply to stutter, and George (Tom Georgeson), the leader of the gang and the only one who knows where the jewels have been hidden after the robbery.

When George is arrested, Mr. Cleese, as Archie Leach (Cary Grant's original name), an uptight barrister, is hired to defend him. Because Wanda thinks that George will tell Archie where the jewels are, she throws herself at the proper barrister with results that aren't entirely surprising.

"A Fish Called Wanda" recalls those radio commercials Mr. Cleese has been doing in this country in behalf of an English candy company. The tone is faux-eccentric and sort of hearty, in the way of someone who pretends to be ingratiatingly odd while delivering an utterly humorless, hard-sell message. In this case, the product being pushed is laughs.

Both as a member of the Monty Python troupe and as the co-writer and co-star of "Fawlty Towers," Mr. Cleese has demonstrated his gift for the comedy of intemperance. The perfect Cleese character is self-obsessed, short-tempered and disconnected. He goes through life convinced that everybody else is crazy.

This sense of elevated madness is missing from his performance in "A Fish Called Wanda," and from the film itself. Each character has some redeeming moments, but the redeeming moments of no two or three characters ever overlap.

The screenplay doesn't seem to have been thought through. Mr. Kline's Otto West is described as being incredibly dumb, though the actor clearly is not. The dialogue *reports* funny things instead of showing them. The movie remains in a limbo halfway between the informed anarchy of Monty Python comedy stripped of all social and political satire, and the comparatively genteel comedy of "The Lavender Hill Mob."

When, toward the end, someone stuffs ketchup-smeared french fries into Mr. Palin's nostrils, "A Fish Called Wanda" seems to have turned into a private joke to be enjoyed only by the members of the cast and crew who made it.

1988 Jl 15, C8:1

Up on the Roof

DIE HARD, directed by John McTiernan; screenplay by Jeb Stuart and Steven E. de Souza, based on the novel by Roderick Thorp; director of photography, Jan De Bont; film editors, Frank J. Urioste and John F. Link; music by Michael Kamen; production designer, Jackson DeGovia; produced by Lawrence Gordon and Joel Silver; released by 20th Century-Fox Film Corporation. At Criterion Center, Broadway between 44th and 45th Streets; Baronet, Third Avenue at 59th Street. Running time: 127 minutes. This film is rated R.

John McClane	Bruce Willis
Holly Gennaro McClane	Bonnie Bedelia
Sgt. Al Powell	Reginald Veljohnson
Hans Gruber	Alan Rickman
Karl	Alexander Godunov
Dwayne T. Robinson	Paul Gleason
Argyle	De'Voreaux White
Thornburg	William Atherton

By CARYN JAMES

"Die Hard," the movie that gambles a $5 million salary on Bruce Willis, has to be the most excessive film around. It piles every known element of the action genre onto the flimsy story of a New York cop who rescues hostages from a Los Angeles office tower on Christmas Eve. Partly an interracial buddy movie, partly the sentimental tale of a ruptured marriage, the film is largely a special-effects carnival full of machine-gun fire, roaring helicopters and an exploding tank. It also has a villain fresh from the Royal Shakespeare Company, a thug from the Bolshoi Ballet and a hero who carries with him the smirks and wisecracks that helped make "Moonlighting" a television hit. The strange thing is, it works: "Die Hard" is exceedingly

Peter Sorel
Heroics In "Die Hard," Bruce Willis portrays a detective trying to rescue hostages in a high-rise building seized by terrorists.

stupid, but escapist fun.

The film's producers and director were also responsible for the Arnold Schwarzenegger hit "Predator." Here they graft the Schwarzenegger-style comic hero onto Mr. Willis's boyish, mischievous "Moonlighting" persona, and send this new creature sauntering into "The Towering Inferno."

●

There is a slow half-hour at the start, when John McClane (Mr. Willis) lands in Los Angeles to visit his estranged wife (Bonnie Bedelia) and goes to her office Christmas party. Minutes later, a group of terrorists shows up, planning to steal $6 million in bonds. The terrorists have to crack a difficult computer code before getting into the vault, so there is plenty of time for McClane to play hero.

Mr. Willis's true expertise is in banter, so the director, John McTiernan, shrewdly blends bursts of action with comic dialogue. McClane races up and down elevator shafts. He kills one terrorist, taking his machine gun and citizens' band radio. Now he can have a running conversation with Al, the sympathetic black cop who arrives first at the scene. Al (played by Reginald Veljohnson) becomes part of the only buddy film where the friends don't meet until the story is over.

Meanwhile, back in the executive suite, there is Hans, the ruthless terrorist leader in a very well-tailored suit. He is the film's best surprise, played by Alan Rickman, who was recently the seductive, manipulative Valmont in the Royal Shakespeare Company's stage production of "Les Liaisons Dangereuses." Here, he makes Hans a perfect snake. "Who are you?" he superciliously asks McClane via radio. "Are you just another American who saw too many movies as a child?"

●

Well, yes, he did. McClane is a movie maverick, who asks to be called Roy, because he always liked Roy Rogers's fancy shirts. Here, he walks around in a sleeveless undershirt, a tattoo on his left bicep, getting sweatier and dirtier and bloodier by the minute. A great part of the film's appeal is in watching the down-and-

dirty cop match wits with the aloof master criminal. The film makers even have the wit to play the "Ode to Joy" when Hans finally walks into the opened vault.

"Die Hard," which opens today at the Baronet and Criterion Center, has more than its share of bloody moments and blasted bodies, and it has some abysmal scenes as well. The former ballet star Alexander Godunov is a conspicuous terrorist, jumping around the set in a basic black costume and flowing blond hair. As the brother of McClane's first victim, he gets to say things like "I want blood!" And when McClane realizes he has been too hard on his wife, he radios an unintentionally funny message to Al: "Tell her that she is the best thing that ever happened to a bum like me."

The final action sequence is not surprising, as F.B.I. helicopters buzz the rooftop and McClane swings down the side of the high-rise and crashes through a window. But the scenes move with such relentless energy and smashing special-effects extravagance that "Die Hard" turns out to be everything action-genre fans, and Bruce Willis's relieved investors, might have hoped for.

1988 Jl 15, C14:5

Nazis and Nightgowns

THE BERLIN AFFAIR, directed by Liliana Cavani; screenplay by Miss Cavani and Roberta Mazzoni, based on the novel "The Buddhist Cross" by Junichiro Tanizaki; director of photography, Dante Spinotti; edited by Ruggero Mastroianni; music by Pino Donaggio; art direction by Luciano Ricceri; produced by Menahem Golan and Yoram Globus; released by the Cannon Group. At Cinema Village, 12th Street east of Fifth Avenue. Running time: 96 minutes. This film is rated R.

Louise von Hollendorf	Gudrun Landgrebe
Heinz von Hollendorf	Kevin McNally
Mitsuko Matsugae	Mio Takaki
Wolf von Hollendorf	Hanns Zischler
Werner von Heiden	Massimo Girotti
Herbert Gessler	Philippe Leroy

Set in World War II Germany, "The Berlin Affair" is the story of a married couple sexually obsessed with a total cipher named Mitsuko. First Mitsuko seduces Louise, the brittle but beautiful hausfrau in her art class. Louise's husband, Heinz, works as a Government minister for the Nazis, and is less upset by his wife's betrayal than by the threat it poses to his career. But eventually he, too, falls for Mitsuko, and from then on she comes to dinner every night and gives Heinz and Louise sleeping potions in their brandy so they'll doze off and not try anything without her.

Made in 1985 by Liliana Cavani, famous for the sadomasochistic "Night Porter" (1974), "The Berlin Affair" may sound provocative. In fact, it is lifeless, perhaps because Mitsuko — jealous, manipulative, plain and petulant — seems totally unappealing to men or women or any combination of the above. We are meant to see that she inspires great passion, but the only exotic thing about her is that she always wears a kimono.

●

In fact, although all the characters seem to sleep with one another, they usually wear their clothes at the time. They sigh, they grapple, they tumble on the floor, but — except for a lingering shot of the elaborate tattoo on Mitsuko's left side — they keep their clothes pretty much in place.

At first this suggests that Ms. Cavani is trying to be titillating; later, one might wonder if it is some fetish. But eventually it just seems careless, and characteristic of a film that lets Louise awaken one morning wearing a different nightgown than the one in which she fell asleep the night before.

The most exploitative aspect of "The Berlin Affair" is the cheap but common use of Nazi Germany as a backdrop for forbidden lust. Its greatest virtue is that it will only be around for two days, today and tomorrow at the Cinema Village.

CARYN JAMES

1988 Jl 15, C12:5

Rohmer's Own View Of the Mind

"Boyfriends and Girlfriends" ("L'Ami de Mon Amie") was shown as part of the recent New York Film Festival. Following are excerpts from Vincent Canby's review, which appeared in The New York Times on Oct. 9, 1987. The French-language film with English subtitles opens today at the Lincoln Plaza 1, Broadway and 63d Street.

Specific places, at specific times of year, have always been key to the methods and the manners of Eric Rohmer's splendidly singular comedies. In "My Night at Maud's," the wintry, nonpicturesque streets and chilly apartments of the city of Clermont-Ferrand had the effect of prompting characters to argue long into the night, as if to stay out of cold, lonely beds. The lush, midsummer Annecy countrysides in "Claire's Knee" were an overwhelming aphrodisiac to an otherwise rational man. In "Pauline at the Beach," the sunlit crispness of the Normandy coast, at the end of the season, required that the characters stop talking around points and come to decisions before facing another autumn at loose ends in Paris.

Mr. Rohmer, the most cerebral, most morally committed of French directors, is also the one who seems most aware of the particular influences of geography and meteorology on people. In a Rohmer movie, the physical world, including architecture, describes the life of the mind.

The spectacular satellite city of Cergy-Pontoise, designed by the Argentine architect Ricardo Bofill, is the unbilled co-star of "L'Ami de Mon Amie," Mr. Rohmer's small, perfectly achieved new addition to the series of films he calls "Comedies and Proverbs."

●

From what Mr. Rohmer shows us, Cergy-Pontoise is a kind of underpopulated, modernist amalgam of Bath, a French Co-op City and a Disney World. The old world — Paris — hovers on the horizon.

Mr. Rohmer, as much as the intense, well-meaning, sometimes seriously muddled lovers in the film itself, is fascinated and rather charmed by this bold architectural attempt to create, at one blow, a perfect environment of office and apart-

Sophie Renoir and Emmanuelle Chaulet in Eric Rohmer's "Boyfriends and Girlfriends."

ment buildings, plazas and parks, shopping areas, theaters, restaurants and a couple of man-made lakes.

Mr. Rohmer remains resolutely unhorrified by it all. He appreciates this particular example of urban planning, while sometimes finding it as exotic as an Eskimo village and as funny as a miniature golf course.

Cergy-Pontoise was designed for community. "It's like a village," Fabien (Eric Viellard) says to Blanche (Emmanuelle Chaulet) about Cergy-Pontoise, after running into Blanche near a shopping center several times within the same afternoon. Fabien is the lover of Léa (Sophie Renoir), Blanche's best friend.

Fabien and Blanche, who scarcely know each other, feel guilty as well as pleased at these chance encounters, dictated not by fate but by the satellite city's layout. In addition, Blanche is more than a little troubled because Léa has confided that she's tired of Fabien, and wishes she could leave him "in easy stages." Léa thinks that Blanche and Fabien would make a fine match.

Blanche, however, thinks she's in love with Alexandre (François-Eric Gendron), an engineer with the local power-and-light company, a man so handsome and self-assured that women chase him. In the course of one idyllic summer in this architec-

tural paradise, Blanche, Fabien, Léa and Alexandre scheme to achieve their own ends without damaging friendships. That they will succeed is no surprise. The fun of "L'Ami de Mon Amie" is watching how close they come to the edge of failure, and the manner in which Cergy-Pontoise reveals character and rules choices.

"L'Ami de Mon Amie" is as clean and functional in appearance as the satellite city, but it's full of unexpected delights. As usual, every member of Mr. Rohmer's cast is very good, but Miss Chaulet may well be a brand-new star. Don't go anticipating a laugh a minute. A friend of mine emerged from the press screening claiming the movie was 16 hours long. I guessed about 90 minutes. In fact, it's 102 minutes; they are all wonderful.

•

"Boyfriends and Girlfriends," which has been rated PG ("Parental Guidance Suggested"), is full of English-subtitled French conversation that will be beyond the comprehension of most small children.

1988 Jl 15, C10:6

Luckiest Makers Of Sows' Ears

MIDNIGHT RUN, directed and produced by Martin Brest; written by George Gallo; director of photography, Donald Thorin; edited by Billy Weber, Chris Lebenzon and Michael Tronick; music by Danny Elfman; production designer, Angelo Graham; released by Universal Pictures.   Running time: 128 minutes. This film is rated R.

Jack Walsh	Robert De Niro
Jonathan Mardukas	Charles Grodin
Alonzo Mosely	Yaphet Kotto
Marvin Dorfler	John Ashton
Jimmy Serrano	Dennis Farina
Eddie Moscone	Joe Pantoliano

By VINCENT CANBY

For Jack Walsh (Robert De Niro), who looks and talks like a mug but is an ex-Chicago cop turned into modern-day bounty hunter, the assignment is an easy way to make $100,000: find Jonathan Mardukas (Charles Grodin), a mild-mannered certified public accountant, and return him to Los Angeles.

Jonathan Mardukas made a name for himself by stealing $15 million from his firm when he learned that it was mob-operated. Jonathan is a save-the-whales sort of fellow. He doesn't smoke or drink and sticks to a low-cholesterol diet. He gave most of his loot to charity and then promptly disappeared.

Jack's employer is the bondsman who stands to forfeit the half million he put up as bail for the accountant.

In fact, Jack finds Jonathan in Manhattan within the first 15 or so minutes of "Midnight Run." That part of it is a snap. There are difficulties, however, in getting the man back to the West Coast before the forfeit deadline. Federal Bureau of Investigation agents, bumbling but persistent, want to make the metaphoric kill themselves. The mob wants Jonathan physically dead.

•

Their journey from New York to Los Angeles involves jumbo jets, biplanes, Amtrak, freight trains, buses, swimming, walking, helicopters and automobiles, borrowed and stolen.

This is the perfectly serviceable premise of "Midnight Run," which might have remained a perfectly forgettable action-comedy if somebody hadn't had the inspiration to cast Mr. De Niro and Mr. Grodin in the leading roles.

"Midnight Run" wastes more talent and money than most movies ever hope to see. The surprise is that there is still plenty of both left on the screen. The movie was directed by Martin Brest ("Beverly Hills Cop" and its sequel) and written by George Gallo. They must be the luckiest manufacturers of sows' ears in Hollywood.

On the Run Charles Grodin portrays a bail-jumping accountant who has embezzled from the mob and Robert De Niro plays the bounty hunter who has captured him in "Midnight Run."

"Midnight Run," which opens today at the National and other theaters, isn't exactly a silk purse, but it contains two performances that are pure gold.

Like most fine actors, Mr. De Niro has never given a good performance that wasn't in some way illuminated by humor, which is not to be confused with laughs. Sometimes it is apparent in what appears to be the self-awareness of the character, as in "Raging Bull" and "The Untouchables." Sometimes it can be seen in the actor's awareness of — and comment on — the character, as in "Taxi Driver" and "King of Comedy."

The fact that humor has always been an aspect of Mr. De Niro's intelligence as an actor should come as no surprise to anyone who remembers him in Brian De Palma's "Greetings" and "Hi, Mom," two sublimely funny underground artifacts of the late 1960's. Now, with "Midnight Run," he has the opportunity to be blatantly funny in a big, expensive, groaningly elaborate Hollywood formula comedy.

He brings to Jack Walsh's double takes, slow burns, furtive smiles and expressions of mock surprise the same degree of intensity with which he played Jake LaMotta in "Raging Bull" and Travis Bickle in "Taxi Driver." Yet he's no Metropolitan Opera star trying to squeeze his tenor voice into the latest Michael Jackson hit. The laughter he prompts is big, open and genuine.

Mr. Grodin is an ideal almost-straight man. His Jonathan Mardukas is Jack Walsh's opposite. He is seemingly cool, utterly sane, an obviously caring individual, but he's also a guy who can ask Jack Walsh, as they are huddling in a freight car heading toward Los Angeles, "Have you ever had sex with an animal?"

Mr. De Niro and Mr. Grodin are lunatic delights, which is somewhat more than can be said for the movie, whose mechanics keep getting in the way of the performances.

That's not being entirely fair. Mr. Gallo has written some funny lines, and Mr. Brest has made sure the movie was photographed in a way to tell a coherent story.

Throughout "Midnight Run," however, the splashy obligations of the conventional, big-budget action-comedy frequently slow things down to a near halt. There are so many automobiles, trains and airplanes that the movie seems to be less about people than about vehicles, which are clearly driven or piloted by others.

Then, just when it seems that the movie is hopelessly lost to the stunt men and second-unit people and when you're convinced that almost any 10 actors in Hollywood could be doing this, Mr. De Niro and Mr. Grodin reappear to give the comedy their own very humane comic dimension.

The members of the supporting cast also do their share of revivifying work, particularly Dennis Farina as the mob boss and Joe Pantoliano as the bondsman.

Great pains went into the physical production. The movie, which is one long cross-country chase from New York to California, was filmed mostly on what are called "actual locations," as well as on one stream in New Zealand. This stands in for some swirling rapids in the American West. Make-believe doesn't come cheap these days.

1988 Jl 20, C15:5

Correction

A film review of "Midnight Run" yesterday misidentified the director of "Beverly Hills Cop II." He is Tony Scott, not Martin Brest.

1988 Jl 21, A3:2

The Burden of Exile

GOD DOESN'T BELIEVE IN US ANYMORE, directed by Axel Corti; written (in German with English subtitles) by Georg Stefan Troller; camera, Wolfgang Treu; distributed by Roxie Releasing. Running time: 110 minutes.

Ferry	Johannes Silberschneider
Gandhi	Armin Mueller-Stahl
Alena	Barbara Petritsch

SANTE FE, directed by Mr. Corti; written (German with English subtitles) by Mr. Troller; camera by Gernot Roll; distributed by Roxie Releasing. Film Forum 1, 57 Watts Street. Running time: 110 minutes. These films have no rating.

Freddy Wolff	Gabriel Barylli
Lissa	Doris Buchrucker
Dr. Treumann	Peter Lühr
Popper	Gideon Singer
Mrs. Shapiro	Monica Bleibtreu

By VINCENT CANBY

"God Doesn't Believe in Us Anymore" and "Santa Fe" are the first two parts of "Where To and Back," a German-Austrian trilogy about the experiences of a small number of Austrian Jews who escape the Nazis in 1938 and make their way to the United States. The nearly-four-hour program opens today at Film Forum 1.

The trilogy concludes with "Welcome in Vienna," shown at the Film Forum in June, in which one of the refugees, who has become an American soldier, returns to Vienna after the war as a member of the army of occupation. The three films, directed by Axel Corti, were written by Georg Stefan Troller, whose own story apparently parallels those he recalls in his screenplays.

I have not seen "Welcome in Vienna," but it is obvious that the three films should be seen in chronological order. Though "God Doesn't Believe in Us Anymore" and "Santa Fe"

make narrative sense on their own, something relating to the compulsion to make the films is lacking. There is no last word.

•

It is to the credit of Mr. Troller and Mr. Corti that, even without a coda, the first two films, produced for television, are as complete and satisfying as they are. ("Welcome in Vienna" was produced for theatrical release.)

"God Doesn't Believe in Us Anymore" and "Santa Fe" don't have the density of written literature. Instead they have the manner of stories recalled orally, casually, around a table. Peripheral details and subsidiary events are often remembered much more vividly than the obligatory big scenes. These are tales told to listeners for whom certain things need not be said and for whom other things cannot be expressed.

"God Doesn't Believe in Us Anymore" is the story of Ferry (Johannes Silberschneider), a Viennese teen-ager whose father is killed trying to escape the Nazis' mass roundup of Jews in November 1938. For a while, Ferry's impulse is to stay in Vienna and try to get along as best he can. He is virtually pushed into flight by a corrupt policeman who, having confiscated Ferry's father's radio, sells the bewildered boy an escape plan.

Once Ferry leaves Vienna, he can't turn back. En route to Prague, then to Paris and, with the fall of France, to Marseilles, always a half-step ahead of the German occupiers, Ferry makes friends with other illicit travelers.

Chief among these are Gandhi (Armin Mueller-Stahl), an anti-Nazi German officer (a gentile) who has escaped Dachau, and Alena (Barbara Petritsch), Gandhi's half-Jewish mistress.

"Santa Fe" opens with Ferry's arrival in New York in late 1940, but then the film picks up the story of another refugee, Freddy (Gabriel Barylli), a switch in heros that may have been dictated by the unavailability of the young actor playing Ferry. "Santa Fe," which takes its title from Freddy's dream to become a cowboy in Santa Fe, N,M., is by far the more successful of the trilogy's first two parts.

"God Doesn't Believe in Us Anymore" is an enlightened "road" movie, mostly about escape, though it seems consciously to resist the temptation to make Ferry's escapes dramatic. Mr. Troller and Mr. Corti are more interested in the psychological burden of exile. Best are the scenes set in Paris, where Ferry and the other refugees live lives measured in visa extensions (of 2 to 14 days each), finally to be interred by the French as enemy aliens in September 1939.

The state of mind of the exile is more fully and affectingly explored in "Santa Fe," set entirely in New York, where the "lucky" ones who have escaped Europe are haunted by all those who didn't.

Sharing Freddy's lot are a hustling photographer, who awaits a job he'll never get on Life magazine, an extroverted ex-actor, a prominent surgeon who isn't allowed to operate and an emotionally crippled woman, slightly older than Freddy, with whom he has a doomed affair.

•

The refugees try to re-create their European cafe life in an East Side coffee shop, but nothing can disguise their enduring loneliness and feelings of humiliation and loss. After some weeks in New York, Freddy must be urged to unpack his suitcase. He still

dreams of Santa Fe, refusing to believe, as a friend says, that New York is the end of the line.

The two films are beautifully photographed in black and white, with a great deal of invention (Trieste's harbor stands in for New York's) and no fanciness. For the most part they are also well acted by the members of the large casts. Mr. Silberschneider and Mr. Barylli, who appear to be the author's surrogates, remain passive observers of the world around them.

Mr. Troller and Mr. Corti have the good sense never to give the impression that they know they are telling an epic story. Both "God Doesn't Believe in Us Anymore" and "Santa Fe" have an air of detachment about them. There are no grand moments that sum up their vision.

Instead Mr. Troller and Mr. Corti attend to specific characters in particular moments and leave the summing up to others. This intense modesty is the strength of the films.

1988 Jl 20, C20:5

Newport's News, 1926

Robert Mitchum

MR. NORTH, directed by Danny Huston; screenplay by Janet Roach, John Huston and James Costigan, based on the novel "Theophilus North" by Thornton Wilder; director of photography, Robin Vidgeon; edited by Roberto Silvi; music by David McHugh; production designer, Eugene Lee; produced by Steven Haft and Skip Steloff; released by The Samuel Goldwyn Company. At 68th Street Playhouse, at Third Avenue. Running time: 92 minutes. This film is rated PG.

Theophilus North	Anthony Edwards
James McHenry Bosworth	Robert Mitchum
Mrs. Amelia Cranston	Lauren Bacall
Henry Simmons	Harry Dean Stanton
Persis Bosworth-Tennyson	Anjelica Huston
Elspeth Skeel	Mary Stuart Masterson
Sally Boffin	Virginia Madsen
Sarah Baily-Lewis	Tammy Grimes
Dr. Angus McPherson	David Warner
Y.M.C.A. clerk	Christopher Durang

By VINCENT CANBY

"Mr. North" is a comic fable about Theophilus North (Anthony Edwards), a clean-cut Yale graduate who has the self-assurance of a crackpot saint. At the height of the 1926 summer season, Theophilus makes his way through the social maze of Newport, R.I., with the aplomb and springy step of a very young, very American Mr. Hulot. He tutors the children of the rich, teaches them tennis, and reads to the elderly in English, French, German, Italian and Hebrew.

He doesn't actually speak Hebrew, but he offers to bone up on it when a client resists his estimate of six weeks to read the Bible in English. Theophilus says that since Hebrew has no vowels, the reading time could be reduced by one third.

Theophilus seems to be not quite of this world, at least partially because he's loaded with static electricity. When he shakes hands without first grounding himself, the other person receives a shock.

In the course of "Mr. North," Theophilus reveals himself to be a con artist, a faith healer and a fixer. He talks himself into jobs he wasn't hired to perform. He cures the migraine headaches of a debutante and the incontinence of an aging, mansion-bound millionaire. He breaks down (temporarily) the caste system that separates the members of Newport's ruling elite from those who attend them.

Theophilus is almost too good to be true, and almost too whimsical to be fun.

But although "Mr. North," which opens today at the 68th Street Playhouse, has some sticky patches, it is a most enjoyable high comedy, a deceptively summery movie that is full of the intimations of autumn.

These are built in.

•

The film, the first to be directed by John Huston's son Danny, was the last with which the elder Huston was to be associated before he died last summer, at age 81, in Newport during the production. The screenplay, written by Janet Roach, John Huston and James Costigan, is based on "Theophilus North," Thornton Wilder's final novel, published in 1973 when Wilder was 76.

Though the film never acknowledges the fact, Theophilus North is a benign WASP dybbuk. He looks to be still in his mid-20's but the youthful body is possessed by the mind, memories and concerns of a man nearing the end of a very long life. Theophilus couldn't care less about contemporary fashion. All of his passions are tempered by an awareness of their transitory nature. Yet, like many remarkable old men, including Huston and Wilder, he remains fascinated by the world. His interests, if not his appetites, are undiminished.

Wilder's novel, said to be his most autobiographical, takes the form of a series of stories recollected by Theophilus North in old age. Because the film has no such immediately identifiable voice, "Mr. North" sometimes seems more detached, more artificial, than would be the case if it were understood that these are reveries of an extraordinary sensibility.

The world they recall is a most seductive one of sunlight, of punishments that fit crimes and of conversation in which sentences are perfectly composed with beginnings, middles and ends. There is order in all things. The society of the butlers, chauffeurs and cooks who serve the rich is as rigidly structured as that of their employers.

•

Theophilus, the outsider, is as much at ease with one group as with the other. He becomes the confidant of a tough, lonely old robber baron (Robert Mitchum), who is being pushed into his grave by his venal daughter (Tammy Grimes) and doctor (David Warner). He aids a pretty, pampered teen-ager (Mary Stuart Masterson) threatened with brain surgery, and is the matchmaker for an Irish parlor maid (Virginia Madsen) who loves above her station.

Beginning with Mr. Edwards and Mr. Mitchum (who plays the role that John Huston was originally going to do), all of the actors are good, and several are knockouts. These include Harry Dean Stanton, never funnier than as an English butler who knows his place; Lauren Bacall, as a one-

time scullery maid who has risen to become the grande dame of boardinghouse keepers, and Christopher Durang (the playwright), as the clerk of Newport's Y.M.C.A., a fellow who does his best to maintain the high tone of his establishment.

In a role even tinier than her role in "A Handful of Dust," Anjelica Huston gives "Mr. North" its final shapeliness, though what she does can't be analyzed. It has to do with the nature of her presence. She is the film's amused benediction.

After the huge success of "The Bridge of San Luis Rey," published in the late 1920's, Thornton Wilder fell on lean times in the 30's, when proletariat literature became the rage. In The New Republic, Mike Gold, the Marxist critic, described Wilder as "the prophet of the genteel Christ." The charge of genteelness will also be made against the film, which, in one crucial courtroom scene, goes soft and silly.

However, "Mr. North" quickly recovers. Class will out.

•

"Mr. North," which has been rated PG ("Parental Guidance Suggested"), has some mildly vulgar language.

1988 Jl 22, C8:4

Mr. Herman's Neighborhood

BIG TOP PEE-WEE, directed by Randal Kleiser; written by Paul Reubens and George McGrath; director of photography, Steven Poster; film editor, Jeff Gourson; music by Danny Elfman; production designer, Stephen Marsh; produced by Mr. Reubens and Debra Hill; released by Paramount Pictures. At Embassy 2, Broadway at 47th Street, and other theaters. Running time: 82 minutes. This film is rated PG.

Pee-wee Herman	Pee-wee Herman
Winnie	Penelope Ann Miller
Mace Montana	Kris Kristofferson
Gina Piccolapupula	Valeria Golino
Voice of Vance the Pig	Wayne White
Midge Montana	Susan Tyrrell
Mr. Ryan	Albert Henderson
Otis	Jack Murdock

You either love Pee-wee Herman or he makes your skin crawl. There are few halfhearted responses to the wildly successful comedian who always plays "himself" — that is, a fictional character who behaves like a child in a skinny gray suit, whose lipstick and eyeliner can seem eerily androgynous to adults and clownish to kids.

Until now, Pee-wee's humor has come from his being bizarrely out of touch with the normal world. His first feature, "Pee-wee's Big Adventure," was a series of encounters between Pee-wee and real life, and his television show, "Pee-wee's Playhouse," surrounds him with a Pee-wee world where a talking chair is nothing strange. But in "Big Top Pee-wee," which opens today at the Embassy 2 and other theaters, he and the circus world meet each other half way, with results that are less outrageous than kiddie-cute.

The film is not realistic by anyone's standards except Pee-wee's. Here he is a farmer and agricultural scientist who has invented a hot-dog tree. His best friend and collaborator — and, we suspect, the brains of the team — is a talking pig named Vance. In the nearby Depression-era town, the general store stocks tartar-control Colgate toothpaste and 2-liter plastic bottles of 7-Up.

Pee-wee Herman finds the girl of his dreams in the trapeze artist Gina Piccolapupula, played by Valeria Golino, in "Big Top Pee-Wee."

Still, there is a definite effort to make Pee-wee himself slightly less eccentric. For one thing, he has toned down his makeup considerably. For another, he likes girls, though in the first film females sent him running in the opposite direction — because of adolescence or personal preference, one never knew.

Now he is engaged to a pretty blond schoolteacher, until the circus literally blows into town during a storm and he is smitten with a beautiful trapeze artist named Gina Piccolapupula. This new, lukewarm, compromised Pee-wee is remarkably unfunny.

The only scenes in which the old Pee-wee emerges — they are the best episodes — are his tête-à-têtes with Vance. Maybe it's just easier to believe that Pee-wee has a good relationship with a talking pig than with a sweet schoolteacher or a sexy circus star. But the Pee-wee you either find uproarious or too creepy for words is the one who holds Vance in his lap and croons in his cracked voice, "Who's my handsome little baby?" and who points to their strange agricultural inventions and says, "Look, Vance, the calla lillies are in bloom again."

Otherwise, "Big Top Pee-wee" (co-produced and co-written under his other name, Paul Reubens) is an uninspired circus film for children. They might, at least, like the lions, elephants and the hippo named Zsa Zsa that wander through Pee-wee's farm.

•

"Big Top Pee-wee" is rated PG ("Parental Guidance Suggested"), though even its strongest double-entendres are harmless.

CARYN JAMES

1988 Jl 22, C10:3

PASCALI'S ISLAND, directed and written by James Dearden, based on the novel by Barry Unsworth; director of photography, Roger Deakins; edited by Edward Marnier; music by Loek Dikker; production designer, Andrew Mollo; produced by Eric Fellner; re-

Ben Kingsley

leased by Avenue Pictures. At Cinema 1, Third Avenue and 60th Street. Running time: 101 minutes. This film is rated PG-13.

Basil Pascali	Ben Kingsley
Anthony Bowles	Charles Dance
Lydia Neuman	Helen Mirren
Izzet Effendi	Stefan Gryff
Herr Gesing	George Murcell
The Pasha	Nadim Sawalha

By CARYN JAMES

The mannered style of "Pascali's Island" perfectly suits its tale of political and emotional intrigue hiding behind a crumbling facade of stability. On a Greek island in 1908, in the fading years of the Ottoman Empire, Greek rebels, Turkish spies and foreign mercenaries mingle in shady hotel bars and winding streets overlooking the sea. Basil Pascali (Ben Kingsley) has been sending unanswered espionage reports to the sultan for 20 years. Anthony Bowles (Charles Dance) is a British archeologist whose purpose in visiting the island is mysterious and suspect. And Lydia Neuman (Helen Mirren) is a bohemian-looking Viennese painter, a woman of a certain age who attracts the two men.

"Pascali's Island," written and directed by James Dearden, who wrote the script for "Fatal Attraction," is an ambitious attempt to explore the psychological dance these three engage in. But the film is as cooly cerebral as "Fatal Attraction" was overheated. That coolness extends to its very heart, which is meant to be full of passion. Slow and stately, "Pascali's Island" never gets beneath its own superficial gentility.

When Bowles arrives on the island, the tall, blond visitor is a handsome contrast to the balding, rather squat Pascali, who introduces himself to the Englishman with the prideful obseqiousness of a Uriah Heep: "I am a well-known figure on the island." Bowles hires Pascali to be his interpreter; Pascali sneaks into Bowles's hotel room and learns the archeologist may be a fraud.

●

A complicated plot unravels — Bowles leases some land from the local pasha, and a series of double- and triple-crosses begins — but this seems much less important than the acting of the three principals. Mr. Kingsley never gives indecisive performances, but this strong one illustrates everything that is wrong with the film. He bugs his eyes; he casts a mournful look when he sees a glance of attraction pass between Bowles and Lydia. It is a performance that points outward instead of in, that telegraphs its messages instead of convincing us that Pascali is lonely and disappointed.

The fault is not with the actors. Their perfectly matched, painstaking performances seem just what the director ordered. Everything is posed and practiced, from the unlikely angle at which Ms. Mirren's robe falls when she lies in bed with Mr. Dance to the deliberate way she peels a pear.

The dialogue, from start to finish, is either empty or obvious, in ways that reveal nothing new about the speakers. "I no longer know what I am," says Pascali, announcing rather than exploring the blatant theme of confused cultural identities. "This island, it's all coming to an end," Lydia warns him. "You must go." He answers quietly, long after she is out of earshot, and with the most pathetic look of self-pity on his face, "I have nowhere to go." Maybe it is daring to create a self-pitying hero we don't much like, but it can't be intentional that we believe so little in Pascali's emotions.

●

Even the look of the film pushes viewers away. Many of the sunny exteriors are shot in yellow-tinged shadows. These scenes are sometimes juxtaposed with blinding, bright views of the sea and pretentious orange suns. And the film's violent climax, in which betrayals lead to death, begins to approach the melodrama of "Fatal Attraction."

Mr. Dearden is clearly capable of creating the psychological undercurrent he aims for and so badly misses in "Pascali's Island" (based on Barry Unsworth's epistolary novel, containing Pascali's letters to the sultan). He succeeded beautifully in "Diversion," his 42-minute film on which "Fatal Attraction" was based, a tale of adultery in which the only violence is emotional. "Pascali's Island," which opens today at Cinema 1, announces Mr. Dearden as a serious film maker. But as with Pascali's identity crisis, the announcement is no substitute for convincing evidence.

●

"Pascali's Island" is rated PG-13 ("Special Parental Guidance for Those Younger Than 13"). There is a flash of partial nudity and some violent deaths.

1988 Jl 22, C16:4

On the Road Deborra-Lee Furness plays the role of Asta Cadell, a lone champion of justice who rides into a remote, tension-filled Australian town astride a motorcycle in "Shame."

Vroooom! Up Roars Ms. Macho

"Shame" was shown as part of the recent "New Directors/New Films" series. Following are excerpts from Caryn James's review, which appeared in The New York Times on March 19. The film opens today at the 57th Street Playhouse, 110 West 57th Street.

It is easy to find soft-headed movies that pretend to be about women's roles in society, and much harder to come across a film as good as "Shame," a tough-minded Australian action story with a smart, sensitive, unsettling macho heroine. In the film's first minutes a black-clothed motorcyclist rides into town, takes off a helmet to reveal long, strawberry blond curls and walks into a grimy bar asking for a room and a mechanic to fix her bike. Is she a tomboy or a femme fatale? A tourist or a drifter? From then on the film provokes several new questions for every one it answers as it takes the B-level action genre seriously enough to turn it on its head and eventually shatter its limits.

Stuck in town while she waits for spare bike parts, the heroine, Asta, is given a room by Tim Curtis, a mechanic. That night Tim's teen-age daughter is brought home, hysterical, angry and frightened. Lizzie has been raped by a gang of teen-age boys who have terrorized and attacked other women in town. But even Lizzie's father doubts her story, buying into a thoughtless convention: the boys are just being boys, and the girls must have provoked them.

Asta believes and befriends Lizzie, confronts the gang members, teaches the women to stand up for themselves. But the film is never polemical or simple-minded. As Asta re-

veals bits about her life, she becomes more than the female reverse of a stereotypical male biker. She can kick and claw her way out of trouble but more often uses her intellect to fight back. Deborra-Lee Furness, who plays Asta, looks strong but soft and resembles Judith Ivey.

●

Though the director, Steve Jodrell, plays off the action genre — two groups of women face off by throwing insults at each other in a supermarket — his style is distinct. He makes us feel the barrenness of life in this town, where most of the women work in a pet-food factory, with no hope of escape. Tim Curtis and his mother look like frail birds, so it is even more remarkable when Tim comes to his daughter's defense, when Lizzie's grandmother looks up to the night sky and confides an old desire to walk on the moon.

It would be easy, and expected, if Asta breezed through the town, vanquishing the bad guys. But "Shame" does not let anyone off that simply; as it goes on, it presents increasingly complex issues. What happens when the law won't keep the gang members away from Lizzie? When is violence the best, or the only, response to violence?

Finally the characters turn more violent, their story tragic and emotional. Action and true emotion rarely mix well, but Mr. Jodrell pulls off a relentless climax, always poised delicately between the exaggerated and the realistic.

Perhaps Asta has been heroic; perhaps she has also been wrongheaded and careless. "Shame" does not offer answers, but an intelligent, stylized way of framing the questions.

1988 Jl 22, C10:6

New Jersey Ennui

HOME REMEDY, directed and written by Maggie Greenwald; director of photography, Thomas H. Jewett; edited by Pamela Scott Arnold; music by Steve Katz; production designer, Robert P. Kracik; produced by Kathie Hersch; released by Kino International Corp. At Film Forum 2, 57 Watts Street. Running time: 91 minutes. This film has no rating.

Richie Rosenbaum	Seth Barrish
Nancy Smith	Maxine Albert
P.J. Smith	Richard Kidney
Moshe	David Feinman
Donnie	John Tsakonas
Mary	Alexa
Bambi	Cynde Kahn

A 30-year-old single man who works at a copy center and lives in a boxy house in suburban New Jersey can't be blamed for saying, as the main character in "Home Remedy" does, "Life is boring and then you die." When Richie attempts to overcome boredom by learning to love it, his attitude is more suspect. He locks himself in the house, reads "Understanding the Kaballah," plays the harmonica and captures it all on videotape. A film about this moribund antihero is bound to run into a classic problem: How does a story about boredom avoid becoming a boring story?

Maggie Greenwald, the film's writer and director, introduces a goofy neighbor: a 40-year-old wife and mother from down the block, a good-natured nosybody who spends her afternoons camped in a chaise longue in Richie's driveway, talking to him through his window. Nancy is a promising caricature, a woman who creates a garden for Richie where flowers grow next to junk from her

basement — plastic party favors, an old guitar, toy dogs and Barbie dolls. But this sort of film can work only by expanding its premise in wildly unexpected ways, and Nancy's brief moments of absurdity don't stretch far enough.

●

"Home Remedy," which opens today at the Film Forum 2, is merely a workmanlike expansion of a satiric idea. Its mundane photography and predictable dialogue give it the low-budget look and feel of a clever student film, although it is not — Ms. Greenwald was a sound and film editor before making this first feature. Seth Barrish is competent as Richie, whose attitude is "What's the use?" Maxine Albert is sympathetic but whiny as Nancy, who can find true enjoyment in a good lunch of franks and beans. Together, they're a tiresome pair.

Nancy's jealous husband finally relieves Richie's stupor. When this blue-collar deus ex machina arrives to tear up the house, he may offer inadvertent salvation for the characters, but he also points out how little logic and wit Ms. Greenwald has brought to this very slight film.

CARYN JAMES

1988 Jl 22, C17:1

Haunted by Ghosts Of Politics Past

THE COLOR OF DESTINY, directed by Jorge Duran; screenplay (in Portuguese with English subtitles) by Nelson Natotti and Mr. Duran with the collaboration of José Joffily; director of photography, José Tadeu Ribeiro; film editor, Dominique Paris; music by David Tygel; art direction, Clóvis Bueno; produced by Mr. Duran; production company, Nativa Filmes; released by Embra Filme. At the Public, 425 Lafayette Street. Running time: 104 minutes. This film has no rating.

Paulo	Guilherme Fontes
Laura	Norma Bengel
Victor	Franklin Caicedo
Patricia	Julia Lemmertz
Helena	Andréa Beltrão

Jorge Duran's "Color of Destiny," the Brazilian film opening today at the Public Theater, has the sincerity of the work of a young director looking for a way to come to terms with a subject that haunts him: the overthrow of Salvador Allende Gossens' Marxist Government in Chile in 1973.

Like Mr. Duran, the film's hero, Paulo (Guilherme Fontes), is a Chilean who has been living in exile in Rio de Janeiro since the coup. Paulo, now a teen-ager who expresses himself through his paintings, remembers those events only through vintage newsreels and through nightmares in which he dreams about his older brother, killed by the military government that succeeded Allende's.

●

Paulo has sympathetic, liberal, loving parents. He also has a girlfriend, who seems to be his first and who is driving him crazy with her idea of fidelity. Helena believes it is possible for a person to be in love with two people at the same time. Paulo is obsessively jealous.

Patricia, 18, Paulo's pretty, slightly older cousin, arrives in Rio after having been imprisoned in Chile for anti-Government activities. Suddenly, in the way of schematic film making, it is possible for Paulo to resolve his sexual and political hang-ups in a single, bold gesture.

"The Color of Destiny" is nicely acted. It is full of what seem to be the clearly remembered details of teenage angst. It is also full of commonplace dream sequences. These tell a chronological story and, like the paintings attributed to Paulo, betray the heavy hand of the film maker making his point.

VINCENT CANBY

1988 Jl 22, C17:1

Pink Ties And White Gloves

CADDYSHACK II, directed by Allan Arkush; written by Harold Ramis and Peter Torokvei; director of photography, Harry Stradling; edited by Bernard Gribble; music by Ira Newborn; production designer, Bill Matthews; produced by Neil Canton; released by Warner Brothers. At Criterion Center, Broadway at 45th Street; Plaza, 58th Street east of Madison Avenue and other theaters. Running time: 103 minutes. This film is rated PG.

Jack Hartounian	Jackie Mason
Ty Webb	Chevy Chase
Captain Tom Everett	Dan Aykroyd
Elizabeth Pearce	Dyan Cannon
Chandler Young	Robert Stack
Cynthia Young	Dina Merrill
Harry	Jonathan Silverman
Miffy Young	Chynna Phillips

By CARYN JAMES

Fans of Jackie Mason's one-man Broadway show should beware of "Caddyshack II," the latest step in the comedian's reborn career.

If the star is smart, he'll claim to have sent a twin brother or a clone off to Hollywood; the film features someone who walks like Jackie Mason, talks like Jackie Mason, does everything except make people laugh like Jackie Mason.

This sequel to the 1980 film that starred Rodney Dangerfield and Bill Murray is set in the same country club, Bushwood. Mr. Mason is a self-made millionaire named Jack Hartounian, whose daughter wants to become a club member along with her Radcliffe roommate, Miffy. The script possibilities amount to this: Mr. Mason wears purple suits with garish pink ties and invades the club, where Miffy's mother (Dina Merrill) always wears white gloves.

On the Links Randy Quaid plays the crafty attorney of Jackie Mason, a self-made millionaire, in "Caddyshack II."

Hartounian has little to do with Mr. Mason's acerbic stage persona, wasting the only opportunity to redeem this humorless script. Instead, he is gauche but the salt of the earth (his company even builds low-rent apartment houses). The rich snobs bar him from the club, of course, so he gets even by buying it and turning it into a theme park called "Jacky's Wacky Golf." Anything that has to tell you it's wacky probably isn't, and this film practically yells in desperation, "I'm wacky! I'm wacky!"

"Caddyshack II," which opened yesterday at the Criterion Center and other theaters, piles on people who have been more successful in films that seem to have had scripts. Dyan Cannon is Miffy's cousin, the only other person at the club as gauche as Jack. Chevy Chase is innocuous as the wealthy man who sells him Bushwood. And Dan Ackroyd has never been more irritating as a former marine hired to eliminate Jack.

●

If Mr. Mason hopes to make the kind of segue from stand-up comedy to movies that Mr. Dangerfield did, he and his advisers better think again. "Caddyshack II" is the kind of film that sends careers spiraling downward.

1988 Jl 23, 16:5

A *Natural* Bartender

COCKTAIL, directed by Roger Donaldson; screenplay by Heywood Gould, based on his novel; director of photography, Dean Semler; edited by Neil Travis; music by J. Peter Robinson; production designer, Mel Bourne; produced by Ted Field and Robert W. Cort; released by Touchstone Pictures. At Cinema 2, Third Avenue at 60th Street, and other theaters. Running time: 100 minutes. This film is rated R.

Brian Flanagan	Tom Cruise
Doug Coughlin	Bryan Brown
Jordan Mooney	Elisabeth Shue
Bonnie	Lisa Banes
Mr. Mooney	Laurence Luckinbill
Kerry Couglin	Kelly Lynch
Coral	Gina Gershon

By VINCENT CANBY

"Cocktail" is an upscale, utterly brainless variation on those efficient old B-movies of the 1930's and 40's about the lives, loves and skills of coal miners, sand hogs and telephone linemen, among others.

Whatever the risky job, it never paid enough, but these were rugged guys. They worked hard, played hard, fought frequently and didn't talk too good, but they were the salt of the earth. In such men-at-work movies, women were treated with the respect due the weaker sex.

As movie language has become rougher over the years, the jobs have become more effete and the characters, though somewhat better educated, more seriously dim.

Take Brian Flanagan (Tom Cruise), the young, on-the-make hero of "Cocktail," which treats the profession of bartending with a lot of the same narrow-focused intensity and none of the intelligence that Howard Hawks brought to tuna-fishing in "Tiger Shark."

Just out of the Army, Brian crosses the East River from Queens to Manhattan with the fond expectation of becoming a Wall Street wheeler-dealer or, at least, an ad agency whiz. Brian, an exceptionally good-looking kid, has a breezy, ingratiating manner and a good wardrobe but no university degrees.

●

Mixmaster

Tom Cruise portrays a cocky bartender named Brian Flanagan who becomes the toast of the Upper East Side in "Cocktail."

Astonished and depressed when he strikes out, Brian takes a job as a bartender in an East Side singles bar. At first, he is all thumbs. He doesn't know a daiquiri from a John Collins. On his first night, the drink orders pile up. Waitresses show marked distress. Customers are rude. Brian is ready to quit when he's taken under the wing of Doug Coughlin (Bryan Brown), a cynical, philosophical veteran who knows all about bartending, women and life.

In no time flat, Brian is mixing four drinks at once, tossing ice cubes into the air and catching them in a glass held behind his back, trading double-entendres with the waitresses and addresses with beautiful patrons at barside.

Brian tries to continue his education during the day, but career pressures become too great. He realizes he has found his true calling. He is that rare pheonomeon, a *natural* bartender: part-performer, part-therapist, part-gigolo. With the help of Coughlin, Brian becomes a star, sought after by women and the owners of other bars. Soon he and Brian are making plans for their own place, to be called Cocktails and Dreams.

"Cocktail," which opens today at the Cinema 2 and other theaters, is "Saturday Night Fever" without John Travolta, the Bee-Gees and dancing. It is an inane romantic drama that only a very young, very naïve bartender could love. How it got that way is difficult to understand.

It was directed by Roger Donaldson, the Australian who made "Smash Palace" (in New Zealand) and last year's stylish hit "No Way Out." It was adapted by Heywood Gould ("Fort Apache: The Bronx," "The Boys From Brazil") from his own ironic, obscenely funny 1984 novel, which the screenplay resembles not at all. In this case, the screenplay has the sort of dopey fatuousness usually found in a so-called novelization of a second-rate screenplay.

The Brian Flanagan in Mr. Gould's first-person novel is tough and self-aware, a young man who loathes much of what he does but who is also too weak and too much of an amused observer to change course easily. Between novel and screenplay, Mr. Gould seems to have been brainwashed. He now accepts Brian and his scene without criticism or comment, at face value. "Cocktail," the movie, celebrates the sleazy life that the novel originally satirized.

Mr. Cruise, who was fine as Paul Newman's cocky co-star in "The Color of Money," doesn't act the role of Brian Flanagan, and maybe no one could. He visits it with a certain amount of good humor, bringing with him a lot of the boyish mannerisms and tics he seems to have picked up

from Mr. Newman. Mr. Brown is no better in a role that is similarly disadvantaged. He has charm as an actor, but this wasn't enough to stifle the derisive laughter I heard during a crucial scene at the preview I attended.

The women in the film, mindless props to be used by the comradely males, include Elisabeth Shue, as a "good" girl, and Lisa Banes as a predator.

If, by chance, you find yourself in a theater watching "Cocktail," resist the temptation to walk out before the end. The final scene is the hoot of the year.

1988 Jl 29, C6:5

Grinning and Grating

Tami Erin

THE NEW ADVENTURES OF PIPPI LONGSTOCKING, directed by Ken Annakin, written by Mr. Annakin, based on the books by Astrid Lindren; director of photography, Roland Smith; edited by Ken Zemke; music by Misha Segal; songs by Harriet Schock and Ms. Segal; production designer, Jack Senter; produced by Gary Mehlman and Walter Moshay. Released by Columbia Pictures. At the Plaza, 58th Street, east of Madison Avenue, and other theaters. 100 minutes. This film is rated G.

Pippi	Tami Erin
Miss Bannister	Eileen Brennan
Mr. Settigren	Dennis Dugan
Mrs. Settigren	Dianne Hull
Mr. Blackhart	George Di Cenzo
Glue Man	Dick Van Patten
Captain Efraim	John Schuck

By JANET MASLIN

While it would be impossible to prove scientifically that "The New Adventures of Pippi Longstocking" is the longest children's film ever made or Pippi herself the most irritating of characters, it would be difficult to persuade any audience otherwise. Pippi is the freckle-faced, irrepressible heroine with the braids that stick out parallel to her shoulders, and one of the film's only points of interest is the star's hairdo. The angle of those stiffly* wired braids varies subtly from scene to scene.

"The New Adventures of Pippi Longstocking," which opens today at the Plaza and other theaters, has a cast of players who deliver each line as if they've just received slight electrical shocks, with Tami Erin even more wide-eyed than the others in the title role; a favorite tic of Miss Erin's is the broad wink accompanied by the open-mouthed smile. A pretty, vixenish 13-year-old actress, Miss Erin appears in brightly colored, ragtag outfits featuring baggy bloomers and garters to hold up her trademark stockings. Done up this way, she seems dressed for another type of film altogether.

Although Pippi's signal quality is her ability to ignore adult rules of decorum and find free-spirited fun in any pursuit — one of the film's big musical numbers is about washing the floor — the film reduces this to a series of food fights. These play better when they're compressed in the montage that closes the film than they do scattered through the other-

wise-uneventful narrative. In any case, such frolicsome scenes and Pippi's way of grinning delightedly at very minor occurrences, like the sight of her pet monkey eating a banana, become grating in a very short time. The film does contain several punchy songs that would sound better in any other context than they do here.

The only sparks of wit come from Elieen Brennan, as the story's requisite meanie. But even she is forced to gush admiringly over Pippi before the film is over. As for the film's adventure scenes, they have been directed in the flattest way imaginable by Ken Annakin ("Those Magnificent Men in Their Flying Machines"). The daring ride by Pippi and two other children through dangerous rapids, for example, involves a churning plastic waterfall and rubber rocks.

1988 Jl 29, C11

Simian Suspense

Jason Beghe plays the role of a law student whose life is changed by a freak accident in "Monkey Shines: An Experiment in Fear."

Myles Aronowitz

Primate to Primate

MONKEY SHINES: AN EXPERIMENT IN FEAR, directed by George A. Romero; written by Mr. Romero, based on the book by Michael Stewart; director of photography, James A Conter; edited by Pasquale Buba; music by David Shire; production designer, Cletus Anderson; produced by Charles Evans. Released by Orion Pictures. At Criterion Center, Broadway at 45th Street, and other theaters. Running time: 113 Minutes. This film is rated R.

Allan Mann ....Jason Beghe
Goeffrey Fisher .... John Pankow
Melanie Parker ....Kate McNeil
Dorothy Mann .... Joyce Van Patten
Maryanne Hodges ....Christine Forrest
Dean Burbage .... Stephan Root
Dr. John Wiseman ....Stanley Tucci

By CARYN JAMES

George A. Romero's "Monkey Shines: An Experiment in Fear" has more coincidences than a Sidney Sheldon mini-series, more clichés than a Jackie Collins potboiler, and one thing they don't have — Ella, the killer monkey. A cute little organ-grinder's monkey, Ella dusts furniture, does windows, and has been injected with an experimental serum made from freeze-dried human brain cells. Trained to help the handicapped, she belongs to a quadriplegic named Allan — he was, of course, a star athlete until he was hit by that truck — and when Ella is not helping Allan with his law-school homework, they are trading telepathic messages. Either the man or the monkey is very angry, as Allan's former girlfriend, careless nurse and nagging mother eventually learn the hard way.

The strangest feature of "Monkey Shines" is not Ella, though. It is the fact that the first half is all calm, and tedious, exposition. Allan's mad-

scientist friend, Geoff, injects Ella with the sinister brain cells; a pretty monkey trainer named Melanie becomes Allan's love interest. There are endless, detailed scenes of Ella helping Allan in his new life. All this from the director who had a zombie stalking around a graveyard in the first 10 minutes of his classic "Night of the Living Dead."

By the time Ella turns nasty, we've seen her grimace threateningly so many times that she cannot inspire shrieks of horror. At the end, however, Allan, overplayed by Jason Beghe, might provoke howls of laughter. "Ella, no!" he says, "Ella, no!" when she's trying to wipe out everyone in sight. These howls are not cruel, because we never doubt that Allan will walk again.

Mr. Romero, who adapted the screenplay from Michael Stewart's novel, wraps up more loose ends than anyone cares about, yet leaves some nagging bits of illogic. Is Ella carrying out Allan's angry impulses? Or is she, the innocent victim of some demented human brain, feeding him dark ideas in the first place? And why do we see Allan grow monkey-fang teeth when Ella gets mad? Would the telepathic connection have been too subtle without this symbol?

"Monkey Shines: An Experiment in Fear," which opens today at the Criterion Center and other theaters, at least has some quirky minor performances. Joyce Van Patten always seems too nice to have a nasty son like Allan. And Christine Forrest's slovenly nurse, padding around the house in fuzzy slippers, is a welcome comic touch in a film that begins in sentimentality and ends in ludicrous melodrama.

1988 Jl 29, C12:4

All Awry

Arsinee Khanjian and Aidan Tierney star in "Family Viewing."

Comical 'Family Viewing'

"Family Viewing" was shown as part of the recent "New Directors/ New Film" series. Following are excerpts from Janet Maslin's review, which appeared in The New York Times on March 23. The film opens today at the Bleecker Street Cinema 1, at La Guardia Place.

Video cameras and monitors watch over the characters in Atom Egoyan's "Family Viewing" with the patience and passivity of vultures, but without the enthusiasm. The advent of this modern technology seems to have drained all vitality out of the participants in Mr. Egoyan's very peculiar black comedy, and it's their listlessness that makes them so funny and sad.

A son affecting a great show of dutifulness, for example, arrives with flowers in hand to pay a visit to his mother in a nursing home, only to be told that the woman at whom he's gazing so lovingly is a complete stranger. The video equipment that watches over this and most other encounters in the film is clearly implicated as a key part of what has gone wrong with these people's lives.

Actually, the idea of lives gone wrong is more passionate than any judgment Mr. Egoyan musters. The film proceeds in a unique and utterly disaffected way, following the bizarre connections that link a teen-age boy named Stan (David Hemblen), his sexy stepmother and his dully unre-

sponsive father. Also in the cast is a blithe young woman who makes a living delivering pornographic messages over the telephone, and who has grown to know Stan's family a lot better than anyone initially realizes.

•

"Family Viewing" has an oddball humor and a sense of contemporary corruption that are very much its own. Its characters seem most alive when they are captured on videotape, and Mr. Egoyan even moves the main action onto videotape from time to time. The film's potential for absurdist humor is thus thoroughly exploited, but it takes on an added pathos when Stan begins struggling to preserve his few scraps of real feeling. He steals videotapes of the mother who abandoned him years earlier, thus angering his father, who has been re-recording homemade porno footage over this material. And in an even more desperate move, Stan eventually steals his own grandmother, who seems immensely grateful to be freed from the film's impersonal, high-tech world.

"Family Viewing" seems hopelessly arch at first, but over time it develops real style and real feeling. Mr. Egoyan is well worth watching in the future.

1988 Jl 29, C10:5

FILM VIEW/Vincent Canby

Calls to the Kidult

"**D**IE HARD," WHICH SOUNDS like a dozen other movies anyone might name, is for that reason, as well as a couple of others, a nearly perfect movie for our time.

Bear with me, plot synopsis and all.

"Die Hard" is about a New York cop, John McClane (Bruce Willis), who faces down a gang of European terrorists on the top floors of a brand-new, computer-controlled, high-rise office building in Los Angeles's Century City.

The time is Christmas Eve. The occasion is the Christmas party of the Nakatomi Corporation. This is a Japanese conglomerate so rich and powerful that it can afford to keep $640 million in negotiable bearer bonds sitting in its climate-controlled safe, gathering neither dust nor interest.

■

John McClane has come to Los Angeles to spend the holidays with his children and his estranged wife, Holly (Bonnie Bedelia), who has chosen to become the Number 2 executive at Nakatomi rather than remain the live-in wife of a New York policeman. The terrorists have come for the bearer bonds.

At the very moment that John McClane is in the men's room, freshening up after his flight from New York, the terrorists crash the party, take the corporate merrymakers hostage and set about to open the unblowable safe. With, at first, nothing more than his Beretta 92, and wearing neither shirt nor shoes, McClane sets about his duty.

The next 12 hours are sheer hell. Nakatomi employes and their guests are subjected to terrible indignities. "It would be a pity to ruin that suit," says the sneering terrorist leader who knows Savile Row tailoring when he sees it. He then shoots his prisoner through the forehead, but the mess seems to splatter more on the glass partition behind the victim than on his suit.

Meanwhile John McClane is running up and down stairwells, crawling through air vents and swinging across elevator shafts. One by one, he picks off terrorists and liberates guns and walkie-talkies as they become available.

It isn't enough that his life is threatened by the terrorists. John's heroic, one-man defense of our way of life is continually undermined by the representatives of the Los Angeles police department, the F.B.I. and the television networks who have gathered around the building in Nakatomi Plaza below. John ranks as a child among the other authority figures at the scene, but he is the only person who knows what to do.

Watching "Die Hard" is like snorting pure oxygen, but it doesn't clear the brain as much as it whistles through it. It leaves no trace whatsoever.

It's an utterly silly movie that has been put

together with scary competence by John McTiernan, the director; Jeb Stuart and Steven E. de Souza, the screenwriters, and the hundreds of other contributors to the project. In all, nearly 400 people are cited in the credits, including Arthur Freed, Nacio Herb Brown, Stevie Wonder, Sammy Cahn, Jule Styne and Tony Kerum, the caterer. For some reason, Beethoven, whose "Ode to Joy" from the Ninth Symphony is used quite prominently, is not mentioned.

That "Die Hard" is becoming one of the box-office hits of the summer is not surprising, at least after the fact. It's as bright, shiny and noisy as a video game, and so fast-paced that even bogus thrills count.

No movie, except one with subtitles, requires that the viewer be able to read, but "Die Hard" renders even basic reasoning skills superfluous. One doesn't have to understand the why's of the story to follow what's going on. At times, one doesn't even have to be sighted. The film's booming soundtrack score describes every image and the appropriate emotion to attach to it.

"Die Hard" has the form of a movie, one made with a great many sophisticated skills, but it works on the audience less as a coherent movie than as an amusement park ride.

The people who came up with the film's ad line understood this: "It will blow you through the back of the theater."

"Die Hard" is not a film for children, nor is it a film for adults. Instead it's a movie for that new, true-blue American of the electronic age, the kidult, who may be 8, 18, 38 or 80.

To backtrack a minute:

In the past, our most popular movies have been those that somehow have managed to appeal to both children and adults, though not necessarily for the same reasons or with the same degree of intensity.

Even recently, with "Close Encounters of the Third Kind," "E.T." and "Empire of the Sun," Steven Spielberg has demonstrated that movies that engage the imagination of the child need not insult the intelligence of "parents and adult guardians." That's the phrase used by the members of the Film Rating Board, those hard-working egg candlers who

look at movies and stamp letters on them according to what they determine to be their audience suitability.

The Spielberg films have always been made on the assumption that there exists a common ground where the interests of children and adults overlap, even though there are vast differences between children and adults in their experience, education and capacity to understand.

Today's hip film makers now realize that's baloney.

In "The Disappearance of Childhood," published in 1984, Neil Postman, a New York University professor of communication arts and

It's a movie designed for the child-adult whose capacities and interests are fixed at an early age.

sciences, argues doomily and persuasively that, in our new society, childhood is becoming obsolete. He suggests that the revolution in communications, begun by Marconi and peaking with television, has so changed the amount and meaning of information available to children that the functional differences between today's children and adults are vanishing.

Childhood, says Mr. Postman, grew out of a kind of cultural necessity. Following the invention of the printing press in the 15th century and the sudden availability of books, the members of the newly influential and ambitious middle class began to put great store by literacy, knowledge and reasoned discourse.

The imperatives of education created that period called childhood, in which children are not seen as miniature adults but as unformed beings in need of care, direction and instruction, not only in books but in religion, sex, manners, what-have-you. Childhood is a time for secrets to be revealed in due order.

Mr. Postman goes on to say that, as a result of televsion's nonstop dissemination of information of every conceivable sort, mostly in easy-to-take little narratives, there are fewer and fewer secrets left to children. The result: impatience with formal education, increasing illiteracy, an inability to reason productively and the effective breakdown of the difference between the manners and prerogatives that once separated child from adult.

As childhood disappears, so does adulthood.

Mr. Postman's arguments are seductive and, as he notes, they are possibly only part of the story behind the extraordinary social changes taking place today.

■

To give a label to what he describes, it might be said that in the place of childhood and adulthood we now have kidulthood, a single, continuing condition that begins about the time that speech is learned and continues into old age.

That may be the only sane way to regard a movie on the order of "Die Hard."

It's a movie designed for, and best

Peter Sorel

Bruce Willis as a New York City detective and Bonnie Bedelia as his estranged wife, in the film about terrorists who take over a Los Angeles skyscraper

appreciated by, the kidult, the amalgamated child-adult whose capacities and interests are fixed at an early age. No longer is there a necessity to find areas in which the interests of the child and the adult overlap. They are the same.

The audiences with which I twice saw "Die Hard" reacted to its mindless thrills with unusual uniformity, as if it were a series of highly pleasurable, near-orgasmic hot-foots. However, it was also clear that the people who put the film on the screen are not only canny but also a lot funnier than that is, perhaps, necessary. Certainly, it is a lot funnier than any kidult watching the film would have to notice to enjoy it.

The humor has nothing to do with the dialogue, which is, most of the time, either standard tough-guy sarcastic or sentimental. The big belly laughs are prompted by explosions, hangings, shootings, bodies dropping 30 stories to the pavement and other forms of cinematically redeeming mayhem.

Yet there is something quite witty in the film's view of the world. It's not by chance that the powerful conglomerate is Japanese, and that the terrorists are Germans.

"Die Hard" appreciates the irony in the confrontation between America's two former enemies, each now more powerful in some ways than they were before they were defeated, squaring off in L.A., a sort of metaphorical Switzerland. All the host city can offer are services, those of its law enforcement agencies, the fire department and Jack McClane, hero.

■

It's also significant, in the film's view of things, that these terrorists, once known for their radical politics, have themselves been corrupted by the profit motive. They couldn't care less about brothers imprisoned in Sri Lanka. They're out for the money and the good things it can buy, probably overseas.

Like other movies in this genre, "Die Hard" expresses a kidult's faith in the limitless wonders of technology and gadgetry. The plot simply could not happen if the computer system that guards the Nakatomi Building "went down" in the sort of unpredictable fainting fits with which the rest of us are all too familiar.

The Nakatomi computers work perfectly, and so can easily be put out of action. All the terrorists have to do is read their instruction manuals and follow the crystal-clear directions. Do I hear a horse-laugh?

The movie's closest approximation to a real person is the one American member of the terrorist gang. He is Theo (Clarence Gilyard Jr.), a jive-talking, hot-shot computer genius. Theo grew up in the computer age and, like many American kids, appears to be having a ball in it.

The movie is also fascinated by weaponry, including Steyr Aug assault rifles, Walther PPK pistols and H & K MP-5, 9-millimeter submachine guns. These are identified in the production notes for, I suppose, the edification of film reviewers for whom the bug bomb is still high-tech.

It's too early yet to know whether "Die Hard" will mean the big break for Mr. Willis, known principally for light comedy as the male lead in the televi-

sion series, "Moonlighting." Considering the material he has to work with (the screenplay and his own personality), he doesn't do badly, though at his toughest he comes across as someone trying very hard to imitate Mickey Rourke.

Alexander Godunov, the former Russian ballet star, is a sight gag in his terrorist costume of basic black, which sets off his long blond hair. Maddened by the death of a fellow terrorist, he shouts, "I want blood!" in one of his few intelligible speeches. For this Mr. Godunov defected.

Only Alan Rickman, the English actor seen here in "Les Liaisons Dangereuses," gives a consistently credible performance as the leader of the terrorists.

However, consistently credible performances, coherence and cinematic style are beside the point of kidult movies. It's enough that they keep moving, exploding, making a lot of noise and, in all other ways, seeming to progress from one story point to the next.

The waves of the future: kidult auteurists. As I walked up the aisle after the showing of "Die Hard" at the Baronet, I followed two aging young men in deep discussion about the movie.

"That scene," said the first fellow, full of impatience, "was a direct steal from 'Lethal Weapon.'"

Said his friend, "I hear what you're saying. I admit that. McTiernan certainly knows that. It was a quote."

Replied the friend, sneering and saying a vulgar word, "You're out of your mind. It wasn't a quote. McTiernan word stole it."

Onwards. □

1988 Jl 31, II:19:1

A World of Symbols That Have Come Alive

ALICE, scripted, designed and edited by Jan Svankmajer; photography by Svatopluk Maly; animator, Bedrich Glaser; produced by Peter-Christian Fueter; a Condor Features Production in association with Film Four International and Hessischer Rundfunk; distributed by First Run Features. At Film Forum 1, 57 Watts Street. Running time: 84 minutes. This film has no rating.

Alice .... Kristyna Kohoutova

By CARYN JAMES

Of all the ways to adapt "Alice in Wonderland," the most perverse, it seems, would be to peel back its genteel Victorian veneer. Without the story's decorum and fairy-tale disguises, the Hatter would seem dangerously mad, the Caterpillar would be a seductive snake, all of Wonderland would be haunted rather than fantastic. That is precisely what Jan Svankmajer, a Czechoslovak animator, has done in "Alice," and though he strips away all sweetness and light, he does not violate Lewis Carroll's story.

Instead, he combines live action with toy figures filmed in remarkably fluid stop-motion and creates an eerie world of magical objects. Brightly alluring on the surface, these rabbits, jam jars and dollhouses are sinister inside. The rabbit eats his own sawdust stuffing, the jam is full of tacks and the dollhouse becomes Alice's prison, as Mr. Svankmajer's extraordinary film explores the story's dark undercurrents.

Wonderland A surreal caterpillar is among the characters seen in the Czechoslovak animator Jan Svankmajer's "Alice," inspired by the Lewis Carroll classic.

Though Alice follows the White Rabbit to a subterranean land where she wanders into a mad tea party, plays croquet with flamingos for mallets and stands trial before the furious Queen of Hearts, the film only loosely follows Carroll's plot, or any plot at all. Mr. Svankmajer moves from one surreal profusion of images to another. His Alice sits in a cluttered playroom next to a small china doll that is her exact double; suddenly a stuffed rabbit kicks its way out of a glass exhibit case, puts on a red coat and escapes to Wonderland through the drawer of an old wooden writing desk.

●

The White Rabbit moves so smoothly, we instantly forget he is an animated toy. But Mr. Svankmajer never lets us forget we are watching a film in which an actress plays Alice telling us a story. Near the start, she faces the camera and says, "Alice thought to herself, 'Now you will see a film. . . .'" She goes on to speak all the characters' voices, and the camera returns time and again to a close-up of her lips reciting.

Her own self-conscious narrator, Alice acts out her story. Following the rabbit into the drawer, she falls down what resembles an elevator shaft, passing shelves filled with objects — like a cup filled with the skulls of baby birds. These things will reappear in Wonderland, which is a series of cramped rooms, suddenly opening onto a barren field where a painted stage backdrop hides more cramped rooms. Wonderland is a place where a rat in royal blue velvet swims across a flooded room and starts a campfire on Alice's head. That, Alice thinks, is going too far, so she dunks her head under water.

In this toyland, Kristyna Kohoutova, as Alice, is the only living creature, which adds to its eeriness. When she drinks a bottle of ink, the live Alice suddenly shrinks and becomes her animated-doll double. She eats a tart, grows and is the live actress again, switching back and forth with sudden and effective dream logic.

●

With its extreme close-ups, its constant motion and its smooth animation, the film is so visually active that it distracts us from a heavy-handed fact — this is a world of symbols come alive. In a room where Alice finds the darning basket from home, socks fill with sawdust and crawl through round holes in the floor. They

look like worms and phallic symbols, but most of all like socks come to life. One sock picks dentures and fake eyeballs out of a glass jar, puts them on and becomes the caterpillar.

Another minor flaw in "Alice" is partly a problem of translation. During the repeated close-ups of Alice's mouth, her voice is conspicuously dubbed into English. The disjunction of lips and voice does not increase the film's surrealism; it jolts us out of its fictive world.

Mr. Svankmajer, who has made short animated films for over 20 years but never before done a full-length feature, has called "Alice" a series of "dialogues with childhood, or expeditions into its landscape." Film Forum 1, where "Alice" opens today, suggests it is "not appropriate for young children." Both are right. "Alice," as it unearths the fears that animate dreams and nightmares, is definitely a film for adults.

1988 Ag 3, C18:4

Poor Spirits

Cyndi Lauper

VIBES, directed by Ken Kwapis; screenplay by Lowell Ganz and Babaloo Mandel, story by Deborah Blum, Mr. Ganz and Mr. Mandel; director of photography, John Bailey; edited by Carol Littleton; music by James Horner; production designer, Richard Sawyer; produced by Miss Blum and Tony Ganz; released by Columbia Pictures. At Sutton, 57th Street at Third Avenue, and other theaters. Running time: 99 minutes. This film is rated PG.

Sylvia Pickel ....Cyndi Lauper
Nick Deezy .... Jeff Goldblum
Dr. Harrison Steele ....Julian Sands
Ingo Swedlin .... Googy Gress
Harry Buscafusco .... Peter Falk

Cyndi Lauper, known for her zany style, is remarkably subdued in "Vibes," in which she and Jeff Goldblum co-star as a pair of psychics who become embroiled in an intrigue plot. The craziest thing she does is to appear in this film at all.

"Vibes," which opens today at the Sutton and other theaters, has all the ingredients of lighthearted adventure-comedy except the essential one: laughs. Its only chuckles are prompted by Peter Falk, who comes so close to reviving the character he played in "The In-Laws" that he creates more than a little nostalgia for that much, much wittier film. As for Miss Lauper and Mr. Goldblum, both appear ready for an explosion of merriment that never comes. Mr. Goldblum in particular seems more than ready for a leading romantic comedy role, but too often here he's virtually acting alone.

● ·

Miss Lauper and Mr. Goldblum are cast as Sylvia Pickel and Nick Deezy, and the film is never any more amusing than those names. This is surprising in view of the sizable comic potential that a two-psychic love story offers; these characters, after all, can pick up a garment and know just who has been touching it and under what circumstances, so the potential for humor is surely there. Instead of making jokes, the screenplay (by Lowell Ganz and Babaloo Mandel) sends its stars to Ecuador in search of lost treasure, and makes Sylvia spend most of her time conversing with a friend from the spirit world. Miss Lauper doesn't do this well, but it's possible that no one could.

If anyone connected with "Vibes" had indeed been psychic, they would have let this material go by.

●

"Vibes" is rated PG ("Parental Guidance Suggested"). It contains some profanity. JANET MASLIN

1988 Ag 5, C6:1

Eating in Public

Kevin Dillon

THE BLOB, directed by Chuck Russell; screenplay by Mr. Russell and Frank Darabont; director of photography, Mark Irwin; edited by Terry Stokes and Tod Feuerman; music by Michael Hoenig; production designer, Craig Stearns; produced by Jack H. Harris and Elliott Kastner; released by Tri Star Pictures. At Criterion Center, Broadway and 45th Street, and other theaters. Running time: 90 minutes. This film is rated R.

Meg Penny	Shawnee Smith
Paul Taylor	Donovan Leitch
Scott Jeskey	Ricky Paull Goldin
Brian Flagg	Kevin Dillon
Sheriff Herb Geller	Jeffrey DeMunn
Fran Hewitt	Candy Clark
Reverend Meeker	Del Close

By JANET MASLIN

Modern technology has yielded at least one definite advance in the last 30 years: a better Blob. Whereas the original 1958 model, a rolling heap of silicone, did little more than wobble and eat, the updated Blob is infinitely more advanced. It can climb to the ceiling and plop down on anyone below. It can choose its victims mischievously, rather than on its predecessor's catch-as-catch-can basis. It can play practical jokes. And it can overtake, subdue and digest its prey right before the audience's very eyes. This *is* progress, after a fashion.

So by any reasonable standard, Chuck Russell's current "Blob" is new and improved. It's a more professional effort in every way. The special effects look sickeningly good, and the actors show signs of being able to act, which could not be said of any members of the original cast — not even Steve McQueen, who was Steven McQueen then and appearing in his first major film role. Yet for reasons having nothing to do with merit, the 1958 film earned a place in history. The remake, enterprising as it is, won't do the same.

The original's very amateurishness had a lot to do with making it memorable. The utter ingenuousness of its small-town Americana remains astounding, and the inadvertent

humor generated by the Blob itself — surely the silliest of all sci-fi creations in an era when silliness was king — is another major plus. Filmed on a very low budget in Pennysluania, the first "Blob" is entirely without Hollywood polish. It's a funny, revealing, often dull and never frightening souvenir of the era in which it was made.

●

The new "Blob," which opens today at the Criterion and other theaters, is very much a film of the moment. It is more violent than the original, more spectacular, more cynical, more patently commercial and more attentive to detail. The plot outline — which, like everything else about the original film, left plenty of room for improvement — remains similar, from the Blob's first arrival via meteor to its various rampages (in a doctor's office, in a movie theater, down the main street of the little town) to its by no means irreversible demise. But within those guidelines, just about everything else has changed.

Gone is the friendly, folksy atmosphere in which a clean-cut teen-ager (Mr. McQueen) joined forces with the grudgingly supportive local police to vanquish the mysterious creature. On the evidence of the new film, nice guys are clearly out of fashion. Donovan Leitch, as a wholesome-looking high-school football player, looks like the film's hero in its early scenes, but he is one of many characters who become very graphic Blob-bait. His cheerleader girlfriend (played by Shawnee Smith) and the town's sneering, motorcycle-riding outcast (Kevin Dillon) are left to battle the creature.

●

Fighting the Blob isn't so simple this time, since the screenplay by Mr. Russell and Frank Darabont adds hostile police, sinister Government scientists and one very peculiar clergyman (Del Close) to the man-versus-Blob dynamic. There are also jokes about condoms and some about medical insurance (the first Blob victim doesn't have any) thrown into the thoroughly contemporary mix. What emerges is a lively, grisly, better-than-average high-tech monster movie that devotes more energy to special effects than to drama.

Among the actors, Mr. Dillon does a good job of projecting a wounded heroism behind his ever-present sneer, and Jeffrey DeMunn makes the local sheriff a genial, reasonable fellow who is in no way prepared for the Blob's incursion. Candy Clark's salt-of-the-earth performance as a waitress comes closest to recalling the earlier film's atmosphere, and Miss Smith's cheerleader strikes the most modern chord. It is she, dressed for combat and furiously cursing the enemy, who proves the most formidable Blob-baiter of them all.

The Blob itself is the most impressive cast member, a genuinely clever creation that's at least as versatile as it is disgusting. Listed in the film's extensive credits, among many other contributors to this movie magic, are three Blob Effects Coordinators, two Blob Shop Foremen, and five Blob Wranglers.

1988 Ag 5, C6:5

War Is Heck

THE RESCUE, directed by Ferdinand Fairfax; written by Jim Thomas and John Thomas; director of photography, Russell Boyd; film editors, David Holden and Carroll Timothy O'Meara; music by Bruce Broughton; production designer, Maurice Cain; produced by Laura Ziskin; released by Touchstone Pictures. At the Plaza, 59th Street east of Madison Avenue, and other theaters. Running time: 98 minutes. This film is rated PG.

J. J. Merrill	Kevin Dillon
Adrian Phillips	Christina Harnos
Max Rothman	Marc Price
Shawn Howard	Ned Vaughn
Bobby Howard	Ian Giatti
Commander Howard	Charles Haid
Commander Merrill	Edward Albert

Kiddie-centrism reaches some new pinnacle with "The Rescue," the story of five brave youngsters who storm their way into North Korea to free their fathers, who have just become prisoners of war for reasons that only the screenwriters (Jim Thomas and John Thomas, also authors of "Predator") would understand. In the process, these young heroes discover that going to war is a lot like visiting an amusement park, except the noises are louder. Parents may not regard this as an ideal lesson for young viewers.

"The Rescue," which opens today at the Plaza and other theaters, does everything it can to re-cast its unremarkable military exploits in teen-pleasing terms. But its manner is so perfunctory that even the film's young target audience may fail to be moved. The screenplay does laughably little to develop character traits of any kind; the parents are stern, the kids love their dads, and that's about all there is to anyone's psyche. Even the potential to turn this into an on-the-march version of "The Breakfast Club" is dissipated when the youngsters fail to strike up interesting friendships with one another.

The manner by which the young characters (four teen-agers and a 10-year-old sidekick) actually execute their rescue mission is quite literally child's play. The film, as directed by Ferdinand Fairfax, proceeds emo-

tionlessly from one gimmick to another. When the youngsters, all Navy brats, band together to discuss their fathers' capture, one of them proves able to eavesdrop electronically on a military meeting at which a plan to rescue the captives is rejected. From here, it is simplicity itself to break into headquarters, steal the rejected documents and tape them back together, making a map of the place where the fathers are imprisoned. If this weren't a military adventure, it would play like Nancy Drew.

●

"The Rescue" panders to its audience so shamelessly that it piles one trick onto another. And when the young people borrow a car as part of their scheme, there's a Chuck Berry song on the radio. They crash the car off the end of a dock, steal a boat, and make their way to a Korean ally who pronounces their exploits "incredible." Later on, they slide down a huge water chute, have an exciting airborne adventure and shoot off rockets that look just like toys.

Though the plot is set up as a way of letting these youngsters win the love and admiration of their heretofore stern fathers (Kevin Dillon, as the toughest of the young heroes, typically calls his father "Sir"), even this is robbed of any feeling by the film's hasty, matter-of-fact style. The editing, which particularly contributes to this flatness, is at times noticeably odd. The screenplay is so weak that it never even comes up with a homecoming line. The film ends with the lamest of freeze-frames.

The young actors, among them Christina Harnos as the lone girl among the heroes and Marc Price as the group's resident wisecracking type, are eager and attractive. But they haven't been given anything to do.

●

"The Rescue" is rated PG ("Parental Guidance Suggested"). It contains some profanity.
JANET MASLIN

1988 Ag 5, C9:1

FILM VIEW/Janet Maslin

The Blob as Social Barometer

FILM LENDS EXTRA POIGNANCY to the passing of time, allowing an instant overview of the arc of a career. The Film Society of Lincoln Center's forthcoming "New Directors/Newer Films" series will make it possible to see these trajectories clearly, to trace the path of a Hector Babenco as he progressed from the raw "Pixote" to the brilliantly realized "Kiss of the Spider Woman" to the sodden "Ironweed." It will show how George Miller went from the fiercely independent "Road Warrior" to the patently commercial "Witches of Eastwick" in only a few years' time, or how Spike Lee

"Steven" McQueen, center, starred in the original version of "The Blob," made in 1958.

Michael Kenworthy and Shawnee Smith cope with a more sophisticated blob in the 1988 remake.

moved on from the short "Joe's Bed-Stuy Barbershop: We Cut Heads" to his mightily self-assured "She's Gotta Have It."

It doesn't take a film festival to underscore such changes. Who, in watching the enchanting rapport between Robert De Niro and Charles Grodin in "Midnight Run," can forget that 15 years ago — at about the time when they were making "Mean Streets" and "The Heartbreak Kid," respectively — it was impossible to imagine these two actors in the same universe, let alone in the same comedy? Yet here they are, greatly mellowed, trading affectionate quips about arteriosclerosis.

Among film luminaries whose careers have evolved noticeably over time, the Blob is worth remembering, too. After all, a lot has changed since the Blob first slithered across the screen 30 years ago. There are physiological advances: in its friskier days the Blob would simply pounce, pause discreetly and then wobble away, leaving behind only a crisp nurse's hat where the whole nurse had been. Today, a new high-tech Blob can be seen digesting every morsel.

Technology has improved greatly since Irvin S. Yeaworth directed the first "Blob" in 1958 (both this and the current remake, which was directed by Chuck Russell, are the work of the same producer, Jack H. Harris). So the present Blob now has veins, bubbles, a taste for practical jokes and an ability to leap from the ceiling. But technical polish was never an essential part of the Blob's appeal, and indeed the innocence of the first film was and is quite touching. It was made for $240,000, has grossed a hundred times that, and no amount of money could duplicate its ingenuous 1950's style.

Both Blob films take place in small middle-American towns and follow the same general lines: the Blob arrives from space and attaches itself to an old man. A teen-age couple comes to the old man's aid and takes him to see a doctor, at which point the Blob's nutritional demands increase greatly. Subsequent exploits take the Blob to a movie theater, a meat locker and finally to a major confrontation with the townspeople, who vanquish this unwelcome visitor by remarkably simple means. Now as then, the Blob hates cold weather.

Anyone who sees both films (the early "Blob" is available on videocassette, and a new print of it was recently shown at the Film Forum's II's fantasy and science fiction series) will be less struck by these surface similarities than by how much the world has changed in 30 years. The town in which the first Blob ran amok was a nice place

filled with clean-cut kids (led by Steven McQueen, as he was then known) and square-jawed, dedicated authority figures. Many non-teens in the cast — a fire chief, a nurse, a waitress — seem to be in uniform, and to take their professionalism very seriously. There is a palpable faith in the ability of officialdom to solve any problem, even the problem of a runaway Blob.

Today's version is infinitely more cynical. The hero, played by Donovan Leitch in a straight-arrow manner echoing Mr. McQueen's, is devoured early in the story, and it falls to the town's motorcycle-riding outcast (played by Kevin Dillon) to save the day. The police, particularly one disgruntled officer, do a lot of sneering at the kids. And there is now a subplot about corrupt government scientists pursuing the Blob for experiments in germ warfare.

Aside from giving the film a look that owes a lot to Steven Spielberg, these scientists underscore another neo-"Blob" quality: the urge to explain. Whereas the townspeople of 1958 took it for granted that a Blob could fall from the sky, hatch, and begin its hunt for nourishment, the audience of today apparently expects the facts. So there is knowing talk of the Blob as "a plasmic lifeform that hunts its prey" and speculation as to its origins. Above all, there is a strong sense that the more we say, the less we know.

Among the things that have clearly improved during the Blob's lifetime is the function of female characters in stories like this. Mr. McQueen's simpering girlfriend in the first film (played by Aneta Corseaut) fretted stupidly over what would become of the old man's little dog, and stood by helplessly while the teen-age boys decided what to do. By contrast, the new film's heroine, played by Shawnee Smith, is out there toting a weapon in the final battle, crying "Come on, you son of a bitch!" at the marauding Blob.

We can only guess as to how confusing this must be from the Blob's point of view. Thirty years ago, the Blob led a simpler life, coping with universal scorn (the doctor examining the story's first victim actually tries to cover the Blob with a blanket) and randomly attacking anyone who might hove into view. Today it's different. The Blob has a moral sense (witnessed by a taste for sexually promiscuous teen-age victims), a hazy sense of purpose and a different brand of enemy behind every tree. Maybe this reflects changing times, and perhaps it's also what 30 years of stardom can do. Come to think of it, the Blob looks jowlier these days, too.   □

1988 Ag 7, II:19:1

From Small Triumph To Small Triumph

CLEAN AND SOBER, directed by Glenn Gordon Caron; written by Tod Carroll; director of photography, Jan Kiesser; editor, Richard Chew; music by Gabriel Yared; production designer, Joel Schiller; produced by Tony Ganz and Deborah Blums; released by Warner Brothers. At Loews 84th Street Six, at Broadway; Beekman, Second Avenue at 66th Street. Running time: 124 minutes. This film is rated R.

Daryl Poynter	Michael Keaton
Charlie Standers	Kathy Baker
Craig	Morgan Freeman
Richard Dirks	M. Emmet Walsh
Donald Towle	Tate Donovan
Richard Dirks	M. Emmet Walsh

By JANET MASLIN

At the start of "Clean and Sober," Daryl Poynter (Michael Keaton) finds himself at rock bottom: he wakes up with a bad hangover, heavy debts and a comatose stranger in his bed. Daryl's alcohol and cocaine habits are the source of all this trouble, and they might have remained out of control indefinitely. But when Daryl's date fails to wake up at all and his irregular bookkeeping practices are in danger of being discovered, he thinks it wise to stage a temporary retreat. A chemical dependency center with a 21-day detoxification program sounds like just the place.

Daryl enters this rehabilitation center with the firm conviction that he does *not* have a problem. The film, directed by Glenn Gordon Caron, works slowly, carefully and finally quite affectingly to trace the process whereby he discovers otherwise. Though it covers only a monthlong period, "Clean and Sober" is so slow and deliberate, approaching its subject in such an intent, realistic manner, that it seems to have spanned several lifetimes.

●

If the changes that Daryl undergoes can be explained very simply, the film nonetheless gives them an unexpected dimension. Much of this comes from the acting, thanks to a terrific supporting cast (including Morgan Freeman, Kathy Baker and M. Emmet Walsh) and Mr. Keaton himself. The perfect actor for a role like this, Mr. Keaton begins the film on a sour, self-interested note, giving a very convincing impersonation of a man who will gladly use anyone or anything to get what he wants. The

Michael Keaton, left, and Kathy Baker, right, in "Clean and Sober," a film about one man's struggle with an alcohol and drug problem.

later parts of the film, in which Daryl quietly evolves into a concerned, affectionate, responsible being, are all the more moving for that reason.

"Clean and Sober," which opens today at the Beekman and other theaters, observes this performance very closely as it captures the full extent of Daryl's change. When first seen, he has an edgy, irritable manner, a very brief attention span and a tendency to blame others for his many problems. He has embezzled money from an escrow account at his office, but he sees this as a minor transgression and expects to make up for it in no time. He is furious with creditors and with unreliable drug dealers who no longer follow orders. And once he checks into the detoxification facility, he is enraged by Craig (Mr. Freeman), a recovering addict who leads the therapy group in which Daryl is enrolled. An arrogant yuppie character through and through, Daryl even screams insults about what he presumes is Craig's contemptibly small salary.

As Craig, Mr. Freeman presides over the group in a wise, watchful manner that gives the entire film extra weight. Without saying much, he seems to understand precisely what each of his charges is going through, and his power to eject them from the center for bad faith or bad behavior becomes daunting to all. The group scenes led by Craig are involvingly staged, and so are Daryl's encounters with Richard Dirks (Mr. Walsh), who becomes his sponsor once he has passed the program's initial stages and gone on to attend Alcoholics Anonymous meetings. Functioning as a guardian angel, Dirks forces Daryl to examine his behavior and cleans up Daryl's apartment with a portable vacuum, getting rid of any leftover drug residue in his bureau drawers.

Though the film sometimes has a faintly didactic tone, offering slides of sick and healthy livers and invoking some of the techniques used by Alcoholics Anonymous, it presents Daryl's progress in highly personal terms. He is greatly helped by a growing affection for Charlie Standers (Miss Baker), a fellow group member whom he likes to call Chuck. Charlie's situation is worse than his own; she has a dead-end factory job and an unhappy living arrangement with a morose man (Luca Bercovici) who has drug problems of his own.

But Daryl, flippant at first, then genuinely concerned for Charlie, manages to wear down her initial resistance and later to lure her over to his newly cleaned-up apartment for dinner. She arrives with a brown bag that she says contains a bottle of tequila, and for a moment Daryl really pauses. Then he sighs with relief. It's Pepsi instead.

The scene in which Charlie and Daryl, neatly dressed, politely eat the dinner that he has cooked and display a genuine, unguarded interest in each other would qualify as run-of-the-mill in most other movies, but in this one it amounts to a small triumph. "Clean and Sober" proceeds in just this way, from one such tiny increment to another, the best way to capture such a giant step forward.

1988 Ag 10, C17:1

A Twist in the Road

A Summer Story directed by Piers Haggard; adapted by Penelope Mortimer from a story by John Galsworthy; director of photography, Kenneth MacMillan; produced by Danton Rissner; released by Atlantic Entertainment Group. At Carnegie Hall Cinema, Sev-

enth Avenue at 57th Street, and other theaters; running time: 95 minutes. This film is rated PG-13.

Megan	Imogen Stubbs
Ashton	James Wilby
Jim	Ken Colley
Stella	Sophie Ward
Mrs. Narracombe	Susannah York
Joe	Jerome Flynn

By JANET MASLIN

Two young gentlemen from London are wandering through the Devon countryside in their walking tweeds on a summer day in 1902 when one of them twists his ankle. In search of help, he looks up to find a beautiful country lass in a simple frock, homespun apron and straw hat. She is carrying a sheaf of wheat.

The girl, named Megan (Imogen Stubbs), takes the apple-cheeked Frank Ashton (James Wilby) home to a stone-walled, thatch-roofed farmhouse nestled in a breathtakingly scenic valley. He rents a room from Megan's Auntie (Susannah York) and settles in to recuperate. He sits by the fireside, reads leather-bound volumes of poetry as the ducks waddle by, eats hearty meals from antique china and observes the household's two little boys with their tousled blond hair, peach complexions and nubby sweaters.

Frank so throws himself into the spirit of things that he attends the local sheep-shearing festivities. That same evening, on a bed of sheep cuttings, that Megan and Frank realize they have fallen in love.

A montage ensues. Frank and Megan bathe in a stream, then the piglets are seen frolicking. The lovers romp in the hayloft and read poetry, and there are shots of cows and ducks. Agricultural note: In the interest of historical accuracy, the film makers have obtained old-fashioned horned cows instead of the modern, hornless kind.

Frank determines to marry Megan, but first he must arrange a brief departure; Megan's Auntie has begun to look askance at Megan's favoring this stranger instead of her own son, Joe (Jerome Flynn), who sometimes clutches a piece of grass when he talks. So Frank leaves, winding up at the seaside resort of Torquay, where seemingly every female in town wears white lace and carries a parasol. He encounters a school chum, decked out in white flannels, blue blazer and straw boater.

Frank confides that he is in love with a country girl. The school chum, having now changed into a maroon dressing gown with a white ascot, confesses that he too once had a great passion for the wrong sort of girl and was lucky enough to get over it.

Frank then falls under the spell of his chum's sister, Stella (Sophie Ward), a cool, flirtatious beauty who plays on Frank's class loyalties almost as skillfully as she plays the piano. "Oh, I love the idea of staying on a farm!" she cries after hearing an extremely abbreviated account of Frank's idyll. "But isn't the reality rather smelly?"

What happens next in "A Summer Story," which opens today at the Carnegie Hall Cinema, should be left undisclosed, but the film aspires to a four-hankie ending. Those hankies had better be pure linen.

Adapted by Penelope Mortimer from a John Galsworthy story and directed by Piers Haggard (who did the television series "Pennies From Heaven"), "A Summer Story" is a relentlessly pretty film that's no more

tough-minded than Frank himself. It could be described as pure hokum if the characters spoke that way, but they don't. They say things like "She's right willful, is our Meg, when she's a mind of it."

The actors in a film like this don't so much act as glow. Miss Stubbs is particularly good at this, and Miss York, affecting a heavy Devonshire accent, is always a pleasure. Mr. Wilby, who had the title role in "Maurice," is ideal as he beams through the story's dewier earlier sections, and less at home in later scenes that call for more distress. All of the actors seem to have thrown themselves wholeheartedly into the film's lulling, decorative spirit. Audiences may well do the same.

●

"A Summer Story" is rated PG-13 ("Special Parental Guidance Suggested for Those Younger Than 13"). It contains brief nudity.

1988 Ag 11, C18:5

The Inner Life Of the Absolute

Harvey Keitel

THE LAST TEMPTATION OF CHRIST, directed by Martin Scorsese; written by Paul Schrader; based on the novel by Nikos Kazantzakis; director of photography, Michael Ballhaus; edited by Thelma Schoonmaker; music by Peter Gabriel; production designer, John Beard; produced by Barbara De Fina; released by Universal Pictures. At the Ziegfeld, Avenue of the Americas and 54th Street. Running time: 160 minutes. This film is rated R.

Jesus	Willem Dafoe
Judas	Harvey Keitel
Mary Magdalene	Barbara Hershey
Saul/Paul	Harry Dean Stanton
Pontius Pilate	David Bowie
John the Baptist	Andre Gregory
Lazarus	Tomas Arana

By JANET MASLIN

NIKOS KAZANTZAKIS'S radical, revisionist novel "The Last Temptation of Christ" redefines divinity through choice. It suggests that if Jesus accepted his destiny triumphantly, in full awareness of another alternative, his spiritual example was thus greatly enhanced by a human dimension. "That part of Christ's nature which was profoundly human," Mr. Kazantzakis wrote in his introduction to this startling volume, "helps us to understand him and love him and to pursue his Passion as though it were our own."

Martin Scorsese's film adaptation of this 1951 novel, which opens today at the Ziegfeld, is also informed by a concept of choice, and the choices the film maker has made cover a wide spectrum. He has elected to shun the conventions of Biblical cinema, underscore the contemporary implications of Mr. Kazantzakis's story, create a heightened historical context for Jesus' teachings and emphasize the visceral aspects of his experience as well. Though the choices that shape this exceptionally ambitious, deeply troubling and, at infrequent moments, genuinely transcendent film are often contradictory, they create an extra dimension. Mr. Scorsese's evident struggle with this material becomes as palpable as the story depicted on the screen.

Faith and sacrifice, guilt and redemption, sin and atonement — these are forceful elements in many of Mr. Scorsese's earlier films, from "Mean Streets" (1973) to "Taxi Driver" (1976) to "Raging Bull" (1980). And these works have established their director as perhaps the most innately religious of major American film makers, certainly one of the best. But paradoxically, the film that finds Mr. Scorsese in such close proximity to the heart of his earlier concerns is often strikingly less spiritual than its secular equivalents. It seems possible, indeed understandable, that for him this monumental subject has had a daunting effect.

The director does not seem constrained by the episodes setting forth Mr. Kazantzakis's most daring constructs; if anything, it is these seemingly irreverent and sometimes very bloody sequences that generate the film's most spontaneous and powerful scenes. "The Last Temptation of Christ" begins with a voice-over (its tone reminiscent of Harvey Keitel's opening inner monologue in "Mean Streets") that presents Jesus as a tormented, worried individual. Soon afterward, he is seen assisting in the crucifixion of a fellow Jew, an act that makes him the object of universal scorn. He is doing this, he then explains, in a passage that typifies the film's unconventional tactics, because he fears and dreads his Messianic destiny. Perhaps he would rather invoke God's wrath than His love.

Soon afterward, he appears transfixed by guilt, sorrow and even longing in the presence of Mary Magdalene (played in fiery style by a tattoo-wearing Barbara Hershey) as he watches her engage in prostitution with an international array of clients. Pained, awkward and self-analytical in these early moments ("What if I say the wrong thing? What if I say the *right* thing?"), the film's Jesus changes markedly as the story progresses. He is seen addressing and conquering his doubts until he at last attains a joyful acceptance of his

A scene from Martin Scorsese's film "The Last Temptation of Christ."

role.

The promise held forth by the film's beginning, a promise to use drastic and unexpected ideas as a means of understanding Jesus' inner life, gradually gives way to something less focused. Though this handsome film was made on a small budget and a streamlined scale, it's big enough to wander from the central thread of its story. The opening sequences, which are abruptly strung together, are closely connected with Jesus' internal struggle, but they give way to a less emotionally compelling central section in which miracle after miracle is re-enacted. This part of the film, working as a kind of greatest hits sequence in which Jesus heals the sick, turns water to wine and raises a handsome young Lazarus from the grave, functions as pageantry without much passion.

•

A lot of the film has this stilted, showy quality, since it's often more apt to announce its ideas than to illustrate them. In contrast with the real spiritual torment conveyed by many of Mr. Scorsese's other characters, his version of Jesus is a controlled, slightly remote figure, despite the screenplay's many allusions to his pain. Fortunately, Willem Dafoe has such a gleaming intensity in this role, so much quiet authority, that the

film's images of Jesus are overwhelming even when the thoughts attributed to him are not. As photographed by Michael Ballhaus and staged by Mr. Scorsese, with many aspects of religious painting in mind, some of the film works better on a visual level than a verbal one. Many of the tableaux that come to life here, like the elaborate Palm Sunday scene, are altogether breathtaking.

The dialogue that accompanies these moments amounts to one of the film's great incongruities, since the language (in a screenplay by Paul Schrader) is often as intentionally flat as the imagery is starkly glorious. Peering out through various odd-looking beards and wigs are actors so identifiable and eccentric that they often upstage the material: though David Bowie makes a strikingly urbane Pontius Pilate, Andre Gregory as a chattering John the Baptist and Harry Dean Stanton as a fast-talking Saul (who becomes Paul) have a more distracting effect. So does Harvey Keitel, with red hair and an enlarged nose to play an eminently down-to-earth Judas, whose betrayal of Jesus is one of the many events that this film re-envisions. When a lion appears to Jesus in the desert and asks, in the voice of Mr. Keitel, "Don't you rekonnize me?", the film is in danger of becoming silly.

•

And yet, despite such maladroit moments, "The Last Temptation of Christ" finally exerts enormous power. What emerges most memorably is its sense of absolute conviction, never more palpable than in the final fantasy sequence that removes Jesus from the cross and creates for him the life of an ordinary man. Though this episode lasts longer than it should and is allowed to wander far afield, it finally has the mightily affirmative, truly visceral impact for which the whole film clearly strives. Anyone who questions the sincerity or seriousness of what Mr. Scorsese has attempted need only see the film to lay those doubts to rest.

1988 Ag 12, C1:1

TUCKER: THE MAN AND HIS DREAM, directed by Francis Ford Coppola; written by Arnold Schulman and David Seidler; cinematography by Vittorio Storaro; film editor, Priscilla Nedd; music by Joe Jackson; production designer, Dean Tavoularis; produced by Fred Roos and Fred Fuchs; released by Paramount Pictures. At Loews New York Twin, Second Avenue at 66th Street, and other theaters. Running time: 105 minutes. This film is rated PG.

Preston Tucker	Jeff Bridges
Vera	Joan Allen
Abe	Martin Landau
Eddie	Frederic Forrest
Jimmy	Mako
Alex	Elias Koteas
Junior	Christian Slater

Jeff Bridges

Glad-handing and gregarious, passionately dedicated to his work, fired by the beauty of a new idea, Preston Tucker in 1945 nearly set the auto industry on its ear. If he had preferred movies to cars, "Tucker" is the kind of film he would have made.

"Tucker: The Man and His Dream," which opens today at Loews New York Twin and other theaters, is instead the work of Francis Ford Coppola, who shares much of his subject's exuberance and all of his love for pie in the sky. Despite this, or perhaps because of it, "Tucker" is the best thing Mr. Coppola has done in years.

The film's cockeyed optimism, manifested by a visual style that makes everything look as brand spanking new and packed with promise as the Tucker automobile itself, becomes something of a secret weapon. Just beneath that sunny, stylized exterior, to which Mr. Coppola characteristically gives much more emphasis than is really necessary, lies a story of disappointment and failure. And the film's compulsive jauntiness, instead of generating easy irony, gives the film a wistful, bittersweet edge. The old photographs of the real Preston Tucker that accompany the film's closing credits seem especially moving in this light.

Jeff Bridges is just the right actor for the title role, capturing both Tucker's relentless snappiness and the hints of disbelief that begin to show through his smile. He gives Tucker's optimism great charm, then turns it into something genuinely heroic once it crashes head-on into the exigencies of American business. Preston Tucker, starting out as a man with boundless energy and an exhilarating new idea, became a casualty of the various corporate practices that interfered with his dream. The film, which rushes through the fine points of this with a Tucker-like breathlessness, strongly suggests that he was a victim of conspiracy as well. (In an inspired bit of casting, Lloyd Bridges makes a cameo appearance with his son as the Senator who apparently spearheads the auto industry's anti-Tucker campaign.)

Preston Tucker is first seen in a mock-promotional film that sets the tone of salesmanship for what will follow. He is then introduced as a family man in Ypsilanti, Mich., the kind of fellow who can come home with 12 new Dalmatians for no particular reason, then invite everyone in the neighborhood to supper. There's a grand, overstated element to his impulsiveness, but he makes it irresistible. So when Tucker begins daydreaming aloud about a new car that will incorporate pioneering safety features, look glorious and run like the wind, he finds many devoted assistants ready to carry out his ideas. "Looks like it's goin' 90 miles per hour standing still," one says admiringly, and it's true: the real Tucker cars used in the film are every bit as beautiful as what Tucker has promised.

To the accompaniment of "Hold That Tiger!" and Joe Jackson's jumping big-band score, Tucker forms a cadre of loyal assistants (led by Martin Landau as his business manager and Joan Allen as his devoted wife) and begins his huge job of salesmanship. As Tucker bursts from one scene into the next and often seems to be in two places at once, Mr. Coppola employs elaborate two-sided sets and stunningly artificial transitions, not only to indulge his own well-established taste for such showmanship, but to convey a hint of all that is double-edged in Tucker's world.

The film's overstatement begins to seem touchingly transparent once Tucker has begun putting his plans into effect and discovering the difficulty of actually putting his car into production. At a key point in this process, the film introduces him to a ghostly Howard Hughes (Dean Stockwell), whose Spruce Goose airplane hovers in the background, offering a hint of Tucker's own future.

Although one of Tucker's many mottos is "Don't let the future pass you by," the film suggests that this is exactly what happened to its hero. The Tucker car, which looks so spectacular in the jubilant sequence that has Tucker and several singing assistants unveiling a prototype for the press, later becomes its most stirring image of defeat. Alone in their factory, surrounded by the few cars they have manufactured and the strong likelihood that there will be no more, Tucker and his men must come to terms with their failure. But Mr. Coppola, typically and stirringly, finally celebrates their limited accomplishment and ends the film with a Tucker parade.

"Tucker" is a both a paean to the inventor's ingenuity and a lament for the lack of understanding that surrounds him. Filling the screen with images of hope and promise, from W.P.A. murals to the actors' sharp new clothes, Mr. Coppola gives the film a buoyant yet impassioned tone. The big-band music keeps on playing even when Tucker finds himself in court on charges of stock fraud, pleading his own case before an image of justice that is noticeably blind. "If Benjamin Franklin were alive today, he'd be arrested for flying a kite without a license." In the film's determinedly one-sided view, Tucker was a victim of this same kind of thinking.

Thanks to Vittorio Storaro's golden-hued cinematography, Dean Tavoularis's elaborate production design and Milena Canonero's handsome costumes, "Tucker" is extravagantly good looking. Mr. Coppola has done things this fancily before, but never with so clear and moving a sense of purpose.

•

"Tucker" is rated PG ("Parental Guidance Suggested"). It includes some strong language.
JANET MASLIN
1988 Ag 12, C8:1

Charmin' Billy

YOUNG GUNS, directed by Christopher Cain; written by John Fusco; director of photography, Dean Semler; edited by Jack Hofstra; music by Anthony Marinelli and Brian Banks; production designer, Jane Musky; produced by Joe Roth and Mr. Cain; released by 20th Century-Fox. At Manhattan Twin,

Western Kiefer Sutherland is in "Young Guns," Christopher Cain's action-adventure tale about six outcasts hired by an English merchant to safeguard his ranch.

Third Avenue at 59th Street, and other theaters. Running time: 97 minutes. This film is rated R.

William H. Bonney (Billy)	Emilio Estevez
Doc Scurlock	Kiefer Sutherland
Chavez Y. Chavez	Lou Diamond Phillips
Dick Brewer	Charlie Sheen
"Dirty Steve" Stephens	Dermot Mulroney
Charley Bowdre	Casey Siemaszko
John Tunstall	Terence Stamp
L. G. Murphy	Jack Palance
Alex McSween	Terry O'Quinn

The western "Young Guns," which opens today at the Manhattan Twin and other theaters, is less like a real movie than an extended photo opportunity for its trendy young stars. Dressing up in badges and holsters has often been an irresistible temptation for groups of photogenic young actors, and this film, in the tradition of "The Long Riders," is happy to watch its cast play cowboy on an elaborate scale. However, "Young Guns" doesn't make the mistake of taking itself too seriously. It's a good-humored exercise, if also a transparent one, and it sustains its spirit of fun right up to the point of a final shootout, in which the young heroes are badly outnumbered. Even so, the film manages to end on a cheery note.

"Young Guns" is, after all, a story of Billy the Kid's early days, the period in which he first made his reputation as a dangerous outlaw. A lot of blood is shed during this formative stage in his career, and the film stages Billy's first killings in a disconcertingly lighthearted way. However, Emilio Estevez gives Billy a convincingly humorous side, and some of the other actors — most notably Kiefer Sutherland as an amusingly sensitive type and Casey Siemaszko as the film's resident cut-up — also help to keep things genial. The stars, who also include Lou Diamond Phillips and Charlie Sheen, appear as the Regulator gang, a group originally deputized to help fight crime, until their enthusiasm got out of hand.

•

As directed by Christopher Cain, "Young Guns" makes no particular effort to strike a note of historical accuracy. Sequences like the one in which the young outlaws drink a peyote potion are staged in distinctly modern terms, and largely played for laughs. The film's look is also casu-

ally anachronistic, with a showy visual style that suggests an old sepia photograph bursting into life as a rock video. Mr. Cain often relies on hand-held camera work, even for a shot of a pheasant skittering across the prairie. The footage is often so stylishly shadowy and high-contrast that the stars' faces are hidden by their cowboy hats, with nothing visible but the tip of a nose.

"Young Guns" is best watched in the playful, none-too-serious spirit in which it was made. Though the film concentrates reverentially on its young stars, it also includes good performances from a few grown-ups, notably Terry O'Quinn as a lawyer and Jack Palance as the story's wild-eyed villain.
JANET MASLIN
1988 Ag 12, C18:1

Torn by Questions Of War and Ideals

Vered Cohen

LATE SUMMER BLUES, directed by Renen Schorr; written (in Hebrew with English subtitles) by Doron Nesher; story by Mr. Schorr; director of photography, Eitan Harris; editor, Shlomo Hazan; music by Rafi Kadishzon; produced by Ilan De Vries, Mr. Schorr and Mr. Nesher; released by Kino International Corporation. At the Bleecker Street Cinema, at La Guardia Place. Running time: 101 minutes. This film has no rating.

Arileh Schechter	Dor Zweigenbom
Mossi Shoval	Yoav Tsafir
Margo	Shahar Segal
Yossi Tsvillich	Omri Dolev
Naomi	Noa Goldberg
Shosh	Vered Cohen
Kobi	Sharon Bar-ziv

By CARYN JAMES

Any film about young men heading off to war is an easy trap for sentimentality, and a semi-autobiographical look at the naïve idealism of high-school days is dangerously prone to myopia. "Late Summer Blues" stumbles into both these pitfalls, as it tells of four Israeli high school graduates about to be drafted in the summer of 1970, when soldiers were dying in the war of attrition over control of land bordering the Suez Canal. Directed by Renen Schorr, who is the exact contemporary of his characters, this painfully sincere film begs us to respond with flashes of nostalgic recognition, to weep at the thought of warriors dying young. But it lacks the artistic vision and historical perspective that might have allowed this loaded material to resonate with true emotion.

The film has the episodic structure and small scale of cinéma vérité, and the narrative frame of a home movie. Each major character has a section named for him. Yossi, known as Joe, is inducted into the Army even before the graduation ceremonies take place; he writes in his diary that he regrets he has not had time to "get a driver's license or sleep with a girl." Three weeks later, he is dead, killed in an accident during training.

Arileh spray paints "Stop the War of Attrition" on every wall he can find. Mossi, the musician, decides they should dedicate the graduation play to Yossi. "A protest show! It'll be terrific!" he says, and the movie audience is forced to sit through a song and dance number that owes everything to "Hair." Margo, an aspiring film maker and a diabetic who is exempt from the draft, wanders through "Late Summer Blues" filming his friends. There is too little difference between his home movies, inserted throughout, and the rest of the film.

•

When Margo looks back three years and says in the final scene, "I can't believe that's how we were — so stupid, so beautiful, so pure," he offers the perspective that should have informed the film all along. Without it, Yossi's diary is merely familiar and banal, Arileh's rebellion seems anachronistic and Mossi's show naïve.

"Late Summer Blues," which opens today at the Bleecker Street Cinema, was a hit in Israel. There, it mirrored the past of many Israelis who, like the director and Arileh, found themelves torn over the war of attrition, questioning their Government for the first time. But even with its obvious parallels to American protests about the Vietnam War, the film (in Hebrew with English subtitles) is not artistically accomplished enough to make the Israeli youths of 1970 come to life for a general audience today.

The single triumph of "Late Summer Blues" is its acting, most by students and amateurs, who are so realistic that the film often feels like a documentary about ingenuous young people. By not acknowledging how familiar such idealism and rebellion have become, Mr. Schorr and the screenwriter, Doron Nesher, seem as innocent as their characters.

1988 Ag 12, C13:1

Amid the Alien Clones

MAC and Me directed by Stewart Raffill; written by Stewart Raffill and Steve Feke; director of photography, Nick McLean; edited by Tom Walls; music by Alan Silvestri; production designer, W. Stewart Campbell; produced by R. J. Louis; released by Orion Pictures. At Guild 50th Street, west of Fifth Avenue; D. W. Griffth, 59th Street, east of Third Avenue. Running time: 99 minutes.

Janet	Christine Ebersole
Michael	Jonathan Ward
Courtney	Katrina Caspary
Debbie	Lauren Stanley
Eric	Jade Calegory
Mitford	Vinnie Torrente
Wickett	Martin West

By CARYN JAMES

If you made a film about a homesick extraterrestrial befriended by a little boy, would you dare to have the creature look like E. T.'s cousin? "MAC and Me" is such a shameless clone that its cute little alien has E. T.'s gangly, prune-skinned body, his elongated arms and fingers, his enormous, mournful eyes — that look of a cross between an infant and his own grandfather. Only a 2-year-old or an amnesiac might be surprised at any of this film's Spielbergian turns. Fortunately, there is some residual charm left in these borrowings, so "MAC and Me" may be mildly amus-

ing to children too impatient to wait for the "E. T." video to be released this fall.

At the start, NASA captures a neat nuclear family — Mama Alien, Papa Alien, sister and baby brother — but they break loose from the space agency's lab. Somehow the littlest alien is separated and finds his way to Los Angeles. There he finds a single mom (Christine Ebersole), with a teen-age son and a younger child named Eric. The furniture is mysteriously rearranged, the television set turns on when it isn't plugged in, and soon Eric discovers MAC — the Mysterious Alien Creature.

The story's only original turn is that Eric is in a wheelchair. For a time this seems like a thoughtful, uncondescending statement about the ability of handicapped people to do everything. Eric is a smart, strong and self-sufficient hero. But it is alarming when he and his chair fall off a cliff and into a river — even if MAC is predictably there to save him from drowning. And by the time the film sends Eric careering into heavy traffic, the apparent thoughtfulness has turned awfully irresponsible.

With its cardboard family and familiar aliens, "MAC and Me" would seem like the generic version of "E. T." if it were not so full of brand-name commercials. Coke is the drink that revives dying aliens. Mom works at Sears, whose logo is all over the place. A huge birthday party takes place at McDonald's, where MAC dances around disguised in a bear suit. His brief dance and a scene in which the reunited family wanders into a supermarket are the film's least derivative and most appealing episodes.

"MAC and Me," which opened yesterday at the Guild and other theaters, has a final police shootout and a fiery explosion in which Eric is the victim. When a doctor announced that Eric was gone, a small boy behind me said, "He ain't dead," with all the calm assurance of an experienced moviegoer who knows perfectly well that if E. T. came back, so would Eric. Cloning is a dangerous thing.

•

"MAC and Me" is rated PG ("Parental Guidance Suggested"). MAC's abandonment and Eric's danger may be too strong for very young children.

1988 Ag 13, 14:1

FILM VIEW

When a Movie Serves a Mickey

By JANET MASLIN

IN "COCKTAIL," UNQUESTIONably the party-hearty movie of the year, the story's bartender hero, Brian Flanagan (Tom Cruise), recites this poem:

I see America drinking the fabulous cocktails I make,
America's getting stinking on something I stir or I shake.
America, you're just devoted to every flavor I've got,
But if you want to get loaded, why don't you just order a shot?

Recited in a crowded bar full of appreciative customers, this little offering brings down the house. Everybody toasts and laughs and cheers. The bartender is greeted with wild appreciation. But in the midst of all this hundred-proof excitement, something is missing: nobody's getting drunk.

That's strange, because the characters in "Cocktail" drink all the time. "Beer is for breakfast around here — drink or be gone!" warns Brian's mentor, Doug Coughlin (Bryan Brown), and the younger man takes this lesson to heart. When he does his homework — in his free time he is taking a business course, although the screenplay emphasizes that he's better off bartending than studying — he keeps a bottle by his side. Yet, Brian's drinking appears to be of little consequence. It has no effect on his demeanor (always genial), his professional style (frisky) or his ultimate goal (to "make a million"). If anything, it's so associated with the power and ease he craves that it may just help him along.

For all the many ways in which Hollywood has depicted serious drinking — and it has returned to this subject again and again, presenting it in far more wrenching and immediate terms than would be possible in other media — it has almost never taken the habit this lightly. The kind of regular drinking that Brian Flanagan does is almost always shown to have some larger impact on a character's life. There have been especially powerful films that

examined the pathology of alcohol addiction, from Billy Wilder's landmark "Lost Weekend" to "Days of Wine and Roses" and the current "Clean and Sober." In the last of these, a cooler, more contemporary look at the subject, Michael Keaton plays a savvy young professional who's been living the "Cocktail" life too long and finds himself in a detoxification center kicking alcohol and cocaine addiction simultaneously.

There have also been films that celebrated the happier side of heavy drinking, from the giddy "Arthur" to the sly, exuberantly raw "Barfly." And at a time when drinking carried more social cachet than it does at present, the "Thin Man" films gave it an aura of pure sophistication; how many mornings found Nick and Nora Charles trading hangover quips as they lounged about in silk pajamas? Alcohol has also had its uses as a dramatic device, freeing the memory and imagination for long reveries, as it did for Jack Nicholson's Francis Phelan in "Ironweed." Or it can play tricks on a character's consciousness, as it did for Jane Fonda in "The Morning After." Even the fraternity boys who threw beer at one another in "Animal House" and so many other food-fight movies seemed to take greater notice of it than Brian Flanagan does.

Films that examine the dangerous aspects of alcoholism often have similar frameworks, regardless of when they were made. Though 1988's "Clean and Sober" is much less melodramatic than 1945's "Lost Weekend" and much less scathing than 1962's unexpectedly enduring "Days of Wine and Roses," it has a great deal in common with each of them.

The latter film, which was directed by Blake Edwards, remains perhaps the saddest and most graphic anatomy of this problem, rendered especially wrenching by the fact that it details alcoholism a deux. The film's hero, a self-loathing public-relations man played by Jack Lemmon, has already acquired the habit of drinking to relieve on-the-job stress when he encounters the sweet young woman played by Lee Remick, a creature so naïve that she thinks a brandy Alexander is chocolate milk. In the early stages of their love affair, as he gradually in-

319

In "Cocktail," Tom Cruise is a bartender—connotations of success and fun

duces her to drink along with him, alcohol becomes central to the deeper intoxication of their romance.

Later on, the film watches carefully as the balance shifts back and forth between them. After these two marry, when their daughter is an infant, the mother chooses not to drink while the father stays out later and later without her. In one of the film's most painful scenes, he comes home soused and angry one night, demanding that his wife — who isn't drinking because she's a nursing mother — stop being a teetotaler and start being a little fun. At the end of the scene, she has agreed to start feeding the baby formula and has resumed her drinking. And not long thereafter she has taken the lead, discouraging her husband when *he* attempts to kick the habit. The film ricochets back and forth from husband to wife, binge to binge, Alcoholics Anonymous meeting to detox center, in detailing the disastrous impact of drinking on these characters' lives.

Here, as in other films treating alcoholism as a grave problem, one major element is the addict's feverish concern with the exact location of whatever drugs or alcohol he or she has been able to hide. One person who often understands this keenly is the bartender himself, traditionally quite a different figure from the "Cocktail" type. In "The Lost Weekend," the fatherly bartender played by Howard Da Silva repeatedly warns Ray Milland that he's got a problem.

Another key ingredient is the turning to petty crime — in "The Lost Weekend," Ray Milland pockets a cleaning woman's wages and steals a handbag in a nightclub — in order to finance the habit. And a third, once the decision to recover has been made, is the helpfulness of supportive outsiders, often explicitly connected with Alcoholics Anonymous, in helping to provide some incentive for change. Together, these ingredients are the backbone of any film choosing to treat substance abuse as a kind of sickness.

And playfulness is essential to any film that chooses to give it a comic spin. The irrepressible Arthur, still cackling wildly at his own jokes in "Arthur 2 on the Rocks," is presented unmistakably as a case of arrested development, which is a lot of what makes him funny. In this, as in the first film, Arthur likes ferrying his martinis around via model electric train and otherwise demonstrating a childish glee; he also favors boyish in-

sults and a charming obliviousness to any possible consequences of his behavior.

Both films shared this obliviousness, the first much more successfully than the second, and it went a long way toward making at least the earlier one funny. The recent sequel, in which Arthur and his wife try to adopt a child and the adoption agency pays little heed to his drinking problem, has a lot more trouble doing this than the first. In both films, though, Dudley Moore's wild glass-waving is reserved for certain key scenes. Most of his performance has an unobtrusively levelheaded side, which makes it much more appealing than non-stop drunkenness would be.

At the very least, even in a film as merry as "Arthur," inebriation signals some loss of control. It suggests an unhappiness with some other aspect of a character's life,

whether it's Arthur's weighty responsibilities in handling the $750 million that he either does or does not have (both screenplays threaten to take it away from him) or the writer's block used by "The Lost Weekend" to explain its hero's downward slide (in the end, he recovers enough to begin writing a novel called "The Bottle"). For Jane Fonda's over-the-hill actress in "The Morning After," drinking is connected with the decline of a career. But neither Brian Flanagan nor "Cocktail" experiences any of these troubling touches, which is what makes the film so peculiar. Brian, who admittedly drinks less than any of these others but is also a good deal younger, is able to regard alcohol as an uncomplicatedly positive thing.

For him, drinking becomes closely associated with friendship (it cements his bond with the dapper Coughlin, who says things like: "A bartender is the aristocrat of the working world"). It's also connected with family; Brian's salt-of-the-earth uncle, who dishes out homilies like "most things in life, good and bad, just kinda happen to you," owns a tavern himself. It has to do with sex, which the film treats almost as casually as it does drinking, since his position as an ice-flinging, glass-juggling show-stopper makes Brian a prime target for his highly available female customers. (However much they drink, neither Brian nor Doug does any damage with the glassware.) Perhaps most important, drinking in "Cocktail" is tied in with Brian's larger notions about making it big.

■

The unusual thing about this is the viewing of alcohol in terms of power and status, rather than in terms of physiology. "Cocktail" treats alcohol chiefly as one of the trappings of 80's-style glamour. As on "Dallas," a TV program that is directed so that characters seem to be pouring or ordering drinks in almost every scene, the use of alcohol is so divorced from the *effects* of alcohol that it takes on a separate meaning.

Lee Remick and Jack Lemmon in Blake Edwards's "Days of Wine and Roses"—perhaps the saddest and most graphic anatomy of problem drinking

It becomes a sign of power and ease, signaling *more* control, rather than less; it becomes a route to success, rather than a hindrance. For Brian, who reads books with titles like "How to Turn Your Idea Into a Million Dollars," the bartender's life will lead to rich, beautiful women, expensive accommodations and general high-rolling playing. Alcohol is just his way of greasing the wheels.

Since Brian, as played by the ever-grinning Mr. Cruise, is one of the most vacant movie characters in memory, it's possible to believe that this is all he sees. In the easygoing, on-the-make scheme of "Cocktail," it is of course possible to drink a lot and face no consequences, just as it's possible to fall in love with a sweet, simple girl and have her turn out to be a heiress all the same. Everything falls effortlessly into place for Brian, and despite one highly melodramatic subplot, there are no real costs. The film begins with Brian's army buddies drunkenly driving along to help him catch his bus to New York, and it ends just as effervescently. Last line: "The bar is open!"

Meanwhile, any audience tempted by the high-spirited, rock-and-rolling silliness of "Cocktail" will be barraged by subliminal information. Alcohol itself, presented as a substance of no particular consequence, inevitably takes on the connotations of success and fun, just it might in an advertising campaign. So, it's a long, painful and essential leap from this to "Clean and Sober," which presents the other side of the story in no uncertain terms. If the contrast between the two films makes anything clear, it's this: Whether alcohol is presented in a tragic light or a funny one, whether it's seen as damaging or delightful, there is nothing more reckless than treating it lightly. Nothing could be worse than pretending it doesn't matter. □

1988 Ag 14, II:1:3

The Bitter and Sweet Of Autumnal Affection

THE WASH, directed by Michael Toshiyuki Uno; written by Philip Kan Gotanda; director of photography, Walt Lloyd; edited by Jay Freund; music by John Morris; production designer, David Wasco; produced by Calvin Skaggs; released by Skouras Pictures. At 57th Street Playhouse, at Avenue of the Americas. Running time: 94 minutes. This film is not rated.

Nobu	Mako
Masi	Nobu McCarthy
Marsha	Patti Yasutake
Judy	Marion Yue
Sadao	Sab Shimono
Kiyoko	Shizuko Hoshi

By CARYN JAMES

A Japanese-American woman in her 60's, so average and middle-class she might have stepped out of a detergent commercial, glares at her stubborn, self-absorbed husband. With a controlled intensity that carries the weight of 40 years, she asks, "Why don't you want me anymore?" That emotionally honest moment at the center of "The Wash" is one of many powerful scenes that shape this story of an older couple's painful separation and funny new romances. Though set in a Japanese section of San Jose, Calif., the small-scale film is less about any ethnic community than it is about the confused feelings that arise when a woman whose generation is more apt to endure unhappy marriages than to rupture them finally changes her life.

"The Wash" begins eight months after Masi has left her husband, Nobu, and she still stops by every week to do his laundry. Gruff, proud and inflexible, he builds kites but never varies the design, because "My old man did it this way." Nobu has found a substitute for Masi in a good-natured, middle-aged waitress named Kiyoko ("She's young," says one of Nobu's daughters. "Tacky, but young."), whom he already takes for granted. He stops by the restaurant to get free meals and yells when Kiyoko serves the wrong kind of pickles.

The husband's unbending character (played by Mako) is limited. It is Masi who changes, and the actress Nobu McCarthy defines her with brilliance and subtlety as a woman who is strong-willed but tentative about her new life.

The most tender, understated moments are between Masi and her suitor, Sadao (Sab Shimono). As they sit stiffly in Masi's living room, Sadao chats about methods of decaffeinating coffee while Masi nervously serves Sanka with nondairy creamer. They are as awkward and touching as adolescents on a first date. Sadao teaches Masi to fish; he takes her to the movies. And eventually when they move into each other's arms it is a natural and lovely gesture that by contrast makes Nobu's bad temper less tolerable than ever. Though Masi has been saddened by her aging physical charms, she is pleased and unsurprised that she is still desirable.

Nobu has saddened her the most. Late in the film, when he asks Masi to

Mako, left, and Nobu McCarthy in a scene from "The Wash."

sleep with him after years of inattention, he can only deflect the real question by asking, "Why don't you cook me breakfast?" The great strength of "The Wash," is that, through Masi, we see Nobu sympathetically, as the victim of his own intolerance. When their daughter Marsha invites her parents to dinner, Nobu is typically silent, except when he's starting a fight. Yet Masi laughingly accepts his skewed version of a compliment and apology as he recalls their youth. "You were a good dancer," he says. "You were! Best in all the relocation camps!"

Masi encourages their younger daughter, Judy, to forgive her father, who has shunned her for marrying a black man. But Masi herself is perfectly capable of yelling at Nobu, "You don't like white people, you don't like black people, you don't like Mexicans; so what *do* you like?"

At times "The Wash," written by Philip Kan Gotanda from his own play, threatens to slide into clichés. Masi proclaims she has "the right to be happy"; Marsha's relationship with her inconsiderate boyfriend too neatly mirrors her parents' marriage, and Nobu has an unlikely last-minute reconciliation with Judy. But in his first feature, the director, Michael Toshiyuki Uno, manages to glide over the script's weaker moments with first-rate performances from the entire cast, including Patti Yasutake as Marsha and Shizuko Hoshi as Kiyoko. Even the suburban design of the film, from the boxy rooms to Masi's housewifely slacks and blouses, is thoroughly believable.

And when it is crucial to avoid sappiness, the film does. Though Masi asks for a divorce so she can marry Sadeo — it is a wrenching, angry confrontation — the film ends with the engaged couple visiting the grave of Sadeo's wife. His own name waits on

the gravestone, a poignant reminder that for all the happiness of their new lives, the claims of the past weigh heavily. At such moments "The Wash," which opens today at the 57th Street Playhouse, is a triumph of intelligent acting and film making.

1988 Ag 17, C17:4

Russian Punk Scene

Film Forum

Konstantin Kinchev, Soviet rock star, in film "The Burglar."

THE BURGLAR, directed by Valery Ogorodnikov; written (Russian with English subtitles) by Valery Priyemykhov; director of photography, Valery Mironov; art director, Viktor Ivanov; produced by Lenfilm Studios. Released by International Film Exchange. At Film Forum 1, 57 Watts Street. Running time: 89 minutes. This film is not rated.

Senka Laushkin	Oleg Yelykomov
Kostya Laushkin	Konstantin Kinchev
Father	Yuri Tsapnik
Sveta	Svetlana Gaitan
Angelina	Polina Petrenko

By JANET MASLIN

Glasnost has made it possible for the Soviet director Valery Ogorodnikov to turn his cameras on a rebellious teen-age culture that must seem shocking by Soviet standards, though to Western eyes it will look relatively tame. Much of it can be found at the community centers where, under very noticeable adult supervision, Leningrad's adolescents gather to sing the rock-and-roll songs that constitute their main means of expressing individuality.

Idiosyncrasies of dress are possible, too — styling mousse has clearly made its way to Soviet shores — but there are distinct limits. A young man who pushes his fashion statement too far may find himself rounded up by police, asked for identification and told to rethink his wardrobe.

"The Burglar," which opens today at the Film Forum 1, reflects a strong Western influence, which must make it all the more startling for Soviet audiences. The musicians who perform in the film, singing what must surely be their own compositions, owe obvious debts to everyone from Elvis Presley to Talking Heads, though their lyrics must lose a great deal in translation (as one song puts it, "Pain and joy have brushed their teeth and gone to bed").

For every musical interlude in which the singers struggle with Anglicisms like "boogie-woogie," the film includes glimpses of more formal Soviet musical training. Dance classes of cookie-cutter-pretty little ballerinas are observed, and the film's young hero, a pensive pre-teen-age boy named Senka Laushkin (Oleg Yelykomov), plays in a boys' band whose teacher has a more traditional sense of music and its importance. "We make people happy, boys," he tells the students. "One false note can spoil the mood of thousands of good people."

•

"The Burglar" explores Senka's relationship with an older brother named Kostya (Konstantin Kinchev), who is deeply involved in local punk society and has the MTV T-shirt to prove it. Eager for contact with the wider world, Kostya and his friends study slides of everything from the assassination attempt on the Pope to a beach scene in Japan, and one of the group has adopted the Westernized word "Howmuch" as his nickname. "He looks like Howmuch," someone remarks, upon seeing a slide of Elvis Presley.

Left on their own after the death of their mother, which has turned their father into a hard-drinking ladies' man, the brothers are seen navigating their way through a society that does little to help them. Kostya has already cast his lot with his rebellious contemporaries. But young Senka is still adrift, and the film greatly underscores the bleakness of his situation. In an earnest but predictably plaintive way, it follows the disastrous route Senka takes in trying to become closer to his brother.

The performances are uncomplicatedly sincere, and the film's only real surprise is that Mr. Kinchev, whose musical performances as Kostya would seem to indicate otherwise, is in fact a big Soviet rock star.

1988 Ag 17, C22:1

A One-Man Career Crusade

THE BEER DRINKER'S GUIDE TO FITNESS AND FILM MAKING, directed, written, produced and edited by Fred G. Sullivan; director of photography, Hal Landen; music by Kenneth Higgins and James Calabrese. Released by Adirondack Alliance Film Corporation. At the Bleecker Street Cinema, at La Guardia Place. Running time: 84 minutes. This film is rated PG.

Fred G.	Fred G. Sullivan
Polly	Polly Sullivan
Tate	Tate Sullivan
Katie	Katie Sullivan
Kirk	Kirk Sullivan
Ricky	Ricky Sullivan
The Temptress	Jan Jalenak

The four little children of Fred G. Sullivan, a k a "Adirondack Fred," do not want to starve. And they don't want to be sold to the gypsies, either. They say as much, several times, during the course of Mr. Sullivan's "Beer Drinker's Guide to Fitness and Film Making," in hopes that this film will let their father strike it rich and stop having to worry about where the next diaper is coming from. But audiences may hope otherwise, despite the fact that Mr. Sullivan's jokey, charmingly ingenuous (and actually very elaborate) home movie happens to be a real delight.

Complain as Mr. Sullivan does about the hardships of film making and family life, there is reason to think that he's still got it made. Not financially, of course; this film, which fully details the life of the director (who is also writer, editor, producer and star), his wife, Polly, and their offspring, makes it clear that theirs is not a conventionally glamorous life. Mr. Sullivan tries his best, suggesting that the family's small, overcrowded house in Saranac Lake, N.Y., be renamed a "bungalow" because that sounds more Hollywood. But in fact, as a speeded-up montage of a day in the life of the Sullivans (with baths, trips in the station wagon, and tricycles all over the front yard) makes clear, things are tough.

They are made tougher by the fact that Fred G., as he's called by various friends and neighbors, insists that he is a film maker, despite strong reasons to think otherwise. Mr. Sullivan's only other feature, something called "Cold River," didn't go far (although he proudly includes footage of a multiplex movie marquee listing "Cold River" right beside "Cheech and Chong's Nice Dreams"). In another part of town, Mr. Sullivan still holes up in his film-making office, spending most of his time answering phone calls from bill collectors (if this footage is to be believed). Refusing to give up, he feels he has no recourse but to make some film, *any* film, to find out whether he's got what it takes. It's nice to be able to report that he does.

"The Beer Drinker's Guide to Fitness and Film Making," which opens today at the Bleecker Street Cinema, is as peculiar as its title, an unpredictable amalgam of Mr. Sullivan's random thoughts about his career, his children, his personal history and his favorite beverages. "With wine, Fred and Polly go for quantity over quality," says one of several merchants interviewed about obscure Sullivania. "To tell you the truth, I haven't thought about him in maybe 20 years," says Fred's coach from high school. "Oh, thank God, I didn't know you then!" says Polly, when the focus turns to Fred's early stabs at film making. Also tottering through the film is a large Russian-speaking bear who prompts various bathroom jokes (Mr. Sullivan tailors the occasional gag to his children's sense of humor) and orders the film maker to take a long hard look at his priorities.

In its last moments, which are suddenly quite touching, "The Beer Drinker's Guide to Fitness and Film Making" makes its purpose clear: to turn a time in the Sullivan children's lives and a portrait of their parents into a live-action family album that will preserve these memories. It's remarkable that Mr. Sullivan does this with so little vanity and so much wry, self-deprecating humor. The scenes involving the fate of "Cold River" first show Mr. Sullivan, dressed in a loin cloth with leather straps across his chest, wandering a burning desert with a film can in either hand; this is his idea of what looking for a distributor was like. After that, he is seen in a tuxedo, having mud slung at him as the reviews come in. Things will be different this time.

•

"The Beer Drinker's Guide to Fitness and Film Making" is rated PG ("Parental Guidance Suggested"). It contains occasional profanity and brief nudity. JANET MASLIN

1988 Ag 19, C6:5

All in the Family Business

Dean Stockwell

MARRIED TO THE MOB, directed by Jonathan Demme; written by Barry Strugatz and Mark R. Burns; director of photography, Tak Fujimoto; edited by Craig McKay; music by David Byrne; production designer, Kristi Zea; produced by Kenneth Utt and Edward Saxon; released by Orion Pictures. At Loews New York Twin, Second Avenue and 66th Street, and other theaters. Running time: 103 minutes. This film is rated R.

Angela De Marco	Michelle Pfeiffer
Mike Downey	Matthew Modine
Tony (The Tiger) Russo	Dean Stockwell
Connie Russo	Mercedes Ruehl
Frank (Cucumber) De Marco	Alec Baldwin
Rose	Joan Cusack
Theresa	Ellen Foley
Phyllis	O-Lan Jones
Joey De Marco	Anthony J. Nici
The Priest	David Johansen
Rita (Hello Gorgeous) Harcourt	Sister Carol East

By JANET MASLIN

Jonathan Demme is the American cinema's king of amusing artifacts: blinding bric-a-brac, the junkiest of jewelry, costumes so frightening they take your breath away. Mr. Demme may joke, but he's also capable of suggesting that the very fabric of American life may be woven of such things, and that it takes a merry and adventurous spirit to make the most of them. In addition, Mr. Demme has an unusually fine ear for musical novelty, and the sounds that waft through his films heighten the visual impression of pure, freewheeling vitality. If making these films is half as much fun as watching them, Mr. Demme must be a happy man.

"Married to the Mob," which opens today at Loews New York Twin and other theaters, is much more lightweight than Mr. Demme's wonderful "Something Wild," but it's in the same exuberant vein. As usual, the director has found himself the perfect theme song, which in this case is "Mambo Italiano," sung by Rosemary Clooney. Close your eyes while this plays during the opening credits and you may well visualize the entire film ahead of time, from its quiet opening in a chandelier-filled corner of Long Island to the climactic sequence set in the Honeymoon Suite of the Eden Roc Hotel in Miami Beach.

In telling a story that hinges on stereotypical Italian gangsters, Mr. Demme conjures up a comic garishness that is really something special. He makes this even funnier by underscoring the aspects of mob-related home life that are, by these standards, utterly mundane. As the wife of "Cucumber," Frank De Marco (Alec Baldwin), the film's heroine Angela (Michelle Pfeiffer) has a home life fraught with problems, not the least of which is wondering how her philandering husband got his nickname. For instance, there's a revolver in the kitchen drawer, in easy reach of the couple's young son (Anthony J. Nici), who's in any case too busy running a three-card monte game in the backyard to notice.

•

There are other mob wives (Joan Cusack, O-Lan Jones, Ellen Foley and Mercedes Ruehl) who pronounce themselves Angela's friends "whether you like it or not." And there's the fact that, as Angela puts it to Frank, "Everything we wear, eat or own fell off a truck." No wonder Angela looks pink-eyed and weepy most of the time.

Frank and an associate are first seen in business suits, waiting for a commuter train as if this were second nature to them. They are there to assassinate another mobster, who is also dressed as if headed for an office job. That same evening, after having neatly knocked off their target, the two hit men meet with the rest of their mob family and are congratulated on "a beautiful ride." The setting for this is a place called the King's Roost, where each arriving mobster gives a pat on the cheek — a *hard* pat on the cheek — to a doorman who wears a full suit of armor. Mr. Demme has a great eye for this sort of detail.

The head of the family is Tony the Tiger (Dean Stockwell), who enters the place grandly bestowing big tips and pieces of his wardrobe — a silk scarf here, a vicuña coat there — on everyone in sight. Later in the evening, when Frank makes the mistake of fooling around with the waitress whom Tony has given a diamond necklace, Tony calmly makes Angela a widow.

•

This becomes the film's excuse for saying goodbye to mob life (after a funeral presided over by the singer David Johansen as a solemn priest) and embarking on a journey of discovery. It follows Angela as she moves to the Lower East Side, searches tremulously for a job, and winds up putting her beautician's skills to use at a place called Hello Gorgeous (run by Sister Carol East, the reggae singer who gave "Something Wild" such a terrific send-off). Unbeknownst to Angela, she does all this under the surveillance of a zany F.B.I. man (Matthew Modine) whose real target is Tony the Tiger. Just because Tony was seen kissing Angela at her husband's funeral, and later gave her various gifts covered in gilt wrap, red hearts and white lovebirds,

Case Thwarted
Michelle Pfeiffer hugs Matthew Modine in "Married to the Mob," Jonathan Demme's comedy about an F.B.I. agent who falls in love with the widow of a murdered Mafia chief.

the F.B.I. thinks Angela may help the agents nail their man.

With a screenplay by Barry Strugatz and Mark R. Burns, "Married to the Mob" works best as a wildly overdecorated screwball farce, given an extra spin by the subplot that sends Connie, Tony's wife (Miss Ruehl), into the most hilarious of jealous rages. It also plays as a gentle romance, and as the story of a woman trying to re-invent her life. Unlike "Something Wild," which sent its two chief characters on a true voyage into the unknown and turned each of them inside out before it was over, "Married to the Mob" has no real breakout quality. A closing montage, composed of glimpses of scenes that have evidently since been cut, suggests there may at some point have been more to it, but the finished film remains amiably thin.

•

Though Mr. Demme's "Something Wild" stars, Jeff Daniels and Melanie Griffith, set off palpable fireworks once the film threw them together, Miss Pfeiffer and Mr. Modine don't connect in the same way. Mr. Modine, a very likable actor, brings a nicely bemused quality to his role, but he doesn't have the game, nutty side suggested by the screenplay. Miss Pfeiffer, who looks utterly ravishing in outfits that set the teeth on edge, turns Angela's plight into something funny, but she seems eminently sane even when the movie does not. Appealing as they are, the two leads are readily upstaged by Miss Ruehl and, especially, by Mr. Stockwell. His shoulder-rolling caricature of this suave, foppish and thoroughly henpecked kingpin is the film's biggest treat.

"Married to the Mob" also draws upon the talents of David Byrne, whose score drifts mischievously through the film, and Tak Fujimoto, Mr. Demme's longtime cameraman, who can imbue the ghastliest settings with full-bodied, jubilant good looks. The Eden Roc's Honeymoon Suite, which, if the film can be believed, has golden dolphins on the walls and tufts of turquoise fluff on the bedspread, is a challenge even for him.

1988 Ag 19, C6:1

Dream the Dreams, Scream the Screams

A NIGHTMARE ON ELM STREET 4: THE DREAM MASTER directed by Renny Harlin; written by Brian Helgeland and Scott Pierce; story by William Kotzwinkle and Mr. Helgeland; director of photography, Steven Fierberg; edited by Michael N. Knue and Chuck Weiss; music by Craig Safan; production designers, Mick Strawn and C. J. Strawn; produced by Robert Shaye and Rachel Talalay; released by New Line Cinema. At Loews

Robert Englund

Astor Plaza, 44th Street and Broadway, and other theaters. Running time: 93 minutes. This film is rated R.

Freddy Krueger	Robert Englund
Joey	Rodney Eastman
Danny	Danny Hassel
Rick	Andras Jones
Kristen	Tuesday Knight
Sheila	Toy Newkirk
Alice	Lisa Wilcox

By CARYN JAMES

The best job on Elm Street must be the undertaker's — business booms and is full of variety, thanks to endless deaths by special effects. The victims of Freddy Krueger are not simply slashed by the burned-to-death child murderer with the razor-clawed gloves who invades their dreams. In "A Nightmare on Elm Street 4: The Dream Master," they are tortured by fire, water, earth and air. A woman burns, a man drowns in his waterbed, someone sinks into quicksand and several fly through the air. Where else would a young woman's arms fall off and be replaced by a bug's feelers, the better for her to be glued to death in a roach motel?

If this transformation of human into bug brings Kafka to mind, don't give it another thought. Though the "Elm Street" series contains the most intelligent premise in current genre films, none of the movies take much advantage of their potential. As Freddy weaves in and out of high school students' dreams, he offers endless possibilities for keeping audiences off guard; you never know when the teen-agers will wake from a nightmare, terrorized but alive, and when Freddy will decide they've dreamed their last and make the nightmare come true. That eerie slide between dream and reality, and the teen-agers' power to pull their friends into their nightmares (as if fighting Freddy is a class trip), is just the kind of twist that allows film makers to redefine a genre.

But the wildly successsful "Elm Street" series has not made its mark by raising unconscious fears. Freddy, in fact, has become an almost-cuddly cult personality, who has his own fan club. Instead, the films rely on ever-

more-shocking special effects, a technique "Elm Street 4" exploits so well it barely needs a plot at all.

The three survivors from "Elm Street 3" meet in Kristen's dream, and are killed off early, but not before she has unwittingly passed her meek friend Alice on to Freddy. Alice has an idea about mastering dreams by thinking pleasant thoughts, a theory so off that the film practically ignores it.

"Elm Street 4" does have an endless onslaught of astonishing, often grotesque special effects, though. At the start Freddy is merely a few bones thrown around the pit where he was last buried. Suddenly the bones move themselves together like magic, Freddy's scarred face emerges from his skull, and he calmly picks up his hat and puts it on with its usual rakish tilt. Freddy has little to say for himself here; even his usual wisecracks are overwhelmed by the film's visual busyness.

In some of the best scenes, Alice watches a movie, which contains the town diner where she works. Suddenly she flies over the theater seats and lands on screen, where Freddy sits at the counter waiting to be served. He gets a large pizza, with the tiny faces of his victims replacing the pepperoni.

When the shy Alice finally battles Freddy one on one, she leaps through a mirror and finds herself in an abandoned church. The souls of murdered children poke out of Freddy's chest, little faces wrapped in flesh, shaping a horrifying bas-relief. It is all technically impressive, and emotionally like being at a stomach-churning circus.

Each "Elm Street" film has had a different director. "Elm Street 4," which opens today at Loews Astor Plaza and other theaters, was done by the young Finnish director Renny Harlin, who has two abysmal films to his credit, the macho "Born American" and the recent horror story "Prison." Mr. Harlin only has to keep things moving, which he does with restless camera work, swirling high above Freddy and his victims. Freddy, who says "I am eternal," seems to be a self-fulfilling prophecy, immune to directors and scripts.

1988 Ag 19, C8:3

THE BIG BLUE directed by Luc Besson; written by Mr. Besson and Robert Garland; director of photography, Carlo Varini; edited by Olivier Mauffroy; production designer, Dan Weil; produced by Patrice Ledoux; released by Columbia Pictures. At Movieland, Broadway at 47th Street; the Sutton, 57th Street at Third Avenue. Running time: 119 minutes. This film is rated PG.

Joanna	Rosanna Arquette
Jacques Mayol	Jean-Marc Barr
Enzo Molinari	Jean Reno
Dr. Laurence	Paul Shenar
Novelli	Sergio Castellito
Uncle Louis	Jean Bouise
Roberto	Marc Duret
Duffy	Griffin Dunne

By JANET MASLIN

At one point in "The Big Blue," Jacques Mayol (Jean-Marc Barr), the not-of-this-world deep sea diver who is the elusive hero of Luc Besson's new film, shows his wallet to a friend. There's a nicely framed picture of a dolphin inside. "That's my family," Jacques says shyly, then he asks, "What kind of man has such a family?" Good question.

"The Big Blue" provides an answer, after a fashion. It also reveals, among other things, what might happen if two men in evening clothes

Rosanna Arquette

practicing the art of free diving (done without air tanks) were to share a bottle of champagne underwater. When the bottle was uncorked, bubbles would escape. When the wine was poured into glasses, some of it would get there without dissolving into water. After that, it would be anyone's guess. So many things are, really.

Although "The Big Blue" was made in English by a French director, it does not show signs of being workable in any tongue, save perhaps for the language of the briny deep. And a lot of what happens here would beggar even a dolphin's understanding. But the film has a handsome, expensive look and a charmingly inscrutable manner that make it easier to take than it would have been staged more solemnly. The scenery is glorious, and that doesn't hurt either.

"The Big Blue" begins in gray, with a prologue showing Jacques as a young boy learning to dive off the craggy coast of Greece; here and in other parts of the film, Mr. Besson uses spectacular helicopter shots that speed bracingly across the surface of the water. Later on, when Jacques has grown up and the footage has blossomed into full color, the film roams from Peru to the Riviera, New York to Sicily in search of purpose. Jacques is reunited with his childhood rival Enzo, now grown into a raffish diving champion (and played very drolly by Jean Reno). He also meets Joanna (Rosanna Arquette), an American insurance executive who is sent by Mr. Besson's devil-may-care story (with a screenplay co-written by Robert Garland) from the midst of a llama herd to the scenic cliffs of Taormina. The film doesn't try overly hard to explain her presence, and that's just as well.

Miss Arquette is attractively game in this role, but the sad fact is that she's playing second fiddle to fish. Jacques is in love with the deep, as is Enzo, and the film's most heartfelt passages are those that observe these two diving rivals as they brave the watery depths. The film's undersea footage has a powerful otherworldly quality, much as if it were unfolding in outer space, as indeed it might be. Mr. Besson clearly intends a mystical element to all this, but the beautifully filmed scenes of Jacques cavorting with dolphins are at least as nutty as they are picturesque.

"The Big Blue" opened yesterday at Loew's 84th Street and a great many other theaters, where it is being advertised as "The Motion Picture Event of the Summer." Since it's not a mainstream film by any stretch of the imagination, this is misleading even by movie-ad standards.

•

"The Big Blue" is rated PG ("Parental Guidance Suggested"). It contains brief nudity.

1988 Ag 20, 11:4

THE NEW YORK TIMES

FILM VIEW/Janet Maslin

Two Directors Put Their Stamp On Their Dreams

BACK IN 1974, FRANCIS FORD Coppola was already mentioning the auto-industry maverick Preston Tucker as a future film subject. And Martin Scorsese had been given a copy of Nikos Kazantzakis's "Last Temptation of Christ" while making "Boxcar Bertha," which was released in 1972. When a project hangs over a film maker's career for a decade and a half, how can it fail to become a monumental albatross? The film maker's decision to keep such an idea in sight must surely indicate that the project has become (to invoke one of Mr. Coppola's much less vital undertakings) one from the heart.

As it happens, Mr. Coppola's new "Tucker" and Mr. Scorsese's "Last Temptation of Christ," which after all those years on the drawing board had the odd fortune to open on the very same day, both display unmistakable signs of the men who made them. The director's individual hallmark can be found in each of these films' depiction of its central character, who reflects more than a little of the film maker's own personality. But the signature touches go well beyond that. It would be possible to see either film without benefit of identifying credits and still know exactly whose work was on the screen.

■

It's especially easy to see why the career trajectory and the upbeat, sunny salesmanship of Preston Tucker held such fascination for Mr. Coppola, since the parallels with his own personality are so clear. The film's Tucker will sound a familiar note for anyone who followed Mr. Coppola's passionately idealistic plans for American Zoetrope, the film studio that he once envisioned as the most innovative, far-reaching facility of its kind. From the sound of it, there was nothing that Zoetrope wouldn't have the high-tech equipment or the high-minded adventuresomeness to try. "Tucker" is filled with this kind of excitement, and also with the idea that its hero's ultimate business failure can be construed as a bittersweet and very backhanded moral victory. Mr. Coppola was forced to sell his studio at auction in 1984 and has lately said that his days of working within the Hollywood system are over.

The portrait that "Tucker" offers feels like Mr. Coppola's best-case version of his own story; in that light, it's all the more startling that he seized on the idea so long ago, before its promise had come true. From the top of the heap, in 1974, just after having made "The Godfather: Part II" and "The Conversation," Mr. Coppola said: "People thought Tucker was a con man, and maybe in some ways he was, but he was also legit. That's a duality that interests me because I've been accused of being a con man in the last five years. People tell me, 'You've been successful because you're a good talker, and you wheel and deal.' " For all that emphasis on breeziness and cunning, the other side of the Tucker coin, the side that forced the collapse

of Tucker's business, must in some way have been in the director's mind.

"Tucker" is Mr. Coppola's best work in years because of that very thread of disappointment, the ominous undercurrent that

pervades even the film's sweetest scenes. Characteristically overdirected, with lavish sets and costumes and an oversupply of attention-getting visual tricks, "Tucker" manages to brim with hope and promise and simultaneously suggest imminent disaster. In the title role, Jeff Bridges is the ideal embodiment of this story's contradictions, registering such boundless hope and enthusiasm in the film's early scenes and such poignant disbelief when things go wrong.

In making "Tucker," Mr. Coppola has returned to his own best subject — the underside of American business, as paradoxically buoyant and golden here as it is darkly ironic in the "Godfather" films — and given it a ruefully personal dimension. "Tucker" combines the elaborate showmanship of the director's recent work with an urgent sense of purpose, and the combined effect gives his work a weight it has long been missing.

Mr. Scorsese's "Last Temptation of Christ" is, if anything, even more closely attuned to its director's own passionate interests, no matter

Ralph Nelson Jr. ("Tucker")

At top, Barbara Hershey, Willem Dafoe and Harvey Keitel in "The Last Temptation of Christ"; above, Joan Allen and Jeff Bridges in "Tucker"

how universal its subject may seem. If the audacious Kazantzakis novel provides the framework for the revisionist portrait of Jesus Christ that is presented here, Mr. Scorsese himself sets a distinctively street-wise tone.

■

The abstract idea of struggle — of a Jesus who learns to embrace his mission by at first attempting to resist it — is amplified by decidedly down-to-earth touches that recall the director's earlier work. This film's questioning tone, its occasional bits of inner monologue, its flashes of unexpected joking and even its determinedly grim and visceral concept of sacrifice are powerfully reminiscent of Mr. Scorsese's earlier work. So is the casting, which is often eccentric (Harvey Keitel as a savvy, conversational Judas; David Bowie as a drily elegant Pontius Pilate) to say the least.

The fact that "The Last Temptation of Christ" presents an extremely urgent and personal vision is in grave danger of being overlooked. If things had gone according to plan and "The Last Temptation of Christ" had premiered at this year's New York Film Festival, it might have played quietly in small, art-house settings, where its experimental methods might have been welcomed and its shortcomings tolerated; its place in the context of Mr. Scorsese's other work would have been readily understood.

As it is, opening in a sideshow atmosphere, this fragile and difficult film risks being badly overexposed. Though the furor surrounding the film's release is indeed ugly, there may be more to this hoopla than issues of censorship and sacrilege. Universal, the film's distributor, is no stranger to controversy, having suffered through equally lucrative shark-sighting reports around the time it first opened "Jaws." □

1988 Ag 21, II:21:1

Thieves' Highway

BANDITS produced and directed by Claude Lelouch; screenplay by Mr. Lelouch and Pierre Uytterhoeven from a story by Mr. Lelouch; cinematographers, Jean-Yves Le Mener Berto and Olivier Bory; edited by Hugue Darmois; music by Francis Lai; art director, Jacques Bufnoir. Released by Films 13 and TF1 Films. At the Paris, 4 West 58th Street. Running time: 98 minutes. This film is not rated.

Simon Verini	Jean Yanne
Marie Sophie	Marie-Sophie L.
"Mozart"	Patrick Bruel
Charlot	Charles Gérard
Manouchka	Corinne Marchand

By CARYN JAMES

The enduring appeal of Claude Lelouch's film "A Man and a Woman" is largely due to its aura of head-over-heels love. However problematic the romance and sentimental the story, falling in love seemed spontaneous and irresistible, beyond anyone's control. Mr. Lelouch has tried and tried in the 22 years since to recapture that film's easy allure (most blatantly in "A Man and a Woman: 20 Years Later") but the job seems to get tougher and tougher. In "Bandits" he contrives a story of jewel thieves and fairy-tale love, and only proves that trying too hard is a sure way to kill romance.

The hero of "Bandits" is Simon Verini (Jean Yanne), first seen fishing with his pretty wife and prettier 12-year-old daughter, Marie-Sophie, near their very pretty country house. A teen-age thief — called Mozart because he committed his first crime at

the age of 5 — drops by, and Verini agrees to fence some jewels for Mozart's gang.

But after Verini gets the jewels, his wife is kidnapped and killed. He takes Marie-Sophie to a Swiss boarding school, where he hands the headmistress a suitcase full of money and says, "Keep her until she's 21 and a princess." Soon he's in prison, writing Marie-Sophie that her mother is alive and living in Brazil. Eventually he confesses his version of the truth — he is a gentleman bandit stealing from the rich (though he seems to have forgotten the part about the poor). Mr. Lelouch barely stops short of scattering magic wands and fairy dust across the screen.

Ten years later, Marie-Sophie (now played by the actress Marie-Sophie L., the coy L presumably standing for Lelouch, to whom she is married) is just what her father ordered. She looks beautiful and slightly prim, like the wholesome women in cosmetics ads with billowing white curtains and open fields in the background. She could be Grace Kelly en route to Monaco, except this is supposed to be the 1980's.

●

When Marie-Sophie is reunited with her father, just released from prison, a curious incestuous undertone creeps in. Mr. Lelouch, fairy-tale style, finds this innocently charming. Marie-Sophie takes piles of her father's letters through customs and calls them "love letters." After spending the day with her father, she asks an old family friend, "Can one fall in love in 12 hours?" The friend,

Bereaved Marie-Sophie L. and Jean Yanne star in Claude Lelouch's "Bandits," about a suave gentleman thief whose wife is slain in a senseless robbery.

expressing the philosophy on which the entire film is based, says, "In 12 seconds," and means it.

This is already too much to believe, so why not pile on Verini's revenge against his wife's murderer and his return to prison — all within two days of his release, more than enough time for Mozart to return and fall in love with Marie-Sophie? Soon Mozart proposes: "If I get your father out, will you marry me?" In less than 12 seconds she answers, "Of course."

Mozart's method of releasing Verini is amusing, and Mr. Lelouch might have done better to stay with the gangsters' saga. Instead, he sends Mozart dashing off after his victory, racing his motorcycle through golden evening light, the Eiffel Tower shimmering in the background. Robbery, murder, terrorism — at least it's all rich-looking and painless to watch, with many scenes shot through car windows as Mr. Lelouch aims for a fuzzy romantic glow. But "Bandits," which opens today at the Paris, suggests that the director is lost in some romantic fog all his own, no longer able to tell the difference between endless love and incurable silliness.

1988 Ag 24, C17:1

Between the Real And the Literary

CROSSING DELANCEY, directed by Joan Micklin Silver; written by Susan Sandler, based on her original play; director of photography, Theo Van de Sande; edited by Rick Shaine; music by Paul Chihara; production designer, Dan Leigh; produced by Michael Nozik; released by Warner Brothers. Plaza 42, East 58th Street. Running time: 97 minutes. This film is rated PG.

Isabelle Grossman	Amy Irving
Sam Posner	Peter Riegert
Bubbie Kantor	Reizl Bozyk
Anton Maes	Jeroen Krabbe
Hannah Mandelbaum	Sylvia Miles
Lionel	George Martin

By JANET MASLIN

Isabelle (Izzy) Grossman's grandmother lives a life steeped in old-world Jewish culture on the Lower East Side of New York. Her parents live, as the grandmother describes it, "in Florida with Red Buttons" (in a retirement community there).

As for where Izzy herself lives, that's harder to say. She has a small, not terribly hospitable apartment on the Upper West Side and doesn't seem to spend much time there. She pays frequent visits to her grand-

mother, fitting determinedly but a little uncomfortably into the life of the Lower East Side. And she also has a job at a fashionable bookstore, an elite place that particularly prides itself on the small soirees that draw celebrated authors. In this world, Izzy is, among other things, a potential party favor.

"Crossing Delancey," which opens today at the Plaza, is about the process whereby 33-year-old Izzy, played charmingly and believably by Amy Irving, finally figures out where she stands. Her past catches up with her in the form of a pickle merchant named Sam Posner (Peter Riegert). Sam is single. He's responsible. He loves old ladies, particularly Isabelle's grandmother, and he's generous almost to a fault. He's also understanding, hardworking, athletic and very patient about Izzy's identity problems. Although he can be found in a little shop where the sign reads, "A joke and a pickle for only a nickel," it's clear that a man like this belongs in the Smithsonian.

Izzy is also courted by a Very Famous Author of the married variety (Jeroen Krabbe), a jaded, world-weary celebrity who woos her with Confucius's words about ripe plums; Izzy is terribly impressed, needless to say. It is encounters like this, and the fact that her job allows her to have Isaac Bashevis Singer's unlisted home telephone number, that keep Izzy in thrall to the literary world. What's more, at the bookstore she's a rising star, and she can give as good as she gets. Momentarily confounded by Confucius, she quickly tells the author: "What I love most about your writing is its deceptive accessibility. It reads like pulp fiction, and then you hear music."

●

It's not hard to tell from this, and from the humorous depiction of the bookstore crowd's snobbery, where the film's heart really lies. But what makes "Crossing Delancey" so appealing is the warm and leisurely way it arrives at its inevitable conclusion. All the different aspects of Izzy's busy, contradiction-filled life are carefully drawn, giving the film a realistic, well-populated feeling and a nicely wry view of the modern world. Yet somehow the director, Joan Micklin Silver, and the writer, Susan Sandler (adapting her own play), manage to combine a down-to-earth, contemporary outlook with the dreaminess of a fairy tale.

There's an element of overstatement to all this, as evidenced by the presence of Sylvia Miles in the role of an old-world marriage broker. "Ya look, ya meet, ya try, ya see," says she, while digging messily into a meal served in Izzy's grandmother's kitchen. Yet somehow in this setting, Miss Miles seems a lot less flamboyant than usual. The film's style is deliberately broad, but the actors give it humor and delicacy. Miss Irving, who's in virtually every scene, gives Izzy a refreshing worldliness, a hint of disappointment and a hard-won wisdom that banish any trace of ingenuousness from the role. Alluring in some scenes and vaguely irritable in others, sometimes with an uptown hauteur that makes the character that much more credible (as in her first meeting with the suitor who's introduced as a pickle merchant), she is able to span the full breadth of this character's crazily inconsistent world.

The film's scene-stealer is 74-year-old Reizl Bozyk, a star of the Yiddish theater who plays Izzy's Bubbie (pronounced to rhyme with Chubby) as a

Amy Irving and Reizl Bozyk: nubile granddaughter and matchmaking grandma

perfect Everygranny, loving, teasing and pestering at the same time. Miss Bozyk also has the film's best lines, like, "Get off your high horse, Miss Universe" (to a matchmaker-resisting Izzy) and, "She lives alone in a room like a dog" (by way of explaining her granddaughter's apartment). "You want to catch the wild monkey, you got to climb the tree," she finally advises, when at long last Izzy realizes she may have condescended to Mr. Right one time too many. The film's ending, though terribly trumped up, nicely affirms Miss Bozyk's efficacy as a grandmotherly Cupid.

"Crossing Delancey" includes several sharply edged supporting performances, with Rosemary Harris as a fully clawed literary lioness, Mr. Krabbe as the lazily seductive writer and Suzzy Roche, of the singing Roche sisters, adding a distinctly modern touch as Izzy's pragmatic, unattached friend. The Roches' warm, gossamer harmonies also weave through the film's opening and closing scenes, heightening the power of its romantic spell.

1988 Ag 24, C15:1

Puppy Love Unleashed

THE YEAR MY VOICE BROKE, directed and written by John Duigan; director of photography, Geoff Burton; edited by Neil Thumpston; production designer, Roger Ford; produced by Terry Hayes, Doug Mitchell and George Miller; released by Avenue Pictures. 68th Street Playhouse, at Third Avenue. Running time: 103 minutes. This film is rated PG-13.

Danny	Noah Taylor
Freya	Loene Carmen
Trevor	Ben Mendelsohn
Nils Olson	Graeme Blundell
Anne Olson	Lynette Curran
Bruce Embling	Malcom Robertson
Sheila Embling	Judi Farr

By CARYN JAMES

Unless a genius comes along to shake up the material, another coming-of-age film does not offer much hope for originality; the best anyone can expect is that it will not seem too stale and that it might even break out with an innovative quirk or two. "The Year My Voice Broke" is certainly not fresh, but it is so pleasant and unpretentious that we can almost forget the total lack of surprise in this deftly acted Australian film.

The setting, a small town in New South Wales in 1962, is itself as strong a character as Danny, the 15-year-old hero, and Freya, the 16-year-old heroine. The town looks typical, or at least common to many Australian films. It is also oddly familiar because it resembles movie sets for old westerns, with shabby little clapboard houses set along a dusty main street and magnificent hills and open plains in the background. This ghost-town atmosphere pervades the film, so it makes perfect sense that a haunted house sits in a lonely space nearby.

Danny (Noah Taylor) is a perfect specimen, straining against his age and the smallness of a town with only one movie theater. Ruddy-cheeked and serious-looking, he has feelings for Freya that have suddenly changed since the childhood days when they played together in a rocky hiding place outside town. Danny dreams of Freya at night and, more inventively, tries to send telepathic messages that coach her to find him irresistible. He begins to kiss her one night after walking her home, but as soon as he puts his arms around her his bike falls over, its childish bell clanging on the ground.

Freya (Loene Carmen) has already moved beyond Danny and entered a world of sexuality she doesn't much understand. From the minute we notice the chipped red polish on her nails and see her twist Danny's arm and wrestle him to the ground with playful innocence, it is clear that Freya is not ready for the leap into womanhood she is instinctively about to make.

John Duigan, the director and writer, makes his characters warm and sympathetic, avoiding any opportunity for adult laughter at their expense. Even when Danny slouches into a school dance, wearing a leather jacket and dark glasses, a cigarette dangling from his mouth, the attempt to impress Freya is more touching than comic. Mr. Taylor never exaggerates Danny, and is best in the scenes when he is forced to watch Freya falling for an older boy, a soccer player who is also the town troublemaker. How can Danny, with all his dreamy plans and paralyzing frustrations, possibly compete?

Miss Carmen is perfectly cast, capturing Freya's bafflement at how fast life is overtaking her. She gets a bad reputation around town; even her younger sister's friend has heard that Freya is "a nymphoniac." But she has warmth and good humor with Danny, even when he tries to hypnotize her. He foolishly believes she is unconscious, then suggests she will wake up and want to make love to him. Freya laughs when she opens her eyes to end the joke, but never makes fun of him.

Some of these touches are charming. Many are just too cute: among other voices from the 1960's, those of Gene Pitney and Lesley Gore are heard in the background, as "The Man Who Shot Liberty Valance" and "That's the Way Boys Are" defines Danny's heroic fantasies and Freya's girlish innocence.

And "The Year My Voice Broke," which opens today at Cinema 2, takes off only toward the end, when adult drama overtakes the characters. When Freya tells Danny she is pregnant, the audience can see it coming. But no one would have expected Mr. Taylor's perfect response, as Danny cries a bit, shakes his head, and simply says, "Hopeless." Then he helps Freya through an ordeal that also moves him beyond boyhood, and finally proves there is some life in coming-of-age stories after all.

●

"The Year My Voice Broke" is rated PG-13 ("Special Parental Guidance Suggested for Those Younger Than 13"). There is some sexual suggestiveness.

1988 Ag 25, C18:1

At the Intersection Of Three Fates: Death

THE THIN BLUE LINE, directed and written by Errol Morris; directors of photography, Stefan Czapsky and Robert Chappell; edited by Paul Barnes; music by Philip Glass; production designer, Ted Bafaloukos; produced by Mark Lipson; released by Miramax Films. Lincoln Plaza Cinemas, 63d Street and Broadway. Running time: 101 minutes. This film is not rated.

WITH: The principals in the case and, in re-enactments, Adam Goldfine, Derek Horton, Ron Thornhill, Marianne Leone, Amanda Caprio and Michael Nicoll.

If Randall Adams and David Harris can agree on anything, it's that fate dealt them a terrible hand when, on Saturday, Nov. 27, 1976, it threw them together. Mr. Adams knows that his whole life would have been different if he hadn't run out of gas that morning, if he hadn't been hitchhiking and if Mr. Harris hadn't picked him up. Mr. Harris, who gave Mr. Adams a ride in a car he had stolen a day earlier, wonders what would have happened if Mr. Adams, who was living in a seedy Dallas motel with his brother, hadn't refused to give him a place to sleep.

But the two men did meet and spend the day together, and they did wind up at a drive-in where a film called "Swinging Cheerleaders" was being shown. Mr. Adams, who was then a 28-year-old drifter, says he didn't like the movie and insisted on going home before it was over, leaving Mr. Harris to roam on his own. Mr. Harris, then a 16-year-old runaway, says the twosome were at the drive-in until midnight or so. The time is crucial, because at 12:30 A.M. a Dallas police officer named Robert Wood saw the stolen car moving with only its parking lights on. He signaled for the car to stop, walked over to talk to the driver, and the driver killed him.

Errol Morris, the director of "The Thin Blue Line," has fashioned a brilliant work of pulp fiction around this

Ned Burgess

Imprisoned Randall Adams, under life sentence for a policeman's murder in 1976, is seen in "The Thin Blue Line."

Loene Carmen, left, Ben Mendelsohn and Noah Taylor in "The Year My Voice Broke."

crime. Mr Morris's film is both an investigation of the murder and a nightmarish meditation on the difference between truth and fiction, an alarming glimpse at the many distortions that have shaped Mr. Adams's destiny. Mr. Adams was tried for the murder, found guilty (in large part because of Mr. Harris's testimony), and given a death sentence that has since been commuted to life imprisonment. Mr. Harris, now on Death Row in connection with another murder, calmly acknowledges at the end of the film that he said what was necessary to save himself, even if it meant blaming a perfect stranger.

•

Aptly enough, Mr. Morris first approached this case through its most Kafkaesque figure, about whom he had planned to make a film. This was the psychiatrist nicknamed Dr. Death, a popular expert witness at capital trials who has regularly testified that defendants are sociopaths who will kill again. (In the Adams case, the defendant's lack of remorse became another damning element, though Mr. Adams claims that he feels no remorse because he didn't commit a crime.) In any case, this psychiatrist's approach to justice exemplifies the skewed but irrefutable logic that the film so hauntingly explores.

"The Thin Blue Line," which opens today at the Lincoln Plaza, re-invents its story even as it re-examines it. Mr. Morris's graceful camera isolates witnesses and evidence against dark backgrounds, glides eerily through re-enactments of certain episodes, and selects and enlarges particular images (huge kernels of popcorn accompany a discussion of whether the drive-in's refreshment stand was really open as late as Mr. Harris said it was; in fact it closed early). In this deliberately artificial context, justice begins to feel as remote for the viewer as it undoubtedly feels to Mr. Adams.

Although actors are used in the re-enactments, the people interviewed here are real participants in the case. But they, too, begin to sound like actors; everyone seems keenly aware of the camera. Mr. Harris in particular affects a beatific look and a candid manner that become all the more chilling as the film explores his lengthy criminal record. Indeed, the police in Mr. Harris's hometown of Vidor, Tex., know him so well by now that they speak of him rather fondly, despite the burglary, kidnapping, and murder charges in his past. Though Mr. Morris avoids making obvious judgments, the section in which Mr. Harris describes his brother's accidental drowning becomes especially startling in view of his equally off-handed accounts of the criminal acts for which he has been convicted.

•

"The Thin Blue Line" is not really structured as an investigation. It's more like a reverie, filled with strangely exaggerated images and colored by the ominous hum of Philip Glass's score. This means that minor details sometimes assume undue importance, upstaging key facts of the case: Mr. Morris's slow-motion image of a milkshake flying through the air becomes much more memorable than the testimony of the policewoman who was drinking the shake, for example. Some striking shots of automobile tail lights distract attention from the process whereby the killer's car was identified. The case itself is so complicated, and so fascinating, that there is reason to wish the facts emerged more clearly.

But Mr. Morris, to his credit, has created something larger and more compelling than the mere particulars. He explores this case and goes well beyond it, to the darker side of justice and to a vision that is both poetic and perverse. Hidden motives, withheld data and questionable interpretations of the facts are everywhere, and each interview invariably creates more questions than it answers. And the more maps, diagrams and key details the director assembles, the more frighteningly the truth slips away
                                    JANET MASLIN

1988 Ag 26, C6:1

Charges

Edén Pastora Gómez, an anti-Sandinista leader.

COVERUP: BEHIND THE IRAN-CONTRA AFFAIR, directed by Barbara Trent; written by Eve Goldberg; edited by David Kaspar and Ms. Goldberg; music by Richard Elliot; produced by Ms. Trent, Gary Meyer and Mr. Kaspar; released by the Empowerment Project. At the Public, 425 Lafayette Street. Running time: 76 minutes. This film is not rated.

Narrator .... Elizabeth Montgomery

By WALTER GOODMAN

"Coverup: Behind the Iran-Contra Affair" loses force as the movie makers run out of evidence that a shadowy right-wing group has been conducting American foreign policy and threatening constitutional rights, and settle for surmise, speculation and the tricks of film making to bolster their case. (Sad but unilluminating pictures of injured Laotians are used to accompany reminders of the C.I.A.'s "secret war" in Laos.) This overreaching exposé, which opens at the Public Theater today, leaves less doubt about the political predilections of its producers, Barbara Trent, Gary Meyer and David Kaspar, than about their allegations.

"Coverup" begins with a charge by Barbara Honegger, who worked for the Reagan-Bush campaign for a while in 1980, that the Republicans promised arms to the Iranians if they delayed returning the hostages taken at the American Embassy in Teheran until after the Presidential election. The hostages were in fact freed in January 1981, and, the movie asserts, American arms began flowing to Iran soon thereafter. Ms. Honegger's analysis is provocative, but she produces no smoking gun.

The solidest part of the documentary is based on the book "The Iran Contra Connection" (South End Press), of which Peter Dale Scott, a professor at the University of California at Berkeley, was one of the authors. The book digs into the backgrounds of the main players, especially former C.I.A. and military officials. Along with the half-dozen like-minded commentators relied on by the producers, Mr. Scott has a weakness for hyperbole (he asserts, for example that an ex-C.I.A. claque was out to run the Reagan Administration), but his reminders of the C.I.A.'s activities in behalf of the Shah of Iran and the Nicaraguan dictator Anastasio Somoza Debayle do support what has since been revealed about the connection between the Iranian arms deal and aid to the contras.

•

Although some of "Coverup's" most effective film comes from the Iran-contra hearings, the hearings themelves are written off as what Mr. Scott calls "damage control." He maintains, for example, that Congress avoided following up leads of extensive drug trafficking by the C.I.A. (The movie makers cannot resist juxtaposing charges of Administration complicity in the drug trade with shots of the President and Nancy Reagan expressing their opposition to drugs.)

Toward the end, the pitch of the accusations grows higher as the level of evidence gets lower. The attempted assassination of Edén Pastora Gómez, the anti-Sandinista leader, is presented as a plot to kill American journalists in order to discredit the Sandinistas. Among the conspirators, we are told, are "some other people leading up to the White House." These charges are leveled mainly by two journalists who have brought a multi-million-dollar suit against several former C.I.A. agents involved in the Iran-contra affair. If there is any evidence that they were implicated in the Pastora assassination attempt, it is not presented here.

•

The lawyer for the journalists, it turns out, is Daniel Sheehan, of the Christic Institute, a public interest group that has been involved in litigation over Three Mile Island and the Karen Silkwood case. Mr. Sheehan has appeared frequently during the documentary to offer his opinions about "a small secret team" stirring up wars for personal profit. The acknowledgement of his direct interest in the journalists' suit requires that everything he has said previously be seen in that light.

The movie ends with vague charges of a plan, involving both Lieut. Col. Oliver L. North and Vice President Bush (whose picture is used at every pretext), to "suspend the American Constitution," and with familiar warnings of the impact of political contributions by right-wing groups. Ms. Trent, who also directed, tends to rely heavily on visual devices and portentous music as the charges outrun the evidence. By the end, you may lose interest in chasing them.

1988 Ag 26, C8:6

Patience, Patience

HERO AND THE TERROR, directed by William Tannen; screenplay by Dennis Shryack and Michael Blodgett, based on the novel by Mr. Blodgett; director of photography, Eric Van Haren Noman; edited by Christian A. Wagner; music by David M. Frank; production designer, Holger Gross; produced by Raymond Wagner; released by the Cannon Group Inc. At Criterion Center, Broadway and 45th Street, and other theaters. Running time: 97 minutes. This film is rated R.

Danny O'Brien	Chuck Norris
Kay	Brynn Thayer
Robinson	Steve James
Simon Moon	Jack O'Halloran
Dwight	Jeffrey Kramer
Mayor	Ron O'Neal
Theater Manager	Murphy Dunne

By CARYN JAMES

Chuck Norris's big problem in "Hero and the Terror" is that he is a police detective who never waits for his backup. As Danny O'Brien, his life is full of other unlikely complications: he feels guilty about undeserved heroism; his pregnant girlfriend, who used to be his psychiatrist, won't marry him; his best friend is killed by a serial murderer just waiting to get Danny next. And the script he lives in seems so perfect for Charles Bronson that the audience wouldn't blink if Mr. Bronson jumped out shooting from behind a parked car. But Danny's big problem is that he's too stupid and impatient to wait for help.

In an opening dream, he flashes back to the day his partner yelled, "Call for backup," and Danny instantly charged into a shack where the killer had stashed his victims' bodies, all female, all at least partly undressed. A chase followed, and the gigantic murderer fell through a shaky rung on a ladder beneath a pier.

Danny wakes up; it's three years later, and the killer — nicknamed the Terror by a peculiarly unimaginative press corps — is in prison. Danny, called Hero, feels bad because he *knows* that wobbly ladder rung thrust heroism upon him unjustly.

In no time, the Terror escapes, and is carting his victims back to hidden passages in an old restored movie theater as if he were the Phantom of the Opera. Danny tracks him for a couple of days, while trying to maintain some kind of personal life. One especially weird juxtaposition cuts from a scene of the killer twisting the partner's neck to a shot of Danny's newborn baby girl. Life goes on, sort of.

So do action heroes, and the more heroic they're meant to be, the dopier their judgments. Just before the big finale, Danny sits outside the movie theater where he knows the Terror waits. He phones headquarters and says he's going in. "Danny," he is told, "you wait for your backup." He never learns. Hero chases the Terror to the roof, where there are plenty of skylights to get smashed.

Despite several well-placed karate kicks, Danny is not the usual macho Chuck Norris role, not the Rambo blood brother who regularly rescues Americans from Vietnam in Mr. Norris's "Missing in Action" films. He is a neatly groomed, middle-class urban warrior, a Bronson-type hero, though "Hero and the Terror," which opens today at the Criterion and other theaters, is considerably less violent than most Bronson movies. (It may just be that snapping a victim's neck is less bloody than blowing him away.)

The camera tends to look up at

Chuck Norris

Danny, making him seem like a looming hero. In fact, he is such a sensitive guy that there is too little action for this film to work as a genre piece, and too much talk by actors who should have waited for backup from the script.

1988 Ag 26, C12:1

Love and Hatred

BETRAYED, directed by Costa-Gravas; written by Joe Eszterhas; director of photography, Patrick Blossier; edited by Joële Van Effenterre; music by Bill Conti; production designer, Patrizia Von Brandenstein; produced by Irwin Winkler; released by United Artists. At Embassy 1, Broadway and 46th Street, and other theaters. Running time: 123 minutes. This film is rated R.

Katie Phillips/Cathy Weaver	Debra Winger
Gary Simmons	Tom Berenger
Michael Carnes	John Heard
Gladys Simmons	Betsy Blair
Shorty	John Mahoney
Wes	Ted Levine
Sam Kraus	Richard Libertini
Rachel Simmons	Maria Valdez

By JANET MASLIN

When a widowed Midwestern farmer named Gary Simmons (Tom Berenger) falls in love with a demure young newcomer named Katie Phillips (Debra Winger), he wants her to know everything about his world. So he takes her camping and hunting, but these prove not to be ordinary recreational outings. The campsite is at a white-supremacist outpost in Montana, where vacationers dress in Ku Klux Klan robes and burn crosses as they gather to sing "Amazing Grace." And at the hunt, which takes place at night and employs vicious dogs and live ammunition, the prey is a terrified black man.

These are the most shocking episodes in "Betrayed," a film directed by Costa-Gavras and written by Joe Eszterhas in a scorching, irony-laden style that strives for the incendiary at every turn. When film makers play this deliberately with fire, they had better do it with a lot more skill and intelligence than are on display here.

"Betrayed," which opens today at the Embassy 1 and other theaters, is indeed grim and unsettling, but beyond that its impact is harder to assess. That's because the film's effect, which is initially so overwhelming, has practically no staying power. Though the premise is startling and the acting good enough to divert attention from the screenplay's many problems, those weaknesses become clearer and clearer as the story un-

folds. The final impression is that someone has drawn out an elephant gun, loaded heavy ammunition, taken aim, and somehow shot himself in the foot.

•

"Betrayed" begins on a chilling note, with the murder of a talk-show host in Chicago. (Here and elsewhere, the film falls back eagerly on real headlines to strengthen its impact; the reference to the 1984 killing of Alan Berg in Denver is clear.) Richard Libertini, who makes a memorable impression as the hatred-fanning host in this brief sequence, avows that it's all right to "let people say what they want, as ugly as it may be," and indeed his call-in guests do exactly that. But the last look on his face, as he realizes he is caught in a deadly ambush, is far more eloquent in suggesting the terrible consequences of encouraging people to do their worst. Cut to a beautiful sunlit wheatfield, the purest embodiment of American's heartland (Costa-Gavras is fond of doing exactly that, whenever the film's ironic underpinnings are in danger of being overlooked). It is here, in an atmosphere of perfect wholesomeness, that Gary Simmons and his two small children live. After Gary meets Katie in a bar, where they do the two-step to "The Yellow Rose of Texas," he invites her home for dinner with his mother. Things look innocent enough, but there's some small talk to the effect that "we have to return America to real Americans." Gary's mother complains about store-bought cake, saying that things just aren't what they used to be. Gary compliments her on her own baking, calling it "the best white cake in the whole white world."

Perhaps Katie would take note of such remarks even if she were not, beneath the gingham dresses and the schoolgirl smile, an F.B.I. agent named Cathy Weaver, sent to infiltrate the local white supremacist movement. As it is, she smiles carefully and waits to see what will happen next. But as she learns more and more about Gary's covert activities, something unexpected (by Cathy, if not by the audience) begins to happen. She and Gary begin to fall in love.

•

Although Miss Winger (an astonishingly natural actress, capable of looking entirely different in each new role) and Mr. Berenger (who's also very good, giving Gary a badly needed down-to-earth quality) make

the attraction convincing, there are story problems even at this early stage. Is there *any* credible way to stage the sequence that has the amorous Gary dragging his new sweetheart along on a racist hunting expedition, insisting "You'll like this" when she protests? Is it possible, after this, that she can still find him attractive? Is the F.B.I. really apt to send a brand-new female agent on such a dangerous mission, to deny her adequate backup and to bully her when she complains? John Heard, who is good as an F.B.I. colleague who's in love with Cathy, is meant to provide the element of sexual jealousy that explains this. But like too much of "Betrayed," it just doesn't make sense.

The screenplay, which specializes in applying Band-Aid touches to major plot problems, gives Cathy a strong attachment to Gary's little daughter (Maria Valdez), by way of explaining why she's still willing to hang around. But a more serious difficulty arises when Cathy, having fallen for Gary, makes no effort to change or understand him. This story might generate real tension if Cathy found herself genuinely affected by Gary's racist ideas (which quickly branch out to include anti-Semitic and anti-homosexual tenets once he feels comfortable enough to let his hair down), or if some perverse side of the romance became apparent. And it would have much more impact if either of the principals underwent any change. But they don't; instead, "Betrayed" becomes little more than an ineptly thought-out suspense story. And Costa-Gavras begins to use easy cynicism, unlikely plot tricks (like a computer printout conveniently detailing an entire network of white racist operatives) and muddy conspiracy theories to get by.

•

The rampant Americana that figures so prominently and ironically in "Betrayed" is especially unconvincing. Do white racists, when gathered at a campground to practice shooting at racially identifiable targets and trade Nazi memorabilia, really sit around the campfire singing "Old Blue" and "Michael Row the Boat Ashore"? Perhaps they do, but surely not in the charmingly uncomplicated manner depicted here. Nor is it likely that the Simmons family would show so few deep-seated effects of Gary's thinking. (When the little girl does parrot some of her father's sentiments, the effect is too false to be disturbing.) And must so many of the

Debra Winger and Tom Berenger in "Betrayed."

328

film's scenes take place at county fairs, on the Fourth of July, in church and to the tune of "America the Beautiful"? In underestimating the aberrance of its characters, "Betrayed" further trivializes its explosive subject.

The actual news events upon which many of the film's developments are based give "Betrayed" an undeniable grip on the attention. And the film's overheated approach to its subject only heightens its potential power. But having summoned its demons, "Betrayed" winds up utterly confounded by them. Though the title refers to some climactic plot developments, this film's real betrayal occurs somewhere between the audience and the screen.

1988 Ag 26, C16:1

Youthful Memories

Jodie Foster

STEALING HOME, written and directed by Steven Kampmann and Will Aldis; director of photography, Bobby Byrne; music by David Foster; art director, Vaughan Edwards; produced by Thom Mount and Hank Moonjean; released by Warner Brothers. At National Twin, Broadway and 44th Street, and other theaters. Running time: 98 minutes. This film is rated PG-13.

Billy Wyatt	Mark Harmon
Billy Wyatt at 16	William McNamara
Katie Chandler	Jodie Foster
Ginny Wyatt	Blair Brown
Sam Wyatt	John Shea
Alan Appleby at 38	Harold Ramis
Alan Appleby at 16	Jonathan Silverman
Young Billy Wyatt	Thacher Goodwin
Laura Appleby	Judith Kahan
Mrs. Parks	Miriam Flynn

You know what kind of girl she was. You probably know what kind of summer it was, too. The light was golden. The beach was clean. He was young and impressionable, she worldly and wise. Whenever he had trouble, she helped get him through, and because of that he can never forget her. Oh yes, he also had a friend, and the friend's every thought was of losing his virginity. There was an older woman on hand who (inevitably) was happy to oblige.

The film is "Stealing Home," and it's the work of a two-man writing and directing partnership (Steven Kampmann and Will Aldis), though not even an entire baseball team's worth of writers and directors could have freed this material from its suffocating sentimentality. Baseball happens to be its real subject, since there's something about Katie (Jodie Foster) that freed Billy Wyatt (Mark Harmon) from his fears and allowed him to become a professional ballplayer. Katie first gave Billy a little gold baseball to wear around his neck when he was a teen-ager (William McNamara). But even when he was a little kid (Thacher Goodwin) she was always encouraging him to have fun and break free.

The fact that the characters in "Stealing Home" frequently change ages, and do this confusingly and unconvincingly, is only one of the film's staging problems. Another is that Katie, though Miss Foster works hard to give her a thrillingly madcap and indelibly romantic side, spends part of the film in an urn. As ashes. Which Billy must brandish very clumsily indeed as he struggles with his grief over Katie's untimely suicide (this grief takes the form of three-day stubble). No actor could play as many scenes as Mr. Harmon does with an urn tucked under his arm and do it well — especially not an urn that is sometimes seen wearing a baseball cap.

"Stealing Home," which opens today at the National and other theaters, is best watched for some of its actors, although the casting is spotty in the extreme. John Shea makes Billy's enthusiastic, baseball-loving father seem terminally silly, but the lovely Blair Brown makes Billy's mother a genuinely sympathetic figure. Jonathan Silverman and Harold Ramis, playing the same friend of Billy's at different ages, prove to be funny and well matched. Judith Kahan has a brief, amusing scene as this same character's sweetly bewildered mother. Another mother gag has the parent (Miriam Flynn) of Billy's first sexual partner wandering into the room just as Billy loses his virginity, and being too preoccupied to notice.

Miss Foster is asked to greatly overstate Katie's allure, but she does this with impressive bravado. Although Billy and Katie are seen reading "The Catcher in the Rye" and "The Group," respectively, the time period remains inconsistent and hazy. The era is simply established as a dreamily idyllic past, thanks to sand dunes at twilight, waves that crash in the distance, shiny red convertibles without seat belts and a musical score that may make you want to weep, for all the wrong reasons.

•

"Stealing Home" is rated PG-13 ("Special Parental Guidance Suggested for Those Younger Than 13"). It includes brief nudity and sexual references. JANET MASLIN

1988 Ag 26, C17:4

Beyond Mr. Ed

HOT TO TROT, directed by Michael Dinner; written by Stephen Neigher and Charlie Peters; cinematographer, Victor J. Kemper; edited by Frank Morriss; production designer, William F. Matthews; animal trainers, Glenn Randall and Corky Randall; produced by Steve Tisch and Wendy Finerman. Released by Warner Brothers. At Criterion Center, Broadway and 45th Street; Eastside Cinema, Third Avenue at 55th Street. Running time: 83 minutes. This film is rated PG.

Fred Chaney	Bob Goldthwait
Walter Sawyer	Dabney Coleman
Boyd Osborne	Jim Metzler
Victoria Peyton	Cindy Pickett
Allison Rowe	Virginia Madsen
Voice of Don	John Candy

By JANET MASLIN

"Hot to Trot," which opened yesterday at the Criterion Center and other theaters, bills itself as "the funniest talking horse movie ever." That's not so very much to live up to. But even so, "Hot to Trot" doesn't qualify, since its biggest innovation is the idea of a horse named Don who's as wise-

cracking, irreverent and messy as the human characters. The film never gets any funnier than a sequence that has Don wrecking the apartment of his human friend, a stockbroker named Fred, with the help of a goat, a pig, a duck and other self-proclaimed party animals.

•

The horse's voice is supplied by John Candy, who sounds exactly the same in this role as he does in any other. The stockbroker Fred, a dim fellow who is locked in a business war with his philandering stepfather (played by Dabney Coleman), is played by Bob Goldthwait. Mr. Goldthwait (formerly Bobcat), with his wide-eyed grimaces and his fingernail-on-blackboard wailing, has a comic style that's an acquired taste at best, and at worst quite incomprehensible. In this role he fidgets constantly, looks strange in a business suit and is easily upstaged by four-legged Don.

•

Although Michael Dinner's direction is noticeably better than the material, the film aims consistently for the lowest common denominator. Mr. Coleman, who's almost always great fun when he's cast as a corporate conniver, this time is made to wear buckteeth and big unsightly glasses. A light bulb appears when Fred has a good idea. The big laugh in a scene that has Fred hanging desperately from a window ledge is the pigeon that comes and pecks at his head. And it takes less than a minute from the film's opening shot for someone to step in horse manure.

"Hot to Trot" is rated PG ("Parental Guidance Suggested"). It contains some rude language.

1988 Ag 27, 11:3

FILM VIEW/Janet Maslin

How Frightfully Well Decorated

WHAT KIND OF FILM works a word like "mangel-wurzel" into the conversation? The kind of film that a lot of us secretly enjoy more than we should. A mangel-wurzel, for the uninitiated, is a variety of large beet used by Europeans as cattle feed, and reference to it is made casually during the pastoral section of "A Summer Story." But what on earth would make such a thing, in this context, so delicious? The fact that it's part of the larger framework of a film filled with natural fibers and rampant Anglophilia, with linen and tweed, with straw hats and walking sticks and — inevitably — white flannel.

■

White flannel films are terrifically popular right now, thanks to the combined influence of PBS, the director James Ivory, the producer Ismail Merchant (the Cecil B. De Mille of this genre, with "The Deceivers," about a British officer and the murderous Indian cult of the 1820's called the Thuggees, opening this week) and, of course, Ralph Lauren. From "Mr. North" to "Pascali's Island," from "White Mischief" to "A Handful of Dust," audiences with happy memories of "Maurice" and "A Room With a View" still intact can be found savoring the proudly recherché hallmarks of this form: the sight of lawn tennis played on grass courts, the look of well-worn leather-bound volumes of poetry, the sound of tea being poured into fine antique china.

It helps when these films are either English or frankly Anglophile, but with the right ingredients even a Danish film like "Babette's Feast" can linger for six months, ostensibly making a point about the enduring beauty of art but in fact thrilling cuisine-minded viewers with its anatomy of a four-star meal. And yes, even American films can play to this same refinement-seeking, luxury-loving sensibility if they really try. Put Robert Mitchum, as "Mr. North" has, in a blue paisley dressing gown with satin lapels, equip him with pocket watch and expensive-ly-coiffed gray hair, send him to Newport, give him lines of dialogue like "I'm a Harvard man myself, class of '76" or "I am very much looking forward to the passage we're to hear today," and you've won the white flannel crowd's heart.

The remarkable thing is that once audiences have been sufficiently lulled by these trappings, they become willing to make extraordinary allowances for the gentlemanly pacing and hazy plotting that often accompany them. Thanks to "Masterpiece Theater," American audiences have developed a patient, even grateful acceptance of certain staging habits that would be frailties anywhere else. It's astonishing to watch an audience sit patiently through the impenetrable "Handful of Dust," a film whose many distortions and misreadings of the Evelyn Waugh novel would perhaps seem more irritating if they were easier to hear. As it is, the film's director, Charles Sturridge (who also directed the mini-series adaptation of Waugh's "Brideshead Revisited"), lets the actors chirp their lines so breezily and inaudibly that they lose much of their meaning.

Viewers who have not read Waugh beforehand will thus miss a great deal of what goes on; as the characters seem to gloss over every nuance; even the novel's horrifying mistaken-identity reference regarding the death of a key character is allowed to glide by. Though the characters indeed say what they should, the visual style of the film often contradicts them, giving a grand look to a house described as acutely uncomfortable, an impeccable old-money patina to a men's club meant to be quite new, a fashionable gloss to a character widely regarded as unsavory. Only Anjelica Huston, making a minor specialty out of turning up in films like this wearing riding habits (she also does this in "Mr. North"), gives the material anything like the ironic edge it needs.

Audiences seem content to enjoy the good breeding on display in films like this, regardless of whether it serves or supplants the larger story. And the actors who have emerged as dreamboats of the genre — like Charles Dance ("Pascali's Island," "White Mischief") or James Wilby ("Maurice," "A Handful of Dust," "A Summer Story") — are at least as notable for their debonair bearing, strawberry-blond good looks and gifts for looking great in straw boaters as for other talents. Mr. Dance can be a sexually magnetic, crisply intelligent presence, but Mr. Wilby is more rosily bland, and in white flannel films that makes him immensely valuable. He's the perfect actor for roles that require a handsome, dull, slightly vacant aristocrat to find himself immensely surprised at the appearance in his life of real passion.

When material of this stripe is not handled as expertly as it has been by Merchant-Ivory (whose "Room With a View" and "Maurice" are the genre at its peak), it's best taken less seriously. That's what helps to make "A Summer Story" a real white flannel treat. Though its story, about the star-crossed love affair between an upper-crust Londoner and a simple country girl, is solemnly told, the film does nothing to insist on the viewer's serious attention and everything to make the film as decorative as possible. Carried to the extreme that it is here, this approach becomes vastly amusing. Pay attention to the story if you must, and to the actors, who do indeed give this material their all. But you will nonetheless be delightfully distracted by white gloves and blue blazers in the film's city scenes, homespun frocks, hearty meals and tousle-haired children in its rustic sections. And mangel-wurzels, too. □

1988 Ag 28, II:23:1

Emile Belcourt, left, and Frederick Westcott in the film version of "The Man Who Mistook His Wife for a Hat."

A Rose Is a Rose Is a 'Convoluted Form'

THE MAN WHO MISTOOK HIS WIFE FOR A HAT, directed by Christopher Rawlence, based on an essay by Oliver Sacks; camera, Christopher Morphet; edited by Howard Sharp; music by Michael Nyman; libretto by Mr. Rawlence; distributed by Films for the Humanities. At Film Forum 1, 57 Watts Street. Running time: 75 minutes. This film has no rating.

The Neurologist	Emile Belcourt
Dr. P.	Frederick Westcott
Mrs. P.	Patricia Hooper
WITH: Oliver Sacks and John Tighe	

By CARYN JAMES

In less than a decade, "The Man Who Mistook His Wife for a Hat" has gone through several startling and successful incarnations — an essay became an opera, which is now a film. Each version reinforces the haunting atmosphere of loss in a story that began with the neurologist Oliver Sacks's 1979 observation of a patient he called Dr. P., a music teacher with an impairment that caused him to see objects without recognizing them. A glove or a rose might be utterly mysterious shapes to him, though he never lost his feeling for music.

Dr. Sacks's account of his two meetings with Dr. P. and his wife became the title essay in his best-selling book, where scientific facts yielded to humanistic probing, all shaped by a storyteller's skill. Dr. Sacks took us into his office, where he examined this most cultivated and knowledgeable man who nonetheless thought his shoe was his foot, and reached for his wife's head instead of his hat before leaving. A later meeting at Dr. P's house allowed Dr. Sacks to ruminate on the incurable case, at the peculiar marvel of everyday knowledge gone askew.

●

The composer Michael Nyman and the librettist Christopher Rawlence transformed the essay into a highly praised one-hour opera for three voices, a work faithful to Dr. Sacks's passion for narrative and Dr. P's for music. And in another extraordinary turn, Mr. Rawlence has directed a film version of the opera that bears no resemblance to ordinary performance films. This version of "The Man Who Mistook His Wife for a Hat," which opens today at the Film Forum, builds richly on the previous layers. But it is so purely conceived as film, with a shifting, sophisticated, shrewdly focused camera eye, that it may rejuvenate the tired term "experimental."

The film begins with Dr. Sacks on camera, telling about the day he saw two cute but rather greenish twins in a stroller; they turned out to be two melons in a shopping cart. There is a little Dr. P. in all of us, he suggests. Throughout the film Mr. Rawlence returns to Dr. Sacks (who in a late scene reveals what he did not know in 1979, that Dr. P. was suffering from the early stages of Alzheimer's disease).

Early on, the director also sets up images that will flash through Dr. P's story. There are extreme close-ups of Chinese figures that reappear on the cups Mrs. P. uses for tea. We see a rose, which Dr. P. will describe as "a convoluted red form with a linear green attachment." As the film moves ahead, a computer screen scrolls by words such as "aphasia" and "musical alexia."

●

Interwoven with these images and narrative fragments is the opera itself. Emile Belcourt sings the role of "The Neurologist," offering a fictionalized version of Dr. Sacks's medical and philosophical observations. Patricia Hooper plays Mrs. P. as a kind and patient woman. And Frederick Westcott is exceptional as Dr. P., his dignified manner and baritone voice giving ironic authority to a character whose cognitive powers are slipping away. When Dr. P. observes the Neurologist — seeing an eye, then a nose, then an ear but never grasping the concepts of face or identity — the camera follows to create Dr. P's off-kilter view.

The repetitive, minimalist quality in Mr. Nyman's score creates tension, and is perfectly suited to the opera's quest, sifting through bits of evidence in Dr. P's case, re-examining this or that image. Often, however, it is so difficult to understand the words as they are sung (they seem overwhelmed by the volume of the music), that it helps to have read Dr. Sacks's essay. Mr. Rawlence's language tends toward bluntness, with too little mockery in phrases such as, "But what of the parietal regions?"

The most touching moment in the film, in fact, is a traditional one that throws into relief the fragmented forms of music, drama and film that mingle here. When Dr. P. sings a Schumann song while his wife accompanies him on the piano, the lyrical music from the "Dichterliebe" comes like a breeze from the past, a reminder of the • Romantic, organic forms that 20th-century art so often leaves behind. Similarly, the small phrases from Schumann that echo through Mr. Nyman's score suggest Dr. P.'s tenuous connection to his former self.

The film is not flawless. There is no need for several grotesque looks at a human brain that has been surgically removed; it is a misguided attempt to rub medical facts in our faces. And even though it is only 75 minutes long, the film drags a bit toward the end. But its flaws are truly minor; its achievement, though not to traditional tastes, is astonishing.

1988 Ag 31, C17:1

Gamblers 8, Baseball 0

EIGHT MEN OUT, directed and written by John Sayles, based on the book by Eliot Asinof; director of photography, Robert Richardson; edited by John Tintori; music by Mason Daring; production design, Nora Chavooshian; produced by Sarah Pillsbury and Midge Sanford; released by the Orion Pictures Corporation. At Loews Tower East, Third Avenue and 72d Street, and other theaters. Running time: 120 minutes. This film is rated PG.

Buck Weaver	John Cusack
Charles Comiskey	Clifton James
Arnold Rothstein	Michael Lerner
Bill Burns	Christopher Lloyd
Kid Gleason	John Mahoney
Hap Felsch	Charlie Sheen
Eddie Cicotte	David Strathairn
Shoeless Joe Jackson	D. B. Sweeney
Ray Schalk	Gordon Clapp
Chick Gandil	Michael Rooker
Billy Maharg	Richard Edson
Abe Attell	Michael Mantell
Sport Sullivan	Kevin Tighe
Ring Lardner	Mr. Sayles
Hugh Fullerton	Studs Terkel

By JANET MASLIN

Of course John Sayles begins "Eight Men Out" with a little boy, with the kid who is the purest and most hopeful of baseball fans, the one whose subsequent plea, "Say it ain't so, Joe!" went down in history. "Eight Men Out" is the story of the 1919 World Series-fixing scheme that shattered the faith of this boy and so many others. As such, it's much more than a film about baseball. It's an amazingly full and heartbreaking vision of the dreams, aspirations and disillusionments of a nation, as filtered through its national pastime.

"Eight Men Out," which opens today at Loews Tower East and other theaters, establishes its scope in a wonderfully edited (by John Tintori) opening ballpark scene that shows how many disparate elements Mr. Sayles will bring into play. There are the Chicago White Sox themselves, just on the verge of winning the pen-

nant and in their full bloom of talent and optimism. There are the White Sox wives and children, bursting with pride, and the fans, whose excitement fills the air. There is also the team's owner, Charles Comiskey (Clifton James), whose stinginess is so extraordinary that he rewards his players for winning the pennant with bottles of flat Champagne.

Also poised in the stadium, ready to bring about the White Sox' downfall, are the various speculators who know how many bets will be riding on this popular team. Realizing that the players' economic dissatisfaction contains the seeds of a big gambling win, these operators lay their plans to subvert the ballplayers one at a time. Ready to record and lament this sad story are the sportswriters, led by Hugh Fullerton (Studs Terkel) and Ring Lardner (played by Mr. Sayles), who wander through the film as a tiny Greek chorus. "Gamblers 8, baseball 0," they say in disgust at this scandal's sorry outcome.

In addition to viewing the events of the Black Sox debacle (as it became known) from so many different angles, Mr. Sayles also sees it with great generosity. The jaunty, deceptively upbeat "Eight Men Out" (with credits in which the camera rises blissfully heavenward, then falls again) resembles the film maker's earlier and more mournfully beautiful "Matewan," not only in using many of the same actors, but also in bringing such far-reaching sympathy to its story. "Eight Men Out" doesn't condemn the White Sox, and would be a far less interesting film if it did. Instead, it regards the players as unwitting losers caught by forces far more powerful than their own winning spirit. Some of the team members are depicted as more eager to take a tumble than others, but all are seen by Mr. Sayles as pawns in a losing game.

The actors have clearly been chosen very carefully, so that their faces alone speak eloquently of America's post-World War I self-image. The ballplayers, even those who prove quickest to betray their game, have strong, clear faces that radiate vitality and dedication, while the gamblers' various looks suggest the network of power, money and opportunism of which they are a part. The players' fine young faces grow ever cloudier and more downcast as the story proceeds.

One of Mr. Sayles's many talents is for drawing striking performances from actors who have never been nearly this memorable in other roles. "Eight Men Out" contains many such small marvels, particularly from John Cusack and David Strathairn as the film's closest approximation of tragic heroes. Mr. Cusack, as Buck Weaver, the team member who most strenuously resisted the fix scheme, conveys an idealism and disappointment that struggle within him visibly as the team's fortunes pivot back and forth. Mr. Strathairn, as the once-honest pitcher Eddie Cicotte who suffers the story's most painful crisis of conscience, captures the full helplessness and misery of a man who sees no choice but to do what he knows is wrong.

There is in this material (with Mr. Sayles's screenplay based on Eliot Asinof's 1963 book) great potential for pious oversimplication, for viewing the White Sox as cardboard victims. Happily, Mr. Sayles avoids this easily, and breathes enormous humanity and variety into this story. The film's snappy manner, aside from capturing the spirit of postwar

buoyancy and soon-to-be-lost innocence, also holds the attention handily, and Robert Richardson's cinematography creates a handsome and evocative look, making meticulous use of light and shadow. Chief among the director's other accomplishments are insuring that the World Series games are genuinely exciting, despite what the audience knows about their ultimate outcome, and making an extremely complicated plot full of bribes, counterbribes and double-crosses seem crystal clear.

Notable in the large and excellent cast of "Eight Men Out" are D. B. Sweeney, who gives Shoeless Joe Jackson the slow, voluptuous Southern naïveté of the young Elvis; Michael Lerner, who plays the formidable gangster Arnold Rothstein with the quietest aplomb; Gordon Clapp as the team's firecracker of a catcher; John Mahoney as the worried manager who senses much more about his players' plans than he would like to, and Michael Rooker as the quintessential bad apple. Charlie Sheen is also good as the team's most suggestible player, the good-natured fellow who isn't sure whether it's worse to be corrupt or to be a fool. The story's delightfully colorful villains are played by Christopher Lloyd and Richard Edson (as the halfway-comic duo who make the first assault on the players), Michael Mantell as the chief gangster's extremely undependable right-hand man, and Kevin Tighe as the Bostonian smoothie who coolly declares: "You know what you feed a dray horse in the morning if you want a day's work out of him? Just enough so he knows he's hungry."

For Mr. Sayles, whose idealism has never been more affecting or apparent than it is in this story of boyish enthusiam gone bad in an all too grown-up world, "Eight Men Out" represents a home run.

●

"Eight Men Out" is rated PG. ("Parental Guidance Suggested"). It contains some strong language.

1988 S 2, C3:1

The Waltons, With Caterers

Suzy Amis

ROCKET GIBRALTAR, directed by Daniel Petrie; written by Amos Poe; photography by Jost Vacano; edited by Melody London; music by Andrew Powell; production designer, Bill Groom; produced by Jeff Weiss. Released by Columbia Pictures. At Regency Cinema, Broadway and 67th Street. Running time: 100 minutes. This film is rated PG.

Levi Rockwell	Burt Lancaster
Aggie Rockwell	Suzy Amis
Rose Black	Patricia Clarkson
Ruby Hanson	Frances Conroy
Amanda (Billi) Rockwell	Sinead Cusack
Rolo Rockwell	John Glover
Crow Black	Bill Pullman

If the Waltons had money, not to mention show-business connections and a large house in the Hamptons, they might be a lot like the Rockwell family of "Rocket Gibraltar," which

Generations Macaulay Culkin and Burt Lancaster play grandson and grandfather in "Rocket Gibraltar."

opens today at the Regency. It is not without irony that the Rockwells have been named, since their picture-perfect happy family tableau harkens back to a simpler time.

Though the addition of such elements as a swimming pool, a portable telephone (which the story's movie-producer character carries with him everywhere) and a party arranged by a French caterer present some contemporary touches, "Rocket Gibraltar" is in fact a heart-tugging tale of simple family values. But it contains a subplot so bizarre that audiences may not know whether to laugh or cry.

The handsome, affluent Rockwell clan has gathered at its beach house to celebrate the 77th birthday of grandfather Levi, the warm and gentle patriarch. Despite the glaring problems of the screenplay (by Amos Poe), Levi is a lovely character, and Burt Lancaster gives a wonderful performance in the role. Wry and reflective, full of love for his family, but none too sugary, Levi is the pivot around whom the whole film revolves. Mr. Lancaster is so touching that he makes it a disappointment every time the story wanders off elsewhere.

Although it's not apparent through the film's early scenes of well-heeled merrymaking, Levi is nearing death and he knows it. This would be a many-hanky premise were it not for the demented subplot that has Levi's little grandchildren planning to surprise the old man with a Viking funeral barge for his birthday.

●

Granted, Levi had made an impassioned moonlit speech about the Viking way of setting the dead out to sea on burning boats. (And the director, Daniel Petrie, replays this speech twice, in the unlikely event that anyone missed it the first time.) But he is alive and well during much of the children's boat-building adventure, and even when they learn of their grandfather's heart trouble (which he keeps secret from his grown children), they seem less moved by grief than excited by the aptness of their birthday offering. Not even the wash of sentimental music on the soundtrack can keep the children's final exploits from seeming regrettably insensitive, to say the least.

Perhaps this is understandable in the context of the Rockwells' general effervescence, which helps them make light of situations another family might view as pathological. The nymphomania of daughter Aggie (who's in fact played appealingly by Suzy Amis) is treated as a good-hearted family joke as they all gather in the kitchen each morning to talk about what Aggie had been heard doing with a brand-new boyfriend the night before. In a less sunny film, Aggie would soon be having an affair with one of her brothers-in-law, but "Rocket Gibraltar" is, except for its preoccupation with the Viking funeral plot, remarkably oblivious to life's darker side.

•

"Rocket Gibraltar" is rated PG ("Parental Guidance Suggested"). It includes some mildly rude language.
JANET MASLIN
1988 S 2, C6:5

Americana

THE WIZARD OF LONELINESS, directed by Jenny Bowen; screenplay by Nancy Larson, based on the novel by John Nichols; additional written material furnished by Miss Bowen; director of photography, Richard Bowen; edited by Lisa Day; music by Michel Colombier; production designer, Jeffrey Beecroft; produced by Philip Porcella and Thom Tyson; released by Skouras Pictures Inc. At 57th Street Playhouse, Avenue of the Americas. Running time: 110 minutes. This film is rated PG-13.

Wendall	Lukas Haas
Sybil	Lea Thompson
Doc	John Randolph
Cornelia	Anne Pitoniak
Duffy	Dylan Baker
John T.	Lance Guest
Tom	Jeremiah Warner
Fred	Steve Hendrickson

By JENNIFER DUNNING

There are enough carefully researched period artifacts to stock a claustrophobically crowded museum. Scene after scene, shot in golden light and crammed with nicely homely faces, looks as if it came straight out of a Norman Rockwell portfolio. But fine performances take hold about a third of the way through "The Wizard of Loneliness," which opens today at the 57th Street Playhouse, and this chronicle of a lonely, bratty young boy adrift in a friendly Vermont village in 1944 becomes genuinely poignant and colorful.

Based on the novel of the same name by John Nichols, the author of "The Milagro Beanfield War," the film tells the story of 12-year-old Wendall Oler, who comes to live with his grandparents after the death of his unloving mother and the departure of his alienated father for the war. At first Wendall's only goal is to steal enough money to run away. But he is drawn irrevocably into the life of the town around him and of his lovably mad extended family. He comes to know his parents a little better and to love his imperturbably affectionate grandfather, his crusty grandmother, his spirited uncle and mysterious aunt and, especially, his little cousin, Tom.

An important catalyst for this gradual thawing is Duffy, his uncle's childhood friend and aunt's secret lover. Presumed dead, Duffy returns from the battlefront to hide out near the village, appearing first on the train taking Wendall to his new home. Sporting an anachronistic-looking beard, Duffy immediately establishes himself as a quiet lunatic. But it is the violence he wreaks with such deceptive gentleness on friends and family that finally yanks Wendall back to life emotionally.

"The Wizard of Loneliness" deals on more than one level with the abandonment of children by their parents. In a metaphor that is delicately conceived and realized, Duffy's destructiveness becomes as much a part of a knowable, natural world as the killing by Wendall's pet rabbit of its newborn babies. By the end of the film, the boy is invoking his fantasy powers as the "wizard of loneliness" not to destroy but to protect.

"The Wizard of Loneliness" hasn't quite the same sense of emotional truth as "Hope and Glory" and "My Life as a Dog," two recent films about a boy's coming of age. This is due in part to some peculiar lapses in authenticity in the screenplay by Nancy Larson. It is hard to believe, for instance, that a young man and woman growing up in a Vermont town in the 1940's would talk so casually of pornography and masturbation. Richard Bowen's photography is lovingly handsome, with one standout sequence that plays with surprising freshness with light and reflections.

•

But it is the actors, directed by Jenny Bowen, who bring "The Wizard of Loneliness" to vibrant life, gradually convincing us of the wonder of that place and time in history. Lukas Haas, who played the son in "Witness," makes Wendall as poignant as he is irritating in a performance of impressive restraint, nuance and detail. Dylan Baker is similarly nuanced as the pathetic Duffy, a cruelly violent madman who never becomes an unsympathetic character. Lea Thompson turns in a performance filled with glints of light and darkness as Wendall's tantalizing Aunt Sybil.

Lance Guest is sweetly madcap as Uncle John T., and Wendall's grandparents are familiar characters played with fresh vigor by John Randolph and Anne Pitoniak. Several of the characters are played by residents of Bristol, Vt., where "The Wizard of Loneliness" was filmed. Chief among them is little Jeremiah Warner, whose unaffectedly charming portrayal of Tom suggests that the town may have a fine young actor in its midst.

Long Ago Lukas Haas portrays a boy growing up during World War II in "The Wizard of Loneliness."

"The Wizard of Loneliness" is rated PG-13 ("Special Parental Guidance for Those Younger Than 13"). It contains one murder scene that could be disturbing to young children.
1988 S 2, C9:1

Straddling 2 Worlds

Pierce Brosnan

THE DECEIVERS, directed by Nicholas Meyer; screenplay by Michael Hirst, based on the novel by John Masters; director of photography, Walter Lassally; edited by Richard Trevor; music by John Scott; production design by Ken Adam; produced by Ismail Merchant; released by Cinecom Pictures. At the Sutton, 57th Street and Third Avenue. Running time: 112 minutes. This film is rated PG-13.

William Savage	Pierce Brosnan
Hussein	Saeed Jaffrey
Chandra Singh	Shashi Kapoor
Sarah Wilson	Helena Michell
Colonel Wilson	Keith Michell
George Anglesmith	David Robb
Feringeea	Tario Yunis
Nawab	Jalal Agha

The intrepid hero of "The Deceivers" is played by Pierce Brosnan, who is seen getting the best of a wild tiger during one of the film's early scenes. Obviously, this William Savage — a fictionalized version of one William Sleeman, a British officer living in the India of the 1820's — is quite a fellow. It develops that he is also a hero of the drawing room, sporting the prettily curled coiffure and red-and-gold-braid uniform peculiar to the time and place, or at least to this slightly fussy production.

William Savage is also revealed as a heroic undercover investigator who, disguising himself as an Indian, infiltrates the ranks of the murderous cult called the Thuggees to discover their secrets. William Sleeman evidently got to the bottom of the Thuggees' mystery; Mr. Brosnan as Savage, on the other hand, doesn't seem remotely plausible as an Indian, not even from the back.

"The Deceivers," which opens today at the Sutton, has an enjoyably touristy flavor and a hint of "Gunga Din," but it's too muddy to make good use of either the mysticism or historical interest inherent in its story. The Thuggees (from whom the word "thug" derives) were professional assassins with the methodology of a religious cult, infiltrating groups of travelers and then murdering them swiftly and terribly, according to certain prescribed forms (worship of the goddess Kali, sacramental eating of sugar and ritual strangulation by handkerchief were all part of the cult's practice). The Thuggees' reign of terror lasted more than 300 years and, according to the film, claimed two million victims.

•

The film, as directed by Nicholas Meyer, concentrates more fully on local color than on clear exposition of the Thuggees' strange story. The tininess of Michael Hirst's screenplay ("It's older than time and just as

Helena Michell in "The Deceivers," a Merchant Ivory production.

mysterious") hardly helps bring this material to life, any more than Mr. Brosnan's unconvincing and (despite several episodes in which he proves himself capable of violent killing) rather passive performance. Though the film observes Thuggee rituals with what is meant to be a growing fascination, it settles for skin-deep exoticism rather than real curiosity. In its own way, "The Deceivers" is oddly old-fashioned.

Fortunately, the presence of Saeed Jaffrey as the cult member induced to aid Savage in his masquerade gives the film added interest, since the excellent Mr. Jaffrey is so much more soulful and animated than anyone else here. Also in the cast, constrained by lavish costumes and even more lavish decorousness, are Helena Michell and Keith Michell, who are father and daughter (and are cast that way, as Savage's commanding officer and his new bride).

The film's most crazily ill-realized sequence finds Mr. Brosnan making love to a prostitute and hallucinating the presence of the two other key women in the story, so that as the three women meld together in his mind, the writhing six-armed female silhouette of the goddess Kali appears behind him on the wall. An unusually strong suspension of disbelief is as necessary to watching the rest of "The Deceivers" as it is here.

•

"The Deceivers" is rated PG-13 ("Special Parental Guidance Suggested for Those Younger Than 13"). It contains considerable violence, and the six-armed silhouette is nude.
JANET MASLIN
1988 S 2, C10:1

A Call-In Killer

Richard Belzer

FREEWAY, directed by Francis Delia; screenplay by Darrell Fetty and Mr. Delia, based on the novel by Deanne Barkley; director of photography, Frank Byers; edited by Philip J. Sgriccia; music by Joe Delia; production designer, Douglas Metrov; produced by Peter S. Davis and William Panzer; released by New World Pictures. At Movieland, Broadway and 47th Street, and Movie Center 5, 125th Street between Powell and Douglass Boulevards. Running time: 91 minutes. This film is rated R.

Sarah "Sunny" Harper .... Darlanne Fluegel
Frank Quinn .... James Russo
Edward Anthony Heller .... Billy Drago
Dr. David Lazarus .... Richard Belzer
Lieutenant Boyle .... Michael Callan
Detective Gomez .... Joey Palese
Lawyer .... Steve Franken

By RICHARD F. SHEPARD

The freeway killer is a maniac, a defrocked priest, a marksman and a fan of call-in radio, but he has apparently never had an automobile accident that was not of his own making. To a New Yorker, who lives in a place where highway traffic rarely loosens up enough to enjoy a wild chase,

"Freeway," the movie that opened yesterday at the Movieland, is the very stuff that Southern California is made of.

That is to say, it has cars and cultism, a beautiful blonde, a lean and dark ex-cop, a couple of encounters in bed and as many car-bumpings as are par for the course at an amusement park dodge 'em rink. "Freeway" draws inspiration from the car shootings that have captured headlines, but it is very much its own thing, which is not necessarily AAA's highest rating.

•

It is about a madman who shoots other drivers on the freeway as he mutters hysterical mystical cant over a car phone to a radio advice-giver. The police believe he is a random killer, but Sunny, the blond heroine, played by Darlanne Fluegel detects a pattern. So does the ex-cop, played by James Russo, and they join forces, and bodies, in the search for the villain who has done away with their spouses.

As a film, this vehicle has inadequate shocks for a stretch of potholed concrete that, in the long run, is more loud and colorful than attention-holding. The screenplay, by Darrell Fetty

and Francis Delia, who is also the director, has the feel of a pre-fab from central casting, down to the dialogue, the waggling of eyebrows and the supporting cast of cops. Billy Drago looks sufficiently spine-chilling, and Richard Belzer is quite credible as the ratings-conscious Dr. Lazarus, who is the psychologist and the only man to whom the evil fellow will speak.

"Freeway" may have its moments for automobile fans, but otherwise it makes a strong case for mass transportation.

1988 S 3, 10:6

FILM VIEW/Janet Maslin

Truth Eludes Fact and Fiction

ONE REASON WHY THE FEAture-length documentary has lately been in decline is that the fiction feature has subsumed its role. We're as apt to get our facts from lightly embroidered versions of real events as from the events themselves. The television movie, which can proudly base itself on a true story and then touch up the story to suit the audience's taste, has paved the way for this development, but television drama in itself is rarely alarming. It doesn't much matter whether a biography of Barbara Hutton starring Farrah Fawcett gets its facts straight — but when the subject is something like white supremacist groups and their murderous activities, that's another story.

Using real events as the basis for quasi-fiction has been a much more acceptable tactic for novelists than it is for film makers; perhaps it's less dangerous on the page, where the impact is less visceral and the reader better able to make distinctions. And the novelist's fictionalizing of real events is more self-evident as a technique than the film maker's equivalent approach may be. So Don DeLillo, going well beyond E. L. Doctorow's methods of intermingling real and fictional figures (in "Ragtime") or imagining the experiences of recognizable ones (in "The Book of Daniel"), goes so far as to include a disclaimer in "Libra," the new novel that extrapolates the life of Lee Harvey Oswald from exhaustive research into Oswald's real history.

"This is a work of imagination," Mr. DeLillo writes, in an afterword, adding: "Any novel about a major unresolved event would aspire to fill some of the blank spaces in the known record. To do this, I've altered and embellished reality, extended real people into imagined space and time, invented incidents, dialogues and characters. Because this book makes no claim to literal truth, because it is only itself, apart and complete, readers may find refuge here — a way of thinking about the assassination without being constrained by half-facts or overwhelmed by possibilities, by the tide of speculation that widens with the years."

■

The author's straightforward statement of purpose is indeed helpful in a book where the line between reality and imagination will be

By differing means, 'Betrayed' and 'The Thin Blue Line' rake over actual events.

indistinguishable to most readers, a book that chronicles well-known aspects of President Kennedy's assassination but also extends to include domestic conversations between Lee Harvey Oswald and his mother. If the reader is inevitably distracted by wondering which parts of this novel arise from research and which are pure invention, a viewer of Costa-Gavras's "Betrayed" is sure to ask the same questions. While "Betrayed" doesn't explain its modus operandi, it clearly combines news-inspired episodes with fictionalized embellishments.

The fiction involves a romance between an undercover F.B.I. agent (Debra Winger) and a hard-working family man (Tom Berenger) who turns out to be the leader of his local white supremacist cadre. The fact-based sections of the film are its most powerful, since they establish the most violent activities of white supremacist groups like the Aryan Nations and the Order; the assassination of a talk-show host, who is obviously modeled on Alan Berg, employs the Order's "ZOG" terminology (for "Zionist Occupied Government"). The section of the film that shows a white racist group staging a bank robbery to finance its activities also has some basis in fact. And even the film's extremely disturbing sequence showing white racists hunting and killing a black man has some connection with these groups' murderous activities.

However, "Betrayed" only uses this basis in fact as the framework for fiction, and not terribly believable fiction at that. After rattling the audience with the film's early shock scenes, Costa-Gavras never really returns to the violent racism that initially appeared to be the film's subject. Instead, he concentrates on the romance.

■

By switching gears in this way, the film does something very dangerous indeed: it stimulates the audience's alarm about real

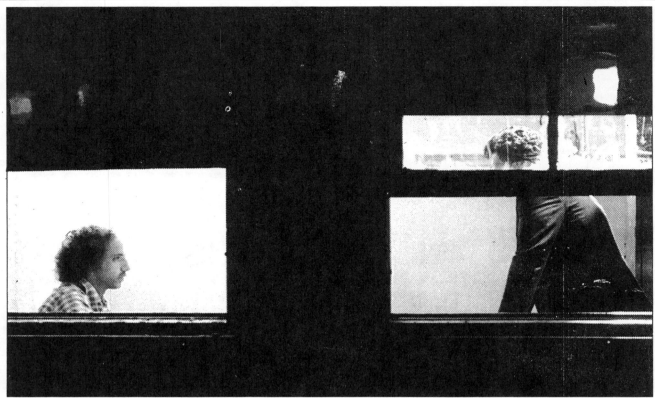

Mark Lipson

Adam Goldfine, portraying a man suspected of an actual murder, is interrogated by Michael Nicoll in "The Thin Blue Line."

events, then makes the events trivial and manageable. One of the principals even comes equipped with a computer listing of white racist operatives all over the country, as well as their potential targets. The film's dismaying implication is that if a list like this can be confiscated and the right villains apprehended, the problems initially used to upset the audience can easily be solved. Here, thanks to the reckless cross-breeding of real and fanciful information, is a ready opportunity for the audience to stop taking an explosive subject seriously.

Audiences can always be expected to wonder where the truth in a partially-true story lies (certainly Paul Schrader's forthcoming "Patty Hearst" will raise the same questions). It's reasonable to hope that a film maker will either make clear where the line between fact and imagination falls or blur the distinction with some larger purpose in mind, as Mr. DeLillo has.

Errol Morris has done it, too, in "The Thin Blue Line," a film that plays in a genuinely original way upon the audience's impulse to discern what is or is not real. This film, which unravels a complicated Texas murder case and even concludes with a virtual confession from a central figure in the investigation, nevertheless becomes more and more nightmarishly bewildering as it goes on.

Using interviews, strikingly enlarged details and stylized re-enactments, Mr. Morris's much better film starts off in search of the facts. But "The Thin Blue Line," carefully shaping evidence and underlining the false ring of much of what is said, intentionally reveals how elusive the truth can be — even when the facts are at the film maker's disposal. Especially then. ☐

1988 S 4, II:17:1

A Movie That Cannily Celebrates The American Businessman As a Hero

John Gross

IF YOU BUILD A BETTER mousetrap than your neighbor, you are quite liable to get your fingers caught in it. In 1946 Preston Tucker set out to produce the car of his dreams, the "Tucker Torpedo" — a vehicle that in terms of design, performance and safety was far in advance of its period. By the time he went out of business, in 1948, he had been forced into bankruptcy and put on trial for fraud: he was acquitted, but his great days were over.

Francis Ford Coppola has taken the Torpedo episode as the basis for his latest movie, "Tucker." A dark enough theme, you might have supposed: a story calculated to prompt sardonic thoughts about the forces by which Tucker was crushed — big business and its political allies — and melancholy reflections about the fate of the pioneer.

The predominant mood that Mr. Coppola establishes, however, is one of brightness. Perhaps "Tucker" ought to be a cautionary tale, but it breezes ahead as though it were a success story, as though the setbacks were only temporary and the villains were ultimately vanquished. It has the pace and high spirits of a celebration.

But what exactly is being celebrated?

In the first place, obviously, the movie's hero. Whatever the real Preston Tucker may have been like, the Tucker played by Jeff Bridges is a paragon of decency no less than of dynamism — good-humored, direct, energetic, limitlessly resilient, as handsome as a Tucker Torpedo.

He is surrounded, too, by a copybook family — loyal wife, cute kids — and by a bunch of inspired, oddball colleagues who have been infected by

Ralph Nelson

Jeff Bridges as the title character in "Tucker," Francis Ford Coppola's study of the auto innovator Preston Tucker—a paragon of decency

his dream (even the downbeat machinist who pretends that he hasn't been). The Tucker home is a comfortable frame house; there are lots of dogs, and a plump cook, and, when morale needs a fillip, collective trips to the local soda fountain. One way and another, it is all rather like a Norman Rockwell come to life.

Are there really no shadows or hidden complexities? None to speak of. In the sequence where Tucker consults Howard Hughes, for example, another director might have implied that he was meeting a macabre counterpart, a dark double. But as Mr. Coppola handles the episode, it is the contrast between the two men that comes across. Where Hughes is a maverick whose ambitions are pushing him close to madness, Tucker remains boyish and unspoiled — an effect heightened by the fact that he is accompanied on the visit by his youngest son.

■

Then there is Tucker's smile. He smiles when he hears good news, and he smiles when he hears bad news. At first this is disconcerting — the man must have something to hide; then you are gradually persuaded that all the smiles are equally honest ones, that smiling in the face of adversity simply signifies defiant optimism. And if he sometimes vents his frustration by punching walls or throwing the phone about — well, even faultless heroes must be allowed one or two faults for the sake of plausibility.

If the movie made any pretense of

being an exercise in documentary realism, its blue-sky presentation of Tucker and his team would soon become cloying and absurd. But it is essentially a myth or fairy tale. An American myth, and a capitalist fairy tale: for its purposes, the two are much the same thing.

The equation is spelled out as plainly as possible in the long courtroom speech toward the end of the film, where Tucker takes charge of his own defense. What he has been trying to do, he tells the jury, embodies "everything the country stands for," and by implication everything the country has recently been fighting for — the larger freedom of which the free enterprise system is an inseparable component.

Americans invented that system, he insists; and if they abandon it they will end up buying their cars and radios from the countries they have just defeated. Not that he really believes that things will ever come to quite such a desperate pass.

It hardly needs to be pointed out that Americans didn't really invent free enterprise, or the market economy, or call it what you will; but it is a measure of how deeply committed the country is to capitalist ideals that a man like Tucker can take it for granted that they did. Nowhere else are businessmen so readily treated as heroes.

Watching the movie, I found my thoughts straying at one point to another film in which technological progress is stifled by entrenched interests, the old Alec Guinness comedy "The Man in the White Suit." The

man in the white suit invents an indestructible fabric — and it is characteristic of the difference between British mythology and American mythology that he should be a technician pure and simple rather than a mixture of technician and entrepreneur.

■

Tucker, by contrast, sees himself as heir to a tradition in which it is hard to tell the two vocations apart. He invokes Edison, the Wright brothers, Henry Ford and finally, unbeatably, the example of a Founding Father: "If Benjamin Franklin were alive today, he'd be arrested for flying a kite without a license."

Today — there's the rub. For Tucker's experiences have convinced him that he grew up "a generation too late." And who is to blame for the decline that has set in, the slow throttling of the American dream? He has no hesitation in naming the guilty men: "the bureaucrats."

But this is in fact a piece of evasion. The prime villain of the movie, the one we actually see, is a politico rather than a bureaucrat, the scheming Senator Ferguson; and behind Ferguson and the forces he mobilizes lurk the big car makers of Detroit. The ultimate enemies at whose hands Tucker suffers defeat are fellow capitalists.

It would be possible, no doubt, to interpret the story as a clash between two phases of capitalist culture: mature corporate capitalism and the earlier capitalism of the self-made innovator. But innovators are

usually in a minority, and men like Tucker are always being made to feel that they have been born too late (or too soon).

In the end the most paradoxical aspect of "Tucker" is the movie's ambivalent attitude toward the period in which it is set. If we judge the story by its outcome, the late 1940's were a gray, unheroic age: there was no longer the scope there had once been for dreamers and pioneers. Yet the feeling that the film conveys is very different. It is one of innocence, confidence and euphoria.

Perhaps the nostalgia with which Mr. Coppola evokes the past is a little tongue in cheek. But only a little. When the movie reminds us of the raucous energies of 40's pop culture, for instance — when we hear the blasts of "Hold That Tiger!", or when the concluding motorcade glides past a movie house showing "Incendiary Blonde" — we feel that they are energies Tucker himself shares, that he is not so much a victim of his period as a representative figure. And when we find that his final vindication, however sentimental it may be, produces the requisite lump in the throat, we may equally well wonder whether he doesn't transcend any one period, and whether Mr. Coppola hasn't tapped something permanent in the American psyche. □

1988 S 4, II:33:1

335

River Phoenix and Martha Plimpton in "Running on Empty."

Running Mates

RUNNING ON EMPTY, directed by Sidney Lumet; written by Naomi Foner; director of photography, Gerry Fisher; film editor, Andrew Mondshein; music by Tony Mottola; production designer, Philip Rosenberg; produced by Amy Robinson and Griffin Dunne; released by Warner Brothers. At National Twin, Broadway and 44th Street, and other theaters. Running time: 115 minutes. This film is rated PG-13.

Annie Pope	Christine Lahti
Danny Pope	River Phoenix
Arthur Pope	Judd Hirsch
Harry Pope	Jonas Abry
Lorna Phillips	Martha Plimpton
Mr. Phillips	Ed Crowley
Gus Winant	L. M. Kit Carson
Mr. Patterson	Steven Hill

By JANET MASLIN

The Pope family knows things that other families don't. For instance, the Popes know how to leave town forever on a moment's notice, abandoning everything, even the family dog. The parents, Arthur (Judd Hirsch) and Annie (Christine Lahti), know how to find new jobs that don't require much experience or attract much attention. The children, Danny (River Phoenix) and Harry (Jonas Abry), know they ought to miss school on the day when class photographs are being taken. All the Popes know how to change the subject smoothly when anyone asks who they are or where they came from.

They have settled into this furtive, peripatetic life for one reason: because 15 years ago, when Arthur and Annie were campus radicals, they blew up a defense research laboratory involved in the manufacturing of napalm and badly injured a man who was inside. This earned them a place on the F.B.I.'s Most Wanted list and sent them deep underground. As "Running on Empty" begins, with a tense, efficient sequence that shows the family staging an emergency departure from a town in Florida, one thing is clear: the Popes are approaching a crisis. They have been living this way too long.

The catalyst for change is 17-year-old Danny, who has been on the run all his life. Now Danny has reached the age where people ask him where he'll be applying to college, and it's a painful question. Though Danny knows his weary, demoralized par-

ents need [their] children to hold them together, he's beginning to long for a place in the wider world. When a girl in the New Jersey town where the Popes have resettled complains that normal life is dreary, Danny can't help saying that it doesn't sound so bad.

•

Were it not for Danny (played outstandingly well by River Phoenix), "Running on Empty," which opens today at the National and other theaters, would be as threadbare as the Popes themselves. The parents' story is much less affecting than their son's. (The second boy, Harry, plays a very minor role in Pope family dynamics, and in the film.) Perhaps Arthur and Annie's paying the consequences of their former radicalism would seem more compelling if the radicalism were believable, but the otherwise good screenplay (by Naomi Foner) rings false about the Popes' past.

Despite their having blown up the lab, and despite Arthur's occasional outbursts (as when he denounces a chamber-music recital that the musically gifted Danny wants to attend as "decadent," "white-skinned" and "privileged"), the Popes seem like ordinary, middle-class parents in all but the obvious ways. If that is indeed the point, then it's a glib one, and the casting doesn't help. Even in a worn black T-shirt and dingy surroundings, delivering abrupt diatribes like the one above, Mr. Hirsch is not easily confused with Abbie Hoffman.

Miss Lahti has been given more to work with, thanks to old newspaper clips that identify her as the "Fugitive Deb" she was in 1971, and to the screenplay's having given her a still-radical old boyfriend (L. M. Kit Carson) and an estranged father (Steven Hill) with whom she can interact. The film shows its histrionic side in encounters like Annie's tearful, difficult meeting with her father. But the actors are often so good that they're able to be real and touching even when the material sounds strained.

•

The heart of "Running on Empty" is the slow-burning romance between Danny and the smart, tomboyish Lorna Phillips (Martha Plimpton), the daughter of the high school music teacher (Ed Crowley) in the New Jer-

sey town where the Popes put down temporary roots. Both father and daughter recognize Danny as an exceptional young man, and the film is at its most warm-hearted as Danny finds all the ordinariness and stability he has lacked in the Phillips household. The courtship between Danny and Lorna is staged especially disarmingly, with Mr. Phoenix and Miss Plimpton conveying a sweet, serious and believably gradual attraction. "You have a lot of secrets, don't you?" Lorna asks after the couple's first physical encounter. "And now you have another one."

"Running on Empty" works best when it plays upon emotions generated by the Popes' unique predicament, something that it often does rather shamelessly. It helps that Sidney Lumet has directed the film in a crisp, handsome style that diminishes the maudlin or unlikely aspects of its story, even when they threaten to intrude. Jarringly convenient details — like Danny's outstanding musical talent, or like the newspaper clipping through which young Harry learns of his family's past for what seems to be the first time — are helpfully downplayed, whenever possible. The film has the ring of a good story, if not the ring of truth.

The casting, for the most part, is very good, as is the emphasis on fascinating minutiae of the Popes' life, like what it takes for one of them to go to a dentist (David Margulies). At other times, as when the Popes and Lorna celebrate a birthday by dancing happily to James Taylor's "Fire and Rain" (doing the Twist to a particularly pained verse, which reflects very indirectly on their own ordeal), the film can sound abruptly stagy notes, too. Luckily, "Running on Empty" has a lot more momentum than its title suggests, enough energy to take an unusual and intriguing premise and see it through.

•

"Running on Empty" is rated PG-13 ("Special Parental Guidance Suggested for Those Younger Than 13"). It contains some harsh language.

1988 S 9, C6:5

Theresa Russell

TRACK 29, directed by Nicolas Roeg; screenplay by Dennis Potter; director of photography, Alex Thomson; music by Stanley Myers; edited by Tony Lawson; production designer, Shuna Harwood; produced by Rick McCallum; released by Island Pictures. At D. W. Griffith, 59th Street east of Third Avenue; Quad Cinema, 13th Street, near Fifth Avenue. Running time: 90 minutes. This film is rated R.

Linda	Theresa Russell
Martin	Gary Oldman
Henry	Christopher Lloyd
Arlanda	Colleen Camp
Nurse Stein	Sandra Bernhard
Dr. Bernard Fairmont	Seymour Cassel

From the fevered and weirdly musical imagination of Dennis Potter ("Pennies From Heaven," "The Singing Detective") comes "Track

Mystery Man Gary Oldman tells a bored Southern housewife he's her long-lost child in "Track 29."

29," the portrait of a deluded, repressed and neglected Southern housewife married to a nasty, infantile doctor who has trains on the brain. (The title comes from the song "Chattanooga Choo-Choo"). This story has found its way into the even more fevered hands of Nicolas Roeg, a director who has done brilliant work when the material was right ("Don't Look Now") and hair-raising work when it wasn't ("Bad Timing: A Sensual Obsession").

Though the screenwriter and the director clearly share certain affinities, their collective efforts on "Track 29," which opens today at the D. W. Griffith and Quad Cinema, amount to overkill, particularly since the direction is so laden with contempt for the characters. The housewife, Linda (played by Theresa Russell, who looks great but speaks with a ridiculous drawl), wears lavender in virtually every scene and is presented as the epitome of brainless, oversexed Americana.

The toy-filled gingerbread house where Linda lives with her husband, Henry (Christopher Lloyd), watching cartoons together as they eat their breakfast cereal, is equally hellish. It has a satellite dish on the lawn, a huge water tower next door and an array of humorlessly hideous knick-knacks inside. Part of the house is devoted to Henry's fantastically intricate computer-operated train set, which matters much more to him than Linda does. And Linda, bored to distraction, spends a lot of time in the backyard swimming pool and sometimes wears a bathing cap at mealtime.

•

The film revolves around the appearance in Linda's life of a mysterious young Englishman named Martin (Gary Oldman), who insists he is the baby Linda conceived at an amusement park when she was a teen-ager, and then gave away. Arriving to the tune of John Lennon's primal "Mother," Martin quickly insinuates himself into Linda's life. "I've come all the way across the pond in search of my Ma-ma," says he, stabbing a knife into a fried egg for emphasis.

Martin quickly worms his way into the very heart of Linda's psyche, as

Mr. Roeg begins to establish that he may only be a figment of her tortured and steamy imagination. This possibility is a good deal more interesting than the film ever allows it to become, since "Track 29" dissolves into a parade of hopelessly condescending images. There is, for instance, the convention of train enthusiasts that is addressed by Henry, who sounds like an evangelist as he declares, "I'm *proud* of my model railroad." The Stars and Stripes waves proudly behind him, the majorettes wiggle and Henry's mistress, a nurse who spanks him (Sandra Bernhard), is moved to tears.

Though Mr. Roeg's films can often be perverse (and startlingly, bracingly so), they are rarely this silly. Nor are they this maddening, since "Track 29" does contain the seeds of something tantalizing. Linda's attempt to come to terms with her past through a wildly unpredictable, even dangerous fantasy has the stamp of Mr. Potter's better material, but it has been made too mindless to have any impact. The real urgency of Mr. Oldman's performance, and the wicked blandness of Mr. Lloyd's, seem regrettably wasted, under the circumstances.   *JANET MASLIN*

                          1988 S 9, C10:3

Banana Republic

MOON OVER PARADOR, produced and directed by Paul Mazursky; screenplay by Leon Capetanos and Mr. Mazursky, based on a story by Charles G. Booth; director of photography, Donald McAlpine; edited by Stuart Pappe; music by Maurice Jarre; production designer, Pato Guzman; released by Universal Pictures. At Beekman, 65th Street and Second Avenue, and other theaters. Running time: 105 minutes. This film is rated PG-13.

Jack Noah	Richard Dreyfuss
Roberto Strausmann	Raul Julia
Madonna	Sonia Braga
Ralph	Jonathan Winters
Alejandro	Fernando Rey
Himself	Sammy Davis Jr.
Clint	Michael Greene
Midge	Polly Holliday
Carlo	Charo
Magda	Marianne Sagebrecht
Momma	Carlotta Gerson (Paul Mazursky)
First Dictator	Lorin Dreyfuss

Parador, the Caribbean dictatorship where Paul Mazursky's new film takes place, is definitely a nice place to visit. The carnivals are colorful, the music lively, and the natives are friendly — even the bottom-pinching dictator and the diabolical, scheming chief of police.

However, for reasons that are difficult to pinpoint, Parador is not a particularly funny place. Though Mr. Mazursky's new "Moon Over Parador" has the makings of a clever satire, it never gets beyond the fond, gentle mood of an amusing travelogue.

The film's comic potential rests entirely in its premise about a so-so actor who gets his very best role when he is asked to impersonate Parador's newly deceased dictator. Jack Noah (Richard Dreyfuss), first seen hanging around the Public Theater in Manhattan and remembering his Paradoran escapade in flashback, was dressed up like Don Johnson to shoot a bad movie in Parador when he happened to meet the country's dictator. Jack bore an eerie resemblance to this leader (whose name was a very un-Paradoran Simms), and a fellow cast member unhelpfully blurted out the news that Jack did a good Simms impersonation. Soon af-

Leading Role Richard Dreyfuss portrays an actor forced to portray a Caribbean dictator in "Moon Over Parador."

terward, Simms had a heart attack and his behind-the-scenes strongman (Raul Julia) recruited Jack Noah for the part.

•

Jack has agreed, but he wants to do this on his own terms. They are actor's terms, and then some. When Jack makes a speech to the assembled Paradoran multitudes, the speech is apt to contain familiar song lyrics (on one occasion, he weaves together "The Impossible Dream" and "September Song"). And he regards televised aerobics as a way of communicating with the Paradoran people, who have been outfitted with T-shirts bearing Simms's picture. When asked a tough question by the press, he waves to the reporters and pretends not to hear over the sound of his nearby helicopter, giving a Reaganesque wave. Understandably, after all this, Jack comes to believe that he has found the role of a lifetime.

"Moon Over Parador," which opens today at the Beekman and other theaters, is more sentimental than comic about this, though its mood is never less than sweetly engaging. It is also somewhat sentimental about Parador itself, an elaborate but oddly shapeless creation. A lot of energy has gone into giving Parador its own flag (peach, white and robin's egg blue), its own national anthem (a glum mix of "O Tannenbaum" and Mendelssohn's wedding march), and its own favorite entertainers, like Sammy Davis Jr. But Mr. Mazursky takes this one step too far by actually producing Mr. Davis, having him sing and make some extemporaneous remarks.

Mr. Mazursky has obviously had fun casting the film, with Charo, Fernando Rey and Marianne Sagebrecht as part of the staff that Jack Noah inherits (the servants immediately recognize him as an actor, but they decide to humor him), and Jonathan Winters as a very peculiar American visitor. The director himself, in a black ruffled dress, looks suitably formidable as the dictator's fashion-plate mother. Sonia Braga shimmies energetically in a number of eye-

catching outfits, but hers is only one of many characters that remain much too vague to be interesting. As the dead man's former mistress, a highly pragmatic sex bomb who easily transfers her affections to Jack Noah, Miss Braga is certainly glamorous. But the film is too ready to concentrate on her wiggling, and too slow to allow her any wit.

The film's jokes about actors are affectionate ("TV is better than it was, right?" Jack asks a colleague, at the possibility of a television job), but its political satire is notably weak. "Vote for whom you want — this is a free dictatorship!" says a Paradoran as Simms runs for election on both of the country's tickets, and the humor never gets much beyond that. The film's closing turn of events, which has the potential to be quite diabolical, is one of many comic opportunites that Mr. Mazursky, very uncharacteristically, lets slip away.

•

"Moon Over Parador" is rated PG-13 ("Special Parental Guidance Suggested for Those Younger Than 13"). It contains numerous scenes of scantily clad Paradoran dancers.
                          JANET MASLIN

                          1988 S 9, C13:1

Life on the Edge

Paul McIsaac

DOC'S KINGDOM, screenplay and direction by Robert Kramer; photography by Robert Machover; edited by Sandrine Cavafian; music by Barre Philips; a Filmagem/Garance Production. At the Public, 425 Lafayette Street. Running time: 90 minutes. This film has no rating.

Doc	Paul McIsaac
Jimmy	Vincent Gallo
César	João César Monteiro
Mr. Ruy	Ruy Furtado

By RICHARD F. SHEPARD

There is a curious morning-after quality about "Doc's Kingdom," the new Robert Kramer movie that opens today at the Public Theater. The night before was 20 years ago, when Doc, the protagonist, was involved in the passionate upheavals of the 1960's

that promised, perhaps threatened, to make the world anew.

Now, Doc is a burned-out ex-radical living in Portugal, where he practices medicine, a profession he took to when he decided that the proper course was to heal, not to destroy. He is a quiet man, the quintessential loner hemmed in by his rejected activist past and unadjusted to his passive present. As an ill and alcoholic Doc, Paul McIsaac creates a tightly wound figure, even at his booziest. He hears that local radicals are out to get him because he is an American, and he wants to meet them, but he keeps a gun to protect himself.

•

Meanwhile, Jimmy, a young man in New Jersey, played no less tensely by Vincent Gallo, is distraught at his mother's death and learns by going through her mail that he has a father, Doc, who is still alive and living in Portugal. He travels there and the two men have an emotional meeting that goes from bellicose hostility to understanding.

Mr. Kramer — who was born in New York but moved to Europe in the late 70's — established himself as a film maker with something to say about the way the world is and how it should be with about a dozen movies, including the 1969 "Ice." "Ice" foretold of urban guerrilla warfare and explained to many the feelings of the Left in those tumultuous times. In "Doc's Kingdom," he offers a moody portrait of disillusionment, yet one that falls short of despair. It is impossible for one to escape the past, even Doc, whose "kingdom," as the film maker describes it, is always on the edge. Doc is always seeking to cut free from any bonds, whether fatherhood or ideology.

The scenes are placed in grayish, murky settings on a gloomy waterfront or in residential regions high above the city. Although these are punctuated with other segments, such as those set in the brisk and noisy atmosphere of Doc's hospital, the atmosphere is one that somehow gives the feeling of a mystery about to happen. There is no mystery, but there is always the sense of impending personal tragedy for Doc.

"Doc's Kingdom" has a European flavor that goes beyond geography. The photography by Robert Machover clings to the actors' faces, giving an emphasis that is somehow reminiscent of silent-film techniques. Mr. Kramer's screenplay is not compelling, nor was it probably so intended, but he has created a haunting picture, one that prompts ruminations about formulas for living and what they come to mean to idealists who are ultimately defeated by their own humanity.

                          1988 S 9, C10:3

FILM VIEW

JANET MASLIN

Baseball Movies Turn Men to Mush

THE LESS ONE KNOWS about baseball — and I happen to know less than almost anybody — the more one is apt to notice in movies about the game. It can be wonderfully liberating to have little idea whether the rookie is really any good, whether the aging manager stands a chance of breathing new life into his career or whether the team has any hope of winning the pennant, since the attention is thus freed to concentrate on more pressing matters. The most salient of these, in almost every film about the game, is baseball's uncanny way of turning otherwise strong men into mush.

After all, Barry Levinson, much admired for the wisecracking humor in films like "Diner" and "Good Morning, Vietnam," was moved to uncharacteristic rapture when he made a film about the national pastime. Mr. Levinson's film of Bernard Malamud's novel "The Natural," which stands as the Cadillac of baseball movies, is best remembered for a prettiness truly baffling to the non-fan.

There were (thanks to Caleb Deschanel's gorgeous cinematography) the beautiful bat-carving sequence, in which the bat got a name ("Wonderboy"); the opening and closing scenes of catch being played in sunlit, windswept wheat fields; and the spectacular slow-motion climax that sends brilliant sparks cascading down upon a winning team.

There was, most remarkably, the scene that had Glenn Close as the hero's sweetheart rising to her feet in the

Bob Marshak

Whooping it up in John Sayles's "Eight Men Out"

bleachers to reveal what seemed to be a light bulb in her hat (the better to create a halo-like glow). And there was the moment in which Robert Redford pitched in slow motion to highlight the extraordinary talents of Mr. Malamud's hero, but such obligatory slow-motion scenes always startle the non-fan. At times like these, even we can tell that Mr. Redford, or Michael Moriarty (in "Bang the Drum Slowly"), or whoever it is, looks a lot more like a movie star than a real player.

Perhaps real baseball aficionados fail to notice such intrusions of reality into the baseball film's myth-making process, just as they also pointedly overlook the sentimental excesses that are peculiar to the subject. In "Stealing Home" (one of several current baseball movies, the others being John Sayles's anatomy of the 1919 Black Sox scandal, "Eight Men Out," and the romantic comedy "Bull Durham"), Jodie Foster plays

the older woman who made an ineradicable impression on the film's young hero when she gave him a little gold baseball necklace, telling him what a great player he would be some day.

The film's crowning bit of sports totemism finds Mark Harmon, as the hero, playing scenes with an urn containing the ashes of Miss Foster, his baseball muse, which is adorned with a baseball cap. Without fully grasping what baseball means to those who love it, we non-fans do understand its unique nature at times like this. A scene in which an urn wore a football helmet would never work at all.

Since baseball serves as such an all-embracing metaphor, it often provides the backdrop for films that aren't really about baseball at all; these, needless to say, are the non-fan's favorite kind. "Bang the Drum Slowly" (1973) is so predominantly a film about friendship — about the love and loyalty between two men, sentiments perhaps expressed more comfortably in the ballpark setting than elsewhere — that it hardly involves any ballplaying at all. The actors, Michael Moriarty as a star pitcher and Robert De Niro as the tobacco-chewing catcher who is dying of Hodgkin's disease, play a lot of scenes in dugouts and locker rooms, but beyond that, the emphasis on baseball is actually slight. The film's footage of these two loping around a stadium to the sad strains of "The Streets of Laredo" is at least as memorable as its ballgame scenes.

"Bull Durham" gives the game much more attention than that, but it, too, is primarily about other things: about the roguishness of the players, the overripe poetry in their souls (and in their conversation), the specialness that lets them live outside life's usual rules. This last conceit is an awfully lucky one, since the Susan Sarandon character — the baseball angel who lives for the game, is a big help at batting practice and obligingly works sex into her training program for new players — would undoubtedly be stoned to death if she ever interacted with anyone other than ballplayers. Friends, neighbors and most team wives and girl-

friends are conveniently invisible during most of the film.

John Sayles's "Eight Men Out" is the rare baseball film that makes the game seem serious and exciting, yet also manages to be

America's national pastime has a way of turning sloppily sentimental on the screen.

about much more. Like the director's earlier and more solemn "Matewan," this film about the 1919 Black Sox scandal tells of working men who are cornered by forces beyond their control, in this case the gamblers who stand to make a killing by inducing the White Sox to throw the World Series. Mr. Sayles tells this story of faith and disillusionment with great sympathy, but "Eight Men Out" is remarkably unsentimental, especially for a film on this subject. The hopeful young faces of the actors who play the White Sox, at first full of promise and later clouded with shame, say as much about baseball's place in the heart of a nation as anything can.

Though mush is mercifully absent here, there are the inescapable touches without which no baseball movie would be worthy of the name. There are little kids in newsboy caps, breathless fans in the bleachers, and base-running that makes the dust really fly. And there is the clarion rendition of the National Anthem by an Irish tenor (Patrick Grant), the perfect embodiment of this film's nostalgia, intelligence and real emotion. □

1988 S 11, II:1:3

Joel Warren

Susan Sarandon and Kevin Costner, pitching woo in "Bull Durham"

Sheila Hancock and Peter Capaldi in "The Love Child."

Cool Flashes

THE LOVE CHILD, directed by Robert Smith; written by Gordon Hann; photographed by Thaddeus O'Sullivan; edited by John Davies; produced by Angela Topping; a British film Institute-Channel 4 presentation of a Frontroom Film. At Film Forum 1, 57 Watts Street. Running time: 102 minutes. This film has no rating.

Edith	Sheila Hancock
Dillon	Peter Capaldi
Maurice	Percy Herbert
Bernadette	Lesley Sharp
The voices	Alexei Sayle

By JANET MASLIN

Dillon (Peter Capaldi) doesn't really know what it's like "when you're a Pink Frog" (to quote a big acid-rock hit of the 1960's), but he thinks perhaps he should. Dillon's father was the leader of the Pink Frogs, but he and Dillon's hippie mother died long before their son ever knew them.

For most of his life, Dillon has lived with his grandmother, Edith (Sheila Hancock), who is a much freer spirit than he. Dillon has grown up to work as a dispirited accounts clerk for a large, faceless corporation, and there's little in his present life to recall his unusual past. There are a few reminders, though, like the fact that inanimate objects — beer cans, public toilets — sometimes talk to him.

Like most of the members of Dillon's family, Edith has never married, and she remains feisty and unconventional. Not so her grandson, who imagines a more or less normal life for himself but who, during the course of Robert Smith's "Love Child," gradually drifts away from that goal. Seen dashing off to work early in the film, then sitting around the office chatting idly with colleagues about Paul McCartney's income, Dillon slowly evolves to the point where he is showing up at work with nail polish on. The film traces this transformation in a thorough and amusing way.

•

"The Love Child," a dry and nicely unpredictable British comedy, is the work of Frontroom Productions, a group whose chief concern is conveying a sense of place. Accordingly, "The Love Child" is loose and leisurely, more intent on depicting a wide range of characters in its Brixton setting than on confining itself to a narrow story. However, the relations between Dillon and his grandmother are outlined in such a lively way that the film never seems to drift.

Mr. Smith and the screenwriter, Gordon Hann, find much wry humor in the clash of manners between this ever more desperate young man and this serene, foxy Granny, who during the course of the film is reunited with Dillon's long-lost grandfather, the family crook. "The Love Child" concludes with a party celebrating this reunion, and has a coda in which two punks discuss the fact that gerbils mate for all of their six-year life span. "That's bearable, I s'pose," says one punk, with a shrug.

"The Love Child," which opens today at the Film Forum 1, is engagingly acted by Mr. Capaldi, who makes Dillon so panicky that even the sight of a fellow train passenger reading about Charles and Diana can raise his anxiety level, and by Miss Hancock, who makes the grandmother a delightfully outspoken creature. Hippie memorabilia scattered through the apartment that grandmother and grandson share also contribute some color, as do incidental characters like Bernadette (Lesley Sharp), an artist who's invited over for a bath one day and later brings out an unexpected side of Dillon's nature by painting him to look like an ancient Egyptian.

Though the mood of the film is always clear, the sound is not. American audiences may have some difficulty in making out some of the film's slangier dialogue.

1988 S 14, C20:5

MILES FROM HOME, directed by Gary Sinise; written by Chris Gerolmo; director of photography, Elliot Davis; edited by Jane Schwartz Jaffe; music by Robert Folk; production designer, David Gropman; produced by Frederick Zollo and Paul Kurta; released by Cinecom Pictures. At Paris, 58th Street, west of Fifth Avenue. Running time: 113 minutes. This film is rated R.

Frank Roberts Sr.	Brian Dennehy
Young Frank	Jason Campbill
Young Terry	Austin Bamgarner
Nikita Khrushchev	Larry Poling
Frank Roberts Jr.	Richard Gere
Terry Roberts	Kevin Anderson
Mark	Terry Kinney
Sally	Penelope Ann Miller
Jennifer	Helen Hunt
Exotic dancer	Laurie Metcalf
Barry Maxwell	John Malkovich

By JANET MASLIN

The farm of the fictitious Roberts family was once such a shining example of American agricultural expertise that when Nikita Khrushchev visited Iowa, it was the Roberts place that he wanted to see. That remarkable moment is captured in the rapturous slow-motion prologue to "Miles From Home," which views Khrushchev's visit through the proud eyes of the two young Roberts boys (with Brian Dennehy making a fleeting appearance as their father). But today, with Frank Roberts Sr. gone and the farm in the hands of his sons, Frank Jr. (Richard Gere) and Terry (Kevin Anderson), the place is on the verge of bankruptcy. What has gone wrong?

The answer, quite literally, is blowing in the wind. It can also be heard in the chirping of the insects, the rustling of the cornstalks, the swelling of the plaintive soundtrack music and any of the other sounds that fill the empty spaces in Gary Sinise's insistently lyrical new film, saying things that the actors seldom can.

•

"Miles From Home," which opens today at the Paris, has an original and articulate screenplay by Chris Gerolmo (reflecting the bleak, mythic heartland of Bruce Springsteen's "Nebraska" album, an acknowledged influence on Mr. Gerolmo), but its style nonetheless seems very terse. That's because so much tongue-tied anguish, so much seething, so much mournful music, so much painful indecisiveness is allowed to overpower the characters' every thought or action.

Although Mr. Sinise, the co-founder and former artistic director of Chicago's Steppenwolf Theater Company, presents a clear vision of these farmers and their tragic predicament, his film is often sidetracked by mood-heightening elements that it doesn't need. The story, sad and inexorable, speaks powerfully enough for itself.

•

After the 1959 prologue (which has been expertly doctored to resemble an old newsreel), the film moves to the present, where it finds the Roberts brothers quite literally awaiting a storm. "It's a big 'un; she's comin' in fast," says Mr. Gere, as Frank, in the film's typically blunt farm dialect. The real storm on the horizon is, of course, a fiscal one, as the bank prepares to call in its loan and the Robertses, in a preliminary fund-raising move, sell off some of their household

goods. "Must be sad to be so broke you gotta sell everything, and everyone knows you got nothin' left," says a pretty, somewhat too radiant customer named Sally (Penelope Ann Miller), not realizing that Terry is one of the farm's embattled owners. In any case, Terry has soon fallen in love with her.

Frank, the older brother, is a fellow of more complex emotions — actually quite a fascinating character, although his nature never emerges quite as clearly as it could. Driven to extraordinary heights of bitterness by his feelings of failure, Frank has the idea of burning down the farm rather than peacefully allowing the bank to foreclose on it. The fire, which is even more spectacularly pretty than the film's waving-wheatfield scenes, has an unexpected side effect as far as the Roberts brothers are concerned. It turns them into heroes in the eyes of their fellow Iowans, who share their rage (and admire their tactics — one of the Robertses' subsequent brainstorms is to steal a Mercedes-Benz from in front of the offices of the Federal Home Administration).

Although Terry, the more passive of the brothers, merely goes along with this and other such exploits, Frank allows his new celebrity to go to his head. Propelled by grief, he begins to show off, as in a bank holdup scene that has Frank and Terry arguing endlessly over whether to rob the place, while the bewildered bank customers simply stand by. At another, equally odd moment, Frank interrupts his necking with Sally's friend Jennifer (Helen Hunt) at a county fair when he hears of an event involving a prize ox. In the rodeo ring, watching the ox's owner pushing his animal way beyond its strength, Frank stuns the crowd by shooting the animal to put it out of its misery.

•

Both Frank and Mr. Gere can be bewildering at such moments, but "Miles From Home" does convey the pain and desperation of this character. Mr. Gere's performance, like Mr. Sinise's direction, incorporates more dilatory, decorative flourishes than are really needed, but its essential urgency comes through, as does its liveliness; leading the life of the outlaw, Frank visibly begins to thrive. Mr. Anderson, though quiet much of the time, does a fine job of conveying the younger brother's worry and uncertainty, and the film — not surprisingly, in view of Mr. Sinise's background — contains some marvelous small performances, too.

Judith Ivey is unexpectedly funny as the chance acquaintance who's

Uprooted

Richard Gere and Kevin Anderson portray brothers dealing with the loss of their once-prosperous farm in "Miles From Home."

thrilled by the Robertses' exploits. And Laurie Metcalf is particularly good as the pragmatic stripper who helps the runaway brothers find their way onto the cover of Rolling Stone. John Malkovich, as the reporter who antagonizes Frank by asking some inevitable questions, manages in one brief scene to convey a sadly cynical, more worldly view of the Roberts brothers that contrasts all too sharply with the adulation of their friends and neighbors.

1988 S 16, C8:4

Getting One's Kicks

Assumpta Serna

MATADOR, directed by Pedro Almodóvar; script (in Spanish with English subtitles) by Mr. Almodóvar and Jesus Ferrero; director of photography, Angel Luis Fernandez; edited by José Salcedo; music by Ernardo Bonezzi; production design by Roman Arango, José Morales and Josep Rosell; released by Cinevista/World Artists. At Cinema Studio, Broadway at 66th Street. Running time: 107 minutes. This film has no rating.

María Cardinal	Assumpta Serna
Angel	Antonio Banderas
Diego	Nacho Martinez
Eva	Eva Cobo
Berta	Julietta Serrano
Pilar	Chus Lampreave
Julia	Carmen Maura
Police detective	Eusebio Poncela
Flower Seller	Bibi Andersen
Designer	Pedro Almodóvar

By VINCENT CANBY

Diego and María have not yet met, but it's clear from the initial sequences of "Matador," Pedro Almodóvar's insistently raffish, 1986 Spanish comedy, that they were made for each other. Each equates the act of killing with an act of sex in which death is the ultimate orgasm.

Even in a society that tolerates virtually anything that consenting adults agree to do, this must lead to certain practical problems for lovers so obsessively bent.

In "Matador," Mr. Almodóvar, who is quickly becoming Spain's most reputable disreputable young film maker, faces this issue with a grand lack of solemnity and a lot of spirited affronts to convention. The film opens today at the Cinema Studio.

With his exhausted eyes and his painful limp, Diego (Nacho Martinez) is still a charismatic personality. He's a former star matador, forced to retire from the ring after being gored by a bull, and is now the master of a school for bullfighters. The handsome, elegant María (Assumpta Serna) is a successful Madrid lawyer.

When first seen in "Matador," Diego is huffing and puffing with erotic anticipation as he sits at home, alone, watching videos of beautiful young women being drowned, beaten, stabbed and decapitated. They remind Diego of past pleasures and those still to be achieved.

Meanwhile, in another part of Madrid, María is having heated sex with

a stranger. At the climactic moment, she pulls out a hatpin and, like a matador, stabs her partner with a quick, clean thrust at the base of the neck between the shoulders.

Diego and María might have gone through life forever unfulfilled were it not for Angel (Antonio Banderas) and Eva (Eva Cobo). Angel, one of Diego's students, is a handsome, moody young man, still a virgin in his 20's, constantly harassed by a pious mother. He also possesses second sight. Eva, who lives in the apartment across the court from Angel, is Diego's pretty young mistress.

One night, after being teased by Diego about his manliness, Angel attempts to rape Eva, unaware of her relationship to Diego. Angel botches the job so wimpishly (he has trouble opening his pocket knife to threaten her) that the haughty Eva refuses to press charges.

When the police decline to arrest him, Angel confesses to the murders he knows to have been carried out by Diego and María. María, in the interests of justice, elects to defend Angel, which provides her introduction to Diego.

In this fashion, Mr. Almodóvar's rather cynical conception of true love is finally served.

On the basis of "What Have I Done to Deserve This?," released here in 1985, and "Law of Desire" (1987), Mr. Almodóvar has been compared, somewhat prematurely, with Luis Buñuel, Billy Wilder and John Waters. There are entertaining hints of each director in Mr. Almodóvar's work but, so far, his films are most memorable for their comically deadpan treatment of supposedly taboo subjects. The movies themselves aren't as consistently funny or invigorating as the points of view they represent.

The films do offer lots of material for interpretation, which, I suspect, amuses Mr. Almodóvar as much as such interpretation used to amuse Buñuel. Considered on its most obvious level, "Matador" can be read as a cautionary tale about the awful impossibility of the love of two matadors. Who sticks whom first? It's also significant for the exuberant heedlessness with which it portrays a society breaking loose from decades of fascist repression.

In the manner of Buñuel's apocryphal "I am an atheist, thank God," Mr. Almodóvar likes to say that his films deny that Franco ever existed, which is, of course, to affirm the Franco heritage.

The best moments of "Matador" have nothing to do with its star-crossed lovers but with its narrative asides. These include a chic Madrid fashion show, titled "Spain Divided," at which the designer (played by the director) goes into a snit when he finds two of his models shooting dope backstage. "Please go to the toilet," he says pettishly. "That's what it's for."

The movie looks terrific and is acted with absolute, straight-faced conviction by the excellent cast headed by Miss Serna, Mr. Martinez and Mr. Banderas. "Matador" is of most interest as another work in the career of a film maker who, possibly, is in the process of refining a singular talent.

Upcoming, and not yet seen by me, is his latest comedy, "Women on the Verge of a Nervous Breakdown," which will open the 1988 New York Film Festival at Lincoln Center next Friday.

1988 S 16, C8:5

Odd Doings As 'Mama Turns 100'

"Mama Turns 100" was shown as part of the 1980 New Spanish Cinema Festival. Following are excerpts from Vincent Canby's review, which appeared in The New York Times Jan. 11, 1980. The film, in Spanish with English subtitles, opens today at the Bleecker Street Cinema, at La Guardia Place.

The big, airy old country house is not especially handsome but it occupies an imposing site atop a high hill and is clearly in charge of all that it surveys. In the distance, one sees the blue silhouette of a modern city that, as yet, has not imposed its needs on the people living here. The family inside the house is not aristocratic but representative of the rich, upper bourgeoisie whose manners and morals have for decades dominated the life of Spain. Time, as it always is in such fiction, is running out.

At the start of Carlos Saura's lugubriously satiric new film, "Mama Turns 100" ("Mamá Cumple 100 Años"), the family is gathering to celebrate the 100th birthday of its matriarch, a garrulous, overweight, peculiarly youthful-looking old woman who spends most of the day in bed. When she does leave her room — to visit the grave of a dead son or to dine with her family — she is carried like a potentate in a sedan chair.

This is no ordinary family but one that glories in its eccentricities. In addition to Mama (Rafaela Aparicio), who can read thoughts and project her own down corridors, around corners and through closed doors, there are the vividly remembered dead son, who was impotent unless wearing one of his collection of military uniforms, and another son, still alive, who lumbers around the estate attempting to hang-glide but often cracking his skull.

•

The only seemingly normal people are two outsiders, Ana (Geraldine Chaplin), the children's former governess, and her husband, Antonio (Norman Brinsky), who have come to the estate for Mama's party and discover what appears to be a plan to murder the old woman.

This is more or less the plot of "Mama Turns 100."

Mr. Saura, one of Spain's most talented film makers, has virtually built his entire career by making films that are about things other than what they seem to be about. Everybody in his movies has two natures, the one we see and the one represented. A household is never a household but a large cross-section of Spanish society. When he is working at the top of his form, as in "Cría" and "La Prima Angélica," Mr. Saura makes the surface scene so compelling that the symbols take care of themselves. The good films yield to as much or to as little interpretation as one cares to make.

This is not true of "Mama Turns 100," which recalls the allegory of Mr. Saura's "Garden of Delights" but with none of the real humor of the earlier film. "Mama Turns 100" has a number of fitfully funny and moving moments, but one is more often aware of the director's scheme to

have one thing stand in for another. Its surreal effects are not short cuts to truth but murky detours through tedium.

1988 S 16, C13:1

Wrong Turn

THE BEAST, directed by Kevin Reynolds; screenplay by William Mastrosimone, based on his play "Nanawatai"; director of photography, Douglas Milsome; music by Mark Isham; art director, Richard James; produced by John Fiedler; released by Columbia Pictures. At the Manhattan Twin, 59th Street east of Third Avenue, and other theaters. Running time: 109 minutes. This film is rated R.

Daskal	George Dzundza
Koverchenko	Jason Patric
Taj	Steven Bauer
Golikov	Stephen Baldwin
Kaminski	Don Harvey
Akbar	Kabir Bedi
Samad	Erick Avari
Moustafa	Haim Gerafi
Sherina	Shosh Marciano

"The Beast," opening today at the Manhattan Twin and other theaters, is a sincere, most peculiar, politically aware action film, a sort of cross between "The Lost Patrol" and a liberal-leaning "Rambo."

The title refers to a Russian tank, whose crew members turn right instead of left in the middle of Afghanistan and find themselves lost behind enemy lines. As the brave but poorly armed Afghan rebels pursue the tank, the Russians, all of whom talk in slangy American English, grow more and more panicky. Analogies to Vietnam are invited.

One good young Russian soldier, played by Jason Patric, becomes disenchanted with the war and, having been left in the desert to die by his commander, joins the Afghan rebels. George Dzundza plays the cruel commander and Steven Bauer is the leader of the Afghan rebels.

The film was directed by Kevin Reynolds — who made his debut with "Fandango" — and adapted by William Mastrosimone from his own play. There's nothing terribly wrong with "The Beast" except that it raises neither one's interest nor one's political consciousness. Though it was shot in Israel, it has the look (except for the color of the photography) of a B-picture made in or near Hollywood 50 years ago.

VINCENT CANBY

1988 S 16, C13:1

Tame Kingdom

Keanu Reeves

THE PRINCE OF PENNSYLVANIA, written and directed by Ron Nyswaner; director of photography, Frank Prinzi; edited by William Scharf; music by Thomas Newman; production designer, Toby Corbett; produced by Joan Fishman; released by New Line Cinema Corporation. At 68th Street Playhouse, at Third Avenue. Running time: 90 minutes. This film is rated R.

Upheaval
Amy Madigan co-stars with Keanu Reeves, Fred Ward and Bonnie Bedelia in "Prince of Pennsylvania."

Carol Rosegg

Gary Marshetta .... Fred Ward
Rupert Marshetta .... Keanu Reeves
Pam Marshetta .... Bonnie Bedelia
Carla Headlee .... Amy Madigan
Jack Sike .... Jeff Hayenga
Lois Sike .... Tracey Ellis
Roger Marshetta .... Joseph De Lisi

The hero of "The Prince of Pennsylvania" is a sullen teen-age boy named Rupert Marshetta (Keanu Reeves), who is locked in battle with his father. Already, there's a problem: the father, a stubborn, difficult, long-suffering coal miner named Gary Marshetta (Fred Ward), is nevertheless a great deal more likable than his loutish and self-involved son. This problem is greatly emphasized when Rupert and an older girlfriend, Carla Headlee (Amy Madigan), decide to kidnap Gary so they can raise enough money to leave their small Pennsylvania town. This scheme will seem both cruel and inefficient to audiences who wish Rupert would get moving in a hurry.

"The Prince of Pennyslvania," which opens today at the 68th Street Playhouse, takes its title from the father's erstwhile hopes for his family (he imagined himself as a king, his wife as a queen, etc.) and its style from any number of films about colorful, small-town eccentrics. What it lacks is the charm that's essential to such a slender premise, as well as any ability to see Rupert in perspective. The film seems to celebrate its hero's exploits because he is a misunderstood teen-ager, and for no other reason; inevitably, this gets a little wearing. So does Mr. Reeves, who slouches belligerently in the role, has an unbecomingly lopsided hairdo and radiates little of the brilliance that other characters ascribe to him. Mr. Reeves, who was extremely good in "River's Edge," appears to have been bushwhacked by the sheer obnoxiousness of the character he plays.

•

"The Prince of Pennsylvania," written and directed by Ron Nyswaner (who comes from Pennsylvania and wrote several drafts of "Swing Shift," as well as the original screenplay for "Mrs. Soffel"), has actors mostly good enough to prevail over the limitations of many of their roles. As Rupert's tough-talking, adulterous mother, Bonnie Bedelia suggests the hopelessness of small-town life but does so with wry humor; as Carla, Miss Madigan is a ragged, furious dynamo. Mr. Ward, always an appealing actor, can't help but give Gary unwarranted charm, even in the scene that shows him learning of his wife's infidelity and angrily beating her. In a blind fury, he tells her not to

expect any more swimming pools or VCR's if she's going to behave this way.

"The Prince of Pennyslania," which strives for droll, idiosyncratic humor, is in its own way as narrow and limited as the small-town life it means to skewer.

JANET MASLIN

1988 S 16, C17:1

Dispatches From a War Zone

DEAR AMERICA: LETTERS HOME FROM VIETNAM, directed by Bill Couturie; screenplay by Richard Dewhurst and Mr. Couturie; cinematographer and original photography by Michael Chin; edited by Stephen Stept; music by Todd Boekelheide; produced by Mr. Couturie and Thomas Bird; released by Corsair Pictures. At Eastside Cinema, Third Avenue at 55th Street. Running time: 86 minutes. This film is rated PG-13.

Readers include Robert De Niro, Michael J. Fox, Kathleen Turner, Ellen Burstyn, Howard Rollins Jr. and Robin Williams.

Bill Couturie's "Dear America: Letters Home From Vietnam" recalls the Vietnam War in the words of the men and women who fought it, in letters written in haste, without self-consciousness and, mostly, without pretense. These are read on the soundtrack by more than two dozen professional actors, some of whose voices are all too familiar, juxtaposed with Vietnam War film, much of which is new to me and all of which remains sad and harrowing.

The documentary feature, originally shown on Home Box Office, opens today at the Eastside Cinema.

When the letters are read straight, with little attempt to dramatize their contents, the effect is devastating. When the actors or actresses attempt

to "act," the immediacy of the emotions becomes lost in performance. The film's low point comes near the end when Ellen Burstyn is allowed to emote her way through a letter written by a mother to her dead son. This isn't even a letter home.

Otherwise the film's letters successfully express the sort of intense feelings never intended to be spoken aloud. Sometimes the thoughts are ghostly, as when the once-official line is heard. One young man writes that he'd rather fight in Vietnam than in Kansas City, adding, "I think it's better to fight and die for freedom in 'Nam than live under oppression and fear."

•

Another man says, "One of the staggering facts is that most men here believe we will not win the war, and yet they stick their necks out every day and carry on as if they were fighting for the continental security of the United States."

Still another says simply, "I want to hold my head between my hands and run screaming away from here." One soldier is specific: "I was carrying that thing" — his leg — "all the way back. I was afraid the whole damn thing would come off."

Mr. Couturie, the director, and his associates have done a first-rate job. For the most part, they don't impose their own order on the war. They follow it chronologically, from the early 1960's until its end in 1973, supplementing the letters with period music, clips from state-side news programs and official statistics relating to the numbers of American troops involved and the casualties.

•

"Dear America: Letters Home From Vietnam," which has been rated PG-13 ("Special Parental Guidance Suggested for Those Younger Than 13"), includes vulgar language, nudity and bloodily graphic shots of wounded men.   VINCENT CANBY

1988 S 16, C18:1

Charles Bronson As Clark Kent

MESSENGER OF DEATH, directed by J. Lee Thompson; screenplay by Paul Jarrico, based on a novel by Rex Burns; director of photography, Gideon Porath; edited by Peter Lee Thompson; music by Robert O. Ragland; art director, W. Brooke Wheeler; produced by Pancho Kohner; released by the Cannon Group Inc. At the Criterion Center, Broadway and 45th Street, and other theaters. Running time: 92 minutes. This film is rated R.

Garret Smith .... Charles Bronson
Jastra Watson .... Trish van Devere
Homer Foxx .... Laurence Luckinbill

In Conflict
Billy Stocks is one of the soldiers seen in "Dear America: Letters Home From Vietnam."

Chief Barney Doyle .... Daniel Benzali
Josephine Fabrizio .... Marilyn Hassett
Orville Beecham .... Charles Dierkop
Willis Beecham .... Jeff Corey
Zenas Beecham .... John Ireland

If "Messenger of Death," the Charles Bronson movie that opened yesterday in neighborhood theaters, were a novel, it could be called a decent page turner, one that holds the eye and makes one wonder whodunit.

As a matter of fact, Paul Jarrico's screenplay did originate in a novel by Rex Burns, on which it is based, and it is set in the scenically overpowering countryside of Colorado, which makes for attractive background. Mr. Bronson plays a reporter for a Denver newspaper and is a considerably laid-back figure compared with the unrelievedly violent characters he often portrays. He is covering the case of the murder by unknowns of the three wives and six children of a farmer, a member of an expelled Mormon sect involved in a bitter family feud.

Mr. Bronson is more a messenger of peace, an intermediary between the warring factions who is more shot upon than shooting. He does not even tote a gun in this movie and, beyond a mere smidgen of brutal kicking (of the bad guy, of course) at the end, he is almost meek in his relentless pursuit of the perpetrators, who, it turns out, are not the ones you might have suspected early on.

Bronson fans need not worry that their hero and his movies are going soft, however. There are enough bodies, car-crushings and lingering scenes of victims crossing over into death to slake any aficionado's thirst for blood.

Under J. Lee Thompson's brisk direction, the characters are well drawn, particularly by Jeff Corey and John Ireland as the cultist brothers and by Laurence Luckinbill as the police chief who aspires to become mayor. "Messenger of Death" may not be the most memorable film in the history of the art, but it is a creditable, professional job.

RICHARD F. SHEPARD

1988 S 17, 12:5

A Crazy Eddie Type Who Goes Crazy

SEVEN HOURS TO JUDGEMENT, directed by Beau Bridges; screenplay by Walter Davis and Elliot Stephens, story by Mr. Davis; director of photography, Hanania Baer; edited by Bill Butler; music by John Debney; production designer, Phedon Papamichael; produced by Mort Abrahams; released by Trans World Entertainment. At Movieland, Broadway and 47th Street. Running time: 100 minutes. This film is rated R.

John Eden .... Beau Bridges
David Reardon .... Ron Leibman
Lisa Eden .... Julianne Phillips
Ira .... Tiny Ron
Danny Larwin .... Al Freeman Jr.
Chino .... Reggie Johnson
Doctor .... Glen-Michael Jones
Victor .... Chris Garcia
Doowa .... Shawn Miller

"Seven Hours to Judgment," directed by and starring Beau Bridges, is a dim suspense drama about a Crazy Eddie-type of Manhattan appliance merchant who goes certifiably crazy when his wife is murdered by a gang of black and Hispanic muggers. To get even, he kidnaps the judge who, for legal reasons, was forced to free the criminals, and the judge's wife.

Mr. Bridges plays the judge and

Ron Liebman the kidnapper, while Seattle stands in for New York. Not one of them is convincing, but Seattle, at least, doesn't give the impression that it has forgotten its dialogue. The screenplay holds less water than a ravaged buttercup.

Reggie Johnson ("Platoon") plays the main mugger, not at all badly, but it's depressing to watch him, as well as the other black and Hispanic actors, and realize that such roles are probably what they're offered most often.

The film opened yesterday at the Movieland Theater.

VINCENT CANBY

1988 S 17, 12:5

similar effect of holding its audience rapt and then raising many questions in retrospect. The story, upon close examination, has been artfully softened, custom-tailored for viewers who can better embrace this material at a sentimental distance than at close range. Sixties radicalism and 80's slickness make strange bedfellows indeed. ☐

1988 S 18, II:25:1

FILM VIEW/Janet Maslin

Sentimentalizing 60's Radicalism

"**R**UNNING ON EMPTY" IS Sidney Lumet's family drama about radicals who, 15 years after blowing up a research laboratory that made napalm, are still on the run. Why is this idea so undeniably compelling? In part it's novelty, since Hollywood has left the radicalism of the 1960's relatively unexplored. And, of course, there's a romantic side to this story of rebels on the run. For baby-boom viewers, the film's ascetic characters and their disdain for materialism — they live in makeshift quarters, throw wonderful birthday parties using paper streamers and tinsel crowns, and get their clothes from lost-and-founds — must seem refreshing, too.

In addition, "Running on Empty" works metaphorically, as an image of people paying the price of decisions they have since outgrown. Feeling trapped by a career, a marriage or any other choice that seems irreversible is sure to help viewers sympathize with the Pope family's plight. Though the Popes, Annie (made warm, real and very moving by Christine Lahti) and Arthur (Judd Hirsch), remain proud of their earlier antiwar activities, they obviously have their regrets. When an old flame shows up to tempt Annie with the thought of running away from Arthur and the children, she says, almost bitterly, "I wish I could."

"Running on Empty" takes this daring premise and grafts onto it a layer of standard Hollywood sentimentality, doing so with great skill. Though the Popes look and feel different from typical movie families, they are allowed by Mr. Lumet and the screenwriter, Naomi Foner, to play upon the heartstrings in traditional, highly effective ways. So, as absorbing, emotional and powerfully acted as it is, "Running on Empty" is also disconcerting at times. The film's mixture of outlaw characters and conventionally sudsy situations can be very peculiar.

Although "Running on Empty" has the ambiance of the old Left (Arthur refers to himself as a "red diaper baby"; Ronnie Gilbert of the Weavers turns up in a small role), its politics are mostly skin-deep. The Popes' domestic style, for instance, isn't really consistent with their radical thinking. Arthur does cook, since he's had some experience in restaurant jobs, but in other respects he is the traditional overbearing patriarch; for her part, Annie is the soft, loving, nurturing Mom of every child's dreams.

One of the film makers' clever touches is to direct Arthur's bombastic outbursts almost exclusively at the couple's 17-year-old son Danny (River Phoenix) and rarely at his Annie. Though a real husband with a temper like Arthur's might well, after 15 years of hardship, be taking his irritation out on his wife, the senior Popes still call one another "Babe" and don't really fight. They aren't terribly affectionate, either. The film, in generating as much sympathy for the Popes as it possibly can, is shrewd in limiting discussions of their politics and ducking the question of how these people really get along.

The film is also clever in its conception of Danny, who is a model child. Danny is a musical prodigy, so talented that an attentive teacher (played enthusiastically by Ed Crowley) singles him out and earmarks him for Juilliard; he is so good that the officials overseeing his Juilliard audition (Elzbieta Czyzewska and Burke Pearson) are visibly moved as they listen to him.

Mr. Lumet, whose prowess with actors means all these smaller roles are well cast and memorably played, has also added another canny touch: Danny's piano teacher turns out to have been Annie herself, instructing him on her old practice board and passing on her talent and her sense of tradition. The film would be less moving if Danny were not so brilliant.

It also helps that Danny is charmingly self-effacing, utterly devoted to his parents, loath to complain about the strains created by life underground, and so considerate that he refuses to sleep with his girlfriend without being entirely candid with her. Danny's impassioned confession to the smart, sympathetic Lorna (Martha Plimpton) marks one of the rare occasions when Mr. Lumet allows the camera to attract attention in any way. Though in this scene it moves intently toward the young lovers, heightening the tension of the moment, the camera is in most scenes extremely discreet. The film's visual style, terse, forceful and subtle, is a great help in creating weight and suspense.

In the end, the mildly melodramatic or convenient notes occasionally sounded by "Running on Empty" are allowed to take over. The last part of the film becomes wholeheartedly tear-jerking as Annie meets with her father (Steven Hill) after not having seen him for 14 years. This scene — well written, restrained, deeply emotional and shamelessly manipulative — captures the entire film's approach in a nutshell. It emphasizes the pain and irony inherent in Annie's situation while overlooking less salable sentiments like bitterness and rage. And it is masterfully executed: When Mr. Hill, impassive through much of the scene, utters an unexpected sob, audiences may find themselves moved to tears. Who, after all, could resist a moment like this?

Though "Running on Empty" is much better than the current "Betrayed," it has the

Natasha Richardson

Reluctant Revolutionary

PATTY HEARST, directed by Paul Schrader; screenplay by Nicholas Kazan, based on the book "Every Secret Thing" by Patricia Campbell Hearst with Alvin Moscow; director of photography, Bojan Bazelli; edited by Michael R. Miller; music by Scott Johnson; production designer, Jane Musky; produced by Marvin Worth; released by Atlantic Releasing Corporation. At Loews 84th Street Six, at Broadway, and other theaters. Running time: 108 minutes. This film is rated R.

Patricia Hearst	Natasha Richardson
Teko	William Forsythe
Cinque	Ving Rhames
Yolanda	Frances Fisher
Wendy	Jodi Long
Fahizah	Olivia Barash
Gelina	Dana Delany
Zoya	Marek Johnson
Gabi	Kitty Swink
Cujo	Pete Kowanko

Patty Hearst, a k a Tania, a member of the self-styled Symbionese Liberation Army, and two of her S.L.A. comrades sit on a bed in an anonymous Los Angeles motel room and watch a "live" telecast as the police storm their S.L.A. hideout in another part of the city. Everyone in the house is finally killed. It's only by chance that Patty and the other two are not in the house.

Says Patty, when the televised siege is all over, "They didn't even try to take us alive."

This sense of eerie disconnection, of being a participant in events while also being detached from them, is not something that is often dramatized with any success. Even when it is, as in Paul Schrader's fine new film "Patty Hearst," it tends to be chilling and off-putting. It doesn't make for the kind of neat movie in which one immediately knows how one is supposed to respond.

The success of "Patty Hearst," directed by Mr. Schrader from the screenplay by Nicholas Kazan, is that it avoids imposing any kind of reassuring order on the harrowing, real-life story of the Hearst publishing company heiress. Instead, the movie makes scary demands on the audience.

On the evening of Feb. 4, 1974, Patricia Campbell Hearst, age 19, was kidnapped by the S.L.A. from her apartment near the campus of the University of California at Berkeley. For the next six weeks she was kept in a closet, blindfolded, and subjected to periodic indoctrination by her captors. She was bullied, ranted at, lied to and threatened with immediate execution if the police should try to free her.

Miss Hearst became a true media event. At the direction of her kidnappers, she sent taped messages to the outside world urging that her father and the state government meet the demands for her release. At one point she urged her mother not to wear black on television all the time. "It doesn't really help things," she said.

Much like someone kept too long in a zero-gravity tank, Miss Hearst lost all sense of direction and identity, though without losing the memory of her earlier life. As she says in her book, "Every Secret Thing," written with Alvin Moscow and published in 1982, she was never unaware of what she was doing.

This is the contradiction with which the courts wrestled when they upheld her conviction for bank robbery and other felonies. It is something movie audiences have to deal with when watching it.

When, finally, the S.L.A. gave Miss Hearst the choice to go free, which she thought might be a trick to kill her, or to join their revolution, she joined. For the next 18 months, she remained with the S.L.A. as a loyal participant in the group's dangerously addled-brained missions.

The story of Miss Hearst — her kidnapping, her transformation into a bank-robbing "urban guerrilla," her capture, trial, sentence and Presidential pardon — remains a haunting one, at least in part because it seems so commonplace, yet inexplicable.

The film's Patty Hearst, played by Natasha Richardson in an absolutely smashing performance, is a decent-natured young woman of average intelligence, emotionally equipped to cope with nothing much more complex than her classes, family life and routine relationships.

However, in the context of fictional movies about ordinary people who are thrown into extraordinary circumstances and subsequently triumph, Patty Hearst looks like a perfect void. To a certain extent, she is.

"Patty Hearst," which opens today at Loews 84th Street and other theaters, is a model of swift, spare, unsentimental film making about a character who can never be known, as most fictional characters are, and about a specific time and circumstances that, with hindsight, seem incredible.

When the film was shown at the Cannes Festival this year, European critics were offended by Mr. Schrader's almost comic portrait of the bumbling methods of the S.L.A. and by what the critics took to be his scorn for revolution in general. In Europe, the spirit of 1968 is still treasured. Students rose in France and West Germany. In Czechoslovakia, an entire nation stood up, and then was crushed. It was a time of great promises and greater sacrifices.

To look at "Patty Hearst" in this way is to miss the pertinent points of the film, which is about the fragility of personality and the sometimes remarkable success that can be gained by fanatics of an initially well-meaning, totally bent nature.

The film is always sympathetic to Miss Richardson's Patty. It is fascinated by, and scathing about, the muddled attempts of the white middle-class revolutionaries to assume the mystical "blackness" of their leader, General Field Marshal Cinque (Ving Rhames), the only black in the eight-man S.L.A. They are pathetic and yet they are killers.

Though made on a comparatively modest budget, "Patty Hearst" is a beautifully produced movie, seen entirely from Patty's limited point of view. It is stylized at times, utterly direct and both shocking and grimly funny.

Beginning with Mr. Rhames, every member of the supporting cast is excellent. Miss Richardson goes beyond that, if possible. There's not a wasted gesture or word. The flat, slightly nasal monotone, which is her California accent, defines the tight-lipped temper of the movie.

"Patty Hearst" would rather say too little than too much.

VINCENT CANBY

1988 S 23, C8:5

Double Trouble

DEAD RINGERS, directed by David Cronenberg; written by Mr. Cronenberg and Norman Snider, based on the book "Twins" by Bari Wood and Jack Geasland; director of photography, Peter Suschitzky; edited by Ronald Sanders; music by Howard Shore; production designer, Carol Spier; produced by Mr. Cronenberg and Marc Boyman; released by 20th Century-Fox Film Corporation. At National Twin, Broadway and 44th Street, and other theaters. Running time: 115 minutes. This film is rated R.

Beverly and Elliot Mantle	Jeremy Irons
Claire Niveau	Genevieve Bujold
Cary	Heidi von Palleske
Danuta	Barbara Gordon
Laura	Shirley Douglas
Anders Wolleck	Stephen Lack
Leo	Nick Nichols
Arlene	Lynn Cormack

By JANET MASLIN

The sleek, icy elegance of "Dead Ringers," David Cronenberg's film about twin gynecologists teetering on the brink of madness, is unexpected. Both the director, whose past films include the much gorier "Scanners" and "Videodrome," and the highly unusual subject suggest a more lurid approach. But Mr. Cronenberg, who has begun to emerge as a master of body-related horrific fantasy (his last film was "The Fly"), clearly understands that a small amount of medical mischief can be more unnerving than conventional grisliness. Even the film's opening credits, which present antiquated obstetrical drawings and strange medical instruments, are enough to make audiences queasy.

Who, then, will be drawn to this spectacle? Anyone with a taste for the macabre wit, the weird poignancy and the shifting notions of identity that lend "Dead Ringers" such fascination. And anyone who cares to see Jeremy Irons's seamless performance, a schizophrenic marvel, in the two title roles. Mr. Cronenberg has shaped a startling tale of physical and psychic disintegration, pivoting on the twins' hopeless interdependence and playing havoc with the viewer's grip on reality. It's a mesmerizing achievement, as well as a terrifi-

Attila Dory

Malpractice Jeremy Irons as Dr. Elliot Mantle, one of the twin gynecologists he portrays in "Dead Ringers."

cally unnerving one.

"Dead Ringers," which opens today at the National and other theaters, owes some of its inspiration to the case of the doctors Cyril and Stewart Marcus, who died in 1975; its nominal source is "Twins," a 1977 novel by Bari Wood and Jack Geasland. Adapting the novel with Norman Snider, Mr. Cronenberg has preserved only a trace of the real Marcus story, preferring to invent a pathology of his own. The twins of "Dead Ringers" descend, as the Marcuses did, into drug addiction, physical squalor and finally violence. But they do this with a cool, brittle detachment that makes their final decline so much more wrenching, and with a painful interweaving of identities that at times becomes as unsettling for the audience as it is for them.

The prologue to "Dead Ringers" shows the pre-adolescent Mantle brothers discussing sex wistfully, regretting the fact that it seems so, well, personal. Creatures that fertilize eggs underwater without physical contact have a much easier lot than humans, they agree. A neighborhood girl, who merely laughs at the brothers when they express sexual curiosity, sends them further along the path to a purely clinical approach, and the film's next scene finds them at medical school, where they invent an instrument that other doctors deem bizarre. Nonetheless, it helps to make their fortune, and the film's first 1988 scene finds the prosperous, urbane Mantles running a private clinic in Toronto. In one of the story's many ironies, these twins have chosen infertility as their specialty.

Though the twins are not often seen on the job, their contemptuous and sometimes nasty approach to their patients is made clear, as is their fondness for gamesmanship; the brothers enjoy changing places on occasion, especially when they embark upon an affair. Without his efforts, the dapper Elliot tells his more introverted brother Beverly, the latter would perhaps never have had any luck with women at all. But the twins' tricks prove to be no match for Claire Niveau (given real substance by Genevieve Bujold), a famous film star who arrives at the clinic as a patient, is promptly wooed by Elliot and

is then passed on to Beverly. Claire becomes the means by which the twins' lifelong bond is destroyed.

One brother falls in love with her, and wants for the first time to keep something for his own. The other brother finds he cannot tolerate this betrayal. And Mr. Irons, who uses few conversational clues to establish which twin he is playing in any given shot, manages to make this conflict as dramatically sharp as it is psychologically riveting. It is always evident which personality Mr. Irons has adopted, a feat even more impressive than the formidable technical tricks that keep the viewer from detecting a split screen. What makes the performance(s) even better is that Mr. Irons invests these bizarre, potentially freakish characters with so much intelligence and so much real feeling.

The ghoulishness of "Dead Ringers" is kept very much in check, even as the story spirals downward. The film's cool, muted visual style helps see to that. There are very few departures from the expensive, high-tech look of the Mantles' clinic and their apartment. And the odd touches, when they do occur, are treated almost offhandedly. Nothing is said, for instance, about the fact that when the Mantles appear in the operating room, the doctors, nurses, orderlies and patients are serenely draped in fabric that is blood red.

Among the film's more hauntingly strange developments are Beverly's invention of a new set of surgical devices, which frighten everyone who sees them; the brothers' growing identification with the Siamese twins Chang and Eng, and the drug addiction that finally leaves one brother utterly oblivious to his sibling's fate. The film's final image, like so many steps along the brothers' route to self-destruction, is not easily forgotten.

1988 S 23, C10:1

Horror in the Country

Henry Thomas

MURDER ONE, directed by Graeme Campbell; written by Fleming B. (Tex) Fuller; director of photography, Ludek Bogner; edited by Michael McMahon; music by Mychael Danna; production designer, Bora Bulajic; produced by Nicolas Stiliadis; released by Miramax Films. At Cine Twin, Seventh Avenue near 47th Street, and other theaters. Running time: 90 minutes. This film is rated R.

Billy Isaacs	Henry Thomas
Carl Isaacs	James Wilder
Wayne Coleman	Stephen Shellen
George Dungee	Errol Slue

By RICHARD F. SHEPARD

A suspenseful, brutal and tautly told tale measures up to the title of the film "Murder One," which opens today at the Cine Twin and other theaters. It is a drama based on the cold-blooded killing of seven people in 1973 during a wild journey through the South by three brothers and their friend.

In 1977, Fleming B. (Tex) Fuller wrote and directed a prize-winning documentary for public television in which he created portraits of Death Row prisoners in North Carolina and Georgia. Among them were the men involved in the 1973 killings. That documentary inspired Mr. Fuller to write this new film. The three who actually pulled triggers were sentenced to death in 1974; two are awaiting retrials and one was convicted again this year of six of the murders. The youngest, who turned state's evidence, is serving a life sentence.

It is a simple, almost mindless, outburst of crime that is tackled here. Two half-brothers, Wayne Coleman and Carl Isaacs, escaped from a Maryland prison with a fellow inmate, George Dungee, and picked up their teen-age brother, Billy Isaacs. The four then set out, restlessly and aimlessly, on a meandering drive that took them through 12 states in 13 days. During that trip, they killed a man who caught them stealing a car and six people whose farmhouse they invaded in Georgia, and did stick-ups as they needed money along the way.

What distinguishes "Murder One" from the easy-thrill sort of escapade the film could easily have degenerated into is the businesslike manner its makers have adopted for the telling. Graeme Campbell, the director, has filmed what is almost a re-enactment of the spree. One cannot do a drama about murder without depicting violence, of course, but there is a minimum of gore and false horror beyond the horror of the deed. People are shown being shot in a relatively nonresistant way, with the shot almost as the coup de grâce, rather than hot-blooded torture. That is horror enough.

•

It is a story told from the point of view of young Billy, the callow youth who admired his brothers at first and then wanted nothing more than to go home, away from the ugliness. Henry Thomas, as the youngster, portrays an appealing figure, a clean-cut boy of decent instincts who is torn by the life he knows he should be leading and the one he is caught up in. The film does not harp on motivation, although it offers significant hints in the depiction of the boozy tramp of a mother who is not interested in her three boys beyond warning Billy not to associate with his brothers. We also see their inability to fit in anywhere in society and the undefined forces that drive them to ever greater excess.

James Wilder, as Carl Isaacs, is a thoroughly malevolent character, one in whom evil rather than insanity seems to prevail. Stephen Shellen makes Wayne Coleman into someone no less driven but with a remnant of feeling for the wretched Georgia family and a love for his little brother. Errol Slue is masterful in his performance as the dimwitted George Dungee, neither good nor bad but always affable and obedient.

Even the chase scenes are not sensationalized, and the car with the four is mostly seen tooling along picturesque country roads to a background of soft, even pleasant music that stops, dramatically, when crimes are in progress. There are no extraneous love affairs, no sentimentalizing and no relief for the tranquil-minded or moral-seeker in "Murder One." It sticks to its point all the way through.

1988 S 23, C15:1

In Trouble Matt Dillon plays the role of an amoral drifter in "Kansas."

The Town And the City

KANSAS, directed by David Stevens; written by Spencer Eastman; director of photography, David Eggby; edited by Robert Barrere; music by Pino Donaggio; produced by George Litto; released by Trans World Entertainment. At Loews 84th Street Six, at Broadway, and other theaters. Running time: 108 minutes. This film is rated R.

Doyle Kennedy	Matt Dillon
Wade Corey	Andrew McCarthy
Lori Bayles	Leslie Hope
Nordquist	Alan Toy
Fleener	Andy Romano
Buckshot	Brent Jennings
Connie	Brynn Thayer

By CARYN JAMES

"Kansas" sets itself up as a suspense story entangled with the people and values of America's heartland. Here is what happens in one supposedly sleepy little town. A wheat field-wholesome young man named Wade (Andrew McCarthy) is on his way to New York City. After his car burns up, he jumps on a freight train where he meets a drifter named Doyle (Matt Dillon) and is so unfazed by his sinister looks — the gold tooth and the panther tattooed on his forearm might have made most folks suspicious — that he hops off the train with his new friend. Following Doyle's lead, the impressionable Wade breaks into a house, goes to a parade where he spots the girl of his dreams and robs a bank. But while he is fleeing the bank, a car carrying the Governor's small daughter falls into the river, so Wade saves the child from drowning, runs away and hides the money — all this before lunchtime. Soon he finds work at a farm owned by the father of the girl of his dreams, a convenient place to roll in the hay, literally, while the town searches for the mystery hero.

•

The plot slows down after that, but does not get less incredible. The characters never become intriguing, though we're supposed to wonder about Wade's moral direction when he hangs onto the money, lies to Doyle and is uncovered as the hero.

For a film so exhaustively loaded with silliness, "Kansas," which opens today at Loews 84th Street Six and other theaters, is remarkably dull. It

was filmed in Kansas by David Stevens, an Australian television director, and the only thing truly Kansan is the scenery. Wade spends a night in a field of sunflowers and there are the inevitable panoramic views of flat, open spaces under the broad sky, but nothing of the heartland intrudes on the paper-thin people who live in a state that might as well be Oz. Wade should have stayed on that train to Manhattan; he would have had a quieter life.

1988 S 23, C17:1

Rustic Rumblings

Don Johnson

SWEET HEARTS DANCE, directed by Robert Greenwald; written by Ernest Thompson; director of photography, Tak Fujimoto; edited by Robert Florio; music by Richard Gibbs; production designer, James Allen; produced by Jeffrey Lurie; released by Tri-Star Pictures. At Criterion Center, Broadway and 45th Street, and other theaters. Running time: 102 minutes. This film is rated R.

Wiley Boon	Don Johnson
Sandra Boon	Susan Sarandon
Sam Manners	Jeff Daniels
Adie Nims	Elizabeth Perkins
Pearne Manners	Kate Reid
Kyle Boon	Justin Henry
Debs Boon	Holly Marie Combs
B. J. Boon	Heather Coleman

Susan Sarandon, Jeff Daniels and Elizabeth Perkins play residents of a small, picturesque, rather too in-grown Vermont village in "Sweet Hearts Dance," and Don Johnson is there, too. So there arise some blunt but inevitable questions: can Mr. Johnson hold his own in this company? Has television stardom made him too much of a commodity to fit comfortably into an ensemble film like this? Will there be large-screen life for him after "Miami Vice"?

It turns out that Mr. Johnson is a disarming, funny and natural actor who appears as much at home in this small-town, no-frills setting as he does at the center of television's drug trade. What's more, the rapport between the film's four principals is so well established that its romantic quadrille about the various ups and downs of two humorously contrasting couples really does come to life.

Mr. Johnson and Miss Sarandon play the story's old marrieds, with three children (among them Justin Henry, who has grown from the adorable tot of "Kramer vs. Kramer" to a large and amusingly sullen teen-ager) and not a lot of fire in their lives. Mr. Daniels and Miss Perkins, on the other hand, play a school principal and a new teacher who are just getting their love affair off to a start, albeit a rocky one. The principal, Sam Manners, does ask the teacher, Adie Nims, to marry him during the story. But, as he assures her while he's asking, he's "just kidding, just kidding."

So "Sweet Hearts Dance," which opens today at the Criterion Center and other theaters, approaches love

Midlife Susan Sarandon stars in "Sweet Hearts Dance," about two couples dealing with changes in their relationships.

as a series of fits and starts. It approaches narrative in much the same way, which would be more of a problem if the film were not so enjoyably loose-jointed anyhow. As written by Ernest Thompson ("On Golden Pond") and directed by Robert Greenwald, the film is structured as a series of cute, breezy episodes tethered to various holidays and generally making the point that love isn't easy. Even the film's more dramatic moments, as when Mr. Johnson's Wiley Boon bursts into tears and tells his friend Sam that he isn't happy with his wife, Sandra, anymore, are handled with a mercifully light touch.

"Sweet Hearts Dance" tends to drift, but it has good humor and an easygoing appeal, not to mention a thoroughly attractive cast. Mr. Daniels, who is always a delight in fall-guy roles, has an especially appealing one here, and Miss Sarandon makes the lot of the long-suffering Mrs. Wiley Boon seem funny and real. Mr. Johnson is nicely self-mocking as a man who gets winded trying to chase egg-throwing teen-agers on Halloween (and a man who'd not-so-secretly like to be out throwing eggs himself). Miss Perkins makes Adie understandably charmed and mildly perplexed as the new arrival to this picture-perfect (and otherwise nicely imperfect) rustic scene.

JANET MASLIN

1988 S 23, C17:1

Animal Rights

GORILLAS IN THE MIST, directed by Michael Apted; screenplay by Anna Hamilton Phelan, story by Miss Phelan and Tab Murphy, based on the work by Dian Fossey and the article by Harold T. P. Hayes; director of photography, John Seale; edited by Stuart Baird; music by Maurice Jarre; production designer, John Graysmark; produced by Arnold Glimcher and Terence Clegg; released by Warner Brothers and Universal Pictures. At the Beekman, Second Avenue at 65th Street. Running time: 125 minutes. This film is rated PG-13.

Dian Fossey	Sigourney Weaver
Bob Campbell	Bryan Brown
Roz Carr	Julie Harris
Sembagare	John Omirah Miluwi
Dr. Louis Leakey	Iain Cuthbertson
Van Vecten	Constantin Alexandrov
Mukara	Waigwa Wachira

Sigourney Weaver as the American naturalist Dian Fossey, in "Gorillas in the Mist."

When Sigourney Weaver, as the naturalist Dian Fossey, is first seen arriving in Africa, she towers over everyone else in view. A trim, impatient, utterly confident white woman, she is instantly at home giving orders to the impoverished black tribesmen who gather around her. This supreme self-assurance of Miss Weaver's, sometimes less than helpful in other films, is perfect for "Gorillas in the Mist," the story of a smart, determined, well-bred and physically commanding woman who brooks no frailty in others. Like Katharine Hepburn, who might well have played this part if Dian Fossey had lived earlier, Miss Weaver was made for such a role.

"Gorillas in the Mist," which opens today at the Beekman, is the story of Miss Fossey's extraordinary exploits among the mountain gorillas that she studied for 18 years. It's a story of stirring and unusual heroism, though not one of many surprises. Indeed, though there is no set formula for films about mountain gorillas, the satisfying and largely unremarkable progress of this one suggests that such a thing might be possible.

As Miss Fossey, Miss Weaver is seen arriving in Africa with the wrong wardrobe and the wrong attitude, demanding that her luggage be carried, and setting up shop at a remote campsite, with a picture of her fiancé from Kentucky by her side. In voice-over, she corresponds with Dr. Louis Leakey, who has commissioned her to conduct a mountain gorilla census. "Surely you didn't expect the poor beggars to come out of the the jungle and line up just so we can count them!" Dr. Leakey writes, when his protégée encounters problems. But soon after this she finds her first fresh gorilla droppings. And soon after *that*, the first gorillas are seen. "So beautiful!" exclaims Miss Weaver, as she will on many occasions throughout the film. Moments like this do have an irresistible appeal.

Like an American friend (Julie Harris) who has lived in Africa long enough to cultivate an astonishingly lush flower garden, Miss Fossey determines to set down roots. She begins hammering out an uneasy truce with local tribesmen, who suspect her of being a witch ("Oh yeah? They wouldn't be the first," says she). She begins to fight the local practice of gorilla poaching, used to supply baby animals to zoos and, more brutally, gorilla heads and hands as trophies for tourists. The scenes depicting these raids on the animals are staged with heart-rending urgency.

Most important, Miss Weaver's Dian Fossey is seen establishing her rapport with the animals themselves, in remarkable scenes that show the gorillas approaching her tentatively and then clambering playfully all over her. (The fact that Rick Baker, the makeup wizard who specializes in simians, has contributed special effects indicates that a little of this footage is artificial, but it all looks utterly convincing.) Though much of the strength of Miss Weaver's fine performance comes from the intelligent, muscular resilience she projects so fiercely, a lot of it also derives from the wit and abandon with which she mimics the gorillas' behavior to win their confidence.

As directed by Michael Apted, "Gorillas in the Mist" has an unusually powerful sense of place. The glimpses of mountainous Rwanda, where these rare gorillas live, are indeed breathtaking, and the local culture is made as palpable as the landscape itself. There are excellent African actors in a couple of key roles: John Omirah Miluwi as Miss Fossey's trusted guide and close friend, and Waigwa Wachira as the local official who expects her to place her ideas about gorilla preservation in the larger context of Rwanda's strapped economy. There is even, when Miss Fossey visits town, a dilapidated-looking Grand Hotel, into which she marches, on one memorable occasion, to berate a gorilla trader in the middle of a crowded dining room. She does this with a baby gorilla in her arms.

"Gorillas in the Mist" takes its title from Miss Fossey's own memoir, and it was to be a film recounting her heartening efforts to save the species from extinction. But her brutal murder, in 1985, has necessitated another ending, one with which the film does not easily cope. The screenplay, by Anna Hamilton Phelan, makes the killing (which is still unsolved) almost an afterthought, and follows the brief sequence detailing the naturalist's death and burial with an incongruously upbeat closing title lauding her achievements. There seems little question that the woman herself was more complicated than this portrait.

"Gorillas in the Mist," an engrossing but long film with a tendency to meander, devotes an idyllic central section to Miss Fossey's affair with Bob Campbell (Bryan Brown), the National Geographic photographer whose films first called attention to her accomplishments. Though this makes for a sunny episode, it is destined to end unhappily when the couple find they have irreconcilable differences. That much is clear when Mr. Campbell brings Miss Fossey, hardly a woman who needs pets, a little dog.

•

"Gorillas in the Mist" is rated PG-13 ("Special Parental Guidance Suggested for Those Younger Than 13"). It contains some profanity and violence. JANET MASLIN

1988 S 23, C19:1

Home, Sweet Home

TIGER WARSAW, produced and directed by Amin Q. Chaudhri; screenplay by Roy London; edited by Brian Smedley-Aston; music by Ernest Troost; production designer, Tom Targownik; released by Sony Pictures. At Cinema 2, Third Avenue at 60th Street, and other theaters. Running time: 92 minutes. This film is rated R.

Chuck (Tiger) Warsaw .... Patrick Swayze
Frances Warsaw .... Piper Laurie
Mitchell Warsaw .... Lee Richardson
Paula Warsaw .... Mary McDonnell
Karen .... Barbara Williams
Tony .... Bobby DiCicco

By WALTER GOODMAN

Patrick Swayze, lately of "Dirty Dancing," gets a chance in "Tiger Warsaw" to be brooding and boyish, soulful and shaky and to show off his chest. He plays a fellow in his early 30's who returns home 15 years after having made a mess of the family household and tries to pick up the pieces. What the young Charles (Tiger) Warsaw did, we gather through quick flashbacks, was shoot his dad after being caught peeping at his sister, who was in her undies at the time. He is eye-wateringly contrite, but the reception is heated rather than warm.

Roy London's nonstarter of a screenplay drifts drearily along until, with about 10 minutes to go, it ends in a rushed wrap, as though somebody suddenly realized that time was up. Until then, it is mainly a series of encounters — between Tiger and his mother (Piper Laurie keeping her chin up), who loves her boy but worries about Dad's reaction to his return; Tiger and his sister, a career woman who holds a grudge; Tiger and a former girlfriend, who welcomes him back into bed, and Tiger and a former buddy, whose hot-and-cold reception is dramatically tepid.

•

None of the characters make a lot of sense. Dad, especially, is an enigma; you can't be sure whether he isn't all there or Lee Richardson's absent performance just makes it seem that way. For a few moments at the start, as the camera introduces us to the working-class neighborhoods of an industrial town in the Midwest, the movie, which opens today at Cinema 2 and other theaters, seems to promise a look into a piece of ethnic America. (The family was named Warsaw by an immigration official who couldn't spell the real name.) But despite a scene at a hometown basketball game and some rough talk, the inhabitants are unanchored, unless it is to the world of the soaps.

The scattershot scene-by-scene confrontations are low caliber. The dialogue is synthetic street talk: "I got nothin' to live for, man." "Tony, I really love you, man." Interested in what working people ask about sex? "That was intense." Amin Q. Chaudhri's direction is intensely dull.

1988 S 23, C20:1

Dead-Film File

Colin Friels

GROUND ZERO, directed by Michael Pattinson and Bruce Myles; written by Mac Gudgeon and Jan Sardi; director of photography, Steve Dobson; edited by David Pulbrook; music by Tom Bahler; production designer, Brian Thomson; produced by Mr. Pattinson; released by Avenue Pictures. At the Sutton, Third Avenue and 57th Street. Running time: 100 minutes. This film is rated PG-13.

Harvey	Colin Friels
Trebilcock	Jack Thompson
Prosper	Donald Pleasence
Pat	Natalie Bate
Charlie	Burnham Burnham
Commission President	Simon Chilvers
Hocking	Neil Fitzpatrick
Walamari	Bob Maza

What connection can there be between a long-buried radioactive airplane and a smart young cinematographer who films dancing chili dogs for a living? It's the kind of connection that's often found in taut, clever conspiracy-theory thrillers, of which the new Australian film "Ground Zero" is a prime example. What's more, the dreadful secret that is revealed in this film by Michael Pattinson and Bruce Myles turns out to be largely true. The closing titles, corroborating information that is unearthed during the course of the story, are sobering indeed.

"Ground Zero," which opens today at the Sutton, sends the boyish cinematographer Harvey Denton (Colin Friels) on a journey of discovery into his own past. An anonymous phone tip, advising him to watch television coverage of a Royal Commission investigation into British nuclear tests conducted during the 1950's, leads Harvey to a terrible surprise. He learns that his own father, who was also a cinematographer, clandestinely filmed events at the Maralinga Air Force base as the atomic tests were conducted. And his father, whose remains are discovered aboard the long-buried airplane, died a violent death soon thereafter.

•

Much of "Ground Zero" concerns Harvey's search for his father's missing film, some of which has mysteriously disappeared; if he can bring this before the Royal Commission, he thinks he may be able to stop the cover-up that is under way. Although the commission has made a show of examining all witnesses to the Maralinga test, the aborigines who watched it are forbidden by their religion to speak of the dead; therefore, they cannot describe the heavy casualties to which the elder Denton's home movie attests. The closing titles, which cite the numbers of servicemen who developed cancer after witnessing the test, say that there are no reliable figures tallying aborgine casualties, since these people were counted together with emus and kangaroo.

Though the paranoid-conspiracy formula is commonplace among American thrillers, it is given an element of novelty in this Australian setting. And the directors approach their story with urgency and conviction, as well as with visual flair and a taste for the high-tech gadgetry that helps keep the film lively. However, since there is often a tendency in films like this to tie up too many loose ends, the screenplay (by Mac Gudgeon and Jan Sardi) adds a subplot about whether Harvey will save his failed marriage to a television news reporter (Natalie Bate), who also becomes involved in the case. This makes the film more fun, but also makes its slickness more apparent.

Mr. Friels shows himself to be an excellent leading man, even in a role that requires him to do little more than look skeptical every time an Australian Government official gives him false information. Also good is Donald Pleasence as the extremely odd hermit who lives in a desert cave and who has waited many years for the Maralinga tragedy to come to light.

•

"Ground Zero" is rated PG-13 *("Special Parental Guidance Suggested for Those Younger Than 13"). It contains some violent sequences.*
JANET MASLIN

1988 S 23, C18:1

A Benign Farce

WOMEN ON THE VERGE OF A NERVOUS BREAKDOWN, directed by Pedro Almodóvar; screenplay (in Spanish with English subtitles) by Mr. Almodóvar; director of photography, José Luis Alcaine; edited by José Salcedo; music by Bernardo Bonezzi; an El Deseo, S.A./Laurenfilm Production; released by Orion Classics. At Alice Tully Hall, 7:45 P.M.; Avery Fisher Hall, 9. Running time: 88 minutes. This film has no rating.

Pepa Marcos	Carmen Maura
Carlos	Antonio Banderas
Lucia	Julieta Serrano
Candela	María Barranco
Marisa	Rossy De Palma
Ivan	Fernando Guillen
Taxi Driver	Guillermo Montesinos

By VINCENT CANBY

It hasn't been Pepa's day, or even week. Ivan, her longtime lover and a male-chauvinist rat, walks out on her, leaving only a bland message on her answering machine. Planning suicide, Pepa spikes a blenderful of garden-fresh gazpacho with sleeping pills, but forgets to drink it.

Pepa's suicide quickly takes on the aspects of a dental check-up: It keeps getting sidetracked.

Saying she really shouldn't smoke, Pepa lights a cigarette and sets her bed ablaze. Her best friend, Candela, who has been having a blissful affair with a man she didn't realize was a Shiite terrorist, comes by looking for refuge from the police.

The first couple to look at Pepa's apartment, which she has put on the market, are Carlos, Ivan's grown son, whom Pepa had never known about, and Marisa, Carlos's toothy girlfriend. When Pepa seeks legal advice, the lawyer happens to be Ivan's newest mistress.

•

These are only some of the delirious ingredients in this most entertaining, deliberately benign new Spanish farce, "Women on the Verge of a Nervous Breakdown." The director is Pedro Almodóvar, better known here for his deliberately scandalous dark comedies ("Matador," "Law of Desire" and "What Have I Done to Deserve This?") in which anything goes, provided that it may offend *somebody's* sensibility.

In "Women on the Verge of a Nervous Breakdown," Mr. Almodóvar sets out to charm rather than shock. That he succeeds should not come as a surprise. The common denominator of all Almodóvar films, even the one that winds up in an ecstatic murder-suicide pact, is their great good humor.

"Women on the Verge of a Nervous Breakdown" will be shown tonight at 7:45 at Alice Tully Hall and at 9 in Avery Fisher Hall to begin the 26th New York Film Festival.

In what may be one of the most cheering programming decisions in the festival's quarter-century, tonight's show begins with "Night of the Living Duck." This is an all-new Merrie Melodies cartoon in which Daffy Duck, who has too long played second fiddle to Disney's Donald, makes a memorable Lincoln Center debut, the first Hollywood cartoon character to be so honored.

In his brisk eight minutes on screen, Daffy sets a pace for priceless nuttiness that is impossible for any feature to follow with complete security.

However, Mr. Almodóvar is not a film maker who can be easily upstaged by a near-classic cartoon. At its best, "Women on the Verge of a Nervous Breakdown" has much of the cheeringly mad intensity of animated shorts produced in Hollywood before the television era.

•

This is exemplified in Carmen Maura's grand performance as Pepa. Miss Maura, who looks a bit like Jeanne Moreau, is to Mr. Almodóvar's cinema what Anna Magnani once was to Roberto Rossellini's. This comparision would come to mind even if the director hadn't said publicly that the inspiration for "Women on the Verge" was Jean Cocteau's short, one-character play "The Human Voice," which was acted by Miss Magnani in the Rossellini screen adaptation.

Julieta Serrano in "Women on the Verge of a Nervous Breakdown."

Though Mr. Almodóvar apparently adores "The Human Voice," or did at one time, his new film is a fiendishly funny sendup of Cocteau's fustian portrait of a desperate woman who, abandoned by her lover, uses the telephone as a blunt instrument just by talking into it. As written and performed, Pepa is every bracing thing that the self-pitying Cocteau character is not.

Miss Maura is wonderful as a woman who simply cannot resist fighting back. The actress has a big, no-nonsense screen personality that perfectly fits Mr. Almodóvar's raffishly deadpan comic method. Watching "Women on the Verge" while remembering "The Human Voice," one experiences the same sense of liberation that Bob Hoskins feels when he leaves Los Angeles and enters Toontown in "Who Framed Roger Rabbit."

•

"Women on the Verge" takes place in its own, very special farcical universe, where outrageous coincidences are the norm and where logic dictates that a forgotten blender full of spiked gazpacho will be drunk by the wrong person. It's also a place where a television anchor is a sweet old grandmother instead of a barely literate sex symbol, and where Pepa, an actress, appears in a commercial for a detergent guaranteed to get the blood out of your killer son's shirt and trousers.

Though feminist in its sympathies, "Women on the Verge" is far from being a tract of any sort. The characters Mr. Almodóvar has written and directed keep asserting idiosyncrasies that do not allow them, or the film, to be so humorlessly categorized.

The pace sometimes flags, and there are scenes in which the comic potential appears to be lost only because the camera is in the wrong place. Farce isn't easy to pull off, but Mr. Almodóvar is well on his way to mastering this most difficult of all screen genres.

For the record, credit should be given also to the auteurs responsible for "Night of the Living Duck," including Greg Ford and Terry Lennon, who did the story and direction. The venerable Mel Blanc is heard as Daffy. Mel Tormé provides Daffy's singing voice and the song "Monsters Lead Such Interesting Lives (They Don't Live 9 to 5)" was written by Virg Dzurinko and Mr. Ford. Pure funniness.

1988 S 23, C25:1

Vulgar vs. Spontaneous

HIGH HOPES, directed and written by Mike Leigh; director of photography, Roger Pratt; film editor, Jon Gregory; produced by Victor Glynn and Simon Channing-Williams. At Alice Tully Hall, as part of the 26th New York Film Festival. Running time: 100 minutes. This film has no rating

Cyril	Philip Davis
Shirley	Ruth Sheen
Mrs. Bender	Edna Dore
Martin	Philip Jackson
Valerie	Heather Tobias
Laetitia	Lesley Manville
Rupert	David Bamber

By JANET MASLIN

A traveler from the country who is lost in London wanders into the flat shared by Cyril (Philip Davis) and Shirley (Ruth Sheen), and he has

Ruth Sheen and Philip Davis in a scene from Mike Leigh's "High Hopes."

such a hard time going home that they wind up nicknaming him "E. T." It's easy to see why the stranger, only a minor character drifting through Mike Leigh's "High Hopes," is so drawn to these two. Cyril and Shirley, who travel about in matching motorcycle leathers, are an utterly spontaneous and unpretentious duo, which sets them in marked contrast to everyone else in Mr. Leigh's astute socioeconomic satire.

The title seemingly refers to Cyril and Shirley's optimism, a sentiment that often seems badly misplaced in view of Mr. Leigh's larger portrait of the England of Margaret Thatcher, for whom Shirley has named her prickliest cactus. The spirit of self-interest can be found everywhere in the film, even in the principals' figurative backyard.

"High Hopes" revolves loosely around the various members of Cyril's family, who represent a wide range of economic conditions. Cyril himself is defiantly impecunious, working as a messenger and refusing Shirley's persistent pleas that they have a child. On the other hand, Cyril's sister, Valerie (Heather Tobias), is loudly and aggressively nouveau riche, with a red sports car and an Afghan hound that wears a sweater. A less self-conscious form of poverty than Cyril's is represented by his mother (Edna Dore), a quietly dejected woman now on the eve of her 70th birthday. The run-down row house where she lives, a neighborhood where gentrification has begun, and the yuppies next door do not take kindly to such a shabby old lady.

•

Although "High Hopes" is mostly a gentle, reflective and personable comedy of manners, it turns sharply funny at the sight of these new neighbors. "I thank God every day I've been blessed with such beautiful

skin," says the wife, Laetitia (Lesley Manville); for his part, her husband, Rupert (David Bamber), declares, "What made this country great is a place for everyone, and everyone in his place."

On one unfortunate occasion, when the ever-more-forgetful old woman loses her money and keys, the neighbors are thrown together with hilarious results. Laetitia, visibly annoyed when the old lady asks to use her bathroom, soon warms to this conversational opportunity. She suggests that Cyril's mother has no business occupying such a large house, and asks her, "Do you have all your original features?" By this she means fireplaces and such, but Cyril's mother is understandably confused.

It seems only fitting that a film containing Rupert and Laetitia should also include a visit to the grave of Karl Marx, where Cyril and Shirley wonder what exactly has gone wrong in their society until a group of Asian tourists interrupts their reverie. The later part of the film, which takes an abruptly more serious tone than its opening, is a serious contemplation of Cyril and Shirley's frustration. There is no better setting for this than the house of Cyril's shrieking sister, the indescribably vulgar setting for the old woman's wretched 70th birthday party. Cyril winds up stealing an imitation-gold banana as a kind of trophy.

•

"High Hopes" manages to be enjoyably whimsical without ever losing its cutting edge. Mr. Leigh, who works with his actors in a quasi-improvisatory way, succeeds especially well in creating the impression that rarely, if ever, does anyone in the film understand anyone else's point of view. The exceptions to this rule are Cyril and Shirley, who understand each other perfectly but in matters regarding their future can seldom

agree. Though the actors are all good, Miss Sheen, a wonderfully empathetic actress with a flair for comic understatement, is outstanding.

"High Hopes" will be shown at 9 P.M. tonight and 4:30 P.M. tomorrow as part of the New York Film Festival.

1988 S 24, 12:4

Panic on the Streets

MAPANTSULA, directed by Oliver Schmitz; screenplay by Mr. Schmitz and Thomas Mogotlane; director of photography, Rod Stewart; edited by Mark Baard; music by the Ouens; art director, Robyn Hofmeyr; produced by Max Montocchio. At Alice Tully Hall, as part of the 26th New York Film Festival. Running time: 105 minutes. This film has no rating.

Panic	Thomas Mogotlane
Pat	Thembi Mtshali
Stander	Marcel Van Heerden
Ma Modise	Dolly Rathebe
Sam	Eugene Majola
Duma	Peter Sephuma

By JANET MASLIN

The insouciant lead character in the South African film "Mapantsula," a thief named Panic, is as talented as he is cool. Panic is such an unflappable pickpocket that he can steal a man's wallet and then stand there, switchblade in hand, rifling through the wallet's contents while silently daring the victim to challenge him. He's such a skilled shoplifter that he can wrap each half of a man's suit tightly around one of his calves, holding the merchandise in place with heavy socks. And Panic is good with the ladies, too. As "Mapantsula" begins, Panic's concerns do not extend much beyond these particular spheres.

This fine and caustic South African film, directed by Oliver Schmitz and written by him and Thomas Mogot-

Thomas Mogotlane as Panic in a scene from "Mapantsula."

lane, the actor who plays Panic, is the story of Panic's transformation. All around him, in the black township where his neighbors are vigorously protesting rent increases, Panic sees the difficult conditions under which others live, but he initially feels himself to be immune. "These people live in a dream," he says contemptuously of those blacks who hold regular jobs in the white community.

And he does his best to see that his girlfriend, Pat (Thembi Mtshali), who works as a maid for a rude and patronizing white woman, will herself lose her job. Panic visits Pat at work, insults the mistress of the house and throws a rock through her window, not so much for political reasons as out of the sheer, unbridled rage that is his guiding emotion.

•

To depict the process whereby Panic is radicalized, Mr. Schmitz gives the film a dual time frame. "Mapantsula" (the title means something like gangster) cuts back and forth between scenes of a freewheeling, unreconstructed Panic on the streets and a warier man who is now in jail, though the circumstances of his arrest are not explained fully until the film's end.

In jail, Panic at first shares the camaraderie of his fellow prisoners, who are there for political reasons, and he shares their jailhouse humor. "At least we have privacy, and we don't have to worry about being arrested any more," one prisoner says.

Panic is treated brutally and insultingly by the white police, but this is only one factor contributing to his conversion. The others can be found on the street as he gradually begins to see past his self-interest to the harsh facts of black South African life. In true renegade spirit, "Mapantsula" was made semicovertly (the script · shown to censors was for an ordinary gangster film); and it feels more authentic and less contrived than other South African films that have been shown here. The interaction between blacks and whites in street scenes, the day-to-day routine of life in a black neighborhood, and the galvanizing spirit of black South African music are all powerfully felt.

•

Mr. Mogotlane makes Panic much more than a symbol, treating him as a raffish, amusingly overconfident figure at first and a visibly shaken man as the film progresses, until at last he utters the single syllable that encapsulates the film's final point. It's a dashing performance, and a fierce one, too. "Mapantsula," acted by a good and forthright South African cast, is also filled with the buoyant, inspirational a cappella music that drives its political message further home.

"Mapantsula" will be shown at 6 P.M. tonight and 2 P. M. tomorrow as part of the New York Film Festival.

1988 S 24, 12:4

Oppressed Chauvinist

FELIX, directed and written by Christel Buschmann, Helke Sander, Helma Sanders-Brahms and Margarethe von Trotta; in German with English subtitles; cinematographers, Frank Brühne, Mike Gast, Martin Gressmann and Franz Rath; edited by Jane Seitz; a Future Film Production. At Alice Tully Hall, as part of the 26th New York Film Festival. Running time: 95 minutes. This film has no rating.

Felix	Ulrich Tukur
Eva	Eva Mattes
Susanne	Annette Uhlen
Danuta	Danuta Lato
Gabi	Gabriela Herz
Luci	Barbara Auer

By VINCENT CANBY

"Felix" was conceived, it seems, as a somewhat solemn stunt of a movie but turns out to be a surprisingly jolly entertainment.

The German film is the work of four women, each of whom wrote and directed one segment in the story of Felix, a charming bounder who feels wrongfully oppressed by the women he uses so casually.

"Felix" will be shown at the New York Film Festival at 1 P.M. today and 7 P.M. tomorrow.

The film isn't exactly seamless, but Ulrich Tukur, who plays Felix, gives such a seamlessly funny performance that the movie has far more cohesion than might be expected. Mr. Tukur, an actor in the William Hurt style, creates a thoroughly plausible male chauvinist, the kind who has no trouble holding two contradictory ideas in his head at the same time.

Felix feels hemmed in by his relationship with Trudy, who is walking out on him as the movie begins. Then he is bereft as well as furious and humiliated. He believes Trudy is the only woman for him but feels she's being unreasonable in expecting him to be faithful.

•

In this, the film's initial segment, written and directed by Helma Sanders-Brahms, Felix paces his chicly underfurnished, white-walled flat, drinking from a bottle of whisky and talking on the telephone to Karen, a close friend of his and Trudy's. When he isn't suggesting that he and Karen get together, he's painting a picture of himself as an artist thwarted by middle-class sensibilities.

"I saw us as Jean-Paul Sartre and Simone de Beauvoir," he tells Karen, but Trudy was too conventional. Felix says he has nothing against bourgeois traditions, preferably at Christmas.

In the film's second segment, written and directed by Helke Sander, Felix is at the seashore. He tries to regain his self-esteem by picking up two very pretty young women who attempt to teach him the joys of sex without the usual physical contact.

Ulrich Tukur and Barbara Auer in a scene from "Felix."

He fails miserably.

Margarethe von Trotta wrote and directed the third segment, the film's best, in which Felix, wandering around town at loose ends, meets Eva (Eva Mattes), a woman despondently eating an ice cream cone. Eva turns to ice cream when she's depressed. Felix takes her to a soda shop. Having been abandoned by her lover, Eva swallows great gobs of ice cream as if they were Seconals.

Felix knows how she feels and suggests, very discreetly, that he might stand in for the lost lover. This is impossible for reasons that are clear when Eva's lover turns up. Miss Mattes and Mr. Tukur are a delight as two intelligent people who manage to make emotional contact without the obligatory sexual finale.

•

In the film's sweetly funny concluding sequence, written and directed by Christel Buschmann, Felix explores Hamburg at night. Involved in this adventure are a not-great Elvis Presley impersonator who is devoted to the entertainer's late, *fat* period, a very drunk barfly who attacks Felix for eating "toxic waste" (a hotdog) and a married couple whose free and easy ways shock the supposedly liberated Felix.

The pleasures of the film accumulate. "Felix" is finally so enjoyable that no one, without being told, would easily identify it as the work of four very different talents.

1988 S 24, 13:1

Fable of Life
On Collective Farm

ASYA'S HAPPINESS, directed by Andrei Konchalovsky; script (Russian with English subtitles) by Yuri Klepikov; camera, Georgi Rerberg; art direction, Mikhail Romadin; a production of Mosfilm-Studio. At Alice Tully Hall, as part of the 26th New York Film Festival. Running time: 95 minutes. This film has no rating.

Asya	Iya Savina
WITH: Aleksandr Surin and Lyubov Sokolova

By VINCENT CANBY

A note at the beginning of "Asya's Happiness," Andrei Konchalovsky's 1967 Russian film, describes it as "the story of a woman who loved a man but did not marry him."

I don't know whether this was intended to prepare 1967 Russian audiences for a comparatively scandalous film, which they were not allowed to see until some years later, or if it was simply Mr. Konchalovsky's way of setting the tone for his offbeat (in 1967 Russian terms) fable of life on a collective farm.

The film, reportedly a favorite of Mikhail S. Gorbachev, the Soviet leader, was finally shown to critics at the 1977 Moscow Film Festival. The New York Film Festival will show it at 3:30 P.M. today at Alice Tully Hall.

Until its final 20 minutes or so, when it becomes almost a parody of stereotypical, idyllically photographed Russian films about the joys of joint endeavor, "Asya's Happiness" is a movie of insight and a good deal of humor. The setting is a collective farm at harvest time and the heroine a pretty young woman who is proudly pregnant by a handsome rascal who has no intention of legitimizing the relationship. The gutsy, independently minded Asya couldn't care less as long as he doesn't run away. He doesn't.

Though Asya, nicely played by Iya Savina, is the focal point of the narrative, Mr. Konchalovsky allows the movie to wander around, poking into the lives and reminiscences of subsidiary characters. These are what give the film its richness and feeling of authenticity. Only three of the actors in the film are professionals, and of them, only Miss Savina is identified with her role in the film's credits.

One man remembers the emotional reception he received when he finally returned home after a prison sentence (for an unspecified crime). The head of the farm, a very busy, take-charge sort of fellow who is a dwarf, tells a moving and funny story about his courtship of the woman he finally married. The times are identified by one young man's curiosity about the Vietnam War, which, as he understands it, is being fought by the members of the North Atlantic Treaty Organization.

After making "Asya's Happiness" as well as an excellent adaptation of "Uncle Vanya" in 1970 and the epic "Siberiade" in 1978, Mr. Konchalovsky moved to the West. None of the films he has directed in this country, including "Runaway Train" and "Shy People," display the ease, compassion and natural humor that are evident throughout "Asya's Happiness." The alien soil does not seem to nourish his talent.

1988 S 24, 13:1

Iya Savina in the title role of "Asya's Happiness."

The World As Her Theater

The New York Times
Susan Sontag

SARAH, written and directed by Edgardo Cozarinsky; edited by Suzanne Baron; camera, Stéphane Adam; music by Jules Massenet, Emmanuel Chabrier, Giuseppe Verdi and Giaccomo Puccini; produced by Nicole Stephane; a French-Belgian co-production. At Alice Tully Hall, as part of the 26th New York Film Festival. Running time: 31 minutes. This film has no rating.

WITH: the voice of Susan Sontag

By CARYN JAMES

She could not recall who the father of her son was, Sarah Bernhardt wrote in her memoir, but she placed Victor Hugo on a short list of possibilities. She once announced she was having a leopard's tail grafted into herself. She continued acting well into old age, a star and a scandal because she adored theatricality on stage and off. "Sarah," Edgardo Cozarinsky's half-hour film about her life and career, is as wonderfully profligate as the actress herself. A rich compilation of photographs and films, it captures the wild variety of Bernhardt's histrionics and the feel of an age when melodrama was a descriptive word, not a dirty one. "Sarah" will be shown at the New York Film Festival tonight at 9:30 and tomorrow at 6:15.

Still photographs — famous ones by Felix Nadir as well as lesser-known shots — show the young beauty, sometimes prim, sometimes seductive, often with eyes rolled toward heaven. Later stills reveal that the aging grand dame had grown quite thick about the middle.

In silent films of Bernhardt on stage, we see the grand gestures of a time when acting could not be too broad. As Camille, she reclines on a couch and flings a hands back over her brow. As Hamlet, she lunges forward in a duel to knock a sword out of her opponent's hand.

We even hear her voice at the start, in a scratchy recording that makes her sound a bit like Glinda the Good Witch. No wonder Mr. Cozarinsky's fictionalized first-person narrative, read in a voice-over by Susan Sontag as Bernhardt, asserts that her true image was not captured on film or recordings, but in "photography, which allows the eye to linger, which authorizes the mind to dream."

The major misstep in "Sarah," however, is this presumptuous monologue, which is straightforward and earnest, two things Bernhardt never was. Mr. Cozarinsky, presumably blending some of Bernhardt's genuine statements with invented ones, is shrewd enough to have her state, "I would turn that thing called 'the world' into a theater, and with this theater invent myself." But even that cogent explanation attacks the enigmatic, alluring image Bernhardt worked so hard to create. Ms. Sontag intelligently avoids imitating Bernhardt's dramatic tone; instead, her voice tends so much toward flatness that we cannot believe she speaks for the actress.

Still, Mr. Cozarinsky allows the eye to linger, and provides magnificent images which the mind can turn to dreams. A line of horse-drawn carriages, each overflowing with flowers, moves slowly ahead at Bernhardt's funeral in 1923. Bits of this film are scattered throughout "Sarah," as if to remind us of the dramatic excess she took to her grave.

1988 S 25, 64:1

Who Was That Masked Man?

LA MASCHERA, directed by Fiorella Infascelli; screenplay (Italian with English subtitles) by Adriano Apra and Miss Infascelli with the collaboration of Ennio De Concini and Enzo Ungari; director of photography, Acacio De Almeida; music by Luis Bacalov; edited by Francesco Malvestito; production designer, Antonello Geleng and Stefania Benelli; produced by Lilia Smecchia and Ettore Rosboch; a RAI Radiotelevisione Italiana RAI Due Instituto Luce — Italnoleggio Cinematografico, Best International Films Production.

Iris	Helena Bonham Carter
Leonardo	Michael Maloney
Leonardo's Father	Feodor Chaliapin
Elia	Roberto Herlitzka
Theater Company Manager	
	Michele de Marchi
Viola	Alberto Cracco
Maria	Valentina Lainati

By VINCENT CANBY

"La Maschera" is the sort of sublimely silly movie that somehow finds its way into every film festival. It is prettily photographed, solemnly acted and so supremely and vacuously irrelevant that it prompts serious thoughts about revolution. Any society that can take it seriously must be in the last stages of decadence. Quick, Angelo, my Fabergé snuffbox!

The Italian film, the first feature to be directed by Fiorella Infascelli, will be shown at the New York Film Festival tonight at 9:30 P.M. and tomorrow evening at 6:15.

"La Maschera" wears its subtext on its sleeve. It's about an 18th-century Italian nobleman, a wastrel named Leonardo (Michael Maloney), a fellow who has been so dissolute for so long that he has lost touch with the real him. It is also about Iris (Helena Bonham Carter), who has her own identity problem. She is a pretty young actress utterly exhausted with role playing and speaking other people's lines.

One night, after watching Iris perform, Leonardo attempts to seduce her. She pushes him away. Iris is supposed to be full of scorn, though all that Miss Bonham Carter is able to register is a severe pout. The furious Leonardo vows revenge. He'll worm his way into her affections and then dump her.

To this end, he disguises himself, minimally, in a series of New Year's Eve masks and courts her. In falling in love with the stranger, Iris escapes from the awful world of theatrical make-believe. It is the film's grand paradox that Leonardo, as he puts on one mask after another, uncovers the man he once was.

"La Maschera" plays like the libretto for an opera for which no music was ever written. The actors are no less inert than the scenery. Miss Infascelli is so fond of shots of fountains, brooks and rivers that, after the press screening, someone asked her if water was her element.

She responded through an English interpreter. "Yes," she said, "water is definitely my element." She added that her next film will be shot in a villa on an island with lots of scenes of water, and even with some underwater scenes.

Quick, Angelo, the tenterhooks.

1988 S 25, 64:4

BIRD directed by Clint Eastwood; written by Joel Oliansky; director of photography, Jack N. Green; film editor, Joel Cox; music score by Lennie Niehaus; production designer, Edward C. Carfagno; produced by Mr. Eastwood; released by Warner Brothers; at Alice Tully Hall as part of the 26th New York Film Festival; running time, 163 minutes. This film is rated R.

Charlie (Bird) Parker	Forest Whitaker
Chan Parker	Diane Venora
Red Rodney	Michael Zelniker
Dizzy Gillespie	Samuel E. Wright
Buster Franklin	Keith David
Brewster	Michael McGuire
Esteves	James Handy

By JANET MASLIN

Although the first scene of "Bird" shows the young Charlie Parker in a rustic setting, the film seldom ventures outdoors after that. Most of "Bird," Clint Eastwood's film biography of the legendary jazz saxophonist, takes place in the smoky nightclubs where Parker played or in the dimly lighted apartments where his unruly private life unfolded. The film's studied, shadowy look, at times so striking that the actors' features can't clearly be seen, becomes its most concerted effort to capture the spirit of Parker's music.

Until Bertrand Tavernier's "'Round Midnight," in which Dexter Gordon served as the purest imaginable embodiment of jazz and its attendant way of life, it might have seemed impossible to convey these things on screen. "Bird," earnest and immense as it is, reinforces the earlier notion of jazz's elusiveness. Though the music is everywhere in Mr. Eastwood's film, heard on the superb soundtrack and seen on every street corner, its essence remains somehow out of reach.

Clearly, enormous reserves of energy and affection have gone into creating the nightclub world of "Bird," in which the music spills out onto the streets at every opportunity. The film creates the enchanting impression that there was a time (the late 1940's and early 50's) and a place (52d Street in Manhattan) in which this music was the galvanizing force in every life. All the great clubs are here, lovingly re-created; even the street's most famous doorman (and most ardent jazz booster) can be found. Yet the figure of Charlie Parker, for all the passionate excitment of this atmosphere, is somehow indistinct.

Forest Whitaker, whose hulking physique and expansive grin give him an uncanny resemblance to Parker at times, is first seen at a crisis point in the musician's life, driven to a suicide attempt by the death of his young daughter and the decline of his career. From this, the film flashes back to tell how this brilliant innovator, whose nickname was "Bird," got his musical start. Though this is a standard way of framing any film biography, it's jarring here because the latter-day Parker takes some getting used to. Nervous and unsteady, grinning yet morose, plagued by a pain the film never fully fathoms, he starts off as a difficult figure and remains that way.

The film's biographical details, faithful but highly selective (Parker's several early marriages are mentioned only in passing), chart the unsteady course of Parker's career and his rocky relationship with Chan Richardson, the tough, beautiful daughter of a show-business family. She off-handedly tells Parker "It's always been musicians" when she first meets him. As Chan, Diane Venora gives the film almost as much of a compass as the real woman must have given Charlie Parker. And whenever the film returns to her smart, no-nonsense characterization, it is on steady ground.

But like Parker himself, this nearly three-hour film does a great deal of wandering. It takes Parker to California, where he finds that be-bop music is ahead of its time; it manages a humorous glimpse at one of his idols, Igor Stravinsky; it travels to the deep South, where Red Rodney (Michael Zelniker), the white member of Park-

Damon Whitaker as the young Charlie Parker in a scene from Clint Eastwood's film biography of the legendary jazz saxophonist, "Bird."

er's band, is passed off as an albino bluesman so he can stay in black hotels. Parker is seen in a hospital ward, waking from his delirium to find that a young doctor wants his autograph. Wherever Parker goes, he is already a great hero to those who have heard him play.

•

Though Mr. Whitaker makes Parker a substantial and sympathetic figure, he doesn't convey much of the man's legendary charm. For instance, Parker's reputation as a ladykiller isn't corroborated by this screen incarnation. And the more complex side of his nature, the musical side that emerges in his collaborations with giants like Dizzy Gillespie (Samuel E. Wright), is better heard on the soundtrack than seen.

What the film does best is capture a general sense of the tight, self-protective and in some ways dangerously insular jazz world. It deals soberingly with Parker's drug habit (he was an addict from his middle teens until his death, in 1955, as a 34-year-old so dissipated that the coroner estimated his age at 50 or 60) and with the ulcers and liver trouble that sometimes made Scotch and milk his drink of choice. Parker's role as, in Nat Hentoff's words, "the paradigm of the jazzman-as-victim" is well-established here, better so than the underlying pressures that led him in that direction.

"Bird" is less moving as a character study than it is as a tribute and as a labor of love. The portrait it offers, though hazy at times, is one Charlie Parker's admirers will recognize.

"Bird" will be shown tonight at 9:15 and tomorrow at 6:15 P.M. as part of the New York Film Festival.

1988 S 26, C19:1

Correction

A film review of "Bird" on Monday, about the jazz saxophonist Charlie Parker, omitted the name of the actor who played Parker as a young man. He is Damon Whitaker.

1988 S 29, A3:2

Mélange à Trois

THE MAN WITH THREE COFFINS, directed by Lee Chang Ho; screenplay (Korean with English subtitles) by Lee Jue Ha, based on his novel "A Wanderer Never Sleeps Even on the Road"; director of photography, Park Seung Bae; music by Lee Chong Ku; produced by Lee Myung Won; released by New Yorker Films. At Alice Tully Hall, as part of the 26th New York Film Festival. Running time: 105 minutes. This film has no rating.

Yang Soon Suk ....Kim Myung Kon
Yang's wife, a nurse, a prostitute . Lee Bo Hee
Shaman ....Woo Ok Joo

By CARYN JAMES

It's a shrewd director who knows the effect of his work as well as Lee Chang Ho. At a press conference after "The Man With Three Coffins," the first South Korean film to be shown at the New York Film Festival, he said through an interpreter, "Thank you for your patience" — a bluntly honest remark. "The Man With Three Coffins" is the kind of film that must be seen twice before it makes sense. But only the most committed and curious students of world cinema may feel that Mr. Lee's artistic rigor is reward enough for struggling through the film's taxing narrative strategy and its obscurity to most Western viewers.

In summary, the plot sounds compelling. Three years after his wife's death, a man travels north to her hometown to scatter her ashes. Along the way he crosses paths more than once with a nurse also heading north with her elderly charge and encounters a prostitute who dies soon after he sleeps with her. All three women, including the wife seen in flashbacks, are played by the same actress, creating mysterious echoes. Is the hero imagining this similarity? Or are the women reincarnations of the wife?

•

The story and subsequent questions do not take shape until halfway through the film, though. In the very first scene, the nurse and the man are walking along a road discussing her contract to care for the aged patient; their allusions make complete sense only when the same scene is repeated at the end. The entire film is a similar series of clues dropped here and picked up there, as the man's memory ranges freely through the past and abruptly returns to the present.

This disjointed manner works against any emotional engagement and turns the film into a puzzle whose most probable solution, given late in the film, seems disappointingly obvious. A fortuneteller has told the nurse, as we learn in awkwardly translated subtitles: "At 30, you'll meet a man with three coffins on the shore. That man is your husband of the previous life."

The film's most consistently interesting feature is the shifting style of its photography. Transitions from present to past are shot in glistening sepia tones that gradually warm up to fill with color. When the man stands on the shore of a lake, with a slender tree to one side of him and a single boat on the horizon, we see an elegantly composed portrait. And in a smoke-filled gambling house, the photography, by Park Seung Bae, refuses to be lyrical.

•

Still, there is little to prepare us for the man's emotional shriek of loss, captured in a freeze-frame at the end, when he discovers that the nurse is lost to him. We see her take part in a Buddhist ritual, though without Mr. Lee's later explanation it would have been hard to grasp that the nurse is becoming a shaman and will devote her life to others. Similarly, though there are references to the old patient heading "as close to the D.M.Z." as he can get, "The Man with Three Coffins" seems very different from the director's assessment of it as a political film calling for the unification of Korea.

"The Man With Three Coffins" will be shown at 9:30 tonight and at 6:15 P.M. tomorrow. Preceding it is "Souvenir," a futile four-minute film shot in blue tones that tries to create the mood of another era as a woman with a Louise Brooks bob lounges in a slip and smokes a cigarette.

1988 S 27, C16:5

Apocalypse As Rock Video

THE LAST OF ENGLAND, directed by Derek Jarman; photography by Mr. Jarman, Christopher Hughes, Cerith Wyn Evans and Richard Heslop; edited by Peter Cartwright, Angus Cook, Sally Yeadon and John Maybury; music by Simon Turner, Andy Gill, Mayo Thompson, Albert Oehlen, Barry Adamson and El Tito; production designer, Christopher Hobbs; produced by James Mackay and Don Boyd. At Alice Tully Hall, as part of the 26th New York Film Festival. Running time: 87 minutes. This film has no rating.

WITH: Tilda Swinton, Spencer Leigh, Spring, Gay Gaynor, Matthew Hawkins, Gerrard McCarthur, John Phillips and the voice of Nigel Terry.

By JANET MASLIN

Surely Derek Jarman's "Last of England" is the longest and gloomiest rock video ever made. Its manifold images of annihilation and misery are assembled in free-associating fashion, without any concern for narrative but with the quick, vigorous, flashy pacing that video audiences understand. The energy level of "The Last of England" is much too high for monotony, but the film's expressionistic leaps are determinedly obscure. Whatever the reason, there were many walkouts during the film's New York Film Festival press screening.

Mr. Jarman, whose earlier films include "The Tempest" and "Caravaggio," intersperses home-movie snippets and male homoerotic imagery with his new film's visions of rubble and despair. A typical fast-moving sequence combines glimpses of long-haired male dancers dressed as ballerinas, red-filtered glimpses of scampering female nudes, shots of frightened hostages held by terrorists and random explosions in the distance. Mr. Jarman returns regularly to each of these motifs in a musical and lulling manner, if not a particularly illuminating one.

•

Shot in Super-8, with the camera often hand-held, "The Last of England" does manage a bleak vitality despite the overwhelming pessimism of its images. Signs of struggle are everywhere. A punk in torn jeans walks through a landscape of destruction, stomping the last vestiges of civilization; a baby lies in a carriage lined with newspapers proclaiming imminent doom. A bride lies dressed in tatters; the groom faces a firing squad. A man dressed as a terrorist and a naked man embrace on a bed covered with a Union Jack, with wine bottles and guns scattered around them. A voice on the soundtrack (that of Nigel Terry) invokes Allen Ginsberg's "Howl."

The cumulative effect of "The Last of England" is affectingly ominous, but it's also indistinct. The film's autobiographical aspects — the polite, happy family seen in the home movie material is Mr. Jarman's, though the film never identifies it as such — help to keep it out of reach. So does the wildly improvised quality of most of the film's sequences; there is no screenplay at all and virtually no dialogue.

At a press conference, Mr. Jarman said that he has tested positive for AIDS antibodies and that several cast members developed the disease after the film was made. But he said he had not intended AIDS to be this film's principal subject; terrorism, the threat of nuclear annihilation and a general breakdown of society are more prominently addressed. Nevertheless, the gaunt men wandering disorientedly through the destruction-littered landscape of "The Last of England" seem to offer a haunting vision of this plague and its ravages.

"The Last of England" will be shown at 9:15 P.M. tonight as part of the New York Film Festival.

1988 S 28, C18:3

One Wild Romance

NANOU, directed and written by Conny Templeman; in French and English with English subtitles; photographed by Martin Fuhrer; produced by Simon Perry and Patrick Sandrin. At Film Forum 1, 57 Watts Street. Running time: 110 minutes. This film has no rating.

Nanou	Imogen Stubbs
Luc	Jean-Philippe Ecoffey
Max	Daniel Day-Lewis

By WALTER GOODMAN

Can a young woman from the British middle class find happiness in France with a working-class youth of radical disposition? That is the question posed and answered in "Nanou," which opens today at Film Forum 1. Produced in French and English, it introduces the work of Conny Templeman, a young British director and writer. Rather like her heroine, Ms. Templeman displays a feeling for French working-class ways as well as an agreeably light approach to her actors and to individual scenes. Unfortunately, the writer has shortchanged the director; once we catch onto the theme, the story saunters along a touch predictably.

It is no strain believing that Imogen Stubbs as Nanou and Jean-Philippe Ecoffey as Luc would fall for each other. He has a pouty-pretty, sullen-sexy look and she is a fresh British beauty. When, in an irritated moment, he criticizes her for getting fat, Nanou sheds her nightie and takes a good look at herself in the mirror, which allows us to confirm that this woman is a bit of all right.

•

After some introductory byplay, their relationship really gets steaming when Nanou, on the bed, caresses the face of Luc, on the floor, with her foot; he responds by chewing on her toes, and you know where that leads. Soon they are on the kitchen table and, taken by a sudden, irrepressible urge in the middle of town, they go dashing into a shed marked plainly "Défense de Stationner."

But, Ms. Templeman is telling us, such early bursts of sexual activity have a way of cooling, particularly as Luc is always leaving Nanou behind while he goes off on mysterious errands that have to do with bringing down the system. Nanou's nice English boyfriend (Daniel Day-Lewis in a brief appearance) is far more attentive and appreciative of her efforts at photography, but he just doesn't get those juices running. The appearance and disappearance of a professional terrorist seems an effort to pump some excitement into an uneventful love story, but the effect is more puzzling than stimulating.

Although Luc chides Nanou for having been spoiled by her proper English family, he accommodates her desire for such bourgeois amenities as curtains and an armchair, and further shows his affection by faking a sip of a rival's urine at her request. But mostly he leaves her to busy herself with this and that while he plays the revolutionary. "I have to get back to work," he mutters, dons his rucksack and disappears. Poor Nanou feels left out. The scene in which she finally accompanies him on a major mission catches the confusion of the amateur terrorists and demonstrates that Ms. Templeman can put together an effective action sequence. But it also calls attention to how little excitement the previous hour has offered.

1988 S 28, C18:5

A Lethal Attack Of Bleeding Hearts

MEMORIES OF ME, directed by Henry Winkler; written by Eric Roth and Billy Crystal; director of photography, Andrew Dintenfass; edited by Peter E. Berger; music by Georges Delerue; production designer, William J. Cassidy; produced by Alan King, Mr. Crystal and Michael Hertzberg; released by Metro-Goldwyn-Mayer Pictures Inc. At Loew's New York Twin, Second Avenue and 66th Street; Loews 84th Street Six, at Broadway, and other theaters. Running time: 104 minutes. This film is rated PG-13.

Abbie	Mr. Crystal
Abe	Mr. King
Lisa	JoBeth Williams
Dorothy Davis	Janet Carroll

By CARYN JAMES

As a Hollywood movie extra named Abe Polin, Alan King dresses in a lobster costume. There is a joke about melted butter. Abe's son, Abbie (Billy Crystal), is visiting from New York, so they go to a bar where the heart-surgeon son quietly drinks Perrier while crass old Dad sits at the piano and belts out "Too Pooped to Pop." He ends by announcing: "No applause. Just throw money."

"Memories of Me" knows that Abe and Abbie are clichés, but seems to like them that way. It may be harder for an audience to warm up to a film so predictable it practically invites us to sing along. "I thought I was immortal," Abbie realizes after he has a heart attack. Because he's not, he flies off to reconcile with that "professional embarrassment," his father. Their story builds to a mawkish finale that aims for the heart but is more likely to make us feel we're being beaten over the head and bullied to the point of tears.

The familiar father-son scenario appeared most recently in Garry Marshall's 1986 film "Nothing in Common," which "Memories of Me" resembles down to the gratuitous role of the son's goody-goody girlfriend (here JoBeth Williams is made to say, "Just be his son!"). Abe, of course, has a not-unexpected illness. The first hint of medical trouble comes when the lobster recites a scene from "Inherit the Wind." And Dad thought he was immortal!

"Nothing in Common" had the nerve to begin with Jackie Gleason and Tom Hanks as a beastly selfish pair. "Memories of Me," written by Mr. Crystal and Eric Roth, is whiny and wimpy, allowing Abe and Abbie's soft-heartedness to show through from the start. It's as if Mr. King and Mr. Crystal, who produced the film along with Michael Hertzberg, were afraid to make either character a little bit unlikable.

•

"Memories of Me," which opens today at Loew's New York Twin and other theaters, was directed by Henry Winkler, the actor, television producer and director. In his first feature, Mr. Winkler seems to aim the camera anywhere and let the actors walk through their roles — until he gets to the fancied-up confrontation scene. Abe and Abbie jump out of a car in a tunnel, arguing about who loves whom the least. As they circle each other threatening to throw punches, the camera twists back and forth, alternately capturing Abe, Abbie and a wall.

The cast should have been able to salvage something from this mess. Mr. Crystal is one of the most inventive comic actors around, Mr. King proved long ago he can be a respectable dramatic actor and JoBeth Williams can be effectively engaging. All

Ron Batzdorff

three seem trapped in "Memories of Me," a film that assumes it's up to the job of dealing with life and death and love, but is not even up to dealing with lobsters.

•

"Memories of Me" is rated PG-13 ("Special Parental Guidance Suggested for Those Younger Than 13"). There is some impolite, though never shocking, language.

1988 S 28, C23:1

Love and Abuse In Liverpool

DISTANT VOICES, STILL LIVES, directed and written by Terence Davies; photography by William Diver and Patrick Duval; edited by Mr. Diver; art directors, Miki van Zwanenberg and Jocelyn James; produced by Jennifer Howarth; a British Film Institute Production in association with Channel 4 Television Ltd. and ZDF. At Alice Tully Hall, as part of the 26th New York Film Festival. Running time: 85 minutes. This film has no rating.

Mother	Freda Dowie
Father	Pete Postlethwaite
Eileen	Angela Walsh
Tony	Dean Williams
Maisie	Lorraine Ashbourne
Eileen as a child	Sally Davies
Tony as a child	Nathan Walsh
Maisie as a chld	Susan Flanagan

By VINCENT CANBY

"I wouldn't say no to a bust like that," a chatty suburban hairdresser says of (I think) Diana Dors.

The hairdresser is Betty, who has a breathing problem, a skin condition that prompts her to scratch a lot and a daughter, Charlene, who remains vague when her mother asks questions about her love life.

Mike Leigh's "Short and the Curlies" is also about Joy, a very bored young woman who works in a chemist's shop and who is being courted by Clive, a skinny, irrepressible young man with a large Adam's apple and a joke for every occasion. Clive asks Joy if she has a hole in her stocking. Joy says no. Says Clive, "Then how do you get your foot in?"

Clive is full of such thigh-slappers. Joy, who is intrigued in spite of herself, is likely to respond by saying she has a mouth ulcer.

•

Being just 18 minutes long, "The Short and the Curlies" is, technically, a short subject. It is, however, so irresistibly funny and wise that it dominates the program that will be shown at the New York Film Festival at 6:15 P.M. today and 5 P.M. Sunday.

I've not yet seen Mr. Leigh's feature "High Hopes," which the festival presented last weekend, but this 18-minute production whets the appetite. "The Short and the Curlies" has

something of the manner of a shaggy-dog story. It also possesses a first-rate film maker's sureness of touch and tone. David Thewlis, as the Ichabod Crane-like Clive, heads the excellent cast, which also includes Alison Steadman, Sylvestra le Touzel and Wendy Nottingham.

•

The feature on the bill is Terence Davies's 85-minute "Distant Voices, Still Lives," which comes to Lincoln Center after having won the Golden Leopard at the Locarno Film Festival and the Critics Prize at the Toronto festival.

The English film is one of those dimly realized personal statements that ultimately says a lot less than the written program notes that accompany it. On the screen is a tight-lipped, elliptical recollection of growing up in a working-class Liverpool family dominated by a possibly psychotic dad who is loving one minute and physically abusive the next. The director says the movie is autobiographical and describes it as an homage to his mother and sisters.

Mr. Davies covered more or less the same ground, though from his own point of view, in his "Trilogy," shown at the 1984 New Directors/New Films festival.

For no organic reason, Mr. Davies divides the film into two parts, "Distant Voices" and "Still Lives," in both of which marriages, deaths, baptisms and other family occasions are remembered in no special chronological order. This leads to redundancies that, I'm sure, are intentionally anti-dramatic.

•

To fill in the narrative gaps, Mr. Davies uses a lot of songs of the 1940's and 50's ("Roll Out the Barrel," "Buttons and Bows" and "Taking a Chance on Love," among others),

David Thewlis in "The Short and the Curlies"

Family Ties

Billy Crystal plays a heart surgeon and JoBeth Williams is the girlfriend helping him mend his relationship with his father in "Memories of Me."

many of them sung a cappella by members of the cast. The songs are sometimes quite nice, but they have none of the force of pop music as used by Dennis Potter in "Pennies From Heaven" and "The Singing Detective."

The songs, presented cold, clearly mean more to the director than they do to an audience that doesn't share his very specific feelings of loss and love. "Distant Voices, Still Lives" has the rigorous, studied look of advanced film-school work. The color photography has a soft, golden hue, and the camera movements are stately, with a lot of pans from right to left and, on occasion, a slow rise toward heaven, as if the film (and the man directing it) were looking up to God.

1988 S 29, C24:3

Rose Petals From Heaven

ASHIK KERIB, directed by Sergei Paradzhanov; screenplay (Russian with English subtitles) by Georgi Badridze, based on themes from "Ashik Kerib" by Mikhail Lermontov; director of photography, Albert Yavuryan; music by Dzhavashir Kuliev; production designers, Shota Gogolashvili and Nikolai Zandukeli; an International Film Exchange Release. At Alice Tully Hall, as part of the 26th New York Film Festival. Running time: 78 minutes. This film has no rating.

WITH: Yuri Goyan, Veronika Metonidze, Levan Natroshvili and Sofiko Chiaureli

By WALTER GOODMAN

The Soviet director Sergei Paradzhanov brings affection, humor and high style to his retelling of "Ashik Kerib," Mikhail Lermontov's fable of a wandering minstrel. Set in the misty past, presumably in the Ukraine or in Armenia, whose folklore has served Mr. Paradzhanov before, "Ashik Kerib" portrays the buffetings that the artist takes at the hands of philistines and despots before being rescued by the magic of his art.

It is easy to find autobiographical overtones in this new work from a director who spent four years in a Soviet prison and was forbidden to make movies for years more. But "Ashik Kerib," which is being shown at the New York Film Festival at 9:15 tonight and at noon Saturday, betrays no bitterness. Set in wildly beautiful country amid ruins that retain glimpses of ancient splendors, filled with lovely details of medieval frescoes and artifacts, sumptuous costumes and stirring folk songs, it is a children's tale as rendered by a sophisticated romantic. The masterfully composed scenes of weddings and funerals, courts and caravans call up the fabulous.

•

The journey of Ashik Kerib (Yuri Goyan), a minstrel with a shaven head, a muscular torso and very sturdy lungs, begins when he is refused the hand of his beloved because he has no money. Her rude father shows what he thinks of the rose petals the minstrel offers as a gift by turning his backside on him. For 1,000 days and nights, the minstrel goes where fate directs, singing his heart out even as he is abused by the worldly and the powerful. (If you are looking for political images, Sultan Aziz, otherwise known as "destroyer of souls," puts him in armor, then demands that he play his lute.) He is chained and rolled up in a carpet, confronted by a tiger with a revolving head and threatened with having his own head cut off.

The minstrel is better appreciated by children and common folk, particularly the handicapped. The blind find their way to the sounds of his lute, and when he sings to the deaf, they burst into dance. He is inspired by a feeble old minstrel who perishes with a remarkably energetic solo. Also, fortunately, Ashik Kerib has a couple of angels to look after him and is carried off in the nick of time by a robust saint on a white horse.

•

Every sequence of this highly stylized work has a ritualistic quality. But faithful though Mr. Paradzhanov may be to ethnic traditions, he is very much the modern, winking at us as he delivers symbols by the bushel — doves and pomegranates are special favorites, but there are also flopping fish, turkeys and a cow. Some of the symbols are obscure, as are some of the incidents, but once you get into the spirit of the movie, that hardly matters.

When, at the start, rice rains down to celebrate Arik's betrothal, it doesn't rain, it pours. The villains, hysterics to a man, owe less to Armenian folklore than to Hollywood's silent-era eye rollers. The castle of the great pasha ("May I be praised!") is guarded by sleepy automatons; the frolicsome ladies of his harem are equipped with machine guns. The mustachioed henchmen are a combination of the Keystone Kops, the Flying Karamazov Brothers and the chorus line from "La Cage aux Folles." That tiger prances straight out of vaudeville.

How Mr. Paradzhanov manages the tricky feat of kidding folk themes yet according them love and respect is his secret. How well he succeeds is here for the rest of us to relish.

1988 S 29, C24:5

Learning to Cope

PELLE THE CONQUEROR, directed by Bille August; adapted by Mr. August from the novel by Martin Andersen Nexo; in Danish with English subtitles; director of photography, Jorgen Persson; edited by Janus Billeskov Jansen; music by Stefan Nilsson; art director, Anna Asp; released by Miramax Films. At Alice Tully Hall, as part of the 26th New York Film Festival. Running time: 150 minutes. This film has no rating.

Lasse	Max von Sydow
Pelle	Pelle Hvenegaard
Manager	Erik Paaske
Anna	Kristina Tornqvists
Trainee	Morten Jorgensen

By VINCENT CANBY

Bille August's "Pelle the Conqueror" is not for people who prefer to take showers. It's for the person who likes to get into a movie as if it were a long hot bath. To hurry it would be to miss its method and its point.

The Danish film, which won the Golden Palm, the top prize, at this year's Cannes Festival, is a vividly re-created, minutely detailed panorama of a particular time (the turn of the century), place (rural Denmark) and circumstance (life on a great farm) in the course of the four seasons. The observer is Pelle (Pelle Hvenegaard), a staunch, wide-eyed Swedish boy who has come to Denmark with his aging, destitute and widowed father, Lasse (Max von Sydow).

Lasse has promised his son that Denmark will be a land of opportunity, a place of plentiful jobs, where pork is served on Sundays and butter is spread on bread. Instead Lasse and Pelle are lucky to be hired as little better than indentured servants, underpaid, underfed and overworked.

•

For the illiterate Lasse, who drinks too much and has no spine to fight, the farm is the end of the line. For Pelle, it is his introduction to an adult world in which rewards and punishments are thoroughly scrambled and arbitrary power is exercised by the few. Mr. August's screenplay is adapted from the first part of Martin Andersen Nexo's Danish novel in which Pelle, when he grows up, goes on to become a union leader.

"Pelle the Conqueror" will be shown at the New York Film Festival tonight at 9:15 and tomorrow at 2:30 P.M.

One of the scandals at the Cannes festival was that Mr. von Sydow did not win the best-actor award, which went to Forest Whitaker for his work in Clint Eastwood's "Bird." The Whitaker performance is acceptable, possibly limited by its rather commonplace context. The von Sydow performance is in a category by itself. It is another highlight in an already extraordinary career, and quite unlike anything that American audiences have seen him do to date.

Lasse is a refinement of the sort of fraudulent, washed-up, but deep-down noble boxer that Wallace Beery exuberantly overacted in "The Champ," a film that "Pelle" doesn't otherwise resemble, except in its close-up of the father-son relationship. Mr. von Sydow is something splendid to see as the boozy, weak-willed, loving Lasse. Though it is a rich performance, full of wit and humor, it is never broad or self-serving.

It is also the backbone of the movie, which sometimes looks too big in terms of landscapes, weather and the crowds of people on screen to have come from the comparatively small though clearly vital Danish film industry. "Pelle" has a kind of Dickensian appreciation for narrative, being packed with subplots perceived in the melodramtic terms of an adolescent boy's imagination.

•

Among the many subsidiary characters, there are the parvenu landowner whose philandering has driven his wife to drink and, finally, to stronger measures of revenge; a malformed boy who is Pelle's age and who dreams of joining a circus as a freak; a kind, sex-starved widow who is partial to Lasse, and another woman, a boistrous farmhand who turns Lasse down as a suitor on the grounds that he's too old to be "dangerous."

Mr. August never indulges the pathos that is built into the story, which is to his credit as a disciplined film maker, though it also keeps the film at a slight remove from the audience. One is never unaware that this is a very long movie. Mr. August brings a cool 20th-century sensibility to what is, at heart, a piece of passionate 19th-century fiction.

•

As played by Mr. Hvenegaard, who looks a bit like the young Dickie Moore in Hollywood's old "Oliver Twist," Pelle is idealized without being softened. Mostly, he is a camera, receiving the images of a childhood that will eventually shape the course of his life.

The scale of the physical production is most impressive. Mr. August and Jorgen Persson, the cinematographer, avoid the picturesque, which is not to say that "Pelle" isn't a beautiful film. It's just that its looks are more than skin deep.

1988 S 30, C8:1

Lost Between Two Cultures

DAUGHTER OF THE NILE, directed by Hou Hsiao-hsien; screenplay (Mandarin with English subtitles) by Chu Tien-wen; cinematography by Chen Hwai-en; edited by Liau Ching-sown; music by Chen Zhi-yuan and Zhang Hong-yi; art directors, Liu Zhi-hua and Lin Ju. At Alice Tully Hall, as part of the 26th New York Film Festival. Running time: 90 minutes. This film has no rating.

Shao Yang	Yang Lin
Shao Fang	Kao Jai
Ah San	Yang Fan
Grandpa	Li Tien-lu
Father	Tsui Fu-sheng
Shao Fang's fiancé	Hsin Shu-fen
Tutor	Wu Nian-zhen

"Daughter of the Nile," directed by the Chinese-born, Taiwanese-bred Hou Hsiao-hsien, is of primary interest as contemporary sociology interpreted as fiction by an earnest film student.

The movie will be shown at the New York Film Festival tonight at 6:15 and Sunday night at 7:30.

The setting is Taipei, where the young people, who have no real roots in the Americanized island they inhabit, zip around the neon-lit city on motorcycles, work at Kentucky Fried Chicken, smoke Marlboros and slip into big trouble without knowing how they got there.

Shao Yang, a pretty, solemn young woman, tries to keep her family together while working as a waitress and going to night school. Her mother and older brother are dead. Her father works out of town. It's up to Shao Yang to take care of her adolescent sister, who has already begun to steal, and another brother who is a burglar and gang member.

The young people aren't deprived of material things. They are without strong interests or direction, caught at equal distances between two cultures. They are vaguely like the much more vivid characters in Jean-Luc Godard's films of the late 1960's and early 70's.

Hou Hsiao-hsien's "Summer at Grandpa's," which was shown at the 1986 New Directors/New Films festival, seemed to have been strongly influenced by François Truffaut's films. His new movie recalls, fleetingly, not only Mr. Godard, but also Yasujiro Ozu. It's a curious combination.

"Daughter of the Nile" contains no tatami shots, in which people are photographed as if seen from a sitting position on the floor, but there are repeated shots of interiors recently vacated or just about to be entered. Shao Yang goes about her bleak life with a very Ozu-like, Japanese resignation, asking only what she can do for others, never thinking of herself.

Though the conditions in which Shao Yang lives may be authentic, her character, and the way the director presents her, appears to be borrowed.

The film's title is a poetic conceit, imposed on the movie to give it resonance. It refers to a comic book character, a young woman who goes back in time to ancient Egypt and, like Shao Yang, winds up feeling neither here nor there.

VINCENT CANBY

1988 S 30, C8:4

Out of the Night

ELVIRA, MISTRESS OF THE DARK, directed by James Signorelli; written by Sam Egan, John Paragon and Cassandra Peterson; director of photography, Hanania Baer; film editor, Battle Davis; music by James Campbell; production designer, John De Cuir Jr.; produced by Eric Gardner and Mark Pierson; released by New World Pictures. At Loews Astor Plaza, Broadway and 44th Street, and other theaters. Running time: 96 minutes. This film is rated PG-13.

Elvira .... Cassandra Peterson
Vincent Talbot .... W. Morgan Sheppard
Bob Redding .... Daniel Greene
Patty .... Susan Kellermann
Travis .... Jeff Conaway
Chastity Pariah .... Edie McClurg

By CARYN JAMES

Elvira's jet-black wig shoots up in a giant beehive shape, then falls like a veil to her waist. Her eyes are so heavy with makeup it's a wonder she can blink. And her slinky black dress might make Cher jealous or Frederick of Hollywood blush. Cut up to her thighs and down to her navel, it is designed to expose Elvira's proudest comic prop, a gravity-defying bosom more believable on Jessica Rabbit than on any real-life woman. Elvira the spoofy-sexy witch (the persona of an actress named Cassandra Peterson) is not what you'd call a class act, but she is a successul one. She began by introducing old horror films on television in Los Angeles, and soon spread her trashy-comic image nationwide in syndication and on video. Like Pee-wee Herman, Elvira is a walking visual joke, a cult figure trying to break through to the mainstream. And if you had to ask about any of this, you don't want to see her movie.

"Elvira, Mistress of the Dark" is a lame attempt to cash in on her character's success. The heroine drives to a small Massachusetts town called Fallwell, which looks like the set from "Peyton Place" — except for the house Elvira has inherited, which resembles the Bates Motel. The puritanical townspeople, led by Mrs. Chastity Pariah, try to drive Elvira away, but the teen-agers love her so much they pitch in and paint the house. She inherits an old recipe book and unwittingly cooks up monsters and love potions, and ends up locked in a sorcerers' battle with her sinister Uncle Vincent (played by W. Morgan Sheppard with the faintly British accent just right for the Vincent Price facsimile).

•

Part horror spoof, part small-town satire, the script by Sam Egan, John Paragon and Ms. Peterson meanders along as if Elvira's Halloween look and endless double-entendres are enough to carry the film. But her one-liners are obvious, and by the end we've grown so accustomed to her costume that she almost looks normal.

There are only a couple of fresh and funny moments. When Elvira inherits a fluffy little white poodle, in no time she turns him into a punked-out dog with a pink Mohawk cut and a studded leather collar. The punk poodle knows how to steal scenes. And in a flashback we peek into a basket left at an orphanage and see a small girl — baby Elvira — in full eye makeup, her tiny fingernails painted black. Otherwise, "Elvira, Mistress of the Dark," which opens today at Loews Astor Plaza and other theaters, turns a trashy idea into an oddly tame film.

1988 S 30, C12:4

A New Place to Dwell

Charlie Schlatter

HEARTBREAK HOTEL, directed and written by Chris Columbus; director of photography, Stephen Dobson; edited by Raja Gosnell; music by Georges Delerue; production designer, John Muto; produced by Lynda Obst and Debra Hill; released by Touchstone Pictures. At D. W. Griffith, 59th Street between Second and Third Avenues, and other theaters. Running time: 90 minutes. This film is rated PG-13.

Elvis Presley .... David Keith
Marie Wolfe .... Tuesday Weld
Johnny Wolfe .... Charlie Schlatter
Pam Wolfe .... Angela Goethals
Rosie Pantangellio .... Jacque Lynn Colton
Steve Ayres .... Chris Mulkey
Irene .... Karen Landry

By JANET MASLIN

Who's the mythic figure in the multicolored suit, the one who descends from on high to grant our wishes and make our troubles easier to bear? Is it Santa Claus? Superman? Or, as opined by the slick and sometimes amusing new comedy "Heartbreak Hotel," is it Elvis Presley?

"Heartbreak Hotel," which was written and directed by Chris Columbus and opens today at the D. W. Griffith and other theaters, presents the notion of a pet Elvis, for audiences to whom the idea of an extraterrestrial in the closet now seems hopelessly passé. After all, when you think about it — and the film *does* think about it, sometimes in funny ways — Elvis is a lot more exotic than that.

•

The film catches up with him in 1972, when he has taken to singing "The Battle Hymn of the Republic" in a gaudy stage show geared to female fans old enough to be his mother. (The particulars of Elvis's real stage act are nicely recapitulated, right down to the scarf handler who supplied the King with souvenirs he could toss to the fans.) In all other ways, it shows the star to be the same sweet, gentlemanly, receptive and clean-living Elvis he always was. After all, this is a fairy tale.

The film's Elvis is a funny fellow, played by David Keith with a flair for mimickry and a fine appreciation for patented Presley mannerisms. (The stage choreography, the shoulder-rolling walk and the speaking voice are just right.) Unfortunately, "Heartbreak Hotel" isn't about Elvis alone. It's also about the Wolfe family, a mother, daughter and teen-age son who kidnap Elvis, bring him home and try to rescue him from has-been status.

•

The film's conception of the Wolfes isn't nearly as enjoyable as its Elvis pastiche. Mom (Tuesday Weld) is becoming dissipated, seeing boyfriends (notably the bully played by Chris Mulkey) who beat her up; teenage son Johnny (Charlie Schlatter) and little daughter Pam (Angela Goethals) are understandably dismayed by this. Since Mom is a longtime Elvis fan, and Elvis is the only thing she seems to care about, Johnny has a brainstorm. Maybe he could import Elvis to his little home town in Ohio! "And I figure, if I can make her happy," Johnny says about his mother, "then maybe I can hold our family together."

A lot of Mr. Columbus's screenplay sounds like this; poor Mom must actually say "You are *something,* Mr. Presley!" later on in the story. But first things first: Johnny and his friends, who have their own rock band and an excess of confidence in their musical abilities, hatch an Elvis-napping scheme. They find a local pizza waitress who looks like Elvis's deceased mother, Gladys, and position her front row center at a Presley concert. This gets Elvis's attention, and so does a note she passes him, signed with Elvis's mother's special nickname. The boys then use their Gladys lookalike to lure Elvis away just as he's been doing what he likes to do after a concert, sitting alone singing spirituals and drinking water. If Elvis is indeed still among us, as his most ardent fans maintain, he's having a particularly good laugh at this.

Mr. Columbus, who previously directed "Adventures in Baby-Sitting" and whose writing credits include "Gremlins" and "The Goonies," sets up this idea well but has no idea where to stop. He pushes the film's slender premise much too far, trying to work miraculous feats of self-improvement upon Johnny, his mother, Marie, and even Elvis himself. Johnny, under Elvis's tutelage, has better luck with girls and knocks everyone dead at his local talent competition (who wouldn't, singing a duet of "Heartbreak Hotel" with Elvis himself?). Marie begins to dress more neatly and ditches the bully. As for Elvis, he paints the Wolfes' house, fixes their lawn mower, cures little Pam's fear of the dark and does every helpful chore he can think of except putting on the snow tires. Perhaps there wasn't time.

As Johnny, Mr. Schlatter is by turns unctuous and petulant, so his constant Elvis-baiting becomes less entertaining than obnoxious. The film's repeated suggestions that the Elvis of 1972 ought to return to his 50's roots are certainly sound, but they become tiresome when delivered by the self-righteous Johnny. And the film is quick to jettison them anyway, once it's ready to send Elvis back to the arms of his Memphis mafia. "Heartbreak Hotel," which gets a lot of mileage trading on bona fide Elvis trivia, is happy to abandon any contact with reality whenever it's convenient to do so.

Parts of "Heartbreak Hotel" are meant to echo scenes from Presley movies, but they haven't been staged as effectively as they could have been. A scene in which Elvis is dared by the bully to sing, for instance, and soon has everyone rolling in the aisles of the local luncheonette, would have looked a lot better in the bright primary colors of the early Presley era then they do with the murky red lighting they've been given here.

•

"Heartbreak Hotel" is rated PG-13 ("Special Parental Guidance Suggested for Those Younger Than 13"). The kids talk dirty, but Elvis does not.

1988 S 30, C18:5

So the One Guy Says To the Other Guy . . .

PUNCHLINE, directed and written by David Seltzer; director of photography, Reynaldo Villalobos; edited by Bruce Green; music by Charles Gross; production design by Jack DeGovia; produced by Daniel Melnick and Michael Rachmil; released by Columbia Pictures. At Coronet, Third Avenue and 59th Street. Running time: 128 minutes. This film is rated R.

Lilah Krytsick .... Sally Field
Steven Gold .... Tom Hanks
John Krytsick .... John Goodman
Romeo .... Mark Rydell
Madeline Urie .... Kim Greist
Arnold .... Paul Mazursky

By VINCENT CANBY

David Seltzer's "Punchline" is a tepid romantic comedy about two aspiring stand-up comics, Steven Gold (Tom Hanks), a failed medical student who can only express himself in one-liners, and Lilah Krytsick (Sally Field), an otherwise happily married New Jersey housewife who dreams of stardom on television and the night-club circuit.

Steven and Lilah meet at the Punchline, a Manhattan club where they work for virtually nothing as they await discovery. Steven's obsessed routines have the audiences rolling in the aisles. Each night when Lilah goes on, she dies a little. Against his better judgment, Steven undertakes to teach Lilah about comedy.

"All of our lives are funny, babe," says Steven. "We're God's animated cartoons."

If you can believe that Lilah (who never stops looking and sounding like Sally Field in "Places in the Heart") can become a smash hit talking about everyday problems with shopping carts and her Polish husband, then you'll believe anything, including "Punchline."

The film, opening today at the Coronet, has a seriously split personality.

As he demonstrated in his breakthrough film, "Big," Mr. Hanks is a fine comic actor. He is full of nervous energy and has the talent to channel it properly. When Mr. Seltzer gives him good material, he's very funny and affecting here. Miss Field also has a sense of humor, though it has nothing to do with stand-up comedy. A big "Punchline" problem is that it's impossible to tell the difference between Miss Field's routines that are *supposed* to be awful, and the awful ones that are supposed to be funny.

There is a credibility gap in both the screenplay and the casting. The driven, ambitious Steven might well fall for Sally Field, the Oscar winner, but he would probably flee from the sight of Lilah, the pushy amateur who is so witless she pays $500 for ancient material. At no point in "Punchline" do Lilah and Steven seem to be made for each other.

This considerably dims the romantic aspect of "Punchline," which suggests that Lilah might run off with Steven and abandon her three small daughters and her insurance-salesman husband (John Goodman) who, as written, is just as colorless as his wife.

"Punchline" has its occasional moments. Mr. Hanks does two stand-up routines that will be as funny to movie audiences as they are to the audiences within the film. (Two other stand-up routines, which are meant to serve the narrative, bend logic and, worse, aren't funny at all.) Miss Field has a couple of nicely nutty sequences

Tom Hanks, as a dropout medical student, and Sally Field, as a suburban housewife, play the aspiring comedians in the movie written and directed by David Seltzer.

as the moonlighting wife-and-mother at home.

The supporting cast includes Mark Rydell, better known as a director ("On Golden Pond"), who appears as the hustling manager of the Punchline, and Paul Mazursky, the director of the current "Moon Over Parador," who plays the old-joke salesman.

1988 S 30, C14:4

'Cane Toads,'

"Cane Toads" was shown as part of the 1988 New Directors/New Films series. Following are excerpts from Janet Maslin's review, which appeared in The New York Times on March 21. The film opens today at the Collective for Living Cinema, 41 White Street, and will be shown there through Oct. 6.

Pet or pest? This is the question posed by "Cane Toads: An Unnatural History," a short Australian documentary that's an absolute delight. It supplies the answers to every conceivable question the viewer may have about the species in question, and a few extras: What can the toad do for tourism? What sort of person goes out of his way to squash cane toads while driving? Who feeds his favorite toads cat food, or thinks they

look nice in baby clothes?

Ugly even by toad standards, the cane toad is revealed to be an amazingly resourceful creature. It was imported to Australia from Hawaii in 1935 — to illustrate this, the director, Mark Lewis, shows glimpses of a train trip across Australia from a toad's-eye view — in hopes that it would destroy a grub that threatened the sugar cane crop. But the toads' lack of interest in eating grubs was matched only by their eagerness to multiply. There are now millions of cane toads in Queensland, descended from an original group of only 101.

Mr. Lewis can hardly be blamed for having some fun at these creatures' expense. He displays a large statue of a toad on a pedestal as one Queensland resident explains why this would be a good tourist attraction, then makes the monument disappear as we learn that the measure was voted down. The bookbinder who sent the Prince and Princess of Wales a volume bound in toadskin for a wedding gift is allowed a chance to show off his wares. Mr. Lewis illustrates the toads' voracious and indiscriminate eating habits by filming one as it hungrily stalks a Ping-Pong ball. He underscores their unusual tenacity by depicting the mating ritual whereby the male attaches himself to the back of a female for a long time. "Strange that the male should be so intent as to fail to notice the female's condition," marvels one scientist, since the female lies squashed in the middle of a road.

"Cane Toads" is funny, but it's also well balanced; it captures the real danger that the toads pose to their new environment. Their skin secretes a deadly poison (which also doubles as a hallucinogenic drug for some Australians), and as a result they have caused great damage to other species. They have also multiplied at a frightening rate, which is why some of those whom Mr. Lewis interviews have such enterprising ways of killing them. Staunchly on the toads' side, on the other hand, is one sweet-faced elderly woman who says, "If anyone tried to hurt one of my toads, there'd be a lot of noise and they'd realize I wasn't a lady."

1988 S 30, C19:1

Splintered Personality

BIG TIME, directed by Chris Blum; director of photography, Daniel Hainey; edited by Glenn Scantlebury; stage show concept by Kathleen Brennan and Tom Waits; produced by Luc Roeg; released by Island Visual Arts. At the Bleecker Street Cinema, at La Guardia Place. Running time: 87 minutes. This film is rated PG.

WITH: Tom Waits, Michael Blair, Ralph Carney, Greg Cohen, Marc Ribot and Willie Schwarz.

By JON PARELES

"Big Time" squanders a rare opportunity: The chance (and budget) to film Tom Waits, one of rock's most aberrant and meticulous character actors, in a theatrical concert tailored to his eccentricities.

For more than a decade, Mr. Waits has been perfecting a gang of overlapping personas, a bunch of derelict philosopher-kings who rasp out romantic metaphors between wisecracks. They inhabit a seedy urban world of pawnshops and tattoos, of cigarette butts and polyester and triple-X movies; given voice by Mr. Waits's songs, they become heroes, or at least anti-heroes. In a tour last fall

Calling the Tune
The singer-songwriter Tom Waits stars in "Big Time," using characters created in songs from several of his albums.

that played Broadway (and at the Warfield Theater in Los Angeles, where "Big Time" was filmed), Mr. Waits staged his recent songs as what he called "un operachi romantico," with low-rent props and a band that could swagger through jazz or blues, wheeze out accordion waltzes or clank and oompah. That production, chopped up according to a dubious concept, is the basis of "Big Time," which opens today at the Bleecker Street Cinema.

The concept seems to be that one incarnation of Mr. Waits, snoring while a Spanish television station blares in his apartment, is dreaming of himself both onstage and as a combination ticket-taker, usher and freelance watch salesman. (All of them wear four or five watches at once.) Instead of filming the concert straightforwardly, which might give Mr. Waits a chance to establish his stage characters and make connections from song to song, Chris Blum shreds the concert with shtick by Mr. Waits's usher persona, television-static effects and ticking watches. The songs are scattered, interrupted by speech and abruptly clipped, derailing any simple enjoyment.

When the songs are allowed to proceed, the camera zeroes in on Mr. Waits's face for relentless, claustrophobia-inducing close-ups; the band, which was onstage, is virtually invisible for the film's first half-hour. The camera captures Mr. Waits's grimaces and odd postures in minute, sweaty detail as he growls and rasps and croons; piano teachers will be shocked by his double-jointed hand positions at the keyboard, with fingers bent upwards. It's clear that he works hard and that even if his characters are weirdos, he knows exactly what he wants to do.

Yet only one sequence, late in the film, captures the production's cockeyed humor and humanity: Mr. Waits stands in a bathtub with a glowing plastic curtain, singing "Innocent When You Dream" while bubbles rise around him. For the rest, even Mr. Waits's considerable cult following is likely to find "Big Time" frustrating and off-putting. By reducing a stage show to endless, clinical close-ups, "Big Time" turns Mr. Waits's performance into a freak show.

●

"Big Time" is rated PG ("Parental Guidance Suggested"). It contains a few profanities.

1988 S 30, C20:1

AVANT GARDE VOICES, a collection of five short films. These films have no rating. At Alice Tully Hall, as part of the 26th New York Film Festival.

I...DREAMING, 7 minutes, by Stan Brakhage

MARILYN'S WINDOW, 7 minutes, by Stan Brakhage

LIVED IN QUOTES, 21 minutes, by Laurie Dunphy

HONOR AND OBEY, 22 minutes, by Warren Sonbert

FAKE FRUIT FACTORY, 30 minutes, by Chick Strand

By CARYN JAMES

In Warren Sonbert's "Honor and Obey," soldiers march in formation, a tiger stalks through the snow, religious processions wind through streets and palm trees wave in a tropical breeze. As brightly colored images of authority figures blend into scenes of cocktail parties, this 22-minute silent film flows along with the grace of a musical score built on complex tensions hidden among the notes. "Whose authority will you obey?" the film seems to ask, as it deftly avoids simple-minded juxtapositions. Instead, we see a mélange of images so full of geography — Notre Dame Cathedral, the Sydney Opera House, Fifth Avenue — that the work mocks the idea of any specific setting. Sooner or later, social and natural laws meet and probably clash, Mr. Sonbert suggests, but in this scenario of discrete images all is apparent harmony.

"Honor and Obey" is by far the most accomplished and rewarding piece in "Avant-Garde Voices," the title covering five works by independent film makers to be shown at the New York Film Festival at 6 o'clock tonight. Varying widely in their aims and their artistic success, the works include a pair of lyrical 7-minute meditations by Stan Brakhage; Laurie Dunphy's ambitious 21-minute sociopolitical essay on South Africa; Chick Strand's tiresome half-hour look at Mexican workers who make fake fruit, and the work by Mr. Sonbert, who at the age of 41 has been making films for over 20 years. But the rubric avant-garde suits them all, and much too comfortably.

●

All come from a solid American avant-garde tradition that goes back nearly half a century, to the films of Maya Deren. Their fragmented forms and repetitions of sounds and images force viewers to become imaginative conspirators piecing together personal versions of what appears on the screen. By experimental standards, such works are mild and accessible; the program's title should not fool anyone into thinking this is a night of radical cinema.

But the disorienting effects of these works can be powerful reminders of how film makers have absolute control over what we see and a tentative influence on what we think. In Ms. Dunphy's "Lived in Quotes," filmed entirely in South Africa, the most dominant of the recurring images shows two black schoolgirls walking down a road. A voice that seems to come from radio eventually informs us that the English cannot say the African "!Click" sound. But the girls make hardly any headway down the road, and the soundtrack moves back to the beginning of the sentence several times for every half-syllable it moves forward.

This thwarted forward motion is intentionally irritating, as Ms. Dunphy forces her audience to experience a small frustration that is nothing compared to the injustice of apartheid. But her images, such as an elephant caged and carried off in a truck, are often too blatant. Quotations from South Africans, presented on title cards, suggest we cannot truly see the faces or hear the voices of South Africa. Its message is heartfelt, and "Lived in Quotes" is not politically or artistically sophisticated enough to match Ms. Dunphy's ambitions.

Stan Brakhage, certainly the best-known name on the program, has made some truly experimental films in the last 30 years. But the two slight films on this program merely create dreamlike moods that give back precisely as much or as little as the viewer is inclined to impose on them. "I ... Dreaming" sets shadowy images of people going to sleep and rising against a lulling, dignified song. Words from the song occasionally flash across the screen. "Marilyn's Window" is a silent film in which the fast-moving camera jumps here and there to show waves breaking, the sun rising and setting and a white-curtained window nestled under a gable.

In Ms. Strand's "Fake Fruit Factory," we see extreme, shaky close-ups of Mexican women painting fruit and hear them talk (in Spanish with English subtitles) about sex and their American boss. One scene holds the camera interminably on a moving car's rear-view mirror, reflecting trees along the highway. This is the kind of wearying work that gives the avant-garde a bad name. But it is the odd film out on a program that is less about innovation than about how palatable the "avant-garde" has become.

1988 O 1, 15:1

All About Myrtle, A Temperamental Star

OPENING NIGHT, directed and written by John Cassavetes; director of photography and producer, Al Ruban; edited by Tom Cornwell; music by Bo Harwood. At Alice Tully Hall, as part of the 26th New York Film Festival. Running time: 144 minutes. This film has no rating.

Myrtle Gordon	Gena Rowlands
Maurice Aarons	John Cassavetes
Manny Victor	Ben Gazzara
Sarah Goode	Joan Blondell
David Samuels	Paul Stewart
Dorothy Victor	Zohra Lampert

By JANET MASLIN

"Opening Night" could be described as John Cassavetes' version of "All About Eve" if Mr. Cassavetes were the sort to be strongly influenced by the work of other film makers, which he most certainly is not. Like the characters who ramble amiably through this sprawling, funny, emotionally raw 1978 film — which has a style that's of a piece with the director's other long films of the 1970's, among them "Minnie and Moskowitz" (1971), "A Woman Under the Influence" (1974) and "The Killing of a Chinese Bookie" (1976) — Mr. Cassavetes displays a remarkably free-spirited point of view.

"Opening Night," previously unreleased in the United States, is a reminder of what has made Mr. Cassavetes' films so appealing, and of what can make them so maddening, too. For all its length — nearly two and three-quarter hours — it's a relatively thin example of the director's work, but a mischievous and inviting one, too.

Gena Rowlands, at her most radiant, totters through the film in the role of Myrtle Gordon, a very famous actress who requires vast reserves of forbearance from anyone who's daring or foolhardy enough to try working with her. As the film begins, Myrtle is in New Haven starring in the final tryouts of a play called "The Second Woman," which is, if God is willing and Myrtle can be held in check, on its way to Broadway.

●

Overseeing the production, and collectively gnashing their teeth when they are not sweet-talking the star, are the play's seasoned director, Manny Victor (Ben Gazzara), and his playful wife (Zohra Lampert), who good-naturedly tells him, "If I had known what a boring man you were when I married you, I wouldn't have gone through all those emotional crises"; a co-star named Maurice Aarons (Mr. Cassavetes), with whom Myrtle goes back a long time; the playwright Sarah Goode (Joan Blondell), who has more reason to worry about Myrtle than anyone else, and the producer David Samuels (Paul Stewart), Sarah's husband, the one who's most apt to bring down the curtain once and for all. Second most apt, actually, since Myrtle is doing everything she can to bring on a disaster.

Miss Rowlands, as she has shown in other films directed by her husband, can be incomparably funny while coming apart at the seams. Drinking and smoking heavily as the film begins, refusing to eat, and on the threshold of some truly major breaks with reality, she has a way of bringing these little eccentricities to bear upon her work. The film, which presents bits and pieces of the play in rehearsal and then gradually lets them evolve into something whole, has a lot of fun with Myrtle's improvisations on stage and their unfortunate effects on her fellow actors.

There is a long episode, for instance, about a scene in which Maurice is supposed to slap Myrtle, something which he would by now like to do anyhow. When Myrtle feels she's being hit too hard, it takes endless cajoling from the others to make her play this scene at all. Finally, when the scene is played before an audience, Myrtle collapses in a heap before Maurice can even complete his swing, then refuses to get up while Maurice nervously improvises a lot of questions about her health. As the film makes clear, anyone who has worked with Myrtle for a long period of time gets used to this sort of thing.

As in "All About Eve," the star's secret fear turns out to be a dread of the aging process, which in this case is the subject of the play she's trying to do; Sarah, the author, says the phrase "the second woman" refers to the person a woman becomes once the pretty, youthful side of her disappears. Myrtle has so much trouble with this idea that she hallucinates a dead fan (Laura Johnson), who has been hit by a car early in the film but returns to haunt Myrtle as a vision of her own lost youth. This device, typically for Mr. Cassavetes, is labored and attenuated but strangely touching anyhow.

•

When Joan Blondell was making "Opening Night" in 1977, she told an interviewer, "I couldn't tell when the actors were having a private conversation and when they were actually changing the lines of the script." The shifting-sands quality that colors Myrtle's performances on stage also extends to the actors in the film, but the cast has a vibrancy that is perhaps a byproduct of this kind of uncertainty. In any case, the actors are finally as steady as their out-of-town tryout is precarious, and the cast does a good job of conveying a tangled web of interrelationships. Mr. Gazzara in particular gives a humorous edge to Manny Victor's superhuman restraint, and Miss Blondell makes the playwright shrewd and sympathetic. As always, Mr. Cassavetes, a figure of wry, unpredictable intelligence and uncertain temper, is as darkly commanding in front of the camera as he is behind it.

"Opening Night" will be shown tonight at 9 P.M. and tomorrow at 1:30 P.M. as part of the New York Film Festival.

1988 O 1, 15:1

A Sexual Expedition

A WINTER TAN, directed by Jackie Burroughs, Louis Clark, John Frizzell, John Walker and Aerlyn Weissman; written by Miss Burroughs, from the book "Give Sorrow Words: Maryse Holder's Letters From Mexico"; cinematographer, Mr. Walker; edited by Alan Lee and Susan Martin; music by Ahmed Hassan and John Lang; produced by Miss Clark; released by Circle Films. At Alice Tully Hall, as part of the 26th New York Film Festival. Running time: 91 minutes. This film has no rating.

WITH: Jackie Burroughs, Erando Gonzalez, Javier Torres Zarragoza, Anita Olanick, Diane D'Aquila, Fernando Perez de Leon, Dulce Kuri and Ruben Dario Hernandez.

By JANET MASLIN

When do businessmen do the tango? More often than you might think, according to "Ray's Male Heterosexual Dance Hall," a wickedly deadpan short film by Bryan Gordon. Mr. Gordon has the novel idea of letting a bevy of dark-suited executives meet at lunchtime in a dance club (with ticker tape over the bar) to run through their paces, which are choreographed to songs like "Begin the Beguine."

By treating this place in an utterly offhanded way, Mr. Gordon (whose film won this year's Oscar for a live-action short) makes it that much funnier. The executives invite one another to dance in the same tones they might use to propose business meetings, and they curry favor shamelessly while whirling across the floor. The most important man in the group dances in his own special spotlight, and has the power to insist that the record ("September Song") be changed. When that happens, underlings compliment him extravagantly on his good taste.

•

The club is seen through the eyes of a young man who is newly out of work and has come to the club to seek his fortune. "If you're smart, you'll stop dancing with me right now," says a small, unattractive bald man, who refers to himself as "dead meat" in the corporate hierarchy. "Quite

frankly, I don't even know what it is I do," says a good-looking younger man, who nonetheless boasts that his job includes "great benefits." "Do you think this is an era of style over substance?" one executive asks another. "Yes — and we're winning," is the reply.

The very unlikely co-feature for this exceptionally droll and polished short is "A Winter Tan," the detailed and explicit portrait of a woman who can be regarded as a defiant sexual adventurer. She can also be seen as an extraordinarily tireless bore. Maryse Holder, whose frank and voluminous letters from Mexico were published by Grove Press under the title "Give Sorrow Words," is the subject of this film by Jackie Burroughs, Louise Clark, John Frizzell, John Walker and Aerlyn Weissman. Five directors were, in this case, either too many or not enough.

•

Miss Burroughs is also this Canadian film's star, playing Miss Holder on the journey of self-discovery and sexual risk-taking that proved to be her last (she was murdered while in Mexico). Much of this awkwardly staged performance consists of Miss Burroughs approaching just about anyone who will listen and reciting endless, intense, self-dramatizing and aggressively sexual passages from Miss Holder's prose. The letters, which are not written in a truly conversational style, are thus shown at a considerable disadvantage.

As played by Miss Burroughs, Miss Holder, a New York schoolteacher, is a gaunt, leathery woman with a nervous grin, someone who attracts attention more through sheer persistence than by any other means. She talks to the camera, to acquaintances and to apparent strangers (who appear almost comically indifferent), describing her self-styled "vacation from feminism," discussing her conquests ad nauseaum ("and then this one, this lovely child, sucking at my lips like a guppy"), explaining exactly what she likes about Mexican men, worrying about how she looks in a bathing suit ("My skin hangs from me like yellow melting wax"), thinking about her life back home with a woman friend ("my intense repressed anxiety re the banality of our domesticity") and on and on. The performance strives for a tone that might be described as achingly vulnerable, but it's the ache viewers are apt to experience most acutely.

1988 O 2, 57:6

Zohra Lampert, left, Ben Gazzara, Paul Stewart and Gena Rowlands portray participants in a theatrical production in "Opening Night," a 1978 film directed by John Cassavetes.

FILM VIEW/Janet Maslin

'Ringers': The Eerier, The Better

IN THE FIRST HALF HOUR OF "PATTY HEARST," AS the blindfolded heiress is systematically berated by one shrill Symbionese Liberation Army member after another, the film tries to convey what Miss Hearst's nightmarish experience must have been like. That it isn't truly able to capture this, either then or later, can be explained only partially by the film's assumption that, as far as Miss Hearst's thought processes were concerned, there was nobody home.

It's really no wonder that, when so many new films take their inspiration from the most bizarre headlines of recent years, a close understanding of their central characters isn't easily achieved. The fact that these people exist far outside the range of so-called normal experience is what has brought them to the screen in the first place. Small wonder, then, that the Dian Fossey of "Gorillas in the Mist" becomes, as played captivatingly by Sigourney Weaver, a tough, dedicated and extraordinarily single-minded naturalist with nothing terribly unusual to her makeup. Enjoyable as the film is, it leaves the impression that the real Miss Fossey must have been a lot more peculiar than this.

Similarly, the white racists of "Betrayed" and the underground radicals of "Running on Empty" are presented as perfectly ordinary, family-minded citizens who just happen to have an offbeat idea or two. It's not hard to understand why this happens, if film makers find themselves caught between an eagerness to adapt outstandingly odd news events and a necessity to tell these stories in terms that audiences will understand. Still, it's a surprise to find that among these current news-derived films, the one that manages to be most interesting, most accessible and most emotionally involving is the one based on the most freakish real story.

The eerie decline of Drs. Stewart and Cyril Marcus, the twin gynecologists who died of barbiturate withdrawal in 1975, is the inspiration for David Cronenberg's "Dead Ringers" (though the film is nominally adapted from "Twins" by Bari Wood and Jack Geasland, a highly fictionalized 1977 version of the Marcus story). The first of many wise moves Mr. Cronenberg has made is to use very little of the real Marcus pathology. This is true even though the brothers in the film, called the Mantles, are indeed successful gynecologists who enjoy trading places to fool their patients. And like the Marcuses, they, too, retreat into heavy drug use and utter isolation. A few real traces of the Marcuses' unpredictable behavior, like the way one of them once appropriated the anesthesia mask of a patient in the operating room, have also found their way into the film.

But beyond this, Mr. Cronenberg and his co-screenwriter, Norman Snider, have invented something much more compelling. Mr. Cronenberg's great achievement in this cleverly restrained film, all the more surprising in someone whose past area of expertise has been pure horror (his earlier work includes "Scanners," "Videodrome" and "The Fly"), is to devise twin characters who are as unbalanced as the Marcuses, yet are vastly sympathetic, too. Jeremy Irons, who plays both twins and gives a dual performance so good that the difficult special effects aspects of his work are never noticeable, gives the Mantles clear and separate personalities. He lets them talk entirely naturally with each another. And he makes them sound as if they've been trading banter in this same dry, debonair way for many years.

■

The first hour of "Dead Ringers" presents a dual portrait so riveting that audiences may forget the film is headed for anything untoward; only the occasional small directorial frisson (somber notes on the soundtrack, red robes in the operating room) signals potential trouble. Quick, witty biographical scenes establish the Mantle brothers as boyish prodigies whose fascination with the mechanics of reproduction is entirely clinical, and who otherwise eschew most forms of human contact. The fact that no family background is ever mentioned makes these self-sufficient twins that much eerier.

One of them, Elliott, is a practiced cad and a shrewd manipulator; the other, Beverly, devotes himself to solitary medical work and remains terribly shy. Only through Elliott's beneficence does Beverly ever have any luck with women, who find the Mantles notoriously difficult to tell apart.

The screenplay introduces a smart, sexy and intuitive actress named Claire Niveau (Genevieve Bujold), who triggers a breakdown of the twins' lifelong modus operandi. Beverly falls in love with her and, for the first time, wants to keep an experience to himself; Elliott is made more jealous by this than even he may realize. "Dead Ringers" contains a marvelous scene in which Claire, having learned very late in the game that she's been seeing two Mantles instead of one, demands a showdown with both brothers. When Claire becomes angry, Elliott insults her and laughs; meanwhile Beverly is so mortified he can barely speak. This scene, played brilliantly and completely convincingly by Mr. Irons, shows just how involving the Mantle brothers can be.

Their decline begins with Claire's departure, but Mr. Cronenberg is careful to give it a gradual pace. He plays down the macabre and makes the Mantles' deterioration an unnervingly reasonable extension of their past experience. Part of why "Dead Ringers" is so haunting is that it finds something universal in the brothers' story, yet also keeps their overriding strangeness in sight. Most films based on unusual real events promise something similar, but few succeed as well as this. □

1988 O 2, II:21:5

The Miseries Of a Gold Miner

JACOB, directed by Mircea Daneliuc; screenplay (Rumanian with English subtitles) by Mr. Daneliuc from the works by Geo Bogza; director of photography, Florin Mihailescu; film editor, Maria Neag; art director, Magdalena Marasescu. At Alice Tully Hall, as part of the 26th New York Film Festival. Running time: 117 minutes. This film has no rating.

WITH: Dorel Visan, Cecilia Birbora, Ion Fiscuteanu, Maria Seles, Livia Baba and Dinu Apetrei.

By VINCENT CANBY

"Jacob," Mircea Daneliuc's new Rumanian film, is about a gold miner whose life is very difficult, in the mines and out.

Jacob is married to the widow of a miner who, despondent, blew himself up at home one night, nearly taking his wife and children with him. That incident haunts Jacob, as well as the suspicion that his wife, who is somewhat younger than he is, might be un-

faithful.

Jacob's best friend has a plan to steal a large hunk of gold from the mine. Jacob is tempted, but at the last minute he refuses to cooperate. The would-be theft is discovered. Though Jacob and his friend are never found guilty of anything, they are reassigned to other jobs, Jacob to a coal mine that is a three-hour walk from his village.

"Jacob" will be shown at the New York Film Festival at 9:15 today and at 6:15 P.M. tomorrow. The film begins with a suicide and manages to become even more bleak as it goes along.

●

The festival's program notes compare "Jacob" to "Wozzeck" and to "Fassbinder's brooding strongmen." This is ridiculous.

Georg Buchner's play "Wozzeck," made into a splendid film by Werner Herzog in 1979, is about a heroic figure, a certifiable nut who is driven to destruction by society as well as by the demons within him. Neither is Jacob comparable to the only so-

called strongman in all of Rainer Werner Fassbinder's work, that is, Franz Biberkopf, the innocent Everyman in Fassbinder's screen adaptation Alfred Doblin's "Berlin Alexanderplatz."

Jacob, well played by Dorel Visan, is not a heroic figure, if only because the film that surrounds him is so uncharacterized and murky. He has moments when he comes to life, as when he slaps his wife around and then asks her why she is crying. "We should be happy," he says. "After all, it is Christmas." Mostly he just seems depressed for good reason. He is beaten by the system from start to finish.

●

The film's English subtitles don't help. They mix contemporary 12-letter obscenities with words otherwise only heard in Scotland ("bairns" for "kids" or "children") and are so inadequate that even basic plot points are fuzzy.

1988 O 3, C24:4

Life on a Mattress

36 FILLETTE, directed by Catherine Breillat; screenplay (French with English subtitles) by Miss Breillat and Roger Salloch; cinematography by Laurent Dailland; edited by Yann Dedet; produced by Emmanuel Schlumberger and Valerie Seydoux; released by Circle Releasing Corporation. At Alice Tully Hall, as part of the 26th New York Film Festival. Running time: 92 minutes. This film has no rating.

Lili .... Delphine Zentout
Maurice .... Etienne Chicot
Bertrand .... Olivier Parniere
Boris Golovine .... Jean-Pierre Léaud
Anne-Marie .... Berta Dominguez D.

By JANET MASLIN

Films about the sexual initiation of adolescent girls have a way of becoming almost as coy as their heroines. Certainly that's the case with Catherine Breillat's "36 Fillette," a film that devotes inordinate attention to stop-and-go sexual maneuvers and slow, heavy breathing. These and other related details are sure to make "36 Fillette" popular with art lovers of a certain stripe.

The title refers to a child's dress size, which the film's heroine, Lili (Delphine Zentout), has unmistakably outgrown. A sullen, uncommunicative 14-year-old vacationing with her family in Biarritz, Lili is clearly ready to strike out on her own. She does so by dressing up in jeans, a corset and a raincoat, then hitching a ride to a local nightclub in search of adventure. Not surprisingly, adventure comes her way.

The director, who is also a novelist, never gets beyond the obvious narrowness of this subject matter, but within these limitations the film works well. Miss Breillat, the screenwriter for Maurice Pialat's "Police," reflects something of Mr. Pialat's intimate yet detached style, suspending judgement as it simply observes Lili's uneasy, ambivalent behavior. Rude and angry, but also profoundly curious, Lili manages to bring as much sexual torment to others as she is experiencing herself. The chief recipient of this is Maurice (Etienne Chicot), a middle-aged playboy who, until meeting Lili, thought he had seen it all.

●

The film is at its most believable in conveying Lili's powerfully mixed feelings toward this man. "If I'd slept with 50 guys, I'm sure I'd like you,"

she tells Maurice on one of the rare occasions that find her trying to be polite. Otherwise, Lili is as bored and insulting as she can be, and as he attempts to seduce her, the jaded Maurice appears equally contemptuous and world-weary. Dubbed into any other language, "36 Fillette" would still be unmistakably French.

The process whereby Lili's resistance and Maurice's dismissiveness blossom into a real passion of sorts has been conveyed so slowly and haltingly that it appears to be taking place in real time. The occasion of their first flirtatious liaison in a disco becomes a teasing, attenuated all-night affair, with Maurice at one point complaining that he hasn't a 14-year-old's stamina or patience for such gamesmanship. This meeting ends in a draw at dawn, with Lili telling Maurice, "I hope you mangle yourself," then kissing him goodbye. The next time they meet, it is Lili who more openly initiates the encounter, with Maurice growing visibly nonplussed as he sees himself losing the upper hand. The film finally arrives at the point where Lili, having acknowledged her feelings of desire, has also found an angry way of minimizing their importance.

●

"36 Fillette" also contains an early sequence in which Lili, on her way to a first date with Maurice, encounters a very famous musician who listens with fascination to her ideas about life and love. Not even Jean-Pierre Léaud, who locates something humorous and real in this spellbound celebrity, can really make Lili seem as interesting as that, although he does deliver the film's one homily. The world, he tells her, is "a giant spring mattress." "You just bounce on it and you land somewhere else," he says." The film is, figuratively speaking, an inordinately thorough account of Lili's first bounce.

As Lili, Miss Zentout suggests a shorter, younger, much more pneumatic Hedy Lamarr, and has the pouty, impenetrable manner the role requires. Mr. Chicot makes Maurice seem a more reflective figure and in some ways a more compelling one, since the audience is given such a graphic sense of what he's up against.

"36 Fillette" will be shown tonight at 9:15 and Friday at 6:15 as part of the New York Film Festival.

1988 O 4, C19:1

Literally Underground

DEBAJO DEL MUNDO, written and directed by Beda Docampo Feijoo and Juan Bautista Stagnaro; in Spanish with English subtitles; director of photography, Frantisek Uldrich; edited by Pablo Mari; music by José Luis Castuneira de Dios; produced by Jorge E. Estrada Mora and Leo Mehl; released by New World Pictures. At the Guild, 33 West 50th Street. Running time: 105 minutes. This film is rated R.

Nachman .... Sergio Renan
Liba .... Barbara Múgica
Smialek .... Víctor La Place
Baruj .... Oscar Ferrigno
Josef .... Gabriel Gibot
Judith .... Paula Canals
Szachna .... Bruno Stagnaro
Raquel .... Gabriela Toscano

By CARYN JAMES

"Debajo del Mundo" ("Under the World") exists in dangerous artistic territory. The film is based on a true story, of Polish Jews who in 1942 escaped to a makeshift hovel dug underground in the woods. For the next two years the family of six moved from one squalid catacomb to another. This subject comes so loaded with emotional power that one dishonest scene could send the film careening into cheapened sentiment, manipulation or self-righteousness. But the exceptional achievement of "Debajo del Mundo" is to display the ugly truth — these hunted people could not take eating or breathing for granted — with a brutal honesty that is enhanced, not evaded, by gracefully composed visual images.

The film defines its role in Holocaust literature modestly and effectively. It is not a philosophical or intellectual examination of evil; it does not take the exhaustive approach of Marcel Ophuls ("The Sorrow and the Pity" and the forthcoming "Hotel Terminus"), in which the overwhelming accretion of details is part of the viewer's experience; and it does not try to engage our sympathies easily by singling out one character, an Anne Frank, with whom we are asked to identify. Instead, it focuses on the daily survival of parents and their sons — three young men and an adolescent boy — for whom heroism is stealing potatos under cover of darkness and drama is lighting a fire that could mean discovery. They are nearly hunted by scavengers who pick up the unbearable smell of excrement that comes from their hiding place.

At the start, the members of the family are called from the farm where they work and ordered to turn themselves in for deportation. Nachman, the father, believes they should go and face the will of God with courage. The idea of living underground offends not only his conscience but also his dignity, "the last thing we can afford to lose," he says. His wife, Liba, and his sons convince him otherwise, and from then on such conversations seem luxuries they cannot afford, as the film redefines dignity to mean tenacious survival.

Wisely, the film rarely presumes to see from the family's point of view; most often we witness the horror of their reactions at close range and are forced into the uneasy position of sympathetic, helpless voyeurs. We view but cannot truly share the gruesome details of the family's underground existence. Lice are attracted by their rotting clothes, so the sons steal sacks that the mother sews into rough tunics, giving the characters a biblical look. As the months go by, the faces we see in extreme close-ups become dirtier, gaunter, filled with blue shadows. When a young woman is killed by the Nazis just outside the shelter's entrance, we hear her cry for help but see only the anguished look on Liba's face.

Late in the film, when the family escapes through the snow to yet another buried shelter, the sudden freedom seems too much for any of them to bear. Nachman collapses and says he cannot go on, and soon they have all fallen against the white background, clasping one another and wailing with exhaustion and fear. It is a moment of total release and emotional force that the film has earned with its cautious restraint. Soon the family moves on, three members carrying the others on their backs through the snow. Eventually, there are deaths that seem more painful for taking place off camera, leaving the details to our imaginations.

On its way to creating such powerful moments, the film overcomes a major obstacle for American viewers. The survivors of the family settled in Argentina after the war; —

two Argentines, Beda Docampo Feijoo and Juan Bautista Stagnaro, learned of the story and together wrote and directed the film. (With the director María Luisa Bemberg, they also wrote "Camila," an Academy Award nominee for best foreign-language film for 1984.) At first it is disorienting to hear Spanish-speaking actors portray Polish Jews, but the strangeness vanishes quickly in this imagistic film.

"Debajo del Mundo," which opens today at the Guild, does not completely avert the dangers of its subject. When Nachman teaches his youngest son about the solar system, for instance, he says: "We are part of the universe, part of God. That's what's so marvelous." The film does not begin to explore how complicted Nachman's faith must be, does not hint that the son might naturally rail against such attitudes. But it convinces us thoroughly that its characters lived, and survived heroically.

1988 O 5, C19:5

From the Holocaust To El Salvador

GOLUB, directed and produced by Jerry Blumenthal and Gordon Quinn; photography by Mr. Quinn; edited by Mr. Blumenthal; music by Tom Sivak. Running time: 54 minutes.

FALKENAU, THE IMPOSSIBLE, directed by Emil Weiss; written (in French with English subtitles) by Mr. Weiss and Samuel Fuller; director of photography, Pierre Boffety; edited by Pascale Suer; music by Teddy Lasry. Running time: 52 minutes. These films have no rating. At Alice Tully Hall, as part of the 26th New York Film Festival.

By CARYN JAMES

"Nothing is impossible with a camera, my boy!" Samuel Fuller bellows at his interviewer in "Faulkenau, the Impossible." The director's voice is still full of bravado at the age of 76. With his lined face and flowing white hair, even smoking a cigar he looks like an aged avenging angel swooping down from the screen to rage against war. Leon Golub, on the other hand, is a slight, bald man of 66. He talks without a trace of pretension about power, politics and art, and often chuckles at mundane details as he goes about his work — painting huge canvases that freeze political assassins, torturers and mercenaries.

"Golub" and "Faulkenau," which will be shown at the New York Film Festival at 6:15 tonight, are both concerned with the way art gives shape to the worst political horrors. Otherwise, they are as different and as provocative as the artists they document, and together they offer a complicated reply to Mr. Fuller's assertion that film can do anything.

"Faulkenau" begins with glimpses of Mr. Fuller's autobiographical 1980 film "The Big Red One," about Americans in the First Infantry Division in World War II. But this documentary is far different from that film and the crime and gangster movies Mr. Fuller churned out in the 1950's. Through much of "Faulkenau" we see the first film the director ever shot, taken when he was a young soldier and his division liberated the concentration camp at Falkenau, Czechoslovakia (now called Sokolov). As Mr. Fuller narrates the brutal scenes of stiff, starved bodies lined up on the ground, an additonal human drama unfolds. The division commander had gone to the town, Mr.

Fuller explains, and taken every man who said he had seen and suspected nothing about the death camp nearby. Those townspeople were forced to witness the bodies being clothed and prepared for burial, were made to carry the victims to their graves. Even then, Mr. Fuller had a director's eye, as his camera pans to show how near the town and the camp were, and he closes in on hands trying to pull clothing onto the naked corpses. These images make "Faulkenau" brutal and as difficult to sit though as it ought to be.

It is also shrewdly directed by Emil Weiss, who throws dramatic light on Mr. Fuller's head like a halo. He indulges Mr. Fuller at the end, allowing him to yell that there should be no war at all, not in Afghanistan, not in Nicaragua. He alllows Mr. Fuller to blather in response to an important question: Can fiction films ever represent horrors like the Holocaust? Yet this excess captures a part of Mr. Fuller's character. "Faulkenau" makes us wonder how Mr. Fuller ever turned his wartime experience into a film like "The Big Red One," a truly goofy drama in which American soldiers deliver an Italian baby in a German tank.

If "Faulkenau" raises many more questions than it can answer, "Golub" is not nearly as complex as the artist himself. It is a well-intentioned, competent film that chronicles the creation of a single painting, "White Squad X," in which two assassins loom over a victim on the ground and one points a gun at his head. Because Mr. Golub is often inspired by photographs and news tape, glimpses of photos and television broadcasts are interspersed throughout. But the effect of seeing death-squad victims in El Salvador next to Mr. Golub's own work diminishes his transformation of politics into art. Perhaps that mysterious process cannot and should not be explained away, but "Golub" sets up comparisons that seem badly suited to the exaggerated figures and bright colors that paradoxically give Mr. Golub's paintings a look of enhanced reality.

At the start Mr. Golub says he aims for disjunction in his painting, an awkwardness among the figures that reflects our fractured times. "The modern world sees things in bits and pieces and funny twists," he says. "Golub" works best when it takes us into galleries and focuses its camera on the awkward and chilling faces Mr. Golub has painted.

1988 O 5, C23:1

Seething Chronicle

HOTEL TERMINUS: THE LIFE AND TIMES OF KLAUS BARBIE, produced and directed by Marcel Ophuls; photography by Michael Davis, Pierre Boffety, Reuben Aaronson, Wilhelm Rosing, Lionel LeGros, Daniel Chabert and Paul Gonon; edited by Albert Jurgenson and Catherine Zins; production company: the Memory Pictures Company; a Samuel Goldwyn release. At Alice Tully Hall as part of the 26th New York Film Festival. Running time: 267 minutes. This film has no rating.

By VINCENT CANBY

Marcel Ophuls's "Hotel Terminus: The Life and Times of Klaus Barbie" begins with a deceptive sense of restraint and calm. In the opening sequence, a friend of Mr. Barbie's recalls a New Year's Eve party at which the former Gestapo officer took offense at some disrespectful remarks made about Hitler. The friend

was amused that Mr. Barbie still might find some subjects *not* funny.

Cut to Lyons, where three former members of the French Resistance are playing pool and talking about Mr. Barbie's forthcoming trial for crimes against humanity, committed in and around Lyons in 1944 and 1945.

The aging Frenchmen now seem philosophical. Terrible things were done, that's true, but it was all such a long time ago. One fellow recalls that he was a 15-year-old bellboy at the Hotel Terminus when it was the Gestapo headquarters in Lyons. Were the Germans good tippers? They were, he says with a smile, "but we also cheated them a bit."

Sitting in front of a Christmas tree, a former American intelligence agent does his best to appear at ease and cooperative. He talks to Mr. Ophuls in a friendly, now-that-you-mention-it manner.

•

Oh, yes, he says, he certainly did use Mr. Barbie, no doubt about that. He worked with him closely, in fact, but he never had the feeling that Mr. Barbie was the sort of man who might be guilty of atrocities. Mr. Barbie was such a devilishly clever fellow that he wouldn't have to lower himself. A very old German farmer

Marcel Ophuls, who directed "Hotel Terminus: The Life and Times of Klaus Barbie."

remembers Klaus as a boy he called "Sonny."

This early testimony is almost genial.

Yet "Hotel Terminus: The Life and Times of Klaus Barbie" quickly gathers the force and the momentum of a freight train that will not be stopped or sidetracked. It is inexorable in its pursuit of truth, not just about Barbie the "butcher of Lyons," but about the moral climate of his world and of ours today.

This spellbinding, four-and-a-half-hour film will be shown at the New York Film Festival today at 6:15 P.M. and on Saturday at 6:30. It starts a commercial engagement Sunday at the Cinema Studio.

In form, "Hotel Terminus" is much like Mr. Ophuls's classic "Sorrow and the Pity" (1970), a vivid, harrowing, minutely detailed recollection of France under the German Occupation as it was experienced in and around the town of Clermont-Ferrand. Like "The Sorrow and the Pity," the new film is composed of dozens and dozens of interviews, each of which evokes another narrative within the principal narrative.

These accumulate, finally, to create a vast historical panorama far beyond the scope of conventional movie fiction. At the center there is the unprepossessing figure of Mr. Barbie himself, self-described as "privileged to act as a small but active member of the Führer's following."

•

A boyhood friend recalls Mr. Barbie as a good pal. In addition, he is, variously, "a Nazi idealist"; a man who would fondle a cat one minute and beat up a young girl the next, and a Nazi survivor who, in the immediate postwar years, was employed by American intelligence, both for his own talents and those of his informants, a network, one man says, stretching "from Portugal to Moscow." Mr. Barbie was a con artist who sold snake oil to his American benefactors.

At the end of his career, in South America before his extradition to Europe in 1983, he was a tireless hustler and deadly crackpot, wheeling and dealing in Bolivia and Peru where he was an active member of the German business communities, hobnobbing with politicians, arms dealers and drug traffickers.

The witnesses to Mr. Barbie's life and times include his victims, his colleagues in the Gestapo (who are less defensive than his colleagues in American intelligence), veterans of the French Resistance, collaborators, historians, janitors, businessmen, leftists, rightists, neighbors, journalists and, the film's most enigmatic character, Jacques Vergès, the man who defended Mr. Barbie at his trial last year.

•

The method is the same that Mr. Ophuls used in "The Sorrow and the Pity," but "Hotel Terminus" is very different from that film and from Claude Lanzmann's "Shoah." "The Sorrow and the Pity" is meditative, a sad but even-tempered film that can find pathos in the desperately frightened face of a woman, a collaborator, having her head shaved in front of an angry mob.

"Shoah" is almost unbearably mournful, not only because of the graphic testimony recalled so matter-of-factly by Mr. Lanzmann's witnesses, but also because there's scarcely a frame of film that doesn't suggest the manner by which time softens the past. "Shoah" says that some things must not be forgotten, but distance blurs the image and, no matter how we try to remember it, pain recedes. The images of a concentration camp as it looks today — a peaceful, ghostly, parklike setting with well-tended grass — are metaphors for the impermanence of all things, including memory.

In "Hotel Terminus" Mr. Ophuls is anything but meditative. He's angry and sarcastic and, as the film goes on, he becomes increasingly impatient. He argues with reluctant witnesses. He pushes his camera into a stranger's face and laughs when the stranger refuses to cooperate. (One such stranger is an ex-President of Bolivia, caught as he's putting out his garbage.)

The tempo of the cross-cutting between witnesses speeds up, on occasion so maddeningly that one forgets the identity of the speaker. At times, it seems as if the director were telling some self-serving interviewee to stop all this nonsense and come clean. At other times, he appears to fear that he simply won't be able to get everything in. The more he digs, the more he finds.

Mr. Ophuls is not dealing with some vague, comfortingly abstract concept of guilt, but with provable guilt, which includes guilt by association, by stupidity, by naïveté and, most of all, by deed.

The film is rich with the details of how people look, sound and behave, and with the details of middle-class décor, from the rugs on the floor to the pictures on the walls. There are plenty of things a film cannot do, but no novelist could possibly set a scene with the inventorying eye of the Ophuls camera.

"Hotel Terminus" leaves certain questions unanswered, but that's all right too. One longs to learn more about the rabidly anti-Communist René Hardy, twice aquitted of charges that he betrayed his Resistance comrades, and about Mr. Vergès, who attempted to defend Mr. Barbie by equating Nazi atrocities with France's colonial policies. In any case, the questions are raised.

The Barbie trial is something of an anti-climax in the film, as it was in fact when Mr. Barbie refused to take the stand. Yet "Hotel Terminus" proceeds to its conclusion with the breathtaking relentlessness of superior fiction. It's a fine, serious work by a film maker unlike any other. Great.

1988 O 6, C25:1

Bitter Tears Of the Industrial Age

HARD TIMES, directed, edited and produced by João Botelho; screenplay (in Portuguese with English subtitles) by Mr. Botelho, from the novel by Charles Dickens; photography by Elso Roque; music by António Pinho Vargas; production companies: Portuguese Film Institute, Portuguese Radio-Television and Calouste Gulbenkian Foundation. At Alice Tully Hall, as part of the 26th New York Film Festival. Running time: 90 minutes. This film has no rating.

Jose Grandela	Henrique Viana
Senhora Vilaverde	Eunice Muñoz
Luisa	Julia Britton
Tomaz Cremalheira	Ruy Furtado
D. Tereza Cremalheira	Isabel de Castro
Sebâstiao	Joaquim Mendes

By JANET MASLIN

Of all the films in this year's New York Film Festival, surely "Hard Times" is the most peculiar. João Botelho's version of the 1854 Charles Dickens novel has been translated into Portuguese and filmed in contemporary settings, but these are actually the least eccentric things about it. Mr. Botelho's other modifications of his material are much more puzzling, and more self-defeating as well.

Although "Hard Times" is one of Dickens' shorter and most sharply focused novels, offering a bitter look at the effects of the industrial revolution on a place called Coketown ("a town of machinery and tall chimneys, out of which interminable serpents of smoke trailed themselves forever and ever, and never got uncoiled"), it is sufficiently Dickensian to have a dense, dramatic plot and an edge of caustic wit. These are exactly the qualities that Mr. Botelho's film chooses to minimize, in favor of an abstract, detached tone.

The film's greatest asset is its starkly beautiful black-and-white cinematography, which is moody and spare. Its greatest mystery is that this visual style is allowed to prevail over everything else, since the story is told in such a terse and dispirited manner. The actors play characters who have been given Portuguese names in Mr. Botelho's screenplay but Dickensian names in the subtitles (so that Mrs. Sparsit is also known as Senhora Vilaverde, and the Gradgrinds are the Cremalheiras). They say little and look dejected. Their mood is better suited to Dickens' overview than to his dialogue.

It's clear that Mr. Botelho does not intend a direct adaptation of "Hard Times," and instead has in mind a kind of commentary on the text. It's also clear that this approach is extremely limited, even for those familiar with the novel, and that for those unacquainted with it the film is sure to be nearly indecipherable. Though Mr. Botelho uses Dickens's dialogue, and is in his own way really very faithful to the novel, he has eliminated large and important sections of it, especially those having to do with the burgeoning labor movement within Coketown (which is called World's End here).

In addition, the film favors such long silences and abbreviated dialogue that it relies on occasional brief voice-overs to hold together a plot of Dickensian complexity. Of all the impossible things "Hard Times" attempts, this last is the most impossible.

The audacity of this film's approach and the handsomeness of its visual style are impressive, but they exist at such cross-purposes to the rest of what goes, with results that are less analytical than simply tedious. When the narrator announces that "Sissy stopped her wild crying" in an early scene, for instance, Sissy looks not much more morose than anyone else in the cast, and she has hardly shed a tear.

"Hard Times" was shown yesterday and can be seen again Saturday at 4 P.M., as part of the New York Film Festival.

1988 O 6, C29:1

Living for Today

IMAGINE: JOHN LENNON, a documentary directed by Andrew Solt; written by Sam Egan and Mr. Solt; edited by Bud Friedgen; produced by David L. Wolper and Mr. Solt; co-produced by Mr. Egan; released by Warner Brothers. At Carnegie Hall Cinema, Seventh Avenue at 57th Street, and other theaters. Running time: 103 minutes. This film is rated R.

By JANET MASLIN

There's a scene in the documentary "Imagine: John Lennon" that finds Lennon face to face with one of his most persistent fans. This dazed-looking young man has been caught trespassing on the grounds of the Lennons' estate in Ascot, England, and is now awestruck to be in the presence of his hero. So he wants to talk about Beatles songs. He thinks that when Lennon sang the line "Boy, you're gonna carry that weight/Carry that weight a long time," he himself was the "Boy" the singer had in mind.

"That's Paul sang that," Lennon says wearily. But the fan remains convinced that Lennon's songwriting is directed specifically at him. Finally, Lennon begins to sound exasperated as he tosses off as good a definition of contemporary popular songwriting as anyone might want. Still, the fan looks dubious; he truly believes that the Beatles touch him in some extraordinarily pure and unprecedented way. An entire generation shared that feeling, to one extent or another, and "Imagine: John Lennon" is a potent reminder of why.

This film is part of the public relations battle now raging around Lennon's memory. In contrast to Albert Goldman's reckless, mean-spirited and nonetheless fascinating biography of Lennon, the film presents a notably more sanitized and superficial portrait. (Lennon's violent temper and drug experiences barely exist, for instance, and the death of the Beatles' manager Brian Epstein is mentioned only momentarily between references to a visit to the Maharishi and the making of "Yellow Submarine.") On the other hand, this film has things no Beatles biographer has yet captured: the pure euphoria of the Beatles' music, the sad spectacle of the group's dissolution and Lennon's defiant yet somehow poignant efforts to strike out on his own.

•

"Imagine: John Lennon," which opens today at the Carnegie Hall Cinema and other theaters, was directed by Andrew Solt, co-director of "This Is Elvis," the amusingly schlocky biography in which the voice of the King says nice things about his Mama, Colonel Tom Parker and so on from beyond the grave. This time, Mr. Solt takes a notably less silly approach. And if he has not made the full transition to serious and incisive documentary-making, he has at least shaped a lively, entertaining film that offers a moving portrait of Lennon and his times.

The film, incorporating a lot of previously unseen home-movie footage, begins with Lennon and Miss Ono installed at Tittenhurst, their bucolic Ascot estate. But it covers all stages of Lennon's varied career. He and the Beatles are seen looking extraordinarily boyish in their early days, then beaming with delight as they catapult to the top. The dizziness of Beatlemania is amply documented, with Lennon merrily delivering his famous insult at a Royal Variety Performance ("Would the people in the cheaper seats clap your hands, and the rest of you just rattle your jewelry"), and with guards at a Beatles concert in America being promised earplugs "so as to keep you from havin' a headache." Later on, the Beatles' recording career is discussed by their outstandingly interesting and articulate record producer, George Martin, who says, "When we did 'Sgt. Pepper' we were given a license to kill, so to speak."

Later on, the film covers Lennon's

John Lennon

post-Beatle collaborations with Yoko Ono, who is seen in the recording studio instructing the technicians on how she would like Lennon to sound when he sings "Oh Yoko," a song ostensibly meant to be airy and care-free. There are also glimpses of the Lennons' well-publicized bedroom activities, from the bed-in for peace to an awkward scene, filmed not long before Lennon's murder, that shows them undressing rather theatrically and beginning to make love. By and large, though, the film presents Lennon and Miss Ono at their most sympathetic, as when they ward off angry attacks from Gloria Emerson of The New York Times (who calls them "vulgar and self-aggrandizing") and from a very hostile Al Capp.

The film also includes touching footage of Lennon playing with his younger son, Sean, to the accompaniment of the song "Beautiful Boy." (Like many of the songs on the soundtrack, it is heard in a version slightly different from the familiar one, which gives the music a steady sense of surprise.) Though the other Beatles are not among the film's interviewees, Sean; the singer's elder son, Julian; Lennon's former wife, Cynthia, and Miss Ono are also interviewed by an off-screen questioner who is clearly ready to accept anything they say. So Lennon's first wife, in describing Julian's childhood, can observe with the film's typical sunniness that "John as a father was forced, I'm afraid, to be a part-time Dad."

"Imagine: John Lennon" isn't terribly penetrating about Lennon's inner makeup, but it doesn't have to be. The sense of his enormously resilient talent and his endlessly changeable nature — he seems to have had a dozen different personalities by the time the film is over — come through without effort. This film does what it means to, recapturing much of what the Beatles meant to their contemporaries and conveying an acute and tragic sense of what was lost when Lennon died. Though this is a film about John Lennon, it's a film about his audience, too.

1988 O 7, C7:1

Children Without Childhood

SALAAM BOMBAY!, directed and produced by Mira Nair; screenplay (Indian with English subtitles) by Sooni Taraporevala, from a story by Miss Nair and Miss Taraporevala; photography by Sandi Sissel; edited by Barry Alexander Brown; music by L. Subramaniam; production designer, Mitch Epstein. A Cinecom Release. At Alice Tully Hall tonight and tomorrow as part of the 26th New York Film Festival; opens Sunday at the Lincoln Plaza 1, 63d Street and Broadway. Running time: 113 minutes. This film has no rating.

Krishna/Chaipau .... Shafiq Syed
Koyla .... Sarfuddin Qurrassi
Keera .... Raju Barnad
Chillum .... Raghubir Yadav
Rekha .... Aneeta Kanwar
Baba .... Nana Patekar
Manju .... Hansa Vithal
Salim .... Mohanraj Babu

By VINCENT CANBY

Krishna, a small, spindly legged 10-year-old country boy, is kicked out of the house by his mother and told not to return until he has 500 rupees to pay for a bicycle he has ruined. Krishna drifts to the nearest big city where, without effort, he is absorbed into Bombay's proliferating population of homeless street kids.

A concerned documentary would probably treat Krishna as one of the faceless mob, important mostly as a representation of a human condition. The film that contained him would be a general statement, and Krishna

Homeless In "Salaam Bombay!" Shafiq Syed portrays an abandoned 10-year-old boy who sells tea in the teeming streets of the city in the hope of earning enough to return to his village.

himself, old beyond his years, would remain unknowable, forever lost. How sad, we would be asked to say, and then, but that's India.

The achievement of "Salaam Bombay!," Mira Nair's remarkably good first fiction feature, is that Krishna has his own identity. He's an utterly specific character. Krishna may be naïve, but he quickly learns how to get along in a world of beggars, prostitutes, drug pushers and vicious rip-off artists, some of whom are quite respectable.

For a film about such hopelessness, "Salaam Bombay!" is surprisingly cheering, not because Miss Nair has sentimentalized the scene but because, being Indian herself, she understands the particular reality of what appears, to us tourists, to be hopelessness. Seen close up, rather than from the window of a taxi cab, despair is not so easily recognized. Life, lived always on the edge of disaster, is coped with, if not always with success.

"Salaam Bombay!" isn't exactly an upper, but neither is it a predigested social treatise. That the film is less nightmarish than Hector Babenco's riveting "Pixote" may have something to do with its being set in India rather than Brazil. There's a kind of ancient sophistication about the Bombay demimonde that is different from life in São Paulo, where widespread poverty and rootlessness are only a little older than the glass-and-steel high-rises of the very rich.

●

"Salaam Bombay!" will be shown at the New York Film Festival tonight at 9:15 and tomorrow at 11:30 A.M. It opens its commercial engagement Sunday at the Lincoln Plaza 1.

Miss Nair, who was born and brought up in India and studied at Harvard as an undergraduate, has made four documentaries, all in India, which obviously helped prepare her for this work of fiction. One doesn't necessarily feed the other, however. "Salaam Bombay!" demonstrates this young director's extraordinary self-control when faced with fiction's manifold possibil-

ities. The movie possesses a free-flowing exuberance not often associated with the documentary form.

Even more unusual is the director's success with her actors. Without the film's program notes, I'm not sure I'd be able to tell the professionals from the non-professionals.

The children, all non-professionals, are splendid, especially Shafiq Syed, the little boy who plays Krishna, and Hansa Vithal, as the tiny, stoic daughter of a Bombay prostitute and her pimp. The exceptionally good pro-actors include Aneeta Kanwar as the prostitute, Nana Patekar as the pimp, and Raghubir Yadav as a God-forsaken drug addict who, early on, befriends Krishna.

"Salaam Bombay!," which was written by Sooni Taraporevala from a story by her and Miss Nair, is rich with self-explanatory incident. Action is character. Dialogue is spare. Even the camera is laconic. Though shot (beautifully by Sandi Sissel) entirely on location in Bombay, under conditions that could not have been easy, the film and its characters are never overwhelmed by local color.

Miss Nair sees Bombay less as a recognizable city than as the ever-present chaos surrounding Krishna and the people who move in and out of his life. Bombay is a place of noise, restless movement and no privacy whatsover. It is squalor accepted as the natural order of things, and thus accommodated.

Miss Nair does not share this fatalism, but in "Salaam Bombay!" she allows us to examine it without panic, and without patronizing it. She is a new film maker to watch.

1988 O 7, C8:1

Strangers In a Strange Land

ALIEN NATION, directed by Graham Baker; written by Rockne S. O'Bannon; director of photography, Adam Greenberg; edited by Kent Beyda; music by Curt Sobel; production designer, Jack T. Collis; produced by Gale Anne Hurd and Richard Kobritz; released by 20th Century-Fox Film Corporation. At Criterion Center, Broadway near 44th Street, and other theaters. Running time: 89 minutes. This film is rated R.

Matthew Sykes .... James Caan
Sam Francisco .... Mandy Patinkin
William Harcourt .... Terence Stamp
Kipling .... Kevyn Major Howard
Cassandra .... Leslie Bevis
Fedorchuk .... Peter Jason
Quint .... George Jenesky

By JANET MASLIN

"Alien Nation" has the best science-fiction idea this side of "The Terminator": it presents a race of extraterrestrials that has already arrived and been absorbed into the population of Los Angeles. How, you may wonder, can anyone tell? In fact the spacelings, called Newcomers, are pretty easy to spot. They have little ingrown ears and bald heads mottled in a pattern like military camouflage fabric. What's more, since sea water affects them the way battery acid affects humans, they have an unnatural fear of going to the beach.

These aliens, according to the film's premise, have in three years' time made great inroads. An introductory section of the film, after first recycling one of President Reagan's more adaptable speeches to make it sound as if he is welcoming the aliens, shows just how far they have come.

Newcomers have been integrated into many different strata of Los Angeles life, so that some are doctors and some are aspiring middle-class types taking dancing lessons. Some are holding up grocery stores.

One of them (Terence Stamp) has even become enough of a credit to his race to be honored by the Mayor at a testimonial dinner. Another, called Sam Francisco (Mandy Patinkin), is the first to have reached the rank of detective in the Los Angeles Police Department. Incidentally, the Newcomers have made some odd choices in adopting what they think are typically earthly names. They are called things like Humphrey Bogart, Harley Davidson and Rudyard Kipling; Sam Francisco is proud to say that he has named his son after President Richard Nixon.

"Alien Nation," which opens today at the Criterion Center and other theaters, introduces Sam as the new partner of a hard-boiled longtime police officer named Matthew Sykes (James Caan), whose close friend and previous partner, Tug (Roger Aaron Brown), has been killed while fighting Newcomer street hoods.

Then it settles down, with remarkable ease, into the routine of a two-cop buddy film, extraterrestrials and all. Matthew and Sam (whom Matthew refuses to address that way, renaming him George) go through all the familiar stages of forging a friendship between partners: cool antipathy, exchanges of insults, growing mutual respect on the job and, finally, an all-night drinking binge to solidify their buddyhood.

Even then, though, the differences between them are unmistakable, since Matthew gets loaded drinking vodka and Sam (or George) achieves the same effect with lumpy sour milk.

"Alien Nation," which was written by Rockne S. O'Bannon and directed by Graham Baker, works as a witty parable about racism for a while, mixing aliens and earthlings with a casualness that, under the circumstances, seems very clever. The places and situations in which the Newcomers turn up are consistent with familiar racial stereotypes. And the progress whereby this highly intelligent and hard-working new ethnic group has infiltrated the Los Angeles population is charted in interesting ways.

Even better, the film also works well on the buddy level, with Mr. Caan very good as a crusty tough-talking veteran, the kind of guy who'll stop his car to have an argument right in the middle of traffic if he feels like it, and Mr. Patinkin is equally excellent as the polite alien whose manners are much more middle class than his partner's. Sam, his wife and his bicycle-riding child already live in a nice little house with a white picket fence, whereas the divorced Matthew lives in typical lonely guy squalor.

Eventually, though it happens later rather than sooner, the conventional aspects of "Alien Nation" overwhelm the novelty. The film is more violent than it has to be, and its biggest disappointment comes with a revelation about secret activities in which the aliens seem to be engaging in right under the earthlings' noses.

Whispering in their native tongue, the aliens indeed seem to be up to something sinister, but this covert activity proves remarkably uninteresting and leads to nothing more than a half-hour's worth of standard action-film gunplay. It turns out, after all, that there's nothing new under the sun.

1988 O 7, C10:6

Odd Couple
Mandy Patinkin, as an
immigrant from another
planet, teams up with
James Caan on
the Los Angeles police
force to hunt a murderer in
"Alien Nation."

A House Is Not a Home

CLARA'S HEART, directed by Robert Mulligan; screenplay by Mark Medoff, based on the novel by Joseph Olshan; director of photography, Freddie Francis; edited by Sidney Levin; music by Dave Grusin; production designer, Jeffrey Howard; produced by Martin Elfand; released by Warner Brothers. At the National, Broadway at 44th Street, and other theaters. Running time: 108 minutes. This film is rated PG-13.

Clara Mayfield	Whoopi Goldberg
Bill Hart	Michael Ontkean
Leona Hart	Kathleen Quinlan
David Hart	Neil Patrick Harris
Peter Epstein	Spalding Gray
Dora	Beverly Todd
Blanche Loudon	Hattie Winston

"Oh Bill," says Leona (Kathleen Quinlan), an attractive and very well-heeled white woman on vacation in Jamaica, "come meet the most wonderful person!" The wonderful person is Clara (Whoopi Goldberg), a black maid working in the hotel where Leona and her husband are staying, on a vacation meant to help them recover from the death of their infant daughter. Since Clara has a sixth sense and probably a seventh sense too, she has perceived this immediately and set out to make Leona feel better. She helps her out of the bathtub, feeds her breakfast, and spends half the morning proving herself a very good listener. Soon Leona and Bill have brought Clara home to an exclusive suburb of Baltimore.

Clara soon takes over the running of the couple's extremely large house. She bakes coconut raisin cookies for breakfast, and she irons Bill's shirts so well that they don't need starch. She pitches in with advice whenever the family has a problem, sometimes doing this with a mop in hand. And when she takes over the raising of the couple's son, David (Neil Patrick Harris, a fine young actor who really holds his own in scenes with Miss Goldberg), she does a much better job than his parents ever could. Really, Clara is a treasure.

"Clara's Heart," which opens today at the National and other theaters, has in Whoopi Goldberg virtually the only actress who could turn Clara from an affront into a likable heroine. Funny and sarcastic in delivering the screenplay's snappy rejoinders, Miss Goldberg is also comfortable with the character's sentimental side. Indeed, she appears at ease in every way, and for the first time seems genuinely to become the character she is playing. That's a lucky thing, since without any charm or verisimilitude from Miss Goldberg, the film would have degenerated into hopeless goo.

•

Directed by Robert Mulligan in an unapologetically sentimental style,

"Clara's Heart" succeeds in tugging the heartstrings only when Clara herself is on screen. Leona and Bill (Michael Ontkean) become thoroughly dislikable characters, even more so than they're meant to be ("I feel I have to put all my energy into helping myself before I can help anyone else," Leona says), and in any case they are made to seem colorless and dull. Even Spalding Gray, who plays Leona's new boyfriend when the couple decide to separate, has been made to lack personality, which can't have been easy.

The screenplay by Mark Medoff (from a novel by Joseph Olshan) doesn't have much of an ear for conventional dialogue ("You want to know the worst of it, Bill? The worst of it is we're not even friends anymore"), but it does well with Clara's wisecracks and with the Jamaican patois she teaches David. Clara and David, after an initial period of extreme rudeness on his part, soon become fast friends. She teaches him valuable lessons, helps him to weather his parents' breakup, and even knows where to draw the line; when David says he wants Clara to be his friend always, she says, "Always is much longer than you're going to need me."

"Clara's Heart," which is notably lacking in any sense of socioeconomic reality, even sends David with Clara into Baltimore's inner city, where he learns more lessons about life and discovers that Clara has a terrible secret. The film is exasperatingly slow in getting to the bottom of this, and the secret itself doesn't do anything to explain Clara's character.

•

"Clara's Heart" is rated PG-13 ("Special Parental Guidance for Those Younger Than 13"). It includes some off-color language.
JANET MASLIN

1988 O 7, C16:5

Bolshevik Days

THE ONSET OF AN UNKNOWN AGE, At Alice Tully Hall as part of the 26th New York Film Festival. Running time: 80 minutes. This film has no rating.

ANGEL, directed by Andrei Smirnov; script (Russian with English subtitles) by Boris Yermolayev, Ilya Suslov and Mikhail Suslov; camera, Pavel Lebeshev; art direction, V. Korovin; music by Alfred Schnitke.
WITH: Leonid Kulagin, Georgi Burkov, Lyudmila Polyakova, Nikolai Gubenko.

HOMELAND OF ELECTRICITY, directed and written by Larisa Shepitko; camera, Dimitri Korzhikhin; art direction, Vladimir Konovalov and Valery Kostrin; music by Roman Ledenev.
WITH: S. Gorbatyuk, Y. Kondratyuk, A. Popova.

By WALTER GOODMAN

The two short movies that make up "The Onset of an Unknown Age" were made in 1967 to commemorate the 50th anniversary of the Bolshevik Revolution, but it was almost the 70th anniversary before Russians were permitted to see them. The program note for the New York Film Festival, where "Unknown Age" is being shown today at 2 P.M., suggests that the depiction of the early days of the Bolshevik regime may have been deemed too negative for a celebration. A reasonable surmise. In both movies one can discern symptoms of talented directors being caught between the demands of their talent and those of their regime.

The first tale, Andrei Smirnov's "Angel," begins on a weary train crowded with weary people trying to get out of the way of the post-revolution civil war. We come to know a few of them: an irascible engine driver and his spunky daughter; a goofy young man traveling with a cow that he believes will bring him fortune; a pregnant farm woman who shows him how the animal should be milked; a take-charge commissar, and an intellectual who squints a lot because, as he explains, "In these days, a man can get himself killed

wearing eyeglasses."

When the train chugs off the tracks, the travelers find themselves in enemy country, and our six are captured by a ragtag band of White Guards under the command of a religious fanatic called Angel. The engine driver's daughter is raped; the commissar is axed to death. "There's your hammer and sickle," chortles the satanic Angel.

"Angel" seems slightly at odds with the Communist myth it is meant to propagate. For example, the commissar, though hard-working and brave, is finally ineffectual; he doesn't even put up much of a fight against Angel's men. Such unorthodox truths are undercut by the last pasted-on scene, when the apolitical intellectual resolves to carry out the commissar's mission and the recently raped girl smiles hopefully as she walks with her comrades into the future.

Even with the slight plot and the ritualistic last-minute effort to conclude on a suitably upbeat 50th-anniversary note, "Angel" manages to convey glimpses of character as well as the harshness and confusion of a grim time.

The second feature, "Homeland of Electricity," also has an inspirational ending that does not much ease a depressing story. Bolshevik headquarters sends a young engineering student to the drought-stricken village of Verchovka for the job of building a generator that can pump water into the parched fields. The peasants, evidently selected for their harshly weathered faces, look on longingly as he goes about his work. They contribute the family samovars and telescopes to the cause, not useful but a sign of comradeship.

The gush of water, when it finally comes, to the accompaniment of clanging church bells, makes a rousing scene. Unfortunately, a few minutes later, the makeshift pump blows up. As everyone is standing around despondently, a voice is heard expressing hope in the future. Could it be the engine driver's daughter?

Despite the simplicity of the story, "Homeland of Electricity" keeps fighting against the rules of Socialist Realism. Through Dimitri Korzhikhin's camera, the peasants in a religious procession or in their fields become white-on-white mirages. At times, we seem to be in the middle of somebody's dream. Roman Ledenev's dissonant score battles reality all the way. The director, Larisa Shepitko, may have invented a new film form: Socialist Unrealism.

Both directors were evidently inhibited as well as inspired by the need to suit their visions to a national holiday. Miss Shepitko died in 1979. Mr. Smirnov is now acting president of the Soviet Film Makers Union, a position that might offer opportunities to relieve his colleagues of clinging inhibitions.

1988 O 8, 14:3

Helpful
Whoopi Goldberg and
Hattie Winston portray old
friends in "Clara's Heart,"
about a Jamaican
housekeeper who helps a
young boy deal with the
trauma of his parents'
divorce.

The Pangs of Old Age

"The Promise" was shown as part of the 1987 New Directors/New Films series. Following are excerpts from Janet Maslin's review, which appeared in The New York Times on March 17, 1987. The film opened yesterday at the Public Theater, 425 Lafayette Street.

A culture may reveal itself most fully through the things it fears. In the fine Japanese film "A Promise," the pain and humiliation of senility take a terrible toll, not only on the elderly but also on the younger relatives whose lives are affected. "A Promise," about an elderly woman found dead in the house of her son and daughter-in-law, addresses the question of euthanasia, since the woman has almost certainly died at the hands of her loved ones. But it is even more disturbing as a study of ways in which the older generation's weakness and debility can affect the younger.

"A Promise" is a well-drawn portrait of an entire family in contemporary Japan, from the sheepish, overlooked grandparents to the harried parents to the children growing up on rock videos. It has been directed by Yoshishige Yoshida in a cool, modern style that seems all the more merciless, under the circumstances. The rituals of Japanese life are seen as stripped of most of their meaning, existing only in the hollowest form. The legacy of order and fastidiousness brings no comfort, and when it comes to facing the unruliness of old age, it may even make life harder.

•

So 50-year-old Yoshi (Choichiro) and his wife, Ritsuko (Orie Sato), who take care of Yoshi's parents, are even more unnerved than they might be by simple facts of the older couple's lives. It is Yoshi's mother, Tatsu (Sachiko Murase), who has become senile, and her lack of bladder control makes her otherwise quite reserved daughter-in-law especially upset. The younger woman's excessive revulsion, and the lack of inner resources it reveals, is not shared by Yoshi, but he suffers in his own way. The physical job of caring for his mother and dealing frankly with her frail, tiny body is almost more than he can bear.

For all the pain that "A Promise" explores, it also has moments of great tenderness and beauty, moments between two elderly actors (Ms. Murase and Rentaro Mikuni as her husband) who play their roles very movingly. The reality of their old age is sweetened by their shared memories of happier times. And Mr. Mikuni, who must embody varying degrees of senility as the story progresses, can make an extremely eloquent gesture out of simply staring quietly at an urban landscape. Choichiro is also quite good as a man whose own moral shortcomings are brought into play by this family crisis and who somehow finds unexpected strength upon which to draw.

1988 O 8, 14:3

FILM VIEW/Vincent Canby

Tory, Tory, Hallelujah!

THERE'S NOTHING LIKE NAKED, undisguised anger to get the creative juices flowing. In this day and age, it's far more effective than love.

Whatever you think of Prime Minister Margaret Thatcher's Tory Government, you have to give it credit as the tormenting inspiration for some exceptionally fine, furious (and often hugely funny) English films, each aimed, in one way or another, at Thatcherism.

There have been Lindsay Anderson's farcical "Britannia Hospital," rather loathed in its own land; Richard Eyre's "Ploughman's Lunch," seen by too few people here, and the two Stephen Frears-Hanif Kureishi collaborations, "My Beautiful Laundrette" and "Sammy and Rosie Get Laid."

Now add "High Hopes" to the list. This is Mike Leigh's immensely sad, bitterly funny new English comedy, which slipped into the 26th New York Film Festival during its first weekend and, without half trying, became the festival's only memorable discovery.

■

The Lincoln Center event, which closes tonight with the presentation of China's "Red Sorghum," has presented a handful of other good films, but no film from a new director to match the singular imagination of Mr. Leigh's modestly designed, major triumph.

"High Hopes" is about Cyril and Shirley, an unmarried, 30-ish, loving couple with roots in London's working class and aspirations to change the world. That is, Cyril would like to change the world, though he has come to the conviction that the cause is hopeless — everybody is making too much money. Shirley shares Cyril's politics but, at the moment, she wants mostly to change Cyril's disinclination to start a family.

With his blond beard, his glasses, his fondness for marijuana and his unwillingness to be anything more than a messenger on a motorcycle to a society he finds corrupt, Cyril looks and behaves like an updated 1960's dropout. He says he can see no point in bringing another child into a world that already is overpopulated, but it could also be that he doesn't want to share Shirley with anyone, including his own baby.

■

As played by Philip Davis and Ruth Sheen, Cyril and Shirley are a sweet, most engaging pair. By nature, intelligence and interests they are semidetached from the class to which they cling. They laugh, fight and talk at cross-purposes but, when the chips are down, they listen to and genuinely respect each other.

Their lives (and their flat) are so easily arranged that, when they find themselves saddled with a homeless, mentally retarded young man, they can put him up for a few nights without major fuss. Cyril's family is something else.

There is his mother (Edna Dore) who, on the eve of her 70th birthday, is becoming forgetful, which everyone takes to be senility but may be only despair. Mum is not easy to get along with under the best of circumstances. There are also Cyril's grossly ambitious and insecure sister, Valerie (Heather Tobias), and Valerie's self-made slob of a husband, Martin (Philip Jacobson).

In one of the film's funniest, most agonizing sequences, poor Mum is the guest of honor at a birthday party where Valerie and Martin, whose main purpose is to show off their house, nearly kill her with their aggressive, nouveau riche kindness. Mum wants tea. They insist on champagne. When Mum declines a piece of birthday cake, Valerie threatens to stuff it down her throat. Valerie has the manner of a deranged nanny. "She has to eat a piece of cake," she says on her way to hysteria, "or her wish goes down the drain!"

"High Hopes" is deadly serious about its despair over a society in which self-interest is seen as enlightenment. The movie doesn't hesitate to speak its mind to the audience, as when Cyril and Shirley visit the grave of Karl Marx and read, "The philosophers only interpret the world in their various ways. The point is to change it."

Yet "High Hopes" seems so spontaneous and is so sure of itself that it can slide effortlessly from such a sequence to others of broad, uproarious satire. There is a viciously comic sendup of Thatcherism at its most condescending when Mum, who has forgotten her keys, must impose on the typical Tory neighbors who are gentrifying her neighborhood.

"Isn't that house rather large for you?" asks Laetitia, sounding exactly like Mrs. Thatcher. "I mean, *three* bedrooms."

Mum is noncommittal. When Laetitia understands that Mum doesn't own the house, she airily advises Mum to buy it, "then resell."

■

Though the Tory couple is played (beautifully) by Lesley Manville and David Bamber with all of the subtlety of performers in a revue sketch, "High Hopes" doesn't go off its track. "High Hopes" embraces contradictory moods and changes of pace that would shatter the work of a less skilled film maker.

"High Hopes" hardly looks avant-garde, yet the style is neither conventional nor especially realistic, compared to most theatrical movies. From the film's opening shots, Mr. Leigh establishes the equivalent to a short-story writer's "voice." His "prose" is spare, direct, matter of fact, without fanciness. Then the occasional oddball word, phrase or observation comes along that characterizes the particular vision of the piece.

Mr. Leigh's camera seems to resist being moved, at least for movement's sake. People walk out of the screen image still talking, to be overheard as if in the next room. The director is parsimonious with his close-ups and with so-called establishing shots, which show the audience who is where in relation to whom. Much of the exposition is ellipsized and, though explanations are kept to a minimum, the narrative is never obscure.

This style is also evident in "The Short and Curlies," an 18-minute Leigh comedy shown by the festival, not with "High Hopes" but with Terence Davies's glumly self-important, autobiographical feature, "Distant Voices, Still Lives." Like "High Hopes," "The Short and Curlies," which is about love and courtship among the lower clases, is so brisk and economical in its telling that it seems to have the freshness of an entirely new form.

Mr. Leigh, 45, comes to films from television and the legitimate theater where, according to his official biography, he composes his plays with the cooperation of the actors. Over very long rehearsal periods (up to nine weeks) the actors improvise and suggest their own characters. His first film, "Bleak Moments," made in 1971, was shown here in 1980 in a retrospective of British films held in connection with the New York festival. It was not well received.

In whatever way that "High Hopes" and "The Short and Curlies" came into being, they are unmistakable originals. ☐

1988 O 9, II:23:1

Orient Expression

RED SORGHUM, directed by Zhang Yimou; screenplay (Mandarin with English subtitles) by Chen Jianyu, Zhu Wei and Mo Yan, based on a story by Mo Yan; photography by Gu Changwei; music by Zhao Jiping; art direction by Yang Gang; production company, Xian Film Studio; released by New Yorker Films. At Alice Tully Hall, as part of the New York Film Festival. Running time: 91 minutes. This film has no rating.

Grandmother; Nine	Gong Li
Grandfather	Jiang Wen
Father	Liu Ji
Luohan	Teng Ru-Jun
Sanpao	Ji Cun Hua

By VINCENT CANBY

"Red Sorghum," Zhang Yimou's new Chinese film, begins very prettily, and with something of the ho-ho-ho joviality exhibited by the members of the chorus in a stock production of "The Student Prince."

The time is the 1920's. A beautiful young woman, concealed inside a bride's traditional sedan chair, is being carried through an arid landscape to her arranged marriage with a rich old wine maker. As they are expected to do, the bearers bounce the sedan chair around a lot and sing naughty songs.

The bride-to-be is miserable, not only with the horseplay but also in anticipation of marriage to a man who is over 50 and who has leprosy. Her father, a farmer, has exchanged her for a new mule.

As the procession passes through a photogenic field of waving sorghum, which looks rather like Kansas corn without ears, a masked bandit jumps out of the foliage and demands the bearers' money. After he has pocketed the coins, he throws back the curtain hiding the young woman and pulls her out.

●

Nine, as she is called, does not resist. She looks at the bandit eye-to-eye. In what is to be the best moment in all of "Red Sorghum," it is realized that, for Nine, rape by a masked bandit is preferable to marriage to a rich, aging leper. Nine has a mind of her own.

Rape, however, is not to be; at least, not right away. Nine is saved by one of the bearers, a big, primitive brute of a man full of passion and elemental force. Once the bandit is skewered, the bearers pulled together, and Nine back inside the sedan chair, the procession continues.

"Red Sorghum," which won the Golden Bear as the best film shown at this year's Berlin Film Festival, is an exotic fable, related by an unseen soundtrack narrator who identifies himself as the grandson of Nine.

"Some people believe the story, and some people don't," says the narrator. He is speaking today, as he recalls the unconventional courtship of his grandmother by his grandfather, who turns out to be the fellow who saved Nine from the bandit.

"Red Sorghum" will be shown tonight at 8:30 at Avery Fisher Hall to close the 26th New York Film Festival. It opens tomorrow at the Lincoln Plaza.

●

The film arrives here already widely praised as one of the best examples of the work now being done by China's "new wave" of film makers, sometimes called "the Fifth Generation." These are the people who have come out of Beijing's Film Academy since 1982, in the first classes to be graduated after the Cultural Revolution.

Not having any knowledge of the sort of films the Chinese were making before, I've no way of knowing exactly why these films (including "The Girl from Hunan," released earlier this year) are regarded as breakthroughs. Seen in the context of the international film scene, "Red Sorghum" is something less than an epiphany.

It is a handsomely produced, finally lugubrious piece of exotica about picturesque peasants who, in the 1930's when the Japanese invade and the chips are down, don't hesitate to make the ultimate sacrifice. Though it's a fable, the point of view is still

Another Time A smiling Gong Li totes a basket of food in "Red Sorghum."

that of social realist cinema.

Nine may not be typical of Chinese women of her time, but she is an idealization of the progressive woman of our time. She's the only affecting character in the film. Yet she is always seen in a metaphorical long shot. She's less an individual than a representation.

●

So, too, is life at the winery, where, even before the Communist Revolution, the work is done as if on a collective. Everybody is on a first-name basis. Life is happy. Even the earthy humor seems generalized, having a lot to do with urinating in unusual places.

Zhang Yimou, a cameraman making his debut as a director, uses a lot of compositions that may look striking to some but just self-conscious to

Bearers carring bride to her wedding in a scene from "Red Sorghum."

others. One favorite: a broad flat landscape with a thin ribbon of sky at the top. He also likes the same sort of color filters with which Joshua Logan punctuated his film version of "South Pacific."

When Nine is eventually raped, not entirely against her will, by the bearer who becomes Grandpa, the soundtrack swells with more romantic music than has been heard in any movie since David Lean's "Ryan's Daughter." The film's most daring character is the comically drunken hero, who represents, apparently, the assertive life force.

Yet he, too, is less a specific character than a representation of a general type. "Red Sorghum" may look avant-garde in terms of movies made during China's Cultural Revolution (1966-1976), but it's supposedly innovative epic style looks decidedly old-fashioned here. The best thing that can be said about the movie is that it's far better than its title.

1988 O 9, 74:1

Evening the Odds

THE BOXER AND DEATH, directed by Peter Solan; screenplay (German and Czech with English subtitles) by Jozef Hen, Tibor Vichta and Mr. Solan, based on the novel by Mr. Hen; director of photography, Tibor Biath; produced by Studio Hranych Filmov, Bratislava. At Film Forum 1, 57 Watts Street. Running time: 107 minutes. This film has no rating.

Kominek	Stefan Kvietik
Kraft	Manfred Krug
Helga	Valentina Thielova
Venzlak	Jozef Kondrat
Willi	Edwin Marian

By JANET MASLIN

Among the starving inmates of a Nazi concentration camp, there is one well-fed and well-muscled man. An accident of fate has placed him in this peculiarly mortifying position. Before the war, both he and the camp's commandant were boxers, and the commandant is now feeling frustrated and alone. So the commandant (Manfred Krug) earmarks this prisoner, Jan Kominek (Stefan Kvietik), as his own personal plaything. Kominek is given special rations, training privileges and anything else that will leave him ready to take a beating in the ring.

The simplicity with which this story is told in "The Boxer and Death," a fine and largely undiscovered 1962 Czechoslovak film by Peter Solan that opens today at the Film Forum 1, amounts to irony. In focusing intensively upon relations between Kominek and his master, and in deliberately ignoring the terrible circumstances that surround them, the film is able to give new immediacy to its subject. The facts of concentration camp life figure only marginally, and thus all the more horrifyingly, in this story. The occasional glances that the commandant Kraft or his sparring partner Kominek will give to a smoking crematorium chimney in the distance are made tremendously powerful by this apparent indifference.

When Kraft first picks Kominek out of a group of prisoners, Kominek is too weak and emaciated to ward off the commandant's blows. This offends Kraft's highly developed sense of fair play, which he applies with wild inappropriateness to many master-prisoner situations. But since

Kraft is astute enough to recognize real boxing talent in this potential adversary, he decides to even the odds. Kominek is told to gain weight, begin training and prepare to hold his own for at least a few rounds.

What will Kominek do with his extra ration of bread? And how will his desperate fellow prisoners feel about such privilege? Kominek proves eager to share, but not all his comrades take him up on the offer. Some are too disheartened, and some see Kominek's chance to fight fairly with the commandant as an opportunity not to be missed. One man says he would prefer ant poison to bread.

The hardships endured by the prisoners, to whom Kraft refers as flies, are interspersed with the progress of Kominek's training program. In one remarkable sequence, which exemplifies both the film's heightened realism and Mr. Solan's gift for understatement, a new group of men, women and children are seen standing silently behind barbed wire as the principals pass by, photographed in the crisp black and white tones that give the film a heightened solemnity. Shortly afterward, when Kominek passes this site again, the crutches and violin cases and baby carriages are still there, but the people are gone. The black smoke billowing in the distance says more than enough about what has happened.

●

"The Boxer and Death" never reduces Kraft to a stereotypical figure of evil, nor does it make Kominek a one-dimensional hero; the relationship between the two men is more complex than that, as are the two excellent leading performances. Kominek's need to suppress his rage in the ring is perhaps less surprising than the commandant's combination of prissiness, authoritarianism and real respect for his new partner. Guided by his ideas of sportsmanlike behavior — ideas that provide the film with its greatest irony of all, in view of the commandant's official duties at the camp — he nonetheless cannot help asserting his authority at the wrong moments. The film's conclusion finds Kraft and Kominek each struggling with his own ideas of what, under these extraordinary circumstances, really constitutes fair play.

Kraft, who has an exercise-loving mistress named Helga (Valentina Thielova), is shown to be appreciably more thoughtful, conscience-ridden and tortured than his frivolous friends. "And this is a *prisoner?*" says one in disbelief when the powerful-looking Kominek arrives for his climactic bout with the commandant. "I always say: Work ennobles," another of Kraft's colleagues idly declares.

1988 O 12, C19:1

ANOTHER WOMAN, written and directed by Woody Allen; director of photography, Sven Nykvist; edited by Susan E. Morse; music by various composers; production designer, Santo Loquasto; produced by Robert Greenhut; released by Orion Pictures. At the Paris, 58th Street, west of Fifth Avenue. Running time: 88 minutes. This film is rated PG.

Marion	Gena Rowlands
Hope	Mia Farrow
Ken	Ian Holm
Lydia	Blythe Danner
Larry	Gene Hackman
Kathy	Betty Buckley
Laura	Martha Plimpton
Marion's Father	John Houseman
Claire	Sandy Dennis
Sam	Philip Bosco
Paul	Harris Yulin
Lynn	Frances Conroy
Donald	Kenneth Welsh
Mark	Bruce Jay Friedman

Gena Rowlands and Gene Hackman in "Another Woman."

By VINCENT CANBY

Woody Allen's "Another Woman," his 17th feature since "Take the Money and Run" in 1969, is about the mid-century crisis of Marion (Gena Rowlands), an intelligent, beautiful, esteemed professor of philosophy who, having just passed what a friend describes as "the big 5-0," is re-examining her life.

Marion doesn't say it but she feels "strangely troubled," which is the style of the syntax in which she thinks aloud on the soundtrack. She is married, she believes happily, to Ken (Ian Holm), the successful cardiologist who is her second husband.

Marion and Ken live in upper-middle-class Manhattan ease amid a circle of equally successful friends. Everyone speaks slightly stilted, epistolary dialogue. The rounded sentences sound as if they'd been written in a French influenced by Flaubert, then translated into English by a lesser student of Constance Garnett.

Marion realizes that something is missing. Children, among other things. Also, possibly more important, passion and a certain recklessness. Even as a child, Marion was disapproving of those less gifted at ego-management. Like Harriet Craig, in George Kelly's "Craig's Wife," who is obsessed with spotless carpets, Marion is unnaturally fastidious about her emotional life. She's a driven woman but, by keeping her feelings at bay, she has maintained the facade of order.

●

Though in the manner of Ingmar Berman, whom Mr. Allen admires and whose cameraman (Sven Nykvist) he uses here, "Another Woman" appears to be his most personal, most self-searching film. It's very much his own work, It is utterly serious and comes from both the head and the heart.

Marion's crises could, with several adjustments, be recognized as those of the film maker. Yet something vital is missing and, without it, "Another Woman" takes the breath away, both for the intensity of its grand aspirations and for the thoroughness of its windy failure.

How did it happen?

The ingredient missing from "Another Woman" is the presence of Mr. Allen himself who, as a character within the film, might have functioned in the way of his Mickey Sachs, the hypochondriacal television pro-

ducer in "Hannah and Her Sisters."

Mickey Sachs was not, as many people thought when the film came out, peripheral to the dramatic cohesion of "Hannah," Mr. Allen's most successfully "serious" film to date. The self-conscious, alternately wise-cracking and suicidal Mickey Sachs acted as a kind of lightning rod in "Hannah," protecting the other characters by grounding the bolts of criticism that will be aimed at those in "Another Woman" with a lot more justification.

Part-adolescent voyager, part-sage, the New York-born-and-bred Mickey Sachs established and made ironic "Hannah's" sometimes flowery literary tone, which is both comic and moving.

Mickey Sachs also helped to set "Hannah" in time and place. Just as Bergman's greatest films are always, in some unstated fashion, a response to life in Sweden and its hermetically sealed welfare state, "Hannah" is a film that could have happened nowhere else except Manhattan, at no other juncture of history.

"Another Woman," also shot entirely in and around Manhattan, seems stateless, partially because Mr. Allen's inward-turning characters discover so little that is either emotionally or dramatically urgent. They are talking automatons. Feelings, for all of the importance the film gives them, are more frequently announced than experienced, and when they are announced, they are contained in sentences that no one except Mickey Sachs or Alvie Singer or any other Woody Allen character could get away with.

●

"We stopped at a gallery and spent some time marveling at the pictures," Marion says on the soundtrack. "I shouldn't have seduced you, intellectually, I mean," says someone else. "I experienced odd feelings of melancholy and loneliness," is another. Everybody sounds alike.

For a while, this arch language seems intended to remove "Another Woman" from mundane realities, to give it a particular, heightened style. That suspicion vanishes forever when someone reads the line, "His kisses were full of desire," from a supposedly successful novel written by one of the film's characters.

Mr. Allen is becoming an immensely sophisticated director, but this screenplay is in need of a merciless literary editor. It's full of an earnest teen-age writer's superfluous words, in addition to flashbacks and a dream sequence that contain material better dealt with in the film's contemporary narrative.

Mr. Allen's literary references (to Rilke here) stand out like sore thumbs, though they are endearing as the expressions of an artist who appreciates knowledge and the process of its acquisition. It's meant as admiration to say that Mr. Allen has never grown up. He is someone who never stops reading, and never ceases to be amazed by his discoveries. His passion is genuine, but his literary references aren't easily understood by an audience that doesn't share his particular pleasures. They're name-dropping.

As his characters here don't seem to be especially connected to time, place or each other, they also exist entirely outside whatever jobs they do. People are labeled "professor," "cardiologist," "novelist," but what they do for most of the day, five or six days a week, is reflected by absolutely nothing in their behavior. They could as easily be clipping coupons.

As usual, Mr. Allen has brought together a cast of superlative actors. Miss Rowlands is a riveting screen image, not for anything she says but for the ravaged beauty and genuine pathos she allows the camera to find in her face and figure. Mia Farrow appears in a comparatively small role, as a near-suicidal analysand whose sessions with her doctor, in the next apartment, are overheard by Marion and are the catalyst for what, in the world of this film, would be called Marion's voyage of self-discovery.

It is significant that in the unreal world of "Another Woman" neither Miss Farrow nor her doctor ever mention the fact that her character is very visibly pregnant, which might have something to do with her state of mind. The film's best vignette features Sandy Dennis as a long-lost friend from Marion's youth. Some of the other good actors who come and go, leaving no lasting impression, are Gene Hackman, Blythe Danner, Martha Plimpton, John Houseman, Harris Yulin and Philip Bosco.

"Another Woman" opens today at the Paris theater.

"Another Woman," which has been rated PG ("Parental Guidance Suggested"), contains some mildly vulgar words.

1988 O 14, C3:3

Rehabilitation

THE LAST EMPEROR, directed by Li Han Hsiang; screenplay (Mandarin with English subtitles) by Mr. Hsiang, based on Li Shu Xian's "Pu Yi and I," "Pu Yi's Latter Life," and "Pu Yi's My Former Life"; a New Kwun Lun Film Production Company (Li Han Hsiang) and China International Television Corporation co-production; released by Southern Films in the Nanyang theater chain. At the Public Theater, 425 Lafayette Street. Running time: 100 minutes. This film has no rating.

Pu Yi	Tony Leung
Li Shu Xian	Pan Hung
Empress Wan Jung	Li Dien Lang
Li Yu Qin	Li Dien Xing

The film opening today at the Public Theater, titled "The Last Emperor," is a double-decker footnote, to history and to movies, specifically, to Bernardo Bertolucci's Oscar-winning "Last Emperor."

The film, made three years ago as a joint venture of movie people in Hong Kong and China, supplements the far more scenic and sweeping Bertolucci epic. The Chinese film includes some interesting archival newsreel film relating to the political upheavals surrounding Pu Yi, China's last emperor, and gives us a recap of how Pu Yi found himself washed up, out of a job and a prisoner of war at the end of World War II.

Its principal interest, however, is Pu Yi's redemption, through the benignity of an all-wise, all-seeing Communism. As played by Tony Leung, Pu Yi has some of the qualities of a Chinese Jimmy Stewart. He's good-humored and all thumbs when, as a freshly indoctrinated, newly demoted absolute monarch, he attempts to cope with the mysteries of a common-place cooking stove.

The movie goes on to recall his last, happy marriage with a pretty nurse, with whom he goes sightseeing in the Forbidden City; his brutal arrest during the Cultural Revolution, and, finally, his death from cancer in 1967.

As the Bertolucci film turned Pu Yi and the members of his entourage into lost, rather Europeanized Bertolucci characters, this "Last Emperor" sees Pu Yi as a winning example of a politically born-again former emperor. This "Last Emperor" doesn't cut deep but Pu Yi's life and times, as well as the manner in which the Chinese have come to treat him officially, remain fascinating.

VINCENT CANBY

1988 O 14, C8:5

You Must Remember This

THE KISS, directed by Pen Densham; screenplay by Stephen Volk and Tom Ropelewski, story by Mr. Volk; director of photography, Francois Portat; edited by Stan Cole; music by J. Peter Robinson; production designer, Roy Forge Smith; produced by Mr. Densham and John Watson; released by Tri-Star Pictures and Astral Film Enterprises. At Criterion Center, Broadway and 45th Street, and other theaters. Running time: 100 minutes. This film is rated R.

Felice	Joanna Pacula
Amy	Meredith Salenger
Brenda	Mimi Kuzyk
Hilary	Pamela Collyer
Jack	Nicholas Kilbertus
Tobin	Jan Rubes

"The Kiss" is the story of a jet-setting Cosmo cover girl (Joanna Pacula) who is actually the essence of evil incarnate. This distinction, it turns out, is not as sharp as one might think.

The film reveals what happens when the witchy, hair-tossing Felice (Miss Pacula) appears on the doorstep of a nice, all-American family in which the mother has just been mangled by a truck. This mother, Hilary (Pamela Collyer), was Felice's long-lost sister. "Your mom and I weren't very close for a while," says Felice, to explain why no one has ever heard of her. There is a similarly likely explanation for Felice's heavy middle-European accent.

The film, which is rich in disgusting special effects and poor in every other regard, follows Felice's efforts to pass on whatever it is that the living dead pass on to the next generation. She attempts to do this orally with her young niece Amy (Meredith Salenger), which explains the film's title. The object being transferred is some kind of a blood-oozing serpent, the sort of thing that would ordinarily command attention. In the overkill of the film's climactic scene, however, the demon snake is upstaged by a fire, an explosion, a blood-tainted swimming pool, a chain saw and a hailstorm.

Though Miss Pacula looks glamorously depraved and Miss Salenger is suitably sweet, the only engaging performance comes from Mimi Kuzyk, as a next-door neighbor named Brenda who lacks the good sense to stay home. In one scene, as Brenda and Amy watch "Blonde Venus" on television, Miss Salenger sees Marlene Dietrich and asks, "How come she's dressed up like a gorilla?" "Style," Miss Kuzyk says.

"The Kiss," a film from Coca-Cola-controlled Tri-Star and opening today at the Criterion Center and other theaters, is loaded with suggestions that it's often nice to relax and have a Coke.

JANET MASLIN

1988 O 14, C11:1

Second Thoughts

THE ACCUSED, directed by Jonathan Kaplan; screenplay by Tom Topor; director of photography, Ralf Bode; edited by Jerry Greenberg and O. Nicholas Brown; music by Brad Fiedel; production designer, Richard Wilcox; produced by Stanley R. Jaffe and Sherry Lansing; released by Paramount Pictures. At Loews Tower East, Third Avenue and 71st Street, and other theaters. Running time: 115 minutes. This film is rated R.

Katheryn Murphy	Kelly McGillis
Sarah Tobias	Jodie Foster
Kenneth Joyce	Bernie Coulson
Sally Frazer	Ann Hearn
Bob Joiner	Steve Antin
Cliff Albrecht	Leo Rossi
Paul Rudolph	Carmen Argenziano

By VINCENT CANBY

"The Accused," written by Tom Topor and directed by Jonathan Kaplan, makes a persuasive case for the proposition that witnesses who encourage a crime are as guilty as the perpetrators. In this case, the crime is a gang rape, committed in the back room of a crowded bar late on a boozy night. The victim is a sexily dressed young woman, not entirely sober and a little high on marijuana, who, as everybody says, "asked for it."

In a departure from most films about rape, "The Accused" has the gumption to suggest that even though a victim might, rather carelessly, have put herself into the situation that leads to the crime, the crime remains a crime. The victim's behavior is not the issue. There are no extenuating circumstances.

"The Accused," which opens today at Loews Tower East and other theaters, is a good, tough melodrama that follows its narrative line with the tight focus of a single-minded beagle. Though not a re-enactment of an actual case, it has the conviction of an unusually laconic docudrama, the sort that attends to the business at hand and allows the audience to find for itself any larger applications.

The film also features a splendid performance by Jodie Foster as the victim, Sarah Tobias, a pretty, tough-talking, not exactly virginal young woman whose aimless life is suddenly brought up short in the back room of a place called the Mill. Kelly McGillis plays Katheryn Murphy, the assistant district attorney who, having allowed the rapists to plea-bargain their way to lesser charges, has second thoughts.

Jodie Foster

To redeem Sarah's self-respect as well as her own, Katheryn brings charges against three of the men who witnessed the rape and who, she sets out to prove, actively encouraged it. It is this trial that is the film's concern.

Though there is little doubt about the trial's outcome, since the film would otherwise have little point, "The Accused" is a consistently engrossing melodrama, modest in its aims and as effective for the clichés it avoids as for the clear eye through which it sees its working-class American lives. Filmed in the state of Washington, it looks and sounds exactly right, from the tacky trailer that Sarah Tobias shares with a lay-about, unemployed musician, to Sarah's richly vulgar language, which is her only defense against the world around her.

Since Miss Foster appeared as the adolescent femme fatale in "Bugsy Malone" and as the teen-age hooker in "Taxi Driver," there's never been much doubt that she's a good actress as well as a vixenish beauty. Now it's clear that she's an exceptionally fine, intelligent, vivid actress whose beauty is undiminished. Here she has the benefit of a very well written role. One day she will get a great one.

Mr. Kaplan ("Over the Edge," "Heart Like a Wheel") is a director of such efficiency that one tends to overlook this as the personal style it is. With the exception of a crashing soundtrack score, which says everything twice, "The Accused" is a model of no-nonsense, tight-lipped movie making.

1988 O 14, C13:1

Piano Harpy

MADAME SOUSATZKA, directed by John Schlesinger; screenplay by Ruth Prawer Jhabvala and Mr. Schlesinger, from the novel by Bernice Rubens; director of photography, Nat Crosby; edited by Peter Honess; music by Gerald Gouriet; production designer, Luciana Arrighi; produced by Robin Dalton; released by Universal. At Baronet, Third Avenue at 59th Street. Running time: 122 minutes. This film is rated PG-13.

Madame Sousatzka	Shirley MacLaine
Lady Emily	Dame Peggy Ashcroft
Jenny	Twiggy
Sushila	Shabana Azmi
Manek Sen	Navin Chowdhry
Ronnie Blum	Leigh Lawson
Cordle	Geoffrey Bayldon
Vincent Pick	Lee Montague

Navin Chowdry and Ms. MacLaine as a duo in the John Schlesinger film.

By JANET MASLIN

Madame Irina Sousatzka (Shirley MacLaine) is a magnificent relic, the kind of creature who can be found only in the memories of her most devoted students, or else on the movie screen. A woman like this would be at a disadvantage in the real world, but Madame barely acknowledges the real world at all. She lives solely for music, surrounded by photographs of great pianists and educating a handpicked group of prodigies, to whom she gives homemade cookies and imparts her own brand of wisdom. "I teach not only how to play the piano, but how to live," says she.

John Schlesinger's "Madame Sousatzka" is as much of an antique as the woman herself and a long, sentimental celebration of the "great pianist and pedagogue," as one of Madame's admirers describes her. It's as affectionate, big-hearted and creaky as any film that ever graced Radio City Music Hall, with leisureliness and dime-store philosophizing to match. And if its insights into Madame's character don't go much deeper than the layer of makeup that transforms Miss MacLaine into a painted harridan, they don't really have to. Like its heroine, "Madame Sousatzka" finds a form of defiance in what otherwise might merely seem dated.

"Madame Sousatzka," which opens today at the Baronet, reserves its greatest enthusiasm for the excesses of the Sousatzka System, which are explained in great detail. (A yellowing chart in her London studio shows precisely how the bones of the fingers are to be held.) Madame will cover a student's eyes when he plays, so the music "can arise from the depths of the very soul to the height of reason." She will declare: "It's all one: the way we dress, the way we speak, the way we play. It's all connected." She will scold: "No, no! The message cannot come to the fingers if you don't open your body and let it through!" And she will snap, in her most brittle tones: "Bartok! As though he could ever play Bartok!," about someone whose talents she does not admire.

•

Shirley MacLaine plays this to the hilt and beyond, which is just what the role requires. She's both a monster and a marvel. Festooned with fringed shawls and clanking beads, walking with a slight hobble, spraying herself furiously with perfume when she becomes flustered, and made up garishly as the very essence of faded glory, Miss MacLaine rivets the attention at every turn. Her catalogue of facial expressions alone is fascinating, since she seems to have captured every possible variation on the withering look. With her icy sidelong glances, her overbearing scowls and her brittle glares of suspicion and disapproval, this Madame Sousatzka is indeed as formidable as she means to be.

The screenplay, by Mr. Schlesinger and Ruth Prawer Jhabvala, brings the character and her friends to life without giving them much of a dramatic raison d'être. It surrounds Madame with colorful neighbors (among them the great Dame Peggy Ashcroft as the sweet old lady next door, and Twiggy as a flirtatious, blithely charming would-be singer upstairs) and gives her a brilliant new protégé (Navin Chowdhry), yet it never succeeds in generating much of a story. The film meanders between Madame's efforts with this new student and her impending eviction from the building in which she has lived for many years. In the end, "Madame Sousatzka" very nearly tears down the building to create the impression that something has changed.

The plot is so weak that one of its significant developments is the discovery of a stray hair in the Indian food that the new student, Manek Sen (Mr. Chowdhry), and his mother, Sushila (Shabana Azmi), have been cooking as part of their catering business. Nonetheless, "Madame Sousatzka" holds the attention through sheer force of personality, if not through any discernible action. Miss

MacLaine's scenes with the very appealing Mr. Chowdhry are particularly enjoyable, as the teacher sheds her sternness and begins showing genuine affection for the boy. Indeed, all the older women in the story appear unaccountably attracted to this young man, not the least of them his own mother.

•

Late in the film, there's a clumsy effort to inject an element of longing into Madame Sousatzka's psyche. When Manek makes his concert debut, she relives the disaster that was her own; on the same occasion, she gazes at a painting of a voluptuous nude and then catches a glimpse of two young lovers. If these touches seem entirely superficial, that's because Miss MacLaine makes the idea of Madame's requiring any greater satisfaction from life seem irrelevant. The character's grand assurance, her sweeping faith in the rectitude of her own opinions, is her own greatest virtue and the film's as well.

The incidental touches are among the best things about "Madame Sousatzka": the wine-dark, portrait-filled apartment that Madame has made a shrine to her art (with a stuffed octopus on the Steinway); the Indian landlady and her friends who've created a home away from home in the apartment downstairs from Manek and his mother; the sign reading "For Distressed Gentlefolk" on a box of things Dame Peggy's character is giving away. Dame Peggy also has a wonderful moment when, as a hospital patient, she exclaims more or less happily over the pudding and macaroni she is being fed, and cites this meal as one of the pleasures of being English.

•

"Madame Sousatzka" is rated PG-13 ("Special Parental Guidance Suggested for Those Younger Than 13"). It contains some strong language and sexual innuendoes.

1988 O 14, C8:5

Walking Shorts

THE 21ST INTERNATIONAL TOURNEE OF ANIMATION, a series of short films produced by Terry Thoren; presented by Expanded Entertainment. At the Festival Theater, 57th Street west of Fifth Avenue. Running time: 105 minutes. These films have no rating.

By CARYN JAMES

Any film that sends vicious M & M's candies skittering up a human foot as if they were African ants and that sets Che Guevara twirling in dance with the Statue of Liberty deserves a livelier title than "The 21st International Tournée of Animation." The latest in this annual series of short animated films is full of wit, sophistication and visual energy — the best way to escape the listlessness and self-importance such anthologies are prone to. These film makers graciously take their technical finesse for granted, and allow the audience to lose itself in the split-second, magical transformations that are the soul of animation.

About half of the 14 pieces tell no stories except visual ones, but as they flash in and out of scenes the films dare us to keep up with them. The Swiss "78 Tours" presents a Chinese-box vision; a grassy park turns out to be printed on the dress of a woman, who sits in a park, and on and on. This cyclical world is in constant motion — a coffee cup turns into a man walking down a spiral staircase, which gives way to a Ferris wheel. The drawn figures are viewed as if a movie camera is swinging around 180 degrees, a technique that blurs the definitions of cartoons and cinema.

"Pas à Deux" is just as dizzying but wildly comic. In vibrant caricatures, unlikely couples dance together and suddenly become even less likely partners. It's hard to say which pair is the strangest of the strange — Don Quixote and Olive Oyl, Tarzan and Snow White or van Gogh and a Playboy bunny. The Pope dances alone.

•

The narrative pieces range from silly to effectively mysterious. In "Arnold Escapes From Church," a clay-animated boy lets his imagination conjure deliciously irreverent, literal responses to Psalm 23. "Thou preparest a table before me in the presence of mine enemies" brings a hatchet-faced schoolmarm to a feast of candy and cake, and "My cup runneth over" sends a coffee cup with legs scampering along the table.

"The Writer," by the Dutch animator Paul Driessen, has a beautifully eerie, Medieval setting. The writer is a blobby, monkish-looking figure created with spare lines, in subdued shades of blue and brown. Bright red,

green and yellow shapes float up from his quill pen to a world in which people can turn into cats or castles and where death roams in the shape of a rickety Halloween skeleton. This deft blend of wit and seriousness owes much more to Ingmar Bergman than to other animators.

•

Even at their most conventional, these films are aware of their animated past and take funny turns on -traditional cartoon styles. "The Cat Came Back" evokes a Tom and Jerry world full of crayon colors, as it illustrates a Canadian folk song about an indestructible cat who turns up on an old man's doorstep. The man chases him into a cave and underwater, only to return and find the cat has eaten the sofa.

The half-hour piece that ends the collection, "The Man Who Planted Trees," is all too much like a bedtime story. It resembles a prettily drawn storybook; in lullaby-low tones Christopher Plummer narrates the tale of a man who singlehandedly planted thousands of trees and reclaimed barren land. It anchors the anthology with solemn reverence, and seems at odds with the generally high spirits of "The 21st International Tournée of Animation," which opens today at the Festival Theater.

1988 O 14, C16:6

FILM VIEW/Janet Maslin

Sex Scenes: Handle With Utmost Care

SINCE THE PLOT OF THE COURT-room drama "The Accused" hinges on the facts of a rape case and the manner in which they will be perceived by a jury, there's a lot riding on how the film depicts the crime. Will the rape be presented in an exploitative way? Will its impact be used to anger and upset the audience? Or will the event be handled so that it does not interfere with the viewer's objective judgment of the case? Where the treatment of this all-important and potentially inflammatory episode is concerned, the film itself is, in a sense, on trial.

On screen, as in life, sexual imagery can be made to say one thing and mean quite another. And nothing can compare with sexuality as a means of leaving film audiences powerfully bewildered. Consider Catherine Breillat's "36 Fillette," the only French entry in this year's New York Film Festival, with a heroine described in festival literature as being "like a Rohmer creature with hormones." In theory, this is an examination of the conflicting feelings of anger and desire that a 14-year-old girl experiences as she stands on the threshold of a sexual awakening.

In fact, it's a symphony of heavy breathing, with the young girl's ambivalence toward her middle-aged lover taking the form of slow, teasing make-out sessions that span a great deal of screen time. Yes, "36 Fillette" happens to be sufficiently well acted to make this interesting for more than the obvious reasons. And no, Miss Breillat does not appear to be using the footage in an exploitative way. But there's an awfully thin line separating this enlightened feminist acknowledgment of the young girl's nascent stirrings from the cheap, sensational use that some male directors might make of these same impulses. Who can blame the viewer for finding this confusing?

"The Accused," which was directed by Jonathan Kaplan, is a much tougher and more forthright film, which makes its handling of sexually volatile material that much more difficult. Certainly Mr. Kaplan has worked hard to achieve a sober and intelligently provocative tone. The film begins with only a searing suggestion of what has occurred, with

'The Accused' shows that on screen, as in life, sexual imagery can be made to say one thing and mean quite another.

Sarah Tobias (Jodie Foster) making her desperate escape from the bar where she has just been attacked by several men (the circumstances of the assault resemble those of the much-publicized rape case in New Bedford, Mass., several years ago). After this, it presents in coolly pragmatic terms the police examination that Sarah undergoes. Miss Foster, who is extraordinarily good in this role, makes certain that the salient emotions any viewer will feel during this part of the film are sympathy and pain.

But when and how will Mr. Kaplan complete the film's account of what happened? "The Accused" quickly introduces Sarah to Katheryn Murphy (Kelly McGillis), the assistant district attorney who will help to unravel the facts of the case. The obvious differences in background between the yuppie Katheryn and the angry, uneducated Sarah give the film an extra element of tension. In fact the contrast between these two women becomes more compelling than the investigation itself, since the film grows more manipulative as it reconstructs the circumstances of the rape.

Sarah's character is established as the kind that won't be helpful in court. She was legally drunk at the time of the rape, and she drove to the bar alone late at night, in a car whose license plates read "Sxy Sadi." What's more, as an irate Katheryn later discovers, Sarah eyed one of her prospective rapists and told a friend that she'd love to sleep with him. Mr. Kaplan and the screenwriter, Tom Topor, release these bits of information into the film gradually, to heighten the suspense. It's a technique that makes perfect sense in building up to the denouement of a mystery story but is more questionable here.

In standard whodunit style, "The Accused" saves its big re-enactment of the rape for the courtroom episode at the end of the film, contrasting the prim, serious-looking figure that Sarah has now become with the slatternly flirt she was at the start. The re-enactment shows her sashaying into the bar, exchanging meaningful glances with every man in the room, dancing provocatively in the middle of the bar, and then seeming extremely surprised when several men take her up on an apparent invitation. The re-enactment abruptly becomes more somber as the attack begins, and Mr. Kaplan avoids any element of luridness in staging the rape itself; this part of the scene is very discreet. But by using this episode as its dramatic crescendo, the film inevitably exploits the rape in its own way.

■

Of course it would have been less effective to let this story unfold in real time, to begin with the full rape sequence and get it over with so that the investigation could begin. And the film makers can hardly be blamed for wanting to present their material in the most gripping manner possible. Still, it's fascinating to watch the film vacillate between seriousness and entertainment, and to notice the ways in which entertainment ultimately wins out.

So Katheryn's career, which hangs in the balance as she risks everything to prosecute this case, becomes as important to the story's outcome as the legal issues. Sarah's helpful transformation into a somber, responsible witness begs the question of how a woman of really disreputable character might fare in court. And the rape itself becomes at least as teasing as it is troubling. In the end, this film, however well intentioned, can't help clouding the issues on which it means to cast light. □

1988 O 16, II:25:1

Rob McEwan

Jodie Foster, left, as a rape victim with Kelly McGillis in "The Accused"

Confessions Of a Shoeshine Man

THINGS CHANGE, directed by David Mamet; written by Mr. Mamet and Shel Silverstein; director of photography, Juan Ruiz Anchia; edited by Trudy Ship; music by Alaric Jans; production designer, Michael Merritt; produced by Michael Hausman; released by Columbia Pictures. At Sutton, Third Avenue and 57th Street. Running time: 100 minutes. This film is rated PG.

Gino	Don Ameche
Jerry	Joe Mantegna
Joseph Vincent	Robert Prosky
Frankie	J. J. Johnston
Mr. Silver	Ricky Jay
Mr. Green	Mike Nussbaum
Frankie	J. J. Macy
Billy Drake	W. H. Macy
Hotel Manager	J. T. Walsh
Jackie Shore	Jonathan Katz

By VINCENT CANBY

The gofer at the Tahoe airport pumps mob-soldier Jerry (Joe Mantegna) about the identity of Jerry's elderly, aloof traveling companion. Says Jerry with offhand cool, his eyebrow lifted a significant millimeter, "He's the guy behind the guy behind the guy." The go-fer is impressed.

So is the staff at Tahoe's gaudy Hotel Galaxy, where Jerry and his companion are housed in neo-Roman splendor on what's called "the Criterion Floor." Under his breath, nodding toward the older man, Jerry tells the manager, "Out here for a little low-profile relaxation." Says the manager, "Your privacy will be respect-

ed."

Jerry's mysterious pal is not, as everyone assumes, some all-powerful don-of-dons, so mighty and awesome that, like God's, his name can't be said aloud. He is Gino (Don Ameche), a hard-working, fatalistic Chicago shoeshine man who, on the promise of a fishing boat and a funded retirement in Sicily, has agreed to confess to a mob murder he didn't commit.

Out of the goodness of his heart, and without the knowledge of his superiors, Jerry has decided that Gino should have his (Jerry's) dream weekend at Lake Tahoe before turning himself in to the Chicago police. What follows is a wonderfully fresh, deadpan comedy of mistaken identities and sentimental gangsters, the sort whose lives are governed by a hierarchy of contradictory loyalties that only a mother could understand.

•

"Things Change," the second film to be directed by David Mamet, is an airier piece than his fine "House of Games," but no less characteristic and oddball. The screenplay is a collaboration between Mr. Mamet, the Pulitzer Prize-winning playwright, and Shel Silverstein, the cartoonist and playwright who may be one of the funniest people alive.

Their film, which opens today at the Sutton, is an enchanted lark about wiseguys and those hustlers who think they are wiseguys, but aren't.

Chief among the latter is Mr. Mantegna's brilliantly funny Jerry who, when first met, is washing the dishes in the don's Chicago mansion. Jerry is being penalized for some unspecified gaffe. He is offered redemption if he takes charge of the bewildered Gino, drills him in all of the things to which Gino must confess, and gets him to the courthouse on time Monday morning.

Jerry is a marvelous character, but I've no idea how much it has to do with the writing and direction and how much with Mr. Mantegna's extraordinary performance. In whatever way Jerry came into being, he is fused funniness.

•

He wants desperately to be a good company man. He seems to be the sort of fellow who has studied hard to be able to look and sound authentic. He has cultivated the vocabulary of the laconic and all of the gestures of the slippery. He has the confidence of someone who can walk through a downpour without getting wet.

Left to his own devices, however, Jerry inevitably gives himself away. He is a flawed hood.

In performance and role, Mr. Mantegna's Jerry is perfectly matched by Mr. Ameche's Gino, who sports a splendid, old-world mustache and accent, along with the kind of great comic aplomb that wins actors awards for other than sentimental reasons. With his superb timing, Mr. Ameche manages somehow to fit into the Mamet universe while always having one foot outside, much like Gino with the mob.

Nothing fazes Gino, not a pair of sweet, imposingly sexy showgirls, who want to take him fishing, and not even the Tahoe don (Robert Prosky) who, suspecting Gino to be a V.I.P., in-

vites him to lunch. Their meeting is a huge success, the don interpreting Gino's earnest remarks about shoe repairing to be sage parables about the loneliness of life at the top.

•

Equally fine are a number of other actors associated with Mr. Mamet's theater work, including J. J. Johnston, W. H. Macy and J. T. Walsh. A particular standout is Jonathan Katz, who co-wrote the original story for "House of Games." Here he appears as a Tahoe comic named Jackie Shore, whose on-stage monologues are so good — so on-target and funny-awful — that the demands of the movie seem to be an untimely interruption.

The dialogue is full of Mr. Mamet's fondness for words and phrases repeated in such a way that their meanings are reduced, as if by long simmering, to something that is essential but still hopelessly and hilariously opaque. Talking isn't communication. It's an exchange of arcane passwords.

Like "House of Games," the new film, photographed by Juan Ruiz Anchia and designed by Michael Merritt, looks to be both realistic and fantastic. This is Mr. Mamet's way as a director. He seems to sidle into scenes, though the scenes themselves are blunt and straightforward.

Also like "House of Games," "Things Change" has an ending problem. As written and directed, the film's final two scenes don't make immediate sense. A last-minute twist is in order, but this twist is so muffed in the placement of the camera and in dramtic emphasis that many people may be as perplexed as I was.

One buys the resolution because

Stephen Vaughan

Joe Mantegna, left, as a Mafia bodyguard, with his charge, Mr. Ameche, in a lavish hotel suite in "Things Change"

one wants to, and because "Things Change" has been so self-assured up to that point that it deserves the benefit of all doubts.

•

"Things Change," which has been rated PG ("Parental Guidance Suggested"), contains some mildly vulgar language.

1988 O 21, C10:5

Spaghetti With Gobs Of Tomato Sauce

THE LAIR OF THE WHITE WORM, written, directed and produced by Ken Russell; adapted from the novel by Bram Stoker; director of photography, Dick Bush; edited by Peter Davies; music by Stanislas Syrewicz; released by Vestron Pictures. At the D. W. Griffith, 59th Street east of Third Avenue, and the Eighth Street Playhouse, off the Avenue of the Americas. Running time: 94 minutes. This film is rated R.

Lady Sylvia Marsh	Amanda Donohoe
Lord James D'Ampton	Hugh Grant
Eve Trent	Catherine Oxenberg
Angus Flint	Peter Capaldi
Mary Trent	Sammi Davis
Peters	Stratford Johns
P. C. Erny	Paul Brooke

By JANET MASLIN

Not a worm is left unturned in Ken Russell's buoyant, mischievous and predictably overwrought new film, loosely based on the last novel by the author of "Dracula," Bram Stoker. "The Lair of the White Worm" (from Stoker's 1911 novel, published in America under the title "The Garden of Evil") incorporates every imagi-

nable worm and serpent double-entendre. Though no film of Mr. Russell's would be anywhere without an overabundance of phallic symbolism, that barely scratches the surface of the imagery to be found in this one.

"Slither in," says a driver (who is secretly a reptile) to a potential passenger. "Name your poison," says another soigné snakeperson, who also declares with bored sophistication, "I actually *hibernate* in winter." Suggestions of snakiness are everywhere, even in the cords of a life-saving vest modeled by a stewardess in one of the film's wild-eyed dream sequences. Of course, spaghetti is the favorite food of all concerned.

The career of Ken Russell appears to be on an unexpected upswing at the moment, after he had all but lost the fiery, passionate momentum of his spectacular early work. Lately, with the gleefully outrageous "Salome's Last Dance" and now with this slyly tongue-in-cheek horror film, a less feverish Mr. Russell seems to have regained some degree of detachment and control without sacrificing his characteristic wickedness.

Though "The Lair of the White Worm," has at least as much potential to give offense as some of the director's more frenzied efforts, it also has a welcome element of droll humor. And the director has once again attracted some excellent actors who share his peculiar sense of fun. Even a perusal of the credits will offer some idea of the film's singular tenor. Among the minor roles listed are six "Maids/Nuns," seven "Soldiers/Witchdoctors," one "Snakewoman," "Lady Sylvia's Stunt Double" and (in a particularly eyebrow-raising fantasy sequence dramatizing the strug-

gle between paganism and Christianity in terms best appreciated by fans of rock video) "Jesus Christ."

"The Lair of the White Worm," which opens today at the D. W. Griffith and the Eighth Street Playhouse, tells of the dread events that are unleashed when a Scottish archeologist named Angus Flint (Peter Capaldi) unearths a large and mysterious worm-shaped skull in the Derbyshire countryside. Angus, who is staying with a simple country lass named Mary Trent (Sammi Davis) and her more glamorous sister Eve (Catherine Oxenberg), soon discovers that worm lore looms large in local history. It seems that Lord James D'Ampton (Hugh Grant) is the descendant of a knight credited with slaying a monstrous serpent, and that this event is still commemorated with an annual worm-themed party at the D'Ampton manse. Mr. Russell has even unearthed a folk song, entitled "The D'Ampton Worm," to accompany these festivities.

The new creature in the neighborhood is Lady Sylvia Marsh, who, as played by Amanda Donohoe, is the very essence of drawing-room naughtiness. That she is also the embodiment of the legendary white worm, or at least some sort of worm-related priestess, is icing on the cake. Miss Donohoe plays the role with a marvelously withering verbal understatement, which is not exactly matched by the film's visual style. She may drive a sports car and wear fashionably deadly looking sunglasses, which suggest normalcy of a certain sort, but she also appears in kinky black underwear to polish off one victim and blue body paint to attack another. Understatement in a film of Mr. Russell's goes only so far.

Mr. Grant, who co-starred in "Maurice," makes D'Ampton the kind of supremely jaded aristocrat who can calmly report, "I think we have another reptile loose on the premises." As his manservant, Stratford Johns shows just the right aplomb in dealing with the worm's presence and the attendant problems this creates. Miss Davis and Mr. Capaldi are wonderfully earnest as they dig for clues to the worm's strange story, and Miss Oxenberg, if less polished than the rest of the cast, looks as bewitching as she's supposed to. It is her job to illustrate one of the film's minor lessons, namely that nice underwear matters. You never know when someone may choose you as a candidate for human sacrifice.

1988 O 21, C14:1

Slices of Life and Love

Julia Roberts

MYSTIC PIZZA, directed by Donald Petrie; screenplay by Amy Jones, Perry Howze, Randy Howze and Alfred Uhry, story by Miss Jones; director of photography, Tim Suhrstedt; edited by Marion Rothman and Don Brochu; music by David McHugh; produced by Mark Levinson and Scott Rosenfelt; released by the Samuel Goldwyn Company. At Gotham, Third Avenue at 58th Street, and other theaters. Running time: 102 minutes. This film is rated R.

Daisy Araujo .... Julia Roberts
Kat Araujo ....Annabeth Gish
Jojo Barboza .... Lili Taylor
Bill Montijo ....Vincent Phillip D'Onofrio
Tim Travers .... William R. Moses
Charles Gordon Winsor ....Adam Storke
Leona Valsouano ....Conchata Ferrell
Phoebe ....Porscha Radcliffe

By JANET MASLIN

It would be easy to think ill of a film that equates life's great mysteries with a secret formula for tomato sauce, but in the case of "Mystic Pizza," it would also be a mistake. Though in essence this is little more than a girls' romance novel brought to life, it has been filled with heart and humor. The place, the people and even the largely predictable situations in which they find themselves are presented in an entirely winning way. "Mystic Pizza" offers warm, inviting and funny glimpses into the lives and loves of three appealing young women, who are just on the threshold of leaving the carefree years of their girlhood behind.

The film's most dubious assumption is that the town of Mystic, Conn., is a desolate backwater, a place that the film's three Portuguese-American heroines cannot wait to leave. But the picturesque scenery contradicts that idea, as does the fact that even low-level jobs in Mystic (the mother of one of the heroines works on a pier, putting rubber bands on the claws of newly caught lobsters) have a certain touristy charm.

The three young women themselves are waitresses at the pizza parlor of the title, sharing hard work and feisty camaraderie. Even the gruff proprietor of the place (Conchata Ferrell) has a friendly and lovable side. There in the restaurant, while slinging pizza and mopping the floor, the voluptuous Daisy Araujo (Julia Roberts), her level-headed kid sister Kat (Annabeth Gish) and their wise-cracking friend Jojo Barboza (Lili Taylor) work their way through the kinds of romantic crises that are the film's real raisons d'être.

•

"Mystic Pizza," which opens today at the Gotham and other theaters, has a real flair for disaster. It begins with a catastrophic wedding at which Jojo, the panicky bride, falls into a swoon just as she reaches the altar; though she loves Bill (Vincent Phillip D'Onofrio), a very long-suffering young fisherman, she's less enthusiastic about the idea of getting married. While the film follows the subsequent comic ups and downs of Bill and Jojo's courtship, which has of course made Bill a local laughingstock, it devotes equal energy to Daisy and Kat's respective problems.

As played by Miss Roberts, a lively and beautiful young actress who resembles her brother Eric more in appearance than in temperament, Daisy is indeed the town bombshell. She doesn't have to work very hard to capture the attention of anyone she meets, and during the course of the story she rivets the eye of the rich ne'er-do-well Charlie (Adam Storke), who like all of the film's stock characters proves capable of a surprise or two. Meanwhile, the hard-working, Yale-bound Kat is hired as a babysitter by a perfect father (William R. Moses) who happens to be married, and finds that proximity to this dreamboat is ruining her hard-won composure.

Although each of these romances works out more or less as expected, "Mystic Pizza" manages to seem fresh anyhow. This is especially remarkable in view of the fact that the film credits four different screenwriters (among them Amy Jones, who wrote the story, and the Pulitzer Prize-winning playwright Alfred Uhry) for a script that never seems choppy. And Donald Petrie, who keeps the film balanced and on track, is a first-time feature director whose work has no aura of inexperience. Instead, the script and direction makes the characters seem attractive and real, and the well-chosen young cast heightens the film's appeal.

Mr. D'Onofrio, who was so extraordinary as the tormented recruit in Stanley Kubrick's "Full Metal Jacket," turns the fisherman Bill into a model of misplaced patience, while Miss Taylor makes Jojo the film's resident cut-up. Miss Gish gives Kat a quiet, substantial presence and a steady, open gaze, qualities very like the ones she admires in the smoothly appealing Mr. Moses. And Mr. Storke holds his ground with the scene-stealing Miss Roberts, which must have been very difficult indeed.

As for the secret tomato sauce recipe, it functions both as a metaphor and as an excuse to introduce a television food critic into the story. Anyone who isn't certain how the pizza parlor will rate with this curmudgeon may be out of tune with the film's blithe and sunny brand of magic.

1988 O 21, C20:6

Whydunit

WITHOUT A CLUE, directed by Thom Eberhardt; written by Gary Murphy and Larry Strawther; director of photography, Alan Hume; edited by Peter Tanner; music by Henri Mancini; production designer, Brian Ackland-Snow; produced by Marc Stirdivant; released by Orion Pictures Corporation. At Guild 50th Street, west of Fifth Avenue, and other theaters. Running time: 107 minutes. This film is rated PG.

Sherlock Holmes ....Michael Caine
Dr. Watson .... Ben Kingsley
Inspector Lestrade ....Jeffrey Jones
Fake Leslie .... Lysette Anthony
Professor Moriarty ....Paul Freeman
Lord Smithwick ....Nigel Davenport
Mrs. Hudson .... Pat Keen

"Without a Clue," opening today at the Guild and other theaters, is an appallingly witless sendup of the Sherlock Holmes-Dr. Watson stories, based on an idea that wouldn't support a five-minute revue sketch, much less a feature film for Michael Caine and Ben Kingsley.

The idea: Dr. Watson is actually the genius-sleuth who, to protect his medical reputation, has credited a fictitious character named Sherlock Holmes with the successes recalled in Watson's popular stories. When the public demands to meet Holmes, Watson (Mr. Kingsley) hires a rummy second-rate actor (Mr. Caine) to play the role.

The acclaim given Holmes leads to bad feelings between the two men. Watson fires Holmes and tries to interest his publishers in a new character, that is, himself, to be known as "the crime doctor." Nobody is interested. In desperation, Watson rehires Holmes for one last caper.

•

This is all there is to "Without a Clue," which is otherwise notable only for Mr. Caine's angry performance as a jolly buffoon. The actor

goes through the film as if he were being held hostage by a terrorist talent agent. He does the slapstick business and says the terrible lines with a minimum of conviction and no sense of fun. He is both gloomy and patronizing. He seems to be saying, "Shoot me if you don't like it."

Mr. Kingsley behaves far more professionally, though he doesn't have to do much except look exasperated with his slobbish employee. For the

record, Thom Eberhardt directed the original screenplay written by Gary Murphy and Larry Strawther. This one belongs near the top of the list of the 10 worst of 1988.

•

"Without a Clue," which has been rated PG ("Parental Guidance Suggested"), includes some naughty words. VINCENT CANBY

1988 O 21, C21:1

Six Hours of Dickens

"Little Dorrit" was shown as part of the recent New Directors/New Films series. Following are excerpts from Vincent Canby's review, which appeared in The New York Times on March 26. The film opens today at the 57th Street Playhouse, 110 West 57th Street.

Television's mini-series have given us a taste for literary adaptations that approximate the entire content of a long work. They've also evolved into what is virtually a new dramatic form. They helped prepare Broadway audiences for the Royal Shakespeare Company's eight-and-a-half-hour version of Charles Dickens's "Nicholas Nickleby" (1981), and they prompt one to anticipate — with a good deal of excitement — Christine Edzard's six-hour adaptation of "Little Dorrit."

Six hours would seem to be more than ample time to re-create the manifold details of this (now) comparatively little-read Dickens work, which George Bernard Shaw called "his masterpiece among many masterpieces."

The film's physical production must be one of the handsomest, most evocative ever given a Dickens novel, and the performances, by some of Britain's finest character actors, are as rich in baroque detail as anyone could hope when anticipating the film.

Considering Dickens's penchant for subplots and extended narrative asides, the novel is straightforward, told in two parts ("Poverty" and "Riches") in chronological order. At its center is the curious love story of the middle-aged Arthur Clennam, brought up by a repressive, religious zealot of a mother, and the much younger, physically stunted, snow-pure Amy Dorrit ("Little Dorrit"), born and raised in the infamous Marshalsea debtors' prison by her mannered, blithely fraudulent old dad.

True transforming love is not immediately recognized by Arthur. The 800-plus-page novel comes perilously close to The End and an Afterword before Arthur and Amy declare themselves. In the meantime, Dickens has given the reader a tumultuous portrait of a doomy Protestant 19th-century England, its unthinkable poverty, lunatic (under the circumstances) optimism, heedless bureaucracy, society snobs, celebrated swindlers and assorted colorful lowlifes. Further complicating matters are a mystery relating to one major character's parentage and another mystery involving a sizable bequest that's been withheld from a rightful heir.

Dickens tells all this in his entertainingly garrulous manner as if sitting on a cloud, observing everything in the most minute, sometimes rueful, sometimes very comic detail. He doesn't much care for going into people's minds. He doesn't have to. Never at a loss for a caustic comment, he remains more of a reporter and social critic than a Freudian analyst.

Miss Edzard, who wrote the screenplay as well as directing the film, has chosen to reveal the novel by rearranging its two sections. In the first, we follow most of the novel's events as seen by Arthur Clennam (Derek Jacobi). Part 2 goes back over these same events, while introducing some additional plot information, as seen through the eyes of Little Dorrit.

The intention, we are told in the film's program notes, is not a "Rashomon" examination of the impossibility of truth. Rather it seems to be an attempt to evoke two different, subjective points of view. Part 1 is dimly lighted. The colors are dark. When it isn't raining, the sky is full of the debris of the Industrial Revolution.

Part 2 is supposedly full of sunshine, light, bright colors. I say "sup-

Odd Couple
Ben Kingsley, far left, portrays the brilliant Dr. Watson and Michael Caine plays Reginald Kincaid, the third-rate actor he hires to become Sherlock Holmes, in "Without a Clue."

Graham Attwood

Twice Told
Sarah Pickering, in the title role, and Derek Jacobi, as the ineffectual Arthur Clennam, star in "Little Dorrit."

posedly" because, after several hours of watching, such subtleties tend to be overlooked unless one is terrifically bored.

Spun out and repeated in this fashion, the movie does a disservice to itself in the cause of a scheme that's of more interest in theory than in fact. It's exhausting. That's the bad news.

The good is that "Little Dorrit" comes to vivid life just often enough to demand attention when one is beginning to think of other things that must be done. The cast, headed by Mr. Jacobi and Alec Guinness as William Dorrit, is spectacular. The film is a montage of memorable images, beginning with Sarah Pickering's small, strained, pretty face as Little Dorrit.

One must cherish the late Joan Greenwood as Arthur's terrible mother; Miriam Margolyes as Flora Finching (who speaks in woozily hilarious, nonstop paragraphs instead of phrases or even sentences); Max Wall as the evil Flintwinch, Patricia Hayes as Affery, Flintwinch's wife; Roshan Seth as the rent collector, Pancks, and Eleanor Bron as Mrs. Merdle, the social-climbing wife of Britain's financial wizard-of-the-moment. Until he goes broke, taking much of the country to ruin with him, Merdle (Michael Elphick) is exalted as "the spirit of the age!"

1988 O 21, C12:3

Out of the Ordinary, The Extraordinary

BAT 21, directed by Peter Markle; screenplay by William C. Anderson and George Gordon, based on the book by Mr. Anderson; director of photography, Mark Irwin; edited by Stephen E. Rivkin; music by Christopher Young; production designer, Vincent Cresci-man; produced by David Fisher, Gary A. Neill and Michael Balson; released by Tri-Star Pictures. At the Criterion Center, Broadway and 45th Street, and other theaters. Running time: 105 minutes. This film is rated R.

Lieut. Col. Iceal Hambleton	Gene Hackman
Capt. Bartholomew Clark	Danny Glover
Col. George Walker	Jerry Reed
Ross Carver	David Marshall Grant
Sgt. Harley Rumbaugh	Clayton Rohner
Maj. Jake Scott	Erich Anderson

Gene Hackman, as Lieut. Col. Iceal Hambleton in "Bat 21," radiates something not usually seen on the faces of war heroes: worry. Hambleton, whose real story is the basis for the film, is seen as a 53-year-old Air Force strategist who was quite literally pulled off the golf course to help out with a reconnaissance mission, during which he was unexpectedly shot down in Vietnam. The film,

which details the elaborate Air Force effort to rescue Hambleton, is more the story of an ordinary man in extraordinary cirumstances than it is a familiar story of war.

It's hard to imagine what the film might have been with anyone other than Mr. Hackman in this role, for this actor's quintessential decency and ordinariness have never seemed more affecting. It's precisely the lack of bravado in Hambleton that makes him an interesting character, and a poignant anti-Rambo. Alone and frightened in the jungle, Hambleton has the adventures that might be expected, but he doesn't become thrill-crazy. When he has to treat a wound, it's painful, not exciting; when he steals some food, he's fearful, not defiant. And when he's forced to kill a Vietnamese man who attacks him, he is deeply remorseful. Watching as the dead man's family discovers his body, Mr. Hackman's Hambleton blurts out a simple but wrenching apology.

"Bat 21," which was shot in Borneo and opens today at the Criterion Center and other theaters, takes its name from the radio code Hambleton uses in his communications with "Bird Dog" (Danny Glover), the pilot at work trying to rescue him. Though the two have never met before, these men become at least temporarily close on the basis of their shared experience. "Bird Dog, I killed a man today," Hambleton confesses. "I don't know you, Bat 21," Bird Dog replies, "but you don't sound like a killer. I'm sure you couldn't stop it from happening. The important thing is to put it behind you."

•

As this may indicate, "Bat 21" has an oversensitive side sometimes bordering on the touchy-feely, as when a

young Vietnamese boy saves Hambleton from a trap, then goes one step further by offering the American his hat during a torrential rainstorm. However, in spite of such occasional excesses, the film has a solid, simple story, an effective cast and a fair amount of grit. Though Mr. Hackman gives the film's outstanding performance, Mr. Glover is good in a more conventional role, as are David Marshall Grant and Clayton Rohner as members of the rescue team. The direction by Peter Markle isn't better than workmanlike, but it gets the job done.

JANET MASLIN
1988 O 21, C22:1

Spooks on the Loose (It's the Season)

HALLOWEEN 4: THE RETURN OF MICHAEL MYERS, directed by Dwight H. Little; screenplay by Alan B. McElroy, story by Dhani Lipsius, Larry Rattner, Benjamin Ruffner and Mr. McElroy; director of photography, Peter Lyons Collister; edited by Curtiss Clayton; music by Alan Howarth; art director, Roger S. Crandall; produced by Paul Freeman; released by Galaxy International Releasing Company. At the Criterion Center, Broadway and 45th Street, and other theaters. Running time: 88 minutes. This film is rated R.

Dr. Loomis	Donald Pleasence
Rachel Carruthers	Ellie Cornell
Jamie Lloyd	Danielle Harris
Michael Myers	George P. Wilbur
Dr. Hoffman	Michael Pataki

By CARYN JAMES

It seems too strange to be true, but Halloween and Friday the 13th and prom nights were not always celebrated with slasher films; those quaint seasonal customs began a mere 10 years ago. Before Jason put on his hockey mask and began strewing bodies around, before Freddy started haunting the dreams of teenagers on Elm Street, in 1978 there was Michael Myers, the killer in John Carpenter's stylish and still scary "Halloween."

Like the bones of some animal captured in a fossil, the pattern is all there. Little Michael, a 6-year-old in a Halloween clown costume, kills his sister for having sex. The story picks up years later, with the adult Michael wearing a stark white mask and stalking a goody-goody teen-age baby sitter played by Jamie Lee Curtis. Now and then he diverts himself by stabbing and impaling her sexually active friends. Donald Pleasence, as the doctor who likes to call Michael "evil incarnate," shoots the villain at the end, and they all live to make "Halloween II."

In Peril
Gene Hackman stars in "Bat 21," based on an the actual rescue during the Vietnam War of Air Force Lieut. Col. Iceal Hambleton.

"Halloween 4: The Return of Michael Myers" opened yesterday on two screens at the Criterion Center and at seven other theaters in Manhattan. It seems the latest stage in some curious evolutionary pattern; the slasher species keeps proliferating and getting weaker at the same time.

These days, the murderer in the white mask is more reminiscent of Broadway's Phantom of the Opera than a serial movie killer. En route to a new mental hospital, Michael escapes and heads for his old hometown. He is after his little niece, Jamie, the daughter of the Jamie Lee Curtis character; this passes for an inside joke.

•

For a short time, his ghostlike ability to appear and disappear — now he's behind you, now he's under the bed, now he's in the closet — promises to keep you off-guard. But before long, "Halloween 4" turns into a series of special effects, including an exploding gas station and an electrocution. Does Michael Myers need all this high-tech help? Isn't it enough just to be a homicidal maniac?

In this film, suspense and psychological horror have given way to superhuman strength and resilience. Michael can now push his thumb through a man's forehead. Jamie falls down a flight of stairs and gets up as if she stumbled in the playground. Her foster sister — the blonde, sexless baby sitter — falls off a roof and takes a little longer to get up and pursue Michael again. Mr. Pleasence, as the doctor, has a limp that slows him down, but he still likes to call Michael "evil." (Ms. Curtis and Mr. Carpenter, lucky for them, had better things to do.)

The one effectively handled scene is the last, which promises a sequel with a feminist twist. A feminist slasher is probably not what the pioneers of the women's movement had in mind. But at least she'll be different.

1988 O 22, 12:4

Free Associating

STREAMS OF CONSCIOUSNESS: NEW AMERICAN ANIMATION, "Parade" by Joey Ahlbum; "Nine Lives" by Karen Aqua; "Suspicious Circumstances" by Jim Blashfield; "Nexus" by Rose Bond; "Face Like a Frog" by Sally Cruikshank; "Tugging the Worm" by Jim Duesing; "Dissipative Fantasies" by David Ehrlich; "Thicket" by George Griffin; "Trap" by Amy Kravitz; "Paradisia" by Marcy Page; "Preludes in Magical Time" by Sara Petty; "Skyheart" by Dennis Pies; "Voices" by Joanna Priestley. Released by Expanded Entertainment. At Film Forum 1, 57 Watts Street. Running time: 87 minutes. This film has no rating.

By CARYN JAMES

In "Voices," Joanna Priestley offers a glimpse of her own fears: her animated face grows fat and old, the world seems to destroy itself. All the while, she races through artistic styles from realistic to mock-symbolic.

Cameras float across the screen amid a jumble of colored shapes that suddenly include Felix the Cat stroking his tail. Meanwhile, Ms. Priestly comments, "I could be very deep and symbolic, and let you guess what I'm trying to say." She has the wit to include that scene only to mock it — a distinction that sets "Voices" above many of the other 12 works in "Streams of Consciousness: New American Animation," which opens today at Film Forum 1.

The idea behind this artsy enigmatic collection seems to be that animated images are the perfect way to dip into deep psychological currents. The practical result is a huge variety of humanized creatures — an uncanny number of them fishy looking — and an onslaught of shifting geometric shapes set to music.

•

A few pieces match "Voices" for freshness and accomplishment and surpass it in ambition. In Sally Cruikshank's bright, eccentric "Face Like a Frog," amphibious types with blue and chartreuse bodies walk on two legs through a fun-house world. A vampish female frog seduces an innocent male through a series of rooms, racing by ghosts, dancing walnuts and a lounge lizard who really is a lizard. She leads him through Miami Beach to hell, where fishy red devils dance in a kind of conga line.

"Face Like a Frog" sets the standard that other works fail to match. The hero of "Tugging the Worm" is a green winged androgynous creature that turns part human and falls in with punks; in "Dissipative Fantasies," large-headed children who resemble the aliens in "Close Encounters of the Third Kind" worry about world peace. Ms. Cruikshank's carefree indulgence in the fun house is far more satisfying than these message-laden works.

The collection's most dazzling piece is Marcy Page's "Paradisia," which begins with an irresistible fantasy. In a castle, a woman with flowing red hair looks in a fountain; soon Michelangelo's David comes to life and dances with her. As this 12-minute fantasia reinvents the story of Eve's discovery of desire, the woman swirls through the air and becomes entwined with mythic and legendary figures, including the serpent in the garden, St. George and Pegasus. She rides into the sky on the back of a lion, which becomes St. Michael, who slowly is fused with a serpent.

"Paradisia" moves with unbroken grace, and is delicately drawn in reds and blues that are vivid enough to avoid being too sentimental and pretty.

"Suspicious Circumstances" animates photographic images in a sophisticated and truly surreal way as it traces the disappearance of a man — bit by bit. Two hands joined at the wrists fly through the air and pull off his ear and his nose.

Cups shaped like Donald Duck along with cans of food zoom around like spaceships. Like so many pieces in "Streams of Consciousness," the work says more about the fluid and polished techniques of animation that it does about the psychological stream it splashes around in.

1988 O 26, C21:1

FILM ACTRESS, directed by Kon Ichikawa; screenplay (Japanese with English subtitles) by Kaneto Shindo, Shinya Hidaka and Mr. Ichikawa; story by Mr. Shindo; cinematography, Yukio Isohata; edited by Chizuko Osada; music by Kensaku Tanigawa; art direction, Shinobu Muraki; produced by Tomoyuki Tanaka and Mr. Ichikawa; a Toho production. At Carnegie Screening Room, Seventh Avenue at 57th Street. Running time: 130 minutes. This film has no rating.

Kinuyo Tanaka	Sayuri Yoshinaga
Shiro Kido	Koji Ishizaka
Hiroshi Shimizu	Toru Watanabe
Mizouchi	Bunta Sugawara
Yae	Mitsuko Mori
Uncle Gentaro	Fujio Tokita
Senkichi Nakama	Mitsuru Hirata

By JANET MASLIN

The moment of triumph depicted at the end of Kon Ichikawa's "Film Actress," which opens today at the Carnegie Screening Room, isn't the sort of pinnacle Western audiences might expect. Though the film outlines the career of a legendary screen star, it involves no joyous acceptance speechs, no paper-thin displays of humility and no tributes from adoring fans.

Instead, the biographical "Film Actress" concludes with some timorous advice delivered by its heroine, the actress Kinuyo Tanaka (played by Sayuri Yoshinaga), to one of Japan's greatest directors, Kenji Mizoguchi, as they begin work on the masterpiece (Mizoguchi's "Life of Oharu," made in 1951) that will mark a turning point in both their careers. Speaking up, for a Japanese actress of Miss Tanaka's era, is victory enough.

"Film Actress" is, among other things, an engrossing study of how the Japanese film industry's way of doing things has differed from Hollywood's methods. The history of Japanese film making is the film's true subject, and Mr. Ichikawa, in his characteristically cool and oblique manner, approaches it in an unexpected fashion. He uses the trajectory of Miss Tanaka's career, which began in 1924 and ended with her death in 1977, to focus attention on the conditions under which she made her reputation.

Though the film is long and deals extensively with Miss Tanaka's life off screen, it has an impersonal feeling. Private life, to the film's characters and seemingly to Mr. Ichikawa as well, cannot compare in importance to what happens on the screen. Besides, the film views Miss Tanaka as an elusive and curiously naïve figure, at least in the early stages of her career. "You're clever, yet virtuously old-fashioned," someone says to her later on.

After a prologue in which technicians are seen developing film stock ("It's a wonderful invention," one exclaims), the young Miss Tanaka is seen with her family, as they nervously prepare a celebratory dinner. The festivities are in honor of the director Hiroshi Shimizu (Toru Watanabe), who has arranged for Miss Tanaka to be hired as a contract player by Japan's powerful Shochiko/ Studio. The family is excited, but for different reasons from those Western audiences might expect. They are glad because this has enabled them to move to Tokyo. And they hope that if Miss Tanaka becomes famous, her long-lost, draft-dodging brother may be induced to return home.

The studio system into which Miss Tanaka is introduced is, by Western standards, a stunningly decorous one. The office of the studio head Shiro Kido (Koji Ishizaka) is an austere book-lined room reminiscent of a high school principal's quarters; the studio executives' credo is, as one puts it, that "entertainment must produce happy feelings."

The wardrobe department features stacks of neatly folded kimonos, and actresses preparing for their roles are gathered into a single dressing room, where together they sew, put on makeup and whisper. And the concept of a casting couch is such anathema that the director Shimizu actually bursts into the actresses' room and challenges the gossip about himself and Miss Tanaka head-on. "Who says I patronize Tanaka for my personal reasons?" he demands to know, after hearing complaints that his protégée is monopolizing too many major roles. "Who?"

Of course, some things are universal; the director and Miss Tanaka do become romantically involved, though the studio head advises that they avoid marriage to preserve the actress's girlish image. Though this union ends disastrously, Miss Tanaka finds herself many years later developing an extracurricular attachment to another of her directors, the brilliant and difficult Mizoguchi.

Mr. Ichikawa, who can be difficult in his own right, chooses to make a slight alteration in the spelling of Mizoguchi's name (the film calls him "Mizouchi") because some of the facts of the film maker's life have been rearranged. He was not a widower when he and Miss Tanaka made "Life of Oharu," for example. More important, he bitterly opposed her subsequently becoming Japan's first female director, and their friendship ended as a result of this schism. "Film Actress" is quirky enough to overlook Miss Tanaka's directorial career altogether.

Shot in color, and making no effort to be faithful to the period in which it takes place, "Film Actress" includes scattered documentary segments detailing the early history of Japanese cinema. These passages, from a 73-year-old director who began his own career as an animator in the 1930's, have enormous resonance. There are glimpses of silent films, early talkies, even a Western-style musical in color; there are excerpts from what a narrator calls the "nihilistic dramas of the 1920's" ("Why are humans mortal?" a character in one such film wants to know. "I wish I could live forever. Even after I die I'll be your wife").

These montages are brief but mesmerizing, and the film also includes discussion of Western influences on Japanese film makers, with excited references to Griffith's "Broken Blossoms" and Chaplin's "Woman of Paris."

The dialogue (the screenplay is by Kaneto Shindo, who wrote a novel about Kinuyo Tanaka, along with Shinya Hidaka and Mr. Ichikawa) can sometimes be expository and stiff ("Ozu, I hear you'll be a director," someone says at one such moment). And the film's pace is determinedly slow. Still, "Film Actress" is fascinating in its ambition and its enthusiasm. And Miss Yoshinaga's shy yet steely performance is a quiet tribute to the woman she plays.

1988 O 28, C8:5

Life-Giving Disgrace

Shima Iwashita

GONZA THE SPEARMAN, directed by Masahiro Shinoda; screenplay (Japanese with English subtitles) by Taeko Tomioka, from a play by Monzaemon Chikamatsu; photography by Kazuo Miyagawa; edited by Sachiko Yamachi; music by Toru Takemitsu; produced by Kiyoshi Iwashita, Tomiyuki Motomichi and Masatake Wakita; a Shochiko Hyogensha production. At the Public, 425 Lafayette Street. Running time: 121 minutes. This film has no rating.

Gonza Sasano	Hiromi Goh
Osai	Shima Iwashita
Bannojo Kawazura	Shohej Hino
Oyuki	Misako Tanaka
Oyuki's Governess	Haruko Kato
Ichinoshin Asaka	Takashi Tsumura
Okiku	Kaori Mizushima

By WALTER GOODMAN

Don't be put off by the title. "Gonza the Spearman" is not an Eastern western. Masahiro Shinoda's stately work, which opens the Public Theater's Autumn in Japan series today, has few duels and only a gout or two of blood. Instead, it is filled with historical imagination, social comment and restrained passion, along with scene after elegantly composed scene of a culture that seems to have been paralyzed in a spare beauty.

The story, based on an 18th-century play by Monzaemon Chikamatsu, is set in the 17th century, during the Tokugawa shogunate. Peace reigns, and an ambitious samurai like young, handsome Gonza can find no employment for his martial arts. Getting ahead now requires mastery of the elaborate tea ceremony, handed down in privileged families from parent to child. In quest of its mysteries, Gonza finds himself in a late-night meeting with the appealing Osai, wife of his absent lord, Ichinoshin. They are discovered by a rival of Gonza and must flee.

For a modern audience, the tranquil, unchanging tea ceremony, rendered here in all its delicate refinement, seems purposefully devoid of content. In its show of deference by youth to age, women to men, subordinate to superior, it expresses in a pure form the society's ideal structure. The charge of adultery against Gonza and Osai, although false, endangers that structure and so they must be hunted down.

•

In his direction, Mr. Shinoda adopts the pace of the tea ceremony itself; the action is controlled, every movement carefully ordered. The pace can be slow, and in a rare slip, Mr. Shinoda stays too long with the grief of Osai's parents and children at her flight, until the scene verges on the maudlin. Even when the story seems to be stretched out, however, the visual rewards keep coming, as Kazuo Miyagawa's camera finds the beauty in stone walls, sliding panels, simple gardens, rich gowns, women's faces. When the action resumes, the strangely powerful music of Toru Takemitsu keeps us on edge.

Once Gonza, played as a callow swashbuckler by Hiromi Goh, meets Osai, in a true and lovely portrayal by Shima Iwashita, she becomes the tale's central figure. Bored with her ritualized life, loyal to her humane husband and concerned for his reputation, lusting for the unsophisticated Gonza yet trained to keep such feelings to herself, she is the catalyst of tragedy.

When, with death a near certainty, she tells Gonza, "I love running away with you," it is a revelation to both of them. For their brief time together, the pair achieve an honesty that was entirely suppressed in their sterile court existences. "We've come so far," she says. They catch the breath of life in time to die.

The philosophic Ichinoshin, bound by rules that he recognizes as cruel and senseless, seems a bridge between centuries. "What a world we live in," he sighs as he sets forth to murder the mother of his children. Osai's final words to her lord, who has just killed her lover, "I have missed you, my husband," is rich in ambiguities yet moving in the most basic way. Back at court, the tea ceremony goes on.

1988 O 28, C15:1

Man With a Mission

ART BLAKEY: THE JAZZ MESSENGER, directed by Dick Fontaine and Pat Hartley. Released by Rhapsody Films. At Film Forum 2, 57 Watts Street. Running time: 78 minutes. This film has no rating.

WITH: Art Blakey, the Jazz Messengers, the Jazz Warriors and others.

By JON PARELES

"The bandstand is the only place I got to go in this world," says the drummer Art Blakey. "If I don't get there, I'm dead." He's giving a new band of Jazz Messengers a pep talk, alternately fatherly and hard-nosed, in one of the most telling sequences of "Art Blakey: The Jazz Messenger," a documentary that has its New York premiere tonight and tomorrow at Film Forum 2 as part of its Jazz Film Festival.

From behind his drums, Mr. Blakey runs an elite jazz school, recruiting promising young musicians as Jazz Messengers and pushing them hard every time they step on a bandstand. He has honed young musicians, from Clifford Brown to Wynton Marsalis, in a career that now extends more than 50 years. The documentary presents Mr. Blakey working with an expanded band in London, then back in New York checking out possible Messengers at Sweet Basil in Greenwich Village and introducing a new group at Mikell's on the Upper West Side. It also·shows musicians who worked with Mr. Blakey during the past six decades explaining his galvanizing effect; the trumpeter Dizzy Gillespie calls him "the volcano." Mr. Blakey himself talks about his self-imposed mission to perpetuate jazz for the next generation. And sooner or later, none of his associates can resist imitating his gravelly voice.

The documentary's ratio of talk to music is rather high; none of the pieces are heard uninterrupted. Instead, there's always one more testimonial or anecdote, even atop rare archival footage of Mr. Blakey with the Billy Eckstine Band at the dawn of be-bop. To confuse matters, musicians and commentators aren't identified until the end of the film. Still, Mr. Blakey's indomitable energy comes through, on and off the bandstand.

On the program with "Art Blakey: The Jazz Messenger" are shorts by its director, Dick Fontaine, including the first New York showing of a 1967 short, "Who Is Sonny Rollins," a fascinating portrait of Mr. Rollins at a time when the great tenor saxophonist had withdrawn from club performances. He plays, instead, with students in Harlem, in the countryside, and on the Williamsburg Bridge to the accompaniment of passing subway trains, his melodic sense as probing and bluesy as ever.

1988 O 28, C16:4

Sex, Murder And Insurance

INTO THE FIRE, directed by Graeme Campbell; written by Jesse Ballard; director of photography, Rhett Morita; edited by Harvey Zlatarits and Marvin Lawrence; music by Andy Thompson; produced by Nicolas Stiliadis; released by Moviestore Entertainment. At Cine 1, Seventh Avenue at 48th Street, and other theaters. Running time: 90 minutes. This film is rated R.

Dirk Winfield	Art Hindle
Liette	Olivia D'Abo
Wade Burnett	Lee Montgomery
Rosalind Winfield	Susan Anspach

By CARYN JAMES

"I saw Jimmy," says Wade, the cute young handyman at snowy Wolf Lodge. "He's in the lake. He's frozen and dead." Yes, he's frozen *and* dead, says the none-too-bright Wade, with all the excitement of someone who has just found his misplaced car keys instead of the previous cute young handyman. "Into the Fire" tries to heat up "The Postman Always Rings Twice" — a truly perverse idea — with quadruple plot twists about who's murdering whom for the insurance money. It adds bloody deaths and prophetic nightmares, so that everything seems too blunt, almost baroque, except for the listless acting.

The story begins when Wade and Jackson, a rock musician and his dog, stop at a diner off a rural road. Before long Wade finds himself caught between two women — both blond, both sexually starved, both attached to hideous dialogue. The young waitress at the diner ("Did you know I was cheerleader and prom queen?" she says, showing him her yearbook) entices him to stay around and work at the lodge for the sadistic-looking Dirk Winfield and his wife, Rosalind. Mrs. Winfield is played by Susan Anspach, who was good in "Five Easy Pieces" and who spends some time here without a blouse and with some nasty bruises on her face. She comes to like Wade and eventually tells him, "I'll meet you in Rio when the insurance company pays off."

"Into the Fire," which opened yesterday at the Cine 1 and other theaters, is heavy on sound effects — every door creaks, every footstep crunches in the snow, and when Mrs. Winfield gulps down a whisky you need earplugs. It never misses a chance to let a character drool blood. What it does not have is any good excuse for being here.

1988 O 29, 18:5

Trainer as Terrorist

FEDS, directed by Dan Goldberg; written by Len Blum and Mr. Goldberg; director of photography, Timothy Suhrstedt; edited by Don Cambern; music by Randy Edelman; produced by Len Blum and Ilona Herzberg; an Ivan Reitman production; released by Warner Brothers. At the Criterion Center, Broadway at 45th Street; the Gemini Twin, Second Avenue at 64th Street, and other theaters. Running time: 83 minutes. This film is rated PG-13.

Ellie DeWitt	Rebecca De Mornay
Janis Zuckerman	Mary Gross
Brent Sheppard	Kenneth Marshall
Howard Butz	Larry Cedar
Sperry	James Luisi
Hupperman	Raymond Singer
Bill Bilecki	Fred Dalton Thompson

By JANET MASLIN

"Feds," a comedy starring Mary Gross and Rebecca De Mornay as two F.B.I. agents in training opened yesterday at the Criterion Center and other theaters. The Criterion was not the best place to see it, however.

The theater advertised a 12:40 P.M. show but patrons arriving at that time found the film had already begun. Very little seemed to have happened. Miss Gross and Miss De Mornay were seen going shopping together, sitting through classes, fraternizing with fellow students and mastering such tactics as wielding guns, slapping on handcuffs and kneeing antagonists in the groin. Then, at 1:25, the film ended.

The audience marched down to the lobby, where it was told that the projectionist had misread his schedule and had started the film 40 minutes early. The next show would not be until 2:30. A ticket taker assured irate patrons that if they went back upstairs, the film would begin again at 1:30. By 1:45, it was clear this was not to be. The audience returned to the lobby, where a manager appeared and declared there would be no show before 2:30 after all.

•

At 1:50, it was suggested that the projectionist show the first half hour of the film, then rewind it for the 2:30 show. He said that this was impossible. Refunds appeared to be the only solution. By 2 the patrons had formed a long line and were beginning to receive their money back. At that point, I left.

The film itself seemed amiably innocuous, no more or less gripping than the average training manual. Miss Gross and Miss De Mornay appeared to have a friendly rapport. Miss Gross in particular sounded mildly funny as she told offenders they were under arrest in that high, wispy voice of hers. Fred Dalton Thompson was also good as the students' gruff, laconic instructor, at one point summoning them in the middle of the night for a training exercise in which he would play a terrorist, take a hostage and be hunted down by teams of students. Not until 1:24 or so, when the chase concluded, was it evident that this was meant to be the film's exciting climactic episode.

"Feds" will no doubt be available on video cassette very soon.

•

"Feds" is rated PG-13 ("Special Parental Guidance Suggested for Those Younger Than 13"). This rating is at least partly attributable to suggestive remarks Miss Gross's character makes to a sailor.

1988 O 29, 18:5

ABOUT THE ARTS/John Gross

'Little Dorrit': Fine Performances, Vivid Faces — Gaunt Cheek by Comfortable Jowl

THE NEW FILM OF "LITtle Dorrit," written and directed by Christine Edzard, must be the most ambitious movie adaptation of a Dickens novel ever made, and, setting aside David Lean's superlative 1946 version of "Great Expectations," the most successful. Moreover, in "Great Expectations" David Lean was working with a relatively compact story, while "Little Dorrit" is a great urban sprawl of book, Dickens at his most profuse.

Faced with the problem of bringing this superabundance of material under control, Miss Edzard's solution has been to divide the story into two sections — each running for three hours — and to regroup the major episodes accordingly. Part 1 is called "Nobody's Fault," which is the title Dickens originally planned to give the novel; Part 2 is called "Little Dorrit's Story."

"Nobody's Fault" centers on Arthur Clennam, who returns to London after 20 years in China — in the first instance, to the dark family home presided over by his harsh, sternly religious mother. Intrigued by the seamstress who works for her, a diminutive young woman called Amy Dorrit, he gets to know her and her family. They have been inmates of the Marshalsea debtors' prison for many years: Amy's father, William Dorrit, is the patriarch of the place, and Amy herself was born there.

Clennam tries to help them as best he can. Then they unexpectedly come into a fortune, and leave the jail for a life of foreign travel and high society — while Clennam, after a business failure, ends up in the Marshalsea himself.

In "Little Dorrit's Story" we retrace the same events through Amy's eyes. We also learn about her early life, and follow her and her family abroad to Italy and back to London in their new post-Marshalsea prosperity.

In particular, we see them entering the opulent world of Merdle, a fraudulent company promoter whose eventual crash drags down thousands of investors with him (Clennam among them). It is only then that Amy and Clennam are united, never again — once Clennam has left the Marshalsea — to be separated.

Susan Tanner as Little Dorrit as a child and Alec Guinness as her father, the selfish, pathetic William

The movie built around these twin narratives is fluent, intelligent and atmospheric. It abounds in pungent performances and memorable faces — gaunt cheek by comfortable jowl; it moves with equal conviction from the jostling streets to the silent gloom of the Clennam house, from the ramshackle poverty of Bleeding Heart Yard to the smooth corridors of the Circumlocution Office. The sounds of the drama are haunting, too, as haunting as the images: above all the restless noises that echo through the Marshalsea.

If you haven't read "Little Dorrit," you may well find that the film makes you want to; and if you do, you will find that for the most part the film is commendably true to the spirit in which Dickens wrote. In one respect, indeed — the depiction of the two central characters — it represents a distinct improvement.

In the novel, where she isn't a blur, Amy Dorrit comes close to being an embarrassment, a stunted Dickensian child-wife of uncertain sexual status. And though the characterization of Arthur Clennam is more successful, he is only half brought to life. It is as though his heavy spirits infected the way Dickens drew him.

In the film, by contrast, both characters are fully realized. Derek Jacobi endows Clennam with the presence that Dickens was only half able to supply; Amy, as played by Sarah Pickering, has the selflessness and sweetness of temper that the novelist was aiming for, without the sentimental haze in which he enveloped her.

A convincing Clennam and Amy are essential to the two-part structure that Christine Edzard has imposed on the story. They provide a unifying principle, each in turn; they lend credibility to the central contrast between the oppression and frustration of Part 1 and the redemption of Part 2.

It says something about the peculiar nature of Dickens's genius that they don't have the same degree of importance in the novel, that their inadequacies don't prevent the book from being a major masterpiece. For many readers it may seem to confirm the view that construction was his weakest point, that his work typically consists, as George Orwell put it, of "rotten architecture and wonderful gargoyles."

But it would be truer to say that there are two kinds of structure in a Dickens novel. There is the plot, often melodramatic and far-fetched; and there is what you might call the poetic structure — a dense network of images and motifs, often linked by the finest verbal filaments, and an underlying narrative rhythm.

In Miss Edzard's rearrangement of "Little Dorrit," some of this rhythm has undoubtedly been disrupted. The Merdles, for example — the financier and his wife — make their first appearance little more than a quarter of the way into the book; and the Merdles represent Dickens at the height of his powers. In the movie, however, Miss Edzard's scheme insures that we don't encounter them until Part 2 — which is one reason why Part 1 starts to drag.

Conversely, there is the public unmasking of Casby, the landlord of Bleeding Heart Yard: a silky-haired, hard-hearted humbug who eventually has his locks sheared and his impostures denounced by Mr. Pancks, his rent collector. This occurs far too early in the film. There isn't time for the requisite build-up, and the contrast between Casby and Pancks gets blunted.

As for the verbal energy of the book, the film can't hope to match it, by its very nature. You can show Merdle looking preoccupied (he is contemplating suicide); you can't show him looking down into his hat "as if it were some 20 feet deep." You can show Pancks bustling about, but you can't show him bustling about "like a little coaly tugboat."

Still, all this simply means that the film must be judged on its own terms; and though it has its slow patches and its occasional lapses, they don't seriously detract from a remarkable achievement.

Who could have foretold, for example, than any film maker would have done as well as Miss Edzard does with the potentially B-movie scenes in Mrs. Clennam's house? The glimmering dark brown interiors take on an almost Rembrandtesque quality; the late Joan Greenwood invests Mrs. Clennam herself with extraordinary power.

Then there is Alec Guinness, whose career stretches back to "Great Expectations" and to the controversial 1948 movie of "Oliver Twist." He has rarely given a more finely judged performance than he does as selfish, pathetic William Dorrit, cadging his "testimonials" from new arrivals in the Marshalsea, reverting to his Marshalsea self (but has he ever escaped from it?) in the unforgettable scene where he breaks down at a Merdle banquet.

But it isn't a question of one or two star performers. Even the least of the characters on screen is apt to have his or her sudden piercing moment; and it is here, in its overflowing detail, and its eye for the rejected and disregarded, that the film is at its most truly Dickensian. □

1988 O 30, II:22:1

FILM VIEW/Janet Maslin

Oscar, Just an Old Softy

ANYONE WHO SEES SHIRLEY MacLaine in "Madame Sousatzka" is sure to feel sorry for her, because Ms. MacLaine looks a fright. Heavy makeup accentuates every line in her face, and the age spots on her hands look conspicuous and real. She walks with a slight limp, weighed down by clattering jewelry, and her costumes give her a thick, ungainly silhouette. However, there's a limit to the sympathy this ought to generate, because next spring Ms. MacLaine is liable to be laughing all the way to the Academy Awards.

In fact, this is exactly the sort of performance that wins prizes, and not only Oscars at that; many a Golden Palm or a Silver Bear has been awarded by a jury swayed by similar considerations. Ms. MacLaine has reached the stage at which lifetime achievements begin to be recognized, and although she is a recent Academy Award winner (for "Terms of Endearment"), she has been a bridesmaid with enough frequency (nominations for "Some Came Running," "The Apartment," "The Turning Point" and "Irma La Douce") to remain eligible for another win.

And her showy, external role in "Madame Sousatzka" is designed to be remembered. Disguising one's appearance is a superficial but foolproof way of indicating a major personality change, and the elaborate means by which Ms. MacLaine transforms herself into an aging, imperious piano teacher is itself a sizable achievement. What's more, the character isn't far from home. The formidable, caustic, defiantly eccentric Madame Sousatzka is recognizable as an extension of the actress's own personality, which underscores the rightness of this role.

There's another thing that makes the performance award-worthy, but within this scheme of things it's relatively minor: the fact that it's actually quite good. However, since Madame Sousatzka needn't seem genuine, undergo real change or even have much inner life to be entertaining, the actress need not do many of the things normally associated with great acting to make a great impression. Awards do acknowledge superb work from time to time, but they have much more to do with luck, sentiment and being in the right place and the right time.

■

What Whoopi Goldberg does in "Clara's Heart" is at least as prize-worthy, if measured by the same criteria, but Ms. Goldberg's luck may not be as strong. "Clara's Heart," though every bit as quaint as "Madame Sousatzka," doesn't provide as effective a backdrop for its star. Unlike Ms. MacLaine, who is surrounded by a colorful group of supporting players to hide the fact that the film has no real story, Ms. Goldberg, playing a similarly heart-warming and attention-getting figure, is largely on her own.

As the motherly, omniscient, good-as-gold Jamaican housekeeper of the title, dispensing the kind of aphorisms that ought to make this a dream role, Ms. Goldberg unfortunately operates in a vacuum. Though Neil Patrick Harris does a good job as the boy whom Clara raises, the adults in the film are too wan to hold their own in any conver-

Shirley MacLaine and Navin Chowdhry in "Madame Sousatzka"

sation with the irrepressible Clara, which leaves Ms. Goldberg sounding overbearing where she ought to sound wise. Still, Ms. Goldberg is warm and funny, and she really does bring this character to life. Her performance might well have emerged as a sentimental favorite if the film itself weren't so thin.

■

Although acting gimmicks have a way of winning prizes, they can also backfire, as may be the case with Jeremy Irons's astonishing pas de deux in "Dead Ringers." If Mr. Irons were a little less good here, the artifice of his performance might be less easily taken for granted (Meryl Streep often has the same problem). As it is, he plays the film's twin brothers so effortlessly that neither his work nor the remarkable technical tricks that make it seamless really stands out. What's more, a film about half-mad, drug-addicted twin gynecologists, no matter how good, is sure to lack something in mass appeal. Though this is easily Mr. Irons's best film work, he will probably go prizeless until a more one-dimensional and likable character comes along.

Either that, or an unexpectedly vicious one; whichever role ("Big" or "Punchline") brings Tom Hanks his Oscar nomination this year, it will be the latter, nastier performance that puts this nice-guy actor over the top. Mr. Hanks in "Big" was a boyish delight as well as a technical marvel, but the manic, bitter energy he brings to the stand-up comic of "Punchline" is sufficiently out of character to look like acting rather than charm.

And the "Punchline" performance has a rough side, which in award-givers' terms often translates as something real. Jodie Foster, another

Whoopi Goldberg in "Clara's Heart"—a quaint role

likely nominee this year, gives a devastating performance in "The Accused," and in terms of awards it helps that the tough-talking rape victim whom she plays has so much grit. Rude, angry and uneducated, she's a clear departure for Ms. Foster, and it helps that much publicity has been focused on the sheer physical arduousness of the role.

Gene Hackman must have experienced his own physical difficulties filming "Bat 21" in the jungles of Malaysia, but Mr. Hackman isn't the sort to let this show. Nor is he awards material by the usual standards (though his "French Connection" character brought him an Oscar). In "Bat 21" and "Another Woman," there's no identifiable quality that makes Mr. Hackman stand out; he simply makes himself outstandingly vital and real. This isn't what wins prizes, but it's something other actors surely understand. □

1988 O 30, II:13:1

4 Films at Once On Holocaust Offer a Dialogue

By CARYN JAMES

Four films about the Holocaust opened in New York almost at once recently, and most filmgoers reacted like Annie Hall. When Woody Allen's character suggests seeing "The Sorrow and the Pity" one more time, Annie replies: "I'm not in the mood for a four-hour documentary about Nazis." Who is ever in the mood for a film about Nazis? The best-intentioned people cannot find the right time to depress themselves. Others roll their eyes as if to say, "We've seen it all before."

All four of those films were artistically fresh and sophisticated; all received extravagant critical praise. But only Marcel Ophuls's "Hotel Terminus: The Life and Times of Klaus Barbie" is still playing, and ticket sales for that documentary, another four-hour-plus event from the director of "The Sorrow and the Pity," are weak.

Without the panache and advance publicity attached to Mr. Ophuls's work, the other films were lucky to open at all.

•

Set in a concentration camp, "The Boxer and Death," is a 1962 Czechoslovak film that had never been shown here; business was awful during its two-week run at Film Forum. "Debajo del Mundo" ("Under the World") sounds all wrong for American audiences — an Argentine film about Polish Jews who hid in an underground tunnel for years. It is, in fact, a powerful, poetic film that did little business in its two weeks at a single New York theater and has not been picked up by any other in the city.

And perhaps the most disturbing of the four, "Faulkenau, the Impossible: Samuel Fuller Bears Witness," was shown at the New York Film Festival. It is a one-hour documentary about the liberation of the Faulkenau death camp in Czechoslovakia, and its length gives it virtually no chance for theatrical release (though it may eventually be shown on television).

But while they were here, viewing these films back-to-back created a kind of dialogue among them, richer than any one alone could have offered. And seen together, they hinted at the way Holocaust films work on their reluctant audiences. It is not only the horror and difficulty of the subject that keeps audiences away. Using shifting points of view, these films force us to be judges, witnesses, voyeurs of horror, intimates of Nazis and of their victims. We are made to share the uneasy visions of the guilty, the innocent and those who cannot tell the difference. It is the direct opposite of movie escapism — what most of us, after all, go to movies for — as we are grabbed by the throat and forced to respond in complicated ways.

Mr. Ophuls's film — the most topical and commercially viable — is also the most rational, the least wrenching. Audiences might expect to leave "Hotel Terminus" feeling emotionally drained; they are more likely to be mentally invigorated. As Mr. Ophuls traces the life of Klaus Barbie from childhood, through his savage treatment of Jews during the war, to his 1987 trial and conviction for crimes against humanity, he constructs an overwhelming pattern of witnesses: a farmer who knew Klaus Barbie as a polite boy; Americans who sit in front of Christmas trees and swimming pools and cooly describe why they employed him after the war; a calm, white-haired woman who speaks with resignation about how Mr. Barbie tortured her and killed her son and husband.

Mr. Ophuls dares his subjects to reveal themselves at their best or worst or most confused. He knows just when to mock a reluctant or lying witness, to relieve the tension of his film. The more than four hours of "Hotel Terminus" zoom by, making it a masterpiece of its type, but its type is judicious and analytical. Mr. Ophuls asks us to sift its relentless flood of evidence, to respond not to history but to memories filtered through time and edited for film. Those memories have the strength to move us, but ultimately we sit in the interviewer's chair with Mr. Ophuls — a relatively safe place to be.

•

Bárbara Múgica, left, Bruno Stagnaro and Gabriel Rovito in "Debajo del Mundo."

Under slightly different circumstances, the true story that became the fictionalized "Debajo del Mundo" might have become a two-minute clip in "Hotel Terminus." The small, emotional drama fills in the details that Mr. Ophuls's subjects can only nod at. The power of "Debajo del Mundo" comes from its intense focus on the day-to-day survival of parents and their four sons hiding underground. We see Nazis and collaborators only when the family is threatened by them. Otherwise, we are as cut off from the course of the war and politics as if we too were living in a tunnel in the woods. Eating and bathing are immediate issues; moral dilemmas are rarely discussed, so the film does not ask us to think very much. Instead, the camera forces us to confront the pain or hunger on the characters' faces and to respond emotionally.

Yet the directors, Beda Docampo Feijoo and Juan Bautista Stagnaro, do not always allow us to share the characters' points of view. Sometimes — when a gunshot above ground tells them a friend has been killed — we come watch them as if we were ghosts hiding in the tunnel. Slightly distanced, we are forced into a more realistic contemporary position — helpless, pained witnesses to the past.

"The Boxer and Death" uses point of view to throw us off balance from the start. The film begins with a boxer working out; only when he exchanges his boxing shorts for an SS uniform do we recoil from the Nazi's perspective that we have unwittingly shared. This film will not allow us to rest easily again, shifting back and forth between Kominek, the Nazi commandant of the camp, and Kraft, a prisoner he saves and puts into training as his sparring partner.

Though Kraft has our sympathy, we must try to understand the personalities of both the Nazi commandant and the prisoner, for we must decide whom to root for in the boxing match that is the film's climax. What we know of the Nazi's character suggests that if Kraft wins the match, he will lose his life. Yet how can we hope he will lose this metaphorical battle with evil, a fight he is desperate to win?

The film is based on a novel by Jozef Hen, and its literary roots show a bit too much in the symbolic weight that is loaded on the boxing match. The metaphor allows some emotional distance, reminds us that though these events might have happened, they are fictional. Yet the film can suddenly turn chilling, in the matter-of-fact way a Nazi soldier shoots an old man who has befriended Kraft. "The Boxer and Death" is disturbing because it shifts so fluidly from the commandant to the prisoner, from metaphor to realism.

The narrative strategy of Emil Weiss's "Faulkenau" drags us into the past and buffets us. The director Samuel Fuller shows a 21-minute film he shot as a young soldier when his regiment liberated a death camp in Faulkenau. Mr. Fuller's comments lead us into his firsthand visual account, where we are surrounded by the inescapable horror of the death camp and disoriented by the shifting points of view.

At Faulkenau, Mr. Fuller says, the captain of the United States regiment

The star of "Faulkenau, the Impossible: Samuel Fuller Bears Witness."

found prominent townspeople who said they knew, heard, smelled nothing from the camp nearby. The captain made these men dress the corpses of the dead. Mr. Fuller's camera shows us emaciated prisoners sitting on a hillside watching the skeletal bodies being clothed for burial. We see close-ups of the bodies being dressed as we share the point of view of the townspeople who pleaded innocence. When these town leaders pull wagons of the dead through the streets to be buried, we seem to be standing with their neighbors watching the procession go by.

When Mr. Weiss asks Mr. Fuller if fiction films can ever represent the Holocaust, Mr. Fuller imagines a ludicrous action movie about a concentration camp. There would be a breakout and a chase, Mr. Fuller says, in terms absolutely true to his own B-movie career and false to the brutal firsthand film we have just seen. In fact, the best answers to Mr. Weiss's question are "Debajo del Mundo" or "The Boxer and Death," fiction films that draw power from their proximity to the historical context of "Faulkenau" or "Hotel Terminus."

Even while describing his glitzy genre piece, though, Mr. Fuller knows how to turn audiences into judges, silent conspirators and victims at once, knows how to direct at them the hideous question, "What would I have done?" Mr. Fuller says: "I would put the audience of the world on trial. I would blame them for letting such a thing happen." And, he adds, though the prisoner in his film might break out: "He never wins. He is the audience, that one man."

1988 N 1, C 17:1

Subliminal Persuasion

THEY LIVE, directed by John Carpenter; screenplay by Frank Armitage (Mr. Carpenter), from the short story "Eight O'Clock in the Morning" by Ray Nelson; director of photography, Gary B. Kibbe; edited by Gib Jaffe and Frank E. Jimenez; music by John Carpenter and Alan Howarth; art directors, William J. Durrell Jr. and Daniel Lomino; produced by Larry Franco; released by Universal Pictures. At Movieland, Broadway at 47th Street, and other theaters. Running time: 115 minutes. This film is rated R.

Nada .... Roddy Piper
Frank .... Keith David
Holly .... Meg Foster
Drifter .... George (Buck) Flower
Gilbert .... Peter Jason
Street Preacher .... Raymond St. Jacques

The idea that alien forces control our media, making subliminal use of billboards, commercials and magazines to subvert our thinking, probably isn't that hard for most of us to believe. So credibility isn't the problem with John Carpenter's "They Live," which opens today at the Movieland and other theaters, but execution is. Mr. Carpenter has directed the film with B-movie bluntness, but with none of the requisite snap. And his screenplay (written under the pseudonym Frank Armitage) makes the principals sound even more tongue-tied than they have to.

B-movie casting is another problem, since the star, Roddy Piper, plays his role like the former wrestler that he is. Mr. Piper appears as John Nada, a generic drifter who finds his way to Los Angeles as the film begins. The best part of "They Live" is its opening, when the story still holds some surprises and the promise that it may catch fire. Nada wanders through Los Angeles, gets a job as a construction worker, and is led by a new buddy named Frank (Keith David) to a shantytown called Justiceville, where he gets his first real inkling that things may not be what they seem.

A street-corner preacher, affiliated with a church next to Justiceville, sounds the first alarm when he warns that "they" are exploiting a sleeping middle class. Later on, when Nada learns that the church is merely a front for a resistance movement, he discovers more. "Our impulses are being redirected," someone warns. "We are living in an artificially induced state of consciousness that resembles sleep."

●

Once Nada stumbles upon a package of special sunglasses, the secret is out. When he wears these glasses, he sees subliminal messages everywhere. "Marry and Reproduce," says a billboard on which a bikini-clad woman pitches vacations in the tropics. "Consume," says a sign advertising a close-out sale. "This Is Your God," says a dollar bill, and on the newsstands magazines put forth slogans like "Honor Apathy" and "Obey."

What's more, the glasses enable Nada to see just who "they" are: the rich and powerful who, through these lenses, become skeleton-faced ghouls with glittering metallic eyes. Even the politician on television who talks of "morning in America" and declares "We don't need pessimism!" is one of "them."

Unfortunately, once this particular cat is out of the bag, the film has nowhere to go. Mr. Piper spends the rest of his time chasing around to no particular purpose, though he does announce with some enthusiasm that the nation needs a wake-up call, which he plans to deliver himself. Mr. David, who is more animated as Nada's ally, teams up with him midway through the film for a noisy attenuated slugfest that seems to have been intended as some sort of comic highlight. It's not.

Since Mr. Carpenter seems to be trying to make a real point here, the flatness of "They Live" is doubly disappointing. So is its crazy inconsistency, since the film stops trying to abide even by its own game plan after a while. Nada and Frank sink beneath the pavement at one point, find themselves in an underground tunnel, follow it to a grand ballroom where aliens and wealthy Earthlings are toasting "the global good life," and from here discover a nearby spaceport from which travelers can shuttle to the alien planet. Even for end-of-the-world fantasy, this is too much.

JANET MASLIN

1988 N 4, C 8:1

Love Amid the Snow And Insect Swarms

RIVER OF FIREFLIES, directed by Eizo Sugawa; screenplay (Japanese with English subtitles) by Kyohei Nakaoka and Mr. Sugawa, from a novel by Teru Miyamoto; photographed by Masahisa Himeda; art director, Iwao Akune; produced by Kiyoshi Fujimoto; distributed by the Shochiku Company. At the Public Theater, 425 Lafayette Street. Running time: 115 minutes. This film has no rating.

Tatsuo .... Takayuki Sakazume
Shigetatsu .... Rentaro Mikuni
Chiyo .... Yukiyo Toake
Eiko .... Tamae Sawada
Harue .... Tomoko Naraoka
Ginzo .... Taiji Tonoyama

By WALTER GOODMAN

When it comes to growing-up-in-the-movies, East and West meet; perhaps they even borrow a little from each another. "River of Fireflies," now at the Public Theater, is a Japanese version of the genre, but the elements will be familiar to moviegoers the world over: a boy's intimations of sex, his loss of childhood friendship and gain of youthful love, his arrival at a more realistic understanding of the weaknesses and strengths of his parents, and the discovery of a new maturity in himself.

The himself here is 14-year-old Tatsuo (Takayuki Sakazume), who lives with his parents in a small city in northern Japan. It is almost spring, the right time of year for Tatsuo to have a crush on pretty Eiko (Tamae Sawada), the most popular girl in school. At home, things are bleak; his father is approaching bankruptcy and does not look at all well.

As for the title, it refers to a tale that Tatsuo once heard from his father — that after a heavy April snowfall, a great swarm of fireflies will appear up in the mountains and any couple who witness their mating will marry. It is snowing and snowing, and Tatsuo can't stop thinking about Eiko and those fireflies.

●

The direction by Eizo Sugawa tends toward the lush. He likes scenic views and fuzzy flashbacks and lays on the Romance music whenever Tatsuo and Eiko meet. He is also given to some pat symbols — a death is noted by the shattering of a mirror. However, he is fortunate in his cast, particularly Rentaro Mikuni as Tatsuo's father, a tough bird whose somewhat dissolute life shows in his ravaged face but who has managed to evoke loyalty in others and who loves his wife and son in his fashion.

The plot is episodic and at times a little odd, as when the father, whom we know as a hard-drinking businessman, acts as sex counselor to a couple who could not wait for the wedding

Savior
Roddy Piper stars in "They Live," about creatures from another world who unleash a force to control the human race.

ceremony. Some of Tatsuo's mild adventures, like his fights with a nasty rival, are standard growing-up fare, but there are fresher scenes, too; the reappearance of the father's first wife is especially touching.

One of the characters observes, "The winter is very long this year." So it seems, as we await the big firefly get-together and the opportunity for Mr. Sugawa to indulge his penchant for mystical effects. When last seen, Tatsuo and Eiko appear to be dissolving among the colorfully mating bugs. Well, that's what growing up is all about.

1988 N 4, C 13:1

Parent, Child And Friend

Diane Keaton

THE GOOD MOTHER, directed by Leonard Nimoy; screenplay by Michael Bortman, based on the novel by Sue Miller; director of photography, David Watkin; film editor, Peter Berger; music by Elmer Bernstein; production designer, Stan Jolley; produced by Arnold Glimcher; released by Touchstone Pictures. At Embassy 1, Broadway and 46th Street, and other theaters. Running time: 104 minutes. This film is rated R.

Anna	Diane Keaton
Leo	Liam Neeson
Muth	Jason Robards
Grandfather	Ralph Bellamy
Grandmother	Teresa Wright
Brian	James Naughton
Molly	Asia Vieira
Frank Williams	Joe Morton
Ursula	Katey Sagal

By JANET MASLIN

The heroine of "The Good Mother" is a flighty, interestingly dressed woman with a scatterbrained manner all her own. She is instantly recognizable as Diane Keaton, though not as Anna Dunlap, the heroine of Sue Miller's phenomenally assured, morally troubling and meticulously precise first novel.

Anna Dunlap is impoverished, recently divorced and completely devoted to the care of her young daughter. It has never occurred to her that her dedication to the child might be called into question. But Miss Miller describes what happens once Anna falls under the spell of a passion strong enough to rival her love for the little girl, when she becomes involved in the first deeply intoxicating sexual relationship of her life. Mesmerized by the new man with whom she has begun an affair, Anna takes leave of her usual caution just long enough to risk losing her daughter forever.

The two essential aspects of this character are her motherly warmth and her capacity for liberating, judgment-clouding abandon. Without these things, "The Good Mother" cannot begin to make much sense on the screen. But the film version, which opens today at the Embassy 1 and other theaters, makes it immediately clear that its aspirations are

very different from those of the novel. Opening with a long, listless passage describing Anna's girlhood vacations with her family in Maine, the film is as self-consciously literary as the book is swift, cinematic and clean.

•

It's not hard to fathom the Hollywood logic whereby Leonard Nimoy, the director of a hit film involving an infant ("Three Men and a Baby"), was designated the man for this particular job. And Mr. Nimoy has dealt with "The Good Mother" in a serious and reasonable way, but still his film is almost entirely devoid of feeling. Even in that early childhood sequence, with Miss Keaton's voice on the soundtrack saying "I *wanted* to be a passionate person," it's clear that some fundamental element of emotion is missing. The little girl playing the young Anna stares blankly ahead of her as this line is read.

When the film moves to the present, to the apartment in Cambridge, Mass., where Anna sets up housekeeping with her daughter, Molly (Asia Vieira), it takes on a different sort of unreality. Miss Keaton and Miss Vieira seem to be exactly what they are, a friendly star and a child actress romping playfully for the benefit of the camera. Never do they suggest a real mother and child, especially not in moments like the one that has Miss Vieira spilling a glass of milk and Miss Keaton finding this an occasion for merry laughter. The film captures none of the day-to-day friction, none of the rituals, none of the small intimacies that would shape a real mother-child relationship.

Molly is given relatively little screen time, so it's not surprising that she never emerges as a strong character; Anna's lover Leo (Liam Neeson), on the other hand, is a powerful presence throughout most of the film. And Mr. Neeson, giving a breakthrough performance here, makes Leo extremely appealing, a charming, sexy and iconoclastic figure whose presence is more than enough to account for the changes he sets off in Anna. Still, Miss Keaton appears to be straining at this stage of the story, and there is only a limited rapport between these two adult principals on screen. So there is no feeling for the uninhibited domestic arrangement that springs up between them as a tribute to Anna's newly awakened sexuality. As a result, the film offers little preparation for the event that threatens Anna and Molly's life together.

•

As is revealed midway through the story, after Anna's ex-husband (James Naughton) has filed charges against her, Leo has allowed the sexually curious Molly to touch his genitals; he did this, in part, because he imagined it was what Anna would have wanted. The film does not depict this incident, and it describes it in terms somewhat more innocent than those of Miss Miller's novel, yet these are not the reasons it seems to lack importance. The episode and its courtroom aftermath feel empty because the film has not convincingly suggested that there's very much at stake.

Though "The Good Mother" improves when it graduates from Anna's emotional awakening to her courtroom defiance (Jason Robards and Joe Morton do well as the two lawyers), by this point the damage has been done. Miss Keaton has spent too much of the film in a relative vac-

uum, seldom making the all-important connections with her co-stars. The scenes that show her working in a medical laboratory make a joke of her trying to talk to a young colleague who wears a radio with headphones and cannot hear her; ignored by him, Miss Keaton's Anna keeps rattling on anyhow. However, her manner with those who are actively listening to her isn't so very different from this, and it frequently upstages the importance of what is being said.

•

"The Good Mother" begins and ends with glimpses of Anna Dunlap's family in Maine, pretty scenes that may suggest some poetic continuity but have little real bearing upon the drama at hand. (Though the family is made to seem absurdly jaunty, it does feature Ralph Bellamy and Teresa Wright as the grandparents whose attitudes help to account for Anna's behavior.) These scenes, which like much of the film are accompanied by easy-listening musical accents, are no doubt meant to place the Cambridge events in perspective, but they don't do this at all. For all its potential to challenge and disturb, "The Good Mother" is finally no more wrenching than a placid Maine landscape on a summer day.

1988 N 4, C15:1

Wide Awake In America

U2: RATTLE AND HUM, directed and edited by Phil Joanou; directors of photography, Robert Brinkmann and Jordan Cronenweth; music produced by Jimmy Iovine; produced by Michael Hamlyn; released by Paramount Pictures. At Loews Astor Plaza, 44th Street west of Broadway, and other theaters. Running time: 99 minutes. This film is rated PG-13.

With: U2.

As a whole new generation of film makers cuts its teeth on rock video, the hardest thing about filming concert documentaries may be insuring that they don't look better than they should. Flashy, high-style concert footage is by now rock's most numbing cliché, and it has a way of destroying any grit or authenticity that exists in the music itself.

Luckily, this isn't much of a liability for "U2: Rattle and Hum," even though its director, Phil Joanou, made an earlier feature ("Three O'Clock High") that invested a schoolyard fight between a nice kid and a bully with the visual importance of a moon launch. This time, Mr. Joanou devises a sinuous black-and-white style that superbly showcases the simplicity and directness of

the group's performing style, and he has the good sense to stay with it.

The temptation to make the film showier is apparent here and there, especially when it bursts into color to capture the excitement of a big U2 stadium appearance. Instead of heightening the film's energy, this episode nearly dispels the remarkable intimacy that Mr. Joanou's gliding black-and-white footage has been able to establish. Indeed, the best parts of "U2: Rattle and Hum," which opens today at Loews Astor Plaza and other theaters, underscore the difference between concert effects designed to please fans at a great distance and cinematic effects that work at very close range. U2 is one of those rare bands capable of casting their full spell on either scale.

If anything, the camera might have lingered longer in close-up on the musicians as they play, since they are at their best when the camera's intensity matches their own. U2's concert performances here, filmed during their American tour last year, are for the most part thrilling, all the more so for the complete absence of posturing in the band's on-stage manner. Instead of acting out the songs that he performs, the singer Bono makes himself a supple, unself-conscious extension of the music itself, and the film captures this beautifully. The band's musicianship also remains astonishingly tight and focused, even in stadium surroundings.

The film captures much more of U2's personality onstage than it does elsewhere, though it includes a number of extracurricular vignettes. The best of these send the band members to Harlem, where they record a spine-tingling version of "I Still Haven't Found What I'm Looking For" with a gospel choir; another sends them to Sun Studios in Memphis to record several songs beneath the likeness of Elvis Presley. The film is on shakier ground when it sends the musicians, like so many tourists, on a visit to Elvis Presley's Graceland, or even when Mr. Joanou sits the musicians down and attempts to ask them questions. U2's music speaks much better than this for itself.

•

"U2: Rattle and Hum" is rated PG-13 ("Special Parental Guidance Suggested for Those Younger Than 13"). It contains mild obscenities, none of which will strike even the youngest rock fans as new.

JANET MASLIN

1988 N 4, C16:1

On the Road
Members of the popular Irish rock band U2 are the focus of the documentary "U2 Rattle and Hum," directed by Phil Joanu.

Colm Henry

Over the Years
Jessica Lange, as a
campus queen, and
Dennis Quaid,
as a football hero, are
followed from the mid-
1950's to the early 80's
in "Everybody's
All-American."

After the Cheers

EVERYBODY'S ALL-AMERICAN, directed by
Taylor Hackford; screenplay by Tom Rickman, from the novel by Frank Deford; director of photography, Stephen Goldblatt; edited
by Don Zimmerman; music by James Newton Howard; production designer, Joe Alves;
produced by Mr. Hackford, Laura Ziskin and
Ian Sander; released by Warner Brothers. At
National Twin, Broadway at 44th Street, and
other theaters. Running time: 122 minutes.
This film is rated R.

Gavin Grey	Dennis Quaid
Babs Rogers	Jessica Lange
Donnie (Cake)	Timothy Hutton
Edward Lawrence	John Goodman
Bolling Kiely	Raymond Baker
Darlene Kiely	Savannah Boucher
Narvel Blue	Carl Lumbly
Leslie	Patricia Clarkson

By JANET MASLIN

Bards from A. E. Housman to
Bruce Springsteen have mourned the
passing of the athlete's glory, but it's
a subject that never goes out of style.
And it has been brought vibrantly to
life in Taylor Hackford's "Everybody's All-American," a film that
matches this director's "Officer and
a Gentleman" in the sharpness of its
sense of place, the sureness of its
storytelling momentum and the larger-than-life performances of its stars.

"Everybody's All-American" is as
resolutely conventional as its characters, but Mr. Hackford turns that into
an old-fashioned virtue. He tells this
story (from a novel by Frank Deford)
in predictably poignant terms, following a Louisiana football hero named
Gavin Grey (Dennis Quaid) as he descends from the top of the heap and
gradually, over the course of 25
years, finds himself over the hill. Con-
currently, the film charts the evolution of Babs Rogers (Jessica Lange),
the voluptuous Magnolia Queen
whose sole ambition, as the film begins, is to become Mrs. Gavin Grey.
"Everybody's All-American" is,
among other things, a bittersweet
warning about the perils of seeing
such wishes come true.

The film spans the period from 1956
to 1981, and during that time everything about it seems to change
(Theadora Van Runkel's costume design, which carries Miss Lange from
clouds of tulle and taffeta to nearly
businesslike clothing, is especially
helpful in effecting this transformation). The one visual constant is
Gavin's flat-top haircut, first seen
above a young, trim face brimming
with exultation and promise. Years
later, beneath that same haircut,
Gavin has become a bloated and
bewildered memory of his former
self, still embarrassingly eager to recite blow-by-blow accounts of his 1956
gridiron season. His college nickname, "The Gray Ghost," has come
to seem all too prophetic by now.

Meanwhile, Babs has blossomed.
Once the quintessential Southern
belle ("I'm majorin' in Gavin and
me," she simpers sweetly to Gavin's
adoring nephew, who is nicknamed
Cake and played by Timothy Hutton),
and a radiant vision of acquiescent
femininity, she settles happily into
the role of beautiful bride. But Babs is
more prescient about her husband's
waning fortunes than he is, and she
steers him into a business career long
before he recognizes this as a necessity. Early in the film, at the peak of his
fame, Gavin denounces a car salesman who seeks his endorsement as
"common." Many years and one
huge financial failure later, he and
Babs are the angry, dissatisfied employees of this same man. Still, Babs
finds beneath her Dixie sweetness the
kind of grit that's needed to reverse
her family's fortunes.

"Everybody's All-American" has a
surprisingly small cast, in view of its
ambition to describe a transitional
period in the life of the American
South. The characters are effective
on their own, yet they work as stereotypes too. Narvel Blue (Carl Lum-
bly), the talented though relatively
uncelebrated black athlete who is a
match for Gavin on the playing field,
becomes a leader of the local civil
rights movement and, eventually, a
pillar of the community. Meanwhile,
Gavin's beefy, big-hearted crony
Lawrence (John Goodman) shows
traces of the racism and corruption
that reflect outmoded Southern attitudes at their most self-destructive.
And Cake, who becomes a professor
of history at a Northern university,
emerges as the one character with
any sense of perspective. The film is
careful not to overstress the symbolic
value of any of this, and so on the simple storytelling level, it works.

Miss Lange gives such a stellar
performance, and also such a technically adroit one, that she emerges in
an entirely new light. At the beginning of the film, projecting a breathless sexual receptiveness that recalls
Marilyn Monroe's, she resembles
something made of spun sugar; later
on, as disappointment sets in, she becomes less of a confection and more
of a touchingly authentic character,
clearly able to turn that erotic magnetism off and on at will. Miss Lange
weathers Babs's many changes
glamorously and without apparent effort.

•

Mr. Quaid is equally good as a man
who's fearful of any change at all. He
too makes a quantum leap here, establishing himself for the first time
as an actor of real weight and muta-
bility. Gavin's pain and disbelief, so
eloquently rendered by Mr. Quaid,
take on genuinely tragic overtones as
the film progresses. Mr. Hutton's role

consists largely of waiting in the
wings, but he manages to do this in an
astute and sympathetic way, always
suggesting the disillusionment that
becomes an essential part of Cake's
affection for his uncle. He also brings
to Cake's periodic encounters with
Babs a distinct sweetness and inevi-
tability.

"Everybody's All-American,"
which opens today at the National
and other theaters, insists on an upbeat Hollywood ending that seems uncharacteristically facile; the rest of it
is much more affecting and genuine
than that. If it's a soap opera, it's a
soap opera in the best sense, a film
about ordinary but inevitable sentiments any viewer will recognize and
understand. If unexpected degrees of
intelligence, perspective and talent
have been brought to bear upon such
a story, so much the better.

1988 N 4, C17:1

A Horse And a Family

FAR NORTH, directed by Sam Shepard;
screenplay by Mr. Shepard; director of
photography, Robbie Greenberg; edited by
Bill Yahraus; music by the Red Clay Ramblers; production designer, Peter Jamison;
produced by Carolyn Pfeiffer and Malcolm R.
Harding; released by Alive Films. At the Festival, 6 West 57th Street. Running time: 90
minutes. This film is rated PG-13.

Kate	Jessica Lange
Bertrum	Charles Durning
Rita	Tess Harper
Uncle Dane	Donald Moffat
Amy	Ann Wedgeworth
Jilly	Patricia Arquette

By JANET MASLIN

"Far North," the first film directed
by the playwright, actor and screenwriter Sam Shepard, begins with footage of a runaway horse and wagon.
By the time the camera has finished
vacillating between the horse's flying
hooves, muscular flank and impassive eye, with a shot or two of wagon
wheels for good measure, it's clear
that the beast itself isn't the only
thing out of control here.

In "Far North," Mr. Shepard shows
himself capable of making great as-
sociative leaps with the camera from
time to time, but the incidental passages are more awkward, shapeless
and uncertain. There is less sense of
what the muted, oblique "Far North"
actually is than of what it might have
been.

It doesn't help that the above-mentioned horse, Mel, happens to have
the film's best role. As some sort of
symbol of rogue masculinity, he gallops across the screen with considerably more abandon than any of the
human actors is able to achieve,
though not for lack of trying. Charles
Durning and Jessica Lange, as the father and daughter locked in a comic
and furious battle over the fate of
Mel, both work hard at breathing life
into the stubborn family conflicts that
are at the heart of Mr. Shepard's
screenplay. When Kate (Ms. Lange),
who has moved to the city, returns to
her family's home in the desolate
northern reaches of the rural Midwest, she finds herself sharply reminded of just why she left in the first
place.

•

Mr. Durning, as Kate's profoundly
intractable father, Bertrum, has
something special in mind for Kate
when she comes to visit; having
landed in the hospital after his buck-

Family Feud Jessica Lange plays
a daughter in conflict with her father
in "Far North," written and
directed by Sam Shepard.

board mishap with Mel, Bertrum
wants to make sure the horse pays
for this outrage. "He's had a grudge
against me since the day he was
foaled," Bertrum tells Kate, by way
of explaining why he expects her to
shoot Mel for revenge's sake. Across
the hall in the same hospital, as a general indicator of the well-being of
Kate's large family, is another relative, her uncle (Donald Moffat). He
too has horses on his mind, but only
because he watches them racing on
television.

The sexes are carefully separated
in "Far North," which opens today at
the Festival. Bertrum intends high
praise when he tells Kate she's tough
enough to kill the horse and lets her
know where he keeps the shotgun.
Back home, the women of the family
are a dizzier but more tenacious
breed. They span four generations,
from Kate's jubilantly promiscuous
niece, Jilly (Patricia Arquette), to
her comically blunt sister, Rita (Tess
Harper), to Kate and Rita's dreamily
disoriented mother, Amy (Ann
Wedgeworth), to the great-grand-
mother of the family (Nina Draxten),
who is celebrating her hundredth
birthday.

The film ricochets busily among
these various family members, generally striking a note of humorous
confusion but occasionally reaching
for much more, as in the scene that
has the bewildered Amy preparing a
huge breakfast for the large masculine family that doesn't exist anymore; in an act of haunting generosity, the camera pans across the breakfast table and shows these long-ab-
sent male relatives eating heartily,
just as they do in Amy's imagination.
In another sequence that successfully
rises above the ordinary, Mr. Shepard
sets most of the principals loose in a
moonlit forest and lets them wander
in circles until their paths finally and
fatefully cross.

Much of "Far North" is less
weighty than this, though it never re-
laxes enough to become as fanciful as
it apparently means to be. Mel the
horse, in addition to serving as the
fulcrum of the screenplay, is one of
the few things in "Far North" more
at home on the screen than on the
stage.

1988 N 9, C18:5

Arthur Penn leading a class for playwrights and directors in a scene from the film "Hello Actors Studio."

Lights, Camera, Did Dad Love Mom?

HELLO ACTORS STUDIO, directed by Annie Tresgot; camera by Michel Brault; released by Actors Studio. At Film Forum 1, 57 Watts Street. Running time: 165 minutes. This film has no rating.

With: Paul Newman, Ellen Burstyn, Eli Wallach, Shelley Winters, Harvey Keitel, Maureen Stapleton, Lee Grant, Gene Wilder, Rod Steiger and Sally Kirkland.

By WALTER GOODMAN

Everything you've always wanted to know about the Actors Studio is now available for the price of admission to Film Forum 1. "Hello Actors Studio" is a three-hour look at the celebrated school that has brought us Marlon Brando, Paul Newman, Robert De Niro and other stars who can also act. No doubt talent, particularly of such degree, will out, Actors Studio or no; still, the testimonials here by the likes of Mr. Newman, its current president ("Whatever I know about acting, I learned in the Actors Studio"), command respect.

Just what the studio gives to performers comes through in the exercises of current hopefuls under the tutelage of such volunteers as Shelley Winters, Arthur Penn, Lee Grant and, most visibly, the artistic director, Ellen Burstyn. If "Hello Actors Studio" seems fan clubby at times, that is in the nature of the premises. The big names subsidize as well as inspire the no-name students, who are admitted by audition and pay nothing.

Elia Kazan tells of the studio's development out of the Group Theater of the 1930's. Under Lee Strasberg, it won fame and influence in the 1950's as the high church of Stanislavsky-derived Method acting, training actors to dig into their own lives for the emotions that would enable them to create the playwright's characters. Today, with Mr. Strasberg gone, his church appears to have been secularized. Ms. Winters says, "The Method is what works for you."

How it works is demonstrated by classes in which teachers and audiences of professionals press the young performers to shun imitation and search for fresh interpretation. These exercises, on which the documentary's director, Annie Tresgot, lingers, are not in themselves compelling; one observer of a two-person scene from a work in progress comments, "I was bored to death." Norman Mailer, in the audience, puts on a better show than the actors. Nonetheless, they show us what the studio is getting at.

No doubt the classroom examples could have been shortened with benefit to the long movie, which, perhaps with television in mind, is divided into three one-hour sections. Still, the classes are more illuminating than much of what such successful alumni as Rod Steiger have to say about acting dangerously and close to the edge.

Perhaps the hackneyed and self-complimenting comments of actors talking about acting is pardonable; their craft is not easily communicated. They do best with specifics, like Gene Wilder's funny and touching account of how he persuaded himself to fall in love with a male sheep for Woody Allen's "Everything You Always Wanted to Know About Sex (but Were Afraid to Ask)."

Evidence that the Method is still susceptible to what the director Sydney Pollack calls "ridiculous fanaticism" comes in the form of two young actresses preparing to play in Genet's "Maids." One reports with great earnestness that they have been developing a relationship by sharing intimate details of their lives, connecting their wrists with a cord and watching pornographic movies together.

Eli Wallach recalls Marilyn Monroe, that shaky sometime student, having trouble completing a scene in "The Misfits" that required her simply to cross a street because she was still trying to work out whether her father loved her mother.

•

Mr. Pollack, who offers the most sensible comments throughout (although he, too, resorts to phrases like "close to the edge"), notes that the Method has "messed up" many students. "The very best is dangerously close to the very worst," he cautions.

How annoying the mannerisms of the Method can be is displayed in a clip of a jittery performance by James Dean as a trapped murderer in a 1953 television show. But we are also treated to a few minutes of Marlon Brando's explosive appearance in "A Streetcar Named Desire" and all is forgiven; it's enough to make you want to sign up.

1988 N 9, C19:1

A Living Doll

CHILD'S PLAY, directed by Tom Holland; screenplay by Don Mancini, John Lafia and Tom Holland; director of photography, Bill Butler; edited by Edward Warschilka and Roy E. Peterson; music by Joe Renzetti; production designer, Daniel A. Lomino; produced by David Kirschner; released by MGM/UA. At the Embassy, Broadway at 47th Street, and other theaters. Running time: 88 minutes. This film is rated R.

Karen Barclay	Catherine Hicks
Mike Norris	Chris Sarandon
Andy Barclay	Alex Vincent
Charles Lee Ray	Brad Dourif
Maggie Peterson	Dinah Manoff
Jack Santos	Tommy Swerdlow
Dr. Ardmore	Jack Colvin

By CARYN JAMES

Even before a killer doll turns up in "Child's Play," you may feel you've dropped into "The Twilight Zone" — the television show, not the place. As a detective chases a murderer down a murky Chicago street and into a toy store, the scene looks so television-perfect, so shallow, artificial and lurid, that you expect the camera to pull back and reveal that we've really been watching television. Though the film never becomes so blatantly ironic, the television look suits Tom Holland's clever, playful thriller. Straddling the line between sendup and suspense, "Child's Play" occupies the narrow, self-conscious space that is truly "Twilight Zone" territory.

When the detective (Chris Sarandon) shoots the scraggly-looking "Lakeshore Strangler" (Brad Dourif), lightning flashes over the toy store and the murderer begins to chant. He throws his departing soul into the nearest available body — a three-foot-tall talking doll called a Good Guy.

Soon, 6-year-old Andy gets a birthday present from his Mom — a Good Guy doll with Mr. Dourif's chilly blue eyes and thin voice. "My name is Chucky and I'm your friend to the end," he tells Andy. He also tells him he wants to stay up and watch the 9 o'clock news, but the baby sitter, Maggie, says no.

"How did Aunt Maggie fall out the window?" Andy's worried mom (Catherine Hicks) asks later. "Chucky did it," the boy blurts out, and instead of being rewarded for his honesty he is branded a bad seed.

•

Mr. Holland, the director and one of the screenwriters, borrows heavily from his own "Fright Night," a 1985 spoof in which a teen-ager spends the first half of the film trying to convince adults that a vampire lives next door and the second half trying to kill off the vampire (played by Mr. Sarandon). Similarly, in "Child's Play," only the audience believes Andy at first. Eventually Chucky bites Mom and tries to slash the detective, so they become less skeptical.

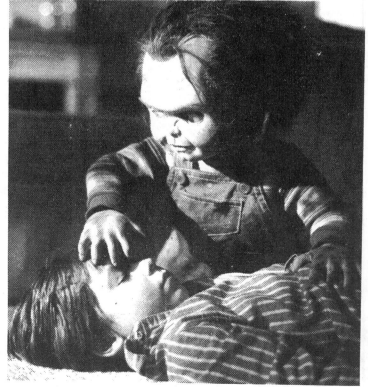

Chucky, a possessed doll, and Alex Vincent in "Child's Play."

Originality is not the point of "Child's Play," though. It's the deft wit and swift editing that keep us off guard, no matter how predictable the plot.

The freshest twist in the film is Andy, who comes to battle Chucky one-on-one. When the doll (the walking, talking Chucky is actually a puppet) arrives at the hospital where Andy is being observed, no one believes the boy's cries that "Chucky is here and he's going to kill me!" In a dark operating room, the 6-year-old's resourcefulness is pitted against the doll's criminal mind. Alex Vincent is wonderfully natural as Andy; he has a crying scene that makes most Method actors look like amateurs.

"Child's Play," which opens today at the Embassy 2 and other theaters, has some limp dialogue among the clever touches. Its appeal is clearly for upscale horror fans rather than a general movie audience. Yet it is a fitting successor to the classic television horror stories it takes off from. As Rod Serling did in "The Twilight Zone," Mr. Holland treats his audience intelligently. *You* don't believe in killer dolls, he suggests, and neither do the perfectly reasonable people in this film; it's all a game. He creates an artifice with just a tiny chink to admit true horror: the most reasonable people on the screen believe in the living, murderous doll.

1988 N 9, C19:1

The Justice Of the Wilderness

Meryl Streep

A CRY IN THE DARK, directed by Fred Schepisi; screenplay by Robert Caswell and Mr. Schepisi, based on the book "Evil Angels" by John Bryson; director of photography, Ian Baker; edited by Jill Bilcock; music by Bruce Smeaton; production designers, Wendy Dickson and George Liddle; produced by Verity Lambert; released by Warner Brothers. At Coronet, Third Avenue at 59th Street, and other theaters. Running time: 121 minutes. This film is rated PG-13.

Lindy Chamberlain	Meryl Streep
Michael Chamberlain	Sam Neill
Muirhead	Charles (Bud) Tingwell
Sturgess	Dennis Miller
Phillips	Neil Fitzpatrick
Tipple	Lewis Fitzgerald
Kirkham	Brendan Higgins

By VINCENT CANBY

Fred Schepisi's "Cry in the Dark" is based on the sort of true story beloved by supermarket tabloids that feature headlines about mothers who boil their babies for breakfast.

In 1980, while on a camping trip in the Australian outback with her parents, 5-week-old Azaria Chamberlain disappeared from the tent while her mother, Lindy Chamberlain, and her father, Michael Chamberlain, a Seventh-Day Adventist minister, were sharing a cookout with friends a few feet away.

Lindy Chamberlain had seen a dingo, the Australian coyote-like wild dog, slipping out of the family's tent and immediately sounded the alarm. In the search that followed, the child's bloody nightdress was found, but not the body. The local coroner ruled that the evidence suggested the baby had been abducted by the animal and probably killed.

The case didn't end there, however. On the basis of forensic evidence that later proved extremely faulty, the case was reopened and, as a result, Lindy Chamberlain was tried for the murder of her baby and her husband as an accessory after the fact.

Helping to whip up the hysteria were newspaper and television reporters. The parents were faulted for not having seemed more distraught immediately after the baby disappeared. The public wanted more tears, more visible signs of grief and torment. The Chamberlains were noticeably "different," possibly because they belonged to what the reporters referred to as a "cult." There were even suggestions the baby had been the victim of a ritual sacrifice.

•

"A Cry in the Dark," which opens today at the Coronet and other theaters, has much of the manner of a television docudrama, ultimately being a rather comforting celebration of personal triumph over travails so dread and so particular that they have no truly disturbing, larger application.

Yet "A Cry in the Dark" is better than that, mostly because of another stunning performance by Meryl Streep, who plays Lindy Chamberlain with the kind of virtuosity that seems to redefine the possibilities of screen acting. If there have been times when Miss Streep's extraordinary work has looked to be too technical, as in the screen version of "Plenty," also directed by Mr. Schepisi, it is because the material (windy and impossibly pretentious in "Plenty") has left her apparently performing in a vacuum.

The screenplay for "A Cry in the Dark," adapted by Robert Caswell and Mr. Schepisi from a book by John Bryson, isn't perfect, but it provides Miss Streep with the kind of raw material that allows her to create a character who, while being perfectly ordinary, is always unexpectedly special.

Wearing what appears to be a not-great black wig, which fits her head like a shower cap, and speaking with a New Zealand accent overlaid with a strong layer of Australian, Miss Streep's Lindy Chamberlain is just reticent and stubborn enough to deflect easy sentimentality. There also seems to be something a little arrogant about her, which is the way most of us react to people with strongly held beliefs we don't share.

•

There is wit, which is not to be confused with humor, in everything she does, from the remarkable accent to the physical mannerisms. Unlike most screen actresses, Miss Streep works on two levels at once. There is, on the surface, the character she is creating within the context of the script. Underneath that, there is the sometimes breathtaking pleasure in watching an actress exercise her talent as she reaches for, and achieves, the high notes.

This is not an especially popular form of screen acting. It has the effect of calling attention to itself, which goes against the grain of realist cinema in which verisimilitude is all. Being able to see and to enjoy an actress act, much as one attends to a diva such as Joan Sutherland, is not something moviegoers take to — unless, like Bette Davis, the actress more or less announces what she's doing with gestures that have become familiar with time.

Miss Streep is an original for our own era.

Though Sam Neill is very good as Lindy Chamberlain's tormented husband, Miss Streep supplies the guts of the melodrama that are missing from the screenplay. Mr. Schepisi has chosen to present the terrible events in the outback in such a way that there's never any doubt in the audience's mind about what happened. The audience doesn't worry about the fate of the Chamberlains as much as it worries about the unconvincing ease with which justice is miscarried.

•

Mr. Schepisi may have followed the facts of the case, but he has not made them comprehensible in terms of the film. The manner by which justice miscarries is the real subject of the movie. In this screenplay, however, it serves only as a pretext for a personal drama that remains chilly and distant.

While watching the film, suspense wars with impatience. As a result, the courtroom confrontations are so weakened that "A Cry in the Dark" becomes virtually a one-character movie. It's Mr. Schepisi's great good fortune that that one character is portrayed by the incomparable Meryl Streep.

•

"A Cry in the Dark," which has been rated PG-13 ("Special Parental Guidance Suggested for Those Younger Than 13"), contains some scenes of emotional panic and loss that might disturb very young children.

1988 N 11, C6:4

The Camera as Means And Mirror of Change

VIOLENCE AT NOON, directed by Nagisa Oshima; screenplay (Japanese with English subtitles) by Tsutomu Tamura, from a story by Taijun Takeda; photographed by Akira Takada; music by Hikaru Hayashi; released by the Shochiku Company. At the Public Theater, 425 Lafayette Street. Running time: 99 minutes. This film has no rating.

Shino	Saeda Kawaguchi
Matsuko	Akiko Koyama
Eisuke	Kei Sato
Genji	Mutsuhiro Toura
Shino's Father	Hosei Komatsu
Shino's Grandmother	Teruko Kishi
School Principal	Taiji Tonoyama
Inagaki	Hideo Kanze

Aficionados of the Japanese cinema will not want to miss "Violence at Noon," Nagisa Oshima's grandly idiosyncratic 1966 film that has its New York theatrical premiere today as part of the Public Theater's retrospective devoted to Japan's Shochiku Studios. Other moviegoers may need extensive program notes.

Mr. Oshima ("In the Realm of the Senses") is known here as the most outspoken and possibly most talented of the directors who constituted Japan's New Wave, a term Mr. Oshima despises. At the time he made "Violence at Noon," the director, then 34 years old, was still enthusiastically experimenting with what is fancily called "film" language," though he was becoming increasingly disillusioned with the use of film for political ends.

"Violence at Noon" is a time-fractured narrative about the members of a youth commune who, six years after their efforts have failed, come to no good end, much in the way that Mr. Oshima saw the failure of the once idealistic Japanese student-radical movement of the early 1960's. The film's interest is not in its narrative but in the director's eccentric use of the Cinemascope screen and in his heady montages employing dozens of cuts to make up even a single, very short sequence.

The camera swirls and swoops. The present gives way to the past, which, in turn gives way to the present, with the speed of a narrator who can't resist interrupting himself. Mr. Oshima has no interest in a shapely story, and no patience for explaining matters that might be immediately apparent to the Japanese audiences of the film's own day.

Though strongly influenced by Jean-Luc Godard, Mr. Oshima never borrowed from his French mentor. He expresses himself in ways that exclusively reflect his Japanese heritage. The Godard influence is most apparent in Mr. Oshima's obsession for using film both as a means of social change and as the instrument for recording it. *VINCENT CANBY*

1988 N 11, C6:4

A 'Dear Jack' Letter

DISTANT THUNDER, directed by Rick Rosenthal; screenplay by Robert Stitzel; director of photography, Ralf Bode; edited by Dennis Virkler; music by Maurice Jarre; art director, Mark S. Freeborn; produced by Robert Schaffel; released by Paramount. At Loews New York Twin, Second Avenue at 66th Street, and other theaters. Running time: 114 minutes. This film is rated R.

Mark Lambert	John Lithgow
Jack Lambert	Ralph Macchio
Char	Kerrie Keane
Moss	Jamey Sheridan
Larry	Denis Arndt
Harvey Nitz	Reb Brown
Barbara	Janet Margolin

By JANET MASLIN

Fate works overtime developing the coincidences that shape "Distant

Chas Gerretsen

Reconciliation In Rick Rosenthal's "Distant Thunder," John Lithgow portrays a disturbed Vietnam veteran living in the wilds who is reunited with his son, played by Ralph Macchio.

Thunder," a film that reunites a shell-shocked Vietnam veteran with his long-lost son, now 18. The veteran, Mark Lambert (John Lithgow), has been living in a remote forest in the state of Washington as the film begins, making his living collecting ferns. It should be noted that Mr. Lithgow is such an unprepossessingly fine actor that he can make any occupation seem credible, even this one.

It must also be noted that not even Mr. Lithgow's wrenching and authentic performance in "Distant Thunder" can keep the film from seeming terribly contrived, especially where the relationship between Mark and his son, Jack (Ralph Macchio), is concerned. As the film begins, Mark makes his way out of the mountains and uneasily lands a job at a lumber mill, where he happens to meet Char (Kerrie Keane), who happens to be extremely sympathetic with the problems of traumatized Vietnam veterans. She "lost a good friend in Vietnam," she explains. By "good friend," she means her father.

It is Char who, seeing the laminated baby picture that Mark carries in his pocket, urges him to re-establish contact with his son. Meanwhile, in Haddon Falls, Ill., Jack is about to graduate from high school with the highest grade point average that anyone in Haddon Falls has ever heard of.

Details like this — and "Distant Thunder" has too many of them — are distinctly unhelpful. Why is it necessary for Jack to be a Presidential scholar instead of just a nice kid who loves and misses his absent father? Aside from making the character less believable, this unnecessary wrinkle makes the role harder for the easygoing Mr. Macchio, who is not the Presidential scholar type.

In any case, Mark writes Jack a letter and Jack is very moved; Jack writes back to his father, and ditto. Jack announces that he is coming to visit, and he arrives at the lumber mill, where Char befriends him and spends the rest of her time implementing the father-son reunion. A certain amount of gruffness keeps Mark and Jack apart for a while, but just as they are about to call it quits, something happens. Fate, which really ought to be down for the count by now, marshals the energy to meddle again.

The two best things about "Distant Thunder," which opens today at Loews New York Twin and other theaters, are its genuine sympathy for the problems faced by Vietnam veterans and the pain and urgency conveyed by Mr. Lithgow's quiet, downcast demeanor. Looking stiffly uncomfortable in almost every scene (except those in which he is roused to unexpected violence), Mr. Lithgow says infinitely more with body language than Robert Stitzel's screenplay says with predictable, unembroidered dialogue. ("Dear Jack, I'm sorry," Mark writes to his son at one point in the story. "Love, Dad.") Rick Rosenthal's direction is no more colorful or passionate than any of this.

One peculiarity about "Distant Thunder" is its reluctance to say much about how Mark, who is first seen in a 1969 prologue during a battle in Vietnam, happened to come home, marry Jack's mother (Janet Margolin), father the child and then disappear into the forest. Another is its title, which has been casually or obliviously borrowed from a better and earlier film (first seen here in 1973) by Satyajit Ray.

1988 N 11, C13:1

Not All-Italian, But Very Pretty

Sasha Mitchell

SPIKE OF BENSONHURST, directed by Paul Morrissey; screenplay by Mr. Morrissey and Alan Bowne; director of photography, Steven Fierberg; edited by Stan Salfas; music by various composers; production designer, Stephen McCabe; produced by David Weisman and Nelson Lyon; released by Filmdallas. At Criterion Center, Broadway at 45th Street, and other theaters. Running time: 101 minutes. This film is rated R.

Spike Fumo	Sasha Mitchell
Baldo Cacetti	Ernest Borgnine
Sylvia Cacetti	Anne DeSalvo
Congresswoman	Sylvia Miles
Helen Fumo	Geraldine Smith
Bandana	Rick Aviles
Angel	Maria Pitillo
India	Talisa Soto
India and Bandana's Mother	Antonia Rey

Paul Morrissey's "Spike of Bensonhurst" would be a comedy of manners if anyone in the film had any. But they don't, which is very much the point. This film, set among Mafia operatives and petty crooks in the Italian neighborhood of Bensonhurst, in Brooklyn, is a humorous look at the way traditional values have deteriorated even here. Spike Fumo (Sasha Mitchell), a would-be prizefighter, is a man in the middle, with an accent and demeanor suited to old-fashioned pursuits like numbers-running, but with the looks of a petulantly perfect male model.

"Spike of Bensonhurst," which opens today at the Criterion and other theaters, shows Spike to be a man with a lot of problems. His family life is a shambles, since his father is in Sing Sing and his mother lives with another woman (though this is considered a useful arrangement, since it keeps Spike's mother from cheating on her husband with other men). His career is going nowhere, since Spike, whose fights are all fixed, isn't much good at winning or losing on cue.

One day, while in the ring, Spike catches the eye of the beautiful blonde Angel (Maria Pitillo), who happens to be the daughter of the neighborhood Mafia kingpin, Baldo Cacetti (Ernest Borgnine). Angel isn't a serious sort (she doesn't like high art, by which she means the Live Aid concert), but Spike doesn't care. He spirits her away from her boyfriend with the kind of blunt Bensonhurst-accented remark in which the screenplay by Mr. Morrissey and Alan Bowne specializes. "Whyn't you lose that square head?" Spike asks. "He's a fazool."

•

Spike's connection with the very halfhearted Angel sends him into and out of Cacetti's good graces. So he winds up spending part of his time in the Puerto Rican community of Red Hook, living with a family that is absolutely thrilled by Spike's Mafia connections. Here, in a slum so wretched that the high school class Spike briefly attends is held in a bathroom, Spike finds another girlfriend, the

gorgeous India (Talisa Soto); her mother (Antonia Rey) is among the film's most successful comic characters. Mr. Morrissey's casting vacillates wildly between beautiful young actors who look great in tight T-shirts, and amusingly overblown grotesques. Sylvia Miles plays Bensonhurst's cocaine-snorting cheerfully corrupt Congresswoman.

"Spike of Bensonhurst," which is accompanied throughout by jaunty Italian bubble-gum pop songs, doesn't have the sharpest satirical edge, but it does have personality. Mr. Morrissey has loaded the film with lively Mafia-connected locals, all of whom lament the fact that things aren't what they used to be. The video-cassette-pirating business, one of several respectable career routes to which Cacetti tries to steer his prospective son-in-law (the trick here, Cacetti explains in a room filled with busy VCR's, is to keep the labels straight and not mix up the porno movies with the cartoons), is no match for a traditional profession like numbers-running.

•

The film's prettier actors, particularly Mr. Mitchell, prove to be a lot more animated than their looks might suggest. And the more broadly comic players are well chosen. Mr. Borgnine strikes the right note of gangster authority coupled with mild bewilderment, and Anne DeSalvo is funny as his younger wife, a woman who advises her broker to invest in high-fat foods. "They're the next craze. Trust me!" she shrieks into her hot-pink telephone.

One of the film's better small touches has the boxing ring announcer telling the Bensonhurst spectators which fighters are of all-Italian parentage and which ones (like Spike, who had an Irish grandparent) are of mixed blood. Within the film's humorously provincial scheme of things, this matters quite a lot.

JANET MASLIN

1988 N 11, C15:1

'Women on the Verge'

"Women on the Verge of a Nervous Breakdown" was shown as part of this year's New York Film Festival. Following are excerpts from Vincent Canby's review, which appeared in The New York Times on Sept. 23. The film opens today at Cinema Studio 1 and 2, Broadway and 66th Street.

It hasn't been Pepa's day, or even week. Ivan, her longtime lover and a male-chauvinist rat, walks out on her, leaving only a bland message on her answering machine. Planning suicide, Pepa spikes a blenderful of garden-fresh gazpacho with sleeping pills, but forgets to drink it.

Pepa's suicide quickly takes on the aspects of a dental checkup: it keeps getting sidetracked.

Saying she really shouldn't smoke, Pepa lights a cigarette and sets her bed ablaze. Her best friend, Candela, who has been having a blissful affair with a man she didn't realize was a Shiite terrorist, comes by looking for refuge from the police.

The first couple to look at Pepa's apartment, which she has put on the market, are Carlos, Ivan's grown son,

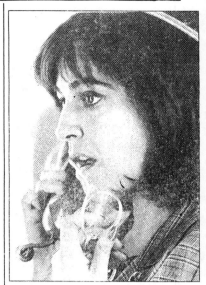

Tossed Aside Carmen Maura stars in "Women on the Verge of a Nervous Breakdown" as the jilted mistress of a married man.

whom Pepa had never known about, and Marisa, Carlos's toothy girlfriend. When Pepa seeks legal advice, the lawyer happens to be Ivan's newest mistress.

These are only some of the delirious ingredients in this most entertaining, deliberately benign new Spanish farce, "Women on the Verge of a Nervous Breakdown." The director is Pedro Almodóvar, better known here for his deliberately scandalous dark comedies ("Matador," "Law of Desire" and "What Have I Done to Deserve This?") in which anything goes, provided that it may offend somebody's sensibility.

•

In "Women on the Verge of a Nervous Breakdown," Mr. Almodóvar sets out to charm rather than shock. That he succeeds should not come as a surprise. The common denominator of all Almodóvar films, even the one that winds up in an ecstatic murder-suicide pact, is their great good humor.

"Women on the Verge of a Nervous Breakdown" has much of the cheeringly mad intensity of animated shorts produced in Hollywood before the television era. This is exemplified in Carmen Maura's grand performance as Pepa. Miss Maura, who looks a bit like Jeanne Moreau, is to Mr. Almodóvar's cinema what Anna Magnani once was to Roberto Rossellini's.

Miss Maura is wonderful as a woman who simply cannot resist fighting back. The actress has a big, no-nonsense screen personality that perfectly fits Mr. Almodóvar's raffishly deadpan comic method.

"Women on the Verge" takes place in its own, very special farcical universe, where outrageous coincidences are the norm and where logic dictates that a forgotten blenderful of spiked gazpacho will be drunk by the wrong person. It's also a place where a television anchor is a sweet old grandmother instead of a barely literate sex symbol, and where Pepa, an actress, appears in a commercial for a detergent guaranteed to get the blood out of your killer son's shirt and trousers.

Though feminist in its sympathies, "Women on the Verge" is far from being a tract of any sort. The characters Mr. Almodóvar has written and directed keep asserting idiosyncrasies that do not allow them, or the film, to be so humorlessly categorized.

The pace sometimes flags, and there are scenes in which the comic potential appears to be lost only because the camera is in the wrong place. Farce isn't easy to pull off, but Mr. Almodóvar is well on his way to mastering this most difficult of all screen genres.

1988 N 11, C16:1

ERNEST SAVES CHRISTMAS, directed by John Cherry; screenplay by B. Kline and Ed Turner; director of photography, Peter Stein; edited by Sharyn L. Ross; music by Mark Snow; art director, Ian Thomas; produced by Stacy Williams and Doug Claybourne; released by Touchstone Pictures. At the Embassy 4, Broadway at 47th Street, and other theaters. Running time: 89 minutes. This film is rated PG.

Ernest P. Worrell	Jim Varney
Santa	Douglas Seale
Joe Carruthers	Oliver Clark
Harmony	Noëlle Parker
Chuck	Gailard Sartain
Mary Morrissey	Billie Bird
Bobby	Bill Byrge
Marty	Robert Lesser

Jim Varney

By CARYN JAMES

"Ernest Saves Christmas" features a credible Santa Claus, live reindeer and, much less surprising, commercials embedded in the scenery. The character of Ernest, a bumbling yokel whose vocabulary consists almost entirely of the words "Hey, Vern!," was born in television commercials, in which he grins widely and intrudes obnoxiously on his neighbors' privacy. The strategy seems to be that you'll buy whatever soft drink or car or hardware Ernest is selling — anything just to get rid of him.

Then, with all the aplomb of breakfast cereals turned into cartoons, Ernest made loads of money with his first feature film, the unfunny slapstick "Ernest Goes to Camp." The strategy for his film career seems to be that Ernest's face is familiar, and there are so few children's movies around that kids will sit through anything. Though the plot of his new film appears to concern Santa Claus, with Ernest it's once a commercial, always a commercial.

Here he is a cabdriver in Florida — where Disney, the company behind the film, just happens to have a studio. Brand names clutter the screen, from the conspicuous logos for an airline and a pen — shown so often they become positively tedious — to glimpses of a rental truck, a beer sign and a billboard advertising a floral delivery service.

Buried among the ads is a story about how Santa is losing his power

and has to find a successor. Ernest picks up the old man at the airport on Dec. 23, and becomes his chauffeur and accomplice in the search. Somehow, Ernest still finds time to do uninspired things like tear down a wall trying to string up Christmas lights.

●

The best that can be said for the film is that it leaves Ernest behind now and then to focus on Santa, who is played by Douglas Seale with sweetness, sincerity and an amazing amount of dignity, considering his surroundings. Ernest also appears in disguises, proving he's even more irritating when gotten up as a snake rancher or an old woman, or when he's doing his John Wayne impersonation. The film's production notes say that on the set Jim Varney, who plays Ernest, would recite scenes from Shakespeare or Harold Pinter. You might want to pay money to see Ernest do Pinter, but not his John Wayne.

"Ernest Saves Christmas," which opens today at the Embassy 4 and other theaters, was directed lifelessly by John Cherry, who also directed the first Ernest film and all those commercials. In the end, everyone — Ernest, the new Santa, a runaway girl Ernest saves — learns the true, altruistic meaning of Christmas. Everyone except the mercenaries who made this film.

●

"Ernest Saves Christmas" is rated PG ("Parental Guidance Suggested"), though there is nothing objectionable about the film except for Ernest's pushy behavior.

1988 N 11, C15:1

A Blue Yonder That's Not So Wild

IRON EAGLE II, directed by Sidney J. Furie; screenplay by Mr. Furie and Kevin Elders; director of photography, Alain Dostie; edited by Rit Wallis; music by Amin Bhatia; art director, Ariel Roshko; produced by Jacob Kotzky, Sharon Harel and John Kemeny; released by Tri-Star. At Loews 84th Street, at

Broadway, and other theaters. Running time: 100 minutes. This film is rated PG.

Chappy	Louis Gossett Jr.
Cooper	Mark Humphrey
Stillmore	Stuart Margolin
Vardovsky	Alan Scarfe
Valeri	Sharon H. Brandon
Downs	Maury Chaykin
Yuri	Colm Feore
Graves	Clark Johnson

By CARYN JAMES

It is meant as the most backhanded sort of compliment, but "Iron Eagle II" is not quite as silly as the original. Of course, it would be hard to match the extreme looniness of that action-fantasy, in which a teen-ager named Doug Masters flies a jet into a Middle Eastern country and rescues his father, a shot-down Air-Force pilot, just hours before he is to be executed. Doug's battle cry, as he turns up the volume on his Walkman and zooms into space, is "rock 'n' roll!"

Luckily for us, with the help of a Soviet fighter, jet twirling, renegade Doug rocks his way to oblivion in the first scene of "Iron Eagle II." What follows is a clone of "Top Gun" without the megastars and glitzy style, which doesn't leave this sequel much to work with.

●

It does have one of those fake political plots that action films use to glue together the special-effects scenes. Gen. Chappy Sinclair is the American in charge of our half of a joint mission with the Soviets. Together, the team has to destroy a nuclear weapon plant built by a fictional country that Soviets and Americans loathe more than they do each other.

The group, as Chappy says, is "the biggest bunch of misfits you could find," though they are well balanced. Along with a claustrophobic pilot and a redneck Communist-hater, there is a black American, a female Russian and a handsome United States pilot named Cooper — what a coincidence, Doug's best friend. Cooper falls for the lone woman, though not before he and his friends drop in a few comments along the lines of "I wonder if she flies like she walks." As Chappy, Louis Gossett Jr. sinks deeper into his post-"Officer and a Gentleman" phase. He glowers, barks orders and gives tough inspirational speeches, in

On the Attack Louis Gossett Jr. appears again as Gen. Charles (Chappy) Sinclair in the sequel "Iron Eagle II." In Sidney J. Furie's action film, Americans and Russians join forces against terrorists

scenes that could be out-takes from "Iron Eagle I."

The action scenes, including the lengthy final attack on the weapon plant, are competent if you like that cut-rate "Top Gun" look. For every shot of jets chasing one another in the air or crashing into the side of a mountain, there is a shot of an instrument panel going haywire and a close-up of a tense-looking pilot.

The music behind these scenes is certainly not up to Doug's volume, but at one point you can make out a voice singing "Livin' on the Edge." "Iron Eagle II," which opened yesterday at the Criterion Center and other theaters, lives much closer to the mediocre middle.

●

"Iron Eagle II" is rated PG. There are some violent deaths in the air.

1988 N 12, 15:3

FILM VIEW/Janet Maslin

Some Images Take a Bite Out of the Truth

IN THE 16 YEARS SINCE "THE CANdidate" first appeared, our standards certainly have shifted. What once seemed to be examples of outrageous media manipulation have come to appear disturbingly routine. No wonder this formerly caustic-seeming glimpse of the American electoral process now looks, at least in some quarters, like a simple blueprint for success. "The idea is to get you in completely natural situations," say the campaign advisers of Robert Redford's Bill McKay as they contrive photo opportunities for his television commercials. "I'm still hoping for a chance to debate you," McKay shouts to his opponent, who pats him paternally and answers, "Don't blame you a bit."

The techniques used by McKay's campaign staff to shape the public perception of their man seemed deeply cynical in 1972, but they've since become second nature. We have grown fully accustomed to five-second remarks pulled out of context, to vapid optimism and empty platitudes, to campaign appearances that reshape any news event to suit a candidate's purposes. ("We've got a fire in Malibu," one of the McKay advisers discovers excitedly. "It's perfect!") We may even have reached the stage of preferring blatantly artificial television imagery to the less flashy, less dramatic facts that we know to be true.

■

This affinity has begun to extend well beyond politics, although the fusion of political and advertising methods that brought about "Morning in America" rhetoric have greatly increased our tolerance for any kind of soft sell. We can now watch news coverage on television and find ourselves subtly swayed by images of a defiant and ingenuous-looking Tawana Brawley insisting on her innocence, even though all the known evidence suggests otherwise. We may be more inclined to accept the conspiracy theories set forth in a mini-series like "Favorite Son" than the less Byzantine, more verifiable facts of recent American history.

Thanks in part to television's pervasive influence, we sometimes seem dangerously eager to reject what we do know in favor of sexier, simpler-minded alternatives. We may also have become correspondingly ready to assume, on the basis of persuasive and highly selective video images, that we know more than we do. Thanks to the dubious advance of allowing cameras into courtrooms, we often find ourselves possessed of strong opinions on the basis of very little real information. So home viewers are happy to draw conclusions about the culpability of a Joel Steinberg, or to make assumptions about the psyche of a Sukhreet Gabel, on the basis of a sound bite or two.

Jumping to conclusions on the basis of slender media-powered evidence has become such a habit, for so many of us, that it's bracing to see this problem explored in a foreign setting. "A Cry in the Dark," Fred Schepisi's film about the Lindy Chamberlain case, tells a bizarre story, the facts of which have not been widely known outside Australia. At home, Mrs. Chamberlain spent years in an unwanted limelight, an easy target for every sort of snap judgment and armchair analysis. But for American audiences steeped in their own local scandals, her story and the media-created fanfare surrounding it will come as a genuine shock.

In 1980, Lindy Chamberlain was on a camping trip with her husband, two sons and 9-week-old daughter, Azaria, at Ayers Rock, Australia's great tourist attraction. Dingoes, or Australian wild dogs, were common at this site. And Mrs. Chamberlain exhibited grotesquely bad judgment when she put the baby to bed in an unguarded tent after nightfall, apparently near a spot where dingoes had recently been seen. The worst happened. A dingo was seen leaving the tent; the baby has never been found.

The biggest surprise about "A Cry in the Dark," and perhaps the best thing about it (except for Meryl Streep's brilliantly self-effacing performance as Lindy Chamberlain), is the film's dispensing quickly with the question of Lindy Chamberlain's guilt. It is Mr. Schepisi's clear assumption that she was party to a terrible accident, not to a crime. At one point in the film, Lindy sarcastically describes the grisly steps she is alleged to have taken and the brief time she would have had to complete them, making it clear that the murder would have been physically as well as psychologically impossible for her.

∎

So "A Cry in the Dark" is not about the facts of this case; it's about public opinion and the reckless ways in which it is formed. Throughout the film, Australians are seen following the Chamberlain case on their television news and in tabloid accounts ("Azaria Anguish" is one headline), freely dispensing their own verdicts on the basis of this limited information. Getting beer from their refrigerators, taking breaks after their tennis games, spending evenings gathered around their television sets, these spectators have made the Chamberlains Topic A. "I'm *not* having an-

"The Candidate" (1972), starring Robert Redford, and the current "Cry in the Dark,"

with Sam Neill and Meryl Streep, illustrate the power of the media.

other dinner party ruined by those people!" one hostess petulantly declares.

In the film's view, Lindy Chamberlain was tried for murder (and subsequently convicted) largely because she did not hold up well under such circumstances. Confronted by reporters, she would harden into an attitude of harsh, contemptuous defiance; in one television interview, she shocked viewers with a calmly gruesome description of the way the

dingo eats its prey. Dingo lovers, of whom Australia has many, were particularly outraged by such behavior.

The chilling and timely message of "A Cry in the Dark" is best captured in the homily delivered by Lindy's father midway through the story: "A lie goes round the world while the truth is still putting its boots on." ☐

1988 N 13, II:13:1

Lizard Lullaby

Littlefoot, from the animated film "The Land Before Time."

THE LAND BEFORE TIME, directed by Don Bluth; screenplay by Stu Krieger, story by Judy Freudberg and Tony Geiss; film editors, Dan Molina and John K. Carr; music by James Horner; production designer, Mr. Bluth; produced by Mr. Bluth, Gary Goldman

and John Pomeroy and Sullivan Bluth Studios; released by Universal Pictures. At the National Twin, Broadway at 44th Street, and other theaters. Running time: 73 minutes. This film is rated G.

Voices:
Narrator and Rooter .... Pat Hingle
Littlefoot's Mother .... Helen Shaver
Littlefoot .... Gabriel Damon
Cera .... Candice Houston
Daddy Topps .... Burke Barnes
Ducky .... Judith Barsi
Petrie .... Will Ryan

By JANET MASLIN

The animated baby dinosaurs in "The Land Before Time" scamper and frolic and gambol just the way animated baby creatures should. In circumstances like these, "cute" cannot be thought of as a term of opprobrium. It's the only way to describe the enchanting behavior of these little beings, and in fact it hardly does

them justice. Where animated cuteness is concerned, these dinosaurs stand just this side of the baby Dumbo, or perhaps Lady and the Tramp's first litter.

"The Land Before Time," which opens today at the National and other theaters, is the work of Don Bluth, whose style of animation harks back to the the best of Disney. Mr. Bluth has come to look like a true purist in the world of modern animation, and this time he sounds a much less saccharine and more traditional note than he did with the earlier "An American Tail." Even better, most of "The Land Before Time" is so authentically geared to the thinking of children that it should charm adults as well.

Audiences that have grown inured to the cost-cutting tactics of much modern animation — the flat and stationary backgrounds, the characters that barely blink, the camera movements that take the place of more expensive and painstaking drawing — should luxuriate in the full-blown, three-dimensional style to be found here. Against rocky purple landscapes and beneath orange skies, this film's dinosaurs lumber elegantly and expressively across the screen. The adult dinosaurs in the film have been cast as loving parents, thus greatly heightening their innate appeal to the imaginations of young viewers. But very early in the story, these parents are traumatically separated from their young.

●

If the look of "The Land Before Time" is attractively old-fashioned, the film's story line is more modern. It owes a debt to the theories of mythology espoused by Joseph Campbell, whose ideas found a pop cultural outlet in George Lucas's "Star Wars" (Mr. Lucas is one of this film's executive producers, along with Steven Spielberg, Kathleen Kennedy and Frank Marshall). In congruence with the patterns Mr. Campbell detected in the myths of many different cultures, the film sets forth the idea that a loved one must die to make possible the exploits of a young hero, in this case a tiny brontosaurus named Littlefoot.

The last of his breed, Littlefoot (with the charmingly childlike voice of Gabriel Damon) is sent forth by his mother (with the voice of Helen Shaver) and grandparents to find a place called the Great Valley, where edible leaves abound. His departure from his leafless, famine-ridden homeland is accompanied by an earthquake and a terrible battle, in which his mother is mortally wounded by a Tyrannosaurus rex. This is staged in a manner that should not be frightening to children, but they may be mystified by the dying mother brontosaurus's declaration that "the great circle of life has begun." Luckily, the film glosses over Littlefoot's loss and concentrates on his adventures en route to the Great Valley.

The film's different species, who call each other names like "longneck" (brontosaurus) and "sharptooth" (tyrannosaurus), are discouraged by the adult dinosaurs from mingling with one another. But once the children are separated from their parents, they form a cheerfully heterogeneous band. Littlefoot teams up with a tiny pterodactyl and members of several other species, chief among them a bratty little triceratops named Cera, who sounds just like a spoiled human 6-year-old. "I knew it was you all along! I knew! I did!" she shrieks, on an occasion when the other dino-babies catch her by surprise.

"The Land Before Time," with a story by Judy Freudberg and Tony Geiss and a screenplay by Stu Krieger, isn't heavily plotted; it doesn't do much more than concentrate on the amusingly lifelike dynamics among the dinosaur children as they make their journey. Luckily, it isn't very long either. At a just-right length of 73 minutes, it ought to win audiences' hearts without wearing out their patience.

1988 N 18, C8:4

OLIVER AND COMPANY, directed by George Scribner; story inspired by Charles Dickens's "Oliver Twist"; animation screenplay by Jim Cox, Timothy J. Disney and James Mangold; edited by Jim Melton and Mark Hester;

Oliver, from the animated film "Oliver and Company."

music by J. A. C. Redford; art director, Dan Hansen; produced in association with Silver Screen Partners; presented by Walt Disney Pictures; distributed by Buena Vista Pictures Distribution Inc. At Guild 50th Street near Fifth Avenue, and other theaters. Running time: 72 minutes. This film is rated G.

Voices:
Oliver .... Joey Lawrence
Dodger .... Billy Joel
Tito .... Cheech Marin
Einstein .... Richard Mulligan
Francis .... Roscoe Lee Browne
Fagin .... Dom DeLuise
Georgette .... Bette Midler
Jenny .... Natalie Gregory
Sykes .... Robert Loggia

By VINCENT CANBY

Bette Midler's talent is radioactive. It can seep through anything except, possibly, a lead shield. Even when she is disguised as a vain Park Avenue poodle, whose territorial instincts are overwhelmed by her sexual needs, Miss Midler and her bigger-than-life performing personality cannot be hidden.

There's no mistaking who is behind the screen as Miss Midler provides the speaking voice for the tempestuous Georgette, a dog with a heart of brass. When she bursts into song with "Perfect Isn't Easy," a funny parody of an old-fashioned Broadway show stopper, she almost bursts through the screen.

It deserves a golden dog biscuit.

Georgette is just one of the anthropomorphic animals with which Walt Disney Pictures has cast its newest animated feature, "Oliver and Company," an extremely loose updated variation on the Charles Dickens classic.

In the film, which opens today at the Guild and other theaters, Oliver is a small, orange-furred kitten, abandoned in mid-Manhattan and forced to fend for himself. He's first adopted by a band of raffish disenfranchised urban dogs led by Dodger (voice by Billy Joel), a cheerful terrier and con artist. The gang's human master is Fagin (voice by Dom DeLuise), a fainthearted failure of an underworld figure who lives in fear of a Mr. Big named Bill Sykes.

●

When Oliver is readopted, not against his will, by a lonely little rich girl named Jenny, the plot complications don't multiply, they accumulate as if they were lint.

In addition to Miss Midler, "Oliver and Company" has a handful of other attractive things to offer — two good songs and the voices. These include Mr. Joel's singing Dodger's big-city creed, "Why Should I Worry?"; Cheech Marin's voice as a hyperactive Chihuahua named Tito, and Mr. DeLuise's as Fagin who, when he's marked for termination by Sykes, warns his canine charges, "Remember, dead men don't buy dog food."

The screenplay, while not great, is certainly serviceable, especially in the way that it allows the actors to express their known personalities within animated figures not of the first order.

●

"Oliver and Company" is being touted as the first in a new series of animated Disney features to use state-of-the-art computer techniques. In whatever way the film was put together, however, "Oliver and Company" looks cheesy and second-rate. The animation is somewhat better than the usual stuff seen on Saturday morning television, but not much.

It is totally without distinctive visual style, suggesting only the sort of bland cartoon drawings one finds in a manual of first-aid instructions. In addition, the animation itself looks cheap, sometimes as primitive as those early pre-Disney black-and-white cartoons in which the foreground characters moved against a frozen backdrop.

It is incomprehensible how "Oliver and Company" could have issued from the studio that set the standards by which all animated films have been judged for nearly 60 years. I should think that Walt Disney, wherever he is, might be having a gigantic all-stops-out Donald Duck-type tantrum. It's not that "Oliver and Company" is not up to par. It actively denies its own unique heritage.

1988 N 18, C8:4

Northward Bound With the Family

WHERE SPRING COMES LATE, directed, created and written by Yoji Yamada; in Japanese with English subtitles; photography by Tetsuo Takahane; music by Masaru Sato; produced by Yoshiharu Mishima; released by the Shochiku Company. At the Public, 425 Lafayette Street. Running time: 106 minutes. This film has no rating.

Tamiko .... Chieko Baisho
Seiichi .... Hisashi Igawa
Genzo .... Chishu Ryu
Tsutomu .... Gin Maeda

Yoji Yamada's "Where Spring Comes Late" is an epic about one man's family's journey to discover the new Japan. They are Seiichi Kazami, a young, out-of-work coal miner; Tamiko, his wife; their two small children, and Genzo, Seiichi's old father.

With high hopes and borrowed funds, the Kazamis set out from their village in southern Japan to become dairy-farming pioneers on the northern island of Hokkaido. In 1970, when the film was made, Hokkaido, to most Japanese, was still a chilly, unknown land, an underpopulated frontier territory.

"Where Spring Comes Late" opens today at the Public Theater as part of the current retrospective devoted to the films of Shochiku Studios.

At first, everything is splendidly new and promising to the Kazamis. They pass through bustling Nagasaki, the largest city any of them have ever seen, and move on to Fukuyama, on the Inland Sea, where they expect to leave old Genzo with Seiichi's brother. In the course of one edgy night with the brother's family, during which everyone is crowded into a tiny house filled with tense adults and noisy children, Seiichi and Tamiko realize that they'll have to take Grandpa with them.

They continue, changing trains at Osaka where they spend a few mar-

velous, exhausting hours at Osaka's Expo 70, before proceeding to Tokyo. It is there that events turn grim and the scheme of the movie begins to show. In a movie of this sort, one death is acceptable and two suggest a plague.

●

In its first half, "Where Spring Comes Late" has a lot of the grit, pathos and humor of an Italian neorealist comedy of the late 1950's. Even the ample soundtrack music sounds Italian, though with a Japanese intonation. After Tokyo, as the Kazamis journey farther and farther north, the movie seems to melt into upbeat sentimentality.

Mr. Yamada, who wrote and directed "Where Spring Comes Late," was considered one of Japan's most promising new directors in the late 1960's, but then became sidetracked, to his own immense financial gain, by the hugely popular series of "Torasan" comedies.

His talent is certainly evident in "Where Spring Comes Late." The film is handsomely shot in Cinemascope (called "Shochiku Grandscope" in my credits), which Japanese film makers used with a poetic authority not matched by directors anywhere else in the world. The large cast, including Chishu Ryu as Genzo, performs with reticent skill.

As long as it is attending to the commonplace details of family life, "Where Spring Comes Late" has real power. As soon as it begins to attend to its epic concerns, the film itself becomes commonplace.

VINCENT CANBY

1988 N 18, C8:4

Shades and Shenanigans

Steve Guttenberg

HIGH SPIRITS, directed and written by Neil Jordan; director of photography, Alex Thomson; edited by Michael Bradsell; music by George Fenton; production designer, Anton Furst; produced by Stephen Woolley and David Saunders; released by Tri-Star Pictures Inc. At Gemini Twin, 64th Street and Second Avenue, and other theaters. Running time: 96 minutes. This film is rated PG-13.

Mary .... Daryl Hannah
Peter Plunkett .... Peter O'Toole
Jack .... Steve Guttenberg
Sharon .... Beverly D'Angelo
Miranda .... Jennifer Tilly
Brother Tony .... Peter Gallagher
Martin .... Liam Neeson
Plunkett Sr. .... Ray McAnally
Mrs. Plunkett .... Liz Smith

By JANET MASLIN

In the comedy "High Spirits," a deadbeat Irish nobleman named Peter Plunkett (Peter O'Toole) contrives a scheme for holding onto his cobwebby ancestral castle: he declares the place haunted, then buses in American tourists to observe the

Spectral Eire

Peter O'Toole stars in "High Spirits," about ghostly goings-on in an Irish castle.

ghosts in action. Weary family retainers are seen hanging from the trees, clanking about in suits of armor and otherwise making sure that things go bump in the night.

Unfortunately there is an unplanned complication, since Castle Plunkett is home to real ghosts as well as fake ones. These ghosts, Martin (Liam Neeson) and Mary (Daryl Hannah) are young, attractive and very tired of re-enacting the same connubial argument every evening. For 200 years, they have been re-living — if that is the word — the wedding-night quarrel in which the jealous Martin bellowed, "So, ya wee harlot!" and stabbed his bride to death. The marriage was apparently never consummated. Two hundred years is a long time to wait.

So "High Spirits" sounds as if it has the makings of a droll farce, enlivened by quiet wit and glimpses of the Irish countryside. This, however, is not the case. The film has been directed as broad, noisy slapstick by Neil Jordan, who was much more at home in the dark, colloquial world of "Mona Lisa" (which he also directed) than he is in this one.

"High Spirits," which opens today at the Gemini and other theaters, is filled with furniture-splintering special effects and busy stuntwork, none of which is executed with any special flair. Tricks like the one that has a canopy bed spinning wildly, rising to the ceiling, crashing through the floor and then sliding down a flight of stairs are much more exhausting than they are funny.

Luckily, "High Spirits" has a good cast and enough joie de vivre to rise above some of its underlying clumsiness. Miss Hannah, wafting through the castle in a diaphanous gown and speaking in the demure tones of an 18th-century Irish maiden, is everything a ghost ought to be, and in addition to that she's also rather amorous. She understandably catches the eye of Jack, a nice-guy American whose wife, Sharon, takes a lot of Valium and refuses to let Jack anywhere near her.

The casting here isn't exactly surprising, but then Steve Guttenberg and Beverly D'Angelo are just right for these light comic roles. Miss D'Angelo has a remarkable knack for making nagging, frigid, uncooperative wives seem a lot more likable than they otherwise might.

Mr. Neeson gallops wildly through the film with a mad gleam in his eye, and when his Martin turns out to be Sharon's idea of Mr. Right, the film develops the zestful symmetry that is its most appealing element. Mr. O'Toole hams his role to the heavens, but he seems to be enjoying himself immensely and his spirit of fun is contagious.

Also good in the cast is Peter Gallagher, as a young candidate for the priesthood who has not yet taken his vows and perhaps never will, since one of the other tourists (Jennifer Tilly) is determined to catch his eye. In one typically broad scene, this cleric finds himself challenged by doubts that appear to him in the form of masked nuns with tiny, gleaming yellow eyes, and he becomes so agitated that his pants begin to steam.

Liz Smith and Ray McAnally play the senior Plunketts, one of whom is alive and one of whom is not. In small roles, the actors who play the Plunketts' Irish retainers do the muttering, grumbling and modest clowning that the film badly needs in larger doses.

•

"High Spirits" is rated PG-13 ("Special Parental Guidance Suggested for Those Younger Than 13"). It includes some fairly blunt sexual references.

1988 N 18, C10:1

That Was a Year That Was

1969, directed and written by Ernest Thompson; director of photography, Jules Brenner; film editor, William Anderson; music by Michael Small; production designer, Marcia Hinds; produced by Daniel Grodnik and Bill Badalato; released by Atlantic Entertainment Group. At Loews New York Twin, Second Avenue and 66th Street, and other theaters. Running time: 95 minutes. This film is rated R.

Ralph	Robert Downey Jr.
Scott	Kiefer Sutherland
Cliff	Bruce Dern
Jessie	Mariette Hartley
Beth	Winona Ryder
Ev	Joanna Cassidy

For Ernest Thompson, the writer and director of "1969," that year represents a state of mind. It is not a state of mind that anyone else might recognize, however. Figuratively speaking, "1969" takes place on Golden Pond (to recall the screenplay of Mr. Thompson's that became a box-office bonanza). It's set in the land of high sentiment, family feuds and generation-gap histrionics, in the kind of small town where such touches seem less quaint than they otherwise might.

In deference to its time, "1969" also includes hippie costumes, drugs, psychedelic drawings, student demonstrations and many timely pop songs by groups like Canned Heat, Cream and Creedence Clearwater Revival. But these things feel like window dressing, nothing more.

The film, which opens today at

Loews New York Twin and other theaters, looks for about five minutes like the story of two footloose college boys, Ralph (Robert Downey Jr.) and Scott (Kiefer Sutherland). It soon develops that they are not so carefree after all, and that each has a melodramatic set of family problems, which are brought to the fore when the boys hitchhike home for Easter vacation.

Scott has clashed with his father, a stern military man (played by Bruce Dern), over the fact that Scott's older brother is a marine being sent to Vietnam. Ralph's problem is his widowed mother (Joanna Cassidy), who wears very short skirts, shrieks excitedly on public occasions and otherwise behaves inexplicably. Later in the story, it becomes clear that she drinks to excess and harbors a very special fondness for Scott's father.

"1969" is awash in the problems that arise from these domestic situations, building up to a painfully self-congratulatory ending in which the whole town where the story takes place rises up in protest against the Vietnam War. The film is lively only insofar as the actors are able to make it so. Mr. Sutherland, not terribly convincing as a reluctant innocent in the midst of the sexual revolution, is likable anyhow, and so is Mr. Downey, even if the screenplay gives each of their characters a cute side. Winona Ryder, the beautiful young actress who plays Mr. Downey's sister, has such fascinatingly offbeat timing that she becomes a lot more interesting than her role.

Some of the players, particularly Miss Cassidy and Mariette Hartley as the two heroes' respective mothers, are made to seem wooden by the one-note manner in which their roles are written. Mr. Dern, unusually laconic here, is unexpectedly moving as the character who seems most confused by changing times.

JANET MASLIN

1988 N 18, C10:5

The Eccentricity of People and Syntax

FRESH HORSES, directed by David Anspaugh; screenplay by Larry Ketron, based on his play; director of photography, Fred Murphy; edited by David Rosenbloom; music by David Foster and Patrick Williams; production designer, Paul Sylbert; produced by Dick Berg; released by Weintraub Entertainment Group. At the Warner, Broadway and 43d Street; the Manhattan Twin, 59th Street east of Third Avenue, and other theaters. Running time: 105 minutes. This film is rated PG-13.

Jewel	Molly Ringwald
Matt	Andrew McCarthy
Jean	Patti D'Arbanville
Tipton	Ben Stiller
Matt's Dad	Leon Russom
Ellen	Molly Hagan
Green	Viggo Mortensen

By VINCENT CANBY

When Matt (Andrew McCarthy), a clean-cut college senior, first sets eyes on Jewel (Molly Ringwald), it is infatuation at first sight. She's in the kitchen of a Kentucky farmhouse where assorted low-lifes and students come together to drink beer, dance and play pool.

Matt asks the pretty flame-haired Jewel if she lives there. "No," she says, "I just come over from next door." In her rural Kentucky syntax she explains that her stepdaddy had gotten into bed with her and tried to fool around.

Jewel has a problem with her verb tenses as well as with her stepfather. By the end of "Fresh Horses," both problems will have been solved.

As acted by Mr. McCarthy and Miss Ringwald, Matt and Jewel are engagingly eccentric characters. He is studying to be an engineer and is interested in designing roller-coasters and board games. She's a high school dropout. She says she is 20, but she could be 16. Matt becomes increasingly obsessed. He dumps his rich upper-crust Cincinnati fiancée, even as he realizes that Jewel is either remarkably naïve or a psychotic liar.

•

"Fresh Horses," a title that means nothing in the context of what happens, is really a comedy, though it's difficult to tell from the solemn, very ordinary production directed by David Anspaugh ("Hoosiers"), and adapted by Larry Ketron from his own Off Broadway play. Mr. Ketron's screenplay has the manner of something that, in the way of Hollywood, has been opened up, fleshed out and improved to the point where most of its original charm has vanished.

The film's narrative is now so shapely that, beginning about halfway through, there's not a scene or scarcely a line of dialogue that cannot be predicted. The performances remain consistently good while the movie winds down around them, being over long before it leaves the screen.

"Fresh Horses" opened yesterday at the Warner and other theaters.

•

"Fresh Horses," which has been rated PG-13 ("parental guidance suggested for those younger than 13"), includes some discreetly photographed sex scenes and vulgar language.

1988 N 19, 15:3

Flower of Youth

Robert Downey Jr. and Kiefer Sutherland portray college students during a turbulent time in "1969," written and directed by Ernest Thompson.

Ghosts and Gangs

TWICE DEAD, directed by Bert Dragin; screenplay by Mr. Dragin and Robert McDonnell; cinematographer, Zoran Hochstatter; edited by Patrick Rand; music by David Bergeaud; production designer, Stephan Rice; produced by Guy J. Louthan and Mr. McDonnell; released by Concorde Inc. At the Criterion Center, Broadway and 45th Street; the Eastside Cinema, Third Avenue at 55th Street, and other theaters. Running time: 90 minutes. This film is rated R.

Scott	Tom Brezhahan
Robin-Myrna	Jill Whitlow
Crip-Tyler	Jonathan Chapin
Silk	Christopher Burgard
Harry	Sam Melville
Sylvia	Brooke Bundy
Petie	Todd Bridges

The title of "Twice Dead" refers to suicides that begin and end the story, but it also astutely describes the two lethally boring plots that collide in this exploitation film. Mom, Dad and their teen-age son and daughter inherit a crumbling house, deserted except for a ghost who hanged himself there. The family arrives to find a street gang with heavily moussed hair blocking their doorway, as if the only thing worse than a haunted house is a haunted house in a really bad neighborhood.

In fact, the director and co-writer, Bert Dragin, has absolutely no wit about this ludicrous premise. Instead, he seems to assume that the double plot will allow him twice as many chances for lurid scenes, like the one in which someone puts the naked female mannequin on the floor and repeatedly drives his motorcycle into it.

•

A deranged-looking gang member gets a crush on the daughter. Dad reaches for his rifle at the slightest excuse — when his son has a bad dream, for instance. The son makes friends with the ghost. All the while, Mr. Dragin — the director of an equally offensive film called "Summer Camp Nightmare," about the sadistic owner of a children's camp — kills time waiting for the onslaught of ugly murders. Someone is decapitated by a dumbwaiter; someone is fried by faulty wiring on an electric blanket during sex.

Of all the low-rent films that have skulked into town recently, "Twice Dead," which opened yesterday at the Criterion Center and other theaters, is the worst.

CARYN JAMES

1988 N 19, 15:3

Lately, Seeing Isn't Believing

By CARYN JAMES

AS THE HEROINE OF "THE GOOD Mother" — with no ambiguity, the film presents Anna as the best-intentioned mom of all time — Diane Keaton walks down a charming street near Harvard Square and suddenly bursts into histrionics. Her lover, Leo, is an artist who has asked angrily why she is not more passionate about her work.

Anna, a part-time piano teacher and the divorced mother of a 4-year-old, fights back with the illogic and defensiveness of someone whose most sensitive nerve has just been hit. "I might have been a composer, or a musician," she screams hysterically. "That was the plan for me, but I wasn't good enough! So I made a different kind of life for myself, with

Molly! And I really hate being told there's no honor in it!"

Forget for a moment the horrendous equation Anna takes for granted: her daughter as compensation for lack of talent. Ms. Keaton's furious cries mask another question. Who told Anna there's no honor in being a mother? Leo has never suggested that; no one in the film has disparaged Anna's motherhood, which is shown to be full of sweetness and shot in silvery light. Yet as Ms. Keaton makes her sham argument, we are meant to cheer Anna on, as if her inflated reaction, so detached from the reality of her life, makes perfect sense.

The scene distills "The Good Mother" in all its incarnations — from Sue Miller's manipulative best-selling novel to Leonard Nimoy's self-important movie to the predictable debates about Anna's goodness that both

book and film set up like a silly riddle. And "The Good Mother" is just the most extreme among recent films that take quirky issues and atypical characters, then try to inflate melodrama to the status of social issues.

Costa-Gavras's "Betrayed" sets itself up as the story of a racist vigilante group whose members seem so ordinary they could be your next-door neighbors; then the film cloaks the issue in a ludicrous plot about the F.B.I. and an assassination attempt. In "Running on Empty," 60's radicals on the lam must let their teen-aged son make his own way the 80's. Though the film is finely acted and thoughtful, it is less about social conscience than family bonds.

■

Not every socially conscious film needs to be as tersely serious as "A World Apart," in

Michael Ginsberg

Asia Vieira and Diane Keaton in "The Good Mother"—Its ads reflect its pretentious veneer.

which the anti-apartheid heroine played by Barbara Hershey is defined by her political activism. But more and more films seem to bait their audiences with universal themes, then reel them in with melodrama.

What is "The Good Mother" actually about, seen without its deceptive rhetoric? Anna loses her frigidity and discovers sexual passion with Leo. One night while they are making love, Molly crawls into bed with them and instantly falls asleep; they quietly continue and do not budge the child.

Another evening, Molly finds Leo in the shower and asks, with a child's curiosity, if she can touch his penis. He says yes, assuming Anna would want him to be unembarrassed about his body. When Molly's father finds out about this, he sues for custody. The question that comes from these particulars is whether Anna has been seriously irresponsible or just momentarily lax.

Yet advertisements for the film accurately reflect its pretentious veneer: "Can a court determine how we should live, how we should love, how we should raise our children?" Both the novel and the film suggest that Anna is being punished for her sexuality. "I don't see how he has a right to sit in judgment on my life like this," Ms. Keaton whines about Brian, her former husband, but nothing in the film allows it to claim such a weighty social theme. Brian is not condemning her active sex life but her decisions about their child.

Despite Anna's talk about "raising Molly freely" — something the film makes little of as we see Anna flip from prude to libertine, literally overnight — "The Good Mother" is not about a woman who brings a lover into her home. It is about a woman without the good sense to carry her sleeping child out of her bed. At most, the story asks whether this odd and misguided woman is punished too severely for a lapse of judgment.

"You let him!" Brian accuses Anna. "You're in charge of her and you let him!" He may overstate her guilt, but at least he recognizes that the real issue is Anna's competence as a mother, not her libido. We see him, of course, only as the buttoned-down villain in boring gray suits. Stacking the case against him, neither the film nor the novel ever admits his point of view.

∎

"Betrayed" works in the same slippery way. Coming from the director of intelligent political thrillers such as "Z" and "State of Siege," it is more disappointing because its aspirations and our expectations are higher. Debra Winger plays an F.B.I. agent sent undercover as a farm worker to track down the vigilantes. She falls in love, nearly at first sight, with an apparently innocent farmer played by Tom Berenger. After he takes her along on a vigilante mission, she runs away, only to be sent back to the farm by her F.B.I. superiors.

An ordinary woman who falls deeply and gradually in love with a man, then discovers the dark side of his character — that situation would have created tough questions about how social injustice permeates everyday life. "Betrayed" would have been far more real, far less commercial and dramatic, if Ms. Winger's character had been a typical worker rather than a Federal agent armed with a plot device that ships her back to a murderer's arms. Yet the heightened romance and tricked-up story undermine every serious point "Betrayed" might have made. In this melodramatic context, the crucial scene of evil — the group hunts and shoots a black man as if he were an animal in season — is maddeningly trivialized.

Oddly, the current film with the greatest potential to exploit a titillating subject takes the most high-minded and effective approach. Jonathan Kaplan's "Accused" vaguely echoes the true case of a woman who was raped in a bar while onlookers cheered, but its fictional working-class heroine comes loaded with liabilities. Sarah is drunk and stoned when she is attacked; barely dressed, she has danced in the bar so lasciviously that her attackers can claim "she asked for it." Yet Jodie Foster makes her a startling character with plenty of tough realism and no self-pity.

∎

"The Accused" might easily have veered away to examine the potentially lurid and cliched details of Sarah's personal life. Instead, it focuses intensely not only on justice for her but on the class divisions that make her distrust the legal system. In one of the film's most telling scenes, Sarah challenges her yuppie lawyer, played by Kelly McGillis. "You ain't gonna defend me cause I'm some low-class bimbo," Ms. Foster says, with all the steely sureness of a woman who knows very well how powerless her social standing makes her.

The film never explores those class issues fully enough. And it takes its own unlikely turn when the lawyer allows the rapists to plead to a lesser crime and later prosecutes the bystanders. But "The Accused" has the courage not to cheat on its social themes and the honesty to admit that Sarah is a problematic heroine.

In fact, Sarah's atypical status is a key to the film's success, as "The Accused" demonstrates that an unusual character can also be universal. "The Good Mother" refuses to recognize that Anna is at all unusual. "The Accused" lets us know that Sarah's behavior has been cavalier and incautious — her judgment is every bit as disastrous as Anna's — yet the film insists that no circumstances can explain or excuse the crime against her. The social theme becomes more powerful when viewed in such complex and real terms. Late in the film, when scenes of the rape are intercut with the trial, they are horrifying; even as Sarah flings herself around the bar, we steel ourselves against the violence we know is about to come.

∎

Self-important melodramas are nothing new, of course, but the latest flurry can be traced back to the innocent "Fatal Attraction," a film that never pretended to be anything more than a thriller about a psychotic woman. Reactions to "Fatal Attraction" spiraled as critics and magazine writers suggested that it meant something serious. Alex, the murder-

Rob McEwan

Jodie Foster and Kelly McGillis in "The Accused," which takes a high-minded and effective approach to its titillating subject

ous rejected lover played by Glenn Close, came to represent single women, and Michael Douglas's adulterous affair with her became a cautionary tale about the age of AIDS.

But how unsettling was "Fatal Attraction," really? Was anyone's life truly changed by it? Were anyone's ideas altered? Did anyone sit up with

a jolt and say, "Oh, my, a metaphor about the consequenses of adultery! I'd better be faithful!"

In fact, films like "Fatal Attraction" and "The Good Mother" provoke debates as shallow and superficial as the movies themselves. Melodramas that pretend to higher

things allow audiences to have it both ways. There is the self-satisfying illusion of having grappled with a serious issue and, at the same time, the reassurance offered by the distance between us and the unbelievable Anna or Alex. If their characters seem to resemble anyone we know, it is not because the films have discovered

the universal qualities beneath their quirks. More likely, we have imposed an easy and comfortable universality on them, and perhaps been duped by a film's sneaky self-importance. □

1988 N 20, II:13:1

FILM VIEW

Japan's Best Movies Don't Travel

By VINCENT CANBY

TOKYO

THROUGHOUT MITSUO YANAGIMACHI'S "Fire Festival" ("Himatsuri"), one of the finest films to be made here in recent years, there recurs a series of images that are initially funny but which, as the film progresses, become increasingly disturbing.

Kimiko, a prostitute at the end of her prime, has returned to the small fishing village where she grew up. She's broke and at her wit's end but unfailingly cheerful as she goes about her bawdy business. When she's all dolled up in short, tight-fitting dresses and spiky high heels, she strides. When she puts on a traditional kimono, with the obi tied in the back, she takes smaller, ladylike steps.

Whatever she's wearing, however, Kimiko can't help but sashay, sometimes more broadly than others. Underneath the frequently hoisted or removed clothing, she is

Could it be that the world that welcomes the country's VCR's finds its finest films too Japanese?

Mitsuo Yanagimachi's "Fire Festival" has the blunt power of Greek tragedy.

the same desperate woman. Only the fashions change.

The story of Kimiko is not the main concern of "Fire Festival," but it reinforces the enormous power of a movie that, above all else, is about the shifting, contradictory impulses shaping contemporary Japan.

More than the films being made in any other country today, Japanese films illustrate, in one way and another, what's happening in this land, but then Japan's growing influence as a great economic power is so apparent that only a mountain hermit could remain untouched. It's evident in every aspect of Japanese life — finance and industry, fast food, appliances and, in particular, the content of their movies.

These come in all sizes, shapes and degrees of awareness: sophisticated satires whose subject is social change itself, poetic, quintessentially Japanese dramas in which ancient Shinto and Buddhist beliefs are tested against the demands of the new society; and cheapie, violence-laden exploitation pictures, exemplied by what are called the "be-bop high school" movies, which glamorize the lives of brainless youth on the rampage.

Such exploitation movies, like those in the United States, haven't a thought in their heads. Yet sitting through something called "Crazy Boys" on a Saturday evening in a Ginza theater is like flipping through a catalogue of evolving Japanese behavioral patterns, seen against the high-tech décor of the new Japan.

Except for the work of Akira Kurosawa, Japanese films have never found a consistently wide audience in America. The classics of Kenji Mizoguchi, Yasujiro Ozu and Mikio Naruse are more often honored in museums than in commercial theaters. Of the

films of contemporary Japanese directors, only those of the satirist Juzo Itami have received something approximating the kind of commercial release that highly praised French or Italian films receive (and of Mr. Itami's films, only one, "Tampopo," was an unqualified commercial hit).

■

The question that Japanese movie people most frequently ask the American visitor is why Japanese films aren't more successful in the United States. There's a certain amount of pride in the way they suggest that Japanese films may be — well — "too Japanese," but there is also immense frustration. Why doesn't a world that welcomes Japan's video cassette recorders respond with equal passion to its movies?

There's no easy answer, since the very particularity of Japanese movies is what the small but faithful group of American moviegoers admire most.

Now it seems that the "Japaneseness" of Japanese movies, which is their glory, might also be subjected to the same sort of pressures that have drastically altered everything else in this country, from the Tokyo skyline to Japanese tourism. (Well-heeled Japanese teen-agers, I'm told, now favor surfing vacations in Bali.)

Other countries have become world leaders over extended intervals of time. Japan's remarkable affluence has been achieved in something less than a decade. Nobody, here or abroad, can be quite sure what this sudden pre-eminence is going to mean in the long run.

Since the Meiji Restoration 120 years ago and the subsequent opening of Japan to out-

side influences, the Japanese have had their share of cultural shocks, none greater (until now) than the physical devastation wreaked during the closing days of World War II, followed by military defeat and the Allied occupation.

The changes taking place in Japan today are far more pleasant but no less profound and disorienting. It's not easy being immaculately rich. It's as if everyone in the country had won the New York State lottery on the same day.

The resulting uncertainty is the concern common to all of the more serious new Japanese films. However, in "Crazy Boys," which is about the often vicious high jinks of some young men who spend their time escaping from (and being put back into) a minimum security prison, the uncertainty is expressed entirely in what looks to be a style borrowed from Southern California — a big-beat soundtrack score, fast cutting and a narrative that, for all of its sex and violence, is no less sentimental than "The Panda Story."

At one point in "Crazy Boys," its swaggering delinquents even go in for marijuana farming, which appears to be a borrowed fantasy since pot is not exactly a common substance of abuse in publicly puritanical Japan, even among the demimonde.

Some people will tell you that the scarcity of drugs is the result of a tacit agreement between the yakuza (gangsters) and the police. That is, the yakuza are given a free hand to exploit various rackets, including prostitution, as long as they keep drugs out. A simpler, more plausible explanation is that there is, as yet, no demand.

Representing Japan at the Hawaii International Film Festival next week will be "So What" by Naoto Yamakawa, whose earlier film, the neo-Godardian "New Morning of Billy the Kid," marked him as one of the more promising of the younger new directors. "So What," like "Crazy Boys," is the Japanese as well as the English title.

One of the film's principal locations is a roadhouse called the Norson Welles (sic), frequented by the film's four protagonists, high school pals who are trying to form a rock band. The Norson Welles stands at the edge of a field near a small town so far from Tokyo that the young heroes feel as if they are in Siberia or, possibly, Alaska, which is a little bit farther away.

Hiroshi, the ringleader, and his friends hang out at the Norson Welles after school, drinking beer and talking about the future. The walls of the barroom are hung with photographs of John Lennon, Jimi Hendrix and other idols who, one boy says with respect, "died for their music."

The four feel misunderstood. Their teachers object to the noise when they practice at school after classes. Their parents are impatient with them. Except for their music, the pals are as aimless as their somewhat older counterparts in Fellini's "I Vitelloni."

The boys lack for nothing in the way of middle-class comforts. Most of the time, they practice in a barn owned by an old farmer who regards their electronically amplified music with baffled resignation, but the cows keep interrupting rehearsals. "If you don't have money," says one of Hiroshi's pals, "you don't have anything."

Somebody suddenly has an inspiration: "Hey, why don't we give a concert!" They do, but the results, while not exactly tragic, do not lead up to a Mickey Rooney-Judy Garland, "Babes in Arms" triumph. The film's ending is muted, much like that of "I Vitelloni."

"So What" has its own big-beat title song, which, I assume, is meant to be taken both as a promotional tool for the film and as a description of a state of mind.

"So What" is certainly not a silly film. It's not a be-bop high school movie, but it seems caught halfway between its genuinely Japanese concerns and a style that could be American or French or Italian, just about anything. Except for the language and the actors, it would appear to be stateless.

Stateless is absolutely the last word one would ever use about Mr. Yanagimachi's "Fire Festival," which I missed when it was shown at the 1985 New York Film Festival and which seems to have had as much trouble finding an audience in Japan as it did in the United States.

This eerie, complex film represents the kind of splendid Japanese work that may be in as much need of support and protection these days as its spectacular southern Honshu landscapes. Though environmental protection could be said to be one of the movie's concerns, it is chiefly interested in Japan's animistic heritage that, as Shintoism, has survived from pre-history to this present age of remarkable transitions.

Mr. Yanagimachi's screenplay takes as its inspiration the bare bones of a true story reported in the newspapers in 1980. An otherwise unremarkable man, living in a small village in southwestern Honshu, murdered the members of his family and then committed suicide for reasons never made clear.

As the director-writer imagines the tale, the man is Tatsuo, a robust lumberman, a decent family man and good-humored, guiltless womanizer who lives in a seaside village about to be developed into a fancy resort. In the course of a series of mysterious epiphanies, in the mountains where he chops trees and at sea where he fishes at night, Tatsuo finds himself in the thrall of the landscape whose gods and demons he has been challenging all his life.

■

Urged by the members of his family to sell out to the developers of the new resort, Tatsuo calmly selects an alternate course.

The title is not great. It suggests a film that is quaintly folkloric, while "Fire Festival" has much of the blunt power of Greek tragedy. Though the landscapes are beautiful, they are not mere scenery. They are the world according to Tatsuo. Tatsuo doesn't fight change. By embracing change in his manner, he affirms his identification with nature.

"Fire Festival" is not a film that could have come from any other culture, in any other time. As with many of the best Japanese films of the past, the foreigner can't possibly comprehend all of the various levels of "Fire Festival" without program notes.

Who wants program notes? I do, at least when the film is of the eccentric richness of "Fire Festival."

The best Japanese films are often acquired tastes. It's not just because the culture and manners are different. Japanese films don't look like the films from any other country. Japanese directors understand the power of close-ups, which they use sparingly. Medium- and long-shots are favored, requiring the audience to search the images for meanings that close-ups would either overstate or misrepresent in other ways. The pacing is slow compared to American films, compared even to most Japanese dramas one sees on television.

These are some of the very general reasons that Japanese films are not more popular abroad. They also are the reasons that Japanese films, at least *some* Japanese films, remain singular achievements. There's no easy way to reach an international market without denying a large portion of a magnificent heritage.

It could be that, as a result of the country's ascending position in the world, the rest of the world will eventually come to look at Japanese films with a better informed eye. That is a higher hope. □

1988 N 20, II:13:1

Short War, Long Movie

HANNA'S WAR, directed by Menahem Golan; written by Mr. Golan and Stanley Mann, based on the books "The Diaries of Hanna Senesh" by Hanna Senesh and "A Great Wind Cometh" by Yoel Palgi; director of photography, Elemer Ragalyi; edited by Alain Jakubowicz; music by Dov Seltzer; art director, Tividar Bertalan; produced by Mr. Golan and Yoram Globus; released by the Cannon Group Inc. At 57th Street Playhouse, at Avenue of the Americas, and other theaters. Running time: 150 minutes. This film is rated PG.

Katalin .... Ellen Burstyn
Hanna .... Maruschka Detmers
McCormack .... Anthony Andrews
Rosza .... Donald Pleasence
Captain Simon .... David Warner
Yoel .... Vincenzo Ricotta
Ruven .... Christopher Fairbank
Peretz .... Rob Jacks
Tony .... Serge el-Baz
Aba .... Eli Gorenstein

By WALTER GOODMAN

Hanna Senesh was a young Hungarian woman who settled in Palestine before World War II and returned to Europe in 1944, by parachute, as a British agent. She was arrested and executed, gaining a place among Jewish heroes and martyrs. "Hanna's War," based in part on her diaries, gives us the hero and martyr but not much of a character.

The Israeli movie maker Menahem Golan evidently took on "Hanna's War," which opens today at the 57th Street Playhouse and other theaters, as his personal contribution to Israeli kitsch. In addition to producing it with his partner, Yoram Globus, he also directed and collaborated on the screenplay.

The movie is awash in sunrise-sunset music and soaked in local color. The scenes in Hanna's kibbutz are idyllic; the kibbutzniks work hard and dance to "Hava Nagila." The Yugoslav partisans are also into folkdancing. Now and then Hanna recites one of her poems, which are as trite as the dialogue.

The script clunks along on recycled lines. When Hanna is recruited to parachute into Yugoslavia, she is told, "This will probably be a suicide mission." To which she responds, "When do we go?" You haven't seen so much shoulder-thumping hand-shaking camaraderie since "Beau Geste."

Hanna's mother (Ellen Burstyn), speaking of Hitler in 1937, remarks airily, "Who cares what such a silly man says?" Ms. Burstyn also gets to compare Hanna to Joan of Arc. A prison guard pleads, "We just follow orders." When the local Fascists prevent Hanna (Maruschka Detmers) from receiving a school honor because she is a Jew, the young poet declaims, "Only now I am beginning to see what it is to be Jewish in a gentile society." She scolds her tormentors, "Hungary learns quickly to bow her head to new masters." Even her big speech to the court is a bore.

The early action scenes offer some excitement, especially the Partisans' capture of a train that turns out to have boxcars filled with human beings. Since Hanna was caught practically as soon as she set foot in Hungary, her war was a short one. She doesn't get a chance to do much on screen after that except be tortured. Ms. Detmers, a Dutch-born French actress, delivers emotions as required; she is brave in action and miserable under torture, but there is nobody there. Ms. Burstyn seems to be wishing that she, too, were somewhere else.

The villains provide what zest there is: Donald Pleasence, doing his nutty number as a sadist with a soft streak ("I love a young girl's fingernails. Yours were so pretty.") and David Warner as the Uriah Heep of Hungarian Fascists ("This will be the last time you will see one another — and I mean the last time"). Anthony Andrews, playing a tough Scottish officer and gentleman, has the good luck to be eliminated fairly early.

1988 N 23, C14:1

Bearing Arms Maruschka Detmers stars in "Hanna's War," a drama based on the true story of Hanna Senesh, a Hungarian Jew who fought the Nazis in World War II.

Fleeing the Police In Paradise

BUSTER, directed by David Green; screenplay by Colin Shindler; director of photography, Tony Imi; edited by Lesley Walker; music by Anne Dudley; production designer, Simon Holland; produced by Norma Heyman; released by the Hemdale Releasing Corporation. At the Beekman, 65th Street at Second Avenue; the Criterion Center, Broadway between 44th and 45th Streets, and other theaters. Running time: 93 minutes. This film is rated R.

Buster	Phil Collins
June	Julie Walters
Bruce	Larry Lamb
Franny	Stephanie Lawrence
Nicky	Ellen Beaven
Harry	Michael Attwell
Ronnie	Ralph Brown
George	Christopher Ellison

By JANET MASLIN

Though Buster Edwards played a role in one of the biggest heists in recent history, he was strictly small-time. His exploits were petty enough to include, for instance, the middle-of-the-night theft of baby clothes, with a shopping list supplied by his pregnant wife. So what makes Buster a fit subject for a feature-length film biography? Perhaps nothing more than Buster's feisty, indefatigable manner, and the fact that he was there.

"Buster," which opens today at the Beekman, has a breezy style that goes a long way toward concealing its fundamental slightness. It also has the idea of treating the Buster Edwards story as a romance instead of a cavalcade of crime. The low-level British gangster Buster, played in hardy salt-of-the-earth style by the singer Phil Collins, is initially seen as a harried family man, worrying about how to make ends meet while the rent collector is almost literally at the door. (In fact, he's outside the window, peering in as the Edwards family cowers behind the living room sofa.) Buster's devotion to his wife, June (Julie Walters), is apparent even during their worst bickering.

"Borrow from a bank!" June shouts, during an argument about whether the growing Edwards family, with one child and another on the way, will ever move from their rental apartment and take a mortgage on a house. "Well, I do borrow from banks," replies Buster. "That's my job!" His work takes him one step further, however, when he and a group of cronies hatch a scheme to detain a mail train carrying a large amount of cash. Thus is Britain's infamous Great Train Robbery of 1963 set in motion.

•

"Buster," which was directed by David Green, a British television director, does what it can to link the robbery and its aftermath to other events unfolding in England at the time, most notably to the embarrassment caused by the Profumo scandal. In the wake of this, the film maintains, the Conservative Government was eager to deflect the headlines and take a tough stand. So the gang of robbers, in which Buster was little more than a junior member, became the target of an enormous manhunt. Most of the thieves were apprehended quickly. But Buster, after a comical close call with a neighbor in his new suburban home, took his family and escaped to Mexico.

The film is at its best in exploring the Edwards's troubles in paradise. Joined in Mexico by one of his partners in crime, Buster had an inordi-

nately hard time adapting to freedom, ease and sunshine. June stubbornly insisted on ordering British staples in Mexican restaurants, and otherwise displayed a homesickness that wouldn't go away. Eventually, she had to choose between the feckless Buster and the mother (played with acerbic intelligence by Sheila Hancock) who understandably wished Buster would leave her daughter alone. And Buster had to decide whether life on the run was really the life he wanted.

Had Buster not made the grand gesture he did, there wouldn't be much to his story. There isn't much to it anyway, but "Buster" profiles him in an easygoing and affectionate manner. Mr. Collins, who makes Buster a shrewd, scrappy figure, is heard singing on the soundtrack, but his performance is good enough to make audiences temporarily forget his career as a pop star. Miss Walters finds humor and humanity in June Edwards's remarkable forbearance. A little extra dividend is the Four Tops song heard on the soundtrack as the Edwardses supposedly live it up in Acapulco. Though the music enthusiastically claims otherwise, it's clear these reluctant visitors are having a perfectly miserable time.

1988 N 23, C12:1

Mideast Misfits

BIG GIRL, written and directed by Nirit Yaron-Gronich; CROWS, written and directed by Ayelet Menahemi; in Hebrew with English subtitles. At Film Forum 1, 57 Watts Street. Running time: 90 minutes. These films have no rating.

"Big Girl" is the more conventional of two Israeli films on the new bill at the Film Forum 1, and also the better. Directed by Nirit Yaron-Gronich, this story of a teen-age girl on the brink of sexual rebellion fits neatly into the tradition of coming-of-age films with heroines who experience inchoate longings that they don't fully understand.

In this case, though, the setting is unusual and the heroine an exceptionally vivid figure. As played by Ruthi Goldberg, the adolescent Ilit is a sparkling, vibrant young woman on the verge of independence, old enough to be hurt by life but yet equipped to fight back.

During the course of the story, Ilit's friendship with a pretty, rebellious schoolmate (Anat Zahor) becomes a source of trouble. Ilit gets involved with drugs, fights off a pass from a male teacher and falls into an affair with a self-involved married man. The film, helped greatly by Miss Goldberg's bright, inquisitive presence, does a good job of chronicling the process whereby Ilit moves from the protected world of her childhood to the dangers lurking beyond.

•

The second film on the program, "Crows," has a beginning that is ideally suited to one of those contests that solicit the opening lines of very unpromising works of fiction. "My father, he doesn't give a damn," the narrator, Maggie (Gili Benousilio), is heard saying. "He wanders around the cows all day long, thinking of my mother."

So Maggie, a farm girl, runs away to Tel Aviv, where she finds life is hard. "People don't invite strangers home," she complains, though her sullen, disoriented manner can

hardly be expected to win new friends. "They just chuck their rubbish out, thinking it makes them stink less."

Eventually, Maggie does find some companions: she falls in with a noisily flamboyant group of Tel Aviv homosexuals, who treat her as a kind of mascot and make her privy to their various problems. They shave Maggie's head. They confide in her about the lovers' quarrels that create rifts in their close-knit group. They dress up wildly and take Maggie along for nights of carousing. They involve her in their most dramatic troubles, like the frequent suicide attempts that threaten to splinter the group once and for all.

•

"Crows" has been described as "a dramatic re-creation of a real-life story, based on the personal experiences of the director and some of the participating actors." Thus the director, a woman named Ayelet Menahemi, seems to find more meaning and emotion in this material than most audiences will. Shock value is the main and perhaps only reason that the punks and transvestites of "Crows" have a claim on the attention; beyond this, their constant bickering is loud, repetitive and shallow. The direction is lively, but its pretentiousness becomes irritating very quickly.
                    JANET MASLIN

1988 N 23, C14:4

Back From Antarea

COCOON: THE RETURN, directed by Daniel Petrie; screenplay by Stephen McPherson, story by Mr. McPherson and Elizabeth Bradley, based on characters created by David Saperstein; director of photography, Tak Fujimoto; edited by Mark Roy Warner; music by James Horner; produced by Richard D. Zanuck, David Brown and Lili Fini Zanuck; released by 20th Century-Fox Film Corporation. Running time: 116 minutes.

Art Selwyn	Don Ameche
Ben Luckett	Wilford Brimley
Sara	Courteney Cox
Joe Finley	Hume Cronyn
Bernie Lefkowitz	Jack Gilford
Jack Bonner	Steve Guttenberg
David	Barret Oliver
Mary Luckett	Maureen Stapleton
Ruby	Elaine Stritch
Alma Finley	Jessica Tandy
Bess McCarthy	Gwen Verdon

By JANET MASLIN

If you, like the characters of "Cocoon," had spent the last several years on the planet Antarea losing track of earthly time, you might well mistake this story's latest installment for a V, a VI or a VII, instead of the mere II that it is. "Cocoon: The Return" is so tired, in fact, that it can barely recapitulate the winning formula of the original hit.

All the same actors are back, and they again appear as elderly people enjoying a delirious resurgence of youth. But since this takes the form of conga lines, surfside romps and Frank Sinatra singing "You Make Me Feel So Young" on the soundtrack, the net effect is one of being on a cruise ship to hell.

•

If the fun never ends, neither does it ever pick up steam. The film simply drifts from one time-wasting episode to the next until it's time to go back to Antarea — or not, as the case may be. Deciding whether they wish to go back to this problem-free planet or linger on Earth with friends, families and the prospect of mortality is the

Bob de Stolfe

Back to the Present Hume Cronyn and Wilford Brimley appear in "Cocoon: The Return," Daniel Petrie's sequel to the 1985 fantasy-drama about elderly Floridians who have a chance at eternal life.

only real dilemma these characters face.

The reason for the return voyage has something to do with "unfinished business," but like everything else about "Cocoon: The Return" it is allowed to remain vague. In any case, the first film's band of geriatric renegades appears on the doorstep of Bernie Lefkowitz (Jack Gilford), a widower who elected to skip the Antarean voyage and is now learning to hook rugs in an old-age home. The three visiting couples — Hume Cronyn and Jessica Tandy, Don Ameche and Gwen Verdon, Wilford Brimley and Maureen Stapleton — decide to help him shake off his gloom, but it isn't easy. While his three elderly male buddies strike up a volleyball game with young girls at the beach, Bernie mopes on the sidelines in his street clothes, then drags the others off to the cemetery for a visit to his wife's grave.

Though the visiting couples travel in a pack, their activities are separate enough to keep the film vacillating awkwardly from one subplot to another. Amid cries of "I feel like a teen-ager!" and "Did you get a load of the sunshine?" one of the couples experiences a fountain-of-youth medical miracle; another faces a life-threatening illness. Bernie Lefkowitz is wooed by a brassy motel operator (Elaine Stritch), who does everything she can to banish his blues.

•

And the Lucketts, played by Mr. Brimley and Miss Stapleton, reacquaint themselves with their relatives, prompting their misunderstood grandson to utter some of the film's more notable lines: "Mom, I don't need to see a shrink. They're not dead — they really *did* go to another planet." Since Mr. Brimley has done everything possible to destroy audience good will with his recent series of overbearing health-conscious cereal commercials, it's nice to find Miss Stapleton in one scene making him bacon for breakfast.

As if this weren't more than enough plot to keep up with, the film must also touch base with a disjointed group of younger characters, including Steve Guttenberg's tour boat operator, who seems even dopier here than he did the first time. Then there are scientists, led by the prettily professional-looking Courteney Cox, who study a silent, glowing Antarean that looks like a very large version of Tinkerbell. "No matter how many times I see that, it's still impressive," one of these scientists says. The screenplay, by Stephen McPherson, isn't often better than that.

Daniel Petrie's direction of "Cocoon: The Return," which opens today at the Gotham and other theaters, is slower, more sentimental and much less genuinely sweet than Ron Howard's direction of the first film. Even so, this weary sequel does have a few things to recommend it. Tak Fujimoto's cinematography gives a crisp, lively look to the Florida scenery. And some of the actors, particularly Mr. Ameche, Mr. Cronyn and Miss Tandy, radiate grace and gallantry even when the material does not.

●

"Cocoon: The Return" is rated PG ("Parental Guidance Suggested"). It includes sexual references of the most innocuous kind.

1988 N 23, C15:1

Southern Reflections

FULL MOON IN BLUE WATER, directed by Peter Masterson; written by Bill Bozzone; director of photography, Fred Murphy; edited by Jill Savitt; music by Phil Marshall; produced by Lawrence Turman, David Foster and John Turman; released by Trans World Entertainment. At the Festival (6 West 57th Street) and other theaters. Running time; 98 minutes. This film is rated R.

Floyd	Gene Hackman
Louise	Teri Garr
The General	Burgess Meredith
Jimmy	Elias Koteas
Charlie	Kevin Cooney
Virgil	David Doty
Baytch	Gil Glasgow
Dorothy	Becky Gelke
Lois	Marietta Marich

In spite of the participation of a number of talented people, "Full Moon in Blue Water" is almost as immediately forgettable as its title. The film is set in a town named Blue Water, on the Gulf Coast of Texas, and it takes place during a full moon. The full moon is seen by the audience, and a character says at one point, "There's a full moon tonight."

That's the kind of movie it is: a throwback to the sort of 1950's "Philco Playhouse" comedy-drama in which characters say exactly what they mean in the poetic, down-home accents of their region. The title is relevant, though not memorable.

Bill Bozzone's screenplay is about people getting in touch with their feelings.

●

They include Floyd (Gene Hackman), the owner of the failing Blue Water Grill, who has been in an emotional stupor for a year, since his wife mysteriously disappeared; Louise (Teri Garr), who drives the school bus and loves Floyd in spite of the ghost he clings to; the General (Burgess Meredith), Floyd's senile, wheelchair-bound father-in-law, and Jimmy (Elias Koteas), the young man who takes care of the General but who is not quite right in the head; every Southern community in fiction seem to have at least one.

In a 24-hour period, Floyd comes to terms with the past, Louise comes to

Service With a Smile Teri Garr co-stars with Gene Hackman and Burgess Meredith in "Full Moon in Blue Water."

terms with the future, the fate of the Blue Water Grill is decided and the General gets a chance to say a lot of alternately balmy and pertinent things that are, somehow, never very surprising.

The film was directed by Peter Masterson ("The Trip to Bountiful") on location on the Texas coast. It looks and sounds authentic without being authentically compelling for a minute. The most interesting character in the movie is Floyd's missing wife, who, though mourned, is never explained. In literature of this loquacious, neo-realist sort, a little taciturnity is most welcome.

"Full Moon in Blue Water" opens today at the Festival and other theaters.
VINCENT CANBY

1988 N 23, C15:1

Cooking One's Goose

SCROOGED, directed by Richard Donner; written by Mitch Glazer and Michael O'Donoghue; director of photography, Michael Chapman; edited by Frederic Steinkamp and William Steinkamp; music by Danny Elfman; production designer, J. Michael Riva; produced by Richard Donner and Art Linson; released by Paramount Pictures. At Loews Astor Plaza, 44th Street west of Broadway; Loews Orpheum, 86th Street near Third Avenue, and other theaters. Running time: 115 minutes. This film is rated PG-13.

Frank Cross	Bill Murray
Claire Phillips	Karen Allen
Lew Hayward	John Forsythe
Brice Cummings	John Glover
Ghost of Christmas Past	David Johansen
Ghost of Christmas Present	Carol Kane
Preston Rhinelander	Robert Mitchum
Himself	John Houseman

By VINCENT CANBY

Locked deep inside Bill Murray there is a small, hyperactive misanthrope fighting to be heard through the large heavy body that contains him. The misanthrope never sleeps. He's a busy demon, peering out through Mr. Murray's squinty eyes, seeing all and remaining actively unimpressed. By the time his nastiest observations fight their way to the surface, however, much of their sting has been absorbed by flesh, leaving a sometimes revivifying but thor-

oughly domesticated skepticism.

Because Mr. Murray is funniest when the big, laid-back, good-natured slob gives in to the furious mini-misanthrope, "Scrooged," an updated variation on Dickens's "Christmas Carol," is best when Mr. Murray is allowed to be his secret self.

As Frank Cross, the ratings-mad program chief of the IBC television network, Mr. Murray's contemporary Scrooge is a joy as long as he's making life miserable for everyone around him. When, finally, Frank sees the error of his ways, the movie succumbs to its heart of jelly. This may well be the secret of Mr. Murray's enormous popularity in a series of similarly second-rate comedies, including "Ghostbusters." In the end Mr. Murray must always deny what has appeared to be, until then, his redeeming offensiveness.

"Scrooged," which opens today at Loew's Astor Plaza and other theaters, has some very funny things in it, including snippets from IBC's big Christmas show, an adaptation of "A Christmas Carol" with a lot of leggy, scantily clad showgirls and a boozy actor (Buddy Hackett) playing a conventional Scrooge.

The actor has trouble with his lines. Standing in the middle of a set representing a Christmas card's vision of 19th-century London, this Scrooge barks out, "Why must I be molested by sea urchins!" The show-within-the-show promises a lot, but it is never allowed to attain the sublime bad taste of the "Springtime for Hitler" number in Mel Brooks's "Producers."

That is not Mr. Murray's style. In spite of the jokes at the expense of television-network censors, there's very little in the film, aside from naughty words, that wouldn't be perfectly acceptable on prime-time television. "Scrooged," written by Mitch Glazer and Michael O'Donoghue and directed by Richard Donner, exemplifies the kind of lazily executed comedies Mr. Murray seems always to make.

"Scrooged" works in fits and starts. The mundane demands of the sentimental story keep interrupting what are, essentially, revue sketches, a few of which are hilarious.

John Shannon

To the Dickens David Johansen is the cabbie; Bill Murray, the passenger in "Scrooged," an updated version of "A Christmas Carol," directed by Richard Donner.

Frank stuns a network staff meeting when he tosses out the Christmas show's trailer, which features an avuncular John Houseman reading from Dickens, and substitutes his own. This is an action-packed montage of clips of freeway killers, airplane terrorists and A-bomb detonations. Says one aide, "It looks like 'The Manson Family Christmas Special.'" Frank dismisses the man on the spot.

When the newspapers report that an old lady has died of a heart attack watching the trailer, Frank says, "You can't buy publicity like this." A production assistant complains that he is unable to fasten a pair of tiny antlers to the head of a mouse. Frank's solution: "Staple them."

John Forsythe appears in an amusing turn as the movie's Marley, Frank's predecessor at the network who died seven years before on the golf course, which explains why the ghost is wearing rotting sports clothes. After Mr. Murray (at least when he's being all-out mean), Carol Kane gives the film's funniest performance, as the Ghost of Christmas Present. Looking like Billie Burke's Glinda in "The Wizard of Oz," she's a pretty, diaphanous creature who alternately reasons with Frank and punches him in the stomach with the force of Muhammad Ali.

No expense has been spared in the film's physical production and casting. The movie looks as if it cost a lot even when it's not necessary; the classiness of the supporting cast, however, is. Robert Mitchum is cool and comic as the network president. He warns Frank to prepare for the day when cats and dogs will be a significant portion of the viewing audience. Karen Allen is charming as the girl Frank leaves behind in his ruthless climb to the top, and John Glover is the ever-smiling, patronizing new boy at the network who, if things go wrong, will be Frank's successor.

"Scrooged" is nothing if not contemporary. Frank Cross's passionately delivered final speech, in which he endorses the power of love and the importance of old-fashioned family values, might have come out of the recent Presidential campaign.

1988 N 23, C16:5

Halloween Party At a Funeral Home

NIGHT OF THE DEMONS, directed by Kevin Tenney; written and produced by Joe Augustyn; director of photography, David Lewis; edited by Daniel Duncan; art director, Ken Aichele; released by Paragon Arts International. At Criterion Center, Broadway at 45th Street, and other theaters. Running time: 89 minutes. This film is rated R.

Suzanne	Linnea Quigley
Judy	Cathy Podewell
Sal	William Gallo
Stooge	Hal Havins
Angela	Mimi Kinkade
Roger	Alvin Alexis

By CARYN JAMES

The cleverest thing about "Night of the Demons" is its advertising campaign. "Angela is having a party," the ads read. "Jason and Freddy are too scared to come." Well, that's partly true. The plot involves a Halloween party at a demonically possessed former funeral home, but my guess is that even the mass-murdering heroes of the "Friday the 13th" and "Nightmare on Elm Street" series would rather stay home and wash their hair than go to this film. And if Jason and Freddy's taste is too good for this, you know what to expect.

The 10 people gathered at the house are supposed to be high school students. None of them look like they've seen high school in years, though they may have graduated from Bad Acting School together. You'd think that demonic possession could only help, until it actually happens. Faces turn into rubbery-looking masks that bring to mind cut-rate costume shops. Angela dances and pulls her dress over her head. Her friend Suzanne seems to think she has wandered into a porno film.

•

"Night of the Demons" is stupid; it is sexist; at 89 minutes it feels unforgivably long. And it is just the most obvious mark of the film's total ineptitude that a story clearly marked for Halloween is arriving in time for Thanksgiving. But at least it gives you something extra to be thankful for — *not* seeing this piece of trash. You might as well be grateful for small favors.

"Night of the Demons" opened yesterday at the Criterion Center and other theaters.

1988 N 24, C16:4

Love in the Ruins

WE THE LIVING, directed by Goffredo Alessandrini; screenplay (Italian with English subtitles) by Anton Giulio Majano, based on the novel by Ayn Rand; adaptation by Corrado Alvaro and Orio Vergani; camera, Giuseppe Caracciolo; edited by Eraldo Da Roma; music by Renzo Rossellini; art direction, Andrea Beloborodoff, Giorgio Abkhasi and Amieto Bonetti; an Angelika Films release of a Scalera Films production. At Carnegie Hall Cinema, Seventh Avenue at 56th Street, and Bleecker Street Cinema, at La Guardia Place. Running time: 170 minutes. This film has no rating.

Kira	Alida Valli
Leo	Rossano Brazzi
Andrei	Fosco Giachetti
Tishenko	Giovanni Grasso
Pavel	Emilio Cigoli

By CARYN JAMES

Made in Italy during World War II, at first approved by the Fascists and then banned from theaters, "We the Living" has lost its political urgency. But it has gained historical interest, not to mention unintended kitsch. Seeing Rossano Brazzi play an aristocratic White Russian, standing in the fakest snow that wartime supplies could buy, may be the most peculiar twist of all in the curious story of how Ayn Rand's autobiographical first novel came to the screen.

In 1942, the director Goffredo Alessandrini helped himself, without any legal right, to Rand's novel, which was set in the years after the Russian Revolution. Even Rand's earliest writing anticipated the self-aggrandizing heroes of her most famous works, "The Fountainhead" and "Atlas Shrugged." A simplistic paean to the lost wealth and freedom of upper-class individuals, "We the Living" is so anti-Communist that it makes "Doctor Zhivago" look like "The Communist Manifesto."

Characters are hitched to ideas and sent scurrying through a crisscrossed plot: Kira, the White Russian heroine who dreams of becoming an engineer, gives herself to the Communist Andrei in order to save the life of her true love, the aristocratic Leo.

Resurrected
Alida Valli and Rossano Brazzi confront a sailor in "We the Living," a 1942 Italian film based on a semi-autobiographical Ayn Rand novel about a woman and her two lovers.

On paper, the novel's anti-Communist theme was acceptable to the state, which controlled film production. But the film follows the book rather faithfully, and to Rand Communism was less a specific political movement than a free-floating governmental fog that suffocated the individual. It took little more than casting Italian actors and changing "comrade" to "compagno," to allow the film to seem a barely veiled attack on Fascism. So lengthy it was released as two separate movies, "We the Living" had a successful five-month run before the Government decided the film's anti-Fascism was more dangerous than its anti-Communism was helpful, and banned it.

•

In 1968, Rand's lawyer bought the rights to the film. A cut-down version of "We the Living," with some portions newly and badly dubbed in Italian, opens today, for the first time in New York, at the Carnegie Hall and Bleecker Street Cinemas. Rand, who died in 1982, helped with the editing, and for once a film's difficult road to the screen is a true sign of its limited appeal. This 2-hour-and-50-minute eccentricity is far more interesting to hear about than to sit through.

As Kira, Alida Valli looks freshly beautiful, even jaunty, as she rides what is meant to be a filthy, overcrowded train back to her hometown: the city that is now Leningrad, was then Petrograd and to Kira "will always be Petersburg." When she meets Leo in front of an abandoned villa — a cardboard-looking set with all that fake snow — they look into each other's eyes and instantly find the kind of true love that only exists in movies.

For a time, Mr. Alessandrini's style is intriguingly varied, veering wildly from almost expressionistic shots of the villa to naturalistic close-ups. But before long that dizzying mix seems arbitrary, interrupted in this version by too many abrupt breaks where chunks of the story have been chopped out.

We are left with romantic scenes punctuated by political statements. The young Rossano Brazzi looks rather like the young Richard Burton; he and Miss Valli emote together in the quaintest, most old-fashioned way. As Kira and Leo try to escape the country by ship, Leo says "We'll be free, Kira, free!" and we look in at them through a porthole and watch them kiss.

Of course they are captured and sent back to Petrograd, to suffer the indignity of poverty. Miss Valli grows wan, but where the novel tells of the squalor of the cramped room Kira and Leo scandalously share, the film shows us a pretty apartment where paintings line the walls. When Leo gets tuberculosis, Kira sleeps with Andrei, her Communist suitor; the money he believes is going to her poor parents is used to send Leo to a sanitarium. But without any real sense of Kira's suffering, her decision — presented as desperate in the novel — seems rather unimaginative, even lazy, on the screen.

Andrei, however, could have been created only by Ayn Rand. The mark of his devotion is that he buys Kira black-market presents. The mark of his redemption is the final speech he gives to his compagni on a panel about to purge him. "You can never kill that thing in men that knows how to say I!"

Mr. Alessandrini's ambitious and ingenious film, once considered so serious and dangerous, looks very much like a giddy period piece today.

1988 N 25, C11:1

FILM VIEW/Janet Maslin

In Today's Animation, It's Dog Eat Doggie

NONE OF US WHO GREW UP whistling while we worked, wishing upon stars and always letting our consciences be our guides can question the persuasive power of animated children's movies. Nor can we fail to notice how much has changed since the great Disney classics first taught their humble lessons. In those days, a children's film was apt to provide a safe, comfortable, middle-class setting for a story about being true to oneself, generous to one's neighbors or loyal to one's friends. Today, ideas like those would quite literally never get off the drawing board.

The messages to be found in children's animation have evolved tellingly over the years. For instance, money and power now matter more than they ever did. And the heroes of these films are as apt to be involved in Messianic, world-saving missions as in being nice to their parents or learning not to lie. In addition, a streetwise sensibility, something that couldn't have been more alien to children's animation during the golden age of Disney, has lately developed a degree of cachet. Thanks to the dubious influence of Ralph Bakshi, whose "Fritz the Cat" and "Heavy Traffic" wedded advanced animation techniques with urban decay, it has become possible to blend a child-oriented visual style with lurid images most children would be hard pressed to understand.

A hint of this self-defeating strategy can be found in "Oliver & Company," the new animated Disney feature that takes place in the alleys, slums and subways of New York City. Evidently, somebody thought this a useful, child-pleasing innovation. "Oliver &

Company," a loose version of "Oliver Twist" with cats and dogs playing the roles of Dickens's urchins, attempts a hip, contemporary style that is at its best in the rock songs (sung by Huey Lewis, Billy Joel and others) that make up its energetic soundtrack. This street-smart mood is at its worst in the scenes that show a canine street gang cheerfully attempting crimes that range from theft to kidnapping.

The Oliver of the title is an antiseptically cute kitten who falls into this doggie demimonde, with the canine gang members representing various ethnic stereotypes (the chihuahua's wise-guy dialogue is supplied by Cheech Marin). The ethnic traits embodied by the dogs in "Lady and the Tramp" weren't any less stereotypical than this, but those earlier characters didn't have phrases like "Chill out, man!" in their lexicons.

■

In any case, the bland little Oliver spends much of the film learning tricks of the trade from these four-legged street hustlers, until he has the good luck to be adopted by a rich little girl named Jenny. The whole gang finds its way into Jenny's mansion, where the dogs admire the expensive art collection owned by Jenny's family.

As the only real child in the film, the blinking, snub-nosed Jenny represents kiddie animation at its most cloying and unauthentic. Real children in films like this were once a rarity, being so much less adaptable than anthropomorphic baby animals; only with Saturday morning television have they caught on. And animated children like Jenny seem much less vivid and fully imagined than their animal counterparts. However, Jenny will still be easier for most children to take than the film's Fagin, who has a Bakshi-inspired five o'clock shadow and large, ugly gaps between his teeth.

In addition to congratulating its characters on their wise-guy criminal instincts and rewarding little Oliver with his new status as a rich girl's coddled kitten, "Oliver & Company" also treats its young audiences to glimpses of sinister adult gangsters gliding ominiously through the city's alleyways. This is certainly a far cry from "Lady and the Tramp," where danger meant a trip to the dog pound, or from "Dumbo," where being laughed at by other elephants was the worst thing little Dumbo could imagine.

■

Along with the questionable role models that "Oliver & Company" presents to children, it also offers the kind of two-dimensional, barely mobile animation that comes to life only because the dogs' roles are read by recognizable actors. Bette Midler's vain, imperious poodle becomes the film's most memorable creation, but this same pooch would hardly amount to much if the film were seen without benefit of Miss Midler's voice. By contrast, the baby dinosaurs of "The Land Before Time," the other new animated film currently in circulation, are able to scamper and wriggle charmingly against backgrounds that actually move behind them. In "Oliver & Company" entirely too much of the film's movement is supplied by the panning of the camera, which does nothing to improve the flatness of the scenery.

The dinosaurs of "The Land Before Time" behave and sound like children of 6 or so, as opposed to the teen-age or adult voices that accompany the "Oliver" dogs. (The itty-bitty child's voice of the kitten Oliver sounds somewhat incongruous, under the circumstances.) The dinosaurs also *think*

Oliver the kitten is filled in by the streetwise Dodger in "Oliver & Company."

like children, which is a great help. Though the plot sends the dinosaurs on a long journey to a leafy valley where their species can thrive — temporarily, anyhow — it allows for considerable little-kid bickering along the way. Like the classic children's films of the past, it takes care to provide young audiences with thoughts and emotions that will make sense to them.

That it also finds mythic dimensions in the death of one dinosaur's mother is a slight but unfortunate intrusion of adult thinking into the children's world. Children have more than enough opportunity to think like adults when they grow up. □

1988 N 27, II:13:1

Another Line of Work

Michelle Pfeiffer

TEQUILA SUNRISE, written and directed by Robert Towne; director of photography, Conrad L. Hall; edited by Claire Simpson; music by Dave Grusin; production designer, Richard Sylbert; produced by Thom Mount; released by Warner Brothers. At the Sutton, Third Avenue at 57th Street, and other theaters. Running time: 116 minutes. This film is rated R.

Dale McKussic	Mel Gibson
Jo Ann Vallenari	Michelle Pfeiffer
Frescia	Kurt Russell
Commandante Escalante	Raul Julia
Maguire	J. T. Walsh

By VINCENT CANBY

Watching Robert Towne's "Tequila Sunrise" is like being allowed into a swinging Hollywood party so chic that, to quote Neil Simon, you're the only person there you've never heard of. All of the guests are dressed to the nines, including those wearing old jeans and T-shirts, which, in fact, are designer-distressed. You don't know the host but the people are friendly. The talk is nasty, clever and funny.

You're in with the in crowd.

Then, little by little, you realize that you aren't.

Because nobody is drinking anything stronger than Chablis, it's clear that when people leave the room, it's not in search of aspirin. The other guests are soon laughing too loud about things that aren't funny, talking intently about things that make no sense. You are forgotten but not gone.

The same thing happens with the film. While the audience looks on with increasing bewilderment, "Tequila Sunrise" sails away on what appears to be a gigantic cocaine high.

•

As long as it sticks around and remains coherent, "Tequila Sunrise" promises to be an entertaining romantic melodrama about a couple of high school friends now on opposite sides of the Los Angeles law.

McKussic (Mel Gibson) is a former cocaine importer making heroic efforts to become a legitimate businessman. His pal is Frescia (Kurt Russell), a narcotics detective whose associates are sure that McKussic is still dealing in drugs, which, at the very beginning, he is. Between the two men is the stunning presence of Michelle Pfeiffer, who plays Jo Ann Vallenari, the beautiful, remarkably self-contained owner of the elegant restaurant where McKussic dines every night.

The police are convinced that McKussic uses the restaurant as his place of business. They set up round-the-clock surveillance teams. They tap the phones. They try to decipher calls that otherwise appear to be harmless ("I'll be late for my reservation, but please hold the table").

Finally, when the police receive word that McKussic is about to receive a big cocaine shipment from his Mexican supplier, there's nothing for Frescia to do but attempt to become friendly with Jo Ann, whom they assume is McKussic's partner.

•

So far, so good. A perfectly workmanlike premise, and one that Mr. Towne, the author of the screenplays for "Shampoo" and "Chinatown," among others, could be expected to doll up with a good deal of hip wit and sophistication. This he does in an early encounter between Frescia and Jo Ann when she notes, correctly, that when the detective smiles, his lips seem to stick to his teeth. He accuses her of having the spontaneity of a maître d', which is also true.

It appears to be instant love, but then it also appears to be love between Jo Ann and McKussic, the erstwhile cocaine dealer. This much I think I know. Almost everything that comes after this, including more than half the film, remains a mystery, even after the closing credits.

What went wrong with "Tequila Sunrise," which opens today at the Sutton and other theaters, can only be guessed. Though Mr. Towne has written a lot of good screenplays of his own, and doctored a number by other people, "Tequila Sunrise" is only his second film as a writer-director, his first having been "Personal Best" in 1981.

Here the problem seems to be the fatal collaboration of a good writer with a director who wasn't strong or overbearing enough to pull him up short. The movie has the fuzzy focus of someone who has stared too long at a light bulb. Narrative points aren't made and the wrong points are emphasized. It could also be that too much footage was shot so that, when the time came for editing, a lot of essential material had to be cut out.

•

In whatever way "Tequila Sunrise" came into being, the result is a long, teasing trailer for a film not yet made. The movie looks very stylish and its principal actors, including Raul Julia (as a Mexican policeman), are all good company, even when they don't seem to have a clue about what's happening. Hard funny lines ("Maybe friendships just wear out, like tires") compete with ones that, under the circumstances, simply sound insincere ("Cocaine is no good for anybody").

Beautifully shot scenes are intercut with others that could have been ordered from a rotten-movie manual. It seems that worlds are about to collide when Mr. Gibson and Mr. Russell, having a commonplace conversation, are silhouetted against the sun as it sinks slowly into the Pacific. One love scene is shot upside down, tastefully. Still other scenes look as if they were afterthoughts, inserted following the first sneak preview to give order to the story.

"Tequila Sunrise" is a hangover, more muddling than painful.

1988 D 2, C8:4

The Bad Guy Cheats At Arm-Wrestling

DAKOTA, directed by Fred Holmes; screenplay by Lynn and Darryl J. Kuntz; camera, Jim Wrenn; music by Chris Christian; art direction, Pat O'Neal; produced by Darryl J. Kuntz and Frank J. Kuntz; released by Miramax Films. At Embassy 4, Broadway at 47th Street, and other theaters. Running time: 96 mintues. This film is rated PG.

Dakota	Lou Diamond Phillips
Aunt Zard	Herta Ware
Molly	DeeDee Norton
Casey	Jordan Burton
Walt	Eli Cummins
Bo	Steven Ruge
Rooster	John Hawkes
Rob	Tom Campitelli

By WALTER GOODMAN

"Dakota" is the sort of movie that demands an addition to the rating code — say, PI2 ("Unfit for Anybody Over Puberty"). It is a finding-yourself show. Eighteen-year-old Dakota (he doesn't like to give out his first name) races away from home troubles into the Western scenery on his motorbike and finds himself on the Diamond Thoroughbred Horse Ranch in Texas. He and Molly, the rancher's nice daughter, find each other, even though she knows about horses and all he knows about is automobiles. Soon they are meeting at Enchanted Rock. Dakota also helps Molly's brave 12-year-old one-legged brother to find himself, while a deeply wise old Indian woman grinds out wisdom.

•

Yup, there is a bully, named Bo, who is bent on giving Dakota a hard time; this hombre even cheats at arm-wrestling. Fortunately for Dakota, if not for the audience, Bo is as ineffectual as the director, Fred Holmes, who goes in for amateur arti-

On His Own Lou Diamond Phillips stars in "Dakota," about a teen-age runaway with no experience handling horses who winds up working on a ranch for thoroughbreds.

ness; every scene drifts on and on like the Texas range, to the accompaniment of what sounds like an unstrung banjo.

Dakota is played without surprises by Lou Diamond Phillips, who is also listed as associate producer. But nobody could have done much with the hammy screenplay by Lynn and Darryl J. Kuntz: "Sometimes a man has to go back to go forward." If you find yourself near Embassy 4 or one of the neighborhood theaters where "Dakota" is playing, go back.

"Dakota" is rated PG ("Parental Guidance Suggested"), possibly because of some mild violence and milder sex.

1988 D 2, C8:5

Radical Chic That's Lost Its Bloom

NOBODY LISTENED, produced, written and directed by Nestor Almendros and Jorge Ulla; in Spanish with English subtitles; director of photography, Orson Ochoa; edited by Gloria Piñeyro and Esther Durán; music by Ignacio Cervantes; presented by the Cuban Human Rights Film Project. At Cinema Studio 2, Broadway and 66th Street. Running time: 117 minutes. This film has no rating.

By JANET MASLIN

"Piece of cake for intellectuals": that is how René Tavernier, a French member of PEN, describes Fidel Castro's Cuba at a conference on human rights violations that is included in "Nobody Listened," a documentary by Nestor Almendros and Jorge Ulla. Mr. Tavernier discusses the appeal held by the Cuban model for ideologues who have grown disillusioned with Communist states elsewhere. "No big power," he says. "No old monster. Castro is a friend of the intellectuals. So he pretends, and we believe him."

"Nobody Listened," which opens today for a limited run at the Cinema Studio 2, is a stinging and trenchant indictment of the kind of radical chic to which Mr. Tavernier refers. Frankly partisan, it collects the extremely persuasive testimony of many Cubans who regard themselves as victims of the Castro regime. Though the film also includes some rare newsreel footage, mostly of the early days of the Castro revolution, much of it is devoted to these witnesses' accounts. A number of key figures from those days, among them Eloy Gutiérrez Menoyo and Huber Matos, have served long terms in Cuban prisons and are given ample

time to describe the horror and indignity of their ordeals.

•

Although "Nobody Listened" includes brief clandestinely shot glimpses of contemporary Cuba, and even a sequence inside what is supposed to be a model Cuban jail (with a beauty shop where female inmates receive haircuts and manicures, "all of course completely free"), the film makers themselves were denied the chance to film in their former country. (Mr. Ulla is a Cuban-born journalist and documentary film maker; Mr. Almendros, the master cinematographer, was born in Spain and educated in Cuba during the 1950's.)

So the film opens cleverly with a sequence in which Mr. Ulla makes repeated telephone calls to various Cuban authorities, requesting permission to make the film; he is put off, misled and finally labeled a traitor. This is immediately followed by official Cuban footage of a sunny touristy land that bears no resemblance to the place that is subsequently described here.

The film's many interviewees describe both the physical misery of captivity and the spiritual agony of realizing that their earlier hopes for a revitalized Cuba would be dashed. If anything, the film covers so many bases that it sometimes glosses too quickly over the larger political framework for these personal accounts.

Among the most indelible reminiscences are those of Alcides Martínez, who describes incarceration with a group of other men in a space so tiny it was known as a drawer; a tiny letter smuggled out under these conditions is held up as a very real trophy. Jorge Valls, a writer, on the other hand, points out that at least "free thinking dwelt behind prison walls; it was truly the free territory of Cuba." As for public free expression at the time of the revolution, Mr. Valls says: "None of that in 1959! Just ex-

traordinary exaltation, fanatical idolatry of the victorious warrior, and rampant folly that made everything acceptable."

•

The capriciousness of Cuban justice in those times is underscored repeatedly here, as various Castro lieutenants describe the minimal disloyalties that sent them to jail for very long sentences. "The whole thing was so devoid of seriousness, so arbitrary, so out of place in a true judicial system that it's only conceivable in a country where the warlord dictates all and the rest merely assent," Mr. Matos says of his trial. When Mr. Ulla asks why justice is so variable in Cuba, Mr. Matos says, "In Castro's hands, the law depends on the highs and lows of his temperament."

Making no attempt to give equal time to pro-Castro partisans, the film makers allow the sheer weight of testimony here to speak for itself. "Nobody Listened" is an urgent and painful litany, measured in its tone but passionately intent on making its point.

1988 D 2, C14:6

Fighting Fish Into the Breach

THE NAKED GUN: FROM THE FILES OF POLICE SQUAD!, directed by David Zucker; written by Jerry Zucker, Jim Abrahams, David Zucker and Pat Proft; director of photography, Robert Stevens; edited by Michael Jablow; music by Ira Newborn; production designer, John J. Lloyd; produced by Robert K. Weiss; released by Paramount Pictures. At Embassy 1, Broadway and 46th Street, and other theaters. Running time: 89 minutes. This film is rated PG-13.

Lieut. Frank Drebin	Leslie Nielsen
Jane Spencer	Priscilla Presley
Victor Ludwig	Ricardo Montalban
Capt. Ed Hocken	George Kennedy
Mayor of Los Angeles	Nancy Marchand
Ludwig's secretary	Charlotte Zucker

The proudly sophomoric comedy style of the Zucker-Abrahams-Zucker writing team, responsible for "Airplane!," "Top Secret!" and now (with Pat Proft) "The Naked Gun: From the Files of Police Squad!," is funniest when it's hardest to second-guess. But this time, in a scattershot detective parody that's a spinoff of the team's television series, things are relatively sane.

It will help if, while watching "The Naked Gun" at Embassy 1 or other neighborhood theaters, viewers can assume a mental age of about 14. The jokes will seem fresher that way, and they will also, much to the writers' credit, seem screamingly funny at times. Bathroom jokes, giddy repetition and calamitous pratfalls are the

Speaking Out Esturmio Mesa-Schuman, a farmer, describes the treatment of political inmates in Cuban prisons in "Nobody Listened."

Elliott Marks

Leslie Nielsen as Lieut. Frank Drebin in "The Naked Gun."

sine qua non of this kind of humor, but "The Naked Gun" gives such things an unexpected sophistication. Much of this can be attributed to the dapper presence of Leslie Nielsen who, as Lieut. Frank Drebin, manages to bring something heroic to the role of a perfectly oblivious fall guy.

First seen at a meeting of hostile world leaders in Beirut, Lebanon ("And don't ever let me catch you guys in America!" he shouts to look-alikes representing Idi Amin, Yasir Arafat, Muammar el-Qaddafi and others), Drebin returns to Los Angeles and finds himself on the hunt for a diabolical businessman named Victor Ludwig (Ricardo Montalban). Drebin, who is more or less outsmarted by Ludwig's tank of expensive fighting fish, isn't much of a match for the man himself.

Nor can he keep up with Drebin's beautiful assistant, Jane Spencer (Priscilla Presley), who has a gift for the double entendre and an unfortunate habit of walking into things.

"The Naked Gun" is so good-natured that it brings out the funny side of performers who, like Miss Presley, have never seemed to have much sense of humor in the past. Also in the cast, and equally well used, are George Kennedy as Drebin's friend and superior, Nancy Marchand as the Mayor of Los Angeles and Charlotte Zucker, who is David and Jerry Zucker's mother.

David Zucker, who directed "The Naked Gun," has given it a cheerful, messy style that never quite matches the ebullience of the writing. But high spirits may be all that a film like this really needs.

One of the more inspired visual gags is the standard young-and-in-love montage that finds Mr. Nielsen and Miss Presley frolicking prettily together and experiencing quite a few physical mishaps themselves. This sequence ends with a small credit in its lower left-hand corner, making it suitable for use on MTV. Later on,

once he and Miss Presley have begun their photogenic romance, she tells him, "I'm a very lucky woman." "So am I," Mr. Nielsen earnestly replies. It's impossible not to see that coming, but it's equally impossible not to laugh.

FILM VIEW/Vincent Canby

Annual Report On the Mob

MEMBERS OF ORGANIZED CRIME HAVEN'T fared all that well in court this year. Yet, in movies, they've come up winners in three odd-ball comedies that are making some observers feel queasy.

In Jonathan Demme's "Married to the Mob," about a young Mafia widow (Michelle Pfeiffer) who attempts to rejoin the straight world, the funniest characters are a murderous but henpecked don (Dean Stockwell) and his furiously jealous wife (Mercedes Ruehl). David Mamet's "Things Change" is a terrifically genial fairy tale about an aging, Sicilian-born Chicago shoeshine man (Don Ameche) who is given a last, Mafia-sponsored fling in Lake Tahoe before taking the rap for a mob murder he didn't commit.

Now comes the strangest and the most politically self-conscious film of the lot, Paul Morrissey's "Spike of Bensonhurst," in which Spike (Sasha Mitchell), the prizefighter-son of a mob soldier, earns the enmity (temporary) of his Mafia sponsor by trying to bust up the neighborhood crack trade.

Some things aren't supposed to be funny, including mob-owned politicians and drug trafficking, but you'd hardly

---

Crime isn't supposed to be funny, but three movies about the Mafia argue otherwise.

---

know it from these engagingly irreverent movies in which, for the most part, explicit violence is avoided. The mayhem, like the mob's business activities, usually remains off-screen. When murders are shown in "Married to the Mob," they have no emotional significance. Rather they are used to fuel the farcical complications of the story.

There's a scene in "Spike of Bensonhurst" in which a character has his hand beaten with the sort of mallet that makes tough steaks tender. The scene is definitely not funny. It is rough even if the camera averts its eye just before the mallet lands. The hand, one must assume, does get cubed. Though the character reappears, the damaged hand, conveniently, is never referred to again. The movie ends shortly afterward on an upbeat note of family reconciliation. In Mr. Morrissey's theology, letting bygones be bygones still is redemption.

Should we be concerned by this rather cavalier approach to a lamentable social problem? Should we go back to an earlier time — say, about 55 years ago — and ask moviemakers not to glorify crime, or not to make it seem harmless by appearing to be funny?

It could be that we are hopelessly decadent, but if we are, we've been on the road for some time.

In one of their now-classic "2,000-Year-Old Man" routines, Carl Reiner, as the interviewer, asks Mel Brooks, as the ancient, what Robin Hood was really like. The 2,000-Year-Old Man answers frankly. Robin Hood, he says, was a phony

"The Naked Gun" is rated PG-13 ("Special Parental Guidance for Those Younger Than 13"). It contains a number of innocently off-color jokes.   JANET MASLIN

1988 D 2, C16:1

and fraud. "He took from the rich. He also took from the poor, and he kept it all for himself."

Out of stuch stuff are legends made.

We've been in the process of humanizing, if not exactly humane-izing, organized crime for as long as I can remember. Though Rico in "Little Caesar" remains unrepentant to the fadeout ("Mother of God, is this the end of Rico?"), Edward G. Robinson's galvanizing performance not only made his career but also helped to give movie gangsters the status of tragic heroes. Their unfortunate flaw was that, for one reason or another, they were forced to operate outside conventional society.

■

Francis Coppola's two back-to-back adaptations of Mario Puzo's "Godfather" further humanized the documented viciousness of organized criminal activities. They set up the Mafia as a kind of alternative society existing separate from, but side-by-side with, the one in which big business functions with somewhat more discretion.

Though the films are loaded with violence, the gang warfare is internecine. No casual strollers-by get caught in the crossfire. The antisocial business of the Mafia is talked about as if it were nothing more destructive than the importation of improperly graded olive oil. Marlon Brando's great don even comes out against drugs. It's not a question of just saying no. The don is pragmatic. "Drugs will destroy us," he says, which, of course, they didn't.

The recent appearance of three Mafia comedies heralds no new cynicism but, instead, a refinement on the sort of gangster comedy that's been around since Frank Capra's "Lady for a Day" (1933) and another Robinson vehicle, based on a play by Howard Lindsay and Damon Runyon, "A Slight Case of Murder" (1937). Lugs can be lovable when they don't shoot straight.

The most insidious aspect of "Married to the Mob," "Things Change" and "Spike of Bensonhurst" is that each, in its own way, is so entertaining. "Married to the Mob," in which Michelle Pfeiffer proves that she can be as funny as she is beautiful, is Americana of the exceptionally high order Mr. Demme has already demonstrated in "Handle With Care," "Melvin and Howard" and "Something Wild."

"Things Change," written by Mr. Mamet with Shel Silverstein, is so firmly funny in its writing and in the performances (by Joe Mantegna and Mr. Ameche, among others) that it avoids the sentimentality into which Capra comedies often capsize. The wild card in this deck is "Spike of Bensonhurst."

Mr. Morrissey is proving himself to be a remarkable stayer. When his "Trash" was released in 1970, I wrote that although he was a talented director, the film, being a parody of itself, represented a dead-end in film making. Wrong. The Morrissey career has been checkered but never fully checked, even with the release earlier this year of the solemn, muddled (I think), unintentionally funny "Beethoven's Nephew."

Andy Warhol, Mr. Morrissey's mentor, has come and gone, but the singular Morrissey films, including "Mixed Blood" (1985), continue to roll off what is virtually a one-man assembly line. He has collaborators — the screenplay for "Spike" was written with Alan Bowne. Yet Mr. Morrissey's work is as immediately apparent from the nearly identical look of the pretty young actors he casts (full-lipped, sullen, seemingly androgynous) as from his screenplays: a dizzy mixture of camp humor, shock effects and what can now be clearly identified as scattershot political conservatism.

Mr. Morrissey has a strong love-hate relationship with squalid locales and inarticulate characters, exemplified in "Trash" by the principal setting, a dingy basement apartment on the Lower East Side, and by Holly Woodlawn, the film's lovelorn female-impersonator heroine, and Joe Dallesandro, her uninterested lover.

■

In "Spike" there is no doubt that Mr. Morrissey blames society, especially its liberal politicians, for the awful state of things that so intrigue him. 'Drugs are honest," says one hood. "There ain't any laws against it. Politicians took care of that." This appears to be Mr. Morrissey's main political point.

"Spike" comes close to mainstream movie making, though nothing in the film is as conventional as the role models it sends up, including "Saturday Night Fever" and maybe even "The Godfather." Spike, well played by Sasha Mitchell (who is a male model), aspires to a career in the ring and will throw any number of fights if it will bring him the sponsorship of the local don (Ernest Borgnine).

The don, however, thinks prizefighting has become "too ethnic," meaning too black and too Hispanic. Spike tries to please the don by running numbers but, when he gets his chance to fight again, he refuses to throw the bout. Though Spike has two girlfriends, one Italian and one Puerto Rican, the most intense relationship in the film is between Spike and the don.

Mr. Borgnine is better than he's been in years as an old-fashioned gangster who simply doesn't understand what is happening in the world. The don notes sadly that his wife is "a tramp" and that Spike's mother is a lesbian, which, he acknowledges, is better than if she were cheating on Spike's father with a man.

"I guess that's the way things are in society today," he says, "but it don't mean I gotta like it."

When Spike is exiled from Bensonhurst and takes up residence in Red Hook with a Puerto Rican family, Spike becomes outraged (and politicized) seeing the damage that the mob's crack dealers are doing to the neighborhood. He takes it upon himself, as a self-styled representative of "a more advanced civilization," to clean up the mess with a baseball bat. The mother (Antonia Rey) of his Puerto Rican girlfriend is enchanted by Spike. "The dream of my life," she says, clasping her hands and swooning, "a Mafia connection!"

Though Mr. Morrissey has never been well known as an actor's director, he obtains excellent performances from the members of his large cast, including Miss Rey, Sylvia Miles as a coke-sniffing liberal Congresswoman, Rick Aviles as one of Spike's boxing partners, Maria Pitillo as Angel, the Mafia princess of Bensonhurst, and Anne DeSalvo as the princess's trampish stepmother.

When asked by Mr. Borgnine why his daughter is late getting ready for a party, Miss DeSalvo delivers a typical Morrissey explanation. Angel, she says, refuses to use a hair dryer. "She wants it to dry natural, or her dye job will oxidize."

It's the sort of thing that Holly Woodlawn, had she not been possibly balding, would have said 18 years ago. □

1988 D 4, II:15:5

Talking Feet

RETRACING STEPS: AMERICAN DANCE SINCE POSTMODERNISM, produced and directed by Michael Blackwood; written by Sally Banes; distributed by Michael Blackwood Productions Inc. Running time: 88 minutes.
WITH: Johanna Boyce, Blondell Cummings, Molissa Fenley, Bill T. Jones and Arnie Zane, Diane Martel, Wendy Perron, Stephen Petronio and Jim Self.

BEEHIVE, directed by Frank Moore and Jim Self; choreography by Mr. Self; cinematography by Barry Shils; music by Man Parrish; costumes, sets and special effects by Mr. Moore. Running time: 15 minutes.
At Film Forum 1, 57 Watts Street. These films have no rating.
WITH: Mr. Self; Teri Weksler

By JENNIFER DUNNING

Michael Blackwood's "Retracing Steps" doesn't have an official rating, but it ought to carry a warning. The new documentary, which opens today for a week's run at Film Forum 1 with "Beehive," a giddily delightful short movie by Frank Moore and Jim Self, contains a good deal of verbiage that may make reasonably sophisticated viewers over 40 feel very old and cynical.

"Retracing Steps" has the clarity and sensitivity one expects from Mr. Blackwood, whose documentaries include "Making Dances," a portrait of seven experimentalist choreographers who came of artistic age in the 1970's and 1980's. In "Retracing Steps," subtitled "American Dance Since Postmodernism," Mr. Blackwood takes on the next generation of modern-dance choreographers, with the help of Sally Banes, the film's writer and consultant and a historian of the postmodernist dance movement. Nine choreographers — Johanna Boyce, Blondell Cummings, Molissa Fenley, Bill T. Jones and Arnie Zane, Diane Martel, Wendy Perron, Stephen Petronio and Mr. Self — talk of their work, their futures and their places in postmodernist dance history.

●

Dance had long been thought of as an art that existed outside the realm of words. But public analysis of work and even the incorporation of that analysis into the work itself became fashionable with the generation of choreographers interviewed in "Making Dances." Much of what is said in "Retracing Steps" suggests that it is time for the talk to stop for a while or to become more focused, plain-spoken and communicative and less self-justifying.

Several of the choreographers seem ill at ease on camera, among them Ms. Perron, Ms. Martel and, less obviously, Mr. Petronio. Some of the talk is predictable. We expect, for example, that Mr. Petronio will allude to deconstructionism, and he does. Ms. Martel mentions Antonin Artaud — or "good old Artaud," as she puts it — while she talks, ad nauseam, of her desire to offend.

Mr. Petronio talks solemnly of building "a three-dimensional model for abandonment" and of his "personal commitment to extending himself," though his description of his dances as "adrenalized situations" is informative, and so are his precise observations on his abstraction of imagery. Ms. Perron speaks of phrases in her dance that allow the performers to improvise and thus help shape the work. But haven't performers been doing that by the mere act of performing since the first choreographed step was taken? And where did Mr. Zane get the idea that anyone has ever thought of modern dance as a "rosy occupation"?

But Mr. Zane and, particularly, Mr. Jones talk interestingly of their discovering and dealing with political themes in dance. Mr. Jones recalls with wry honesty their early, innocent artistic elitism. His comments about his childhood and his entry into dance are revealing, as are those of Ms. Boyce, Ms. Cummings and Mr. Self. There are informative discussions of work processes from Ms. Boyce and Mr. Self, and Ms. Boyce touches provocatively on the make-or-break nature of a choreographic career today.

A very moving high point of "Retracing Steps" occurs when Ms. Cummings, who is black, talks of performing her "Chicken Soup" for a black audience that brings a special understanding to the solo. Tears suddenly well up in her eyes, but she continues, speaking as calmly and steadily as she has throughout the film. That moment sheds additional light on her dances.

But the well-chosen and sensitively filmed dance shown in "Retracing Steps," shot in a variety of pristine studios and on the stage, needs little explanation. It is, as the film's preamble states, physically explosive, ironic, elegant, outrageous and dramatic. It is also welldanced — and an appropriate monument to the choreographers of what might be termed the post-postmodernist generation.

1988 D 7, C24:5

Footwork

Molissa Fenley is one of nine young choreographers seen in Michael Blackwood's "Retracing Steps: American Dance Since Postmodernism."

Jack Mitchell

Without Chatter

AMERIKA, TERRA INCOGNITA, directed by Diego Rísquez; screenplay by Luis A. Duque and Mr. Rísquez; edited by Leonardo Henríquez; director of cinematography, Andrés Agusti; music by Alejandro Blanco Uribe; produced by Lidia Córdoba; a Coralie Films International Zanzibar Release. At the Bleecker Street Cinema, 144 Bleecker Street. Running time: 90 minutes. This film has no rating.

European Princess .... María Luisa Mosquera
Indian Chief .... Alberto Martín
Astrologer .... Hugo Márquez
Conquistador .... Luis M. Trujillo

By CARYN JAMES

"Amerika, Terra Incognita" is a brightly colored parade of familiar but skewed images. Conquistadors march through the lush forests of the New World to their ship filled with loot — exotic plants, glowing jewels, a crocodile made of gold and a captive Indian, stony with dignity. They arrive at the overwrought Spanish court, where an artist who is almost, but not quite, Velázquez paints a version of "Las Meninas" ("The Maids of Honor") that makes you wonder, "What's wrong with this picture?"

And at a court musicale, Vivaldi wears a long red hair ribbon and conducts a composition of his own, though the music sounds far more like John Cage's. These always pretty and sometimes parodic pictures are the whole of this ambitious and chaotic film. Dislocated images are so much the point that there is no dialogue at all — only stately music, appropriate sound effects and some brief lines spoken at the musicale.

The film is the third in a trilogy by Diego Rísquez, a Venezuelan director, examining the European conquest of South America. The first two films, never released in New York — "Bolívar, Sifonía, Tropikal" and "Orinoko, Nueva Mundo" — are also free of spoken words.

But if Mr. Rísquez, who has also been a photographer and a painter, seems to distrust language, he is even warier of the static images that have been passed down to us through history books and art. "Amerika, Terra Incognita," which opens today at the Bleecker Street Cinema, aims to shake us free from those imagined scenes.

●

At first, the conquistadors look like a crayon-colored history lesson, a high school pageant come to life. The characters' unnatural silence enhances the effect of a tableau set in motion. So the film becomes amiably goofy when mermaids suddenly escort the ship out to sea, and it seems self-mocking when the camera shoots a very tight close-up of a wave then swings topsy-turvy for a minute to suggest the long voyage to Spain.

Yet as Mr. Rísquez follows the Indian — clearly noble and nothing like a savage — through the Spanish court, the film's tone veers so wildly from straightforward to ironic that the director quickly loses control. There are scenes we laugh with — like the Monty Pythonesque musical — and others we laugh at. The Indian teaches the Spaniards how to pot plants; they don't seem to know the roots must go in, not on, the soil.

At his best, Mr. Rísquez can create eerie allusions. As Velázquez works on his famous painting of the infanta and her maids, the mirror that hangs in the background of that painting suddenly turns black in a way that suggests a television screen; then the Indian's face appears in the mirror to replace the faces of the royal couple.

The small boy in the painting rests his foot not on a dog but on the golden crocodile. Strangeness intrudes on this familiar image in an unsettling way.

•

But even the strongest of these images ultimately seem weightless. The captive Indian appears to have magical powers, but that ghost of a theme remains hidden. And in a truly silly ending, a Spanish princess seduces the Indian — he had, after all, been wandering around in little more than a loincloth and a huge mother-of-pearl necklace — and bears him a child made of gold.

It is hard to see how that golden child is different from the golden crocodile. "Amerika, Terra Incognita" can't support even that much rational investigation. But this gracefully designed and insistently visual film is at least original and never dull in the way it entertains the eye.

1988 D 9, C10:6

3 Murders, 2 Agents, One Long Hot Summer

Gene Hackman

MISSISSIPPI BURNING, directed by Alan Parker; written by Chris Gerolmo; director of photography, Peter Biziou; edited by Gerry Hambling; music by Trevor Jones; production designers, Philip Harrison and Geoffrey Kirkland; produced by Frederick Zollo and Robert F. Colesberry; released by Orion Pictures. At Loews Tower East, Third Avenue and 72d Street, and Loews 84th Street

Six, at Broadway. Running time: 127 minutes. This film is rated R.

Anderson	Gene Hackman
Ward	Willem Dafoe
Mrs. Pell	Frances McDormand
Deputy Pell	Brad Dourif
Mayor Tilman	R. Lee Ermey
Sheriff Stuckey	Gailard Sartain
Townley	Stephen Tobolowsky

By VINCENT CANBY

On the night of Sunday, June 21, 1964, the civil-rights workers James Chaney, a local black man, and Andrew Goodman and Michael Schwerner, both white and from New York, disappeared after being held a few hours on a bogus traffic charge in the Philadelphia, Miss., jail. For some months, Mr. Schwerner had been conspicuous in and around east-central Mississippi as a leading member of one of the volunteer teams coming to the South to help register black voters.

It promised to be a violent summer. The United States Senate had just passed a far-reaching Civil Rights Act. Many college students were

planning to go South to aid the integration movement. Outraged Southern editorial writers warned of the coming "invasion."

The disappearance of Chaney, Goodman and Schwerner was immediately called a publicity stunt by the white supremacists. It was something concocted by the Rev. Dr. Martin Luther King Jr., they said. The local police weren't much interested in pursuing the matter. People disappeared every day. Why should these men be considered more important? The favored story was that Chaney, Goodman and Schwerner had slipped away to the North and were hiding out, laughing at all the fuss they were causing.

•

The Federal Bureau of Investigation, which at that time didn't have one black agent, stepped in. Six weeks later, after a certain amount of luck and the payment of a sizable amount of cash to informants, the bodies of the three men were found buried in a dam not far from Philadelphia.

A scene from Alan Parker's film, — "I'm trying to reach a generation who knows nothing of that historical event," *says the director.*

Charged with interfering with the victims' civil rights (there was no Federal murder statute) were members of the Ku Klux Klan, as well as the county sheriff and his deputy.

Taking the bare bones of this true story, Chris Gerolmo, the screenwriter, and Alan Parker, the director, have come up with one of the toughest, straightest, most effective fiction films yet made about bigotry and racial violence, whether in this country or anywhere else in the world.

"Mississippi Burning," which opens today at Loews Tower East and Loews 84th Street Six, avoids the pieties and the subterfuges of such films as "Cry Freedom" and "A World Apart." In attempting to dramatize the fight against South African apartheid, both "Cry Freedom" and, to a lesser extent, "A World Apart" lose sight of the real subject, which eventually becomes mere background detail.

"Mississippi Burning" never makes that mistake. It is relentless in the way it maintains its focus. Virtually every image says that this is the way things were, and may still be. Think about it.

The film doesn't pretend to be about the civil-rights workers themselves. It's almost as if Mr. Parker and Mr. Gerolmo respected the victims, their ideals and their fate too much to reinvent them through the use of fiction.

"Mississippi Burning" is, instead, a fictionalized account of the investigation into their disappearance. Some of the imagined twists and turns of the investigation go rather far off the track, but never for a minute does the film sacrifice the honesty of time, temper and place. More important, the fictional characters exist and come to vivid life entirely within the context of the events recalled by the film. This is not only good movie making, it also honors the steadfastness of the legions of people who once fought for social change.

•

The film's principal characters are two F.B.I. men sent down to fictional Jessup County, Miss., to look into the reported disappearance of the civil-rights workers. The leader of the two-man team is Ward (Willem Dafoe), a straight-backed, neatly pressed young agent who goes by the book.

His partner, and the film's volatile center, is a not easily categorized fellow named Anderson (Gene Hackman). A Mississippi redneck, as well as a former Mississippi county sheriff, Anderson is one of those independently minded Southerners who confound all out-of-state preconceptions about Mississippi, or any other place in the supposedly solid South. (Another would be William Bradford Huie, the crusading Alabama-born-and-bred journalist, author of "Three Lives for Mississippi" (1965), one of the first books about the Chaney-Goodman-Schwerner case.)

The tensions that develop between Ward and Anderson are not entirely unpredictable. The film's resolution also depends on two rather unlikely character transformations. Yet nothing long deters the accumulating dramatic momentum as "Mississippi Burning" proceeds and as the defense of the good, psalm-singing, white Christian murderers unravels.

"Mississippi Burning" looks and sounds utterly authentic. It's a measure of some remarkable progress that it was filmed entirely in Mississippi, with the Governor's apparent blessing, and in Alabama. Though it is mesmerizing, it would be difficult to describe it as an entertainment.

The violence it depicts in such graphic detail — the beatings of innocents, the burnings of houses, schools and churches, the civil chaos — is sometimes so rough and harrowing that one looks for a way out of the film, seizing on minor discrepancies to relieve the tension.

"Mississippi Burning" is so full of conviction in other ways, however, that its drama cannot be easily ignored.

Mr. Hackman has possibly the best-written role of his career as the scratchy, rumpled, down-home-talking redneck, who himself has murder in his heart. He is sensational. He seems to creep up on Anderson, allowing the character to take shape gradually though, quite early on, he reveals what becomes the — for lack of a better word — subtext for everything the audience sees.

By comparison, Mr. Dafoe's agent Ward is far more functional, a sort of necessity to keep things moving. Frances McDormand is surprisingly moving as another plot function, the unhappy, bewildered wife of one of the murderers. The superior supporting cast includes Brad Dourif, Gailard Sartain and Michael Rooker, all of whom play Southern types who could have stepped out of newsreels of the period.

Peter Biziou's camerawork is so evocative that, I suspect, one could hear dogs barking in the distance, freight trains passing in the night and tree toads and crickets even without a soundtrack.

"Mississippi Burning" is first-rate.

1988 D 9, C12:1

Student of Cooking And Kidding

MY STEPMOTHER IS AN ALIEN, directed by Richard Benjamin; written by Jerico and Herschel Weingrod and Timothy Harris and Jonathan Reynolds; director of photography, Richard H. Kline; film editor, Jacqueline Cambas; music by Alan Silvestri; production designer, Charles Rosen; produced by Franklin R. Levy and Ronald Parker; released by the Weintraub Entertainment Group. At the Manhattan Twin, 59th Street east of Third Avenue, and other theaters. Running time: 108 minutes. This film is rated PG-13.

Dr. Steve Mills	Dan Aykroyd
Celeste	Kim Basinger
Ron Mills	Jon Lovitz
Jessie Mills	Alyson Hannigan
Dr. Lucas Budlong	Joseph Maher
Fred Glass	Seth Green
Grady	Wesley Mann
The Voice of Bag	Ann Prentiss
The Voice of Carl Sagan	Harry Shearer

By JANET MASLIN

In "My Stepmother Is an Alien," Kim Basinger plays a creature from another galaxy who is sent to Earth to sweet-talk a scientist into revealing secrets that will save her planet. The alien, called Celeste, is supposed to be an outstandingly brilliant individual who is well qualified for the task at hand. Her methods: cooking elaborate meals for the scientist, going to bed with him and wowing him with her delightfully birdbrained manner. When this doesn't do the trick, Celeste consults with three male elders from her planet, who recommend she turn on even more charm.

Of all the dizzy dames to be found on movie screens this Christmas — and there are quite a lot of them — Celeste stands in a class by herself. She's a formidable paradox, since she's as winningly played as she is annoyingly written. She is also, where giddy women in form-fitting outfits are concerned, something of a wild extreme. What's more, Celeste is outstandingly ill-situated, since she is expected to work her formidable wiles on a man who hardly seems to warrant the effort. Dan Aykroyd, who plays the scientist, isn't the least bit funny in this role, nor is he remotely suited to playing a romantic lead.

"My Stepmother Is an Alien," which was directed by Richard Benjamin and opens today at the Manhattan Twin and other theaters, begins with a lengthy sequence setting up the scientist, Dr. Steve Mills; his playboy brother (Jon Lovitz, who makes a scene-stealing sleazeball); his lovable teen-age daughter (Alyson Hannigan) by a wife who is conveniently deceased, and the experiment that paves the way for Celeste's arrival. This experiment is depicted on a computer screen as if it were a video game, which may give some idea of the audience at which the film is aimed.

After the experiment goes awry, Celeste is dispatched to Earth, where she lands on a beach and wiggles her toes giddily in the sand. Then she slithers into a party where the plump, disheveled Dr. Mills can be found, and delivers some adorable non sequiturs meant to illustrate her faulty knowledge of Earth customs ("Do you have any spinach — my hands are freezing!" she remarks, just after trying to light a carrot as if it were a cigarette). Dr. Mills is delighted, especially since Celeste has taken the trouble to wear red, his favorite color.

Unlike the screenwriters, who often cross the thin line between wit and silliness as they outline Celeste's neo-"I Love Lucy"-isms, Miss Basinger reveals unfailingly sound instincts for comedy. Enchantingly eccentric, outfitted in a series of outstandingly strange and funny costumes (by Aggie Guerard Rodgers), Miss Basinger ought to be more than enough to make the film interesting. But unfortunately, she's not alone. And the romantic scenes between Miss Basinger and Mr. Aykroyd play like a game of What's Wrong With This Picture?

•

The film tries to get a lot of mileage out of Celeste's efforts to understand essential earthly practices, like cooking and kissing. To master the former, she appropriates a restaurant menu and makes everything on it for the astonished Dr. Mills; as for the latter, she studies a montage of filmed embraces, featuring everyone from Soviet leaders to Dracula, and when she subsequently tries to learn about sex, she treats the porno film "Debbie Does Dallas" as an educa-

tional tool. Celeste is given guidance in these matters by the talking snake she carries in her pocketbook, a creation that is of more psychiatric than comic interest.

"My Stepmother Is an Alien" winds up on a sentimental note, as Celeste takes stock of all the earthly pleasures she has been experiencing and decides that humans have it made. A book of Shirley MacLaine's turns out to provide Celeste with one of her most memorable earthly laughs.

•

"My Stepmother Is an Alien" is rated PG-13 ("Special Parental Guidance Suggested for Those Younger Than 13"). It includes several bedroom scenes and sexual innuendoes.

1988 D 9, C17:1

Odd Couple

TWINS, produced and directed by Ivan Reitman; written by William Davies, William Osborne, Timothy Harris and Herschel Weingrod; director of photography, Andrzej Bartkowiak; edited by Sheldon Kahn and Donn Cambern; music by Georges Delerue; production designer, James D. Bissell; released by Universal Pictures. At the National Twin, Broadway and 44th Street, and other theaters. Running time: 115 minutes. This film is rated PG.

Julius Benedict	Arnold Schwarzenegger
Vincent Benedict	Danny DeVito
Marnie Mason	Kelly Preston
Linda Mason	Chloe Webb
Mary Ann Benedict	Bonnie Bartlett
Webster	Marshall Bell
Beetroot McKinley	Trey Wilson

By VINCENT CANBY

The reports that Arnold Schwarzenegger has a gift for comedy, based on isolated double-entendres he has delivered in such films as "Red Heat" and "The Terminator," turn out to have been premature.

In his new film, "Twins," which is supposed to be funny, the former Mr. Universe and pint-sized Danny DeVito play twins, the result of a genetic experiment that went awry. To the extent that "Twins" is carried by anybody, it is carried by Mr. DeVito. Mr. Schwarzenegger is dead weight.

The gimmick is this: having been separated at birth, the brothers finally meet 35 years later in Los Angeles. The big joke is that Julius (Mr. Schwarzenegger), raised on an idyllic desert island, is a perfect specimen of a man, a genius, pure in body as well as spirit. He is also — hold on to your sides — a *virgin*!

Vincent (Mr. DeVito), self-described as "genetic trash," is Julius's opposite. Kicked out of the orphanage

Out of the Blue
Dan Aykroyd plays a widowed scientist and Kim Basinger the extraterrestrial he marries in "My Stepmother Is an Alien."

Sharing Genes
In "Twins," Arnold Schwarzenegger and Danny DeVito star as, yes, twins separated at birth, who meet as adults and try to find their mother.

Bruce McBroom

at age 14 after getting a nun into trouble, Vincent is a womanizing con artist, car thief and fast-talker. He also has enormous aplomb. While running down the street to escape an irate husband, he uses an electric razor to take off his 5 o'clock shadow.

In the past, Mr. Schwarzenegger's chief asset has been a willingness to send up what is taken to be the body builder's arrogance and self-assurance. It's something else to play a naïf, which is as far out of his range as "Henry V." He's also beginning to look physically reconstituted. It's one of the oddities of "Twins" that though Mr. DeVito is balding, overweight and undergrown, he appears to be younger than his twin.

The film is the latest in the list of sloppy comic extravaganzas directed by Ivan Reitman, the auteur who earlier brought us "Meatballs," "Stripes," "Legal Eagles" and "Ghostbusters." The direction is no less lame than the screenplay, which has to do with the brothers' search for their parents, with industrial espionage, with Mr. Schwarzenegger's losing his virginity and, in one scene, with Mr. DeVito's teaching his co-star how to waltz.

"Twins," which opens today at the National and other theaters, is the sort of movie that seems to be made of Styrofoam. It's instantly disposable but it won't quickly disappear.

•

"Twins," which has been rated PG ("Parental Guidance Suggested"), contains some mildly vulgar language.

1988 D 9, C18:1

Strangers On a Plane

Michael Lacascio, left, and Burt Wright in "Troma's War."

TROMA'S WAR, directed by Michael Herz and Samuel Weil; screenplay by Mitchell Dana with Lloyd Kaufman, based on a story by Mr. Kaufman; director of photography, James London; edited by Brian Sternkopf; music Chris DeMarco; produced by Mr. Kaufman and Mr. Herz; released by Troma Inc. At Cine Twin, 711 Seventh Avenue, at 48th Street, and

Movie Center 5, 125th Street near Powell Boulevard. Running time: 95 minutes. This film is rated R.

Lydia	Carolyn Beauchamp
Taylor	Sean Bowen
Parker	Michael Ryder
Kirkland	Patrick Weathers
Dottie	Jessica Dublin
Marshall	Steven Crossley
Siamese Twin	Burt Wright
Siamese Twin	Michael Locascio

Troma Inc. has by now made a number of films (like "Squeeze Play," "The Toxic Avenger" and "Surf Nazis Must Die") without compromising its amateur status in the slightest. So sex, gore, bathroom jokes, putrescence and idiot humor remain the hallmarks of the Troma style. In "Troma's War," the balance has shifted slightly to favor burning stuntmen and gruesome (if cheesily unconvincing) makeup effects, but the sensibility remains the same. It's hard to imagine who, other than Troma relatives and Troma friends, makes up the audience for these things.

In "Troma's War," which opens today at the Cine Twin and Movie Center 5, a group of assorted miscreants is stranded on a desert island after a plane crash (the directors, Michael Herz and Samuel Weil, linger lovingly over shots of charred bodies and blood-spattered wreckage). They are mistaken for guerrilla fighters — even the women, whose costumes suggest another line of work entirely — and captured by a sadistic band of neo-Nazis and neo-Rambos. Much fighting accompanies all this, replete with the obligatory close-ups of spurting blood bags. There is so much machine-gunning that the entire cast appears to have died twice.

However, even viewers with a taste for hard-core violence will be put off by the uniquely Tromaesque manner in which these events are staged. The emphasis on stupidity is finally a lot more noxious than the abundant blood and guts. One wounded man is given amateur stitches by a woman with a sewing kit; the mother of a missing baby is presented with the child's dirty diaper; a team searching a corpse for weapons finds condoms instead. A man with AIDS, covered with sores, surveys the ranks of female prisoners deciding which of them to infect first. Several rapes later, one of these women shoots the AIDS patient in the groin.

It's clear Troma makes and markets its films with real enthusiasm, and it's also clear that independent film making is to be valued even under the worst of circumstances. But circumstances don't get much worse than this. *JANET MASLIN*

1988 D 9, C23:1

FILM VIEW/Janet Maslin

Under the Tree, The Laughs Are Scarce

FILM COMEDIES USED TO BE easier to identify than they are today. For one thing, they were usually funny. And they generally arrived in warmer weather, when the laughing reflex presumably functions most freely. But this year Santa had some trouble with his calendar, and the result is a group of Christmas films designed with humor in mind. The stars, premises and marketing campaigns associated with each of these films suggest comedy. But here is one area in which the creature that looks like a duck, quacks like a duck and waddles like a duck may not be a duck at all.

"Twins," for example, looks from a distance like the Duck of the Year. It has the season's funniest poster, which should guarantee it an audience. And it has a premise that can be explained in 10 words or less ("Schwarzenegger turns out to be DeVito's long-lost twin brother" — all right, 11 words if you use first names). What's more, Mr. DeVito is an actor who's funny no matter what he's doing, and even Mr. Schwarzenegger is beginning to seem more amusing than frightening. So how is it possible to sit through "Twins" with hardly a chuckle?

"Twins" turns out to be, among other things, sad evidence that witty direction is becoming a dying art. Having assembled the ingredients of a halfway funny film, Ivan Reitman has handled them with all the delicacy of a traffic cop. "Twins" is so clumsy that a scene in which Mr. Schwarzenegger gets into a car has him blocking the camera with his suitcase; a scene in which a woman trips requires a close-up of her ankles. When it comes to more elaborate tricks, Mr. Reitman seems to have expended so much effort in executing the stunt that he's lost track of its original purpose.

"Twins" looks expensive, and there's nothing funny about that, either. The scenery, the seeping light, the irrelevant sequences — like those about Mr. Schwarzenegger as an innocent conducting his first love affair — distill the humor instead of heightening it. The comedy inherent in these two incongruous figures' being twins is thoroughly overwhelmed by a cluttered screenplay. When a film gets one of its bigger laughs by having a sweet-looking woman punch someone in the nose, it's beyond help.

"My Stepmother is an Alien" is another would-be comedy whose makers seem to have lost track of their goal, which was presumably to make people laugh. The premise (again saleably compact): Beautiful spaceling arrives to make Earth widower an adorable wife. And Kim Basinger, as the alien, again establishes herself as a wonderfully dizzy comic talent. So the film is fun as long as Miss Basinger is skittering from one crisis to another, or showing off an enjoyably weird wardrobe.

■

However, there's a trace of the concubine in this eager-to-please character, which makes the screenplay's claims that she is the most intelligent creature in her galaxy seem rather thin. (Two of the four screenwriters here are also the authors of "Twins," prompting questions about which galaxy new comedy writers are coming from.) And even if the film worked as a sexier, updated "I Love Lucy," it has serious problems where Dan Aykroyd, who plays the widower, is

Christmas is bringing an unusual number of comedies, but the humor is in short supply.

concerned. He, like so many staples of contemporary film humor, manages to connote comedy without being funny at all.

Bill Murray, on the other hand, can be funny under almost any circumstances, and his may be the perfect comic sensibility for the 80's: casually cynical, serenely mean-spirited, strictly out for number one. Though this is surely a minority opinion, I found much of "Scrooged" hilarious and wasn't much bothered by the sections that are saccharine or slow. "Scrooged" may have its problems, but it's also got a timely idea: this is a fine moment for updating Dickens's tale of greed and retribution, and network television seems just the place to locate a contemporary Scrooge. What's more, the insouciantly nasty dialogue is often priceless, Mr. Murray's Scrooge character reacting to the news that he will be visited tomorrow by the Ghost of Christmas Past: "Tomorrow's bad for me — maybe lunch next Thursday. You, me and the ghost — Trader Vic's?"

Reviews of "Scrooged" have cited the problem that the first part of the film is almost too funny, since the rest of it can't keep up the pace. Some problem. In a season like this, real laughs are welcome wherever they can be found. So "The Naked Gun," from the Zucker-Abrahams-Zucker "Airplane!" team, is welcome even as a pale throwback to the writers' zanier work. The jokes are silly, even stupid at times, and there aren't many that you can't see coming from miles away. There are, however, so many gags that the writers inevitably hit their target from time to time. And there's something delightful about the utter shamelessness of everyone involved.

"The Naked Gun" and even "Scrooged" are raw enough so that audiences will at least know whether they've been entertained. With "Twins," it won't be so simple. Nature abhors a vacuum. Movie audiences, convinced by advertising and high hopes that they're witnessing something funny when they aren't, can sometimes turn one into a hit.

1988 D 11, II:13

Bruce McBroom

Bonnie Bartlett with Danny DeVito and Arnold Schwarzenegger in Ivan Reitman's "Twins" — sad evidence that witty direction is becoming a dying art

Dreams Unrealized

TORCH SONG TRILOGY, directed by Paul Bogart; screenplay by Harvey Fierstein, based on his play; director of photography, Mikael Salomon; edited by Nicholas C. Smith; music adapted by Peter Matz; production designer, Richard Hoover; produced by Howard Gottfried; released by New Line Cinema. At Carnegie Hall Cinema, Seventh Avenue and 57th Street; Gemini Twin, 64th Street and Second Avenue, and other theaters. Running time: 126 minutes. This film is rated R.

Arnold	Harvey Fierstein
Ma	Anne Bancroft
Alan	Matthew Broderick
Ed	Brian Kerwin
Laurel	Karen Young
David	Eddie Castrodad
Murray	Ken Page
Bertha Venation	Charles Pierce
Marina Del Rey	Axel Vera

By JANET MASLIN

The climactic confrontation between Arnold Beckoff (Harvey Fierstein) and his mother (Anne Bancroft) at the end of "Torch Song Trilogy" isn't really as drastic as it appears. Though mother and son argue bitterly about their clash in values, in fact they aren't very far apart. Yes, the mother would like to see her son settle down and lead a so-called normal life, but then so would he. The fact that Arnold makes a living as a drag queen (under names like "Virginia Hamn") has done nothing to make him any less conventional than his nagging Jewish mother.

As the centerpiece of "Torch Song Trilogy," which opens today at the Gemini and other theaters, Arnold embodies the naughty-but-nice view of homosexual life. He's looking for love, a stable home life and even children (one of Arnold's mother's complaints is that her son has adopted a teen-ager named David, supposedly a young delinquent but in fact as sweet a guy as Arnold himself). Arnold talks about passionate sex but seems more at home in bunny-rabbit bedroom slippers, padding around his nicely decorated apartment. Even his stage act, in which he dresses up and sings about subjects like bulimia, takes some trouble to avoid the risqué.

•

Like "La Cage aux Folles," "Torch Song Trilogy" presents a homosexual world that any mother, with the possible exception of Arnold Beckoff's, would love. Greatly shortened from Mr. Fierstein's long-running, Tony Award-winning play, the film version emphasizes the lovable at every turn, but the surprise is that it does this entertainingly and well. Mr. Fierstein, whose larger-than-life character might have been expected to wear out his welcome under the close scrutiny of the movie camera, instead emerges as an enjoyably wise-cracking figure. As hammy as his on-stage alter ego, Mr. Fierstein's Arnold nonetheless manages to complain about his messy love life in lively and amusing detail.

The film, which confines itself to the 1970's (after a brief prologue in which tiny Arnold gives his mother a funny inkling of what she can look forward to) and thus avoids the specter of AIDS, divides itself into sections on the basis of the men with whom Arnold becomes involved. First there is Ed (Brian Kerwin), a dreamboat who turns out to have too many heterosex-

ual predilections for Arnold's taste.

In the beginning, their courtship brings out the impetuous romantic in Arnold, who joyfully celebrates a two-week anniversary and leaps out of bed to beautify himself just before Ed wakes up in the morning. Later, when Arnold learns that Ed is interested in women, he rails against hypocrisy in the kind of high-minded outburst that gives "Torch Song Trilogy" an occasional semblance of seriousness. This outburst, however, like most of Arnold's others, isn't about much more than hurt feelings.

•

Next comes Alan, played by Matthew Broderick, who early in his career played Arnold's adopted teen-age son Off Broadway. "Every guy I meet takes one look at me and all he wants is sex," Alan says, and if Mr. Broderick isn't precisely right for this role, he plays it gamely enough to make him seem young and eager. Arnold falls hard for Alan, who works as a male model and is capable of occasional errant behavior, but here again sorrow is in the wings. Arnold is at his most vituperative in decrying the fate that befalls Alan.

Luckily, even the blunter sentiments expressed in "Torch Song Trilogy" are couched in the self-deprecating humor that is the material's saving grace. "Face it: a thing of beauty is a joy till sunrise," Arnold says in the film's introduction. "Then wham bam you're writin' letters to Dear Abby and you're burnin' black candles at midnight." Later on, Arnold's mother, who has her own brand of sarcasm, gets off a bus yelling, "It was a pleasure meeting you all, not one of whom would give me a seat."

Lines like this aren't made to be said softly, and so everything in "Torch Song Trilogy" is delivered at top volume. Miss Bancroft, playing in a manner that might seem scenery-chewing in another context, is exactly right in what she does here. And Mr. Fierstein matches her arm-wave for arm-wave, grimace for grimace, decibel for decibel.

1988 D 14, C19:1

Seeking a Purpose

SIERRA LEONE, produced and directed by Uwe Schrader; written (in German with English subtitles) by Klaus Müller-Laue and Mr. Schrader; photography by Mr. Müller-Laue. At Film Forum 1, 57 Watts Street. Running time: 92 minutes. This film has no rating.

Fred	Christian Redl
Alma	Ann Gisel Glass
Vera	Rita Russek
Rita	Constanze Engelbrecht

By CARYN JAMES

As so many German films have done in the last 20 years, Uwe Schrader's "Sierra Leone" practically dares you to like it. Its hero, Fred, who has returned to West Germany after working for three years in Africa, is self-centered, shallow and boorish. He is the kind of man who never bothered to call or write his wife all the time he was gone yet seems genuinely surprised that she is not glad to see him again. He had, after all, kept sending her checks.

If this pale, balding, middle-aged man is conspicuously out of place in the film's opening scenes at a street market in Sierra Leone, on his return he quickly discovers that the industrial German landscape has become an equally alien place. For most of the film he wanders through a series

Anne Bancroft and Harvey Fierstein in "Torch Song Trilogy."

of sleazy bars and dingy hotel rooms wearing a grimy shirt and not bothering to stop smoking while he eats his fast-food meals. Fred meanders along, making a halfhearted search for some point to his life, and the film meanders with him as Mr. Schrader effectively immerses the viewer in a tawdry, working-class existence.

Fred finds it impossible to settle back into his old life. The factory where he once worked is laying off people. In bars his old friends seem even less inspired than he. They get drunk and promise to change their lives — one man swears he will quit his job as a cabdriver — or explain their pasts by saying things like: "I had a wife once. She divorced me. I shot her dog."

•

Fred tries to find solace in women. After his wife sends him away, he has a short fling with a former girlfriend, then spirals downward to pick up Alma, a pathetically trampy clerk at his hotel. But none of these women mean much to him, or to the film, which is far more intent on describing the increasingly tacky ambiance in which Fred finds them. The girlfriend works in a cafeteria and has a decent apartment. Alma hangs out at a video-game arcade and when working behind the hotel bar will, on request, nonchalantly open her blouse to reveal the tattoo on her breast. She will then calmly change the cassette on the bar's cheap portable tape player. Since there's nothing left for Fred in his hometown, he and Alma take off on a trip to nowhere in particular, often eating and sleeping in the car.

Mr. Schrader has a tendency to jump into a scene and let crucial information emerge toward the end of the sequence. We do not immediately learn the identity of Fred's wife's, the complications with the old girlfriend, or the secret in Alma's past. And the film as a whole mirrors this technique, with an affecting turn at the very end. Fred looks at a shuffling, balding old bartender in another nondescript hotel and announces he is afraid of turning into that man. The entire film suggests how likely a possibility that is. Fred's final action may come as a relief; after all his meandering at least it's action. But it

comes at the end of an overlong, though artfully depressing, trek.

Ultimately, Mr. Schrader, who wrote and directed the film, has nothing new to say about German society, however effectively he decribes its marginal lives. At 35 years old, he comes from a slightly younger generation than Werner Herzog or Rainer Werner Fassbinder, whose work sends slight echoes through this film. At times "Sierra Leone," opening today at the Film Forum, seems like a perverse version of Mr. Herzog's already-bizarre black comedy "Stroszek," in which a German wanders through the tacky back roads of the American Midwest. But Mr. Schrader has none of Mr. Herzog's humor. He does have Fassbinder's eye for the lurid, though, and "Sierra Leone" creates an atmosphere as dark and meaningless as it intends. To that extent, it succeeds on its own stubborn, uningratiating terms.

1988 D 14, C28:5

Cads Suave And Slovenly

DIRTY ROTTEN SCOUNDRELS, directed by Frank Oz; written by Dale Launer and Stanley Shapiro and Paul Henning; director of photography, Michael Ballhaus; edited by Stephen A. Rotter and William Scharf; music by Miles Goodman; production designer, Roy Walker; produced by Bernard Williams; released by Orion Pictures Corporation. At Embassy 4, Broadway at 47th Street; Guild 50th Street, west of Fifth Avenue, and other theaters. Running time: 110 minutes. This film is rated PG.

Freddy Benson	Steve Martin
Lawrence Jamieson	Michael Caine
Janet Colgate	Glenne Headly
Inspector Andre	Anton Rodgers
Fanny Eubanks	Barbara Harris
Arthur	Ian McDiarmid
Mrs. Reed	Dana Ivey

By VINCENT CANBY

Lawrence Jamieson (Michael Caine) is a haberdasher's dream, the sort of man who could make Oleg Cassini look like a panhandler. Lawrence wears clothes well, has a gourmet's palate, impeccable manners and lives in splendor on the French Riviera in a magnificent villa over-

looking the sea.

He's also a superior con artist. Most of the time he passes himself off as a prince in mufti, a deposed royal in need of money to liberate his homeland from the yoke of Communism. Rich women of a certain age find Lawrence irresistible.

Freddy Benson (Steve Martin) wears baggy gray trousers, a green T-shirt and a Panama hat. He's a self-satisfied klutz who aspires to be a con artist. His ploy is to tell rich women that his grandmother needs an operation. Sometimes Freddy receives a "loan." More often it's the price of a meal, which, on the French Riviera, isn't necessarily modest. Compared with Lawrence, Freddy is small change.

•

At the beginning of "Dirty Rotten Scoundrels," one of the season's most cheerful, most satisfying new comedies, Freddy is on a train en route to the South of France, trying to psych himself up to the task at hand. He asks himself why he shouldn't prey on women. Men, he reasons, suffer "more heart attacks than women, more strokes and more prostate problems." Men are entitled to whatever they can get.

That thought prompts Freddy to grin with eager anticipation and utterly unwarranted confidence in his own malevolent schemes.

Freddy's mistake is to settle in the fictitious Riviera town of Beaumont-sur-Mur, which is Lawrence's exclusive turf. After some initial sparring, Freddy blackmails the elegant Lawrence into teaching him the tricks of the trade. They make a bet: the first man to swindle a woman out of $50,000 can keep the money and the territory.

•

All of this may sound familiar. "Dirty Rotten Scoundrels" is a remake of the 1964 comedy "Bedtime Story," which was written by Stanley

Shapiro and Paul Henning and which starred David Niven and Marlon Brando in the roles now being played by Mr. Caine and Mr. Martin.

Except for its title, the earlier film has receded from memory, but I can't imagine that it could have been anywhere near as entertaining as the blithe, seemingly all-new, laugh-out-loud escapade opening today at the Embassy 4 and other theaters.

Their comic methods are different, but from their first unequal encounter until the very last in a series of twist endings, Mr. Caine and Mr. Martin work together with an exuberant ease that's a joy to watch.

Don't mistake what Mr. Caine does with the work of a straight man. Like Jack Benny, whom he otherwise resembles not at all, Mr. Caine is a sneaky master of the pregnant reaction shot. This is a superb comic performance, seeming laid-back but larcenous in effect. Looking exceptionally fit, well-fed and intimidatingly grand, Mr. Caine nearly walks off with the movie, mostly by appearing to be politely appalled by the gauche Freddy Benson.

•

Playing to (and for) his co-star, Mr. Martin gives a performance of inspired goofiness. As an American innocent who sets out to bag big game with a BB gun, he is the last hilariously enfeebled embodiment of 19th-century frontier optimism. No matter how often his Freddy Benson fails, he's ever ready to get up, brush himself off and start all over again.

Lawrence announces loftily that he never takes advantage of the poor or the virtuous. Freddy likes nothing better than a sitting target. His career depends on it.

"Dirty Rotten Scoundrels" was directed by Frank Oz, one of the Muppet wizards who went on to make the film adaptation of "The Little Shop of Horrors," and written by Dale Launer ("Ruthless People"), with

Michael Caine, rear, and Steve Martin in "Dirty Rotten Scoundrels."

equal credit going to Mr. Shapiro and Mr. Henning. Line by line, the dialogue isn't all that quotable, but there is consistently funny life on the screen. The film's comic timing is nearly flawless.

The object of the $50,000 bet between the two men is the pretty, gullible young Janet Colgate (charmingly played by Glenne Headly), known as "the American soap queen," a sitting target if there ever was one. Freddy attempts to play on her sympathies by passing himself off as a paralyzed naval officer on six weeks of "medical trauma leave."

He has been unable to walk, he explains, ever since his fiancée ran off with the television host of "Dance, U.S.A."

The more urbane Lawrence, not to be outdone, identifies himself to the heiress as a famous Viennese psychiatrist, the only man in the world who is known to be able to cure such psychosomatic illnesses.

●

Among the other women who come into the lives of the desperate competitors are a romantic husky-voiced Nebraska widow (Barbara Harris) and an Oklahoma millionairess (Dana Ivey). When the latter falls for Lawrence, she makes firm plans to have "the biggest royal wedding Tulsa has ever seen."

Each and every one of them is a delight. In this season of lazy, fat, mistimed and misdirected comedies, exemplified by "Scrooged" and "Twins," "Dirty Rotten Scoundrels" is an enchanted featherweight folly.

●

"Dirty Rotten Scoundrels," which has been rated PG ("Parental Guidance Suggested"), includes some vulgar language and one amusingly gross scatalogical joke.

1988 D 14, C21:4

Correction

A film review on Wednesday about "Dirty Rotten Scoundrels" misidentified the actress who plays an Oklahoma millionaire. She is Meagen Fay, not Dana Ivey.

1988 D 16, A3:2

Brothers of the Road

Tom Cruise

RAIN MAN, directed by Barry Levinson; screenplay by Ronald Bass and Barry Morrow, story by Mr. Morrow; director of photography, John Seale; edited by Stu Linder; music by Hans Zimmer; production designer, Ida Random; produced by Mark Johnson; released by United Artists. At Loews Paramount, Broadway at 61st Street, and other theaters. Running time: 130 minutes. This film is rated R.

Raymond Babbitt	Dustin Hoffman
Charlie Babbitt	Tom Cruise
Susanna	Valeria Golino
Dr. Bruner	Jerry Molen
John Mooney	Jack Murdock
Vern	Michael D. Roberts
Lenny	Ralph Seymour

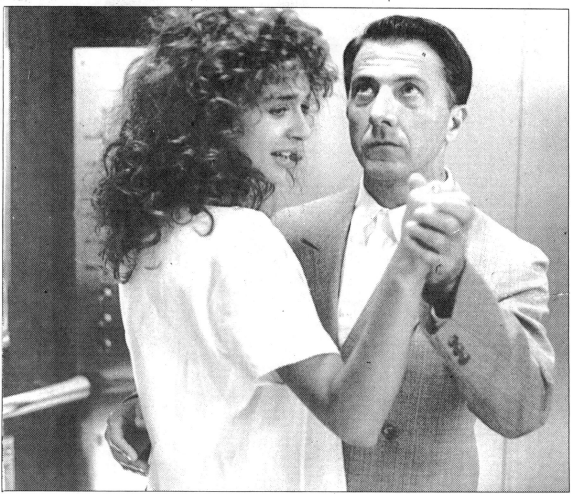

Stephen Vaughan

Valeria Golino, as Charlie's girlfriend, treats Raymond to a dance in a Las Vegas hotel elevator.

By VINCENT CANBY

When Charlie Babbitt (Tom Cruise), a fast-talking automobile salesman in Los Angeles, returns to Cincinnati for his father's funeral, he finds that he has inherited a pocket watch and a 1949 Buick Roadmaster convertible. The pocket watch and Roadmaster are in mint condition, and Charlie had been estranged from his father for years, but still he is disappointed.

The disappointment turns to fury when Charlie learns that his father's $3 million fortune has been left to Raymond (Dustin Hoffman), Charlie's autistic older brother of whose existence he has been completely ignorant. To get his hands on the money, Charlie kidnaps the helpless Raymond, who has been confined to an institution, and sets off for Los Angeles, aiming to have himself declared Raymond's legal guardian.

"Rain Man," directed by Barry Levinson from the screenplay by Ronald Bass and Barry Morrow, is both a road movie and the oddest of this year's brother-movies in which one brother, a sophisticated hustler, and the other, an innocent abroad, realize they are good for each other.

The difference, however, is that Mr. Hoffman's innocent exists in a never-ending mental twilight, lit by occasional flashes of lightning. Raymond is not only autistic, which doctors say is the result of metabolic and neurological disorders, he is also an autistic savant.

●

Though he goes through life preoccupied by self, obsessed by routine and hedged in by inexplicable anxieties, he is also capable of feats beyond the powers of genius. He can't make emotional contact with the people around him but, given a few hours, he memorizes the Cincinnati telephone book, "A" through "G." He glances at a pile of matches and correctly calculates their total number.

For Mr. Hoffman, "Rain Man" is a star's dream of a role.

From the moment Raymond comes onto the screen, a slight, small buttoned-up figure, avoiding eye contact, speaking in tight little sentences that match the steps he takes, Mr. Hoffman demands that attention be paid to his intelligence, invention and research as an actor.

The performance is a display of sustained virtuosity but, like Raymond, it makes no lasting connections with the emotions. Its end effect depends largely on one's susceptibility to the sight of an actor acting nonstop and extremely well, but to no particularly urgent dramatic purpose.

The performance is so remarkable, in fact, that it overwhelms what is otherwise a becomingly modest, decently thought-out, sometimes funny film. For reasons I don't quite understand, the dead-seriousness of Mr. Hoffman's efforts don't add heft to "Rain Man." In much the way that Raymond stays detached, the performance seems to exist outside the film but, instead of illuminating "Rain Man," it upstages the work of everyone else involved.

This is partly because Raymond remains pretty much the same exotic creature from the beginning to the end. He can't change in any important measure. He can only reveal additional aspects of himself as the movie goes along.

The film's true central character, though he's not the center of attention, is the confused, economically and emotionally desperate Charlie, beautifully played by Mr. Cruise, even when he is put into the position of acting as straight-man to his costar. It may be no accident that Charlie (and Mr. Cruise) manage to survive "Rain Man" as well as they do.

Charlie is a lot like the edgy, self-deluding heroes who have turned up in other Levinson films, most memorably as played by Richard Dreyfuss in "Tin Men."

The brothers' "road" adventures begin with their first abortive attempt to leave Cincinnati. At the last minute, Raymond refuses to board the airplane on which they are booked, citing the airline's safety record. The only airline he'll consider is Australia's Qantas, which, of course, doesn't fly between Cincinnati and Los Angeles.

Charlie puts Raymond into the Roadmaster and they start to drive, but even driving has its problems. They spend several days in a Midwestern motel because Raymond won't go outside when it rains.

By the time they reach Las Vegas, Charlie has realized that Raymond has special mental skills. After instructing Raymond in the basics of blackjack, Charlie takes him into a casino for the sort of results any gambler would die for.

These scenes are funny, but the humor becomes uncomfortable when Charlie decides that Raymond should learn something about women. In a scene that duplicates the one played by Danny DeVito and Arnold Schwarzenegger in ''Twins,'' Charlie teaches Raymond how to dance. This appears to be stretching Raymond's potential for growth since, early on, the point has been made that he hates being touched.

The supporting cast is headed by Valeria Golino, the Italian actress who made her American film debut in ''Big Top Pee-wee.'' She's very good but the movie, a star vehicle, hasn't much time for her.

''Rain Man'' opens today at the Paramount and other theaters.

1988 D 16, C12:5

After a Death In the Family

THE HOUSE OF BERNARDA ALBA, (LA CASA DE BERNARDA ALBA), directed by Mario Camus; screenplay (Spanish with English subtitles) by Mr. Camus and Antonio Larreta, based on the play by Federico García Lorca; director of photography, Fernando Arribas; film editor, José M. Biurrun; art director, Rafael Palmero; released by Paraiso Producciones. At the Public, 425 Lafayette Street. Running time: 106 minutes. This film has no rating.

Bernarda .... Irene Gutiérrez Caba
Adela .... Ana Belén
Poncia .... Florinda Chico
Angustias .... Enriqueta Carballeira
Martirio .... Vicky Peña
Magdalena .... Aurora Pastor
Amelia .... Mercedes Lezcano

By JANET MASLIN

''The House of Bernarda Alba'' begins with the funeral of a man who surely wielded little influence, since his widow, Bernarda Alba (Irene Gutiérrez Caba), is such a formidable tyrant. Feared by her five daughters, hated by her servants, Bernarda Alba rules her household with an iron hand.

Upon the death of her husband, the widow declares a lengthy mourning period during which her daughters are forbidden any contact with men. So the important male character in the drama, the handsome and calculating young Pepe el Romano, is never allowed to appear. Instead, Pepe lingers at the edges of the story, appearing at the window of one daughter or another in the middle of the night, and serving as the catalyst who drives the women to the edge of rebellion.

The hothouse atmosphere of Federico García Lorca's play is intense enough to give the daughters' obsessive trousseau-making an edge of madness, and to give the entire play a starkly symbolic dimension. The stern, unyielding Bernarda Alba becomes the essence of dictatorial repression, finding her only satisfactions in imposing rules and denying the happiness of others. The frustration of her daughters goes far beyond the hardship of women denied male companionship, suggesting powerlessness and frustration of a more universal kind.

•

The daughters' fates seem to hinge on the whims of the changeable Pepe, who openly courts the eldest and wealthiest of the girls while secretly wooing the youngest and prettiest (Ana Belén) as well. The young women's susceptibility to this suitor's capriciousness is also emphasized, though not as evidence of the larger helplessness of women in Spain's patriarchal society. Bernarda Alba's absolute power, within her own household and even in orchestrating events on the outside, is much too palpable to support that.

Mario Camus's film version of ''The House of Bernarda Alba,'' which opens today at the Public Theater, is a serious and generally faithful adaptation, one that conveys both the simplicity and the symbolism of the material. Mr. Camus, who also directed ''The Holy Innocents,'' has also made this a somewhat decorous version, so that the occasional earthiness of the young women's dialogue is eclipsed by the pretty spectacle of the actresses sewing petticoats.

The cast members playing the five daughters are uniformly attractive, though the characters themselves are meant to differ in this regard; Angustias, the eldest, who is half-sister to the others and has a sizable inheritance from her father, is described as having ''looked like a dressed-up stick at 20, so what can she look like now, now that she's 40?'' Yet the actress who plays Angustias, Enriqueta Carballeira, is as attractive as everything else about the film.

The good looks of Mr. Camus's film do not prevent the material from building to a frenzied and tragic conclusion, as the young women's subjugation and delusion bring at least one of them to the breaking point, and rupture the sanctity of Bernarda Alba's power. This ending has some force, but had the production been grittier, it would have had more.

1988 D 16, C14:6

Family Ties

Ana Belen appears in ''The House of Bernarda Alba.''

America Through Alien Eyes

SINCE THE LATE 1950'S, AMERIcan directors have roamed the world, mostly mindlessly in search of pretty scenery; but only recently have European directors been working in this country in any numbers.

One of the first was Louis Malle, who makes movies as gracefully here (''Pretty Baby,'' ''Atlantic City'') as he does in his native France (''Au Revoir les Enfants''). Wim Wenders is as at home in America (''Paris, Texas'') as he is in Germany (''Wings of Desire''). Though Barbet Schroeder is French, one of his best films is entirely American — ''Barfly,'' shot on Los Angeles's Skid Row. Werner Herzog, the usually dour German director, filmed his only comedy, ''Stroszek,'' mostly on location in northern Wisconsin and Minnesota.

''Bagdad Cafe,'' shot in the American West by Percy Adlon, another German director (''Sugarbaby''), is well on its way to becoming one of this year's cult favorites.

Location shooting has added a valuable dimension to European movie production, giv-

'Mississippi Burning' is the latest interpretation of American life by foreign directors.

ing directors an international mobility previously unheard of.

Sometimes the rewards are real. Sometimes we still seem to be caught in the kind of provincial past that could produce the French-made camp classic of the 1950's, ''I Spit on Your Grave,'' about race relations in the United States. ''I Spit on Your Grave'' remains memorable today for its climax, in which an American black man, seeking sanctuary in the North, is shot dead attempting to cross the infamous armed border known as the Mason-Dixon line.

Now compare the just-opened ''Mississippi Burning,'' Alan Parker's fictionalized account of the investigation into the real-life murders of three civil rights workers in Mississippi in 1964, with ''Betrayed,'' Costa-Gavras's fictionalized investigation into the same sort of bigotry as it exists in this country today.

The London-born Mr. Parker's film is both uncomfortably brutal and utterly convincing. The melodrama by the Greek-born, French-bred Costa-Gavras looks as overripely American as a Norman Rockwell illustration and, for sheer absurdity, approaches ''I Spit on Your Grave.''

The interesting thing is that Costa-Gavras, possibly to his own detriment, has a far stronger (or, at least, a far more easily defined) personality as a film maker than Mr. Parker. Even when the Costa-Gavras films, including "The Confession," "State of Seige" and "Missing," haven't been quite as truthful as claimed, they have demonstrated the director's gift for stunning melodrama as well as his consistently absorbing obsession with political intrigue and conspiracy. All by himself he has pioneered what is virtually a new movie genre — muckraking political quasi-journalism.

By comparison, Mr. Parker's choice of film material in the past would seem dilettantish: a witty musical parody of gangster movies ("Bugsy Malone"), an over-wrought melodrama torn from the headlines on page 15 ("Midnight Express"), a very good comedy-drama about a marriage ("Shoot the Moon"), a first-rate adaptation of a seriously fanciful novel ("Birdy") and a ludicrous exploration of the occult ("Angel Heart").

■

Why, then, is Mr. Parker's film so much more effective than Costa-Gavras's? It isn't only because Mr. Parker has spent more time working in this country than Costa-Gavras, who is very much a man of the world. It's also not enough to say that Chris Gerolmo's screenplay for "Mississippi Burning" is better than Joe Eszterhas's for "Betrayed," though it is.

"Mississippi Burning" never allows the foreground story to get in the way of, or to be separated from, the real subject of the film, which is the war that was fought in the 1960's to implement racial integration and the various civil rights reforms.

Even more important, perhaps, is Mr. Parker's eclecticism as a movie maker. Like the contract directors in the days of the great Hollywood studios, he comes to "Mississippi Burning" unencumbered by any commitment except to honor his own intelligence as well as the work at hand, with all of the facility at his command. He also seems to remain firmly unsurprised by anything in the American scene, which is not to say that he's nonjudgmental.

■

"Mississippi Burning" succeeds *just* because Mr. Parker approaches the subject neither as a zealot, out to demonstrate his own truth, nor as a film maker locked

into a particular style. His manner, though slick, is also self-effacing. It's that of the inquiring journalist who wants to recall a time and place as honestly he can, with as few distortions as possible.

In the end, some facts are ignored and some are distorted, but nothing in "Mississippi Burning" seriously damages the film's validity as a melodrama or as an evocation of recent history. It is also acted to the hilt by Gene Hackman, Willem Dafoe and the members of the large cast of supporting performers.

Costa-Gavras could argue, with some reason, that the subject of "Mississippi Burning" is a far safer and easier one to handle than his own attempt to portray the face of bigotry in America today. This is a potentially sensational subject, but it's not well served by "Betrayed," which, like almost all Costa-Gavras films, is inspired by an actual event, the 1984 assassination of Alan Berg, an audience-baiting, Denver talk-show host.

■

After that prologue, vividly staged and full of disorienting menace, "Betrayed" strays off into cloud-cuckoo-land. Debra Winger, playing an undercover agent for the Federal Bureau of Investigation, hires herself out as a farmhand in the Middle West. In less time than it takes to feed the chickens, she infiltrates the Ku Klux Klan, observes a lynching, discovers a conspiracy to overthrow the Federal Government and finds herself deeply torn between her love for the key conspirator and her own ideals (to say nothing of her job).

Costa-Gavras's bigots are not double-named Southern rednecks. They are Americans caught in an economic squeeze they cannot comprehend. Except for a tendency to blame their troubles on blacks, Jews and Roman Catholics, they are as ideally American as apple pie or store-bought white cake.

"They don't make white cake like they used to," a gentle, loving farm mom says in a meaningful speech that sets the film's instep-high irony level. Mom also talks about how America is going to the dogs and

knows that when her handsome, Vietnam-vet son (Tom Berenger) goes hunting on the weekend, he is shooting black men for sport and practice.

■

Costa-Gavras is too hip not to be aware of the astonishing implausibilities in "Betrayed." He doesn't ignore them out of arrogance or ignorance, I suspect, but in his passion to make a film that dramatizes, in personal terms, what he sees to be a major social-political problem in this country today.

Underneath all of the surface nonsense in "Betrayed," there is legitimate concern about the widening gap between America's haves and have-nots, and about a casually accepted, murderous hatred that can wear a look of such disarming Christian innocence.

Costa-Gavras must know that European audiences, especially European critics, will attend to this concern first and worry about plausibility later. Americans approach movies the other way around. We want to be coaxed into believing before we'll think.

Every now and then, a film on the order of "Mississippi Burning" comes along that allows us to think and believe at the same time. Also, to chew gum. □

1988 D 18, II:13:1

Class Differences In a Classless Society

A FORGOTTEN TUNE FOR THE FLUTE, directed by Eldar Ryazanov; screenplay (Russian with English subtitles) by Emil Braginsky and Mr. Ryazanov; cinematography, Vadim Alisov; music, Andrei Petrov; art direction, Aleksandr Borisov; released by Fries Entertainment. At Bleecker Street Cinema, west of La Guardia Place, and Carnegie Hall Screening Room, Seventh Avenue at 56th Street. Running time: 118 minutes. This film has no rating.

Leonid .... Leonid Filatov
Lida .... Tatyana Dogileva
Leonid's wife .... Irina Kupchenko

By WALTER GOODMAN

Add a dash of social criticism, the Soviet Union's popular new spice, to a borsch of an old-fashioned romantic comedy, and you have "A Forgotten Tune for the Flute." Eldar Ryazanov's bright and funny movie, which opens today at the Carnegie Hall Screening Room and the Bleecker Street Cinema, is as nourishing as the broth served up by Hollywood in the

1930's. The comments on Soviet bureaucracy and class privilege in the classless society are sharp enough to give a censor a touch of heartburn.

The plot is not flagrantly novel. Leonid (Leonid Filatov) is an important official in the Leisure Time Directorate, which is dedicated to the rule that "Nothing's to be permitted; everything's to be refused." He day-dreams about breaking his bureaucratic bonds and telling off his fuddy-duddy boss, but the lures of perks and privileges are too much for him. Then he meets luscious Lida (Tatyana Dogileva), a nurse who makes house calls, and begins daydreaming about leaving his somewhat bossy wife (Irina Kupchenko), whose big-shot father is the source of his good fortune. Of course, that would end Leonid's chances of taking over the Directorate.

●

What gives this triangle its lift is the movie maker's shrewd view of the social conventions by which its enagingly developed characters operate. Leonid is a hangdog charmer; in the office he is all careerist, but when, under Lida's inspiration, he takes out the dusty flute he played in the years before success struck, he is sheer wistfulness. The predicaments in which he keeps finding himself bring out the desperate comic in him. When his wife walks in on Lida dancing to the strains of his flute, he explains, "The doctor said I needed exercise."

Both the women between whom Leonid bounces, besides being beauties, have stronger characters than he does but are no less emotionally needy. The comedy, which manages to stay this side of farce, has an element of rue. In a last-ditch plea, Leonid's wife tells him that "thousands of men live with wives they don't love, and they're happy."

Mr. Ryazanov, who collaborated on the consistently clever script, fills the screen with droll asides. A women's chorus, which has become a nuisance to the Leisure Directorate, is consigned to an endless tour far from Moscow. We see the plump women, got up in extravagant ethnic costumes, bringing the sound of music to a Black Sea resort, to a Navy ship, to sheep herders in what seem to be the outer reaches of Mongolia. The song that constitutes their entire repertory (lyrics by Yevgeny Yevtushenko), goes like this: "On a spring night, think of me. On a summer night, think of me." And so on, into the long Russian winter.

●

When the bureaucrats visit an art exhibition, the paintings are so atrocious, the prices so exorbitant, that you almost sympathize with their lament that "the time of bulldozers is over."

Breaking Out
Leonid Filatov stars in "A Forgotten Tune for the Flute" as a Soviet official who rediscovers the man beneath the bureaucrat.

Everybody involved here, from the time-servers in Leonid's gossipy office to an old lady who bustles amiably about Lida's crowded quarters to the members of an amateur acting group that performs a racy version of Gogol's "Inspector General," has a flash of color. The contrast between ordinary folk and the upper echelons, with their big apartments, new cars, real caviar and fur coats, bubbles through the story; when a crowded bus stops in this movie, the masses come catapulting out.

The question for Leonid, of course, is whether to give up all the pleasures of power for life with Lida, assuming she will have him. While worrying about it, he has a comic-opera dream in which he and his colleagues are reduced to begging — except that "In our socialist country, there cannot be beggary." That fortunate country will be further enriched by "A Forgotten Tune for the Flute."

1988 D 21, C20:6

Revenge and Lust
In the Drawing Room

DANGEROUS LIAISONS, directed by Stephen Frears; screenplay by Christopher Hampton, based on his play, adapted from the novel "Les Liaisons Dangereuses" by Choderlos de Laclos; director of photography, Philippe Rousselot; film editor, Mick Audsley; music by George Fenton; production designer, Stuart Craig; produced by Norma Heyman and Hank Moonjean; released by Warner Brothers. At 68th Street Playhouse, at Third Avenue. Running time: 118 minutes. This film is rated R.

Marquise de Merteuil .... Glenn Close
Vicomte de Valmont .... John Malkovich
Madame de Tourvel .... Michelle Pfeiffer
Madame de Volanges .... Swoosie Kurtz
Chevalier Danceny .... Keanu Reeves
Madame de Rosemonde .... Mildred Natwick

By VINCENT CANBY

Like the elaborate dresses into which she has been fitted with a good deal of help, the Marquise de Merteuil (Glenn Close) seems always about to burst, not because of any engineering failure but in anticipation of some delightful new viciousness, a plot of such subtlety that only she can appreciate it. She keeps control of herself and simply smiles.

In the fashion·of the day, the Marquise's waist is cinched to the point where her generous bust has no place to go but up, and possibly out. It can't be comfortable but, among other things, the Marquise has learned that to be a successful woman in France in the 1780's, the last decade of the ancien régime, one has to put up with a certain amount of pain. The pleasure will follow.

Pleasure also follows a certain amount of time spent becoming accustomed to the stylized mannerisms of "Dangerous Liaisons," Stephen Frears's handsome, intelligent adaptation of Christopher Hampton's London and Broadway play, "Les Liaisons Dangereuses."

The source material is the classic 18th-century epistolary novel by Choderlos de Laclos, adapted and updated in 1959 by Roger Vadim as a vehicle for Gérard Philippe and Jeanne Moreau. (The Vadim film was not released here until 1961, after the censors demanded that the lighting in several scenes be dimmed to obscure the nudity.)

Though I have fond, fuzzy memories of that film, I can't imagine that it could come anywhere near the Frears-Hampton version in terms of witty, entertaining, if occasionally overripe decadence.

"Dangerous Liaisons," which opens today at the 68th Street Playhouse, is comparatively small in physical scope, having been filmed with a handful of actors, mostly indoors, though in some of France's most magnificent chateaus. Whenever it does go outside, it resolutely avoids looking at the conditions that, a few years later, will result in the first great bloody revolution of the modern age.

Mr. Frears and Mr. Hampton resist the temptations of hindsight, as they also resist the unimaginative movie maker's desire to open up the play. Instead, "Dangerous Liaisons" unfolds as a kind of lethal drawing-room comedy with occasional more or less obligatory visits to various bedchambers. History's echoes are there, but they're heard mostly in the hollow sounds of footsteps on parquet floors.

At the center of the film are the Marquise de Merteuil and Vicomte de Valmont, (John Malkovich), her rich, aristocratic former lover, who now devote themselves to the pursuit of sexual liaisons, not necessarily for pleasure but for the power they confer on the one who is loved but does not love. Power is all. It's apparent in the film's opening sequence that, since Valmont still has a passion for the Marquise, she holds the advantage.

The Marquise has a plan: to even the score with a lover who has left her, she asks Valmont to seduce the man's virginal, convent-bred fiancée. Valmont has his own plan. He has set his sights on a faithful young wife whose husband is serving abroad. Valmont's idea of pleasure is to persuade the wife to surrender herself to him without, for a moment, abandoning her principles.

When seduction has become such a commonplace pastime, refinements in betrayal are immensely important.

The Marquise insists that Valmont undertake her mission and, to keep him interested, agrees to spend one night with him if he can prove that he has also been successful with the faithful wife. Valmont accepts, but he makes a fatal mistake. He falls in love along the way.

From time to time, Mr. Hampton's dialogue comes perilously close to camp, especially at the beginning. When the ear gets used to it and to actors for whom, like Mr. Malkovich, this sort of dialogue initially seems as foreign as Eskimo, the film takes off in the breathless pursuit of its scheming seducers.

Nothing Miss Close has done on the screen before approaches the richness and comic delicacy of her work as the Marquise. She was exceptionally good in "Fatal Attraction" but, compared with her elegant performance as the Marquise, her abandoned mistress in the earlier film is a dreadnought plowing across a sea no bigger than a bathtub.

The Marquise is a wonderfully written role of almost classical dimensions. When she spars with Valmont, finally admitting that her game is cruelty rather than betrayal, she assumes command of the movie, hanging onto it until the very last shot.

Valmont would not seem to be a role that Mr. Malkovich was born to play. He looks and sounds more like 20th-century Pittsburgh than 18th-century Paris. Yet once the shock of seeing him in powdered wigs recedes, he is unexpectedly fine. The intelligence and strength of the actor shape the audience's response to him. He's no mincing fop but a man caught in what is finally an unequal struggle.

Michelle Pfeiffer, whose brightly colored, contemporary beauty seems to have been muted by camera filters, is another happy surprise as the pure wife who is romantically swindled by Valmont. Equally good are Uma Thurman as the convent girl who takes to sin with enthusiasm, Swoosie Kurtz as her worried mother and the indefatigable Mildred Natwick as Valmont's old aunt.

The film looks great, in part, I assume, because of the contributions of Stuart Craig, the production designer, and Philippe Rousselot, the cameraman. "Dangerous Liaisons" seems to use a lot of two-shots, in which one character is seen instead of two, the rest of the image being filled with details of décor. For Mr. Frears ("My Beautiful Laundrette," "Sammy and Rosie Get Laid"), environment doesn't have to be working-class to be important.

1988 D 21, C22:1

Cinderella
In a Business Suit

WORKING GIRL, directed by Mike Nichols; written by Kevin Wade; director of photography, Michael Ballhaus; edited by Sam O'Steen; music by Carly Simon; production designer, Patrizia Von Brandenstein; produced by Douglas Wick; released by 20th Century-Fox Film Corporation. At Criterion Center, Broadway between 44th and 45th Streets; Coronet, Third Avenue at 59th Street, and other theaters. Running time: 115 minutes. This film is rated R.

Jack Trainer .... Harrison Ford
Katharine Parker .... Sigourney Weaver
Tess McGill .... Melanie Griffith
Mick Dugan .... Alec Baldwin
Cyn .... Joan Cusack
Oren Trask .... Philip Bosco
Ginny .... Nora Dunn

By JANET MASLIN

In "Working Girl," Tess McGill (Melanie Griffith) first appears wearing the hairdo that Farrah forgot: a teased, bleached, badly outdated coiffure that immediately places her at the bottom of the corporate totem pole. Tess is a secretary who lives on Staten Island, works in Manhattan and has no idea how large a gulf exists, at least in this film's scheme of things, between the states of mind represented by those two places.

But she's about to find out. "Working Girl" presents Tess with one of the best opportunities for wish fulfillment this side of "Cinderella," an opportunity that's conceived in contemporary terms and goes well beyond Prince Charming. Tess is given a chance to prove herself in the professional arena, undergo a much-needed fashion overhaul and move up from a romance based on animal magnetism to one that very pointedly mixes business with pleasure. Though it isn't likely that an innocent like Tess could accomplish all this in a few weeks' time, "Working Girl" is enjoyable even when it isn't credible, which is most of the time. The film, like its heroine, has a genius for getting by on pure charm.

"Working Girl," which opens today at the Coronet and other theaters, derives a lot of its charm from the performance of Melanie Griffith, the baby-voiced bombshell who gives Tess an unbeatable mixture of street smarts, business sense and sex appeal. Tess's crazy-like-a-fox approach to career advancement is demonstrated early in the story when she rejects a pass from an obnoxious arbitrager and spitefully impugns the manliness of one boss with a gesture that none of her co-workers could possibly miss.

Yet under the right circumstances, Tess can become the very essence of cooperation. Her big mistake in "Working Girl" is to suppose that her new boss, a thrillingly flirtatious and encouraging female executive, is de-

Glenn Close and John Malkovich in "Dangerous Liaisons."

Melanie Griffith in a scene from "Working Girl."

serving of all the helpfulness and loyalty a good secretary can give.

The first half-hour of the film, which also establishes Tess's dismal home life on Staten Island — with a tattooed boyfriend, played amusingly by Alec Baldwin, who never manages to give Tess anything she can wear outside the bedroom — works wonderfully. This is especially true of the delightful sequence that has Tess being bowled over by Katharine Parker (Sigourney Weaver), who soon after hiring Tess breezily quotes Coco Chanel and makes it known that she is younger than her secretary, if only by two weeks.

Under Katharine's tutelage, Tess comes up with new ideas, like a suggestion that dim sum be served at a business reception. "I'd love to help you," Katharine whispers smoothly to the perspiring Tess, "but we can't busy the quarterback with passing out the Gatorade."

It's essential to "Working Girl" that Tess quickly find reason to reassess her admiration for Katharine, and that Katharine quite literally break a leg. With this, the film's fairy tale aspects are set in motion. Tess decides to masquerade as an executive in order to sell the idea she thinks Katharine was stealing, and she arranges a head-to-toe overnight transformation without needing help from a fairy godmother.

Thanks to Katharine's trust, Tess even has access to the right wardrobe, though viewers would do well to ignore the fact that Miss Griffith and Miss Weaver aren't remotely the same size. Or that no one in the office spots Tess wearing Katharine's clothes, commandeering her desk and using a very nonsecretarial manner to answer the telephone.

The screenplay, by Kevin Wade, has a sly wit, but it is also surprisingly primitive. So the plot contains distracting holes, and the details of Tess's scheme to succeed seem crude, even for a film as lighthearted as this. Mike Nichols, who directed "Working Girl," also displays an uncharacteristically blunt touch, and in its later stages the story remains lively but seldom has the perceptiveness or acuity of Mr. Nichols's best

work. When Tess crashes the wedding of a C.E.O.'s daughter to help promote her idea, for instance, the C.E.O. is made gullible, the guests unattractive, and the party so full of fake tropical scenery that it looks much more idiotic than it has to.

"Working Girl" combines romance with satire when it introduces Tess to Jack Trainer (Harrison Ford), an executive who wears so many hats here that he serves the screenplay as a kind of all-purpose generic male. Mr. Ford, who plays Jack in a foggy and rather faraway manner, never sets off many sparks with Miss Griffith, but perhaps that's not the point. One of the many things that mark "Working Girl" as an 80's creation is its way of regarding business and sex as almost interchangeable pursuits and suggesting that life's greatest happiness can be achieved by combining the two.

"Working Girl," always fun even when at its most frivolous, has the benefit of the cinematographer Michael Ballhaus's sharp visual sense of board room chic, and of supporting characters who help carry its class distinctions beyond simple caricature. Chief among these, along with Mr. Baldwin, is Joan Cusack as the no-nonsense Staten Island girlfriend who lets Tess know that she takes a dim view of magical transformations. "Sometimes I sing and dance around the house in my underwear," she says witheringly. "Doesn't make me Madonna. Never will."

1988 D 21, C22:4

Water Under The Bridge

BEACHES, directed by Garry Marshall; screenplay by Mary Agnes Donoghue, based on the novel by Iris Rainer Dart; director of photography, Dante Spinotti; edited by Richard Halsey; music by Georges Delerue; production designer, Albert Brenner; produced by Bonnie Bruckheimer-Martell, Bette Midler and Margaret Jennings South; released by Touchstone Pictures. At Cinema 1, Third Avenue and 60th Street; Gramercy, 23d Street and Lexington Avenue. Running time: 120 minutes. This film is rated PG-13.

C. C. Bloom	Bette Midler
Hillary Whitney Essex	Barbara Hershey
John Pierce	John Heard
Dr. Richard Milstein	Spalding Gray
Leona Bloom	Lainie Kazan
Michael Essex	James Read
Victoria Essex	Grace Johnston
C. C. (age 11)	Mayim Bialik
Hillary (age 11)	Marcie Leeds

By JANET MASLIN

There are a few indications that "Beaches," the story of a long and checkered friendship between two women, takes place in the 1980's. There is the fact, for instance, that when one of the friends, a wealthy Californian named Hillary Whitney (Barbara Hershey) announces that she plans to have a baby and raise it alone, the other friend, a vivacious singer named C. C. Bloom (Bette Midler), says this will be just wonderful. In other respects, though, "Beaches" is strictly a 40's saga, complete with bitter feuds, tearful recriminations, loving affirmations and, of course, the kind of fatal illness that can drag on endlessly without altering the afflicted's good looks.

Those who go to see "Beaches," which was directed by Garry Marshall and which opens today at Cinema I and other theaters, ought to know what they'll be getting, and that they'll be getting quite a lot of it. "Beaches" — which has a couple of key scenes at the beach but otherwise never justifies that title except perhaps with the vague view that we are all life's driftwood — is pure soap from beginning to end.

Though its stars work hard to hold the attention, they are asked to play this story absolutely straight. Even viewers with a taste for melodrama will doubtlessly expect more irony or perspective on the genre that "Beaches" has to offer.

•

Of course, there is a flashback: C. C. Bloom, now a big star rehearsing a concert at the Hollywood Bowl (Miss Midler sings a sultry version of "Under the Boardwalk"), suddenly receives shocking news. She drives off in a terrible rainstorm, heading we know not where. Cut to C. C.'s girlhood, to an Atlantic City sojourn during which the brassy little redhead (played by Mayim Bialik, who does a wicked imitation of the adult Miss M.) makes friends with the rich over-

protected Hillary. Perhaps they do not know that this friendship will last a lifetime, but we, of course, do.

C. C. and Hillary become loyal pen pals. (C. C. in New York: "I'm on my own now and I've got a flat, a can of Mace and a subscription to Variety. I'm all set.") They keep this up until, in their early 20's, they are reunited as New York roommates, banging on the radiators with the kind of pluck that only New York movie roommates have. As opposites, C. C. and Hillary do make an appealing if pat combination, Miss Hershey looking the demure debutante and Miss Midler brazening her way through every situation. Together, they make the friendship convincing and the story a lot more interesting than it otherwise would be.

•

Each of the heroines is allowed one marriage (though one of the husbands, John Heard as a theater director, manages to become involved with both of the friends). After this, though, men mostly fade out of the story, leaving C. C. and Hillary to confront age, rivalry, success and finally mortality. By the time "Beaches" arrives at the inevitable tragic and bittersweet note, though, it seems to have run through several different preliminary endings. Any one of these would have sufficed.

Miss Midler gets to sing a lot, which is a big help. In the supporting cast, Spalding Gray looks mildly stunned at having to play the dreamboat doctor who nearly takes C. C. away from her life of glitter, but he does have one of the film's few memorable lines. "I don't understand it," he says when things go wrong. "I mean, just yesterday she was telling me she wanted to be a nurse."

•

"Beaches" is rated PG-13 ("Special Parental Guidance Suggested for Children Younger Than 13"). It includes some off-color language and one mildly risqué musical routine.

1988 D 21, C28:4

Taking the Air(waves)

TALK RADIO, directed by Oliver Stone; screenplay by Eric Bogosian and Mr. Stone, based on the play created by Mr. Bogosian and Tad Savinar and written by Mr. Bogosian, and on the book "Talked to Death: The Life

Jane O'Neal

Bette Midler as C. C. Bloom in the film "Beaches."

and Murder of Alan Berg," by Stephen Singular; director of photography, Robert Richardson; edited by David Brenner; music by Stewart Copeland; production designer, Bruno Rubeo; produced by Edward R. Pressman and A. Kitman Ho; released by Universal Pictures. At Beekman, Second Avenue and 65th Street. Running time: 110 minutes. This film is rated R.

Barry	Eric Bogosian
Ellen	Ellen Greene
Laura	Leslie Hope
Stu	John C. McGinley
Dan	Alec Baldwin
Dietz	John Pankow
Kent	Michael Wincott
Sheila Fleming	Linda Atkinson
Jeffrey Fisher	Robert Trebor

VINCENT CANBY

"Talk Radio," Eric Bogosian's short Off Broadway play, was performed without an intermission, being a single, uninterrupted night in the life of Barry Champlain, a manic talk-show host headed, it seems, for a nervous breakdown and the junk heap.

Nobody is really worried. For every Barry Champlain on the air, there are probably half a dozen waiting in the wings, ready to insult the lonely, the forlorn, the obsessed and the often half-crazy people who call in.

As much as the play is about Barry, it's also about the time that produced him. He is not a mainstream character, but his is the kind of arrogance that convinces frequently mindless listeners that they too ought to be heard, which, indeed, they can be on talk radio.

Eric Bogosian as Barry Champlain in "Talk Radio."

In addition, they've grafted onto the play elements from the real-life story of Alan Berg, the Denver talk-show host who was murdered in 1984 by a white supremacist group — the same event used by Costa-Gavras as the starting point for his recent film, "Betrayed."

Mr. Bogosian repeats his stage performance as Barry with a lot of furious energy but no real payoff. He keeps being interrupted by the dopey demands of the dreadful screenplay that now bears Mr. Stone's name as well as his.

The movie still takes place mostly in one night. The tension, however, is reduced to zero by the introduction of a wife and by a series of flashbacks written to explain how he got his start and what happened to the marriage. There's also some overheated emphasis on the fact that Barry's producers ask him to tone down his abrasive personality for a national audience.

Taking this compact piece of contemporary Americana, less a drama than a small slice of bizarre life, Mr. Bogosian and Oliver Stone, the director, have made a mess of a movie that comes complete with a conventional beginning, middle and end, and long, spongy flashbacks.

•

"Talk Radio," opening today at the Beekman, is a nearly perfect example of how *not* to make a movie of a play. Mr. Stone has fancied it up not only with empty narrative asides but also with idiotic camerawork, exemplified by his use, toward the end, of the Lazy Susan shot. Barry, sitting at his microphone, earphones in place, is studied by the camera as the studio turns around him. It's enough to make one dizzy, but is that enough?

A lot of Mr. Bogosian's sharper lines remain in the script, but its nihilism now seems unearned. It is also at odds with the orderliness of the new narrative.

Among the other actors who appear are Ellen Greene as Barry's wife, Leslie Hope as his producer and mistress and John C. McGinley as his engineer.

1988 D 21, C28:4

Growing Up in Denmark

"Pelle the Conqueror" was shown as part of the New York Film Festival this fall. Following are excerpts from Vincent Canby's review, which appeared in The New York Times on Sept. 30. The film, in Danish with English subtitles, opens today at Lincoln Plaza Cinema, Broadway at 63d Street.

Bille August's "Pelle the Conqueror" is not for people who prefer to take showers. It's for the person who likes to get into a movie as if it were a long hot bath. To hurry it would be to miss its method and its point.

The Danish film, which won the Golden Palm, the top prize, at this year's Cannes Festival, is a vividly re-created, minutely detailed panorama of a particular time (the turn of the century), place (rural Denmark) and circumstance (life on a great

Father and son share a moment together outside school in Bille August's "Pelle the Conqueror."

farm) in the course of the four seasons. The observer is Pelle (Pelle Hvenegaard), a staunch, wide-eyed Swedish boy who has come to Denmark with his aging, destitute and widowed father, Lasse (Max von Sydow).

Lasse has promised his son that Denmark will be a land of opportunity, a place of plentiful jobs where pork is served on Sundays and butter is spread on bread. Instead Lasse and Pelle are lucky to be hired as little better than indentured servants, underpaid, underfed and overworked.

For the illiterate Lasse, who drinks too much and has no spine to fight, the farm is the end of the line. For Pelle, it is his introduction to an adult world in which rewards and punishments are thoroughly scrambled and arbitrary power is exercised by the few. Mr. August's screenplay is adapted from the first part of Martin Andersen Nexo's Danish novel in which Pelle, when he grows up, goes on to become a union leader.

Mr. von Sydow is something splendid to see as the boozy, weak-willed, loving Lasse. Though it is a rich performance full of wit and humor, it is never broad or self-serving.

It is also the backbone of the movie, which sometimes looks too big in terms of landscapes, weather and the crowds of people on screen to have come from the comparatively small though clearly vital Danish film industry. "Pelle" has a kind of Dickensian appreciation for narrative, being packed with subplots perceived in the melodramtic terms of an adolescent boy's imagination.

•

Mr. August never indulges the pathos that is built into the story, which is to his credit as a disciplined film maker, though it also keeps the film at a slight remove from the audience. One is never unaware that this is a very long movie. Mr. August brings a cool 20th-century sensibility to what is, at heart, a piece of passionate 19th-century fiction.

As played by Mr. Hvenegaard, who looks a bit like the young Dickie Moore in Hollywood's old "Oliver Twist," Pelle is idealized without being softened. Mostly, he is a camera, receiving the images of a childhood that will eventually shape the course of his life.

The scale of the physical production is most impressive. Mr. August and Jorgen Persson, the cinematographer, avoid the picturesque, which is not to say that "Pelle" isn't a beautiful film. It's just that its looks are more than skin deep.

1988 D 21, C28:5

Emotional Ties
Alan Bates and Evie the dog play leading roles in "We Think the World of You," about love in London in the 1950's.

WE THINK THE WORLD OF YOU, directed by Colin Gregg; screenplay by Hugh Stoddart; director of photography, Mike Garfath; edited by Peter Delfgou; production designer, Jamie Leonard; produced by Tomasso Jandelli; released by Cinecom Pictures. At Cinema Third Avenue, Third and 60th Street. Running time: 94 minutes. This film is rated PG.

Frank .... Alan Bates
Johnny .... Gary Oldman
Megan .... Frances Barber
Millie .... Liz Smith
Tom .... Max Wall
Rita .... Kerry Wise

By JANET MASLIN

"We Think the World of You" is almost certainly the only film ever made about two men who fall in love with the same dog, a German shepherd named Evie. Evie is, needless to say, the beneficiary of emotions that her human admirers have difficulty expressing in other ways. Originally the prized pet of Johnny, a working-class fellow whose housebreaking has landed him in prison, Evie is sent to live with Johnny's mother, Millie, and stepfather, Tom, while her master is away. For Frank, the older and better-bred man who is desperately fixated on Johnny, this is simply too much to bear.

•

Though Frank is openly contemptuous of Johnny's wife and children, he is on good terms with Millie, who used to be his cleaning woman. So he begins to pay her visits, and during one of these interludes Evie catches his eye. Evie immediately reminds Frank of all the inequities that color his relationship with Johnny, like the fact that the younger man's much-hated wife has more opportunities to pay prison visits than his homosexual lover does. All of this somehow turns Frank into the dog's devoted champion. So when Frank learns that Millie refuses to walk the large and unruly Evie, and that Tom sometimes canes her, he decides to go to war.

"We Think the World of You," which opens today at Cinema Third Avenue, is based on a 1960 novel by J. R. Ackerley, the dog fancier whose earlier "My Dog Tulip" has earned its place in many a heart. The novel is a considerably less gentle effort, since it accentuates the bitter, resentful and snobbish aspects of Mr. Ackerley's semi-autobiographical Frank. Frank's vehement defense of Evie becomes his only means of expressing indignation, and the book is written as an outpouring of petty complaints, occasionally punctuated by rhapsodies on Evie's intelligence and beauty. It's impossible to capture the tone of this on screen.

The film, which was directed by Colin Gregg, is notably less bitchy than the novel, which means that it makes much less sense. Alan Bates, who has some of Frank's irritable hauteur but little of his aggrieved and fiercely jealous side, mostly just goes through the motions of arguing with Millie over how and when Evie will have her walks. The particulars of this, the negotiations for doggie visitation rights and the fights over opportunities to see Johnny begin to seem remarkably mundane and tedious when robbed of their sexual urgency. Since Mr. Bates isn't terribly convincing as Johnny's lover, it becomes difficult to see why he or anyone else should go to all this trouble.

"We Think the World of You" is faithful to the events of the novel without capturing any of the undercurrents that set them in motion. Under these circumstances, the cast is mostly at sea. The excellent Gary Oldman makes Johnny reasonably compelling, but he doesn't make him the handsome young sex object whom Frank can't forget. As the unthinking lug who repeatedly employs the pious working-class platitude of the title, Mr. Oldman inevitably seems too smart for his role.

•

Frances Barber makes Johnny's wife an eerie and faintly sinister figure, but neither she nor anyone else in the cast conveys the full and peculiar flavor of Johnny's domestic arrangements. Only Liz Smith, as the chatterbox Millie who keeps busy taking care of one of Johnny's children (a "howling little oaf," as Frank thinks of him in the novel), has the right mixture of dottiness and cunning.

Betsy, who plays Evie, seems a perfectly nice dog but never the paragon that Frank so lovingly imagines.

1988 D 22, C15:1

Love My Son, Love Me

David Eberts as Edmund in "Burning Secret."

BURNING SECRET, written and directed by Andrew Birkin; director of photography, Ernest Day; edited by Paul Green; music by Hans Zimmer; production designer, Bernd Lepel; produced by Norma Heyman, Eberhard Junkersdorf and Carol Lynn Greene; released by Vestron Pictures. At 57th Street Playhouse, at Avenue of the Americas. Running time: 107 minutes. This film is rated PG.

Edmund .... David Eberts
Sonya .... Faye Dunaway
Baron .... Klaus Maria Brandauer
The Father .... Ian Richardson
Dr. Weiss .... John Nettleton

---

By VINCENT CANBY

"Burning Secret" is a small, minutely observed emotional drama about the rude coming-of-age of a sheltered 12-year-old boy.

The time is 1919. Edmund is the asthmatic son of the American ambassador to Austria and his some-

what younger, beautiful, very proper wife, Sonya.

During a winter stay in the mountains, at a fine Old World hotel adjacent to the sanitarium where he is being treated for his asthma, Edmund is befriended by a charming, cynical former officer in the Austro-Hungarian army. He is Baron Alexander Maria von Hauenschild. Edmund is enchanted by the baron, by his bayonet scar and by his grim war stories. Then, gradually, Edmund realizes that the baron has transferred his affections to his mother, and that these two trusted adults, in their mutual infatuation, have abandoned him.

"Burning Secret," which opens today at the 57th Street Playhouse, is "Masterpiece Cinema."

It is handsomely photographed, set and costumed, and acted with conviction by two of the three leading performers. The screenplay sounds as carefully modulated as the voice of a speech student. It is full of pregnant thoughts expressed in perfectly rounded sentences that never ring quite real or sincere.

The film is the first feature to be directed by Andrew Birkin, who also wrote the screenplay based on the Stefan Zweig short story "Brennendes Geheimnis." It's possible that Mr. Birkin has made just the sort of film he intended — tasteful, rather literary and remote in time in a way that is soothing and escapist.

David Eberts, who has never acted before, is exceptionally good as the bewildered boy. Edmund has every right to be outraged by the manner in which he has been betrayed. Mr. Birkin's screenplay is so clumsy in presenting these incidents that they make the baron and the boy's mother appear to be more willfully cruel than merely thoughtless.

Klaus Maria Brandauer's baron is also a fully conceived character, though the screenplay overstates the baron's inability to feel anything deeply, including affection for the boy and love for his mother. Since his own ghastly betrayal by Austria's defeat in the war, he is among the walking wounded. At one point the baron sticks a pin through his numb bayonet scar. Still later he holds his hand over a candle until the flesh begins to burn. It's not a difficult idea to grasp.

Faye Dunaway is less successful as Sonya. When she has material to act against, such as the title role in "Mommie Dearest" or the Skid Row drunk in "Barfly," Miss Dunaway can be an unusually interesting, surprising actress. She needs challenges.

When playing a genteel lady, as she does here, she becomes very actressy. Toward the end of "Burning Secret," she begins to behave like her own, very funny, very nasty interpretation of Joan Crawford playing a lady in "Mommie Dearest." She is completely bogus, but wears clothes well.

•

"Burning Secret" has been rated PG ("Parental Guidance Suggested"). It includes material that might be disturbing to very young children.

1988 D 22, C16:5

Leaving No Footprints

THE ACCIDENTAL TOURIST, directed by Lawrence Kasdan; screenplay by Frank Galati and Mr. Kasdan, based on the book by Anne Tyler; director of photography, John Bailey; edited by Carol Littleton; music by John Williams; production designer, Bo Welch; produced by Mr. Kasdan, Charles Okun and

William Hurt as Macon Leary in "The Accidental Tourist."

Michael Grillo; released by Warner Brothers. At Cinema 2, Third Avenue at 60th Street. Running time: 122 minutes. This film is rated PG.

Macon	William Hurt
Sarah	Kathleen Turner
Muriel	Geena Davis
Rose	Amy Wright
Porter	David Ogden Stiers
Charles	Ed Begley Jr.
Julian	Bill Pullman
Alexander	Robert Gorman

By JANET MASLIN

Anne Tyler's fiction is as revealing of the tiny intimacies that bind people together as of the larger gaps that keep them apart. A key revelation of character, in one of Miss Tyler's novels, is more apt to occur while someone is driving a car or putting away groceries than during a more conventionally dramatic situation. Her writing is beautifully attuned to the minutiae of daily routines, to the seemingly trivial habits that both define and circumscribe her characters' lives. But in the film version of "The Accidental Tourist," which opens today at Cinema 2, it's the broad strokes that stand out.

"The Accidental Tourist," which was unaccountably voted the best film of 1988 by the New York Film Critics' Circle this month, is about a man whose professional life defines his psyche: Macon Leary (Willam Hurt), who has written a series of travel guides for businessmen who wish they could stay home. He roams the world in search of soft bedspreads and American-style restaurants, considering it a victory to "locate a meal in London not much different from a meal in Cleveland."

Macon has trained himself to travel light and leave no footprints, and he has channeled all of his fastidiousness into perfecting this as a science. "There are very few necessities in this world," he has written, "that do not come in travel-sized packets." Macon is also, at the time that the story begins, mourning the loss of his only child, a 12-year-old boy who was shot in a restaurant holdup; as a consequence of this, Macon's long marriage to Sarah (Kathleen Turner) has come to an end. But there is reason to believe that this quiet, methodical, pleasure-denying loner wasn't substantially different before these tragedies occurred.

•

"The Accidental Tourist" observes the long, slow reawakening that occurs in Macon after he has hit rock bottom. Though this process is presented in tiny, artful increments in Miss Tyler's novel, it's not the kind of transformation that can easily be captured on the screen. For one thing, Macon barely seems to change at all until this lengthy and meandering film is almost over. Mr. Hurt flinches his way through the story with a pained morose expression that doesn't lift until the film's final moments.

"The Accidental Tourist," which was directed by Lawrence Kasdan, is the kind of literary adaptation that forgets that films have a language of their own. A lot of Miss Tyler's dialogue is used in the film, but its effect here is very different from its effect on the page. "There's something muffled about the way you experience things," Sarah tells him. "It's as if you were trying to slip through life unchanged." Speaking of the design on the cover of Macon's travel books, she says, "That traveling armchair isn't just your logo. It's you."

A novel can successfully incorporate such pronouncements into its larger scheme, but a film is better off conveying the same ideas in more visual and indirect ways. But "The Accidental Tourist" often relies on Miss Tyler's methods without tempering them, and gives a tone of crashing obviousness to material that need not have seemed that way. In addition, the screenplay by Mr. Kasdan and Frank Galati doesn't do much to compensate for moments when Miss Tyler's dialogue lacks a conversational ring.

If "The Accidental Tourist" is essentially a one-theme story, it nonetheless has a diffuse and rambling plot. Abandoned by Sarah, and living at home with a very unruly dog, Macon eventually breaks his leg and moves in with the rest of his family. In the ancestral house, presided over by Macon's prematurely middle-aged sister, Rose (Amy Wright, who turns this contentedly eccentric character into the film's brightest light), the other Leary brothers have already come home to roost.

•

Together, the siblings alphabetize things in the pantry, play card games no one else can understand, refuse to answer their telephone and otherwise reinforce the habits that have made it impossible for them to live with anyone else. Only in these family scenes (with David Ogden Stiers and Ed Begley Jr. playing Macon's brothers) does this dark, somber film have any glimmer of vitality or humor.

Also on the scene is a dog trainer named Muriel Pritchett, a pushy, loudly dressed woman whose nonstop chatter serves as the conversational equivalent of shooting herself in the foot. Muriel doesn't hold much allure for Macon at first, but this doesn't stop her; she sets her cap for him anyhow and hounds him until she breaks down his resistance.

The novel treats Muriel as a charmingly offbeat character, but she's abrasively cute even on the page. On film, in the person of Geena Davis (who tries hard but is sandbagged by her role), she is quite insufferable, as is the notion that she represents Macon's emotional salvation.

Kathleen Turner is a welcome presence in the film, but her scenes with Mr. Hurt never suggest the weariness and familiarity of a 20-year union; without this, the wife's function in the story is less clear than it could be. Bill Pullman is nicely enterprising as Macon's publisher, who visits the Leary household as a curiosity seeker and winds up with a lot more than he bargained for.

•

"The Accidental Tourist" is rated PG ("Parental Guidance Suggested"). It includes discreet bedroom scenes and mildly off-color language.

1988 D 23, C12:5

Life in the Fastest Of Lanes

James Woods

THE BOOST, directed by Harold Becker; screenplay by Darryl Ponicsan, based on the book "'Ludes" by Benjamin Stein; director of photography, Howard Atherton; music by Stanley Myers; produced by Daniel H. Blatt; released by Hemdale Film Corporation. At D. W. Griffith, 59th Street east of Third Avenue. Running time: 95 minutes. This film is rated R.

Lenny	James Woods
Linda	Sean Young
Joel	John Kapelos
Max	Steven Hill
Rochelle	Kelle Kerr
Ned	John Rothman
Barbara	Amanda Blake
Sheryl	Grace Zabriskie

By VINCENT CANBY

The illegal substance of choice in "The Boost" is cocaine, but when first seen, Lenny Brown (James Woods) is so manic he seems to be headed for disaster long before he becomes hooked on drugs.

Lenny is happily married to the beautiful, patient Linda (Sean Young), a paralegal assistant in a Manhattan law firm. Linda pays the bills while Lenny hustles around town looking for a job. Though he's "a born salesman" (he says), he comes on so strong that he manages to fast-talk his way out of every opportunity, especially with Ivy League types. Lenny's grasp of reality is tenuous. He leaves someone on the street, saying "I have to catch a cab," then walks directly down the steps to the subway.

The promise of a great future arrives in an offer from a California magnate named Max (Steven Hill). If the Devil lived in California and sold real estate, he would probably look like the genial, blunt-spoken Max. He's a little too heavy, perhaps, but lightly, fashionably tanned and dressed in the perfect taste that has nothing to do with Brooks Brothers. Max sees Lenny's potential as a West Coast operator.

"Southern California real estate never goes bad," Max tells his willing disciple. Max installs Lenny and Linda in a pretty, utterly characterless hilltop house (rented by the week), with their own Mercedes (leased by the month). Lenny is an immediate smash. In his first day on the job, selling land mostly for tax-shelter purposes, he makes more money than he did in a year in New York.

•

"The Boost," directed by Harold Becker from Darryl Ponicsan's screenplay, is far better and far more convincing as a picture of a very ephemeral kind of southern California culture than as a demonstration of the psychological and emotional havoc caused by drugs.

The director and the writer obviously know their territory, its manners and the arcane language, which Lenny picks up with ease. Lenny looks around a pool party and announces to Linda, "The discretionary spending power here is enormous." He points out a guest as "a young guy with 42 car washes and mega-tax problems."

Lenny can't believe his good fortune, though even he is occasionally surprised by some of the customs. When a client pays $75,000 in cash for a piece of property, he asks the man what business he's in. The answer, "Leisure activities."

It's these leisure activities that finally wreck the lives of Lenny and Linda, as well as the movie. A threat by the Government to close tax-shelter loopholes ends the real-estate boom. Lenny, who has bought his own airplane and is speculating in real estate himself, is left high and dry. He is without a job and $700,000 in debt.

•

When a pal offers him a snort of cocaine to lift his spirits, Lenny accepts. In less time than it takes to buy a bag of popcorn, Linda is also hooked. From that point forward, "The Boost" becomes a movie about the awful things that addicted people do to themselves and to one another, whether they drink, sniff or shoot up.

Ms. Young ("No Way Out"), playing it as straight as possible, is effective in a role that's more victim than victimizer. Mr. Woods also is good, though he begins the film on such a hysterical level that he's hard put to achieve new peaks in hysteria when Lenny falls into the abyss. Looking on, at first with amusement, then with chilly distaste, Mr. Hill gives the film's most sophisticated performance as Max, the sort of fellow, one is sure, who will prove to be earthquake-proof, when that day comes.

"The Boost" opens today at the D. W. Griffith theater.

1988 D 23, C16:6

HELLBOUND: HELLRAISER II, directed by Tony Randel; screenplay by Peter Atkins; director of photography, Robin Vidgeon; edited by Richard Marden; music by Christopher Young; production design, Mike Buchanan; produced by Christopher Figg; released by New World Pictures. At Movieland, Broadway and 47th Street, and other theaters. Running time: 98 minutes. This film is rated R.

Julia	Clare Higgins
Kirsty	Ashley Laurence
Channard	Kenneth Cranham
Tiffany	Imogen Boorman
Frank	Sean Chapman
Kyle	William Hope
Pinhead	Doug Bradley

By CARYN JAMES

You might find "Hellbound: Hellraiser II" provocative if, and only if, you badly want to know what people look like after they have been stripped of their skins by evil powers. As it turns out, they look very much like walking, talking candied apples, with a shiny red coating that covers their entire bodies. That effect looks even sillier than it sounds, though it's meant to carry a slight sadomasochistic erotic thrill.

Miscalculating what might be titillating for most human beings is just one of the problems with this sequel to "Hellraiser," last year's commercially successful film written and directed by the English horror writer Clive Barker. Though the script for "Hellbound" is related to the Barker story, the film drops its plot whenever a fake-looking monster walks on the screen. Ogling strange creatures is the film's true reason for being.

As the halfhearted story begins, Kirsty, the heroine, wakes up in a psychiatric hospital, having seen her family literally go to the devils in "Hellraiser." The sequel contains generous flashbacks to the original, so you'll know Kirsty has seen her dear father, evil uncle and wicked stepmother taken away by the Cenobites — dead souls who worship the Devil and look like skinheads brought back from the grave. They have pasty white faces, wear lots of black leather, and at least one of them — the one who stares back from subway posters — has nails sticking out of his face.

It takes a while for "Hellbound" to get to the Cenobites, though. First the skinned stepmother returns from the dead, and even though she looks like a candied apple, manages to seduce Kirsty's doctor. This is supposed to be the gory-sexy part.

Next comes the supposedly suspenseful part, which is, in fact, quite dull. The doctor owns dozens of the little boxlike puzzles whose solution will open the doors to the Cenobites' cavernous, hell-like home. The only person who can solve the puzzle is Kirsty's fellow psychiatric patient, Tiffany.

Midway through the movie, Tiffany solves the puzzle while sitting in the doctor's study. Glass jars shatter, sending eyeballs and fetuses flying around the room. From then on, the film is a barrage of loud music and icky special effects — "icky" is the mot juste here — while Kirsty helps Tiffany escape from the land of the Cenobites. Each blinding flash of light, every view of the Cenobites, every run down the cavernous corridors seems to be repeated a half-dozen times.

"Hellbound," which opens today at Movieland and other theaters, has been directed by Tony Randel. This Tony Randel was a production executive on "Hellraiser," and unfortunately is not the actor who played Felix Unger on "The Odd Couple." Too bad; the thought of too-neat Felix directing flayed people is a much better idea than anything in "Hellbound."

1988 D 23, C18:1

A House Divided

GENESIS, directed by Mrinal Sen; screenplay (Hindi with English subtitles) by Mr. Sen with Mohit Chattopadhya, from a novella by Samaresh Basu; camera, Carlo Varini; edited by Elizabeth Waelchli; music by Ravi Shankar; art director, Nitish Roy; produced by Scarabee Films (France), Mrinal Sen PLRT Productions (India), Les Films de la Drève (Belgium), Cactus Film (Switzerland). At the Public Theater, 425 Lafayette Street. Running time: 108 minutes. This film has no rating.

The Woman .... Shabana Azmi
The Farmer .... Naseeruddin Shah
The Weaver .... Om Puri
The Trader .... M. K. Raina

By WALTER GOODMAN

Rest easy. Despite the title, "Genesis" is not a biblical extravaganza. The Indian director Mrinal Sen's 1986 movie, now at the Public Theater, is a simply conceived, artfully rendered parable of love and jealousy, freedom and slavery. The tale is rudimentary, its themes a touch obvious, yet the telling, done with grave humanity, carries meanings of its own.

A weaver and a farmer, in flight from exploitation, settle near a desert, where they live like brothers. The weaver supports the bare and smoky household by exchanges with an itinerant trader, the movie's one ambiguous figure. The farmer tends the land. Life goes so well that the two can delude themselves that "we are slaves to no one, we are our own masters."

Into their sparse Eden comes a teen-aged woman with a lantern, a needless symbol for so luminous an actress as Shabana Azmi. She proves a hard worker who scrubs the sandy floor and also scrubs away some of the men's crudeness. She softens their lives and joins in their play.

They compete in their efforts to please her, and you will not be surprised to learn that this means trouble. As the worldly trader warns, "There are two of them and one of you." She tries to give fair shares — "I accepted you both because you needed me," she tells them in pure affection — but it doesn't do. Here, as in the Old Testament Genesis, the brothers are riven.

Although Miss Azmi has an angel-with-a-dirty-face quality, Mr. Sen, who wrote the screenplay, keeps his characters down to earth. They stand for human beings through the ages, unable to master either their own emotions or life's circumstances. Now and then there is a frightening roar overhead, the sound of the world, that sends them cowering.

Mr. Sen's evident intention to connect man's inner and outer forms of slavery does not click. Even if this two-man-one-woman community could have continued amiably, it would still have been destroyed by the bulldozers brought in by the trader. The director's final reliance on destruction ex machina stems from his politics rather than from his characters' passions. Yet with the help of Carlo Varini's camera and Ravi Shankar's music, "Genesis" brings home the sparseness, beauty and perils of existence at a basic level.

Although Mrinal Sen has made about 25 movies in India, for American audiences "Genesis" marks a notable beginning.

1988 D 23, C18:6

Seeking Oneself

A HUNGARIAN FAIRY TALE, directed by Gyula Gazdag; written (Hungarian with English subtitles) by Mr. Gazdag and Miklos Gyorffy; photography by Elemer Ragalyi. At Film Forum 1, 57 Watts Street. Running time: 97 minutes. This film has no rating.

Andris .... David Vermes
Maria .... Maria Varga
Orban .... Frantisek Husak
Young woman .... Eszter Csakanyi

By JANET MASLIN

The title of Gyula Gazdag's haunting fable amounts to a slight redundancy, since the story of "A Hungarian Fairy Tale" could not take place anywhere else. It grows luxuriantly out of a unique peculiarity of Hungarian law, one that requires the birth certificate of an illegitimate child to bear some paternal name, *any* paternal name, once the child reaches 3 years of age. A name must be fabricated even if the real father's identity is unknown.

Mr. Gazdag uses the inspired unreasonableness of this edict as the jumping-off point for an elegantly realized black-and-white daydream. His film begins on a near-magical note, with the romantic, wordless meeting of a beautiful young woman and a handsome stranger at a performance of "The Magic Flute," an encounter that results in the birth of Andris (David Vermes). As Andris's lovely mother (Maria Varga) explains to a local registry clerk (Frantisek Husak), there is no father's name to be listed. So she and the clerk collaborate on inventing a name, address and even an occupation — bricklayer — for the nonexistent man.

Years later, bricks again play a role in this eerie and fanciful tale. Andris's smiling mother strolls down the street on a sunny day, looking perfectly serene, when a brick falls out of the sky. The boy is left alone in the world, but he does not know that. He believes that the man listed on the birth certificate can be found, and he sets out to locate him.

The journey on which Andris embarks signals a departure from the mainstream, a break with the kind of restrictive culture that produces absurdities like the birth-certificate rule in the first place. As the boy frees himself, the film breaks loose in its own way. It becomes more and more dreamlike, progressing in a breathless and sometimes briskly elliptical style, as a couple of the characters who played important roles in Andris's early days now reappear and join him in his rebellion. Mr. Gazdag re-shapes these characters' frustrations into an exhilarating taste of freedom.

The film's springy pace and liberating energy lift it beyond the realm of mere fantasy. Mr. Gazdag, whose other films include the documentary "Package Tour," succeeds this time in creating a delicate mixture of dreamy reverie and harsh fact. "A Hungarian Fairy Tale," which opens today at the Film Forum 1, manages to capture the poignancy of Andris's plight without losing sight of its allegorical dimensions, thanks to the

A scene from "A Hungarian Fairy Tale," Gyula Gazdag's film about the pitfalls of bureaucracy.

mundane if peculiar touches that punctuate his story. For a time, he is cared for by a seemingly normal family with striking problems of its own; in another part of the film, he falls in with a troop of scouts armed with live ammunition. In the end, as the danger around him heightens, he joins forces with an impromptu new family and quite literally takes flight.

"A Hungarian Fairy Tale" has been photographed in a handsome, bright and yet vaguely mysterious style that gives free reign to Mr. Gazdag's far-reaching imagination.

1988 D 28, C17:1

Wake-Up Time

LIFE IS A DREAM, directed by Raúl Ruiz; screenplay (in French with English subtitles) by Mr. Ruiz based on Pedro Calderón de la Barca's play (excerpts translated by Jean-Louis Schefer); camera, Jacques Bouquin; edited by Martine Bouquin and Rodolpho We-deles; art direction, Christian Olivares; produced by the Maison de La Culture du Havre and the Institut National de la Communication Audiovisuelle. At the Public, 425 Lafayette Street, at Astor Place. Running time: 100 minutes. This film has no rating.

WITH: Sylvain Thirolle, Roch Leibovici, Bénédicte Sire, Jean-Bernard Guillard, Jean-Pierre Agazar, Alain Hall Halle, Jean-François Lapalus and Alain Rimoux.

By VINCENT CANBY

In "Life Is a Dream," a 1986 film by Raúl Ruiz, the expatriate Chilean film maker now living in France, a youngish revolutionary returns secretly to Chile for reasons that are never clear. Lying on the bed in his hotel room in Valparaiso, the man recalls that 10 years earlier he had memorized the names of 1,500 members of an anti-junta movement.

This he accomplished through mnemonics, associating each name with a line from the classic Spanish drama "Life Is a Dream," written by the 17th-century playwright Pedro Calderón de la Barca.

The film incorporates some scenes from the Calderón drama, which Mr. Ruiz once staged for the Avignon Theater Festival. The movie is, however, less about the Calderón play or about the Chilean opposition than about the philosophical concept stated by the title. Mr. Ruiz might just as well have used the round "Row, Row, Row Your Boat" as a jumping-off place for this film, which the director's admirers describe as surreal or fabulist but which to the rest of us seems uninspired, semi-literate camp.

In Mr. Ruiz's "Life Is a Dream," the hero goes to the Valparaiso movie theater where he spent long hours of his youth. As he watches the same movies he watched years ago (which are actually Mr. Ruiz's own dim parodies of B-movies), the reality of the movies becomes hopelessly and humorlessly mixed with the man's consciousness of what is or is not the real world.

Mr. Ruiz's cinematic gifts are not astonishing. The imagery is commonplace, possibly on purpose, as is his fondness for switching from full-color to black and white to monochrome, when everything is seen as either green, blue or amber. The wit and wisdom of the dialogue may lose something in the English subtitles: "What is it like to be Chilean?" "To be dead." Or, "Women love nonexistent things. It's their nature."

Mr. Ruiz's films have been compared favorably to the early work of Jean-Luc Godard. This is sheer baloney. Mr. Godard's films are the work of a man who is not only literate, but also so aggressively innovative that, even today, Mr. Ruiz and others have yet to catch up.

"Life Is a Dream" opens today at the Public Theater.

1988 D 30, C10:6

FILM VIEW/Vincent Canby

Eventually — Plenty to Laugh About

WHILE 1988 WAS PUSHING its way from January to December, it never seemed an especially funny year. It was a grind. There wasn't time to analyze what was happening since there were too many movies to be looked at: 419 this year compared to 388 in 1987. This sets a new record for the Reagan decade, one that will probably stick, since, according to trade observers, the production boom prompted by the home video market has peaked.

The year initially appeared to be memorable only for the dizzy rate at which movies were opening and closing: in the theater one week and coming to your corner video store the next.

The logical reason that 1988 didn't seem to be strong on funny stuff is that, until June, it wasn't. Most of the good comedies opened in the year's second half, but these more than made up for the earlier scarcity. Six of the films on the 1988 10-best list are comedies, as are 5 of the 10 runners-up.

The year has had its other pleasures. Meryl Streep gives one of the best performances of her career in "A Cry in the Dark," though the movie never matches her quality. Jonathan Kaplan's "Accused" is good, efficient film making, made special by Jodie Foster, who may well receive an Oscar nomination. Greta Scacchi probably won't receive an Oscar nomination for her work, frequently unclothed, in "White Mischief," though she's one of 1988's most cherished memories as what, in G-rated conversation, would be called a b-i-t-c-h.

The actors had a better time of it. That is, the year's best performances by actors were in films that tended to be the equal of the performances. One notable exception: Daniel Day Lewis's expert clowning in "Stars and Bars," which was one of the few 1988 films that deserved to stay around longer than it did.

Two other exceptions are Michael Caine and Steve Martin, who are so splendidly funny in "Dirty Rotten Scoundrels," the remake of the 1964 "Bedtime Story," directed by Frank Oz from the original Stanley Shapiro-Paul Henning screenplay updated by Dale Launer. This isn't to say that there isn't a lot of talent behind the scenes in "Dirty Rotten Scoundrels," only that Mr. Caine and Mr. Martin make their comparatively conventional material look great.

■

Dennis Potter's "Singing Detective" is *not* included on the 10-best list, even though the film, made for television and originally shown in New York on Channel 13, now officially qualifies as a theatrical release because of its engagement at the Public Theater. "The Singing Detective" remains the year's most innovative and original film, but, after all, it was conceived as a television work. More power to television.

The 10 best films of the year, in alphabetical order, are:

¶"Au Revoir les Enfants." This is Louis Malle's moving, unsentimental evocation of the Nazi occupation of France as seen through the eyes of a 12-year-old schoolboy, remembering his friendship with a Jewish classmate. Mr. Malle treats the emotionally charged material with the kind of simplicity and ease that are achieved only with

Gaspard Manesse and Raphaël Fejtö in "Au Revoir les Enfants"—a moving, unsentimental evocation

Bob Hoskins and client in "Who Framed Roger Rabbit"—live action and animation integrated by wizards

Simone LaGrange in "Hotel Terminus: The Life and Times of Klaus Barbie"—a fascinating mosaic

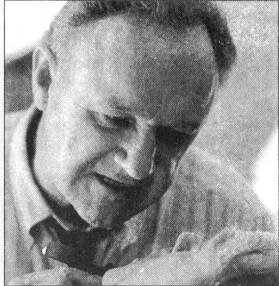
Gene Hackman in "Mississippi Burning"—a time recalled with extraordinary conviction and sorrow

enormous self-discipline. Nothing is overstated.

The cast is headed by Gaspard Manesse and Raphaël Fejtö, as the schoolboys and by François Negret, who is exceptionally fine as a pint-sized collaborator from the working class.

¶"Hotel Terminus: The Life and Times of and Klaus Barbie." A companion film to his epic "The Sorrow and the Pity" (1970), Marcel Ophuls's "Hotel Terminus" is angrier and more far-reaching in its implications. It's not only about the career of Barbie, the Nazi "Butcher of Lyons," it's also an indictment of all the people, including American intelligence agents, who protected Barbie after the war and used him to fight the cold war.

The 4½-hour film is a fascinating mosaic

composed of dozens of interviews (sometimes very spiky) with Barbie's childhood friends, his World War II colleagues and victims, and his postwar friends, including some of the politicians, businessmen and drug traffickers who made possible his later affluence in South America. Though a documentary, "Hotel Terminus" has the resonance of great fiction.

¶"Married to the Mob." Jonathan Demme, a specialist in documenting the eccentrics who make America great ("Handle With Care," "Melvin and Howard," "Something Wild"), is in top form in this straight-faced farce starring Michelle Pfeiffer, Matthew Modine, Dean Stockwell and Mercedes Ruehl. It's about a spunky young woman (Miss Pfeiffer) who attempts to escape the

413

Carmen Maura in "Women on the Verge of a Nervous Breakdwon"—a delightful farce

Don Ameche in "Things Change"—The movie never really falters.

Andrew Schwartz

Melanie Griffith and Harrison Ford in "Working Girl"—classy Manhattan comedy

San Francisco Examiner/Fran Ortiz

Natasha Richardson in "Patty Hearst"—The victim's point of view gives it eerie power.

mob after her husband, a Mafia hit man, dies prematurely of bullet wounds.

The movie is a nearly perfect mix of first-rate performances, screenplay and direction, plus the sort of proudly overstated architecture and interior décor that celebrate America's great good taste.

¶"Mississippi Burning." Alan Parker, the eclectic, sometimes erratic English director ("Bugsy Malone," "Shoot the Moon," "Angel Heart"), doesn't allow piety and good thoughts to soften this fictionalized recapitulation of the real-life lynching of three civil rights workers in Mississippi in 1964. Chris Gerolmo's excellent screenplay concentrates on the investigation that followed the lynching. It's an often tough-to-watch, violent melodrama in which time, temper and place are recalled with extraordinary conviction and sorrow.

The film also gives Gene Hackman the best role he's had in eons, that of a Federal Bureau of Investigation agent, a former Mississippi county sheriff whose rage is a match for the states' righters. Mr. Hackman is is a sure

Oscar nominee and, very likely, a winner.

¶"Patty Hearst." Paul Schrader, who writes screenplays ("Taxi," "The Last Temptation of Christ") more often than he directs them ("Blue Collar," "Mishima"), hits his stride as a director with "Patty Hearst." Based on Nicholas Kazan's screenplay, the film is a cool, nonjudgmental, unsurprised dramatization of the events surrounding the kidnapping of Patricia Hearst by members of the Symbionese Liberation Army in 1974.

Mr. Schrader and Mr. Kazin recall the events entirely from the victim's limited point of view. This gives "Patty Hearst" its eerie power, in that it demands that the audience either enter the film — participate, really — or turn away. Most audiences seem to have turned away. It was a flop at the box office. In the title role, Nastasha Richardson gives one of the year's three or four top performances by an actress.

¶"A Taxing Woman." Having

made an unexpected pile of money from his first two comedies ("The Funeral" and "Tampopo"), only to see it grabbed by the tax people, Juzo Itami, Japan's most original new satirist, turned his attention to Japan's equivalent of the Internal Revenue Service. The result is a very funny, furiously witty movie about a rather ordinary middle-class woman (played with hilarious intensity by Nobuko Miyamoto), who discovers that, as a tax collector, she has the gifts of an artist. Her target is a suave, completely ruthless real estate operator, played with elegant, comic ease by Tsutomu Yamazaki.

Like Mr. Itami's earlier films, "A Taxing Woman" is dense with comic detail. Every image contains a wealth of information, much of it extremely funny and a lot of it unexpectedly sad. Mr. Itami is a brilliant observer of the social scene.

■

¶"Things Change." After making his directorial debut with "House of Games," a sharp-edged, quite dark comedy, David Mamet looks at the Mafia with a gentler eye in "Things Change." The fine screenplay, written with Shel Silverstein, is about an aging Chicago shoeshine man (Don Ameche) who, for a price, agrees to take the rap for a mob murder he didn't commit. To ease the way, a Mafia soldier (Joe Mantegna) decides to give the old man a wild weekend of fun and games at the casinos in Lake Tahoe.

Mr. Ameche and Mr. Mantegna are superb as the mismatched pals whose identities are mistaken and who, for several nights, live high off the hog in the mob's Never Never Land. Mr. Mamet flubs the ending, but everything that precedes it is so fine that the movie never really falters.

¶"Who Framed Roger Rabbit" Under the direction of Robert Zemeckis, this may be the most successfully executed, as well as the funniest, comedy ever to mix live action and animation techniques. Bob Hoskins is great as a shabby, short-tempered private eye who, though he hates "Toons," finds himself trying to save the neck of a cartoon star named Roger Rabbit. The setting is Hollywood and the time 1947.

The screenplay is by Jeffrey Price and Peter S. Seaman, and the integration of animated material with live-action footage is by wizards. Though "Roger Rabbit" is brand-new, with a strictly 1980's sensibility, it successfully evokes everything that made cartoons seem so enchanting when we were children.

■

¶"Women on the Verge of a Nervous Breakdown." Pedro Almodóvar, the young Spanish director best known for his deliberately scandalous comedies, edges into the mainstream with this delightful farce. Among other things, it's about a lovesick radio actress, a blenderful of garden-fresh gazpacho laced with sleeping pills, some bumbling policemen, a woman psychiatrist, terrorists from the Middle East, telephones and telephone answering machines.

The entire cast is super. However, Carmen Maura is superb as the abandoned actress who behaves a little bit the way Anna Magnani might had she ever sniffed glue.

¶"Working Girl." Kevin Wade ("Key Exchange") wrote and Mike Nichols directed this classy Manhattan comedy about a young woman from the wrong side of the tracks in Staten Island who aspires to wheel and deal with the Ivy Leaguers on Wall Street. Melanie Griffith is pure pleasure as the ambitious one who is taught all she needs to known about rotten ethics by her immediate boss. The latter is a self-assured career woman played by Sigourney Weaver with all nails sharpened.

Harrison Ford is the man who happens to be in the lives of both women, and Philip Bosco plays the closest thing that Wall Street might ever have to a Santa Claus. The comedy is classic Nichols, as is the richness of the physical production that begins with an airborne close-up of Miss Liberty and stays aloft, metaphorically speaking, until everything is straightened out, sort of.

■

The runners-up, in no particular order of preference, are Mr. Nichols's

equally smooth screen adaptation of Neil Simon's "Biloxi Blues"; the hilarious "Naked Gun," "torn'" as the ads say, "from the files of Police Squad" by Jerry Zucker, Jim Abrahams and David Zucker, the people who made "Airplane," with the assistance of Pat Proft; John Waters's 1960's musical, "Hairspray," with Divine and others; Gabriel Axel's Danish-French meditation on art and food, "Babette's Feast," this year's winner of the foreign-language Oscar.

Also Errol Morris's "Thin Blue Line," a handsome, probing documentary about a real-life Texas murder; Ron Shelton's baseball comedy, "Bull Durham," with Kevin Costner, Susan Sarandon and Tim Robbins; David Cronenberg's "Dead Ringers," with Jeremy Irons as lethally dependent, identical twins; Eric Rohmer's "Boyfriends and Girlfriends," about love in a new, not-quite-perfect environment; Mira Nair's "Salaam Bombay," about Bombay's resilient street kids; and "Pelle the Conqueror," Bille August's beautiful Danish period epic, with Max von Sydow never better as a spineless drunk who's also a loving father.   □

1988 D25, II:9:1

Ken Regan

Michelle Pfeiffer and Matthew Modine in "Married to the Mob"—a nearly perfect mix

Durham." Chris Menges, the cinematographer who made his directorial debut with "A World Apart," was voted best director. The best cinematography award went to Henri Alekan for his work on "Wings of Desire." "The Thin Blue Line," Errol Morris's examination of a Texas murder case, was voted best documentary.

The awards will be presented on Jan. 15 in a ceremony at Sardi's restaurant.

The 29 members of the New York Film Critics' Circle are:

Peter Travers, People — Chairman.
David Ansen, Newsweek.
Joy Gould Boyum, Glamor.
Dwight Brown, The Black American/Hollywood Reporter.
Georgia Brown, Seven Days.
Vincent Canby, The New York Times.
Kathleen Carroll, New York Daily News.

Richard Corliss, Time.
Judith Crist, Coming Attractions.
Lynn Darling, Newsday.
David Denby, New York Magazine.
David Edelstein, The New York Post.
Richard Freedman, Newhouse Newspapers.
Joseph Gelmis, Newsday.
Molly Haskell, Vogue.
J. Hoberman, The Village Voice.
Pauline Kael, The New Yorker.
Jack Kroll, Newsweek.
Janet Maslin, The New York Times.
Mike McGrady, Newsday.
Terrence Rafferty, The New Yorker.
Rex Reed, The New York Observer.
Julie Salamon, The Wall Street Journal.
Andrew Sarris, The Village Voice.
Richard Schickel, Time.
John Simon, National Review.
David Sterritt, Christian Science Monitor.
Armond White, The City Sun.
Bruce Williamson, Playboy.

1988 D 16, C12:1

'Unbearable Lightness' Gets Film Prize

"The Unbearable Lightness of Being," the film version of the novel by Milan Kundera, was voted the best film of 1988 yesterday by the National Society of Film Critics, a 39-member group that includes critics from New York, Chicago, Los Angeles and other cities. Philip Kaufman was voted best director for his work on that film.

Michael Keaton was voted best actor for both "Beetlejuice" and "Clean and Sober," and Judy Davis was voted best actress for "High Tide." Mercedes Ruehl and Dean Stockwell were voted best support-

ing actress and actor, respectively, for "Married to the Mob."

Ron Shelton's screenplay for "Bull Durham" was voted the year's best, and Errol Morris's "Thin Blue Line" was voted best documentary. Henri Alekan was voted best cinematographer for "Wings of Desire."

The group also voted a special award "for his originality" to Pedro Almodovar, director of "Women on the Verge of a Nervous Breakdown" and "Matador."

1989 Ja 9, C14:5

'Accidental Tourist' Wins Critics' Award

By JANET MASLIN

"The Accidental Tourist," the screen adaptation of the novel by Anne Tyler in which a lonely, methodical man rediscovers his capacity for love, was voted the best film of 1988 by the New York Film Critics' Circle. Like each of the group's choices, in a year when no film won more than a single award, it was a far from unanimous one.

"A World Apart," a film about a white journalist and her daughter in South Africa, received the same number of votes as "The Accidental Tourist." But because the group votes weighted ballots — with members allotting one, two or three points to their choices for third, second or first place — and only "The Accidental Tourist" appeared on a majority of ballots, a tie was not declared.

The same thing happened in the best actor category, where Jeremy Irons was declared the winner for his performance as twin brothers in "Dead Ringers." Dustin Hoffman, who received an equal number of votes for his role as an autistic savant in "Rain Man," appeared on less than a majority of ballots and so was not considered a co-winner.

Meryl Streep was voted best actress for "A Cry in the Dark," and Diane Venora was chosen best supporting actress for her role as Charlie Parker's common-law wife in "Bird." Dean Stockwell was voted best supporting actor for both "Married to the Mob," in which he plays a gangster, and "Tucker," in which he appears briefly as Howard Hughes.

The Spanish comedy "Women on the Verge of a Nervous Breakdown" was voted best foreign film, and the best screenplay award went to "Bull

'Rain Man' Wins Oscar as Best Film

By ALJEAN HARMETZ

Special to The New York Times

HOLLYWOOD, March 29 — "Rain Man," a drama about a car salesman who tries to trick his handicapped brother out of his inheritance, won four major Oscars tonight: best picture, actor, director and original screenplay.

At the 61st annual Academy Awards ceremonies, Dustin Hoffman walked off with his second Oscar, for his role as an autistic savant who can memorize telephone books and count the cards at blackjack. Mr. Hoffman won in 1979 for "Kramer vs. Kramer."

Barry Levinson, who was the fourth director to be offered "Rain Man," won his first Oscar for the movie.

The Oscar for best actress went to Jodie Foster for her portayal of a flamboyant waitress who is gang raped, in "The Accused." At the age of 13, Ms. Foster won a supporting ac-

tress nomination for her performance as a teen-age prostitute in "Taxi Driver." Miss Foster reached the stage laughing. "This is such a big deal, and my life is so simple," she said.

For her performance as an eccentric dog trainer who forces her passive lover to re-engage with life in "The Accidental Tourist," Geena Davis won the Oscar as best supporting actress at the 61st Academy Awards presentations tonight.

A major surprise, Ms. Davis's victory broke a pattern that started in 1938 when Fay Bainter was nominated in both the star and supporting categories and won as supporting actress. This year Sigourney Weaver had been nominated for the supporting-actress prize for "Working Girl" as well as for the best-actress award for "Gorillas in the Mist." Each of the four times an actor or actress had been nominated in both star and supporting categories, the performer won the supporting Oscar.

Geena Davis, who was named best supporting actress, in a scene from "The Accidental Tourist"; Dustin Hoffman, who was selected as best actor, in center photo at right with

Tom Cruise in a scene from "Rain Man."

With a poise that is unusual among winners, Miss Davis said, "I sort of can't believe I have to go first." She started by thanking Anne Tyler for writing the novel "The Accidental Tourist," and ended by thanking "my acting coach and darling husband, Jeff Goldblum."

In another surprise, the matching Oscar for best supporting actor went to Kevin Kline for his performance as a dangerous but lethally dumb gangster in "A Fish Called Wanda." The sentimental favorite was Martin Landau for his role as a loyal financier to a visionary car designer in "Tucker: The Man and His dream." For the last three years the supporting Oscar was won by a grizzled actor — Don Ameche, Michael Caine and Sean Connery — who had paid his dues over the decades but had never won the golden statuette. Mr. Caine and Mr. Connery presented the award.

In his acceptance speech, Mr. Kline recounted how John Cleese had told him he wanted "to write a movie where you get run over by a steamroller and eat a lot of Michael Palin's tropical fish." He then saluted the other nominees.

The award for best foreign-language film went to "Pelle the Conqueror," the saga of a Swedish emigrant — played by Max von Sydow — who struggles to earn a living and bring up his son in Denmark. Directed by Bille August, "Pelle" was the favorite. The winner of last year's foreign-language award, "Babette's Feast," was also from Denmark.

Broadcast to Soviet Union

Tonight's ceremony, which was held at the Shrine Civic Auditorium in downtown Los Angeles, was broadcast by ABC to 91 countries, including, for the first time, the Soviet Union.

In the early technical awards, the Oscar for sound was given to Clint Eastwood's "Bird," a movie based on

the life of the jazz musician Charlie Parker. "Who Framed Roger Rabbit," in which cartoon characters driving cartoon vehicles crashed against live co-stars, was honored for sound-effects editing. The decaying ghosts of "Beetlejuice" earned the makeup award.

"Dangerous Liaisons" was the first film to take home two of the golden statues. "Liaisons" won the art-direction Oscar for its re-creation of the sumptuous world of 18th-century

French aristocracy, and James Acheson's corsets and waistcoats won for costume design.

The award for visual effects was won by "Roger Rabbit."

A Musical Surprise

In another surprise in an evening that started with surprises, the award for original score was won by Dave Grusin for "The Milagro Beanfield War."

Among the most ebullient of the winners and, from the applause, one

Kevin Kline, who won the award as best supporting actor, in "A Fish Called Wanda."

of the most popular, was Carly Simon, who won for best song — "Let the River Run" — from the movie "Working Girl." Ms. Simon thanked her husband "for writing the best lines in the song."

A few of the winners did not have to wait in suspense. The academy's board of governors had voted a special award to Richard Williams, the animator who created Jessica and Roger Rabbit and then managed to make the cartoon characters interact with live actors in "Who Framed

The Oscar Winners

FILM: "Rain Man" (United Artists).
FOREIGN-LANGUAGE FILM: "Pelle the Conqueror" (Bille August, Denmark).
DIRECTOR: Barry Levinson, for "Rain Man."
ACTOR: Dustin Hoffman, for "Rain Man."
ACTRESS: Jodie Foster, for "The Accused."
SUPPORTING ACTOR: Kevin Kline, for "A Fish Named Wanda."
SUPPORTING ACTRESS: Geena Davis, for "The Accidental Tourist."
ORIGINAL SCREENPLAY: Ronald Bass and Barry Morrow, for "Rain Man."
SCREENPLAY ADAPTATION: Christopher Hampton, for "Dangerous Liaisons."
CINEMATOGRAPHY: Peter Biziou, for "Mississippi Burning."
EDITING: Arthur Schmidt, for "Who Framed Roger Rabbit."
ORIGINAL SCORE: Dave Grusin, for "The Milagro Beanfield War."
ORIGINAL SONG: Carly Simon, for "Let the River Run" ("Working Girl").
ART DIRECTION: Stuart Craig, art direction, and Gerard James, set decoration, for "Dangerous Liaisons."
COSTUME DESIGN: James Acheson, for "Dangerous Liaisons."
SOUND: Les Fresholtz, Dick Alexander, Vern Poore and Willie D. Burton, for "Bird."

SOUND EDITING: Charles L. Campbell and Louis L. Edemann, for "Who Framed Roger Rabbit."
MAKEUP: Ve Neill, Steve La Porte and Robert Short, for "Beetlejuice."
VISUAL EFFECTS: Ken Ralston, Richard Williams, Edward Jones and George Gibbs, for "Who Framed Roger Rabbit."
DOCUMENTARY, FEATURE: "Hotel Terminus: The Life and Times of Klaus Barbie," Marcel Ophuls, producer.
DOCUMENTARY, SHORT SUBJECT: "You Don't Have to Die," William Guttentag and Malcolm Clarke, producers.
SHORT FILM, ANIMATED: "Tin Toy," John Lasseter and William Reeves.
SHORT FILM, LIVE: "The Appointments of Dennis Jennings," Dean Parisot and Steven Wright.
HONORARY AWARD: The National Film Board of Canada, for 50 years of commitment and excellence in film.
HONORARY AWARD: Eastman Kodak Company, for 100 years of service and achievement.
SPECIAL ACHIEVEMENT: Richard Williams, for animation direction and creation of the cartoon characters in "Who Framed Roger Rabbit."
MERIT AWARD: Ray Dolby and Ioan Allen of Dolby Laboratories, for contributions to motion-picture sound.
GORDON E. SAWYER AWARD: Gordon Henry Cook, for work in zoom-lens design.

Roger Rabbit.'' In 1972, Mr. Williams won an Oscar for his cartoon version of Dickens's "Christmas Carol.''

Special Oscars were also voted to the National Film Board of Canada on the occasion of its 50th birthday and to the Eastman Kodak Company, which is celebrating its centennial. The National Film Board has received a total of 52 nominations and has won 8 Oscars for its documen-taries, cartoons, and live-action shorts.

The Gordon E. Sawyer Award, which is presented for outstanding contributions to the science or technology of motion pictures, went to Gordon Henry Cook for his work in zoom-lens design.

A special Oscar for technical achievement went to Ray Dolby and Ioan Allen of Dolby Laboratories for their contributions to motion-picture sound.

The academy is divided into 13 branches, and each branch makes nominations for achievements in its own field. For example, film editors make nominations for film editing, and cinematographers for photography. The 4,661 voting members include 1,297 actors, 261 art directors and costume designers, 109 cinema-tographers, 265 directors, 337 executives, 185 film editors, 246 musicians, 363 producers, 312 publicists, 214 makers of short films, 326 sound editors, 374 writers, and 372 members-at-large.

Everyone nominates for best picture, and all 4,661 are entitled to vote for the winners in most categories.

1989 Mr 30, C 17:1

417

Index

This index covers all the film reviews included in this volume. It is divided into three sections: Titles, Personal Names, and Corporate Names.

The Titles Index lists each film reviewed by title. The Persons Index lists by name every performer, producer, director, screenwriter, etc. mentioned in the reviews, with the function in parentheses following the name, and the titles of the movies with which the person was connected, in chronological order. The Corporate Names Index lists all performing arts groups and organizations, and producing, distributing, and otherwise participating companies mentioned in reviews by name, again with the function in parentheses following the name, and the titles of the movies with which they were associated, in chronological order.

Citations in this index are by year, month, day, section of newspaper (if applicable), page and column; for example, 1983 Ja 11,II,12:1. Since the reviews appear in chronological order, the date is the key locator. The citations also serve to locate the reviews in bound volumes and microfilm editions of The Times.

In the citations, the months are abbreviated as follows:

Ja - January	My - May	S - September
F - February	Je - June	O - October
Mr - March	Jl - July	N - November
Ap - April	Ag - August	D - December

TITLES INDEX

All films reviewed are listed alphabetically by title. Titles are inverted only if they begin with an article ("Doctor Glas" is listed under D, not G; but "The Graduate" is listed under G, not T). Titles beginning with a number are alphabetized as though the number were spelled out in English. Wherever possible, foreign films are entered under both the English and foreign-language title. Titles given incorrectly in the review appear correctly here. Films reviewed more than once and films with identical titles are given multiple listings.

PERSONAL NAMES INDEX

All persons included in the credits are listed alphabetically, last name first. Their function in the films is listed after the name in parentheses: Original Author, Screenwriter, Director, Producer, Cinematographer, Composer, Narrator, Miscellaneous. In entries where no such qualifier appears, the person was a performer (actor, actress, singer). A person with multiple functions will have multiple entries; for example, an actor who later turned producer or director will have two listings. A person having two functions in the same film will also have two listings. Functions that are none of the above, such as editors, costume designers, art directors, etc., are given as miscellaneous.

Names beginning with Mc are alphabetized as though spelled Mac.

Names beginning with St. are alphabetized as though spelled Saint.

Entries under each name are by title of film, in chronological order.

CORPORATE NAMES INDEX

All companies mentioned in reviews as involved in the production or distribution of the film or in some other major function connected with it, such as performing arts groups and organizations, are listed here alphabetically. Company names are not inverted unless they start with a personal forename (for example, J Arthur Rank Organization is listed as Rank, J Arthur, Organization). The function of the company is given in parentheses, abbreviated as follows:

Prod. - Producer
Distr. - Distributor
Misc. - Miscellaneous

Misc. is used when the function is uncommon or not precisely defined in the review; it is also used for performing arts groups and organizations. A company that has more than one function is given more than one listing; thus a user who has completed scanning a long listing under RKO (Distr.) will then find an additional listing under RKO (Prod.).

Abbreviations in names are alphabetized as though they were words (RKO as Rko).

Entries under each company name are by title of film, in chronological order.

I

J

K

L

M

N

B

My Stepmother Is an Alien 1988,D 11,II,13:1
Baskin, Sonny (Miscellaneous)
Overboard 1987,D 16,C,22:3
Bass, Ronald (Screenwriter)
Black Widow 1987,F 6,C,3:1
Gardens of Stone 1987,My 8,C,32:1
Rain Man 1988,D 16,C,12:5
Bassett, Linda
Waiting for the Moon 1987,Mr 6,C,14:5
Bassin, Roberta
Barfly 1987,S 30,C,18:1
Bassinson, Kevin (Composer)
Jackie Chan's Police Story 1987,S 26,12:3
Bastiani, Billy
Salvation! 1987,My 31,51:1
Bastien, Fanny
Wolf at the Door, The 1987,Jl 31,C,8:5
Basu, Samaresh (Original Author)
Genesis 1988,D 23,C,18:6
Bate, Natalie
Ground Zero 1988,S 23,C,18:1
Bateman, Jason
Teen Wolf Too 1987,N 20,C,14:6
Bateman, Justine
Satisfaction 1988,F 13,15:1
Bateman, Kent (Producer)
Teen Wolf Too 1987,N 20,C,14:6
Bates, Alan
Duet for One 1987,F 13,C,10:4
Prayer for the Dying, A 1987,S 11,C,11:1
We Think the World of You 1988,D 22,C,15:1
Bates, Kathy
Summer Heat 1987,My 29,C,8:4
Batinkoff, Randall
For Keeps 1988,Ja 15,C,17:3
Battista, Franco (Miscellaneous)
Crazy Moon 1988,F 8,C,18:5
Bauchau, Patrick
Friendship's Death 1988,Mr 25,C,22:4
Baudour, Michel (Cinematographer)
Vie Est Belle, La 1987,N 18,C,21:1
Bauer, Belinda
Rosary Murders, The 1987,Ag 28,C,12:3
Bauer, Mary (Miscellaneous)
Summer Heat 1987,My 29,C,8:4
Bauer, Richard
Sicilian, The 1987,O 23,C,4:5
Bauer, Steven
Beast, The 1988,S 16,C,13:1
Baxley, Craig R (Director)
Action Jackson 1988,F 12,C,10:1
Baye, Nathalie
Honeymoon 1987,N 20,C,24:1
Beethoven's Nephew 1988,Je 10,C,12:6
Bayldon, Geoffrey
Madame Sousatzka 1988,O 14,C,8:5
Bayly, Stephen (Director)
Coming Up Roses 1987,S 11,C,9:1
Baz, Serge el-
Hanna's War 1988,N 23,C,14:1
Bazelli, Bojan (Cinematographer)
China Girl 1987,S 25,C,16:6
Patty Hearst 1988,S 23,C,8:5
Bazin, Janine (Producer)
Jean Renoir, the Boss 1987,N 20,C,23:1
Bazzoni, Camillo (Cinematographer)
Summer Night with Greek Profile, Almond Eyes and Scent of
Basil 1987,Je 19,C,12:6
Two Lives of Mattia Pascal, The 1988,Mr 18,C,8:5
Beach, Michael
End of the Line 1988,F 26,C,15:1
In a Shallow Grave 1988,My 6,C,21:1
Beadle, Gary
Playing Away 1987,Mr 13,C,19:1
Playing Away 1988,Ap 1,C,4:4
Bean, Sean
Stormy Monday 1988,Ap 22,C,3:5
Stormy Monday 1988,My 1,II,23:1
Beard, John (Miscellaneous)
Siesta 1987,N 11,C,23:3
Last Temptation of Christ, The 1988,Ag 12,C,1:1
Beart, Emmanuelle
Manon of the Spring 1987,N 6,C,25:1
Date with an Angel 1987,N 21,14:5
Beato, Alfonso (Cinematographer)
Big Easy, The 1987,Ag 21,C,6:3
Beaton, Norman
Playing Away 1987,Mr 13,C,19:1
Playing Away 1988,Ap 1,C,4:4
Beatty, Ned
Big Easy, The 1987,Ag 21,C,6:3

Fourth Protocol, The 1987,Ag 28,C,19:1
Trouble with Spies, The 1987,D 4,C,5:1
Switching Channels 1988,Mr 4,C,10:4
Unholy, The 1988,Ap 23,18:4
Midnight Crossing 1988,My 14,16:5
Beatty, Warren
Ishtar 1987,My 15,C,3:1
Ishtar 1987,Je 7,II,24:1
Beatty, Warren (Producer)
Ishtar 1987,My 15,C,3:1
Beauchamp, Carolyn
Troma's War 1988,D 9,C,23:1
Beauman, Nicholas (Miscellaneous)
High Tide 1988,F 19,C,5:1
Beaumont, Gabrielle (Director)
He's My Girl 1987,S 11,C,5:1
Beaune, Michel
Honeymoon 1987,N 20,C,24:1
Beaven, Ellen
Buster 1988,N 23,C,12:1
Beaver, Terry
Funland 1988,Je 1,C,17:1
Bebel, Andrea
Big Shots 1987,O 2,C,17:1
Bebey, Francis (Composer)
Choice, The 1988,Mr 24,C,26:6
Bechtler, Hildegard (Miscellaneous)
Coming Up Roses 1987,S 11,C,9:1
Beck, John
Deadly Illusion 1987,O 31,10:5
Beckendorff, Ghita (Miscellaneous)
Dark Side of the Moon, The 1987,Mr 19,C,28:1
Becker, Barbara (Miscellaneous)
Lord of the Dance/Destroyer of Illusion 1987,D 26,14:4
Becker, Desiree
Good Morning, Babylon 1987,Jl 15,C,18:5
Becker, Harold (Director)
Boost, The 1988,D 23,C,16:6
Beckerman, Sidney (Producer)
Inside Out 1987,Ag 21,C,11:1
Beckhaus, Friedrich
Wannsee Conference, The 1987,N 18,C,29:3
Bedelia, Bonnie
Die Hard 1988,Jl 15,C,14:5
Die Hard 1988,Jl 31,II,19:1
Prince of Pennsylvania, The 1988,S 16,C,17:1
Bedi, Kabir
Beast, The 1988,S 16,C,13:1
Bednarski, Robert
Wild Thing 1987,Ap 17,C,13:1
Beecroft, Jeffrey (Miscellaneous)
Wizard of Loneliness, The 1988,S 2,C,9:1
Beeman, Greg (Director)
License to Drive 1988,Jl 6,C,17:1
Beers, Francine
Three Men and a Baby 1987,N 25,C,24:3
Beeson, Lana
Pinocchio and the Emperor of the Night 1987,D 25,C,6:5
Beethoven, Ludwig van (Composer)
Beethoven's Nephew 1988,Je 10,C,12:6
Beghe, Jason
Monkey Shines: An Experiment in Fear 1988,Jl 29,C,12:4
Begley, Ed, Jr
Amazon Women on the Moon 1987,S 18,C,12:6
Amazon Women on the Moon 1987,O 4,II,23:1
Accidental Tourist, The 1988,D 23,C,12:5
Belcher, Joe
Link 1987,Ap 24,C,10:4
Belcourt, Emile
Man Who Mistook His Wife for a Hat, The 1988,Ag
31,C,17:1
Belefonte, Gina
Tokyo Pop 1988,Ap 15,C,4:4
Belen, Ana
House of Bernarda Alba, The (Casa de Bernarda Alba, La)
1988,D 16,C,14:6
Beliard, Florence
Love Is a Dog from Hell 1988,Mr 18,C,15:1
Love Is a Dog from Hell 1988,Ap 23,14:5
Belizon, Antonio (Miscellaneous)
Sur, El (South, The) 1988,Ja 15,C,11:1
Belkodja, Catherine
Black and White 1987,Mr 13,C,20:4
Bell, Marlene
Fringe Dwellers, The 1987,Ja 23,C,13:3
Bell, Marshall
Twins 1988,D 9,C,18:1
Bell, Tom
Wish You Were Here 1987,Jl 24,C,7:2

Bellamy, Ralph
Disorderlies 1987,Ag 15,13:1
Amazon Women on the Moon 1987,S 18,C,12:6
Coming to America 1988,Je 29,C,20:5
Good Mother, The 1988,N 4,C,15:1
Belleville, Francoise (Miscellaneous)
Mes Petites Amoureuses 1987,Ja 30,C,16:1
Belling, Kylie
Fringe Dwellers, The 1987,Ja 23,C,13:3
Bellis, Andreas (Cinematographer)
Sweet Country 1987,Ja 23,C,6:5
Bellocchio, Marco (Director)
Devil in the Flesh 1987,My 29,C,3:1
Devil in the Flesh 1987,Je 28,II,18:5
Bellocchio, Marco (Screenwriter)
Devil in the Flesh 1987,My 29,C,3:1
Bellon, Roger (Composer)
Unholy, The 1988,Ap 23,18:4
Belmont, Vera (Producer)
Vie Est Belle, La 1987,N 18,C,21:1
Beloborodoff, Andrea (Miscellaneous)
We the Living 1988,N 25,C,11:1
Belson, Jerry (Director)
Surrender 1987,O 9,C,10:6
Belson, Jerry (Producer)
For Keeps 1988,Ja 15,C,17:3
Belson, Jerry (Screenwriter)
Surrender 1987,O 9,C,10:6
Beltran, Robert
Gaby—A True Story 1987,O 30,C,10:4
Beltrao, Andrea
Color of Destiny, The 1988,Jl 22,C,17:1
Belushi, James
Principal, The 1987,S 18,C,14:6
Red Heat 1988,Je 17,C,14:5
Red Heat 1988,Je 19,II,23:1
Belzer, Richard
Wrong Guys, The 1988,Je 4,12:3
Freeway 1988,S 3,10:6
Ben Amotz, Dahn (Original Author)
I Don't Give a Damn 1988,My 20,C,22:5
Benchley, Peter (Miscellaneous)
Jaws: The Revenge 1987,Jl 18,15:4
Bender, Michael (Producer)
Beetlejuice 1988,Mr 30,C,18:6
Bendico, Silvia D'Amico (Producer)
Dark Eyes 1987,S 25,C,26:5
Two Lives of Mattia Pascal, The 1988,Mr 18,C,8:5
Benedetto, Bob (Screenwriter)
Aloha Summer 1988,F 26,C,8:1
Benedict, Paul
Arthur 2 on the Rocks 1988,Jl 8,C,8:1
Benelli, Stefania (Miscellaneous)
Maschera, La 1988,S 25,64:4
Bengel, Norma
Color of Destiny, The 1988,Jl 22,C,17:1
Bengtsson, Christina
Dark Side of the Moon, The 1987,Mr 19,C,28:1
Benguigui, Jean
Buffet Froid (Cold Cuts) 1987,S 4,C,5:4
Bening, Annette
Great Outdoors, The 1988,Je 17,C,12:6
Benitez, Tomas (Screenwriter)
Salsa 1988,My 7,13:1
Benjamin, Randy (Miscellaneous)
Kiss Daddy Good Night 1988,My 20,C,11:1
Benjamin, Richard (Director)
Little Nikita 1988,Mr 18,C,26:5
My Stepmother Is an Alien 1988,D 9,C,17:1
Benji
Benji the Hunted 1987,Je 17,C,18:6
Benner, Dick (Director)
Too Outrageous 1987,O 16,C,12:1
Benner, Dick (Screenwriter)
Too Outrageous 1987,O 16,C,12:1
Bennett, Alan
Little Dorrit 1988,Mr 26,11:1
Bennett, Alan (Screenwriter)
Prick Up Your Ears 1987,Ap 17,C,17:1
Bennett, Bill (Director)
Backlash 1987,Mr 26,C,14:4
Backlash 1987,Ag 27,C,18:3
Bennett, Bill (Producer)
Backlash 1987,Mr 26,C,14:4
Backlash 1987,Ag 27,C,18:3
Bennett, Bill (Screenwriter)
Backlash 1987,Mr 26,C,14:4
Backlash 1987,Ag 27,C,18:3
Bennett, Brian (Composer)
Riders of the Storm 1988,My 7,12:3

Brodek, Thomas H (Producer)
  Principal, The 1987,S 18,C,14:6
Broderick, Matthew
  Project X 1987,Ap 17,C,15:1
  Biloxi Blues 1988,Mr 25,C,1:1
  Torch Song Trilogy 1988,D 14,C,19:1
Brodie, Bill (Miscellaneous)
  Short Circuit 2 1988,Jl 6,C,18:5
Bromberg, Dave (Miscellaneous)
  Sleepwalk 1987,Mr 20,C,15:1
  Sleepwalk 1987,Jl 3,C,5:1
Bromet, Frans (Cinematographer)
  Broken Mirrors 1987,Mr 4,C,21:1
  Pointsman, The 1988,Ap 8,C,22:1
Bromfield, Rex (Director)
  Home Is Where the Hart Is 1987,D 5,14:4
Bromfield, Rex (Screenwriter)
  Home Is Where the Hart Is 1987,D 5,14:4
Bromfield, Valri
  Home Is Where the Hart Is 1987,D 5,14:4
Bron, Eleanor
  Little Dorrit 1988,Mr 26,11:1
  Little Dorrit 1988,O 21,C,12:3
Bronett, Henry
  Mozart Brothers, The 1987,S 18,C,21:1
Bronson, Charles
  Assassination 1987,Ja 10,13:1
  Death Wish 4: The Crackdown 1987,N 7,14:1
  Messenger of Death 1988,S 17,12:5
Brook, Irina
  Captive 1987,Ap 3,C,8:1
Brooke, Paul
  Lair of the White Worm, The 1988,O 21,C,14:1
Brooks, Albert
  Broadcast News 1987,D 16,C,21:4
  Broadcast News 1987,D 20,II,25:5
Brooks, Annabel
  Nightflyers 1987,O 24,17:1
Brooks, Carroll
  Bad Blood 1987,S 30,C,20:5
Brooks, Claude
  Hiding Out 1987,N 6,C,21:1
Brooks, David Allen
  Kindred, The 1987,Ja 10,13:1
Brooks, James L (Director)
  Broadcast News 1987,D 16,C,21:4
  Broadcast News 1987,D 20,II,25:5
Brooks, James L (Producer)
  Broadcast News 1987,D 16,C,21:4
  Broadcast News 1987,D 20,II,25:5
Brooks, James L (Screenwriter)
  Broadcast News 1987,D 16,C,21:4
  Broadcast News 1987,D 20,II,25:5
Brooks, Maggie (Screenwriter)
  Loose Connections 1988,Jl 8,C,11:1
Brooks, Mel
  Spaceballs 1987,Je 24,C,23:1
Brooks, Mel (Director)
  Spaceballs 1987,Je 24,C,23:1
Brooks, Mel (Producer)
  Spaceballs 1987,Je 24,C,23:1
Brooks, Mel (Screenwriter)
  Spaceballs 1987,Je 24,C,23:1
Brooks, Randi
  Cop 1988,F 5,C,19:3
Brooks, Randy
  Assassination 1987,Ja 10,13:1
  Colors 1988,Ap 15,C,4:1
Brooks, Richard
  Shakedown 1988,My 6,C,20:1
Brooks, Richard (Cinematographer)
  Morgan Stewart's Coming Home 1987,Je 4,C,16:4
Broomfield, Nicholas (Director)
  Lily Tomlin 1987,Mr 6,C,8:5
Broomfield, Nicholas (Miscellaneous)
  Lily Tomlin 1987,Mr 6,C,8:5
Broomfield, Nicholas (Producer)
  Lily Tomlin 1987,Mr 6,C,8:5
Brosnan, Pierce
  Fourth Protocol, The 1987,Ag 28,C,19:1
  Deceivers, The 1988,S 2,C,10:1
Brou, Kouadio
  Faces of Women 1987,F 13,C,22:1
Broughton, Bruce (Composer)
  Square Dance 1987,F 20,C,4:5
  Harry and the Hendersons 1987,Je 5,C,14:5
  Monster Squad 1987,Ag 14,C,15:1
  Big Shots 1987,O 2,C,17:1
  Cross My Heart 1987,N 13,C,21:1
  Presidio, The 1988,Je 10,C,15:1

Rescue, The 1988,Ag 5,C,9:1
Brown, Amelda
  Little Dorrit 1988,Mr 26,11:1
Brown, Andrew (Producer)
  Prick Up Your Ears 1987,Ap 17,C,17:1
Brown, Barry Alexander (Miscellaneous)
  School Daze 1988,F 12,C,11:1
  Salaam Bombay! 1988,O 7,C,8:1
Brown, Blair
  Stealing Home 1988,Ag 26,C,17:4
Brown, Bryan
  Good Wife, The 1987,F 20,C,19:3
  Cocktail 1988,Jl 29,C,6:5
  Cocktail 1988,Ag 14,II,1:3
  Gorillas in the Mist 1988,S 23,C,19:1
Brown, Clancy
  Extreme Prejudice 1987,Ap 24,C,8:5
  Shoot to Kill 1988,F 12,C,8:5
Brown, David (Producer)
  Cocoon: The Return 1988,N 23,C,15:1
Brown, Ernie
  In the Mood 1987,S 16,C,27:1
Brown, H J (Cinematographer)
  Hero's Journey, A: The World of Joseph Campbell 1987,Mr
    22,62:1
  Hero's Journey, A: The World of Joseph Campbell 1987,D
    4,C,18:1
Brown, Jim
  Running Man, The 1987,N 13,C,10:5
Brown, Michael (Miscellaneous)
  Jaws: The Revenge 1987,Jl 18,15:4
  Above the Law 1988,Ap 8,C,26:4
Brown, Nacio Herb (Miscellaneous)
  Die Hard 1988,Jl 31,II,19:1
Brown, O Nicholas (Miscellaneous)
  Project X 1987,Ap 17,C,15:1
  Rambo III 1988,My 25,C,15:1
  Accused, The 1988,O 14,C,13:1
Brown, Ralph
  Withnail and I 1987,Mr 27,C,9:1
  Withnail and I 1987,Je 19,C,10:1
  Buster 1988,N 23,C,12:1
Brown, Reb
  Distant Thunder 1988,N 11,C,13:1
Brown, Robert
  Living Daylights, The 1987,Jl 31,C,3:5
Brown, Robert (Miscellaneous)
  Lost Boys, The 1987,Jl 31,C,21:1
  Permanent Record 1988,Ap 22,C,10:1
Brown, Roger Aaron
  Alien Nation 1988,O 7,C,10:6
Brown, Sharon
  For Keeps 1988,Ja 15,C,17:3
Browne, Leslie
  Dancers 1987,O 9,C,24:1
Browne, Roscoe Lee
  Oliver and Company 1988,N 18,C,8:4
Bruce, James (Director)
  Suicide Club, The 1988,My 21,54:5
Bruce, James (Producer)
  Suicide Club, The 1988,My 21,54:5
Brucker, Jane
  Dirty Dancing 1987,Ag 21,C,3:4
Bruckheimer, Jerry (Producer)
  Beverly Hills Cop II 1987,My 20,C,28:1
  Beverly Hills Cop II 1987,Je 7,II,24:1
Bruckheimer-Martell, Bonnie (Producer)
  Beaches 1988,D 21,C,28:4
Bruel, Patrick
  Bandits 1988,Ag 24,C,17:1
Brugmans, George (Screenwriter)
  Pointsman, The 1988,Ap 8,C,22:1
Bruhne, Frank (Cinematographer)
  Felix 1988,S 24,13:1
Bruner, James (Screenwriter)
  Braddock: Missing in Action III 1988,Ja 22,C,9:1
Bruno, Tamara
  Pickup Artist, The 1987,S 18,C,23:1
Bruns, Philip
  Return of the Living Dead Part II 1988,Ja 15,C,11:1
Bruus, Morten (Cinematographer)
  Dark Side of the Moon, The 1987,Mr 19,C,28:1
Bruzdowicz, Joanna (Composer)
  Jupon Rouge, Le (Manuela's Loves) 1988,Mr 21,C,17:1
Bryceland, Yvonne
  World Apart, A 1988,Je 17,C,10:4
Bryden, Bill (Director)
  Aria 1988,My 21,54:3
Bryden, Bill (Screenwriter)
  Aria 1988,My 21,54:3

Bryson, John (Original Author)
  Cry in the Dark, A 1988,N 11,C,6:4
Buarque, Chico (Composer)
  Opera do Malandro 1987,Ja 30,C,6:5
Buarque, Chico (Miscellaneous)
  Opera do Malandro 1987,Ja 30,C,6:5
Buarque, Chico (Original Author)
  Opera do Malandro 1987,Ja 30,C,6:5
Buarque, Chico (Screenwriter)
  Opera do Malandro 1987,Ja 30,C,6:5
Buba, Pasquale (Miscellaneous)
  Monkey Shines: An Experiment in Fear 1988,Jl 29,C,12:4
Bucci, Flavio
  Two Lives of Mattia Pascal, The 1988,Mr 18,C,8:5
Buchanan, Michael (Miscellaneous)
  Hellraiser 1987,S 20,85:5
  Salome's Last Dance 1988,My 6,C,8:5
  Hellbound: Hellraiser II 1988,D 23,C,18:1
Buchanan, Simone
  Shame 1988,Mr 19,10:3
Buchrucker, Doris
  Santa Fe 1988,Jl 20,C,20:5
Buckley, Betty
  Wild Thing 1987,Ap 17,C,13:1
  Frantic 1988,F 26,C,3:4
  Another Woman 1988,O 14,C,3:3
Buckman, Peter (Screenwriter)
  Appointment with Death 1988,Ap 15,C,4:5
Budd, Barbara
  Three Men and a Baby 1987,N 25,C,24:3
Buechler, John Carl (Director)
  Friday the 13th, Part VII—The New Blood 1988,My 15,56:5
Bueno, Clovis (Miscellaneous)
  Color of Destiny, The 1988,Jl 22,C,17:1
Bueno, Gustavo
  City and the Dogs, The 1987,Ja 7,C,20:5
Buff, Conrad (Miscellaneous)
  Spaceballs 1987,Je 24,C,23:1
  Short Circuit 2 1988,Jl 6,C,18:5
Bufnoir, Jacques (Miscellaneous)
  Bandits 1988,Ag 24,C,17:1
Buhai, Jeff (Miscellaneous)
  Revenge of the Nerds II: Nerds in Paradise 1987,Jl 11,18:4
Buhai, Jeff (Screenwriter)
  Johnny Be Good 1988,Mr 25,C,29:1
Bujold, Genevieve
  Moderns, The 1988,Ap 15,C,21:1
  Dead Ringers 1988,S 23,C,10:1
  Dead Ringers 1988,O 2,II,21:5
Bukowski, Bobby (Cinematographer)
  Anna 1987,O 2,C,11:1
  Kiss Daddy Good Night 1988,My 20,C,11:1
Bukowski, Charles (Original Author)
  Love Is a Dog from Hell 1988,Mr 18,C,15:1
  Love Is a Dog from Hell 1988,Ap 23,14:5
Bukowski, Charles (Screenwriter)
  Barfly 1987,S 30,C,18:1
  Barfly 1987,O 11,II,25:5
  Barfly 1987,N 8,II,25:1
  Barfly 1987,N 22,II,23:5
Bulajic, Bora (Miscellaneous)
  Murder One 1988,S 23,C,15:1
Bulgari (Miscellaneous)
  Summer Night with Greek Profile, Almond Eyes and Scent of
    Basil 1987,Je 19,C,12:6
Bumatai, Andy
  Aloha Summer 1988,F 26,C,8:1
Bumstead, Henry (Miscellaneous)
  Time of Destiny, A 1988,Ap 22,C,29:1
  Funny Farm 1988,Je 3,C,14:6
Bundy, Brooke
  Nightmare on Elm Street 3, A: Dream Warriors 1987,F
    27,C,15:3
  Twice Dead 1988,N 19,15:3
Bunker, Jon (Miscellaneous)
  Bellman and True 1988,Ap 1,C,4:4
Bunuel, Luis (Director)
  Ambiciosos, Los (Ambitious Ones, The) 1988,F 12,C,13:1
Bunuel, Luis (Screenwriter)
  Ambiciosos, Los (Ambitious Ones, The) 1988,F 12,C,13:1
Burchill, Andrea
  Housekeeping 1987,N 25,C,11:1
Burg, Mark (Producer)
  Bull Durham 1988,Je 15,C,20:5
Burgard, Christopher
  Twice Dead 1988,N 19,15:3
Burgess, Don (Cinematographer)
  Death Before Dishonor 1987,F 20,C,10:1
  Summer Camp Nightmare 1987,Ap 17,C,30:5
  World Gone Wild 1988,My 22,49:5

C

Month in the Country, A 1988,F 19,C,10:5

Carter, Ron (Composer)
Beatrice 1988,Mr 18,C,25:1

Carter, Ruth (Screenwriter)
Coming Up Roses 1987,S 11,C,9:1

Carter, T K
He's My Girl 1987,S 11,C,5:1

Cartland, Barbara
Where the Heart Roams 1987,Ag 19,C,17:1

Cartlidge, William (Producer)
Consuming Passions 1988,Ap 6,C,18:3

Cartwright, Jon
Shadey 1987,Je 5,C,10:1

Cartwright, Nancy
Chipmunk Adventure, The 1987,My 22,C,10:5

Cartwright, Peter (Miscellaneous)
Last of England, The 1988,S 28,C,18:3

Cartwright, Veronica
Wisdom 1987,Ja 1,9:5
Witches of Eastwick, The 1987,Je 12,C,3:4

Caruso, David
China Girl 1987,S 25,C,16:6

Carvalho, Lucy
Barravento (Turning Wind, The) 1987,F 20,C,5:1

Carver, Mary
Best Seller 1987,S 25,C,24:1

Carver, Raymond (Original Author)
Feathers 1988,Mr 21,C,15:1

Carver, Steve (Director)
Bulletproof 1988,My 16,C,13:1

Carvey, Dana
Moving 1988,Mr 5,16:4

Casal, Jorge (Cinematographer)
Sera Posible el Sur: Un Viaje por Argentina de la Mano de
Mercedes Sosa (South Will Be Possible, The: A Trip Through
Argentina with Mercedes Sosa) 1987,S 11,C,15:1

Casale, Gerald V (Composer)
Revenge of the Nerds II: Nerds in Paradise 1987,Jl 11,18:4
Slaughterhouse Rock 1988,My 22,49:5

Casden, Ron (Director)
Campus Man 1987,My 4,C,17:1

Casey, Audeen
Positive ID 1987,Mr 14,13:1

Casey, Bernie
Steele Justice 1987,My 8,C,12:4
Rent-a-Cop 1988,Ja 15,C,13:1

Cash, Jim (Screenwriter)
Secret of My Success, The 1987,Ap 10,C,14:4

Casile, Demetrio (Miscellaneous)
Boy from Calabria, A 1987,N 20,C,21:1

Caspary, Katrina
MAC and Me 1988,Ag 13,14:1

Caspary, Tina
Can't Buy Me Love 1987,Ag 14,C,13:1

Cassavetes, John
Opening Night 1988,O 1,15:1

Cassavetes, John (Director)
Opening Night 1988,O 1,15:1

Cassavetes, John (Screenwriter)
Opening Night 1988,O 1,15:1

Cassel, Seymour
Tin Men 1987,Mr 6,C,3:1
Johnny Be Good 1988,Mr 25,C,29:1
Plain Clothes 1988,Ap 16,18:1
Track 29 1988,S 9,C,10:3

Cassese, Andrew
Revenge of the Nerds II: Nerds in Paradise 1987,Jl 11,18:4

Cassidy, Jay (Miscellaneous)
Aloha Summer 1988,F 26,C,8:1

Cassidy, Joanna
Fourth Protocol, The 1987,Ag 28,C,19:1
Who Framed Roger Rabbit 1988,Je 22,C,17:2
1969 1988,N 18,C,10:5

Cassidy, William J (Miscellaneous)
Happy New Year 1987,Ag 7,C,10:6
For Keeps 1988,Ja 15,C,17:3
Memories of Me 1988,S 28,C,23:1

Cassini, Stephania
Belly of an Architect, The 1987,O 1,C,22:5

Castaldo, Robert J (Miscellaneous)
Positive ID 1987,Mr 14,13:1

Castellito, Sergio
Big Blue, The 1988,Ag 20,11:4

Castineira de Dios, Jose Luis (Composer)
Night of the Pencils, The 1987,Mr 14,13:1
Debajo del Mundo (Under the World) 1988,O 5,C,19:5

Castro, Emmanuelle (Miscellaneous)
Au Revoir les Enfants (Goodbye, Children) 1988,F 12,C,15:1

Castrodad, Eddie
Torch Song Trilogy 1988,D 14,C,19:1

Castro Vasquez, Marie (Miscellaneous)
Wedding in Galilee 1988,Mr 11,C,23:1

Caswell, Robert (Screenwriter)
Cry in the Dark, A 1988,N 11,C,6:4

Cates, Phoebe
Date with an Angel 1987,N 21,14:5
Bright Lights, Big City 1988,Ap 1,C,22:5

Cattrall, Kim
Mannequin 1987,F 13,C,8:6
Masquerade 1988,Mr 11,C,8:5
Midnight Crossing 1988,My 14,16:5

Cavafian, Sandrine (Miscellaneous)
Doc's Kingdom 1988,S 9,C,10:3

Cavalcanti, Emmanuel
Amulet of Ogum 1987,F 6,C,4:3

Cavallo, Robert (Producer)
Sign o' the Times 1987,N 20,C,14:1

Cavani, Liliana (Director)
Berlin Affair, The 1988,Jl 15,C,12:5

Cavani, Liliana (Screenwriter)
Berlin Affair, The 1988,Jl 15,C,12:5

Caven, Ingrid
Mes Petites Amoureuses 1987,Ja 30,C,16:1

Cavett, Dick
Beetlejuice 1988,Mr 30,C,18:6

Cavina, Gianni
Traffic Jam 1988,Mr 4,C,14:6

Caziot, Jean-Jacques (Miscellaneous)
Annee des Meduses, L' 1987,Ap 24,C,9:1

Ceballos, Rafael (Miscellaneous)
Ambiciosos, Los (Ambitious Ones, The) 1988,F 12,C,13:1

Cecchini, Mimi
Eat and Run 1987,F 20,C,5:1

Cecil, Jane
Summer Heat 1987,My 29,C,8:4
September 1987,D 18,C,3:1

Cedar, Larry
Feds 1988,O 29,18:5

Cei, Pina
Dark Eyes 1987,S 25,C,26:5

Celio, Teco
No Man's Land 1987,F 13,C,14:6

Cellier, Caroline
Annee des Meduses, L' 1987,Ap 24,C,9:1

Celozzi, Nicholas
Slaughterhouse Rock 1988,My 22,49:5

Celulari, Edson
Opera do Malandro 1987,Ja 30,C,6:5

Cenet, Michel (Cinematographer)
I Hate Actors! 1988,Ap 29,C,22:1

Cepek, Petr
My Sweet Little Village 1987,Ja 9,C, 6:5

Cervantes, Ignacio (Composer)
Nobody Listened 1988,D 2,C,14:6

Cervenka, Exene
Salvation! 1987,My 31,51:1

Cerveris, Mike
Tokyo Pop 1988,Ap 15,C,4:4

Cestero, Carlos Augusto
Gran Fiesta, La 1987,Jl 17,C,17:1

Cetinkaya, Yavuzer
Dark Side of the Moon, The 1987,Mr 19,C,28:1

Chabert, Daniel (Cinematographer)
Hotel Terminus: The Life and Times of Klaus Barbie 1988,O
6,C,25:1

Chabrier, Emmanuel (Composer)
Sarah 1988,S 25,64:1

Chaffee, Suzy
Fire and Ice 1987,N 6,C,14:6

Chakir, Amid
Love Is a Dog from Hell 1988,Mr 18,C,15:1
Love Is a Dog from Hell 1988,Ap 23,14:5

Chalaris, Christodoulos (Composer)
Photograph, The 1988,Mr 17,C,26:3

Chalem, Brent
Monster Squad 1987,Ag 14,C,15:1

Chaliapin, Feodor
Moonstruck 1987,D 16,C,22:3
Maschera, La 1988,S 25,64:4

Chamberlain, Richard
Allan Quatermain and the Lost City of Gold 1987,Ja 31,14:5
Allan Quatermain and the Lost City of Gold 1988,Ja 3,II,15:1

Champel, Marcel
Jean de Florette 1987,Je 26,C,3:1

Chan, Jackie
Jackie Chan's Police Story 1987,S 26,12:3

Chan, Jackie (Director)
Jackie Chan's Police Story 1987,S 26,12:3

Chandler, Estee
Teen Wolf Too 1987,N 20,C,14:6

Chandler, Michael (Miscellaneous)
Julia and Julia 1988,F 5,C,5:1

Chang, Sari
China Girl 1987,S 25,C,16:6

Channing, Stockard
Time of Destiny, A 1988,Ap 22,C,29:1

Channing-Williams, Simon (Producer)
High Hopes 1988,S 24,12:4

Chao, Rosalind
Slamdance 1987,N 6,C,10:5

Chapin, Jonathan
Twice Dead 1988,N 19,15:3

Chaplin, Geraldine
Moderns, The 1988,Ap 15,C,21:1
White Mischief 1988,Ap 22,C,20:1
Mama Turns 100 (Mama Cumple 100 Anos) 1988,S 16,C,13:1

Chaplin, Patrice (Original Author)
Siesta 1987,N 11,C,23:3

Chapman, Judith
And God Created Woman 1988,Mr 4,C,22:4

Chapman, Michael (Cinematographer)
Lost Boys, The 1987,Jl 31,C,21:1
Shoot to Kill 1988,F 12,C,8:5
Scrooged 1988,N 23,C,16:5

Chapman, Sean
Hellraiser 1987,S 20,85:5
Hellbound: Hellraiser II 1988,D 23,C,18:1

Chappell, Robert (Cinematographer)
Thin Blue Line, The 1988,Ag 26,C,6:1

Charbonneau, Patricia
Shakedown 1988,My 6,C,20:1
Call Me 1988,My 20,C,11:1

Charlebois, Robert (Composer)
Honeymoon 1987,N 20,C,24:1

Charney, Eva
My Demon Lover 1987,Ap 24,C,14:1

Charo
Moon over Parador 1988,S 9,C,13:1

Charpentier, Gustave (Composer)
Aria 1988,My 21,54:3

Chase, Chevy
Funny Farm 1988,Je 3,C,14:6
Caddyshack II 1988,Jl 23,16:5

Chase, Gary (Composer)
Summer Camp Nightmare 1987,Ap 17,C,30:5

Chase, Thomas (Composer)
And God Created Woman 1988,Mr 4,C,22:4
Bulletproof 1988,My 16,C,13:1

Chaskin, David (Screenwriter)
Curse, The 1987,S 11,C,13:4

Chattaway, Jay (Composer)
Braddock: Missing in Action III 1988,Ja 22,C,9:1
Maniac Cop 1988,My 14,16:5

Chatto, Daniel
Little Dorrit 1988,Mr 26,11:1

Chattopadhya, Mohit (Screenwriter)
Genesis 1988,D 23,C,18:6

Chaudhri, Amin Q (Director)
Tiger Warsaw 1988,S 23,C,20:1

Chaudhri, Amin Q (Producer)
Tiger Warsaw 1988,S 23,C,20:1

Chaulet, Emmanuelle
Ami de Mon Amie, L' (My Girlfriend's Boyfriend) 1987,O
9,C,4:5
Boyfriends and Girlfriends (Ami de Mon Amie, L') 1988,Jl
15,C,10:6

Chaumette, Monique
Beatrice 1988,Mr 18,C,25:1

Chaves, Richard
Predator 1987,Je 12,C,6:4

Chavooshian, Nora (Miscellaneous)
Eight Men Out 1988,S 2,C,3:1

Chaykin, Maury
Wild Thing 1987,Ap 17,C,13:1
Stars and Bars 1988,Mr 18,C,3:1
Iron Eagle II 1988,N 12,15:3

Cheadle, Don
Hamburger Hill 1987,Ag 28,C,16:5
Colors 1988,Ap 15,C,4:1

Chekhov, Anton (Original Author)
Dark Eyes 1987,S 25,C,26:5
Trois Soeurs (Paura e Amore) 1988,My 22,II,21:5

Chen, Joan
Last Emperor, The 1987,N 20,C,3:4

Chen, Steven
Sleepwalk 1987,Mr 20,C,15:1

Chen Hwai-en (Cinematographer)
Daughter of the Nile 1988,S 30,C,8:4

Chen Jianyu (Screenwriter)
Red Sorghum 1988,O 9,74:1

Corbellini, Vanni
  Belly of an Architect, The 1987,O 1,C,22:5
Corbett, Toby (Miscellaneous)
  Prince of Pennsylvania, The 1988,S 16,C,17:1
Corbin, Barry
  Critters 2: The Main Course 1988,Ap 29,C,6:6
Cordoba, Lidia (Producer)
  Amerika, Terra Incognita 1988,D 9,C,10:6
Corey, Jeff
  Messenger of Death 1988,S 17,12:5
Corfman, Caris
  Funny Farm 1988,Je 3,C,14:6
Corke, Penny (Producer)
  Gothic 1987,Ap 10,C,16:3
  Salome's Last Dance 1988,My 6,C,8:5
Cormack, Lynne
  Too Outrageous 1987,O 16,C,12:1
  Dead Ringers 1988,S 23,C,10:1
Corman, Julie (Producer)
  Da 1988,Ap 29,C,10:1
Corman, Maddie
  Some Kind of Wonderful 1987,F 27,C,17:3
Corman, Roger (Producer)
  Daddy's Boys 1988,Je 10,C,13:1
Cornell, Dan
  Bell Diamond 1988,Mr 17,C,30:1
Cornell, Ellie
  Halloween 4: The Return of Michael Myers 1988,O 22,12:4
Cornell, John (Director)
  Crocodile Dundee II 1988,My 25,C,15:3
Cornell, John (Producer)
  Crocodile Dundee II 1988,My 25,C,15:3
Cornfeld, Stuart (Producer)
  Moving 1988,Mr 5,16:4
Cornuelle, Jenny
  Deadly Illusion 1987,O 31,10:5
Cornwell, Tom (Miscellaneous)
  Opening Night 1988,O 1,15:1
Coromina, Pepon (Producer)
  Anguish 1988,Ja 29,C,15:1
Corradi, Pio (Cinematographer)
  Alpine Fire 1987,F 20,C,20:1
  Candy Mountain 1988,Je 10,C,6:5
Corrao, Angelo (Miscellaneous)
  Pickup Artist, The 1987,S 18,C,23:1
Correa, Rubens W
  Man Facing Southeast 1987,Mr 13,C,4:5
Correll, Charles (Cinematographer)
  Revenge of the Nerds II: Nerds in Paradise 1987,Jl 11,18:4
Corriveau, Andre (Miscellaneous)
  Blind Trust 1987,N 7,13:1
Corriveau, Jean (Composer)
  Night Zoo 1988,Mr 30,C,20:5
Corso, John W (Miscellaneous)
  She's Having a Baby 1988,F 5,C,18:1
  Great Outdoors, The 1988,Je 17,C,12:6
Cort, Robert W (Producer)
  Critical Condition 1987,Ja 16,C,16:4
  Outrageous Fortune 1987,Ja 30,C,5:1
  Revenge of the Nerds II: Nerds in Paradise 1987,Jl 11,18:4
  Three Men and a Baby 1987,N 25,C,24:3
  Seventh Sign, The 1988,Ap 1,C,20:3
  Cocktail 1988,Jl 29,C,6:5
Cortese, Joe
  Deadly Illusion 1987,O 31,10:5
Cortez, Raul
  Vera 1987,O 16,C,4:5
Corti, Axel (Director)
  Welcome in Vienna 1988,Je 1,C,17:1
  God Doesn't Believe in Us Anymore 1988,Jl 20,C,20:5
  Santa Fe 1988,Jl 20,C,20:5
Corti, Axel (Screenwriter)
  Welcome in Vienna 1988,Je 1,C,17:1
Cosby, Bill
  Leonard Part 6 1987,D 18,C,30:1
Cosby, Bill (Miscellaneous)
  Leonard Part 6 1987,D 18,C,30:1
Cosby, Bill (Producer)
  Leonard Part 6 1987,D 18,C,30:1
Coscarelli, Don (Director)
  Phantasm II 1988,Jl 8,C,11:1
Coscarelli, Don (Screenwriter)
  Phantasm II 1988,Jl 8,C,11:1
Cosma, Vladimir (Composer)
  Levy and Goliath 1988,Mr 17,C,20:4
Cossu, Scott (Composer)
  Islands 1987,O 16,C,26:4
Costa-Gavras (Director)
  Family Business 1987,S 6,66:2
  Betrayed 1988,Ag 26,C,16:1

Betrayed 1988,S 4,II,17:1
Betrayed 1988,N 20,II,13:1
Betrayed 1988,D 18,II,13:1
Costa-Gavras (Screenwriter)
  Family Business 1987,S 6,66:2
Costello, Elvis
  Straight to Hell 1987,Je 26,C,8:5
Costello, George (Miscellaneous)
  Wrong Guys, The 1988,Je 4,12:3
Costigan, George
  Rita, Sue and Bob Too 1987,Jl 17,C,18:1
Costigan, James (Screenwriter)
  Mr North 1988,Jl 22,C,8:4
Costner, Kevin
  Untouchables, The 1987,Je 3,C,17:1
  Untouchables, The 1987,Je 21,II,19:5
  Untouchables, The 1987,Je 28,II,31:1
  No Way Out 1987,Ag 14,C,3:1
  Bull Durham 1988,Je 15,C,20:5
  Bull Durham 1988,Jl 3,II,1:3
  Bull Durham 1988,S 11,II,1:3
Cotnoir, Brian (Miscellaneous)
  Radium City 1987,S 26,9:4
Cotterill, Ralph
  Burke and Wills 1987,Je 12,C,10:1
  Right Hand Man, The 1987,O 2,C,13:1
  Howling III 1987,N 13,C,5:1
Cotton, Oliver
  Hiding Out 1987,N 6,C,21:1
Cottrell, Pierre (Producer)
  Mes Petites Amoureuses 1987,Ja 30,C,16:1
Cottrell, Vincent (Miscellaneous)
  Mes Petites Amoureuses 1987,Ja 30,C,16:1
Coulibaly, Dounamba (Miscellaneous)
  Yeelen 1987,O 8,C,37:1
Coulson, Bernie
  Accused, The 1988,O 14,C,13:1
Coulson, David (Miscellaneous)
  Death in the Family, A 1987,O 21,C,24:5
Coulson, Peter (Miscellaneous)
  Handful of Dust, A 1988,Je 24,C,14:1
Coulter, Michael (Cinematographer)
  Good Father, The 1987,F 11,C,23:1
  Housekeeping 1987,N 25,C,11:1
Court, Jason
  Night in the Life of Jimmy Reardon, A 1988,F 27,20:1
Courtenay, Margaret
  Duet for One 1987,F 13,C,10:4
Courtenay, Tom
  Happy New Year 1987,Ag 7,C,10:6
  Leonard Part 6 1987,D 18,C,30:1
Coustet, Marita (Producer)
  Beethoven's Nephew 1988,Je 10,C,12:6
Couture, Charlelie
  Moderns, The 1988,Ap 15,C,21:1
Couturie, Bill (Director)
  Dear America: Letters Home from Vietnam 1988,S 16,C,18:1
Couturie, Bill (Producer)
  Dear America: Letters Home from Vietnam 1988,S 16,C,18:1
Couturie, Bill (Screenwriter)
  Dear America: Letters Home from Vietnam 1988,S 16,C,18:1
Cowan, Paul (Producer)
  Riders of the Storm 1988,My 7,12:3
Cowles, Matthew
  Stars and Bars 1988,Mr 18,C,3:1
Cox, Alex (Director)
  Straight to Hell 1987,Je 26,C,8:5
  Walker 1987,D 4,C,36:1
  Straight to Hell 1988,Ja 3,II,15:1
Cox, Alex (Miscellaneous)
  Walker 1987,D 4,C,36:1
Cox, Alex (Screenwriter)
  Straight to Hell 1987,Je 26,C,8:5
Cox, Andy (Composer)
  Tin Men 1987,Mr 6,C,3:1
Cox, Courteney
  Masters of the Universe 1987,Ag 8,50:1
  Cocoon: The Return 1988,N 23,C,15:1
Cox, Jim (Screenwriter)
  Oliver and Company 1988,N 18,C,8:4
Cox, Joel (Miscellaneous)
  Bird 1988,S 26,C,19:1
Cox, Paul (Cinematographer)
  Vincent: The Life and Death of Vincent Van Gogh 1988,Mr
    16,C,25:1
Cox, Paul (Director)
  Vincent: The Life and Death of Vincent Van Gogh 1988,Mr
    16,C,25:1
Cox, Paul (Miscellaneous)
  Vincent: The Life and Death of Vincent Van Gogh 1988,Mr
    16,C,25:1

Cox, Paul (Screenwriter)
  Vincent: The Life and Death of Vincent Van Gogh 1988,Mr
    16,C,25:1
Cox, Ronny
  Steele Justice 1987,My 8,C,12:4
  Beverly Hills Cop II 1987,My 20,C,28:1
  Robocop 1987,Jl 17,C,10:1
  Robocop 1987,Ag 2,II,23:5
Coyote, Peter
  Outrageous Fortune 1987,Ja 30,C,5:1
  Man in Love, A 1987,Jl 31,C,10:6
  Stacking 1988,Ja 15,C,15:1
Cozarinsky, Edgardo (Director)
  Sarah 1988,S 25,64:1
Cozarinsky, Edgardo (Screenwriter)
  Sarah 1988,S 25,64:1
Crabe, James (Cinematographer)
  Happy New Year 1987,Ag 7,C,10:6
  For Keeps 1988,Ja 15,C,17:3
Cracco, Alberto
  Maschera, La 1988,S 25,64:4
Craddock, Malcolm (Producer)
  Ping Pong 1987,Jl 17,C,10:6
Crafford, Ian (Miscellaneous)
  Hope and Glory 1987,O 9,C,23:1
Craig, Alan S
  Bagdad Cafe 1988,Ap 22,C,19:1
Craig, Diane
  Traveling North 1988,F 12,C,10:1
Craig, Stuart (Miscellaneous)
  Cry Freedom 1987,N 6,C,14:3
  Stars and Bars 1988,Mr 18,C,3:1
  Dangerous Liaisons 1988,D 21,C,22:1
Craigie, Ingrid
  Dead, The 1987,D 17,C,19:4
  Da 1988,Ap 29,C,10:1
Crandall, Roger S (Miscellaneous)
  Halloween 4: The Return of Michael Myers 1988,O 22,12:4
Cranham, Kenneth
  Hellbound: Hellraiser II 1988,D 23,C,18:1
Cranna, Jim
  Living on Tokyo Time 1987,Ag 14,C,20:1
Craven, Garth (Miscellaneous)
  Gaby—A True Story 1987,O 30,C,10:4
  Shoot to Kill 1988,F 12,C,8:5
Craven, Matt
  Tin Men 1987,Mr 6,C,3:1
Craven, Wes (Director)
  Serpent and the Rainbow, The 1988,F 5,C,3:4
Craven, Wes (Screenwriter)
  Nightmare on Elm Street 3, A: Dream Warriors 1987,F 27,C,15:3
Crawford, Robert L (Producer)
  Funny Farm 1988,Je 3,C,14:6
Cray, Robert
  Chuck Berry: Hail! Hail! Rock 'n' Roll 1987,O 3,10:5
Creber, William J (Miscellaneous)
  Hot Pursuit 1987,My 11,C,14:5
Crenna, Richard
  Rambo III 1988,My 25,C,15:1
  Rambo III 1988,Je 19,II,23:1
Crenshaw, Marshall
  Bamba, La 1987,Jl 24,C,4:3
Cresciman, Vincent (Screenwriter)
  Bamba, La 1987,Jl 24,C,4:3
  Bat 21 1988,O 21,C,22:1
Crew, Carl
  Blood Diner 1987,S 4,C,6:5
Crichton, Charles (Director)
  Fish Called Wanda, A 1988,Jl 15,C,8:1
Crichton, Charles (Miscellaneous)
  Fish Called Wanda, A 1988,Jl 15,C,8:1
Crisman, Steve (Producer)
  Suicide Club, The 1988,My 21,54:5
Cristante, Ivo (Miscellaneous)
  Amazon Women on the Moon 1987,S 18,C,12:6
  Bad Dreams 1988,Ap 8,C,10:1
Cristiani, Gabriella (Miscellaneous)
  Last Emperor, The 1987,N 20,C,3:4
  High Season 1988,Mr 25,C,12:6
Cristofer, Michael (Screenwriter)
  Witches of Eastwick, The 1987,Je 12,C,3:4
Crivelli, Carlo (Composer)
  Devil in the Flesh 1987,My 29,C,3:1
Crombie, Jonathan
  Housekeeper, The 1987,Ap 24,C,7:1
Cronauer, Gail
  Positive ID 1987,Mr 14,13:1
Cronenberg, David (Director)
  Dead Ringers 1988,S 23,C,10:1
  Dead Ringers 1988,O 2,II,21:5

D

Dean, Phil
Shame 1988,Mr 19,10:3
de Angelis, Ricardo (Cinematographer)
Man Facing Southeast 1987,Mr 13,C,4:5
de Antonio, Emile
Andy Warhol 1987,Je 9,C,20:1
Dear, William (Director)
Harry and the Hendersons 1987,Je 5,C,14:5
Harry and the Hendersons 1987,Jl 12,II,19:1
Dear, William (Producer)
Harry and the Hendersons 1987,Je 5,C,14:5
Dear, William (Screenwriter)
Harry and the Hendersons 1987,Je 5,C,14:5
Dearden, James (Director)
Pascali's Island 1988,Jl 22,C,16:4
Dearden, James (Screenwriter)
Fatal Attraction 1987,S 18,C,10:5
Fatal Attraction 1987,S 27,II,22:1
Fatal Attraction 1988,Ja 31,II,19:1
Pascali's Island 1988,Jl 22,C,16:4
Deats, Danyl
River's Edge 1987,My 8,C,28:4
De Baer, Jean
84 Charing Cross Road 1987,F 13,C,10:4
Debassige, Diane
Loyalties 1987,Mr 21,14:3
Loyalties 1987,N 20,C,21:1
Debney, John (Composer)
Curse, The 1987,S 11,C,13:4
Wild Pair, The 1987,D 12,19:1
Seven Hours to Judgement 1988,S 17,12:5
de Boer, Caspar
Assault, The 1987,F 6,C,8:1
DeBont, Jan (Cinematographer)
Who's That Girl 1987,Ag 8,16:1
Leonard Part 6 1987,D 18,C,30:1
Die Hard 1988,Jl 15,C,14:5
Dec, Ba Nam Sa
Karma 1987,Jl 8,C,22:5
Decamp, Kyle
She Must Be Seeing Things 1988,Ap 13,C,20:4
De Carlo, Yvonne
American Gothic 1988,Je 4,12:6
de Castro, Isabel
Hard Times 1988,O 6,C,29:1
De Ceresa, Ferruccio
Mass Is Ended, The 1988,My 6,C,18:6
DeClue, Denise (Screenwriter)
For Keeps 1988,Ja 15,C,17:3
De Concini, Ennio (Screenwriter)
Devil in the Flesh 1987,My 29,C,3:1
Two Lives of Mattia Pascal, The 1988,Mr 18,C,8:5
Maschera, La 1988,S 25,64:4
De Cuir, John, Jr (Miscellaneous)
Elvira, Mistress of the Dark 1988,S 30,C,12:4
Dedek, Tomasz
Great Race, The 1988,Mr 12,19:1
Dedet, Yann
Under Satan's Sun 1987,O 3,13:1
Dedet, Yann (Miscellaneous)
Under Satan's Sun 1987,O 3,13:1
36 Fillette 1988,O 4,C,19:1
Dees, Rick
Bamba, La 1987,Jl 24,C,4:3
Deese, Frank (Screenwriter)
Principal, The 1987,S 18,C,14:6
Deezen, Eddie
Million Dollar Mystery 1987,Je 12,C,6:4
De Fina, Barbara (Producer)
Last Temptation of Christ, The 1988,Ag 12,C,1:1
Deford, Frank (Original Author)
Everybody's All American 1988,N 4,C,17:1
DeForest, Calvert
My Demon Lover 1987,Ap 24,C,14:1
de Ganay, Thierry (Producer)
Someone to Watch Over Me 1987,O 9,C,40:1
de Giacomo, Franco (Cinematographer)
Dark Eyes 1987,S 25,C,26:5
Degli Schiavi, Antonio
History 1988,Je 3,C,15:1
de Goros, Jean-Claude
Man in Love, A 1987,Jl 31,C,10:6
DeGovia, Jackson (Miscellaneous)
Roxanne 1987,Je 19,C,3:4
Die Hard 1988,Jl 15,C,14:5
Punchline 1988,S 30,C,14:4
De Groot, Andrew (Cinematographer)
Dogs in Space 1987,O 9,C,7:1
de Guzman, Michael (Screenwriter)
Jaws: The Revenge 1987,Jl 18,15:4

de Haas, Wim
Assault, The 1987,F 6,C,8:1
DeHaven, Carter (Producer)
Hoosiers 1987,F 27,C,10:3
Best Seller 1987,S 25,C,24:1
Dehn, Mura
In a Jazz Way: A Portrait of Mura Dehn 1987,D 16,22:5
Dehn, Mura (Director)
Spirit Moves, The: A History of Black Social Dance on Film 1987,D 16,C,22:5
Dehn, Mura (Producer)
Spirit Moves, The: A History of Black Social Dance on Film 1987,D 16,C,22:5
Deimel, Mark (Director)
Perfect Match 1988,Je 4,12:3
Deimel, Mark (Producer)
Perfect Match 1988,Je 4,12:3
Deimel, Mark (Screenwriter)
Perfect Match 1988,Je 4,12:3
Deitz, James
Who's That Girl 1987,Ag 8,16:1
de Jonge, Marc
Rambo III 1988,My 25,C,15:1
de Keyzer, Bruno (Cinematographer)
Beatrice 1988,Mr 18,C,25:1
Little Dorrit 1988,Mr 26,11:1
Dekker, Fred (Director)
Monster Squad 1987,Ag 14,C,15:1
Dekker, Fred (Screenwriter)
Monster Squad 1987,Ag 14,C,15:1
De Klein, John (Screenwriter)
Care Bears' Adventure in Wonderland, The 1987,Ag 7,C,21:1
de La Bouillerie, Hubert C (Miscellaneous)
Police Academy 5: Assignment Miami Beach 1988,Mr 19,13:3
Delachau, Christophe
Mammame 1988,Ja 29,C,10:4
de la Iglesia, Eloy (Director)
Colegas (Pals) 1987,Ag 14,C,15:1
de la Iglesia, Eloy (Screenwriter)
Colegas (Pals) 1987,Ag 14,C,15:1
Del Amo, Pablo G (Miscellaneous)
Tasio 1987,Mr 27,C,15:1
Sur, El (South, The) 1988,Ja 15,C,11:1
Delaney, Kim
Campus Man 1987,My 4,C,17:1
Drifter, The 1988,Je 5,59:1
Delano, Laura
Gran Fiesta, La 1987,Jl 17,C,17:1
Delany, Cathleen
Dead, The 1987,D 17,C,19:4
Delany, Dana
Masquerade 1988,Mr 11,C,8:5
Patty Hearst 1988,S 23,C,8:5
De La Paz, Danny
Gaby—A True Story 1987,O 30,C,10:4
Wild Pair, The 1987,D 12,19:1
de la Torre, Amelia
Padre Nuestro 1987,Ap 22,C,24:1
Delect, Ovida
Call Me Madame 1988,Mr 12,14:4
Call Me Madame 1988,Mr 27,II,29:1
Call Me Madame 1988,Je 10,C,16:6
de Leon, Carlos
Hotel Colonial 1987,S 19,16:3
Delerue, Georges (Composer)
Man in Love, A 1987,Jl 31,C,10:6
Maid to Order 1987,Ag 28,C,6:1
Family Business 1987,S 6,66:2
Pickup Artist, The 1987,S 18,C,23:1
Lonely Passion of Judith Hearne, The 1987,D 23,C,15:1
House on Carroll Street, The 1988,Mr 4,C,23:1
Biloxi Blues 1988,Mr 25,C,1:1
Memories of Me 1988,S 28,C,23:1
Heartbreak Hotel 1988,S 30,C,18:5
Twins 1988,D 9,C,18:1
Beaches 1988,D 21,C,28:4
Delfgou, Peter (Miscellaneous)
We Think the World of You 1988,D 22,C,15:1
Delia, Francis (Director)
Freeway 1988,S 3,10:6
Delia, Francis (Screenwriter)
Freeway 1988,S 3,10:6
Delia, Joe (Composer)
China Girl 1987,S 25,C,16:6
Freeway 1988,S 3,10:6
de Lint, Derek
Assault, The 1987,F 6,C,8:1
Unbearable Lightness of Being, The 1988,F 5,C,8:5
De Lisi, Joseph
Prince of Pennsylvania, The 1988,S 16,C,17:1

Delivoria, Marina
Tree We Hurt, The 1988,Ja 29,C,11:1
Delmont
Angele 1988,F 26,C,19:1
Del Monte, Peter (Director)
Julia and Julia 1988,F 5,C,5:1
Del Monte, Peter (Miscellaneous)
Julia and Julia 1988,F 5,C,5:1
Del Monte, Peter (Screenwriter)
Julia and Julia 1988,F 5,C,5:1
DeLongis, Anthony
Chipmunk Adventure, The 1987,My 22,C,10:5
Delora, Jennifer
Deranged 1987,O 31,12:3
Delpy, Julie
Bad Blood 1987,S 30,C,20:5
Beatrice 1988,Mr 18,C,25:1
Del Rey, Pedro (Miscellaneous)
Padre Nuestro 1987,Ap 22,C,24:1
Del Rosario, Linda (Miscellaneous)
Family Viewing 1988,Mr 23,C,20:5
Del Ruth, Thomas (Cinematographer)
Running Man, The 1987,N 13,C,10:5
Cross My Heart 1987,N 13,C,21:1
Satisfaction 1988,F 13,15:1
Del Sol, Laura
Two Lives of Mattia Pascal, The 1988,Mr 18,C,8:5
Del Testa, Guido
Cammina Cammina (Keep Walking, Keep Walking) 1988,Jl 10,43:5
Deluc, Xavier
Captive 1987,Ap 3,C,8:1
Good Weather, But Stormy Late This Afternoon 1987,My 20,C,20:3
De Luca, Rudy (Screenwriter)
Million Dollar Mystery 1987,Je 12,C,6:4
DeLuise, Dom
Oliver and Company 1988,N 18,C,8:4
de Luze, Herve (Miscellaneous)
Jean de Florette 1987,Je 26,C,3:1
Manon of the Spring 1987,N 6,C,25:1
de Malberg, Stanislas Carre
Au Revoir les Enfants (Goodbye, Children) 1988,F 12,C,15:1
de Marchi, Michele
Maschera, La 1988,S 25,64:4
DeMarco, Chris (Composer)
Troma's War 1988,D 9,C,23:1
Demazis, Orane
Angele 1988,F 26,C,19:1
de Medeiros, Maria
Sorceress 1988,Ap 1,C,23:1
De Meo, Paul (Screenwriter)
Wrong Guys, The 1988,Je 4,12:3
Deming, Peter (Cinematographer)
Evil Dead 2: Dead by Dawn 1987,Mr 13,C,18:1
Hollywood Shuffle 1987,Mr 20,C,8:1
Demme, Jonathan (Director)
Swimming to Cambodia 1987,Mr 13,C,8:1
Swimming to Cambodia 1987,Mr 22,II,19:1
Married to the Mob 1988,Ag 19,C,6:1
Married to the Mob 1988,D 4,II,15:5
Demme, Jonathan (Miscellaneous)
Eat the Peach 1987,Jl 17,C,6:1
De Mornay, Rebecca
And God Created Woman 1988,Mr 4,C,22:4
Feds 1988,O 29,18:5
De Moss, Darcy
Can't Buy Me Love 1987,Ag 14,C,13:1
Dempsey, Patrick
Can't Buy Me Love 1987,Ag 14,C,13:1
In the Mood 1987,S 16,C,27:1
In a Shallow Grave 1988,My 6,C,21:1
DeMunn, Jeffrey
Blob, The 1988,Ag 5,C,6:5
Dench, Judi
84 Charing Cross Road 1987,F 13,C,10:4
Handful of Dust, A 1988,Je 24,C,14:1
De Negri, Giuliani (Producer)
Good Morning, Babylon 1987,Jl 15,C,18:5
Deneuve, Catherine
Scene of the Crime 1987,Ja 23,C,14:1
Scene of the Crime 1987,F 8,II,21:1
Dengel, Jake
Ironweed 1987,D 18,C,24:5
Deng Xiaotuang
Girl from Hunan 1988,Mr 4,C,22:4
Denham, Maurice
84 Charing Cross Road 1987,F 13,C,10:4
De Niro, Robert
Angel Heart 1987,Mr 6,C,5:1

E

F

Fountas, Costas (Miscellaneous)
Tree We Hurt, The 1988,Ja 29,C,11:1
Fowler, Peggy (Producer)
Campus Man 1987,My 4,C,17:1
Fox, Charles (Composer)
Short Circuit 2 1988,Jl 6,C,18:5
Fox, Colin
Care Bears' Adventure in Wonderland, The 1987,Ag 7,C,21:1
Fox, James
Whistle Blower, The 1987,Jl 10,C,4:2
High Season 1988,Mr 25,C,12:6
Fox, James (Original Author)
White Mischief 1988,Ap 22,C,20:1
White Mischief 1988,My 22,II,43:1
Fox, Jennifer (Director)
Beirut: The Last Home Movie 1988,Je 29,C,19:1
Fox, Jennifer (Producer)
Beirut: The Last Home Movie 1988,Je 29,C,19:1
Fox, Jennifer (Screenwriter)
Beirut: The Last Home Movie 1988,Je 29,C,19:1
Fox, Michael J
Light of Day 1987,F 6,C,4:3
Secret of My Success, The 1987,Ap 10,C,14:4
Secret of My Success, The 1987,Ap 12,II,17:1
Bright Lights, Big City 1988,Ap 1,C,22:5
Fox, Michael J (Narrator)
Dear America: Letters Home from Vietnam 1988,S 16,C,18:1
Fox, Tom (Producer)
Return of the Living Dead Part II 1988,Ja 15,C,11:1
Fraker, William A (Cinematographer)
Burglar 1987,Mr 20,C,10:4
Baby Boom 1987,O 7,C,24:5
Frances, Cornelia
Return to Snowy River 1988,Ap 15,C,8:1
Francescato, Alberto
Long Live the Lady! 1987,O 16,C,26:5
Francis, Eric
Little Dorrit 1988,Mr 26,11:1
Francis, Freddie (Cinematographer)
Memed, My Hawk 1987,My 4,C,17:1
Clara's Heart 1988,O 7,C,16:5
Francis, Mike
Benji the Hunted 1987,Je 17,C,18:6
Francis, Nancy
Benji the Hunted 1987,Je 17,C,18:6
Francis-Bruce, Richard (Miscellaneous)
Witches of Eastwick, The 1987,Je 12,C,3:4
Francks, Cree Summer
Wild Thing 1987,Ap 17,C,13:1
Francks, Don
Big Town, The 1987,S 25,C,20:4
Franco, Larry (Producer)
Prince of Darkness 1987,O 23,C,26:1
They Live 1988,N 4,C,8:1
Francois, Guy Claude (Miscellaneous)
Beatrice 1988,Mr 18,C,25:1
Franenberg, Barry (Miscellaneous)
Summer Camp Nightmare 1987,Ap 17,C,30:5
Frank, A Scott (Screenwriter)
Plain Clothes 1988,Ap 16,18:1
Frank, Charles
Russkies 1987,N 6,C,12:3
Frank, Christopher (Director)
Annee des Meduses, L' 1987,Ap 24,C,9:1
Frank, Christopher (Original Author)
Annee des Meduses, L' 1987,Ap 24,C,9:1
Frank, Christopher (Screenwriter)
Annee des Meduses, L' 1987,Ap 24,C,9:1
Malone 1987,My 4,C,17:4
Frank, David (Composer)
Above the Law 1988,Ap 8,C,26:4
Call Me 1988,My 20,C,11:1
Hero and the Terror 1988,Ag 26,C,12:1
Frank, Gary
Enemy Territory 1987,My 22,C,7:1
Frank, Laurie (Screenwriter)
Making Mr Right 1987,Ap 10,C,16:5
Frank, Peter C (Miscellaneous)
Dirty Dancing 1987,Ag 21,C,3:4
Hello Again 1987,N 6,C,21:1
Frank, Robert (Director)
Candy Mountain 1988,Je 10,C,6:5
Franken, Steve
Freeway 1988,S 3,10:6
Frankenheimer, John (Director)
Manchurian Candidate, The 1988,Ap 24,II,23:5
Franklin, David
Shame 1988,Mr 19,10:3
Franklin, Howard (Screenwriter)
Someone to Watch Over Me 1987,O 9,C,40:1

Franklin, Jeff (Miscellaneous)
Summer School 1987,Jl 22,C,22:1
Franklin, Jeff (Screenwriter)
Summer School 1987,Jl 22,C,22:1
Franklin, Richard (Director)
Link 1987,Ap 24,C,10:4
Franklin, Richard (Producer)
Link 1987,Ap 24,C,10:4
Franz, Elizabeth
Secret of My Success, The 1987,Ap 10,C,14:4
Frappat, Francois
Black and White 1987,Mr 13,C,20:4
Frappier, Roger (Producer)
Blind Trust 1987,N 7,13:1
Night Zoo 1988,Mr 30,C,20:5
Fraser, Bill
Little Dorrit 1988,Mr 26,11:1
Frazer, Rupert
Empire of the Sun 1987,D 9,C,25:1
Frazier, Ronald E (Producer)
Wrong Guys, The 1988,Je 4,12:3
Frears, Stephen (Director)
Prick Up Your Ears 1987,Ap 17,C,17:1
Sammy and Rosie Get Laid 1987,O 30,C,5:1
Dangerous Liaisons 1988,D 21,C,22:1
Frechette, Peter
Kindred, The 1987,Ja 10,13:1
Frederick, Jesse (Composer)
Aloha Summer 1988,F 26,C,8:1
Free, William (Director)
Hero's Journey, A: The World of Joseph Campbell 1987,Mr 22,62:1
Hero's Journey, A: The World of Joseph Campbell 1987,D 4,C,18:1
Free, William (Producer)
Hero's Journey, A: The World of Joseph Campbell 1987,Mr 22,62:1
Hero's Journey, A: The World of Joseph Campbell 1987,D 4,C,18:1
Freeborn, Mark S (Miscellaneous)
Distant Thunder 1988,N 11,C,13:1
Freed, Arthur (Miscellaneous)
Die Hard 1988,Jl 31,II,19:1
Freed, Reuben (Miscellaneous)
Blue Monkey, The 1987,O 16,C,12:6
Freed, Rona
Penitent, The 1988,My 27,C,13:1
Freed, Sam
Call Me 1988,My 20,C,11:1
Freeman, Al, Jr
Seven Hours to Judgement 1988,S 17,12:5
Freeman, Damita Jo
Bad Dreams 1988,Ap 8,C,10:1
Freeman, David (Screenwriter)
Street Smart 1987,Mr 27,C,8:1
Freeman, Jeff (Miscellaneous)
Bad Dreams 1988,Ap 8,C,10:1
Bulletproof 1988,My 16,C,13:1
Freeman, Joan (Director)
Satisfaction 1988,F 13,15:1
Freeman, Kathleen
Dragnet 1987,Je 26,C,3:1
In the Mood 1987,S 16,C,27:1
Freeman, Morgan
Street Smart 1987,Mr 27,C,8:1
Clean and Sober 1988,Ag 10,C,17:1
Freeman, Paul
Without a Clue 1988,O 21,C,21:1
Freeman, Paul (Producer)
Halloween 4: The Return of Michael Myers 1988,O 22,12:4
Freeman-Fox, Lois (Miscellaneous)
Like Father Like Son 1987,O 2,C,8:5
Freilino, Brian
Good Morning, Babylon 1987,Jl 15,C,18:5
Frenck, Jenny (Miscellaneous)
Yeelen 1987,O 8,C,37:1
Fresson, Josephine
Black and White 1987,Mr 13,C,20:4
Freudberg, Judy (Miscellaneous)
Land Before Time, The 1988,N 18,C,8:4
Freund, Jay (Miscellaneous)
Forever, Lulu 1987,Ap 24,C,10:4
Wash, The 1988,Ag 17,C,17:4
Frey, Sami
Black Widow 1987,F 6,C,3:1
Fridley, Tom
Summer Camp Nightmare 1987,Ap 17,C,30:5
Fried, Paul (Miscellaneous)
Shakedown 1988,My 6,C,20:1
Call Me 1988,My 20,C,11:1

Friedgen, Bud (Miscellaneous)
Imagine: John Lennon 1988,O 7,C,7:1
Friedman, Bruce Jay
Another Woman 1988,O 14,C,3:3
Friedman, Peter
Seventh Sign, The 1988,Ap 1,C,20:3
Friedman, Richard (Miscellaneous)
Mondo New York 1988,Ap 22,C,23:1
Friedman, Stephen (Producer)
Touch and Go 1987,Ja 14,C,20:5
Morgan Stewart's Coming Home 1987,Je 4,C,16:4
Big Easy, The 1987,Ag 21,C,6:3
Friedson, Adam (Producer)
Fire from the Mountain 1987,O 10,19:4
Friels, Colin
Kangaroo 1987,Mr 13,C,12:5
High Tide 1988,F 19,C,5:1
Ground Zero 1988,S 23,C,18:1
Friend, Michael (Miscellaneous)
Hearst Metrotone Newsreel Show 1987,My 6,C,18:1
Fries, Thomas (Producer)
Flowers in the Attic 1987,N 21,12:5
Frishberg, Dave
Someone to Love 1988,Ap 21,C,20:4
Frize, Nicolas (Composer)
Mix-Up 1987,Jl 24,C,12:6
Frizzell, John (Director)
Winter Tan, A 1988,O 2,57:6
Froemke, Susan (Director)
Horowitz Plays Mozart 1987,O 8,C,37:1
Froemke, Susan (Producer)
Horowitz Plays Mozart 1987,O 8,C,37:1
Islands 1987,O 16,C,26:4
Froman, David
Steele Justice 1987,My 8,C,12:4
Fromholz, Steve
Positive ID 1987,Mr 14,13:1
Froom, Mitchell (Composer)
Slamdance 1987,N 6,C,10:5
Frost, Lindsay
Dead Heat 1988,My 7,13:1
Frost, Mark (Screenwriter)
Believers, The 1987,Je 10,C,22:5
Frot, Catherine
Sorceress 1988,Ap 1,C,23:1
Frot-Coutaz, Gerard (Director)
Good Weather, But Stormy Late This Afternoon 1987,My 20,C,20:3
Frot-Coutaz, Gerard (Screenwriter)
Good Weather, But Stormy Late This Afternoon 1987,My 20,C,20:3
Fruet, Michael (Miscellaneous)
Blue Monkey, The 1987,O 16,C,12:6
Fruet, William (Director)
Blue Monkey, The 1987,O 16,C,12:6
Frumkes, Roy (Producer)
Street Trash 1987,S 16,C,27:3
Frumkes, Roy (Screenwriter)
Street Trash 1987,S 16,C,27:3
Frye, Sean
For Keeps 1988,Ja 15,C,17:3
Fuchs, Fred (Producer)
Tucker: The Man and His Dream 1988,Ag 12,C,8:1
Fuchs, Jozef
Everything for Sale 1987,Mr 13,C,15:1
Fuchs, Leo L (Producer)
Malone 1987,My 4,C,17:4
Fudge, Allen
My Demon Lover 1987,Ap 24,C,14:1
Fueter, Peter-Christian (Producer)
Alice 1988,Ag 3,C,18:4
Fuhrer, Martin (Cinematographer)
Nanou 1988,S 28,C,18:5
Fujii, Hideo (Cinematographer)
Dark Hair 1987,Mr 22,62:1
Fujimine, Sadatoshi (Producer)
Sorekara (And Then) 1987,Ap 8,C,23:1
Fujimoto, Kiyoshi (Producer)
River of Fireflies 1988,N 4,C,13:1
Fujimoto, Tak (Cinematographer)
Married to the Mob 1988,Ag 19,C,6:1
Sweet Hearts Dance 1988,S 23,C,17:1
Cocoon: The Return 1988,N 23,C,15:1
Fu Jingshen (Cinematographer)
Girl from Hunan 1988,Mr 4,C,22:4
Fujioka, John
Steel Dawn 1987,N 6,C,33:1
Fujitani, Miwako
Sorekara (And Then) 1987,Ap 8,C,23:1
Fulford, Christopher
Prayer for the Dying, A 1987,S 11,C,11:1

G

Gazzara, Ben
Opening Night 1988,O 1,15:1
Gazzarri, Bill
Decline of Western Civilization Part II, The: The Metal Years 1988,Je 17,C,14:4
Geary, Anthony
Disorderlies 1987,Ag 15,13:1
You Can't Hurry Love 1988,Ja 29,C,11:1
Geasland, Jack (Original Author)
Dead Ringers 1988,S 23,C,10:1
Dead Ringers 1988,O 2,II,21:5
Gedrick, Jason
Stacking 1988,Ja 15,C,15:1
Promised Land 1988,Ja 22,C,13:1
Gee, Timothy (Miscellaneous)
Salome's Last Dance 1988,My 6,C,8:5
Gee, Zand (Cinematographer)
Living on Tokyo Time 1987,Ag 14,C,20:1
Geiss, Tony (Miscellaneous)
Land Before Time, The 1988,N 18,C,8:4
Gelb, Larry (Composer)
Dances Sacred and Profane 1987,Je 13,13:1
Gelb, Peter (Producer)
Horowitz Plays Mozart 1987,O 8,C,37:1
Geldzahler, Henry
Andy Warhol 1987,Je 9,C,20:1
Geleng, Antonello (Miscellaneous)
Maschera, La 1988,S 25,64:4
Gelin, Xavier (Producer)
Honeymoon 1987,N 20,C,24:1
Gelke, Becky
Full Moon in Blue Water 1988,N 23,C,15:1
Gems, Jonathan (Screenwriter)
White Mischief 1988,Ap 22,C,20:1
White Mischief 1988,My 22,II,43:1
Gence, Denise
Buffet Froid (Cold Cuts) 1987,S 4,C,5:4
Gendron, Francois-Eric
Ami de Mon Amie, L' (My Girlfriend's Boyfriend) 1987,O 9,C,4:5
Boyfriends and Girlfriends (Ami de Mon Amie, L') 1988,Jl 15,C,10:6
Gendron, Pierre (Producer)
Night Zoo 1988,Mr 30,C,20:5
Genkins, Harvey (Cinematographer)
Garbage Pail Kids 1987,Ag 22,14:5
Genny, Lily
Field of Honor (Champ d'Honneur) 1988,Mr 18,C,24:5
Genovese, Mike
Invisible Kid, The 1988,Mr 31,C,16:4
Gentil, Dominique (Cinematographer)
Faces of Women 1987,F 13,C,22:1
Geoffray, Gerald (Producer)
Witchboard 1987,Mr 15,61:1
Geoffrion, Robert (Screenwriter)
Honeymoon 1987,N 20,C,24:1
George, Louis (Producer)
Slaughterhouse Rock 1988,My 22,49:5
George, Peter (Director)
Surf Nazis Must Die 1987,O 2,C,24:5
Georgeson, Tom
Fish Called Wanda, A 1988,Jl 15,C,8:1
Gerafi, Haim
Beast, The 1988,S 16,C,13:1
Gerard, Charles
Bandits 1988,Ag 24,C,17:1
Gerber, Helena (Miscellaneous)
Alpine Fire 1987,F 20,C,20:1
Gerdes, George
Squeeze, The 1987,Jl 10,C,24:1
Gere, Richard
No Mercy 1987,Ja 4,II,17:1
Miles from Home 1988,S 16,C,8:4
German, Aleksei (Director)
My Friend Ivan Lapshin 1987,Mr 24,C,14:5
German, Yuri (Original Author)
My Friend Ivan Lapshin 1987,Mr 24,C,14:5
Gerolmo, Chris (Screenwriter)
Miles from Home 1988,S 16,C,8:4
Mississippi Burning 1988,D 9,C,12:1
Mississippi Burning 1988,D 18,II,13:1
Gerroll, Daniel
84 Charing Cross Road 1987,F 13,C,10:4
Big Business 1988,Je 10,C,10:4
Gershon, Gina
Red Heat 1988,Je 17,C,14:5
Cocktail 1988,Jl 29,C,6:5
Gerstein, Ellen
Daddy's Boys 1988,Je 10,C,13:1
Gertz, Jami
Lost Boys, The 1987,Jl 31,C,21:1

Less Than Zero 1987,N 6,C,23:1
Getty, Estelle
Mannequin 1987,F 13,C,8:6
Ghaffari, Earl (Miscellaneous)
Kindred, The 1987,Ja 10,13:1
Decline of Western Civilization Part II, The: The Metal Years 1988,Je 17,C,14:4
Ghaffari, Earl (Screenwriter)
Kindred, The 1987,Ja 10,13:1
Gheilardini, Tersilio
Cammina Cammina (Keep Walking, Keep Walking) 1988,Jl 10,43:5
Ghertler, Louise (Director)
In a Jazz Way: A Portrait of Mura Dehn 1987,D 16,22:5
Ghir, Kulvinder
Rita, Sue and Bob Too 1987,Jl 17,C,18:1
Giachetti, Fosco
We the Living 1988,N 25,C,11:1
Giambalvo, Louis
Bad Dreams 1988,Ap 8,C,10:1
Gian, Joey
Death Before Dishonor 1987,F 20,C,10:1
Gianikian, Yervant (Director)
From the Pole to the Equator 1988,Ap 6,C,18:3
Gianikian, Yervant (Producer)
From the Pole to the Equator 1988,Ap 6,C,18:3
Giannoti, Anna-Maria
Night Zoo 1988,Mr 30,C,20:5
Giatti, Ian
Great Outdoors, The 1988,Je 17,C,12:6
Rescue, The 1988,Ag 5,C,9:1
Gibb, Cynthia
Malone 1987,My 4,C,17:4
Jack's Back 1988,My 6,C,19:1
Short Circuit 2 1988,Jl 6,C,18:5
Gibb, Donald
Revenge of the Nerds II: Nerds in Paradise 1987,Jl 11,18:4
Gibbs, Antony (Miscellaneous)
Russkies 1987,N 6,C,12:3
Gibbs, Michael (Composer)
Heat 1987,Mr 13,C,33:1
Housekeeping 1987,N 25,C,11:1
Gibbs, Richard (Composer)
Sweet Hearts Dance 1988,S 23,C,17:1
Gibbs, Timothy
Kindred, The 1987,Ja 10,13:1
Gibot, Gabriel
Debajo del Mundo (Under the World) 1988,O 5,C,19:5
Gibson, Henry
Monster in the Closet 1987,My 15,C,9:1
Switching Channels 1988,Mr 4,C,10:4
Gibson, Mel
Lethal Weapon 1987,Mr 6,C,7:1
Lethal Weapon 1987,My 10,II,17:1
Tequila Sunrise 1988,D 2,C,8:4
Gideon, Raynold (Producer)
Made in Heaven 1987,N 6,C,16:1
Gidley, Pamela
Permanent Record 1988,Ap 22,C,10:1
Blue Iguana, The 1988,Ap 23,18:2
Gielgud, John
Whistle Blower, The 1987,Jl 10,C,4:2
Appointment with Death 1988,Ap 15,C,4:5
Arthur 2 on the Rocks 1988,Jl 8,C,8:1
Giercke, Franz-Christoph (Producer)
Lord of the Dance/Destroyer of Illusion 1987,D 26,14:4
Gift, Roland
Sammy and Rosie Get Laid 1987,O 30,C,5:1
Gignoux, Hubert
Melo 1987,O 5,C,19:5
Melo 1988,Ja 31,55:1
Gil, Gilberto (Composer)
Subway to the Stars 1988,Mr 25,C,14:6
Gilbert, Brian (Director)
Vice Versa 1988,Mr 11,C,12:6
Gilbert, Gabrielle (Miscellaneous)
Invisible Kid, The 1988,Mr 31,C,16:4
Gilbert, Ronnie
Running on Empty 1988,S 18,II,25:1
Gilford, Jack
Cocoon: The Return 1988,N 23,C,15:1
Gill, Andy (Composer)
Last of England, The 1988,S 28,C,18:3
Gill, Joumana
Friendship's Death 1988,Mr 25,C,22:4
Gillert, Patrick
Singing the Blues in Red 1988,Ja 29,C,8:5
Gillespie, Dizzy
Art Blakey: The Jazz Messenger 1988,O 28,C,16:4

Gillette, Pierre (Miscellaneous)
Man in the Silk Hat, The 1988,Ap 1,C,10:5
Gillin, Hugh
Wanted Dead or Alive 1987,Ja 16,C,17:2
Gilpin, Jack
Funny Farm 1988,Je 3,C,14:6
Giltaij, Goert (Cinematographer)
Pointsman, The 1988,Ap 8,C,22:1
Gilula, Steve (Producer)
Computer Animation Show, The 1988,F 5,C,14:5
Gilyard, Clarence, Jr
Die Hard 1988,Jl 31,II,19:1
Gimenez, Claudia
Opera do Malandro 1987,Ja 30,C,6:5
Gimignani, Alberto
Family, The 1988,Ja 22,C,11:1
Ginzberg, Valeri (Cinematographer)
Commissar 1988,Je 17,C,16:4
Giono, Jean (Original Author)
Angele 1988,F 26,C,19:1
Giordano, Martine (Miscellaneous)
Scene of the Crime 1987,Ja 23,C,14:1
Vie Est Belle, La 1987,N 18,C,21:1
Rendez-Vous 1987,D 25,C,6:5
Giorgobiani, Edisher
Repentance 1987,D 4,C,11:1
Giraldi, Bob (Director)
Hiding Out 1987,N 6,C,21:1
Girardot, Annie
Traffic Jam 1988,Mr 4,C,14:6
Girardot, Hippolyte
Manon of the Spring 1987,N 6,C,25:1
Giraudeau, Bernard
Annee des Meduses, L' 1987,Ap 24,C,9:1
Giraudi, Nicolas
Scene of the Crime 1987,Ja 23,C,14:1
Scene of the Crime 1987,F 8,II,21:1
Giron, Ali
Moderns, The 1988,Ap 15,C,21:1
Girotti, Massimo
Berlin Affair, The 1988,Jl 15,C,12:5
Gish, Annabeth
Hiding Out 1987,N 6,C,21:1
Mystic Pizza 1988,O 21,C,20:6
Gish, Lillian
Whales of August, The 1987,O 16,C,3:1
Gislason, Thomas (Miscellaneous)
Element of Crime, The 1987,My 1,C,11:1
Gittes, Harry (Producer)
Little Nikita 1988,Mr 18,C,26:5
Giulini, Carlo Maria (Miscellaneous)
Horowitz Plays Mozart 1987,O 8,C,37:1
Giza, Hanna
Woman from the Provinces, A 1987,Mr 22,62:2
Gladstone, Andi (Producer)
Working Girls 1987,F 27,C,8:5
Gladstone, Dana
Presidio, The 1988,Je 10,C,15:1
Glanzelius, Anton
My Life as a Dog 1987,Mr 24,C,14:3
My Life as a Dog 1987,My 1,C,16:1
Glaser, Bedrich (Miscellaneous)
Alice 1988,Ag 3,C,18:4
Glaser, Etienne
Mozart Brothers, The 1987,S 18,C,21:1
Glaser, Etienne (Miscellaneous)
Mozart Brothers, The 1987,S 18,C,21:1
Glaser, Etienne (Screenwriter)
Mozart Brothers, The 1987,S 18,C,21:1
Glaser, Paul Michael (Director)
Running Man, The 1987,N 13,C,10:5
Glasgow, Gil
Full Moon in Blue Water 1988,N 23,C,15:1
Glass, Ann Gisel
Sierra Leone 1988,D 14,C,28:5
Glass, Philip (Composer)
Hamburger Hill 1987,Ag 28,C,16:5
Powaqqatsi 1988,Ap 29,C,20:4
Thin Blue Line, The 1988,Ag 26,C,6:1
Glatzeder, Winfried
Rosa Luxemburg 1987,My 1,C,10:5
Glazer, Mitch (Screenwriter)
Scrooged 1988,N 23,C,16:5
Gleason, Michael (Director)
Summer Heat 1987,My 29,C,8:4
Gleason, Michael (Screenwriter)
Summer Heat 1987,My 29,C,8:4
Gleason, Paul
Forever, Lulu 1987,Ap 24,C,10:4
Morgan Stewart's Coming Home 1987,Je 4,C,16:4

Johnny Be Good 1988,Mr 25,C,29:1
Die Hard 1988,Jl 15,C,14:5
Gleeson, Patrick (Composer)
Bedroom Window, The 1987,Ja 16,C,6:4
Deadly Illusion 1987,O 31,10:5
Stacking 1988,Ja 15,C,15:1
Gleizer, Michele
Beatrice 1988,Mr 18,C,25:1
Glemnitz, Reinhard
Wannsee Conference, The 1987,N 18,C,29:3
Glen, John (Director)
Living Daylights, The 1987,Jl 31,C,3:5
Glenn, Scott
Man on Fire 1987,O 10,18:4
Off Limits 1988,Mr 11,C,8:5
Glennon, James (Cinematographer)
Time of Destiny, A 1988,Ap 22,C,29:1
Glick, Stacey
Three O'Clock High 1987,O 9,C,16:3
Glickenhaus, James (Director)
Shakedown 1988,My 6,C,20:1
Glickenhaus, James (Screenwriter)
Shakedown 1988,My 6,C,20:1
Glimcher, Arnold (Producer)
Gorillas in the Mist 1988,S 23,C,19:1
Good Mother, The 1988,N 4,C,15:1
Glinski, Robert (Director)
Sunday Pranks 1988,Mr 13,57:1
Glinski, Robert (Screenwriter)
Sunday Pranks 1988,Mr 13,57:1
Globus, Yoram (Producer)
Allan Quatermain and the Lost City of Gold 1987,Ja 31,14:5
Over the Top 1987,F 12,C,21:2
Duet for One 1987,F 13,C,10:4
Street Smart 1987,Mr 27,C,8:1
Hanoi Hilton, The 1987,Mr 27,C,13:1
Superman IV: The Quest for Peace 1987,Jl 25,13:2
Masters of the Universe 1987,Ag 8,50:1
Tough Guys Don't Dance 1987,S 18,C,14:1
Dancers 1987,O 9,C,24:1
King Lear 1988,Ja 22,C,6:1
Braddock: Missing in Action III 1988,Ja 22,C,9:1
Salsa 1988,My 7,13:1
Shy People 1988,Jl 1,C,8:5
Berlin Affair, The 1988,Jl 15,C,12:5
Hanna's War 1988,N 23,C,14:1
Glover, Crispin
River's Edge 1987,My 8,C,28:4
River's Edge 1987,Je 14,II,23:5
Glover, Danny
Lethal Weapon 1987,Mr 6,C,7:1
Lethal Weapon 1987,My 10,II,17:1
Bat 21 1988,O 21,C,22:1
Glover, John
Masquerade 1988,Mr 11,C,8:5
Rocket Gibraltar 1988,S 2,C,6:5
Scrooged 1988,N 23,C,16:5
Glover, Julian
Fourth Protocol, The 1987,Ag 28,C,19:1
Glover, Kara
Beat, The 1988,Je 3,C,10:6
Gluck, Wolfgang (Director)
38: Vienna Before the Fall 1988,My 6,C,17:1
Gluck, Wolfgang (Screenwriter)
38: Vienna Before the Fall 1988,My 6,C,17:1
Glueckman, Alan Jay (Screenwriter)
Russkies 1987,N 6,C,12:3
Glynn, Carlin
Gardens of Stone 1987,My 8,C,32:1
Glynn, Victor (Producer)
High Hopes 1988,S 24,12:4
Go, Hiromi
Comic Magazine (Komikku Zasshi) 1987,Ja 16,C,14:6
Goberman, John (Producer)
Distant Harmony 1988,F 4,C,15:1
Godard, Jean-Luc
King Lear 1988,Ja 22,C,6:1
Godard, Jean-Luc (Director)
King Lear 1988,Ja 22,C,6:1
Aria 1988,My 21,54:3
Godard, Jean-Luc (Screenwriter)
King Lear 1988,Ja 22,C,6:1
Aria 1988,My 21,54:3
Goddard, Alan
Bell Diamond 1988,Mr 17,C,30:1
Goddard, Gary (Director)
Masters of the Universe 1987,Ag 8,50:1
Goded, Angel (Cinematographer)
Realm of Fortune, The 1987,Mr 17,C,14:1
Frida 1988,F 17,C,18:5

Godin, Jacques
Blind Trust 1987,N 7,13:1
Godmilow, Jill (Director)
Waiting for the Moon 1987,Mr 6,C,14:5
Godmilow, Jill (Miscellaneous)
Waiting for the Moon 1987,Mr 6,C,14:5
Godunov, Alexander
Die Hard 1988,Jl 15,C,14:5
Die Hard 1988,Jl 31,II,19:1
Godwin, Christopher
Handful of Dust, A 1988,Je 24,C,14:1
Goethals, Angela
Heartbreak Hotel 1988,S 30,C,18:5
Gogolashvili, Shota (Miscellaneous)
Ashik Kerib 1988,S 29,C,24:5
Goh, Hiromi
Gonza the Spearman 1988,O 28,C,15:1
Goicoechea, Enrique
Tasio 1987,Mr 27,C,15:1
Golan, Menahem (Director)
Over the Top 1987,F 12,C,21:2
Over the Top 1987,Mr 1,II,21:1
Hanna's War 1988,N 23,C,14:1
Golan, Menahem (Producer)
Allan Quatermain and the Lost City of Gold 1987,Ja 31,14:5
Over the Top 1987,F 12,C,21:2
Duet for One 1987,F 13,C,10:4
Street Smart 1987,Mr 27,C,8:1
Hanoi Hilton, The 1987,Mr 27,C,13:1
Superman IV: The Quest for Peace 1987,Jl 25,13:2
Masters of the Universe 1987,Ag 8,50:1
Tough Guys Don't Dance 1987,S 18,C,14:1
Dancers 1987,O 9,C,24:1
King Lear 1988,Ja 22,C,6:1
Braddock: Missing in Action III 1988,Ja 22,C,9:1
Salsa 1988,My 7,13:1
Shy People 1988,Jl 1,C,8:5
Berlin Affair, The 1988,Jl 15,C,12:5
Hanna's War 1988,N 23,C,14:1
Golan, Menahem (Screenwriter)
Hanna's War 1988,N 23,C,14:1
Goldberg, Barry (Composer)
Three for the Road 1987,Ap 10,C,5:1
Goldberg, Dan (Director)
Feds 1988,O 29,18:5
Goldberg, Dan (Screenwriter)
Feds 1988,O 29,18:5
Goldberg, Eve (Miscellaneous)
Coverup: Behind the Iran-Contra Affair 1988,Ag 26,C,8:6
Goldberg, Eve (Screenwriter)
Coverup: Behind the Iran-Contra Affair 1988,Ag 26,C,8:6
Goldberg, Noa
Late Summer Blues 1988,Ag 12,C,13:1
Goldberg, Ruthi
Big Girl 1988,N 23,C,14:4
Goldberg, Whoopi
Burglar 1987,Mr 20,C,10:4
Fatal Beauty 1987,O 30,C,8:5
Telephone, The 1988,F 14,77:1
Clara's Heart 1988,O 7,C,16:5
Clara's Heart 1988,O 30,II,13:1
Goldblatt, Mark (Director)
Dead Heat 1988,My 7,13:1
Goldblatt, Stephen (Cinematographer)
Lethal Weapon 1987,Mr 6,C,7:1
Everybody's All American 1988,N 4,C,17:1
Goldblum, Jeff
Beyond Therapy 1987,F 27,C,8:5
Vibes 1988,Ag 5,C,6:1
Golden, Annie
Forever, Lulu 1987,Ap 24,C,10:4
Goldenberg, Billy (Composer)
Eighteen Again 1988,Ap 8,C,12:1
Goldenberg, Mark (Composer)
Teen Wolf Too 1987,N 20,C,14:6
Goldfine, Adam
Thin Blue Line, The 1988,Ag 26,C,6:1
Thin Blue Line, The 1988,S 4,II,17:1
Goldfinger, Ron (Miscellaneous)
Kiss Daddy Good Night 1988,My 20,C,11:1
Goldin, Ricky Paull
Blob, The 1988,Ag 5,C,6:5
Goldman, B J (Screenwriter)
Bulletproof 1988,My 16,C,13:1
Goldman, Bo (Screenwriter)
Little Nikita 1988,Mr 18,C,26:5
Goldman, Gary (Producer)
Land Before Time, The 1988,N 18,C,8:4
Goldman, Mia (Miscellaneous)
Big Easy, The 1987,Ag 21,C,6:3

Cross My Heart 1987,N 13,C,21:1
Goldman, Michael
One Woman or Two 1987,F 6,C,18:1
Goldman, Michal (Director)
Jumpin' Night in the Garden of Eden, A 1988,Mr 2,C,20:1
Goldman, Michal (Producer)
Jumpin' Night in the Garden of Eden, A 1988,Mr 2,C,20:1
Goldman, Shepard (Screenwriter)
Salsa 1988,My 7,13:1
Goldman, Wendy (Original Author)
Casual Sex? 1988,Ap 22,C,24:1
Goldman, Wendy (Screenwriter)
Casual Sex? 1988,Ap 22,C,24:1
Goldman, William (Original Author)
Heat 1987,Mr 13,C,33:1
Princess Bride, The 1987,S 25,C,10:5
Goldman, William (Screenwriter)
Heat 1987,Mr 13,C,33:1
Princess Bride, The 1987,S 25,C,10:5
Goldsmith, George (Screenwriter)
Blue Monkey, The 1987,O 16,C,12:6
Goldsmith, Jerry (Composer)
Hoosiers 1987,F 27,C,10:3
Extreme Prejudice 1987,Ap 24,C,8:5
Link 1987,Ap 24,C,10:4
Innerspace 1987,Jl 1,C,17:1
Rent-a-Cop 1988,Ja 15,C,13:1
Rambo III 1988,My 25,C,15:1
Goldsmith, Paul H (Cinematographer)
Killing Time, The 1987,O 23,C,14:3
Goldstein, Jenette
Near Dark 1987,O 4,67:2
Goldstein, Josh (Screenwriter)
Eighteen Again 1988,Ap 8,C,12:1
Goldstein, Steve
House of Games 1987,O 11,94:1
Goldstein, William (Composer)
Hello Again 1987,N 6,C,21:1
Goldthwait, Bob
Burglar 1987,Mr 20,C,10:4
Police Academy 4: Citizens on Patrol 1987,Ap 4,12:5
Hot to Trot 1988,Ag 27,11:3
Goldwyn, Tony
Gaby—A True Story 1987,O 30,C,10:4
Golia, David (Cinematographer)
Rosary Murders, The 1987,Ag 28,C,12:3
Golin, Steven (Producer)
Blue Iguana, The 1988,Ap 23,18:2
Golino, Valeria
Trois Soeurs (Paura e Amore) 1988,My 22,II,21:5
Big Top Pee-wee 1988,Jl 22,C,10:3
Rain Man 1988,D 16,C,12:5
Golub, Leon
Golub 1988,O 5,C,23:1
Gomez, Paulina
Gaby—A True Story 1987,O 30,C,10:4
Gomez Cruz, Ernesto
Realm of Fortune, The 1987,Mr 17,C,14:1
Goncalves, Milton
Subway to the Stars 1988,Mr 25,C,14:6
Gong Li
Red Sorghum 1988,O 9,74:1
Gonon, Paul (Cinematographer)
Hotel Terminus: The Life and Times of Klaus Barbie 1988,O 6,C,25:1
Gonzales, Federico
Hotel Colonial 1987,S 19,16:3
Gonzalez, Antonio
Colegas (Pals) 1987,Ag 14,C,15:1
Gonzalez, Cordelia
Gran Fiesta, La 1987,Jl 17,C,17:1
Gonzalez, Erando
Winter Tan, A 1988,O 2,57:6
Gonzalez, Rosario
Colegas (Pals) 1987,Ag 14,C,15:1
Goodman, Dody
Chipmunk Adventure, The 1987,My 22,C,10:5
Goodman, Joel (Miscellaneous)
Satisfaction 1988,F 13,15:1
Goodman, John
Raising Arizona 1987,Mr 11,C,24:5
Burglar 1987,Mr 20,C,10:4
Big Easy, The 1987,Ag 21,C,6:3
Wrong Guys, The 1988,Je 4,12:3
Punchline 1988,S 30,C,14:4
Everybody's All American 1988,N 4,C,17:1
Goodman, Karen (Director)
No Applause, Just Throw Money 1988,Mr 12,14:4
Goodman, Karen (Producer)
No Applause, Just Throw Money 1988,Mr 12,14:4

H

Overboard 1988,F 14,II,1:1
Haworth, Ted (Miscellaneous)
Batteries Not Included 1987,D 18,C,12:5
Hawthorne, Denys (Narrator)
Oscar Wilde: Spendthrift of Genius 1988,Je 15,C,19:3
Hayashi, Dennis (Producer)
Living on Tokyo Time 1987,Ag 14,C,20:1
Hayashi, Hikaru (Composer)
Violence at Noon 1988,N 11,C,6:4
Hayden, Karl
Da 1988,Ap 29,C,10:1
Hayden, Mathew (Producer)
Unholy, The 1988,Ap 23,18:4
Midnight Crossing 1988,My 14,16:5
Hayenga, Jeff
Prince of Pennsylvania, The 1988,S 16,C,17:1
Hayes, Gloria
Witchboard 1987,Mr 15,61:1
Hayes, Harold T P (Original Author)
Gorillas in the Mist 1988,S 23,C,19:1
Hayes, Patricia
Little Dorrit 1988,Mr 26,11:1
Willow 1988,My 20,C,8:4
Fish Called Wanda, A 1988,Jl 15,C,8:1
Little Dorrit 1988,O 21,C,12:3
Hayes, Terry (Producer)
Year My Voice Broke, The 1988,Ag 25,C,18:1
Haygarth, Tony
Month in the Country, A 1987,S 27,67:1
Month in the Country, A 1988,F 19,C,10:5
Hayman, David
Gospel According to Vic 1987,Mr 13,C,13:1
Hope and Glory 1987,O 9,C,23:1
Hayman, James (Cinematographer)
Tokyo Pop 1988,Ap 15,C,4:4
Haynes, Tiger
Enemy Territory 1987,My 22,C,7:1
Apprentice to Murder 1988,F 26,C,14:1
Haywood, Chris
Burke and Wills 1987,Je 12,C,10:1
Dogs in Space 1987,O 9,C,7:1
Tale of Ruby Rose, The 1988,My 25,C,18:6
Hazan, Shlomo (Miscellaneous)
Late Summer Blues 1988,Ag 12,C,13:1
Head, Murray
White Mischief 1988,Ap 22,C,20:1
Headley, Shari
Coming to America 1988,Je 29,C,20:5
Headly, Glenne
Making Mr Right 1987,Ap 10,C,16:5
Nadine 1987,Ag 7,C,8:3
Stars and Bars 1988,Mr 18,C,3:1
Dirty Rotten Scoundrels 1988,D 14,C,21:4
Heald, Anthony
Outrageous Fortune 1987,Ja 30,C,5:1
Orphans 1987,S 18,C,3:1
Healey, Leslie (Miscellaneous)
Second Victory, The 1987,My 27,C,22:3
Healey, Mary
Consuming Passions 1988,Ap 6,C,18:3
Heard, John
Telephone, The 1988,F 14,77:1
Milagro Beanfield War, The 1988,Mr 18,C,17:1
Big 1988,Je 3,C,8:4
Betrayed 1988,Ag 26,C,16:1
Beaches 1988,D 21,C,28:4
Hearn, Ann
Accused, The 1988,O 14,C,13:1
Hearst, Patricia Campbell (Original Author)
Patty Hearst 1988,S 23,C,8:5
Hecht, Ben (Original Author)
Switching Channels 1988,Mr 4,C,10:4
I Hate Actors! 1988,Ap 29,C,22:1
Heckert, James (Miscellaneous)
Assassination 1987,Ja 10,13:1
Heeley, Bryan
Rita, Sue and Bob Too 1987,Jl 17,C,18:1
Hehir, Peter
Kangaroo 1987,Mr 13,C,12:5
Heiden, Ira
Nightmare on Elm Street 3, A: Dream Warriors 1987,F
27,C,15:3
Heim, Alan (Miscellaneous)
Funny Farm 1988,Je 3,C,14:6
Heinisch, Christian
Class Relations 1987,F 27,C,16:1
Heinl, Bernd (Cinematographer)
Bagdad Cafe 1988,Ap 22,C,19:1
Heinrich, Juergen
Judgment in Berlin 1988,My 6,C,13:1

Helfer, Daniel (Director)
Record, The 1988,My 13,C,15:1
Helfer, Daniel (Screenwriter)
Record, The 1988,My 13,C,15:1
Helfrich, Mark (Miscellaneous)
Predator 1987,Je 12,C,6:4
Action Jackson 1988,F 12,C,10:1
Helgeland, Brian (Miscellaneous)
Nightmare on Elm Street 4, A: The Dream Master 1988,Ag
19,C,8:3
Helgeland, Brian (Screenwriter)
Nightmare on Elm Street 4, A: The Dream Master 1988,Ag
19,C,8:3
Heller, Bill (Composer)
Deranged 1987,O 31,12:3
Heller, Paul M (Producer)
Withnail and I 1987,Mr 27,C,9:1
Withnail and I 1987,Je 19,C,10:1
Heller, Rosilyn (Producer)
Who's That Girl 1987,Ag 8,16:1
Hellwig, Juergen (Producer)
Filming Othello 1987,F 4,C,24:3
Hellwig, Klaus (Producer)
Filming Othello 1987,F 4,C,24:3
Helm, Levon
End of the Line 1988,F 26,C,15:1
Helman, Geoffrey (Producer)
84 Charing Cross Road 1987,F 13,C,10:4
Helmond, Katherine
Shadey 1987,Je 5,C,10:1
Overboard 1987,D 16,C,22:3
Lady in White 1988,My 13,C,10:3
Helmy, Michael (Miscellaneous)
Back to the Beach 1987,Ag 8,16:5
Helou, Tony
Dogs in Space 1987,O 9,C,7:1
Helpern, David (Producer)
Dead Heat 1988,My 7,13:1
Helvey, Laszlo
Singing on the Treadmill 1987,Jl 31,C,11:1
Hemblen, David
Family Viewing 1988,Mr 23,C,20:5
Short Circuit 2 1988,Jl 6,C,18:5
Family Viewing 1988,Jl 29,C,10:5
Hembrow, Mark
Return to Snowy River 1988,Ap 15,C,8:1
Hemingway, Mariel
Superman IV: The Quest for Peace 1987,Jl 25,13:2
Sunset 1988,Ap 29,C,13:1
Suicide Club, The 1988,My 21,54:5
Hemingway, Mariel (Producer)
Suicide Club, The 1988,My 21,54:5
Hen, Jozef (Original Author)
Boxer and Death, The 1988,O 12,C,19:1
Boxer and Death, The 1988,N 1,C,17:1
Hen, Jozef (Screenwriter)
Boxer and Death, The 1988,O 12,C,19:1
Henderickx, Guido (Miscellaneous)
Love Is a Dog from Hell 1988,Mr 18,C,15:1
Love Is a Dog from Hell 1988,Ap 23,14:5
Henderson, Albert
Big Top Pee-wee 1988,Jl 22,C,10:3
Hendrickson, Benjamin
Russkies 1987,N 6,C,12:3
Hendrickson, Stephen (Miscellaneous)
Wall Street 1987,D 11,C,3:4
Hendrickson, Steve
Wizard of Loneliness, The 1988,S 2,C,9:1
Henenlotter, Frank (Director)
Brain Damage 1988,Ap 15,C,16:5
Henenlotter, Frank (Miscellaneous)
Brain Damage 1988,Ap 15,C,16:5
Henenlotter, Frank (Screenwriter)
Brain Damage 1988,Ap 15,C,16:5
Henkin, Hilary (Screenwriter)
Fatal Beauty 1987,O 30,C,8:5
Hennessey, Dan
Care Bears' Adventure in Wonderland, The 1987,Ag 7,C,21:1
Henning, Eva
Three Strange Loves (Torst) 1988,Ja 20,C,20:1
Henning, Paul (Screenwriter)
Dirty Rotten Scoundrels 1988,D 14,C,21:4
Henning-Jensen, Astrid
Element of Crime, The 1987,My 1,C,11:1
Henriksen, Finn (Miscellaneous)
Babette's Feast 1987,O 1,C,22:5
Babette's Feast 1988,Mr 4,C,12:6
Henriksen, Lance
Near Dark 1987,O 4,67:2

Henriquez, Leonardo (Miscellaneous)
Amerika, Terra Incognita 1988,D 9,C,10:6
Henry, Buck
Aria 1988,My 21,54:3
Henry, Deanne
Home Is Where the Hart Is 1987,D 5,14:4
Henry, Justin
Sweet Hearts Dance 1988,S 23,C,17:1
Henry, Lenny
Suicide Club, The 1988,My 21,54:5
Henshaw, Jim
Care Bears' Adventure in Wonderland, The 1987,Ag 7,C,21:1
Hepburn, Doreen
Da 1988,Ap 29,C,10:1
Hepton, Bernard
Shadey 1987,Je 5,C,10:1
He Qun (Miscellaneous)
Big Parade, The 1988,Mr 15,C,16:5
Herbert, James (Cinematographer)
Athens, Ga—Inside/Out 1987,My 29,C,14:1
Herbert, Jocelyn (Miscellaneous)
Whales of August, The 1987,O 16,C,3:1
Herbert, Percy
Love Child, The 1988,S 14,C,20:5
Herbst, Rick
Brain Damage 1988,Ap 15,C,16:5
Hercules, Evan (Miscellaneous)
Prayer for the Dying, A 1987,S 11,C,11:1
Riders of the Storm 1988,My 7,12:3
Herlitzka, Roberto
Summer Night with Greek Profile, Almond Eyes and Scent of
Basil 1987,Je 19,C,12:6
Dark Eyes 1987,S 25,C,26:5
Maschera, La 1988,S 25,64:4
Herman, Pee-wee
Back to the Beach 1987,Ag 8,16:5
Big Top Pee-wee 1988,Jl 22,C,10:3
Hernandez, Humberto (Producer)
Parting of the Ways (Lejanja) 1987,S 23,C,22:6
Herr, Michael (Screenwriter)
Full Metal Jacket 1987,Je 26,C,3:1
Full Metal Jacket 1987,Jl 5,II,17:5
Herring, Pembroke (Miscellaneous)
Who's That Girl 1987,Ag 8,16:1
Herrington, David (Cinematographer)
Housekeeper, The 1987,Ap 24,C,7:1
Herrington, Rowdy (Director)
Jack's Back 1988,My 6,C,19:1
Herrington, Rowdy (Screenwriter)
Jack's Back 1988,My 6,C,19:1
Herrmann, Edward
Lost Boys, The 1987,Jl 31,C,21:1
Overboard 1987,D 16,C,22:3
Big Business 1988,Je 10,C,10:4
Hersch, Kathie (Producer)
Home Remedy 1988,Jl 22,C,17:1
Herschlag, Alex
Living on Tokyo Time 1987,Ag 14,C,20:1
Hershey, Barbara
Hoosiers 1987,F 27,C,10:3
Tin Men 1987,Mr 6,C,3:1
World Apart, A 1988,Je 17,C,10:4
Shy People 1988,Jl 1,C,8:5
Last Temptation of Christ, The 1988,Ag 12,C,1:1
Last Temptation of Christ, The 1988,Ag 21,II,21:1
Beaches 1988,D 21,C,28:4
Hertzberg, Michael (Producer)
Memories of Me 1988,S 28,C,23:1
Hertzberg, Paul (Producer)
Bulletproof 1988,My 16,C,13:1
Herz, Gabriela
Felix 1988,S 24,13:1
Herz, Michael (Director)
Troma's War 1988,D 9,C,23:1
Herz, Michael (Producer)
Troma's War 1988,D 9,C,23:1
Herzberg, Ilona (Producer)
Casual Sex? 1988,Ap 22,C,24:1
Feds 1988,O 29,18:5
Herzner, Norbert (Miscellaneous)
Bagdad Cafe 1988,Ap 22,C,19:1
Herzog, John (Cinematographer)
Hello Mary Lou 1987,O 17,16:5
Heschong, Albert (Miscellaneous)
Extreme Prejudice 1987,Ap 24,C,8:5
Hesketh-Harvey, Kit (Screenwriter)
Maurice 1987,S 18,C,18:5
Heslop, Richard (Cinematographer)
Last of England, The 1988,S 28,C,18:3
Hesseman, Howard
Heat 1987,Mr 13,C,33:1

J

K

Kabilio, Alfi (Composer)
Girl, The 1987,Ag 7,C,10:6
Kaczender, George (Director)
Prettykill 1987,Mr 27,C,13:3
Kaczmarek,Jane
Vice Versa 1988,Mr 11,C,12:6
DOA 1988,Mr 18,C,8:5
Kadi, Charlotte
Annee des Meduses, L' 1987,Ap 24,C,9:1
Kadishzon, Rafi (Composer)
Late Summer Blues 1988,Ag 12,C,13:1
Kafka, Franz (Original Author)
Class Relations 1987,F 27,C,16:1
Kahan, Judith
Stealing Home 1988,Ag 26,C,17:4
Kahn, Cynde
Home Remedy 1988,Jl 22,C,17:1
Kahn, Michael (Miscellaneous)
Wisdom 1987,Ja 1,9:5
Fatal Attraction 1987,S 18,C,10:5
Empire of the Sun 1987,D 9,C,25:1
Arthur 2 on the Rocks 1988,Jl 8,C,8:1
Kahn, Sheldon (Miscellaneous)
Bamba, La 1987,Jl 24,C,4:3
Big Shots 1987,O 2,C,17:1
Casual Sex? 1988,Ap 22,C,24:1
Twins 1988,D 9,C,18:1
Kahn, Sheldon (Producer)
Casual Sex? 1988,Ap 22,C,24:1
Kalashnikov, Leonid (Cinematographer)
Theme, The 1987,S 28,C,18:1
Kalem, Toni
Billy Galvin 1987,F 20,C,8:5
Kalinowski, Tadeusz
Everything for Sale 1987,Mr 13,C,15:1
Kalipha, Stefan
Playing Away 1987,Mr 13,C,19:1
Playing Away 1988,Ap 1,C,4:4
Kalle, Pepe
Vie Est Belle, La 1987,N 18,C,21:1
Kalogeras, Savas (Cinematographer)
Crazy Moon 1988,F 8,C,18:5
Kamen, Michael (Composer)
Lethal Weapon 1987,Mr 6,C,7:1
Adventures in Baby-Sitting 1987,Jl 1,C,24:3
Rita, Sue and Bob Too 1987,Jl 17,C,18:1
Someone to Watch Over Me 1987,O 9,C,40:1
Suspect 1987,O 23,C,14:3
Action Jackson 1988,F 12,C,10:1
Die Hard 1988,Jl 15,C,14:5
Kamino, Brenda
I've Heard the Mermaids Singing 1987,S 11,C,8:1
Kaminsky, Stuart (Miscellaneous)
Enemy Territory 1987,My 22,C,7:1
Kaminsky, Stuart (Screenwriter)
Enemy Territory 1987,My 22,C,7:1
Kamiyama, Shigeru
Sea and Poison, The 1987,Jl 22,C,18:3
Kampmann, Steven
Tiger's Tale, A 1988,F 12,C,9:1
Kampmann, Steven (Director)
Stealing Home 1988,Ag 26,C,17:4
Kampmann, Steven (Screenwriter)
Couch Trip, The 1988,Ja 15,C,8:1
Stealing Home 1988,Ag 26,C,17:4
Kan, Victor
Ping Pong 1987,Jl 17,C,10:6
Kanazawa, Masatsugi (Miscellaneous)
Comic Magazine (Komikku Zasshi) 1987,Ja 16,C,14:6
Kane, Carol
Ishtar 1987,My 15,C,3:1
Princess Bride, The 1987,S 25,C,10:5
Sticky Fingers 1988,My 6,C,28:5
License to Drive 1988,Jl 6,C,17:1
Scrooged 1988,N 23,C,16:5
Kane, Issiaka
Yeelen 1987,O 8,C,37:1
Kane, Ivan
Prison 1988,Mr 4,C,33:1
Kani, John
Saturday Night at the Palace 1988,My 20,C,16:1
Kanievska, Marek (Director)
Less Than Zero 1987,N 6,C,23:1
Less Than Zero 1987,N 22,II,23:5

Kanwar, Aneeta
Salaam Bombay! 1988,O 7,C,8:1
Kanze, Hideo
Violence at Noon 1988,N 11,C,6:4
Kao Jai
Daughter of the Nile 1988,S 30,C,8:4
Kapelos, John
Roxanne 1987,Je 19,C,3:4
Boost, The 1988,D 23,C,16:6
Kaplan, George (Screenwriter)
Seventh Sign, The 1988,Ap 1,C,20:3
Kaplan, Jonathan (Director)
Project X 1987,Ap 17,C,15:1
Accused, The 1988,O 14,C,13:1
Accused, The 1988,O 16,II,25:1
Accused, The 1988,N 20,II,13:1
Kaplan, Mike (Producer)
Whales of August, The 1987,O 16,C,3:1
Kapoor, Shashi
Sammy and Rosie Get Laid 1987,O 30,C,5:1
Deceivers, The 1988,S 2,C,10:1
Kaprisky, Valerie
Annee des Meduses, L' 1987,Ap 24,C,9:1
Karaman, Bushra
Wedding in Galilee 1988,Mr 11,C,23:1
Karen, James
Return of the Living Dead Part II 1988,Ja 15,C,11:1
Karman, Janice
Chipmunk Adventure, The 1987,My 22,C,10:5
Karman, Janice (Director)
Chipmunk Adventure, The 1987,My 22,C,10:5
Karman, Janice (Screenwriter)
Chipmunk Adventure, The 1987,My 22,C,10:5
Karmento, Eva (Miscellaneous)
Diary for My Loved Ones 1987,S 26,12:3
Karmitz, Marin (Producer)
Opera do Malandro 1987,Ja 30,C,6:5
No Man's Land 1987,F 13,C,14:6
Melo 1987,O 5,C,19:5
Melo 1988,Ja 31,55:1
Karpinski, Maciej (Screenwriter)
Woman Alone, A 1987,Mr 15,61:1
Karvan, Claudia
High Tide 1988,F 19,C,5:1
Karyo, Michel
Sorceress 1988,Ap 1,C,23:1
Karyo, Tcheky
Sorceress 1988,Ap 1,C,23:1
Kasarda, John (Miscellaneous)
Masquerade 1988,Mr 11,C,8:5
Kasdan, Lawrence (Director)
Accidental Tourist, The 1988,D 23,C,12:5
Kasdan, Lawrence (Producer)
Cross My Heart 1987,N 13,C,21:1
Accidental Tourist, The 1988,D 23,C,12:5
Kasdan, Lawrence (Screenwriter)
Accidental Tourist, The 1988,D 23,C,12:5
Kasongo, Kanku
Vie Est Belle, La 1987,N 18,C,21:1
Kaspar, David (Miscellaneous)
Coverup: Behind the Iran-Contra Affair 1988,Ag 26,C,8:6
Kaspar, David (Producer)
Coverup: Behind the Iran-Contra Affair 1988,Ag 26,C,8:6
Kastner, Elliott (Producer)
Angel Heart 1987,Mr 6,C,5:1
Absolution 1988,Jl 1,C,8:5
Blob, The 1988,Ag 5,C,6:5
Kataoka, Tsurutaro
Comic Magazine (Komikku Zasshi) 1987,Ja 16,C,14:6
Kath, Camelia
Killing Time, The 1987,O 23,C,14:3
Katims, Robert
Broadcast News 1987,D 16,C,21:4
Kato, Haruko
Gonza the Spearman 1988,O 28,C,15:1
Kato, Yoshi
Tampopo 1987,Mr 26,C,21:1
Tampopo 1987,My 22,C,17:1
Profound Desire of the Gods, The 1988,My 6,C,10:1
Katsourides, Dinos (Miscellaneous)
Sweet Country 1987,Ja 23,C,6:5
Katsulas, Andreas
Someone to Watch Over Me 1987,O 9,C,40:1
Katz, Elia
Man in Love, A 1987,Jl 31,C,10:6
Katz, Jonathan
Things Change 1988,O 21,C,10:5
Katz, Jonathan (Miscellaneous)
House of Games 1987,O 11,94:1

Katz, Lyuba
Commissar 1988,Je 17,C,16:4
Katz, Pamela (Director)
In a Jazz Way: A Portrait of Mura Dehn 1987,D 16,22:5
Katz, Robert (Producer)
Telephone, The 1988,F 14,77:1
Katz, Robert (Screenwriter)
Hotel Colonial 1987,S 19,16:3
Katz, Stephen M (Cinematographer)
And God Created Woman 1988,Mr 4,C,22:4
Eighteen Again 1988,Ap 8,C,12:1
Katz, Steve (Composer)
Home Remedy 1988,Jl 22,C,17:1
Katzin, Lee H (Director)
World Gone Wild 1988,My 22,49:5
Kaufman, Lloyd (Miscellaneous)
Troma's War 1988,D 9,C,23:1
Kaufman, Lloyd (Producer)
Troma's War 1988,D 9,C,23:1
Kaufman, Lloyd (Screenwriter)
Troma's War 1988,D 9,C,23:1
Kaufman, Philip (Director)
Unbearable Lightness of Being, The 1988,F 5,C,8:5
Unbearable Lightness of Being, The 1988,F 14,II,1:1
Kaufman, Philip (Screenwriter)
Unbearable Lightness of Being, The 1988,F 5,C,8:5
Kaufmann, Christine
Bagdad Cafe 1988,Ap 22,C,19:1
Kava, Caroline
Little Nikita 1988,Mr 18,C,26:5
Kavanagh, John
Bellman and True 1988,Ap 1,C,4:4
Kavner, Julie
Radio Days 1987,Ja 30,C,1:1
Radio Days 1987,F 1,II,21:1
Surrender 1987,O 9,C,10:6
Kavur, Fuad (Producer)
Memed, My Hawk 1987,My 4,C,17:1
Kawaguchi, Saeda
Violence at Noon 1988,N 11,C,6:4
Kawahara, Takashi
Eat the Peach 1987,Jl 17,C,6:1
Kawarazaki, Choichiro
Profound Desire of the Gods, The 1988,My 6,C,10:1
Kay, Karyn (Screenwriter)
Call Me 1988,My 20,C,11:1
Kay, Sandra (Screenwriter)
Working Girls 1987,F 27,C,8:5
Kaye, Norman (Composer)
Vincent: The Life and Death of Vincent Van Gogh 1988,Mr 16,C,25:1
Kaye, Stubby
Who Framed Roger Rabbit 1988,Je 22,C,17:2
Kaye-Mason, Clarissa
Good Wife, The 1987,F 20,C,19:3
Kayle, Jack
Aria 1988,My 21,54:3
Kazan, Elia
Hello Actors Studio 1988,N 9,C,19:1
Kazan, Lainie
Harry and the Hendersons 1987,Je 5,C,14:5
Beaches 1988,D 21,C,28:4
Kazan, Nicholas (Screenwriter)
Patty Hearst 1988,My 22,II,21:5
Patty Hearst 1988,S 23,C,8:5
Kazantzakis, Nikos (Original Author)
Last Temptation of Christ, The 1988,Ag 12,C,1:1
Last Temptation of Christ, The 1988,Ag 21,II,21:1
Kazurinsky, Tim
Police Academy 4: Citizens on Patrol 1987,Ap 4,12:5
Kazurinsky, Tim (Screenwriter)
For Keeps 1988,Ja 15,C,17:3
Kean, Marie
Dead, The 1987,D 17,C,19:4
Lonely Passion of Judith Hearne, The 1987,D 23,C,15:1
Keane, John (Composer)
Kitchen Toto, The 1988,Jl 8,C,12:5
Keane, Kerrie
Distant Thunder 1988,N 11,C,13:1
Kearney, Stephen
Rikky and Pete 1988,My 20,C,9:1
Keaton, Diane
Radio Days 1987,Ja 30,C,1:1
Heaven 1987,Ap 17,C,8:5
Baby Boom 1987,O 7,C,24:5
Good Mother, The 1988,N 4,C,15:1
Good Mother, The 1988,N 20,II,13:1
Keaton, Diane (Director)
Heaven 1987,Ap 17,C,8:5

Keaton, Michael
  Touch and Go 1987,Ja 14,C,20:5
  Squeeze, The 1987,Jl 10,C,24:1
  Beetlejuice 1988,Mr 30,C,18:6
  Beetlejuice 1988,My 8,II,19:1
  Clean and Sober 1988,Ag 10,C,17:1
Keays-Byrne, Hugh
  Kangaroo 1987,Mr 13,C,12:5
Keen, Pat
  Without a Clue 1988,O 21,C,21:1
Keener, Eliott
  Angel Heart 1987,Mr 6,C,5:1
Keir, Andrew
  Absolution 1988,Jl 1,C,8:5
Keister, Shane (Composer)
  Ernest Goes to Camp 1987,My 23,15:4
Keita, Balla Moussa
  Yeelen 1987,O 8,C,37:1
Keita, Salif (Miscellaneous)
  Yeelen 1987,O 8,C,37:1
Keitel, Harvey
  Pickup Artist, The 1987,S 18,C,23:1
  Last Temptation of Christ, The 1988,Ag 12,C,1:1
  Last Temptation of Christ, The 1988,Ag 21,II,21:1
  Hello Actors Studio 1988,N 9,C,19:1
Keith, Brian
  Death Before Dishonor 1987,F 20,C,10:1
Keith, David
  White of the Eye 1988,My 20,C,22:5
  Heartbreak Hotel 1988,S 30,C,18:5
Keith, David (Director)
  Curse, The 1987,S 11,C,13:4
Keith, Harvey (Director)
  Mondo New York 1988,Ap 22,C,23:1
Keith, Harvey (Screenwriter)
  Mondo New York 1988,Ap 22,C,23:1
Keklikian, Selma
  Family Viewing 1988,Mr 23,C,20:5
Kelleher, John (Producer)
  Eat the Peach 1987,Jl 17,C,6:1
Kelleher, John (Screenwriter)
  Eat the Peach 1987,Jl 17,C,6:1
Keller, Laurie (Producer)
  Riders of the Storm 1988,My 7,12:3
Keller, Marthe
  Dark Eyes 1987,S 25,C,26:5
Kellerman, Sally
  Three for the Road 1987,Ap 10,C,5:1
  You Can't Hurry Love 1988,Ja 29,C,11:1
  Someone to Love 1988,Ap 21,C,20:4
Kellermann, Susan
  Elvira, Mistress of the Dark 1988,S 30,C,12:4
Kelley, David E (Miscellaneous)
  From the Hip 1987,F 6,C,10:4
Kelley, David E (Screenwriter)
  From the Hip 1987,F 6,C,10:4
Kellogg, John
  Orphans 1987,S 18,C,3:1
Kelly, Chris (Miscellaneous)
  Shadey 1987,Je 5,C,10:1
Kelly, Joe (Cinematographer)
  Heaven 1987,Ap 17,C,8:5
Kelly, Joe (Producer)
  Heaven 1987,Ap 17,C,8:5
Kemal, Yashar (Original Author)
  Memed, My Hawk 1987,My 4,C,17:1
Kemeny, John (Producer)
  Iron Eagle II 1988,N 12,15:3
Kemp, Brandis
  South of Reno 1988,Je 3,C,15:1
Kemper, Victor J (Cinematographer)
  Hot to Trot 1988,Ag 27,11:3
Kempf, Angie
  Pickup Artist, The 1987,S 18,C,23:1
Kempinski, Tom (Original Author)
  Duet for One 1987,F 13,C,10:4
Kempinski, Tom (Screenwriter)
  Duet for One 1987,F 13,C,10:4
Kempster, Victor (Miscellaneous)
  And God Created Woman 1988,Mr 4,C,22:4
Kendall, David (Director)
  Luggage of the Gods 1987,Je 19,C,12:6
Kendall, David (Screenwriter)
  Luggage of the Gods 1987,Je 19,C,12:6
Kenna, Peter (Screenwriter)
  Good Wife, The 1987,F 20,C,19:3
Kennedy, Anne (Screenwriter)
  Jewel's Darl 1987,O 21,C,24:5
Kennedy, Burt (Director)
  Trouble with Spies, The 1987,D 4,C,5:1

Kennedy, Burt (Producer)
  Trouble with Spies, The 1987,D 4,C,5:1
Kennedy, Burt (Screenwriter)
  Trouble with Spies, The 1987,D 4,C,5:1
Kennedy, George
  Creepshow 2 1987,My 4,C,17:1
  Naked Gun, The 1988,D 2,C,16:1
Kennedy, Graham
  Traveling North 1988,F 12,C,10:1
Kennedy, Kathleen (Producer)
  Empire of the Sun 1987,D 9,C,25:1
  Batteries Not Included 1987,D 18,C,12:5
  Land Before Time, The 1988,N 18,C,8:4
Kennedy, Kristina
  Baby Boom 1987,O 7,C,24:5
Kennedy, Michelle
  Baby Boom 1987,O 7,C,24:5
Kennedy, Patrick (Miscellaneous)
  In the Mood 1987,S 16,C,27:1
  Plain Clothes 1988,Ap 16,18:1
Kennedy, William (Original Author)
  Ironweed 1987,D 18,C,24:5
Kennedy, William (Screenwriter)
  Ironweed 1987,D 18,C,24:5
Kennelly, Sheila
  Tale of Ruby Rose, The 1988,My 25,C,18:6
Kenney, Bill (Miscellaneous)
  Big Town, The 1987,S 25,C,20:4
  Rambo III 1988,My 25,C,15:1
Kenny, Francis (Cinematographer)
  Campus Man 1987,My 4,C,17:1
  Salvation! 1987,My 31,51:1
Kent, Jessie
  Summer Heat 1987,My 29,C,8:4
Kent, Julie
  Dancers 1987,O 9,C,24:1
Kenworthy, Michael
  Blob, The 1988,Ag 7,II,19:1
Kepinska, Elzbieta
  Everything for Sale 1987,Mr 13,C,15:1
Keramidas, Harry (Miscellaneous)
  Squeeze, The 1987,Jl 10,C,24:1
  Big Business 1988,Je 10,C,10:4
Kerber, Randy (Composer)
  Date with an Angel 1987,N 21,14:5
Kerlow, Max
  Frida 1988,F 17,C,18:5
Kern, David (Miscellaneous)
  Maniac Cop 1988,My 14,16:5
Kerner, Jordan (Producer)
  Less Than Zero 1987,N 6,C,23:1
Kernochan, Sarah (Screenwriter)
  Dancers 1987,O 9,C,24:1
Kerns, Joanna
  Cross My Heart 1987,N 13,C,21:1
Kerr, Bill
  Lighthorsemen, The 1988,My 13,C,14:1
Kerr, E Katherine
  Suspect 1987,O 23,C,14:3
Kerr, Kelle
  Boost, The 1988,D 23,C,16:6
Kerum, Tony (Miscellaneous)
  Die Hard 1988,Jl 31,II,19:1
Kerwin, Brian
  Torch Song Trilogy 1988,D 14,C,19:1
Kessler, Lyle (Original Author)
  Orphans 1987,S 18,C,3:1
  Orphans 1987,O 4,II,23:1
Kessler, Lyle (Screenwriter)
  Orphans 1987,S 18,C,3:1
  Orphans 1987,O 4,II,23:1
Kessler, M L (Screenwriter)
  Allnighter, The 1987,My 4,C,16:1
Kesten, Christian
  Virus Knows No Morals, A 1987,Je 19,C,10:4
Kesten, Stephen F (Producer)
  Million Dollar Mystery 1987,Je 12,C,6:4
Kesterman, Rolf (Cinematographer)
  Disorderlies 1987,Ag 15,13:1
  Surf Nazis Must Die 1987,O 2,C,24:5
  Casual Sex? 1988,Ap 22,C,24:1
Ketron, Larry (Original Author)
  Fresh Horses 1988,N 19,15:3
Ketron, Larry (Screenwriter)
  Permanent Record 1988,Ap 22,C,10:1
  Fresh Horses 1988,N 19,15:3
Khamis, Juliano Mer
  Wedding in Galilee 1988,Mr 11,C,23:1
Khanjian, Arsinee
  Family Viewing 1988,Mr 23,C,20:5

Family Viewing 1988,Jl 29,C,10:5
Khleifi, Michel (Director)
  Wedding in Galilee 1988,Mr 11,C,23:1
  Wedding in Galilee 1988,Je 24,C,11:1
Khleifi, Michel (Screenwriter)
  Wedding in Galilee 1988,Mr 11,C,23:1
  Wedding in Galilee 1988,Je 24,C,11:1
Khouri, Makram
  Wedding in Galilee 1988,Mr 11,C,23:1
Kia, Blaine
  Aloha Summer 1988,F 26,C,8:1
Kibbe, Gary B (Cinematographer)
  Prince of Darkness 1987,O 23,C,26:1
  They Live 1988,N 4,C,8:1
Kiberd, Declan (Screenwriter)
  Samuel Beckett: Silence to Silence 1987,Ap 15,C,22:1
Kidder, Margot
  Superman IV: The Quest for Peace 1987,Jl 25,13:2
Kidney, Richard
  Home Remedy 1988,Jl 22,C,17:1
Kienzle, William X (Original Author)
  Rosary Murders, The 1987,Ag 28,C,12:3
Kieslowski, Krzysztof (Director)
  No End 1987,Mr 6,C,17:2
Kieslowski, Krzysztof (Screenwriter)
  No End 1987,Mr 6,C,17:2
Kiesser, Jan (Cinematographer)
  Some Kind of Wonderful 1987,F 27,C,17:3
  Made in Heaven 1987,N 6,C,16:1
  Clean and Sober 1988,Ag 10,C,17:1
Kiger, Robby
  Monster Squad 1987,Ag 14,C,15:1
Kilalea, Rory
  Allan Quatermain and the Lost City of Gold 1987,Ja 31,14:5
Kilar, Wojciech (Composer)
  Land of Promise 1988,F 5,C,13:6
Kilbertus, Nicholas
  Kiss, The 1988,O 14,C,11:1
Kilik, Jon (Producer)
  Beat, The 1988,Je 3,C,10:6
Kilmer, Val
  Willow 1988,My 20,C,8:4
Kilpatrick, Lincoln
  Prison 1988,Mr 4,C,33:1
Kilpatrick, Patrick
  Russkies 1987,N 6,C,12:3
Kim, Evan C
  Dead Pool 1988,Jl 13,C,22:1
Kim, Miki
  Braddock: Missing in Action III 1988,Ja 22,C,9:1
Kimball, Jeffrey L (Cinematographer)
  Beverly Hills Cop II 1987,My 20,C,28:1
Kimbrough, Charles
  Switching Channels 1988,Mr 4,C,10:4
Kim Myung Kon
  Man with Three Coffins, The 1988,S 27,C,16:5
Kinberg, Michael (Director)
  Class (Growing Pains) 1987,Je 24,C,18:4
Kincaid, Tim (Producer)
  Enemy Territory 1987,My 22,C,7:1
Kinchev, Konstantin
  Burglar, The 1988,Ag 17,C,22:1
King, Alan
  You Talkin' to Me? 1987,S 25,C,14:1
  Memories of Me 1988,S 28,C,23:1
King, Alan (Producer)
  Memories of Me 1988,S 28,C,23:1
King, Carole
  Russkies 1987,N 6,C,12:3
King, Don
  Heaven 1987,Ap 17,C,8:5
King, Don (Composer)
  Kiss Daddy Good Night 1988,My 20,C,11:1
King, Erik
  Street Smart 1987,Mr 27,C,8:1
King, Jan (Composer)
  Invisible Kid, The 1988,Mr 31,C,16:4
King, Joel (Cinematographer)
  Club Life 1987,Ap 3,C,9:1
King, Pascal
  Gothic 1987,Ap 10,C,16:3
King, Rick (Director)
  Killing Time, The 1987,O 23,C,14:3
King, Stephen
  Creepshow 2 1987,My 4,C,17:1
King, Stephen (Original Author)
  Creepshow 2 1987,My 4,C,17:1
  Running Man, The 1987,N 13,C,10:5
King, Zalman (Director)
  Two Moon Junction 1988,Ap 30,17:1

L

Mannequin 1987,F 13,C,8:6
Burglar 1987,Mr 20,C,10:4
Levels, Calvin
Adventures in Baby-Sitting 1987,Jl 1,C,24:3
Levesque, Michael (Miscellaneous)
Plain Clothes 1988,Ap 16,18:1
Permanent Record 1988,Ap 22,C,10:1
Levin, G Roy
House of Games 1987,O 11,94:1
Levin, Pavlik
Commissar 1988,Je 17,C,16:4
Levin, Rachel
Gaby—A True Story 1987,O 30,C,10:4
Gaby—A True Story 1987,N 8,II,25:1
Levin, Sidney (Miscellaneous)
Nuts 1987,N 20,C,16:6
Clara's Heart 1988,O 7,C,16:5
Levin, Sy (Producer)
Flowers in the Attic 1987,N 21,12:5
Levine, Floyd
Braddock: Missing in Action III 1988,Ja 22,C,9:1
Levine, Jerry
Casual Sex? 1988,Ap 22,C,24:1
Levine, Robert
Dominick and Eugene 1988,Mr 18,C,20:1
Levine, Ted
Betrayed 1988,Ag 26,C,16:1
Levinson, Art (Producer)
Mannequin 1987,F 13,C,8:6
Levinson, Barry (Director)
Tin Men 1987,Mr 6,C,3:1
Tin Men 1987,Ap 12,II,17:1
Good Morning, Vietnam 1987,D 23,C,11:1
Good Morning, Vietnam 1988,Ja 10,II,21:1
Rain Man 1988,D 16,C,12:5
Levinson, Barry (Screenwriter)
Tin Men 1987,Mr 6,C,3:1
Tin Men 1987,Ap 12,II,17:1
Levinson, Larry (Miscellaneous)
Braddock: Missing in Action III 1988,Ja 22,C,9:1
Levinson, Mark (Producer)
Russkies 1987,N 6,C,12:3
Mystic Pizza 1988,O 21,C,20:6
Levry, Carmen
Faces of Women 1987,F 13,C,22:1
Levy, David (Producer)
Monster in the Closet 1987,My 15,C,9:1
Levy, Franklin R (Producer)
My Stepmother Is an Alien 1988,D 9,C,17:1
Levy, Marty
Slamdance 1987,N 6,C,10:5
Levy, Michael I (Producer)
Gardens of Stone 1987,My 8,C,32:1
Masquerade 1988,Mr 11,C,8:5
Levy, Robert L (Producer)
Killing Time, The 1987,O 23,C,14:3
Levy, Sandra (Producer)
High Tide 1988,F 19,C,5:1
Levy, Shawn
Wild Thing 1987,Ap 17,C,13:1
Lewis, David (Cinematographer)
Night of the Demons 1988,N 24,C,16:4
Lewis, Elbert
Square Dance 1987,F 20,C,4:5
Lewis, Fiona
Innerspace 1987,Jl 1,C,17:1
Lewis, Huey
Oliver and Company 1988,N 27,II,13:1
Lewis, Jerry Lee
Chuck Berry: Hail! Hail! Rock 'n' Roll 1987,O 3,10:5
Lewis, Mark (Director)
Cane Toads: An Unnatural History 1988,Mr 21,C,15:1
Cane Toads: An Unnatural History 1988,Mr 27,II,29:1
Cane Toads: An Unnatural History 1988,S 30,C,19:1
Lewis, Mark (Screenwriter)
Cane Toads: An Unnatural History 1988,Mr 21,C,15:1
Lewis, Richard
Wrong Guys, The 1988,Je 4,12:3
Lewis, Robert
Hello Again 1987,N 6,C,21:1
Lewitt, Elliott (Producer)
Zelly and Me 1988,Ap 15,C,4:4
Lezcano, Mercedes
House of Bernarda Alba, The (Casa de Bernarda Alba, La) 1988,D 16,C,14:6
Lhomme, Pierre (Cinematographer)
Maurice 1987,S 18,C,18:5
Liau Ching-sown (Miscellaneous)
Daughter of the Nile 1988,S 30,C,8:4
Libertini, Richard
Betrayed 1988,Ag 26,C,16:1

Libowitzky, Herwig (Miscellaneous)
38: Vienna Before the Fall 1988,My 6,C,17:1
Licht, Andrew (Producer)
License to Drive 1988,Jl 6,C,17:1
Lichtenberg, Nic (Director)
Karen Blixen 1987,Ap 15,C,22:1
Liddell, Bobby (Screenwriter)
Enemy Territory 1987,My 22,C,7:1
Liddle, Alice (Screenwriter)
Permanent Record 1988,Ap 22,C,10:1
Liddle, George (Miscellaneous)
Cry in the Dark, A 1988,N 11,C,6:4
Liden, Anki
My Life as a Dog 1987,Mr 24,C,14:3
My Life as a Dog 1987,My 1,C,16:1
Li Dien Lang
Last Emperor, The 1988,O 14,C,8:5
Li Dien Xing
Last Emperor, The 1988,O 14,C,8:5
Lieber, Ed (Composer)
Anita—Dances of Vice 1987,O 3,15:1
Lieberson, Sandy (Producer)
Rita, Sue and Bob Too 1987,Jl 17,C,18:1
Stars and Bars 1988,Mr 18,C,3:1
Liegens, Alfred
In a Jazz Way: A Portrait of Mura Dehn 1987,D 16,22:5
Lier, Johanna
Alpine Fire 1987,F 20,C,20:1
Li Han Hsiang (Director)
Last Emperor, The 1988,O 14,C,8:5
Li Han Hsiang (Screenwriter)
Last Emperor, The 1988,O 14,C,8:5
Lillie, Ronald (Producer)
Loyalties 1987,Mr 21,14:3
Loyalties 1987,N 20,C,21:1
Lim, Kay Tong
Off Limits 1988,Mr 11,C,8:5
Lima, Noel (Miscellaneous)
Vampires in Havana 1987,Ag 5,C,23:1
Lima, Valdemar (Cinematographer)
Barravento (Turning Wind, The) 1987,F 20,C,5:1
Limpach, H (Screenwriter)
Anita—Dances of Vice 1987,O 3,15:1
Lin, Bridget
Jackie Chan's Police Story 1987,S 26,12:3
Lin, Traci
Tiger's Tale, A 1988,F 12,C,9:1
Lincoln, Lar Park
House II: The Second Story 1987,Ag 29,11:1
Friday the 13th, Part VII—The New Blood 1988,My 15,56:5
Linda, Boguslaw
Woman Alone, A 1987,Mr 15,61:1
Linden, Hal
New Life, A 1988,Mr 25,C,5:2
Linder, Cec
Honeymoon 1987,N 20,C,24:1
Linder, George (Producer)
Running Man, The 1987,N 13,C,10:5
Linder, Maud (Director)
Man in the Silk Hat, The 1988,Ap 1,C,10:5
Linder, Maud (Narrator)
Man in the Silk Hat, The 1988,Ap 1,C,10:5
Linder, Maud (Producer)
Man in the Silk Hat, The 1988,Ap 1,C,10:5
Linder, Maud (Screenwriter)
Man in the Silk Hat, The 1988,Ap 1,C,10:5
Linder, Max
Man in the Silk Hat, The 1988,Ap 1,C,10:5
Linder, Stu (Miscellaneous)
Tin Men 1987,Mr 6,C,3:1
Good Morning, Vietnam 1987,D 23,C,11:1
Rain Man 1988,D 16,C,12:5
Lindfors, Viveca
Unfinished Business 1987,My 29,C,8:4
Lindfors, Viveca (Director)
Unfinished Business 1987,My 29,C,8:4
Lindfors, Viveca (Screenwriter)
Unfinished Business 1987,My 29,C,8:4
Lindh, Bjorn Json (Composer)
Mozart Brothers, The 1987,S 18,C,21:1
Lindley, John (Cinematographer)
Stepfather, The 1987,My 8,C,9:1
In the Mood 1987,S 16,C,27:1
Serpent and the Rainbow, The 1988,F 5,C,3:4
Shakedown 1988,My 6,C,20:1
Lindon, Vincent
Man in Love, A 1987,Jl 31,C,10:6
Lindren, Astrid (Original Author)
New Adventures of Pippi Longstocking, The 1988,Jl 29,C,11

Lindsay, Arto (Composer)
Kiss Daddy Good Night 1988,My 20,C,11:1
Lindsay, Helen
Playing Away 1987,Mr 13,C,19:1
Playing Away 1988,Ap 1,C,4:4
Line, Helga
Law of Desire 1987,Mr 27,C,15:1
Ling, Barbara (Miscellaneous)
Making Mr Right 1987,Ap 10,C,16:5
Less Than Zero 1987,N 6,C,23:1
Ling, Barbara Yu
Ping Pong 1987,Jl 17,C,10:6
Lin Ju (Miscellaneous)
Daughter of the Nile 1988,S 30,C,8:4
Link, John F (Miscellaneous)
Predator 1987,Je 12,C,6:4
Die Hard 1988,Jl 15,C,14:5
Linke, Paul
Daddy's Boys 1988,Je 10,C,13:1
Linn, Michael (Composer)
Allan Quatermain and the Lost City of Gold 1987,Ja 31,14:5
Linnman, Susanne (Miscellaneous)
My Life as a Dog 1987,Mr 24,C,14:3
My Life as a Dog 1987,My 1,C,16:1
Linson, Art (Producer)
Untouchables, The 1987,Je 3,C,17:1
Scrooged 1988,N 23,C,16:5
Linthorst, Kees (Miscellaneous)
Assault, The 1987,F 6,C,8:1
Liotard, Therese
Boy from Calabria, A 1987,N 20,C,21:1
Liotta, Ray
Dominick and Eugene 1988,Mr 18,C,20:1
Dominick and Eugene 1988,Ap 3,II,26:5
Lipinski, Eugene
Riders of the Storm 1988,My 7,12:3
Lipp, Jeremy (Screenwriter)
Duet for One 1987,F 13,C,10:4
Lippin, Renee
Radio Days 1987,Ja 30,C,1:1
Lippman, Jane (Director)
Rights and Reactions: Lesbian and Gay Rights on Trial 1988,Je 15,C,19:3
Lippman, Jane (Miscellaneous)
Rights and Reactions: Lesbian and Gay Rights on Trial 1988,Je 15,C,19:3
Lippman, Jane (Producer)
Rights and Reactions: Lesbian and Gay Rights on Trial 1988,Je 15,C,19:3
Lipsius, Dhani (Miscellaneous)
Halloween 4: The Return of Michael Myers 1988,O 22,12:4
Lipson, Mark (Producer)
Thin Blue Line, The 1988,Ag 26,C,6:1
Lisberger, Steven (Director)
Hot Pursuit 1987,My 11,C,14:5
Lisberger, Steven (Miscellaneous)
Hot Pursuit 1987,My 11,C,14:5
Lisberger, Steven (Screenwriter)
Hot Pursuit 1987,My 11,C,14:5
Li Shin Yu (Miscellaneous)
Sleepwalk 1987,Mr 20,C,15:1
Sleepwalk 1987,Jl 3,C,5:1
Li Shu Xian (Original Author)
Last Emperor, The 1988,O 14,C,8:5
Lispector, Clarice (Original Author)
Hour of the Star, The 1987,Ja 21,C,22:1
Lissek, Leon
Personal Services 1987,My 15,C,4:5
Lister, Tom (Tiny), Jr
Prison 1988,Mr 4,C,33:1
Lithgow, John
Harry and the Hendersons 1987,Je 5,C,14:5
Distant Thunder 1988,N 11,C,13:1
Li Tien-lu
Daughter of the Nile 1988,S 30,C,8:4
Little, Dwight H (Director)
Halloween 4: The Return of Michael Myers 1988,O 22,12:4
Little, Michelle
My Demon Lover 1987,Ap 24,C,14:1
Little, Russ (Composer)
Too Outrageous 1987,O 16,C,12:1
Little Richard
Chuck Berry: Hail! Hail! Rock 'n' Roll 1987,O 3,10:5
Littleton, Carol (Miscellaneous)
Swimming to Cambodia 1987,Mr 13,C,8:1
Vibes 1988,Ag 5,C,6:1
Accidental Tourist, The 1988,D 23,C,12:5
Littlewood, Joan
Hungry Feeling, A: The Life and Death of Brendan Behan 1988,Ap 28,C,20:3

M

Martin, Peter (Composer)
Hope and Glory 1987,O 9,C,23:1
Martin, Remi
Family Business 1987,S 6,66:2
Martin, Sandy
Barfly 1987,S 30,C,18:1
Martin, Steve
Roxanne 1987,Je 19,C,3:4
Planes, Trains and Automobiles 1987,N 25,C,19:1
Dirty Rotten Scoundrels 1988,D 14,C,21:4
Martin, Steve (Screenwriter)
Roxanne 1987,Je 19,C,3:4
Martin, Susan (Miscellaneous)
Winter Tan, A 1988,O 2,57:6
Martin, Troy Kennedy (Screenwriter)
Red Heat 1988,Je 17,C,14:5
Martin, Vera
Loyalties 1987,Mr 21,14:3
Loyalties 1987,N 20,C,21:1
Martin, Vincent
Field of Honor (Champ d'Honneur) 1988,Mr 18,C,24:5
Martin, William E (Screenwriter)
Harry and the Hendersons 1987,Je 5,C,14:5
Martinez, Alcides
Nobody Listened 1988,D 2,C,14:6
Martinez, Nacho
Tasio 1987,Mr 27,C,15:1
Law of Desire 1987,Mr 27,C,15:1
Half of Heaven 1988,Ja 21,C,24:3
Matador 1988,S 16,C,8:5
Martini, Richard (Director)
You Can't Hurry Love 1988,Ja 29,C,11:1
Martini, Richard (Miscellaneous)
Three for the Road 1987,Ap 10,C,5:1
Martini, Richard (Screenwriter)
Three for the Road 1987,Ap 10,C,5:1
You Can't Hurry Love 1988,Ja 29,C,11:1
Marx, Sue (Director)
Young in Heart 1987,O 8,C,37:1
Masciari, Eugenio
Mass Is Ended, The 1988,My 6,C,18:6
Mascolo, Dionys
Mes Petites Amoureuses 1987,Ja 30,C,16:1
Mascolo, Joe
Heat 1987,Mr 13,C,33:1
Maslansky, Paul (Producer)
Police Academy 4: Citizens on Patrol 1987,Ap 4,12:5
Police Academy 5: Assignment Miami Beach 1988,Mr 19,13:3
Maslon, Jimmy (Producer)
Blood Diner 1987,S 4,C,6:5
Mason, Jackie
Caddyshack II 1988,Jl 23,16:5
Mason, Nick (Composer)
White of the Eye 1988,My 20,C,22:5
Mason, Paul (Producer)
Wild Pair, The 1987,D 12,19:1
Mason, Steve (Cinematographer)
Tale of Ruby Rose, The 1988,My 25,C,18:6
Mason, Thomas Boyd
In a Shallow Grave 1988,My 6,C,21:1
Masrevery, Jean
Boy from Calabria, A 1987,N 20,C,21:1
Massenet, Jules (Composer)
Sarah 1988,S 25,64:1
Masters, Ben
Making Mr Right 1987,Ap 10,C,16:5
Masters, John (Original Author)
Deceivers, The 1988,S 2,C,10:1
Masters, Tony (Miscellaneous)
Rent-a-Cop 1988,Ja 15,C,13:1
Masterson, Mary Stuart
Some Kind of Wonderful 1987,F 27,C,17:3
Some Kind of Wonderful 1987,Mr 15,II,21:1
Gardens of Stone 1987,My 8,C,32:1
Mr North 1988,Jl 22,C,8:4
Masterson, Peter
Gardens of Stone 1987,My 8,C,32:1
Masterson, Peter (Director)
Full Moon in Blue Water 1988,N 23,C,15:1
Mastrantonio, Mary Elizabeth
Slamdance 1987,N 6,C,10:5
Mastroianni, Marcello
Dark Eyes 1987,S 25,C,26:5
Dark Eyes 1987,O 4,II,23:1
Traffic Jam 1988,Mr 4,C,14:6
Two Lives of Mattia Pascal, The 1988,Mr 18,C,8:5
Mastroianni, Ruggero (Miscellaneous)
Two Lives of Mattia Pascal, The 1988,Mr 18,C,8:5
Berlin Affair, The 1988,Jl 15,C,12:5

Mastropasqua, Corrado
Night Zoo 1988,Mr 30,C,20:5
Mastrosimone, William (Original Author)
Beast, The 1988,S 16,C,13:1
Mastrosimone, William (Screenwriter)
Beast, The 1988,S 16,C,13:1
Masur, Richard
Believers, The 1987,Je 10,C,22:5
Walker 1987,D 4,C,36:1
Rent-a-Cop 1988,Ja 15,C,13:1
Shoot to Kill 1988,F 12,C,8:5
License to Drive 1988,Jl 6,C,17:1
Matheron, Marie
Grand Highway, The 1988,Ja 22,C,17:1
Mathers, James
Aria 1988,My 21,54:3
Matheson, Richard Christian (Screenwriter)
Three O'Clock High 1987,O 9,C,16:3
Mathews, Thom
Return of the Living Dead Part II 1988,Ja 15,C,11:1
Mathias, Harry (Cinematographer)
Ernest Goes to Camp 1987,My 23,15:4
Matlin, Marlee
Walker 1987,D 4,C,36:1
Matos, Huber
Nobody Listened 1988,D 2,C,14:6
Matson, Sasha (Composer)
Daddy's Boys 1988,Je 10,C,13:1
Matsuda, Yusaku
Sorekara (And Then) 1987,Ap 8,C,23:1
Matsui, Yasuko
Profound Desire of the Gods, The 1988,My 6,C,10:1
Mattausch, Dietrich
Wannsee Conference, The 1987,N 18,C,29:3
Matter, Herbert (Cinematographer)
Spirit Moves, The: A History of Black Social Dance on Film 1987,D 16,C,22:5
Mattes, Eva
Felix 1988,S 24,13:1
Matteson, Pam
Million Dollar Mystery 1987,Je 12,C,6:4
Matthau, Walter
Couch Trip, The 1988,Ja 15,C,8:1
Matthews, Al
Riders of the Storm 1988,My 7,12:3
Matthews, Bill (Miscellaneous)
Caddyshack II 1988,Jl 23,16:5
Matthews, Sue
Living on Tokyo Time 1987,Ag 14,C,20:1
Matthews, William F (Miscellaneous)
Three O'Clock High 1987,O 9,C,16:3
Hot to Trot 1988,Ag 27,11:3
Mattick, Michael
Summer Heat 1987,My 29,C,8:4
Mattsson, Arne (Director)
Girl, The 1987,Ag 7,C,10:6
Mattsson, Arne (Producer)
Girl, The 1987,Ag 7,C,10:6
Matula, Jerzy (Composer)
Great Race, The 1988,Mr 12,19:1
Matz, Peter (Miscellaneous)
Torch Song Trilogy 1988,D 14,C,19:1
Mauch, Thomas (Cinematographer)
Deadline 1987,S 11,C,4:4
Mauffroy, Olivier (Miscellaneous)
Big Blue, The 1988,Ag 20,11:4
Maura, Carmen
Law of Desire 1987,Mr 27,C,15:1
Dark Habits 1988,My 6,C,28:5
Matador 1988,S 16,C,8:5
Women on the Verge of a Nervous Breakdown 1988,S 23,C,25:1
Women on the Verge of a Nervous Breakdown 1988,N 11,C,16:1
Maureen, Mollie
Little Dorrit 1988,Mr 26,11:1
Maus, Rodger (Miscellaneous)
Sunset 1988,Ap 29,C,13:1
Maximowna, Ita
Theater in Ruins 1987,Je 5,C,10:4
Maxwell, Richard (Screenwriter)
Serpent and the Rainbow, The 1988,F 5,C,3:4
May, Bradford (Cinematographer)
Monster Squad 1987,Ag 14,C,15:1
May, Brian (Composer)
Death Before Dishonor 1987,F 20,C,10:1
Steel Dawn 1987,N 6,C,33:1
May, Elaine (Director)
Ishtar 1987,My 15,C,3:1
Ishtar 1987,Je 7,II,24:1

May, Elaine (Miscellaneous)
Ishtar 1987,My 15,C,3:1
May, Elaine (Screenwriter)
Ishtar 1987,My 15,C,3:1
May, Jim (Cinematographer)
Ernest Goes to Camp 1987,My 23,15:4
May, Jodhi
World Apart, A 1988,Je 17,C,10:4
Maybury, John (Miscellaneous)
Last of England, The 1988,S 28,C,18:3
Mayer, Frederic
Field of Honor (Champ d'Honneur) 1988,Mr 18,C,24:5
Mayersberg, Paul (Director)
Captive 1987,Ap 3,C,8:1
Mayersberg, Paul (Screenwriter)
Captive 1987,Ap 3,C,8:1
Mayer-Woppermann, Katharina (Miscellaneous)
Dragon Chow 1988,My 27,C,10:5
Maynard, Doug (Composer)
Patti Rocks 1988,Ja 15,C,12:1
Mayron, Melanie
Sticky Fingers 1988,My 6,C,28:5
Sticky Fingers 1988,My 15,II,27:1
Mayron, Melanie (Producer)
Sticky Fingers 1988,My 6,C,28:5
Mayron, Melanie (Screenwriter)
Sticky Fingers 1988,My 6,C,28:5
Sticky Fingers 1988,My 15,II,27:1
Maysles, Albert (Cinematographer)
Horowitz Plays Mozart 1987,O 8,C,37:1
Islands 1987,O 16,C,26:4
Maysles, Albert (Director)
Horowitz Plays Mozart 1987,O 8,C,37:1
Islands 1987,O 16,C,26:4
Maysles, David (Cinematographer)
Islands 1987,O 16,C,26:4
Maysles, David (Director)
Islands 1987,O 16,C,26:4
Mayuzumi, Toshiro (Composer)
Pornographers, The 1987,My 22,C,10:5
Profound Desire of the Gods, The 1988,My 6,C,10:1
Maza, Bob
Fringe Dwellers, The 1987,Ja 23,C,13:3
Ground Zero 1988,S 23,C,18:1
Mazurowna, Ernestine
Jean de Florette 1987,Je 26,C,3:1
Mazursky, Paul
Moon over Parador 1988,S 9,C,13:1
Punchline 1988,S 30,C,14:4
Mazursky, Paul (Director)
Moon over Parador 1988,S 9,C,13:1
Mazursky, Paul (Producer)
Moon over Parador 1988,S 9,C,13:1
Mazursky, Paul (Screenwriter)
Moon over Parador 1988,S 9,C,13:1
Mazzoni, Roberta (Screenwriter)
Berlin Affair, The 1988,Jl 15,C,12:5
Mead, Abigail (Composer)
Full Metal Jacket 1987,Je 26,C,3:1
Meat Loaf
Squeeze, The 1987,Jl 10,C,24:1
Medina, Ofelia
Frida 1988,F 17,C,18:5
Medjuck, Joe (Producer)
Big Shots 1987,O 2,C,17:1
Medoff, Mark (Screenwriter)
Clara's Heart 1988,O 7,C,16:5
Meehan, Thomas (Screenwriter)
Spaceballs 1987,Je 24,C,23:1
Meerson, Steve (Screenwriter)
Back to the Beach 1987,Ag 8,16:5
Meffre, Armand
Jean de Florette 1987,Je 26,C,3:1
Manon of the Spring 1987,N 6,C,25:1
Megino, Luis (Producer)
Half of Heaven 1988,Ja 21,C,24:3
Megino, Luis (Screenwriter)
Half of Heaven 1988,Ja 21,C,24:3
Meheux, Phil (Cinematographer)
Fourth Protocol, The 1987,Ag 28,C,19:1
Mehl, Leo (Producer)
Debajo del Mundo (Under the World) 1988,O 5,C,19:5
Mehlman, Gary (Producer)
New Adventures of Pippi Longstocking, The 1988,Jl 29,C,11
Meillon, John
Crocodile Dundee II 1988,My 25,C,15:3
Mejia, Gerardo
Colors 1988,Ap 15,C,4:1
Melamed, Fred
Suspect 1987,O 23,C,14:3

Patty Hearst 1988,S 23,C,8:5
Miller, Penelope Ann
Adventures in Baby-Sitting 1987,Jl 1,C,24:3
Biloxi Blues 1988,Mr 25,C,1:1
Big Top Pee-wee 1988,Jl 22,C,10:3
Miles from Home 1988,S 16,C,8:4
Miller, Shawn
Seven Hours to Judgement 1988,S 17,12:5
Miller, Stephen E
Stepfather, The 1987,My 8,C,9:1
Home Is Where the Hart Is 1987,D 5,14:4
Miller, Sue (Original Author)
Good Mother, The 1988,N 4,C,15:1
Good Mother, The 1988,N 20,II,13:1
Miller, Susan (Screenwriter)
Lady Beware 1987,S 18,C,23:1
Miller, Ty
Slaughterhouse Rock 1988,My 22,49:5
Millette, Jean-Louis
Blind Trust 1987,N 7,13:1
Milliken, Sue (Producer)
Fringe Dwellers, The 1987,Ja 23,C,13:3
Millo, Mario (Composer)
Shame 1988,Mr 19,10:3
Lighthorsemen, The 1988,My 13,C,14:1
Mills, Alec (Cinematographer)
Living Daylights, The 1987,Jl 31,C,3:5
Mills, Hayley
Appointment with Death 1988,Ap 15,C,4:5
Mills, John
Who's That Girl 1987,Ag 8,16:1
When the Wind Blows 1988,Mr 11,C,19:1
Milo (Miscellaneous)
Stand and Deliver 1988,Mr 18,C,14:1
Milsome, Douglas (Cinematographer)
Full Metal Jacket 1987,Je 26,C,3:1
Beast, The 1988,S 16,C,13:1
Miluwi, John Omirah
Gorillas in the Mist 1988,S 23,C,19:1
Minch, Michelle (Miscellaneous)
Two Moon Junction 1988,Ap 30,17:1
Minchenberg, Richard
Wisdom 1987,Ja 1,9:5
Miner, Michael (Screenwriter)
Robocop 1987,Jl 17,C,10:1
Robocop 1987,Ag 2,II,23:5
Minervini, Gianni (Producer)
Summer Night with Greek Profile, Almond Eyes and Scent of
Basil 1987,Je 19,C,12:6
Minh, Ho Quang (Director)
Karma 1987,Jl 8,C,22:5
Minh, Ho Quang (Screenwriter)
Karma 1987,Jl 8,C,22:5
Minion, Joe (Director)
Daddy's Boys 1988,Je 10,C,13:1
Minnelli, Liza
Rent-a-Cop 1988,Ja 15,C,13:1
Arthur 2 on the Rocks 1988,Jl 8,C,8:1
Minoff, Marvin (Producer)
Dominick and Eugene 1988,Mr 18,C,20:1
Minott, Sugar
Cool Running: The Reggae Movie 1988,Ap 22,C,36:5
Minsker, Andy
Broken Noses 1987,N 4,C,28:5
Mintz, Larry
Burglar 1987,Mr 20,C,10:4
Mioteris, Nikos
Tree We Hurt, The 1988,Ja 29,C,11:1
Miou Miou
Traffic Jam 1988,Mr 4,C,14:6
Miqueau, Marie-Catherine (Miscellaneous)
Yeelen 1987,O 8,C,37:1
Mirkovich, Steve (Miscellaneous)
Death Before Dishonor 1987,F 20,C,10:1
Prince of Darkness 1987,O 23,C,26:1
Deadly Illusion 1987,O 31,10:5
Mironov, Andrei
My Friend Ivan Lapshin 1987,Mr 24,C,14:5
Mironov, Valery (Cinematographer)
Burglar, The 1988,Ag 17,C,22:1
Mironova, Olga
Come and See 1987,F 6,C,4:4
Mirren, Helen
Gospel According to Vic 1987,Mr 13,C,13:1
Pascali's Island 1988,Jl 22,C,16:4
Mishima, Yoshiharu (Producer)
Where Spring Comes Late 1988,N 18,C,8:4
Miski, Giselle (Miscellaneous)
Faces of Women 1987,F 13,C,22:1
Misrachi, Paul (Composer)
Ambiciosos, Los (Ambitious Ones, The) 1988,F 12,C,13:1

Mitchell, Donna
Less Than Zero 1987,N 6,C,23:1
Mitchell, Doug (Producer)
Year My Voice Broke, The 1988,Ag 25,C,18:1
Mitchell, James (Miscellaneous)
Monster Squad 1987,Ag 14,C,15:1
Presidio, The 1988,Je 10,C,15:1
Mitchell, Jennifer Lee
Kiss Daddy Good Night 1988,My 20,C,11:1
Mitchell, John
Gospel According to Vic 1987,Mr 13,C,13:1
Mitchell, Ruth
Little Dorrit 1988,Mr 26,11:1
Mitchell, Sasha
Death Before Dishonor 1987,F 20,C,10:1
Spike of Bensonhurst 1988,N 11,C,15:1
Spike of Bensonhurst 1988,D 4,II,15:5
Mitchell, Sollace (Director)
Call Me 1988,My 20,C,11:1
Mitchell, Willie
Gospel According to Al Green 1987,S 9,C,18:5
Mitchum, Robert
Broken Noses 1987,N 4,C,28:5
Mr North 1988,Jl 22,C,8:4
Scrooged 1988,N 23,C,16:5
Mittleman, Steve
Roxanne 1987,Je 19,C,3:4
Miura, Kazuyoshi
Comic Magazine (Komikku Zasshi) 1987,Ja 16,C,14:6
Miyagawa, Kazuo (Cinematographer)
Love Suicides at Sonezaki, The 1988,Jl 13,C,22:1
Gonza the Spearman 1988,O 28,C,15:1
Miyamoto, Nobuko
Tampopo 1987,Mr 26,C,21:1
Tampopo 1987,My 22,C,17:1
Taxing Woman, A 1987,S 26,9:1
Funeral, The 1987,O 23,C,14:3
Taxing Woman, A 1988,My 13,C,14:3
Miyamoto, Teru (Original Author)
River of Fireflies 1988,N 4,C,13:1
Miyauchi, Fukiko (Screenwriter)
Promise, A 1987,Mr 17,C,14:4
Mizushima, Kaori
Gonza the Spearman 1988,O 28,C,15:1
Modine, Matthew
Full Metal Jacket 1987,Je 26,C,3:1
Full Metal Jacket 1987,Jl 5,II,17:5
Orphans 1987,S 18,C,3:1
Orphans 1987,O 4,II,23:1
Married to the Mob 1988,Ag 19,C,6:1
Modugno, Enrica Maria
Mass Is Ended, The 1988,My 6,C,18:6
Moeller, J David
Square Dance 1987,F 20,C,4:5
Moffat, Donald
Monster in the Closet 1987,My 15,C,9:1
Far North 1988,N 9,C,18:5
Moffett, D W
Black Widow 1987,F 6,C,3:1
Moffiatt, Mary (Composer)
High Tide 1988,F 19,C,5:1
Mogotlane, Thomas
Mapantsula 1988,S 24,12:4
Mogotlane, Thomas (Screenwriter)
Mapantsula 1988,S 24,12:4
Mokae, Zakes
Cry Freedom 1987,N 6,C,14:3
Serpent and the Rainbow, The 1988,F 5,C,3:4
Mokri, Amir (Cinematographer)
Slamdance 1987,N 6,C,10:5
Molen, Jerry
Rain Man 1988,D 16,C,12:5
Molin, Bud (Miscellaneous)
Summer School 1987,Jl 22,C,22:1
Molina, Alfred
Prick Up Your Ears 1987,Ap 17,C,17:1
Molina, Angela
Half of Heaven 1988,Ja 21,C,24:3
Traffic Jam 1988,Mr 4,C,14:6
Molina, Dan (Miscellaneous)
Land Before Time, The 1988,N 18,C,8:4
Molina, Miguel
Law of Desire 1987,Mr 27,C,15:1
Molina, Monica
Half of Heaven 1988,Ja 21,C,24:3
Molinero, Juana
Penitent, The 1988,My 27,C,13:1
Mollin, Fred (Composer)
Friday the 13th, Part VII—The New Blood 1988,My 15,56:5

Mollinger, Ursula (Miscellaneous)
Wannsee Conference, The 1987,N 18,C,29:3
Mollo, Andrew (Miscellaneous)
Pascali's Island 1988,Jl 22,C,16:4
Mommertz, Paul (Screenwriter)
Wannsee Conference, The 1987,N 18,C,29:3
Monahan, Dan
From the Hip 1987,F 6,C,10:4
Mondshein, Andrew (Miscellaneous)
Making Mr Right 1987,Ap 10,C,16:5
Running on Empty 1988,S 9,C,6:5
Mones, Paul (Director)
Beat, The 1988,Je 3,C,10:6
Mones, Paul (Screenwriter)
Beat, The 1988,Je 3,C,10:6
Monette, Richard
I've Heard the Mermaids Singing 1987,S 11,C,8:1
Hello Mary Lou 1987,O 17,16:5
Monge, Ray
Mala Noche 1988,My 4,C,20:5
Monicelli, Mario (Director)
Two Lives of Mattia Pascal, The 1988,Mr 18,C,8:5
Monicelli, Mario (Screenwriter)
Two Lives of Mattia Pascal, The 1988,Mr 18,C,8:5
Monje Berbel, Jose Ma
Night of the Pencils, The 1987,Mr 14,13:1
Monori, Lili
Singing on the Treadmill 1987,Jl 31,C,11:1
Monoson, Lawrence
Gaby—A True Story 1987,O 30,C,10:4
Monsigny, Jean (Cinematographer)
Choice, The 1988,Mr 24,C,26:6
Montague, Lee
Madame Sousatzka 1988,O 14,C,8:5
Montalban, Ricardo
Naked Gun, The 1988,D 2,C,16:1
Montand, Yves
Jean de Florette 1987,Je 26,C,3:1
Manon of the Spring 1987,N 6,C,25:1
Monteiro, Joao Cesar
Doc's Kingdom 1988,S 9,C,10:3
Monteleone, Enzo (Screenwriter)
Hotel Colonial 1987,S 19,16:3
Montenegro, Fernanda
Hour of the Star, The 1987,Ja 21,C,22:1
Montero, Germaine
Sur, El (South, The) 1988,Ja 15,C,11:1
Montesinos, Guillermo
Women on the Verge of a Nervous Breakdown 1988,S
23,C,25:1
Montezuma, Magdalena
Rose King, The 1987,D 30,C,10:5
Montezuma, Magdalena (Screenwriter)
Rose King, The 1987,D 30,C,10:5
Montgomery, Elizabeth (Narrator)
Coverup: Behind the Iran-Contra Affair 1988,Ag 26,C,8:6
Montgomery, Julia
Kindred, The 1987,Ja 10,13:1
South of Reno 1988,Je 3,C,15:1
Montgomery, Lee
Into the Fire 1988,O 29,18:5
Montocchio, Max (Producer)
Mapantsula 1988,S 24,12:4
Mooney, Paul
Hollywood Shuffle 1987,Mr 20,C,8:1
Moonjean, Hank (Producer)
Stealing Home 1988,Ag 26,C,17:4
Dangerous Liaisons 1988,D 21,C,22:1
Moore, Brian (Original Author)
Lonely Passion of Judith Hearne, The 1987,D 23,C,15:1
Moore, Demi
Wisdom 1987,Ja 1,9:5
Seventh Sign, The 1988,Ap 1,C,20:3
Moore, Dudley
Like Father Like Son 1987,O 2,C,8:5
Arthur 2 on the Rocks 1988,Jl 8,C,8:1
Moore, Frank
Mondo New York 1988,Ap 22,C,23:1
Moore, Frank (Director)
Beehive 1988,D 7,C,24:5
Moore, Frank (Miscellaneous)
Beehive 1988,D 7,C,24:5
Moore, Juanita
Two Moon Junction 1988,Ap 30,17:1
Moore, Tim (Producer)
Jack's Back 1988,My 6,C,19:1
Moore, Tracey
Care Bears' Adventure in Wonderland, The 1987,Ag 7,C,21:1
Moore, Wesley (Screenwriter)
Apprentice to Murder 1988,F 26,C,14:1

Mundi, Coati
Who's That Girl 1987,Ag 8,16:1
Mundy, Meg
Fatal Attraction 1987,S 18,C,10:5
Munoz, Eunice
Hard Times 1988,O 6,C,29:1
Munro, Neil
John and the Missus 1987,O 24,17:1
Murai, Kunihiko (Composer)
Tampopo 1987,Mr 26,C,21:1
Tampopo 1987,My 22,C,17:1
Murakami, Jimmy T (Director)
When the Wind Blows 1988,Mr 11,C,19:1
Muraki, Shinobu (Miscellaneous)
Film Actress 1988,O 28,C,8:5
Murase, Sachiko
Promise, A 1987,Mr 17,C,14:4
Promise, A 1988,O 8,14:3
Murcell, George
Pascali's Island 1988,Jl 22,C,16:4
Murch, Walter (Miscellaneous)
Unbearable Lightness of Being, The 1988,F 5,C,8:5
Murcott, Derek
Eat and Run 1987,F 20,C,5:1
Murdock, Jack
Big Top Pee-wee 1988,Jl 22,C,10:3
Rain Man 1988,D 16,C,12:5
Murer, Fredi M (Director)
Alpine Fire 1987,F 20,C,20:1
Murer, Fredi M (Screenwriter)
Alpine Fire 1987,F 20,C,20:1
Murney, Christopher
Secret of My Success, The 1987,Ap 10,C,14:4
Muro, Jim (Director)
Street Trash 1987,S 16,C,27:3
Murota, Hideo
Taxing Woman, A 1987,S 26,9:1
Murphy, Eddie
Golden Child, The 1987,F 15,II,19:1
Beverly Hills Cop II 1987,My 20,C,28:1
Beverly Hills Cop II 1987,Je 7,II,24:1
Eddie Murphy Raw 1987,D 19,18:4
Raw 1988,Ja 10,II,21:1
Coming to America 1988,Je 29,C,20:5
Murphy, Eddie (Miscellaneous)
Beverly Hills Cop II 1987,My 20,C,28:1
Coming to America 1988,Je 29,C,20:5
Murphy, Eddie (Screenwriter)
Eddie Murphy Raw 1987,D 19,18:4
Murphy, Fred (Cinematographer)
Hoosiers 1987,F 27,C,10:3
Best Seller 1987,S 25,C,24:1
Dead, The 1987,D 17,C,19:4
Five Corners 1988,Ja 22,C,18:1
Fresh Horses 1988,N 19,15:3
Full Moon in Blue Water 1988,N 23,C,15:1
Murphy, Gary (Screenwriter)
Without a Clue 1988,O 21,C,21:1
Murphy, Roger (Cinematographer)
Andy Warhol 1987,Je 9,C,20:1
Murphy, Rosemary
September 1987,D 18,C,3:1
Murphy, Tab (Miscellaneous)
Gorillas in the Mist 1988,S 23,C,19:1
Murray, Bill
Scrooged 1988,N 23,C,16:5
Scrooged 1988,D 11,II,13:1
Murray, Don
Made in Heaven 1987,N 6,C,16:1
Murray, Forrest (Producer)
Five Corners 1988,Ja 22,C,18:1
Murray, Graeme (Miscellaneous)
Malone 1987,My 4,C,17:4
Murray-Leach, Roger (Miscellaneous)
Fish Called Wanda, A 1988,Jl 15,C,8:1
Murtaugh, James
Rosary Murders, The 1987,Ag 28,C,12:3
Musafar, Fakir
Dances Sacred and Profane 1987,Je 13,13:1
Musca, Tom (Miscellaneous)
Little Nikita 1988,Mr 18,C,26:5
Musca, Tom (Producer)
Stand and Deliver 1988,Mr 18,C,14:1
Musca, Tom (Screenwriter)
Stand and Deliver 1988,Mr 18,C,14:1
Musky, Jane (Miscellaneous)
Young Guns 1988,Ag 12,C,18:1
Patty Hearst 1988,S 23,C,8:5
Mutabaruka
Cool Running: The Reggae Movie 1988,Ap 22,C,36:5

Muto, John (Miscellaneous)
River's Edge 1987,My 8,C,28:4
Nightflyers 1987,O 24,17:1
Flowers in the Attic 1987,N 21,12:5
Heartbreak Hotel 1988,S 30,C,18:5
Muu, Tran Dinh (Cinematographer)
Karma 1987,Jl 8,C,22:5
Mvusi, Linda
World Apart, A 1988,Je 17,C,10:4
Mweze, Ngangura (Director)
Vie Est Belle, La 1987,N 18,C,21:1
Mweze, Ngangura (Screenwriter)
Vie Est Belle, La 1987,N 18,C,21:1
Myers, Stanley (Composer)
Prick Up Your Ears 1987,Ap 17,C,17:1
Second Victory, The 1987,My 27,C,22:3
Wish You Were Here 1987,Jl 24,C,7:2
Stars and Bars 1988,Mr 18,C,3:1
Absolution 1988,Jl 1,C,8:5
Track 29 1988,S 9,C,10:3
Boost, The 1988,D 23,C,16:6
Myerson, Alan (Director)
Police Academy 5: Assignment Miami Beach 1988,Mr 19,13:3
Myles, Bruce (Director)
Ground Zero 1988,S 23,C,18:1
Myles, Lynda (Producer)
Defense of the Realm 1987,Ja 16,C,6:5
Myrow, Fred (Composer)
Phantasm II 1988,Jl 8,C,11:1

N

Nabeshima, Jun (Miscellaneous)
Emperor's Naked Army Marches On, The 1988,Mr 15,C,15:1
Nagari, Benni (Composer)
I Don't Give a Damn 1988,My 20,C,22:5
Nahrebecka, Anna
Land of Promise 1988,F 5,C,13:6
Naidu, Ajay
Touch and Go 1987,Ja 14,C,20:5
Nair, Mira (Director)
Salaam Bombay! 1988,O 7,C,8:1
Nair, Mira (Miscellaneous)
Salaam Bombay! 1988,O 7,C,8:1
Nair, Mira (Producer)
Salaam Bombay! 1988,O 7,C,8:1
Naito, Akira (Miscellaneous)
Love Suicides at Sonezaki, The 1988,Jl 13,C,22:1
Nakagawa, Ken
Living on Tokyo Time 1987,Ag 14,C,20:1
Nakagawa, Scott
Aloha Summer 1988,F 26,C,8:1
Nakamura, Ganjiro
Pornographers, The 1987,My 22,C,10:5
Nakamura, Katsuo
Sorekara (And Then) 1987,Ap 8,C,23:1
Nakamura, Senjaku
Dark Hair 1987,Mr 22,62:1
Nakaoka, Kyohei (Screenwriter)
River of Fireflies 1988,N 4,C,13:1
Nance, Jack
Barfly 1987,S 30,C,18:1
Nankin, Michael (Screenwriter)
Russkies 1987,N 6,C,12:3
Napier, Eve
Crazy Moon 1988,F 8,C,18:5
Napolitano, Silvia (Miscellaneous)
Julia and Julia 1988,F 5,C,5:1
Napolitano, Silvia (Screenwriter)
Julia and Julia 1988,F 5,C,5:1
Naraoka, Tomoko
River of Fireflies 1988,N 4,C,13:1
Na Renhua
Girl from Hunan 1988,Mr 4,C,22:4
Narita, Hiro (Cinematographer)
No Man's Land 1987,O 23,C,10:5
Nasatir, Marcia (Producer)
Hamburger Hill 1987,Ag 28,C,16:5
Ironweed 1987,D 18,C,24:5
Nash, Chris
Satisfaction 1988,F 13,15:1
Nathan, James (Screenwriter)
Killing Time, The 1987,O 23,C,14:3
Natotti, Nelson (Screenwriter)
Color of Destiny, The 1988,Jl 22,C,17:1

Natroshvili, Levan
Ashik Kerib 1988,S 29,C,24:5
Natsume, Soseki (Original Author)
Sorekara (And Then) 1987,Ap 8,C,23:1
Natwick, Mildred
Dangerous Liaisons 1988,D 21,C,22:1
Naughton, James
Glass Menagerie, The 1987,O 23,C,14:3
Good Mother, The 1988,N 4,C,15:1
Nava, Gregory (Director)
Time of Destiny, A 1988,Ap 22,C,29:1
Nava, Gregory (Screenwriter)
Time of Destiny, A 1988,Ap 22,C,29:1
Navarro, Emile (Cinematographer)
Mix-Up 1987,Jl 24,C,12:6
Navarro, Liliana
City and the Dogs, The 1987,Ja 7,C,20:5
Nayyar, Harsh
Making Mr Right 1987,Ap 10,C,16:5
Neag, Maria (Miscellaneous)
Jacob 1988,O 3,C,24:4
Neame, Christopher
Steel Dawn 1987,N 6,C,33:1
DOA 1988,Mr 18,C,8:5
Neame, Christopher (Producer)
Bellman and True 1988,Ap 1,C,4:4
Neau, Andre (Cinematographer)
Waiting for the Moon 1987,Mr 6,C,14:5
Nebout, Claire
Scene of the Crime 1987,Ja 23,C,14:1
Nechayeva, Yevgeniya
Theme, The 1987,S 28,C,18:1
Nedaskovskaya, Raisa
Commissar 1988,Je 17,C,16:4
Nedd, Priscilla (Miscellaneous)
Street Smart 1987,Mr 27,C,8:1
Tucker: The Man and His Dream 1988,Ag 12,C,8:1
Needles, Nique
Dogs in Space 1987,O 9,C,7:1
Neeley, Ted (Composer)
Summer Camp Nightmare 1987,Ap 17,C,30:5
Neely, Gail
Million Dollar Mystery 1987,Je 12,C,6:4
Surf Nazis Must Die 1987,O 2,C,24:5
Neeson, Liam
Duet for One 1987,F 13,C,10:4
Prayer for the Dying, A 1987,S 11,C,11:1
Suspect 1987,O 23,C,14:3
Satisfaction 1988,F 13,15:1
Dead Pool 1988,Jl 13,C,22:1
Good Mother, The 1988,N 4,C,15:1
High Spirits 1988,N 18,C,10:1
Negret, Francois
Au Revoir les Enfants (Goodbye, Children) 1988,F 12,C,15:1
Negulesco, Julian
Jupon Rouge, Le (Manuela's Loves) 1988,Mr 21,C,17:1
Nehm, Kristina
Fringe Dwellers, The 1987,Ja 23,C,13:3
Neidorf, David
Bull Durham 1988,Je 15,C,20:5
Neigher, Stephen (Screenwriter)
Hot to Trot 1988,Ag 27,11:3
Neill, Gary A (Producer)
Bat 21 1988,O 21,C,22:1
Neill, Sam
Good Wife, The 1987,F 20,C,19:3
Cry in the Dark, A 1988,N 11,C,6:4
Cry in the Dark, A 1988,N 13,II,13:1
Nellessen, Eric (Producer)
Dragon Chow 1988,My 27,C,10:5
Nelska, Liliana
Welcome in Vienna 1988,Je 1,C,17:1
Nelson, Craig T
Action Jackson 1988,F 12,C,10:1
Nelson, Gary (Director)
Allan Quatermain and the Lost City of Gold 1987,Ja 31,14:5
Nelson, Judd
From the Hip 1987,F 6,C,10:4
Nelson, Mildred
Hoxsey: Quacks Who Cure Cancer? 1988,F 3,C,21:4
Nelson, Mimi
Three Strange Loves (Torst) 1988,Ja 20,C,20:1
Nelson, Peter (Producer)
Lonely Passion of Judith Hearne, The 1987,D 23,C,15:1
Nelson, Peter (Screenwriter)
Lonely Passion of Judith Hearne, The 1987,D 23,C,15:1
Nelson, Ray (Original Author)
They Live 1988,N 4,C,8:1
Nemec, Jan
Unbearable Lightness of Being, The 1988,F 5,C,8:5

P

Paradisi, Giulio
Cammina Cammina (Keep Walking, Keep Walking) 1988,Jl 10,43:5

Paradzhanov, Sergei (Director)
Legend of Suram Fortress, The 1987,F 18,C,18:5
Ashik Kerib 1988,S 29,C,24:5

Paragon, John (Screenwriter)
Elvira, Mistress of the Dark 1988,S 30,C,12:4

Pare, Michael
World Gone Wild 1988,My 22,49:5

Paredes, Marisa
Dark Habits 1988,My 6,C,28:5

Parent, Gail (Screenwriter)
Cross My Heart 1987,N 13,C,21:1

Parer, Damien (Producer)
Shame 1988,Mr 19,10:3

Parfitt, Judy
Maurice 1987,S 18,C,18:5

Paris, Dominique (Miscellaneous)
Color of Destiny, The 1988,Jl 22,C,17:1

Parker, Alan (Composer)
American Gothic 1988,Je 4,12:6

Parker, Alan (Director)
Angel Heart 1987,Mr 6,C,5:1
Mississippi Burning 1988,D 9,C,12:1
Mississippi Burning 1988,D 18,II,13:1

Parker, Alan (Screenwriter)
Angel Heart 1987,Mr 6,C,5:1

Parker, Corey
Biloxi Blues 1988,Mr 25,C,1:1

Parker, David (Cinematographer)
Rikky and Pete 1988,My 20,C,9:1

Parker, David (Producer)
Rikky and Pete 1988,My 20,C,9:1

Parker, David (Screenwriter)
Rikky and Pete 1988,My 20,C,9:1

Parker, Jameson
Prince of Darkness 1987,O 23,C,26:1

Parker, Lindsay
Flowers in the Attic 1987,N 21,12:5

Parker, Monica
He's My Girl 1987,S 11,C,5:1

Parker, Noelle
Ernest Saves Christmas 1988,N 11,C,15:1

Parker, Ray, Jr
Enemy Territory 1987,My 22,C,7:1

Parker, Ronald (Producer)
My Stepmother Is an Alien 1988,D 9,C,17:1

Parks, Michael
Club Life 1987,Ap 3,C,9:1

Parks, Van Dyke (Composer)
Casual Sex? 1988,Ap 22,C,24:1

Park Seung Bae (Cinematographer)
Man with Three Coffins, The 1988,S 27,C,16:5

Parniere, Olivier
36 Fillette 1988,O 4,C,19:1

Parodi, Alejandro
Realm of Fortune, The 1987,Mr 17,C,14:1

Parrish, Man (Composer)
Beehive 1988,D 7,C,24:5

Parros, Peter
Death Before Dishonor 1987,F 20,C,10:1

Parsekian, Tom
Club Life 1987,Ap 3,C,9:1

Pas, Michael
Love Is a Dog from Hell 1988,Mr 18,C,15:1
Love Is a Dog from Hell 1988,Ap 23,14:5

Pascal, Christine
Grand Highway, The 1988,Ja 22,C,17:1

Pascali, Consuelo
Family, The 1988,Ja 22,C,11:1

Pascual, Cristina S
Dark Habits 1988,My 6,C,28:5

Pasdar, Adrian
Near Dark 1987,O 4,67:2

Pastor, Aurora
House of Bernarda Alba, The (Casa de Bernarda Alba, La) 1988,D 16,C,14:6

Pastor, Julian
Gran Fiesta, La 1987,Jl 17,C,17:1

Pataki, Eva (Screenwriter)
Diary for My Loved Ones 1987,S 26,12:3

Pataki, Michael
Halloween 4: The Return of Michael Myers 1988,O 22,12:4

Pate, Michael
Howling III 1987,N 13,C,5:1

Patekar, Nana
Salaam Bombay! 1988,O 7,C,8:1

Paterson, Bill
Coming Up Roses 1987,S 11,C,9:1

Paterson, Iain (Producer)
Friday the 13th, Part VII—The New Blood 1988,My 15,56:5

Paterson, Owen (Miscellaneous)
Traveling North 1988,F 12,C,10:1

Paterson, Robert
Gospel According to Vic 1987,Mr 13,C,13:1

Patinkin, Mandy
Princess Bride, The 1987,S 25,C,10:5
House on Carroll Street, The 1988,Mr 4,C,23:1
Alien Nation 1988,O 7,C,10:6

Patou, Candice
Caviar Rouge, Le 1988,Mr 25,C,10:5

Patric, Jason
Lost Boys, The 1987,Jl 31,C,21:1
Beast, The 1988,S 16,C,13:1

Patterson, Frank
Dead, The 1987,D 17,C,19:4

Patterson, Jay
Street Smart 1987,Mr 27,C,8:1
Nadine 1987,Ag 7,C,8:3
DOA 1988,Mr 18,C,8:5

Pattinson, Michael (Director)
Ground Zero 1988,S 23,C,18:1

Pattinson, Michael (Producer)
Ground Zero 1988,S 23,C,18:1

Patton, Will
No Way Out 1987,Ag 14,C,3:1
Stars and Bars 1988,Mr 18,C,3:1

Paul, Alexandra
Dragnet 1987,Je 26,C,3:1

Paul, Don Michael
Aloha Summer 1988,F 26,C,8:1

Paul, Stefan (Director)
Sera Posible el Sur: Un Viaje por Argentina de la Mano de Mercedes Sosa (South Will Be Possible, The: A Trip Through Argentina with Mercedes Sosa) 1987,S 11,C,15:1

Paulino dos Santos, Luis (Screenwriter)
Barravento (Turning Wind, The) 1987,F 20,C,5:1

Paull, Lawrence G (Miscellaneous)
Project X 1987,Ap 17,C,15:1
Cross My Heart 1987,N 13,C,21:1
License to Drive 1988,Jl 6,C,17:1

Paulsen, Rob
Perfect Match 1988,Je 4,12:3

Pavarotti, Luciano
Distant Harmony 1988,F 4,C,15:1

Pawluskiewicz, Jan Kanty (Composer)
Woman Alone, A 1987,Mr 15,61:1

Paxton, Bill
Near Dark 1987,O 4,67:2

Paymar, Michelle (Director)
Sippie 1987,S 5,11:1

Payne, Cynthia (Miscellaneous)
Personal Services 1987,My 15,C,4:5

Pays, Amanda
Kindred, The 1987,Ja 10,13:1
Off Limits 1988,Mr 11,C,8:5

Peaks, John
Evil Dead 2: Dead by Dawn 1987,Mr 13,C,18:1

Pearce, Richard (Director)
No Mercy 1987,Ja 4,II,17:1

Pearl, Daniel (Cinematographer)
Amazon Women on the Moon 1987,S 18,C,12:6
Deadly Illusion 1987,O 31,10:5
Hiding Out 1987,N 6,C,21:1

Pearl, Linda (Miscellaneous)
Russkies 1987,N 6,C,12:3

Pearson, Burke
Running on Empty 1988,S 18,II,25:1

Pearson, Durk (Miscellaneous)
Dead Pool 1988,Jl 13,C,22:1

Pearson, Julie (Sunny)
Barfly 1987,S 30,C,18:1

Peccianti, Lucia
Cammina Cammina (Keep Walking, Keep Walking) 1988,Jl 10,43:5

Peck, Bob
Kitchen Toto, The 1988,Jl 8,C,12:5

Peck, Gregory
Amazing Grace and Chuck 1987,My 22,C,30:4

Peeples, Nia
North Shore 1987,Ag 14,C,6:6

Pegram, Nigel
Riders of the Storm 1988,My 7,12:3

Pekny, Romuald
38: Vienna Before the Fall 1988,My 6,C,17:1

Peled, Hanan (Miscellaneous)
Deadline 1987,S 11,C,4:4

Peled, Hanan (Screenwriter)
Deadline 1987,S 11,C,4:4

I Don't Give a Damn 1988,My 20,C,22:5

Pellay, Lanah
Eat the Rich 1988,Ap 22,C,4:4

Pellegrino, Frank
Too Outrageous 1987,O 16,C,12:1

Peltier, Kenout (Miscellaneous)
Opera do Malandro 1987,Ja 30,C,6:5

Pelton, Dale Allan (Miscellaneous)
Return of the Living Dead Part II 1988,Ja 15,C,11:1

Pena, Angel (Composer)
Gran Fiesta, La 1987,Jl 17,C,17:1

Pena, Elizabeth
Bamba, La 1987,Jl 24,C,4:3
Batteries Not Included 1987,D 18,C,12:5

Pena, Vicky
House of Bernarda Alba, The (Casa de Bernarda Alba, La) 1988,D 16,C,14:6

Penalver, Diana
Padre Nuestro 1987,Ap 22,C,24:1

Pendleton, Austin
Hello Again 1987,N 6,C,21:1

Penella, Emma
Padre Nuestro 1987,Ap 22,C,24:1

Penn, Arthur
Hello Actors Studio 1988,N 9,C,19:1

Penn, Arthur (Director)
Dead of Winter 1987,F 6,C,4:3
Dead of Winter 1988,Ja 3,II,15:1

Penn, Edward
Lady Beware 1987,S 18,C,23:1

Penn, Leo (Director)
Judgment in Berlin 1988,My 6,C,13:1

Penn, Leo (Screenwriter)
Judgment in Berlin 1988,My 6,C,13:1

Penn, Sean
Colors 1988,Ap 15,C,4:1
Judgment in Berlin 1988,My 6,C,13:1

Penney, Alan
Howling III 1987,N 13,C,5:1

Penney, John (Miscellaneous)
Kindred, The 1987,Ja 10,13:1

Penney, John (Screenwriter)
Kindred, The 1987,Ja 10,13:1

Penney, Julian (Cinematographer)
Traveling North 1988,F 12,C,10:1

Penzer, Jean (Cinematographer)
Buffet Froid (Cold Cuts) 1987,S 4,C,5:4

Peploe, Clare (Director)
High Season 1988,Mr 25,C,12:6

Peploe, Clare (Screenwriter)
High Season 1988,Mr 25,C,12:6

Peploe, Mark (Screenwriter)
Last Emperor, The 1987,N 20,C,3:4
High Season 1988,Mr 25,C,12:6

Peranio, Vincent (Miscellaneous)
Hairspray 1988,F 26,C,17:1

Percy, Lee (Miscellaneous)
Slamdance 1987,N 6,C,10:5

Pereira dos Santos, Nelson (Director)
Amulet of Ogum 1987,F 6,C,4:3

Pereira dos Santos, Nelson (Miscellaneous)
Barravento (Turning Wind, The) 1987,F 20,C,5:1

Pereira dos Santos, Nelson (Screenwriter)
Amulet of Ogum 1987,F 6,C,4:3

Perez de Leon, Fernando
Winter Tan, A 1988,O 2,57:6

Pergament, Robert (Miscellaneous)
Blind Date 1987,Mr 27,C,11:1
Sunset 1988,Ap 29,C,13:1

Pergola, James (Cinematographer)
Police Academy 5: Assignment Miami Beach 1988,Mr 19,13:3

Perico Ortiz, Luis (Composer)
Mondo New York 1988,Ap 22,C,23:1

Perkins, Elizabeth
From the Hip 1987,F 6,C,10:4
Big 1988,Je 3,C,8:4
Big 1988,Je 12,II,29:1
Sweet Hearts Dance 1988,S 23,C,17:1

Perkins, Millie
Slamdance 1987,N 6,C,10:5
Wall Street 1987,D 11,C,3:4
Two Moon Junction 1988,Ap 30,17:1

Permut, David (Producer)
Dragnet 1987,Je 26,C,3:1

Perpignani, Roberto (Miscellaneous)
Good Morning, Babylon 1987,Jl 15,C,18:5

Perrimond, Maurice (Cinematographer)
Call Me Madame 1988,Mr 12,14:4

Perrin, Bryce (Miscellaneous)
Tale of Ruby Rose, The 1988,My 25,C,18:6

R

Qu Xiaosong (Composer)
Horse Thief, The 1988,Ja 6,C,15:1
Big Parade, The 1988,Mr 15,C,16:5
Qvistgaard, Berthe
Dark Side of the Moon, The 1987,Mr 19,C,28:1

Raab, Kurt
Record, The 1988,My 13,C,15:1
Raacke, Catarina
Record, The 1988,My 13,C,15:1
Rabal, Francisco
Padre Nuestro 1987,Ap 22,C,24:1
Time of Destiny, A 1988,Ap 22,C,29:1
History 1988,Je 3,C,15:1
Rabattoni, Toni (Cinematographer)
Barravento (Turning Wind, The) 1987,F 20,C,5:1
Rabbett, Martin
Allan Quatermain and the Lost City of Gold 1987,Ja 31,14:5
Raben, Peer (Composer)
Inside Out 1987,Ag 21,C,11:1
Racette, Francine
Au Revoir les Enfants (Goodbye, Children) 1988,F 12,C,15:1
Rachini, Pasquale (Cinematographer)
Last Minute, The 1988,F 26,C,10:5
Rachmil, Michael (Producer)
Roxanne 1987,Je 19,C,3:4
Punchline 1988,S 30,C,14:4
Racimo, Victoria
Ernest Goes to Camp 1987,My 23,15:4
Rackman, Steve
Crocodile Dundee II 1988,My 25,C,15:3
Radakovic, Goran
Hey Babu Riba 1987,Mr 15,60:1
Hey Babu Riba 1987,S 18,C,24:1
Radcliffe, Porscha
Mystic Pizza 1988,O 21,C,20:6
Radclyffe, Sarah (Producer)
Wish You Were Here 1987,Jl 24,C,7:2
Sammy and Rosie Get Laid 1987,O 30,C,5:1
World Apart, A 1988,Je 17,C,10:4
Rademakers, Fons (Director)
Assault, The 1987,F 6,C,8:1
Rademakers, Fons (Producer)
Assault, The 1987,F 6,C,8:1
Rader, Jack
Braddock: Missing in Action III 1988,Ja 22,C,9:1
Radford, Michael (Director)
White Mischief 1988,Ap 22,C,20:1
White Mischief 1988,My 22,II,43:1
Radford, Michael (Screenwriter)
White Mischief 1988,Ap 22,C,20:1
White Mischief 1988,My 22,II,43:1
Radstrom, Niklas (Miscellaneous)
Mozart Brothers, The 1987,S 18,C,21:1
Radstrom, Niklas (Screenwriter)
Mozart Brothers, The 1987,S 18,C,21:1
Radziwilowicz, Jerzy
No End 1987,Mr 6,C,17:2
Rafelson, Bob (Director)
Black Widow 1987,F 6,C,3:1
Raffe, Alexandra (Producer)
I've Heard the Mermaids Singing 1987,S 11,C,8:1
Raffill, Stewart (Director)
MAC and Me 1988,Ag 13,14:1
Raffill, Stewart (Screenwriter)
MAC and Me 1988,Ag 13,14:1
Ragalyi, Elemer (Cinematographer)
Package Tour 1987,Ja 23,C,7:1
Singing on the Treadmill 1987,Jl 31,C,11:1
Hanna's War 1988,N 23,C,14:1
Hungarian Fairy Tale, A 1988,D 28,C,17:1
Ragland, Robert O (Composer)
Assassination 1987,Ja 10,13:1
Prettykill 1987,Mr 27,C,13:3
Messenger of Death 1988,S 17,12:5
Rahbani, Ziad (Composer)
Beirut: The Last Home Movie 1988,Je 29,C,19:1
Railsback, Steve
Blue Monkey, The 1987,O 16,C,12:6
Raimi, Sam (Director)
Evil Dead 2: Dead by Dawn 1987,Mr 13,C,18:1
Raimi, Sam (Screenwriter)
Evil Dead 2: Dead by Dawn 1987,Mr 13,C,18:1
Raimi, Theodore
Evil Dead 2: Dead by Dawn 1987,Mr 13,C,18:1

Raina, M K
Genesis 1988,D 23,C,18:6
Rainer, Josef
Campus Man 1987,My 4,C,17:1
Rajski, Peggy (Producer)
Matewan 1987,Ag 28,C,3:4
Rall, Thomas
Dancers 1987,O 9,C,24:1
Ramalho, Elba
Opera do Malandro 1987,Ja 30,C,6:5
Rameau, Jean Philippe (Composer)
Aria 1988,My 21,54:3
Ramis, Harold
Baby Boom 1987,O 7,C,24:5
Stealing Home 1988,Ag 26,C,17:4
Ramis, Harold (Screenwriter)
Caddyshack II 1988,Jl 23,16:5
Ramos, Loyda
Salsa 1988,My 7,13:1
Ramos, Rudy
Colors 1988,Ap 15,C,4:1
Ramos, Santiago
Half of Heaven 1988,Ja 21,C,24:3
Rampling, Charlotte
Angel Heart 1987,Mr 6,C,5:1
DOA 1988,Mr 18,C,8:5
Ramsay, Remak
House on Carroll Street, The 1988,Mr 4,C,23:1
Ramsay, Todd (Miscellaneous)
Malone 1987,My 4,C,17:4
Ramsey, Anne
Throw Momma from the Train 1987,D 11,C,15:1
Ramsey, Marion
Police Academy 4: Citizens on Patrol 1987,Ap 4,12:5
Police Academy 5: Assignment Miami Beach 1988,Mr 19,13:3
Rand, Ayn (Original Author)
We the Living 1988,N 25,C,11:1
Rand, Patrick (Miscellaneous)
Twice Dead 1988,N 19,15:3
Randall, Charles
Enemy Territory 1987,My 22,C,7:1
Randall, Corky (Miscellaneous)
Hot to Trot 1988,Ag 27,11:3
Randall, Glenn (Miscellaneous)
Hot to Trot 1988,Ag 27,11:3
Randel, Tony (Director)
Hellbound: Hellraiser II 1988,D 23,C,18:1
Randolph, John
Wizard of Loneliness, The 1988,S 2,C,9:1
Randolph, Virginia (Miscellaneous)
Action Jackson 1988,F 12,C,10:1
Random, Ida (Miscellaneous)
Who's That Girl 1987,Ag 8,16:1
Throw Momma from the Train 1987,D 11,C,15:1
Rain Man 1988,D 16,C,12:5
Ransohoff, Martin (Producer)
Big Town, The 1987,S 25,C,20:4
Switching Channels 1988,Mr 4,C,10:4
Rapp, Anthony
Adventures in Baby-Sitting 1987,Jl 1,C,24:3
Rappaport, Ezra D (Screenwriter)
Harry and the Hendersons 1987,Je 5,C,14:5
Rappaport, Mark (Miscellaneous)
Ira, You'll Get into Trouble 1987,F 20,C,4:5
Rappeneau, Elisabeth (Screenwriter)
One Woman or Two 1987,F 6,C,18:1
Rascoe, Stephanie
Positive ID 1987,Mr 14,13:1
Positive ID 1987,O 27,C,16:1
Rash, Steve (Director)
Can't Buy Me Love 1987,Ag 14,C,13:1
Rasulala, Thalmus
Bulletproof 1988,My 16,C,13:1
Rath, Franz (Cinematographer)
Felix 1988,S 24,13:1
Rathborne, Tina (Director)
Zelly and Me 1988,Ap 15,C,4:4
Rathborne, Tina (Producer)
Zelly and Me 1988,Ap 15,C,4:4
Rathborne, Tina (Screenwriter)
Zelly and Me 1988,Ap 15,C,4:4
Rathebe, Dolly
Mapantsula 1988,S 24,12:4
Rattner, Larry (Miscellaneous)
Halloween 4: The Return of Michael Myers 1988,O 22,12:4
Ratzenberger, John
House II: The Second Story 1987,Ag 29,11:1
Raubertas, Peter Paul (Miscellaneous)
Slaughterhouse Rock 1988,My 22,49:5

Raven, Elsa
Moderns, The 1988,Ap 15,C,21:1
Rawi, Ousama (Director)
Housekeeper, The 1987,Ap 24,C,7:1
Rawlence, Christopher (Director)
Man Who Mistook His Wife for a Hat, The 1988,Ag 31,C,17:1
Rawlence, Christopher (Screenwriter)
Man Who Mistook His Wife for a Hat, The 1988,Ag 31,C,17:1
Rawlings, Terry (Miscellaneous)
Lonely Passion of Judith Hearne, The 1987,D 23,C,15:1
White of the Eye 1988,My 20,C,22:5
Rawlins, David (Miscellaneous)
Police Academy 4: Citizens on Patrol 1987,Ap 4,12:5
Ray, David (Miscellaneous)
Glass Menagerie, The 1987,O 23,C,14:3
Ray, James
She's Having a Baby 1988,F 5,C,18:1
Ray, Leslie (Screenwriter)
My Demon Lover 1987,Ap 24,C,14:1
Ray-Gavras, Michele (Producer)
Family Business 1987,S 6,66:2
Raynal, Jackie (Miscellaneous)
Jean Renoir, the Boss 1987,N 20,C,23:1
Rayner, Eddie (Composer)
Rikky and Pete 1988,My 20,C,9:1
Rea, Stephen
Loose Connections 1988,Jl 8,C,11:1
Read, James
Beaches 1988,D 21,C,28:4
Red, Eric (Screenwriter)
Near Dark 1987,O 4,67:2
Redbone, Leon
Candy Mountain 1988,Je 10,C,6:5
Reddy, Don (Cinematographer)
Benji the Hunted 1987,Je 17,C,18:6
Redford, J A C (Composer)
Oliver and Company 1988,N 18,C,8:4
Redford, Robert (Director)
Milagro Beanfield War, The 1988,Mr 18,C,17:1
Milagro Beanfield War, The 1988,Ap 3,II,26:5
Redford, Robert (Producer)
Milagro Beanfield War, The 1988,Mr 18,C,17:1
Redglare, Rockets
Salvation! 1987,My 31,51:1
Redgrave, Lynn
Morgan Stewart's Coming Home 1987,Je 4,C,16:4
Redgrave, Vanessa
Prick Up Your Ears 1987,Ap 17,C,17:1
Consuming Passions 1988,Ap 6,C,18:3
Redl, Christian
Sierra Leone 1988,D 14,C,28:5
Redman, Anthony (Miscellaneous)
China Girl 1987,S 25,C,16:6
Reed, Bruce
Club Life 1987,Ap 3,C,9:1
Reed, Jerry
Bat 21 1988,O 21,C,22:1
Reed, Les (Composer)
Creepshow 2 1987,My 4,C,17:1
Reed, Oliver
Captive 1987,Ap 3,C,8:1
Rees, Oreet (Miscellaneous)
Distant Harmony 1988,F 4,C,15:1
Reese, Barbara
Housekeeping 1987,N 25,C,11:1
Reeve, Christopher
Street Smart 1987,Mr 27,C,8:1
Superman IV: The Quest for Peace 1987,Jl 25,13:2
Switching Channels 1988,Mr 4,C,10:4
Reeve, Christopher (Miscellaneous)
Superman IV: The Quest for Peace 1987,Jl 25,13:2
Reeve, Geoffrey (Producer)
Whistle Blower, The 1987,Jl 10,C,4:2
Reeves, Keanu
River's Edge 1987,My 8,C,28:4
River's Edge 1987,Je 14,II,23:5
Permanent Record 1988,Ap 22,C,10:1
Prince of Pennsylvania, The 1988,S 16,C,17:1
Dangerous Liaisons 1988,D 21,C,22:1
Regan, Kerry (Miscellaneous)
Shame 1988,Mr 19,10:3
Regehr, Duncan
Monster Squad 1987,Ag 14,C,15:1
Regent, Benoit
Black and White 1987,Mr 13,C,20:4
Reggiani, Serge
Bad Blood 1987,S 30,C,20:5
Reggio, Godfrey (Director)
Powaqqatsi 1988,Ap 29,C,20:4

Ricotta, Vincenzo
  Hanna's War 1988,N 23,C,14:1
Ridsdale, Chris (Miscellaneous)
  Eat the Rich 1988,Ap 22,C,4:4
Riegert, Peter
  Man in Love, A 1987,Jl 31,C,10:6
  Crossing Delancey 1988,Ag 24,C,15:1
Rieneck, Claudia (Miscellaneous)
  Welcome in Vienna 1988,Je 1,C,17:1
Riesner, Dean (Screenwriter)
  Fatal Beauty 1987,O 30,C,8:5
Rigollier, Claire
  Black and White 1987,Mr 13,C,20:4
Riis, Sharon (Miscellaneous)
  Loyalties 1987,Mr 21,14:3
  Loyalties 1987,N 20,C,21:1
Riis, Sharon (Screenwriter)
  Loyalties 1987,Mr 21,14:3
  Loyalties 1987,N 20,C,21:1
Rijxman, Lineke
  Broken Mirrors 1987,Mr 4,C,21:1
Riley, Gary
  Summer School 1987,Jl 22,C,22:1
Riley, Terry (Composer)
  No Man's Land 1987,F 13,C,14:6
Rimmer, Meredith
  Loyalties 1987,Mr 21,14:3
  Loyalties 1987,N 20,C,21:1
Rimoux, Alain
  Life Is a Dream 1988,D 30,C,10:6
Ringel, Israel (Producer)
  I Don't Give a Damn 1988,My 20,C,22:5
Ringwald, Molly
  Pickup Artist, The 1987,S 18,C,23:1
  For Keeps 1988,Ja 15,C,17:3
  For Keeps 1988,Ja 17,II,18:5
  King Lear 1988,Ja 22,C,6:1
  Fresh Horses 1988,N 19,15:3
Rinpoche, Trulshig
  Lord of the Dance/Destroyer of Illusion 1987,D 26,14:4
Rinzler, Lisa (Cinematographer)
  Forever, Lulu 1987,Ap 24,C,10:4
  John Huston and the Dubliners 1988,Mr 19,8:3
Ripka, William (Producer)
  Kiss Daddy Good Night 1988,My 20,C,11:1
Ripstein, Arturo (Director)
  Realm of Fortune, The 1987,Mr 17,C,14:1
  Hell Without Limits 1987,O 28,C,25:1
Ripstein, Arturo (Screenwriter)
  Hell Without Limits 1987,O 28,C,25:1
Riquelme, Carlos
  Milagro Beanfield War, The 1988,Mr 18,C,17:1
Risquez, Diego (Director)
  Amerika, Terra Incognita 1988,D 9,C,10:6
Risquez, Diego (Screenwriter)
  Amerika, Terra Incognita 1988,D 9,C,10:6
Rissner, Danton (Producer)
  Summer Story, A 1988,Ag 11,C,18:5
Ritchie, Michael (Director)
  Couch Trip, The 1988,Ja 15,C,8:1
Ritt, Martin (Director)
  Nuts 1987,N 20,C,16:6
Riva, J Michael (Miscellaneous)
  Scrooged 1988,N 23,C,16:5
Rivers, Joan
  Spaceballs 1987,Je 24,C,23:1
Rivet, Pascal
  Au Revoir les Enfants (Goodbye, Children) 1988,F 12,C,15:1
Rivette, Jacques (Director)
  Jean Renoir, the Boss 1987,N 20,C,23:1
Rivkin, Stephen E (Miscellaneous)
  Bat 21 1988,O 21,C,22:1
Rizzo, Jilly
  Pickup Artist, The 1987,S 18,C,23:1
Rizzoli, Angelo (Producer)
  Trois Soeurs (Paura e Amore) 1988,My 22,II,21:5
Roach, Adriana
  Honeymoon 1987,N 20,C,24:1
Roach, Janet (Screenwriter)
  Mr North 1988,Jl 22,C,8:4
Roach, Pat
  Willow 1988,My 20,C,8:4
Robards, Jason
  Square Dance 1987,F 20,C,4:5
  Bright Lights, Big City 1988,Ap 1,C,22:5
  Good Mother, The 1988,N 4,C,15:1
Robb, David
  Deceivers, The 1988,S 2,C,10:1
Robbins, Matthew (Director)
  Batteries Not Included 1987,D 18,C,12:5

Robbins, Matthew (Screenwriter)
  Batteries Not Included 1987,D 18,C,12:5
Robbins, Richard (Composer)
  Maurice 1987,S 18,C,18:5
Robbins, Tim
  Five Corners 1988,Ja 22,C,18:1
  Bull Durham 1988,Je 15,C,20:5
  Bull Durham 1988,Jl 3,II,1:3
Robbins, Tom
  Made in Heaven 1987,N 6,C,16:1
Robert, Genevieve (Director)
  Casual Sex? 1988,Ap 22,C,24:1
Roberts, Andy (Composer)
  Loose Connections 1988,Jl 8,C,11:1
Roberts, Conrad
  Serpent and the Rainbow, The 1988,F 5,C,3:4
Roberts, Julia
  Satisfaction 1988,F 13,15:1
  Mystic Pizza 1988,O 21,C,20:6
Roberts, Michael D
  Rain Man 1988,D 16,C,12:5
Roberts, Pascale
  Grand Highway, The 1988,Ja 22,C,17:1
Roberts, Scott (Screenwriter)
  Riders of the Storm 1988,My 7,12:3
Roberts, Tony
  Radio Days 1987,Ja 30,C,1:1
  Eighteen Again 1988,Ap 8,C,12:1
Robertson, B A (Composer)
  Gospel According to Vic 1987,Mr 13,C,13:1
Robertson, Cliff
  Malone 1987,My 4,C,17:4
Robertson, Malcom
  Year My Voice Broke, The 1988,Ag 25,C,18:1
Robertson, Tim
  Kangaroo 1987,Mr 13,C,12:5
Robertston, Eric N (Composer)
  Home Is Where the Hart Is 1987,D 5,14:4
Robins, Laila
  Planes, Trains and Automobiles 1987,N 25,C,19:1
Robinson, Amy (Producer)
  Running on Empty 1988,S 9,C,6:5
Robinson, Andrew
  Hellraiser 1987,S 20,85:5
  Shoot to Kill 1988,F 12,C,8:5
Robinson, Bruce (Director)
  Withnail and I 1987,Mr 27,C,9:1
  Withnail and I 1987,Je 19,C,10:1
Robinson, Bruce (Screenwriter)
  Withnail and I 1987,Mr 27,C,9:1
  Withnail and I 1987,Je 19,C,10:1
Robinson, David (Director)
  Keeping Love Alive 1988,Mr 13,57:1
  Keeping Love Alive 1988,Mr 27,II,29:1
Robinson, David (Producer)
  Keeping Love Alive 1988,Mr 13,57:1
Robinson, J Peter (Composer)
  Believers, The 1987,Je 10,C,22:5
  Return of the Living Dead Part II 1988,Ja 15,C,11:1
  Cocktail 1988,Jl 29,C,6:5
  Kiss, The 1988,O 14,C,11:1
Robinson, Marilynne (Original Author)
  Housekeeping 1987,N 25,C,11:1
Robinson, Mark
  Girl, The 1987,Ag 7,C,10:6
Robinson, Phil Alden (Director)
  In the Mood 1987,S 16,C,27:1
Robinson, Phil Alden (Miscellaneous)
  In the Mood 1987,S 16,C,27:1
Robinson, Phil Alden (Screenwriter)
  In the Mood 1987,S 16,C,27:1
Robinson, Tom (Screenwriter)
  Salvation! 1987,My 31,51:1
Robson, Wayne
  Dead of Winter 1987,F 6,C,4:3
  Housekeeping 1987,N 25,C,11:1
Rocard, Pascale
  Field of Honor (Champ d'Honneur) 1988,Mr 18,C,24:5
Rocco, Alex
  Lady in White 1988,My 13,C,10:3
Rocha, Annecy
  Amulet of Ogum 1987,F 6,C,4:3
Rocha, Glauber (Director)
  Barravento (Turning Wind, The) 1987,F 20,C,5:1
Rocha, Glauber (Screenwriter)
  Barravento (Turning Wind, The) 1987,F 20,C,5:1
Roche, Suzzy
  Crossing Delancey 1988,Ag 24,C,15:1
Rochon, Lela
  Wild Pair, The 1987,D 12,19:1

Rockett, Rikki
  Decline of Western Civilization Part II, The: The Metal Years
    1988,Je 17,C,14:4
Roddam, Franc (Director)
  Aria 1988,My 21,54:3
Roddam, Franc (Screenwriter)
  Aria 1988,My 21,54:3
Rodgers, Aggie Guerard (Miscellaneous)
  My Stepmother Is an Alien 1988,D 9,C,17:1
Rodgers, Anton
  Fourth Protocol, The 1987,Ag 28,C,19:1
  Dirty Rotten Scoundrels 1988,D 14,C,21:4
Rodgers, Nile (Composer)
  Coming to America 1988,Je 29,C,20:5
Rodionov, Aleksei (Cinematographer)
  Come and See 1987,F 6,C,4:4
Rodriguez, Paul
  Born in East LA 1987,Ag 24,C,14:5
Rodriguez, Valente
  Salsa 1988,My 7,13:1
Rodriguez Solis, Leonardo (Cinematographer)
  Night of the Pencils, The 1987,Mr 14,13:1
Roebuck, Daniel
  Project X 1987,Ap 17,C,15:1
  River's Edge 1987,My 8,C,28:4
  River's Edge 1987,Je 14,II,23:5
  Dudes 1988,Je 24,C,9:1
Roeg, Luc (Producer)
  Big Time 1988,S 30,C,20:1
Roeg, Nicolas (Director)
  Aria 1988,My 21,54:3
  Track 29 1988,S 9,C,10:3
Roeg, Nicolas (Screenwriter)
  Aria 1988,My 21,54:3
Rogers, Mimi
  Street Smart 1987,Mr 27,C,8:1
  Someone to Watch Over Me 1987,O 9,C,40:1
Rogers, Stuart
  Summer Camp Nightmare 1987,Ap 17,C,30:5
Rogers, Wayne
  Killing Time, The 1987,O 23,C,14:3
Rohmer, Eric (Director)
  Ami de Mon Amie, L' (My Girlfriend's Boyfriend) 1987,O
    9,C,4:5
  Ami de Mon Amie, L' 1987,O 18,II,25:1
  Boyfriends and Girlfriends (Ami de Mon Amie, L') 1988,Jl
    15,C,10:6
Rohmer, Eric (Screenwriter)
  Ami de Mon Amie, L' (My Girlfriend's Boyfriend) 1987,O
    9,C,4:5
Rohner, Clayton
  Bat 21 1988,O 21,C,22:1
Roland, Eugenie Cisse
  Faces of Women 1987,F 13,C,22:1
Rolf, Frederick
  Street Smart 1987,Mr 27,C,8:1
Rolf, Tom (Miscellaneous)
  Outrageous Fortune 1987,Ja 30,C,5:1
  Stakeout 1987,Ag 5,C,21:1
  Great Outdoors, The 1988,Je 17,C,12:6
Roll, Gernot (Cinematographer)
  Welcome in Vienna 1988,Je 1,C,17:1
  Santa Fe 1988,Jl 20,C,20:5
Rollins, Howard, Jr (Narrator)
  Dear America: Letters Home from Vietnam 1988,S 16,C,18:1
Rollins, Sonny
  Sonny Rollins: Saxophone Colossus 1987,S 1,C,14:4
  Who Is Sonny Rollins 1988,O 28,C,16:4
Rolston, Mark
  Weeds 1987,O 16,C,10:5
Romadin, Mikhail (Miscellaneous)
  Asya's Happiness 1988,S 24,13:1
Romand, Francoise (Director)
  Mix-Up 1987,Jl 24,C,12:6
  Call Me Madame 1988,Mr 12,14:4
  Call Me Madame 1988,Mr 27,II,29:1
  Call Me Madame 1988,Je 10,C,16:6
Romani, Augusto
  Joan of Arc at the Stake 1987,O 6,C,14:3
Romano, Andy
  Kansas 1988,S 23,C,17:1
Romano, Carlos
  Hotel Colonial 1987,S 19,16:3
Romanowska, Halina
  Sunday Pranks 1988,Mr 13,57:1
Romanus, Richard
  Couch Trip, The 1988,Ja 15,C,8:1
Romero, George A (Director)
  Monkey Shines: An Experiment in Fear 1988,Jl 29,C,12:4
Romero, George A (Screenwriter)
  Creepshow 2 1987,My 4,C,17:1

Monkey Shines: An Experiment in Fear 1988,Jl 29,C,12:4
Romor, Laurent
　Family Business 1987,S 6,66:2
Rondinella, Clelia
　Two Lives of Mattia Pascal, The 1988,Mr 18,C,8:5
Rongier, Robert (Miscellaneous)
　Honeymoon 1987,N 20,C,24:1
Ronstadt, Linda
　Return of Ruben Blades, The 1987,S 7,9:3
　Chuck Berry: Hail! Hail! Rock 'n' Roll 1987,O 3,10:5
Rooker, Michael
　Eight Men Out 1988,S 2,C,3:1
　Mississippi Burning 1988,D 9,C,12:1
Rooney, Cindy Kaplan (Miscellaneous)
　Zelly and Me 1988,Ap 15,C,4:4
Roos, Fred (Producer)
　Barfly 1987,S 30,C,18:1
　Tucker: The Man and His Dream 1988,Ag 12,C,8:1
Roose, Ronald (Miscellaneous)
　My Demon Lover 1987,Ap 24,C,14:1
Roose-Evans, James (Miscellaneous)
　84 Charing Cross Road 1987,F 13,C,10:4
Root, Stephan
　Monkey Shines: An Experiment in Fear 1988,Jl 29,C,12:4
Ropelewski, Tom (Screenwriter)
　Kiss, The 1988,O 14,C,11:1
Roque, Elso (Cinematographer)
　Hard Times 1987,O 6,C,29:1
Rosa, Robby
　Salsa 1988,My 7,13:1
Rosboch, Ettore (Producer)
　Maschera, La 1988,S 25,64:4
Rose, Alexandra (Producer)
　Overboard 1987,D 16,C,22:3
Rose, Barbara
　Andy Warhol 1987,Je 9,C,20:1
Rose, Clifford
　Girl, The 1987,Ag 7,C,10:6
Rose, Cristine
　Singing the Blues in Red 1988,Ja 29,C,8:5
Rose, Gabrielle
　Family Viewing 1988,Mr 23,C,20:5
Rosell, Josep (Miscellaneous)
　Matador 1988,S 16,C,8:5
Rosen, Charles (Miscellaneous)
　Broadcast News 1987,D 16,C,21:4
　My Stepmother Is an Alien 1988,D 9,C,17:1
Rosen, Martin (Director)
　Stacking 1988,Ja 15,C,15:1
Rosen, Martin (Producer)
　Stacking 1988,Ja 15,C,15:1
Rosen, Robert (Director)
　Hearst Metrotone Newsreel Show 1987,My 6,C,18:1
Rosen, Robert L (Producer)
　World Gone Wild 1988,My 22,49:5
Rosenberg, Alan
　White of the Eye 1988,My 20,C,22:5
Rosenberg, Harold
　Andy Warhol 1987,Je 9,C,20:1
Rosenberg, Mark (Producer)
　Bright Lights, Big City 1988,Ap 1,C,22:5
Rosenberg, Philip (Miscellaneous)
　Moonstruck 1987,D 16,C,22:3
　Running on Empty 1988,S 9,C,6:5
Rosenbloom, David (Miscellaneous)
　Best Seller 1987,S 25,C,24:1
　Fresh Horses 1988,N 19,15:3
Rosenblum, Steven (Miscellaneous)
　Wild Thing 1987,Ap 17,C,13:1
　Steele Justice 1987,My 8,C,12:4
Rosenfelt, Scott (Producer)
　Russkies 1987,N 6,C,12:3
　Mystic Pizza 1988,O 21,C,20:6
Rosenquist, James
　Wall Street 1987,D 11,C,3:4
Rosenstock, Harvey (Miscellaneous)
　Teen Wolf Too 1987,N 20,C,14:6
　Dead Heat 1988,My 7,13:1
Rosenthal, Mark (Miscellaneous)
　Superman IV: The Quest for Peace 1987,Jl 25,13:2
Rosenthal, Mark (Screenwriter)
　Superman IV: The Quest for Peace 1987,Jl 25,13:2
Rosenthal, Rick (Director)
　Russkies 1987,N 6,C,12:3
　Distant Thunder 1988,N 11,C,13:1
Roshko, Ariel (Miscellaneous)
　Iron Eagle II 1988,N 12,15:3
Rosing, Wilhelm (Cinematographer)
　Hotel Terminus: The Life and Times of Klaus Barbie 1988,O 6,C,25:1

Rosovsky, Ivy (Miscellaneous)
　Brain Damage 1988,Ap 15,C,16:5
Ross, Chelcie
　Hoosiers 1987,F 27,C,10:3
Ross, Gary (Screenwriter)
　Big 1988,Je 3,C,8:4
Ross, Herbert (Director)
　Secret of My Success, The 1987,Ap 10,C,14:4
　Secret of My Success, The 1987,Ap 12,II,17:1
　Dancers 1987,O 9,C,24:1
Ross, Herbert (Producer)
　Secret of My Success, The 1987,Ap 10,C,14:4
Ross, Sharyn L (Miscellaneous)
　Ernest Saves Christmas 1988,N 11,C,15:1
Ross, Steven (Cinematographer)
　Luggage of the Gods 1987,Je 19,C,12:6
Ross, Willie
　Rita, Sue and Bob Too 1987,Jl 17,C,18:1
Rossellini, Isabella
　Tough Guys Don't Dance 1987,S 18,C,14:1
　Siesta 1987,N 11,C,23:3
　Zelly and Me 1988,Ap 15,C,4:4
Rossellini, Renzo (Composer)
　Human Voice, The 1987,O 6,C,14:3
　We the Living 1988,N 25,C,11:1
Rossellini, Roberto (Director)
　Joan of Arc at the Stake 1987,O 6,C,14:3
　Human Voice, The 1987,O 6,C,14:3
Rossellini, Roberto (Producer)
　Human Voice, The 1987,O 6,C,14:3
Rossellini, Roberto (Screenwriter)
　Human Voice, The 1987,O 6,C,14:3
Rossi, Leo
　Black Widow 1987,F 6,C,3:1
　Accused, The 1988,O 14,C,13:1
Rossini, Gioacchino (Composer)
　Vincent: The Life and Death of Vincent Van Gogh 1988,Mr 16,C,25:1
Rossovich, Rick
　Roxanne 1987,Je 19,C,3:4
Rostand, Edmond (Original Author)
　Roxanne 1987,Je 19,C,3:4
Roth, Dena (Miscellaneous)
　Eighteen Again 1988,Ap 8,C,12:1
Roth, Eric (Screenwriter)
　Suspect 1987,O 23,C,14:3
　Memories of Me 1988,S 28,C,23:1
Roth, Ivan E
　Blue Monkey, The 1987,O 16,C,12:6
Roth, Joe (Director)
　Revenge of the Nerds II: Nerds in Paradise 1987,Jl 11,18:4
Roth, Joe (Producer)
　Young Guns 1988,Ag 12,C,18:1
Roth, Marty (Miscellaneous)
　Filming Othello 1987,F 4,C,24:3
Rothberg, Jeff (Producer)
　Hiding Out 1987,N 6,C,21:1
Rothberg, Jeff (Screenwriter)
　Hiding Out 1987,N 6,C,21:1
Rothman, John
　Boost, The 1988,D 23,C,16:6
Rothman, Marion (Miscellaneous)
　Mystic Pizza 1988,O 21,C,20:6
Rotman, Keith (Producer)
　Heat 1987,Mr 13,C,33:1
Rotter, Stephen A (Miscellaneous)
　Ishtar 1987,My 15,C,3:1
　Dirty Rotten Scoundrels 1988,D 14,C,21:4
Rotundo, Nick (Miscellaneous)
　Hello Mary Lou 1987,O 17,16:5
Rotunno, Giuseppe (Cinematographer)
　Hotel Colonial 1987,S 19,16:3
　Rent-a-Cop 1988,Ja 15,C,13:1
　Julia and Julia 1988,F 5,C,5:1
Rouchand, Dominique (Producer)
　Mix-Up 1987,Jl 24,C,12:6
Rougerie, Jean
　Buffet Froid (Cold Cuts) 1987,S 4,C,5:4
Rougeul, Jean
　Hypothesis of a Stolen Painting 1987,N 13,C,15:1
Roundtree, Richard
　Maniac Cop 1988,My 14,16:5
Rourke, Mickey
　Angel Heart 1987,Mr 6,C,5:1
　Prayer for the Dying, A 1987,S 11,C,11:1
　Barfly 1987,S 30,C,18:1
　Barfly 1987,O 4,II,23:1
　Barfly 1987,O 11,II,25:5
　Angel Heart 1988,Ja 3,II,15:1

Rouse, Russell (Miscellaneous)
　DOA 1988,Mr 18,C,8:5
Rousselot, Philippe (Cinematographer)
　Hope and Glory 1987,O 9,C,23:1
　Dangerous Liaisons 1988,D 21,C,22:1
Rovito, Gabriel
　Debajo del Mundo (Under the World) 1988,N 1,C,17:1
Rowe, Douglas
　In the Mood 1987,S 16,C,27:1
Rowe, Glenys (Producer)
　Dogs in Space 1987,O 9,C,7:1
Rowell, Victoria
　Leonard Part 6 1987,D 18,C,30:1
Rowland, Bruce (Composer)
　Return to Snowy River 1988,Ap 15,C,8:1
Rowland, Oscar
　Promised Land 1988,Ja 22,C,13:1
Rowlands, Gena
　Light of Day 1987,F 6,C,4:3
　Opening Night 1988,O 1,15:1
　Another Woman 1988,O 14,C,3:3
Roy, Nitish (Miscellaneous)
　Genesis 1988,D 23,C,18:6
Royer, Patrice (Miscellaneous)
　Hypothesis of a Stolen Painting 1987,N 13,C,15:1
Rozema, Patricia (Director)
　I've Heard the Mermaids Singing 1987,S 11,C,8:1
Rozema, Patricia (Miscellaneous)
　I've Heard the Mermaids Singing 1987,S 11,C,8:1
Rozema, Patricia (Producer)
　I've Heard the Mermaids Singing 1987,S 11,C,8:1
Rozema, Patricia (Screenwriter)
　I've Heard the Mermaids Singing 1987,S 11,C,8:1
Ruane, John (Director)
　Feathers 1988,Mr 21,C,15:1
Ruane, John (Screenwriter)
　Feathers 1988,Mr 21,C,15:1
Rubach, Claire (Producer)
　Miss . . . or Myth? 1987,S 16,C,28:3
Ruban, Al (Cinematographer)
　Opening Night 1988,O 1,15:1
Ruban, Al (Producer)
　Opening Night 1988,O 1,15:1
Rubbert, Rainer (Composer)
　Anita—Dances of Vice 1987,O 3,15:1
Rubel, Marc (Screenwriter)
　Big Business 1988,Je 10,C,10:4
Ruben, Joseph (Director)
　Stepfather, The 1987,My 8,C,9:1
Rubens, Bernice (Original Author)
　Madame Sousatzka 1988,O 14,C,8:5
Rubeo, Bruno (Miscellaneous)
　Walker 1987,D 4,C,36:1
　Talk Radio 1988,D 21,C,28:4
Rubes, Jan
　Dead of Winter 1987,F 6,C,4:3
　Kiss, The 1988,O 14,C,11:1
Rubin, Jennifer
　Nightmare on Elm Street 3, A: Dream Warriors 1987,F 27,C,15:3
　Bad Dreams 1988,Ap 8,C,10:1
　Permanent Record 1988,Ap 22,C,10:1
Rubin, Rick (Composer)
　Less Than Zero 1987,N 6,C,23:1
Rubinstein, Arthur B (Composer)
　Stakeout 1987,Ag 5,C,21:1
Rubinstein, John
　Someone to Watch Over Me 1987,O 9,C,40:1
Rubinstein, Zelda
　Anguish 1988,Ja 29,C,15:1
　Poltergeist III 1988,Je 10,C,17:1
Ruck, Alan
　Three for the Road 1987,Ap 10,C,5:1
Rucker, Steve (Composer)
　And God Created Woman 1988,Mr 4,C,22:4
　Bulletproof 1988,My 16,C,13:1
Rude, Dick
　Straight to Hell 1987,Je 26,C,8:5
Rude, Dick (Screenwriter)
　Straight to Hell 1987,Je 26,C,8:5
Rudnick, Regina
　Virus Knows No Morals, A 1987,Je 19,C,10:4
Rudolf, Gene (Miscellaneous)
　Best Seller 1987,S 25,C,24:1
Rudolph, Alan (Director)
　Made in Heaven 1987,N 6,C,16:1
　Made in Heaven 1987,N 22,II,23:5
　Moderns, The 1988,Ap 15,C,21:1
Rudolph, Alan (Screenwriter)
　Moderns, The 1988,Ap 15,C,21:1

S

Salinas, Martin (Screenwriter)
Gaby—A True Story 1987,O 30,C,10:4
Sall, Fatou
Faces of Women 1987,F 13,C,22:1
Salloch, Roger (Screenwriter)
36 Fillette 1988,O 4,C,19:1
Sallows, Ken (Miscellaneous)
Rikky and Pete 1988,My 20,C,9:1
Tale of Ruby Rose, The 1988,My 25,C,18:6
Salomon, Amnon (Cinematographer)
Deadline 1987,S 11,C,4:4
Salomon, Mikael (Cinematographer)
Wolf at the Door, The 1987,Jl 31,C,8:5
Zelly and Me 1988,Ap 15,C,4:4
Torch Song Trilogy 1988,D 14,C,19:1
Salonia, Adriana
Night of the Pencils, The 1987,Mr 14,13:1
Salvay, Bennett (Composer)
Aloha Summer 1988,F 26,C,8:1
Salveson, Catherine (Producer)
Hoxsey: Quacks Who Cure Cancer? 1988,F 3,C,21:4
Samano, Jose (Producer)
Hail Hazana 1988,Je 10,C,18:1
Samano, Jose (Screenwriter)
Hail Hazana 1988,Je 10,C,18:1
Samminiatesi, Renzo
Cammina Cammina (Keep Walking, Keep Walking) 1988,Jl 10,43:5
Sampaio, Antonio
Barravento (Turning Wind, The) 1987,F 20,C,5:1
Sams, Coke (Screenwriter)
Ernest Goes to Camp 1987,My 23,15:4
Samuel, Stephen
Singing the Blues in Red 1988,Ja 29,C,8:5
Sana, Madi
Choice, The 1988,Mr 24,C,26:6
Sanchez, Rodolfo (Cinematographer)
Vera 1987,O 16,C,4:5
Blue Iguana, The 1988,Ap 23,18:2
Sand, Bob (Screenwriter)
Touch and Go 1987,Ja 14,C,20:5
Sand, Paul
Teen Wolf Too 1987,N 20,C,14:6
Sandell, William (Miscellaneous)
Robocop 1987,Jl 17,C,10:1
Big Business 1988,Je 10,C,10:4
Sander, Helke (Director)
Felix 1988,S 24,13:1
Sander, Helke (Screenwriter)
Felix 1988,S 24,13:1
Sander, Ian (Producer)
DOA 1988,Mr 18,C,8:5
Everybody's All American 1988,N 4,C,17:1
Sander, Otto
Rosa Luxemburg 1987,My 1,C,10:5
Wings of Desire 1988,Ap 29,C,15:1
Sanders, Ronald (Miscellaneous)
Dead Ringers 1988,S 23,C,10:1
Sanders-Brahms, Helma (Director)
Felix 1988,S 24,13:1
Sanders-Brahms, Helma (Screenwriter)
Felix 1988,S 24,13:1
Sanderson, Martyn
Tale of Ruby Rose, The 1988,My 25,C,18:6
Sandler, Susan (Original Author)
Crossing Delancey 1988,Ag 24,C,15:1
Sandler, Susan (Screenwriter)
Crossing Delancey 1988,Ag 24,C,15:1
Sandlund, Debra
Tough Guys Don't Dance 1987,S 18,C,14:1
Sandoval, Miguel
Straight to Hell 1987,Je 26,C,8:5
Sandrelli, Stefania
Family, The 1988,Ja 22,C,11:1
Traffic Jam 1988,Mr 4,C,14:6
Sandrey, Robert
Field of Honor (Champ d'Honneur) 1988,Mr 18,C,24:5
Sandrin, Patrick (Producer)
Nanou 1988,S 28,C,18:5
Sandrock, Carla (Miscellaneous)
Saturday Night at the Palace 1988,My 20,C,16:1
Sands, Julian
Gothic 1987,Ap 10,C,16:3
Siesta 1987,N 11,C,23:3
Siesta 1987,N 22,II,23:5
Vibes 1988,Ag 5,C,6:1
Sanford, Midge (Producer)
River's Edge 1987,My 8,C,28:4
Eight Men Out 1988,S 2,C,3:1
San Francisco, Enrique
Colegas (Pals) 1987,Ag 14,C,15:1

Hail Hazana 1988,Je 10,C,18:1
Sangare, Aoua
Yeelen 1987,O 8,C,37:1
Sangare, Koke
Yeelen 1987,O 8,C,37:1
Sanogo, Niamanto
Yeelen 1987,O 8,C,37:1
Sansom, Ken
Chipmunk Adventure, The 1987,My 22,C,10:5
Santa Lucia, Daniel
Hotel Colonial 1987,S 19,16:3
Santana, Carlos (Composer)
Bamba, La 1987,Jl 24,C,4:3
Sant'Anna, Ney
Amulet of Ogum 1987,F 6,C,4:3
Santarelli, Silvio
Joan of Arc at the Stake 1987,O 6,C,14:3
Santeiro, Gilberto (Miscellaneous)
Subway to the Stars 1988,Mr 25,C,14:6
Santiago, Flavio
Subway to the Stars 1988,Mr 25,C,14:6
Santos, Francisco (Miscellaneous)
Amulet of Ogum 1987,F 6,C,4:3
Santos, Isabel
Parting of the Ways (Lejanja) 1987,S 23,C,22:6
Sanvoisin, Michel (Miscellaneous)
Little Dorrit 1988,Mr 26,11:1
Sanz, Margarita
Realm of Fortune, The 1987,Mr 17,C,14:1
Saperstein, David (Miscellaneous)
Cocoon: The Return 1988,N 23,C,15:1
Sapin, Luis (Screenwriter)
Ambiciosos, Los (Ambitious Ones, The) 1988,F 12,C,13:1
Sapoznik, Henry
Jumpin' Night in the Garden of Eden, A 1988,Mr 2,C,20:1
Sara, Mia
Apprentice to Murder 1988,F 26,C,14:1
Sarandon, Chris
Princess Bride, The 1987,S 25,C,10:5
Child's Play 1988,N 9,C,19:1
Sarandon, Susan
Witches of Eastwick, The 1987,Je 12,C,3:4
Bull Durham 1988,Je 15,C,20:5
Bull Durham 1988,Jl 3,II,1:3
Bull Durham 1988,S 11,II,1:3
Sweet Hearts Dance 1988,S 23,C,17:1
Sarda, Yves (Miscellaneous)
Black and White 1987,Mr 13,C,20:4
Sarde, Alain (Producer)
Buffet Froid (Cold Cuts) 1987,S 4,C,5:4
Sarde, Philippe (Composer)
Scene of the Crime 1987,Ja 23,C,14:1
Rendez-Vous 1987,D 25,C,6:5
Sardi, Jan (Screenwriter)
Ground Zero 1988,S 23,C,18:1
Sargent, Alvin (Screenwriter)
Nuts 1987,N 20,C,16:6
Dominick and Eugene 1988,Mr 18,C,20:1
Sargent, Joseph (Director)
Jaws: The Revenge 1987,Jl 18,15:4
Sargent, Joseph (Producer)
Jaws: The Revenge 1987,Jl 18,15:4
Sarin, Vic (Cinematographer)
Loyalties 1987,Mr 21,14:3
Loyalties 1987,N 20,C,21:1
Sarkisyan, Rose
Family Viewing 1988,Mr 23,C,20:5
Sarr, Ismaila
Yeelen 1987,O 8,C,37:1
Sartain, Gailard
Ernest Goes to Camp 1987,My 23,15:4
Ernest Saves Christmas 1988,N 11,C,15:1
Mississippi Burning 1988,D 9,C,12:1
Sato, Kei
Violence at Noon 1988,N 11,C,6:4
Sato, Masaru (Composer)
Where Spring Comes Late 1988,N 18,C,8:4
Sato, Orie
Promise, A 1987,Mr 17,C,14:4
Promise, A 1988,O 8,14:3
Sauder, Peter (Miscellaneous)
Care Bears' Adventure in Wonderland, The 1987,Ag 7,C,21:1
Saulnier, Jacques (Miscellaneous)
Melo 1987,O 5,C,19:5
Melo 1988,Ja 31,55:1
Saunders, David (Producer)
High Spirits 1988,N 18,C,10:1
Saunders, Don (Miscellaneous)
Right Hand Man, The 1987,O 2,C,13:1

Saunders, Justine
Fringe Dwellers, The 1987,Ja 23,C,13:3
Saura, Carlos (Director)
El Dorado 1988,My 22,II,21:5
Mama Turns 100 (Mama Cumple 100 Anos) 1988,S 16,C,13:1
Savage, Carlos (Miscellaneous)
Realm of Fortune, The 1987,Mr 17,C,14:1
Savage, Fred
Princess Bride, The 1987,S 25,C,10:5
Vice Versa 1988,Mr 11,C,12:6
Savage, John
Hotel Colonial 1987,S 19,16:3
Beat, The 1988,Je 3,C,10:6
Savant, Doug
Masquerade 1988,Mr 11,C,8:5
Savident, John
Little Dorrit 1988,Mr 26,11:1
Saville, Philip (Director)
Shadey 1987,Je 5,C,10:1
Savina, Iya
Asya's Happiness 1988,S 24,13:1
Savinar, Tad (Miscellaneous)
Talk Radio 1988,D 21,C,28:4
Savini, Tom
Creepshow 2 1987,My 4,C,17:1
Savitt, Jill (Miscellaneous)
Full Moon in Blue Water 1988,N 23,C,15:1
Sawada, Tamae
River of Fireflies 1988,N 4,C,13:1
Sawadogo, Ousmane
Choice, The 1988,Mr 24,C,26:6
Sawalha, Nadim
Pascali's Island 1988,Jl 22,C,16:4
Sawyer, Richard (Miscellaneous)
Vibes 1988,Ag 5,C,6:1
Sawyer, Shirley
Gap-Toothed Women 1987,S 16,C,28:3
Saxon, Edward (Producer)
Married to the Mob 1988,Ag 19,C,6:1
Sayle, Alexei
Siesta 1987,N 11,C,23:3
Love Child, The 1988,S 14,C,20:5
Sayles, John
Matewan 1987,Ag 28,C,3:4
Eight Men Out 1988,S 2,C,3:1
Sayles, John (Director)
Matewan 1987,Ag 28,C,3:4
Eight Men Out 1988,S 2,C,3:1
Eight Men Out 1988,S 11,II,1:3
Sayles, John (Miscellaneous)
Wild Thing 1987,Ap 17,C,13:1
Sayles, John (Screenwriter)
Wild Thing 1987,Ap 17,C,13:1
Matewan 1987,Ag 28,C,3:4
Eight Men Out 1988,S 2,C,3:1
Sbaraglia, Leonardo
Night of the Pencils, The 1987,Mr 14,13:1
Sbarge, Stephen A (Cinematographer)
Ira, You'll Get into Trouble 1987,F 20,C,4:5
Sbarge, Stephen A (Director)
Ira, You'll Get into Trouble 1987,F 20,C,4:5
Sbarge, Stephen A (Producer)
Ira, You'll Get into Trouble 1987,F 20,C,4:5
Scacchi, Greta
Defense of the Realm 1987,Ja 16,C,6:5
Burke and Wills 1987,Je 12,C,10:1
Good Morning, Babylon 1987,Jl 15,C,18:5
Man in Love, A 1987,Jl 31,C,10:6
White Mischief 1988,Ap 22,C,20:1
Trois Soeurs (Paura e Amore) 1988,My 22,II,21:5
Scales, Prunella
Lonely Passion of Judith Hearne, The 1987,D 23,C,15:1
Consuming Passions 1988,Ap 6,C,18:3
Scanlon, Toni
High Tide 1988,F 19,C,5:1
Scannell, Kevin
Shoot to Kill 1988,F 12,C,8:5
Scantlebury, Glenn (Miscellaneous)
Big Time 1988,S 30,C,20:1
Scarfe, Alan
Iron Eagle II 1988,N 12,15:3
Scarfiotti, Ferdinando (Miscellaneous)
Last Emperor, The 1987,N 20,C,3:4
Scarpa, Renato
Julia and Julia 1988,F 5,C,5:1
Scarpelli, Furio (Screenwriter)
Family, The 1988,Ja 22,C,11:1
Scarwid, Diana
Heat 1987,Mr 13,C,33:1
Schaal, Wendy
Innerspace 1987,Jl 1,C,17:1

Scott-Justice, Jessica (Miscellaneous)
Sticky Fingers 1988,My 6,C,28:5
Scotto, Vincent (Composer)
Angele 1988,F 26,C,19:1
Scotton, Giorgio (Producer)
Family, The 1988,Ja 22,C,11:1
Scott Thomas, Kristin
Handful of Dust, A 1988,Je 24,C,14:1
Scribner, George (Director)
Oliver and Company 1988,N 18,C,8:4
Scrimm, Angus
Phantasm II 1988,Jl 8,C,11:1
Sculthorpe, Peter (Composer)
Burke and Wills 1987,Je 12,C,10:1
Seacat, Sondra
Promised Land 1988,Ja 22,C,13:1
Seagal, Steven
Above the Law 1988,Ap 8,C,26:4
Seagal, Steven (Miscellaneous)
Above the Law 1988,Ap 8,C,26:4
Seagal, Steven (Producer)
Above the Law 1988,Ap 8,C,26:4
Seagrove, Jenny
Appointment with Death 1988,Ap 15,C,4:5
Seale, Douglas
Ernest Saves Christmas 1988,N 11,C,15:1
Seale, John (Cinematographer)
Stakeout 1987,Ag 5,C,21:1
Gorillas in the Mist 1988,S 23,C,19:1
Rain Man 1988,D 16,C,12:5
Seaman, Peter S (Screenwriter)
Who Framed Roger Rabbit 1988,Je 22,C,17:2
Who Framed Roger Rabbit 1988,Jl 3,II,1:3
Sebesky, Don (Composer)
Rosary Murders, The 1987,Ag 28,C,12:3
Secrist, Kim (Miscellaneous)
Teen Wolf Too 1987,N 20,C,14:6
Seda, Dori
Gap-Toothed Women 1987,S 16,C,28:3
Seferchian, Marc (Cinematographer)
Call Me Madame 1988,Mr 12,14:4
Segal, Gilles
Jupon Rouge, Le (Manuela's Loves) 1988,Mr 21,C,17:1
Segal, Misha (Composer)
Steele Justice 1987,My 8,C,12:4
New Adventures of Pippi Longstocking, The 1988,Jl 29,C,11
Segal, Misha (Miscellaneous)
New Adventures of Pippi Longstocking, The 1988,Jl 29,C,11
Segal, Shahar
Late Summer Blues 1988,Ag 12,C,13:1
Segura, Francois
Field of Honor (Champ d'Honneur) 1988,Mr 18,C,24:5
Seidelman, Susan (Director)
Making Mr Right 1987,Ap 10,C,16:5
Making Mr Right 1988,Ja 3,II,15:1
Seidler, David (Screenwriter)
Tucker: The Man and His Dream 1988,Ag 12,C,8:1
Seigner, Emmanuelle
Frantic 1988,F 26,C,3:4
Seiler, Paul
My Life for Zarah Leander 1987,My 29,C,8:1
Seipp, Michele
Blue Iguana, The 1988,Ap 23,18:2
Seitz, Jane (Miscellaneous)
Felix 1988,S 24,13:1
Seles, Maria
Jacob 1988,O 3,C,24:4
Selezyova, Nataliya
Theme, The 1987,S 28,C,18:1
Self, Jim
Retracing Steps: American Dance Since Postmodemism
1988,D 7,C,24:5
Beehive 1988,D 7,C,24:5
Self, Jim (Director)
Beehive 1988,D 7,C,24:5
Self, Jim (Miscellaneous)
Beehive 1988,D 7,C,24:5
Sellars, Peter
King Lear 1988,Ja 22,C,6:1
Selleck, Tom
Three Men and a Baby 1987,N 25,C,24:3
Three Men and a Baby 1987,D 6,II,23:5
Three Men and a Baby 1988,Ja 31,II,19:1
Sellers, Victoria
Heaven 1987,Ap 17,C,8:5
Seltzer, David (Director)
Punchline 1988,S 30,C,14:4
Seltzer, David (Screenwriter)
Punchline 1988,S 30,C,14:4
Seltzer, Dov (Composer)
Hanna's War 1988,N 23,C,14:1

Semler, Dean (Cinematographer)
Lighthorsemen, The 1988,My 13,C,14:1
Cocktail 1988,Jl 29,C,6:5
Young Guns 1988,Ag 12,C,18:1
Semler, Peter
Caviar Rouge, Le 1988,Mr 25,C,10:5
Sen, Mrinal (Director)
Genesis 1988,D 23,C,18:6
Sen, Mrinal (Screenwriter)
Genesis 1988,D 23,C,18:6
Senesh, Hanna (Original Author)
Hanna's War 1988,N 23,C,14:1
Senia, Jean-Marie (Composer)
Wedding in Galilee 1988,Mr 11,C,23:1
Man in the Silk Hat, The 1988,Ap 1,C,10:5
Senna, Orlando (Screenwriter)
Opera do Malandro 1987,Ja 30,C,6:5
Senter, Jack (Miscellaneous)
New Adventures of Pippi Longstocking, The 1988,Jl 29,C,11
Seoane, Maria (Original Author)
Night of the Pencils, The 1987,Mr 14,13:1
Sephuma, Peter
Mapantsula 1988,S 24,12:4
Ser, Randy (Miscellaneous)
Casual Sex? 1988,Ap 22,C,24:1
Seresin, Michael (Cinematographer)
Angel Heart 1987,Mr 6,C,5:1
Serna, Assumpta
Matador 1988,S 16,C,8:5
Serra, Noun (Miscellaneous)
Lord of the Dance/Destroyer of Illusion 1987,D 26,14:4
Serra, Pablo
City and the Dogs, The 1987,Ja 7,C,20:5
Serra, Raymond
Forever, Lulu 1987,Ap 24,C,10:4
Serrano, Julieta
Dark Habits 1988,My 6,C,28:5
Matador 1988,S 16,C,8:5
Women on the Verge of a Nervous Breakdown 1988,S
23,C,25:1
Serrano, Tina
Night of the Pencils, The 1987,Mr 14,13:1
Serrault, Michel
Buffet Froid (Cold Cuts) 1987,S 4,C,5:4
Serreau, Coline (Original Author)
Three Men and a Baby 1987,N 25,C,24:3
Three Men and a Baby 1987,D 6,II,23:5
Serry, Viviane
Mammame 1988,Ja 29,C,10:4
Servais, Jean
Ambiciosos, Los (Ambitious Ones, The) 1988,F 12,C,13:1
Angele 1988,F 26,C,19:1
Setbon, Philippe (Miscellaneous)
Honeymoon 1987,N 20,C,24:1
Setbon, Philippe (Screenwriter)
Honeymoon 1987,N 20,C,24:1
Seth, Roshan
Little Dorrit 1988,Mr 26,11:1
Little Dorrit 1988,O 21,C,12:3
Setzer, Brian
Bamba, La 1987,Jl 24,C,4:3
Seweryn, Andrzej
Land of Promise 1988,F 5,C,13:6
Sex, John
Mondo New York 1988,Ap 22,C,23:1
Sexton, John (Producer)
Burke and Wills 1987,Je 12,C,10:1
Seydoux, Michel (Producer)
Man in Love, A 1987,Jl 31,C,10:6
Seydoux, Valerie (Producer)
36 Fillette 1988,O 4,C,19:1
Seyfried, Robert
Mammame 1988,Ja 29,C,10:4
Seymour, Lynn
Dancers 1987,O 9,C,24:1
Seymour, Ralph
Rain Man 1988,D 16,C,12:5
Sgriccia, Philip J (Miscellaneous)
Freeway 1988,S 3,10:6
Shadix, Glenn
Beetlejuice 1988,Mr 30,C,18:6
Shaffer, Anthony (Screenwriter)
Appointment with Death 1988,Ap 15,C,4:5
Absolution 1988,Jl 1,C,8:5
Shaffer, Deborah (Director)
Fire from the Mountain 1987,O 10,19:4
Shaffer, Deborah (Producer)
Fire from the Mountain 1987,O 10,19:4
Shaffer, Ralph (Miscellaneous)
Care Bears' Adventure in Wonderland, The 1987,Ag
7,C,21:1

Shafransky, R A (Producer)
Swimming to Cambodia 1987,Mr 13,C,8:1
Shagan, Steve (Screenwriter)
Sicilian, The 1987,O 23,C,4:5
Shah, Naseeruddin
Genesis 1988,D 23,C,18:6
Shaine, Rick (Miscellaneous)
Dead of Winter 1987,F 6,C,4:3
Crossing Delancey 1988,Ag 24,C,15:1
Shakespeare, William (Original Author)
King Lear 1988,Ja 22,C,6:1
Shakhov, V
Commissar 1988,Je 17,C,16:4
Shamberg, Michael (Producer)
Fish Called Wanda, A 1988,Jl 15,C,8:1
Shambert, Michael H (Producer)
Salvation! 1987,My 31,51:1
Shanahan, James (Miscellaneous)
Overboard 1987,D 16,C,22:3
Shankar, Ravi (Composer)
Genesis 1988,D 23,C,18:6
Shanley, John Patrick (Screenwriter)
Moonstruck 1987,D 16,C,22:3
Five Corners 1988,Ja 22,C,18:1
Shannon, Al
No Man's Land 1987,O 23,C,10:5
Drifter, The 1988,Je 5,59:1
Shanta, James Anthony
Allnighter, The 1987,My 4,C,16:1
Shapiro, George (Producer)
Summer School 1987,Jl 22,C,22:1
Shapiro, Robert (Producer)
Arthur 2 on the Rocks 1988,Jl 8,C,8:1
Shapiro, Stanley (Screenwriter)
Dirty Rotten Scoundrels 1988,D 14,C,21:4
Shapiro, Stuart S (Producer)
Mondo New York 1988,Ap 22,C,23:1
Sharkey, Bill Ray
Dudes 1988,Je 24,C,9:1
Sharon, Steve (Miscellaneous)
Dead Pool 1988,Jl 13,C,22:1
Sharon, Steve (Screenwriter)
Dead Pool 1988,Jl 13,C,22:1
Sharp, Howard (Miscellaneous)
Man Who Mistook His Wife for a Hat, The 1988,Ag
31,C,17:1
Sharp, Jan (Producer)
Good Wife, The 1987,F 20,C,19:3
Sharp, Lesley
Rita, Sue and Bob Too 1987,Jl 17,C,18:1
Love Child, The 1988,S 14,C,20:5
Shaver, Helen
Believers, The 1987,Je 10,C,22:5
Land Before Time, The 1988,N 18,C,8:4
Shaw, Penelope (Miscellaneous)
Hanoi Hilton, The 1987,Mr 27,C,13:1
Shaw, Sandy (Miscellaneous)
Dead Pool 1988,Jl 13,C,22:1
Shaw, Sebastian
High Season 1988,Mr 25,C,12:6
Shawn, Dick
Maid to Order 1987,Ag 28,C,6:1
Shawn, Wallace
Bedroom Window, The 1987,Ja 16,C,6:4
Radio Days 1987,Ja 30,C,1:1
Radio Days 1987,F 1,II,21:1
Bedroom Window, The 1987,F 8,II,21:1
Prick Up Your Ears 1987,Ap 17,C,17:1
Princess Bride, The 1987,S 25,C,10:5
Modems, The 1988,Ap 15,C,21:1
Shaye, Robert (Producer)
Nightmare on Elm Street 3, A: Dream Warriors 1987,F
27,C,15:3
My Demon Lover 1987,Ap 24,C,14:1
Hidden, The 1987,O 30,C,19:1
Nightmare on Elm Street 4, A: The Dream Master 1988,Ag
19,C,8:3
Shea, John
Honeymoon 1987,N 20,C,24:1
New Life, A 1988,Mr 25,C,5:2
Light Years 1988,My 15,56:1
Stealing Home 1988,Ag 26,C,17:4
Shearer, Harry
My Stepmother Is an Alien 1988,D 9,C,17:1
Sheedy, Ally
Maid to Order 1987,Ag 28,C,6:1
Sheen, Charlie
Platoon 1987,Ja 11,II,21:1
Three for the Road 1987,Ap 10,C,5:1
No Man's Land 1987,O 23,C,10:5

Sobel, Curt (Composer)
  Alien Nation 1988,O 7,C,10:6
Sobocinski, Witold (Cinematographer)
  Everything for Sale 1987,Mr 13,C,15:1
  Land of Promise 1988,F 5,C,13:6
  Frantic 1988,F 26,C,3:4
Soeteman, Gerard (Screenwriter)
  Assault, The 1987,F 6,C,8:1
Sofonova, Elena
  Dark Eyes 1987,S 25,C,26:5
Sofr, Jaromir (Cinematographer)
  My Sweet Little Village 1987,Ja 9,C, 6:5
Sohar, Ika
  I Don't Give a Damn 1988,My 20,C,22:5
Sokolova, Lyubov
  Asya's Happiness 1988,S 24,13:1
Solan, Peter (Director)
  Boxer and Death, The 1988,O 12,C,19:1
Solan, Peter (Screenwriter)
  Boxer and Death, The 1988,O 12,C,19:1
Solano, Isidro Jose
  Tasio 1987,Mr 27,C,15:1
Soler, Andres
  Ambiciosos, Los (Ambitious Ones, The) 1988,F 12,C,13:1
Soler, Domingo
  Ambiciosos, Los (Ambitious Ones, The) 1988,F 12,C,13:1
Solo, Robert (Producer)
  Colors 1988,Ap 15,C,4:1
Solomon, Maribeth (Composer)
  Care Bears' Adventure in Wonderland, The 1987,Ag 7,C,21:1
Solt, Andrew (Director)
  Imagine: John Lennon 1988,O 7,C,7:1
Solt, Andrew (Producer)
  Imagine: John Lennon 1988,O 7,C,7:1
Solt, Andrew (Screenwriter)
  Imagine: John Lennon 1988,O 7,C,7:1
Sommer, Josef
  Rosary Murders, The 1987,Ag 28,C,12:3
Son, Trinh Cong (Composer)
  Karma 1987,Jl 8,C,22:5
Sonbert, Warren (Director)
  Honor and Obey (Avant Garde Voices) 1988,O 1,15:1
Sones, Sonya (Miscellaneous)
  River's Edge 1987,My 8,C,28:4
Sonnenfeld, Barry (Cinematographer)
  Raising Arizona 1987,Mr 11,C,24:5
  Throw Momma from the Train 1987,D 11,C,15:1
  Big 1988,Je 3,C,8:4
Sonnenfeld, Barry (Miscellaneous)
  Three O'Clock High 1987,O 9,C,16:3
Sontag, Susan (Narrator)
  Sarah 1988,S 25,64:1
Sonye, Michael
  Surf Nazis Must Die 1987,O 2,C,24:5
Soon-Teck Oh
  Death Wish 4: The Crackdown 1987,N 7,14:1
Soon-Teck Oh (Narrator)
  Steele Justice 1987,My 8,C,12:4
Sordi, Alberto
  Traffic Jam 1988,Mr 4,C,14:6
Sosa, Mercedes
  Sera Posible el Sur: Un Viaje por Argentina de la Mano de
    Mercedes Sosa (South Will Be Possible, The: A Trip
    Through Argentina with Mercedes Sosa) 1987,S 11,C,15:1
Sothern, Ann
  Whales of August, The 1987,O 16,C,3:1
Soto, Hugo
  Man Facing Southeast 1987,Mr 13,C,4:5
Soto, Talisa
  Spike of Bensonhurst 1988,N 11,C,15:1
Soul, David
  Hanoi Hilton, The 1987,Mr 27,C,13:1
  Appointment with Death 1988,Ap 15,C,4:5
Soule, Allen
  House of Games 1987,O 11,94:1
Soutendijk, Renee
  Second Victory, The 1987,My 27,C,22:3
South, Margaret Jennings (Producer)
  Beaches 1988,D 21,C,28:4
Southern, Terry (Screenwriter)
  Telephone, The 1988,F 14,77:1
Southon, Mike (Cinematographer)
  Gothic 1987,Ap 10,C,16:3
Sova, Peter (Cinematographer)
  Tin Men 1987,Mr 6,C,3:1
  Good Morning, Vietnam 1987,D 23,C,11:1
Sowder, Cynthia (Miscellaneous)
  Allnighter, The 1987,My 4,C,16:1
  Blue Iguana, The 1988,Ap 23,18:2
Spada, Andrea
  History 1988,Je 3,C,15:1

Spader, James
  Mannequin 1987,F 13,C,8:6
  Baby Boom 1987,O 7,C,24:5
  Less Than Zero 1987,N 6,C,23:1
  Jack's Back 1988,My 6,C,19:1
Spall, Timothy
  Gothic 1987,Ap 10,C,16:3
Spang, Ron (Miscellaneous)
  Dead Pool 1988,Jl 13,C,22:1
Spano, Anthony (Miscellaneous)
  Cop 1988,F 5,C,19:3
Spano, Vincent
  Good Morning, Babylon 1987,Jl 15,C,18:5
  And God Created Woman 1988,Mr 4,C,22:4
Sparks, Adrian
  Apprentice to Murder 1988,F 26,C,14:1
Spelling, Aaron (Producer)
  Surrender 1987,O 9,C,10:6
  Satisfaction 1988,F 13,15:1
Spence, Bruce
  Rikky and Pete 1988,My 20,C,9:1
Spence, Michael (Miscellaneous)
  Summer Camp Nightmare 1987,Ap 17,C,30:5
Spence, Peter
  Crazy Moon 1988,F 8,C,18:5
Spencer, Brenton (Cinematographer)
  Blue Monkey, The 1987,O 16,C,12:6
Spencer, James H (Miscellaneous)
  Innerspace 1987,Jl 1,C,17:1
Sperling, David (Cinematographer)
  Street Trash 1987,S 16,C,27:3
  Drifter, The 1988,Je 5,59:1
Spheeris, Penelope (Director)
  Decline of Western Civilization Part II, The: The Metal Years
    1988,Je 17,C,14:4
  Dudes 1988,Je 24,C,9:1
  Decline of Western Civilization Part II, The: The Metal Years
    1988,Je 26,II,21:1
Spheeris, Penelope (Screenwriter)
  Summer Camp Nightmare 1987,Ap 17,C,30:5
Spicer, Michael (Composer)
  Backlash 1987,Mr 26,C,14:4
  Backlash 1987,Ag 27,C,18:3
Spiegel, Scott (Screenwriter)
  Evil Dead 2: Dead by Dawn 1987,Mr 13,C,18:1
Spielberg, Anne (Screenwriter)
  Big 1988,Je 3,C,8:4
Spielberg, Steven (Director)
  Empire of the Sun 1987,D 9,C,25:1
  Empire of the Sun 1988,F 7,II,21:1
Spielberg, Steven (Producer)
  American Tail, An 1987,Ja 18,II,19:1
  Empire of the Sun 1987,D 9,C,25:1
  Batteries Not Included 1987,D 18,C,12:5
  Land Before Time, The 1988,N 18,C,8:4
Spier, Carol (Miscellaneous)
  Dead Ringers 1988,S 23,C,10:1
Spiers, David (Miscellaneous)
  Ping Pong 1987,Jl 17,C,10:6
  Promised Land 1988,Ja 22,C,13:1
Spinell, Joe
  Deadly Illusion 1987,O 31,10:5
Spinelli, Philip J (Producer)
  Invisible Kid, The 1988,Mr 31,C,16:4
Spinotti, Dante (Cinematographer)
  From the Hip 1987,F 6,C,10:4
  Berlin Affair, The 1988,Jl 15,C,12:5
  Beaches 1988,D 21,C,28:4
Spisak, Neil (Miscellaneous)
  End of the Line 1988,F 26,C,15:1
Spottiswoode, Roger (Director)
  Shoot to Kill 1988,F 12,C,8:5
Sprenger, Wolf-Dieter
  Dragon Chow 1988,My 27,C,10:5
Spring
  Last of England, The 1988,S 28,C,18:3
Springsteen, Bruce
  Chuck Berry: Hail! Hail! Rock 'n' Roll 1987,O 3,10:5
Springsteen, Bruce (Composer)
  Light of Day 1987,F 6,C,4:3
Sprott, Eion (Miscellaneous)
  Moonstruck 1987,D 16,C,22:3
Squires, Buddy (Cinematographer)
  No Applause, Just Throw Money 1988,Mr 12,14:4
Stack, Robert
  Plain Clothes 1988,Ap 16,18:1
  Caddyshack II 1988,Jl 23,16:5
Stadlbauer, Hans
  Bagdad Cafe 1988,Ap 22,C,19:1

Stafford-Clark, Nigel (Producer)
  Stormy Monday 1988,Ap 22,C,3:5
Stagnaro, Bruno
  Debajo del Mundo (Under the World) 1988,O 5,C,19:5
  Debajo del Mundo (Under the World) 1988,N 1,C,17:1
Stagnaro, Juan Bautista (Director)
  Debajo del Mundo (Under the World) 1988,O 5,C,19:5
  Debajo del Mundo (Under the World) 1988,N 1,C,17:1
Stagnaro, Juan Bautista (Screenwriter)
  Debajo del Mundo (Under the World) 1988,O 5,C,19:5
Stakis, Anastassia
  Siesta 1987,N 11,C,23:3
Staley, James
  Assassination 1987,Ja 10,13:1
Stallone, Frank
  Barfly 1987,S 30,C,18:1
Stallone, Sylvester
  Over the Top 1987,F 12,C,21:2
  Over the Top 1987,Mr 1,II,21:1
  Over the Top 1987,My 10,II,17:1
  Over the Top 1988,Ja 3,II,15:1
  Rambo III 1988,My 25,C,15:1
  Rambo III 1988,Je 19,II,23:1
Stallone, Sylvester (Screenwriter)
  Over the Top 1987,F 12,C,21:2
  Over the Top 1987,Mr 1,II,21:1
  Rambo III 1988,My 25,C,15:1
  Rambo III 1988,Je 19,II,23:1
Stamp, Terence
  Link 1987,Ap 24,C,10:4
  Sicilian, The 1987,O 23,C,4:5
  Wall Street 1987,D 11,C,3:4
  Young Guns 1988,Ag 12,C,18:1
  Alien Nation 1988,O 7,C,10:6
Stamper, Larry (Miscellaneous)
  Wild Thing 1987,Ap 17,C,13:1
Stanczak, Wadeck
  Scene of the Crime 1987,Ja 23,C,14:1
  Rendez-Vous 1987,D 25,C,6:5
Standing, John
  Nightflyers 1987,O 24,17:1
Stanier, John (Cinematographer)
  Rambo III 1988,My 25,C,15:1
Stanley, Lauren
  MAC and Me 1988,Ag 13,14:1
Stanley, Paul
  Decline of Western Civilization Part II, The: The Metal Years
    1988,Je 17,C,14:4
Stanton, Charlotte
  Square Dance 1987,F 20,C,4:5
Stanton, Harry Dean
  Slamdance 1987,N 6,C,10:5
  Stars and Bars 1988,Mr 18,C,3:1
  Mr North 1988,Jl 22,C,8:4
  Last Temptation of Christ, The 1988,Ag 12,C,1:1
Stanton, John
  Rent-a-Cop 1988,Ja 15,C,13:1
Stapleton, Maureen
  Made in Heaven 1987,N 6,C,16:1
  Nuts 1987,N 20,C,16:6
  Hello Actors Studio 1988,N 9,C,19:1
  Cocoon: The Return 1988,N 23,C,15:1
Stapleton, Oliver (Cinematographer)
  Prick Up Your Ears 1987,Ap 17,C,17:1
  Chuck Berry: Hail! Hail! Rock 'n' Roll 1987,O 3,10:5
  Sammy and Rosie Get Laid 1987,O 30,C,5:1
Stark, Graham
  Blind Date 1987,Mr 27,C,11:1
Stark, Jonathan
  Project X 1987,Ap 17,C,15:1
  House II: The Second Story 1987,Ag 29,11:1
Stark, Ray (Producer)
  Biloxi Blues 1988,Mr 25,C,1:1
Stassen, Willy (Cinematographer)
  Love Is a Dog from Hell 1988,Mr 18,C,15:1
  Love Is a Dog from Hell 1988,Ap 23,14:5
Stavrou, Aris (Cinematographer)
  Photograph, The 1988,Mr 17,C,26:3
Steadman, Alison
  Short and the Curlies, The 1988,S 29,C,24:3
Steadman, Robert (Cinematographer)
  Above the Law 1988,Ap 8,C,26:4
Steagall, Rod
  Benji the Hunted 1987,Je 17,C,18:6
Stearns, Craig (Miscellaneous)
  Date with an Angel 1987,N 21,14:5
  Dead Heat 1988,My 7,13:1
  Blob, The 1988,Ag 5,C,6:5
Steele, David (Composer)
  Tin Men 1987,Mr 6,C,3:1

T

Torque, Henry (Composer)
Mammame 1988,Ja 29,C,10:4
Torrance, Robert (Cinematographer)
Perfect Match 1988,Je 4,12:3
Torrance, Robert (Producer)
Perfect Match 1988,Je 4,12:3
Torrance, Tim (Composer)
Perfect Match 1988,Je 4,12:3
Torrens, Pip
Handful of Dust, A 1988,Je 24,C,14:1
Torrente, Vinnie
MAC and Me 1988,Ag 13,14:1
Torres, Michelle
Fringe Dwellers, The 1987,Ja 23,C,13:3
Torres Zarragoza, Javier
Winter Tan, A 1988,O 2,57:6
Torrini, Cinzia TH (Director)
Hotel Colonial 1987,S 19,16:3
Torrini, Cinzia TH (Screenwriter)
Hotel Colonial 1987,S 19,16:3
Torruella, Magi (Cinematographer)
Hail Hazana 1988,Je 10,C,18:1
Torzecki, Grzegorz (Cinematographer)
Sunday Pranks 1988,Mr 13,57:1
Torzecki, Grzegorz (Screenwriter)
Sunday Pranks 1988,Mr 13,57:1
Toscano, Gabriela
Debajo del Mundo (Under the World) 1988,O 5,C,19:5
Tosi, Tarcisio
Long Live the Lady! 1987,O 16,C,26:5
Toura, Mutsuhiro
Violence at Noon 1988,N 11,C,6:4
Towey, John Madden
Invisible Kid, The 1988,Mr 31,C,16:4
Towne, Robert
Pickup Artist, The 1987,S 18,C,23:1
Towne, Robert (Director)
Tequila Sunrise 1988,D 2,C,8:4
Towne, Robert (Screenwriter)
Tequila Sunrise 1988,D 2,C,8:4
Towns, Colin (Composer)
Shadey 1987,Je 5,C,10:1
Bellman and True 1988,Ap 1,C,4:4
Townsend, Robert
Hollywood Shuffle 1987,Mr 20,C,8:1
Townsend, Robert (Director)
Hollywood Shuffle 1987,Mr 20,C,8:1
Eddie Murphy Raw 1987,D 19,18:4
Townsend, Robert (Producer)
Hollywood Shuffle 1987,Mr 20,C,8:1
Townsend, Robert (Screenwriter)
Hollywood Shuffle 1987,Mr 20,C,8:1
Toy, Alan
Kansas 1988,S 23,C,17:1
Tracey, Ian
Stakeout 1987,Ag 5,C,21:1
Tracy, Margaret (Original Author)
White of the Eye 1988,My 20,C,22:5
Trafankowska, Daria
Sunday Pranks 1988,Mr 13,57:1
Trainor, Mary Ellen
Monster Squad 1987,Ag 14,C,15:1
Tran, Tung Thanh
Good Morning, Vietnam 1987,D 23,C,11:1
Traore, Soumba
Yeelen 1987,O 8,C,37:1
Trapaga, Monica
High Tide 1988,F 19,C,5:1
Travanti, Daniel J
Midnight Crossing 1988,My 14,16:5
Travers, Nigel
Burke and Wills 1987,Je 12,C,10:1
Travis, Nancy
Three Men and a Baby 1987,N 25,C,24:3
Travis, Neil (Miscellaneous)
No Way Out 1987,Ag 14,C,3:1
Cocktail 1988,Jl 29,C,6:5
Travnecek, Claudia (Miscellaneous)
Fire and Ice 1987,N 6,C,14:6
Travolta, Joey
Amazon Women on the Moon 1987,S 18,C,12:6
Trebor, Robert
Making Mr Right 1987,Ap 10,C,16:5
My Demon Lover 1987,Ap 24,C,14:1
Talk Radio 1988,D 21,C,28:4
Trent, Barbara (Director)
Coverup: Behind the Iran-Contra Affair 1988,Ag 26,C,8:6
Trent, Barbara (Producer)
Coverup: Behind the Iran-Contra Affair 1988,Ag 26,C,8:6
Tresgot, Annie (Director)
Hello Actors Studio 1988,N 9,C,19:1

Treu, Wolfgang (Cinematographer)
God Doesn't Believe in Us Anymore 1988,Jl 20,C,20:5
Trevor, Richard (Miscellaneous)
Deceivers, The 1988,S 2,C,10:1
Tribiger, Alexander
Loyalties 1987,Mr 21,14:3
Loyalties 1987,N 20,C,21:1
Tribiger, Jonathan
Loyalties 1987,Mr 21,14:3
Loyalties 1987,N 20,C,21:1
Trigg, Derek (Miscellaneous)
Girl, The 1987,Ag 7,C,10:6
Trinchet, Jorge
Parting of the Ways (Lejanja) 1987,S 23,C,22:6
Trindade, Ze
Subway to the Stars 1988,Mr 25,C,14:6
Trintignant, Jean-Louis
Rendez-Vous 1987,D 25,C,6:5
Tristan, Dorothy (Screenwriter)
Weeds 1987,O 16,C,10:5
Trixner, Heinz
38: Vienna Before the Fall 1988,My 6,C,17:1
Troch, Ludo (Miscellaneous)
Love Is a Dog from Hell 1988,Mr 18,C,15:1
Love Is a Dog from Hell 1988,Ap 23,14:5
Trodd, Kenith (Producer)
Month in the Country, A 1987,S 27,67:1
Month in the Country, A 1988,F 19,C,10:5
Troisi, Massimo
Hotel Colonial 1987,S 19,16:3
Troller, Georg Stefan (Screenwriter)
Welcome in Vienna 1988,Je 1,C,17:1
God Doesn't Believe in Us Anymore 1988,Jl 20,C,20:5
Santa Fe 1988,Jl 20,C,20:5
Tronick, Michael (Miscellaneous)
Beverly Hills Cop II 1987,My 20,C,28:1
Midnight Run 1988,Jl 20,C,15:5
Troost, Ernest (Composer)
Dead Heat 1988,My 7,13:1
Tiger Warsaw 1988,S 23,C,20:1
Trovaioli, Armando (Composer)
Family, The 1988,Ja 22,C,11:1
Trujillo, Luis M
Amerika, Terra Incognita 1988,D 9,C,10:6
Truxa, Erik
Dark Side of the Moon, The 1987,Mr 19,C,28:1
Tsafir, Yoav
Late Summer Blues 1988,Ag 12,C,13:1
Tsakonas, John
Home Remedy 1988,Jl 22,C,17:1
Tsangas, Christos
Photograph, The 1988,Mr 17,C,26:3
Tsapnik, Yuri
Burglar, The 1988,Ag 17,C,22:1
Tselios, Paris
High Season 1988,Mr 25,C,12:6
Tseshang Rigzin
Horse Thief, The 1988,Ja 6,C,15:1
Tsugawa, Masahiko
Tampopo 1987,Mr 26,C,21:1
Taxing Woman, A 1987,S 26,9:1
Tsui Fu-sheng
Daughter of the Nile 1988,S 30,C,8:4
Tsui Hark (Producer)
Chinese Ghost Story, A 1988,Mr 23,C,20:5
Tsumura, Takashi
Gonza the Spearman 1988,O 28,C,15:1
Tsutsui, Tomomi (Screenwriter)
Sorekara (And Then) 1987,Ap 8,C,23:1
Tuber, Joel (Producer)
Making Mr Right 1987,Ap 10,C,16:5
Tucci, Maria
Touch and Go 1987,Ja 14,C,20:5
Tucci, Stanley
Monkey Shines: An Experiment in Fear 1988,Jl 29,C,12:4
Tucker, Ken
Gospel According to Al Green 1987,S 9,C,18:5
Tucker, Michael
Radio Days 1987,Ja 30,C,1:1
Tin Men 1987,Mr 6,C,3:1
Tukur, Ulrich
Felix 1988,S 24,13:1
Tullis, Dan, Jr
Extreme Prejudice 1987,Ap 24,C,8:5
Tung, Bill
Jackie Chan's Police Story 1987,S 26,12:3
Turman, John (Producer)
Full Moon in Blue Water 1988,N 23,C,15:1
Turman, Lawrence (Producer)
Short Circuit 2 1988,Jl 6,C,18:5

Full Moon in Blue Water 1988,N 23,C,15:1
Turner, Bonnie (Screenwriter)
Funland 1988,Je 1,C,17:1
Turner, Ed (Screenwriter)
Emest Saves Christmas 1988,N 11,C,15:1
Turner, Kathleen
Julia and Julia 1988,F 5,C,5:1
Switching Channels 1988,Mr 4,C,10:4
Who Framed Roger Rabbit 1988,Je 22,C,17:2
Accidental Tourist, The 1988,D 23,C,12:5
Turner, Kathleen (Narrator)
Dear America: Letters Home from Vietnam 1988,S 16,C,18:1
Turner, Simon (Composer)
Last of England, The 1988,S 28,C,18:3
Turner, Terry (Screenwriter)
Funland 1988,Je 1,C,17:1
Turrin, Joseph (Composer)
New Life, A 1988,Mr 25,C,5:2
Turturro, John
Sicilian, The 1987,O 23,C,4:5
Five Corners 1988,Ja 22,C,18:1
Tushingham, Rita
Housekeeper, The 1987,Ap 24,C,7:1
Twiggy
Madame Sousatzka 1988,O 14,C,8:5
Twohy, D T (Screenwriter)
Critters 2: The Main Course 1988,Ap 29,C,6:6
Tygel, David (Composer)
Color of Destiny, The 1988,Jl 22,C,17:1
Tyler, Anne (Original Author)
Accidental Tourist, The 1988,D 23,C,12:5
Tyler, Steven
Decline of Western Civilization Part II, The: The Metal Years
1988,Je 17,C,14:4
Tyner, Harold
Best Seller 1987,S 25,C,24:1
Tyrrell, Susan
Chipmunk Adventure, The 1987,My 22,C,10:5
Big Top Pee-wee 1988,Jl 22,C,10:3
Tyson, Cathy
Serpent and the Rainbow, The 1988,F 5,C,3:4
Tyson, Richard
Three O'Clock High 1987,O 9,C,16:3
Two Moon Junction 1988,Ap 30,17:1
Tyson, Thom (Producer)
Wizard of Loneliness, The 1988,S 2,C,9:1
Tyszkiewicz, Beata
Everything for Sale 1987,Mr 13,C,15:1
Tyzack, Margaret
Prick Up Your Ears 1987,Ap 17,C,17:1
Tzafrir, Shlomo (Miscellaneous)
I Don't Give a Damn 1988,My 20,C,22:5

U

Ubarry, Hechter
Crocodile Dundee II 1988,My 25,C,15:3
Ubell, Marc (Miscellaneous)
Deranged 1987,O 31,12:3
Uchida, Yuya
Comic Magazine (Komikku Zasshi) 1987,Ja 16,C,14:6
Uchida, Yuya (Screenwriter)
Comic Magazine (Komikku Zasshi) 1987,Ja 16,C,14:6
Udenio, Fabiana
Summer School 1987,Jl 22,C,22:1
Udy, Helene
Nightflyers 1987,O 24,17:1
Ugresic, Dubravke (Screenwriter)
In the Jaws of Life 1987,Mr 20,C,15:1
Uhlen, Annette
Felix 1988,S 24,13:1
Uhler, Laurent (Miscellaneous)
No Man's Land 1987,F 13,C,14:6
Uhry, Alfred (Screenwriter)
Mystic Pizza 1988,O 21,C,20:6
U Lan (Director)
Girl from Hunan 1988,Mr 4,C,22:4
Uldrich, Frantisek (Cinematographer)
Debajo del Mundo (Under the World) 1988,O 5,C,19:5
Ulfik, Rick (Composer)
Street Trash 1987,S 16,C,27:3
Ulla, Jorge (Director)
Nobody Listened 1988,D 2,C,14:6
Ulla, Jorge (Producer)
Nobody Listened 1988,D 2,C,14:6
Ulla, Jorge (Screenwriter)
Nobody Listened 1988,D 2,C,14:6

W

One Woman or Two 1988,Ja 3,II,15:1
Gorillas in the Mist 1988,S 23,C,19:1
Working Girl 1988,D 21,C,22:4
Weaving, Hugo
Right Hand Man, The 1987,O 2,C,13:1
Webb, Chloe
Belly of an Architect, The 1987,O 1,C,22:5
Twins 1988,D 9,C,18:1
Webb, Jimmy (Composer)
Hanoi Hilton, The 1987,Mr 27,C,13:1
Webb, Simon (Composer)
Playing Away 1987,Mr 13,C,19:1
Playing Away 1988,Ap 1,C,4:4
Webber, Robert
Nuts 1987,N 20,C,16:6
Webber, Timothy
John and the Missus 1987,O 24,17:1
Weber, Billy (Miscellaneous)
Beverly Hills Cop II 1987,My 20,C,28:1
Midnight Run 1988,Jl 20,C,15:5
Weber, Bruce (Director)
Broken Noses 1987,N 4,C,28:5
Wechsler, Nick (Producer)
Beat, The 1988,Je 3,C,10:6
Wechsler, Richard (Producer)
Plain Clothes 1988,Ap 16,18:1
Wedeles, Rodolpho (Miscellaneous)
Life Is a Dream 1988,D 30,C,10:6
Wedgeworth, Ann
Made in Heaven 1987,N 6,C,16:1
Tiger's Tale, A 1988,F 12,C,9:1
Far North 1988,N 9,C,18:5
Wei, Rex
Ping Pong 1987,Jl 17,C,10:6
Weil, Dan (Miscellaneous)
Big Blue, The 1988,Ag 20,11:4
Weil, Samuel (Director)
Troma's War 1988,D 9,C,23:1
Weiland, Paul (Director)
Leonard Part 6 1987,D 18,C,30:1
Weinberg, Joanna
Saturday Night at the Palace 1988,My 20,C,16:1
Weincke, Jan (Cinematographer)
Dead of Winter 1987,F 6,C,4:3
Weeds 1987,O 16,C,10:5
Hello Again 1987,N 6,C,21:1
Weingrod, Herschel (Screenwriter)
My Stepmother Is an Alien 1988,D 9,C,17:1
Twins 1988,D 9,C,18:1
Weinstein, Bob (Producer)
Light Years 1988,My 15,56:1
Weinstock, Jane (Miscellaneous)
Sleepwalk 1987,Mr 20,C,15:1
Sleepwalk 1987,Jl 3,C,5:1
Weintraub, Jerry (Producer)
Happy New Year 1987,Ag 7,C,10:6
Weiser, Doug
Midnight Crossing 1988,My 14,16:5
Weiser, Doug (Producer)
Midnight Crossing 1988,My 14,16:5
Weiser, Doug (Screenwriter)
Midnight Crossing 1988,My 14,16:5
Weiser, Stanley (Miscellaneous)
Project X 1987,Ap 17,C,15:1
Weiser, Stanley (Screenwriter)
Project X 1987,Ap 17,C,15:1
Wall Street 1987,D 11,C,3:4
Weisman, David (Producer)
Spike of Bensonhurst 1988,N 11,C,15:1
Weisman, Matthew (Miscellaneous)
Teen Wolf Too 1987,N 20,C,14:6
Weisman, Matthew (Screenwriter)
Burglar 1987,Mr 20,C,10:4
Weiss, Adam (Miscellaneous)
Bull Durham 1988,Je 15,C,20:5
Weiss, Chuck (Miscellaneous)
Nightmare on Elm Street 4, A: The Dream Master 1988,Ag 19,C,8:3
Weiss, Emil (Director)
Faulkenau, the Impossible 1988,O 5,C,23:1
Faulkenau, the Impossible: Samuel Fuller Bears Witness 1988,N 1,C,17:1
Weiss, Emil (Screenwriter)
Faulkenau, the Impossible 1988,O 5,C,23:1
Weiss, Jeff (Producer)
Rocket Gibraltar 1988,S 2,C,6:5
Weiss, Robert K (Director)
Amazon Women on the Moon 1987,S 18,C,12:6
Weiss, Robert K (Producer)
Dragnet 1987,Je 26,C,3:1

Amazon Women on the Moon 1987,S 18,C,12:6
Naked Gun, The 1988,D 2,C,16:1
Weissman, Aerlyn (Director)
Winter Tan, A 1988,O 2,57:6
Weksler, Teri
Beehive 1988,D 7,C,24:5
Welch, Bo (Miscellaneous)
Lost Boys, The 1987,Jl 31,C,21:1
Accidental Tourist, The 1988,D 23,C,12:5
Welch, Elisabeth
Keeping Love Alive 1988,Mr 13,57:1
Keeping Love Alive 1988,Mr 27,II,29:1
Weld, Tuesday
Heartbreak Hotel 1988,S 30,C,18:5
Welin, Hans (Cinematographer)
Mozart Brothers, The 1987,S 18,C,21:1
Welker, Frank
Chipmunk Adventure, The 1987,My 22,C,10:5
Pinocchio and the Emperor of the Night 1987,D 25,C,6:5
Wellburn, Tim (Miscellaneous)
Fringe Dwellers, The 1987,Ja 23,C,13:3
Burke and Wills 1987,Je 12,C,10:1
Weller, Elly
Assault, The 1987,F 6,C,8:1
Weller, Peter
Robocop 1987,Jl 17,C,10:1
Robocop 1987,Ag 2,II,23:5
Shakedown 1988,My 6,C,20:1
Welles, Gwen
Sticky Fingers 1988,My 6,C,28:5
Welles, Orson
Filming Othello 1987,F 4,C,24:3
Someone to Love 1988,Ap 21,C,20:4
Welles, Orson (Director)
Filming Othello 1987,F 4,C,24:3
Wells, Jerold
Element of Crime, The 1987,My 1,C,11:1
Wells, John
Consuming Passions 1988,Ap 6,C,18:3
Wells, Peter (Director)
Death in the Family, A 1987,O 21,C,24:5
Jewel's Darl 1987,O 21,C,24:5
Wells, Peter (Screenwriter)
Death in the Family, A 1987,O 21,C,24:5
Jewel's Darl 1987,O 21,C,24:5
Wells, Vernon
Innerspace 1987,Jl 1,C,17:1
Welsh, John
Campus Man 1987,My 4,C,17:1
Welsh, Kenneth
Loyalties 1987,Mr 21,14:3
Loyalties 1987,N 20,C,21:1
House on Carroll Street, The 1988,Mr 4,C,23:1
Crocodile Dundee II 1988,My 25,C,15:3
Another Woman 1988,O 14,C,3:3
Wemba, Papa
Vie Est Belle, La 1987,N 18,C,21:1
Wemba, Papa (Composer)
Vie Est Belle, La 1987,N 18,C,21:1
Wemyss, Graeme (Stig)
Shame 1988,Mr 19,10:3
Wenders, Wim (Director)
Wings of Desire 1988,Ap 29,C,15:1
Wenders, Wim (Producer)
Wings of Desire 1988,Ap 29,C,15:1
Wenders, Wim (Screenwriter)
Wings of Desire 1988,Ap 29,C,15:1
Wendt, George
Plain Clothes 1988,Ap 16,18:1
Wenning, Katherine (Miscellaneous)
Maurice 1987,S 18,C,18:5
Wentz, Kip
Poltergeist III 1988,Je 10,C,17:1
Werner, Dennis (Miscellaneous)
Street Trash 1987,S 16,C,27:3
Werner, Peter (Director)
No Man's Land 1987,O 23,C,10:5
Wert, Timothy
Consuming Passions 1988,Ap 6,C,18:3
Wertmuller, Lina (Director)
Summer Night with Greek Profile, Almond Eyes and Scent of Basil 1987,Je 19,C,12:6
Wertmuller, Lina (Screenwriter)
Summer Night with Greek Profile, Almond Eyes and Scent of Basil 1987,Je 19,C,12:6
Wertmuller, Massimo
Summer Night with Greek Profile, Almond Eyes and Scent of Basil 1987,Je 19,C,12:6
Wesley, Kassie
Evil Dead 2: Dead by Dawn 1987,Mr 13,C,18:1

West, Brian (Cinematographer)
84 Charing Cross Road 1987,F 13,C,10:4
West, Howard (Producer)
Summer School 1987,Jl 22,C,22:1
West, Martin
MAC and Me 1988,Ag 13,14:1
West, Morris (Screenwriter)
Second Victory, The 1987,My 27,C,22:3
West, Tegan
Hamburger Hill 1987,Ag 28,C,16:5
Westbury, Ken (Cinematographer)
Bellman and True 1988,Ap 1,C,4:4
Westcott, Frederick
Man Who Mistook His Wife for a Hat, The 1988,Ag 31,C,17:1
Westheimer, Dr Ruth
One Woman or Two 1987,F 6,C,18:1
Forever, Lulu 1987,Ap 24,C,10:4
One Woman or Two 1988,Ja 3,II,15:1
Westlake, Donald E (Miscellaneous)
Stepfather, The 1987,My 8,C,9:1
Westlake, Donald E (Screenwriter)
Stepfather, The 1987,My 8,C,9:1
Westlake, Hilary
Gold Diggers, The 1988,F 12,C,22:1
Weston, Jack
Ishtar 1987,My 15,C,3:1
Dirty Dancing 1987,Ag 21,C,3:4
Short Circuit 2 1988,Jl 6,C,18:5
Wetanson, Burt (Screenwriter)
American Gothic 1988,Je 4,12:6
Wexler, Haskell (Cinematographer)
Matewan 1987,Ag 28,C,3:4
Colors 1988,Ap 15,C,4:1
Colors 1988,My 1,II,23:1
Weyers, Marius
Saturday Night at the Palace 1988,My 20,C,16:1
Whalley, Joanne
Good Father, The 1987,F 11,C,23:1
Willow 1988,My 20,C,8:4
Wheatley, Thomas
Living Daylights, The 1987,Jl 31,C,3:5
Wheaton, Amy
Curse, The 1987,S 11,C,13:4
Wheaton, Wil
Curse, The 1987,S 11,C,13:4
Wheeler, Anne (Director)
Loyalties 1987,Mr 21,14:3
Loyalties 1987,N 20,C,21:1
Wheeler, Anne (Miscellaneous)
Loyalties 1987,Mr 21,14:3
Loyalties 1987,N 20,C,21:1
Wheeler, Ira
September 1987,D 18,C,3:1
Wheeler, John W (Miscellaneous)
Million Dollar Mystery 1987,Je 12,C,6:4
Wheeler, Whitney Brooke (Miscellaneous)
Death Wish 4: The Crackdown 1987,N 7,14:1
Messenger of Death 1988,S 17,12:5
Whitaker, Charlotte (Miscellaneous)
Patti Rocks 1988,Ja 15,C,12:1
Whitaker, Damon
Bird 1988,S 26,C,19:1
Whitaker, Forest
Stakeout 1987,Ag 5,C,21:1
Good Morning, Vietnam 1987,D 23,C,11:1
Bird 1988,S 26,C,19:1
Whitcraft, Elizabeth
Angel Heart 1987,Mr 6,C,5:1
White, April
Positive ID 1987,Mr 14,13:1
White, De'Voreaux
Die Hard 1988,Jl 15,C,14:5
White, Erin
Positive ID 1987,Mr 14,13:1
White, Ron
Too Outrageous 1987,O 16,C,12:1
White, Timothy (Producer)
Feathers 1988,Mr 21,C,15:1
White, Wayne
Big Top Pee-wee 1988,Jl 22,C,10:3
Whitelaw, Billie
Samuel Beckett: Silence to Silence 1987,Ap 15,C,22:1
Shadey 1987,Je 5,C,10:1
Maurice 1987,S 18,C,18:5
Whitemore, Hugh (Screenwriter)
84 Charing Cross Road 1987,F 13,C,10:4
Whitfield, Lynn
Jaws: The Revenge 1987,Jl 18,15:4
Whitford, Bradley
Adventures in Baby-Sitting 1987,Jl 1,C,24:3

Revenge of the Nerds II: Nerds in Paradise 1987,Jl 11,18:4
Whitlock, Graham (Miscellaneous)
Playing Away 1987,Mr 13,C,19:1
Playing Away 1988,Ap 1,C,4:4
Whitlow, Jill
Twice Dead 1988,N 19,15:3
Whitmore, James
Nuts 1987,N 20,C,16:6
Whitrow, Benjamin
Personal Services 1987,My 15,C,4:5
Whittingham, Christopher
Little Dorrit 1988,Mr 26,11:1
Whitton, Margaret
Secret of My Success, The 1987,Ap 10,C,14:4
Ironweed 1987,D 18,C,24:5
Whybrow, Arthur
Bellman and True 1988,Ap 1,C,4:4
Wichniarz, Kazimierz
Woman from the Provinces, A 1987,Mr 22,62:2
Wick, Douglas (Producer)
Working Girl 1988,D 21,C,22:4
Wicket, W W (Screenwriter)
Seventh Sign, The 1988,Ap 1,C,20:3
Wicks, Victoria
Ping Pong 1987,Jl 17,C,10:6
Wiederhorn, Ken (Director)
Return of the Living Dead Part II 1988,Ja 15,C,11:1
Wiederhorn, Ken (Screenwriter)
Return of the Living Dead Part II 1988,Ja 15,C,11:1
Wiest, Dianne
Radio Days 1987,Ja 30,C,1:1
Radio Days 1987,F 1,II,21:1
Lost Boys, The 1987,Jl 31,C,21:1
September 1987,D 18,C,3:1
Bright Lights, Big City 1988,Ap 1,C,22:5
Wigutow, Daniel (Producer)
Distant Harmony 1988,F 4,C,15:1
Wilbur, George P
Halloween 4: The Return of Michael Myers 1988,O 22,12:4
Wilby, James
Maurice 1987,S 18,C,18:5
Handful of Dust, A 1988,Je 24,C,14:1
Summer Story, A 1988,Ag 11,C,18:5
Handful of Dust, A 1988,Ag 28,II,23:1
Wilcox, Lisa
Nightmare on Elm Street 4, A: The Dream Master 1988,Ag 19,C,8:3
Wilcox, Richard (Miscellaneous)
Accused, The 1988,O 14,C,13:1
Wild, Jamie
Overboard 1987,D 16,C,22:3
Wilde, Oscar (Original Author)
Salome's Last Dance 1988,My 6,C,8:5
Salome's Last Dance 1988,My 22,II,43:1
Wilder, Gene
Hello Actors Studio 1988,N 9,C,19:1
Wilder, James
Murder One 1988,S 23,C,15:1
Wilder, Thornton (Original Author)
Mr North 1988,Jl 22,C,8:4
Wildgruber, Ulrich
Dragon Chow 1988,My 27,C,10:5
Wilding, Michael, Jr
Deadly Illusion 1987,O 31,10:5
Wildsmith, Dawn
Surf Nazis Must Die 1987,O 2,C,24:5
Wiley, Ethan (Director)
House II: The Second Story 1987,Ag 29,11:1
Wiley, Ethan (Screenwriter)
House II: The Second Story 1987,Ag 29,11:1
Wilheim, Ladislav (Miscellaneous)
Braddock: Missing in Action III 1988,Ja 22,C,9:1
Wilhoite, Kathleen
Witchboard 1987,Mr 15,61:1
Campus Man 1987,My 4,C,17:1
Wilk, Scott (Composer)
Plain Clothes 1988,Ap 16,18:1
Wilkinson, Marc (Composer)
Day on the Grand Canal with the Emperor of China (or Surface Is Illusion But So Is Depth), A 1988,Mr 19,8:3
Willard, Fred
Roxanne 1987,Je 19,C,3:4
Willcox, Pete
Dudes 1988,Je 24,C,9:1
Williams, Barbara
Tiger Warsaw 1988,S 23,C,20:1
Williams, Bernard (Producer)
Wisdom 1987,Ja 1,9:5
Who's That Girl 1987,Ag 8,16:1
Dirty Rotten Scoundrels 1988,D 14,C,21:4

Williams, Billy (Cinematographer)
Suspect 1987,O 23,C,14:3
Williams, Billy Dee
Deadly Illusion 1987,O 31,10:5
Williams, Dean
Distant Voices, Still Lives 1988,S 29,C,24:3
Williams, Dick Anthony
Gardens of Stone 1987,My 8,C,32:1
Williams, Heathcote
Wish You Were Here 1987,Jl 24,C,7:2
Williams, JoBeth
Memories of Me 1988,S 28,C,23:1
Williams, John (Composer)
Witches of Eastwick, The 1987,Je 12,C,3:4
Superman IV: The Quest for Peace 1987,Jl 25,13:2
Empire of the Sun 1987,D 9,C,25:1
Accidental Tourist, The 1988,D 23,C,12:5
Williams, Patrick (Composer)
Fresh Horses 1988,N 19,15:3
Williams, Paul (Composer)
Ishtar 1987,My 15,C,3:1
Williams, Robin
Good Morning, Vietnam 1987,D 23,C,11:1
Good Morning, Vietnam 1988,Ja 10,II,21:1
Williams, Robin (Narrator)
Dear America: Letters Home from Vietnam 1988,S 16,C,18:1
Williams, Stacy (Producer)
Ernest Goes to Camp 1987,My 23,15:4
Ernest Saves Christmas 1988,N 11,C,15:1
Williams, Tennessee (Original Author)
Glass Menagerie, The 1987,O 23,C,14:3
Williams, Terri Lyn
Bell Diamond 1988,Mr 17,C,30:1
Williams, Treat
Dead Heat 1988,My 7,13:1
Williams, Trevor (Miscellaneous)
Revenge of the Nerds II: Nerds in Paradise 1987,Jl 11,18:4
Police Academy 5: Assignment Miami Beach 1988,Mr 19,13:3
Williams, Vanessa
Pickup Artist, The 1987,S 18,C,23:1
Williamson, David (Original Author)
Traveling North 1988,F 12,C,10:1
Williamson, David (Screenwriter)
Traveling North 1988,F 12,C,10:1
Williamson, John
Positive ID 1987,Mr 14,13:1
Williamson, Mykel T
You Talkin' to Me? 1987,S 25,C,14:1
Williamson, Nicol
Black Widow 1987,F 6,C,3:1
Willingham, Noble
Summer Heat 1987,My 29,C,8:4
Good Morning, Vietnam 1987,D 23,C,11:1
Willis, Bruce
Blind Date 1987,Mr 27,C,11:1
Blind Date 1987,My 3,II,19:1
Sunset 1988,Ap 29,C,13:1
Sunset 1988,My 8,II,19:1
Die Hard 1988,Jl 15,C,14:5
Die Hard 1988,Jl 31,II,19:1
Willis, Gordon (Cinematographer)
Pickup Artist, The 1987,S 18,C,23:1
Bright Lights, Big City 1988,Ap 1,C,22:5
Wilmore, Duncan
Project X 1987,Ap 17,C,15:1
Wilms, Andre
Field of Honor (Champ d'Honneur) 1988,Mr 18,C,24:5
Wilson, David (Miscellaneous)
Eat the Peach 1987,Jl 17,C,6:1
Wilson, Earl (Miscellaneous)
Midnight Crossing 1988,My 14,16:5
Wilson, Elizabeth
Believers, The 1987,Je 10,C,22:5
Wilson, Hugh (Director)
Burglar 1987,Mr 20,C,10:4
Wilson, Hugh (Screenwriter)
Burglar 1987,Mr 20,C,10:4
Wilson, Ian (Cinematographer)
Wish You Were Here 1987,Jl 24,C,7:2
Wilson, John (Miscellaneous)
Belly of an Architect, The 1987,O 1,C,22:5
Wilson, Kara
Gospel According to Vic 1987,Mr 13,C,13:1
Wilson, Lambert
Belly of an Architect, The 1987,O 1,C,22:5
Rendez-Vous 1987,D 25,C,6:5
History 1988,Je 3,C,15:1
Wilson, Larry (Miscellaneous)
Beetlejuice 1988,Mr 30,C,18:6

Wilson, Larry (Producer)
Beetlejuice 1988,Mr 30,C,18:6
Wilson, Michael G (Producer)
Living Daylights, The 1987,Jl 31,C,3:5
Wilson, Michael G (Screenwriter)
Living Daylights, The 1987,Jl 31,C,3:5
Wilson, S S (Screenwriter)
Batteries Not Included 1987,D 18,C,12:5
Short Circuit 2 1988,Jl 6,C,18:5
Wilson, Scott
Malone 1987,My 4,C,17:4
Wilson, Snoo (Screenwriter)
Shadey 1987,Je 5,C,10:1
Wilson, Thomas F
Action Jackson 1988,F 12,C,10:1
Wilson, Tony (Cinematographer)
Backlash 1987,Mr 26,C,14:4
Backlash 1987,Ag 27,C,18:3
Wilson, Trey
Raising Arizona 1987,Mr 11,C,24:5
Bull Durham 1988,Je 15,C,20:5
Twins 1988,D 9,C,18:1
Wiltgen, Ana Beatriz
Subway to the Stars 1988,Mr 25,C,14:6
Wilton, Penelope
Cry Freedom 1987,N 6,C,14:3
Cry Freedom 1987,N 15,II,25:5
Wimble, Chris (Miscellaneous)
84 Charing Cross Road 1987,F 13,C,10:4
Winans, Sam (Composer)
Enemy Territory 1987,My 22,C,7:1
Winbush, Troy
Principal, The 1987,S 18,C,14:6
Wincer, Simon (Director)
Lighthorsemen, The 1988,My 13,C,14:1
Wincer, Simon (Producer)
Lighthorsemen, The 1988,My 13,C,14:1
Wincott, Michael
Talk Radio 1988,D 21,C,28:4
Winding, Genevieve (Miscellaneous)
Field of Honor (Champ d'Honneur) 1988,Mr 18,C,24:5
Windisch, Ingrid (Producer)
Judgment in Berlin 1988,My 6,C,13:1
Windom, William
Planes, Trains and Automobiles 1987,N 25,C,19:1
Pinocchio and the Emperor of the Night 1987,D 25,C,6:5
She's Having a Baby 1988,F 5,C,18:1
Funland 1988,Je 1,C,17:1
Winfield, Paul
Death Before Dishonor 1987,F 20,C,10:1
Big Shots 1987,O 2,C,17:1
Serpent and the Rainbow, The 1988,F 5,C,3:4
Wingate, William (Original Author)
Malone 1987,My 4,C,17:4
Winger, Debra
Black Widow 1987,F 6,C,3:1
Made in Heaven 1987,N 6,C,16:1
Betrayed 1988,Ag 26,C,16:1
Betrayed 1988,S 4,II,17:1
Betrayed 1988,N 20,II,13:1
Betrayed 1988,D 18,II,13:1
Winkler, Charles (Director)
You Talkin' to Me? 1987,S 25,C,14:1
Winkler, Charles (Screenwriter)
You Talkin' to Me? 1987,S 25,C,14:1
Winkler, Henry (Director)
Memories of Me 1988,S 28,C,23:1
Winkler, Irwin (Producer)
Betrayed 1988,Ag 26,C,16:1
Winner, Michael (Director)
Appointment with Death 1988,Ap 15,C,4:5
Winner, Michael (Producer)
Appointment with Death 1988,Ap 15,C,4:5
Winner, Michael (Screenwriter)
Appointment with Death 1988,Ap 15,C,4:5
Winningham, Mare
Made in Heaven 1987,N 6,C,16:1
Shy People 1988,Jl 1,C,8:5
Winslow, Michael
Police Academy 4: Citizens on Patrol 1987,Ap 4,12:5
Spaceballs 1987,Je 24,C,23:1
Police Academy 5: Assignment Miami Beach 1988,Mr 19,13:3
Winston, Hattie
Clara's Heart 1988,O 7,C,16:5
Winter, Edward
From the Hip 1987,F 6,C,10:4
Winters, Jerry (Producer)
Levy and Goliath 1988,Mr 17,C,20:4
Winters, Jonathan
Moon over Parador 1988,S 9,C,13:1

Winters, Shelley
Hello Actors Studio 1988,N 9,C,19:1
Wirth, Billy
Lost Boys, The 1987,Jl 31,C,21:1
Wise, Alfie
Heat 1987,Mr 13,C,33:1
Wise, Jonathan
Three O'Clock High 1987,O 9,C,16:3
Wise, Kerry
We Think the World of You 1988,D 22,C,15:1
Wise, Mike (Producer)
Making Mr Right 1987,Ap 10,C,16:5
Wise, Pam (Miscellaneous)
Horowitz Plays Mozart 1987,O 8,C,37:1
Wise, Peter
Enemy Territory 1987,My 22,C,7:1
Wise, Ray
Robocop 1987,Jl 17,C,10:1
Wiseman, Andrew (Producer)
Tale of Ruby Rose, The 1988,My 25,C,18:6
Wiseman, Frederick (Director)
Blind 1987,D 2,C,18:4
Wiseman, Frederick (Producer)
Blind 1987,D 2,C,18:4
Wiseman, Jeffrey
Overboard 1987,D 16,C,22:3
Wisniak, Alain (Composer)
Annee des Meduses, L' 1987,Ap 24,C,9:1
Wisniewski, Andreas
Gothic 1987,Ap 10,C,16:3
Living Daylights, The 1987,Jl 31,C,3:5
Witczak, Pawel
Woman Alone, A 1987,Mr 15,61:1
Witherspoon, John
Hollywood Shuffle 1987,Mr 20,C,8:1
Withrow, Glenn
Nightflyers 1987,O 24,17:1
Dudes 1988,Je 24,C,9:1
Witter, Karen
Perfect Match 1988,Je 4,12:3
Wivesson, Gudmar
Babette's Feast 1987,O 1,C,22:5
Babette's Feast 1988,Mr 4,C,12:6
Wodoslawsky, Stefan (Producer)
Crazy Moon 1988,F 8,C,18:5
Wodoslawsky, Stefan (Screenwriter)
Crazy Moon 1988,F 8,C,18:5
Wohlbruck, John (Screenwriter)
End of the Line 1988,F 26,C,15:1
Wolf, Dick (Producer)
No Man's Land 1987,O 23,C,10:5
Wolf, Dick (Screenwriter)
No Man's Land 1987,O 23,C,10:5
Masquerade 1988,Mr 11,C,8:5
Wolf, Gary K (Original Author)
Who Framed Roger Rabbit 1988,Je 22,C,17:2
Wolf, Jeffrey (Miscellaneous)
Heat 1987,Mr 13,C,33:1
Wolfe, Adam (Miscellaneous)
Athens, Ga—Inside/Out 1987,My 29,C,14:1
Wolfe, Traci
Lethal Weapon 1987,Mr 6,C,7:1
Wolinsky, Sidney (Miscellaneous)
Maid to Order 1987,Ag 28,C,6:1
Wollen, Peter (Director)
Friendship's Death 1988,Mr 25,C,22:4
Wollen, Peter (Screenwriter)
Friendship's Death 1988,Mr 25,C,22:4
Wolper, David L (Producer)
Imagine: John Lennon 1988,O 7,C,7:1
Wolters-Alfs, Elisabeth (Producer)
Deadline 1987,S 11,C,4:4
Wo Ma
Chinese Ghost Story, A 1988,Mr 23,C,20:5
Wonder, Stevie (Miscellaneous)
Die Hard 1988,Jl 31,II,19:1
Wong, James (Composer)
Chinese Ghost Story, A 1988,Mr 23,C,20:5
Wong, Leonard (Cinematographer)
Mondo New York 1988,Ap 22,C,23:1
Wong, Russell
China Girl 1987,S 25,C,16:6
Wong, Victor
Prince of Darkness 1987,O 23,C,26:1
Last Emperor, The 1987,N 20,C,3:4
Wong Tsu Hsien
Chinese Ghost Story, A 1988,Mr 23,C,20:5
Wong Wing Hang (Cinematographer)
Chinese Ghost Story, A 1988,Mr 23,C,20:5
Wood, Bari (Original Author)
Dead Ringers 1988,S 23,C,10:1

Dead Ringers 1988,O 2,II,21:5
Woodcock, Mark (Cinematographer)
Andy Warhol 1987,Je 9,C,20:1
Woodruff, Tom, Jr
Monster Squad 1987,Ag 14,C,15:1
Woods, Donald (Original Author)
Cry Freedom 1987,N 6,C,14:3
Cry Freedom 1987,N 8,II,25:1
Cry Freedom 1987,N 15,II,25:5
Woods, James
Best Seller 1987,S 25,C,24:1
Cop 1988,F 5,C,19:3
Cop 1988,F 14,II,1:1
Boost, The 1988,D 23,C,16:6
Woods, James (Producer)
Cop 1988,F 5,C,19:3
Woods, Michael
Lady Beware 1987,S 18,C,23:1
Woodward, Allison
Deadly Illusion 1987,O 31,10:5
Woodward, Joanne
Glass Menagerie, The 1987,O 23,C,14:3
Woodward, Tim
Personal Services 1987,My 15,C,4:5
Woodyard, Gary (Miscellaneous)
Return to Snowy River 1988,Ap 15,C,8:1
Wooldridge, Susan
Loyalties 1987,Mr 21,14:3
Hope and Glory 1987,O 9,C,23:1
Loyalties 1987,N 20,C,21:1
Wooley, Sheb
Hoosiers 1987,F 27,C,10:3
Wooll, Nigel (Producer)
Willow 1988,My 20,C,8:4
Woolley, Stephen (Producer)
High Spirits 1988,N 18,C,10:1
Woo Ok Joo
Man with Three Coffins, The 1988,S 27,C,16:5
Wooster, Arthur (Cinematographer)
Eat the Peach 1987,Jl 17,C,6:1
Woronov, Mary
Black Widow 1987,F 6,C,3:1
Worth, Marvin (Producer)
Patty Hearst 1988,S 23,C,8:5
Wosiewicz, Leszek (Director)
Case of Herman the Stoker, The 1988,Mr 13,57:1
Case of Herman the Stoker, The 1988,Mr 27,II,29:1
Wosiewicz, Leszek (Screenwriter)
Case of Herman the Stoker, The 1988,Mr 13,57:1
Case of Herman the Stoker, The 1988,Mr 27,II,29:1
Wozniak, Victoria (Miscellaneous)
Patti Rocks 1988,Ja 15,C,12:1
Wrenn, Jim (Cinematographer)
Dakota 1988,D 2,C,8:5
Wright, Amy
Telephone, The 1988,F 14,77:1
Accidental Tourist, The 1988,D 23,C,12:5
Wright, Burt
Troma's War 1988,D 9,C,23:1
Wright, Clive (Composer)
South of Reno 1988,Je 3,C,15:1
Wright, Jenny
Near Dark 1987,O 4,67:2
Wright, John (Miscellaneous)
Running Man, The 1987,N 13,C,10:5
Wright, Max
Touch and Go 1987,Ja 14,C,20:5
Wright, Michael
Principal, The 1987,S 18,C,14:6
Wright, Robin
Princess Bride, The 1987,S 25,C,10:5
Wright, Samuel E
Bird 1988,S 26,C,19:1
Wright, Teresa
Good Mother, The 1988,N 4,C,15:1
Wright, Tom
Creepshow 2 1987,My 4,C,17:1
Wuhl, Robert
Good Morning, Vietnam 1987,D 23,C,11:1
Bull Durham 1988,Je 15,C,20:5
Wu Nian-zhen
Daughter of the Nile 1988,S 30,C,8:4
Wurlitzer, Rudy (Director)
Candy Mountain 1988,Je 10,C,6:5
Wurlitzer, Rudy (Screenwriter)
Walker 1987,D 4,C,36:1
Candy Mountain 1988,Je 10,C,6:5
Wu Roufu
Big Parade, The 1988,Mr 15,C,16:5

Wurtzel, Stuart (Miscellaneous)
Suspect 1987,O 23,C,14:3
House on Carroll Street, The 1988,Mr 4,C,23:1
Wu Tao
Last Emperor, The 1987,N 20,C,3:4
Wu Tianming (Producer)
Horse Thief, The 1988,Ja 6,C,15:1
Wyhowski, Hugo Luczyc (Miscellaneous)
Sammy and Rosie Get Laid 1987,O 30,C,5:1
Wyman, Brad (Producer)
White of the Eye 1988,My 20,C,22:5
Wyner, George
Spaceballs 1987,Je 24,C,23:1
Wyrodek, Halina
Woman from the Provinces, A 1987,Mr 22,62:2
Wyss, Sarah
Bell Diamond 1988,Mr 17,C,30:1

X

Xarhakos, Stavros (Composer)
Sweet Country 1987,Ja 23,C,6:5
Xie Fei (Director)
Girl from Hunan 1988,Mr 4,C,22:4
Xing Zheng (Miscellaneous)
Girl from Hunan 1988,Mr 4,C,22:4
Xin Ming
Wild Mountains 1987,Mr 19,C,26:4
Xu Shouli
Wild Mountains 1987,Mr 19,C,26:4
Xu Youfu (Composer)
Wild Mountains 1987,Mr 19,C,26:4

Y

Yablans, Irwin (Miscellaneous)
Prison 1988,Mr 4,C,33:1
Yablans, Irwin (Producer)
Prison 1988,Mr 4,C,33:1
Yaccelini, Alberto (Miscellaneous)
Mes Petites Amoureuses 1987,Ja 30,C,16:1
Yadav, Raghubir
Salaam Bombay! 1988,O 7,C,8:1
Yaguchi, Yoko
Most Beautiful, The 1987,Je 12,C,14:5
Yahraus, Bill (Miscellaneous)
Far North 1988,N 9,C,18:5
Yakusho, Koji
Tampopo 1987,Mr 26,C,21:1
Tampopo 1987,My 22,C,17:1
Yaltkaya, Cengiz (Composer)
Luggage of the Gods 1987,Je 19,C,12:6
Yamachi, Sachiko (Miscellaneous)
Gonza the Spearman 1988,O 28,C,15:1
Yamada, Yoji (Director)
Where Spring Comes Late 1988,N 18,C,8:4
Yamada, Yoji (Miscellaneous)
Where Spring Comes Late 1988,N 18,C,8:4
Yamada, Yoji (Screenwriter)
Where Spring Comes Late 1988,N 18,C,8:4
Yamakawa, Naoto (Director)
So What 1988,N 20,II,13:1
Yamamoto, Issei (Producer)
Pornographers, The 1987,My 22,C,10:5
Yamashita, Daisuke
Taxing Woman, A 1987,S 26,9:1
Yamazaki, Tsutomu
Tampopo 1987,Mr 26,C,21:1
Tampopo 1987,My 22,C,17:1
Taxing Woman, A 1987,S 26,9:1
Funeral, The 1987,O 23,C,14:3
Taxing Woman, A 1988,My 13,C,14:3
Yamazaki, Yoshihiro (Cinematographer)
Promise, A 1987,Mr 17,C,14:4
Yanagimachi, Mitsuo (Director)
Fire Festival (Himatsuri) 1988,N 20,II,13:1
Yanagimachi, Mitsuo (Screenwriter)
Fire Festival (Himatsuri) 1988,N 20,II,13:1
Yanchenko, Oleg (Composer)
Come and See 1987,F 6,C,4:4
Yanez, Ernesto
Realm of Fortune, The 1987,Mr 17,C,14:1
Yang Fan
Daughter of the Nile 1988,S 30,C,8:4

Z

Zimmel, Harv (Miscellaneous)
Shoot to Kill 1988,F 12,C,8:5
Zimmel, Harv (Screenwriter)
Shoot to Kill 1988,F 12,C,8:5
Zimmer, Hans (Composer)
World Apart, A 1988,Je 17,C,10:4
Rain Man 1988,D 16,C,12:5
Burning Secret 1988,D 22,C,16:5
Zimmerman, Don (Miscellaneous)
Over the Top 1987,F 12,C,21:2
Fatal Beauty 1987,O 30,C,8:5
Everybody's All American 1988,N 4,C,17:1
Zimmerman, Jeff (Cinematographer)
Decline of Western Civilization Part II, The: The Metal Years
1988,Je 17,C,14:4
Zimmerman, Paul D (Screenwriter)
Consuming Passions 1988,Ap 6,C,18:3
Zinnemann, Tim (Producer)
Running Man, The 1987,N 13,C,10:5
Zins, Catherine (Miscellaneous)
Hotel Terminus: The Life and Times of Klaus Barbie 1988,O
6,C,25:1
Zischler, Hanns
Berlin Affair, The 1988,Jl 15,C,12:5
Ziskin, Laura (Producer)
No Way Out 1987,Ag 14,C,3:1
DOA 1988,Mr 18,C,8:5
Rescue, The 1988,Ag 5,C,9:1
Everybody's All American 1988,N 4,C,17:1
Zitzermann, Bernard (Cinematographer)
No Man's Land 1987,F 13,C,14:6
Man in Love, A 1987,Jl 31,C,10:6
Zivkovic, Brane (Composer)
In the Jaws of Life 1987,Mr 20,C,15:1
Zlatarits, Harvey (Miscellaneous)
Into the Fire 1988,O 29,18:5
Zobel, Richard
From the Hip 1987,F 6,C,10:4
Zollo, Frederick (Producer)
Miles from Home 1988,S 16,C,8:4
Mississippi Burning 1988,D 9,C,12:1
Zolnay, Pal
Diary for My Loved Ones 1987,S 26,12:3
Zorn, John (Composer)
She Must Be Seeing Things 1988,Ap 13,C,20:4
Zourdoumis, Leonidas (Cinematographer)
Powaqqatsi 1988,Ap 29,C,20:4
Zsigmond, Vilmos (Cinematographer)
Witches of Eastwick, The 1987,Je 12,C,3:4
Zuanic, Rod
Tale of Ruby Rose, The 1988,My 25,C,18:6
Zucker, Charlotte
Naked Gun, The 1988,D 2,C,16:1
Zucker, David (Director)
Naked Gun, The 1988,D 2,C,16:1
Naked Gun, The 1988,D 11,II,13:1
Zucker, David (Screenwriter)
Naked Gun, The 1988,D 2,C,16:1
Naked Gun, The 1988,D 11,II,13:1
Zucker, Jerry (Screenwriter)
Naked Gun, The 1988,D 2,C,16:1
Naked Gun, The 1988,D 11,II,13:1
Zuehlke, Joshua
Amazing Grace and Chuck 1987,My 22,C,30:4
Zumwalt, Rick
Over the Top 1987,F 12,C,21:2
Zuniga, Daphne
Spaceballs 1987,Je 24,C,23:1
Zupanic, Ladislav
My Sweet Little Village 1987,Ja 9,C, 6:5
Zurinaga, Marcos (Cinematographer)
Gran Fiesta, La 1987,Jl 17,C,17:1
Zurinaga, Marcos (Director)
Gran Fiesta, La 1987,Jl 17,C,17:1
Zurinaga, Marcos (Screenwriter)
Gran Fiesta, La 1987,Jl 17,C,17:1
Zutic, Milos
Hey Babu Riba 1987,Mr 15,60:1
Hey Babu Riba 1987,S 18,C,24:1
Zweibel, Alan (Screenwriter)
Dragnet 1987,Je 26,C,3:1
Zweig, Stefan (Original Author)
Burning Secret 1988,D 22,C,16:5
Zweigenbom, Dor
Late Summer Blues 1988,Ag 12,C,13:1
Zwerin, Charlotte (Director)
Horowitz Plays Mozart 1987,O 8,C,37:1
Islands 1987,O 16,C,26:4
Zwickler, Phil (Director)
Rights and Reactions: Lesbian and Gay Rights on Trial
1988,Je 15,C,19:3

Zwickler, Phil (Producer)
Rights and Reactions: Lesbian and Gay Rights on Trial
1988,Je 15,C,19:3

E

F

G

N

O

P

Some Kind of Wonderful 1987,F 27,C,17:3
Campus Man 1987,My 4,C,17:1
Hot Pursuit 1987,My 11,C,14:5
Beverly Hills Cop II 1987,My 20,C,28:1
Untouchables, The 1987,Je 3,C,17:1
Summer School 1987,Jl 22,C,22:1
Back to the Beach 1987,Ag 8,16:5
Hamburger Hill 1987,Ag 28,C,16:5
Fatal Attraction 1987,S 18,C,10:5
Planes, Trains and Automobiles 1987,N 25,C,19:1
She's Having a Baby 1988,F 5,C,18:1
New Life, A 1988,Mr 25,C,5:2
Plain Clothes 1988,Ap 16,18:1
Permanent Record 1988,Ap 22,C,10:1
Blue Iguana, The 1988,Ap 23,18:2
Friday the 13th, Part VII—The New Blood 1988,My 15,56:5
Crocodile Dundee II 1988,My 25,C,15:3
Presidio, The 1988,Je 10,C,15:1
Coming to America 1988,Je 29,C,20:5
Big Top Pee-wee 1988,Jl 22,C,10:3
Tucker: The Man and His Dream 1988,Ag 12,C,8:1
Accused, The 1988,O 14,C,13:1
U2: Rattle and Hum 1988,N 4,C,16:1
Distant Thunder 1988,N 11,C,13:1
Scrooged 1988,N 23,C,16:5
Naked Gun, The 1988,D 2,C,16:1
Platinum Pictures Inc (Dist.)
Deranged 1987,O 31,12:3
Pogues, The (Misc.)
Straight to Hell 1987,Je 26,C,8:5
Polish Television, "X" Film Unit (Prod.)
Great Race, The 1988,Mr 12,19:1
Portuguese Film Institute (Prod.)
Hard Times 1988,O 6,C,29:1
Portuguese Radio-Television (Prod.)
Hard Times 1988,O 6,C,29:1
Probst Films (Prod.)
Dragon Chow 1988,My 27,C,10:5
Pussycat Club (Misc.)
Comic Magazine (Komikku Zasshi) 1987,Ja 16,C,14:6

R

R5/S8 (Dist.)
Love Suicides at Sonezaki, The 1988,Jl 13,C,22:1
RAI Channel 1 (Prod.)
Long Live the Lady! 1987,O 16,C,26:5
Boy from Calabria, A 1987,N 20,C,21:1
Family, The 1988,Ja 22,C,11:1
Last Minute, The 1988,F 26,C,10:5
Two Lives of Mattia Pascal, The 1988,Mr 18,C,8:5
RAI Channel 2 (Prod.)
Jean de Florette 1987,Je 26,C,3:1
Maschera, La 1988,S 25,64:4
RAI Radiotelevisione Italiana (Prod.)
Long Live the Lady! 1987,O 16,C,26:5
Julia and Julia 1988,F 5,C,5:1
Cammina Cammina (Keep Walking, Keep Walking) 1988,Jl 10,43:5
Maschera, La 1988,S 25,64:4
Rearguard Pictures (Dist.)
Wannsee Conference, The 1987,N 18,C,29:3
Red Clay Ramblers (Misc.)
Far North 1988,N 9,C,18:5
Reel Movies International (Dist.)
Element of Crime, The 1987,My 1,C,11:1
Regina Films (Prod.)
Amulet of Ogum 1987,F 6,C,4:3
Renn Productions (Prod.)
Jean de Florette 1987,Je 26,C,3:1
Reteitalia Spa (Misc.)
Summer Night with Greek Profile, Almond Eyes and Scent of Basil 1987,Je 19,C,12:6
Rhapsody Films (Dist.)
Art Blakey: The Jazz Messenger 1988,O 28,C,16:4
Road Movies (Prod.)
Anita—Dances of Vice 1987,O 3,15:1
Rosebud Releasing Corporation (Dist.)
Evil Dead 2: Dead by Dawn 1987,Mr 13,C,18:1
Roxie Releasing (Dist.)
Welcome in Vienna 1988,Je 1,C,17:1
God Doesn't Believe in Us Anymore 1988,Jl 20,C,20:5
Santa Fe 1988,Jl 20,C,20:5

S

Sandstar (Dist.)
Perfect Match 1988,Je 4,12:3
Sara Films (Prod.)
Buffet Froid (Cold Cuts) 1987,S 4,C,5:4
Scalera Films (Prod.)
We the Living 1988,N 25,C,11:1
Scarabee Films (Prod.)
Genesis 1988,D 23,C,18:6
Scotti Brothers Pictures Inc (Dist.)
He's My Girl 1987,S 11,C,5:1
Lady Beware 1987,S 18,C,23:1
Seibu Saison Group (Prod.)
Promise, A 1987,Mr 17,C,14:4
Seis del Solar (Misc.)
Return of Ruben Blades, The 1987,S 7,9:3
Selena(Prod.)
Field of Honor (Champ d'Honneur) 1988,Mr 18,C,24:5
Sen, Mrinal, PLRT Productions(Prod.)
Genesis 1988,D 23,C,18:6
Septembre Productions (Prod.)
I Hate Actors! 1988,Ap 29,C,22:1
Shapiro Entertainment (Dist.)
Girl, The 1987,Ag 7,C,10:6
Shapiro Glickenhaus Entertainment Corporation (Dist.)
Maniac Cop 1988,My 14,16:5
Shisso Production, Tokyo (Prod.)
Emperor's Naked Army Marches On, The 1988,Mr 15,C,15:1
Shochiku Company (Dist.)
I Lived, But . . . 1987,Ap 1,C,25:1
River of Fireflies 1988,N 4,C,13:1
Violence at Noon 1988,N 11,C,6:4
Where Spring Comes Late 1988,N 18,C,8:4
Shochiko Company (Prod.)
Gonza the Spearman 1988,O 28,C,15:1
Silver Screen Partners (Misc.)
Oliver and Company 1988,N 18,C,8:4
Simon & Goodman Picture Company (Prod.)
No Applause, Just Throw Money 1988,Mr 12,14:4
Skatalites, The (Misc.)
Cool Running: The Reggae Movie 1988,Ap 22,C,36:5
Skouras Pictures Inc (Dist.)
Good Father, The 1987,F 11,C,23:1
Waiting for the Moon 1987,Mr 6,C,14:5
Gospel According to Vic 1987,Mr 13,C,13:1
Shadey 1987,Je 5,C,10:1
Eat the Peach 1987,Jl 17,C,6:1
Living on Tokyo Time 1987,Ag 14,C,20:1
Coming Up Roses 1987,S 11,C,9:1
Deadline 1987,S 11,C,4:4
Dogs in Space 1987,O 9,C,7:1
Half of Heaven 1988,Ja 21,C,24:3
In a Shallow Grave 1988,My 6,C,21:1
Wash, The 1988,Ag 17,C,17:4
Wizard of Loneliness, The 1988,S 2,C,9:1
Sled Reynolds and Gideon (Misc.)
Benji the Hunted 1987,Je 17,C,18:6
Slotint SA (Prod.)
Caviar Rouge, Le 1988,Mr 25,C,10:5
Sofica Creations (Prod.)
Under Satan's Sun 1987,O 3,13:1
Sofica Investimage (Prod.)
Under Satan's Sun 1987,O 3,13:1
Sony Pictures (Dist.)
Tiger Warsaw 1988,S 23,C,20:1
Soprofilms (Prod.)
Bad Blood 1987,S 30,C,20:5
Southern Films (Dist.)
Last Emperor, The 1988,O 14,C,8:5
Spectrafilm (Dist.)
Prettykill 1987,Mr 27,C,13:3
Blue Monkey, The 1987,O 16,C,12:6
Too Outrageous 1987,O 16,C,12:1
Stacking 1988,Ja 15,C,15:1
Anguish 1988,Ja 29,C,15:1
Aloha Summer 1988,F 26,C,8:1
Tokyo Pop 1988,Ap 15,C,4:4
Sticky Fingers 1988,My 6,C,28:5
Squalls (Misc.)
Athens, Ga—Inside/Out 1987,My 29,C,14:1
Square Pictures (Dist.)
Howling III 1987,N 13,C,5:1
Stella Film GmbH (Prod.)
Au Revoir les Enfants (Goodbye, Children) 1988,F 12,C,15:1

Stillman International (Dist.)
Hail Hazana 1988,Je 10,C,18:1
Studio Hranych Filmov (Prod.)
Boxer and Death, The 1988,O 12,C,19:1
Sullivan Bluth Studios (Prod.)
Land Before Time, The 1988,N 18,C,8:4
Sunsplash Filmworks Limited (Prod.)
Cool Running: The Reggae Movie 1988,Ap 22,C,36:5
Svensk Filmindustri (Dist.)
My Life as a Dog 1987,My 1,C,16:1
Svensk Filmindustri (Prod.)
My Life as a Dog 1987,Mr 24,C,14:3
Swedish Information Service (Misc.)
Three Strange Loves (Torst) 1988,Ja 20,C,20:1
Swiss Television Zurich (Misc.)
Record, The 1988,My 13,C,15:1

T

Taft Entertainment Pictures (Dist.)
Light of Day 1987,F 6,C,4:3
Tangerine Dream (Misc.)
Near Dark 1987,O 4,67:2
Three O'Clock High 1987,O 9,C,16:3
Shy People 1988,Jl 1,C,8:5
Tapestry International (Dist.)
Rights and Reactions: Lesbian and Gay Rights on Trial 1988,Je 15,C,19:3
Taurus Entertainment Company (Dist.)
Invisible Kid, The 1988,Mr 31,C,16:4
Slaughterhouse Rock 1988,My 22,49:5
Telemunchen(Prod.)
Two Lives of Mattia Pascal, The 1988,Mr 18,C,8:5
Television Suisse-Romande (Prod.)
No Man's Land 1988,F 13,C,14:6
Caviar Rouge, Le 1988,Mr 25,C,10:5
Tevere Film (Prod.)
Human Voice, The 1987,O 6,C,14:3
TF1 Films (Dist.)
Bandits 1988,Ag 24,C,17:1
TF1 Films (Prod.)
Opera do Malandro 1987,Ja 30,C,6:5
Call Me Madame 1988,Mr 12,14:4
Theatre de la Ville de Paris (Prod.)
Mammame 1988,Ja 29,C,10:4
Third World (Misc.)
Cool Running: The Reggae Movie 1988,Ap 22,C,36:5
Thunder Basin Films (Prod.)
Dances Sacred and Profane 1987,Je 13,13:1
Tinc Productions (Dist.)
Land of Promise 1988,F 5,C,13:6
Tito, El (Misc.)
Last of England, The 1988,S 28,C,18:3
Toho (Prod.)
Film Actress 1988,O 28,C,8:5
Tokyo Symphony Orchestra (Misc.)
Sea and Poison, The 1987,Jl 22,C,18:3
Touchstone Pictures (Dist.)
Outrageous Fortune 1987,Ja 30,C,5:1
Ernest Goes to Camp 1987,My 23,15:4
Adventures in Baby-Sitting 1987,Jl 1,C,24:3
Stakeout 1987,Ag 5,C,21:1
Can't Buy Me Love 1987,Ag 14,C,13:1
Good Morning, Vietnam 1987,D 23,C,11:1
Shoot to Kill 1988,F 12,C,8:5
DOA 1988,Mr 18,C,8:5
Big Business 1988,Je 10,C,10:4
Who Framed Roger Rabbit 1988,Je 22,C,17:2
Cocktail 1988,Jl 29,C,6:5
Rescue, The 1988,Ag 5,C,9:1
Heartbreak Hotel 1988,S 30,C,18:5
Good Mother, The 1988,N 4,C,15:1
Ernest Saves Christmas 1988,N 11,C,15:1
Beaches 1988,D 21,C,28:4
Touchstone Pictures (Prod.)
Tin Men 1987,Mr 6,C,3:1
Trans World Entertainment (Dist.)
Curse, The 1987,S 11,C,13:4
Wild Pair, The 1987,D 12,19:1
I Don't Give a Damn 1988,My 20,C,22:5
Absolution 1988,Jl 1,C,8:5
Seven Hours to Judgement 1988,S 17,12:5
Kansas 1988,S 23,C,17:1
Full Moon in Blue Water 1988,N 23,C,15:1
Tri-Star Pictures (Dist.)
Touch and Go 1987,Ja 14,C,20:5

V

W

X

Z